# THE
# XPRESS
# LOCOMOTIVE
# REGISTER
## PART 3
# BR : EASTERN (ex-LNER) REGIONS
## 1950 - 1960

*In memory of*
**A.J. SOMERS**
*Who not only worked, serviced and managed many of
the engines in this book but took a delight in them.*

Part three of the Register follows the format of part two by showing a datum line for January and August (Winter and Summer position) for each locomotive with any alterations made in between entered in bold type with the month and year. The listing of locomotives is broadly numerical although where a class is broken into subdivisions (the A2 Pacifics for example) each part immediately follows the main entry. Similarly where a class has been significantly rebuilt, such as the A3 class, two entries are shown. BR Standard locomotives, main line diesel and electric engines, diesel shunters and LMS designs allocated to ex-LNER sheds have been included towards the rear of the book.

As with previous volumes, the data used has been extracted from BTC documents issued to the compilers at the time and every effort has been taken to ensure accuracy of reproduction.

*Acknowledgements and thanks for assistance with text, illustrations and general advice are due to C. Bentley, A. Rush, P. Webb, A. J. Somers, J.T.S. Cat, M. Bentley, R. Tagg, A.W. Fitch, R. Bell, H. Townley, W.T. Stubbs and J. Wooders.*

A4 60020 'Guillemot' of Gateshead runs into Durham with a Kings Cross express during 1963, the last year in which the class was on active East Coast duty. Not only did the engine spent the whole of the 1950's at Gateshead but its entire twenty-six year career was based on Tyneside although it was allocated to Heaton MPD for almost a year in 1944/5. The Gateshead A4's had the widest operating range of any A4's and were diagrammed to work north of Newcastle to Edinburgh and south to Grantham and occasionally Kings Cross, especially during the years from 1959 onwards when acting as substitutes for the rather unreliable 2000hp diesel-electrics. 60020 was withdrawn in March 1964.

The most nomadic of all the east coast Pacifics were the Tyneside A3's which rotated in pairs between Gateshead and Darlington sheds, principally to act as passenger pilot for any express failures on the main line between Newcastle and York. 60071 'Tranquil' stands at Darlington in September 1956, its companion at the time being 60038 'Firdaussi'.

A4 4-6-2 (1935)

| | 60001 | 60002 | 60003 | 60004 | 60005 | 60006 | 60007 | 60008 | 60009 |
|---|---|---|---|---|---|---|---|---|---|
| Aug-50 | GATESHEAD - 52A | GATESHEAD - 52A | KINGS CROSS - 34A | HAYMARKET - 64B | GATESHEAD - 52A | KINGS CROSS - 34A | KINGS CROSS - 34A | KINGS CROSS - 34A | HAYMARKET - 64B |
| Jan-51 | GATESHEAD - 52A | GATESHEAD - 52A | KINGS CROSS - 34A | HAYMARKET - 64B | GATESHEAD - 52A | KINGS CROSS - 34A | KINGS CROSS - 34A | KINGS CROSS - 34A | HAYMARKET - 64B |
| Aug-51 | GATESHEAD - 52A | GATESHEAD - 52A | KINGS CROSS - 34A | HAYMARKET - 64B | GATESHEAD - 52A | KINGS CROSS - 34A | KINGS CROSS - 34A | KINGS CROSS - 34A | HAYMARKET - 64B |
| Jan-52 | GATESHEAD - 52A | GATESHEAD - 52A | KINGS CROSS - 34A | HAYMARKET - 64B | GATESHEAD - 52A | KINGS CROSS - 34A | KINGS CROSS - 34A | KINGS CROSS - 34A | HAYMARKET - 64B |
| Aug-52 | GATESHEAD - 52A | GATESHEAD - 52A | KINGS CROSS - 34A | HAYMARKET - 64B | GATESHEAD - 52A | KINGS CROSS - 34A | KINGS CROSS - 34A | KINGS CROSS - 34A | HAYMARKET - 64B |
| Jan-53 | GATESHEAD - 52A | GATESHEAD - 52A | KINGS CROSS - 34A | HAYMARKET - 64B | GATESHEAD - 52A | KINGS CROSS - 34A | KINGS CROSS - 34A | KINGS CROSS - 34A | HAYMARKET - 64B |
| Aug-53 | GATESHEAD - 52A | GATESHEAD - 52A | KINGS CROSS - 34A | HAYMARKET - 64B | GATESHEAD - 52A | KINGS CROSS - 34A | KINGS CROSS - 34A | KINGS CROSS - 34A | HAYMARKET - 64B |
| Jan-54 | GATESHEAD - 52A | GATESHEAD - 52A | KINGS CROSS - 34A | HAYMARKET - 64B | GATESHEAD - 52A | KINGS CROSS - 34A | KINGS CROSS - 34A | KINGS CROSS - 34A | HAYMARKET - 64B |
| Aug-54 | GATESHEAD - 52A | GATESHEAD - 52A | KINGS CROSS - 34A | HAYMARKET - 64B | GATESHEAD - 52A | KINGS CROSS - 34A | KINGS CROSS - 34A | KINGS CROSS - 34A | HAYMARKET - 64B |
| Jan-55 | GATESHEAD - 52A | GATESHEAD - 52A | KINGS CROSS - 34A | HAYMARKET - 64B | GATESHEAD - 52A | KINGS CROSS - 34A | KINGS CROSS - 34A | KINGS CROSS - 34A | HAYMARKET - 64B |
| Aug-55 | GATESHEAD - 52A | GATESHEAD - 52A | KINGS CROSS - 34A | HAYMARKET - 64B | GATESHEAD - 52A | KINGS CROSS - 34A | KINGS CROSS - 34A | KINGS CROSS - 34A | HAYMARKET - 64B |
| Jan-56 | GATESHEAD - 52A | GATESHEAD - 52A | KINGS CROSS - 34A | HAYMARKET - 64B | GATESHEAD - 52A | KINGS CROSS - 34A | KINGS CROSS - 34A | KINGS CROSS - 34A | HAYMARKET - 64B |
| Aug-56 | GATESHEAD - 52A | GATESHEAD - 52A | KINGS CROSS - 34A | HAYMARKET - 64B | GATESHEAD - 52A | KINGS CROSS - 34A | KINGS CROSS - 34A | KINGS CROSS - 34A | HAYMARKET - 64B |
| Jan-57 | GATESHEAD - 52A | GATESHEAD - 52A | **4/57 : GRAN - 35B** | HAYMARKET - 64B | GATESHEAD - 52A | KINGS CROSS - 34A | KINGS CROSS - 34A | **4/57 : GRAN - 35B** | HAYMARKET - 64B |
| Aug-57 | GATESHEAD - 52A | GATESHEAD - 52A | **9/57 : KX - 34A** | HAYMARKET - 64B | GATESHEAD - 52A | KINGS CROSS - 34A | KINGS CROSS - 34A | **9/57 : KX - 34A** | HAYMARKET - 64B |
| Jan-58 | GATESHEAD - 52A | GATESHEAD - 52A | KINGS CROSS - 34A | HAYMARKET - 64B | GATESHEAD - 52A | KINGS CROSS - 34A | KINGS CROSS - 34A | KINGS CROSS - 34A | HAYMARKET - 64B |
| Aug-58 | GATESHEAD - 52A | GATESHEAD - 52A | KINGS CROSS - 34A | HAYMARKET - 64B | GATESHEAD - 52A | KINGS CROSS - 34A | KINGS CROSS - 34A | KINGS CROSS - 34A | HAYMARKET - 64B |
| Jan-59 | GATESHEAD - 52A | GATESHEAD - 52A | KINGS CROSS - 34A | HAYMARKET - 64B | GATESHEAD - 52A | KINGS CROSS - 34A | KINGS CROSS - 34A | KINGS CROSS - 34A | HAYMARKET - 64B |
| Aug-59 | GATESHEAD - 52A | GATESHEAD - 52A | KINGS CROSS - 34A | HAYMARKET - 64B | GATESHEAD - 52A | KINGS CROSS - 34A | KINGS CROSS - 34A | KINGS CROSS - 34A | HAYMARKET - 64B |
| Nov-59 | GATESHEAD - 52A | GATESHEAD - 52A | KINGS CROSS - 34A | HAYMARKET - 64B | GATESHEAD - 52A | KINGS CROSS - 34A | KINGS CROSS - 34A | KINGS CROSS - 34A | HAYMARKET - 64B |
| Jan-60 | GATESHEAD - 52A | GATESHEAD - 52A | KINGS CROSS - 34A | HAYMARKET - 64B | GATESHEAD - 52A | KINGS CROSS - 34A | KINGS CROSS - 34A | KINGS CROSS - 34A | HAYMARKET - 64B |
| Apr-60 | GATESHEAD - 52A | GATESHEAD - 52A | KINGS CROSS - 34A | HAYMARKET - 64B | GATESHEAD - 52A | KINGS CROSS - 34A | KINGS CROSS - 34A | KINGS CROSS - 34A | HAYMARKET - 64B |
| Aug-60 | GATESHEAD - 52A | GATESHEAD - 52A | KINGS CROSS - 34A | HAYMARKET - 64B | GATESHEAD - 52A | KINGS CROSS - 34A | KINGS CROSS - 34A | KINGS CROSS - 34A | HAYMARKET - 64B |
| Nov-60 | GATESHEAD - 52A | GATESHEAD - 52A | KINGS CROSS - 34A | HAYMARKET - 64B | GATESHEAD - 52A | KINGS CROSS - 34A | KINGS CROSS - 34A | KINGS CROSS - 34A | HAYMARKET - 64B |

| | 60010 | 60011 | 60012 | 60013 | 60014 | 60015 | 60016 | 60017 | 60018 |
|---|---|---|---|---|---|---|---|---|---|
| Aug-50 | KINGS CROSS - 34A | HAYMARKET - 64B | HAYMARKET - 64B | KINGS CROSS - 34A | KINGS CROSS - 34A | GRANTHAM - 35B | GATESHEAD - 52A | KINGS CROSS - 34A | GATESHEAD - 52A |
| Jan-51 | KINGS CROSS - 34A | HAYMARKET - 64B | HAYMARKET - 64B | KINGS CROSS - 34A | KINGS CROSS - 34A | GRANTHAM - 35B | GATESHEAD - 52A | KINGS CROSS - 34A | GATESHEAD - 52A |
| Aug-51 | KINGS CROSS - 34A | HAYMARKET - 64B | HAYMARKET - 64B | KINGS CROSS - 34A | KINGS CROSS - 34A | **9/51 K.X. - 34A** | GATESHEAD - 52A | KINGS CROSS - 34A | GATESHEAD - 52A |
| Jan-52 | KINGS CROSS - 34A | HAYMARKET - 64B | HAYMARKET - 64B | KINGS CROSS - 34A | KINGS CROSS - 34A | KINGS CROSS - 34A | GATESHEAD - 52A | KINGS CROSS - 34A | GATESHEAD - 52A |
| Aug-52 | KINGS CROSS - 34A | HAYMARKET - 64B | HAYMARKET - 64B | KINGS CROSS - 34A | KINGS CROSS - 34A | KINGS CROSS - 34A | GATESHEAD - 52A | KINGS CROSS - 34A | GATESHEAD - 52A |
| Jan-53 | KINGS CROSS - 34A | HAYMARKET - 64B | HAYMARKET - 64B | KINGS CROSS - 34A | KINGS CROSS - 34A | KINGS CROSS - 34A | GATESHEAD - 52A | KINGS CROSS - 34A | GATESHEAD - 52A |
| Aug-53 | KINGS CROSS - 34A | HAYMARKET - 64B | HAYMARKET - 64B | KINGS CROSS - 34A | KINGS CROSS - 34A | KINGS CROSS - 34A | GATESHEAD - 52A | KINGS CROSS - 34A | GATESHEAD - 52A |
| Jan-54 | KINGS CROSS - 34A | HAYMARKET - 64B | HAYMARKET - 64B | KINGS CROSS - 34A | KINGS CROSS - 34A | KINGS CROSS - 34A | GATESHEAD - 52A | KINGS CROSS - 34A | GATESHEAD - 52A |
| Aug-54 | KINGS CROSS - 34A | HAYMARKET - 64B | HAYMARKET - 64B | KINGS CROSS - 34A | KINGS CROSS - 34A | KINGS CROSS - 34A | GATESHEAD - 52A | KINGS CROSS - 34A | GATESHEAD - 52A |
| Jan-55 | KINGS CROSS - 34A | HAYMARKET - 64B | HAYMARKET - 64B | KINGS CROSS - 34A | KINGS CROSS - 34A | KINGS CROSS - 34A | GATESHEAD - 52A | KINGS CROSS - 34A | GATESHEAD - 52A |
| Aug-55 | KINGS CROSS - 34A | HAYMARKET - 64B | HAYMARKET - 64B | KINGS CROSS - 34A | KINGS CROSS - 34A | KINGS CROSS - 34A | GATESHEAD - 52A | KINGS CROSS - 34A | GATESHEAD - 52A |
| Jan-56 | KINGS CROSS - 34A | HAYMARKET - 64B | HAYMARKET - 64B | KINGS CROSS - 34A | KINGS CROSS - 34A | KINGS CROSS - 34A | GATESHEAD - 52A | KINGS CROSS - 34A | GATESHEAD - 52A |
| Aug-56 | KINGS CROSS - 34A | HAYMARKET - 64B | HAYMARKET - 64B | KINGS CROSS - 34A | KINGS CROSS - 34A | KINGS CROSS - 34A | GATESHEAD - 52A | KINGS CROSS - 34A | GATESHEAD - 52A |
| Jan-57 | **4/57 : GRAN - 35B** | HAYMARKET - 64B | HAYMARKET - 64B | KINGS CROSS - 34A | KINGS CROSS - 34A | KINGS CROSS - 34A | GATESHEAD - 52A | KINGS CROSS - 34A | GATESHEAD - 52A |
| Aug-57 | **9/57 : KX - 34A** | HAYMARKET - 64B | HAYMARKET - 64B | KINGS CROSS - 34A | KINGS CROSS - 34A | KINGS CROSS - 34A | GATESHEAD - 52A | KINGS CROSS - 34A | GATESHEAD - 52A |
| Jan-58 | KINGS CROSS - 34A | HAYMARKET - 64B | HAYMARKET - 64B | KINGS CROSS - 34A | KINGS CROSS - 34A | KINGS CROSS - 34A | GATESHEAD - 52A | KINGS CROSS - 34A | GATESHEAD - 52A |
| Aug-58 | KINGS CROSS - 34A | HAYMARKET - 64B | HAYMARKET - 64B | KINGS CROSS - 34A | KINGS CROSS - 34A | KINGS CROSS - 34A | GATESHEAD - 52A | KINGS CROSS - 34A | GATESHEAD - 52A |
| Jan-59 | KINGS CROSS - 34A | HAYMARKET - 64B | HAYMARKET - 64B | KINGS CROSS - 34A | KINGS CROSS - 34A | KINGS CROSS - 34A | GATESHEAD - 52A | KINGS CROSS - 34A | GATESHEAD - 52A |
| Aug-59 | KINGS CROSS - 34A | HAYMARKET - 64B | HAYMARKET - 64B | KINGS CROSS - 34A | KINGS CROSS - 34A | KINGS CROSS - 34A | GATESHEAD - 52A | KINGS CROSS - 34A | GATESHEAD - 52A |
| Nov-59 | KINGS CROSS - 34A | HAYMARKET - 64B | HAYMARKET - 64B | KINGS CROSS - 34A | KINGS CROSS - 34A | KINGS CROSS - 34A | GATESHEAD - 52A | KINGS CROSS - 34A | GATESHEAD - 52A |
| Jan-60 | KINGS CROSS - 34A | HAYMARKET - 64B | HAYMARKET - 64B | KINGS CROSS - 34A | KINGS CROSS - 34A | KINGS CROSS - 34A | GATESHEAD - 52A | KINGS CROSS - 34A | GATESHEAD - 52A |
| Apr-60 | KINGS CROSS - 34A | HAYMARKET - 64B | HAYMARKET - 64B | KINGS CROSS - 34A | KINGS CROSS - 34A | KINGS CROSS - 34A | GATESHEAD - 52A | KINGS CROSS - 34A | GATESHEAD - 52A |
| Aug-60 | KINGS CROSS - 34A | HAYMARKET - 64B | HAYMARKET - 64B | KINGS CROSS - 34A | KINGS CROSS - 34A | KINGS CROSS - 34A | GATESHEAD - 52A | KINGS CROSS - 34A | GATESHEAD - 52A |
| Nov-60 | KINGS CROSS - 34A | HAYMARKET - 64B | HAYMARKET - 64B | KINGS CROSS - 34A | KINGS CROSS - 34A | KINGS CROSS - 34A | GATESHEAD - 52A | KINGS CROSS - 34A | GATESHEAD - 52A |

| | 60019 | 60020 | 60021 | 60022 | 60023 | 60024 | 60025 | 60026 | 60027 |
|---|---|---|---|---|---|---|---|---|---|
| Aug-50 | GATESHEAD - 52A | GATESHEAD - 52A | KINGS CROSS - 34A | KINGS CROSS - 34A | GATESHEAD - 52A | HAYMARKET - 64B | KINGS CROSS - 34A | GRANTHAM - 35B | HAYMARKET - 64B |
| Jan-51 | GATESHEAD - 52A | GATESHEAD - 52A | KINGS CROSS - 34A | KINGS CROSS - 34A | GATESHEAD - 52A | HAYMARKET - 64B | KINGS CROSS - 34A | GRANTHAM - 35B | HAYMARKET - 64B |
| Aug-51 | GATESHEAD - 52A | GATESHEAD - 52A | KINGS CROSS - 34A | KINGS CROSS - 34A | GATESHEAD - 52A | HAYMARKET - 64B | KINGS CROSS - 34A | **9/51 K.X. - 34A** | HAYMARKET - 64B |
| Jan-52 | GATESHEAD - 52A | GATESHEAD - 52A | KINGS CROSS - 34A | KINGS CROSS - 34A | GATESHEAD - 52A | HAYMARKET - 64B | KINGS CROSS - 34A | KINGS CROSS - 34A | HAYMARKET - 64B |
| Aug-52 | GATESHEAD - 52A | GATESHEAD - 52A | KINGS CROSS - 34A | KINGS CROSS - 34A | GATESHEAD - 52A | HAYMARKET - 64B | KINGS CROSS - 34A | KINGS CROSS - 34A | HAYMARKET - 64B |
| Jan-53 | GATESHEAD - 52A | GATESHEAD - 52A | KINGS CROSS - 34A | KINGS CROSS - 34A | GATESHEAD - 52A | HAYMARKET - 64B | KINGS CROSS - 34A | KINGS CROSS - 34A | HAYMARKET - 64B |
| Aug-53 | GATESHEAD - 52A | GATESHEAD - 52A | KINGS CROSS - 34A | KINGS CROSS - 34A | GATESHEAD - 52A | HAYMARKET - 64B | KINGS CROSS - 34A | KINGS CROSS - 34A | HAYMARKET - 64B |
| Jan-54 | GATESHEAD - 52A | GATESHEAD - 52A | KINGS CROSS - 34A | KINGS CROSS - 34A | GATESHEAD - 52A | HAYMARKET - 64B | KINGS CROSS - 34A | KINGS CROSS - 34A | HAYMARKET - 64B |
| Aug-54 | GATESHEAD - 52A | GATESHEAD - 52A | KINGS CROSS - 34A | KINGS CROSS - 34A | GATESHEAD - 52A | HAYMARKET - 64B | KINGS CROSS - 34A | KINGS CROSS - 34A | HAYMARKET - 64B |
| Jan-55 | GATESHEAD - 52A | GATESHEAD - 52A | KINGS CROSS - 34A | KINGS CROSS - 34A | GATESHEAD - 52A | HAYMARKET - 64B | KINGS CROSS - 34A | KINGS CROSS - 34A | HAYMARKET - 64B |
| Aug-55 | GATESHEAD - 52A | GATESHEAD - 52A | KINGS CROSS - 34A | KINGS CROSS - 34A | GATESHEAD - 52A | HAYMARKET - 64B | KINGS CROSS - 34A | KINGS CROSS - 34A | HAYMARKET - 64B |
| Jan-56 | GATESHEAD - 52A | GATESHEAD - 52A | KINGS CROSS - 34A | KINGS CROSS - 34A | GATESHEAD - 52A | HAYMARKET - 64B | KINGS CROSS - 34A | KINGS CROSS - 34A | HAYMARKET - 64B |
| Aug-56 | GATESHEAD - 52A | GATESHEAD - 52A | KINGS CROSS - 34A | KINGS CROSS - 34A | GATESHEAD - 52A | HAYMARKET - 64B | KINGS CROSS - 34A | KINGS CROSS - 34A | HAYMARKET - 64B |
| Jan-57 | GATESHEAD - 52A | GATESHEAD - 52A | KINGS CROSS - 34A | KINGS CROSS - 34A | GATESHEAD - 52A | HAYMARKET - 64B | KINGS CROSS - 34A | KINGS CROSS - 34A | HAYMARKET - 64B |
| Aug-57 | GATESHEAD - 52A | GATESHEAD - 52A | KINGS CROSS - 34A | KINGS CROSS - 34A | GATESHEAD - 52A | HAYMARKET - 64B | KINGS CROSS - 34A | KINGS CROSS - 34A | HAYMARKET - 64B |
| Jan-58 | GATESHEAD - 52A | GATESHEAD - 52A | KINGS CROSS - 34A | KINGS CROSS - 34A | GATESHEAD - 52A | HAYMARKET - 64B | KINGS CROSS - 34A | KINGS CROSS - 34A | HAYMARKET - 64B |
| Aug-58 | GATESHEAD - 52A | GATESHEAD - 52A | KINGS CROSS - 34A | KINGS CROSS - 34A | GATESHEAD - 52A | HAYMARKET - 64B | KINGS CROSS - 34A | KINGS CROSS - 34A | HAYMARKET - 64B |
| Jan-59 | GATESHEAD - 52A | GATESHEAD - 52A | KINGS CROSS - 34A | KINGS CROSS - 34A | GATESHEAD - 52A | HAYMARKET - 64B | KINGS CROSS - 34A | KINGS CROSS - 34A | HAYMARKET - 64B |
| Aug-59 | GATESHEAD - 52A | GATESHEAD - 52A | KINGS CROSS - 34A | KINGS CROSS - 34A | GATESHEAD - 52A | HAYMARKET - 64B | KINGS CROSS - 34A | KINGS CROSS - 34A | HAYMARKET - 64B |
| Nov-59 | GATESHEAD - 52A | GATESHEAD - 52A | KINGS CROSS - 34A | KINGS CROSS - 34A | GATESHEAD - 52A | HAYMARKET - 64B | KINGS CROSS - 34A | KINGS CROSS - 34A | HAYMARKET - 64B |
| Jan-60 | GATESHEAD - 52A | GATESHEAD - 52A | KINGS CROSS - 34A | KINGS CROSS - 34A | GATESHEAD - 52A | HAYMARKET - 64B | KINGS CROSS - 34A | KINGS CROSS - 34A | HAYMARKET - 64B |
| Apr-60 | GATESHEAD - 52A | GATESHEAD - 52A | KINGS CROSS - 34A | KINGS CROSS - 34A | GATESHEAD - 52A | HAYMARKET - 64B | KINGS CROSS - 34A | KINGS CROSS - 34A | HAYMARKET - 64B |
| Aug-60 | GATESHEAD - 52A | GATESHEAD - 52A | KINGS CROSS - 34A | KINGS CROSS - 34A | GATESHEAD - 52A | HAYMARKET - 64B | KINGS CROSS - 34A | KINGS CROSS - 34A | HAYMARKET - 64B |
| Nov-60 | GATESHEAD - 52A | GATESHEAD - 52A | KINGS CROSS - 34A | KINGS CROSS - 34A | GATESHEAD - 52A | HAYMARKET - 64B | KINGS CROSS - 34A | KINGS CROSS - 34A | HAYMARKET - 64B |

| | 60028 | 60029 | 60030 | 60031 | 60032 | 60033 | 60034 | Double Chimneys | |
|---|---|---|---|---|---|---|---|---|---|
| Aug-50 | KINGS CROSS - 34A | KINGS CROSS - 34A | KINGS CROSS - 34A | HAYMARKET - 64B | KINGS CROSS - 34A | KINGS CROSS - 34A | KINGS CROSS - 34A | 60001 - 4/58 | 60025 - 9/58 |
| Jan-51 | KINGS CROSS - 34A | KINGS CROSS - 34A | KINGS CROSS - 34A | HAYMARKET - 64B | KINGS CROSS - 34A | KINGS CROSS - 34A | KINGS CROSS - 34A | 60002 - 7/57 | 60026 - 8/57 |
| Aug-51 | KINGS CROSS - 34A | KINGS CROSS - 34A | KINGS CROSS - 34A | HAYMARKET - 64B | KINGS CROSS - 34A | KINGS CROSS - 34A | KINGS CROSS - 34A | 60003 - 7/57 | 60027 - 2/58 |
| Jan-52 | KINGS CROSS - 34A | KINGS CROSS - 34A | KINGS CROSS - 34A | HAYMARKET - 64B | KINGS CROSS - 34A | KINGS CROSS - 34A | KINGS CROSS - 34A | 60004 - 12/57 | 60028 - 11/57 |
| Aug-52 | KINGS CROSS - 34A | KINGS CROSS - 34A | KINGS CROSS - 34A | HAYMARKET - 64B | KINGS CROSS - 34A | KINGS CROSS - 34A | KINGS CROSS - 34A | 60005 - 6/38* | 60029 - 10/58 |
| Jan-53 | KINGS CROSS - 34A | KINGS CROSS - 34A | KINGS CROSS - 34A | HAYMARKET - 64B | KINGS CROSS - 34A | KINGS CROSS - 34A | KINGS CROSS - 34A | 60006 - 9/57 | 60030 - 5/58 |
| Aug-53 | KINGS CROSS - 34A | KINGS CROSS - 34A | KINGS CROSS - 34A | HAYMARKET - 64B | KINGS CROSS - 34A | KINGS CROSS - 34A | KINGS CROSS - 34A | 60007 - 12/57 | 60031 - 3/58 |
| Jan-54 | KINGS CROSS - 34A | KINGS CROSS - 34A | KINGS CROSS - 34A | HAYMARKET - 64B | KINGS CROSS - 34A | KINGS CROSS - 34A | KINGS CROSS - 34A | 60008 - 8/58 | 60032 - 11/58 |
| Aug-54 | KINGS CROSS - 34A | KINGS CROSS - 34A | KINGS CROSS - 34A | HAYMARKET - 64B | KINGS CROSS - 34A | KINGS CROSS - 34A | KINGS CROSS - 34A | 60009 - 11/58 | 60033 - 6/38* |
| Jan-55 | KINGS CROSS - 34A | KINGS CROSS - 34A | KINGS CROSS - 34A | HAYMARKET - 64B | KINGS CROSS - 34A | KINGS CROSS - 34A | KINGS CROSS - 34A | 60010 - 12/57 | 60034 - 7/38* |
| Aug-55 | KINGS CROSS - 34A | KINGS CROSS - 34A | KINGS CROSS - 34A | HAYMARKET - 64B | KINGS CROSS - 34A | KINGS CROSS - 34A | KINGS CROSS - 34A | 60011 - 1/58 | **d/c when built* |
| Jan-56 | KINGS CROSS - 34A | KINGS CROSS - 34A | KINGS CROSS - 34A | HAYMARKET - 64B | KINGS CROSS - 34A | KINGS CROSS - 34A | KINGS CROSS - 34A | 60012 - 7/58 | |
| Aug-56 | KINGS CROSS - 34A | KINGS CROSS - 34A | KINGS CROSS - 34A | HAYMARKET - 64B | KINGS CROSS - 34A | KINGS CROSS - 34A | KINGS CROSS - 34A | 60013 - 7/58 | |
| Jan-57 | KINGS CROSS - 34A | KINGS CROSS - 34A | **4/57 : GRAN - 35B** | HAYMARKET - 64B | KINGS CROSS - 34A | KINGS CROSS - 34A | KINGS CROSS - 34A | 60014 - 10/57 | |
| Aug-57 | KINGS CROSS - 34A | KINGS CROSS - 34A | **9/57 : KX - 34A** | HAYMARKET - 64B | KINGS CROSS - 34A | KINGS CROSS - 34A | KINGS CROSS - 34A | 60015 - 8/57 | |
| Jan-58 | KINGS CROSS - 34A | KINGS CROSS - 34A | KINGS CROSS - 34A | HAYMARKET - 64B | KINGS CROSS - 34A | KINGS CROSS - 34A | KINGS CROSS - 34A | 60016 - 6/57 | |
| Aug-58 | KINGS CROSS - 34A | KINGS CROSS - 34A | KINGS CROSS - 34A | HAYMARKET - 64B | KINGS CROSS - 34A | KINGS CROSS - 34A | KINGS CROSS - 34A | 60017 - 5/57 | |
| Jan-59 | KINGS CROSS - 34A | KINGS CROSS - 34A | KINGS CROSS - 34A | HAYMARKET - 64B | KINGS CROSS - 34A | KINGS CROSS - 34A | KINGS CROSS - 34A | 60018 - 10/57 | |
| Aug-59 | KINGS CROSS - 34A | KINGS CROSS - 34A | KINGS CROSS - 34A | HAYMARKET - 64B | KINGS CROSS - 34A | KINGS CROSS - 34A | KINGS CROSS - 34A | 60019 - 9/57 | |
| Nov-59 | KINGS CROSS - 34A | KINGS CROSS - 34A | KINGS CROSS - 34A | HAYMARKET - 64B | KINGS CROSS - 34A | KINGS CROSS - 34A | KINGS CROSS - 34A | 60020 - 11/57 | |
| Jan-60 | KINGS CROSS - 34A | KINGS CROSS - 34A | KINGS CROSS - 34A | HAYMARKET - 64B | KINGS CROSS - 34A | KINGS CROSS - 34A | KINGS CROSS - 34A | 60021 - 4/58 | |
| Apr-60 | KINGS CROSS - 34A | KINGS CROSS - 34A | KINGS CROSS - 34A | HAYMARKET - 64B | KINGS CROSS - 34A | KINGS CROSS - 34A | KINGS CROSS - 34A | 60022 - 3/38* | |
| Aug-60 | KINGS CROSS - 34A | KINGS CROSS - 34A | KINGS CROSS - 34A | HAYMARKET - 64B | KINGS CROSS - 34A | KINGS CROSS - 34A | KINGS CROSS - 34A | 60023 - 9/58 | |
| Nov-60 | KINGS CROSS - 34A | KINGS CROSS - 34A | KINGS CROSS - 34A | HAYMARKET - 64B | KINGS CROSS - 34A | KINGS CROSS - 34A | KINGS CROSS - 34A | 60024 - 8/58 | |

A3 (REBUILD) : 1958

| | 60035 | 60036 | 60037 | 60038 | 60039 | 60040 | 60041 | 60042 | 60043 |
|---|---|---|---|---|---|---|---|---|---|
| Jan-58 | | | | | | | | | |
| Aug-58 | | | | | | | | 9/58: GHD - 52A | |
| Jan-59 | 1/59: HAY - 64B | 11/58: N. HILL - 50B | 10/58: HAY - 64B | | | | | GATESHEAD-52A | 2/59: HAY - 64B |
| Aug-59 | HAYMARKET-64B | NEVILLE HILL-50B | HAYMARKET-64B | | 7/59: KX - 34A | | 7/59: HAY - 64B | GATESHEAD-52A | HAYMARKET-64B |
| Nov-59 | HAYMARKET-64B | NEVILLE HILL-50B | HAYMARKET-64B | 9/59: GHD - 52A | KINGS CROSS-34A | 10/59: GHD - 52A | HAYMARKET-64B | GATESHEAD-52A | HAYMARKET-64B |
| Jan-60 | HAYMARKET-64B | NEVILLE HILL-50B | HAYMARKET-64B | GATESHEAD-52A | KINGS CROSS-34A | 12/59: DARL - 51A | HAYMARKET-64B | GATESHEAD-52A | HAYMARKET-64B |
| Apr-60 | HAYMARKET-64B | NEVILLE HILL-55H | HAYMARKET-64B | 4/60 : HBCK - 55A | KINGS CROSS-34A | DARLINGTON-51A | HAYMARKET-64B | GATESHEAD-52A | HAYMARKET-64B |
| Aug-60 | HAYMARKET-64B | NEVILLE HILL-55H | HAYMARKET-64B | HOLBECK-55A | KINGS CROSS-34A | 8/60: GHD - 52A | 8/60: ST M: 64A | GATESHEAD-52A | HAYMARKET-64B |
| Nov-60 | HAYMARKET-64B | NEVILLE HILL-55H | HAYMARKET-64B | HOLBECK-55A | KINGS CROSS-34A | GATESHEAD-52A | EDINBURGH (SM) - 64A | GATESHEAD-52A | HAYMARKET-64B |

| | 60044 | 60045 | 60046 | 60047 | 60048 | 60049 | 60050 | 60051 | 60052 |
|---|---|---|---|---|---|---|---|---|---|
| Jan-58 | | | | | | | | | |
| Aug-58 | | | 8/58: DCR - 36A | | | | | | |
| Jan-59 | | | DONCASTER-36A | | | 3/59: GRAN - 34F | 4/59: GRAN - 34F | | 11/58: GHD - 52A |
| Aug-59 | 6/59: KX - 34A | | 6/59: GRAN - 34F | 7/59: GRAN - 34F | 5/59: GRAN - 34F | GRANTHAM-34F | GRANTHAM-34F | 8/59: GHD - 52A | GATESHEAD-52A |
| Nov-59 | KINGS CROSS-34A | 10/59: GHD - 52A | GRANTHAM-34F | GRANTHAM-34F | GRANTHAM-34F | GRANTHAM-34F | GRANTHAM-34F | GATESHEAD-52A | GATESHEAD-52A |
| Jan-60 | KINGS CROSS-34A | GATESHEAD-52A | GRANTHAM-34F | GRANTHAM-34F | GRANTHAM-34F | GRANTHAM-34F | GRANTHAM-34F | GATESHEAD-52A | GATESHEAD-52A |
| Apr-60 | KINGS CROSS-34A | GATESHEAD-52A | GRANTHAM-34F | GRANTHAM-34F | GRANTHAM-34F | GRANTHAM-34F | GRANTHAM-34F | GATESHEAD-52A | GATESHEAD-52A |
| Aug-60 | KINGS CROSS-34A | GATESHEAD-52A | GRANTHAM-34F | GRANTHAM-34F | GRANTHAM-34F | GRANTHAM-34F | GRANTHAM-34F | 7/60: DARL - 51A | 7/60: DARL - 51A |
| Nov-60 | KINGS CROSS-34A | GATESHEAD-52A | GRANTHAM-34F | GRANTHAM-34F | GRANTHAM-34F | GRANTHAM-34F | GRANTHAM-34F | DARLINGTON-51A | DARLINGTON-51A |

| | 60053 | 60054 | 60055 | 60056 | 60057 | 60058 | 60059 | 60060 | 60061 |
|---|---|---|---|---|---|---|---|---|---|
| Jan-58 | | | | | | | | | |
| Aug-58 | 11/58: GHD - 52A | 8/58: GRAN - 34F | 6/58: KX - 34A | | 9/58: HAY - 64B | 10/58: GHD - 52A | 7/58: KX - 34A | | 10/58: GRAN - 34F |
| Jan-59 | 12/58: DARL - 51A | GRANTHAM-34F | KINGS CROSS-34A | | HAYMARKET-64B | 11/58: DARL - 51A | KINGS CROSS-34A | 3/59: GHD - 52A | 1/59: DCTR - 36A |
| Aug-59 | 6/59: GHD - 52A | GRANTHAM-34F | KINGS CROSS-34A | 7/59: KX - 34A | HAYMARKET-64B | 6/59: GHD - 52A | KINGS CROSS-34A | GATESHEAD-52A | 4/59: KX - 34A |
| Nov-59 | GATESHEAD-52A | GRANTHAM-34F | KINGS CROSS-34A | KINGS CROSS-34A | HAYMARKET-64B | GATESHEAD-52A | KINGS CROSS-34A | GATESHEAD-52A | 9/59: NEW E - 34E |
| Jan-60 | GATESHEAD-52A | GRANTHAM-34F | KINGS CROSS-34A | KINGS CROSS-34A | HAYMARKET-64B | GATESHEAD-52A | KINGS CROSS-34A | GATESHEAD-52A | 11/59: KX - 34A |
| Apr-60 | GATESHEAD-52A | GRANTHAM-34F | KINGS CROSS-34A | KINGS CROSS-34A | HAYMARKET-64B | GATESHEAD-52A | KINGS CROSS-34A | GATESHEAD-52A | KINGS CROSS-34A |
| Aug-60 | GATESHEAD-52A | GRANTHAM-34F | KINGS CROSS-34A | KINGS CROSS-34A | HAYMARKET-64B | GATESHEAD-52A | KINGS CROSS-34A | GATESHEAD-52A | KINGS CROSS-34A |
| Nov-60 | GATESHEAD-52A | GRANTHAM-34F | KINGS CROSS-34A | KINGS CROSS-34A | HAYMARKET-64B | GATESHEAD-52A | KINGS CROSS-34A | GATESHEAD-52A | KINGS CROSS-34A |

| | 60062 | 60063 | 60064 | 60065 | 60066 | 60067 | 60068 | 60069 | 60070 |
|---|---|---|---|---|---|---|---|---|---|
| Jan-58 | | | | | | | | | |
| Aug-58 | | | | 10/58: GRAN - 34F | 10/58: KX - 34A | | | | |
| Jan-59 | 2/59: KX - 34A | 2/59: GRAN - 34F | | GRANTHAM-34F | 11/58: DCTR - 36A | 4/59: DCR - 36A | 4/59: CAR - 12C | | 4/59: GHD - 52A |
| Aug-59 | KINGS CROSS-34A | GRANTHAM-34F | 6/59: GRAN - 34F | GRANTHAM-34F | 4/59: KX - 34A | 6/59: GRAN - 34F | CARLISLE (C) - 12C | 9/59: TWEED - 52D | 6/59: DARL - 51A |
| Nov-59 | KINGS CROSS-34A | GRANTHAM-34F | GRANTHAM-34F | GRANTHAM-34F | 9/59: NEW E: 34E | 9/59: NEW E: 34E | CARLISLE (C) - 12C | TWEEDMOUTH-52D | DARLINGTON-51A |
| Jan-60 | KINGS CROSS-34A | GRANTHAM-34F | GRANTHAM-34F | GRANTHAM-34F | 10/59: KX - 34A | 10/59: KX - 34A | CARLISLE (C) - 12C | TWEEDMOUTH-52D | 12/59: GHD - 52A |
| Apr-60 | KINGS CROSS-34A | GRANTHAM-34F | GRANTHAM-34F | GRANTHAM-34F | KINGS CROSS-34A | KINGS CROSS-34A | CARLISLE (C) - 12C | TWEEDMOUTH-52D | GATESHEAD-52A |
| Aug-60 | KINGS CROSS-34A | GRANTHAM-34F | GRANTHAM-34F | GRANTHAM-34F | KINGS CROSS-34A | KINGS CROSS-34A | CARLISLE (C) - 12C | 6/60: COP H: 56C | 6/60: COP H: 56C |
| Nov-60 | KINGS CROSS-34A | 11/60: KX - 34A | GRANTHAM-34F | GRANTHAM-34F | KINGS CROSS-34A | KINGS CROSS-34A | CARLISLE (C) - 12C | COPLEY HILL-56C | COPLEY HILL-56C |

| | 60071 | 60072 | 60073 | 60074 | 60075 | 60076 | 60077 | 60078 | 60079 |
|---|---|---|---|---|---|---|---|---|---|
| Jan-58 | | | | | | | | | |
| Aug-58 | 7/58: GHD - 52A | | 8/58: HTN - 52B | | | | | | |
| Jan-59 | GATESHEAD-52A | | HEATON-52B | 3/59: N. HILL - 50B | | | | 2/59: GHD - 52A | |
| Aug-59 | GATESHEAD-52A | 7/59: TWEED - 52D | HEATON-52B | NEVILLE HILL-50B | 8/59: GHD - 52A | 6/59: GHD - 52A | 4/59: HTN - 52B | GATESHEAD-52A | |
| Nov-59 | 12/59: DARL - 51A | TWEEDMOUTH-52D | HEATON-52B | NEVILLE HILL-50B | GATESHEAD-52A | GATESHEAD-52A | HEATON-52B | GATESHEAD-52A | |
| Jan-60 | DARLINGTON-51A | TWEEDMOUTH-52D | HEATON-52B | NEVILLE HILL-50B | GATESHEAD-52A | GATESHEAD-52A | HEATON-52B | GATESHEAD-52A | 1/60: CAR - 12C |
| Apr-60 | DARLINGTON-51A | TWEEDMOUTH-52D | HEATON-52B | NEVILLE HILL-55H | GATESHEAD-52A | GATESHEAD-52A | 3/60: HOLB - 55A | GATESHEAD-52A | CARLISLE (C) - 12C |
| Aug-60 | 7/60: GHD - 52A | 6/60: COP H: 56C | HEATON-52B | NEVILLE HILL-55H | GATESHEAD-52A | GATESHEAD-52A | HOLBECK-55A | GATESHEAD-52A | CARLISLE (C) - 12C |
| Nov-60 | GATESHEAD-52A | COPLEY HILL-56C | HEATON-52B | NEVILLE HILL-55H | GATESHEAD-52A | GATESHEAD-52A | HOLBECK-55A | GATESHEAD-52A | CARLISLE (C) - 12C |

| | 60080 | 60081 | 60082 | 60083 | 60084 | 60085 | 60086 | 60087 | 60088 |
|---|---|---|---|---|---|---|---|---|---|
| Jan-58 | | | | | | | | | |
| Aug-58 | | | | | 7/58: N.HILL - 50B | | | 8/58: HAY - 64B | |
| Jan-59 | | 10/58: N. HILL - 50B | | | NEVILLE HILL-50B | 11/58: HTN - 52B | | HAYMARKET-64B | |
| Aug-59 | | NEVILLE HILL-50B | 9/59: HTN - 52B | 9/59: HTN - 52B | NEVILLE HILL-50B | HEATON-52B | 6/59: N.HILL - 50B | HAYMARKET-64B | 7/59: HTN - 52B |
| Nov-59 | 10/59: HTN - 52B | NEVILLE HILL-50B | HEATON-52B | HEATON-52B | NEVILLE HILL-50B | HEATON-52B | NEVILLE HILL-50B | HAYMARKET-64B | HEATON-52B |
| Jan-60 | HEATON-52B | NEVILLE HILL-50B | HEATON-52B | HEATON-52B | NEVILLE HILL-50B | HEATON-52B | NEVILLE HILL-50B | HAYMARKET-64B | HEATON-52B |
| Apr-60 | 5/60: HOLB - 55A | NEVILLE HILL-55H | 5/60: HOLB - 55A | HEATON-52B | NEVILLE HILL-55H | HEATON-52B | NEVILLE HILL-55H | HAYMARKET-64B | 5/60: HOLB - 55A |
| Aug-60 | HOLBECK-55A | NEVILLE HILL-55H | HOLBECK-55A | HEATON-52B | NEVILLE HILL-55H | HEATON-52B | NEVILLE HILL-55H | 8/60: ST M - 64A | HOLBECK-55A |
| Nov-60 | HOLBECK-55A | NEVILLE HILL-55H | HOLBECK-55A | HEATON-52B | NEVILLE HILL-55H | HEATON-52B | NEVILLE HILL-55H | EDINBURGH (SM) - 64A | HOLBECK-55A |

| | 60089 | 60090 | 60091 | 60092 | 60093 | 60094 | 60095 | 60096 | 60098 |
|---|---|---|---|---|---|---|---|---|---|
| Jan-58 | | | | | | | | | |
| Aug-58 | | 8/58: HAY - 64B | | | | | | 7/58: HAY - 64B | |
| Jan-59 | | HAYMARKET-64B | 3/59: GHD - 52A | | 12/58: CAR - 12C | | 2/59: CAR - 12C | HAYMARKET-64B | |
| Aug-59 | | HAYMARKET-64B | 6/59: DARL - 51A | | CARLISLE (C) - 12C | 8/59: HAY - 64B | CARLISLE (C) - 12C | HAYMARKET-64B | 7/59: HAY - 64B |
| Nov-59 | 10/59: HAY - 64B | HAYMARKET-64B | DARLINGTON-51A | 11/59: HTN - 52B | CARLISLE (C) - 12C | HAYMARKET-64B | CARLISLE (C) - 12C | HAYMARKET-64B | HAYMARKET-64B |
| Jan-60 | HAYMARKET-64B | HAYMARKET-64B | 12/59: GHD - 52A | HEATON-52B | CARLISLE (C) - 12C | HAYMARKET-64B | CARLISLE (C) - 12C | HAYMARKET-64B | HAYMARKET-64B |
| Apr-60 | HAYMARKET-64B | HAYMARKET-64B | GATESHEAD-52A | 5/60: HOLB - 55A | CARLISLE (C) - 12C | HAYMARKET-64B | CARLISLE (C) - 12C | HAYMARKET-64B | HAYMARKET-64B |
| Aug-60 | HAYMARKET-64B | HAYMARKET-64B | GATESHEAD-52A | HOLBECK-55A | CARLISLE (C) - 12C | HAYMARKET-64B | CARLISLE (C) - 12C | HAYMARKET-64B | HAYMARKET-64B |
| Nov-60 | HAYMARKET-64B | HAYMARKET-64B | GATESHEAD-52A | HOLBECK-55A | CARLISLE (C) - 12C | HAYMARKET-64B | CARLISLE (C) - 12C | HAYMARKET-64B | HAYMARKET-64B |

| | 60099 | 60100 | 60101 | 60102 | 60103 | 60104 | 60105 | 60106 | 60107 |
|---|---|---|---|---|---|---|---|---|---|
| Jan-58 | | | | | | | | | |
| Aug-58 | 7/58: HAY - 64B | 9/58: HAY - 64B | | | | | | | |
| Jan-59 | HAYMARKET-64B | HAYMARKET-64B | 2/59: HAY - 64B | 4/59: DCR - 36A | 1/59: KX - 34A | 4/59: DCR - 36A | 3/59: GRAN - 34F | 11/58: GRAN - 34F | |
| Aug-59 | HAYMARKET-64B | HAYMARKET-64B | HAYMARKET-64B | 6/59: GRAN - 34F | KINGS CROSS-34A | 6/59: GRAN - 34F | GRANTHAM-34F | GRANTHAM-34F | 6/59 : GRAN - 34F |
| Nov-59 | HAYMARKET-64B | HAYMARKET-64B | HAYMARKET-64B | GRANTHAM-34F | KINGS CROSS-34A | 10/59: KX - 34A | GRANTHAM-34F | GRANTHAM-34F | GRANTHAM-34F |
| Jan-60 | HAYMARKET-64B | HAYMARKET-64B | HAYMARKET-64B | GRANTHAM-34F | KINGS CROSS-34A | W/D 12/59 | GRANTHAM-34F | GRANTHAM-34F | GRANTHAM-34F |
| Apr-60 | HAYMARKET-64B | HAYMARKET-64B | HAYMARKET-64B | GRANTHAM-34F | KINGS CROSS-34A | | GRANTHAM-34F | GRANTHAM-34F | GRANTHAM-34F |
| Aug-60 | HAYMARKET-64B | HAYMARKET-64B | HAYMARKET-64B | GRANTHAM-34F | KINGS CROSS-34A | | GRANTHAM-34F | GRANTHAM-34F | GRANTHAM-34F |
| Nov-60 | HAYMARKET-64B | HAYMARKET-64B | HAYMARKET-64B | 10/60: KX - 34A | KINGS CROSS-34A | | GRANTHAM-34F | GRANTHAM-34F | 10/60: KX - 34A |

| | 60108 | 60109 | 60110 | 60111 | 60112 |
|---|---|---|---|---|---|
| Jan-58 | | | | | 7/58: DCR - 36A |
| Aug-58 | | | | | DONCASTER-36A |
| Jan-59 | | 3/59: DCR - 36A | 5/59: KX - 34A | 6/59: GRAN - 34F | DONCASTER-36A |
| Aug-59 | 5/59: KX - 34A | 4/59: KX - 34A | KINGS CROSS-34A | GRANTHAM-34F | 6/59: GRAN - 34F |
| Nov-59 | KINGS CROSS-34A | KINGS CROSS-34A | KINGS CROSS-34A | GRANTHAM-34F | GRANTHAM-34F |
| Jan-60 | KINGS CROSS-34A | KINGS CROSS-34A | KINGS CROSS-34A | GRANTHAM-34F | GRANTHAM-34F |
| Apr-60 | KINGS CROSS-34A | KINGS CROSS-34A | KINGS CROSS-34A | GRANTHAM-34F | GRANTHAM-34F |
| Aug-60 | KINGS CROSS-34A | KINGS CROSS-34A | KINGS CROSS-34A | GRANTHAM-34F | GRANTHAM-34F |
| Nov-60 | KINGS CROSS-34A | KINGS CROSS-34A | KINGS CROSS-34A | GRANTHAM-34F | GRANTHAM-34F |

Of the five types of 8P LNER Pacifics (121 locomotives including the W1 4-6-4), the A4's were regarded as a class apart and in spite of the more modern A1 and A2 designs continued as the backbone of east coast haulage until displaced by diesels in the early 1960s. Divided between Kings Cross, Gateshead and Haymarket sheds, it is interesting to note that none were allocated to the Leeds (GN) district although several services between London and Leeds Central were diagrammed to Kings Cross representatives of the class. A further point of interest lies in the parochiality of diagramming – Grantham, Newcastle and Edinburgh were regarded as locomotive staging posts – which resulted in Kings Cross engines being very largely restricted to services between London and Grantham whilst the Gateshead allocation worked either from Newcastle to Grantham or from Newcastle to Edinburgh. Haymarket engines did not normally work south of Newcastle although they could be seen on services from Edinburgh to Glasgow, Dundee and Perth. This policy of engine changing had its roots in post war maintenance difficulties and, apart from a relatively small number of prestige services, remained in force until the arrival of diesels.

In addition to allowing local management to keep a close eye on their engines, the policy also promoted high mileages. Typically a Kings Cross Pacific would perform two return trips between London and Grantham (420 miles) and thus beat the (rather more publicised) 393 daily mileage of the non-stop run to Edinburgh performed during the summer months by engines from Kings Cross and Haymarket sheds. In order to keep the London-based engines

A3 4-6-2 (1922)

| | 60035 | 60036 | 60037 | 60038 | 60039 | 60040 | 60041 | 60042 | 60043 |
|---|---|---|---|---|---|---|---|---|---|
| Aug-50 | HAYMARKET - 64B | NEVILLE HILL - 50B | HAYMARKET - 64B | GATESHEAD - 52A | KINGS CROSS - 34A | GATESHEAD - 52A | HAYMARKET - 64B | GATESHEAD - 52A | HAYMARKET - 64B |
| Jan-51 | HAYMARKET - 64B | NEVILLE HILL - 50B | HAYMARKET - 64B | GATESHEAD - 52A | KINGS CROSS - 34A | GATESHEAD - 52A | HAYMARKET - 64B | GATESHEAD - 52A | HAYMARKET - 64B |
| Aug-51 | HAYMARKET - 64B | NEVILLE HILL - 50B | HAYMARKET - 64B | GATESHEAD - 52A | 9/51: GRAN: 35B | GATESHEAD - 52A | HAYMARKET - 64B | GATESHEAD - 52A | HAYMARKET - 64B |
| Jan-52 | HAYMARKET - 64B | NEVILLE HILL - 50B | HAYMARKET - 64B | GATESHEAD - 52A | GRANTHAM - 35B | GATESHEAD - 52A | HAYMARKET - 64B | GATESHEAD - 52A | HAYMARKET - 64B |
| Aug-52 | HAYMARKET - 64B | NEVILLE HILL - 50B | HAYMARKET - 64B | GATESHEAD - 52A | GRANTHAM - 35B | GATESHEAD - 52A | HAYMARKET - 64B | GATESHEAD - 52A | HAYMARKET - 64B |
| Jan-53 | HAYMARKET - 64B | NEVILLE HILL - 50B | HAYMARKET - 64B | 2/53: DARL - 51A | GRANTHAM - 35B | GATESHEAD - 52A | HAYMARKET - 64B | 3/53: DARL - 51A | HAYMARKET - 64B |
| Aug-53 | HAYMARKET - 64B | NEVILLE HILL - 50B | HAYMARKET - 64B | 8/53: GHD - 52A | GRANTHAM - 35B | GATESHEAD - 52A | HAYMARKET - 64B | DARLINGTON - 51A | HAYMARKET - 64B |
| Jan-54 | HAYMARKET - 64B | NEVILLE HILL - 50B | 3/54: CARL - 68E | GATESHEAD - 52A | GRANTHAM - 35B | 10/53: DARL - 51A | HAYMARKET - 64B | 10/53: GHD - 52A | HAYMARKET - 64B |
| Aug-54 | HAYMARKET - 64B | NEVILLE HILL - 50B | 4/54: HAY - 64B | GATESHEAD - 52A | GRANTHAM - 35B | 3/54: GHD - 52A | HAYMARKET - 64B | 3/54: DARL - 51A | HAYMARKET - 64B |
| Jan-55 | HAYMARKET - 64B | NEVILLE HILL - 50B | HAYMARKET - 64B | GATESHEAD - 52A | GRANTHAM - 35B | GATESHEAD - 52A | HAYMARKET - 64B | 9/54: GHD - 52A | HAYMARKET - 64B |
| Aug-55 | HAYMARKET - 64B | NEVILLE HILL - 50B | HAYMARKET - 64B | GATESHEAD - 52A | GRANTHAM - 35B | 8/55: DARL - 51A | HAYMARKET - 64B | GATESHEAD - 52A | HAYMARKET - 64B |
| Jan-56 | HAYMARKET - 64B | NEVILLE HILL - 50B | HAYMARKET - 64B | GATESHEAD - 52A | GRANTHAM - 35B | 2/56: GHD - 52A | HAYMARKET - 64B | GATESHEAD - 52A | HAYMARKET - 64B |
| Aug-56 | HAYMARKET - 64B | NEVILLE HILL - 50B | HAYMARKET - 64B | 8/56: DARL - 51A | GRANTHAM - 35B | GATESHEAD - 52A | HAYMARKET - 64B | GATESHEAD - 52A | HAYMARKET - 64B |
| Jan-57 | HAYMARKET - 64B | NEVILLE HILL - 50B | HAYMARKET - 64B | 3/57: GHD - 52A | 10/56: LTR - 38C | GATESHEAD - 52A | HAYMARKET - 64B | 11/56: DARL - 51A | HAYMARKET - 64B |
| Aug-57 | HAYMARKET - 64B | NEVILLE HILL - 50B | HAYMARKET - 64B | GATESHEAD - 52A | 4/57: KX - 34A | GATESHEAD - 52A | HAYMARKET - 64B | 5/57: GHD _ 52A | HAYMARKET - 64B |
| Jan-58 | HAYMARKET - 64B | NEVILLE HILL - 50B | HAYMARKET - 64B | GATESHEAD - 52A | KINGS CROSS - 34A | 11/57: DARL - 51A | HAYMARKET - 64B | GATESHEAD - 52A | HAYMARKET - 64B |
| Aug-58 | HAYMARKET - 64B | NEVILLE HILL - 50B | HAYMARKET - 64B | GATESHEAD - 52A | KINGS CROSS - 34A | 5/58: GHD - 52A | HAYMARKET - 64B | R/B 9/58 | HAYMARKET - 64B |
| Jan-59 | R/B 1/59 | R/B 11/58 | R/B 10/58 | GATESHEAD - 52A | KINGS CROSS - 34A | GATESHEAD - 52A | HAYMARKET - 64B | | R/B 2/59 |
| Aug-59 | | | | GATESHEAD - 52A | R/B 7/59 | GATESHEAD - 52A | R/B 7/59 | | |
| Nov-59 | | | | R/B 9/59 | | R/B 10/59 | | | |
| Jan-60 | | | | | | | | | |
| Apr-60 | | | | | | | | | |
| Aug-60 | | | | | | | | | |
| Nov-60 | | | | | | | | | |

| | 60044 | 60045 | 60046 | 60047 | 60048 | 60049 | 60050 | 60051 | 60052 |
|---|---|---|---|---|---|---|---|---|---|
| Aug-50 | COPLEY HILL - 37B | GATESHEAD - 52A | COPLEY HILL - 37B | DONCASTER - 36A | LEICESTER (GC) - 38C | LEICESTER (GC) - 38C | NEASDEN - 34E | NEASDEN - 34E | LEICESTER (GC) - 38C |
| Jan-51 | COPLEY HILL - 37B | GATESHEAD - 52A | COPLEY HILL - 37B | 1/51: KX - 34A | LEICESTER (GC) - 38C | LEICESTER (GC) - 38C | NEASDEN - 34E | NEASDEN - 34E | LEICESTER (GC) - 38C |
| Aug-51 | 9/51: DCTR - 36A | GATESHEAD - 52A | 9/51: DCTR - 36A | 9/51: GRAN: 35B | LEICESTER (GC) - 38C | LEICESTER (GC) - 38C | NEASDEN - 34E | NEASDEN - 34E | LEICESTER (GC) - 38C |
| Jan-52 | DONCASTER - 36A | GATESHEAD - 52A | DONCASTER - 36A | GRANTHAM - 35B | LEICESTER (GC) - 38C | LEICESTER (GC) - 38C | NEASDEN - 34E | NEASDEN - 34E | LEICESTER (GC) - 38C |
| Aug-52 | DONCASTER - 36A | GATESHEAD - 52A | DONCASTER - 36A | GRANTHAM - 35B | LEICESTER (GC) - 38C | LEICESTER (GC) - 38C | NEASDEN - 34E | NEASDEN - 34E | LEICESTER (GC) - 38C |
| Jan-53 | DONCASTER - 36A | GATESHEAD - 52A | DONCASTER - 36A | GRANTHAM - 35B | LEICESTER (GC) - 38C | LEICESTER (GC) - 38C | NEASDEN - 34E | NEASDEN - 34E | LEICESTER (GC) - 38C |
| Aug-53 | DONCASTER - 36A | GATESHEAD - 52A | DONCASTER - 36A | GRANTHAM - 35B | LEICESTER (GC) - 38C | LEICESTER (GC) - 38C | NEASDEN - 34E | NEASDEN - 34E | LEICESTER (GC) - 38C |
| Jan-54 | 12/53: LEIC - 38C | 3/54: DARL - 51A | DONCASTER - 36A | GRANTHAM - 35B | 12/53: DCTR - 36A | LEICESTER (GC) - 38C | NEASDEN - 34E | 12/53: GRAN - 36B | LEICESTER (GC) - 38C |
| Aug-54 | LEICESTER (GC) - 38C | DARLINGTON - 51A | DONCASTER - 36A | 6/54: KX - 34A | DONCASTER - 36A | LEICESTER (GC) - 38C | NEASDEN - 34E | 5/54: C. HILL - 37B | 6/54: NEAS: 34E |
| Jan-55 | LEICESTER (GC) - 38C | 11/54: GHD - 52A | DONCASTER - 36A | 11/54: GRAN - 35B | DONCASTER - 36A | LEICESTER (GC) - 38C | NEASDEN - 34E | COPLEY HILL - 37B | 12/54: LEIC - 38C |
| Aug-55 | 4.55: NEAS - 34E | GATESHEAD - 52A | DONCASTER - 36A | GRANTHAM - 35B | DONCASTER - 36A | 6/55: KX - 34A | 7/55: KX - 34A | COPLEY HILL - 37B | 9/55: C. HILL - 37B |
| Jan-56 | NEASDEN - 34E | 11/55: DARL - 51A | DONCASTER - 36A | GRANTHAM - 35B | DONCASTER - 36A | 11/55: LEIC - 38C | 11/55: NEAS - 34E | COPLEY HILL - 37B | COPLEY HILL - 37B |
| Aug-56 | 3/56: KX - 34A | 5/56: GHD - 52A | DONCASTER - 36A | GRANTHAM - 35B | DONCASTER - 36A | LEICESTER (GC) - 38C | 6/56: KX - 34A | COPLEY HILL - 56C | COPLEY HILL - 56C |
| Jan-57 | 10/56: GRAN - 35B | GATESHEAD - 52A | DONCASTER - 36A | GRANTHAM - 35B | DONCASTER - 36A | LEICESTER (GC) - 38C | 10/56: GRAN - 35B | COPLEY HILL - 56C | COPLEY HILL - 56C |
| Aug-57 | 4/57: KX - 34A | GATESHEAD - 52A | DONCASTER - 36A | GRANTHAM - 35B | DONCASTER - 36A | 9/57: GRAN - 35B | GRANTHAM - 35B | 9/57: HTN - 52B | COPLEY HILL - 56C |
| Jan-58 | KINGS CROSS - 34A | GATESHEAD - 52A | DONCASTER - 36A | GRANTHAM - 35B | DONCASTER - 36A | GRANTHAM - 35B | GRANTHAM - 35B | 1/58: GHD - 52A | 1/58: GHD - 52A |
| Aug-58 | KINGS CROSS - 34A | 5/58: DARL - 51A | R/B 8/58 | GRANTHAM - 34F | 6/58: KX - 34A | GRANTHAM - 34F | GRANTHAM - 34F | 6/58: DARL - 51A | GATESHEAD - 52A |
| Jan-59 | KINGS CROSS - 34A | 11/58: GHD - 52A | | GRANTHAM - 34F | 1/59: GRAN - 34F | R/B 3/59 | R/B 4/59 | 12/58: GHD - 52A | R/B 11/58 |
| Aug-59 | R/B 6/59 | GATESHEAD - 52A | | R/B 7/59 | R/B 5/59 | | | R/B 8/59 | |
| Nov-59 | | R/B 10/59 | | | | | | | |
| Jan-60 | | | | | | | | | |
| Apr-60 | | | | | | | | | |
| Aug-60 | | | | | | | | | |
| Nov-60 | | | | | | | | | |

| | 60053 | 60054 | 60055 | 60056 | 60057 | 60058 | 60059 | 60060 | 60061 |
|---|---|---|---|---|---|---|---|---|---|
| Aug-50 | GRANTHAM - 35B | LEICESTER (GC) - 38C | DONCASTER - 36A | COPLEY HILL - 37B | HAYMARKET - 64B | DONCASTER - 36A | KINGS CROSS - 34A | GATESHEAD - 52A | DONCASTER - 36A |
| Jan-51 | GRANTHAM - 35B | LEICESTER (GC) - 38C | DONCASTER - 36A | COPLEY HILL - 37B | HAYMARKET - 64B | 10/50: KX - 34A | 3/51: LEIC - 38C | GATESHEAD - 52A | 11/50: C. HILL - 37B |
| Aug-51 | GRANTHAM - 35B | LEICESTER (GC) - 38C | DONCASTER - 36A | 9/51: DCTR - 36A | HAYMARKET - 64B | 11/50: DCTR - 36A | LEICESTER (GC) - 38C | GATESHEAD - 52A | 2/51: KX - 34A |
| Jan-52 | GRANTHAM - 35B | LEICESTER (GC) - 38C | DONCASTER - 36A | 10/51: GRAN - 36B | HAYMARKET - 64B | DONCASTER - 36A | LEICESTER (GC) - 38C | 2/52: DARL - 51A | KINGS CROSS - 34A |
| Aug-52 | GRANTHAM - 35B | LEICESTER (GC) - 38C | DONCASTER - 36A | 6/52: DCTR - 36A | HAYMARKET - 64B | DONCASTER - 36A | LEICESTER (GC) - 38C | 9/52: GHD - 52A | KINGS CROSS - 34A |
| Jan-53 | GRANTHAM - 35B | LEICESTER (GC) - 38C | DONCASTER - 36A | 7/52: KX - 34A | HAYMARKET - 64B | DONCASTER - 36A | LEICESTER (GC) - 38C | GATESHEAD - 52A | 2/53: GRAN - 36B |
| Aug-53 | GRANTHAM - 35B | LEICESTER (GC) - 38C | DONCASTER - 36A | 2/53: GRAN - 36B | HAYMARKET - 64B | DONCASTER - 36A | LEICESTER (GC) - 38C | GATESHEAD - 52A | GRANTHAM - 35B |
| Jan-54 | GRANTHAM - 35B | LEICESTER (GC) - 38C | DONCASTER - 36A | GRANTHAM - 35B | HAYMARKET - 64B | DONCASTER - 36A | LEICESTER (GC) - 38C | GATESHEAD - 52A | GRANTHAM - 35B |
| Aug-54 | 5/54: C. HILL - 37B | LEICESTER (GC) - 38C | DONCASTER - 36A | GRANTHAM - 35B | HAYMARKET - 64B | 6/54: C.HILL - 37B | LEICESTER (GC) - 38C | GATESHEAD - 52A | 8/54: KX - 34A |
| Jan-55 | COPLEY HILL - 37B | LEICESTER (GC) - 38C | DONCASTER - 36A | GRANTHAM - 35B | HAYMARKET - 64B | COPLEY HILL - 37B | LEICESTER (GC) - 38C | GATESHEAD - 52A | 11/54: GRAN - 35B |
| Aug-55 | COPLEY HILL - 37B | LEICESTER (GC) - 38C | DONCASTER - 36A | GRANTHAM - 35B | HAYMARKET - 64B | COPLEY HILL - 37B | LEICESTER (GC) - 38C | 5/55: DARL - 51A | GRANTHAM - 35B |
| Jan-56 | COPLEY HILL - 37B | LEICESTER (GC) - 38C | DONCASTER - 36A | GRANTHAM - 35B | HAYMARKET - 64B | COPLEY HILL - 37B | LEICESTER (GC) - 38C | 10/55: GHD - 52A | GRANTHAM - 35B |
| Aug-56 | COPLEY HILL - 56C | 6/56: KX - 34A | 6/56: KX - 34A | 6/56: KX - 34A | HAYMARKET - 64B | COPLEY HILL - 56C | LEICESTER (GC) - 38C | GATESHEAD - 52A | GRANTHAM - 35B |
| Jan-57 | COPLEY HILL - 56C | KINGS CROSS - 34A | KINGS CROSS - 34A | KINGS CROSS - 34A | HAYMARKET - 64B | COPLEY HILL - 56C | LEICESTER (GC) - 38C | GATESHEAD - 52A | GRANTHAM - 35B |
| Aug-57 | 9/57: GHD - 52A | 6/57: GRAN - 35B | KINGS CROSS - 34A | KINGS CROSS - 34A | HAYMARKET - 64B | 9/57: GHD - 52A | 4/57: KX - 34A | 6/57: DARL - 51A | GRANTHAM - 35B |
| Jan-58 | GATESHEAD - 52A | GRANTHAM - 35B | KINGS CROSS - 34A | KINGS CROSS - 34A | HAYMARKET - 64B | GATESHEAD - 52A | KINGS CROSS - 34A | 12/57: GHD - 52A | GRANTHAM - 35B |
| Aug-58 | R/B 11/58 | R/B 8/58 | R/B 6/58 | KINGS CROSS - 34A | R/B 9/58 | R/B 10/58 | R/B 7/58 | GATESHEAD - 52A | R/B 10/58 |
| Jan-59 | | | | KINGS CROSS - 34A | | | | R/B 3/59 | |
| Aug-59 | | | | R/B 7/59 | | | | | |
| Nov-59 | | | | | | | | | |
| Jan-60 | | | | | | | | | |
| Apr-60 | | | | | | | | | |
| Aug-60 | | | | | | | | | |
| Nov-60 | | | | | | | | | |

| | 60062 | 60063 | 60064 | 60065 | 60066 | 60067 | 60068 | 60069 | 60070 |
|---|---|---|---|---|---|---|---|---|---|
| Aug-50 | COPLEY HILL - 37B | KINGS CROSS - 34A | DONCASTER - 36A | KINGS CROSS - 34A | DONCASTER - 36A | KINGS CROSS - 34A | CARLISLE (C) - 12B | HEATON - 52B | DARLINGTON - 51A |
| Jan-51 | COPLEY HILL - 37B | KINGS CROSS - 34A | DONCASTER - 36A | KINGS CROSS - 34A | 10/50: KX - 34A | KINGS CROSS - 34A | CARLISLE (C) - 12B | HEATON - 52B | DARLINGTON - 51A |
| Aug-51 | 9/51: DCTR - 36A | 9/51: GRAN - 35B | DONCASTER - 36A | 9/51: GRAN - 35B | 11/50: DCTR - 36A | 9/51: GRAN - 35B | CARLISLE (C) - 68E | HEATON - 52B | DARLINGTON - 51A |
| Jan-52 | DONCASTER - 36A | GRANTHAM - 35B | DONCASTER - 36A | GRANTHAM - 35B | DONCASTER - 36A | 6/52: DCTR - 36A | CARLISLE (C) - 68E | HEATON - 52B | 2/52: GHD - 52A |
| Aug-52 | DONCASTER - 36A | GRANTHAM - 35B | DONCASTER - 36A | GRANTHAM - 35B | DONCASTER - 36A | 7/52: KX - 34A | CARLISLE (C) - 68E | HEATON - 52B | GATESHEAD - 52A |
| Jan-53 | 2/53: GRAN - 35B | 2/53: NEAS - 34E | DONCASTER - 36A | GRANTHAM - 35B | DONCASTER - 36A | KINGS CROSS - 34A | CARLISLE (C) - 68E | HEATON - 52B | GATESHEAD - 52A |
| Aug-53 | GRANTHAM - 35B | NEASDEN - 34E | DONCASTER - 36A | GRANTHAM - 35B | DONCASTER - 36A | KINGS CROSS - 34A | CARLISLE (C) - 68E | HEATON - 52B | 8/53: DARL - 51A |
| Jan-54 | 11/53: KX - 34A | NEASDEN - 34E | DONCASTER - 36A | GRANTHAM - 35B | DONCASTER - 36A | 11/53: DCTR - 36A | CARLISLE (C) - 68E | HEATON - 52B | DARLINGTON - 51A |
| Aug-54 | KINGS CROSS - 34A | NEASDEN - 34E | DONCASTER - 36A | GRANTHAM - 35B | DONCASTER - 36A | DONCASTER - 36A | CARLISLE (C) - 68E | HEATON - 52B | 3/54: GHD - 52A |
| Jan-55 | KINGS CROSS - 34A | 3/55: KX - 34A | DONCASTER - 36A | GRANTHAM - 35B | DONCASTER - 36A | DONCASTER - 36A | CARLISLE (C) - 68E | HEATON - 52B | GATESHEAD - 52A |
| Aug-55 | KINGS CROSS - 34A | KINGS CROSS - 34A | DONCASTER - 36A | GRANTHAM - 35B | DONCASTER - 36A | DONCASTER - 36A | CARLISLE (C) - 68E | HEATON - 52B | GATESHEAD - 52A |
| Jan-56 | KINGS CROSS - 34A | 3/56: NEAS - 34E | DONCASTER - 36A | GRANTHAM - 35B | DONCASTER - 36A | DONCASTER - 36A | CARLISLE (C) - 68E | HEATON - 52B | GATESHEAD - 52A |
| Aug-56 | KINGS CROSS - 34A | 6/56: KX - 34A | DONCASTER - 36A | GRANTHAM - 35B | 8/56: DCTR - 36A | DONCASTER - 36A | CARLISLE (C) - 68E | HEATON - 52B | GATESHEAD - 52A |
| Jan-57 | KINGS CROSS - 34A | 10/56: GRAN - 35B | DONCASTER - 36A | GRANTHAM - 35B | DONCASTER - 36A | DONCASTER - 36A | CARLISLE (C) - 68E | HEATON - 52B | GATESHEAD - 52A |
| Aug-57 | KINGS CROSS - 34A | GRANTHAM - 35B | DONCASTER - 36A | GRANTHAM - 35B | 6/57: KX - 34A | DONCASTER - 36A | CARLISLE (C) - 68E | HEATON - 52B | 5/57: DARL - 51A |
| Jan-58 | KINGS CROSS - 34A | GRANTHAM - 35B | DONCASTER - 36A | GRANTHAM - 35B | KINGS CROSS - 34A | DONCASTER - 36A | CARLISLE (C) - 68E | HEATON - 52B | 11/57: GHD - 52A |
| Aug-58 | KINGS CROSS - 34A | GRANTHAM - 34F | DONCASTER - 36A | GRANTHAM - 34F | KINGS CROSS - 34A | DONCASTER - 36A | CARLISLE (C) - 12C | 9/58: TWEED - 52D | GATESHEAD - 52A |
| Jan-59 | R/B 2/59 | R/B 2/59 | DONCASTER - 36A | R/B 10/58 | R/B 10/58 | R/B 4/59 | R/B 4/59 | TWEEDMOUTH - 52D | R/B 4/59 |
| Aug-59 | | | R/B 6/59 | | | | | R/B 9/59 | |
| Nov-59 | | | | | | | | | |
| Jan-60 | | | | | | | | | |
| Apr-60 | | | | | | | | | |
| Aug-60 | | | | | | | | | |
| Nov-60 | | | | | | | | | |

fully occupied some of the Grantham trips had to include the stopping trains, a facility that allowed penurious enthusiasts living at places such as St Neots to sample the best of east coast motive power for the price of a return ticket to Sandy or Huntingdon. Nowhere else in the country could such lordly engines be found on such lowly duties.

Second fiddle to the A4's was played by the A1 locomotives which could be found all over the system and especially on the Leeds – Kings Cross workings which tended to be monopolised by Copley Hill shed. The allocation of Pacific engines to the Leeds (GN) area was a post-war innovation since for much of its history Wakefield viaduct had restricted the passage of 4-6-2's whilst at the same time most of the London – Leeds trains ran as expresses

| | 60071 | 60072 | 60073 | 60074 | 60075 | 60076 | 60077 | 60078 | 60079 |
|---|---|---|---|---|---|---|---|---|---|
| Aug-50 | GATESHEAD - 52A | HEATON - 52B | HEATON - 52B | NEVILLE HILL - 50B | GATESHEAD - 52A | DARLINGTON - 51A | HEATON - 52B | GATESHEAD - 52A | CARLISLE (C) - 12B |
| Jan-51 | GATESHEAD - 52A | HEATON - 52B | HEATON - 52B | **11/50 : YORK : 50A** | GATESHEAD - 52A | DARLINGTON - 51A | HEATON - 52B | GATESHEAD - 52A | CARLISLE (C) - 12B |
| Aug-51 | GATESHEAD - 52A | HEATON - 52B | HEATON - 52B | **12/50 : N. HILL - 50B** | GATESHEAD - 52A | DARLINGTON - 51A | HEATON - 52B | GATESHEAD - 52A | CARLISLE (C) - 68E |
| Jan-52 | **2/52: DARL - 51A** | HEATON - 52B | HEATON - 52B | NEVILLE HILL - 50B | GATESHEAD - 52A | **2/52: GHD - 52A** | HEATON - 52B | GATESHEAD - 52A | CARLISLE (C) - 68E |
| Aug-52 | **3/52: GHD - 52A** | HEATON - 52B | HEATON - 52B | NEVILLE HILL - 50B | **9/52: DARL - 51A** | **3/52: DARL - 51A** | HEATON - 52B | GATESHEAD - 52A | CARLISLE (C) - 68E |
| Jan-53 | GATESHEAD - 52A | HEATON - 52B | HEATON - 52B | NEVILLE HILL - 50B | **2/53: GHD - 52A** | **10/52: GHD - 52A** | HEATON - 52B | GATESHEAD - 52A | CARLISLE (C) - 68E |
| Aug-53 | GATESHEAD - 52A | HEATON - 52B | HEATON - 52B | NEVILLE HILL - 50B | GATESHEAD - 52A | GATESHEAD - 52A | HEATON - 52B | GATESHEAD - 52A | CARLISLE (C) - 68E |
| Jan-54 | GATESHEAD - 52A | HEATON - 52B | HEATON - 52B | NEVILLE HILL - 50B | GATESHEAD - 52A | GATESHEAD - 52A | HEATON - 52B | GATESHEAD - 52A | CARLISLE (C) - 68E |
| Aug-54 | **9/54: DARL - 51A** | HEATON - 52B | HEATON - 52B | NEVILLE HILL - 50B | GATESHEAD - 52A | GATESHEAD - 52A | HEATON - 52B | GATESHEAD - 52A | CARLISLE (C) - 68E |
| Jan-55 | **2/55: GHD - 52A** | HEATON - 52B | HEATON - 52B | NEVILLE HILL - 50B | **11/54: DARL - 51A** | GATESHEAD - 52A | HEATON - 52B | **2/55: DARL - 51A** | CARLISLE (C) - 68E |
| Aug-55 | **5/56: DARL - 51A** | HEATON - 52B | HEATON - 52B | NEVILLE HILL - 50B | **5/55: GHD - 52A** | GATESHEAD - 52A | HEATON - 52B | **8/55: GHD - 52A** | CARLISLE (C) - 68E |
| Jan-56 | DARLINGTON - 51A | HEATON - 52B | HEATON - 52B | NEVILLE HILL - 50B | GATESHEAD - 52A | **2/56: DARL - 51A** | HEATON - 52B | GATESHEAD - 52A | CARLISLE (C) - 68E |
| Aug-56 | **11/56: GHD - 52A** | HEATON - 52B | HEATON - 52B | NEVILLE HILL - 50B | GATESHEAD - 52A | **8/56: GHD - 52A** | HEATON - 52B | GATESHEAD - 52A | CARLISLE (C) - 68E |
| Jan-57 | **3/57: DARL - 51A** | HEATON - 52B | HEATON - 52B | NEVILLE HILL - 50B | GATESHEAD - 52A | GATESHEAD - 52A | HEATON - 52B | GATESHEAD - 52A | CARLISLE (C) - 68E |
| Aug-57 | **6/57: GHD - 52A** | HEATON - 52B | HEATON - 52B | NEVILLE HILL - 50B | GATESHEAD - 52A | GATESHEAD - 52A | HEATON - 52B | GATESHEAD - 52A | CARLISLE (C) - 68E |
| Jan-58 | GATESHEAD - 52A | HEATON - 52B | HEATON - 52B | NEVILLE HILL - 50B | GATESHEAD - 52A | **12/57: DARL - 51A** | HEATON - 52B | **R/B 2/59** | CARLISLE (C) - 68E |
| Aug-58 | **R/B 7/58** | **9/58:TWEED - 52D** | **R/B 8/58** | NEVILLE HILL - 50B | GATESHEAD - 52A | **6/58: GHD - 52A** | HEATON - 52B | | CARLISLE (C) - 12C |
| Jan-59 | | TWEEDMOUTH - 52D | | **R/B 3/59** | GATESHEAD - 52A | GATESHEAD - 52A | HEATON - 52B | | CARLISLE (C) - 12C |
| Aug-59 | | **R/B 7/59** | | | **R/B 8/59** | **R/B 6/59** | **R/B 4/59** | | CARLISLE (C) - 12C |
| Nov-59 | | | | | | | | | CARLISLE (C) - 12C |
| Jan-60 | | | | | | | | | **R/B 1/60** |
| Apr-60 | | | | | | | | | |
| Aug-60 | | | | | | | | | |
| Nov-60 | | | | | | | | | |

| | 60080 | 60081 | 60082 | 60083 | 60084 | 60085 | 60086 | 60087 | 60088 |
|---|---|---|---|---|---|---|---|---|---|
| Aug-50 | HEATON - 52B | NEVILLE HILL - 50B | GATESHEAD - 52A | HEATON - 52B | NEVILLE HILL - 50B | HEATON - 52B | NEVILLE HILL - 50B | HAYMARKET - 64B | HEATON - 52B |
| Jan-51 | HEATON - 52B | NEVILLE HILL - 50B | GATESHEAD - 52A | HEATON - 52B | NEVILLE HILL - 50B | HEATON - 52B | NEVILLE HILL - 50B | HAYMARKET - 64B | HEATON - 52B |
| Aug-51 | HEATON - 52B | NEVILLE HILL - 50B | GATESHEAD - 52A | HEATON - 52B | NEVILLE HILL - 50B | HEATON - 52B | NEVILLE HILL - 50B | HAYMARKET - 64B | HEATON - 52B |
| Jan-52 | HEATON - 52B | NEVILLE HILL - 50B | GATESHEAD - 52A | HEATON - 52B | NEVILLE HILL - 50B | HEATON - 52B | NEVILLE HILL - 50B | HAYMARKET - 64B | HEATON - 52B |
| Aug-52 | HEATON - 52B | NEVILLE HILL - 50B | **10/52: DARL: 51A** | HEATON - 52B | NEVILLE HILL - 50B | HEATON - 52B | NEVILLE HILL - 50B | HAYMARKET - 64B | HEATON - 52B |
| Jan-53 | HEATON - 52B | NEVILLE HILL - 50B | **3/53: GHD - 52A** | HEATON - 52B | NEVILLE HILL - 50B | HEATON - 52B | NEVILLE HILL - 50B | HAYMARKET - 64B | HEATON - 52B |
| Aug-53 | HEATON - 52B | NEVILLE HILL - 50B | GATESHEAD - 52A | HEATON - 52B | NEVILLE HILL - 50B | HEATON - 52B | NEVILLE HILL - 50B | HAYMARKET - 64B | HEATON - 52B |
| Jan-54 | HEATON - 52B | NEVILLE HILL - 50B | GATESHEAD - 52A | HEATON - 52B | NEVILLE HILL - 50B | HEATON - 52B | NEVILLE HILL - 50B | HAYMARKET - 64B | HEATON - 52B |
| Aug-54 | HEATON - 52B | NEVILLE HILL - 50B | GATESHEAD - 52A | HEATON - 52B | NEVILLE HILL - 50B | HEATON - 52B | NEVILLE HILL - 50B | HAYMARKET - 64B | HEATON - 52B |
| Jan-55 | HEATON - 52B | NEVILLE HILL - 50B | GATESHEAD - 52A | HEATON - 52B | NEVILLE HILL - 50B | HEATON - 52B | NEVILLE HILL - 50B | HAYMARKET - 64B | HEATON - 52B |
| Aug-55 | HEATON - 52B | NEVILLE HILL - 50B | GATESHEAD - 52A | HEATON - 52B | NEVILLE HILL - 50B | HEATON - 52B | NEVILLE HILL - 50B | HAYMARKET - 64B | HEATON - 52B |
| Jan-56 | HEATON - 52B | NEVILLE HILL - 50B | GATESHEAD - 52A | HEATON - 52B | NEVILLE HILL - 50B | HEATON - 52B | NEVILLE HILL - 50B | HAYMARKET - 64B | HEATON - 52B |
| Aug-56 | HEATON - 52B | NEVILLE HILL - 50B | **5/56: HTN: 52B** | HEATON - 52B | NEVILLE HILL - 50B | HEATON - 52B | NEVILLE HILL - 50B | HAYMARKET - 64B | HEATON - 52B |
| Jan-57 | HEATON - 52B | NEVILLE HILL - 50B | HEATON - 52B | HEATON - 52B | NEVILLE HILL - 50B | HEATON - 52B | NEVILLE HILL - 50B | HAYMARKET - 64B | HEATON - 52B |
| Aug-57 | HEATON - 52B | NEVILLE HILL - 50B | HEATON - 52B | HEATON - 52B | NEVILLE HILL - 50B | HEATON - 52B | NEVILLE HILL - 50B | HAYMARKET - 64B | HEATON - 52B |
| Jan-58 | HEATON - 52B | NEVILLE HILL - 50B | HEATON - 52B | HEATON - 52B | NEVILLE HILL - 50B | HEATON - 52B | NEVILLE HILL - 50B | HAYMARKET - 64B | HEATON - 52B |
| Aug-58 | HEATON - 52B | NEVILLE HILL - 50B | HEATON - 52B | HEATON - 52B | **R/B 7/58** | HEATON - 52B | NEVILLE HILL - 50B | **R/B 8/58** | HEATON - 52B |
| Jan-59 | HEATON - 52B | **R/B 10/58** | HEATON - 52B | HEATON - 52B | | **R/B 11/58** | NEVILLE HILL - 50B | | HEATON - 52B |
| Aug-59 | HEATON - 52B | | HEATON - 52B | HEATON - 52B | | | **R/B 6/59** | | **R/B 7/59** |
| Nov-59 | **R/B 10/59** | | **R/B 9/59** | **R/B 9/59** | | | | | |
| Jan-60 | | | | | | | | | |
| Apr-60 | | | | | | | | | |
| Aug-60 | | | | | | | | | |
| Nov-60 | | | | | | | | | |

| | 60089 | 60090 | 60091 | 60092 | 60093 | 60094 | 60095 | 60096 | 60097 |
|---|---|---|---|---|---|---|---|---|---|
| Aug-50 | KINGS CROSS - 34A | HAYMARKET - 64B | HEATON - 52B | HEATON - 52B | CARLISLE (C) - 12B | HAYMARKET - 64B | CARLISLE (C) - 12B | HAYMARKET - 64B | HAYMARKET - 64B |
| Jan-51 | **2/51: HMKT - 64B** | HAYMARKET - 64B | HEATON - 52B | HEATON - 52B | CARLISLE (C) - 12B | HAYMARKET - 64B | CARLISLE (C) - 12B | HAYMARKET - 64B | HAYMARKET - 64B |
| Aug-51 | HAYMARKET - 64B | HAYMARKET - 64B | HEATON - 52B | HEATON - 52B | CARLISLE (C) - 68E | HAYMARKET - 64B | CARLISLE (C) - 68E | HAYMARKET - 64B | HAYMARKET - 64B |
| Jan-52 | HAYMARKET - 64B | HAYMARKET - 64B | HEATON - 52B | HEATON - 52B | CARLISLE (C) - 68E | HAYMARKET - 64B | CARLISLE (C) - 68E | HAYMARKET - 64B | HAYMARKET - 64B |
| Aug-52 | HAYMARKET - 64B | HAYMARKET - 64B | HEATON - 52B | HEATON - 52B | CARLISLE (C) - 68E | HAYMARKET - 64B | CARLISLE (C) - 68E | HAYMARKET - 64B | HAYMARKET - 64B |
| Jan-53 | HAYMARKET - 64B | HAYMARKET - 64B | HEATON - 52B | HEATON - 52B | CARLISLE (C) - 68E | HAYMARKET - 64B | CARLISLE (C) - 68E | HAYMARKET - 64B | HAYMARKET - 64B |
| Aug-53 | HAYMARKET - 64B | HAYMARKET - 64B | HEATON - 52B | HEATON - 52B | CARLISLE (C) - 68E | HAYMARKET - 64B | CARLISLE (C) - 68E | HAYMARKET - 64B | **1/54: CARLISLE - 68E** |
| Jan-54 | HAYMARKET - 64B | HAYMARKET - 64B | HEATON - 52B | HEATON - 52B | CARLISLE (C) - 68E | HAYMARKET - 64B | CARLISLE (C) - 68E | HAYMARKET - 64B | **2/54: HMKT - 64B** |
| Aug-54 | HAYMARKET - 64B | HAYMARKET - 64B | HEATON - 52B | HEATON - 52B | CARLISLE (C) - 68E | HAYMARKET - 64B | CARLISLE (C) - 68E | HAYMARKET - 64B | HAYMARKET - 64B |
| Jan-55 | HAYMARKET - 64B | HAYMARKET - 64B | HEATON - 52B | HEATON - 52B | CARLISLE (C) - 68E | HAYMARKET - 64B | CARLISLE (C) - 68E | HAYMARKET - 64B | HAYMARKET - 64B |
| Aug-55 | HAYMARKET - 64B | HAYMARKET - 64B | HEATON - 52B | HEATON - 52B | CARLISLE (C) - 68E | HAYMARKET - 64B | CARLISLE (C) - 68E | HAYMARKET - 64B | HAYMARKET - 64B |
| Jan-56 | HAYMARKET - 64B | HAYMARKET - 64B | HEATON - 52B | HEATON - 52B | CARLISLE (C) - 68E | HAYMARKET - 64B | CARLISLE (C) - 68E | HAYMARKET - 64B | HAYMARKET - 64B |
| Aug-56 | HAYMARKET - 64B | HAYMARKET - 64B | HEATON - 52B | HEATON - 52B | CARLISLE (C) - 68E | HAYMARKET - 64B | CARLISLE (C) - 68E | HAYMARKET - 64B | HAYMARKET - 64B |
| Jan-57 | HAYMARKET - 64B | HAYMARKET - 64B | HEATON - 52B | HEATON - 52B | CARLISLE (C) - 68E | HAYMARKET - 64B | CARLISLE (C) - 68E | HAYMARKET - 64B | HAYMARKET - 64B |
| Aug-57 | HAYMARKET - 64B | HAYMARKET - 64B | HEATON - 52B | HEATON - 52B | CARLISLE (C) - 68E | HAYMARKET - 64B | CARLISLE (C) - 68E | HAYMARKET - 64B | HAYMARKET - 64B |
| Jan-58 | HAYMARKET - 64B | HAYMARKET - 64B | HEATON - 52B | HEATON - 52B | CARLISLE (C) - 68E | HAYMARKET - 64B | CARLISLE (C) - 68E | HAYMARKET - 64B | HAYMARKET - 64B |
| Aug-58 | HAYMARKET - 64B | **R/B 8/58** | **7/58: GHD - 52A** | HEATON - 52B | CARLISLE (C) - 12C | HAYMARKET - 64B | CARLISLE (C) - 12C | **R/B 7/58** | HAYMARKET - 64B |
| Jan-59 | HAYMARKET - 64B | | **R/B 3/59** | HEATON - 52B | **R/B 12/58** | HAYMARKET - 64B | **R/B 2/59** | | HAYMARKET - 64B |
| Aug-59 | HAYMARKET - 64B | | | HEATON - 52B | | **R/B 8/59** | | | HAYMARKET - 64B |
| Nov-59 | **R/B 10/59** | | | **R/B 11/59** | | | | | HAYMARKET - 64B |
| Jan-60 | | | | | | | | | HAYMARKET - 64B |
| Apr-60 | | | | | | | | | HAYMARKET - 64B |
| Aug-60 | | | | | | | | | HAYMARKET - 64B |
| Nov-60 | | | | | | | | | HAYMARKET - 64B |

| | 60098 | 60099 | 60100 | 60101 | 60102 | 60103 | 60104 | 60105 | 60106 |
|---|---|---|---|---|---|---|---|---|---|
| Aug-50 | HAYMARKET - 64B | HAYMARKET - 64B | HAYMARKET - 64B | HAYMARKET - 64B | LEICESTER (GC) - 38C | LEICESTER (GC) - 38C | LEICESTER (GC) - 38C | KINGS CROSS - 34A | GRANTHAM - 35B |
| Jan-51 | HAYMARKET - 64B | HAYMARKET - 64B | HAYMARKET - 64B | HAYMARKET - 64B | LEICESTER (GC) - 38C | LEICESTER (GC) - 38C | LEICESTER (GC) - 38C | KINGS CROSS - 34A | GRANTHAM - 35B |
| Aug-51 | HAYMARKET - 64B | HAYMARKET - 64B | HAYMARKET - 64B | HAYMARKET - 64B | LEICESTER (GC) - 38C | LEICESTER (GC) - 38C | LEICESTER (GC) - 38C | **9/51 : GRAN - 35B** | GRANTHAM - 35B |
| Jan-52 | HAYMARKET - 64B | HAYMARKET - 64B | HAYMARKET - 64B | HAYMARKET - 64B | LEICESTER (GC) - 38C | LEICESTER (GC) - 38C | LEICESTER (GC) - 38C | GRANTHAM - 35B | GRANTHAM - 35B |
| Aug-52 | HAYMARKET - 64B | HAYMARKET - 64B | HAYMARKET - 64B | HAYMARKET - 64B | LEICESTER (GC) - 38C | LEICESTER (GC) - 38C | LEICESTER (GC) - 38C | GRANTHAM - 35B | GRANTHAM - 35B |
| Jan-53 | HAYMARKET - 64B | HAYMARKET - 64B | HAYMARKET - 64B | HAYMARKET - 64B | LEICESTER (GC) - 38C | LEICESTER (GC) - 38C | LEICESTER (GC) - 38C | GRANTHAM - 35B | **2/53: KX - 34A** |
| Aug-53 | HAYMARKET - 64B | HAYMARKET - 64B | HAYMARKET - 64B | HAYMARKET - 64B | LEICESTER (GC) - 38C | LEICESTER (GC) - 38C | LEICESTER (GC) - 38C | GRANTHAM - 35B | KINGS CROSS - 34A |
| Jan-54 | HAYMARKET - 64B | HAYMARKET - 64B | HAYMARKET - 64B | HAYMARKET - 64B | LEICESTER (GC) - 38C | **12/53: GRAN - 35B** | LEICESTER (GC) - 38C | GRANTHAM - 35B | **11/53: GRAN - 35B** |
| Aug-54 | HAYMARKET - 64B | HAYMARKET - 64B | HAYMARKET - 64B | HAYMARKET - 64B | **6/54: NEAS - 34E** | **6/54: KX - 34A** | **6/54: NEAS - 34E** | GRANTHAM - 35B | **5/54: C. HILL - 37B** |
| Jan-55 | HAYMARKET - 64B | HAYMARKET - 64B | HAYMARKET - 64B | HAYMARKET - 64B | **12/54: LEIC - 38C** | **8/54: GRAN - 35B** | **1/55: LEIC - 38C** | GRANTHAM - 35B | COPLEY HILL - 37B |
| Aug-55 | HAYMARKET - 64B | HAYMARKET - 64B | HAYMARKET - 64B | HAYMARKET - 64B | LEICESTER (GC) - 38C | GRANTHAM - 35B | LEICESTER (GC) - 38C | GRANTHAM - 35B | **9/55: LEIC - 38C** |
| Jan-56 | HAYMARKET - 64B | HAYMARKET - 64B | HAYMARKET - 64B | HAYMARKET - 64B | LEICESTER (GC) - 38C | GRANTHAM - 35B | LEICESTER (GC) - 38C | GRANTHAM - 35B | LEICESTER (GC) - 38C |
| Aug-56 | HAYMARKET - 64B | HAYMARKET - 64B | HAYMARKET - 64B | HAYMARKET - 64B | LEICESTER (GC) - 38C | GRANTHAM - 35B | LEICESTER (GC) - 38C | GRANTHAM - 35B | LEICESTER (GC) - 38C |
| Jan-57 | HAYMARKET - 64B | HAYMARKET - 64B | HAYMARKET - 64B | HAYMARKET - 64B | LEICESTER (GC) - 38C | GRANTHAM - 35B | LEICESTER (GC) - 38C | GRANTHAM - 35B | LEICESTER (GC) - 38C |
| Aug-57 | HAYMARKET - 64B | HAYMARKET - 64B | HAYMARKET - 64B | HAYMARKET - 64B | **9/57: KX - 34A** | **4/57: KX - 34A** | **9/57: KX - 34A** | GRANTHAM - 35B | **9/57: GRAN - 35B** |
| Jan-58 | HAYMARKET - 64B | HAYMARKET - 64B | HAYMARKET - 64B | HAYMARKET - 64B | **10/57: DCTR - 36A** | KINGS CROSS - 34A | **10/57: DCTR - 36A** | GRANTHAM - 35B | GRANTHAM - 35B |
| Aug-58 | HAYMARKET - 64B | **R/B 7/58** | **R/B 9/58** | HAYMARKET - 64B | DONCASTER - 36A | KINGS CROSS - 34A | DONCASTER - 36A | GRANTHAM - 34F | GRANTHAM - 34F |
| Jan-59 | HAYMARKET - 64B | | | **R/B 2/59** | **R/B 4/59** | **R/B 1/59** | **R/V 4/59** | GRANTHAM - 34F | **R/B 11/58** |
| Aug-59 | **R/B 7/59** | | | | | | | **R/B 3/59** | |
| Nov-59 | | | | | | | | | |
| Jan-60 | | | | | | | | | |
| Apr-60 | | | | | | | | | |
| Aug-60 | | | | | | | | | |
| Nov-60 | | | | | | | | | |

only as far as Doncaster where they were broken up into components for Hull, York and Wakefield; the latter being divided at Westgate into Bradford and Leeds sections and worked, as often as not, from Doncaster by elderly GCR 4-6-0's.

The expansion of east coast services – a 35% increase in main line services from Kings Cross between 1950 and 1958 - during the 1950s was remarkable and almost certainly could not have been attempted without the presence of the 90 postwar Pacific locomotives. The loads and timings of most of these workings called for an engine of 8P classification and as a result the older A3 locomotives, as a class 7P, were very largely relegated to secondary express services, especially north of York and Leeds. As a rule of thumb, for every ten trains leaving Kings Cross in the mid-1950s, six would be worked

*Regrets that the classic Great Northern look of the A3's disappeared with their rebuilding in the late 1950's had to be balanced by an astonishing increase in performance which effectively brought the class up to 8P standards. The German smoke deflectors were added a year or two after the blastpipe alterations and were noted as being amongst the few deflectors that actually did their job. Exactly forty years old, 60112 'St Simon' stands at its home shed of Grantham in September 1963.*

## DISTRIBUTION OF 8P & 7P LOCOMOTIVES : 1957

| | A1 | A2 | A2/1 | A2/2 | A2/3 | A3 | A4 | W1 | V2 | Total |
|---|---|---|---|---|---|---|---|---|---|---|
| Gateshead | 14 | 1 | | | 3 | 8 | 8 | | 11 | 45 |
| Haymarket | 5 | 6 | 3 | | 1 | 15 | 7 | | 4 | 41 |
| Kings Cross | 3 | | | | | 4 | 19 | | 13 | 39 |
| York | 5 | 1 | | 3 | 4 | | | | 26 | 39 |
| Heaton | 3 | 1 | | | 2 | 11 | | | 20 | 37 |
| New England | | 1 | 1 | 3 | 5 | | | | 23 | 34 |
| Doncaster | | | | | | 7 | | 1 | 17 | 25 |
| Grantham | 10 | | | | | 9 | | | | 19 |
| Copley Hill | 8 | | | | | 4 | | | 5 | 17 |
| St Margarets | | | | | | | | | 17 | 17 |
| Ferryhill | | 3 | | | | | | | 11 | 14 |
| Dundee | | 2 | | | | | | | 11 | 13 |
| Leicester | | | | | | 8 | | | 2 | 10 |
| Arsdley | 2 | | | | | | | | 4 | 6 |
| March | | | | | | | | | 6 | 6 |
| Tweedmouth | | | | | | | | | 6 | 6 |
| Woodford | | | | | | | | | 6 | 6 |
| N. Hill | | | | | | 5 | | | | 5 |
| Carlisle (C) | | | | | | 4 | | | | 4 |
| Neasden | | | | | | 1 | | | 2 | 3 |
| Darlington | | | | | | 2 | | | | 2 |

## DISTRIBUTION OF MIXED TRAFFIC ENGINES : 1957

| | B1 | B12 | B16 | B17 | B2 | BR5 | K1 | K2 | K3 | K4 | Total |
|---|---|---|---|---|---|---|---|---|---|---|---|
| Stratford | 24 | 7 | | 17 | 1 | | | | 18 | | 67 |
| York | 11 | | 43 | | | | 10 | | | | 64 |
| March | | | 12 | | | | 24 | | 17 | | 53 |
| Colwick | 19 | | | | | | | 14 | 12 | | 45 |
| Immingham | 23 | | | | | | | 3 | 14 | | 40 |
| St Margarets | 17 | | | | | | | | 23 | | 40 |
| Doncaster | 30 | | | | | | | | 4 | | 34 |
| Darnall | 23 | | | | | | | 7 | 4 | | 34 |
| Eastfield | 9 | | | 7 | | | | 13 | | 5 | 34 |
| Dairycoates | 3 | | | | | | | 25 | | | 28 |
| Ipswich | 10 | 10 | | 8 | | | | | | | 28 |
| Neville Hill | 12 | 15 | | | | | | | | | 27 |
| Darlington | 19 | | | | | 8 | | | | | 27 |
| Norwich | 9 | 6 | | | | | | | 10 | | 25 |
| Lincoln | 7 | | | | | | | 4 | 13 | | 24 |
| Cambridge | 5 | | | 8 | 10 | | | | | | 23 |
| N. England | 15 | | | | | | | | 3 | | 18 |
| Heaton | | | | 7 | | | | | 9 | | 16 |
| Carlisle (C) | 7 | | | | | | | | 8 | | 15 |
| Kittybrewster | 14 | | | | | | | 1 | | | 15 |
| Stockton | 8 | | | | | 6 | | | | | 14 |
| Blaydon | | | | 1 | 13 | | | | | | 14 |
| Boston | | | | | | | | 13 | 1 | | 14 |
| Tweedmouth | 5 | | | | | | | | 7 | | 12 |
| Ardsley | 12 | | | | | | | | | | 12 |
| Thornton Jcn | 11 | | | | | | | 1 | | | 12 |
| Colchester | 3 | | | 8 | | | | | | | 11 |
| Kings Cross | 9 | | | 1 | | | | | | | 10 |
| Neasden | 10 | | | 5 | | | | | | | 10 |
| Parkeston | 9 | | | | | | | | | | 9 |
| Leicester | 9 | | | | | | | | 6 | | 9 |
| Gorton | 3 | | | | | | | | 6 | | 9 |
| Haymarket | 9 | | | | | | | | | | 9 |
| Dundee | 9 | | | | | | | | | | 9 |
| Hitchin | 8 | | | | | | | | | | 8 |
| Yarmouth (ST) | | | 6 | | | | | 2 | | | 8 |
| Woodford | 3 | | | | | | | | 5 | | 8 |
| Mexborough | 5 | | | | | | 1 | | 3 | | 8 |
| Keith | 3 | | | | | | | 5 | | | 8 |
| Bot Gdns | 7 | | | | | | | | | | 7 |
| Bradford | 7 | | | | | | | | | | 7 |
| Ft William | | | | | | | 6 | 1 | | | 7 |
| Copley Hill | 6 | | | | | | | | | | 6 |
| Retford | 6 | | | | | | | | | | 6 |
| Gateshead | 5 | | | | | | | | | | 5 |
| Lowestoft | | | | | | | | 5 | | | 5 |
| Dunfermline | 1 | | | | | | | 3 | | | 4 |
| Parkhead | 1 | | | | | | | 3 | | | 4 |
| Spital Bge | 1 | 2 | | | | | | | | | 3 |
| Annesley | | | | | | | | | 3 | | 3 |
| Selby | | | 2 | | | | | | | | 2 |
| Bor Gdns | 2 | | | | | | | | | | 2 |
| Hav Hill | | | | | | | 2 | | | | 2 |
| Grantham | | 2 | | | | | | | | | 2 |
| Dalry Rd | 2 | | | | | | | | | | 2 |
| Starbeck | | | | 1 | | | | | | | 1 |
| W. Hartlepool | 1 | | | | | | | | | | 1 |
| Northallerton | | | | | | | 1 | | | | 1 |
| Scarborough | | | 1 | | | | | | | | 1 |
| Yarmouth (B) | | | 1 | | | | | | | | 1 |

| | 60107 | 60108 | 60109 | 60110 | 60111 | 60112 | A1 4-6-2 (1945) 60113 | A1 4-6-2 (1948) 60114 | 60115 |
|---|---|---|---|---|---|---|---|---|---|
| Aug-50 | LEICESTER (GC) - 38C | KINGS CROSS - 34A | KINGS CROSS - 34A | KINGS CROSS - 34A | NEASDEN - 34E | COPLEY HILL - 37B | NEWENGLAND - 35A | COPLEY HILL - 37B | GATESHEAD - 52A |
| Jan-51 | LEICESTER (GC) - 38C | 1/51: DCTR - 36A | KINGS CROSS - 34A | KINGS CROSS - 34A | NEASDEN - 34E | 11/50: DCTR - 36A | NEWENGLAND - 35A | COPLEY HILL - 37B | GATESHEAD - 52A |
| Aug-51 | LEICESTER (GC) - 38C | DONCASTER - 36A | 9/51: GRAN - 35B | 9/51: GRAN - 35B | NEASDEN - 34E | 4/51: C. HILL - 37B | 9/51: GRAN - 35B | COPLEY HILL - 37B | GATESHEAD - 52A |
| Jan-52 | LEICESTER (GC) - 38C | DONCASTER - 36A | GRANTHAM - 35B | GRANTHAM - 35B | NEASDEN - 34E | 9/51: DCTR - 36A | GRANTHAM - 35B | COPLEY HILL - 37B | GATESHEAD - 52A |
| Aug-52 | LEICESTER (GC) - 38C | 7/52: KX - 34A | GRANTHAM - 35B | GRANTHAM - 35B | NEASDEN - 34E | GRANTHAM - 35B | GRANTHAM - 35B | COPLEY HILL - 37B | GATESHEAD - 52A |
| Jan-53 | LEICESTER (GC) - 38C | 9/52: NEAS: 34E | GRANTHAM - 35B | GRANTHAM - 35B | NEASDEN - 34E | 2/53: DCTR - 36A | GRANTHAM - 35B | 2/53: GRAN - 35B | GATESHEAD - 52A |
| Aug-53 | LEICESTER (GC) - 38C | 5/53: KX - 34A | GRANTHAM - 35B | GRANTHAM - 35B | NEASDEN - 34E | DONCASTER - 36A | GRANTHAM - 35B | GRANTHAM - 35B | GATESHEAD - 52A |
| Jan-54 | LEICESTER (GC) - 38C | 12/53: NEAS - 34E | 11/53: DCTR - 36A | GRANTHAM - 35B | NEASDEN - 34E | DONCASTER - 36A | GRANTHAM - 35B | GRANTHAM - 35B | GATESHEAD - 52A |
| Aug-54 | LEICESTER (GC) - 38C | NEASDEN - 34E | DONCASTER - 36A | GRANTHAM - 35B | NEASDEN - 34E | DONCASTER - 36A | GRANTHAM - 35B | GRANTHAM - 35B | GATESHEAD - 52A |
| Jan-55 | LEICESTER (GC) - 38C | NEASDEN - 34E | DONCASTER - 36A | GRANTHAM - 35B | NEASDEN - 34E | DONCASTER - 36A | GRANTHAM - 35B | GRANTHAM - 35B | GATESHEAD - 52A |
| Aug-55 | LEICESTER (GC) - 38C | 7/55: KX - 34A | DONCASTER - 36A | GRANTHAM - 35B | 4/55: LEIC - 38C | DONCASTER - 36A | GRANTHAM - 35B | GRANTHAM - 35B | GATESHEAD - 52A |
| Jan-56 | LEICESTER (GC) - 38C | 11/55: NEAS - 34E | DONCASTER - 36A | GRANTHAM - 35B | LEICESTER (GC) - 38C | DONCASTER - 36A | GRANTHAM - 35B | GRANTHAM - 35B | GATESHEAD - 52A |
| Aug-56 | LEICESTER (GC) - 38C | NEASDEN - 34E | DONCASTER - 36A | GRANTHAM - 35B | LEICESTER (GC) - 38C | DONCASTER - 36A | GRANTHAM - 35B | GRANTHAM - 35B | GATESHEAD - 52A |
| Jan-57 | LEICESTER (GC) - 38C | 2/57: KX - 34A | DONCASTER - 36A | GRANTHAM - 35B | LEICESTER (GC) - 38C | DONCASTER - 36A | GRANTHAM - 35B | GRANTHAM - 35B | GATESHEAD - 52A |
| Aug-57 | 9/57: GRAN - 35B | KINGS CROSS - 34A | DONCASTER - 36A | 6/57: KX - 34A | 9/57: GRAN - 35B | DONCASTER - 36A | 9/57: KX - 34A | 9/57: DCTR - 36A | GATESHEAD - 52A |
| Jan-58 | GRANTHAM - 35B | KINGS CROSS - 34A | DONCASTER - 36A | KINGS CROSS - 34A | GRANTHAM - 35B | DONCASTER - 36A | 10/57: DCTR - 36A | DONCASTER - 36A | GATESHEAD - 52A |
| Aug-58 | GRANTHAM - 34F | 10/58: DCTR - 36A | 6/58: KX - 34A | KINGS CROSS - 34A | GRANTHAM - 34F | R/B 7/58 | DONCASTER - 36A | DONCASTER - 36A | GATESHEAD - 52A |
| Jan-59 | GRANTHAM - 34F | 11/58: KX - 34A | 10/58: DCTR - 36A | KINGS CROSS - 34A | GRANTHAM - 34F | | DONCASTER - 36A | DONCASTER - 36A | GATESHEAD - 52A |
| Aug-59 | R/B 6/59 | R/B 5/59 | R/B 3/59 | R/B 5/59 | R/B 6/59 | | DONCASTER - 36A | DONCASTER - 36A | GATESHEAD - 52A |
| Nov-59 | | | | | | | DONCASTER - 36A | DONCASTER - 36A | GATESHEAD - 52A |
| Jan-60 | | | | | | | DONCASTER - 36A | DONCASTER - 36A | GATESHEAD - 52A |
| Apr-60 | | | | | | | DONCASTER - 36A | DONCASTER - 36A | GATESHEAD - 52A |
| Aug-60 | | | | | | | DONCASTER - 36A | DONCASTER - 36A | GATESHEAD - 52A |
| Nov-60 | | | | | | | DONCASTER - 36A | DONCASTER - 36A | GATESHEAD - 52A |

| | 60116 | 60117 | 60118 | 60119 | 60120 | 60121 | 60122 | 60123 | 60124 |
|---|---|---|---|---|---|---|---|---|---|
| Aug-50 | HEATON - 52B | COPLEY HILL - 37B | COPLEY HILL - 37B | COPLEY HILL - 37B | COPLEY HILL - 37B | YORK - 50A | KINGS CROSS - 34A | COPLEY HILL - 37B | GATESHEAD - 52A |
| Jan-51 | HEATON - 52B | COPLEY HILL - 37B | COPLEY HILL - 37B | COPLEY HILL - 37B | COPLEY HILL - 37B | YORK - 50A | KINGS CROSS - 34A | COPLEY HILL - 37B | GATESHEAD - 52A |
| Aug-51 | HEATON - 52B | COPLEY HILL - 37B | COPLEY HILL - 37B | COPLEY HILL - 37B | COPLEY HILL - 37B | YORK - 50A | 9/51: GRAN - 35B | 9/51: ARDS - 37A | GATESHEAD - 52A |
| Jan-52 | HEATON - 52B | COPLEY HILL - 37B | COPLEY HILL - 37B | COPLEY HILL - 37B | COPLEY HILL - 37B | YORK - 50A | GRANTHAM - 35B | ARDSLEY - 37A | GATESHEAD - 52A |
| Aug-52 | HEATON - 52B | 6/52: GRAN - 35B | COPLEY HILL - 37B | COPLEY HILL - 37B | COPLEY HILL - 37B | YORK - 50A | GRANTHAM - 35B | ARDSLEY - 37A | GATESHEAD - 52A |
| Jan-53 | HEATON - 52B | 1/53: C.HILL - 37B | COPLEY HILL - 37B | COPLEY HILL - 37B | COPLEY HILL - 37B | YORK - 50A | GRANTHAM - 35B | ARDSLEY - 37A | GATESHEAD - 52A |
| Aug-53 | HEATON - 52B | COPLEY HILL - 37B | COPLEY HILL - 37B | COPLEY HILL - 37B | COPLEY HILL - 37B | YORK - 50A | GRANTHAM - 35B | ARDSLEY - 37A | GATESHEAD - 52A |
| Jan-54 | HEATON - 52B | COPLEY HILL - 37B | COPLEY HILL - 37B | COPLEY HILL - 37B | COPLEY HILL - 37B | YORK - 50A | 11/53: C.HILL - 37B | ARDSLEY - 37A | GATESHEAD - 52A |
| Aug-54 | HEATON - 52B | COPLEY HILL - 37B | COPLEY HILL - 37B | COPLEY HILL - 37B | COPLEY HILL - 37B | YORK - 50A | COPLEY HILL - 37B | ARDSLEY - 37A | GATESHEAD - 52A |
| Jan-55 | HEATON - 52B | COPLEY HILL - 37B | COPLEY HILL - 37B | COPLEY HILL - 37B | COPLEY HILL - 37B | YORK - 50A | COPLEY HILL - 37B | ARDSLEY - 37A | GATESHEAD - 52A |
| Aug-55 | HEATON - 52B | COPLEY HILL - 37B | COPLEY HILL - 37B | COPLEY HILL - 37B | COPLEY HILL - 37B | YORK - 50A | 9/55: GRAN - 35B | ARDSLEY - 37A | GATESHEAD - 52A |
| Jan-56 | HEATON - 52B | COPLEY HILL - 37B | COPLEY HILL - 37B | 12/55: GRAN - 35B | COPLEY HILL - 37B | YORK - 50A | GRANTHAM - 35B | ARDSLEY - 37A | GATESHEAD - 52A |
| Aug-56 | HEATON - 52B | COPLEY HILL - 56C | COPLEY HILL - 56C | GRANTHAM - 35B | COPLEY HILL - 56C | YORK - 50A | GRANTHAM - 35B | ARDSLEY - 56B | GATESHEAD - 52A |
| Jan-57 | HEATON - 52B | COPLEY HILL - 56C | COPLEY HILL - 56C | GRANTHAM - 35B | COPLEY HILL - 56C | YORK - 50A | GRANTHAM - 35B | ARDSLEY - 56B | GATESHEAD - 52A |
| Aug-57 | HEATON - 52B | COPLEY HILL - 56C | COPLEY HILL - 56C | 9/57: KX - 34A | COPLEY HILL - 56C | YORK - 50A | 9/57: KX - 34A | 9/57: C.HILL - 56C | GATESHEAD - 52A |
| Jan-58 | HEATON - 52B | COPLEY HILL - 56C | COPLEY HILL - 56C | KINGS CROSS - 34A | COPLEY HILL - 56C | YORK - 50A | KINGS CROSS - 34A | COPLEY HILL - 56C | GATESHEAD - 52A |
| Aug-58 | HEATON - 52B | COPLEY HILL - 56C | COPLEY HILL - 56C | 8/58: DCTR - 36A | COPLEY HILL - 56C | YORK - 50A | KINGS CROSS - 34A | COPLEY HILL - 56C | GATESHEAD - 52A |
| Jan-59 | HEATON - 52B | COPLEY HILL - 56C | COPLEY HILL - 56C | DONCASTER - 36A | COPLEY HILL - 56C | YORK - 50A | KINGS CROSS - 34A | COPLEY HILL - 56C | GATESHEAD - 52A |
| Aug-59 | HEATON - 52B | COPLEY HILL - 56C | COPLEY HILL - 56C | DONCASTER - 36A | COPLEY HILL - 56C | YORK - 50A | 4/59: DCTR - 36A | COPLEY HILL - 56C | GATESHEAD - 52A |
| Nov-59 | HEATON - 52B | COPLEY HILL - 56C | COPLEY HILL - 56C | DONCASTER - 36A | COPLEY HILL - 56C | YORK - 50A | DONCASTER - 36A | COPLEY HILL - 56C | GATESHEAD - 52A |
| Jan-60 | HEATON - 52B | COPLEY HILL - 56C | COPLEY HILL - 56C | DONCASTER - 36A | COPLEY HILL - 56C | YORK - 50A | DONCASTER - 36A | COPLEY HILL - 56C | GATESHEAD - 52A |
| Apr-60 | HEATON - 52B | COPLEY HILL - 56C | COPLEY HILL - 56C | DONCASTER - 36A | COPLEY HILL - 56C | YORK - 50A | DONCASTER - 36A | COPLEY HILL - 56C | GATESHEAD - 52A |
| Aug-60 | HEATON - 52B | COPLEY HILL - 56C | COPLEY HILL - 56C | DONCASTER - 36A | COPLEY HILL - 56C | YORK - 50A | DONCASTER - 36A | COPLEY HILL - 56C | 9/60: HTN - 52B |
| Nov-60 | HEATON - 52B | COPLEY HILL - 56C | COPLEY HILL - 56C | DONCASTER - 36A | COPLEY HILL - 56C | YORK - 50A | DONCASTER - 36A | COPLEY HILL - 56C | HEATON - 52B |

| | 60125 | 60126 | 60127 | 60128 | 60129 | 60130 | 60131 | 60132 | 60133 |
|---|---|---|---|---|---|---|---|---|---|
| Aug-50 | COPLEY HILL - 37B | HEATON - 52B | HEATON - 52B | KINGS CROSS - 34A | GATESHEAD - 52A | KINGS CROSS - 34A | KINGS CROSS - 34A | GATESHEAD - 52A | COPLEY HILL - 37B |
| Jan-51 | COPLEY HILL - 37B | HEATON - 52B | HEATON - 52B | KINGS CROSS - 34A | GATESHEAD - 52A | KINGS CROSS - 34A | KINGS CROSS - 34A | GATESHEAD - 52A | COPLEY HILL - 37B |
| Aug-51 | COPLEY HILL - 37B | HEATON - 52B | HEATON - 52B | 9/51: GRAN - 35B | GATESHEAD - 52A | 9/51: GRAN - 35B | 9/51: GRAN - 35B | GATESHEAD - 52A | COPLEY HILL - 37B |
| Jan-52 | COPLEY HILL - 37B | HEATON - 52B | HEATON - 52B | GRANTHAM - 35B | GATESHEAD - 52A | GRANTHAM - 35B | GRANTHAM - 35B | GATESHEAD - 52A | COPLEY HILL - 37B |
| Aug-52 | COPLEY HILL - 37B | HEATON - 52B | HEATON - 52B | GRANTHAM - 35B | GATESHEAD - 52A | GRANTHAM - 35B | GRANTHAM - 35B | GATESHEAD - 52A | COPLEY HILL - 37B |
| Jan-53 | 2/53: GRAN - 35B | HEATON - 52B | HEATON - 52B | GRANTHAM - 35B | GATESHEAD - 52A | 2/53: ARDS - 37A | 2/53: C.HILL - 37B | GATESHEAD - 52A | COPLEY HILL - 37B |
| Aug-53 | 7/53: C.HILL - 37B | HEATON - 52B | HEATON - 52B | GRANTHAM - 35B | GATESHEAD - 52A | ARDSLEY - 37A | COPLEY HILL - 37B | GATESHEAD - 52A | COPLEY HILL - 37B |
| Jan-54 | COPLEY HILL - 37B | HEATON - 52B | HEATON - 52B | GRANTHAM - 35B | GATESHEAD - 52A | ARDSLEY - 37A | COPLEY HILL - 37B | GATESHEAD - 52A | COPLEY HILL - 37B |
| Aug-54 | 5/54: GRAN - 35B | HEATON - 52B | HEATON - 52B | GRANTHAM - 35B | GATESHEAD - 52A | ARDSLEY - 37A | COPLEY HILL - 37B | GATESHEAD - 52A | COPLEY HILL - 37B |
| Jan-55 | GRANTHAM - 35B | HEATON - 52B | HEATON - 52B | GRANTHAM - 35B | GATESHEAD - 52A | ARDSLEY - 37A | COPLEY HILL - 37B | GATESHEAD - 52A | COPLEY HILL - 37B |
| Aug-55 | GRANTHAM - 35B | HEATON - 52B | HEATON - 52B | GRANTHAM - 35B | GATESHEAD - 52A | ARDSLEY - 37A | COPLEY HILL - 37B | GATESHEAD - 52A | COPLEY HILL - 37B |
| Jan-56 | GRANTHAM - 35B | HEATON - 52B | HEATON - 52B | GRANTHAM - 35B | GATESHEAD - 52A | ARDSLEY - 37A | COPLEY HILL - 37B | GATESHEAD - 52A | COPLEY HILL - 37B |
| Aug-56 | GRANTHAM - 35B | HEATON - 52B | HEATON - 52B | GRANTHAM - 35B | GATESHEAD - 52A | ARDSLEY - 56B | COPLEY HILL - 56C | GATESHEAD - 52A | COPLEY HILL - 56C |
| Jan-57 | GRANTHAM - 35B | HEATON - 52B | HEATON - 52B | GRANTHAM - 35B | GATESHEAD - 52A | ARDSLEY - 56B | COPLEY HILL - 56C | GATESHEAD - 52A | COPLEY HILL - 56C |
| Aug-57 | 6/57: KX - 34A | HEATON - 52B | HEATON - 52B | 9/57: KX - 34A | GATESHEAD - 52A | 9/57: C.HILL - 56C | COPLEY HILL - 56C | GATESHEAD - 52A | COPLEY HILL - 56C |
| Jan-58 | 1/58: DCTR - 36A | HEATON - 52B | HEATON - 52B | KINGS CROSS - 34A | GATESHEAD - 52A | COPLEY HILL - 56C | COPLEY HILL - 56C | GATESHEAD - 52A | COPLEY HILL - 56C |
| Aug-58 | DONCASTER - 36A | HEATON - 52B | HEATON - 52B | KINGS CROSS - 34A | GATESHEAD - 52A | COPLEY HILL - 56C | COPLEY HILL - 56C | GATESHEAD - 52A | COPLEY HILL - 56C |
| Jan-59 | DONCASTER - 36A | HEATON - 52B | HEATON - 52B | KINGS CROSS - 34A | GATESHEAD - 52A | COPLEY HILL - 56C | COPLEY HILL - 56C | GATESHEAD - 52A | COPLEY HILL - 56C |
| Aug-59 | DONCASTER - 36A | HEATON - 52B | HEATON - 52B | 4/59: DCTR - 36A | GATESHEAD - 52A | COPLEY HILL - 56C | COPLEY HILL - 56C | GATESHEAD - 52A | COPLEY HILL - 56C |
| Nov-59 | DONCASTER - 36A | HEATON - 52B | HEATON - 52B | DONCASTER - 36A | GATESHEAD - 52A | COPLEY HILL - 56C | COPLEY HILL - 56C | GATESHEAD - 52A | COPLEY HILL - 56C |
| Jan-60 | DONCASTER - 36A | HEATON - 52B | HEATON - 52B | DONCASTER - 36A | GATESHEAD - 52A | COPLEY HILL - 56C | COPLEY HILL - 56C | GATESHEAD - 52A | COPLEY HILL - 56C |
| Apr-60 | DONCASTER - 36A | HEATON - 52B | HEATON - 52B | DONCASTER - 36A | GATESHEAD - 52A | COPLEY HILL - 56C | COPLEY HILL - 56C | GATESHEAD - 52A | COPLEY HILL - 56C |
| Aug-60 | DONCASTER - 36A | HEATON - 52B | HEATON - 52B | DONCASTER - 36A | 9/60: HTN - 52B | COPLEY HILL - 56C | COPLEY HILL - 56C | 8/60: HTN - 52B | COPLEY HILL - 56C |
| Nov-60 | DONCASTER - 36A | HEATON - 52B | HEATON - 52B | DONCASTER - 36A | HEATON - 52B | COPLEY HILL - 56C | COPLEY HILL - 56C | HEATON - 52B | COPLEY HILL - 56C |

| | 60134 | 60135 | 60136 | 60137 | 60138 | 60139 | 60140 | 60141 | 60142 |
|---|---|---|---|---|---|---|---|---|---|
| Aug-50 | COPLEY HILL - 37B | GATESHEAD - 52A | KINGS CROSS - 34A | GATESHEAD - 52A | YORK - 50A | KINGS CROSS - 34A | YORK - 50A | COPLEY HILL - 37B | GATESHEAD - 52A |
| Jan-51 | COPLEY HILL - 37B | GATESHEAD - 52A | KINGS CROSS - 34A | GATESHEAD - 52A | YORK - 50A | KINGS CROSS - 34A | YORK - 50A | COPLEY HILL - 37B | GATESHEAD - 52A |
| Aug-51 | COPLEY HILL - 37B | GATESHEAD - 52A | 9/51: GRAN - 35B | GATESHEAD - 52A | YORK - 50A | KINGS CROSS - 34A | YORK - 50A | COPLEY HILL - 37B | GATESHEAD - 52A |
| Jan-52 | COPLEY HILL - 37B | GATESHEAD - 52A | GRANTHAM - 35B | GATESHEAD - 52A | YORK - 50A | KINGS CROSS - 34A | YORK - 50A | COPLEY HILL - 37B | GATESHEAD - 52A |
| Aug-52 | COPLEY HILL - 37B | GATESHEAD - 52A | GRANTHAM - 35B | GATESHEAD - 52A | YORK - 50A | KINGS CROSS - 34A | YORK - 50A | COPLEY HILL - 37B | GATESHEAD - 52A |
| Jan-53 | COPLEY HILL - 37B | GATESHEAD - 52A | GRANTHAM - 35B | GATESHEAD - 52A | YORK - 50A | KINGS CROSS - 34A | YORK - 50A | COPLEY HILL - 37B | GATESHEAD - 52A |
| Aug-53 | COPLEY HILL - 37B | GATESHEAD - 52A | GRANTHAM - 35B | GATESHEAD - 52A | YORK - 50A | KINGS CROSS - 34A | YORK - 50A | COPLEY HILL - 37B | GATESHEAD - 52A |
| Jan-54 | COPLEY HILL - 37B | GATESHEAD - 52A | GRANTHAM - 35B | GATESHEAD - 52A | YORK - 50A | KINGS CROSS - 34A | YORK - 50A | COPLEY HILL - 37B | GATESHEAD - 52A |
| Aug-54 | COPLEY HILL - 37B | GATESHEAD - 52A | GRANTHAM - 35B | GATESHEAD - 52A | YORK - 50A | KINGS CROSS - 34A | YORK - 50A | COPLEY HILL - 37B | GATESHEAD - 52A |
| Jan-55 | COPLEY HILL - 37B | GATESHEAD - 52A | GRANTHAM - 35B | GATESHEAD - 52A | YORK - 50A | KINGS CROSS - 34A | YORK - 50A | COPLEY HILL - 37B | GATESHEAD - 52A |
| Aug-55 | COPLEY HILL - 37B | GATESHEAD - 52A | GRANTHAM - 35B | GATESHEAD - 52A | YORK - 50A | KINGS CROSS - 34A | YORK - 50A | COPLEY HILL - 37B | GATESHEAD - 52A |
| Jan-56 | COPLEY HILL - 37B | GATESHEAD - 52A | GRANTHAM - 35B | GATESHEAD - 52A | YORK - 50A | 12/55: GRAN - 35B | YORK - 50A | COPLEY HILL - 37B | GATESHEAD - 52A |
| Aug-56 | COPLEY HILL - 56C | GATESHEAD - 52A | GRANTHAM - 35B | GATESHEAD - 52A | YORK - 50A | GRANTHAM - 35B | YORK - 50A | COPLEY HILL - 56C | GATESHEAD - 52A |
| Jan-57 | COPLEY HILL - 56C | GATESHEAD - 52A | GRANTHAM - 35B | GATESHEAD - 52A | YORK - 50A | GRANTHAM - 35B | YORK - 50A | COPLEY HILL - 56C | GATESHEAD - 52A |
| Aug-57 | COPLEY HILL - 56C | GATESHEAD - 52A | 4/57: KX - 34A | GATESHEAD - 52A | YORK - 50A | 4/57: KX - 34A | YORK - 50A | COPLEY HILL - 56C | GATESHEAD - 52A |
| Jan-58 | COPLEY HILL - 56C | GATESHEAD - 52A | 4/58: DCTR - 36A | GATESHEAD - 52A | YORK - 50A | KINGS CROSS - 34A | YORK - 50A | COPLEY HILL - 56C | GATESHEAD - 52A |
| Aug-58 | COPLEY HILL - 56C | GATESHEAD - 52A | 8/58: KX - 34A | GATESHEAD - 52A | YORK - 50A | KINGS CROSS - 34A | YORK - 50A | COPLEY HILL - 56C | GATESHEAD - 52A |
| Jan-59 | COPLEY HILL - 56C | GATESHEAD - 52A | KINGS CROSS - 34A | GATESHEAD - 52A | YORK - 50A | KINGS CROSS - 34A | YORK - 50A | COPLEY HILL - 56C | GATESHEAD - 52A |
| Aug-59 | COPLEY HILL - 56C | GATESHEAD - 52A | 4/59: DCTR - 36A | GATESHEAD - 52A | YORK - 50A | 4/59: DCTR - 36A | YORK - 50A | COPLEY HILL - 56C | GATESHEAD - 52A |
| Nov-59 | COPLEY HILL - 56C | GATESHEAD - 52A | DONCASTER - 36A | GATESHEAD - 52A | YORK - 50A | DONCASTER - 36A | YORK - 50A | COPLEY HILL - 56C | GATESHEAD - 52A |
| Jan-60 | COPLEY HILL - 56C | GATESHEAD - 52A | DONCASTER - 36A | GATESHEAD - 52A | YORK - 50A | DONCASTER - 36A | YORK - 50A | COPLEY HILL - 56C | GATESHEAD - 52A |
| Apr-60 | COPLEY HILL - 56C | GATESHEAD - 52A | DONCASTER - 36A | 6/60: HTN - 52B | YORK - 50A | DONCASTER - 36A | YORK - 50A | COPLEY HILL - 56C | GATESHEAD - 52A |
| Aug-60 | COPLEY HILL - 56C | GATESHEAD - 52A | DONCASTER - 36A | HEATON - 52B | YORK - 50A | DONCASTER - 36A | YORK - 50A | COPLEY HILL - 56C | 9/60: HTN - 52B |
| Nov-60 | COPLEY HILL - 56C | GATESHEAD - 52A | DONCASTER - 36A | HEATON - 52B | YORK - 50A | DONCASTER - 36A | YORK - 50A | COPLEY HILL - 56C | HEATON - 52B |

by A1 Pacifics, three by A4's and the remainder an A3 or A2; a number of the last mentioned being stationed at New England for Peterborough-based workings.

The decline of the A3's was not permanent and late in the 1950s the class was brought up to 8P level by being equipped with Kylchap double-blastpipes, a modest rebuilding which brought the class to the fore in large numbers during the final three or four years of steam.

Although a New England A2 had been diagrammed for the working early in the 1950's, during the latter part of the decade the 10.00 Edinburgh - Kings Cross 'Flying Scotsman' was booked to a Kings Cross A4 which worked northwards with the previous days 16.45 'Tees-Tyne Pullman' from London; the engine working through to Newcastle. A1 Pacifics were not a regular feature of the working although the use of English Electric Type 4 diesels from 1959 and their seeming reluctance to complete a round trip increased their chances of appearing, as happened on 19th April 1960 when Gateshead replaced a failed diesel with A1 60155 'Borderer'. Such was the urgency to replace one engine with another than the headboard was affixed facing inwards. The train is seen passing Peterborough North on the final leg of the journey.

Designed during an era when express services routinely loaded up to 600 tons but ran at modest speeds, the A2 Pacifics fell short of unqualified acceptance during the changed conditions of the later 1950's. Driver's representatives complained about poor riding, that nothing remained tight on the engines for long and before long the class - which consisted of five variations on a common theme - was relegated to rather second division express working; fifteen covering the Edinburgh - Dundee - Aberdeen services (where their high tractive effort was put to good use) with a similar number operating between Newcastle and York. The balance was based at New England where they were largely employed on the stopping trains to and from Kings Cross. One of the few east coast workings that the class held for a significant period was the up Aberdonian and the down Heart of Midlothian between Newcastle and Kings Cross, worked alternately by New England and Heaton engines. 60531 'Bahram', pulls away from Dundee after taking over an Edinburgh - Aberdeen express.

| | 60143 | 60144 | 60145 | 60146 | 60147 | 60148 | 60149 | 60150 | 60151 |
|---|---|---|---|---|---|---|---|---|---|
| Aug-50 | GATESHEAD-52A | KINGS CROSS-34A | GATESHEAD-52A | YORK-50A | GATESHEAD-52A | KINGS CROSS-34A | KINGS CROSS-34A | GATESHEAD-52A | GATESHEAD-52A |
| Jan-51 | GATESHEAD-52A | KINGS CROSS-34A | GATESHEAD-52A | YORK-50A | GATESHEAD-52A | KINGS CROSS-34A | KINGS CROSS-34A | GATESHEAD-52A | GATESHEAD-52A |
| Aug-51 | GATESHEAD-52A | 9/51: ARDS - 37A | GATESHEAD-52A | YORK-50A | GATESHEAD-52A | 9/51: GRAN - 35B | 9/51: GRAN - 35B | GATESHEAD-52A | GATESHEAD-52A |
| Jan-52 | GATESHEAD-52A | ARDSLEY-37A | GATESHEAD-52A | YORK-50A | GATESHEAD-52A | GRANTHAM-35B | GRANTHAM-35B | GATESHEAD-52A | GATESHEAD-52A |
| Aug-52 | GATESHEAD-52A | ARDSLEY-37A | GATESHEAD-52A | YORK-50A | GATESHEAD-52A | GRANTHAM-35B | GRANTHAM-35B | GATESHEAD-52A | GATESHEAD-52A |
| Jan-53 | GATESHEAD-52A | 2/53: GRAN - 35B | GATESHEAD-52A | YORK-50A | GATESHEAD-52A | GRANTHAM-35B | GRANTHAM-35B | GATESHEAD-52A | GATESHEAD-52A |
| Aug-53 | GATESHEAD-52A | GRANTHAM-35B | GATESHEAD-52A | YORK-50A | GATESHEAD-52A | GRANTHAM-35B | GRANTHAM-35B | GATESHEAD-52A | GATESHEAD-52A |
| Jan-54 | GATESHEAD-52A | GRANTHAM-35B | GATESHEAD-52A | YORK-50A | GATESHEAD-52A | 11/53: C.HILL - 37B | GRANTHAM-35B | GATESHEAD-52A | GATESHEAD-52A |
| Aug-54 | GATESHEAD-52A | GRANTHAM-35B | GATESHEAD-52A | YORK-50A | GATESHEAD-52A | 5/54: GRAN - 35B | GRANTHAM-35B | GATESHEAD-52A | GATESHEAD-52A |
| Jan-55 | GATESHEAD-52A | GRANTHAM-35B | GATESHEAD-52A | YORK-50A | GATESHEAD-52A | GRANTHAM-35B | GRANTHAM-35B | GATESHEAD-52A | GATESHEAD-52A |
| Aug-55 | GATESHEAD-52A | GRANTHAM-35B | GATESHEAD-52A | YORK-50A | GATESHEAD-52A | 9/55: C.HILL - 37B | GRANTHAM-35B | GATESHEAD-52A | GATESHEAD-52A |
| Jan-56 | GATESHEAD-52A | GRANTHAM-35B | GATESHEAD-52A | YORK-50A | GATESHEAD-52A | COPLEYHILL-37B | GRANTHAM-35B | GATESHEAD-52A | GATESHEAD-52A |
| Aug-56 | GATESHEAD-52A | GRANTHAM-35B | GATESHEAD-52A | YORK-50A | GATESHEAD-52A | COPLEYHILL-56C | 10/56: KX - 34A | GATESHEAD-52A | GATESHEAD-52A |
| Jan-57 | GATESHEAD-52A | GRANTHAM-35B | GATESHEAD-52A | YORK-50A | GATESHEAD-52A | COPLEYHILL-56C | KINGS CROSS-34A | GATESHEAD-52A | GATESHEAD-52A |
| Aug-57 | GATESHEAD-52A | 9/57: KX - 34A | GATESHEAD-52A | YORK-50A | GATESHEAD-52A | COPLEYHILL-56C | KINGS CROSS-34A | GATESHEAD-52A | GATESHEAD-52A |
| Jan-58 | GATESHEAD-52A | 11/57: DCTR - 36A | GATESHEAD-52A | YORK-50A | GATESHEAD-52A | COPLEYHILL-56C | KINGS CROSS-34A | GATESHEAD-52A | GATESHEAD-52A |
| Aug-58 | GATESHEAD-52A | DONCASTER-36A | GATESHEAD-52A | YORK-50A | GATESHEAD-52A | COPLEYHILL-56C | 10/58: DCTR - 36A | GATESHEAD-52A | GATESHEAD-52A |
| Jan-59 | GATESHEAD-52A | DONCASTER-36A | GATESHEAD-52A | YORK-50A | GATESHEAD-52A | COPLEYHILL-56C | DONCASTER-36A | GATESHEAD-52A | GATESHEAD-52A |
| Aug-59 | GATESHEAD-52A | DONCASTER-36A | GATESHEAD-52A | YORK-50A | GATESHEAD-52A | COPLEYHILL-56C | DONCASTER-36A | GATESHEAD-52A | GATESHEAD-52A |
| Nov-59 | GATESHEAD-52A | DONCASTER-36A | GATESHEAD-52A | YORK-50A | GATESHEAD-52A | COPLEYHILL-56C | DONCASTER-36A | GATESHEAD-52A | GATESHEAD-52A |
| Jan-60 | GATESHEAD-52A | DONCASTER-36A | GATESHEAD-52A | YORK-50A | GATESHEAD-52A | COPLEYHILL-56C | DONCASTER-36A | GATESHEAD-52A | GATESHEAD-52A |
| Apr-60 | 6/60: HTN - 52B | DONCASTER-36A | GATESHEAD-52A | YORK-50A | GATESHEAD-52A | COPLEYHILL-56C | DONCASTER-36A | GATESHEAD-52A | 6/60: HTN - 52B |
| Aug-60 | HEATON-52B | DONCASTER-36A | GATESHEAD-52A | YORK-50A | 9/60: HTN - 52B | COPLEYHILL-56C | DONCASTER-36A | GATESHEAD-52A | HEATON-52B |
| Nov-60 | HEATON-52B | DONCASTER-36A | GATESHEAD-52A | YORK-50A | HEATON-52B | COPLEYHILL-56C | DONCASTER-36A | GATESHEAD-52A | HEATON-52B |

| | 60152 | 60153 | 60154 | 60155 | 60156 | 60157 | 60158 | 60159 | 60160 |
|---|---|---|---|---|---|---|---|---|---|
| Aug-50 | HAYMARKET-64B | YORK-50A | GATESHEAD-52A | GATESHEAD-52A | KINGS CROSS-34A | KINGS CROSS-34A | KINGS CROSS-34A | HAYMARKET-64B | HAYMARKET-64B |
| Jan-51 | 1/51: POLM - 66A | YORK-50A | GATESHEAD-52A | GATESHEAD-52A | KINGS CROSS-34A | KINGS CROSS-34A | KINGS CROSS-34A | HAYMARKET-64B | 1/51: POLM - 66A |
| Aug-51 | 3/51: HMKT - 64B | YORK-50A | GATESHEAD-52A | GATESHEAD-52A | 9/51: GRAN - 35B | 9/51: GRAN - 35B | 9/51: GRAN - 35B | HAYMARKET-64B | 3/51: HMKT - 64B |
| Jan-52 | HAYMARKET-64B | YORK-50A | GATESHEAD-52A | GATESHEAD-52A | GRANTHAM-35B | GRANTHAM-35B | GRANTHAM-35B | HAYMARKET-64B | 10/51: POLM - 66A |
| Aug-52 | HAYMARKET-64B | YORK-50A | GATESHEAD-52A | GATESHEAD-52A | GRANTHAM-35B | GRANTHAM-35B | GRANTHAM-35B | HAYMARKET-64B | 2/52: HMKT - 64B |
| Jan-53 | 1/53: POLM - 66A | YORK-50A | GATESHEAD-52A | GATESHEAD-52A | GRANTHAM-35B | GRANTHAM-35B | GRANTHAM-35B | HAYMARKET-64B | HAYMARKET-64B |
| Aug-53 | 7/53: HMKT - 64B | YORK-50A | GATESHEAD-52A | GATESHEAD-52A | GRANTHAM-35B | GRANTHAM-35B | 7/53: C.HILL - 37B | HAYMARKET-64B | HAYMARKET-64B |
| Jan-54 | HAYMARKET-64B | YORK-50A | GATESHEAD-52A | GATESHEAD-52A | GRANTHAM-35B | GRANTHAM-35B | COPLEYHILL-37B | HAYMARKET-64B | HAYMARKET-64B |
| Aug-54 | HAYMARKET-64B | YORK-50A | GATESHEAD-52A | GATESHEAD-52A | GRANTHAM-35B | GRANTHAM-35B | 5/54: GRAN - 35B | HAYMARKET-64B | HAYMARKET-64B |
| Jan-55 | HAYMARKET-64B | YORK-50A | GATESHEAD-52A | GATESHEAD-52A | GRANTHAM-35B | GRANTHAM-35B | GRANTHAM-35B | HAYMARKET-64B | HAYMARKET-64B |
| Aug-55 | HAYMARKET-64B | YORK-50A | GATESHEAD-52A | GATESHEAD-52A | GRANTHAM-35B | GRANTHAM-35B | GRANTHAM-35B | HAYMARKET-64B | HAYMARKET-64B |
| Jan-56 | HAYMARKET-64B | YORK-50A | GATESHEAD-52A | GATESHEAD-52A | GRANTHAM-35B | GRANTHAM-35B | GRANTHAM-35B | HAYMARKET-64B | HAYMARKET-64B |
| Aug-56 | HAYMARKET-64B | YORK-50A | GATESHEAD-52A | GATESHEAD-52A | GRANTHAM-35B | GRANTHAM-35B | GRANTHAM-35B | HAYMARKET-64B | HAYMARKET-64B |
| Jan-57 | HAYMARKET-64B | YORK-50A | GATESHEAD-52A | GATESHEAD-52A | 10/56: KX - 34A | 10/56: KX - 34A | GRANTHAM-35B | HAYMARKET-64B | HAYMARKET-64B |
| Aug-57 | HAYMARKET-64B | YORK-50A | GATESHEAD-52A | GATESHEAD-52A | KINGS CROSS-34A | KINGS CROSS-34A | 6/57: KX - 34A | HAYMARKET-64B | HAYMARKET-64B |
| Jan-58 | HAYMARKET-64B | YORK-50A | GATESHEAD-52A | GATESHEAD-52A | KINGS CROSS-34A | KINGS CROSS-34A | KINGS CROSS-34A | HAYMARKET-64B | HAYMARKET-64B |
| Aug-58 | HAYMARKET-64B | YORK-50A | GATESHEAD-52A | GATESHEAD-52A | KINGS CROSS-34A | KINGS CROSS-34A | 10/58: DCTR - 36A | HAYMARKET-64B | HAYMARKET-64B |
| Jan-59 | HAYMARKET-64B | YORK-50A | GATESHEAD-52A | GATESHEAD-52A | KINGS CROSS-34A | KINGS CROSS-34A | DONCASTER-36A | HAYMARKET-64B | HAYMARKET-64B |
| Aug-59 | HAYMARKET-64B | YORK-50A | GATESHEAD-52A | GATESHEAD-52A | 4/59: DCTR - 36A | 4/59: DCTR - 36A | DONCASTER-36A | HAYMARKET-64B | HAYMARKET-64B |
| Nov-59 | HAYMARKET-64B | YORK-50A | GATESHEAD-52A | GATESHEAD-52A | DONCASTER-36A | DONCASTER-36A | DONCASTER-36A | HAYMARKET-64B | HAYMARKET-64B |
| Jan-60 | HAYMARKET-64B | YORK-50A | GATESHEAD-52A | GATESHEAD-52A | DONCASTER-36A | DONCASTER-36A | DONCASTER-36A | HAYMARKET-64B | HAYMARKET-64B |
| Apr-60 | HAYMARKET-64B | YORK-50A | GATESHEAD-52A | GATESHEAD-52A | DONCASTER-36A | DONCASTER-36A | DONCASTER-36A | HAYMARKET-64B | HAYMARKET-64B |
| Aug-60 | HAYMARKET-64B | YORK-50A | GATESHEAD-52A | 9/60: HTN - 52B | DONCASTER-36A | DONCASTER-36A | DONCASTER-36A | HAYMARKET-64B | HAYMARKET-64B |
| Nov-60 | HAYMARKET-64B | YORK-50A | GATESHEAD-52A | HEATON-52B | DONCASTER-36A | DONCASTER-36A | DONCASTER-36A | HAYMARKET-64B | HAYMARKET-64B |

| | | | A2/3 4-6-2 (1946) | | | | | | |
|---|---|---|---|---|---|---|---|---|---|
| | 60161 | 60162 | 60500 | 60511 | 60512 | 60513 | 60514 | 60515 | 60516 |
| Aug-50 | HAYMARKET-64B | HAYMARKET-64B | NEWENGLAND-35A | HEATON-52B | HEATON-52B | NEWENGLAND-35A | NEWENGLAND-35A | HEATON-52B | HEATON-52B |
| Jan-51 | 1/51: POLM - 66A | HAYMARKET-64B | NEWENGLAND-35A | HEATON-52B | HEATON-52B | NEWENGLAND-35A | NEWENGLAND-35A | HEATON-52B | HEATON-52B |
| Aug-51 | 3/51: HMKT - 64B | HAYMARKET-64B | NEWENGLAND-35A | HEATON-52B | HEATON-52B | NEWENGLAND-35A | NEWENGLAND-35A | HEATON-52B | HEATON-52B |
| Jan-52 | 10/51: POLM - 66A | HAYMARKET-64B | NEWENGLAND-35A | HEATON-52B | HEATON-52B | NEWENGLAND-35A | NEWENGLAND-35A | HEATON-52B | HEATON-52B |
| Aug-52 | POLMADIE-66A | HAYMARKET-64B | NEWENGLAND-35A | HEATON-52B | HEATON-52B | NEWENGLAND-35A | NEWENGLAND-35A | 7/52: GHD - 52A | 7/52: GHD - 52A |
| Jan-53 | POLMADIE-66A | HAYMARKET-64B | NEWENGLAND-35A | HEATON-52B | 12/52: YORK - 50A | NEWENGLAND-35A | NEWENGLAND-35A | 12/52: YORK - 50A | GATESHEAD-52A |
| Aug-53 | 7/53: HMKT - 64B | HAYMARKET-64B | NEWENGLAND-35A | HEATON-52B | YORK-50A | NEWENGLAND-35A | NEWENGLAND-35A | YORK-50A | GATESHEAD-52A |
| Jan-54 | HAYMARKET-64B | HAYMARKET-64B | NEWENGLAND-35A | HEATON-52B | YORK-50A | NEWENGLAND-35A | NEWENGLAND-35A | YORK-50A | GATESHEAD-52A |
| Aug-54 | HAYMARKET-64B | HAYMARKET-64B | NEWENGLAND-35A | HEATON-52B | YORK-50A | NEWENGLAND-35A | NEWENGLAND-35A | YORK-50A | GATESHEAD-52A |
| Jan-55 | HAYMARKET-64B | HAYMARKET-64B | NEWENGLAND-35A | HEATON-52B | YORK-50A | NEWENGLAND-35A | NEWENGLAND-35A | YORK-50A | GATESHEAD-52A |
| Aug-55 | HAYMARKET-64B | HAYMARKET-64B | NEWENGLAND-35A | HEATON-52B | YORK-50A | NEWENGLAND-35A | NEWENGLAND-35A | YORK-50A | GATESHEAD-52A |
| Jan-56 | HAYMARKET-64B | HAYMARKET-64B | NEWENGLAND-35A | HEATON-52B | YORK-50A | NEWENGLAND-35A | NEWENGLAND-35A | YORK-50A | GATESHEAD-52A |
| Aug-56 | HAYMARKET-64B | HAYMARKET-64B | NEWENGLAND-35A | HEATON-52B | YORK-50A | NEWENGLAND-35A | NEWENGLAND-35A | YORK-50A | GATESHEAD-52A |
| Jan-57 | HAYMARKET-64B | HAYMARKET-64B | NEWENGLAND-35A | HEATON-52B | YORK-50A | NEWENGLAND-35A | NEWENGLAND-35A | YORK-50A | GATESHEAD-52A |
| Aug-57 | HAYMARKET-64B | HAYMARKET-64B | NEWENGLAND-35A | HEATON-52B | YORK-50A | NEWENGLAND-35A | NEWENGLAND-35A | YORK-50A | GATESHEAD-52A |
| Jan-58 | HAYMARKET-64B | HAYMARKET-64B | NEWENGLAND-35A | HEATON-52B | YORK-50A | NEWENGLAND-35A | NEWENGLAND-35A | YORK-50A | GATESHEAD-52A |
| Aug-58 | HAYMARKET-64B | HAYMARKET-64B | NEWENGLAND-34E | HEATON-52B | YORK-50A | 6/58: GRAN - 34F | NEWENGLAND-34E | YORK-50A | GATESHEAD-52A |
| Jan-59 | HAYMARKET-64B | HAYMARKET-64B | NEWENGLAND-34E | HEATON-52B | YORK-50A | GRANTHAM-34F | NEWENGLAND-34E | YORK-50A | GATESHEAD-52A |
| Aug-59 | HAYMARKET-64B | HAYMARKET-64B | NEWENGLAND-34E | HEATON-52B | YORK-50A | 6/59: NEWE - 34E | NEWENGLAND-34E | YORK-50A | GATESHEAD-52A |
| Nov-59 | HAYMARKET-64B | HAYMARKET-64B | NEWENGLAND-34E | HEATON-52B | YORK-50A | NEWENGLAND-34E | NEWENGLAND-34E | YORK-50A | GATESHEAD-52A |
| Jan-60 | HAYMARKET-64B | HAYMARKET-64B | NEWENGLAND-34E | HEATON-52B | YORK-50A | NEWENGLAND-34E | NEWENGLAND-34E | YORK-50A | GATESHEAD-52A |
| Apr-60 | HAYMARKET-64B | HAYMARKET-64B | NEWENGLAND-34E | HEATON-52B | YORK-50A | NEWENGLAND-34E | NEWENGLAND-34E | YORK-50A | 5/60: HTN - 52B |
| Aug-60 | HAYMARKET-64B | HAYMARKET-64B | NEWENGLAND-34E | HEATON-52B | YORK-50A | NEWENGLAND-34E | NEWENGLAND-34E | YORK-50A | YORK-50A |
| Nov-60 | HAYMARKET-64B | HAYMARKET-64B | NEWENGLAND-34E | HEATON-52B | YORK-50A | NEWENGLAND-34E | NEWENGLAND-34E | YORK-50A | YORK-50A |

| | | | | | | | | | A2/2 4-6-2 (1943) |
|---|---|---|---|---|---|---|---|---|---|
| | 60517 | 60518 | 60519 | 60520 | 60521 | 60522 | 60523 | 60524 | 60501 |
| Aug-50 | HEATON-52B | GATESHEAD-52A | HAYMARKET-64B | NEWENGLAND-35A | GATESHEAD-52A | YORK-50A | NEWENGLAND-35A | YORK-50A | YORK-50A |
| Jan-51 | HEATON-52B | GATESHEAD-52A | HAYMARKET-64B | NEWENGLAND-35A | GATESHEAD-52A | YORK-50A | NEWENGLAND-35A | YORK-50A | 11/50: N.HILL - 50B |
| Aug-51 | HEATON-52B | GATESHEAD-52A | HAYMARKET-64B | NEWENGLAND-35A | GATESHEAD-52A | YORK-50A | NEWENGLAND-35A | YORK-50A | 12/50: YORK - 50A |
| Jan-52 | HEATON-52B | GATESHEAD-52A | HAYMARKET-64B | NEWENGLAND-35A | GATESHEAD-52A | YORK-50A | NEWENGLAND-35A | YORK-50A | YORK-50A |
| Aug-52 | HEATON-52B | GATESHEAD-52A | HAYMARKET-64B | NEWENGLAND-35A | GATESHEAD-52A | YORK-50A | NEWENGLAND-35A | YORK-50A | YORK-50A |
| Jan-53 | HEATON-52B | GATESHEAD-52A | HAYMARKET-64B | NEWENGLAND-35A | GATESHEAD-52A | YORK-50A | NEWENGLAND-35A | YORK-50A | YORK-50A |
| Aug-53 | HEATON-52B | GATESHEAD-52A | HAYMARKET-64B | NEWENGLAND-35A | GATESHEAD-52A | YORK-50A | NEWENGLAND-35A | YORK-50A | YORK-50A |
| Jan-54 | HEATON-52B | GATESHEAD-52A | HAYMARKET-64B | NEWENGLAND-35A | GATESHEAD-52A | YORK-50A | NEWENGLAND-35A | YORK-50A | YORK-50A |
| Aug-54 | HEATON-52B | GATESHEAD-52A | HAYMARKET-64B | NEWENGLAND-35A | GATESHEAD-52A | YORK-50A | NEWENGLAND-35A | YORK-50A | YORK-50A |
| Jan-55 | HEATON-52B | GATESHEAD-52A | HAYMARKET-64B | NEWENGLAND-35A | GATESHEAD-52A | YORK-50A | NEWENGLAND-35A | YORK-50A | YORK-50A |
| Aug-55 | HEATON-52B | GATESHEAD-52A | HAYMARKET-64B | NEWENGLAND-35A | GATESHEAD-52A | YORK-50A | NEWENGLAND-35A | YORK-50A | YORK-50A |
| Jan-56 | HEATON-52B | GATESHEAD-52A | HAYMARKET-64B | NEWENGLAND-35A | GATESHEAD-52A | YORK-50A | NEWENGLAND-35A | YORK-50A | YORK-50A |
| Aug-56 | HEATON-52B | GATESHEAD-52A | HAYMARKET-64B | NEWENGLAND-35A | GATESHEAD-52A | YORK-50A | NEWENGLAND-35A | YORK-50A | YORK-50A |
| Jan-57 | HEATON-52B | GATESHEAD-52A | HAYMARKET-64B | NEWENGLAND-35A | GATESHEAD-52A | YORK-50A | NEWENGLAND-35A | YORK-50A | YORK-50A |
| Aug-57 | HEATON-52B | GATESHEAD-52A | HAYMARKET-64B | 9/57: GRAN - 35B | GATESHEAD-52A | YORK-50A | NEWENGLAND-35A | YORK-50A | YORK-50A |
| Jan-58 | HEATON-52B | GATESHEAD-52A | HAYMARKET-64B | GRANTHAM-35B | GATESHEAD-52A | YORK-50A | NEWENGLAND-35A | YORK-50A | YORK-50A |
| Aug-58 | HEATON-52B | GATESHEAD-52A | HAYMARKET-64B | GRANTHAM-34F | GATESHEAD-52A | YORK-50A | NEWENGLAND-34E | YORK-50A | YORK-50A |
| Jan-59 | HEATON-52B | GATESHEAD-52A | HAYMARKET-64B | GRANTHAM-34F | GATESHEAD-52A | YORK-50A | 12/58: GRAN - 34F | YORK-50A | YORK-50A |
| Aug-59 | HEATON-52B | GATESHEAD-52A | HAYMARKET-64B | 6/59: NEWE - 34E | GATESHEAD-52A | YORK-50A | 4/59: NEWE - 34E | YORK-50A | YORK-50A |
| Nov-59 | HEATON-52B | GATESHEAD-52A | HAYMARKET-64B | NEWENGLAND-34E | GATESHEAD-52A | YORK-50A | NEWENGLAND-34E | YORK-50A | YORK-50A |
| Jan-60 | HEATON-52B | GATESHEAD-52A | HAYMARKET-64B | 1/60: DCTR - 36A | GATESHEAD-52A | YORK-50A | 1/60: DCTR - 36A | YORK-50A | YORK-50A |
| Apr-60 | HEATON-52B | 5/60: HTN - 52B | HAYMARKET-64B | DONCASTER-36A | GATESHEAD-52A | YORK-50A | DONCASTER-36A | YORK-50A | 2/60: W/D |
| Aug-60 | HEATON-52B | 6/60: YORK - 50A | HAYMARKET-64B | DONCASTER-36A | 6/60: HTN - 52B | YORK-50A | DONCASTER-36A | YORK-50A | |
| Nov-60 | HEATON-52B | YORK-50A | HAYMARKET-64B | DONCASTER-36A | HEATON-52B | YORK-50A | DONCASTER-36A | YORK-50A | |

If for most of the decade the A3's found themselves excluded from the principal services, they could still be found in respectable numbers on the relief duties which formed a significant element of east coast mileage. (On any normal weekday during the 1950's something like half a dozen additional services to Leeds, Newcastle or Edinburgh would be booked to run from Kings Cross, with double or triple that number at weekends). A single relief

Although the A1 Pacifics were especially associated with the Leeds - Kings Cross workings, five of the class were sent to Haymarket where they were intended as replacements for some of the A3's at that shed. They worked express traffic over all the former NB main lines but were rarely seen south of Newcastle. 60161 'North British', seen above at Haymarket in October 1953, had the distinction, together with two other A1's, of being allocated for a short period to Polmadie, working over the CR/LNW to Carlisle and Crewe.

Rebuilt during the war from the P2 2-8-2's of 1934, the six A2/2 4-6-2's were the forerunners of an attempt to construct a new fleet of Pacifics for the LNER. They were not especially successful and being found wanting on the former P2 diagrams, Edinburgh - Dundee - Aberdeen, were sent south to York and New England, each shed having three engines apiece. Neither depot played a major role in east coast express working and much of the work performed by the engines consisted of excursion, semi-fast and fitted goods duties. 60501 'Cock o' the North' turns at Haymarket in June 1951.

| | 60502 | 60503 | 60504 | 60505 | 60506 | A2/1 4-6-2 (1944) 60507 | 60508 | 60509 | 60510 |
|---|---|---|---|---|---|---|---|---|---|
| Aug-50 | YORK-50A | YORK-50A | NEWENGLAND-35A | NEWENGLAND-35A | NEWENGLAND-35A | HAYMARKET-64B | NEWENGLAND-35A | HAYMARKET-64B | HAYMARKET-64B |
| Jan-51 | YORK-50A | 11/50: N.HILL - 50B | NEWENGLAND-35A | NEWENGLAND-35A | NEWENGLAND-35A | HAYMARKET-64B | NEWENGLAND-35A | HAYMARKET-64B | HAYMARKET-64B |
| Aug-51 | YORK-50A | 12/50: YORK - 50A | NEWENGLAND-35A | NEWENGLAND-35A | NEWENGLAND-35A | HAYMARKET-64B | NEWENGLAND-35A | HAYMARKET-64B | HAYMARKET-64B |
| Jan-52 | YORK-50A | YORK-50A | NEWENGLAND-35A | NEWENGLAND-35A | NEWENGLAND-35A | HAYMARKET-64B | NEWENGLAND-35A | HAYMARKET-64B | HAYMARKET-64B |
| Aug-52 | YORK-50A | YORK-50A | NEWENGLAND-35A | NEWENGLAND-35A | NEWENGLAND-35A | HAYMARKET-64B | NEWENGLAND-35A | HAYMARKET-64B | HAYMARKET-64B |
| Jan-53 | YORK-50A | YORK-50A | NEWENGLAND-35A | NEWENGLAND-35A | NEWENGLAND-35A | HAYMARKET-64B | NEWENGLAND-35A | HAYMARKET-64B | HAYMARKET-64B |
| Aug-53 | YORK-50A | YORK-50A | NEWENGLAND-35A | NEWENGLAND-35A | NEWENGLAND-35A | HAYMARKET-64B | NEWENGLAND-35A | HAYMARKET-64B | HAYMARKET-64B |
| Jan-54 | YORK-50A | YORK-50A | 1/54: GRAN - 35B | NEWENGLAND-35A | 1/54: GRAN - 35B | HAYMARKET-64B | NEWENGLAND-35A | HAYMARKET-64B | HAYMARKET-64B |
| Aug-54 | YORK-50A | YORK-50A | 6/54: NEW.E - 35A | NEWENGLAND-35A | 6/54: NEW.E - 35A | HAYMARKET-64B | NEWENGLAND-35A | HAYMARKET-64B | HAYMARKET-64B |
| Jan-55 | YORK-50A | YORK-50A | NEWENGLAND-35A | NEWENGLAND-35A | NEWENGLAND-35A | 7/55:FHILL - 61B | NEWENGLAND-35A | HAYMARKET-64B | HAYMARKET-64B |
| Aug-55 | YORK-50A | YORK-50A | NEWENGLAND-35A | NEWENGLAND-35A | NEWENGLAND-35A | 8/55: HMKT - 64B | NEWENGLAND-35A | HAYMARKET-64B | HAYMARKET-64B |
| Jan-56 | YORK-50A | YORK-50A | NEWENGLAND-35A | NEWENGLAND-35A | NEWENGLAND-35A | HAYMARKET-64B | NEWENGLAND-35A | HAYMARKET-64B | HAYMARKET-64B |
| Aug-56 | YORK-50A | YORK-50A | NEWENGLAND-35A | NEWENGLAND-35A | NEWENGLAND-35A | HAYMARKET-64B | NEWENGLAND-35A | HAYMARKET-64B | HAYMARKET-64B |
| Jan-57 | YORK-50A | YORK-50A | NEWENGLAND-35A | NEWENGLAND-35A | NEWENGLAND-35A | HAYMARKET-64B | NEWENGLAND-35A | HAYMARKET-64B | HAYMARKET-64B |
| Aug-57 | YORK-50A | YORK-50A | NEWENGLAND-35A | NEWENGLAND-35A | NEWENGLAND-35A | HAYMARKET-64B | NEWENGLAND-35A | HAYMARKET-64B | HAYMARKET-64B |
| Jan-58 | YORK-50A | YORK-50A | NEWENGLAND-35A | NEWENGLAND-35A | NEWENGLAND-35A | HAYMARKET-64B | NEWENGLAND-35A | HAYMARKET-64B | HAYMARKET-64B |
| Aug-58 | YORK-50A | YORK-50A | NEWENGLAND-34E | NEWENGLAND-34E | NEWENGLAND-34E | HAYMARKET-64B | NEWENGLAND-34E | HAYMARKET-64B | HAYMARKET-64B |
| Jan-59 | YORK-50A | YORK-50A | NEWENGLAND-34E | NEWENGLAND-34E | NEWENGLAND-34E | HAYMARKET-64B | NEWENGLAND-34E | HAYMARKET-64B | HAYMARKET-64B |
| Aug-59 | YORK-50A | YORK-50A | NEWENGLAND-34E | NEWENGLAND-34E | NEWENGLAND-34E | HAYMARKET-64B | NEWENGLAND-34E | HAYMARKET-64B | HAYMARKET-64B |
| Nov-59 | YORK-50A | 11/59: W/D | NEWENGLAND-34E | 10/59: W/D | NEWENGLAND-34E | HAYMARKET-64B | NEWENGLAND-34E | HAYMARKET-64B | HAYMARKET-64B |
| Jan-60 | YORK-50A | | NEWENGLAND-34E | | NEWENGLAND-34E | HAYMARKET-64B | NEWENGLAND-34E | HAYMARKET-64B | HAYMARKET-64B |
| Apr-60 | YORK-50A | | NEWENGLAND-34E | | NEWENGLAND-34E | HAYMARKET-64B | NEWENGLAND-34E | HAYMARKET-64B | HAYMARKET-64B |
| Aug-60 | YORK-50A | | NEWENGLAND-34E | | NEWENGLAND-34E | 8/60: ST M - 64A | NEWENGLAND-34E | 9/60: W/D | HAYMARKET-64B |
| Nov-60 | YORK-50A | | NEWENGLAND-34E | | NEWENGLAND-34E | EDINBURGH(SM) - 64A | NEWENGLAND-34E | | HAYMARKET-64B |

| | A2 4-6-2 (1947) 60525 | 60526 | 60527 | 60528 | 60529 | 60530 | 60531 | 60532 | 60533 |
|---|---|---|---|---|---|---|---|---|---|
| Aug-50 | FERRYHILL-61B | YORK-50A | DUNDEE-62B | DUNDEE-62B | HAYMARKET-64B | HAYMARKET-64B | FERRYHILL-61B | HAYMARKET-64B | NEWENGLAND-35A |
| Jan-51 | FERRYHILL-61B | YORK-50A | DUNDEE-62B | DUNDEE-62B | HAYMARKET-64B | HAYMARKET-64B | FERRYHILL-61B | 1/51: FHILL - 61B | NEWENGLAND-35A |
| Aug-51 | FERRYHILL-61B | YORK-50A | DUNDEE-62B | DUNDEE-62B | HAYMARKET-64B | HAYMARKET-64B | FERRYHILL-61B | FERRYHILL-61B | NEWENGLAND-35A |
| Jan-52 | FERRYHILL-61B | YORK-50A | DUNDEE-62B | DUNDEE-62B | HAYMARKET-64B | HAYMARKET-64B | FERRYHILL-61B | FERRYHILL-61B | NEWENGLAND-35A |
| Aug-52 | FERRYHILL-61B | YORK-50A | DUNDEE-62B | DUNDEE-62B | HAYMARKET-64B | HAYMARKET-64B | FERRYHILL-61B | FERRYHILL-61B | NEWENGLAND-35A |
| Jan-53 | FERRYHILL-61B | YORK-50A | DUNDEE-62B | DUNDEE-62B | HAYMARKET-64B | HAYMARKET-64B | FERRYHILL-61B | FERRYHILL-61B | NEWENGLAND-35A |
| Aug-53 | FERRYHILL-61B | YORK-50A | DUNDEE-62B | DUNDEE-62B | HAYMARKET-64B | HAYMARKET-64B | FERRYHILL-61B | FERRYHILL-61B | NEWENGLAND-35A |
| Jan-54 | FERRYHILL-61B | YORK-50A | DUNDEE-62B | DUNDEE-62B | HAYMARKET-64B | HAYMARKET-64B | FERRYHILL-61B | FERRYHILL-61B | NEWENGLAND-35A |
| Aug-54 | FERRYHILL-61B | YORK-50A | DUNDEE-62B | DUNDEE-62B | HAYMARKET-64B | HAYMARKET-64B | FERRYHILL-61B | FERRYHILL-61B | 6/54: GRAM - 35B |
| Jan-55 | FERRYHILL-61B | YORK-50A | DUNDEE-62B | DUNDEE-62B | HAYMARKET-64B | HAYMARKET-64B | FERRYHILL-61B | FERRYHILL-61B | GRANTHAM-35B |
| Aug-55 | FERRYHILL-61B | YORK-50A | DUNDEE-62B | DUNDEE-62B | HAYMARKET-64B | HAYMARKET-64B | FERRYHILL-61B | FERRYHILL-61B | GRANTHAM-35B |
| Jan-56 | FERRYHILL-61B | YORK-50A | DUNDEE-62B | DUNDEE-62B | HAYMARKET-64B | HAYMARKET-64B | FERRYHILL-61B | FERRYHILL-61B | GRANTHAM-35B |
| Aug-56 | FERRYHILL-61B | YORK-50A | DUNDEE-62B | DUNDEE-62B | HAYMARKET-64B | HAYMARKET-64B | FERRYHILL-61B | FERRYHILL-61B | GRANTHAM-35B |
| Jan-57 | FERRYHILL-61B | YORK-50A | DUNDEE-62B | DUNDEE-62B | HAYMARKET-64B | HAYMARKET-64B | FERRYHILL-61B | FERRYHILL-61B | 10/56: NEW E - 35A |
| Aug-57 | FERRYHILL-61B | YORK-50A | DUNDEE-62B | DUNDEE-62B | HAYMARKET-64B | HAYMARKET-64B | FERRYHILL-61B | FERRYHILL-61B | 9/57: GRAN - 35B |
| Jan-58 | FERRYHILL-61B | YORK-50A | DUNDEE-62B | DUNDEE-62B | HAYMARKET-64B | HAYMARKET-64B | FERRYHILL-61B | FERRYHILL-61B | GRANTHAM-35B |
| Aug-58 | FERRYHILL-61B | YORK-50A | DUNDEE-62B | DUNDEE-62B | HAYMARKET-64B | HAYMARKET-64B | FERRYHILL-61B | FERRYHILL-61B | 6/58: KX - 34A |
| Jan-59 | FERRYHILL-61B | YORK-50A | DUNDEE-62B | DUNDEE-62B | HAYMARKET-64B | HAYMARKET-64B | FERRYHILL-61B | FERRYHILL-61B | 12/58: GRAN - 34F |
| Aug-59 | FERRYHILL-61B | YORK-50A | DUNDEE-62B | DUNDEE-62B | HAYMARKET-64B | HAYMARKET-64B | FERRYHILL-61B | FERRYHILL-61B | 6/59: NEW E - 34E |
| Nov-59 | FERRYHILL-61B | YORK-50A | DUNDEE-62B | DUNDEE-62B | HAYMARKET-64B | HAYMARKET-64B | FERRYHILL-61B | FERRYHILL-61B | NEWENGLAND-34E |
| Jan-60 | FERRYHILL-61B | YORK-50A | DUNDEE-62B | DUNDEE-62B | HAYMARKET-64B | HAYMARKET-64B | FERRYHILL-61B | FERRYHILL-61B | 1/60: DCTR - 36A |
| Apr-60 | FERRYHILL-61B | YORK-50A | 5/60: PERTH - 63A | 5/60: PERTH - 63A | HAYMARKET-64B | HAYMARKET-64B | FERRYHILL-61B | FERRYHILL-61B | DONCASTER-36A |
| Aug-60 | FERRYHILL-61B | YORK-50A | 6/60: FHILL: 61B | 6/60: FHILL: 61B | HAYMARKET-64B | HAYMARKET-64B | FERRYHILL-61B | FERRYHILL-61B | DONCASTER-36A |
| Nov-60 | FERRYHILL-61B | YORK-50A | FERRYHILL-61B | FERRYHILL-61B | HAYMARKET-64B | HAYMARKET-64B | FERRYHILL-61B | FERRYHILL-61B | DONCASTER-36A |

| | 60534 | 60535 | 60536 | 60537 | 60538 | 60539 | W1 4-6-2 (1937) 60700 | V2 2-6-2 (1936) 60800 | 60801 |
|---|---|---|---|---|---|---|---|---|---|
| Aug-50 | HAYMARKET-64B | HAYMARKET-64B | HAYMARKET-64B | FERRYHILL-61B | GATESHEAD-52A | HEATON-52B | KINGS CROSS-34A | KINGS CROSS-34A | HEATON-52B |
| Jan-51 | HAYMARKET-64B | HAYMARKET-64B | HAYMARKET-64B | 1/51: HMKT - 64B | GATESHEAD-52A | HEATON-52B | KINGS CROSS-34A | KINGS CROSS-34A | HEATON-52B |
| Aug-51 | HAYMARKET-64B | HAYMARKET-64B | HAYMARKET-64B | HAYMARKET-64B | GATESHEAD-52A | HEATON-52B | KINGS CROSS-34A | KINGS CROSS-34A | HEATON-52B |
| Jan-52 | HAYMARKET-64B | HAYMARKET-64B | HAYMARKET-64B | HAYMARKET-64B | GATESHEAD-52A | HEATON-52B | KINGS CROSS-34A | KINGS CROSS-34A | HEATON-52B |
| Aug-52 | HAYMARKET-64B | HAYMARKET-64B | HAYMARKET-64B | HAYMARKET-64B | GATESHEAD-52A | HEATON-52B | KINGS CROSS-34A | KINGS CROSS-34A | HEATON-52B |
| Jan-53 | HAYMARKET-64B | HAYMARKET-64B | HAYMARKET-64B | HAYMARKET-64B | GATESHEAD-52A | HEATON-52B | KINGS CROSS-34A | 5/53: WOOD - 38E | 12/52: TWEED - 52D |
| Aug-53 | HAYMARKET-64B | HAYMARKET-64B | HAYMARKET-64B | HAYMARKET-64B | GATESHEAD-52A | HEATON-52B | KINGS CROSS-34A | 7/53: KX - 34A | 5/53: GHD - 52A |
| Jan-54 | HAYMARKET-64B | HAYMARKET-64B | HAYMARKET-64B | HAYMARKET-64B | GATESHEAD-52A | HEATON-52B | 11/53: DCTR - 36A | KINGS CROSS-34A | 11/53: HTN - 52B |
| Aug-54 | HAYMARKET-64B | HAYMARKET-64B | HAYMARKET-64B | HAYMARKET-64B | GATESHEAD-52A | HEATON-52B | DONCASTER-36A | KINGS CROSS-34A | HEATON-52B |
| Jan-55 | HAYMARKET-64B | HAYMARKET-64B | HAYMARKET-64B | HAYMARKET-64B | GATESHEAD-52A | HEATON-52B | DONCASTER-36A | KINGS CROSS-34A | HEATON-52B |
| Aug-55 | HAYMARKET-64B | HAYMARKET-64B | HAYMARKET-64B | HAYMARKET-64B | GATESHEAD-52A | HEATON-52B | DONCASTER-36A | KINGS CROSS-34A | 5/55: TWEED - 52D |
| Jan-56 | HAYMARKET-64B | HAYMARKET-64B | HAYMARKET-64B | HAYMARKET-64B | GATESHEAD-52A | HEATON-52B | DONCASTER-36A | KINGS CROSS-34A | TWEEDMOUTH-52D |
| Aug-56 | HAYMARKET-64B | HAYMARKET-64B | HAYMARKET-64B | HAYMARKET-64B | GATESHEAD-52A | HEATON-52B | DONCASTER-36A | KINGS CROSS-34A | TWEEDMOUTH-52D |
| Jan-57 | HAYMARKET-64B | HAYMARKET-64B | HAYMARKET-64B | HAYMARKET-64B | GATESHEAD-52A | HEATON-52B | DONCASTER-36A | KINGS CROSS-34A | TWEEDMOUTH-52D |
| Aug-57 | HAYMARKET-64B | HAYMARKET-64B | HAYMARKET-64B | HAYMARKET-64B | GATESHEAD-52A | HEATON-52B | DONCASTER-36A | KINGS CROSS-34A | TWEEDMOUTH-52D |
| Jan-58 | HAYMARKET-64B | HAYMARKET-64B | HAYMARKET-64B | HAYMARKET-64B | GATESHEAD-52A | HEATON-52B | DONCASTER-36A | KINGS CROSS-34A | TWEEDMOUTH-52D |
| Aug-58 | HAYMARKET-64B | HAYMARKET-64B | HAYMARKET-64B | HAYMARKET-64B | GATESHEAD-52A | HEATON-52B | DONCASTER-36A | KINGS CROSS-34A | TWEEDMOUTH-52D |
| Jan-59 | HAYMARKET-64B | HAYMARKET-64B | HAYMARKET-64B | HAYMARKET-64B | GATESHEAD-52A | HEATON-52B | DONCASTER-36A | KINGS CROSS-34A | TWEEDMOUTH-52D |
| Aug-59 | HAYMARKET-64B | HAYMARKET-64B | HAYMARKET-64B | HAYMARKET-64B | GATESHEAD-52A | HEATON-52B | 6/59: W/D | KINGS CROSS-34A | TWEEDMOUTH-52D |
| Nov-59 | HAYMARKET-64B | HAYMARKET-64B | HAYMARKET-64B | HAYMARKET-64B | GATESHEAD-52A | HEATON-52B | | KINGS CROSS-34A | TWEEDMOUTH-52D |
| Jan-60 | HAYMARKET-64B | HAYMARKET-64B | HAYMARKET-64B | HAYMARKET-64B | GATESHEAD-52A | HEATON-52B | | KINGS CROSS-34A | TWEEDMOUTH-52D |
| Apr-60 | HAYMARKET-64B | HAYMARKET-64B | HAYMARKET-64B | HAYMARKET-64B | GATESHEAD-52A | HEATON-52B | | KINGS CROSS-34A | TWEEDMOUTH-52D |
| Aug-60 | HAYMARKET-64B | HAYMARKET-64B | HAYMARKET-64B | HAYMARKET-64B | 6/60: HTN - 52B | HEATON-52B | | KINGS CROSS-34A | TWEEDMOUTH-52D |
| Nov-60 | HAYMARKET-64B | HAYMARKET-64B | HAYMARKET-64B | HAYMARKET-64B | HEATON-52B | HEATON-52B | | KINGS CROSS-34A | TWEEDMOUTH-52D |

| | 60802 | 60803 | 60804 | 60825 | 60836 | 60807 | 60808 | 60809 | 60810 |
|---|---|---|---|---|---|---|---|---|---|
| Aug-50 | HEATON-52B | NEWENGLAND-35A | DUNDEE-62B | HEATON-52B | HEATON-52B | HEATON-52B | HEATON-52B | HEATON-52B | HEATON-52B |
| Jan-51 | HEATON-52B | NEWENGLAND-35A | DUNDEE-62B | HEATON-52B | HEATON-52B | HEATON-52B | HEATON-52B | HEATON-52B | HEATON-52B |
| Aug-51 | 7/51: GHD - 52A | NEWENGLAND-35A | DUNDEE-62B | HEATON-52B | HEATON-52B | HEATON-52B | HEATON-52B | 7/51: GHD - 52A | 7/51: GHD - 52A |
| Jan-52 | GATESHEAD-52A | NEWENGLAND-35A | DUNDEE-62B | HEATON-52B | HEATON-52B | HEATON-52B | HEATON-52B | GATESHEAD-52A | 9/51: HTN - 52B |
| Aug-52 | GATESHEAD-52A | 6/52: MARCH - 31B | DUNDEE-62B | HEATON-52B | HEATON-52B | HEATON-52B | HEATON-52B | GATESHEAD-52A | HEATON-52B |
| Jan-53 | GATESHEAD-52A | 5/53: NEW E - 35A | DUNDEE-62B | HEATON-52B | 1/53: TWEED - 52D | 3/53: TWEED - 52D | 3/53: TWEED - 52D | GATESHEAD-52A | HEATON-52B |
| Aug-53 | GATESHEAD-52A | 7/53: MARCH - 31B | DUNDEE-62B | HEATON-52B | 3/53: HTN - 52B | 5/53: GHD - 52A | TWEEDMOUTH-52D | GATESHEAD-52A | HEATON-52B |
| Jan-54 | GATESHEAD-52A | MARCH-31B | DUNDEE-62B | 1/54: TWEED - 52D | HEATON-52B | GATESHEAD-52A | TWEEDMOUTH-52D | GATESHEAD-52A | HEATON-52B |
| Aug-54 | GATESHEAD-52A | MARCH-31B | DUNDEE-62B | TWEEDMOUTH-52D | HEATON-52B | GATESHEAD-52A | TWEEDMOUTH-52D | GATESHEAD-52A | HEATON-52B |
| Jan-55 | GATESHEAD-52A | MARCH-31B | DUNDEE-62B | TWEEDMOUTH-52D | HEATON-52B | GATESHEAD-52A | TWEEDMOUTH-52D | GATESHEAD-52A | HEATON-52B |
| Aug-55 | GATESHEAD-52A | MARCH-31B | 11/55: FYHL - 61B | TWEEDMOUTH-52D | HEATON-52B | GATESHEAD-52A | TWEEDMOUTH-52D | GATESHEAD-52A | HEATON-52B |
| Jan-56 | GATESHEAD-52A | MARCH-31B | 1/56: DUND - 62B | TWEEDMOUTH-52D | HEATON-52B | GATESHEAD-52A | TWEEDMOUTH-52D | GATESHEAD-52A | HEATON-52B |
| Aug-56 | 4/56: HTN - 52B | MARCH-31B | DUNDEE-62B | TWEEDMOUTH-52D | HEATON-52B | GATESHEAD-52A | TWEEDMOUTH-52D | 4/56: HTN - 52B | HEATON-52B |
| Jan-57 | HEATON-52B | MARCH-31B | DUNDEE-62B | TWEEDMOUTH-52D | HEATON-52B | GATESHEAD-52A | TWEEDMOUTH-52D | HEATON-52B | HEATON-52B |
| Aug-57 | HEATON-52B | MARCH-31B | DUNDEE-62B | 6/57: GHD - 52A | HEATON-52B | GATESHEAD-52A | TWEEDMOUTH-52D | 6/57: GHD - 52A | HEATON-52B |
| Jan-58 | HEATON-52B | MARCH-31B | DUNDEE-62B | GATESHEAD-52A | HEATON-52B | GATESHEAD-52A | TWEEDMOUTH-52D | GATESHEAD-52A | HEATON-52B |
| Aug-58 | HEATON-52B | MARCH-31B | DUNDEE-62B | GATESHEAD-52A | HEATON-52B | GATESHEAD-52A | 6/58: HTN - 52B | GATESHEAD-52A | HEATON-52B |
| Jan-59 | HEATON-52B | MARCH-31B | DUNDEE-62B | GATESHEAD-52A | HEATON-52B | GATESHEAD-52A | HEATON-52B | GATESHEAD-52A | HEATON-52B |
| Aug-59 | HEATON-52B | MARCH-31B | DUNDEE-62B | GATESHEAD-52A | HEATON-52B | GATESHEAD-52A | HEATON-52B | GATESHEAD-52A | HEATON-52B |
| Nov-59 | HEATON-52B | MARCH-31B | DUNDEE-62B | GATESHEAD-52A | HEATON-52B | GATESHEAD-52A | HEATON-52B | GATESHEAD-52A | HEATON-52B |
| Jan-60 | HEATON-52B | MARCH-31B | DUNDEE-62B | 1/60: HTN - 52B | HEATON-52B | 1/60: HTN - 52B | HEATON-52B | 12/59: HTN - 52B | HEATON-52B |
| Apr-60 | HEATON-52B | MARCH-31B | DUNDEE-62B | HEATON-52B | HEATON-52B | HEATON-52B | 7/60: C.HILL - 56C | 7/60: C.HILL - 56C | HEATON-52B |
| Aug-60 | HEATON-52B | MARCH-31B | DUNDEE-62B | HEATON-52B | 6/60: TNBY - 51L | HEATON-52B | 9/60: TNBY - 51L | 9/60: TNBY - 51L | 6/60: YORK - 50A |
| Nov-60 | HEATON-52B | MARCH-31B | DUNDEE-62B | HEATON-52B | THORNABY-51L | HEATON-52B | THORNABY-51L | THORNABY-51L | YORK-50A |

service to Aberdeen, for example, might require engines from Kings Cross, Grantham, Gateshead, Haymarket and Dundee; a circumstance that not only kept many A3's in regular employment but brought the V2 2-6-2's into front line service.

*In and out of the plant. A2/2 60501 'Cock o' the North' waits at Doncaster to enter the works whilst V2 2-6-2 60870 returns to work after an overhaul. Both views were taken on 12 July 1956*

| | 60811 | 60812 | 60813 | 60814 | 60815 | 60816 | 60817 | 60818 | 60819 |
|---|---|---|---|---|---|---|---|---|---|
| Aug-50 | HEATON - 52B | HEATON - 52B | KINGS CROSS - 34A | KINGS CROSS - 34A | W.HALSE - 38E | HAYMARKET - 64B | W.HALSE - 38E | W.HALSE - 38E | FERRYHILL - 61B |
| Jan-51 | HEATON - 52B | HEATON - 52B | **2/51: STM - 64A** | KINGS CROSS - 34A | W.HALSE - 38E | HAYMARKET - 64B | W.HALSE - 38E | **1/51: KX - 34A** | FERRYHILL - 61B |
| Aug-51 | HEATON - 52B | HEATON - 52B | EDINBURGH (SM) - 64A | **6/51: STM - 64A** | **6/51: DCTR - 36A** | HAYMARKET - 64B | W.HALSE - 38E | KINGS CROSS - 34A | FERRYHILL - 61B |
| Jan-52 | HEATON - 52B | HEATON - 52B | EDINBURGH (SM) - 64A | EDINBURGH (SM) - 64A | DONCASTER - 36A | HAYMARKET - 64B | W.HALSE - 38E | KINGS CROSS - 34A | FERRYHILL - 61B |
| Aug-52 | HEATON - 52B | HEATON - 52B | EDINBURGH (SM) - 64A | EDINBURGH (SM) - 64A | DONCASTER - 36A | HAYMARKET - 64B | W.HALSE - 38E | KINGS CROSS - 34A | FERRYHILL - 61B |
| Jan-53 | **12/52: TWEED - 52D** | HEATON - 52B | EDINBURGH (SM) - 64A | **2/53: KX - 34A** | DONCASTER - 36A | HAYMARKET - 64B | W.HALSE - 38E | **2/53: STM - 64A** | FERRYHILL - 61B |
| Aug-53 | **3/53: HTN - 52B** | HEATON - 52B | EDINBURGH (SM) - 64A | KINGS CROSS - 34A | DONCASTER - 36A | HAYMARKET - 64B | W.HALSE - 38E | EDINBURGH (SM) - 64A | FERRYHILL - 61B |
| Jan-54 | HEATON - 52B | HEATON - 52B | EDINBURGH (SM) - 64A | KINGS CROSS - 34A | DONCASTER - 36A | HAYMARKET - 64B | W.HALSE - 38E | EDINBURGH (SM) - 64A | FERRYHILL - 61B |
| Aug-54 | HEATON - 52B | HEATON - 52B | EDINBURGH (SM) - 64A | KINGS CROSS - 34A | DONCASTER - 36A | HAYMARKET - 64B | W.HALSE - 38E | EDINBURGH (SM) - 64A | FERRYHILL - 61B |
| Jan-55 | HEATON - 52B | HEATON - 52B | EDINBURGH (SM) - 64A | KINGS CROSS - 34A | DONCASTER - 36A | HAYMARKET - 64B | W.HALSE - 38E | EDINBURGH (SM) - 64A | FERRYHILL - 61B |
| Aug-55 | HEATON - 52B | HEATON - 52B | EDINBURGH (SM) - 64A | KINGS CROSS - 34A | DONCASTER - 36A | HAYMARKET - 64B | W.HALSE - 38E | EDINBURGH (SM) - 64A | FERRYHILL - 61B |
| Jan-56 | HEATON - 52B | HEATON - 52B | EDINBURGH (SM) - 64A | KINGS CROSS - 34A | **11/55: WOOD - 38E** | HAYMARKET - 64B | W.HALSE - 38E | EDINBURGH (SM) - 64A | FERRYHILL - 61B |
| Aug-56 | HEATON - 52B | HEATON - 52B | EDINBURGH (SM) - 64A | KINGS CROSS - 34A | W.HALSE - 38E | HAYMARKET - 64B | W.HALSE - 38E | EDINBURGH (SM) - 64A | FERRYHILL - 61B |
| Jan-57 | HEATON - 52B | HEATON - 52B | EDINBURGH (SM) - 64A | KINGS CROSS - 34A | W.HALSE - 38E | HAYMARKET - 64B | W.HALSE - 38E | EDINBURGH (SM) - 64A | FERRYHILL - 61B |
| Aug-57 | HEATON - 52B | HEATON - 52B | EDINBURGH (SM) - 64A | KINGS CROSS - 34A | **11/57: LEIC - 38C** | HAYMARKET - 64B | **5/57: DCTR - 36A** | EDINBURGH (SM) - 64A | FERRYHILL - 61B |
| Jan-58 | HEATON - 52B | HEATON - 52B | EDINBURGH (SM) - 64A | KINGS CROSS - 34A | **12/57: WOOD - 38E** | **11/57: STM - 64A** | DONCASTER - 36A | EDINBURGH (SM) - 64A | FERRYHILL - 61B |
| Aug-58 | HEATON - 52B | HEATON - 52B | EDINBURGH (SM) - 64A | KINGS CROSS - 34A | W.HALSE - 2F | **8/58: HMKT - 64B** | DONCASTER - 36A | EDINBURGH (SM) - 64A | FERRYHILL - 61B |
| Jan-59 | HEATON - 52B | HEATON - 52B | EDINBURGH (SM) - 64A | KINGS CROSS - 34A | W.HALSE - 2F | HAYMARKET - 64B | DONCASTER - 36A | EDINBURGH (SM) - 64A | **1/59: HMKT - 64B** |
| Aug-59 | HEATON - 52B | HEATON - 52B | EDINBURGH (SM) - 64A | KINGS CROSS - 34A | **8/59: LEIC - 15E** | HAYMARKET - 64B | DONCASTER - 36A | EDINBURGH (SM) - 64A | HAYMARKET - 64B |
| Nov-59 | HEATON - 52B | HEATON - 52B | EDINBURGH (SM) - 64A | KINGS CROSS - 34A | LEICESTER (GC) - 15E | **11/59: STM - 64A** | DONCASTER - 36A | EDINBURGH (SM) - 64A | **11/59: STM - 64A** |
| Jan-60 | HEATON - 52B | HEATON - 52B | EDINBURGH (SM) - 64A | KINGS CROSS - 34A | LEICESTER (GC) - 15E | **11/59: STM - 64A** | DONCASTER - 36A | EDINBURGH (SM) - 64A | EDINBURGH (SM) - 64A |
| Apr-60 | HEATON - 52B | HEATON - 52B | EDINBURGH (SM) - 64A | KINGS CROSS - 34A | LEICESTER (GC) - 15E | EDINBURGH (SM) - 64A | DONCASTER - 36A | EDINBURGH (SM) - 64A | EDINBURGH (SM) - 64A |
| Aug-60 | HEATON - 52B | HEATON - 52B | EDINBURGH (SM) - 64A | KINGS CROSS - 34A | LEICESTER (GC) - 15E | EDINBURGH (SM) - 64A | DONCASTER - 36A | **8/60: EAST - 65A** | EDINBURGH (SM) - 64A |
| Nov-60 | HEATON - 52B | HEATON - 52B | EDINBURGH (SM) - 64A | KINGS CROSS - 34A | LEICESTER (GC) - 15E | EDINBURGH (SM) - 64A | DONCASTER - 36A | EASTFIELD - 65A | EDINBURGH (SM) - 64A |

| | 60820 | 60821 | 60822 | 60823 | 60824 | 60825 | 60826 | 60827 | 60828 |
|---|---|---|---|---|---|---|---|---|---|
| Aug-50 | W.HALSE - 38E | KINGS CROSS - 34A | FERRYHILL - 61B | KINGS CROSS - 34A | FERRYHILL - 61B | EDINBURGH (SM) - 64A | W.HALSE - 38E | FERRYHILL - 61B | NEWENGLAND - 35A |
| Jan-51 | **1/51: NEWE - 35A** | KINGS CROSS - 34A | **11/50: DUND - 62B** | KINGS CROSS - 34A | FERRYHILL - 61B | EDINBURGH (SM) - 64A | **3/51: NEWE - 35A** | FERRYHILL - 61B | NEWENGLAND - 35A |
| Aug-51 | NEWENGLAND - 35A | **4/51: STM - 64A** | DUNDEE - 62B | EDINBURGH (SM) - 64A | FERRYHILL - 61B | EDINBURGH (SM) - 64A | **6/51: MARCH - 31B** | FERRYHILL - 61B | NEWENGLAND - 35A |
| Jan-52 | NEWENGLAND - 35A | EDINBURGH (SM) - 64A | DUNDEE - 62B | EDINBURGH (SM) - 64A | FERRYHILL - 61B | EDINBURGH (SM) - 64A | **9/51: C.HILL - 37B** | FERRYHILL - 61B | NEWENGLAND - 35A |
| Aug-52 | NEWENGLAND - 35A | EDINBURGH (SM) - 64A | DUNDEE - 62B | EDINBURGH (SM) - 64A | FERRYHILL - 61B | EDINBURGH (SM) - 64A | COPLEYHILL - 37B | FERRYHILL - 61B | NEWENGLAND - 35A |
| Jan-53 | **2/53: WOOD - 38E** | **2/53: KX - 34A** | DUNDEE - 62B | EDINBURGH (SM) - 64A | FERRYHILL - 61B | EDINBURGH (SM) - 64A | COPLEYHILL - 37B | FERRYHILL - 61B | NEWENGLAND - 35A |
| Aug-53 | **5/53: LEIC - 38C** | KINGS CROSS - 34A | DUNDEE - 62B | EDINBURGH (SM) - 64A | FERRYHILL - 61B | EDINBURGH (SM) - 64A | COPLEYHILL - 37B | FERRYHILL - 61B | NEWENGLAND - 35A |
| Jan-54 | LEICESTER (GC) - 38C | KINGS CROSS - 34A | DUNDEE - 62B | EDINBURGH (SM) - 64A | FERRYHILL - 61B | EDINBURGH (SM) - 64A | **11/53: ARDS - 37A** | FERRYHILL - 61B | NEWENGLAND - 35A |
| Aug-54 | LEICESTER (GC) - 38C | KINGS CROSS - 34A | DUNDEE - 62B | EDINBURGH (SM) - 64A | FERRYHILL - 61B | EDINBURGH (SM) - 64A | ARDSLEY - 37A | FERRYHILL - 61B | **6/54: NEWE - 35A** |
| Jan-55 | LEICESTER (GC) - 38C | KINGS CROSS - 34A | DUNDEE - 62B | EDINBURGH (SM) - 64A | FERRYHILL - 61B | EDINBURGH (SM) - 64A | ARDSLEY - 37A | FERRYHILL - 61B | KINGS CROSS - 34A |
| Aug-55 | LEICESTER (GC) - 38C | KINGS CROSS - 34A | DUNDEE - 62B | EDINBURGH (SM) - 64A | FERRYHILL - 61B | EDINBURGH (SM) - 64A | **4/55: NEWE - 35A** | FERRYHILL - 61B | **7/55: NEAS - 34E** |
| Jan-56 | **5/56: NEAS - 34E** | KINGS CROSS - 34A | DUNDEE - 62B | EDINBURGH (SM) - 64A | FERRYHILL - 61B | EDINBURGH (SM) - 64A | NEWENGLAND - 35A | FERRYHILL - 61B | **11/55: KX - 34A** |
| Aug-56 | **5/56: KX - 34A** | **8/56: NEWE - 35A** | DUNDEE - 62B | EDINBURGH (SM) - 64A | FERRYHILL - 61B | EDINBURGH (SM) - 64A | NEWENGLAND - 35A | FERRYHILL - 61B | KINGS CROSS - 34A |
| Jan-57 | **6/56: NEAS - 34E** | NEWENGLAND - 35A | DUNDEE - 62B | EDINBURGH (SM) - 64A | FERRYHILL - 61B | EDINBURGH (SM) - 64A | NEWENGLAND - 35A | FERRYHILL - 61B | KINGS CROSS - 34A |
| Aug-57 | **5/57: KX - 34A** | **8/57: GRAN - 35B** | DUNDEE - 62B | EDINBURGH (SM) - 64A | FERRYHILL - 61B | EDINBURGH (SM) - 64A | NEWENGLAND - 35A | FERRYHILL - 61B | KINGS CROSS - 34A |
| Jan-58 | KINGS CROSS - 34A | GRANTHAM - 35B | DUNDEE - 62B | EDINBURGH (SM) - 64A | FERRYHILL - 61B | EDINBURGH (SM) - 64A | NEWENGLAND - 35A | FERRYHILL - 61B | **1/58: LEIC - 15E** |
| Aug-58 | KINGS CROSS - 34A | GRANTHAM - 34F | DUNDEE - 62B | EDINBURGH (SM) - 64A | FERRYHILL - 61B | EDINBURGH (SM) - 64A | NEWENGLAND - 34E | FERRYHILL - 61B | LEICESTER (GC) - 15E |
| Jan-59 | KINGS CROSS - 34A | **12/58: NEWE - 34E** | DUNDEE - 62B | EDINBURGH (SM) - 64A | **1/59: HMKT - 64B** | EDINBURGH (SM) - 64A | NEWENGLAND - 34E | **1/59: HMKT - 64B** | **11/58: YORK - 50A** |
| Aug-59 | **9/59: NEWE - 34E** | NEWENGLAND - 34E | DUNDEE - 62B | EDINBURGH (SM) - 64A | HAYMARKET - 64B | EDINBURGH (SM) - 64A | NEWENGLAND - 34E | HAYMARKET - 64B | YORK - 50A |
| Nov-59 | NEWENGLAND - 34E | NEWENGLAND - 34E | DUNDEE - 62B | EDINBURGH (SM) - 64A | **11/59: STM - 64A** | EDINBURGH (SM) - 64A | **10/59: DCTR - 36A** | **11/59: STM - 64A** | YORK - 50A |
| Jan-60 | NEWENGLAND - 34E | NEWENGLAND - 34E | DUNDEE - 62B | EDINBURGH (SM) - 64A | EDINBURGH (SM) - 64A | EDINBURGH (SM) - 64A | DONCASTER - 36A | EDINBURGH (SM) - 64A | YORK - 50A |
| Apr-60 | NEWENGLAND - 34E | NEWENGLAND - 34E | DUNDEE - 62B | EDINBURGH (SM) - 64A | EDINBURGH (SM) - 64A | EDINBURGH (SM) - 64A | DONCASTER - 36A | EDINBURGH (SM) - 64A | YORK - 50A |
| Aug-60 | NEWENGLAND - 34E | NEWENGLAND - 34E | DUNDEE - 62B | **6/60: PRTH - 63A** | EDINBURGH (SM) - 64A | EDINBURGH (SM) - 64A | DONCASTER - 36A | EDINBURGH (SM) - 64A | YORK - 50A |
| Nov-60 | NEWENGLAND - 34E | NEWENGLAND - 34E | DUNDEE - 62B | PERTH - 63A | EDINBURGH (SM) - 64A | EDINBURGH (SM) - 64A | DONCASTER - 36A | EDINBURGH (SM) - 64A | YORK - 50A |

| | 60829 | 60830 | 60831 | 60832 | 60833 | 60834 | 60835 | 60836 | 60837 |
|---|---|---|---|---|---|---|---|---|---|
| Aug-50 | NEWENGLAND - 35A | W.HALSE - 38E | W.HALSE - 38E | W.HALSE - 38E | HEATON - 52B | HAYMARKET - 64B | HEATON - 52B | EDINBURGH (SM) - 64A | YORK - 50A |
| Jan-51 | NEWENGLAND - 35A | W.HALSE - 38E | W.HALSE - 38E | **2/51: NEWE - 35A** | HEATON - 52B | **11/50: DUND - 62B** | HEATON - 52B | **1/51: HMKT - 64B** | YORK - 50A |
| Aug-51 | NEWENGLAND - 35A | NEWENGLAND - 35A | W.HALSE - 38E | NEWENGLAND - 35A | HEATON - 52B | DUNDEE - 62B | HEATON - 52B | **3/51: STM - 64A** | YORK - 50A |
| Jan-52 | NEWENGLAND - 35A | NEWENGLAND - 35A | W.HALSE - 38E | NEWENGLAND - 35A | HEATON - 52B | DUNDEE - 62B | HEATON - 52B | EDINBURGH (SM) - 64A | YORK - 50A |
| Aug-52 | NEWENGLAND - 35A | **6/52: MARCH - 31B** | W.HALSE - 38E | NEWENGLAND - 35A | HEATON - 52B | DUNDEE - 62B | **12/52: TWEED - 52D** | EDINBURGH (SM) - 64A | YORK - 50A |
| Jan-53 | NEWENGLAND - 35A | MARCH - 31B | **3/53: LEIC - 38C** | NEWENGLAND - 35A | HEATON - 52B | DUNDEE - 62B | **3/53: HTN - 52B** | EDINBURGH (SM) - 64A | YORK - 50A |
| Aug-53 | NEWENGLAND - 35A | MARCH - 31B | **5/53: KX - 34A** | NEWENGLAND - 35A | HEATON - 52B | DUNDEE - 62B | HEATON - 52B | EDINBURGH (SM) - 64A | YORK - 50A |
| Jan-54 | NEWENGLAND - 35A | MARCH - 31B | **7/53: WOOD - 38E** | NEWENGLAND - 35A | HEATON - 52B | DUNDEE - 62B | HEATON - 52B | EDINBURGH (SM) - 64A | YORK - 50A |
| Aug-54 | NEWENGLAND - 35A | MARCH - 31B | W.HALSE - 38E | NEWENGLAND - 35A | HEATON - 52B | DUNDEE - 62B | HEATON - 52B | EDINBURGH (SM) - 64A | YORK - 50A |
| Jan-55 | NEWENGLAND - 35A | MARCH - 31B | W.HALSE - 38E | NEWENGLAND - 35A | HEATON - 52B | DUNDEE - 62B | HEATON - 52B | EDINBURGH (SM) - 64A | YORK - 50A |
| Aug-55 | NEWENGLAND - 35A | MARCH - 31B | W.HALSE - 38E | NEWENGLAND - 35A | **9/55: GHD - 52A** | DUNDEE - 62B | HEATON - 52B | EDINBURGH (SM) - 64A | **6/55: DARL - 51A** |
| Jan-56 | NEWENGLAND - 35A | MARCH - 31B | W.HALSE - 38E | NEWENGLAND - 35A | GATESHEAD - 52A | DUNDEE - 62B | HEATON - 52B | EDINBURGH (SM) - 64A | **9/55: YORK - 50A** |
| Aug-56 | NEWENGLAND - 35A | MARCH - 31B | W.HALSE - 38E | NEWENGLAND - 35A | GATESHEAD - 52A | DUNDEE - 62B | HEATON - 52B | EDINBURGH (SM) - 64A | YORK - 50A |
| Jan-57 | NEWENGLAND - 35A | MARCH - 31B | OODFORD HALSE - 38E | NEWENGLAND - 35A | GATESHEAD - 52A | DUNDEE - 62B | HEATON - 52B | EDINBURGH (SM) - 64A | YORK - 50A |
| Aug-57 | NEWENGLAND - 35A | MARCH - 31B | **9/57: LEIC - 38C** | NEWENGLAND - 35A | GATESHEAD - 52A | DUNDEE - 62B | HEATON - 52B | EDINBURGH (SM) - 64A | YORK - 50A |
| Jan-58 | NEWENGLAND - 35A | MARCH - 31B | LEICESTER (GC) - 38C | NEWENGLAND - 35A | GATESHEAD - 52A | DUNDEE - 62B | HEATON - 52B | EDINBURGH (SM) - 64A | YORK - 50A |
| Aug-58 | NEWENGLAND - 34E | MARCH - 31B | LEICESTER (GC) - 15E | NEWENGLAND - 34E | GATESHEAD - 52A | DUNDEE - 62B | HEATON - 52B | EDINBURGH (SM) - 64A | YORK - 50A |
| Jan-59 | NEWENGLAND - 34E | MARCH - 31B | LEICESTER (GC) - 15E | NEWENGLAND - 34E | GATESHEAD - 52A | DUNDEE - 62B | HEATON - 52B | EDINBURGH (SM) - 64A | YORK - 50A |
| Aug-59 | NEWENGLAND - 34E | MARCH - 31B | **8/59: YORK - 50A** | NEWENGLAND - 34E | GATESHEAD - 52A | DUNDEE - 62B | HEATON - 52B | EDINBURGH (SM) - 64A | **6/59: C.HILL - 56C** |
| Nov-59 | NEWENGLAND - 34E | MARCH - 31B | YORK - 50A | NEWENGLAND - 34E | GATESHEAD - 52A | DUNDEE - 62B | HEATON - 52B | EDINBURGH (SM) - 64A | **10/59: YORK - 50A** |
| Jan-60 | NEWENGLAND - 34E | MARCH - 31B | YORK - 50A | NEWENGLAND - 34E | **1/60: HTN - 52B** | DUNDEE - 62B | HEATON - 52B | EDINBURGH (SM) - 64A | YORK - 50A |
| Apr-60 | NEWENGLAND - 34E | MARCH - 31B | YORK - 50A | NEWENGLAND - 34E | HEATON - 52B | DUNDEE - 62B | HEATON - 52B | EDINBURGH (SM) - 64A | YORK - 50A |
| Aug-60 | NEWENGLAND - 34E | MARCH - 31B | YORK - 50A | NEWENGLAND - 34E | HEATON - 52B | DUNDEE - 62B | HEATON - 52B | **8/60: EAST - 65A** | YORK - 50A |
| Nov-60 | NEWENGLAND - 34E | MARCH - 31B | YORK - 50A | NEWENGLAND - 34E | HEATON - 52B | DUNDEE - 62B | HEATON - 52B | EASTFIELD - 65A | YORK - 50A |

| | 60838 | 60839 | 60840 | 60841 | 60842 | 60843 | 60844 | 60845 | 60846 |
|---|---|---|---|---|---|---|---|---|---|
| Aug-50 | DUNDEE - 62B | YORK - 50A | DUNDEE - 62B | NEWENGLAND - 35A | NEWENGLAND - 35A | YORK - 50A | DUNDEE - 62B | W.HALSE - 38E | DONCASTER - 36A |
| Jan-51 | DUNDEE - 62B | YORK - 50A | DUNDEE - 62B | NEWENGLAND - 35A | NEWENGLAND - 35A | YORK - 50A | DUNDEE - 62B | W.HALSE - 38E | DONCASTER - 36A |
| Aug-51 | DUNDEE - 62B | YORK - 50A | DUNDEE - 62B | NEWENGLAND - 35A | NEWENGLAND - 35A | YORK - 50A | DUNDEE - 62B | **9/51: NEWE - 35A** | **9/51: C.HILL - 37B** |
| Jan-52 | DUNDEE - 62B | YORK - 50A | DUNDEE - 62B | NEWENGLAND - 35A | NEWENGLAND - 35A | YORK - 50A | DUNDEE - 62B | NEWENGLAND - 35A | COPLEYHILL - 37B |
| Aug-52 | DUNDEE - 62B | YORK - 50A | DUNDEE - 62B | NEWENGLAND - 35A | NEWENGLAND - 35A | YORK - 50A | DUNDEE - 62B | **5/52: SWINDON - 82C** | COPLEYHILL - 37B |
| Jan-53 | DUNDEE - 62B | YORK - 50A | **11/52: STM - 64A** | NEWENGLAND - 35A | NEWENGLAND - 35A | YORK - 50A | DUNDEE - 62B | SWINDON - 82C | COPLEYHILL - 37B |
| Aug-53 | DUNDEE - 62B | YORK - 50A | EDINBURGH (SM) - 64A | NEWENGLAND - 35A | NEWENGLAND - 35A | YORK - 50A | DUNDEE - 62B | **5/53: NEWE - 35A** | **7/53: ARDS - 37A** |
| Jan-54 | DUNDEE - 62B | YORK - 50A | EDINBURGH (SM) - 64A | NEWENGLAND - 35A | NEWENGLAND - 35A | YORK - 50A | DUNDEE - 62B | NEWENGLAND - 35A | ARDSLEY - 37A |
| Aug-54 | DUNDEE - 62B | YORK - 50A | EDINBURGH (SM) - 64A | NEWENGLAND - 35A | NEWENGLAND - 35A | YORK - 50A | DUNDEE - 62B | NEWENGLAND - 35A | ARDSLEY - 37A |
| Jan-55 | DUNDEE - 62B | YORK - 50A | EDINBURGH (SM) - 64A | NEWENGLAND - 35A | NEWENGLAND - 35A | YORK - 50A | DUNDEE - 62B | NEWENGLAND - 35A | ARDSLEY - 37A |
| Aug-55 | DUNDEE - 62B | YORK - 50A | EDINBURGH (SM) - 64A | **9/55: C.HILL - 37B** | NEWENGLAND - 35A | YORK - 50A | DUNDEE - 62B | **9/55: GRAN - 35B** | ARDSLEY - 37A |
| Jan-56 | DUNDEE - 62B | YORK - 50A | EDINBURGH (SM) - 64A | COPLEYHILL - 37B | NEWENGLAND - 35A | YORK - 50A | DUNDEE - 62B | GRANTHAM - 35B | ARDSLEY - 37A |
| Aug-56 | DUNDEE - 62B | YORK - 50A | EDINBURGH (SM) - 64A | COPLEYHILL - 56C | NEWENGLAND - 35A | YORK - 50A | DUNDEE - 62B | **10/56: NEWE - 35A** | ARDSLEY - 56B |
| Jan-57 | DUNDEE - 62B | YORK - 50A | EDINBURGH (SM) - 64A | COPLEYHILL - 56C | NEWENGLAND - 35A | YORK - 50A | DUNDEE - 62B | NEWENGLAND - 35A | ARDSLEY - 56B |
| Aug-57 | DUNDEE - 62B | YORK - 50A | EDINBURGH (SM) - 64A | COPLEYHILL - 56C | **8/57: GRAN - 35B** | YORK - 50A | DUNDEE - 62B | NEWENGLAND - 35A | ARDSLEY - 56B |
| Jan-58 | DUNDEE - 62B | YORK - 50A | EDINBURGH (SM) - 64A | COPLEYHILL - 56C | **9/57: LEIC - 38C** | YORK - 50A | DUNDEE - 62B | NEWENGLAND - 35A | ARDSLEY - 56B |
| Aug-58 | DUNDEE - 62B | YORK - 50A | EDINBURGH (SM) - 64A | COPLEYHILL - 56C | LEICESTER (GC) - 15E | **6/59: C.HILL - 56C** | DUNDEE - 62B | NEWENGLAND - 34E | **9/58: HTN - 52B** |
| Jan-59 | DUNDEE - 62B | YORK - 50A | EDINBURGH (SM) - 64A | COPLEYHILL - 56C | LEICESTER (GC) - 15E | **9/58: TWEED - 52D** | DUNDEE - 62B | NEWENGLAND - 34E | HEATON - 52B |
| Aug-59 | DUNDEE - 62B | YORK - 50A | EDINBURGH (SM) - 64A | COPLEYHILL - 56C | **8/59: YORK - 50A** | TWEEDMOUTH - 52D | DUNDEE - 62B | NEWENGLAND - 34E | HEATON - 52B |
| Nov-59 | DUNDEE - 62B | YORK - 50A | EDINBURGH (SM) - 64A | COPLEYHILL - 56C | YORK - 50A | TWEEDMOUTH - 52D | DUNDEE - 62B | NEWENGLAND - 34E | HEATON - 52B |
| Jan-60 | DUNDEE - 62B | YORK - 50A | EDINBURGH (SM) - 64A | COPLEYHILL - 56C | YORK - 50A | TWEEDMOUTH - 52D | DUNDEE - 62B | NEWENGLAND - 34E | HEATON - 52B |
| Apr-60 | DUNDEE - 62B | YORK - 50A | EDINBURGH (SM) - 64A | **6/60: GRAN - 34F** | YORK - 50A | TWEEDMOUTH - 52D | DUNDEE - 62B | NEWENGLAND - 34E | HEATON - 52B |
| Aug-60 | DUNDEE - 62B | YORK - 50A | EDINBURGH (SM) - 64A | **10/60: NEWE - 34E** | YORK - 50A | TWEEDMOUTH - 52D | DUNDEE - 62B | NEWENGLAND - 34E | **7/60: TNBY - 51L** |
| Nov-60 | DUNDEE - 62B | YORK - 50A | EDINBURGH (SM) - 64A | NEWENGLAND - 34E | YORK - 50A | TWEEDMOUTH - 52D | DUNDEE - 62B | NEWENGLAND - 34E | THORNABY - 51L |

Although intended as a replacement for the K3 2-6-0's on main line express goods services, the V2's very quickly displayed an aptitude for express passenger work and were the favoured substitute for an A4 at times of shortage. An ever fruitful source of express work for V2's was New England shed which, whenever it had to find a replacement for one of its A2 allocation – a not infrequent occurrence – would have no qualms about booking one of its 2-6-2's into the diagram. (Since New England covered the down Heart of Midlothian between Peterborough and Newcastle and the Up Aberdonian, their V2's could, when allowed, cover very respectable distances). In the North East, where long distance relief trains often approached the volume of booked originating services, there was rarely a shortage of express work for A3's and V2's. On a day picked at random no less than sixteen such workings were arranged: most running from Newcastle to Kings Cross or Edinburgh but with a number of gems such as the 19.48 Alnwick to Marylebone and 21.45

| | 60847 | 60848 | 60849 | 60850 | 60851 | 60852 | 60853 | 60854 | 60855 |
|---|---|---|---|---|---|---|---|---|---|
| Aug-50 | YORK - 50A | EDINBURGH (SM) - 64A | DONCASTER - 36A | NEWENGLAND - 35A | FERRYHILL - 61B | DONCASTER - 36A | WOODFORD HALSE - 38E | NEWENGLAND - 35A | NEWENGLAND - 35A |
| Jan-51 | YORK - 50A | EDINBURGH (SM) - 64A | DONCASTER - 36A | NEWENGLAND - 35A | FERRYHILL - 61B | DONCASTER - 36A | WOODFORD HALSE - 38E | NEWENGLAND - 35A | NEWENGLAND - 35A |
| Aug-51 | YORK - 50A | EDINBURGH (SM) - 64A | DONCASTER - 36A | NEWENGLAND - 35A | FERRYHILL - 61B | DONCASTER - 36A | **9/51: NEW E - 35A** | NEWENGLAND - 35A | NEWENGLAND - 35A |
| Jan-52 | YORK - 50A | EDINBURGH (SM) - 64A | DONCASTER - 36A | NEWENGLAND - 35A | FERRYHILL - 61B | DONCASTER - 36A | NEWENGLAND - 35A | NEWENGLAND - 35A | NEWENGLAND - 35A |
| Aug-52 | YORK - 50A | EDINBURGH (SM) - 64A | DONCASTER - 36A | NEWENGLAND - 35A | FERRYHILL - 61B | DONCASTER - 36A | NEWENGLAND - 35A | NEWENGLAND - 35A | NEWENGLAND - 35A |
| Jan-53 | YORK - 50A | EDINBURGH (SM) - 64A | DONCASTER - 36A | NEWENGLAND - 35A | FERRYHILL - 61B | DONCASTER - 36A | NEWENGLAND - 35A | NEWENGLAND - 35A | NEWENGLAND - 35A |
| Aug-53 | YORK - 50A | EDINBURGH (SM) - 64A | DONCASTER - 36A | NEWENGLAND - 35A | FERRYHILL - 61B | DONCASTER - 36A | NEWENGLAND - 35A | NEWENGLAND - 35A | NEWENGLAND - 35A |
| Jan-54 | YORK - 50A | EDINBURGH (SM) - 64A | DONCASTER - 36A | NEWENGLAND - 35A | FERRYHILL - 61B | DONCASTER - 36A | NEWENGLAND - 35A | NEWENGLAND - 35A | **12/53: KX - 34A** |
| Aug-54 | YORK - 50A | EDINBURGH (SM) - 64A | DONCASTER - 36A | NEWENGLAND - 35A | FERRYHILL - 61B | DONCASTER - 36A | NEWENGLAND - 35A | NEWENGLAND - 35A | KINGS CROSS - 34A |
| Jan-55 | YORK - 50A | EDINBURGH (SM) - 64A | DONCASTER - 36A | NEWENGLAND - 35A | FERRYHILL - 61B | DONCASTER - 36A | NEWENGLAND - 35A | NEWENGLAND - 35A | KINGS CROSS - 34A |
| Aug-55 | YORK - 50A | EDINBURGH (SM) - 64A | DONCASTER - 36A | NEWENGLAND - 35A | FERRYHILL - 61B | DONCASTER - 36A | NEWENGLAND - 35A | NEWENGLAND - 35A | **7/55: NEAS - 34E** |
| Jan-56 | YORK - 50A | EDINBURGH (SM) - 64A | DONCASTER - 36A | NEWENGLAND - 35A | FERRYHILL - 61B | DONCASTER - 36A | NEWENGLAND - 35A | NEWENGLAND - 35A | **11/55: KX - 34A** |
| Aug-56 | YORK - 50A | **9/56: GHD - 52A** | DONCASTER - 36A | NEWENGLAND - 35A | FERRYHILL - 61B | DONCASTER - 36A | NEWENGLAND - 35A | NEWENGLAND - 35A | KINGS CROSS - 34A |
| Jan-57 | YORK - 50A | GATESHEAD - 52A | DONCASTER - 36A | NEWENGLAND - 35A | FERRYHILL - 61B | DONCASTER - 36A | NEWENGLAND - 35A | NEWENGLAND - 35A | KINGS CROSS - 34A |
| Aug-57 | YORK - 50A | **9/57: YORK - 50A** | DONCASTER - 36A | NEWENGLAND - 35A | FERRYHILL - 61B | DONCASTER - 36A | NEWENGLAND - 35A | **6/57: GRAN - 35B** | **10/57: NEAS - 34E** |
| Jan-58 | YORK - 50A | YORK - 50A | DONCASTER - 36A | NEWENGLAND - 35A | FERRYHILL - 61B | DONCASTER - 36A | NEWENGLAND - 35A | **9/57: LEIC - 38C** | NEASDEN - 34E |
| Aug-58 | YORK - 50A | **6/58: DARL - 51A** | DONCASTER - 36A | NEWENGLAND - 34E | FERRYHILL - 61B | DONCASTER - 36A | NEWENGLAND - 34E | **3/58: KX - 34A** | NEASDEN - 14D |
| Jan-59 | YORK - 50A | DARLINGTON - 51A | DONCASTER - 36A | NEWENGLAND - 34E | FERRYHILL - 61B | DONCASTER - 36A | NEWENGLAND - 34E | KINGS CROSS - 34A | **11/58: YORK - 50A** |
| Aug-59 | YORK - 50A | DARLINGTON - 51A | DONCASTER - 36A | NEWENGLAND - 34E | FERRYHILL - 61B | DONCASTER - 36A | NEWENGLAND - 34E | KINGS CROSS - 34A | YORK - 50A |
| Nov-59 | YORK - 50A | DARLINGTON - 51A | DONCASTER - 36A | **10/59: DCTR - 36A** | FERRYHILL - 61B | DONCASTER - 36A | NEWENGLAND - 34E | KINGS CROSS - 34A | YORK - 50A |
| Jan-60 | YORK - 50A | DARLINGTON - 51A | DONCASTER - 36A | DONCASTER - 36A | FERRYHILL - 61B | DONCASTER - 36A | NEWENGLAND - 34E | KINGS CROSS - 34A | YORK - 50A |
| Apr-60 | YORK - 50A | DARLINGTON - 51A | DONCASTER - 36A | DONCASTER - 36A | FERRYHILL - 61B | DONCASTER - 36A | NEWENGLAND - 34E | KINGS CROSS - 34A | YORK - 50A |
| Aug-60 | YORK - 50A | DARLINGTON - 51A | DONCASTER - 36A | DONCASTER - 36A | FERRYHILL - 61B | DONCASTER - 36A | NEWENGLAND - 34E | KINGS CROSS - 34A | YORK - 50A |
| Nov-60 | YORK - 50A | DARLINGTON - 51A | DONCASTER - 36A | DONCASTER - 36A | FERRYHILL - 61B | DONCASTER - 36A | NEWENGLAND - 34E | KINGS CROSS - 34A | YORK - 50A |

| | 60856 | 60857 | 60858 | 60859 | 60860 | 60861 | 60862 | 60863 | 60864 |
|---|---|---|---|---|---|---|---|---|---|
| Aug-50 | YORK - 50A | DONCASTER - 36A | NEWENGLAND - 35A | NEWENGLAND - 35A | HEATON - 52B | DONCASTER - 36A | KINGS CROSS - 34A | NEWENGLAND - 35A | YORK - 50A |
| Jan-51 | YORK - 50A | DONCASTER - 36A | NEWENGLAND - 35A | **2/51: WOOD - 38E** | HEATON - 52B | DONCASTER - 36A | KINGS CROSS - 34A | **3/51: WOOD - 38E** | YORK - 50A |
| Aug-51 | YORK - 50A | DONCASTER - 36A | NEWENGLAND - 35A | WOODFORD HALSE - 38E | **7/51: GHD - 52A** | **9/51: C.HILL - 37B** | KINGS CROSS - 34A | WOODFORD HALSE - 38E | YORK - 50A |
| Jan-52 | YORK - 50A | DONCASTER - 36A | NEWENGLAND - 35A | WOODFORD HALSE - 38E | **9/51: HTN - 52B** | COPLEY HILL - 37B | KINGS CROSS - 34A | WOODFORD HALSE - 38E | YORK - 50A |
| Aug-52 | YORK - 50A | DONCASTER - 36A | **6/52: MARCH - 31B** | WOODFORD HALSE - 38E | HEATON - 52B | COPLEY HILL - 37B | KINGS CROSS - 34A | WOODFORD HALSE - 38E | YORK - 50A |
| Jan-53 | YORK - 50A | DONCASTER - 36A | MARCH - 31B | WOODFORD HALSE - 38E | **3/53: TWEED - 52D** | COPLEY HILL - 37B | KINGS CROSS - 34A | WOODFORD HALSE - 38E | YORK - 50A |
| Aug-53 | YORK - 50A | DONCASTER - 36A | MARCH - 31B | WOODFORD HALSE - 38E | TWEEDMOUTH - 52D | **7/53: ARDS - 37A** | KINGS CROSS - 34A | **5/53: LEIC - 38C** | YORK - 50A |
| Jan-54 | YORK - 50A | DONCASTER - 36A | MARCH - 31B | **1/54: C.HILL - 37B** | TWEEDMOUTH - 52D | ARDSLEY - 37A | KINGS CROSS - 34A | LEICESTER (GC) - 38C | YORK - 50A |
| Aug-54 | YORK - 50A | DONCASTER - 36A | MARCH - 31B | COPLEY HILL - 37B | TWEEDMOUTH - 52D | ARDSLEY - 37A | KINGS CROSS - 34A | LEICESTER (GC) - 38C | YORK - 50A |
| Jan-55 | YORK - 50A | DONCASTER - 36A | MARCH - 31B | COPLEY HILL - 37B | TWEEDMOUTH - 52D | ARDSLEY - 37A | KINGS CROSS - 34A | LEICESTER (GC) - 38C | YORK - 50A |
| Aug-55 | YORK - 50A | DONCASTER - 36A | MARCH - 31B | COPLEY HILL - 37B | TWEEDMOUTH - 52D | ARDSLEY - 37A | KINGS CROSS - 34A | LEICESTER (GC) - 38C | YORK - 50A |
| Jan-56 | YORK - 50A | DONCASTER - 36A | MARCH - 31B | COPLEY HILL - 37B | TWEEDMOUTH - 52D | ARDSLEY - 37A | KINGS CROSS - 34A | LEICESTER (GC) - 38C | YORK - 50A |
| Aug-56 | YORK - 50A | DONCASTER - 36A | MARCH - 31B | COPLEY HILL - 56C | TWEEDMOUTH - 52D | ARDSLEY - 56B | KINGS CROSS - 34A | LEICESTER (GC) - 38C | YORK - 50A |
| Jan-57 | YORK - 50A | DONCASTER - 36A | MARCH - 31B | COPLEY HILL - 56C | TWEEDMOUTH - 52D | ARDSLEY - 56B | KINGS CROSS - 34A | LEICESTER (GC) - 38C | YORK - 50A |
| Aug-57 | YORK - 50A | DONCASTER - 36A | MARCH - 31B | COPLEY HILL - 56C | **6/57: GHD - 52A** | ARDSLEY - 56B | KINGS CROSS - 34A | **6/57: GRAN - 35B** | YORK - 50A |
| Jan-58 | YORK - 50A | DONCASTER - 36A | MARCH - 31B | COPLEY HILL - 56C | GATESHEAD - 52A | ARDSLEY - 56B | KINGS CROSS - 34A | **9/57: LEIC - 38C** | YORK - 50A |
| Aug-58 | YORK - 50A | DONCASTER - 36A | MARCH - 31B | COPLEY HILL - 56C | GATESHEAD - 52A | ARDSLEY - 56B | KINGS CROSS - 34A | LEICESTER (GC) - 15E | YORK - 50A |
| Jan-59 | YORK - 50A | DONCASTER - 36A | MARCH - 31B | COPLEY HILL - 56C | GATESHEAD - 52A | ARDSLEY - 56B | KINGS CROSS - 34A | LEICESTER (GC) - 15E | YORK - 50A |
| Aug-59 | YORK - 50A | DONCASTER - 36A | MARCH - 31B | COPLEY HILL - 56C | GATESHEAD - 52A | ARDSLEY - 56B | KINGS CROSS - 34A | LEICESTER (GC) - 15E | **6/59: C.HILL - 56C** |
| Nov-59 | YORK - 50A | DONCASTER - 36A | MARCH - 31B | COPLEY HILL - 56C | GATESHEAD - 52A | ARDSLEY - 56B | KINGS CROSS - 34A | LEICESTER (GC) - 15E | **10/59: YORK - 50A** |
| Jan-60 | YORK - 50A | DONCASTER - 36A | MARCH - 31B | COPLEY HILL - 56C | **1/60: HTN - 52B** | ARDSLEY - 56B | KINGS CROSS - 34A | LEICESTER (GC) - 15E | YORK - 50A |
| Apr-60 | YORK - 50A | DONCASTER - 36A | MARCH - 31B | COPLEY HILL - 56C | HEATON - 52B | ARDSLEY - 56B | KINGS CROSS - 34A | LEICESTER (GC) - 15E | YORK - 50A |
| Aug-60 | YORK - 50A | **6/60: GRAN - 34F** | MARCH - 31B | **9/60: TNBY - 51L** | HEATON - 52B | ARDSLEY - 56B | KINGS CROSS - 34A | LEICESTER (GC) - 15E | YORK - 50A |
| Nov-60 | YORK - 50A | **10/60: DCTR - 36A** | MARCH - 31B | THORNABY - 51L | HEATON - 52B | ARDSLEY - 56B | KINGS CROSS - 34A | LEICESTER (GC) - 15E | YORK - 50A |

| | 60865 | 60866 | 60867 | 60868 | 60869 | 60870 | 60871 | 60872 | 60873 |
|---|---|---|---|---|---|---|---|---|---|
| Aug-50 | NEWENGLAND - 35A | NEWENGLAND - 35A | DONCASTER - 36A | HEATON - 52B | NEWENGLAND - 35A | DONCASTER - 36A | NEWENGLAND - 35A | DONCASTER - 36A | KINGS CROSS - 34A |
| Jan-51 | NEWENGLAND - 35A | NEWENGLAND - 35A | DONCASTER - 36A | HEATON - 52B | NEWENGLAND - 35A | DONCASTER - 36A | **1/51: WOOD - 38E** | DONCASTER - 36A | KINGS CROSS - 34A |
| Aug-51 | **6/51: MARCH - 31B** | NEWENGLAND - 35A | DONCASTER - 36A | HEATON - 52B | NEWENGLAND - 35A | DONCASTER - 36A | WOODFORD HALSE - 38E | DONCASTER - 36A | **4/51: ST M - 64A** |
| Jan-52 | **9/51: C.HILL - 37B** | NEWENGLAND - 35A | DONCASTER - 36A | HEATON - 52B | NEWENGLAND - 35A | DONCASTER - 36A | WOODFORD HALSE - 38E | DONCASTER - 36A | EDINBURGH (SM) - 64A |
| Aug-52 | COPLEY HILL - 37B | NEWENGLAND - 35A | DONCASTER - 36A | **7/52: GHD - 52A** | NEWENGLAND - 35A | DONCASTER - 36A | **8/52: LEIC - 38C** | DONCASTER - 36A | EDINBURGH (SM) - 64A |
| Jan-53 | COPLEY HILL - 37B | NEWENGLAND - 35A | DONCASTER - 36A | GATESHEAD - 52A | NEWENGLAND - 35A | DONCASTER - 36A | **9/52: WOOD - 38E** | DONCASTER - 36A | EDINBURGH (SM) - 64A |
| Aug-53 | COPLEY HILL - 37B | NEWENGLAND - 35A | DONCASTER - 36A | GATESHEAD - 52A | NEWENGLAND - 35A | DONCASTER - 36A | WOODFORD HALSE - 38E | DONCASTER - 36A | EDINBURGH (SM) - 64A |
| Jan-54 | COPLEY HILL - 37B | NEWENGLAND - 35A | DONCASTER - 36A | GATESHEAD - 52A | NEWENGLAND - 35A | DONCASTER - 36A | WOODFORD HALSE - 38E | DONCASTER - 36A | EDINBURGH (SM) - 64A |
| Aug-54 | COPLEY HILL - 37B | NEWENGLAND - 35A | DONCASTER - 36A | GATESHEAD - 52A | NEWENGLAND - 35A | DONCASTER - 36A | WOODFORD HALSE - 38E | DONCASTER - 36A | EDINBURGH (SM) - 64A |
| Jan-55 | COPLEY HILL - 37B | NEWENGLAND - 35A | DONCASTER - 36A | GATESHEAD - 52A | NEWENGLAND - 35A | DONCASTER - 36A | WOODFORD HALSE - 38E | DONCASTER - 36A | EDINBURGH (SM) - 64A |
| Aug-55 | COPLEY HILL - 37B | NEWENGLAND - 35A | **9/55: NEW E - 35A** | GATESHEAD - 52A | NEWENGLAND - 35A | DONCASTER - 36A | WOODFORD HALSE - 38E | DONCASTER - 36A | EDINBURGH (SM) - 64A |
| Jan-56 | COPLEY HILL - 37B | NEWENGLAND - 35A | NEWENGLAND - 35A | GATESHEAD - 52A | NEWENGLAND - 35A | DONCASTER - 36A | **11/55: DCTR - 36A** | DONCASTER - 36A | EDINBURGH (SM) - 64A |
| Aug-56 | COPLEY HILL - 56C | NEWENGLAND - 35A | NEWENGLAND - 35A | GATESHEAD - 52A | NEWENGLAND - 35A | DONCASTER - 36A | **8/56: KX - 34A** | DONCASTER - 36A | EDINBURGH (SM) - 64A |
| Jan-57 | COPLEY HILL - 56C | NEWENGLAND - 35A | NEWENGLAND - 35A | GATESHEAD - 52A | NEWENGLAND - 35A | DONCASTER - 36A | KINGS CROSS - 34A | DONCASTER - 36A | EDINBURGH (SM) - 64A |
| Aug-57 | COPLEY HILL - 56C | NEWENGLAND - 35A | NEWENGLAND - 35A | GATESHEAD - 52A | NEWENGLAND - 35A | DONCASTER - 36A | KINGS CROSS - 34A | DONCASTER - 36A | EDINBURGH (SM) - 64A |
| Jan-58 | COPLEY HILL - 56C | NEWENGLAND - 35A | NEWENGLAND - 35A | GATESHEAD - 52A | NEWENGLAND - 35A | DONCASTER - 36A | KINGS CROSS - 34A | DONCASTER - 36A | EDINBURGH (SM) - 64A |
| Aug-58 | **9/58: TWEED - 52D** | NEWENGLAND - 34E | NEWENGLAND - 34E | GATESHEAD - 52A | NEWENGLAND - 34E | DONCASTER - 36A | KINGS CROSS - 34A | DONCASTER - 36A | EDINBURGH (SM) - 64A |
| Jan-59 | TWEEDMOUTH - 52D | **11/58: DCTR - 36A** | NEWENGLAND - 34E | GATESHEAD - 52A | NEWENGLAND - 34E | DONCASTER - 36A | KINGS CROSS - 34A | DONCASTER - 36A | EDINBURGH (SM) - 64A |
| Aug-59 | TWEEDMOUTH - 52D | DONCASTER - 36A | NEWENGLAND - 34E | GATESHEAD - 52A | NEWENGLAND - 34E | DONCASTER - 36A | KINGS CROSS - 34A | DONCASTER - 36A | EDINBURGH (SM) - 64A |
| Nov-59 | TWEEDMOUTH - 52D | DONCASTER - 36A | NEWENGLAND - 34E | GATESHEAD - 52A | NEWENGLAND - 34E | DONCASTER - 36A | KINGS CROSS - 34A | DONCASTER - 36A | EDINBURGH (SM) - 64A |
| Jan-60 | TWEEDMOUTH - 52D | DONCASTER - 36A | NEWENGLAND - 34E | **1/60: HTN - 52B** | NEWENGLAND - 34E | DONCASTER - 36A | KINGS CROSS - 34A | DONCASTER - 36A | EDINBURGH (SM) - 64A |
| Apr-60 | TWEEDMOUTH - 52D | DONCASTER - 36A | NEWENGLAND - 34E | HEATON - 52B | NEWENGLAND - 34E | DONCASTER - 36A | KINGS CROSS - 34A | DONCASTER - 36A | EDINBURGH (SM) - 64A |
| Aug-60 | TWEEDMOUTH - 52D | DONCASTER - 36A | NEWENGLAND - 34E | HEATON - 52B | NEWENGLAND - 34E | DONCASTER - 36A | KINGS CROSS - 34A | DONCASTER - 36A | EDINBURGH (SM) - 64A |
| Nov-60 | TWEEDMOUTH - 52D | DONCASTER - 36A | NEWENGLAND - 34E | HEATON - 52B | NEWENGLAND - 34E | DONCASTER - 36A | KINGS CROSS - 34A | DONCASTER - 36A | EDINBURGH (SM) - 64A |

| | 60874 | 60875 | 60876 | 60877 | 60878 | 60879 | 60880 | 60881 | 60882 |
|---|---|---|---|---|---|---|---|---|---|
| Aug-50 | NEWENGLAND - 35A | DONCASTER - 36A | NEWENGLAND - 35A | DONCASTER - 36A | NEWENGLAND - 35A | NEWENGLAND - 35A | DONCASTER - 36A | DONCASTER - 36A | HAYMARKET - 64B |
| Jan-51 | NEWENGLAND - 35A | DONCASTER - 36A | NEWENGLAND - 35A | DONCASTER - 36A | NEWENGLAND - 35A | NEWENGLAND - 35A | DONCASTER - 36A | DONCASTER - 36A | **3/51: ST M - 64A** |
| Aug-51 | NEWENGLAND - 35A | DONCASTER - 36A | **9/51: WOD - 38E** | DONCASTER - 36A | NEWENGLAND - 35A | **6/51: WOOD - 38E** | DONCASTER - 36A | DONCASTER - 36A | EDINBURGH (SM) - 64A |
| Jan-52 | NEWENGLAND - 35A | DONCASTER - 36A | WOODFORD HALSE - 38E | DONCASTER - 36A | NEWENGLAND - 35A | WOODFORD HALSE - 38E | DONCASTER - 36A | DONCASTER - 36A | EDINBURGH (SM) - 64A |
| Aug-52 | NEWENGLAND - 35A | DONCASTER - 36A | WOODFORD HALSE - 38E | DONCASTER - 36A | NEWENGLAND - 35A | WOODFORD HALSE - 38E | DONCASTER - 36A | DONCASTER - 36A | EDINBURGH (SM) - 64A |
| Jan-53 | NEWENGLAND - 35A | DONCASTER - 36A | WOODFORD HALSE - 38E | DONCASTER - 36A | NEWENGLAND - 35A | WOODFORD HALSE - 38E | DONCASTER - 36A | DONCASTER - 36A | EDINBURGH (SM) - 64A |
| Aug-53 | NEWENGLAND - 35A | DONCASTER - 36A | WOODFORD HALSE - 38E | DONCASTER - 36A | NEWENGLAND - 35A | WOODFORD HALSE - 38E | DONCASTER - 36A | DONCASTER - 36A | EDINBURGH (SM) - 64A |
| Jan-54 | NEWENGLAND - 35A | DONCASTER - 36A | **12/53: KX - 34A** | DONCASTER - 36A | **3/54: LEIC - 38C** | WOODFORD HALSE - 38E | DONCASTER - 36A | DONCASTER - 36A | EDINBURGH (SM) - 64A |
| Aug-54 | NEWENGLAND - 35A | DONCASTER - 36A | KINGS CROSS - 34A | DONCASTER - 36A | LEICESTER (GC) - 38C | WOODFORD HALSE - 38E | DONCASTER - 36A | DONCASTER - 36A | EDINBURGH (SM) - 64A |
| Jan-55 | NEWENGLAND - 35A | DONCASTER - 36A | KINGS CROSS - 34A | DONCASTER - 36A | LEICESTER (GC) - 38C | WOODFORD HALSE - 38E | DONCASTER - 36A | DONCASTER - 36A | EDINBURGH (SM) - 64A |
| Aug-55 | NEWENGLAND - 35A | DONCASTER - 36A | KINGS CROSS - 34A | DONCASTER - 36A | LEICESTER (GC) - 38C | WOODFORD HALSE - 38E | DONCASTER - 36A | **6/55: KX - 34A** | EDINBURGH (SM) - 64A |
| Jan-56 | NEWENGLAND - 35A | **12/55: NEW E - 35A** | KINGS CROSS - 34A | **5/56: KX - 34A** | LEICESTER (GC) - 38C | WOODFORD HALSE - 38E | DONCASTER - 36A | **11/55: DCTR - 36A** | EDINBURGH (SM) - 64A |
| Aug-56 | NEWENGLAND - 35A | NEWENGLAND - 35A | KINGS CROSS - 34A | **6/56: NEAS - 34E** | LEICESTER (GC) - 38C | WOODFORD HALSE - 38E | DONCASTER - 36A | DONCASTER - 36A | EDINBURGH (SM) - 64A |
| Jan-57 | NEWENGLAND - 35A | NEWENGLAND - 35A | **5/57: NEAS - 34E** | **3/57: KX - 34A** | LEICESTER (GC) - 38C | WOODFORD HALSE - 38E | DONCASTER - 36A | DONCASTER - 36A | EDINBURGH (SM) - 64A |
| Aug-57 | NEWENGLAND - 35A | NEWENGLAND - 35A | **7/57: KX - 34A** | KINGS CROSS - 34A | LEICESTER (GC) - 38C | **6/57: LEIC - 38C** | DONCASTER - 36A | DONCASTER - 36A | EDINBURGH (SM) - 64A |
| Jan-58 | NEWENGLAND - 35A | NEWENGLAND - 35A | **10/57: NEAS - 34E** | **10/57: NEAS - 34E** | LEICESTER (GC) - 38C | LEICESTER (GC) - 38C | DONCASTER - 36A | DONCASTER - 36A | EDINBURGH (SM) - 64A |
| Aug-58 | NEWENGLAND - 34E | NEWENGLAND - 34E | NEASDEN - 14D | NEASDEN - 14D | LEICESTER (GC) - 15E | LEICESTER (GC) - 15E | DONCASTER - 36A | DONCASTER - 36A | EDINBURGH (SM) - 64A |
| Jan-59 | NEWENGLAND - 34E | NEWENGLAND - 34E | **11/58: YORK - 50A** | **11/58: YORK - 50A** | **11/58: YORK - 50A** | LEICESTER (GC) - 15E | DONCASTER - 36A | DONCASTER - 36A | EDINBURGH (SM) - 64A |
| Aug-59 | NEWENGLAND - 34E | **6/59: GRAN - 34F** | YORK - 50A | **6/59: C.HILL - 56C** | YORK - 50A | **8/59: YORK - 50A** | DONCASTER - 36A | DONCASTER - 36A | EDINBURGH (SM) - 64A |
| Nov-59 | NEWENGLAND - 34E | **9/59: DCTR - 36A** | YORK - 50A | **10/59: YORK - 50A** | YORK - 50A | YORK - 50A | DONCASTER - 36A | DONCASTER - 36A | EDINBURGH (SM) - 64A |
| Jan-60 | NEWENGLAND - 34E | DONCASTER - 36A | YORK - 50A | YORK - 50A | YORK - 50A | YORK - 50A | DONCASTER - 36A | DONCASTER - 36A | EDINBURGH (SM) - 64A |
| Apr-60 | NEWENGLAND - 34E | DONCASTER - 36A | YORK - 50A | YORK - 50A | YORK - 50A | YORK - 50A | DONCASTER - 36A | DONCASTER - 36A | EDINBURGH (SM) - 64A |
| Aug-60 | NEWENGLAND - 34E | DONCASTER - 36A | YORK - 50A | YORK - 50A | YORK - 50A | YORK - 50A | DONCASTER - 36A | DONCASTER - 36A | EDINBURGH (SM) - 64A |
| Nov-60 | NEWENGLAND - 34E | DONCASTER - 36A | YORK - 50A | YORK - 50A | YORK - 50A | YORK - 50A | DONCASTER - 36A | DONCASTER - 36A | EDINBURGH (SM) - 64A |

Darlington to Paignton. Since the trains were timed long before an engine could be diagrammed, the timing office generally assumed for the sake of their calculations V2 haulage for long distance specials and nine times out of ten the diagramming office would follow suit. It was a strange day when a couple of hours spent at an east coast location did not produce at least one 2-6-2 on a main line working.

| | 60883 | 60884 | 60885 | 60886 | 60887 | 60888 | 60889 | 60890 | 60891 |
|---|---|---|---|---|---|---|---|---|---|
| Aug-50 | GATESHEAD - 52A | GATESHEAD - 52A | GATESHEAD - 52A | HEATON - 52B | HEATON - 52B | FERRYHILL - 61B | DONCASTER - 36A | DONCASTER - 36A | HEATON - 52B |
| Jan-51 | GATESHEAD - 52A | **11/50: HTN - 52B** | **11/50: HTN - 52B** | HEATON - 52B | HEATON - 52B | FERRYHILL - 61B | DONCASTER - 36A | DONCASTER - 36A | HEATON - 52B |
| Aug-51 | GATESHEAD - 52A | **5/51: TWEED - 52D** | **5/51: TWEED - 52D** | **5/51: TWEED - 52D** | **5/51: TWEED - 52D** | FERRYHILL - 61B | DONCASTER - 36A | **6/51: WOOD - 38E** | HEATON - 52B |
| Jan-52 | GATESHEAD - 52A | TWEEDMOUTH - 52D | **1/52: HTN - 52B** | **1/52: HTN - 52B** | **1/52: HTN - 52B** | FERRYHILL - 61B | DONCASTER - 36A | WOODFORD HALSE - 38E | HEATON - 52B |
| Aug-52 | GATESHEAD - 52A | TWEEDMOUTH - 52D | **7/52: GHD - 52A** | **7/52: GHD - 52A** | **7/52: GHD - 52A** | FERRYHILL - 61B | DONCASTER - 36A | WOODFORD HALSE - 38E | HEATON - 52B |
| Jan-53 | GATESHEAD - 52A | TWEEDMOUTH - 52D | GATESHEAD - 52A | GATESHEAD - 52A | **2/53: HTN - 52B** | FERRYHILL - 61B | DONCASTER - 36A | **3/53: LEIC - 83C** | HEATON - 52B |
| Aug-53 | GATESHEAD - 52A | TWEEDMOUTH - 52D | GATESHEAD - 52A | GATESHEAD - 52A | HEATON - 52B | FERRYHILL - 61B | DONCASTER - 36A | **5/53: WOOD - 38E** | HEATON - 52B |
| Jan-54 | GATESHEAD - 52A | TWEEDMOUTH - 52D | **11/53: HTN - 52B** | **11/53: HTN - 52B** | HEATON - 52B | FERRYHILL - 61B | DONCASTER - 36A | WOODFORD HALSE - 38E | HEATON - 52B |
| Aug-54 | GATESHEAD - 52A | TWEEDMOUTH - 52D | HEATON - 52B | HEATON - 52B | HEATON - 52B | FERRYHILL - 61B | DONCASTER - 36A | WOODFORD HALSE - 38E | HEATON - 52B |
| Jan-55 | GATESHEAD - 52A | TWEEDMOUTH - 52D | HEATON - 52B | HEATON - 52B | HEATON - 52B | FERRYHILL - 61B | DONCASTER - 36A | WOODFORD HALSE - 38E | HEATON - 52B |
| Aug-55 | GATESHEAD - 52A | **5/55: HTN - 52B** | HEATON - 52B | HEATON - 52B | **9/55: GHD - 52A** | FERRYHILL - 61B | DONCASTER - 36A | WOODFORD HALSE - 38E | HEATON - 52B |
| Jan-56 | **4/56: HTN - 52B** | HEATON - 52B | HEATON - 52B | HEATON - 52B | GATESHEAD - 52A | FERRYHILL - 61B | DONCASTER - 36A | WOODFORD HALSE - 38E | HEATON - 52B |
| Aug-56 | GATESHEAD - 52A | **10/56: ARDS - 56B** | HEATON - 52B | HEATON - 52B | GATESHEAD - 52A | FERRYHILL - 61B | DONCASTER - 36A | WOODFORD HALSE - 38E | HEATON - 52B |
| Jan-57 | **8/56: ST M - 64A** | ARDSLEY - 56B | **10/56: C.HILL - 56C** | HEATON - 52B | GATESHEAD - 52A | FERRYHILL - 61B | DONCASTER - 36A | WOODFORD HALSE - 38E | HEATON - 52B |
| Aug-57 | EDINBURGH (SM) - 64A | ARDSLEY - 56B | COPLEYHILL - 56C | HEATON - 52B | **9/57: YORK - 50A** | FERRYHILL - 61B | DONCASTER - 36A | WOODFORD HALSE - 38E | HEATON - 52B |
| Jan-58 | EDINBURGH (SM) - 64A | ARDSLEY - 56B | COPLEYHILL - 56C | HEATON - 52B | YORK - 50A | FERRYHILL - 61B | DONCASTER - 36A | WOODFORD HALSE - 38E | HEATON - 52B |
| Aug-58 | EDINBURGH (SM) - 64A | ARDSLEY - 56B | COPLEYHILL - 56C | HEATON - 52B | YORK - 50A | FERRYHILL - 61B | DONCASTER - 36A | WOODFORD HALSE - 2F | HEATON - 52B |
| Jan-59 | EDINBURGH (SM) - 64A | ARDSLEY - 56B | COPLEYHILL - 56C | HEATON - 52B | YORK - 50A | FERRYHILL - 61B | DONCASTER - 36A | WOODFORD HALSE - 2F | HEATON - 52B |
| Aug-59 | EDINBURGH (SM) - 64A | ARDSLEY - 56B | COPLEYHILL - 56C | HEATON - 52B | YORK - 50A | FERRYHILL - 61B | DONCASTER - 36A | **8/59: LEIC - 15E** | HEATON - 52B |
| Nov-59 | EDINBURGH (SM) - 64A | ARDSLEY - 56B | **11/59: TNBY - 51L** | HEATON - 52B | YORK - 50A | FERRYHILL - 61B | DONCASTER - 36A | LEICESTER (GC) - 15E | HEATON - 52B |
| Jan-60 | EDINBURGH (SM) - 64A | ARDSLEY - 56B | THORNABY - 51L | HEATON - 52B | YORK - 50A | FERRYHILL - 61B | DONCASTER - 36A | LEICESTER (GC) - 15E | HEATON - 52B |
| Apr-60 | EDINBURGH (SM) - 64A | ARDSLEY - 56B | THORNABY - 51L | HEATON - 52B | YORK - 50A | FERRYHILL - 61B | DONCASTER - 36A | LEICESTER (GC) - 15E | HEATON - 52B |
| Aug-60 | EDINBURGH (SM) - 64A | ARDSLEY - 56B | THORNABY - 51L | HEATON - 52B | YORK - 50A | FERRYHILL - 61B | DONCASTER - 36A | LEICESTER (GC) - 15E | HEATON - 52B |
| Nov-60 | EDINBURGH (SM) - 64A | ARDSLEY - 56B | THORNABY - 51L | HEATON - 52B | YORK - 50A | FERRYHILL - 61B | DONCASTER - 36A | LEICESTER (GC) - 15E | HEATON - 52B |

| | 60892 | 60893 | 60894 | 60895 | 60896 | 60897 | 60898 | 60899 | 60900 |
|---|---|---|---|---|---|---|---|---|---|
| Aug-50 | KINGS CROSS - 34A | NEWENGLAND - 35A | EDINBURGH (SM) - 64A | HEATON - 52B | DONCASTER - 36A | NEWENGLAND - 35A | FERRYHILL - 61B | NEWENGLAND - 35A | KINGS CROSS - 34A |
| Jan-51 | **2/51: ST M - 64A** | NEWENGLAND - 35A | **1/51: HMKT - 64B** | HEATON - 52B | DONCASTER - 36A | NEWENGLAND - 35A | FERRYHILL - 61B | NEWENGLAND - 35A | KINGS CROSS - 34A |
| Aug-51 | EDINBURGH (SM) - 64A | NEWENGLAND - 35A | **3/51: ST M - 64A** | HEATON - 52B | DONCASTER - 36A | NEWENGLAND - 35A | FERRYHILL - 61B | NEWENGLAND - 35A | KINGS CROSS - 34A |
| Jan-52 | EDINBURGH (SM) - 64A | NEWENGLAND - 35A | EDINBURGH (SM) - 64A | HEATON - 52B | DONCASTER - 36A | NEWENGLAND - 35A | FERRYHILL - 61B | NEWENGLAND - 35A | KINGS CROSS - 34A |
| Aug-52 | EDINBURGH (SM) - 64A | NEWENGLAND - 35A | EDINBURGH (SM) - 64A | HEATON - 52B | DONCASTER - 36A | NEWENGLAND - 35A | FERRYHILL - 61B | **6/52: MARCH - 31B** | KINGS CROSS - 34A |
| Jan-53 | EDINBURGH (SM) - 64A | NEWENGLAND - 35A | EDINBURGH (SM) - 64A | HEATON - 52B | DONCASTER - 36A | NEWENGLAND - 35A | FERRYHILL - 61B | MARCH - 31B | **2/53: ST M - 64A** |
| Aug-53 | EDINBURGH (SM) - 64A | NEWENGLAND - 35A | EDINBURGH (SM) - 64A | **7/53: DARL - 51A** | DONCASTER - 36A | NEWENGLAND - 35A | FERRYHILL - 61B | MARCH - 31B | EDINBURGH (SM) - 64A |
| Jan-54 | EDINBURGH (SM) - 64A | NEWENGLAND - 35A | EDINBURGH (SM) - 64A | **10/53: YORK - 50A** | DONCASTER - 36A | NEWENGLAND - 35A | FERRYHILL - 61B | MARCH - 31B | EDINBURGH (SM) - 64A |
| Aug-54 | EDINBURGH (SM) - 64A | NEWENGLAND - 35A | EDINBURGH (SM) - 64A | YORK - 50A | DONCASTER - 36A | NEWENGLAND - 35A | FERRYHILL - 61B | MARCH - 31B | EDINBURGH (SM) - 64A |
| Jan-55 | EDINBURGH (SM) - 64A | NEWENGLAND - 35A | EDINBURGH (SM) - 64A | YORK - 50A | DONCASTER - 36A | NEWENGLAND - 35A | FERRYHILL - 61B | MARCH - 31B | EDINBURGH (SM) - 64A |
| Aug-55 | EDINBURGH (SM) - 64A | NEWENGLAND - 35A | EDINBURGH (SM) - 64A | YORK - 50A | DONCASTER - 36A | NEWENGLAND - 35A | FERRYHILL - 61B | MARCH - 31B | EDINBURGH (SM) - 64A |
| Jan-56 | EDINBURGH (SM) - 64A | NEWENGLAND - 35A | EDINBURGH (SM) - 64A | YORK - 50A | DONCASTER - 36A | NEWENGLAND - 35A | FERRYHILL - 61B | MARCH - 31B | EDINBURGH (SM) - 64A |
| Aug-56 | EDINBURGH (SM) - 64A | NEWENGLAND - 35A | EDINBURGH (SM) - 64A | YORK - 50A | DONCASTER - 36A | NEWENGLAND - 35A | FERRYHILL - 61B | MARCH - 31B | EDINBURGH (SM) - 64A |
| Jan-57 | EDINBURGH (SM) - 64A | NEWENGLAND - 35A | EDINBURGH (SM) - 64A | YORK - 50A | DONCASTER - 36A | NEWENGLAND - 35A | FERRYHILL - 61B | MARCH - 31B | EDINBURGH (SM) - 64A |
| Aug-57 | EDINBURGH (SM) - 64A | **10/57: GRAN - 35B** | EDINBURGH (SM) - 64A | YORK - 50A | DONCASTER - 36A | NEWENGLAND - 35A | FERRYHILL - 61B | **6/57: KX - 34A** | EDINBURGH (SM) - 64A |
| Jan-58 | EDINBURGH (SM) - 64A | GRANTHAM - 35B | EDINBURGH (SM) - 64A | YORK - 50A | DONCASTER - 36A | NEWENGLAND - 35A | FERRYHILL - 61B | **9/57: DCTR - 36A** | EDINBURGH (SM) - 64A |
| Aug-58 | EDINBURGH (SM) - 64A | GRANTHAM - 34F | EDINBURGH (SM) - 64A | YORK - 50A | DONCASTER - 36A | NEWENGLAND - 34E | FERRYHILL - 61B | DONCASTER - 36A | EDINBURGH (SM) - 64A |
| Jan-59 | EDINBURGH (SM) - 64A | **12/58: NEWE - 34E** | EDINBURGH (SM) - 64A | YORK - 50A | DONCASTER - 36A | NEWENGLAND - 34E | FERRYHILL - 61B | DONCASTER - 36A | EDINBURGH (SM) - 64A |
| Aug-59 | EDINBURGH (SM) - 64A | NEWENGLAND - 34E | EDINBURGH (SM) - 64A | YORK - 50A | DONCASTER - 36A | NEWENGLAND - 34E | FERRYHILL - 61B | DONCASTER - 36A | EDINBURGH (SM) - 64A |
| Nov-59 | EDINBURGH (SM) - 64A | NEWENGLAND - 34E | EDINBURGH (SM) - 64A | YORK - 50A | DONCASTER - 36A | NEWENGLAND - 34E | FERRYHILL - 61B | DONCASTER - 36A | EDINBURGH (SM) - 64A |
| Jan-60 | EDINBURGH (SM) - 64A | NEWENGLAND - 34E | EDINBURGH (SM) - 64A | YORK - 50A | DONCASTER - 36A | NEWENGLAND - 34E | FERRYHILL - 61B | DONCASTER - 36A | EDINBURGH (SM) - 64A |
| Apr-60 | EDINBURGH (SM) - 64A | NEWENGLAND - 34E | EDINBURGH (SM) - 64A | YORK - 50A | **6/60: GRAN - 34F** | NEWENGLAND - 34E | FERRYHILL - 61B | DONCASTER - 36A | EDINBURGH (SM) - 64A |
| Aug-60 | EDINBURGH (SM) - 64A | NEWENGLAND - 34E | EDINBURGH (SM) - 64A | YORK - 50A | **10/60: DCTR - 36A** | NEWENGLAND - 34E | FERRYHILL - 61B | DONCASTER - 36A | EDINBURGH (SM) - 64A |
| Nov-60 | EDINBURGH (SM) - 64A | NEWENGLAND - 34E | EDINBURGH (SM) - 64A | YORK - 50A | DONCASTER - 36A | NEWENGLAND - 34E | FERRYHILL - 61B | DONCASTER - 36A | EDINBURGH (SM) - 64A |

| | 60901 | 60902 | 60903 | 60904 | 60905 | 60906 | 60907 | 60908 | 60909 |
|---|---|---|---|---|---|---|---|---|---|
| Aug-50 | YORK - 50A | DONCASTER - 36A | KINGS CROSS - 34A | YORK - 50A | NEWENGLAND - 35A | NEWENGLAND - 35A | YORK - 50A | NEWENGLAND - 35A | KINGS CROSS - 34A |
| Jan-51 | YORK - 50A | DONCASTER - 36A | KINGS CROSS - 34A | YORK - 50A | NEWENGLAND - 35A | NEWENGLAND - 35A | YORK - 50A | NEWENGLAND - 35A | KINGS CROSS - 34A |
| Aug-51 | YORK - 50A | DONCASTER - 36A | KINGS CROSS - 34A | YORK - 50A | NEWENGLAND - 35A | NEWENGLAND - 35A | YORK - 50A | NEWENGLAND - 35A | KINGS CROSS - 34A |
| Jan-52 | YORK - 50A | DONCASTER - 36A | KINGS CROSS - 34A | YORK - 50A | NEWENGLAND - 35A | NEWENGLAND - 35A | YORK - 50A | NEWENGLAND - 35A | KINGS CROSS - 34A |
| Aug-52 | **7/52: DARL - 51A** | DONCASTER - 36A | KINGS CROSS - 34A | YORK - 50A | NEWENGLAND - 35A | NEWENGLAND - 35A | **7/52: DARL - 51A** | NEWENGLAND - 35A | KINGS CROSS - 34A |
| Jan-53 | **10/52: YORK - 50A** | **5/53: KX - 34A** | KINGS CROSS - 34A | YORK - 50A | NEWENGLAND - 35A | NEWENGLAND - 35A | **10/52: YORK - 50A** | NEWENGLAND - 35A | **5/53: DCTR - 36A** |
| Aug-53 | YORK - 50A | **7/53: DCTR - 36A** | KINGS CROSS - 34A | YORK - 50A | NEWENGLAND - 35A | NEWENGLAND - 35A | YORK - 50A | NEWENGLAND - 35A | **7/53: KX - 34A** |
| Jan-54 | YORK - 50A | DONCASTER - 36A | KINGS CROSS - 34A | YORK - 50A | NEWENGLAND - 35A | NEWENGLAND - 35A | YORK - 50A | NEWENGLAND - 35A | KINGS CROSS - 34A |
| Aug-54 | YORK - 50A | DONCASTER - 36A | KINGS CROSS - 34A | YORK - 50A | NEWENGLAND - 35A | NEWENGLAND - 35A | YORK - 50A | NEWENGLAND - 35A | KINGS CROSS - 34A |
| Jan-55 | YORK - 50A | DONCASTER - 36A | KINGS CROSS - 34A | YORK - 50A | NEWENGLAND - 35A | NEWENGLAND - 35A | YORK - 50A | NEWENGLAND - 35A | KINGS CROSS - 34A |
| Aug-55 | YORK - 50A | **7/55: KX - 34A** | KINGS CROSS - 34A | YORK - 50A | NEWENGLAND - 35A | NEWENGLAND - 35A | YORK - 50A | NEWENGLAND - 35A | **7/55: DCTR - 36A** |
| Jan-56 | YORK - 50A | KINGS CROSS - 34A | KINGS CROSS - 34A | YORK - 50A | **12/55: DCTR - 36A** | NEWENGLAND - 35A | YORK - 50A | NEWENGLAND - 35A | DONCASTER - 36A |
| Aug-56 | **6/56: HTN - 52B** | KINGS CROSS - 34A | KINGS CROSS - 34A | YORK - 50A | DONCASTER - 36A | NEWENGLAND - 35A | YORK - 50A | NEWENGLAND - 35A | DONCASTER - 36A |
| Jan-57 | HEATON - 52B | KINGS CROSS - 34A | KINGS CROSS - 34A | YORK - 50A | DONCASTER - 36A | NEWENGLAND - 35A | YORK - 50A | NEWENGLAND - 35A | DONCASTER - 36A |
| Aug-57 | HEATON - 52B | KINGS CROSS - 34A | KINGS CROSS - 34A | YORK - 50A | DONCASTER - 36A | NEWENGLAND - 35A | YORK - 50A | NEWENGLAND - 35A | DONCASTER - 36A |
| Jan-58 | HEATON - 52B | KINGS CROSS - 34A | KINGS CROSS - 34A | YORK - 50A | DONCASTER - 36A | NEWENGLAND - 35A | YORK - 50A | NEWENGLAND - 35A | DONCASTER - 36A |
| Aug-58 | HEATON - 52B | KINGS CROSS - 34A | KINGS CROSS - 34A | **6/58: GHD - 52A** | DONCASTER - 36A | NEWENGLAND - 34E | YORK - 50A | NEWENGLAND - 34E | DONCASTER - 36A |
| Jan-59 | HEATON - 52B | KINGS CROSS - 34A | KINGS CROSS - 34A | GATESHEAD - 52A | DONCASTER - 36A | NEWENGLAND - 34E | YORK - 50A | NEWENGLAND - 34E | DONCASTER - 36A |
| Aug-59 | HEATON - 52B | KINGS CROSS - 34A | KINGS CROSS - 34A | GATESHEAD - 52A | DONCASTER - 36A | NEWENGLAND - 34E | YORK - 50A | **6/59: GRAN - 34F** | DONCASTER - 36A |
| Nov-59 | HEATON - 52B | KINGS CROSS - 34A | KINGS CROSS - 34A | GATESHEAD - 52A | DONCASTER - 36A | NEWENGLAND - 34E | YORK - 50A | **9/59: DCTR - 36A** | DONCASTER - 36A |
| Jan-60 | HEATON - 52B | KINGS CROSS - 34A | KINGS CROSS - 34A | **1/60: HTN - 52B** | DONCASTER - 36A | NEWENGLAND - 34E | YORK - 50A | DONCASTER - 36A | DONCASTER - 36A |
| Apr-60 | **6/60: DARL - 51A** | KINGS CROSS - 34A | KINGS CROSS - 34A | HEATON - 52B | DONCASTER - 36A | NEWENGLAND - 34E | YORK - 50A | DONCASTER - 36A | **6/60: GRAN - 34F** |
| Aug-60 | **9/60 : TNBY - 51L** | KINGS CROSS - 34A | KINGS CROSS - 34A | HEATON - 52B | DONCASTER - 36A | NEWENGLAND - 34E | YORK - 50A | DONCASTER - 36A | **10.60: DCTR - 36A** |
| Nov-60 | THORNABY - 51L | KINGS CROSS - 34A | KINGS CROSS - 34A | HEATON - 52B | DONCASTER - 36A | NEWENGLAND - 34E | YORK - 50A | DONCASTER - 36A | DONCASTER - 36A |

| | 60910 | 60911 | 60912 | 60913 | 60914 | 60915 | 60916 | 60917 | 60918 |
|---|---|---|---|---|---|---|---|---|---|
| Aug-50 | HEATON - 52B | NEWENGLAND - 35A | NEWENGLAND - 35A | NEWENGLAND - 35A | KINGS CROSS - 34A | KINGS CROSS - 34A | NEWENGLAND - 35A | DONCASTER - 36A | YORK - 50A |
| Jan-51 | HEATON - 52B | NEWENGLAND - 35A | NEWENGLAND - 35A | NEWENGLAND - 35A | KINGS CROSS - 34A | 1/51: WOOD - 38E | NEWENGLAND - 35A | DONCASTER - 36A | YORK - 50A |
| Aug-51 | HEATON - 52B | NEWENGLAND - 35A | NEWENGLAND - 35A | **6/51: MARCH - 31B** | KINGS CROSS - 34A | WOODFORD HALSE - 38E | NEWENGLAND - 35A | DONCASTER - 36A | YORK - 50A |
| Jan-52 | HEATON - 52B | NEWENGLAND - 35A | NEWENGLAND - 35A | **9/51: C.HILL - 37B** | KINGS CROSS - 34A | WOODFORD HALSE - 38E | NEWENGLAND - 35A | DONCASTER - 36A | YORK - 50A |
| Aug-52 | HEATON - 52B | NEWENGLAND - 35A | NEWENGLAND - 35A | COPLEYHILL - 37B | KINGS CROSS - 34A | WOODFORD HALSE - 38E | NEWENGLAND - 35A | DONCASTER - 36A | YORK - 50A |
| Jan-53 | HEATON - 52B | NEWENGLAND - 35A | NEWENGLAND - 35A | COPLEYHILL - 37B | KINGS CROSS - 34A | WOODFORD HALSE - 38E | NEWENGLAND - 35A | DONCASTER - 36A | YORK - 50A |
| Aug-53 | HEATON - 52B | NEWENGLAND - 35A | NEWENGLAND - 35A | COPLEYHILL - 37B | KINGS CROSS - 34A | WOODFORD HALSE - 38E | NEWENGLAND - 35A | DONCASTER - 36A | YORK - 50A |
| Jan-54 | HEATON - 52B | NEWENGLAND - 35A | NEWENGLAND - 35A | COPLEYHILL - 37B | KINGS CROSS - 34A | WOODFORD HALSE - 38E | NEWENGLAND - 35A | DONCASTER - 36A | YORK - 50A |
| Aug-54 | HEATON - 52B | NEWENGLAND - 35A | NEWENGLAND - 35A | COPLEYHILL - 37B | KINGS CROSS - 34A | WOODFORD HALSE - 38E | NEWENGLAND - 35A | DONCASTER - 36A | YORK - 50A |
| Jan-55 | HEATON - 52B | NEWENGLAND - 35A | NEWENGLAND - 35A | COPLEYHILL - 37B | KINGS CROSS - 34A | WOODFORD HALSE - 38E | NEWENGLAND - 35A | DONCASTER - 36A | YORK - 50A |
| Aug-55 | HEATON - 52B | NEWENGLAND - 35A | NEWENGLAND - 35A | COPLEYHILL - 37B | KINGS CROSS - 34A | WOODFORD HALSE - 38E | **4/55: ARDS - 37A** | DONCASTER - 36A | YORK - 50A |
| Jan-56 | HEATON - 52B | NEWENGLAND - 35A | NEWENGLAND - 35A | COPLEYHILL - 37B | KINGS CROSS - 34A | WOODFORD HALSE - 38E | ARDSLEY - 37A | DONCASTER - 36A | YORK - 50A |
| Aug-56 | HEATON - 52B | NEWENGLAND - 35A | NEWENGLAND - 35A | COPLEYHILL - 56C | KINGS CROSS - 34A | WOODFORD HALSE - 38E | ARDSLEY - 56B | DONCASTER - 36A | YORK - 50A |
| Jan-57 | HEATON - 52B | NEWENGLAND - 35A | NEWENGLAND - 35A | COPLEYHILL - 56C | KINGS CROSS - 34A | WOODFORD HALSE - 38E | ARDSLEY - 56B | DONCASTER - 36A | YORK - 50A |
| Aug-57 | HEATON - 52B | **6/57: GRAN - 35B** | NEWENGLAND - 35A | COPLEYHILL - 56C | KINGS CROSS - 34A | WOODFORD HALSE - 38E | ARDSLEY - 56B | DONCASTER - 36A | YORK - 50A |
| Jan-58 | HEATON - 52B | **9/57: LEIC - 38C** | NEWENGLAND - 35A | COPLEYHILL - 56C | KINGS CROSS - 34A | WOODFORD HALSE - 38E | ARDSLEY - 56B | DONCASTER - 36A | YORK - 50A |
| Aug-58 | HEATON - 52B | LEICESTER (GC) - 15E | NEWENGLAND - 34E | **9/58: TWEED - 52D** | KINGS CROSS - 34A | WOODFORD HALSE - 2F | ARDSLEY - 56B | DONCASTER - 36A | YORK - 50A |
| Jan-59 | HEATON - 52B | LEICESTER (GC) - 15E | NEWENGLAND - 34E | TWEEDMOUTH - 52D | KINGS CROSS - 34A | WOODFORD HALSE - 2F | ARDSLEY - 56B | DONCASTER - 36A | YORK - 50A |
| Aug-59 | HEATON - 52B | **8/59: YORK - 50A** | **6/59: GRAN - 34F** | TWEEDMOUTH - 52D | **9/59: NEWE - 34E** | **8/59: LEIC - 15E** | ARDSLEY - 56B | DONCASTER - 36A | YORK - 50A |
| Nov-59 | HEATON - 52B | YORK - 50A | **9/59: DCTR - 36A** | TWEEDMOUTH - 52D | NEWENGLAND - 34E | **9/59: YORK - 50A** | ARDSLEY - 56B | DONCASTER - 36A | YORK - 50A |
| Jan-60 | HEATON - 52B | YORK - 50A | DONCASTER - 36A | TWEEDMOUTH - 52D | NEWENGLAND - 34E | YORK - 50A | ARDSLEY - 56B | DONCASTER - 36A | YORK - 50A |
| Apr-60 | HEATON - 52B | YORK - 50A | DONCASTER - 36A | TWEEDMOUTH - 52D | NEWENGLAND - 34E | YORK - 50A | ARDSLEY - 56B | DONCASTER - 36A | YORK - 50A |
| Aug-60 | HEATON - 52B | YORK - 50A | DONCASTER - 36A | TWEEDMOUTH - 52D | NEWENGLAND - 34E | YORK - 50A | **9/60: TNBY - 51L** | DONCASTER - 36A | YORK - 50A |
| Nov-60 | HEATON - 52B | YORK - 50A | DONCASTER - 36A | TWEEDMOUTH - 52D | NEWENGLAND - 34E | YORK - 50A | THORNABY - 51L | DONCASTER - 36A | YORK - 50A |

*The 1950's was quite an eventful decade for V2 60913 which started the period at New England but moved north via March and Copley Hill to start the 1960's at Tweedmouth, Berwick. The engine is seen at Gateshead MPD in August 1963.*

*Doncaster is generally thought of an East Coast shed although in fact a large proportion of its work was concerned with Great Central traffic to Sheffield and Cleethorpes, duties than many of its thirty-odd B1 4-6-0's were heavily engaged upon. 61036 'Ralph Assheton', which was based at Doncaster throughout the decade, prepares to leave Sheffield Victoria in the summer of 1960.*

| | 60919 | 60920 | 60921 | 60922 | 60923 | 60924 | 60925 | 60926 | 60927 |
|---|---|---|---|---|---|---|---|---|---|
| Aug-50 | FERRYHILL - 61B | DUNDEE - 62B | DONCASTER - 36A | KINGS CROSS - 34A | GATESHEAD - 52A | NEWENGLAND - 35A | YORK - 50A | GATESHEAD - 52A | HAYMARKET - 64B |
| Jan-51 | FERRYHILL - 61B | DUNDEE - 62B | DONCASTER - 36A | **1/51: ST M - 64A** | GATESHEAD - 52A | NEWENGLAND - 35A | YORK - 50A | **11/50: HTN - 52B** | HAYMARKET - 64B |
| Aug-51 | FERRYHILL - 61B | DUNDEE - 62B | DONCASTER - 36A | EDINBURGH(SM) - 64A | GATESHEAD - 52A | NEWENGLAND - 35A | YORK - 50A | HEATON - 52B | HAYMARKET - 64B |
| Jan-52 | FERRYHILL - 61B | DUNDEE - 62B | DONCASTER - 36A | EDINBURGH(SM) - 64A | GATESHEAD - 52A | NEWENGLAND - 35A | YORK - 50A | HEATON - 52B | HAYMARKET - 64B |
| Aug-52 | FERRYHILL - 61B | DUNDEE - 62B | DONCASTER - 36A | EDINBURGH(SM) - 64A | GATESHEAD - 52A | NEWENGLAND - 35A | YORK - 50A | HEATON - 52B | HAYMARKET - 64B |
| Jan-53 | FERRYHILL - 61B | DUNDEE - 62B | DONCASTER - 36A | EDINBURGH(SM) - 64A | GATESHEAD - 52A | NEWENGLAND - 35A | YORK - 50A | **12/52: TWEED - 52D** | HAYMARKET - 64B |
| Aug-53 | FERRYHILL - 61B | DUNDEE - 62B | DONCASTER - 36A | EDINBURGH(SM) - 64A | GATESHEAD - 52A | NEWENGLAND - 35A | YORK - 50A | TWEEDMOUTH - 52D | HAYMARKET - 64B |
| Jan-54 | FERRYHILL - 61B | DUNDEE - 62B | DONCASTER - 36A | EDINBURGH(SM) - 64A | GATESHEAD - 52A | NEWENGLAND - 35A | YORK - 50A | TWEEDMOUTH - 52D | HAYMARKET - 64B |
| Aug-54 | FERRYHILL - 61B | DUNDEE - 62B | DONCASTER - 36A | EDINBURGH(SM) - 64A | GATESHEAD - 52A | NEWENGLAND - 35A | YORK - 50A | TWEEDMOUTH - 52D | HAYMARKET - 64B |
| Jan-55 | FERRYHILL - 61B | DUNDEE - 62B | DONCASTER - 36A | EDINBURGH(SM) - 64A | GATESHEAD - 52A | NEWENGLAND - 35A | YORK - 50A | TWEEDMOUTH - 52D | HAYMARKET - 64B |
| Aug-55 | FERRYHILL - 61B | DUNDEE - 62B | DONCASTER - 36A | EDINBURGH(SM) - 64A | GATESHEAD - 52A | NEWENGLAND - 35A | YORK - 50A | TWEEDMOUTH - 52D | HAYMARKET - 64B |
| Jan-56 | FERRYHILL - 61B | DUNDEE - 62B | DONCASTER - 36A | EDINBURGH(SM) - 64A | GATESHEAD - 52A | NEWENGLAND - 35A | YORK - 50A | TWEEDMOUTH - 52D | HAYMARKET - 64B |
| Aug-56 | FERRYHILL - 61B | DUNDEE - 62B | DONCASTER - 36A | **9/56: HTN - 52B** | GATESHEAD - 52A | NEWENGLAND - 35A | YORK - 50A | TWEEDMOUTH - 52D | HAYMARKET - 64B |
| Jan-57 | FERRYHILL - 61B | DUNDEE - 62B | DONCASTER - 36A | HEATON - 52B | GATESHEAD - 52A | NEWENGLAND - 35A | YORK - 50A | TWEEDMOUTH - 52D | HAYMARKET - 64B |
| Aug-57 | FERRYHILL - 61B | DUNDEE - 62B | DONCASTER - 36A | HEATON - 52B | GATESHEAD - 52A | NEWENGLAND - 35A | YORK - 50A | TWEEDMOUTH - 52D | HAYMARKET - 64B |
| Jan-58 | FERRYHILL - 61B | DUNDEE - 62B | DONCASTER - 36A | HEATON - 52B | GATESHEAD - 52A | NEWENGLAND - 35A | YORK - 50A | TWEEDMOUTH - 52D | **11/57: ST M - 64A** |
| Aug-58 | FERRYHILL - 61B | DUNDEE - 62B | DONCASTER - 36A | HEATON - 52B | GATESHEAD - 52A | NEWENGLAND - 35A | YORK - 50A | TWEEDMOUTH - 52D | **5/58: HMKT - 64B** |
| Jan-59 | FERRYHILL - 61B | **1/59: HMKT - 62B** | DONCASTER - 36A | HEATON - 52B | GATESHEAD - 52A | NEWENGLAND - 34E | YORK - 50A | TWEEDMOUTH - 52D | HAYMARKET - 64B |
| Aug-59 | FERRYHILL - 61B | HAYMARKET - 64B | DONCASTER - 36A | HEATON - 52B | GATESHEAD - 52A | NEWENGLAND - 34E | YORK - 50A | TWEEDMOUTH - 52D | HAYMARKET - 64B |
| Nov-59 | FERRYHILL - 61B | **11/59: ST M - 64A** | DONCASTER - 36A | HEATON - 52B | GATESHEAD - 52A | NEWENGLAND - 34E | YORK - 50A | TWEEDMOUTH - 52D | HAYMARKET - 64B |
| Jan-60 | FERRYHILL - 61B | EDINBURGH(SM) - 64A | DONCASTER - 36A | HEATON - 52B | GATESHEAD - 52A | NEWENGLAND - 34E | YORK - 50A | TWEEDMOUTH - 52D | HAYMARKET - 64B |
| Apr-60 | FERRYHILL - 61B | EDINBURGH(SM) - 64A | DONCASTER - 36A | HEATON - 52B | GATESHEAD - 52A | NEWENGLAND - 34E | YORK - 50A | TWEEDMOUTH - 52D | HAYMARKET - 64B |
| Aug-60 | FERRYHILL - 61B | EDINBURGH(SM) - 64A | DONCASTER - 36A | HEATON - 52B | GATESHEAD - 52A | NEWENGLAND - 34E | YORK - 50A | TWEEDMOUTH - 52D | **6/60: ST M - 64A** |
| Nov-60 | FERRYHILL - 61B | EDINBURGH(SM) - 64A | DONCASTER - 36A | HEATON - 52B | GATESHEAD - 52A | NEWENGLAND - 34E | YORK - 50A | TWEEDMOUTH - 52D | EDINBURGH(SM) - 64A |

| | 60928 | 60929 | 60930 | 60931 | 60932 | 60933 | 60934 | 60935 | 60936 |
|---|---|---|---|---|---|---|---|---|---|
| Aug-50 | DONCASTER - 36A | YORK - 50A | DONCASTER - 36A | DUNDEE - 62B | TWEEDMOUTH - 52D | YORK - 50A | YORK - 50A | DONCASTER - 36A | NEWENGLAND - 35A |
| Jan-51 | DONCASTER - 36A | YORK - 50A | DONCASTER - 36A | DUNDEE - 62B | TWEEDMOUTH - 52D | YORK - 50A | YORK - 50A | DONCASTER - 36A | NEWENGLAND - 35A |
| Aug-51 | DONCASTER - 36A | YORK - 50A | DONCASTER - 36A | DUNDEE - 62B | TWEEDMOUTH - 52D | YORK - 50A | YORK - 50A | DONCASTER - 36A | NEWENGLAND - 35A |
| Jan-52 | DONCASTER - 36A | YORK - 50A | DONCASTER - 36A | DUNDEE - 62B | TWEEDMOUTH - 52D | YORK - 50A | YORK - 50A | DONCASTER - 36A | NEWENGLAND - 35A |
| Aug-52 | DONCASTER - 36A | **7/52: DARL - 51A** | DONCASTER - 36A | DUNDEE - 62B | TWEEDMOUTH - 52D | YORK - 50A | YORK - 50A | DONCASTER - 36A | NEWENGLAND - 35A |
| Jan-53 | DONCASTER - 36A | **10/52: YORK - 50A** | DONCASTER - 36A | DUNDEE - 62B | TWEEDMOUTH - 52D | **12/52: ST M - 64A** | YORK - 50A | DONCASTER - 36A | NEWENGLAND - 35A |
| Aug-53 | DONCASTER - 36A | YORK - 50A | DONCASTER - 36A | DUNDEE - 62B | TWEEDMOUTH - 52D | EDINBURGH(SM) - 64A | YORK - 50A | DONCASTER - 36A | NEWENGLAND - 35A |
| Jan-54 | DONCASTER - 36A | YORK - 50A | DONCASTER - 36A | DUNDEE - 62B | TWEEDMOUTH - 52D | EDINBURGH(SM) - 64A | YORK - 50A | DONCASTER - 36A | NEWENGLAND - 35A |
| Aug-54 | DONCASTER - 36A | YORK - 50A | DONCASTER - 36A | DUNDEE - 62B | TWEEDMOUTH - 52D | EDINBURGH(SM) - 64A | YORK - 50A | DONCASTER - 36A | NEWENGLAND - 35A |
| Jan-55 | DONCASTER - 36A | YORK - 50A | DONCASTER - 36A | DUNDEE - 62B | TWEEDMOUTH - 52D | EDINBURGH(SM) - 64A | YORK - 50A | DONCASTER - 36A | NEWENGLAND - 35A |
| Aug-55 | DONCASTER - 36A | YORK - 50A | DONCASTER - 36A | DUNDEE - 62B | TWEEDMOUTH - 52D | EDINBURGH(SM) - 64A | YORK - 50A | DONCASTER - 36A | NEWENGLAND - 35A |
| Jan-56 | DONCASTER - 36A | YORK - 50A | DONCASTER - 36A | DUNDEE - 62B | TWEEDMOUTH - 52D | EDINBURGH(SM) - 64A | YORK - 50A | DONCASTER - 36A | NEWENGLAND - 35A |
| Aug-56 | DONCASTER - 36A | YORK - 50A | DONCASTER - 36A | DUNDEE - 62B | TWEEDMOUTH - 52D | EDINBURGH(SM) - 64A | YORK - 50A | DONCASTER - 36A | NEWENGLAND - 35A |
| Jan-57 | DONCASTER - 36A | YORK - 50A | DONCASTER - 36A | DUNDEE - 62B | TWEEDMOUTH - 52D | EDINBURGH(SM) - 64A | YORK - 50A | DONCASTER - 36A | NEWENGLAND - 35A |
| Aug-57 | DONCASTER - 36A | YORK - 50A | DONCASTER - 36A | DUNDEE - 62B | TWEEDMOUTH - 52D | EDINBURGH(SM) - 64A | YORK - 50A | DONCASTER - 36A | NEWENGLAND - 35A |
| Jan-58 | DONCASTER - 36A | YORK - 50A | DONCASTER - 36A | DUNDEE - 62B | TWEEDMOUTH - 52D | EDINBURGH(SM) - 64A | YORK - 50A | DONCASTER - 36A | NEWENGLAND - 35A |
| Aug-58 | DONCASTER - 36A | **8/58: GHD - 52A** | DONCASTER - 36A | **10/58: ST M - 64A** | **6/58: HTN - 52B** | EDINBURGH(SM) - 64A | **6/58: GHD - 52A** | DONCASTER - 36A | NEWENGLAND - 34E |
| Jan-59 | DONCASTER - 36A | GATESHEAD - 52A | DONCASTER - 36A | EDINBURGH(SM) - 64A | HEATON - 52B | EDINBURGH(SM) - 64A | GATESHEAD - 52A | DONCASTER - 36A | **11/58: DCTR - 36A** |
| Aug-59 | DONCASTER - 36A | GATESHEAD - 52A | DONCASTER - 36A | EDINBURGH(SM) - 64A | HEATON - 52B | EDINBURGH(SM) - 64A | GATESHEAD - 52A | DONCASTER - 36A | DONCASTER - 36A |
| Nov-59 | DONCASTER - 36A | GATESHEAD - 52A | DONCASTER - 36A | EDINBURGH(SM) - 64A | HEATON - 52B | EDINBURGH(SM) - 64A | GATESHEAD - 52A | DONCASTER - 36A | DONCASTER - 36A |
| Jan-60 | DONCASTER - 36A | GATESHEAD - 52A | DONCASTER - 36A | EDINBURGH(SM) - 64A | HEATON - 52B | EDINBURGH(SM) - 64A | GATESHEAD - 52A | DONCASTER - 36A | DONCASTER - 36A |
| Apr-60 | DONCASTER - 36A | GATESHEAD - 52A | DONCASTER - 36A | EDINBURGH(SM) - 64A | HEATON - 52B | EDINBURGH(SM) - 64A | GATESHEAD - 52A | DONCASTER - 36A | **6/60: NEWE - 34E** |
| Aug-60 | DONCASTER - 36A | GATESHEAD - 52A | DONCASTER - 36A | **8/60: EAST - 65A** | HEATON - 52B | **8/60: EAST - 65A** | GATESHEAD - 52A | DONCASTER - 36A | **10/60: DCTR - 36A** |
| Nov-60 | DONCASTER - 36A | GATESHEAD - 52A | DONCASTER - 36A | EASTFIELD - 65A | HEATON - 52B | EASTFIELD - 65A | GATESHEAD - 52A | DONCASTER - 36A | DONCASTER - 36A |

| | 60937 | 60938 | 60939 | 60940 | 60941 | 60942 | 60943 | 60944 | 60945 |
|---|---|---|---|---|---|---|---|---|---|
| Aug-50 | DUNDEE - 62B | NEWENGLAND - 35A | HEATON - 52B | GATESHEAD - 52A | YORK - 50A | HEATON - 52B | DONCASTER - 36A | HEATON - 52B | HEATON - 52B |
| Jan-51 | DUNDEE - 62B | NEWENGLAND - 35A | HEATON - 52B | GATESHEAD - 52A | YORK - 50A | **10/50: HTN - 52B** | DONCASTER - 36A | HEATON - 52B | HEATON - 52B |
| Aug-51 | DUNDEE - 62B | NEWENGLAND - 35A | HEATON - 52B | GATESHEAD - 52A | YORK - 50A | **3/51: GHD - 52A** | DONCASTER - 36A | **7/51: GHD - 52A** | HEATON - 52B |
| Jan-52 | DUNDEE - 62B | NEWENGLAND - 35A | HEATON - 52B | GATESHEAD - 52A | YORK - 50A | **9/51: HTN - 52B** | DONCASTER - 36A | **9/51: HTN - 52B** | HEATON - 52B |
| Aug-52 | DUNDEE - 62B | **6/52: MARCH - 31B** | HEATON - 52B | GATESHEAD - 52A | YORK - 50A | HEATON - 52B | DONCASTER - 36A | HEATON - 52B | **7/52: GHD - 52A** |
| Jan-53 | DUNDEE - 62B | **5/53: DCTR - 36A** | HEATON - 52B | GATESHEAD - 52A | YORK - 50A | HEATON - 52B | DONCASTER - 36A | HEATON - 52B | GATESHEAD - 52A |
| Aug-53 | DUNDEE - 62B | **7/53: MARCH - 31B** | HEATON - 52B | GATESHEAD - 52A | YORK - 50A | HEATON - 52B | DONCASTER - 36A | HEATON - 52B | GATESHEAD - 52A |
| Jan-54 | DUNDEE - 62B | MARCH - 31B | HEATON - 52B | GATESHEAD - 52A | YORK - 50A | HEATON - 52B | DONCASTER - 36A | HEATON - 52B | **11/53: HTN - 52B** |
| Aug-54 | DUNDEE - 62B | MARCH - 31B | HEATON - 52B | GATESHEAD - 52A | YORK - 50A | HEATON - 52B | DONCASTER - 36A | HEATON - 52B | HEATON - 52B |
| Jan-55 | DUNDEE - 62B | MARCH - 31B | HEATON - 52B | GATESHEAD - 52A | YORK - 50A | HEATON - 52B | DONCASTER - 36A | HEATON - 52B | HEATON - 52B |
| Aug-55 | DUNDEE - 62B | MARCH - 31B | HEATON - 52B | GATESHEAD - 52A | **6/55: DARL - 51A** | HEATON - 52B | **6/55: KX - 34A** | HEATON - 52B | HEATON - 52B |
| Jan-56 | DUNDEE - 62B | MARCH - 31B | HEATON - 52B | GATESHEAD - 52A | **9/55: YORK - 50A** | HEATON - 52B | KINGS CROSS - 34A | HEATON - 52B | HEATON - 52B |
| Aug-56 | DUNDEE - 62B | MARCH - 31B | HEATON - 52B | GATESHEAD - 52A | YORK - 50A | HEATON - 52B | KINGS CROSS - 34A | HEATON - 52B | HEATON - 52B |
| Jan-57 | DUNDEE - 62B | MARCH - 31B | HEATON - 52B | GATESHEAD - 52A | YORK - 50A | HEATON - 52B | KINGS CROSS - 34A | HEATON - 52B | HEATON - 52B |
| Aug-57 | DUNDEE - 62B | MARCH - 31B | **9/57: YORK - 50A** | GATESHEAD - 52A | YORK - 50A | **6/57: GHD - 52A** | **10/57: NEWE - 35A** | HEATON - 52B | HEATON - 52B |
| Jan-58 | DUNDEE - 62B | MARCH - 31B | YORK - 50A | GATESHEAD - 52A | YORK - 50A | GATESHEAD - 52A | **11/57: DCTR - 36A** | HEATON - 52B | HEATON - 52B |
| Aug-58 | **10/58: ST M - 64A** | MARCH - 31B | YORK - 50A | GATESHEAD - 52A | YORK - 50A | GATESHEAD - 52A | DONCASTER - 36A | HEATON - 52B | HEATON - 52B |
| Jan-59 | EDINBURGH(SM) - 64A | MARCH - 31B | YORK - 50A | GATESHEAD - 52A | YORK - 50A | GATESHEAD - 52A | DONCASTER - 36A | HEATON - 52B | HEATON - 52B |
| Aug-59 | EDINBURGH(SM) - 64A | MARCH - 31B | **6/59: C.HILL - 56C** | GATESHEAD - 52A | YORK - 50A | GATESHEAD - 52A | DONCASTER - 36A | HEATON - 52B | HEATON - 52B |
| Nov-59 | EDINBURGH(SM) - 64A | MARCH - 31B | **10/59: YORK - 50A** | **12/59: HTN - 52B** | YORK - 50A | GATESHEAD - 52A | DONCASTER - 36A | HEATON - 52B | HEATON - 52B |
| Jan-60 | EDINBURGH(SM) - 64A | MARCH - 31B | YORK - 50A | HEATON - 52B | YORK - 50A | GATESHEAD - 52A | DONCASTER - 36A | HEATON - 52B | HEATON - 52B |
| Apr-60 | EDINBURGH(SM) - 64A | MARCH - 31B | YORK - 50A | HEATON - 52B | YORK - 50A | GATESHEAD - 52A | DONCASTER - 36A | HEATON - 52B | HEATON - 52B |
| Aug-60 | EDINBURGH(SM) - 64A | MARCH - 31B | YORK - 50A | HEATON - 52B | YORK - 50A | GATESHEAD - 52A | DONCASTER - 36A | HEATON - 52B | HEATON - 52B |
| Nov-60 | EDINBURGH(SM) - 64A | MARCH - 31B | YORK - 50A | HEATON - 52B | YORK - 50A | GATESHEAD - 52A | DONCASTER - 36A | HEATON - 52B | HEATON - 52B |

| | 60946 | 60947 | 60948 | 60949 | 60950 | 60951 | 60952 | 60953 | 60954 |
|---|---|---|---|---|---|---|---|---|---|
| Aug-50 | YORK - 50A | HEATON - 52B | DONCASTER - 36A | HEATON - 52B | NEWENGLAND - 35A | HAYMARKET - 64B | HEATON - 52B | EDINBURGH(SM) - 64A | YORK - 50A |
| Jan-51 | YORK - 50A | HEATON - 52B | DONCASTER - 36A | HEATON - 52B | NEWENGLAND - 35A | HAYMARKET - 64B | HEATON - 52B | EDINBURGH(SM) - 64A | YORK - 50A |
| Aug-51 | YORK - 50A | HEATON - 52B | DONCASTER - 36A | **7/51: GHD - 52A** | NEWENGLAND - 35A | HAYMARKET - 64B | HEATON - 52B | EDINBURGH(SM) - 64A | YORK - 50A |
| Jan-52 | YORK - 50A | HEATON - 52B | DONCASTER - 36A | GATESHEAD - 52A | NEWENGLAND - 35A | HAYMARKET - 64B | HEATON - 52B | EDINBURGH(SM) - 64A | YORK - 50A |
| Aug-52 | YORK - 50A | **7/52: GHD - 52A** | DONCASTER - 36A | GATESHEAD - 52A | NEWENGLAND - 35A | HAYMARKET - 64B | **7/52: GHD - 52A** | EDINBURGH(SM) - 64A | YORK - 50A |
| Jan-53 | YORK - 50A | GATESHEAD - 52A | DONCASTER - 36A | GATESHEAD - 52A | NEWENGLAND - 35A | HAYMARKET - 64B | GATESHEAD - 52A | EDINBURGH(SM) - 64A | YORK - 50A |
| Aug-53 | YORK - 50A | GATESHEAD - 52A | **10/53: MARCH - 31B** | GATESHEAD - 52A | NEWENGLAND - 35A | HAYMARKET - 64B | GATESHEAD - 52A | EDINBURGH(SM) - 64A | YORK - 50A |
| Jan-54 | YORK - 50A | GATESHEAD - 52A | MARCH - 31B | GATESHEAD - 52A | NEWENGLAND - 35A | HAYMARKET - 64B | **11/53: HTN - 52B** | EDINBURGH(SM) - 64A | YORK - 50A |
| Aug-54 | YORK - 50A | GATESHEAD - 52A | MARCH - 31B | GATESHEAD - 52A | NEWENGLAND - 35A | HAYMARKET - 64B | HEATON - 52B | EDINBURGH(SM) - 64A | YORK - 50A |
| Jan-55 | YORK - 50A | GATESHEAD - 52A | MARCH - 31B | GATESHEAD - 52A | NEWENGLAND - 35A | HAYMARKET - 64B | HEATON - 52B | EDINBURGH(SM) - 64A | YORK - 50A |
| Aug-55 | **6/55: DARL - 51A** | GATESHEAD - 52A | MARCH - 31B | GATESHEAD - 52A | NEWENGLAND - 35A | HAYMARKET - 64B | HEATON - 52B | EDINBURGH(SM) - 64A | YORK - 50A |
| Jan-56 | **9/55: YORK - 50A** | GATESHEAD - 52A | MARCH - 31B | GATESHEAD - 52A | NEWENGLAND - 35A | HAYMARKET - 64B | HEATON - 52B | EDINBURGH(SM) - 64A | YORK - 50A |
| Aug-56 | YORK - 50A | GATESHEAD - 52A | MARCH - 31B | GATESHEAD - 52A | **8/56: KX - 34A** | HAYMARKET - 64B | HEATON - 52B | EDINBURGH(SM) - 64A | YORK - 50A |
| Jan-57 | YORK - 50A | GATESHEAD - 52A | MARCH - 31B | GATESHEAD - 52A | KINGS CROSS - 34A | HAYMARKET - 64B | HEATON - 52B | EDINBURGH(SM) - 64A | YORK - 50A |
| Aug-57 | YORK - 50A | GATESHEAD - 52A | MARCH - 31B | GATESHEAD - 52A | KINGS CROSS - 34A | HAYMARKET - 64B | HEATON - 52B | EDINBURGH(SM) - 64A | YORK - 50A |
| Jan-58 | YORK - 50A | GATESHEAD - 52A | MARCH - 31B | GATESHEAD - 52A | KINGS CROSS - 34A | **11/57: ST M - 64A** | YORK - 50A | EDINBURGH(SM) - 64A | YORK - 50A |
| Aug-58 | YORK - 50A | GATESHEAD - 52A | MARCH - 31B | GATESHEAD - 52A | KINGS CROSS - 34A | **5/58: HMKT - 64B** | **6/58: GHD - 52A** | EDINBURGH(SM) - 64A | YORK - 50A |
| Jan-59 | YORK - 50A | GATESHEAD - 52A | MARCH - 31B | GATESHEAD - 52A | KINGS CROSS - 34A | HAYMARKET - 64B | GATESHEAD - 52A | EDINBURGH(SM) - 64A | YORK - 50A |
| Aug-59 | **6/59: DARL - 51A** | GATESHEAD - 52A | MARCH - 31B | GATESHEAD - 52A | KINGS CROSS - 34A | HAYMARKET - 64B | GATESHEAD - 52A | EDINBURGH(SM) - 64A | YORK - 50A |
| Nov-59 | **9/59: TNBY - 51L** | GATESHEAD - 52A | MARCH - 31B | GATESHEAD - 52A | KINGS CROSS - 34A | HAYMARKET - 64B | GATESHEAD - 52A | EDINBURGH(SM) - 64A | YORK - 50A |
| Jan-60 | THORNABY - 51L | GATESHEAD - 52A | MARCH - 31B | GATESHEAD - 52A | KINGS CROSS - 34A | HAYMARKET - 64B | GATESHEAD - 52A | EDINBURGH(SM) - 64A | YORK - 50A |
| Apr-60 | THORNABY - 51L | GATESHEAD - 52A | MARCH - 31B | GATESHEAD - 52A | KINGS CROSS - 34A | HAYMARKET - 64B | GATESHEAD - 52A | EDINBURGH(SM) - 64A | YORK - 50A |
| Aug-60 | THORNABY - 51L | GATESHEAD - 52A | MARCH - 31B | GATESHEAD - 52A | KINGS CROSS - 34A | **6/60: ST M - 64A** | GATESHEAD - 52A | EDINBURGH(SM) - 64A | YORK - 50A |
| Nov-60 | THORNABY - 51L | GATESHEAD - 52A | MARCH - 31B | GATESHEAD - 52A | KINGS CROSS - 34A | EDINBURGH(SM) - 64A | GATESHEAD - 52A | EDINBURGH(SM) - 64A | YORK - 50A |

| | 60955 | 60956 | 60957 | 60958 | 60959 | 60960 | 60961 | 60962 | 60963 |
|---|---|---|---|---|---|---|---|---|---|
| Aug-50 | FERRYHILL - 61B | DONCASTER - 36A | HEATON - 52B | DUNDEE - 62B | HAYMARKET - 64B | YORK - 50A | YORK - 50A | YORK - 50A | YORK - 50A |
| Jan-51 | FERRYHILL - 61B | DONCASTER - 36A | HEATON - 52B | DUNDEE - 62B | HAYMARKET - 64B | YORK - 50A | YORK - 50A | YORK - 50A | YORK - 50A |
| Aug-51 | FERRYHILL - 61B | DONCASTER - 36A | HEATON - 52B | DUNDEE - 62B | HAYMARKET - 64B | YORK - 50A | YORK - 50A | YORK - 50A | YORK - 50A |
| Jan-52 | FERRYHILL - 61B | DONCASTER - 36A | HEATON - 52B | DUNDEE - 62B | HAYMARKET - 64B | YORK - 50A | YORK - 50A | YORK - 50A | YORK - 50A |
| Aug-52 | FERRYHILL - 61B | DONCASTER - 36A | 7/52: GHD - 52A | DUNDEE - 62B | HAYMARKET - 64B | YORK - 50A | YORK - 50A | YORK - 50A | YORK - 50A |
| Jan-53 | FERRYHILL - 61B | DONCASTER - 36A | GATESHEAD - 52A | DUNDEE - 62B | HAYMARKET - 64B | YORK - 50A | YORK - 50A | YORK - 50A | YORK - 50A |
| Aug-53 | FERRYHILL - 61B | DONCASTER - 36A | GATESHEAD - 52A | DUNDEE - 62B | HAYMARKET - 64B | YORK - 50A | YORK - 50A | YORK - 50A | YORK - 50A |
| Jan-54 | FERRYHILL - 61B | DONCASTER - 36A | GATESHEAD - 52A | DUNDEE - 62B | HAYMARKET - 64B | YORK - 50A | YORK - 50A | YORK - 50A | YORK - 50A |
| Aug-54 | FERRYHILL - 61B | DONCASTER - 36A | GATESHEAD - 52A | DUNDEE - 62B | HAYMARKET - 64B | YORK - 50A | YORK - 50A | YORK - 50A | YORK - 50A |
| Jan-55 | FERRYHILL - 61B | DONCASTER - 36A | GATESHEAD - 52A | DUNDEE - 62B | HAYMARKET - 64B | YORK - 50A | YORK - 50A | YORK - 50A | YORK - 50A |
| Aug-55 | FERRYHILL - 61B | DONCASTER - 36A | GATESHEAD - 52A | DUNDEE - 62B | HAYMARKET - 64B | YORK - 50A | YORK - 50A | YORK - 50A | YORK - 50A |
| Jan-56 | FERRYHILL - 61B | DONCASTER - 36A | 4/56: HTN - 52B | DUNDEE - 62B | HAYMARKET - 64B | YORK - 50A | YORK - 50A | YORK - 50A | YORK - 50A |
| Aug-56 | FERRYHILL - 61B | DONCASTER - 36A | 9/56: STM - 64A | DUNDEE - 62B | HAYMARKET - 64B | YORK - 50A | YORK - 50A | 6/56: HTN - 52B | YORK - 50A |
| Jan-57 | FERRYHILL - 61B | DONCASTER - 36A | EDINBURGH(SM) - 64A | DUNDEE - 62B | HAYMARKET - 64B | YORK - 50A | YORK - 50A | HEATON - 52B | YORK - 50A |
| Aug-57 | FERRYHILL - 61B | DONCASTER - 36A | EDINBURGH(SM) - 64A | DUNDEE - 62B | HAYMARKET - 64B | YORK - 50A | YORK - 50A | HEATON - 52B | YORK - 50A |
| Jan-58 | FERRYHILL - 61B | DONCASTER - 36A | EDINBURGH(SM) - 64A | DUNDEE - 62B | 11/57: STM - 64A | YORK - 50A | YORK - 50A | HEATON - 52B | YORK - 50A |
| Aug-58 | FERRYHILL - 61B | DONCASTER - 36A | EDINBURGH(SM) - 64A | 10/58: STM - 64A | 5/58: HMKT - 64B | YORK - 50A | YORK - 50A | HEATON - 52B | YORK - 50A |
| Jan-59 | FERRYHILL - 61B | DONCASTER - 36A | EDINBURGH(SM) - 64A | EDINBURGH(SM) - 64A | HAYMARKET - 64B | YORK - 50A | YORK - 50A | HEATON - 52B | YORK - 50A |
| Aug-59 | FERRYHILL - 61B | DONCASTER - 36A | EDINBURGH(SM) - 64A | EDINBURGH(SM) - 64A | HAYMARKET - 64B | 6/59: DARL - 51A | YORK - 50A | HEATON - 52B | YORK - 50A |
| Nov-59 | FERRYHILL - 61B | DONCASTER - 36A | EDINBURGH(SM) - 64A | EDINBURGH(SM) - 64A | HAYMARKET - 64B | 9/59: TNBY - 51L | YORK - 50A | HEATON - 52B | YORK - 50A |
| Jan-60 | FERRYHILL - 61B | DONCASTER - 36A | EDINBURGH(SM) - 64A | EDINBURGH(SM) - 64A | HAYMARKET - 64B | THORNABY - 51L | YORK - 50A | HEATON - 52B | YORK - 50A |
| Apr-60 | FERRYHILL - 61B | DONCASTER - 36A | EDINBURGH(SM) - 64A | EDINBURGH(SM) - 64A | HAYMARKET - 64B | THORNABY - 51L | YORK - 50A | HEATON - 52B | YORK - 50A |
| Aug-60 | FERRYHILL - 61B | 6/60: NEWE - 34E | EDINBURGH(SM) - 64A | EDINBURGH(SM) - 64A | 6/60: STM - 64A | THORNABY - 51L | YORK - 50A | HEATON - 52B | YORK - 50A |
| Nov-60 | FERRYHILL - 61B | NEWENGLAND - 34E | EDINBURGH(SM) - 64A | EDINBURGH(SM) - 64A | EDINBURGH(SM) - 64A | THORNABY - 51L | YORK - 50A | HEATON - 52B | YORK - 50A |

| | 60964 | 60965 | 60966 | 60967 | 60968 | 60969 | 60970 | 60971 | 60972 |
|---|---|---|---|---|---|---|---|---|---|
| Aug-50 | GATESHEAD - 52A | GATESHEAD - 52A | NEWENGLAND - 35A | GATESHEAD - 52A | YORK - 50A | DUNDEE - 62B | FERRYHILL - 61B | DUNDEE - 62B | HAYMARKET - 64B |
| Jan-51 | GATESHEAD - 52A | GATESHEAD - 52A | NEWENGLAND - 35A | GATESHEAD - 52A | YORK - 50A | DUNDEE - 62B | FERRYHILL - 61B | DUNDEE - 62B | 1/51: DUND - 62B |
| Aug-51 | GATESHEAD - 52A | GATESHEAD - 52A | 9/51: WFD.H - 38E | GATESHEAD - 52A | YORK - 50A | DUNDEE - 62B | FERRYHILL - 61B | DUNDEE - 62B | DUNDEE - 62B |
| Jan-52 | GATESHEAD - 52A | GATESHEAD - 52A | W.HALSE - 38E | GATESHEAD - 52A | YORK - 50A | DUNDEE - 62B | FERRYHILL - 61B | DUNDEE - 62B | DUNDEE - 62B |
| Aug-52 | GATESHEAD - 52A | GATESHEAD - 52A | W.HALSE - 38E | GATESHEAD - 52A | YORK - 50A | DUNDEE - 62B | FERRYHILL - 61B | DUNDEE - 62B | DUNDEE - 62B |
| Jan-53 | GATESHEAD - 52A | 12/52: STM - 64A | 2/53: NEWE - 35A | GATESHEAD - 52A | YORK - 50A | DUNDEE - 62B | FERRYHILL - 61B | DUNDEE - 62B | DUNDEE - 62B |
| Aug-53 | GATESHEAD - 52A | EDINBURGH(SM) - 64A | NEWENGLAND - 35A | GATESHEAD - 52A | YORK - 50A | DUNDEE - 62B | FERRYHILL - 61B | DUNDEE - 62B | DUNDEE - 62B |
| Jan-54 | GATESHEAD - 52A | EDINBURGH(SM) - 64A | NEWENGLAND - 35A | GATESHEAD - 52A | YORK - 50A | DUNDEE - 62B | FERRYHILL - 61B | DUNDEE - 62B | DUNDEE - 62B |
| Aug-54 | GATESHEAD - 52A | EDINBURGH(SM) - 64A | NEWENGLAND - 35A | GATESHEAD - 52A | YORK - 50A | DUNDEE - 62B | FERRYHILL - 61B | DUNDEE - 62B | DUNDEE - 62B |
| Jan-55 | GATESHEAD - 52A | EDINBURGH(SM) - 64A | NEWENGLAND - 35A | GATESHEAD - 52A | YORK - 50A | DUNDEE - 62B | FERRYHILL - 61B | DUNDEE - 62B | DUNDEE - 62B |
| Aug-55 | GATESHEAD - 52A | EDINBURGH(SM) - 64A | 9/55: GRAN - 35B | GATESHEAD - 52A | YORK - 50A | DUNDEE - 62B | FERRYHILL - 61B | DUNDEE - 62B | DUNDEE - 62B |
| Jan-56 | GATESHEAD - 52A | EDINBURGH(SM) - 64A | GRANTHAM - 35B | GATESHEAD - 52A | YORK - 50A | DUNDEE - 62B | FERRYHILL - 61B | DUNDEE - 62B | 1/56: FYHL - 61B |
| Aug-56 | GATESHEAD - 52A | EDINBURGH(SM) - 64A | 10/56: NEWE - 35A | GATESHEAD - 52A | YORK - 50A | DUNDEE - 62B | FERRYHILL - 61B | DUNDEE - 62B | FERRYHILL - 61B |
| Jan-57 | GATESHEAD - 52A | EDINBURGH(SM) - 64A | NEWENGLAND - 35A | GATESHEAD - 52A | YORK - 50A | DUNDEE - 62B | FERRYHILL - 61B | DUNDEE - 62B | FERRYHILL - 61B |
| Aug-57 | GATESHEAD - 52A | EDINBURGH(SM) - 64A | 10/57: GRAN - 35B | GATESHEAD - 52A | YORK - 50A | DUNDEE - 62B | FERRYHILL - 61B | DUNDEE - 62B | FERRYHILL - 61B |
| Jan-58 | GATESHEAD - 52A | EDINBURGH(SM) - 64A | GRANTHAM - 35B | GATESHEAD - 52A | YORK - 50A | DUNDEE - 62B | FERRYHILL - 61B | DUNDEE - 62B | FERRYHILL - 61B |
| Aug-58 | GATESHEAD - 52A | EDINBURGH(SM) - 64A | GRANTHAM - 34F | GATESHEAD - 52A | YORK - 50A | 10/58: STM - 64A | FERRYHILL - 61B | 10/58: STM - 64A | FERRYHILL - 61B |
| Jan-59 | GATESHEAD - 52A | EDINBURGH(SM) - 64A | 12/58: NEWE - 34E | GATESHEAD - 52A | YORK - 50A | EDINBURGH(SM) - 64A | FERRYHILL - 61B | EDINBURGH(SM) - 64A | FERRYHILL - 61B |
| Aug-59 | GATESHEAD - 52A | EDINBURGH(SM) - 64A | NEWENGLAND - 34E | GATESHEAD - 52A | YORK - 50A | EDINBURGH(SM) - 64A | FERRYHILL - 61B | EDINBURGH(SM) - 64A | FERRYHILL - 61B |
| Nov-59 | GATESHEAD - 52A | EDINBURGH(SM) - 64A | NEWENGLAND - 34E | GATESHEAD - 52A | YORK - 50A | EDINBURGH(SM) - 64A | FERRYHILL - 61B | EDINBURGH(SM) - 64A | FERRYHILL - 61B |
| Jan-60 | GATESHEAD - 52A | EDINBURGH(SM) - 64A | NEWENGLAND - 34E | GATESHEAD - 52A | YORK - 50A | EDINBURGH(SM) - 64A | FERRYHILL - 61B | EDINBURGH(SM) - 64A | FERRYHILL - 61B |
| Apr-60 | GATESHEAD - 52A | EDINBURGH(SM) - 64A | NEWENGLAND - 34E | GATESHEAD - 52A | YORK - 50A | EDINBURGH(SM) - 64A | FERRYHILL - 61B | EDINBURGH(SM) - 64A | FERRYHILL - 61B |
| Aug-60 | GATESHEAD - 52A | EDINBURGH(SM) - 64A | NEWENGLAND - 34E | 6/60: TNBY - 51L | YORK - 50A | EDINBURGH(SM) - 64A | 7/60: PERTH - 63A | EDINBURGH(SM) - 64A | FERRYHILL - 61B |
| Nov-60 | GATESHEAD - 52A | EDINBURGH(SM) - 64A | NEWENGLAND - 34E | THORNABY - 51L | YORK - 50A | EDINBURGH(SM) - 64A | PERTH - 63A | EDINBURGH(SM) - 64A | FERRYHILL - 61B |

| | 60973 | 60974 | 60975 | 60976 | 60977 | 60978 | 60979 | 60980 | 60981 |
|---|---|---|---|---|---|---|---|---|---|
| Aug-50 | FERRYHILL - 61B | YORK - 50A | YORK - 50A | YORK - 50A | YORK - 50A | YORK - 50A | YORK - 50A | EDINBURGH(SM) - 64A | YORK - 50A |
| Jan-51 | FERRYHILL - 61B | YORK - 50A | YORK - 50A | YORK - 50A | YORK - 50A | YORK - 50A | YORK - 50A | 1/51: HMKT - 64B | YORK - 50A |
| Aug-51 | FERRYHILL - 61B | YORK - 50A | YORK - 50A | YORK - 50A | YORK - 50A | YORK - 50A | YORK - 50A | 3/51: STM - 64A | YORK - 50A |
| Jan-52 | FERRYHILL - 61B | YORK - 50A | YORK - 50A | YORK - 50A | YORK - 50A | YORK - 50A | YORK - 50A | EDINBURGH(SM) - 64A | YORK - 50A |
| Aug-52 | FERRYHILL - 61B | YORK - 50A | YORK - 50A | YORK - 50A | YORK - 50A | YORK - 50A | YORK - 50A | EDINBURGH(SM) - 64A | YORK - 50A |
| Jan-53 | FERRYHILL - 61B | YORK - 50A | YORK - 50A | YORK - 50A | YORK - 50A | YORK - 50A | YORK - 50A | EDINBURGH(SM) - 64A | YORK - 50A |
| Aug-53 | FERRYHILL - 61B | YORK - 50A | YORK - 50A | YORK - 50A | YORK - 50A | YORK - 50A | YORK - 50A | EDINBURGH(SM) - 64A | 7/53: DARL - 51A |
| Jan-54 | FERRYHILL - 61B | YORK - 50A | YORK - 50A | YORK - 50A | YORK - 50A | YORK - 50A | YORK - 50A | EDINBURGH(SM) - 64A | 10/53: YORK - 50A |
| Aug-54 | FERRYHILL - 61B | YORK - 50A | YORK - 50A | YORK - 50A | YORK - 50A | YORK - 50A | YORK - 50A | EDINBURGH(SM) - 64A | YORK - 50A |
| Jan-55 | FERRYHILL - 61B | YORK - 50A | YORK - 50A | YORK - 50A | YORK - 50A | YORK - 50A | YORK - 50A | EDINBURGH(SM) - 64A | YORK - 50A |
| Aug-55 | FERRYHILL - 61B | YORK - 50A | YORK - 50A | YORK - 50A | YORK - 50A | YORK - 50A | YORK - 50A | EDINBURGH(SM) - 64A | YORK - 50A |
| Jan-56 | FERRYHILL - 61B | YORK - 50A | YORK - 50A | YORK - 50A | YORK - 50A | YORK - 50A | YORK - 50A | EDINBURGH(SM) - 64A | YORK - 50A |
| Aug-56 | FERRYHILL - 61B | YORK - 50A | YORK - 50A | YORK - 50A | YORK - 50A | 6/56: HTN - 52B | 6/56: HTN - 52B | EDINBURGH(SM) - 64A | YORK - 50A |
| Jan-57 | FERRYHILL - 61B | YORK - 50A | YORK - 50A | YORK - 50A | YORK - 50A | HEATON - 52B | HEATON - 52B | EDINBURGH(SM) - 64A | YORK - 50A |
| Aug-57 | FERRYHILL - 61B | YORK - 50A | YORK - 50A | YORK - 50A | YORK - 50A | HEATON - 52B | HEATON - 52B | EDINBURGH(SM) - 64A | YORK - 50A |
| Jan-58 | FERRYHILL - 61B | YORK - 50A | YORK - 50A | YORK - 50A | YORK - 50A | HEATON - 52B | HEATON - 52B | EDINBURGH(SM) - 64A | YORK - 50A |
| Aug-58 | FERRYHILL - 61B | YORK - 50A | YORK - 50A | 6/58: C.HILL - 56C | YORK - 50A | HEATON - 52B | 7/58: GHD - 52A | EDINBURGH(SM) - 64A | YORK - 50A |
| Jan-59 | FERRYHILL - 61B | YORK - 50A | YORK - 50A | 9/58: HTN - 52B | YORK - 50A | HEATON - 52B | GATESHEAD - 52A | EDINBURGH(SM) - 64A | YORK - 50A |
| Aug-59 | FERRYHILL - 61B | YORK - 50A | YORK - 50A | HEATON - 52B | YORK - 50A | HEATON - 52B | GATESHEAD - 52A | EDINBURGH(SM) - 64A | YORK - 50A |
| Nov-59 | FERRYHILL - 61B | YORK - 50A | YORK - 50A | HEATON - 52B | YORK - 50A | HEATON - 52B | GATESHEAD - 52A | EDINBURGH(SM) - 64A | YORK - 50A |
| Jan-60 | FERRYHILL - 61B | YORK - 50A | YORK - 50A | HEATON - 52B | YORK - 50A | HEATON - 52B | GATESHEAD - 52A | EDINBURGH(SM) - 64A | YORK - 50A |
| Apr-60 | FERRYHILL - 61B | YORK - 50A | YORK - 50A | HEATON - 52B | YORK - 50A | HEATON - 52B | GATESHEAD - 52A | EDINBURGH(SM) - 64A | YORK - 50A |
| Aug-60 | 6/60: PERTH - 63A | YORK - 50A | YORK - 50A | HEATON - 52B | YORK - 50A | HEATON - 52B | GATESHEAD - 52A | EDINBURGH(SM) - 64A | YORK - 50A |
| Nov-60 | PERTH - 63A | YORK - 50A | YORK - 50A | HEATON - 52B | YORK - 50A | HEATON - 52B | GATESHEAD - 52A | EDINBURGH(SM) - 64A | YORK - 50A |

| | 60982 | 60983 | B1 4-6-0 (1942) 61000 | 61001 | 61002 | 61003 | 61004 | 61005 | 61006 |
|---|---|---|---|---|---|---|---|---|---|
| Aug-50 | YORK - 50A | KINGS CROSS - 34A | STRATFORD - 30A | STRATFORD - 30A | EDINBURGH(SM) - 64A | PARKESTON - 30F | PARKESTON - 30F | PARKESTON - 30F | PARKESTON - 30F |
| Jan-51 | YORK - 50A | KINGS CROSS - 34A | STRATFORD - 30A | STRATFORD - 30A | 3/51: DAL RD - 64C | PARKESTON - 30F | PARKESTON - 30F | PARKESTON - 30F | PARKESTON - 30F |
| Aug-51 | YORK - 50A | KINGS CROSS - 34A | STRATFORD - 30A | STRATFORD - 30A | 9/51: DARL - 51A | PARKESTON - 30F | PARKESTON - 30F | PARKESTON - 30F | PARKESTON - 30F |
| Jan-52 | YORK - 50A | KINGS CROSS - 34A | STRATFORD - 30A | STRATFORD - 30A | 11/51: YORK - 50A | PARKESTON - 30F | PARKESTON - 30F | PARKESTON - 30F | PARKESTON - 30F |
| Aug-52 | YORK - 50A | KINGS CROSS - 34A | STRATFORD - 30A | 7/52: NEAS - 34E | YORK - 50A | PARKESTON - 30F | PARKESTON - 30F | PARKESTON - 30F | PARKESTON - 30F |
| Jan-53 | YORK - 50A | KINGS CROSS - 34A | STRATFORD - 30A | NEASDEN - 34E | YORK - 50A | PARKESTON - 30F | PARKESTON - 30F | PARKESTON - 30F | PARKESTON - 30F |
| Aug-53 | 7/53: DARL - 51A | KINGS CROSS - 34A | STRATFORD - 30A | NEASDEN - 34E | YORK - 50A | PARKESTON - 30F | PARKESTON - 30F | PARKESTON - 30F | PARKESTON - 30F |
| Jan-54 | 10/53: YORK - 50A | KINGS CROSS - 34A | STRATFORD - 30A | NEASDEN - 34E | YORK - 50A | PARKESTON - 30F | PARKESTON - 30F | PARKESTON - 30F | PARKESTON - 30F |
| Aug-54 | YORK - 50A | KINGS CROSS - 34A | STRATFORD - 30A | NEASDEN - 34E | YORK - 50A | PARKESTON - 30F | PARKESTON - 30F | PARKESTON - 30F | PARKESTON - 30F |
| Jan-55 | YORK - 50A | KINGS CROSS - 34A | STRATFORD - 30A | NEASDEN - 34E | YORK - 50A | PARKESTON - 30F | PARKESTON - 30F | PARKESTON - 30F | PARKESTON - 30F |
| Aug-55 | 6/55: DARL - 51A | KINGS CROSS - 34A | STRATFORD - 30A | NEASDEN - 34E | YORK - 50A | PARKESTON - 30F | PARKESTON - 30F | PARKESTON - 30F | PARKESTON - 30F |
| Jan-56 | 9/55: YORK - 50A | KINGS CROSS - 34A | STRATFORD - 30A | NEASDEN - 34E | YORK - 50A | PARKESTON - 30F | PARKESTON - 30F | PARKESTON - 30F | PARKESTON - 30F |
| Aug-56 | YORK - 50A | KINGS CROSS - 34A | STRATFORD - 30A | NEASDEN - 34E | YORK - 50A | PARKESTON - 30F | PARKESTON - 30F | 10/56: NEWE - 35A | 10/56: NEWE - 35A |
| Jan-57 | YORK - 50A | KINGS CROSS - 34A | 2/57: COL - 30E | 2/57: S.BGE - 35C | YORK - 50A | PARKESTON - 30F | PARKESTON - 30F | 2/57: S.BGE - 35C | 2/57: S.BGE - 35C |
| Aug-57 | YORK - 50A | KINGS CROSS - 34A | COLCHESTER - 30E | 3/57: IPS - 32B | YORK - 50A | PARKESTON - 30F | PARKESTON - 30F | 6/57: STRAT - 30A | 6/57: STRAT - 30A |
| Jan-58 | YORK - 50A | KINGS CROSS - 34A | COLCHESTER - 30E | IPSWICH - 32B | YORK - 50A | PARKESTON - 30F | 3/58I STRAT - 30A | STRATFORD - 30A | STRATFORD - 30A |
| Aug-58 | YORK - 50A | KINGS CROSS - 34A | COLCHESTER - 30E | IPSWICH - 32B | YORK - 50A | PARKESTON - 30F | 4/58: PARK - 30F | STRATFORD - 30A | STRATFORD - 30A |
| Jan-59 | YORK - 50A | KINGS CROSS - 34A | COLCHESTER - 30E | IPSWICH - 32B | YORK - 50A | PARKESTON - 30F | PARKESTON - 30F | 1/59: PARK - 30F | 1/59: PARK - 30F |
| Aug-59 | YORK - 50A | KINGS CROSS - 34A | COLCHESTER - 30E | 9/59: NORW - 32A | YORK - 50A | 10/59: MARCH - 31B | PARKESTON - 30F | PARKESTON - 30F | PARKESTON - 30F |
| Nov-59 | YORK - 50A | KINGS CROSS - 34A | 10/59: MARCH - 31B | 12/59: DCTR - 36A | YORK - 50A | 11/59: DCTR - 36A | 12/59: MARCH - 31B | 10/59: MARCH - 31B | 10/59: MARCH - 31B |
| Jan-60 | YORK - 50A | KINGS CROSS - 34A | 12/59: DCTR - 36A | DONCASTER - 36A | YORK - 50A | DONCASTER - 36A | 1/60: DARN - 41A | MARCH - 31B | MARCH - 31B |
| Apr-60 | YORK - 50A | KINGS CROSS - 34A | DONCASTER - 36A | DONCASTER - 36A | YORK - 50A | DONCASTER - 36A | DARNALL - 41A | MARCH - 31B | MARCH - 31B |
| Aug-60 | YORK - 50A | KINGS CROSS - 34A | 6/60: CLWK - 40E | DONCASTER - 36A | YORK - 50A | DONCASTER - 36A | DARNALL - 41A | MARCH - 31B | MARCH - 31B |
| Nov-60 | YORK - 50A | KINGS CROSS - 34A | COLWICK - 40E | DONCASTER - 36A | YORK - 50A | DONCASTER - 36A | DARNALL - 41A | MARCH - 31B | MARCH - 31B |

Unlike the rest of the country where the 4-6-0 was virtually the standard wheel arrangement for most main line traffic, the type had a relatively limited use on the ER especially on the Great Northern section where services were handled by Pacifics at one extreme and by 2-6-4 or 0-6-2 tanks at the other. The few G.N. gaps which remained for 4-6-0's consisted of Cambridge and Baldock services for which a handful of B1 engines were provided; the Cambridge-based workings sometimes being worked by B17 or B2 4-6-0's. Between Hitchin and Doncaster appearances by 4-6-0's were generally confined to connecting services although two services in each direction between Kings Cross and Cleethorpes were booked to a pair of Immingham B1 4-6-0's. It is interesting to note that after allowing for the fact that most of the Doncaster and Colwick B1's worked over the Great Central section, the number of the class allocated to GN services was, at about fifty, numerically the smallest of any Eastern Region component.

| | 61007 | 61008 | 61009 | 61010 | 61011 | 61012 | 61013 | 61014 | 61015 |
|---|---|---|---|---|---|---|---|---|---|
| Aug-50 | HAYMARKET - 64B | STRATFORD - 30A | STRATFORD - 30A | BOTANIC GARDENS - 53B | GATESHEAD - 52A | GATESHEAD - 52A | GATESHEAD - 52A | GATESHEAD - 52A | YORK - 50A |
| Jan-51 | HAYMARKET - 64B | STRATFORD - 30A | STRATFORD - 30A | BOTANIC GARDENS - 53B | GATESHEAD - 52A | GATESHEAD - 52A | GATESHEAD - 52A | GATESHEAD - 52A | YORK - 50A |
| Aug-51 | HAYMARKET - 64B | STRATFORD - 30A | STRATFORD - 30A | BOTANIC GARDENS - 53B | GATESHEAD - 52A | GATESHEAD - 52A | GATESHEAD - 52A | GATESHEAD - 52A | YORK - 50A |
| Jan-52 | HAYMARKET - 64B | STRATFORD - 30A | STRATFORD - 30A | BOTANIC GARDENS - 53B | GATESHEAD - 52A | GATESHEAD - 52A | GATESHEAD - 52A | GATESHEAD - 52A | YORK - 50A |
| Aug-52 | HAYMARKET - 64B | STRATFORD - 30A | **7/52: NEAS - 34E** | BOTANIC GARDENS - 53B | GATESHEAD - 52A | GATESHEAD - 52A | GATESHEAD - 52A | GATESHEAD - 52A | YORK - 50A |
| Jan-53 | HAYMARKET - 64B | STRATFORD - 30A | NEASDEN - 34E | BOTANIC GARDENS - 53B | GATESHEAD - 52A | GATESHEAD - 52A | GATESHEAD - 52A | GATESHEAD - 52A | YORK - 50A |
| Aug-53 | HAYMARKET - 64B | STRATFORD - 30A | NEASDEN - 34E | BOTANIC GARDENS - 53B | GATESHEAD - 52A | GATESHEAD - 52A | GATESHEAD - 52A | GATESHEAD - 52A | **11/53: N.HILL - 50B** |
| Jan-54 | HAYMARKET - 64B | STRATFORD - 30A | NEASDEN - 34E | BOTANIC GARDENS - 53B | GATESHEAD - 52A | GATESHEAD - 52A | GATESHEAD - 52A | **1/54: TWEED - 56D** | **2/54: YORK - 50A** |
| Aug-54 | HAYMARKET - 64B | STRATFORD - 30A | **8/54: LEIC - 38C** | BOTANIC GARDENS - 53B | GATESHEAD - 52A | GATESHEAD - 52A | GATESHEAD - 52A | TWEEDMOUTH - 52D | YORK - 50A |
| Jan-55 | HAYMARKET - 64B | STRATFORD - 30A | **12/54: NEAS - 34E** | BOTANIC GARDENS - 53B | GATESHEAD - 52A | GATESHEAD - 52A | GATESHEAD - 52A | TWEEDMOUTH - 52D | YORK - 50A |
| Aug-55 | HAYMARKET - 64B | STRATFORD - 30A | NEASDEN - 34E | BOTANIC GARDENS - 53B | GATESHEAD - 52A | GATESHEAD - 52A | GATESHEAD - 52A | TWEEDMOUTH - 52D | **9/55: DARL - 51A** |
| Jan-56 | HAYMARKET - 64B | **11/55: KX - 34A** | NEASDEN - 34E | BOTANIC GARDENS - 53B | GATESHEAD - 52A | GATESHEAD - 52A | GATESHEAD - 52A | TWEEDMOUTH - 52D | DARLINGTON - 51A |
| Aug-56 | HAYMARKET - 64B | **6/56: LEIC - 38C** | **6/56: DARN - 41A** | BOTANIC GARDENS - 53B | **10/56: ARDS - 56B** | GATESHEAD - 52A | **10/56: ARDS - 56B** | TWEEDMOUTH - 52D | DARLINGTON - 51A |
| Jan-57 | HAYMARKET - 64B | LEICESTER (GC) - 38C | DARNALL - 41A | BOTANIC GARDENS - 53B | ARDSLEY - 56B | GATESHEAD - 52A | ARDSLEY - 56B | TWEEDMOUTH - 52D | DARLINGTON - 51A |
| Aug-57 | HAYMARKET - 64B | LEICESTER (GC) - 38C | **10/57: DCTR - 36A** | BOTANIC GARDENS - 53B | ARDSLEY - 56B | GATESHEAD - 52A | ARDSLEY - 56B | TWEEDMOUTH - 52D | DARLINGTON - 51A |
| Jan-58 | HAYMARKET - 64B | LEICESTER (GC) - 38C | **11/57: LINC - 40A** | BOTANIC GARDENS - 53B | ARDSLEY - 56B | GATESHEAD - 52A | ARDSLEY - 56B | TWEEDMOUTH - 52D | DARLINGTON - 51A |
| Aug-58 | HAYMARKET - 64B | LEICESTER (GC) - 15E | LINCOLN - 40A | BOTANIC GARDENS - 53B | ARDSLEY - 56B | GATESHEAD - 52A | ARDSLEY - 56B | TWEEDMOUTH - 52D | **6/58: WAKE - 56A** |
| Jan-59 | HAYMARKET - 64B | LEICESTER (GC) - 15E | LINCOLN - 40A | BOTANIC GARDENS - 53B | **2/59: WAKE - 56A** | GATESHEAD - 52A | ARDSLEY - 56B | TWEEDMOUTH - 52D | WAKEFIELD - 56A |
| Aug-59 | HAYMARKET - 64B | **9/59: AGE - 26B** | LINCOLN - 40A | **6/59: DYCTS - 53A** | **4/59: MIRF - 56D** | GATESHEAD - 52A | ARDSLEY - 56B | **6/59: GHD - 52A** | WAKEFIELD - 56A |
| Nov-59 | HAYMARKET - 64B | AGECROFT - 26B | LINCOLN - 40A | DAIRYCOATES - 53A | MIRFIELD - 56D | GATESHEAD - 52A | ARDSLEY - 56B | GATESHEAD - 52A | WAKEFIELD - 56A |
| Jan-60 | HAYMARKET - 64B | AGECROFT - 26B | LINCOLN - 40A | DAIRYCOATES - 53A | MIRFIELD - 56D | GATESHEAD - 52A | ARDSLEY - 56B | GATESHEAD - 52A | WAKEFIELD - 56A |
| Apr-60 | HAYMARKET - 64B | AGECROFT - 26B | LINCOLN - 40A | DAIRYCOATES - 50B | MIRFIELD - 56D | GATESHEAD - 52A | ARDSLEY - 56B | GATESHEAD - 52A | WAKEFIELD - 56A |
| Aug-60 | **7/60: DAL RD - 64C** | AGECROFT - 26B | LINCOLN - 40A | DAIRYCOATES - 50B | **7/60: GORT - 9G** | **8/60: DYCTS - 50B** | ARDSLEY - 56B | GATESHEAD - 52A | WAKEFIELD - 56A |
| Nov-60 | DALRY ROAD - 64C | AGECROFT - 26B | LINCOLN - 40A | DAIRYCOATES - 50B | GORTON - 9G | DAIRYCOATES - 50B | ARDSLEY - 56B | GATESHEAD - 52A | WAKEFIELD - 56A |

| | 61016 | 61017 | 61018 | 61019 | 61020 | 61021 | 61022 | 61023 | 61024 |
|---|---|---|---|---|---|---|---|---|---|
| Aug-50 | YORK - 50A | STOCKTON - 51E | STOCKTON - 51E | TWEEDMOUTH - 52D | YORK - 50A | DARLINGTON - 51A | DARLINGTON - 51A | DARLINGTON - 51A | TWEEDMOUTH - 52D |
| Jan-51 | YORK - 50A | STOCKTON - 51E | STOCKTON - 51E | TWEEDMOUTH - 52D | YORK - 50A | DARLINGTON - 51A | DARLINGTON - 51A | DARLINGTON - 51A | TWEEDMOUTH - 52D |
| Aug-51 | YORK - 50A | STOCKTON - 51E | STOCKTON - 51E | TWEEDMOUTH - 52D | YORK - 50A | DARLINGTON - 51A | DARLINGTON - 51A | DARLINGTON - 51A | **7/51: GHD - 52A** |
| Jan-52 | YORK - 50A | STOCKTON - 51E | STOCKTON - 51E | TWEEDMOUTH - 52D | YORK - 50A | DARLINGTON - 51A | DARLINGTON - 51A | DARLINGTON - 51A | **9/51: DAR - 51A** |
| Aug-52 | YORK - 50A | STOCKTON - 51E | STOCKTON - 51E | TWEEDMOUTH - 52D | YORK - 50A | **7/52: GHD - 52A** | **7/52: YORK - 50A** | **7/52: GHD - 52A** | **7/52: YORK - 50A** |
| Jan-53 | YORK - 50A | STOCKTON - 51E | STOCKTON - 51E | TWEEDMOUTH - 52D | YORK - 50A | **10/52: DARL - 51A** | **10/52: DARL - 51A** | **10/52: DARL - 51A** | **10/52: DARL - 51A** |
| Aug-53 | YORK - 50A | **8/53: N. HILL - 50B** | STOCKTON - 51E | TWEEDMOUTH - 52D | **11/[illegible].HILL - 50B** | DARLINGTON - 51A | **7/53: GHD - 52A** | DARLINGTON - 51A | DARLINGTON - 51A |
| Jan-54 | YORK - 50A | NEVILLE HILL - 50B | STOCKTON - 51E | **1/54: GHD - 52A** | **2/54: YORK - 50A** | DARLINGTON - 51A | GATESHEAD - 52A | DARLINGTON - 51A | DARLINGTON - 51A |
| Aug-54 | YORK - 50A | NEVILLE HILL - 50B | STOCKTON - 51E | GATESHEAD - 52A | YORK - 50A | DARLINGTON - 51A | GATESHEAD - 52A | DARLINGTON - 51A | DARLINGTON - 51A |
| Jan-55 | YORK - 50A | NEVILLE HILL - 50B | STOCKTON - 51E | GATESHEAD - 52A | YORK - 50A | DARLINGTON - 51A | GATESHEAD - 52A | DARLINGTON - 51A | DARLINGTON - 51A |
| Aug-55 | YORK - 50A | NEVILLE HILL - 50B | STOCKTON - 51E | GATESHEAD - 52A | **9/55: DARL - 51A** | **6/55: YORK - 50A** | GATESHEAD - 52A | **6/55: YORK - 50A** | DARLINGTON - 51A |
| Jan-56 | YORK - 50A | **11/55: YORK - 50A** | STOCKTON - 51E | GATESHEAD - 52A | DARLINGTON - 51A | **9/55: DARL - 51A** | GATESHEAD - 52A | **9/55: DARL - 51A** | DARLINGTON - 51A |
| Aug-56 | YORK - 50A | YORK - 50A | STOCKTON - 51E | GATESHEAD - 52A | DARLINGTON - 51A | DARLINGTON - 51A | GATESHEAD - 52A | DARLINGTON - 51A | DARLINGTON - 51A |
| Jan-57 | YORK - 50A | YORK - 50A | STOCKTON - 51E | **2/57: BLAY - 52C** | DARLINGTON - 51A | DARLINGTON - 51A | GATESHEAD - 52A | DARLINGTON - 51A | DARLINGTON - 51A |
| Aug-57 | **5/57: N.HILL - 50B** | YORK - 50A | STOCKTON - 51E | BLAYDON - 52C | DARLINGTON - 51A | DARLINGTON - 51A | GATESHEAD - 52A | DARLINGTON - 51A | DARLINGTON - 51A |
| Jan-58 | NEVILLE HILL - 50B | YORK - 50A | STOCKTON - 51E | BLAYDON - 52C | DARLINGTON - 51A | DARLINGTON - 51A | GATESHEAD - 52A | DARLINGTON - 51A | DARLINGTON - 51A |
| Aug-58 | NEVILLE HILL - 50B | **6/58: C.HILL - 56C** | **6/58: H.HILL - 51G** | BLAYDON - 52C | **6/58: LOWM - 56F** | **6/58: H.HILL - 51G** | GATESHEAD - 52A | **6/58: LOWM - 56F** | **6/58: H.HILL - 51G** |
| Jan-59 | NEVILLE HILL - 50B | **2/59: WAKE - 56A** | HAVERTON HILL - 51G | BLAYDON - 52C | LOWMOOR - 56F | HAVERTON HILL - 51G | GATESHEAD - 52A | LOWMOOR - 56F | HAVERTON HILL - 51G |
| Aug-59 | NEVILLE HILL - 50B | WAKEFIELD - 56A | **6/59: TNBY - 51L** | BLAYDON - 52C | LOWMOOR - 56F | **6/59: TNBY - 51L** | GATESHEAD - 52A | LOWMOOR - 56F | **6/59: TNBY - 51L** |
| Nov-59 | NEVILLE HILL - 50B | WAKEFIELD - 56A | **9/59: DAR - 51A** | **10/59: GHD - 52A** | **11/59: WAKE - 56A** | **9/59: DAR - 51A** | GATESHEAD - 52A | **11/59: ARDS - 56B** | **9/59: DAR - 51A** |
| Jan-60 | NEVILLE HILL - 50B | WAKEFIELD - 56A | DARLINGTON - 51A | GATESHEAD - 52A | WAKEFIELD - 56A | DARLINGTON - 51A | GATESHEAD - 52A | ARDSLEY - 56B | DARLINGTON - 51A |
| Apr-60 | NEVILLE HILL - 55H | WAKEFIELD - 56A | **6/60: WAKE - 56A** | GATESHEAD - 52A | WAKEFIELD - 56A | **6/60: WAKE - 56A** | GATESHEAD - 52A | ARDSLEY - 56B | **6/60: WAKE - 56A** |
| Aug-60 | NEVILLE HILL - 55H | WAKEFIELD - 56A | **8/60: YORK - 50A** | GATESHEAD - 52A | **9/60: YORK - 50A** | **8/60: YORK - 50A** | GATESHEAD - 52A | ARDSLEY - 56B | WAKEFIELD - 56A |
| Nov-60 | NEVILLE HILL - 55H | WAKEFIELD - 56A | YORK - 50A | GATESHEAD - 52A | YORK - 50A | YORK - 50A | GATESHEAD - 52A | ARDSLEY - 56B | WAKEFIELD - 56A |

| | 61025 | 61026 | 61027 | 61028 | 61029 | 61030 | 61031 | 61032 | 61033 |
|---|---|---|---|---|---|---|---|---|---|
| Aug-50 | TWEEDMOUTH - 52D | DONCASTER - 36A | NEW ENGLAND - 35A | NEASDEN - 34E | ARDSLEY - 37A | STOCKTON - 51E | ARDSLEY - 37A | STOCKTON - 51E | ARDSLEY - 37A |
| Jan-51 | TWEEDMOUTH - 52D | DONCASTER - 36A | NEW ENGLAND - 35A | NEASDEN - 34E | **9/50: C.HILL - 37B** | STOCKTON - 51E | ARDSLEY - 37A | STOCKTON - 51E | **10/50: C.HILL - 37B** |
| Aug-51 | TWEEDMOUTH - 52D | DONCASTER - 36A | NEW ENGLAND - 35A | NEASDEN - 34E | **2/51: ARDS - 37A** | STOCKTON - 51E | **5/51: BRAD - 37C** | STOCKTON - 51E | COPLEY HILL - 37B |
| Jan-52 | TWEEDMOUTH - 52D | DONCASTER - 36A | NEW ENGLAND - 35A | NEASDEN - 34E | **12/51: DARN - 39B** | STOCKTON - 51E | BRADFORD - 37C | STOCKTON - 51E | **2/52: ARDS - 37A** |
| Aug-52 | TWEEDMOUTH - 52D | DONCASTER - 36A | NEW ENGLAND - 35A | NEASDEN - 34E | DARNALL - 39B | STOCKTON - 51E | BRADFORD - 37C | STOCKTON - 51E | **9/52: STRAT - 30A** |
| Jan-53 | TWEEDMOUTH - 52D | DONCASTER - 36A | NEW ENGLAND - 35A | NEASDEN - 34E | DARNALL - 39B | STOCKTON - 51E | BRADFORD - 37C | STOCKTON - 51E | **10/52: COLW - 38A** |
| Aug-53 | TWEEDMOUTH - 52D | DONCASTER - 36A | **5/53: HITCH - 34D** | NEASDEN - 34E | **9/53: ST M - 64A** | STOCKTON - 51E | BRADFORD - 37C | STOCKTON - 51E | COLWICK - 38A |
| Jan-54 | TWEEDMOUTH - 52D | DONCASTER - 36A | HITCHIN - 34D | NEASDEN - 34E | EDINBURGH (SM) - 64A | STOCKTON - 51E | BRADFORD - 37C | STOCKTON - 51E | COLWICK - 38A |
| Aug-54 | TWEEDMOUTH - 52D | DONCASTER - 36A | HITCHIN - 34D | **6/54: LEIC - 38C** | EDINBURGH (SM) - 64A | STOCKTON - 51E | BRADFORD - 37C | STOCKTON - 51E | COLWICK - 38A |
| Jan-55 | TWEEDMOUTH - 52D | DONCASTER - 36A | HITCHIN - 34D | **12/54: NEAS - 34E** | EDINBURGH (SM) - 64A | STOCKTON - 51E | BRADFORD - 37C | STOCKTON - 51E | **11/54: CAMB - 31A** |
| Aug-55 | TWEEDMOUTH - 52D | DONCASTER - 36A | HITCHIN - 34D | NEASDEN - 34E | EDINBURGH (SM) - 64A | STOCKTON - 51E | BRADFORD - 37C | STOCKTON - 51E | CAMBRIDGE - 31A |
| Jan-56 | TWEEDMOUTH - 52D | DONCASTER - 36A | HITCHIN - 34D | NEASDEN - 34E | EDINBURGH (SM) - 64A | STOCKTON - 51E | BRADFORD - 37C | STOCKTON - 51E | CAMBRIDGE - 31A |
| Aug-56 | TWEEDMOUTH - 52D | DONCASTER - 36A | HITCHIN - 34D | NEASDEN - 34E | EDINBURGH (SM) - 64A | STOCKTON - 51E | BRADFORD - 56G | STOCKTON - 51E | CAMBRIDGE - 31A |
| Jan-57 | TWEEDMOUTH - 52D | DONCASTER - 36A | HITCHIN - 34D | NEASDEN - 34E | EDINBURGH (SM) - 64A | STOCKTON - 51E | BRADFORD - 56G | STOCKTON - 51E | **11/56: DARN - 41A** |
| Aug-57 | TWEEDMOUTH - 52D | DONCASTER - 36A | HITCHIN - 34D | NEASDEN - 34E | EDINBURGH (SM) - 64A | STOCKTON - 51E | BRADFORD - 56G | STOCKTON - 51E | DARNALL - 41A |
| Jan-58 | TWEEDMOUTH - 52D | **11/57: LINC - 40A** | HITCHIN - 34D | NEASDEN - 34E | EDINBURGH (SM) - 64A | STOCKTON - 51E | **1/58: LOWM - 56F** | STOCKTON - 51E | DARNALL - 41A |
| Aug-58 | TWEEDMOUTH - 52D | LINCOLN - 40A | HITCHIN - 34D | NEASDEN - 14D | EDINBURGH (SM) - 64A | STOCKTON - 51E | **9/58: DAR - 51A** | STOCKTON - 51E | DARNALL - 41A |
| Jan-59 | TWEEDMOUTH - 52D | LINCOLN - 40A | HITCHIN - 34D | **2/59: LEIC - 15E** | EDINBURGH (SM) - 64A | STOCKTON - 51E | **12/58: TNBY - 51L** | STOCKTON - 51E | DARNALL - 41A |
| Aug-59 | TWEEDMOUTH - 52D | LINCOLN - 40A | **6/59: DARN - 41A** | **6/59: WOOD - 2F** | EDINBURGH (SM) - 64A | **6/59: TNBY - 51L** | THORNABY - 51L | **6/59: TNBY - 51L** | DARNALL - 41A |
| Nov-59 | TWEEDMOUTH - 52D | **12/59: IMM - 40B** | DARNALL - 41A | WOODFORD HALSE - 2F | EDINBURGH (SM) - 64A | **9/59: DARL - 51A** | THORNABY - 51L | **9/59: DARL - 51A** | DARNALL - 41A |
| Jan-60 | TWEEDMOUTH - 52D | IMMINGHAM - 40B | DARNALL - 41A | WOODFORD HALSE - 2F | EDINBURGH (SM) - 64A | DARLINGTON - 51A | THORNABY - 51L | DARLINGTON - 51A | DARNALL - 41A |
| Apr-60 | **6/60: BLAY - 52C** | **3/60: LINC - 40A** | DARNALL - 41A | WOODFORD HALSE - 2F | EDINBURGH (SM) - 64A | DARLINGTON - 51A | THORNABY - 51L | DARLINGTON - 51A | DARNALL - 41A |
| Aug-60 | BLAYDON - 52C | LINCOLN - 40A | DARNALL - 41A | WOODFORD HALSE - 2F | EDINBURGH (SM) - 64A | DARLINGTON - 51A | **9/60: YORK - 50A** | DARLINGTON - 51A | DARNALL - 41A |
| Nov-60 | BLAYDON - 52C | LINCOLN - 40A | DARNALL - 41A | WOODFORD HALSE - 2F | EDINBURGH (SM) - 64A | DARLINGTON - 51A | YORK - 50A | DARLINGTON - 51A | DARNALL - 41A |

| | 61034 | 61035 | 61036 | 61037 | 61038 | 61039 | 61040 | 61041 | 61042 |
|---|---|---|---|---|---|---|---|---|---|
| Aug-50 | STOCKTON - 51E | NEVILLE HILL - 50B | DONCASTER - 36A | STOCKTON - 51E | YORK - 50A | DARLINGTON - 51A | NORWICH - 32A | NORWICH - 32A | NORWICH - 32A |
| Jan-51 | STOCKTON - 51E | NEVILLE HILL - 50B | DONCASTER - 36A | STOCKTON - 51E | YORK - 50A | DARLINGTON - 51A | NORWICH - 32A | NORWICH - 32A | NORWICH - 32A |
| Aug-51 | STOCKTON - 51E | NEVILLE HILL - 50B | DONCASTER - 36A | STOCKTON - 51E | YORK - 50A | DARLINGTON - 51A | **9/51: DARL - 51A** | NORWICH - 32A | NORWICH - 32A |
| Jan-52 | STOCKTON - 51E | NEVILLE HILL - 50B | DONCASTER - 36A | STOCKTON - 51E | YORK - 50A | DARLINGTON - 51A | DARLINGTON - 51A | NORWICH - 32A | NORWICH - 32A |
| Aug-52 | STOCKTON - 51E | NEVILLE HILL - 50B | DONCASTER - 36A | STOCKTON - 51E | YORK - 50A | **7/52: YORK - 50A** | **7/52: YORK - 50A** | NORWICH - 32A | NORWICH - 32A |
| Jan-53 | STOCKTON - 51E | NEVILLE HILL - 50B | DONCASTER - 36A | STOCKTON - 51E | YORK - 50A | **10/52: DAR - 51A** | **10/52: DAR - 51A** | NORWICH - 32A | NORWICH - 32A |
| Aug-53 | STOCKTON - 51E | NEVILLE HILL - 50B | DONCASTER - 36A | STOCKTON - 51E | YORK - 50A | DARLINGTON - 51A | DARLINGTON - 51A | **7/53: DARN - 39B** | NORWICH - 32A |
| Jan-54 | STOCKTON - 51E | NEVILLE HILL - 50B | DONCASTER - 36A | STOCKTON - 51E | YORK - 50A | DARLINGTON - 51A | DARLINGTON - 51A | DARNALL - 39B | NORWICH - 32A |
| Aug-54 | STOCKTON - 51E | NEVILLE HILL - 50B | DONCASTER - 36A | STOCKTON - 51E | YORK - 50A | DARLINGTON - 51A | DARLINGTON - 51A | DARNALL - 39B | NORWICH - 32A |
| Jan-55 | STOCKTON - 51E | NEVILLE HILL - 50B | DONCASTER - 36A | STOCKTON - 51E | YORK - 50A | DARLINGTON - 51A | DARLINGTON - 51A | DARNALL - 39B | NORWICH - 32A |
| Aug-55 | STOCKTON - 51E | NEVILLE HILL - 50B | DONCASTER - 36A | STOCKTON - 51E | YORK - 50A | DARLINGTON - 51A | DARLINGTON - 51A | DARNALL - 39B | NORWICH - 32A |
| Jan-56 | STOCKTON - 51E | NEVILLE HILL - 50B | DONCASTER - 36A | STOCKTON - 51E | YORK - 50A | DARLINGTON - 51A | DARLINGTON - 51A | DARNALL - 41A | NORWICH - 32A |
| Aug-56 | STOCKTON - 51E | NEVILLE HILL - 50B | DONCASTER - 36A | STOCKTON - 51E | YORK - 50A | DARLINGTON - 51A | DARLINGTON - 51A | DARNALL - 41A | NORWICH - 32A |
| Jan-57 | STOCKTON - 51E | NEVILLE HILL - 50B | DONCASTER - 36A | STOCKTON - 51E | YORK - 50A | DARLINGTON - 51A | DARLINGTON - 51A | DARNALL - 41A | **2/57: YAR (ST) - 32D** |
| Aug-57 | STOCKTON - 51E | NEVILLE HILL - 50B | DONCASTER - 36A | STOCKTON - 51E | **5/57: N.HILL - 50B** | DARLINGTON - 51A | DARLINGTON - 51A | DARNALL - 41A | **3/57: NORW - 32A** |
| Jan-58 | STOCKTON - 51E | NEVILLE HILL - 50B | DONCASTER - 36A | STOCKTON - 51E | NEVILLE HILL - 50B | DARLINGTON - 51A | DARLINGTON - 51A | DARNALL - 41A | NORWICH - 32A |
| Aug-58 | STOCKTON - 51E | NEVILLE HILL - 50B | DONCASTER - 36A | **6/58: H.HILL - 51G** | NEVILLE HILL - 50B | **6/58: LOWM - 56F** | **6/58: LOWM - 56F** | DARNALL - 41A | NORWICH - 32A |
| Jan-59 | STOCKTON - 51E | NEVILLE HILL - 50B | DONCASTER - 36A | HAVERTON HILL - 51G | NEVILLE HILL - 50B | LOWMOOR - 56F | **3/59: WAKE - 56A** | DARNALL - 41A | NORWICH - 32A |
| Aug-59 | **6/59: TNBY - 51L** | NEVILLE HILL - 50B | DONCASTER - 36A | **6/59: TNBY - 51L** | NEVILLE HILL - 50B | LOWMOOR - 56F | **4/59@ MIRF - 56D** | DARNALL - 41A | NORWICH - 32A |
| Nov-59 | THORNABY - 51L | NEVILLE HILL - 50B | DONCASTER - 36A | THORNABY - 51L | NEVILLE HILL - 50B | 11/59: ARDS - 56B | MIRFIELD - 56D | DARNALL - 41A | **12/59: MARCH - 31B** |
| Jan-60 | THORNABY - 51L | NEVILLE HILL - 50B | DONCASTER - 36A | THORNABY - 51L | NEVILLE HILL - 50B | ARDSLEY - 56B | MIRFIELD - 56D | DARNALL - 41A | MARCH - 31B |
| Apr-60 | THORNABY - 51L | NEVILLE HILL - 55H | DONCASTER - 36A | THORNABY - 51L | NEVILLE HILL - 55H | ARDSLEY - 56B | MIRFIELD - 56D | DARNALL - 41A | **3/60: LINC - 40A** |
| Aug-60 | THORNABY - 51L | NEVILLE HILL - 55H | DONCASTER - 36A | **9/60: DAR - 51A** | NEVILLE HILL - 55H | **9/60: YORK - 50A** | MIRFIELD - 56D | DARNALL - 41A | LINCOLN - 40A |
| Nov-60 | THORNABY - 51L | NEVILLE HILL - 55H | DONCASTER - 36A | DARLINGTON - 51A | NEVILLE HILL - 55H | YORK - 50A | MIRFIELD - 56D | DARNALL - 41A | LINCOLN - 40A |

For a brief period between their introduction and the arrival of Britannia Pacifics, B1's were the principal engines on the Great Eastern and although they were displaced very quickly from the Norwich expresses, over sixty of the class remained on the district working in consort with the B2, B17 and B12's where from the timing point of view, no distinction was drawn between any of the 4-6-0 classes. On the Lea Valley route for example the nine coach non-stop booking from Liverpool Street to Cambridge was sixty-eight minutes for a 4-6-0 as against only four minutes less for a Britannia. With a heavier twelve coach service the bookings were seventy-three minutes for a B1, B2 or B17 and sixty-six for a Pacific.

Perhaps the most grateful recipient of the B1 4-6-0's was the Great Central which saw in them the first new engines it had had in significant numbers for many years. Over eighty of the class were allocated to GC sheds – notably Darnall and Immingham – with many of the thirty Doncaster engines being

| | 61043 | 61044 | 61045 | 61046 | 61047 | 61048 | 61049 | 61050 | 61051 |
|---|---|---|---|---|---|---|---|---|---|
| Aug-50 | NORWICH - 32A | NORWICH - 32A | NORWICH - 32A | NORWICH - 32A | NORWICH - 32A | NORWICH - 32A | NORWICH - 32A | NORWICH - 32A | NORWICH - 32A |
| Jan-51 | NORWICH - 32A | NORWICH - 32A | NORWICH - 32A | NORWICH - 32A | **5/51: LINC - 40A** | NORWICH - 32A | NORWICH - 32A | NORWICH - 32A | NORWICH - 32A |
| Aug-51 | NORWICH - 32A | NORWICH - 32A | NORWICH - 32A | NORWICH - 32A | **6/51: NORW - 32A** | NORWICH - 32A | **9/51: DARL - 51A** | **5/51: ARDS - 37A** | **5/51: ARDS - 37A** |
| Jan-52 | NORWICH - 32A | NORWICH - 32A | NORWICH - 32A | NORWICH - 32A | NORWICH - 32A | NORWICH - 32A | DARLINGTON - 51A | **10/51: NORW - 32A** | **12/51: NORW - 32A** |
| Aug-52 | NORWICH - 32A | NORWICH - 32A | NORWICH - 32A | NORWICH - 32A | NORWICH - 32A | NORWICH - 32A | DARLINGTON - 51A | NORWICH - 32A | NORWICH - 32A |
| Jan-53 | NORWICH - 32A | NORWICH - 32A | NORWICH - 32A | NORWICH - 32A | NORWICH - 32A | NORWICH - 32A | DARLINGTON - 51A | NORWICH - 32A | NORWICH - 32A |
| Aug-53 | NORWICH - 32A | **7/53: DARN - 39B** | NORWICH - 32A | NORWICH - 32A | NORWICH - 32A | NORWICH - 32A | DARLINGTON - 51A | NORWICH - 32A | NORWICH - 32A |
| Jan-54 | NORWICH - 32A | DARNALL - 39B | NORWICH - 32A | NORWICH - 32A | **11/53: NEWE - 35A** | NORWICH - 32A | DARLINGTON - 51A | NORWICH - 32A | NORWICH - 32A |
| Aug-54 | NORWICH - 32A | DARNALL - 39B | NORWICH - 32A | NORWICH - 32A | NEWENGLAND - 35A | NORWICH - 32A | DARLINGTON - 51A | NORWICH - 32A | NORWICH - 32A |
| Jan-55 | NORWICH - 32A | DARNALL - 39B | NORWICH - 32A | NORWICH - 32A | NEWENGLAND - 35A | NORWICH - 32A | DARLINGTON - 51A | NORWICH - 32A | NORWICH - 32A |
| Aug-55 | NORWICH - 32A | DARNALL - 39B | NORWICH - 32A | NORWICH - 32A | NEWENGLAND - 35A | NORWICH - 32A | DARLINGTON - 51A | NORWICH - 32A | NORWICH - 32A |
| Jan-56 | NORWICH - 32A | DARNALL - 41A | NORWICH - 32A | NORWICH - 32A | **12/55: S.BGE - 35C** | NORWICH - 32A | DARLINGTON - 51A | NORWICH - 32A | NORWICH - 32A |
| Aug-56 | NORWICH - 32A | DARNALL - 41A | NORWICH - 32A | NORWICH - 32A | SPITALBGE - 35C | NORWICH - 32A | DARLINGTON - 51A | **6/56: DARN - 41A** | **6/56: DARN - 41A** |
| Jan-57 | NORWICH - 32A | DARNALL - 41A | NORWICH - 32A | NORWICH - 32A | SPITALBGE - 35C | NORWICH - 32A | DARLINGTON - 51A | DARNALL - 41A | DARNALL - 41A |
| Aug-57 | NORWICH - 32A | DARNALL - 41A | NORWICH - 32A | NORWICH - 32A | SPITALBGE - 35C | NORWICH - 32A | DARLINGTON - 51A | DARNALL - 41A | DARNALL - 41A |
| Jan-58 | NORWICH - 32A | DARNALL - 41A | NORWICH - 32A | NORWICH - 32A | SPITALBGE - 35C | NORWICH - 32A | DARLINGTON - 51A | DARNALL - 41A | DARNALL - 41A |
| Aug-58 | NORWICH - 32A | DARNALL - 41A | NORWICH - 32A | NORWICH - 32A | SPITALBGE - 31F | NORWICH - 32A | **6/58: LOWM - 56F** | DARNALL - 41A | DARNALL - 41A |
| Jan-59 | NORWICH - 32A | DARNALL - 41A | NORWICH - 32A | NORWICH - 32A | **12/58: IMM - 40B** | NORWICH - 32A | LOWMOOR - 56F | DARNALL - 41A | DARNALL - 41A |
| Aug-59 | NORWICH - 32A | DARNALL - 41A | NORWICH - 32A | NORWICH - 32A | IMMINGHAM - 40B | NORWICH - 32A | LOWMOOR - 56F | DARNALL - 41A | DARNALL - 41A |
| Nov-59 | NORWICH - 32A | DARNALL - 41A | NORWICH - 32A | NORWICH - 32A | IMMINGHAM - 40B | NORWICH - 32A | **11/59: MIRF - 56D** | DARNALL - 41A | DARNALL - 41A |
| Jan-60 | NORWICH - 32A | DARNALL - 41A | NORWICH - 32A | NORWICH - 32A | IMMINGHAM - 40B | NORWICH - 32A | MIRFIELD - 56D | DARNALL - 41A | DARNALL - 41A |
| Apr-60 | NORWICH - 32A | DARNALL - 41A | NORWICH - 32A | NORWICH - 32A | IMMINGHAM - 40B | NORWICH - 32A | MIRFIELD - 56D | DARNALL - 41A | DARNALL - 41A |
| Aug-60 | NORWICH - 32A | DARNALL - 41A | NORWICH - 32A | **6/60: CAMB - 31A** | IMMINGHAM - 40B | **6/60: CAMB - 31A** | **7/60: YORK - 50A** | DARNALL - 41A | DARNALL - 41A |
| Nov-60 | NORWICH - 32A | DARNALL - 41A | NORWICH - 32A | CAMBRIDGE - 31A | IMMINGHAM - 40B | CAMBRIDGE - 31A | YORK - 50A | DARNALL - 41A | DARNALL - 41A |

| | 61052 | 61053 | 61054 | 61055 | 61056 | 61058 | 61059 | 61060 | 61061 |
|---|---|---|---|---|---|---|---|---|---|
| Aug-50 | NORWICH - 32A | IPSWICH - 32B | IPSWICH - 32B | IPSWICH - 32B | IPSWICH - 32B | IPSWICH - 32B | IPSWICH - 32B | DAIRYCOATES - 53A | EDINBURGH(SM) - 64A |
| Jan-51 | **9/50: IPS - 32B** | IPSWICH - 32B | IPSWICH - 32B | IPSWICH - 32B | IPSWICH - 32B | IPSWICH - 32B | IPSWICH - 32B | DAIRYCOATES - 53A | EDINBURGH(SM) - 64A |
| Aug-51 | IPSWICH - 32B | **9/51: YORK - 50A** | IPSWICH - 32B | IPSWICH - 32B | **5/51: ARDS - 37A** | IPSWICH - 32B | IPSWICH - 32B | DAIRYCOATES - 53A | **9/51: DARL - 51A** |
| Jan-52 | IPSWICH - 32B | YORK - 50A | IPSWICH - 32B | IPSWICH - 32B | **12/51: IPS - 32B** | IPSWICH - 32B | IPSWICH - 32B | DAIRYCOATES - 53A | DARLINGTON - 51A |
| Aug-52 | IPSWICH - 32B | YORK - 50A | IPSWICH - 32B | IPSWICH - 32B | **7/52: COLW - 38A** | IPSWICH - 32B | IPSWICH - 32B | DAIRYCOATES - 53A | DARLINGTON - 51A |
| Jan-53 | IPSWICH - 32B | YORK - 50A | IPSWICH - 32B | IPSWICH - 32B | COLWICK - 38A | IPSWICH - 32B | IPSWICH - 32B | DAIRYCOATES - 53A | DARLINGTON - 51A |
| Aug-53 | IPSWICH - 32B | YORK - 50A | IPSWICH - 32B | IPSWICH - 32B | COLWICK - 38A | IPSWICH - 32B | IPSWICH - 32B | DAIRYCOATES - 53A | DARLINGTON - 51A |
| Jan-54 | IPSWICH - 32B | YORK - 50A | IPSWICH - 32B | IPSWICH - 32B | COLWICK - 38A | IPSWICH - 32B | IPSWICH - 32B | DAIRYCOATES - 53A | DARLINGTON - 51A |
| Aug-54 | IPSWICH - 32B | YORK - 50A | IPSWICH - 32B | IPSWICH - 32B | COLWICK - 38A | IPSWICH - 32B | IPSWICH - 32B | DAIRYCOATES - 53A | DARLINGTON - 51A |
| Jan-55 | IPSWICH - 32B | YORK - 50A | IPSWICH - 32B | IPSWICH - 32B | COLWICK - 38A | IPSWICH - 32B | IPSWICH - 32B | DAIRYCOATES - 53A | DARLINGTON - 51A |
| Aug-55 | IPSWICH - 32B | YORK - 50A | IPSWICH - 32B | IPSWICH - 32B | COLWICK - 38A | IPSWICH - 32B | IPSWICH - 32B | DAIRYCOATES - 53A | DARLINGTON - 51A |
| Jan-56 | IPSWICH - 32B | YORK - 50A | IPSWICH - 32B | IPSWICH - 32B | COLWICK - 38A | IPSWICH - 32B | IPSWICH - 32B | DAIRYCOATES - 53A | DARLINGTON - 51A |
| Aug-56 | IPSWICH - 32B | YORK - 50A | IPSWICH - 32B | IPSWICH - 32B | COLWICK - 38A | IPSWICH - 32B | IPSWICH - 32B | DAIRYCOATES - 53A | DARLINGTON - 51A |
| Jan-57 | IPSWICH - 32B | YORK - 50A | IPSWICH - 32B | IPSWICH - 32B | COLWICK - 38A | IPSWICH - 32B | IPSWICH - 32B | **3/57: GRAN - 35B** | DARLINGTON - 51A |
| Aug-57 | IPSWICH - 32B | YORK - 50A | IPSWICH - 32B | IPSWICH - 32B | **10/57: IPS - 32B** | IPSWICH - 32B | IPSWICH - 32B | **10/57: NEWE - 35A** | DARLINGTON - 51A |
| Jan-58 | IPSWICH - 32B | YORK - 50A | IPSWICH - 32B | IPSWICH - 32B | IPSWICH - 32B | IPSWICH - 32B | IPSWICH - 32B | NEWENGLAND - 35A | **6/58: LOWM - 56F** |
| Aug-58 | IPSWICH - 32B | YORK - 50A | IPSWICH - 32B | IPSWICH - 32B | IPSWICH - 32B | IPSWICH - 32B | IPSWICH - 32B | NEWENGLAND - 34E | **9/58: DARL - 51A** |
| Jan-59 | IPSWICH - 32B | YORK - 50A | IPSWICH - 32B | IPSWICH - 32B | IPSWICH - 32B | IPSWICH - 32B | IPSWICH - 32B | NEWENGLAND - 34E | **10/58: W.HPL - 51C** |
| Aug-59 | IPSWICH - 32B | YORK - 50A | **8/59: NORW - 32A** | IPSWICH - 32B | IPSWICH - 32B | IPSWICH - 32B | IPSWICH - 32B | NEWENGLAND - 34E | W.HARTLEPOOL - 51C |
| Nov-59 | **10/59: MARCH - 31B** | YORK - 50A | NORWICH - 32A | **10/59: DCTR - 36A** | **11/59: MARCH - 31B** | **11/59: MARCH - 31B** | **12/59: MARCH - 31B** | NEWENGLAND - 34E | W.HARTLEPOOL - 51C |
| Jan-60 | MARCH - 31B | YORK - 50A | NORWICH - 32A | DONCASTER - 36A | **2/60: DARN - 41A** | MARCH - 31B | **2/60: K.LYNN - 31C** | NEWENGLAND - 34E | W.HARTLEPOOL - 51C |
| Apr-60 | MARCH - 31B | YORK - 50A | **4/60: LOW - 32C** | DONCASTER - 36A | DARNALL - 41A | **4/60: LINC - 40A** | KINGS LYNN - 31C | NEWENGLAND - 34E | W.HARTLEPOOL - 51C |
| Aug-60 | MARCH - 31B | YORK - 50A | **9/60: NORW - 32A** | DONCASTER - 36A | DARNALL - 41A | LINCOLN - 40A | **7/60: MARCH - 31B** | NEWENGLAND - 34E | W.HARTLEPOOL - 51C |
| Nov-60 | MARCH - 31B | YORK - 50A | NORWICH - 32A | DONCASTER - 36A | DARNALL - 41A | LINCOLN - 40A | MARCH - 31B | NEWENGLAND - 34E | W.HARTLEPOOL - 51C |

| | 61062 | 61063 | 61064 | 61065 | 61066 | 61067 | 61068 | 61069 | 61070 |
|---|---|---|---|---|---|---|---|---|---|
| Aug-50 | NEVILLEHILL - 50B | ANNESLEY - 38B | EASTFIELD - 65A | NEVILLEHILL - 50B | ANNESLEY - 38B | EDINBURGH(SM) - 64A | DAIRYCOATES - 53A | NEVILLEHILL - 50B | NEWENGLAND - 35A |
| Jan-51 | NEVILLEHILL - 50B | ANNESLEY - 38B | EASTFIELD - 65A | **11/50: HTN - 52B** | ANNESLEY - 38B | EDINBURGH(SM) - 64A | DAIRYCOATES - 53A | NEVILLEHILL - 50B | NEWENGLAND - 35A |
| Aug-51 | NEVILLEHILL - 50B | ANNESLEY - 38B | EASTFIELD - 65A | **1/51: N.HILL - 50B** | ANNESLEY - 38B | EDINBURGH(SM) - 64A | DAIRYCOATES - 53A | NEVILLEHILL - 50B | NEWENGLAND - 35A |
| Jan-52 | NEVILLEHILL - 50B | ANNESLEY - 38B | EASTFIELD - 65A | NEVILLEHILL - 50B | ANNESLEY - 38B | EDINBURGH(SM) - 64A | DAIRYCOATES - 53A | NEVILLEHILL - 50B | NEWENGLAND - 35A |
| Aug-52 | NEVILLEHILL - 50B | ANNESLEY - 38B | EASTFIELD - 65A | NEVILLEHILL - 50B | ANNESLEY - 38B | EDINBURGH(SM) - 64A | DAIRYCOATES - 53A | NEVILLEHILL - 50B | NEWENGLAND - 35A |
| Jan-53 | NEVILLEHILL - 50B | ANNESLEY - 38B | EASTFIELD - 65A | NEVILLEHILL - 50B | ANNESLEY - 38B | EDINBURGH(SM) - 64A | DAIRYCOATES - 53A | NEVILLEHILL - 50B | NEWENGLAND - 35A |
| Aug-53 | NEVILLEHILL - 50B | ANNESLEY - 38B | EASTFIELD - 65A | NEVILLEHILL - 50B | ANNESLEY - 38B | EDINBURGH(SM) - 64A | DAIRYCOATES - 53A | NEVILLEHILL - 50B | NEWENGLAND - 35A |
| Jan-54 | NEVILLEHILL - 50B | ANNESLEY - 38B | EASTFIELD - 65A | NEVILLEHILL - 50B | ANNESLEY - 38B | EDINBURGH(SM) - 64A | **2/54: B.GDNS - 53B** | NEVILLEHILL - 50B | NEWENGLAND - 35A |
| Aug-54 | NEVILLEHILL - 50B | ANNESLEY - 38B | EASTFIELD - 65A | NEVILLEHILL - 50B | ANNESLEY - 38B | EDINBURGH(SM) - 64A | BOTGDNS - 53B | NEVILLEHILL - 50B | NEWENGLAND - 35A |
| Jan-55 | NEVILLEHILL - 50B | ANNESLEY - 38B | EASTFIELD - 65A | NEVILLEHILL - 50B | ANNESLEY - 38B | EDINBURGH(SM) - 64A | BOTGDNS - 53B | NEVILLEHILL - 50B | NEWENGLAND - 35A |
| Aug-55 | NEVILLEHILL - 50B | ANNESLEY - 38B | **5/55: CANAL - 68E** | NEVILLEHILL - 50B | ANNESLEY - 38B | EDINBURGH(SM) - 64A | BOTGDNS - 53B | NEVILLEHILL - 50B | NEWENGLAND - 35A |
| Jan-56 | NEVILLEHILL - 50B | ANNESLEY - 38B | CARLISLE(C) - 68E | NEVILLEHILL - 50B | ANNESLEY - 38B | EDINBURGH(SM) - 64A | BOTGDNS - 53B | NEVILLEHILL - 50B | NEWENGLAND - 35A |
| Aug-56 | NEVILLEHILL - 50B | **10/56: COLW - 38A** | CARLISLE(C) - 68E | NEVILLEHILL - 50B | **10/56: COLW - 38A** | EDINBURGH(SM) - 64A | BOTGDNS - 53B | NEVILLEHILL - 50B | NEWENGLAND - 35A |
| Jan-57 | NEVILLEHILL - 50B | **11/56: LEIC - 38C** | CARLISLE(C) - 68E | NEVILLEHILL - 50B | COLWICK - 38A | EDINBURGH(SM) - 64A | BOTGDNS - 53B | NEVILLEHILL - 50B | NEWENGLAND - 35A |
| Aug-57 | NEVILLEHILL - 50B | LEICESTER(GC) - 38C | CARLISLE(C) - 68E | **9/57: GHD - 52A** | **10/57: CAMB - 31A** | EDINBURGH(SM) - 64A | BOTGDNS - 53B | NEVILLEHILL - 50B | NEWENGLAND - 35A |
| Jan-58 | NEVILLEHILL - 50B | LEICESTER(GC) - 38C | CARLISLE(C) - 68E | GATESHEAD - 52A | CAMBRIDGE - 31A | EDINBURGH(SM) - 64A | BOTGDNS - 53B | NEVILLEHILL - 50B | NEWENGLAND - 35A |
| Aug-58 | NEVILLEHILL - 50B | LEICESTER(GC) - 15E | CARLISLE(C) - 12C | **9/58: DYCTS - 53A** | CAMBRIDGE - 31A | EDINBURGH(SM) - 64A | BOTGDNS - 53B | NEVILLEHILL - 50B | NEWENGLAND - 34E |
| Jan-59 | NEVILLEHILL - 50B | LEICESTER(GC) - 15E | CARLISLE(C) - 12C | DAIRYCOATES - 53A | CAMBRIDGE - 31A | EDINBURGH(SM) - 64A | BOTGDNS - 53B | **2/59: YORK - 50A** | NEWENGLAND - 34E |
| Aug-59 | NEVILLEHILL - 50B | LEICESTER(GC) - 15E | CARLISLE(C) - 12C | DAIRYCOATES - 53A | CAMBRIDGE - 31A | EDINBURGH(SM) - 64A | **6/59: SCAR - 55E** | YORK - 50A | NEWENGLAND - 34E |
| Nov-59 | **10/59: TNBY - 51L** | LEICESTER(GC) - 15E | CARLISLE(C) - 12C | DAIRYCOATES - 53A | CAMBRIDGE - 31A | EDINBURGH(SM) - 64A | SCARBOROUGH - 55E | YORK - 50A | NEWENGLAND - 34E |
| Jan-60 | THORNABY - 51L | LEICESTER(GC) - 15E | CARLISLE(C) - 12C | DAIRYCOATES - 53A | CAMBRIDGE - 31A | EDINBURGH(SM) - 64A | SCARBOROUGH - 55E | YORK - 50A | NEWENGLAND - 34E |
| Apr-60 | THORNABY - 51L | **3/60: NEAS - 34E** | CARLISLE(C) - 12C | DAIRYCOATES - 50B | CAMBRIDGE - 31A | EDINBURGH(SM) - 64A | **4/60: DARL - 51A** | YORK - 50A | NEWENGLAND - 34E |
| Aug-60 | **9/60: YORK - 50A** | **10/60: LEIC - 15E** | CARLISLE(C) - 12C | DAIRYCOATES - 50B | CAMBRIDGE - 31A | EDINBURGH(SM) - 64A | **5/60: TNBY - 51L** | YORK - 50A | NEWENGLAND - 34E |
| Nov-60 | YORK - 50A | LEICESTER(GC) - 15E | CARLISLE(C) - 12C | DAIRYCOATES - 50B | CAMBRIDGE - 31A | EDINBURGH(SM) - 64A | **9/60: YORK - 50A** | YORK - 50A | NEWENGLAND - 34E |

| | 61071 | 61072 | 61073 | 61074 | 61075 | 61076 | 61077 | 61078 | 61079 |
|---|---|---|---|---|---|---|---|---|---|
| Aug-50 | YORK - 50A | THORNTONJCN - 62A | NEWENGLAND - 35A | DAIRYCOATES - 53A | NEWENGLAND - 35A | HAYMARKET - 64B | NEASDEN - 34E | COLWICK - 38A | IMMINGHAM - 40B |
| Jan-51 | YORK - 50A | THORNTONJCN - 62A | NEWENGLAND - 35A | DAIRYCOATES - 53A | NEWENGLAND - 35A | HAYMARKET - 64B | NEASDEN - 34E | COLWICK - 38A | IMMINGHAM - 40B |
| Aug-51 | YORK - 50A | THORNTONJCN - 62A | NEWENGLAND - 35A | DAIRYCOATES - 53A | NEWENGLAND - 35A | HAYMARKET - 64B | NEASDEN - 34E | COLWICK - 38A | IMMINGHAM - 40B |
| Jan-52 | YORK - 50A | THORNTONJCN - 62A | NEWENGLAND - 35A | DAIRYCOATES - 53A | NEWENGLAND - 35A | HAYMARKET - 64B | NEASDEN - 34E | **3/52: LEIC - 38C** | IMMINGHAM - 40B |
| Aug-52 | YORK - 50A | THORNTONJCN - 62A | NEWENGLAND - 35A | DAIRYCOATES - 53A | NEWENGLAND - 35A | HAYMARKET - 64B | NEASDEN - 34E | **6/52: WOOD - 38E** | IMMINGHAM - 40B |
| Jan-53 | YORK - 50A | THORNTONJCN - 62A | NEWENGLAND - 35A | DAIRYCOATES - 53A | NEWENGLAND - 35A | HAYMARKET - 64B | NEASDEN - 34E | W HALSE - 38E | IMMINGHAM - 40B |
| Aug-53 | YORK - 50A | THORNTONJCN - 62A | NEWENGLAND - 35A | DAIRYCOATES - 53A | NEWENGLAND - 35A | HAYMARKET - 64B | NEASDEN - 34E | W HALSE - 38E | IMMINGHAM - 40B |
| Jan-54 | YORK - 50A | THORNTONJCN - 62A | NEWENGLAND - 35A | DAIRYCOATES - 53A | NEWENGLAND - 35A | HAYMARKET - 64B | NEASDEN - 34E | W HALSE - 38E | IMMINGHAM - 40B |
| Aug-54 | YORK - 50A | THORNTONJCN - 62A | NEWENGLAND - 35A | DAIRYCOATES - 53A | **6/54: KX - 34A** | HAYMARKET - 64B | NEASDEN - 34E | W HALSE - 38E | IMMINGHAM - 40B |
| Jan-55 | YORK - 50A | THORNTONJCN - 62A | NEWENGLAND - 35A | DAIRYCOATES - 53A | KINGS CROSS - 34A | HAYMARKET - 64B | NEASDEN - 34E | W HALSE - 38E | IMMINGHAM - 40B |
| Aug-55 | YORK - 50A | THORNTONJCN - 62A | NEWENGLAND - 35A | DAIRYCOATES - 53A | KINGS CROSS - 34A | HAYMARKET - 64B | NEASDEN - 34E | W HALSE - 38E | IMMINGHAM - 40B |
| Jan-56 | YORK - 50A | THORNTONJCN - 62A | NEWENGLAND - 35A | DAIRYCOATES - 53A | KINGS CROSS - 34A | HAYMARKET - 64B | NEASDEN - 34E | W HALSE - 38E | IMMINGHAM - 40B |
| Aug-56 | YORK - 50A | THORNTONJCN - 62A | NEWENGLAND - 35A | DAIRYCOATES - 53A | KINGS CROSS - 34A | HAYMARKET - 64B | NEASDEN - 34E | W HALSE - 38E | IMMINGHAM - 40B |
| Jan-57 | YORK - 50A | THORNTONJCN - 62A | NEWENGLAND - 35A | **3/57: GRAN - 35B** | KINGS CROSS - 34A | HAYMARKET - 64B | NEASDEN - 34E | W HALSE - 38E | IMMINGHAM - 40B |
| Aug-57 | YORK - 50A | THORNTONJCN - 62A | NEWENGLAND - 35A | **10/57: NEWE - 35A** | KINGS CROSS - 34A | HAYMARKET - 64B | NEASDEN - 34E | W HALSE - 38E | IMMINGHAM - 40B |
| Jan-58 | YORK - 50A | THORNTONJCN - 62A | NEWENGLAND - 35A | NEWENGLAND - 35A | KINGS CROSS - 34A | HAYMARKET - 64B | NEASDEN - 34E | W HALSE - 38E | IMMINGHAM - 40B |
| Aug-58 | YORK - 50A | **9/58: DUNF - 62C** | NEWENGLAND - 34E | NEWENGLAND - 34E | KINGS CROSS - 34A | HAYMARKET - 64B | NEASDEN - 14D | W HALSE - 2F | IMMINGHAM - 40B |
| Jan-59 | YORK - 50A | DUNFERMLINE - 62C | NEWENGLAND - 34E | NEWENGLAND - 34E | KINGS CROSS - 34A | HAYMARKET - 64B | NEASDEN - 14D | W HALSE - 2F | IMMINGHAM - 40B |
| Aug-59 | YORK - 50A | DUNFERMLINE - 62C | NEWENGLAND - 34E | NEWENGLAND - 34E | KINGS CROSS - 34A | HAYMARKET - 64B | NEASDEN - 14D | W HALSE - 2F | IMMINGHAM - 40B |
| Nov-59 | YORK - 50A | DUNFERMLINE - 62C | NEWENGLAND - 34E | NEWENGLAND - 34E | KINGS CROSS - 34A | HAYMARKET - 64B | NEASDEN - 14D | W HALSE - 2F | IMMINGHAM - 40B |
| Jan-60 | YORK - 50A | DUNFERMLINE - 62C | NEWENGLAND - 34E | NEWENGLAND - 34E | KINGS CROSS - 34A | HAYMARKET - 64B | NEASDEN - 14D | W HALSE - 2F | IMMINGHAM - 40B |
| Apr-60 | YORK - 50A | DUNFERMLINE - 62C | NEWENGLAND - 34E | NEWENGLAND - 34E | KINGS CROSS - 34A | HAYMARKET - 64B | NEASDEN - 14D | W HALSE - 2F | IMMINGHAM - 40B |
| Aug-60 | YORK - 50A | DUNFERMLINE - 62C | NEWENGLAND - 34E | NEWENGLAND - 34E | **10/60: NEWE - 34E** | HAYMARKET - 64B | NEASDEN - 14D | W HALSE - 2F | IMMINGHAM - 40B |
| Nov-60 | YORK - 50A | DUNFERMLINE - 62C | NEWENGLAND - 34E | NEWENGLAND - 34E | NEWENGLAND - 34E | HAYMARKET - 64B | NEASDEN - 14D | W HALSE - 2F | IMMINGHAM - 40B |

used on the route to North East Lincolnshire. The type was also popular on the London extension and although Neasden, Woodford and Leicester had about twenty A3 and V2 locomotives for the principal services, B1's took charge of a large proportion of residual workings to and from Marylebone.

As elsewhere, the Great Central ran its share of relief trains – which relied heavily on B1 4-6-0's – and a typical summer weekend in the early 1950s would see three additional services from Marylebone to Manchester, one to Nottingham and two night services to Edinburgh: a commitment which called for eleven addition engine workings. This, however, was small beer compared to the GC traffic moved in North Lincolnshire, the same day seeing no less than twenty five additional services being booked to run from the West Riding and the Nottingham mining area to Cleethorpes alone. When the total number of additional trains – let alone booked services – run on the section is taken into account, it becomes clear why sheds such as Darnall and Immingham had such large allocations of mixed traffic engines.

*Varying standards of appearance. For some reason an usual amount of effort is being made to get B1 4-6-0 61395 into a presentable condition at Carlisle Canal on 19th June 1960. Further down the line K3 2-6-0 61858 waits its turn for cleaning. Much of Canal's work involved trains to Edinburgh via Hawick although its seven B1's tended to be used on the NER route to Newcastle.*

| | 61080 | 61081 | 61082 | 61083 | 61084 | 61085 | 61086 | 61087 | 61088 |
|---|---|---|---|---|---|---|---|---|---|
| Aug-50 | DAIRYCOATES-53A | HAYMARKET-64B | IMMINGHAM-40B | NEASDEN-34E | YORK-50A | ARDSLEY-37A | DONCASTER-36A | DONCASTER-36A | LEICESTER (GC)-38C |
| Jan-51 | DAIRYCOATES-53A | HAYMARKET-64B | IMMINGHAM-40B | NEASDEN-34E | YORK-50A | ARDSLEY-37A | DONCASTER-36A | DONCASTER-36A | LEICESTER (GC)-38C |
| Aug-51 | DAIRYCOATES-53A | HAYMARKET-64B | IMMINGHAM-40B | NEASDEN-34E | YORK-50A | ARDSLEY-37A | DONCASTER-36A | DONCASTER-36A | LEICESTER (GC)-38C |
| Jan-52 | DAIRYCOATES-53A | HAYMARKET-64B | IMMINGHAM-40B | NEASDEN-34E | YORK-50A | ARDSLEY-37A | 2/52: N.HILL-50B | DONCASTER-36A | LEICESTER (GC)-38C |
| Aug-52 | DAIRYCOATES-53A | HAYMARKET-64B | IMMINGHAM-40B | NEASDEN-34E | YORK-50A | ARDSLEY-37A | NEVILLE HILL-50B | DONCASTER-36A | LEICESTER (GC)-38C |
| Jan-53 | DAIRYCOATES-53A | HAYMARKET-64B | IMMINGHAM-40B | NEASDEN-34E | YORK-50A | ARDSLEY-37A | NEVILLE HILL-50B | DONCASTER-36A | LEICESTER (GC)-38C |
| Aug-53 | DAIRYCOATES-53A | HAYMARKET-64B | IMMINGHAM-40B | NEASDEN-34E | YORK-50A | 10/53: NEWE-35A | NEVILLE HILL-50B | DONCASTER-36A | LEICESTER (GC)-38C |
| Jan-54 | DAIRYCOATES-53A | HAYMARKET-64B | IMMINGHAM-40B | NEASDEN-34E | YORK-50A | NEWENGLAND-35A | NEVILLE HILL-50B | DONCASTER-36A | LEICESTER (GC)-38C |
| Aug-54 | DAIRYCOATES-53A | HAYMARKET-64B | IMMINGHAM-40B | NEASDEN-34E | YORK-50A | NEWENGLAND-35A | NEVILLE HILL-50B | DONCASTER-36A | LEICESTER (GC)-38C |
| Jan-55 | DAIRYCOATES-53A | HAYMARKET-64B | IMMINGHAM-40B | NEASDEN-34E | YORK-50A | NEWENGLAND-35A | NEVILLE HILL-50B | DONCASTER-36A | LEICESTER (GC)-38C |
| Aug-55 | DAIRYCOATES-53A | HAYMARKET-64B | IMMINGHAM-40B | NEASDEN-34E | YORK-50A | 6/55: LINC-40A | NEVILLE HILL-50B | DONCASTER-36A | LEICESTER (GC)-38C |
| Jan-56 | DAIRYCOATES-53A | HAYMARKET-64B | IMMINGHAM-40B | NEASDEN-34E | YORK-50A | LINCOLN-40A | NEVILLE HILL-50B | DONCASTER-36A | LEICESTER (GC)-38C |
| Aug-56 | DAIRYCOATES-53A | HAYMARKET-64B | IMMINGHAM-40B | NEASDEN-34E | YORK-50A | LINCOLN-40A | NEVILLE HILL-50B | DONCASTER-36A | LEICESTER (GC)-38C |
| Jan-57 | DAIRYCOATES-53A | HAYMARKET-64B | IMMINGHAM-40B | 2/57: S.BGE-35C | YORK-50A | LINCOLN-40A | NEVILLE HILL-50B | DONCASTER-36A | 11/56: COLW-38A |
| Aug-57 | DAIRYCOATES-53A | HAYMARKET-64B | IMMINGHAM-40B | SPITAL BRIDGE-35C | YORK-50A | LINCOLN-40A | NEVILLE HILL-50B | DONCASTER-36A | COLWICK-38A |
| Jan-58 | 12/57: B.GDNS-53B | HAYMARKET-64B | IMMINGHAM-40B | SPITAL BRIDGE-35C | YORK-50A | LINCOLN-40A | NEVILLE HILL-50B | DONCASTER-36A | COLWICK-38A |
| Aug-58 | BOTANIC GARDENS-53B | HAYMARKET-64B | IMMINGHAM-40B | SPITAL BRIDGE-31F | YORK-50A | 6/58: LEIC-15E | NEVILLE HILL-50B | DONCASTER-36A | COLWICK-40E |
| Jan-59 | BOTANIC GARDENS-53B | HAYMARKET-64B | IMMINGHAM-40B | 12/58: IMM-40B | YORK-50A | LEICESTER (GC)-15E | 1/59: YORK-50A | DONCASTER-36A | COLWICK-40E |
| Aug-59 | 6/59: DYCTS-53A | HAYMARKET-64B | IMMINGHAM-40B | 6/59: MEX-41F | YORK-50A | LEICESTER (GC)-15E | YORK-50A | DONCASTER-36A | COLWICK-40E |
| Nov-59 | DAIRYCOATES-53A | HAYMARKET-64B | IMMINGHAM-40B | MEXBOROUGH-41F | YORK-50A | 11/59: WOOD-2F | YORK-50A | DONCASTER-36A | COLWICK-40E |
| Jan-60 | DAIRYCOATES-53A | HAYMARKET-64B | IMMINGHAM-40B | MEXBOROUGH-41F | YORK-50A | WOODFORD HALSE-2F | YORK-50A | DONCASTER-36A | COLWICK-40E |
| Apr-60 | DAIRYCOATES-53A | HAYMARKET-64B | IMMINGHAM-40B | MEXBOROUGH-41F | YORK-50A | WOODFORD HALSE-2F | YORK-50A | DONCASTER-36A | COLWICK-40E |
| Aug-60 | DAIRYCOATES-50B | HAYMARKET-64B | IMMINGHAM-40B | MEXBOROUGH-41F | YORK-50A | 10/60: LEIC-15E | YORK-50A | DONCASTER-36A | COLWICK-40E |
| Nov-60 | DAIRYCOATES-50B | HAYMARKET-64B | IMMINGHAM-40B | MEXBOROUGH-41F | YORK-50A | LEICESTER (GC)-15E | YORK-50A | DONCASTER-36A | COLWICK-40E |

| | 61089 | 61090 | 61091 | 61092 | 61093 | 61094 | 61095 | 61096 | 61097 |
|---|---|---|---|---|---|---|---|---|---|
| Aug-50 | STRATFORD-30A | HITCHIN-34D | HITCHIN-34D | LEICESTER (GC)-38C | HITCHIN-34D | HITCHIN-34D | HITCHIN-34D | ARDSLEY-37A | HITCHIN-34D |
| Jan-51 | STRATFORD-30A | 5/51: IMM-40B | HITCHIN-34D | LEICESTER (GC)-38C | HITCHIN-34D | HITCHIN-34D | HITCHIN-34D | ARDSLEY-37A | HITCHIN-34D |
| Aug-51 | 6/51: STRAT-30A | HITCHIN-34D | HITCHIN-34D | LEICESTER (GC)-38C | HITCHIN-34D | HITCHIN-34D | HITCHIN-34D | ARDSLEY-37A | HITCHIN-34D |
| Jan-52 | STRATFORD-30A | HITCHIN-34D | HITCHIN-34D | LEICESTER (GC)-38C | HITCHIN-34D | HITCHIN-34D | 12/51: IPS-32B | HITCHIN-34D | HITCHIN-34D |
| Aug-52 | STRATFORD-30A | HITCHIN-34D | HITCHIN-34D | LEICESTER (GC)-38C | HITCHIN-34D | HITCHIN-34D | IPSWICH-32B | HITCHIN-34D | HITCHIN-34D |
| Jan-53 | STRATFORD-30A | HITCHIN-34D | HITCHIN-34D | LEICESTER (GC)-38C | HITCHIN-34D | HITCHIN-34D | IPSWICH-32B | HITCHIN-34D | HITCHIN-34D |
| Aug-53 | STRATFORD-30A | HITCHIN-34D | HITCHIN-34D | LEICESTER (GC)-38C | HITCHIN-34D | 5/53: NEWE-35A | IPSWICH-32B | HITCHIN-34D | HITCHIN-34D |
| Jan-54 | STRATFORD-30A | HITCHIN-34D | HITCHIN-34D | LEICESTER (GC)-38C | HITCHIN-34D | NEWENGLAND-35A | IPSWICH-32B | HITCHIN-34D | HITCHIN-34D |
| Aug-54 | STRATFORD-30A | HITCHIN-34D | HITCHIN-34D | LEICESTER (GC)-38C | HITCHIN-34D | NEWENGLAND-35A | IPSWICH-32B | HITCHIN-34D | HITCHIN-34D |
| Jan-55 | STRATFORD-30A | HITCHIN-34D | HITCHIN-34D | 1/55: COLW-38A | HITCHIN-34D | NEWENGLAND-35A | IPSWICH-32B | HITCHIN-34D | HITCHIN-34D |
| Aug-55 | STRATFORD-30A | HITCHIN-34D | HITCHIN-34D | COLWICK-38A | HITCHIN-34D | NEWENGLAND-35A | IPSWICH-32B | HITCHIN-34D | HITCHIN-34D |
| Jan-56 | STRATFORD-30A | HITCHIN-34D | HITCHIN-34D | COLWICK-38A | HITCHIN-34D | NEWENGLAND-35A | IPSWICH-32B | HITCHIN-34D | HITCHIN-34D |
| Aug-56 | STRATFORD-30A | HITCHIN-34D | HITCHIN-34D | COLWICK-38A | HITCHIN-34D | NEWENGLAND-35A | IPSWICH-32B | HITCHIN-34D | HITCHIN-34D |
| Jan-57 | 2/57: COL-30E | HITCHIN-34D | HITCHIN-34D | COLWICK-38A | HITCHIN-34D | HITCHIN-34D | 3/57: S.BGE-35C | HITCHIN-34D | HITCHIN-34D |
| Aug-57 | 10/57: STRAT-30A | HITCHIN-34D | HITCHIN-34D | COLWICK-38A | HITCHIN-34D | HITCHIN-34D | SPITAL BRIDGE-35C | 10/57: CAMB-31A | HITCHIN-34D |
| Jan-58 | STRATFORD-30A | HITCHIN-34D | HITCHIN-34D | COLWICK-40E | HITCHIN-34D | HITCHIN-34D | SPITAL BRIDGE-35C | CAMBRIDGE-31A | HITCHIN-34D |
| Aug-58 | STRATFORD-30A | HITCHIN-34D | HITCHIN-34D | COLWICK-40E | HITCHIN-34D | HITCHIN-34D | SPITAL BRIDGE-31F | CAMBRIDGE-31A | HITCHIN-34D |
| Jan-59 | STRATFORD-30A | HITCHIN-34D | HITCHIN-34D | COLWICK-40E | HITCHIN-34D | HITCHIN-34D | SPITAL BRIDGE-31F | 12/58: S.BGE-35C | HITCHIN-34D |
| Aug-59 | STRATFORD-30A | 6/59: MEX-41F | HITCHIN-34D | COLWICK-40E | 6/59: MEX-41F | 9/59: DARN-41A | SPITAL BRIDGE-31F | SPITAL BRIDGE-31F | HITCHIN-34D |
| Nov-59 | STRATFORD-30A | MEXBOROUGH-41F | HITCHIN-34D | COLWICK-40E | MEXBOROUGH-41F | DARNALL-41A | 2/60: MARCH-31B | 2/60: MARCH-31B | HITCHIN-34D |
| Jan-60 | STRATFORD-30A | MEXBOROUGH-41F | HITCHIN-34D | COLWICK-40E | MEXBOROUGH-41F | DARNALL-41A | MARCH-31B | MARCH-31B | HITCHIN-34D |
| Apr-60 | STRATFORD-30A | 5/60: DARN-41A | HITCHIN-34D | COLWICK-40E | MEXBOROUGH-41F | DARNALL-41A | MARCH-31B | MARCH-31B | HITCHIN-34D |
| Aug-60 | STRATFORD-30A | DARNALL-41A | 8/60: NEWE-34E | COLWICK-40E | MEXBOROUGH-41F | DARNALL-41A | MARCH-31B | MARCH-31B | 8/60: NEWE-34E |
| Nov-60 | STRATFORD-30A | DARNALL-41A | NEWENGLAND-34E | COLWICK-40E | MEXBOROUGH-41F | DARNALL-41A | MARCH-31B | MARCH-31B | NEWENGLAND-34E |

| | 61098 | 61099 | 61100 | 61101 | 61102 | 61103 | 61104 | 61105 | 61106 |
|---|---|---|---|---|---|---|---|---|---|
| Aug-50 | STRATFORD-30A | HITCHIN-34D | GATESHEAD-52A | DUNDEE-62B | DUNDEE-62B | THORNTON JCN-62A | STRATFORD-30A | HITCHIN-34D | LEICESTER (GC)-38C |
| Jan-51 | STRATFORD-30A | HITCHIN-34D | GATESHEAD-52A | DUNDEE-62B | DUNDEE-62B | THORNTON JCN-62A | STRATFORD-30A | HITCHIN-34D | LEICESTER (GC)-38C |
| Aug-51 | 9/51: IMM-40B | HITCHIN-34D | GATESHEAD-52A | DUNDEE-62B | DUNDEE-62B | THORNTON JCN-62A | STRATFORD-30A | HITCHIN-34D | LEICESTER (GC)-38C |
| Jan-52 | IMMINGHAM-40B | HITCHIN-34D | GATESHEAD-52A | DUNDEE-62B | DUNDEE-62B | THORNTON JCN-62A | STRATFORD-30A | HITCHIN-34D | 10/52: COLW-38A |
| Aug-52 | IMMINGHAM-40B | HITCHIN-34D | GATESHEAD-52A | DUNDEE-62B | DUNDEE-62B | THORNTON JCN-62A | STRATFORD-30A | HITCHIN-34D | LEICESTER (GC)-38C |
| Jan-53 | IMMINGHAM-40B | 1/53: KX-34A | GATESHEAD-52A | DUNDEE-62B | DUNDEE-62B | THORNTON JCN-62A | STRATFORD-30A | 1/53: KX-34A | 10/52: COLW-38A |
| Aug-53 | IMMINGHAM-40B | 9/53: STM-64A | GATESHEAD-52A | DUNDEE-62B | DUNDEE-62B | THORNTON JCN-62A | STRATFORD-30A | KINGS CROSS-34A | 2/53: LEIC-38C |
| Jan-54 | IMMINGHAM-40B | EDINBURGH (SM)-64A | GATESHEAD-52A | DUNDEE-62B | DUNDEE-62B | THORNTON JCN-62A | STRATFORD-30A | KINGS CROSS-34A | LEICESTER (GC)-38C |
| Aug-54 | IMMINGHAM-40B | EDINBURGH (SM)-64A | GATESHEAD-52A | DUNDEE-62B | DUNDEE-62B | THORNTON JCN-62A | STRATFORD-30A | 6/54: HIT-34D | 3/54: COLW-38A |
| Jan-55 | IMMINGHAM-40B | EDINBURGH (SM)-64A | GATESHEAD-52A | 5/55: DUNF-62C | DUNDEE-62B | THORNTON JCN-62A | STRATFORD-30A | HITCHIN-34D | COLWICK-38A |
| Aug-55 | IMMINGHAM-40B | EDINBURGH (SM)-64A | GATESHEAD-52A | DUNFERMLINE-62C | DUNDEE-62B | THORNTON JCN-62A | STRATFORD-30A | HITCHIN-34D | COLWICK-38A |
| Jan-56 | IMMINGHAM-40B | EDINBURGH (SM)-64A | GATESHEAD-52A | DUNFERMLINE-62C | DUNDEE-62B | THORNTON JCN-62A | STRATFORD-30A | HITCHIN-34D | COLWICK-38A |
| Aug-56 | IMMINGHAM-40B | EDINBURGH (SM)-64A | GATESHEAD-52A | DUNFERMLINE-62C | DUNDEE-62B | THORNTON JCN-62A | STRATFORD-30A | HITCHIN-34D | COLWICK-38A |
| Jan-57 | IMMINGHAM-40B | 2/57: BLAY-52C | GATESHEAD-52A | DUNFERMLINE-62C | DUNDEE-62B | THORNTON JCN-62A | STRATFORD-30A | HITCHIN-34D | COLWICK-38A |
| Aug-57 | IMMINGHAM-40B | BLAYDON-52C | GATESHEAD-52A | DUNFERMLINE-62C | DUNDEE-62B | THORNTON JCN-62A | STRATFORD-30A | HITCHIN-34D | 12/57: LEIC-38C |
| Jan-58 | IMMINGHAM-40B | BLAYDON-52C | GATESHEAD-52A | DUNFERMLINE-62C | DUNDEE-62B | THORNTON JCN-62A | STRATFORD-30A | 7/58: DARN-41A | LEICESTER (GC)-38C |
| Aug-58 | IMMINGHAM-40B | BLAYDON-52C | GATESHEAD-52A | DUNFERMLINE-62C | DUNDEE-62B | THORNTON JCN-62A | STRATFORD-30A | DARNALL-41A | LEICESTER (GC)-15E |
| Jan-59 | IMMINGHAM-40B | BLAYDON-52C | GATESHEAD-52A | DUNFERMLINE-62C | DUNDEE-62B | THORNTON JCN-62A | 1/59: CAMB-31A | DARNALL-41A | LEICESTER (GC)-15E |
| Aug-59 | IMMINGHAM-40B | BLAYDON-52C | GATESHEAD-52A | DUNFERMLINE-62C | DUNDEE-62B | THORNTON JCN-62A | 5/59: DARN-41A | DARNALL-41A | LEICESTER (GC)-15E |
| Nov-59 | IMMINGHAM-40B | 10/59: GHD-52A | GATESHEAD-52A | DUNFERMLINE-62C | DUNDEE-62B | THORNTON JCN-62A | 12/59: MEX-41F | DARNALL-41A | 11/59: WOOD-2F |
| Jan-60 | IMMINGHAM-40B | GATESHEAD-52A | GATESHEAD-52A | DUNFERMLINE-62C | DUNDEE-62B | THORNTON JCN-62A | 1/60: DARN-41A | DARNALL-41A | WOODFORD HALSE-2F |
| Apr-60 | IMMINGHAM-40B | GATESHEAD-52A | GATESHEAD-52A | DUNFERMLINE-62C | DUNDEE-62B | THORNTON JCN-62A | DARNALL-41A | DARNALL-41A | WOODFORD HALSE-2F |
| Aug-60 | IMMINGHAM-40B | GATESHEAD-52A | GATESHEAD-52A | DUNFERMLINE-62C | DUNDEE-62B | THORNTON JCN-62A | DARNALL-41A | DARNALL-41A | WOODFORD HALSE-2F |
| Nov-60 | IMMINGHAM-40B | GATESHEAD-52A | GATESHEAD-52A | DUNFERMLINE-62C | DUNDEE-62B | THORNTON JCN-62A | DARNALL-41A | DARNALL-41A | WOODFORD HALSE-2F |

| | 61107 | 61108 | 61109 | 61110 | 61111 | 61112 | 61113 | 61114 | 61115 |
|---|---|---|---|---|---|---|---|---|---|
| Aug-50 | DONCASTER-36A | LEICESTER (GC)-38C | STRATFORD-30A | COLWICK-38A | COLWICK-38A | LINCOLN-40A | KINGS CROSS-34A | GORTON-39A | YORK-50A |
| Jan-51 | DONCASTER-36A | LEICESTER (GC)-38C | STRATFORD-30A | COLWICK-38A | COLWICK-38A | LINCOLN-40A | KINGS CROSS-34A | GORTON-39A | YORK-50A |
| Aug-51 | 10/51: IMM-40B | LEICESTER (GC)-38C | STRATFORD-30A | 10/51: WOOD-38E | COLWICK-38A | 10/51: NORW-32A | KINGS CROSS-34A | GORTON-39A | YORK-50A |
| Jan-52 | 11/51: DCTR-36A | LEICESTER (GC)-38C | STRATFORD-30A | 12/51: NORW-32A | COLWICK-38A | 3/52: LINC-40A | KINGS CROSS-34A | GORTON-39A | YORK-50A |
| Aug-52 | DONCASTER-36A | LEICESTER (GC)-38C | STRATFORD-30A | 3/52: ARDS-37A | COLWICK-38A | LINCOLN-40A | KINGS CROSS-34A | 10/52: STRAT-30A | YORK-50A |
| Jan-53 | DONCASTER-36A | LEICESTER (GC)-38C | STRATFORD-30A | ARDSLEY-37A | 1/53: LEIC-38C | LINCOLN-40A | 1/53: NEWE-35A | STRATFORD-30A | YORK-50A |
| Aug-53 | DONCASTER-36A | 9/53: STM-64A | STRATFORD-30A | ARDSLEY-37A | 2/53: COLW-38A | LINCOLN-40A | NEWENGLAND-35A | STRATFORD-30A | YORK-50A |
| Jan-54 | DONCASTER-36A | EDINBURGH (SM)-64A | STRATFORD-30A | ARDSLEY-37A | COLWICK-38A | 11/53: MEX-36B | NEWENGLAND-35A | 3/54: DCTR-36A | YORK-50A |
| Aug-54 | DONCASTER-36A | EDINBURGH (SM)-64A | STRATFORD-30A | ARDSLEY-37A | COLWICK-38A | MEXBOROUGH-36B | NEWENGLAND-35A | DONCASTER-36A | YORK-50A |
| Jan-55 | DONCASTER-36A | EDINBURGH (SM)-64A | STRATFORD-30A | ARDSLEY-37A | 1/55: LEIC-38C | MEXBOROUGH-36B | NEWENGLAND-35A | DONCASTER-36A | YORK-50A |
| Aug-55 | DONCASTER-36A | EDINBURGH (SM)-64A | STRATFORD-30A | ARDSLEY-37A | 2/55: COLW-38A | MEXBOROUGH-36B | NEWENGLAND-35A | DONCASTER-36A | YORK-50A |
| Jan-56 | DONCASTER-36A | EDINBURGH (SM)-64A | STRATFORD-30A | ARDSLEY-37A | COLWICK-38A | MEXBOROUGH-36B | NEWENGLAND-35A | DONCASTER-36A | YORK-50A |
| Aug-56 | DONCASTER-36A | EDINBURGH (SM)-64A | STRATFORD-30A | ARDSLEY-56B | 10/56: KX-34A | MEXBOROUGH-36B | NEWENGLAND-35A | DONCASTER-36A | YORK-50A |
| Jan-57 | DONCASTER-36A | EDINBURGH (SM)-64A | STRATFORD-30A | ARDSLEY-56B | 12/56: NEAS-34E | MEXBOROUGH-36B | NEWENGLAND-35A | DONCASTER-36A | YORK-50A |
| Aug-57 | DONCASTER-36A | EDINBURGH (SM)-64A | STRATFORD-30A | ARDSLEY-56B | 2/57: STRAT-30A | MEXBOROUGH-36B | NEWENGLAND-35A | DONCASTER-36A | YORK-50A |
| Jan-58 | DONCASTER-36A | EDINBURGH (SM)-64A | STRATFORD-30A | ARDSLEY-56B | STRATFORD-30A | MEXBOROUGH-36B | NEWENGLAND-34E | DONCASTER-36A | 6/58: C.HILL-56C |
| Aug-58 | DONCASTER-36A | EDINBURGH (SM)-64A | STRATFORD-30A | ARDSLEY-56B | STRATFORD-30A | MEXBOROUGH-41F | NEWENGLAND-34E | DONCASTER-36A | COPLEY HILL-56C |
| Jan-59 | DONCASTER-36A | EDINBURGH (SM)-64A | STRATFORD-30A | ARDSLEY-56B | 1/59: PARK-30F | MEXBOROUGH-41F | NEWENGLAND-34E | DONCASTER-36A | COPLEY HILL-56C |
| Aug-59 | DONCASTER-36A | EDINBURGH (SM)-64A | STRATFORD-30A | ARDSLEY-56B | 6/59: DARN-41A | 6/59: DARN-41A | NEWENGLAND-34E | 12/59: IMM-40B | COPLEY HILL-56C |
| Nov-59 | DONCASTER-36A | EDINBURGH (SM)-64A | STRATFORD-30A | ARDSLEY-56B | DARNALL-41A | DARNALL-41A | NEWENGLAND-34E | DONCASTER-36A | COPLEY HILL-56C |
| Jan-60 | DONCASTER-36A | EDINBURGH (SM)-64A | STRATFORD-30A | ARDSLEY-56B | DARNALL-41A | DARNALL-41A | NEWENGLAND-34E | IMMINGHAM-40B | COPLEY HILL-56C |
| Apr-60 | DONCASTER-36A | EDINBURGH (SM)-64A | STRATFORD-30A | ARDSLEY-56B | DARNALL-41A | DARNALL-41A | NEWENGLAND-34E | IMMINGHAM-40B | COPLEY HILL-56C |
| Aug-60 | DONCASTER-36A | EDINBURGH (SM)-64A | STRATFORD-30A | ARDSLEY-56B | DARNALL-41A | DARNALL-41A | NEWENGLAND-34E | IMMINGHAM-40B | COPLEY HILL-56C |
| Nov-60 | DONCASTER-36A | EDINBURGH (SM)-64A | STRATFORD-30A | ARDSLEY-56B | DARNALL-41A | DARNALL-41A | NEWENGLAND-34E | IMMINGHAM-40B | COPLEY HILL-56C |

Although a mixed traffic class, the B1's primary role was as a replacement for the several classes of pregrouping passenger engines whose duties did not call for the output of a Pacific or V2. Inevitably the class worked a considerable amount of goods traffic – one diagram called for a through working between Kings Cross and Hull with a fast freight – but they were not the equal of a K3 2-6-0 in this respect which, in the case of a fitted goods from Kings Cross to Doncaster for example, could take the full line limit of sixty vehicles as opposed to only forty-five by a B1.

Where the B1 was a standard locomotive with examples allocated the length and breadth of the system, the handful of other 4-6-0 classes were, by the mid 1950s, confined to fairly strict geographical areas. Most of the B16's were concentrated around the southern parts of the North Eastern working

| | 61116 | 61117 | 61118 | 61119 | 61120 | 61121 | 61122 | 61123 | 61124 |
|---|---|---|---|---|---|---|---|---|---|
| Aug-50 | EASTFIELD - 65A | EASTFIELD - 65A | THORNTONJCN - 62A | STRATFORD - 30A | DONCASTER - 36A | CAMBRIDGE - 31A | COLWICK - 38A | COLWICK - 38A | DONCASTER - 36A |
| Jan-51 | EASTFIELD - 65A | EASTFIELD - 65A | THORNTONJCN - 62A | STRATFORD - 30A | DONCASTER - 36A | CAMBRIDGE - 31A | COLWICK - 38A | COLWICK - 38A | DONCASTER - 36A |
| Aug-51 | EASTFIELD - 65A | EASTFIELD - 65A | THORNTONJCN - 62A | STRATFORD - 30A | DONCASTER - 36A | CAMBRIDGE - 31A | 10/51: ARDS - 37A | 10/51: ARDS - 37A | DONCASTER - 36A |
| Jan-52 | EASTFIELD - 65A | EASTFIELD - 65A | THORNTONJCN - 62A | STRATFORD - 30A | DONCASTER - 36A | CAMBRIDGE - 31A | ARDSLEY - 37A | ARDSLEY - 37A | DONCASTER - 36A |
| Aug-52 | 6/52: NEAS - 34E | EASTFIELD - 65A | THORNTONJCN - 62A | STRATFORD - 30A | DONCASTER - 36A | CAMBRIDGE - 31A | ARDSLEY - 37A | ARDSLEY - 37A | DONCASTER - 36A |
| Jan-53 | NEASDEN - 34E | EASTFIELD - 65A | THORNTONJCN - 62A | STRATFORD - 30A | DONCASTER - 36A | CAMBRIDGE - 31A | ARDSLEY - 37A | ARDSLEY - 37A | DONCASTER - 36A |
| Aug-53 | NEASDEN - 34E | EASTFIELD - 65A | THORNTONJCN - 62A | STRATFORD - 30A | DONCASTER - 36A | CAMBRIDGE - 31A | 10/53: NEWE - 35A | ARDSLEY - 37A | DONCASTER - 36A |
| Jan-54 | NEASDEN - 34E | EASTFIELD - 65A | THORNTONJCN - 62A | STRATFORD - 30A | DONCASTER - 36A | CAMBRIDGE - 31A | NEWENGLAND - 35A | ARDSLEY - 37A | DONCASTER - 36A |
| Aug-54 | NEASDEN - 34E | EASTFIELD - 65A | THORNTONJCN - 62A | STRATFORD - 30A | DONCASTER - 36A | CAMBRIDGE - 31A | NEWENGLAND - 35A | ARDSLEY - 37A | DONCASTER - 36A |
| Jan-55 | NEASDEN - 34E | EASTFIELD - 65A | THORNTONJCN - 62A | STRATFORD - 30A | DONCASTER - 36A | CAMBRIDGE - 31A | NEWENGLAND - 35A | ARDSLEY - 37A | DONCASTER - 36A |
| Aug-55 | NEASDEN - 34E | EASTFIELD - 65A | THORNTONJCN - 62A | STRATFORD - 30A | DONCASTER - 36A | CAMBRIDGE - 31A | 6/55: DARN - 41A | ARDSLEY - 37A | DONCASTER - 36A |
| Jan-56 | NEASDEN - 34E | 11/55: PKHD - 65C | THORNTONJCN - 62A | STRATFORD - 30A | DONCASTER - 36A | CAMBRIDGE - 31A | 11/55: DCTR - 36A | ARDSLEY - 37A | DONCASTER - 36A |
| Aug-56 | NEASDEN - 34E | PARKHEAD - 65C | THORNTONJCN - 62A | STRATFORD - 30A | DONCASTER - 36A | CAMBRIDGE - 31A | DONCASTER - 36A | ARDSLEY - 56B | DONCASTER - 36A |
| Jan-57 | NEASDEN - 34E | PARKHEAD - 65C | THORNTONJCN - 62A | STRATFORD - 30A | DONCASTER - 36A | 11/56: DCTR - 36A | DONCASTER - 36A | ARDSLEY - 56B | DONCASTER - 36A |
| Aug-57 | NEASDEN - 34E | PARKHEAD - 65C | THORNTONJCN - 62A | STRATFORD - 30A | DONCASTER - 36A | DONCASTER - 36A | DONCASTER - 36A | ARDSLEY - 56B | DONCASTER - 36A |
| Jan-58 | NEASDEN - 34E | PARKHEAD - 65C | THORNTONJCN - 62A | STRATFORD - 30A | DONCASTER - 36A | DONCASTER - 36A | DONCASTER - 36A | ARDSLEY - 56B | DONCASTER - 36A |
| Aug-58 | NEASDEN - 14D | PARKHEAD - 65C | THORNTONJCN - 62A | STRATFORD - 30A | DONCASTER - 36A | DONCASTER - 36A | DONCASTER - 36A | ARDSLEY - 56B | DONCASTER - 36A |
| Jan-59 | NEASDEN - 14D | PARKHEAD - 65C | THORNTONJCN - 62A | STRATFORD - 30A | DONCASTER - 36A | DONCASTER - 36A | DONCASTER - 36A | ARDSLEY - 56B | DONCASTER - 36A |
| Aug-59 | 9/59: LEIC - 15E | PARKHEAD - 65C | THORNTONJCN - 62A | STRATFORD - 30A | DONCASTER - 36A | DONCASTER - 36A | DONCASTER - 36A | ARDSLEY - 56B | DONCASTER - 36A |
| Nov-59 | 11/59: NEAS - 14D | PARKHEAD - 65C | THORNTONJCN - 62A | STRATFORD - 30A | 11/59: RET - 36E | DONCASTER - 36A | DONCASTER - 36A | ARDSLEY - 56B | DONCASTER - 36A |
| Jan-60 | NEASDEN - 14D | PARKHEAD - 65C | THORNTONJCN - 62A | STRATFORD - 30A | RETFORD - 36E | DONCASTER - 36A | DONCASTER - 36A | ARDSLEY - 56B | DONCASTER - 36A |
| Apr-60 | NEASDEN - 14D | PARKHEAD - 65C | THORNTONJCN - 62A | STRATFORD - 30A | RETFORD - 36E | DONCASTER - 36A | DONCASTER - 36A | ARDSLEY - 56B | DONCASTER - 36A |
| Aug-60 | 10/60: LEIC - 15E | PARKHEAD - 65C | THORNTONJCN - 62A | STRATFORD - 30A | RETFORD - 36E | DONCASTER - 36A | DONCASTER - 36A | ARDSLEY - 56B | DONCASTER - 36A |
| Nov-60 | 11/60: NEAS - 14D | PARKHEAD - 65C | THORNTONJCN - 62A | STRATFORD - 30A | RETFORD - 36E | DONCASTER - 36A | DONCASTER - 36A | ARDSLEY - 56B | DONCASTER - 36A |

| | 61125 | 61126 | 61127 | 61128 | 61129 | 61130 | 61131 | 61132 | 61133 |
|---|---|---|---|---|---|---|---|---|---|
| Aug-50 | DONCASTER - 36A | DONCASTER - 36A | DONCASTER - 36A | DONCASTER - 36A | KINGS CROSS - 34A | STRATFORD - 30A | COLWICK - 38A | FERRYHILL - 61B | FERRYHILL - 61B |
| Jan-51 | DONCASTER - 36A | 12/50: RET - 36E | DONCASTER - 36A | DONCASTER - 36A | KINGS CROSS - 34A | STRATFORD - 30A | COLWICK - 38A | 1/51: DUND - 62B | FERRYHILL - 61B |
| Aug-51 | DONCASTER - 36A | RETFORD - 36E | DONCASTER - 36A | DONCASTER - 36A | KINGS CROSS - 34A | 9/51: IMM - 40B | COLWICK - 38A | DUNDEE - 62B | 9/51: KITTY - 61A |
| Jan-52 | DONCASTER - 36A | RETFORD - 36E | DONCASTER - 36A | DONCASTER - 36A | 11/51: ARDS - 37A | IMMINGHAM - 40B | COLWICK - 38A | DUNDEE - 62B | KITTYBREWSTER - 61A |
| Aug-52 | DONCASTER - 36A | RETFORD - 36E | DONCASTER - 36A | DONCASTER - 36A | 7/52: C.HILL - 37B | IMMINGHAM - 40B | 9/52: STRAT - 30A | DUNDEE - 62B | KITTYBREWSTER - 61A |
| Jan-53 | DONCASTER - 36A | RETFORD - 36E | DONCASTER - 36A | DONCASTER - 36A | COPLEYHILL - 37B | IMMINGHAM - 40B | 10/52: ARDS - 37A | DUNDEE - 62B | 1/53: EAST - 65A |
| Aug-53 | DONCASTER - 36A | RETFORD - 36E | DONCASTER - 36A | DONCASTER - 36A | COPLEYHILL - 37B | IMMINGHAM - 40B | ARDSLEY - 37A | DUNDEE - 62B | EASTFIELD - 65A |
| Jan-54 | DONCASTER - 36A | RETFORD - 36E | DONCASTER - 36A | DONCASTER - 36A | COPLEYHILL - 37B | IMMINGHAM - 40B | ARDSLEY - 37A | DUNDEE - 62B | EASTFIELD - 65A |
| Aug-54 | DONCASTER - 36A | RETFORD - 36E | DONCASTER - 36A | DONCASTER - 36A | COPLEYHILL - 37B | IMMINGHAM - 40B | ARDSLEY - 37A | DUNDEE - 62B | EASTFIELD - 65A |
| Jan-55 | DONCASTER - 36A | RETFORD - 36E | DONCASTER - 36A | DONCASTER - 36A | COPLEYHILL - 37B | IMMINGHAM - 40B | ARDSLEY - 37A | DUNDEE - 62B | EASTFIELD - 65A |
| Aug-55 | DONCASTER - 36A | RETFORD - 36E | DONCASTER - 36A | DONCASTER - 36A | COPLEYHILL - 37B | IMMINGHAM - 40B | ARDSLEY - 37A | DUNDEE - 62B | EASTFIELD - 65A |
| Jan-56 | DONCASTER - 36A | RETFORD - 36E | DONCASTER - 36A | DONCASTER - 36A | COPLEYHILL - 37B | IMMINGHAM - 40B | ARDSLEY - 37A | DUNDEE - 62B | 2/56: TH JCN - 62A |
| Aug-56 | DONCASTER - 36A | RETFORD - 36E | DONCASTER - 36A | DONCASTER - 36A | COPLEYHILL - 56C | IMMINGHAM - 40B | ARDSLEY - 56B | DUNDEE - 62B | THORNTONJCN - 62A |
| Jan-57 | DONCASTER - 36A | RETFORD - 36E | DONCASTER - 36A | DONCASTER - 36A | COPLEYHILL - 56C | IMMINGHAM - 40B | ARDSLEY - 56B | DUNDEE - 62B | THORNTONJCN - 62A |
| Aug-57 | DONCASTER - 36A | RETFORD - 36E | DONCASTER - 36A | DONCASTER - 36A | COPLEYHILL - 56C | IMMINGHAM - 40B | 9/57: BRAD - 56G | DUNDEE - 62B | THORNTONJCN - 62A |
| Jan-58 | DONCASTER - 36A | RETFORD - 36E | DONCASTER - 36A | DONCASTER - 36A | COPLEYHILL - 56C | IMMINGHAM - 40B | 2/58: LOW M - 56F | DUNDEE - 62B | THORNTONJCN - 62A |
| Aug-58 | DONCASTER - 36A | RETFORD - 36E | DONCASTER - 36A | DONCASTER - 36A | COPLEYHILL - 56C | IMMINGHAM - 40B | LOWMOOR - 56F | DUNDEE - 62B | THORNTONJCN - 62A |
| Jan-59 | DONCASTER - 36A | RETFORD - 36E | DONCASTER - 36A | DONCASTER - 36A | COPLEYHILL - 56C | IMMINGHAM - 40B | 2/59: WAKE - 56A | DUNDEE - 62B | THORNTONJCN - 62A |
| Aug-59 | DONCASTER - 36A | RETFORD - 36E | DONCASTER - 36A | DONCASTER - 36A | COPLEYHILL - 56C | IMMINGHAM - 40B | WAKEFIELD - 56A | DUNDEE - 62B | THORNTONJCN - 62A |
| Nov-59 | DONCASTER - 36A | RETFORD - 36E | DONCASTER - 36A | DONCASTER - 36A | COPLEYHILL - 56C | IMMINGHAM - 40B | WAKEFIELD - 56A | DUNDEE - 62B | THORNTONJCN - 62A |
| Jan-60 | DONCASTER - 36A | RETFORD - 36E | DONCASTER - 36A | DONCASTER - 36A | COPLEYHILL - 56C | IMMINGHAM - 40B | WAKEFIELD - 56A | 1/60: TH JCN - 62A | THORNTONJCN - 62A |
| Apr-60 | DONCASTER - 36A | RETFORD - 36E | DONCASTER - 36A | DONCASTER - 36A | COPLEYHILL - 56C | IMMINGHAM - 40B | WAKEFIELD - 56A | THORNTONJCN - 62A | THORNTONJCN - 62A |
| Aug-60 | DONCASTER - 36A | RETFORD - 36E | DONCASTER - 36A | DONCASTER - 36A | COPLEYHILL - 56C | IMMINGHAM - 40B | WAKEFIELD - 56A | THORNTONJCN - 62A | THORNTONJCN - 62A |
| Nov-60 | DONCASTER - 36A | RETFORD - 36E | DONCASTER - 36A | DONCASTER - 36A | COPLEYHILL - 56C | IMMINGHAM - 40B | WAKEFIELD - 56A | THORNTONJCN - 62A | THORNTONJCN - 62A |

| | 61134 | 61135 | 61136 | 61137 | 61138 | 61139 | 61140 | 61141 | 61142 |
|---|---|---|---|---|---|---|---|---|---|
| Aug-50 | KITTYBREWSTER - 61A | PARKESTON - 30F | KINGS CROSS - 34A | KINGS CROSS - 34A | KINGS CROSS - 34A | KINGS CROSS - 34A | NEASDEN - 34E | LEICESTER (GC) - 38C | IMMINGHAM - 40B |
| Jan-51 | KITTYBREWSTER - 61A | PARKESTON - 30F | KINGS CROSS - 34A | KINGS CROSS - 34A | KINGS CROSS - 34A | KINGS CROSS - 34A | NEASDEN - 34E | LEICESTER (GC) - 38C | IMMINGHAM - 40B |
| Aug-51 | KITTYBREWSTER - 61A | PARKESTON - 30F | KINGS CROSS - 34A | KINGS CROSS - 34A | KINGS CROSS - 34A | KINGS CROSS - 34A | NEASDEN - 34E | LEICESTER (GC) - 38C | IMMINGHAM - 40B |
| Jan-52 | KITTYBREWSTER - 61A | PARKESTON - 30F | KINGS CROSS - 34A | KINGS CROSS - 34A | KINGS CROSS - 34A | KINGS CROSS - 34A | NEASDEN - 34E | LEICESTER (GC) - 38C | IMMINGHAM - 40B |
| Aug-52 | KITTYBREWSTER - 61A | PARKESTON - 30F | 6/52: NEAS - 34E | KINGS CROSS - 34A | KINGS CROSS - 34A | KINGS CROSS - 34A | 6/52: EAST - 65A | LEICESTER (GC) - 38C | IMMINGHAM - 40B |
| Jan-53 | 3/53: EAST - 65A | PARKESTON - 30F | NEASDEN - 34E | 1/53: DCTR - 36A | 1/53: NEWE - 35A | 1/53: NEWE - 35A | EASTFIELD - 65A | LEICESTER (GC) - 38C | IMMINGHAM - 40B |
| Aug-53 | EASTFIELD - 65A | PARKESTON - 30F | NEASDEN - 34E | DONCASTER - 36A | NEWENGLAND - 35A | 3/53: K X - 34A | EASTFIELD - 65A | LEICESTER (GC) - 38C | IMMINGHAM - 40B |
| Jan-54 | EASTFIELD - 65A | PARKESTON - 30F | NEASDEN - 34E | DONCASTER - 36A | NEWENGLAND - 35A | KINGS CROSS - 34A | EASTFIELD - 65A | LEICESTER (GC) - 38C | IMMINGHAM - 40B |
| Aug-54 | EASTFIELD - 65A | PARKESTON - 30F | NEASDEN - 34E | DONCASTER - 36A | NEWENGLAND - 35A | KINGS CROSS - 34A | EASTFIELD - 65A | LEICESTER (GC) - 38C | IMMINGHAM - 40B |
| Jan-55 | EASTFIELD - 65A | PARKESTON - 30F | NEASDEN - 34E | DONCASTER - 36A | NEWENGLAND - 35A | KINGS CROSS - 34A | EASTFIELD - 65A | LEICESTER (GC) - 38C | IMMINGHAM - 40B |
| Aug-55 | EASTFIELD - 65A | PARKESTON - 30F | NEASDEN - 34E | DONCASTER - 36A | 6/55: DARN - 41A | KINGS CROSS - 34A | EASTFIELD - 65A | LEICESTER (GC) - 38C | IMMINGHAM - 40B |
| Jan-56 | 2/56: TH JCN - 62A | PARKESTON - 30F | NEASDEN - 34E | DONCASTER - 36A | DARNALL - 41A | KINGS CROSS - 34A | EASTFIELD - 65A | LEICESTER (GC) - 38C | IMMINGHAM - 40B |
| Aug-56 | THORNTONJCN - 62A | PARKESTON - 30F | NEASDEN - 34E | DONCASTER - 36A | DARNALL - 41A | KINGS CROSS - 34A | EASTFIELD - 65A | LEICESTER (GC) - 38C | IMMINGHAM - 40B |
| Jan-57 | THORNTONJCN - 62A | PARKESTON - 30F | NEASDEN - 34E | DONCASTER - 36A | DARNALL - 41A | KINGS CROSS - 34A | EASTFIELD - 65A | 11/56: COLW - 38A | IMMINGHAM - 40B |
| Aug-57 | THORNTONJCN - 62A | PARKESTON - 30F | NEASDEN - 34E | DONCASTER - 36A | DARNALL - 41A | KINGS CROSS - 34A | EASTFIELD - 65A | COLWICK - 38A | IMMINGHAM - 40B |
| Jan-58 | THORNTONJCN - 62A | 3/58: STRAT - 30A | NEASDEN - 34E | DONCASTER - 36A | DARNALL - 41A | KINGS CROSS - 34A | EASTFIELD - 65A | COLWICK - 38A | IMMINGHAM - 40B |
| Aug-58 | THORNTONJCN - 62A | STRATFORD - 30A | NEASDEN - 14D | DONCASTER - 36A | DARNALL - 41A | KINGS CROSS - 34A | EASTFIELD - 65A | COLWICK - 40E | IMMINGHAM - 40B |
| Jan-59 | THORNTONJCN - 62A | 1/59: PARK - 30F | NEASDEN - 14D | 12/58: LEIC - 15E | DARNALL - 41A | 1/59: HIT - 34D | EASTFIELD - 65A | COLWICK - 40E | IMMINGHAM - 40B |
| Aug-59 | THORNTONJCN - 62A | PARKESTON - 30F | 9/59: LEIC - 15E | LEICESTER (GC) - 15E | DARNALL - 41A | 6/59: DARN - 41A | EASTFIELD - 65A | COLWICK - 40E | IMMINGHAM - 40B |
| Nov-59 | THORNTONJCN - 62A | 10/59: DCTR - 36A | 11/59: NEAS - 14D | LEICESTER (GC) - 15E | 12/59: MILL - 41C | DARNALL - 41A | EASTFIELD - 65A | COLWICK - 40E | 12/59: COLW - 40E |
| Jan-60 | THORNTONJCN - 62A | DONCASTER - 36A | NEASDEN - 14D | LEICESTER (GC) - 15E | 2/60: CANK - 41D | DARNALL - 41A | EASTFIELD - 65A | COLWICK - 40E | COLWICK - 40E |
| Apr-60 | 6/60: EAST - 65A | DONCASTER - 36A | NEASDEN - 14D | LEICESTER (GC) - 15E | CANKLOW - 41D | DARNALL - 41A | EASTFIELD - 65A | COLWICK - 40E | COLWICK - 40E |
| Aug-60 | EASTFIELD - 65A | DONCASTER - 36A | NEASDEN - 14D | LEICESTER (GC) - 15E | CANKLOW - 41D | DARNALL - 41A | EASTFIELD - 65A | COLWICK - 40E | COLWICK - 40E |
| Nov-60 | EASTFIELD - 65A | DONCASTER - 36A | NEASDEN - 14D | LEICESTER (GC) - 15E | CANKLOW - 41D | DARNALL - 41A | EASTFIELD - 65A | COLWICK - 40E | COLWICK - 40E |

| | 61143 | 61144 | 61145 | 61146 | 61147 | 61148 | 61149 | 61150 | 61151 |
|---|---|---|---|---|---|---|---|---|---|
| Aug-50 | NEWENGLAND - 35A | STRATFORD - 30A | DARNALL - 39B | THORNTONJCN - 62A | DUNDEE - 62B | THORNTONJCN - 62A | PARKESTON - 30F | DARNALL - 39B | DARNALL - 39B |
| Jan-51 | NEWENGLAND - 35A | STRATFORD - 30A | DARNALL - 39B | THORNTONJCN - 62A | DUNDEE - 62B | THORNTONJCN - 62A | PARKESTON - 30F | DARNALL - 39B | DARNALL - 39B |
| Aug-51 | 5/51: GRAN - 35B | 9/51: IMM - 40B | 10/51: ARDS - 37A | THORNTONJCN - 62A | 10/51: TH JCN - 62A | THORNTONJCN - 62A | PARKESTON - 30F | DARNALL - 39B | DARNALL - 39B |
| Jan-52 | 9/51: NEWE - 35A | IMMINGHAM - 40B | 11/51: BRAD - 37C | THORNTONJCN - 62A | THORNTONJCN - 62A | THORNTONJCN - 62A | PARKESTON - 30F | DARNALL - 39B | DARNALL - 39B |
| Aug-52 | NEWENGLAND - 35A | IMMINGHAM - 40B | BRADFORD - 37C | THORNTONJCN - 62A | THORNTONJCN - 62A | THORNTONJCN - 62A | PARKESTON - 30F | DARNALL - 39B | DARNALL - 39B |
| Jan-53 | NEWENGLAND - 35A | IMMINGHAM - 40B | BRADFORD - 37C | THORNTONJCN - 62A | THORNTONJCN - 62A | THORNTONJCN - 62A | PARKESTON - 30F | DARNALL - 39B | DARNALL - 39B |
| Aug-53 | NEWENGLAND - 35A | IMMINGHAM - 40B | BRADFORD - 37C | THORNTONJCN - 62A | THORNTONJCN - 62A | THORNTONJCN - 62A | PARKESTON - 30F | DARNALL - 39B | DARNALL - 39B |
| Jan-54 | NEWENGLAND - 35A | IMMINGHAM - 40B | 12/53: DCTR - 36A | THORNTONJCN - 62A | THORNTONJCN - 62A | THORNTONJCN - 62A | PARKESTON - 30F | DARNALL - 39B | DARNALL - 39B |
| Aug-54 | NEWENGLAND - 35A | IMMINGHAM - 40B | DONCASTER - 36A | THORNTONJCN - 62A | THORNTONJCN - 62A | THORNTONJCN - 62A | PARKESTON - 30F | DARNALL - 39B | DARNALL - 39B |
| Jan-55 | NEWENGLAND - 35A | IMMINGHAM - 40B | DONCASTER - 36A | THORNTONJCN - 62A | THORNTONJCN - 62A | THORNTONJCN - 62A | PARKESTON - 30F | DARNALL - 39B | DARNALL - 39B |
| Aug-55 | 6/55: LINC - 40A | IMMINGHAM - 40B | DONCASTER - 36A | THORNTONJCN - 62A | THORNTONJCN - 62A | THORNTONJCN - 62A | PARKESTON - 30F | DARNALL - 39B | DARNALL - 39B |
| Jan-56 | LINCOLN - 40A | IMMINGHAM - 40B | DONCASTER - 36A | THORNTONJCN - 62A | THORNTONJCN - 62A | THORNTONJCN - 62A | PARKESTON - 30F | DARNALL - 41A | DARNALL - 41A |
| Aug-56 | LINCOLN - 40A | IMMINGHAM - 40B | DONCASTER - 36A | THORNTONJCN - 62A | THORNTONJCN - 62A | THORNTONJCN - 62A | PARKESTON - 30F | DARNALL - 41A | DARNALL - 41A |
| Jan-57 | LINCOLN - 40A | IMMINGHAM - 40B | DONCASTER - 36A | THORNTONJCN - 62A | THORNTONJCN - 62A | THORNTONJCN - 62A | PARKESTON - 30F | DARNALL - 41A | DARNALL - 41A |
| Aug-57 | LINCOLN - 40A | IMMINGHAM - 40B | DONCASTER - 36A | THORNTONJCN - 62A | THORNTONJCN - 62A | THORNTONJCN - 62A | PARKESTON - 30F | DARNALL - 41A | DARNALL - 41A |
| Jan-58 | 11/57: IMM - 40B | IMMINGHAM - 40B | DONCASTER - 36A | THORNTONJCN - 62A | THORNTONJCN - 62A | THORNTONJCN - 62A | PARKESTON - 30F | DARNALL - 41A | DARNALL - 41A |
| Aug-58 | IMMINGHAM - 40B | IMMINGHAM - 40B | DONCASTER - 36A | THORNTONJCN - 62A | THORNTONJCN - 62A | THORNTONJCN - 62A | PARKESTON - 30F | DARNALL - 41A | DARNALL - 41A |
| Jan-59 | IMMINGHAM - 40B | IMMINGHAM - 40B | DONCASTER - 36A | THORNTONJCN - 62A | THORNTONJCN - 62A | THORNTONJCN - 62A | PARKESTON - 30F | DARNALL - 41A | DARNALL - 41A |
| Aug-59 | IMMINGHAM - 40B | IMMINGHAM - 40B | DONCASTER - 36A | THORNTONJCN - 62A | THORNTONJCN - 62A | THORNTONJCN - 62A | PARKESTON - 30F | DARNALL - 41A | DARNALL - 41A |
| Nov-59 | IMMINGHAM - 40B | IMMINGHAM - 40B | DONCASTER - 36A | THORNTONJCN - 62A | THORNTONJCN - 62A | THORNTONJCN - 62A | PARKESTON - 30F | DARNALL - 41A | DARNALL - 41A |
| Jan-60 | IMMINGHAM - 40B | IMMINGHAM - 40B | DONCASTER - 36A | THORNTONJCN - 62A | THORNTONJCN - 62A | THORNTONJCN - 62A | PARKESTON - 30F | DARNALL - 41A | DARNALL - 41A |
| Apr-60 | IMMINGHAM - 40B | IMMINGHAM - 40B | DONCASTER - 36A | THORNTONJCN - 62A | THORNTONJCN - 62A | THORNTONJCN - 62A | PARKESTON - 30F | DARNALL - 41A | DARNALL - 41A |
| Aug-60 | IMMINGHAM - 40B | IMMINGHAM - 40B | DONCASTER - 36A | 9/60: DAL RD - 64C | THORNTONJCN - 62A | THORNTONJCN - 62A | PARKESTON - 30F | DARNALL - 41A | DARNALL - 41A |
| Nov-60 | IMMINGHAM - 40B | IMMINGHAM - 40B | DONCASTER - 36A | DALRYROAD - 64C | THORNTONJCN - 62A | THORNTONJCN - 62A | PARKESTON - 30F | DARNALL - 41A | DARNALL - 41A |

across the Leeds – York – Scarborough axis with appearances south of Doncaster being uncommon enough to become a talking point. (Curiously, one of their most regular southern appearances took place on the Great Central. One of the York allocation had a freight working to Woodford Halse and could occasionally be seen at Neasden on a filling-in duty). The B17 (and B2 derivatives) were confined to the Great Eastern – the last of the Great Central batch having been transferred in late 1951- where they could be found on almost any type of main line service. The B12's were, apart from a couple of engines at Grantham, similarly confined to the Great Eastern; the last of the GNoS engines having been withdrawn in 1953.

| | 61152 | 61153 | 61154 | 61155 | 61156 | 61157 | 61158 | 61159 | 61160 |
|---|---|---|---|---|---|---|---|---|---|
| Aug-50 | DARNALL - 39B | DARNALL - 39B | DARNALL - 39B | GORTON - 39A | GORTON - 39A | GORTON - 39A | GORTON - 39A | GORTON - 39A | GORTON - 39A |
| Jan-51 | DARNALL - 39B | DARNALL - 39B | DARNALL - 39B | GORTON - 39A | GORTON - 39A | GORTON - 39A | GORTON - 39A | GORTON - 39A | GORTON - 39A |
| Aug-51 | DARNALL - 39B | DARNALL - 39B | DARNALL - 39B | GORTON - 39A | GORTON - 39A | GORTON - 39A | GORTON - 39A | GORTON - 39A | GORTON - 39A |
| Jan-52 | DARNALL - 39B | DARNALL - 39B | DARNALL - 39B | GORTON - 39A | GORTON - 39A | GORTON - 39A | GORTON - 39A | GORTON - 39A | GORTON - 39A |
| Aug-52 | DARNALL - 39B | DARNALL - 39B | DARNALL - 39B | GORTON - 39A | GORTON - 39A | GORTON - 39A | GORTON - 39A | GORTON - 39A | GORTON - 39A |
| Jan-53 | DARNALL - 39B | DARNALL - 39B | DARNALL - 39B | GORTON - 39A | GORTON - 39A | **10/52: DCTR - 36A** | GORTON - 39A | GORTON - 39A | GORTON - 39A |
| Aug-53 | DARNALL - 39B | DARNALL - 39B | DARNALL - 39B | GORTON - 39A | GORTON - 39A | DONCASTER - 36A | GORTON - 39A | GORTON - 39A | GORTON - 39A |
| Jan-54 | DARNALL - 39B | DARNALL - 39B | DARNALL - 39B | GORTON - 39A | GORTON - 39A | DONCASTER - 36A | **11/53: DCTR - 36A** | GORTON - 39A | GORTON - 39A |
| Aug-54 | DARNALL - 39B | DARNALL - 39B | DARNALL - 39B | **6/54: C.HILL - 37B** | GORTON - 39A | DONCASTER - 36A | DONCASTER - 36A | **6/54: IMM - 40B** | **6/54: CAMB - 31A** |
| Jan-55 | DARNALL - 39B | DARNALL - 39B | DARNALL - 39B | **12/54: DCTR - 36A** | GORTON - 39A | DONCASTER - 36A | DONCASTER - 36A | IMMINGHAM - 40B | CAMBRIDGE - 31A |
| Aug-55 | DARNALL - 39B | DARNALL - 39B | DARNALL - 39B | DONCASTER - 36A | GORTON - 39A | DONCASTER - 36A | DONCASTER - 36A | IMMINGHAM - 40B | CAMBRIDGE - 31A |
| Jan-56 | DARNALL - 41A | DARNALL - 41A | DARNALL - 41A | DONCASTER - 36A | GORTON - 39A | DONCASTER - 36A | DONCASTER - 36A | IMMINGHAM - 40B | CAMBRIDGE - 31A |
| Aug-56 | DARNALL - 41A | DARNALL - 41A | DARNALL - 41A | DONCASTER - 36A | GORTON - 39A | DONCASTER - 36A | DONCASTER - 36A | IMMINGHAM - 40B | CAMBRIDGE - 31A |
| Jan-57 | DARNALL - 41A | DARNALL - 41A | DARNALL - 41A | DONCASTER - 36A | GORTON - 39A | DONCASTER - 36A | DONCASTER - 36A | IMMINGHAM - 40B | **11/56: COLW - 38A** |
| Aug-57 | **10/57: DCTR - 36A** | DARNALL - 41A | DARNALL - 41A | DONCASTER - 36A | GORTON - 39A | DONCASTER - 36A | DONCASTER - 36A | IMMINGHAM - 40B | COLWICK - 38A |
| Jan-58 | **11/57: DARN - 41A** | DARNALL - 41A | DARNALL - 41A | DONCASTER - 36A | **10/57: S BGE - 35C** | DONCASTER - 36A | DONCASTER - 36A | IMMINGHAM - 40B | **10/57: IPS - 32B** |
| Aug-58 | DARNALL - 41A | DARNALL - 41A | DARNALL - 41A | DONCASTER - 36A | SPITALBRIDGE - 31F | DONCASTER - 36A | DONCASTER - 36A | IMMINGHAM - 40B | IPSWICH - 32B |
| Jan-59 | DARNALL - 41A | DARNALL - 41A | DARNALL - 41A | DONCASTER - 36A | SPITALBRIDGE - 31F | DONCASTER - 36A | DONCASTER - 36A | IMMINGHAM - 40B | IPSWICH - 32B |
| Aug-59 | DARNALL - 41A | DARNALL - 41A | DARNALL - 41A | DONCASTER - 36A | SPITALBRIDGE - 31F | DONCASTER - 36A | DONCASTER - 36A | IMMINGHAM - 40B | 8/59: LOPW - 32C |
| Nov-59 | **10/59: MILL - 41C** | DARNALL - 41A | DARNALL - 41A | DONCASTER - 36A | SPITALBRIDGE - 31F | DONCASTER - 36A | DONCASTER - 36A | IMMINGHAM - 40B | LOWESTOFT - 32C |
| Jan-60 | MILLHOUSES - 41C | DARNALL - 41A | DARNALL - 41A | DONCASTER - 36A | **2/60: MARCH - 31B** | DONCASTER - 36A | DONCASTER - 36A | IMMINGHAM - 40B | LOWESTOFT - 32C |
| Apr-60 | MILLHOUSES - 41C | DARNALL - 41A | DARNALL - 41A | **6/60: DARN - 41A** | MARCH - 31B | DONCASTER - 36A | DONCASTER - 36A | IMMINGHAM - 40B | **3/60: LINC - 40A** |
| Aug-60 | MILLHOUSES - 41C | DARNALL - 41A | DARNALL - 41A | DARNALL - 41A | MARCH - 31B | DONCASTER - 36A | DONCASTER - 36A | IMMINGHAM - 40B | LINCOLN - 40A |
| Nov-60 | MILLHOUSES - 41C | **11/60: LANG - 41J** | DARNALL - 41A | DARNALL - 41A | MARCH - 31B | DONCASTER - 36A | DONCASTER - 36A | IMMINGHAM - 40B | LINCOLN - 40A |

| | 61161 | 61162 | 61163 | 61164 | 61165 | 61166 | 61167 | 61168 | 61169 |
|---|---|---|---|---|---|---|---|---|---|
| Aug-50 | GORTON - 39A | GORTON - 39A | NEASDEN - 34E | NEASDEN - 34E | MEXBOROUGH - 36B | MEXBOROUGH - 36B | MEXBOROUGH - 36B | MEXBOROUGH - 36B | DARNALL - 39B |
| Jan-51 | GORTON - 39A | GORTON - 39A | NEASDEN - 34E | NEASDEN - 34E | MEXBOROUGH - 36B | MEXBOROUGH - 36B | MEXBOROUGH - 36B | MEXBOROUGH - 36B | DARNALL - 39B |
| Aug-51 | GORTON - 39A | GORTON - 39A | NEASDEN - 34E | NEASDEN - 34E | MEXBOROUGH - 36B | MEXBOROUGH - 36B | MEXBOROUGH - 36B | MEXBOROUGH - 36B | DARNALL - 39B |
| Jan-52 | GORTON - 39A | GORTON - 39A | NEASDEN - 34E | NEASDEN - 34E | MEXBOROUGH - 36B | MEXBOROUGH - 36B | MEXBOROUGH - 36B | MEXBOROUGH - 36B | DARNALL - 39B |
| Aug-52 | GORTON - 39A | GORTON - 39A | NEASDEN - 34E | NEASDEN - 34E | MEXBOROUGH - 36B | MEXBOROUGH - 36B | MEXBOROUGH - 36B | MEXBOROUGH - 36B | DARNALL - 39B |
| Jan-53 | GORTON - 39A | GORTON - 39A | NEASDEN - 34E | NEASDEN - 34E | MEXBOROUGH - 36B | MEXBOROUGH - 36B | MEXBOROUGH - 36B | MEXBOROUGH - 36B | DARNALL - 39B |
| Aug-53 | GORTON - 39A | GORTON - 39A | NEASDEN - 34E | NEASDEN - 34E | MEXBOROUGH - 36B | MEXBOROUGH - 36B | **7/53: IMM - 40B** | **7/53: IMM - 40B** | DARNALL - 39B |
| Jan-54 | GORTON - 39A | GORTON - 39A | NEASDEN - 34E | NEASDEN - 34E | MEXBOROUGH - 36B | MEXBOROUGH - 36B | **11/53: MEX - 36B** | IMMINGHAM - 40B | DARNALL - 39B |
| Aug-54 | GORTON - 39A | **6/54: C.HILL - 37B** | **6/54: LEIC - 38C** | NEASDEN - 34E | MEXBOROUGH - 36B | MEXBOROUGH - 36B | MEXBOROUGH - 36B | IMMINGHAM - 40B | DARNALL - 39B |
| Jan-55 | GORTON - 39A | **11/54: DCTR - 36A** | **1/55: COLW - 38A** | NEASDEN - 34E | MEXBOROUGH - 36B | MEXBOROUGH - 36B | MEXBOROUGH - 36B | IMMINGHAM - 40B | DARNALL - 39B |
| Aug-55 | GORTON - 39A | DONCASTER - 36A | COLWICK - 38A | NEASDEN - 34E | MEXBOROUGH - 36B | MEXBOROUGH - 36B | MEXBOROUGH - 36B | IMMINGHAM - 40B | DARNALL - 39B |
| Jan-56 | GORTON - 39A | DONCASTER - 36A | COLWICK - 38A | NEASDEN - 34E | MEXBOROUGH - 36B | MEXBOROUGH - 36B | MEXBOROUGH - 36B | IMMINGHAM - 40B | DARNALL - 41A |
| Aug-56 | GORTON - 39A | DONCASTER - 36A | COLWICK - 38A | NEASDEN - 34E | MEXBOROUGH - 36B | MEXBOROUGH - 36B | MEXBOROUGH - 36B | IMMINGHAM - 40B | DARNALL - 41A |
| Jan-57 | GORTON - 39A | DONCASTER - 36A | COLWICK - 38A | **1/57: STRAT - 30A** | MEXBOROUGH - 36B | MEXBOROUGH - 36B | MEXBOROUGH - 36B | IMMINGHAM - 40B | DARNALL - 41A |
| Aug-57 | GORTON - 39A | DONCASTER - 36A | COLWICK - 38A | STRATFORD - 30A | MEXBOROUGH - 36B | MEXBOROUGH - 36B | MEXBOROUGH - 36B | IMMINGHAM - 40B | DARNALL - 41A |
| Jan-58 | GORTON - 39A | DONCASTER - 36A | COLWICK - 38A | STRATFORD - 30A | MEXBOROUGH - 36B | MEXBOROUGH - 36B | MEXBOROUGH - 36B | IMMINGHAM - 40B | DARNALL - 41A |
| Aug-58 | GORTON - 9G | DONCASTER - 36A | COLWICK - 40E | STRATFORD - 30A | MEXBOROUGH - 41F | MEXBOROUGH - 41F | MEXBOROUGH - 41F | IMMINGHAM - 40B | DARNALL - 41A |
| Jan-59 | **6/59: LEIC - 15E** | **1/59: IMM - 40B** | COLWICK - 40E | STRATFORD - 30A | MEXBOROUGH - 41F | MEXBOROUGH - 41F | MEXBOROUGH - 41F | IMMINGHAM - 40B | DARNALL - 41A |
| Aug-59 | **9/59: GORT - 9G** | IMMINGHAM - 40B | COLWICK - 40E | **5/59: DARN - 41A** | MEXBOROUGH - 41F | MEXBOROUGH - 41F | MEXBOROUGH - 41F | IMMINGHAM - 40B | DARNALL - 41A |
| Nov-59 | GORTON - 9G | IMMINGHAM - 40B | COLWICK - 40E | DARNALL - 41A | MEXBOROUGH - 41F | MEXBOROUGH - 41F | MEXBOROUGH - 41F | IMMINGHAM - 40B | DARNALL - 41A |
| Jan-60 | GORTON - 9G | IMMINGHAM - 40B | COLWICK - 40E | DARNALL - 41A | MEXBOROUGH - 41F | MEXBOROUGH - 41F | MEXBOROUGH - 41F | IMMINGHAM - 40B | DARNALL - 41A |
| Apr-60 | GORTON - 9G | IMMINGHAM - 40B | COLWICK - 40E | DARNALL - 41A | MEXBOROUGH - 41F | MEXBOROUGH - 41F | MEXBOROUGH - 41F | IMMINGHAM - 40B | DARNALL - 41A |
| Aug-60 | **6/60: MIRF - 56D** | IMMINGHAM - 40B | COLWICK - 40E | DARNALL - 41A | MEXBOROUGH - 41F | MEXBOROUGH - 41F | MEXBOROUGH - 41F | IMMINGHAM - 40B | DARNALL - 41A |
| Nov-60 | MIRFIELD - 56D | IMMINGHAM - 40B | COLWICK - 40E | DARNALL - 41A | MEXBOROUGH - 41F | MEXBOROUGH - 41F | MEXBOROUGH - 41F | IMMINGHAM - 40B | DARNALL - 41A |

| | 61170 | 61171 | 61172 | 61173 | 61174 | 61175 | 61176 | 61177 | 61178 |
|---|---|---|---|---|---|---|---|---|---|
| Aug-50 | DONCASTER - 36A | STRATFORD - 30A | EASTFIELD - 65A | DARLINGTON - 51A | MEXBOROUGH - 36B | STRATFORD - 30A | DARLINGTON - 51A | STRATFORD - 30A | HAYMARKET - 64B |
| Jan-51 | DONCASTER - 36A | STRATFORD - 30A | EASTFIELD - 65A | DARLINGTON - 51A | MEXBOROUGH - 36B | STRATFORD - 30A | DARLINGTON - 51A | STRATFORD - 30A | HAYMARKET - 64B |
| Aug-51 | DONCASTER - 36A | **9/51: LINC - 40A** | EASTFIELD - 65A | DARLINGTON - 51A | MEXBOROUGH - 36B | **9/51: IMM - 40B** | DARLINGTON - 51A | **9/51: LINC - 40A** | HAYMARKET - 64B |
| Jan-52 | DONCASTER - 36A | LINCOLN - 40A | EASTFIELD - 65A | **11/51: STOCK - 51E** | MEXBOROUGH - 36B | IMMINGHAM - 40B | DARLINGTON - 51A | LINCOLN - 40A | HAYMARKET - 64B |
| Aug-52 | DONCASTER - 36A | LINCOLN - 40A | EASTFIELD - 65A | STOCKTON - 51E | **3/52: DARN - 41A** | IMMINGHAM - 40B | DARLINGTON - 51A | LINCOLN - 40A | HAYMARKET - 64B |
| Jan-53 | DONCASTER - 36A | LINCOLN - 40A | EASTFIELD - 65A | STOCKTON - 51E | DARNALL - 39B | IMMINGHAM - 40B | DARLINGTON - 51A | LINCOLN - 40A | HAYMARKET - 64B |
| Aug-53 | DONCASTER - 36A | LINCOLN - 40A | EASTFIELD - 65A | STOCKTON - 51E | DARNALL - 39B | IMMINGHAM - 40B | **7/53: YORK - 50A** | LINCOLN - 40A | HAYMARKET - 64B |
| Jan-54 | DONCASTER - 36A | LINCOLN - 40A | EASTFIELD - 65A | STOCKTON - 51E | DARNALL - 39B | IMMINGHAM - 40B | YORK - 50A | LINCOLN - 40A | HAYMARKET - 64B |
| Aug-54 | DONCASTER - 36A | LINCOLN - 40A | EASTFIELD - 65A | STOCKTON - 51E | DARNALL - 39B | IMMINGHAM - 40B | YORK - 50A | LINCOLN - 40A | HAYMARKET - 64B |
| Jan-55 | DONCASTER - 36A | **1/55: DCTR - 36A** | EASTFIELD - 65A | STOCKTON - 51E | DARNALL - 39B | IMMINGHAM - 40B | YORK - 50A | LINCOLN - 40A | HAYMARKET - 64B |
| Aug-55 | DONCASTER - 36A | DONCASTER - 36A | EASTFIELD - 65A | STOCKTON - 51E | DARNALL - 39B | IMMINGHAM - 40B | **9/55: DARL - 51A** | LINCOLN - 40A | HAYMARKET - 64B |
| Jan-56 | DONCASTER - 36A | DONCASTER - 36A | **2/56: DUND - 62B** | STOCKTON - 51E | DARNALL - 41A | IMMINGHAM - 40B | DARLINGTON - 51A | **11/55: CAMB - 31A** | HAYMARKET - 64B |
| Aug-56 | DONCASTER - 36A | DONCASTER - 36A | DUNDEE - 62B | STOCKTON - 51E | DARNALL - 41A | IMMINGHAM - 40B | DARLINGTON - 51A | CAMBRIDGE - 31A | HAYMARKET - 64B |
| Jan-57 | DONCASTER - 36A | DONCASTER - 36A | DUNDEE - 62B | STOCKTON - 51E | DARNALL - 41A | IMMINGHAM - 40B | DARLINGTON - 51A | **11/56: COLW - 38A** | HAYMARKET - 64B |
| Aug-57 | DONCASTER - 36A | **6/57: STRAT - 30A** | DUNDEE - 62B | STOCKTON - 51E | DARNALL - 41A | IMMINGHAM - 40B | DARLINGTON - 51A | COLWICK - 38A | HAYMARKET - 64B |
| Jan-58 | DONCASTER - 36A | STRATFORD - 30A | DUNDEE - 62B | STOCKTON - 51E | DARNALL - 41A | IMMINGHAM - 40B | DARLINGTON - 51A | COLWICK - 38A | HAYMARKET - 64B |
| Aug-58 | DONCASTER - 36A | STRATFORD - 30A | DUNDEE - 62B | STOCKTON - 51E | **10/58: KX - 34A** | IMMINGHAM - 40B | DARLINGTON - 51A | COLWICK - 40E | HAYMARKET - 64B |
| Jan-59 | DONCASTER - 36A | STRATFORD - 30A | DUNDEE - 62B | STOCKTON - 51E | KINGS CROSS - 34A | IMMINGHAM - 40B | DARLINGTON - 51A | COLWICK - 40E | HAYMARKET - 64B |
| Aug-59 | DONCASTER - 36A | **4/59: CAMB - 31A** | DUNDEE - 62B | **6/59: TNBY - 51L** | KINGS CROSS - 34A | IMMINGHAM - 40B | DARLINGTON - 51A | COLWICK - 40E | HAYMARKET - 64B |
| Nov-59 | DONCASTER - 36A | CAMBRIDGE - 31A | DUNDEE - 62B | THORNABY - 51L | KINGS CROSS - 34A | IMMINGHAM - 40B | DARLINGTON - 51A | COLWICK - 40E | HAYMARKET - 64B |
| Jan-60 | DONCASTER - 36A | CAMBRIDGE - 31A | DUNDEE - 62B | THORNABY - 51L | KINGS CROSS - 34A | IMMINGHAM - 40B | DARLINGTON - 51A | COLWICK - 40E | HAYMARKET - 64B |
| Apr-60 | DONCASTER - 36A | CAMBRIDGE - 31A | DUNDEE - 62B | THORNABY - 51L | KINGS CROSS - 34A | IMMINGHAM - 40B | DARLINGTON - 51A | COLWICK - 40E | HAYMARKET - 64B |
| Aug-60 | DONCASTER - 36A | CAMBRIDGE - 31A | DUNDEE - 62B | THORNABY - 51L | KINGS CROSS - 34A | IMMINGHAM - 40B | DARLINGTON - 51A | COLWICK - 40E | HAYMARKET - 64B |
| Nov-60 | DONCASTER - 36A | CAMBRIDGE - 31A | DUNDEE - 62B | THORNABY - 51L | **10/60: NEWE - 34E** | **11/60: COLW - 40E** | DARLINGTON - 51A | COLWICK - 40E | HAYMARKET - 64B |

| | 61179 | 61180 | 61181 | 61182 | 61183 | 61184 | 61185 | 61186 | 61187 |
|---|---|---|---|---|---|---|---|---|---|
| Aug-50 | DARNALL - 39B | EASTFIELD - 65A | DARNALL - 39B | GORTON - 39A | DARNALL - 39B | GORTON - 39A | LEICESTER (GC) - 38C | LEICESTER (GC) - 38C | LEICESTER (GC) - 38C |
| Jan-51 | DARNALL - 39B | EASTFIELD - 65A | DARNALL - 39B | GORTON - 39A | DARNALL - 39B | GORTON - 39A | LEICESTER (GC) - 38C | LEICESTER (GC) - 38C | LEICESTER (GC) - 38C |
| Aug-51 | DARNALL - 39B | EASTFIELD - 65A | DARNALL - 39B | **10/51@ NORW - 32A** | DARNALL - 39B | GORTON - 39A | LEICESTER (GC) - 38C | LEICESTER (GC) - 38C | LEICESTER (GC) - 38C |
| Jan-52 | DARNALL - 39B | EASTFIELD - 65A | DARNALL - 39B | **3/52: GORT - 39A** | DARNALL - 39B | GORTON - 39A | LEICESTER (GC) - 38C | LEICESTER (GC) - 38C | LEICESTER (GC) - 38C |
| Aug-52 | DARNALL - 39B | EASTFIELD - 65A | DARNALL - 39B | GORTON - 39A | DARNALL - 39B | GORTON - 39A | LEICESTER (GC) - 38C | LEICESTER (GC) - 38C | LEICESTER (GC) - 38C |
| Jan-53 | DARNALL - 39B | EASTFIELD - 65A | DARNALL - 39B | GORTON - 39A | DARNALL - 39B | GORTON - 39A | LEICESTER (GC) - 38C | **2/53: COLW - 38A** | LEICESTER (GC) - 38C |
| Aug-53 | DARNALL - 39B | EASTFIELD - 65A | DARNALL - 39B | GORTON - 39A | DARNALL - 39B | **9/53: ST M - 64A** | LEICESTER (GC) - 38C | COLWICK - 38A | LEICESTER (GC) - 38C |
| Jan-54 | DARNALL - 39B | EASTFIELD - 65A | DARNALL - 39B | GORTON - 39A | DARNALL - 39B | EDINBURGH (SM) - 64A | LEICESTER (GC) - 38C | COLWICK - 38A | LEICESTER (GC) - 38C |
| Aug-54 | DARNALL - 39B | EASTFIELD - 65A | DARNALL - 39B | **6/54: IMM - 40B** | DARNALL - 39B | EDINBURGH (SM) - 64A | LEICESTER (GC) - 38C | COLWICK - 38A | LEICESTER (GC) - 38C |
| Jan-55 | DARNALL - 39B | EASTFIELD - 65A | DARNALL - 39B | IMMINGHAM - 40B | DARNALL - 39B | EDINBURGH (SM) - 64A | LEICESTER (GC) - 38C | COLWICK - 38A | **1/55: NEAS - 34E** |
| Aug-55 | DARNALL - 39B | **7/55: DUND - 62B** | DARNALL - 39B | IMMINGHAM - 40B | DARNALL - 39B | EDINBURGH (SM) - 64A | LEICESTER (GC) - 38C | COLWICK - 38A | NEASDEN - 34E |
| Jan-56 | DARNALL - 41A | DUNDEE - 62B | DARNALL - 41A | IMMINGHAM - 40B | DARNALL - 41A | EDINBURGH (SM) - 64A | LEICESTER (GC) - 38C | COLWICK - 38A | NEASDEN - 34E |
| Aug-56 | DARNALL - 41A | DUNDEE - 62B | DARNALL - 41A | IMMINGHAM - 40B | DARNALL - 41A | EDINBURGH (SM) - 64A | LEICESTER (GC) - 38C | COLWICK - 38A | NEASDEN - 34E |
| Jan-57 | DARNALL - 41A | DUNDEE - 62B | DARNALL - 41A | **2/57: STRAT - 30A** | DARNALL - 41A | EDINBURGH (SM) - 64A | **11/56: COLW - 38A** | COLWICK - 38A | NEASDEN - 34E |
| Aug-57 | DARNALL - 41A | DUNDEE - 62B | DARNALL - 41A | STRATFORD - 30A | DARNALL - 41A | EDINBURGH (SM) - 64A | COLWICK - 38A | **9/57: WOOD - 38E** | NEASDEN - 34E |
| Jan-58 | DARNALL - 41A | DUNDEE - 62B | DARNALL - 41A | STRATFORD - 30A | DARNALL - 41A | EDINBURGH (SM) - 64A | COLWICK - 38A | WOODFORD HALSE - 38E | NEASDEN - 34E |
| Aug-58 | **10/58: KX - 34A** | DUNDEE - 62B | DARNALL - 41A | **8/58: CAMB - 31A** | DARNALL - 41A | EDINBURGH (SM) - 64A | COLWICK - 40E | WOODFORD HALSE - 2F | NEASDEN - 14D |
| Jan-59 | KINGS CROSS - 34A | DUNDEE - 62B | DARNALL - 41A | CAMBRIDGE - 31A | DARNALL - 41A | EDINBURGH (SM) - 64A | COLWICK - 40E | WOODFORD HALSE - 2F | NEASDEN - 14D |
| Aug-59 | KINGS CROSS - 34A | DUNDEE - 62B | DARNALL - 41A | CAMBRIDGE - 31A | DARNALL - 41A | EDINBURGH (SM) - 64A | COLWICK - 40E | WOODFORD HALSE - 2F | **9/59: WOOD - 2F** |
| Nov-59 | KINGS CROSS - 34A | DUNDEE - 62B | DARNALL - 41A | CAMBRIDGE - 31A | DARNALL - 41A | EDINBURGH (SM) - 64A | COLWICK - 40E | WOODFORD HALSE - 2F | WOODFORD HALSE - 2F |
| Jan-60 | KINGS CROSS - 34A | DUNDEE - 62B | DARNALL - 41A | CAMBRIDGE - 31A | DARNALL - 41A | EDINBURGH (SM) - 64A | **12/59: IMM - 40B** | WOODFORD HALSE - 2F | WOODFORD HALSE - 2F |
| Apr-60 | KINGS CROSS - 34A | DUNDEE - 62B | DARNALL - 41A | CAMBRIDGE - 31A | DARNALL - 41A | EDINBURGH (SM) - 64A | IMMINGHAM - 40B | WOODFORD HALSE - 2F | WOODFORD HALSE - 2F |
| Aug-60 | KINGS CROSS - 34A | DUNDEE - 62B | DARNALL - 41A | CAMBRIDGE - 31A | DARNALL - 41A | EDINBURGH (SM) - 64A | IMMINGHAM - 40B | WOODFORD HALSE - 2F | WOODFORD HALSE - 2F |
| Nov-60 | KINGS CROSS - 34A | DUNDEE - 62B | DARNALL - 41A | CAMBRIDGE - 31A | DARNALL - 41A | EDINBURGH (SM) - 64A | IMMINGHAM - 40B | WOODFORD HALSE - 2F | WOODFORD HALSE - 2F |

One of the effects of the large fleet of class 7 and 8 locomotives was to reduce the number of duties for 2-6-0's on the main line and engines that had once been the mainstay of the many fast goods services from Kings Cross found themselves ousted by V2 2-6-2's to be sent to the Great Eastern, Lincoln and Hull districts. (The benefits of the V2's on express goods services was largely limited to a better turn of speed and a more comfortable ride for the crew since their goods loading classification was the same as that for a K3. The K3's on the other hand were no substitute for a Pacific when passenger duties beckoned although they did a considerable amount of work on secondary and cross-country excursion services).

| | 61188 | 61189 | 61190 | 61191 | 61192 | 61193 | 61194 | 61195 | 61196 |
|---|---|---|---|---|---|---|---|---|---|
| Aug-50 | LEICESTER (GC) - 38C | STOCKTON - 51E | IMMINGHAM - 40B | IMMINGHAM - 40B | STRATFORD - 30A | DONCASTER - 36A | MEXBOROUGH - 36B | IMMINGHAM - 40B | DONCASTER - 36A |
| Jan-51 | LEICESTER (GC) - 38C | STOCKTON - 51E | IMMINGHAM - 40B | IMMINGHAM - 40B | STRATFORD - 30A | DONCASTER - 36A | MEXBOROUGH - 36B | IMMINGHAM - 40B | DONCASTER - 36A |
| Aug-51 | LEICESTER (GC) - 38C | STOCKTON - 51E | IMMINGHAM - 40B | 9/51: STRAT - 30A | STRATFORD - 30A | DONCASTER - 36A | MEXBOROUGH - 36B | IMMINGHAM - 40B | DONCASTER - 36A |
| Jan-52 | LEICESTER (GC) - 38C | STOCKTON - 51E | IMMINGHAM - 40B | STRATFORD - 30A | STRATFORD - 30A | DONCASTER - 36A | MEXBOROUGH - 36B | IMMINGHAM - 40B | DONCASTER - 36A |
| Aug-52 | LEICESTER (GC) - 38C | STOCKTON - 51E | IMMINGHAM - 40B | STRATFORD - 30A | 7/52: COLW - 38A | DONCASTER - 36A | MEXBOROUGH - 36B | IMMINGHAM - 40B | DONCASTER - 36A |
| Jan-53 | 1/53: COLW - 38A | STOCKTON - 51E | IMMINGHAM - 40B | STRATFORD - 30A | COLWICK - 38A | DONCASTER - 36A | MEXBOROUGH - 36B | IMMINGHAM - 40B | DONCASTER - 36A |
| Aug-53 | COLWICK - 38A | STOCKTON - 51E | IMMINGHAM - 40B | 9/53: ST M - 64A | COLWICK - 38A | DONCASTER - 36A | MEXBOROUGH - 36B | IMMINGHAM - 40B | DONCASTER - 36A |
| Jan-54 | COLWICK - 38A | STOCKTON - 51E | IMMINGHAM - 40B | EDINBURGH (SM) - 64A | COLWICK - 38A | DONCASTER - 36A | MEXBOROUGH - 36B | IMMINGHAM - 40B | DONCASTER - 36A |
| Aug-54 | COLWICK - 38A | STOCKTON - 51E | IMMINGHAM - 40B | EDINBURGH (SM) - 64A | 6/54: WOOD - 38E | DONCASTER - 36A | MEXBOROUGH - 36B | IMMINGHAM - 40B | DONCASTER - 36A |
| Jan-55 | COLWICK - 38A | STOCKTON - 51E | IMMINGHAM - 40B | EDINBURGH (SM) - 64A | W. HALSE - 38E | DONCASTER - 36A | MEXBOROUGH - 36B | IMMINGHAM - 40B | DONCASTER - 36A |
| Aug-55 | COLWICK - 38A | STOCKTON - 51E | IMMINGHAM - 40B | EDINBURGH (SM) - 64A | W. HALSE - 38E | DONCASTER - 36A | MEXBOROUGH - 36B | IMMINGHAM - 40B | DONCASTER - 36A |
| Jan-56 | COLWICK - 38A | STOCKTON - 51E | IMMINGHAM - 40B | EDINBURGH (SM) - 64A | W. HALSE - 38E | DONCASTER - 36A | MEXBOROUGH - 36B | IMMINGHAM - 40B | DONCASTER - 36A |
| Aug-56 | COLWICK - 38A | STOCKTON - 51E | IMMINGHAM - 40B | EDINBURGH (SM) - 64A | W. HALSE - 38E | DONCASTER - 36A | MEXBOROUGH - 36B | IMMINGHAM - 40B | DONCASTER - 36A |
| Jan-57 | COLWICK - 38A | 10/56: ARDS - 56B | IMMINGHAM - 40B | EDINBURGH (SM) - 64A | W. HALSE - 38E | DONCASTER - 36A | MEXBOROUGH - 36B | IMMINGHAM - 40B | DONCASTER - 36A |
| Aug-57 | COLWICK - 38A | ARDSLEY - 56B | IMMINGHAM - 40B | EDINBURGH (SM) - 64A | W. HALSE - 38E | DONCASTER - 36A | MEXBOROUGH - 36B | IMMINGHAM - 40B | DONCASTER - 36A |
| Jan-58 | COLWICK - 38A | ARDSLEY - 56B | IMMINGHAM - 40B | EDINBURGH (SM) - 64A | W. HALSE - 38E | DONCASTER - 36A | MEXBOROUGH - 36B | IMMINGHAM - 40B | DONCASTER - 36A |
| Aug-58 | 6/58: LEIC - 15E | ARDSLEY - 56B | IMMINGHAM - 40B | EDINBURGH (SM) - 64A | W. HALSE - 2F | DONCASTER - 36A | MEXBOROUGH - 41F | IMMINGHAM - 40B | DONCASTER - 36A |
| Jan-59 | 9/58: COLW - 40E | 2/59: C.HILL - 56C | IMMINGHAM - 40B | EDINBURGH (SM) - 64A | W. HALSE - 2F | DONCASTER - 36A | MEXBOROUGH - 41F | IMMINGHAM - 40B | DONCASTER - 36A |
| Aug-59 | COLWICK - 40E | COPLEY HILL - 56C | IMMINGHAM - 40B | EDINBURGH (SM) - 64A | W. HALSE - 2F | DONCASTER - 36A | MEXBOROUGH - 41F | IMMINGHAM - 40B | DONCASTER - 36A |
| Nov-59 | COLWICK - 40E | COPLEY HILL - 56C | IMMINGHAM - 40B | EDINBURGH (SM) - 64A | W. HALSE - 2F | DONCASTER - 36A | MEXBOROUGH - 41F | IMMINGHAM - 40B | DONCASTER - 36A |
| Jan-60 | COLWICK - 40E | COPLEY HILL - 56C | IMMINGHAM - 40B | EDINBURGH (SM) - 64A | W. HALSE - 2F | DONCASTER - 36A | MEXBOROUGH - 41F | IMMINGHAM - 40B | DONCASTER - 36A |
| Apr-60 | COLWICK - 40E | COPLEY HILL - 56C | IMMINGHAM - 40B | EDINBURGH (SM) - 64A | W. HALSE - 2F | DONCASTER - 36A | MEXBOROUGH - 41F | IMMINGHAM - 40B | DONCASTER - 36A |
| Aug-60 | COLWICK - 40E | COPLEY HILL - 56C | IMMINGHAM - 40B | EDINBURGH (SM) - 64A | W. HALSE - 2F | DONCASTER - 36A | MEXBOROUGH - 41F | IMMINGHAM - 40B | DONCASTER - 36A |
| Nov-60 | COLWICK - 40E | COPLEY HILL - 56C | IMMINGHAM - 40B | EDINBURGH (SM) - 64A | 10/60: LEIC - 15E | DONCASTER - 36A | MEXBOROUGH - 41F | IMMINGHAM - 40B | DONCASTER - 36A |

| | 61197 | 61198 | 61199 | 61200 | 61201 | 61202 | 61203 | 61204 | 61205 |
|---|---|---|---|---|---|---|---|---|---|
| Aug-50 | EASTFIELD - 65A | DARLINGTON - 51A | TWEEDMOUTH - 52D | KINGS CROSS - 34A | IPSWICH - 32B | IMMINGHAM - 40B | KINGS CROSS - 34A | IMMINGHAM - 40B | STRATFORD - 30A |
| Jan-51 | EASTFIELD - 65A | DARLINGTON - 51A | TWEEDMOUTH - 52D | KINGS CROSS - 34A | IPSWICH - 32B | IMMINGHAM - 40B | KINGS CROSS - 34A | IMMINGHAM - 40B | STRATFORD - 30A |
| Aug-51 | EASTFIELD - 65A | DARLINGTON - 51A | 7/51: GHD - 52A | KINGS CROSS - 34A | IPSWICH - 32B | IMMINGHAM - 40B | KINGS CROSS - 34A | IMMINGHAM - 40B | STRATFORD - 30A |
| Jan-52 | EASTFIELD - 65A | DARLINGTON - 51A | GATESHEAD - 52A | KINGS CROSS - 34A | IPSWICH - 32B | IMMINGHAM - 40B | KINGS CROSS - 34A | IMMINGHAM - 40B | STRATFORD - 30A |
| Aug-52 | EASTFIELD - 65A | DARLINGTON - 51A | GATESHEAD - 52A | KINGS CROSS - 34A | IPSWICH - 32B | IMMINGHAM - 40B | KINGS CROSS - 34A | IMMINGHAM - 40B | STRATFORD - 30A |
| Jan-53 | EASTFIELD - 65A | DARLINGTON - 51A | GATESHEAD - 52A | KINGS CROSS - 34A | IPSWICH - 32B | IMMINGHAM - 40B | KINGS CROSS - 34A | IMMINGHAM - 40B | STRATFORD - 30A |
| Aug-53 | EASTFIELD - 65A | DARLINGTON - 51A | GATESHEAD - 52A | KINGS CROSS - 34A | 10/53: COLW - 38A | 5/53: LINC - 40A | KINGS CROSS - 34A | 10/53: NEW E - 35A | 10/53: NEW E - 35A |
| Jan-54 | EASTFIELD - 65A | DARLINGTON - 51A | GATESHEAD - 52A | KINGS CROSS - 34A | COLWICK - 38A | LINCOLN - 40A | KINGS CROSS - 34A | NEWENGLAND - 35A | NEWENGLAND - 35A |
| Aug-54 | EASTFIELD - 65A | DARLINGTON - 51A | GATESHEAD - 52A | KINGS CROSS - 34A | COLWICK - 38A | LINCOLN - 40A | KINGS CROSS - 34A | NEWENGLAND - 35A | NEWENGLAND - 35A |
| Jan-55 | EASTFIELD - 65A | DARLINGTON - 51A | GATESHEAD - 52A | KINGS CROSS - 34A | 1/55: LEIC - 38C | LINCOLN - 40A | KINGS CROSS - 34A | NEWENGLAND - 35A | NEWENGLAND - 35A |
| Aug-55 | EASTFIELD - 65A | DARLINGTON - 51A | 9/55: TWEED - 56D | KINGS CROSS - 34A | 2/55: COLW - 38A | LINCOLN - 40A | KINGS CROSS - 34A | NEWENGLAND - 35A | NEWENGLAND - 35A |
| Jan-56 | EASTFIELD - 65A | DARLINGTON - 51A | TWEEDMOUTH - 52D | KINGS CROSS - 34A | COLWICK - 38A | LINCOLN - 40A | KINGS CROSS - 34A | NEWENGLAND - 35A | NEWENGLAND - 35A |
| Aug-56 | EASTFIELD - 65A | DARLINGTON - 51A | TWEEDMOUTH - 52D | KINGS CROSS - 34A | COLWICK - 38A | LINCOLN - 40A | KINGS CROSS - 34A | NEWENGLAND - 35A | NEWENGLAND - 35A |
| Jan-57 | EASTFIELD - 65A | DARLINGTON - 51A | TWEEDMOUTH - 52D | KINGS CROSS - 34A | COLWICK - 38A | LINCOLN - 40A | KINGS CROSS - 34A | NEWENGLAND - 35A | NEWENGLAND - 35A |
| Aug-57 | EASTFIELD - 65A | DARLINGTON - 51A | TWEEDMOUTH - 52D | KINGS CROSS - 34A | COLWICK - 38A | LINCOLN - 40A | 10/57: CAMB - 31A | 6/57: S.BGE - 35C | 6/57: S.BGE - 35C |
| Jan-58 | EASTFIELD - 65A | DARLINGTON - 51A | TWEEDMOUTH - 52D | KINGS CROSS - 34A | COLWICK - 38A | LINCOLN - 40A | CAMBRIDGE - 31A | SPITAL BGE - 35C | SPITAL BGE - 35C |
| Aug-58 | EASTFIELD - 65A | DARLINGTON - 51A | TWEEDMOUTH - 52D | KINGS CROSS - 34A | 10/58: LEIC - 15E | LINCOLN - 40A | CAMBRIDGE - 31A | SPITAL BGE - 31F | SPITAL BGE - 31F |
| Jan-59 | EASTFIELD - 65A | 6/59: LOW M - 56F | TWEEDMOUTH - 52D | KINGS CROSS - 34A | LEICESTER (GC) - 15E | LINCOLN - 40A | CAMBRIDGE - 31A | SPITAL BGE - 31F | SPITAL BGE - 31F |
| Aug-59 | EASTFIELD - 65A | 8/59: YORK - 50A | TWEEDMOUTH - 52D | 4/59: NEW E - 34E | 8/59: AGE - 26B | LINCOLN - 40A | CAMBRIDGE - 31A | SPITAL BGE - 31F | SPITAL BGE - 31F |
| Nov-59 | EASTFIELD - 65A | YORK - 50A | TWEEDMOUTH - 52D | NEWENGLAND - 34E | AGECROFT - 26B | LINCOLN - 40A | CAMBRIDGE - 31A | SPITAL BGE - 31F | SPITAL BGE - 31F |
| Jan-60 | EASTFIELD - 65A | YORK - 50A | TWEEDMOUTH - 52D | NEWENGLAND - 34E | AGECROFT - 26B | LINCOLN - 40A | CAMBRIDGE - 31A | 2/60: MARCH - 31B | 2/60: MARCH - 31B |
| Apr-60 | EASTFIELD - 65A | YORK - 50A | TWEEDMOUTH - 52D | 4/60: KX - 34A | AGECROFT - 26B | LINCOLN - 40A | CAMBRIDGE - 31A | MARCH - 31B | MARCH - 31B |
| Aug-60 | EASTFIELD - 65A | YORK - 50A | 6/60: BLAY - 52C | KINGS CROSS - 34A | AGECROFT - 26B | LINCOLN - 40A | 9/60: MARCH - 31B | MARCH - 31B | MARCH - 31B |
| Nov-60 | EASTFIELD - 65A | YORK - 50A | BLAYDON - 52C | KINGS CROSS - 34A | AGECROFT - 26B | LINCOLN - 40A | MARCH - 31B | MARCH - 31B | MARCH - 31B |

| | 61206 | 61207 | 61208 | 61209 | 61210 | 61211 | 61212 | 61213 | 61214 |
|---|---|---|---|---|---|---|---|---|---|
| Aug-50 | NEWENGLAND - 35A | NEWENGLAND - 35A | RETFORD - 36E | ANNESLEY - 38B | NEWENGLAND - 35A | RETFORD - 36E | RETFORD - 36E | RETFORD - 36E | STOCKTON - 51E |
| Jan-51 | NEWENGLAND - 35A | NEWENGLAND - 35A | RETFORD - 36E | ANNESLEY - 38B | NEWENGLAND - 35A | RETFORD - 36E | RETFORD - 36E | RETFORD - 36E | STOCKTON - 51E |
| Aug-51 | NEWENGLAND - 35A | NEWENGLAND - 35A | RETFORD - 36E | ANNESLEY - 38B | NEWENGLAND - 35A | RETFORD - 36E | RETFORD - 36E | RETFORD - 36E | STOCKTON - 51E |
| Jan-52 | NEWENGLAND - 35A | NEWENGLAND - 35A | RETFORD - 36E | ANNESLEY - 38B | NEWENGLAND - 35A | RETFORD - 36E | RETFORD - 36E | RETFORD - 36E | STOCKTON - 51E |
| Aug-52 | NEWENGLAND - 35A | NEWENGLAND - 35A | RETFORD - 36E | ANNESLEY - 38B | NEWENGLAND - 35A | RETFORD - 36E | RETFORD - 36E | RETFORD - 36E | STOCKTON - 51E |
| Jan-53 | 1/53: KX - 34A | NEWENGLAND - 35A | RETFORD - 36E | ANNESLEY - 38B | 1/53: KX - 34A | RETFORD - 36E | RETFORD - 36E | RETFORD - 36E | STOCKTON - 51E |
| Aug-53 | 7/53: NEAS - 34E | NEWENGLAND - 35A | RETFORD - 36E | ANNESLEY - 38B | 3/53: NEW E - 35A | RETFORD - 36E | RETFORD - 36E | RETFORD - 36E | STOCKTON - 51E |
| Jan-54 | NEASDEN - 34E | NEWENGLAND - 35A | RETFORD - 36E | ANNESLEY - 38B | NEWENGLAND - 35A | RETFORD - 36E | RETFORD - 36E | RETFORD - 36E | STOCKTON - 51E |
| Aug-54 | NEASDEN - 34E | NEWENGLAND - 35A | RETFORD - 36E | ANNESLEY - 38B | NEWENGLAND - 35A | RETFORD - 36E | RETFORD - 36E | RETFORD - 36E | STOCKTON - 51E |
| Jan-55 | NEASDEN - 34E | NEWENGLAND - 35A | RETFORD - 36E | ANNESLEY - 38B | NEWENGLAND - 35A | RETFORD - 36E | RETFORD - 36E | RETFORD - 36E | STOCKTON - 51E |
| Aug-55 | NEASDEN - 34E | NEWENGLAND - 35A | RETFORD - 36E | ANNESLEY - 38B | NEWENGLAND - 35A | RETFORD - 36E | RETFORD - 36E | RETFORD - 36E | STOCKTON - 51E |
| Jan-56 | NEASDEN - 34E | NEWENGLAND - 35A | RETFORD - 36E | ANNESLEY - 38B | NEWENGLAND - 35A | RETFORD - 36E | RETFORD - 36E | RETFORD - 36E | STOCKTON - 51E |
| Aug-56 | NEASDEN - 34E | NEWENGLAND - 35A | RETFORD - 36E | 10/56: COLW - 38A | NEWENGLAND - 35A | RETFORD - 36E | RETFORD - 36E | RETFORD - 36E | 10/56: C.HILL - 56C |
| Jan-57 | NEASDEN - 34E | NEWENGLAND - 35A | RETFORD - 36E | COLWICK - 38A | NEWENGLAND - 35A | RETFORD - 36E | RETFORD - 36E | RETFORD - 36E | COPLEY HILL - 56C |
| Aug-57 | NEASDEN - 34E | NEWENGLAND - 35A | RETFORD - 36E | COLWICK - 38A | NEWENGLAND - 35A | RETFORD - 36E | RETFORD - 36E | RETFORD - 36E | COPLEY HILL - 56C |
| Jan-58 | NEASDEN - 34E | NEWENGLAND - 35A | RETFORD - 36E | COLWICK - 38A | NEWENGLAND - 35A | RETFORD - 36E | RETFORD - 36E | RETFORD - 36E | COPLEY HILL - 56C |
| Aug-58 | NEASDEN - 14D | NEWENGLAND - 34E | RETFORD - 36E | COLWICK - 40E | NEWENGLAND - 34E | RETFORD - 36E | RETFORD - 36E | RETFORD - 36E | COPLEY HILL - 56C |
| Jan-59 | NEASDEN - 14D | NEWENGLAND - 34E | RETFORD - 36E | COLWICK - 40E | NEWENGLAND - 34E | RETFORD - 36E | RETFORD - 36E | 11/58: DCTR - 36A | COPLEY HILL - 56C |
| Aug-59 | NEASDEN - 14D | NEWENGLAND - 34E | RETFORD - 36E | COLWICK - 40E | NEWENGLAND - 34E | RETFORD - 36E | RETFORD - 36E | DONCASTER - 36A | COPLEY HILL - 56C |
| Nov-59 | NEASDEN - 14D | NEWENGLAND - 34E | RETFORD - 36E | COLWICK - 40E | NEWENGLAND - 34E | RETFORD - 36E | RETFORD - 36E | 11/59: RET - 36E | COPLEY HILL - 56C |
| Jan-60 | NEASDEN - 14D | NEWENGLAND - 34E | RETFORD - 36E | COLWICK - 40E | NEWENGLAND - 34E | RETFORD - 36E | RETFORD - 36E | RETFORD - 36E | COPLEY HILL - 56C |
| Apr-60 | NEASDEN - 14D | NEWENGLAND - 34E | RETFORD - 36E | COLWICK - 40E | NEWENGLAND - 34E | RETFORD - 36E | RETFORD - 36E | RETFORD - 36E | COPLEY HILL - 56C |
| Aug-60 | NEASDEN - 14D | NEWENGLAND - 34E | RETFORD - 36E | COLWICK - 40E | NEWENGLAND - 34E | RETFORD - 36E | RETFORD - 36E | RETFORD - 36E | COPLEY HILL - 56C |
| Nov-60 | NEASDEN - 14D | NEWENGLAND - 34E | RETFORD - 36E | COLWICK - 40E | NEWENGLAND - 34E | RETFORD - 36E | RETFORD - 36E | RETFORD - 36E | COPLEY HILL - 56C |

| | 61215 | 61216 | 61217 | 61218 | 61219 | 61220 | 61221 | 61222 | 61223 |
|---|---|---|---|---|---|---|---|---|---|
| Aug-50 | BOT GDNS - 53B | NEVILLE HILL - 50B | CARLISLE (C) - 12B | NEVILLE HILL - 50B | CARLISLE (C) - 12B | STOCKTON - 51E | HAYMARKET - 64B | CARLISLE (C) - 12B | GORTON - 39A |
| Jan-51 | BOT GDNS - 53B | NEVILLE HILL - 50B | CARLISLE (C) - 12B | NEVILLE HILL - 50B | CARLISLE (C) - 12B | STOCKTON - 51E | HAYMARKET - 64B | CARLISLE (C) - 12B | GORTON - 39A |
| Aug-51 | BOT GDNS - 53B | NEVILLE HILL - 50B | CARLISLE (C) - 68E | NEVILLE HILL - 50B | CARLISLE (C) - 68E | STOCKTON - 51E | HAYMARKET - 64B | CARLISLE (C) - 68E | GORTON - 39A |
| Jan-52 | BOT GDNS - 53B | NEVILLE HILL - 50B | CARLISLE (C) - 68E | NEVILLE HILL - 50B | CARLISLE (C) - 68E | STOCKTON - 51E | HAYMARKET - 64B | CARLISLE (C) - 68E | GORTON - 39A |
| Aug-52 | BOT GDNS - 53B | NEVILLE HILL - 50B | CARLISLE (C) - 68E | NEVILLE HILL - 50B | CARLISLE (C) - 68E | STOCKTON - 51E | HAYMARKET - 64B | CARLISLE (C) - 68E | GORTON - 39A |
| Jan-53 | BOT GDNS - 53B | NEVILLE HILL - 50B | CARLISLE (C) - 68E | NEVILLE HILL - 50B | CARLISLE (C) - 68E | STOCKTON - 51E | HAYMARKET - 64B | CARLISLE (C) - 68E | GORTON - 39A |
| Aug-53 | BOT GDNS - 53B | NEVILLE HILL - 50B | CARLISLE (C) - 68E | NEVILLE HILL - 50B | CARLISLE (C) - 68E | STOCKTON - 51E | HAYMARKET - 64B | CARLISLE (C) - 68E | GORTON - 39A |
| Jan-54 | BOT GDNS - 53B | NEVILLE HILL - 50B | CARLISLE (C) - 68E | NEVILLE HILL - 50B | CARLISLE (C) - 68E | STOCKTON - 51E | HAYMARKET - 64B | CARLISLE (C) - 68E | GORTON - 39A |
| Aug-54 | BOT GDNS - 53B | NEVILLE HILL - 50B | CARLISLE (C) - 68E | NEVILLE HILL - 50B | CARLISLE (C) - 68E | STOCKTON - 51E | HAYMARKET - 64B | CARLISLE (C) - 68E | 6/54: CAMB - 31A |
| Jan-55 | BOT GDNS - 53B | NEVILLE HILL - 50B | CARLISLE (C) - 68E | NEVILLE HILL - 50B | CARLISLE (C) - 68E | STOCKTON - 51E | HAYMARKET - 64B | CARLISLE (C) - 68E | CAMBRIDGE - 31A |
| Aug-55 | BOT GDNS - 53B | NEVILLE HILL - 50B | CARLISLE (C) - 68E | NEVILLE HILL - 50B | CARLISLE (C) - 68E | STOCKTON - 51E | HAYMARKET - 64B | CARLISLE (C) - 68E | CAMBRIDGE - 31A |
| Jan-56 | BOT GDNS - 53B | NEVILLE HILL - 50B | CARLISLE (C) - 68E | NEVILLE HILL - 50B | CARLISLE (C) - 68E | STOCKTON - 51E | HAYMARKET - 64B | CARLISLE (C) - 68E | CAMBRIDGE - 31A |
| Aug-56 | BOT GDNS - 53B | NEVILLE HILL - 50B | CARLISLE (C) - 68E | NEVILLE HILL - 50B | CARLISLE (C) - 68E | STOCKTON - 51E | HAYMARKET - 64B | CARLISLE (C) - 68E | 6/56: NORW - 32A |
| Jan-57 | BOT GDNS - 53B | NEVILLE HILL - 50B | CARLISLE (C) - 68E | NEVILLE HILL - 50B | CARLISLE (C) - 68E | STOCKTON - 51E | HAYMARKET - 64B | CARLISLE (C) - 68E | NORWICH - 32A |
| Aug-57 | BOT GDNS - 53B | NEVILLE HILL - 50B | CARLISLE (C) - 68E | NEVILLE HILL - 50B | CARLISLE (C) - 68E | STOCKTON - 51E | HAYMARKET - 64B | CARLISLE (C) - 68E | NORWICH - 32A |
| Jan-58 | BOT GDNS - 53B | NEVILLE HILL - 50B | CARLISLE (C) - 68E | NEVILLE HILL - 50B | 12/57: HMKT - 64B | STOCKTON - 51E | HAYMARKET - 64B | CARLISLE (C) - 68E | 12/57: YAR (ST) - 32D |
| Aug-58 | BOT GDNS - 53B | NEVILLE HILL - 50B | CARLISLE (C) - 12C | NEVILLE HILL - 50B | HAYMARKET - 64B | STOCKTON - 51E | HAYMARKET - 64B | CARLISLE (C) - 12C | 9/58: NORW - 32A |
| Jan-59 | BOT GDNS - 53B | NEVILLE HILL - 50B | CARLISLE (C) - 12C | NEVILLE HILL - 50B | HAYMARKET - 64B | STOCKTON - 51E | HAYMARKET - 64B | CARLISLE (C) - 12C | NORWICH - 32A |
| Aug-59 | 6/59: DYCTS - 53A | NEVILLE HILL - 50B | CARLISLE (C) - 12C | NEVILLE HILL - 50B | HAYMARKET - 64B | STOCKTON - 51E | HAYMARKET - 64B | CARLISLE (C) - 12C | 5/59: LOW - 32C |
| Nov-59 | DAIRYCOATES - 53A | NEVILLE HILL - 50B | CARLISLE (C) - 12C | NEVILLE HILL - 50B | HAYMARKET - 64B | STOCKTON - 51E | HAYMARKET - 64B | CARLISLE (C) - 12C | LOWESTOFT - 32C |
| Jan-60 | DAIRYCOATES - 53A | NEVILLE HILL - 50B | CARLISLE (C) - 12C | NEVILLE HILL - 50B | HAYMARKET - 64B | STOCKTON - 51E | HAYMARKET - 64B | CARLISLE (C) - 12C | LOWESTOFT - 32C |
| Apr-60 | DAIRYCOATES - 50B | NEVILLE HILL - 55H | CARLISLE (C) - 12C | NEVILLE HILL - 55H | HAYMARKET - 64B | STOCKTON - 51E | HAYMARKET - 64B | CARLISLE (C) - 12C | 3/60: LINC - 40A |
| Aug-60 | DAIRYCOATES - 50B | NEVILLE HILL - 55H | CARLISLE (C) - 12C | NEVILLE HILL - 55H | HAYMARKET - 64B | STOCKTON - 51E | HAYMARKET - 64B | CARLISLE (C) - 12C | LINCOLN - 40A |
| Nov-60 | DAIRYCOATES - 50B | NEVILLE HILL - 55H | CARLISLE (C) - 12C | NEVILLE HILL - 55H | HAYMARKET - 64B | STOCKTON - 51E | HAYMARKET - 64B | CARLISLE (C) - 12C | LINCOLN - 40A |

| | 61224 | 61225 | 61226 | 61227 | 61228 | 61229 | 61230 | 61231 | 61232 |
|---|---|---|---|---|---|---|---|---|---|
| Aug-50 | DARLINGTON - 51A | GORTON - 39A | PARKESTON - 30F | STRATFORD - 30A | GORTON - 39A | BRADFORD - 37C | BRADFORD - 37C | RETFORD - 36E | PARKESTON - 30F |
| Jan-51 | DARLINGTON - 51A | GORTON - 39A | **10/50: MARCH - 31B** | **3/51: CAMB - 31A** | GORTON - 39A | BRADFORD - 37C | BRADFORD - 37C | RETFORD - 36E | PARKESTON - 30F |
| Aug-51 | DARLINGTON - 51A | GORTON - 39A | **12/50: PARK - 30F** | **5/51: STRAT - 30A** | GORTON - 39A | BRADFORD - 37C | BRADFORD - 37C | RETFORD - 36E | PARKESTON - 30F |
| Jan-52 | DARLINGTON - 51A | GORTON - 39A | PARKESTON - 30F | STRATFORD - 30A | GORTON - 39A | BRADFORD - 37C | BRADFORD - 37C | RETFORD - 36E | PARKESTON - 30F |
| Aug-52 | DARLINGTON - 51A | **7/52: DARN - 39B** | PARKESTON - 30F | STRATFORD - 30A | GORTON - 39A | BRADFORD - 37C | BRADFORD - 37C | RETFORD - 36E | PARKESTON - 30F |
| Jan-53 | DARLINGTON - 51A | DARNALL - 39B | PARKESTON - 30F | STRATFORD - 30A | GORTON - 39A | BRADFORD - 37C | BRADFORD - 37C | RETFORD - 36E | PARKESTON - 30F |
| Aug-53 | **7/53: YORK - 50A** | DARNALL - 39B | PARKESTON - 30F | STRATFORD - 30A | GORTON - 39A | BRADFORD - 37C | BRADFORD - 37C | RETFORD - 36E | PARKESTON - 30F |
| Jan-54 | YORK - 50A | DARNALL - 39B | PARKESTON - 30F | STRATFORD - 30A | GORTON - 39A | BRADFORD - 37C | BRADFORD - 37C | RETFORD - 36E | PARKESTON - 30F |
| Aug-54 | YORK - 50A | DARNALL - 39B | PARKESTON - 30F | STRATFORD - 30A | **6/54: IPS - 32B** | BRADFORD - 37C | BRADFORD - 37C | RETFORD - 36E | PARKESTON - 30F |
| Jan-55 | YORK - 50A | DARNALL - 39B | PARKESTON - 30F | STRATFORD - 30A | IPSWICH - 32B | BRADFORD - 37C | BRADFORD - 37C | RETFORD - 36E | PARKESTON - 30F |
| Aug-55 | **9/55: DARL - 51A** | DARNALL - 39B | PARKESTON - 30F | STRATFORD - 30A | IPSWICH - 32B | BRADFORD - 37C | BRADFORD - 37C | RETFORD - 36E | PARKESTON - 30F |
| Jan-56 | DARLINGTON - 51A | **11/55: DCTR - 36A** | PARKESTON - 30F | STRATFORD - 30A | IPSWICH - 32B | BRADFORD - 37C | BRADFORD - 37C | RETFORD - 36E | PARKESTON - 30F |
| Aug-56 | DARLINGTON - 51A | DONCASTER - 36A | PARKESTON - 30F | STRATFORD - 30A | IPSWICH - 32B | BRADFORD - 56G | BRADFORD - 56G | RETFORD - 36E | PARKESTON - 30F |
| Jan-57 | DARLINGTON - 51A | DONCASTER - 36A | PARKESTON - 30F | **11/56: PARK - 30F** | IPSWICH - 32B | BRADFORD - 56G | BRADFORD - 56G | RETFORD - 36E | PARKESTON - 30F |
| Aug-57 | DARLINGTON - 51A | DONCASTER - 36A | PARKESTON - 30F | PARKESTON - 30F | IPSWICH - 32B | BRADFORD - 56G | BRADFORD - 56G | RETFORD - 36E | PARKESTON - 30F |
| Jan-58 | DARLINGTON - 51A | DONCASTER - 36A | PARKESTON - 30F | PARKESTON - 30F | IPSWICH - 32B | **2/58: LOW M - 56F** | **2/58: LOW M - 56F** | RETFORD - 36E | PARKESTON - 30F |
| Aug-58 | DARLINGTON - 51A | DONCASTER - 36A | PARKESTON - 30F | PARKESTON - 30F | IPSWICH - 32B | **9/58: DARL - 51A** | LOWMOOR - 56F | RETFORD - 36E | PARKESTON - 30F |
| Jan-59 | DARLINGTON - 51A | DONCASTER - 36A | PARKESTON - 30F | PARKESTON - 30F | IPSWICH - 32B | DARLINGTON - 51A | LOWMOOR - 56F | RETFORD - 36E | PARKESTON - 30F |
| Aug-59 | DARLINGTON - 51A | DONCASTER - 36A | PARKESTON - 30F | PARKESTON - 30F | **9/59: NORW - 32A** | **6/59: YORK - 50A** | LOWMOOR - 56F | RETFORD - 36E | PARKESTON - 30F |
| Nov-59 | DARLINGTON - 51A | DONCASTER - 36A | PARKESTON - 30F | PARKESTON - 30F | NORWICH - 32A | YORK - 50A | **11/59: MIRF - 56D** | RETFORD - 36E | PARKESTON - 30F |
| Jan-60 | DARLINGTON - 51A | **2/60: RET - 36E** | PARKESTON - 30F | PARKESTON - 30F | **2/60: DARN - 41A** | YORK - 50A | MIRFIELD - 56D | RETFORD - 36E | PARKESTON - 30F |
| Apr-60 | DARLINGTON - 51A | RETFORD - 36E | PARKESTON - 30F | PARKESTON - 30F | DARNALL - 41A | YORK - 50A | MIRFIELD - 56D | RETFORD - 36E | PARKESTON - 30F |
| Aug-60 | DARLINGTON - 51A | RETFORD - 36E | PARKESTON - 30F | PARKESTON - 30F | DARNALL - 41A | YORK - 50A | MIRFIELD - 56D | RETFORD - 36E | PARKESTON - 30F |
| Nov-60 | DARLINGTON - 51A | RETFORD - 36E | PARKESTON - 30F | PARKESTON - 30F | DARNALL - 41A | YORK - 50A | MIRFIELD - 56D | RETFORD - 36E | PARKESTON - 30F |

| | 61233 | 61234 | 61235 | 61236 | 61237 | 61238 | 61239 | 61240 | 61241 |
|---|---|---|---|---|---|---|---|---|---|
| Aug-50 | STRATFORD - 30A | STRATFORD - 30A | STRATFORD - 30A | STRATFORD - 30A | NEVILLE HILL - 50B | GATESHEAD - 52A | YORK - 50A | NEVILLE HILL - 50B | TWEEDMOUTH - 52D |
| Jan-51 | STRATFORD - 30A | STRATFORD - 30A | STRATFORD - 30A | STRATFORD - 30A | NEVILLE HILL - 50B | GATESHEAD - 52A | YORK - 50A | NEVILLE HILL - 50B | TWEEDMOUTH - 52D |
| Aug-51 | STRATFORD - 30A | STRATFORD - 30A | STRATFORD - 30A | STRATFORD - 30A | NEVILLE HILL - 50B | GATESHEAD - 52A | YORK - 50A | NEVILLE HILL - 50B | TWEEDMOUTH - 52D |
| Jan-52 | STRATFORD - 30A | STRATFORD - 30A | STRATFORD - 30A | STRATFORD - 30A | NEVILLE HILL - 50B | GATESHEAD - 52A | YORK - 50A | NEVILLE HILL - 50B | TWEEDMOUTH - 52D |
| Aug-52 | STRATFORD - 30A | STRATFORD - 30A | STRATFORD - 30A | STRATFORD - 30A | NEVILLE HILL - 50B | GATESHEAD - 52A | YORK - 50A | NEVILLE HILL - 50B | TWEEDMOUTH - 52D |
| Jan-53 | STRATFORD - 30A | STRATFORD - 30A | STRATFORD - 30A | STRATFORD - 30A | NEVILLE HILL - 50B | GATESHEAD - 52A | YORK - 50A | NEVILLE HILL - 50B | TWEEDMOUTH - 52D |
| Aug-53 | STRATFORD - 30A | STRATFORD - 30A | STRATFORD - 30A | STRATFORD - 30A | NEVILLE HILL - 50B | GATESHEAD - 52A | YORK - 50A | NEVILLE HILL - 50B | TWEEDMOUTH - 52D |
| Jan-54 | STRATFORD - 30A | STRATFORD - 30A | STRATFORD - 30A | STRATFORD - 30A | NEVILLE HILL - 50B | GATESHEAD - 52A | **10/53: CANAL - 68E** | NEVILLE HILL - 50B | TWEEDMOUTH - 52D |
| Aug-54 | STRATFORD - 30A | STRATFORD - 30A | STRATFORD - 30A | STRATFORD - 30A | NEVILLE HILL - 50B | GATESHEAD - 52A | CARLISLE(CANAL) - 68E | NEVILLE HILL - 50B | TWEEDMOUTH - 52D |
| Jan-55 | STRATFORD - 30A | STRATFORD - 30A | STRATFORD - 30A | STRATFORD - 30A | NEVILLE HILL - 50B | GATESHEAD - 52A | CARLISLE(CANAL) - 68E | NEVILLE HILL - 50B | TWEEDMOUTH - 52D |
| Aug-55 | STRATFORD - 30A | STRATFORD - 30A | STRATFORD - 30A | STRATFORD - 30A | NEVILLE HILL - 50B | GATESHEAD - 52A | CARLISLE(CANAL) - 68E | NEVILLE HILL - 50B | TWEEDMOUTH - 52D |
| Jan-56 | STRATFORD - 30A | STRATFORD - 30A | STRATFORD - 30A | STRATFORD - 30A | NEVILLE HILL - 50B | GATESHEAD - 52A | CARLISLE(CANAL) - 68E | NEVILLE HILL - 50B | TWEEDMOUTH - 52D |
| Aug-56 | STRATFORD - 30A | STRATFORD - 30A | STRATFORD - 30A | STRATFORD - 30A | NEVILLE HILL - 50B | GATESHEAD - 52A | CARLISLE(CANAL) - 68E | NEVILLE HILL - 50B | TWEEDMOUTH - 52D |
| Jan-57 | STRATFORD - 30A | STRATFORD - 30A | STRATFORD - 30A | STRATFORD - 30A | NEVILLE HILL - 50B | **1/57: BLAY - 52C** | CARLISLE(CANAL) - 68E | NEVILLE HILL - 50B | TWEEDMOUTH - 52D |
| Aug-57 | STRATFORD - 30A | STRATFORD - 30A | STRATFORD - 30A | STRATFORD - 30A | NEVILLE HILL - 50B | BLAYDON - 52C | CARLISLE(CANAL) - 68E | NEVILLE HILL - 50B | TWEEDMOUTH - 52D |
| Jan-58 | STRATFORD - 30A | STRATFORD - 30A | STRATFORD - 30A | STRATFORD - 30A | NEVILLE HILL - 50B | BLAYDON - 52C | CARLISLECANAL - 68E | NEVILLE HILL - 50B | TWEEDMOUTH - 52D |
| Aug-58 | STRATFORD - 30A | STRATFORD - 30A | **10/58: NORW - 32A** | STRATFORD - 30A | NEVILLE HILL - 50B | BLAYDON - 52C | CARLISLECANAL - 12C | NEVILLE HILL - 50B | TWEEDMOUTH - 52D |
| Jan-59 | STRATFORD - 30A | STRATFORD - 30A | NORWICH - 32A | STRATFORD - 30A | NEVILLE HILL - 50B | BLAYDON - 52C | CARLISLECANAL - 12C | NEVILLE HILL - 50B | TWEEDMOUTH - 52D |
| Aug-59 | STRATFORD - 30A | **5/59: DARN - 41A** | NORWICH - 32A | **4/59: CAMB - 31A** | NEVILLE HILL - 50B | **6/59: GHD - 52A** | CARLISLECANAL - 12C | NEVILLE HILL - 50B | TWEEDMOUTH - 52D |
| Nov-59 | STRATFORD - 30A | DARNALL - 41A | NORWICH - 32A | CAMBRIDGE - 31A | NEVILLE HILL - 50B | GATESHEAD - 52A | CARLISLECANAL - 12C | **10/59: TNBY - 51L** | TWEEDMOUTH - 52D |
| Jan-60 | STRATFORD - 30A | DARNALL - 41A | **IMMINGHAM - 40B** | CAMBRIDGE - 31A | NEVILLE HILL - 50B | GATESHEAD - 52A | CARLISLECANAL - 12C | THORNABY - 51L | TWEEDMOUTH - 52D |
| Apr-60 | STRATFORD - 30A | DARNALL - 41A | IMMINGHAM - 40B | CAMBRIDGE - 31A | NEVILLE HILL - 55H | GATESHEAD - 52A | CARLISLECANAL - 12C | THORNABY - 51L | TWEEDMOUTH - 52D |
| Aug-60 | STRATFORD - 30A | DARNALL - 41A | IMMINGHAM - 40B | CAMBRIDGE - 31A | NEVILLE HILL - 55H | GATESHEAD - 52A | CARLISLECANAL - 12C | **9/60: YORK - 50A** | **6/60: BLAY - 52C** |
| Nov-60 | STRATFORD - 30A | DARNALL - 41A | IMMINGHAM - 40B | CAMBRIDGE - 31A | NEVILLE HILL - 55H | GATESHEAD - 52A | CARLISLECANAL - 12C | YORK - 50A | BLAYDON - 52C |

| | 61242 | 61243 | 61244 | 61245 | 61246 | 61247 | 61248 | 61249 | 61250 |
|---|---|---|---|---|---|---|---|---|---|
| Aug-50 | EDINBURGH(SM) - 64A | EASTFIELD - 65A | HAYMARKET - 64B | HAYMARKET - 64B | DONCASTER - 36A | DONCASTER - 36A | DONCASTER - 36A | DONCASTER - 36A | DONCASTER - 36A |
| Jan-51 | EDINBURGH(SM) - 64A | EASTFIELD - 65A | HAYMARKET - 64B | HAYMARKET - 64B | DONCASTER - 36A | DONCASTER - 36A | DONCASTER - 36A | DONCASTER - 36A | DONCASTER - 36A |
| Aug-51 | **4/51: DAL RD - 64C** | EASTFIELD - 65A | HAYMARKET - 64B | HAYMARKET - 64B | DONCASTER - 36A | DONCASTER - 36A | DONCASTER - 36A | DONCASTER - 36A | DONCASTER - 36A |
| Jan-52 | **10/51: KEITH - 61C** | EASTFIELD - 65A | HAYMARKET - 64B | HAYMARKET - 64B | DONCASTER - 36A | DONCASTER - 36A | DONCASTER - 36A | DONCASTER - 36A | DONCASTER - 36A |
| Aug-52 | KEITH - 61C | EASTFIELD - 65A | HAYMARKET - 64B | HAYMARKET - 64B | DONCASTER - 36A | DONCASTER - 36A | DONCASTER - 36A | DONCASTER - 36A | DONCASTER - 36A |
| Jan-53 | KEITH - 61C | EASTFIELD - 65A | HAYMARKET - 64B | HAYMARKET - 64B | DONCASTER - 36A | DONCASTER - 36A | DONCASTER - 36A | DONCASTER - 36A | DONCASTER - 36A |
| Aug-53 | KEITH - 61C | EASTFIELD - 65A | HAYMARKET - 64B | HAYMARKET - 64B | **9/53: ST M - 64A** | DONCASTER - 36A | DONCASTER - 36A | DONCASTER - 36A | DONCASTER - 36A |
| Jan-54 | KEITH - 61C | EASTFIELD - 65A | HAYMARKET - 64B | HAYMARKET - 64B | EDINBURGH(SM) - 64A | DONCASTER - 36A | DONCASTER - 36A | **3/54: STRAT - 30A** | DONCASTER - 36A |
| Aug-54 | KEITH - 61C | EASTFIELD - 65A | HAYMARKET - 64B | HAYMARKET - 64B | EDINBURGH(SM) - 64A | DONCASTER - 36A | DONCASTER - 36A | STRATFORD - 30A | DONCASTER - 36A |
| Jan-55 | KEITH - 61C | EASTFIELD - 65A | HAYMARKET - 64B | HAYMARKET - 64B | EDINBURGH(SM) - 64A | DONCASTER - 36A | **1/55: LINC - 40A** | STRATFORD - 30A | DONCASTER - 36A |
| Aug-55 | KEITH - 61C | EASTFIELD - 65A | HAYMARKET - 64B | HAYMARKET - 64B | EDINBURGH(SM) - 64A | DONCASTER - 36A | **5/55: IMM - 40B** | STRATFORD - 30A | DONCASTER - 36A |
| Jan-56 | KEITH - 61C | EASTFIELD - 65A | HAYMARKET - 64B | HAYMARKET - 64B | **2/56: DAL RD - 64C** | DONCASTER - 36A | **2/56: LINC - 40A** | STRATFORD - 30A | DONCASTER - 36A |
| Aug-56 | KEITH - 61C | EASTFIELD - 65A | HAYMARKET - 64B | HAYMARKET - 64B | DALRYROAD - 64C | DONCASTER - 36A | LINCOLN - 40A | STRATFORD - 30A | DONCASTER - 36A |
| Jan-57 | **2/57: KITTY - 61A** | EASTFIELD - 65A | HAYMARKET - 64B | HAYMARKET - 64B | DALRYROAD - 64C | DONCASTER - 36A | LINCOLN - 40A | STRATFORD - 30A | DONCASTER - 36A |
| Aug-57 | KITTYBREWSTER - 61A | EASTFIELD - 65A | HAYMARKET - 64B | HAYMARKET - 64B | DALRYROAD - 64C | DONCASTER - 36A | LINCOLN - 40A | STRATFORD - 30A | DONCASTER - 36A |
| Jan-58 | KITTYBREWSTER - 61A | EASTFIELD - 65A | HAYMARKET - 64B | HAYMARKET - 64B | **2/58: ST M - 64A** | DONCASTER - 36A | LINCOLN - 40A | STRATFORD - 30A | DONCASTER - 36A |
| Aug-58 | KITTYBREWSTER - 61A | EASTFIELD - 65A | HAYMARKET - 64B | HAYMARKET - 64B | EDINBURGH(SM) - 64A | DONCASTER - 36A | LINCOLN - 40A | STRATFORD - 30A | DONCASTER - 36A |
| Jan-59 | KITTYBREWSTER - 61A | EASTFIELD - 65A | HAYMARKET - 64B | HAYMARKET - 64B | EDINBURGH(SM) - 64A | DONCASTER - 36A | LINCOLN - 40A | **1/59: PARK - 30F** | DONCASTER - 36A |
| Aug-59 | KITTYBREWSTER - 61A | EASTFIELD - 65A | HAYMARKET - 64B | HAYMARKET - 64B | EDINBURGH(SM) - 64A | DONCASTER - 36A | LINCOLN - 40A | **6/59: DARN - 41A** | DONCASTER - 36A |
| Nov-59 | KITTYBREWSTER - 61A | EASTFIELD - 65A | HAYMARKET - 64B | HAYMARKET - 64B | EDINBURGH(SM) - 64A | DONCASTER - 36A | **11/59: IMM - 40B** | DARNALL - 41A | DONCASTER - 36A |
| Jan-60 | KITTYBREWSTER - 61A | EASTFIELD - 65A | HAYMARKET - 64B | HAYMARKET - 64B | EDINBURGH(SM) - 64A | DONCASTER - 36A | IMMINGHAM - 40B | DARNALL - 41A | DONCASTER - 36A |
| Apr-60 | KITTYBREWSTER - 61A | EASTFIELD - 65A | HAYMARKET - 64B | HAYMARKET - 64B | EDINBURGH(SM) - 64A | DONCASTER - 36A | IMMINGHAM - 40B | DARNALL - 41A | DONCASTER - 36A |
| Aug-60 | KITTYBREWSTER - 61A | EASTFIELD - 65A | **7/60: DAL RD - 64C** | HAYMARKET - 64B | EDINBURGH(SM) - 64A | **6/60: COLW - 40E** | IMMINGHAM - 40B | DARNALL - 41A | DONCASTER - 36A |
| Nov-60 | KITTYBREWSTER - 61A | EASTFIELD - 65A | DALRYROAD - 64C | HAYMARKET - 64B | EDINBURGH(SM) - 64A | COLWICK - 40E | IMMINGHAM - 40B | DARNALL - 41A | DONCASTER - 36A |

| | 61251 | 61252 | 61253 | 61254 | 61255 | 61256 | 61257 | 61258 | 61259 |
|---|---|---|---|---|---|---|---|---|---|
| Aug-50 | KINGS CROSS - 34A | IPSWICH - 32B | IPSWICH - 32B | IPSWICH - 32B | DARLINGTON - 51A | NEVILLE HILL - 50B | NEVILLE HILL - 50B | NEVILLE HILL - 50B | NEVILLE HILL - 50B |
| Jan-51 | KINGS CROSS - 34A | IPSWICH - 32B | IPSWICH - 32B | IPSWICH - 32B | DARLINGTON - 51A | NEVILLE HILL - 50B | NEVILLE HILL - 50B | NEVILLE HILL - 50B | NEVILLE HILL - 50B |
| Aug-51 | KINGS CROSS - 34A | IPSWICH - 32B | IPSWICH - 32B | IPSWICH - 32B | DARLINGTON - 51A | NEVILLE HILL - 50B | NEVILLE HILL - 50B | NEVILLE HILL - 50B | NEVILLE HILL - 50B |
| Jan-52 | KINGS CROSS - 34A | IPSWICH - 32B | IPSWICH - 32B | IPSWICH - 32B | DARLINGTON - 51A | NEVILLE HILL - 50B | NEVILLE HILL - 50B | **1/52: DCTR - 36A** | NEVILLE HILL - 50B |
| Aug-52 | KINGS CROSS - 34A | IPSWICH - 32B | IPSWICH - 32B | IPSWICH - 32B | DARLINGTON - 51A | NEVILLE HILL - 50B | NEVILLE HILL - 50B | **7/52: LINC - 40A** | NEVILLE HILL - 50B |
| Jan-53 | KINGS CROSS - 34A | IPSWICH - 32B | IPSWICH - 32B | IPSWICH - 32B | DARLINGTON - 51A | NEVILLE HILL - 50B | NEVILLE HILL - 50B | LINCOLN - 40A | NEVILLE HILL - 50B |
| Aug-53 | KINGS CROSS - 34A | IPSWICH - 32B | IPSWICH - 32B | IPSWICH - 32B | DARLINGTON - 51A | NEVILLE HILL - 50B | NEVILLE HILL - 50B | LINCOLN - 40A | NEVILLE HILL - 50B |
| Jan-54 | KINGS CROSS - 34A | IPSWICH - 32B | IPSWICH - 32B | IPSWICH - 32B | DARLINGTON - 51A | NEVILLE HILL - 50B | NEVILLE HILL - 50B | LINCOLN - 40A | NEVILLE HILL - 50B |
| Aug-54 | **6/54: HITCH - 34D** | IPSWICH - 32B | IPSWICH - 32B | IPSWICH - 32B | DARLINGTON - 51A | NEVILLE HILL - 50B | NEVILLE HILL - 50B | LINCOLN - 40A | NEVILLE HILL - 50B |
| Jan-55 | HITCHIN - 34D | IPSWICH - 32B | IPSWICH - 32B | IPSWICH - 32B | DARLINGTON - 51A | NEVILLE HILL - 50B | NEVILLE HILL - 50B | LINCOLN - 40A | NEVILLE HILL - 50B |
| Aug-55 | HITCHIN - 34D | IPSWICH - 32B | IPSWICH - 32B | IPSWICH - 32B | DARLINGTON - 51A | NEVILLE HILL - 50B | NEVILLE HILL - 50B | LINCOLN - 40A | NEVILLE HILL - 50B |
| Jan-56 | HITCHIN - 34D | IPSWICH - 32B | IPSWICH - 32B | IPSWICH - 32B | DARLINGTON - 51A | NEVILLE HILL - 50B | NEVILLE HILL - 50B | LINCOLN - 40A | NEVILLE HILL - 50B |
| Aug-56 | HITCHIN - 34D | IPSWICH - 32B | IPSWICH - 32B | IPSWICH - 32B | DARLINGTON - 51A | NEVILLE HILL - 50B | NEVILLE HILL - 50B | LINCOLN - 40A | NEVILLE HILL - 50B |
| Jan-57 | HITCHIN - 34D | IPSWICH - 32B | IPSWICH - 32B | IPSWICH - 32B | DARLINGTON - 51A | NEVILLE HILL - 50B | NEVILLE HILL - 50B | LINCOLN - 40A | NEVILLE HILL - 50B |
| Aug-57 | HITCHIN - 34D | IPSWICH - 32B | IPSWICH - 32B | IPSWICH - 32B | DARLINGTON - 51A | **9/57: GHD - 52A** | NEVILLE HILL - 50B | LINCOLN - 40A | NEVILLE HILL - 50B |
| Jan-58 | HITCHIN - 34D | IPSWICH - 32B | IPSWICH - 32B | IPSWICH - 32B | DARLINGTON - 51A | GATESHEAD - 52A | NEVILLE HILL - 50B | LINCOLN - 40A | NEVILLE HILL - 50B |
| Aug-58 | HITCHIN - 34D | IPSWICH - 32B | IPSWICH - 32B | IPSWICH - 32B | DARLINGTON - 51A | **9/58: DYCTS - 53A** | NEVILLE HILL - 50B | LINCOLN - 40A | NEVILLE HILL - 50B |
| Jan-59 | HITCHIN - 34D | IPSWICH - 32B | IPSWICH - 32B | IPSWICH - 32B | **2/59: H.HILL - 51G** | DAIRYCOATES - 53A | NEVILLE HILL - 50B | LINCOLN - 40A | NEVILLE HILL - 50B |
| Aug-59 | **6/59: GRAN - 34F** | IPSWICH - 32B | IPSWICH - 32B | IPSWICH - 32B | **6/59: TNBY - 51L** | DAIRYCOATES - 53A | NEVILLE HILL - 50B | LINCOLN - 40A | NEVILLE HILL - 50B |
| Nov-59 | GRANTHAM - 34F | **10/59: IPS - 32B** | **10/59: MARCH - 31B** | **10/59: MARCH - 31B** | THORNABY - 51L | DAIRYCOATES - 53A | THORNABY - 51L | LINCOLN - 40A | NEVILLE HILL - 50B |
| Jan-60 | GRANTHAM - 34F | **1/60: CAMB - 31A** | **1/60: CAMB - 31A** | **1/60: CAMB - 31A** | THORNABY - 51L | DAIRYCOATES - 53A | THORNABY - 51L | LINCOLN - 40A | NEVILLE HILL - 55H |
| Apr-60 | GRANTHAM - 34F | CAMBRIDGE - 31A | CAMBRIDGE - 31A | CAMBRIDGE - 31A | THORNABY - 51L | DAIRYCOATES - 50B | THORNABY - 51L | LINCOLN - 40A | NEVILLE HILL - 55H |
| Aug-60 | GRANTHAM - 34F | CAMBRIDGE - 31A | CAMBRIDGE - 31A | CAMBRIDGE - 31A | THORNABY - 51L | DAIRYCOATES - 50B | THORNABY - 51L | LINCOLN - 40A | NEVILLE HILL - 55H |
| Nov-60 | GRANTHAM - 34F | CAMBRIDGE - 31A | CAMBRIDGE - 31A | CAMBRIDGE - 31A | THORNABY - 51L | DAIRYCOATES - 50B | THORNABY - 51L | LINCOLN - 40A | NEVILLE HILL - 55H |

K3 2-6-0 61962 of Heaton stands at Edinburgh Haymarket on 10 March 1951 between the 23.35 Heaton - Niddrie and the 21.48 Cadder - Heaton fitted goods workings.

Dairycoates K3 2-6-0 61869 makes an appear at Springhead (H&B) shed on 28th August 1952. Lacking an allocation of mixed traffic engines, any special fast goods services from the Docks coming within the orbit of Springhead's operations were often covered by engines from Dairycoates shed.

| | 61260 | 61261 | 61262 | 61263 | 61264 | 61265 | 61266 | 61267 | 61268 |
|---|---|---|---|---|---|---|---|---|---|
| Aug-50 | EASTFIELD - 65A | EASTFIELD - 65A | THORNTON JCN - 62A | DUNDEE - 62B | PARKESTON - 30F | DONCASTER - 36A | KINGS CROSS - 34A | BRADFORD - 37C | BRADFORD - 37C |
| Jan-51 | EASTFIELD - 65A | EASTFIELD - 65A | THORNTON JCN - 62A | DUNDEE - 62B | PARKESTON - 30F | DONCASTER - 36A | KINGS CROSS - 34A | BRADFORD - 37C | BRADFORD - 37C |
| Aug-51 | EASTFIELD - 65A | EASTFIELD - 65A | THORNTON JCN - 62A | DUNDEE - 62B | PARKESTON - 30F | DONCASTER - 36A | KINGS CROSS - 34A | BRADFORD - 37C | BRADFORD - 37C |
| Jan-52 | EASTFIELD - 65A | EASTFIELD - 65A | THORNTON JCN - 62A | DUNDEE - 62B | PARKESTON - 30F | DONCASTER - 36A | KINGS CROSS - 34A | BRADFORD - 37C | BRADFORD - 37C |
| Aug-52 | EASTFIELD - 65A | EASTFIELD - 65A | THORNTON JCN - 62A | DUNDEE - 62B | PARKESTON - 30F | DONCASTER - 36A | KINGS CROSS - 34A | BRADFORD - 37C | BRADFORD - 37C |
| Jan-53 | EASTFIELD - 65A | EASTFIELD - 65A | THORNTON JCN - 62A | DUNDEE - 62B | PARKESTON - 30F | DONCASTER - 36A | **1/53: DCTR - 36A** | BRADFORD - 37C | BRADFORD - 37C |
| Aug-53 | EASTFIELD - 65A | EASTFIELD - 65A | THORNTON JCN - 62A | DUNDEE - 62B | PARKESTON - 30F | DONCASTER - 36A | DONCASTER - 36A | BRADFORD - 37C | BRADFORD - 37C |
| Jan-54 | EASTFIELD - 65A | EASTFIELD - 65A | THORNTON JCN - 62A | DUNDEE - 62B | PARKESTON - 30F | DONCASTER - 36A | DONCASTER - 36A | BRADFORD - 37C | BRADFORD - 37C |
| Aug-54 | EASTFIELD - 65A | EASTFIELD - 65A | THORNTON JCN - 62A | DUNDEE - 62B | PARKESTON - 30F | **6/54: GORT - 39A** | DONCASTER - 36A | BRADFORD - 37C | BRADFORD - 37C |
| Jan-55 | EASTFIELD - 65A | EASTFIELD - 65A | THORNTON JCN - 62A | DUNDEE - 62B | PARKESTON - 30F | GORTON - 39A | DONCASTER - 36A | BRADFORD - 37C | BRADFORD - 37C |
| Aug-55 | EASTFIELD - 65A | EASTFIELD - 65A | THORNTON JCN - 62A | DUNDEE - 62B | PARKESTON - 30F | GORTON - 39A | DONCASTER - 36A | BRADFORD - 37C | BRADFORD - 37C |
| Jan-56 | EASTFIELD - 65A | EASTFIELD - 65A | THORNTON JCN - 62A | DUNDEE - 62B | PARKESTON - 30F | GORTON - 39A | DONCASTER - 36A | BRADFORD - 37C | BRADFORD - 37C |
| Aug-56 | EASTFIELD - 65A | EASTFIELD - 65A | THORNTON JCN - 62A | DUNDEE - 62B | PARKESTON - 30F | GORTON - 39A | DONCASTER - 36A | BRADFORD - 56G | BRADFORD - 56G |
| Jan-57 | **3/57: ST M - 64A** | **3/57: ST M - 64A** | THORNTON JCN - 62A | DUNDEE - 62B | PARKESTON - 30F | GORTON - 39A | DONCASTER - 36A | BRADFORD - 56G | BRADFORD - 56G |
| Aug-57 | EDINBURGH (SM) - 64A | EDINBURGH (SM) - 64A | THORNTON JCN - 62A | DUNDEE - 62B | PARKESTON - 30F | GORTON - 39A | DONCASTER - 36A | **6/57: WAKE - 56A** | **6/57: WAKE - 56A** |
| Jan-58 | EDINBURGH (SM) - 64A | EDINBURGH (SM) - 64A | THORNTON JCN - 62A | DUNDEE - 62B | PARKESTON - 30F | GORTON - 39A | DONCASTER - 36A | **9/57: C.HILL - 56C** | WAKEFIELD - 56A |
| Aug-58 | EDINBURGH (SM) - 64A | EDINBURGH (SM) - 64A | THORNTON JCN - 62A | DUNDEE - 62B | PARKESTON - 30F | GORTON - 9G | DONCASTER - 36A | **9/58: W.HPL - 51C** | WAKEFIELD - 56A |
| Jan-59 | EDINBURGH (SM) - 64A | **1/59: EAST - 65A** | THORNTON JCN - 62A | DUNDEE - 62B | PARKESTON - 30F | **6/59: LEIC - 15E** | DONCASTER - 36A | W. HARTLEPOOL - 51C | WAKEFIELD - 56A |
| Aug-59 | EDINBURGH (SM) - 64A | EASTFIELD - 65A | THORNTON JCN - 62A | DUNDEE - 62B | PARKESTON - 30F | **8/59: GORT - 9G** | DONCASTER - 36A | W. HARTLEPOOL - 51C | WAKEFIELD - 56A |
| Nov-59 | EDINBURGH (SM) - 64A | EASTFIELD - 65A | THORNTON JCN - 62A | DUNDEE - 62B | PARKESTON - 30F | GORTON - 9G | DONCASTER - 36A | W. HARTLEPOOL - 51C | WAKEFIELD - 56A |
| Jan-60 | EDINBURGH (SM) - 64A | EASTFIELD - 65A | THORNTON JCN - 62A | DUNDEE - 62B | PARKESTON - 30F | GORTON - 9G | DONCASTER - 36A | W. HARTLEPOOL - 51C | WAKEFIELD - 56A |
| Apr-60 | EDINBURGH (SM) - 64A | EASTFIELD - 65A | THORNTON JCN - 62A | DUNDEE - 62B | PARKESTON - 30F | GORTON - 9G | DONCASTER - 36A | W. HARTLEPOOL - 51C | WAKEFIELD - 56A |
| Aug-60 | **6/60: DAL RD - 64C** | EASTFIELD - 65A | **6/60: DUND - 62B** | DUNDEE - 62B | PARKESTON - 30F | GORTON - 9G | **6/60: DARN - 41A** | W. HARTLEPOOL - 51C | WAKEFIELD - 56A |
| Nov-60 | DALRY ROAD - 64C | EASTFIELD - 65A | DUNDEE - 62B | DUNDEE - 62B | PARKESTON - 30F | GORTON - 9G | DARNALL - 41A | W. HARTLEPOOL - 51C | WAKEFIELD - 56A |

| | 61269 | 61270 | 61271 | 61272 | 61273 | 61274 | 61275 | 61276 | 61277 |
|---|---|---|---|---|---|---|---|---|---|
| Aug-50 | LINCOLN - 40A | NORWICH - 32A | NORWICH - 32A | NORWICH - 32A | DARLINGTON - 51A | DARLINGTON - 51A | DARLINGTON - 51A | DARLINGTON - 51A | EDINBURGH (SM) - 64A |
| Jan-51 | LINCOLN - 40A | NORWICH - 32A | NORWICH - 32A | NORWICH - 32A | DARLINGTON - 51A | DARLINGTON - 51A | DARLINGTON - 51A | DARLINGTON - 51A | EDINBURGH (SM) - 64A |
| Aug-51 | LINCOLN - 40A | NORWICH - 32A | NORWICH - 32A | NORWICH - 32A | DARLINGTON - 51A | DARLINGTON - 51A | DARLINGTON - 51A | DARLINGTON - 51A | EDINBURGH (SM) - 64A |
| Jan-52 | **5/52: COLW - 38A** | NORWICH - 32A | NORWICH - 32A | NORWICH - 32A | DARLINGTON - 51A | DARLINGTON - 51A | **11/51: STOCK - 51E** | DARLINGTON - 51A | EDINBURGH (SM) - 64A |
| Aug-52 | **6/52: LINC - 40A** | NORWICH - 32A | NORWICH - 32A | NORWICH - 32A | DARLINGTON - 51A | DARLINGTON - 51A | STOCKTON - 51E | DARLINGTON - 51A | EDINBURGH (SM) - 64A |
| Jan-53 | LINCOLN - 40A | NORWICH - 32A | NORWICH - 32A | NORWICH - 32A | DARLINGTON - 51A | DARLINGTON - 51A | STOCKTON - 51E | DARLINGTON - 51A | EDINBURGH (SM) - 64A |
| Aug-53 | LINCOLN - 40A | NORWICH - 32A | **10/53: COLW - 38A** | **10/53: COLW - 38A** | DARLINGTON - 51A | DARLINGTON - 51A | STOCKTON - 51E | DARLINGTON - 51A | EDINBURGH (SM) - 64A |
| Jan-54 | **11/53: COLW - 38A** | NORWICH - 32A | COLWICK - 38A | COLWICK - 38A | DARLINGTON - 51A | DARLINGTON - 51A | STOCKTON - 51E | DARLINGTON - 51A | EDINBURGH (SM) - 64A |
| Aug-54 | COLWICK - 38A | NORWICH - 32A | COLWICK - 38A | COLWICK - 38A | DARLINGTON - 51A | DARLINGTON - 51A | STOCKTON - 51E | DARLINGTON - 51A | EDINBURGH (SM) - 64A |
| Jan-55 | COLWICK - 38A | NORWICH - 32A | COLWICK - 38A | **1/55: LEIC - 38C** | DARLINGTON - 51A | DARLINGTON - 51A | **12/54: WHPL - 51C** | DARLINGTON - 51A | EDINBURGH (SM) - 64A |
| Aug-55 | COLWICK - 38A | **8/55: IPS - 32B** | COLWICK - 38A | **2/55: COLW - 38A** | DARLINGTON - 51A | **6/55: YORK - 50A** | W. HARTLEPOOL - 51C | DARLINGTON - 51A | EDINBURGH (SM) - 64A |
| Jan-56 | COLWICK - 38A | **11/55: NORW - 32A** | COLWICK - 38A | COLWICK - 38A | DARLINGTON - 51A | **9/55: DARL - 51A** | W. HARTLEPOOL - 51C | DARLINGTON - 51A | EDINBURGH (SM) - 64A |
| Aug-56 | COLWICK - 38A | NORWICH - 32A | COLWICK - 38A | COLWICK - 38A | DARLINGTON - 51A | DARLINGTON - 51A | W. HARTLEPOOL - 51C | DARLINGTON - 51A | EDINBURGH (SM) - 64A |
| Jan-57 | **11/56: LEIC - 38C** | NORWICH - 32A | COLWICK - 38A | **1/57: ANN - 38B** | DARLINGTON - 51A | DARLINGTON - 51A | W. HARTLEPOOL - 51C | DARLINGTON - 51A | EDINBURGH (SM) - 64A |
| Aug-57 | LEICESTER (GC) - 38C | NORWICH - 32A | **6/57: WOOD - 38E** | ANNESLEY - 38B | DARLINGTON - 51A | DARLINGTON - 51A | W. HARTLEPOOL - 51C | DARLINGTON - 51A | **5/57 : TH JCN - 62A** |
| Jan-58 | LEICESTER (GC) - 38C | NORWICH - 32A | WOODFORD HALSE - 38E | **1/58: DARN - 41A** | DARLINGTON - 51A | DARLINGTON - 51A | W. HARTLEPOOL - 51C | DARLINGTON - 51A | THORNTON JCN - 62A |
| Aug-58 | LEICESTER (GC) - 15E | NORWICH - 32A | WOODFORD HALSE - 2F | **10/58: KX - 34A** | DARLINGTON - 51A | DARLINGTON - 51A | W. HARTLEPOOL - 51C | DARLINGTON - 51A | THORNTON JCN - 62A |
| Jan-59 | LEICESTER (GC) - 15E | NORWICH - 32A | WOODFORD HALSE - 2F | KINGS CROSS - 34A | DARLINGTON - 51A | DARLINGTON - 51A | W. HARTLEPOOL - 51C | DARLINGTON - 51A | THORNTON JCN - 62A |
| Aug-59 | **9/59: AGEC - 26B** | **10/59: DCTR - 36A** | WOODFORD HALSE - 2F | **4/59: NEWE - 34E** | **6/59: YORK - 50A** | **6/59: LOW M - 56F** | W. HARTLEPOOL - 51C | **6/59: YORK - 50A** | THORNTON JCN - 62A |
| Nov-59 | AGECROFT - 26B | DONCASTER - 36A | WOODFORD HALSE - 2F | NEW ENGLAND - 34E | YORK - 50A | LOW MOOR - 56F | W. HARTLEPOOL - 51C | YORK - 50A | THORNTON JCN - 62A |
| Jan-60 | AGECROFT - 26B | DONCASTER - 36A | WOODFORD HALSE - 2F | NEW ENGLAND - 34E | YORK - 50A | LOW MOOR - 56F | W. HARTLEPOOL - 51C | YORK - 50A | THORNTON JCN - 62A |
| Apr-60 | AGECROFT - 26B | DONCASTER - 36A | WOODFORD HALSE - 2F | NEW ENGLAND - 34E | YORK - 50A | LOW MOOR - 56F | W. HARTLEPOOL - 51C | YORK - 50A | THORNTON JCN - 62A |
| Aug-60 | AGECROFT - 26B | DONCASTER - 36A | WOODFORD HALSE - 2F | NEW ENGLAND - 34E | YORK - 50A | LOW MOOR - 56F | W. HARTLEPOOL - 51C | YORK - 50A | **6/60: DUND - 62B** |
| Nov-60 | AGECROFT - 26B | DONCASTER - 36A | WOODFORD HALSE - 2F | NEW ENGLAND - 34E | YORK - 50A | LOW MOOR - 56F | W. HARTLEPOOL - 51C | YORK - 50A | DUNDEE - 62B |

| | 61278 | 61279 | 61280 | 61281 | 61282 | 61283 | 61284 | 61285 | 61286 |
|---|---|---|---|---|---|---|---|---|---|
| Aug-50 | DUNDEE - 62B | LINCOLN - 40A | LINCOLN - 40A | LINCOLN - 40A | STRATFORD - 30A | COLWICK - 38A | IMMINGHAM - 40B | CAMBRIDGE - 31A | CAMBRIDGE - 31A |
| Jan-51 | DUNDEE - 62B | LINCOLN - 40A | LINCOLN - 40A | LINCOLN - 40A | STRATFORD - 30A | COLWICK - 38A | IMMINGHAM - 40B | CAMBRIDGE - 31A | CAMBRIDGE - 31A |
| Aug-51 | DUNDEE - 62B | LINCOLN - 40A | LINCOLN - 40A | LINCOLN - 40A | STRATFORD - 30A | COLWICK - 38A | IMMINGHAM - 40B | CAMBRIDGE - 31A | CAMBRIDGE - 31A |
| Jan-52 | DUNDEE - 62B | LINCOLN - 40A | **5/52: COLW - 38A** | LINCOLN - 40A | STRATFORD - 30A | COLWICK - 38A | IMMINGHAM - 40B | CAMBRIDGE - 31A | CAMBRIDGE - 31A |
| Aug-52 | DUNDEE - 62B | LINCOLN - 40A | **6/52: LINC - 40A** | LINCOLN - 40A | STRATFORD - 30A | COLWICK - 38A | IMMINGHAM - 40B | CAMBRIDGE - 31A | CAMBRIDGE - 31A |
| Jan-53 | DUNDEE - 62B | LINCOLN - 40A | **9/52: STRAT - 30A** | LINCOLN - 40A | STRATFORD - 30A | COLWICK - 38A | IMMINGHAM - 40B | CAMBRIDGE - 31A | CAMBRIDGE - 31A |
| Aug-53 | DUNDEE - 62B | LINCOLN - 40A | STRATFORD - 30A | LINCOLN - 40A | STRATFORD - 30A | COLWICK - 38A | IMMINGHAM - 40B | CAMBRIDGE - 31A | CAMBRIDGE - 31A |
| Jan-54 | DUNDEE - 62B | LINCOLN - 40A | STRATFORD - 30A | LINCOLN - 40A | **11/53: NEWE - 35A** | COLWICK - 38A | IMMINGHAM - 40B | CAMBRIDGE - 31A | CAMBRIDGE - 31A |
| Aug-54 | DUNDEE - 62B | **8/54: NORW - 32A** | STRATFORD - 30A | LINCOLN - 40A | NEW ENGLAND - 35A | **11/54: WOOD - 38E** | IMMINGHAM - 40B | CAMBRIDGE - 31A | CAMBRIDGE - 31A |
| Jan-55 | DUNDEE - 62B | **12/54: LINC - 40A** | STRATFORD - 30A | LINCOLN - 40A | NEW ENGLAND - 35A | **2/55: COLW - 38A** | IMMINGHAM - 40B | CAMBRIDGE - 31A | CAMBRIDGE - 31A |
| Aug-55 | DUNDEE - 62B | LINCOLN - 40A | STRATFORD - 30A | LINCOLN - 40A | NEW ENGLAND - 35A | COLWICK - 38A | IMMINGHAM - 40B | CAMBRIDGE - 31A | CAMBRIDGE - 31A |
| Jan-56 | DUNDEE - 62B | LINCOLN - 40A | STRATFORD - 30A | **2/56: IMM - 40B** | NEW ENGLAND - 35A | COLWICK - 38A | IMMINGHAM - 40B | CAMBRIDGE - 31A | CAMBRIDGE - 31A |
| Aug-56 | DUNDEE - 62B | LINCOLN - 40A | STRATFORD - 30A | IMMINGHAM - 40B | NEW ENGLAND - 35A | **11/56: LEIC - 38C** | IMMINGHAM - 40B | CAMBRIDGE - 31A | CAMBRIDGE - 31A |
| Jan-57 | DUNDEE - 62B | **2/57: STRAT - 30A** | STRATFORD - 30A | IMMINGHAM - 40B | NEW ENGLAND - 35A | **12/56: COLW - 38A** | IMMINGHAM - 40B | **11/56: DCTR - 36A** | CAMBRIDGE - 31A |
| Aug-57 | DUNDEE - 62B | STRATFORD - 30A | STRATFORD - 30A | IMMINGHAM - 40B | NEW ENGLAND - 35A | **5/57: KX - 34A** | IMMINGHAM - 40B | DONCASTER - 36A | CAMBRIDGE - 31A |
| Jan-58 | DUNDEE - 62B | STRATFORD - 30A | STRATFORD - 30A | IMMINGHAM - 40B | NEW ENGLAND - 35A | **10/57: CAMB - 31A** | IMMINGHAM - 40B | DONCASTER - 36A | CAMBRIDGE - 31A |
| Aug-58 | DUNDEE - 62B | **8/58: NORW - 32A** | STRATFORD - 30A | **6/58: COLW - 40E** | NEW ENGLAND - 34E | CAMBRIDGE - 31A | IMMINGHAM - 40B | DONCASTER - 36A | CAMBRIDGE - 31A |
| Jan-59 | DUNDEE - 62B | NORWICH - 32A | **1/59: PARK - 30F** | COLWICK - 40E | NEW ENGLAND - 34E | CAMBRIDGE - 31A | IMMINGHAM - 40B | DONCASTER - 36A | CAMBRIDGE - 31A |
| Aug-59 | DUNDEE - 62B | **9/59: DCTR - 36A** | **4/59: CAMB - 31A** | COLWICK - 40E | NEW ENGLAND - 34E | CAMBRIDGE - 31A | IMMINGHAM - 40B | DONCASTER - 36A | CAMBRIDGE - 31A |
| Nov-59 | DUNDEE - 62B | DONCASTER - 36A | CAMBRIDGE - 31A | COLWICK - 40E | NEW ENGLAND - 34E | CAMBRIDGE - 31A | **11/59: LINC - 40A** | DONCASTER - 36A | CAMBRIDGE - 31A |
| Jan-60 | DUNDEE - 62B | DONCASTER - 36A | CAMBRIDGE - 31A | COLWICK - 40E | NEW ENGLAND - 34E | CAMBRIDGE - 31A | LINCOLN - 40A | DONCASTER - 36A | CAMBRIDGE - 31A |
| Apr-60 | DUNDEE - 62B | DONCASTER - 36A | CAMBRIDGE - 31A | COLWICK - 40E | NEW ENGLAND - 34E | CAMBRIDGE - 31A | LINCOLN - 40A | DONCASTER - 36A | CAMBRIDGE - 31A |
| Aug-60 | DUNDEE - 62B | DONCASTER - 36A | CAMBRIDGE - 31A | COLWICK - 40E | NEW ENGLAND - 34E | CAMBRIDGE - 31A | LINCOLN - 40A | **6/60: COW - 40E** | CAMBRIDGE - 31A |
| Nov-60 | DUNDEE - 62B | DONCASTER - 36A | CAMBRIDGE - 31A | COLWICK - 40E | NEW ENGLAND - 34E | CAMBRIDGE - 31A | LINCOLN - 40A | COLWICK - 40E | CAMBRIDGE - 31A |

| | 61287 | 61288 | 61289 | 61290 | 61291 | 61292 | 61293 | 61294 | 61295 |
|---|---|---|---|---|---|---|---|---|---|
| Aug-50 | CAMBRIDGE - 31A | YORK - 50A | DARLINGTON - 51A | STOCKTON - 51E | DARLINGTON - 51A | DUNDEE - 62B | DUNDEE - 62B | BRADFORD - 37C | COPLEY HILL - 37B |
| Jan-51 | CAMBRIDGE - 31A | YORK - 50A | DARLINGTON - 51A | STOCKTON - 51E | DARLINGTON - 51A | DUNDEE - 62B | DUNDEE - 62B | BRADFORD - 37C | COPLEY HILL - 37B |
| Aug-51 | CAMBRIDGE - 31A | YORK - 50A | DARLINGTON - 51A | STOCKTON - 51E | DARLINGTON - 51A | DUNDEE - 62B | DUNDEE - 62B | BRADFORD - 37C | COPLEY HILL - 37B |
| Jan-52 | CAMBRIDGE - 31A | YORK - 50A | DARLINGTON - 51A | STOCKTON - 51E | DARLINGTON - 51A | DUNDEE - 62B | DUNDEE - 62B | BRADFORD - 37C | COPLEY HILL - 37B |
| Aug-52 | CAMBRIDGE - 31A | YORK - 50A | DARLINGTON - 51A | STOCKTON - 51E | DARLINGTON - 51A | DUNDEE - 62B | DUNDEE - 62B | BRADFORD - 37C | COPLEY HILL - 37B |
| Jan-53 | CAMBRIDGE - 31A | YORK - 50A | DARLINGTON - 51A | STOCKTON - 51E | DARLINGTON - 51A | DUNDEE - 62B | DUNDEE - 62B | BRADFORD - 37C | COPLEY HILL - 37B |
| Aug-53 | CAMBRIDGE - 31A | YORK - 50A | DARLINGTON - 51A | **10/53: CANAL - 68E** | DARLINGTON - 51A | DUNDEE - 62B | DUNDEE - 62B | **9/53: EAST - 65A** | COPLEY HILL - 37B |
| Jan-54 | CAMBRIDGE - 31A | YORK - 50A | DARLINGTON - 51A | CARLISLE (CANAL) - 68E | DARLINGTON - 51A | DUNDEE - 62B | DUNDEE - 62B | EASTFIELD - 65A | **11/53: ARDS - 37A** |
| Aug-54 | CAMBRIDGE - 31A | YORK - 50A | DARLINGTON - 51A | CARLISLE (CANAL) - 68E | DARLINGTON - 51A | DUNDEE - 62B | DUNDEE - 62B | **6/54: KITTY - 61A** | ARDSLEY - 37A |
| Jan-55 | CAMBRIDGE - 31A | YORK - 50A | DARLINGTON - 51A | CARLISLE (CANAL) - 68E | DARLINGTON - 51A | DUNDEE - 62B | DUNDEE - 62B | KITTYBREWSTER - 61A | ARDSLEY - 37A |
| Aug-55 | CAMBRIDGE - 31A | YORK - 50A | DARLINGTON - 51A | CARLISLE (CANAL) - 68E | **6/55: YORK - 50A** | DUNDEE - 62B | DUNDEE - 62B | KITTYBREWSTER - 61A | ARDSLEY - 37A |
| Jan-56 | CAMBRIDGE - 31A | YORK - 50A | DARLINGTON - 51A | CARLISLE (CANAL) - 68E | **9/55: DARL - 51A** | DUNDEE - 62B | DUNDEE - 62B | KITTYBREWSTER - 61A | ARDSLEY - 37A |
| Aug-56 | CAMBRIDGE - 31A | YORK - 50A | DARLINGTON - 51A | CARLISLE (CANAL) - 68E | DARLINGTON - 51A | DUNDEE - 62B | DUNDEE - 62B | KITTYBREWSTER - 61A | ARDSLEY - 56B |
| Jan-57 | CAMBRIDGE - 31A | YORK - 50A | **1/57: B GDNS - 53B** | CARLISLE (CANAL) - 68E | DARLINGTON - 51A | DUNDEE - 62B | DUNDEE - 62B | KITTYBREWSTER - 61A | ARDSLEY - 56B |
| Aug-57 | CAMBRIDGE - 31A | YORK - 50A | BOTANIC GARDENS - 53B | CARLISLE (CANAL) - 68E | DARLINGTON - 51A | DUNDEE - 62B | DUNDEE - 62B | KITTYBREWSTER - 61A | ARDSLEY - 56B |
| Jan-58 | CAMBRIDGE - 31A | YORK - 50A | BOTANIC GARDENS - 53B | CARLISLE CANAL - 68E | DARLINGTON - 51A | DUNDEE - 62B | DUNDEE - 62B | KITTYBREWSTER - 61A | ARDSLEY - 56B |
| Aug-58 | CAMBRIDGE - 31A | YORK - 50A | BOTANIC GARDENS - 53B | CARLISLE CANAL - 12C | DARLINGTON - 51A | DUNDEE - 62B | DUNDEE - 62B | KITTYBREWSTER - 61A | ARDSLEY - 56B |
| Jan-59 | CAMBRIDGE - 31A | YORK - 50A | BOTANIC GARDENS - 53B | CARLISLE CANAL - 12C | DARLINGTON - 51A | DUNDEE - 62B | DUNDEE - 62B | KITTYBREWSTER - 61A | ARDSLEY - 56B |
| Aug-59 | CAMBRIDGE - 31A | YORK - 50A | **6/59: DYCTS - 53A** | CARLISLE CANAL - 12C | **6/59: YORK - 50A** | DUNDEE - 62B | DUNDEE - 62B | KITTYBREWSTER - 61A | ARDSLEY - 56B |
| Nov-59 | CAMBRIDGE - 31A | YORK - 50A | DAIRYCOATES - 53A | CARLISLE CANAL - 12C | YORK - 50A | DUNDEE - 62B | DUNDEE - 62B | KITTYBREWSTER - 61A | ARDSLEY - 56B |
| Jan-60 | CAMBRIDGE - 31A | YORK - 50A | DAIRYCOATES - 53A | CARLISLE CANAL - 12C | YORK - 50A | DUNDEE - 62B | DUNDEE - 62B | KITTYBREWSTER - 61A | ARDSLEY - 56B |
| Apr-60 | CAMBRIDGE - 31A | YORK - 50A | DAIRYCOATES - 50B | CARLISLE CANAL - 12C | YORK - 50A | DUNDEE - 62B | DUNDEE - 62B | KITTYBREWSTER - 61A | ARDSLEY - 56B |
| Aug-60 | CAMBRIDGE - 31A | YORK - 50A | DAIRYCOATES - 50B | CARLISLE CANAL - 12C | YORK - 50A | DUNDEE - 62B | DUNDEE - 62B | **6/60: ST M - 64A** | ARDSLEY - 56B |
| Nov-60 | CAMBRIDGE - 31A | YORK - 50A | DAIRYCOATES - 50B | CARLISLE CANAL - 12C | YORK - 50A | DUNDEE - 62B | DUNDEE - 62B | EDINBURGH (SM) - 64A | ARDSLEY - 56B |

## Table 1 (61296–61304)

| | 61296 | 61297 | 61298 | 61299 | 61300 | 61301 | 61302 | 61303 | 61304 |
|---|---|---|---|---|---|---|---|---|---|
| Aug-50 | BRADFORD-37C | ARDSLEY-37A | LEICESTER (GC)-38C | LEICESTER (GC)-38C | CAMBRIDGE-31A | CAMBRIDGE-31A | CAMBRIDGE-31A | STOCKTON-51E | B.GDNS-53B |
| Jan-51 | BRADFORD-37C | ARDSLEY-37A | LEICESTER (GC)-38C | LEICESTER (GC)-38C | CAMBRIDGE-31A | CAMBRIDGE-31A | CAMBRIDGE-31A | STOCKTON-51E | B.GDNS-53B |
| Aug-51 | BRADFORD-37C | ARDSLEY-37A | LEICESTER (GC)-38C | LEICESTER (GC)-38C | CAMBRIDGE-31A | CAMBRIDGE-31A | CAMBRIDGE-31A | STOCKTON-51E | B.GDNS-53B |
| Jan-52 | BRADFORD-37C | ARDSLEY-37A | LEICESTER (GC)-38C | LEICESTER (GC)-38C | CAMBRIDGE-31A | CAMBRIDGE-31A | CAMBRIDGE-31A | STOCKTON-51E | B.GDNS-53B |
| Aug-52 | BRADFORD-37C | ARDSLEY-37A | LEICESTER (GC)-38C | LEICESTER (GC)-38C | CAMBRIDGE-31A | CAMBRIDGE-31A | CAMBRIDGE-31A | STOCKTON-51E | B.GDNS-53B |
| Jan-53 | BRADFORD-37C | ARDSLEY-37A | LEICESTER (GC)-38C | LEICESTER (GC)-38C | CAMBRIDGE-31A | CAMBRIDGE-31A | CAMBRIDGE-31A | STOCKTON-51E | B.GDNS-53B |
| Aug-53 | BRADFORD-37C | ARDSLEY-37A | LEICESTER (GC)-38C | LEICESTER (GC)-38C | CAMBRIDGE-31A | CAMBRIDGE-31A | CAMBRIDGE-31A | STOCKTON-51E | B.GDNS-53B |
| Jan-54 | BRADFORD-37C | ARDSLEY-37A | LEICESTER (GC)-38C | LEICESTER (GC)-38C | CAMBRIDGE-31A | CAMBRIDGE-31A | CAMBRIDGE-31A | STOCKTON-51E | B.GDNS-53B |
| Aug-54 | BRADFORD-37C | ARDSLEY-37A | LEICESTER (GC)-38C | LEICESTER (GC)-38C | CAMBRIDGE-31A | CAMBRIDGE-31A | CAMBRIDGE-31A | STOCKTON-51E | B.GDNS-53B |
| Jan-55 | BRADFORD-37C | ARDSLEY-37A | LEICESTER (GC)-38C | LEICESTER (GC)-38C | CAMBRIDGE-31A | CAMBRIDGE-31A | CAMBRIDGE-31A | STOCKTON-51E | B.GDNS-53B |
| Aug-55 | BRADFORD-37C | ARDSLEY-37A | LEICESTER (GC)-38C | LEICESTER (GC)-38C | CAMBRIDGE-31A | CAMBRIDGE-31A | CAMBRIDGE-31A | STOCKTON-51E | B.GDNS-53B |
| Jan-56 | BRADFORD-37C | ARDSLEY-37A | LEICESTER (GC)-38C | LEICESTER (GC)-38C | CAMBRIDGE-31A | CAMBRIDGE-31A | CAMBRIDGE-31A | STOCKTON-51E | B.GDNS-53B |
| Aug-56 | BRADFORD-56G | ARDSLEY-56B | LEICESTER (GC)-38C | LEICESTER (GC)-38C | CAMBRIDGE-31A | CAMBRIDGE-31A | 10/56: NEWE-35A | STOCKTON-51E | B.GDNS-53B |
| Jan-57 | BRADFORD-56G | ARDSLEY-56B | LEICESTER (GC)-38C | LEICESTER (GC)-38C | CAMBRIDGE-31A | CAMBRIDGE-31A | NEWENGLAND-35A | STOCKTON-51E | B.GDNS-53B |
| Aug-57 | 6/57: WAKE-56A | ARDSLEY-56B | LEICESTER (GC)-38C | LEICESTER (GC)-38C | CAMBRIDGE-31A | CAMBRIDGE-31A | NEWENGLAND-35A | STOCKTON-51E | B.GDNS-53B |
| Jan-58 | WAKEFIELD-56A | ARDSLEY-56B | LEICESTER (GC)-38C | 11/57: COLW-38A | CAMBRIDGE-31A | CAMBRIDGE-31A | NEWENGLAND-35A | STOCKTON-51E | B.GDNS-53B |
| Aug-58 | WAKEFIELD-56A | ARDSLEY-56B | LEICESTER (GC)-15E | COLWICK-40E | CAMBRIDGE-31A | CAMBRIDGE-31A | NEWENGLAND-34E | STOCKTON-51E | B.GDNS-53B |
| Jan-59 | WAKEFIELD-56A | ARDSLEY-56B | LEICESTER (GC)-15E | COLWICK-40E | 12/58: COL-30E | CAMBRIDGE-31A | NEWENGLAND-34E | STOCKTON-51E | B.GDNS-53B |
| Aug-59 | WAKEFIELD-56A | ARDSLEY-56B | 9/59: AGEC-26B | COLWICK-40E | COLCHESTER-30E | CAMBRIDGE-31A | NEWENGLAND-34E | 6/59: TNBY-51L | 6/59: SCAR-50E |
| Nov-59 | WAKEFIELD-56A | ARDSLEY-56B | AGECROFT-26B | COLWICK-40E | 12/59: MARCH-31B | CAMBRIDGE-31A | NEWENGLAND-34E | THORNABY-51L | SCARBOROUGH-50E |
| Jan-60 | WAKEFIELD-56A | ARDSLEY-56B | AGECROFT-26B | COLWICK-40E | 1/60: CAMB-31A | CAMBRIDGE-31A | NEWENGLAND-34E | THORNABY-51L | SCARBOROUGH-50E |
| Apr-60 | WAKEFIELD-56A | ARDSLEY-56B | AGECROFT-26B | COLWICK-40E | CAMBRIDGE-31A | CAMBRIDGE-31A | NEWENGLAND-34E | THORNABY-51L | 4/60: DARL-51A |
| Aug-60 | WAKEFIELD-56A | ARDSLEY-56B | AGECROFT-26B | COLWICK-40E | CAMBRIDGE-31A | CAMBRIDGE-31A | NEWENGLAND-34E | THORNABY-51L | DARLINGTON-51A |
| Nov-60 | WAKEFIELD-56A | ARDSLEY-56B | AGECROFT-26B | COLWICK-40E | CAMBRIDGE-31A | CAMBRIDGE-31A | NEWENGLAND-34E | THORNABY-51L | DARLINGTON-51A |

## Table 2 (61305–61313)

| | 61305 | 61306 | 61307 | 61308 | 61309 | 61310 | 61311 | 61312 | 61313 |
|---|---|---|---|---|---|---|---|---|---|
| Aug-50 | B.GDNS-53B | B.GDNS-53B | KITTYBREWSTER-61A | KEITH-61C | ARDSLEY-37A | ARDSLEY-37A | DARNALL-39B | DARNALL-39B | DARNALL-39B |
| Jan-51 | B.GDNS-53B | B.GDNS-53B | KITTYBREWSTER-61A | KEITH-61C | ARDSLEY-37A | 2/51: C.HILL-37B | DARNALL-39B | DARNALL-39B | DARNALL-39B |
| Aug-51 | B.GDNS-53B | B.GDNS-53B | KITTYBREWSTER-61A | KEITH-61C | 8/51: C.HILL-37B | COPLEYHILL-37B | DARNALL-39B | DARNALL-39B | DARNALL-39B |
| Jan-52 | B.GDNS-53B | B.GDNS-53B | KITTYBREWSTER-61A | KEITH-61C | COPLEYHILL-37B | 2/52: ARDS-37A | DARNALL-39B | DARNALL-39B | DARNALL-39B |
| Aug-52 | B.GDNS-53B | B.GDNS-53B | KITTYBREWSTER-61A | KEITH-61C | COPLEYHILL-37B | ARDSLEY-37A | DARNALL-39B | DARNALL-39B | DARNALL-39B |
| Jan-53 | B.GDNS-53B | B.GDNS-53B | KITTYBREWSTER-61A | KEITH-61C | COPLEYHILL-37B | ARDSLEY-37A | DARNALL-39B | DARNALL-39B | DARNALL-39B |
| Aug-53 | B.GDNS-53B | B.GDNS-53B | KITTYBREWSTER-61A | KEITH-61C | COPLEYHILL-37B | ARDSLEY-37A | DARNALL-39B | DARNALL-39B | DARNALL-39B |
| Jan-54 | B.GDNS-53B | B.GDNS-53B | KITTYBREWSTER-61A | KEITH-61C | COPLEYHILL-37B | ARDSLEY-37A | DARNALL-39B | DARNALL-39B | DARNALL-39B |
| Aug-54 | B.GDNS-53B | B.GDNS-53B | 7/54: KEITH-61C | KEITH-61C | COPLEYHILL-37B | ARDSLEY-37A | 10/54: LINC-40A | 10/54: NORW-32A | DARNALL-39B |
| Jan-55 | B.GDNS-53B | B.GDNS-53B | KEITH-61C | KEITH-61C | COPLEYHILL-37B | ARDSLEY-37A | LINCOLN-40A | NORWICH-32A | DARNALL-39B |
| Aug-55 | B.GDNS-53B | B.GDNS-53B | KEITH-61C | KEITH-61C | COPLEYHILL-37B | ARDSLEY-37A | LINCOLN-40A | NORWICH-32A | DARNALL-39B |
| Jan-56 | B.GDNS-53B | B.GDNS-53B | KEITH-61C | KEITH-61C | COPLEYHILL-37B | ARDSLEY-37A | LINCOLN-40A | 1/56: YAR (ST)-32D | DARNALL-39B |
| Aug-56 | B.GDNS-53B | B.GDNS-53B | KEITH-61C | KEITH-61C | COPLEYHILL-56C | ARDSLEY-56B | 10/56: KX-34A | 4/56: NORW-32A | DARNALL-41A |
| Jan-57 | B.GDNS-53B | B.GDNS-53B | 2/57: KITTY-61A | 2/57: KITTY-61A | COPLEYHILL-56C | ARDSLEY-56B | 2/57: STRAT-30A | NORWICH-32A | DARNALL-41A |
| Aug-57 | B.GDNS-53B | B.GDNS-53B | 8/57: STM-64A | 9/57: STM-64A | COPLEYHILL-56C | ARDSLEY-56B | STRATFORD-30A | NORWICH-32A | DARNALL-41A |
| Jan-58 | B.GDNS-53B | B.GDNS-53B | EDINBURGH (SM)-64A | EDINBURGH (SM)-64A | COPLEYHILL-56C | ARDSLEY-56B | STRATFORD-30A | NORWICH-32A | DARNALL-41A |
| Aug-58 | B.GDNS-53B | B.GDNS-53B | EDINBURGH (SM)-64A | EDINBURGH (SM)-64A | COPLEYHILL-56C | ARDSLEY-56B | 8/58: PARK-30F | NORWICH-32A | DARNALL-41A |
| Jan-59 | B.GDNS-53B | B.GDNS-53B | EDINBURGH (SM)-64A | EDINBURGH (SM)-64A | COPLEYHILL-56C | ARDSLEY-56B | 12/58: COL-30E | NORWICH-32A | DARNALL-41A |
| Aug-59 | 6/59: SCAR-50E | 6/59: DYCTS-53A | EDINBURGH (SM)-64A | EDINBURGH (SM)-64A | COPLEYHILL-56C | ARDSLEY-56B | COLCHESTER-30E | 5/59: DARN-41A | DARNALL-41A |
| Nov-59 | SCARBOROUGH-50E | DAIRYCOATES-53A | EDINBURGH (SM)-64A | EDINBURGH (SM)-64A | COPLEYHILL-56C | ARDSLEY-56B | 10/59: PARK-30F | DARNALL-41A | DARNALL-41A |
| Jan-60 | SCARBOROUGH-50E | DAIRYCOATES-50B | EDINBURGH (SM)-64A | EDINBURGH (SM)-64A | COPLEYHILL-56C | ARDSLEY-56B | PARKESTON-30F | DARNALL-41A | DARNALL-41A |
| Apr-60 | 4/60: DYCTS-50B | DAIRYCOATES-50B | EDINBURGH (SM)-64A | EDINBURGH (SM)-64A | COPLEYHILL-56C | ARDSLEY-56B | PARKESTON-30F | DARNALL-41A | DARNALL-41A |
| Aug-60 | DAIRYCOATES-50B | DAIRYCOATES-50B | 7/60: KITTY-61A | 7/60: KITTY-61A | COPLEYHILL-56C | ARDSLEY-56B | PARKESTON-30F | DARNALL-41A | DARNALL-41A |
| Nov-60 | DAIRYCOATES-50B | DAIRYCOATES-50B | KITTYBREWSTER-61A | KITTYBREWSTER-61A | COPLEYHILL-56C | ARDSLEY-56B | PARKESTON-30F | DARNALL-41A | DARNALL-41A |

## Table 3 (61314–61322)

| | 61314 | 61315 | 61316 | 61317 | 61318 | 61319 | 61320 | 61321 | 61322 |
|---|---|---|---|---|---|---|---|---|---|
| Aug-50 | DARNALL-39B | DARNALL-39B | DARNALL-39B | DARNALL-39B | IMMINGHAM-40B | BORO'GDNS-54C | BORO'GDNS-54C | BORO'GDNS-54C | TWEEDMOUTH-52D |
| Jan-51 | DARNALL-39B | DARNALL-39B | DARNALL-39B | DARNALL-39B | IMMINGHAM-40B | BORO'GDNS-54C | BORO'GDNS-54C | BORO'GDNS-54C | TWEEDMOUTH-52D |
| Aug-51 | DARNALL-39B | DARNALL-39B | DARNALL-39B | DARNALL-39B | IMMINGHAM-40B | BORO'GDNS-54C | BORO'GDNS-54C | BORO'GDNS-54C | TWEEDMOUTH-52D |
| Jan-52 | DARNALL-39B | DARNALL-39B | DARNALL-39B | DARNALL-39B | IMMINGHAM-40B | BORO'GDNS-54C | BORO'GDNS-54C | BORO'GDNS-54C | TWEEDMOUTH-52D |
| Aug-52 | DARNALL-39B | DARNALL-39B | DARNALL-39B | DARNALL-39B | IMMINGHAM-40B | BORO'GDNS-54C | BORO'GDNS-54C | BORO'GDNS-54C | TWEEDMOUTH-52D |
| Jan-53 | DARNALL-39B | DARNALL-39B | DARNALL-39B | DARNALL-39B | IMMINGHAM-40B | BORO'GDNS-54C | BORO'GDNS-54C | BORO'GDNS-54C | TWEEDMOUTH-52D |
| Aug-53 | DARNALL-39B | DARNALL-39B | DARNALL-39B | DARNALL-39B | IMMINGHAM-40B | BORO'GDNS-54C | BORO'GDNS-54C | BORO'GDNS-54C | TWEEDMOUTH-52D |
| Jan-54 | DARNALL-39B | DARNALL-39B | DARNALL-39B | DARNALL-39B | IMMINGHAM-40B | BORO'GDNS-54C | BORO'GDNS-54C | BORO'GDNS-54C | TWEEDMOUTH-52D |
| Aug-54 | DARNALL-39B | DARNALL-39B | DARNALL-39B | 8/54: NORW-32A | IMMINGHAM-40B | BORO'GDNS-54C | BORO'GDNS-54C | BORO'GDNS-54C | TWEEDMOUTH-52D |
| Jan-55 | DARNALL-39B | DARNALL-39B | DARNALL-39B | NORWICH-32A | IMMINGHAM-40B | BORO'GDNS-54C | BORO'GDNS-54C | BORO'GDNS-54C | TWEEDMOUTH-52D |
| Aug-55 | DARNALL-39B | DARNALL-39B | DARNALL-39B | NORWICH-32A | IMMINGHAM-40B | BORO'GDNS-54C | BORO'GDNS-54C | BORO'GDNS-54C | TWEEDMOUTH-52D |
| Jan-56 | DARNALL-41A | DARNALL-41A | DARNALL-41A | NORWICH-32A | IMMINGHAM-40B | BORO'GDNS-54C | BORO'GDNS-54C | BORO'GDNS-54C | TWEEDMOUTH-52D |
| Aug-56 | DARNALL-41A | DARNALL-41A | DARNALL-41A | NORWICH-32A | IMMINGHAM-40B | BORO'GDNS-54C | 10/56: BRAD-56G | BORO'GDNS-54C | TWEEDMOUTH-52D |
| Jan-57 | DARNALL-41A | DARNALL-41A | DARNALL-41A | NORWICH-32A | IMMINGHAM-40B | BORO'GDNS-54C | 6/57: WAKE-56A | BORO'GDNS-54C | TWEEDMOUTH-52D |
| Aug-57 | 10/57: CAMB-31A | DARNALL-41A | DARNALL-41A | NORWICH-32A | IMMINGHAM-40B | BORO'GDNS-54C | 9/57: C.HILL-56C | BORO'GDNS-54C | TWEEDMOUTH-52D |
| Jan-58 | CAMBRIDGE-31A | DARNALL-41A | DARNALL-41A | NORWICH-32A | IMMINGHAM-40B | BORO'GDNS-54C | COPLEYHILL-56C | BORO'GDNS-54C | TWEEDMOUTH-52D |
| Aug-58 | CAMBRIDGE-31A | DARNALL-41A | DARNALL-41A | NORWICH-32A | IMMINGHAM-40B | 6/58: WAKE-56A | COPLEYHILL-56C | 6/58: WAKE-56A | TWEEDMOUTH-52D |
| Jan-59 | CAMBRIDGE-31A | DARNALL-41A | DARNALL-41A | NORWICH-32A | IMMINGHAM-40B | 9/58: DARL-51A | COPLEYHILL-56C | 9/58: DARL-51A | TWEEDMOUTH-52D |
| Aug-59 | CAMBRIDGE-31A | DARNALL-41A | DARNALL-41A | NORWICH-32A | IMMINGHAM-40B | 6/59: YORK-50A | COPLEYHILL-56C | DARLINGTON-51A | TWEEDMOUTH-52D |
| Nov-59 | 10/59: DCTR-36A | DARNALL-41A | DARNALL-41A | NORWICH-32A | IMMINGHAM-40B | YORK-50A | COPLEYHILL-56C | DARLINGTON-51A | TWEEDMOUTH-52D |
| Jan-60 | DONCASTER-36A | DARNALL-41A | DARNALL-41A | DARNALL-41A | IMMINGHAM-40B | YORK-50A | COPLEYHILL-56C | DARLINGTON-51A | TWEEDMOUTH-52D |
| Apr-60 | DONCASTER-36A | DARNALL-41A | 5/60: MEX-41F | 4/60: LINC-40A | IMMINGHAM-40B | YORK-50A | COPLEYHILL-56C | DARLINGTON-51A | TWEEDMOUTH-52D |
| Aug-60 | DONCASTER-36A | DARNALL-41A | MEXBOROUGH-41F | IMMINGHAM-40B | IMMINGHAM-40B | YORK-50A | COPLEYHILL-56C | DARLINGTON-51A | 6/60: BLAY-52C |
| Nov-60 | DONCASTER-36A | DARNALL-41A | MEXBOROUGH-41F | IMMINGHAM-40B | IMMINGHAM-40B | YORK-50A | COPLEYHILL-56C | DARLINGTON-51A | BLAYDON-52C |

## Table 4 (61323–61331)

| | 61323 | 61324 | 61325 | 61326 | 61327 | 61328 | 61329 | 61330 | 61331 |
|---|---|---|---|---|---|---|---|---|---|
| Aug-50 | KITTYBREWSTER-61A | KITTYBREWSTER-61A | IMMINGHAM-40B | NEWTON HEATH-26A | DARNALL-39B | IMMINGHAM-40B | LINCOLN-40A | NEWENGLAND-35A | NEWENGLAND-35A |
| Jan-51 | KITTYBREWSTER-61A | KITTYBREWSTER-61A | IMMINGHAM-40B | 9/50: GORT-39A | DARNALL-39B | IMMINGHAM-40B | LINCOLN-40A | NEWENGLAND-35A | NEWENGLAND-35A |
| Aug-51 | KITTYBREWSTER-61A | KITTYBREWSTER-61A | IMMINGHAM-40B | GORTON-39A | DARNALL-39B | IMMINGHAM-40B | 9/51: STRAT-30A | NEWENGLAND-35A | NEWENGLAND-35A |
| Jan-52 | KITTYBREWSTER-61A | KITTYBREWSTER-61A | IMMINGHAM-40B | GORTON-39A | DARNALL-39B | IMMINGHAM-40B | STRATFORD-30A | NEWENGLAND-35A | NEWENGLAND-35A |
| Aug-52 | KITTYBREWSTER-61A | KITTYBREWSTER-61A | IMMINGHAM-40B | GORTON-39A | DARNALL-39B | IMMINGHAM-40B | STRATFORD-30A | NEWENGLAND-35A | NEWENGLAND-35A |
| Jan-53 | KITTYBREWSTER-61A | KITTYBREWSTER-61A | IMMINGHAM-40B | GORTON-39A | DARNALL-39B | IMMINGHAM-40B | STRATFORD-30A | 1/53: KX-34A | NEWENGLAND-35A |
| Aug-53 | KITTYBREWSTER-61A | KITTYBREWSTER-61A | IMMINGHAM-40B | GORTON-39A | DARNALL-39B | IMMINGHAM-40B | STRATFORD-30A | 9/53: STM-64A | NEWENGLAND-35A |
| Jan-54 | KITTYBREWSTER-61A | KITTYBREWSTER-61A | IMMINGHAM-40B | GORTON-39A | DARNALL-39B | IMMINGHAM-40B | STRATFORD-30A | EDINBURGH (SM)-64A | KINGS CROSS-34A |
| Aug-54 | KITTYBREWSTER-61A | KITTYBREWSTER-61A | IMMINGHAM-40B | 6/54: DCTR-36A | DARNALL-39B | IMMINGHAM-40B | STRATFORD-30A | EDINBURGH (SM)-64A | KINGS CROSS-34A |
| Jan-55 | KITTYBREWSTER-61A | KITTYBREWSTER-61A | IMMINGHAM-40B | DONCASTER-36A | DARNALL-39B | IMMINGHAM-40B | STRATFORD-30A | 12/54: CARS-64D | KINGS CROSS-34A |
| Aug-55 | KITTYBREWSTER-61A | KITTYBREWSTER-61A | IMMINGHAM-40B | DONCASTER-36A | DARNALL-39B | IMMINGHAM-40B | STRATFORD-30A | CARSTAIRS-64D | KINGS CROSS-34A |
| Jan-56 | KITTYBREWSTER-61A | KITTYBREWSTER-61A | IMMINGHAM-40B | DONCASTER-36A | DARNALL-39B | IMMINGHAM-40B | STRATFORD-30A | CARSTAIRS-64D | KINGS CROSS-34A |
| Aug-56 | KITTYBREWSTER-61A | KITTYBREWSTER-61A | IMMINGHAM-40B | DONCASTER-36A | DARNALL-41A | IMMINGHAM-40B | STRATFORD-30A | 3/56: STM-64A | KINGS CROSS-34A |
| Jan-57 | 3/57: SBGE-35C | KITTYBREWSTER-61A | IMMINGHAM-40B | DONCASTER-36A | DARNALL-41A | IMMINGHAM-40B | STRATFORD-30A | EDINBURGH (SM)-64A | KINGS CROSS-34A |
| Aug-57 | SPITAL BRIDGE-35C | KITTYBREWSTER-61A | IMMINGHAM-40B | DONCASTER-36A | DARNALL-41A | IMMINGHAM-40B | STRATFORD-30A | 5/57: THJN-62A | KINGS CROSS-34A |
| Jan-58 | SPITAL BRIDGE-35C | KITTYBREWSTER-61A | IMMINGHAM-40B | DONCASTER-36A | DARNALL-41A | IMMINGHAM-40B | STRATFORD-30A | THORNTON JCN-62A | KINGS CROSS-34A |
| Aug-58 | SPITAL BRIDGE-31F | KITTYBREWSTER-61A | IMMINGHAM-40B | DONCASTER-36A | DARNALL-41A | IMMINGHAM-40B | STRATFORD-30A | THORNTON JCN-62A | KINGS CROSS-34A |
| Jan-59 | SPITAL BRIDGE-31F | KITTYBREWSTER-61A | IMMINGHAM-40B | DONCASTER-36A | DARNALL-41A | IMMINGHAM-40B | STRATFORD-30A | THORNTON JCN-62A | KINGS CROSS-34A |
| Aug-59 | SPITAL BRIDGE-31F | KITTYBREWSTER-61A | IMMINGHAM-40B | DONCASTER-36A | DARNALL-41A | IMMINGHAM-40B | STRATFORD-30A | THORNTON JCN-62A | KINGS CROSS-34A |
| Nov-59 | SPITAL BRIDGE-31F | KITTYBREWSTER-61A | IMMINGHAM-40B | DONCASTER-36A | DARNALL-41A | IMMINGHAM-40B | STRATFORD-30A | THORNTON JCN-62A | KINGS CROSS-34A |
| Jan-60 | 2/60: MARCH-31B | KITTYBREWSTER-61A | IMMINGHAM-40B | DONCASTER-36A | DARNALL-41A | IMMINGHAM-40B | STRATFORD-30A | THORNTON JCN-62A | KINGS CROSS-34A |
| Apr-60 | MARCH-31B | KITTYBREWSTER-61A | IMMINGHAM-40B | DONCASTER-36A | DARNALL-41A | IMMINGHAM-40B | STRATFORD-30A | THORNTON JCN-62A | 4/60: NEWE-34E |
| Aug-60 | MARCH-31B | KITTYBREWSTER-61A | IMMINGHAM-40B | DONCASTER-36A | DARNALL-41A | IMMINGHAM-40B | STRATFORD-30A | THORNTON JCN-62A | NEWENGLAND-34E |
| Nov-60 | MARCH-31B | KITTYBREWSTER-61A | IMMINGHAM-40B | DONCASTER-36A | DARNALL-41A | IMMINGHAM-40B | STRATFORD-30A | THORNTON JCN-62A | NEWENGLAND-34E |

| | 60955 | 60956 | 60957 | 60958 | 60959 | 60960 | 60961 | 60962 | 60963 |
|---|---|---|---|---|---|---|---|---|---|
| Aug-50 | FERRYHILL-61B | DONCASTER-36A | HEATON-52B | DUNDEE-62B | HAYMARKET-64B | YORK-50A | YORK-50A | YORK-50A | YORK-50A |
| Jan-51 | FERRYHILL-61B | DONCASTER-36A | HEATON-52B | DUNDEE-62B | HAYMARKET-64B | YORK-50A | YORK-50A | YORK-50A | YORK-50A |
| Aug-51 | FERRYHILL-61B | DONCASTER-36A | HEATON-52B | DUNDEE-62B | HAYMARKET-64B | YORK-50A | YORK-50A | YORK-50A | YORK-50A |
| Jan-52 | FERRYHILL-61B | DONCASTER-36A | HEATON-52B | DUNDEE-62B | HAYMARKET-64B | YORK-50A | YORK-50A | YORK-50A | YORK-50A |
| Aug-52 | FERRYHILL-61B | DONCASTER-36A | 7/52: GHD-52A | DUNDEE-62B | HAYMARKET-64B | YORK-50A | YORK-50A | YORK-50A | YORK-50A |
| Jan-53 | FERRYHILL-61B | DONCASTER-36A | GATESHEAD-52A | DUNDEE-62B | HAYMARKET-64B | YORK-50A | YORK-50A | YORK-50A | YORK-50A |
| Aug-53 | FERRYHILL-61B | DONCASTER-36A | GATESHEAD-52A | DUNDEE-62B | HAYMARKET-64B | YORK-50A | YORK-50A | YORK-50A | YORK-50A |
| Jan-54 | FERRYHILL-61B | DONCASTER-36A | GATESHEAD-52A | DUNDEE-62B | HAYMARKET-64B | YORK-50A | YORK-50A | YORK-50A | YORK-50A |
| Aug-54 | FERRYHILL-61B | DONCASTER-36A | GATESHEAD-52A | DUNDEE-62B | HAYMARKET-64B | YORK-50A | YORK-50A | YORK-50A | YORK-50A |
| Jan-55 | FERRYHILL-61B | DONCASTER-36A | GATESHEAD-52A | DUNDEE-62B | HAYMARKET-64B | YORK-50A | YORK-50A | YORK-50A | YORK-50A |
| Aug-55 | FERRYHILL-61B | DONCASTER-36A | GATESHEAD-52A | DUNDEE-62B | HAYMARKET-64B | YORK-50A | YORK-50A | YORK-50A | YORK-50A |
| Jan-56 | FERRYHILL-61B | DONCASTER-36A | 4/56: HTN-52B | DUNDEE-62B | HAYMARKET-64B | YORK-50A | YORK-50A | YORK-50A | YORK-50A |
| Aug-56 | FERRYHILL-61B | DONCASTER-36A | 9/56: ST M-64A | DUNDEE-62B | HAYMARKET-64B | YORK-50A | YORK-50A | 6/56: HTN-52B | YORK-50A |
| Jan-57 | FERRYHILL-61B | DONCASTER-36A | EDINBURGH(SM)-64A | DUNDEE-62B | HAYMARKET-64B | YORK-50A | YORK-50A | HEATON-52B | YORK-50A |
| Aug-57 | FERRYHILL-61B | DONCASTER-36A | EDINBURGH(SM)-64A | DUNDEE-62B | HAYMARKET-64B | YORK-50A | YORK-50A | HEATON-52B | YORK-50A |
| Jan-58 | FERRYHILL-61B | DONCASTER-36A | EDINBURGH(SM)-64A | DUNDEE-62B | 11/57: ST M-64A | YORK-50A | YORK-50A | HEATON-52B | YORK-50A |
| Aug-58 | FERRYHILL-61B | DONCASTER-36A | EDINBURGH(SM)-64A | 10/58: ST M-64A | 5/58: HMKT-64B | YORK-50A | YORK-50A | HEATON-52B | YORK-50A |
| Jan-59 | FERRYHILL-61B | DONCASTER-36A | EDINBURGH(SM)-64A | EDINBURGH(SM)-64A | HAYMARKET-64B | YORK-50A | YORK-50A | HEATON-52B | YORK-50A |
| Aug-59 | FERRYHILL-61B | DONCASTER-36A | EDINBURGH(SM)-64A | EDINBURGH(SM)-64A | HAYMARKET-64B | YORK-50A | 6/59: DARL-51A | HEATON-52B | YORK-50A |
| Nov-59 | FERRYHILL-61B | DONCASTER-36A | EDINBURGH(SM)-64A | EDINBURGH(SM)-64A | HAYMARKET-64B | YORK-50A | 9/59: TNBY-51L | HEATON-52B | YORK-50A |
| Jan-60 | FERRYHILL-61B | DONCASTER-36A | EDINBURGH(SM)-64A | EDINBURGH(SM)-64A | HAYMARKET-64B | YORK-50A | THORNABY-51L | HEATON-52B | YORK-50A |
| Apr-60 | FERRYHILL-61B | DONCASTER-36A | EDINBURGH(SM)-64A | EDINBURGH(SM)-64A | HAYMARKET-64B | YORK-50A | THORNABY-51L | HEATON-52B | YORK-50A |
| Aug-60 | FERRYHILL-61B | 6/60: NEWE-34E | EDINBURGH(SM)-64A | EDINBURGH(SM)-64A | 6/60: ST M-64A | YORK-50A | THORNABY-51L | HEATON-52B | YORK-50A |
| Nov-60 | FERRYHILL-61B | NEWENGLAND-34E | EDINBURGH(SM)-64A | EDINBURGH(SM)-64A | EDINBURGH(SM)-64A | YORK-50A | THORNABY-51L | HEATON-52B | YORK-50A |

| | 60964 | 60965 | 60966 | 60967 | 60968 | 60969 | 60970 | 60971 | 60972 |
|---|---|---|---|---|---|---|---|---|---|
| Aug-50 | GATESHEAD-52A | GATESHEAD-52A | NEWENGLAND-35A | GATESHEAD-52A | YORK-50A | DUNDEE-62B | FERRYHILL-61B | DUNDEE-62B | HAYMARKET-64B |
| Jan-51 | GATESHEAD-52A | GATESHEAD-52A | NEWENGLAND-35A | GATESHEAD-52A | YORK-50A | DUNDEE-62B | FERRYHILL-61B | DUNDEE-62B | 1/51: DUND-62B |
| Aug-51 | GATESHEAD-52A | GATESHEAD-52A | 9/51: WFD.H-38E | GATESHEAD-52A | YORK-50A | DUNDEE-62B | FERRYHILL-61B | DUNDEE-62B | DUNDEE-62B |
| Jan-52 | GATESHEAD-52A | GATESHEAD-52A | W.HALSE-38E | GATESHEAD-52A | YORK-50A | DUNDEE-62B | FERRYHILL-61B | DUNDEE-62B | DUNDEE-62B |
| Aug-52 | GATESHEAD-52A | GATESHEAD-52A | W.HALSE-38E | GATESHEAD-52A | YORK-50A | DUNDEE-62B | FERRYHILL-61B | DUNDEE-62B | DUNDEE-62B |
| Jan-53 | GATESHEAD-52A | 12/52: ST M-64A | 2/53: NEWE-35A | GATESHEAD-52A | YORK-50A | DUNDEE-62B | FERRYHILL-61B | DUNDEE-62B | DUNDEE-62B |
| Aug-53 | GATESHEAD-52A | EDINBURGH(SM)-64A | NEWENGLAND-35A | GATESHEAD-52A | YORK-50A | DUNDEE-62B | FERRYHILL-61B | DUNDEE-62B | DUNDEE-62B |
| Jan-54 | GATESHEAD-52A | EDINBURGH(SM)-64A | NEWENGLAND-35A | GATESHEAD-52A | YORK-50A | DUNDEE-62B | FERRYHILL-61B | DUNDEE-62B | DUNDEE-62B |
| Aug-54 | GATESHEAD-52A | EDINBURGH(SM)-64A | NEWENGLAND-35A | GATESHEAD-52A | YORK-50A | DUNDEE-62B | FERRYHILL-61B | DUNDEE-62B | DUNDEE-62B |
| Jan-55 | GATESHEAD-52A | EDINBURGH(SM)-64A | NEWENGLAND-35A | GATESHEAD-52A | YORK-50A | DUNDEE-62B | FERRYHILL-61B | DUNDEE-62B | DUNDEE-62B |
| Aug-55 | GATESHEAD-52A | EDINBURGH(SM)-64A | 9/55: GRAN-35B | GATESHEAD-52A | YORK-50A | DUNDEE-62B | FERRYHILL-61B | DUNDEE-62B | DUNDEE-62B |
| Jan-56 | GATESHEAD-52A | EDINBURGH(SM)-64A | GRANTHAM-35B | GATESHEAD-52A | YORK-50A | DUNDEE-62B | FERRYHILL-61B | DUNDEE-62B | 1/56: FYHL-61B |
| Aug-56 | GATESHEAD-52A | EDINBURGH(SM)-64A | 10/56: NEWE-35A | GATESHEAD-52A | YORK-50A | DUNDEE-62B | FERRYHILL-61B | DUNDEE-62B | FERRYHILL-61B |
| Jan-57 | GATESHEAD-52A | EDINBURGH(SM)-64A | NEWENGLAND-35A | GATESHEAD-52A | YORK-50A | DUNDEE-62B | FERRYHILL-61B | DUNDEE-62B | FERRYHILL-61B |
| Aug-57 | GATESHEAD-52A | EDINBURGH(SM)-64A | 10/57: GRAN-35B | GATESHEAD-52A | YORK-50A | DUNDEE-62B | FERRYHILL-61B | DUNDEE-62B | FERRYHILL-61B |
| Jan-58 | GATESHEAD-52A | EDINBURGH(SM)-64A | GRANTHAM-35B | GATESHEAD-52A | YORK-50A | DUNDEE-62B | FERRYHILL-61B | DUNDEE-62B | FERRYHILL-61B |
| Aug-58 | GATESHEAD-52A | EDINBURGH(SM)-64A | GRANTHAM-35B | GATESHEAD-52A | YORK-50A | 10/58: ST M-64A | FERRYHILL-61B | 10/58: ST M-64A | FERRYHILL-61B |
| Jan-59 | GATESHEAD-52A | EDINBURGH(SM)-64A | 12/58: NEWE-34E | GATESHEAD-52A | YORK-50A | EDINBURGH(SM)-64A | FERRYHILL-61B | EDINBURGH(SM)-64A | FERRYHILL-61B |
| Aug-59 | GATESHEAD-52A | EDINBURGH(SM)-64A | NEWENGLAND-34E | GATESHEAD-52A | YORK-50A | EDINBURGH(SM)-64A | FERRYHILL-61B | EDINBURGH(SM)-64A | FERRYHILL-61B |
| Nov-59 | GATESHEAD-52A | EDINBURGH(SM)-64A | NEWENGLAND-34E | GATESHEAD-52A | YORK-50A | EDINBURGH(SM)-64A | FERRYHILL-61B | EDINBURGH(SM)-64A | FERRYHILL-61B |
| Jan-60 | GATESHEAD-52A | EDINBURGH(SM)-64A | NEWENGLAND-34E | GATESHEAD-52A | YORK-50A | EDINBURGH(SM)-64A | FERRYHILL-61B | EDINBURGH(SM)-64A | FERRYHILL-61B |
| Apr-60 | GATESHEAD-52A | EDINBURGH(SM)-64A | NEWENGLAND-34E | GATESHEAD-52A | YORK-50A | EDINBURGH(SM)-64A | FERRYHILL-61B | EDINBURGH(SM)-64A | FERRYHILL-61B |
| Aug-60 | GATESHEAD-52A | EDINBURGH(SM)-64A | NEWENGLAND-34E | 6/60: TNBY-51L | YORK-50A | EDINBURGH(SM)-64A | 7/60: PERTH-63A | EDINBURGH(SM)-64A | FERRYHILL-61B |
| Nov-60 | GATESHEAD-52A | EDINBURGH(SM)-64A | NEWENGLAND-34E | THORNABY-51L | YORK-50A | EDINBURGH(SM)-64A | PERTH-63A | EDINBURGH(SM)-64A | FERRYHILL-61B |

| | 60973 | 60974 | 60975 | 60976 | 60977 | 60978 | 60979 | 60980 | 60981 |
|---|---|---|---|---|---|---|---|---|---|
| Aug-50 | FERRYHILL-61B | YORK-50A | YORK-50A | YORK-50A | YORK-50A | YORK-50A | YORK-50A | EDINBURGH(SM)-64A | YORK-50A |
| Jan-51 | FERRYHILL-61B | YORK-50A | YORK-50A | YORK-50A | YORK-50A | YORK-50A | YORK-50A | 1/51: HMKT-64B | YORK-50A |
| Aug-51 | FERRYHILL-61B | YORK-50A | YORK-50A | YORK-50A | YORK-50A | YORK-50A | YORK-50A | 3/51: ST M-64A | YORK-50A |
| Jan-52 | FERRYHILL-61B | YORK-50A | YORK-50A | YORK-50A | YORK-50A | YORK-50A | YORK-50A | EDINBURGH(SM)-64A | YORK-50A |
| Aug-52 | FERRYHILL-61B | YORK-50A | YORK-50A | YORK-50A | YORK-50A | YORK-50A | YORK-50A | EDINBURGH(SM)-64A | YORK-50A |
| Jan-53 | FERRYHILL-61B | YORK-50A | YORK-50A | YORK-50A | YORK-50A | YORK-50A | YORK-50A | EDINBURGH(SM)-64A | YORK-50A |
| Aug-53 | FERRYHILL-61B | YORK-50A | YORK-50A | YORK-50A | YORK-50A | YORK-50A | YORK-50A | EDINBURGH(SM)-64A | YORK-50A |
| Jan-54 | FERRYHILL-61B | YORK-50A | YORK-50A | YORK-50A | YORK-50A | YORK-50A | YORK-50A | EDINBURGH(SM)-64A | 7/53: DARL-51A |
| Aug-54 | FERRYHILL-61B | YORK-50A | YORK-50A | YORK-50A | YORK-50A | YORK-50A | YORK-50A | EDINBURGH(SM)-64A | 10/53: YORK-50A |
| Jan-55 | FERRYHILL-61B | YORK-50A | YORK-50A | YORK-50A | YORK-50A | YORK-50A | YORK-50A | EDINBURGH(SM)-64A | YORK-50A |
| Aug-55 | FERRYHILL-61B | YORK-50A | YORK-50A | YORK-50A | YORK-50A | YORK-50A | YORK-50A | EDINBURGH(SM)-64A | YORK-50A |
| Jan-56 | FERRYHILL-61B | YORK-50A | YORK-50A | YORK-50A | YORK-50A | YORK-50A | YORK-50A | EDINBURGH(SM)-64A | YORK-50A |
| Aug-56 | FERRYHILL-61B | YORK-50A | YORK-50A | YORK-50A | YORK-50A | 6/56: HTN-52B | 6/56: HTN-52B | EDINBURGH(SM)-64A | YORK-50A |
| Jan-57 | FERRYHILL-61B | YORK-50A | YORK-50A | YORK-50A | YORK-50A | HEATON-52B | HEATON-52B | EDINBURGH(SM)-64A | YORK-50A |
| Aug-57 | FERRYHILL-61B | YORK-50A | YORK-50A | YORK-50A | YORK-50A | HEATON-52B | HEATON-52B | EDINBURGH(SM)-64A | YORK-50A |
| Jan-58 | FERRYHILL-61B | YORK-50A | YORK-50A | YORK-50A | YORK-50A | HEATON-52B | HEATON-52B | EDINBURGH(SM)-64A | YORK-50A |
| Aug-58 | FERRYHILL-61B | YORK-50A | YORK-50A | 6/58: C.HILL-56C | YORK-50A | HEATON-52B | 7/58: GHD-52A | EDINBURGH(SM)-64A | YORK-50A |
| Jan-59 | FERRYHILL-61B | YORK-50A | YORK-50A | 9/58: HTN-52B | YORK-50A | HEATON-52B | GATESHEAD-52A | EDINBURGH(SM)-64A | YORK-50A |
| Aug-59 | FERRYHILL-61B | YORK-50A | YORK-50A | HEATON-52B | YORK-50A | HEATON-52B | GATESHEAD-52A | EDINBURGH(SM)-64A | YORK-50A |
| Nov-59 | FERRYHILL-61B | YORK-50A | YORK-50A | HEATON-52B | YORK-50A | HEATON-52B | GATESHEAD-52A | EDINBURGH(SM)-64A | YORK-50A |
| Jan-60 | FERRYHILL-61B | YORK-50A | YORK-50A | HEATON-52B | YORK-50A | HEATON-52B | GATESHEAD-52A | EDINBURGH(SM)-64A | YORK-50A |
| Apr-60 | FERRYHILL-61B | YORK-50A | YORK-50A | HEATON-52B | YORK-50A | HEATON-52B | GATESHEAD-52A | EDINBURGH(SM)-64A | YORK-50A |
| Aug-60 | 6/60: PERTH-63A | YORK-50A | YORK-50A | HEATON-52B | YORK-50A | HEATON-52B | GATESHEAD-52A | EDINBURGH(SM)-64A | YORK-50A |
| Nov-60 | PERTH-63A | YORK-50A | YORK-50A | HEATON-52B | YORK-50A | HEATON-52B | GATESHEAD-52A | EDINBURGH(SM)-64A | YORK-50A |

| | 60982 | 60983 | B1 4-6-0 (1942) 61000 | 61001 | 61002 | 61003 | 61004 | 61005 | 61006 |
|---|---|---|---|---|---|---|---|---|---|
| Aug-50 | YORK-50A | KINGS CROSS-34A | STRATFORD-30A | STRATFORD-30A | EDINBURGH(SM)-64A | PARKESTON-30F | PARKESTON-30F | PARKESTON-30F | PARKESTON-30F |
| Jan-51 | YORK-50A | KINGS CROSS-34A | STRATFORD-30A | STRATFORD-30A | 3/51: DAL RD-64C | PARKESTON-30F | PARKESTON-30F | PARKESTON-30F | PARKESTON-30F |
| Aug-51 | YORK-50A | KINGS CROSS-34A | STRATFORD-30A | STRATFORD-30A | 9/51: DARL-51A | PARKESTON-30F | PARKESTON-30F | PARKESTON-30F | PARKESTON-30F |
| Jan-52 | YORK-50A | KINGS CROSS-34A | STRATFORD-30A | STRATFORD-30A | 11/51: YORK-50A | PARKESTON-30F | PARKESTON-30F | PARKESTON-30F | PARKESTON-30F |
| Aug-52 | YORK-50A | KINGS CROSS-34A | STRATFORD-30A | 7/52: NEAS-34E | YORK-50A | PARKESTON-30F | PARKESTON-30F | PARKESTON-30F | PARKESTON-30F |
| Jan-53 | YORK-50A | KINGS CROSS-34A | STRATFORD-30A | NEASDEN-34E | YORK-50A | PARKESTON-30F | PARKESTON-30F | PARKESTON-30F | PARKESTON-30F |
| Aug-53 | 7/53: DARL-51A | KINGS CROSS-34A | STRATFORD-30A | NEASDEN-34E | YORK-50A | PARKESTON-30F | PARKESTON-30F | PARKESTON-30F | PARKESTON-30F |
| Jan-54 | 10/53: YORK-50A | KINGS CROSS-34A | STRATFORD-30A | NEASDEN-34E | YORK-50A | PARKESTON-30F | PARKESTON-30F | PARKESTON-30F | PARKESTON-30F |
| Aug-54 | YORK-50A | KINGS CROSS-34A | STRATFORD-30A | NEASDEN-34E | YORK-50A | PARKESTON-30F | PARKESTON-30F | PARKESTON-30F | PARKESTON-30F |
| Jan-55 | YORK-50A | KINGS CROSS-34A | STRATFORD-30A | NEASDEN-34E | YORK-50A | PARKESTON-30F | PARKESTON-30F | PARKESTON-30F | PARKESTON-30F |
| Aug-55 | YORK-50A | KINGS CROSS-34A | STRATFORD-30A | NEASDEN-34E | YORK-50A | PARKESTON-30F | PARKESTON-30F | PARKESTON-30F | PARKESTON-30F |
| Jan-56 | YORK-50A | KINGS CROSS-34A | STRATFORD-30A | NEASDEN-34E | YORK-50A | PARKESTON-30F | PARKESTON-30F | PARKESTON-30F | PARKESTON-30F |
| Aug-56 | YORK-50A | KINGS CROSS-34A | STRATFORD-30A | NEASDEN-34E | YORK-50A | PARKESTON-30F | PARKESTON-30F | 10/56: NEWE-35A | 10/56: NEWE-35A |
| Jan-57 | YORK-50A | KINGS CROSS-34A | 2/57: COL-30E | 2/57: COL-30E | YORK-50A | PARKESTON-30F | PARKESTON-30F | 2/57: S.BGE-35C | 2/57: S.BGE-35C |
| Aug-57 | YORK-50A | KINGS CROSS-34A | COLCHESTER-30E | 3/57: IPS-32B | YORK-50A | PARKESTON-30F | PARKESTON-30F | 6/57: STRAT-30A | 6/57: STRAT-30A |
| Jan-58 | YORK-50A | KINGS CROSS-34A | COLCHESTER-30E | IPSWICH-32B | YORK-50A | PARKESTON-30F | PARKESTON-30F | STRATFORD-30A | STRATFORD-30A |
| Aug-58 | YORK-50A | KINGS CROSS-34A | COLCHESTER-30E | IPSWICH-32B | YORK-50A | PARKESTON-30F | 3/58: STRAT-30A | STRATFORD-30A | STRATFORD-30A |
| Jan-59 | YORK-50A | KINGS CROSS-34A | COLCHESTER-30E | IPSWICH-32B | YORK-50A | PARKESTON-30F | 4/58: PARK-30F | 1/59: PARK-30F | 1/59: PARK-30F |
| Aug-59 | YORK-50A | KINGS CROSS-34A | COLCHESTER-30E | 9/59: NORW-32A | YORK-50A | PARKESTON-30F | PARKESTON-30F | PARKESTON-30F | PARKESTON-30F |
| Nov-59 | YORK-50A | KINGS CROSS-34A | 10/59: MARCH-31B | 12/59: DCTR-36A | YORK-50A | 10/59: MARCH-31B | 11/59: DCTR-36A | 10/59: MARCH-31B | 10/59: MARCH-31B |
| Jan-60 | YORK-50A | KINGS CROSS-34A | 12/59: DCTR-36A | DONCASTER-36A | YORK-50A | 12/59: DCTR-36A | 1/60: DARN-41A | MARCH-31B | MARCH-31B |
| Apr-60 | YORK-50A | KINGS CROSS-34A | DONCASTER-36A | DONCASTER-36A | YORK-50A | DONCASTER-36A | DARNALL-41A | MARCH-31B | MARCH-31B |
| Aug-60 | YORK-50A | KINGS CROSS-34A | 6/60: CLWK-40E | DONCASTER-36A | YORK-50A | DONCASTER-36A | DARNALL-41A | MARCH-31B | MARCH-31B |
| Nov-60 | YORK-50A | KINGS CROSS-34A | COLWICK-40E | DONCASTER-36A | YORK-50A | DONCASTER-36A | DARNALL-41A | MARCH-31B | MARCH-31B |

Unlike the rest of the country where the 4-6-0 was virtually the standard wheel arrangement for most main line traffic, the type had a relatively limited use on the ER especially on the Great Northern section where services were handled by Pacifics at one extreme and by 2-6-4 or 0-6-2 tanks at the other. The few G.N. gaps which remained for 4-6-0's consisted of Cambridge and Baldock services for which a handful of B1 engines were provided; the Cambridge-based workings sometimes being worked by B17 or B2 4-6-0's. Between Hitchin and Doncaster appearances by 4-6-0's were generally confined to connecting services although two services in each direction between Kings Cross and Cleethorpes were booked to a pair of Immingham B1 4-6-0's. It is interesting to note that after allowing for the fact that most of the Doncaster and Colwick B1's worked over the Great Central section, the number of the class allocated to GN services was, at about fifty, numerically the smallest of any Eastern Region component.

| | 61007 | 61008 | 61009 | 61010 | 61011 | 61012 | 61013 | 61014 | 61015 |
|---|---|---|---|---|---|---|---|---|---|
| Aug-50 | HAYMARKET-64B | STRATFORD-30A | STRATFORD-30A | BOTANIC GARDENS-53B | GATESHEAD-52A | GATESHEAD-52A | GATESHEAD-52A | GATESHEAD-52A | YORK-50A |
| Jan-51 | HAYMARKET-64B | STRATFORD-30A | STRATFORD-30A | BOTANIC GARDENS-53B | GATESHEAD-52A | GATESHEAD-52A | GATESHEAD-52A | GATESHEAD-52A | YORK-50A |
| Aug-51 | HAYMARKET-64B | STRATFORD-30A | STRATFORD-30A | BOTANIC GARDENS-53B | GATESHEAD-52A | GATESHEAD-52A | GATESHEAD-52A | GATESHEAD-52A | YORK-50A |
| Jan-52 | HAYMARKET-64B | STRATFORD-30A | STRATFORD-30A | BOTANIC GARDENS-53B | GATESHEAD-52A | GATESHEAD-52A | GATESHEAD-52A | GATESHEAD-52A | YORK-50A |
| Aug-52 | HAYMARKET-64B | STRATFORD-30A | 7/52: NEAS-34E | BOTANIC GARDENS-53B | GATESHEAD-52A | GATESHEAD-52A | GATESHEAD-52A | GATESHEAD-52A | YORK-50A |
| Jan-53 | HAYMARKET-64B | STRATFORD-30A | NEASDEN-34E | BOTANIC GARDENS-53B | GATESHEAD-52A | GATESHEAD-52A | GATESHEAD-52A | GATESHEAD-52A | YORK-50A |
| Aug-53 | HAYMARKET-64B | STRATFORD-30A | NEASDEN-34E | BOTANIC GARDENS-53B | GATESHEAD-52A | GATESHEAD-52A | GATESHEAD-52A | GATESHEAD-52A | YORK-50A |
| Jan-54 | HAYMARKET-64B | STRATFORD-30A | NEASDEN-34E | BOTANIC GARDENS-53B | GATESHEAD-52A | GATESHEAD-52A | GATESHEAD-52A | 1/54: TWEED-52D | 11/53: N.HILL-50B |
| Aug-54 | HAYMARKET-64B | STRATFORD-30A | 8/54: LEIC-38C | BOTANIC GARDENS-53B | GATESHEAD-52A | GATESHEAD-52A | GATESHEAD-52A | TWEEDMOUTH-52D | 2/54: YORK-50A |
| Jan-55 | HAYMARKET-64B | STRATFORD-30A | 12/54: NEAS-34E | BOTANIC GARDENS-53B | GATESHEAD-52A | GATESHEAD-52A | GATESHEAD-52A | TWEEDMOUTH-52D | YORK-50A |
| Aug-55 | HAYMARKET-64B | STRATFORD-30A | NEASDEN-34E | BOTANIC GARDENS-53B | GATESHEAD-52A | GATESHEAD-52A | GATESHEAD-52A | TWEEDMOUTH-52D | 9/55: DARL-51A |
| Jan-56 | HAYMARKET-64B | STRATFORD-30A | NEASDEN-34E | BOTANIC GARDENS-53B | GATESHEAD-52A | GATESHEAD-52A | GATESHEAD-52A | TWEEDMOUTH-52D | DARLINGTON-51A |
| Aug-56 | HAYMARKET-64B | 6/56: LEIC-38C | 6/56: DARN-41A | BOTANIC GARDENS-53B | 10/56: ARDS-56B | GATESHEAD-52A | 10/56: ARDS-56B | TWEEDMOUTH-52D | DARLINGTON-51A |
| Jan-57 | HAYMARKET-64B | LEICESTER (GC)-38C | DARNALL-41A | BOTANIC GARDENS-53B | ARDSLEY-56B | GATESHEAD-52A | ARDSLEY-56B | TWEEDMOUTH-52D | DARLINGTON-51A |
| Aug-57 | HAYMARKET-64B | LEICESTER (GC)-38C | 10/57: DCTR-36A | BOTANIC GARDENS-53B | ARDSLEY-56B | GATESHEAD-52A | ARDSLEY-56B | TWEEDMOUTH-52D | DARLINGTON-51A |
| Jan-58 | HAYMARKET-64B | LEICESTER (GC)-38C | 11/57: LINC-40A | BOTANIC GARDENS-53B | ARDSLEY-56B | GATESHEAD-52A | ARDSLEY-56B | TWEEDMOUTH-52D | 6/58: WAKE-56A |
| Aug-58 | HAYMARKET-64B | LEICESTER (GC)-15E | LINCOLN-40A | BOTANIC GARDENS-53B | ARDSLEY-56B | GATESHEAD-52A | ARDSLEY-56B | TWEEDMOUTH-52D | WAKEFIELD-56A |
| Jan-59 | HAYMARKET-64B | LEICESTER (GC)-15E | LINCOLN-40A | BOTANIC GARDENS-53B | 2/59: WAKE-56A | GATESHEAD-52A | ARDSLEY-56B | TWEEDMOUTH-52D | WAKEFIELD-56A |
| Aug-59 | HAYMARKET-64B | 9/59: AGE-26B | LINCOLN-40A | 6/59: DYCTS-53A | 4/59: MIRF-56D | GATESHEAD-52A | ARDSLEY-56B | 6/59: GHD-52A | WAKEFIELD-56A |
| Nov-59 | HAYMARKET-64B | AGECROFT-26B | LINCOLN-40A | DAIRYCOATES-53A | MIRFIELD-56D | GATESHEAD-52A | ARDSLEY-56B | GATESHEAD-52A | WAKEFIELD-56A |
| Jan-60 | HAYMARKET-64B | AGECROFT-26B | LINCOLN-40A | DAIRYCOATES-53A | MIRFIELD-56D | GATESHEAD-52A | ARDSLEY-56B | GATESHEAD-52A | WAKEFIELD-56A |
| Apr-60 | HAYMARKET-64B | AGECROFT-26B | LINCOLN-40A | DAIRYCOATES-50B | MIRFIELD-56D | GATESHEAD-52A | ARDSLEY-56B | GATESHEAD-52A | WAKEFIELD-56A |
| Aug-60 | 7/60: DAL RD-64C | AGECROFT-26B | LINCOLN-40A | DAIRYCOATES-50B | 7/60: GORT-9G | 8/60: DYCTS-50B | ARDSLEY-56B | GATESHEAD-52A | WAKEFIELD-56A |
| Nov-60 | DALRY ROAD-64C | AGECROFT-26B | LINCOLN-40A | DAIRYCOATES-50B | GORTON-9G | DAIRYCOATES-50B | ARDSLEY-56B | GATESHEAD-52A | WAKEFIELD-56A |

| | 61016 | 61017 | 61018 | 61019 | 61020 | 61021 | 61022 | 61023 | 61024 |
|---|---|---|---|---|---|---|---|---|---|
| Aug-50 | YORK-50A | STOCKTON-51E | STOCKTON-51E | TWEEDMOUTH-52D | YORK-50A | DARLINGTON-51A | DARLINGTON-51A | DARLINGTON-51A | TWEEDMOUTH-52D |
| Jan-51 | YORK-50A | STOCKTON-51E | STOCKTON-51E | TWEEDMOUTH-52D | YORK-50A | DARLINGTON-51A | DARLINGTON-51A | DARLINGTON-51A | TWEEDMOUTH-52D |
| Aug-51 | YORK-50A | STOCKTON-51E | STOCKTON-51E | TWEEDMOUTH-52D | YORK-50A | DARLINGTON-51A | DARLINGTON-51A | 7/51: GHD-52A | 9/51: DAR-51A |
| Jan-52 | YORK-50A | STOCKTON-51E | STOCKTON-51E | TWEEDMOUTH-52D | YORK-50A | DARLINGTON-51A | DARLINGTON-51A | DARLINGTON-51A | DARLINGTON-51A |
| Aug-52 | YORK-50A | STOCKTON-51E | STOCKTON-51E | TWEEDMOUTH-52D | YORK-50A | 7/52: GHD-52A | 7/52: YORK-50A | 7/52: GHD-52A | 7/52: YORK-50A |
| Jan-53 | YORK-50A | STOCKTON-51E | STOCKTON-51E | TWEEDMOUTH-52D | YORK-50A | 10/52: DARL-51A | 10/52: DARL-51A | 10/52: DARL-51A | 10/52: DARL-51A |
| Aug-53 | YORK-50A | 8/53: N.HILL-50B | STOCKTON-51E | TWEEDMOUTH-52D | 11/53: N.HILL-50B | DARLINGTON-51A | DARLINGTON-51A | DARLINGTON-51A | DARLINGTON-51A |
| Jan-54 | YORK-50A | NEVILLE HILL-50B | STOCKTON-51E | 1/54: GHD-52A | 2/54: YORK-50A | DARLINGTON-51A | GATESHEAD-52A | DARLINGTON-51A | DARLINGTON-51A |
| Aug-54 | YORK-50A | NEVILLE HILL-50B | STOCKTON-51E | GATESHEAD-52A | YORK-50A | DARLINGTON-51A | GATESHEAD-52A | DARLINGTON-51A | DARLINGTON-51A |
| Jan-55 | YORK-50A | NEVILLE HILL-50B | STOCKTON-51E | GATESHEAD-52A | YORK-50A | DARLINGTON-51A | GATESHEAD-52A | DARLINGTON-51A | DARLINGTON-51A |
| Aug-55 | YORK-50A | NEVILLE HILL-50B | STOCKTON-51E | GATESHEAD-52A | 9/55: DARL-51A | 6/55: YORK-50A | GATESHEAD-52A | 6/55: YORK-50A | DARLINGTON-51A |
| Jan-56 | YORK-50A | 11/55: YORK-50A | STOCKTON-51E | GATESHEAD-52A | DARLINGTON-51A | 9/55: DARL-51A | GATESHEAD-52A | 9/55: DARL-51A | DARLINGTON-51A |
| Aug-56 | YORK-50A | YORK-50A | STOCKTON-51E | GATESHEAD-52A | DARLINGTON-51A | DARLINGTON-51A | GATESHEAD-52A | DARLINGTON-51A | DARLINGTON-51A |
| Jan-57 | YORK-50A | YORK-50A | STOCKTON-51E | 2/57: BLAY-52C | DARLINGTON-51A | DARLINGTON-51A | GATESHEAD-52A | DARLINGTON-51A | DARLINGTON-51A |
| Aug-57 | 5/57: N.HILL-50B | YORK-50A | STOCKTON-51E | BLAYDON-52C | DARLINGTON-51A | DARLINGTON-51A | GATESHEAD-52A | DARLINGTON-51A | DARLINGTON-51A |
| Jan-58 | NEVILLE HILL-50B | YORK-50A | STOCKTON-51E | BLAYDON-52C | DARLINGTON-51A | DARLINGTON-51A | GATESHEAD-52A | DARLINGTON-51A | DARLINGTON-51A |
| Aug-58 | NEVILLE HILL-50B | 6/58: C.HILL-56C | 6/58: H.HILL-51G | BLAYDON-52C | 6/58: LOW M-56F | 6/58: H.HILL-51G | GATESHEAD-52A | 6/58: LOW M-56F | 6/58: H.HILL-51G |
| Jan-59 | NEVILLE HILL-50B | 2/59: WAKE-56A | HAVERTON HILL-51G | BLAYDON-52C | LOWMOOR-56F | HAVERTON HILL-51G | GATESHEAD-52A | LOWMOOR-56F | HAVERTON HILL-51G |
| Aug-59 | NEVILLE HILL-50B | WAKEFIELD-56A | 6/59: TNBY-51L | BLAYDON-52C | LOWMOOR-56F | 6/59: TNBY-51L | GATESHEAD-52A | LOWMOOR-56F | 6/59: TNBY-51L |
| Nov-59 | NEVILLE HILL-50B | WAKEFIELD-56A | 9/59: DAR-51A | 10/59: GHD-52A | 11/59: WAKE-56A | 9/59: DAR-51A | GATESHEAD-52A | 11/59: ARDS-56B | 9/59: DAR-51A |
| Jan-60 | NEVILLE HILL-50B | WAKEFIELD-56A | DARLINGTON-51A | GATESHEAD-52A | WAKEFIELD-56A | DARLINGTON-51A | GATESHEAD-52A | ARDSLEY-56B | DARLINGTON-51A |
| Apr-60 | NEVILLE HILL-55H | WAKEFIELD-56A | 6/60: WAKE-56A | GATESHEAD-52A | WAKEFIELD-56A | 6/60: WAKE-56A | GATESHEAD-52A | ARDSLEY-56B | 6/60: WAKE-56A |
| Aug-60 | NEVILLE HILL-55H | WAKEFIELD-56A | 8/60: YORK-50A | GATESHEAD-52A | 9/60: YORK-50A | 8/60: YORK-50A | GATESHEAD-52A | ARDSLEY-56B | WAKEFIELD-56A |
| Nov-60 | NEVILLE HILL-55H | WAKEFIELD-56A | YORK-50A | GATESHEAD-52A | YORK-50A | YORK-50A | GATESHEAD-52A | ARDSLEY-56B | WAKEFIELD-56A |

| | 61025 | 61026 | 61027 | 61028 | 61029 | 61030 | 61031 | 61032 | 61033 |
|---|---|---|---|---|---|---|---|---|---|
| Aug-50 | TWEEDMOUTH-52D | DONCASTER-36A | NEWENGLAND-35A | NEASDEN-34E | ARDSLEY-37A | STOCKTON-51E | ARDSLEY-37A | STOCKTON-51E | ARDSLEY-37A |
| Jan-51 | TWEEDMOUTH-52D | DONCASTER-36A | NEWENGLAND-35A | NEASDEN-34E | 9/50: C.HILL-37B | STOCKTON-51E | ARDSLEY-37A | STOCKTON-51E | 10/50: C.HILL-37B |
| Aug-51 | TWEEDMOUTH-52D | DONCASTER-36A | NEWENGLAND-35A | NEASDEN-34E | 2/51: ARDS-37A | STOCKTON-51E | 5/51: BRAD-37C | STOCKTON-51E | COPLEYHILL-37B |
| Jan-52 | TWEEDMOUTH-52D | DONCASTER-36A | NEWENGLAND-35A | NEASDEN-34E | 12/51: DARN-39B | STOCKTON-51E | BRADFORD-37C | STOCKTON-51E | 2/52: ARDS-37A |
| Aug-52 | TWEEDMOUTH-52D | DONCASTER-36A | NEWENGLAND-35A | NEASDEN-34E | DARNALL-39B | STOCKTON-51E | BRADFORD-37C | STOCKTON-51E | 9/52: STRAT-30A |
| Jan-53 | TWEEDMOUTH-52D | DONCASTER-36A | 5/53: HITCH-34D | NEASDEN-34E | DARNALL-39B | STOCKTON-51E | BRADFORD-37C | STOCKTON-51E | 10/52: COLW-38A |
| Aug-53 | TWEEDMOUTH-52D | DONCASTER-36A | HITCHIN-34D | NEASDEN-34E | 9/53: STM-64A | STOCKTON-51E | BRADFORD-37C | STOCKTON-51E | COLWICK-38A |
| Jan-54 | TWEEDMOUTH-52D | DONCASTER-36A | HITCHIN-34D | NEASDEN-34E | EDINBURGH (SM)-64A | STOCKTON-51E | BRADFORD-37C | STOCKTON-51E | COLWICK-38A |
| Aug-54 | TWEEDMOUTH-52D | DONCASTER-36A | HITCHIN-34D | 6/54: LEIC-38C | EDINBURGH (SM)-64A | STOCKTON-51E | BRADFORD-37C | STOCKTON-51E | COLWICK-38A |
| Jan-55 | TWEEDMOUTH-52D | DONCASTER-36A | HITCHIN-34D | 12/54: NEAS-34E | EDINBURGH (SM)-64A | STOCKTON-51E | BRADFORD-37C | STOCKTON-51E | 11/54: CAMB-31A |
| Aug-55 | TWEEDMOUTH-52D | DONCASTER-36A | HITCHIN-34D | NEASDEN-34E | EDINBURGH (SM)-64A | STOCKTON-51E | BRADFORD-37C | STOCKTON-51E | CAMBRIDGE-31A |
| Jan-56 | TWEEDMOUTH-52D | DONCASTER-36A | HITCHIN-34D | NEASDEN-34E | EDINBURGH (SM)-64A | STOCKTON-51E | BRADFORD-37C | STOCKTON-51E | CAMBRIDGE-31A |
| Aug-56 | TWEEDMOUTH-52D | DONCASTER-36A | HITCHIN-34D | NEASDEN-34E | EDINBURGH (SM)-64A | STOCKTON-51E | BRADFORD-56G | STOCKTON-51E | CAMBRIDGE-31A |
| Jan-57 | TWEEDMOUTH-52D | DONCASTER-36A | HITCHIN-34D | NEASDEN-34E | EDINBURGH (SM)-64A | STOCKTON-51E | BRADFORD-56G | STOCKTON-51E | 11/56: DARN-41A |
| Aug-57 | TWEEDMOUTH-52D | DONCASTER-36A | HITCHIN-34D | NEASDEN-34E | EDINBURGH (SM)-64A | STOCKTON-51E | BRADFORD-56G | STOCKTON-51E | DARNALL-41A |
| Jan-58 | TWEEDMOUTH-52D | 11/57: LINC-40A | HITCHIN-34D | NEASDEN-34E | EDINBURGH (SM)-64A | STOCKTON-51E | 1/58: LOW M-56F | STOCKTON-51E | DARNALL-41A |
| Aug-58 | TWEEDMOUTH-52D | LINCOLN-40A | HITCHIN-34D | NEASDEN-14D | EDINBURGH (SM)-64A | STOCKTON-51E | 9/58: DAR-51A | STOCKTON-51E | DARNALL-41A |
| Jan-59 | TWEEDMOUTH-52D | LINCOLN-40A | HITCHIN-34D | 2/59: LEIC-15E | EDINBURGH (SM)-64A | STOCKTON-51E | 12/58: TNBY-51L | STOCKTON-51E | DARNALL-41A |
| Aug-59 | TWEEDMOUTH-52D | LINCOLN-40A | 6/59: DARN-41A | 6/59: WOOD-2F | EDINBURGH (SM)-64A | 6/59: TNBY-51L | THORNABY-51L | 9/59: TNBY-51L | DARNALL-41A |
| Nov-59 | TWEEDMOUTH-52D | 12/59: IMM-40B | DARNALL-41A | WOODFORD HALSE-2F | EDINBURGH (SM)-64A | 9/59: DARL-51A | THORNABY-51L | 9/59: DARL-51A | DARNALL-41A |
| Jan-60 | TWEEDMOUTH-52D | IMMINGHAM-40B | DARNALL-41A | WOODFORD HALSE-2F | EDINBURGH (SM)-64A | DARLINGTON-51A | THORNABY-51L | DARLINGTON-51A | DARNALL-41A |
| Apr-60 | 6/60: BLAY-52C | 3/60: LINC-40A | DARNALL-41A | WOODFORD HALSE-2F | EDINBURGH (SM)-64A | DARLINGTON-51A | THORNABY-51L | DARLINGTON-51A | DARNALL-41A |
| Aug-60 | BLAYDON-52C | LINCOLN-40A | DARNALL-41A | WOODFORD HALSE-2F | EDINBURGH (SM)-64A | DARLINGTON-51A | 9/60: YORK-50A | DARLINGTON-51A | DARNALL-41A |
| Nov-60 | BLAYDON-52C | LINCOLN-40A | DARNALL-41A | WOODFORD HALSE-2F | EDINBURGH (SM)-64A | DARLINGTON-51A | YORK-50A | DARLINGTON-51A | DARNALL-41A |

| | 61034 | 61035 | 61036 | 61037 | 61038 | 61039 | 61040 | 61041 | 61042 |
|---|---|---|---|---|---|---|---|---|---|
| Aug-50 | STOCKTON-51E | NEVILLE HILL-50B | DONCASTER-36A | STOCKTON-51E | YORK-50A | DARLINGTON-51A | NORWICH-32A | NORWICH-32A | NORWICH-32A |
| Jan-51 | STOCKTON-51E | NEVILLE HILL-50B | DONCASTER-36A | STOCKTON-51E | YORK-50A | DARLINGTON-51A | NORWICH-32A | NORWICH-32A | NORWICH-32A |
| Aug-51 | STOCKTON-51E | NEVILLE HILL-50B | DONCASTER-36A | STOCKTON-51E | YORK-50A | DARLINGTON-51A | 9/51: DAR-51A | NORWICH-32A | NORWICH-32A |
| Jan-52 | STOCKTON-51E | NEVILLE HILL-50B | DONCASTER-36A | STOCKTON-51E | YORK-50A | DARLINGTON-51A | DARLINGTON-51A | NORWICH-32A | NORWICH-32A |
| Aug-52 | STOCKTON-51E | NEVILLE HILL-50B | DONCASTER-36A | STOCKTON-51E | YORK-50A | 7/52: YORK-50A | 7/52: YORK-50A | NORWICH-32A | NORWICH-32A |
| Jan-53 | STOCKTON-51E | NEVILLE HILL-50B | DONCASTER-36A | STOCKTON-51E | YORK-50A | 10/52: DAR-51A | 10/52: DAR-51A | NORWICH-32A | NORWICH-32A |
| Aug-53 | STOCKTON-51E | NEVILLE HILL-50B | DONCASTER-36A | STOCKTON-51E | YORK-50A | DARLINGTON-51A | DARLINGTON-51A | 7/53: DARN-39B | NORWICH-32A |
| Jan-54 | STOCKTON-51E | NEVILLE HILL-50B | DONCASTER-36A | STOCKTON-51E | YORK-50A | DARLINGTON-51A | DARLINGTON-51A | DARNALL-39B | NORWICH-32A |
| Aug-54 | STOCKTON-51E | NEVILLE HILL-50B | DONCASTER-36A | STOCKTON-51E | YORK-50A | DARLINGTON-51A | DARLINGTON-51A | DARNALL-39B | NORWICH-32A |
| Jan-55 | STOCKTON-51E | NEVILLE HILL-50B | DONCASTER-36A | STOCKTON-51E | YORK-50A | DARLINGTON-51A | DARLINGTON-51A | DARNALL-39B | NORWICH-32A |
| Aug-55 | STOCKTON-51E | NEVILLE HILL-50B | DONCASTER-36A | STOCKTON-51E | YORK-50A | DARLINGTON-51A | DARLINGTON-51A | DARNALL-41A | NORWICH-32A |
| Jan-56 | STOCKTON-51E | NEVILLE HILL-50B | DONCASTER-36A | STOCKTON-51E | YORK-50A | DARLINGTON-51A | DARLINGTON-51A | DARNALL-41A | NORWICH-32A |
| Aug-56 | STOCKTON-51E | NEVILLE HILL-50B | DONCASTER-36A | STOCKTON-51E | YORK-50A | DARLINGTON-51A | DARLINGTON-51A | DARNALL-41A | NORWICH-32A |
| Jan-57 | STOCKTON-51E | NEVILLE HILL-50B | DONCASTER-36A | STOCKTON-51E | YORK-50A | DARLINGTON-51A | DARLINGTON-51A | DARNALL-41A | 2/57: YAR (ST)-32D |
| Aug-57 | STOCKTON-51E | NEVILLE HILL-50B | DONCASTER-36A | STOCKTON-51E | 5/57: N.HILL-50B | DARLINGTON-51A | DARLINGTON-51A | DARNALL-41A | 3/57: NORW-32A |
| Jan-58 | STOCKTON-51E | NEVILLE HILL-50B | DONCASTER-36A | STOCKTON-51E | NEVILLE HILL-50B | DARLINGTON-51A | DARLINGTON-51A | DARNALL-41A | NORWICH-32A |
| Aug-58 | STOCKTON-51E | NEVILLE HILL-50B | DONCASTER-36A | 6/58: H.HILL-51G | NEVILLE HILL-50B | 6/58: LOW M-56F | 6/58: LOW M-56F | DARNALL-41A | NORWICH-32A |
| Jan-59 | STOCKTON-51E | NEVILLE HILL-50B | DONCASTER-36A | HAVERTON HILL-51G | NEVILLE HILL-50B | LOWMOOR-56F | 3/59: WAKE-56A | DARNALL-41A | NORWICH-32A |
| Aug-59 | 6/59: TNBY-51L | NEVILLE HILL-50B | DONCASTER-36A | 6/59: TNBY-51L | NEVILLE HILL-50B | LOWMOOR-56F | 4/59@ MIRF-56D | DARNALL-41A | NORWICH-32A |
| Nov-59 | THORNABY-51L | NEVILLE HILL-50B | DONCASTER-36A | THORNABY-51L | NEVILLE HILL-50B | 11/59: ARDS-56B | MIRFIELD-56D | DARNALL-41A | 12/59: MARCH-31B |
| Jan-60 | THORNABY-51L | NEVILLE HILL-50B | DONCASTER-36A | THORNABY-51L | NEVILLE HILL-50B | ARDSLEY-56B | MIRFIELD-56D | DARNALL-41A | MARCH-31B |
| Apr-60 | THORNABY-51L | NEVILLE HILL-50B | DONCASTER-36A | THORNABY-51L | NEVILLE HILL-55H | ARDSLEY-56B | MIRFIELD-56D | DARNALL-41A | 3/60: LINC-40A |
| Aug-60 | THORNABY-51L | NEVILLE HILL-55H | DONCASTER-36A | 9/60: DAR-51A | NEVILLE HILL-55H | 9/60: YORK-50A | MIRFIELD-56D | DARNALL-41A | LINCOLN-40A |
| Nov-60 | THORNABY-51L | NEVILLE HILL-55H | DONCASTER-36A | DARLINGTON-51A | NEVILLE HILL-55H | YORK-50A | MIRFIELD-56D | DARNALL-41A | LINCOLN-40A |

For a brief period between their introduction and the arrival of Britannia Pacifics, B1's were the principal engines on the Great Eastern and although they were displaced very quickly from the Norwich expresses, over sixty of the class remained on the district working in consort with the B2, B17 and B12's where from the timing point of view, no distinction was drawn between any of the 4-6-0 classes. On the Lea Valley route for example the nine coach non-stop booking from Liverpool Street to Cambridge was sixty-eight minutes for a 4-6-0 as against only four minutes less for a Britannia. With a heavier twelve coach service the bookings were seventy-three minutes for a B1, B2 or B17 and sixty-six for a Pacific.

Perhaps the most grateful recipient of the B1 4-6-0's was the Great Central which saw in them the first new engines it had had in significant numbers for many years. Over eighty of the class were allocated to GC sheds – notably Darnall and Immingham – with many of the thirty Doncaster engines being

| Aug-50 | 61043 | 61044 | 61045 | 61046 | 61047 | 61048 | 61049 | 61050 | 61051 |
|---|---|---|---|---|---|---|---|---|---|
| Aug-50 | NORWICH-32A | NORWCH-32A | NORWICH-32A | NORWICH-32A | NORWICH-32A | NORWICH-32A | NORWICH-32A | NORWCH-32A | NORWICH-32A |
| Jan-51 | NORWCH-32A | NORWCH-32A | NORWICH-32A | NORWICH-32A | 5/51: LINC-40A | NORWICH-32A | NORWICH-32A | NORWCH-32A | NORWICH-32A |
| Aug-51 | NORWICH-32A | NORWCH-32A | NORWICH-32A | NORWICH-32A | 6/51: NORW-32A | NORWICH-32A | 9/51: DARL-51A | 5/51: ARDS-37A | 5/51: ARDS-37A |
| Jan-52 | NORWCH-32A | NORWCH-32A | NORWICH-32A | NORWICH-32A | NORWICH-32A | NORWICH-32A | DARLINGTON-51A | 10/51: NORW-32A | 12/51: NORW-32A |
| Aug-52 | NORWCH-32A | NORWCH-32A | NORWICH-32A | NORWICH-32A | NORWICH-32A | NORWICH-32A | DARLINGTON-51A | NORWCH-32A | NORWCH-32A |
| Jan-53 | NORWCH-32A | NORWCH-32A | NORWICH-32A | NORWICH-32A | NORWICH-32A | NORWICH-32A | DARLINGTON-51A | NORWCH-32A | NORWCH-32A |
| Aug-53 | NORWCH-32A | 7/53: DARN-39B | NORWICH-32A | NORWICH-32A | NORWICH-32A | NORWICH-32A | DARLINGTON-51A | NORWCH-32A | NORWCH-32A |
| Jan-54 | NORWICH-32A | DARNALL-39B | NORWICH-32A | NORWICH-32A | 11/53: NEWE-35A | NORWICH-32A | DARLINGTON-51A | NORWCH-32A | NORWCH-32A |
| Aug-54 | NORWICH-32A | DARNALL-39B | NORWICH-32A | NORWICH-32A | NEWENGLAND-35A | NORWICH-32A | DARLINGTON-51A | NORWICH-32A | NORWCH-32A |
| Jan-55 | NORWICH-32A | DARNALL-39B | NORWICH-32A | NORWICH-32A | NEWENGLAND-35A | NORWICH-32A | DARLINGTON-51A | NORWICH-32A | NORWCH-32A |
| Aug-55 | NORWICH-32A | DARNALL-39B | NORWICH-32A | NORWICH-32A | NEWENGLAND-35A | NORWICH-32A | DARLINGTON-51A | NORWICH-32A | NORWCH-32A |
| Jan-56 | NORWICH-32A | DARNALL-41A | NORWICH-32A | NORWICH-32A | 12/55: S.BGE-35C | NORWCH-32A | DARLINGTON-51A | NORWICH-32A | NORWCH-32A |
| Aug-56 | NORWICH-32A | DARNALL-41A | NORWICH-32A | NORWICH-32A | SPITALBGE-35C | NORWCH-32A | DARLINGTON-51A | 6/56: DARN-41A | 6/56: DARN-41A |
| Jan-57 | NORWICH-32A | DARNALL-41A | NORWICH-32A | NORWICH-32A | SPITALBGE-35C | NORWICH-32A | DARLINGTON-51A | DARNALL-41A | DARNALL-41A |
| Aug-57 | NORWICH-32A | DARNALL-41A | NORWICH-32A | NORWICH-32A | SPITALBGE-35C | NORWICH-32A | DARLINGTON-51A | DARNALL-41A | DARNALL-41A |
| Jan-58 | NORWICH-32A | DARNALL-41A | NORWICH-32A | NORWICH-32A | SPITALBGE-31F | NORWICH-32A | DARLINGTON-51A | DARNALL-41A | DARNALL-41A |
| Aug-58 | NORWICH-32A | DARNALL-41A | NORWICH-32A | NORWICH-32A | SPITALBGE-31F | NORWICH-32A | 6/58: LOW M-56F | DARNALL-41A | DARNALL-41A |
| Jan-59 | NORWICH-32A | DARNALL-41A | NORWICH-32A | NORWICH-32A | 12/58: IMM-40B | NORWICH-32A | LOWMOOR-56F | DARNALL-41A | DARNALL-41A |
| Aug-59 | NORWICH-32A | DARNALL-41A | NORWICH-32A | NORWICH-32A | IMMINGHAM-40B | NORWICH-32A | LOWMOOR-56F | DARNALL-41A | DARNALL-41A |
| Nov-59 | NORWICH-32A | DARNALL-41A | NORWICH-32A | NORWICH-32A | IMMINGHAM-40B | NORWICH-32A | 11/59: MIRF-56D | DARNALL-41A | DARNALL-41A |
| Jan-60 | NORWICH-32A | DARNALL-41A | NORWICH-32A | NORWICH-32A | IMMINGHAM-40B | NORWICH-32A | MIRFIELD-56D | DARNALL-41A | DARNALL-41A |
| Apr-60 | NORWICH-32A | DARNALL-41A | NORWICH-32A | NORWICH-32A | IMMINGHAM-40B | NORWICH-32A | MIRFIELD-56D | DARNALL-41A | DARNALL-41A |
| Aug-60 | NORWICH-32A | DARNALL-41A | NORWICH-32A | 6/60: CAMB-31A | IMMINGHAM-40B | 6/60: CAMB-31A | 7/60: YORK-50A | DARNALL-41A | DARNALL-41A |
| Nov-60 | NORWICH-32A | DARNALL-41A | NORWICH-32A | CAMBRIDGE-31A | IMMINGHAM-40B | CAMBRIDGE-31A | YORK-50A | DARNALL-41A | DARNALL-41A |

| | 61052 | 61053 | 61054 | 61055 | 61056 | 61058 | 61059 | 61060 | 61061 |
|---|---|---|---|---|---|---|---|---|---|
| Aug-50 | NORWCH-32A | IPSWICH-32B | IPSWICH-32B | IPSWICH-32B | IPSWICH-32B | IPSWICH-32B | IPSWICH-32B | DAIRYCOATES-53A | EDINBURGH(SM)-64A |
| Jan-51 | 9/50: IPS-32B | IPSWICH-32B | IPSWICH-32B | IPSWICH-32B | IPSWICH-32B | IPSWICH-32B | IPSWICH-32B | DAIRYCOATES-53A | EDINBURGH(SM)-64A |
| Aug-51 | IPSWICH-32B | 9/51: YORK-50A | IPSWICH-32B | IPSWICH-32B | 5/51: ARDS-37A | IPSWICH-32B | IPSWICH-32B | DAIRYCOATES-53A | 9/51: DARL-51A |
| Jan-52 | IPSWICH-32B | YORK-50A | IPSWICH-32B | IPSWICH-32B | 12/51: IPS-32B | IPSWICH-32B | IPSWICH-32B | DAIRYCOATES-53A | DARLINGTON-51A |
| Aug-52 | IPSWICH-32B | YORK-50A | IPSWICH-32B | IPSWICH-32B | 7/52: COLW-38A | IPSWICH-32B | IPSWICH-32B | DAIRYCOATES-53A | DARLINGTON-51A |
| Jan-53 | IPSWICH-32B | YORK-50A | IPSWICH-32B | IPSWICH-32B | COLWICK-38A | IPSWICH-32B | IPSWICH-32B | DAIRYCOATES-53A | DARLINGTON-51A |
| Aug-53 | IPSWICH-32B | YORK-50A | IPSWICH-32B | IPSWICH-32B | COLWICK-38A | IPSWICH-32B | IPSWICH-32B | DAIRYCOATES-53A | DARLINGTON-51A |
| Jan-54 | IPSWICH-32B | YORK-50A | IPSWICH-32B | IPSWICH-32B | COLWICK-38A | IPSWICH-32B | IPSWICH-32B | DAIRYCOATES-53A | DARLINGTON-51A |
| Aug-54 | IPSWICH-32B | YORK-50A | IPSWICH-32B | IPSWICH-32B | COLWICK-38A | IPSWICH-32B | IPSWICH-32B | DAIRYCOATES-53A | DARLINGTON-51A |
| Jan-55 | IPSWICH-32B | YORK-50A | IPSWICH-32B | IPSWICH-32B | COLWICK-38A | IPSWICH-32B | IPSWICH-32B | DAIRYCOATES-53A | DARLINGTON-51A |
| Aug-55 | IPSWICH-32B | YORK-50A | IPSWICH-32B | IPSWICH-32B | COLWICK-38A | IPSWICH-32B | IPSWICH-32B | DAIRYCOATES-53A | DARLINGTON-51A |
| Jan-56 | IPSWICH-32B | YORK-50A | IPSWICH-32B | IPSWICH-32B | COLWICK-38A | IPSWICH-32B | IPSWICH-32B | DAIRYCOATES-53A | DARLINGTON-51A |
| Aug-56 | IPSWICH-32B | YORK-50A | IPSWICH-32B | IPSWICH-32B | COLWICK-38A | IPSWICH-32B | IPSWICH-32B | DAIRYCOATES-53A | DARLINGTON-51A |
| Jan-57 | IPSWICH-32B | YORK-50A | IPSWICH-32B | IPSWICH-32B | COLWICK-38A | IPSWICH-32B | IPSWICH-32B | 3/57: GRAN-35B | DARLINGTON-51A |
| Aug-57 | IPSWICH-32B | YORK-50A | IPSWICH-32B | IPSWICH-32B | 10/57: IPS-32B | IPSWICH-32B | IPSWICH-32B | 10/57: NEWE-35A | DARLINGTON-51A |
| Jan-58 | IPSWICH-32B | YORK-50A | IPSWICH-32B | IPSWICH-32B | IPSWICH-32B | IPSWICH-32B | IPSWICH-32B | NEWENGLAND-35A | 6/58: LOW M-56F |
| Aug-58 | IPSWICH-32B | YORK-50A | IPSWICH-32B | IPSWICH-32B | IPSWICH-32B | IPSWICH-32B | IPSWICH-32B | NEWENGLAND-35A | 9/58: DARL-51A |
| Jan-59 | IPSWICH-32B | YORK-50A | IPSWICH-32B | IPSWICH-32B | IPSWICH-32B | IPSWICH-32B | IPSWICH-32B | NEWENGLAND-34E | 10/58: W.HPL-51C |
| Aug-59 | IPSWICH-32B | YORK-50A | 8/59: NORW-32A | IPSWICH-32B | IPSWICH-32B | IPSWICH-32B | IPSWICH-32B | NEWENGLAND-34E | W HARTLEPOOL-51C |
| Nov-59 | 10/59: MARCH-31B | YORK-50A | NORWICH-32A | 10/59: DCTR-36A | 11/59: MARCH-31B | 11/59: MARCH-31B | 12/59: MARCH-31B | NEWENGLAND-34E | W HARTLEPOOL-51C |
| Jan-60 | MARCH-31B | YORK-50A | NORWICH-32A | DONCASTER-36A | 2/60: DARN-41A | MARCH-31B | 2/60: K.LYNN-31C | NEWENGLAND-34E | W HARTLEPOOL-51C |
| Apr-60 | MARCH-31B | YORK-50A | 4/60: LOW-32C | DONCASTER-36A | DARNALL-41A | 4/60: LINC-40A | KINGS LYNN-31C | NEWENGLAND-34E | W HARTLEPOOL-51C |
| Aug-60 | MARCH-31B | YORK-50A | 9/60: NORW-32A | DONCASTER-36A | DARNALL-41A | LINCOLN-40A | 7/60: MARCH-31B | NEWENGLAND-34E | W HARTLEPOOL-51C |
| Nov-60 | MARCH-31B | YORK-50A | NORWICH-32A | DONCASTER-36A | DARNALL-41A | LINCOLN-40A | MARCH-31B | NEWENGLAND-34E | W HARTLEPOOL-51C |

| | 61062 | 61063 | 61064 | 61065 | 61066 | 61067 | 61068 | 61069 | 61070 |
|---|---|---|---|---|---|---|---|---|---|
| Aug-50 | NEVILLEHILL-50B | ANNESLEY-38B | EASTFIELD-65A | NEVILLEHILL-50B | ANNESLEY-38B | EDINBURGH(SM)-64A | DAIRYCOATES-53A | NEVILLEHILL-50B | NEWENGLAND-35A |
| Jan-51 | NEVILLEHILL-50B | ANNESLEY-38B | EASTFIELD-65A | 11/50: HTN-52B | ANNESLEY-38B | EDINBURGH(SM)-64A | DAIRYCOATES-53A | NEVILLEHILL-50B | NEWENGLAND-35A |
| Aug-51 | NEVILLEHILL-50B | ANNESLEY-38B | EASTFIELD-65A | 1/51: N.HILL-50B | ANNESLEY-38B | EDINBURGH(SM)-64A | DAIRYCOATES-53A | NEVILLEHILL-50B | NEWENGLAND-35A |
| Jan-52 | NEVILLEHILL-50B | ANNESLEY-38B | EASTFIELD-65A | NEVILLEHILL-50B | ANNESLEY-38B | EDINBURGH(SM)-64A | DAIRYCOATES-53A | NEVILLEHILL-50B | NEWENGLAND-35A |
| Aug-52 | NEVILLEHILL-50B | ANNESLEY-38B | EASTFIELD-65A | NEVILLEHILL-50B | ANNESLEY-38B | EDINBURGH(SM)-64A | DAIRYCOATES-53A | NEVILLEHILL-50B | NEWENGLAND-35A |
| Jan-53 | NEVILLEHILL-50B | ANNESLEY-38B | EASTFIELD-65A | NEVILLEHILL-50B | ANNESLEY-38B | EDINBURGH(SM)-64A | DAIRYCOATES-53A | NEVILLEHILL-50B | NEWENGLAND-35A |
| Aug-53 | NEVILLEHILL-50B | ANNESLEY-38B | EASTFIELD-65A | NEVILLEHILL-50B | ANNESLEY-38B | EDINBURGH(SM)-64A | DAIRYCOATES-53A | NEVILLEHILL-50B | NEWENGLAND-35A |
| Jan-54 | NEVILLEHILL-50B | ANNESLEY-38B | EASTFIELD-65A | NEVILLEHILL-50B | ANNESLEY-38B | EDINBURGH(SM)-64A | 2/54: B.GDNS-53B | NEVILLEHILL-50B | NEWENGLAND-35A |
| Aug-54 | NEVILLEHILL-50B | ANNESLEY-38B | EASTFIELD-65A | NEVILLEHILL-50B | ANNESLEY-38B | EDINBURGH(SM)-64A | BOTGDNS-53B | NEVILLEHILL-50B | NEWENGLAND-35A |
| Jan-55 | NEVILLEHILL-50B | ANNESLEY-38B | EASTFIELD-65A | NEVILLEHILL-50B | ANNESLEY-38B | EDINBURGH(SM)-64A | BOTGDNS-53B | NEVILLEHILL-50B | NEWENGLAND-35A |
| Aug-55 | NEVILLEHILL-50B | ANNESLEY-38B | 5/55: CANAL-68E | NEVILLEHILL-50B | ANNESLEY-38B | EDINBURGH(SM)-64A | BOTGDNS-53B | NEVILLEHILL-50B | NEWENGLAND-35A |
| Jan-56 | NEVILLEHILL-50B | ANNESLEY-38B | CARLISLE(C)-68E | NEVILLEHILL-50B | ANNESLEY-38B | EDINBURGH(SM)-64A | BOTGDNS-53B | NEVILLEHILL-50B | NEWENGLAND-35A |
| Aug-56 | NEVILLEHILL-50B | 10/56: COLW-38A | CARLISLE(C)-68E | NEVILLEHILL-50B | 10/56: COLW-38A | EDINBURGH(SM)-64A | BOTGDNS-53B | NEVILLEHILL-50B | NEWENGLAND-35A |
| Jan-57 | NEVILLEHILL-50B | 11/56: LEIC-38C | CARLISLE(C)-68E | NEVILLEHILL-50B | COLWICK-38A | EDINBURGH(SM)-64A | BOTGDNS-53B | NEVILLEHILL-50B | NEWENGLAND-35A |
| Aug-57 | NEVILLEHILL-50B | LEICESTER(GC)-38C | CARLISLE(C)-68E | 9/57: GHD-52A | 10/57: CAMB-31A | EDINBURGH(SM)-64A | BOTGDNS-53B | NEVILLEHILL-50B | NEWENGLAND-35A |
| Jan-58 | NEVILLEHILL-50B | LEICESTER(GC)-38C | CARLISLE(C)-68E | GATESHEAD-52A | CAMBRIDGE-31A | EDINBURGH(SM)-64A | BOTGDNS-53B | NEVILLEHILL-50B | NEWENGLAND-35A |
| Aug-58 | NEVILLEHILL-50B | LEICESTER(GC)-15E | CARLISLE(C)-12C | 9/58: DYCTS-53A | CAMBRIDGE-31A | EDINBURGH(SM)-64A | BOTGDNS-53B | NEVILLEHILL-50B | NEWENGLAND-34E |
| Jan-59 | NEVILLEHILL-50B | LEICESTER(GC)-15E | CARLISLE(C)-12C | DAIRYCOATES-53A | CAMBRIDGE-31A | EDINBURGH(SM)-64A | BOTGDNS-53B | 2/59: YORK-50A | NEWENGLAND-34E |
| Aug-59 | NEVILLEHILL-50B | LEICESTER(GC)-15E | CARLISLE(C)-12C | DAIRYCOATES-53A | CAMBRIDGE-31A | EDINBURGH(SM)-64A | 6/59: SCAR-55E | YORK-50A | NEWENGLAND-34E |
| Nov-59 | 10/59: TNBY-51L | LEICESTER(GC)-15E | CARLISLE(C)-12C | DAIRYCOATES-53A | CAMBRIDGE-31A | EDINBURGH(SM)-64A | SCARBOROUGH-55E | YORK-50A | NEWENGLAND-34E |
| Jan-60 | THORNABY-51L | LEICESTER(GC)-15E | CARLISLE(C)-12C | DAIRYCOATES-53A | CAMBRIDGE-31A | EDINBURGH(SM)-64A | SCARBOROUGH-55E | YORK-50A | NEWENGLAND-34E |
| Apr-60 | THORNABY-51L | 3/60: NEAS-34E | CARLISLE(C)-12C | DAIRYCOATES-53A | CAMBRIDGE-31A | EDINBURGH(SM)-64A | 4/60: DARL-51A | YORK-50A | NEWENGLAND-34E |
| Aug-60 | 9/60: YORK-50A | 10/60: LEIC-15E | CARLISLE(C)-12C | DAIRYCOATES-50B | CAMBRIDGE-31A | EDINBURGH(SM)-64A | 5/60: TNBY-51L | YORK-50A | NEWENGLAND-34E |
| Nov-60 | YORK-50A | LEICESTER(GC)-15E | CARLISLE(C)-12C | DAIRYCOATES-50B | CAMBRIDGE-31A | EDINBURGH(SM)-64A | 9/60: YORK-50A | YORK-50A | NEWENGLAND-34E |

| | 61071 | 61072 | 61073 | 61074 | 61075 | 61076 | 61077 | 61078 | 61079 |
|---|---|---|---|---|---|---|---|---|---|
| Aug-50 | YORK-50A | THORNTONJCN-62A | NEWENGLAND-35A | DAIRYCOATES-53A | NEWENGLAND-35A | HAYMARKET-64B | NEASDEN-34E | COLWICK-38A | IMMINGHAM-40B |
| Jan-51 | YORK-50A | THORNTONJCN-62A | NEWENGLAND-35A | DAIRYCOATES-53A | NEWENGLAND-35A | HAYMARKET-64B | NEASDEN-34E | COLWICK-38A | IMMINGHAM-40B |
| Aug-51 | YORK-50A | THORNTONJCN-62A | NEWENGLAND-35A | DAIRYCOATES-53A | NEWENGLAND-35A | HAYMARKET-64B | NEASDEN-34E | COLWICK-38A | IMMINGHAM-40B |
| Jan-52 | YORK-50A | THORNTONJCN-62A | NEWENGLAND-35A | DAIRYCOATES-53A | NEWENGLAND-35A | HAYMARKET-64B | NEASDEN-34E | 3/52: LEIC-38C | IMMINGHAM-40B |
| Aug-52 | YORK-50A | THORNTONJCN-62A | NEWENGLAND-35A | DAIRYCOATES-53A | NEWENGLAND-35A | HAYMARKET-64B | NEASDEN-34E | 6/52: WOOD-38E | IMMINGHAM-40B |
| Jan-53 | YORK-50A | THORNTONJCN-62A | NEWENGLAND-35A | DAIRYCOATES-53A | NEWENGLAND-35A | HAYMARKET-64B | NEASDEN-34E | W HALSE-38E | IMMINGHAM-40B |
| Aug-53 | YORK-50A | THORNTONJCN-62A | NEWENGLAND-35A | DAIRYCOATES-53A | NEWENGLAND-35A | HAYMARKET-64B | NEASDEN-34E | W HALSE-38E | IMMINGHAM-40B |
| Jan-54 | YORK-50A | THORNTONJCN-62A | NEWENGLAND-35A | DAIRYCOATES-53A | NEWENGLAND-35A | HAYMARKET-64B | NEASDEN-34E | W HALSE-38E | IMMINGHAM-40B |
| Aug-54 | YORK-50A | THORNTONJCN-62A | NEWENGLAND-35A | DAIRYCOATES-53A | 6/54: KX-34A | HAYMARKET-64B | NEASDEN-34E | W HALSE-38E | IMMINGHAM-40B |
| Jan-55 | YORK-50A | THORNTONJCN-62A | NEWENGLAND-35A | DAIRYCOATES-53A | KINGS CROSS-34A | HAYMARKET-64B | NEASDEN-34E | W HALSE-38E | IMMINGHAM-40B |
| Aug-55 | YORK-50A | THORNTONJCN-62A | NEWENGLAND-35A | DAIRYCOATES-53A | KINGS CROSS-34A | HAYMARKET-64B | NEASDEN-34E | W HALSE-38E | IMMINGHAM-40B |
| Jan-56 | YORK-50A | THORNTONJCN-62A | NEWENGLAND-35A | DAIRYCOATES-53A | KINGS CROSS-34A | HAYMARKET-64B | NEASDEN-34E | W HALSE-38E | IMMINGHAM-40B |
| Aug-56 | YORK-50A | THORNTONJCN-62A | NEWENGLAND-35A | DAIRYCOATES-53A | KINGS CROSS-34A | HAYMARKET-64B | NEASDEN-34E | W HALSE-38E | IMMINGHAM-40B |
| Jan-57 | YORK-50A | THORNTONJCN-62A | NEWENGLAND-35A | 3/57: GRAN-35B | KINGS CROSS-34A | HAYMARKET-64B | NEASDEN-34E | W HALSE-38E | IMMINGHAM-40B |
| Aug-57 | YORK-50A | THORNTONJCN-62A | NEWENGLAND-35A | 10/57: NEWE-35A | KINGS CROSS-34A | HAYMARKET-64B | NEASDEN-34E | W HALSE-38E | IMMINGHAM-40B |
| Jan-58 | YORK-50A | THORNTONJCN-62A | NEWENGLAND-35A | NEWENGLAND-35A | KINGS CROSS-34A | HAYMARKET-64B | NEASDEN-34E | W HALSE-38E | IMMINGHAM-40B |
| Aug-58 | YORK-50A | 9/58: DUNF-62C | NEWENGLAND-34E | NEWENGLAND-34E | KINGS CROSS-34A | HAYMARKET-64B | NEASDEN-14D | W HALSE-2F | IMMINGHAM-40B |
| Jan-59 | YORK-50A | DUNFERMLINE-62C | NEWENGLAND-34E | NEWENGLAND-34E | KINGS CROSS-34A | HAYMARKET-64B | NEASDEN-14D | W HALSE-2F | IMMINGHAM-40B |
| Aug-59 | YORK-50A | DUNFERMLINE-62C | NEWENGLAND-34E | NEWENGLAND-34E | KINGS CROSS-34A | HAYMARKET-64B | NEASDEN-14D | W HALSE-2F | IMMINGHAM-40B |
| Nov-59 | YORK-50A | DUNFERMLINE-62C | NEWENGLAND-34E | NEWENGLAND-34E | KINGS CROSS-34A | HAYMARKET-64B | NEASDEN-14D | W HALSE-2F | IMMINGHAM-40B |
| Jan-60 | YORK-50A | DUNFERMLINE-62C | NEWENGLAND-34E | NEWENGLAND-34E | KINGS CROSS-34A | HAYMARKET-64B | NEASDEN-14D | W HALSE-2F | IMMINGHAM-40B |
| Apr-60 | YORK-50A | DUNFERMLINE-62C | NEWENGLAND-34E | NEWENGLAND-34E | KINGS CROSS-34A | HAYMARKET-64B | NEASDEN-14D | W HALSE-2F | IMMINGHAM-40B |
| Aug-60 | YORK-50A | DUNFERMLINE-62C | NEWENGLAND-34E | NEWENGLAND-34E | 10/60: NEWE-34E | HAYMARKET-64B | NEASDEN-14D | W HALSE-2F | IMMINGHAM-40B |
| Nov-60 | YORK-50A | DUNFERMLINE-62C | NEWENGLAND-34E | NEWENGLAND-34E | NEWENGLAND-34E | HAYMARKET-64B | NEASDEN-14D | W HALSE-2F | IMMINGHAM-40B |

used on the route to North East Lincolnshire. The type was also popular on the London extension and although Neasden, Woodford and Leicester had about twenty A3 and V2 locomotives for the principal services, B1's took charge of a large proportion of residual workings to and from Marylebone.

As elsewhere, the Great Central ran its share of relief trains – which relied heavily on B1 4-6-0's – and a typical summer weekend in the early 1950s would see three additional services from Marylebone to Manchester, one to Nottingham and two night services to Edinburgh: a commitment which called for eleven addition engine workings. This, however, was small beer compared to the GC traffic moved in North Lincolnshire, the same day seeing no less than twenty five additional services being booked to run from the West Riding and the Nottingham mining area to Cleethorpes alone. When the total number of additional trains – let alone booked services – run on the section is taken into account, it becomes clear why sheds such as Darnall and Immingham had such large allocations of mixed traffic engines.

*Varying standards of appearance. For some reason an usual amount of effort is being made to get B1 4-6-0 61395 into a presentable condition at Carlisle Canal on 19th June 1960. Further down the line K3 2-6-0 61858 waits its turn for cleaning. Much of Canal's work involved trains to Edinburgh via Hawick although its seven B1's tended to be used on the NER route to Newcastle.*

| | 61080 | 61081 | 61082 | 61083 | 61084 | 61085 | 61086 | 61087 | 61088 |
|---|---|---|---|---|---|---|---|---|---|
| Aug-50 | DAIRYCOATES-53A | HAYMARKET-64B | IMMINGHAM-40B | NEASDEN-34E | YORK-50A | ARDSLEY-37A | DONCASTER-36A | DONCASTER-36A | LEICESTER (GC)-38C |
| Jan-51 | DAIRYCOATES-53A | HAYMARKET-64B | IMMINGHAM-40B | NEASDEN-34E | YORK-50A | ARDSLEY-37A | DONCASTER-36A | DONCASTER-36A | LEICESTER (GC)-38C |
| Aug-51 | DAIRYCOATES-53A | HAYMARKET-64B | IMMINGHAM-40B | NEASDEN-34E | YORK-50A | ARDSLEY-37A | DONCASTER-36A | DONCASTER-36A | LEICESTER (GC)-38C |
| Jan-52 | DAIRYCOATES-53A | HAYMARKET-64B | IMMINGHAM-40B | NEASDEN-34E | YORK-50A | ARDSLEY-37A | 2/52: N.HILL-50B | DONCASTER-36A | LEICESTER (GC)-38C |
| Aug-52 | DAIRYCOATES-53A | HAYMARKET-64B | IMMINGHAM-40B | NEASDEN-34E | YORK-50A | ARDSLEY-37A | NEVILLE HILL-50B | DONCASTER-36A | LEICESTER (GC)-38C |
| Jan-53 | DAIRYCOATES-53A | HAYMARKET-64B | IMMINGHAM-40B | NEASDEN-34E | YORK-50A | ARDSLEY-37A | NEVILLE HILL-50B | DONCASTER-36A | LEICESTER (GC)-38C |
| Aug-53 | DAIRYCOATES-53A | HAYMARKET-64B | IMMINGHAM-40B | NEASDEN-34E | YORK-50A | 10/53: NEW E-35A | NEVILLE HILL-50B | DONCASTER-36A | LEICESTER (GC)-38C |
| Jan-54 | DAIRYCOATES-53A | HAYMARKET-64B | IMMINGHAM-40B | NEASDEN-34E | YORK-50A | NEWENGLAND-35A | NEVILLE HILL-50B | DONCASTER-36A | LEICESTER (GC)-38C |
| Aug-54 | DAIRYCOATES-53A | HAYMARKET-64B | IMMINGHAM-40B | NEASDEN-34E | YORK-50A | NEWENGLAND-35A | NEVILLE HILL-50B | DONCASTER-36A | LEICESTER (GC)-38C |
| Jan-55 | DAIRYCOATES-53A | HAYMARKET-64B | IMMINGHAM-40B | NEASDEN-34E | YORK-50A | 6/55: LINC-40A | NEVILLE HILL-50B | DONCASTER-36A | LEICESTER (GC)-38C |
| Aug-55 | DAIRYCOATES-53A | HAYMARKET-64B | IMMINGHAM-40B | NEASDEN-34E | YORK-50A | LINCOLN-40A | NEVILLE HILL-50B | DONCASTER-36A | LEICESTER (GC)-38C |
| Jan-56 | DAIRYCOATES-53A | HAYMARKET-64B | IMMINGHAM-40B | NEASDEN-34E | YORK-50A | LINCOLN-40A | NEVILLE HILL-50B | DONCASTER-36A | LEICESTER (GC)-38C |
| Aug-56 | DAIRYCOATES-53A | HAYMARKET-64B | IMMINGHAM-40B | NEASDEN-34E | YORK-50A | LINCOLN-40A | NEVILLE HILL-50B | DONCASTER-36A | LEICESTER (GC)-38C |
| Jan-57 | DAIRYCOATES-53A | HAYMARKET-64B | IMMINGHAM-40B | 2/57: S.B GE-35C | YORK-50A | LINCOLN-40A | NEVILLE HILL-50B | DONCASTER-36A | 11/56: COLW-38A |
| Aug-57 | DAIRYCOATES-53A | HAYMARKET-64B | IMMINGHAM-40B | SPITAL BRIDGE-35C | YORK-50A | LINCOLN-40A | NEVILLE HILL-50B | DONCASTER-36A | COLWICK-38A |
| Jan-58 | 12/57: B.GDNS-53B | HAYMARKET-64B | IMMINGHAM-40B | SPITAL BRIDGE-35C | YORK-50A | LINCOLN-40A | NEVILLE HILL-50B | DONCASTER-36A | COLWICK-40E |
| Aug-58 | BOTANIC GARDENS-53B | HAYMARKET-64B | IMMINGHAM-40B | SPITAL BRIDGE-31F | YORK-50A | 6/58: LEIC-15E | NEVILLE HILL-50B | DONCASTER-36A | COLWICK-40E |
| Jan-59 | BOTANIC GARDENS-53B | HAYMARKET-64B | IMMINGHAM-40B | 12/58: IMM-40B | YORK-50A | LEICESTER (GC)-15E | 1/59: YORK-50A | DONCASTER-36A | COLWICK-40E |
| Aug-59 | 6/59: DYCTS-53A | HAYMARKET-64B | IMMINGHAM-40B | 6/59: MEX-41F | YORK-50A | LEICESTER (GC)-15E | YORK-50A | DONCASTER-36A | COLWICK-40E |
| Nov-59 | DAIRYCOATES-53A | HAYMARKET-64B | IMMINGHAM-40B | MEXBOROUGH-41F | YORK-50A | 11/59: WOOD-2F | YORK-50A | DONCASTER-36A | COLWICK-40E |
| Jan-60 | DAIRYCOATES-53A | HAYMARKET-64B | IMMINGHAM-40B | MEXBOROUGH-41F | YORK-50A | WOODFORD HALSE-2F | YORK-50A | DONCASTER-36A | COLWICK-40E |
| Apr-60 | DAIRYCOATES-50B | HAYMARKET-64B | IMMINGHAM-40B | MEXBOROUGH-41F | YORK-50A | WOODFORD HALSE-2F | YORK-50A | DONCASTER-36A | COLWICK-40E |
| Aug-60 | DAIRYCOATES-50B | HAYMARKET-64B | IMMINGHAM-40B | MEXBOROUGH-41F | YORK-50A | 10/60: LEIC-15E | YORK-50A | DONCASTER-36A | COLWICK-40E |
| Nov-60 | DAIRYCOATES-50B | HAYMARKET-64B | IMMINGHAM-40B | MEXBOROUGH-41F | YORK-50A | LEICESTER (GC)-15E | YORK-50A | DONCASTER-36A | COLWICK-40E |

| | 61089 | 61090 | 61091 | 61092 | 61093 | 61094 | 61095 | 61096 | 61097 |
|---|---|---|---|---|---|---|---|---|---|
| Aug-50 | STRATFORD-30A | HITCHIN-34D | HITCHIN-34D | LEICESTER (GC)-38C | HITCHIN-34D | HITCHIN-34D | HITCHIN-34D | ARDSLEY-37A | HITCHIN-34D |
| Jan-51 | 5/51: IMM-40B | HITCHIN-34D | HITCHIN-34D | LEICESTER (GC)-38C | HITCHIN-34D | HITCHIN-34D | HITCHIN-34D | ARDSLEY-37A | HITCHIN-34D |
| Aug-51 | 6/51: STRAT-30A | HITCHIN-34D | HITCHIN-34D | LEICESTER (GC)-38C | HITCHIN-34D | HITCHIN-34D | HITCHIN-34D | ARDSLEY-37A | HITCHIN-34D |
| Jan-52 | STRATFORD-30A | HITCHIN-34D | HITCHIN-34D | LEICESTER (GC)-38C | HITCHIN-34D | HITCHIN-34D | 12/51: IPS-32B | HITCHIN-34D | HITCHIN-34D |
| Aug-52 | STRATFORD-30A | HITCHIN-34D | HITCHIN-34D | LEICESTER (GC)-38C | HITCHIN-34D | HITCHIN-34D | IPSWICH-32B | HITCHIN-34D | HITCHIN-34D |
| Jan-53 | STRATFORD-30A | HITCHIN-34D | HITCHIN-34D | LEICESTER (GC)-38C | HITCHIN-34D | HITCHIN-34D | IPSWICH-32B | HITCHIN-34D | HITCHIN-34D |
| Aug-53 | STRATFORD-30A | HITCHIN-34D | HITCHIN-34D | LEICESTER (GC)-38C | HITCHIN-34D | 5/53: NEW E-35A | IPSWICH-32B | HITCHIN-34D | HITCHIN-34D |
| Jan-54 | STRATFORD-30A | HITCHIN-34D | HITCHIN-34D | LEICESTER (GC)-38C | HITCHIN-34D | NEWENGLAND-35A | IPSWICH-32B | HITCHIN-34D | HITCHIN-34D |
| Aug-54 | STRATFORD-30A | HITCHIN-34D | HITCHIN-34D | LEICESTER (GC)-38C | HITCHIN-34D | NEWENGLAND-35A | IPSWICH-32B | HITCHIN-34D | HITCHIN-34D |
| Jan-55 | STRATFORD-30A | HITCHIN-34D | HITCHIN-34D | 1/55: COLW-38A | HITCHIN-34D | NEWENGLAND-35A | IPSWICH-32B | HITCHIN-34D | HITCHIN-34D |
| Aug-55 | STRATFORD-30A | HITCHIN-34D | HITCHIN-34D | COLWICK-38A | HITCHIN-34D | NEWENGLAND-35A | IPSWICH-32B | HITCHIN-34D | HITCHIN-34D |
| Jan-56 | STRATFORD-30A | HITCHIN-34D | HITCHIN-34D | COLWICK-38A | HITCHIN-34D | NEWENGLAND-35A | IPSWICH-32B | HITCHIN-34D | HITCHIN-34D |
| Aug-56 | STRATFORD-30A | HITCHIN-34D | HITCHIN-34D | COLWICK-38A | HITCHIN-34D | NEWENGLAND-35A | IPSWICH-32B | HITCHIN-34D | HITCHIN-34D |
| Jan-57 | 2/57: COL-30E | HITCHIN-34D | HITCHIN-34D | COLWICK-38A | HITCHIN-34D | HITCHIN-34D | 3/57: S.B GE-35C | HITCHIN-34D | HITCHIN-34D |
| Aug-57 | 10/57: STRAT-30A | HITCHIN-34D | HITCHIN-34D | COLWICK-38A | HITCHIN-34D | HITCHIN-34D | SPITAL BRIDGE-35C | 10/57: CAMB-31A | HITCHIN-34D |
| Jan-58 | STRATFORD-30A | HITCHIN-34D | HITCHIN-34D | COLWICK-40E | HITCHIN-34D | HITCHIN-34D | SPITAL BRIDGE-35C | CAMBRIDGE-31A | HITCHIN-34D |
| Aug-58 | STRATFORD-30A | HITCHIN-34D | HITCHIN-34D | COLWICK-40E | HITCHIN-34D | HITCHIN-34D | SPITAL BRIDGE-31F | CAMBRIDGE-31A | HITCHIN-34D |
| Jan-59 | STRATFORD-30A | HITCHIN-34D | HITCHIN-34D | COLWICK-40E | HITCHIN-34D | HITCHIN-34D | SPITAL BRIDGE-31F | 12/58: S.B GE-35C | HITCHIN-34D |
| Aug-59 | STRATFORD-30A | 6/59: MEX-41F | HITCHIN-34D | COLWICK-40E | 6/59: MEX-41F | 9/59: DARN-41A | SPITAL BRIDGE-31F | SPITAL BRIDGE-31F | HITCHIN-34D |
| Nov-59 | STRATFORD-30A | MEXBOROUGH-41F | HITCHIN-34D | COLWICK-40E | MEXBOROUGH-41F | DARNALL-41A | SPITAL BRIDGE-31F | SPITAL BRIDGE-31F | HITCHIN-34D |
| Jan-60 | STRATFORD-30A | MEXBOROUGH-41F | HITCHIN-34D | COLWICK-40E | MEXBOROUGH-41F | DARNALL-41A | 2/60: MARCH-31B | 2/60: MARCH-31B | HITCHIN-34D |
| Apr-60 | STRATFORD-30A | 5/60: DARN-41A | HITCHIN-34D | COLWICK-40E | MEXBOROUGH-41F | DARNALL-41A | MARCH-31B | MARCH-31B | HITCHIN-34D |
| Aug-60 | STRATFORD-30A | DARNALL-41A | 8/60: NEW E-34E | COLWICK-40E | MEXBOROUGH-41F | DARNALL-41A | MARCH-31B | MARCH-31B | 8/60: NEW E-34E |
| Nov-60 | STRATFORD-30A | DARNALL-41A | NEWENGLAND-34E | COLWICK-40E | MEXBOROUGH-41F | DARNALL-41A | MARCH-31B | MARCH-31B | NEWENGLAND-34E |

| | 61098 | 61099 | 61100 | 61101 | 61102 | 61103 | 61104 | 61105 | 61106 |
|---|---|---|---|---|---|---|---|---|---|
| Aug-50 | STRATFORD-30A | HITCHIN-34D | GATESHEAD-52A | DUNDEE-62B | DUNDEE-62B | THORNTON JCN-62A | STRATFORD-30A | HITCHIN-34D | LEICESTER (GC)-38C |
| Jan-51 | STRATFORD-30A | HITCHIN-34D | GATESHEAD-52A | DUNDEE-62B | DUNDEE-62B | THORNTON JCN-62A | STRATFORD-30A | HITCHIN-34D | LEICESTER (GC)-38C |
| Aug-51 | 9/51: IMM-40B | HITCHIN-34D | GATESHEAD-52A | DUNDEE-62B | DUNDEE-62B | THORNTON JCN-62A | STRATFORD-30A | HITCHIN-34D | LEICESTER (GC)-38C |
| Jan-52 | IMMINGHAM-40B | HITCHIN-34D | GATESHEAD-52A | DUNDEE-62B | DUNDEE-62B | THORNTON JCN-62A | STRATFORD-30A | HITCHIN-34D | LEICESTER (GC)-38C |
| Aug-52 | IMMINGHAM-40B | HITCHIN-34D | GATESHEAD-52A | DUNDEE-62B | DUNDEE-62B | THORNTON JCN-62A | STRATFORD-30A | HITCHIN-34D | 10/52: COLW-38A |
| Jan-53 | IMMINGHAM-40B | 1/53: KX-34A | GATESHEAD-52A | DUNDEE-62B | DUNDEE-62B | THORNTON JCN-62A | STRATFORD-30A | 1/53: KX-34A | 2/53: LEIC (GC)-38C |
| Aug-53 | IMMINGHAM-40B | 9/53: ST M-64A | GATESHEAD-52A | DUNDEE-62B | DUNDEE-62B | THORNTON JCN-62A | STRATFORD-30A | KINGS CROSS-34A | LEICESTER (GC)-38C |
| Jan-54 | IMMINGHAM-40B | EDINBURGH (SM)-64A | GATESHEAD-52A | DUNDEE-62B | DUNDEE-62B | THORNTON JCN-62A | STRATFORD-30A | KINGS CROSS-34A | 3/54: COLW-38A |
| Aug-54 | IMMINGHAM-40B | EDINBURGH (SM)-64A | GATESHEAD-52A | DUNDEE-62B | DUNDEE-62B | THORNTON JCN-62A | STRATFORD-30A | 6/54: HIT-34D | COLWICK-38A |
| Jan-55 | IMMINGHAM-40B | EDINBURGH (SM)-64A | GATESHEAD-52A | DUNDEE-62B | DUNDEE-62B | THORNTON JCN-62A | STRATFORD-30A | HITCHIN-34D | COLWICK-38A |
| Aug-55 | IMMINGHAM-40B | EDINBURGH (SM)-64A | GATESHEAD-52A | 5/55: DUNF-62C | DUNDEE-62B | THORNTON JCN-62A | STRATFORD-30A | HITCHIN-34D | COLWICK-38A |
| Jan-56 | IMMINGHAM-40B | EDINBURGH (SM)-64A | GATESHEAD-52A | DUNFERMLINE-62C | DUNDEE-62B | THORNTON JCN-62A | STRATFORD-30A | HITCHIN-34D | COLWICK-38A |
| Aug-56 | IMMINGHAM-40B | EDINBURGH (SM)-64A | GATESHEAD-52A | DUNFERMLINE-62C | DUNDEE-62B | THORNTON JCN-62A | STRATFORD-30A | HITCHIN-34D | COLWICK-38A |
| Jan-57 | IMMINGHAM-40B | EDINBURGH (SM)-64A | 2/57: BLAY-52C | DUNFERMLINE-62C | DUNDEE-62B | THORNTON JCN-62A | STRATFORD-30A | HITCHIN-34D | COLWICK-38A |
| Aug-57 | IMMINGHAM-40B | EDINBURGH (SM)-64A | BLAYDON-52C | DUNFERMLINE-62C | DUNDEE-62B | THORNTON JCN-62A | STRATFORD-30A | HITCHIN-34D | COLWICK-38A |
| Jan-58 | IMMINGHAM-40B | EDINBURGH (SM)-64A | BLAYDON-52C | DUNFERMLINE-62C | DUNDEE-62B | THORNTON JCN-62A | STRATFORD-30A | HITCHIN-34D | 12/57: LEIC-38C |
| Aug-58 | IMMINGHAM-40B | EDINBURGH (SM)-64A | BLAYDON-52C | DUNFERMLINE-62C | DUNDEE-62B | THORNTON JCN-62A | STRATFORD-30A | 7/58: DARN-41A | LEICESTER (GC)-15E |
| Jan-59 | IMMINGHAM-40B | EDINBURGH (SM)-64A | BLAYDON-52C | DUNFERMLINE-62C | DUNDEE-62B | THORNTON JCN-62A | 1/59: CAMB-31A | DARNALL-41A | LEICESTER (GC)-15E |
| Aug-59 | IMMINGHAM-40B | EDINBURGH (SM)-64A | BLAYDON-52C | DUNFERMLINE-62C | DUNDEE-62B | THORNTON JCN-62A | 5/59: DARN-41A | DARNALL-41A | LEICESTER (GC)-15E |
| Nov-59 | IMMINGHAM-40B | EDINBURGH (SM)-64A | 10/59: GHD-52A | DUNFERMLINE-62C | DUNDEE-62B | THORNTON JCN-62A | 12/59: MEX-41F | DARNALL-41A | 11/59: WOOD-2F |
| Jan-60 | IMMINGHAM-40B | EDINBURGH (SM)-64A | GATESHEAD-52A | DUNFERMLINE-62C | DUNDEE-62B | THORNTON JCN-62A | 1/60: DARN-41A | DARNALL-41A | WOODFORD HALSE-2F |
| Apr-60 | IMMINGHAM-40B | EDINBURGH (SM)-64A | GATESHEAD-52A | DUNFERMLINE-62C | DUNDEE-62B | THORNTON JCN-62A | DARNALL-41A | DARNALL-41A | WOODFORD HALSE-2F |
| Aug-60 | IMMINGHAM-40B | EDINBURGH (SM)-64A | GATESHEAD-52A | DUNFERMLINE-62C | DUNDEE-62B | THORNTON JCN-62A | DARNALL-41A | DARNALL-41A | WOODFORD HALSE-2F |
| Nov-60 | IMMINGHAM-40B | EDINBURGH (SM)-64A | GATESHEAD-52A | DUNFERMLINE-62C | DUNDEE-62B | THORNTON JCN-62A | DARNALL-41A | DARNALL-41A | WOODFORD HALSE-2F |

| | 61107 | 61108 | 61109 | 61110 | 61111 | 61112 | 61113 | 61114 | 61115 |
|---|---|---|---|---|---|---|---|---|---|
| Aug-50 | DONCASTER-36A | LEICESTER (GC)-38C | STRATFORD-30A | COLWICK-38A | COLWICK-38A | LINCOLN-40A | KINGS CROSS-34A | GORTON-39A | YORK-50A |
| Jan-51 | DONCASTER-36A | LEICESTER (GC)-38C | STRATFORD-30A | COLWICK-38A | COLWICK-38A | LINCOLN-40A | KINGS CROSS-34A | GORTON-39A | YORK-50A |
| Aug-51 | 10/51: IMM-40B | LEICESTER (GC)-38C | STRATFORD-30A | 10/51: WOOD-38E | COLWICK-38A | 10/51: NORW-32A | KINGS CROSS-34A | GORTON-39A | YORK-50A |
| Jan-52 | 11/51: DCTR-36A | LEICESTER (GC)-38C | STRATFORD-30A | 12/51: NORW-32A | COLWICK-38A | 3/52: LINC-40A | KINGS CROSS-34A | GORTON-39A | YORK-50A |
| Aug-52 | DONCASTER-36A | LEICESTER (GC)-38C | STRATFORD-30A | 3/52: ARDS-37A | COLWICK-38A | LINCOLN-40A | KINGS CROSS-34A | 10/52: STRAT-30A | YORK-50A |
| Jan-53 | DONCASTER-36A | LEICESTER (GC)-38C | ARDSLEY-37A | 1/53: LEIC-38C | 1/53: LEIC-38C | LINCOLN-40A | 1/53: NEW E-35A | STRATFORD-30A | YORK-50A |
| Aug-53 | DONCASTER-36A | 9/53: ST M-64A | ARDSLEY-37A | 2/53: COLW-38A | 2/53: COLW-38A | LINCOLN-40A | NEWENGLAND-35A | STRATFORD-30A | YORK-50A |
| Jan-54 | DONCASTER-36A | EDINBURGH (SM)-64A | ARDSLEY-37A | COLWICK-38A | COLWICK-38A | 11/53: MEX-36B | NEWENGLAND-35A | 3/54: DCTR-36A | YORK-50A |
| Aug-54 | DONCASTER-36A | EDINBURGH (SM)-64A | ARDSLEY-37A | COLWICK-38A | COLWICK-38A | MEXBOROUGH-36B | 8/54: NORW-32A | DONCASTER-36A | YORK-50A |
| Jan-55 | DONCASTER-36A | EDINBURGH (SM)-64A | ARDSLEY-37A | 1/55: LEIC-38C | COLWICK-38A | MEXBOROUGH-36B | 12/54: NEW E-35A | DONCASTER-36A | YORK-50A |
| Aug-55 | DONCASTER-36A | EDINBURGH (SM)-64A | ARDSLEY-37A | 2/55: COLW-38A | COLWICK-38A | MEXBOROUGH-36B | NEWENGLAND-35A | DONCASTER-36A | YORK-50A |
| Jan-56 | DONCASTER-36A | EDINBURGH (SM)-64A | ARDSLEY-37A | COLWICK-38A | COLWICK-38A | MEXBOROUGH-36B | NEWENGLAND-35A | DONCASTER-36A | YORK-50A |
| Aug-56 | DONCASTER-36A | EDINBURGH (SM)-64A | ARDSLEY-56B | 10/56: KX-34A | COLWICK-38A | MEXBOROUGH-36B | NEWENGLAND-35A | DONCASTER-36A | YORK-50A |
| Jan-57 | DONCASTER-36A | EDINBURGH (SM)-64A | ARDSLEY-56B | 12/56: NEAS-34E | COLWICK-38A | MEXBOROUGH-36B | NEWENGLAND-35A | DONCASTER-36A | YORK-50A |
| Aug-57 | DONCASTER-36A | EDINBURGH (SM)-64A | ARDSLEY-56B | 2/57: STRAT-30A | COLWICK-38A | MEXBOROUGH-36B | NEWENGLAND-35A | DONCASTER-36A | YORK-50A |
| Jan-58 | DONCASTER-36A | EDINBURGH (SM)-64A | ARDSLEY-56B | STRATFORD-30A | COLWICK-38A | MEXBOROUGH-36B | NEWENGLAND-35A | DONCASTER-36A | 6/58: C.HILL-56C |
| Aug-58 | DONCASTER-36A | EDINBURGH (SM)-64A | ARDSLEY-56B | STRATFORD-30A | MEXBOROUGH-41F | MEXBOROUGH-41F | NEWENGLAND-34E | DONCASTER-36A | COPLEY HILL-56C |
| Jan-59 | DONCASTER-36A | EDINBURGH (SM)-64A | ARDSLEY-56B | 1/59: PARK-30F | MEXBOROUGH-41F | MEXBOROUGH-41F | NEWENGLAND-34E | DONCASTER-36A | COPLEY HILL-56C |
| Aug-59 | DONCASTER-36A | EDINBURGH (SM)-64A | ARDSLEY-56B | 6/59: DARN-41A | 6/59: DARN-41A | 6/59: DARN-41A | NEWENGLAND-34E | DONCASTER-36A | COPLEY HILL-56C |
| Nov-59 | DONCASTER-36A | EDINBURGH (SM)-64A | ARDSLEY-56B | DARNALL-41A | DARNALL-41A | DARNALL-41A | NEWENGLAND-34E | 12/59: IMM-40B | COPLEY HILL-56C |
| Jan-60 | DONCASTER-36A | EDINBURGH (SM)-64A | ARDSLEY-56B | DARNALL-41A | DARNALL-41A | DARNALL-41A | NEWENGLAND-34E | IMMINGHAM-40B | COPLEY HILL-56C |
| Apr-60 | DONCASTER-36A | EDINBURGH (SM)-64A | ARDSLEY-56B | DARNALL-41A | DARNALL-41A | DARNALL-41A | NEWENGLAND-34E | IMMINGHAM-40B | COPLEY HILL-56C |
| Aug-60 | DONCASTER-36A | EDINBURGH (SM)-64A | ARDSLEY-56B | DARNALL-41A | DARNALL-41A | DARNALL-41A | NEWENGLAND-34E | IMMINGHAM-40B | COPLEY HILL-56C |
| Nov-60 | DONCASTER-36A | EDINBURGH (SM)-64A | ARDSLEY-56B | DARNALL-41A | DARNALL-41A | DARNALL-41A | NEWENGLAND-34E | IMMINGHAM-40B | COPLEY HILL-56C |

Although a mixed traffic class, the B1's primary role was as a replacement for the several classes of pregrouping passenger engines whose duties did not call for the output of a Pacific or V2. Inevitably the class worked a considerable amount of goods traffic – one diagram called for a through working between Kings Cross and Hull with a fast freight – but they were not the equal of a K3 2-6-0 in this respect which, in the case of a fitted goods from Kings Cross to Doncaster for example, could take the full line limit of sixty vehicles as opposed to only forty-five by a B1.

Where the B1 was a standard locomotive with examples allocated the length and breadth of the system, the handful of other 4-6-0 classes were, by the mid 1950s, confined to fairly strict geographical areas. Most of the B16's were concentrated around the southern parts of the North Eastern working

| | 61116 | 61117 | 61118 | 61119 | 61120 | 61121 | 61122 | 61123 | 61124 |
|---|---|---|---|---|---|---|---|---|---|
| Aug-50 | EASTFIELD - 65A | EASTFIELD - 65A | THORNTONJCN - 62A | STRATFORD - 30A | DONCASTER - 36A | CAMBRIDGE - 31A | COLWICK - 38A | COLWICK - 38A | DONCASTER - 36A |
| Jan-51 | EASTFIELD - 65A | EASTFIELD - 65A | THORNTONJCN - 62A | STRATFORD - 30A | DONCASTER - 36A | CAMBRIDGE - 31A | COLWICK - 38A | COLWICK - 38A | DONCASTER - 36A |
| Aug-51 | EASTFIELD - 65A | EASTFIELD - 65A | THORNTONJCN - 62A | STRATFORD - 30A | DONCASTER - 36A | CAMBRIDGE - 31A | **10/51: ARDS - 37A** | **10/51: ARDS - 37A** | DONCASTER - 36A |
| Jan-52 | EASTFIELD - 65A | EASTFIELD - 65A | THORNTONJCN - 62A | STRATFORD - 30A | DONCASTER - 36A | CAMBRIDGE - 31A | ARDSLEY - 37A | ARDSLEY - 37A | DONCASTER - 36A |
| Aug-52 | **6/52: NEAS - 34E** | EASTFIELD - 65A | THORNTONJCN - 62A | STRATFORD - 30A | DONCASTER - 36A | CAMBRIDGE - 31A | ARDSLEY - 37A | ARDSLEY - 37A | DONCASTER - 36A |
| Jan-53 | NEASDEN - 34E | EASTFIELD - 65A | THORNTONJCN - 62A | STRATFORD - 30A | DONCASTER - 36A | CAMBRIDGE - 31A | ARDSLEY - 37A | ARDSLEY - 37A | DONCASTER - 36A |
| Aug-53 | NEASDEN - 34E | EASTFIELD - 65A | THORNTONJCN - 62A | STRATFORD - 30A | DONCASTER - 36A | CAMBRIDGE - 31A | **10/53: NEWE - 35A** | ARDSLEY - 37A | DONCASTER - 36A |
| Jan-54 | NEASDEN - 34E | EASTFIELD - 65A | THORNTONJCN - 62A | STRATFORD - 30A | DONCASTER - 36A | CAMBRIDGE - 31A | NEWENGLAND - 35A | ARDSLEY - 37A | DONCASTER - 36A |
| Aug-54 | NEASDEN - 34E | EASTFIELD - 65A | THORNTONJCN - 62A | STRATFORD - 30A | DONCASTER - 36A | CAMBRIDGE - 31A | NEWENGLAND - 35A | ARDSLEY - 37A | DONCASTER - 36A |
| Jan-55 | NEASDEN - 34E | EASTFIELD - 65A | THORNTONJCN - 62A | STRATFORD - 30A | DONCASTER - 36A | CAMBRIDGE - 31A | NEWENGLAND - 35A | ARDSLEY - 37A | DONCASTER - 36A |
| Aug-55 | NEASDEN - 34E | EASTFIELD - 65A | THORNTONJCN - 62A | STRATFORD - 30A | DONCASTER - 36A | CAMBRIDGE - 31A | **6/55: DARN - 41A** | ARDSLEY - 37A | DONCASTER - 36A |
| Jan-56 | NEASDEN - 34E | **11/55: PKHD - 65C** | THORNTONJCN - 62A | STRATFORD - 30A | DONCASTER - 36A | CAMBRIDGE - 31A | **11/55: DCTR - 36A** | ARDSLEY - 37A | DONCASTER - 36A |
| Aug-56 | NEASDEN - 34E | PARKHEAD - 65C | THORNTONJCN - 62A | STRATFORD - 30A | DONCASTER - 36A | CAMBRIDGE - 31A | DONCASTER - 36A | ARDSLEY - 37A | DONCASTER - 36A |
| Jan-57 | NEASDEN - 34E | PARKHEAD - 65C | THORNTONJCN - 62A | STRATFORD - 30A | DONCASTER - 36A | **11/56: DCTR - 36A** | DONCASTER - 36A | ARDSLEY - 56B | DONCASTER - 36A |
| Aug-57 | NEASDEN - 34E | PARKHEAD - 65C | THORNTONJCN - 62A | STRATFORD - 30A | DONCASTER - 36A | DONCASTER - 36A | DONCASTER - 36A | ARDSLEY - 56B | DONCASTER - 36A |
| Jan-58 | NEASDEN - 34E | PARKHEAD - 65C | THORNTONJCN - 62A | STRATFORD - 30A | DONCASTER - 36A | DONCASTER - 36A | DONCASTER - 36A | ARDSLEY - 56B | DONCASTER - 36A |
| Aug-58 | NEASDEN - 14D | PARKHEAD - 65C | THORNTONJCN - 62A | STRATFORD - 30A | DONCASTER - 36A | DONCASTER - 36A | DONCASTER - 36A | ARDSLEY - 56B | DONCASTER - 36A |
| Jan-59 | NEASDEN - 14D | PARKHEAD - 65C | THORNTONJCN - 62A | STRATFORD - 30A | DONCASTER - 36A | DONCASTER - 36A | DONCASTER - 36A | ARDSLEY - 56B | DONCASTER - 36A |
| Aug-59 | **9/59: LEIC - 15E** | PARKHEAD - 65C | THORNTONJCN - 62A | STRATFORD - 30A | DONCASTER - 36A | DONCASTER - 36A | DONCASTER - 36A | ARDSLEY - 56B | DONCASTER - 36A |
| Nov-59 | **11/59: NEAS - 14D** | PARKHEAD - 65C | THORNTONJCN - 62A | STRATFORD - 30A | **11/59: RET - 36E** | DONCASTER - 36A | DONCASTER - 36A | ARDSLEY - 56B | DONCASTER - 36A |
| Jan-60 | NEASDEN - 14D | PARKHEAD - 65C | THORNTONJCN - 62A | STRATFORD - 30A | RETFORD - 36E | DONCASTER - 36A | DONCASTER - 36A | ARDSLEY - 56B | DONCASTER - 36A |
| Apr-60 | NEASDEN - 14D | PARKHEAD - 65C | THORNTONJCN - 62A | STRATFORD - 30A | RETFORD - 36E | DONCASTER - 36A | DONCASTER - 36A | ARDSLEY - 56B | DONCASTER - 36A |
| Aug-60 | **10/60: LEIC - 15E** | PARKHEAD - 65C | THORNTONJCN - 62A | STRATFORD - 30A | RETFORD - 36E | DONCASTER - 36A | DONCASTER - 36A | ARDSLEY - 56B | DONCASTER - 36A |
| Nov-60 | **11/60: NEAS - 14D** | PARKHEAD - 65C | THORNTONJCN - 62A | STRATFORD - 30A | RETFORD - 36E | DONCASTER - 36A | DONCASTER - 36A | ARDSLEY - 56B | DONCASTER - 36A |

| | 61125 | 61126 | 61127 | 61128 | 61129 | 61130 | 61131 | 61132 | 61133 |
|---|---|---|---|---|---|---|---|---|---|
| Aug-50 | DONCASTER - 36A | DONCASTER - 36A | DONCASTER - 36A | DONCASTER - 36A | KINGS CROSS - 34A | STRATFORD - 30A | COLWICK - 38A | FERRYHILL - 61B | FERRYHILL - 61B |
| Jan-51 | DONCASTER - 36A | **12/50: RET - 36E** | DONCASTER - 36A | DONCASTER - 36A | KINGS CROSS - 34A | STRATFORD - 30A | COLWICK - 38A | **1/51: DUND - 62B** | FERRYHILL - 61B |
| Aug-51 | DONCASTER - 36A | RETFORD - 36E | DONCASTER - 36A | DONCASTER - 36A | KINGS CROSS - 34A | **9/51: IMM - 40B** | COLWICK - 38A | DUNDEE - 62B | **9/51: KITTY - 61A** |
| Jan-52 | DONCASTER - 36A | RETFORD - 36E | DONCASTER - 36A | DONCASTER - 36A | **11/51: ARDS - 37A** | IMMINGHAM - 40B | COLWICK - 38A | DUNDEE - 62B | KITTYBREWSTER - 61A |
| Aug-52 | DONCASTER - 36A | RETFORD - 36E | DONCASTER - 36A | DONCASTER - 36A | **7/52: C.HILL - 37B** | IMMINGHAM - 40B | **9/52: STRAT - 30A** | DUNDEE - 62B | KITTYBREWSTER - 61A |
| Jan-53 | DONCASTER - 36A | RETFORD - 36E | DONCASTER - 36A | DONCASTER - 36A | COPLEYHILL - 37B | IMMINGHAM - 40B | **10/52: ARDS - 37A** | DUNDEE - 62B | **1/53: EAST - 65A** |
| Aug-53 | DONCASTER - 36A | RETFORD - 36E | DONCASTER - 36A | DONCASTER - 36A | COPLEYHILL - 37B | IMMINGHAM - 40B | ARDSLEY - 37A | DUNDEE - 62B | EASTFIELD - 65A |
| Jan-54 | DONCASTER - 36A | RETFORD - 36E | DONCASTER - 36A | DONCASTER - 36A | COPLEYHILL - 37B | IMMINGHAM - 40B | ARDSLEY - 37A | DUNDEE - 62B | EASTFIELD - 65A |
| Aug-54 | DONCASTER - 36A | RETFORD - 36E | DONCASTER - 36A | DONCASTER - 36A | COPLEYHILL - 37B | IMMINGHAM - 40B | ARDSLEY - 37A | DUNDEE - 62B | EASTFIELD - 65A |
| Jan-55 | DONCASTER - 36A | RETFORD - 36E | DONCASTER - 36A | DONCASTER - 36A | COPLEYHILL - 37B | IMMINGHAM - 40B | ARDSLEY - 37A | DUNDEE - 62B | EASTFIELD - 65A |
| Aug-55 | DONCASTER - 36A | RETFORD - 36E | DONCASTER - 36A | DONCASTER - 36A | COPLEYHILL - 37B | IMMINGHAM - 40B | ARDSLEY - 37A | DUNDEE - 62B | EASTFIELD - 65A |
| Jan-56 | DONCASTER - 36A | RETFORD - 36E | DONCASTER - 36A | DONCASTER - 36A | COPLEYHILL - 37B | IMMINGHAM - 40B | ARDSLEY - 37A | DUNDEE - 62B | **2/56: TH JCN - 62A** |
| Aug-56 | DONCASTER - 36A | RETFORD - 36E | DONCASTER - 36A | DONCASTER - 36A | COPLEYHILL - 56C | IMMINGHAM - 40B | ARDSLEY - 56B | DUNDEE - 62B | THORNTONJCN - 62A |
| Jan-57 | DONCASTER - 36A | RETFORD - 36E | DONCASTER - 36A | DONCASTER - 36A | COPLEYHILL - 56C | IMMINGHAM - 40B | ARDSLEY - 56B | DUNDEE - 62B | THORNTONJCN - 62A |
| Aug-57 | DONCASTER - 36A | RETFORD - 36E | DONCASTER - 36A | DONCASTER - 36A | COPLEYHILL - 56C | IMMINGHAM - 40B | **9/57: BRAD - 56G** | DUNDEE - 62B | THORNTONJCN - 62A |
| Jan-58 | DONCASTER - 36A | RETFORD - 36E | DONCASTER - 36A | DONCASTER - 36A | COPLEYHILL - 56C | IMMINGHAM - 40B | **2/58: LOW M - 56F** | DUNDEE - 62B | THORNTONJCN - 62A |
| Aug-58 | DONCASTER - 36A | RETFORD - 36E | DONCASTER - 36A | DONCASTER - 36A | COPLEYHILL - 56C | IMMINGHAM - 40B | LOWMOOR - 56F | DUNDEE - 62B | THORNTONJCN - 62A |
| Jan-59 | DONCASTER - 36A | RETFORD - 36E | DONCASTER - 36A | DONCASTER - 36A | COPLEYHILL - 56C | IMMINGHAM - 40B | **2/59: WAKE - 56A** | DUNDEE - 62B | THORNTONJCN - 62A |
| Aug-59 | DONCASTER - 36A | RETFORD - 36E | DONCASTER - 36A | DONCASTER - 36A | COPLEYHILL - 56C | IMMINGHAM - 40B | WAKEFIELD - 56A | DUNDEE - 62B | THORNTONJCN - 62A |
| Nov-59 | DONCASTER - 36A | RETFORD - 36E | DONCASTER - 36A | DONCASTER - 36A | COPLEYHILL - 56C | IMMINGHAM - 40B | WAKEFIELD - 56A | DUNDEE - 62B | THORNTONJCN - 62A |
| Jan-60 | DONCASTER - 36A | RETFORD - 36E | DONCASTER - 36A | DONCASTER - 36A | COPLEYHILL - 56C | IMMINGHAM - 40B | WAKEFIELD - 56A | **1/60: TH JCN - 62A** | THORNTONJCN - 62A |
| Apr-60 | DONCASTER - 36A | RETFORD - 36E | DONCASTER - 36A | DONCASTER - 36A | COPLEYHILL - 56C | IMMINGHAM - 40B | WAKEFIELD - 56A | THORNTONJCN - 62A | THORNTONJCN - 62A |
| Aug-60 | DONCASTER - 36A | RETFORD - 36E | DONCASTER - 36A | DONCASTER - 36A | COPLEYHILL - 56C | IMMINGHAM - 40B | WAKEFIELD - 56A | THORNTONJCN - 62A | THORNTONJCN - 62A |
| Nov-60 | DONCASTER - 36A | RETFORD - 36E | DONCASTER - 36A | DONCASTER - 36A | COPLEYHILL - 56C | IMMINGHAM - 40B | WAKEFIELD - 56A | THORNTONJCN - 62A | THORNTONJCN - 62A |

| | 61134 | 61135 | 61136 | 61137 | 61138 | 61139 | 61140 | 61141 | 61142 |
|---|---|---|---|---|---|---|---|---|---|
| Aug-50 | KITTYBREWSTER - 61A | PARKESTON - 30F | KINGS CROSS - 34A | KINGS CROSS - 34A | KINGS CROSS - 34A | KINGS CROSS - 34A | NEASDEN - 34E | LEICESTER (GC) - 38C | IMMINGHAM - 40B |
| Jan-51 | KITTYBREWSTER - 61A | PARKESTON - 30F | KINGS CROSS - 34A | KINGS CROSS - 34A | KINGS CROSS - 34A | KINGS CROSS - 34A | NEASDEN - 34E | LEICESTER (GC) - 38C | IMMINGHAM - 40B |
| Aug-51 | KITTYBREWSTER - 61A | PARKESTON - 30F | KINGS CROSS - 34A | KINGS CROSS - 34A | KINGS CROSS - 34A | KINGS CROSS - 34A | NEASDEN - 34E | LEICESTER (GC) - 38C | IMMINGHAM - 40B |
| Jan-52 | KITTYBREWSTER - 61A | PARKESTON - 30F | KINGS CROSS - 34A | KINGS CROSS - 34A | KINGS CROSS - 34A | KINGS CROSS - 34A | NEASDEN - 34E | LEICESTER (GC) - 38C | IMMINGHAM - 40B |
| Aug-52 | KITTYBREWSTER - 61A | PARKESTON - 30F | **6/52: NEAS - 34E** | KINGS CROSS - 34A | KINGS CROSS - 34A | KINGS CROSS - 34A | **6/52: EAST - 65A** | LEICESTER (GC) - 38C | IMMINGHAM - 40B |
| Jan-53 | **3/53: EAST - 65A** | PARKESTON - 30F | NEASDEN - 34E | **1/53: DCTR - 36A** | **1/53: NEWE - 35A** | **1/53: NEWE - 35A** | EASTFIELD - 65A | LEICESTER (GC) - 38C | IMMINGHAM - 40B |
| Aug-53 | EASTFIELD - 65A | PARKESTON - 30F | NEASDEN - 34E | DONCASTER - 36A | NEWENGLAND - 35A | **3/53: K X - 34A** | EASTFIELD - 65A | LEICESTER (GC) - 38C | IMMINGHAM - 40B |
| Jan-54 | EASTFIELD - 65A | PARKESTON - 30F | NEASDEN - 34E | DONCASTER - 36A | NEWENGLAND - 35A | KINGS CROSS - 34A | EASTFIELD - 65A | LEICESTER (GC) - 38C | IMMINGHAM - 40B |
| Aug-54 | EASTFIELD - 65A | PARKESTON - 30F | NEASDEN - 34E | DONCASTER - 36A | NEWENGLAND - 35A | KINGS CROSS - 34A | EASTFIELD - 65A | LEICESTER (GC) - 38C | IMMINGHAM - 40B |
| Jan-55 | EASTFIELD - 65A | PARKESTON - 30F | NEASDEN - 34E | DONCASTER - 36A | NEWENGLAND - 35A | KINGS CROSS - 34A | EASTFIELD - 65A | LEICESTER (GC) - 38C | IMMINGHAM - 40B |
| Aug-55 | EASTFIELD - 65A | PARKESTON - 30F | NEASDEN - 34E | DONCASTER - 36A | **6/55: DARN - 41A** | KINGS CROSS - 34A | EASTFIELD - 65A | LEICESTER (GC) - 38C | IMMINGHAM - 40B |
| Jan-56 | **2/56: TH JCN - 62A** | PARKESTON - 30F | NEASDEN - 34E | DONCASTER - 36A | DARNALL - 41A | KINGS CROSS - 34A | EASTFIELD - 65A | LEICESTER (GC) - 38C | IMMINGHAM - 40B |
| Aug-56 | THORNTONJCN - 62A | PARKESTON - 30F | NEASDEN - 34E | DONCASTER - 36A | DARNALL - 41A | KINGS CROSS - 34A | EASTFIELD - 65A | LEICESTER (GC) - 38C | IMMINGHAM - 40B |
| Jan-57 | THORNTONJCN - 62A | PARKESTON - 30F | NEASDEN - 34E | DONCASTER - 36A | DARNALL - 41A | KINGS CROSS - 34A | EASTFIELD - 65A | **11/56: COLW - 38A** | IMMINGHAM - 40B |
| Aug-57 | THORNTONJCN - 62A | PARKESTON - 30F | NEASDEN - 34E | DONCASTER - 36A | DARNALL - 41A | KINGS CROSS - 34A | EASTFIELD - 65A | COLWICK - 38A | IMMINGHAM - 40B |
| Jan-58 | THORNTONJCN - 62A | **3/58: STRAT - 30A** | NEASDEN - 34E | DONCASTER - 36A | DARNALL - 41A | KINGS CROSS - 34A | EASTFIELD - 65A | COLWICK - 38A | IMMINGHAM - 40B |
| Aug-58 | THORNTONJCN - 62A | STRATFORD - 30A | NEASDEN - 14D | DONCASTER - 36A | DARNALL - 41A | KINGS CROSS - 34A | EASTFIELD - 65A | COLWICK - 40E | IMMINGHAM - 40B |
| Jan-59 | THORNTONJCN - 62A | **1/59: PARK - 30F** | NEASDEN - 14D | **12/58: LEIC - 15E** | DARNALL - 41A | **1/59: HIT - 34D** | EASTFIELD - 65A | COLWICK - 40E | IMMINGHAM - 40B |
| Aug-59 | THORNTONJCN - 62A | PARKESTON - 30F | **9/59: LEIC - 15E** | LEICESTER (GC) - 15E | DARNALL - 41A | **6/59: DARN - 41A** | EASTFIELD - 65A | COLWICK - 40E | IMMINGHAM - 40B |
| Nov-59 | THORNTONJCN - 62A | **10/59: DCTR - 36A** | **11/59: NEAS - 14D** | LEICESTER (GC) - 15E | **12/59: MILL - 41C** | DARNALL - 41A | EASTFIELD - 65A | COLWICK - 40E | **12/59: COLW - 40E** |
| Jan-60 | THORNTONJCN - 62A | DONCASTER - 36A | NEASDEN - 14D | LEICESTER (GC) - 15E | **2/60: CANK - 41D** | DARNALL - 41A | EASTFIELD - 65A | COLWICK - 40E | COLWICK - 40E |
| Apr-60 | **6/60: EAST - 65A** | DONCASTER - 36A | NEASDEN - 14D | LEICESTER (GC) - 15E | CANKLOW - 41D | DARNALL - 41A | EASTFIELD - 65A | COLWICK - 40E | COLWICK - 40E |
| Aug-60 | EASTFIELD - 65A | DONCASTER - 36A | NEASDEN - 14D | LEICESTER (GC) - 15E | CANKLOW - 41D | DARNALL - 41A | EASTFIELD - 65A | COLWICK - 40E | COLWICK - 40E |
| Nov-60 | EASTFIELD - 65A | DONCASTER - 36A | NEASDEN - 14D | LEICESTER (GC) - 15E | CANKLOW - 41D | DARNALL - 41A | EASTFIELD - 65A | COLWICK - 40E | COLWICK - 40E |

| | 61143 | 61144 | 61145 | 61146 | 61147 | 61148 | 61149 | 61150 | 61151 |
|---|---|---|---|---|---|---|---|---|---|
| Aug-50 | NEWENGLAND - 35A | STRATFORD - 30A | DARNALL - 39B | THORNTONJCN - 62A | DUNDEE - 62B | THORNTONJCN - 62A | PARKESTON - 30F | DARNALL - 39B | DARNALL - 39B |
| Jan-51 | NEWENGLAND - 35A | STRATFORD - 30A | DARNALL - 39B | THORNTONJCN - 62A | DUNDEE - 62B | THORNTONJCN - 62A | PARKESTON - 30F | DARNALL - 39B | DARNALL - 39B |
| Aug-51 | **5/51: GRAN - 35B** | **9/51: IMM - 40B** | **10/51: ARDS - 37A** | THORNTONJCN - 62A | **10/51: TH JCN - 62A** | THORNTONJCN - 62A | PARKESTON - 30F | DARNALL - 39B | DARNALL - 39B |
| Jan-52 | **9/51: NEWE - 35A** | IMMINGHAM - 40B | **11/51: BRAD - 37C** | THORNTONJCN - 62A | THORNTONJCN - 62A | THORNTONJCN - 62A | PARKESTON - 30F | DARNALL - 39B | DARNALL - 39B |
| Aug-52 | NEWENGLAND - 35A | IMMINGHAM - 40B | BRADFORD - 37C | THORNTONJCN - 62A | THORNTONJCN - 62A | THORNTONJCN - 62A | PARKESTON - 30F | DARNALL - 39B | DARNALL - 39B |
| Jan-53 | NEWENGLAND - 35A | IMMINGHAM - 40B | BRADFORD - 37C | THORNTONJCN - 62A | THORNTONJCN - 62A | THORNTONJCN - 62A | PARKESTON - 30F | DARNALL - 39B | DARNALL - 39B |
| Aug-53 | NEWENGLAND - 35A | IMMINGHAM - 40B | BRADFORD - 37C | THORNTONJCN - 62A | THORNTONJCN - 62A | THORNTONJCN - 62A | PARKESTON - 30F | DARNALL - 39B | DARNALL - 39B |
| Jan-54 | NEWENGLAND - 35A | IMMINGHAM - 40B | **12/53: DCTR - 36A** | THORNTONJCN - 62A | THORNTONJCN - 62A | THORNTONJCN - 62A | PARKESTON - 30F | DARNALL - 39B | DARNALL - 39B |
| Aug-54 | NEWENGLAND - 35A | IMMINGHAM - 40B | DONCASTER - 36A | THORNTONJCN - 62A | THORNTONJCN - 62A | THORNTONJCN - 62A | PARKESTON - 30F | DARNALL - 39B | DARNALL - 39B |
| Jan-55 | NEWENGLAND - 35A | IMMINGHAM - 40B | DONCASTER - 36A | THORNTONJCN - 62A | THORNTONJCN - 62A | THORNTONJCN - 62A | PARKESTON - 30F | DARNALL - 39B | DARNALL - 39B |
| Aug-55 | **6/55: LINC - 40A** | IMMINGHAM - 40B | DONCASTER - 36A | THORNTONJCN - 62A | THORNTONJCN - 62A | THORNTONJCN - 62A | PARKESTON - 30F | DARNALL - 39B | DARNALL - 39B |
| Jan-56 | LINCOLN - 40A | IMMINGHAM - 40B | DONCASTER - 36A | THORNTONJCN - 62A | THORNTONJCN - 62A | THORNTONJCN - 62A | PARKESTON - 30F | DARNALL - 41A | DARNALL - 41A |
| Aug-56 | LINCOLN - 40A | IMMINGHAM - 40B | DONCASTER - 36A | THORNTONJCN - 62A | THORNTONJCN - 62A | THORNTONJCN - 62A | PARKESTON - 30F | DARNALL - 41A | DARNALL - 41A |
| Jan-57 | LINCOLN - 40A | IMMINGHAM - 40B | DONCASTER - 36A | THORNTONJCN - 62A | THORNTONJCN - 62A | THORNTONJCN - 62A | PARKESTON - 30F | DARNALL - 41A | DARNALL - 41A |
| Aug-57 | LINCOLN - 40A | IMMINGHAM - 40B | DONCASTER - 36A | THORNTONJCN - 62A | THORNTONJCN - 62A | THORNTONJCN - 62A | PARKESTON - 30F | DARNALL - 41A | DARNALL - 41A |
| Jan-58 | **11/57: IMM - 40B** | IMMINGHAM - 40B | DONCASTER - 36A | THORNTONJCN - 62A | THORNTONJCN - 62A | THORNTONJCN - 62A | PARKESTON - 30F | DARNALL - 41A | DARNALL - 41A |
| Aug-58 | IMMINGHAM - 40B | IMMINGHAM - 40B | DONCASTER - 36A | THORNTONJCN - 62A | THORNTONJCN - 62A | THORNTONJCN - 62A | PARKESTON - 30F | DARNALL - 41A | DARNALL - 41A |
| Jan-59 | IMMINGHAM - 40B | IMMINGHAM - 40B | DONCASTER - 36A | THORNTONJCN - 62A | THORNTONJCN - 62A | THORNTONJCN - 62A | PARKESTON - 30F | DARNALL - 41A | DARNALL - 41A |
| Aug-59 | IMMINGHAM - 40B | IMMINGHAM - 40B | DONCASTER - 36A | THORNTONJCN - 62A | THORNTONJCN - 62A | THORNTONJCN - 62A | PARKESTON - 30F | DARNALL - 41A | DARNALL - 41A |
| Nov-59 | IMMINGHAM - 40B | IMMINGHAM - 40B | DONCASTER - 36A | THORNTONJCN - 62A | THORNTONJCN - 62A | THORNTONJCN - 62A | PARKESTON - 30F | DARNALL - 41A | DARNALL - 41A |
| Jan-60 | IMMINGHAM - 40B | IMMINGHAM - 40B | DONCASTER - 36A | THORNTONJCN - 62A | THORNTONJCN - 62A | THORNTONJCN - 62A | PARKESTON - 30F | DARNALL - 41A | DARNALL - 41A |
| Apr-60 | IMMINGHAM - 40B | IMMINGHAM - 40B | DONCASTER - 36A | THORNTONJCN - 62A | THORNTONJCN - 62A | THORNTONJCN - 62A | PARKESTON - 30F | DARNALL - 41A | DARNALL - 41A |
| Aug-60 | IMMINGHAM - 40B | IMMINGHAM - 40B | DONCASTER - 36A | **9/60: DAL RD - 64C** | THORNTONJCN - 62A | THORNTONJCN - 62A | PARKESTON - 30F | DARNALL - 41A | DARNALL - 41A |
| Nov-60 | IMMINGHAM - 40B | IMMINGHAM - 40B | DONCASTER - 36A | DALRYROAD - 64C | THORNTONJCN - 62A | THORNTONJCN - 62A | PARKESTON - 30F | DARNALL - 41A | DARNALL - 41A |

across the Leeds – York – Scarborough axis with appearances south of Doncaster being uncommon enough to become a talking point. (Curiously, one of their most regular southern appearances took place on the Great Central. One of the York allocation had a freight working to Woodford Halse and could occasionally be seen at Neasden on a filling-in duty). The B17 (and B2 derivatives) were confined to the Great Eastern – the last of the Great Central batch having been transferred in late 1951- where they could be found on almost any type of main line service. The B12's were, apart from a couple of engines at Grantham, similarly confined to the Great Eastern; the last of the GNoS engines having been withdrawn in 1953.

Allocation table for locomotives 61152–61187 (August 1950 – November 1960).

| | 61152 | 61153 | 61154 | 61155 | 61156 | 61157 | 61158 | 61159 | 61160 |
|---|---|---|---|---|---|---|---|---|---|
| Aug-50 | DARNALL-39B | DARNALL-39B | DARNALL-39B | GORTON-39A | GORTON-39A | GORTON-39A | GORTON-39A | GORTON-39A | GORTON-39A |
| Jan-51 | DARNALL-39B | DARNALL-39B | DARNALL-39B | GORTON-39A | GORTON-39A | GORTON-39A | GORTON-39A | GORTON-39A | GORTON-39A |
| Aug-51 | DARNALL-39B | DARNALL-39B | DARNALL-39B | GORTON-39A | GORTON-39A | GORTON-39A | GORTON-39A | GORTON-39A | GORTON-39A |
| Jan-52 | DARNALL-39B | DARNALL-39B | DARNALL-39B | GORTON-39A | GORTON-39A | GORTON-39A | GORTON-39A | GORTON-39A | GORTON-39A |
| Aug-52 | DARNALL-39B | DARNALL-39B | DARNALL-39B | GORTON-39A | GORTON-39A | GORTON-39A | GORTON-39A | GORTON-39A | GORTON-39A |
| Jan-53 | DARNALL-39B | DARNALL-39B | DARNALL-39B | GORTON-39A | GORTON-39A | 10/52: DCTR-36A | GORTON-39A | GORTON-39A | GORTON-39A |
| Aug-53 | DARNALL-39B | DARNALL-39B | DARNALL-39B | GORTON-39A | GORTON-39A | DONCASTER-36A | GORTON-39A | GORTON-39A | GORTON-39A |
| Jan-54 | DARNALL-39B | DARNALL-39B | DARNALL-39B | GORTON-39A | GORTON-39A | DONCASTER-36A | 11/53: DCTR-36A | GORTON-39A | GORTON-39A |
| Aug-54 | DARNALL-39B | DARNALL-39B | DARNALL-39B | 6/54: C.HILL-37B | GORTON-39A | DONCASTER-36A | DONCASTER-36A | 6/54: IMM-40B | 6/54: CAMB-31A |
| Jan-55 | DARNALL-39B | DARNALL-39B | DARNALL-39B | 12/54: DCTR-36A | GORTON-39A | DONCASTER-36A | DONCASTER-36A | IMMINGHAM-40B | CAMBRIDGE-31A |
| Aug-55 | DARNALL-39B | DARNALL-39B | DARNALL-39B | DONCASTER-36A | GORTON-39A | DONCASTER-36A | DONCASTER-36A | IMMINGHAM-40B | CAMBRIDGE-31A |
| Jan-56 | DARNALL-41A | DARNALL-41A | DARNALL-41A | DONCASTER-36A | GORTON-39A | DONCASTER-36A | DONCASTER-36A | IMMINGHAM-40B | CAMBRIDGE-31A |
| Aug-56 | DARNALL-41A | DARNALL-41A | DARNALL-41A | DONCASTER-36A | GORTON-39A | DONCASTER-36A | DONCASTER-36A | IMMINGHAM-40B | CAMBRIDGE-31A |
| Jan-57 | DARNALL-41A | DARNALL-41A | DARNALL-41A | DONCASTER-36A | GORTON-39A | DONCASTER-36A | DONCASTER-36A | IMMINGHAM-40B | 11/56: COLW-38A |
| Aug-57 | 10/57: DCTR-36A | DARNALL-41A | DARNALL-41A | DONCASTER-36A | GORTON-39A | DONCASTER-36A | DONCASTER-36A | IMMINGHAM-40B | COLWICK-38A |
| Jan-58 | 11/57: DARN-41A | DARNALL-41A | DARNALL-41A | DONCASTER-36A | 10/57: S BGE-35C | DONCASTER-36A | DONCASTER-36A | IMMINGHAM-40B | 10/57: IPS-32B |
| Aug-58 | DARNALL-41A | DARNALL-41A | DARNALL-41A | DONCASTER-36A | SPITALBRIDGE-31F | DONCASTER-36A | DONCASTER-36A | IMMINGHAM-40B | IPSWICH-32B |
| Jan-59 | DARNALL-41A | DARNALL-41A | DARNALL-41A | DONCASTER-36A | SPITALBRIDGE-31F | DONCASTER-36A | DONCASTER-36A | IMMINGHAM-40B | IPSWICH-32B |
| Aug-59 | DARNALL-41A | DARNALL-41A | DARNALL-41A | DONCASTER-36A | SPITALBRIDGE-31F | DONCASTER-36A | DONCASTER-36A | IMMINGHAM-40B | 8/59: LOW-32C |
| Nov-59 | 10/59: MILL-41C | DARNALL-41A | DARNALL-41A | DONCASTER-36A | SPITALBRIDGE-31F | DONCASTER-36A | DONCASTER-36A | IMMINGHAM-40B | LOWESTOFT-32C |
| Jan-60 | MILLHOUSES-41C | DARNALL-41A | DARNALL-41A | DONCASTER-36A | 2/60: MARCH-31B | DONCASTER-36A | DONCASTER-36A | IMMINGHAM-40B | LOWESTOFT-32C |
| Apr-60 | MILLHOUSES-41C | DARNALL-41A | DARNALL-41A | 6/60: DARN-41A | MARCH-31B | DONCASTER-36A | DONCASTER-36A | IMMINGHAM-40B | 3/60: LINC-40A |
| Aug-60 | MILLHOUSES-41C | DARNALL-41A | DARNALL-41A | DARNALL-41A | MARCH-31B | DONCASTER-36A | DONCASTER-36A | IMMINGHAM-40B | LINCOLN-40A |
| Nov-60 | MILLHOUSES-41C | 11/60: LANG-41J | DARNALL-41A | DARNALL-41A | MARCH-31B | DONCASTER-36A | DONCASTER-36A | IMMINGHAM-40B | LINCOLN-40A |

| | 61161 | 61162 | 61163 | 61164 | 61165 | 61166 | 61167 | 61168 | 61169 |
|---|---|---|---|---|---|---|---|---|---|
| Aug-50 | GORTON-39A | GORTON-39A | NEASDEN-34E | NEASDEN-34E | MEXBOROUGH-36B | MEXBOROUGH-36B | MEXBOROUGH-36B | MEXBOROUGH-36B | DARNALL-39B |
| Jan-51 | GORTON-39A | GORTON-39A | NEASDEN-34E | NEASDEN-34E | MEXBOROUGH-36B | MEXBOROUGH-36B | MEXBOROUGH-36B | MEXBOROUGH-36B | DARNALL-39B |
| Aug-51 | GORTON-39A | GORTON-39A | NEASDEN-34E | NEASDEN-34E | MEXBOROUGH-36B | MEXBOROUGH-36B | MEXBOROUGH-36B | MEXBOROUGH-36B | DARNALL-39B |
| Jan-52 | GORTON-39A | GORTON-39A | NEASDEN-34E | NEASDEN-34E | MEXBOROUGH-36B | MEXBOROUGH-36B | MEXBOROUGH-36B | MEXBOROUGH-36B | DARNALL-39B |
| Aug-52 | GORTON-39A | GORTON-39A | NEASDEN-34E | NEASDEN-34E | MEXBOROUGH-36B | MEXBOROUGH-36B | MEXBOROUGH-36B | MEXBOROUGH-36B | DARNALL-39B |
| Jan-53 | GORTON-39A | GORTON-39A | NEASDEN-34E | NEASDEN-34E | MEXBOROUGH-36B | MEXBOROUGH-36B | MEXBOROUGH-36B | MEXBOROUGH-36B | DARNALL-39B |
| Aug-53 | GORTON-39A | GORTON-39A | NEASDEN-34E | NEASDEN-34E | MEXBOROUGH-36B | MEXBOROUGH-36B | 7/53: IMM-40B | 7/53: IMM-40B | DARNALL-39B |
| Jan-54 | GORTON-39A | GORTON-39A | NEASDEN-34E | NEASDEN-34E | MEXBOROUGH-36B | MEXBOROUGH-36B | 11/53: MEX-36B | IMMINGHAM-40B | DARNALL-39B |
| Aug-54 | GORTON-39A | 6/54: C.HILL-37B | 6/54: LEIC-38C | NEASDEN-34E | MEXBOROUGH-36B | MEXBOROUGH-36B | MEXBOROUGH-36B | IMMINGHAM-40B | DARNALL-39B |
| Jan-55 | GORTON-39A | 11/54: DCTR-36A | 1/55: COLW-38A | NEASDEN-34E | MEXBOROUGH-36B | MEXBOROUGH-36B | MEXBOROUGH-36B | IMMINGHAM-40B | DARNALL-39B |
| Aug-55 | GORTON-39A | DONCASTER-36A | COLWICK-38A | NEASDEN-34E | MEXBOROUGH-36B | MEXBOROUGH-36B | MEXBOROUGH-36B | IMMINGHAM-40B | DARNALL-39B |
| Jan-56 | GORTON-39A | DONCASTER-36A | COLWICK-38A | NEASDEN-34E | MEXBOROUGH-36B | MEXBOROUGH-36B | MEXBOROUGH-36B | IMMINGHAM-40B | DARNALL-41A |
| Aug-56 | GORTON-39A | DONCASTER-36A | COLWICK-38A | NEASDEN-34E | MEXBOROUGH-36B | MEXBOROUGH-36B | MEXBOROUGH-36B | IMMINGHAM-40B | DARNALL-41A |
| Jan-57 | GORTON-39A | DONCASTER-36A | COLWICK-38A | 1/57: STRAT-30A | MEXBOROUGH-36B | MEXBOROUGH-36B | MEXBOROUGH-36B | IMMINGHAM-40B | DARNALL-41A |
| Aug-57 | GORTON-39A | DONCASTER-36A | COLWICK-38A | STRATFORD-30A | MEXBOROUGH-36B | MEXBOROUGH-36B | MEXBOROUGH-36B | IMMINGHAM-40B | DARNALL-41A |
| Jan-58 | GORTON-39A | DONCASTER-36A | COLWICK-38A | STRATFORD-30A | MEXBOROUGH-36B | MEXBOROUGH-36B | MEXBOROUGH-36B | IMMINGHAM-40B | DARNALL-41A |
| Aug-58 | GORTON-9G | DONCASTER-36A | COLWICK-40E | STRATFORD-30A | MEXBOROUGH-41F | MEXBOROUGH-41F | MEXBOROUGH-41F | IMMINGHAM-40B | DARNALL-41A |
| Jan-59 | GORTON-9G | 1/59: IMM-40B | COLWICK-40E | STRATFORD-30A | MEXBOROUGH-41F | MEXBOROUGH-41F | MEXBOROUGH-41F | IMMINGHAM-40B | DARNALL-41A |
| Aug-59 | 6/59: LEIC-15E | IMMINGHAM-40B | COLWICK-40E | 5/59: DARN-41A | MEXBOROUGH-41F | MEXBOROUGH-41F | MEXBOROUGH-41F | IMMINGHAM-40B | DARNALL-41A |
| Nov-59 | 9/59: GORT-9G | IMMINGHAM-40B | COLWICK-40E | DARNALL-41A | MEXBOROUGH-41F | MEXBOROUGH-41F | MEXBOROUGH-41F | IMMINGHAM-40B | DARNALL-41A |
| Jan-60 | GORTON-9G | IMMINGHAM-40B | COLWICK-40E | DARNALL-41A | MEXBOROUGH-41F | MEXBOROUGH-41F | MEXBOROUGH-41F | IMMINGHAM-40B | DARNALL-41A |
| Apr-60 | GORTON-9G | IMMINGHAM-40B | COLWICK-40E | DARNALL-41A | MEXBOROUGH-41F | MEXBOROUGH-41F | MEXBOROUGH-41F | IMMINGHAM-40B | DARNALL-41A |
| Aug-60 | 6/60: MIRF-56D | IMMINGHAM-40B | COLWICK-40E | DARNALL-41A | MEXBOROUGH-41F | MEXBOROUGH-41F | MEXBOROUGH-41F | IMMINGHAM-40B | DARNALL-41A |
| Nov-60 | MIRFIELD-56D | IMMINGHAM-40B | COLWICK-40E | DARNALL-41A | MEXBOROUGH-41F | MEXBOROUGH-41F | MEXBOROUGH-41F | IMMINGHAM-40B | DARNALL-41A |

| | 61170 | 61171 | 61172 | 61173 | 61174 | 61175 | 61176 | 61177 | 61178 |
|---|---|---|---|---|---|---|---|---|---|
| Aug-50 | DONCASTER-36A | STRATFORD-30A | EASTFIELD-65A | DARLINGTON-51A | MEXBOROUGH-36B | STRATFORD-30A | DARLINGTON-51A | STRATFORD-30A | HAYMARKET-64B |
| Jan-51 | DONCASTER-36A | STRATFORD-30A | EASTFIELD-65A | DARLINGTON-51A | MEXBOROUGH-36B | STRATFORD-30A | DARLINGTON-51A | STRATFORD-30A | HAYMARKET-64B |
| Aug-51 | DONCASTER-36A | 9/51: LINC-40A | EASTFIELD-65A | DARLINGTON-51A | MEXBOROUGH-36B | 9/51: IMM-40B | DARLINGTON-51A | 9/51: LINC-40A | HAYMARKET-64B |
| Jan-52 | DONCASTER-36A | LINCOLN-40A | EASTFIELD-65A | 11/51: STOCK-51E | MEXBOROUGH-36B | IMMINGHAM-40B | DARLINGTON-51A | LINCOLN-40A | HAYMARKET-64B |
| Aug-52 | DONCASTER-36A | LINCOLN-40A | EASTFIELD-65A | STOCKTON-51E | 3/52: DARN-39B | IMMINGHAM-40B | DARLINGTON-51A | LINCOLN-40A | HAYMARKET-64B |
| Jan-53 | DONCASTER-36A | LINCOLN-40A | EASTFIELD-65A | STOCKTON-51E | DARNALL-39B | IMMINGHAM-40B | DARLINGTON-51A | LINCOLN-40A | HAYMARKET-64B |
| Aug-53 | DONCASTER-36A | LINCOLN-40A | EASTFIELD-65A | STOCKTON-51E | DARNALL-39B | IMMINGHAM-40B | 7/53: YORK-50A | LINCOLN-40A | HAYMARKET-64B |
| Jan-54 | DONCASTER-36A | LINCOLN-40A | EASTFIELD-65A | STOCKTON-51E | DARNALL-39B | IMMINGHAM-40B | YORK-50A | LINCOLN-40A | HAYMARKET-64B |
| Aug-54 | DONCASTER-36A | LINCOLN-40A | EASTFIELD-65A | STOCKTON-51E | DARNALL-39B | IMMINGHAM-40B | YORK-50A | LINCOLN-40A | HAYMARKET-64B |
| Jan-55 | DONCASTER-36A | 1/55: DCTR-36A | EASTFIELD-65A | STOCKTON-51E | DARNALL-39B | IMMINGHAM-40B | YORK-50A | LINCOLN-40A | HAYMARKET-64B |
| Aug-55 | DONCASTER-36A | DONCASTER-36A | EASTFIELD-65A | STOCKTON-51E | DARNALL-39B | IMMINGHAM-40B | 9/55: DARL-51A | LINCOLN-40A | HAYMARKET-64B |
| Jan-56 | DONCASTER-36A | DONCASTER-36A | 2/56: DUND-62B | STOCKTON-51E | DARNALL-41A | IMMINGHAM-40B | DARLINGTON-51A | 11/55: CAMB-31A | HAYMARKET-64B |
| Aug-56 | DONCASTER-36A | DONCASTER-36A | DUNDEE-62B | STOCKTON-51E | DARNALL-41A | IMMINGHAM-40B | DARLINGTON-51A | CAMBRIDGE-31A | HAYMARKET-64B |
| Jan-57 | DONCASTER-36A | DONCASTER-36A | DUNDEE-62B | STOCKTON-51E | DARNALL-41A | IMMINGHAM-40B | DARLINGTON-51A | 11/56: COLW-38A | HAYMARKET-64B |
| Aug-57 | DONCASTER-36A | 6/57: STRAT-30A | DUNDEE-62B | STOCKTON-51E | DARNALL-41A | IMMINGHAM-40B | DARLINGTON-51A | COLWICK-38A | HAYMARKET-64B |
| Jan-58 | DONCASTER-36A | STRATFORD-30A | DUNDEE-62B | STOCKTON-51E | DARNALL-41A | IMMINGHAM-40B | DARLINGTON-51A | COLWICK-38A | HAYMARKET-64B |
| Aug-58 | DONCASTER-36A | STRATFORD-30A | DUNDEE-62B | STOCKTON-51E | 10/58: KX-34A | IMMINGHAM-40B | DARLINGTON-51A | COLWICK-40E | HAYMARKET-64B |
| Jan-59 | DONCASTER-36A | STRATFORD-30A | DUNDEE-62B | STOCKTON-51E | KINGS CROSS-34A | IMMINGHAM-40B | DARLINGTON-51A | COLWICK-40E | HAYMARKET-64B |
| Aug-59 | DONCASTER-36A | 4/59: CAMB-31A | DUNDEE-62B | 6/59: TNBY-51L | KINGS CROSS-34A | IMMINGHAM-40B | DARLINGTON-51A | COLWICK-40E | HAYMARKET-64B |
| Nov-59 | DONCASTER-36A | CAMBRIDGE-31A | DUNDEE-62B | THORNABY-51L | KINGS CROSS-34A | IMMINGHAM-40B | DARLINGTON-51A | COLWICK-40E | HAYMARKET-64B |
| Jan-60 | DONCASTER-36A | CAMBRIDGE-31A | DUNDEE-62B | THORNABY-51L | KINGS CROSS-34A | IMMINGHAM-40B | DARLINGTON-51A | COLWICK-40E | HAYMARKET-64B |
| Apr-60 | DONCASTER-36A | CAMBRIDGE-31A | DUNDEE-62B | THORNABY-51L | KINGS CROSS-34A | IMMINGHAM-40B | DARLINGTON-51A | COLWICK-40E | HAYMARKET-64B |
| Aug-60 | DONCASTER-36A | CAMBRIDGE-31A | DUNDEE-62B | THORNABY-51L | KINGS CROSS-34A | IMMINGHAM-40B | DARLINGTON-51A | COLWICK-40E | HAYMARKET-64B |
| Nov-60 | DONCASTER-36A | CAMBRIDGE-31A | DUNDEE-62B | THORNABY-51L | 10/60: NEWE-34E | 11/60: COLW-40E | DARLINGTON-51A | COLWICK-40E | HAYMARKET-64B |

| | 61179 | 61180 | 61181 | 61182 | 61183 | 61184 | 61185 | 61186 | 61187 |
|---|---|---|---|---|---|---|---|---|---|
| Aug-50 | DARNALL-39B | EASTFIELD-65A | DARNALL-39B | GORTON-39A | DARNALL-39B | GORTON-39A | LEICESTER(GC)-38C | LEICESTER(GC)-38C | LEICESTER(GC)-38C |
| Jan-51 | DARNALL-39B | EASTFIELD-65A | DARNALL-39B | GORTON-39A | DARNALL-39B | GORTON-39A | LEICESTER(GC)-38C | LEICESTER(GC)-38C | LEICESTER(GC)-38C |
| Aug-51 | DARNALL-39B | EASTFIELD-65A | DARNALL-39B | 10/51: NORW-32A | DARNALL-39B | GORTON-39A | LEICESTER(GC)-38C | LEICESTER(GC)-38C | LEICESTER(GC)-38C |
| Jan-52 | DARNALL-39B | EASTFIELD-65A | DARNALL-39B | 3/52: GORT-39A | DARNALL-39B | GORTON-39A | LEICESTER(GC)-38C | LEICESTER(GC)-38C | LEICESTER(GC)-38C |
| Aug-52 | DARNALL-39B | EASTFIELD-65A | DARNALL-39B | GORTON-39A | DARNALL-39B | GORTON-39A | LEICESTER(GC)-38C | LEICESTER(GC)-38C | LEICESTER(GC)-38C |
| Jan-53 | DARNALL-39B | EASTFIELD-65A | DARNALL-39B | GORTON-39A | DARNALL-39B | GORTON-39A | 2/53: COLW-38A | LEICESTER(GC)-38C | LEICESTER(GC)-38C |
| Aug-53 | DARNALL-39B | EASTFIELD-65A | DARNALL-39B | GORTON-39A | DARNALL-39B | 9/53: ST M-64A | COLWICK-38A | LEICESTER(GC)-38C | LEICESTER(GC)-38C |
| Jan-54 | DARNALL-39B | EASTFIELD-65A | DARNALL-39B | GORTON-39A | DARNALL-39B | EDINBURGH(SM)-64A | COLWICK-38A | LEICESTER(GC)-38C | LEICESTER(GC)-38C |
| Aug-54 | DARNALL-39B | EASTFIELD-65A | DARNALL-39B | 6/54: IMM-40B | DARNALL-39B | EDINBURGH(SM)-64A | COLWICK-38A | LEICESTER(GC)-38C | LEICESTER(GC)-38C |
| Jan-55 | DARNALL-39B | EASTFIELD-65A | DARNALL-39B | IMMINGHAM-40B | DARNALL-39B | EDINBURGH(SM)-64A | COLWICK-38A | LEICESTER(GC)-38C | 1/55: NEAS-34E |
| Aug-55 | DARNALL-39B | 7/55: DUND-62B | DARNALL-39B | IMMINGHAM-40B | DARNALL-39B | EDINBURGH(SM)-64A | COLWICK-38A | LEICESTER(GC)-38C | NEASDEN-34E |
| Jan-56 | DARNALL-41A | DUNDEE-62B | DARNALL-41A | IMMINGHAM-40B | DARNALL-41A | EDINBURGH(SM)-64A | COLWICK-38A | LEICESTER(GC)-38C | NEASDEN-34E |
| Aug-56 | DARNALL-41A | DUNDEE-62B | DARNALL-41A | IMMINGHAM-40B | DARNALL-41A | EDINBURGH(SM)-64A | COLWICK-38A | LEICESTER(GC)-38C | NEASDEN-34E |
| Jan-57 | DARNALL-41A | DUNDEE-62B | DARNALL-41A | 2/57: STRAT-30A | DARNALL-41A | EDINBURGH(SM)-64A | COLWICK-38A | 11/56: COLW-38A | NEASDEN-34E |
| Aug-57 | DARNALL-41A | DUNDEE-62B | DARNALL-41A | STRATFORD-30A | DARNALL-41A | EDINBURGH(SM)-64A | COLWICK-38A | 9/57: WOOD-38E | NEASDEN-34E |
| Jan-58 | DARNALL-41A | DUNDEE-62B | DARNALL-41A | STRATFORD-30A | DARNALL-41A | EDINBURGH(SM)-64A | COLWICK-38A | WOODFORD HALSE-2F | NEASDEN-34E |
| Aug-58 | 10/58: KX-34A | DUNDEE-62B | DARNALL-41A | 8/58: CAMB-31A | DARNALL-41A | EDINBURGH(SM)-64A | COLWICK-40E | WOODFORD HALSE-2F | NEASDEN-14D |
| Jan-59 | KINGS CROSS-34A | DUNDEE-62B | DARNALL-41A | CAMBRIDGE-31A | DARNALL-41A | EDINBURGH(SM)-64A | COLWICK-40E | WOODFORD HALSE-2F | NEASDEN-14D |
| Aug-59 | KINGS CROSS-34A | DUNDEE-62B | DARNALL-41A | CAMBRIDGE-31A | DARNALL-41A | EDINBURGH(SM)-64A | COLWICK-40E | WOODFORD HALSE-2F | 9/59: WOOD-2F |
| Nov-59 | KINGS CROSS-34A | DUNDEE-62B | DARNALL-41A | CAMBRIDGE-31A | DARNALL-41A | EDINBURGH(SM)-64A | COLWICK-40E | WOODFORD HALSE-2F | WOODFORD HALSE-2F |
| Jan-60 | KINGS CROSS-34A | DUNDEE-62B | DARNALL-41A | CAMBRIDGE-31A | DARNALL-41A | 12/59: IMM-40B | COLWICK-40E | WOODFORD HALSE-2F | WOODFORD HALSE-2F |
| Apr-60 | KINGS CROSS-34A | DUNDEE-62B | DARNALL-41A | CAMBRIDGE-31A | DARNALL-41A | IMMINGHAM-40B | IMMINGHAM-40B | WOODFORD HALSE-2F | WOODFORD HALSE-2F |
| Aug-60 | KINGS CROSS-34A | DUNDEE-62B | DARNALL-41A | CAMBRIDGE-31A | DARNALL-41A | IMMINGHAM-40B | IMMINGHAM-40B | WOODFORD HALSE-2F | WOODFORD HALSE-2F |
| Nov-60 | KINGS CROSS-34A | DUNDEE-62B | DARNALL-41A | CAMBRIDGE-31A | DARNALL-41A | IMMINGHAM-40B | IMMINGHAM-40B | WOODFORD HALSE-2F | WOODFORD HALSE-2F |

One of the effects of the large fleet of class 7 and 8 locomotives was to reduce the number of duties for 2-6-0's on the main line and engines that had once been the mainstay of the many fast goods services from Kings Cross found themselves ousted by V2 2-6-2's to be sent to the Great Eastern, Lincoln and Hull districts. (The benefits of the V2's on express goods services was largely limited to a better turn of speed and a more comfortable ride for the crew since their goods loading classification was the same as that for a K3. The K3's on the other hand were no substitute for a Pacific when passenger duties beckoned although they did a considerable amount of work on secondary and cross-country excursion services).

| | 61188 | 61189 | 61190 | 61191 | 61192 | 61193 | 61194 | 61195 | 61196 |
|---|---|---|---|---|---|---|---|---|---|
| Aug-50 | LEICESTER (GC) - 38C | STOCKTON - 51E | IMMINGHAM - 40B | IMMINGHAM - 40B | STRATFORD - 30A | DONCASTER - 36A | MEXBOROUGH - 36B | IMMINGHAM - 40B | DONCASTER - 36A |
| Jan-51 | LEICESTER (GC) - 38C | STOCKTON - 51E | IMMINGHAM - 40B | IMMINGHAM - 40B | STRATFORD - 30A | DONCASTER - 36A | MEXBOROUGH - 36B | IMMINGHAM - 40B | DONCASTER - 36A |
| Aug-51 | LEICESTER (GC) - 38C | STOCKTON - 51E | IMMINGHAM - 40B | **9/51: STRAT - 30A** | STRATFORD - 30A | DONCASTER - 36A | MEXBOROUGH - 36B | IMMINGHAM - 40B | DONCASTER - 36A |
| Jan-52 | LEICESTER (GC) - 38C | STOCKTON - 51E | IMMINGHAM - 40B | STRATFORD - 30A | STRATFORD - 30A | DONCASTER - 36A | MEXBOROUGH - 36B | IMMINGHAM - 40B | DONCASTER - 36A |
| Aug-52 | LEICESTER (GC) - 38C | STOCKTON - 51E | IMMINGHAM - 40B | STRATFORD - 30A | **7/52: COLW - 38A** | DONCASTER - 36A | MEXBOROUGH - 36B | IMMINGHAM - 40B | DONCASTER - 36A |
| Jan-53 | **1/53: COLW - 38A** | STOCKTON - 51E | IMMINGHAM - 40B | STRATFORD - 30A | COLWICK - 38A | DONCASTER - 36A | MEXBOROUGH - 36B | IMMINGHAM - 40B | DONCASTER - 36A |
| Aug-53 | COLWICK - 38A | STOCKTON - 51E | IMMINGHAM - 40B | **9/53: STM - 64A** | COLWICK - 38A | DONCASTER - 36A | MEXBOROUGH - 36B | IMMINGHAM - 40B | DONCASTER - 36A |
| Jan-54 | COLWICK - 38A | STOCKTON - 51E | IMMINGHAM - 40B | EDINBURGH (SM) - 64A | COLWICK - 38A | DONCASTER - 36A | MEXBOROUGH - 36B | IMMINGHAM - 40B | DONCASTER - 36A |
| Aug-54 | COLWICK - 38A | STOCKTON - 51E | IMMINGHAM - 40B | EDINBURGH (SM) - 64A | **6/54: WOOD - 38E** | DONCASTER - 36A | MEXBOROUGH - 36B | IMMINGHAM - 40B | DONCASTER - 36A |
| Jan-55 | COLWICK - 38A | STOCKTON - 51E | IMMINGHAM - 40B | EDINBURGH (SM) - 64A | W. HALSE - 38E | DONCASTER - 36A | MEXBOROUGH - 36B | IMMINGHAM - 40B | DONCASTER - 36A |
| Aug-55 | COLWICK - 38A | STOCKTON - 51E | IMMINGHAM - 40B | EDINBURGH (SM) - 64A | W. HALSE - 38E | DONCASTER - 36A | MEXBOROUGH - 36B | IMMINGHAM - 40B | DONCASTER - 36A |
| Jan-56 | COLWICK - 38A | STOCKTON - 51E | IMMINGHAM - 40B | EDINBURGH (SM) - 64A | W. HALSE - 38E | DONCASTER - 36A | MEXBOROUGH - 36B | IMMINGHAM - 40B | DONCASTER - 36A |
| Aug-56 | COLWICK - 38A | STOCKTON - 51E | IMMINGHAM - 40B | EDINBURGH (SM) - 64A | W. HALSE - 38E | DONCASTER - 36A | MEXBOROUGH - 36B | IMMINGHAM - 40B | DONCASTER - 36A |
| Jan-57 | COLWICK - 38A | **10/56: ARDS - 56B** | IMMINGHAM - 40B | EDINBURGH (SM) - 64A | W. HALSE - 38E | DONCASTER - 36A | MEXBOROUGH - 36B | IMMINGHAM - 40B | DONCASTER - 36A |
| Aug-57 | COLWICK - 38A | ARDSLEY - 56B | IMMINGHAM - 40B | EDINBURGH (SM) - 64A | W. HALSE - 38E | DONCASTER - 36A | MEXBOROUGH - 36B | IMMINGHAM - 40B | DONCASTER - 36A |
| Jan-58 | COLWICK - 38A | ARDSLEY - 56B | IMMINGHAM - 40B | EDINBURGH (SM) - 64A | W. HALSE - 38E | DONCASTER - 36A | MEXBOROUGH - 36B | IMMINGHAM - 40B | DONCASTER - 36A |
| Aug-58 | **6/58: LEIC - 15E** | ARDSLEY - 56B | IMMINGHAM - 40B | EDINBURGH (SM) - 64A | W. HALSE - 2F | DONCASTER - 36A | MEXBOROUGH - 41F | IMMINGHAM - 40B | DONCASTER - 36A |
| Jan-59 | **9/58: COLW - 40E** | **2/59: C.HILL - 56C** | IMMINGHAM - 40B | EDINBURGH (SM) - 64A | W. HALSE - 2F | DONCASTER - 36A | MEXBOROUGH - 41F | IMMINGHAM - 40B | DONCASTER - 36A |
| Aug-59 | COLWICK - 40E | COPLEYHILL - 56C | IMMINGHAM - 40B | EDINBURGH (SM) - 64A | W. HALSE - 2F | DONCASTER - 36A | MEXBOROUGH - 41F | IMMINGHAM - 40B | DONCASTER - 36A |
| Nov-59 | COLWICK - 40E | COPLEYHILL - 56C | IMMINGHAM - 40B | EDINBURGH (SM) - 64A | W. HALSE - 2F | DONCASTER - 36A | MEXBOROUGH - 41F | IMMINGHAM - 40B | DONCASTER - 36A |
| Jan-60 | COLWICK - 40E | COPLEYHILL - 56C | IMMINGHAM - 40B | EDINBURGH (SM) - 64A | W. HALSE - 2F | DONCASTER - 36A | MEXBOROUGH - 41F | IMMINGHAM - 40B | DONCASTER - 36A |
| Apr-60 | COLWICK - 40E | COPLEYHILL - 56C | IMMINGHAM - 40B | EDINBURGH (SM) - 64A | W. HALSE - 2F | DONCASTER - 36A | MEXBOROUGH - 41F | IMMINGHAM - 40B | DONCASTER - 36A |
| Aug-60 | COLWICK - 40E | COPLEYHILL - 56C | IMMINGHAM - 40B | EDINBURGH (SM) - 64A | W. HALSE - 2F | DONCASTER - 36A | MEXBOROUGH - 41F | IMMINGHAM - 40B | DONCASTER - 36A |
| Nov-60 | COLWICK - 40E | COPLEYHILL - 56C | IMMINGHAM - 40B | EDINBURGH (SM) - 64A | **10/60: LEIC - 15E** | DONCASTER - 36A | MEXBOROUGH - 41F | IMMINGHAM - 40B | DONCASTER - 36A |

| | 61197 | 61198 | 61199 | 61200 | 61201 | 61202 | 61203 | 61204 | 61205 |
|---|---|---|---|---|---|---|---|---|---|
| Aug-50 | EASTFIELD - 65A | DARLINGTON - 51A | TWEEDMOUTH - 52D | KINGS CROSS - 34A | IPSWICH - 32B | IMMINGHAM - 40B | KINGS CROSS - 34A | IMMINGHAM - 40B | STRATFORD - 30A |
| Jan-51 | EASTFIELD - 65A | DARLINGTON - 51A | TWEEDMOUTH - 52D | KINGS CROSS - 34A | IPSWICH - 32B | IMMINGHAM - 40B | KINGS CROSS - 34A | IMMINGHAM - 40B | STRATFORD - 30A |
| Aug-51 | EASTFIELD - 65A | DARLINGTON - 51A | **7/51: GHD - 52A** | KINGS CROSS - 34A | IPSWICH - 32B | IMMINGHAM - 40B | KINGS CROSS - 34A | IMMINGHAM - 40B | STRATFORD - 30A |
| Jan-52 | EASTFIELD - 65A | DARLINGTON - 51A | GATESHEAD - 52A | KINGS CROSS - 34A | IPSWICH - 32B | IMMINGHAM - 40B | KINGS CROSS - 34A | IMMINGHAM - 40B | STRATFORD - 30A |
| Aug-52 | EASTFIELD - 65A | DARLINGTON - 51A | GATESHEAD - 52A | KINGS CROSS - 34A | IPSWICH - 32B | IMMINGHAM - 40B | KINGS CROSS - 34A | IMMINGHAM - 40B | STRATFORD - 30A |
| Jan-53 | EASTFIELD - 65A | DARLINGTON - 51A | GATESHEAD - 52A | KINGS CROSS - 34A | IPSWICH - 32B | IMMINGHAM - 40B | KINGS CROSS - 34A | IMMINGHAM - 40B | STRATFORD - 30A |
| Aug-53 | EASTFIELD - 65A | DARLINGTON - 51A | GATESHEAD - 52A | KINGS CROSS - 34A | **10/53: COLW - 38A** | **5/53: LINC - 40A** | KINGS CROSS - 34A | **10/53: NEWE - 35A** | **10/53: NEWE - 35A** |
| Jan-54 | EASTFIELD - 65A | DARLINGTON - 51A | GATESHEAD - 52A | KINGS CROSS - 34A | COLWICK - 38A | LINCOLN - 40A | KINGS CROSS - 34A | NEWENGLAND - 35A | NEWENGLAND - 35A |
| Aug-54 | EASTFIELD - 65A | DARLINGTON - 51A | GATESHEAD - 52A | KINGS CROSS - 34A | COLWICK - 38A | LINCOLN - 40A | KINGS CROSS - 34A | NEWENGLAND - 35A | NEWENGLAND - 35A |
| Jan-55 | EASTFIELD - 65A | DARLINGTON - 51A | GATESHEAD - 52A | KINGS CROSS - 34A | **1/55: LEIC - 38C** | LINCOLN - 40A | KINGS CROSS - 34A | NEWENGLAND - 35A | NEWENGLAND - 35A |
| Aug-55 | EASTFIELD - 65A | DARLINGTON - 51A | **9/55: TWEED - 56D** | KINGS CROSS - 34A | **2/55: COLW - 38A** | LINCOLN - 40A | KINGS CROSS - 34A | NEWENGLAND - 35A | NEWENGLAND - 35A |
| Jan-56 | EASTFIELD - 65A | DARLINGTON - 51A | TWEEDMOUTH - 52D | KINGS CROSS - 34A | COLWICK - 38A | LINCOLN - 40A | KINGS CROSS - 34A | NEWENGLAND - 35A | NEWENGLAND - 35A |
| Aug-56 | EASTFIELD - 65A | DARLINGTON - 51A | TWEEDMOUTH - 52D | KINGS CROSS - 34A | COLWICK - 38A | LINCOLN - 40A | KINGS CROSS - 34A | NEWENGLAND - 35A | NEWENGLAND - 35A |
| Jan-57 | EASTFIELD - 65A | DARLINGTON - 51A | TWEEDMOUTH - 52D | KINGS CROSS - 34A | COLWICK - 38A | LINCOLN - 40A | KINGS CROSS - 34A | NEWENGLAND - 35A | NEWENGLAND - 35A |
| Aug-57 | EASTFIELD - 65A | DARLINGTON - 51A | TWEEDMOUTH - 52D | KINGS CROSS - 34A | COLWICK - 38A | LINCOLN - 40A | **10/57: CAMB - 31A** | **6/57:S.BGE - 35C** | **6/57:S.BGE - 35C** |
| Jan-58 | EASTFIELD - 65A | DARLINGTON - 51A | TWEEDMOUTH - 52D | KINGS CROSS - 34A | COLWICK - 38A | LINCOLN - 40A | CAMBRIDGE - 31A | SPITAL BGE - 35C | SPITAL BGE - 35C |
| Aug-58 | EASTFIELD - 65A | DARLINGTON - 51A | TWEEDMOUTH - 52D | KINGS CROSS - 34A | **10/58: LEIC - 15E** | LINCOLN - 40A | CAMBRIDGE - 31A | SPITAL BGE - 31F | SPITAL BGE - 31F |
| Jan-59 | EASTFIELD - 65A | **6/59: LOWM - 56F** | TWEEDMOUTH - 52D | KINGS CROSS - 34A | LEICESTER (GC) - 15E | LINCOLN - 40A | CAMBRIDGE - 31A | SPITAL BGE - 31F | SPITAL BGE - 31F |
| Aug-59 | EASTFIELD - 65A | **8/59: YORK - 50A** | TWEEDMOUTH - 52D | **4/59: NEWE - 34E** | **8/59: AGE - 26B** | LINCOLN - 40A | CAMBRIDGE - 31A | SPITAL BGE - 31F | SPITAL BGE - 31F |
| Nov-59 | EASTFIELD - 65A | YORK - 50A | TWEEDMOUTH - 52D | NEWENGLAND - 34E | AGECROFT - 26B | LINCOLN - 40A | CAMBRIDGE - 31A | SPITAL BGE - 31F | SPITAL BGE - 31F |
| Jan-60 | EASTFIELD - 65A | YORK - 50A | TWEEDMOUTH - 52D | NEWENGLAND - 34E | AGECROFT - 26B | LINCOLN - 40A | CAMBRIDGE - 31A | **2/60: MARCH - 31B** | **2/60: MARCH - 31B** |
| Apr-60 | EASTFIELD - 65A | YORK - 50A | TWEEDMOUTH - 52D | **4/60: KX - 34A** | AGECROFT - 26B | LINCOLN - 40A | CAMBRIDGE - 31A | MARCH - 31B | MARCH - 31B |
| Aug-60 | EASTFIELD - 65A | YORK - 50A | **6/60: BLAY - 52C** | KINGS CROSS - 34A | AGECROFT - 26B | LINCOLN - 40A | **9/60: MARCH - 31B** | MARCH - 31B | MARCH - 31B |
| Nov-60 | EASTFIELD - 65A | YORK - 50A | BLAYDON - 52C | KINGS CROSS - 34A | AGECROFT - 26B | LINCOLN - 40A | MARCH - 31B | MARCH - 31B | MARCH - 31B |

| | 61206 | 61207 | 61208 | 61209 | 61210 | 61211 | 61212 | 61213 | 61214 |
|---|---|---|---|---|---|---|---|---|---|
| Aug-50 | NEWENGLAND - 35A | NEWENGLAND - 35A | RETFORD - 36E | ANNESLEY - 38B | NEWENGLAND - 35A | RETFORD - 36E | RETFORD - 36E | RETFORD - 36E | STOCKTON - 51E |
| Jan-51 | NEWENGLAND - 35A | NEWENGLAND - 35A | RETFORD - 36E | ANNESLEY - 38B | NEWENGLAND - 35A | RETFORD - 36E | RETFORD - 36E | RETFORD - 36E | STOCKTON - 51E |
| Aug-51 | NEWENGLAND - 35A | NEWENGLAND - 35A | RETFORD - 36E | ANNESLEY - 38B | NEWENGLAND - 35A | RETFORD - 36E | RETFORD - 36E | RETFORD - 36E | STOCKTON - 51E |
| Jan-52 | NEWENGLAND - 35A | NEWENGLAND - 35A | RETFORD - 36E | ANNESLEY - 38B | NEWENGLAND - 35A | RETFORD - 36E | RETFORD - 36E | RETFORD - 36E | STOCKTON - 51E |
| Aug-52 | NEWENGLAND - 35A | NEWENGLAND - 35A | RETFORD - 36E | ANNESLEY - 38B | NEWENGLAND - 35A | RETFORD - 36E | RETFORD - 36E | RETFORD - 36E | STOCKTON - 51E |
| Jan-53 | **1/53: KX - 34A** | NEWENGLAND - 35A | RETFORD - 36E | ANNESLEY - 38B | 1/53: KX - 34A | RETFORD - 36E | RETFORD - 36E | RETFORD - 36E | STOCKTON - 51E |
| Aug-53 | **7/53: NEAS - 34E** | NEWENGLAND - 35A | RETFORD - 36E | ANNESLEY - 38B | **3/53: NEWE - 35A** | RETFORD - 36E | RETFORD - 36E | RETFORD - 36E | STOCKTON - 51E |
| Jan-54 | NEASDEN - 34E | NEWENGLAND - 35A | RETFORD - 36E | ANNESLEY - 38B | NEWENGLAND - 35A | RETFORD - 36E | RETFORD - 36E | RETFORD - 36E | STOCKTON - 51E |
| Aug-54 | NEASDEN - 34E | NEWENGLAND - 35A | RETFORD - 36E | ANNESLEY - 38B | NEWENGLAND - 35A | RETFORD - 36E | RETFORD - 36E | RETFORD - 36E | STOCKTON - 51E |
| Jan-55 | NEASDEN - 34E | NEWENGLAND - 35A | RETFORD - 36E | ANNESLEY - 38B | NEWENGLAND - 35A | RETFORD - 36E | RETFORD - 36E | RETFORD - 36E | STOCKTON - 51E |
| Aug-55 | NEASDEN - 34E | NEWENGLAND - 35A | RETFORD - 36E | ANNESLEY - 38B | NEWENGLAND - 35A | RETFORD - 36E | RETFORD - 36E | RETFORD - 36E | STOCKTON - 51E |
| Jan-56 | NEASDEN - 34E | NEWENGLAND - 35A | RETFORD - 36E | ANNESLEY - 38B | NEWENGLAND - 35A | RETFORD - 36E | RETFORD - 36E | RETFORD - 36E | STOCKTON - 51E |
| Aug-56 | NEASDEN - 34E | NEWENGLAND - 35A | RETFORD - 36E | **10/56: COLW - 38A** | NEWENGLAND - 35A | RETFORD - 36E | RETFORD - 36E | RETFORD - 36E | **10/56: C.HILL - 56C** |
| Jan-57 | NEASDEN - 34E | NEWENGLAND - 35A | RETFORD - 36E | COLWICK - 38A | NEWENGLAND - 35A | RETFORD - 36E | RETFORD - 36E | RETFORD - 36E | COPLEYHILL - 56C |
| Aug-57 | NEASDEN - 34E | NEWENGLAND - 35A | RETFORD - 36E | COLWICK - 38A | NEWENGLAND - 35A | RETFORD - 36E | RETFORD - 36E | RETFORD - 36E | COPLEYHILL - 56C |
| Jan-58 | NEASDEN - 34E | NEWENGLAND - 35A | RETFORD - 36E | COLWICK - 38A | NEWENGLAND - 35A | RETFORD - 36E | RETFORD - 36E | RETFORD - 36E | COPLEYHILL - 56C |
| Aug-58 | NEASDEN - 14D | NEWENGLAND - 34E | RETFORD - 36E | COLWICK - 40E | NEWENGLAND - 34E | RETFORD - 36E | RETFORD - 36E | RETFORD - 36E | COPLEYHILL - 56C |
| Jan-59 | NEASDEN - 14D | NEWENGLAND - 34E | RETFORD - 36E | COLWICK - 40E | NEWENGLAND - 34E | RETFORD - 36E | RETFORD - 36E | **11/58: DCTR - 36A** | COPLEYHILL - 56C |
| Aug-59 | NEASDEN - 14D | NEWENGLAND - 34E | RETFORD - 36E | COLWICK - 40E | NEWENGLAND - 34E | RETFORD - 36E | RETFORD - 36E | DONCASTER - 36A | COPLEYHILL - 56C |
| Nov-59 | NEASDEN - 14D | NEWENGLAND - 34E | RETFORD - 36E | COLWICK - 40E | NEWENGLAND - 34E | RETFORD - 36E | RETFORD - 36E | **11/59: RET - 36E** | COPLEYHILL - 56C |
| Jan-60 | NEASDEN - 14D | NEWENGLAND - 34E | RETFORD - 36E | COLWICK - 40E | NEWENGLAND - 34E | RETFORD - 36E | RETFORD - 36E | RETFORD - 36E | COPLEYHILL - 56C |
| Apr-60 | NEASDEN - 14D | NEWENGLAND - 34E | RETFORD - 36E | COLWICK - 40E | NEWENGLAND - 34E | RETFORD - 36E | RETFORD - 36E | RETFORD - 36E | COPLEYHILL - 56C |
| Aug-60 | NEASDEN - 14D | NEWENGLAND - 34E | RETFORD - 36E | COLWICK - 40E | NEWENGLAND - 34E | RETFORD - 36E | RETFORD - 36E | RETFORD - 36E | COPLEYHILL - 56C |
| Nov-60 | NEASDEN - 14D | NEWENGLAND - 34E | RETFORD - 36E | COLWICK - 40E | NEWENGLAND - 34E | RETFORD - 36E | RETFORD - 36E | RETFORD - 36E | COPLEYHILL - 56C |

| | 61215 | 61216 | 61217 | 61218 | 61219 | 61220 | 61221 | 61222 | 61223 |
|---|---|---|---|---|---|---|---|---|---|
| Aug-50 | BOTGDNS - 53B | NEVILLE HILL - 50B | CARLISLE (C) - 12B | NEVILLE HILL - 50B | CARLISLE (C) - 12B | STOCKTON - 51E | HAYMARKET - 64B | CARLISLE (C) - 12B | GORTON - 39A |
| Jan-51 | BOTGDNS - 53B | NEVILLE HILL - 50B | CARLISLE (C) - 12B | NEVILLE HILL - 50B | CARLISLE (C) - 12B | STOCKTON - 51E | HAYMARKET - 64B | CARLISLE (C) - 12B | GORTON - 39A |
| Aug-51 | BOTGDNS - 53B | NEVILLE HILL - 50B | CARLISLE (C) - 68E | NEVILLE HILL - 50B | CARLISLE (C) - 68E | STOCKTON - 51E | HAYMARKET - 64B | CARLISLE (C) - 68E | GORTON - 39A |
| Jan-52 | BOTGDNS - 53B | NEVILLE HILL - 50B | CARLISLE (C) - 68E | NEVILLE HILL - 50B | CARLISLE (C) - 68E | STOCKTON - 51E | HAYMARKET - 64B | CARLISLE (C) - 68E | GORTON - 39A |
| Aug-52 | BOTGDNS - 53B | NEVILLE HILL - 50B | CARLISLE (C) - 68E | NEVILLE HILL - 50B | CARLISLE (C) - 68E | STOCKTON - 51E | HAYMARKET - 64B | CARLISLE (C) - 68E | GORTON - 39A |
| Jan-53 | BOTGDNS - 53B | NEVILLE HILL - 50B | CARLISLE (C) - 68E | NEVILLE HILL - 50B | CARLISLE (C) - 68E | STOCKTON - 51E | HAYMARKET - 64B | CARLISLE (C) - 68E | GORTON - 39A |
| Aug-53 | BOTGDNS - 53B | NEVILLE HILL - 50B | CARLISLE (C) - 68E | NEVILLE HILL - 50B | CARLISLE (C) - 68E | STOCKTON - 51E | HAYMARKET - 64B | CARLISLE (C) - 68E | GORTON - 39A |
| Jan-54 | BOTGDNS - 53B | NEVILLE HILL - 50B | CARLISLE (C) - 68E | NEVILLE HILL - 50B | CARLISLE (C) - 68E | STOCKTON - 51E | HAYMARKET - 64B | CARLISLE (C) - 68E | GORTON - 39A |
| Aug-54 | BOTGDNS - 53B | NEVILLE HILL - 50B | CARLISLE (C) - 68E | NEVILLE HILL - 50B | CARLISLE (C) - 68E | STOCKTON - 51E | HAYMARKET - 64B | CARLISLE (C) - 68E | **6/54: CAMB - 31A** |
| Jan-55 | BOTGDNS - 53B | NEVILLE HILL - 50B | CARLISLE (C) - 68E | NEVILLE HILL - 50B | CARLISLE (C) - 68E | STOCKTON - 51E | HAYMARKET - 64B | CARLISLE (C) - 68E | CAMBRIDGE - 31A |
| Aug-55 | BOTGDNS - 53B | NEVILLE HILL - 50B | CARLISLE (C) - 68E | NEVILLE HILL - 50B | CARLISLE (C) - 68E | STOCKTON - 51E | HAYMARKET - 64B | CARLISLE (C) - 68E | CAMBRIDGE - 31A |
| Jan-56 | BOTGDNS - 53B | NEVILLE HILL - 50B | CARLISLE (C) - 68E | NEVILLE HILL - 50B | CARLISLE (C) - 68E | STOCKTON - 51E | HAYMARKET - 64B | CARLISLE (C) - 68E | CAMBRIDGE - 31A |
| Aug-56 | BOTGDNS - 53B | NEVILLE HILL - 50B | CARLISLE (C) - 68E | NEVILLE HILL - 50B | CARLISLE (C) - 68E | STOCKTON - 51E | HAYMARKET - 64B | CARLISLE (C) - 68E | **6/56: NORW - 32A** |
| Jan-57 | BOTGDNS - 53B | NEVILLE HILL - 50B | CARLISLE (C) - 68E | NEVILLE HILL - 50B | CARLISLE (C) - 68E | STOCKTON - 51E | HAYMARKET - 64B | CARLISLE (C) - 68E | NORWICH - 32A |
| Aug-57 | BOTGDNS - 53B | NEVILLE HILL - 50B | CARLISLE (C) - 68E | NEVILLE HILL - 50B | CARLISLE (C) - 68E | STOCKTON - 51E | HAYMARKET - 64B | CARLISLE (C) - 68E | NORWICH - 32A |
| Jan-58 | BOTGDNS - 53B | NEVILLE HILL - 50B | CARLISLE (C) - 68E | NEVILLE HILL - 50B | **12/57: HMKT - 64B** | STOCKTON - 51E | HAYMARKET - 64B | CARLISLE (C) - 68E | **12/57: YAR (ST) - 32D** |
| Aug-58 | BOTGDNS - 53B | NEVILLE HILL - 50B | CARLISLE (C) - 12C | NEVILLE HILL - 50B | HAYMARKET - 64B | STOCKTON - 51E | HAYMARKET - 64B | CARLISLE (C) - 12C | **9/58: NORW - 32A** |
| Jan-59 | BOTGDNS - 53B | NEVILLE HILL - 50B | CARLISLE (C) - 12C | NEVILLE HILL - 50B | HAYMARKET - 64B | STOCKTON - 51E | HAYMARKET - 64B | CARLISLE (C) - 12C | NORWICH - 32A |
| Aug-59 | **6/59: DYCTS - 53A** | NEVILLE HILL - 50B | CARLISLE (C) - 12C | NEVILLE HILL - 50B | HAYMARKET - 64B | STOCKTON - 51E | HAYMARKET - 64B | CARLISLE (C) - 12C | **5/59: LOW - 32C** |
| Nov-59 | DAIRYCOATES - 53A | NEVILLE HILL - 50B | CARLISLE (C) - 12C | NEVILLE HILL - 50B | HAYMARKET - 64B | STOCKTON - 51E | HAYMARKET - 64B | CARLISLE (C) - 12C | LOWESTOFT - 32C |
| Jan-60 | DAIRYCOATES - 53A | NEVILLE HILL - 50B | CARLISLE (C) - 12C | NEVILLE HILL - 50B | HAYMARKET - 64B | STOCKTON - 51E | HAYMARKET - 64B | CARLISLE (C) - 12C | LOWESTOFT - 32C |
| Apr-60 | DAIRYCOATES - 50B | NEVILLE HILL - 55H | CARLISLE (C) - 12C | NEVILLE HILL - 55H | HAYMARKET - 64B | STOCKTON - 51E | HAYMARKET - 64B | CARLISLE (C) - 12C | **3/60: LINC - 40A** |
| Aug-60 | DAIRYCOATES - 50B | NEVILLE HILL - 55H | CARLISLE (C) - 12C | NEVILLE HILL - 55H | HAYMARKET - 64B | STOCKTON - 51E | HAYMARKET - 64B | CARLISLE (C) - 12C | LINCOLN - 40A |
| Nov-60 | DAIRYCOATES - 50B | NEVILLE HILL - 55H | CARLISLE (C) - 12C | NEVILLE HILL - 55H | HAYMARKET - 64B | STOCKTON - 51E | HAYMARKET - 64B | CARLISLE (C) - 12C | LINCOLN - 40A |

| | 61224 | 61225 | 61226 | 61227 | 61228 | 61229 | 61230 | 61231 | 61232 |
|---|---|---|---|---|---|---|---|---|---|
| Aug-50 | DARLINGTON - 51A | GORTON - 39A | PARKESTON - 30F | STRATFORD - 30A | GORTON - 39A | BRADFORD - 37C | BRADFORD - 37C | RETFORD - 36E | PARKESTON - 30F |
| Jan-51 | DARLINGTON - 51A | GORTON - 39A | **10/50: MARCH - 31B** | **3/51: CAMB - 31A** | GORTON - 39A | BRADFORD - 37C | BRADFORD - 37C | RETFORD - 36E | PARKESTON - 30F |
| Aug-51 | DARLINGTON - 51A | GORTON - 39A | **12/50: PARK - 30F** | **5/51: STRAT - 30A** | GORTON - 39A | BRADFORD - 37C | BRADFORD - 37C | RETFORD - 36E | PARKESTON - 30F |
| Jan-52 | DARLINGTON - 51A | GORTON - 39A | PARKESTON - 30F | STRATFORD - 30A | GORTON - 39A | BRADFORD - 37C | BRADFORD - 37C | RETFORD - 36E | PARKESTON - 30F |
| Aug-52 | DARLINGTON - 51A | **7/52: DARN - 39B** | PARKESTON - 30F | STRATFORD - 30A | GORTON - 39A | BRADFORD - 37C | BRADFORD - 37C | RETFORD - 36E | PARKESTON - 30F |
| Jan-53 | DARLINGTON - 51A | DARNALL - 39B | PARKESTON - 30F | STRATFORD - 30A | GORTON - 39A | BRADFORD - 37C | BRADFORD - 37C | RETFORD - 36E | PARKESTON - 30F |
| Aug-53 | **7/53: YORK - 50A** | DARNALL - 39B | PARKESTON - 30F | STRATFORD - 30A | GORTON - 39A | BRADFORD - 37C | BRADFORD - 37C | RETFORD - 36E | PARKESTON - 30F |
| Jan-54 | YORK - 50A | DARNALL - 39B | PARKESTON - 30F | STRATFORD - 30A | GORTON - 39A | BRADFORD - 37C | BRADFORD - 37C | RETFORD - 36E | PARKESTON - 30F |
| Aug-54 | YORK - 50A | DARNALL - 39B | PARKESTON - 30F | STRATFORD - 30A | **6/54: IPS - 32B** | BRADFORD - 37C | BRADFORD - 37C | RETFORD - 36E | PARKESTON - 30F |
| Jan-55 | YORK - 50A | DARNALL - 39B | PARKESTON - 30F | STRATFORD - 30A | IPSWICH - 32B | BRADFORD - 37C | BRADFORD - 37C | RETFORD - 36E | PARKESTON - 30F |
| Aug-55 | **9/55: DARL - 51A** | DARNALL - 39B | PARKESTON - 30F | STRATFORD - 30A | IPSWICH - 32B | BRADFORD - 37C | BRADFORD - 37C | RETFORD - 36E | PARKESTON - 30F |
| Jan-56 | DARLINGTON - 51A | **11/55: DCTR - 36A** | PARKESTON - 30F | STRATFORD - 30A | IPSWICH - 32B | BRADFORD - 37C | BRADFORD - 37C | RETFORD - 36E | PARKESTON - 30F |
| Aug-56 | DARLINGTON - 51A | DONCASTER - 36A | PARKESTON - 30F | STRATFORD - 30A | IPSWICH - 32B | BRADFORD - 56G | BRADFORD - 56G | RETFORD - 36E | PARKESTON - 30F |
| Jan-57 | DARLINGTON - 51A | DONCASTER - 36A | PARKESTON - 30F | **11/56: PARK - 30F** | IPSWICH - 32B | BRADFORD - 56G | BRADFORD - 56G | RETFORD - 36E | PARKESTON - 30F |
| Aug-57 | DARLINGTON - 51A | DONCASTER - 36A | PARKESTON - 30F | PARKESTON - 30F | IPSWICH - 32B | BRADFORD - 56G | BRADFORD - 56G | RETFORD - 36E | PARKESTON - 30F |
| Jan-58 | DARLINGTON - 51A | DONCASTER - 36A | PARKESTON - 30F | PARKESTON - 30F | IPSWICH - 32B | **2/58: LOW M - 56F** | **2/58: LOW M - 56F** | RETFORD - 36E | PARKESTON - 30F |
| Aug-58 | DARLINGTON - 51A | DONCASTER - 36A | PARKESTON - 30F | PARKESTON - 30F | IPSWICH - 32B | **9/58: DARL - 51A** | LOWMOOR - 56F | RETFORD - 36E | PARKESTON - 30F |
| Jan-59 | DARLINGTON - 51A | DONCASTER - 36A | PARKESTON - 30F | PARKESTON - 30F | IPSWICH - 32B | DARLINGTON - 51A | LOWMOOR - 56F | RETFORD - 36E | PARKESTON - 30F |
| Aug-59 | DARLINGTON - 51A | DONCASTER - 36A | PARKESTON - 30F | PARKESTON - 30F | **9/59: NORW - 32A** | **6/59: YORK - 50A** | LOWMOOR - 56F | RETFORD - 36E | PARKESTON - 30F |
| Nov-59 | DARLINGTON - 51A | DONCASTER - 36A | PARKESTON - 30F | PARKESTON - 30F | NORWICH - 32A | YORK - 50A | **11/59: MIRF - 56D** | RETFORD - 36E | PARKESTON - 30F |
| Jan-60 | DARLINGTON - 51A | **2/60: RET - 36E** | PARKESTON - 30F | PARKESTON - 30F | **2/60: DARN - 41A** | YORK - 50A | MIRFIELD - 56D | RETFORD - 36E | PARKESTON - 30F |
| Apr-60 | DARLINGTON - 51A | RETFORD - 36E | PARKESTON - 30F | PARKESTON - 30F | DARNALL - 41A | YORK - 50A | MIRFIELD - 56D | RETFORD - 36E | PARKESTON - 30F |
| Aug-60 | DARLINGTON - 51A | RETFORD - 36E | PARKESTON - 30F | PARKESTON - 30F | DARNALL - 41A | YORK - 50A | MIRFIELD - 56D | RETFORD - 36E | PARKESTON - 30F |
| Nov-60 | DARLINGTON - 51A | RETFORD - 36E | PARKESTON - 30F | PARKESTON - 30F | DARNALL - 41A | YORK - 50A | MIRFIELD - 56D | RETFORD - 36E | PARKESTON - 30F |

| | 61233 | 61234 | 61235 | 61236 | 61237 | 61238 | 61239 | 61240 | 61241 |
|---|---|---|---|---|---|---|---|---|---|
| Aug-50 | STRATFORD - 30A | STRATFORD - 30A | STRATFORD - 30A | STRATFORD - 30A | NEVILLE HILL - 50B | GATESHEAD - 52A | YORK - 50A | NEVILLE HILL - 50B | TWEEDMOUTH - 52D |
| Jan-51 | STRATFORD - 30A | STRATFORD - 30A | STRATFORD - 30A | STRATFORD - 30A | NEVILLE HILL - 50B | GATESHEAD - 52A | YORK - 50A | NEVILLE HILL - 50B | TWEEDMOUTH - 52D |
| Aug-51 | STRATFORD - 30A | STRATFORD - 30A | STRATFORD - 30A | STRATFORD - 30A | NEVILLE HILL - 50B | GATESHEAD - 52A | YORK - 50A | NEVILLE HILL - 50B | TWEEDMOUTH - 52D |
| Jan-52 | STRATFORD - 30A | STRATFORD - 30A | STRATFORD - 30A | STRATFORD - 30A | NEVILLE HILL - 50B | GATESHEAD - 52A | YORK - 50A | NEVILLE HILL - 50B | TWEEDMOUTH - 52D |
| Aug-52 | STRATFORD - 30A | STRATFORD - 30A | STRATFORD - 30A | STRATFORD - 30A | NEVILLE HILL - 50B | GATESHEAD - 52A | YORK - 50A | NEVILLE HILL - 50B | TWEEDMOUTH - 52D |
| Jan-53 | STRATFORD - 30A | STRATFORD - 30A | STRATFORD - 30A | STRATFORD - 30A | NEVILLE HILL - 50B | GATESHEAD - 52A | YORK - 50A | NEVILLE HILL - 50B | TWEEDMOUTH - 52D |
| Aug-53 | STRATFORD - 30A | STRATFORD - 30A | STRATFORD - 30A | STRATFORD - 30A | NEVILLE HILL - 50B | GATESHEAD - 52A | YORK - 50A | NEVILLE HILL - 50B | TWEEDMOUTH - 52D |
| Jan-54 | STRATFORD - 30A | STRATFORD - 30A | STRATFORD - 30A | STRATFORD - 30A | NEVILLE HILL - 50B | GATESHEAD - 52A | **10/53: CANAL - 68E** | NEVILLE HILL - 50B | TWEEDMOUTH - 52D |
| Aug-54 | STRATFORD - 30A | STRATFORD - 30A | STRATFORD - 30A | STRATFORD - 30A | NEVILLE HILL - 50B | GATESHEAD - 52A | CARLISLE(CANAL) - 68E | NEVILLE HILL - 50B | TWEEDMOUTH - 52D |
| Jan-55 | STRATFORD - 30A | STRATFORD - 30A | STRATFORD - 30A | STRATFORD - 30A | NEVILLE HILL - 50B | GATESHEAD - 52A | CARLISLE(CANAL) - 68E | NEVILLE HILL - 50B | TWEEDMOUTH - 52D |
| Aug-55 | STRATFORD - 30A | STRATFORD - 30A | STRATFORD - 30A | STRATFORD - 30A | NEVILLE HILL - 50B | GATESHEAD - 52A | CARLISLE(CANAL) - 68E | NEVILLE HILL - 50B | TWEEDMOUTH - 52D |
| Jan-56 | STRATFORD - 30A | STRATFORD - 30A | STRATFORD - 30A | STRATFORD - 30A | NEVILLE HILL - 50B | GATESHEAD - 52A | CARLISLE(CANAL) - 68E | NEVILLE HILL - 50B | TWEEDMOUTH - 52D |
| Aug-56 | STRATFORD - 30A | STRATFORD - 30A | STRATFORD - 30A | STRATFORD - 30A | NEVILLE HILL - 50B | GATESHEAD - 52A | CARLISLE(CANAL) - 68E | NEVILLE HILL - 50B | TWEEDMOUTH - 52D |
| Jan-57 | STRATFORD - 30A | STRATFORD - 30A | STRATFORD - 30A | STRATFORD - 30A | NEVILLE HILL - 50B | **1/57: BLAY - 52C** | CARLISLE(CANAL) - 68E | NEVILLE HILL - 50B | TWEEDMOUTH - 52D |
| Aug-57 | STRATFORD - 30A | STRATFORD - 30A | STRATFORD - 30A | STRATFORD - 30A | NEVILLE HILL - 50B | BLAYDON - 52C | CARLISLE(CANAL) - 68E | NEVILLE HILL - 50B | TWEEDMOUTH - 52D |
| Jan-58 | STRATFORD - 30A | STRATFORD - 30A | STRATFORD - 30A | STRATFORD - 30A | NEVILLE HILL - 50B | BLAYDON - 52C | CARLISLECANAL - 68E | NEVILLE HILL - 50B | TWEEDMOUTH - 52D |
| Aug-58 | STRATFORD - 30A | STRATFORD - 30A | **10/58: NORW - 32A** | STRATFORD - 30A | NEVILLE HILL - 50B | BLAYDON - 52C | CARLISLECANAL - 12C | NEVILLE HILL - 50B | TWEEDMOUTH - 52D |
| Jan-59 | STRATFORD - 30A | STRATFORD - 30A | NORWICH - 32A | STRATFORD - 30A | NEVILLE HILL - 50B | BLAYDON - 52C | CARLISLECANAL - 12C | NEVILLE HILL - 50B | TWEEDMOUTH - 52D |
| Aug-59 | STRATFORD - 30A | **5/59: DARN - 41A** | NORWICH - 32A | **4/59: CAMB - 31A** | NEVILLE HILL - 50B | **6/59: GHD - 52A** | CARLISLECANAL - 12C | NEVILLE HILL - 50B | TWEEDMOUTH - 52D |
| Nov-59 | STRATFORD - 30A | DARNALL - 41A | NORWICH - 32A | CAMBRIDGE - 31A | NEVILLE HILL - 50B | GATESHEAD - 52A | CARLISLECANAL - 12C | **10/59: TNBY - 51L** | TWEEDMOUTH - 52D |
| Jan-60 | STRATFORD - 30A | DARNALL - 41A | **IMMINGHAM - 40B** | CAMBRIDGE - 31A | NEVILLE HILL - 50B | GATESHEAD - 52A | CARLISLECANAL - 12C | THORNABY - 51L | TWEEDMOUTH - 52D |
| Apr-60 | STRATFORD - 30A | DARNALL - 41A | IMMINGHAM - 40B | CAMBRIDGE - 31A | NEVILLE HILL - 55H | GATESHEAD - 52A | CARLISLECANAL - 12C | THORNABY - 51L | TWEEDMOUTH - 52D |
| Aug-60 | STRATFORD - 30A | DARNALL - 41A | IMMINGHAM - 40B | CAMBRIDGE - 31A | NEVILLE HILL - 55H | GATESHEAD - 52A | CARLISLECANAL - 12C | **9/60: YORK - 50A** | **6/60: BLAY - 52C** |
| Nov-60 | STRATFORD - 30A | DARNALL - 41A | IMMINGHAM - 40B | CAMBRIDGE - 31A | NEVILLE HILL - 55H | GATESHEAD - 52A | CARLISLECANAL - 12C | YORK - 50A | BLAYDON - 52C |

| | 61242 | 61243 | 61244 | 61245 | 61246 | 61247 | 61248 | 61249 | 61250 |
|---|---|---|---|---|---|---|---|---|---|
| Aug-50 | EDINBURGH(SM) - 64A | EASTFIELD - 65A | HAYMARKET - 64B | HAYMARKET - 64B | DONCASTER - 36A | DONCASTER - 36A | DONCASTER - 36A | DONCASTER - 36A | DONCASTER - 36A |
| Jan-51 | EDINBURGH(SM) - 64A | EASTFIELD - 65A | HAYMARKET - 64B | HAYMARKET - 64B | DONCASTER - 36A | DONCASTER - 36A | DONCASTER - 36A | DONCASTER - 36A | DONCASTER - 36A |
| Aug-51 | **4/51: DAL RD - 64C** | EASTFIELD - 65A | HAYMARKET - 64B | HAYMARKET - 64B | DONCASTER - 36A | DONCASTER - 36A | DONCASTER - 36A | DONCASTER - 36A | DONCASTER - 36A |
| Jan-52 | **10/51: KEITH - 61C** | EASTFIELD - 65A | HAYMARKET - 64B | HAYMARKET - 64B | DONCASTER - 36A | DONCASTER - 36A | DONCASTER - 36A | DONCASTER - 36A | DONCASTER - 36A |
| Aug-52 | KEITH - 61C | EASTFIELD - 65A | HAYMARKET - 64B | HAYMARKET - 64B | DONCASTER - 36A | DONCASTER - 36A | DONCASTER - 36A | DONCASTER - 36A | DONCASTER - 36A |
| Jan-53 | KEITH - 61C | EASTFIELD - 65A | HAYMARKET - 64B | HAYMARKET - 64B | DONCASTER - 36A | DONCASTER - 36A | DONCASTER - 36A | DONCASTER - 36A | DONCASTER - 36A |
| Aug-53 | KEITH - 61C | EASTFIELD - 65A | HAYMARKET - 64B | HAYMARKET - 64B | **9/53: S T M - 64A** | DONCASTER - 36A | DONCASTER - 36A | DONCASTER - 36A | DONCASTER - 36A |
| Jan-54 | KEITH - 61C | EASTFIELD - 65A | HAYMARKET - 64B | HAYMARKET - 64B | EDINBURGH(SM) - 64A | DONCASTER - 36A | DONCASTER - 36A | **3/54: STRAT - 30A** | DONCASTER - 36A |
| Aug-54 | KEITH - 61C | EASTFIELD - 65A | HAYMARKET - 64B | HAYMARKET - 64B | EDINBURGH(SM) - 64A | DONCASTER - 36A | DONCASTER - 36A | STRATFORD - 30A | DONCASTER - 36A |
| Jan-55 | KEITH - 61C | EASTFIELD - 65A | HAYMARKET - 64B | HAYMARKET - 64B | EDINBURGH(SM) - 64A | DONCASTER - 36A | **1/55: LINC - 40A** | STRATFORD - 30A | DONCASTER - 36A |
| Aug-55 | KEITH - 61C | EASTFIELD - 65A | HAYMARKET - 64B | HAYMARKET - 64B | EDINBURGH(SM) - 64A | DONCASTER - 36A | **5/55: IMM - 40B** | STRATFORD - 30A | DONCASTER - 36A |
| Jan-56 | KEITH - 61C | EASTFIELD - 65A | HAYMARKET - 64B | HAYMARKET - 64B | **2/56: DAL RD - 64C** | DONCASTER - 36A | **2/56: LINC - 40A** | STRATFORD - 30A | DONCASTER - 36A |
| Aug-56 | KEITH - 61C | EASTFIELD - 65A | HAYMARKET - 64B | HAYMARKET - 64B | DALRYROAD - 64C | DONCASTER - 36A | LINCOLN - 40A | STRATFORD - 30A | DONCASTER - 36A |
| Jan-57 | **2/57: KITTY - 61A** | EASTFIELD - 65A | HAYMARKET - 64B | HAYMARKET - 64B | DALRYROAD - 64C | DONCASTER - 36A | LINCOLN - 40A | STRATFORD - 30A | DONCASTER - 36A |
| Aug-57 | KITTYBREWSTER - 61A | EASTFIELD - 65A | HAYMARKET - 64B | HAYMARKET - 64B | DALRYROAD - 64C | DONCASTER - 36A | LINCOLN - 40A | STRATFORD - 30A | DONCASTER - 36A |
| Jan-58 | KITTYBREWSTER - 61A | EASTFIELD - 65A | HAYMARKET - 64B | HAYMARKET - 64B | **2/58: S T M - 64A** | DONCASTER - 36A | LINCOLN - 40A | STRATFORD - 30A | DONCASTER - 36A |
| Aug-58 | KITTYBREWSTER - 61A | EASTFIELD - 65A | HAYMARKET - 64B | HAYMARKET - 64B | EDINBURGH(SM) - 64A | DONCASTER - 36A | LINCOLN - 40A | STRATFORD - 30A | DONCASTER - 36A |
| Jan-59 | KITTYBREWSTER - 61A | EASTFIELD - 65A | HAYMARKET - 64B | HAYMARKET - 64B | EDINBURGH(SM) - 64A | DONCASTER - 36A | LINCOLN - 40A | **1/59: PARK - 30F** | DONCASTER - 36A |
| Aug-59 | KITTYBREWSTER - 61A | EASTFIELD - 65A | HAYMARKET - 64B | HAYMARKET - 64B | EDINBURGH(SM) - 64A | DONCASTER - 36A | LINCOLN - 40A | **6/59: DARN - 41A** | DONCASTER - 36A |
| Nov-59 | KITTYBREWSTER - 61A | EASTFIELD - 65A | HAYMARKET - 64B | HAYMARKET - 64B | EDINBURGH(SM) - 64A | DONCASTER - 36A | **11/59: IMM - 40B** | DARNALL - 41A | DONCASTER - 36A |
| Jan-60 | KITTYBREWSTER - 61A | EASTFIELD - 65A | HAYMARKET - 64B | HAYMARKET - 64B | EDINBURGH(SM) - 64A | DONCASTER - 36A | IMMINGHAM - 40B | DARNALL - 41A | DONCASTER - 36A |
| Apr-60 | KITTYBREWSTER - 61A | EASTFIELD - 65A | HAYMARKET - 64B | HAYMARKET - 64B | EDINBURGH(SM) - 64A | DONCASTER - 36A | IMMINGHAM - 40B | DARNALL - 41A | DONCASTER - 36A |
| Aug-60 | KITTYBREWSTER - 61A | EASTFIELD - 65A | **7/60: DAL RD - 64C** | HAYMARKET - 64B | EDINBURGH(SM) - 64A | **6/60: COLW - 40E** | IMMINGHAM - 40B | DARNALL - 41A | DONCASTER - 36A |
| Nov-60 | KITTYBREWSTER - 61A | EASTFIELD - 65A | DALRYROAD - 64C | HAYMARKET - 64B | EDINBURGH(SM) - 64A | COLWICK - 40E | IMMINGHAM - 40B | DARNALL - 41A | DONCASTER - 36A |

| | 61251 | 61252 | 61253 | 61254 | 61255 | 61256 | 61257 | 61258 | 61259 |
|---|---|---|---|---|---|---|---|---|---|
| Aug-50 | KINGS CROSS - 34A | IPSWICH - 32B | IPSWICH - 32B | IPSWICH - 32B | DARLINGTON - 51A | NEVILLE HILL - 50B | NEVILLE HILL - 50B | NEVILLE HILL - 50B | NEVILLE HILL - 50B |
| Jan-51 | KINGS CROSS - 34A | IPSWICH - 32B | IPSWICH - 32B | IPSWICH - 32B | DARLINGTON - 51A | NEVILLE HILL - 50B | NEVILLE HILL - 50B | NEVILLE HILL - 50B | NEVILLE HILL - 50B |
| Aug-51 | KINGS CROSS - 34A | IPSWICH - 32B | IPSWICH - 32B | IPSWICH - 32B | DARLINGTON - 51A | NEVILLE HILL - 50B | NEVILLE HILL - 50B | NEVILLE HILL - 50B | NEVILLE HILL - 50B |
| Jan-52 | KINGS CROSS - 34A | IPSWICH - 32B | IPSWICH - 32B | IPSWICH - 32B | DARLINGTON - 51A | NEVILLE HILL - 50B | NEVILLE HILL - 50B | **1/52: DCTR - 36A** | NEVILLE HILL - 50B |
| Aug-52 | KINGS CROSS - 34A | IPSWICH - 32B | IPSWICH - 32B | IPSWICH - 32B | DARLINGTON - 51A | NEVILLE HILL - 50B | NEVILLE HILL - 50B | **7/52: LINC - 40A** | NEVILLE HILL - 50B |
| Jan-53 | KINGS CROSS - 34A | IPSWICH - 32B | IPSWICH - 32B | IPSWICH - 32B | DARLINGTON - 51A | NEVILLE HILL - 50B | NEVILLE HILL - 50B | LINCOLN - 40A | NEVILLE HILL - 50B |
| Aug-53 | KINGS CROSS - 34A | IPSWICH - 32B | IPSWICH - 32B | IPSWICH - 32B | DARLINGTON - 51A | NEVILLE HILL - 50B | NEVILLE HILL - 50B | LINCOLN - 40A | NEVILLE HILL - 50B |
| Jan-54 | KINGS CROSS - 34A | IPSWICH - 32B | IPSWICH - 32B | IPSWICH - 32B | DARLINGTON - 51A | NEVILLE HILL - 50B | NEVILLE HILL - 50B | LINCOLN - 40A | NEVILLE HILL - 50B |
| Aug-54 | **6/54: HITCH - 34D** | IPSWICH - 32B | IPSWICH - 32B | IPSWICH - 32B | DARLINGTON - 51A | NEVILLE HILL - 50B | NEVILLE HILL - 50B | LINCOLN - 40A | NEVILLE HILL - 50B |
| Jan-55 | HITCHIN - 34D | IPSWICH - 32B | IPSWICH - 32B | IPSWICH - 32B | DARLINGTON - 51A | NEVILLE HILL - 50B | NEVILLE HILL - 50B | LINCOLN - 40A | NEVILLE HILL - 50B |
| Aug-55 | HITCHIN - 34D | IPSWICH - 32B | IPSWICH - 32B | IPSWICH - 32B | DARLINGTON - 51A | NEVILLE HILL - 50B | NEVILLE HILL - 50B | LINCOLN - 40A | NEVILLE HILL - 50B |
| Jan-56 | HITCHIN - 34D | IPSWICH - 32B | IPSWICH - 32B | IPSWICH - 32B | DARLINGTON - 51A | NEVILLE HILL - 50B | NEVILLE HILL - 50B | LINCOLN - 40A | NEVILLE HILL - 50B |
| Aug-56 | HITCHIN - 34D | IPSWICH - 32B | IPSWICH - 32B | IPSWICH - 32B | DARLINGTON - 51A | NEVILLE HILL - 50B | NEVILLE HILL - 50B | LINCOLN - 40A | NEVILLE HILL - 50B |
| Jan-57 | HITCHIN - 34D | IPSWICH - 32B | IPSWICH - 32B | IPSWICH - 32B | DARLINGTON - 51A | NEVILLE HILL - 50B | NEVILLE HILL - 50B | LINCOLN - 40A | NEVILLE HILL - 50B |
| Aug-57 | HITCHIN - 34D | IPSWICH - 32B | IPSWICH - 32B | IPSWICH - 32B | DARLINGTON - 51A | **9/57: GHD - 52A** | NEVILLE HILL - 50B | LINCOLN - 40A | NEVILLE HILL - 50B |
| Jan-58 | HITCHIN - 34D | IPSWICH - 32B | IPSWICH - 32B | IPSWICH - 32B | DARLINGTON - 51A | GATESHEAD - 52A | NEVILLE HILL - 50B | LINCOLN - 40A | NEVILLE HILL - 50B |
| Aug-58 | HITCHIN - 34D | IPSWICH - 32B | IPSWICH - 32B | IPSWICH - 32B | DARLINGTON - 51A | **9/58: DYCTS - 53A** | NEVILLE HILL - 50B | LINCOLN - 40A | NEVILLE HILL - 50B |
| Jan-59 | HITCHIN - 34D | IPSWICH - 32B | IPSWICH - 32B | IPSWICH - 32B | **2/59: H.HILL - 51G** | DAIRYCOATES - 53A | NEVILLE HILL - 50B | LINCOLN - 40A | NEVILLE HILL - 50B |
| Aug-59 | **6/59: GRAN - 34F** | IPSWICH - 32B | IPSWICH - 32B | IPSWICH - 32B | **6/59: TNBY - 51L** | DAIRYCOATES - 53A | NEVILLE HILL - 50B | LINCOLN - 40A | NEVILLE HILL - 50B |
| Nov-59 | GRANTHAM - 34F | **10/59: IPS - 32B** | **10/59: MARCH - 31B** | **10/59: MARCH - 31B** | THORNABY - 51L | DAIRYCOATES - 53A | THORNABY - 51L | LINCOLN - 40A | NEVILLE HILL - 50B |
| Jan-60 | GRANTHAM - 34F | **1/60: CAMB - 31A** | **1/60: CAMB - 31A** | **1/60: CAMB - 31A** | THORNABY - 51L | DAIRYCOATES - 53A | THORNABY - 51L | LINCOLN - 40A | NEVILLE HILL - 50B |
| Apr-60 | GRANTHAM - 34F | CAMBRIDGE - 31A | CAMBRIDGE - 31A | CAMBRIDGE - 31A | THORNABY - 51L | DAIRYCOATES - 50B | THORNABY - 51L | LINCOLN - 40A | NEVILLE HILL - 55H |
| Aug-60 | GRANTHAM - 34F | CAMBRIDGE - 31A | CAMBRIDGE - 31A | CAMBRIDGE - 31A | THORNABY - 51L | DAIRYCOATES - 50B | THORNABY - 51L | LINCOLN - 40A | NEVILLE HILL - 55H |
| Nov-60 | GRANTHAM - 34F | CAMBRIDGE - 31A | CAMBRIDGE - 31A | CAMBRIDGE - 31A | THORNABY - 51L | DAIRYCOATES - 50B | THORNABY - 51L | LINCOLN - 40A | NEVILLE HILL - 55H |

K3 2-6-0 61962 of Heaton stands at Edinburgh Haymarket on 10 March 1951 between the 23.35 Heaton - Niddrie and the 21.48 Cadder - Heaton fitted goods workings.

Dairycoates K3 2-6-0 61869 makes an appear at Springhead (H&B) shed on 28th August 1952. Lacking an allocation of mixed traffic engines, any special fast goods services from the Docks coming within the orbit of Springhead's operations were often covered by engines from Dairycoates shed.

| | 61260 | 61261 | 61262 | 61263 | 61264 | 61265 | 61266 | 61267 | 61268 |
|---|---|---|---|---|---|---|---|---|---|
| Aug-50 | EASTFIELD - 65A | EASTFIELD - 65A | THORNTON JCN - 62A | DUNDEE - 62B | PARKESTON - 30F | DONCASTER - 36A | KINGS CROSS - 34A | BRADFORD - 37C | BRADFORD - 37C |
| Jan-51 | EASTFIELD - 65A | EASTFIELD - 65A | THORNTON JCN - 62A | DUNDEE - 62B | PARKESTON - 30F | DONCASTER - 36A | KINGS CROSS - 34A | BRADFORD - 37C | BRADFORD - 37C |
| Aug-51 | EASTFIELD - 65A | EASTFIELD - 65A | THORNTON JCN - 62A | DUNDEE - 62B | PARKESTON - 30F | DONCASTER - 36A | KINGS CROSS - 34A | BRADFORD - 37C | BRADFORD - 37C |
| Jan-52 | EASTFIELD - 65A | EASTFIELD - 65A | THORNTON JCN - 62A | DUNDEE - 62B | PARKESTON - 30F | DONCASTER - 36A | KINGS CROSS - 34A | BRADFORD - 37C | BRADFORD - 37C |
| Aug-52 | EASTFIELD - 65A | EASTFIELD - 65A | THORNTON JCN - 62A | DUNDEE - 62B | PARKESTON - 30F | DONCASTER - 36A | KINGS CROSS - 34A | BRADFORD - 37C | BRADFORD - 37C |
| Jan-53 | EASTFIELD - 65A | EASTFIELD - 65A | THORNTON JCN - 62A | DUNDEE - 62B | PARKESTON - 30F | DONCASTER - 36A | **1/53: DCTR - 36A** | BRADFORD - 37C | BRADFORD - 37C |
| Aug-53 | EASTFIELD - 65A | EASTFIELD - 65A | THORNTON JCN - 62A | DUNDEE - 62B | PARKESTON - 30F | DONCASTER - 36A | DONCASTER - 36A | BRADFORD - 37C | BRADFORD - 37C |
| Jan-54 | EASTFIELD - 65A | EASTFIELD - 65A | THORNTON JCN - 62A | DUNDEE - 62B | PARKESTON - 30F | DONCASTER - 36A | DONCASTER - 36A | BRADFORD - 37C | BRADFORD - 37C |
| Aug-54 | EASTFIELD - 65A | EASTFIELD - 65A | THORNTON JCN - 62A | DUNDEE - 62B | PARKESTON - 30F | **6/54: GORT - 39A** | DONCASTER - 36A | BRADFORD - 37C | BRADFORD - 37C |
| Jan-55 | EASTFIELD - 65A | EASTFIELD - 65A | THORNTON JCN - 62A | DUNDEE - 62B | PARKESTON - 30F | GORTON - 39A | DONCASTER - 36A | BRADFORD - 37C | BRADFORD - 37C |
| Aug-55 | EASTFIELD - 65A | EASTFIELD - 65A | THORNTON JCN - 62A | DUNDEE - 62B | PARKESTON - 30F | GORTON - 39A | DONCASTER - 36A | BRADFORD - 37C | BRADFORD - 37C |
| Jan-56 | EASTFIELD - 65A | EASTFIELD - 65A | THORNTON JCN - 62A | DUNDEE - 62B | PARKESTON - 30F | GORTON - 39A | DONCASTER - 36A | BRADFORD - 37C | BRADFORD - 37C |
| Aug-56 | EASTFIELD - 65A | EASTFIELD - 65A | THORNTON JCN - 62A | DUNDEE - 62B | PARKESTON - 30F | GORTON - 39A | DONCASTER - 36A | BRADFORD - 56G | BRADFORD - 56G |
| Jan-57 | **3/57: ST M - 64A** | **3/57: ST M - 64A** | THORNTON JCN - 62A | DUNDEE - 62B | PARKESTON - 30F | GORTON - 39A | DONCASTER - 36A | BRADFORD - 56G | BRADFORD - 56G |
| Aug-57 | EDINBURGH (SM) - 64A | EDINBURGH (SM) - 64A | THORNTON JCN - 62A | DUNDEE - 62B | PARKESTON - 30F | GORTON - 39A | DONCASTER - 36A | **6/57: WAKE - 56A** | **6/57: WAKE - 56A** |
| Jan-58 | EDINBURGH (SM) - 64A | EDINBURGH (SM) - 64A | THORNTON JCN - 62A | DUNDEE - 62B | PARKESTON - 30F | GORTON - 39A | DONCASTER - 36A | **9/57: C.HILL - 56C** | WAKEFIELD - 56A |
| Aug-58 | EDINBURGH (SM) - 64A | EDINBURGH (SM) - 64A | THORNTON JCN - 62A | DUNDEE - 62B | PARKESTON - 30F | GORTON - 9G | DONCASTER - 36A | **9/58: W.HPL - 51C** | WAKEFIELD - 56A |
| Jan-59 | EDINBURGH (SM) - 64A | **1/59: EAST - 65A** | THORNTON JCN - 62A | DUNDEE - 62B | PARKESTON - 30F | **6/59: LEIC - 15E** | DONCASTER - 36A | W. HARTLEPOOL - 51C | WAKEFIELD - 56A |
| Aug-59 | EDINBURGH (SM) - 64A | EASTFIELD - 65A | THORNTON JCN - 62A | DUNDEE - 62B | PARKESTON - 30F | **8/59: GORT - 9G** | DONCASTER - 36A | W. HARTLEPOOL - 51C | WAKEFIELD - 56A |
| Nov-59 | EDINBURGH (SM) - 64A | EASTFIELD - 65A | THORNTON JCN - 62A | DUNDEE - 62B | PARKESTON - 30F | GORTON - 9G | DONCASTER - 36A | W. HARTLEPOOL - 51C | WAKEFIELD - 56A |
| Jan-60 | EDINBURGH (SM) - 64A | EASTFIELD - 65A | THORNTON JCN - 62A | DUNDEE - 62B | PARKESTON - 30F | GORTON - 9G | DONCASTER - 36A | W. HARTLEPOOL - 51C | WAKEFIELD - 56A |
| Apr-60 | EDINBURGH (SM) - 64A | EASTFIELD - 65A | THORNTON JCN - 62A | DUNDEE - 62B | PARKESTON - 30F | GORTON - 9G | DONCASTER - 36A | W. HARTLEPOOL - 51C | WAKEFIELD - 56A |
| Aug-60 | **6/60: DAL RD - 64C** | EASTFIELD - 65A | **6/60: DUND - 62B** | DUNDEE - 62B | PARKESTON - 30F | GORTON - 9G | **6/60: DARN - 41A** | W. HARTLEPOOL - 51C | WAKEFIELD - 56A |
| Nov-60 | DALRY ROAD - 64C | EASTFIELD - 65A | DUNDEE - 62B | DUNDEE - 62B | PARKESTON - 30F | GORTON - 9G | DARNALL - 41A | W. HARTLEPOOL - 51C | WAKEFIELD - 56A |

| | 61269 | 61270 | 61271 | 61272 | 61273 | 61274 | 61275 | 61276 | 61277 |
|---|---|---|---|---|---|---|---|---|---|
| Aug-50 | LINCOLN - 40A | NORWICH - 32A | NORWICH - 32A | NORWICH - 32A | DARLINGTON - 51A | DARLINGTON - 51A | DARLINGTON - 51A | DARLINGTON - 51A | EDINBURGH (SM) - 64A |
| Jan-51 | LINCOLN - 40A | NORWICH - 32A | NORWICH - 32A | NORWICH - 32A | DARLINGTON - 51A | DARLINGTON - 51A | DARLINGTON - 51A | DARLINGTON - 51A | EDINBURGH (SM) - 64A |
| Aug-51 | LINCOLN - 40A | NORWICH - 32A | NORWICH - 32A | NORWICH - 32A | DARLINGTON - 51A | DARLINGTON - 51A | DARLINGTON - 51A | DARLINGTON - 51A | EDINBURGH (SM) - 64A |
| Jan-52 | **5/52: COLW - 38A** | NORWICH - 32A | NORWICH - 32A | NORWICH - 32A | DARLINGTON - 51A | DARLINGTON - 51A | **11/51: STOCK - 51E** | DARLINGTON - 51A | EDINBURGH (SM) - 64A |
| Aug-52 | **6/52: LINC - 40A** | NORWICH - 32A | NORWICH - 32A | NORWICH - 32A | DARLINGTON - 51A | DARLINGTON - 51A | STOCKTON - 51E | DARLINGTON - 51A | EDINBURGH (SM) - 64A |
| Jan-53 | LINCOLN - 40A | NORWICH - 32A | NORWICH - 32A | NORWICH - 32A | DARLINGTON - 51A | DARLINGTON - 51A | STOCKTON - 51E | DARLINGTON - 51A | EDINBURGH (SM) - 64A |
| Aug-53 | LINCOLN - 40A | NORWICH - 32A | **10/53: COLW - 38A** | **10/53: COLW - 38A** | DARLINGTON - 51A | DARLINGTON - 51A | STOCKTON - 51E | DARLINGTON - 51A | EDINBURGH (SM) - 64A |
| Jan-54 | **11/53: COLW - 38A** | NORWICH - 32A | COLWICK - 38A | COLWICK - 38A | DARLINGTON - 51A | DARLINGTON - 51A | STOCKTON - 51E | DARLINGTON - 51A | EDINBURGH (SM) - 64A |
| Aug-54 | COLWICK - 38A | NORWICH - 32A | COLWICK - 38A | COLWICK - 38A | DARLINGTON - 51A | DARLINGTON - 51A | STOCKTON - 51E | DARLINGTON - 51A | EDINBURGH (SM) - 64A |
| Jan-55 | COLWICK - 38A | NORWICH - 32A | COLWICK - 38A | **1/55: LEIC - 38C** | DARLINGTON - 51A | DARLINGTON - 51A | **12/54: WHPL - 51C** | DARLINGTON - 51A | EDINBURGH (SM) - 64A |
| Aug-55 | COLWICK - 38A | **8/55: IPS - 32B** | COLWICK - 38A | **2/55: COLW - 38A** | DARLINGTON - 51A | **6/55: YORK - 50A** | W. HARTLEPOOL - 51C | DARLINGTON - 51A | EDINBURGH (SM) - 64A |
| Jan-56 | COLWICK - 38A | **11/55: NORW - 32A** | COLWICK - 38A | COLWICK - 38A | DARLINGTON - 51A | **9/55: DARL - 51A** | W. HARTLEPOOL - 51C | DARLINGTON - 51A | EDINBURGH (SM) - 64A |
| Aug-56 | COLWICK - 38A | NORWICH - 32A | COLWICK - 38A | COLWICK - 38A | DARLINGTON - 51A | DARLINGTON - 51A | W. HARTLEPOOL - 51C | DARLINGTON - 51A | EDINBURGH (SM) - 64A |
| Jan-57 | **11/56: LEIC - 38C** | NORWICH - 32A | COLWICK - 38A | **1/57: ANN - 38B** | DARLINGTON - 51A | DARLINGTON - 51A | W. HARTLEPOOL - 51C | DARLINGTON - 51A | EDINBURGH (SM) - 64A |
| Aug-57 | LEICESTER (GC) - 38C | NORWICH - 32A | **6/57: WOOD - 38E** | ANNESLEY - 38B | DARLINGTON - 51A | DARLINGTON - 51A | W. HARTLEPOOL - 51C | DARLINGTON - 51A | **5/57: TH JCN - 62A** |
| Jan-58 | LEICESTER (GC) - 38C | NORWICH - 32A | WOODFORD HALSE - 38E | **1/58: DARN - 41A** | DARLINGTON - 51A | DARLINGTON - 51A | W. HARTLEPOOL - 51C | DARLINGTON - 51A | THORNTON JCN - 62A |
| Aug-58 | LEICESTER (GC) - 15E | NORWICH - 32A | WOODFORD HALSE - 2F | **10/58: KX - 34A** | DARLINGTON - 51A | DARLINGTON - 51A | W. HARTLEPOOL - 51C | DARLINGTON - 51A | THORNTON JCN - 62A |
| Jan-59 | LEICESTER (GC) - 15E | NORWICH - 32A | WOODFORD HALSE - 2F | KINGS CROSS - 34A | DARLINGTON - 51A | DARLINGTON - 51A | W. HARTLEPOOL - 51C | DARLINGTON - 51A | THORNTON JCN - 62A |
| Aug-59 | **9/59: AGEC - 26B** | **10/59: DCTR - 36A** | WOODFORD HALSE - 2F | **4/59: NEWE - 34E** | **6/59: YORK - 50A** | **6/59: LOW M - 56F** | W. HARTLEPOOL - 51C | **6/59: YORK - 50A** | THORNTON JCN - 62A |
| Nov-59 | AGECROFT - 26B | DONCASTER - 36A | WOODFORD HALSE - 2F | NEWENGLAND - 34E | YORK - 50A | LOWMOOR - 56F | W. HARTLEPOOL - 51C | YORK - 50A | THORNTON JCN - 62A |
| Jan-60 | AGECROFT - 26B | DONCASTER - 36A | WOODFORD HALSE - 2F | NEWENGLAND - 34E | YORK - 50A | LOWMOOR - 56F | W. HARTLEPOOL - 51C | YORK - 50A | THORNTON JCN - 62A |
| Apr-60 | AGECROFT - 26B | DONCASTER - 36A | WOODFORD HALSE - 2F | NEWENGLAND - 34E | YORK - 50A | LOWMOOR - 56F | W. HARTLEPOOL - 51C | YORK - 50A | THORNTON JCN - 62A |
| Aug-60 | AGECROFT - 26B | DONCASTER - 36A | WOODFORD HALSE - 2F | NEWENGLAND - 34E | YORK - 50A | LOWMOOR - 56F | W. HARTLEPOOL - 51C | YORK - 50A | **6/60: DUND - 62B** |
| Nov-60 | AGECROFT - 26B | DONCASTER - 36A | WOODFORD HALSE - 2F | NEWENGLAND - 34E | YORK - 50A | LOWMOOR - 56F | W. HARTLEPOOL - 51C | YORK - 50A | DUNDEE - 62B |

| | 61278 | 61279 | 61280 | 61281 | 61282 | 61283 | 61284 | 61285 | 61286 |
|---|---|---|---|---|---|---|---|---|---|
| Aug-50 | DUNDEE - 62B | LINCOLN - 40A | LINCOLN - 40A | LINCOLN - 40A | STRATFORD - 30A | COLWICK - 38A | IMMINGHAM - 40B | CAMBRIDGE - 31A | CAMBRIDGE - 31A |
| Jan-51 | DUNDEE - 62B | LINCOLN - 40A | LINCOLN - 40A | LINCOLN - 40A | STRATFORD - 30A | COLWICK - 38A | IMMINGHAM - 40B | CAMBRIDGE - 31A | CAMBRIDGE - 31A |
| Aug-51 | DUNDEE - 62B | LINCOLN - 40A | LINCOLN - 40A | LINCOLN - 40A | STRATFORD - 30A | COLWICK - 38A | IMMINGHAM - 40B | CAMBRIDGE - 31A | CAMBRIDGE - 31A |
| Jan-52 | DUNDEE - 62B | LINCOLN - 40A | **5/52: COLW - 38A** | LINCOLN - 40A | STRATFORD - 30A | COLWICK - 38A | IMMINGHAM - 40B | CAMBRIDGE - 31A | CAMBRIDGE - 31A |
| Aug-52 | DUNDEE - 62B | LINCOLN - 40A | **6/52: LINC - 40A** | LINCOLN - 40A | STRATFORD - 30A | COLWICK - 38A | IMMINGHAM - 40B | CAMBRIDGE - 31A | CAMBRIDGE - 31A |
| Jan-53 | DUNDEE - 62B | LINCOLN - 40A | **9/52: STRAT - 30A** | LINCOLN - 40A | STRATFORD - 30A | COLWICK - 38A | IMMINGHAM - 40B | CAMBRIDGE - 31A | CAMBRIDGE - 31A |
| Aug-53 | DUNDEE - 62B | LINCOLN - 40A | STRATFORD - 30A | LINCOLN - 40A | STRATFORD - 30A | COLWICK - 38A | IMMINGHAM - 40B | CAMBRIDGE - 31A | CAMBRIDGE - 31A |
| Jan-54 | DUNDEE - 62B | LINCOLN - 40A | STRATFORD - 30A | LINCOLN - 40A | **11/53: NEWE - 35A** | COLWICK - 38A | IMMINGHAM - 40B | CAMBRIDGE - 31A | CAMBRIDGE - 31A |
| Aug-54 | DUNDEE - 62B | **8/54: NORW - 32A** | STRATFORD - 30A | LINCOLN - 40A | NEWENGLAND - 35A | **11/54: WOOD - 38E** | IMMINGHAM - 40B | CAMBRIDGE - 31A | CAMBRIDGE - 31A |
| Jan-55 | DUNDEE - 62B | **12/54: LINC - 40A** | STRATFORD - 30A | LINCOLN - 40A | NEWENGLAND - 35A | **2/55: COLW - 38A** | IMMINGHAM - 40B | CAMBRIDGE - 31A | CAMBRIDGE - 31A |
| Aug-55 | DUNDEE - 62B | LINCOLN - 40A | STRATFORD - 30A | LINCOLN - 40A | NEWENGLAND - 35A | COLWICK - 38A | IMMINGHAM - 40B | CAMBRIDGE - 31A | CAMBRIDGE - 31A |
| Jan-56 | DUNDEE - 62B | LINCOLN - 40A | STRATFORD - 30A | **2/56: IMM - 40B** | NEWENGLAND - 35A | COLWICK - 38A | IMMINGHAM - 40B | CAMBRIDGE - 31A | CAMBRIDGE - 31A |
| Aug-56 | DUNDEE - 62B | LINCOLN - 40A | STRATFORD - 30A | IMMINGHAM - 40B | NEWENGLAND - 35A | **11/56: LEIC - 38C** | IMMINGHAM - 40B | CAMBRIDGE - 31A | CAMBRIDGE - 31A |
| Jan-57 | DUNDEE - 62B | **2/57: STRAT - 30A** | STRATFORD - 30A | IMMINGHAM - 40B | NEWENGLAND - 35A | **12/56: COLW - 38A** | IMMINGHAM - 40B | **11/56: DCTR - 36A** | CAMBRIDGE - 31A |
| Aug-57 | DUNDEE - 62B | STRATFORD - 30A | STRATFORD - 30A | IMMINGHAM - 40B | NEWENGLAND - 35A | **5/57: KX - 34A** | IMMINGHAM - 40B | DONCASTER - 36A | CAMBRIDGE - 31A |
| Jan-58 | DUNDEE - 62B | STRATFORD - 30A | STRATFORD - 30A | IMMINGHAM - 40B | NEWENGLAND - 35A | **10/57: CAMB - 31A** | IMMINGHAM - 40B | DONCASTER - 36A | CAMBRIDGE - 31A |
| Aug-58 | DUNDEE - 62B | **8/58: NORW - 32A** | STRATFORD - 30A | **6/58: COLW - 40E** | NEWENGLAND - 34E | CAMBRIDGE - 31A | IMMINGHAM - 40B | DONCASTER - 36A | CAMBRIDGE - 31A |
| Jan-59 | DUNDEE - 62B | NORWICH - 32A | **1/59: PARK - 30F** | COLWICK - 40E | NEWENGLAND - 34E | CAMBRIDGE - 31A | IMMINGHAM - 40B | DONCASTER - 36A | CAMBRIDGE - 31A |
| Aug-59 | DUNDEE - 62B | **9/59: DCTR - 36A** | **4/59: CAMB - 31A** | COLWICK - 40E | NEWENGLAND - 34E | CAMBRIDGE - 31A | IMMINGHAM - 40B | DONCASTER - 36A | CAMBRIDGE - 31A |
| Nov-59 | DUNDEE - 62B | DONCASTER - 36A | CAMBRIDGE - 31A | COLWICK - 40E | NEWENGLAND - 34E | CAMBRIDGE - 31A | **11/59: LINC - 40A** | DONCASTER - 36A | CAMBRIDGE - 31A |
| Jan-60 | DUNDEE - 62B | DONCASTER - 36A | CAMBRIDGE - 31A | COLWICK - 40E | NEWENGLAND - 34E | CAMBRIDGE - 31A | LINCOLN - 40A | DONCASTER - 36A | CAMBRIDGE - 31A |
| Apr-60 | DUNDEE - 62B | DONCASTER - 36A | CAMBRIDGE - 31A | COLWICK - 40E | NEWENGLAND - 34E | CAMBRIDGE - 31A | LINCOLN - 40A | DONCASTER - 36A | CAMBRIDGE - 31A |
| Aug-60 | DUNDEE - 62B | DONCASTER - 36A | CAMBRIDGE - 31A | COLWICK - 40E | NEWENGLAND - 34E | CAMBRIDGE - 31A | LINCOLN - 40A | **6/60: COW - 40E** | CAMBRIDGE - 31A |
| Nov-60 | DUNDEE - 62B | DONCASTER - 36A | CAMBRIDGE - 31A | COLWICK - 40E | NEWENGLAND - 34E | CAMBRIDGE - 31A | LINCOLN - 40A | COLWICK - 40E | CAMBRIDGE - 31A |

| | 61287 | 61288 | 61289 | 61290 | 61291 | 61292 | 61293 | 61294 | 61295 |
|---|---|---|---|---|---|---|---|---|---|
| Aug-50 | CAMBRIDGE - 31A | YORK - 50A | DARLINGTON - 51A | STOCKTON - 51E | DARLINGTON - 51A | DUNDEE - 62B | DUNDEE - 62B | BRADFORD - 37C | COPLEYHILL - 37B |
| Jan-51 | CAMBRIDGE - 31A | YORK - 50A | DARLINGTON - 51A | STOCKTON - 51E | DARLINGTON - 51A | DUNDEE - 62B | DUNDEE - 62B | BRADFORD - 37C | COPLEYHILL - 37B |
| Aug-51 | CAMBRIDGE - 31A | YORK - 50A | DARLINGTON - 51A | STOCKTON - 51E | DARLINGTON - 51A | DUNDEE - 62B | DUNDEE - 62B | BRADFORD - 37C | COPLEYHILL - 37B |
| Jan-52 | CAMBRIDGE - 31A | YORK - 50A | DARLINGTON - 51A | STOCKTON - 51E | DARLINGTON - 51A | DUNDEE - 62B | DUNDEE - 62B | BRADFORD - 37C | COPLEYHILL - 37B |
| Aug-52 | CAMBRIDGE - 31A | YORK - 50A | DARLINGTON - 51A | STOCKTON - 51E | DARLINGTON - 51A | DUNDEE - 62B | DUNDEE - 62B | BRADFORD - 37C | COPLEYHILL - 37B |
| Jan-53 | CAMBRIDGE - 31A | YORK - 50A | DARLINGTON - 51A | STOCKTON - 51E | DARLINGTON - 51A | DUNDEE - 62B | DUNDEE - 62B | BRADFORD - 37C | COPLEYHILL - 37B |
| Aug-53 | CAMBRIDGE - 31A | YORK - 50A | DARLINGTON - 51A | **10/53: CANAL - 68E** | DARLINGTON - 51A | DUNDEE - 62B | DUNDEE - 62B | **9/53: EAST - 65A** | COPLEYHILL - 37B |
| Jan-54 | CAMBRIDGE - 31A | YORK - 50A | DARLINGTON - 51A | CARLISLE (CANAL) - 68E | DARLINGTON - 51A | DUNDEE - 62B | DUNDEE - 62B | EASTFIELD - 65A | **11/53: ARDS - 37A** |
| Aug-54 | CAMBRIDGE - 31A | YORK - 50A | DARLINGTON - 51A | CARLISLE (CANAL) - 68E | DARLINGTON - 51A | DUNDEE - 62B | DUNDEE - 62B | **6/54: KITTY - 61A** | ARDSLEY - 37A |
| Jan-55 | CAMBRIDGE - 31A | YORK - 50A | DARLINGTON - 51A | CARLISLE (CANAL) - 68E | DARLINGTON - 51A | DUNDEE - 62B | DUNDEE - 62B | KITTYBREWSTER - 61A | ARDSLEY - 37A |
| Aug-55 | CAMBRIDGE - 31A | YORK - 50A | DARLINGTON - 51A | CARLISLE (CANAL) - 68E | **6/55: YORK - 50A** | DUNDEE - 62B | DUNDEE - 62B | KITTYBREWSTER - 61A | ARDSLEY - 37A |
| Jan-56 | CAMBRIDGE - 31A | YORK - 50A | DARLINGTON - 51A | CARLISLE (CANAL) - 68E | **9/55: DARL - 51A** | DUNDEE - 62B | DUNDEE - 62B | KITTYBREWSTER - 61A | ARDSLEY - 37A |
| Aug-56 | CAMBRIDGE - 31A | YORK - 50A | DARLINGTON - 51A | CARLISLE (CANAL) - 68E | DARLINGTON - 51A | DUNDEE - 62B | DUNDEE - 62B | KITTYBREWSTER - 61A | ARDSLEY - 56B |
| Jan-57 | CAMBRIDGE - 31A | YORK - 50A | **1/57: B GDNS - 53B** | CARLISLE (CANAL) - 68E | DARLINGTON - 51A | DUNDEE - 62B | DUNDEE - 62B | KITTYBREWSTER - 61A | ARDSLEY - 56B |
| Aug-57 | CAMBRIDGE - 31A | YORK - 50A | BOTANIC GARDENS - 53B | CARLISLE (CANAL) - 68E | DARLINGTON - 51A | DUNDEE - 62B | DUNDEE - 62B | KITTYBREWSTER - 61A | ARDSLEY - 56B |
| Jan-58 | CAMBRIDGE - 31A | YORK - 50A | BOTANIC GARDENS - 53B | CARLISLECANAL - 68E | DARLINGTON - 51A | DUNDEE - 62B | DUNDEE - 62B | KITTYBREWSTER - 61A | ARDSLEY - 56B |
| Aug-58 | CAMBRIDGE - 31A | YORK - 50A | BOTANIC GARDENS - 53B | CARLISLECANAL - 12C | DARLINGTON - 51A | DUNDEE - 62B | DUNDEE - 62B | KITTYBREWSTER - 61A | ARDSLEY - 56B |
| Jan-59 | CAMBRIDGE - 31A | YORK - 50A | BOTANIC GARDENS - 53B | CARLISLECANAL - 12C | DARLINGTON - 51A | DUNDEE - 62B | DUNDEE - 62B | KITTYBREWSTER - 61A | ARDSLEY - 56B |
| Aug-59 | CAMBRIDGE - 31A | YORK - 50A | **6/59: DYCTS - 53A** | CARLISLECANAL - 12C | **6/59: YORK - 50A** | DUNDEE - 62B | DUNDEE - 62B | KITTYBREWSTER - 61A | ARDSLEY - 56B |
| Nov-59 | CAMBRIDGE - 31A | YORK - 50A | DAIRYCOATES - 53A | CARLISLECANAL - 12C | YORK - 50A | DUNDEE - 62B | DUNDEE - 62B | KITTYBREWSTER - 61A | ARDSLEY - 56B |
| Jan-60 | CAMBRIDGE - 31A | YORK - 50A | DAIRYCOATES - 53A | CARLISLECANAL - 12C | YORK - 50A | DUNDEE - 62B | DUNDEE - 62B | KITTYBREWSTER - 61A | ARDSLEY - 56B |
| Apr-60 | CAMBRIDGE - 31A | YORK - 50A | DAIRYCOATES - 50B | CARLISLECANAL - 12C | YORK - 50A | DUNDEE - 62B | DUNDEE - 62B | KITTYBREWSTER - 61A | ARDSLEY - 56B |
| Aug-60 | CAMBRIDGE - 31A | YORK - 50A | DAIRYCOATES - 50B | CARLISLECANAL - 12C | YORK - 50A | DUNDEE - 62B | DUNDEE - 62B | **6/60: ST M - 64A** | ARDSLEY - 56B |
| Nov-60 | CAMBRIDGE - 31A | YORK - 50A | DAIRYCOATES - 50B | CARLISLECANAL - 12C | YORK - 50A | DUNDEE - 62B | DUNDEE - 62B | EDINBURGH (SM) - 64A | ARDSLEY - 56B |

| | 61296 | 61297 | 61298 | 61299 | 61300 | 61301 | 61302 | 61303 | 61304 |
|---|---|---|---|---|---|---|---|---|---|
| Aug-50 | BRADFORD - 37C | ARDSLEY - 37A | LEICESTER (GC) - 38C | LEICESTER (GC) - 38C | CAMBRIDGE - 31A | CAMBRIDGE - 31A | CAMBRIDGE - 31A | STOCKTON - 51E | B.GDNS - 53B |
| Jan-51 | BRADFORD - 37C | ARDSLEY - 37A | LEICESTER (GC) - 38C | LEICESTER (GC) - 38C | CAMBRIDGE - 31A | CAMBRIDGE - 31A | CAMBRIDGE - 31A | STOCKTON - 51E | B.GDNS - 53B |
| Aug-51 | BRADFORD - 37C | ARDSLEY - 37A | LEICESTER (GC) - 38C | LEICESTER (GC) - 38C | CAMBRIDGE - 31A | CAMBRIDGE - 31A | CAMBRIDGE - 31A | STOCKTON - 51E | B.GDNS - 53B |
| Jan-52 | BRADFORD - 37C | ARDSLEY - 37A | LEICESTER (GC) - 38C | LEICESTER (GC) - 38C | CAMBRIDGE - 31A | CAMBRIDGE - 31A | CAMBRIDGE - 31A | STOCKTON - 51E | B.GDNS - 53B |
| Aug-52 | BRADFORD - 37C | ARDSLEY - 37A | LEICESTER (GC) - 38C | LEICESTER (GC) - 38C | CAMBRIDGE - 31A | CAMBRIDGE - 31A | CAMBRIDGE - 31A | STOCKTON - 51E | B.GDNS - 53B |
| Jan-53 | BRADFORD - 37C | ARDSLEY - 37A | LEICESTER (GC) - 38C | LEICESTER (GC) - 38C | CAMBRIDGE - 31A | CAMBRIDGE - 31A | CAMBRIDGE - 31A | STOCKTON - 51E | B.GDNS - 53B |
| Aug-53 | BRADFORD - 37C | ARDSLEY - 37A | LEICESTER (GC) - 38C | LEICESTER (GC) - 38C | CAMBRIDGE - 31A | CAMBRIDGE - 31A | CAMBRIDGE - 31A | STOCKTON - 51E | B.GDNS - 53B |
| Jan-54 | BRADFORD - 37C | ARDSLEY - 37A | LEICESTER (GC) - 38C | LEICESTER (GC) - 38C | CAMBRIDGE - 31A | CAMBRIDGE - 31A | CAMBRIDGE - 31A | STOCKTON - 51E | B.GDNS - 53B |
| Aug-54 | BRADFORD - 37C | ARDSLEY - 37A | LEICESTER (GC) - 38C | LEICESTER (GC) - 38C | CAMBRIDGE - 31A | CAMBRIDGE - 31A | CAMBRIDGE - 31A | STOCKTON - 51E | B.GDNS - 53B |
| Jan-55 | BRADFORD - 37C | ARDSLEY - 37A | LEICESTER (GC) - 38C | LEICESTER (GC) - 38C | CAMBRIDGE - 31A | CAMBRIDGE - 31A | CAMBRIDGE - 31A | STOCKTON - 51E | B.GDNS - 53B |
| Aug-55 | BRADFORD - 37C | ARDSLEY - 37A | LEICESTER (GC) - 38C | LEICESTER (GC) - 38C | CAMBRIDGE - 31A | CAMBRIDGE - 31A | CAMBRIDGE - 31A | STOCKTON - 51E | B.GDNS - 53B |
| Jan-56 | BRADFORD - 37C | ARDSLEY - 37A | LEICESTER (GC) - 38C | LEICESTER (GC) - 38C | CAMBRIDGE - 31A | CAMBRIDGE - 31A | CAMBRIDGE - 31A | STOCKTON - 51E | B.GDNS - 53B |
| Aug-56 | BRADFORD - 56G | ARDSLEY - 56B | LEICESTER (GC) - 38C | LEICESTER (GC) - 38C | CAMBRIDGE - 31A | CAMBRIDGE - 31A | **10/56: NEWE - 35A** | STOCKTON - 51E | B.GDNS - 53B |
| Jan-57 | BRADFORD - 56G | ARDSLEY - 56B | LEICESTER (GC) - 38C | LEICESTER (GC) - 38C | CAMBRIDGE - 31A | CAMBRIDGE - 31A | NEWENGLAND - 35A | STOCKTON - 51E | B.GDNS - 53B |
| Aug-57 | **6/57: WAKE - 56A** | ARDSLEY - 56B | LEICESTER (GC) - 38C | LEICESTER (GC) - 38C | CAMBRIDGE - 31A | CAMBRIDGE - 31A | NEWENGLAND - 35A | STOCKTON - 51E | B.GDNS - 53B |
| Jan-58 | WAKEFIELD - 56A | ARDSLEY - 56B | LEICESTER (GC) - 38C | **11/57: COLW - 38A** | CAMBRIDGE - 31A | CAMBRIDGE - 31A | NEWENGLAND - 35A | STOCKTON - 51E | B.GDNS - 53B |
| Aug-58 | WAKEFIELD - 56A | ARDSLEY - 56B | LEICESTER (GC) - 15E | COLWICK - 40E | CAMBRIDGE - 31A | CAMBRIDGE - 31A | NEWENGLAND - 34E | STOCKTON - 51E | B.GDNS - 53B |
| Jan-59 | WAKEFIELD - 56A | ARDSLEY - 56B | LEICESTER (GC) - 15E | COLWICK - 40E | **12/58: COL - 30E** | CAMBRIDGE - 31A | NEWENGLAND - 34E | STOCKTON - 51E | B.GDNS - 53B |
| Aug-59 | WAKEFIELD - 56A | ARDSLEY - 56B | **9/59: AGEC - 26B** | COLWICK - 40E | COLCHESTER - 30E | CAMBRIDGE - 31A | NEWENGLAND - 34E | **6/59: TNBY - 51L** | **6/59: SCAR - 50E** |
| Nov-59 | WAKEFIELD - 56A | ARDSLEY - 56B | AGECROFT - 26B | COLWICK - 40E | **12/59: MARCH - 31B** | CAMBRIDGE - 31A | NEWENGLAND - 34E | THORNABY - 51L | SCARBOROUGH - 50E |
| Jan-60 | WAKEFIELD - 56A | ARDSLEY - 56B | AGECROFT - 26B | COLWICK - 40E | **1/60: CAMB - 31A** | CAMBRIDGE - 31A | NEWENGLAND - 34E | THORNABY - 51L | SCARBOROUGH - 50E |
| Apr-60 | WAKEFIELD - 56A | ARDSLEY - 56B | AGECROFT - 26B | COLWICK - 40E | CAMBRIDGE - 31A | CAMBRIDGE - 31A | NEWENGLAND - 34E | THORNABY - 51L | **4/60: DARL - 51A** |
| Aug-60 | WAKEFIELD - 56A | ARDSLEY - 56B | AGECROFT - 26B | COLWICK - 40E | CAMBRIDGE - 31A | CAMBRIDGE - 31A | NEWENGLAND - 34E | THORNABY - 51L | DARLINGTON - 51A |
| Nov-60 | WAKEFIELD - 56A | ARDSLEY - 56B | AGECROFT - 26B | COLWICK - 40E | CAMBRIDGE - 31A | CAMBRIDGE - 31A | NEWENGLAND - 34E | THORNABY - 51L | DARLINGTON - 51A |

| | 61305 | 61306 | 61307 | 61308 | 61309 | 61310 | 61311 | 61312 | 61313 |
|---|---|---|---|---|---|---|---|---|---|
| Aug-50 | B.GDNS - 53B | B.GDNS - 53B | KITTYBREWSTER - 61A | KEITH - 61C | ARDSLEY - 37A | ARDSLEY - 37A | DARNALL - 39B | DARNALL - 39B | DARNALL - 39B |
| Jan-51 | B.GDNS - 53B | B.GDNS - 53B | KITTYBREWSTER - 61A | KEITH - 61C | ARDSLEY - 37A | **2/51: C.HILL - 37B** | DARNALL - 39B | DARNALL - 39B | DARNALL - 39B |
| Aug-51 | B.GDNS - 53B | B.GDNS - 53B | KITTYBREWSTER - 61A | KEITH - 61C | **8/51: C.HILL - 37B** | COPLEYHILL - 37B | DARNALL - 39B | DARNALL - 39B | DARNALL - 39B |
| Jan-52 | B.GDNS - 53B | B.GDNS - 53B | KITTYBREWSTER - 61A | KEITH - 61C | COPLEYHILL - 37B | **2/52: ARDS - 37A** | DARNALL - 39B | DARNALL - 39B | DARNALL - 39B |
| Aug-52 | B.GDNS - 53B | B.GDNS - 53B | KITTYBREWSTER - 61A | KEITH - 61C | COPLEYHILL - 37B | ARDSLEY - 37A | DARNALL - 39B | DARNALL - 39B | DARNALL - 39B |
| Jan-53 | B.GDNS - 53B | B.GDNS - 53B | KITTYBREWSTER - 61A | KEITH - 61C | COPLEYHILL - 37B | ARDSLEY - 37A | DARNALL - 39B | DARNALL - 39B | DARNALL - 39B |
| Aug-53 | B.GDNS - 53B | B.GDNS - 53B | KITTYBREWSTER - 61A | KEITH - 61C | COPLEYHILL - 37B | ARDSLEY - 37A | DARNALL - 39B | DARNALL - 39B | DARNALL - 39B |
| Jan-54 | B.GDNS - 53B | B.GDNS - 53B | KITTYBREWSTER - 61A | KEITH - 61C | COPLEYHILL - 37B | ARDSLEY - 37A | DARNALL - 39B | DARNALL - 39B | DARNALL - 39B |
| Aug-54 | B.GDNS - 53B | B.GDNS - 53B | **7/54: KEITH - 61C** | KEITH - 61C | COPLEYHILL - 37B | ARDSLEY - 37A | **10/54: LINC - 40A** | **10/54: NORW - 32A** | DARNALL - 39B |
| Jan-55 | B.GDNS - 53B | B.GDNS - 53B | KEITH - 61C | KEITH - 61C | COPLEYHILL - 37B | ARDSLEY - 37A | LINCOLN - 40A | NORWICH - 32A | DARNALL - 39B |
| Aug-55 | B.GDNS - 53B | B.GDNS - 53B | KEITH - 61C | KEITH - 61C | COPLEYHILL - 37B | ARDSLEY - 37A | LINCOLN - 40A | NORWICH - 32A | DARNALL - 39B |
| Jan-56 | B.GDNS - 53B | B.GDNS - 53B | KEITH - 61C | KEITH - 61C | COPLEYHILL - 37B | ARDSLEY - 37A | LINCOLN - 40A | **1/56: YAR (ST) - 32D** | DARNALL - 41A |
| Aug-56 | B.GDNS - 53B | B.GDNS - 53B | KEITH - 61C | KEITH - 61C | COPLEYHILL - 56C | ARDSLEY - 56B | **10/56: KX - 34A** | **4/56: NORW - 32A** | DARNALL - 41A |
| Jan-57 | B.GDNS - 53B | B.GDNS - 53B | **2/57: KITTY - 61A** | **2/57: KITTY - 61A** | COPLEYHILL - 56C | ARDSLEY - 56B | **2/57: STRAT - 30A** | NORWICH - 32A | DARNALL - 41A |
| Aug-57 | B.GDNS - 53B | B.GDNS - 53B | **8/57: ST M - 64A** | **9/57: ST M - 64A** | COPLEYHILL - 56C | ARDSLEY - 56B | STRATFORD - 30A | NORWICH - 32A | DARNALL - 41A |
| Jan-58 | B.GDNS - 53B | B.GDNS - 53B | EDINBURGH (SM) - 64A | EDINBURGH (SM) - 64A | COPLEYHILL - 56C | ARDSLEY - 56B | STRATFORD - 30A | NORWICH - 32A | DARNALL - 41A |
| Aug-58 | B.GDNS - 53B | B.GDNS - 53B | EDINBURGH (SM) - 64A | EDINBURGH (SM) - 64A | COPLEYHILL - 56C | ARDSLEY - 56B | **8/58: PARK - 30F** | NORWICH - 32A | DARNALL - 41A |
| Jan-59 | B.GDNS - 53B | B.GDNS - 53B | EDINBURGH (SM) - 64A | EDINBURGH (SM) - 64A | COPLEYHILL - 56C | ARDSLEY - 56B | **12/58: COL - 30E** | NORWICH - 32A | DARNALL - 41A |
| Aug-59 | **6/59: SCAR - 50E** | **6/59: DYCTS - 53A** | EDINBURGH (SM) - 64A | EDINBURGH (SM) - 64A | COPLEYHILL - 56C | ARDSLEY - 56B | COLCHESTER - 30E | **5/59: DARN - 41A** | DARNALL - 41A |
| Nov-59 | SCARBOROUGH - 50E | DAIRYCOATES - 53A | EDINBURGH (SM) - 64A | EDINBURGH (SM) - 64A | COPLEYHILL - 56C | ARDSLEY - 56B | **10/59: PARK - 30F** | **9/59: STAVE - 41H** | DARNALL - 41A |
| Jan-60 | SCARBOROUGH - 50E | DAIRYCOATES - 53A | EDINBURGH (SM) - 64A | EDINBURGH (SM) - 64A | COPLEYHILL - 56C | ARDSLEY - 56B | PARKESTON - 30F | **1/60: CANK - 41D** | DARNALL - 41A |
| Apr-60 | **4/60: DYCTS - 50B** | DAIRYCOATES - 50B | EDINBURGH (SM) - 64A | EDINBURGH (SM) - 64A | COPLEYHILL - 56C | ARDSLEY - 56B | PARKESTON - 30F | CANKLOW - 41D | DARNALL - 41A |
| Aug-60 | DAIRYCOATES - 50B | DAIRYCOATES - 50B | EDINBURGH (SM) - 64A | **7/60: KITTY - 61A** | COPLEYHILL - 56C | ARDSLEY - 56B | PARKESTON - 30F | CANKLOW - 41D | DARNALL - 41A |
| Nov-60 | DAIRYCOATES - 50B | DAIRYCOATES - 50B | EDINBURGH (SM) - 64A | KITTYBREWSTER - 61A | COPLEYHILL - 56C | ARDSLEY - 56B | PARKESTON - 30F | CANKLOW - 41D | DARNALL - 41A |

| | 61314 | 61315 | 61316 | 61317 | 61318 | 61319 | 61320 | 61321 | 61322 |
|---|---|---|---|---|---|---|---|---|---|
| Aug-50 | DARNALL - 39B | DARNALL - 39B | DARNALL - 39B | DARNALL - 39B | IMMINGHAM - 40B | BORO' GDNS - 54C | BORO' GDNS - 54C | BORO' GDNS - 54C | TWEEDMOUTH - 52D |
| Jan-51 | DARNALL - 39B | DARNALL - 39B | DARNALL - 39B | DARNALL - 39B | IMMINGHAM - 40B | BORO' GDNS - 54C | BORO' GDNS - 54C | BORO' GDNS - 54C | TWEEDMOUTH - 52D |
| Aug-51 | DARNALL - 39B | DARNALL - 39B | DARNALL - 39B | DARNALL - 39B | IMMINGHAM - 40B | BORO' GDNS - 54C | BORO' GDNS - 54C | BORO' GDNS - 54C | TWEEDMOUTH - 52D |
| Jan-52 | DARNALL - 39B | DARNALL - 39B | DARNALL - 39B | DARNALL - 39B | IMMINGHAM - 40B | BORO' GDNS - 54C | BORO' GDNS - 54C | BORO' GDNS - 54C | TWEEDMOUTH - 52D |
| Aug-52 | DARNALL - 39B | DARNALL - 39B | DARNALL - 39B | DARNALL - 39B | IMMINGHAM - 40B | BORO' GDNS - 54C | BORO' GDNS - 54C | BORO' GDNS - 54C | TWEEDMOUTH - 52D |
| Jan-53 | DARNALL - 39B | DARNALL - 39B | DARNALL - 39B | DARNALL - 39B | IMMINGHAM - 40B | BORO' GDNS - 54C | BORO' GDNS - 54C | BORO' GDNS - 54C | TWEEDMOUTH - 52D |
| Aug-53 | DARNALL - 39B | DARNALL - 39B | DARNALL - 39B | DARNALL - 39B | IMMINGHAM - 40B | BORO' GDNS - 54C | BORO' GDNS - 54C | BORO' GDNS - 54C | TWEEDMOUTH - 52D |
| Jan-54 | DARNALL - 39B | DARNALL - 39B | DARNALL - 39B | DARNALL - 39B | IMMINGHAM - 40B | BORO' GDNS - 54C | BORO' GDNS - 54C | BORO' GDNS - 54C | TWEEDMOUTH - 52D |
| Aug-54 | DARNALL - 39B | DARNALL - 39B | DARNALL - 39B | **8/54: NORW - 32A** | IMMINGHAM - 40B | BORO' GDNS - 54C | BORO' GDNS - 54C | BORO' GDNS - 54C | TWEEDMOUTH - 52D |
| Jan-55 | DARNALL - 39B | DARNALL - 39B | DARNALL - 39B | NORWICH - 32A | IMMINGHAM - 40B | BORO' GDNS - 54C | BORO' GDNS - 54C | BORO' GDNS - 54C | TWEEDMOUTH - 52D |
| Aug-55 | DARNALL - 39B | DARNALL - 39B | DARNALL - 39B | NORWICH - 32A | IMMINGHAM - 40B | BORO' GDNS - 54C | BORO' GDNS - 54C | BORO' GDNS - 54C | TWEEDMOUTH - 52D |
| Jan-56 | DARNALL - 41A | DARNALL - 41A | DARNALL - 41A | NORWICH - 32A | IMMINGHAM - 40B | BORO' GDNS - 54C | BORO' GDNS - 54C | BORO' GDNS - 54C | TWEEDMOUTH - 52D |
| Aug-56 | DARNALL - 41A | DARNALL - 41A | DARNALL - 41A | NORWICH - 32A | IMMINGHAM - 40B | BORO' GDNS - 54C | BORO' GDNS - 54C | BORO' GDNS - 54C | TWEEDMOUTH - 52D |
| Jan-57 | DARNALL - 41A | DARNALL - 41A | DARNALL - 41A | NORWICH - 32A | IMMINGHAM - 40B | BORO' GDNS - 54C | **10/56:BRAD - 56G** | BORO' GDNS - 54C | TWEEDMOUTH - 52D |
| Aug-57 | **10/57: CAMB - 31A** | DARNALL - 41A | DARNALL - 41A | NORWICH - 32A | IMMINGHAM - 40B | BORO' GDNS - 54C | **6/57: WAKE - 56A** | BORO' GDNS - 54C | TWEEDMOUTH - 52D |
| Jan-58 | CAMBRIDGE - 31A | DARNALL - 41A | DARNALL - 41A | NORWICH - 32A | IMMINGHAM - 40B | BORO' GDNS - 54C | **9/57: C.HILL - 56C** | BORO' GDNS - 54C | TWEEDMOUTH - 52D |
| Aug-58 | CAMBRIDGE - 31A | DARNALL - 41A | DARNALL - 41A | NORWICH - 32A | IMMINGHAM - 40B | **6/58: WAKE - 56A** | COPLEYHILL - 56C | **6/58: WAKE - 56A** | TWEEDMOUTH - 52D |
| Jan-59 | CAMBRIDGE - 31A | DARNALL - 41A | DARNALL - 41A | NORWICH - 32A | IMMINGHAM - 40B | **9/58: DARL - 51A** | COPLEYHILL - 56C | **9/58: DARL - 51A** | TWEEDMOUTH - 52D |
| Aug-59 | CAMBRIDGE - 31A | DARNALL - 41A | DARNALL - 41A | NORWICH - 32A | IMMINGHAM - 40B | **6/59: YORK - 50A** | COPLEYHILL - 56C | DARLINGTON - 51A | TWEEDMOUTH - 52D |
| Nov-59 | **10/59: DCTR - 36A** | DARNALL - 41A | DARNALL - 41A | NORWICH - 32A | IMMINGHAM - 40B | YORK - 50A | COPLEYHILL - 56C | DARLINGTON - 51A | TWEEDMOUTH - 52D |
| Jan-60 | DONCASTER - 36A | DARNALL - 41A | DARNALL - 41A | **4/60: LINC - 40A** | IMMINGHAM - 40B | YORK - 50A | COPLEYHILL - 56C | DARLINGTON - 51A | TWEEDMOUTH - 52D |
| Apr-60 | DONCASTER - 36A | DARNALL - 41A | **5/60: MEX - 41F** | **4/60: IMM - 40B** | IMMINGHAM - 40B | YORK - 50A | COPLEYHILL - 56C | DARLINGTON - 51A | TWEEDMOUTH - 52D |
| Aug-60 | DONCASTER - 36A | DARNALL - 41A | MEXBOROUGH - 41F | IMMINGHAM - 40B | IMMINGHAM - 40B | YORK - 50A | COPLEYHILL - 56C | DARLINGTON - 51A | **6/60: BLAY - 52C** |
| Nov-60 | DONCASTER - 36A | DARNALL - 41A | MEXBOROUGH - 41F | IMMINGHAM - 40B | IMMINGHAM - 40B | YORK - 50A | COPLEYHILL - 56C | DARLINGTON - 51A | BLAYDON - 52C |

| | 61323 | 61324 | 61325 | 61326 | 61327 | 61328 | 61329 | 61330 | 61331 |
|---|---|---|---|---|---|---|---|---|---|
| Aug-50 | KITTYBREWSTER - 61A | KITTYBREWSTER - 61A | IMMINGHAM - 40B | NEWTON HEATH - 26A | DARNALL - 39B | IMMINGHAM - 40B | LINCOLN - 40A | NEWENGLAND - 35A | NEWENGLAND - 35A |
| Jan-51 | KITTYBREWSTER - 61A | KITTYBREWSTER - 61A | IMMINGHAM - 40B | **9/50: GORT - 39A** | DARNALL - 39B | IMMINGHAM - 40B | LINCOLN - 40A | NEWENGLAND - 35A | NEWENGLAND - 35A |
| Aug-51 | KITTYBREWSTER - 61A | KITTYBREWSTER - 61A | IMMINGHAM - 40B | GORTON - 39A | DARNALL - 39B | IMMINGHAM - 40B | **9/51: STRAT - 30A** | NEWENGLAND - 35A | NEWENGLAND - 35A |
| Jan-52 | KITTYBREWSTER - 61A | KITTYBREWSTER - 61A | IMMINGHAM - 40B | GORTON - 39A | DARNALL - 39B | IMMINGHAM - 40B | STRATFORD - 30A | NEWENGLAND - 35A | NEWENGLAND - 35A |
| Aug-52 | KITTYBREWSTER - 61A | KITTYBREWSTER - 61A | IMMINGHAM - 40B | GORTON - 39A | DARNALL - 39B | IMMINGHAM - 40B | STRATFORD - 30A | NEWENGLAND - 35A | NEWENGLAND - 35A |
| Jan-53 | KITTYBREWSTER - 61A | KITTYBREWSTER - 61A | IMMINGHAM - 40B | GORTON - 39A | DARNALL - 39B | IMMINGHAM - 40B | STRATFORD - 30A | NEWENGLAND - 35A | **1/53: KX - 34A** |
| Aug-53 | KITTYBREWSTER - 61A | KITTYBREWSTER - 61A | IMMINGHAM - 40B | GORTON - 39A | DARNALL - 39B | IMMINGHAM - 40B | STRATFORD - 30A | **9/53: ST M - 64A** | KINGS CROSS - 34A |
| Jan-54 | KITTYBREWSTER - 61A | KITTYBREWSTER - 61A | IMMINGHAM - 40B | GORTON - 39A | DARNALL - 39B | IMMINGHAM - 40B | STRATFORD - 30A | EDINBURGH (SM) - 64A | KINGS CROSS - 34A |
| Aug-54 | KITTYBREWSTER - 61A | KITTYBREWSTER - 61A | IMMINGHAM - 40B | **6/54: DCTR - 36A** | DARNALL - 39B | IMMINGHAM - 40B | STRATFORD - 30A | EDINBURGH (SM) - 64A | KINGS CROSS - 34A |
| Jan-55 | KITTYBREWSTER - 61A | KITTYBREWSTER - 61A | IMMINGHAM - 40B | DONCASTER - 36A | DARNALL - 39B | IMMINGHAM - 40B | STRATFORD - 30A | **12/54: CARS - 64D** | KINGS CROSS - 34A |
| Aug-55 | KITTYBREWSTER - 61A | KITTYBREWSTER - 61A | IMMINGHAM - 40B | DONCASTER - 36A | DARNALL - 39B | IMMINGHAM - 40B | STRATFORD - 30A | CARSTAIRS - 64D | KINGS CROSS - 34A |
| Jan-56 | KITTYBREWSTER - 61A | KITTYBREWSTER - 61A | IMMINGHAM - 40B | DONCASTER - 36A | DARNALL - 41A | IMMINGHAM - 40B | STRATFORD - 30A | **3/56: ST M - 64A** | KINGS CROSS - 34A |
| Aug-56 | KITTYBREWSTER - 61A | KITTYBREWSTER - 61A | IMMINGHAM - 40B | DONCASTER - 36A | DARNALL - 41A | IMMINGHAM - 40B | STRATFORD - 30A | EDINBURGH (SM) - 64A | KINGS CROSS - 34A |
| Jan-57 | **3/57: S BGE - 35C** | KITTYBREWSTER - 61A | IMMINGHAM - 40B | DONCASTER - 36A | DARNALL - 41A | IMMINGHAM - 40B | STRATFORD - 30A | EDINBURGH (SM) - 64A | KINGS CROSS - 34A |
| Aug-57 | SPITALBRIDGE - 35C | KITTYBREWSTER - 61A | IMMINGHAM - 40B | DONCASTER - 36A | DARNALL - 41A | IMMINGHAM - 40B | STRATFORD - 30A | **5/57: TH JN - 62A** | KINGS CROSS - 34A |
| Jan-58 | SPITAL BRIDGE - 35C | KITTYBREWSTER - 61A | IMMINGHAM - 40B | DONCASTER - 36A | DARNALL - 41A | IMMINGHAM - 40B | STRATFORD - 30A | THORNTON JCN - 62A | KINGS CROSS - 34A |
| Aug-58 | SPITAL BRIDGE - 31F | KITTYBREWSTER - 61A | IMMINGHAM - 40B | DONCASTER - 36A | DARNALL - 41A | IMMINGHAM - 40B | STRATFORD - 30A | THORNTON JCN - 62A | KINGS CROSS - 34A |
| Jan-59 | SPITAL BRIDGE - 31F | KITTYBREWSTER - 61A | IMMINGHAM - 40B | DONCASTER - 36A | DARNALL - 41A | IMMINGHAM - 40B | STRATFORD - 30A | THORNTON JCN - 62A | KINGS CROSS - 34A |
| Aug-59 | SPITAL BRIDGE - 31F | KITTYBREWSTER - 61A | IMMINGHAM - 40B | DONCASTER - 36A | DARNALL - 41A | IMMINGHAM - 40B | STRATFORD - 30A | THORNTON JCN - 62A | KINGS CROSS - 34A |
| Nov-59 | SPITAL BRIDGE - 31F | KITTYBREWSTER - 61A | IMMINGHAM - 40B | DONCASTER - 36A | DARNALL - 41A | IMMINGHAM - 40B | STRATFORD - 30A | THORNTON JCN - 62A | KINGS CROSS - 34A |
| Jan-60 | **2/60: MARCH - 31B** | KITTYBREWSTER - 61A | IMMINGHAM - 40B | DONCASTER - 36A | DARNALL - 41A | IMMINGHAM - 40B | STRATFORD - 30A | THORNTON JCN - 62A | KINGS CROSS - 34A |
| Apr-60 | MARCH - 31B | KITTYBREWSTER - 61A | IMMINGHAM - 40B | DONCASTER - 36A | DARNALL - 41A | IMMINGHAM - 40B | STRATFORD - 30A | THORNTON JCN - 62A | **4/60: NEWE - 34E** |
| Aug-60 | MARCH - 31B | KITTYBREWSTER - 61A | IMMINGHAM - 40B | DONCASTER - 36A | DARNALL - 41A | IMMINGHAM - 40B | STRATFORD - 30A | THORNTON JCN - 62A | NEWENGLAND - 34E |
| Nov-60 | MARCH - 31B | KITTYBREWSTER - 61A | IMMINGHAM - 40B | DONCASTER - 36A | DARNALL - 41A | IMMINGHAM - 40B | STRATFORD - 30A | THORNTON JCN - 62A | NEWENGLAND - 34E |

| | 61332 | 61333 | 61334 | 61335 | 61336 | 61337 | 61338 | 61339 | 61340 |
|---|---|---|---|---|---|---|---|---|---|
| Aug-50 | NORWICH - 32A | CAMBRIDGE - 31A | CAMBRIDGE - 31A | STRATFORD - 30A | STRATFORD - 30A | YORK - 50A | NEVILLE HILL - 50B | NEVILLE HILL - 50B | EASTFIELD - 65A |
| Jan-51 | NORWICH - 32A | CAMBRIDGE - 31A | CAMBRIDGE - 31A | STRATFORD - 30A | STRATFORD - 30A | YORK - 50A | **11/50: HTN - 52B** | NEVILLE HILL - 50B | EASTFIELD - 65A |
| Aug-51 | NORWICH - 32A | CAMBRIDGE - 31A | CAMBRIDGE - 31A | STRATFORD - 30A | STRATFORD - 30A | YORK - 50A | **1/51: N.HILL - 50B** | **9/51: YORK - 50A** | EASTFIELD - 65A |
| Jan-52 | NORWICH - 32A | CAMBRIDGE - 31A | CAMBRIDGE - 31A | STRATFORD - 30A | STRATFORD - 30A | YORK - 50A | **9/51: YORK - 50A** | YORK - 50A | EASTFIELD - 65A |
| Aug-52 | NORWICH - 32A | CAMBRIDGE - 31A | CAMBRIDGE - 31A | STRATFORD - 30A | STRATFORD - 30A | YORK - 50A | YORK - 50A | YORK - 50A | EASTFIELD - 65A |
| Jan-53 | NORWICH - 32A | CAMBRIDGE - 31A | CAMBRIDGE - 31A | STRATFORD - 30A | STRATFORD - 30A | YORK - 50A | YORK - 50A | YORK - 50A | EASTFIELD - 65A |
| Aug-53 | **9/53: STM - 64A** | **9/53: STM - 64A** | CAMBRIDGE - 31A | STRATFORD - 30A | STRATFORD - 30A | YORK - 50A | YORK - 50A | YORK - 50A | EASTFIELD - 65A |
| Jan-54 | EDINBURGH(SM) - 64A | **3/54: BATH - 64F** | CAMBRIDGE - 31A | STRATFORD - 30A | STRATFORD - 30A | YORK - 50A | YORK - 50A | YORK - 50A | EASTFIELD - 65A |
| Aug-54 | EDINBURGH(SM) - 64A | **4/54: EAST - 65A** | CAMBRIDGE - 31A | STRATFORD - 30A | STRATFORD - 30A | YORK - 50A | YORK - 50A | YORK - 50A | EASTFIELD - 65A |
| Jan-55 | EDINBURGH(SM) - 64A | **6/54: KITTY - 61A** | CAMBRIDGE - 31A | STRATFORD - 30A | STRATFORD - 30A | YORK - 50A | YORK - 50A | YORK - 50A | EASTFIELD - 65A |
| Aug-55 | EDINBURGH(SM) - 64A | KITTYBREWSTER - 61A | CAMBRIDGE - 31A | STRATFORD - 30A | STRATFORD - 30A | YORK - 50A | **9/55: DARL - 51A** | YORK - 50A | EASTFIELD - 65A |
| Jan-56 | EDINBURGH(SM) - 64A | KITTYBREWSTER - 61A | CAMBRIDGE - 31A | STRATFORD - 30A | STRATFORD - 30A | YORK - 50A | DARLINGTON - 51A | YORK - 50A | EASTFIELD - 65A |
| Aug-56 | EDINBURGH(SM) - 64A | KITTYBREWSTER - 61A | CAMBRIDGE - 31A | STRATFORD - 30A | STRATFORD - 30A | YORK - 50A | DARLINGTON - 51A | YORK - 50A | EASTFIELD - 65A |
| Jan-57 | EDINBURGH(SM) - 64A | KITTYBREWSTER - 61A | **11/56: DARN - 41A** | STRATFORD - 30A | **2/57: COL - 30E** | YORK - 50A | DARLINGTON - 51A | YORK - 50A | EASTFIELD - 65A |
| Aug-57 | EDINBURGH(SM) - 64A | **8/57: STM - 64A** | DARNALL - 41A | STRATFORD - 30A | COLCHESTER - 30E | YORK - 50A | DARLINGTON - 51A | YORK - 50A | EASTFIELD - 65A |
| Jan-58 | EDINBURGH(SM) - 64A | **11/57: HMKT - 64B** | DARNALL - 41A | STRATFORD - 30A | COLCHESTER - 30E | YORK - 50A | DARLINGTON - 51A | YORK - 50A | EASTFIELD - 65A |
| Aug-58 | EDINBURGH(SM) - 64A | HAYMARKET - 64B | DARNALL - 41A | STRATFORD - 30A | COLCHESTER - 30E | YORK - 50A | DARLINGTON - 51A | **6/58: C. HILL - 56C** | EASTFIELD - 65A |
| Jan-59 | EDINBURGH(SM) - 64A | **1/59: EAST - 65A** | DARNALL - 41A | STRATFORD - 30A | COLCHESTER - 30E | YORK - 50A | DARLINGTON - 51A | COPLEY HILL - 56C | EASTFIELD - 65A |
| Aug-59 | EDINBURGH(SM) - 64A | **2/59: PARK - 65C** | DARNALL - 41A | STRATFORD - 30A | COLCHESTER - 30E | YORK - 50A | DARLINGTON - 51A | COPLEY HILL - 56C | EASTFIELD - 65A |
| Nov-59 | EDINBURGH(SM) - 64A | PARKHEAD - 65C | **10/59: MILL - 41C** | STRATFORD - 30A | **12/59: PARK - 30F** | YORK - 50A | DARLINGTON - 51A | COPLEY HILL - 56C | EASTFIELD - 65A |
| Jan-60 | EDINBURGH(SM) - 64A | PARKHEAD - 65C | **1/60: CANK - 41D** | STRATFORD - 30A | PARKESTON - 30F | YORK - 50A | DARLINGTON - 51A | COPLEY HILL - 56C | EASTFIELD - 65A |
| Apr-60 | EDINBURGH(SM) - 64A | PARKHEAD - 65C | CANKLOW - 41D | STRATFORD - 30A | PARKESTON - 30F | YORK - 50A | DARLINGTON - 51A | COPLEY HILL - 56C | EASTFIELD - 65A |
| Aug-60 | EDINBURGH(SM) - 64A | PARKHEAD - 65C | CANKLOW - 41D | STRATFORD - 30A | PARKESTON - 30F | YORK - 50A | DARLINGTON - 51A | COPLEY HILL - 56C | EASTFIELD - 65A |
| Nov-60 | EDINBURGH(SM) - 64A | PARKHEAD - 65C | CANKLOW - 41D | STRATFORD - 30A | PARKESTON - 30F | YORK - 50A | DARLINGTON - 51A | COPLEY HILL - 56C | EASTFIELD - 65A |

| | 61341 | 61342 | 61343 | 61344 | 61345 | 61346 | 61347 | 61348 | 61349 |
|---|---|---|---|---|---|---|---|---|---|
| Aug-50 | EDINBURGH(SM) - 64A | EASTFIELD - 65A | KITTYBREWSTER - 61A | EASTFIELD - 65A | KITTYBREWSTER - 61A | KEITH - 61C | KEITH - 61C | KITTYBREWSTER - 61A | KITTYBREWSTER - 61A |
| Jan-51 | EDINBURGH(SM) - 64A | EASTFIELD - 65A | KITTYBREWSTER - 61A | EASTFIELD - 65A | KITTYBREWSTER - 61A | **12/50: KITTY - 61A** | **12/50: KITTY - 61A** | KITTYBREWSTER - 61A | KITTYBREWSTER - 61A |
| Aug-51 | EDINBURGH(SM) - 64A | EASTFIELD - 65A | KITTYBREWSTER - 61A | EASTFIELD - 65A | KITTYBREWSTER - 61A | KITTYBREWSTER - 61A | KITTYBREWSTER - 61A | KITTYBREWSTER - 61A | KITTYBREWSTER - 61A |
| Jan-52 | EDINBURGH(SM) - 64A | EASTFIELD - 65A | KITTYBREWSTER - 61A | EASTFIELD - 65A | KITTYBREWSTER - 61A | KITTYBREWSTER - 61A | KITTYBREWSTER - 61A | KITTYBREWSTER - 61A | KITTYBREWSTER - 61A |
| Aug-52 | EDINBURGH(SM) - 64A | EASTFIELD - 65A | KITTYBREWSTER - 61A | EASTFIELD - 65A | KITTYBREWSTER - 61A | KITTYBREWSTER - 61A | KITTYBREWSTER - 61A | KITTYBREWSTER - 61A | KITTYBREWSTER - 61A |
| Jan-53 | EDINBURGH(SM) - 64A | EASTFIELD - 65A | KITTYBREWSTER - 61A | EASTFIELD - 65A | KITTYBREWSTER - 61A | KITTYBREWSTER - 61A | KITTYBREWSTER - 61A | KITTYBREWSTER - 61A | KITTYBREWSTER - 61A |
| Aug-53 | EDINBURGH(SM) - 64A | EASTFIELD - 65A | KITTYBREWSTER - 61A | EASTFIELD - 65A | KITTYBREWSTER - 61A | KITTYBREWSTER - 61A | KITTYBREWSTER - 61A | KITTYBREWSTER - 61A | KITTYBREWSTER - 61A |
| Jan-54 | EDINBURGH(SM) - 64A | EASTFIELD - 65A | KITTYBREWSTER - 61A | EASTFIELD - 65A | KITTYBREWSTER - 61A | KITTYBREWSTER - 61A | KITTYBREWSTER - 61A | KITTYBREWSTER - 61A | KITTYBREWSTER - 61A |
| Aug-54 | EDINBURGH(SM) - 64A | EASTFIELD - 65A | KITTYBREWSTER - 61A | EASTFIELD - 65A | KITTYBREWSTER - 61A | KITTYBREWSTER - 61A | KITTYBREWSTER - 61A | KITTYBREWSTER - 61A | KITTYBREWSTER - 61A |
| Jan-55 | EDINBURGH(SM) - 64A | EASTFIELD - 65A | KITTYBREWSTER - 61A | EASTFIELD - 65A | KITTYBREWSTER - 61A | KITTYBREWSTER - 61A | KITTYBREWSTER - 61A | KITTYBREWSTER - 61A | KITTYBREWSTER - 61A |
| Aug-55 | EDINBURGH(SM) - 64A | EASTFIELD - 65A | KITTYBREWSTER - 61A | EASTFIELD - 65A | KITTYBREWSTER - 61A | KITTYBREWSTER - 61A | KITTYBREWSTER - 61A | KITTYBREWSTER - 61A | KITTYBREWSTER - 61A |
| Jan-56 | EDINBURGH(SM) - 64A | EASTFIELD - 65A | KITTYBREWSTER - 61A | EASTFIELD - 65A | KITTYBREWSTER - 61A | KITTYBREWSTER - 61A | KITTYBREWSTER - 61A | KITTYBREWSTER - 61A | KITTYBREWSTER - 61A |
| Aug-56 | EDINBURGH(SM) - 64A | EASTFIELD - 65A | KITTYBREWSTER - 61A | EASTFIELD - 65A | KITTYBREWSTER - 61A | KITTYBREWSTER - 61A | KITTYBREWSTER - 61A | KITTYBREWSTER - 61A | KITTYBREWSTER - 61A |
| Jan-57 | EDINBURGH(SM) - 64A | EASTFIELD - 65A | KITTYBREWSTER - 61A | EASTFIELD - 65A | KITTYBREWSTER - 61A | KITTYBREWSTER - 61A | KITTYBREWSTER - 61A | **3/57: S BGE - 35C** | KITTYBREWSTER - 61A |
| Aug-57 | EDINBURGH(SM) - 64A | EASTFIELD - 65A | KITTYBREWSTER - 61A | EASTFIELD - 65A | KITTYBREWSTER - 61A | KITTYBREWSTER - 61A | KITTYBREWSTER - 61A | SPITAL BRIDGE - 35C | **9/57: STM - 64A** |
| Jan-58 | EDINBURGH(SM) - 64A | EASTFIELD - 65A | KITTYBREWSTER - 61A | **11/57: PARK : 65C** | KITTYBREWSTER - 61A | KITTYBREWSTER - 61A | KITTYBREWSTER - 61A | SPITAL BRIDGE - 35C | EDINBURGH(SM) - 64A |
| Aug-58 | EDINBURGH(SM) - 64A | EASTFIELD - 65A | KITTYBREWSTER - 61A | PARKHEAD - 65C | KITTYBREWSTER - 61A | KITTYBREWSTER - 61A | KITTYBREWSTER - 61A | SPITAL BRIDGE - 31F | EDINBURGH(SM) - 64A |
| Jan-59 | EDINBURGH(SM) - 64A | EASTFIELD - 65A | KITTYBREWSTER - 61A | PARKHEAD - 65C | KITTYBREWSTER - 61A | KITTYBREWSTER - 61A | KITTYBREWSTER - 61A | SPITAL BRIDGE - 31F | EDINBURGH(SM) - 64A |
| Aug-59 | EDINBURGH(SM) - 64A | EASTFIELD - 65A | **4/59: TH JN - 62A** | PARKHEAD - 65C | KITTYBREWSTER - 61A | KITTYBREWSTER - 61A | KITTYBREWSTER - 61A | SPITAL BRIDGE - 31F | EDINBURGH(SM) - 64A |
| Nov-59 | EDINBURGH(SM) - 64A | EASTFIELD - 65A | THORNTON JCN - 62A | PARKHEAD - 65C | KITTYBREWSTER - 61A | KITTYBREWSTER - 61A | KITTYBREWSTER - 61A | SPITAL BRIDGE - 31F | EDINBURGH(SM) - 64A |
| Jan-60 | EDINBURGH(SM) - 64A | EASTFIELD - 65A | THORNTON JCN - 62A | PARKHEAD - 65C | KITTYBREWSTER - 61A | KITTYBREWSTER - 61A | KITTYBREWSTER - 61A | **2/60: MARCH - 31B** | EDINBURGH(SM) - 64A |
| Apr-60 | EDINBURGH(SM) - 64A | EASTFIELD - 65A | THORNTON JCN - 62A | PARKHEAD - 65C | KITTYBREWSTER - 61A | KITTYBREWSTER - 61A | KITTYBREWSTER - 61A | **4/60: LINC - 40A** | EDINBURGH(SM) - 64A |
| Aug-60 | EDINBURGH(SM) - 64A | EASTFIELD - 65A | THORNTON JCN - 62A | PARKHEAD - 65C | KITTYBREWSTER - 61A | KITTYBREWSTER - 61A | KITTYBREWSTER - 61A | LINCOLN - 40A | EDINBURGH(SM) - 64A |
| Nov-60 | EDINBURGH(SM) - 64A | EASTFIELD - 65A | THORNTON JCN - 62A | PARKHEAD - 65C | KITTYBREWSTER - 61A | KITTYBREWSTER - 61A | KITTYBREWSTER - 61A | LINCOLN - 40A | EDINBURGH(SM) - 64A |

| | 61350 | 61351 | 61352 | 61353 | 61354 | 61355 | 61356 | 61357 | 61358 |
|---|---|---|---|---|---|---|---|---|---|
| Aug-50 | KITTYBREWSTER - 61A | KITTYBREWSTER - 61A | KITTYBREWSTER - 61A | KEITH - 61C | EDINBURGH(SM) - 64A | EDINBURGH(SM) - 64A | EDINBURGH(SM) - 64A | EDINBURGH(SM) - 64A | EDINBURGH(SM) - 64A |
| Jan-51 | KITTYBREWSTER - 61A | KITTYBREWSTER - 61A | KITTYBREWSTER - 61A | **10/50: Rugby Test** | EDINBURGH(SM) - 64A | EDINBURGH(SM) - 64A | EDINBURGH(SM) - 64A | EDINBURGH(SM) - 64A | EDINBURGH(SM) - 64A |
| Aug-51 | KITTYBREWSTER - 61A | KITTYBREWSTER - 61A | KITTYBREWSTER - 61A | **9/51: DARL - 51A** | EDINBURGH(SM) - 64A | EDINBURGH(SM) - 64A | EDINBURGH(SM) - 64A | EDINBURGH(SM) - 64A | EDINBURGH(SM) - 64A |
| Jan-52 | KITTYBREWSTER - 61A | KITTYBREWSTER - 61A | KITTYBREWSTER - 61A | DARLINGTON - 51A | EDINBURGH(SM) - 64A | EDINBURGH(SM) - 64A | EDINBURGH(SM) - 64A | EDINBURGH(SM) - 64A | EDINBURGH(SM) - 64A |
| Aug-52 | KITTYBREWSTER - 61A | KITTYBREWSTER - 61A | KITTYBREWSTER - 61A | DARLINGTON - 51A | EDINBURGH(SM) - 64A | EDINBURGH(SM) - 64A | EDINBURGH(SM) - 64A | EDINBURGH(SM) - 64A | EDINBURGH(SM) - 64A |
| Jan-53 | KITTYBREWSTER - 61A | KITTYBREWSTER - 61A | KITTYBREWSTER - 61A | DARLINGTON - 51A | EDINBURGH(SM) - 64A | EDINBURGH(SM) - 64A | EDINBURGH(SM) - 64A | EDINBURGH(SM) - 64A | EDINBURGH(SM) - 64A |
| Aug-53 | KITTYBREWSTER - 61A | KITTYBREWSTER - 61A | KITTYBREWSTER - 61A | DARLINGTON - 51A | EDINBURGH(SM) - 64A | EDINBURGH(SM) - 64A | EDINBURGH(SM) - 64A | EDINBURGH(SM) - 64A | EDINBURGH(SM) - 64A |
| Jan-54 | KITTYBREWSTER - 61A | KITTYBREWSTER - 61A | KITTYBREWSTER - 61A | DARLINGTON - 51A | EDINBURGH(SM) - 64A | EDINBURGH(SM) - 64A | EDINBURGH(SM) - 64A | EDINBURGH(SM) - 64A | EDINBURGH(SM) - 64A |
| Aug-54 | KITTYBREWSTER - 61A | KITTYBREWSTER - 61A | KITTYBREWSTER - 61A | DARLINGTON - 51A | EDINBURGH(SM) - 64A | **9/54: HMKT - 64B** | EDINBURGH(SM) - 64A | EDINBURGH(SM) - 64A | EDINBURGH(SM) - 64A |
| Jan-55 | KITTYBREWSTER - 61A | KITTYBREWSTER - 61A | KITTYBREWSTER - 61A | DARLINGTON - 51A | EDINBURGH(SM) - 64A | HAYMARKET - 64B | EDINBURGH(SM) - 64A | **1/55: CARS - 64D** | EDINBURGH(SM) - 64A |
| Aug-55 | KITTYBREWSTER - 61A | KITTYBREWSTER - 61A | KITTYBREWSTER - 61A | DARLINGTON - 51A | EDINBURGH(SM) - 64A | HAYMARKET - 64B | EDINBURGH(SM) - 64A | **4/55: STM - 64A** | EDINBURGH(SM) - 64A |
| Jan-56 | KITTYBREWSTER - 61A | KITTYBREWSTER - 61A | KITTYBREWSTER - 61A | DARLINGTON - 51A | EDINBURGH(SM) - 64A | HAYMARKET - 64B | EDINBURGH(SM) - 64A | EDINBURGH(SM) - 64A | EDINBURGH(SM) - 64A |
| Aug-56 | KITTYBREWSTER - 61A | KITTYBREWSTER - 61A | KITTYBREWSTER - 61A | DARLINGTON - 51A | EDINBURGH(SM) - 64A | HAYMARKET - 64B | EDINBURGH(SM) - 64A | EDINBURGH(SM) - 64A | EDINBURGH(SM) - 64A |
| Jan-57 | KITTYBREWSTER - 61A | KITTYBREWSTER - 61A | KITTYBREWSTER - 61A | DARLINGTON - 51A | EDINBURGH(SM) - 64A | HAYMARKET - 64B | EDINBURGH(SM) - 64A | EDINBURGH(SM) - 64A | EDINBURGH(SM) - 64A |
| Aug-57 | KITTYBREWSTER - 61A | **9/57: STM - 64A** | KITTYBREWSTER - 61A | DARLINGTON - 51A | EDINBURGH(SM) - 64A | HAYMARKET - 64B | EDINBURGH(SM) - 64A | EDINBURGH(SM) - 64A | **5/57: TH JN - 62A** |
| Jan-58 | KITTYBREWSTER - 61A | EDINBURGH(SM) - 64A | KITTYBREWSTER - 61A | DARLINGTON - 51A | EDINBURGH(SM) - 64A | HAYMARKET - 64B | EDINBURGH(SM) - 64A | EDINBURGH(SM) - 64A | THORNTON JCN - 62A |
| Aug-58 | KITTYBREWSTER - 61A | EDINBURGH(SM) - 64A | KITTYBREWSTER - 61A | DARLINGTON - 51A | EDINBURGH(SM) - 64A | HAYMARKET - 64B | EDINBURGH(SM) - 64A | EDINBURGH(SM) - 64A | THORNTON JCN - 62A |
| Jan-59 | KITTYBREWSTER - 61A | EDINBURGH(SM) - 64A | KITTYBREWSTER - 61A | DARLINGTON - 51A | EDINBURGH(SM) - 64A | **1/59: EAST - 65A** | EDINBURGH(SM) - 64A | EDINBURGH(SM) - 64A | THORNTON JCN - 62A |
| Aug-59 | KITTYBREWSTER - 61A | EDINBURGH(SM) - 64A | KITTYBREWSTER - 61A | DARLINGTON - 51A | EDINBURGH(SM) - 64A | EASTFIELD - 65A | EDINBURGH(SM) - 64A | EDINBURGH(SM) - 64A | THORNTON JCN - 62A |
| Nov-59 | KITTYBREWSTER - 61A | EDINBURGH(SM) - 64A | KITTYBREWSTER - 61A | DARLINGTON - 51A | EDINBURGH(SM) - 64A | EASTFIELD - 65A | EDINBURGH(SM) - 64A | EDINBURGH(SM) - 64A | THORNTON JCN - 62A |
| Jan-60 | KITTYBREWSTER - 61A | EDINBURGH(SM) - 64A | KITTYBREWSTER - 61A | DARLINGTON - 51A | EDINBURGH(SM) - 64A | EASTFIELD - 65A | EDINBURGH(SM) - 64A | EDINBURGH(SM) - 64A | THORNTON JCN - 62A |
| Apr-60 | KITTYBREWSTER - 61A | EDINBURGH(SM) - 64A | KITTYBREWSTER - 61A | DARLINGTON - 51A | EDINBURGH(SM) - 64A | EASTFIELD - 65A | EDINBURGH(SM) - 64A | EDINBURGH(SM) - 64A | THORNTON JCN - 62A |
| Aug-60 | KITTYBREWSTER - 61A | EDINBURGH(SM) - 64A | KITTYBREWSTER - 61A | DARLINGTON - 51A | EDINBURGH(SM) - 64A | EASTFIELD - 65A | EDINBURGH(SM) - 64A | EDINBURGH(SM) - 64A | THORNTON JCN - 62A |
| Nov-60 | KITTYBREWSTER - 61A | EDINBURGH(SM) - 64A | KITTYBREWSTER - 61A | DARLINGTON - 51A | EDINBURGH(SM) - 64A | EASTFIELD - 65A | EDINBURGH(SM) - 64A | EDINBURGH(SM) - 64A | THORNTON JCN - 62A |

| | 61359 | 61360 | 61361 | 61362 | 61363 | 61364 | 61365 | 61366 | 61367 |
|---|---|---|---|---|---|---|---|---|---|
| Aug-50 | EDINBURGH(SM) - 64A | STRATFORD - 30A | STRATFORD - 30A | STRATFORD - 30A | STRATFORD - 30A | LINCOLN - 40A | IMMINGHAM - 40B | IMMINGHAM - 40B | COLWICK - 38A |
| Jan-51 | EDINBURGH(SM) - 64A | STRATFORD - 30A | STRATFORD - 30A | STRATFORD - 30A | STRATFORD - 30A | LINCOLN - 40A | IMMINGHAM - 40B | IMMINGHAM - 40B | **5/51: WOOD - 38E** |
| Aug-51 | EDINBURGH(SM) - 64A | STRATFORD - 30A | STRATFORD - 30A | STRATFORD - 30A | STRATFORD - 30A | LINCOLN - 40A | IMMINGHAM - 40B | IMMINGHAM - 40B | **2/52: COLW - 38A** |
| Jan-52 | EDINBURGH(SM) - 64A | STRATFORD - 30A | STRATFORD - 30A | STRATFORD - 30A | STRATFORD - 30A | LINCOLN - 40A | IMMINGHAM - 40B | IMMINGHAM - 40B | **3/52: LEIC - 38C** |
| Aug-52 | EDINBURGH(SM) - 64A | STRATFORD - 30A | STRATFORD - 30A | STRATFORD - 30A | STRATFORD - 30A | LINCOLN - 40A | IMMINGHAM - 40B | IMMINGHAM - 40B | **6/52: COLW - 38A** |
| Jan-53 | EDINBURGH(SM) - 64A | STRATFORD - 30A | STRATFORD - 30A | STRATFORD - 30A | STRATFORD - 30A | LINCOLN - 40A | IMMINGHAM - 40B | IMMINGHAM - 40B | COLWICK - 38A |
| Aug-53 | EDINBURGH(SM) - 64A | STRATFORD - 30A | STRATFORD - 30A | STRATFORD - 30A | STRATFORD - 30A | **10/53: NEWE - 35A** | IMMINGHAM - 40B | IMMINGHAM - 40B | COLWICK - 38A |
| Jan-54 | EDINBURGH(SM) - 64A | STRATFORD - 30A | STRATFORD - 30A | STRATFORD - 30A | STRATFORD - 30A | NEW ENGLAND - 35A | **12/53: DCTR - 36A** | IMMINGHAM - 40B | COLWICK - 38A |
| Aug-54 | EDINBURGH(SM) - 64A | STRATFORD - 30A | STRATFORD - 30A | STRATFORD - 30A | STRATFORD - 30A | NEW ENGLAND - 35A | DONCASTER - 36A | IMMINGHAM - 40B | COLWICK - 38A |
| Jan-55 | EDINBURGH(SM) - 64A | STRATFORD - 30A | STRATFORD - 30A | STRATFORD - 30A | STRATFORD - 30A | **2/55 : NEWE - 35A** | DONCASTER - 36A | IMMINGHAM - 40B | COLWICK - 38A |
| Aug-55 | EDINBURGH(SM) - 64A | STRATFORD - 30A | STRATFORD - 30A | STRATFORD - 30A | STRATFORD - 30A | KINGS CROSS - 34A | DONCASTER - 36A | IMMINGHAM - 40B | COLWICK - 38A |
| Jan-56 | EDINBURGH(SM) - 64A | STRATFORD - 30A | STRATFORD - 30A | STRATFORD - 30A | STRATFORD - 30A | KINGS CROSS - 34A | DONCASTER - 36A | IMMINGHAM - 40B | COLWICK - 38A |
| Aug-56 | EDINBURGH(SM) - 64A | STRATFORD - 30A | STRATFORD - 30A | STRATFORD - 30A | STRATFORD - 30A | KINGS CROSS - 34A | DONCASTER - 36A | IMMINGHAM - 40B | COLWICK - 38A |
| Jan-57 | EDINBURGH(SM) - 64A | **1/57: COL - 30E** | **1/57: COL - 30E** | STRATFORD - 30A | **2/57: COL - 30E** | KINGS CROSS - 34A | DONCASTER - 36A | IMMINGHAM - 40B | **5/57: KX - 34A** |
| Aug-57 | EDINBURGH(SM) - 64A | COLCHESTER - 30E | COLCHESTER - 30E | STRATFORD - 30A | COLCHESTER - 30E | KINGS CROSS - 34A | DONCASTER - 36A | IMMINGHAM - 40B | **10/57: NEWE - 35A** |
| Jan-58 | EDINBURGH(SM) - 64A | COLCHESTER - 30E | COLCHESTER - 30E | STRATFORD - 30A | COLCHESTER - 30E | KINGS CROSS - 34A | DONCASTER - 36A | IMMINGHAM - 40B | **2/58: HIT - 34D** |
| Aug-58 | EDINBURGH(SM) - 64A | COLCHESTER - 30E | COLCHESTER - 30E | STRATFORD - 30A | COLCHESTER - 30E | KINGS CROSS - 34A | DONCASTER - 36A | IMMINGHAM - 40B | HITCHIN - 34D |
| Jan-59 | EDINBURGH(SM) - 64A | COLCHESTER - 30E | COLCHESTER - 30E | **1/59: PARK - 30F** | COLCHESTER - 30E | KINGS CROSS - 34A | DONCASTER - 36A | IMMINGHAM - 40B | HITCHIN - 34D |
| Aug-59 | EDINBURGH(SM) - 64A | **4/59: CAMB - 31A** | COLCHESTER - 30E | PARKESTON - 30F | COLCHESTER - 30E | KINGS CROSS - 34A | DONCASTER - 36A | IMMINGHAM - 40B | **6/59: GRAN - 34F** |
| Nov-59 | EDINBURGH(SM) - 64A | **10/59: DCTR - 36A** | **12/59: PARK - 30F** | PARKESTON - 30F | **12/59: MARCH - 31B** | KINGS CROSS - 34A | DONCASTER - 36A | IMMINGHAM - 40B | GRANTHAM - 34F |
| Jan-60 | EDINBURGH(SM) - 64A | DONCASTER - 36A | PARKESTON - 30F | PARKESTON - 30F | **1/60: CAMB - 31A** | KINGS CROSS - 34A | DONCASTER - 36A | IMMINGHAM - 40B | GRANTHAM - 34F |
| Apr-60 | EDINBURGH(SM) - 64A | DONCASTER - 36A | PARKESTON - 30F | PARKESTON - 30F | CAMBRIDGE - 31A | KINGS CROSS - 34A | DONCASTER - 36A | IMMINGHAM - 40B | GRANTHAM - 34F |
| Aug-60 | EDINBURGH(SM) - 64A | DONCASTER - 36A | PARKESTON - 30F | PARKESTON - 30F | CAMBRIDGE - 31A | KINGS CROSS - 34A | DONCASTER - 36A | IMMINGHAM - 40B | GRANTHAM - 34F |
| Nov-60 | EDINBURGH(SM) - 64A | DONCASTER - 36A | PARKESTON - 30F | PARKESTON - 30F | CAMBRIDGE - 31A | KINGS CROSS - 34A | DONCASTER - 36A | IMMINGHAM - 40B | GRANTHAM - 34F |

| | 61368 | 61369 | 61370 | 61371 | 61372 | 61373 | 61374 | 61375 | 61376 |
|---|---|---|---|---|---|---|---|---|---|
| Aug-50 | COLWICK - 38A | COLWICK - 38A | 10/50: LINC - 40A | 10/50: LINC - 40A | 12/50: IMM - 40B | 12/50: IMM - 40B | | | |
| Jan-51 | COLWICK - 38A | COLWICK - 38A | 3/51: NEWE - 35A | LINCOLN - 40A | IMMINGHAM - 40B | 3/51: NEWE - 35A | 2/51: IMM - 40B | 2/51: IMM - 40B | 4/51: COLW - 38A |
| Aug-51 | 5/51: WOOD - 38E | COLWICK - 38A | 4/51: MARCH - 31B | LINCOLN - 40A | 9/51: STRAT - 30A | 4/51: MARCH - 31B | IMMINGHAM - 40B | 9/51: STRAT - 30A | 10/51: WOOD - 38E |
| Jan-52 | WOODFORD HALSE - 38E | COLWICK - 38A | 9/51: STRAT - 30A | LINCOLN - 40A | STRATFORD - 30A | 9/51: STRAT - 30A | IMMINGHAM - 40B | STRATFORD - 30A | 2/51: COLW - 38A |
| Aug-52 | WOODFORD HALSE - 38E | COLWICK - 38A | STRATFORD - 30A | LINCOLN - 40A | STRATFORD - 30A | STRATFORD - 30A | IMMINGHAM - 40B | STRATFORD - 30A | COLWICK - 38A |
| Jan-53 | WOODFORD HALSE - 38E | 10/52: LEIC - 38C | STRATFORD - 30A | LINCOLN - 40A | STRATFORD - 30A | STRATFORD - 30A | IMMINGHAM - 40B | STRATFORD - 30A | COLWICK - 38A |
| Aug-53 | WOODFORD HALSE - 38E | LEICESTER (GC) - 38C | STRATFORD - 30A | LINCOLN - 40A | STRATFORD - 30A | STRATFORD - 30A | IMMINGHAM - 40B | STRATFORD - 30A | COLWICK - 38A |
| Jan-54 | WOODFORD HALSE - 38E | LEICESTER (GC) - 38C | STRATFORD - 30A | LINCOLN - 40A | STRATFORD - 30A | STRATFORD - 30A | IMMINGHAM - 40B | STRATFORD - 30A | COLWICK - 38A |
| Aug-54 | WOODFORD HALSE - 38E | LEICESTER (GC) - 38C | STRATFORD - 30A | LINCOLN - 40A | STRATFORD - 30A | STRATFORD - 30A | IMMINGHAM - 40B | STRATFORD - 30A | COLWICK - 38A |
| Jan-55 | WOODFORD HALSE - 38E | LEICESTER (GC) - 38C | STRATFORD - 30A | LINCOLN - 40A | STRATFORD - 30A | STRATFORD - 30A | IMMINGHAM - 40B | STRATFORD - 30A | COLWICK - 38A |
| Aug-55 | WOODFORD HALSE - 38E | LEICESTER (GC) - 38C | STRATFORD - 30A | LINCOLN - 40A | STRATFORD - 30A | STRATFORD - 30A | IMMINGHAM - 40B | STRATFORD - 30A | COLWICK - 38A |
| Jan-56 | WOODFORD HALSE - 38E | LEICESTER (GC) - 38C | STRATFORD - 30A | 11/55: CAMB - 31A | STRATFORD - 30A | STRATFORD - 30A | IMMINGHAM - 40B | STRATFORD - 30A | COLWICK - 38A |
| Aug-56 | WOODFORD HALSE - 38E | LEICESTER (GC) - 38C | STRATFORD - 30A | CAMBRIDGE - 31A | STRATFORD - 30A | STRATFORD - 30A | IMMINGHAM - 40B | STRATFORD - 30A | COLWICK - 38A |
| Jan-57 | WOODFORD HALSE - 38E | LEICESTER (GC) - 38C | 2/57: COL - 30E | CAMBRIDGE - 31A | STRATFORD - 30A | 2/57: COL - 30E | IMMINGHAM - 40B | STRATFORD - 30A | 12/56: LEIC - 38C |
| Aug-57 | WOODFORD HALSE - 38E | LEICESTER (GC) - 38C | COLCHESTER - 30E | CAMBRIDGE - 31A | STRATFORD - 30A | COLCHESTER - 30E | IMMINGHAM - 40B | STRATFORD - 30A | LEICESTER (GC) - 38C |
| Jan-58 | WOODFORD HALSE - 38E | LEICESTER (GC) - 38C | COLCHESTER - 30E | CAMBRIDGE - 31A | STRATFORD - 30A | COLCHESTER - 30E | IMMINGHAM - 40B | STRATFORD - 30A | LEICESTER (GC) - 38C |
| Aug-58 | WOODFORD HALSE - 2F | LEICESTER (GC) - 15E | COLCHESTER - 30E | CAMBRIDGE - 31A | STRATFORD - 30A | COLCHESTER - 30E | IMMINGHAM - 40B | STRATFORD - 30A | LEICESTER (GC) - 15E |
| Jan-59 | WOODFORD HALSE - 2F | LEICESTER (GC) - 15E | COLCHESTER - 30E | CAMBRIDGE - 31A | 1/59: PARK - 30F | COLCHESTER - 30E | IMMINGHAM - 40B | STRATFORD - 30A | LEICESTER (GC) - 15E |
| Aug-59 | WOODFORD HALSE - 2F | LEICESTER (GC) - 15E | 6/59: DARN - 41A | CAMBRIDGE - 31A | PARKESTON - 30F | COLCHESTER - 30E | IMMINGHAM - 40B | STRATFORD - 30A | LEICESTER (GC) - 15E |
| Nov-59 | WOODFORD HALSE - 2F | 10/59: AGEC - 26B | DARNALL - 41A | CAMBRIDGE - 31A | PARKESTON - 30F | 10/59: PARK - 30F | IMMINGHAM - 40B | STRATFORD - 30A | LEICESTER (GC) - 15E |
| Jan-60 | WOODFORD HALSE - 2F | AGECROFT - 26B | DARNALL - 41A | CAMBRIDGE - 31A | PARKESTON - 30F | PARKESTON - 30F | IMMINGHAM - 40B | STRATFORD - 30A | LEICESTER (GC) - 15E |
| Apr-60 | WOODFORD HALSE - 2F | AGECROFT - 26B | 4/60: CANK - 41D | CAMBRIDGE - 31A | PARKESTON - 30F | PARKESTON - 30F | IMMINGHAM - 40B | STRATFORD - 30A | LEICESTER (GC) - 15E |
| Aug-60 | WOODFORD HALSE - 2F | AGECROFT - 26B | CANKLOW - 41D | CAMBRIDGE - 31A | PARKESTON - 30F | PARKESTON - 30F | IMMINGHAM - 40B | STRATFORD - 30A | LEICESTER (GC) - 15E |
| Nov-60 | WOODFORD HALSE - 2F | AGECROFT - 26B | CANKLOW - 41D | CAMBRIDGE - 31A | PARKESTON - 30F | PARKESTON - 30F | IMMINGHAM - 40B | STRATFORD - 30A | LEICESTER (GC) - 15E |

| | 61377 | 61378 | 61379 | 61380 | 61381 | 61382 | 61383 | 61384 | 61385 |
|---|---|---|---|---|---|---|---|---|---|
| Aug-50 | | | | | | | | | |
| Jan-51 | 4/51: COLW - 38A | 5/51: COLW - 38A | 6/51: COLW - 38A | | | | | | |
| Aug-51 | 12/51: NORW - 32A | COLWICK - 38A | COLWICK - 38A | 8/51: COLW - 38A | 9/51: COLW - 38A | 9/51: ARDS - 37A | 10/51: ARDS - 37A | 9/51: ARDS - 37A | 9/51: ARDS - 37A |
| Jan-52 | 3/52: ARD - 37A | COLWICK - 38A | COLWICK - 38A | COLWICK - 38A | 11/51: WOOD - 38E | ARDSLEY - 37A | ARDSLEY - 37A | ARDSLEY - 37A | ARDSLEY - 37A |
| Aug-52 | 7/52: C.HILL - 37B | 10/52: STRAT - 30A | COLWICK - 38A | COLWICK - 38A | WOODFORD HALSE - 38E | ARDSLEY - 37A | ARDSLEY - 37A | 9/52: BRAD - 37C | ARDSLEY - 37A |
| Jan-53 | COPLEYHILL - 37B | STRATFORD - 30A | COLWICK - 38A | 2/53: LEIC - 38C | WOODFORD HALSE - 38E | ARDSLEY - 37A | ARDSLEY - 37A | 10/52: STRAT - 30A | ARDSLEY - 37A |
| Aug-53 | COPLEYHILL - 37B | STRATFORD - 30A | COLWICK - 38A | LEICESTER (GC) - 38C | WOODFORD HALSE - 38E | ARDSLEY - 37A | ARDSLEY - 37A | STRATFORD - 30A | ARDSLEY - 37A |
| Jan-54 | 3/54: ARDS - 37A | STRATFORD - 30A | COLWICK - 38A | LEICESTER (GC) - 38C | 3/54: LEIC - 38C | ARDSLEY - 37A | ARDSLEY - 37A | STRATFORD - 30A | ARDSLEY - 37A |
| Aug-54 | ARDSLEY - 37A | STRATFORD - 30A | COLWICK - 38A | LEICESTER (GC) - 38C | 11/54: WOOD - 38E | ARDSLEY - 37A | ARDSLEY - 37A | STRATFORD - 30A | ARDSLEY - 37A |
| Jan-55 | ARDSLEY - 37A | STRATFORD - 30A | COLWICK - 38A | LEICESTER (GC) - 38C | 2/55: LEIC - 38C | ARDSLEY - 37A | ARDSLEY - 37A | STRATFORD - 30A | ARDSLEY - 37A |
| Aug-55 | ARDSLEY - 37A | STRATFORD - 30A | COLWICK - 38A | LEICESTER (GC) - 38C | LEICESTER (GC) - 38C | ARDSLEY - 37A | ARDSLEY - 37A | STRATFORD - 30A | ARDSLEY - 37A |
| Jan-56 | 12/55: DCTR - 36A | STRATFORD - 30A | COLWICK - 38A | LEICESTER (GC) - 38C | LEICESTER (GC) - 38C | ARDSLEY - 37A | ARDSLEY - 37A | STRATFORD - 30A | ARDSLEY - 37A |
| Aug-56 | DONCASTER - 36A | STRATFORD - 30A | COLWICK - 38A | LEICESTER (GC) - 38C | LEICESTER (GC) - 38C | ARDSLEY - 56B | ARDSLEY - 56B | STRATFORD - 30A | ARDSLEY - 56B |
| Jan-57 | DONCASTER - 36A | STRATFORD - 30A | COLWICK - 38A | LEICESTER (GC) - 38C | LEICESTER (GC) - 38C | ARDSLEY - 56B | ARDSLEY - 56B | 10/56: PARK - 30F | ARDSLEY - 56B |
| Aug-57 | DONCASTER - 36A | STRATFORD - 30A | COLWICK - 38A | LEICESTER (GC) - 38C | LEICESTER (GC) - 38C | 9/57: BRAD - 56G | 9/57: BRAD - 56G | PARKESTON - 30F | ARDSLEY - 56B |
| Jan-58 | DONCASTER - 36A | STRATFORD - 30A | COLWICK - 38A | LEICESTER (GC) - 38C | LEICESTER (GC) - 38C | 2/58: LOWM - 56F | 2/58: LOWM - 56F | PARKESTON - 30F | ARDSLEY - 56B |
| Aug-58 | DONCASTER - 36A | STRATFORD - 30A | COLWICK - 40E | LEICESTER (GC) - 15E | LEICESTER (GC) - 15E | 9/58: DARL - 51A | LOWMOOR - 56F | PARKESTON - 30F | ARDSLEY - 56B |
| Jan-59 | DONCASTER - 36A | 1/59: PARK - 30F | COLWICK - 40E | LEICESTER (GC) - 15E | LEICESTER (GC) - 15E | DARLINGTON - 51A | LOWMOOR - 56F | PARKESTON - 30F | 2/59: WAKE - 56A |
| Aug-59 | DONCASTER - 36A | PARKESTON - 30F | COLWICK - 40E | LEICESTER (GC) - 15E | LEICESTER (GC) - 15E | DARLINGTON - 51A | LOWMOOR - 56F | PARKESTON - 30F | WAKEFIELD - 56A |
| Nov-59 | DONCASTER - 36A | PARKESTON - 30F | COLWICK - 40E | LEICESTER (GC) - 15E | LEICESTER (GC) - 15E | DARLINGTON - 51A | LOWMOOR - 56F | PARKESTON - 30F | WAKEFIELD - 56A |
| Jan-60 | DONCASTER - 36A | PARKESTON - 30F | COLWICK - 40E | LEICESTER (GC) - 15E | LEICESTER (GC) - 15E | DARLINGTON - 51A | LOWMOOR - 56F | PARKESTON - 30F | WAKEFIELD - 56A |
| Apr-60 | 6/60: DARN - 41A | PARKESTON - 30F | COLWICK - 40E | LEICESTER (GC) - 15E | LEICESTER (GC) - 15E | DARLINGTON - 51A | LOWMOOR - 56F | 5/60: LINC - 40A | WAKEFIELD - 56A |
| Aug-60 | DARNALL - 41A | PARKESTON - 30F | COLWICK - 40E | LEICESTER (GC) - 15E | LEICESTER (GC) - 15E | DARLINGTON - 51A | LOWMOOR - 56F | LINCOLN - 40A | WAKEFIELD - 56A |
| Nov-60 | DARNALL - 41A | PARKESTON - 30F | COLWICK - 40E | LEICESTER (GC) - 15E | LEICESTER (GC) - 15E | DARLINGTON - 51A | LOWMOOR - 56F | LINCOLN - 40A | WAKEFIELD - 56A |

| | 61386 | 61387 | 61388 | 61389 | 61390 | 61391 | 61392 | 61393 | 61394 |
|---|---|---|---|---|---|---|---|---|---|
| Aug-50 | | | | | | | | | |
| Jan-51 | | | | | | | | | |
| Aug-51 | 10/51: ARDS - 37A | 10/51: ARDS - 37A | | | | | | | |
| Jan-52 | 2/52: C.HILL - 37B | 2/52: C.HILL - 37B | 11/51: ARDS - 37A | 11/51: NEWE - 35A | 12/51: NEWE - 35A | 12/51: NEWE - 35A | 12/51: NEWE - 35A | 1/52: DCTR - 36A | 1/52: DCTR - 36A |
| Aug-52 | COPLEYHILL - 37B | COPLEYHILL - 37B | ARDSLEY - 37A | NEWENGLAND - 35A | 7/52: COLW - 38A | NEWENGLAND - 35A | NEWENGLAND - 35A | DONCASTER - 36A | DONCASTER - 36A |
| Jan-53 | COPLEYHILL - 37B | COPLEYHILL - 37B | 11/52: C. HILL - 37B | NEWENGLAND - 35A | COLWICK - 38A | NEWENGLAND - 35A | NEWENGLAND - 35A | 1/53: KX - 34A | 1/53: KX - 34A |
| Aug-53 | COPLEYHILL - 37B | COPLEYHILL - 37B | COPLEYHILL - 37B | NEWENGLAND - 35A | COLWICK - 38A | NEWENGLAND - 35A | NEWENGLAND - 35A | 2/53: HIT - 34D | 2/53: HIT - 34D |
| Jan-54 | COPLEYHILL - 37B | COPLEYHILL - 37B | COPLEYHILL - 37B | NEWENGLAND - 35A | COLWICK - 38A | NEWENGLAND - 35A | NEWENGLAND - 35A | HITCHIN - 34D | HITCHIN - 34D |
| Aug-54 | COPLEYHILL - 37B | COPLEYHILL - 37B | COPLEYHILL - 37B | NEWENGLAND - 35A | COLWICK - 38A | NEWENGLAND - 35A | NEWENGLAND - 35A | 6/54: KX - 34A | 6/54: KX - 34A |
| Jan-55 | COPLEYHILL - 37B | COPLEYHILL - 37B | COPLEYHILL - 37B | NEWENGLAND - 35A | 11/54: IMM - 40B | NEWENGLAND - 35A | NEWENGLAND - 35A | KINGS CROSS - 34A | KINGS CROSS - 34A |
| Aug-55 | COPLEYHILL - 37B | COPLEYHILL - 37B | COPLEYHILL - 37B | NEWENGLAND - 35A | IMMINGHAM - 40B | NEWENGLAND - 35A | NEWENGLAND - 35A | KINGS CROSS - 34A | KINGS CROSS - 34A |
| Jan-56 | COPLEYHILL - 37B | COPLEYHILL - 37B | COPLEYHILL - 37B | NEWENGLAND - 35A | IMMINGHAM - 40B | NEWENGLAND - 35A | 3/56: CAMB - 31A | KINGS CROSS - 34A | KINGS CROSS - 34A |
| Aug-56 | COPLEYHILL - 56C | COPLEYHILL - 56C | COPLEYHILL - 56C | NEWENGLAND - 35A | IMMINGHAM - 40B | NEWENGLAND - 35A | 10/56: NEWE - 35A | KINGS CROSS - 34A | KINGS CROSS - 34A |
| Jan-57 | COPLEYHILL - 56C | COPLEYHILL - 56C | COPLEYHILL - 56C | NEWENGLAND - 35A | IMMINGHAM - 40B | NEWENGLAND - 35A | NEWENGLAND - 35A | KINGS CROSS - 34A | 4/57: NEAS - 34E |
| Aug-57 | COPLEYHILL - 56C | COPLEYHILL - 56C | COPLEYHILL - 56C | 10/57: GRAN - 35B | IMMINGHAM - 40B | NEWENGLAND - 35A | 10/57: GRAN - 35B | KINGS CROSS - 34A | 5/57: KX - 34A |
| Jan-58 | COPLEYHILL - 56C | COPLEYHILL - 56C | COPLEYHILL - 56C | GRANTHAM - 35B | IMMINGHAM - 40B | NEWENGLAND - 35A | GRANTHAM - 35B | KINGS CROSS - 34A | KINGS CROSS - 34A |
| Aug-58 | COPLEYHILL - 56C | 9/58: DARL - 51A | COPLEYHILL - 56C | GRANTHAM - 34F | IMMINGHAM - 40B | NEWENGLAND - 34E | GRANTHAM - 34F | KINGS CROSS - 34A | KINGS CROSS - 34A |
| Jan-59 | COPLEYHILL - 56C | DARLINGTON - 51A | COPLEYHILL - 56C | GRANTHAM - 34F | IMMINGHAM - 40B | NEWENGLAND - 34E | GRANTHAM - 34F | KINGS CROSS - 34A | KINGS CROSS - 34A |
| Aug-59 | COPLEYHILL - 56C | 6/59: LOWM - 56F | 8/59: YORK - 50A | GRANTHAM - 34F | IMMINGHAM - 40B | NEWENGLAND - 34E | GRANTHAM - 34F | KINGS CROSS - 34A | KINGS CROSS - 34A |
| Nov-59 | COPLEYHILL - 56C | LOWMOOR - 56F | YORK - 50A | GRANTHAM - 34F | 12/59: DCTR - 36A | NEWENGLAND - 34E | GRANTHAM - 34F | 10/59: NEWE - 34E | KINGS CROSS - 34A |
| Jan-60 | COPLEYHILL - 56C | LOWMOOR - 56F | YORK - 50A | GRANTHAM - 34F | DONCASTER - 36A | NEWENGLAND - 34E | GRANTHAM - 34F | 2/60: KX - 34A | KINGS CROSS - 34A |
| Apr-60 | COPLEYHILL - 56C | LOWMOOR - 56F | YORK - 50A | GRANTHAM - 34F | 6/60: COLW - 40E | NEWENGLAND - 34E | GRANTHAM - 34F | KINGS CROSS - 34A | KINGS CROSS - 34A |
| Aug-60 | COPLEYHILL - 56C | LOWMOOR - 56F | YORK - 50A | GRANTHAM - 34F | COLWICK - 40E | NEWENGLAND - 34E | GRANTHAM - 34F | KINGS CROSS - 34A | KINGS CROSS - 34A |
| Nov-60 | COPLEYHILL - 56C | LOWMOOR - 56F | YORK - 50A | GRANTHAM - 34F | COLWICK - 40E | NEWENGLAND - 34E | GRANTHAM - 34F | KINGS CROSS - 34A | KINGS CROSS - 34A |

| | 61395 | 61396 | 61397 | 61398 | 61399 | 61400 | 61401 | 61402 | 61403 |
|---|---|---|---|---|---|---|---|---|---|
| Aug-50 | | | | | | KITTYBREWSTER - 61A | KITTYBREWSTER - 61A | DUNDEE - 62B | DUNDEE - 62B |
| Jan-51 | | | | | | KITTYBREWSTER - 61A | KITTYBREWSTER - 61A | DUNDEE - 62B | DUNDEE - 62B |
| Aug-51 | | | | | | KITTYBREWSTER - 61A | KITTYBREWSTER - 61A | DUNDEE - 62B | DUNDEE - 62B |
| Jan-52 | | | | | | KITTYBREWSTER - 61A | KITTYBREWSTER - 61A | DUNDEE - 62B | DUNDEE - 62B |
| Aug-52 | 2/52: CANAL - 68E | 2/52: CANAL - 68E | 3/52: ST M - 64A | 4/52: ST M - 64A | 4/52: DCTR - 36A | KITTYBREWSTER - 61A | KITTYBREWSTER - 61A | DUNDEE - 62B | DUNDEE - 62B |
| Jan-53 | CARLISLE (CANAL) - 68E | EASTFIELD - 65A | EDINBURGH (SM) - 64A | EDINBURGH (SM) - 64A | 10/52: STRAT - 30A | KITTYBREWSTER - 61A | KITTYBREWSTER - 61A | DUNDEE - 62B | DUNDEE - 62B |
| Aug-53 | CARLISLE (CANAL) - 68E | EASTFIELD - 65A | EDINBURGH (SM) - 64A | EDINBURGH (SM) - 64A | STRATFORD - 30A | KITTYBREWSTER - 61A | KITTYBREWSTER - 61A | DUNDEE - 62B | DUNDEE - 62B |
| Jan-54 | CARLISLE (CANAL) - 68E | EASTFIELD - 65A | EDINBURGH (SM) - 64A | EDINBURGH (SM) - 64A | STRATFORD - 30A | KITTYBREWSTER - 61A | KITTYBREWSTER - 61A | DUNDEE - 62B | DUNDEE - 62B |
| Aug-54 | CARLISLE (CANAL) - 68E | EASTFIELD - 65A | EDINBURGH (SM) - 64A | EDINBURGH (SM) - 64A | STRATFORD - 30A | KITTYBREWSTER - 61A | KITTYBREWSTER - 61A | DUNDEE - 62B | DUNDEE - 62B |
| Jan-55 | CARLISLE (CANAL) - 68E | EASTFIELD - 65A | EDINBURGH (SM) - 64A | 11/54: CARS - 64D | STRATFORD - 30A | KITTYBREWSTER - 61A | KITTYBREWSTER - 61A | DUNDEE - 62B | 3/55: TH JN - 62A |
| Aug-55 | CARLISLE (CANAL) - 68E | EASTFIELD - 65A | EDINBURGH (SM) - 64A | CARSTAIRS - 64D | STRATFORD - 30A | KITTYBREWSTER - 61A | KITTYBREWSTER - 61A | DUNDEE - 62B | THORNTON JCN - 62A |
| Jan-56 | CARLISLE (CANAL) - 68E | EASTFIELD - 65A | EDINBURGH (SM) - 64A | 2/56: ST M - 64A | STRATFORD - 30A | KITTYBREWSTER - 61A | KITTYBREWSTER - 61A | DUNDEE - 62B | THORNTON JCN - 62A |
| Aug-56 | CARLISLE (CANAL) - 68E | EASTFIELD - 65A | EDINBURGH (SM) - 64A | EDINBURGH (SM) - 64A | STRATFORD - 30A | KITTYBREWSTER - 61A | 10/56: TH JN - 62A | DUNDEE - 62B | THORNTON JCN - 62A |
| Jan-57 | CARLISLE (CANAL) - 68E | EASTFIELD - 65A | EDINBURGH (SM) - 64A | EDINBURGH (SM) - 64A | STRATFORD - 30A | KITTYBREWSTER - 61A | THORNTON JCN - 62A | DUNDEE - 62B | THORNTON JCN - 62A |
| Aug-57 | CARLISLE (CANAL) - 68E | EASTFIELD - 65A | EDINBURGH (SM) - 64A | EDINBURGH (SM) - 64A | STRATFORD - 30A | KITTYBREWSTER - 61A | THORNTON JCN - 62A | DUNDEE - 62B | THORNTON JCN - 62A |
| Jan-58 | CARLISLE CANAL - 68E | EASTFIELD - 65A | EDINBURGH (SM) - 64A | EDINBURGH (SM) - 64A | STRATFORD - 30A | KITTYBREWSTER - 61A | THORNTON JCN - 62A | DUNDEE - 62B | THORNTON JCN - 62A |
| Aug-58 | CARLISLE CANAL - 12C | EASTFIELD - 65A | EDINBURGH (SM) - 64A | EDINBURGH (SM) - 64A | STRATFORD - 30A | KITTYBREWSTER - 61A | THORNTON JCN - 62A | DUNDEE - 62B | THORNTON JCN - 62A |
| Jan-59 | CARLISLE CANAL - 12C | EASTFIELD - 65A | EDINBURGH (SM) - 64A | EDINBURGH (SM) - 64A | 1/59: NOR - 30A | KITTYBREWSTER - 61A | THORNTON JCN - 62A | DUNDEE - 62B | THORNTON JCN - 62A |
| Aug-59 | CARLISLE CANAL - 12C | EASTFIELD - 65A | EDINBURGH (SM) - 64A | EDINBURGH (SM) - 64A | NORWICH - 32A | KITTYBREWSTER - 61A | THORNTON JCN - 62A | DUNDEE - 62B | THORNTON JCN - 62A |
| Nov-59 | CARLISLE CANAL - 12C | EASTFIELD - 65A | EDINBURGH (SM) - 64A | EDINBURGH (SM) - 64A | NORWICH - 32A | KITTYBREWSTER - 61A | THORNTON JCN - 62A | DUNDEE - 62B | THORNTON JCN - 62A |
| Jan-60 | CARLISLE CANAL - 12C | EASTFIELD - 65A | EDINBURGH (SM) - 64A | EDINBURGH (SM) - 64A | 2/60: DARN - 41A | KITTYBREWSTER - 61A | THORNTON JCN - 62A | DUNDEE - 62B | THORNTON JCN - 62A |
| Apr-60 | CARLISLE CANAL - 12C | EASTFIELD - 65A | EDINBURGH (SM) - 64A | EDINBURGH (SM) - 64A | DARNALL - 41A | KITTYBREWSTER - 61A | 6/60: EAST 65A | DUNDEE - 62B | 4/60: EAST - 65A |
| Aug-60 | CARLISLE CANAL - 12C | EASTFIELD - 65A | EDINBURGH (SM) - 64A | EDINBURGH (SM) - 64A | DARNALL - 41A | KITTYBREWSTER - 61A | EASTFIELD - 65A | DUNDEE - 62B | EASTFIELD - 65A |
| Nov-60 | CARLISLE CANAL - 12C | EASTFIELD - 65A | EDINBURGH (SM) - 64A | EDINBURGH (SM) - 64A | DARNALL - 41A | KITTYBREWSTER - 61A | EASTFIELD - 65A | DUNDEE - 62B | EASTFIELD - 65A |

| | 61404 | 61405 | 61406 | 61407 | 61408 | 61409 | B 16 4-6-0 (1920)<br>61410 | 61411 | 61412 |
|---|---|---|---|---|---|---|---|---|---|
| Aug-50 | KITTYBREWSTER - 61A | LINCOLN - 40A | IMMINGHAM - 40B | IMMINGHAM - 40B | IMMINGHAM - 40B | IMMINGHAM - 40B | NEVILLE HILL - 50B | NEVILLE HILL - 50B | NEVILLE HILL - 50B |
| Jan-51 | 11/50: HMKT - 64B | LINCOLN - 40A | IMMINGHAM - 40B | IMMINGHAM - 40B | IMMINGHAM - 40B | IMMINGHAM - 40B | NEVILLE HILL - 50B | NEVILLE HILL - 50B | NEVILLE HILL - 50B |
| Aug-51 | HAYMARKET - 64B | LINCOLN - 40A | IMMINGHAM - 40B | IMMINGHAM - 40B | IMMINGHAM - 40B | IMMINGHAM - 40B | NEVILLE HILL - 50B | NEVILLE HILL - 50B | NEVILLE HILL - 50B |
| Jan-52 | HAYMARKET - 64B | LINCOLN - 40A | IMMINGHAM - 40B | IMMINGHAM - 40B | IMMINGHAM - 40B | IMMINGHAM - 40B | NEVILLE HILL - 50B | NEVILLE HILL - 50B | NEVILLE HILL - 50B |
| Aug-52 | HAYMARKET - 64B | LINCOLN - 40A | IMMINGHAM - 40B | IMMINGHAM - 40B | IMMINGHAM - 40B | IMMINGHAM - 40B | NEVILLE HILL - 50B | NEVILLE HILL - 50B | NEVILLE HILL - 50B |
| Jan-53 | HAYMARKET - 64B | LINCOLN - 40A | IMMINGHAM - 40B | IMMINGHAM - 40B | IMMINGHAM - 40B | IMMINGHAM - 40B | NEVILLE HILL - 50B | NEVILLE HILL - 50B | NEVILLE HILL - 50B |
| Aug-53 | HAYMARKET - 64B | LINCOLN - 40A | IMMINGHAM - 40B | 9/53: STM - 64A | IMMINGHAM - 40B | IMMINGHAM - 40B | NEVILLE HILL - 50B | NEVILLE HILL - 50B | NEVILLE HILL - 50B |
| Jan-54 | HAYMARKET - 64B | LINCOLN - 40A | IMMINGHAM - 40B | EDINBURGH (SM) - 64A | IMMINGHAM - 40B | IMMINGHAM - 40B | NEVILLE HILL - 50B | NEVILLE HILL - 50B | NEVILLE HILL - 50B |
| Aug-54 | HAYMARKET - 64B | LINCOLN - 40A | IMMINGHAM - 40B | EDINBURGH (SM) - 64A | IMMINGHAM - 40B | IMMINGHAM - 40B | NEVILLE HILL - 50B | NEVILLE HILL - 50B | NEVILLE HILL - 50B |
| Jan-55 | HAYMARKET - 64B | LINCOLN - 40A | IMMINGHAM - 40B | EDINBURGH (SM) - 64A | IMMINGHAM - 40B | IMMINGHAM - 40B | NEVILLE HILL - 50B | NEVILLE HILL - 50B | NEVILLE HILL - 50B |
| Aug-55 | HAYMARKET - 64B | LINCOLN - 40A | IMMINGHAM - 40B | EDINBURGH (SM) - 64A | IMMINGHAM - 40B | IMMINGHAM - 40B | 9/55: HTN - 52B | NEVILLE HILL - 50B | NEVILLE HILL - 50B |
| Jan-56 | HAYMARKET - 64B | LINCOLN - 40A | IMMINGHAM - 40B | 2/56: DYRD - 64C | IMMINGHAM - 40B | IMMINGHAM - 40B | HEATON - 52B | NEVILLE HILL - 50B | NEVILLE HILL - 50B |
| Aug-56 | HAYMARKET - 64B | LINCOLN - 40A | IMMINGHAM - 40B | DALRY ROAD - 64C | IMMINGHAM - 40B | IMMINGHAM - 40B | HEATON - 52B | NEVILLE HILL - 50B | NEVILLE HILL - 50B |
| Jan-57 | HAYMARKET - 64B | LINCOLN - 40A | IMMINGHAM - 40B | DALRY ROAD - 64C | IMMINGHAM - 40B | IMMINGHAM - 40B | HEATON - 52B | NEVILLE HILL - 50B | NEVILLE HILL - 50B |
| Aug-57 | HAYMARKET - 64B | LINCOLN - 40A | IMMINGHAM - 40B | 4/57: DUNF - 62C | IMMINGHAM - 40B | IMMINGHAM - 40B | HEATON - 52B | NEVILLE HILL - 50B | NEVILLE HILL - 50B |
| Jan-58 | HAYMARKET - 64B | LINCOLN - 40A | IMMINGHAM - 40B | DUNFERMLINE - 62C | IMMINGHAM - 40B | IMMINGHAM - 40B | HEATON - 52B | NEVILLE HILL - 50B | NEVILLE HILL - 50B |
| Aug-58 | HAYMARKET - 64B | LINCOLN - 40A | IMMINGHAM - 40B | DUNFERMLINE - 62C | IMMINGHAM - 40B | IMMINGHAM - 40B | 6/58: YORK - 50A | NEVILLE HILL - 50B | NEVILLE HILL - 50B |
| Jan-59 | 1/59: STRX - 65B | LINCOLN - 40A | IMMINGHAM - 40B | DUNFERMLINE - 62C | IMMINGHAM - 40B | IMMINGHAM - 40B | YORK - 50A | NEVILLE HILL - 50B | NEVILLE HILL - 50B |
| Aug-59 | 4/59: PARK - 65C | LINCOLN - 40A | IMMINGHAM - 40B | DUNFERMLINE - 62C | IMMINGHAM - 40B | IMMINGHAM - 40B | YORK - 50A | NEVILLE HILL - 50B | NEVILLE HILL - 50B |
| Nov-59 | PARKHEAD - 65C | LINCOLN - 40A | IMMINGHAM - 40B | DUNFERMLINE - 62C | IMMINGHAM - 40B | 12/59: LINC - 40A | YORK - 50A | NEVILLE HILL - 50B | NEVILLE HILL - 50B |
| Jan-60 | PARKHEAD - 65C | LINCOLN - 40A | IMMINGHAM - 40B | DUNFERMLINE - 62C | IMMINGHAM - 40B | LINCOLN - 40A | YORK - 50A | NEVILLE HILL - 50B | NEVILLE HILL - 50B |
| Apr-60 | PARKHEAD - 65C | LINCOLN - 40A | IMMINGHAM - 40B | DUNFERMLINE - 62C | IMMINGHAM - 40B | LINCOLN - 40A | YORK - 50A | NEVILLE HILL - 55H | NEVILLE HILL - 55H |
| Aug-60 | PARKHEAD - 65C | LINCOLN - 40A | IMMINGHAM - 40B | DUNFERMLINE - 62C | IMMINGHAM - 40B | LINCOLN - 40A | YORK - 50A | NEVILLE HILL - 55H | NEVILLE HILL - 55H |
| Nov-60 | PARKHEAD - 65C | LINCOLN - 40A | IMMINGHAM - 40B | DUNFERMLINE - 62C | IMMINGHAM - 40B | LINCOLN - 40A | 10/60: W/D | NEVILLE HILL - 55H | NEVILLE HILL - 55H |

| | 61413 | 61414 | 61415 | 61416 | 61419 | 61422 | 61423 | 61424 | 61425 |
|---|---|---|---|---|---|---|---|---|---|
| Aug-50 | NEVILLE HILL - 50B | NEVILLE HILL - 50B | NEVILLE HILL - 50B | YORK - 50A | YORK - 50A | YORK - 50A | YORK - 50A | YORK - 50A | NEVILLE HILL - 50B |
| Jan-51 | NEVILLE HILL - 50B | NEVILLE HILL - 50B | NEVILLE HILL - 50B | YORK - 50A | YORK - 50A | YORK - 50A | YORK - 50A | YORK - 50A | NEVILLE HILL - 50B |
| Aug-51 | NEVILLE HILL - 50B | NEVILLE HILL - 50B | NEVILLE HILL - 50B | 5/51: N. HILL - 50B | 5/51: N. HILL - 50B | 5/51: N. HILL - 50B | YORK - 50A | 5/51: N.HILL - 50B | NEVILLE HILL - 50B |
| Jan-52 | NEVILLE HILL - 50B | NEVILLE HILL - 50B | NEVILLE HILL - 50B | 10/51: YORK - 50A | 2/52: YORK - 50A | NEVILLE HILL - 50B | YORK - 50A | NEVILLE HILL - 50B | NEVILLE HILL - 50B |
| Aug-52 | NEVILLE HILL - 50B | NEVILLE HILL - 50B | NEVILLE HILL - 50B | YORK - 50A | YORK - 50A | NEVILLE HILL - 50B | YORK - 50A | NEVILLE HILL - 50B | NEVILLE HILL - 50B |
| Jan-53 | NEVILLE HILL - 50B | NEVILLE HILL - 50B | NEVILLE HILL - 50B | YORK - 50A | YORK - 50A | NEVILLE HILL - 50B | YORK - 50A | NEVILLE HILL - 50B | NEVILLE HILL - 50B |
| Aug-53 | NEVILLE HILL - 50B | NEVILLE HILL - 50B | NEVILLE HILL - 50B | YORK - 50A | YORK - 50A | 5/53: SELBY - 50C | YORK - 50A | 11/53: YORK - 50A | NEVILLE HILL - 50B |
| Jan-54 | NEVILLE HILL - 50B | NEVILLE HILL - 50B | NEVILLE HILL - 50B | YORK - 50A | YORK - 50A | SELBY - 50C | YORK - 50A | 3/54: N. HILL - 50B | NEVILLE HILL - 50B |
| Aug-54 | NEVILLE HILL - 50B | NEVILLE HILL - 50B | NEVILLE HILL - 50B | YORK - 50A | YORK - 50A | SELBY - 50C | YORK - 50A | 8/54: YORK - 50A | NEVILLE HILL - 50B |
| Jan-55 | NEVILLE HILL - 50B | NEVILLE HILL - 50B | NEVILLE HILL - 50B | YORK - 50A | YORK - 50A | SELBY - 50C | YORK - 50A | YORK - 50A | NEVILLE HILL - 50B |
| Aug-55 | 9/55: HTN - 52B | 9/55: HTN - 52B | 9/55: HTN - 52B | YORK - 50A | YORK - 50A | 6/55: YORK - 50A | YORK - 50A | YORK - 50A | NEVILLE HILL - 50B |
| Jan-56 | HEATON - 52B | 5/56: BLAY - 52C | HEATON - 52B | YORK - 50A | YORK - 50A | YORK - 50A | YORK - 50A | YORK - 50A | NEVILLE HILL - 50B |
| Aug-56 | HEATON - 52B | 6/56: N.HILL - 50B | 6/56: N.HILL - 50B | YORK - 50A | YORK - 50A | YORK - 50A | YORK - 50A | YORK - 50A | NEVILLE HILL - 50B |
| Jan-57 | HEATON - 52B | NEVILLE HILL - 50B | NEVILLE HILL - 50B | YORK - 50A | YORK - 50A | YORK - 50A | YORK - 50A | YORK - 50A | NEVILLE HILL - 50B |
| Aug-57 | HEATON - 52B | NEVILLE HILL - 50B | NEVILLE HILL - 50B | YORK - 50A | 7/57: SELBY - 50C | YORK - 50A | YORK - 50A | YORK - 50A | NEVILLE HILL - 50B |
| Jan-58 | HEATON - 52B | NEVILLE HILL - 50B | NEVILLE HILL - 50B | YORK - 50A | 9/57: YORK - 50A | YORK - 50A | YORK - 50A | YORK - 50A | NEVILLE HILL - 50B |
| Aug-58 | 6/58: YORK - 50A | NEVILLE HILL - 50B | NEVILLE HILL - 50B | YORK - 50A | YORK - 50A | YORK - 50A | YORK - 50A | YORK - 50A | NEVILLE HILL - 50B |
| Jan-59 | YORK - 50A | NEVILLE HILL - 50B | NEVILLE HILL - 50B | YORK - 50A | YORK - 50A | YORK - 50A | YORK - 50A | YORK - 50A | NEVILLE HILL - 50B |
| Aug-59 | YORK - 50A | NEVILLE HILL - 50B | NEVILLE HILL - 50B | YORK - 50A | YORK - 50A | YORK - 50A | YORK - 50A | YORK - 50A | NEVILLE HILL - 50B |
| Nov-59 | YORK - 50A | NEVILLE HILL - 50B | NEVILLE HILL - 50B | YORK - 50A | YORK - 50A | YORK - 50A | YORK - 50A | YORK - 50A | NEVILLE HILL - 50B |
| Jan-60 | YORK - 50A | NEVILLE HILL - 50B | NEVILLE HILL - 50B | YORK - 50A | YORK - 50A | YORK - 50A | YORK - 50A | YORK - 50A | NEVILLE HILL - 50B |
| Apr-60 | YORK - 50A | NEVILLE HILL - 55H | NEVILLE HILL - 55H | YORK - 50A | YORK - 50A | YORK - 50A | YORK - 50A | YORK - 50A | 3/60: YORK - 50A |
| Aug-60 | YORK - 50A | NEVILLE HILL - 55H | NEVILLE HILL - 55H | YORK - 50A | YORK - 50A | YORK - 50A | YORK - 50A | YORK - 50A | YORK - 50A |
| Nov-60 | YORK - 50A | NEVILLE HILL - 55H | NEVILLE HILL - 55H | YORK - 50A | YORK - 50A | YORK - 50A | YORK - 50A | 10/60: W/D | YORK - 50A |

| | 61426 | 61427 | 61428 | 61429 | 61430 | 61431 | 61432 | 61433 | 61436 |
|---|---|---|---|---|---|---|---|---|---|
| Aug-50 | YORK - 50A | NEVILLE HILL - 50B | NEVILLE HILL - 50B | NEVILLE HILL - 50B | YORK - 50A | NEVILLE HILL - 50B | NEVILLE HILL - 50B | NEVILLE HILL - 50B | YORK - 50A |
| Jan-51 | YORK - 50A | NEVILLE HILL - 50B | NEVILLE HILL - 50B | NEVILLE HILL - 50B | YORK - 50A | NEVILLE HILL - 50B | NEVILLE HILL - 50B | NEVILLE HILL - 50B | YORK - 50A |
| Aug-51 | 5/51: N.HILL - 50B | NEVILLE HILL - 50B | NEVILLE HILL - 50B | NEVILLE HILL - 50B | YORK - 50A | NEVILLE HILL - 50B | NEVILLE HILL - 50B | NEVILLE HILL - 50B | 5/51: N.HILL - 50B |
| Jan-52 | 10/51: YORK - 50A | NEVILLE HILL - 50B | NEVILLE HILL - 50B | NEVILLE HILL - 50B | YORK - 50A | NEVILLE HILL - 50B | NEVILLE HILL - 50B | NEVILLE HILL - 50B | 2/52: YORK - 50A |
| Aug-52 | YORK - 50A | NEVILLE HILL - 50B | NEVILLE HILL - 50B | NEVILLE HILL - 50B | YORK - 50A | NEVILLE HILL - 50B | NEVILLE HILL - 50B | NEVILLE HILL - 50B | YORK - 50A |
| Jan-53 | YORK - 50A | NEVILLE HILL - 50B | NEVILLE HILL - 50B | NEVILLE HILL - 50B | YORK - 50A | NEVILLE HILL - 50B | NEVILLE HILL - 50B | NEVILLE HILL - 50B | YORK - 50A |
| Aug-53 | YORK - 50A | NEVILLE HILL - 50B | NEVILLE HILL - 50B | NEVILLE HILL - 50B | YORK - 50A | NEVILLE HILL - 50B | NEVILLE HILL - 50B | NEVILLE HILL - 50B | YORK - 50A |
| Jan-54 | YORK - 50A | NEVILLE HILL - 50B | NEVILLE HILL - 50B | NEVILLE HILL - 50B | YORK - 50A | NEVILLE HILL - 50B | NEVILLE HILL - 50B | NEVILLE HILL - 50B | YORK - 50A |
| Aug-54 | YORK - 50A | NEVILLE HILL - 50B | NEVILLE HILL - 50B | NEVILLE HILL - 50B | YORK - 50A | NEVILLE HILL - 50B | NEVILLE HILL - 50B | NEVILLE HILL - 50B | YORK - 50A |
| Jan-55 | YORK - 50A | NEVILLE HILL - 50B | NEVILLE HILL - 50B | NEVILLE HILL - 50B | YORK - 50A | NEVILLE HILL - 50B | NEVILLE HILL - 50B | NEVILLE HILL - 50B | YORK - 50A |
| Aug-55 | YORK - 50A | NEVILLE HILL - 50B | NEVILLE HILL - 50B | NEVILLE HILL - 50B | YORK - 50A | NEVILLE HILL - 50B | NEVILLE HILL - 50B | NEVILLE HILL - 50B | YORK - 50A |
| Jan-56 | YORK - 50A | NEVILLE HILL - 50B | NEVILLE HILL - 50B | NEVILLE HILL - 50B | YORK - 50A | NEVILLE HILL - 50B | NEVILLE HILL - 50B | NEVILLE HILL - 50B | YORK - 50A |
| Aug-56 | YORK - 50A | NEVILLE HILL - 50B | NEVILLE HILL - 50B | NEVILLE HILL - 50B | YORK - 50A | NEVILLE HILL - 50B | NEVILLE HILL - 50B | 10/56: SELBY - 50C | YORK - 50A |
| Jan-57 | YORK - 50A | NEVILLE HILL - 50B | NEVILLE HILL - 50B | NEVILLE HILL - 50B | YORK - 50A | NEVILLE HILL - 50B | NEVILLE HILL - 50B | SELBY - 50C | YORK - 50A |
| Aug-57 | YORK - 50A | NEVILLE HILL - 50B | NEVILLE HILL - 50B | NEVILLE HILL - 50B | YORK - 50A | NEVILLE HILL - 50B | NEVILLE HILL - 50B | SELBY - 50C | YORK - 50A |
| Jan-58 | YORK - 50A | NEVILLE HILL - 50B | NEVILLE HILL - 50B | NEVILLE HILL - 50B | YORK - 50A | NEVILLE HILL - 50B | NEVILLE HILL - 50B | SELBY - 50C | YORK - 50A |
| Aug-58 | YORK - 50A | NEVILLE HILL - 50B | NEVILLE HILL - 50B | NEVILLE HILL - 50B | YORK - 50A | NEVILLE HILL - 50B | NEVILLE HILL - 50B | SELBY - 50C | YORK - 50A |
| Jan-59 | YORK - 50A | NEVILLE HILL - 50B | NEVILLE HILL - 50B | NEVILLE HILL - 50B | YORK - 50A | NEVILLE HILL - 50B | NEVILLE HILL - 50B | SELBY - 50C | YORK - 50A |
| Aug-59 | 9/59: W/D | NEVILLE HILL - 50B | NEVILLE HILL - 50B | NEVILLE HILL - 50B | YORK - 50A | NEVILLE HILL - 50B | NEVILLE HILL - 50B | 6/59: YORK - 50A | YORK - 50A |
| Nov-59 | | NEVILLE HILL - 50B | NEVILLE HILL - 50B | NEVILLE HILL - 50B | 10/59: W/D | NEVILLE HILL - 50B | NEVILLE HILL - 50B | 11/59: W/D | YORK - 50A |
| Jan-60 | | NEVILLE HILL - 50B | NEVILLE HILL - 50B | NEVILLE HILL - 50B | | NEVILLE HILL - 50B | NEVILLE HILL - 50B | | YORK - 50A |
| Apr-60 | | 3/60: W/D | NEVILLE HILL - 55H | NEVILLE HILL - 55H | | 3/60: YORK - 50A | NEVILLE HILL - 55H | | YORK - 50A |
| Aug-60 | | | NEVILLE HILL - 55H | NEVILLE HILL - 55H | | YORK - 50A | NEVILLE HILL - 55H | | YORK - 50A |
| Nov-60 | | | 11/60: W/D | NEVILLE HILL - 55H | | YORK - 50A | NEVILLE HILL - 55H | | YORK - 50A |

| | 61437 | 61440 | 61441 | 61442 | 61443 | 61445 | 61446 | 61447 | 61450 |
|---|---|---|---|---|---|---|---|---|---|
| Aug-50 | YORK - 50A | NEVILLE HILL - 50B | YORK - 50A | NEVILLE HILL - 50B | YORK - 50A | NEVILLE HILL - 50B | NEVILLE HILL - 50B | NEVILLE HILL - 50B | YORK - 50A |
| Jan-51 | YORK - 50A | NEVILLE HILL - 50B | YORK - 50A | NEVILLE HILL - 50B | YORK - 50A | NEVILLE HILL - 50B | NEVILLE HILL - 50B | NEVILLE HILL - 50B | YORK - 50A |
| Aug-51 | YORK - 50A | NEVILLE HILL - 50B | 5/51: N. HILL - 50B | NEVILLE HILL - 50B | 5/51: N. HILL - 50B | 7/51: SCAR - 50E | NEVILLE HILL - 50B | NEVILLE HILL - 50B | YORK - 50A |
| Jan-52 | YORK - 50A | NEVILLE HILL - 50B | 10/51: YORK - 50A | NEVILLE HILL - 50B | 2/52: YORK - 50A | SCARBOROUGH - 50E | NEVILLE HILL - 50B | NEVILLE HILL - 50B | YORK - 50A |
| Aug-52 | YORK - 50A | NEVILLE HILL - 50B | YORK - 50A | NEVILLE HILL - 50B | YORK - 50A | SCARBOROUGH - 50E | NEVILLE HILL - 50B | NEVILLE HILL - 50B | YORK - 50A |
| Jan-53 | YORK - 50A | NEVILLE HILL - 50B | YORK - 50A | NEVILLE HILL - 50B | YORK - 50A | SCARBOROUGH - 50E | NEVILLE HILL - 50B | NEVILLE HILL - 50B | YORK - 50A |
| Aug-53 | YORK - 50A | NEVILLE HILL - 50B | YORK - 50A | 5/53: STAR - 50D | YORK - 50A | SCARBOROUGH - 50E | NEVILLE HILL - 50B | NEVILLE HILL - 50B | YORK - 50A |
| Jan-54 | YORK - 50A | NEVILLE HILL - 50B | YORK - 50A | STARBECK - 50D | YORK - 50A | SCARBOROUGH - 50E | NEVILLE HILL - 50B | NEVILLE HILL - 50B | YORK - 50A |
| Aug-54 | YORK - 50A | NEVILLE HILL - 50B | YORK - 50A | STARBECK - 50D | YORK - 50A | SCARBOROUGH - 50E | NEVILLE HILL - 50B | NEVILLE HILL - 50B | YORK - 50A |
| Jan-55 | YORK - 50A | NEVILLE HILL - 50B | YORK - 50A | STARBECK - 50D | YORK - 50A | SCARBOROUGH - 50E | NEVILLE HILL - 50B | NEVILLE HILL - 50B | YORK - 50A |
| Aug-55 | YORK - 50A | 9/55: HTN - 52C | YORK - 50A | 5/55: N. HILL - 50B | YORK - 50A | SCARBOROUGH - 50E | NEVILLE HILL - 50B | 9/55: HTN - 52B | YORK - 50A |
| Jan-56 | YORK - 50A | HEATON - 52B | YORK - 50A | NEVILLE HILL - 50B | YORK - 50A | SCARBOROUGH - 50E | NEVILLE HILL - 50B | HEATON - 52B | YORK - 50A |
| Aug-56 | YORK - 50A | HEATON - 52B | YORK - 50A | NEVILLE HILL - 50B | YORK - 50A | SCARBOROUGH - 50E | NEVILLE HILL - 50B | 6/56: N. HILL - 50B | YORK - 50A |
| Jan-57 | YORK - 50A | HEATON - 52B | YORK - 50A | NEVILLE HILL - 50B | YORK - 50A | SCARBOROUGH - 50E | NEVILLE HILL - 50B | NEVILLE HILL - 50B | YORK - 50A |
| Aug-57 | YORK - 50A | HEATON - 52B | YORK - 50A | NEVILLE HILL - 50B | YORK - 50A | SCARBOROUGH - 50E | NEVILLE HILL - 50B | NEVILLE HILL - 50B | YORK - 50A |
| Jan-58 | YORK - 50A | HEATON - 52B | YORK - 50A | NEVILLE HILL - 50B | YORK - 50A | SCARBOROUGH - 50E | NEVILLE HILL - 50B | NEVILLE HILL - 50B | YORK - 50A |
| Aug-58 | YORK - 50A | 6/58: YORK - 50A | YORK - 50A | NEVILLE HILL - 50B | YORK - 50A | SCARBOROUGH - 50E | NEVILLE HILL - 50B | NEVILLE HILL - 50B | YORK - 50A |
| Jan-59 | YORK - 50A | YORK - 50A | YORK - 50A | NEVILLE HILL - 50B | YORK - 50A | SCARBOROUGH - 50E | NEVILLE HILL - 50B | NEVILLE HILL - 50B | YORK - 50A |
| Aug-59 | YORK - 50A | YORK - 50A | YORK - 50A | NEVILLE HILL - 50B | YORK - 50A | SCARBOROUGH - 50E | NEVILLE HILL - 50B | NEVILLE HILL - 50B | YORK - 50A |
| Nov-59 | YORK - 50A | YORK - 50A | 10/59: W/D | NEVILLE HILL - 50B | YORK - 50A | SCARBOROUGH - 50E | NEVILLE HILL - 50B | NEVILLE HILL - 50B | YORK - 50A |
| Jan-60 | YORK - 50A | YORK - 50A | | 2/60: W/D | YORK - 50A | SCARBOROUGH - 50E | NEVILLE HILL - 50B | NEVILLE HILL - 50B | YORK - 50A |
| Apr-60 | YORK - 50A | YORK - 50A | | | YORK - 50A | SCARBOROUGH - 50E | NEVILLE HILL - 55H | NEVILLE HILL - 55H | YORK - 50A |
| Aug-60 | YORK - 50A | 8/60: W/D | | | YORK - 50A | SCARBOROUGH - 50E | NEVILLE HILL - 55H | NEVILLE HILL - 55H | YORK - 50A |
| Nov-60 | YORK - 50A | | | | YORK - 50A | SCARBOROUGH - 50E | NEVILLE HILL - 55H | NEVILLE HILL - 55H | YORK - 50A |

## Section 1

| | 61451 | 61452 | 61456 | 61458 | 61459 | 61460 | 61462 | 61465 | 61466 |
|---|---|---|---|---|---|---|---|---|---|
| Aug-50 | YORK-50A | YORK-50A | YORK-50A | YORK-50A | YORK-50A | YORK-50A | YORK-50A | YORK-50A | YORK-50A |
| Jan-51 | YORK-50A | YORK-50A | YORK-50A | YORK-50A | YORK-50A | YORK-50A | YORK-50A | YORK-50A | YORK-50A |
| Aug-51 | 5/51:N.HILL-50B | 5/51:N.HILL-50B | 5/51:N.HILL-50B | 5/51:N.HILL-50B | 5/51:N.HILL-50B | 5/51:N.HILL-50B | 5/51:N.HILL-50B | 5/51:N.HILL-50B | 5/51:N.HILL-50B |
| Jan-52 | 11/51:SCAR-50E | NEVILLE HILL-50B | 10/51:YORK-50A | NEVILLE HILL-50B | 10/51:YORK-50A | 2/52:YORK-50A | NEVILLE HILL-50B | NEVILLE HILL-50B | NEVILLE HILL-50B |
| Aug-52 | 2/52:YORK-50A | NEVILLE HILL-50B | YORK-50A | NEVILLE HILL-50B | YORK-50A | YORK-50A | YORK-50A | YORK-50A | NEVILLE HILL-50B |
| Jan-53 | YORK-50A | NEVILLE HILL-50B | YORK-50A | NEVILLE HILL-50B | YORK-50A | YORK-50A | NEVILLE HILL-50B | NEVILLE HILL-50B | NEVILLE HILL-50B |
| Aug-53 | YORK-50A | 11/53:YORK-50A | YORK-50A | 11/53:YORK-50A | YORK-50A | YORK-50A | 11/53:YORK-50A | 11/53:YORK-50A | NEVILLE HILL-50B |
| Jan-54 | YORK-50A | 3/54:N.HILL-50B | YORK-50A | 3/54:N.HILL-50B | YORK-50A | YORK-50A | 3/54:N.HILL-50B | 3/54:N.HILL-50B | NEVILLE HILL-50B |
| Aug-54 | YORK-50A | 8/54:YORK-50A | YORK-50A | 8/54:YORK-50A | YORK-50A | YORK-50A | 8/54:YORK-50A | 8/54:YORK-50A | 8/54:YORK-50A |
| Jan-55 | YORK-50A | YORK-50A | YORK-50A | YORK-50A | YORK-50A | YORK-50A | YORK-50A | YORK-50A | YORK-50A |
| Aug-55 | YORK-50A | YORK-50A | YORK-50A | YORK-50A | YORK-50A | YORK-50A | YORK-50A | YORK-50A | YORK-50A |
| Jan-56 | 11/55:HTN-52B | YORK-50A | 11/55:HTN-52B | 11/55:HTN-52B | YORK-50A | YORK-50A | YORK-50A | YORK-50A | YORK-50A |
| Aug-56 | HEATON-52B | YORK-50A | HEATON-52B | HEATON-52B | YORK-50A | YORK-50A | YORK-50A | YORK-50A | YORK-50A |
| Jan-57 | HEATON-52B | YORK-50A | HEATON-52B | HEATON-52B | YORK-50A | YORK-50A | YORK-50A | YORK-50A | YORK-50A |
| Aug-57 | HEATON-52B | YORK-50A | HEATON-52B | HEATON-52B | 7/57:SELBY-50C | YORK-50A | YORK-50A | YORK-50A | YORK-50A |
| Jan-58 | HEATON-52B | YORK-50A | HEATON-52B | HEATON-52B | SELBY-50C | YORK-50A | YORK-50A | YORK-50A | 2/58:SELBY-50C |
| Aug-58 | 6/58:YORK-50B | YORK-50A | 6/58:SELBY-50C | 6/58:SELBY-50C | SELBY-50C | YORK-50A | YORK-50A | YORK-50A | SELBY-50C |
| Jan-59 | YORK-50A | YORK-50A | SELBY-50C | SELBY-50C | SELBY-50C | YORK-50A | YORK-50A | YORK-50A | SELBY-50C |
| Aug-59 | YORK-50A | YORK-50A | 6/59:YORK-50A | 6/59:YORK-50A | 6/59:YORK-50A | YORK-50A | YORK-50A | YORK-50A | 9/59:YORK-50A |
| Nov-59 | YORK-50A | YORK-50A | YORK-50A | 11/59:W/D | YORK-50A | YORK-50A | YORK-50A | YORK-50A | YORK-50A |
| Jan-60 | YORK-50A | YORK-50A | YORK-50A | | YORK-50A | YORK-50A | YORK-50A | 2/60:W/D | YORK-50A |
| Apr-60 | YORK-50A | YORK-50A | YORK-50A | | YORK-50A | YORK-50A | YORK-50A | | YORK-50A |
| Aug-60 | YORK-50A | YORK-50A | 8/60:W/D | | YORK-50A | YORK-50A | YORK-50A | | YORK-50A |
| Nov-60 | YORK-50A | YORK-50A | | | YORK-50A | YORK-50A | YORK-50A | | YORK-50A |

## Section 2

| | 61469 | 61470 | 61471 | 61473 | 61474 | 61477 | 61478 | B 16 4-6-0 (1937) 61421 | 61435 |
|---|---|---|---|---|---|---|---|---|---|
| Aug-50 | NEVILLE HILL-50B | NEVILLE HILL-50B | NEVILLE HILL-50B | YORK-50A | YORK-50A | YORK-50A | NEVILLE HILL-50B | YORK-50A | YORK-50A |
| Jan-51 | NEVILLE HILL-50B | NEVILLE HILL-50B | NEVILLE HILL-50B | YORK-50A | YORK-50A | YORK-50A | NEVILLE HILL-50B | YORK-50A | YORK-50A |
| Aug-51 | NEVILLE HILL-50B | NEVILLE HILL-50B | NEVILLE HILL-50B | 5/51:N.HILL-50B | 5/51:N.HILL-50B | YORK-50A | NEVILLE HILL-50B | YORK-50A | YORK-50A |
| Jan-52 | NEVILLE HILL-50B | NEVILLE HILL-50B | NEVILLE HILL-50B | NEVILLE HILL-50B | NEVILLE HILL-50B | YORK-50A | NEVILLE HILL-50B | YORK-50A | YORK-50A |
| Aug-52 | NEVILLE HILL-50B | NEVILLE HILL-50B | NEVILLE HILL-50B | NEVILLE HILL-50B | NEVILLE HILL-50B | YORK-50A | NEVILLE HILL-50B | YORK-50A | YORK-50A |
| Jan-53 | NEVILLE HILL-50B | NEVILLE HILL-50B | NEVILLE HILL-50B | NEVILLE HILL-50B | NEVILLE HILL-50B | YORK-50A | NEVILLE HILL-50B | YORK-50A | YORK-50A |
| Aug-53 | NEVILLE HILL-50B | NEVILLE HILL-50B | NEVILLE HILL-50B | 11/53:YORK-50A | 11/53:YORK-50A | YORK-50A | NEVILLE HILL-50B | YORK-50A | YORK-50A |
| Jan-54 | NEVILLE HILL-50B | NEVILLE HILL-50B | NEVILLE HILL-50B | 3/54:N.HILL-50B | 3/54:N.HILL-50B | YORK-50A | NEVILLE HILL-50B | YORK-50A | YORK-50A |
| Aug-54 | NEVILLE HILL-50B | NEVILLE HILL-50B | NEVILLE HILL-50B | 8/54:YORK-50A | 8/54:YORK-50A | YORK-50A | NEVILLE HILL-50B | YORK-50A | YORK-50A |
| Jan-55 | NEVILLE HILL-50B | NEVILLE HILL-50B | NEVILLE HILL-50B | YORK-50A | YORK-50A | YORK-50A | NEVILLE HILL-50B | YORK-50A | YORK-50A |
| Aug-55 | 9/55:HTN-52B | NEVILLE HILL-50B | NEVILLE HILL-50B | YORK-50A | 6/55:SELBY-50C | YORK-50A | 5/55:STAR-50D | YORK-50A | YORK-50A |
| Jan-56 | 5/56:BLAY-52C | NEVILLE HILL-50B | NEVILLE HILL-50B | YORK-50A | SELBY-50C | YORK-50A | STARBECK-50D | YORK-50A | YORK-50A |
| Aug-56 | 7/56:HTN-52B | NEVILLE HILL-50B | NEVILLE HILL-50B | YORK-50A | SELBY-50C | YORK-50A | STARBECK-50D | YORK-50A | YORK-50A |
| Jan-57 | HEATON-52B | NEVILLE HILL-50B | NEVILLE HILL-50B | YORK-50A | SELBY-50C | YORK-50A | STARBECK-50D | YORK-50A | YORK-50A |
| Aug-57 | HEATON-52B | NEVILLE HILL-50B | NEVILLE HILL-50B | YORK-50A | SELBY-50C | YORK-50A | STARBECK-50D | YORK-50A | YORK-50A |
| Jan-58 | HEATON-52B | NEVILLE HILL-50B | NEVILLE HILL-50B | YORK-50A | 1/58:W/D | YORK-50A | STARBECK-50D | YORK-50A | YORK-50A |
| Aug-58 | 6/58:SELBY-50C | NEVILLE HILL-50B | NEVILLE HILL-50B | YORK-50A | | YORK-50A | STARBECK-50D | YORK-50A | YORK-50A |
| Jan-59 | SELBY-50C | NEVILLE HILL-50B | NEVILLE HILL-50B | YORK-50A | | YORK-50A | STARBECK-50D | YORK-50A | YORK-50A |
| Aug-59 | 9/59:YORK-50A | NEVILLE HILL-50B | NEVILLE HILL-50B | YORK-50A | | YORK-50A | 6/59:YORK-50A | YORK-50A | YORK-50A |
| Nov-59 | YORK-50A | 11/59:W/D | NEVILLE HILL-50B | YORK-50A | | YORK-50A | YORK-50A | YORK-50A | YORK-50A |
| Jan-60 | YORK-50A | | NEVILLE HILL-50B | YORK-50A | | YORK-50A | YORK-50A | YORK-50A | YORK-50A |
| Apr-60 | YORK-50A | | NEVILLE HILL-50B | YORK-50A | | 2/60:W/D | YORK-50A | YORK-50A | YORK-50A |
| Aug-60 | YORK-50A | | NEVILLE HILL-55H | YORK-50A | | | YORK-50A | YORK-50A | YORK-50A |
| Nov-60 | 11/60:W/D | | 9/60:W/D | YORK-50A | | | YORK-50A | YORK-50A | YORK-50A |

## Section 3

| | 61438 | 61455 | 61457 | 61475 | B 16 4-6-0 (1944) 61417 | 61418 | 61420 | 61434 | 61439 |
|---|---|---|---|---|---|---|---|---|---|
| Aug-50 | YORK-50A | YORK-50A | YORK-50A | YORK-50A | YORK-50A | YORK-50A | YORK-50A | YORK-50A | YORK-50A |
| Jan-51 | YORK-50A | YORK-50A | YORK-50A | YORK-50A | YORK-50A | YORK-50A | YORK-50A | YORK-50A | YORK-50A |
| Aug-51 | YORK-50A | YORK-50A | YORK-50A | YORK-50A | YORK-50A | YORK-50A | YORK-50A | YORK-50A | YORK-50A |
| Jan-52 | YORK-50A | YORK-50A | YORK-50A | YORK-50A | YORK-50A | YORK-50A | YORK-50A | YORK-50A | YORK-50A |
| Aug-52 | YORK-50A | YORK-50A | YORK-50A | YORK-50A | YORK-50A | YORK-50A | YORK-50A | YORK-50A | YORK-50A |
| Jan-53 | YORK-50A | YORK-50A | YORK-50A | YORK-50A | YORK-50A | YORK-50A | YORK-50A | YORK-50A | YORK-50A |
| Aug-53 | YORK-50A | YORK-50A | YORK-50A | YORK-50A | YORK-50A | YORK-50A | YORK-50A | YORK-50A | YORK-50A |
| Jan-54 | YORK-50A | YORK-50A | YORK-50A | YORK-50A | YORK-50A | YORK-50A | YORK-50A | YORK-50A | YORK-50A |
| Aug-54 | YORK-50A | YORK-50A | YORK-50A | YORK-50A | YORK-50A | YORK-50A | YORK-50A | YORK-50A | YORK-50A |
| Jan-55 | YORK-50A | YORK-50A | YORK-50A | YORK-50A | YORK-50A | YORK-50A | YORK-50A | YORK-50A | YORK-50A |
| Aug-55 | YORK-50A | YORK-50A | YORK-50A | YORK-50A | YORK-50A | YORK-50A | YORK-50A | YORK-50A | YORK-50A |
| Jan-56 | YORK-50A | YORK-50A | YORK-50A | YORK-50A | YORK-50A | YORK-50A | YORK-50A | YORK-50A | YORK-50A |
| Aug-56 | YORK-50A | YORK-50A | YORK-50A | YORK-50A | YORK-50A | YORK-50A | YORK-50A | YORK-50A | YORK-50A |
| Jan-57 | YORK-50A | YORK-50A | YORK-50A | YORK-50A | YORK-50A | YORK-50A | YORK-50A | YORK-50A | YORK-50A |
| Aug-57 | YORK-50A | YORK-50A | YORK-50A | YORK-50A | YORK-50A | YORK-50A | YORK-50A | YORK-50A | YORK-50A |
| Jan-58 | YORK-50A | YORK-50A | YORK-50A | YORK-50A | YORK-50A | YORK-50A | YORK-50A | YORK-50A | YORK-50A |
| Aug-58 | YORK-50A | YORK-50A | YORK-50A | YORK-50A | YORK-50A | YORK-50A | YORK-50A | YORK-50A | YORK-50A |
| Jan-59 | YORK-50A | YORK-50A | YORK-50A | YORK-50A | YORK-50A | YORK-50A | YORK-50A | YORK-50A | YORK-50A |
| Aug-59 | YORK-50A | YORK-50A | YORK-50A | YORK-50A | YORK-50A | YORK-50A | YORK-50A | YORK-50A | YORK-50A |
| Nov-59 | YORK-50A | YORK-50A | YORK-50A | YORK-50A | YORK-50A | YORK-50A | YORK-50A | YORK-50A | YORK-50A |
| Jan-60 | YORK-50A | YORK-50A | YORK-50A | YORK-50A | YORK-50A | YORK-50A | YORK-50A | YORK-50A | YORK-50A |
| Apr-60 | YORK-50A | YORK-50A | YORK-50A | YORK-50A | YORK-50A | YORK-50A | YORK-50A | YORK-50A | YORK-50A |
| Aug-60 | YORK-50A | YORK-50A | YORK-50A | YORK-50A | YORK-50A | YORK-50A | YORK-50A | YORK-50A | YORK-50A |
| Nov-60 | YORK-50A | YORK-50A | YORK-50A | YORK-50A | YORK-50A | YORK-50A | YORK-50A | YORK-50A | YORK-50A |

## Section 4

| | 61444 | 61448 | 61449 | 61453 | 61454 | 61461 | 61463 | 61464 | 61467 |
|---|---|---|---|---|---|---|---|---|---|
| Aug-50 | YORK-50A | YORK-50A | YORK-50A | YORK-50A | YORK-50A | YORK-50A | YORK-50A | YORK-50A | YORK-50A |
| Jan-51 | YORK-50A | YORK-50A | YORK-50A | YORK-50A | YORK-50A | YORK-50A | YORK-50A | YORK-50A | YORK-50A |
| Aug-51 | YORK-50A | YORK-50A | YORK-50A | YORK-50A | YORK-50A | YORK-50A | YORK-50A | YORK-50A | YORK-50A |
| Jan-52 | YORK-50A | YORK-50A | YORK-50A | YORK-50A | YORK-50A | YORK-50A | YORK-50A | YORK-50A | YORK-50A |
| Aug-52 | YORK-50A | YORK-50A | YORK-50A | YORK-50A | YORK-50A | YORK-50A | YORK-50A | YORK-50A | YORK-50A |
| Jan-53 | YORK-50A | YORK-50A | YORK-50A | YORK-50A | YORK-50A | YORK-50A | YORK-50A | YORK-50A | YORK-50A |
| Aug-53 | YORK-50A | YORK-50A | YORK-50A | YORK-50A | YORK-50A | YORK-50A | YORK-50A | YORK-50A | YORK-50A |
| Jan-54 | YORK-50A | YORK-50A | YORK-50A | YORK-50A | YORK-50A | YORK-50A | YORK-50A | YORK-50A | YORK-50A |
| Aug-54 | YORK-50A | YORK-50A | YORK-50A | YORK-50A | YORK-50A | YORK-50A | YORK-50A | YORK-50A | YORK-50A |
| Jan-55 | YORK-50A | YORK-50A | YORK-50A | YORK-50A | YORK-50A | YORK-50A | YORK-50A | YORK-50A | YORK-50A |
| Aug-55 | YORK-50A | YORK-50A | YORK-50A | YORK-50A | YORK-50A | YORK-50A | YORK-50A | YORK-50A | YORK-50A |
| Jan-56 | YORK-50A | YORK-50A | YORK-50A | YORK-50A | YORK-50A | YORK-50A | YORK-50A | YORK-50A | YORK-50A |
| Aug-56 | YORK-50A | YORK-50A | YORK-50A | YORK-50A | YORK-50A | YORK-50A | YORK-50A | YORK-50A | YORK-50A |
| Jan-57 | YORK-50A | YORK-50A | YORK-50A | YORK-50A | YORK-50A | YORK-50A | YORK-50A | YORK-50A | YORK-50A |
| Aug-57 | YORK-50A | YORK-50A | YORK-50A | YORK-50A | YORK-50A | YORK-50A | YORK-50A | YORK-50A | YORK-50A |
| Jan-58 | YORK-50A | YORK-50A | YORK-50A | YORK-50A | YORK-50A | YORK-50A | YORK-50A | YORK-50A | YORK-50A |
| Aug-58 | YORK-50A | YORK-50A | YORK-50A | YORK-50A | YORK-50A | YORK-50A | YORK-50A | YORK-50A | YORK-50A |
| Jan-59 | YORK-50A | YORK-50A | YORK-50A | YORK-50A | YORK-50A | YORK-50A | YORK-50A | YORK-50A | YORK-50A |
| Aug-59 | YORK-50A | YORK-50A | YORK-50A | YORK-50A | YORK-50A | YORK-50A | YORK-50A | YORK-50A | YORK-50A |
| Nov-59 | YORK-50A | YORK-50A | YORK-50A | YORK-50A | YORK-50A | YORK-50A | YORK-50A | YORK-50A | YORK-50A |
| Jan-60 | YORK-50A | YORK-50A | YORK-50A | YORK-50A | YORK-50A | YORK-50A | YORK-50A | YORK-50A | YORK-50A |
| Apr-60 | YORK-50A | YORK-50A | YORK-50A | YORK-50A | YORK-50A | YORK-50A | YORK-50A | YORK-50A | YORK-50A |
| Aug-60 | YORK-50A | YORK-50A | YORK-50A | YORK-50A | YORK-50A | YORK-50A | YORK-50A | YORK-50A | YORK-50A |
| Nov-60 | YORK-50A | YORK-50A | YORK-50A | YORK-50A | YORK-50A | YORK-50A | YORK-50A | YORK-50A | YORK-50A |

Locomotive allocation table — B 4 and B 12 classes

**Section 1**

| | 61468 | 61472 | 61476 | B 4 4-6-0 (1906) 61482 | B 12 4-6-0 (1911) 61501 | 61502 | 61503 | 61521 | 61528 |
|---|---|---|---|---|---|---|---|---|---|
| Aug-50 | YORK-50A | YORK-50A | YORK-50A | ARDSLEY-37A | KEITH-61C | KEITH-61C | KEITH-61C | KITTYBREWSTER-61A | KITTYBREWSTER-61A |
| Jan-51 | YORK-50A | YORK-50A | YORK-50A | 11/50: W/D | KEITH-61C | KEITH-61C | KEITH-61C | KITTYBREWSTER-61A | KITTYBREWSTER-61A |
| Aug-51 | YORK-50A | YORK-50A | YORK-50A | | KEITH-61C | KEITH-61C | 6/51: W/D | KITTYBREWSTER-61A | KITTYBREWSTER-61A |
| Jan-52 | YORK-50A | YORK-50A | YORK-50A | | KEITH-61C | KEITH-61C | | KITTYBREWSTER-61A | KITTYBREWSTER-61A |
| Aug-52 | YORK-50A | YORK-50A | YORK-50A | | KEITH-61C | KEITH-61C | | 7/52: W/D | KITTYBREWSTER-61A |
| Jan-53 | YORK-50A | YORK-50A | YORK-50A | | KEITH-61C | KEITH-61C | | | KITTYBREWSTER-61A |
| Aug-53 | YORK-50A | YORK-50A | YORK-50A | | 5/53: W/D | KEITH-61C | | | 7/53: W/D |
| Jan-54 | YORK-50A | YORK-50A | YORK-50A | | | KEITH-61C | | | |
| Aug-54 | YORK-50A | YORK-50A | YORK-50A | | | 4/54: W/D | | | |
| Jan-55 | YORK-50A | YORK-50A | YORK-50A | | | | | | |
| Aug-55 | YORK-50A | YORK-50A | YORK-50A | | | | | | |
| Jan-56 | YORK-50A | YORK-50A | YORK-50A | | | | | | |
| Aug-56 | YORK-50A | YORK-50A | YORK-50A | | | | | | |
| Jan-57 | YORK-50A | YORK-50A | YORK-50A | | | | | | |
| Aug-57 | YORK-50A | YORK-50A | YORK-50A | | | | | | |
| Jan-58 | YORK-50A | YORK-50A | YORK-50A | | | | | | |
| Aug-58 | YORK-50A | YORK-50A | YORK-50A | | | | | | |
| Jan-59 | YORK-50A | YORK-50A | YORK-50A | | | | | | |
| Aug-59 | YORK-50A | YORK-50A | YORK-50A | | | | | | |
| Nov-59 | YORK-50A | YORK-50A | YORK-50A | | | | | | |
| Jan-60 | YORK-50A | YORK-50A | YORK-50A | | | | | | |
| Apr-60 | YORK-50A | YORK-50A | YORK-50A | | | | | | |
| Aug-60 | YORK-50A | YORK-50A | YORK-50A | | | | | | |
| Nov-60 | YORK-50A | YORK-50A | YORK-50A | | | | | | |

**Section 2**

| | 61539 | 61543 | 61552 | 61560 | 61563 | B 12 4-6-0 (1932) 61512 | 61514 | 61515 | 61516 |
|---|---|---|---|---|---|---|---|---|---|
| Aug-50 | KITTYBREWSTER-61A | KITTYBREWSTER-61A | KITTYBREWSTER-61A | KITTYBREWSTER-61A | KITTYBREWSTER-61A | COLCHESTER-30E | STRATFORD-30A | STRATFORD-30A | STRATFORD-30A |
| Jan-51 | KITTYBREWSTER-61A | KITTYBREWSTER-61A | KITTYBREWSTER-61A | KITTYBREWSTER-61A | KITTYBREWSTER-61A | COLCHESTER-30E | STRATFORD-30A | STRATFORD-30A | STRATFORD-30A |
| Aug-51 | KITTYBREWSTER-61A | KITTYBREWSTER-61A | KITTYBREWSTER-61A | KITTYBREWSTER-61A | KITTYBREWSTER-61A | COLCHESTER-30E | 5/51: YAR (ST)-32D | 7/51: COL-30E | STRATFORD-30A |
| Jan-52 | KITTYBREWSTER-61A | KITTYBREWSTER-61A | KITTYBREWSTER-61A | KITTYBREWSTER-61A | KITTYBREWSTER-61A | COLCHESTER-30E | YARMOUTH(ST)-32D | 11/51: W/D | STRATFORD-30A |
| Aug-52 | KITTYBREWSTER-61A | KITTYBREWSTER-61A | 7/52: W/D | 4/52: W/D | KITTYBREWSTER-61A | COLCHESTER-30E | YARMOUTH(ST)-32D | | STRATFORD-30A |
| Jan-53 | KITTYBREWSTER-61A | KITTYBREWSTER-61A | | | KITTYBREWSTER-61A | COLCHESTER-30E | YARMOUTH(ST)-32D | | STRATFORD-30A |
| Aug-53 | 4/53: KEITH-61C | 6/53: W/D | | | 4/53: W/D | COLCHESTER-30E | YARMOUTH(ST)-32D | | STRATFORD-30A |
| Jan-54 | KEITH-61C | | | | | 1/54: STRAT-30A | YARMOUTH(ST)-32D | | STRATFORD-30A |
| Aug-54 | 11/54: W/D | | | | | STRATFORD-30A | 1/55: NORW-32A | | STRATFORD-30A |
| Jan-55 | | | | | | STRATFORD-30A | 3/55: YAR (ST)-32D | | STRATFORD-30A |
| Aug-55 | | | | | | STRATFORD-30A | 6/55: NORW-30A | | STRATFORD-30A |
| Jan-56 | | | | | | STRATFORD-30A | NORWICH-32A | | STRATFORD-30A |
| Aug-56 | | | | | | STRATFORD-30A | NORWICH-32A | | STRATFORD-30A |
| Jan-57 | | | | | | 1/57: W/D | NORWICH-32A | | 2/57: GRAN-35B |
| Aug-57 | | | | | | | NORWICH-32A | | 4/57: K.LYNN-31C |
| Jan-58 | | | | | | | NORWICH-32A | | 10/57: CAMB-31A |
| Aug-58 | | | | | | | NORWICH-32A | | 7/58: W/D |
| Jan-59 | | | | | | | NORWICH-32A | | |
| Aug-59 | | | | | | | NORWICH-32A | | |
| Nov-59 | | | | | | | 10/59: W/D | | |
| Jan-60 | | | | | | | | | |
| Apr-60 | | | | | | | | | |
| Aug-60 | | | | | | | | | |
| Nov-60 | | | | | | | | | |

**Section 3**

| | 61519 | 61520 | 61523 | 61525 | 61530 | 61533 | 61535 | 61537 | 61538 |
|---|---|---|---|---|---|---|---|---|---|
| Aug-50 | STRATFORD-30A | YARMOUTH(B)-32F | COLCHESTER-30E | STRATFORD-30A | YARMOUTH(B)-32F | SOUTHLYNN-31D | IPSWICH-32B | SOUTHLYNN-31D | GRANTHAM-35B |
| Jan-51 | STRATFORD-30A | YARMOUTH(B)-32F | COLCHESTER-30E | STRATFORD-30A | 10/50: IPS-32B | SOUTHLYNN-31D | IPSWICH-32B | SOUTHLYNN-31D | GRANTHAM-35B |
| Aug-51 | STRATFORD-30A | YARMOUTH(B)-32F | COLCHESTER-30E | 8/51: W/D | 2/51: NOR-30A | SOUTHLYNN-31D | IPSWICH-32B | SOUTHLYNN-31D | GRANTHAM-35B |
| Jan-52 | STRATFORD-30A | YARMOUTH(B)-32F | COLCHESTER-30E | | 5/51: YAR (B)-32F | SOUTHLYNN-31D | IPSWICH-32B | SOUTHLYNN-31D | GRANTHAM-35B |
| Aug-52 | STRATFORD-30A | YARMOUTH(B)-32F | COLCHESTER-30E | | YARMOUTH(B)-32F | 7/52: IPS-32B | IPSWICH-32B | SOUTHLYNN-31D | GRANTHAM-35B |
| Jan-53 | STRATFORD-30A | YARMOUTH(B)-32F | COLCHESTER-30E | | YARMOUTH(B)-32F | 10/52: S.LYNN-31D | IPSWICH-32B | SOUTHLYNN-31D | GRANTHAM-35B |
| Aug-53 | STRATFORD-30A | YARMOUTH(B)-32F | COLCHESTER-30E | | YARMOUTH(B)-32F | 5/53: YAR (ST)-32D | IPSWICH-32B | SOUTHLYNN-31D | GRANTHAM-35B |
| Jan-54 | STRATFORD-30A | YARMOUTH(B)-32F | 1/54: STRAT-30A | | 10/53: NOR-32A | 2/54: IPS-32B | IPSWICH-32B | SOUTHLYNN-31D | GRANTHAM-35B |
| Aug-54 | STRATFORD-30A | YARMOUTH(B)-32F | STRATFORD-30A | | 5/54: YAR (B)-32F | 4/54: IPS-32B | IPSWICH-32B | 8/54: IPS-32B | GRANTHAM-35B |
| Jan-55 | STRATFORD-30A | 3/55: NOR-32A | STRATFORD-30A | | YARMOUTH(B)-32F | 1/55: NOR-32A | IPSWICH-32B | IPSWICH-32B | GRANTHAM-35B |
| Aug-55 | STRATFORD-30A | NORWICH-32A | 3/55: W/D | | YARMOUTH(B)-32F | 8/55: IPS-32B | IPSWICH-32B | IPSWICH-32B | 7/55: S.BGE-35C |
| Jan-56 | STRATFORD-30A | NORWICH-32A | | | YARMOUTH(B)-32F | IPSWICH-32B | IPSWICH-32B | IPSWICH-32B | SPITALBRIDGE-35C |
| Aug-56 | STRATFORD-30A | NORWICH-32A | | | YARMOUTH(B)-32F | IPSWICH-32B | IPSWICH-32B | IPSWICH-32B | SPITALBRIDGE-35C |
| Jan-57 | 2/57: NOR-32A | NORWICH-32A | | | YARMOUTH(B)-32F | IPSWICH-32B | IPSWICH-32B | IPSWICH-32B | 1/57: W/D |
| Aug-57 | NORWICH-32A | 6/57: W/D | | | YARMOUTH(B)-32F | IPSWICH-32B | IPSWICH-32B | 4/57: W/D | |
| Jan-58 | 12/57: W/D | | | | YARMOUTH(B)-32F | 11/57: YAR (B)-32F | IPSWICH-32B | | |
| Aug-58 | | | | | YARMOUTH(B)-32F | YARMOUTH(B)-32F | IPSWICH-32B | | |
| Jan-59 | | | | | 1/59: NOR-32A | 1/59: NOR-32A | 1/59: NOR-32A | | |
| Aug-59 | | | | | 6/59: CAMB-31A | 6/59: CAMB-31A | 10/59: NOR-32A | | |
| Nov-59 | | | | | 11/59: W/D | 11/59: W/D | 12/59: W/D | | |
| Jan-60 | | | | | | | | | |
| Apr-60 | | | | | | | | | |
| Aug-60 | | | | | | | | | |
| Nov-60 | | | | | | | | | |

**Section 4**

| | 61540 | 61541 | 61542 | 61545 | 61546 | 61547 | 61549 | 61550 | 61553 |
|---|---|---|---|---|---|---|---|---|---|
| Aug-50 | SOUTHLYNN-31D | GRANTHAM-35B | STRATFORD-30A | YARMOUTH(B)-32F | STRATFORD-30A | SOUTHLYNN-31D | STRATFORD-30A | STRATFORD-30A | GRANTHAM-35B |
| Jan-51 | SOUTHLYNN-31D | GRANTHAM-35B | 5/51: NOR-32A | 10/50: NOR-32A | STRATFORD-30A | SOUTHLYNN-31D | STRATFORD-30A | STRATFORD-30A | GRANTHAM-35B |
| Aug-51 | SOUTHLYNN-31D | GRANTHAM-35B | 6/51: YAR (ST)-32D | 1/51: YAR (ST)-32D | STRATFORD-30A | SOUTHLYNN-31D | STRATFORD-30A | STRATFORD-30A | GRANTHAM-35B |
| Jan-52 | SOUTHLYNN-31D | GRANTHAM-35B | YARMOUTH(ST)-32D | 6/51: YAR (B)-32F | STRATFORD-30A | SOUTHLYNN-31D | STRATFORD-30A | STRATFORD-30A | GRANTHAM-35B |
| Aug-52 | SOUTHLYNN-31D | GRANTHAM-35B | YARMOUTH(ST)-32D | YARMOUTH(B)-32F | STRATFORD-30A | SOUTHLYNN-31D | STRATFORD-30A | STRATFORD-30A | GRANTHAM-35B |
| Jan-53 | SOUTHLYNN-31D | GRANTHAM-35B | YARMOUTH(ST)-32D | YARMOUTH(B)-32F | STRATFORD-30A | SOUTHLYNN-31D | STRATFORD-30A | STRATFORD-30A | GRANTHAM-35B |
| Aug-53 | SOUTHLYNN-31D | GRANTHAM-35B | YARMOUTH(ST)-32D | YARMOUTH(B)-32F | STRATFORD-30A | SOUTHLYNN-31D | STRATFORD-30A | STRATFORD-30A | GRANTHAM-35B |
| Jan-54 | SOUTHLYNN-31D | GRANTHAM-35B | YARMOUTH(ST)-32D | 6/54: YAR )ST)-32D | STRATFORD-30A | SOUTHLYNN-31D | STRATFORD-30A | STRATFORD-30A | GRANTHAM-35B |
| Aug-54 | 6/54: NOR-32A | GRANTHAM-35B | YARMOUTH(ST)-32D | 8/54: NOR-32A | STRATFORD-30A | 10/54: NOR-32A | STRATFORD-30A | STRATFORD-30A | GRANTHAM-35B |
| Jan-55 | NORWICH-32A | 1/55: NOR-32A | 1/55: NOR-32A | 1/55: YAR (B)-32F | STRATFORD-30A | NORWICH-32A | STRATFORD-30A | STRATFORD-30A | GRANTHAM-35B |
| Aug-55 | NORWICH-32A | GRANTHAM-35B | NORWICH-32A | YARMOUTH(B)-32F | STRATFORD-30A | NORWICH-32A | STRATFORD-30A | STRATFORD-30A | GRANTHAM-35B |
| Jan-56 | NORWICH-32A | GRANTHAM-35B | NORWICH-32A | YARMOUTH(B)-32F | STRATFORD-30A | NORWICH-32A | STRATFORD-30A | STRATFORD-30A | GRANTHAM-35B |
| Aug-56 | NORWICH-32A | GRANTHAM-35B | NORWICH-32A | YARMOUTH(B)-32F | STRATFORD-30A | NORWICH-32A | STRATFORD-30A | STRATFORD-30A | GRANTHAM-35B |
| Jan-57 | 2/57: YAR (B)-32F | 1/57: W/D | NORWICH-32A | 1/57: W/D | 2/57: MARCH-31B | NORWICH-32A | 2/57: MARCH-31B | 1/57: W/D | 4/57: CAMB-31A |
| Aug-57 | YARMOUTH(B)-32F | | NORWICH-32A | | 5/57: BURY-31E | NORWICH-32A | MARCH-31B | | 5/57: BURY-31E |
| Jan-58 | 10/57: W/D | | NORWICH-32A | | BURYSTEDMUNDS-31E | NORWICH-32A | MARCH-31B | | BURYSTEDMUNDS-31E |
| Aug-58 | | | 7/58: W/D | | BURYSTEDMUNDS-31E | 10/58: W/D | MARCH-31B | | 8/58: W/D |
| Jan-59 | | | | | 1/59: CAMB-31A | | 1/59: W/D | | |
| Aug-59 | | | | | 5/59: W/D | | | | |
| Nov-59 | | | | | | | | | |
| Jan-60 | | | | | | | | | |
| Apr-60 | | | | | | | | | |
| Aug-60 | | | | | | | | | |
| Nov-60 | | | | | | | | | |

*Although more than fifty miles north of the border Haymarket was very much a meeting of north and south, a location where 4-4-0's of the types peculiar to Scotland rubbed shoulders with Pacifics and Green Arrows more familiar to English eyes. In the upper view a fairly representative group of Haymarket engines pause between workings whilst, below, D30 4-4-0 62437 'Adam Woodcock' and J83 0-6-0T 68473 stand on the pit roads.*

| | 61554 | 61555 | 61556 | 61557 | 61558 | 61559 | 61561 | 61562 | 61564 |
|---|---|---|---|---|---|---|---|---|---|
| Aug-50 | GRANTHAM-35B | COLCHESTER-30E | COLCHESTER-30E | COLCHESTER-30E | COLCHESTER-30E | STRATFORD-30A | IPSWICH-32B | IPSWICH-32B | IPSWICH-32B |
| Jan-51 | GRANTHAM-35B | COLCHESTER-30E | COLCHESTER-30E | COLCHESTER-30E | COLCHESTER-30E | STRATFORD-30A | IPSWICH-32B | IPSWICH-32B | IPSWICH-32B |
| Aug-51 | GRANTHAM-35B | COLCHESTER-30E | COLCHESTER-30E | COLCHESTER-30E | COLCHESTER-30E | 5/51: COL-30E | IPSWICH-32B | IPSWICH-32B | IPSWICH-32B |
| Jan-52 | GRANTHAM-35B | COLCHESTER-30E | COLCHESTER-30E | COLCHESTER-30E | COLCHESTER-30E | 9/51: W/D | IPSWICH-32B | IPSWICH-32B | IPSWICH-32B |
| Aug-52 | GRANTHAM-35B | COLCHESTER-30E | COLCHESTER-30E | COLCHESTER-30E | COLCHESTER-30E | | IPSWICH-32B | IPSWICH-32B | IPSWICH-32B |
| Jan-53 | GRANTHAM-35B | COLCHESTER-30E | COLCHESTER-30E | COLCHESTER-30E | COLCHESTER-30E | | IPSWICH-32B | IPSWICH-32B | IPSWICH-32B |
| Aug-53 | GRANTHAM-35B | COLCHESTER-30E | COLCHESTER-30E | COLCHESTER-30E | COLCHESTER-30E | | IPSWICH-32B | IPSWICH-32B | IPSWICH-32B |
| Jan-54 | GRANTHAM-35B | 1/54: STRAT-30A | COLCHESTER-30E | COLCHESTER-30E | 1/54: STRAT-30A | | IPSWICH-32B | IPSWICH-32B | IPSWICH-32B |
| Aug-54 | GRANTHAM-35B | STRATFORD-30A | COLCHESTER-30E | COLCHESTER-30E | STRATFORD-30A | | IPSWICH-32B | IPSWICH-32B | IPSWICH-32B |
| Jan-55 | GRANTHAM-35B | STRATFORD-30A | COLCHESTER-30E | COLCHESTER-30E | STRATFORD-30A | | IPSWICH-32B | IPSWICH-32B | IPSWICH-32B |
| Aug-55 | GRANTHAM-35B | STRATFORD-30A | COLCHESTER-30E | COLCHESTER-30E | STRATFORD-30A | | IPSWICH-32B | 8/55: W/D | IPSWICH-32B |
| Jan-56 | 3/56: S.BGE-35C | STRATFORD-30A | COLCHESTER-30E | COLCHESTER-30E | STRATFORD-30A | | IPSWICH-32B | | IPSWICH-32B |
| Aug-56 | SPITALBRIDGE-35C | 11/56: COL-30E | 11/56: COL-30E | COLCHESTER-30E | 11/56: COL-30E | | IPSWICH-32B | | IPSWICH-32B |
| Jan-57 | 3/57: CAMB-31A | 2/57: GRAN-35B | 2/57: NOR-32A | 1/57: W/D | 2/57: S.BGE-35C | | IPSWICH-32B | | IPSWICH-32B |
| Aug-57 | 5/57: BURY-31E | 4/57: CAMB-31A | NORWICH-32A | | 4/57: K.LYNN-31C | | IPSWICH-32B | | IPSWICH-32B |
| Jan-58 | BURYSTEDMUNDS-31E | 10/57: W/D | 12/57: W/D | | 11/57: CAMB-31A | | IPSWICH-32B | | IPSWICH-32B |
| Aug-58 | 9/58: W/D | | | | CAMBRIDGE-31A | | 8/58: W/D | | IPSWICH-32B |
| Jan-59 | | | | | CAMBRIDGE-31A | | | | 11/58:W/D |
| Aug-59 | | | | | 4/59: W/D | | | | |
| Nov-59 | | | | | | | | | |
| Jan-60 | | | | | | | | | |
| Apr-60 | | | | | | | | | |
| Aug-60 | | | | | | | | | |
| Nov-60 | | | | | | | | | |

| | 61565 | 61566 | 61567 | 61568 | 61569 | 61570 | 61571 | 61572 | 61573 |
|---|---|---|---|---|---|---|---|---|---|
| Aug-50 | GRANTHAM-35B | IPSWICH-32B | STRATFORD-30A | STRATFORD-30A | IPSWICH-32B | IPSWICH-32B | STRATFORD-30A | STRATFORD-30A | STRATFORD-30A |
| Jan-51 | GRANTHAM-35B | IPSWICH-32B | STRATFORD-30A | 5/51: IPS-32B | IPSWICH-32B | IPSWICH-32B | STRATFORD-30A | STRATFORD-30A | STRATFORD-30A |
| Aug-51 | GRANTHAM-35B | IPSWICH-32B | 5/51: COL-30E | 7/51: NOR-32A | IPSWICH-32B | IPSWICH-32B | STRATFORD-30A | STRATFORD-30A | STRATFORD-30A |
| Jan-52 | GRANTHAM-35B | IPSWICH-32B | 11/51: STRAT-30A | NORWICH-32A | IPSWICH-32B | IPSWICH-32B | STRATFORD-30A | STRATFORD-30A | STRATFORD-30A |
| Aug-52 | GRANTHAM-35B | IPSWICH-32B | STRATFORD-30A | NORWICH-32A | IPSWICH-32B | IPSWICH-32B | 2/53: GRAN-35B | 2/53: GRAN-35B | STRATFORD-30A |
| Jan-53 | GRANTHAM-35B | IPSWICH-32B | 2/53: GRAN-35B | 7/53: YAR(B)-32F | IPSWICH-32B | IPSWICH-32B | 3/53: IPS-32B | 3/53: IPS-32B | STRATFORD-30A |
| Aug-53 | GRANTHAM-35B | IPSWICH-32B | GRANTHAM-35B | 10/53: YAR(ST)-32D | IPSWICH-32B | IPSWICH-32B | IPSWICH-32B | IPSWICH-32B | STRATFORD-30A |
| Jan-54 | GRANTHAM-35B | IPSWICH-32B | GRANTHAM-35B | 2/54: IPS-32B | IPSWICH-32B | IPSWICH-32B | IPSWICH-32B | IPSWICH-32B | STRATFORD-30A |
| Aug-54 | GRANTHAM-35B | IPSWICH-32B | GRANTHAM-35B | 8/54: NOR-32A | IPSWICH-32B | IPSWICH-32B | IPSWICH-32B | IPSWICH-32B | STRATFORD-30A |
| Jan-55 | GRANTHAM-35B | IPSWICH-32B | GRANTHAM-35B | NORWICH-32A | IPSWICH-32B | IPSWICH-32B | IPSWICH-32B | IPSWICH-32B | STRATFORD-30A |
| Aug-55 | 7/55: S.BGE-35C | IPSWICH-32B | GRANTHAM-35B | NORWICH-32A | IPSWICH-32B | IPSWICH-32B | IPSWICH-32B | IPSWICH-32B | STRATFORD-30A |
| Jan-56 | SPITALBRIDGE-35C | IPSWICH-32B | GRANTHAM-35B | NORWICH-32A | IPSWICH-32B | IPSWICH-32B | IPSWICH-32B | IPSWICH-32B | STRATFORD-30A |
| Aug-56 | SPITALBRIDGE-35C | IPSWICH-32B | 9/56: S.BGE-35C | NORWICH-32A | IPSWICH-32B | IPSWICH-32B | IPSWICH-32B | IPSWICH-32B | STRATFORD-30A |
| Jan-57 | 1/57: W/D | IPSWICH-32B | 3/57: CAMB-31A | NORWICH-32A | 1/57: W/D | IPSWICH-32B | IPSWICH-32B | IPSWICH-32B | 2/57: CAMB-31A |
| Aug-57 | | IPSWICH-32B | 5/57: BURY-31E | NORWICH-32A | | IPSWICH-32B | IPSWICH-32B | IPSWICH-32B | 5/57: BURY-31E |
| Jan-58 | | IPSWICH-32B | BURYSTEDMUNDS-31E | NORWICH-32A | | IPSWICH-32B | 11/57: NOR-32A | IPSWICH-32B | BURYSTEDMUNDS-31E |
| Aug-58 | | 6/58: NOR-32A | BURYSTEDMUNDS-31E | NORWICH-32A | | 4/58: W/D | NORWICH-32A | IPSWICH-32B | BURYSTEDMUNDS-31E |
| Jan-59 | | 1/59: W/D | 11/58: W/D | NORWICH-32A | | | NORWICH-32A | IPSWICH-32B | 1/59: W/D |
| Aug-59 | | | | 8/59: W/D | | | NORWICH-32A | IPSWICH-32B | |
| Nov-59 | | | | | | | 12/59: W/D | 10/59: NOR-32A | |
| Jan-60 | | | | | | | | NORWICH-32A | |
| Apr-60 | | | | | | | | NORWICH-32A | |
| Aug-60 | | | | | | | | NORWICH-32A | |
| Nov-60 | | | | | | | | NORWICH-32A | |

B 12 4-6-0 (1943) — 61505, 61507

| | 61574 | 61575 | 61576 | 61577 | 61578 | 61579 | 61580 | 61505 | 61507 |
|---|---|---|---|---|---|---|---|---|---|
| Aug-50 | STRATFORD-30A | STRATFORD-30A | STRATFORD-30A | IPSWICH-32B | STRATFORD-30A | STRATFORD-30A | STRATFORD-30A | KITTYBREWSTER-61A | KITTYBREWSTER-61A |
| Jan-51 | STRATFORD-30A | STRATFORD-30A | STRATFORD-30A | IPSWICH-32B | STRATFORD-30A | STRATFORD-30A | STRATFORD-30A | KITTYBREWSTER-61A | KITTYBREWSTER-61A |
| Aug-51 | STRATFORD-30A | STRATFORD-30A | STRATFORD-30A | IPSWICH-32B | STRATFORD-30A | 5/51: COL-30E | 9/51: COL-30E | KITTYBREWSTER-61A | 9/51: KEITH-61C |
| Jan-52 | STRATFORD-30A | STRATFORD-30A | STRATFORD-30A | IPSWICH-32B | STRATFORD-30A | 11/51: COL-30E | 11/51: STRAT-30A | KITTYBREWSTER-61A | KEITH-61C |
| Aug-52 | STRATFORD-30A | STRATFORD-30A | STRATFORD-30A | IPSWICH-32B | STRATFORD-30A | COLCHESTER-30E | STRATFORD-30A | 3/52: W/D | KEITH-61C |
| Jan-53 | 2/53: GRAN-35B | STRATFORD-30A | STRATFORD-30A | IPSWICH-32B | STRATFORD-30A | COLCHESTER-30E | 2/53: GRAN-35B | | 3/53: W/D |
| Aug-53 | GRANTHAM-35B | STRATFORD-30A | STRATFORD-30A | IPSWICH-32B | STRATFORD-30A | COLCHESTER-30E | GRANTHAM-35B | | |
| Jan-54 | GRANTHAM-35B | STRATFORD-30A | STRATFORD-30A | IPSWICH-32B | STRATFORD-30A | 1/54: STRAT-30A | GRANTHAM-35B | | |
| Aug-54 | GRANTHAM-35B | STRATFORD-30A | STRATFORD-30A | IPSWICH-32B | STRATFORD-30A | STRATFORD-30A | GRANTHAM-35B | | |
| Jan-55 | GRANTHAM-35B | STRATFORD-30A | STRATFORD-30A | IPSWICH-32B | STRATFORD-30A | STRATFORD-30A | GRANTHAM-35B | | |
| Aug-55 | GRANTHAM-35B | STRATFORD-30A | STRATFORD-30A | IPSWICH-32B | STRATFORD-30A | STRATFORD-30A | GRANTHAM-35B | | |
| Jan-56 | GRANTHAM-35B | STRATFORD-30A | STRATFORD-30A | IPSWICH-32B | STRATFORD-30A | STRATFORD-30A | GRANTHAM-35B | | |
| Aug-56 | GRANTHAM-35B | STRATFORD-30A | STRATFORD-30A | IPSWICH-32B | STRATFORD-30A | STRATFORD-30A | GRANTHAM-35B | | |
| Jan-57 | 1/57: W/D | 2/57: MARCH-31B | 2/57: MARCH-31B | IPSWICH-32B | 1/57: W/D | 1/57: W/D | 4/57: CAMB-31A | | |
| Aug-57 | | 4/57: K.LYNN-31C | 5/57: BURY-31E | IPSWICH-32B | | | CAMBRIDGE-31A | | |
| Jan-58 | | 10/57: CAMB-31A | BURYSTEDMUNDS-31E | IPSWICH-32B | | | CAMBRIDGE-31A | | |
| Aug-58 | | CAMBRIDGE-31A | BURYSTEDMUNDS-31E | 8/58: NOR-32A | | | 3/59: W/D | | |
| Jan-59 | | CAMBRIDGE-31A | 1/59: W/D | 4/59: CAMB-31A | | | | | |
| Aug-59 | | 4/59: W/D | | 8/59: W/D | | | | | |
| Nov-59 | | | | | | | | | |
| Jan-60 | | | | | | | | | |
| Apr-60 | | | | | | | | | |
| Aug-60 | | | | | | | | | |
| Nov-60 | | | | | | | | | |

B 17 4-6-0 (1927) — 61601, 61602, 61604

| | 61508 | 61511 | 61513 | 61524 | 61526 | 61532 | 61601 | 61602 | 61604 |
|---|---|---|---|---|---|---|---|---|---|
| Aug-50 | KITTYBREWSTER-61A | KITTYBREWSTER-61A | KITTYBREWSTER-61A | KITTYBREWSTER-61A | KITTYBREWSTER-61A | KITTYBREWSTER-61A | IPSWICH-32B | STRATFORD-30A | IPSWICH-32B |
| Jan-51 | KITTYBREWSTER-61A | KITTYBREWSTER-61A | KITTYBREWSTER-61A | KITTYBREWSTER-61A | KITTYBREWSTER-61A | KITTYBREWSTER-61A | IPSWICH-32B | STRATFORD-30A | IPSWICH-32B |
| Aug-51 | KITTYBREWSTER-61A | KITTYBREWSTER-61A | KITTYBREWSTER-61A | KITTYBREWSTER-61A | KITTYBREWSTER-61A | KITTYBREWSTER-61A | IPSWICH-32B | STRATFORD-30A | IPSWICH-32B |
| Jan-52 | KITTYBREWSTER-61A | KITTYBREWSTER-61A | KITTYBREWSTER-61A | KITTYBREWSTER-61A | 9/51:W/D | KITTYBREWSTER-61A | IPSWICH-32B | STRATFORD-30A | IPSWICH-32B |
| Aug-52 | KITTYBREWSTER-61A | 4/52: W/D | KITTYBREWSTER-61A | KITTYBREWSTER-61A | | KITTYBREWSTER-61A | IPSWICH-32B | STRATFORD-30A | 7/52: STRAT-30A |
| Jan-53 | 6/52: KEITH-61C | | KITTYBREWSTER-61A | KITTYBREWSTER-61A | | 4/53: KEITH-61C | 2/53: STRAT-30A | STRATFORD-30A | STRATFORD-30A |
| Aug-53 | KEITH-61C | | KITTYBREWSTER-61A | 7/53:KEITH-61C | | 7/53: W/D | STRATFORD-30A | STRATFORD-30A | 8/53: W/D |
| Jan-54 | 5/53: W/D | | 2/53: W/D | 11/53: W/D | | | STRATFORD-30A | STRATFORD-30A | |
| Aug-54 | | | | | | | STRATFORD-30A | STRATFORD-30A | |
| Jan-55 | | | | | | | STRATFORD-30A | STRATFORD-30A | |
| Aug-55 | | | | | | | STRATFORD-30A | STRATFORD-30A | |
| Jan-56 | | | | | | | STRATFORD-30A | STRATFORD-30A | |
| Aug-56 | | | | | | | STRATFORD-30A | STRATFORD-30A | |
| Jan-57 | | | | | | | STRATFORD-30A | STRATFORD-30A | |
| Aug-57 | | | | | | | 2/57: MARCH-31B | 2/57: YAR(ST)-32D | |
| Jan-58 | | | | | | | 6/57: STRAT-30A | YARMOUTH(ST)-32D | |
| Aug-58 | | | | | | | 1/58: W/D | 1/58: W/D | |
| Jan-59 | | | | | | | | | |
| Aug-59 | | | | | | | | | |
| Nov-59 | | | | | | | | | |
| Jan-60 | | | | | | | | | |
| Apr-60 | | | | | | | | | |
| Aug-60 | | | | | | | | | |
| Nov-60 | | | | | | | | | |

## 61605–61618

| | 61605 | 61606 | 61608 | 61609 | 61610 | 61611 | 61612 | 61613 | 61618 |
|---|---|---|---|---|---|---|---|---|---|
| Aug-50 | STRATFORD-30A | STRATFORD-30A | STRATFORD-30A | NORWCH-32A | STRATFORD-30A | STRATFORD-30A | STRATFORD-30A | STRATFORD-30A | IPSWCH-32B |
| Jan-51 | STRATFORD-30A | STRATFORD-30A | STRATFORD-30A | NORWCH-32A | STRATFORD-30A | STRATFORD-30A | STRATFORD-30A | STRATFORD-30A | IPSWCH-32B |
| Aug-51 | STRATFORD-30A | STRATFORD-30A | STRATFORD-30A | NORWCH-32A | STRATFORD-30A | STRATFORD-30A | STRATFORD-30A | STRATFORD-30A | IPSWCH-32B |
| Jan-52 | 3/52: MARCH-31B | STRATFORD-30A | STRATFORD-30A | NORWCH-32A | STRATFORD-30A | STRATFORD-30A | STRATFORD-30A | STRATFORD-30A | IPSWCH-32B |
| Aug-52 | 9/52: STRAT-30A | STRATFORD-30A | STRATFORD-30A | NORWCH-32A | STRATFORD-30A | STRATFORD-30A | STRATFORD-30A | STRATFORD-30A | IPSWCH-32B |
| Jan-53 | STRATFORD-30A | STRATFORD-30A | STRATFORD-30A | 2/53: STRAT-30A | STRATFORD-30A | STRATFORD-30A | STRATFORD-30A | STRATFORD-30A | IPSWCH-32B |
| Aug-53 | STRATFORD-30A | STRATFORD-30A | STRATFORD-30A | STRATFORD-30A | STRATFORD-30A | STRATFORD-30A | STRATFORD-30A | STRATFORD-30A | 11/53: STRAT-30A |
| Jan-54 | STRATFORD-30A | STRATFORD-30A | STRATFORD-30A | STRATFORD-30A | STRATFORD-30A | STRATFORD-30A | STRATFORD-30A | STRATFORD-30A | 1/54: IPS-32B |
| Aug-54 | STRATFORD-30A | STRATFORD-30A | STRATFORD-30A | STRATFORD-30A | STRATFORD-30A | STRATFORD-30A | STRATFORD-30A | STRATFORD-30A | IPSWCH-32B |
| Jan-55 | STRATFORD-30A | STRATFORD-30A | STRATFORD-30A | STRATFORD-30A | STRATFORD-30A | STRATFORD-30A | STRATFORD-30A | STRATFORD-30A | IPSWCH-32B |
| Aug-55 | STRATFORD-30A | STRATFORD-30A | STRATFORD-30A | STRATFORD-30A | STRATFORD-30A | STRATFORD-30A | STRATFORD-30A | STRATFORD-30A | IPSWCH-32B |
| Jan-56 | STRATFORD-30A | STRATFORD-30A | STRATFORD-30A | STRATFORD-30A | STRATFORD-30A | STRATFORD-30A | STRATFORD-30A | STRATFORD-30A | IPSWCH-32B |
| Aug-56 | STRATFORD-30A | 11/56: COL-30E | 11/56: COL-30E | STRATFORD-30A | STRATFORD-30A | STRATFORD-30A | STRATFORD-30A | STRATFORD-30A | IPSWCH-32B |
| Jan-57 | STRATFORD-30A | 2/57: STRAT-30A | 2/57: STRAT-30A | STRATFORD-30A | STRATFORD-30A | 2/57: IPS-32B | STRATFORD-30A | STRATFORD-30A | IPSWCH-32B |
| Aug-57 | STRATFORD-30A | STRATFORD-30A | STRATFORD-30A | STRATFORD-30A | STRATFORD-30A | IPSWICH-32B | STRATFORD-30A | STRATFORD-30A | IPSWCH-32B |
| Jan-58 | STRATFORD-30A | STRATFORD-30A | STRATFORD-30A | 5/58: IPS-32B | STRATFORD-30A | IPSWICH-32B | 6/58: COL-30E | 6/58: COL-30E | IPSWCH-32B |
| Aug-58 | 5/58: W/D | 6/58: COL-30E | 6/58: COL-30E | 6/58: W/D | 5/58: MARCH-31B | IPSWICH-32B | 7/58: IPS-32B | 9/58: STRAT-30A | IPSWCH-32B |
| Jan-59 | | 9/58: W/D | 12/58: CAMB-31A | | MARCH-31B | IPSWICH-32B | IPSWICH-32B | 1/59: CAMB-31A | IPSWCH-32B |
| Aug-59 | | | CAMBRIDGE-31A | | MARCH-31B | 8/59: NOR-32A | 8/59: NOR-32A | CAMBRIDGE-31A | IPSWCH-32B |
| Nov-59 | | | CAMBRIDGE-31A | | MARCH-31B | 10/59: W/D | 10/59: W/D | 12/59: W/D | 10/59: CAMB-31A |
| Jan-60 | | | CAMBRIDGE-31A | | 12/59: W/D | | | | 2/60: W/D |
| Apr-60 | | | W/D | | | | | | |
| Aug-60 | | | 2/60: W/D | | | | | | |
| Nov-60 | | | | | | | | | |

## 61619–61627

| | 61619 | 61620 | 61621 | 61622 | 61623 | 61624 | 61625 | 61626 | 61627 |
|---|---|---|---|---|---|---|---|---|---|
| Aug-50 | CAMBRIDGE-31A | CAMBRIDGE-31A | CAMBRIDGE-31A | CAMBRIDGE-31A | CAMBRIDGE-31A | CAMBRIDGE-31A | CAMBRIDGE-31A | MARCH-31B | CAMBRIDGE-31A |
| Jan-51 | CAMBRIDGE-31A | CAMBRIDGE-31A | 9/50: STRAT-30A | CAMBRIDGE-31A | CAMBRIDGE-31A | CAMBRIDGE-31A | CAMBRIDGE-31A | MARCH-31B | CAMBRIDGE-31A |
| Aug-51 | CAMBRIDGE-31A | CAMBRIDGE-31A | 6/51: MARCH-31B | CAMBRIDGE-31A | CAMBRIDGE-31A | CAMBRIDGE-31A | CAMBRIDGE-31A | MARCH-31B | CAMBRIDGE-31A |
| Jan-52 | CAMBRIDGE-31A | CAMBRIDGE-31A | MARCH-31B | CAMBRIDGE-31A | CAMBRIDGE-31A | CAMBRIDGE-31A | CAMBRIDGE-31A | MARCH-31B | CAMBRIDGE-31A |
| Aug-52 | CAMBRIDGE-31A | CAMBRIDGE-31A | MARCH-31B | CAMBRIDGE-31A | CAMBRIDGE-31A | CAMBRIDGE-31A | CAMBRIDGE-31A | MARCH-31B | CAMBRIDGE-31A |
| Jan-53 | 10/52: MARCH-31B | 10/52: MARCH-31B | MARCH-31B | MARCH-31B | CAMBRIDGE-31A | 10/52: MARCH-31B | CAMBRIDGE-31A | MARCH-31B | CAMBRIDGE-31A |
| Aug-53 | MARCH-31B | MARCH-31B | 7/53: IPS-32B | 7/53: YAR(ST)-32D | CAMBRIDGE-31A | 3/53: W/D | 7/53: IPS-32B | MARCH-31B | CAMBRIDGE-31A |
| Jan-54 | MARCH-31B | MARCH-31B | 11/53: STRAT-30A | YARMOUTH(ST)-32D | CAMBRIDGE-31A | | IPSWICH-32B | MARCH-31B | CAMBRIDGE-31A |
| Aug-54 | MARCH-31B | MARCH-31B | 1/54: MARCH-31B | YARMOUTH(ST)-32D | CAMBRIDGE-31A | | IPSWICH-32B | MARCH-31B | 6/54: MARCH-31B |
| Jan-55 | MARCH-31B | MARCH-31B | MARCH-31B | YARMOUTH(ST)-32D | CAMBRIDGE-31A | | IPSWICH-32B | MARCH-31B | MARCH-31B |
| Aug-55 | MARCH-31B | MARCH-31B | MARCH-31B | YARMOUTH(ST)-32D | CAMBRIDGE-31A | | IPSWICH-32B | MARCH-31B | MARCH-31B |
| Jan-56 | MARCH-31B | MARCH-31B | MARCH-31B | YARMOUTH(ST)-32D | CAMBRIDGE-31A | | IPSWICH-32B | MARCH-31B | MARCH-31B |
| Aug-56 | MARCH-31B | MARCH-31B | MARCH-31B | YARMOUTH(ST)-32D | CAMBRIDGE-31A | | IPSWICH-32B | MARCH-31B | MARCH-31B |
| Jan-57 | MARCH-31B | MARCH-31B | MARCH-31B | YARMOUTH(ST)-32D | CAMBRIDGE-31A | | IPSWICH-32B | MARCH-31B | MARCH-31B |
| Aug-57 | MARCH-31B | MARCH-31B | MARCH-31B | YARMOUTH(ST)-32D | CAMBRIDGE-31A | | IPSWICH-32B | MARCH-31B | MARCH-31B |
| Jan-58 | MARCH-31B | MARCH-31B | MARCH-31B | YARMOUTH(ST)-32D | CAMBRIDGE-31A | | IPSWICH-32B | MARCH-31B | MARCH-31B |
| Aug-58 | 8/58: W/D | MARCH-31B | MARCH-31B | 9/58: W/D | CAMBRIDGE-31A | | IPSWICH-32B | MARCH-31B | MARCH-31B |
| Jan-59 | | MARCH-31B | 11/58: W/D | | CAMBRIDGE-31A | | IPSWICH-32B | 12/58: K.LYNN-31C | MARCH-31B |
| Aug-59 | | 4/59: K.LYNN-31C | | | 7/59: W/D | | 10/59: CAMB-31A | 4/59: MARCH-31B | 7/59: W/D |
| Nov-59 | | KINGS LYNN-31C | | | | | 11/59: W/D | 12/59: W/D | |
| Jan-60 | | 2/60: W/D | | | | | | | |
| Apr-60 | | | | | | | | | |
| Aug-60 | | | | | | | | | |
| Nov-60 | | | | | | | | | |

## 61628–61637

| | 61628 | 61629 | 61630 | 61631 | 61633 | 61634 | 61635 | 61636 | 61637 |
|---|---|---|---|---|---|---|---|---|---|
| Aug-50 | CAMBRIDGE-31A | NORWCH-32A | MARCH-31B | CAMBRIDGE-31A | MARCH-31B | IPSWICH-32B | MARCH-31B | CAMBRIDGE-31A | CAMBRIDGE-31A |
| Jan-51 | CAMBRIDGE-31A | NORWCH-32A | MARCH-31B | CAMBRIDGE-31A | MARCH-31B | IPSWICH-32B | MARCH-31B | CAMBRIDGE-31A | CAMBRIDGE-31A |
| Aug-51 | CAMBRIDGE-31A | NORWCH-32A | MARCH-31B | 10/51: MARCH-31B | MARCH-31B | IPSWICH-32B | MARCH-31B | CAMBRIDGE-31A | CAMBRIDGE-31A |
| Jan-52 | CAMBRIDGE-31A | NORWCH-32A | 3/52: STRAT-30A | 6/52: CAMB-31A | MARCH-31B | IPSWICH-32B | MARCH-31B | 2/52: STRAT-30A | CAMBRIDGE-31A |
| Aug-52 | 9/52: W/D | NORWCH-32A | STRATFORD-30A | 7/52: STRAT-30A | MARCH-31B | IPSWICH-32B | MARCH-31B | 3/52: CAMB-31A | CAMBRIDGE-31A |
| Jan-53 | | NORWCH-32A | 3/53: CAMB-31A | 2/53: IPS-32B | MARCH-31B | IPSWICH-32B | MARCH-31B | CAMBRIDGE-31A | CAMBRIDGE-31A |
| Aug-53 | | NORWCH-32A | 5/53: STRAT-30A | IPSWICH-32B | MARCH-31B | 11/53: STRAT-30A | MARCH-31B | CAMBRIDGE-31A | 7/53: IPS-32B |
| Jan-54 | | NORWCH-32A | 1/54: MARCH-31B | IPSWICH-32B | MARCH-31B | 1/54: COL-30E | MARCH-31B | CAMBRIDGE-31A | IPSWICH-32B |
| Aug-54 | | 8/54: YAR (ST)-32D | 6/54: STRAT 30A | IPSWICH-32B | MARCH-31B | 5/54: STRAT-30A | MARCH-31B | CAMBRIDGE-31A | IPSWICH-32B |
| Jan-55 | | 1/55: NOR-32A | STRATFORD-30A | IPSWICH-32B | MARCH-31B | STRATFORD-30A | MARCH-31B | CAMBRIDGE-31A | IPSWICH-32B |
| Aug-55 | | 8/55: IPS-32B | STRATFORD-30A | IPSWICH-32B | MARCH-31B | STRATFORD-30A | MARCH-31B | CAMBRIDGE-31A | IPSWICH-32B |
| Jan-56 | | IPSWICH-32B | STRATFORD-30A | IPSWICH-32B | 3/56: CAMB-31A | 3/56: CAMB-31A | MARCH-31B | CAMBRIDGE-31A | IPSWICH-32B |
| Aug-56 | | IPSWICH-32B | STRATFORD-30A | IPSWICH-32B | CAMBRIDGE-31A | CAMBRIDGE-31A | MARCH-31B | CAMBRIDGE-31A | IPSWICH-32B |
| Jan-57 | | IPSWICH-32B | STRATFORD-30A | IPSWICH-32B | 12/56: MARCH-31B | CAMBRIDGE-31A | MARCH-31B | CAMBRIDGE-31A | IPSWICH-32B |
| Aug-57 | | IPSWICH-32B | STRATFORD-30A | IPSWICH-32B | MARCH-31B | 11/57: MARCH-31B | MARCH-31B | CAMBRIDGE-31A | IPSWICH-32B |
| Jan-58 | | IPSWICH-32B | STRATFORD-30A | IPSWICH-32B | MARCH-31B | 8/58: W/D | MARCH-31B | CAMBRIDGE-31A | IPSWICH-32B |
| Aug-58 | | IPSWICH-32B | 7/58: MARCH-31B | IPSWICH-32B | MARCH-31B | | MARCH-31B | 7/58: NOR-32A | IPSWICH-32B |
| Jan-59 | | IPSWICH-32B | 9/58: W/D | IPSWICH-32B | MARCH-31B | | 1/59: W/D | NORWICH-32A | IPSWICH-32B |
| Aug-59 | | 9/59: W/D | | 4/59: W/D | MARCH-31B | | | NORWICH-32A | 9/59: W/D |
| Nov-59 | | | | | 9/59: W/D | | | 10/59: W/D | |
| Jan-60 | | | | | | | | | |
| Apr-60 | | | | | | | | | |
| Aug-60 | | | | | | | | | |
| Nov-60 | | | | | | | | | |

## 61638–61648

| | 61638 | 61640 | 61641 | 61642 | 61643 | 61645 | 61646 | 61647 | 61648 |
|---|---|---|---|---|---|---|---|---|---|
| Aug-50 | CAMBRIDGE-31A | | MARCH-31B | CAMBRIDGE-31A | CAMBRIDGE-31A | IPSWICH-32B | MARCH-31B | IPSWICH-32B | STRATFORD-30A |
| Jan-51 | CAMBRIDGE-31A | CAMBRIDGE-31A | MARCH-31B | CAMBRIDGE-31A | CAMBRIDGE-31A | IPSWICH-32B | MARCH-31B | IPSWICH-32B | STRATFORD-30A |
| Aug-51 | 9/51: MARCH-31B | CAMBRIDGE-31A | MARCH-31B | CAMBRIDGE-31A | CAMBRIDGE-31A | IPSWICH-32B | MARCH-31B | IPSWICH-32B | STRATFORD-30A |
| Jan-52 | MARCH-31B | CAMBRIDGE-31A | MARCH-31B | CAMBRIDGE-31A | 1/52: STRAT-30A | IPSWICH-32B | 3/52: STRAT-30A | IPSWICH-32B | STRATFORD-30A |
| Aug-52 | MARCH-31B | CAMBRIDGE-31A | MARCH-31B | CAMBRIDGE-31A | 9/52: CAMB-31A | IPSWICH-32B | STRATFORD-30A | IPSWICH-32B | STRATFORD-30A |
| Jan-53 | MARCH-31B | CAMBRIDGE-31A | MARCH-31B | CAMBRIDGE-31A | 1/53: MARCH-31B | IPSWICH-32B | STRATFORD-30A | IPSWICH-32B | STRATFORD-30A |
| Aug-53 | MARCH-31B | CAMBRIDGE-31A | MARCH-31B | CAMBRIDGE-31A | MARCH-31B | 11/53: STRAT-30A | STRATFORD-30A | IPSWICH-32B | STRATFORD-30A |
| Jan-54 | MARCH-31B | CAMBRIDGE-31A | MARCH-31B | CAMBRIDGE-31A | MARCH-31B | 1/54: COL-30E | 1/54: COL-30E | IPSWICH-32B | STRATFORD-30A |
| Aug-54 | MARCH-31B | CAMBRIDGE-31A | MARCH-31B | CAMBRIDGE-31A | MARCH-31B | COLCHESTER-30E | COLCHESTER-30E | IPSWICH-32B | STRATFORD-30A |
| Jan-55 | MARCH-31B | CAMBRIDGE-31A | MARCH-31B | CAMBRIDGE-31A | MARCH-31B | COLCHESTER-30E | COLCHESTER-30E | IPSWICH-32B | STRATFORD-30A |
| Aug-55 | MARCH-31B | CAMBRIDGE-31A | MARCH-31B | CAMBRIDGE-31A | MARCH-31B | 5/55: STRAT-30A | COLCHESTER-30E | IPSWICH-32B | STRATFORD-30A |
| Jan-56 | MARCH-31B | CAMBRIDGE-31A | MARCH-31B | CAMBRIDGE-31A | MARCH-31B | 6/56: COL-30E | COLCHESTER-30E | IPSWICH-32B | STRATFORD-30A |
| Aug-56 | MARCH-31B | CAMBRIDGE-31A | MARCH-31B | CAMBRIDGE-31A | MARCH-31B | 10/56: CAMB-31A | 10/56: CAMB-31A | IPSWICH-32B | 6/56: COL-30E |
| Jan-57 | MARCH-31B | CAMBRIDGE-31A | MARCH-31B | CAMBRIDGE-31A | MARCH-31B | 12/56: MARCH-31B | CAMBRIDGE-31A | IPSWICH-32B | 10/56: STRAT-30A |
| Aug-57 | MARCH-31B | CAMBRIDGE-31A | MARCH-31B | CAMBRIDGE-31A | MARCH-31B | MARCH-31B | 11/57: MARCH-31B | IPSWICH-32B | STRATFORD-30A |
| Jan-58 | MARCH-31B | CAMBRIDGE-31A | MARCH-31B | CAMBRIDGE-31A | MARCH-31B | MARCH-31B | MARCH-31B | IPSWICH-32B | STRATFORD-30A |
| Aug-58 | 3/58: W/D | CAMBRIDGE-31A | MARCH-31B | 9/58: W/D | 7/58: W/D | MARCH-31B | MARCH-31B | IPSWICH-32B | STRATFORD-30A |
| Jan-59 | | 11/58: W/D | MARCH-31B | | | 2/59: W/D | 1/59: W/D | IPSWICH-32B | 12/58: W/D |
| Aug-59 | | | MARCH-31B | | | | | IPSWICH-32B | |
| Nov-59 | | | MARCH-31B | | | | | 10/59: CAMB-31A | |
| Jan-60 | | | MARCH-31B | | | | | 11/59: W/D | |
| Apr-60 | | | 2/60:: W/D | | | | | | |
| Aug-60 | | | | | | | | | |
| Nov-60 | | | | | | | | | |

| | 61649 | 61650 | 61651 | 61652 | 61653 | 61654 | 61655 | 61656 | 61657 |
|---|---|---|---|---|---|---|---|---|---|
| Aug-50 | IPSWICH - 32B | WOODFORD HALSE - 38E | WOODFORD HALSE - 38E | COLWICK - 38A | COLWICK - 38A | STRATFORD - 30A | STRATFORD - 30A | MARCH - 31B | COLWICK - 38A |
| Jan-51 | IPSWICH - 32B | WOODFORD HALSE - 38E | WOODFORD HALSE - 38E | **12/50: CAMB - 31A** | **12/50: CAMB - 31A** | STRATFORD - 30A | **9/50: CAMB - 31A** | MARCH - 31B | **3/51: CAMB - 31A** |
| Aug-51 | IPSWICH - 32B | **5/51: STRAT - 30A** | **10/51: COLW - 38A** | CAMBRIDGE - 31A | CAMBRIDGE - 31A | STRATFORD - 30A | CAMBRIDGE - 31A | MARCH - 31B | CAMBRIDGE - 31A |
| Jan-52 | IPSWICH - 32B | STRATFORD - 30A | **11/51: STRAT - 30A** | CAMBRIDGE - 31A | CAMBRIDGE - 31A | STRATFORD - 30A | CAMBRIDGE - 31A | MARCH - 31B | CAMBRIDGE - 31A |
| Aug-52 | IPSWICH - 32B | STRATFORD - 30A | STRATFORD - 30A | CAMBRIDGE - 31A | CAMBRIDGE - 31A | STRATFORD - 30A | **7/52: STRAT - 30A** | MARCH - 31B | CAMBRIDGE - 31A |
| Jan-53 | IPSWICH - 32B | STRATFORD - 30A | STRATFORD - 30A | CAMBRIDGE - 31A | CAMBRIDGE - 31A | STRATFORD - 30A | STRATFORD - 30A | **10/52: CAMB - 31A** | CAMBRIDGE - 31A |
| Aug-53 | IPSWICH - 32B | STRATFORD - 30A | STRATFORD - 30A | CAMBRIDGE - 31A | CAMBRIDGE - 31A | STRATFORD - 30A | STRATFORD - 30A | **7/53: NOR - 32A** | CAMBRIDGE - 31A |
| Jan-54 | IPSWICH - 32B | **1/54: COL - 30E** | **1/54: COL - 30E** | CAMBRIDGE - 31A | CAMBRIDGE - 31A | STRATFORD - 30A | STRATFORD - 30A | NORWICH - 32A | CAMBRIDGE - 31A |
| Aug-54 | IPSWICH - 32B | COLCHESTER - 30E | COLCHESTER - 30E | CAMBRIDGE - 31A | CAMBRIDGE - 31A | STRATFORD - 30A | STRATFORD - 30A | NORWICH - 32A | CAMBRIDGE - 31A |
| Jan-55 | IPSWICH - 32B | COLCHESTER - 30E | COLCHESTER - 30E | CAMBRIDGE - 31A | CAMBRIDGE - 31A | STRATFORD - 30A | STRATFORD - 30A | **1/55: YAR(ST) - 32D** | CAMBRIDGE - 31A |
| Aug-55 | IPSWICH - 32B | COLCHESTER - 30E | COLCHESTER - 30E | CAMBRIDGE - 31A | CAMBRIDGE - 31A | **6/55: COL - 30E** | STRATFORD - 30A | YARMOUTH(ST) - 32D | CAMBRIDGE - 31A |
| Jan-56 | IPSWICH - 32B | COLCHESTER - 30E | COLCHESTER - 30E | CAMBRIDGE - 31A | CAMBRIDGE - 31A | **11/55: STRAT - 30A** | STRATFORD - 30A | YARMOUTH(ST) - 32D | **3/56: MARCH - 31B** |
| Aug-56 | IPSWICH - 32B | COLCHESTER - 30E | COLCHESTER - 30E | CAMBRIDGE - 31A | CAMBRIDGE - 31A | STRATFORD - 30A | STRATFORD - 30A | YARMOUTH(ST) - 32D | MARCH - 31B |
| Jan-57 | IPSWICH - 32B | COLCHESTER - 30E | COLCHESTER - 30E | CAMBRIDGE - 31A | CAMBRIDGE - 31A | STRATFORD - 30A | STRATFORD - 30A | YARMOUTH(ST) - 32D | MARCH - 31B |
| Aug-57 | IPSWICH - 32B | COLCHESTER - 30E | COLCHESTER - 30E | CAMBRIDGE - 31A | CAMBRIDGE - 31A | STRATFORD - 30A | STRATFORD - 30A | YARMOUTH(ST) - 32D | MARCH - 31B |
| Jan-58 | IPSWICH - 32B | COLCHESTER - 30E | COLCHESTER - 30E | CAMBRIDGE - 31A | **11/57: MARCH - 31B** | STRATFORD - 30A | STRATFORD - 30A | YARMOUTH(ST) - 32D | MARCH - 31B |
| Aug-58 | IPSWICH - 32B | **9/58: W/D** | COLCHESTER - 30E | CAMBRIDGE - 31A | MARCH - 31B | **7/58: IPS - 32B** | STRATFORD - 30A | YARMOUTH(ST) - 32D | MARCH - 31B |
| Jan-59 | **2/59: W/D** | | **CAMBRIDGE - 31A** | CAMBRIDGE - 31A | MARCH - 31B | IPSWICH - 32B | **1/59: CAMB - 31A** | YARMOUTH(ST) - 32D | MARCH - 31B |
| Aug-59 | | | **8/59: W/D** | CAMBRIDGE - 31A | MARCH - 31B | IPSWICH - 32B | **4/59: W/D** | **9/59: NOR - 32A** | MARCH - 31B |
| Nov-59 | | | | **9/59: W/D** | MARCH - 31B | **11/59: W/D** | | NORWICH - 32A | MARCH - 31B |
| Jan-60 | | | | | MARCH - 31B | | | **1/60: MARCH - 31B** | MARCH - 31B |
| Apr-60 | | | | | **2/60: W/D** | | | **2/60: W/D** | **5/60: W/D** |
| Aug-60 | | | | | | | | | |
| Nov-60 | | | | | | | | | |

| | 61658 | 61659 | 61660 | 61661 | 61662 | 61663 | 61664 | 61665 | 61666 |
|---|---|---|---|---|---|---|---|---|---|
| Aug-50 | STRATFORD - 30A | NORWICH - 32A | MARCH - 31B | YARMOUTH(ST) - 32D | COLWICK - 38A | CAMBRIDGE - 31A | WOODFORD HALSE - 38E | YARMOUTH(ST) - 32D | MARCH - 31B |
| Jan-51 | STRATFORD - 30A | NORWICH - 32A | MARCH - 31B | YARMOUTH(ST) - 32D | COLWICK - 38A | CAMBRIDGE - 31A | WOODFORD HALSE - 38E | YARMOUTH(ST) - 32D | MARCH - 31B |
| Aug-51 | **6/51: MARCH - 31B** | **7/51: YAR(ST) - 32D** | **6/51: STRAT - 30A** | **7/51: NOR - 32A** | COLWICK - 38A | CAMBRIDGE - 31A | **5/51: STRAT - 30A** | **7/51: NOR - 32A** | MARCH - 31B |
| Jan-52 | MARCH - 31B | **3/52: NOR - 32A** | STRATFORD - 30A | **9/51: STRAT - 30A** | **11/51: STRAT - 30A** | CAMBRIDGE - 31A | **9/51: NOR - 32A** | **3/52: YAR(ST) - 32D** | MARCH - 31B |
| Aug-52 | MARCH - 31B | NORWICH - 32A | STRATFORD - 30A | STRATFORD - 30A | STRATFORD - 30A | CAMBRIDGE - 31A | **3/52: YAR(ST) - 32D** | YARMOUTH(ST) - 32D | **7/52: STRAT - 30A** |
| Jan-53 | MARCH - 31B | NORWICH - 32A | STRATFORD - 30A | STRATFORD - 30A | STRATFORD - 30A | CAMBRIDGE - 31A | YARMOUTH(ST) - 32D | YARMOUTH(ST) - 32D | **3/53: MARCH - 31B** |
| Aug-53 | MARCH - 31B | **5/53: YAR (ST) - 32D** | STRATFORD - 30A | STRATFORD - 30A | STRATFORD - 30A | **7/53: STRAT - 30A** | **5/53: NOR - 32A** | **5/53: NOR - 32A** | **7/53: STRAT - 30A** |
| Jan-54 | MARCH - 31B | YARMOUTH(ST) - 32D | STRATFORD - 30A | STRATFORD - 30A | **1/54: COL - 30E** | STRATFORD - 30A | NORWICH - 32A | NORWICH - 32A | STRATFORD - 30A |
| Aug-54 | MARCH - 31B | YARMOUTH(ST) - 32D | STRATFORD - 30A | STRATFORD - 30A | COLCHESTER - 30E | STRATFORD - 30A | **1/55: YAR(ST) - 32D** | NORWICH - 32A | **5/54: COL - 30E** |
| Jan-55 | MARCH - 31B | YARMOUTH(ST) - 32D | STRATFORD - 30A | STRATFORD - 30A | COLCHESTER - 30E | STRATFORD - 30A | **3/55: NOR - 32A** | **1/55: YAR(ST) - 32D** | COLCHESTER - 30E |
| Aug-55 | **5/55: STRAT - 30A** | YARMOUTH(ST) - 32D | STRATFORD - 30A | STRATFORD - 30A | COLCHESTER - 30E | STRATFORD - 30A | **6/55: YAR(ST) - 32D** | YARMOUTH(ST) - 32D | COLCHESTER - 30E |
| Jan-56 | STRATFORD - 30A | YARMOUTH(ST) - 32D | STRATFORD - 30A | STRATFORD - 30A | COLCHESTER - 30E | STRATFORD - 30A | YARMOUTH(ST) - 32D | YARMOUTH(ST) - 32D | COLCHESTER - 30E |
| Aug-56 | STRATFORD - 30A | YARMOUTH(ST) - 32D | **6/56: COL - 30E** | STRATFORD - 30A | COLCHESTER - 30E | STRATFORD - 30A | YARMOUTH(ST) - 32D | YARMOUTH(ST) - 32D | COLCHESTER - 30E |
| Jan-57 | STRATFORD - 30A | YARMOUTH(ST) - 32D | **10/56: STRAT - 30A** | STRATFORD - 30A | COLCHESTER - 30E | STRATFORD - 30A | YARMOUTH(ST) - 32D | YARMOUTH(ST) - 32D | COLCHESTER - 30E |
| Aug-57 | STRATFORD - 30A | YARMOUTH(ST) - 32D | STRATFORD - 30A | STRATFORD - 30A | COLCHESTER - 30E | STRATFORD - 30A | YARMOUTH(ST) - 32D | YARMOUTH(ST) - 32D | COLCHESTER - 30E |
| Jan-58 | STRATFORD - 30A | YARMOUTH(ST) - 32D | STRATFORD - 30A | **6/58: COL - 30E** | COLCHESTER - 30E | STRATFORD - 30A | YARMOUTH(ST) - 32D | YARMOUTH(ST) - 32D | COLCHESTER - 30E |
| Aug-58 | **12/58: STRAT - 30A** | YARMOUTH(ST) - 32D | **5/58: YAR(ST) - 32D** | **9/58: STRAT - 30A** | COLCHESTER - 30E | STRATFORD - 30A | YARMOUTH(ST) - 32D | YARMOUTH(ST) - 32D | COLCHESTER - 30E |
| Jan-59 | 1/59: COL - 30E | **12/58: LOW - 32C** | **12/58: LOW - 32C** | **1/59: CAMB - 31A** | COLCHESTER - 30E | **12/58: COL - 30E** | **6/59: NOR - 32A** | YARMOUTH(ST) - 32D | COLCHESTER - 30E |
| Aug-59 | **10/59: STRAT - 30A** | LOWESTOFT - 32C | LOWESTOFT - 32C | **7/59: W/D** | **10/59: STRAT - 30A** | COLCHESTER - 30E | **9/59: YAR(ST) - 32D** | **4/59: W/D** | COLCHESTER - 30E |
| Nov-59 | **11/59: W/D** | LOWESTOFT - 32C | LOWESTOFT - 32C | | **11/59: W/D** | **12/59: STRAT - 30A** | **10/59: LOW - 32C** | | **10/59: STRAT - 30A** |
| Jan-60 | | LOWESTOFT - 32C | **1/60: MARCH - 31B** | | | STRATFORD - 30A | **1/60: MARCH - 31B** | | STRATFORD - 30A |
| Apr-60 | | **3/60: W/D** | **5/60: W/D** | | | **3/60: W/D** | **5/60: W/D** | | **3/60: W/D** |
| Aug-60 | | | | | | | | | |
| Nov-60 | | | | | | | | | |

| | 61667 | 61668 | 61669 | 61670 | 61672 | B2 4-6-0 (1945) 61600 | 61603 | 61607 | 61614 |
|---|---|---|---|---|---|---|---|---|---|
| Aug-50 | WOODFORD HALSE - 38E | IPSWICH - 32B | IPSWICH - 32B | NORWICH - 32A | MARCH - 31B | IPSWICH - 32B | COLCHESTER - 30E | COLCHESTER - 30E | COLCHESTER - 30E |
| Jan-51 | WOODFORD HALSE - 38E | IPSWICH - 32B | IPSWICH - 32B | NORWICH - 32A | MARCH - 31B | IPSWICH - 32B | COLCHESTER - 30E | COLCHESTER - 30E | COLCHESTER - 30E |
| Aug-51 | **10/51: COLW - 38A** | IPSWICH - 32B | IPSWICH - 32B | **7/51: YAR(ST) - 32D** | **6/51: STRAT - 30A** | IPSWICH - 32B | COLCHESTER - 30E | COLCHESTER - 30E | COLCHESTER - 30E |
| Jan-52 | **11/51: STRAT - 30A** | IPSWICH - 32B | IPSWICH - 32B | **3/52: NOR - 32A** | STRATFORD - 30A | IPSWICH - 32B | COLCHESTER - 30E | COLCHESTER - 30E | COLCHESTER - 30E |
| Aug-52 | STRATFORD - 30A | IPSWICH - 32B | IPSWICH - 32B | NORWICH - 32A | STRATFORD - 30A | IPSWICH - 32B | COLCHESTER - 30E | COLCHESTER - 30E | COLCHESTER - 30E |
| Jan-53 | STRATFORD - 30A | **2/53: STRAT - 30A** | IPSWICH - 32B | NORWICH - 32A | STRATFORD - 30A | **1/53: STRAT - 30A** | COLCHESTER - 30E | COLCHESTER - 30E | COLCHESTER - 30E |
| Aug-53 | STRATFORD - 30A | STRATFORD - 30A | IPSWICH - 32B | **5/53: YAR(ST) - 32D** | STRATFORD - 30A | STRATFORD - 30A | COLCHESTER - 30E | COLCHESTER - 30E | COLCHESTER - 30E |
| Jan-54 | **1/54: COL - 30E** | STRATFORD - 30A | IPSWICH - 32B | YARMOUTH(ST) - 32D | STRATFORD - 30A | STRATFORD - 30A | COLCHESTER - 30E | COLCHESTER - 30E | COLCHESTER - 30E |
| Aug-54 | COLCHESTER - 30E | STRATFORD - 30A | IPSWICH - 32B | YARMOUTH(ST) - 32D | STRATFORD - 30A | STRATFORD - 30A | COLCHESTER - 30E | COLCHESTER - 30E | COLCHESTER - 30E |
| Jan-55 | COLCHESTER - 30E | STRATFORD - 30A | IPSWICH - 32B | YARMOUTH(ST) - 32D | STRATFORD - 30A | STRATFORD - 30A | COLCHESTER - 30E | COLCHESTER - 30E | COLCHESTER - 30E |
| Aug-55 | COLCHESTER - 30E | **6/55: COL - 30E** | IPSWICH - 32B | YARMOUTH(ST) - 32D | **6/55: COL - 30E** | STRATFORD - 30A | COLCHESTER - 30E | COLCHESTER - 30E | COLCHESTER - 30E |
| Jan-56 | COLCHESTER - 30E | **11/55: STRAT - 30A** | IPSWICH - 32B | YARMOUTH(ST) - 32D | **11/55: STRAT - 30A** | STRATFORD - 30A | COLCHESTER - 30E | COLCHESTER - 30E | COLCHESTER - 30E |
| Aug-56 | COLCHESTER - 30E | STRATFORD - 30A | IPSWICH - 32B | YARMOUTH(ST) - 32D | STRATFORD - 30A | STRATFORD - 30A | COLCHESTER - 30E | COLCHESTER - 30E | COLCHESTER - 30E |
| Jan-57 | COLCHESTER - 30E | STRATFORD - 30A | IPSWICH - 32B | YARMOUTH(ST) - 32D | STRATFORD - 30A | **2/57: MARCH - 31B** | **11/56: CAMB - 31A** | **11/56: CAMB - 31A** | **11/56: CAMB - 31A** |
| Aug-57 | **10/57: STRAT - 30A** | STRATFORD - 30A | IPSWICH - 32B | YARMOUTH(ST) - 32D | STRATFORD - 30A | **6/57: STRAT - 30A** | CAMBRIDGE - 31A | CAMBRIDGE - 31A | CAMBRIDGE - 31A |
| Jan-58 | **5/58: CAMB - 31A** | STRATFORD - 30A | IPSWICH - 32B | YARMOUTH(ST) - 32D | STRATFORD - 30A | STRATFORD - 30A | CAMBRIDGE - 31A | CAMBRIDGE - 31A | CAMBRIDGE - 31A |
| Aug-58 | **6/58: W/D** | STRATFORD - 30A | **9/58: W/D** | YARMOUTH(ST) - 32D | STRATFORD - 30A | **7/58: W/D** | **9/58: W/D** | CAMBRIDGE - 31A | CAMBRIDGE - 31A |
| Jan-59 | | **12/58: COL - 30E** | | YARMOUTH(ST) - 32D | **11/58: IPS - 32B** | | | CAMBRIDGE - 31A | CAMBRIDGE - 31A |
| Aug-59 | | COLCHESTER - 30E | | YARMOUTH(ST) - 32D | **6/59: LOW - 32C** | | | CAMBRIDGE - 31A | |
| Nov-59 | | **12/59: STRAT - 30A** | | **10/59: LOW - 32C** | LOWESTOFT - 32C | | | **12/59: W/D** | |
| Jan-60 | | STRATFORD - 30A | | LOWESTOFT - 32C | LOWESTOFT - 32C | | | | |
| Apr-60 | | STRATFORD - 30A | | **3/60: W/D** | **3/60: W/D** | | | | |
| Aug-60 | | **9/60: W/D** | | | | | | | |
| Nov-60 | | | | | | | | | |

| | 61615 | 61616 | 61617 | 61632 | 61639 | 61644 | 61671 | B 13 4-6-0 (1899) 61699 | V4 2-6-2 (1941) 61700 |
|---|---|---|---|---|---|---|---|---|---|
| Aug-50 | COLCHESTER - 30E | COLCHESTER - 30E | CAMBRIDGE - 31A | COLCHESTER - 30E | COLCHESTER - 30E | COLCHESTER - 30E | CAMBRIDGE - 31A | Rugby Test | EASTFIELD - 65A |
| Jan-51 | COLCHESTER - 30E | COLCHESTER - 30E | CAMBRIDGE - 31A | COLCHESTER - 30E | COLCHESTER - 30E | COLCHESTER - 30E | CAMBRIDGE - 31A | Rugby Test | EASTFIELD - 65A |
| Aug-51 | COLCHESTER - 30E | COLCHESTER - 30E | CAMBRIDGE - 31A | COLCHESTER - 30E | COLCHESTER - 30E | COLCHESTER - 30E | CAMBRIDGE - 31A | **5/51: W/D** | EASTFIELD - 65A |
| Jan-52 | COLCHESTER - 30E | COLCHESTER - 30E | CAMBRIDGE - 31A | COLCHESTER - 30E | COLCHESTER - 30E | COLCHESTER - 30E | CAMBRIDGE - 31A | | EASTFIELD - 65A |
| Aug-52 | COLCHESTER - 30E | COLCHESTER - 30E | CAMBRIDGE - 31A | COLCHESTER - 30E | COLCHESTER - 30E | COLCHESTER - 30E | CAMBRIDGE - 31A | | EASTFIELD - 65A |
| Jan-53 | COLCHESTER - 30E | COLCHESTER - 30E | CAMBRIDGE - 31A | COLCHESTER - 30E | COLCHESTER - 30E | COLCHESTER - 30E | CAMBRIDGE - 31A | | EASTFIELD - 65A |
| Aug-53 | COLCHESTER - 30E | COLCHESTER - 30E | CAMBRIDGE - 31A | COLCHESTER - 30E | COLCHESTER - 30E | COLCHESTER - 30E | CAMBRIDGE - 31A | | EASTFIELD - 65A |
| Jan-54 | COLCHESTER - 30E | COLCHESTER - 30E | CAMBRIDGE - 31A | COLCHESTER - 30E | COLCHESTER - 30E | COLCHESTER - 30E | CAMBRIDGE - 31A | | EASTFIELD - 65A |
| Aug-54 | COLCHESTER - 30E | COLCHESTER - 30E | CAMBRIDGE - 31A | COLCHESTER - 30E | COLCHESTER - 30E | COLCHESTER - 30E | CAMBRIDGE - 31A | | **6/54: FYHIL - 61B** |
| Jan-55 | COLCHESTER - 30E | COLCHESTER - 30E | CAMBRIDGE - 31A | COLCHESTER - 30E | COLCHESTER - 30E | COLCHESTER - 30E | CAMBRIDGE - 31A | | FERRYHILL - 61B |
| Aug-55 | COLCHESTER - 30E | COLCHESTER - 30E | CAMBRIDGE - 31A | COLCHESTER - 30E | COLCHESTER - 30E | COLCHESTER - 30E | CAMBRIDGE - 31A | | FERRYHILL - 61B |
| Jan-56 | COLCHESTER - 30E | COLCHESTER - 30E | CAMBRIDGE - 31A | COLCHESTER - 30E | COLCHESTER - 30E | COLCHESTER - 30E | CAMBRIDGE - 31A | | FERRYHILL - 61B |
| Aug-56 | COLCHESTER - 30E | COLCHESTER - 30E | CAMBRIDGE - 31A | COLCHESTER - 30E | COLCHESTER - 30E | COLCHESTER - 30E | CAMBRIDGE - 31A | | FERRYHILL - 61B |
| Jan-57 | **11/56: CAMB - 31A** | **11/56: CAMB - 31A** | CAMBRIDGE - 31A | **11/56: CAMB - 31A** | **11/56: CAMB - 31A** | **11/56: CAMB - 31A** | CAMBRIDGE - 31A | | **3/57: W/D** |
| Aug-57 | CAMBRIDGE - 31A | CAMBRIDGE - 31A | CAMBRIDGE - 31A | CAMBRIDGE - 31A | CAMBRIDGE - 31A | CAMBRIDGE - 31A | CAMBRIDGE - 31A | | |
| Jan-58 | CAMBRIDGE - 31A | CAMBRIDGE - 31A | CAMBRIDGE - 31A | CAMBRIDGE - 31A | CAMBRIDGE - 31A | CAMBRIDGE - 31A | CAMBRIDGE - 31A | | |
| Aug-58 | CAMBRIDGE - 31A | CAMBRIDGE - 31A | **8/58: W/D** | CAMBRIDGE - 31A | CAMBRIDGE - 31A | CAMBRIDGE - 31A | **9/58: W/D** | | |
| Jan-59 | CAMBRIDGE - 31A | CAMBRIDGE - 31A | | **2/59: W/D** | CAMBRIDGE - 31A | CAMBRIDGE - 31A | | | |
| Aug-59 | | **9/59: W/D** | | | **5/59: W/D** | CAMBRIDGE - 31A | | | |
| Nov-59 | | | | | | **11/59: W/D** | | | |
| Jan-60 | | | | | | | | | |
| Apr-60 | | | | | | | | | |
| Aug-60 | | | | | | | | | |
| Nov-60 | | | | | | | | | |

## K2 2-6-0 (1912)

| | 61701 | 61720 | 61721 | 61722 | 61723 | 61724 | 61725 | 61726 | 61727 |
|---|---|---|---|---|---|---|---|---|---|
| Aug-50 | EASTFIELD-65A | IMMINGHAM-40B | STRATFORD-30A | IMMINGHAM-40B | COLWICK-38A | IMMINGHAM-40B | BOSTON-40F | COLWICK-38A | IMMINGHAM-40B |
| Jan-51 | EASTFIELD-65A | IMMINGHAM-40B | STRATFORD-30A | 3/51: EAST-65A | COLWICK-38A | IMMINGHAM-40B | BOSTON-40F | COLWICK-38A | IMMINGHAM-40B |
| Aug-51 | EASTFIELD-65A | IMMINGHAM-40B | 6/51: EAST-65A | EASTFIELD-65A | COLWICK-38A | IMMINGHAM-40B | BOSTON-40F | COLWICK-38A | IMMINGHAM-40B |
| Jan-52 | EASTFIELD-65A | IMMINGHAM-40B | 1/52: DUNF-62C | 3/52: PARK-65C | COLWICK-38A | IMMINGHAM-40B | BOSTON-40F | COLWICK-38A | IMMINGHAM-40B |
| Aug-52 | EASTFIELD-65A | IMMINGHAM-40B | DUNFERMLINE-62C | PARKHEAD-65C | COLWICK-38A | IMMINGHAM-40B | BOSTON-40F | COLWICK-38A | IMMINGHAM-40B |
| Jan-53 | EASTFIELD-65A | IMMINGHAM-40B | DUNFERMLINE-62C | PARKHEAD-65C | COLWICK-38A | IMMINGHAM-40B | BOSTON-40F | COLWICK-38A | IMMINGHAM-40B |
| Aug-53 | EASTFIELD-65A | IMMINGHAM-40B | DUNFERMLINE-62C | PARKHEAD-65C | COLWICK-38A | IMMINGHAM-40B | BOSTON-40F | COLWICK-38A | IMMINGHAM-40B |
| Jan-54 | EASTFIELD-65A | IMMINGHAM-40B | DUNFERMLINE-62C | PARKHEAD-65C | COLWICK-38A | IMMINGHAM-40B | BOSTON-40F | COLWICK-38A | IMMINGHAM-40B |
| Aug-54 | 6/54: FYHIL-61B | IMMINGHAM-40B | DUNFERMLINE-62C | PARKHEAD-65C | COLWICK-38A | IMMINGHAM-40B | BOSTON-40F | COLWICK-38A | IMMINGHAM-40B |
| Jan-55 | FERRYHILL-61B | IMMINGHAM-40B | DUNFERMLINE-62C | PARKHEAD-65C | COLWICK-38A | IMMINGHAM-40B | BOSTON-40F | COLWICK-38A | IMMINGHAM-40B |
| Aug-55 | FERRYHILL-61B | 7/55: BOS-40F | DUNFERMLINE-62C | 9/55: W/D | COLWICK-38A | 7/55: DARN-41A | BOSTON-40F | COLWICK-38A | IMMINGHAM-40B |
| Jan-56 | FERRYHILL-61B | BOSTON-40F | DUNFERMLINE-62C | | COLWICK-38A | DARNALL-41A | BOSTON-40F | COLWICK-38A | 6/56: W/D |
| Aug-56 | FERRYHILL-61B | 6/56: W/D | DUNFERMLINE-62C | | COLWICK-38A | DARNALL-41A | BOSTON-40F | COLWICK-38A | |
| Jan-57 | FERRYHILL-61B | | DUNFERMLINE-62C | | COLWICK-38A | DARNALL-41A | BOSTON-40F | COLWICK-38A | |
| Aug-57 | 10/57: W/D | | DUNFERMLINE-62C | | COLWICK-38A | DARNALL-41A | BOSTON-40F | 5/57: W/D | |
| Jan-58 | | | DUNFERMLINE-62C | | COLWICK-38A | 1/58: W/D | 1/58: W/D | | |
| Aug-58 | | | DUNFERMLINE-62C | | COLWICK-40E | | | | |
| Jan-59 | | | DUNFERMLINE-62C | | COLWICK-40E | | | | |
| Aug-59 | | | DUNFERMLINE-62C | | COLWICK-40E | | | | |
| Nov-59 | | | DUNFERMLINE-62C | | 11/59: W/D | | | | |
| Jan-60 | | | 2/60: W/D | | | | | | |
| Apr-60 | | | | | | | | | |
| Aug-60 | | | | | | | | | |
| Nov-60 | | | | | | | | | |

| | 61728 | 61729 | 61730 | 61731 | 61732 | 61733 | 61734 | 61735 | 61736 |
|---|---|---|---|---|---|---|---|---|---|
| Aug-50 | IMMINGHAM-40B | NEWENGLAND-35A | NEWENGLAND-35A | BOSTON-40F | COLWICK-38A | IMMINGHAM-40B | STRATFORD-30A | NEWENGLAND-35A | NEWENGLAND-35A |
| Jan-51 | IMMINGHAM-40B | 11/50: GRAN-38A | 10/50: NOR-32A | BOSTON-40F | COLWICK-38A | 1/51: PARK-65C | STRATFORD-30A | 1/51: PARK-65C | NEWENGLAND-35A |
| Aug-51 | IMMINGHAM-40B | 1/51: COLW-38A | 3/51: IMM-40B | BOSTON-40F | COLWICK-38A | PARKHEAD-65C | 6/51: EAST-65A | PARKHEAD-65C | 5/51: IMM-40B |
| Jan-52 | IMMINGHAM-40B | COLWICK-38A | IMMINGHAM-40B | 1/52: TH JCN-62A | COLWICK-38A | PARKHEAD-65C | 2/52: DUNF-62C | PARKHEAD-65C | IMMINGHAM-40B |
| Aug-52 | IMMINGHAM-40B | COLWICK-38A | IMMINGHAM-40B | THORNTONJCN-62A | COLWICK-38A | PARKHEAD-65C | DUNFERMLINE-62C | PARKHEAD-65C | IMMINGHAM-40B |
| Jan-53 | 3/53: BOST-40F | COLWICK-38A | IMMINGHAM-40B | THORNTONJCN-62A | COLWICK-38A | PARKHEAD-65C | 12/52: TH JCN-62A | PARKHEAD-65C | IMMINGHAM-40B |
| Aug-53 | BOSTON-40F | COLWICK-38A | IMMINGHAM-40B | THORNTONJCN-62A | COLWICK-38A | PARKHEAD-65C | 5/53: FERRY-61B | PARKHEAD-65C | IMMINGHAM-40B |
| Jan-54 | BOSTON-40F | COLWICK-38A | IMMINGHAM-40B | THORNTONJCN-62A | COLWICK-38A | PARKHEAD-65C | FERRYHILL-61B | PARKHEAD-65C | IMMINGHAM-40B |
| Aug-54 | BOSTON-40F | COLWICK-38A | IMMINGHAM-40B | THORNTONJCN-62A | COLWICK-38A | PARKHEAD-65C | 7/54: KEITH-61C | PARKHEAD-65C | IMMINGHAM-40B |
| Jan-55 | BOSTON-40F | COLWICK-38A | IMMINGHAM-40B | THORNTONJCN-62A | COLWICK-38A | PARKHEAD-65C | KEITH-61C | PARKHEAD-65C | IMMINGHAM-40B |
| Aug-55 | 7/55: DARN-41A | COLWICK-38A | IMMINGHAM-40B | THORNTONJCN-62A | COLWICK-38A | PARKHEAD-65C | KEITH-61C | PARKHEAD-65C | IMMINGHAM-40B |
| Jan-56 | DARNALL-41A | COLWICK-38A | IMMINGHAM-40B | THORNTONJCN-62A | COLWICK-38A | PARKHEAD-65C | 7/56: W/D | PARKHEAD-65C | IMMINGHAM-40B |
| Aug-56 | DARNALL-41A | COLWICK-38A | IMMINGHAM-40B | 9/56: BOST-40F | COLWICK-38A | PARKHEAD-65C | | PARKHEAD-65C | IMMINGHAM-40B |
| Jan-57 | DARNALL-41A | COLWICK-38A | IMMINGHAM-40B | BOSTON-40F | COLWICK-38A | PARKHEAD-65C | | 1/57: W/D | IMMINGHAM-40B |
| Aug-57 | DARNALL-41A | 6/57: W/D | IMMINGHAM-40B | BOSTON-40F | 4/57: TH JCN:62A | PARKHEAD-65C | | | 5/57: W/D |
| Jan-58 | DARNALL-41A | | IMMINGHAM-40B | BOSTON-40F | THORNTONJCN-62A | 10/57: W/D | | | |
| Aug-58 | DARNALL-41A | | IMMINGHAM-40B | BOSTON-40F | THORNTONJCN-62A | | | | |
| Jan-59 | DARNALL-41A | | IMMINGHAM-40B | BOSTON-40F | THORNTONJCN-62A | | | | |
| Aug-59 | DARNALL-41A | | IMMINGHAM-40B | 6/59: W/D | THORNTONJCN-62A | | | | |
| Nov-59 | DARNALL-41A | | IMMINGHAM-40B | | THORNTONJCN-62A | | | | |
| Jan-60 | DARNALL-41A | | IMMINGHAM-40B | | THORNTONJCN-62A | | | | |
| Apr-60 | DARNALL-41A | | IMMINGHAM-40B | | THORNTONJCN-62A | | | | |
| Aug-60 | DARNALL-41A | | IMMINGHAM-40B | | THORNTONJCN-62A | | | | |
| Nov-60 | DARNALL-41A | | IMMINGHAM-40B | | THORNTONJCN-62A | | | | |

| | 61737 | 61738 | 61739 | 61740 | 61741 | 61742 | 61743 | 61744 | 61745 |
|---|---|---|---|---|---|---|---|---|---|
| Aug-50 | STRATFORD-30A | SOUTH LYNN-31D | NEWENGLAND-35A | NEWENGLAND-35A | COLWICK-38A | SOUTHLYNN-31D | SOUTHLYNN-31D | BOSTON-40F | STRATFORD-30A |
| Jan-51 | STRATFORD-30A | SOUTH LYNN-31D | 1/51: BOST-40F | 1/51: IMM-40B | 1/51: EAST-65A | SOUTHLYNN-31D | SOUTHLYNN-31D | BOSTON-40F | STRATFORD-30A |
| Aug-51 | STRATFORD-30A | 4/51: COLW-38A | 5/51: IMM-40B | IMMINGHAM-40B | EASTFIELD-65A | SOUTHLYNN-31D | 10/51: MARCH-31B | BOSTON-40F | STRATFORD-30A |
| Jan-52 | STRATFORD-30A | COLWICK-38A | IMMINGHAM-40B | IMMINGHAM-40B | EASTFIELD-65A | SOUTHLYNN-31D | MARCH-31B | BOSTON-40F | STRATFORD-30A |
| Aug-52 | STRATFORD-30A | COLWICK-38A | IMMINGHAM-40B | IMMINGHAM-40B | EASTFIELD-65A | 10/52: MARCH-31B | MARCH-31B | BOSTON-40F | 10/52: LINC-40A |
| Jan-53 | 10/52: COLW-38A | COLWICK-38A | 2/53: TH JCN-62A | IMMINGHAM-40B | EASTFIELD-65A | MARCH-31B | 10/53: LINC-40A | 10/53: LINC-40A | 3/53: BOST-40F |
| Aug-53 | COLWICK-38A | COLWICK-38A | 4/53: IMM-40B | IMMINGHAM-40B | EASTFIELD-65A | 10/53: LINC-40A | LINCOLN-40A | LINCOLN-40A | BOSTON-40F |
| Jan-54 | COLWICK-38A | COLWICK-38A | IMMINGHAM-40B | IMMINGHAM-40B | EASTFIELD-65A | LINCOLN-40A | LINCOLN-40A | LINCOLN-40A | BOSTON-40F |
| Aug-54 | COLWICK-38A | COLWICK-38A | IMMINGHAM-40B | IMMINGHAM-40B | EASTFIELD-65A | 10/54: IMM-40B | LINCOLN-40A | LINCOLN-40A | BOSTON-40F |
| Jan-55 | COLWICK-38A | COLWICK-38A | IMMINGHAM-40B | IMMINGHAM-40B | EASTFIELD-65A | 11/54: BOST-40F | 2/55: BOST-40F | BOSTON-40F | BOSTON-40F |
| Aug-55 | 6/55: DARN-41A | COLWICK-38A | 7/55: DARN-39B | IMMINGHAM-40B | EASTFIELD-65A | BOSTON-40F | BOSTON-40F | BOSTON-40F | BOSTON-40F |
| Jan-56 | DARNALL-41A | COLWICK-38A | DARNALL-41A | IMMINGHAM-40B | EASTFIELD-65A | BOSTON-40F | BOSTON-40F | BOSTON-40F | BOSTON-40F |
| Aug-56 | DARNALL-41A | COLWICK-38A | DARNALL-41A | IMMINGHAM-40B | EASTFIELD-65A | BOSTON-40F | BOSTON-40F | BOSTON-40F | BOSTON-40F |
| Jan-57 | 11/56: W/D | COLWICK-38A | DARNALL-41A | IMMINGHAM-40B | 3/57: KITTY-61A | BOSTON-40F | BOSTON-40F | 1/57: W/D | BOSTON-40F |
| Aug-57 | | COLWICK-38A | 6/57: COLW-38A | IMMINGHAM-40B | KITTYBREWSTER-61A | BOSTON-40F | BOSTON-40F | | BOSTON-40F |
| Jan-58 | | COLWICK-38A | COLWICK-38A | IMMINGHAM-40B | KITTYBREWSTER-61A | BOSTON-40F | BOSTON-40F | | BOSTON-40F |
| Aug-58 | | COLWICK-40E | COLWICK-40E | IMMINGHAM-40B | KITTYBREWSTER-61A | BOSTON-40F | BOSTON-40F | | BOSTON-40F |
| Jan-59 | | COLWICK-40E | 2/59: W/D | IMMINGHAM-40B | KITTYBREWSTER-61A | BOSTON-40F | BOSTON-40F | | 3/59: IMM-40B |
| Aug-59 | | 7/59: W/D | | IMMINGHAM-40B | KITTYBREWSTER-61A | BOSTON-40F | | | IMMINGHAM-40B |
| Nov-59 | | | | IMMINGHAM-40B | KITTYBREWSTER-61A | BOSTON-40F | | | IMMINGHAM-40B |
| Jan-60 | | | | IMMINGHAM-40B | KITTYBREWSTER-61A | BOSTON-40F | | | IMMINGHAM-40B |
| Apr-60 | | | | IMMINGHAM-40B | 3/60: W/D | BOSTON-40F | | | IMMINGHAM-40B |
| Aug-60 | | | | 6/60: COLW-40E | | BOSTON-40F | | | IMMINGHAM-40B |
| Nov-60 | | | | COLWICK-40E | | BOSTON-40F | | | IMMINGHAM-40B |

| | 61746 | 61747 | 61748 | 61749 | 61750 | 61751 | 61752 | 61753 | 61754 |
|---|---|---|---|---|---|---|---|---|---|
| Aug-50 | STRATFORD-30A | NEWENGLAND-35A | SOUTHLYNN-31D | COLWICK-38A | BOSTON-40F | COLWICK-38A | STRATFORD-30A | STRATFORD-30A | STRATFORD-30A |
| Jan-51 | STRATFORD-30A | 10/50: YAR(B)-32F | SOUTHLYNN-31D | COLWICK-38A | BOSTON-40F | COLWICK-38A | STRATFORD-30A | STRATFORD-30A | STRATFORD-30A |
| Aug-51 | STRATFORD-30A | 12/50: NORW-32A | SOUTHLYNN-31D | COLWICK-38A | BOSTON-40F | COLWICK-38A | STRATFORD-30A | STRATFORD-30A | STRATFORD-30A |
| Jan-52 | STRATFORD-30A | 3/51: COLW-38A | SOUTHLYNN-31D | COLWICK-38A | BOSTON-40F | COLWICK-38A | STRATFORD-30A | STRATFORD-30A | STRATFORD-30A |
| Aug-52 | 10/52: LINC-40A | COLWICK-38A | SOUTHLYNN-31D | COLWICK-38A | BOSTON-40F | COLWICK-38A | 10/52: COLW-38A | 10/52: COLW-38A | 10/52: COLW-38A |
| Jan-53 | LINCOLN-40A | COLWICK-38A | 10/53: LINC-40A | COLWICK-38A | BOSTON-40F | COLWICK-38A | COLWICK-38A | COLWICK-38A | COLWICK-38A |
| Aug-53 | LINCOLN-40A | COLWICK-38A | LINCOLN-40A | COLWICK-38A | BOSTON-40F | COLWICK-38A | COLWICK-38A | COLWICK-38A | COLWICK-38A |
| Jan-54 | LINCOLN-40A | COLWICK-38A | LINCOLN-40A | COLWICK-38A | BOSTON-40F | COLWICK-38A | COLWICK-38A | COLWICK-38A | COLWICK-38A |
| Aug-54 | LINCOLN-40A | COLWICK-38A | LINCOLN-40A | COLWICK-38A | BOSTON-40F | COLWICK-38A | COLWICK-38A | COLWICK-38A | COLWICK-38A |
| Jan-55 | LINCOLN-40A | COLWICK-38A | LINCOLN-40A | COLWICK-38A | BOSTON-40F | COLWICK-38A | COLWICK-38A | COLWICK-38A | COLWICK-38A |
| Aug-55 | LINCOLN-40A | 6/55: DARN-41A | 7/55: BOST-40F | 6/55: DARN-39B | BOSTON-40F | COLWICK-38A | COLWICK-38A | COLWICK-38A | COLWICK-38A |
| Jan-56 | LINCOLN-40A | DARNALL-41A | BOSTON-40F | DARNALL-41A | BOSTON-40F | COLWICK-38A | COLWICK-38A | COLWICK-38A | COLWICK-38A |
| Aug-56 | LINCOLN-40A | DARNALL-41A | BOSTON-40F | DARNALL-41A | BOSTON-40F | 6/56: LINC-40A | COLWICK-38A | COLWICK-38A | COLWICK-38A |
| Jan-57 | LINCOLN-40A | DARNALL-41A | BOSTON-40F | 6/57: COLW-38A | BOSTON-40F | LINCOLN-40A | COLWICK-38A | COLWICK-38A | COLWICK-38A |
| Aug-57 | LINCOLN-40A | DARNALL-41A | BOSTON-40F | COLWICK-38A | BOSTON-40F | LINCOLN-40A | COLWICK-38A | COLWICK-38A | COLWICK-38A |
| Jan-58 | BOSTON-40F | DARNALL-41A | BOSTON-40F | COLWICK-38A | BOSTON-40F | 2/58: BOST-40F | COLWICK-38A | COLWICK-38A | COLWICK-38A |
| Aug-58 | BOSTON-40F | DARNALL-41A | BOSTON-40F | COLWICK-40E | BOSTON-40F | BOSTON-40F | COLWICK-40E | COLWICK-40E | COLWICK-40E |
| Jan-59 | BOSTON-40F | DARNALL-41A | BOSTON-40F | 1/59: W/D | BOSTON-40F | BOSTON-40F | COLWICK-40E | COLWICK-40E | COLWICK-40E |
| Aug-59 | | DARNALL-41A | | | 6/59: W/D | 6/59: W/D | COLWICK-40E | 9/59: W/D | COLWICK-40E |
| Nov-59 | | DARNALL-41A | | | | | 12/59: W/D | | 12/59: W/D |
| Jan-60 | | DARNALL-41A | | | | | | | |
| Apr-60 | | DARNALL-41A | | | | | | | |
| Aug-60 | | DARNALL-41A | | | | | | | |
| Nov-60 | | DARNALL-41A | | | | | | | |

| | 61755 | 61756 | 61757 | 61758 | 61759 | 61760 | 61761 | 61762 | 61763 |
|---|---|---|---|---|---|---|---|---|---|
| Aug-50 | BOSTON - 40F | BOSTON - 40F | SOUTH LYNN - 31D | COLWICK - 38A | STRATFORD - 30A | BOSTON - 40F | STRATFORD - 30A | BOSTON - 40F | COLWICK - 38A |
| Jan-51 | 2/51: EAST - 65A | BOSTON - 40F | SOUTH LYNN - 31D | COLWICK - 38A | STRATFORD - 30A | BOSTON - 40F | STRATFORD - 30A | BOSTON - 40F | COLWICK - 38A |
| Aug-51 | EASTFIELD - 65A | BOSTON - 40F | 9/51: MARCH - 31B | 4/51: EAST - 65A | STRATFORD - 30A | BOSTON - 40F | STRATFORD - 30A | BOSTON - 40F | COLWICK - 38A |
| Jan-52 | 1/52: TH JN - 62A | BOSTON - 40F | MARCH - 31B | 1/52: DUNF - 62C | STRATFORD - 30A | BOSTON - 40F | STRATFORD - 30A | BOSTON - 40F | COLWICK - 38A |
| Aug-52 | THORNTON JCN - 62A | BOSTON - 40F | 7/52: BOST - 40F | DUNFERMLINE - 62C | 10/52: COLW - 38A | BOSTON - 40F | 10/52: LINC - 40A | BOSTON - 40F | COLWICK - 38A |
| Jan-53 | THORNTON JCN - 62A | BOSTON - 40F | BOSTON - 40F | DUNFERMLINE - 62C | COLWICK - 38A | BOSTON - 40F | LINCOLN - 40A | BOSTON - 40F | COLWICK - 38A |
| Aug-53 | THORNTON JCN - 62A | BOSTON - 40F | BOSTON - 40F | DUNFERMLINE - 62C | COLWICK - 38A | BOSTON - 40F | LINCOLN - 40A | BOSTON - 40F | COLWICK - 38A |
| Jan-54 | THORNTON JCN - 62A | BOSTON - 40F | BOSTON - 40F | DUNFERMLINE - 62C | COLWICK - 38A | BOSTON - 40F | LINCOLN - 40A | BOSTON - 40F | COLWICK - 38A |
| Aug-54 | THORNTON JCN - 62A | BOSTON - 40F | BOSTON - 40F | DUNFERMLINE - 62C | COLWICK - 38A | BOSTON - 40F | LINCOLN - 40A | BOSTON - 40F | COLWICK - 38A |
| Jan-55 | THORNTON JCN - 62A | BOSTON - 40F | BOSTON - 40F | DUNFERMLINE - 62C | COLWICK - 38A | BOSTON - 40F | 2/55: BOST - 40F | BOSTON - 40F | COLWICK - 38A |
| Aug-55 | THORNTON JCN - 62A | BOSTON - 40F | BOSTON - 40F | DUNFERMLINE - 62C | 6/55: DARN - 39B | 7/55: DARN - 39B | 7/55: DARN - 39B | BOSTON - 40F | COLWICK - 38A |
| Jan-56 | THORNTON JCN - 62A | BOSTON - 40F | BOSTON - 40F | DUNFERMLINE - 62C | DARNALL - 41A | DARNALL - 41A | DARNALL - 41A | BOSTON - 40F | COLWICK - 38A |
| Aug-56 | THORNTON JCN - 62A | BOSTON - 40F | BOSTON - 40F | DUNFERMLINE - 62C | 6/56: LINC - 40A | DARNALL - 41A | DARNALL - 41A | BOSTON - 40F | COLWICK - 38A |
| Jan-57 | 2/57: KITTY - 61A | BOSTON - 40F | BOSTON - 40F | DUNFERMLINE - 62C | LINCOLN - 40A | DARNALL - 41A | DARNALL - 41A | BOSTON - 40F | COLWICK - 38A |
| Aug-57 | 3/57: KEITH - 61C | BOSTON - 40F | BOSTON - 40F | DUNFERMLINE - 62C | LINCOLN - 40A | DARNALL - 41A | DARNALL - 41A | BOSTON - 40F | COLWICK - 38A |
| Jan-58 | KEITH - 61C | BOSTON - 40F | BOSTON - 40F | DUNFERMLINE - 62C | 12/57: BOST - 40F | DARNALL - 41A | DARNALL - 41A | BOSTON - 40F | COLWICK - 38A |
| Aug-58 | KEITH - 61C | BOSTON - 40F | BOSTON - 40F | DUNFERMLINE - 62C | BOSTON - 40F | DARNALL - 41A | DARNALL - 41A | BOSTON - 40F | COLWICK - 40E |
| Jan-59 | KEITH - 61C | 3/59: IMM - 40B | 2/59: W/D | DUNFERMLINE - 62C | BOSTON - 40F | DARNALL - 41A | DARNALL - 41A | BOSTON - 40F | 3/59: IMM - 40B |
| Aug-59 | KEITH - 61C | IMMINGHAM - 40B | | 6/59: W/D | 4/59: NEW E - 34E | DARNALL - 41A | DARNALL - 41A | 6/59: W/D | IMMINGHAM - 40B |
| Nov-59 | 11/59: W/D | IMMINGHAM - 40B | | | NEW ENGLAND - 34E | DARNALL - 41A | DARNALL - 41A | | 11/59: NEW E - 34E |
| Jan-60 | | IMMINGHAM - 40B | | | 12/59: W/D | DARNALL - 41A | DARNALL - 41A | | NEW ENGLAND - 34E |
| Apr-60 | | IMMINGHAM - 40B | | | | DARNALL - 41A | DARNALL - 41A | | NEW ENGLAND - 34E |
| Aug-60 | | 6/60: COLW - 40E | | | | DARNALL - 41A | DARNALL - 41A | | NEW ENGLAND - 34E |
| Nov-60 | | COLWICK - 40E | | | | DARNALL - 41A | DARNALL - 41A | | NEW ENGLAND - 34E |

| | 61764 | 61765 | 61766 | 61767 | 61768 | 61769 | 61770 | 61771 | 61772 |
|---|---|---|---|---|---|---|---|---|---|
| Aug-50 | EASTFIELD - 65A | STRATFORD - 30A | SOUTH LYNN - 31D | STRATFORD - 30A | COLWICK - 38A | COLWICK - 38A | BOSTON - 40F | COLWICK - 38A | PARKHEAD - 65C |
| Jan-51 | EASTFIELD - 65A | STRATFORD - 30A | SOUTH LYNN - 31D | STRATFORD - 30A | COLWICK - 38A | COLWICK - 38A | 1/51: EAST - 65A | COLWICK - 38A | PARKHEAD - 65C |
| Aug-51 | EASTFIELD - 65A | STRATFORD - 30A | SOUTH LYNN - 31D | STRATFORD - 30A | COLWICK - 38A | 5/51: EAST - 65A | EASTFIELD - 65A | COLWICK - 38A | PARKHEAD - 65C |
| Jan-52 | EASTFIELD - 65A | STRATFORD - 30A | SOUTH LYNN - 31D | STRATFORD - 30A | COLWICK - 38A | 3/52: PARK - 65C | 1/52: TH JN - 62A | COLWICK - 38A | PARKHEAD - 65C |
| Aug-52 | EASTFIELD - 65A | 10/52: LINC - 40A | 7/52: BOST - 40F | LINCOLN - 40A | COLWICK - 38A | PARKHEAD - 65C | 9/52: DUNF - 62C | COLWICK - 38A | PARKHEAD - 65C |
| Jan-53 | EASTFIELD - 65A | LINCOLN - 40A | 2/53: TH JCN - 62A | LINCOLN - 40A | COLWICK - 38A | PARKHEAD - 65C | DUNFERMLINE - 62C | COLWICK - 38A | PARKHEAD - 65C |
| Aug-53 | EASTFIELD - 65A | LINCOLN - 40A | 4/53: BOST - 40F | LINCOLN - 40A | COLWICK - 38A | PARKHEAD - 65C | DUNFERMLINE - 62C | COLWICK - 38A | PARKHEAD - 65C |
| Jan-54 | EASTFIELD - 65A | LINCOLN - 40A | BOSTON - 40F | LINCOLN - 40A | COLWICK - 38A | PARKHEAD - 65C | DUNFERMLINE - 62C | COLWICK - 38A | PARKHEAD - 65C |
| Aug-54 | EASTFIELD - 65A | LINCOLN - 40A | BOSTON - 40F | 6/54: BOST - 40F | COLWICK - 38A | PARKHEAD - 65C | DUNFERMLINE - 62C | COLWICK - 38A | PARKHEAD - 65C |
| Jan-55 | EASTFIELD - 65A | LINCOLN - 40A | BOSTON - 40F | BOSTON - 40F | COLWICK - 38A | PARKHEAD - 65C | DUNFERMLINE - 62C | COLWICK - 38A | PARKHEAD - 65C |
| Aug-55 | EASTFIELD - 65A | 7/55: BOST - 40F | BOSTON - 40F | BOSTON - 40F | COLWICK - 38A | PARKHEAD - 65C | DUNFERMLINE - 62C | COLWICK - 38A | PARKHEAD - 65C |
| Jan-56 | EASTFIELD - 65A | BOSTON - 40F | BOSTON - 40F | BOSTON - 40F | COLWICK - 38A | PARKHEAD - 65C | DUNFERMLINE - 62C | COLWICK - 38A | PARKHEAD - 65C |
| Aug-56 | EASTFIELD - 65A | BOSTON - 40F | BOSTON - 40F | BOSTON - 40F | COLWICK - 38A | PARKHEAD - 65C | DUNFERMLINE - 62C | COLWICK - 38A | PARKHEAD - 65C |
| Jan-57 | EASTFIELD - 65A | BOSTON - 40F | BOSTON - 40F | BOSTON - 40F | COLWICK - 38A | PARKHEAD - 65C | DUNFERMLINE - 62C | COLWICK - 38A | PARKHEAD - 65C |
| Aug-57 | EASTFIELD - 65A | BOSTON - 40F | BOSTON - 40F | BOSTON - 40F | COLWICK - 38A | PARKHEAD - 65C | DUNFERMLINE - 62C | COLWICK - 38A | PARKHEAD - 65C |
| Jan-58 | EASTFIELD - 65A | BOSTON - 40F | BOSTON - 40F | BOSTON - 40F | COLWICK - 38A | PARKHEAD - 65C | DUNFERMLINE - 62C | 3/58: BOST - 40F | PARKHEAD - 65C |
| Aug-58 | EASTFIELD - 65A | 5/58: W/D | BOSTON - 40F | BOSTON - 40F | COLWICK - 40E | PARKHEAD - 65C | DUNFERMLINE - 62C | BOSTON - 40F | PARKHEAD - 65C |
| Jan-59 | EASTFIELD - 65A | | 3/59: IMM - 40B | 3/59: IMM - 40B | 1/59: W/D | PARKHEAD - 65C | DUNFERMLINE - 62C | 3/59: IMM - 40B | PARKHEAD - 65C |
| Aug-59 | EASTFIELD - 65A | | IMMINGHAM - 40B | IMMINGHAM - 40B | | PARKHEAD - 65C | 7/59: W/D | IMMINGHAM - 40B | PARKHEAD - 65C |
| Nov-59 | EASTFIELD - 65A | | IMMINGHAM - 40B | IMMINGHAM - 40B | | PARKHEAD - 65C | | IMMINGHAM - 40B | 12/59: W/D |
| Jan-60 | EASTFIELD - 65A | | IMMINGHAM - 40B | IMMINGHAM - 40B | | PARKHEAD - 65C | | IMMINGHAM - 40B | |
| Apr-60 | EASTFIELD - 65A | | IMMINGHAM - 40B | IMMINGHAM - 40B | | PARKHEAD - 65C | | IMMINGHAM - 40B | |
| Aug-60 | EASTFIELD - 65A | | 6/60: COLW - 40E | 6/60: COLW - 40E | | PARKHEAD - 65C | | 9/60: COLW - 40E | |
| Nov-60 | EASTFIELD - 65A | | COLWICK - 40E | COLWICK - 40E | | 11/60: W/D | | COLWICK - 40E | |

| | 61773 | 61774 | 61775 | 61776 | 61777 | 61778 | 61779 | 61780 | 61781 |
|---|---|---|---|---|---|---|---|---|---|
| Aug-50 | COLWICK - 38A | EASTFIELD - 65A | EASTFIELD - 65A | EASTFIELD - 65A | STRATFORD - 30A | STRATFORD - 30A | EASTFIELD - 65A | STRATFORD - 30A | EASTFIELD - 65A |
| Jan-51 | COLWICK - 38A | EASTFIELD - 65A | EASTFIELD - 65A | EASTFIELD - 65A | STRATFORD - 30A | STRATFORD - 30A | EASTFIELD - 65A | STRATFORD - 30A | EASTFIELD - 65A |
| Aug-51 | COLWICK - 38A | EASTFIELD - 65A | EASTFIELD - 65A | EASTFIELD - 65A | STRATFORD - 30A | STRATFORD - 30A | EASTFIELD - 65A | STRATFORD - 30A | EASTFIELD - 65A |
| Jan-52 | COLWICK - 38A | EASTFIELD - 65A | EASTFIELD - 65A | EASTFIELD - 65A | STRATFORD - 30A | STRATFORD - 30A | EASTFIELD - 65A | STRATFORD - 30A | EASTFIELD - 65A |
| Aug-52 | COLWICK - 38A | EASTFIELD - 65A | EASTFIELD - 65A | EASTFIELD - 65A | 10/52: COILW - 38A | 10/52: LINC - 40A | EASTFIELD - 65A | 10/52: COLW - 38A | EASTFIELD - 65A |
| Jan-53 | COLWICK - 38A | EASTFIELD - 65A | EASTFIELD - 65A | EASTFIELD - 65A | COLWICK - 38A | LINCOLN - 40A | 11/52: KITTY - 61A | COLWICK - 38A | EASTFIELD - 65A |
| Aug-53 | COLWICK - 38A | EASTFIELD - 65A | EASTFIELD - 65A | EASTFIELD - 65A | COLWICK - 38A | LINCOLN - 40A | KITTYBREWSTER - 61A | COLWICK - 38A | EASTFIELD - 65A |
| Jan-54 | COLWICK - 38A | EASTFIELD - 65A | EASTFIELD - 65A | EASTFIELD - 65A | COLWICK - 38A | LINCOLN - 40A | KITTYBREWSTER - 61A | COLWICK - 38A | EASTFIELD - 65A |
| Aug-54 | COLWICK - 38A | EASTFIELD - 65A | EASTFIELD - 65A | EASTFIELD - 65A | COLWICK - 38A | LINCOLN - 40A | 7/54: KEITH - 61C | COLWICK - 38A | EASTFIELD - 65A |
| Jan-55 | COLWICK - 38A | EASTFIELD - 65A | EASTFIELD - 65A | EASTFIELD - 65A | COLWICK - 38A | 3/55: BOST - 40F | KEITH - 61C | COLWICK - 38A | EASTFIELD - 65A |
| Aug-55 | COLWICK - 38A | EASTFIELD - 65A | EASTFIELD - 65A | EASTFIELD - 65A | COLWICK - 38A | 4/55: LINC - 40A | KEITH - 61C | COLWICK - 38A | EASTFIELD - 65A |
| Jan-56 | COLWICK - 38A | EASTFIELD - 65A | EASTFIELD - 65A | EASTFIELD - 65A | COLWICK - 38A | LINCOLN - 40A | KEITH - 61C | COLWICK - 38A | EASTFIELD - 65A |
| Aug-56 | COLWICK - 38A | EASTFIELD - 65A | EASTFIELD - 65A | EASTFIELD - 65A | COLWICK - 38A | LINCOLN - 40A | KEITH - 61C | COLWICK - 38A | EASTFIELD - 65A |
| Jan-57 | COLWICK - 38A | EASTFIELD - 65A | EASTFIELD - 65A | EASTFIELD - 65A | COLWICK - 38A | LINCOLN - 40A | KEITH - 61C | COLWICK - 38A | EASTFIELD - 65A |
| Aug-57 | COLWICK - 38A | EASTFIELD - 65A | EASTFIELD - 65A | EASTFIELD - 65A | 8/57: NEW E - 35A | 6/57: IMM - 40B | KEITH - 61C | COLWICK - 38A | EASTFIELD - 65A |
| Jan-58 | COLWICK - 38A | EASTFIELD - 65A | EASTFIELD - 65A | EASTFIELD - 65A | NEW ENGLAND - 35A | IMMINGHAM - 40B | KEITH - 61C | COLWICK - 38A | EASTFIELD - 65A |
| Aug-58 | COLWICK - 40E | 4/58: W/D | 5/58: W/D | EASTFIELD - 65A | NEW ENGLAND - 34E | IMMINGHAM - 40B | KEITH - 61C | COLWICK - 40E | EASTFIELD - 65A |
| Jan-59 | 11/58: BOST - 40F | | | 3/59: W/D | NEW ENGLAND - 34E | IMMINGHAM - 40B | KEITH - 61C | COLWICK - 40E | 12/58: W/D |
| Aug-59 | 3/59: IMM - 40B | | | | 5/59: W/D | IMMINGHAM - 40B | KEITH - 61C | COLWICK - 40E | |
| Nov-59 | IMMINGHAM - 40B | | | | | 10/59: W/D | KEITH - 61C | 10/59: W/D | |
| Jan-60 | IMMINGHAM - 40B | | | | | | KEITH - 61C | | |
| Apr-60 | IMMINGHAM - 40B | | | | | | KEITH - 61C | | |
| Aug-60 | 9/60: COLW - 40E | | | | | | 6/60: W/D | | |
| Nov-60 | COLWICK - 40E | | | | | | | | |

| | 61782 | 61783 | 61784 | 61785 | 61786 | 61787 | 61788 | 61789 | 61790 |
|---|---|---|---|---|---|---|---|---|---|
| Aug-50 | FORT WILLIAM - 63D | FORT WILLIAM - 63D | EASTFIELD - 65A | EASTFIELD - 65A | EASTFIELD - 65A | FORT WILLIAM - 63D | FORT WILLIAM - 63D | FORT WILLIAM - 63D | FORT WILLIAM - 63D |
| Jan-51 | FORT WILLIAM - 63D | FORT WILLIAM - 63D | EASTFIELD - 65A | EASTFIELD - 65A | EASTFIELD - 65A | FORT WILLIAM - 63D | FORT WILLIAM - 63D | FORT WILLIAM - 63D | FORT WILLIAM - 63D |
| Aug-51 | FORT WILLIAM - 63D | FORT WILLIAM - 63D | EASTFIELD - 65A | EASTFIELD - 65A | EASTFIELD - 65A | FORT WILLIAM - 63D | FORT WILLIAM - 63D | FORT WILLIAM - 63D | FORT WILLIAM - 63D |
| Jan-52 | FORT WILLIAM - 63D | FORT WILLIAM - 63D | EASTFIELD - 65A | EASTFIELD - 65A | EASTFIELD - 65A | FORT WILLIAM - 63D | FORT WILLIAM - 63D | FORT WILLIAM - 63D | FORT WILLIAM - 63D |
| Aug-52 | 6/52: EAST - 65A | FORT WILLIAM - 63D | EASTFIELD - 65A | EASTFIELD - 65A | EASTFIELD - 65A | FORT WILLIAM - 63D | FORT WILLIAM - 63D | 6/52: EAST - 65A | FORT WILLIAM - 63D |
| Jan-53 | 11/52: KITTY - 61A | 5/53: EAST - 65A | EASTFIELD - 65A | EASTFIELD - 65A | EASTFIELD - 65A | FORT WILLIAM - 63D | 5/53: EAST - 65A | EASTFIELD - 65A | 5/53: EAST - 65A |
| Aug-53 | KITTYBREWSTER - 61A | 7/53: FORT W - 63D | EASTFIELD - 65A | EASTFIELD - 65A | EASTFIELD - 65A | FORT WILLIAM - 63D | 7/53: FORT W - 63C | EASTFIELD - 65A | 7/53: FORT W - 63D |
| Jan-54 | KITTYBREWSTER - 61A | FORT WILLIAM - 63D | EASTFIELD - 65A | EASTFIELD - 65A | EASTFIELD - 65A | FORT WILLIAM - 63D | FORT WILLIAM - 63D | EASTFIELD - 65A | FORT WILLIAM - 63D |
| Aug-54 | 7/54: KEITH - 61C | 6/54: KITTY - 61A | EASTFIELD - 65A | EASTFIELD - 65A | EASTFIELD - 65A | FORT WILLIAM - 63D | FORT WILLIAM - 63D | EASTFIELD - 65A | 6/54: KITTY - 61A |
| Jan-55 | KEITH - 61C | KITTYBREWSTER - 61A | EASTFIELD - 65A | EASTFIELD - 65A | EASTFIELD - 65A | FORT WILLIAM - 63D | FORT WILLIAM - 63D | EASTFIELD - 65A | KITTYBREWSTER - 61A |
| Aug-55 | KEITH - 61C | KITTYBREWSTER - 61A | EASTFIELD - 65A | EASTFIELD - 65A | EASTFIELD - 65A | FORT WILLIAM - 63D | FORT WILLIAM - 63D | EASTFIELD - 65A | KITTYBREWSTER - 61A |
| Jan-56 | KEITH - 61C | KITTYBREWSTER - 61A | EASTFIELD - 65A | EASTFIELD - 65A | EASTFIELD - 65A | FORT WILLIAM - 63D | FORT WILLIAM - 63D | EASTFIELD - 65A | KITTYBREWSTER - 61A |
| Aug-56 | KEITH - 61C | 9/56: KEITH - 61C | EASTFIELD - 65A | EASTFIELD - 65A | EASTFIELD - 65A | 5/56: EAST - 65A | 5/56: EAST - 65A | EASTFIELD - 65A | KITTYBREWSTER - 61A |
| Jan-57 | KEITH - 61C | KEITH - 61C | EASTFIELD - 65A | EASTFIELD - 65A | EASTFIELD - 65A | EASTFIELD - 65A | EASTFIELD - 65A | EASTFIELD - 65A | KITTYBREWSTER - 61A |
| Aug-57 | KEITH - 61C | KEITH - 61C | 6/57: FORT W - 63D | EASTFIELD - 65A | EASTFIELD - 65A | EASTFIELD - 65A | EASTFIELD - 65A | EASTFIELD - 65A | KITTYBREWSTER - 61A |
| Jan-58 | KEITH - 61C | KEITH - 61C | FORT WILLIAM - 63D | EASTFIELD - 65A | EASTFIELD - 65A | EASTFIELD - 65A | EASTFIELD - 65A | EASTFIELD - 65A | KITTYBREWSTER - 61A |
| Aug-58 | KEITH - 61C | KEITH - 61C | FORT WILLIAM - 63D | EASTFIELD - 65A | EASTFIELD - 65A | EASTFIELD - 65A | EASTFIELD - 65A | EASTFIELD - 65A | KITTYBREWSTER - 61A |
| Jan-59 | KEITH - 61C | KEITH - 61C | FORT WILLIAM - 63D | EASTFIELD - 65A | EASTFIELD - 65A | EASTFIELD - 65A | EASTFIELD - 65A | EASTFIELD - 65A | KITTYBREWSTER - 61A |
| Aug-59 | KEITH - 61C | 6/59: W/D | FORT WILLIAM - 63D | 4/59: W/D | EASTFIELD - 65A | EASTFIELD - 65A | EASTFIELD - 65A | EASTFIELD - 65A | KITTYBREWSTER - 61A |
| Nov-59 | KEITH - 61C | | FORT WILLIAM - 63D | | 12/59: W/D | 10/59: W/D | EASTFIELD - 65A | 9/59: W/D | 11/59: W/D |
| Jan-60 | KEITH - 61C | | FORT WILLIAM - 63D | | | | EASTFIELD - 65A | | |
| Apr-60 | KEITH - 61C | | FORT WILLIAM - 63B | | | | EASTFIELD - 65A | | |
| Aug-60 | 8/60: W/D | | FORT WILLIAM - 63B | | | | EASTFIELD - 65A | | |
| Nov-60 | | | FORT WILLIAM - 63B | | | | EASTFIELD - 65A | | |

| | 61791 | 61792 | 61793 | 61794 | K3 2-6-0 (1924) 61800 | 61801 | 61802 | 61803 | 61804 |
|---|---|---|---|---|---|---|---|---|---|
| Aug-50 | FORT WILLIAM - 63D | EASTFIELD - 65A | EASTFIELD - 65A | EASTFIELD - 65A | IMMINGHAM - 40B | STRATFORD - 30A | IMMINGHAM - 40B | IMMINGHAM - 40B | NEW ENGLAND - 35A |
| Jan-51 | FORT WILLIAM - 63D | EASTFIELD - 65A | EASTFIELD - 65A | EASTFIELD - 65A | IMMINGHAM - 40B | STRATFORD - 30A | IMMINGHAM - 40B | IMMINGHAM - 40B | NEW ENGLAND - 35A |
| Aug-51 | FORT WILLIAM - 63D | EASTFIELD - 65A | EASTFIELD - 65A | EASTFIELD - 65A | IMMINGHAM - 40B | STRATFORD - 30A | IMMINGHAM - 40B | IMMINGHAM - 40B | NEW ENGLAND - 35A |
| Jan-52 | FORT WILLIAM - 63D | EASTFIELD - 65A | EASTFIELD - 65A | EASTFIELD - 65A | IMMINGHAM - 40B | STRATFORD - 30A | IMMINGHAM - 40B | IMMINGHAM - 40B | NEW ENGLAND - 35A |
| Aug-52 | FORT WILLIAM - 63D | EASTFIELD - 65A | **9/52: KITTY - 61A** | EASTFIELD - 65A | IMMINGHAM - 40B | STRATFORD - 30A | IMMINGHAM - 40B | IMMINGHAM - 40B | NEW ENGLAND - 35A |
| Jan-53 | **5/53: EAST - 65A** | **11/52: KITTY - 61A** | KITTYBREWSTER - 61A | EASTFIELD - 65A | IMMINGHAM - 40B | STRATFORD - 30A | IMMINGHAM - 40B | IMMINGHAM - 40B | NEW ENGLAND - 35A |
| Aug-53 | **7/53: FORT W - 63D** | KITTYBREWSTER - 61A | KITTYBREWSTER - 61A | EASTFIELD - 65A | IMMINGHAM - 40B | STRATFORD - 30A | IMMINGHAM - 40B | IMMINGHAM - 40B | **10/53: MARCH - 31B** |
| Jan-54 | FORT WILLIAM - 63D | KITTYBREWSTER - 61A | KITTYBREWSTER - 61A | EASTFIELD - 65A | IMMINGHAM - 40B | STRATFORD - 30A | IMMINGHAM - 40B | IMMINGHAM - 40B | MARCH - 31B |
| Aug-54 | FORT WILLIAM - 63D | **7/54: KEITH - 61C** | **7/54: KEITH - 61C** | EASTFIELD - 65A | IMMINGHAM - 40B | **6/54: LINC - 40A** | IMMINGHAM - 40B | IMMINGHAM - 40B | MARCH - 31B |
| Jan-55 | FORT WILLIAM - 63D | KEITH - 61C | KEITH - 61C | EASTFIELD - 65A | IMMINGHAM - 40B | **11/54: STRAT - 30A** | IMMINGHAM - 40B | IMMINGHAM - 40B | MARCH - 31B |
| Aug-55 | FORT WILLIAM - 63D | KEITH - 61C | KEITH - 61C | EASTFIELD - 65A | IMMINGHAM - 40B | STRATFORD - 30A | IMMINGHAM - 40B | IMMINGHAM - 40B | MARCH - 31B |
| Jan-56 | FORT WILLIAM - 63D | KEITH - 61C | KEITH - 61C | EASTFIELD - 65A | IMMINGHAM - 40B | STRATFORD - 30A | IMMINGHAM - 40B | IMMINGHAM - 40B | MARCH - 31B |
| Aug-56 | FORT WILLIAM - 63D | KEITH - 61C | KEITH - 61C | EASTFIELD - 65A | IMMINGHAM - 40B | STRATFORD - 30A | **6/56: LINC - 40A** | IMMINGHAM - 40B | **7/56: LINC - 40A** |
| Jan-57 | FORT WILLIAM - 63D | KEITH - 61C | KEITH - 61C | EASTFIELD - 65A | IMMINGHAM - 40B | **2/57: MARCH - 31B** | LINCOLN - 40A | IMMINGHAM - 40B | **2/57: COLW - 38A** |
| Aug-57 | FORT WILLIAM - 63D | KEITH - 61C | KEITH - 61C | EASTFIELD - 65A | IMMINGHAM - 40B | MARCH - 31B | LINCOLN - 40A | IMMINGHAM - 40B | **6/57: WOOD - 38E** |
| Jan-58 | FORT WILLIAM - 63D | KEITH - 61C | KEITH - 61C | EASTFIELD - 65A | IMMINGHAM - 40B | MARCH - 31B | LINCOLN - 40A | IMMINGHAM - 40B | WOODFORD HALSE - 38E |
| Aug-58 | FORT WILLIAM - 63D | KEITH - 61C | KEITH - 61C | EASTFIELD - 65A | IMMINGHAM - 40B | MARCH - 31B | LINCOLN - 40A | IMMINGHAM - 40B | WOODFORD HALSE - 2F |
| Jan-59 | FORT WILLIAM - 63D | KEITH - 61C | **2/59: W/D** | EASTFIELD - 65A | **1/59: DCTR - 36A** | MARCH - 31B | **6/59: LOW - 32C** | **1/59: DCTR - 36A** | WOODFORD HALSE - 2F |
| Aug-59 | FORT WILLIAM - 63D | KEITH - 61C | | EASTFIELD - 65A | DONCASTER - 36A | MARCH - 31B | 8/59: LINC - 40A | DONCASTER - 36A | WOODFORD HALSE - 2F |
| Nov-59 | FORT WILLIAM - 63D | KEITH - 61C | | EASTFIELD - 65A | DONCASTER - 36A | **12/59: CAMB - 31A** | LINCOLN - 40A | DONCASTER - 36A | WOODFORD HALSE - 2F |
| Jan-60 | FORT WILLIAM - 63D | KEITH - 61C | | EASTFIELD - 65A | DONCASTER - 36A | CAMBRIDGE - 31A | LINCOLN - 40A | DONCASTER - 36A | WOODFORD HALSE - 2F |
| Apr-60 | **4/60: W/D** | KEITH - 61C | | EASTFIELD - 65A | DONCASTER - 36A | CAMBRIDGE - 31A | **3/60: W/D** | DONCASTER - 36A | WOODFORD HALSE - 2F |
| Aug-60 | | KEITH - 61C | | **8/60: W/D** | DONCASTER - 36A | CAMBRIDGE - 31A | | DONCASTER - 36A | WOODFORD HALSE - 2F |
| Nov-60 | | **11/60: W/D** | | | DONCASTER - 36A | CAMBRIDGE - 31A | | DONCASTER - 36A | WOODFORD HALSE - 2F |

| | 61805 | 61806 | 61807 | 61808 | 61809 | 61810 | 61811 | 61812 | 61813 |
|---|---|---|---|---|---|---|---|---|---|
| Aug-50 | STRATFORD - 30A | IMMINGHAM - 40B | LINCOLN - 40A | GORTON - 39A | GORTON - 39A | STRATFORD - 30A | NEW ENGLAND - 35A | COLWICK - 38A | DAIRYCOATES - 53A |
| Jan-51 | STRATFORD - 30A | IMMINGHAM - 40B | LINCOLN - 40A | GORTON - 39A | GORTON - 39A | STRATFORD - 30A | NEW ENGLAND - 35A | COLWICK - 38A | DAIRYCOATES - 53A |
| Aug-51 | STRATFORD - 30A | IMMINGHAM - 40B | **12/51: IMM - 40B** | GORTON - 39A | GORTON - 39A | STRATFORD - 30A | NEW ENGLAND - 35A | COLWICK - 38A | DAIRYCOATES - 53A |
| Jan-52 | STRATFORD - 30A | IMMINGHAM - 40B | **3/52: LINC - 40A** | GORTON - 39A | GORTON - 39A | STRATFORD - 30A | NEW ENGLAND - 35A | **3/52: GOR - 39A** | DAIRYCOATES - 53A |
| Aug-52 | STRATFORD - 30A | IMMINGHAM - 40B | LINCOLN - 40A | GORTON - 39A | GORTON - 39A | STRATFORD - 30A | NEW ENGLAND - 35A | GORTON - 39A | DAIRYCOATES - 53A |
| Jan-53 | STRATFORD - 30A | IMMINGHAM - 40B | LINCOLN - 40A | GORTON - 39A | GORTON - 39A | STRATFORD - 30A | NEW ENGLAND - 35A | GORTON - 39A | DAIRYCOATES - 53A |
| Aug-53 | STRATFORD - 30A | IMMINGHAM - 40B | LINCOLN - 40A | GORTON - 39A | GORTON - 39A | STRATFORD - 30A | **10/53: MARCH - 31B** | GORTON - 39A | DAIRYCOATES - 53A |
| Jan-54 | STRATFORD - 30A | IMMINGHAM - 40B | LINCOLN - 40A | GORTON - 39A | GORTON - 39A | STRATFORD - 30A | MARCH - 31B | GORTON - 39A | DAIRYCOATES - 53A |
| Aug-54 | STRATFORD - 30A | IMMINGHAM - 40B | LINCOLN - 40A | GORTON - 39A | **6/54: COLW - 38A** | STRATFORD - 30A | MARCH - 31B | **6/54: LINC - 40A** | DAIRYCOATES - 53A |
| Jan-55 | STRATFORD - 30A | IMMINGHAM - 40B | LINCOLN - 40A | GORTON - 39A | COLWICK - 38A | STRATFORD - 30A | MARCH - 31B | LINCOLN - 40A | DAIRYCOATES - 53A |
| Aug-55 | STRATFORD - 30A | IMMINGHAM - 40B | LINCOLN - 40A | GORTON - 39A | COLWICK - 38A | STRATFORD - 30A | MARCH - 31B | LINCOLN - 40A | DAIRYCOATES - 53A |
| Jan-56 | STRATFORD - 30A | IMMINGHAM - 40B | LINCOLN - 40A | GORTON - 39A | COLWICK - 38A | STRATFORD - 30A | MARCH - 31B | LINCOLN - 40A | DAIRYCOATES - 53A |
| Aug-56 | STRATFORD - 30A | IMMINGHAM - 40B | LINCOLN - 40A | GORTON - 39A | COLWICK - 38A | STRATFORD - 30A | MARCH - 31B | **6/56: NOR - 32A** | DAIRYCOATES - 53A |
| Jan-57 | **2/57: NEW E - 35A** | IMMINGHAM - 40B | LINCOLN - 40A | GORTON - 39A | COLWICK - 38A | STRATFORD - 30A | MARCH - 31B | **2/57: DCTR - 36A** | DAIRYCOATES - 53A |
| Aug-57 | NEW ENGLAND - 35A | IMMINGHAM - 40B | LINCOLN - 40A | **11/57: WOOD - 38E** | COLWICK - 38A | STRATFORD - 30A | MARCH - 31B | DONCASTER - 36A | DAIRYCOATES - 53A |
| Jan-58 | NEW ENGLAND - 35A | IMMINGHAM - 40B | LINCOLN - 40A | **12/57: COLW - 40E** | **1/58: WOOD - 2G** | STRATFORD - 30A | MARCH - 31B | DONCASTER - 36A | DAIRYCOATES - 53A |
| Aug-58 | NEW ENGLAND - 34E | IMMINGHAM - 40B | LINCOLN - 40A | COLWICK - 40E | WOODFORD HALSE - 2F | STRATFORD - 30A | MARCH - 31B | DONCASTER - 36A | DAIRYCOATES - 53A |
| Jan-59 | NEW ENGLAND - 34E | **11/58: LINC - 40A** | LINCOLN - 40A | **6/59: MARCH - 31B** | WOODFORD HALSE - 2F | **12/58: MARCH - 31B** | MARCH - 31B | DONCASTER - 36A | DAIRYCOATES - 53A |
| Aug-59 | NEW ENGLAND - 34E | LINCOLN - 40A | LINCOLN - 40A | **8/59: COLW - 40E** | WOODFORD HALSE - 2F | MARCH - 31B | MARCH - 31B | DONCASTER - 36A | DAIRYCOATES - 53A |
| Nov-59 | NEW ENGLAND - 34E | LINCOLN - 40A | LINCOLN - 40A | COLWICK - 40E | WOODFORD HALSE - 2F | MARCH - 31B | MARCH - 31B | DONCASTER - 36A | DAIRYCOATES - 53A |
| Jan-60 | NEW ENGLAND - 34E | LINCOLN - 40A | LINCOLN - 40A | COLWICK - 40E | WOODFORD HALSE - 2F | MARCH - 31B | MARCH - 31B | DONCASTER - 36A | DAIRYCOATES - 53A |
| Apr-60 | NEW ENGLAND - 34E | **3/60: W/D** | LINCOLN - 40A | COLWICK - 40E | WOODFORD HALSE - 2F | MARCH - 31B | **5/60: STAVE - 41H** | DONCASTER - 36A | DAIRYCOATES - 50B |
| Aug-60 | NEW ENGLAND - 34E | | LINCOLN - 40A | COLWICK - 40E | WOODFORD HALSE - 2F | MARCH - 31B | STAVELEY - 41H | DONCASTER - 36A | DAIRYCOATES - 50B |
| Nov-60 | NEW ENGLAND - 34E | | LINCOLN - 40A | COLWICK - 40E | WOODFORD HALSE - 2F | MARCH - 31B | STAVELEY - 41H | DONCASTER - 36A | DAIRYCOATES - 50B |

| | 61814 | 61815 | 61816 | 61817 | 61818 | 61819 | 61820 | 61821 | 61822 |
|---|---|---|---|---|---|---|---|---|---|
| Aug-50 | DAIRYCOATES - 53A | STRATFORD - 30A | COLWICK - 38A | STRATFORD - 30A | HEATON - 52B | DAIRYCOATES - 53A | STRATFORD - 30A | COLWICK - 38A | LINCOLN - 40A |
| Jan-51 | DAIRYCOATES - 53A | STRATFORD - 30A | COLWICK - 38A | STRATFORD - 30A | HEATON - 52B | DAIRYCOATES - 53A | STRATFORD - 30A | COLWICK - 38A | **10/50: COLW - 38A** |
| Aug-51 | DAIRYCOATES - 53A | STRATFORD - 30A | COLWICK - 38A | STRATFORD - 30A | HEATON - 52B | DAIRYCOATES - 53A | STRATFORD - 30A | COLWICK - 38A | COLWICK - 38A |
| Jan-52 | DAIRYCOATES - 53A | STRATFORD - 30A | COLWICK - 38A | STRATFORD - 30A | HEATON - 52B | DAIRYCOATES - 53A | STRATFORD - 30A | COLWICK - 38A | COLWICK - 38A |
| Aug-52 | DAIRYCOATES - 53A | STRATFORD - 30A | COLWICK - 38A | STRATFORD - 30A | HEATON - 52B | DAIRYCOATES - 53A | STRATFORD - 30A | COLWICK - 38A | COLWICK - 38A |
| Jan-53 | DAIRYCOATES - 53A | STRATFORD - 30A | COLWICK - 38A | STRATFORD - 30A | HEATON - 52B | DAIRYCOATES - 53A | STRATFORD - 30A | COLWICK - 38A | COLWICK - 38A |
| Aug-53 | DAIRYCOATES - 53A | STRATFORD - 30A | **10/53: MARCH - 31B** | STRATFORD - 30A | HEATON - 52B | DAIRYCOATES - 53A | STRATFORD - 30A | COLWICK - 38A | COLWICK - 38A |
| Jan-54 | DAIRYCOATES - 53A | STRATFORD - 30A | MARCH - 31B | STRATFORD - 30A | HEATON - 52B | DAIRYCOATES - 53A | STRATFORD - 30A | COLWICK - 38A | **11/53: MARCH - 31B** |
| Aug-54 | DAIRYCOATES - 53A | **6/54: LINC - 40A** | MARCH - 31B | STRATFORD - 30A | HEATON - 52B | DAIRYCOATES - 53A | STRATFORD - 30A | COLWICK - 38A | MARCH - 31B |
| Jan-55 | DAIRYCOATES - 53A | **10/54: STRAT - 30A** | MARCH - 31B | STRATFORD - 30A | HEATON - 52B | DAIRYCOATES - 53A | STRATFORD - 30A | COLWICK - 38A | MARCH - 31B |
| Aug-55 | DAIRYCOATES - 53A | STRATFORD - 30A | MARCH - 31B | STRATFORD - 30A | HEATON - 52B | DAIRYCOATES - 53A | STRATFORD - 30A | COLWICK - 38A | MARCH - 31B |
| Jan-56 | DAIRYCOATES - 53A | STRATFORD - 30A | MARCH - 31B | STRATFORD - 30A | HEATON - 52B | DAIRYCOATES - 53A | STRATFORD - 30A | COLWICK - 38A | MARCH - 31B |
| Aug-56 | DAIRYCOATES - 53A | STRATFORD - 30A | MARCH - 31B | STRATFORD - 30A | HEATON - 52B | DAIRYCOATES - 53A | STRATFORD - 30A | COLWICK - 38A | MARCH - 31B |
| Jan-57 | DAIRYCOATES - 53A | STRATFORD - 30A | MARCH - 31B | STRATFORD - 30A | HEATON - 52B | DAIRYCOATES - 53A | STRATFORD - 30A | COLWICK - 38A | MARCH - 31B |
| Aug-57 | DAIRYCOATES - 53A | STRATFORD - 30A | MARCH - 31B | STRATFORD - 30A | HEATON - 52B | DAIRYCOATES - 53A | STRATFORD - 30A | COLWICK - 38A | MARCH - 31B |
| Jan-58 | DAIRYCOATES - 53A | **3/58: PARK - 30F** | MARCH - 31B | STRATFORD - 30A | HEATON - 52B | DAIRYCOATES - 53A | **3/58: PARK - 30F** | COLWICK - 38A | MARCH - 31B |
| Aug-58 | DAIRYCOATES - 53A | PARKESTON - 30F | MARCH - 31B | STRATFORD - 30A | HEATON - 52B | DAIRYCOATES - 53A | PARKESTON - 30F | COLWICK - 40E | MARCH - 31B |
| Jan-59 | DAIRYCOATES - 53A | PARKESTON - 30F | **3/59: DARN - 41A** | **12/58: CAMB - 31A** | HEATON - 52B | DAIRYCOATES - 53A | PARKESTON - 30F | COLWICK - 40E | MARCH - 31B |
| Aug-59 | DAIRYCOATES - 53A | PARKESTON - 30F | DARNALL - 41A | CAMBRIDGE - 31A | HEATON - 52B | DAIRYCOATES - 53A | PARKESTON - 30F | COLWICK - 40E | MARCH - 31B |
| Nov-59 | DAIRYCOATES - 53A | **10/59: STRAT - 30A** | DARNALL - 41A | CAMBRIDGE - 31A | HEATON - 52B | DAIRYCOATES - 53A | **10/59: STRAT - 30A** | COLWICK - 40E | MARCH - 31B |
| Jan-60 | DAIRYCOATES - 53A | STRATFORD - 30A | DARNALL - 41A | CAMBRIDGE - 31A | HEATON - 52B | DAIRYCOATES - 53A | STRATFORD - 30A | COLWICK - 40E | MARCH - 31B |
| Apr-60 | DAIRYCOATES - 50B | STRATFORD - 30A | DARNALL - 41A | CAMBRIDGE - 31A | HEATON - 52B | DAIRYCOATES - 50B | **4/60: STAVE - 41H** | COLWICK - 40E | **4.60: STAVE - 41H** |
| Aug-60 | DAIRYCOATES - 50B | **6/60: W/D** | DARNALL - 41A | CAMBRIDGE - 31A | HEATON - 52B | DAIRYCOATES - 50B | **6/60: MEX - 41F** | COLWICK - 40E | **6/60: MEX - 41F** |
| Nov-60 | DAIRYCOATES - 50B | | DARNALL - 41A | CAMBRIDGE - 31A | HEATON - 52B | DAIRYCOATES - 50B | MEXBOROUGH - 41F | COLWICK - 40E | MEXBOROUGH - 41F |

| | 61823 | 61824 | 61825 | 61826 | 61827 | 61828 | 61829 | 61830 | 61831 |
|---|---|---|---|---|---|---|---|---|---|
| Aug-50 | EDINBURGH (SM) - 64A | COLWICK - 38A | IMMINGHAM - 40B | COLWICK - 38A | IMMINGHAM - 40B | GORTON - 39A | GORTON - 39A | STRATFORD - 30A | STRATFORD - 30A |
| Jan-51 | EDINBURGH (SM) - 64A | COLWICK - 38A | IMMINGHAM - 40B | COLWICK - 38A | IMMINGHAM - 40B | GORTON - 39A | GORTON - 39A | STRATFORD - 30A | STRATFORD - 30A |
| Aug-51 | EDINBURGH (SM) - 64A | COLWICK - 38A | IMMINGHAM - 40B | COLWICK - 38A | IMMINGHAM - 40B | GORTON - 39A | GORTON - 39A | STRATFORD - 30A | STRATFORD - 30A |
| Jan-52 | EDINBURGH (SM) - 64A | COLWICK - 38A | IMMINGHAM - 40B | COLWICK - 38A | IMMINGHAM - 40B | GORTON - 39A | GORTON - 39A | STRATFORD - 30A | STRATFORD - 30A |
| Aug-52 | EDINBURGH (SM) - 64A | COLWICK - 38A | IMMINGHAM - 40B | COLWICK - 38A | IMMINGHAM - 40B | GORTON - 39A | GORTON - 39A | STRATFORD - 30A | STRATFORD - 30A |
| Jan-53 | EDINBURGH (SM) - 64A | COLWICK - 38A | IMMINGHAM - 40B | COLWICK - 38A | IMMINGHAM - 40B | GORTON - 39A | GORTON - 39A | STRATFORD - 30A | STRATFORD - 30A |
| Aug-53 | EDINBURGH (SM) - 64A | **11/53: MARCH - 31B** | IMMINGHAM - 40B | **10/53: MARCH - 31B** | **11/53: MARCH - 31B** | GORTON - 39A | GORTON - 39A | STRATFORD - 30A | STRATFORD - 30A |
| Jan-54 | EDINBURGH (SM) - 64A | **1/54: COLW - 38A** | IMMINGHAM - 40B | MARCH - 31B | MARCH - 31B | GORTON - 39A | GORTON - 39A | STRATFORD - 30A | STRATFORD - 30A |
| Aug-54 | EDINBURGH (SM) - 64A | COLWICK - 38A | IMMINGHAM - 40B | MARCH - 31B | MARCH - 31B | **6/54: MARCH - 31B** | **6/54: DARN - 39B** | STRATFORD - 30A | STRATFORD - 30A |
| Jan-55 | EDINBURGH (SM) - 64A | COLWICK - 38A | IMMINGHAM - 40B | MARCH - 31B | MARCH - 31B | LINCOLN - 40A | **11/54: LINC - 40A** | STRATFORD - 30A | STRATFORD - 30A |
| Aug-55 | EDINBURGH (SM) - 64A | COLWICK - 38A | IMMINGHAM - 40B | MARCH - 31B | MARCH - 31B | LINCOLN - 40A | LINCOLN - 40A | STRATFORD - 30A | STRATFORD - 30A |
| Jan-56 | EDINBURGH (SM) - 64A | COLWICK - 38A | IMMINGHAM - 40B | MARCH - 31B | MARCH - 31B | LINCOLN - 40A | LINCOLN - 40A | STRATFORD - 30A | STRATFORD - 30A |
| Aug-56 | EDINBURGH (SM) - 64A | COLWICK - 38A | IMMINGHAM - 40B | MARCH - 31B | MARCH - 31B | LINCOLN - 40A | **6/56: NOR - 32A** | STRATFORD - 30A | STRATFORD - 30A |
| Jan-57 | EDINBURGH (SM) - 64A | COLWICK - 38A | IMMINGHAM - 40B | MARCH - 31B | MARCH - 31B | LINCOLN - 40A | **2/57: DCTR - 36A** | **2/57: NEW E - 35A** | **2/57: MARCH - 31B** |
| Aug-57 | EDINBURGH (SM) - 64A | COLWICK - 38A | IMMINGHAM - 40B | MARCH - 31B | MARCH - 31B | LINCOLN - 40A | DONCASTER - 36A | NEW ENGLAND - 35A | MARCH - 31B |
| Jan-58 | EDINBURGH (SM) - 64A | **1/58: WOOD - 2G** | **11/57: DARN - 41A** | MARCH - 31B | MARCH - 31B | LINCOLN - 40A | DONCASTER - 36A | NEW ENGLAND - 35A | MARCH - 31B |
| Aug-58 | EDINBURGH (SM) - 64A | WOODFORD HALSE - 2F | DARNALL - 41A | **6/58: NOR - 32A** | MARCH - 31B | LINCOLN - 40A | DONCASTER - 36A | NEW ENGLAND - 34E | MARCH - 31B |
| Jan-59 | EDINBURGH (SM) - 64A | WOODFORD HALSE - 2F | DARNALL - 41A | NORWICH - 32A | MARCH - 31B | LINCOLN - 40A | DONCASTER - 36A | NEW ENGLAND - 34E | MARCH - 31B |
| Aug-59 | EDINBURGH (SM) - 64A | WOODFORD HALSE - 2F | DARNALL - 41A | NORWICH - 32A | MARCH - 31B | LINCOLN - 40A | DONCASTER - 36A | NEW ENGLAND - 34E | MARCH - 31B |
| Nov-59 | EDINBURGH (SM) - 64A | WOODFORD HALSE - 2F | DARNALL - 41A | NORWICH - 32A | MARCH - 31B | LINCOLN - 40A | DONCASTER - 36A | NEW ENGLAND - 34E | MARCH - 31B |
| Jan-60 | **2/60: W/D** | WOODFORD HALSE - 2F | DARNALL - 41A | **2/60: STAVE - 41H** | MARCH - 31B | LINCOLN - 40A | DONCASTER - 36A | NEW ENGLAND - 34E | MARCH - 31B |
| Apr-60 | | WOODFORD HALSE - 2F | DARNALL - 41A | STAVELEY - 41H | MARCH - 31B | LINCOLN - 40A | DONCASTER - 36A | NEW ENGLAND - 34E | MARCH - 31B |
| Aug-60 | | WOODFORD HALSE - 2F | DARNALL - 41A | STAVELEY - 41H | MARCH - 31B | LINCOLN - 40A | DONCASTER - 36A | NEW ENGLAND - 34E | MARCH - 31B |
| Nov-60 | | WOODFORD HALSE - 2F | DARNALL - 41A | STAVELEY - 41H | MARCH - 31B | LINCOLN - 40A | DONCASTER - 36A | NEW ENGLAND - 34E | MARCH - 31B |

The K3 'Jazzers' had a high tractive effort and in theory had an edge over the B1 4-6-0's for express goods services where haulage mattered more than speed. Inclined to be rough at speed they were concentrated at sheds with a preponderance of goods traffic but relatively little express passenger traffic such as Hull Dairycoates which had one of the largest allocations of the class. Having deputised for a B1, Dairycoates K3 61857 backs out of Sheffield Victoria to Darnall shed after having handed over the 09.35 Hull - Liverpool to an EM2 electric in 1960.

The curse of motive power operations were undiagrammed special trains because one could never be sure when (or if) the engine would be returned. March MPD was especially plagued with such workings when in the autumn dozens of long distance sugar beet specials operated, most of them without proper engine diagrams. The Ely - Alscot (Shrewsbury) service presented especial problems since crew would be relieved at Colwick, Burton and Crewe without anyone wishing to change the engine en route. There were no return workings and thus K1 62032 of March finds itself languishing, unbalanced, at Crewe South with no obvious means of getting back to the Great Eastern. Meanwhile March loco was an engine short for its workings.

| | 61832 | 61833 | 61834 | 61835 | 61836 | 61837 | 61838 | 61839 | 61840 |
|---|---|---|---|---|---|---|---|---|---|
| Aug-50 | GORTON - 39A | COLWICK - 38A | STRATFORD - 30A | STRATFORD - 30A | IMMINGHAM - 40B | IMMINGHAM - 40B | IMMINGHAM - 40B | GORTON - 39A | STRATFORD - 30A |
| Jan-51 | GORTON - 39A | COLWICK - 38A | STRATFORD - 30A | STRATFORD - 30A | IMMINGHAM - 40B | IMMINGHAM - 40B | IMMINGHAM - 40B | GORTON - 39A | STRATFORD - 30A |
| Aug-51 | GORTON - 39A | COLWICK - 38A | STRATFORD - 30A | STRATFORD - 30A | IMMINGHAM - 40B | IMMINGHAM - 40B | IMMINGHAM - 40B | **5/51: IMM - 40B** | STRATFORD - 30A |
| Jan-52 | GORTON - 39A | COLWICK - 38A | STRATFORD - 30A | STRATFORD - 30A | IMMINGHAM - 40B | IMMINGHAM - 40B | IMMINGHAM - 40B | IMMINGHAM - 40B | STRATFORD - 30A |
| Aug-52 | GORTON - 39A | COLWICK - 38A | STRATFORD - 30A | STRATFORD - 30A | IMMINGHAM - 40B | IMMINGHAM - 40B | IMMINGHAM - 40B | IMMINGHAM - 40B | STRATFORD - 30A |
| Jan-53 | GORTON - 39A | COLWICK - 38A | STRATFORD - 30A | STRATFORD - 30A | IMMINGHAM - 40B | IMMINGHAM - 40B | IMMINGHAM - 40B | IMMINGHAM - 40B | STRATFORD - 30A |
| Aug-53 | GORTON - 39A | COLWICK - 38A | STRATFORD - 30A | STRATFORD - 30A | IMMINGHAM - 40B | IMMINGHAM - 40B | IMMINGHAM - 40B | IMMINGHAM - 40B | STRATFORD - 30A |
| Jan-54 | GORTON - 39A | COLWICK - 38A | STRATFORD - 30A | **11/53: MARCH - 31B** | IMMINGHAM - 40B | IMMINGHAM - 40B | IMMINGHAM - 40B | IMMINGHAM - 40B | STRATFORD - 30A |
| Aug-54 | GORTON - 39A | COLWICK - 38A | STRATFORD - 30A | MARCH - 31B | IMMINGHAM - 40B | IMMINGHAM - 40B | IMMINGHAM - 40B | IMMINGHAM - 40B | STRATFORD - 30A |
| Jan-55 | GORTON - 39A | COLWICK - 38A | STRATFORD - 30A | MARCH - 31B | IMMINGHAM - 40B | IMMINGHAM - 40B | IMMINGHAM - 40B | IMMINGHAM - 40B | STRATFORD - 30A |
| Aug-55 | GORTON - 39A | COLWICK - 38A | STRATFORD - 30A | MARCH - 31B | IMMINGHAM - 40B | IMMINGHAM - 40B | IMMINGHAM - 40B | IMMINGHAM - 40B | STRATFORD - 30A |
| Jan-56 | GORTON - 39A | COLWICK - 38A | STRATFORD - 30A | MARCH - 31B | IMMINGHAM - 40B | IMMINGHAM - 40B | IMMINGHAM - 40B | IMMINGHAM - 40B | STRATFORD - 30A |
| Aug-56 | GORTON - 39A | COLWICK - 38A | STRATFORD - 30A | MARCH - 31B | IMMINGHAM - 40B | IMMINGHAM - 40B | IMMINGHAM - 40B | IMMINGHAM - 40B | STRATFORD - 30A |
| Jan-57 | GORTON - 39A | COLWICK - 38A | STRATFORD - 30A | MARCH - 31B | IMMINGHAM - 40B | IMMINGHAM - 40B | **2/57: COLW - 38A** | IMMINGHAM - 40B | STRATFORD - 30A |
| Aug-57 | GORTON - 39A | COLWICK - 38A | STRATFORD - 30A | MARCH - 31B | IMMINGHAM - 40B | IMMINGHAM - 40B | **6/57: WOOD - 38E** | IMMINGHAM - 40B | STRATFORD - 30A |
| Jan-58 | GORTON - 39A | COLWICK - 38A | **3/58: PARK - 30F** | MARCH - 31B | IMMINGHAM - 40B | 1/58: COLW - 40E | WOODFORD HALSE - 38E | IMMINGHAM - 40B | STRATFORD - 30A |
| Aug-58 | GORTON - 9G | COLWICK - 40E | **8/58: CAMB - 31A** | MARCH - 31B | IMMINGHAM - 40B | COLWICK - 40E | WOODFORD HALSE - 2F | IMMINGHAM - 40B | **12/58: PARK - 30F** |
| Jan-59 | GORTON - 9G | COLWICK - 40E | CAMBRIDGE - 31A | MARCH - 31B | **1/59: MEX - 41F** | COLWICK - 40E | WOODFORD HALSE - 2F | **1/59: MEX - 41F** | **1/59: MARCH - 31B** |
| Aug-59 | **6/59: WOOD - 2F** | COLWICK - 40E | CAMBRIDGE - 31A | MARCH - 31B | **6/59: DCTR - 36A** | COLWICK - 40E | WOODFORD HALSE - 2F | **6/59: DCTR - 36A** | MARCH - 31B |
| Nov-59 | WOODFORD HALSE - 2F | COLWICK - 40E | CAMBRIDGE - 31A | MARCH - 31B | DONCASTER - 36A | COLWICK - 40E | WOODFORD HALSE - 2F | DONCASTER - 36A | MARCH - 31B |
| Jan-60 | WOODFORD HALSE - 2F | COLWICK - 40E | CAMBRIDGE - 31A | MARCH - 31B | DONCASTER - 36A | COLWICK - 40E | WOODFORD HALSE - 2F | DONCASTER - 36A | MARCH - 31B |
| Apr-60 | WOODFORD HALSE - 2F | COLWICK - 40E | CAMBRIDGE - 31A | MARCH - 31B | **2/60: W/D** | COLWICK - 40E | **3/60: W/D** | DONCASTER - 36A | MARCH - 31B |
| Aug-60 | WOODFORD HALSE - 2F | COLWICK - 40E | CAMBRIDGE - 31A | MARCH - 31B | | COLWICK - 40E | | DONCASTER - 36A | MARCH - 31B |
| Nov-60 | WOODFORD HALSE - 2F | COLWICK - 40E | CAMBRIDGE - 31A | MARCH - 31B | | COLWICK - 40E | | DONCASTER - 36A | MARCH - 31B |

| | 61841 | 61842 | 61843 | 61844 | 61845 | 61846 | 61847 | 61848 | 61849 |
|---|---|---|---|---|---|---|---|---|---|
| Aug-50 | NEW ENGLAND - 35A | IMMINGHAM - 40B | NEW ENGLAND - 35A | MARCH - 31B | IMMINGHAM - 40B | MARCH - 31B | MARCH - 31B | GORTON - 39A | STRATFORD - 30A |
| Jan-51 | NEW ENGLAND - 35A | IMMINGHAM - 40B | NEW ENGLAND - 35A | **10/50: LOW - 32C** | IMMINGHAM - 40B | MARCH - 31B | MARCH - 31B | GORTON - 39A | STRATFORD - 30A |
| Aug-51 | NEW ENGLAND - 35A | IMMINGHAM - 40B | NEW ENGLAND - 35A | **12/50: MARCH - 31B** | IMMINGHAM - 40B | **9/51: DAIRY - 53A** | **9/51: DAIRY - 53A** | GORTON - 39A | STRATFORD - 30A |
| Jan-52 | NEW ENGLAND - 35A | IMMINGHAM - 40B | NEW ENGLAND - 35A | **9/51: DAIRY - 53A** | IMMINGHAM - 40B | DAIRYCOATES - 53A | DAIRYCOATES - 53A | GORTON - 39A | STRATFORD - 30A |
| Aug-52 | NEW ENGLAND - 35A | IMMINGHAM - 40B | NEW ENGLAND - 35A | DAIRYCOATES - 53A | IMMINGHAM - 40B | DAIRYCOATES - 53A | DAIRYCOATES - 53A | GORTON - 39A | STRATFORD - 30A |
| Jan-53 | NEW ENGLAND - 35A | IMMINGHAM - 40B | NEW ENGLAND - 35A | DAIRYCOATES - 53A | IMMINGHAM - 40B | DAIRYCOATES - 53A | DAIRYCOATES - 53A | GORTON - 39A | STRATFORD - 30A |
| Aug-53 | **10/53: MARCH - 31B** | IMMINGHAM - 40B | NEW ENGLAND - 35A | DAIRYCOATES - 53A | **5/53: LINC - 40A** | DAIRYCOATES - 53A | DAIRYCOATES - 53A | GORTON - 39A | STRATFORD - 30A |
| Jan-54 | MARCH - 31B | **11/53: MARCH - 31B** | **10/53: MARCH - 31B** | DAIRYCOATES - 53A | **11/53: MARCH - 31B** | DAIRYCOATES - 53A | DAIRYCOATES - 53A | GORTON - 39A | STRATFORD - 30A |
| Aug-54 | MARCH - 31B | MARCH - 31B | MARCH - 31B | DAIRYCOATES - 53A | MARCH - 31B | DAIRYCOATES - 53A | DAIRYCOATES - 53A | **6/54: DARN - 39B** | STRATFORD - 30A |
| Jan-55 | MARCH - 31B | MARCH - 31B | MARCH - 31B | DAIRYCOATES - 53A | MARCH - 31B | DAIRYCOATES - 53A | DAIRYCOATES - 53A | **10/54: LINC - 40A** | STRATFORD - 30A |
| Aug-55 | MARCH - 31B | MARCH - 31B | MARCH - 31B | DAIRYCOATES - 53A | MARCH - 31B | DAIRYCOATES - 53A | DAIRYCOATES - 53A | LINCOLN - 40A | STRATFORD - 30A |
| Jan-56 | MARCH - 31B | MARCH - 31B | MARCH - 31B | DAIRYCOATES - 53A | MARCH - 31B | DAIRYCOATES - 53A | DAIRYCOATES - 53A | LINCOLN - 40A | STRATFORD - 30A |
| Aug-56 | **10/56: WOOD - 38E** | **10/56: WOOD - 38E** | **10/56: WOD - 38E** | **10/56: HTN - 52B** | MARCH - 31B | DAIRYCOATES - 53A | DAIRYCOATES - 53A | LINCOLN - 40A | STRATFORD - 30A |
| Jan-57 | WOODFORD HALSE - 38E | WOODFORD HALSE - 38E | WOODFORD HALSE - 38E | HEATON - 52B | MARCH - 31B | DAIRYCOATES - 53A | DAIRYCOATES - 53A | LINCOLN - 40A | STRATFORD - 30A |
| Aug-57 | WOODFORD HALSE - 38E | WOODFORD HALSE - 38E | WOODFORD HALSE - 38E | HEATON - 52B | MARCH - 31B | DAIRYCOATES - 53A | DAIRYCOATES - 53A | LINCOLN - 40A | STRATFORD - 30A |
| Jan-58 | WOODFORD HALSE - 38E | WOODFORD HALSE - 38E | WOODFORD HALSE - 38E | HEATON - 52B | MARCH - 31B | DAIRYCOATES - 53A | DAIRYCOATES - 53A | LINCOLN - 40A | STRATFORD - 30A |
| Aug-58 | WOODFORD HALSE - 2F | WOODFORD HALSE - 2F | WOODFORD HALSE - 2F | HEATON - 52B | MARCH - 31B | DAIRYCOATES - 53A | DAIRYCOATES - 53A | LINCOLN - 40A | STRATFORD - 30A |
| Jan-59 | WOODFORD HALSE - 2F | WOODFORD HALSE - 2F | WOODFORD HALSE - 2F | HEATON - 52B | MARCH - 31B | DAIRYCOATES - 53A | DAIRYCOATES - 53A | LINCOLN - 40A | **12/58: PARK - 30F** |
| Aug-59 | WOODFORD HALSE - 2F | WOODFORD HALSE - 2F | WOODFORD HALSE - 2F | HEATON - 52B | **8/59: MARCH - 31B** | DAIRYCOATES - 53A | DAIRYCOATES - 53A | LINCOLN - 40A | **3/59: CAMB - 31A** |
| Nov-59 | WOODFORD HALSE - 2F | WOODFORD HALSE - 2F | WOODFORD HALSE - 2F | HEATON - 52B | MARCH - 31B | DAIRYCOATES - 53A | DAIRYCOATES - 53A | LINCOLN - 40A | CAMBRIDGE - 31A |
| Jan-60 | WOODFORD HALSE - 2F | WOODFORD HALSE - 2F | WOODFORD HALSE - 2F | HEATON - 52B | MARCH - 31B | DAIRYCOATES - 53A | DAIRYCOATES - 53A | LINCOLN - 40A | CAMBRIDGE - 31A |
| Apr-60 | WOODFORD HALSE - 2F | WOODFORD HALSE - 2F | WOODFORD HALSE - 2F | HEATON - 52B | MARCH - 31B | DAIRYCOATES - 50B | DAIRYCOATES - 50B | LINCOLN - 40A | CAMBRIDGE - 31A |
| Aug-60 | WOODFORD HALSE - 2F | WOODFORD HALSE - 2F | WOODFORD HALSE - 2F | **9/60: TWEED - 52D** | MARCH - 31B | DAIRYCOATES - 50B | DAIRYCOATES - 50B | LINCOLN - 40A | CAMBRIDGE - 31A |
| Nov-60 | WOODFORD HALSE - 2F | WOODFORD HALSE - 2F | WOODFORD HALSE - 2F | TWEEDMOUTH - 52D | MARCH - 31B | DAIRYCOATES - 50B | DAIRYCOATES - 50B | LINCOLN - 40A | CAMBRIDGE - 31A |

| | 61850 | 61851 | 61852 | 61853 | 61854 | 61855 | 61856 | 61857 | 61858 |
|---|---|---|---|---|---|---|---|---|---|
| Aug-50 | NEW ENGLAND - 35A | CARLISLE (C) - 12B | GORTON - 39A | NEW ENGLAND - 35A | CARLISLE (C) - 12B | EDINBURGH (SM) - 64A | GORTON - 39A | EDINBURGH (SM) - 64A | CARLISLE (C) - 12B |
| Jan-51 | NEW ENGLAND - 35A | CARLISLE (C) - 12B | GORTON - 39A | NEW ENGLAND - 35A | CARLISLE (C) - 12B | EDINBURGH (SM) - 64A | GORTON - 39A | EDINBURGH (SM) - 64A | CARLISLE (C) - 12B |
| Aug-51 | NEW ENGLAND - 35A | CARLISLE (C) - 68E | GORTON - 39A | NEW ENGLAND - 35A | CARLISLE (C) - 68E | EDINBURGH (SM) - 64A | GORTON - 39A | EDINBURGH (SM) - 64A | CARLISLE (C) - 68E |
| Jan-52 | NEW ENGLAND - 35A | CARLISLE (C) - 68E | GORTON - 39A | NEW ENGLAND - 35A | CARLISLE (C) - 68E | EDINBURGH (SM) - 64A | GORTON - 39A | EDINBURGH (SM) - 64A | CARLISLE (C) - 68E |
| Aug-52 | NEW ENGLAND - 35A | CARLISLE (C) - 68E | GORTON - 39A | NEW ENGLAND - 35A | CARLISLE (C) - 68E | EDINBURGH (SM) - 64A | GORTON - 39A | EDINBURGH (SM) - 64A | CARLISLE (C) - 68E |
| Jan-53 | NEW ENGLAND - 35A | CARLISLE (C) - 68E | GORTON - 39A | NEW ENGLAND - 35A | CARLISLE (C) - 68E | EDINBURGH (SM) - 64A | GORTON - 39A | EDINBURGH (SM) - 64A | CARLISLE (C) - 68E |
| Aug-53 | NEW ENGLAND - 35A | CARLISLE (C) - 68E | GORTON - 39A | **10/53: MARCH - 31B** | CARLISLE (C) - 68E | EDINBURGH (SM) - 64A | GORTON - 39A | EDINBURGH (SM) - 64A | CARLISLE (C) - 68E |
| Jan-54 | **10/53: MARCH - 31B** | CARLISLE (C) - 68E | GORTON - 39A | MARCH - 31B | CARLISLE (C) - 68E | EDINBURGH (SM) - 64A | GORTON - 39A | EDINBURGH (SM) - 64A | CARLISLE (C) - 68E |
| Aug-54 | MARCH - 31B | CARLISLE (C) - 68E | **6/54: INC - 40A** | MARCH - 31B | CARLISLE (C) - 68E | EDINBURGH (SM) - 64A | **6/54: COLW - 38A** | EDINBURGH (SM) - 64A | CARLISLE (C) - 68E |
| Jan-55 | MARCH - 31B | CARLISLE (C) - 68E | LINCOLN - 40A | MARCH - 31B | CARLISLE (C) - 68E | EDINBURGH (SM) - 64A | **1/55: ANN - 38B** | EDINBURGH (SM) - 64A | CARLISLE (C) - 68E |
| Aug-55 | MARCH - 31B | CARLISLE (C) - 68E | **5/55: IMM - 40B** | MARCH - 31B | CARLISLE (C) - 68E | EDINBURGH (SM) - 64A | ANNESLEY - 38B | EDINBURGH (SM) - 64A | CARLISLE (C) - 68E |
| Jan-56 | MARCH - 31B | CARLISLE (C) - 68E | IMMINGHAM - 40B | MARCH - 31B | CARLISLE (C) - 68E | EDINBURGH (SM) - 64A | ANNESLEY - 38B | EDINBURGH (SM) - 64A | CARLISLE (C) - 68E |
| Aug-56 | **10/56: MEX - 36B** | CARLISLE (C) - 68E | IMMINGHAM - 40B | **10/56: WOOD - 38E** | CARLISLE (C) - 68E | EDINBURGH (SM) - 64A | ANNESLEY - 38B | EDINBURGH (SM) - 64A | CARLISLE (C) - 68E |
| Jan-57 | MEXBOROUGH - 36B | CARLISLE (C) - 68E | IMMINGHAM - 40B | WOODFORD HALSE - 38E | **3/57: DAIRY - 53A** | EDINBURGH (SM) - 64A | ANNESLEY - 38B | **3/57: DAIRY - 53A** | CARLISLE (C) - 68E |
| Aug-57 | MEXBOROUGH - 36B | CARLISLE (C) - 68E | IMMINGHAM - 40B | WOODFORD HALSE - 38E | DAIRYCOATES - 53A | EDINBURGH (SM) - 64A | ANNESLEY - 38B | DAIRYCOATES - 53A | CARLISLE (C) - 68E |
| Jan-58 | MEXBOROUGH - 36B | CARLISLE CANAL - 68E | **1/58: COL - 38A** | WOODFORD HALSE - 38E | DAIRYCOATES - 53A | EDINBURGH (SM) - 64A | ANNESLEY - 38B | DAIRYCOATES - 53A | CARLISLE CANAL - 68E |
| Aug-58 | MEXBOROUGH - 41F | CARLISLE CANAL - 12C | COLWICK - 40E | WOODFORD HALSE - 2F | **6/58: TWEED - 52D** | EDINBURGH (SM) - 64A | ANNESLEY - 16D | DAIRYCOATES - 53A | CARLISLE CANAL - 12C |
| Jan-59 | MEXBOROUGH - 41F | CARLISLE CANAL - 12C | COLWICK - 40E | WOODFORD HALSE - 2F | TWEEDMOUTH - 52D | EDINBURGH (SM) - 64A | ANNESLEY - 16D | DAIRYCOATES - 53A | CARLISLE CANAL - 12C |
| Aug-59 | **6/59: DCTR - 36A** | **6/59: MARCH - 31B** | COLWICK - 40E | **4/59: ARDS - 56B** | TWEEDMOUTH - 52D | **7/59: W/D** | **4/59: ARDS - 56B** | DAIRYCOATES - 53A | CARLISLE CANAL - 12C |
| Nov-59 | DONCASTER - 36A | MARCH - 31B | COLWICK - 40E | ARDSLEY - 56B | TWEEDMOUTH - 52D | | ARDSLEY - 56B | DAIRYCOATES - 53A | CARLISLE CANAL - 12C |
| Jan-60 | DONCASTER - 36A | MARCH - 31B | COLWICK - 40E | ARDSLEY - 56B | TWEEDMOUTH - 52D | | ARDSLEY - 56B | DAIRYCOATES - 53A | CARLISLE CANAL - 12C |
| Apr-60 | DONCASTER - 36A | **3/60: CANAL - 12C** | COLWICK - 40E | ARDSLEY - 56B | TWEEDMOUTH - 52D | | ARDSLEY - 56B | DAIRYCOATES - 50B | CARLISLE CANAL - 12C |
| Aug-60 | DONCASTER - 36A | **6/60: WOOD - 2F** | COLWICK - 40E | ARDSLEY - 56B | TWEEDMOUTH - 52D | | ARDSLEY - 56B | DAIRYCOATES - 50B | CARLISLE CANAL - 12C |
| Nov-60 | DONCASTER - 36A | WOODFORD HALSE - 2F | COLWICK - 40E | ARDSLEY - 56B | TWEEDMOUTH - 52D | | ARDSLEY - 56B | DAIRYCOATES - 50B | CARLISLE CANAL - 12C |

| | 61859 | 61860 | 61861 | 61862 | 61864 | 61865 | 61866 | 61867 | 61868 |
|---|---|---|---|---|---|---|---|---|---|
| Aug-50 | LINCOLN - 40A | MARCH - 31B | DONCASTER - 36A | NEW ENGLAND - 35A | MARCH - 31B | GORTON - 39A | MARCH - 31B | NEW ENGLAND - 35A | NEW ENGLAND - 35A |
| Jan-51 | LINCOLN - 40A | MARCH - 31B | DONCASTER - 36A | NEW ENGLAND - 35A | **10/50: LOW - 32C** | GORTON - 39A | MARCH - 31B | NEW ENGLAND - 35A | NEW ENGLAND - 35A |
| Aug-51 | LINCOLN - 40A | MARCH - 31B | DONCASTER - 36A | NEW ENGLAND - 35A | **12/50: COLW - 38A** | GORTON - 39A | MARCH - 31B | NEW ENGLAND - 35A | NEW ENGLAND - 35A |
| Jan-52 | LINCOLN - 40A | MARCH - 31B | DONCASTER - 36A | NEW ENGLAND - 35A | COLWICK - 38A | GORTON - 39A | MARCH - 31B | NEW ENGLAND - 35A | NEW ENGLAND - 35A |
| Aug-52 | LINCOLN - 40A | MARCH - 31B | DONCASTER - 36A | **7/52: LINC - 40A** | COLWICK - 38A | GORTON - 39A | MARCH - 31B | NEW ENGLAND - 35A | NEW ENGLAND - 35A |
| Jan-53 | LINCOLN - 40A | MARCH - 31B | DONCASTER - 36A | **10/52: STRAT - 30A** | COLWICK - 38A | GORTON - 39A | MARCH - 31B | NEW ENGLAND - 35A | NEW ENGLAND - 35A |
| Aug-53 | LINCOLN - 40A | MARCH - 31B | DONCASTER - 36A | STRATFORD - 30A | COLWICK - 38A | GORTON - 39A | MARCH - 31B | NEW ENGLAND - 35A | NEW ENGLAND - 35A |
| Jan-54 | LINCOLN - 40A | MARCH - 31B | **11/53: MARCH - 31B** | STRATFORD - 30A | **10/53: MARCH - 31B** | GORTON - 39A | MARCH - 31B | **10/53: MARCH - 31B** | **10/53: MARCH - 31B** |
| Aug-54 | LINCOLN - 40A | MARCH - 31B | MARCH - 31B | STRATFORD - 30A | MARCH - 31B | GORTON - 39A | MARCH - 31B | MARCH - 31B | MARCH - 31B |
| Jan-55 | LINCOLN - 40A | MARCH - 31B | MARCH - 31B | STRATFORD - 30A | MARCH - 31B | GORTON - 39A | MARCH - 31B | MARCH - 31B | MARCH - 31B |
| Aug-55 | LINCOLN - 40A | MARCH - 31B | MARCH - 31B | STRATFORD - 30A | MARCH - 31B | GORTON - 39A | MARCH - 31B | MARCH - 31B | MARCH - 31B |
| Jan-56 | LINCOLN - 40A | MARCH - 31B | MARCH - 31B | STRATFORD - 30A | MARCH - 31B | GORTON - 39A | MARCH - 31B | MARCH - 31B | MARCH - 31B |
| Aug-56 | LINCOLN - 40A | MARCH - 31B | MARCH - 31B | STRATFORD - 30A | MARCH - 31B | GORTON - 39A | **10/56: WOOD - 38E** | **10/56: MEX - 36B** | **10/56: MEX - 36B** |
| Jan-57 | LINCOLN - 40A | MARCH - 31B | MARCH - 31B | STRATFORD - 30A | **11/56: NEW E - 35A** | GORTON - 39A | WOODFORD HALSE - 38E | MEXBOROUGH - 36B | MEXBOROUGH - 36B |
| Aug-57 | LINCOLN - 40A | MARCH - 31B | MARCH - 31B | STRATFORD - 30A | NEW ENGLAND - 35A | GORTON - 39A | WOODFORD HALSE - 38E | MEXBOROUGH - 36B | MEXBOROUGH - 36B |
| Jan-58 | LINCOLN - 40A | MARCH - 31B | MARCH - 31B | STRATFORD - 30A | NEW ENGLAND - 35A | GORTON - 39A | **1/58: IMM - 40B** | MEXBOROUGH - 36B | MEXBOROUGH - 36B |
| Aug-58 | LINCOLN - 40A | MARCH - 31B | MARCH - 31B | STRATFORD - 30A | NEW ENGLAND - 34E | GORTON - 9G | IMMINGHAM - 40B | MEXBOROUGH - 41F | MEXBOROUGH - 41F |
| Jan-59 | LINCOLN - 40A | MARCH - 31B | MARCH - 31B | **12/58: PARK - 30F** | NEW ENGLAND - 34E | GORTON - 9G | IMMINGHAM - 40B | **6/59: MARCH - 31B** | MEXBOROUGH - 41F |
| Aug-59 | LINCOLN - 40A | MARCH - 31B | MARCH - 31B | PARKESTON - 30F | NEW ENGLAND - 34E | GORTON - 9G | IMMINGHAM - 40B | **8/59: DCTR - 36A** | **6/59: DCTR - 36A** |
| Nov-59 | LINCOLN - 40A | MARCH - 31B | MARCH - 31B | PARKESTON - 30F | NEW ENGLAND - 34E | GORTON - 9G | IMMINGHAM - 40B | DONCASTER - 36A | DONCASTER - 36A |
| Jan-60 | LINCOLN - 40A | MARCH - 31B | MARCH - 31B | PARKESTON - 30F | NEW ENGLAND - 34E | GORTON - 9G | IMMINGHAM - 40B | DONCASTER - 36A | DONCASTER - 36A |
| Apr-60 | LINCOLN - 40A | MARCH - 31B | MARCH - 31B | PARKESTON - 30F | NEW ENGLAND - 34E | **4/60: WOOD - 2F** | IMMINGHAM - 40B | DONCASTER - 36A | DONCASTER - 36A |
| Aug-60 | LINCOLN - 40A | MARCH - 31B | MARCH - 31B | **6/60: MARCH - 31B** | NEW ENGLAND - 34E | WOODFORD HALSE - 2F | IMMINGHAM - 40B | DONCASTER - 36A | DONCASTER - 36A |
| Nov-60 | LINCOLN - 40A | MARCH - 31B | MARCH - 31B | MARCH - 31B | NEW ENGLAND - 34E | WOODFORD HALSE - 2F | IMMINGHAM - 40B | DONCASTER - 36A | DONCASTER - 36A |

| | 61869 | 61870 | 61871 | 61872 | 61873 | 61874 | 61875 | 61876 | 61877 |
|---|---|---|---|---|---|---|---|---|---|
| Aug-50 | MARCH - 31B | GORTON - 39A | DAIRYCOATES - 53A | DAIRYCOATES - 53A | MARCH - 31B | DAIRYCOATES - 53A | HEATON - 52B | EDINBURGH (SM) - 64A | GORTON - 39A |
| Jan-51 | MARCH - 31B | GORTON - 39A | DAIRYCOATES - 53A | DAIRYCOATES - 53A | MARCH - 31B | DAIRYCOATES - 53A | HEATON - 52B | EDINBURGH (SM) - 64A | **3/51: NOR - 32A** |
| Aug-51 | **9/51: DAIRY - 53A** | GORTON - 39A | DAIRYCOATES - 53A | DAIRYCOATES - 53A | MARCH - 31B | DAIRYCOATES - 53A | HEATON - 52B | EDINBURGH (SM) - 64A | **5/51: MARCH - 31B** |
| Jan-52 | DAIRYCOATES - 53A | GORTON - 39A | DAIRYCOATES - 53A | DAIRYCOATES - 53A | MARCH - 31B | DAIRYCOATES - 53A | HEATON - 52B | EDINBURGH (SM) - 64A | **9/51: LOW - 32C** |
| Aug-52 | DAIRYCOATES - 53A | GORTON - 39A | DAIRYCOATES - 53A | DAIRYCOATES - 53A | MARCH - 31B | DAIRYCOATES - 53A | HEATON - 52B | EDINBURGH (SM) - 64A | **12/51: NOR - 32A** |
| Jan-53 | DAIRYCOATES - 53A | GORTON - 39A | DAIRYCOATES - 53A | DAIRYCOATES - 53A | MARCH - 31B | DAIRYCOATES - 53A | HEATON - 52B | EDINBURGH (SM) - 64A | NORWICH - 32A |
| Aug-53 | DAIRYCOATES - 53A | GORTON - 39A | DAIRYCOATES - 53A | DAIRYCOATES - 53A | MARCH - 31B | DAIRYCOATES - 53A | HEATON - 52B | EDINBURGH (SM) - 64A | NORWICH - 32A |
| Jan-54 | DAIRYCOATES - 53A | GORTON - 39A | DAIRYCOATES - 53A | DAIRYCOATES - 53A | MARCH - 31B | DAIRYCOATES - 53A | HEATON - 52B | EDINBURGH (SM) - 64A | NORWICH - 32A |
| Aug-54 | DAIRYCOATES - 53A | **6/54: COLW - 38A** | DAIRYCOATES - 53A | DAIRYCOATES - 53A | MARCH - 31B | DAIRYCOATES - 53A | HEATON - 52B | EDINBURGH (SM) - 64A | NORWICH - 32A |
| Jan-55 | DAIRYCOATES - 53A | COLWICK - 38A | DAIRYCOATES - 53A | DAIRYCOATES - 53A | MARCH - 31B | DAIRYCOATES - 53A | HEATON - 52B | EDINBURGH (SM) - 64A | NORWICH - 32A |
| Aug-55 | DAIRYCOATES - 53A | COLWICK - 38A | DAIRYCOATES - 53A | DAIRYCOATES - 53A | MARCH - 31B | DAIRYCOATES - 53A | HEATON - 52B | EDINBURGH (SM) - 64A | NORWICH - 32A |
| Jan-56 | DAIRYCOATES - 53A | COLWICK - 38A | DAIRYCOATES - 53A | DAIRYCOATES - 53A | MARCH - 31B | DAIRYCOATES - 53A | HEATON - 52B | EDINBURGH (SM) - 64A | NORWICH - 32A |
| Aug-56 | **10/56: HTN - 52B** | COLWICK - 38A | DAIRYCOATES - 53A | DAIRYCOATES - 53A | **10/56: COL - 38A** | DAIRYCOATES - 53A | HEATON - 52B | EDINBURGH (SM) - 64A | NORWICH - 32A |
| Jan-57 | HEATON - 52B | COLWICK - 38A | DAIRYCOATES - 53A | DAIRYCOATES - 53A | COLWICK - 38A | DAIRYCOATES - 53A | HEATON - 52B | EDINBURGH (SM) - 64A | NORWICH - 32A |
| Aug-57 | HEATON - 52B | COLWICK - 38A | DAIRYCOATES - 53A | DAIRYCOATES - 53A | COLWICK - 38A | DAIRYCOATES - 53A | HEATON - 52B | EDINBURGH (SM) - 64A | NORWICH - 32A |
| Jan-58 | HEATON - 52B | COLWICK - 38A | DAIRYCOATES - 53A | DAIRYCOATES - 53A | COLWICK - 38A | DAIRYCOATES - 53A | HEATON - 52B | EDINBURGH (SM) - 64A | NORWICH - 32A |
| Aug-58 | HEATON - 52B | COLWICK - 40E | DAIRYCOATES - 53A | DAIRYCOATES - 53A | COLWICK - 40E | DAIRYCOATES - 53A | HEATON - 52B | EDINBURGH (SM) - 64A | NORWICH - 32A |
| Jan-59 | HEATON - 52B | COLWICK - 40E | DAIRYCOATES - 53A | DAIRYCOATES - 53A | COLWICK - 40E | DAIRYCOATES - 53A | HEATON - 52B | EDINBURGH (SM) - 64A | NORWICH - 32A |
| Aug-59 | HEATON - 52B | COLWICK - 40E | DAIRYCOATES - 53A | DAIRYCOATES - 53A | COLWICK - 40E | DAIRYCOATES - 53A | HEATON - 52B | EDINBURGH (SM) - 64A | NORWICH - 32A |
| Nov-59 | HEATON - 52B | COLWICK - 40E | DAIRYCOATES - 53A | DAIRYCOATES - 53A | COLWICK - 40E | DAIRYCOATES - 53A | HEATON - 52B | **9/59: W/D** | NORWICH - 32A |
| Jan-60 | **2/60: DAIRY - 53A** | COLWICK - 40E | DAIRYCOATES - 53A | DAIRYCOATES - 53A | COLWICK - 40E | DAIRYCOATES - 53A | **2/60: DAIRY - 50B** | | **2/60: STAVE - 41H** |
| Apr-60 | DAIRYCOATES - 50B | COLWICK - 40E | DAIRYCOATES - 50B | DAIRYCOATES - 50B | COLWICK - 40E | DAIRYCOATES - 50B | DAIRYCOATES - 50B | | **4/60: LINC - 40A** |
| Aug-60 | DAIRYCOATES - 50B | COLWICK - 40E | DAIRYCOATES - 50B | DAIRYCOATES - 50B | COLWICK - 40E | DAIRYCOATES - 50B | DAIRYCOATES - 50B | | **8/60: IMM - 40B** |
| Nov-60 | DAIRYCOATES - 50B | COLWICK - 40E | DAIRYCOATES - 50B | DAIRYCOATES - 50B | COLWICK - 40E | DAIRYCOATES - 50B | DAIRYCOATES - 50B | | IMMINGHAM - 40B |

| | 61878 | 61879 | 61880 | 61881 | 61882 | 61883 | 61884 | 61885 | 61886 |
|---|---|---|---|---|---|---|---|---|---|
| Aug-50 | EDINBURGH (SM) - 64A | EDINBURGH (SM) - 64A | STRATFORD - 30A | EDINBURGH (SM) - 64A | CARLISLE (CANAL) - 12B | DAIRYCOATES - 53A | HEATON - 52B | EDINBURGH (SM) - 64A | MARCH - 31B |
| Jan-51 | EDINBURGH (SM) - 64A | EDINBURGH (SM) - 64A | STRATFORD - 30A | EDINBURGH (SM) - 64A | CARLISLE (CANAL) - 12B | DAIRYCOATES - 53A | HEATON - 52B | EDINBURGH (SM) - 64A | MARCH - 31B |
| Aug-51 | EDINBURGH (SM) - 64A | EDINBURGH (SM) - 64A | STRATFORD - 30A | EDINBURGH (SM) - 64A | CARLISE (CANAL) - 68E | DAIRYCOATES - 53A | HEATON - 52B | EDINBURGH (SM) - 64A | MARCH - 31B |
| Jan-52 | EDINBURGH (SM) - 64A | EDINBURGH (SM) - 64A | STRATFORD - 30A | EDINBURGH (SM) - 64A | CARLISE (CANAL) - 68E | DAIRYCOATES - 53A | HEATON - 52B | EDINBURGH (SM) - 64A | MARCH - 31B |
| Aug-52 | EDINBURGH (SM) - 64A | EDINBURGH (SM) - 64A | STRATFORD - 30A | EDINBURGH (SM) - 64A | CARLISE (CANAL) - 68E | DAIRYCOATES - 53A | HEATON - 52B | EDINBURGH (SM) - 64A | MARCH - 31B |
| Jan-53 | EDINBURGH (SM) - 64A | EDINBURGH (SM) - 64A | STRATFORD - 30A | EDINBURGH (SM) - 64A | CARLISE (CANAL) - 68E | DAIRYCOATES - 53A | HEATON - 52B | EDINBURGH (SM) - 64A | MARCH - 31B |
| Aug-53 | EDINBURGH (SM) - 64A | EDINBURGH (SM) - 64A | STRATFORD - 30A | EDINBURGH (SM) - 64A | CARLISE (CANAL) - 68E | DAIRYCOATES - 53A | **4/53: DAIRY - 53A** | EDINBURGH (SM) - 64A | MARCH - 31B |
| Jan-54 | EDINBURGH (SM) - 64A | EDINBURGH (SM) - 64A | STRATFORD - 30A | EDINBURGH (SM) - 64A | CARLISE (CANAL) - 68E | DAIRYCOATES - 53A | DAIRYCOATES - 53A | EDINBURGH (SM) - 64A | MARCH - 31B |
| Aug-54 | EDINBURGH (SM) - 64A | EDINBURGH (SM) - 64A | STRATFORD - 30A | EDINBURGH (SM) - 64A | CARLISE (CANAL) - 68E | DAIRYCOATES - 53A | DAIRYCOATES - 53A | EDINBURGH (SM) - 64A | MARCH - 31B |
| Jan-55 | EDINBURGH (SM) - 64A | EDINBURGH (SM) - 64A | STRATFORD - 30A | EDINBURGH (SM) - 64A | CARLISE (CANAL) - 68E | DAIRYCOATES - 53A | DAIRYCOATES - 53A | EDINBURGH (SM) - 64A | MARCH - 31B |
| Aug-55 | EDINBURGH (SM) - 64A | EDINBURGH (SM) - 64A | STRATFORD - 30A | EDINBURGH (SM) - 64A | CARLISE (CANAL) - 68E | DAIRYCOATES - 53A | DAIRYCOATES - 53A | EDINBURGH (SM) - 64A | MARCH - 31B |
| Jan-56 | EDINBURGH (SM) - 64A | EDINBURGH (SM) - 64A | STRATFORD - 30A | EDINBURGH (SM) - 64A | CARLISE (CANAL) - 68E | DAIRYCOATES - 53A | DAIRYCOATES - 53A | EDINBURGH (SM) - 64A | MARCH - 31B |
| Aug-56 | EDINBURGH (SM) - 64A | EDINBURGH (SM) - 64A | STRATFORD - 30A | EDINBURGH (SM) - 64A | CARLISE (CANAL) - 68E | DAIRYCOATES - 53A | DAIRYCOATES - 53A | EDINBURGH (SM) - 64A | MARCH - 31B |
| Jan-57 | EDINBURGH (SM) - 64A | EDINBURGH (SM) - 64A | STRATFORD - 30A | EDINBURGH (SM) - 64A | CARLISE (CANAL) - 68E | DAIRYCOATES - 53A | DAIRYCOATES - 53A | EDINBURGH (SM) - 64A | MARCH - 31B |
| Aug-57 | EDINBURGH (SM) - 64A | EDINBURGH (SM) - 64A | STRATFORD - 30A | EDINBURGH (SM) - 64A | CARLISE (CANAL) - 68E | DAIRYCOATES - 53A | DAIRYCOATES - 53A | EDINBURGH (SM) - 64A | MARCH - 31B |
| Jan-58 | EDINBURGH (SM) - 64A | EDINBURGH (SM) - 64A | STRATFORD - 30A | EDINBURGH (SM) - 64A | CARLISLE CANAL - 68E | DAIRYCOATES - 53A | DAIRYCOATES - 53A | EDINBURGH (SM) - 64A | MARCH - 31B |
| Aug-58 | EDINBURGH (SM) - 64A | EDINBURGH (SM) - 64A | **12/58: PARK - 30F** | EDINBURGH (SM) - 64A | CARLISLE CANAL - 12C | DAIRYCOATES - 53A | **9/58: HTN - 52B** | EDINBURGH (SM) - 64A | MARCH - 31B |
| Jan-59 | EDINBURGH (SM) - 64A | EDINBURGH (SM) - 64A | **1/59: CAMB - 31A** | EDINBURGH (SM) - 64A | CARLISLE CANAL - 12C | DAIRYCOATES - 53A | HEATON - 52B | EDINBURGH (SM) - 64A | MARCH - 31B |
| Aug-59 | **8/59: W/D** | **6/59: W/D** | CAMBRIDGE - 31A | EDINBURGH (SM) - 64A | **4/59: WOOD - 2F** | DAIRYCOATES - 53A | HEATON - 52B | EDINBURGH (SM) - 64A | MARCH - 31B |
| Nov-59 | | | CAMBRIDGE - 31A | EDINBURGH (SM) - 64A | WOODFORD HALSE - 2F | DAIRYCOATES - 53A | HEATON - 52B | **11/59: W/D** | MARCH - 31B |
| Jan-60 | | | CAMBRIDGE - 31A | EDINBURGH (SM) - 64A | WOODFORD HALSE - 2F | DAIRYCOATES - 53A | HEATON - 52B | | MARCH - 31B |
| Apr-60 | | | CAMBRIDGE - 31A | EDINBURGH (SM) - 64A | WOODFORD HALSE - 2F | DAIRYCOATES - 50B | HEATON - 52B | | MARCH - 31B |
| Aug-60 | | | CAMBRIDGE - 31A | **5/60: W/D** | **6/60: W/D** | DAIRYCOATES - 50B | HEATON - 52B | | MARCH - 31B |
| Nov-60 | | | CAMBRIDGE - 31A | | | DAIRYCOATES - 50B | HEATON - 52B | | MARCH - 31B |

| | 61887 | 61888 | 61889 | 61890 | 61891 | 61892 | 61893 | 61894 | 61895 |
|---|---|---|---|---|---|---|---|---|---|
| Aug-50 | MARCH - 31B | MARCH - 31B | MARCH - 31B | NEW ENGLAND - 35A | IMMINGHAM - 40B | DAIRYCOATES - 53A | MARCH - 31B | LINCOLN - 40A | MARCH - 31B |
| Jan-51 | MARCH - 31B | MARCH - 31B | MARCH - 31B | NEW ENGLAND - 35A | IMMINGHAM - 40B | DAIRYCOATES - 53A | MARCH - 31B | LINCOLN - 40A | MARCH - 31B |
| Aug-51 | MARCH - 31B | MARCH - 31B | MARCH - 31B | NEW ENGLAND - 35A | IMMINGHAM - 40B | DAIRYCOATES - 53A | **9/51: DAIRY - 53A** | LINCOLN - 40A | MARCH - 31B |
| Jan-52 | MARCH - 31B | MARCH - 31B | MARCH - 31B | NEW ENGLAND - 35A | IMMINGHAM - 40B | DAIRYCOATES - 53A | DAIRYCOATES - 53A | LINCOLN - 40A | MARCH - 31B |
| Aug-52 | MARCH - 31B | MARCH - 31B | MARCH - 31B | NEW ENGLAND - 35A | IMMINGHAM - 40B | DAIRYCOATES - 53A | DAIRYCOATES - 53A | LINCOLN - 40A | MARCH - 31B |
| Jan-53 | MARCH - 31B | MARCH - 31B | MARCH - 31B | NEW ENGLAND - 35A | IMMINGHAM - 40B | DAIRYCOATES - 53A | DAIRYCOATES - 53A | LINCOLN - 40A | MARCH - 31B |
| Aug-53 | MARCH - 31B | MARCH - 31B | MARCH - 31B | **10/53: MARCH - 31B** | IMMINGHAM - 40B | DAIRYCOATES - 53A | DAIRYCOATES - 53A | LINCOLN - 40A | MARCH - 31B |
| Jan-54 | MARCH - 31B | MARCH - 31B | MARCH - 31B | MARCH - 31B | IMMINGHAM - 40B | DAIRYCOATES - 53A | DAIRYCOATES - 53A | LINCOLN - 40A | MARCH - 31B |
| Aug-54 | MARCH - 31B | MARCH - 31B | **8/54: LINC - 40A** | MARCH - 31B | IMMINGHAM - 40B | DAIRYCOATES - 53A | DAIRYCOATES - 53A | LINCOLN - 40A | MARCH - 31B |
| Jan-55 | MARCH - 31B | MARCH - 31B | LINCOLN - 40A | MARCH - 31B | IMMINGHAM - 40B | DAIRYCOATES - 53A | DAIRYCOATES - 53A | LINCOLN - 40A | MARCH - 31B |
| Aug-55 | MARCH - 31B | MARCH - 31B | LINCOLN - 40A | MARCH - 31B | IMMINGHAM - 40B | DAIRYCOATES - 53A | DAIRYCOATES - 53A | LINCOLN - 40A | MARCH - 31B |
| Jan-56 | MARCH - 31B | MARCH - 31B | LINCOLN - 40A | MARCH - 31B | IMMINGHAM - 40B | DAIRYCOATES - 53A | DAIRYCOATES - 53A | LINCOLN - 40A | MARCH - 31B |
| Aug-56 | MARCH - 31B | MARCH - 31B | LINCOLN - 40A | MARCH - 31B | IMMINGHAM - 40B | DAIRYCOATES - 53A | DAIRYCOATES - 53A | LINCOLN - 40A | **10/56: DCTR - 36A** |
| Jan-57 | **10/56: DCTR - 36A** | **10/56: COLW - 38A** | LINCOLN - 40A | MARCH - 31B | IMMINGHAM - 40B | DAIRYCOATES - 53A | DAIRYCOATES - 53A | LINCOLN - 40A | DONCASTER - 36A |
| Aug-57 | DONCASTER - 36A | COLWICK - 38A | LINCOLN - 40A | MARCH - 31B | IMMINGHAM - 40B | DAIRYCOATES - 53A | DAIRYCOATES - 53A | LINCOLN - 40A | DONCASTER - 36A |
| Jan-58 | DONCASTER - 36A | COLWICK - 38A | LINCOLN - 40A | MARCH - 31B | IMMINGHAM - 40B | DAIRYCOATES - 53A | DAIRYCOATES - 53A | LINCOLN - 40A | DONCASTER - 36A |
| Aug-58 | DONCASTER - 36A | COLWICK - 40E | LINCOLN - 40A | MARCH - 31B | IMMINGHAM - 40B | DAIRYCOATES - 53A | DAIRYCOATES - 53A | LINCOLN - 40A | DONCASTER - 36A |
| Jan-59 | DONCASTER - 36A | COLWICK - 40E | LINCOLN - 40A | MARCH - 31B | IMMINGHAM - 40B | DAIRYCOATES - 53A | DAIRYCOATES - 53A | LINCOLN - 40A | DONCASTER - 36A |
| Aug-59 | DONCASTER - 36A | COLWICK - 40E | LINCOLN - 40A | MARCH - 31B | IMMINGHAM - 40B | DAIRYCOATES - 53A | DAIRYCOATES - 53A | LINCOLN - 40A | DONCASTER - 36A |
| Nov-59 | DONCASTER - 36A | COLWICK - 40E | LINCOLN - 40A | MARCH - 31B | IMMINGHAM - 40B | DAIRYCOATES - 53A | DAIRYCOATES - 53A | LINCOLN - 40A | DONCASTER - 36A |
| Jan-60 | DONCASTER - 36A | COLWICK - 40E | LINCOLN - 40A | MARCH - 31B | IMMINGHAM - 40B | DAIRYCOATES - 53A | DAIRYCOATES - 53A | LINCOLN - 40A | DONCASTER - 36A |
| Apr-60 | DONCASTER - 36A | COLWICK - 40E | LINCOLN - 40A | MARCH - 31B | IMMINGHAM - 40B | DAIRYCOATES - 50B | DAIRYCOATES - 50B | LINCOLN - 40A | DONCASTER - 36A |
| Aug-60 | DONCASTER - 36A | COLWICK - 40E | LINCOLN - 40A | MARCH - 31B | IMMINGHAM - 40B | DAIRYCOATES - 50B | DAIRYCOATES - 50B | LINCOLN - 40A | DONCASTER - 36A |
| Nov-60 | DONCASTER - 36A | COLWICK - 40E | **11/60: COLW - 40E** | MARCH - 31B | IMMINGHAM - 40B | DAIRYCOATES - 50B | DAIRYCOATES - 50B | **11/60: COLW - 40E** | DONCASTER - 36A |

| | 61896 | 61897 | 61898 | 61899 | 61900 | 61901 | 61902 | 61903 | 61904 |
|---|---|---|---|---|---|---|---|---|---|
| Aug-50 | GORTON - 39A | EDINBURGH (SM) - 64A | CARLISLE (CANAL) - 12B | DAIRYCOATES - 53A | EDINBURGH (SM) - 64A | HEATON - 52B | DAIRYCOATES - 53A | DAIRYCOATES - 53A | HEATON - 52B |
| Jan-51 | GORTON - 39A | EDINBURGH (SM) - 64A | CARLISLE (CANAL) - 12B | DAIRYCOATES - 53A | EDINBURGH (SM) - 64A | HEATON - 52B | DAIRYCOATES - 53A | DAIRYCOATES - 53A | HEATON - 52B |
| Aug-51 | GORTON - 39A | EDINBURGH (SM) - 64A | CARLISE (CANAL) - 68E | DAIRYCOATES - 53A | EDINBURGH (SM) - 64A | HEATON - 52B | DAIRYCOATES - 53A | DAIRYCOATES - 53A | HEATON - 52B |
| Jan-52 | GORTON - 39A | EDINBURGH (SM) - 64A | CARLISE (CANAL) - 68E | DAIRYCOATES - 53A | EDINBURGH (SM) - 64A | **1/52: TWEED - 52D** | DAIRYCOATES - 53A | DAIRYCOATES - 53A | HEATON - 52B |
| Aug-52 | GORTON - 39A | EDINBURGH (SM) - 64A | CARLISE (CANAL) - 68E | DAIRYCOATES - 53A | EDINBURGH (SM) - 64A | TWEEDMOUTH - 52D | DAIRYCOATES - 53A | DAIRYCOATES - 53A | HEATON - 52B |
| Jan-53 | GORTON - 39A | EDINBURGH (SM) - 64A | CARLISE (CANAL) - 68E | **12/52: TWEED - 52D** | EDINBURGH (SM) - 64A | TWEEDMOUTH - 52D | DAIRYCOATES - 53A | DAIRYCOATES - 53A | HEATON - 52B |
| Aug-53 | GORTON - 39A | EDINBURGH (SM) - 64A | CARLISE (CANAL) - 68E | TWEEDMOUTH - 52D | EDINBURGH (SM) - 64A | TWEEDMOUTH - 52D | DAIRYCOATES - 53A | DAIRYCOATES - 53A | HEATON - 52B |
| Jan-54 | GORTON - 39A | EDINBURGH (SM) - 64A | CARLISE (CANAL) - 68E | TWEEDMOUTH - 52D | EDINBURGH (SM) - 64A | TWEEDMOUTH - 52D | DAIRYCOATES - 53A | DAIRYCOATES - 53A | HEATON - 52B |
| Aug-54 | COLWICK - 38A | EDINBURGH (SM) - 64A | CARLISE (CANAL) - 68E | TWEEDMOUTH - 52D | EDINBURGH (SM) - 64A | TWEEDMOUTH - 52D | DAIRYCOATES - 53A | DAIRYCOATES - 53A | HEATON - 52B |
| Jan-55 | COLWICK - 38A | EDINBURGH (SM) - 64A | CARLISE (CANAL) - 68E | TWEEDMOUTH - 52D | EDINBURGH (SM) - 64A | TWEEDMOUTH - 52D | DAIRYCOATES - 53A | DAIRYCOATES - 53A | HEATON - 52B |
| Aug-55 | COLWICK - 38A | EDINBURGH (SM) - 64A | CARLISE (CANAL) - 68E | **8/55: DAIRY - 53A** | EDINBURGH (SM) - 64A | TWEEDMOUTH - 52D | DAIRYCOATES - 53A | DAIRYCOATES - 53A | **9/55: DAIRY - 53A** |
| Jan-56 | COLWICK - 38A | EDINBURGH (SM) - 64A | CARLISE (CANAL) - 68E | DAIRYCOATES - 53A | EDINBURGH (SM) - 64A | TWEEDMOUTH - 52D | DAIRYCOATES - 53A | DAIRYCOATES - 53A | DAIRYCOATES - 53A |
| Aug-56 | COLWICK - 38A | EDINBURGH (SM) - 64A | CARLISE (CANAL) - 68E | DAIRYCOATES - 53A | EDINBURGH (SM) - 64A | TWEEDMOUTH - 52D | DAIRYCOATES - 53A | DAIRYCOATES - 53A | DAIRYCOATES - 53A |
| Jan-57 | COLWICK - 38A | **3/57: DAIRY - 53A** | CARLISE (CANAL) - 68E | DAIRYCOATES - 53A | EDINBURGH (SM) - 64A | TWEEDMOUTH - 52D | DAIRYCOATES - 53A | DAIRYCOATES - 53A | DAIRYCOATES - 53A |
| Aug-57 | COLWICK - 38A | DAIRYCOATES - 53A | CARLISE (CANAL) - 68E | DAIRYCOATES - 53A | EDINBURGH (SM) - 64A | TWEEDMOUTH - 52D | DAIRYCOATES - 53A | DAIRYCOATES - 53A | DAIRYCOATES - 53A |
| Jan-58 | COLWICK - 38A | DAIRYCOATES - 53A | CARLISLE CANAL - 68E | DAIRYCOATES - 53A | EDINBURGH (SM) - 64A | TWEEDMOUTH - 52D | DAIRYCOATES - 53A | DAIRYCOATES - 53A | DAIRYCOATES - 53A |
| Aug-58 | COLWICK - 40E | DAIRYCOATES - 53A | CARLISLE CANAL - 12C | DAIRYCOATES - 53A | EDINBURGH (SM) - 64A | TWEEDMOUTH - 52D | DAIRYCOATES - 53A | DAIRYCOATES - 53A | DAIRYCOATES - 53A |
| Jan-59 | COLWICK - 40E | DAIRYCOATES - 53A | **2/59: W/D** | DAIRYCOATES - 53A | EDINBURGH (SM) - 64A | TWEEDMOUTH - 52D | DAIRYCOATES - 53A | DAIRYCOATES - 53A | DAIRYCOATES - 53A |
| Aug-59 | COLWICK - 40E | DAIRYCOATES - 53A | | DAIRYCOATES - 53A | EDINBURGH (SM) - 64A | TWEEDMOUTH - 52D | DAIRYCOATES - 53A | DAIRYCOATES - 53A | DAIRYCOATES - 53A |
| Nov-59 | COLWICK - 40E | DAIRYCOATES - 53A | | DAIRYCOATES - 53A | EDINBURGH (SM) - 64A | TWEEDMOUTH - 52D | DAIRYCOATES - 53A | DAIRYCOATES - 53A | DAIRYCOATES - 53A |
| Jan-60 | COLWICK - 40E | DAIRYCOATES - 53A | | DAIRYCOATES - 53A | EDINBURGH (SM) - 64A | TWEEDMOUTH - 52D | DAIRYCOATES - 53A | DAIRYCOATES - 53A | DAIRYCOATES - 53A |
| Apr-60 | COLWICK - 40E | DAIRYCOATES - 50B | | DAIRYCOATES - 50B | **3/60: W/D** | TWEEDMOUTH - 52D | DAIRYCOATES - 50B | DAIRYCOATES - 50B | DAIRYCOATES - 50B |
| Aug-60 | COLWICK - 40E | DAIRYCOATES - 50B | | DAIRYCOATES - 50B | | TWEEDMOUTH - 52D | DAIRYCOATES - 50B | DAIRYCOATES - 50B | DAIRYCOATES - 50B |
| Nov-60 | COLWICK - 40E | DAIRYCOATES - 50B | | DAIRYCOATES - 50B | | TWEEDMOUTH - 52D | DAIRYCOATES - 50B | DAIRYCOATES - 50B | DAIRYCOATES - 50B |

| | 61905 | 61906 | 61907 | 61908 | 61909 | 61910 | 61911 | 61912 | 61913 |
|---|---|---|---|---|---|---|---|---|---|
| **Aug-50** | IMMINGHAM - 40B | HEATON - 52B | DONCASTER - 36A | GORTON - 39A | EDINBURGH(SM) - 64A | GORTON - 39A | EDINBURGH(SM) - 64A | IMMINGHAM - 40B | GORTON - 39A |
| **Jan-51** | IMMINGHAM - 40B | HEATON - 52B | DONCASTER - 36A | **3/51: NOR +DO99 - 32A** | EDINBURGH(SM) - 64A | GORTON - 39A | EDINBURGH(SM) - 64A | IMMINGHAM - 40B | GORTON - 39A |
| **Aug-51** | IMMINGHAM - 40B | HEATON - 52B | DONCASTER - 36A | **5/51: MARCH - 31B** | EDINBURGH(SM) - 64A | GORTON - 39A | EDINBURGH(SM) - 64A | IMMINGHAM - 40B | GORTON - 39A |
| **Jan-52** | IMMINGHAM - 40B | HEATON - 52B | DONCASTER - 36A | **9/51: LOW - 32C** | EDINBURGH(SM) - 64A | GORTON - 39A | EDINBURGH(SM) - 64A | IMMINGHAM - 40B | GORTON - 39A |
| **Aug-52** | IMMINGHAM - 40B | HEATON - 52B | DONCASTER - 36A | **12/51: NOR - 32A** | EDINBURGH(SM) - 64A | GORTON - 39A | EDINBURGH(SM) - 64A | IMMINGHAM - 40B | GORTON - 39A |
| **Jan-53** | IMMINGHAM - 40B | HEATON - 52B | DONCASTER - 36A | NORWICH - 32A | EDINBURGH(SM) - 64A | GORTON - 39A | EDINBURGH(SM) - 64A | IMMINGHAM - 40B | GORTON - 39A |
| **Aug-53** | IMMINGHAM - 40B | HEATON - 52B | DONCASTER - 36A | NORWICH - 32A | EDINBURGH(SM) - 64A | GORTON - 39A | EDINBURGH(SM) - 64A | IMMINGHAM - 40B | GORTON - 39A |
| **Jan-54** | IMMINGHAM - 40B | HEATON - 52B | **11/53: MARCH - 31B** | NORWICH - 32A | EDINBURGH(SM) - 64A | GORTON - 39A | EDINBURGH(SM) - 64A | IMMINGHAM - 40B | GORTON - 39A |
| **Aug-54** | IMMINGHAM - 40B | HEATON - 52B | MARCH - 31B | NORWICH - 32A | EDINBURGH(SM) - 64A | GORTON - 39A | EDINBURGH(SM) - 64A | IMMINGHAM - 40B | GORTON - 39A |
| **Jan-55** | IMMINGHAM - 40B | HEATON - 52B | MARCH - 31B | NORWICH - 32A | EDINBURGH(SM) - 64A | GORTON - 39A | EDINBURGH(SM) - 64A | IMMINGHAM - 40B | GORTON - 39A |
| **Aug-55** | IMMINGHAM - 40B | HEATON - 52B | MARCH - 31B | NORWICH - 32A | EDINBURGH(SM) - 64A | GORTON - 39A | EDINBURGH(SM) - 64A | IMMINGHAM - 40B | GORTON - 39A |
| **Jan-56** | IMMINGHAM - 40B | HEATON - 52B | MARCH - 31B | NORWICH - 32A | EDINBURGH(SM) - 64A | GORTON - 39A | EDINBURGH(SM) - 64A | IMMINGHAM - 40B | GORTON - 39A |
| **Aug-56** | IMMINGHAM - 40B | HEATON - 52B | **10/56: DARN - 41A** | NORWICH - 32A | EDINBURGH(SM) - 64A | GORTON - 39A | EDINBURGH(SM) - 64A | IMMINGHAM - 40B | GORTON - 39A |
| **Jan-57** | IMMINGHAM - 40B | HEATON - 52B | DARNALL - 41A | NORWICH - 32A | EDINBURGH(SM) - 64A | GORTON - 39A | EDINBURGH(SM) - 64A | IMMINGHAM - 40B | GORTON - 39A |
| **Aug-57** | IMMINGHAM - 40B | HEATON - 52B | DARNALL - 41A | NORWICH - 32A | EDINBURGH(SM) - 64A | GORTON - 39A | EDINBURGH(SM) - 64A | IMMINGHAM - 40B | GORTON - 39A |
| **Jan-58** | IMMINGHAM - 40B | HEATON - 52B | DARNALL - 41A | NORWICH - 32A | EDINBURGH(SM) - 64A | GORTON - 39A | EDINBURGH(SM) - 64A | IMMINGHAM - 40B | GORTON - 39A |
| **Aug-58** | IMMINGHAM - 40B | HEATON - 52B | DARNALL - 41A | NORWICH - 32A | EDINBURGH(SM) - 64A | GORTON - 9G | EDINBURGH(SM) - 64A | IMMINGHAM - 40B | GORTON - 9G |
| **Jan-59** | IMMINGHAM - 40B | HEATON - 52B | DARNALL - 41A | NORWICH - 32A | EDINBURGH(SM) - 64A | GORTON - 9G | EDINBURGH(SM) - 64A | IMMINGHAM - 40B | GORTON - 9G |
| **Aug-59** | IMMINGHAM - 40B | HEATON - 52B | DARNALL - 41A | NORWICH - 32A | EDINBURGH(SM) - 64A | GORTON - 9G | EDINBURGH(SM) - 64A | IMMINGHAM - 40B | **8/59: WOOD - 2F** |
| **Nov-59** | IMMINGHAM - 40B | HEATON - 52B | DARNALL - 41A | NORWICH - 32A | EDINBURGH(SM) - 64A | GORTON - 9G | EDINBURGH(SM) - 64A | IMMINGHAM - 40B | WOODFORD HALSE - 2F |
| **Jan-60** | IMMINGHAM - 40B | HEATON - 52B | **12/59: COLW - 40E** | **2/60: MARCH - 31B** | EDINBURGH(SM) - 64A | GORTON - 9G | **12/59: W/D** | IMMINGHAM - 40B | WOODFORD HALSE - 2F |
| **Apr-60** | IMMINGHAM - 40B | HEATON - 52B | COLWICK - 40E | **3/60: STAVE - 41H** | **4/60: W/D** | **3/60: WOOD - 2F** | | IMMINGHAM - 40B | WOODFORD HALSE - 2F |
| **Aug-60** | IMMINGHAM - 40B | HEATON - 52B | COLWICK - 40E | STAVELEY(GC) - 41H | | WOODFORD HALSE - 2F | | IMMINGHAM - 40B | WOODFORD HALSE - 2F |
| **Nov-60** | IMMINGHAM - 40B | HEATON - 52B | COLWICK - 40E | STAVELEY(GC) - 41H | | WOODFORD HALSE - 2F | | IMMINGHAM - 40B | WOODFORD HALSE - 2F |

| | 61914 | 61915 | 61916 | 61917 | 61918 | 61919 | 61920 | 61921 | 61922 |
|---|---|---|---|---|---|---|---|---|---|
| **Aug-50** | GORTON - 39A | NEW ENGLAND - 35A | EDINBURGH(SM) - 64A | HEATON - 52B | DONCASTER - 36A | GORTON - 39A | DAIRYCOATES - 53A | NORWICH - 32A | DAIRYCOATES - 53A |
| **Jan-51** | GORTON - 39A | NEW ENGLAND - 35A | EDINBURGH(SM) - 64A | HEATON - 52B | DONCASTER - 36A | GORTON - 39A | DAIRYCOATES - 53A | NORWICH - 32A | DAIRYCOATES - 53A |
| **Aug-51** | GORTON - 39A | NEW ENGLAND - 35A | **7/51: CANAL - 68E** | HEATON - 52B | DONCASTER - 36A | GORTON - 39A | DAIRYCOATES - 53A | **6/51: MARCH - 31B** | DAIRYCOATES - 53A |
| **Jan-52** | GORTON - 39A | **3/52: DCTR - 36A** | CARLISE(CANAL) - 68E | **1/52: TWEED - 52D** | DONCASTER - 36A | GORTON - 39A | DAIRYCOATES - 53A | MARCH - 31B | DAIRYCOATES - 53A |
| **Aug-52** | GORTON - 39A | DONCASTER - 36A | CARLISE(CANAL) - 68E | TWEEDMOUTH - 52D | DONCASTER - 36A | GORTON - 39A | DAIRYCOATES - 53A | **7/52: LINC - 40A** | DAIRYCOATES - 53A |
| **Jan-53** | GORTON - 39A | DONCASTER - 36A | CARLISE(CANAL) - 68E | TWEEDMOUTH - 52D | DONCASTER - 36A | GORTON - 39A | DAIRYCOATES - 53A | **10/52: STRAT - 30A** | DAIRYCOATES - 53A |
| **Aug-53** | GORTON - 39A | DONCASTER - 36A | CARLISE(CANAL) - 68E | TWEEDMOUTH - 52D | DONCASTER - 36A | GORTON - 39A | DAIRYCOATES - 53A | STRATFORD - 30A | DAIRYCOATES - 53A |
| **Jan-54** | GORTON - 39A | **11/53: MARCH - 31B** | CARLISE(CANAL) - 68E | TWEEDMOUTH - 52D | **11/53: NOR - 32A** | GORTON - 39A | DAIRYCOATES - 53A | STRATFORD - 30A | DAIRYCOATES - 53A |
| **Aug-54** | **6/54: COLW - 38A** | MARCH - 31B | CARLISE(CANAL) - 68E | TWEEDMOUTH - 52D | NORWICH - 32A | **6/54: LINC - 40A** | DAIRYCOATES - 53A | STRATFORD - 30A | DAIRYCOATES - 53A |
| **Jan-55** | COLWICK - 38A | MARCH - 31B | CARLISE(CANAL) - 68E | TWEEDMOUTH - 52D | NORWICH - 32A | LINCOLN - 40A | DAIRYCOATES - 53A | STRATFORD - 30A | DAIRYCOATES - 53A |
| **Aug-55** | COLWICK - 38A | MARCH - 31B | CARLISE(CANAL) - 68E | TWEEDMOUTH - 52D | **11/55: LOW - 32C** | LINCOLN - 40A | DAIRYCOATES - 53A | STRATFORD - 30A | DAIRYCOATES - 53A |
| **Jan-56** | COLWICK - 38A | MARCH - 31B | CARLISE(CANAL) - 68E | TWEEDMOUTH - 52D | **2/56: NOR - 32A** | LINCOLN - 40A | DAIRYCOATES - 53A | STRATFORD - 30A | DAIRYCOATES - 53A |
| **Aug-56** | COLWICK - 38A | MARCH - 31B | CARLISE(CANAL) - 68E | TWEEDMOUTH - 52D | **3/56: LOW - 32C** | LINCOLN - 40A | DAIRYCOATES - 53A | STRATFORD - 30A | DAIRYCOATES - 53A |
| **Jan-57** | COLWICK - 38A | MARCH - 31B | CARLISE(CANAL) - 68E | TWEEDMOUTH - 52D | **5/56: NOR - 32A** | LINCOLN - 40A | DAIRYCOATES - 53A | STRATFORD - 30A | DAIRYCOATES - 53A |
| **Aug-57** | COLWICK - 38A | MARCH - 31B | CARLISE(CANAL) - 68E | TWEEDMOUTH - 52D | NORWICH - 32A | LINCOLN - 40A | DAIRYCOATES - 53A | STRATFORD - 30A | DAIRYCOATES - 53A |
| **Jan-58** | COLWICK - 38A | MARCH - 31B | CARLISLECANAL - 68E | TWEEDMOUTH - 52D | NORWICH - 32A | LINCOLN - 40A | DAIRYCOATES - 53A | **3/58: PARK - 30F** | DAIRYCOATES - 53A |
| **Aug-58** | COLWICK - 40E | MARCH - 31B | CARLISLECANAL - 12C | TWEEDMOUTH - 52D | NORWICH - 32A | LINCOLN - 40A | DAIRYCOATES - 53A | PARKESTON - 30F | DAIRYCOATES - 53A |
| **Jan-59** | COLWICK - 40E | MARCH - 31B | CARLISLECANAL - 12C | TWEEDMOUTH - 52D | NORWICH - 32A | LINCOLN - 40A | DAIRYCOATES - 53A | PARKESTON - 30F | DAIRYCOATES - 53A |
| **Aug-59** | COLWICK - 40E | MARCH - 31B | CARLISLECANAL - 12C | TWEEDMOUTH - 52D | NORWICH - 32A | LINCOLN - 40A | DAIRYCOATES - 53A | PARKESTON - 30F | DAIRYCOATES - 53A |
| **Nov-59** | COLWICK - 40E | MARCH - 31B | CARLISLECANAL - 12C | TWEEDMOUTH - 52D | NORWICH - 32A | LINCOLN - 40A | DAIRYCOATES - 53A | PARKESTON - 30F | DAIRYCOATES - 53A |
| **Jan-60** | COLWICK - 40E | MARCH - 31B | CARLISLECANAL - 12C | TWEEDMOUTH - 52D | NORWICH - 32A | LINCOLN - 40A | DAIRYCOATES - 53A | PARKESTON - 30F | DAIRYCOATES - 53A |
| **Apr-60** | COLWICK - 40E | MARCH - 31B | CARLISLECANAL - 12C | TWEEDMOUTH - 52D | NORWICH - 32A | LINCOLN - 40A | DAIRYCOATES - 50B | PARKESTON - 30F | DAIRYCOATES - 50B |
| **Aug-60** | **8/60: IMM - 40B** | MARCH - 31B | CARLISLECANAL - 12C | TWEEDMOUTH - 52D | **6/60: MARCH - 31B** | LINCOLN - 40A | DAIRYCOATES - 50B | **6/60: MARCH - 31B** | DAIRYCOATES - 50B |
| **Nov-60** | IMMINGHAM - 40B | MARCH - 31B | CARLISLECANAL - 12C | TWEEDMOUTH - 52D | MARCH - 31B | LINCOLN - 40A | DAIRYCOATES - 50B | MARCH - 31B | DAIRYCOATES - 50B |

| | 61923 | 61924 | 61925 | 61926 | 61927 | 61928 | 61929 | 61930 | 61931 |
|---|---|---|---|---|---|---|---|---|---|
| **Aug-50** | DAIRYCOATES - 53A | EDINBURGH(SM) - 64A | LINCOLN - 40A | LOWESTOFT - 32C | DAIRYCOATES - 53A | EDINBURGH(SM) - 64A | NEW ENGLAND - 35A | HEATON - 52B | EDINBURGH(SM) - 64A |
| **Jan-51** | DAIRYCOATES - 53A | EDINBURGH(SM) - 64A | LINCOLN - 40A | LOWESTOFT - 32C | DAIRYCOATES - 53A | EDINBURGH(SM) - 64A | NEW ENGLAND - 35A | HEATON - 52B | EDINBURGH(SM) - 64A |
| **Aug-51** | DAIRYCOATES - 53A | EDINBURGH(SM) - 64A | LINCOLN - 40A | LOWESTOFT - 32C | DAIRYCOATES - 53A | EDINBURGH(SM) - 64A | NEW ENGLAND - 35A | HEATON - 52B | EDINBURGH(SM) - 64A |
| **Jan-52** | DAIRYCOATES - 53A | EDINBURGH(SM) - 64A | LINCOLN - 40A | LOWESTOFT - 32C | DAIRYCOATES - 53A | EDINBURGH(SM) - 64A | NEW ENGLAND - 35A | **1/52: TWEED - 52D** | EDINBURGH(SM) - 64A |
| **Aug-52** | DAIRYCOATES - 53A | EDINBURGH(SM) - 64A | LINCOLN - 40A | LOWESTOFT - 32C | DAIRYCOATES - 53A | EDINBURGH(SM) - 64A | NEW ENGLAND - 35A | TWEEDMOUTH - 52D | EDINBURGH(SM) - 64A |
| **Jan-53** | DAIRYCOATES - 53A | EDINBURGH(SM) - 64A | LINCOLN - 40A | LOWESTOFT - 32C | **10./52: HTN - 52B** | EDINBURGH(SM) - 64A | NEW ENGLAND - 35A | TWEEDMOUTH - 52D | EDINBURGH(SM) - 64A |
| **Aug-53** | DAIRYCOATES - 53A | EDINBURGH(SM) - 64A | LINCOLN - 40A | LOWESTOFT - 32C | HEATON - 52B | EDINBURGH(SM) - 64A | NEW ENGLAND - 35A | TWEEDMOUTH - 52D | EDINBURGH(SM) - 64A |
| **Jan-54** | DAIRYCOATES - 53A | EDINBURGH(SM) - 64A | LINCOLN - 40A | LOWESTOFT - 32C | HEATON - 52B | EDINBURGH(SM) - 64A | **10/53: MARCH - 31B** | TWEEDMOUTH - 52D | EDINBURGH(SM) - 64A |
| **Aug-54** | DAIRYCOATES - 53A | EDINBURGH(SM) - 64A | LINCOLN - 40A | LOWESTOFT - 32C | HEATON - 52B | EDINBURGH(SM) - 64A | MARCH - 31B | TWEEDMOUTH - 52D | EDINBURGH(SM) - 64A |
| **Jan-55** | DAIRYCOATES - 53A | EDINBURGH(SM) - 64A | LINCOLN - 40A | LOWESTOFT - 32C | HEATON - 52B | EDINBURGH(SM) - 64A | MARCH - 31B | TWEEDMOUTH - 52D | EDINBURGH(SM) - 64A |
| **Aug-55** | DAIRYCOATES - 53A | EDINBURGH(SM) - 64A | LINCOLN - 40A | LOWESTOFT - 32C | HEATON - 52B | EDINBURGH(SM) - 64A | MARCH - 31B | TWEEDMOUTH - 52D | EDINBURGH(SM) - 64A |
| **Jan-56** | DAIRYCOATES - 53A | EDINBURGH(SM) - 64A | LINCOLN - 40A | LOWESTOFT - 32C | HEATON - 52B | EDINBURGH(SM) - 64A | MARCH - 31B | TWEEDMOUTH - 52D | EDINBURGH(SM) - 64A |
| **Aug-56** | DAIRYCOATES - 53A | EDINBURGH(SM) - 64A | LINCOLN - 40A | LOWESTOFT - 32C | HEATON - 52B | EDINBURGH(SM) - 64A | MARCH - 31B | TWEEDMOUTH - 52D | EDINBURGH(SM) - 64A |
| **Jan-57** | DAIRYCOATES - 53A | EDINBURGH(SM) - 64A | LINCOLN - 40A | LOWESTOFT - 32C | HEATON - 52B | EDINBURGH(SM) - 64A | MARCH - 31B | TWEEDMOUTH - 52D | EDINBURGH(SM) - 64A |
| **Aug-57** | DAIRYCOATES - 53A | EDINBURGH(SM) - 64A | LINCOLN - 40A | LOWESTOFT - 32C | HEATON - 52B | EDINBURGH(SM) - 64A | MARCH - 31B | TWEEDMOUTH - 52D | EDINBURGH(SM) - 64A |
| **Jan-58** | DAIRYCOATES - 53A | EDINBURGH(SM) - 64A | **11/57: DCTR - 36A** | LOWESTOFT - 32C | HEATON - 52B | EDINBURGH(SM) - 64A | MARCH - 31B | TWEEDMOUTH - 52D | EDINBURGH(SM) - 64A |
| **Aug-58** | **9/58: HTN - 52B** | EDINBURGH(SM) - 64A | DONCASTER - 36A | LOWESTOFT - 32C | HEATON - 52B | EDINBURGH(SM) - 64A | MARCH - 31B | TWEEDMOUTH - 52D | EDINBURGH(SM) - 64A |
| **Jan-59** | HEATON - 52B | EDINBURGH(SM) - 64A | DONCASTER - 36A | LOWESTOFT - 32C | HEATON - 52B | EDINBURGH(SM) - 64A | MARCH - 31B | TWEEDMOUTH - 52D | EDINBURGH(SM) - 64A |
| **Aug-59** | HEATON - 52B | EDINBURGH(SM) - 64A | DONCASTER - 36A | LOWESTOFT - 32C | HEATON - 52B | EDINBURGH(SM) - 64A | MARCH - 31B | TWEEDMOUTH - 52D | **7/59: W/D** |
| **Nov-59** | HEATON - 52B | EDINBURGH(SM) - 64A | DONCASTER - 36A | **11/59: NOR - 32A** | HEATON - 52B | EDINBURGH(SM) - 64A | MARCH - 31B | TWEEDMOUTH - 52D | |
| **Jan-60** | **2/60: DAIRY - 50B** | EDINBURGH(SM) - 64A | DONCASTER - 36A | **2/60: MARCH - 31B** | **2/60: DAIRY - 53A** | EDINBURGH(SM) - 64A | MARCH - 31B | TWEEDMOUTH - 52D | |
| **Apr-60** | DAIRYCOATES - 50B | EDINBURGH(SM) - 64A | DONCASTER - 36A | **3/60: STAVE - 41H** | DAIRYCOATES - 50B | **3/60: W/D** | MARCH - 31B | TWEEDMOUTH - 52D | |
| **Aug-60** | DAIRYCOATES - 50B | EDINBURGH(SM) - 64A | DONCASTER - 36A | **4/60: LIN - 40A** | DAIRYCOATES - 50B | | MARCH - 31B | TWEEDMOUTH - 52D | |
| **Nov-60** | DAIRYCOATES - 50B | EDINBURGH(SM) - 64A | DONCASTER - 36A | LINCOLN - 40A | DAIRYCOATES - 50B | | MARCH - 31B | TWEEDMOUTH - 52D | |

| | 61932 | 61933 | 61934 | 61935 | 61936 | 61937 | 61938 | 61939 | 61940 |
|---|---|---|---|---|---|---|---|---|---|
| **Aug-50** | DAIRYCOATES - 53A | EDINBURGH(SM) - 64A | DAIRYCOATES - 53A | DAIRYCOATES - 53A | CARLISLE(CANAL) - 12B | CARLISLE(CANAL) - 12B | MARCH - 31B | NORWICH - 32A | MARCH - 31B |
| **Jan-51** | DAIRYCOATES - 53A | EDINBURGH(SM) - 64A | DAIRYCOATES - 53A | DAIRYCOATES - 53A | CARLISLE(CANAL) - 12B | CARLISLE(CANAL) - 12B | MARCH - 31B | NORWICH - 32A | MARCH - 31B |
| **Aug-51** | DAIRYCOATES - 53A | EDINBURGH(SM) - 64A | DAIRYCOATES - 53A | DAIRYCOATES - 53A | CARLISE(CANAL) - 68E | CARLISE(CANAL) - 68E | MARCH - 31B | NORWICH - 32A | MARCH - 31B |
| **Jan-52** | DAIRYCOATES - 53A | EDINBURGH(SM) - 64A | DAIRYCOATES - 53A | DAIRYCOATES - 53A | CARLISE(CANAL) - 68E | CARLISE(CANAL) - 68E | MARCH - 31B | NORWICH - 32A | MARCH - 31B |
| **Aug-52** | **10/52: HTN - 52B** | EDINBURGH(SM) - 64A | DAIRYCOATES - 53A | DAIRYCOATES - 53A | CARLISE(CANAL) - 68E | CARLISE(CANAL) - 68E | MARCH - 31B | NORWICH - 32A | MARCH - 31B |
| **Jan-53** | **12/52: TWEED - 52D** | EDINBURGH(SM) - 64A | DAIRYCOATES - 53A | DAIRYCOATES - 53A | CARLISE(CANAL) - 68E | CARLISE(CANAL) - 68E | MARCH - 31B | NORWICH - 32A | MARCH - 31B |
| **Aug-53** | TWEEDMOUTH - 52D | EDINBURGH(SM) - 64A | DAIRYCOATES - 53A | DAIRYCOATES - 53A | CARLISE(CANAL) - 68E | CARLISE(CANAL) - 68E | MARCH - 31B | NORWICH - 32A | MARCH - 31B |
| **Jan-54** | **1/54: HTN - 52B** | EDINBURGH(SM) - 64A | DAIRYCOATES - 53A | DAIRYCOATES - 53A | CARLISE(CANAL) - 68E | CARLISE(CANAL) - 68E | MARCH - 31B | NORWICH - 32A | MARCH - 31B |
| **Aug-54** | HEATON - 52B | EDINBURGH(SM) - 64A | DAIRYCOATES - 53A | DAIRYCOATES - 53A | CARLISE(CANAL) - 68E | CARLISE(CANAL) - 68E | MARCH - 31B | NORWICH - 32A | MARCH - 31B |
| **Jan-55** | HEATON - 52B | EDINBURGH(SM) - 64A | DAIRYCOATES - 53A | DAIRYCOATES - 53A | CARLISE(CANAL) - 68E | CARLISE(CANAL) - 68E | MARCH - 31B | NORWICH - 32A | MARCH - 31B |
| **Aug-55** | **9/55: DAIRY - 53A** | EDINBURGH(SM) - 64A | DAIRYCOATES - 53A | DAIRYCOATES - 53A | CARLISE(CANAL) - 68E | CARLISE(CANAL) - 68E | MARCH - 31B | NORWICH - 32A | MARCH - 31B |
| **Jan-56** | DAIRYCOATES - 53A | EDINBURGH(SM) - 64A | DAIRYCOATES - 53A | DAIRYCOATES - 53A | CARLISE(CANAL) - 68E | CARLISE(CANAL) - 68E | MARCH - 31B | NORWICH - 32A | MARCH - 31B |
| **Aug-56** | DAIRYCOATES - 53A | EDINBURGH(SM) - 64A | DAIRYCOATES - 53A | DAIRYCOATES - 53A | CARLISE(CANAL) - 68E | CARLISE(CANAL) - 68E | **10/56: DARNALL - 41A** | NORWICH - 32A | **10/56: DCTR - 36A** |
| **Jan-57** | DAIRYCOATES - 53A | EDINBURGH(SM) - 64A | DAIRYCOATES - 53A | DAIRYCOATES - 53A | CARLISE(CANAL) - 68E | CARLISE(CANAL) - 68E | DARNALL - 41A | NORWICH - 32A | DONCASTER - 36A |
| **Aug-57** | DAIRYCOATES - 53A | EDINBURGH(SM) - 64A | DAIRYCOATES - 53A | DAIRYCOATES - 53A | CARLISE(CANAL) - 68E | CARLISE(CANAL) - 68E | DARNALL - 41A | NORWICH - 32A | DONCASTER - 36A |
| **Jan-58** | DAIRYCOATES - 53A | EDINBURGH(SM) - 64A | DAIRYCOATES - 53A | DAIRYCOATES - 53A | CARLISLECANAL - 68E | CARLISLECANAL - 68E | DARNALL - 41A | NORWICH - 32A | DONCASTER - 36A |
| **Aug-58** | DAIRYCOATES - 53A | EDINBURGH(SM) - 64A | **6/58: TWEED - 52D** | DAIRYCOATES - 53A | CARLISLECANAL - 12C | CARLISLECANAL - 12C | DARNALL - 41A | NORWICH - 32A | DONCASTER - 36A |
| **Jan-59** | DAIRYCOATES - 53A | EDINBURGH(SM) - 64A | TWEEDMOUTH - 52D | DAIRYCOATES - 53A | CARLISLECANAL - 12C | CARLISLECANAL - 12C | DARNALL - 41A | NORWICH - 32A | DONCASTER - 36A |
| **Aug-59** | DAIRYCOATES - 53A | EDINBURGH(SM) - 64A | TWEEDMOUTH - 52D | DAIRYCOATES - 53A | CARLISLECANAL - 12C | **6/59: MARCH - 31B** | DARNALL - 41A | NORWICH - 32A | DONCASTER - 36A |
| **Nov-59** | DAIRYCOATES - 53A | EDINBURGH(SM) - 64A | TWEEDMOUTH - 52D | DAIRYCOATES - 53A | CARLISLECANAL - 12C | MARCH - 31B | DARNALL - 41A | NORWICH - 32A | DONCASTER - 36A |
| **Jan-60** | DAIRYCOATES - 53A | EDINBURGH(SM) - 64A | TWEEDMOUTH - 52D | DAIRYCOATES - 53A | CARLISLECANAL - 12C | **2/60: CANAL - 12C** | DARNALL - 41A | NORWICH - 32A | DONCASTER - 36A |
| **Apr-60** | DAIRYCOATES - 50B | EDINBURGH(SM) - 64A | TWEEDMOUTH - 52D | DAIRYCOATES - 50B | CARLISLECANAL - 12C | **3/60: W/D** | DARNALL - 41A | NORWICH - 32A | DONCASTER - 36A |
| **Aug-60** | DAIRYCOATES - 50B | EDINBURGH(SM) - 64A | TWEEDMOUTH - 52D | DAIRYCOATES - 50B | CARLISLECANAL - 12C | | DARNALL - 41A | NORWICH - 32A | DONCASTER - 36A |
| **Nov-60** | DAIRYCOATES - 50B | **11/60: W/D** | TWEEDMOUTH - 52D | DAIRYCOATES - 50B | CARLISLECANAL - 12C | | DARNALL - 41A | NORWICH - 32A | DONCASTER - 36A |

| | 61941 | 61942 | 61943 | 61944 | 61945 | 61946 | 61947 | 61948 | 61949 |
|---|---|---|---|---|---|---|---|---|---|
| Aug-50 | DAIRYCOATES - 53A | NORWICH - 32A | ANNESLEY - 38B | LINCOLN - 40A | DAIRYCOATES - 53A | MARCH - 31B | NORWICH - 32A | MARCH - 31B | LOWESTOFT - 32C |
| Jan-51 | DAIRYCOATES - 53A | NORWICH - 32A | ANNESLEY - 38B | LINCOLN - 40A | DAIRYCOATES - 53A | MARCH - 31B | NORWICH - 32A | MARCH - 31B | LOWESTOFT - 32C |
| Aug-51 | DAIRYCOATES - 53A | **6/51: MARCH - 31B** | ANNESLEY - 38B | LINCOLN - 40A | DAIRYCOATES - 53A | MARCH - 31B | **6/51: MARCH - 31B** | MARCH - 31B | LOWESTOFT - 32C |
| Jan-52 | DAIRYCOATES - 53A | MARCH - 31B | ANNESLEY - 38B | LINCOLN - 40A | DAIRYCOATES - 53A | MARCH - 31B | MARCH - 31B | MARCH - 31B | LOWESTOFT - 32C |
| Aug-52 | DAIRYCOATES - 53A | **7/52: LINC - 40A** | ANNESLEY - 38B | LINCOLN - 40A | DAIRYCOATES - 53A | MARCH - 31B | MARCH - 31B | MARCH - 31B | LOWESTOFT - 32C |
| Jan-53 | DAIRYCOATES - 53A | **10/52: STRAT - 30A** | ANNESLEY - 38B | LINCOLN - 40A | DAIRYCOATES - 53A | MARCH - 31B | MARCH - 31B | MARCH - 31B | LOWESTOFT - 32C |
| Aug-53 | DAIRYCOATES - 53A | STRATFORD - 30A | **10/53: MARCH - 31B** | LINCOLN - 40A | DAIRYCOATES - 53A | **10/53: DCTR - 36A** | MARCH - 31B | MARCH - 31B | LOWESTOFT - 32C |
| Jan-54 | DAIRYCOATES - 53A | STRATFORD - 30A | MARCH - 31B | LINCOLN - 40A | DAIRYCOATES - 53A | **11/53: MARCH - 31B** | MARCH - 31B | MARCH - 31B | LOWESTOFT - 32C |
| Aug-54 | DAIRYCOATES - 53A | STRATFORD - 30A | MARCH - 31B | LINCOLN - 40A | DAIRYCOATES - 53A | MARCH - 31B | MARCH - 31B | MARCH - 31B | LOWESTOFT - 32C |
| Jan-55 | DAIRYCOATES - 53A | STRATFORD - 30A | MARCH - 31B | LINCOLN - 40A | DAIRYCOATES - 53A | MARCH - 31B | MARCH - 31B | MARCH - 31B | LOWESTOFT - 32C |
| Aug-55 | DAIRYCOATES - 53A | STRATFORD - 30A | **7/55: BOST - 40F** | LINCOLN - 40A | DAIRYCOATES - 53A | MARCH - 31B | MARCH - 31B | MARCH - 31B | LOWESTOFT - 32C |
| Jan-56 | DAIRYCOATES - 53A | STRATFORD - 30A | BOSTON - 40F | LINCOLN - 40A | DAIRYCOATES - 53A | MARCH - 31B | MARCH - 31B | MARCH - 31B | LOWESTOFT - 32C |
| Aug-56 | DAIRYCOATES - 53A | STRATFORD - 30A | BOSTON - 40F | LINCOLN - 40A | DAIRYCOATES - 53A | MARCH - 31B | **10/56: COLW - 38A** | MARCH - 31B | LOWESTOFT - 32C |
| Jan-57 | DAIRYCOATES - 53A | STRATFORD - 30A | BOSTON - 40F | LINCOLN - 40A | DAIRYCOATES - 53A | MARCH - 31B | COLWICK - 38A | MARCH - 31B | LOWESTOFT - 32C |
| Aug-57 | DAIRYCOATES - 53A | STRATFORD - 30A | BOSTON - 40F | LINCOLN - 40A | DAIRYCOATES - 53A | MARCH - 31B | COLWICK - 38A | MARCH - 31B | LOWESTOFT - 32C |
| Jan-58 | DAIRYCOATES - 53A | **3/58: PARK - 30F** | **11/57: DARN - 41A** | LINCOLN - 40A | DAIRYCOATES - 53A | MARCH - 31B | COLWICK - 38A | MARCH - 31B | LOWESTOFT - 32C |
| Aug-58 | DAIRYCOATES - 53A | PARKESTON - 30F | DARNALL - 41A | LINCOLN - 40A | DAIRYCOATES - 53A | MARCH - 31B | COLWICK - 40E | MARCH - 31B | LOWESTOFT - 32C |
| Jan-59 | DAIRYCOATES - 53A | PARKESTON - 30F | DARNALL - 41A | LINCOLN - 40A | DAIRYCOATES - 53A | MARCH - 31B | COLWICK - 40E | MARCH - 31B | **12/58: NOR - 32A** |
| Aug-59 | DAIRYCOATES - 53A | PARKESTON - 30F | DARNALL - 41A | LINCOLN - 40A | DAIRYCOATES - 53A | MARCH - 31B | COLWICK - 40E | MARCH - 31B | NORWICH - 32A |
| Nov-59 | DAIRYCOATES - 53A | PARKESTON - 30F | **12/59: COLW - 40E** | LINCOLN - 40A | DAIRYCOATES - 53A | MARCH - 31B | COLWICK - 40E | MARCH - 31B | NORWICH - 32A |
| Jan-60 | DAIRYCOATES - 53A | PARKESTON - 30F | COLWICK - 40E | LINCOLN - 40A | DAIRYCOATES - 53A | MARCH - 31B | COLWICK - 40E | MARCH - 31B | NORWICH - 32A |
| Apr-60 | DAIRYCOATES - 50B | PARKESTON - 30F | COLWICK - 40E | LINCOLN - 40A | DAIRYCOATES - 50B | MARCH - 31B | COLWICK - 40E | MARCH - 31B | NORWICH - 32A |
| Aug-60 | DAIRYCOATES - 50B | **6/60: MARCH - 31B** | COLWICK - 40E | LINCOLN - 40A | DAIRYCOATES - 50B | MARCH - 31B | COLWICK - 40E | MARCH - 31B | NORWICH - 32A |
| Nov-60 | DAIRYCOATES - 50B | MARCH - 31B | COLWICK - 40E | LINCOLN - 40A | DAIRYCOATES - 50B | MARCH - 31B | COLWICK - 40E | MARCH - 31B | NORWICH - 32A |

| | 61950 | 61951 | 61952 | 61953 | 61954 | 6195S | 61956 | 61957 | 61958 |
|---|---|---|---|---|---|---|---|---|---|
| Aug-50 | GORTON - 39A | NEWENGLAND - 35A | HEATON - 52B | NORWICH - 32A | NEWENGLAND - 35A | EDINBURGH(SM) - 64A | GORTON - 39A | NORWICH - 32A | LOWESTOFT - 32C |
| Jan-51 | GORTON - 39A | NEWENGLAND - 35A | HEATON - 52B | NORWICH - 32A | NEWENGLAND - 35A | EDINBURGH(SM) - 64A | GORTON - 39A | NORWICH - 32A | LOWESTOFT - 32C |
| Aug-51 | GORTON - 39A | NEWENGLAND - 35A | HEATON - 52B | NORWICH - 32A | NEWENGLAND - 35A | EDINBURGH(SM) - 64A | **5/51: IMM - 40B** | NORWICH - 32A | LOWESTOFT - 32C |
| Jan-52 | GORTON - 39A | NEWENGLAND - 35A | HEATON - 52B | NORWICH - 32A | NEWENGLAND - 35A | EDINBURGH(SM) - 64A | IMMINGHAM - 40B | NORWICH - 32A | LOWESTOFT - 32C |
| Aug-52 | GORTON - 39A | **10/52: STRAT - 30A** | HEATON - 52B | NORWICH - 32A | NEWENGLAND - 35A | EDINBURGH(SM) - 64A | IMMINGHAM - 40B | NORWICH - 32A | LOWESTOFT - 32C |
| Jan-53 | GORTON - 39A | STRATFORD - 30A | **12/52: TWEED - 52D** | NORWICH - 32A | NEWENGLAND - 35A | EDINBURGH(SM) - 64A | IMMINGHAM - 40B | NORWICH - 32A | LOWESTOFT - 32C |
| Aug-53 | GORTON - 39A | STRATFORD - 30A | TWEEDMOUTH - 52D | **11/53: LOW - 32C** | **10/53: MARCH - 31B** | EDINBURGH(SM) - 64A | IMMINGHAM - 40B | NORWICH - 32A | LOWESTOFT - 32C |
| Jan-54 | GORTON - 39A | STRATFORD - 30A | TWEEDMOUTH - 52D | **1/54: NOR - 32A** | MARCH - 31B | EDINBURGH(SM) - 64A | IMMINGHAM - 40B | NORWICH - 32A | LOWESTOFT - 32C |
| Aug-54 | **6/54: DARN - 39B** | STRATFORD - 30A | TWEEDMOUTH - 52D | NORWICH - 32A | MARCH - 31B | EDINBURGH(SM) - 64A | IMMINGHAM - 40B | NORWICH - 32A | LOWESTOFT - 32C |
| Jan-55 | **10/54: LINC - 40A** | STRATFORD - 30A | TWEEDMOUTH - 52D | NORWICH - 32A | MARCH - 31B | EDINBURGH(SM) - 64A | IMMINGHAM - 40B | NORWICH - 32A | LOWESTOFT - 32C |
| Aug-55 | **5/55: IMM - 40B** | STRATFORD - 30A | TWEEDMOUTH - 52D | NORWICH - 32A | MARCH - 31B | EDINBURGH(SM) - 64A | IMMINGHAM - 40B | NORWICH - 32A | LOWESTOFT - 32C |
| Jan-56 | IMMINGHAM - 40B | STRATFORD - 30A | TWEEDMOUTH - 52D | NORWICH - 32A | MARCH - 31B | EDINBURGH(SM) - 64A | IMMINGHAM - 40B | NORWICH - 32A | LOWESTOFT - 32C |
| Aug-56 | IMMINGHAM - 40B | STRATFORD - 30A | TWEEDMOUTH - 52D | NORWICH - 32A | **10/56: DARN - 41A** | EDINBURGH(SM) - 64A | IMMINGHAM - 40B | **1/57: YAR (ST) - 32D** | LOWESTOFT - 32C |
| Jan-57 | IMMINGHAM - 40B | STRATFORD - 30A | TWEEDMOUTH - 52D | NORWICH - 32A | DARNALL - 41A | EDINBURGH(SM) - 64A | IMMINGHAM - 40B | **2/57: NOR - 32A** | LOWESTOFT - 32C |
| Aug-57 | IMMINGHAM - 40B | STRATFORD - 30A | TWEEDMOUTH - 52D | NORWICH - 32A | DARNALL - 41A | EDINBURGH(SM) - 64A | IMMINGHAM - 40B | **6/57: LOW - 32C** | LOWESTOFT - 32C |
| Jan-58 | IMMINGHAM - 40B | **3/58: APRK - 30F** | TWEEDMOUTH - 52D | NORWICH - 32A | DARNALL - 41A | EDINBURGH(SM) - 64A | IMMINGHAM - 40B | **11/57: NOR - 32A** | LOWESTOFT - 32C |
| Aug-58 | IMMINGHAM - 40B | PARKESTON - 30F | TWEEDMOUTH - 52D | NORWICH - 32A | **3/59: MARCH - 31B** | EDINBURGH(SM) - 64A | IMMINGHAM - 40B | NORWICH - 32A | LOWESTOFT - 32C |
| Jan-59 | IMMINGHAM - 40B | PARKESTON - 30F | TWEEDMOUTH - 52D | NORWICH - 32A | **5/59: NOR - 32A** | EDINBURGH(SM) - 64A | IMMINGHAM - 40B | NORWICH - 32A | LOWESTOFT - 32C |
| Aug-59 | IMMINGHAM - 40B | PARKESTON - 30F | TWEEDMOUTH - 52D | NORWICH - 32A | **8/59: MARCH - 31B** | EDINBURGH(SM) - 64A | IMMINGHAM - 40B | NORWICH - 32A | LOWESTOFT - 32C |
| Nov-59 | IMMINGHAM - 40B | PARKESTON - 30F | TWEEDMOUTH - 52D | NORWICH - 32A | MARCH - 31B | EDINBURGH(SM) - 64A | IMMINGHAM - 40B | NORWICH - 32A | LOWESTOFT - 32C |
| Jan-60 | IMMINGHAM - 40B | PARKESTON - 30F | TWEEDMOUTH - 52D | NORWICH - 32A | MARCH - 31B | EDINBURGH(SM) - 64A | IMMINGHAM - 40B | NORWICH - 32A | LOWESTOFT - 32C |
| Apr-60 | IMMINGHAM - 40B | PARKESTON - 30F | TWEEDMOUTH - 52D | NORWICH - 32A | MARCH - 31B | EDINBURGH(SM) - 64A | IMMINGHAM - 40B | NORWICH - 32A | **3/60: STAVE - 41H** |
| Aug-60 | IMMINGHAM - 40B | PARKESTON - 30F | TWEEDMOUTH - 52D | NORWICH - 32A | MARCH - 31B | **6/60: W/D** | IMMINGHAM - 40B | NORWICH - 32A | STAVELEY(GC) - 41H |
| Nov-60 | IMMINGHAM - 40B | PARKESTON - 30F | TWEEDMOUTH - 52D | NORWICH - 32A | MARCH - 31B | | IMMINGHAM - 40B | NORWICH - 32A | STAVELEY(GC) - 41H |

| | 61959 | 61960 | 61961 | 61962 | 61963 | 61964 | 61965 | 61966 | 61967 |
|---|---|---|---|---|---|---|---|---|---|
| Aug-50 | LOWESTOFT - 32C | LINCOLN - 40A | MARCH - 31B | HEATON - 52B | IMMINGHAM - 40B | LINCOLN - 40A | DAIRYCOATES - 53A | LINCOLN - 40A | NEWENGLAND - 35A |
| Jan-51 | LOWESTOFT - 32C | LINCOLN - 40A | **10/50: LOW - 32C** | HEATON - 52B | IMMINGHAM - 40B | LINCOLN - 40A | DAIRYCOATES - 53A | LINCOLN - 40A | NEWENGLAND - 35A |
| Aug-51 | LOWESTOFT - 32C | LINCOLN - 40A | **12/50: MARCH - 31B** | HEATON - 52B | IMMINGHAM - 40B | LINCOLN - 40A | DAIRYCOATES - 53A | LINCOLN - 40A | NEWENGLAND - 35A |
| Jan-52 | LOWESTOFT - 32C | LINCOLN - 40A | MARCH - 31B | **1/52: TWEED - 52D** | IMMINGHAM - 40B | LINCOLN - 40A | DAIRYCOATES - 53A | **3/52: GORT - 39A** | NEWENGLAND - 35A |
| Aug-52 | LOWESTOFT - 32C | LINCOLN - 40A | MARCH - 31B | TWEEDMOUTH - 52D | **7/52: LINC - 40A** | LINCOLN - 40A | DAIRYCOATES - 53A | GORTON - 39A | NEWENGLAND - 35A |
| Jan-53 | LOWESTOFT - 32C | LINCOLN - 40A | MARCH - 31B | TWEEDMOUTH - 52D | **10/52: STRAT - 30A** | LINCOLN - 40A | DAIRYCOATES - 53A | GORTON - 39A | NEWENGLAND - 35A |
| Aug-53 | LOWESTOFT - 32C | LINCOLN - 40A | MARCH - 31B | TWEEDMOUTH - 52D | STRATFORD - 30A | LINCOLN - 40A | DAIRYCOATES - 53A | GORTON - 39A | **10/53: MARCH - 31B** |
| Jan-54 | LOWESTOFT - 32C | LINCOLN - 40A | MARCH - 31B | TWEEDMOUTH - 52D | STRATFORD - 30A | LINCOLN - 40A | DAIRYCOATES - 53A | GORTON - 39A | MARCH - 31B |
| Aug-54 | LOWESTOFT - 32C | LINCOLN - 40A | MARCH - 31B | TWEEDMOUTH - 52D | STRATFORD - 30A | LINCOLN - 40A | DAIRYCOATES - 53A | GORTON - 39A | MARCH - 31B |
| Jan-55 | LOWESTOFT - 32C | LINCOLN - 40A | MARCH - 31B | TWEEDMOUTH - 52D | STRATFORD - 30A | LINCOLN - 40A | DAIRYCOATES - 53A | GORTON - 39A | MARCH - 31B |
| Aug-55 | LOWESTOFT - 32C | LINCOLN - 40A | MARCH - 31B | TWEEDMOUTH - 52D | STRATFORD - 30A | LINCOLN - 40A | DAIRYCOATES - 53A | GORTON - 39A | MARCH - 31B |
| Jan-56 | LOWESTOFT - 32C | LINCOLN - 40A | MARCH - 31B | TWEEDMOUTH - 52D | STRATFORD - 30A | LINCOLN - 40A | DAIRYCOATES - 53A | GORTON - 39A | MARCH - 31B |
| Aug-56 | LOWESTOFT - 32C | LINCOLN - 40A | **10/56: DCTR - 36A** | TWEEDMOUTH - 52D | STRATFORD - 30A | LINCOLN - 40A | DAIRYCOATES - 53A | GORTON - 39A | **10/56: DARN - 41A** |
| Jan-57 | LOWESTOFT - 32C | LINCOLN - 40A | DONCASTER - 36A | TWEEDMOUTH - 52D | STRATFORD - 30A | LINCOLN - 40A | DAIRYCOATES - 53A | GORTON - 39A | DARNALL - 41A |
| Aug-57 | LOWESTOFT - 32C | LINCOLN - 40A | DONCASTER - 36A | TWEEDMOUTH - 52D | STRATFORD - 30A | LINCOLN - 40A | DAIRYCOATES - 53A | **11/57: WOOD - 38E** | DARNALL - 41A |
| Jan-58 | LOWESTOFT - 32C | LINCOLN - 40A | DONCASTER - 36A | TWEEDMOUTH - 52D | STRATFORD - 30A | **11/57: DCTR - 36A** | DAIRYCOATES - 53A | 1/58: IMM - 40B | DARNALL - 41A |
| Aug-58 | LOWESTOFT - 32C | LINCOLN - 40A | DONCASTER - 36A | **9/58: HTN - 52B** | STRATFORD - 30A | DONCASTER - 36A | DAIRYCOATES - 53A | IMMINGHAM - 40B | DARNALL - 41A |
| Jan-59 | LOWESTOFT - 32C | LINCOLN - 40A | DONCASTER - 36A | HEATON - 52B | **12/58: PARK - 30F** | DONCASTER - 36A | DAIRYCOATES - 53A | IMMINGHAM - 40B | DARNALL - 41A |
| Aug-59 | LOWESTOFT - 32C | LINCOLN - 40A | DONCASTER - 36A | HEATON - 52B | PARKESTON - 30F | DONCASTER - 36A | DAIRYCOATES - 53A | IMMINGHAM - 40B | DARNALL - 41A |
| Nov-59 | LOWESTOFT - 32C | LINCOLN - 40A | DONCASTER - 36A | HEATON - 52B | PARKESTON - 30F | DONCASTER - 36A | DAIRYCOATES - 53A | IMMINGHAM - 40B | DARNALL - 41A |
| Jan-60 | LOWESTOFT - 32C | LINCOLN - 40A | DONCASTER - 36A | HEATON - 52B | PARKESTON - 30F | DONCASTER - 36A | DAIRYCOATES - 53A | IMMINGHAM - 40B | DARNALL - 41A |
| Apr-60 | **3/60: STAVE - 41H** | LINCOLN - 40A | DONCASTER - 36A | HEATON - 52B | PARKESTON - 30F | DONCASTER - 36A | DAIRYCOATES - 50B | IMMINGHAM - 40B | DARNALL - 41A |
| Aug-60 | **6/60: MEX - 41F** | LINCOLN - 40A | DONCASTER - 36A | **9/60: TWEED - 52D** | **6/60: MARCH - 31B** | DONCASTER - 36A | DAIRYCOATES - 50B | IMMINGHAM - 40B | DARNALL - 41A |
| Nov-60 | MEXBOROUGH - 41F | LINCOLN - 40A | DONCASTER - 36A | TWEEDMOUTH - 52D | MARCH - 31B | DONCASTER - 36A | DAIRYCOATES - 50B | IMMINGHAM - 40B | DARNALL - 41A |

| | 61968 | 61969 | 61970 | 61971 | 61972 | 61973 | 61974 | 61975 | 61976 |
|---|---|---|---|---|---|---|---|---|---|
| Aug-50 | EDINBURGH(SM) - 64A | HEATON - 52B | NORWICH - 32A | NORWICH - 32A | NEWENGLAND - 35A | LOWESTOFT - 32C | ANNESLEY - 38B | ANNESLEY - 38B | ANNESLEY - 38B |
| Jan-51 | EDINBURGH(SM) - 64A | HEATON - 52B | NORWICH - 32A | **11/50: YAR(B) - 32F** | NEWENGLAND - 35A | LOWESTOFT - 32C | ANNESLEY - 38B | ANNESLEY - 38B | ANNESLEY - 38B |
| Aug-51 | EDINBURGH(SM) - 64A | HEATON - 52B | NORWICH - 32A | **12/50: NOR - 32A** | NEWENGLAND - 35A | LOWESTOFT - 32C | ANNESLEY - 38B | ANNESLEY - 38B | ANNESLEY - 38B |
| Jan-52 | EDINBURGH(SM) - 64A | HEATON - 52B | NORWICH - 32A | NORWICH - 32A | NEWENGLAND - 35A | LOWESTOFT - 32C | ANNESLEY - 38B | ANNESLEY - 38B | ANNESLEY - 38B |
| Aug-52 | EDINBURGH(SM) - 64A | HEATON - 52B | NORWICH - 32A | NORWICH - 32A | NEWENGLAND - 35A | LOWESTOFT - 32C | ANNESLEY - 38B | ANNESLEY - 38B | ANNESLEY - 38B |
| Jan-53 | EDINBURGH(SM) - 64A | **12/52: TWEED - 52D** | NORWICH - 32A | NORWICH - 32A | NEWENGLAND - 35A | LOWESTOFT - 32C | ANNESLEY - 38B | ANNESLEY - 38B | ANNESLEY - 38B |
| Aug-53 | EDINBURGH(SM) - 64A | TWEEDMOUTH - 52D | NORWICH - 32A | NORWICH - 32A | **10/53: MARCH - 31B** | LOWESTOFT - 32C | ANNESLEY - 38B | ANNESLEY - 38B | ANNESLEY - 38B |
| Jan-54 | EDINBURGH(SM) - 64A | TWEEDMOUTH - 52D | NORWICH - 32A | NORWICH - 32A | MARCH - 31B | LOWESTOFT - 32C | ANNESLEY - 38B | ANNESLEY - 38B | **11/53: MARCH - 31B** |
| Aug-54 | EDINBURGH(SM) - 64A | TWEEDMOUTH - 52D | NORWICH - 32A | NORWICH - 32A | MARCH - 31B | LOWESTOFT - 32C | ANNESLEY - 38B | ANNESLEY - 38B | MARCH - 31B |
| Jan-55 | EDINBURGH(SM) - 64A | TWEEDMOUTH - 52D | NORWICH - 32A | NORWICH - 32A | MARCH - 31B | LOWESTOFT - 32C | **2/55: COLW - 38A** | ANNESLEY - 38B | MARCH - 31B |
| Aug-55 | EDINBURGH(SM) - 64A | TWEEDMOUTH - 52D | NORWICH - 32A | NORWICH - 32A | MARCH - 31B | LOWESTOFT - 32C | COLWICK - 38A | ANNESLEY - 38B | MARCH - 31B |
| Jan-56 | EDINBURGH(SM) - 64A | TWEEDMOUTH - 52D | **5/56: YAR(ST) - 32D** | NORWICH - 32A | MARCH - 31B | LOWESTOFT - 32C | COLWICK - 38A | ANNESLEY - 38B | MARCH - 31B |
| Aug-56 | EDINBURGH(SM) - 64A | TWEEDMOUTH - 52D | **7/56: NOR - 32A** | NORWICH - 32A | MARCH - 31B | LOWESTOFT - 32C | COLWICK - 38A | **10/56: COLW - 38A** | MARCH - 31B |
| Jan-57 | EDINBURGH(SM) - 64A | TWEEDMOUTH - 52D | **1/57: YAR(ST) - 32D** | NORWICH - 32A | MARCH - 31B | LOWESTOFT - 32C | COLWICK - 38A | **11/56: ANN - 38B** | MARCH - 31B |
| Aug-57 | EDINBURGH(SM) - 64A | TWEEDMOUTH - 52D | **2/57: NOR - 32A** | NORWICH - 32A | MARCH - 31B | LOWESTOFT - 32C | COLWICK - 38A | ANNESLEY - 38B | MARCH - 31B |
| Jan-58 | EDINBURGH(SM) - 64A | TWEEDMOUTH - 52D | NORWICH - 32A | NORWICH - 32A | MARCH - 31B | LOWESTOFT - 32C | COLWICK - 38A | ANNESLEY - 38B | MARCH - 31B |
| Aug-58 | EDINBURGH(SM) - 64A | TWEEDMOUTH - 52D | **6/58: LOW - 32C** | NORWICH - 32A | MARCH - 31B | LOWESTOFT - 32C | COLWICK - 40E | ANNESLEY - 16D | MARCH - 31B |
| Jan-59 | EDINBURGH(SM) - 64A | TWEEDMOUTH - 52D | **9/58: NOR - 32A** | NORWICH - 32A | MARCH - 31B | **12/58: NOR - 32A** | COLWICK - 40E | ANNESLEY - 16D | MARCH - 31B |
| Aug-59 | EDINBURGH(SM) - 64A | TWEEDMOUTH - 52D | NORWICH - 32A | NORWICH - 32A | MARCH - 31B | NORWICH - 32A | COLWICK - 40E | **4/59: ARDS - 56B** | MARCH - 31B |
| Nov-59 | EDINBURGH(SM) - 64A | TWEEDMOUTH - 52D | NORWICH - 32A | NORWICH - 32A | MARCH - 31B | NORWICH - 32A | COLWICK - 40E | ARDSLEY - 56B | MARCH - 31B |
| Jan-60 | EDINBURGH(SM) - 64A | TWEEDMOUTH - 52D | NORWICH - 32A | NORWICH - 32A | MARCH - 31B | NORWICH - 32A | COLWICK - 40E | ARDSLEY - 56B | MARCH - 31B |
| Apr-60 | EDINBURGH(SM) - 64A | TWEEDMOUTH - 52D | NORWICH - 32A | NORWICH - 32A | MARCH - 31B | **5/60: STAVE -41H** | COLWICK - 40E | ARDSLEY - 56B | **4/60: STAVE - 41H** |
| Aug-60 | EDINBURGH(SM) - 64A | TWEEDMOUTH - 52D | NORWICH - 32A | NORWICH - 32A | MARCH - 31B | STAVELEY - 41H | COLWICK - 40E | ARDSLEY - 56B | STAVELEY(GC) - 41H |
| Nov-60 | EDINBURGH(SM) - 64A | TWEEDMOUTH - 52D | NORWICH - 32A | NORWICH - 32A | MARCH - 31B | STAVELEY - 41H | COLWICK - 40E | ARDSLEY - 56B | STAVELEY(GC) - 41H |

| | 61977 | 61978 | 61979 | 61980 | 61981 | 61982 | 61983 | 61984 | 61985 |
|---|---|---|---|---|---|---|---|---|---|
| Aug-50 | ANNESLEY-38B | DONCASTER-36A | ANNESLEY-38B | ANNESLEY-38B | NORWICH-32A | LINCOLN-40A | EDINBURGH(SM)-64A | HEATON-52B | HEATON-52B |
| Jan-51 | ANNESLEY-38B | DONCASTER-36A | ANNESLEY-38B | ANNESLEY-38B | **5/51: MARCH - 31B** | **10/50: COLW - 38A** | EDINBURGH(SM)-64A | HEATON-52B | HEATON-52B |
| Aug-51 | ANNESLEY-38B | DONCASTER-36A | ANNESLEY-38B | ANNESLEY-38B | **9/51: LOW - 32C** | COLWICK-38A | EDINBURGH(SM)-64A | HEATON-52B | HEATON-52B |
| Jan-52 | **3/52: COLW - 38A** | DONCASTER-36A | ANNESLEY-38B | ANNESLEY-38B | **12/51: NOR - 32A** | COLWICK-38A | EDINBURGH(SM)-64A | HEATON-52B | **1/52: TWEED - 52D** |
| Aug-52 | **10/52: STRAT - 30A** | DONCASTER-36A | ANNESLEY-38B | ANNESLEY-38B | **10/52: LOW - 32C** | **10/52: STRAT - 30A** | EDINBURGH(SM)-64A | HEATON-52B | TWEEDMOUTH-52D |
| Jan-53 | STRATFORD-30A | DONCASTER-36A | ANNESLEY-38B | ANNESLEY-38B | **10/52: LOW - 32C** | STRATFORD-30A | EDINBURGH(SM)-64A | HEATON-52B | TWEEDMOUTH-52D |
| Aug-53 | STRATFORD-30A | DONCASTER-36A | **10/53: MARCH - 31B** | ANNESLEY-38B | **5/53: NOR - 32A** | STRATFORD-30A | EDINBURGH(SM)-64A | HEATON-52B | TWEEDMOUTH-52D |
| Jan-54 | STRATFORD-30A | **11/53: MARCH - 31B** | MARCH-31B | ANNESLEY-38B | NORWICH-32A | **11/53: MARCH - 31B** | EDINBURGH(SM)-64A | HEATON-52B | TWEEDMOUTH-52D |
| Aug-54 | STRATFORD-30A | MARCH-31B | MARCH-31B | ANNESLEY-38B | NORWICH-32A | MARCH-31B | EDINBURGH(SM)-64A | HEATON-52B | TWEEDMOUTH-52D |
| Jan-55 | STRATFORD-30A | MARCH-31B | MARCH-31B | ANNESLEY-38B | NORWICH-32A | MARCH-31B | EDINBURGH(SM)-64A | HEATON-52B | TWEEDMOUTH-52D |
| Aug-55 | STRATFORD-30A | MARCH-31B | MARCH-31B | ANNESLEY-38B | NORWICH-32A | MARCH-31B | EDINBURGH(SM)-64A | HEATON-52B | TWEEDMOUTH-52D |
| Jan-56 | STRATFORD-30A | MARCH-31B | MARCH-31B | ANNESLEY-38B | NORWICH-32A | MARCH-31B | EDINBURGH(SM)-64A | HEATON-52B | TWEEDMOUTH-52D |
| Aug-56 | STRATFORD-30A | MARCH-31B | MARCH-31B | ANNESLEY-38B | NORWICH-32A | **10/56: COLW - 38A** | EDINBURGH(SM)-64A | HEATON-52B | TWEEDMOUTH-52D |
| Jan-57 | STRATFORD-30A | **11/56: NEWE - 35A** | **11/56: NEWE - 35A** | ANNESLEY-38B | NORWICH-32A | COLWICK-38A | EDINBURGH(SM)-64A | HEATON-52B | TWEEDMOUTH-52D |
| Aug-57 | STRATFORD-30A | NEWENGLAND-35A | NEWENGLAND-35A | ANNESLEY-38B | NORWICH-32A | COLWICK-38A | EDINBURGH(SM)-64A | HEATON-52B | TWEEDMOUTH-52D |
| Jan-58 | STRATFORD-30A | NEWENGLAND-35A | NEWENGLAND-35A | ANNESLEY-38B | NORWICH-32A | COLWICK-38A | EDINBURGH(SM)-64A | HEATON-52B | TWEEDMOUTH-52D |
| Aug-58 | STRATFORD-30A | NEWENGLAND-34E | NEWENGLAND-34E | ANNESLEY-16D | NORWICH-32A | COLWICK-40E | EDINBURGH(SM)-64A | HEATON-52B | TWEEDMOUTH-52D |
| Jan-59 | **12/58: PARK - 30F** | NEWENGLAND-34E | NEWENGLAND-34E | **4/59: ARDS - 56B** | NORWICH-32A | COLWICK-40E | EDINBURGH(SM)-64A | HEATON-52B | TWEEDMOUTH-52D |
| Aug-59 | PARKESTON-30F | NEWENGLAND-34E | NEWENGLAND-34E | ARDSLEY-56B | NORWICH-32A | COLWICK-40E | **7/59: W/D** | HEATON-52B | TWEEDMOUTH-52D |
| Nov-59 | PARKESTON-30F | NEWENGLAND-34E | NEWENGLAND-34E | ARDSLEY-56B | NORWICH-32A | COLWICK-40E | | HEATON-52B | TWEEDMOUTH-52D |
| Jan-60 | PARKESTON-30F | NEWENGLAND-34E | NEWENGLAND-34E | ARDSLEY-56B | NORWICH-32A | COLWICK-40E | | HEATON-52B | TWEEDMOUTH-52D |
| Apr-60 | PARKESTON-30F | NEWENGLAND-34E | NEWENGLAND-34E | ARDSLEY-56B | **3/60: STAVE - 41H** | COLWICK-40E | | HEATON-52B | TWEEDMOUTH-52D |
| Aug-60 | PARKESTON-30F | NEWENGLAND-34E | NEWENGLAND-34E | ARDSLEY-56B | STAVELEY(GC)-41H | COLWICK-40E | | **9/60: TWEED - 52D** | TWEEDMOUTH-52D |
| Nov-60 | PARKESTON-30F | NEWENGLAND-34E | NEWENGLAND-34E | ARDSLEY-56B | STAVELEY(GC)-41H | COLWICK-40E | | TWEEDMOUTH-52D | TWEEDMOUTH-52D |

| | | | | | | | | K5 2-6-0 (1945) | K4 2-6-0 (1937) |
|---|---|---|---|---|---|---|---|---|---|
| | 61986 | 61987 | 61988 | 61989 | 61990 | 61991 | 61992 | 61863 | 61993 |
| Aug-50 | HEATON-52B | HEATON-52B | EDINBURGH(SM)-64A | NORWICH-32A | EDINBURGH(SM)-64A | EDINBURGH(SM)-64A | EDINBURGH(SM)-64A | NEWENGLAND-35A | EASTFIELD-65A |
| Jan-51 | HEATON-52B | HEATON-52B | EDINBURGH(SM)-64A | NORWICH-32A | EDINBURGH(SM)-64A | EDINBURGH(SM)-64A | EDINBURGH(SM)-64A | NEWENGLAND-35A | EASTFIELD-65A |
| Aug-51 | HEATON-52B | HEATON-52B | EDINBURGH(SM)-64A | NORWICH-32A | EDINBURGH(SM)-64A | EDINBURGH(SM)-64A | EDINBURGH(SM)-64A | NEWENGLAND-35A | EASTFIELD-65A |
| Jan-52 | HEATON-52B | HEATON-52B | EDINBURGH(SM)-64A | NORWICH-32A | EDINBURGH(SM)-64A | EDINBURGH(SM)-64A | EDINBURGH(SM)-64A | NEWENGLAND-35A | EASTFIELD-65A |
| Aug-52 | HEATON-52B | HEATON-52B | EDINBURGH(SM)-64A | NORWICH-32A | EDINBURGH(SM)-64A | EDINBURGH(SM)-64A | EDINBURGH(SM)-64A | **10/52: STRAT - 30A** | EASTFIELD-65A |
| Jan-53 | HEATON-52B | HEATON-52B | EDINBURGH(SM)-64A | NORWICH-32A | EDINBURGH(SM)-64A | EDINBURGH(SM)-64A | EDINBURGH(SM)-64A | STRATFORD-30A | EASTFIELD-65A |
| Aug-53 | HEATON-52B | HEATON-52B | EDINBURGH(SM)-64A | **11/53: LOW - 32C** | EDINBURGH(SM)-64A | EDINBURGH(SM)-64A | EDINBURGH(SM)-64A | STRATFORD-30A | EASTFIELD-65A |
| Jan-54 | HEATON-52B | HEATON-52B | EDINBURGH(SM)-64A | 1/54: NOR-32A | EDINBURGH(SM)-64A | EDINBURGH(SM)-64A | EDINBURGH(SM)-64A | STRATFORD-30A | EASTFIELD-65A |
| Aug-54 | HEATON-52B | HEATON-52B | EDINBURGH(SM)-64A | **8/54: LOW - 32C** | EDINBURGH(SM)-64A | EDINBURGH(SM)-64A | EDINBURGH(SM)-64A | STRATFORD-30A | EASTFIELD-65A |
| Jan-55 | HEATON-52B | HEATON-52B | EDINBURGH(SM)-64A | **11/54: NOR - 32A** | EDINBURGH(SM)-64A | EDINBURGH(SM)-64A | EDINBURGH(SM)-64A | STRATFORD-30A | EASTFIELD-65A |
| Aug-55 | HEATON-52B | HEATON-52B | EDINBURGH(SM)-64A | NORWICH-32A | EDINBURGH(SM)-64A | EDINBURGH(SM)-64A | EDINBURGH(SM)-64A | STRATFORD-30A | EASTFIELD-65A |
| Jan-56 | HEATON-52B | HEATON-52B | EDINBURGH(SM)-64A | NORWICH-32A | EDINBURGH(SM)-64A | EDINBURGH(SM)-64A | EDINBURGH(SM)-64A | STRATFORD-30A | EASTFIELD-65A |
| Aug-56 | HEATON-52B | HEATON-52B | EDINBURGH(SM)-64A | NORWICH-32A | EDINBURGH(SM)-64A | EDINBURGH(SM)-64A | EDINBURGH(SM)-64A | STRATFORD-30A | EASTFIELD-65A |
| Jan-57 | HEATON-52B | HEATON-52B | EDINBURGH(SM)-64A | NORWICH-32A | EDINBURGH(SM)-64A | EDINBURGH(SM)-64A | EDINBURGH(SM)-64A | STRATFORD-30A | EASTFIELD-65A |
| Aug-57 | HEATON-52B | HEATON-52B | EDINBURGH(SM)-64A | **12/57: YAR(ST) - 32D** | EDINBURGH(SM)-64A | EDINBURGH(SM)-64A | EDINBURGH(SM)-64A | STRATFORD-30A | EASTFIELD-65A |
| Jan-58 | HEATON-52B | HEATON-52B | EDINBURGH(SM)-64A | **2/58: NOR - 32A** | EDINBURGH(SM)-64A | EDINBURGH(SM)-64A | EDINBURGH(SM)-64A | STRATFORD-30A | EASTFIELD-65A |
| Aug-58 | HEATON-52B | HEATON-52B | EDINBURGH(SM)-64A | NORWICH-32A | EDINBURGH(SM)-64A | EDINBURGH(SM)-64A | EDINBURGH(SM)-64A | STRATFORD-30A | EASTFIELD-65A |
| Jan-59 | HEATON-52B | HEATON-52B | EDINBURGH(SM)-64A | NORWICH-32A | EDINBURGH(SM)-64A | EDINBURGH(SM)-64A | EDINBURGH(SM)-64A | STRATFORD-30A | EASTFIELD-65A |
| Aug-59 | HEATON-52B | HEATON-52B | EDINBURGH(SM)-64A | NORWICH-32A | EDINBURGH(SM)-64A | **5/59: W/D** | EDINBURGH(SM)-64A | STRATFORD-30A | **5/59: TH JN - 62A** |
| Nov-59 | HEATON-52B | HEATON-52B | **11/59: W/D** | NORWICH-32A | EDINBURGH(SM)-64A | | EDINBURGH(SM)-64A | STRATFORD-30A | THORNTONJCN-62A |
| Jan-60 | HEATON-52B | HEATON-52B | | NORWICH-32A | EDINBURGH(SM)-64A | | EDINBURGH(SM)-64A | STRATFORD-30A | THORNTONJCN-62A |
| Apr-60 | HEATON-52B | HEATON-52B | | **4/60: STAVE - 41H** | EDINBURGH(SM)-64A | | EDINBURGH(SM)-64A | **5/60: W/D** | THORNTONJCN-62A |
| Aug-60 | HEATON-52B | HEATON-52B | | STAVELEY(GC)-41H | EDINBURGH(SM)-64A | | **8/60: W/D** | | THORNTONJCN-62A |
| Nov-60 | HEATON-52B | HEATON-52B | | STAVELEY(GC)-41H | **11/60: W/D** | | | | THORNTONJCN-62A |

| | | | | | K1 2-6-0 (1945) | K1 2-6-0 (1949) | | | |
|---|---|---|---|---|---|---|---|---|---|
| | 61994 | 61995 | 61996 | 61998 | 61997 | 62001 | 62002 | 62003 | 62004 |
| Aug-50 | EASTFIELD-65A | FORTWILLIAM-63D | FORTWILLIAM-63D | EASTFIELD-65A | EASTFIELD-65A | STOCKTON-51E | HEATON-52B | HEATON-52B | DARLINGTON-51A |
| Jan-51 | EASTFIELD-65A | FORTWILLIAM-63D | FORTWILLIAM-63D | EASTFIELD-65A | EASTFIELD-65A | STOCKTON-51E | HEATON-52B | HEATON-52B | DARLINGTON-51A |
| Aug-51 | EASTFIELD-65A | FORTWILLIAM-63D | FORTWILLIAM-63D | EASTFIELD-65A | EASTFIELD-65A | STOCKTON-51E | HEATON-52B | HEATON-52B | DARLINGTON-51A |
| Jan-52 | EASTFIELD-65A | FORTWILLIAM-63D | FORTWILLIAM-63D | EASTFIELD-65A | EASTFIELD-65A | **11/51: DARL - 51A** | HEATON-52B | HEATON-52B | DARLINGTON-51A |
| Aug-52 | EASTFIELD-65A | FORTWILLIAM-63D | FORTWILLIAM-63D | EASTFIELD-65A | EASTFIELD-65A | DARLINGTON-51A | **7/52: BLAY - 52C** | **7/52: DARL - 51A** | DARLINGTON-51A |
| Jan-53 | EASTFIELD-65A | FORTWILLIAM-63D | FORTWILLIAM-63D | EASTFIELD-65A | EASTFIELD-65A | DARLINGTON-51A | BLAYDON-52C | DARLINGTON-51A | DARLINGTON-51A |
| Aug-53 | EASTFIELD-65A | FORTWILLIAM-63D | FORTWILLIAM-63D | EASTFIELD-65A | EASTFIELD-65A | DARLINGTON-51A | BLAYDON-52C | DARLINGTON-51A | DARLINGTON-51A |
| Jan-54 | EASTFIELD-65A | FORTWILLIAM-63D | FORTWILLIAM-63D | EASTFIELD-65A | EASTFIELD-65A | DARLINGTON-51A | BLAYDON-52C | DARLINGTON-51A | DARLINGTON-51A |
| Aug-54 | EASTFIELD-65A | **6/54: EAST - 65A** | **6/54: EAST - 65A** | EASTFIELD-65A | **6/54: FORT W: 63D** | DARLINGTON-51A | BLAYDON-52C | DARLINGTON-51A | DARLINGTON-51A |
| Jan-55 | EASTFIELD-65A | EASTFIELD-65A | EASTFIELD-65A | EASTFIELD-65A | FORTWILLIAM-63D | DARLINGTON-51A | BLAYDON-52C | DARLINGTON-51A | DARLINGTON-51A |
| Aug-55 | EASTFIELD-65A | EASTFIELD-65A | EASTFIELD-65A | EASTFIELD-65A | FORTWILLIAM-63D | DARLINGTON-51A | BLAYDON-52C | DARLINGTON-51A | DARLINGTON-51A |
| Jan-56 | EASTFIELD-65A | EASTFIELD-65A | EASTFIELD-65A | EASTFIELD-65A | FORTWILLIAM-63D | DARLINGTON-51A | BLAYDON-52C | DARLINGTON-51A | DARLINGTON-51A |
| Aug-56 | EASTFIELD-65A | EASTFIELD-65A | EASTFIELD-65A | EASTFIELD-65A | FORTWILLIAM-63D | DARLINGTON-51A | BLAYDON-52C | DARLINGTON-51A | DARLINGTON-51A |
| Jan-57 | EASTFIELD-65A | EASTFIELD-65A | EASTFIELD-65A | EASTFIELD-65A | FORTWILLIAM-63D | DARLINGTON-51A | BLAYDON-52C | DARLINGTON-51A | DARLINGTON-51A |
| Aug-57 | EASTFIELD-65A | EASTFIELD-65A | EASTFIELD-65A | EASTFIELD-65A | FORTWILLIAM-63D | DARLINGTON-51A | BLAYDON-52C | DARLINGTON-51A | DARLINGTON-51A |
| Jan-58 | EASTFIELD-65A | EASTFIELD-65A | EASTFIELD-65A | EASTFIELD-65A | FORTWILLIAM-63D | DARLINGTON-51A | BLAYDON-52C | DARLINGTON-51A | DARLINGTON-51A |
| Aug-58 | EASTFIELD-65A | EASTFIELD-65A | EASTFIELD-65A | EASTFIELD-65A | FORTWILLIAM-63D | **9/58: STOCK - 51E** | BLAYDON-52C | **9/58: STOCK - 51E** | DARLINGTON-51A |
| Jan-59 | EASTFIELD-65A | EASTFIELD-65A | EASTFIELD-65A | EASTFIELD-65A | FORTWILLIAM-63D | STOCKTON-51E | BLAYDON-52C | STOCKTON-51E | DARLINGTON-51A |
| Aug-59 | EASTFIELD-65A | EASTFIELD-65A | **5/59: TH JN - 62A** | EASTFIELD-65A | FORTWILLIAM-63D | **6/59: TNBY - 51L** | BLAYDON-52C | **6/59: TNBY - 51L** | DARLINGTON-51A |
| Nov-59 | **12/59: DUNF - 62C** | **12/59: DUNF - 62C** | THORNTONJCN-62A | **12/59: DUNF - 62C** | FORTWILLIAM-63D | THORNABY-51L | BLAYDON-52C | THORNABY-51L | DARLINGTON-51A |
| Jan-60 | DUNFERMLINE-62C | DUNFERMLINE-62C | THORNTONJCN-62A | DUNFERMLINE-62C | FORTWILLIAM-63D | THORNABY-51L | BLAYDON-52C | THORNABY-51L | DARLINGTON-51A |
| Apr-60 | DUNFERMLINE-62C | DUNFERMLINE-62C | THORNTONJCN-62A | DUNFERMLINE-62C | FORTWILLIAM-63B | THORNABY-51L | BLAYDON-52C | **5/60 : NLTN - 51J** | DARLINGTON-51A |
| Aug-60 | DUNFERMLINE-62C | DUNFERMLINE-62C | THORNTONJCN-62A | DUNFERMLINE-62C | FORTWILLIAM-63B | THORNABY-51L | BLAYDON-52C | NORTHALLERTON-51J | DARLINGTON-51A |
| Nov-60 | DUNFERMLINE-62C | DUNFERMLINE-62C | THORNTONJCN-62A | DUNFERMLINE-62C | FORTWILLIAM-63B | THORNABY-51L | BLAYDON-52C | NORTHALLERTON-51J | DARLINGTON-51A |

| | 62005 | 62006 | 62007 | 62008 | 62009 | 62010 | 62011 | 62012 | 62013 |
|---|---|---|---|---|---|---|---|---|---|
| Aug-50 | HEATON-52B | DARLINGTON-51A | HEATON-52B | DARLINGTON-51A | DARLINGTON-51A | HEATON-52B | MARCH-31B | MARCH-31B | MARCH-31B |
| Jan-51 | HEATON-52B | DARLINGTON-51A | HEATON-52B | DARLINGTON-51A | DARLINGTON-51A | HEATON-52B | MARCH-31B | MARCH-31B | MARCH-31B |
| Aug-51 | HEATON-52B | DARLINGTON-51A | HEATON-52B | DARLINGTON-51A | DARLINGTON-51A | HEATON-52B | MARCH-31B | MARCH-31B | MARCH-31B |
| Jan-52 | HEATON-52B | DARLINGTON-51A | HEATON-52B | DARLINGTON-51A | DARLINGTON-51A | HEATON-52B | **2/52: EAST - 65A** | **2/52: EAST - 65A** | MARCH-31B |
| Aug-52 | **7/52: DARL - 51A** | DARLINGTON-51A | **7/52: DARL - 51A** | DARLINGTON-51A | DARLINGTON-51A | **7/52: BLAY - 52C** | **6/52: FORT W - 63D** | **6/52: FORT W - 63D** | MARCH-31B |
| Jan-53 | DARLINGTON-51A | DARLINGTON-51A | DARLINGTON-51A | DARLINGTON-51A | DARLINGTON-51A | BLAYDON-52C | FORTWILLIAM-63D | FORTWILLIAM-63D | MARCH-31B |
| Aug-53 | DARLINGTON-51A | DARLINGTON-51A | DARLINGTON-51A | DARLINGTON-51A | DARLINGTON-51A | BLAYDON-52C | FORTWILLIAM-63D | FORTWILLIAM-63D | MARCH-31B |
| Jan-54 | DARLINGTON-51A | **2/54: BLAY - 52C** | DARLINGTON-51A | DARLINGTON-51A | DARLINGTON-51A | BLAYDON-52C | FORTWILLIAM-63D | FORTWILLIAM-63D | MARCH-31B |
| Aug-54 | DARLINGTON-51A | BLAYDON-52C | DARLINGTON-51A | DARLINGTON-51A | DARLINGTON-51A | BLAYDON-52C | FORTWILLIAM-63D | FORTWILLIAM-63D | MARCH-31B |
| Jan-55 | DARLINGTON-51A | BLAYDON-52C | DARLINGTON-51A | DARLINGTON-51A | DARLINGTON-51A | BLAYDON-52C | FORTWILLIAM-63D | FORTWILLIAM-63D | MARCH-31B |
| Aug-55 | DARLINGTON-51A | BLAYDON-52C | DARLINGTON-51A | DARLINGTON-51A | DARLINGTON-51A | BLAYDON-52C | FORTWILLIAM-63D | FORTWILLIAM-63D | MARCH-31B |
| Jan-56 | DARLINGTON-51A | BLAYDON-52C | DARLINGTON-51A | DARLINGTON-51A | DARLINGTON-51A | BLAYDON-52C | FORTWILLIAM-63D | FORTWILLIAM-63D | MARCH-31B |
| Aug-56 | DARLINGTON-51A | BLAYDON-52C | DARLINGTON-51A | DARLINGTON-51A | DARLINGTON-51A | BLAYDON-52C | FORTWILLIAM-63D | FORTWILLIAM-63D | MARCH-31B |
| Jan-57 | DARLINGTON-51A | BLAYDON-52C | DARLINGTON-51A | DARLINGTON-51A | DARLINGTON-51A | BLAYDON-52C | FORTWILLIAM-63D | FORTWILLIAM-63D | MARCH-31B |
| Aug-57 | DARLINGTON-51A | BLAYDON-52C | DARLINGTON-51A | DARLINGTON-51A | DARLINGTON-51A | BLAYDON-52C | FORTWILLIAM-63D | FORTWILLIAM-63D | MARCH-31B |
| Jan-58 | DARLINGTON-51A | BLAYDON-52C | DARLINGTON-51A | DARLINGTON-51A | DARLINGTON-51A | BLAYDON-52C | FORTWILLIAM-63D | FORTWILLIAM-63D | MARCH-31B |
| Aug-58 | DARLINGTON-51A | BLAYDON-52C | DARLINGTON-51A | DARLINGTON-51A | DARLINGTON-51A | BLAYDON-52C | FORTWILLIAM-63D | FORTWILLIAM-63D | MARCH-31B |
| Jan-59 | **6/59: ARDS - 56B** | BLAYDON-52C | DARLINGTON-51A | DARLINGTON-51A | **6/59: ARDS - 56B** | BLAYDON-52C | FORTWILLIAM-63D | FORTWILLIAM-63D | **12/58: STRAT - 30A** |
| Aug-59 | **8/59: YORK - 50A** | BLAYDON-52C | DARLINGTON-51A | DARLINGTON-51A | **8/59: YORK - 50A** | BLAYDON-52C | FORTWILLIAM-63D | FORTWILLIAM-63D | STRATFORD-30A |
| Nov-59 | YORK-50A | BLAYDON-52C | DARLINGTON-51A | DARLINGTON-51A | YORK-50A | BLAYDON-52C | FORTWILLIAM-63D | FORTWILLIAM-63D | STRATFORD-30A |
| Jan-60 | YORK-50A | BLAYDON-52C | DARLINGTON-51A | DARLINGTON-51A | YORK-50A | BLAYDON-52C | FORTWILLIAM-63D | FORTWILLIAM-63D | **2/60: FROD - 36C** |
| Apr-60 | YORK-50A | BLAYDON-52C | DARLINGTON-51A | DARLINGTON-51A | YORK-50A | BLAYDON-52C | FORTWILLIAM-63B | FORTWILLIAM-63B | FRODINGHAM-36C |
| Aug-60 | YORK-50A | BLAYDON-52C | DARLINGTON-51A | DARLINGTON-51A | YORK-50A | BLAYDON-52C | FORTWILLIAM-63B | FORTWILLIAM-63B | FRODINGHAM-36C |
| Nov-60 | YORK-50A | BLAYDON-52C | DARLINGTON-51A | DARLINGTON-51A | YORK-50A | BLAYDON-52C | FORTWILLIAM-63B | FORTWILLIAM-63B | FRODINGHAM-36C |

| | 62014 | 62015 | 62016 | 62017 | 62018 | 62019 | 62020 | 62021 | 62022 |
|---|---|---|---|---|---|---|---|---|---|
| Aug-50 | MARCH - 31B | MARCH - 31B | MARCH - 31B | MARCH - 31B | MARCH - 31B | MARCH - 31B | MARCH - 31B | BLAYDON - 52C | BLAYDON - 52C |
| Jan-51 | MARCH - 31B | MARCH - 31B | MARCH - 31B | MARCH - 31B | MARCH - 31B | MARCH - 31B | MARCH - 31B | BLAYDON - 52C | BLAYDON - 52C |
| Aug-51 | MARCH - 31B | MARCH - 31B | MARCH - 31B | MARCH - 31B | MARCH - 31B | MARCH - 31B | MARCH - 31B | BLAYDON - 52C | BLAYDON - 52C |
| Jan-52 | MARCH - 31B | MARCH - 31B | MARCH - 31B | MARCH - 31B | MARCH - 31B | MARCH - 31B | MARCH - 31B | BLAYDON - 52C | BLAYDON - 52C |
| Aug-52 | MARCH - 31B | MARCH - 31B | MARCH - 31B | MARCH - 31B | MARCH - 31B | MARCH - 31B | MARCH - 31B | BLAYDON - 52C | BLAYDON - 52C |
| Jan-53 | MARCH - 31B | MARCH - 31B | MARCH - 31B | MARCH - 31B | MARCH - 31B | MARCH - 31B | MARCH - 31B | BLAYDON - 52C | BLAYDON - 52C |
| Aug-53 | MARCH - 31B | MARCH - 31B | MARCH - 31B | MARCH - 31B | MARCH - 31B | MARCH - 31B | MARCH - 31B | BLAYDON - 52C | BLAYDON - 52C |
| Jan-54 | MARCH - 31B | MARCH - 31B | MARCH - 31B | MARCH - 31B | MARCH - 31B | MARCH - 31B | MARCH - 31B | BLAYDON - 52C | BLAYDON - 52C |
| Aug-54 | MARCH - 31B | MARCH - 31B | MARCH - 31B | MARCH - 31B | MARCH - 31B | MARCH - 31B | MARCH - 31B | BLAYDON - 52C | BLAYDON - 52C |
| Jan-55 | MARCH - 31B | MARCH - 31B | MARCH - 31B | MARCH - 31B | MARCH - 31B | MARCH - 31B | MARCH - 31B | BLAYDON - 52C | BLAYDON - 52C |
| Aug-55 | MARCH - 31B | MARCH - 31B | MARCH - 31B | MARCH - 31B | MARCH - 31B | MARCH - 31B | MARCH - 31B | BLAYDON - 52C | BLAYDON - 52C |
| Jan-56 | MARCH - 31B | MARCH - 31B | MARCH - 31B | MARCH - 31B | MARCH - 31B | MARCH - 31B | MARCH - 31B | BLAYDON - 52C | BLAYDON - 52C |
| Aug-56 | MARCH - 31B | MARCH - 31B | MARCH - 31B | MARCH - 31B | MARCH - 31B | MARCH - 31B | MARCH - 31B | BLAYDON - 52C | BLAYDON - 52C |
| Jan-57 | MARCH - 31B | MARCH - 31B | MARCH - 31B | MARCH - 31B | MARCH - 31B | MARCH - 31B | MARCH - 31B | BLAYDON - 52C | BLAYDON - 52C |
| Aug-57 | MARCH - 31B | MARCH - 31B | MARCH - 31B | MARCH - 31B | MARCH - 31B | MARCH - 31B | MARCH - 31B | BLAYDON - 52C | BLAYDON - 52C |
| Jan-58 | MARCH - 31B | MARCH - 31B | MARCH - 31B | MARCH - 31B | MARCH - 31B | MARCH - 31B | MARCH - 31B | BLAYDON - 52C | BLAYDON - 52C |
| Aug-58 | MARCH - 31B | MARCH - 31B | MARCH - 31B | MARCH - 31B | MARCH - 31B | MARCH - 31B | MARCH - 31B | BLAYDON - 52C | BLAYDON - 52C |
| Jan-59 | **12/58: STRAT - 30A** | **12/58: STRAT - 30A** | MARCH - 31B | MARCH - 31B | MARCH - 31B | **12/58: STRAT - 30A** | MARCH - 31B | BLAYDON - 52C | BLAYDON - 52C |
| Aug-59 | STRATFORD - 30A | STRATFORD - 30A | MARCH - 31B | MARCH - 31B | MARCH - 31B | STRATFORD - 30A | MARCH - 31B | BLAYDON - 52C | BLAYDON - 52C |
| Nov-59 | STRATFORD - 30A | STRATFORD - 30A | MARCH - 31B | MARCH - 31B | MARCH - 31B | STRATFORD - 30A | MARCH - 31B | BLAYDON - 52C | BLAYDON - 52C |
| Jan-60 | **2/60: FROD - 36C** | **2/60: FROD - 36C** | MARCH - 31B | MARCH - 31B | **1/60: FROD - 36C** | STRATFORD - 30A | **1/60: FROD - 36C** | BLAYDON - 52C | BLAYDON - 52C |
| Apr-60 | FRODINGHAM - 36C | STRATFORD - 30A | MARCH - 31B | MARCH - 31B | FRODINGHAM - 36C | STRATFORD - 30A | FRODINGHAM - 36C | BLAYDON - 52C | BLAYDON - 52C |
| Aug-60 | FRODINGHAM - 36C | STRATFORD - 30A | MARCH - 31B | MARCH - 31B | FRODINGHAM - 36C | STRATFORD - 30A | FRODINGHAM - 36C | BLAYDON - 52C | BLAYDON - 52C |
| Nov-60 | FRODINGHAM - 36C | STRATFORD - 30A | MARCH - 31B | MARCH - 31B | FRODINGHAM - 36C | STRATFORD - 30A | FRODINGHAM - 36C | BLAYDON - 52C | BLAYDON - 52C |

| | 62023 | 62024 | 62025 | 62026 | 62027 | 62028 | 62029 | 62030 | 62031 |
|---|---|---|---|---|---|---|---|---|---|
| Aug-50 | BLAYDON - 52C | BLAYDON - 52C | BLAYDON - 52C | BLAYDON - 52C | BLAYDON - 52C | BLAYDON - 52C | BLAYDON - 52C | BLAYDON - 52C | MARCH - 31B |
| Jan-51 | BLAYDON - 52C | BLAYDON - 52C | BLAYDON - 52C | BLAYDON - 52C | BLAYDON - 52C | BLAYDON - 52C | BLAYDON - 52C | BLAYDON - 52C | MARCH - 31B |
| Aug-51 | BLAYDON - 52C | BLAYDON - 52C | BLAYDON - 52C | BLAYDON - 52C | BLAYDON - 52C | BLAYDON - 52C | BLAYDON - 52C | BLAYDON - 52C | MARCH - 31B |
| Jan-52 | BLAYDON - 52C | BLAYDON - 52C | BLAYDON - 52C | BLAYDON - 52C | BLAYDON - 52C | BLAYDON - 52C | BLAYDON - 52C | BLAYDON - 52C | **2/52: EAST - 65A** |
| Aug-52 | BLAYDON - 52C | BLAYDON - 52C | BLAYDON - 52C | BLAYDON - 52C | BLAYDON - 52C | BLAYDON - 52C | BLAYDON - 52C | BLAYDON - 52C | EASTFIELD - 65A |
| Jan-53 | BLAYDON - 52C | BLAYDON - 52C | BLAYDON - 52C | BLAYDON - 52C | BLAYDON - 52C | BLAYDON - 52C | BLAYDON - 52C | BLAYDON - 52C | EASTFIELD - 65A |
| Aug-53 | BLAYDON - 52C | BLAYDON - 52C | BLAYDON - 52C | BLAYDON - 52C | BLAYDON - 52C | BLAYDON - 52C | BLAYDON - 52C | BLAYDON - 52C | EASTFIELD - 65A |
| Jan-54 | BLAYDON - 52C | BLAYDON - 52C | BLAYDON - 52C | BLAYDON - 52C | BLAYDON - 52C | BLAYDON - 52C | BLAYDON - 52C | BLAYDON - 52C | EASTFIELD - 65A |
| Aug-54 | BLAYDON - 52C | BLAYDON - 52C | BLAYDON - 52C | BLAYDON - 52C | BLAYDON - 52C | BLAYDON - 52C | BLAYDON - 52C | BLAYDON - 52C | **6/54: FORT W - 63D** |
| Jan-55 | BLAYDON - 52C | BLAYDON - 52C | BLAYDON - 52C | BLAYDON - 52C | BLAYDON - 52C | BLAYDON - 52C | BLAYDON - 52C | BLAYDON - 52C | FORTWILLIAM - 63D |
| Aug-55 | BLAYDON - 52C | BLAYDON - 52C | BLAYDON - 52C | BLAYDON - 52C | BLAYDON - 52C | BLAYDON - 52C | BLAYDON - 52C | BLAYDON - 52C | FORTWILLIAM - 63D |
| Jan-56 | BLAYDON - 52C | BLAYDON - 52C | BLAYDON - 52C | BLAYDON - 52C | BLAYDON - 52C | BLAYDON - 52C | BLAYDON - 52C | BLAYDON - 52C | FORTWILLIAM - 63D |
| Aug-56 | BLAYDON - 52C | BLAYDON - 52C | BLAYDON - 52C | BLAYDON - 52C | BLAYDON - 52C | BLAYDON - 52C | BLAYDON - 52C | BLAYDON - 52C | FORTWILLIAM - 63D |
| Jan-57 | BLAYDON - 52C | BLAYDON - 52C | BLAYDON - 52C | BLAYDON - 52C | BLAYDON - 52C | BLAYDON - 52C | BLAYDON - 52C | BLAYDON - 52C | FORTWILLIAM - 63D |
| Aug-57 | BLAYDON - 52C | BLAYDON - 52C | BLAYDON - 52C | BLAYDON - 52C | BLAYDON - 52C | BLAYDON - 52C | BLAYDON - 52C | BLAYDON - 52C | FORTWILLIAM - 63D |
| Jan-58 | BLAYDON - 52C | BLAYDON - 52C | BLAYDON - 52C | BLAYDON - 52C | BLAYDON - 52C | BLAYDON - 52C | BLAYDON - 52C | BLAYDON - 52C | FORTWILLIAM - 63D |
| Aug-58 | BLAYDON - 52C | BLAYDON - 52C | BLAYDON - 52C | BLAYDON - 52C | BLAYDON - 52C | BLAYDON - 52C | BLAYDON - 52C | BLAYDON - 52C | FORTWILLIAM - 63D |
| Jan-59 | BLAYDON - 52C | BLAYDON - 52C | BLAYDON - 52C | BLAYDON - 52C | BLAYDON - 52C | BLAYDON - 52C | BLAYDON - 52C | BLAYDON - 52C | FORTWILLIAM - 63D |
| Aug-59 | BLAYDON - 52C | BLAYDON - 52C | BLAYDON - 52C | BLAYDON - 52C | BLAYDON - 52C | BLAYDON - 52C | BLAYDON - 52C | BLAYDON - 52C | FORTWILLIAM - 63D |
| Nov-59 | BLAYDON - 52C | BLAYDON - 52C | BLAYDON - 52C | BLAYDON - 52C | BLAYDON - 52C | BLAYDON - 52C | BLAYDON - 52C | BLAYDON - 52C | FORTWILLIAM - 63D |
| Jan-60 | BLAYDON - 52C | BLAYDON - 52C | BLAYDON - 52C | BLAYDON - 52C | BLAYDON - 52C | BLAYDON - 52C | BLAYDON - 52C | BLAYDON - 52C | FORTWILLIAM - 63D |
| Apr-60 | BLAYDON - 52C | BLAYDON - 52C | BLAYDON - 52C | BLAYDON - 52C | BLAYDON - 52C | BLAYDON - 52C | BLAYDON - 52C | BLAYDON - 52C | FORTWILLIAM - 63B |
| Aug-60 | BLAYDON - 52C | BLAYDON - 52C | BLAYDON - 52C | BLAYDON - 52C | BLAYDON - 52C | BLAYDON - 52C | BLAYDON - 52C | BLAYDON - 52C | FORTWILLIAM - 63B |
| Nov-60 | BLAYDON - 52C | BLAYDON - 52C | BLAYDON - 52C | BLAYDON - 52C | BLAYDON - 52C | BLAYDON - 52C | BLAYDON - 52C | BLAYDON - 52C | FORTWILLIAM - 63B |

| | 62032 | 62033 | 62034 | 62035 | 62036 | 62037 | 62038 | 62039 | 62040 |
|---|---|---|---|---|---|---|---|---|---|
| Aug-50 | MARCH - 31B | MARCH - 31B | MARCH - 31B | MARCH - 31B | MARCH - 31B | MARCH - 31B | MARCH - 31B | MARCH - 31B | MARCH - 31B |
| Jan-51 | MARCH - 31B | MARCH - 31B | MARCH - 31B | MARCH - 31B | **3/51 : CAMB - 31A** | MARCH - 31B | MARCH - 31B | **3/51 : CAMB - 31A** | MARCH - 31B |
| Aug-51 | MARCH - 31B | MARCH - 31B | MARCH - 31B | MARCH - 31B | **4/51: MARCH - 31B** | MARCH - 31B | MARCH - 31B | **4/51: MEX - 36B** | MARCH - 31B |
| Jan-52 | MARCH - 31B | MARCH - 31B | **2/52: EAST - 65A** | MARCH - 31B | MARCH - 31B | MARCH - 31B | MARCH - 31B | MEXBOROUGH - 36B | MARCH - 31B |
| Aug-52 | MARCH - 31B | MARCH - 31B | EASTFIELD - 65A | MARCH - 31B | MARCH - 31B | MARCH - 31B | MARCH - 31B | MEXBOROUGH - 36B | MARCH - 31B |
| Jan-53 | MARCH - 31B | MARCH - 31B | EASTFIELD - 65A | MARCH - 31B | MARCH - 31B | MARCH - 31B | MARCH - 31B | MEXBOROUGH - 36B | MARCH - 31B |
| Aug-53 | MARCH - 31B | MARCH - 31B | EASTFIELD - 65A | MARCH - 31B | MARCH - 31B | MARCH - 31B | MARCH - 31B | MEXBOROUGH - 36B | MARCH - 31B |
| Jan-54 | MARCH - 31B | MARCH - 31B | EASTFIELD - 65A | MARCH - 31B | MARCH - 31B | MARCH - 31B | MARCH - 31B | MEXBOROUGH - 36B | MARCH - 31B |
| Aug-54 | MARCH - 31B | MARCH - 31B | **6/54: FORT W - 63D** | MARCH - 31B | MARCH - 31B | MARCH - 31B | MARCH - 31B | MEXBOROUGH - 36B | MARCH - 31B |
| Jan-55 | MARCH - 31B | MARCH - 31B | FORTWILLIAM - 63D | MARCH - 31B | MARCH - 31B | MARCH - 31B | MARCH - 31B | MEXBOROUGH - 36B | MARCH - 31B |
| Aug-55 | MARCH - 31B | MARCH - 31B | FORTWILLIAM - 63D | MARCH - 31B | MARCH - 31B | MARCH - 31B | MARCH - 31B | MEXBOROUGH - 36B | MARCH - 31B |
| Jan-56 | MARCH - 31B | MARCH - 31B | FORTWILLIAM - 63D | MARCH - 31B | MARCH - 31B | MARCH - 31B | MARCH - 31B | MEXBOROUGH - 36B | MARCH - 31B |
| Aug-56 | MARCH - 31B | MARCH - 31B | FORTWILLIAM - 63D | MARCH - 31B | MARCH - 31B | MARCH - 31B | MARCH - 31B | MEXBOROUGH - 36B | MARCH - 31B |
| Jan-57 | MARCH - 31B | MARCH - 31B | FORTWILLIAM - 63D | MARCH - 31B | MARCH - 31B | MARCH - 31B | MARCH - 31B | MEXBOROUGH - 36B | MARCH - 31B |
| Aug-57 | MARCH - 31B | MARCH - 31B | FORTWILLIAM - 63D | MARCH - 31B | MARCH - 31B | MARCH - 31B | MARCH - 31B | MEXBOROUGH - 36B | MARCH - 31B |
| Jan-58 | MARCH - 31B | MARCH - 31B | FORTWILLIAM - 63D | MARCH - 31B | MARCH - 31B | MARCH - 31B | MARCH - 31B | MEXBOROUGH - 36B | MARCH - 31B |
| Aug-58 | MARCH - 31B | MARCH - 31B | FORTWILLIAM - 63D | MARCH - 31B | MARCH - 31B | MARCH - 31B | MARCH - 31B | MEXBOROUGH - 41F | MARCH - 31B |
| Jan-59 | MARCH - 31B | MARCH - 31B | FORTWILLIAM - 63D | MARCH - 31B | **12/58: STRAT - 30A** | MARCH - 31B | MARCH - 31B | MEXBOROUGH - 41F | MARCH - 31B |
| Aug-59 | MARCH - 31B | MARCH - 31B | FORTWILLIAM - 63D | MARCH - 31B | STRATFORD - 30A | MARCH - 31B | MARCH - 31B | MEXBOROUGH - 41F | MARCH - 31B |
| Nov-59 | MARCH - 31B | MARCH - 31B | FORTWILLIAM - 63D | MARCH - 31B | STRATFORD - 30A | MARCH - 31B | MARCH - 31B | MEXBOROUGH - 41F | MARCH - 31B |
| Jan-60 | **2/60: FROD - 36C** | MARCH - 31B | FORTWILLIAM - 63D | MARCH - 31B | STRATFORD - 30A | MARCH - 31B | MARCH - 31B | MEXBOROUGH - 41F | MARCH - 31B |
| Apr-60 | FRODINGHAM - 36C | MARCH - 31B | FORTWILLIAM - 63B | MARCH - 31B | STRATFORD - 30A | MARCH - 31B | MARCH - 31B | MEXBOROUGH - 41F | MARCH - 31B |
| Aug-60 | FRODINGHAM - 36C | MARCH - 31B | FORTWILLIAM - 63B | MARCH - 31B | STRATFORD - 30A | MARCH - 31B | MARCH - 31B | MEXBOROUGH - 41F | MARCH - 31B |
| Nov-60 | FRODINGHAM - 36C | MARCH - 31B | FORTWILLIAM - 63B | MARCH - 31B | STRATFORD - 30A | MARCH - 31B | MARCH - 31B | MEXBOROUGH - 41F | MARCH - 31B |

| | 62041 | 62042 | 62043 | 62044 | 6204S | 62046 | 62047 | 62048 | 62049 |
|---|---|---|---|---|---|---|---|---|---|
| Aug-50 | STOCKTON - 51E | STOCKTON - 51E | STOCKTON - 51E | DARLINGTON - 51A | DARLINGTON - 51A | DARLINGTON - 51A | DARLINGTON - 51A | DARLINGTON - 51A | DARLINGTON - 51A |
| Jan-51 | STOCKTON - 51E | STOCKTON - 51E | STOCKTON - 51E | DARLINGTON - 51A | DARLINGTON - 51A | DARLINGTON - 51A | DARLINGTON - 51A | **11/50: HTN - 52B** | **11/50: HTN - 52B** |
| Aug-51 | STOCKTON - 51E | STOCKTON - 51E | STOCKTON - 51E | DARLINGTON - 51A | DARLINGTON - 51A | DARLINGTON - 51A | DARLINGTON - 51A | **1/51: DARL - 51A** | **6/51: DARL - 51A** |
| Jan-52 | STOCKTON - 51E | STOCKTON - 51E | STOCKTON - 51E | DARLINGTON - 51A | DARLINGTON - 51A | DARLINGTON - 51A | DARLINGTON - 51A | **9/51: H.HILL - 51G** | DARLINGTON - 51A |
| Aug-52 | STOCKTON - 51E | STOCKTON - 51E | STOCKTON - 51E | DARLINGTON - 51A | DARLINGTON - 51A | DARLINGTON - 51A | DARLINGTON - 51A | HAVERTON HILL - 51G | DARLINGTON - 51A |
| Jan-53 | STOCKTON - 51E | STOCKTON - 51E | STOCKTON - 51E | DARLINGTON - 51A | DARLINGTON - 51A | DARLINGTON - 51A | DARLINGTON - 51A | HAVERTON HILL - 51G | DARLINGTON - 51A |
| Aug-53 | STOCKTON - 51E | STOCKTON - 51E | STOCKTON - 51E | **5/53: NLTN - 51J** | DARLINGTON - 51A | DARLINGTON - 51A | DARLINGTON - 51A | HAVERTON HILL - 51G | DARLINGTON - 51A |
| Jan-54 | STOCKTON - 51E | STOCKTON - 51E | STOCKTON - 51E | NORTHALLERTON - 51J | DARLINGTON - 51A | DARLINGTON - 51A | DARLINGTON - 51A | HAVERTON HILL - 51G | DARLINGTON - 51A |
| Aug-54 | STOCKTON - 51E | STOCKTON - 51E | STOCKTON - 51E | NORTHALLERTON - 51J | DARLINGTON - 51A | DARLINGTON - 51A | DARLINGTON - 51A | HAVERTON HILL - 51G | DARLINGTON - 51A |
| Jan-55 | STOCKTON - 51E | STOCKTON - 51E | STOCKTON - 51E | NORTHALLERTON - 51J | DARLINGTON - 51A | DARLINGTON - 51A | DARLINGTON - 51A | HAVERTON HILL - 51G | DARLINGTON - 51A |
| Aug-55 | STOCKTON - 51E | STOCKTON - 51E | STOCKTON - 51E | NORTHALLERTON - 51J | DARLINGTON - 51A | DARLINGTON - 51A | DARLINGTON - 51A | HAVERTON HILL - 51G | DARLINGTON - 51A |
| Jan-56 | STOCKTON - 51E | STOCKTON - 51E | STOCKTON - 51E | NORTHALLERTON - 51J | DARLINGTON - 51A | DARLINGTON - 51A | DARLINGTON - 51A | HAVERTON HILL - 51G | DARLINGTON - 51A |
| Aug-56 | STOCKTON - 51E | STOCKTON - 51E | STOCKTON - 51E | NORTHALLERTON - 51J | DARLINGTON - 51A | **6/56: YORK - 50A** | **6/56: YORK - 50A** | **6/56: YORK - 50A** | **6/56: YORK - 50A** |
| Jan-57 | STOCKTON - 51E | STOCKTON - 51E | **6/57: ARDS - 56B** | NORTHALLERTON - 51J | DARLINGTON - 51A | YORK - 50A | YORK - 50A | YORK - 50A | YORK - 50A |
| Aug-57 | STOCKTON - 51E | STOCKTON - 51E | **9/57: DARL - 51A** | NORTHALLERTON - 51J | DARLINGTON - 51A | YORK - 50A | YORK - 50A | YORK - 50A | YORK - 50A |
| Jan-58 | STOCKTON - 51E | STOCKTON - 51E | DARLINGTON - 51A | NORTHALLERTON - 51J | DARLINGTON - 51A | YORK - 50A | YORK - 50A | YORK - 50A | YORK - 50A |
| Aug-58 | STOCKTON - 51E | STOCKTON - 51E | DARLINGTON - 51A | NORTHALLERTON - 51J | DARLINGTON - 51A | YORK - 50A | **9/58: DARL - 51A** | YORK - 50A | YORK - 50A |
| Jan-59 | **6/59: TNBY - 51L** | STOCKTON - 51E | DARLINGTON - 51A | NORTHALLERTON - 51J | DARLINGTON - 51A | YORK - 50A | **12/58: STOCK - 51E** | YORK - 50A | YORK - 50A |
| Aug-59 | **8/59: DAR - 51A** | **6/59: TNBY - 51L** | DARLINGTON - 51A | NORTHALLERTON - 51J | DARLINGTON - 51A | YORK - 50A | 6/59: LOWM - 56F | **10/59: DARL - 51A** | YORK - 50A |
| Nov-59 | DARLINGTON - 51A | THORNABY - 51L | DARLINGTON - 51A | NORTHALLERTON - 51J | DARLINGTON - 51A | YORK - 50A | **8/59: YORK - 50A** | DARLINGTON - 51A | YORK - 50A |
| Jan-60 | DARLINGTON - 51A | THORNABY - 51L | DARLINGTON - 51A | NORTHALLERTON - 51J | DARLINGTON - 51A | YORK - 50A | YORK - 50A | DARLINGTON - 51A | YORK - 50A |
| Apr-60 | DARLINGTON - 51A | THORNABY - 51L | DARLINGTON - 51A | NORTHALLERTON - 51J | DARLINGTON - 51A | YORK - 50A | YORK - 50A | DARLINGTON - 51A | YORK - 50A |
| Aug-60 | DARLINGTON - 51A | THORNABY - 51L | DARLINGTON - 51A | NORTHALLERTON - 51J | DARLINGTON - 51A | YORK - 50A | YORK - 50A | DARLINGTON - 51A | YORK - 50A |
| Nov-60 | DARLINGTON - 51A | THORNABY - 51L | DARLINGTON - 51A | NORTHALLERTON - 51J | DARLINGTON - 51A | YORK - 50A | YORK - 50A | DARLINGTON - 51A | YORK - 50A |

| | 62050 | 62051 | 62052 | 62053 | 62054 | 62055 | 62056 | 62057 | 62058 |
|---|---|---|---|---|---|---|---|---|---|
| Aug-50 | DARLINGTON-51A | MARCH-31B | MARCH-31B | MARCH-31B | MARCH-31B | MARCH-31B | DARLINGTON-51A | DARLINGTON-51A | DARLINGTON-51A |
| Jan-51 | HEATON-52B | MARCH-31B | MARCH-31B | MARCH-31B | MARCH-31B | MARCH-31B | 1/51: H.HILL-51G | 1/51: H.HILL-51G | DARLINGTON-51A |
| Aug-51 | DARLINGTON-51A | MARCH-31B | MARCH-31B | MARCH-31B | MARCH-31B | MARCH-31B | HAVERTON HILL-51G | HAVERTON HILL-51G | 9/51: H.HIL-51G |
| Jan-52 | HAVERTON HILL-51G | MARCH-31B | 2/52: EAST-65A | MARCH-31B | MARCH-31B | MARCH-31B | HAVERTON HILL-51G | HAVERTON HILL-51G | HAVERTON HILL-51G |
| Aug-52 | HAVERTON HILL-51G | MARCH-31B | EASTFIELD-65A | MARCH-31B | MARCH-31B | MARCH-31B | HAVERTON HILL-51G | HAVERTON HILL-51G | HAVERTON HILL-51G |
| Jan-53 | HAVERTON HILL-51G | MARCH-31B | EASTFIELD-65A | MARCH-31B | MARCH-31B | MARCH-31B | HAVERTON HILL-51G | HAVERTON HILL-51G | HAVERTON HILL-51G |
| Aug-53 | HAVERTON HILL-51G | MARCH-31B | EASTFIELD-65A | MARCH-31B | MARCH-31B | MARCH-31B | HAVERTON HILL-51G | HAVERTON HILL-51G | HAVERTON HILL-51G |
| Jan-54 | HAVERTON HILL-51G | MARCH-31B | EASTFIELD-65A | MARCH-31B | MARCH-31B | MARCH-31B | HAVERTON HILL-51G | HAVERTON HILL-51G | HAVERTON HILL-51G |
| Aug-54 | HAVERTON HILL-51G | MARCH-31B | 6/54: FORT W-63D | MARCH-31B | MARCH-31B | MARCH-31B | HAVERTON HILL-51G | HAVERTON HILL-51G | HAVERTON HILL-51G |
| Jan-55 | HAVERTON HILL-51G | MARCH-31B | FORT WILLIAM-63D | MARCH-31B | MARCH-31B | MARCH-31B | HAVERTON HILL-51G | HAVERTON HILL-51G | HAVERTON HILL-51G |
| Aug-55 | HAVERTON HILL-51G | MARCH-31B | FORT WILLIAM-63D | MARCH-31B | MARCH-31B | MARCH-31B | HAVERTON HILL-51G | HAVERTON HILL-51G | HAVERTON HILL-51G |
| Jan-56 | HAVERTON HILL-51G | MARCH-31B | FORT WILLIAM-63D | MARCH-31B | MARCH-31B | MARCH-31B | HAVERTON HILL-51G | HAVERTON HILL-51G | HAVERTON HILL-51G |
| Aug-56 | 6/56: YORK-50A | MARCH-31B | FORT WILLIAM-63D | MARCH-31B | MARCH-31B | MARCH-31B | 6/56: YORK-50A | 6/56: YORK-50A | HAVERTON HILL-51G |
| Jan-57 | YORK-50A | MARCH-31B | FORT WILLIAM-63D | MARCH-31B | MARCH-31B | MARCH-31B | YORK-50A | YORK-50A | HAVERTON HILL-51G |
| Aug-57 | YORK-50A | MARCH-31B | FORT WILLIAM-63D | MARCH-31B | MARCH-31B | MARCH-31B | YORK-50A | YORK-50A | 6/57: STOCK-51E |
| Jan-58 | YORK-50A | MARCH-31B | FORT WILLIAM-63D | MARCH-31B | MARCH-31B | MARCH-31B | YORK-50A | YORK-50A | STOCKTON-51E |
| Aug-58 | YORK-50A | MARCH-31B | FORT WILLIAM-63D | MARCH-31B | MARCH-31B | MARCH-31B | YORK-50A | YORK-50A | 6/58: DARL-51A |
| Jan-59 | YORK-50A | MARCH-31B | FORT WILLIAM-63D | 12/58: STRAT-30A | MARCH-31B | MARCH-31B | YORK-50A | YORK-50A | DARLINGTON-51A |
| Aug-59 | YORK-50A | MARCH-31B | FORT WILLIAM-63D | STRATFORD-30A | MARCH-31B | MARCH-31B | YORK-50A | YORK-50A | DARLINGTON-51A |
| Nov-59 | 10/59: BLAY-52C | MARCH-31B | FORT WILLIAM-63D | STRATFORD-30A | MARCH-31B | MARCH-31B | YORK-50A | YORK-50A | DARLINGTON-51A |
| Jan-60 | BLAYDON-52C | MARCH-31B | FORT WILLIAM-63D | STRATFORD-30A | MARCH-31B | MARCH-31B | YORK-50A | YORK-50A | DARLINGTON-51A |
| Apr-60 | BLAYDON-52C | MARCH-31B | FORT WILLIAM-63B | STRATFORD-30A | MARCH-31B | MARCH-31B | YORK-50A | YORK-50A | DARLINGTON-51A |
| Aug-60 | BLAYDON-52C | MARCH-31B | FORT WILLIAM-63B | STRATFORD-30A | MARCH-31B | MARCH-31B | YORK-50A | YORK-50A | DARLINGTON-51A |
| Nov-60 | BLAYDON-52C | MARCH-31B | FORT WILLIAM-63B | STRATFORD-30A | MARCH-31B | MARCH-31B | YORK-50A | YORK-50A | DARLINGTON-51A |

| | 62059 | 62060 | 62061 | 62062 | 62063 | 62064 | 62065 | 62066 | 62067 |
|---|---|---|---|---|---|---|---|---|---|
| Aug-50 | DARLINGTON-51A | STOCKTON-51E | DARLINGTON-51A | DARLINGTON-51A | STOCKTON-51E | STOCKTON-51E | STOCKTON-51E | MARCH-31B | MARCH-31B |
| Jan-51 | DARLINGTON-51A | STOCKTON-51E | DARLINGTON-51A | DARLINGTON-51A | STOCKTON-51E | STOCKTON-51E | STOCKTON-51E | MARCH-31B | MARCH-31B |
| Aug-51 | 9/51: H.HIL-51G | STOCKTON-51E | 10/51: H.HIL-51G | DARLINGTON-51A | STOCKTON-51E | STOCKTON-51E | STOCKTON-51E | MARCH-31B | MARCH-31B |
| Jan-52 | HAVERTON HILL-51G | STOCKTON-51E | HAVERTON HILL-51G | DARLINGTON-51A | 11/51: DARL-51A | STOCKTON-51E | STOCKTON-51E | MARCH-31B | MARCH-31B |
| Aug-52 | HAVERTON HILL-51G | STOCKTON-51E | HAVERTON HILL-51G | DARLINGTON-51A | DARLINGTON-51A | STOCKTON-51E | STOCKTON-51E | MARCH-31B | MARCH-31B |
| Jan-53 | HAVERTON HILL-51G | STOCKTON-51E | HAVERTON HILL-51G | DARLINGTON-51A | DARLINGTON-51A | STOCKTON-51E | STOCKTON-51E | MARCH-31B | MARCH-31B |
| Aug-53 | HAVERTON HILL-51G | STOCKTON-51E | HAVERTON HILL-51G | DARLINGTON-51A | DARLINGTON-51A | STOCKTON-51E | STOCKTON-51E | MARCH-31B | MARCH-31B |
| Jan-54 | HAVERTON HILL-51G | STOCKTON-51E | HAVERTON HILL-51G | DARLINGTON-51A | DARLINGTON-51A | STOCKTON-51E | STOCKTON-51E | MARCH-31B | MARCH-31B |
| Aug-54 | HAVERTON HILL-51G | STOCKTON-51E | HAVERTON HILL-51G | DARLINGTON-51A | DARLINGTON-51A | STOCKTON-51E | STOCKTON-51E | MARCH-31B | MARCH-31B |
| Jan-55 | HAVERTON HILL-51G | STOCKTON-51E | HAVERTON HILL-51G | DARLINGTON-51A | DARLINGTON-51A | STOCKTON-51E | STOCKTON-51E | MARCH-31B | MARCH-31B |
| Aug-55 | HAVERTON HILL-51G | STOCKTON-51E | HAVERTON HILL-51G | DARLINGTON-51A | DARLINGTON-51A | STOCKTON-51E | STOCKTON-51E | MARCH-31B | MARCH-31B |
| Jan-56 | HAVERTON HILL-51G | STOCKTON-51E | HAVERTON HILL-51G | DARLINGTON-51A | DARLINGTON-51A | STOCKTON-51E | STOCKTON-51E | MARCH-31B | MARCH-31B |
| Aug-56 | HAVERTON HILL-51G | STOCKTON-51E | 6/56: YORK-50A | 6/56: YORK-50A | 6/56: YORK-50A | STOCKTON-51E | STOCKTON-51E | MARCH-31B | MARCH-31B |
| Jan-57 | HAVERTON HILL-51G | STOCKTON-51E | YORK-50A | YORK-50A | YORK-50A | STOCKTON-51E | STOCKTON-51E | MARCH-31B | MARCH-31B |
| Aug-57 | 6/57: ARDS-56B | STOCKTON-51E | YORK-50A | YORK-50A | YORK-50A | STOCKTON-51E | STOCKTON-51E | MARCH-31B | MARCH-31B |
| Jan-58 | 9/57: DARL-51A | STOCKTON-51E | YORK-50A | YORK-50A | YORK-50A | STOCKTON-51E | STOCKTON-51E | MARCH-31B | MARCH-31B |
| Aug-58 | DARLINGTON-51A | 6/58: B.GDNS-54C | YORK-50A | YORK-50A | YORK-50A | 6/58: DARL-51A | STOCKTON-51E | MARCH-31B | MARCH-31B |
| Jan-59 | DARLINGTON-51A | BOROUGH GARDENS-52J | YORK-50A | YORK-50A | YORK-50A | DARLINGTON-51A | 6/59: LOW M-56F | MARCH-31B | MARCH-31B |
| Aug-59 | DARLINGTON-51A | 6/59: YORK-50A | YORK-50A | 10/59: DARL-51A | YORK-50A | DARLINGTON-51A | 8/59: YORK-50A | MARCH-31B | MARCH-31B |
| Nov-59 | DARLINGTON-51A | 10/59: BLAY-52C | YORK-50A | DARLINGTON-51A | YORK-50A | DARLINGTON-51A | YORK-50A | MARCH-31B | MARCH-31B |
| Jan-60 | DARLINGTON-51A | BLAYDON-52C | YORK-50A | DARLINGTON-51A | YORK-50A | DARLINGTON-51A | YORK-50A | MARCH-31B | MARCH-31B |
| Apr-60 | DARLINGTON-51A | BLAYDON-52C | YORK-50A | DARLINGTON-51A | YORK-50A | DARLINGTON-51A | YORK-50A | MARCH-31B | MARCH-31B |
| Aug-60 | DARLINGTON-51A | BLAYDON-52C | YORK-50A | DARLINGTON-51A | YORK-50A | DARLINGTON-51A | YORK-50A | MARCH-31B | MARCH-31B |
| Nov-60 | DARLINGTON-51A | BLAYDON-52C | YORK-50A | DARLINGTON-51A | YORK-50A | DARLINGTON-51A | YORK-50A | MARCH-31B | MARCH-31B |

| | 62068 | 62069 | 62070 | D31 4-4-0 (1890) 62281 | 62283 | D3 4-4-0 (1896) 62000 | 62132 | 62148 | D2 4-4-0 (1897) 62154 |
|---|---|---|---|---|---|---|---|---|---|
| Aug-50 | MARCH-31B | MARCH-31B | MARCH-31B | CARLISLE (CANAL)-12B | BATHGATE-64F | GRANTHAM-35B | LOUTH-40C | COLWICK-38A | BOSTON-40F |
| Jan-51 | MARCH-31B | MARCH-31B | MARCH-31B | CARLISLE (CANAL)-12B | BATHGATE-64F | GRANTHAM-35B | 11/50: B OS-40F | 11/50: W/D | 11/50: W/D |
| Aug-51 | MARCH-31B | MARCH-31B | MARCH-31B | CARLISE (CANAL)-68E | 2/51: W/D | 9/51: W/D | 12/50: W/D | | |
| Jan-52 | MARCH-31B | MARCH-31B | MARCH-31B | CARLISE (CANAL)-68E | | | | | |
| Aug-52 | MARCH-31B | MARCH-31B | MARCH-31B | CARLISE (CANAL)-68E | | | | | |
| Jan-53 | MARCH-31B | MARCH-31B | MARCH-31B | 12/52: W/D | | | | | |
| Aug-53 | MARCH-31B | MARCH-31B | MARCH-31B | | | | | | |
| Jan-54 | MARCH-31B | MARCH-31B | MARCH-31B | | | | | | |
| Aug-54 | MARCH-31B | MARCH-31B | MARCH-31B | | | | | | |
| Jan-55 | MARCH-31B | MARCH-31B | MARCH-31B | | | | | | |
| Aug-55 | MARCH-31B | MARCH-31B | MARCH-31B | | | | | | |
| Jan-56 | MARCH-31B | MARCH-31B | MARCH-31B | | | | | | |
| Aug-56 | MARCH-31B | MARCH-31B | MARCH-31B | | | | | | |
| Jan-57 | MARCH-31B | MARCH-31B | MARCH-31B | | | | | | |
| Aug-57 | MARCH-31B | MARCH-31B | MARCH-31B | | | | | | |
| Jan-58 | MARCH-31B | MARCH-31B | MARCH-31B | | | | | | |
| Aug-58 | MARCH-31B | MARCH-31B | MARCH-31B | | | | | | |
| Jan-59 | MARCH-31B | MARCH-31B | MARCH-31B | | | | | | |
| Aug-59 | MARCH-31B | MARCH-31B | 6/59: STRAT-30A | | | | | | |
| Nov-59 | MARCH-31B | MARCH-31B | STRATFORD-30A | | | | | | |
| Jan-60 | MARCH-31B | MARCH-31B | STRATFORD-30A | | | | | | |
| Apr-60 | MARCH-31B | MARCH-31B | STRATFORD-30A | | | | | | |
| Aug-60 | MARCH-31B | MARCH-31B | STRATFORD-30A | | | | | | |
| Nov-60 | MARCH-31B | MARCH-31B | STRATFORD-30A | | | | | | |

| | 62172 | 62181 | D1 4-4-0 (1911) 62209 | D4 4-4-0 (1893) 62225 | 62227 | 62228 | 62229 | 62230 | 62231 |
|---|---|---|---|---|---|---|---|---|---|
| Aug-50 | COLWICK-38A | BOSTON-40F | STIRLING-63B | KITTYBREWSTER-61A | KEITH-61C | KITTYBREWSTER-61A | KITTYBREWSTER-61A | KITTYBREWSTER-61A | KEITH-61C |
| Jan-51 | COLWICK-38A | 11/50: W/D | 11/50: W/D | 12/50: KEITH-61C | KEITH-61C | KITTYBREWSTER-61A | KITTYBREWSTER-61A | 12/50: KEITH-61C | KEITH-61C |
| Aug-51 | 6/51: W/D | | | KEITH-61C | 3/51: W/D | 9/51: KEITH-61C | KITTYBREWSTER-61A | KEITH-61C | KEITH-61C |
| Jan-52 | | | | KEITH-61C | | KEITH-61C | 12/51: W/D | 3/52: W/D | KEITH-61C |
| Aug-52 | | | | KEITH-61C | | 2/52: W/D | | | KEITH-61C |
| Jan-53 | | | | KEITH-61C | | | | | 10/52: W/D |
| Aug-53 | | | | 2/53: W/D | | | | | |
| Jan-54 | | | | | | | | | |
| Aug-54 | | | | | | | | | |
| Jan-55 | | | | | | | | | |
| Aug-55 | | | | | | | | | |
| Jan-56 | | | | | | | | | |
| Aug-56 | | | | | | | | | |
| Jan-57 | | | | | | | | | |
| Aug-57 | | | | | | | | | |
| Jan-58 | | | | | | | | | |
| Aug-58 | | | | | | | | | |
| Jan-59 | | | | | | | | | |
| Aug-59 | | | | | | | | | |
| Nov-59 | | | | | | | | | |
| Jan-60 | | | | | | | | | |
| Apr-60 | | | | | | | | | |
| Aug-60 | | | | | | | | | |
| Nov-60 | | | | | | | | | |

Although there were pockets where the type survived, 4-4-0's were not a strong feature of the ex LNER unless one happened to be in Scotland or the northern half of the Great Eastern. By the 1950's the type was all but unknown on the Great Northern main line south of Doncaster yet one could spend a day riding the Great Eastern main lines north of Cambridge and be hauled by nothing else. Quite a number remained on the books of North British sheds, although many of their duties had been taken over by B1 4-6-0's, whilst local trains based on the Harrogate Leeds and York districts made frequent use of the relatively recent D49's. All disappeared with the introduction of diesel multiple units from 1956 onwards.

| | 62232 | 62241 | 62242 | 62243 | 62246 | 62247 | 62248 | 62249 | 62251 |
|---|---|---|---|---|---|---|---|---|---|
| Aug-50 | K'BREWSTER-61A | K'BREWSTER-61A | KEITH-61C | KEITH-61C | KEITH-61C | KEITH-61C | KEITH-61C | KEITH-61C | KEITH-61C |
| Jan-51 | 12/50: KEITH - 61C | K'BREWSTER-61A | KEITH-61C | 1/51: W/D | KEITH-61C | 10/50: W/D | KEITH-61C | 10/50: W/D | KEITH-61C |
| Aug-51 | 9/51: W/D | K'BREWSTER-61A | KEITH-61C | | 8/51: W/D | | KEITH-61C | | 6/51: W/D |
| Jan-52 | | K'BREWSTER-61A | KEITH-61C | | | | KEITH-61C | | |
| Aug-52 | | K'BREWSTER-61A | KEITH-61C | | | | KEITH-61C | | |
| Jan-53 | | K'BREWSTER-61A | KEITH-61C | | | | 10/52: W/D | | |
| Aug-53 | | 3/53: W/D | 3/53: W/D | | | | | | |

**D40 4-4-0 (1899)**

| | 62252 | 62255 | 62256 | 62260 | 62261 | 62262 | 62264 | 62265 | 62267 |
|---|---|---|---|---|---|---|---|---|---|
| Aug-50 | KEITH-61C | KEITH-61C | KEITH-61C | K'BREWSTER-61A | K'BREWSTER-61A | KEITH-61C | KEITH-61C | K'BREWSTER-61A | KEITH-61C |
| Jan-51 | KEITH-61C | KEITH-61C | KEITH-61C | K'BREWSTER-61A | K'BREWSTER-61A | KEITH-61C | KEITH-61C | K'BREWSTER-61A | KEITH-61C |
| Aug-51 | KEITH-61C | KEITH-61C | KEITH-61C | K'BREWSTER-61A | K'BREWSTER-61A | KEITH-61C | KEITH-61C | K'BREWSTER-61A | KEITH-61C |
| Jan-52 | 11/51: W/D | KEITH-61C | KEITH-61C | K'BREWSTER-61A | K'BREWSTER-61A | KEITH-61C | KEITH-61C | 10/51: KEITH - 61C | KEITH-61C |
| Aug-52 | | | KEITH-61C | K'BREWSTER-61A | 7/52: KEITH - 61C | KEITH-61C | KEITH-61C | KEITH-61C | KEITH-61C |
| Jan-53 | | | 12/52: W/D | K'BREWSTER-61A | KEITH-61C | KEITH-61C | KEITH-61C | KEITH-61C | KEITH-61C |
| Aug-53 | | | | 8/53: W/D | 3/53: W/D | KEITH-61C | KEITH-61C | KEITH-61C | KEITH-61C |
| Jan-54 | | | | | | KEITH-61C | KEITH-61C | KEITH-61C | KEITH-61C |
| Aug-54 | | | | | | KEITH-61C | KEITH-61C | KEITH-61C | KEITH-61C |
| Jan-55 | | | | | | KEITH-61C | KEITH-61C | KEITH-61C | KEITH-61C |
| Aug-55 | | | | | | KEITH-61C | KEITH-61C | KEITH-61C | KEITH-61C |
| Jan-56 | | | | | | 10/55: W/D | KEITH-61C | KEITH-61C | KEITH-61C |
| Aug-56 | | | | | | | KEITH-61C | KEITH-61C | 8/56: W/D |
| Jan-57 | | | | | | | KEITH-61C | 12/56: W/D | |
| Aug-57 | | | | | | | 3/57: W/D | | |

| | 62268 | 62269 | 62270 | 62271 | 62272 | 62273 | 62274 | 62275 | 62276 |
|---|---|---|---|---|---|---|---|---|---|
| Aug-50 | K'BREWSTER-61A | KEITH-61C | K'BREWSTER-61A | KEITH-61C | K'BREWSTER-61A | K'BREWSTER-61A | K'BREWSTER-61A | K'BREWSTER-61A | K'BREWSTER-61A |
| Jan-51 | K'BREWSTER-61A | KEITH-61C | K'BREWSTER-61A | KEITH-61C | K'BREWSTER-61A | K'BREWSTER-61A | K'BREWSTER-61A | K'BREWSTER-61A | K'BREWSTER-61A |
| Aug-51 | 9/51: KEITH - 61C | KEITH-61C | K'BREWSTER-61A | KEITH-61C | K'BREWSTER-61A | K'BREWSTER-61A | K'BREWSTER-61A | K'BREWSTER-61A | K'BREWSTER-61A |
| Jan-52 | KEITH-61C | KEITH-61C | 10/51: KEITH - 61C | KEITH-61C | 11/51: KEITH - 61C | 2/52: KEITH - 61C | 1/52: KEITH - 61C | K'BREWSTER-61A | K'BREWSTER-61A |
| Aug-52 | KEITH-61C | KEITH-61C | KEITH-61C | KEITH-61C | KEITH-61C | KEITH-61C | KEITH-61C | 4/52: KEITH - 61C | K'BREWSTER-61A |
| Jan-53 | KEITH-61C | KEITH-61C | 4/53: KITTY - 61A | KEITH-61C | KEITH-61C | KEITH-61C | KEITH-61C | KEITH-61C | K'BREWSTER-61A |
| Aug-53 | KEITH-61C | KEITH-61C | 9/53: W/D | KEITH-61C | KEITH-61C | KEITH-61C | KEITH-61C | KEITH-61C | K'BREWSTER-61A |
| Jan-54 | KEITH-61C | KEITH-61C | | KEITH-61C | KEITH-61C | KEITH-61C | KEITH-61C | KEITH-61C | K'BREWSTER-61A |
| Aug-54 | KEITH-61C | KEITH-61C | | KEITH-61C | KEITH-61C | KEITH-61C | 8/54: KITTY - 61A | KEITH-61C | K'BREWSTER-61A |
| Jan-55 | KEITH-61C | KEITH-61C | | KEITH-61C | KEITH-61C | 1/55: W/D | K'BREWSTER-61A | KEITH-61C | K'BREWSTER-61A |
| Aug-55 | KEITH-61C | 9/55: W/D | | KEITH-61C | 3/55: W/D | | K'BREWSTER-61A | 12/55: W/D | K'BREWSTER-61A |
| Jan-56 | KEITH-61C | | | KEITH-61C | | | 8/55: W/D | | 10/55: W/D |
| Aug-56 | 7/56: W/D | | | KEITH-61C | | | | | |
| Jan-57 | | | | 11/56: W/D | | | | | |

**D20 4-4-0 (1899)**

| | 62277 | 62278 | 62279 | 62340 | 62341 | 62342 | 62343 | 62344 | 62345 |
|---|---|---|---|---|---|---|---|---|---|
| Aug-50 | K'BREWSTER-61A | K'BREWSTER-61A | K'BREWSTER-61A | SELBY-50C | SELBY-50C | STARBECK-50D | STARBECK-50D | TWEEDMOUTH-52D | BOTANIC GARDENS - 53B |
| Jan-51 | K'BREWSTER-61A | K'BREWSTER-61A | K'BREWSTER-61A | SELBY-50C | SELBY-50C | 10/50: SELBY - 50C | 10/50: SELBY - 50C | 10/50: ALN - 52D | 1/51: SELBY - 50C |
| Aug-51 | 7/51: KEITH - 61C | K'BREWSTER-61A | K'BREWSTER-61A | 2/51: W/D | 3/51: W/D | 3/51: W/D | 8/51: PICK - 50F | 3/51: W/D | 8/51: YORK - 50A |
| Jan-52 | KEITH-61C | K'BREWSTER-61A | K'BREWSTER-61A | | | | PICKERING-50F | | YORK-50A |
| Aug-52 | KEITH-61C | K'BREWSTER-61A | K'BREWSTER-61A | | | | PICKERING-50F | | YORK-50A |
| Jan-53 | KEITH-61C | K'BREWSTER-61A | K'BREWSTER-61A | | | | 2/53: N.HILL - 50B | | YORK-50A |
| Aug-53 | KEITH-61C | K'BREWSTER-61A | K'BREWSTER-61A | | | | NEVILLE HILL - 50B | | YORK-50A |
| Jan-54 | KEITH-61C | K'BREWSTER-61A | K'BREWSTER-61A | | | | NEVILLE HILL - 50B | | YORK-50A |
| Aug-54 | KEITH-61C | K'BREWSTER-61A | K'BREWSTER-61A | | | | NEVILLE HILL - 50B | | YORK-50A |
| Jan-55 | KEITH-61C | K'BREWSTER-61A | K'BREWSTER-61A | | | | 12/54: SELBY - 50C | | YORK-50A |
| Aug-55 | KEITH-61C | 7/55: W/D | 5/55: W/D | | | | SELBY-50C | | 2/56: SELBY - 50C |
| Jan-56 | KEITH-61C | | | | | | SELBY-50C | | SELBY-50C |
| Aug-56 | KEITH-61C | | | | | | SELBY-50C | | 10/56: W/D |
| Jan-57 | KEITH-61C | | | | | | 10/56: W/D | | |
| Aug-57 | KEITH-61C | | | | | | | | |
| Jan-58 | KEITH-61C | | | | | | | | |
| Aug-58 | 6/58: W/D | | | | | | | | |

### DISTRIBUTION OF CLASS 2P/4P LOCOMOTIVES : 1957

| | D11 | D16 | D20 | D30 | D34 | D41 | D49 | E4 | LM4 | LM2 | Total | | D11 | D16 | D20 | D30 | D34 | D40 | D49 | E4 | LM4 | LM2 | Total |
|---|---|---|---|---|---|---|---|---|---|---|---|---|---|---|---|---|---|---|---|---|---|---|---|
| Eastfield | 14 | | | | 4 | | | | 3 | | 21 | Spital Bge | | 4 | | | | | | | 2 | | 6 |
| New England | | | | | | | | | 19 | | 19 | Bridlington | | 1 | | | | | 5 | | | | 6 |
| Haymarket | 10 | | | 1 | | | 6 | | | | 17 | Middlesbrough | | | | | | | 6 | | | | 6 |
| Melton C | | 5 | | | | | 11 | | | | 16 | Lincoln | 5 | | | | | | | | | | 5 |
| Thornton Jcn | | | 5 | 5 | 5 | | | | | | 15 | Northwich | 5 | | | | | | | | | | 5 |
| South Lynn | | | | | | | 14 | | | | 14 | Neville Hill | | | | | | | 4 | | 1 | | 5 |
| Cambridge | | 8 | | | | 3 | | 3 | | | 14 | West Auckland | | | | | | | | | 4 | | 4 |
| Botanic Gdns | | | 2 | | | | 12 | | | | 14 | Bathgate | | | 1 | 1 | | | | | 1 | | 3 |
| Selby | | | 2 | | | | 4 | 7 | | | 13 | Dunfermline | | | 3 | | | | | | | | 3 |
| Starbeck | | | | | | | 13 | | | | 13 | Stirling | | | 1 | | | | 2 | | | | 3 |
| St Margarets | | | 3 | 2 | | | | | | 2 | 12 | Keith | | | 1 | 2 | | | | | | | 3 |
| K. Lynn | | 11 | | | | | | | | | 11 | Carlisle (C) | | | | | | | 2 | | 1 | | 3 |
| Hull (D) | | | | | | | 10 | | | | 10 | Goole | | | | | | | | 3 | | | 3 |
| Darlington | | | | | | | 3 | 7 | | | 10 | Woodford H. | | | | | | | 2 | | | | 2 |
| Heaton | | | | | | | 10 | | | | 10 | Perth | | | | 2 | | | | | | | 2 |
| Kitty brewster | | | | 7 | 1 | | | | | 1 | 9 | Polmont | | | | | | | 2 | | | | 2 |
| Hawick | | | 8 | | | | | | | | 8 | Hitchin | | 1 | | | | | | 1 | | | 2 |
| Norwich | | 8 | | | | | | | | | 8 | Colchester | | | | | | | | | 2 | | 2 |
| Yarmouth (ST) | | 8 | | | | | | | | | 8 | Alnmouth | | | 2 | | | | | | | | 2 |
| Yarmouth (B) | | 2 | | | | | 6 | | | | 8 | Tweedmouth | | | | | | | 2 | | | | 2 |
| York | | 1 | | | | | 7 | | | | 8 | W. Hartlepool | | | | | | | 2 | | | | 2 |
| Scarborough | | | | | | | 8 | | | | 8 | Kirkby Stephen | | | | | | | | | 2 | | 2 |
| Dundee | | | 2 | 1 | 2 | | | 2 | | 2 | 7 | Trafford Park | 1 | | | | | | | | | | 1 |
| March | | 7 | | | | | | | | | 7 | Lowestoft | | | | | | | | 1 | | | 1 |
| Bury St E | | 6 | | | | | | | | | 6 | | | | | | | | | | | | |

| | 62347 | 62348 | 62349 | 62351 | 62352 | 62353 | 62354 | 62355 | 62357 |
|---|---|---|---|---|---|---|---|---|---|
| Aug-50 | NORTHALLERTON-51J | SELBY-50C | ALNWICK-52D | ALNWICK-52D | ALNWICK-52D | BRIDLINGTON-53D | ALNWICK-52D | BRIDLINGTON-53D | ALNWICK-52D |
| Jan-51 | NORTHALLERTON-51J | SELBY-50C | ALNMOUTH-52D | ALNMOUTH-52D | ALNMOUTH-52D | BRIDLINGTON-53D | ALNMOUTH-52D | BRIDLINGTON-53D | 1/51: W/D |
| Aug-51 | NORTHALLERTON-51J | 2/51: W/D | ALNMOUTH-52D | ALNMOUTH-52D | ALNMOUTH-52D | 4/51: W/D | 4/51: W/D | 6/51: ALN-52D | |
| Jan-52 | NORTHALLERTON-51J | | ALNMOUTH-52D | ALNMOUTH-52D | ALNMOUTH-52D | | | ALNMOUTH-52D | |
| Aug-52 | NORTHALLERTON-51J | | ALNMOUTH-52D | ALNMOUTH-52D | ALNMOUTH-52D | | | ALNMOUTH-52D | |
| Jan-53 | NORTHALLERTON-51J | | ALNMOUTH-52D | ALNMOUTH-52D | 5/53: HTN-52B | | | ALNMOUTH-52D | |
| Aug-53 | NORTHALLERTON-51J | | 5/53: GHD-52A | ALNMOUTH-52D | 10/53: ALN-52D | | | ALNMOUTH-52D | |
| Jan-54 | NORTHALLERTON-51J | | 10/53: ALN-52D | ALNMOUTH-52D | 6/54: W/D | | | ALNMOUTH-52D | |
| Aug-54 | NORTHALLERTON-51J | | 5/54: BLAY-52C | ALNMOUTH-52D | | | | ALNMOUTH-52D | |
| Jan-55 | 11/54: W/D | | BLAYDON-52C | 11/54: W/D | | | | ALNMOUTH-52D | |
| Aug-55 | | | 6/55: SELBY-50C | | | | | ALNMOUTH-52D | |
| Jan-56 | | | SELBY-50C | | | | | 11/55: W/D | |
| Aug-56 | | | 2/56: W/D | | | | | | |
| Jan-57 | | | | | | | | | |
| Aug-57 | | | | | | | | | |
| Jan-58 | | | | | | | | | |
| Aug-58 | | | | | | | | | |
| Jan-59 | | | | | | | | | |
| Aug-59 | | | | | | | | | |
| Nov-59 | | | | | | | | | |
| Jan-60 | | | | | | | | | |
| Apr-60 | | | | | | | | | |
| Aug-60 | | | | | | | | | |
| Nov-60 | | | | | | | | | |

| | 62358 | 62359 | 62360 | 62361 | 62362 | 62363 | 62365 | 62366 | 62369 |
|---|---|---|---|---|---|---|---|---|---|
| Aug-50 | ALNWICK-52D | NORTHALLERTON-51J | ALNWICK-52D | SELBY-50C | ALNWICK-52D | SELBY-50C | BRIDLINGTON-53D | SELBY-50C | YORK-50A |
| Jan-51 | ALNMOUTH-52D | NORTHALLERTON-51J | ALNMOUTH-52D | SELBY-50C | ALNMOUTH-52D | SELBY-50C | 11/50: ALN-52D | SELBY-50C | 9/50: STAR-50D |
| Aug-51 | 4/51: ALN-52D | NORTHALLERTON-51J | ALNMOUTH-52D | 2/51: W/D | 4/51: W/D | 3/51: W/D | 4/51: W/D | 3/51: W/D | 3/51: W/D |
| Jan-52 | ALNMOUTH-52D | NORTHALLERTON-51J | ALNMOUTH-52D | | | | | | |
| Aug-52 | ALNMOUTH-52D | 10/52: W.AUCK-51J | ALNMOUTH-52D | | | | | | |
| Jan-53 | ALNMOUTH-52D | 11/52: W.HPL-51C | ALNMOUTH-52D | | | | | | |
| Aug-53 | ALNMOUTH-52D | W.HARTLEPOOL-51C | 5/53: GHD-52A | | | | | | |
| Jan-54 | ALNMOUTH-52D | W.HARTLEPOOL-51C | 10/53: ALN-52D | | | | | | |
| Aug-54 | ALNMOUTH-52D | 5/54: NLTN-51J | 6/54: GHD-52A | | | | | | |
| Jan-55 | 10/54: W/D | NORTHALLERTON-51J | 11/54: ALN-52D | | | | | | |
| Aug-55 | | 6/55: N.HILL-50B | ALNMOUTH-52D | | | | | | |
| Jan-56 | | 10/55: W/D | ALNMOUTH-52D | | | | | | |
| Aug-56 | | | ALNMOUTH-52D | | | | | | |
| Jan-57 | | | 10/56: W/D | | | | | | |
| Aug-57 | | | | | | | | | |
| Jan-58 | | | | | | | | | |
| Aug-58 | | | | | | | | | |
| Jan-59 | | | | | | | | | |
| Aug-59 | | | | | | | | | |
| Nov-59 | | | | | | | | | |
| Jan-60 | | | | | | | | | |
| Apr-60 | | | | | | | | | |
| Aug-60 | | | | | | | | | |
| Nov-60 | | | | | | | | | |

| | 62370 | 62371 | 62372 | 62373 | 62374 | 62375 | 62376 | 62378 | 62379 |
|---|---|---|---|---|---|---|---|---|---|
| Aug-50 | STARBECK-50D | ALNWICK-52D | W.HARTLEPOOL-51C | STARBECK-50D | SELBY-50C | BRIDLINGTON-53D | SELBY-50C | SELBY-50C | W.HARTLEPOOL-51C |
| Jan-51 | STARBECK-50D | ALNMOUTH-52D | W.HARTLEPOOL-51C | STARBECK-50D | SELBY-50C | BRIDLINGTON-53D | SELBY-50C | SELBY-50C | W.HARTLEPOOL-51C |
| Aug-51 | 4/51: W/D | ALNMOUTH-52D | 6/51: NLTN-51J | 6/51: NLTN-51J | SELBY-50C | 6/51: ALN-52D | 2/51: W/D | SELBY-50C | 4/51: W/D |
| Jan-52 | | ALNMOUTH-52D | NORTHALLERTON-51J | NORTHALLERTON-51J | SELBY-50C | ALNMOUTH-52D | | SELBY-50C | |
| Aug-52 | | ALNMOUTH-52D | NORTHALLERTON-51J | NORTHALLERTON-51J | SELBY-50C | ALNMOUTH-52D | | SELBY-50C | |
| Jan-53 | | 2/53: TWEED-52D | NORTHALLERTON-51J | 2/53: W/D | SELBY-50C | 5/53: GHD-52A | | SELBY-50C | |
| Aug-53 | | 5/53: GHD-52A | NORTHALLERTON-51J | | SELBY-50C | 10/53: ALN-52D | | SELBY-50C | |
| Jan-54 | | 10/53: ALN-52D | 12/53: W.HPL-51C | | SELBY-50C | 6/54: GHD-52A | | SELBY-50C | |
| Aug-54 | | ALNMOUTH-52D | W.HARTLEPOOL-51C | | SELBY-50C | 11/54: ALN-52D | | SELBY-50C | |
| Jan-55 | | 10/54: W/D | W.HARTLEPOOL-51C | | 10/54: W/D | ALNMOUTH-52D | | SELBY-50C | |
| Aug-55 | | | 6/55: N.HILL-50B | | | ALNMOUTH-52D | | SELBY-50C | |
| Jan-56 | | | NEVILLE HILL-50B | | | ALNMOUTH-52D | | SELBY-50C | |
| Aug-56 | | | 6/56: BRID-53D | | | ALNMOUTH-52D | | SELBY-50C | |
| Jan-57 | | | 11/56: W/D | | | ALNMOUTH-52D | | 11/56: W/D | |
| Aug-57 | | | | | | 5/57: W/D | | | |
| Jan-58 | | | | | | | | | |
| Aug-58 | | | | | | | | | |
| Jan-59 | | | | | | | | | |
| Aug-59 | | | | | | | | | |
| Nov-59 | | | | | | | | | |
| Jan-60 | | | | | | | | | |
| Apr-60 | | | | | | | | | |
| Aug-60 | | | | | | | | | |
| Nov-60 | | | | | | | | | |

| | 62380 | 62381 | 62382 | 62383 | 62384 | 62386 | 62387 | 62388 | 62389 |
|---|---|---|---|---|---|---|---|---|---|
| Aug-50 | ALNWICK-52D | SELBY-50C | SELBY-50C | BOTANIC GARDENS-53B | BOTANIC GARDENS-53B | SELBY-50C | ALNWICK-52D | NORTHALLERTON-51J | STARBECK-50D |
| Jan-51 | ALNMOUTH-52D | SELBY-50C | SELBY-50C | BOTANIC GARDENS-53B | 10/50: SELBY-50C | SELBY-50C | ALNMOUTH-52D | NORTHALLERTON-51J | STARBECK-50D |
| Aug-51 | ALNMOUTH-52D | SELBY-50C | 2/51: W/D | 6/51: ALN-52D | SELBY-50C | SELBY-50C | ALNMOUTH-52D | 6/51: W/HPL-51C | 6/51: SELBY-50C |
| Jan-52 | ALNMOUTH-52D | SELBY-50C | | ALNMOUTH-52D | SELBY-50C | SELBY-50C | ALNMOUTH-52D | W.HARTLEPOOL-51C | SELBY-50C |
| Aug-52 | ALNMOUTH-52D | SELBY-50C | | ALNMOUTH-52D | SELBY-50C | SELBY-50C | ALNMOUTH-52D | 11/52: NLTN-51J | 7/52: N.HILL-50B |
| Jan-53 | ALNMOUTH-52D | SELBY-50C | | ALNMOUTH-52D | SELBY-50C | SELBY-50C | 5/53: HTN-52B | 1/53: TYNE D-54B | NEVILLE HILL-50B |
| Aug-53 | ALNMOUTH-52D | SELBY-50C | | ALNMOUTH-52D | SELBY-50C | SELBY-50C | HEATON-52B | 2/53: NLTN-51J | NEVILLE HILL-50B |
| Jan-54 | ALNMOUTH-52D | SELBY-50C | | ALNMOUTH-52D | SELBY-50C | SELBY-50C | HEATON-52B | NORTHALLERTON-51J | NEVILLE HILL-50B |
| Aug-54 | 6/54: GHD-52A | SELBY-50C | | ALNMOUTH-52D | SELBY-50C | SELBY-50C | HEATON-52B | 4/54: W/D | 9/54: W/D |
| Jan-55 | 9/54: W/D | SELBY-50C | | ALNMOUTH-52D | SELBY-50C | SELBY-50C | 6/55: SELBY-50C | | |
| Aug-55 | | SELBY-50C | | ALNMOUTH-52D | 8/55: W/D | SELBY-50C | SELBY-50C | | |
| Jan-56 | | SELBY-50C | | ALNMOUTH-52D | | SELBY-50C | SELBY-50C | | |
| Aug-56 | | 6/56: B.GDNS-53B | | ALNMOUTH-52D | | SELBY-50C | SELBY-50C | | |
| Jan-57 | | BOTANIC GARDENS-53B | | ALNMOUTH-52D | | 10/56: W/D | SELBY-50C | | |
| Aug-57 | | 9/57: ALN-52D | | 5/57: W/D | | | 6/57: ALN-52D | | |
| Jan-58 | | 11/57: W/D | | | | | 9/57: W/D | | |
| Aug-58 | | | | | | | | | |
| Jan-59 | | | | | | | | | |
| Aug-59 | | | | | | | | | |
| Nov-59 | | | | | | | | | |
| Jan-60 | | | | | | | | | |
| Apr-60 | | | | | | | | | |
| Aug-60 | | | | | | | | | |
| Nov-60 | | | | | | | | | |

**D29 4-4-0 (1909):** 62405, 62410, 62411  
**D30 4-4-0 (1912):** 62417

| Date | 62391 | 62392 | 62395 | 62396 | 62397 | 62405 | 62410 | 62411 | 62417 |
|---|---|---|---|---|---|---|---|---|---|
| Aug-50 | NORTHALLERTON-51J | STARBECK-50D | SELBY-50C | BOT. GDNS-53B | STARBECK-50D | HAYMARKET-64B | THORNTON JCN-62A | THORNTON JCN-62A | HAWICK-64G |
| Jan-51 | NORTHALLERTON-51J | STARBECK-50D | SELBY-50C | BOT. GDNS-53B | 9/50: YORK-50A | HAYMARKET-64B | THORNTON JCN-62A | THORNTON JCN-62A | 1/51: W/D |
| Aug-51 | 6/51: W/D | 6/51: SELBY-50C | SELBY-50C | 6/51: ALN-52D | 10/50: SELBY-50C | 2/51: W/D | THORNTON JCN-62A | THORNTON JCN-62A | |
| Jan-52 | | SELBY-50C | SELBY-50C | ALNMOUTH-52D | 7/52: N.HILL-50B | | 1/52: W/D | THORNTON JCN-62A | |
| Aug-52 | | SELBY-50C | SELBY-50C | 7/52: TWEED-52D | NEVILLE HILL-50B | | | THORNTON JCN-62A | |
| Jan-53 | | SELBY-50C | SELBY-50C | 2/53: ALN-52D | NEVILLE HILL-50B | | | 10/52: W/D | |
| Aug-53 | | SELBY-50C | SELBY-50C | ALNMOUTH-52D | NEVILLE HILL-50B | | | | |
| Jan-54 | | SELBY-50C | SELBY-50C | ALNMOUTH-52D | NEVILLE HILL-50B | | | | |
| Aug-54 | | 5/54: W/D | SELBY-50C | 6/54: GHD-52A | NEVILLE HILL-50B | | | | |
| Jan-55 | | | SELBY-50C | 11/54: ALN-52D | NEVILLE HILL-50B | | | | |
| Aug-55 | | | SELBY-50C | 6/55: SELBY-50C | SELBY-50C | | | | |
| Jan-56 | | | SELBY-50C | SELBY-50C | 6/56: BRID-53D | | | | |
| Aug-56 | | | SELBY-50C | SELBY-50C | BRIDLINGTON-53D | | | | |
| Jan-57 | | | 12/56: YORK-50A | 12/56: BOT. GDNS-53B | 2/57: W/D | | | | |
| Aug-57 | | | 6/57: ALN-52D | 6/57: ALN-52D | | | | | |
| Jan-58 | | | 11/57: W/D | 11/57: W/D | | | | | |

| Date | 62418 | 62419 | 62420 | 62421 | 62422 | 62423 | 62424 | 62425 | 62426 |
|---|---|---|---|---|---|---|---|---|---|
| Aug-50 | THORNTON JCN-62A | THORNTON JCN-62A | HAWICK-64G | EDINBURGH(SM)-64A | HAWICK-64G | HAWICK-64G | EDINBURGH(SM)-64A | HAWICK-64G | STIRLING-63B |
| Jan-51 | THORNTON JCN-62A | THORNTON JCN-62A | HAWICK-64G | EDINBURGH(SM)-64A | HAWICK-64G | HAWICK-64G | EDINBURGH(SM)-64A | HAWICK-64G | STIRLING-63B |
| Aug-51 | THORNTON JCN-62A | THORNTON JCN-62A | HAWICK-64G | EDINBURGH(SM)-64A | HAWICK-64G | HAWICK-64G | EDINBURGH(SM)-64A | HAWICK-64G | STIRLING-63B |
| Jan-52 | THORNTON JCN-62A | THORNTON JCN-62A | HAWICK-64G | EDINBURGH(SM)-64A | HAWICK-64G | HAWICK-64G | EDINBURGH(SM)-64A | HAWICK-64G | STIRLING-63B |
| Aug-52 | THORNTON JCN-62A | THORNTON JCN-62A | HAWICK-64G | EDINBURGH(SM)-64A | HAWICK-64G | HAWICK-64G | EDINBURGH(SM)-64A | HAWICK-64G | STIRLING-63B |
| Jan-53 | THORNTON JCN-62A | THORNTON JCN-62A | HAWICK-64G | EDINBURGH(SM)-64A | HAWICK-64G | HAWICK-64G | EDINBURGH(SM)-64A | HAWICK-64G | STIRLING-63B |
| Aug-53 | THORNTON JCN-62A | THORNTON JCN-62A | HAWICK-64G | EDINBURGH(SM)-64A | HAWICK-64G | HAWICK-64G | EDINBURGH(SM)-64A | HAWICK-64G | STIRLING-63B |
| Jan-54 | THORNTON JCN-62A | THORNTON JCN-62A | HAWICK-64G | EDINBURGH(SM)-64A | HAWICK-64G | HAWICK-64G | EDINBURGH(SM)-64A | HAWICK-64G | STIRLING-63B |
| Aug-54 | THORNTON JCN-62A | THORNTON JCN-62A | HAWICK-64G | EDINBURGH(SM)-64A | HAWICK-64G | HAWICK-64G | EDINBURGH(SM)-64A | HAWICK-64G | STIRLING-63B |
| Jan-55 | THORNTON JCN-62A | THORNTON JCN-62A | HAWICK-64G | EDINBURGH(SM)-64A | HAWICK-64G | HAWICK-64G | EDINBURGH(SM)-64A | HAWICK-64G | STIRLING-63B |
| Aug-55 | THORNTON JCN-62A | THORNTON JCN-62A | HAWICK-64G | EDINBURGH(SM)-64A | HAWICK-64G | HAWICK-64G | EDINBURGH(SM)-64A | HAWICK-64G | STIRLING-63B |
| Jan-56 | THORNTON JCN-62A | THORNTON JCN-62A | HAWICK-64G | EDINBURGH(SM)-64A | HAWICK-64G | HAWICK-64G | EDINBURGH(SM)-64A | HAWICK-64G | STIRLING-63B |
| Aug-56 | THORNTON JCN-62A | THORNTON JCN-62A | HAWICK-64G | EDINBURGH(SM)-64A | HAWICK-64G | HAWICK-64G | EDINBURGH(SM)-64A | HAWICK-64G | STIRLING-63B |
| Jan-57 | THORNTON JCN-62A | THORNTON JCN-62A | HAWICK-64G | EDINBURGH(SM)-64A | HAWICK-64G | HAWICK-64G | EDINBURGH(SM)-64A | HAWICK-64G | STIRLING-63B |
| Aug-57 | THORNTON JCN-62A | THORNTON JCN-62A | 5/57: W/D | EDINBURGH(SM)-64A | HAWICK-64G | HAWICK-64G | 8/57: W/D | HAWICK-64G | STIRLING-63B |
| Jan-58 | THORNTON JCN-62A | 9/57: W/D | | EDINBURGH(SM)-64A | HAWICK-64G | 12/57: W/D | | HAWICK-64G | STIRLING-63B |
| Aug-58 | THORNTON JCN-62A | | | EDINBURGH(SM)-64A | HAWICK-64G | | | 7/58: W/D | STIRLING-63B |
| Jan-59 | THORNTON JCN-62A | | | EDINBURGH(SM)-64A | 12/58: W/D | | | | STIRLING-63B |
| Aug-59 | 8/59: W/D | | | EDINBURGH(SM)-64A | | | | | STIRLING-63B |
| Nov-59 | | | | EDINBURGH(SM)-64A | | | | | STIRLING-63B |
| Jan-60 | | | | EDINBURGH(SM)-64A | | | | | STIRLING-63B |
| Apr-60 | | | | EDINBURGH(SM)-64A | | | | | STIRLING-65J |
| Aug-60 | | | | 8/60: W/D | | | | | 8/60: W/D |
| Nov-60 | | | | | | | | | |

| Date | 62427 | 62428 | 62429 | 62430 | 62431 | 62432 | 62434 | 62435 | 62436 |
|---|---|---|---|---|---|---|---|---|---|
| Aug-50 | DUNDEE-62B | HAWICK-64G | THORNTON JCN-62A | THORNTON JCN-62A | THORNTON JCN-62A | HAWICK-64G | DUNDEE-62B | EDINBURGH(SM)-64A | DUNDEE-62B |
| Jan-51 | DUNDEE-62B | HAWICK-64G | THORNTON JCN-62A | THORNTON JCN-62A | THORNTON JCN-62A | HAWICK-64G | DUNDEE-62B | 1/51: HWCK-64G | DUNDEE-62B |
| Aug-51 | DUNDEE-62B | HAWICK-64G | THORNTON JCN-62A | THORNTON JCN-62A | THORNTON JCN-62A | HAWICK-64G | DUNDEE-62B | HAWICK-64G | DUNDEE-62B |
| Jan-52 | DUNDEE-62B | HAWICK-64G | THORNTON JCN-62A | THORNTON JCN-62A | THORNTON JCN-62A | HAWICK-64G | DUNDEE-62B | HAWICK-64G | 10/51: DUNF-62C |
| Aug-52 | DUNDEE-62B | HAWICK-64G | THORNTON JCN-62A | THORNTON JCN-62A | THORNTON JCN-62A | HAWICK-64G | DUNDEE-62B | HAWICK-64G | DUNFERMLINE-62C |
| Jan-53 | DUNDEE-62B | HAWICK-64G | THORNTON JCN-62A | THORNTON JCN-62A | THORNTON JCN-62A | HAWICK-64G | DUNDEE-62B | HAWICK-64G | DUNFERMLINE-62C |
| Aug-53 | DUNDEE-62B | HAWICK-64G | THORNTON JCN-62A | THORNTON JCN-62A | THORNTON JCN-62A | HAWICK-64G | DUNDEE-62B | HAWICK-64G | DUNFERMLINE-62C |
| Jan-54 | 10/53: DUNF-62C | HAWICK-64G | THORNTON JCN-62A | THORNTON JCN-62A | THORNTON JCN-62A | HAWICK-64G | DUNDEE-62B | HAWICK-64G | DUNFERMLINE-62C |
| Aug-54 | DUNFERMLINE-62C | HAWICK-64G | THORNTON JCN-62A | THORNTON JCN-62A | THORNTON JCN-62A | HAWICK-64G | DUNDEE-62B | HAWICK-64G | DUNFERMLINE-62C |
| Jan-55 | DUNFERMLINE-62C | HAWICK-64G | THORNTON JCN-62A | THORNTON JCN-62A | THORNTON JCN-62A | HAWICK-64G | DUNDEE-62B | HAWICK-64G | DUNFERMLINE-62C |
| Aug-55 | DUNFERMLINE-62C | HAWICK-64G | THORNTON JCN-62A | THORNTON JCN-62A | THORNTON JCN-62A | HAWICK-64G | DUNDEE-62B | HAWICK-64G | DUNFERMLINE-62C |
| Jan-56 | DUNFERMLINE-62C | HAWICK-64G | THORNTON JCN-62A | THORNTON JCN-62A | THORNTON JCN-62A | HAWICK-64G | DUNDEE-62B | HAWICK-64G | DUNFERMLINE-62C |
| Aug-56 | DUNFERMLINE-62C | HAWICK-64G | THORNTON JCN-62A | THORNTON JCN-62A | THORNTON JCN-62A | HAWICK-64G | DUNDEE-62B | HAWICK-64G | DUNFERMLINE-62C |
| Jan-57 | DUNFERMLINE-62C | HAWICK-64G | THORNTON JCN-62A | 1/57: W/D | THORNTON JCN-62A | HAWICK-64G | DUNDEE-62B | HAWICK-64G | DUNFERMLINE-62C |
| Aug-57 | DUNFERMLINE-62C | HAWICK-64G | 8/57: W/D | | THORNTON JCN-62A | HAWICK-64G | DUNDEE-62B | 12/57: W/D | DUNFERMLINE-62C |
| Jan-58 | DUNFERMLINE-62C | HAWICK-64G | | | THORNTON JCN-62A | HAWICK-64G | 4/58: W/D | | DUNFERMLINE-62C |
| Aug-58 | DUNFERMLINE-62C | HAWICK-64G | | | THORNTON JCN-62A | HAWICK-64G | | | DUNFERMLINE-62C |
| Jan-59 | DUNFERMLINE-62C | 12/58: W/D | | | 10/58: W/D | 12/58: W/D | | | DUNFERMLINE-62C |
| Aug-59 | 4/59: W/D | | | | | | | | 6/59: W/D |

**D32 4-4-0 (1906):** 62451  
**D33 4-4-0 (1909):** 62457, 62459

| Date | 62437 | 62438 | 62439 | 62440 | 62441 | 62442 | 62451 | 62457 | 62459 |
|---|---|---|---|---|---|---|---|---|---|
| Aug-50 | HAYMARKET-64B | DUNDEE-62B | BATHGATE-64F | HAWICK-64G | DUNFERMLINE-62C | THORNTON JCN-62A | EDINBURGH(SM)-64A | DUNDEE-62B | DUNFERMLINE-62C |
| Jan-51 | HAYMARKET-64B | DUNDEE-62B | BATHGATE-64F | HAWICK-64G | DUNFERMLINE-62C | THORNTON JCN-62A | EDINBURGH(SM)-64A | DUNDEE-62B | DUNFERMLINE-62C |
| Aug-51 | HAYMARKET-64B | DUNDEE-62B | BATHGATE-64F | HAWICK-64G | DUNFERMLINE-62C | THORNTON JCN-62A | 3/51: W/D | 4/51: DUN-62C | DUNFERMLINE-62C |
| Jan-52 | HAYMARKET-64B | DUNDEE-62B | BATHGATE-64F | HAWICK-64G | DUNFERMLINE-62C | THORNTON JCN-62A | | DUNFERMLINE-62C | 10/51: W/D |
| Aug-52 | HAYMARKET-64B | DUNDEE-62B | BATHGATE-64F | HAWICK-64G | DUNFERMLINE-62C | THORNTON JCN-62A | | 6/52: W/D | |
| Jan-53 | HAYMARKET-64B | DUNDEE-62B | BATHGATE-64F | HAWICK-64G | DUNFERMLINE-62C | THORNTON JCN-62A | | | |
| Aug-53 | HAYMARKET-64B | DUNDEE-62B | BATHGATE-64F | HAWICK-64G | DUNFERMLINE-62C | THORNTON JCN-62A | | | |
| Jan-54 | HAYMARKET-64B | DUNDEE-62B | BATHGATE-64F | HAWICK-64G | DUNFERMLINE-62C | THORNTON JCN-62A | | | |
| Aug-54 | HAYMARKET-64B | DUNDEE-62B | BATHGATE-64F | HAWICK-64G | DUNFERMLINE-62C | THORNTON JCN-62A | | | |
| Jan-55 | HAYMARKET-64B | DUNDEE-62B | BATHGATE-64F | HAWICK-64G | DUNFERMLINE-62C | THORNTON JCN-62A | | | |
| Aug-55 | HAYMARKET-64B | DUNDEE-62B | BATHGATE-64F | HAWICK-64G | DUNFERMLINE-62C | THORNTON JCN-62A | | | |
| Jan-56 | HAYMARKET-64B | DUNDEE-62B | BATHGATE-64F | HAWICK-64G | DUNFERMLINE-62C | THORNTON JCN-62A | | | |
| Aug-56 | HAYMARKET-64B | DUNDEE-62B | BATHGATE-64F | HAWICK-64G | DUNFERMLINE-62C | THORNTON JCN-62A | | | |
| Jan-57 | HAYMARKET-64B | DUNDEE-62B | BATHGATE-64F | HAWICK-64G | DUNFERMLINE-62C | THORNTON JCN-62A | | | |
| Aug-57 | HAYMARKET-64B | DUNDEE-62B | BATHGATE-64F | HAWICK-64G | DUNFERMLINE-62C | THORNTON JCN-62A | | | |
| Jan-58 | HAYMARKET-64B | 10/57: W/D | BATHGATE-64F | HAWICK-64G | DUNFERMLINE-62C | THORNTON JCN-62A | | | |
| Aug-58 | 6/58: W/D | | BATHGATE-64F | 7/58: W/D | 8/58: W/D | 6/58: W/D | | | |
| Jan-59 | | | BATHGATE-64F | | | | | | |
| Aug-59 | | | BATHGATE-64F | | | | | | |
| Nov-59 | | | 10/59: W/D | | | | | | |

| | 62460 | 62461 | 62462 | 62464 | 62466 | D34 4-4-0 (1913)<br>62467 | 62468 | 62469 | 62470 |
|---|---|---|---|---|---|---|---|---|---|
| Aug-50 | EASTFIELD - 65A | STIRLING - 63B | EASTFIELD - 65A | DUNFERMLINE - 62C | DUNDEE - 62B | THORNTON JCN - 62A | THORNTON JCN - 62A | EASTFIELD - 65A | EASTFIELD - 65A |
| Jan-51 | EASTFIELD - 65A | STIRLING - 63B | EASTFIELD - 65A | DUNFERMLINE - 62C | 9/50: DUNF - 62C | THORNTON JCN - 62A | THORNTON JCN - 62A | EASTFIELD - 65A | EASTFIELD - 65A |
| Aug-51 | 8/51: W/D | 6/51: W/D | EASTFIELD - 65A | DUNFERMLINE - 62C | DUNFERMLINE - 62C | THORNTON JCN - 62A | THORNTON JCN - 62A | EASTFIELD - 65A | EASTFIELD - 65A |
| Jan-52 | | | EASTFIELD - 65A | DUNFERMLINE - 62C | 9/51: W/D | THORNTON JCN - 62A | THORNTON JCN - 62A | EASTFIELD - 65A | EASTFIELD - 65A |
| Aug-52 | | | EASTFIELD - 65A | DUNFERMLINE - 62C | | THORNTON JCN - 62A | THORNTON JCN - 62A | EASTFIELD - 65A | EASTFIELD - 65A |
| Jan-53 | | | 11/52: W/D | DUNFERMLINE - 62C | | THORNTON JCN - 62A | THORNTON JCN - 62A | EASTFIELD - 65A | EASTFIELD - 65A |
| Aug-53 | | | | DUNFERMLINE - 62C | | THORNTON JCN - 62A | THORNTON JCN - 62A | 4/53: KITTY - 61A | EASTFIELD - 65A |
| Jan-54 | | | | 9/53: W/D | | THORNTON JCN - 62A | THORNTON JCN - 62A | KITTYBREWSTER - 61A | 10/53: PERTH - 63A |
| Aug-54 | | | | | | THORNTON JCN - 62A | THORNTON JCN - 62A | KITTYBREWSTER - 61A | PERTH - 63A |
| Jan-55 | | | | | | THORNTON JCN - 62A | THORNTON JCN - 62A | KITTYBREWSTER - 61A | PERTH - 63A |
| Aug-55 | | | | | | THORNTON JCN - 62A | THORNTON JCN - 62A | KITTYBREWSTER - 61A | PERTH - 63A |
| Jan-56 | | | | | | THORNTON JCN - 62A | THORNTON JCN - 62A | 2/56: KEITH - 61C | PERTH - 63A |
| Aug-56 | | | | | | THORNTON JCN - 62A | THORNTON JCN - 62A | KEITH - 61C | PERTH - 63A |
| Jan-57 | | | | | | THORNTON JCN - 62A | THORNTON JCN - 62A | KEITH - 61C | PERTH - 63A |
| Aug-57 | | | | | | THORNTON JCN - 62A | THORNTON JCN - 62A | KEITH - 61C | PERTH - 63A |
| Jan-58 | | | | | | THORNTON JCN - 62A | THORNTON JCN - 62A | KEITH - 61C | PERTH - 63A |
| Aug-58 | | | | | | THORNTON JCN - 62A | THORNTON JCN - 62A | KEITH - 61C | PERTH - 63A |
| Jan-59 | | | | | | THORNTON JCN - 62A | 9/58:W/D | KEITH - 61C | PERTH - 63A |
| Aug-59 | | | | | | THORNTON JCN - 62A | | 8/59: W/D | 5/59: W/D |
| Nov-59 | | | | | | THORNTON JCN - 62A | | | |
| Jan-60 | | | | | | THORNTON JCN - 62A | | | |
| Apr-60 | | | | | | THORNTON JCN - 62A | | | |
| Aug-60 | | | | | | THORNTON JCN - 62A | | | |
| Nov-60 | | | | | | 9/60: W/D | | | |

| | 62471 | 62472 | 62474 | 62475 | 62477 | 62478 | 62479 | 62480 | 62482 |
|---|---|---|---|---|---|---|---|---|---|
| Aug-50 | EDINBURGH (SM) - 64A | EASTFIELD - 65A | EASTFIELD - 65A | THORNTON JCN - 62A | EASTFIELD - 65A | THORNTON JCN - 62A | EASTFIELD - 65A | EASTFIELD - 65A | EASTFIELD - 65A |
| Jan-51 | EDINBURGH (SM) - 64A | EASTFIELD - 65A | EASTFIELD - 65A | THORNTON JCN - 62A | EASTFIELD - 65A | THORNTON JCN - 62A | EASTFIELD - 65A | EASTFIELD - 65A | EASTFIELD - 65A |
| Aug-51 | EDINBURGH (SM) - 64A | EASTFIELD - 65A | EASTFIELD - 65A | THORNTON JCN - 62A | EASTFIELD - 65A | THORNTON JCN - 62A | EASTFIELD - 65A | EASTFIELD - 65A | EASTFIELD - 65A |
| Jan-52 | EDINBURGH (SM) - 64A | EASTFIELD - 65A | EASTFIELD - 65A | THORNTON JCN - 62A | EASTFIELD - 65A | THORNTON JCN - 62A | EASTFIELD - 65A | EASTFIELD - 65A | EASTFIELD - 65A |
| Aug-52 | EDINBURGH (SM) - 64A | EASTFIELD - 65A | EASTFIELD - 65A | THORNTON JCN - 62A | EASTFIELD - 65A | THORNTON JCN - 62A | EASTFIELD - 65A | EASTFIELD - 65A | EASTFIELD - 65A |
| Jan-53 | EDINBURGH (SM) - 64A | EASTFIELD - 65A | EASTFIELD - 65A | THORNTON JCN - 62A | EASTFIELD - 65A | THORNTON JCN - 62A | 2/53: KITTY - 61A | EASTFIELD - 65A | EASTFIELD - 65A |
| Aug-53 | EDINBURGH (SM) - 64A | EASTFIELD - 65A | EASTFIELD - 65A | THORNTON JCN - 62A | EASTFIELD - 65A | THORNTON JCN - 62A | KITTYBREWSTER - 61A | EASTFIELD - 65A | EASTFIELD - 65A |
| Jan-54 | EDINBURGH (SM) - 64A | EASTFIELD - 65A | EASTFIELD - 65A | THORNTON JCN - 62A | EASTFIELD - 65A | THORNTON JCN - 62A | KITTYBREWSTER - 61A | 10/53: KITTY - 61A | 10/53: KITTY - 61A |
| Aug-54 | EDINBURGH (SM) - 64A | EASTFIELD - 65A | EASTFIELD - 65A | THORNTON JCN - 62A | EASTFIELD - 65A | THORNTON JCN - 62A | KITTYBREWSTER - 61A | KITTYBREWSTER - 61A | KITTYBREWSTER - 61A |
| Jan-55 | EDINBURGH (SM) - 64A | EASTFIELD - 65A | EASTFIELD - 65A | THORNTON JCN - 62A | EASTFIELD - 65A | THORNTON JCN - 62A | KITTYBREWSTER - 61A | KITTYBREWSTER - 61A | KITTYBREWSTER - 61A |
| Aug-55 | EDINBURGH (SM) - 64A | EASTFIELD - 65A | EASTFIELD - 65A | THORNTON JCN - 62A | EASTFIELD - 65A | THORNTON JCN - 62A | KITTYBREWSTER - 61A | KITTYBREWSTER - 61A | KITTYBREWSTER - 61A |
| Jan-56 | EDINBURGH (SM) - 64A | EASTFIELD - 65A | EASTFIELD - 65A | THORNTON JCN - 62A | EASTFIELD - 65A | THORNTON JCN - 62A | KITTYBREWSTER - 61A | KITTYBREWSTER - 61A | KITTYBREWSTER - 61A |
| Aug-56 | EDINBURGH (SM) - 64A | EASTFIELD - 65A | EASTFIELD - 65A | THORNTON JCN - 62A | EASTFIELD - 65A | THORNTON JCN - 62A | KITTYBREWSTER - 61A | KITTYBREWSTER - 61A | KITTYBREWSTER - 61A |
| Jan-57 | EDINBURGH (SM) - 64A | EASTFIELD - 65A | EASTFIELD - 65A | THORNTON JCN - 62A | EASTFIELD - 65A | THORNTON JCN - 62A | KITTYBREWSTER - 61A | KITTYBREWSTER - 61A | KITTYBREWSTER - 61A |
| Aug-57 | EDINBURGH (SM) - 64A | EASTFIELD - 65A | EASTFIELD - 65A | THORNTON JCN - 62A | EASTFIELD - 65A | THORNTON JCN - 62A | KITTYBREWSTER - 61A | KITTYBREWSTER - 61A | KITTYBREWSTER - 61A |
| Jan-58 | EDINBURGH (SM) - 64A | EASTFIELD - 65A | EASTFIELD - 65A | THORNTON JCN - 62A | EASTFIELD - 65A | THORNTON JCN - 62A | KITTYBREWSTER - 61A | KITTYBREWSTER - 61A | KITTYBREWSTER - 61A |
| Aug-58 | EDINBURGH (SM) - 64A | EASTFIELD - 65A | EASTFIELD - 65A | THORNTON JCN - 62A | EASTFIELD - 65A | THORNTON JCN - 62A | KITTYBREWSTER - 61A | KITTYBREWSTER - 61A | KITTYBREWSTER - 61A |
| Jan-59 | EDINBURGH (SM) - 64A | EASTFIELD - 65A | EASTFIELD - 65A | THORNTON JCN - 62A | EASTFIELD - 65A | THORNTON JCN - 62A | KITTYBREWSTER - 61A | KITTYBREWSTER - 61A | KITTYBREWSTER - 61A |
| Aug-59 | EDINBURGH (SM) - 64A | EASTFIELD - 65A | EASTFIELD - 65A | 6/59: W/D | EASTFIELD - 65A | THORNTON JCN - 62A | KITTYBREWSTER - 61A | KITTYBREWSTER - 61A | KITTYBREWSTER - 61A |
| Nov-59 | EDINBURGH (SM) - 64A | 10/59: W/D | EASTFIELD - 65A | | 10/59: W/D | THORNTON JCN - 62A | KITTYBREWSTER - 61A | 10/59: W/D | KITTYBREWSTER - 61A |
| Jan-60 | EDINBURGH (SM) - 64A | | EASTFIELD - 65A | | | 12/59: W/D | KITTYBREWSTER - 61A | | KITTYBREWSTER - 61A |
| Apr-60 | 4/60: W/D | | EASTFIELD - 65A | | | | KITTYBREWSTER - 61A | | 3/60: W/D |
| Aug-60 | | | EASTFIELD - 65A | | | | KITTYBREWSTER - 61A | | |
| Nov-60 | | | EASTFIELD - 65A | | | | KITTYBREWSTER - 61A | | |

| | 62483 | 62484 | 62485 | 62487 | 62488 | 62489 | 62490 | 62492 | 62493 |
|---|---|---|---|---|---|---|---|---|---|
| Aug-50 | EDINBURGH (SM) - 64A | EDINBURGH (SM) - 64A | DUNDEE - 62B | EDINBURGH (SM) - 64A | EDINBURGH (SM) - 64A | EASTFIELD - 65A | EDINBURGH (SM) - 64A | THORNTON JCN - 62A | EASTFIELD - 65A |
| Jan-51 | EDINBURGH (SM) - 64A | EDINBURGH (SM) - 64A | DUNDEE - 62B | EDINBURGH (SM) - 64A | EDINBURGH (SM) - 64A | EASTFIELD - 65A | EDINBURGH (SM) - 64A | THORNTON JCN - 62A | EASTFIELD - 65A |
| Aug-51 | EDINBURGH (SM) - 64A | EDINBURGH (SM) - 64A | DUNDEE - 62B | EDINBURGH (SM) - 64A | EDINBURGH (SM) - 64A | EASTFIELD - 65A | EDINBURGH (SM) - 64A | THORNTON JCN - 62A | EASTFIELD - 65A |
| Jan-52 | EDINBURGH (SM) - 64A | EDINBURGH (SM) - 64A | DUNDEE - 62B | EDINBURGH (SM) - 64A | EDINBURGH (SM) - 64A | EASTFIELD - 65A | EDINBURGH (SM) - 64A | THORNTON JCN - 62A | EASTFIELD - 65A |
| Aug-52 | EDINBURGH (SM) - 64A | EDINBURGH (SM) - 64A | DUNDEE - 62B | EDINBURGH (SM) - 64A | EDINBURGH (SM) - 64A | EASTFIELD - 65A | EDINBURGH (SM) - 64A | THORNTON JCN - 62A | EASTFIELD - 65A |
| Jan-53 | EDINBURGH (SM) - 64A | EDINBURGH (SM) - 64A | DUNDEE - 62B | EDINBURGH (SM) - 64A | EDINBURGH (SM) - 64A | 2/53: KITTY - 61A | EDINBURGH (SM) - 64A | THORNTON JCN - 62A | 1/53: KITTY - 61A |
| Aug-53 | EDINBURGH (SM) - 64A | 8/53: PERTH - 63A | DUNDEE - 62B | EDINBURGH (SM) - 64A | EDINBURGH (SM) - 64A | KITTYBREWSTER - 61A | EDINBURGH (SM) - 64A | THORNTON JCN - 62A | KITTYBREWSTER - 61A |
| Jan-54 | EDINBURGH (SM) - 64A | PERTH - 63A | DUNDEE - 62B | EDINBURGH (SM) - 64A | EDINBURGH (SM) - 64A | KITTYBREWSTER - 61A | EDINBURGH (SM) - 64A | THORNTON JCN - 62A | KITTYBREWSTER - 61A |
| Aug-54 | EDINBURGH (SM) - 64A | PERTH - 63A | DUNDEE - 62B | EDINBURGH (SM) - 64A | EDINBURGH (SM) - 64A | KITTYBREWSTER - 61A | EDINBURGH (SM) - 64A | THORNTON JCN - 62A | KITTYBREWSTER - 61A |
| Jan-55 | EDINBURGH (SM) - 64A | PERTH - 63A | DUNDEE - 62B | EDINBURGH (SM) - 64A | EDINBURGH (SM) - 64A | KITTYBREWSTER - 61A | EDINBURGH (SM) - 64A | THORNTON JCN - 62A | KITTYBREWSTER - 61A |
| Aug-55 | EDINBURGH (SM) - 64A | PERTH - 63A | DUNDEE - 62B | EDINBURGH (SM) - 64A | EDINBURGH (SM) - 64A | KITTYBREWSTER - 61A | EDINBURGH (SM) - 64A | THORNTON JCN - 62A | KITTYBREWSTER - 61A |
| Jan-56 | EDINBURGH (SM) - 64A | PERTH - 63A | DUNDEE - 62B | EDINBURGH (SM) - 64A | EDINBURGH (SM) - 64A | KITTYBREWSTER - 61A | EDINBURGH (SM) - 64A | THORNTON JCN - 62A | KITTYBREWSTER - 61A |
| Aug-56 | EDINBURGH (SM) - 64A | PERTH - 63A | DUNDEE - 62B | EDINBURGH (SM) - 64A | EDINBURGH (SM) - 64A | KITTYBREWSTER - 61A | EDINBURGH (SM) - 64A | THORNTON JCN - 62A | KITTYBREWSTER - 61A |
| Jan-57 | EDINBURGH (SM) - 64A | PERTH - 63A | DUNDEE - 62B | EDINBURGH (SM) - 64A | EDINBURGH (SM) - 64A | KITTYBREWSTER - 61A | EDINBURGH (SM) - 64A | THORNTON JCN - 62A | KITTYBREWSTER - 61A |
| Aug-57 | EDINBURGH (SM) - 64A | PERTH - 63A | DUNDEE - 62B | EDINBURGH (SM) - 64A | EDINBURGH (SM) - 64A | KITTYBREWSTER - 61A | EDINBURGH (SM) - 64A | THORNTON JCN - 62A | KITTYBREWSTER - 61A |
| Jan-58 | 2/58: HWCK - 64G | PERTH - 63A | DUNDEE - 62B | EDINBURGH (SM) - 64A | EDINBURGH (SM) - 64A | KITTYBREWSTER - 61A | EDINBURGH (SM) - 64A | THORNTON JCN - 62A | KITTYBREWSTER - 61A |
| Aug-58 | HAWICK - 64G | PERTH - 63A | DUNDEE - 62B | EDINBURGH (SM) - 64A | EDINBURGH (SM) - 64A | KITTYBREWSTER - 61A | EDINBURGH (SM) - 64A | THORNTON JCN - 62A | KITTYBREWSTER - 61A |
| Jan-59 | HAWICK - 64G | PERTH - 63A | DUNDEE - 62B | EDINBURGH (SM) - 64A | EDINBURGH (SM) - 64A | KITTYBREWSTER - 61A | EDINBURGH (SM) - 64A | THORNTON JCN - 62A | KITTYBREWSTER - 61A |
| Aug-59 | 4/59: W/D | PERTH - 63A | 8/59: DUNF - 62C | EDINBURGH (SM) - 64A | EDINBURGH (SM) - 64A | KITTYBREWSTER - 61A | 2/59: W/D | 6/59: W/D | KITTYBREWSTER - 61A |
| Nov-59 | | PERTH - 63A | DUNFERMLINE - 62C | 9/59: W/D | 11/59: HWCK - 64G | KITTYBREWSTER - 61A | | | KITTYBREWSTER - 61A |
| Jan-60 | | PERTH - 63A | DUNFERMLINE - 62C | | HAWICK - 64G | 12/59: W/D | | | KITTYBREWSTER - 61A |
| Apr-60 | | PERTH - 63A | 4/60: W/D | | HAWICK - 64G | | | | KITTYBREWSTER - 61A |
| Aug-60 | | PERTH - 63A | | | HAWICK - 64G | | | | 8/60: W/D |
| Nov-60 | | PERTH - 63A | | | HAWICK - 64G | | | | |

| | 62494 | 62495 | 62496 | 62497 | 62498 | D15 4-4-0 (1904)<br>62501 | 62502 | 62503 | 62505 |
|---|---|---|---|---|---|---|---|---|---|
| Aug-50 | EDINBURGH (SM) - 64A | BATHGATE - 64F | EASTFIELD - 65A | EASTFIELD - 65A | EASTFIELD - 65A | KINGS LYNN - 31C | KINGS LYNN - 31C | BURY ST EDMUNDS - 31E | KINGS LYNN - 31C |
| Jan-51 | EDINBURGH (SM) - 64A | BATHGATE - 64F | EASTFIELD - 65A | EASTFIELD - 65A | EASTFIELD - 65A | KINGS LYNN - 31C | KINGS LYNN - 31C | BURY ST EDMUNDS - 31E | KINGS LYNN - 31C |
| Aug-51 | EDINBURGH (SM) - 64A | BATHGATE - 64F | EASTFIELD - 65A | EASTFIELD - 65A | EASTFIELD - 65A | 6/51:W/D | KINGS LYNN - 31C | 2/51: W/D | KINGS LYNN - 31C |
| Jan-52 | EDINBURGH (SM) - 64A | BATHGATE - 64F | EASTFIELD - 65A | EASTFIELD - 65A | EASTFIELD - 65A | | KINGS LYNN - 31C | | 11/51: W/D |
| Aug-52 | EDINBURGH (SM) - 64A | BATHGATE - 64F | EASTFIELD - 65A | EASTFIELD - 65A | EASTFIELD - 65A | | 2/52: W/D | | |
| Jan-53 | EDINBURGH (SM) - 64A | BATHGATE - 64F | EASTFIELD - 65A | EASTFIELD - 65A | EASTFIELD - 65A | | | | |
| Aug-53 | EDINBURGH (SM) - 64A | BATHGATE - 64F | EASTFIELD - 65A | 6/53: KITTY - 61A | EASTFIELD - 65A | | | | |
| Jan-54 | EDINBURGH (SM) - 64A | BATHGATE - 64F | EASTFIELD - 65A | KITTYBREWSTER - 61A | EASTFIELD - 65A | | | | |
| Aug-54 | EDINBURGH (SM) - 64A | BATHGATE - 64F | EASTFIELD - 65A | KITTYBREWSTER - 61A | 5/54: KITTY - 61C | | | | |
| Jan-55 | EDINBURGH (SM) - 64A | BATHGATE - 64F | EASTFIELD - 65A | KITTYBREWSTER - 61A | KITTYBREWSTER - 61A | | | | |
| Aug-55 | EDINBURGH (SM) - 64A | BATHGATE - 64F | EASTFIELD - 65A | KITTYBREWSTER - 61A | KITTYBREWSTER - 61A | | | | |
| Jan-56 | EDINBURGH (SM) - 64A | BATHGATE - 64F | EASTFIELD - 65A | KITTYBREWSTER - 61A | KITTYBREWSTER - 61A | | | | |
| Aug-56 | EDINBURGH (SM) - 64A | BATHGATE - 64F | EASTFIELD - 65A | KITTYBREWSTER - 61A | KITTYBREWSTER - 61A | | | | |
| Jan-57 | EDINBURGH (SM) - 64A | BATHGATE - 64F | EASTFIELD - 65A | KITTYBREWSTER - 61A | KITTYBREWSTER - 61A | | | | |
| Aug-57 | EDINBURGH (SM) - 64A | BATHGATE - 64F | EASTFIELD - 65A | KITTYBREWSTER - 61A | KITTYBREWSTER - 61A | | | | |
| Jan-58 | 2/58: HWCK - 64G | BATHGATE - 64F | EASTFIELD - 65A | KITTYBREWSTER - 61A | KITTYBREWSTER - 61A | | | | |
| Aug-58 | HAWICK - 64G | BATHGATE - 64F | EASTFIELD - 65A | KITTYBREWSTER - 61A | KITTYBREWSTER - 61A | | | | |
| Jan-59 | HAWICK - 64G | BATHGATE - 64F | EASTFIELD - 65A | KITTYBREWSTER - 61A | KITTYBREWSTER - 61A | | | | |
| Aug-59 | 4/59: W/D | BATHGATE - 64F | EASTFIELD - 65A | KITTYBREWSTER - 61A | KITTYBREWSTER - 61A | | | | |
| Nov-59 | | BATHGATE - 64F | EASTFIELD - 65A | KITTYBREWSTER - 61A | KITTYBREWSTER - 61A | | | | |
| Jan-60 | | BATHGATE - 64F | EASTFIELD - 65A | KITTYBREWSTER - 61A | KITTYBREWSTER - 61A | | | | |
| Apr-60 | | BATHGATE - 64F | EASTFIELD - 65A | 3/60: W/D | 4/60: W/D | | | | |
| Aug-60 | | BATHGATE - 64F | EASTFIELD - 65A | | | | | | |
| Nov-60 | | BATHGATE - 64F | EASTFIELD - 65A | | | | | | |

Locomotive allocation history (D16 class, LNER/BR).

## Block 1

*62510 and 62511 are under the heading: D16 4-4-0 (1923)*

| | 62506 | 62507 | 62508 | 62509 | 62520 | 62528 | 62538 | 62510 | 62511 |
|---|---|---|---|---|---|---|---|---|---|
| Aug-50 | KINGS LYNN-31C | KINGS LYNN-31C | BURY St.E.-31E | MELTON C-32G | MELTON C-32G | MELTON C-32G | MELTON C-32G | NORWICH-32A | YARMOUTH(ST)-32D |
| Jan-51 | KINGS LYNN-31C | 11/50: S.LYNN - 31D | 10/50: W/D | MELTON C-32G | MELTON C-32G | MELTON C-32G | MELTON C-32G | NORWICH-32A | YARMOUTH(ST)-32D |
| Aug-51 | KINGS LYNN-31C | 7/51: K.LYNN - 31C | | MELTON C-32G | MELTON C-32G | 6/51: W/D | MELTON C-32G | NORWICH-32A | YARMOUTH(ST)-32D |
| Jan-52 | KINGS LYNN-31C | KINGS LYNN-31C | | 3/52: NOR - 32A | 9/51: W/D | | 3/52: NOR - 32A | NORWICH-32A | YARMOUTH(ST)-32D |
| Aug-52 | 4/52: W/D | 4/52: W/D | | NORWICH-32A | | | 4/52: W/D | NORWICH-32A | YARMOUTH(ST)-32D |
| Jan-53 | | | | 9/52: W/D | | | | NORWICH-32A | YARMOUTH(ST)-32D |
| Aug-53 | | | | | | | | NORWICH-32A | YARMOUTH(ST)-32D |
| Jan-54 | | | | | | | | NORWICH-32A | YARMOUTH(ST)-32D |
| Aug-54 | | | | | | | | NORWICH-32A | YARMOUTH(ST)-32D |
| Jan-55 | | | | | | | | NORWICH-32A | YARMOUTH(ST)-32D |
| Aug-55 | | | | | | | | NORWICH-32A | YARMOUTH(ST)-32D |
| Jan-56 | | | | | | | | NORWICH-32A | YARMOUTH(ST)-32D |
| Aug-56 | | | | | | | | 6/56: CAMB - 31A | YARMOUTH(ST)-32D |
| Jan-57 | | | | | | | | 2/57: K.LYNN - 31C | YARMOUTH(ST)-32D |
| Aug-57 | | | | | | | | KINGS LYNN-31C | 6/57: NOR - 32A |
| Jan-58 | | | | | | | | 10/57: W/D | NORWICH-32A |
| Aug-58 | | | | | | | | | NORWICH-32A |
| Jan-59 | | | | | | | | | NORWICH-32A |
| Aug-59 | | | | | | | | | NORWICH-32A |
| Nov-59 | | | | | | | | | 12/59: W/D |
| Jan-60 | | | | | | | | | |
| Apr-60 | | | | | | | | | |
| Aug-60 | | | | | | | | | |
| Nov-60 | | | | | | | | | |

## Block 2

| | 62513 | 62514 | 62515 | 62516 | 62517 | 62518 | 62519 | 62521 | 62522 |
|---|---|---|---|---|---|---|---|---|---|
| Aug-50 | KINGS LYNN-31C | KINGS LYNN-31C | MELTON C-32G | CAMBRIDGE-31A | YARMOUTH(ST)-32D | KINGS LYNN-31C | MELTON C-32G | YARMOUTH(ST)-32D | NORWICH-32A |
| Jan-51 | KINGS LYNN-31C | KINGS LYNN-31C | MELTON C-32G | CAMBRIDGE-31A | YARMOUTH(ST)-32D | KINGS LYNN-31C | MELTON C-32G | YARMOUTH(ST)-32D | NORWICH-32A |
| Aug-51 | BURY St.E.-31E | KINGS LYNN-31C | MELTON C-32G | CAMBRIDGE-31A | YARMOUTH(ST)-32D | KINGS LYNN-31C | MELTON C-32G | YARMOUTH(ST)-32D | NORWICH-32A |
| Jan-52 | BURY St.E.-31E | KINGS LYNN-31C | MELTON C-32G | 11/51: K.LYNN - 31C | YARMOUTH(ST)-32D | 11/51: CAMB - 31A | MELTON C-32G | YARMOUTH(ST)-32D | NORWICH-32A |
| Aug-52 | BURY St.E.-31E | KINGS LYNN-31C | MELTON C-32G | KINGS LYNN-31C | YARMOUTH(ST)-32D | 3/52: K.LYNN - 31C | MELTON C-32G | YARMOUTH(ST)-32D | NORWICH-32A |
| Jan-53 | BURY St.E.-31E | KINGS LYNN-31C | MELTON C-32G | KINGS LYNN-31C | YARMOUTH(ST)-32D | KINGS LYNN-31C | MELTON C-32G | 5/53: CAMB - 31A | NORWICH-32A |
| Aug-53 | BURY St.E.-31E | KINGS LYNN-31C | MELTON C-32G | KINGS LYNN-31C | YARMOUTH(ST)-32D | KINGS LYNN-31C | MELTON C-32G | CAMBRIDGE-31A | NORWICH-32A |
| Jan-54 | BURY St.E.-31E | KINGS LYNN-31C | MELTON C-32G | KINGS LYNN-31C | 2/54: LOW - 32C | KINGS LYNN-31C | MELTON C-32G | CAMBRIDGE-31A | NORWICH-32A |
| Aug-54 | BURY St.E.-31E | KINGS LYNN-31C | MELTON C-32G | KINGS LYNN-31C | 4/54: YAR(ST) - 32D | KINGS LYNN-31C | MELTON C-32G | CAMBRIDGE-31A | NORWICH-32A |
| Jan-55 | BURY St.E.-31E | KINGS LYNN-31C | MELTON C-32G | KINGS LYNN-31C | YARMOUTH(ST)-32D | KINGS LYNN-31C | MELTON C-32G | CAMBRIDGE-31A | NORWICH-32A |
| Aug-55 | BURY St.E.-31E | KINGS LYNN-31C | MELTON C-32G | KINGS LYNN-31C | YARMOUTH(ST)-32D | KINGS LYNN-31C | MELTON C-32G | CAMBRIDGE-31A | NORWICH-32A |
| Jan-56 | BURY St.E.-31E | KINGS LYNN-31C | MELTON C-32G | KINGS LYNN-31C | YARMOUTH(ST)-32D | KINGS LYNN-31C | MELTON C-32G | CAMBRIDGE-31A | 1/56: K.LYNN - 31C |
| Aug-56 | BURY St.E.-31E | KINGS LYNN-31C | MELTON C-32G | KINGS LYNN-31C | 8/56: YAR(B) - 32F | KINGS LYNN-31C | MELTON C-32G | CAMBRIDGE-31A | KINGS LYNN-31C |
| Jan-57 | 5/57: CAMB - 31A | KINGS LYNN-31C | MELTON C-32G | KINGS LYNN-31C | YARMOUTH(B)-32F | KINGS LYNN-31C | 1/57: W/D | 2/57: K.LYNN - 31C | KINGS LYNN-31C |
| Aug-57 | 6/57: MARCH - 31B | 3/57: W/D | MELTON C-32G | 8/57: W/D | YARMOUTH(B)-32F | KINGS LYNN-31C | | 4/57: CAMB - 31A | KINGS LYNN-31C |
| Jan-58 | MARCH-31B | | MELTON C-32G | | YARMOUTH(B)-32F | KINGS LYNN-31C | | 6/57: K.LYNN - 31C | KINGS LYNN-31C |
| Aug-58 | 8/58: CAMB - 31A | | 4/58: W/D | | YARMOUTH(B)-32F | KINGS LYNN-31C | | KINGS LYNN-31C | 6/58: CAMB - 31A |
| Jan-59 | 11/58: W/D | | | | 1/59: NOR - 32A | 10/58: W/D | | 2/58: W/D | 8/58: W/D |
| Aug-59 | | | | | 6/59: MARCH - 31B | | | | |
| Nov-59 | | | | | 9/59: W/D | | | | |
| Jan-60 | | | | | | | | | |
| Apr-60 | | | | | | | | | |
| Aug-60 | | | | | | | | | |
| Nov-60 | | | | | | | | | |

## Block 3

| | 62523 | 62524 | 62525 | 62526 | 62527 | 62529 | 62530 | 62531 | 62532 |
|---|---|---|---|---|---|---|---|---|---|
| Aug-50 | MELTON C-32G | YARMOUTH(ST)-32D | CAMBRIDGE-31A | IPSWICH-32B | CAMBRIDGE-31A | MARCH-31B | CAMBRIDGE-31A | CAMBRIDGE-31A | TRAFFORD PARK - 9E |
| Jan-51 | MELTON C-32G | YARMOUTH(ST)-32D | CAMBRIDGE-31A | IPSWICH-32B | CAMBRIDGE-31A | MARCH-31B | CAMBRIDGE-31A | CAMBRIDGE-31A | TRAFFORD PARK - 9E |
| Aug-51 | MELTON C-32G | YARMOUTH(ST)-32D | CAMBRIDGE-31A | IPSWICH-32B | CAMBRIDGE-31A | MARCH-31B | CAMBRIDGE-31A | CAMBRIDGE-31A | TRAFFORD PARK - 9E |
| Jan-52 | MELTON C-32G | YARMOUTH(ST)-32D | CAMBRIDGE-31A | IPSWICH-32B | CAMBRIDGE-31A | MARCH-31B | CAMBRIDGE-31A | CAMBRIDGE-31A | TRAFFORD PARK - 9E |
| Aug-52 | 3/52: NOR - 32A | YARMOUTH(ST)-32D | 5/52: K.LYNN - 31C | IPSWICH-32B | 7/52: W/D | MARCH-31B | CAMBRIDGE-31A | CAMBRIDGE-31A | 6/52: CAMB - 31A |
| Jan-53 | NORWICH-32A | YARMOUTH(ST)-32D | 10/52: CAMB - 31A | IPSWICH-32B | | MARCH-31B | CAMBRIDGE-31A | CAMBRIDGE-31A | 10/52: S.BGE - 35C |
| Aug-53 | NORWICH-32A | YARMOUTH(ST)-32D | CAMBRIDGE-31A | 7/53: MARCH - 31B | | MARCH-31B | CAMBRIDGE-31A | CAMBRIDGE-31A | SPITAL BRIDGE - 35C |
| Jan-54 | NORWICH-32A | YARMOUTH(ST)-32D | CAMBRIDGE-31A | MARCH-31B | | MARCH-31B | CAMBRIDGE-31A | CAMBRIDGE-31A | 10/53: CAMB - 31A |
| Aug-54 | NORWICH-32A | YARMOUTH(ST)-32D | CAMBRIDGE-31A | MARCH-31B | | MARCH-31B | CAMBRIDGE-31A | CAMBRIDGE-31A | CAMBRIDGE-31A |
| Jan-55 | NORWICH-32A | YARMOUTH(ST)-32D | CAMBRIDGE-31A | MARCH-31B | | MARCH-31B | CAMBRIDGE-31A | 3/55: W/D | CAMBRIDGE-31A |
| Aug-55 | NORWICH-32A | YARMOUTH(ST)-32D | 9/55: W/D | MARCH-31B | | MARCH-31B | CAMBRIDGE-31A | | CAMBRIDGE-31A |
| Jan-56 | NORWICH-32A | YARMOUTH(ST)-32D | | MARCH-31B | | MARCH-31B | CAMBRIDGE-31A | | CAMBRIDGE-31A |
| Aug-56 | NORWICH-32A | YARMOUTH(ST)-32D | | MARCH-31B | | MARCH-31B | CAMBRIDGE-31A | | 11/56: W/D |
| Jan-57 | NORWICH-32A | YARMOUTH(ST)-32D | | MARCH-31B | | MARCH-31B | CAMBRIDGE-31A | | |
| Aug-57 | NORWICH-32A | YARMOUTH(ST)-32D | | 5/57: W/D | | MARCH-31B | CAMBRIDGE-31A | | |
| Jan-58 | NORWICH-32A | 8/58: YAR(B) - 32F | | | | MARCH-31B | 11/57: MARCH - 31B | | |
| Aug-58 | 8/58: W/D | 1/59: NOR - 32A | | | | MARCH-31B | MARCH-31B | | |
| Jan-59 | | NORWICH-32A | | | | MARCH-31B | 9/58: W/D | | |
| Aug-59 | | NORWICH-32A | | | | MARCH-31B | | | |
| Nov-59 | | NORWICH-32A | | | | 11/59: W/D | | | |
| Jan-60 | | NORWICH-32A | | | | | | | |
| Apr-60 | | 3/60: W/D | | | | | | | |
| Aug-60 | | | | | | | | | |
| Nov-60 | | | | | | | | | |

## Block 4

| | 62533 | 62534 | 62535 | 62536 | 62539 | 62540 | 62541 | 62542 | 62543 |
|---|---|---|---|---|---|---|---|---|---|
| Aug-50 | MELTON C-32G | SOUTH LYNN-31D | TRAFFORD PARK - 9E | TRAFFORD PARK - 9E | MARCH-31B | NORWICH-32A | MARCH-31B | MARCH-31B | SOUTH LYNN-31D |
| Jan-51 | MELTON C-32G | SOUTH LYNN-31D | TRAFFORD PARK - 9E | TRAFFORD PARK - 9E | MARCH-31B | NORWICH-32A | MARCH-31B | MARCH-31B | 11/50: CAMB - 31A |
| Aug-51 | MELTON C-32G | 4/51: K.LYNN - 31C | TRAFFORD PARK - 9E | TRAFFORD PARK - 9E | MARCH-31B | NORWICH-32A | MARCH-31B | MARCH-31B | CAMBRIDGE-31A |
| Jan-52 | MELTON C-32G | KINGS LYNN-31C | TRAFFORD PARK - 9E | TRAFFORD PARK - 9E | MARCH-31B | NORWICH-32A | 3/52: BURY - 31E | MARCH-31B | CAMBRIDGE-31A |
| Aug-52 | MELTON C-32G | KINGS LYNN-31C | 6/52: CAMB - 31A | 6/52: CAMB - 31A | MARCH-31B | NORWICH-32A | BURY St.E-31E | MARCH-31B | 9/52: BURY - 31E |
| Jan-53 | MELTON C-32G | KINGS LYNN-31C | 10/52: S.BGE - 35C | 10/52: S.BGE - 35C | MARCH-31B | NORWICH-32A | BURY St.E-31E | MARCH-31B | BURY St.E-31E |
| Aug-53 | MELTON C-32G | KINGS LYNN-31C | SPITAL BRIDGE - 35C | SPITAL BRIDGE - 35C | MARCH-31B | NORWICH-32A | BURY St.E-31E | MARCH-31B | BURY St.E-31E |
| Jan-54 | MELTON C-32G | KINGS LYNN-31C | SPITAL BRIDGE - 35C | SPITAL BRIDGE - 35C | MARCH-31B | NORWICH-32A | 3/54: CAMB - 31A | MARCH-31B | BURY St.E-31E |
| Aug-54 | MELTON C-32G | KINGS LYNN-31C | SPITAL BRIDGE - 35C | SPITAL BRIDGE - 35C | MARCH-31B | NORWICH-32A | CAMBRIDGE-31A | MARCH-31B | BURY St.E-31E |
| Jan-55 | MELTON C-32G | KINGS LYNN-31C | SPITAL BRIDGE - 35C | SPITAL BRIDGE - 35C | MARCH-31B | NORWICH-32A | CAMBRIDGE-31A | MARCH-31B | BURY St.E-31E |
| Aug-55 | MELTON C-32G | KINGS LYNN-31C | SPITAL BRIDGE - 35C | 7/55: W/D | MARCH-31B | NORWICH-32A | 10/55: W/D | MARCH-31B | BURY St.E-31E |
| Jan-56 | MELTON C-32G | KINGS LYNN-31C | SPITAL BRIDGE - 35C | | MARCH-31B | NORWICH-32A | | MARCH-31B | BURY St.E-31E |
| Aug-56 | MELTON C-32G | KINGS LYNN-31C | SPITAL BRIDGE - 35C | | 4/56: CAMB - 31A | NORWICH-32A | | MARCH-31B | BURY St.E-31E |
| Jan-57 | MELTON C-32G | 4/57: CAMB - 31A | SPITAL BRIDGE - 35C | | CAMBRIDGE-31A | NORWICH-32A | | 9/56: W/D | BURY St.E-31E |
| Aug-57 | MELTON C-32G | 8/57: K.LYNN - 31C | 4/57: LINC - 40A | | CAMBRIDGE-31A | NORWICH-32A | | | BURY St.E-31E |
| Jan-58 | 9/57: W/D | KINGS LYNN-31C | 11/57: W/D | | 10/57: W/D | NORWICH-32A | | | 11/57: MARCH - 31B |
| Aug-58 | | 10/58: CAMB - 31A | | | | NORWICH-32A | | | MARCH-31B |
| Jan-59 | | 11/58: W/D | | | | NORWICH-32A | | | 10/58: W/D |
| Aug-59 | | | | | | 8/59: W/D | | | |
| Nov-59 | | | | | | | | | |
| Jan-60 | | | | | | | | | |
| Apr-60 | | | | | | | | | |
| Aug-60 | | | | | | | | | |
| Nov-60 | | | | | | | | | |

| | 62544 | 62545 | 62546 | 62547 | 62548 | 62549 | 62551 | 62552 | 62553 |
|---|---|---|---|---|---|---|---|---|---|
| Aug-50 | YARMOUTH(ST)-32D | NORWCH-32A | YARMOUTH(ST)-32D | MARCH-31B | MARCH-31B | CAMBRIDGE-31A | CAMBRIDGE-31A | NORWCH-32A | NORWCH-32A |
| Jan-51 | YARMOUTH(ST)-32D | NORWCH-32A | YARMOUTH(ST)-32D | 2/51: W/D | MARCH-31B | CAMBRIDGE-31A | CAMBRIDGE-31A | NORWCH-32A | NORWCH-32A |
| Aug-51 | YARMOUTH(ST)-32D | NORWCH-32A | YARMOUTH(ST)-32D | | MARCH-31B | CAMBRIDGE-31A | CAMBRIDGE-31A | NORWCH-32A | NORWCH-32A |
| Jan-52 | YARMOUTH(ST)-32D | NORWCH-32A | YARMOUTH(ST)-32D | | MARCH-31B | CAMBRIDGE-31A | 5/52: K.LYNN-31C | 3/52: IPS-32B | NORWCH-32A |
| Aug-52 | YARMOUTH(ST)-32D | 7/52: LOW-32C | YARMOUTH(ST)-32D | | MARCH-31B | CAMBRIDGE-31A | 6/52: CAMB-31A | IPSWICH-32B | NORWCH-32A |
| Jan-53 | YARMOUTH(ST)-32D | 9/52: NOR-32A | YARMOUTH(ST)-32D | | MARCH-31B | CAMBRIDGE-31A | 9/52: K.LYNN-31C | IPSWICH-32B | NORWCH-32A |
| Aug-53 | YARMOUTH(ST)-32D | 7/53: BURY-31E | YARMOUTH(ST)-32D | | MARCH-31B | CAMBRIDGE-31A | 10/52: CAMB-31A | 7/53: NOR-32A | NORWCH-32A |
| Jan-54 | YARMOUTH(ST)-32D | 3/54: CAMB-31A | YARMOUTH(ST)-32D | | MARCH-31B | CAMBRIDGE-31A | 1/54: S.BGE-35C | NORWCH-32A | NORWCH-32A |
| Aug-54 | YARMOUTH(ST)-32D | CAMBRIDGE-31A | YARMOUTH(ST)-32D | | MARCH-31B | CAMBRIDGE-31A | SPITAL BRIDGE-35C | 6/54: IPS-32B | NORWCH-32A |
| Jan-55 | YARMOUTH(ST)-32D | 3/55: K.LYNN-31C | YARMOUTH(ST)-32D | | MARCH-31B | CAMBRIDGE-31A | SPITAL BRIDGE-35C | IPSWICH-32B | NORWCH-32A |
| Aug-55 | YARMOUTH(ST)-32D | KINGS LYNN-31C | YARMOUTH(ST)-32D | | MARCH-31B | CAMBRIDGE-31A | SPITAL BRIDGE-35C | IPSWICH-32B | 11/55: CAMB-31A |
| Jan-56 | YARMOUTH(ST)-32D | KINGS LYNN-31C | YARMOUTH(ST)-32D | | MARCH-31B | 12/55: W/D | SPITAL BRIDGE-35C | 10/55: W/D | CAMBRIDGE-31A |
| Aug-56 | YARMOUTH(ST)-32D | KINGS LYNN-31C | YARMOUTH(ST)-32D | | MARCH-31B | | 7/56: W/D | | |
| Jan-57 | YARMOUTH(ST)-32D | KINGS LYNN-31C | YARMOUTH(ST)-32D | | MARCH-31B | | | | 1/57: W/D |
| Aug-57 | 6/57: NOR-32A | 4/57: CAMB-31A | 6/57: W/D | | MARCH-31B | | | | |
| Jan-58 | NORWCH-32A | 10/57: K.LYNN-31C | | | 10/57: W/D | | | | |
| Aug-58 | NORWCH-32A | KINGS LYNN-31C | | | | | | | |
| Jan-59 | NORWCH-32A | 9/58: W/D | | | | | | | |
| Aug-59 | NORWCH-32A | | | | | | | | |
| Nov-59 | 11/59: W/D | | | | | | | | |
| Jan-60 | | | | | | | | | |
| Apr-60 | | | | | | | | | |
| Aug-60 | | | | | | | | | |
| Nov-60 | | | | | | | | | |

| | 62554 | 62555 | 62556 | 62557 | 62558 | 62559 | 62561 | 62562 | 62564 |
|---|---|---|---|---|---|---|---|---|---|
| Aug-50 | NORWCH-32A | NORWCH-32A | NORWCH-32A | CAMBRIDGE-31A | SOUTH LYNN-31D | KINGS LYNN-31C | YARMOUTH(B)-32F | MELTON C.-32G | YARMOUTH(B)-32F |
| Jan-51 | NORWCH-32A | NORWCH-32A | 11/50: LOW-32C | CAMBRIDGE-31A | 4/51: CAMB-31A | KINGS LYNN-31C | YARMOUTH(B)-32F | MELTON C.-32G | YARMOUTH(B)-32F |
| Aug-51 | NORWCH-32A | NORWCH-32A | 4/51: NOR-32A | CAMBRIDGE-31A | 9/51: K.LYNN-31C | KINGS LYNN-31C | YARMOUTH(B)-32F | MELTON C.-32G | YARMOUTH(B)-32F |
| Jan-52 | NORWCH-32A | NORWCH-32A | NORWCH-32A | 3/52: K.LYNN-31C | 3/52: CAMB-31A | KINGS LYNN-31C | YARMOUTH(B)-32F | 5/52: NOR-32A | YARMOUTH(B)-32F |
| Aug-52 | NORWCH-32A | NORWCH-32A | NORWCH-32A | NORWCH-32A | 6/52: K.LYNN-31C | KINGS LYNN-31C | 9/52: NOR-32A | 7/52: CAMB-31A | 9/52: NOR-32A |
| Jan-53 | NORWCH-32A | NORWCH-32A | NORWCH-32A | 10/52: CAMB-31A | 10/52: CAMB-31A | KINGS LYNN-31C | NORWCH-32A | 8/52: K.LYNN-31C | NORWCH-32A |
| Aug-53 | NORWCH-32A | NORWCH-32A | NORWCH-32A | CAMBRIDGE-31A | CAMBRIDGE-31A | KINGS LYNN-31C | NORWCH-32A | 9/52: S.BGE-35C | NORWCH-32A |
| Jan-54 | NORWCH-32A | NORWCH-32A | NORWCH-32A | CAMBRIDGE-31A | CAMBRIDGE-31A | KINGS LYNN-31C | NORWCH-32A | 10/52: CAMB-31A | 5/54: MELTON-32G |
| Aug-54 | NORWCH-32A | NORWCH-32A | NORWCH-32A | CAMBRIDGE-31A | CAMBRIDGE-31A | KINGS LYNN-31C | NORWCH-32A | 3/54: MARCH-31B | 6/54: NOR-32A |
| Jan-55 | NORWCH-32A | NORWCH-32A | NORWCH-32A | CAMBRIDGE-31A | CAMBRIDGE-31A | KINGS LYNN-31C | NORWCH-32A | MARCH-31B | 4/55: NOR-32A |
| Aug-55 | NORWCH-32A | NORWCH-32A | NORWCH-32A | CAMBRIDGE-31A | CAMBRIDGE-31A | KINGS LYNN-31C | 9/55: MELTON-32G | MARCH-31B | 11/55: YAR(B)-32F |
| Jan-56 | 11/55: W/D | NORWCH-32A | NORWCH-32A | 10/55: W/D | 11/55: K.LYNN-31C | 12/55: W/D | MELTON C.-32G | MARCH-31B | 12/55: NOR-32A |
| Aug-56 | | NORWCH-32A | NORWCH-32A | | KINGS LYNN-31C | | MELTON C.-32G | MARCH-31B | |
| Jan-57 | | NORWCH-32A | 1/57: W/D | | KINGS LYNN-31C | | MELTON C.-32G | MARCH-31B | 2/57: CAMB-31A |
| Aug-57 | | NORWCH-32A | | | 5/57: W/D | | MELTON C.-32G | MARCH-31B | 4/57: LINC-40A |
| Jan-58 | | NORWCH-32A | | | | | MELTON C.-32G | 10/57: W/D | LINCOLN-40A |
| Aug-58 | | 3/58: W/D | | | | | 2/58: W/D | | 3/58: W/D |
| Jan-59 | | | | | | | | | |
| Aug-59 | | | | | | | | | |
| Nov-59 | | | | | | | | | |
| Jan-60 | | | | | | | | | |
| Apr-60 | | | | | | | | | |
| Aug-60 | | | | | | | | | |
| Nov-60 | | | | | | | | | |

| | 62565 | 62566 | 62567 | 62568 | 62569 | 62570 | 62571 | 62572 | 62573 |
|---|---|---|---|---|---|---|---|---|---|
| Aug-50 | STRATFORD-30A | BURY St.ED-31E | CAMBRIDGE-31A | TRAFFORD PARK-9E | KINGS LYNN-31C | NORWCH-32A | CAMBRIDGE-31A | COLCHESTER-30E | SOUTH LYNN-31D |
| Jan-51 | 5/51: CAMB-31A | BURY St.ED-31E | CAMBRIDGE-31A | TRAFFORD PARK-9E | KINGS LYNN-31C | NORWCH-32A | CAMBRIDGE-31A | 11/50: STRAT-30A | 11/50: BURY-31E |
| Aug-51 | 8/51: K.LYNN-31C | BURY St.ED-31E | CAMBRIDGE-31A | TRAFFORD PARK-9E | KINGS LYNN-31C | NORWCH-32A | CAMBRIDGE-31A | 5/51: CAMB-31A | BURY St.ED-31E |
| Jan-52 | KINGS LYNN-31C | BURY St.ED-31E | CAMBRIDGE-31A | 6/52: NOR-32A | KINGS LYNN-31C | NORWCH-32A | CAMBRIDGE-31A | 7/51: K.LYNN-31C | BURY St.ED-31E |
| Aug-52 | KINGS LYNN-31C | BURY St.ED-31E | CAMBRIDGE-31A | 7/52: CAMB-31A | KINGS LYNN-31C | NORWCH-32A | CAMBRIDGE-31A | 9/51: MARCH-31B | 5/52: K.LYNN-31C |
| Jan-53 | KINGS LYNN-31C | BURY St.ED-31E | CAMBRIDGE-31A | 9/52: S.LYNN-31D | KINGS LYNN-31C | NORWCH-32A | CAMBRIDGE-31A | MARCH-31B | KINGS LYNN-31C |
| Aug-53 | KINGS LYNN-31C | BURY St.ED-31E | CAMBRIDGE-31A | 10/52: S.BGE-35C | KINGS LYNN-31C | 7/53: CAMB-31A | CAMBRIDGE-31A | MARCH-31B | KINGS LYNN-31C |
| Jan-54 | KINGS LYNN-31C | BURY St.ED-31E | CAMBRIDGE-31A | SPITAL BRIDGE-35C | KINGS LYNN-31C | CAMBRIDGE-31A | CAMBRIDGE-31A | MARCH-31B | KINGS LYNN-31C |
| Aug-54 | KINGS LYNN-31C | BURY St.ED-31E | CAMBRIDGE-31A | SPITAL BRIDGE-35C | KINGS LYNN-31C | CAMBRIDGE-31A | CAMBRIDGE-31A | MARCH-31B | KINGS LYNN-31C |
| Jan-55 | KINGS LYNN-31C | BURY St.ED-31E | CAMBRIDGE-31A | SPITAL BRIDGE-35C | KINGS LYNN-31C | CAMBRIDGE-31A | CAMBRIDGE-31A | MARCH-31B | KINGS LYNN-31C |
| Aug-55 | KINGS LYNN-31C | BURY St.ED-31E | CAMBRIDGE-31A | SPITAL BRIDGE-35C | KINGS LYNN-31C | CAMBRIDGE-31A | CAMBRIDGE-31A | MARCH-31B | KINGS LYNN-31C |
| Jan-56 | KINGS LYNN-31C | BURY St.ED-31E | CAMBRIDGE-31A | SPITAL BRIDGE-35C | KINGS LYNN-31C | CAMBRIDGE-31A | CAMBRIDGE-31A | MARCH-31B | 10/55: W/D |
| Aug-56 | KINGS LYNN-31C | BURY St.ED-31E | CAMBRIDGE-31A | SPITAL BRIDGE-35C | KINGS LYNN-31C | CAMBRIDGE-31A | CAMBRIDGE-31A | MARCH-31B | |
| Jan-57 | 1/57: W/D | BURY St.ED-31E | 12/56: W/D | SPITAL BRIDGE-35C | 11/56: W/D | CAMBRIDGE-31A | CAMBRIDGE-31A | MARCH-31B | |
| Aug-57 | | 6/57: K.LYNN-31C | | 4/57: LINC-40A | | 7/57: YAR(ST)-32D | 4/57: LINC-40A | MARCH-31B | |
| Jan-58 | | KINGS LYNN-31C | | LINCOLN-40A | | YARMOUTH(ST)-32D | LINCOLN-40A | MARCH-31B | |
| Aug-58 | | KINGS LYNN-31C | | 4/58: W/D | | YARMOUTH(ST)-32D | LINCOLN-40A | 7/58: W/D | |
| Jan-59 | | 12/58: W/D | | | | YARMOUTH(ST)-32D | 1/59: W/D | | |
| Aug-59 | | | | | | 6/59: MARCH-31B | | | |
| Nov-59 | | | | | | 11/59: W/D | | | |
| Jan-60 | | | | | | | | | |
| Apr-60 | | | | | | | | | |
| Aug-60 | | | | | | | | | |
| Nov-60 | | | | | | | | | |

| | 62574 | 62575 | 62576 | 62577 | 62578 | 62579 | 62580 | 62581 | 62582 |
|---|---|---|---|---|---|---|---|---|---|
| Aug-50 | CAMBRIDGE-31A | KINGS LYNN-31C | YARMOUTH(ST)-32D | NORWCH-32A | MELTON C.-32G | MARCH-31B | YARMOUTH(ST)-32D | NORWCH-32A | KINGS LYNN-31C |
| Jan-51 | CAMBRIDGE-31A | KINGS LYNN-31C | YARMOUTH(ST)-32D | NORWCH-32A | MELTON C.-32G | 3/51: K.LYNN-31C | YARMOUTH(ST)-32D | NORWCH-32A | KINGS LYNN-31C |
| Aug-51 | CAMBRIDGE-31A | KINGS LYNN-31C | YARMOUTH(ST)-32D | NORWCH-32A | MELTON C.-32G | KINGS LYNN-31C | YARMOUTH(ST)-32D | NORWCH-32A | KINGS LYNN-31C |
| Jan-52 | CAMBRIDGE-31A | KINGS LYNN-31C | YARMOUTH(ST)-32D | NORWCH-32A | MELTON C.-32G | KINGS LYNN-31C | YARMOUTH(ST)-32D | NORWCH-32A | KINGS LYNN-31C |
| Aug-52 | CAMBRIDGE-31A | KINGS LYNN-31C | YARMOUTH(ST)-32D | NORWCH-32A | MELTON C.-32G | KINGS LYNN-31C | YARMOUTH(ST)-32D | NORWCH-32A | KINGS LYNN-31C |
| Jan-53 | CAMBRIDGE-31A | KINGS LYNN-31C | YARMOUTH(ST)-32D | NORWCH-32A | MELTON C.-32G | KINGS LYNN-31C | YARMOUTH(ST)-32D | NORWCH-32A | KINGS LYNN-31C |
| Aug-53 | CAMBRIDGE-31A | KINGS LYNN-31C | 7/53: CAMB-31A | NORWCH-32A | MELTON C.-32G | KINGS LYNN-31C | YARMOUTH(ST)-32D | 3/53: W/D | KINGS LYNN-31C |
| Jan-54 | CAMBRIDGE-31A | KINGS LYNN-31C | 3/54: BURY-31E | NORWCH-32A | MELTON C.-32G | KINGS LYNN-31C | YARMOUTH(ST)-32D | | KINGS LYNN-31C |
| Aug-54 | CAMBRIDGE-31A | KINGS LYNN-31C | BURY St.ED-31E | NORWCH-32A | MELTON C.-32G | KINGS LYNN-31C | YARMOUTH(ST)-32D | | KINGS LYNN-31C |
| Jan-55 | CAMBRIDGE-31A | KINGS LYNN-31C | BURY St.ED-31E | NORWCH-32A | MELTON C.-32G | KINGS LYNN-31C | YARMOUTH(ST)-32D | | KINGS LYNN-31C |
| Aug-55 | CAMBRIDGE-31A | KINGS LYNN-31C | BURY St.ED-31E | NORWCH-32A | MELTON C.-32G | 3/55: W/D | YARMOUTH(ST)-32D | | KINGS LYNN-31C |
| Jan-56 | 12/55: W/D | KINGS LYNN-31C | BURY St.ED-31E | NORWCH-32A | MELTON C.-32G | | YARMOUTH(ST)-32D | | KINGS LYNN-31C |
| Aug-56 | | KINGS LYNN-31C | BURY St.ED-31E | NORWCH-32A | MELTON C.-32G | | YARMOUTH(ST)-32D | | KINGS LYNN-31C |
| Jan-57 | | KINGS LYNN-31C | BURY St.ED-31E | 10/56: W/D | MELTON C.-32G | | 1/57: CAMB-31A | | KINGS LYNN-31C |
| Aug-57 | | 5/57: W/D | 5/57: CAMB-31A | | MELTON C.-32G | | 5/57: K.LYNN-31C | | KINGS LYNN-31C |
| Jan-58 | | | 9/57: W/D | | 10/57: W/D | | KINGS LYNN-31C | | KINGS LYNN-31C |
| Aug-58 | | | | | | | 6/58: W/D | | 10/58: CAMB-31A |
| Jan-59 | | | | | | | | | 1/59: W/D |
| Aug-59 | | | | | | | | | |
| Nov-59 | | | | | | | | | |
| Jan-60 | | | | | | | | | |
| Apr-60 | | | | | | | | | |
| Aug-60 | | | | | | | | | |
| Nov-60 | | | | | | | | | |

| | 62584 | 62585 | 62586 | 62587 | 62588 | 62589 | 62590 | 62592 | 62593 |
|---|---|---|---|---|---|---|---|---|---|
| Aug-50 | NORWICH-32A | NORWICH-32A | YARMOUTH(ST)-32D | TRAFFORD PARK-9E | TRAFFORD PARK-9E | MARCH-31B | IPSWICH-32B | YARMOUTH BEACH-32F | NORWICH-32A |
| Jan-51 | NORWICH-32A | NORWICH-32A | YARMOUTH(ST)-32D | TRAFFORD PARK-9E | TRAFFORD PARK-9E | MARCH-31B | IPSWICH-32B | YARMOUTH BEACH-32F | NORWICH-32A |
| Aug-51 | NORWICH-32A | NORWICH-32A | YARMOUTH(ST)-32D | TRAFFORD PARK-9E | TRAFFORD PARK-9E | MARCH-31B | IPSWICH-32B | YARMOUTH BEACH-32F | NORWICH-32A |
| Jan-52 | NORWICH-32A | 7/52: CAMB-31A | YARMOUTH(ST)-32D | TRAFFORD PARK-9E | 6/52: NOR-32A | MARCH-31B | 1/52: W/D | YARMOUTH BEACH-32F | NORWICH-32A |
| Aug-52 | NORWICH-32A | 9/52: BURY-31E | YARMOUTH(ST)-32D | 10/52: S.BGE-35C | 7/52: MARCH-31B | MARCH-31B | | 9/52: NOR-32A | NORWICH-32A |
| Jan-53 | NORWICH-32A | 10/52: CAMB-31A | YARMOUTH(ST)-32D | SPITAL BRIDGE-35C | 10/52: S.BGE-35C | MARCH-31B | | NORWICH-32A | NORWICH-32A |
| Aug-53 | NORWICH-32A | CAMBRIDGE-31A | YARMOUTH(ST)-32D | SPITAL BRIDGE-35C | MARCH-31B | MARCH-31B | | 7/53: MELTON-32G | NORWICH-32A |
| Jan-54 | NORWICH-32A | CAMBRIDGE-31A | YARMOUTH(ST)-32D | SPITAL BRIDGE-35C | 3/54: BURY-31E | MARCH-31B | | 10/53: NOR-32A | NORWICH-32A |
| Aug-54 | NORWICH-32A | CAMBRIDGE-31A | YARMOUTH(ST)-32D | SPITAL BRIDGE-35C | BURY ST EDMUNDS-31E | MARCH-31B | | NORWICH-32A | NORWICH-32A |
| Jan-55 | NORWICH-32A | CAMBRIDGE-31A | YARMOUTH(ST)-32D | SPITAL BRIDGE-35C | BURY ST EDMUNDS-31E | MARCH-31B | | 1/55: MELTON-32G | NORWICH-32A |
| Aug-55 | NORWICH-32A | 4/55: W/D | YARMOUTH(ST)-32D | SPITAL BRIDGE-35C | BURY ST EDMUNDS-31E | MARCH-31B | | 2/55: YAR(B)-32F | NORWICH-32A |
| Jan-56 | NORWICH-32A | | YARMOUTH(ST)-32D | SPITAL BRIDGE-35C | BURY ST EDMUNDS-31E | MARCH-31B | | 5/55: NOR-32A | NORWICH-32A |
| Aug-56 | 6/56: CAMB-31A | | YARMOUTH(ST)-32D | 12/56: W/D | BURY ST EDMUNDS-31E | MARCH-31B | | NORWICH-32A | NORWICH-32A |
| Jan-57 | 12/56: HIT-34D | | YARMOUTH(ST)-32D | | BURY ST EDMUNDS-31E | MARCH-31B | | 2/57: CAMB-31A | NORWICH-32A |
| Aug-57 | HITCHIN-34D | | 6/57: NOR-32A | | 5/57: CAMB-31A | MARCH-31B | | 4/57: K.LYNN-31C | NORWICH-32A |
| Jan-58 | 12/57: W/D | | NORWICH-32A | | 3/58: K.LYNN-31C | MARCH-31B | | KINGS LYNN-31C | 10/57: W/D |
| Aug-58 | | | 3/58: W/D | | 6/58: CAMB-31A | MARCH-31B | | 4/58: W/D | |
| Jan-59 | | | | | 10/58: W/D | MARCH-31B | | | |
| Aug-59 | | | | | | 5/59: W/D | | | |
| Nov-59 | | | | | | | | | |
| Jan-60 | | | | | | | | | |
| Apr-60 | | | | | | | | | |
| Aug-60 | | | | | | | | | |
| Nov-60 | | | | | | | | | |

| | 62596 | 62597 | 62598 | 62599 | 62601 | 62603 | 62604 | 62605 | 62606 |
|---|---|---|---|---|---|---|---|---|---|
| Aug-50 | YARMOUTH BEACH-32F | YARMOUTH(ST)-32D | COLCHESTER-30E | TRAFFORD PARK-9E | KINGS LYNN-31C | MARCH-31B | YARMOUTH(ST)-32D | MARCH-31B | NORWICH-32A |
| Jan-51 | YARMOUTH BEACH-32F | YARMOUTH(ST)-32D | COLCHESTER-30E | TRAFFORD PARK-9E | KINGS LYNN-31C | 12/50: CAMB-31A | YARMOUTH(ST)-32D | MARCH-31B | NORWICH-32A |
| Aug-51 | YARMOUTH BEACH-32F | YARMOUTH(ST)-32D | 5/51: NOR-32A | TRAFFORD PARK-9E | KINGS LYNN-31C | CAMBRIDGE-31A | YARMOUTH(ST)-32D | MARCH-31B | NORWICH-32A |
| Jan-52 | YARMOUTH BEACH-32F | YARMOUTH(ST)-32D | NORWICH-32A | TRAFFORD PARK-9E | KINGS LYNN-31C | 9/51: W/D | YARMOUTH(ST)-32D | MARCH-31B | NORWICH-32A |
| Aug-52 | 9/52: NOR-32A | YARMOUTH(ST)-32D | 5/52: W/D | 6/52: NOR-32A | KINGS LYNN-31C | | YARMOUTH(ST)-32D | MARCH-31B | NORWICH-32A |
| Jan-53 | NORWICH-32A | YARMOUTH(ST)-32D | | 10/52: S.BGE-35C | KINGS LYNN-31C | | YARMOUTH(ST)-32D | MARCH-31B | NORWICH-32A |
| Aug-53 | 12/53: MELTON-32G | YARMOUTH(ST)-32D | | SPITAL BRIDGE-35C | KINGS LYNN-31C | | YARMOUTH(ST)-32D | MARCH-31B | 7/53: K.LYNN-31C |
| Jan-54 | 1/54: NOR-32A | YARMOUTH(ST)-32D | | SPITAL BRIDGE-35C | KINGS LYNN-31C | | YARMOUTH(ST)-32D | MARCH-31B | KINGS LYNN-31C |
| Aug-54 | NORWICH-32A | YARMOUTH(ST)-32D | | SPITAL BRIDGE-35C | KINGS LYNN-31C | | YARMOUTH(ST)-32D | MARCH-31B | KINGS LYNN-31C |
| Jan-55 | NORWICH-32A | YARMOUTH(ST)-32D | | SPITAL BRIDGE-35C | KINGS LYNN-31C | | YARMOUTH(ST)-32D | MARCH-31B | KINGS LYNN-31C |
| Aug-55 | NORWICH-32A | YARMOUTH(ST)-32D | | SPITAL BRIDGE-35C | KINGS LYNN-31C | | YARMOUTH(ST)-32D | MARCH-31B | KINGS LYNN-31C |
| Jan-56 | NORWICH-32A | YARMOUTH(ST)-32D | | SPITAL BRIDGE-35C | KINGS LYNN-31C | | YARMOUTH(ST)-32D | 12/55: CAMB-31A | KINGS LYNN-31C |
| Aug-56 | NORWICH-32A | YARMOUTH(ST)-32D | | SPITAL BRIDGE-35C | KINGS LYNN-31C | | YARMOUTH(ST)-32D | CAMBRIDGE-31A | KINGS LYNN-31C |
| Jan-57 | NORWICH-32A | 10/56: YAR(B)-32F | | SPITAL BRIDGE-35C | 1/57: W/D | | YARMOUTH(ST)-32D | 10/56: MARCH-31B | KINGS LYNN-31C |
| Aug-57 | NORWICH-32A | 5/57: MELTON-32G | | 4/57: LINC-40A | | | YARMOUTH(ST)-32D | 6/57: W/D | KINGS LYNN-31C |
| Jan-58 | 10/57: W/D | MELTON CONSTABLE-32G | | LINCOLN-40A | | | YARMOUTH(ST)-32D | | KINGS LYNN-31C |
| Aug-58 | | MELTON CONSTABLE-32G | | LINCOLN-40A | | | YARMOUTH(ST)-32D | | KINGS LYNN-31C |
| Jan-59 | | 3/59: NOR-32A | | 9/58: W/D | | | YARMOUTH(ST)-32D | | KINGS LYNN-31C |
| Aug-59 | | SPITAL BRIDGE-31F | | | | | YARMOUTH(ST)-32D | | KINGS LYNN-31C |
| Nov-59 | | SPITAL BRIDGE-31F | | | | | 10/59: LOW-32C | | 9/59: W/D |
| Jan-60 | | 12/59: W/D | | | | | LOWESTOFT-32C | | |
| Apr-60 | | | | | | | 2/60: W/D | | |
| Aug-60 | | | | | | | | | |
| Nov-60 | | | | | | | | | |

| | 62607 | 62608 | 62609 | 62610 | 62611 | 62612 | 62613 | 62614 | 62615 |
|---|---|---|---|---|---|---|---|---|---|
| Aug-50 | BURY ST EDMUNDS-31E | COLCHESTER-30E | TRAFFORD PARK-9E | NORWICH-32A | YARMOUTH(ST)-32D | NORWICH-32A | YARMOUTH(ST)-32D | KINGS LYNN-31C | BURY ST EDMUNDS-31E |
| Jan-51 | BURY ST EDMUNDS-31E | 5/51: NOR-32A | TRAFFORD PARK-9E | NORWICH-32A | YARMOUTH(ST)-32D | NORWICH-32A | YARMOUTH(ST)-32D | KINGS LYNN-31C | BURY ST EDMUNDS-31E |
| Aug-51 | BURY ST EDMUNDS-31E | 6/51: MELTON-32G | TRAFFORD PARK-9E | 8/51: MELTON-32G | YARMOUTH(ST)-32D | NORWICH-32A | YARMOUTH(ST)-32D | KINGS LYNN-31C | 4/51: CAMB-31A |
| Jan-52 | BURY ST EDMUNDS-31E | 12/51: NOR-32A | 6/52: CAMB-31A | 11/51: NOR-32A | YARMOUTH(ST)-32D | NORWICH-32A | YARMOUTH(ST)-32D | KINGS LYNN-31C | CAMBRIDGE-31A |
| Aug-52 | BURY ST EDMUNDS-31E | NORWICH-32A | 7/52: S.LYNN-31D | NORWICH-32A | YARMOUTH(ST)-32D | NORWICH-32A | YARMOUTH(ST)-32D | KINGS LYNN-31C | 9/52: BURY-31E |
| Jan-53 | BURY ST EDMUNDS-31E | NORWICH-32A | 10/52: S.BGE-35C | NORWICH-32A | YARMOUTH(ST)-32D | NORWICH-32A | YARMOUTH(ST)-32D | KINGS LYNN-31C | BURY ST EDMUNDS-31E |
| Aug-53 | BURY ST EDMUNDS-31E | NORWICH-32A | 10/53: CAMB-31A | NORWICH-32A | YARMOUTH(ST)-32D | NORWICH-32A | YARMOUTH(ST)-32D | KINGS LYNN-31C | BURY ST EDMUNDS-31E |
| Jan-54 | BURY ST EDMUNDS-31E | NORWICH-32A | 12/53: S.BGE-35C | NORWICH-32A | YARMOUTH(ST)-32D | NORWICH-32A | YARMOUTH(ST)-32D | KINGS LYNN-31C | BURY ST EDMUNDS-31E |
| Aug-54 | BURY ST EDMUNDS-31E | NORWICH-32A | SPITAL BRIDGE-35C | NORWICH-32A | YARMOUTH(ST)-32D | NORWICH-32A | YARMOUTH(ST)-32D | KINGS LYNN-31C | BURY ST EDMUNDS-31E |
| Jan-55 | 11/54: CAMB-31A | NORWICH-32A | SPITAL BRIDGE-35C | NORWICH-32A | YARMOUTH(ST)-32D | NORWICH-32A | YARMOUTH(ST)-32D | KINGS LYNN-31C | BURY ST EDMUNDS-31E |
| Aug-55 | CAMBRIDGE-31A | NORWICH-32A | SPITAL BRIDGE-35C | NORWICH-32A | YARMOUTH(ST)-32D | NORWICH-32A | YARMOUTH(ST)-32D | KINGS LYNN-31C | BURY ST EDMUNDS-31E |
| Jan-56 | 11/55: W/D | 11/55: CAMB-31A | 11/55: CAMB-31A | 11/55: CAMB-31A | YARMOUTH(ST)-32D | NORWICH-32A | YARMOUTH(ST)-32D | KINGS LYNN-31C | BURY ST EDMUNDS-31E |
| Aug-56 | | CAMBRIDGE-31A | CAMBRIDGE-31A | CAMBRIDGE-31A | YARMOUTH(ST)-32D | NORWICH-32A | YARMOUTH(ST)-32D | KINGS LYNN-31C | BURY ST EDMUNDS-31E |
| Jan-57 | | 1/57: W/D | SPITAL BRIDGE-35C | CAMBRIDGE-31A | 1/57: W/D | NORWICH-32A | YARMOUTH(ST)-32D | KINGS LYNN-31C | 4/57: CAMB-31A |
| Aug-57 | | | 2/57: W/D | 10/57: K.LYNN-31C | | NORWICH-32A | YARMOUTH(ST)-32D | KINGS LYNN-31C | 6/57: MARCH-31B |
| Jan-58 | | | | KINGS LYNN-31C | | NORWICH-32A | YARMOUTH(ST)-32D | KINGS LYNN-31C | MARCH-31B |
| Aug-58 | | | | 1/59: W/D | | NORWICH-32A | YARMOUTH(ST)-32D | 8/58: W/D | 10/58: W/D |
| Jan-59 | | | | | | NORWICH-32A | YARMOUTH(ST)-32D | | |
| Aug-59 | | | | | | 4/59: S.BGE-35C | 4/59: S.BGE-35C | | |
| Nov-59 | | | | | | 11/59: W/D | SPITAL BRIDGE-31F | | |
| Jan-60 | | | | | | | 1/60: MARCH-31B | | |
| Apr-60 | | | | | | | MARCH-31B | | |
| Aug-60 | | | | | | | MARCH-31B | | |
| Nov-60 | | | | | | | 11/60: W/D | | |

D10 4-4-0 (1913)

| | 62616 | 62617 | 62618 | 62619 | 62620 | 62650 | 62651 | 62652 | 62653 |
|---|---|---|---|---|---|---|---|---|---|
| Aug-50 | NORWICH-32A | NORWICH-32A | CAMBRIDGE-31A | NORWICH-32A | MELTON CONSTABLE-32G | NORTHWICH-9G | TRAFFORD PARK-9E | NORTHWICH-9G | TRAFFORD PARK-9E |
| Jan-51 | NORWICH-32A | NORWICH-32A | CAMBRIDGE-31A | NORWICH-32A | MELTON CONSTABLE-32G | NORTHWICH-9G | 2/51: NORTH-9G | NORTHWICH-9G | TRAFFORD PARK-9E |
| Aug-51 | NORWICH-32A | 6/51: MELTON-32G | CAMBRIDGE-31A | NORWICH-32A | MELTON CONSTABLE-32G | NORTHWICH-9G | NORTHWICH-9G | NORTHWICH-9G | TRAFFORD PARK-9E |
| Jan-52 | 3/52: CAMB-31A | MELTON CONSTABLE-32G | CAMBRIDGE-31A | NORWICH-32A | MELTON CONSTABLE-32G | NORTHWICH-9G | NORTHWICH-9G | NORTHWICH-9G | TRAFFORD PARK-9E |
| Aug-52 | CAMBRIDGE-31A | MELTON CONSTABLE-32G | CAMBRIDGE-31A | NORWICH-32A | MELTON CONSTABLE-32G | NORTHWICH-9G | NORTHWICH-9G | NORTHWICH-9G | TRAFFORD PARK-9E |
| Jan-53 | CAMBRIDGE-31A | MELTON CONSTABLE-32G | CAMBRIDGE-31A | NORWICH-32A | MELTON CONSTABLE-32G | NORTHWICH-9G | NORTHWICH-9G | NORTHWICH-9G | TRAFFORD PARK-9E |
| Aug-53 | 2/53: W/D | MELTON CONSTABLE-32G | CAMBRIDGE-31A | NORWICH-32A | MELTON CONSTABLE-32G | NORTHWICH-9G | 2/53: W/D | NORTHWICH-9G | TRAFFORD PARK-9E |
| Jan-54 | | MELTON CONSTABLE-32G | CAMBRIDGE-31A | NORWICH-32A | MELTON CONSTABLE-32G | 2/54: W/D | | NORTHWICH-9G | 2/54: NORTH-9G |
| Aug-54 | | MELTON CONSTABLE-32G | CAMBRIDGE-31A | NORWICH-32A | MELTON CONSTABLE-32G | | | 5/54: W/D | NORTHWICH-9G |
| Jan-55 | | MELTON CONSTABLE-32G | CAMBRIDGE-31A | NORWICH-32A | MELTON CONSTABLE-32G | | | | NORTHWICH-9G |
| Aug-55 | | MELTON CONSTABLE-32G | CAMBRIDGE-31A | NORWICH-32A | MELTON CONSTABLE-32G | | | | 9/55: W/D |
| Jan-56 | | MELTON CONSTABLE-32G | CAMBRIDGE-31A | NORWICH-32A | 10/55: W/D | | | | |
| Aug-56 | | MELTON CONSTABLE-32G | CAMBRIDGE-31A | NORWICH-32A | | | | | |
| Jan-57 | | MELTON CONSTABLE-32G | CAMBRIDGE-31A | NORWICH-32A | | | | | |
| Aug-57 | | 5/57: W/D | CAMBRIDGE-31A | NORWICH-32A | | | | | |
| Jan-58 | | | 3/58: K.LYNN-31C | 10/57: W/D | | | | | |
| Aug-58 | | | KINGS LYNN-31C | | | | | | |
| Jan-59 | | | 12/58: MARCH-31B | | | | | | |
| Aug-59 | | | MARCH-31B | | | | | | |
| Nov-59 | | | 11/59: W/D | | | | | | |
| Jan-60 | | | | | | | | | |
| Apr-60 | | | | | | | | | |
| Aug-60 | | | | | | | | | |
| Nov-60 | | | | | | | | | |

| | | | | | | | D11 4-4-0 (1920) | | |
|---|---|---|---|---|---|---|---|---|---|
| | 62654 | 62655 | 62656 | 62657 | 62658 | 62659 | 62660 | 62661 | 62662 |
| Aug-50 | TRAFFORD PARK - 9E | NORTHWICH - 9G | TRAFFORD PARK - 9E | TRAFFORD PARK - 9E | TRAFFORD PARK - 9E | TRAFFORD PARK - 9E | IMMINGHAM - 40B | IMMINGHAM - 40B | IMMINGHAM - 40B |
| Jan-51 | TRAFFORD PARK - 9E | NORTHWICH - 9G | TRAFFORD PARK - 9E | TRAFFORD PARK - 9E | TRAFFORD PARK - 9E | TRAFFORD PARK - 9E | IMMINGHAM - 40B | IMMINGHAM - 40B | 10/50: T.PARK - 9E |
| Aug-51 | TRAFFORD PARK - 9E | NORTHWICH - 9G | TRAFFORD PARK - 9E | TRAFFORD PARK - 9E | TRAFFORD PARK - 9E | TRAFFORD PARK - 9E | 3/51: T.PARK - 9E | 3/51: T.PARK - 9E | TRAFFORD PARK - 9E |
| Jan-52 | TRAFFORD PARK - 9E | NORTHWICH - 9G | TRAFFORD PARK - 9E | TRAFFORD PARK - 9E | TRAFFORD PARK - 9E | TRAFFORD PARK - 9E | TRAFFORD PARK - 9E | TRAFFORD PARK - 9E | TRAFFORD PARK - 9E |
| Aug-52 | TRAFFORD PARK - 9E | NORTHWICH - 9G | TRAFFORD PARK - 9E | TRAFFORD PARK - 9E | TRAFFORD PARK - 9E | TRAFFORD PARK - 9E | TRAFFORD PARK - 9E | TRAFFORD PARK - 9E | TRAFFORD PARK - 9E |
| Jan-53 | TRAFFORD PARK - 9E | NORTHWICH - 9G | TRAFFORD PARK - 9E | TRAFFORD PARK - 9E | TRAFFORD PARK - 9E | 2/53: NORTH - 9G | TRAFFORD PARK - 9E | TRAFFORD PARK - 9E | TRAFFORD PARK - 9E |
| Aug-53 | 8/53: W/D | 8/53: W/D | 9/53: NORTH - 9G | 2/53: W/D | TRAFFORD PARK - 9E | NORTHWICH - 9G | TRAFFORD PARK - 9E | TRAFFORD PARK - 9E | TRAFFORD PARK - 9E |
| Jan-54 | | | NORTHWICH - 9G | | TRAFFORD PARK - 9E | NORTHWICH - 9G | 11/53: LINC - 40A | TRAFFORD PARK - 9E | TRAFFORD PARK - 9E |
| Aug-54 | | | NORTHWICH - 9G | | 5/54: NORTH - 9G | NORTHWICH - 9G | LINCOLN - 40A | TRAFFORD PARK - 9E | TRAFFORD PARK - 9E |
| Jan-55 | | | 1/55: W/D | | NORTHWICH - 9G | 11/54: W/D | LINCOLN - 40A | TRAFFORD PARK - 9E | TRAFFORD PARK - 9E |
| Aug-55 | | | | | 8/55: W/D | | LINCOLN - 40A | 3/55: NORTH - 9G | 10/55: NORTH - 9G |
| Jan-56 | | | | | | | LINCOLN - 40A | NORTHWICH - 9G | NORTHWICH - 9G |
| Aug-56 | | | | | | | LINCOLN - 40A | NORTHWICH - 9G | NORTHWICH - 9G |
| Jan-57 | | | | | | | LINCOLN - 40A | NORTHWICH - 9G | NORTHWICH - 9G |
| Aug-57 | | | | | | | 4/57: DARN - 41A | NORTHWICH - 9G | NORTHWICH - 9G |
| Jan-58 | | | | | | | DARNALL - 41A | NORTHWICH - 9G | NORTHWICH - 9G |
| Aug-58 | | | | | | | DARNALL - 41A | 5/58: DARN - 41A | 5/58: DARN - 41A |
| Jan-59 | | | | | | | DARNALL - 41A | DARNALL - 41A | DARNALL - 41A |
| Aug-59 | | | | | | | DARNALL - 41A | 6/59: STAVE - 41H | DARNALL - 41A |
| Nov-59 | | | | | | | DARNALL - 41A | STAVELEY (GC) - 41H | DARNALL - 41A |
| Jan-60 | | | | | | | DARNALL - 41A | STAVELEY (GC) - 41H | DARNALL - 41A |
| Apr-60 | | | | | | | DARNALL - 41A | STAVELEY (GC) - 41H | DARNALL - 41A |
| Aug-60 | | | | | | | DARNALL - 41A | STAVELEY (GC) - 41H | 8/60: W/D |
| Nov-60 | | | | | | | 11/60: W/D | STAVELEY (GC) - 41H | |

| | | | | | | | | | D11 4-4-0 (1924) |
|---|---|---|---|---|---|---|---|---|---|
| | 62663 | 62664 | 62665 | 62666 | 62667 | 62668 | 62669 | 62670 | 62671 |
| Aug-50 | HEATON MERSEY - 9F | IMMINGHAM - 40B | HEATON MERSEY - 9F | IMMINGHAM - 40B | IMMINGHAM - 40B | IMMINGHAM - 40B | IMMINGHAM - 40B | TRAFFORD PARK - 9E | EASTFIELD - 65A |
| Jan-51 | HEATON MERSEY - 9F | 1/51: T.PARK - 9E | HEATON MERSEY - 9F | 10/50: T.PARK - 9E | 1/51: T.PARK - 9E | 10/50: T.PARK - 9E | TRAFFORD PARK - 9E | TRAFFORD PARK - 9E | EASTFIELD - 65A |
| Aug-51 | HEATON MERSEY - 9F | TRAFFORD PARK - 9E | HEATON MERSEY - 9F | TRAFFORD PARK - 9E | TRAFFORD PARK - 9E | TRAFFORD PARK - 9E | TRAFFORD PARK - 9E | TRAFFORD PARK - 9E | EASTFIELD - 65A |
| Jan-52 | HEATON MERSEY - 9F | TRAFFORD PARK - 9E | HEATON MERSEY - 9F | TRAFFORD PARK - 9E | TRAFFORD PARK - 9E | TRAFFORD PARK - 9E | TRAFFORD PARK - 9E | TRAFFORD PARK - 9E | EASTFIELD - 65A |
| Aug-52 | HEATON MERSEY - 9F | TRAFFORD PARK - 9E | HEATON MERSEY - 9F | TRAFFORD PARK - 9E | 2/53: IMM - 40B | TRAFFORD PARK - 9E | NORTHWICH - 9G | TRAFFORD PARK - 9E | EASTFIELD - 65A |
| Jan-53 | HEATON MERSEY - 9F | TRAFFORD PARK - 9E | HEATON MERSEY - 9F | 2/53: IMM - 40B | 3/53: BOST - 40F | TRAFFORD PARK - 9E | NORTHWICH - 9G | TRAFFORD PARK - 9E | EASTFIELD - 65A |
| Aug-53 | HEATON MERSEY - 9F | TRAFFORD PARK - 9E | HEATON MERSEY - 9F | 7/53: MEX - 36B | 7/53: MEX - 36B | TRAFFORD PARK - 9E | NORTHWICH - 9G | TRAFFORD PARK - 9E | EASTFIELD - 65A |
| Jan-54 | HEATON MERSEY - 9F | TRAFFORD PARK - 9E | HEATON MERSEY - 9F | 11/53: LINC - 40A | 11/53: LINC - 40A | TRAFFORD PARK - 9E | NORTHWICH - 9G | 11/53: IMM - 40B | EASTFIELD - 65A |
| Aug-54 | 8/54: LINC - 40A | TRAFFORD PARK - 9E | HEATON MERSEY - 9F | LINCOLN - 40A | LINCOLN - 40A | TRAFFORD PARK - 9E | NORTHWICH - 9G | IMMINGHAM - 40B | EASTFIELD - 65A |
| Jan-55 | LINCOLN - 40A | TRAFFORD PARK - 9E | 11/54: NORTH - 9G | LINCOLN - 40A | LINCOLN - 40A | TRAFFORD PARK - 9E | NORTHWICH - 9G | IMMINGHAM - 40B | EASTFIELD - 65A |
| Aug-55 | LINCOLN - 40A | 3/55: NORTH - 9G | NORTHWICH - 9G | LINCOLN - 40A | LINCOLN - 40A | TRAFFORD PARK - 9E | NORTHWICH - 9G | IMMINGHAM - 40B | EASTFIELD - 65A |
| Jan-56 | LINCOLN - 40A | NORTHWICH - 9G | NORTHWICH - 9G | LINCOLN - 40A | LINCOLN - 40A | TRAFFORD PARK - 9E | NORTHWICH - 9G | IMMINGHAM - 40B | EASTFIELD - 65A |
| Aug-56 | LINCOLN - 40A | NORTHWICH - 9G | NORTHWICH - 9G | LINCOLN - 40A | LINCOLN - 40A | TRAFFORD PARK - 9E | NORTHWICH - 9G | 5/56: LINC - 40A | EASTFIELD - 65A |
| Jan-57 | LINCOLN - 40A | NORTHWICH - 9G | NORTHWICH - 9G | LINCOLN - 40A | LINCOLN - 40A | TRAFFORD PARK - 9E | NORTHWICH - 9G | LINCOLN - 40A | EASTFIELD - 65A |
| Aug-57 | 4/57: DARN - 41A | NORTHWICH - 9G | NORTHWICH - 9G | 4/57: DARN - 41A | 4/57: DARN - 41A | TRAFFORD PARK - 9E | NORTHWICH - 9G | 5/57: DARN - 41A | EASTFIELD - 65A |
| Jan-58 | DARNALL - 41A | NORTHWICH - 9G | NORTHWICH - 9G | DARNALL - 41A | DARNALL - 41A | TRAFFORD PARK - 9E | NORTHWICH - 9G | DARNALL - 41A | EASTFIELD - 65A |
| Aug-58 | 4/58: STAVE - 41H | 5/58: DARN - 41A | 5/58: DARN - 41A | DARNALL - 41A | DARNALL - 41A | 5/58: DARN - 41A | 5/58: DARN - 41A | DARNALL - 41A | EASTFIELD - 65A |
| Jan-59 | STAVELEY (GC) - 41H | DARNALL - 41A | DARNALL - 41A | DARNALL - 41A | DARNALL - 41A | DARNALL - 41A | DARNALL - 41A | DARNALL - 41A | EASTFIELD - 65A |
| Aug-59 | STAVELEY (GC) - 41H | DARNALL - 41A | 5/59: W/D | DARNALL - 41A | DARNALL - 41A | DARNALL - 41A | DARNALL - 41A | DARNALL - 41A | EASTFIELD - 65A |
| Nov-59 | STAVELEY (GC) - 41H | DARNALL - 41A | | DARNALL - 41A | DARNALL - 41A | DARNALL - 41A | DARNALL - 41A | DARNALL - 41A | EASTFIELD - 65A |
| Jan-60 | STAVELEY (GC) - 41H | DARNALL - 41A | | DARNALL - 41A | DARNALL - 41A | DARNALL - 41A | DARNALL - 41A | DARNALL - 41A | EASTFIELD - 65A |
| Apr-60 | STAVELEY (GC) - 41H | DARNALL - 41A | | DARNALL - 41A | DARNALL - 41A | DARNALL - 41A | DARNALL - 41A | DARNALL - 41A | EASTFIELD - 65A |
| Aug-60 | 5/60: W/D | 8/60: W/D | | DARNALL - 41A | 8/60: W/D | DARNALL - 41A | 8/60: W/D | DARNALL - 41A | EASTFIELD - 65A |
| Nov-60 | | | | DARNALL - 41A | | DARNALL - 41A | | DARNALL - 41A | EASTFIELD - 65A |

| | 62672 | 62673 | 62674 | 62675 | 62676 | 62677 | 62678 | 62679 | 62680 |
|---|---|---|---|---|---|---|---|---|---|
| Aug-50 | EASTFIELD - 65A | EASTFIELD - 65A | EASTFIELD - 65A | EASTFIELD - 65A | EASTFIELD - 65A | HAYMARKET - 64B | HAYMARKET - 64B | HAYMARKET - 64B | EASTFIELD - 65A |
| Jan-51 | EASTFIELD - 65A | EASTFIELD - 65A | EASTFIELD - 65A | EASTFIELD - 65A | EASTFIELD - 65A | HAYMARKET - 64B | HAYMARKET - 64B | HAYMARKET - 64B | EASTFIELD - 65A |
| Aug-51 | EASTFIELD - 65A | EASTFIELD - 65A | EASTFIELD - 65A | EASTFIELD - 65A | EASTFIELD - 65A | HAYMARKET - 64B | HAYMARKET - 64B | HAYMARKET - 64B | EASTFIELD - 65A |
| Jan-52 | EASTFIELD - 65A | EASTFIELD - 65A | EASTFIELD - 65A | EASTFIELD - 65A | EASTFIELD - 65A | HAYMARKET - 64B | HAYMARKET - 64B | HAYMARKET - 64B | EASTFIELD - 65A |
| Aug-52 | EASTFIELD - 65A | EASTFIELD - 65A | EASTFIELD - 65A | EASTFIELD - 65A | EASTFIELD - 65A | HAYMARKET - 64B | HAYMARKET - 64B | HAYMARKET - 64B | EASTFIELD - 65A |
| Jan-53 | EASTFIELD - 65A | EASTFIELD - 65A | EASTFIELD - 65A | EASTFIELD - 65A | EASTFIELD - 65A | HAYMARKET - 64B | HAYMARKET - 64B | HAYMARKET - 64B | EASTFIELD - 65A |
| Aug-53 | EASTFIELD - 65A | EASTFIELD - 65A | EASTFIELD - 65A | EASTFIELD - 65A | EASTFIELD - 65A | HAYMARKET - 64B | HAYMARKET - 64B | HAYMARKET - 64B | EASTFIELD - 65A |
| Jan-54 | EASTFIELD - 65A | EASTFIELD - 65A | EASTFIELD - 65A | EASTFIELD - 65A | EASTFIELD - 65A | HAYMARKET - 64B | HAYMARKET - 64B | HAYMARKET - 64B | EASTFIELD - 65A |
| Aug-54 | EASTFIELD - 65A | EASTFIELD - 65A | EASTFIELD - 65A | EASTFIELD - 65A | EASTFIELD - 65A | HAYMARKET - 64B | HAYMARKET - 64B | HAYMARKET - 64B | EASTFIELD - 65A |
| Jan-55 | EASTFIELD - 65A | EASTFIELD - 65A | EASTFIELD - 65A | EASTFIELD - 65A | EASTFIELD - 65A | HAYMARKET - 64B | HAYMARKET - 64B | HAYMARKET - 64B | EASTFIELD - 65A |
| Aug-55 | EASTFIELD - 65A | EASTFIELD - 65A | EASTFIELD - 65A | EASTFIELD - 65A | EASTFIELD - 65A | HAYMARKET - 64B | HAYMARKET - 64B | HAYMARKET - 64B | EASTFIELD - 65A |
| Jan-56 | EASTFIELD - 65A | EASTFIELD - 65A | EASTFIELD - 65A | EASTFIELD - 65A | EASTFIELD - 65A | HAYMARKET - 64B | HAYMARKET - 64B | HAYMARKET - 64B | EASTFIELD - 65A |
| Aug-56 | EASTFIELD - 65A | EASTFIELD - 65A | EASTFIELD - 65A | EASTFIELD - 65A | EASTFIELD - 65A | HAYMARKET - 64B | HAYMARKET - 64B | HAYMARKET - 64B | EASTFIELD - 65A |
| Jan-57 | EASTFIELD - 65A | EASTFIELD - 65A | EASTFIELD - 65A | EASTFIELD - 65A | EASTFIELD - 65A | HAYMARKET - 64B | HAYMARKET - 64B | HAYMARKET - 64B | EASTFIELD - 65A |
| Aug-57 | EASTFIELD - 65A | EASTFIELD - 65A | EASTFIELD - 65A | EASTFIELD - 65A | EASTFIELD - 65A | 5/57: TH JN - 62A | 5/57: TH JN - 62A | 5/57: TH JN - 62A | EASTFIELD - 65A |
| Jan-58 | EASTFIELD - 65A | EASTFIELD - 65A | EASTFIELD - 65A | EASTFIELD - 65A | EASTFIELD - 65A | THORNTON JCN - 62A | THORNTON JCN - 62A | THORNTON JCN - 62A | EASTFIELD - 65A |
| Aug-58 | EASTFIELD - 65A | EASTFIELD - 65A | EASTFIELD - 65A | EASTFIELD - 65A | EASTFIELD - 65A | THORNTON JCN - 62A | THORNTON JCN - 62A | THORNTON JCN - 62A | EASTFIELD - 65A |
| Jan-59 | EASTFIELD - 65A | EASTFIELD - 65A | EASTFIELD - 65A | EASTFIELD - 65A | EASTFIELD - 65A | 6/59: DUNF - 62C | THORNTON JCN - 62A | 9/58: W/D | EASTFIELD - 65A |
| Aug-59 | EASTFIELD - 65A | 7/59: W/D | EASTFIELD - 65A | EASTFIELD - 65A | EASTFIELD - 65A | 8/59: W/D | 3/59: W/D | | EASTFIELD - 65A |
| Nov-59 | EASTFIELD - 65A | | EASTFIELD - 65A | 10/59: W/D | 10/59: W/D | | | | EASTFIELD - 65A |
| Jan-60 | EASTFIELD - 65A | | EASTFIELD - 65A | | | | | | EASTFIELD - 65A |
| Apr-60 | EASTFIELD - 65A | | EASTFIELD - 65A | | | | | | EASTFIELD - 65A |
| Aug-60 | EASTFIELD - 65A | | EASTFIELD - 65A | | | | | | EASTFIELD - 65A |
| Nov-60 | EASTFIELD - 65A | | EASTFIELD - 65A | | | | | | EASTFIELD - 65A |

| | 62681 | 62682 | 62683 | 62684 | 62685 | 62686 | 62687 | 62688 | 62689 |
|---|---|---|---|---|---|---|---|---|---|
| Aug-50 | EASTFIELD - 65A | EASTFIELD - 65A | HAYMARKET - 64B | EASTFIELD - 65A | HAYMARKET - 64B | EASTFIELD - 65A | EASTFIELD - 65A | EASTFIELD - 65A | EASTFIELD - 65A |
| Jan-51 | EASTFIELD - 65A | EASTFIELD - 65A | HAYMARKET - 64B | EASTFIELD - 65A | HAYMARKET - 64B | EASTFIELD - 65A | EASTFIELD - 65A | EASTFIELD - 65A | EASTFIELD - 65A |
| Aug-51 | EASTFIELD - 65A | EASTFIELD - 65A | HAYMARKET - 64B | EASTFIELD - 65A | HAYMARKET - 64B | EASTFIELD - 65A | EASTFIELD - 65A | EASTFIELD - 65A | EASTFIELD - 65A |
| Jan-52 | EASTFIELD - 65A | EASTFIELD - 65A | HAYMARKET - 64B | EASTFIELD - 65A | HAYMARKET - 64B | EASTFIELD - 65A | EASTFIELD - 65A | EASTFIELD - 65A | EASTFIELD - 65A |
| Aug-52 | EASTFIELD - 65A | EASTFIELD - 65A | HAYMARKET - 64B | EASTFIELD - 65A | HAYMARKET - 64B | EASTFIELD - 65A | EASTFIELD - 65A | EASTFIELD - 65A | EASTFIELD - 65A |
| Jan-53 | EASTFIELD - 65A | EASTFIELD - 65A | HAYMARKET - 64B | EASTFIELD - 65A | HAYMARKET - 64B | EASTFIELD - 65A | EASTFIELD - 65A | EASTFIELD - 65A | EASTFIELD - 65A |
| Aug-53 | EASTFIELD - 65A | EASTFIELD - 65A | HAYMARKET - 64B | EASTFIELD - 65A | HAYMARKET - 64B | EASTFIELD - 65A | EASTFIELD - 65A | EASTFIELD - 65A | EASTFIELD - 65A |
| Jan-54 | EASTFIELD - 65A | EASTFIELD - 65A | HAYMARKET - 64B | EASTFIELD - 65A | HAYMARKET - 64B | EASTFIELD - 65A | EASTFIELD - 65A | EASTFIELD - 65A | EASTFIELD - 65A |
| Aug-54 | EASTFIELD - 65A | EASTFIELD - 65A | HAYMARKET - 64B | EASTFIELD - 65A | HAYMARKET - 64B | EASTFIELD - 65A | EASTFIELD - 65A | EASTFIELD - 65A | EASTFIELD - 65A |
| Jan-55 | EASTFIELD - 65A | EASTFIELD - 65A | HAYMARKET - 64B | EASTFIELD - 65A | HAYMARKET - 64B | EASTFIELD - 65A | EASTFIELD - 65A | EASTFIELD - 65A | EASTFIELD - 65A |
| Aug-55 | EASTFIELD - 65A | EASTFIELD - 65A | HAYMARKET - 64B | EASTFIELD - 65A | HAYMARKET - 64B | EASTFIELD - 65A | EASTFIELD - 65A | EASTFIELD - 65A | EASTFIELD - 65A |
| Jan-56 | EASTFIELD - 65A | EASTFIELD - 65A | HAYMARKET - 64B | EASTFIELD - 65A | HAYMARKET - 64B | EASTFIELD - 65A | EASTFIELD - 65A | EASTFIELD - 65A | EASTFIELD - 65A |
| Aug-56 | EASTFIELD - 65A | EASTFIELD - 65A | HAYMARKET - 64B | EASTFIELD - 65A | HAYMARKET - 64B | EASTFIELD - 65A | EASTFIELD - 65A | EASTFIELD - 65A | EASTFIELD - 65A |
| Jan-57 | EASTFIELD - 65A | EASTFIELD - 65A | HAYMARKET - 64B | EASTFIELD - 65A | HAYMARKET - 64B | EASTFIELD - 65A | EASTFIELD - 65A | EASTFIELD - 65A | EASTFIELD - 65A |
| Aug-57 | EASTFIELD - 65A | EASTFIELD - 65A | HAYMARKET - 64B | EASTFIELD - 65A | HAYMARKET - 64B | EASTFIELD - 65A | EASTFIELD - 65A | EASTFIELD - 65A | EASTFIELD - 65A |
| Jan-58 | EASTFIELD - 65A | EASTFIELD - 65A | HAYMARKET - 64B | EASTFIELD - 65A | HAYMARKET - 64B | EASTFIELD - 65A | EASTFIELD - 65A | EASTFIELD - 65A | EASTFIELD - 65A |
| Aug-58 | EASTFIELD - 65A | EASTFIELD - 65A | HAYMARKET - 64B | EASTFIELD - 65A | HAYMARKET - 64B | EASTFIELD - 65A | EASTFIELD - 65A | EASTFIELD - 65A | EASTFIELD - 65A |
| Jan-59 | EASTFIELD - 65A | EASTFIELD - 65A | 9/58: W/D | EASTFIELD - 65A | HAYMARKET - 64B | EASTFIELD - 65A | EASTFIELD - 65A | EASTFIELD - 65A | EASTFIELD - 65A |
| Aug-59 | EASTFIELD - 65A | EASTFIELD - 65A | | EASTFIELD - 65A | HAYMARKET - 64B | EASTFIELD - 65A | EASTFIELD - 65A | EASTFIELD - 65A | EASTFIELD - 65A |
| Nov-59 | EASTFIELD - 65A | EASTFIELD - 65A | | 10/59: W/D | HAYMARKET - 64B | EASTFIELD - 65A | EASTFIELD - 65A | EASTFIELD - 65A | EASTFIELD - 65A |
| Jan-60 | EASTFIELD - 65A | EASTFIELD - 65A | | | HAYMARKET - 64B | EASTFIELD - 65A | EASTFIELD - 65A | EASTFIELD - 65A | 2/60: STM - 64A |
| Apr-60 | EASTFIELD - 65A | EASTFIELD - 65A | | | HAYMARKET - 64B | EASTFIELD - 65A | EASTFIELD - 65A | EASTFIELD - 65A | EDINBURGH (SM) - 64A |
| Aug-60 | EASTFIELD - 65A | EASTFIELD - 65A | | | HAYMARKET - 64B | EASTFIELD - 65A | EASTFIELD - 65A | EASTFIELD - 65A | 7/60: EAST - 65A |
| Nov-60 | EASTFIELD - 65A | EASTFIELD - 65A | | | HAYMARKET - 64B | EASTFIELD - 65A | EASTFIELD - 65A | EASTFIELD - 65A | EASTFIELD - 65A |

For a line whose London route had a very limited service whilst the rest of the system made do with stopping trains, the Great Central in its last twenty-five years produced an interestingly wide range of express passenger locomotives, starting with Atlantics and 4-4-0's and - when their six coupled designs fell short on expectation - back to 4-4-0's in the shape of the D10 'Director' class which took to the rails in 1913. Although reasonably successful they had not been designed with wartime conditions in mind and four years after their introduction a further, rather unspectacular, attempt to produce an express 4-6-0 was made with the result that in 1919 the D10 design was perpetuated as the D11 'Improved Director' class and, after the grouping, further expanded by the LNER for duties on the North British section. The remarkable career of both classes has been fully documented elsewhere and there is neither the room nor need to repeat the details except to draw attention to the pleasing irony that as Gresley 4-6-0's were being drafted onto the Great Central, a batch of D11's was sent to the Great Northern to work the Queen of Scots Pullman: no easy retirement. In their final years both classes were despatched to the CLC working occasionally from Manchester to Liverpool but more regularly between Chester and Manchester and it was on one of the latter workings that D10 62659 'Worsley Taylor' was captured at Manchester Central in 1954, its last year of service. Below, D11 62660 'Butler-Henderson' calls at Newark in March 1957 during the period that it was working over the Midland Railway.

| | 62690 | 62691 | 62692 | 62693 | 62694 | D49 4-4-0 (1927) 62700 | 62701 | 62702 | 62703 |
|---|---|---|---|---|---|---|---|---|---|
| Aug-50 | HAYMARKET - 64B | HAYMARKET - 64B | HAYMARKET - 64B | HAYMARKET - 64B | HAYMARKET - 64B | BOT.GDNS - 53B | BRIDLINGTON - 53D | EDINBURGH(SM) - 64A | BOT.GDNS - 53B |
| Jan-51 | HAYMARKET - 64B | HAYMARKET - 64B | HAYMARKET - 64B | HAYMARKET - 64B | HAYMARKET - 64B | BOT.GDNS - 53B | BRIDLINGTON - 53D | EDINBURGH(SM) - 64A | **11/50: BRID - 53D** |
| Aug-51 | HAYMARKET - 64B | HAYMARKET - 64B | HAYMARKET - 64B | HAYMARKET - 64B | HAYMARKET - 64B | BOT.GDNS - 53B | BRIDLINGTON - 53D | EDINBURGH(SM) - 64A | BRIDLINGTON - 53D |
| Jan-52 | HAYMARKET - 64B | HAYMARKET - 64B | HAYMARKET - 64B | HAYMARKET - 64B | HAYMARKET - 64B | BOT.GDNS - 53B | BRIDLINGTON - 53D | EDINBURGH(SM) - 64A | BRIDLINGTON - 53D |
| Aug-52 | HAYMARKET - 64B | HAYMARKET - 64B | HAYMARKET - 64B | HAYMARKET - 64B | HAYMARKET - 64B | BOT.GDNS - 53B | BRIDLINGTON - 53D | **3/52: YORK - 50A** | BRIDLINGTON - 53D |
| Jan-53 | HAYMARKET - 64B | HAYMARKET - 64B | **3/53: BATH - 64F** | HAYMARKET - 64B | HAYMARKET - 64B | BOT.GDNS - 53B | BRIDLINGTON - 53D | YORK - 50A | BRIDLINGTON - 53D |
| Aug-53 | HAYMARKET - 64B | HAYMARKET - 64B | **6/53: HMKT+AU99 - 64B** | HAYMARKET - 64B | HAYMARKET - 64B | BOT.GDNS - 53B | BRIDLINGTON - 53D | YORK - 50A | BRIDLINGTON - 53D |
| Jan-54 | HAYMARKET - 64B | HAYMARKET - 64B | HAYMARKET - 64B | HAYMARKET - 64B | HAYMARKET - 64B | BOT.GDNS - 53B | BRIDLINGTON - 53D | YORK - 50A | BRIDLINGTON - 53D |
| Aug-54 | HAYMARKET - 64B | HAYMARKET - 64B | HAYMARKET - 64B | HAYMARKET - 64B | HAYMARKET - 64B | BOT.GDNS - 53B | BRIDLINGTON - 53D | YORK - 50A | BRIDLINGTON - 53D |
| Jan-55 | HAYMARKET - 64B | HAYMARKET - 64B | HAYMARKET - 64B | HAYMARKET - 64B | HAYMARKET - 64B | BOT.GDNS - 53B | **1/55: B.GDNS - 53B** | YORK - 50A | BRIDLINGTON - 53D |
| Aug-55 | HAYMARKET - 64B | HAYMARKET - 64B | HAYMARKET - 64B | HAYMARKET - 64B | HAYMARKET - 64B | BOT.GDNS - 53B | **6/55: BRID - 53D** | YORK - 50A | BRIDLINGTON - 53D |
| Jan-56 | HAYMARKET - 64B | HAYMARKET - 64B | HAYMARKET - 64B | HAYMARKET - 64B | HAYMARKET - 64B | BOT.GDNS - 53B | BRIDLINGTON - 53D | YORK - 50A | BRIDLINGTON - 53D |
| Aug-56 | HAYMARKET - 64B | HAYMARKET - 64B | HAYMARKET - 64B | HAYMARKET - 64B | HAYMARKET - 64B | BOT.GDNS - 53B | BRIDLINGTON - 53D | YORK - 50A | BRIDLINGTON - 53D |
| Jan-57 | HAYMARKET - 64B | HAYMARKET - 64B | HAYMARKET - 64B | HAYMARKET - 64B | HAYMARKET - 64B | **10/56: BRID - 53D** | BRIDLINGTON - 53D | YORK - 50A | BRIDLINGTON - 53D |
| Aug-57 | HAYMARKET - 64B | HAYMARKET - 64B | HAYMARKET - 64B | HAYMARKET - 64B | HAYMARKET - 64B | **9/57: B.GDNS - 53B** | **9/57: B.GDNS - 53B** | YORK - 50A | **9/57: B.GDNS - 53B** |
| Jan-58 | HAYMARKET - 64B | HAYMARKET - 64B | HAYMARKET - 64B | HAYMARKET - 64B | HAYMARKET - 64B | BOT.GDNS - 53B | BOT.GDNS - 53B | YORK - 50A | BOT.GDNS - 53B |
| Aug-58 | HAYMARKET - 64B | HAYMARKET - 64B | HAYMARKET - 64B | HAYMARKET - 64B | HAYMARKET - 64B | BOT.GDNS - 53B | BOT.GDNS - 53B | **8/58: N.HILL - 50B** | **6/58: W/D** |
| Jan-59 | HAYMARKET - 64B | HAYMARKET - 64B | HAYMARKET - 64B | HAYMARKET - 64B | HAYMARKET - 64B | **10/58: W/D** | BOT.GDNS - 53B | **11/58: W/D** | |
| Aug-59 | HAYMARKET - 64B | HAYMARKET - 64B | HAYMARKET - 64B | HAYMARKET - 64B | HAYMARKET - 64B | | **6/59: DAIRY - 53A** | | |
| Nov-59 | HAYMARKET - 64B | HAYMARKET - 64B | **11/59: W/D** | HAYMARKET - 64B | **11/59: W/D** | | **9/59 : W/D** | | |
| Jan-60 | HAYMARKET - 64B | HAYMARKET - 64B | | **2/60: STM - 64A** | | | | | |
| Apr-60 | HAYMARKET - 64B | HAYMARKET - 64B | | EDINBURGH(SM) - 64A | | | | | |
| Aug-60 | HAYMARKET - 64B | HAYMARKET - 64B | | **7/60: HMKT - 64B** | | | | | |
| Nov-60 | HAYMARKET - 64B | HAYMARKET - 64B | | HAYMARKET - 64B | | | | | |

| | 62704 | 62705 | 62706 | 62707 | 62708 | 62709 | 62710 | 62711 | 62712 |
|---|---|---|---|---|---|---|---|---|---|
| Aug-50 | THORNTONJCN - 62A | HAYMARKET - 64B | HAYMARKET - 64B | BRIDLINGTON - 53D | THORNTONJCN - 62A | HAYMARKET - 64B | BOT.GDNS - 53B | EDINBURGH(SM) - 64A | EDINBURGH(SM) - 64A |
| Jan-51 | THORNTONJCN - 62A | HAYMARKET - 64B | HAYMARKET - 64B | BRIDLINGTON - 53D | THORNTONJCN - 62A | HAYMARKET - 64B | BOT.GDNS - 53B | EDINBURGH(SM) - 64A | EDINBURGH(SM) - 64A |
| Aug-51 | THORNTONJCN - 62A | HAYMARKET - 64B | HAYMARKET - 64B | BRIDLINGTON - 53D | THORNTONJCN - 62A | HAYMARKET - 64B | BOT.GDNS - 53B | EDINBURGH(SM) - 64A | EDINBURGH(SM) - 64A |
| Jan-52 | THORNTONJCN - 62A | HAYMARKET - 64B | HAYMARKET - 64B | BRIDLINGTON - 53D | THORNTONJCN - 62A | HAYMARKET - 64B | BOT.GDNS - 53B | EDINBURGH(SM) - 64A | EDINBURGH(SM) - 64A |
| Aug-52 | THORNTONJCN - 62A | HAYMARKET - 64B | HAYMARKET - 64B | BRIDLINGTON - 53D | THORNTONJCN - 62A | HAYMARKET - 64B | BOT.GDNS - 53B | EDINBURGH(SM) - 64A | EDINBURGH(SM) - 64A |
| Jan-53 | THORNTONJCN - 62A | HAYMARKET - 64B | HAYMARKET - 64B | BRIDLINGTON - 53D | THORNTONJCN - 62A | HAYMARKET - 64B | BOT.GDNS - 53B | EDINBURGH(SM) - 64A | EDINBURGH(SM) - 64A |
| Aug-53 | THORNTONJCN - 62A | HAYMARKET - 64B | HAYMARKET - 64B | BRIDLINGTON - 53D | THORNTONJCN - 62A | HAYMARKET - 64B | BOT.GDNS - 53B | EDINBURGH(SM) - 64A | EDINBURGH(SM) - 64A |
| Jan-54 | THORNTONJCN - 62A | HAYMARKET - 64B | HAYMARKET - 64B | BRIDLINGTON - 53D | THORNTONJCN - 62A | HAYMARKET - 64B | BOT.GDNS - 53B | EDINBURGH(SM) - 64A | EDINBURGH(SM) - 64A |
| Aug-54 | THORNTONJCN - 62A | HAYMARKET - 64B | HAYMARKET - 64B | BRIDLINGTON - 53D | THORNTONJCN - 62A | HAYMARKET - 64B | **10/54: BRID - 53D** | EDINBURGH(SM) - 64A | EDINBURGH(SM) - 64A |
| Jan-55 | THORNTONJCN - 62A | HAYMARKET - 64B | HAYMARKET - 64B | **1/55: B.GDNS - 53B** | THORNTONJCN - 62A | HAYMARKET - 64B | **1/55: B. GDNS - 53B** | EDINBURGH(SM) - 64A | EDINBURGH(SM) - 64A |
| Aug-55 | THORNTONJCN - 62A | HAYMARKET - 64B | HAYMARKET - 64B | **6/55: BRID - 53D** | THORNTONJCN - 62A | HAYMARKET - 64B | BOT.GDNS - 53B | EDINBURGH(SM) - 64A | EDINBURGH(SM) - 64A |
| Jan-56 | THORNTONJCN - 62A | HAYMARKET - 64B | HAYMARKET - 64B | BRIDLINGTON - 53D | THORNTONJCN - 62A | HAYMARKET - 64B | BOT.GDNS - 53B | EDINBURGH(SM) - 64A | EDINBURGH(SM) - 64A |
| Aug-56 | THORNTONJCN - 62A | HAYMARKET - 64B | HAYMARKET - 64B | **6/56: B.GDNS - 53B** | THORNTONJCN - 62A | HAYMARKET - 64B | BOT.GDNS - 53B | EDINBURGH(SM) - 64A | EDINBURGH(SM) - 64A |
| Jan-57 | THORNTONJCN - 62A | HAYMARKET - 64B | HAYMARKET - 64B | **10/56: BRID - 53D** | THORNTONJCN - 62A | HAYMARKET - 64B | BOT.GDNS - 53B | EDINBURGH(SM) - 64A | EDINBURGH(SM) - 64A |
| Aug-57 | THORNTONJCN - 62A | HAYMARKET - 64B | **5/57: TH JN - 62A** | **9/57: B.GDNS - 53B** | THORNTONJCN - 62A | HAYMARKET - 64B | BOT.GDNS - 53B | EDINBURGH(SM) - 64A | EDINBURGH(SM) - 64A |
| Jan-58 | THORNTONJCN - 62A | HAYMARKET - 64B | **2/58: W/D** | BOT.GDNS - 53B | THORNTONJCN - 62A | HAYMARKET - 64B | BOT.GDNS - 53B | EDINBURGH(SM) - 64A | **2/58: TH JN - 62A** |
| Aug-58 | **8/58: W/D** | HAYMARKET - 64B | | BOT.GDNS - 53B | THORNTONJCN - 62A | HAYMARKET - 64B | BOT.GDNS - 53B | EDINBURGH(SM) - 64A | THORNTONJCN - 62A |
| Jan-59 | | HAYMARKET - 64B | | BOT.GDNS - 53B | THORNTONJCN - 62A | HAYMARKET - 64B | BOT.GDNS - 53B | EDINBURGH(SM) - 64A | THORNTONJCN - 62A |
| Aug-59 | | HAYMARKET - 64B | | **6/59: DAIRY - 53A** | **5/59: W/D** | HAYMARKET - 64B | **6/59: DAIRY - 53A** | EDINBURGH(SM) - 64A | THORNTONJCN - 62A |
| Nov-59 | | HAYMARKET - 64B | | **10/59: W/D** | | HAYMARKET - 64B | DAIRYCOATES - 53A | EDINBURGH(SM) - 64A | THORNTONJCN - 62A |
| Jan-60 | | **12/59: W/D** | | | | HAYMARKET - 64B | DAIRYCOATES - 53A | EDINBURGH(SM) - 64A | THORNTONJCN - 62A |
| Apr-60 | | | | | | **2/60: W/D** | DAIRYCOATES - 50B | EDINBURGH(SM) - 64A | **4/60: HWCK - 64G** |
| Aug-60 | | | | | | | DAIRYCOATES - 50B | EDINBURGH(SM) - 64A | HAWICK - 64G |
| Nov-60 | | | | | | | **10/60: W/D** | EDINBURGH(SM) - 64A | HAWICK - 64G |

| | 62713 | 62714 | 62715 | 62716 | 62717 | 62718 | 62719 | 62720 | 62721 |
|---|---|---|---|---|---|---|---|---|---|
| Aug-50 | DUNDEE - 62B | PERTH - 63A | EDINBURGH(SM) - 64A | THORNTONJCN - 62A | THORNTONJCN - 62A | DUNDEE - 62B | HAYMARKET - 64B | BOT.GDNS - 53B | EDINBURGH(SM) - 64A |
| Jan-51 | **10/50: TH JN - 62A** | PERTH - 63A | EDINBURGH(SM) - 64A | THORNTONJCN - 62A | **1/51: B.GDNS - 53B** | DUNDEE - 62B | HAYMARKET - 64B | BOT.GDNS - 53B | EDINBURGH(SM) - 64A |
| Aug-51 | THORNTONJCN - 62A | PERTH - 63A | EDINBURGH(SM) - 64A | THORNTONJCN - 62A | BOT.GDNS - 53B | DUNDEE - 62B | HAYMARKET - 64B | BOT.GDNS - 53B | EDINBURGH(SM) - 64A |
| Jan-52 | THORNTONJCN - 62A | STIRLING - 63B | EDINBURGH(SM) - 64A | THORNTONJCN - 62A | BOT.GDNS - 53B | **3/52: STM - 64A** | HAYMARKET - 64B | BOT.GDNS - 53B | EDINBURGH(SM) - 64A |
| Aug-52 | THORNTONJCN - 62A | STIRLING - 63B | EDINBURGH(SM) - 64A | THORNTONJCN - 62A | BOT.GDNS - 53B | EDINBURGH(SM) - 64A | HAYMARKET - 64B | BOT.GDNS - 53B | EDINBURGH(SM) - 64A |
| Jan-53 | THORNTONJCN - 62A | STIRLING - 63B | EDINBURGH(SM) - 64A | THORNTONJCN - 62A | BOT.GDNS - 53B | EDINBURGH(SM) - 64A | HAYMARKET - 64B | BOT.GDNS - 53B | EDINBURGH(SM) - 64A |
| Aug-53 | THORNTONJCN - 62A | STIRLING - 63B | EDINBURGH(SM) - 64A | THORNTONJCN - 62A | BOT.GDNS - 53B | EDINBURGH(SM) - 64A | HAYMARKET - 64B | BOT.GDNS - 53B | EDINBURGH(SM) - 64A |
| Jan-54 | THORNTONJCN - 62A | STIRLING - 63B | EDINBURGH(SM) - 64A | THORNTONJCN - 62A | BOT.GDNS - 53B | EDINBURGH(SM) - 64A | HAYMARKET - 64B | BOT.GDNS - 53B | EDINBURGH(SM) - 64A |
| Aug-54 | THORNTONJCN - 62A | STIRLING - 63B | EDINBURGH(SM) - 64A | THORNTONJCN - 62A | BOT.GDNS - 53B | EDINBURGH(SM) - 64A | HAYMARKET - 64B | BOT.GDNS - 53B | EDINBURGH(SM) - 64A |
| Jan-55 | THORNTONJCN - 62A | STIRLING - 63B | EDINBURGH(SM) - 64A | THORNTONJCN - 62A | BOT.GDNS - 53B | EDINBURGH(SM) - 64A | HAYMARKET - 64B | BOT.GDNS - 53B | EDINBURGH(SM) - 64A |
| Aug-55 | THORNTONJCN - 62A | STIRLING - 63B | EDINBURGH(SM) - 64A | THORNTONJCN - 62A | BOT.GDNS - 53B | EDINBURGH(SM) - 64A | HAYMARKET - 64B | BOT.GDNS - 53B | EDINBURGH(SM) - 64A |
| Jan-56 | THORNTONJCN - 62A | STIRLING - 63B | EDINBURGH(SM) - 64A | THORNTONJCN - 62A | BOT.GDNS - 53B | EDINBURGH(SM) - 64A | HAYMARKET - 64B | BOT.GDNS - 53B | EDINBURGH(SM) - 64A |
| Aug-56 | THORNTONJCN - 62A | STIRLING - 63B | EDINBURGH(SM) - 64A | THORNTONJCN - 62A | BOT.GDNS - 53B | EDINBURGH(SM) - 64A | HAYMARKET - 64B | BOT.GDNS - 53B | EDINBURGH(SM) - 64A |
| Jan-57 | THORNTONJCN - 62A | STIRLING - 63B | EDINBURGH(SM) - 64A | THORNTONJCN - 62A | BOT.GDNS - 53B | EDINBURGH(SM) - 64A | HAYMARKET - 64B | BOT.GDNS - 53B | EDINBURGH(SM) - 64A |
| Aug-57 | THORNTONJCN - 62A | STIRLING - 63B | EDINBURGH(SM) - 64A | THORNTONJCN - 62A | BOT.GDNS - 53B | EDINBURGH(SM) - 64A | HAYMARKET - 64B | BOT.GDNS - 53B | EDINBURGH(SM) - 64A |
| Jan-58 | **9/57: W/D** | STIRLING - 63B | EDINBURGH(SM) - 64A | THORNTONJCN - 62A | BOT.GDNS - 53B | EDINBURGH(SM) - 64A | HAYMARKET - 64B | BOT.GDNS - 53B | EDINBURGH(SM) - 64A |
| Aug-58 | | STIRLING - 63B | EDINBURGH(SM) - 64A | THORNTONJCN - 62A | BOT.GDNS - 53B | EDINBURGH(SM) - 64A | HAYMARKET - 64B | BOT.GDNS - 53B | **8/58: W/D** |
| Jan-59 | | STIRLING - 63B | EDINBURGH(SM) - 64A | THORNTONJCN - 62A | BOT.GDNS - 53B | EDINBURGH(SM) - 64A | HAYMARKET - 64B | BOT.GDNS - 53B | |
| Aug-59 | | **8/59: W/D** | **7/59: W/D** | THORNTONJCN - 62A | **6/59: DAIRY - 53A** | EDINBURGH(SM) - 64A | HAYMARKET - 64B | **6/59: DAIRY - 53A** | |
| Nov-59 | | | | THORNTONJCN - 62A | DAIRYCOATES - 53A | EDINBURGH(SM) - 64A | **11/59: HWCK - 64G** | **10/59: W/D** | |
| Jan-60 | | | | THORNTONJCN - 62A | DAIRYCOATES - 53A | EDINBURGH(SM) - 64A | HAWICK - 64G | | |
| Apr-60 | | | | THORNTONJCN - 62A | DAIRYCOATES - 50B | EDINBURGH(SM) - 64A | **2/60: W/D** | | |
| Aug-60 | | | | **6/60: TH JN - 62A** | DAIRYCOATES - 50B | EDINBURGH(SM) - 64A | | | |
| Nov-60 | | | | EDINBURGH(SM) - 64A | DAIRYCOATES - 50B | EDINBURGH(SM) - 64A | | | |

| | 62722 | 62723 | 62724 | 62725 | 62726 | 62727 | 62728 | 62729 | 62730 |
|---|---|---|---|---|---|---|---|---|---|
| Aug-50 | BOT.GDNS - 53B | BOT.GDNS - 53B | BOT.GDNS - 53B | PERTH - 63A | YORK - 50A | YORK - 50A | DUNDEE - 62B | THORNTONJCN - 62A | CARLISLE(CANAL) - 12B |
| Jan-51 | BOT.GDNS - 53B | BOT.GDNS - 53B | BOT.GDNS - 53B | PERTH - 63A | YORK - 50A | **10/50: STAR - 50D** | DUNDEE - 62B | THORNTONJCN - 62A | **9/50: STAR - 50D** |
| Aug-51 | BOT.GDNS - 53B | BOT.GDNS - 53B | BOT.GDNS - 53B | PERTH - 63A | YORK - 50A | STARBECK - 50D | DUNDEE - 62B | THORNTONJCN - 62A | **10/50: YORK - 50A** |
| Jan-52 | BOT.GDNS - 53B | BOT.GDNS - 53B | BOT.GDNS - 53B | PERTH - 63A | YORK - 50A | STARBECK - 50D | DUNDEE - 62B | THORNTONJCN - 62A | YORK - 50A |
| Aug-52 | BOT.GDNS - 53B | BOT.GDNS - 53B | BOT.GDNS - 53B | PERTH - 63A | YORK - 50A | STARBECK - 50D | DUNDEE - 62B | THORNTONJCN - 62A | YORK - 50A |
| Jan-53 | BOT.GDNS - 53B | BOT.GDNS - 53B | BOT.GDNS - 53B | PERTH - 63A | YORK - 50A | STARBECK - 50D | DUNDEE - 62B | THORNTONJCN - 62A | YORK - 50A |
| Aug-53 | BOT.GDNS - 53B | BOT.GDNS - 53B | BOT.GDNS - 53B | **10/53: STIR - 63B** | **10/53: SCAR - 50E** | STARBECK - 50D | DUNDEE - 62B | THORNTONJCN - 62A | YORK - 50A |
| Jan-54 | BOT.GDNS - 53B | BOT.GDNS - 53B | BOT.GDNS - 53B | STIRLING - 63B | SCARBOROUGH - 50E | STARBECK - 50D | DUNDEE - 62B | THORNTONJCN - 62A | YORK - 50A |
| Aug-54 | BOT.GDNS - 53B | BOT.GDNS - 53B | BOT.GDNS - 53B | STIRLING - 63B | SCARBOROUGH - 50E | STARBECK - 50D | DUNDEE - 62B | THORNTONJCN - 62A | YORK - 50A |
| Jan-55 | BOT.GDNS - 53B | BOT.GDNS - 53B | BOT.GDNS - 53B | STIRLING - 63B | SCARBOROUGH - 50E | STARBECK - 50D | DUNDEE - 62B | THORNTONJCN - 62A | YORK - 50A |
| Aug-55 | BOT.GDNS - 53B | BOT.GDNS - 53B | BOT.GDNS - 53B | STIRLING - 63B | SCARBOROUGH - 50E | STARBECK - 50D | DUNDEE - 62B | THORNTONJCN - 62A | YORK - 50A |
| Jan-56 | BOT.GDNS - 53B | BOT.GDNS - 53B | BOT.GDNS - 53B | STIRLING - 63B | SCARBOROUGH - 50E | STARBECK - 50D | DUNDEE - 62B | THORNTONJCN - 62A | YORK - 50A |
| Aug-56 | BOT.GDNS - 53B | BOT.GDNS - 53B | BOT.GDNS - 53B | STIRLING - 63B | SCARBOROUGH - 50E | STARBECK - 50D | DUNDEE - 62B | THORNTONJCN - 62A | YORK - 50A |
| Jan-57 | BOT.GDNS - 53B | BOT.GDNS - 53B | BOT.GDNS - 53B | STIRLING - 63B | SCARBOROUGH - 50E | STARBECK - 50D | **2/57: TH JN - 62A** | THORNTONJCN - 62A | YORK - 50A |
| Aug-57 | BOT.GDNS - 53B | BOT.GDNS - 53B | BOT.GDNS - 53B | STIRLING - 63B | SCARBOROUGH - 50E | STARBECK - 50D | THORNTONJCN - 62A | THORNTONJCN - 62A | YORK - 50A |
| Jan-58 | BOT.GDNS - 53B | BOT.GDNS - 53B | **12/57: W/D** | STIRLING - 63B | **1/58: W/D** | STARBECK - 50D | THORNTONJCN - 62A | THORNTONJCN - 62A | YORK - 50A |
| Aug-58 | BOT.GDNS - 53B | BOT.GDNS - 53B | | STIRLING - 63B | | STARBECK - 50D | THORNTONJCN - 62A | THORNTONJCN - 62A | **8/58: SELBY - 50C** |
| Jan-59 | BOT.GDNS - 53B | BOT.GDNS - 53B | | **11/58: W/D** | | STARBECK - 50D | THORNTONJCN - 62A | THORNTONJCN - 62A | **12/58: W/D** |
| Aug-59 | **6/59: DAIRY - 53A** | **6/59: DAIRY - 53A** | | | | **9/59: DAIRY - 53A** | THORNTONJCN - 62A | THORNTONJCN - 62A | |
| Nov-59 | **10/59: W/D** | DAIRYCOATES - 53A | | | | DAIRYCOATES - 53A | **10/59: W/D** | THORNTONJCN - 62A | |
| Jan-60 | | DAIRYCOATES - 53A | | | | DAIRYCOATES - 53A | | THORNTONJCN - 62A | |
| Apr-60 | | DAIRYCOATES - 50B | | | | DAIRYCOATES - 50B | | **4/60: STM - 64A** | |
| Aug-60 | | DAIRYCOATES - 50B | | | | DAIRYCOATES - 50B | | EDINBURGH(SM) - 64A | |
| Nov-60 | | DAIRYCOATES - 50B | | | | DAIRYCOATES - 50B | | EDINBURGH(SM) - 64A | |

| | 62731 | 62732 | 62733 | 62734 | 62735 | 62736 | 62737 | 62738 | 62739 |
|---|---|---|---|---|---|---|---|---|---|
| Aug-50 | CARLISLE(C) - 12B | CARLISLE(C) - 12B | HAYMARKET - 64B | CARLISLE(C) - 12B | CARLISLE(C) - 12B | YORK - 50A | BOT. GDNS - 53B | STARBECK - 50D | NEVILLE HILL - 50B |
| Jan-51 | 9/50: STAR - 50D | 10/50: YORK - 50A | HAYMARKET - 64B | 10/50: YORK - 50A | 9/50: STAR - 50D | 10/50: STAR - 50D | BOT. GDNS - 53B | STARBECK - 50D | NEVILLE HILL - 50B |
| Aug-51 | 10/50: YORK - 50A | 7/51: CANAL - 12B | HAYMARKET - 64B | 7/51: CANAL - 12B | 10/50: YORK - 50A | STARBECK - 50D | BOT. GDNS - 53B | STARBECK - 50D | 7/51: SCAR - 50E |
| Jan-52 | 7/52: SCAR - 50E | CARLISLE(C) - 12B | HAYMARKET - 64B | CARLISLE(C) - 12B | YORK - 50A | STARBECK - 50D | BOT. GDNS - 53B | STARBECK - 50D | SCARBOROUGH - 50E |
| Aug-52 | 10/52: PICK - 50F | CARLISLE(C) - 12B | HAYMARKET - 64B | CARLISLE(C) - 12B | YORK - 50A | STARBECK - 50D | BOT. GDNS - 53B | STARBECK - 50D | SCARBOROUGH - 50E |
| Jan-53 | 2/53: N.HIL - 50B | CARLISLE(C) - 12B | HAYMARKET - 64B | CARLISLE(C) - 12B | YORK - 50A | STARBECK - 50D | BOT. GDNS - 53B | STARBECK - 50D | SCARBOROUGH - 50E |
| Aug-53 | NEVILLE HILL - 50B | CARLISLE(C) - 12B | HAYMARKET - 64B | CARLISLE(C) - 12B | YORK - 50A | STARBECK - 50D | BOT. GDNS - 53B | STARBECK - 50D | SCARBOROUGH - 50E |
| Jan-54 | NEVILLE HILL - 50B | CARLISLE(C) - 12B | HAYMARKET - 64B | CARLISLE(C) - 12B | YORK - 50A | STARBECK - 50D | BOT. GDNS - 53B | STARBECK - 50D | SCARBOROUGH - 50E |
| Aug-54 | NEVILLE HILL - 50B | CARLISLE(C) - 12B | HAYMARKET - 64B | CARLISLE(C) - 12B | 4/54: SCAR - 50E | STARBECK - 50D | BOT. GDNS - 53B | STARBECK - 50D | SCARBOROUGH - 50E |
| Jan-55 | 1/55: STAR - 50D | CARLISLE(C) - 12B | HAYMARKET - 64B | CARLISLE(C) - 12B | SCARBOROUGH - 50E | STARBECK - 50D | BOT. GDNS - 53B | STARBECK - 50D | SCARBOROUGH - 50E |
| Aug-55 | 6/55: YORK - 50A | CARLISLE(C) - 12B | HAYMARKET - 64B | CARLISLE(C) - 12B | SCARBOROUGH - 50E | STARBECK - 50D | BOT. GDNS - 53B | STARBECK - 50D | SCARBOROUGH - 50E |
| Jan-56 | YORK - 50A | CARLISLE(C) - 12B | HAYMARKET - 64B | CARLISLE(C) - 12B | SCARBOROUGH - 50E | STARBECK - 50D | BOT. GDNS - 53B | STARBECK - 50D | SCARBOROUGH - 50E |
| Aug-56 | YORK - 50A | CARLISLE(C) - 12B | HAYMARKET - 64B | CARLISLE(C) - 12B | SCARBOROUGH - 50E | STARBECK - 50D | BOT. GDNS - 53B | STARBECK - 50D | SCARBOROUGH - 50E |
| Jan-57 | YORK - 50A | CARLISLE(C) - 12B | HAYMARKET - 64B | CARLISLE(C) - 12B | SCARBOROUGH - 50E | STARBECK - 50D | BOT. GDNS - 53B | STARBECK - 50D | SCARBOROUGH - 50E |
| Aug-57 | 6/57: SELBY - 50C | CARLISLE(C) - 12B | HAYMARKET - 64B | CARLISLE(C) - 12B | SCARBOROUGH - 50E | STARBECK - 50D | BOT. GDNS - 53B | STARBECK - 50D | SCARBOROUGH - 50E |
| Jan-58 | SELBY - 50C | CARLISLE(C) - 12B | 2/58: TH JN - 62A | CARLISLE(C) - 12B | SCARBOROUGH - 50E | STARBECK - 50D | 1/58: W/D | STARBECK - 50D | SCARBOROUGH - 50E |
| Aug-58 | SELBY - 50C | 10/58: DARL - 51A | THORNTON JCN - 62A | CARLISLE(C) - 12B | 8/58: W/D | 6/58: W/D | | STARBECK - 50D | SCARBOROUGH - 50E |
| Jan-59 | SELBY - 50C | 11/58: W/D | THORNTON JCN - 62A | CARLISLE(C) - 12B | | | | STARBECK - 50D | SCARBOROUGH - 50E |
| Aug-59 | 4/59: W/D | | THORNTON JCN - 62A | CARLISLE(C) - 12B | | | | STARBECK - 50D | SCARBOROUGH - 50E |
| Nov-59 | | | THORNTON JCN - 62A | CARLISLE(C) - 12B | | | | 9/59: W/D | SCARBOROUGH - 50E |
| Jan-60 | | | THORNTON JCN - 62A | CARLISLE(C) - 12B | | | | | SCARBOROUGH - 50E |
| Apr-60 | | | 6/60 : STM - 64A | CARLISLE(C) - 12B | | | | | SCARBOROUGH - 50E |
| Aug-60 | | | EDINBURGH (SM) - 64A | CARLISLE(C) - 12B | | | | | SCARBOROUGH - 50E |
| Nov-60 | | | EDINBURGH (SM) - 64A | CARLISLE(C) - 12B | | | | | 10/60: W/D |

| | 62740 | 62741 | 62742 | 62743 | 62744 | 62745 | 62746 | 62747 | 62748 |
|---|---|---|---|---|---|---|---|---|---|
| Aug-50 | YORK - 50A | BOT. GDNS - 53B | YORK - 50A | BOT. GDNS - 53B | YORK - 50A | YORK - 50A | NEVILLE HILL - 50B | BLAYDON - 52C | NEVILLE HILL - 50B |
| Jan-51 | 10/50: STAR - 50D | BOT. GDNS - 53B | 10/50: N.HILL - 50B | 1/51: HMKT - 64B | YORK - 50A | YORK - 50A | NEVILLE HILL - 50B | BLAYDON - 52C | NEVILLE HILL - 50B |
| Aug-51 | STARBECK - 50D | BOT. GDNS - 53B | NEVILLE HILL - 50B | HAYMARKET - 64B | YORK - 50A | YORK - 50A | 8/51: YORK - 50A | BLAYDON - 52C | NEVILLE HILL - 50B |
| Jan-52 | STARBECK - 50D | BOT. GDNS - 53B | NEVILLE HILL - 50B | HAYMARKET - 64B | 3/52: DUND - 62B | YORK - 50A | YORK - 50A | BLAYDON - 52C | NEVILLE HILL - 50B |
| Aug-52 | STARBECK - 50D | BOT. GDNS - 53B | NEVILLE HILL - 50B | HAYMARKET - 64B | DUNDEE - 62B | YORK - 50A | YORK - 50A | BLAYDON - 52C | NEVILLE HILL - 50B |
| Jan-53 | STARBECK - 50D | BOT. GDNS - 53B | NEVILLE HILL - 50B | HAYMARKET - 64B | DUNDEE - 62B | YORK - 50A | 11/52: STAR - 50D | BLAYDON - 52C | NEVILLE HILL - 50B |
| Aug-53 | STARBECK - 50D | BOT. GDNS - 53B | NEVILLE HILL - 50B | HAYMARKET - 64B | DUNDEE - 62B | YORK - 50A | STARBECK - 50D | BLAYDON - 52C | NEVILLE HILL - 50B |
| Jan-54 | STARBECK - 50D | BOT. GDNS - 53B | NEVILLE HILL - 50B | HAYMARKET - 64B | DUNDEE - 62B | YORK - 50A | STARBECK - 50D | BLAYDON - 52C | NEVILLE HILL - 50B |
| Aug-54 | STARBECK - 50D | BOT. GDNS - 53B | NEVILLE HILL - 50B | HAYMARKET - 64B | DUNDEE - 62B | YORK - 50A | STARBECK - 50D | BLAYDON - 52C | NEVILLE HILL - 50B |
| Jan-55 | STARBECK - 50D | BOT. GDNS - 53B | NEVILLE HILL - 50B | HAYMARKET - 64B | DUNDEE - 62B | 1/55: STAR - 50D | STARBECK - 50D | BLAYDON - 52C | NEVILLE HILL - 50B |
| Aug-55 | STARBECK - 50D | BOT. GDNS - 53B | NEVILLE HILL - 50B | HAYMARKET - 64B | DUNDEE - 62B | 6/55: YORK - 50A | STARBECK - 50D | BLAYDON - 52C | NEVILLE HILL - 50B |
| Jan-56 | STARBECK - 50D | BOT. GDNS - 53B | NEVILLE HILL - 50B | HAYMARKET - 64B | DUNDEE - 62B | YORK - 50A | STARBECK - 50D | BLAYDON - 52C | NEVILLE HILL - 50B |
| Aug-56 | 7/56: N.HILL - 50B | BOT. GDNS - 53B | NEVILLE HILL - 50B | HAYMARKET - 64B | DUNDEE - 62B | YORK - 50A | STARBECK - 50D | 6/56: YORK - 50A | NEVILLE HILL - 50B |
| Jan-57 | NEVILLE HILL - 50B | BOT. GDNS - 53B | NEVILLE HILL - 50B | HAYMARKET - 64B | 2/57: TH JN - 62A | YORK - 50A | STARBECK - 50D | YORK - 50A | NEVILLE HILL - 50B |
| Aug-57 | NEVILLE HILL - 50B | BOT. GDNS - 53B | NEVILLE HILL - 50B | HAYMARKET - 64B | THORNTON JCN - 62A | YORK - 50A | STARBECK - 50D | YORK - 50A | NEVILLE HILL - 50B |
| Jan-58 | NEVILLE HILL - 50B | BOT. GDNS - 53B | NEVILLE HILL - 50B | HAYMARKET - 64B | THORNTON JCN - 62A | YORK - 50A | STARBECK - 50D | YORK - 50A | 1/58: W/D |
| Aug-58 | NEVILLE HILL - 50B | BOT. GDNS - 53B | NEVILLE HILL - 50B | HAYMARKET - 64B | THORNTON JCN - 62A | 8/58: SCAR - 50E | 5/58: W/D | YORK - 50A | |
| Jan-59 | 12/58: YORK - 50A | 10/58: W/D | 11/58: W/D | HAYMARKET - 64B | THORNTON JCN - 62A | SCARBOROUGH - 50E | | 11/58: CANAL - 12C | |
| Aug-59 | 6/59: SELBY - 50C | | | HAYMARKET - 64B | THORNTON JCN - 62A | 3/59: W/D | | CARLISLE(C) - 12C | |
| Nov-59 | 9/59: DAIRY - 53A | | | HAYMARKET - 64B | THORNTON JCN - 62A | | | CARLISLE(C) - 12C | |
| Jan-60 | DAIRYCOATES - 53A | | | HAYMARKET - 64B | THORNTON JCN - 62A | | | CARLISLE(C) - 12C | |
| Apr-60 | DAIRYCOATES - 50B | | | HAYMARKET - 64B | 4/60: HWCK - 64G | | | CARLISLE(C) - 12C | |
| Aug-60 | 8/60: W/D | | | 6/60: W/D | HAWICK - 64G | | | CARLISLE(C) - 12C | |
| Nov-60 | | | | | HAWICK - 64G | | | CARLISLE(C) - 12C | |

| | 62749 | 62750 | 62751 | 62752 | 62753 | 62754 | 62755 | 62756 | 62757 |
|---|---|---|---|---|---|---|---|---|---|
| Aug-50 | STARBECK - 50D | BRIDLINGTON - 53D | SCARBOROUGH - 50E | STARBECK - 50D | STARBECK - 50D | BOT. GDNS - 53B | STARBECK - 50D | NEVILLE HILL - 50B | BOT. GDNS - 53B |
| Jan-51 | STARBECK - 50D | BRIDLINGTON - 53D | SCARBOROUGH - 50E | STARBECK - 50D | STARBECK - 50D | BOT. GDNS - 53B | STARBECK - 50D | NEVILLE HILL - 50B | BOT. GDNS - 53B |
| Aug-51 | STARBECK - 50D | BRIDLINGTON - 53D | SCARBOROUGH - 50E | STARBECK - 50D | STARBECK - 50D | BOT. GDNS - 53B | STARBECK - 50D | 7/51: SCAR - 50E | BOT. GDNS - 53B |
| Jan-52 | STARBECK - 50D | BRIDLINGTON - 53D | SCARBOROUGH - 50E | STARBECK - 50D | STARBECK - 50D | BOT. GDNS - 53B | STARBECK - 50D | SCARBOROUGH - 50E | BOT. GDNS - 53B |
| Aug-52 | STARBECK - 50D | BRIDLINGTON - 53D | SCARBOROUGH - 50E | STARBECK - 50D | STARBECK - 50D | BOT. GDNS - 53B | STARBECK - 50D | SCARBOROUGH - 50E | BOT. GDNS - 53B |
| Jan-53 | STARBECK - 50D | BRIDLINGTON - 53D | SCARBOROUGH - 50E | STARBECK - 50D | STARBECK - 50D | BOT. GDNS - 53B | STARBECK - 50D | SCARBOROUGH - 50E | BOT. GDNS - 53B |
| Aug-53 | STARBECK - 50D | BRIDLINGTON - 53D | SCARBOROUGH - 50E | STARBECK - 50D | STARBECK - 50D | BOT. GDNS - 53B | STARBECK - 50D | SCARBOROUGH - 50E | BOT. GDNS - 53B |
| Jan-54 | STARBECK - 50D | BRIDLINGTON - 53D | SCARBOROUGH - 50E | STARBECK - 50D | STARBECK - 50D | BOT. GDNS - 53B | STARBECK - 50D | SCARBOROUGH - 50E | BOT. GDNS - 53B |
| Aug-54 | STARBECK - 50D | BRIDLINGTON - 53D | SCARBOROUGH - 50E | STARBECK - 50D | STARBECK - 50D | BOT. GDNS - 53B | STARBECK - 50D | SCARBOROUGH - 50E | BOT. GDNS - 53B |
| Jan-55 | STARBECK - 50D | 1/55: B. GDNS - 53B | SCARBOROUGH - 50E | STARBECK - 50D | STARBECK - 50D | BOT. GDNS - 53B | STARBECK - 50D | SCARBOROUGH - 50E | BOT. GDNS - 53B |
| Aug-55 | STARBECK - 50D | 8/55: BRID - 53D | SCARBOROUGH - 50E | STARBECK - 50D | STARBECK - 50D | BOT. GDNS - 53B | STARBECK - 50D | SCARBOROUGH - 50E | BOT. GDNS - 53B |
| Jan-56 | 12/55: N.HILL - 50B | BRIDLINGTON - 53D | SCARBOROUGH - 50E | STARBECK - 50D | STARBECK - 50D | BOT. GDNS - 53B | STARBECK - 50D | SCARBOROUGH - 50E | BOT. GDNS - 53B |
| Aug-56 | NEVILLE HILL - 50B | BRIDLINGTON - 53D | SCARBOROUGH - 50E | STARBECK - 50D | STARBECK - 50D | BOT. GDNS - 53B | 6/56: N. HILL - 50B | SCARBOROUGH - 50E | BOT. GDNS - 53B |
| Jan-57 | NEVILLE HILL - 50B | BRIDLINGTON - 53D | SCARBOROUGH - 50E | STARBECK - 50D | STARBECK - 50D | BOT. GDNS - 53B | 10/56: SELBY - 50C | SCARBOROUGH - 50E | BOT. GDNS - 53B |
| Aug-57 | NEVILLE HILL - 50B | 9/57: B. GDNS - 53B | SCARBOROUGH - 50E | STARBECK - 50D | STARBECK - 50D | BOT. GDNS - 53B | SELBY - 50C | SCARBOROUGH - 50E | BOT. GDNS - 53B |
| Jan-58 | NEVILLE HILL - 50B | BOT. GDNS - 53B | SCARBOROUGH - 50E | STARBECK - 50D | STARBECK - 50D | BOT. GDNS - 53B | SELBY - 50C | SCARBOROUGH - 50E | 12/57 : W/D |
| Aug-58 | 7/58: W/D | BOT. GDNS - 53B | SCARBOROUGH - 50E | 7/58: W/D | STARBECK - 50D | BOT. GDNS - 53B | SELBY - 50C | 4/58: W/D | |
| Jan-59 | | 11/58: W/D | SCARBOROUGH - 50E | | STARBECK - 50D | 11/58: W/D | 11/58: W/D | | |
| Aug-59 | | | 3/59: W/D | | STARBECK - 50D | | | | |
| Nov-59 | | | | | 9/59: W/D | | | | |
| Jan-60 | | | | | | | | | |
| Apr-60 | | | | | | | | | |
| Aug-60 | | | | | | | | | |
| Nov-60 | | | | | | | | | |

| | 62758 | 62759 | 62760 | 62761 | 62762 | 62763 | 62764 | 62765 | 62766 |
|---|---|---|---|---|---|---|---|---|---|
| Aug-50 | STARBECK - 50D | YORK - 50A | YORK - 50A | YORK - 50A | STARBECK - 50D | STARBECK - 50D | SCARBOROUGH - 50E | STARBECK - 50D | BRIDLINGTON - 53D |
| Jan-51 | STARBECK - 50D | YORK - 50A | YORK - 50A | 10/50: STAR - 50D | STARBECK - 50D | STARBECK - 50D | SCARBOROUGH - 50E | STARBECK - 50D | BRIDLINGTON - 53D |
| Aug-51 | STARBECK - 50D | YORK - 50A | YORK - 50A | STARBECK - 50D | STARBECK - 50D | STARBECK - 50D | SCARBOROUGH - 50E | STARBECK - 50D | BRIDLINGTON - 53D |
| Jan-52 | STARBECK - 50D | YORK - 50A | YORK - 50A | STARBECK - 50D | STARBECK - 50D | STARBECK - 50D | SCARBOROUGH - 50E | STARBECK - 50D | BRIDLINGTON - 53D |
| Aug-52 | STARBECK - 50D | YORK - 50A | YORK - 50A | STARBECK - 50D | STARBECK - 50D | STARBECK - 50D | SCARBOROUGH - 50E | STARBECK - 50D | BRIDLINGTON - 53D |
| Jan-53 | STARBECK - 50D | YORK - 50A | YORK - 50A | STARBECK - 50D | STARBECK - 50D | STARBECK - 50D | SCARBOROUGH - 50E | STARBECK - 50D | BRIDLINGTON - 53D |
| Aug-53 | STARBECK - 50D | YORK - 50A | YORK - 50A | STARBECK - 50D | STARBECK - 50D | STARBECK - 50D | SCARBOROUGH - 50E | STARBECK - 50D | BRIDLINGTON - 53D |
| Jan-54 | STARBECK - 50D | YORK - 50A | YORK - 50A | STARBECK - 50D | STARBECK - 50D | STARBECK - 50D | SCARBOROUGH - 50E | STARBECK - 50D | BRIDLINGTON - 53D |
| Aug-54 | STARBECK - 50D | YORK - 50A | YORK - 50A | STARBECK - 50D | STARBECK - 50D | STARBECK - 50D | SCARBOROUGH - 50E | STARBECK - 50D | BRIDLINGTON - 53D |
| Jan-55 | STARBECK - 50D | 1/55: STAR - 50D | YORK - 50A | STARBECK - 50D | STARBECK - 50D | STARBECK - 50D | SCARBOROUGH - 50E | STARBECK - 50D | 1/55: B.GDNS - 53D |
| Aug-55 | STARBECK - 50D | STARBECK - 50D | YORK - 50A | STARBECK - 50D | STARBECK - 50D | STARBECK - 50D | SCARBOROUGH - 50E | STARBECK - 50D | 6/55: BRID - 53D |
| Jan-56 | STARBECK - 50D | STARBECK - 50D | YORK - 50A | STARBECK - 50D | STARBECK - 50D | STARBECK - 50D | SCARBOROUGH - 50E | STARBECK - 50D | BRIDLINGTON - 53D |
| Aug-56 | STARBECK - 50D | STARBECK - 50D | YORK - 50A | 7/56: N.HILL - 50B | STARBECK - 50D | STARBECK - 50D | SCARBOROUGH - 50E | STARBECK - 50D | 6/56: B. GDNS - 53B |
| Jan-57 | STARBECK - 50D | STARBECK - 50D | YORK - 50A | 10/56: SELBY - 50C | STARBECK - 50D | STARBECK - 50D | SCARBOROUGH - 50E | STARBECK - 50D | BOT. GDNS - 53B |
| Aug-57 | STARBECK - 50D | STARBECK - 50D | YORK - 50A | SELBY - 50C | STARBECK - 50D | STARBECK - 50D | SCARBOROUGH - 50E | STARBECK - 50D | BOT. GDNS - 53B |
| Jan-58 | 12/57: W/D | STARBECK - 50D | YORK - 50A | 12/57: W/D | STARBECK - 50D | STARBECK - 50D | SCARBOROUGH - 50E | STARBECK - 50D | BOT. GDNS - 53B |
| Aug-58 | | STARBECK - 50D | 6/58: BRID - 53B | | 6/58: SCAR - 50E | STARBECK - 50D | SCARBOROUGH - 50E | STARBECK - 50D | 9/58: W/D |
| Jan-59 | | STARBECK - 50D | BRIDLINGTON - 53B | | SCARBOROUGH - 50E | STARBECK - 50D | 11/58: W/D | STARBECK - 50D | |
| Aug-59 | | 9/59: DAIRY - 53A | 6/59: DAIRY - 53A | | SCARBOROUGH - 50E | 9/59: DAIRY - 53A | | 6/59: SELBY - 50B | |
| Nov-59 | | DAIRYCOATES - 53A | 10/59: W/D | | SCARBOROUGH - 50E | DAIRYCOATES - 53A | | 9/59: DAIRY - 53A | |
| Jan-60 | | DAIRYCOATES - 53A | | | SCARBOROUGH - 50E | DAIRYCOATES - 53A | | DAIRYCOATES - 53A | |
| Apr-60 | | DAIRYCOATES - 50B | | | SCARBOROUGH - 50E | DAIRYCOATES - 50B | | DAIRYCOATES - 50B | |
| Aug-60 | | DAIRYCOATES - 50B | | | SCARBOROUGH - 50E | DAIRYCOATES - 50B | | DAIRYCOATES - 50B | |
| Nov-60 | | DAIRYCOATES - 50B | | | 10/60: W/D | DAIRYCOATES - 50B | | DAIRYCOATES - 50B | |

Ask any Great Eastern engineman for his choice of engine and the answer was usually unhesitating : a Claud. The popularity of the class was more than fortuitous since whilst the influx of Britannia's and B1's had done a great deal for the main lines into London, little had been done for the dozens of secondary trains in north Norfolk and Cambridge; a situation that resulted in the D16 4-4-0's shouldering a high proportion of services in the rural areas of East Anglia until the arrival of diesel multiple units. Following the return of eight engines from Trafford Park in mid-1952, most of the class was based at sheds outside the London area of the Great Eastern, the exception being an M&GN allocation which, following the influx of LMS 2-6-0's declined from fifteen to seven between 1950 and 1957. 62596, one of the M&GN engines until being moved to Norwich in January 1954, stands on Yarmouth Beach shed in 1950.

Amongst the blessings bestowed by the restricted branches of East Anglia was the retention of the E4 2-4-0's which survived on the Colchester and Mildenhall branches until being displaced by diesel railbuses in the late 1950's. The class was well spoken of - some had worked on the Kirkby Stephen route from Darlington in LNER days - but any doubts as to their abilities on the main line were settled on a day in late 1955 when one of the class had to take over at short notice from an LMS 2MT 2-6-0 on the 16.55 Cambridge - Kettering. Having only a skeleton diagram which indicated that the engine stayed overnight at Kettering to return with the next day's 08.33 to Cambridge, there seemed no reason why 62786 should not cope. Unfortunately the Midland had interposed a trip to Leicester between the two Cambridge workings and the 2-4-0 found itself trying cope with five coaches over the very hilly Midland main line, losing twenty minutes to Leicester and a further forty minutes on the return trip which was via the Melton 'back road'. By the time the 2-4-0 found itself returning to Cambridge the fire was in such bad shape that a further hour and a half was lost when the crew threw the towel in at Kimbolton and called for a fresh engine.

**E4 2-4-0 (1891)** — class heading for 62780–62788

| | 62767 | 62768 | 62769 | 62770 | 62771 | 62772 | 62773 | 62774 | 62775 |
|---|---|---|---|---|---|---|---|---|---|
| Aug-50 | BOT.GDNS-53B | STARBECK-50D | SCARBOROUGH-50E | SCARBOROUGH-50E | BLAYDON-52C | STARBECK-50D | STARBECK-50D | PICKERING-50F | NEVILLE HILL-50B |
| Jan-51 | BOT.GDNS-53B | STARBECK-50D | SCARBOROUGH-50E | SCARBOROUGH-50E | BLAYDON-52C | STARBECK-50D | STARBECK-50D | PICKERING-50F | NEVILLE HILL-50B |
| Aug-51 | BOT.GDNS-53B | STARBECK-50D | SCARBOROUGH-50E | SCARBOROUGH-50E | BLAYDON-52C | STARBECK-50D | STARBECK-50D | 9/51: YORK-50A | NEVILLE HILL-50B |
| Jan-52 | BOT.GDNS-53B | STARBECK-50D | SCARBOROUGH-50E | SCARBOROUGH-50E | BLAYDON-52C | STARBECK-50D | STARBECK-50D | YORK-50A | NEVILLE HILL-50B |
| Aug-52 | BOT.GDNS-53B | STARBECK-50D | SCARBOROUGH-50E | SCARBOROUGH-50E | BLAYDON-52C | STARBECK-50D | STARBECK-50D | YORK-50A | NEVILLE HILL-50B |
| Jan-53 | BOT.GDNS-53B | 10/52: W/D | SCARBOROUGH-50E | SCARBOROUGH-50E | BLAYDON-52C | STARBECK-50D | STARBECK-50D | YORK-50A | NEVILLE HILL-50B |
| Aug-53 | BOT.GDNS-53B | | SCARBOROUGH-50E | SCARBOROUGH-50E | BLAYDON-52C | STARBECK-50D | STARBECK-50D | YORK-50A | NEVILLE HILL-50B |
| Jan-54 | BOT.GDNS-53B | | SCARBOROUGH-50E | SCARBOROUGH-50E | BLAYDON-52C | STARBECK-50D | STARBECK-50D | YORK-50A | NEVILLE HILL-50B |
| Aug-54 | BOT.GDNS-53B | | SCARBOROUGH-50E | SCARBOROUGH-50E | BLAYDON-52C | STARBECK-50D | STARBECK-50D | YORK-50A | NEVILLE HILL-50B |
| Jan-55 | BOT.GDNS-53B | | SCARBOROUGH-50E | SCARBOROUGH-50E | BLAYDON-52C | STARBECK-50D | STARBECK-50D | 1/55: STAR-50D | NEVILLE HILL-50B |
| Aug-55 | BOT.GDNS-53B | | SCARBOROUGH-50E | SCARBOROUGH-50E | BLAYDON-52C | STARBECK-50D | STARBECK-50D | STARBECK-50D | NEVILLE HILL-50B |
| Jan-56 | BOT.GDNS-53B | | SCARBOROUGH-50E | SCARBOROUGH-50E | BLAYDON-52C | STARBECK-50D | STARBECK-50D | STARBECK-50D | NEVILLE HILL-50B |
| Aug-56 | BOT.GDNS-53B | | SCARBOROUGH-50E | SCARBOROUGH-50E | 6/56: YORK-50A | STARBECK-50D | STARBECK-50D | STARBECK-50D | NEVILLE HILL-50B |
| Jan-57 | BOT.GDNS-53B | | SCARBOROUGH-50E | SCARBOROUGH-50E | YORK-50A | 10/56: SELBY-50C | STARBECK-50D | STARBECK-50D | 10/56: SELBY-50C |
| Aug-57 | BOT.GDNS-53B | | SCARBOROUGH-50E | SCARBOROUGH-50E | YORK-50A | SELBY-50C | 6/57: N.HILL-50B | 6/57: N.HILL-50B | SELBY-50C |
| Jan-58 | BOT.GDNS-53B | | SCARBOROUGH-50E | SCARBOROUGH-50E | YORK-50A | SELBY-50C | NEVILLE HILL-50B | NEVILLE HILL-50B | SELBY-50C |
| Aug-58 | BOT.GDNS-53B | | SCARBOROUGH-50E | SCARBOROUGH-50E | YORK-50A | SELBY-50C | 8/58: W/D | NEVILLE HILL-50B | SELBY-50C |
| Jan-59 | 10/58: W/D | | 9/58: W/D | SCARBOROUGH-50E | 10/58: W/D | 9/58: W/D | | 11/58: W/D | 12/58: W/D |
| Aug-59 | | | | 6/59: SELBY-50C | | | | | |
| Nov-59 | | | | 9/59: W/D | | | | | |
| Jan-60 | | | | | | | | | |
| Apr-60 | | | | | | | | | |
| Aug-60 | | | | | | | | | |
| Nov-60 | | | | | | | | | |

**E4 2-4-0 (1891)**

| | 62780 | 62781 | 62782 | 62783 | 62784 | 62785 | 62786 | 62787 | 62788 |
|---|---|---|---|---|---|---|---|---|---|
| Aug-50 | NORWICH-32A | CAMBRIDGE-31A | NORWICH-32A | CAMBRIDGE-31A | CAMBRIDGE-31A | CAMBRIDGE-31A | BURY St.E-31E | NORWICH-32A | CAMBRIDGE-31A |
| Jan-51 | NORWICH-32A | CAMBRIDGE-31A | NORWICH-32A | CAMBRIDGE-31A | CAMBRIDGE-31A | CAMBRIDGE-31A | BURY St.E-31E | NORWICH-32A | CAMBRIDGE-31A |
| Aug-51 | 9/51: CAMB-31A | CAMBRIDGE-31A | NORWICH-32A | CAMBRIDGE-31A | CAMBRIDGE-31A | CAMBRIDGE-31A | BURY St.E-31E | NORWICH-32A | 9/51: NOR-32A |
| Jan-52 | CAMBRIDGE-31A | CAMBRIDGE-31A | NORWICH-32A | CAMBRIDGE-31A | CAMBRIDGE-31A | CAMBRIDGE-31A | 3/52: CAMB-31A | NORWICH-32A | NORWICH-32A |
| Aug-52 | CAMBRIDGE-31A | CAMBRIDGE-31A | NORWICH-32A | 7/52: BURY-31E | CAMBRIDGE-31A | CAMBRIDGE-31A | CAMBRIDGE-31A | NORWICH-32A | NORWICH-32A |
| Jan-53 | CAMBRIDGE-31A | CAMBRIDGE-31A | NORWICH-32A | BURY STEDMUNDS-31E | CAMBRIDGE-31A | CAMBRIDGE-31A | CAMBRIDGE-31A | NORWICH-32A | NORWICH-32A |
| Aug-53 | CAMBRIDGE-31A | CAMBRIDGE-31A | NORWICH-32A | 5/53: CAMB-31A | CAMBRIDGE-31A | CAMBRIDGE-31A | CAMBRIDGE-31A | NORWICH-32A | NORWICH-32A |
| Jan-54 | CAMBRIDGE-31A | CAMBRIDGE-31A | NORWICH-32A | CAMBRIDGE-31A | CAMBRIDGE-31A | CAMBRIDGE-31A | CAMBRIDGE-31A | NORWICH-32A | NORWICH-32A |
| Aug-54 | CAMBRIDGE-31A | CAMBRIDGE-31A | NORWICH-32A | CAMBRIDGE-31A | CAMBRIDGE-31A | CAMBRIDGE-31A | CAMBRIDGE-31A | NORWICH-32A | NORWICH-32A |
| Jan-55 | CAMBRIDGE-31A | CAMBRIDGE-31A | 11/54: W/D | 12/54: W/D | CAMBRIDGE-31A | 12/54: HIT-34D | CAMBRIDGE-31A | NORWICH-32A | NORWICH-32A |
| Aug-55 | CAMBRIDGE-31A | CAMBRIDGE-31A | | | 5/55: W/D | HITCHIN-34D | CAMBRIDGE-31A | NORWICH-32A | NORWICH-32A |
| Jan-56 | 9/55: W/D | 1/56: W/D | | | | HITCHIN-34D | CAMBRIDGE-31A | NORWICH-32A | NORWICH-32A |
| Aug-56 | | | | | | HITCHIN-34D | 7/56: W/D | 8/56: CAMB-31A | 7/56: CAMB-31A |
| Jan-57 | | | | | | HITCHIN-34D | | 11/56: W/D | CAMBRIDGE-31A |
| Aug-57 | | | | | | 5/57: CAMB-31A | | | CAMBRIDGE-31A |
| Jan-58 | | | | | | CAMBRIDGE-31A | | | 3/58: W/D |
| Aug-58 | | | | | | CAMBRIDGE-31A | | | |
| Jan-59 | | | | | | CAMBRIDGE-31A | | | |
| Aug-59 | | | | | | CAMBRIDGE-31A | | | |
| Nov-59 | | | | | | | | | |
| Jan-60 | | | | | | 12/59: W/D | | | |
| Apr-60 | | | | | | | | | |
| Aug-60 | | | | | | | | | |
| Nov-60 | | | | | | | | | |

| | 62789 | 62790 | 62791 | 62792 | 62793 | 62794 | 62795 | 62796 | 62797 |
|---|---|---|---|---|---|---|---|---|---|
| Aug-50 | NORWICH-32A | CAMBRIDGE-31A | STRATFORD-30A | NORWICH-32A | NORWICH-32A | CAMBRIDGE-31A | BURY St.E-31E | NORWICH-32A | NORWICH-32A |
| Jan-51 | NORWICH-32A | 11/50: K.LYNN-31C | STRATFORD-30A | NORWICH-32A | NORWICH-32A | CAMBRIDGE-31A | BURY St.E-31E | NORWICH-32A | NORWICH-32A |
| Aug-51 | NORWICH-32A | KINGS LYNN-31C | 3/51: COL-30E | NORWICH-32A | NORWICH-32A | CAMBRIDGE-31A | 9/51: CAMB-31A | NORWICH-32A | NORWICH-32A |
| Jan-52 | NORWICH-32A | KINGS LYNN-31C | COLCHESTER-30E | NORWICH-32A | NORWICH-32A | 3/52: BURY-31E | 3/52: BURY-31E | NORWICH-32A | NORWICH-32A |
| Aug-52 | NORWICH-32A | 7/52: CAMB-31A | 11/52: CAMB-31A | NORWICH-32A | NORWICH-32A | 6/52: CAMB-31A | CAMBRIDGE-31A | NORWICH-32A | NORWICH-32A |
| Jan-53 | NORWICH-32A | CAMBRIDGE-31A | 5/53: BURY-31E | NORWICH-32A | NORWICH-32A | CAMBRIDGE-31A | CAMBRIDGE-31A | NORWICH-32A | NORWICH-32A |
| Aug-53 | NORWICH-32A | CAMBRIDGE-31A | 7/53: CAMB-31A | NORWICH-32A | NORWICH-32A | CAMBRIDGE-31A | CAMBRIDGE-31A | NORWICH-32A | NORWICH-32A |
| Jan-54 | NORWICH-32A | CAMBRIDGE-31A | CAMBRIDGE-31A | NORWICH-32A | NORWICH-32A | CAMBRIDGE-31A | CAMBRIDGE-31A | NORWICH-32A | NORWICH-32A |
| Aug-54 | NORWICH-32A | CAMBRIDGE-31A | CAMBRIDGE-31A | NORWICH-32A | NORWICH-32A | CAMBRIDGE-31A | CAMBRIDGE-31A | NORWICH-32A | 6/54: LOW-32C |
| Jan-55 | NORWICH-32A | CAMBRIDGE-31A | CAMBRIDGE-31A | NORWICH-32A | NORWICH-32A | CAMBRIDGE-31A | CAMBRIDGE-31A | NORWICH-32A | LOWESTOFT-32C |
| Aug-55 | NORWICH-32A | CAMBRIDGE-31A | 4/55: W/D | 8/55: CAMB-31A | 2/55: W/D | 8/55: W/D | 3/55: W/D | 8/55: CAMB-31A | LOWESTOFT-32C |
| Jan-56 | NORWICH-32A | 1/56: W/D | | CAMBRIDGE-31A | | | | CAMBRIDGE-31A | LOWESTOFT-32C |
| Aug-56 | 8/56: CAMB-31A | | | 6/56: W/D | | | | CAMBRIDGE-31A | LOWESTOFT-32C |
| Jan-57 | CAMBRIDGE-31A | | | | | | | CAMBRIDGE-31A | LOWESTOFT-32C |
| Aug-57 | CAMBRIDGE-31A | | | | | | | 5/57: W/D | 6/57: CAMB-31A |
| Jan-58 | 12/57: W/D | | | | | | | | 3/58: W/D |
| Aug-58 | | | | | | | | | |
| Jan-59 | | | | | | | | | |
| Aug-59 | | | | | | | | | |
| Nov-59 | | | | | | | | | |
| Jan-60 | | | | | | | | | |
| Apr-60 | | | | | | | | | |
| Aug-60 | | | | | | | | | |
| Nov-60 | | | | | | | | | |

**C1 4-4-2 (1902)**: 62822 — **C4 4-4-2 (1902)**: 62900, 62901, 62908, 62909, 62918, 62919 — **Q4 0-8-0 (1902)**: 63201, 63202

| | 62822 | 62900 | 62901 | 62908 | 62909 | 62918 | 62919 | 63201 | 63202 |
|---|---|---|---|---|---|---|---|---|---|
| Aug-50 | GRANTHAM-35B | BOSTON-40F | BOSTON-40F | LINCOLN-40A | IMMINGHAM-40B | LINCOLN-40A | IMMINGHAM-40B | BARNSLEY-36D | ARDSLEY-37A |
| Jan-51 | 11/50: W/D | 11/50: W/D | 11/50: W/D | 11/50: W/D | 11/50: W/D | 12/50: W/D | 11/50: W/D | 1/51: W/D | ARDSLEY-37A |
| Aug-51 | | | | | | | | | ARDSLEY-37A |
| Jan-52 | | | | | | | | | 9/51: W/D |
| Aug-52 | | | | | | | | | |
| Jan-53 | | | | | | | | | |

The object of the **Gresley Society** is to promote interest in the work of Sir Nigel Gresley and pursues this aim through a regular programme of meetings, preservation work and its quarterly journal, **The Gresley Observer**: a 68 page illustrated magazine devoted to matters LNER and packed with articles by those who worked with Gresley locomotives and by those who either remember them or have an interest in them..

**Contact Dr Geoffrey Hughes, 5 Whitby Court, Maryland Gardens, Milford on Sea, Hants. SO41 0WB**
**(01590 - 645369)**

| | 63203 | 63204 | 63205 | 63217 | 63220 | 63221 | 63223 | 63225 | 63226 |
|---|---|---|---|---|---|---|---|---|---|
| Aug-50 | BARNSLEY - 36D | ARDSLEY - 37A | ARDSLEY - 37A | ARDSLEY - 37A | BARNSLEY - 36D | ARDSLEY - 37A | ARDSLEY - 37A | ARDSLEY - 37A | ARDSLEY - 37A |
| Jan-51 | 11/50: W/D | ARDSLEY - 37A | 12/50: W/D | ARDSLEY - 37A | BARNSLEY - 36D | 12/50: W/D | ARDSLEY - 37A | ARDSLEY - 37A | 10/50: W/D |
| Aug-51 | | 6/51: W/D | WD | 3/51: W/D | 3/51: W/D | | 6/51: W/D | ARDSLEY - 37A | |
| Jan-52 | | | | | | | | 9/51: W/D | |

| | | | | | | | Q5 0-8-0 ( 1901 ) | | |
|---|---|---|---|---|---|---|---|---|---|
| | 63227 | 63229 | 63234 | 63235 | 63236 | 63240 | 63243 | 63251 | 63257 |
| Aug-50 | ARDSLEY - 37A | BARNSLEY - 36D | ARDSLEY - 37A | BARNSLEY - 36D | ARDSLEY - 37A | ARDSLEY - 37A | ARDSLEY - 37A | BOROUGH GARDENS - 54C | BOROUGH GARDENS - 54C |
| Jan-51 | ARDSLEY - 37A | 12/50: W/D | ARDSLEY - 37A | BARNSLEY - 36D | ARDSLEY - 37A | ARDSLEY - 37A | ARDSLEY - 37A | 12/50: W/D | 11/50: W/D |
| Aug-51 | 5/51: W/D | | 3/51: W/D | 5/51: W/D | 5/51: W/D | 6/51: W/D | ARDSLEY - 37A | | |
| Jan-52 | | | | | | | 9/51: W/D | | |

| | 63259 | 63261 | 63267 | 63270 | 63271 | 63274 | 63280 | 63282 | 63283 |
|---|---|---|---|---|---|---|---|---|---|
| Aug-50 | BOROUGH GARDENS - 54C | BOROUGH GARDENS - 54C | BOROUGH GARDENS - 54C | YORK - 50A | BOROUGH GARDENS - 54C | NEWPORT - 51B | SELBY - 50C | MIDDLESBROUGH - 51D | MIDDLESBROUGH - 51D |
| Jan-51 | BOROUGH GARDENS - 54C | 10/50: W/D | BOROUGH GARDENS - 54C | 1/51: MALT - 50F | 11/50: W/D | 9/50: W/D | 10/50: W.D | 12/50: W/D | 12/50: W/D |
| Aug-51 | 5/51: W/D | | 6/51: W/D | 3/51: YORK - 50A | | | | | |
| Jan-52 | | | | 8/51: W/D | | | | | |

| | 63284 | 63285 | 63287 | 63303 | 63311 | 63314 | 63319 | 63326 | 63328 |
|---|---|---|---|---|---|---|---|---|---|
| Aug-50 | BOROUGH GARDENS - 54C | SELBY - 50C | BOROUGH GARDENS - 54C | BOROUGH GARDENS - 54C | HAVERTON HILL - 51G | HAVERTON HILL - 51G | SELBY - 50C | BOROUGH GARDENS - 54C | MIDDLESBROUGH - 51D |
| Jan-51 | BOROUGH GARDENS - 54C | 9/50: W/D | 8/50: W/D | BOROUGH GARDENS - 54C | HAVERTON HILL - 51G | HAVERTON HILL - 51G | SELBY - 50C | BOROUGH GARDENS - 54C | 1/51: W/D |
| Aug-51 | 6/51: W/D | | | 4/51: W/D | HAVERTON HILL - 51G | HAVERTON HILL - 51G | 4/51: W/D | BOROUGH GARDENS - 54C | |
| Jan-52 | | | | | 9/51: W/D | 9/51: W/D | | 10/51: W/D | |

A comparative league table of the more important – i.e. revenue generating – areas of the region can be compiled in several ways although basing assessments on eight-coupled engines is probably as good as any since it shows where the mineral activity was at its height and, in doing so, brings to the fore several locations that might not otherwise suggest themselves as centres of special importance.

In passenger terms Nottingham was more closely associated with the Great Central than the Great Northern yet the greatest volume of large mineral engines was to be found at Colwick, partly to work the many GN colliery trips in the district but also to operate the very heavy flow of coal traffic to New England and Whitemoor. Associated with this movement were the allocations at March and New England whose engines and crews worked the traffic forward to Temple Mills and Ferme Park respectively. It will be noted from the adjacent table that neither Stratford or Ferme Park took much of an interest in the working of this traffic; their concern lying with the continuation across London or to local destinations.

Much of the Nottingham (GN) business was concerned with originating trade and most of the through traffic – together with a good deal of coal from local pits – was conducted by the adjacent Great Central with its allocation of over fifty eight coupled locomotives at Annesley. In spite of the grouping GN and GC activities continued to operate as formerly: Colwick being the focal point of GN operations with Annesley having a similar role for the GC.

The Great Central may have had rather a miserable passenger timetable but its importance in terms of mineral traffic is difficult to overstate and can be demonstrated by the fact that its allocation of heavy goods locomotives was greater than that of the GN, GE and NBR districts combined. (Its competitive position in respect to the LMR is usually sited as the reason for the paucity of express trains to and from Marylebone. In actual fact the volume of goods traffic was of such density that there was virtually no capacity on the system available for additional passenger workings).

Annesley and the Nottingham coalfield was, however, only one element in the Great Central's mineral programme and the greatest activity was to be seen on the Sheffield – Doncaster – Cleethorpes section which was allocated in excess of one hundred 2-8-0's at Immingham and Frodingham together with a further seventy at Mexborough. Added to this total was a proportion of the sixty locomotives based at Doncaster.

Not shown in the distribution table is the importance of Gorton which prior to electrification had over fifty eight-couple engines (and, for its fitted goods services, twenty K3 2-6-0's). The introduction of electric locomotives between Wath and Mottram saw Gorton's allocation reduced by almost thirty 2-8-0's with twenty also being transferred away from Mexborough. Since many of the services from Sheffield and Wath contained through loads for destinations west of Mottram, Gorton retained about thirty O4 2-8-0's with which took over from electric power at either Mottram or Ashbury's.

Until the opening of Thornaby shed in 1958, the North Eastern had tended to spread its mineral fleet fairly broadly over the system, the only large allocations being held by Newport and Tyne Dock. There were two areas of concentration, one being the Tees/Wear area which had over one hundred and sixty eight-coupled engines divided between nine sheds; the other being Hull where nearly fifty Austerities were more or less evenly split between the North Eastern and the Hull & Barnsley workings. Tyneside was relatively quiet with about forty-five engines dispersed amongst four sheds whilst York, Harrogate and Leeds, where mineral activity was low, could barely muster ten eight coupled locomotives between them. The coal that the North Eastern did move from the West Ridings area centred upon Gascoigne Wood, Selby, where fifteen engines were based for local trip workings and services to and from Hull.

In contrast to the Great Northern and Great Central, the North Eastern was bounded to the north and south by coal producing areas which meant that most of the local output had to be used locally. The result was a rather self contained system in which mineral trains worked direct from the pit to the consumer. (The coal traffic that did move from the North East to the south of England generally did so by sea, the railway playing no greater part than tripping it to the port of embarkation).

The North British was similarly self contained with the bulk of the Fife output being consumed in the Clyde and Firth Valley although residual tonnages were worked to the North West of England, principally via the Caledonian. The volume of coal mined more than warranted a sizeable fleet of eight coupled engines but because of line restrictions on large engines, which would have filled a small book, 0-6-0's were preferred because of their wider availability and only about forty Austerities were allocated to the section; the majority being based at Thornton Junction, Dundee and Dunfermline.

The influence of the Austerity 2-8-0's was at its greatest on the ex LNER where in some parts they (and the 9F 2-10-0's which followed then) completely ousted older locomotives. On the GN main line south of Peterborough for example almost all mineral traffic was in the hands of WD 2-8-0's and 9F 'Spaceships'. The only area not to have modernised its mineral fleet to anybgreat extent was the North Eastern whose Q6 0-8-0's remained at large until the last days of steam.

| DISTRIBUTION OF HEAVY FREIGHT LOCOMOTIVES : 1957 | | | | | | | | | | | | | | | | | | | | |
|---|---|---|---|---|---|---|---|---|---|---|---|---|---|---|---|---|---|---|---|---|
| | O1 | O2 | O4 | Q1 | Q6 | Q7 | T1 | WD | 9F | Total | | O1 | O2 | O4 | Q1 | Q6 | Q7 | T1 | WD | 9F | Total |
| Colwick | | | 18 | | | | | 60 | | 78 | W. Hartlepool | | | | | 12 | | 5 | | | 17 |
| Mexborough | 1 | | 38 | | | | | 30 | | 69 | Selby | | 2 | 12 | 1 | | | | | | 15 |
| Doncaster | | 35 | 5 | | | | | 3 | 17 | 60 | Grantham | 14 | | | | | | | | | 14 |
| Frodingham | | | 28 | 6 | | | | 21 | | 55 | Consett | | | | | 11 | 1 | | | | 12 |
| Annesley | 53 | | 2 | | | | | | | 55 | Haverton Hill | | | | | 11 | | | | | 11 |
| New England | | | | | | | | 36 | 15 | 51 | Ardsley | | 10 | | | | | | | | 10 |
| Newport | | | | | 9 | | 2 | 37 | | 48 | Stockton | | | | | | 2 | 7 | | | 9 |
| Langwith Jcn | | | 25 | 2 | | | | 18 | | 45 | Dunfermline | | | | | | | 8 | | | 8 |
| Immingham | | | 27 | | | | | 18 | | 45 | N. Blyth | | | | | 6 | | | | | 6 |
| March | | | | | | | | 38 | 5 | 43 | Dundee | | | | | | | 6 | | | 6 |
| Darnall | | | 38 | | | | | | | 38 | Neville Hill | | | 2 | | | | 3 | | | 5 |
| Tyne Dock | 5 | | | | 6 | 5 | 1 | 6 | 10 | 33 | Darlington | | | | | | | 5 | | | 5 |
| Retford | | 17 | 10 | | | | | | | 27 | Stratford | | | | | | | 4 | | | 4 |
| Gorton | | | 26 | | | | | | | 26 | Plaistow | | | | | | | 4 | | | 4 |
| Woodford | | | | | | | | 25 | | 25 | Sunderland | | | | | 3 | | | | | 3 |
| Staveley | | | 18 | | | | | 5 | | 23 | York | | | | | | 3 | | | | 3 |
| Dairycoates | | | | | | | | 23 | | 23 | Dawsholme | | | | | | | 3 | | | 3 |
| Springhead | | | | | | | | 21 | | 21 | Ferryhill | | | | | | | 3 | | | 3 |
| Middlesbrough | | | | | 21 | | | | | 21 | Starbeck | | | | | | | 2 | | | 2 |
| Barnsley | | | 19 | | | | | | | 19 | W. Auckland | | | | | 2 | | | | | 2 |
| Blaydon | | | | | 11 | 7 | | | | 18 | Eastfield | | | | | | | 2 | | | 2 |
| Thornton Jcn | | | | | | | | 18 | | 18 | Bradford | | 1 | | | | | | | | 1 |
| Borough G. | | | 17 | | | | | | | 17 | Grangemouth | | | | | | | 1 | | | 1 |
| | | | | | | | | | | GC : 382, NER : 271, GN : 259 : GE/LTSR : 51, NB : 41 | | | | | | | | | | |

| | | | Q6 0-8-0 (1913) | | | | | | |
|---|---|---|---|---|---|---|---|---|---|
| | 63333 | 63336 | 63340 | 63341 | 63342 | 63343 | 63344 | 63345 | 63346 |
| Aug-50 | MIDDLESBROUGH-51D | SELBY-50C | HAVERTONHILL-51G | NEWPORT-51B | BOR.GDNS-54C | NEWPORT-51B | NEWPORT-51B | NEWPORT-51B | CONSETT-54D |
| Jan-51 | **12/50: W/D** | **10/50: W/D** | 1/51: MBRO-51D | NEWPORT-51B | BOR.GDNS-54C | NEWPORT-51B | NEWPORT-51B | NEWPORT-51B | CONSETT-54D |
| Aug-51 | | | MIDDLESBROUGH-51D | NEWPORT-51B | BOR.GDNS-54C | NEWPORT-51B | NEWPORT-51B | NEWPORT-51B | CONSETT-54D |
| Jan-52 | | | MIDDLESBROUGH-51D | NEWPORT-51B | BOR.GDNS-54C | NEWPORT-51B | NEWPORT-51B | NEWPORT-51B | CONSETT-54D |
| Aug-52 | | | MIDDLESBROUGH-51D | NEWPORT-51B | BOR.GDNS-54C | NEWPORT-51B | NEWPORT-51B | NEWPORT-51B | CONSETT-54D |
| Jan-53 | | | MIDDLESBROUGH-51D | NEWPORT-51B | BOR.GDNS-54C | NEWPORT-51B | NEWPORT-51B | NEWPORT-51B | CONSETT-54D |
| Aug-53 | | | MIDDLESBROUGH-51D | NEWPORT-51B | BOR.GDNS-54C | NEWPORT-51B | NEWPORT-51B | NEWPORT-51B | CONSETT-54D |
| Jan-54 | | | MIDDLESBROUGH-51D | NEWPORT-51B | BOR.GDNS-54C | NEWPORT-51B | NEWPORT-51B | NEWPORT-51B | CONSETT-54D |
| Aug-54 | | | MIDDLESBROUGH-51D | NEWPORT-51B | BOR.GDNS-54C | NEWPORT-51B | NEWPORT-51B | NEWPORT-51B | CONSETT-54D |
| Jan-55 | | | MIDDLESBROUGH-51D | NEWPORT-51B | BOR.GDNS-54C | NEWPORT-51B | NEWPORT-51B | NEWPORT-51B | CONSETT-54D |
| Aug-55 | | | MIDDLESBROUGH-51D | NEWPORT-51B | BOR.GDNS-54C | NEWPORT-51B | NEWPORT-51B | NEWPORT-51B | CONSETT-54D |
| Jan-56 | | | MIDDLESBROUGH-51D | NEWPORT-51B | BOR.GDNS-54C | NEWPORT-51B | NEWPORT-51B | NEWPORT-51B | CONSETT-54D |
| Aug-56 | | | MIDDLESBROUGH-51D | **6/56: H.HILL-51G** | BOR.GDNS-54C | **6/56: H.HILL-51G** | **6/56: H.HILL-51G** | **6/56: H.HILL-51G** | **6/56: B.GDNS-54C** |
| Jan-57 | | | MIDDLESBROUGH-51D | HAVERTONHILL-51G | BOR.GDNS-54C | HAVERTONHILL-51G | HAVERTONHILL-51G | HAVERTONHILL-51G | BOR.GDNS-54C |
| Aug-57 | | | MIDDLESBROUGH-51D | HAVERTONHILL-51G | BOR.GDNS-54C | HAVERTONHILL-51G | HAVERTONHILL-51G | HAVERTONHILL-51G | BOR.GDNS-54C |
| Jan-58 | | | MIDDLESBROUGH-51D | HAVERTONHILL-51G | BOR.GDNS-54C | HAVERTONHILL-51G | HAVERTONHILL-51G | HAVERTONHILL-51G | BOR.GDNS-54C |
| Aug-58 | | | **10/58: W.AUCK-51F** | HAVERTONHILL-51G | BOR.GDNS-54C | HAVERTONHILL-51G | HAVERTONHILL-51G | HAVERTONHILL-51G | BOR.GDNS-54C |
| Jan-59 | | | W.AUCKLAND-51F | HAVERTONHILL-51G | BOR.GDNS-52J | HAVERTONHILL-51G | HAVERTONHILL-51G | **2/59: CON-52K** | BOR.GDNS-52J |
| Aug-59 | | | W.AUCKLAND-51F | **6/59: TNBY-51L** | **6/59: CON-52K** | **6/59: TNBY-51L** | **6/59: TNBY-51L** | CONSETT-52K | **6/59: CON-52K** |
| Nov-59 | | | W.AUCKLAND-51F | THORNABY-51L | CONSETT-52K | THORNABY-51L | THORNABY-51L | CONSETT-52K | CONSETT-52K |
| Jan-60 | | | W.AUCKLAND-51F | THORNABY-51L | CONSETT-52K | THORNABY-51L | THORNABY-51L | CONSETT-52K | CONSETT-52K |
| Apr-60 | | | W.AUCKLAND-51F | THORNABY-51L | CONSETT-52K | THORNABY-51L | THORNABY-51L | CONSETT-52K | CONSETT-52K |
| Aug-60 | | | W.AUCKLAND-51F | THORNABY-51L | CONSETT-52K | THORNABY-51L | THORNABY-51L | CONSETT-52K | CONSETT-52K |
| Nov-60 | | | W.AUCKLAND-51F | THORNABY-51L | CONSETT-52K | THORNABY-51L | THORNABY-51L | CONSETT-52K | CONSETT-52K |

| | 63347 | 63348 | 63349 | 63350 | 63351 | 63352 | 63353 | 63354 | 63355 |
|---|---|---|---|---|---|---|---|---|---|
| Aug-50 | NEWPORT-51B | SELBY-50C | MIDDLESBROUGH-51D | BOR.GDNS-54C | MIDDLESBROUGH-51D | TYNE DOCK-54B | BLAYDON-52C | BOR.GDNS-54C | W.HARTLEPOOL-51C |
| Jan-51 | NEWPORT-51B | SELBY-50C | MIDDLESBROUGH-51D | BOR.GDNS-54C | MIDDLESBROUGH-51D | TYNE DOCK-54B | BLAYDON-52C | BOR.GDNS-54C | W.HARTLEPOOL-51C |
| Aug-51 | NEWPORT-51B | SELBY-50C | MIDDLESBROUGH-51D | BOR.GDNS-54C | MIDDLESBROUGH-51D | TYNE DOCK-54B | BLAYDON-52C | BOR.GDNS-54C | W.HARTLEPOOL-51C |
| Jan-52 | NEWPORT-51B | SELBY-50C | MIDDLESBROUGH-51D | BOR.GDNS-54C | MIDDLESBROUGH-51D | TYNE DOCK-54B | BLAYDON-52C | BOR.GDNS-54C | W.HARTLEPOOL-51C |
| Aug-52 | NEWPORT-51B | SELBY-50C | MIDDLESBROUGH-51D | BOR.GDNS-54C | MIDDLESBROUGH-51D | TYNE DOCK-54B | BLAYDON-52C | BOR.GDNS-54C | **10/52: MBRO-51D** |
| Jan-53 | NEWPORT-51B | **2/53: N.HILL-50B** | MIDDLESBROUGH-51D | BOR.GDNS-54C | MIDDLESBROUGH-51D | TYNE DOCK-54B | BLAYDON-52C | BOR.GDNS-54C | MIDDLESBROUGH-51D |
| Aug-53 | NEWPORT-51B | NEVILLE HILL-50B | MIDDLESBROUGH-51D | BOR.GDNS-54C | MIDDLESBROUGH-51D | TYNE DOCK-54B | BLAYDON-52C | BOR.GDNS-54C | MIDDLESBROUGH-51D |
| Jan-54 | NEWPORT-51B | NEVILLE HILL-50B | MIDDLESBROUGH-51D | BOR.GDNS-54C | MIDDLESBROUGH-51D | TYNE DOCK-54B | BLAYDON-52C | BOR.GDNS-54C | MIDDLESBROUGH-51D |
| Aug-54 | NEWPORT-51B | NEVILLE HILL-50B | MIDDLESBROUGH-51D | BOR.GDNS-54C | **9/54: W.AUCK-51F** | TYNE DOCK-54B | BLAYDON-52C | BOR.GDNS-54C | MIDDLESBROUGH-51D |
| Jan-55 | NEWPORT-51B | NEVILLE HILL-50B | MIDDLESBROUGH-51D | BOR.GDNS-54C | W.AUCKLAND-51F | TYNE DOCK-54B | BLAYDON-52C | BOR.GDNS-54C | **4/55: KY ST-51H** |
| Aug-55 | NEWPORT-51B | NEVILLE HILL-50B | MIDDLESBROUGH-51D | BOR.GDNS-54C | W.AUCKLAND-51F | TYNE DOCK-54B | BLAYDON-52C | BOR.GDNS-54C | **6/55: MBRO-51D** |
| Jan-56 | NEWPORT-51B | NEVILLE HILL-50B | MIDDLESBROUGH-51D | BOR.GDNS-54C | W.AUCKLAND-51F | TYNE DOCK-54B | BLAYDON-52C | BOR.GDNS-54C | MIDDLESBROUGH-51D |
| Aug-56 | **6/56: H.HILL-51G** | NEVILLE HILL-50B | MIDDLESBROUGH-51D | BOR.GDNS-54C | W.AUCKLAND-51F | TYNE DOCK-54B | **7/56: N.BLYTH-52F** | BOR.GDNS-54C | MIDDLESBROUGH-51D |
| Jan-57 | HAVERTONHILL-51G | NEVILLE HILL-50B | MIDDLESBROUGH-51D | BOR.GDNS-54C | W.AUCKLAND-51F | TYNE DOCK-54B | NORTH BLYTH-52F | BOR.GDNS-54C | MIDDLESBROUGH-51D |
| Aug-57 | HAVERTONHILL-51G | **6/57: SELBY-50C** | MIDDLESBROUGH-51D | BOR.GDNS-54C | W.AUCKLAND-51F | TYNE DOCK-54B | **10/57: NWPT-51B** | BOR.GDNS-54C | MIDDLESBROUGH-51D |
| Jan-58 | HAVERTONHILL-51G | SELBY-50C | MIDDLESBROUGH-51D | BOR.GDNS-54C | W.AUCKLAND-51F | TYNE DOCK-54B | NEWPORT-51B | BOR.GDNS-54C | MIDDLESBROUGH-51D |
| Aug-58 | HAVERTONHILL-51G | SELBY-50C | **6/58: TNBY-51L** | BOR.GDNS-54C | W.AUCKLAND-51F | TYNE DOCK-54B | **6/58: W/AUCK-51F** | BOR.GDNS-54C | **6/58: TNBY-51L** |
| Jan-59 | HAVERTONHILL-51G | SELBY-50C | THORNABY-51L | BOR.GDNS-52J | W.AUCKLAND-51F | **2/59: BLAY-52C** | W.AUCKLAND-51F | BOR.GDNS-52J | THORNABY-51L |
| Aug-59 | **6/59: TNBY-51L** | **9/59: YORK-50A** | THORNABY-51L | **6/59: T.DCK-52H** | W.AUCKLAND-51F | BLAYDON-52C | W.AUCKLAND-51F | **6/59: T.DCK-52H** | THORNABY-51L |
| Nov-59 | THORNABY-51L | **12/59: N.HILL-50B** | THORNABY-51L | TYNE DOCK-52H | W.AUCKLAND-51F | BLAYDON-52C | W.AUCKLAND-51F | **12/59: CON-52K** | THORNABY-51L |
| Jan-60 | THORNABY-51L | NEVILLE HILL-50B | THORNABY-51L | TYNE DOCK-52H | W.AUCKLAND-51F | BLAYDON-52C | W.AUCKLAND-51F | CONSETT-52K | THORNABY-51L |
| Apr-60 | THORNABY-51L | NEVILLE HILL-55H | THORNABY-51L | TYNE DOCK-52H | W.AUCKLAND-51F | BLAYDON-52C | W.AUCKLAND-51F | CONSETT-52K | THORNABY-51L |
| Aug-60 | THORNABY-51L | NEVILLE HILL-55H | THORNABY-51L | TYNE DOCK-52H | W.AUCKLAND-51F | BLAYDON-52C | W.AUCKLAND-51F | CONSETT-52K | THORNABY-51L |
| Nov-60 | THORNABY-51L | NEVILLE HILL-55H | THORNABY-51L | TYNE DOCK-52H | W.AUCKLAND-51F | BLAYDON-52C | W.AUCKLAND-51F | CONSETT-52K | THORNABY-51L |

| | 63356 | 63357 | 63358 | 63359 | 63360 | 63361 | 63362 | 63363 | 63364 |
|---|---|---|---|---|---|---|---|---|---|
| Aug-50 | BLAYDON-52C | CONSETT-54D | BOR.GDNS-54C | CONSETT-54D | NEWPORT-51B | CONSETT-54D | NEVILLE HILL-50B | TYNE DOCK-54B | MIDDLESBROUGH-51D |
| Jan-51 | BLAYDON-52C | CONSETT-54D | BOR.GDNS-54C | **1/51: W.HPL-51C** | NEWPORT-51B | CONSETT-54D | **12/50: SELBY-50C** | **11/50: SELBY-50C** | MIDDLESBROUGH-51D |
| Aug-51 | BLAYDON-52C | CONSETT-54D | BOR.GDNS-54C | W.HARTLEPOOL-51C | NEWPORT-51B | CONSETT-54D | SELBY-50C | SELBY-50C | MIDDLESBROUGH-51D |
| Jan-52 | BLAYDON-52C | CONSETT-54D | BOR.GDNS-54C | W.HARTLEPOOL-51C | NEWPORT-51B | CONSETT-54D | SELBY-50C | SELBY-50C | MIDDLESBROUGH-51D |
| Aug-52 | BLAYDON-52C | CONSETT-54D | BOR.GDNS-54C | **7/52: T.DCK-54B** | NEWPORT-51B | CONSETT-54D | SELBY-50C | SELBY-50C | MIDDLESBROUGH-51D |
| Jan-53 | BLAYDON-52C | CONSETT-54D | BOR.GDNS-54C | TYNE DOCK-54B | NEWPORT-51B | CONSETT-54D | SELBY-50C | SELBY-50C | MIDDLESBROUGH-51D |
| Aug-53 | BLAYDON-52C | CONSETT-54D | BOR.GDNS-54C | TYNE DOCK-54B | NEWPORT-51B | CONSETT-54D | SELBY-50C | **10/53: BLAY-52C** | MIDDLESBROUGH-51D |
| Jan-54 | BLAYDON-52C | CONSETT-54D | BOR.GDNS-54C | TYNE DOCK-54B | NEWPORT-51B | CONSETT-54D | SELBY-50C | BLAYDON-52C | MIDDLESBROUGH-51D |
| Aug-54 | BLAYDON-52C | CONSETT-54D | BOR.GDNS-54C | TYNE DOCK-54B | NEWPORT-51B | CONSETT-54D | **6/54: T.DCK-54B** | BLAYDON-52C | MIDDLESBROUGH-51D |
| Jan-55 | BLAYDON-52C | CONSETT-54D | BOR.GDNS-54C | **3/55: CON-54D** | NEWPORT-51B | CONSETT-54D | TYNE DOCK-54B | BLAYDON-52C | MIDDLESBROUGH-51D |
| Aug-55 | BLAYDON-52C | CONSETT-54D | BOR.GDNS-54C | CONSETT-54D | NEWPORT-51B | CONSETT-54D | TYNE DOCK-54B | BLAYDON-52C | MIDDLESBROUGH-51D |
| Jan-56 | BLAYDON-52C | CONSETT-54D | BOR.GDNS-54C | CONSETT-54D | NEWPORT-51B | CONSETT-54D | TYNE DOCK-54B | BLAYDON-52C | MIDDLESBROUGH-51D |
| Aug-56 | BLAYDON-52C | CONSETT-54D | BOR.GDNS-54C | CONSETT-54D | NEWPORT-51B | CONSETT-54D | TYNE DOCK-54B | BLAYDON-52C | MIDDLESBROUGH-51D |
| Jan-57 | BLAYDON-52C | CONSETT-54D | BOR.GDNS-54C | CONSETT-54D | NEWPORT-51B | CONSETT-54D | TYNE DOCK-54B | BLAYDON-52C | MIDDLESBROUGH-51D |
| Aug-57 | BLAYDON-52C | CONSETT-54D | BOR.GDNS-54C | CONSETT-54D | NEWPORT-51B | CONSETT-54D | TYNE DOCK-54B | BLAYDON-52C | MIDDLESBROUGH-51D |
| Jan-58 | BLAYDON-52C | CONSETT-54D | BOR.GDNS-54C | CONSETT-54D | NEWPORT-51B | **4/58: T.DCK-54B** | TYNE DOCK-54B | BLAYDON-52C | MIDDLESBROUGH-51D |
| Aug-58 | BLAYDON-52C | CONSETT-54D | BOR.GDNS-54C | CONSETT-54D | **6/58: TNBY-51L** | **6.58: STOCK-51E** | TYNE DOCK-54B | BLAYDON-52C | **6/58: TNBY-51L** |
| Jan-59 | BLAYDON-52C | CONSETT-52K | BOR.GDNS-52J | CONSETT-52K | THORNABY-51L | **10/58: H.HILL-51G** | **2/59: BLAY-52C** | BLAYDON-52C | THORNABY-51L |
| Aug-59 | BLAYDON-52C | CONSETT-52K | **6/59: T.DCK-52H** | CONSETT-52K | THORNABY-51L | **6/59: TNBY-51L** | BLAYDON-52C | BLAYDON-52C | THORNABY-51L |
| Nov-59 | BLAYDON-52C | CONSETT-52K | TYNE DOCK-52H | CONSETT-52K | THORNABY-51L | THORNABY-51L | BLAYDON-52C | BLAYDON-52C | THORNABY-51L |
| Jan-60 | BLAYDON-52C | CONSETT-52K | TYNE DOCK-52H | CONSETT-52K | THORNABY-51L | THORNABY-51L | BLAYDON-52C | BLAYDON-52C | THORNABY-51L |
| Apr-60 | BLAYDON-52C | CONSETT-52K | TYNE DOCK-52H | CONSETT-52K | THORNABY-51L | THORNABY-51L | BLAYDON-52C | BLAYDON-52C | THORNABY-51L |
| Aug-60 | BLAYDON-52C | CONSETT-52K | TYNE DOCK-52H | CONSETT-52K | THORNABY-51L | THORNABY-51L | BLAYDON-52C | BLAYDON-52C | THORNABY-51L |
| Nov-60 | BLAYDON-52C | CONSETT-52K | TYNE DOCK-52H | CONSETT-52K | THORNABY-51L | THORNABY-51L | BLAYDON-52C | BLAYDON-52C | THORNABY-51L |

| | 63365 | 63366 | 63367 | 63368 | 63369 | 63370 | 63371 | 63372 | 63373 |
|---|---|---|---|---|---|---|---|---|---|
| Aug-50 | CONSETT-54D | BOR.GDNS-54C | HAVERTONHILL-51G | MIDDLESBROUGH-51D | MIDDLESBROUGH-51D | NEWPORT-51B | NEWPORT-51B | CONSETT-54D | MIDDLESBROUGH-51D |
| Jan-51 | CONSETT-54D | BOR.GDNS-54C | HAVERTONHILL-51G | MIDDLESBROUGH-51D | MIDDLESBROUGH-51D | NEWPORT-51B | NEWPORT-51B | CONSETT-54D | MIDDLESBROUGH-51D |
| Aug-51 | CONSETT-54D | BOR.GDNS-54C | HAVERTONHILL-51G | MIDDLESBROUGH-51D | MIDDLESBROUGH-51D | NEWPORT-51B | NEWPORT-51B | CONSETT-54D | MIDDLESBROUGH-51D |
| Jan-52 | CONSETT-54D | BOR.GDNS-54C | HAVERTONHILL-51G | MIDDLESBROUGH-51D | MIDDLESBROUGH-51D | NEWPORT-51B | NEWPORT-51B | CONSETT-54D | MIDDLESBROUGH-51D |
| Aug-52 | CONSETT-54D | BOR.GDNS-54C | HAVERTONHILL-51G | MIDDLESBROUGH-51D | MIDDLESBROUGH-51D | NEWPORT-51B | NEWPORT-51B | CONSETT-54D | MIDDLESBROUGH-51D |
| Jan-53 | CONSETT-54D | BOR.GDNS-54C | HAVERTONHILL-51G | MIDDLESBROUGH-51D | MIDDLESBROUGH-51D | NEWPORT-51B | NEWPORT-51B | CONSETT-54D | MIDDLESBROUGH-51D |
| Aug-53 | CONSETT-54D | BOR.GDNS-54C | HAVERTONHILL-51G | MIDDLESBROUGH-51D | MIDDLESBROUGH-51D | NEWPORT-51B | NEWPORT-51B | CONSETT-54D | MIDDLESBROUGH-51D |
| Jan-54 | CONSETT-54D | BOR.GDNS-54C | HAVERTONHILL-51G | MIDDLESBROUGH-51D | MIDDLESBROUGH-51D | NEWPORT-51B | NEWPORT-51B | CONSETT-54D | MIDDLESBROUGH-51D |
| Aug-54 | CONSETT-54D | BOR.GDNS-54C | HAVERTONHILL-51G | MIDDLESBROUGH-51D | MIDDLESBROUGH-51D | NEWPORT-51B | NEWPORT-51B | CONSETT-54D | MIDDLESBROUGH-51D |
| Jan-55 | CONSETT-54D | BOR.GDNS-54C | HAVERTONHILL-51G | MIDDLESBROUGH-51D | MIDDLESBROUGH-51D | NEWPORT-51B | NEWPORT-51B | CONSETT-54D | **4/55I KY. ST-51D** |
| Aug-55 | CONSETT-54D | BOR.GDNS-54C | HAVERTONHILL-51G | MIDDLESBROUGH-51D | MIDDLESBROUGH-51D | NEWPORT-51B | NEWPORT-51B | CONSETT-54D | **6/55: MBRO-51D** |
| Jan-56 | CONSETT-54D | BOR.GDNS-54C | HAVERTONHILL-51G | MIDDLESBROUGH-51D | MIDDLESBROUGH-51D | NEWPORT-51B | NEWPORT-51B | CONSETT-54D | MIDDLESBROUGH-51D |
| Aug-56 | CONSETT-54D | BOR.GDNS-54C | HAVERTONHILL-51G | MIDDLESBROUGH-51D | MIDDLESBROUGH-51D | NEWPORT-51B | NEWPORT-51B | CONSETT-54D | MIDDLESBROUGH-51D |
| Jan-57 | CONSETT-54D | BOR.GDNS-54C | HAVERTONHILL-51G | MIDDLESBROUGH-51D | MIDDLESBROUGH-51D | NEWPORT-51B | NEWPORT-51B | CONSETT-54D | MIDDLESBROUGH-51D |
| Aug-57 | CONSETT-54D | BOR.GDNS-54C | HAVERTONHILL-51G | MIDDLESBROUGH-51D | MIDDLESBROUGH-51D | NEWPORT-51B | NEWPORT-51B | CONSETT-54D | MIDDLESBROUGH-51D |
| Jan-58 | CONSETT-54D | BOR.GDNS-54C | HAVERTONHILL-51G | MIDDLESBROUGH-51D | MIDDLESBROUGH-51D | NEWPORT-51B | NEWPORT-51B | CONSETT-54D | MIDDLESBROUGH-51D |
| Aug-58 | CONSETT-54D | BOR.GDNS-54C | HAVERTONHILL-51G | **6/58: TNBY-51L** | **6/58: TNBY-51L** | **6/58: TNBY-51L** | **6/58: TNBY-51L** | CONSETT-54D | **6/58: TNBY-51L** |
| Jan-59 | CONSETT-52K | BOR.GDNS-52J | HAVERTONHILL-51G | THORNABY-51L | THORNABY-51L | THORNABY-51L | THORNABY-51L | CONSETT-52K | THORNABY-51L |
| Aug-59 | CONSETT-52K | **6/59: BLAY-52C** | **6/59: TNBY-51L** | THORNABY-51L | THORNABY-51L | THORNABY-51L | THORNABY-51L | CONSETT-52K | THORNABY-51L |
| Nov-59 | CONSETT-52K | BLAYDON-52C | THORNABY-51L | **11/59: BLAY-52C** | THORNABY-51L | THORNABY-51L | THORNABY-51L | CONSETT-52K | THORNABY-51L |
| Jan-60 | CONSETT-52K | BLAYDON-52C | THORNABY-51L | BLAYDON-52C | THORNABY-51L | THORNABY-51L | THORNABY-51L | CONSETT-52K | THORNABY-51L |
| Apr-60 | CONSETT-52K | BLAYDON-52C | THORNABY-51L | BLAYDON-52C | THORNABY-51L | THORNABY-51L | THORNABY-51L | CONSETT-52K | THORNABY-51L |
| Aug-60 | CONSETT-52K | BLAYDON-52C | THORNABY-51L | BLAYDON-52C | THORNABY-51L | THORNABY-51L | THORNABY-51L | **5/60: W/D** | THORNABY-51L |
| Nov-60 | CONSETT-52K | BLAYDON-52C | THORNABY-51L | BLAYDON-52C | THORNABY-51L | THORNABY-51L | THORNABY-51L | | THORNABY-51L |

| | 63374 | 63375 | 63376 | 63377 | 63378 | 63379 | 63380 | 63381 | 63382 |
|---|---|---|---|---|---|---|---|---|---|
| Aug-50 | HAVERTON HILL - 51G | MIDDLESBROUGH - 51D | BLAYDON - 52C | BOR.GDNS - 54C | SELBY - 50C | TYNE DOCK - 54B | MIDDLESBROUGH - 51D | BLAYDON - 52C | SELBY - 50C |
| Jan-51 | HAVERTON HILL - 51G | MIDDLESBROUGH - 51D | BLAYDON - 52C | BOR.GDNS - 54C | SELBY - 50C | TYNE DOCK - 54B | MIDDLESBROUGH - 51D | BLAYDON - 52C | SELBY - 50C |
| Aug-51 | HAVERTON HILL - 51G | MIDDLESBROUGH - 51D | BLAYDON - 52C | BOR.GDNS - 54C | SELBY - 50C | TYNE DOCK - 54B | MIDDLESBROUGH - 51D | BLAYDON - 52C | SELBY - 50C |
| Jan-52 | HAVERTON HILL - 51G | MIDDLESBROUGH - 51D | BLAYDON - 52C | BOR.GDNS - 54C | SELBY - 50C | TYNE DOCK - 54B | MIDDLESBROUGH - 51D | BLAYDON - 52C | SELBY - 50C |
| Aug-52 | HAVERTON HILL - 51G | MIDDLESBROUGH - 51D | BLAYDON - 52C | BOR.GDNS - 54C | SELBY - 50C | TYNE DOCK - 54B | MIDDLESBROUGH - 51D | BLAYDON - 52C | SELBY - 50C |
| Jan-53 | HAVERTON HILL - 51G | MIDDLESBROUGH - 51D | BLAYDON - 52C | BOR.GDNS - 54C | SELBY - 50C | TYNE DOCK - 54B | MIDDLESBROUGH - 51D | BLAYDON - 52C | SELBY - 50C |
| Aug-53 | HAVERTON HILL - 51G | MIDDLESBROUGH - 51D | BLAYDON - 52C | BOR.GDNS - 54C | **4/53: WHITBY - 50G** | TYNE DOCK - 54B | MIDDLESBROUGH - 51D | BLAYDON - 52C | SELBY - 50C |
| Jan-54 | HAVERTON HILL - 51G | MIDDLESBROUGH - 51D | BLAYDON - 52C | BOR.GDNS - 54C | **11/53: SELBY - 50C** | TYNE DOCK - 54B | MIDDLESBROUGH - 51D | BLAYDON - 52C | SELBY - 50C |
| Aug-54 | HAVERTON HILL - 51G | MIDDLESBROUGH - 51D | BLAYDON - 52C | BOR.GDNS - 54C | SELBY - 50C | TYNE DOCK - 54B | MIDDLESBROUGH - 51D | BLAYDON - 52C | SELBY - 50C |
| Jan-55 | HAVERTON HILL - 51G | MIDDLESBROUGH - 51D | BLAYDON - 52C | BOR.GDNS - 54C | SELBY - 50C | TYNE DOCK - 54B | MIDDLESBROUGH - 51D | BLAYDON - 52C | SELBY - 50C |
| Aug-55 | HAVERTON HILL - 51G | MIDDLESBROUGH - 51D | BLAYDON - 52C | BOR.GDNS - 54C | SELBY - 50C | TYNE DOCK - 54B | MIDDLESBROUGH - 51D | BLAYDON - 52C | SELBY - 50C |
| Jan-56 | HAVERTON HILL - 51G | MIDDLESBROUGH - 51D | BLAYDON - 52C | BOR.GDNS - 54C | SELBY - 50C | TYNE DOCK - 54B | MIDDLESBROUGH - 51D | BLAYDON - 52C | SELBY - 50C |
| Aug-56 | HAVERTON HILL - 51G | MIDDLESBROUGH - 51D | BLAYDON - 52C | BOR.GDNS - 54C | SELBY - 50C | TYNE DOCK - 54B | MIDDLESBROUGH - 51D | BLAYDON - 52C | SELBY - 50C |
| Jan-57 | HAVERTON HILL - 51G | MIDDLESBROUGH - 51D | BLAYDON - 52C | BOR.GDNS - 54C | SELBY - 50C | TYNE DOCK - 54B | MIDDLESBROUGH - 51D | BLAYDON - 52C | SELBY - 50C |
| Aug-57 | HAVERTON HILL - 51G | MIDDLESBROUGH - 51D | BLAYDON - 52C | BOR.GDNS - 54C | **6/57: T.DCK - 54B** | TYNE DOCK - 54B | MIDDLESBROUGH - 51D | BLAYDON - 52C | SELBY - 50C |
| Jan-58 | HAVERTON HILL - 51G | MIDDLESBROUGH - 51D | BLAYDON - 52C | BOR.GDNS - 54C | TYNE DOCK - 54B | TYNE DOCK - 54B | MIDDLESBROUGH - 51D | BLAYDON - 52C | SELBY - 50C |
| Aug-58 | HAVERTON HILL - 51G | **6/58: TNBY - 51L** | BLAYDON - 52C | BOR.GDNS - 54C | **9/58: BLAY - 52C** | TYNE DOCK - 54B | **6/58: TNBY - 51L** | BLAYDON - 52C | **6/58: STOCK - 51E** |
| Jan-59 | HAVERTON HILL - 51G | THORNABY - 51L | BLAYDON - 52C | BOR.GDNS - 52J | BLAYDON - 52C | TYNE DOCK - 52H | THORNABY - 51L | BLAYDON - 52C | **10/58: H.HIL - 51G** |
| Aug-59 | **6/59: TBY - 51L** | THORNABY - 51L | BLAYDON - 52C | **6/59: BLAY - 52C** | BLAYDON - 52C | TYNE DOCK - 52H | THORNABY - 51L | BLAYDON - 52C | **6/59: TNBY - 51L** |
| Nov-59 | THORNABY - 51L | THORNABY - 51L | BLAYDON - 52C | BLAYDON - 52C | BLAYDON - 52C | TYNE DOCK - 52H | THORNABY - 51L | BLAYDON - 52C | THORNABY - 51L |
| Jan-60 | THORNABY - 51L | THORNABY - 51L | BLAYDON - 52C | BLAYDON - 52C | BLAYDON - 52C | TYNE DOCK - 52H | THORNABY - 51L | BLAYDON - 52C | THORNABY - 51L |
| Apr-60 | THORNABY - 51L | THORNABY - 51L | BLAYDON - 52C | BLAYDON - 52C | BLAYDON - 52C | TYNE DOCK - 52H | THORNABY - 51L | BLAYDON - 52C | THORNABY - 51L |
| Aug-60 | THORNABY - 51L | THORNABY - 51L | BLAYDON - 52C | BLAYDON - 52C | BLAYDON - 52C | TYNE DOCK - 52H | THORNABY - 51L | BLAYDON - 52C | THORNABY - 51L |
| Nov-60 | THORNABY - 51L | THORNABY - 51L | BLAYDON - 52C | BLAYDON - 52C | BLAYDON - 52C | TYNE DOCK - 52H | THORNABY - 51L | BLAYDON - 52C | THORNABY - 51L |

| | 63383 | 63384 | 63385 | 63386 | 63387 | 63388 | 63389 | 63390 | 63391 |
|---|---|---|---|---|---|---|---|---|---|
| Aug-50 | W.HARTLEPOOL - 51C | BOR.GDNS - 54C | BLAYDON - 52C | BOR.GDNS - 54C | SELBY - 50C | NEWPORT - 51B | NEWPORT - 51B | BLAYDON - 52C | BLAYDON - 52C |
| Jan-51 | W.HARTLEPOOL - 51C | BOR.GDNS - 54C | BLAYDON - 52C | BOR.GDNS - 54C | SELBY - 50C | NEWPORT - 51B | NEWPORT - 51B | BLAYDON - 52C | BLAYDON - 52C |
| Aug-51 | W.HARTLEPOOL - 51C | BOR.GDNS - 54C | BLAYDON - 52C | BOR.GDNS - 54C | SELBY - 50C | NEWPORT - 51B | NEWPORT - 51B | BLAYDON - 52C | BLAYDON - 52C |
| Jan-52 | W.HARTLEPOOL - 51C | BOR.GDNS - 54C | BLAYDON - 52C | BOR.GDNS - 54C | SELBY - 50C | NEWPORT - 51B | NEWPORT - 51B | BLAYDON - 52C | BLAYDON - 52C |
| Aug-52 | W.HARTLEPOOL - 51C | BOR.GDNS - 54C | BLAYDON - 52C | BOR.GDNS - 54C | SELBY - 50C | NEWPORT - 51B | NEWPORT - 51B | BLAYDON - 52C | BLAYDON - 52C |
| Jan-53 | W.HARTLEPOOL - 51C | BOR.GDNS - 54C | BLAYDON - 52C | BOR.GDNS - 54C | TYNE DOCK - 54B | NEWPORT - 51B | NEWPORT - 51B | BLAYDON - 52C | BLAYDON - 52C |
| Aug-53 | W.HARTLEPOOL - 51C | BOR.GDNS - 54C | BLAYDON - 52C | BOR.GDNS - 54C | TYNE DOCK - 54B | NEWPORT - 51B | NEWPORT - 51B | BLAYDON - 52C | BLAYDON - 52C |
| Jan-54 | W.HARTLEPOOL - 51C | BOR.GDNS - 54C | BLAYDON - 52C | BOR.GDNS - 54C | TYNE DOCK - 54B | NEWPORT - 51B | NEWPORT - 51B | BLAYDON - 52C | BLAYDON - 52C |
| Aug-54 | W.HARTLEPOOL - 51C | BOR.GDNS - 54C | BLAYDON - 52C | BOR.GDNS - 54C | TYNE DOCK - 54B | NEWPORT - 51B | NEWPORT - 51B | BLAYDON - 52C | BLAYDON - 52C |
| Jan-55 | W.HARTLEPOOL - 51C | BOR.GDNS - 54C | BLAYDON - 52C | BOR.GDNS - 54C | TYNE DOCK - 54B | NEWPORT - 51B | NEWPORT - 51B | BLAYDON - 52C | BLAYDON - 52C |
| Aug-55 | W.HARTLEPOOL - 51C | BOR.GDNS - 54C | BLAYDON - 52C | BOR.GDNS - 54C | TYNE DOCK - 54B | NEWPORT - 51B | NEWPORT - 51B | BLAYDON - 52C | BLAYDON - 52C |
| Jan-56 | W.HARTLEPOOL - 51C | BOR.GDNS - 54C | BLAYDON - 52C | BOR.GDNS - 54C | TYNE DOCK - 54B | NEWPORT - 51B | NEWPORT - 51B | BLAYDON - 52C | BLAYDON - 52C |
| Aug-56 | W.HARTLEPOOL - 51C | BOR.GDNS - 54C | BLAYDON - 52C | BOR.GDNS - 54C | TYNE DOCK - 54B | NEWPORT - 51B | NEWPORT - 51B | BLAYDON - 52C | **7/56: N.BLYTH - 52F** |
| Jan-57 | W.HARTLEPOOL - 51C | BOR.GDNS - 54C | BLAYDON - 52C | BOR.GDNS - 54C | TYNE DOCK - 54B | NEWPORT - 51B | NEWPORT - 51B | BLAYDON - 52C | NORTH BLYTH - 52F |
| Aug-57 | W.HARTLEPOOL - 51C | BOR.GDNS - 54C | BLAYDON - 52C | BOR.GDNS - 54C | TYNE DOCK - 54B | NEWPORT - 51B | NEWPORT - 51B | BLAYDON - 52C | **6/57: H.HILL - 51G** |
| Jan-58 | W.HARTLEPOOL - 51C | BOR.GDNS - 54C | BLAYDON - 52C | BOR.GDNS - 54C | TYNE DOCK - 54B | NEWPORT - 51B | NEWPORT - 51B | BLAYDON - 52C | HAVERTON HILL - 51G |
| Aug-58 | W.HARTLEPOOL - 51C | BOR.GDNS - 54C | BLAYDON - 52C | BOR.GDNS - 54C | TYNE DOCK - 54B | **6/58: TNBY - 51L** | **6/58: TNBY - 51L** | BLAYDON - 52C | **6/58: W.HTPL - 51C** |
| Jan-59 | W.HARTLEPOOL - 51C | BOR.GDNS - 52J | BLAYDON - 52C | BOR.GDNS - 52J | TYNE DOCK - 52H | THORNABY - 51L | THORNABY - 51L | BLAYDON - 52C | W.HARTLEPOOL - 51C |
| Aug-59 | W.HARTLEPOOL - 51C | **6/59: BLAY - 52C** | BLAYDON - 52C | **6/59: BLAY - 52C** | TYNE DOCK - 52H | THORNABY - 51L | THORNABY - 51L | BLAYDON - 52C | W.HARTLEPOOL - 51C |
| Nov-59 | W.HARTLEPOOL - 51C | BLAYDON - 52C | BLAYDON - 52C | BLAYDON - 52C | **10/59: CON - 52K** | THORNABY - 51L | THORNABY - 51L | BLAYDON - 52C | W.HARTLEPOOL - 51C |
| Jan-60 | W.HARTLEPOOL - 51C | BLAYDON - 52C | BLAYDON - 52C | BLAYDON - 52C | CONSETT - 52K | THORNABY - 51L | THORNABY - 51L | BLAYDON - 52C | W.HARTLEPOOL - 51C |
| Apr-60 | W.HARTLEPOOL - 51C | BLAYDON - 52C | BLAYDON - 52C | BLAYDON - 52C | CONSETT - 52K | THORNABY - 51L | THORNABY - 51L | BLAYDON - 52C | W.HARTLEPOOL - 51C |
| Aug-60 | W.HARTLEPOOL - 51C | BLAYDON - 52C | BLAYDON - 52C | BLAYDON - 52C | **9/60: BLAY - 52C** | THORNABY - 51L | THORNABY - 51L | BLAYDON - 52C | W.HARTLEPOOL - 51C |
| Nov-60 | W.HARTLEPOOL - 51C | BLAYDON - 52C | BLAYDON - 52C | BLAYDON - 52C | BLAYDON - 52C | THORNABY - 51L | THORNABY - 51L | BLAYDON - 52C | W.HARTLEPOOL - 51C |

| | 63392 | 63393 | 63394 | 63395 | 63396 | 63397 | 63398 | 63399 | 63400 |
|---|---|---|---|---|---|---|---|---|---|
| Aug-50 | W.HARTLEPOOL - 51C | MIDDLESBROUGH - 51D | BLAYDON - 52C | SELBY - 50C | W.HARTLEPOOL - 51C | W.HARTLEPOOL - 51C | BLAYDON - 52C | BLAYDON - 52C | BOR.GDNS - 54C |
| Jan-51 | W.HARTLEPOOL - 51C | MIDDLESBROUGH - 51D | BLAYDON - 52C | SELBY - 50C | W.HARTLEPOOL - 51C | W.HARTLEPOOL - 51C | BLAYDON - 52C | BLAYDON - 52C | BOR.GDNS - 54C |
| Aug-51 | W.HARTLEPOOL - 51C | MIDDLESBROUGH - 51D | BLAYDON - 52C | SELBY - 50C | W.HARTLEPOOL - 51C | W.HARTLEPOOL - 51C | BLAYDON - 52C | BLAYDON - 52C | BOR.GDNS - 54C |
| Jan-52 | W.HARTLEPOOL - 51C | MIDDLESBROUGH - 51D | BLAYDON - 52C | SELBY - 50C | W.HARTLEPOOL - 51C | W.HARTLEPOOL - 51C | BLAYDON - 52C | BLAYDON - 52C | BOR.GDNS - 54C |
| Aug-52 | W.HARTLEPOOL - 51C | MIDDLESBROUGH - 51D | BLAYDON - 52C | SELBY - 50C | W.HARTLEPOOL - 51C | W.HARTLEPOOL - 51C | BLAYDON - 52C | BLAYDON - 52C | BOR.GDNS - 54C |
| Jan-53 | W.HARTLEPOOL - 51C | MIDDLESBROUGH - 51D | BLAYDON - 52C | SELBY - 50C | W.HARTLEPOOL - 51C | W.HARTLEPOOL - 51C | BLAYDON - 52C | BLAYDON - 52C | BOR.GDNS - 54C |
| Aug-53 | W.HARTLEPOOL - 51C | MIDDLESBROUGH - 51D | BLAYDON - 52C | SELBY - 50C | W.HARTLEPOOL - 51C | W.HARTLEPOOL - 51C | BLAYDON - 52C | BLAYDON - 52C | BOR.GDNS - 54C |
| Jan-54 | W.HARTLEPOOL - 51C | MIDDLESBROUGH - 51D | BLAYDON - 52C | SELBY - 50C | W.HARTLEPOOL - 51C | W.HARTLEPOOL - 51C | BLAYDON - 52C | BLAYDON - 52C | BOR.GDNS - 54C |
| Aug-54 | W.HARTLEPOOL - 51C | MIDDLESBROUGH - 51D | BLAYDON - 52C | SELBY - 50C | W.HARTLEPOOL - 51C | W.HARTLEPOOL - 51C | BLAYDON - 52C | BLAYDON - 52C | BOR.GDNS - 54C |
| Jan-55 | W.HARTLEPOOL - 51C | MIDDLESBROUGH - 51D | BLAYDON - 52C | SELBY - 50C | W.HARTLEPOOL - 51C | W.HARTLEPOOL - 51C | BLAYDON - 52C | BLAYDON - 52C | BOR.GDNS - 54C |
| Aug-55 | W.HARTLEPOOL - 51C | MIDDLESBROUGH - 51D | BLAYDON - 52C | SELBY - 50C | **8/55: MBRO - 51D** | W.HARTLEPOOL - 51C | BLAYDON - 52C | BLAYDON - 52C | BOR.GDNS - 54C |
| Jan-56 | W.HARTLEPOOL - 51C | MIDDLESBROUGH - 51D | BLAYDON - 52C | SELBY - 50C | MIDDLESBROUGH - 51D | W.HARTLEPOOL - 51C | BLAYDON - 52C | BLAYDON - 52C | BOR.GDNS - 54C |
| Aug-56 | W.HARTLEPOOL - 51C | MIDDLESBROUGH - 51D | BLAYDON - 52C | SELBY - 50C | MIDDLESBROUGH - 51D | W.HARTLEPOOL - 51C | **7/56: N.BLYTH - 52F** | **7/56: N.BLYTH - 52F** | BOR.GDNS - 54C |
| Jan-57 | W.HARTLEPOOL - 51C | MIDDLESBROUGH - 51D | BLAYDON - 52C | SELBY - 50C | MIDDLESBROUGH - 51D | W.HARTLEPOOL - 51C | NORTH BLYTH - 52F | NORTH BLYTH - 52F | BOR.GDNS - 54C |
| Aug-57 | W.HARTLEPOOL - 51C | MIDDLESBROUGH - 51D | BLAYDON - 52C | SELBY - 50C | MIDDLESBROUGH - 51D | W.HARTLEPOOL - 51C | NORTH BLYTH - 52F | **7/57: BLAY - 52C** | BOR.GDNS - 54C |
| Jan-58 | W.HARTLEPOOL - 51C | MIDDLESBROUGH - 51D | BLAYDON - 52C | SELBY - 50C | MIDDLESBROUGH - 51D | W.HARTLEPOOL - 51C | **10/57: NPRT - 51B** | BLAYDON - 52C | BOR.GDNS - 54C |
| Aug-58 | W.HARTLEPOOL - 51C | **6/58: TNBY - 51L** | BLAYDON - 52C | SELBY - 50C | **6/58: TNBY - 51L** | W.HARTLEPOOL - 51C | **6/58: W.AUCK - 51F** | BLAYDON - 52C | BOR.GDNS - 54C |
| Jan-59 | W.HARTLEPOOL - 51C | THORNABY - 51L | BLAYDON - 52C | SELBY - 50C | THORNABY - 51L | W.HARTLEPOOL - 51C | W.AUCKLAND - 51F | BLAYDON - 52C | BOR.GDNS - 52J |
| Aug-59 | W.HARTLEPOOL - 51C | THORNABY - 51L | BLAYDON - 52C | **6/59: DARL - 51A** | THORNABY - 51L | W.HARTLEPOOL - 51C | W.AUCKLAND - 51F | BLAYDON - 52C | **6/59: BLAY - 52C** |
| Nov-59 | W.HARTLEPOOL - 51C | THORNABY - 51L | BLAYDON - 52C | DARLINGTON - 51A | THORNABY - 51L | W.HARTLEPOOL - 51C | W.AUCKLAND - 51F | **11/59: TNBY - 51L** | BLAYDON - 52C |
| Jan-60 | W.HARTLEPOOL - 51C | THORNABY - 51L | BLAYDON - 52C | DARLINGTON - 51A | THORNABY - 51L | W.HARTLEPOOL - 51C | W.AUCKLAND - 51F | THORNABY - 51L | BLAYDON - 52C |
| Apr-60 | W.HARTLEPOOL - 51C | THORNABY - 51L | BLAYDON - 52C | DARLINGTON - 51A | THORNABY - 51L | W.HARTLEPOOL - 51C | W.AUCKLAND - 51F | THORNABY - 51L | BLAYDON - 52C |
| Aug-60 | W.HARTLEPOOL - 51C | THORNABY - 51L | BLAYDON - 52C | DARLINGTON - 51A | THORNABY - 51L | W.HARTLEPOOL - 51C | W.AUCKLAND - 51F | THORNABY - 51L | BLAYDON - 52C |
| Nov-60 | W.HARTLEPOOL - 51C | THORNABY - 51L | BLAYDON - 52C | DARLINGTON - 51A | THORNABY - 51L | W.HARTLEPOOL - 51C | W.AUCKLAND - 51F | THORNABY - 51L | BLAYDON - 52C |

| | 63401 | 63402 | 63403 | 63404 | 63405 | 63406 | 63407 | 63408 | 63409 |
|---|---|---|---|---|---|---|---|---|---|
| Aug-50 | W.HARTLEPOOL - 51C | BOR.GDNS - 54C | BLAYDON - 52C | CONSETT - 54D | HAVERTON HILL - 51G | SELBY - 50C | HAVERTON HILL - 51G | SELBY - 50C | MIDDLESBROUGH - 51D |
| Jan-51 | W.HARTLEPOOL - 51C | BOR.GDNS - 54C | BLAYDON - 52C | CONSETT - 54D | **1/51: MBRO - 51D** | SELBY - 50C | HAVERTON HILL - 51G | SELBY - 50C | MIDDLESBROUGH - 51D |
| Aug-51 | W.HARTLEPOOL - 51C | BOR.GDNS - 54C | BLAYDON - 52C | CONSETT - 54D | MIDDLESBROUGH - 51D | SELBY - 50C | HAVERTON HILL - 51G | SELBY - 50C | MIDDLESBROUGH - 51D |
| Jan-52 | W.HARTLEPOOL - 51C | BOR.GDNS - 54C | BLAYDON - 52C | CONSETT - 54D | MIDDLESBROUGH - 51D | SELBY - 50C | HAVERTON HILL - 51G | **2/52: B.GDNS - 54C** | MIDDLESBROUGH - 51D |
| Aug-52 | **9/52: MBRO - 51D** | BOR.GDNS - 54C | BLAYDON - 52C | CONSETT - 54D | MIDDLESBROUGH - 51D | SELBY - 50C | HAVERTON HILL - 51G | BOR.GDNS - 54C | MIDDLESBROUGH - 51D |
| Jan-53 | MIDDLESBROUGH - 51D | BOR.GDNS - 54C | BLAYDON - 52C | CONSETT - 54D | MIDDLESBROUGH - 51D | SELBY - 50C | HAVERTON HILL - 51G | BOR.GDNS - 54C | MIDDLESBROUGH - 51D |
| Aug-53 | MIDDLESBROUGH - 51D | BOR.GDNS - 54C | BLAYDON - 52C | CONSETT - 54D | MIDDLESBROUGH - 51D | SELBY - 50C | HAVERTON HILL - 51G | BOR.GDNS - 54C | MIDDLESBROUGH - 51D |
| Jan-54 | MIDDLESBROUGH - 51D | BOR.GDNS - 54C | BLAYDON - 52C | CONSETT - 54D | MIDDLESBROUGH - 51D | SELBY - 50C | HAVERTON HILL - 51G | BOR.GDNS - 54C | MIDDLESBROUGH - 51D |
| Aug-54 | MIDDLESBROUGH - 51D | BOR.GDNS - 54C | BLAYDON - 52C | CONSETT - 54D | MIDDLESBROUGH - 51D | SELBY - 50C | HAVERTON HILL - 51G | BOR.GDNS - 54C | MIDDLESBROUGH - 51D |
| Jan-55 | MIDDLESBROUGH - 51D | BOR.GDNS - 54C | BLAYDON - 52C | CONSETT - 54D | MIDDLESBROUGH - 51D | SELBY - 50C | HAVERTON HILL - 51G | BOR.GDNS - 54C | MIDDLESBROUGH - 51D |
| Aug-55 | MIDDLESBROUGH - 51D | BOR.GDNS - 54C | BLAYDON - 52C | CONSETT - 54D | MIDDLESBROUGH - 51D | SELBY - 50C | HAVERTON HILL - 51G | BOR.GDNS - 54C | MIDDLESBROUGH - 51D |
| Jan-56 | MIDDLESBROUGH - 51D | BOR.GDNS - 54C | BLAYDON - 52C | CONSETT - 54D | MIDDLESBROUGH - 51D | SELBY - 50C | HAVERTON HILL - 51G | BOR.GDNS - 54C | MIDDLESBROUGH - 51D |
| Aug-56 | MIDDLESBROUGH - 51D | BOR.GDNS - 54C | **7/56: N.BLYTH - 52F** | CONSETT - 54D | MIDDLESBROUGH - 51D | SELBY - 50C | HAVERTON HILL - 51G | BOR.GDNS - 54C | MIDDLESBROUGH - 51D |
| Jan-57 | MIDDLESBROUGH - 51D | BOR.GDNS - 54C | NORTH BLYTH - 52F | CONSETT - 54D | MIDDLESBROUGH - 51D | SELBY - 50C | HAVERTON HILL - 51G | BOR.GDNS - 54C | MIDDLESBROUGH - 51D |
| Aug-57 | MIDDLESBROUGH - 51D | BOR.GDNS - 54C | NORTH BLYTH - 52F | CONSETT - 54D | MIDDLESBROUGH - 51D | **6/57: T.DCK - 54B** | HAVERTON HILL - 51G | BOR.GDNS - 54C | MIDDLESBROUGH - 51D |
| Jan-58 | MIDDLESBROUGH - 51D | BOR.GDNS - 54C | **10/57: NPRT - 51B** | CONSETT - 54D | MIDDLESBROUGH - 51D | TYNE DOCK - 54B | HAVERTON HILL - 51G | BOR.GDNS - 54C | MIDDLESBROUGH - 51D |
| Aug-58 | **6/58: TNBY - 51L** | BOR.GDNS - 54C | THORNABY - 51L | CONSETT - 54D | **6/58: TNBY - 51L** | TYNE DOCK - 54B | HAVERTON HILL - 51G | BOR.GDNS - 54C | **6/58: TNBY - 51L** |
| Jan-59 | THORNABY - 51L | BOR.GDNS - 52J | **10/58: W.AUCK - 51F** | CONSETT - 52K | THORNABY - 51L | **1/59: CON - 52K** | HAVERTON HILL - 51G | BOR.GDNS - 52J | THORNABY - 51L |
| Aug-59 | THORNABY - 51L | **6/59: BLAY - 52C** | W.AUCKLAND - 51F | CONSETT - 52K | THORNABY - 51L | CONSETT - 52K | **6/59: W.AUCK - 51F** | **6/59: BLAY - 52C** | THORNABY - 51L |
| Nov-59 | THORNABY - 51L | BLAYDON - 52C | W.AUCKLAND - 51F | CONSETT - 52K | THORNABY - 51L | CONSETT - 52K | W.AUCKLAND - 51F | BLAYDON - 52C | THORNABY - 51L |
| Jan-60 | THORNABY - 51L | BLAYDON - 52C | W.AUCKLAND - 51F | CONSETT - 52K | THORNABY - 51L | CONSETT - 52K | W.AUCKLAND - 51F | BLAYDON - 52C | THORNABY - 51L |
| Apr-60 | THORNABY - 51L | BLAYDON - 52C | W.AUCKLAND - 51F | CONSETT - 52K | THORNABY - 51L | CONSETT - 52K | W.AUCKLAND - 51F | BLAYDON - 52C | THORNABY - 51L |
| Aug-60 | THORNABY - 51L | BLAYDON - 52C | W.AUCKLAND - 51F | CONSETT - 52K | THORNABY - 51L | CONSETT - 52K | W.AUCKLAND - 51F | BLAYDON - 52C | THORNABY - 51L |
| Nov-60 | THORNABY - 51L | BLAYDON - 52C | W.AUCKLAND - 51F | CONSETT - 52K | THORNABY - 51L | CONSETT - 52K | W.AUCKLAND - 51F | BLAYDON - 52C | THORNABY - 51L |

| | 63410 | 63411 | 63412 | 63413 | 63414 | 63415 | 63416 | 63417 | 63418 |
|---|---|---|---|---|---|---|---|---|---|
| Aug-50 | W.HARTLEPOOL-51C | MIDDLESBROUGH-51D | BLAYDON-52C | BLAYDON-52C | W.HARTLEPOOL-51C | W.HARTLEPOOL-51C | HAVERTON HILL-51G | MIDDLESBROUGH-51D | CONSETT-54D |
| Jan-51 | W.HARTLEPOOL-51C | MIDDLESBROUGH-51D | BLAYDON-52C | BLAYDON-52C | W.HARTLEPOOL-51C | W.HARTLEPOOL-51C | HAVERTON HILL-51G | MIDDLESBROUGH-51D | CONSETT-54D |
| Aug-51 | W.HARTLEPOOL-51C | MIDDLESBROUGH-51D | BLAYDON-52C | BLAYDON-52C | W.HARTLEPOOL-51C | W.HARTLEPOOL-51C | HAVERTON HILL-51G | MIDDLESBROUGH-51D | CONSETT-54D |
| Jan-52 | W.HARTLEPOOL-51C | MIDDLESBROUGH-51D | BLAYDON-52C | BLAYDON-52C | W.HARTLEPOOL-51C | W.HARTLEPOOL-51C | HAVERTON HILL-51G | MIDDLESBROUGH-51D | CONSETT-54D |
| Aug-52 | W.HARTLEPOOL-51C | MIDDLESBROUGH-51D | BLAYDON-52C | BLAYDON-52C | W.HARTLEPOOL-51C | W.HARTLEPOOL-51C | HAVERTON HILL-51G | MIDDLESBROUGH-51D | CONSETT-54D |
| Jan-53 | W.HARTLEPOOL-51C | MIDDLESBROUGH-51D | BLAYDON-52C | BLAYDON-52C | W.HARTLEPOOL-51C | W.HARTLEPOOL-51C | HAVERTON HILL-51G | MIDDLESBROUGH-51D | CONSETT-54D |
| Aug-53 | W.HARTLEPOOL-51C | MIDDLESBROUGH-51D | BLAYDON-52C | BLAYDON-52C | W.HARTLEPOOL-51C | W.HARTLEPOOL-51C | HAVERTON HILL-51G | MIDDLESBROUGH-51D | CONSETT-54D |
| Jan-54 | W.HARTLEPOOL-51C | MIDDLESBROUGH-51D | BLAYDON-52C | BLAYDON-52C | W.HARTLEPOOL-51C | W.HARTLEPOOL-51C | HAVERTON HILL-51G | MIDDLESBROUGH-51D | CONSETT-54D |
| Aug-54 | W.HARTLEPOOL-51C | MIDDLESBROUGH-51D | BLAYDON-52C | BLAYDON-52C | W.HARTLEPOOL-51C | W.HARTLEPOOL-51C | HAVERTON HILL-51G | MIDDLESBROUGH-51D | CONSETT-54D |
| Jan-55 | W.HARTLEPOOL-51C | MIDDLESBROUGH-51D | BLAYDON-52C | BLAYDON-52C | W.HARTLEPOOL-51C | W.HARTLEPOOL-51C | HAVERTON HILL-51G | MIDDLESBROUGH-51D | CONSETT-54D |
| Aug-55 | W.HARTLEPOOL-51C | MIDDLESBROUGH-51D | BLAYDON-52C | BLAYDON-52C | W.HARTLEPOOL-51C | W.HARTLEPOOL-51C | HAVERTON HILL-51G | MIDDLESBROUGH-51D | CONSETT-54D |
| Jan-56 | W.HARTLEPOOL-51C | MIDDLESBROUGH-51D | BLAYDON-52C | BLAYDON-52C | W.HARTLEPOOL-51C | W.HARTLEPOOL-51C | HAVERTON HILL-51G | MIDDLESBROUGH-51D | CONSETT-54D |
| Aug-56 | W.HARTLEPOOL-51C | MIDDLESBROUGH-51D | BLAYDON-52C | BLAYDON-52C | W.HARTLEPOOL-51C | W.HARTLEPOOL-51C | HAVERTON HILL-51G | MIDDLESBROUGH-51D | CONSETT-54D |
| Jan-57 | W.HARTLEPOOL-51C | MIDDLESBROUGH-51D | BLAYDON-52C | BLAYDON-52C | W.HARTLEPOOL-51C | W.HARTLEPOOL-51C | HAVERTON HILL-51G | MIDDLESBROUGH-51D | CONSETT-54D |
| Aug-57 | W.HARTLEPOOL-51C | MIDDLESBROUGH-51D | HAVERTON HILL-51G | BLAYDON-52C | W.HARTLEPOOL-51C | W.HARTLEPOOL-51C | HAVERTON HILL-51G | MIDDLESBROUGH-51D | CONSETT-54D |
| Jan-58 | W.HARTLEPOOL-51C | MIDDLESBROUGH-51D | HAVERTON HILL-51G | BLAYDON-52C | W.HARTLEPOOL-51C | W.HARTLEPOOL-51C | HAVERTON HILL-51G | MIDDLESBROUGH-51D | CONSETT-54D |
| Aug-58 | W.HARTLEPOOL-51C | **6/58: TNBY - 51L** | **6/58: W.HTPL - 51C** | BLAYDON-52C | W.HARTLEPOOL-51C | W.HARTLEPOOL-51C | HAVERTON HILL-51G | **6/58: TNBY - 51L** | CONSETT-54D |
| Jan-59 | W.HARTLEPOOL-51C | THORNABY-51L | W.HARTLEPOOL-51C | BLAYDON-52C | W.HARTLEPOOL-51C | W.HARTLEPOOL-51C | HAVERTON HILL-51G | THORNABY-51L | CONSETT-52K |
| Aug-59 | W.HARTLEPOOL-51C | THORNABY-51L | W.HARTLEPOOL-51C | BLAYDON-52C | W.HARTLEPOOL-51C | W.HARTLEPOOL-51C | **6/59: TNBY - 51L** | THORNABY-51L | CONSETT-52K |
| Nov-59 | W.HARTLEPOOL-51C | THORNABY-51L | W.HARTLEPOOL-51C | BLAYDON-52C | W.HARTLEPOOL-51C | W.HARTLEPOOL-51C | THORNABY-51L | THORNABY-51L | CONSETT-52K |
| Jan-60 | W.HARTLEPOOL-51C | THORNABY-51L | W.HARTLEPOOL-51C | BLAYDON-52C | W.HARTLEPOOL-51C | W.HARTLEPOOL-51C | THORNABY-51L | THORNABY-51L | CONSETT-52K |
| Apr-60 | W.HARTLEPOOL-51C | THORNABY-51L | W.HARTLEPOOL-51C | BLAYDON-52C | W.HARTLEPOOL-51C | W.HARTLEPOOL-51C | THORNABY-51L | THORNABY-51L | CONSETT-52K |
| Aug-60 | W.HARTLEPOOL-51C | THORNABY-51L | W.HARTLEPOOL-51C | BLAYDON-52C | W.HARTLEPOOL-51C | W.HARTLEPOOL-51C | THORNABY-51L | THORNABY-51L | CONSETT-52K |
| Nov-60 | W.HARTLEPOOL-51C | THORNABY-51L | W.HARTLEPOOL-51C | BLAYDON-52C | W.HARTLEPOOL-51C | W.HARTLEPOOL-51C | THORNABY-51L | THORNABY-51L | CONSETT-52K |

| | 63419 | 63420 | 63421 | 63422 | 63423 | 63424 | 63425 | 63426 | 63427 |
|---|---|---|---|---|---|---|---|---|---|
| Aug-50 | W.HARTLEPOOL-51C | MIDDLESBROUGH-51D | W.HARTLEPOOL-51C | W.HARTLEPOOL-51C | HAVERTON HILL-51G | W.HARTLEPOOL-51C | HAVERTON HILL-51G | NEWPORT-51B | W.HARTLEPOOL-51C |
| Jan-51 | W.HARTLEPOOL-51C | MIDDLESBROUGH-51D | W.HARTLEPOOL-51C | W.HARTLEPOOL-51C | **9/50: SELBY - 50C** | W.HARTLEPOOL-51C | **9/50: SELBY - 50C** | NEWPORT-51B | **1/51 : CON - 54D** |
| Aug-51 | W.HARTLEPOOL-51C | MIDDLESBROUGH-51D | W.HARTLEPOOL-51C | W.HARTLEPOOL-51C | SELBY-50C | W.HARTLEPOOL-51C | SELBY-50C | NEWPORT-51B | CONSETT-54D |
| Jan-52 | W.HARTLEPOOL-51C | MIDDLESBROUGH-51D | W.HARTLEPOOL-51C | W.HARTLEPOOL-51C | SELBY-50C | W.HARTLEPOOL-51C | SELBY-50C | NEWPORT-51B | CONSETT-54D |
| Aug-52 | W.HARTLEPOOL-51C | MIDDLESBROUGH-51D | W.HARTLEPOOL-51C | W.HARTLEPOOL-51C | SELBY-50C | W.HARTLEPOOL-51C | SELBY-50C | NEWPORT-51B | CONSETT-54D |
| Jan-53 | W.HARTLEPOOL-51C | MIDDLESBROUGH-51D | W.HARTLEPOOL-51C | W.HARTLEPOOL-51C | SELBY-50C | W.HARTLEPOOL-51C | SELBY-50C | NEWPORT-51B | CONSETT-54D |
| Aug-53 | W.HARTLEPOOL-51C | MIDDLESBROUGH-51D | W.HARTLEPOOL-51C | W.HARTLEPOOL-51C | SELBY-50C | W.HARTLEPOOL-51C | SELBY-50C | NEWPORT-51B | CONSETT-54D |
| Jan-54 | W.HARTLEPOOL-51C | MIDDLESBROUGH-51D | W.HARTLEPOOL-51C | W.HARTLEPOOL-51C | SELBY-50C | W.HARTLEPOOL-51C | SELBY-50C | NEWPORT-51B | CONSETT-54D |
| Aug-54 | W.HARTLEPOOL-51C | MIDDLESBROUGH-51D | W.HARTLEPOOL-51C | W.HARTLEPOOL-51C | SELBY-50C | W.HARTLEPOOL-51C | SELBY-50C | NEWPORT-51B | CONSETT-54D |
| Jan-55 | W.HARTLEPOOL-51C | MIDDLESBROUGH-51D | W.HARTLEPOOL-51C | W.HARTLEPOOL-51C | SELBY-50C | W.HARTLEPOOL-51C | SELBY-50C | NEWPORT-51B | CONSETT-54D |
| Aug-55 | W.HARTLEPOOL-51C | MIDDLESBROUGH-51D | W.HARTLEPOOL-51C | W.HARTLEPOOL-51C | SELBY-50C | **8/55: MBRO - 51D** | SELBY-50C | NEWPORT-51B | CONSETT-54D |
| Jan-56 | W.HARTLEPOOL-51C | MIDDLESBROUGH-51D | W.HARTLEPOOL-51C | W.HARTLEPOOL-51C | SELBY-50C | MIDDLESBROUGH-51D | SELBY-50C | NEWPORT-51B | CONSETT-54D |
| Aug-56 | W.HARTLEPOOL-51C | MIDDLESBROUGH-51D | W.HARTLEPOOL-51C | W.HARTLEPOOL-51C | SELBY-50C | MIDDLESBROUGH-51D | SELBY-50C | NEWPORT-51B | CONSETT-54D |
| Jan-57 | W.HARTLEPOOL-51C | MIDDLESBROUGH-51D | W.HARTLEPOOL-51C | W.HARTLEPOOL-51C | SELBY-50C | MIDDLESBROUGH-51D | SELBY-50C | NEWPORT-51B | CONSETT-54D |
| Aug-57 | W.HARTLEPOOL-51C | MIDDLESBROUGH-51D | W.HARTLEPOOL-51C | W.HARTLEPOOL-51C | SELBY-50C | MIDDLESBROUGH-51D | **6/57: T.DCK - 54B** | NEWPORT-51B | CONSETT-54D |
| Jan-58 | W.HARTLEPOOL-51C | MIDDLESBROUGH-51D | W.HARTLEPOOL-51C | W.HARTLEPOOL-51C | SELBY-50C | MIDDLESBROUGH-51D | TYNE DOCK-54B | NEWPORT-51B | CONSETT-54D |
| Aug-58 | W.HARTLEPOOL-51C | **6/58: TNBY - 51L** | W.HARTLEPOOL-51C | W.HARTLEPOOL-51C | SELBY-50C | **6/58: TNBY - 51L** | TYNE DOCK-54B | **6/58: TNBY - 51L** | CONSETT-54D |
| Jan-59 | W.HARTLEPOOL-51C | THORNABY-51L | W.HARTLEPOOL-51C | W.HARTLEPOOL-51C | SELBY-50C | THORNABY-51L | TYNE DOCK-52H | THORNABY-51L | CONSETT-52K |
| Aug-59 | W.HARTLEPOOL-51C | THORNABY-51L | W.HARTLEPOOL-51C | W.HARTLEPOOL-51C | **6/59: DARL - 51A** | THORNABY-51L | TYNE DOCK-52H | THORNABY-51L | CONSETT-52K |
| Nov-59 | W.HARTLEPOOL-51C | THORNABY-51L | W.HARTLEPOOL-51C | W.HARTLEPOOL-51C | DARLINGTON-51A | THORNABY-51L | TYNE DOCK-52H | THORNABY-51L | CONSETT-52K |
| Jan-60 | W.HARTLEPOOL-51C | THORNABY-51L | W.HARTLEPOOL-51C | W.HARTLEPOOL-51C | DARLINGTON-51A | THORNABY-51L | TYNE DOCK-52H | THORNABY-51L | CONSETT-52K |
| Apr-60 | W.HARTLEPOOL-51C | THORNABY-51L | W.HARTLEPOOL-51C | W.HARTLEPOOL-51C | DARLINGTON-51A | THORNABY-51L | TYNE DOCK-52H | THORNABY-51L | CONSETT-52K |
| Aug-60 | W.HARTLEPOOL-51C | THORNABY-51L | W.HARTLEPOOL-51C | W.HARTLEPOOL-51C | DARLINGTON-51A | THORNABY-51L | TYNE DOCK-52H | THORNABY-51L | CONSETT-52K |
| Nov-60 | W.HARTLEPOOL-51C | THORNABY-51L | W.HARTLEPOOL-51C | W.HARTLEPOOL-51C | DARLINGTON-51A | THORNABY-51L | TYNE DOCK-52H | THORNABY-51L | CONSETT-52K |

| | 63428 | 63429 | 63430 | 63431 | 63432 | 63433 | 63434 | 63435 | 63436 |
|---|---|---|---|---|---|---|---|---|---|
| Aug-50 | BLAYDON-52C | SELBY-50C | NEWPORT-51B | SELBY-50C | BLAYDON-52C | CONSETT-54D | BOR.GDNS-54C | W.HARTLEPOOL-51C | SELBY-50C |
| Jan-51 | BLAYDON-52C | SELBY-50C | NEWPORT-51B | SELBY-50C | BLAYDON-52C | CONSETT-54D | BOR.GDNS-54C | W.HARTLEPOOL-51C | SELBY-50C |
| Aug-51 | BLAYDON-52C | SELBY-50C | NEWPORT-51B | SELBY-50C | BLAYDON-52C | CONSETT-54D | BOR.GDNS-54C | W.HARTLEPOOL-51C | SELBY-50C |
| Jan-52 | BLAYDON-52C | SELBY-50C | NEWPORT-51B | **2/52: B.GDNS - 54C** | BLAYDON-52C | CONSETT-54D | BOR.GDNS-54C | W.HARTLEPOOL-51C | SELBY-50C |
| Aug-52 | BLAYDON-52C | SELBY-50C | NEWPORT-51B | BOR.GDNS-54C | BLAYDON-52C | CONSETT-54D | BOR.GDNS-54C | W.HARTLEPOOL-51C | SELBY-50C |
| Jan-53 | BLAYDON-52C | SELBY-50C | NEWPORT-51B | BOR.GDNS-54C | BLAYDON-52C | CONSETT-54D | BOR.GDNS-54C | **10/52: MBRO - 51D** | **2/53: N.HILL - 50B** |
| Aug-53 | BLAYDON-52C | SELBY-50C | NEWPORT-51B | BOR.GDNS-54C | BLAYDON-52C | CONSETT-54D | BOR.GDNS-54C | MIDDLESBROUGH-51D | NEVILLE HILL-50B |
| Jan-54 | BLAYDON-52C | SELBY-50C | NEWPORT-51B | BOR.GDNS-54C | BLAYDON-52C | CONSETT-54D | BOR.GDNS-54C | MIDDLESBROUGH-51D | NEVILLE HILL-50B |
| Aug-54 | BLAYDON-52C | SELBY-50C | NEWPORT-51B | BOR.GDNS-54C | BLAYDON-52C | CONSETT-54D | BOR.GDNS-54C | MIDDLESBROUGH-51D | NEVILLE HILL-50B |
| Jan-55 | BLAYDON-52C | SELBY-50C | NEWPORT-51B | BOR.GDNS-54C | BLAYDON-52C | CONSETT-54D | BOR.GDNS-54C | MIDDLESBROUGH-51D | NEVILLE HILL-50B |
| Aug-55 | BLAYDON-52C | SELBY-50C | NEWPORT-51B | BOR.GDNS-54C | BLAYDON-52C | CONSETT-54D | BOR.GDNS-54C | MIDDLESBROUGH-51D | NEVILLE HILL-50B |
| Jan-56 | BLAYDON-52C | SELBY-50C | NEWPORT-51B | BOR.GDNS-54C | BLAYDON-52C | CONSETT-54D | BOR.GDNS-54C | MIDDLESBROUGH-51D | NEVILLE HILL-50B |
| Aug-56 | **7/56: N.BLYTH - 52F** | SELBY-50C | NEWPORT-51B | BOR.GDNS-54C | BLAYDON-52C | CONSETT-54D | BOR.GDNS-54C | MIDDLESBROUGH-51D | NEVILLE HILL-50B |
| Jan-57 | NORTH BLYTH-52F | SELBY-50C | NEWPORT-51B | BOR.GDNS-54C | BLAYDON-52C | CONSETT-54D | BOR.GDNS-54C | MIDDLESBROUGH-51D | NEVILLE HILL-50B |
| Aug-57 | NORTH BLYTH-52F | SELBY-50C | NEWPORT-51B | BOR.GDNS-54C | **9/57: NPRT - 51B** | CONSETT-54D | BOR.GDNS-54C | MIDDLESBROUGH-51D | **6/57: SELBY - 50C** |
| Jan-58 | **10/57: NPRT - 51B** | SELBY-50C | NEWPORT-51B | BOR.GDNS-54C | **11/57: SELBY - 50C** | CONSETT-54D | BOR.GDNS-54C | MIDDLESBROUGH-51D | SELBY-50C |
| Aug-58 | **6/58: TNBY - 51L** | SELBY-50C | **6/58: TNBY - 51L** | BOR.GDNS-54C | **6/58: STOCK - 51E** | CONSETT-54D | BOR.GDNS-54C | **6/58: TNBY - 51L** | SELBY-50C |
| Jan-59 | THORNABY-51L | SELBY-50C | THORNABY-51L | BOR.GDNS-52J | **10/58: H.HILL - 51G** | CONSETT-52K | BOR.GDNS-52J | THORNABY-51L | SELBY-50C |
| Aug-59 | THORNABY-51L | **9/59: T.DCK - 52H** | THORNABY-51L | **6/59: BLAY - 52C** | **6/59: TNBY - 51L** | CONSETT-52K | **6/59: BLAY - 52C** | THORNABY-51L | **9/59: YORK - 50A** |
| Nov-59 | THORNABY-51L | TYNE DOCK-52H | THORNABY-51L | BLAYDON-52C | THORNABY-51L | CONSETT-52K | BLAYDON-52C | THORNABY-51L | **12/59: N.HILL - 50B** |
| Jan-60 | THORNABY-51L | TYNE DOCK-52H | THORNABY-51L | BLAYDON-52C | THORNABY-51L | CONSETT-52K | BLAYDON-52C | THORNABY-51L | NEVILLE HILL-50B |
| Apr-60 | THORNABY-51L | TYNE DOCK-52H | THORNABY-51L | BLAYDON-52C | THORNABY-51L | CONSETT-52K | BLAYDON-52C | THORNABY-51L | NEVILLE HILL-55H |
| Aug-60 | THORNABY-51L | TYNE DOCK-52H | THORNABY-51L | BLAYDON-52C | THORNABY-51L | CONSETT-52K | BLAYDON-52C | THORNABY-51L | NEVILLE HILL-55H |
| Nov-60 | THORNABY-51L | TYNE DOCK-52H | THORNABY-51L | BLAYDON-52C | THORNABY-51L | CONSETT-52K | BLAYDON-52C | THORNABY-51L | NEVILLE HILL-55H |

| | 63437 | 63438 | 63439 | 63440 | 63441 | 63442 | 63443 | 63444 | 63445 |
|---|---|---|---|---|---|---|---|---|---|
| Aug-50 | TYNE DOCK-54B | W.HARTLEPOOL-51C | CONSETT-54D | SELBY-50C | BLAYDON-52C | MIDDLESBROUGH-51D | HAVERTON HILL-51G | BLAYDON-52C | NEWPORT-51B |
| Jan-51 | TYNE DOCK-54B | W.HARTLEPOOL-51C | CONSETT-54D | SELBY-50C | BLAYDON-52C | MIDDLESBROUGH-51D | HAVERTON HILL-51G | **12/50: B.GDNS - 54C** | NEWPORT-51B |
| Aug-51 | TYNE DOCK-54B | W.HARTLEPOOL-51C | CONSETT-54D | SELBY-50C | BLAYDON-52C | MIDDLESBROUGH-51D | HAVERTON HILL-51G | BOR.GDNS-54C | NEWPORT-51B |
| Jan-52 | TYNE DOCK-54B | W.HARTLEPOOL-51C | CONSETT-54D | SELBY-50C | BLAYDON-52C | MIDDLESBROUGH-51D | HAVERTON HILL-51G | BOR.GDNS-54C | NEWPORT-51B |
| Aug-52 | TYNE DOCK-54B | W.HARTLEPOOL-51C | CONSETT-54D | **8/52: WHITBY - 50G** | BLAYDON-52C | MIDDLESBROUGH-51D | HAVERTON HILL-51G | BOR.GDNS-54C | NEWPORT-51B |
| Jan-53 | TYNE DOCK-54B | W.HARTLEPOOL-51C | CONSETT-54D | **12/52: SELBY - 50C** | BLAYDON-52C | MIDDLESBROUGH-51D | HAVERTON HILL-51G | BOR.GDNS-54C | NEWPORT-51B |
| Aug-53 | TYNE DOCK-54B | W.HARTLEPOOL-51C | CONSETT-54D | SELBY-50C | BLAYDON-52C | MIDDLESBROUGH-51D | HAVERTON HILL-51G | BOR.GDNS-54C | NEWPORT-51B |
| Jan-54 | TYNE DOCK-54B | W.HARTLEPOOL-51C | CONSETT-54D | SELBY-50C | BLAYDON-52C | MIDDLESBROUGH-51D | HAVERTON HILL-51G | BOR.GDNS-54C | NEWPORT-51B |
| Aug-54 | TYNE DOCK-54B | W.HARTLEPOOL-51C | CONSETT-54D | SELBY-50C | BLAYDON-52C | MIDDLESBROUGH-51D | HAVERTON HILL-51G | BOR.GDNS-54C | NEWPORT-51B |
| Jan-55 | TYNE DOCK-54B | W.HARTLEPOOL-51C | CONSETT-54D | SELBY-50C | BLAYDON-52C | MIDDLESBROUGH-51D | HAVERTON HILL-51G | BOR.GDNS-54C | NEWPORT-51B |
| Aug-55 | TYNE DOCK-54B | W.HARTLEPOOL-51C | CONSETT-54D | SELBY-50C | BLAYDON-52C | MIDDLESBROUGH-51D | HAVERTON HILL-51G | BOR.GDNS-54C | NEWPORT-51B |
| Jan-56 | TYNE DOCK-54B | W.HARTLEPOOL-51C | CONSETT-54D | SELBY-50C | BLAYDON-52C | MIDDLESBROUGH-51D | HAVERTON HILL-51G | BOR.GDNS-54C | NEWPORT-51B |
| Aug-56 | TYNE DOCK-54B | W.HARTLEPOOL-51C | CONSETT-54D | SELBY-50C | BLAYDON-52C | MIDDLESBROUGH-51D | HAVERTON HILL-51G | BOR.GDNS-54C | NEWPORT-51B |
| Jan-57 | TYNE DOCK-54B | W.HARTLEPOOL-51C | CONSETT-54D | SELBY-50C | BLAYDON-52C | MIDDLESBROUGH-51D | HAVERTON HILL-51G | BOR.GDNS-54C | NEWPORT-51B |
| Aug-57 | TYNE DOCK-54B | W.HARTLEPOOL-51C | CONSETT-54D | SELBY-50C | BLAYDON-52C | MIDDLESBROUGH-51D | HAVERTON HILL-51G | BOR.GDNS-54C | NEWPORT-51B |
| Jan-58 | TYNE DOCK-54B | W.HARTLEPOOL-51C | CONSETT-54D | SELBY-50C | BLAYDON-52C | MIDDLESBROUGH-51D | HAVERTON HILL-51G | BOR.GDNS-54C | NEWPORT-51B |
| Aug-58 | TYNE DOCK-54B | W.HARTLEPOOL-51C | CONSETT-54D | **6/58: STOCK - 51E** | BLAYDON-52C | **6/58: TNBY - 51L** | HAVERTON HILL-51G | BOR.GDNS-54C | **6/58: TNBY - 51L** |
| Jan-59 | TYNE DOCK-52H | W.HARTLEPOOL-51C | CONSETT-52K | **9/58: W.HTPL - 51C** | BLAYDON-52C | THORNABY-51L | HAVERTON HILL-51G | BOR.GDNS-52J | THORNABY-51L |
| Aug-59 | TYNE DOCK-52H | W.HARTLEPOOL-51C | CONSETT-52K | W.HARTLEPOOL-51C | BLAYDON-52C | THORNABY-51L | **6/59: W.AUCK - 51F** | **6/59: BLAY - 52C** | THORNABY-51L |
| Nov-59 | **12/59: CON - 52K** | W.HARTLEPOOL-51C | CONSETT-52K | W.HARTLEPOOL-51C | BLAYDON-52C | THORNABY-51L | W.AUCKLAND-51F | BLAYDON-52C | THORNABY-51L |
| Jan-60 | CONSETT-52K | W.HARTLEPOOL-51C | CONSETT-52K | W.HARTLEPOOL-51C | BLAYDON-52C | THORNABY-51L | W.AUCKLAND-51F | BLAYDON-52C | THORNABY-51L |
| Apr-60 | CONSETT-52K | W.HARTLEPOOL-51C | CONSETT-52K | W.HARTLEPOOL-51C | BLAYDON-52C | THORNABY-51L | W.AUCKLAND-51F | BLAYDON-52C | THORNABY-51L |
| Aug-60 | **9/60: BLAY - 52C** | W.HARTLEPOOL-51C | CONSETT-52K | W.HARTLEPOOL-51C | BLAYDON-52C | THORNABY-51L | W.AUCKLAND-51F | BLAYDON-52C | THORNABY-51L |
| Nov-60 | BLAYDON-52C | W.HARTLEPOOL-51C | CONSETT-52K | W.HARTLEPOOL-51C | BLAYDON-52C | THORNABY-51L | W.AUCKLAND-51F | BLAYDON-52C | THORNABY-51L |

| | 63446 | 63447 | 63440 | 63449 | 63450 | 63451 | 63452 | 63453 | 63454 |
|---|---|---|---|---|---|---|---|---|---|
| Aug-50 | HAVERTON HILL-51G | NEWPORT-51B | SELBY-50C | SELBY-50C | NEVILLE HILL-50B | SELBY-50C | W.HARTLEPOOL-51C | HAVERTON HILL-51G | W.HARTLEPOOL-51C |
| Jan-51 | HAVERTON HILL-51G | NEWPORT-51B | SELBY-50C | SELBY-50C | NEVILLE HILL-50B | SELBY-50C | W.HARTLEPOOL-51C | **9/50: SELBY - 50C** | W.HARTLEPOOL-51C |
| Aug-51 | HAVERTON HILL-51G | NEWPORT-51B | SELBY-50C | SELBY-50C | NEVILLE HILL-50B | SELBY-50C | W.HARTLEPOOL-51C | SELBY-50C | W.HARTLEPOOL-51C |
| Jan-52 | HAVERTON HILL-51G | NEWPORT-51B | SELBY-50C | SELBY-50C | **2/52: SELBY - 50C** | SELBY-50C | W.HARTLEPOOL-51C | SELBY-50C | W.HARTLEPOOL-51C |
| Aug-52 | HAVERTON HILL-51G | NEWPORT-51B | SELBY-50C | SELBY-50C | SELBY-50C | SELBY-50C | W.HARTLEPOOL-51C | **9/52: T.DCK - 54B** | W.HARTLEPOOL-51C |
| Jan-53 | HAVERTON HILL-51G | NEWPORT-51B | SELBY-50C | SELBY-50C | SELBY-50C | SELBY-50C | **10/52: MBRO - 51D** | TYNE DOCK-54B | W.HARTLEPOOL-51C |
| Aug-53 | HAVERTON HILL-51G | NEWPORT-51B | SELBY-50C | SELBY-50C | SELBY-50C | SELBY-50C | MIDDLESBROUGH-51D | TYNE DOCK-54B | W.HARTLEPOOL-51C |
| Jan-54 | HAVERTON HILL-51G | NEWPORT-51B | SELBY-50C | SELBY-50C | SELBY-50C | SELBY-50C | MIDDLESBROUGH-51D | TYNE DOCK-54B | W.HARTLEPOOL-51C |
| Aug-54 | HAVERTON HILL-51G | NEWPORT-51B | SELBY-50C | SELBY-50C | SELBY-50C | SELBY-50C | MIDDLESBROUGH-51D | TYNE DOCK-54B | W.HARTLEPOOL-51C |
| Jan-55 | HAVERTON HILL-51G | NEWPORT-51B | SELBY-50C | SELBY-50C | SELBY-50C | SELBY-50C | MIDDLESBROUGH-51D | TYNE DOCK-54B | W.HARTLEPOOL-51C |
| Aug-55 | HAVERTON HILL-51G | NEWPORT-51B | SELBY-50C | SELBY-50C | SELBY-50C | SELBY-50C | MIDDLESBROUGH-51D | TYNE DOCK-54B | W.HARTLEPOOL-51C |
| Jan-56 | HAVERTON HILL-51G | NEWPORT-51B | SELBY-50C | SELBY-50C | SELBY-50C | SELBY-50C | MIDDLESBROUGH-51D | TYNE DOCK-54B | W.HARTLEPOOL-51C |
| Aug-56 | HAVERTON HILL-51G | NEWPORT-51B | SELBY-50C | SELBY-50C | SELBY-50C | SELBY-50C | MIDDLESBROUGH-51D | TYNE DOCK-54B | W.HARTLEPOOL-51C |
| Jan-57 | HAVERTON HILL-51G | NEWPORT-51B | SELBY-50C | SELBY-50C | SELBY-50C | SELBY-50C | MIDDLESBROUGH-51D | TYNE DOCK-54B | W.HARTLEPOOL-51C |
| Aug-57 | HAVERTON HILL-51G | NEWPORT-51B | SELBY-50C | SELBY-50C | SELBY-50C | SELBY-50C | MIDDLESBROUGH-51D | **9/57: CON - 54D** | W.HARTLEPOOL-51C |
| Jan-58 | HAVERTON HILL-51G | NEWPORT-51B | SELBY-50C | SELBY-50C | SELBY-50C | SELBY-50C | MIDDLESBROUGH-51D | CONSETT-54D | W.HARTLEPOOL-51C |
| Aug-58 | HAVERTON HILL-51G | **6/58: TNBY - 51L** | SELBY-50C | SELBY-50C | SELBY-50C | SELBY-50C | **6/58: TNBY - 51L** | **7/58: B.GDNS - 54C** | W.HARTLEPOOL-51C |
| Jan-59 | HAVERTON HILL-51G | THORNABY-51L | SELBY-50C | SELBY-50C | SELBY-50C | SELBY-50C | THORNABY-51L | **2/59: BLAY - 52C** | W.HARTLEPOOL-51C |
| Aug-59 | **6/59: W.AUCK - 51F** | THORNABY-51L | **9/59: T.DCK - 52H** | **9/59: YORK - 50A** | **6/59: TNBY - 51L** | THORNABY-51L | THORNABY-51L | BLAYDON-52C | W.HARTLEPOOL-51C |
| Nov-59 | W.AUCKLAND-51F | THORNABY-51L | **12/59: CON - 52K** | **12/59: N.HILL - 50B** | THORNABY-51L | THORNABY-51L | THORNABY-51L | BLAYDON-52C | W.HARTLEPOOL-51C |
| Jan-60 | W.AUCKLAND-51F | THORNABY-51L | CONSETT-52K | NEVILLE HILL-50B | THORNABY-51L | THORNABY-51L | THORNABY-51L | BLAYDON-52C | W.HARTLEPOOL-51C |
| Apr-60 | W.AUCKLAND-51F | THORNABY-51L | CONSETT-52K | NEVILLE HILL-55H | THORNABY-51L | THORNABY-51L | THORNABY-51L | BLAYDON-52C | W.HARTLEPOOL-51C |
| Aug-60 | W.AUCKLAND-51F | THORNABY-51L | CONSETT-52K | NEVILLE HILL-55H | THORNABY-51L | THORNABY-51L | THORNABY-51L | BLAYDON-52C | W.HARTLEPOOL-51C |
| Nov-60 | W.AUCKLAND-51F | THORNABY-51L | CONSETT-52K | NEVILLE HILL-55H | THORNABY-51L | THORNABY-51L | THORNABY-51L | BLAYDON-52C | W.HARTLEPOOL-51C |

| | 63455 | 63456 | 63457 | 63458 | 63459 | Q7 0-8-0 (1919) 63460 | 63461 | 63462 | 63463 |
|---|---|---|---|---|---|---|---|---|---|
| Aug-50 | CONSETT-54D | SELBY-50C | W.HARTLEPOOL-51C | BOR.GDNS-54C | MIDDLESBROUGH-51D | TYNE DOCK-54B | TYNE DOCK-54B | TYNE DOCK-54B | TYNE DOCK-54B |
| Jan-51 | CONSETT-54D | SELBY-50C | W.HARTLEPOOL-51C | BOR.GDNS-54C | MIDDLESBROUGH-51D | TYNE DOCK-54B | TYNE DOCK-54B | TYNE DOCK-54B | TYNE DOCK-54B |
| Aug-51 | CONSETT-54D | SELBY-50C | W.HARTLEPOOL-51C | BOR.GDNS-54C | MIDDLESBROUGH-51D | TYNE DOCK-54B | TYNE DOCK-54B | TYNE DOCK-54B | TYNE DOCK-54B |
| Jan-52 | CONSETT-54D | **2/52: B.GDNS - 54C** | W.HARTLEPOOL-51C | BOR.GDNS-54C | MIDDLESBROUGH-51D | TYNE DOCK-54B | TYNE DOCK-54B | TYNE DOCK-54B | TYNE DOCK-54B |
| Aug-52 | CONSETT-54D | BOR.GDNS-54C | W.HARTLEPOOL-51C | BOR.GDNS-54C | MIDDLESBROUGH-51D | TYNE DOCK-54B | TYNE DOCK-54B | TYNE DOCK-54B | TYNE DOCK-54B |
| Jan-53 | CONSETT-54D | BOR.GDNS-54C | W.HARTLEPOOL-51C | BOR.GDNS-54C | MIDDLESBROUGH-51D | TYNE DOCK-54B | TYNE DOCK-54B | TYNE DOCK-54B | TYNE DOCK-54B |
| Aug-53 | CONSETT-54D | BOR.GDNS-54C | W.HARTLEPOOL-51C | BOR.GDNS-54C | MIDDLESBROUGH-51D | TYNE DOCK-54B | TYNE DOCK-54B | TYNE DOCK-54B | TYNE DOCK-54B |
| Jan-54 | CONSETT-54D | BOR.GDNS-54C | W.HARTLEPOOL-51C | BOR.GDNS-54C | MIDDLESBROUGH-51D | TYNE DOCK-54B | TYNE DOCK-54B | TYNE DOCK-54B | TYNE DOCK-54B |
| Aug-54 | CONSETT-54D | BOR.GDNS-54C | W.HARTLEPOOL-51C | BOR.GDNS-54C | **9/54: W..AUCK - 51F** | TYNE DOCK-54B | TYNE DOCK-54B | TYNE DOCK-54B | TYNE DOCK-54B |
| Jan-55 | CONSETT-54D | BOR.GDNS-54C | W.HARTLEPOOL-51C | BOR.GDNS-54C | W.AUCKLAND-51F | TYNE DOCK-54B | TYNE DOCK-54B | TYNE DOCK-54B | TYNE DOCK-54B |
| Aug-55 | CONSETT-54D | BOR.GDNS-54C | W.HARTLEPOOL-51C | BOR.GDNS-54C | W.AUCKLAND-51F | TYNE DOCK-54B | TYNE DOCK-54B | TYNE DOCK-54B | TYNE DOCK-54B |
| Jan-56 | CONSETT-54D | BOR.GDNS-54C | W.HARTLEPOOL-51C | BOR.GDNS-54C | W.AUCKLAND-51F | TYNE DOCK-54B | TYNE DOCK-54B | TYNE DOCK-54B | TYNE DOCK-54B |
| Aug-56 | CONSETT-54D | BOR.GDNS-54C | W.HARTLEPOOL-51C | BOR.GDNS-54C | W.AUCKLAND-51F | TYNE DOCK-54B | **6/56: BLAY - 52C** | **6/56: BLAY - 52C** | TYNE DOCK-54B |
| Jan-57 | CONSETT-54D | BOR.GDNS-54C | W.HARTLEPOOL-51C | BOR.GDNS-54C | W.AUCKLAND-51F | TYNE DOCK-54B | BLAYDON-52C | BLAYDON-52C | TYNE DOCK-54B |
| Aug-57 | CONSETT-54D | BOR.GDNS-54C | W.HARTLEPOOL-51C | BOR.GDNS-54C | W.AUCKLAND-51F | TYNE DOCK-54B | **6/57: T.DCK - 54B** | BLAYDON-52C | TYNE DOCK-54B |
| Jan-58 | CONSETT-54D | BOR.GDNS-54C | W.HARTLEPOOL-51C | BOR.GDNS-54C | W.AUCKLAND-51F | TYNE DOCK-54B | TYNE DOCK-54B | BLAYDON-52C | TYNE DOCK-54B |
| Aug-58 | CONSETT-54D | BOR.GDNS-54C | W.HARTLEPOOL-51C | BOR.GDNS-54C | W.AUCKLAND-51F | TYNE DOCK-54B | TYNE DOCK-54B | BLAYDON-52C | TYNE DOCK-54B |
| Jan-59 | CONSETT-52K | BOR.GDNS-52J | W.HARTLEPOOL-51C | BOR.GDNS-52J | W.AUCKLAND-51F | TYNE DOCK-52H | TYNE DOCK-52H | **2/59: T.DOCK - 54B** | TYNE DOCK-52H |
| Aug-59 | CONSETT-52K | **6/59: BLAY - 52C** | W.HARTLEPOOL-51C | **6/59: BLAY - 52C** | W.AUCKLAND-51F | TYNE DOCK-52H | TYNE DOCK-52H | TYNE DOCK-52H | **6/59: SUND - 52G** |
| Nov-59 | CONSETT-52K | **9/59: CON - 52K** | W.HARTLEPOOL-51C | BLAYDON-52C | W.AUCKLAND-51F | TYNE DOCK-52H | TYNE DOCK-52H | TYNE DOCK-52H | SUNDERLAND-52G |
| Jan-60 | CONSETT-52K | CONSETT-52K | W.HARTLEPOOL-51C | BLAYDON-52C | W.AUCKLAND-51F | TYNE DOCK-52H | TYNE DOCK-52H | TYNE DOCK-52H | **12/59: T.DCK - 52H** |
| Apr-60 | CONSETT-52K | CONSETT-52K | W.HARTLEPOOL-51C | BLAYDON-52C | W.AUCKLAND-51F | TYNE DOCK-52H | TYNE DOCK-52H | TYNE DOCK-52H | TYNE DOCK-52H |
| Aug-60 | CONSETT-52K | CONSETT-52K | W.HARTLEPOOL-51C | BLAYDON-52C | W.AUCKLAND-51F | TYNE DOCK-52H | TYNE DOCK-52H | TYNE DOCK-52H | TYNE DOCK-52H |
| Nov-60 | CONSETT-52K | CONSETT-52K | W.HARTLEPOOL-51C | BLAYDON-52C | W.AUCKLAND-51F | TYNE DOCK-52H | TYNE DOCK-52H | TYNE DOCK-52H | TYNE DOCK-52H |

| | 63464 | 63465 | 63466 | 63467 | 63468 | 63469 | 63470 | 63471 | 63472 |
|---|---|---|---|---|---|---|---|---|---|
| Aug-50 | TYNE DOCK-54B | TYNE DOCK-54B | TYNE DOCK-54B | TYNE DOCK-54B | TYNE DOCK-54B | TYNE DOCK-54B | TYNE DOCK-54B | TYNE DOCK-54B | TYNE DOCK-54B |
| Jan-51 | TYNE DOCK-54B | TYNE DOCK-54B | TYNE DOCK-54B | TYNE DOCK-54B | TYNE DOCK-54B | TYNE DOCK-54B | TYNE DOCK-54B | TYNE DOCK-54B | TYNE DOCK-54B |
| Aug-51 | TYNE DOCK-54B | TYNE DOCK-54B | TYNE DOCK-54B | TYNE DOCK-54B | TYNE DOCK-54B | TYNE DOCK-54B | TYNE DOCK-54B | TYNE DOCK-54B | TYNE DOCK-54B |
| Jan-52 | TYNE DOCK-54B | TYNE DOCK-54B | TYNE DOCK-54B | TYNE DOCK-54B | TYNE DOCK-54B | TYNE DOCK-54B | TYNE DOCK-54B | TYNE DOCK-54B | TYNE DOCK-54B |
| Aug-52 | TYNE DOCK-54B | TYNE DOCK-54B | TYNE DOCK-54B | TYNE DOCK-54B | TYNE DOCK-54B | TYNE DOCK-54B | TYNE DOCK-54B | TYNE DOCK-54B | TYNE DOCK-54B |
| Jan-53 | TYNE DOCK-54B | TYNE DOCK-54B | TYNE DOCK-54B | TYNE DOCK-54B | TYNE DOCK-54B | TYNE DOCK-54B | TYNE DOCK-54B | TYNE DOCK-54B | TYNE DOCK-54B |
| Aug-53 | TYNE DOCK-54B | TYNE DOCK-54B | TYNE DOCK-54B | TYNE DOCK-54B | TYNE DOCK-54B | TYNE DOCK-54B | TYNE DOCK-54B | TYNE DOCK-54B | TYNE DOCK-54B |
| Jan-54 | TYNE DOCK-54B | TYNE DOCK-54B | TYNE DOCK-54B | TYNE DOCK-54B | TYNE DOCK-54B | TYNE DOCK-54B | TYNE DOCK-54B | TYNE DOCK-54B | TYNE DOCK-54B |
| Aug-54 | TYNE DOCK-54B | TYNE DOCK-54B | TYNE DOCK-54B | TYNE DOCK-54B | TYNE DOCK-54B | TYNE DOCK-54B | TYNE DOCK-54B | TYNE DOCK-54B | TYNE DOCK-54B |
| Jan-55 | TYNE DOCK-54B | TYNE DOCK-54B | TYNE DOCK-54B | TYNE DOCK-54B | TYNE DOCK-54B | TYNE DOCK-54B | TYNE DOCK-54B | TYNE DOCK-54B | TYNE DOCK-54B |
| Aug-55 | TYNE DOCK-54B | TYNE DOCK-54B | TYNE DOCK-54B | TYNE DOCK-54B | TYNE DOCK-54B | TYNE DOCK-54B | TYNE DOCK-54B | TYNE DOCK-54B | TYNE DOCK-54B |
| Jan-56 | TYNE DOCK-54B | TYNE DOCK-54B | TYNE DOCK-54B | TYNE DOCK-54B | TYNE DOCK-54B | TYNE DOCK-54B | TYNE DOCK-54B | TYNE DOCK-54B | TYNE DOCK-54B |
| Aug-56 | **6/56: BLAY - 52C** | TYNE DOCK-54B | TYNE DOCK-54B | TYNE DOCK-54B | **6/56: BLAY - 52C** | TYNE DOCK-54B | **6/56: BLAY - 52C** | **6/56: BLAY - 52C** | **6/56: BLAY - 52C** |
| Jan-57 | BLAYDON-52C | TYNE DOCK-54B | **10/56: SUND - 54A** | **10/56: SUND - 54A** | BLAYDON-52C | TYNE DOCK-54B | BLAYDON-52C | BLAYDON-52C | BLAYDON-52C |
| Aug-57 | BLAYDON-52C | TYNE DOCK-54B | SUNDERLAND-54A | SUNDERLAND-54A | **6/57: T.DCK - 54B** | TYNE DOCK-54B | BLAYDON-52C | BLAYDON-52C | BLAYDON-52C |
| Jan-58 | BLAYDON-52C | TYNE DOCK-54B | SUNDERLAND-54A | SUNDERLAND-54A | TYNE DOCK-54B | TYNE DOCK-54B | BLAYDON-52C | BLAYDON-52C | BLAYDON-52C |
| Aug-58 | BLAYDON-52C | TYNE DOCK-54B | SUNDERLAND-54A | SUNDERLAND-54A | TYNE DOCK-54B | TYNE DOCK-54B | **6/58: T.DCK - 54B** | BLAYDON-52C | BLAYDON-52C |
| Jan-59 | **2/59: SUND - 52G** | TYNE DOCK-52H | SUNDERLAND-52G | SUNDERLAND-52G | TYNE DOCK-52H | **2/59: SUND - 52G** | TYNE DOCK-52H | **#REF!** | **#REF!** |
| Aug-59 | SUNDERLAND-52G | TYNE DOCK-52H | SUNDERLAND-52G | SUNDERLAND-52G | TYNE DOCK-52H | SUNDERLAND-52G | TYNE DOCK-52H | TYNE DOCK-52H | TYNE DOCK-52H |
| Nov-59 | SUNDERLAND-52G | TYNE DOCK-52H | SUNDERLAND-52G | SUNDERLAND-52G | TYNE DOCK-52H | SUNDERLAND-52G | TYNE DOCK-52H | TYNE DOCK-52H | TYNE DOCK-52H |
| Jan-60 | **12/59: T.DCK - 52H** | TYNE DOCK-52H | **12/59: T.DCK - 52H** | SUNDERLAND-52G | TYNE DOCK-52H | SUNDERLAND-52G | TYNE DOCK-52H | TYNE DOCK-52H | TYNE DOCK-52H |
| Apr-60 | TYNE DOCK-52H | TYNE DOCK-52H | TYNE DOCK-52H | SUNDERLAND-52G | TYNE DOCK-52H | SUNDERLAND-52G | TYNE DOCK-52H | TYNE DOCK-52H | TYNE DOCK-52H |
| Aug-60 | TYNE DOCK-52H | TYNE DOCK-52H | TYNE DOCK-52H | SUNDERLAND-52G | TYNE DOCK-52H | SUNDERLAND-52G | TYNE DOCK-52H | TYNE DOCK-52H | TYNE DOCK-52H |
| Nov-60 | TYNE DOCK-52H | TYNE DOCK-52H | TYNE DOCK-52H | SUNDERLAND-52G | TYNE DOCK-52H | SUNDERLAND-52G | TYNE DOCK-52H | TYNE DOCK-52H | TYNE DOCK-52H |

| | 63473 | 63474 | O3 2-8-0 (1913) 63475 | 63476 | 63477 | 63478 | 63479 | 63480 | 63481 |
|---|---|---|---|---|---|---|---|---|---|
| Aug-50 | TYNE DOCK-54B | TYNE DOCK-54B | RETFORD-36E | DONCASTER-36A | DONCASTER-36A | DONCASTER-36A | DONCASTER-36A | DONCASTER-36A | DONCASTER-36A |
| Jan-51 | TYNE DOCK-54B | TYNE DOCK-54B | RETFORD-36E | **2/51: RET - 36E** | **3/51: RET - 36E** | **12/50: RET - 36E** | **3/51: RET - 36E** | **2/51: RET - 36E** | DONCASTER-36A |
| Aug-51 | TYNE DOCK-54B | TYNE DOCK-54B | RETFORD-36E | RETFORD-36E | RETFORD-36E | RETFORD-36E | **5/51: W/D** | **3/51: W/D** | **4/51: W/D** |
| Jan-52 | TYNE DOCK-54B | TYNE DOCK-54B | RETFORD-36E | RETFORD-36E | **9/51: W/D** | **9/51: W/D** | | | |
| Aug-52 | TYNE DOCK-54B | TYNE DOCK-54B | RETFORD-36E | **3/52: W/D** | | | | | |
| Jan-53 | TYNE DOCK-54B | TYNE DOCK-54B | **1/53: W/D** | | | | | | |
| Aug-53 | TYNE DOCK-54B | TYNE DOCK-54B | | | | | | | |
| Jan-54 | TYNE DOCK-54B | TYNE DOCK-54B | | | | | | | |
| Aug-54 | TYNE DOCK-54B | TYNE DOCK-54B | | | | | | | |
| Jan-55 | TYNE DOCK-54B | TYNE DOCK-54B | | | | | | | |
| Aug-55 | TYNE DOCK-54B | TYNE DOCK-54B | | | | | | | |
| Jan-56 | TYNE DOCK-54B | TYNE DOCK-54B | | | | | | | |
| Aug-56 | TYNE DOCK-54B | TYNE DOCK-54B | | | | | | | |
| Jan-57 | TYNE DOCK-54B | **10/56: SUND - 54A** | | | | | | | |
| Aug-57 | TYNE DOCK-54B | SUNDERLAND-54A | | | | | | | |
| Jan-58 | TYNE DOCK-54B | SUNDERLAND-54A | | | | | | | |
| Aug-58 | TYNE DOCK-54B | SUNDERLAND-54A | | | | | | | |
| Jan-59 | TYNE DOCK-52H | SUNDERLAND-52G | | | | | | | |
| Aug-59 | **6/59: SUND - 52G** | SUNDERLAND-52G | | | | | | | |
| Nov-59 | SUNDERLAND-52G | SUNDERLAND-52G | | | | | | | |
| Jan-60 | **12/59: T.DCK - 52H** | SUNDERLAND-52G | | | | | | | |
| Apr-60 | TYNE DOCK-52H | SUNDERLAND-52G | | | | | | | |
| Aug-60 | TYNE DOCK-52H | SUNDERLAND-52G | | | | | | | |
| Nov-60 | TYNE DOCK-52H | SUNDERLAND-52G | | | | | | | |

| | 63482 | 63483 | 63484 | 63485 | 63486 | 63488 | 63491 | 63493 | O1 2-8-0 (1944)<br>63571 |
|---|---|---|---|---|---|---|---|---|---|
| Aug-50 | RETFORD - 36E | DONCASTER - 36A | DONCASTER - 36A | DONCASTER - 36A | DONCASTER - 36A | DONCASTER - 36A | DONCASTER - 36A | DONCASTER - 36A | ANNESLEY - 38B |
| Jan-51 | RETFORD - 36E | DONCASTER - 36A | 2/51: RET - 36E | 3/51: RET - 36E | DONCASTER - 36A | 12/50: RET - 36E | 12/50: W/D | DONCASTER - 36A | ANNESLEY - 38B |
| Aug-51 | RETFORD - 36E | DONCASTER - 36A | RETFORD - 36E | RETFORD - 36E | 2/51: W/D | RETFORD - 36E | | 2/51: W/D | ANNESLEY - 38B |
| Jan-52 | 1/52: W/D | DONCASTER - 36A | RETFORD - 36E | 9/51: W/D | | 2/51: W/D | | | ANNESLEY - 38B |
| Aug-52 | | DONCASTER - 36A | 9/52: DCTR - 36A | | | | | | ANNESLEY - 38B |
| Jan-53 | | 1/53: W/D | 12/52: W/D | | | | | | ANNESLEY - 38B |
| Aug-53 | | | | | | | | | ANNESLEY - 38B |
| Jan-54 | | | | | | | | | ANNESLEY - 38B |
| Aug-54 | | | | | | | | | ANNESLEY - 38B |
| Jan-55 | | | | | | | | | ANNESLEY - 38B |
| Aug-55 | | | | | | | | | ANNESLEY - 38B |
| Jan-56 | | | | | | | | | ANNESLEY - 38B |
| Aug-56 | | | | | | | | | ANNESLEY - 38B |
| Jan-57 | | | | | | | | | 3/57: MARCH - 31B |
| Aug-57 | | | | | | | | | MARCH - 31B |
| Jan-58 | | | | | | | | | MARCH - 31B |
| Aug-58 | | | | | | | | | MARCH - 31B |
| Jan-59 | | | | | | | | | MARCH - 31B |
| Aug-59 | | | | | | | | | MARCH - 31B |
| Nov-59 | | | | | | | | | MARCH - 31B |
| Jan-60 | | | | | | | | | 1/60: STAVE - 41H |
| Apr-60 | | | | | | | | | STAVELEY (GC) - 41H |
| Aug-60 | | | | | | | | | STAVELEY (GC) - 41H |
| Nov-60 | | | | | | | | | STAVELEY (GC) - 41H |

| | 63578 | 63579 | 63589 | 63590 | 63591 | 63592 | 63594 | 63596 | 63610 |
|---|---|---|---|---|---|---|---|---|---|
| Aug-50 | ANNESLEY - 38B | ANNESLEY - 38B | ANNESLEY - 38B | GORTON - 39A | GORTON - 39A | GORTON - 39A | ANNESLEY - 38B | ANNESLEY - 38B | ANNESLEY - 38B |
| Jan-51 | ANNESLEY - 38B | ANNESLEY - 38B | ANNESLEY - 38B | 11/50: ANN - 38B | 11/50: ANN - 38B | 11/50: ANN - 38B | ANNESLEY - 38B | ANNESLEY - 38B | ANNESLEY - 38B |
| Aug-51 | ANNESLEY - 38B | ANNESLEY - 38B | ANNESLEY - 38B | ANNESLEY - 38B | ANNESLEY - 38B | ANNESLEY - 38B | ANNESLEY - 38B | ANNESLEY - 38B | ANNESLEY - 38B |
| Jan-52 | ANNESLEY - 38B | ANNESLEY - 38B | ANNESLEY - 38B | ANNESLEY - 38B | ANNESLEY - 38B | ANNESLEY - 38B | ANNESLEY - 38B | ANNESLEY - 38B | ANNESLEY - 38B |
| Aug-52 | ANNESLEY - 38B | ANNESLEY - 38B | ANNESLEY - 38B | ANNESLEY - 38B | ANNESLEY - 38B | ANNESLEY - 38B | ANNESLEY - 38B | ANNESLEY - 38B | ANNESLEY - 38B |
| Jan-53 | ANNESLEY - 38B | ANNESLEY - 38B | ANNESLEY - 38B | ANNESLEY - 38B | ANNESLEY - 38B | ANNESLEY - 38B | ANNESLEY - 38B | ANNESLEY - 38B | ANNESLEY - 38B |
| Aug-53 | ANNESLEY - 38B | ANNESLEY - 38B | ANNESLEY - 38B | ANNESLEY - 38B | ANNESLEY - 38B | ANNESLEY - 38B | ANNESLEY - 38B | ANNESLEY - 38B | ANNESLEY - 38B |
| Jan-54 | ANNESLEY - 38B | ANNESLEY - 38B | ANNESLEY - 38B | ANNESLEY - 38B | ANNESLEY - 38B | ANNESLEY - 38B | ANNESLEY - 38B | ANNESLEY - 38B | ANNESLEY - 38B |
| Aug-54 | ANNESLEY - 38B | ANNESLEY - 38B | ANNESLEY - 38B | ANNESLEY - 38B | ANNESLEY - 38B | ANNESLEY - 38B | ANNESLEY - 38B | ANNESLEY - 38B | ANNESLEY - 38B |
| Jan-55 | ANNESLEY - 38B | ANNESLEY - 38B | ANNESLEY - 38B | ANNESLEY - 38B | ANNESLEY - 38B | ANNESLEY - 38B | ANNESLEY - 38B | ANNESLEY - 38B | ANNESLEY - 38B |
| Aug-55 | ANNESLEY - 38B | ANNESLEY - 38B | ANNESLEY - 38B | ANNESLEY - 38B | ANNESLEY - 38B | ANNESLEY - 38B | ANNESLEY - 38B | ANNESLEY - 38B | ANNESLEY - 38B |
| Jan-56 | ANNESLEY - 38B | ANNESLEY - 38B | ANNESLEY - 38B | ANNESLEY - 38B | ANNESLEY - 38B | ANNESLEY - 38B | ANNESLEY - 38B | ANNESLEY - 38B | ANNESLEY - 38B |
| Aug-56 | ANNESLEY - 38B | ANNESLEY - 38B | ANNESLEY - 38B | ANNESLEY - 38B | ANNESLEY - 38B | ANNESLEY - 38B | ANNESLEY - 38B | ANNESLEY - 38B | ANNESLEY - 38B |
| Jan-57 | ANNESLEY - 38B | 3/57: MARCH - 31B | ANNESLEY - 38B | 3/57: MARCH - 31B | ANNESLEY - 38B | ANNESLEY - 38B | ANNESLEY - 38B | 2/57: MARCH - 31B | ANNESLEY - 38B |
| Aug-57 | ANNESLEY - 38B | 4/57: ANN - 38B | ANNESLEY - 38B | MARCH - 31B | ANNESLEY - 38B | ANNESLEY - 38B | ANNESLEY - 38B | MARCH - 31B | ANNESLEY - 38B |
| Jan-58 | ANNESLEY - 38B | ANNESLEY - 38B | 11/57: COLW - 38A | MARCH - 31B | ANNESLEY - 38B | 11/57: COLW - 38A | 11/57: COLW - 38A | MARCH - 31B | ANNESLEY - 38B |
| Aug-58 | ANNESLEY - 16D | ANNESLEY - 16D | COLWICK - 40E | MARCH - 31B | ANNESLEY - 16D | COLWICK - 40E | COLWICK - 40E | MARCH - 31B | ANNESLEY - 16D |
| Jan-59 | ANNESLEY - 16D | ANNESLEY - 16D | COLWICK - 40E | MARCH - 31B | ANNESLEY - 16D | COLWICK - 40E | COLWICK - 40E | MARCH - 31B | ANNESLEY - 16D |
| Aug-59 | ANNESLEY - 16D | ANNESLEY - 16D | COLWICK - 40E | MARCH - 31B | ANNESLEY - 16D | COLWICK - 40E | COLWICK - 40E | MARCH - 31B | ANNESLEY - 16D |
| Nov-59 | ANNESLEY - 16D | ANNESLEY - 16D | COLWICK - 40E | 11/59: STAVE - 41H | ANNESLEY - 16D | COLWICK - 40E | COLWICK - 40E | MARCH - 31B | ANNESLEY - 16D |
| Jan-60 | ANNESLEY - 16D | ANNESLEY - 16D | COLWICK - 40E | STAVELEY (GC) - 41H | ANNESLEY - 16D | COLWICK - 40E | COLWICK - 40E | 1/60: STAVE - 41H | ANNESLEY - 16D |
| Apr-60 | ANNESLEY - 16D | ANNESLEY - 16D | COLWICK - 40E | STAVELEY (GC) - 41H | ANNESLEY - 16D | COLWICK - 40E | COLWICK - 40E | STAVELEY (GC) - 41H | ANNESLEY - 16D |
| Aug-60 | ANNESLEY - 16D | ANNESLEY - 16D | COLWICK - 40E | STAVELEY (GC) - 41H | ANNESLEY - 16D | COLWICK - 40E | COLWICK - 40E | STAVELEY (GC) - 41H | ANNESLEY - 16D |
| Nov-60 | ANNESLEY - 16D | ANNESLEY - 16D | COLWICK - 40E | STAVELEY (GC) - 41H | ANNESLEY - 16D | COLWICK - 40E | COLWICK - 40E | STAVELEY (GC) - 41H | ANNESLEY - 16D |

| | 63619 | 63630 | 63646 | 63650 | 63652 | 63663 | 63670 | 63676 | 63678 |
|---|---|---|---|---|---|---|---|---|---|
| Aug-50 | GORTON - 39A | GORTON - 39A | ANNESLEY - 38B | GORTON - 39A | GORTON - 39A | GORTON - 39A | GORTON - 39A | DAIRYCOATES - 53A | GORTON - 39A |
| Jan-51 | 11/50: ANN - 38B | 11/50: ANN - 38B | ANNESLEY - 38B | 11/50: ANN - 38B | 11/50: ANN - 38B | 11/50: ANN - 38B | 11/50: ANN - 38B | DAIRYCOATES - 53A | 11/50: ANN - 38B |
| Aug-51 | ANNESLEY - 38B | ANNESLEY - 38B | ANNESLEY - 38B | ANNESLEY - 38B | ANNESLEY - 38B | ANNESLEY - 38B | ANNESLEY - 38B | 9/51: ANN - 38B | ANNESLEY - 38B |
| Jan-52 | ANNESLEY - 38B | ANNESLEY - 38B | ANNESLEY - 38B | ANNESLEY - 38B | ANNESLEY - 38B | ANNESLEY - 38B | ANNESLEY - 38B | ANNESLEY - 38B | ANNESLEY - 38B |
| Aug-52 | ANNESLEY - 38B | ANNESLEY - 38B | ANNESLEY - 38B | ANNESLEY - 38B | ANNESLEY - 38B | ANNESLEY - 38B | ANNESLEY - 38B | ANNESLEY - 38B | ANNESLEY - 38B |
| Jan-53 | ANNESLEY - 38B | ANNESLEY - 38B | ANNESLEY - 38B | ANNESLEY - 38B | ANNESLEY - 38B | ANNESLEY - 38B | ANNESLEY - 38B | ANNESLEY - 38B | ANNESLEY - 38B |
| Aug-53 | ANNESLEY - 38B | ANNESLEY - 38B | ANNESLEY - 38B | ANNESLEY - 38B | ANNESLEY - 38B | ANNESLEY - 38B | ANNESLEY - 38B | ANNESLEY - 38B | ANNESLEY - 38B |
| Jan-54 | ANNESLEY - 38B | ANNESLEY - 38B | ANNESLEY - 38B | ANNESLEY - 38B | ANNESLEY - 38B | ANNESLEY - 38B | ANNESLEY - 38B | ANNESLEY - 38B | ANNESLEY - 38B |
| Aug-54 | ANNESLEY - 38B | ANNESLEY - 38B | ANNESLEY - 38B | ANNESLEY - 38B | ANNESLEY - 38B | ANNESLEY - 38B | ANNESLEY - 38B | ANNESLEY - 38B | ANNESLEY - 38B |
| Jan-55 | ANNESLEY - 38B | ANNESLEY - 38B | ANNESLEY - 38B | ANNESLEY - 38B | ANNESLEY - 38B | ANNESLEY - 38B | ANNESLEY - 38B | ANNESLEY - 38B | ANNESLEY - 38B |
| Aug-55 | ANNESLEY - 38B | ANNESLEY - 38B | ANNESLEY - 38B | ANNESLEY - 38B | ANNESLEY - 38B | ANNESLEY - 38B | ANNESLEY - 38B | ANNESLEY - 38B | ANNESLEY - 38B |
| Jan-56 | ANNESLEY - 38B | ANNESLEY - 38B | ANNESLEY - 38B | ANNESLEY - 38B | ANNESLEY - 38B | ANNESLEY - 38B | ANNESLEY - 38B | ANNESLEY - 38B | ANNESLEY - 38B |
| Aug-56 | ANNESLEY - 38B | ANNESLEY - 38B | ANNESLEY - 38B | ANNESLEY - 38B | ANNESLEY - 38B | ANNESLEY - 38B | ANNESLEY - 38B | ANNESLEY - 38B | ANNESLEY - 38B |
| Jan-57 | 3/57: MARCH - 31B | 3/57: MARCH - 31B | 3/57: MARCH - 31B | 2/57: MARCH - 31B | 2/57: MARCH - 31B | 3/57: MARCH - 31B | 2/57: MARCH - 31B | ANNESLEY - 38B | 3/57: MARCH - 31B |
| Aug-57 | MARCH - 31B | MARCH - 31B | MARCH - 31B | MARCH - 31B | MARCH - 31B | MARCH - 31B | MARCH - 31B | ANNESLEY - 38B | MARCH - 31B |
| Jan-58 | MARCH - 31B | MARCH - 31B | MARCH - 31B | MARCH - 31B | MARCH - 31B | MARCH - 31B | MARCH - 31B | ANNESLEY - 38B | MARCH - 31B |
| Aug-58 | MARCH - 31B | MARCH - 31B | MARCH - 31B | MARCH - 31B | MARCH - 31B | MARCH - 31B | MARCH - 31B | ANNESLEY - 16D | MARCH - 31B |
| Jan-59 | MARCH - 31B | MARCH - 31B | MARCH - 31B | MARCH - 31B | MARCH - 31B | MARCH - 31B | MARCH - 31B | ANNESLEY - 16D | MARCH - 31B |
| Aug-59 | MARCH - 31B | MARCH - 31B | MARCH - 31B | MARCH - 31B | MARCH - 31B | MARCH - 31B | MARCH - 31B | ANNESLEY - 16D | MARCH - 31B |
| Nov-59 | MARCH - 31B | MARCH - 31B | MARCH - 31B | MARCH - 31B | MARCH - 31B | 11/59: STAVE - 41H | MARCH - 31B | ANNESLEY - 16D | MARCH - 31B |
| Jan-60 | 2/60: STAVE - 41H | 2/60: STAVE - 41H | 2/60: STAVE - 41H | 2/60: STAVE - 41H | 3/60: STAVE - 41H | STAVELEY (GC) - 41H | 3/60: STAVE - 41H | ANNESLEY - 16D | 3/60: STAVE - 41H |
| Apr-60 | STAVELEY (GC) - 41H | STAVELEY (GC) - 41H | STAVELEY (GC) - 41H | STAVELEY (GC) - 41H | STAVELEY (GC) - 41H | STAVELEY (GC) - 41H | STAVELEY (GC) - 41H | ANNESLEY - 16D | STAVELEY (GC) - 41H |
| Aug-60 | STAVELEY (GC) - 41H | STAVELEY (GC) - 41H | STAVELEY (GC) - 41H | STAVELEY (GC) - 41H | STAVELEY (GC) - 41H | STAVELEY (GC) - 41H | STAVELEY (GC) - 41H | ANNESLEY - 16D | STAVELEY (GC) - 41H |
| Nov-60 | STAVELEY (GC) - 41H | STAVELEY (GC) - 41H | STAVELEY (GC) - 41H | STAVELEY (GC) - 41H | STAVELEY (GC) - 41H | STAVELEY (GC) - 41H | STAVELEY (GC) - 41H | ANNESLEY - 16D | STAVELEY (GC) - 41H |

| | 63687 | 63689 | 63711 | 63712 | 63725 | 63740 | 63746 | 63752 | 63755 |
|---|---|---|---|---|---|---|---|---|---|
| Aug-50 | ANNESLEY - 38B | ANNESLEY - 38B | GORTON - 39A | DAIRYCOATES - 53A | GORTON - 39A | DAIRYCOATES - 53A | ANNESLEY - 38B | ANNESLEY - 38B | DAIRYCOATES - 53A |
| Jan-51 | ANNESLEY - 38B | ANNESLEY - 38B | 11/50: ANN - 38B | DAIRYCOATES - 53A | 11/50: ANN - 38B | DAIRYCOATES - 53A | ANNESLEY - 38B | ANNESLEY - 38B | DAIRYCOATES - 53A |
| Aug-51 | ANNESLEY - 38B | ANNESLEY - 38B | ANNESLEY - 38B | 9/51: T.DCK - 54B | ANNESLEY - 38B | 9/51: ANN - 38B | ANNESLEY - 38B | ANNESLEY - 38B | 9/51: T.DCK - 54B |
| Jan-52 | ANNESLEY - 38B | ANNESLEY - 38B | ANNESLEY - 38B | TYNE DOCK 54B | ANNESLEY - 38B | ANNESLEY - 38B | ANNESLEY - 38B | ANNESLEY - 38B | TYNE DOCK 54B |
| Aug-52 | ANNESLEY - 38B | ANNESLEY - 38B | ANNESLEY - 38B | TYNE DOCK 54B | ANNESLEY - 38B | ANNESLEY - 38B | ANNESLEY - 38B | ANNESLEY - 38B | TYNE DOCK 54B |
| Jan-53 | ANNESLEY - 38B | ANNESLEY - 38B | ANNESLEY - 38B | TYNE DOCK 54B | ANNESLEY - 38B | ANNESLEY - 38B | ANNESLEY - 38B | ANNESLEY - 38B | TYNE DOCK 54B |
| Aug-53 | ANNESLEY - 38B | ANNESLEY - 38B | ANNESLEY - 38B | TYNE DOCK 54B | ANNESLEY - 38B | ANNESLEY - 38B | ANNESLEY - 38B | ANNESLEY - 38B | TYNE DOCK 54B |
| Jan-54 | ANNESLEY - 38B | ANNESLEY - 38B | ANNESLEY - 38B | TYNE DOCK 54B | ANNESLEY - 38B | ANNESLEY - 38B | ANNESLEY - 38B | ANNESLEY - 38B | TYNE DOCK 54B |
| Aug-54 | ANNESLEY - 38B | ANNESLEY - 38B | ANNESLEY - 38B | TYNE DOCK 54B | ANNESLEY - 38B | ANNESLEY - 38B | ANNESLEY - 38B | ANNESLEY - 38B | TYNE DOCK 54B |
| Jan-55 | ANNESLEY - 38B | ANNESLEY - 38B | ANNESLEY - 38B | TYNE DOCK 54B | ANNESLEY - 38B | ANNESLEY - 38B | ANNESLEY - 38B | ANNESLEY - 38B | TYNE DOCK 54B |
| Aug-55 | ANNESLEY - 38B | ANNESLEY - 38B | ANNESLEY - 38B | TYNE DOCK 54B | ANNESLEY - 38B | ANNESLEY - 38B | ANNESLEY - 38B | ANNESLEY - 38B | TYNE DOCK 54B |
| Jan-56 | ANNESLEY - 38B | ANNESLEY - 38B | ANNESLEY - 38B | TYNE DOCK 54B | ANNESLEY - 38B | ANNESLEY - 38B | ANNESLEY - 38B | ANNESLEY - 38B | TYNE DOCK 54B |
| Aug-56 | ANNESLEY - 38B | ANNESLEY - 38B | ANNESLEY - 38B | TYNE DOCK 54B | 7/56: W'BORO - 15A | ANNESLEY - 38B | ANNESLEY - 38B | ANNESLEY - 38B | TYNE DOCK 54B |
| Jan-57 | 2/57: MARCH - 31B | ANNESLEY - 38B | ANNESLEY - 38B | TYNE DOCK 54B | 12/56: ANN - 38B | ANNESLEY - 38B | 3/57: MARCH - 31B | ANNESLEY - 38B | TYNE DOCK 54B |
| Aug-57 | MARCH - 31B | ANNESLEY - 38B | ANNESLEY - 38B | TYNE DOCK 54B | 3/57: MARCH - 31B | ANNESLEY - 38B | MARCH - 31B | ANNESLEY - 38B | TYNE DOCK 54B |
| Jan-58 | MARCH - 31B | ANNESLEY - 38B | ANNESLEY - 38B | TYNE DOCK 54B | MARCH - 31B | ANNESLEY - 38B | MARCH - 31B | ANNESLEY - 38B | TYNE DOCK 54B |
| Aug-58 | MARCH - 31B | ANNESLEY - 16D | ANNESLEY - 16D | TYNE DOCK 54B | MARCH - 31B | ANNESLEY - 16D | MARCH - 31B | ANNESLEY - 16D | TYNE DOCK 54B |
| Jan-59 | MARCH - 31B | ANNESLEY - 16D | ANNESLEY - 16D | TYNE DOCK - 52H | MARCH - 31B | ANNESLEY - 16D | MARCH - 31B | ANNESLEY - 16D | TYNE DOCK - 52H |
| Aug-59 | MARCH - 31B | ANNESLEY - 16D | ANNESLEY - 16D | TYNE DOCK - 52H | MARCH - 31B | ANNESLEY - 16D | MARCH - 31B | ANNESLEY - 16D | TYNE DOCK - 52H |
| Nov-59 | MARCH - 31B | ANNESLEY - 16D | ANNESLEY - 16D | TYNE DOCK - 52H | MARCH - 31B | ANNESLEY - 16D | MARCH - 31B | ANNESLEY - 16D | TYNE DOCK - 52H |
| Jan-60 | MARCH - 31B | ANNESLEY - 16D | ANNESLEY - 16D | TYNE DOCK - 52H | MARCH - 31B | ANNESLEY - 16D | MARCH - 31B | ANNESLEY - 16D | TYNE DOCK - 52H |
| Apr-60 | MARCH - 31B | ANNESLEY - 16D | ANNESLEY - 16D | TYNE DOCK - 52H | MARCH - 31B | ANNESLEY - 16D | MARCH - 31B | ANNESLEY - 16D | TYNE DOCK - 52H |
| Aug-60 | MARCH - 31B | ANNESLEY - 16D | ANNESLEY - 16D | TYNE DOCK - 52H | MARCH - 31B | ANNESLEY - 16D | MARCH - 31B | ANNESLEY - 16D | TYNE DOCK - 52H |
| Nov-60 | MARCH - 31B | ANNESLEY - 16D | ANNESLEY - 16D | TYNE DOCK - 52H | MARCH - 31B | ANNESLEY - 16D | MARCH - 31B | ANNESLEY - 16D | TYNE DOCK - 52H |

| | 63756 | 63760 | 63768 | 63773 | 63777 | 63780 | 63784 | 63786 | 63789 |
|---|---|---|---|---|---|---|---|---|---|
| Aug-50 | COLWICK - 38A | DAIRYCOATES - 53A | GORTON - 39A | GORTON - 39A | GORTON - 39A | GORTON - 39A | GORTON - 39A | GORTON - 39A | GORTON - 39A |
| Jan-51 | COLWICK - 38A | DAIRYCOATES - 53A | 11/50: ANN - 38B | 11/50: ANN - 38B | 10/50: ANN - 38B | 10/50: ANN - 38B | 11/50: ANN - 38B | 10/50: ANN - 38B | 11/50: ANN - 38B |
| Aug-51 | COLWICK - 38A | 9/51: T.DCK - 54B | ANNESLEY - 38B | ANNESLEY - 38B | ANNESLEY - 38B | ANNESLEY - 38B | ANNESLEY - 38B | ANNESLEY - 38B | ANNESLEY - 38B |
| Jan-52 | COLWICK - 38A | TYNEDOCK 54B | ANNESLEY - 38B | ANNESLEY - 38B | ANNESLEY - 38B | ANNESLEY - 38B | ANNESLEY - 38B | ANNESLEY - 38B | ANNESLEY - 38B |
| Aug-52 | COLWICK - 38A | TYNEDOCK 54B | ANNESLEY - 38B | ANNESLEY - 38B | ANNESLEY - 38B | ANNESLEY - 38B | ANNESLEY - 38B | ANNESLEY - 38B | ANNESLEY - 38B |
| Jan-53 | COLWICK - 38A | TYNEDOCK 54B | ANNESLEY - 38B | ANNESLEY - 38B | ANNESLEY - 38B | ANNESLEY - 38B | ANNESLEY - 38B | ANNESLEY - 38B | ANNESLEY - 38B |
| Aug-53 | COLWICK - 38A | TYNEDOCK 54B | ANNESLEY - 38B | ANNESLEY - 38B | ANNESLEY - 38B | ANNESLEY - 38B | ANNESLEY - 38B | ANNESLEY - 38B | ANNESLEY - 38B |
| Jan-54 | COLWICK - 38A | TYNEDOCK 54B | ANNESLEY - 38B | ANNESLEY - 38B | ANNESLEY - 38B | ANNESLEY - 38B | ANNESLEY - 38B | ANNESLEY - 38B | ANNESLEY - 38B |
| Aug-54 | COLWICK - 38A | TYNEDOCK 54B | ANNESLEY - 38B | ANNESLEY - 38B | ANNESLEY - 38B | ANNESLEY - 38B | ANNESLEY - 38B | ANNESLEY - 38B | ANNESLEY - 38B |
| Jan-55 | COLWICK - 38A | TYNEDOCK 54B | ANNESLEY - 38B | ANNESLEY - 38B | ANNESLEY - 38B | ANNESLEY - 38B | ANNESLEY - 38B | ANNESLEY - 38B | ANNESLEY - 38B |
| Aug-55 | COLWICK - 38A | TYNEDOCK 54B | ANNESLEY - 38B | ANNESLEY - 38B | ANNESLEY - 38B | ANNESLEY - 38B | ANNESLEY - 38B | ANNESLEY - 38B | ANNESLEY - 38B |
| Jan-56 | 1/56: MEX - 36B | TYNEDOCK 54B | ANNESLEY - 38B | ANNESLEY - 38B | ANNESLEY - 38B | ANNESLEY - 38B | ANNESLEY - 38B | ANNESLEY - 38B | ANNESLEY - 38B |
| Aug-56 | MEXBOROUGH - 36B | TYNEDOCK 54B | ANNESLEY - 38B | ANNESLEY - 38B | ANNESLEY - 38B | ANNESLEY - 38B | ANNESLEY - 38B | ANNESLEY - 38B | ANNESLEY - 38B |
| Jan-57 | MEXBOROUGH - 36B | TYNEDOCK 54B | ANNESLEY - 38B | 3/57: MARCH - 31B | ANNESLEY - 38B | 2/57: MARCH - 31B | ANNESLEY - 38B | 3/57: MARCH - 31B | ANNESLEY - 38B |
| Aug-57 | MEXBOROUGH - 36B | TYNEDOCK 54B | ANNESLEY - 38B | MARCH - 31B | ANNESLEY - 38B | MARCH - 31B | 6/57: MARCH - 31B | MARCH - 31B | ANNESLEY - 38B |
| Jan-58 | MEXBOROUGH - 36B | TYNEDOCK 54B | 11/57: COLW - 38A | MARCH - 31B | ANNESLEY - 38B | MARCH - 31B | MARCH - 31B | MARCH - 31B | ANNESLEY - 38B |
| Aug-58 | MEXBOROUGH - 41F | TYNEDOCK 54B | COLWICK - 40E | MARCH - 31B | ANNESLEY - 16D | MARCH - 31B | MARCH - 31B | MARCH - 31B | ANNESLEY - 16D |
| Jan-59 | MEXBOROUGH - 41F | TYNEDOCK - 52H | COLWICK - 40E | MARCH - 31B | ANNESLEY - 16D | MARCH - 31B | MARCH - 31B | MARCH - 31B | ANNESLEY - 16D |
| Aug-59 | 6/59: W/D | TYNEDOCK - 52H | COLWICK - 40E | MARCH - 31B | ANNESLEY - 16D | MARCH - 31B | MARCH - 31B | MARCH - 31B | ANNESLEY - 16D |
| Nov-59 | | TYNEDOCK - 52H | COLWICK - 40E | 12/59: STAVE - 41H | ANNESLEY - 16D | MARCH - 31B | 12/59: STAVE - 41H | MARCH - 31B | ANNESLEY - 16D |
| Jan-60 | | TYNEDOCK - 52H | COLWICK - 40E | STAVELEY(GC) - 41H | ANNESLEY - 16D | MARCH - 31B | STAVELEY(GC) - 41H | MARCH - 31B | ANNESLEY - 16D |
| Apr-60 | | TYNEDOCK - 52H | COLWICK - 40E | STAVELEY(GC) - 41H | ANNESLEY - 16D | MARCH - 31B | STAVELEY(GC) - 41H | MARCH - 31B | ANNESLEY - 16D |
| Aug-60 | | TYNEDOCK - 52H | COLWICK - 40E | STAVELEY(GC) - 41H | ANNESLEY - 16D | MARCH - 31B | STAVELEY(GC) - 41H | MARCH - 31B | ANNESLEY - 16D |
| Nov-60 | | TYNEDOCK - 52H | COLWICK - 40E | STAVELEY(GC) - 41H | ANNESLEY - 16D | MARCH - 31B | STAVELEY(GC) - 41H | MARCH - 31B | ANNESLEY - 16D |

| | 63792 | 63795 | 63796 | 63803 | 63806 | 63808 | 63817 | 63838 | 63854 |
|---|---|---|---|---|---|---|---|---|---|
| Aug-50 | ANNESLEY - 38B | ANNESLEY - 38B | GORTON - 39A | ANNESLEY - 38B | ANNESLEY - 38B | ANNESLEY - 38B | GORTON - 39A | ANNESLEY - 38B | GORTON - 39A |
| Jan-51 | ANNESLEY - 38B | ANNESLEY - 38B | 10/50: ANN - 38B | ANNESLEY - 38B | ANNESLEY - 38B | ANNESLEY - 38B | 11/50: ANN - 38B | ANNESLEY - 38B | 11/50: ANN - 38B |
| Aug-51 | ANNESLEY - 38B | ANNESLEY - 38B | ANNESLEY - 38B | ANNESLEY - 38B | ANNESLEY - 38B | ANNESLEY - 38B | ANNESLEY - 38B | ANNESLEY - 38B | ANNESLEY - 38B |
| Jan-52 | ANNESLEY - 38B | ANNESLEY - 38B | ANNESLEY - 38B | ANNESLEY - 38B | ANNESLEY - 38B | ANNESLEY - 38B | ANNESLEY - 38B | ANNESLEY - 38B | ANNESLEY - 38B |
| Aug-52 | ANNESLEY - 38B | ANNESLEY - 38B | ANNESLEY - 38B | ANNESLEY - 38B | ANNESLEY - 38B | ANNESLEY - 38B | ANNESLEY - 38B | ANNESLEY - 38B | ANNESLEY - 38B |
| Jan-53 | ANNESLEY - 38B | ANNESLEY - 38B | ANNESLEY - 38B | ANNESLEY - 38B | ANNESLEY - 38B | ANNESLEY - 38B | ANNESLEY - 38B | ANNESLEY - 38B | ANNESLEY - 38B |
| Aug-53 | ANNESLEY - 38B | ANNESLEY - 38B | ANNESLEY - 38B | ANNESLEY - 38B | ANNESLEY - 38B | ANNESLEY - 38B | ANNESLEY - 38B | ANNESLEY - 38B | ANNESLEY - 38B |
| Jan-54 | ANNESLEY - 38B | ANNESLEY - 38B | ANNESLEY - 38B | ANNESLEY - 38B | ANNESLEY - 38B | ANNESLEY - 38B | ANNESLEY - 38B | ANNESLEY - 38B | ANNESLEY - 38B |
| Aug-54 | ANNESLEY - 38B | ANNESLEY - 38B | ANNESLEY - 38B | ANNESLEY - 38B | ANNESLEY - 38B | ANNESLEY - 38B | ANNESLEY - 38B | ANNESLEY - 38B | ANNESLEY - 38B |
| Jan-55 | ANNESLEY - 38B | ANNESLEY - 38B | ANNESLEY - 38B | ANNESLEY - 38B | ANNESLEY - 38B | ANNESLEY - 38B | ANNESLEY - 38B | ANNESLEY - 38B | ANNESLEY - 38B |
| Aug-55 | ANNESLEY - 38B | ANNESLEY - 38B | ANNESLEY - 38B | ANNESLEY - 38B | ANNESLEY - 38B | ANNESLEY - 38B | ANNESLEY - 38B | ANNESLEY - 38B | ANNESLEY - 38B |
| Jan-56 | ANNESLEY - 38B | ANNESLEY - 38B | ANNESLEY - 38B | ANNESLEY - 38B | ANNESLEY - 38B | ANNESLEY - 38B | ANNESLEY - 38B | ANNESLEY - 38B | ANNESLEY - 38B |
| Aug-56 | ANNESLEY - 38B | ANNESLEY - 38B | ANNESLEY - 38B | ANNESLEY - 38B | ANNESLEY - 38B | ANNESLEY - 38B | ANNESLEY - 38B | ANNESLEY - 38B | ANNESLEY - 38B |
| Jan-57 | ANNESLEY - 38B | 2/57: MARCH - 31B | 2/57: MARCH - 31B | 2/57: MARCH - 31B | ANNESLEY - 38B | ANNESLEY - 38B | ANNESLEY - 38B | ANNESLEY - 38B | ANNESLEY - 38B |
| Aug-57 | ANNESLEY - 38B | MARCH - 31B | 4/57: ANN - 38B | MARCH - 31B | ANNESLEY - 38B | ANNESLEY - 38B | ANNESLEY - 38B | ANNESLEY - 38B | ANNESLEY - 38B |
| Jan-58 | ANNESLEY - 38B | MARCH - 31B | ANNESLEY - 38B | MARCH - 31B | ANNESLEY - 38B | ANNESLEY - 38B | ANNESLEY - 38B | ANNESLEY - 38B | ANNESLEY - 38B |
| Aug-58 | ANNESLEY - 16D | MARCH - 31B | ANNESLEY - 16D | MARCH - 31B | ANNESLEY - 16D | ANNESLEY - 16D | ANNESLEY - 16D | ANNESLEY - 16D | ANNESLEY - 16D |
| Jan-59 | ANNESLEY - 16D | MARCH - 31B | ANNESLEY - 16D | MARCH - 31B | ANNESLEY - 16D | ANNESLEY - 16D | ANNESLEY - 16D | ANNESLEY - 16D | ANNESLEY - 16D |
| Aug-59 | ANNESLEY - 16D | MARCH - 31B | ANNESLEY - 16D | MARCH - 31B | ANNESLEY - 16D | ANNESLEY - 16D | ANNESLEY - 16D | ANNESLEY - 16D | ANNESLEY - 16D |
| Nov-59 | ANNESLEY - 16D | 12/59: STAVE - 41H | ANNESLEY - 16D | MARCH - 31B | ANNESLEY - 16D | ANNESLEY - 16D | ANNESLEY - 16D | ANNESLEY - 16D | ANNESLEY - 16D |
| Jan-60 | ANNESLEY - 16D | STAVELEY(GC) - 41H | ANNESLEY - 16D | MARCH - 31B | ANNESLEY - 16D | ANNESLEY - 16D | ANNESLEY - 16D | ANNESLEY - 16D | ANNESLEY - 16D |
| Apr-60 | ANNESLEY - 16D | STAVELEY(GC) - 41H | ANNESLEY - 16D | MARCH - 31B | ANNESLEY - 16D | ANNESLEY - 16D | ANNESLEY - 16D | ANNESLEY - 16D | ANNESLEY - 16D |
| Aug-60 | ANNESLEY - 16D | STAVELEY(GC) - 41H | ANNESLEY - 16D | MARCH - 31B | ANNESLEY - 16D | ANNESLEY - 16D | ANNESLEY - 16D | ANNESLEY - 16D | ANNESLEY - 16D |
| Nov-60 | ANNESLEY - 16D | STAVELEY(GC) - 41H | ANNESLEY - 16D | MARCH - 31B | ANNESLEY - 16D | ANNESLEY - 16D | ANNESLEY - 16D | ANNESLEY - 16D | ANNESLEY - 16D |

| | 63856 | 63863 | 63865 | 63867 | 63868 | 63869 | 63872 | 63874 | 63879 |
|---|---|---|---|---|---|---|---|---|---|
| Aug-50 | DAIRYCOATES - 53A | ANNESLEY - 38B | GORTON - 39A | ANNESLEY - 38B | ANNESLEY - 38B | ANNESLEY - 38B | GORTON - 39A | DAIRYCOATES - 53A | ANNESLEY - 38B |
| Jan-51 | DAIRYCOATES - 53A | ANNESLEY - 38B | 11/50: ANN - 38B | ANNESLEY - 38B | ANNESLEY - 38B | ANNESLEY - 38B | 11/50: ANN - 38B | DAIRYCOATES - 53A | ANNESLEY - 38B |
| Aug-51 | 9/51: T.DCK - 54B | ANNESLEY - 38B | ANNESLEY - 38B | ANNESLEY - 38B | ANNESLEY - 38B | ANNESLEY - 38B | ANNESLEY - 38B | 9/51: T.DCK - 54B | ANNESLEY - 38B |
| Jan-52 | TYNEDOCK 54B | ANNESLEY - 38B | ANNESLEY - 38B | ANNESLEY - 38B | ANNESLEY - 38B | ANNESLEY - 38B | ANNESLEY - 38B | TYNEDOCK 54B | ANNESLEY - 38B |
| Aug-52 | TYNEDOCK 54B | ANNESLEY - 38B | ANNESLEY - 38B | ANNESLEY - 38B | ANNESLEY - 38B | ANNESLEY - 38B | ANNESLEY - 38B | TYNEDOCK 54B | ANNESLEY - 38B |
| Jan-53 | TYNEDOCK 54B | ANNESLEY - 38B | ANNESLEY - 38B | ANNESLEY - 38B | ANNESLEY - 38B | ANNESLEY - 38B | ANNESLEY - 38B | TYNEDOCK 54B | ANNESLEY - 38B |
| Aug-53 | TYNEDOCK 54B | ANNESLEY - 38B | ANNESLEY - 38B | ANNESLEY - 38B | ANNESLEY - 38B | ANNESLEY - 38B | ANNESLEY - 38B | TYNEDOCK 54B | ANNESLEY - 38B |
| Jan-54 | TYNEDOCK 54B | ANNESLEY - 38B | ANNESLEY - 38B | ANNESLEY - 38B | ANNESLEY - 38B | ANNESLEY - 38B | ANNESLEY - 38B | TYNEDOCK 54B | ANNESLEY - 38B |
| Aug-54 | TYNEDOCK 54B | ANNESLEY - 38B | ANNESLEY - 38B | ANNESLEY - 38B | ANNESLEY - 38B | ANNESLEY - 38B | ANNESLEY - 38B | TYNEDOCK 54B | ANNESLEY - 38B |
| Jan-55 | TYNEDOCK 54B | ANNESLEY - 38B | ANNESLEY - 38B | ANNESLEY - 38B | ANNESLEY - 38B | ANNESLEY - 38B | ANNESLEY - 38B | TYNEDOCK 54B | ANNESLEY - 38B |
| Aug-55 | TYNEDOCK 54B | ANNESLEY - 38B | ANNESLEY - 38B | ANNESLEY - 38B | ANNESLEY - 38B | ANNESLEY - 38B | ANNESLEY - 38B | TYNEDOCK 54B | ANNESLEY - 38B |
| Jan-56 | TYNEDOCK 54B | ANNESLEY - 38B | ANNESLEY - 38B | ANNESLEY - 38B | ANNESLEY - 38B | ANNESLEY - 38B | ANNESLEY - 38B | TYNEDOCK 54B | ANNESLEY - 38B |
| Aug-56 | TYNEDOCK 54B | ANNESLEY - 38B | ANNESLEY - 38B | ANNESLEY - 38B | ANNESLEY - 38B | ANNESLEY - 38B | ANNESLEY - 38B | TYNEDOCK 54B | ANNESLEY - 38B |
| Jan-57 | TYNEDOCK 54B | ANNESLEY - 38B | ANNESLEY - 38B | ANNESLEY - 38B | 2/57: MARCH - 31B | ANNESLEY - 38B | ANNESLEY - 38B | TYNEDOCK 54B | 2/57: MARCH - 31B |
| Aug-57 | TYNEDOCK 54B | ANNESLEY - 38B | ANNESLEY - 38B | ANNESLEY - 38B | MARCH - 31B | ANNESLEY - 38B | 6/57: MARCH - 31B | TYNEDOCK 54B | MARCH - 31B |
| Jan-58 | TYNEDOCK 54B | 11/57: COLW - 38A | ANNESLEY - 38B | ANNESLEY - 38B | MARCH - 31B | ANNESLEY - 38B | MARCH - 31B | TYNEDOCK 54B | MARCH - 31B |
| Aug-58 | TYNEDOCK 54B | COLWICK - 40E | ANNESLEY - 16D | ANNESLEY - 16D | MARCH - 31B | ANNESLEY - 16D | MARCH - 31B | TYNEDOCK 54B | MARCH - 31B |
| Jan-59 | TYNEDOCK - 52H | COLWICK - 40E | ANNESLEY - 16D | ANNESLEY - 16D | MARCH - 31B | ANNESLEY - 16D | MARCH - 31B | TYNEDOCK - 52H | MARCH - 31B |
| Aug-59 | TYNEDOCK - 52H | COLWICK - 40E | ANNESLEY - 16D | ANNESLEY - 16D | MARCH - 31B | ANNESLEY - 16D | MARCH - 31B | TYNEDOCK - 52H | MARCH - 31B |
| Nov-59 | TYNEDOCK - 52H | COLWICK - 40E | ANNESLEY - 16D | ANNESLEY - 16D | MARCH - 31B | ANNESLEY - 16D | MARCH - 31B | TYNEDOCK - 52H | MARCH - 31B |
| Jan-60 | TYNEDOCK - 52H | COLWICK - 40E | ANNESLEY - 16D | ANNESLEY - 16D | MARCH - 31B | ANNESLEY - 16D | MARCH - 31B | TYNEDOCK - 52H | MARCH - 31B |
| Apr-60 | TYNEDOCK - 52H | COLWICK - 40E | ANNESLEY - 16D | ANNESLEY - 16D | MARCH - 31B | ANNESLEY - 16D | MARCH - 31B | TYNEDOCK - 52H | MARCH - 31B |
| Aug-60 | TYNEDOCK - 52H | COLWICK - 40E | ANNESLEY - 16D | ANNESLEY - 16D | MARCH - 31B | ANNESLEY - 16D | MARCH - 31B | TYNEDOCK - 52H | MARCH - 31B |
| Nov-60 | TYNEDOCK - 52H | COLWICK - 40E | ANNESLEY - 16D | ANNESLEY - 16D | MARCH - 31B | ANNESLEY - 16D | MARCH - 31B | TYNEDOCK - 52H | MARCH - 31B |

| | 63886 | 63887 | 63890 | 63901 | O4 2-8-0 (1944) 63575 | 63604 | 63606 | 63607 | 63612 |
|---|---|---|---|---|---|---|---|---|---|
| Aug-50 | GORTON - 39A | GORTON - 39A | GORTON - 39A | ANNESLEY - 38B | GORTON - 39A | DARNALL - 39B | FRODINGHAM - 36C | IMMINGHAM - 40B | MEXBOROUGH - 36B |
| Jan-51 | 10/50: ANN - 38B | 11/50: ANN - 38B | 11/50: ANN - 38B | ANNESLEY - 38B | GORTON - 39A | DARNALL - 39B | FRODINGHAM - 36C | IMMINGHAM - 40B | MEXBOROUGH - 36B |
| Aug-51 | ANNESLEY - 38B | ANNESLEY - 38B | ANNESLEY - 38B | ANNESLEY - 38B | GORTON - 39A | DARNALL - 39B | FRODINGHAM - 36C | IMMINGHAM - 40B | MEXBOROUGH - 36B |
| Jan-52 | ANNESLEY - 38B | ANNESLEY - 38B | ANNESLEY - 38B | ANNESLEY - 38B | GORTON - 39A | DARNALL - 39B | FRODINGHAM - 36C | IMMINGHAM - 40B | MEXBOROUGH - 36B |
| Aug-52 | ANNESLEY - 38B | ANNESLEY - 38B | ANNESLEY - 38B | ANNESLEY - 38B | 9/52: IMM - 40B | DARNALL - 39B | FRODINGHAM - 36C | IMMINGHAM - 40B | MEXBOROUGH - 36B |
| Jan-53 | ANNESLEY - 38B | ANNESLEY - 38B | ANNESLEY - 38B | ANNESLEY - 38B | IMMINGHAM - 40B | DARNALL - 39B | FRODINGHAM - 36C | IMMINGHAM - 40B | MEXBOROUGH - 36B |
| Aug-53 | ANNESLEY - 38B | ANNESLEY - 38B | ANNESLEY - 38B | ANNESLEY - 38B | 10/53: GOR - 39A | DARNALL - 39B | FRODINGHAM - 36C | 10/53: DARN - 40B | MEXBOROUGH - 36B |
| Jan-54 | ANNESLEY - 38B | ANNESLEY - 38B | ANNESLEY - 38B | ANNESLEY - 38B | GORTON - 39A | DARNALL - 39B | FRODINGHAM - 36C | DARNALL - 39B | MEXBOROUGH - 36B |
| Aug-54 | ANNESLEY - 38B | ANNESLEY - 38B | ANNESLEY - 38B | ANNESLEY - 38B | GORTON - 39A | DARNALL - 39B | FRODINGHAM - 36C | DARNALL - 39B | MEXBOROUGH - 36B |
| Jan-55 | ANNESLEY - 38B | ANNESLEY - 38B | ANNESLEY - 38B | ANNESLEY - 38B | GORTON - 39A | DARNALL - 39B | FRODINGHAM - 36C | 1/55: IMM - 40B | MEXBOROUGH - 36B |
| Aug-55 | ANNESLEY - 38B | ANNESLEY - 38B | ANNESLEY - 38B | ANNESLEY - 38B | GORTON - 39A | DARNALL - 39B | FRODINGHAM - 36C | IMMINGHAM - 40B | MEXBOROUGH - 36B |
| Jan-56 | ANNESLEY - 38B | ANNESLEY - 38B | ANNESLEY - 38B | ANNESLEY - 38B | GORTON - 39A | DARNALL - 41A | FRODINGHAM - 36C | IMMINGHAM - 40B | MEXBOROUGH - 36B |
| Aug-56 | ANNESLEY - 38B | ANNESLEY - 38B | ANNESLEY - 38B | ANNESLEY - 38B | GORTON - 39A | DARNALL - 41A | FRODINGHAM - 36C | IMMINGHAM - 40B | MEXBOROUGH - 36B |
| Jan-57 | ANNESLEY - 38B | 4/57: MARCH - 31B | 4/57: MARCH - 31B | ANNESLEY - 38B | GORTON - 39A | DARNALL - 41A | FRODINGHAM - 36C | IMMINGHAM - 40B | 12/56: BARN - 36D |
| Aug-57 | ANNESLEY - 38B | MARCH - 31B | MARCH - 31B | ANNESLEY - 38B | GORTON - 39A | DARNALL - 41A | FRODINGHAM - 36C | IMMINGHAM - 40B | BARNSLEY - 36D |
| Jan-58 | ANNESLEY - 38B | MARCH - 31B | MARCH - 31B | ANNESLEY - 38B | GORTON - 39A | DARNALL - 41A | FRODINGHAM - 36C | IMMINGHAM - 40B | BARNSLEY - 36D |
| Aug-58 | ANNESLEY - 16D | MARCH - 31B | MARCH - 31B | ANNESLEY - 16D | GORTON - 9G | DARNALL - 41A | FRODINGHAM - 36C | IMMINGHAM - 40B | BARNSLEY - 41G |
| Jan-59 | ANNESLEY - 16D | MARCH - 31B | MARCH - 31B | ANNESLEY - 16D | GORTON - 9G | DARNALL - 41A | FRODINGHAM - 36C | 1/59: LANG JN - 41J | BARNSLEY - 41G |
| Aug-59 | ANNESLEY - 16D | MARCH - 31B | MARCH - 31B | ANNESLEY - 16D | GORTON - 9G | DARNALL - 41A | FRODINGHAM - 36C | LANGWITHJCN - 41J | BARNSLEY - 41G |
| Nov-59 | ANNESLEY - 16D | MARCH - 31B | MARCH - 31B | ANNESLEY - 16D | GORTON - 9G | DARNALL - 41A | FRODINGHAM - 36C | LANGWITHJCN - 41J | 12/59: LANG JN - 41J |
| Jan-60 | ANNESLEY - 16D | MARCH - 31B | MARCH - 31B | ANNESLEY - 16D | GORTON - 9G | DARNALL - 41A | FRODINGHAM - 36C | LANGWITHJCN - 41J | LANGWITHJCN - 41J |
| Apr-60 | ANNESLEY - 16D | MARCH - 31B | MARCH - 31B | ANNESLEY - 16D | GORTON - 9G | DARNALL - 41A | FRODINGHAM - 36C | 5/60: IMM - 40B | 5/60: MEX - 41F |
| Aug-60 | ANNESLEY - 16D | MARCH - 31B | MARCH - 31B | ANNESLEY - 16D | GORTON - 9G | DARNALL - 41A | FRODINGHAM - 36C | IMMINGHAM - 40B | MEXBOROUGH - 41F |
| Nov-60 | ANNESLEY - 16D | MARCH - 31B | MARCH - 31B | ANNESLEY - 16D | GORTON - 9G | DARNALL - 41A | FRODINGHAM - 36C | IMMINGHAM - 40B | 10/60: STAVE - 41H |

| | 63613 | 63628 | 63633 | 63639 | 63644 | 63651 | 63653 | 63683 | 63703 |
|---|---|---|---|---|---|---|---|---|---|
| Aug-50 | STAVELEY - 38D | DAIRYCOATES - 53A | GORTON - 39A | ANNESLEY - 38B | LANGWITH JCN - 40E | IMMINGHAM - 40B | FRODINGHAM - 36C | LANGWITH JCN - 40E | LANGWITH JCN - 40E |
| Jan-51 | STAVELEY - 38D | DAIRYCOATES - 53A | GORTON - 39A | ANNESLEY - 38B | **3/51: TUX - 40D** | IMMINGHAM - 40B | FRODINGHAM - 36C | LANGWITH JCN - 40E | LANGWITH JCN - 40E |
| Aug-51 | STAVELEY - 38D | **9/51: COW - 38A** | GORTON - 39A | ANNESLEY - 38B | **5/51: LANG JN - 40E** | IMMINGHAM - 40B | FRODINGHAM - 36C | LANGWITH JCN - 40E | LANGWITH JCN - 40E |
| Jan-52 | STAVELEY - 38D | COLWICK - 38A | GORTON - 39A | ANNESLEY - 38B | LANGWITH JCN - 40E | IMMINGHAM - 40B | FRODINGHAM - 36C | LANGWITH JCN - 40E | LANGWITH JCN - 40E |
| Aug-52 | STAVELEY - 38D | COLWICK - 38A | **9/52: ARDS - 37A** | **9/52: COW - 38A** | LANGWITH JCN - 40E | IMMINGHAM - 40B | FRODINGHAM - 36C | LANGWITH JCN - 40E | LANGWITH JCN - 40E |
| Jan-53 | STAVELEY - 38D | COLWICK - 38A | ARDSLEY - 37A | COLWICK - 38A | LANGWITH JCN - 40E | IMMINGHAM - 40B | FRODINGHAM - 36C | LANGWITH JCN - 40E | LANGWITH JCN - 40E |
| Aug-53 | STAVELEY - 38D | COLWICK - 38A | ARDSLEY - 37A | COLWICK - 38A | LANGWITH JCN - 40E | IMMINGHAM - 40B | FRODINGHAM - 36C | LANGWITH JCN - 40E | LANGWITH JCN - 40E |
| Jan-54 | STAVELEY - 38D | COLWICK - 38A | ARDSLEY - 37A | COLWICK - 38A | LANGWITH JCN - 40E | IMMINGHAM - 40B | FRODINGHAM - 36C | LANGWITH JCN - 40E | LANGWITH JCN - 40E |
| Aug-54 | COLWICK - 38A | COLWICK - 38A | ARDSLEY - 37A | COLWICK - 38A | LANGWITH JCN - 40E | IMMINGHAM - 40B | FRODINGHAM - 36C | LANGWITH JCN - 40E | LANGWITH JCN - 40E |
| Jan-55 | COLWICK - 38A | COLWICK - 38A | ARDSLEY - 37A | COLWICK - 38A | LANGWITH JCN - 40E | IMMINGHAM - 40B | FRODINGHAM - 36C | **1/55: IMM - 40B** | LANGWITH JCN - 40E |
| Aug-55 | COLWICK - 38A | COLWICK - 38A | ARDSLEY - 37A | COLWICK - 38A | **8/55: IMM - 40B** | IMMINGHAM - 40B | FRODINGHAM - 36C | IMMINGHAM - 40B | LANGWITH JCN - 40E |
| Jan-56 | **1/56: DCTR - 36A** | **1/56: MEX - 36B** | ARDSLEY - 37A | **1/56: ANN - 38B** | IMMINGHAM - 40B | IMMINGHAM - 40B | FRODINGHAM - 36C | IMMINGHAM - 40B | LANGWITH JCN - 40E |
| Aug-56 | DONCASTER - 36A | MEXBOROUGH - 36B | ARDSLEY - 56B | **6/56: COLW - 38A** | IMMINGHAM - 40B | IMMINGHAM - 40B | FRODINGHAM - 36C | IMMINGHAM - 40B | LANGWITH JCN - 40E |
| Jan-57 | DONCASTER - 36A | MEXBOROUGH - 36B | ARDSLEY - 56B | COLWICK - 38A | IMMINGHAM - 40B | IMMINGHAM - 40B | FRODINGHAM - 36C | IMMINGHAM - 40B | LANGWITH JCN - 40E |
| Aug-57 | DONCASTER - 36A | MEXBOROUGH - 36B | ARDSLEY - 56B | COLWICK - 38A | IMMINGHAM - 40B | IMMINGHAM - 40B | FRODINGHAM - 36C | IMMINGHAM - 40B | LANGWITH JCN - 40E |
| Jan-58 | DONCASTER - 36A | MEXBOROUGH - 36B | ARDSLEY - 56B | COLWICK - 38A | IMMINGHAM - 40B | IMMINGHAM - 40B | FRODINGHAM - 36C | IMMINGHAM - 40B | LANGWITH JCN - 40E |
| Aug-58 | DONCASTER - 36A | MEXBOROUGH - 41F | ARDSLEY - 56B | COLWICK - 40E | IMMINGHAM - 40B | IMMINGHAM - 40B | FRODINGHAM - 36C | IMMINGHAM - 40B | LANGWITH JCN - 41J |
| Jan-59 | DONCASTER - 36A | MEXBOROUGH - 41F | ARDSLEY - 56B | COLWICK - 40E | IMMINGHAM - 40B | IMMINGHAM - 40B | FRODINGHAM - 36C | **1/59: LANG JN - 41J** | LANGWITH JCN - 41J |
| Aug-59 | DONCASTER - 36A | MEXBOROUGH - 41F | ARDSLEY - 56B | COLWICK - 40E | IMMINGHAM - 40B | IMMINGHAM - 40B | FRODINGHAM - 36C | LANGWITH JCN - 41J | LANGWITH JCN - 41J |
| Nov-59 | DONCASTER - 36A | MEXBOROUGH - 41F | ARDSLEY - 56B | COLWICK - 40E | IMMINGHAM - 40B | IMMINGHAM - 40B | FRODINGHAM - 36C | LANGWITH JCN - 41J | LANGWITH JCN - 41J |
| Jan-60 | DONCASTER - 36A | MEXBOROUGH - 41F | ARDSLEY - 56B | COLWICK - 40E | IMMINGHAM - 40B | IMMINGHAM - 40B | FRODINGHAM - 36C | LANGWITH JCN - 41J | LANGWITH JCN - 41J |
| Apr-60 | DONCASTER - 36A | MEXBOROUGH - 41F | ARDSLEY - 56B | COLWICK - 40E | **5/60: COLW - 40E** | IMMINGHAM - 40B | FRODINGHAM - 36C | LANGWITH JCN - 41J | LANGWITH JCN - 41J |
| Aug-60 | DONCASTER - 36A | MEXBOROUGH - 41F | ARDSLEY - 56B | COLWICK - 40E | COLWICK - 40E | IMMINGHAM - 40B | FRODINGHAM - 36C | LANGWITH JCN - 41J | LANGWITH JCN - 41J |
| Nov-60 | DONCASTER - 36A | MEXBOROUGH - 41F | ARDSLEY - 56B | COLWICK - 40E | COLWICK - 40E | IMMINGHAM - 40B | FRODINGHAM - 36C | LANGWITH JCN - 41J | LANGWITH JCN - 41J |

| | 63704 | 63721 | 63738 | 63750 | 63763 | 63785 | 63802 | 63805 | 63807 |
|---|---|---|---|---|---|---|---|---|---|
| Aug-50 | MARCH - 31B | ANNESLEY - 38B | IMMINGHAM - 40B | LANGWITH JCN - 40E | RETFORD - 36E | RETFORD - 36E | IMMINGHAM - 40B | GORTON - 39A | LANGWITH JCN - 40E |
| Jan-51 | MARCH - 31B | **10/50: GOR - 39A** | IMMINGHAM - 40B | LANGWITH JCN - 40E | **3/51: BARN - 36D** | RETFORD - 36E | IMMINGHAM - 40B | GORTON - 39A | LANGWITH JCN - 40E |
| Aug-51 | MARCH - 31B | GORTON - 39A | IMMINGHAM - 40B | LANGWITH JCN - 40E | BARNSLEY - 36D | RETFORD - 36E | IMMINGHAM - 40B | GORTON - 39A | LANGWITH JCN - 40E |
| Jan-52 | **10/51: MEX - 36B** | GORTON - 39A | IMMINGHAM - 40B | LANGWITH JCN - 40E | BARNSLEY - 36D | RETFORD - 36E | IMMINGHAM - 40B | GORTON - 39A | **12/51: IMM - 40B** |
| Aug-52 | MEXBOROUGH - 36B | GORTON - 39A | IMMINGHAM - 40B | LANGWITH JCN - 40E | BARNSLEY - 36D | RETFORD - 36E | IMMINGHAM - 40B | GORTON - 39A | **3/53: LANG JN - 40E** |
| Jan-53 | MEXBOROUGH - 36B | GORTON - 39A | IMMINGHAM - 40B | LANGWITH JCN - 40E | BARNSLEY - 36D | RETFORD - 36E | IMMINGHAM - 40B | GORTON - 39A | **7/53: IMM - 40B** |
| Aug-53 | MEXBOROUGH - 36B | GORTON - 39A | IMMINGHAM - 40B | LANGWITH JCN - 40E | BARNSLEY - 36D | RETFORD - 36E | IMMINGHAM - 40B | GORTON - 39A | **10/53: COLW - 38A** |
| Jan-54 | MEXBOROUGH - 36B | GORTON - 39A | IMMINGHAM - 40B | LANGWITH JCN - 40E | BARNSLEY - 36D | RETFORD - 36E | IMMINGHAM - 40B | GORTON - 39A | **4/54: GOR - 39A** |
| Aug-54 | MEXBOROUGH - 36B | GORTON - 39A | IMMINGHAM - 40B | LANGWITH JCN - 40E | BARNSLEY - 36D | RETFORD - 36E | IMMINGHAM - 40B | GORTON - 39A | **8/54: FROD - 36C** |
| Jan-55 | **2/55: BARN - 36D** | GORTON - 39A | IMMINGHAM - 40B | LANGWITH JCN - 40E | BARNSLEY - 36D | RETFORD - 36E | IMMINGHAM - 40B | GORTON - 39A | FRODINGHAM - 36C |
| Aug-55 | BARNSLEY - 36D | GORTON - 39A | IMMINGHAM - 40B | LANGWITH JCN - 40E | BARNSLEY - 36D | RETFORD - 36E | IMMINGHAM - 40B | GORTON - 39A | FRODINGHAM - 36C |
| Jan-56 | BARNSLEY - 36D | GORTON - 39A | IMMINGHAM - 40B | LANGWITH JCN - 40E | BARNSLEY - 36D | RETFORD - 36E | IMMINGHAM - 40B | GORTON - 39A | FRODINGHAM - 36C |
| Aug-56 | BARNSLEY - 36D | GORTON - 39A | IMMINGHAM - 40B | LANGWITH JCN - 40E | BARNSLEY - 36D | RETFORD - 36E | IMMINGHAM - 40B | GORTON - 39A | FRODINGHAM - 36C |
| Jan-57 | BARNSLEY - 36D | GORTON - 39A | IMMINGHAM - 40B | LANGWITH JCN - 40E | BARNSLEY - 36D | RETFORD - 36E | IMMINGHAM - 40B | GORTON - 39A | FRODINGHAM - 36C |
| Aug-57 | BARNSLEY - 36D | GORTON - 39A | IMMINGHAM - 40B | LANGWITH JCN - 40E | BARNSLEY - 36D | RETFORD - 36E | IMMINGHAM - 40B | GORTON - 39A | FRODINGHAM - 36C |
| Jan-58 | BARNSLEY - 36D | GORTON - 39A | IMMINGHAM - 40B | LANGWITH JCN - 40E | BARNSLEY - 36D | RETFORD - 36E | IMMINGHAM - 40B | GORTON - 39A | FRODINGHAM - 36C |
| Aug-58 | BARNSLEY - 41G | GORTON - 9G | IMMINGHAM - 40B | LANGWITH JCN - 40E | BARNSLEY - 41G | RETFORD - 36E | BARNSLEY - 41G | GORTON - 9G | FRODINGHAM - 36C |
| Jan-59 | BARNSLEY - 41G | GORTON - 9G | IMMINGHAM - 40B | LANGWITH JCN - 40E | BARNSLEY - 41G | RETFORD - 36E | BARNSLEY - 41G | GORTON - 9G | FRODINGHAM - 36C |
| Aug-59 | BARNSLEY - 41G | GORTON - 9G | IMMINGHAM - 40B | LANGWITH JCN - 40E | BARNSLEY - 41G | RETFORD - 36E | BARNSLEY - 41G | GORTON - 9G | FRODINGHAM - 36C |
| Nov-59 | **12/59: LANG JN - 41J** | GORTON - 9G | IMMINGHAM - 40B | LANGWITH JCN - 40E | **12/59: LANG JN - 41J** | RETFORD - 36E | BARNSLEY - 41G | GORTON - 9G | FRODINGHAM - 36C |
| Jan-60 | LANGWITH JCN - 41J | GORTON - 9G | IMMINGHAM - 40B | LANGWITH JCN - 40E | LANGWITH JCN - 41J | RETFORD - 36E | **1/60: MEX - 41F** | GORTON - 9G | FRODINGHAM - 36C |
| Apr-60 | **5/60: MEX - 41F** | GORTON - 9G | IMMINGHAM - 40B | **5/60: COLW - 40E** | LANGWITH JCN - 41J | RETFORD - 36E | MEXBOROUGH - 41F | GORTON - 9G | FRODINGHAM - 36C |
| Aug-60 | MEXBOROUGH - 41F | GORTON - 9G | IMMINGHAM - 40B | COLWICK - 40E | LANGWITH JCN - 41J | RETFORD - 36E | MEXBOROUGH - 41F | GORTON - 9G | FRODINGHAM - 36C |
| Nov-60 | MEXBOROUGH - 41F | GORTON - 9G | IMMINGHAM - 40B | COLWICK - 40E | LANGWITH JCN - 41J | RETFORD - 36E | MEXBOROUGH - 41F | GORTON - 9G | FRODINGHAM - 36C |

| | 63818 | 63819 | 63827 | 63828 | 63836 | 63837 | 63853 | 63858 | 63873 |
|---|---|---|---|---|---|---|---|---|---|
| Aug-50 | FRODINGHAM - 36C | IMMINGHAM - 40B | ANNESLEY - 38B | DAIRYCOATES - 53A | IMMINGHAM - 40B | LANGWITH JCN - 40E | ANNESLEY - 38B | ANNESLEY - 38B | ANNESLEY - 38B |
| Jan-51 | FRODINGHAM - 36C | IMMINGHAM - 40B | **9/50: STAVE - 38D** | DAIRYCOATES - 53A | IMMINGHAM - 40B | **3/51: TUX - 40D** | **11/50: GOR - 39A** | **11/50: GOR - 39A** | **11/50: GOR - 39A** |
| Aug-51 | FRODINGHAM - 36C | IMMINGHAM - 40B | STAVELEY - 38D | **8/51: DCTR - 36A** | IMMINGHAM - 40B | **5/51: LANG - JN - 40E** | GORTON - 39A | **9/51: DCTR - 36A** | GORTON - 39A |
| Jan-52 | FRODINGHAM - 36C | IMMINGHAM - 40B | STAVELEY - 38D | **10/51: MEX - 36B** | IMMINGHAM - 40B | LANGWITH JCN - 40E | GORTON - 39A | DONCASTER - 36A | GORTON - 39A |
| Aug-52 | FRODINGHAM - 36C | IMMINGHAM - 40B | STAVELEY - 38D | **9/52: IMM - 40B** | IMMINGHAM - 40B | LANGWITH JCN - 40E | GORTON - 39A | DONCASTER - 36A | GORTON - 39A |
| Jan-53 | FRODINGHAM - 36C | IMMINGHAM - 40B | STAVELEY - 38D | **10/52: MEX - 36B** | IMMINGHAM - 40B | LANGWITH JCN - 40E | GORTON - 39A | DONCASTER - 36A | GORTON - 39A |
| Aug-53 | FRODINGHAM - 36C | IMMINGHAM - 40B | STAVELEY - 38D | MEXBOROUGH - 36B | IMMINGHAM - 40B | LANGWITH JCN - 40E | GORTON - 39A | DONCASTER - 36A | GORTON - 39A |
| Jan-54 | FRODINGHAM - 36C | IMMINGHAM - 40B | STAVELEY - 38D | MEXBOROUGH - 36B | IMMINGHAM - 40B | LANGWITH JCN - 40E | GORTON - 39A | DONCASTER - 36A | GORTON - 39A |
| Aug-54 | FRODINGHAM - 36C | IMMINGHAM - 40B | STAVELEY - 38D | MEXBOROUGH - 36B | IMMINGHAM - 40B | LANGWITH JCN - 40E | **6/54: FROD - 36C** | DONCASTER - 36A | COLWICK - 38A |
| Jan-55 | FRODINGHAM - 36C | IMMINGHAM - 40B | STAVELEY - 38D | MEXBOROUGH - 36B | IMMINGHAM - 40B | LANGWITH JCN - 40E | FRODINGHAM - 36C | DONCASTER - 36A | COLWICK - 38A |
| Aug-55 | FRODINGHAM - 36C | IMMINGHAM - 40B | STAVELEY - 38D | MEXBOROUGH - 36B | IMMINGHAM - 40B | **8/55: IMM - 40B** | FRODINGHAM - 36C | DONCASTER - 36A | COLWICK - 38A |
| Jan-56 | FRODINGHAM - 36C | IMMINGHAM - 40B | STAVELEY - 38D | MEXBOROUGH - 36B | IMMINGHAM - 40B | IMMINGHAM - 40B | FRODINGHAM - 36C | DONCASTER - 36A | COLWICK - 38A |
| Aug-56 | FRODINGHAM - 36C | IMMINGHAM - 40B | STAVELEY - 38D | MEXBOROUGH - 36B | IMMINGHAM - 40B | IMMINGHAM - 40B | FRODINGHAM - 36C | DONCASTER - 36A | COLWICK - 38A |
| Jan-57 | FRODINGHAM - 36C | IMMINGHAM - 40B | STAVELEY - 38D | MEXBOROUGH - 36B | IMMINGHAM - 40B | IMMINGHAM - 40B | FRODINGHAM - 36C | DONCASTER - 36A | COLWICK - 38A |
| Aug-57 | FRODINGHAM - 36C | IMMINGHAM - 40B | STAVELEY - 38D | MEXBOROUGH - 36B | IMMINGHAM - 40B | IMMINGHAM - 40B | FRODINGHAM - 36C | DONCASTER - 36A | COLWICK - 38A |
| Jan-58 | FRODINGHAM - 36C | IMMINGHAM - 40B | STAVELEY - 38D | MEXBOROUGH - 36B | **2/58: BARN - 41G** | IMMINGHAM - 40B | FRODINGHAM - 36C | DONCASTER - 36A | COLWICK - 38A |
| Aug-58 | **7/58: RET - 36E** | IMMINGHAM - 40B | STAVELEY (GC) - 41H | MEXBOROUGH - 41F | BARNSLEY - 41G | IMMINGHAM - 40B | FRODINGHAM - 36C | DONCASTER - 36A | COLWICK - 40E |
| Jan-59 | RETFORD - 36E | IMMINGHAM - 40B | STAVELEY (GC) - 41H | MEXBOROUGH - 41F | BARNSLEY - 41G | IMMINGHAM - 40B | **1/59: LANG JN - 41J** | DONCASTER - 36A | COLWICK - 40E |
| Aug-59 | RETFORD - 36E | **9/59: COLW - 40E** | STAVELEY (GC) - 41H | MEXBOROUGH - 41F | BARNSLEY - 41G | IMMINGHAM - 40B | LANGWITH JCN - 41J | DONCASTER - 36A | COLWICK - 40E |
| Nov-59 | RETFORD - 36E | COLWICK - 40E | STAVELEY (GC) - 41H | MEXBOROUGH - 41F | **10/59: FROD - 36C** | IMMINGHAM - 40B | LANGWITH JCN - 41J | DONCASTER - 36A | COLWICK - 40E |
| Jan-60 | RETFORD - 36E | COLWICK - 40E | STAVELEY (GC) - 41H | MEXBOROUGH - 41F | FRODINGHAM - 36C | IMMINGHAM - 40B | LANGWITH JCN - 41J | DONCASTER - 36A | COLWICK - 40E |
| Apr-60 | RETFORD - 36E | COLWICK - 40E | STAVELEY (GC) - 41H | MEXBOROUGH - 41F | FRODINGHAM - 36C | IMMINGHAM - 40B | LANGWITH JCN - 41J | DONCASTER - 36A | COLWICK - 40E |
| Aug-60 | RETFORD - 36E | COLWICK - 40E | STAVELEY (GC) - 41H | MEXBOROUGH - 41F | FRODINGHAM - 36C | IMMINGHAM - 40B | LANGWITH JCN - 41J | DONCASTER - 36A | COLWICK - 40E |
| Nov-60 | RETFORD - 36E | COLWICK - 40E | STAVELEY (GC) - 41H | MEXBOROUGH - 41F | FRODINGHAM - 36C | IMMINGHAM - 40B | LANGWITH JCN - 41J | DONCASTER - 36A | COLWICK - 40E |

| | | | | | **O4 2-8-0 (1911)** | | | | |
|---|---|---|---|---|---|---|---|---|---|
| | 63882 | 63893 | 63895 | 63914 | 63570 | 63572 | 63573 | 63574 | 63576 |
| Aug-50 | DARNALL - 39B | ANNESLEY - 38B | GORTON - 39A | RETFORD - 36E | TUXFORD - 40D | FRODINGHAM - 36C | COLWICK - 38A | DARNALL - 39B | FRODINGHAM - 36C |
| Jan-51 | DARNALL - 39B | **10/50: COLW - 38A** | GORTON - 39A | RETFORD - 36E | TUXFORD - 40D | FRODINGHAM - 36C | **9/50: ANN - 38B** | DARNALL - 39B | FRODINGHAM - 36C |
| Aug-51 | DARNALL - 39B | COLWICK - 38A | GORTON - 39A | RETFORD - 36E | TUXFORD - 40D | FRODINGHAM - 36C | **11/50: GOR - 39A** | DARNALL - 39B | FRODINGHAM - 36C |
| Jan-52 | DARNALL - 39B | COLWICK - 38A | GORTON - 39A | RETFORD - 36E | TUXFORD - 40D | FRODINGHAM - 36C | GORTON - 39A | DARNALL - 39B | FRODINGHAM - 36C |
| Aug-52 | DARNALL - 39B | **6/52: LANG JN - 40E** | GORTON - 39A | RETFORD - 36E | TUXFORD - 40D | FRODINGHAM - 36C | GORTON - 39A | DARNALL - 39B | FRODINGHAM - 36C |
| Jan-53 | DARNALL - 39B | LANGWITH JCN - 40E | GORTON - 39A | RETFORD - 36E | TUXFORD - 40D | FRODINGHAM - 36C | GORTON - 39A | DARNALL - 39B | FRODINGHAM - 36C |
| Aug-53 | DARNALL - 39B | LANGWITH JCN - 40E | GORTON - 39A | RETFORD - 36E | TUXFORD - 40D | FRODINGHAM - 36C | GORTON - 39A | DARNALL - 39B | FRODINGHAM - 36C |
| Jan-54 | DARNALL - 39B | LANGWITH JCN - 40E | GORTON - 39A | RETFORD - 36E | **10/53: ARDS - 37A** | FRODINGHAM - 36C | GORTON - 39A | DARNALL - 39B | FRODINGHAM - 36C |
| Aug-54 | DARNALL - 39B | LANGWITH JCN - 40E | GORTON - 39A | RETFORD - 36E | ARDSLEY - 37A | FRODINGHAM - 36C | GORTON - 39A | DARNALL - 39B | FRODINGHAM - 36C |
| Jan-55 | DARNALL - 39B | **1/55: IMM - 40B** | GORTON - 39A | RETFORD - 36E | ARDSLEY - 37A | FRODINGHAM - 36C | GORTON - 39A | DARNALL - 39B | FRODINGHAM - 36C |
| Aug-55 | DARNALL - 39B | IMMINGHAM - 40B | GORTON - 39A | RETFORD - 36E | ARDSLEY - 37A | FRODINGHAM - 36C | GORTON - 39A | DARNALL - 39B | FRODINGHAM - 36C |
| Jan-56 | DARNALL - 41A | IMMINGHAM - 40B | GORTON - 39A | RETFORD - 36E | ARDSLEY - 37A | FRODINGHAM - 36C | GORTON - 39A | DARNALL - 41A | FRODINGHAM - 36C |
| Aug-56 | DARNALL - 41A | IMMINGHAM - 40B | GORTON - 39A | RETFORD - 36E | ARDSLEY - 56B | FRODINGHAM - 36C | GORTON - 39A | DARNALL - 41A | FRODINGHAM - 36C |
| Jan-57 | DARNALL - 41A | IMMINGHAM - 40B | GORTON - 39A | RETFORD - 36E | ARDSLEY - 56B | FRODINGHAM - 36C | GORTON - 39A | DARNALL - 41A | FRODINGHAM - 36C |
| Aug-57 | DARNALL - 41A | IMMINGHAM - 40B | GORTON - 39A | RETFORD - 36E | ARDSLEY - 56B | FRODINGHAM - 36C | GORTON - 39A | DARNALL - 41A | FRODINGHAM - 36C |
| Jan-58 | DARNALL - 41A | IMMINGHAM - 40B | GORTON - 39A | RETFORD - 36E | ARDSLEY - 56B | FRODINGHAM - 36C | GORTON - 39A | DARNALL - 41A | FRODINGHAM - 36C |
| Aug-58 | DARNALL - 41A | IMMINGHAM - 40B | GORTON - 9G | RETFORD - 36E | ARDSLEY - 56B | FRODINGHAM - 36C | GORTON - 9G | DARNALL - 41A | FRODINGHAM - 36C |
| Jan-59 | DARNALL - 41A | **1/59: LANG JN - 41J** | GORTON - 9G | RETFORD - 36E | ARDSLEY - 56B | FRODINGHAM - 36C | GORTON - 9G | DARNALL - 41A | FRODINGHAM - 36C |
| Aug-59 | DARNALL - 41A | LANGWITH JCN - 41J | GORTON - 9G | RETFORD - 36E | ARDSLEY - 56B | FRODINGHAM - 36C | GORTON - 9G | DARNALL - 41A | FRODINGHAM - 36C |
| Nov-59 | DARNALL - 41A | LANGWITH JCN - 41J | GORTON - 9G | RETFORD - 36E | ARDSLEY - 56B | **11/59: W/D** | GORTON - 9G | DARNALL - 41A | FRODINGHAM - 36C |
| Jan-60 | DARNALL - 41A | LANGWITH JCN - 41J | GORTON - 9G | RETFORD - 36E | ARDSLEY - 56B | | GORTON - 9G | DARNALL - 41A | FRODINGHAM - 36C |
| Apr-60 | DARNALL - 41A | LANGWITH JCN - 41J | GORTON - 9G | RETFORD - 36E | ARDSLEY - 56B | | GORTON - 9G | DARNALL - 41A | FRODINGHAM - 36C |
| Aug-60 | DARNALL - 41A | LANGWITH JCN - 41J | GORTON - 9G | RETFORD - 36E | ARDSLEY - 56B | | GORTON - 9G | DARNALL - 41A | FRODINGHAM - 36C |
| Nov-60 | DARNALL - 41A | LANGWITH JCN - 41J | GORTON - 9G | RETFORD - 36E | ARDSLEY - 56B | | GORTON - 9G | DARNALL - 41A | FRODINGHAM - 36C |

| | 63577 | 63580 | 63581 | 63582 | 63583 | 63584 | 63585 | 63586 | 63587 |
|---|---|---|---|---|---|---|---|---|---|
| Aug-50 | LANGWITHJCN-40E | ANNESLEY-38B | DARNALL-39B | GORTON-39A | DARNALL-39B | FRODINGHAM-36C | LANGWITHJCN-40E | IMMINGHAM-40B | FRODINGHAM-36C |
| Jan-51 | LANGWITHJCN-40E | **11/50: GOR - 39A** | DARNALL-39B | GORTON-39A | DARNALL-39B | FRODINGHAM-36C | LANGWITHJCN-40E | IMMINGHAM-40B | **3/51: STAVE - 38D** |
| Aug-51 | LANGWITHJCN-40E | GORTON-39A | DARNALL-39B | GORTON-39A | DARNALL-39B | **7/51: DARN - 39B** | LANGWITHJCN-40E | IMMINGHAM-40B | STAVELEY-38D |
| Jan-52 | LANGWITHJCN-40E | GORTON-39A | DARNALL-39B | GORTON-39A | DARNALL-39B | DARNALL-39B | LANGWITHJCN-40E | **12/51: MEX - 36B** | STAVELEY-38D |
| Aug-52 | LANGWITHJCN-40E | **2/52: W/D** | DARNALL-39B | GORTON-39A | DARNALL-39B | DARNALL-39B | LANGWITHJCN-40E | MEXBOROUGH-36B | STAVELEY-38D |
| Jan-53 | LANGWITHJCN-40E | | DARNALL-39B | GORTON-39A | DARNALL-39B | DARNALL-39B | LANGWITHJCN-40E | MEXBOROUGH-36B | STAVELEY-38D |
| Aug-53 | LANGWITHJCN-40E | | DARNALL-39B | GORTON-39A | DARNALL-39B | DARNALL-39B | LANGWITHJCN-40E | MEXBOROUGH-36B | STAVELEY-38D |
| Jan-54 | LANGWITHJCN-40E | | DARNALL-39B | GORTON-39A | DARNALL-39B | **1/54: ARDS - 37A** | LANGWITHJCN-40E | MEXBOROUGH-36B | STAVELEY-38D |
| Aug-54 | LANGWITHJCN-40E | | DARNALL-39B | GORTON-39A | DARNALL-39B | ARDSLEY-37A | LANGWITHJCN-40E | MEXBOROUGH-36B | STAVELEY-38D |
| Jan-55 | LANGWITHJCN-40E | | DARNALL-39B | GORTON-39A | DARNALL-39B | ARDSLEY-37A | LANGWITHJCN-40E | MEXBOROUGH-36B | STAVELEY-38D |
| Aug-55 | LANGWITHJCN-40E | | DARNALL-39B | GORTON-39A | DARNALL-39B | ARDSLEY-37A | LANGWITHJCN-40E | MEXBOROUGH-36B | STAVELEY-38D |
| Jan-56 | LANGWITHJCN-40E | | DARNALL-41A | GORTON-39A | DARNALL-41A | ARDSLEY-37A | LANGWITHJCN-40E | MEXBOROUGH-36B | **1/56: COLW - 38A** |
| Aug-56 | LANGWITHJCN-40E | | DARNALL-41A | GORTON-39A | DARNALL-41A | ARDSLEY-56B | LANGWITHJCN-40E | MEXBOROUGH-36B | COLWICK-38A |
| Jan-57 | LANGWITHJCN-40E | | DARNALL-41A | GORTON-39A | DARNALL-41A | ARDSLEY-56B | LANGWITHJCN-40E | MEXBOROUGH-36B | COLWICK-38A |
| Aug-57 | LANGWITHJCN-40E | | DARNALL-41A | GORTON-39A | DARNALL-41A | ARDSLEY-56B | LANGWITHJCN-40E | MEXBOROUGH-36B | COLWICK-38A |
| Jan-58 | LANGWITHJCN-40E | | DARNALL-41A | GORTON-39A | DARNALL-41A | ARDSLEY-56B | LANGWITHJCN-40E | MEXBOROUGH-36B | COLWICK-38A |
| Aug-58 | LANGWITHJCN-41J | | DARNALL-41A | GORTON-9G | DARNALL-41A | ARDSLEY-56B | LANGWITHJCN-41J | MEXBOROUGH-41F | COLWICK-40E |
| Jan-59 | LANGWITHJCN-41J | | DARNALL-41A | GORTON-9G | DARNALL-41A | ARDSLEY-56B | **10/58: COLW - 40E** | MEXBOROUGH-41F | COLWICK-40E |
| Aug-59 | LANGWITHJCN-41J | | **2/59: W/D** | **8/59: W/D** | **6/59: W/D** | ARDSLEY-56B | COLWICK-40E | MEXBOROUGH-41F | COLWICK-40E |
| Nov-59 | LANGWITHJCN-41J | | | | | ARDSLEY-56B | COLWICK-40E | MEXBOROUGH-41F | COLWICK-40E |
| Jan-60 | LANGWITHJCN-41J | | | | | ARDSLEY-56B | COLWICK-40E | MEXBOROUGH-41F | COLWICK-40E |
| Apr-60 | LANGWITHJCN-41J | | | | | ARDSLEY-56B | COLWICK-40E | MEXBOROUGH-41F | COLWICK-40E |
| Aug-60 | LANGWITHJCN-41J | | | | | ARDSLEY-56B | COLWICK-40E | MEXBOROUGH-41F | COLWICK-40E |
| Nov-60 | LANGWITHJCN-41J | | | | | ARDSLEY-56B | COLWICK-40E | MEXBOROUGH-41F | COLWICK-40E |

| | 63588 | 63593 | 63595 | 63597 | 63598 | 63599 | 63600 | 63601 | 63602 |
|---|---|---|---|---|---|---|---|---|---|
| Aug-50 | TUXFORD-40D | IMMINGHAM-40B | FRODINGHAM-36C | LANGWITHJCN-40E | GORTON-39A | COLWICK-38A | GORTON-39A | FRODINGHAM-36C | FRODINGHAM-36C |
| Jan-51 | TUXFORD-40D | IMMINGHAM-40B | FRODINGHAM-36C | LANGWITHJCN-40E | GORTON-39A | COLWICK-38A | GORTON-39A | FRODINGHAM-36C | **3/51: COLW - 38A** |
| Aug-51 | TUXFORD-40D | IMMINGHAM-40B | FRODINGHAM-36C | LANGWITHJCN-40E | GORTON-39A | COLWICK-38A | GORTON-39A | **5/51: IMM - 40B** | COLWICK-38A |
| Jan-52 | TUXFORD-40D | **12/51: MEX - 36B** | FRODINGHAM-36C | LANGWITHJCN-40E | GORTON-39A | COLWICK-38A | GORTON-39A | IMMINGHAM-40B | COLWICK-38A |
| Aug-52 | TUXFORD-40D | MEXBOROUGH-36B | FRODINGHAM-36C | LANGWITHJCN-40E | GORTON-39A | COLWICK-38A | GORTON-39A | IMMINGHAM-40B | COLWICK-38A |
| Jan-53 | TUXFORD-40D | MEXBOROUGH-36B | FRODINGHAM-36C | LANGWITHJCN-40E | GORTON-39A | COLWICK-38A | GORTON-39A | IMMINGHAM-40B | COLWICK-38A |
| Aug-53 | TUXFORD-40D | MEXBOROUGH-36B | FRODINGHAM-36C | LANGWITHJCN-40E | GORTON-39A | COLWICK-38A | GORTON-39A | IMMINGHAM-40B | COLWICK-38A |
| Jan-54 | **11/53: ARDS - 37A** | MEXBOROUGH-36B | FRODINGHAM-36C | LANGWITHJCN-40E | GORTON-39A | **6/54: COLW - 38A** | GORTON-39A | **10/53: GOR - 39A** | COLWICK-38A |
| Aug-54 | ARDSLEY-37A | MEXBOROUGH-36B | FRODINGHAM-36C | LANGWITHJCN-40E | GORTON-39A | **8/54: DARN - 39B** | GORTON-39A | **8/54: FROD - 36C** | COLWICK-38A |
| Jan-55 | ARDSLEY-37A | MEXBOROUGH-36B | FRODINGHAM-36C | **1/55: IMM - 40B** | GORTON-39A | DARNALL-39B | GORTON-39A | FRODINGHAM-36C | COLWICK-38A |
| Aug-55 | ARDSLEY-37A | MEXBOROUGH-36B | FRODINGHAM-36C | IMMINGHAM-40B | GORTON-39A | DARNALL-39B | GORTON-39A | FRODINGHAM-36C | COLWICK-38A |
| Jan-56 | ARDSLEY-37A | MEXBOROUGH-36B | FRODINGHAM-36C | IMMINGHAM-40B | GORTON-39A | DARNALL-41A | GORTON-39A | FRODINGHAM-36C | **1/56: ANN - 38B** |
| Aug-56 | ARDSLEY-56B | MEXBOROUGH-36B | FRODINGHAM-36C | IMMINGHAM-40B | GORTON-39A | DARNALL-41A | GORTON-39A | FRODINGHAM-36C | ANNESLEY-38B |
| Jan-57 | ARDSLEY-56B | MEXBOROUGH-36B | FRODINGHAM-36C | IMMINGHAM-40B | GORTON-39A | DARNALL-41A | GORTON-39A | FRODINGHAM-36C | **11/56: COLW - 38A** |
| Aug-57 | ARDSLEY-56B | MEXBOROUGH-36B | FRODINGHAM-36C | IMMINGHAM-40B | GORTON-39A | DARNALL-41A | GORTON-39A | FRODINGHAM-36C | COLWICK-38A |
| Jan-58 | ARDSLEY-56B | MEXBOROUGH-36B | FRODINGHAM-36C | IMMINGHAM-40B | GORTON-39A | DARNALL-41A | GORTON-39A | FRODINGHAM-36C | COLWICK-38A |
| Aug-58 | ARDSLEY-56B | MEXBOROUGH-41F | FRODINGHAM-36C | IMMINGHAM-40B | GORTON-9G | DARNALL-41A | GORTON-9G | FRODINGHAM-36C | COLWICK-40E |
| Jan-59 | **2/59: WAKE - 56A** | MEXBOROUGH-41F | FRODINGHAM-36C | **1/59: LANG JN - 41J** | GORTON-9G | DARNALL-41A | GORTON-9G | FRODINGHAM-36C | COLWICK-40E |
| Aug-59 | WAKEFIELD-56A | MEXBOROUGH-41F | FRODINGHAM-36C | LANGWITHJCN-41J | GORTON-9G | DARNALL-41A | GORTON-9G | FRODINGHAM-36C | **6/59: FROD - 36C** |
| Nov-59 | WAKEFIELD-56A | MEXBOROUGH-41F | FRODINGHAM-36C | LANGWITHJCN-41J | GORTON-9G | DARNALL-41A | GORTON-9G | FRODINGHAM-36C | FRODINGHAM-36C |
| Jan-60 | WAKEFIELD-56A | MEXBOROUGH-41F | FRODINGHAM-36C | LANGWITHJCN-41J | GORTON-9G | DARNALL-41A | GORTON-9G | FRODINGHAM-36C | **2/60: RET - 36E** |
| Apr-60 | WAKEFIELD-56A | MEXBOROUGH-41F | FRODINGHAM-36C | LANGWITHJCN-41J | GORTON-9G | DARNALL-41A | GORTON-9G | FRODINGHAM-36C | RETFORD-36E |
| Aug-60 | WAKEFIELD-56A | MEXBOROUGH-41F | FRODINGHAM-36C | LANGWITHJCN-41J | GORTON-9G | DARNALL-41A | GORTON-9G | FRODINGHAM-36C | RETFORD-36E |
| Nov-60 | WAKEFIELD-56A | MEXBOROUGH-41F | FRODINGHAM-36C | LANGWITHJCN-41J | GORTON-9G | DARNALL-41A | GORTON-9G | FRODINGHAM-36C | RETFORD-36E |

| | 63603 | 63605 | 63608 | 63609 | 63611 | 63614 | 63615 | 63616 | 63617 |
|---|---|---|---|---|---|---|---|---|---|
| Aug-50 | DAIRYCOATES-53A | DARNALL-39B | RETFORD-36E | DARNALL-39B | MEXBOROUGH-36B | ANNESLEY-38B | LANGWITHJCN-40E | IMMINGHAM-40B | FRODINGHAM-36C |
| Jan-51 | DAIRYCOATES-53A | DARNALL-39B | RETFORD-36E | DARNALL-39B | MEXBOROUGH-36B | **11/50: GOR - 39A** | LANGWITHJCN-40E | IMMINGHAM-40B | FRODINGHAM-36C |
| Aug-51 | **9/51: ANG JN - 40E** | DARNALL-39B | RETFORD-36E | DARNALL-39B | MEXBOROUGH-36B | GORTON-39A | LANGWITHJCN-40E | IMMINGHAM-40B | FRODINGHAM-36C |
| Jan-52 | LANGWITHJCN-40E | DARNALL-39B | RETFORD-36E | DARNALL-39B | MEXBOROUGH-36B | GORTON-39A | LANGWITHJCN-40E | IMMINGHAM-40B | FRODINGHAM-36C |
| Aug-52 | LANGWITHJCN-40E | DARNALL-39B | RETFORD-36E | DARNALL-39B | MEXBOROUGH-36B | GORTON-39A | LANGWITHJCN-40E | IMMINGHAM-40B | FRODINGHAM-36C |
| Jan-53 | LANGWITHJCN-40E | DARNALL-39B | RETFORD-36E | DARNALL-39B | MEXBOROUGH-36B | GORTON-39A | LANGWITHJCN-40E | IMMINGHAM-40B | FRODINGHAM-36C |
| Aug-53 | LANGWITHJCN-40E | DARNALL-39B | RETFORD-36E | DARNALL-39B | MEXBOROUGH-36B | GORTON-39A | LANGWITHJCN-40E | IMMINGHAM-40B | FRODINGHAM-36C |
| Jan-54 | **10/53: GOR - 39A** | **1/54: ARDS - 37A** | RETFORD-36E | DARNALL-39B | MEXBOROUGH-36B | GORTON-39A | LANGWITHJCN-40E | IMMINGHAM-40B | FRODINGHAM-36C |
| Aug-54 | GORTON-39A | ARDSLEY-37A | RETFORD-36E | DARNALL-39B | MEXBOROUGH-36B | **6/54: COLW - 38A** | LANGWITHJCN-40E | IMMINGHAM-40B | FRODINGHAM-36C |
| Jan-55 | GORTON-39A | ARDSLEY-37A | RETFORD-36E | DARNALL-39B | MEXBOROUGH-36B | COLWICK-38A | LANGWITHJCN-40E | IMMINGHAM-40B | FRODINGHAM-36C |
| Aug-55 | GORTON-39A | ARDSLEY-37A | RETFORD-36E | DARNALL-39B | MEXBOROUGH-36B | COLWICK-38A | **8/55: IMM - 40B** | IMMINGHAM-40B | FRODINGHAM-36C |
| Jan-56 | GORTON-39A | ARDSLEY-37A | RETFORD-36E | DARNALL-41A | MEXBOROUGH-36B | COLWICK-38A | IMMINGHAM-40B | IMMINGHAM-40B | FRODINGHAM-36C |
| Aug-56 | GORTON-39A | ARDSLEY-56B | RETFORD-36E | DARNALL-41A | MEXBOROUGH-36B | COLWICK-38A | IMMINGHAM-40B | IMMINGHAM-40B | FRODINGHAM-36C |
| Jan-57 | GORTON-39A | ARDSLEY-56B | RETFORD-36E | DARNALL-41A | MEXBOROUGH-36B | COLWICK-38A | IMMINGHAM-40B | IMMINGHAM-40B | FRODINGHAM-36C |
| Aug-57 | GORTON-39A | ARDSLEY-56B | RETFORD-36E | DARNALL-41A | MEXBOROUGH-36B | COLWICK-38A | IMMINGHAM-40B | IMMINGHAM-40B | FRODINGHAM-36C |
| Jan-58 | GORTON-39A | ARDSLEY-56B | RETFORD-36E | DARNALL-41A | MEXBOROUGH-36B | COLWICK-38A | IMMINGHAM-40B | IMMINGHAM-40B | FRODINGHAM-36C |
| Aug-58 | GORTON-9G | ARDSLEY-56B | RETFORD-36E | DARNALL-41A | MEXBOROUGH-41F | COLWICK-40E | IMMINGHAM-40B | IMMINGHAM-40B | FRODINGHAM-36C |
| Jan-59 | GORTON-9G | ARDSLEY-56B | RETFORD-36E | DARNALL-41A | MEXBOROUGH-41F | COLWICK-40E | IMMINGHAM-40B | IMMINGHAM-40B | FRODINGHAM-36C |
| Aug-59 | GORTON-9G | ARDSLEY-56B | RETFORD-36E | DARNALL-41A | MEXBOROUGH-41F | **4/59: W/D** | IMMINGHAM-40B | IMMINGHAM-40B | FRODINGHAM-36C |
| Nov-59 | GORTON-9G | ARDSLEY-56B | RETFORD-36E | DARNALL-41A | MEXBOROUGH-41F | | IMMINGHAM-40B | IMMINGHAM-40B | FRODINGHAM-36C |
| Jan-60 | GORTON-9G | ARDSLEY-56B | RETFORD-36E | DARNALL-41A | MEXBOROUGH-41F | | IMMINGHAM-40B | IMMINGHAM-40B | FRODINGHAM-36C |
| Apr-60 | GORTON-9G | ARDSLEY-56B | RETFORD-36E | DARNALL-41A | MEXBOROUGH-41F | | IMMINGHAM-40B | **5/60: COLW - 40E** | FRODINGHAM-36C |
| Aug-60 | GORTON-9G | ARDSLEY-56B | RETFORD-36E | DARNALL-41A | MEXBOROUGH-41F | | IMMINGHAM-40B | COLWICK-40E | FRODINGHAM-36C |
| Nov-60 | GORTON-9G | ARDSLEY-56B | RETFORD-36E | DARNALL-41A | MEXBOROUGH-41F | | IMMINGHAM-40B | COLWICK-40E | FRODINGHAM-36C |

| | 63618 | 63620 | 63621 | 63622 | 63623 | 63624 | 63625 | 63626 | 63627 |
|---|---|---|---|---|---|---|---|---|---|
| Aug-50 | ANNESLEY-38B | CUDWORTH-53E | IMMINGHAM-40B | DARNALL-39B | BARNSLEY-36D | IMMINGHAM-40B | LANGWITHJCN-40E | FRODINGHAM-36C | MEXBOROUGH-36B |
| Jan-51 | **10/50: COLW - 38A** | **1/51: DAIRY - 53A** | IMMINGHAM-40B | DARNALL-39B | BARNSLEY-36D | IMMINGHAM-40B | **9/50: RET - 36E** | FRODINGHAM-36C | **9/50: LANG JN - 40E** |
| Aug-51 | **10/51: ANN - 38B** | DAIRYCOATES-53A | IMMINGHAM-40B | DARNALL-39B | BARNSLEY-36D | IMMINGHAM-40B | **12/50: BARN - 36D** | FRODINGHAM-36C | LANGWITHJCN-40E |
| Jan-52 | **3/52: COLW - 38A** | **9/51: IMM - 40B** | IMMINGHAM-40B | DARNALL-39B | BARNSLEY-36D | IMMINGHAM-40B | BARNSLEY-36D | FRODINGHAM-36C | LANGWITHJCN-40E |
| Aug-52 | COLWICK-38A | IMMINGHAM-40B | IMMINGHAM-40B | DARNALL-39B | BARNSLEY-36D | IMMINGHAM-40B | BARNSLEY-36D | FRODINGHAM-36C | **2/52: W/D** |
| Jan-53 | COLWICK-38A | IMMINGHAM-40B | **3/53: LANG JN - 40E** | DARNALL-39B | BARNSLEY-36D | **3/53: LANG JN - 40E** | BARNSLEY-36D | FRODINGHAM-36C | |
| Aug-53 | COLWICK-38A | IMMINGHAM-40B | **7/53: IMM - 40B** | DARNALL-39B | BARNSLEY-36D | **7/53: IMM - 40B** | BARNSLEY-36D | FRODINGHAM-36C | |
| Jan-54 | COLWICK-38A | **10/53: DARN - 39B** | **10/53: DARN - 39B** | DARNALL-39B | BARNSLEY-36D | **10/53: DARN - 39B** | BARNSLEY-36D | FRODINGHAM-36C | |
| Aug-54 | COLWICK-38A | DARNALL-39B | DARNALL-39B | DARNALL-39B | BARNSLEY-36D | DARNALL-39B | BARNSLEY-36D | FRODINGHAM-36C | |
| Jan-55 | COLWICK-38A | DARNALL-39B | DARNALL-39B | **1/55: IMM - 40B** | BARNSLEY-36D | DARNALL-39B | BARNSLEY-36D | FRODINGHAM-36C | |
| Aug-55 | COLWICK-38A | DARNALL-39B | DARNALL-39B | IMMINGHAM-40B | BARNSLEY-36D | DARNALL-39B | BARNSLEY-36D | FRODINGHAM-36C | |
| Jan-56 | **1/56: DCTR - 36A** | DARNALL-41A | DARNALL-41A | IMMINGHAM-40B | BARNSLEY-36D | DARNALL-41A | BARNSLEY-36D | FRODINGHAM-36C | |
| Aug-56 | DONCASTER-36A | DARNALL-41A | DARNALL-41A | IMMINGHAM-40B | BARNSLEY-36D | DARNALL-41A | BARNSLEY-36D | FRODINGHAM-36C | |
| Jan-57 | DONCASTER-36A | DARNALL-41A | DARNALL-41A | IMMINGHAM-40B | BARNSLEY-36D | DARNALL-41A | BARNSLEY-36D | FRODINGHAM-36C | |
| Aug-57 | DONCASTER-36A | DARNALL-41A | DARNALL-41A | IMMINGHAM-40B | BARNSLEY-36D | DARNALL-41A | BARNSLEY-36D | FRODINGHAM-36C | |
| Jan-58 | DONCASTER-36A | DARNALL-41A | DARNALL-41A | IMMINGHAM-40B | BARNSLEY-36D | DARNALL-41A | BARNSLEY-36D | FRODINGHAM-36C | |
| Aug-58 | DONCASTER-36A | DARNALL-41A | DARNALL-41A | IMMINGHAM-40B | BARNSLEY-41G | DARNALL-41A | BARNSLEY-41G | FRODINGHAM-36C | |
| Jan-59 | DONCASTER-36A | DARNALL-41A | DARNALL-41A | **1/59: LANG JN - 41J** | BARNSLEY-41G | DARNALL-41A | BARNSLEY-41G | FRODINGHAM-36C | |
| Aug-59 | DONCASTER-36A | **2/59: W/D** | DARNALL-41A | LANGWITHJCN-41J | BARNSLEY-41G | DARNALL-41A | **4/59: W/D** | FRODINGHAM-36C | |
| Nov-59 | DONCASTER-36A | | DARNALL-41A | **12/59: BARN - 41G** | BARNSLEY-41G | DARNALL-41A | | FRODINGHAM-36C | |
| Jan-60 | DONCASTER-36A | | DARNALL-41A | **1/60: MEX - 41F** | **1/60: MEX - 41F** | DARNALL-41A | | **1/60: MEX - 41F** | |
| Apr-60 | DONCASTER-36A | | DARNALL-41A | MEXBOROUGH-41F | MEXBOROUGH-41F | DARNALL-41A | | MEXBOROUGH-41F | |
| Aug-60 | DONCASTER-36A | | DARNALL-41A | MEXBOROUGH-41F | MEXBOROUGH-41F | DARNALL-41A | | MEXBOROUGH-41F | |
| Nov-60 | DONCASTER-36A | | DARNALL-41A | MEXBOROUGH-41F | MEXBOROUGH-41F | DARNALL-41A | | MEXBOROUGH-41F | |

| | 63629 | 63631 | 63632 | 63634 | 63635 | 63636 | 63637 | 63638 | 63640 |
|---|---|---|---|---|---|---|---|---|---|
| Aug-50 | DARNALL - 39B | GORTON - 39A | LANGWITHJCN - 40E | TUXFORD - 40D | ANNESLEY - 38B | COLWICK - 38A | RETFORD - 36E | GORTON - 39A | FRODINGHAM - 36C |
| Jan-51 | DARNALL - 39B | GORTON - 39A | LANGWITHJCN - 40E | TUXFORD - 40D | **11/50: GOR - 39A** | COLWICK - 38A | RETFORD - 36E | GORTON - 39A | FRODINGHAM - 36C |
| Aug-51 | DARNALL - 39B | GORTON - 39A | LANGWITHJCN - 40E | TUXFORD - 40D | GORTON - 39A | COLWICK - 38A | RETFORD - 36E | GORTON - 39A | **7/51: DARN - 39B** |
| Jan-52 | DARNALL - 39B | GORTON - 39A | LANGWITHJCN - 40E | TUXFORD - 40D | GORTON - 39A | COLWICK - 38A | RETFORD - 36E | GORTON - 39A | DARNALL - 39B |
| Aug-52 | DARNALL - 39B | GORTON - 39A | LANGWITHJCN - 40E | TUXFORD - 40D | GORTON - 39A | **6/5: LANG JN - 40E** | RETFORD - 36E | GORTON - 39A | DARNALL - 39B |
| Jan-53 | DARNALL - 39B | GORTON - 39A | LANGWITHJCN - 40E | TUXFORD - 40D | GORTON - 39A | LANGWITHJCN - 40E | RETFORD - 36E | GORTON - 39A | DARNALL - 39B |
| Aug-53 | DARNALL - 39B | GORTON - 39A | LANGWITHJCN - 40E | TUXFORD - 40D | GORTON - 39A | LANGWITHJCN - 40E | RETFORD - 36E | GORTON - 39A | DARNALL - 39B |
| Jan-54 | DARNALL - 39B | GORTON - 39A | LANGWITHJCN - 40E | **11/53: LANG JN - 40E** | GORTON - 39A | LANGWITHJCN - 40E | RETFORD - 36E | GORTON - 39A | DARNALL - 39B |
| Aug-54 | DARNALL - 39B | GORTON - 39A | LANGWITHJCN - 40E | LANGWITHJCN - 40E | **6/54: DAR - 39B** | LANGWITHJCN - 40E | RETFORD - 36E | **6/54: COLW - 38A** | DARNALL - 39B |
| Jan-55 | DARNALL - 39B | GORTON - 39A | LANGWITHJCN - 40E | LANGWITHJCN - 40E | **1/55: IMM - 40B** | LANGWITHJCN - 40E | RETFORD - 36E | COLWICK - 38A | DARNALL - 39B |
| Aug-55 | DARNALL - 39B | GORTON - 39A | LANGWITHJCN - 40E | LANGWITHJCN - 40E | IMMINGHAM - 40B | LANGWITHJCN - 40E | RETFORD - 36E | COLWICK - 38A | DARNALL - 39B |
| Jan-56 | DARNALL - 41A | GORTON - 39A | LANGWITHJCN - 40E | LANGWITHJCN - 40E | IMMINGHAM - 40B | LANGWITHJCN - 40E | RETFORD - 36E | COLWICK - 38A | DARNALL - 41A |
| Aug-56 | DARNALL - 41A | GORTON - 39A | LANGWITHJCN - 40E | LANGWITHJCN - 40E | IMMINGHAM - 40B | LANGWITHJCN - 40E | RETFORD - 36E | COLWICK - 38A | DARNALL - 41A |
| Jan-57 | DARNALL - 41A | GORTON - 39A | LANGWITHJCN - 40E | LANGWITHJCN - 40E | IMMINGHAM - 40B | LANGWITHJCN - 40E | RETFORD - 36E | COLWICK - 38A | DARNALL - 41A |
| Aug-57 | DARNALL - 41A | GORTON - 39A | LANGWITHJCN - 40E | LANGWITHJCN - 40E | IMMINGHAM - 40B | LANGWITHJCN - 40E | RETFORD - 36E | COLWICK - 38A | DARNALL - 41A |
| Jan-58 | DARNALL - 41A | GORTON - 39A | LANGWITHJCN - 40E | LANGWITHJCN - 40E | IMMINGHAM - 40B | LANGWITHJCN - 40E | RETFORD - 36E | COLWICK - 38A | DARNALL - 41A |
| Aug-58 | DARNALL - 41A | GORTON - 9G | LANGWITHJCN - 41J | LANGWITHJCN - 41J | IMMINGHAM - 40B | LANGWITHJCN - 41J | RETFORD - 36E | COLWICK - 40E | DARNALL - 41A |
| Jan-59 | DARNALL - 41A | GORTON - 9G | LANGWITHJCN - 41J | LANGWITHJCN - 41J | **1/59: LANG JN - 41J** | LANGWITHJCN - 41J | RETFORD - 36E | COLWICK - 40E | DARNALL - 41A |
| Aug-59 | **2/59: W/D** | GORTON - 9G | LANGWITHJCN - 41J | LANGWITHJCN - 41J | LANGWITHJCN - 41J | LANGWITHJCN - 41J | RETFORD - 36E | **3/59: W/D** | **5/59: W/D** |
| Nov-59 | | GORTON - 9G | **12/59: BARN - 41G** | LANGWITHJCN - 41J | LANGWITHJCN - 41J | LANGWITHJCN - 41J | RETFORD - 36E | | |
| Jan-60 | | GORTON - 9G | **1/60: MEX - 41F** | LANGWITHJCN - 41J | LANGWITHJCN - 41J | LANGWITHJCN - 41J | RETFORD - 36E | | |
| Apr-60 | | GORTON - 9G | MEXBOROUGH - 41F | **5/60: IMM - 40B** | LANGWITHJCN - 41J | LANGWITHJCN - 41J | RETFORD - 36E | | |
| Aug-60 | | GORTON - 9G | MEXBOROUGH - 41F | IMMINGHAM - 40B | LANGWITHJCN - 41J | LANGWITHJCN - 41J | RETFORD - 36E | | |
| Nov-60 | | GORTON - 9G | MEXBOROUGH - 41F | IMMINGHAM - 40B | LANGWITHJCN - 41J | LANGWITHJCN - 41J | RETFORD - 36E | | |

| | 63641 | 63642 | 63643 | 63645 | 63647 | 63648 | 63649 | 63654 | 63655 |
|---|---|---|---|---|---|---|---|---|---|
| Aug-50 | GORTON - 39A | FRODINGHAM - 36C | FRODINGHAM - 36C | FRODINGHAM - 36C | IMMINGHAM - 40B | LANGWITHJCN - 40E | FRODINGHAM - 36C | RETFORD - 36E | FRODINGHAM - 36C |
| Jan-51 | GORTON - 39A | FRODINGHAM - 36C | **9/50: LANG JN - 40E** | FRODINGHAM - 36C | IMMINGHAM - 40B | LANGWITHJCN - 40E | FRODINGHAM - 36C | RETFORD - 36E | FRODINGHAM - 36C |
| Aug-51 | GORTON - 39A | FRODINGHAM - 36C | LANGWITHJCN - 40E | **7/51: DARN - 39B** | IMMINGHAM - 40B | LANGWITHJCN - 40E | **5/51: IMM - 40B** | RETFORD - 36E | FRODINGHAM - 36C |
| Jan-52 | GORTON - 39A | FRODINGHAM - 36C | LANGWITHJCN - 40E | DARNALL - 39B | IMMINGHAM - 40B | **12/51: STAVE - 38D** | IMMINGHAM - 40B | RETFORD - 36E | FRODINGHAM - 36C |
| Aug-52 | GORTON - 39A | FRODINGHAM - 36C | LANGWITHJCN - 40E | DARNALL - 39B | IMMINGHAM - 40B | STAVELEY - 38D | IMMINGHAM - 40B | RETFORD - 36E | FRODINGHAM - 36C |
| Jan-53 | GORTON - 39A | FRODINGHAM - 36C | LANGWITHJCN - 40E | DARNALL - 39B | IMMINGHAM - 40B | STAVELEY - 38D | IMMINGHAM - 40B | RETFORD - 36E | FRODINGHAM - 36C |
| Aug-53 | GORTON - 39A | FRODINGHAM - 36C | LANGWITHJCN - 40E | DARNALL - 39B | IMMINGHAM - 40B | STAVELEY - 38D | IMMINGHAM - 40B | RETFORD - 36E | FRODINGHAM - 36C |
| Jan-54 | GORTON - 39A | FRODINGHAM - 36C | LANGWITHJCN - 40E | DARNALL - 39B | **10/53: COLW - 38A** | STAVELEY - 38D | **10/53: COLW - 38A** | RETFORD - 36E | FRODINGHAM - 36C |
| Aug-54 | GORTON - 39A | FRODINGHAM - 36C | LANGWITHJCN - 40E | DARNALL - 39B | COLWICK - 38A | STAVELEY - 38D | COLWICK - 38A | RETFORD - 36E | FRODINGHAM - 36C |
| Jan-55 | GORTON - 39A | FRODINGHAM - 36C | **1/55: IMM - 40B** | DARNALL - 39B | COLWICK - 38A | STAVELEY - 38D | **12/54: GOR - 39A** | RETFORD - 36E | **2/55: RET - 36E** |
| Aug-55 | GORTON - 39A | FRODINGHAM - 36C | IMMINGHAM - 40B | DARNALL - 39B | COLWICK - 38A | STAVELEY - 38D | GORTON - 39A | RETFORD - 36E | RETFORD - 36E |
| Jan-56 | GORTON - 39A | FRODINGHAM - 36C | IMMINGHAM - 40B | DARNALL - 41A | COLWICK - 38A | STAVELEY - 38D | GORTON - 39A | RETFORD - 36E | RETFORD - 36E |
| Aug-56 | GORTON - 39A | FRODINGHAM - 36C | IMMINGHAM - 40B | DARNALL - 41A | COLWICK - 38A | STAVELEY - 38D | GORTON - 39A | RETFORD - 36E | RETFORD - 36E |
| Jan-57 | GORTON - 39A | FRODINGHAM - 36C | IMMINGHAM - 40B | DARNALL - 41A | COLWICK - 38A | STAVELEY - 38D | GORTON - 39A | RETFORD - 36E | RETFORD - 36E |
| Aug-57 | GORTON - 39A | FRODINGHAM - 36C | IMMINGHAM - 40B | DARNALL - 41A | COLWICK - 38A | STAVELEY - 38D | GORTON - 39A | RETFORD - 36E | RETFORD - 36E |
| Jan-58 | GORTON - 39A | FRODINGHAM - 36C | IMMINGHAM - 40B | DARNALL - 41A | COLWICK - 38A | STAVELEY - 38D | GORTON - 39A | **2/58: FROD - 36C** | RETFORD - 36E |
| Aug-58 | GORTON - 9G | FRODINGHAM - 36C | IMMINGHAM - 40B | DARNALL - 41A | COLWICK - 40E | STAVELEY(GC) - 41H | GORTON - 9G | FRODINGHAM - 36C | RETFORD - 36E |
| Jan-59 | GORTON - 9G | FRODINGHAM - 36C | **1/59: LANG JN - 41J** | DARNALL - 41A | COLWICK - 40E | STAVELEY(GC) - 41H | GORTON - 9G | FRODINGHAM - 36C | RETFORD - 36E |
| Aug-59 | GORTON - 9G | FRODINGHAM - 36C | LANGWITHJCN - 41J | DARNALL - 41A | **6/59: FROD - 36C** | STAVELEY(GC) - 41H | GORTON - 9G | **6/59: W/D** | RETFORD - 36E |
| Nov-59 | GORTON - 9G | **11/59: W/D** | LANGWITHJCN - 41J | DARNALL - 41A | FRODINGHAM - 36C | STAVELEY(GC) - 41H | GORTON - 9G | | RETFORD - 36E |
| Jan-60 | GORTON - 9G | | LANGWITHJCN - 41J | DARNALL - 41A | **2/60: RET - 36E** | **2/60: MEX - 41F** | GORTON - 9G | | RETFORD - 36E |
| Apr-60 | GORTON - 9G | | **5/60: IMM - 40B** | DARNALL - 41A | RETFORD - 36E | MEXBOROUGH - 41F | GORTON - 9G | | RETFORD - 36E |
| Aug-60 | GORTON - 9G | | IMMINGHAM - 40B | DARNALL - 41A | RETFORD - 36E | MEXBOROUGH - 41F | GORTON - 9G | | RETFORD - 36E |
| Nov-60 | GORTON - 9G | | IMMINGHAM - 40B | DARNALL - 41A | RETFORD - 36E | MEXBOROUGH - 41F | GORTON - 9G | | RETFORD - 36E |

| | 63656 | 63657 | 63658 | 63659 | 63660 | 63661 | 63662 | 63664 | 63665 |
|---|---|---|---|---|---|---|---|---|---|
| Aug-50 | LANGWITHJCN - 40E | IMMINGHAM - 40B | LANGWITHJCN - 40E | FRODINGHAM - 36C | FRODINGHAM - 36C | DARNALL - 39B | ANNESLEY - 38B | DAIRYCOATES - 53A | LANGWITHJCN - 40E |
| Jan-51 | **9/50: RET - 36E** | IMMINGHAM - 40B | IMMINGHAM - 40B | FRODINGHAM - 36C | FRODINGHAM - 36C | DARNALL - 39B | **11/50: GOR - 39A** | DAIRYCOATES - 53A | IMMINGHAM - 40B |
| Aug-51 | **12/50: BARN - 36D** | IMMINGHAM - 40B | IMMINGHAM - 40B | FRODINGHAM - 36C | FRODINGHAM - 36C | DARNALL - 39B | GORTON - 39A | **9/51: LANG JN - 40E** | IMMINGHAM - 40B |
| Jan-52 | BARNSLEY - 36D | IMMINGHAM - 40B | IMMINGHAM - 40B | FRODINGHAM - 36C | FRODINGHAM - 36C | DARNALL - 39B | GORTON - 39A | LANGWITHJCN - 40E | IMMINGHAM - 40B |
| Aug-52 | BARNSLEY - 36D | IMMINGHAM - 40B | IMMINGHAM - 40B | FRODINGHAM - 36C | FRODINGHAM - 36C | DARNALL - 39B | GORTON - 39A | LANGWITHJCN - 40E | IMMINGHAM - 40B |
| Jan-53 | BARNSLEY - 36D | IMMINGHAM - 40B | IMMINGHAM - 40B | FRODINGHAM - 36C | FRODINGHAM - 36C | DARNALL - 39B | GORTON - 39A | LANGWITHJCN - 40E | IMMINGHAM - 40B |
| Aug-53 | BARNSLEY - 36D | IMMINGHAM - 40B | IMMINGHAM - 40B | FRODINGHAM - 36C | FRODINGHAM - 36C | DARNALL - 39B | GORTON - 39A | LANGWITHJCN - 40E | IMMINGHAM - 40B |
| Jan-54 | BARNSLEY - 36D | **10/53: COLW - 38A** | **10/53: COLW - 38A** | FRODINGHAM - 36C | FRODINGHAM - 36C | DARNALL - 39B | GORTON - 39A | LANGWITHJCN - 40E | IMMINGHAM - 40B |
| Aug-54 | BARNSLEY - 36D | COLWICK - 38A | **8/54: DARN - 39B** | FRODINGHAM - 36C | FRODINGHAM - 36C | DARNALL - 39B | **6/54: FROD - 36C** | LANGWITHJCN - 40E | IMMINGHAM - 40B |
| Jan-55 | BARNSLEY - 36D | COLWICK - 38A | DARNALL - 39B | FRODINGHAM - 36C | FRODINGHAM - 36C | DARNALL - 39B | FRODINGHAM - 36C | LANGWITHJCN - 40E | IMMINGHAM - 40B |
| Aug-55 | BARNSLEY - 36D | COLWICK - 38A | DARNALL - 39B | FRODINGHAM - 36C | FRODINGHAM - 36C | DARNALL - 39B | FRODINGHAM - 36C | LANGWITHJCN - 40E | IMMINGHAM - 40B |
| Jan-56 | BARNSLEY - 36D | COLWICK - 38A | DARNALL - 41A | **11/55: BARN - 36D** | FRODINGHAM - 36C | DARNALL - 41A | FRODINGHAM - 36C | LANGWITHJCN - 40E | **3/56: IMM - 40B** |
| Aug-56 | BARNSLEY - 36D | COLWICK - 38A | DARNALL - 41A | BARNSLEY - 36D | FRODINGHAM - 36C | DARNALL - 41A | FRODINGHAM - 36C | LANGWITHJCN - 40E | IMMINGHAM - 40B |
| Jan-57 | BARNSLEY - 36D | COLWICK - 38A | DARNALL - 41A | BARNSLEY - 36D | FRODINGHAM - 36C | DARNALL - 41A | FRODINGHAM - 36C | LANGWITHJCN - 40E | IMMINGHAM - 40B |
| Aug-57 | BARNSLEY - 36D | COLWICK - 38A | DARNALL - 41A | BARNSLEY - 36D | FRODINGHAM - 36C | DARNALL - 41A | FRODINGHAM - 36C | LANGWITHJCN - 40E | IMMINGHAM - 40B |
| Jan-58 | BARNSLEY - 36D | COLWICK - 38A | DARNALL - 41A | BARNSLEY - 36D | FRODINGHAM - 36C | DARNALL - 41A | FRODINGHAM - 36C | LANGWITHJCN - 40E | IMMINGHAM - 40B |
| Aug-58 | BARNSLEY - 41G | COLWICK - 40E | DARNALL - 41A | BARNSLEY - 41G | FRODINGHAM - 36C | DARNALL - 41A | FRODINGHAM - 36C | LANGWITHJCN - 41J | IMMINGHAM - 40B |
| Jan-59 | BARNSLEY - 41G | COLWICK - 40E | DARNALL - 41A | BARNSLEY - 41G | FRODINGHAM - 36C | DARNALL - 41A | FRODINGHAM - 36C | LANGWITHJCN - 41J | **1/59: LANG JN - 41J** |
| Aug-59 | BARNSLEY - 41G | COLWICK - 40E | DARNALL - 41A | BARNSLEY - 41G | FRODINGHAM - 36C | DARNALL - 41A | FRODINGHAM - 36C | LANGWITHJCN - 41J | LANGWITHJCN - 41J |
| Nov-59 | BARNSLEY - 41G | COLWICK - 40E | DARNALL - 41A | BARNSLEY - 41G | **9/59: W/D** | DARNALL - 41A | FRODINGHAM - 36C | LANGWITHJCN - 41J | **9/59: FROD - 36C** |
| Jan-60 | **1/60: MEX - 41F** | COLWICK - 40E | DARNALL - 41A | **1/60: MEX - 41F** | | DARNALL - 41A | FRODINGHAM - 36C | LANGWITHJCN - 41J | FRODINGHAM - 36C |
| Apr-60 | MEXBOROUGH - 41F | COLWICK - 40E | DARNALL - 41A | MEXBOROUGH - 41F | | **4/60: STAVE - 41H** | FRODINGHAM - 36C | LANGWITHJCN - 41J | FRODINGHAM - 36C |
| Aug-60 | MEXBOROUGH - 41F | COLWICK - 40E | DARNALL - 41A | MEXBOROUGH - 41F | | STAVELEY(GC) - 41H | FRODINGHAM - 36C | LANGWITHJCN - 41J | FRODINGHAM - 36C |
| Nov-60 | **10/60: STAVE - 41H** | COLWICK - 40E | DARNALL - 41A | MEXBOROUGH - 41F | | STAVELEY(GC) - 41H | FRODINGHAM - 36C | LANGWITHJCN - 41J | FRODINGHAM - 36C |

| | 63666 | 63667 | 63668 | 63669 | 63671 | 63672 | 63673 | 63674 | 63675 |
|---|---|---|---|---|---|---|---|---|---|
| Aug-50 | LANGWITHJCN - 40E | CUDWORTH - 53E | MEXBOROUGH - 36B | FRODINGHAM - 36C | FRODINGHAM - 36C | MEXBOROUGH - 36B | DAIRYCOATES - 53A | ANNESLEY - 38B | DARNALL - 39B |
| Jan-51 | **9/50: MEX - 36B** | **4/51: DAIRY - 53A** | MEXBOROUGH - 36B | FRODINGHAM - 36C | FRODINGHAM - 36C | MEXBOROUGH - 36B | DAIRYCOATES - 53A | ANNESLEY - 38B | DARNALL - 39B |
| Aug-51 | MEXBOROUGH - 36B | **9/51: LANG JN - 40E** | MEXBOROUGH - 36B | FRODINGHAM - 36C | FRODINGHAM - 36C | MEXBOROUGH - 36B | **9/51: COLW - 38A** | ANNESLEY - 38B | DARNALL - 39B |
| Jan-52 | MEXBOROUGH - 36B | LANGWITHJCN - 40E | MEXBOROUGH - 36B | **3/52: BARN - 36D** | FRODINGHAM - 36C | MEXBOROUGH - 36B | COLWICK - 38A | ANNESLEY - 38B | DARNALL - 39B |
| Aug-52 | **9/52: IMM - 40B** | LANGWITHJCN - 40E | MEXBOROUGH - 36B | BARNSLEY - 36D | FRODINGHAM - 36C | MEXBOROUGH - 36B | COLWICK - 38A | **9/52: COLW - 38A** | **5/52: STAVE - 38D** |
| Jan-53 | **10/52: MEX - 36B** | LANGWITHJCN - 40E | MEXBOROUGH - 36B | BARNSLEY - 36D | FRODINGHAM - 36C | MEXBOROUGH - 36B | COLWICK - 38A | **2/53: STAVE - 38D** | STAVELEY - 38D |
| Aug-53 | MEXBOROUGH - 36B | LANGWITHJCN - 40E | MEXBOROUGH - 36B | BARNSLEY - 36D | FRODINGHAM - 36C | MEXBOROUGH - 36B | COLWICK - 38A | **5/53: COLW - 38A** | STAVELEY - 38D |
| Jan-54 | MEXBOROUGH - 36B | LANGWITHJCN - 40E | MEXBOROUGH - 36B | BARNSLEY - 36D | FRODINGHAM - 36C | MEXBOROUGH - 36B | COLWICK - 38A | COLWICK - 38A | STAVELEY - 38D |
| Aug-54 | MEXBOROUGH - 36B | LANGWITHJCN - 40E | MEXBOROUGH - 36B | BARNSLEY - 36D | FRODINGHAM - 36C | MEXBOROUGH - 36B | COLWICK - 38A | COLWICK - 38A | STAVELEY - 38D |
| Jan-55 | MEXBOROUGH - 36B | LANGWITHJCN - 40E | MEXBOROUGH - 36B | BARNSLEY - 36D | FRODINGHAM - 36C | MEXBOROUGH - 36B | COLWICK - 38A | COLWICK - 38A | STAVELEY - 38D |
| Aug-55 | MEXBOROUGH - 36B | LANGWITHJCN - 40E | MEXBOROUGH - 36B | BARNSLEY - 36D | FRODINGHAM - 36C | MEXBOROUGH - 36B | COLWICK - 38A | **7/55: STAVE - 38D** | STAVELEY - 38D |
| Jan-56 | MEXBOROUGH - 36B | LANGWITHJCN - 40E | MEXBOROUGH - 36B | BARNSLEY - 36D | FRODINGHAM - 36C | MEXBOROUGH - 36B | **1/56: MEX - 36B** | **1/56: COLW - 38A** | **1/56: COLW - 38A** |
| Aug-56 | MEXBOROUGH - 36B | LANGWITHJCN - 40E | MEXBOROUGH - 36B | BARNSLEY - 36D | FRODINGHAM - 36C | MEXBOROUGH - 36B | MEXBOROUGH - 36B | COLWICK - 38A | COLWICK - 38A |
| Jan-57 | MEXBOROUGH - 36B | LANGWITHJCN - 40E | MEXBOROUGH - 36B | BARNSLEY - 36D | FRODINGHAM - 36C | MEXBOROUGH - 36B | MEXBOROUGH - 36B | COLWICK - 38A | COLWICK - 38A |
| Aug-57 | MEXBOROUGH - 36B | LANGWITHJCN - 40E | MEXBOROUGH - 36B | BARNSLEY - 36D | FRODINGHAM - 36C | MEXBOROUGH - 36B | MEXBOROUGH - 36B | COLWICK - 38A | COLWICK - 38A |
| Jan-58 | MEXBOROUGH - 36B | LANGWITHJCN - 40E | MEXBOROUGH - 36B | BARNSLEY - 36D | FRODINGHAM - 36C | MEXBOROUGH - 36B | MEXBOROUGH - 36B | COLWICK - 38A | COLWICK - 38A |
| Aug-58 | MEXBOROUGH - 41F | LANGWITHJCN - 41J | MEXBOROUGH - 41F | BARNSLEY - 41G | FRODINGHAM - 36C | MEXBOROUGH - 41F | MEXBOROUGH - 41F | COLWICK - 40E | COLWICK - 40E |
| Jan-59 | MEXBOROUGH - 41F | **1/59: W/D** | **12/58: W/D** | BARNSLEY - 41G | FRODINGHAM - 36C | MEXBOROUGH - 41F | MEXBOROUGH - 41F | COLWICK - 40E | COLWICK - 40E |
| Aug-59 | MEXBOROUGH - 41F | | | BARNSLEY - 41G | FRODINGHAM - 36C | MEXBOROUGH - 41F | **5/59: W/D** | COLWICK - 40E | COLWICK - 40E |
| Nov-59 | MEXBOROUGH - 41F | | | BARNSLEY - 41G | FRODINGHAM - 36C | MEXBOROUGH - 41F | | COLWICK - 40E | COLWICK - 40E |
| Jan-60 | **1/60: FROD - 36C** | | | **1/60: MEX - 41F** | FRODINGHAM - 36C | MEXBOROUGH - 41F | | COLWICK - 40E | COLWICK - 40E |
| Apr-60 | FRODINGHAM - 36C | | | MEXBOROUGH - 41F | FRODINGHAM - 36C | MEXBOROUGH - 41F | | COLWICK - 40E | COLWICK - 40E |
| Aug-60 | FRODINGHAM - 36C | | | MEXBOROUGH - 41F | FRODINGHAM - 36C | MEXBOROUGH - 41F | | COLWICK - 40E | COLWICK - 40E |
| Nov-60 | FRODINGHAM - 36C | | | MEXBOROUGH - 41F | FRODINGHAM - 36C | MEXBOROUGH - 41F | | COLWICK - 40E | COLWICK - 40E |

| | 63677 | 63679 | 63680 | 63681 | 63682 | 63684 | 63685 | 63686 | 63688 |
|---|---|---|---|---|---|---|---|---|---|
| Aug-50 | LANGWITH JCN - 40E | LANGWITH JCN - 40E | DARNALL - 39B | ANNESLEY - 38B | MEXBOROUGH - 36B | FRODINGHAM - 36C | DARNALL - 39B | GORTON - 39A | RETFORD - 36E |
| Jan-51 | **9/50: TUX - 40D** | LANGWITH JCN - 40E | DARNALL - 39B | **11/50: GORT - 39A** | **9/50: LANG JN - 40E** | FRODINGHAM - 36C | DARNALL - 39B | GORTON - 39A | RETFORD - 36E |
| Aug-51 | TUXFORD - 40D | LANGWITH JCN - 40E | DARNALL - 39B | GORTON - 39A | **3/51: GORT - 39A** | **3/51: COLW - 38A** | DARNALL - 39B | GORTON - 39A | RETFORD - 36E |
| Jan-52 | TUXFORD - 40D | LANGWITH JCN - 40E | DARNALL - 39B | GORTON - 39A | **4/51: DARN - 39B** | COLWICK - 38A | DARNALL - 39B | GORTON - 39A | RETFORD - 36E |
| Aug-52 | TUXFORD - 40D | LANGWITH JCN - 40E | DARNALL - 39B | GORTON - 39A | DARNALL - 39B | COLWICK - 38A | DARNALL - 39B | GORTON - 39A | RETFORD - 36E |
| Jan-53 | TUXFORD - 40D | LANGWITH JCN - 40E | DARNALL - 39B | GORTON - 39A | DARNALL - 39B | COLWICK - 38A | DARNALL - 39B | GORTON - 39A | RETFORD - 36E |
| Aug-53 | TUXFORD - 40D | LANGWITH JCN - 40E | DARNALL - 39B | GORTON - 39A | DARNALL - 39B | COLWICK - 38A | DARNALL - 39B | GORTON - 39A | RETFORD - 36E |
| Jan-54 | **11/53: ARDS - 37A** | LANGWITH JCN - 40E | DARNALL - 39B | GORTON - 39A | DARNALL - 39B | COLWICK - 38A | DARNALL - 39B | GORTON - 39A | RETFORD - 36E |
| Aug-54 | ARDSLEY - 37A | LANGWITH JCN - 40E | DARNALL - 39B | GORTON - 39A | DARNALL - 39B | COLWICK - 38A | DARNALL - 39B | GORTON - 39A | RETFORD - 36E |
| Jan-55 | ARDSLEY - 37A | LANGWITH JCN - 40E | DARNALL - 39B | GORTON - 39A | DARNALL - 39B | COLWICK - 38A | DARNALL - 39B | GORTON - 39A | RETFORD - 36E |
| Aug-55 | ARDSLEY - 37A | LANGWITH JCN - 40E | DARNALL - 39B | GORTON - 39A | DARNALL - 39B | COLWICK - 38A | DARNALL - 39B | GORTON - 39A | RETFORD - 36E |
| Jan-56 | **12/55: MEX - 36B** | LANGWITH JCN - 40E | DARNALL - 41A | GORTON - 39A | DARNALL - 41A | **1/56: MEX - 36B** | DARNALL - 41A | GORTON - 39A | RETFORD - 36E |
| Aug-56 | MEXBOROUGH - 36B | LANGWITH JCN - 40E | DARNALL - 41A | GORTON - 39A | DARNALL - 41A | MEXBOROUGH - 36B | DARNALL - 41A | GORTON - 39A | RETFORD - 36E |
| Jan-57 | MEXBOROUGH - 36B | LANGWITH JCN - 40E | DARNALL - 41A | GORTON - 39A | DARNALL - 41A | MEXBOROUGH - 36B | DARNALL - 41A | GORTON - 39A | RETFORD - 36E |
| Aug-57 | MEXBOROUGH - 36B | LANGWITH JCN - 40E | DARNALL - 41A | GORTON - 39A | DARNALL - 41A | MEXBOROUGH - 36B | DARNALL - 41A | GORTON - 39A | RETFORD - 36E |
| Jan-58 | MEXBOROUGH - 36B | LANGWITH JCN - 40E | DARNALL - 41A | GORTON - 39A | DARNALL - 41A | MEXBOROUGH - 36B | DARNALL - 41A | GORTON - 39A | RETFORD - 36E |
| Aug-58 | MEXBOROUGH - 41F | LANGWITH JCN - 40E | DARNALL - 41A | GORTON - 9G | DARNALL - 41A | MEXBOROUGH - 41F | DARNALL - 41A | GORTON - 9G | RETFORD - 36E |
| Jan-59 | **3/59: DCTR - 36A** | LANGWITH JCN - 40E | DARNALL - 41A | GORTON - 9G | DARNALL - 41A | MEXBOROUGH - 41F | DARNALL - 41A | GORTON - 9G | RETFORD - 36E |
| Aug-59 | DONCASTER - 36A | LANGWITH JCN - 40E | DARNALL - 41A | GORTON - 9G | **3/59: W/D** | MEXBOROUGH - 41F | DARNALL - 41A | GORTON - 9G | RETFORD - 36E |
| Nov-59 | DONCASTER - 36A | LANGWITH JCN - 40E | **9/59: W/D** | GORTON - 9G | | MEXBOROUGH - 41F | DARNALL - 41A | GORTON - 9G | RETFORD - 36E |
| Jan-60 | DONCASTER - 36A | LANGWITH JCN - 40E | | GORTON - 9G | | MEXBOROUGH - 41F | DARNALL - 41A | GORTON - 9G | RETFORD - 36E |
| Apr-60 | DONCASTER - 36A | LANGWITH JCN - 40E | | GORTON - 9G | | MEXBOROUGH - 41F | DARNALL - 41A | GORTON - 9G | RETFORD - 36E |
| Aug-60 | DONCASTER - 36A | LANGWITH JCN - 40E | | GORTON - 9G | | MEXBOROUGH - 41F | DARNALL - 41A | GORTON - 9G | RETFORD - 36E |
| Nov-60 | DONCASTER - 36A | LANGWITH JCN - 40E | | GORTON - 9G | | MEXBOROUGH - 41F | DARNALL - 41A | GORTON - 9G | RETFORD - 36E |

| | 63690 | 63691 | 63692 | 63693 | 63694 | 63695 | 63696 | 63697 | 63698 |
|---|---|---|---|---|---|---|---|---|---|
| Aug-50 | FRODINGHAM - 36C | TUXFORD - 40D | IMMINGHAM - 40B | IMMINGHAM - 40B | STAVELEY - 38D | GORTON - 39A | FRODINGHAM - 36C | BARNSLEY - 36D | IMMINGHAM - 40B |
| Jan-51 | FRODINGHAM - 36C | TUXFORD - 40D | IMMINGHAM - 40B | IMMINGHAM - 40B | STAVELEY - 38D | GORTON - 39A | FRODINGHAM - 36C | BARNSLEY - 36D | IMMINGHAM - 40B |
| Aug-51 | FRODINGHAM - 36C | TUXFORD - 40D | IMMINGHAM - 40B | IMMINGHAM - 40B | STAVELEY - 38D | GORTON - 39A | FRODINGHAM - 36C | BARNSLEY - 36D | IMMINGHAM - 40B |
| Jan-52 | FRODINGHAM - 36C | TUXFORD - 40D | IMMINGHAM - 40B | **12/51: ANN - 38B** | STAVELEY - 38D | GORTON - 39A | FRODINGHAM - 36C | BARNSLEY - 36D | **12/51: ANN - 38B** |
| Aug-52 | FRODINGHAM - 36C | TUXFORD - 40D | IMMINGHAM - 40B | ANNESLEY - 38B | STAVELEY - 38D | GORTON - 39A | FRODINGHAM - 36C | BARNSLEY - 36D | ANNESLEY - 38B |
| Jan-53 | FRODINGHAM - 36C | TUXFORD - 40D | IMMINGHAM - 40B | ANNESLEY - 38B | STAVELEY - 38D | GORTON - 39A | FRODINGHAM - 36C | BARNSLEY - 36D | ANNESLEY - 38B |
| Aug-53 | FRODINGHAM - 36C | **11/53: ARDS - 37A** | IMMINGHAM - 40B | ANNESLEY - 38B | STAVELEY - 38D | GORTON - 39A | FRODINGHAM - 36C | BARNSLEY - 36D | ANNESLEY - 38B |
| Jan-54 | FRODINGHAM - 36C | **1/54: DARN - 39B** | IMMINGHAM - 40B | ANNESLEY - 38B | STAVELEY - 38D | GORTON - 39A | FRODINGHAM - 36C | BARNSLEY - 36D | ANNESLEY - 38B |
| Aug-54 | FRODINGHAM - 36C | DARNALL - 39B | IMMINGHAM - 40B | ANNESLEY - 38B | STAVELEY - 38D | **6/54: DARN - 39B** | FRODINGHAM - 36C | BARNSLEY - 36D | ANNESLEY - 38B |
| Jan-55 | FRODINGHAM - 36C | **1/55: IMM - 40B** | IMMINGHAM - 40B | ANNESLEY - 38B | STAVELEY - 38D | DARNALL - 39B | FRODINGHAM - 36C | BARNSLEY - 36D | ANNESLEY - 38B |
| Aug-55 | FRODINGHAM - 36C | IMMINGHAM - 40B | IMMINGHAM - 40B | ANNESLEY - 38B | STAVELEY - 38D | DARNALL - 39B | FRODINGHAM - 36C | BARNSLEY - 36D | ANNESLEY - 38B |
| Jan-56 | FRODINGHAM - 36C | IMMINGHAM - 40B | IMMINGHAM - 40B | ANNESLEY - 38B | **1/56: COLW - 38A** | DARNALL - 41A | FRODINGHAM - 36C | BARNSLEY - 36D | ANNESLEY - 38B |
| Aug-56 | FRODINGHAM - 36C | IMMINGHAM - 40B | IMMINGHAM - 40B | ANNESLEY - 38B | COLWICK - 38A | DARNALL - 41A | FRODINGHAM - 36C | BARNSLEY - 36D | ANNESLEY - 38B |
| Jan-57 | FRODINGHAM - 36C | IMMINGHAM - 40B | IMMINGHAM - 40B | ANNESLEY - 38B | COLWICK - 38A | DARNALL - 41A | FRODINGHAM - 36C | BARNSLEY - 36D | ANNESLEY - 38B |
| Aug-57 | FRODINGHAM - 36C | IMMINGHAM - 40B | IMMINGHAM - 40B | ANNESLEY - 38B | COLWICK - 38A | DARNALL - 41A | FRODINGHAM - 36C | BARNSLEY - 36D | ANNESLEY - 38B |
| Jan-58 | FRODINGHAM - 36C | IMMINGHAM - 40B | IMMINGHAM - 40B | ANNESLEY - 38B | COLWICK - 38A | DARNALL - 41A | FRODINGHAM - 36C | BARNSLEY - 36D | ANNESLEY - 38B |
| Aug-58 | FRODINGHAM - 36C | IMMINGHAM - 40B | IMMINGHAM - 40B | ANNESLEY - 16D | COLWICK - 40E | DARNALL - 41A | FRODINGHAM - 36C | BARNSLEY - 41G | ANNESLEY - 16D |
| Jan-59 | FRODINGHAM - 36C | **1/59: LANG JN - 41J** | IMMINGHAM - 40B | **3/59: DCTR - 36A** | COLWICK - 40E | DARNALL - 41A | FRODINGHAM - 36C | BARNSLEY - 41G | ANNESLEY - 16D |
| Aug-59 | FRODINGHAM - 36C | LANGWITH JCN - 41J | IMMINGHAM - 40B | DONCASTER - 36A | COLWICK - 40E | DARNALL - 41A | **4/59: W/D** | BARNSLEY - 41G | **4/59: DCTR - 36A** |
| Nov-59 | FRODINGHAM - 36C | LANGWITH JCN - 41J | IMMINGHAM - 40B | DONCASTER - 36A | **10/59: W/D** | DARNALL - 41A | | **12/59: LANG JN - 41J** | DONCASTER - 36A |
| Jan-60 | FRODINGHAM - 36C | LANGWITH JCN - 41J | IMMINGHAM - 40B | DONCASTER - 36A | | DARNALL - 41A | | LANGWITH JCN - 41J | DONCASTER - 36A |
| Apr-60 | FRODINGHAM - 36C | LANGWITH JCN - 41J | IMMINGHAM - 40B | DONCASTER - 36A | | DARNALL - 41A | | LANGWITH JCN - 41J | DONCASTER - 36A |
| Aug-60 | FRODINGHAM - 36C | LANGWITH JCN - 41J | IMMINGHAM - 40B | DONCASTER - 36A | | DARNALL - 41A | | LANGWITH JCN - 41J | DONCASTER - 36A |
| Nov-60 | FRODINGHAM - 36C | LANGWITH JCN - 41J | IMMINGHAM - 40B | DONCASTER - 36A | | DARNALL - 41A | | LANGWITH JCN - 41J | DONCASTER - 36A |

| | 63699 | 63700 | 63701 | 63702 | 63705 | 63706 | 63707 | 63708 | 63709 |
|---|---|---|---|---|---|---|---|---|---|
| Aug-50 | ANNESLEY - 38B | ANNESLEY - 38B | MARCH - 31B | STAVELEY - 38D | GORTON - 39A | ANNESLEY - 38B | LANGWITH JCN - 40E | GORTON - 39A | LANGWITH JCN - 40E |
| Jan-51 | **10/50: COLW - 38A** | **11/50: GORT - 39A** | MARCH - 31B | **10/50: ANN - 36B** | GORTON - 39A | **11/50: GORT - 39A** | LANGWITH JCN - 40E | GORTON - 39A | LANGWITH JCN - 40E |
| Aug-51 | **10/51: ANN - 38B** | GORTON - 39A | MARCH - 31B | **11/50: GORT - 39A** | GORTON - 39A | GORTON - 39A | LANGWITH JCN - 40E | GORTON - 39A | LANGWITH JCN - 40E |
| Jan-52 | **11/51: COLW - 38B** | GORTON - 39A | **10/51: MEX - 36B** | **3/52: STAVE - 38D** | **3/52: STAVE - 38D** | **11/51: STAVE - 38D** | LANGWITH JCN - 40E | GORTON - 39A | LANGWITH JCN - 40E |
| Aug-52 | COLWICK - 38A | GORTON - 39A | MEXBOROUGH - 36B | STAVELEY - 38D | STAVELEY - 38D | STAVELEY - 38D | LANGWITH JCN - 40E | GORTON - 39A | LANGWITH JCN - 40E |
| Jan-53 | COLWICK - 38A | GORTON - 39A | MEXBOROUGH - 36B | STAVELEY - 38D | STAVELEY - 38D | STAVELEY - 38D | LANGWITH JCN - 40E | GORTON - 39A | LANGWITH JCN - 40E |
| Aug-53 | COLWICK - 38A | GORTON - 39A | MEXBOROUGH - 36B | STAVELEY - 38D | STAVELEY - 38D | STAVELEY - 38D | LANGWITH JCN - 40E | GORTON - 39A | LANGWITH JCN - 40E |
| Jan-54 | COLWICK - 38A | GORTON - 39A | MEXBOROUGH - 36B | STAVELEY - 38D | STAVELEY - 38D | STAVELEY - 38D | LANGWITH JCN - 40E | GORTON - 39A | **10/53: GORT - 39A** |
| Aug-54 | COLWICK - 38A | GORTON - 39A | MEXBOROUGH - 36B | STAVELEY - 38D | STAVELEY - 38D | **6/54: COLW - 38A** | LANGWITH JCN - 40E | **6/54: DARN - 39B** | GORTON - 39A |
| Jan-55 | COLWICK - 38A | GORTON - 39A | MEXBOROUGH - 36B | STAVELEY - 38D | STAVELEY - 38D | COLWICK - 38A | LANGWITH JCN - 40E | DARNALL - 39B | GORTON - 39A |
| Aug-55 | COLWICK - 38A | GORTON - 39A | MEXBOROUGH - 36B | STAVELEY - 38D | STAVELEY - 38D | **7/55: STAVE - 38D** | LANGWITH JCN - 40E | DARNALL - 39B | GORTON - 39A |
| Jan-56 | COLWICK - 38A | GORTON - 39A | MEXBOROUGH - 36B | STAVELEY - 38D | STAVELEY - 38D | STAVELEY - 38D | LANGWITH JCN - 40E | DARNALL - 41A | GORTON - 39A |
| Aug-56 | COLWICK - 38A | GORTON - 39A | MEXBOROUGH - 36B | STAVELEY - 38D | STAVELEY - 38D | STAVELEY - 38D | LANGWITH JCN - 40E | DARNALL - 41A | GORTON - 39A |
| Jan-57 | COLWICK - 38A | GORTON - 39A | MEXBOROUGH - 36B | STAVELEY - 38D | STAVELEY - 38D | STAVELEY - 38D | LANGWITH JCN - 40E | **10/56: IMM - 40B** | GORTON - 39A |
| Aug-57 | COLWICK - 38A | GORTON - 39A | MEXBOROUGH - 36B | STAVELEY - 38D | STAVELEY - 38D | STAVELEY - 38D | LANGWITH JCN - 40E | IMMINGHAM - 40B | GORTON - 39A |
| Jan-58 | COLWICK - 38A | GORTON - 39A | MEXBOROUGH - 36B | STAVELEY - 38D | STAVELEY - 38D | STAVELEY - 38D | LANGWITH JCN - 40E | IMMINGHAM - 40B | GORTON - 39A |
| Aug-58 | COLWICK - 40E | GORTON - 9G | MEXBOROUGH - 41F | STAVELEY(GC) - 41H | STAVELEY(GC) - 41H | STAVELEY(GC) - 41H | LANGWITH JCN - 40E | IMMINGHAM - 40B | GORTON - 9G |
| Jan-59 | COLWICK - 40E | GORTON - 9G | MEXBOROUGH - 41F | STAVELEY(GC) - 41H | STAVELEY(GC) - 41H | STAVELEY(GC) - 41H | LANGWITH JCN - 40E | IMMINGHAM - 40B | GORTON - 9G |
| Aug-59 | **6/59: W/D** | GORTON - 9G | MEXBOROUGH - 41F | STAVELEY(GC) - 41H | STAVELEY(GC) - 41H | STAVELEY(GC) - 41H | LANGWITH JCN - 40E | IMMINGHAM - 40B | GORTON - 9G |
| Nov-59 | | GORTON - 9G | MEXBOROUGH - 41F | STAVELEY(GC) - 41H | STAVELEY(GC) - 41H | STAVELEY(GC) - 41H | LANGWITH JCN - 40E | IMMINGHAM - 40B | GORTON - 9G |
| Jan-60 | | GORTON - 9G | MEXBOROUGH - 41F | STAVELEY(GC) - 41H | STAVELEY(GC) - 41H | STAVELEY(GC) - 41H | LANGWITH JCN - 40E | IMMINGHAM - 40B | GORTON - 9G |
| Apr-60 | | GORTON - 9G | MEXBOROUGH - 41F | STAVELEY(GC) - 41H | STAVELEY(GC) - 41H | STAVELEY(GC) - 41H | LANGWITH JCN - 40E | IMMINGHAM - 40B | GORTON - 9G |
| Aug-60 | | GORTON - 9G | MEXBOROUGH - 41F | STAVELEY(GC) - 41H | STAVELEY(GC) - 41H | STAVELEY(GC) - 41H | LANGWITH JCN - 40E | IMMINGHAM - 40B | GORTON - 9G |
| Nov-60 | | GORTON - 9G | MEXBOROUGH - 41F | STAVELEY(GC) - 41H | STAVELEY(GC) - 41H | STAVELEY(GC) - 41H | LANGWITH JCN - 40E | IMMINGHAM - 40B | GORTON - 9G |

| | 63710 | 63713 | 63714 | 63715 | 63716 | 63717 | 63718 | 63719 | 63720 |
|---|---|---|---|---|---|---|---|---|---|
| Aug-50 | DARNALL - 39B | GORTON - 39A | DARNALL - 39B | LANGWITH JCN - 40E | ANNESLEY - 38B | LANGWITH JCN - 40E | FRODINGHAM - 36C | GORTON - 39A | STAVELEY - 38D |
| Jan-51 | DARNALL - 39B | GORTON - 39A | DARNALL - 39B | LANGWITH JCN - 40E | **11/50: GOR - 39A** | LANGWITH JCN - 40E | FRODINGHAM - 36C | GORTON - 39A | STAVELEY - 38D |
| Aug-51 | DARNALL - 39B | GORTON - 39A | DARNALL - 39B | LANGWITH JCN - 40E | GORTON - 39A | LANGWITH JCN - 40E | FRODINGHAM - 36C | GORTON - 39A | STAVELEY - 38D |
| Jan-52 | DARNALL - 39B | GORTON - 39A | DARNALL - 39B | LANGWITH JCN - 40E | GORTON - 39A | LANGWITH JCN - 40E | FRODINGHAM - 36C | GORTON - 39A | STAVELEY - 38D |
| Aug-52 | DARNALL - 39B | GORTON - 39A | DARNALL - 39B | LANGWITH JCN - 40E | GORTON - 39A | LANGWITH JCN - 40E | **9/52: BARN - 36D** | GORTON - 39A | STAVELEY - 38D |
| Jan-53 | DARNALL - 39B | GORTON - 39A | DARNALL - 39B | LANGWITH JCN - 40E | GORTON - 39A | LANGWITH JCN - 40E | BARNSLEY - 36D | GORTON - 39A | STAVELEY - 38D |
| Aug-53 | DARNALL - 39B | GORTON - 39A | DARNALL - 39B | LANGWITH JCN - 40E | GORTON - 39A | LANGWITH JCN - 40E | BARNSLEY - 36D | GORTON - 39A | STAVELEY - 38D |
| Jan-54 | DARNALL - 39B | GORTON - 39A | DARNALL - 39B | LANGWITH JCN - 40E | GORTON - 39A | LANGWITH JCN - 40E | BARNSLEY - 36D | GORTON - 39A | STAVELEY - 38D |
| Aug-54 | DARNALL - 39B | GORTON - 39A | DARNALL - 39B | LANGWITH JCN - 40E | GORTON - 39A | LANGWITH JCN - 40E | BARNSLEY - 36D | GORTON - 39A | STAVELEY - 38D |
| Jan-55 | DARNALL - 39B | GORTON - 39A | DARNALL - 39B | LANGWITH JCN - 40E | GORTON - 39A | LANGWITH JCN - 40E | BARNSLEY - 36D | GORTON - 39A | STAVELEY - 38D |
| Aug-55 | DARNALL - 39B | GORTON - 39A | DARNALL - 39B | LANGWITH JCN - 40E | GORTON - 39A | LANGWITH JCN - 40E | BARNSLEY - 36D | GORTON - 39A | STAVELEY - 38D |
| Jan-56 | DARNALL - 41A | GORTON - 39A | DARNALL - 41A | LANGWITH JCN - 40E | GORTON - 39A | LANGWITH JCN - 40E | BARNSLEY - 36D | GORTON - 39A | STAVELEY - 38D |
| Aug-56 | DARNALL - 41A | GORTON - 39A | DARNALL - 41A | LANGWITH JCN - 40E | GORTON - 39A | LANGWITH JCN - 40E | BARNSLEY - 36D | GORTON - 39A | STAVELEY - 38D |
| Jan-57 | DARNALL - 41A | GORTON - 39A | DARNALL - 41A | LANGWITH JCN - 40E | GORTON - 39A | LANGWITH JCN - 40E | BARNSLEY - 36D | GORTON - 39A | STAVELEY - 38D |
| Aug-57 | DARNALL - 41A | GORTON - 39A | DARNALL - 41A | LANGWITH JCN - 40E | GORTON - 39A | LANGWITH JCN - 40E | BARNSLEY - 36D | GORTON - 39A | STAVELEY - 38D |
| Jan-58 | DARNALL - 41A | GORTON - 39A | DARNALL - 41A | LANGWITH JCN - 40E | GORTON - 39A | LANGWITH JCN - 40E | BARNSLEY - 36D | GORTON - 39A | STAVELEY - 38D |
| Aug-58 | DARNALL - 41A | GORTON - 9G | DARNALL - 41A | LANGWITH JCN - 41J | GORTON - 9G | LANGWITH JCN - 40E | BARNSLEY - 41G | GORTON - 9G | STAVELEY(GC) - 41H |
| Jan-59 | DARNALL - 41A | GORTON - 9G | DARNALL - 41A | LANGWITH JCN - 41J | GORTON - 9G | LANGWITH JCN - 40E | BARNSLEY - 41G | GORTON - 9G | STAVELEY(GC) - 41H |
| Aug-59 | **7/59: W/D** | GORTON - 9G | **3/59: W/D** | LANGWITH JCN - 41J | GORTON - 9G | LANGWITH JCN - 40E | BARNSLEY - 41G | GORTON - 9G | STAVELEY(GC) - 41H |
| Nov-59 | | GORTON - 9G | | LANGWITH JCN - 41J | GORTON - 9G | LANGWITH JCN - 40E | **12/59: LANG JN ; 41J** | GORTON - 9G | STAVELEY(GC) - 41H |
| Jan-60 | | GORTON - 9G | | LANGWITH JCN - 41J | GORTON - 9G | LANGWITH JCN - 40E | LANGWITH JCN - 41J | GORTON - 9G | STAVELEY(GC) - 41H |
| Apr-60 | | GORTON - 9G | | LANGWITH JCN - 41J | GORTON - 9G | LANGWITH JCN - 40E | **3/60: MEX - 41F** | GORTON - 9G | STAVELEY(GC) - 41H |
| Aug-60 | | GORTON - 9G | | LANGWITH JCN - 41J | **8/60: W/D** | LANGWITH JCN - 40E | MEXBOROUGH - 41F | GORTON - 9G | STAVELEY(GC) - 41H |
| Nov-60 | | GORTON - 9G | | LANGWITH JCN - 41J | | LANGWITH JCN - 40E | MEXBOROUGH - 41F | GORTON - 9G | STAVELEY(GC) - 41H |

| | 63722 | 63723 | 63724 | 63726 | 63727 | 63728 | 63729 | 63730 | 63731 |
|---|---|---|---|---|---|---|---|---|---|
| Aug-50 | ANNESLEY - 38B | ANNESLEY - 38B | LANGWITH JCN - 40E | FRODINGHAM - 36C | BARNSLEY - 36D | FRODINGHAM - 36C | COLWICK - 38A | MARCH - 31B | FRODINGHAM - 36C |
| Jan-51 | **11/50: GOR - 39A** | **10/50: COLW - 38A** | LANGWITH JCN - 40E | FRODINGHAM - 36C | BARNSLEY - 36D | FRODINGHAM - 36C | COLWICK - 38A | MARCH - 31B | FRODINGHAM - 36C |
| Aug-51 | GORTON - 39A | COLWICK - 38A | LANGWITH JCN - 40E | FRODINGHAM - 36C | BARNSLEY - 36D | FRODINGHAM - 36C | COLWICK - 38A | MARCH - 31B | FRODINGHAM - 36C |
| Jan-52 | GORTON - 39A | COLWICK - 38A | **3/52: MARCH - 31B** | FRODINGHAM - 36C | BARNSLEY - 36D | FRODINGHAM - 36C | COLWICK - 38A | **10/51: MEX - 36B** | FRODINGHAM - 36C |
| Aug-52 | GORTON - 39A | COLWICK - 38A | **5/52: LANG JN - 40E** | **9/52: BARN - 36D** | BARNSLEY - 36D | FRODINGHAM - 36C | **6/52:IMM - 40B** | MEXBOROUGH - 36B | **9/52: BARN - 36D** |
| Jan-53 | GORTON - 39A | COLWICK - 38A | **11/52: TUX - 40D** | BARNSLEY - 36D | BARNSLEY - 36D | FRODINGHAM - 36C | IMMINGHAM - 40B | MEXBOROUGH - 36B | BARNSLEY - 36D |
| Aug-53 | GORTON - 39A | COLWICK - 38A | TUXFORD - 40D | BARNSLEY - 36D | BARNSLEY - 36D | FRODINGHAM - 36C | IMMINGHAM - 40B | MEXBOROUGH - 36B | BARNSLEY - 36D |
| Jan-54 | GORTON - 39A | COLWICK - 38A | **11/53: ARDS - 37A** | BARNSLEY - 36D | BARNSLEY - 36D | FRODINGHAM - 36C | **10/53: COLW - 38A** | MEXBOROUGH - 36B | BARNSLEY - 36D |
| Aug-54 | **8/54: DARN - 39B** | COLWICK - 38A | ARDSLEY - 37A | BARNSLEY - 36D | BARNSLEY - 36D | FRODINGHAM - 36C | COLWICK - 38A | MEXBOROUGH - 36B | BARNSLEY - 36D |
| Jan-55 | **1/55: IMM - 40B** | COLWICK - 38A | ARDSLEY - 37A | BARNSLEY - 36D | BARNSLEY - 36D | FRODINGHAM - 36C | COLWICK - 38A | MEXBOROUGH - 36B | BARNSLEY - 36D |
| Aug-55 | IMMINGHAM - 40B | COLWICK - 38A | ARDSLEY - 37A | BARNSLEY - 36D | BARNSLEY - 36D | FRODINGHAM - 36C | COLWICK - 38A | MEXBOROUGH - 36B | BARNSLEY - 36D |
| Jan-56 | IMMINGHAM - 40B | **1/56: MEX - 36B** | ARDSLEY - 37A | BARNSLEY - 36D | BARNSLEY - 36D | FRODINGHAM - 36C | COLWICK - 38A | MEXBOROUGH - 36B | BARNSLEY - 36D |
| Aug-56 | IMMINGHAM - 40B | MEXBOROUGH - 36B | ARDSLEY - 56B | BARNSLEY - 36D | BARNSLEY - 36D | FRODINGHAM - 36C | COLWICK - 38A | MEXBOROUGH - 36B | BARNSLEY - 36D |
| Jan-57 | IMMINGHAM - 40B | MEXBOROUGH - 36B | ARDSLEY - 56B | BARNSLEY - 36D | BARNSLEY - 36D | FRODINGHAM - 36C | COLWICK - 38A | MEXBOROUGH - 36B | BARNSLEY - 36D |
| Aug-57 | IMMINGHAM - 40B | MEXBOROUGH - 36B | ARDSLEY - 56B | BARNSLEY - 36D | BARNSLEY - 36D | FRODINGHAM - 36C | COLWICK - 38A | MEXBOROUGH - 36B | BARNSLEY - 36D |
| Jan-58 | IMMINGHAM - 40B | MEXBOROUGH - 36B | ARDSLEY - 56B | BARNSLEY - 36D | BARNSLEY - 36D | FRODINGHAM - 36C | COLWICK - 38A | MEXBOROUGH - 36B | BARNSLEY - 36D |
| Aug-58 | IMMINGHAM - 40B | MEXBOROUGH - 41F | ARDSLEY - 56B | BARNSLEY - 41G | BARNSLEY - 41G | FRODINGHAM - 36C | COLWICK - 40E | MEXBOROUGH - 41F | BARNSLEY - 41G |
| Jan-59 | **1/59: LANG JN - 41J** | MEXBOROUGH - 41F | ARDSLEY - 56B | BARNSLEY - 41G | BARNSLEY - 41G | FRODINGHAM - 36C | COLWICK - 40E | MEXBOROUGH - 41F | BARNSLEY - 41G |
| Aug-59 | LANGWITH JCN - 41J | MEXBOROUGH - 41F | ARDSLEY - 56B | BARNSLEY - 41G | BARNSLEY - 41G | FRODINGHAM - 36C | **3/59: W/D** | MEXBOROUGH - 41F | BARNSLEY - 41G |
| Nov-59 | **12/59: BARN - 41G** | **11/59: W/D** | ARDSLEY - 56B | BARNSLEY - 41G | BARNSLEY - 41G | FRODINGHAM - 36C | | MEXBOROUGH - 41F | **12/59: LANG JN - 41J** |
| Jan-60 | **1/60: MEX - 41F** | | ARDSLEY - 56B | **1/60: MEX - 41F** | **1/60: MEX - 41F** | FRODINGHAM - 36C | | **1/60: FROD - 36C** | LANGWITH JCN - 41J |
| Apr-60 | **3/60: LANG JN - 41J** | | ARDSLEY - 56B | MEXBOROUGH - 41F | MEXBOROUGH - 41F | FRODINGHAM - 36C | | FRODINGHAM - 36C | LANGWITH JCN - 41J |
| Aug-60 | LANGWITH JCN - 41J | | ARDSLEY - 56B | MEXBOROUGH - 41F | MEXBOROUGH - 41F | FRODINGHAM - 36C | | FRODINGHAM - 36C | LANGWITH JCN - 41J |
| Nov-60 | LANGWITH JCN - 41J | | ARDSLEY - 56B | MEXBOROUGH - 41F | MEXBOROUGH - 41F | FRODINGHAM - 36C | | FRODINGHAM - 36C | LANGWITH JCN - 41J |

| | 63732 | 63733 | 63734 | 63735 | 63736 | 63737 | 63739 | 63741 | 63742 |
|---|---|---|---|---|---|---|---|---|---|
| Aug-50 | DAIRYCOATES - 53A | DARNALL - 39B | DARNALL - 39B | COLWICK - 38A | RETFORD - 36E | DARNALL - 39B | ANNESLEY - 38B | LANGWITH JCN - 40E | ANNESLEY - 38B |
| Jan-51 | DAIRYCOATES - 53A | DARNALL - 39B | DARNALL - 39B | COLWICK - 38A | RETFORD - 36E | DARNALL - 39B | **10/50: GORT - 39A** | **9/50: FROD - 36C** | **10/50: GORT - 39A** |
| Aug-51 | **9/51: LANG JN - 40E** | DARNALL - 39B | DARNALL - 39B | COLWICK - 38A | RETFORD - 36E | DARNALL - 39B | GORTON - 39A | FRODINGHAM - 36C | GORTON - 39A |
| Jan-52 | LANGWITH JCN - 40E | DARNALL - 39B | DARNALL - 39B | **3/52: MARCH - 31B** | RETFORD - 36E | DARNALL - 39B | GORTON - 39A | FRODINGHAM - 36C | GORTON - 39A |
| Aug-52 | LANGWITH JCN - 40E | DARNALL - 39B | DARNALL - 39B | **5/52: COLW - 38A** | RETFORD - 36E | DARNALL - 39B | GORTON - 39A | FRODINGHAM - 36C | GORTON - 39A |
| Jan-53 | LANGWITH JCN - 40E | DARNALL - 39B | DARNALL - 39B | COLWICK - 38A | RETFORD - 36E | DARNALL - 39B | GORTON - 39A | FRODINGHAM - 36C | GORTON - 39A |
| Aug-53 | LANGWITH JCN - 40E | DARNALL - 39B | DARNALL - 39B | COLWICK - 38A | RETFORD - 36E | DARNALL - 39B | GORTON - 39A | FRODINGHAM - 36C | GORTON - 39A |
| Jan-54 | LANGWITH JCN - 40E | DARNALL - 39B | DARNALL - 39B | **1/54: STAVE - 38D** | RETFORD - 36E | DARNALL - 39B | GORTON - 39A | FRODINGHAM - 36C | GORTON - 39A |
| Aug-54 | LANGWITH JCN - 40E | DARNALL - 39B | DARNALL - 39B | STAVELEY - 38D | RETFORD - 36E | DARNALL - 39B | GORTON - 39A | FRODINGHAM - 36C | **6/54: DARN - 39B** |
| Jan-55 | LANGWITH JCN - 40E | DARNALL - 39B | DARNALL - 39B | STAVELEY - 38D | RETFORD - 36E | DARNALL - 39B | GORTON - 39A | FRODINGHAM - 36C | DARNALL - 39B |
| Aug-55 | LANGWITH JCN - 40E | DARNALL - 39B | DARNALL - 39B | STAVELEY - 38D | RETFORD - 36E | DARNALL - 39B | GORTON - 39A | FRODINGHAM - 36C | DARNALL - 39B |
| Jan-56 | LANGWITH JCN - 40E | DARNALL - 41A | DARNALL - 41A | STAVELEY - 38D | RETFORD - 36E | DARNALL - 41A | **12/55: LANG JN - 40E** | FRODINGHAM - 36C | DARNALL - 41A |
| Aug-56 | LANGWITH JCN - 40E | DARNALL - 41A | DARNALL - 41A | STAVELEY - 38D | RETFORD - 36E | DARNALL - 41A | LANGWITH JCN - 40E | FRODINGHAM - 36C | DARNALL - 41A |
| Jan-57 | LANGWITH JCN - 40E | DARNALL - 41A | DARNALL - 41A | STAVELEY - 38D | RETFORD - 36E | DARNALL - 41A | LANGWITH JCN - 40E | FRODINGHAM - 36C | DARNALL - 41A |
| Aug-57 | LANGWITH JCN - 40E | DARNALL - 41A | DARNALL - 41A | STAVELEY - 38D | RETFORD - 36E | DARNALL - 41A | LANGWITH JCN - 40E | FRODINGHAM - 36C | DARNALL - 41A |
| Jan-58 | LANGWITH JCN - 40E | DARNALL - 41A | DARNALL - 41A | STAVELEY - 38D | RETFORD - 36E | DARNALL - 41A | LANGWITH JCN - 40E | FRODINGHAM - 36C | DARNALL - 41A |
| Aug-58 | LANGWITH JCN - 41J | DARNALL - 41A | DARNALL - 41A | STAVELEY(GC) - 41H | RETFORD - 36E | DARNALL - 41A | LANGWITH JCN - 41J | FRODINGHAM - 36C | DARNALL - 41A |
| Jan-59 | LANGWITH JCN - 41J | DARNALL - 41A | DARNALL - 41A | STAVELEY(GC) - 41H | RETFORD - 36E | DARNALL - 41A | LANGWITH JCN - 41J | FRODINGHAM - 36C | DARNALL - 41A |
| Aug-59 | LANGWITH JCN - 41J | DARNALL - 41A | DARNALL - 41A | STAVELEY(GC) - 41H | RETFORD - 36E | DARNALL - 41A | LANGWITH JCN - 41J | FRODINGHAM - 36C | DARNALL - 41A |
| Nov-59 | LANGWITH JCN - 41J | **12/59: W/D** | DARNALL - 41A | STAVELEY(GC) - 41H | RETFORD - 36E | DARNALL - 41A | LANGWITH JCN - 41J | FRODINGHAM - 36C | DARNALL - 41A |
| Jan-60 | LANGWITH JCN - 41J | | DARNALL - 41A | STAVELEY(GC) - 41H | RETFORD - 36E | DARNALL - 41A | LANGWITH JCN - 41J | FRODINGHAM - 36C | DARNALL - 41A |
| Apr-60 | LANGWITH JCN - 41J | | DARNALL - 41A | STAVELEY(GC) - 41H | RETFORD - 36E | DARNALL - 41A | LANGWITH JCN - 41J | FRODINGHAM - 36C | DARNALL - 41A |
| Aug-60 | LANGWITH JCN - 41J | | DARNALL - 41A | STAVELEY(GC) - 41H | RETFORD - 36E | DARNALL - 41A | LANGWITH JCN - 41J | FRODINGHAM - 36C | DARNALL - 41A |
| Nov-60 | LANGWITH JCN - 41J | | DARNALL - 41A | STAVELEY(GC) - 41H | RETFORD - 36E | DARNALL - 41A | LANGWITH JCN - 41J | FRODINGHAM - 36C | DARNALL - 41A |

| | 63743 | 63744 | 63745 | 63747 | 63748 | 63749 | 63751 | 63753 | 63754 |
|---|---|---|---|---|---|---|---|---|---|
| Aug-50 | ANNESLEY - 38B | FRODINGHAM - 36C | FRODINGHAM - 36C | FRODINGHAM - 36C | ANNESLEY - 38B | STAVELEY - 38D | CUDWORTH - 53E | DAIRYCOATES - 53A | DAIRYCOATES - 53A |
| Jan-51 | **10/50: GORT - 39A** | FRODINGHAM - 36C | FRODINGHAM - 36C | FRODINGHAM - 36C | **11/50: GORT - 39A** | STAVELEY - 38D | CUDWORTH - 53E | **4/51: SPRING - 53C** | **11/50: CUD - 53E** |
| Aug-51 | GORTON - 39A | FRODINGHAM - 36C | FRODINGHAM - 36C | FRODINGHAM - 36C | GORTON - 39A | STAVELEY - 38D | **7/51: ROYS - 20C** | **9/51: DCTR - 36A** | **7/51: ROYS - 20C** |
| Jan-52 | GORTON - 39A | FRODINGHAM - 36C | FRODINGHAM - 36C | FRODINGHAM - 36C | GORTON - 39A | STAVELEY - 38D | **9/51: COLW - 38A** | **10/51: MEX - 36B** | **9/51: COLW - 38A** |
| Aug-52 | GORTON - 39A | FRODINGHAM - 36C | FRODINGHAM - 36C | FRODINGHAM - 36C | GORTON - 39A | STAVELEY - 38D | COLWICK - 38A | MEXBOROUGH - 36B | COLWICK - 38A |
| Jan-53 | GORTON - 39A | FRODINGHAM - 36C | FRODINGHAM - 36C | FRODINGHAM - 36C | GORTON - 39A | STAVELEY - 38D | COLWICK - 38A | MEXBOROUGH - 36B | COLWICK - 38A |
| Aug-53 | GORTON - 39A | FRODINGHAM - 36C | **7/53: IMM - 40B** | FRODINGHAM - 36C | GORTON - 39A | STAVELEY - 38D | **11/53: ANN - 38B** | MEXBOROUGH - 36B | COLWICK - 38A |
| Jan-54 | GORTON - 39A | FRODINGHAM - 36C | **10/53: COLW - 38A** | FRODINGHAM - 36C | GORTON - 39A | STAVELEY - 38D | **1/54: COLW - 38A** | MEXBOROUGH - 36B | COLWICK - 38A |
| Aug-54 | GORTON - 39A | FRODINGHAM - 36C | COLWICK - 38A | FRODINGHAM - 36C | **6/54: DARN - 39B** | STAVELEY - 38D | COLWICK - 38A | **12/54: DCTR - 36A** | COLWICK - 38A |
| Jan-55 | GORTON - 39A | FRODINGHAM - 36C | COLWICK - 38A | FRODINGHAM - 36C | DARNALL - 39B | STAVELEY - 38D | COLWICK - 38A | **2/55: MEX - 36B** | COLWICK - 38A |
| Aug-55 | GORTON - 39A | FRODINGHAM - 36C | COLWICK - 38A | FRODINGHAM - 36C | DARNALL - 39B | STAVELEY - 38D | COLWICK - 38A | MEXBOROUGH - 36B | COLWICK - 38A |
| Jan-56 | GORTON - 39A | FRODINGHAM - 36C | **1/56: MEX - 36B** | FRODINGHAM - 36C | DARNALL - 41A | STAVELEY - 38D | **1/56: MEX - 36B** | MEXBOROUGH - 36B | COLWICK - 38A |
| Aug-56 | GORTON - 39A | FRODINGHAM - 36C | MEXBOROUGH - 36B | FRODINGHAM - 36C | DARNALL - 41A | STAVELEY - 38D | MEXBOROUGH - 36B | MEXBOROUGH - 36B | COLWICK - 38A |
| Jan-57 | GORTON - 39A | FRODINGHAM - 36C | MEXBOROUGH - 36B | FRODINGHAM - 36C | DARNALL - 41A | STAVELEY - 38D | MEXBOROUGH - 36B | MEXBOROUGH - 36B | COLWICK - 38A |
| Aug-57 | GORTON - 39A | FRODINGHAM - 36C | MEXBOROUGH - 36B | FRODINGHAM - 36C | DARNALL - 41A | STAVELEY - 38D | MEXBOROUGH - 36B | MEXBOROUGH - 36B | COLWICK - 38A |
| Jan-58 | GORTON - 39A | FRODINGHAM - 36C | MEXBOROUGH - 36B | FRODINGHAM - 36C | DARNALL - 41A | STAVELEY - 38D | MEXBOROUGH - 36B | MEXBOROUGH - 36B | COLWICK - 38A |
| Aug-58 | GORTON - 9G | FRODINGHAM - 36C | MEXBOROUGH - 41F | FRODINGHAM - 36C | DARNALL - 41A | STAVELEY(GC) - 41H | MEXBOROUGH - 41F | MEXBOROUGH - 41F | COLWICK - 40E |
| Jan-59 | GORTON - 9G | FRODINGHAM - 36C | MEXBOROUGH - 41F | FRODINGHAM - 36C | DARNALL - 41A | STAVELEY(GC) - 41H | MEXBOROUGH - 41F | MEXBOROUGH - 41F | COLWICK - 40E |
| Aug-59 | GORTON - 9G | FRODINGHAM - 36C | **4/59: W/D** | FRODINGHAM - 36C | **9/59: FROD - 36C** | STAVELEY(GC) - 41H | **3/59: W/D** | MEXBOROUGH - 41F | COLWICK - 40E |
| Nov-59 | GORTON - 9G | FRODINGHAM - 36C | | FRODINGHAM - 36C | FRODINGHAM - 36C | **10/59: W/D** | | **11/59: W/D** | COLWICK - 40E |
| Jan-60 | GORTON - 9G | FRODINGHAM - 36C | | FRODINGHAM - 36C | FRODINGHAM - 36C | | | | COLWICK - 40E |
| Apr-60 | GORTON - 9G | FRODINGHAM - 36C | | FRODINGHAM - 36C | FRODINGHAM - 36C | | | | COLWICK - 40E |
| Aug-60 | GORTON - 9G | FRODINGHAM - 36C | | FRODINGHAM - 36C | FRODINGHAM - 36C | | | | COLWICK - 40E |
| Nov-60 | GORTON - 9G | FRODINGHAM - 36C | | FRODINGHAM - 36C | FRODINGHAM - 36C | | | | COLWICK - 40E |

| | 63757 | 63758 | 63759 | 63761 | 63762 | 63764 | 63765 | 63766 | 63767 |
|---|---|---|---|---|---|---|---|---|---|
| Aug-50 | LANGWITH JCN - 40E | LANGWITH JCN - 40E | LANGWITH JCN - 40E | COLWICK - 38A | COLWICK - 38A | DAIRYCOATES - 53A | LANGWITH JCN - 40E | DARNALL - 39B | ANNESLEY - 38B |
| Jan-51 | **9/50: MEX - 36B** | LANGWITH JCN - 40E | LANGWITH JCN - 40E | **10/50: ANN - 38B** | COLWICK - 38A | DAIRYCOATES - 53A | LANGWITH JCN - 40E | DARNALL - 39B | ANNESLEY - 38B |
| Aug-51 | MEXBOROUGH - 36B | LANGWITH JCN - 40E | LANGWITH JCN - 40E | **10/50: GORT - 39A** | **9/51: STAVE - 38D** | **9/51: DCTR - 36A** | LANGWITH JCN - 40E | DARNALL - 39B | ANNESLEY - 38B |
| Jan-52 | MEXBOROUGH - 36B | LANGWITH JCN - 40E | LANGWITH JCN - 40E | GORTON - 39A | STAVELEY - 38D | DONCASTER - 36A | LANGWITH JCN - 40E | DARNALL - 39B | **11/51: GORT - 39A** |
| Aug-52 | MEXBOROUGH - 36B | LANGWITH JCN - 40E | LANGWITH JCN - 40E | GORTON - 39A | STAVELEY - 38D | DONCASTER - 36A | LANGWITH JCN - 40E | DARNALL - 39B | GORTON - 39A |
| Jan-53 | MEXBOROUGH - 36B | LANGWITH JCN - 40E | LANGWITH JCN - 40E | GORTON - 39A | STAVELEY - 38D | DONCASTER - 36A | LANGWITH JCN - 40E | DARNALL - 39B | GORTON - 39A |
| Aug-53 | MEXBOROUGH - 36B | LANGWITH JCN - 40E | LANGWITH JCN - 40E | GORTON - 39A | STAVELEY - 38D | DONCASTER - 36A | LANGWITH JCN - 40E | **7/53: COLW - 38A** | GORTON - 39A |
| Jan-54 | MEXBOROUGH - 36B | LANGWITH JCN - 40E | LANGWITH JCN - 40E | GORTON - 39A | STAVELEY - 38D | DONCASTER - 36A | LANGWITH JCN - 40E | COLWICK - 38A | GORTON - 39A |
| Aug-54 | MEXBOROUGH - 36B | LANGWITH JCN - 40E | LANGWITH JCN - 40E | **6/54: FROD - 36C** | STAVELEY - 38D | DONCASTER - 36A | LANGWITH JCN - 40E | COLWICK - 38A | GORTON - 39A |
| Jan-55 | MEXBOROUGH - 36B | **1/55: IMM - 40B** | LANGWITH JCN - 40E | FRODINGHAM - 36C | STAVELEY - 38D | DONCASTER - 36A | LANGWITH JCN - 40E | **12/54: GORT - 39A** | GORTON - 39A |
| Aug-55 | MEXBOROUGH - 36B | IMMINGHAM - 40B | LANGWITH JCN - 40E | FRODINGHAM - 36C | STAVELEY - 38D | **5/55: MEX - 36B** | LANGWITH JCN - 40E | GORTON - 39A | GORTON - 39A |
| Jan-56 | MEXBOROUGH - 36B | IMMINGHAM - 40B | LANGWITH JCN - 40E | FRODINGHAM - 36C | STAVELEY - 38D | MEXBOROUGH - 36B | LANGWITH JCN - 40E | GORTON - 39A | GORTON - 39A |
| Aug-56 | MEXBOROUGH - 36B | IMMINGHAM - 40B | LANGWITH JCN - 40E | FRODINGHAM - 36C | STAVELEY - 38D | MEXBOROUGH - 36B | LANGWITH JCN - 40E | GORTON - 39A | GORTON - 39A |
| Jan-57 | MEXBOROUGH - 36B | IMMINGHAM - 40B | LANGWITH JCN - 40E | FRODINGHAM - 36C | STAVELEY - 38D | MEXBOROUGH - 36B | LANGWITH JCN - 40E | GORTON - 39A | GORTON - 39A |
| Aug-57 | MEXBOROUGH - 36B | IMMINGHAM - 40B | LANGWITH JCN - 40E | FRODINGHAM - 36C | STAVELEY - 38D | MEXBOROUGH - 36B | LANGWITH JCN - 40E | GORTON - 39A | GORTON - 39A |
| Jan-58 | MEXBOROUGH - 36B | IMMINGHAM - 40B | LANGWITH JCN - 40E | FRODINGHAM - 36C | STAVELEY - 38D | MEXBOROUGH - 36B | LANGWITH JCN - 40E | GORTON - 39A | GORTON - 39A |
| Aug-58 | MEXBOROUGH - 41F | IMMINGHAM - 40B | LANGWITH JCN - 40E | FRODINGHAM - 36C | STAVELEY(GC) - 41H | MEXBOROUGH - 41F | LANGWITH JCN - 41J | GORTON - 9G | GORTON - 9G |
| Jan-59 | MEXBOROUGH - 41F | **1/59: LANG JN - 41J** | LANGWITH JCN - 40E | FRODINGHAM - 36C | STAVELEY(GC) - 41H | MEXBOROUGH - 41F | LANGWITH JCN - 41J | GORTON - 9G | GORTON - 9G |
| Aug-59 | MEXBOROUGH - 41F | LANGWITH JCN - 41J | LANGWITH JCN - 40E | **6/59: W/D** | STAVELEY(GC) - 41H | MEXBOROUGH - 41F | LANGWITH JCN - 41J | GORTON - 9G | GORTON - 9G |
| Nov-59 | MEXBOROUGH - 41F | LANGWITH JCN - 41J | LANGWITH JCN - 40E | | STAVELEY(GC) - 41H | MEXBOROUGH - 41F | LANGWITH JCN - 41J | GORTON - 9G | GORTON - 9G |
| Jan-60 | MEXBOROUGH - 41F | LANGWITH JCN - 41J | LANGWITH JCN - 40E | | STAVELEY(GC) - 41H | **1/60: FROD - 36C** | LANGWITH JCN - 41J | GORTON - 9G | GORTON - 9G |
| Apr-60 | MEXBOROUGH - 41F | **5/60: IMM - 40B** | LANGWITH JCN - 40E | | STAVELEY(GC) - 41H | FRODINGHAM - 36C | LANGWITH JCN - 41J | GORTON - 9G | GORTON - 9G |
| Aug-60 | MEXBOROUGH - 41F | IMMINGHAM - 40B | LANGWITH JCN - 40E | | STAVELEY(GC) - 41H | FRODINGHAM - 36C | LANGWITH JCN - 41J | GORTON - 9G | GORTON - 9G |
| Nov-60 | MEXBOROUGH - 41F | IMMINGHAM - 40B | LANGWITH JCN - 40E | | STAVELEY(GC) - 41H | FRODINGHAM - 36C | LANGWITH JCN - 41J | GORTON - 9G | GORTON - 9G |

| | 63769 | 63770 | 63771 | 63772 | 63774 | 63775 | 63776 | 63778 | 63779 |
|---|---|---|---|---|---|---|---|---|---|
| Aug-50 | DAIRYCOATES - 53A | DAIRYCOATES - 53A | DARNALL - 39B | DAIRYCOATES - 53A | MEXBOROUGH - 36B | MEXBOROUGH - 36B | LANGWITH JCN - 40E | FRODINGHAM - 36C | MEXBOROUGH - 36B |
| Jan-51 | DAIRYCOATES - 53A | **4/51: SPRING - 53C** | DARNALL - 39B | **5/51: CUD - 53E** | MEXBOROUGH - 36B | MEXBOROUGH - 36B | LANGWITH JCN - 40E | FRODINGHAM - 36C | MEXBOROUGH - 36B |
| Aug-51 | **9/51: DCTR - 36A** | **9/51: IMM - 40B** | DARNALL - 39B | **7/51: ROYS - 20C** | MEXBOROUGH - 36B | MEXBOROUGH - 36B | LANGWITH JCN - 40E | FRODINGHAM - 36C | MEXBOROUGH - 36B |
| Jan-52 | DONCASTER - 36A | IMMINGHAM - 40B | DARNALL - 39B | **9/51: COLW - 38A** | MEXBOROUGH - 36B | MEXBOROUGH - 36B | LANGWITH JCN - 40E | FRODINGHAM - 36C | MEXBOROUGH - 36B |
| Aug-52 | DONCASTER - 36A | IMMINGHAM - 40B | DARNALL - 39B | **6/52: STAVE - 38D** | MEXBOROUGH - 36B | MEXBOROUGH - 36B | LANGWITH JCN - 40E | **2/52: W/D** | MEXBOROUGH - 36B |
| Jan-53 | DONCASTER - 36A | IMMINGHAM - 40B | DARNALL - 39B | STAVELEY - 38D | MEXBOROUGH - 36B | MEXBOROUGH - 36B | LANGWITH JCN - 40E | | MEXBOROUGH - 36B |
| Aug-53 | DONCASTER - 36A | IMMINGHAM - 40B | DARNALL - 39B | STAVELEY - 38D | MEXBOROUGH - 36B | MEXBOROUGH - 36B | LANGWITH JCN - 40E | | MEXBOROUGH - 36B |
| Jan-54 | DONCASTER - 36A | IMMINGHAM - 40B | DARNALL - 39B | STAVELEY - 38D | MEXBOROUGH - 36B | MEXBOROUGH - 36B | LANGWITH JCN - 40E | | MEXBOROUGH - 36B |
| Aug-54 | DONCASTER - 36A | IMMINGHAM - 40B | DARNALL - 39B | STAVELEY - 38D | MEXBOROUGH - 36B | MEXBOROUGH - 36B | LANGWITH JCN - 40E | | MEXBOROUGH - 36B |
| Jan-55 | DONCASTER - 36A | IMMINGHAM - 40B | DARNALL - 39B | STAVELEY - 38D | MEXBOROUGH - 36B | MEXBOROUGH - 36B | LANGWITH JCN - 40E | | MEXBOROUGH - 36B |
| Aug-55 | DONCASTER - 36A | IMMINGHAM - 40B | DARNALL - 39B | STAVELEY - 38D | MEXBOROUGH - 36B | MEXBOROUGH - 36B | LANGWITH JCN - 40E | | MEXBOROUGH - 36B |
| Jan-56 | DONCASTER - 36A | IMMINGHAM - 40B | DARNALL - 41A | STAVELEY - 38D | MEXBOROUGH - 36B | MEXBOROUGH - 36B | LANGWITH JCN - 40E | | MEXBOROUGH - 36B |
| Aug-56 | DONCASTER - 36A | IMMINGHAM - 40B | DARNALL - 41A | STAVELEY - 38D | MEXBOROUGH - 36B | MEXBOROUGH - 36B | LANGWITH JCN - 40E | | MEXBOROUGH - 36B |
| Jan-57 | DONCASTER - 36A | IMMINGHAM - 40B | DARNALL - 41A | STAVELEY - 38D | MEXBOROUGH - 36B | **2/57: GORT - 39A** | LANGWITH JCN - 40E | | MEXBOROUGH - 36B |
| Aug-57 | DONCASTER - 36A | IMMINGHAM - 40B | DARNALL - 41A | STAVELEY - 38D | MEXBOROUGH - 36B | GORTON - 39A | LANGWITH JCN - 40E | | MEXBOROUGH - 36B |
| Jan-58 | DONCASTER - 36A | IMMINGHAM - 40B | DARNALL - 41A | STAVELEY - 38D | MEXBOROUGH - 36B | GORTON - 39A | LANGWITH JCN - 40E | | MEXBOROUGH - 36B |
| Aug-58 | DONCASTER - 36A | IMMINGHAM - 40B | DARNALL - 41A | STAVELEY (GC) - 41H | MEXBOROUGH - 41F | GORTON - 9G | LANGWITH JCN - 41J | | MEXBOROUGH - 41F |
| Jan-59 | DONCASTER - 36A | **12/58: COLW - 40E** | DARNALL - 41A | STAVELEY (GC) - 41H | MEXBOROUGH - 41F | GORTON - 9G | LANGWITH JCN - 41J | | MEXBOROUGH - 41F |
| Aug-59 | **3/59: W/D** | COLWICK - 40E | DARNALL - 41A | STAVELEY (GC) - 41H | MEXBOROUGH - 41F | GORTON - 9G | LANGWITH JCN - 41J | | MEXBOROUGH - 41F |
| Nov-59 | | COLWICK - 40E | DARNALL - 41A | STAVELEY (GC) - 41H | MEXBOROUGH - 41F | GORTON - 9G | LANGWITH JCN - 41J | | MEXBOROUGH - 41F |
| Jan-60 | | COLWICK - 40E | **2/60: MEX - 41F** | **2/60: MEX - 41F** | MEXBOROUGH - 41F | GORTON - 9G | LANGWITH JCN - 41J | | MEXBOROUGH - 41F |
| Apr-60 | | COLWICK - 40E | MEXBOROUGH - 41F | MEXBOROUGH - 41F | MEXBOROUGH - 41F | GORTON - 9G | LANGWITH JCN - 41J | | MEXBOROUGH - 41F |
| Aug-60 | | COLWICK - 40E | MEXBOROUGH - 41F | MEXBOROUGH - 41F | MEXBOROUGH - 41F | GORTON - 9G | LANGWITH JCN - 41J | | MEXBOROUGH - 41F |
| Nov-60 | | COLWICK - 40E | MEXBOROUGH - 41F | MEXBOROUGH - 41F | MEXBOROUGH - 41F | GORTON - 9G | LANGWITH JCN - 41J | | MEXBOROUGH - 41F |

| | 63781 | 63782 | 63783 | 63787 | 63788 | 63790 | 63791 | 63793 | 63794 |
|---|---|---|---|---|---|---|---|---|---|
| Aug-50 | COLWICK - 38A | RETFORD - 36E | DARNALL - 39B | COLWICK - 38A | FRODINGHAM - 36C | DARNALL - 39B | MEXBOROUGH - 36B | FRODINGHAM - 36C | GORTON - 39A |
| Jan-51 | **9/50: ANN - 38B** | RETFORD - 36E | DARNALL - 39B | **10.50: ANN - 38B** | FRODINGHAM - 36C | DARNALL - 39B | MEXBOROUGH - 36B | FRODINGHAM - 36C | GORTON - 39A |
| Aug-51 | **11/50: GORT - 39A** | RETFORD - 36E | DARNALL - 39B | **11/50: GORT - 39A** | FRODINGHAM - 36C | DARNALL - 39B | MEXBOROUGH - 36B | FRODINGHAM - 36C | GORTON - 39A |
| Jan-52 | GORTON - 39A | RETFORD - 36E | DARNALL - 39B | GORTON - 39A | FRODINGHAM - 36C | DARNALL - 39B | MEXBOROUGH - 36B | FRODINGHAM - 36C | GORTON - 39A |
| Aug-52 | GORTON - 39A | RETFORD - 36E | DARNALL - 39B | **6/52: STAVE - 38D** | FRODINGHAM - 36C | DARNALL - 39B | MEXBOROUGH - 36B | FRODINGHAM - 36C | GORTON - 39A |
| Jan-53 | GORTON - 39A | RETFORD - 36E | DARNALL - 39B | STAVELEY - 38D | FRODINGHAM - 36C | DARNALL - 39B | MEXBOROUGH - 36B | FRODINGHAM - 36C | GORTON - 39A |
| Aug-53 | GORTON - 39A | RETFORD - 36E | DARNALL - 39B | STAVELEY - 38D | FRODINGHAM - 36C | DARNALL - 39B | MEXBOROUGH - 36B | FRODINGHAM - 36C | GORTON - 39A |
| Jan-54 | GORTON - 39A | RETFORD - 36E | DARNALL - 39B | STAVELEY - 38D | FRODINGHAM - 36C | DARNALL - 39B | MEXBOROUGH - 36B | FRODINGHAM - 36C | GORTON - 39A |
| Aug-54 | **COLWICK - 38A** | RETFORD - 36E | DARNALL - 39B | STAVELEY - 38D | FRODINGHAM - 36C | DARNALL - 39B | MEXBOROUGH - 36B | FRODINGHAM - 36C | GORTON - 39A |
| Jan-55 | COLWICK - 38A | RETFORD - 36E | DARNALL - 39B | STAVELEY - 38D | FRODINGHAM - 36C | DARNALL - 39B | MEXBOROUGH - 36B | FRODINGHAM - 36C | GORTON - 39A |
| Aug-55 | COLWICK - 38A | RETFORD - 36E | DARNALL - 39B | STAVELEY - 38D | FRODINGHAM - 36C | DARNALL - 39B | MEXBOROUGH - 36B | FRODINGHAM - 36C | GORTON - 39A |
| Jan-56 | **1/56: MEX - 36B** | RETFORD - 36E | DARNALL - 41A | STAVELEY - 38D | FRODINGHAM - 36C | DARNALL - 41A | MEXBOROUGH - 36B | FRODINGHAM - 36C | GORTON - 39A |
| Aug-56 | MEXBOROUGH - 36B | RETFORD - 36E | DARNALL - 41A | STAVELEY - 38D | FRODINGHAM - 36C | DARNALL - 41A | MEXBOROUGH - 36B | FRODINGHAM - 36C | GORTON - 39A |
| Jan-57 | MEXBOROUGH - 36B | RETFORD - 36E | DARNALL - 41A | STAVELEY - 38D | FRODINGHAM - 36C | DARNALL - 41A | MEXBOROUGH - 36B | FRODINGHAM - 36C | GORTON - 39A |
| Aug-57 | MEXBOROUGH - 36B | RETFORD - 36E | DARNALL - 41A | STAVELEY - 38D | FRODINGHAM - 36C | DARNALL - 41A | MEXBOROUGH - 36B | FRODINGHAM - 36C | GORTON - 39A |
| Jan-58 | MEXBOROUGH - 36B | RETFORD - 36E | DARNALL - 41A | STAVELEY - 38D | FRODINGHAM - 36C | DARNALL - 41A | MEXBOROUGH - 36B | FRODINGHAM - 36C | GORTON - 39A |
| Aug-58 | MEXBOROUGH - 41F | RETFORD - 36E | DARNALL - 41A | STAVELEY (GC) - 41H | FRODINGHAM - 36C | DARNALL - 41A | MEXBOROUGH - 41F | FRODINGHAM - 36C | GORTON - 9G |
| Jan-59 | **12/58: FROD - 36C** | RETFORD - 36E | DARNALL - 41A | STAVELEY (GC) - 41H | FRODINGHAM - 36C | DARNALL - 41A | MEXBOROUGH - 41F | FRODINGHAM - 36C | GORTON - 9G |
| Aug-59 | FRODINGHAM - 36C | RETFORD - 36E | DARNALL - 41A | STAVELEY (GC) - 41H | FRODINGHAM - 36C | **3/59: W/D** | MEXBOROUGH - 41F | FRODINGHAM - 36C | GORTON - 9G |
| Nov-59 | FRODINGHAM - 36C | RETFORD - 36E | DARNALL - 41A | STAVELEY (GC) - 41H | FRODINGHAM - 36C | | MEXBOROUGH - 41F | FRODINGHAM - 36C | GORTON - 9G |
| Jan-60 | FRODINGHAM - 36C | RETFORD - 36E | DARNALL - 41A | STAVELEY (GC) - 41H | FRODINGHAM - 36C | | MEXBOROUGH - 41F | FRODINGHAM - 36C | GORTON - 9G |
| Apr-60 | FRODINGHAM - 36C | RETFORD - 36E | DARNALL - 41A | STAVELEY (GC) - 41H | FRODINGHAM - 36C | | MEXBOROUGH - 41F | FRODINGHAM - 36C | GORTON - 9G |
| Aug-60 | FRODINGHAM - 36C | RETFORD - 36E | DARNALL - 41A | STAVELEY (GC) - 41H | FRODINGHAM - 36C | | MEXBOROUGH - 41F | FRODINGHAM - 36C | GORTON - 9G |
| Nov-60 | FRODINGHAM - 36C | RETFORD - 36E | DARNALL - 41A | STAVELEY (GC) - 41H | FRODINGHAM - 36C | | MEXBOROUGH - 41F | FRODINGHAM - 36C | GORTON - 9G |

| | 63797 | 63798 | 63799 | 63800 | 63801 | 63804 | 63809 | 63812 | 63813 |
|---|---|---|---|---|---|---|---|---|---|
| Aug-50 | DARNALL - 39B | ANNESLEY - 38B | ANNESLEY - 38B | LANGWITH JCN - 40E | COLWICK - 38A | COLWICK - 38A | LANGWITH JCN - 40E | DAIRYCOATES - 53A | MEXBOROUGH - 36B |
| Jan-51 | DARNALL - 39B | ANNESLEY - 38B | **10/50: GORT - 39A** | LANGWITH JCN - 40E | **9/51: ANN - 38B** | COLWICK - 38A | LANGWITH JCN - 40E | DAIRYCOATES - 53A | MEXBOROUGH - 36B |
| Aug-51 | DARNALL - 39B | ANNESLEY - 38B | GORTON - 39A | LANGWITH JCN - 40E | **11/51: COLW - 38A** | COLWICK - 38A | LANGWITH JCN - 40E | **8/51: COLW - 38A** | MEXBOROUGH - 36B |
| Jan-52 | DARNALL - 39B | ANNESLEY - 38B | GORTON - 39A | LANGWITH JCN - 40E | **8/52: STAVE - 38D** | COLWICK - 38A | LANGWITH JCN - 40E | COLWICK - 38A | MEXBOROUGH - 36B |
| Aug-52 | DARNALL - 39B | **9/52: COLW - 38A** | GORTON - 39A | LANGWITH JCN - 40E | 9/52:COLW - 38A | COLWICK - 38A | **2/52: W/D** | COLWICK - 38A | MEXBOROUGH - 36B |
| Jan-53 | DARNALL - 39B | COLWICK - 38A | GORTON - 39A | LANGWITH JCN - 40E | **10/52: STAVE - 38D** | COLWICK - 38A | | COLWICK - 38A | MEXBOROUGH - 36B |
| Aug-53 | DARNALL - 39B | COLWICK - 38A | GORTON - 39A | LANGWITH JCN - 40E | STAVELEY - 38D | COLWICK - 38A | | COLWICK - 38A | MEXBOROUGH - 36B |
| Jan-54 | DARNALL - 39B | COLWICK - 38A | GORTON - 39A | LANGWITH JCN - 40E | STAVELEY - 38D | COLWICK - 38A | | COLWICK - 38A | MEXBOROUGH - 36B |
| Aug-54 | DARNALL - 39B | COLWICK - 38A | **6/54: FROD - 36C** | LANGWITH JCN - 40E | STAVELEY - 38D | COLWICK - 38A | | COLWICK - 38A | MEXBOROUGH - 36B |
| Jan-55 | DARNALL - 39B | COLWICK - 38A | FRODINGHAM - 36C | LANGWITH JCN - 40E | STAVELEY - 38D | **12/54: STAVE - 38D** | | COLWICK - 38A | MEXBOROUGH - 36B |
| Aug-55 | DARNALL - 39B | COLWICK - 38A | FRODINGHAM - 36C | LANGWITH JCN - 40E | STAVELEY - 38D | STAVELEY - 38D | | COLWICK - 38A | MEXBOROUGH - 36B |
| Jan-56 | DARNALL - 41A | **1/56: MEX - 36B** | FRODINGHAM - 36C | LANGWITH JCN - 40E | STAVELEY - 38D | STAVELEY - 38D | | **1/56: MEX - 36B** | MEXBOROUGH - 36B |
| Aug-56 | DARNALL - 41A | MEXBOROUGH - 36B | FRODINGHAM - 36C | LANGWITH JCN - 40E | STAVELEY - 38D | STAVELEY - 38D | | MEXBOROUGH - 36B | MEXBOROUGH - 36B |
| Jan-57 | DARNALL - 41A | MEXBOROUGH - 36B | FRODINGHAM - 36C | LANGWITH JCN - 40E | STAVELEY - 38D | STAVELEY - 38D | | MEXBOROUGH - 36B | MEXBOROUGH - 36B |
| Aug-57 | DARNALL - 41A | MEXBOROUGH - 36B | FRODINGHAM - 36C | LANGWITH JCN - 40E | STAVELEY - 38D | STAVELEY - 38D | | MEXBOROUGH - 36B | MEXBOROUGH - 36B |
| Jan-58 | DARNALL - 41A | MEXBOROUGH - 36B | FRODINGHAM - 36C | LANGWITH JCN - 40E | STAVELEY - 38D | STAVELEY - 38D | | MEXBOROUGH - 36B | MEXBOROUGH - 36B |
| Aug-58 | DARNALL - 41A | MEXBOROUGH - 41F | FRODINGHAM - 36C | LANGWITH JCN - 40E | STAVELEY (GC) - 41H | STAVELEY (GC) - 41H | | MEXBOROUGH - 41F | MEXBOROUGH - 41F |
| Jan-59 | DARNALL - 41A | MEXBOROUGH - 41F | FRODINGHAM - 36C | LANGWITH JCN - 40E | STAVELEY (GC) - 41H | STAVELEY (GC) - 41H | | MEXBOROUGH - 41F | MEXBOROUGH - 41F |
| Aug-59 | **2/59: W/D** | MEXBOROUGH - 41F | FRODINGHAM - 36C | LANGWITH JCN - 40E | STAVELEY (GC) - 41H | STAVELEY (GC) - 41H | | **5/59: W/D** | MEXBOROUGH - 41F |
| Nov-59 | | MEXBOROUGH - 41F | FRODINGHAM - 36C | LANGWITH JCN - 40E | **11/59: LANG JN - 41J** | **11/59: W/D** | | | MEXBOROUGH - 41F |
| Jan-60 | | MEXBOROUGH - 41F | FRODINGHAM - 36C | LANGWITH JCN - 40E | LANGWITH JCN - 41J | | | | MEXBOROUGH - 41F |
| Apr-60 | | MEXBOROUGH - 41F | FRODINGHAM - 36C | LANGWITH JCN - 40E | LANGWITH JCN - 41J | | | | MEXBOROUGH - 41F |
| Aug-60 | | MEXBOROUGH - 41F | FRODINGHAM - 36C | LANGWITH JCN - 40E | LANGWITH JCN - 41J | | | | MEXBOROUGH - 41F |
| Nov-60 | | MEXBOROUGH - 41F | FRODINGHAM - 36C | LANGWITH JCN - 40E | LANGWITH JCN - 41J | | | | MEXBOROUGH - 41F |

| | 63816 | 63821 | 63822 | 63823 | 63824 | 63829 | 63832 | 63833 | 63835 |
|---|---|---|---|---|---|---|---|---|---|
| Aug-50 | DAIRYCOATES - 53A | DARNALL - 39B | DARNALL - 39B | DAIRYCOATES - 53A | FRODINGHAM - 36C | COLWICK - 38A | FRODINGHAM - 36C | LANGWITH JCN - 40E | DAIRYCOATES - 53A |
| Jan-51 | DAIRYCOATES - 53A | DARNALL - 39B | DARNALL - 39B | DAIRYCOATES - 53A | FRODINGHAM - 36C | **10/50: ANN - 38B** | FRODINGHAM - 36C | LANGWITH JCN - 40E | DAIRYCOATES - 53A |
| Aug-51 | **8/51: COLW - 38A** | DARNALL - 39B | DARNALL - 39B | **8/51: IMM - 40B** | FRODINGHAM - 36C | **11/50: GORT - 39A** | **5/51: IMM - 40B** | LANGWITH JCN - 40E | **9/51: COLW - 38A** |
| Jan-52 | COLWICK - 38A | DARNALL - 39B | DARNALL - 39B | IMMINGHAM - 40B | **3/52: BARN - 36D** | GORTON - 39A | IMMINGHAM - 40B | LANGWITH JCN - 40E | COLWICK - 38A |
| Aug-52 | COLWICK - 38A | DARNALL - 39B | DARNALL - 39B | IMMINGHAM - 40B | BARNSLEY - 36D | GORTON - 39A | IMMINGHAM - 40B | LANGWITH JCN - 40E | COLWICK - 38A |
| Jan-53 | COLWICK - 38A | DARNALL - 39B | DARNALL - 39B | **11/52: TUX - 40D** | BARNSLEY - 36D | GORTON - 39A | IMMINGHAM - 40B | LANGWITH JCN - 40E | COLWICK - 38A |
| Aug-53 | COLWICK - 38A | DARNALL - 39B | DARNALL - 39B | TUXFORD - 40D | BARNSLEY - 36D | GORTON - 39A | IMMINGHAM - 40B | LANGWITH JCN - 40E | COLWICK - 38A |
| Jan-54 | COLWICK - 38A | DARNALL - 39B | DARNALL - 39B | **11/53: ARDS - 37A** | BARNSLEY - 36D | GORTON - 39A | **10/53: COLW - 38A** | LANGWITH JCN - 40E | **4/54: GORT - 39A** |
| Aug-54 | COLWICK - 38A | DARNALL - 39B | DARNALL - 39B | ARDSLEY - 37A | BARNSLEY - 36D | **6/54: COLW - 38A** | COLWICK - 38A | LANGWITH JCN - 40E | **6/54: COLW - 38A** |
| Jan-55 | COLWICK - 38A | DARNALL - 39B | DARNALL - 39B | ARDSLEY - 37A | BARNSLEY - 36D | COLWICK - 38A | COLWICK - 38A | LANGWITH JCN - 40E | COLWICK - 38A |
| Aug-55 | COLWICK - 38A | DARNALL - 39B | DARNALL - 39B | ARDSLEY - 37A | BARNSLEY - 36D | COLWICK - 38A | COLWICK - 38A | LANGWITH JCN - 40E | COLWICK - 38A |
| Jan-56 | COLWICK - 38A | DARNALL - 41A | DARNALL - 41A | ARDSLEY - 37A | BARNSLEY - 36D | COLWICK - 38A | **1/56: MEX - 36B** | LANGWITH JCN - 40E | **1/56: MEX - 36B** |
| Aug-56 | COLWICK - 38A | DARNALL - 41A | DARNALL - 41A | ARDSLEY - 56B | BARNSLEY - 36D | COLWICK - 38A | MEXBOROUGH - 36B | LANGWITH JCN - 40E | MEXBOROUGH - 36B |
| Jan-57 | COLWICK - 38A | DARNALL - 41A | DARNALL - 41A | ARDSLEY - 56B | BARNSLEY - 36D | COLWICK - 38A | MEXBOROUGH - 36B | LANGWITH JCN - 40E | MEXBOROUGH - 36B |
| Aug-57 | COLWICK - 38A | DARNALL - 41A | DARNALL - 41A | ARDSLEY - 56B | BARNSLEY - 36D | COLWICK - 38A | MEXBOROUGH - 36B | LANGWITH JCN - 40E | MEXBOROUGH - 36B |
| Jan-58 | COLWICK - 38A | DARNALL - 41A | DARNALL - 41A | ARDSLEY - 56B | BARNSLEY - 36D | COLWICK - 38A | MEXBOROUGH - 36B | LANGWITH JCN - 40E | MEXBOROUGH - 36B |
| Aug-58 | COLWICK - 40E | DARNALL - 41A | DARNALL - 41A | ARDSLEY - 56B | BARNSLEY - 41G | COLWICK - 40E | MEXBOROUGH - 41F | LANGWITH JCN - 40E | MEXBOROUGH - 41F |
| Jan-59 | COLWICK - 40E | DARNALL - 41A | DARNALL - 41A | ARDSLEY - 56B | BARNSLEY - 41G | **10/58: LANG JN - 41J** | MEXBOROUGH - 41F | LANGWITH JCN - 40E | MEXBOROUGH - 41F |
| Aug-59 | COLWICK - 40E | DARNALL - 41A | DARNALL - 41A | ARDSLEY - 56B | BARNSLEY - 41G | LANGWITH JCN - 41J | MEXBOROUGH - 41F | LANGWITH JCN - 40E | **2/59: W/D** |
| Nov-59 | COLWICK - 40E | DARNALL - 41A | DARNALL - 41A | ARDSLEY - 56B | **11/59: FROD - 36C** | LANGWITH JCN - 41J | MEXBOROUGH - 41F | LANGWITH JCN - 40E | |
| Jan-60 | COLWICK - 40E | DARNALL - 41A | DARNALL - 41A | ARDSLEY - 56B | **1/60: RET - 36E** | LANGWITH JCN - 41J | MEXBOROUGH - 41F | LANGWITH JCN - 40E | |
| Apr-60 | COLWICK - 40E | DARNALL - 41A | DARNALL - 41A | ARDSLEY - 56B | RETFORD - 36E | LANGWITH JCN - 41J | MEXBOROUGH - 41F | LANGWITH JCN - 40E | |
| Aug-60 | COLWICK - 40E | DARNALL - 41A | DARNALL - 41A | ARDSLEY - 56B | RETFORD - 36E | LANGWITH JCN - 41J | MEXBOROUGH - 41F | LANGWITH JCN - 40E | |
| Nov-60 | COLWICK - 40E | DARNALL - 41A | DARNALL - 41A | ARDSLEY - 56B | RETFORD - 36E | LANGWITH JCN - 41J | MEXBOROUGH - 41F | LANGWITH JCN - 40E | |

| | 63839 | 63840 | 63841 | 63842 | 63843 | 63845 | 63846 | 63847 | 63848 |
|---|---|---|---|---|---|---|---|---|---|
| Aug-50 | GORTON - 39A | LANGWITH JCN - 40E | ANNESLEY - 38B | LANGWITH JCN - 40E | BOTANIC GARDENS - 53B | DAIRYCOATES - 53A | DARNALL - 39B | FRODINGHAM - 36C | GORTON - 39A |
| Jan-51 | **4/51: DARN - 39B** | LANGWITH JCN - 40E | GORTON - 39A | LANGWITH JCN - 40E | **9/50: CUD - 53E** | **11/50: CUD - 53E** | DARNALL - 39B | **3/51: STAVE - 38D** | GORTON - 39A |
| Aug-51 | **6/51: COLW - 38A** | LANGWITH JCN - 40E | GORTON - 39A | LANGWITH JCN - 40E | **1/51: DAIRY - 53A** | **7/51: ROY - 20C** | DARNALL - 39B | STAVELEY - 38D | GORTON - 39A |
| Jan-52 | COLWICK - 38A | LANGWITH JCN - 40E | GORTON - 39A | LANGWITH JCN - 40E | **9/51: DCTR - 36A** | **9/51: COLW - 38A** | DARNALL - 39B | STAVELEY - 38D | GORTON - 39A |
| Aug-52 | COLWICK - 38A | LANGWITH JCN - 40E | GORTON - 39A | LANGWITH JCN - 40E | **10/51: MEX - 36B** | COLWICK - 38A | DARNALL - 39B | STAVELEY - 38D | GORTON - 39A |
| Jan-53 | COLWICK - 38A | LANGWITH JCN - 40E | GORTON - 39A | LANGWITH JCN - 40E | MEXBOROUGH - 36B | COLWICK - 38A | DARNALL - 39B | STAVELEY - 38D | GORTON - 39A |
| Aug-53 | COLWICK - 38A | LANGWITH JCN - 40E | GORTON - 39A | LANGWITH JCN - 40E | MEXBOROUGH - 36B | COLWICK - 38A | DARNALL - 39B | STAVELEY - 38D | GORTON - 39A |
| Jan-54 | COLWICK - 38A | LANGWITH JCN - 40E | GORTON - 39A | LANGWITH JCN - 40E | MEXBOROUGH - 36B | COLWICK - 38A | DARNALL - 39B | STAVELEY - 38D | GORTON - 39A |
| Aug-54 | COLWICK - 38A | LANGWITH JCN - 40E | **6/54: COLW - 38A** | LANGWITH JCN - 40E | MEXBOROUGH - 36B | COLWICK - 38A | DARNALL - 39B | STAVELEY - 38D | GORTON - 39A |
| Jan-55 | COLWICK - 38A | LANGWITH JCN - 40E | COLWICK - 38A | LANGWITH JCN - 40E | MEXBOROUGH - 36B | COLWICK - 38A | DARNALL - 39B | STAVELEY - 38D | GORTON - 39A |
| Aug-55 | COLWICK - 38A | LANGWITH JCN - 40E | COLWICK - 38A | LANGWITH JCN - 40E | MEXBOROUGH - 36B | COLWICK - 38A | DARNALL - 39B | STAVELEY - 38D | GORTON - 39A |
| Jan-56 | COLWICK - 38A | LANGWITH JCN - 40E | **1/56: MEX - 36B** | LANGWITH JCN - 40E | MEXBOROUGH - 36B | **1/56: ANN - 38B** | DARNALL - 41A | STAVELEY - 38D | GORTON - 39A |
| Aug-56 | COLWICK - 38A | LANGWITH JCN - 40E | MEXBOROUGH - 36B | LANGWITH JCN - 40E | MEXBOROUGH - 36B | ANNESLEY - 38B | DARNALL - 41A | STAVELEY - 38D | GORTON - 39A |
| Jan-57 | COLWICK - 38A | LANGWITH JCN - 40E | MEXBOROUGH - 36B | LANGWITH JCN - 40E | MEXBOROUGH - 36B | **11/56: STAVE - 38D** | DARNALL - 41A | STAVELEY - 38D | GORTON - 39A |
| Aug-57 | COLWICK - 38A | LANGWITH JCN - 40E | MEXBOROUGH - 36B | LANGWITH JCN - 40E | MEXBOROUGH - 36B | STAVELEY - 38D | DARNALL - 41A | STAVELEY - 38D | GORTON - 39A |
| Jan-58 | COLWICK - 38A | LANGWITH JCN - 40E | MEXBOROUGH - 36B | LANGWITH JCN - 40E | MEXBOROUGH - 36B | STAVELEY - 38D | DARNALL - 41A | STAVELEY - 38D | GORTON - 39A |
| Aug-58 | COLWICK - 40E | LANGWITH JCN - 40E | MEXBOROUGH - 41F | LANGWITH JCN - 41J | MEXBOROUGH - 41F | STAVELEY (GC) - 41H | DARNALL - 41A | STAVELEY (GC) - 41H | GORTON - 9G |
| Jan-59 | COLWICK - 40E | LANGWITH JCN - 40E | MEXBOROUGH - 41F | LANGWITH JCN - 41J | MEXBOROUGH - 41F | STAVELEY (GC) - 41H | DARNALL - 41A | STAVELEY (GC) - 41H | GORTON - 9G |
| Aug-59 | **4/59: W/D** | LANGWITH JCN - 40E | MEXBOROUGH - 41F | LANGWITH JCN - 41J | MEXBOROUGH - 41F | STAVELEY (GC) - 41H | DARNALL - 41A | **5/59: W/D** | GORTON - 9G |
| Nov-59 | | LANGWITH JCN - 40E | MEXBOROUGH - 41F | LANGWITH JCN - 41J | MEXBOROUGH - 41F | STAVELEY (GC) - 41H | DARNALL - 41A | | GORTON - 9G |
| Jan-60 | | LANGWITH JCN - 40E | MEXBOROUGH - 41F | LANGWITH JCN - 41J | MEXBOROUGH - 41F | STAVELEY (GC) - 41H | DARNALL - 41A | | GORTON - 9G |
| Apr-60 | | LANGWITH JCN - 40E | MEXBOROUGH - 41F | LANGWITH JCN - 41J | MEXBOROUGH - 41F | STAVELEY (GC) - 41H | DARNALL - 41A | | GORTON - 9G |
| Aug-60 | | LANGWITH JCN - 40E | MEXBOROUGH - 41F | LANGWITH JCN - 41J | MEXBOROUGH - 41F | STAVELEY (GC) - 41H | DARNALL - 41A | | GORTON - 9G |
| Nov-60 | | LANGWITH JCN - 40E | MEXBOROUGH - 41F | LANGWITH JCN - 41J | MEXBOROUGH - 41F | STAVELEY (GC) - 41H | DARNALL - 41A | | GORTON - 9G |

| | 63849 | 63850 | 63851 | 63852 | 63855 | 63857 | 63859 | 63860 | 63861 |
|---|---|---|---|---|---|---|---|---|---|
| Aug-50 | CUDWORTH - 53E | DARNALL - 39B | COLWICK - 38A | TUXFORD - 40D | DAIRYCOATES - 53A | DAIRYCOATES - 53A | STAVELEY - 38D | DARNALL - 39B | TUXFORD - 40D |
| Jan-51 | CUDWORTH - 53E | DARNALL - 39B | **10/50: ANN - 38B** | TUXFORD - 40D | DAIRYCOATES - 53A | **11/50: CUD - 53E** | **9/50: ANN - 38B** | DARNALL - 39B | TUXFORD - 40D |
| Aug-51 | **7/51: ROYS - 20C** | DARNALL - 39B | ANNESLEY - 38B | TUXFORD - 40D | **9/51: DCTR - 36A** | **7/51: ROYS - 20C** | **11/50: GORT - 39A** | DARNALL - 39B | TUXFORD - 40D |
| Jan-52 | **9/51: COLW - 38A** | DARNALL - 39B | ANNESLEY - 38B | TUXFORD - 40D | DONCASTER - 36A | **9/51: COLW - 38A** | GORTON - 39A | DARNALL - 39B | TUXFORD - 40D |
| Aug-52 | **2/51: W/D** | DARNALL - 39B | **9/52: COLW - 38A** | TUXFORD - 40D | DONCASTER - 36A | **9/52: ARDS - 37A** | GORTON - 39A | DARNALL - 39B | TUXFORD - 40D |
| Jan-53 | | DARNALL - 39B | COLWICK - 38A | TUXFORD - 40D | DONCASTER - 36A | ARDSLEY - 37A | GORTON - 39A | DARNALL - 39B | TUXFORD - 40D |
| Aug-53 | | DARNALL - 39B | COLWICK - 38A | **11/53: ARDS - 37A** | DONCASTER - 36A | ARDSLEY - 37A | GORTON - 39A | DARNALL - 39B | TUXFORD - 40D |
| Jan-54 | | DARNALL - 39B | COLWICK - 38A | **1/54: DARN - 39B** | DONCASTER - 36A | ARDSLEY - 37A | GORTON - 39A | DARNALL - 39B | **11/53: LANG JN - 40E** |
| Aug-54 | | DARNALL - 39B | COLWICK - 38A | DARNALL - 39B | DONCASTER - 36A | ARDSLEY - 37A | **6/54: COLW - 38A** | DARNALL - 39B | LANGWITH JCN - 40E |
| Jan-55 | | DARNALL - 39B | COLWICK - 38A | DARNALL - 39B | DONCASTER - 36A | ARDSLEY - 37A | COLWICK - 38A | DARNALL - 39B | LANGWITH JCN - 40E |
| Aug-55 | | DARNALL - 39B | COLWICK - 38A | DARNALL - 39B | DONCASTER - 36A | ARDSLEY - 37A | COLWICK - 38A | DARNALL - 39B | LANGWITH JCN - 40E |
| Jan-56 | | DARNALL - 41A | **1/56: MEX - 36B** | DARNALL - 41A | DONCASTER - 36A | ARDSLEY - 37A | COLWICK - 38A | DARNALL - 41A | LANGWITH JCN - 40E |
| Aug-56 | | DARNALL - 41A | MEXBOROUGH - 36B | DARNALL - 41A | DONCASTER - 36A | ARDSLEY - 56B | COLWICK - 38A | DARNALL - 41A | LANGWITH JCN - 40E |
| Jan-57 | | DARNALL - 41A | MEXBOROUGH - 36B | DARNALL - 41A | DONCASTER - 36A | ARDSLEY - 56B | COLWICK - 38A | **10/56: IMM - 40B** | LANGWITH JCN - 40E |
| Aug-57 | | DARNALL - 41A | MEXBOROUGH - 36B | DARNALL - 41A | DONCASTER - 36A | ARDSLEY - 56B | COLWICK - 38A | IMMINGHAM - 40B | LANGWITH JCN - 40E |
| Jan-58 | | DARNALL - 41A | MEXBOROUGH - 36B | DARNALL - 41A | DONCASTER - 36A | ARDSLEY - 56B | COLWICK - 38A | IMMINGHAM - 40B | LANGWITH JCN - 40E |
| Aug-58 | | DARNALL - 41A | MEXBOROUGH - 41F | DARNALL - 41A | DONCASTER - 36A | ARDSLEY - 56B | COLWICK - 40E | IMMINGHAM - 40B | LANGWITH JCN - 41J |
| Jan-59 | | DARNALL - 41A | MEXBOROUGH - 41F | DARNALL - 41A | DONCASTER - 36A | **2/59: WAKE - 56A** | COLWICK - 40E | IMMINGHAM - 40B | LANGWITH JCN - 41J |
| Aug-59 | | DARNALL - 41A | **4/59: W/D** | DARNALL - 41A | **3/59: W/D** | WAKEFIELD - 56A | COLWICK - 40E | IMMINGHAM - 40B | LANGWITH JCN - 41J |
| Nov-59 | | DARNALL - 41A | | DARNALL - 41A | | WAKEFIELD - 56A | COLWICK - 40E | IMMINGHAM - 40B | LANGWITH JCN - 41J |
| Jan-60 | | DARNALL - 41A | | DARNALL - 41A | | WAKEFIELD - 56A | COLWICK - 40E | IMMINGHAM - 40B | LANGWITH JCN - 41J |
| Apr-60 | | DARNALL - 41A | | DARNALL - 41A | | WAKEFIELD - 56A | COLWICK - 40E | **5/60: IMM - 40E** | LANGWITH JCN - 41J |
| Aug-60 | | DARNALL - 41A | | DARNALL - 41A | | WAKEFIELD - 56A | COLWICK - 40E | COLWICK - 40E | LANGWITH JCN - 41J |
| Nov-60 | | DARNALL - 41A | | DARNALL - 41A | | WAKEFIELD - 56A | COLWICK - 40E | COLWICK - 40E | LANGWITH JCN - 41J |

| | 63862 | 63864 | 63870 | 63876 | 63877 | 63878 | 63880 | 63881 | 63883 |
|---|---|---|---|---|---|---|---|---|---|
| Aug-50 | GORTON - 39A | GORTON - 39A | LANGWITH JCN - 40E | GORTON - 39A | RETFORD - 36E | IMMINGHAM - 40B | GORTON - 39A | DAIRYCOATES - 53A | BARNSLEY - 36D |
| Jan-51 | GORTON - 39A | GORTON - 39A | LANGWITH JCN - 40E | GORTON - 39A | **9/50: LANG JN - 40E** | IMMINGHAM - 40B | GORTON - 39A | DAIRYCOATES - 53A | BARNSLEY - 36D |
| Aug-51 | GORTON - 39A | GORTON - 39A | LANGWITH JCN - 40E | GORTON - 39A | **3/51: GORT - 39A** | IMMINGHAM - 40B | GORTON - 39A | **9/51: IMM - 40B** | BARNSLEY - 36D |
| Jan-52 | GORTON - 39A | GORTON - 39A | LANGWITH JCN - 40E | GORTON - 39A | **4/51: DARN - 39B** | IMMINGHAM - 40B | GORTON - 39A | IMMINGHAM - 40B | BARNSLEY - 36D |
| Aug-52 | GORTON - 39A | **9/52: ARDS - 37A** | LANGWITH JCN - 40E | GORTON - 39A | **6/51: COLW - 38A** | IMMINGHAM - 40B | GORTON - 39A | IMMINGHAM - 40B | BARNSLEY - 36D |
| Jan-53 | GORTON - 39A | ARDSLEY - 37A | LANGWITH JCN - 40E | GORTON - 39A | COLWICK - 38A | IMMINGHAM - 40B | GORTON - 39A | IMMINGHAM - 40B | BARNSLEY - 36D |
| Aug-53 | GORTON - 39A | ARDSLEY - 37A | LANGWITH JCN - 40E | GORTON - 39A | COLWICK - 38A | IMMINGHAM - 40B | GORTON - 39A | IMMINGHAM - 40B | BARNSLEY - 36D |
| Jan-54 | GORTON - 39A | ARDSLEY - 37A | LANGWITH JCN - 40E | GORTON - 39A | COLWICK - 38A | IMMINGHAM - 40B | GORTON - 39A | **10/53: COLW - 38A** | BARNSLEY - 36D |
| Aug-54 | GORTON - 39A | ARDSLEY - 37A | LANGWITH JCN - 40E | **6/54: COLW - 38A** | COLWICK - 38A | IMMINGHAM - 40B | **6/54: FROD - 36C** | **4/54: DARN - 39B** | BARNSLEY - 36D |
| Jan-55 | GORTON - 39A | ARDSLEY - 37A | LANGWITH JCN - 40E | COLWICK - 38A | COLWICK - 38A | IMMINGHAM - 40B | FRODINGHAM - 36C | DARNALL - 39B | BARNSLEY - 36D |
| Aug-55 | GORTON - 39A | ARDSLEY - 37A | LANGWITH JCN - 40E | COLWICK - 38A | COLWICK - 38A | IMMINGHAM - 40B | FRODINGHAM - 36C | DARNALL - 39B | BARNSLEY - 36D |
| Jan-56 | GORTON - 39A | ARDSLEY - 37A | LANGWITH JCN - 40E | **1/56: MEX - 36B** | **1/56: STAVE - 38D** | IMMINGHAM - 40B | FRODINGHAM - 36C | DARNALL - 41A | BARNSLEY - 36D |
| Aug-56 | GORTON - 39A | ARDSLEY - 56B | LANGWITH JCN - 40E | MEXBOROUGH - 36B | STAVELEY - 38D | IMMINGHAM - 40B | FRODINGHAM - 36C | DARNALL - 41A | BARNSLEY - 36D |
| Jan-57 | GORTON - 39A | ARDSLEY - 56B | LANGWITH JCN - 40E | MEXBOROUGH - 36B | STAVELEY - 38D | IMMINGHAM - 40B | FRODINGHAM - 36C | DARNALL - 41A | BARNSLEY - 36D |
| Aug-57 | GORTON - 39A | ARDSLEY - 56B | LANGWITH JCN - 40E | MEXBOROUGH - 36B | STAVELEY - 38D | IMMINGHAM - 40B | FRODINGHAM - 36C | DARNALL - 41A | BARNSLEY - 36D |
| Jan-58 | GORTON - 39A | ARDSLEY - 56B | LANGWITH JCN - 40E | MEXBOROUGH - 36B | STAVELEY - 38D | IMMINGHAM - 40B | FRODINGHAM - 36C | DARNALL - 41A | BARNSLEY - 36D |
| Aug-58 | GORTON - 9G | ARDSLEY - 56B | LANGWITH JCN - 41J | MEXBOROUGH - 41F | STAVELEY (GC) - 41H | IMMINGHAM - 40B | FRODINGHAM - 36C | DARNALL - 41A | BARNSLEY - 41G |
| Jan-59 | GORTON - 9G | **2/59: WAKE - 56A** | LANGWITH JCN - 41J | MEXBOROUGH - 41F | STAVELEY (GC) - 41H | IMMINGHAM - 40B | FRODINGHAM - 36C | DARNALL - 41A | BARNSLEY - 41G |
| Aug-59 | GORTON - 9G | WAKEFIELD - 56A | LANGWITH JCN - 41J | **3/59: W/D** | STAVELEY (GC) - 41H | IMMINGHAM - 40B | FRODINGHAM - 36C | DARNALL - 41A | BARNSLEY - 41G |
| Nov-59 | GORTON - 9G | WAKEFIELD - 56A | LANGWITH JCN - 41J | | STAVELEY (GC) - 41H | IMMINGHAM - 40B | FRODINGHAM - 36C | DARNALL - 41A | BARNSLEY - 41G |
| Jan-60 | GORTON - 9G | WAKEFIELD - 56A | LANGWITH JCN - 41J | | **2/60: MEX - 41F** | IMMINGHAM - 40B | FRODINGHAM - 36C | DARNALL - 41A | **1/60: MEX - 41F** |
| Apr-60 | GORTON - 9G | WAKEFIELD - 56A | LANGWITH JCN - 41J | | MEXBOROUGH - 41F | IMMINGHAM - 40B | FRODINGHAM - 36C | DARNALL - 41A | MEXBOROUGH - 41F |
| Aug-60 | GORTON - 9G | WAKEFIELD - 56A | LANGWITH JCN - 41J | | MEXBOROUGH - 41F | IMMINGHAM - 40B | FRODINGHAM - 36C | DARNALL - 41A | MEXBOROUGH - 41F |
| Nov-60 | GORTON - 9G | WAKEFIELD - 56A | LANGWITH JCN - 41J | | MEXBOROUGH - 41F | IMMINGHAM - 40B | FRODINGHAM - 36C | DARNALL - 41A | MEXBOROUGH - 41F |

| | 63884 | 63885 | 63888 | 63889 | 63891 | 63894 | 63897 | 63898 | 63899 |
|---|---|---|---|---|---|---|---|---|---|
| Aug-50 | LANGWITH JCN - 40E | TUXFORD - 40D | DARNALL - 39B | DARNALL - 39B | GORTON - 39A | COLWICK - 38A | MARCH - 31B | MEXBOROUGH - 36B | GORTON - 39A |
| Jan-51 | LANGWITH JCN - 40E | TUXFORD - 40D | DARNALL - 39B | DARNALL - 39B | GORTON - 39A | COLWICK - 38A | MARCH - 31B | MEXBOROUGH - 36B | GORTON - 39A |
| Aug-51 | LANGWITH JCN - 40E | TUXFORD - 40D | DARNALL - 39B | DARNALL - 39B | GORTON - 39A | **9/51: ANN - 38B** | MARCH - 31B | MEXBOROUGH - 36B | GORTON - 39A |
| Jan-52 | **12/51: STAVE - 38D** | TUXFORD - 40D | DARNALL - 39B | DARNALL - 39B | GORTON - 39A | ANNESLEY - 38B | **10/51: MEX - 36B** | MEXBOROUGH - 36B | GORTON - 39A |
| Aug-52 | STAVELEY - 38D | TUXFORD - 40D | DARNALL - 39B | DARNALL - 39B | GORTON - 39A | **9/52: COLW - 38A** | MEXBOROUGH - 36B | MEXBOROUGH - 36B | GORTON - 39A |
| Jan-53 | STAVELEY - 38D | TUXFORD - 40D | DARNALL - 39B | DARNALL - 39B | GORTON - 39A | COLWICK - 38A | MEXBOROUGH - 36B | MEXBOROUGH - 36B | GORTON - 39A |
| Aug-53 | STAVELEY - 38D | TUXFORD - 40D | DARNALL - 39B | DARNALL - 39B | GORTON - 39A | COLWICK - 38A | MEXBOROUGH - 36B | MEXBOROUGH - 36B | COLWICK - 38A |
| Jan-54 | STAVELEY - 38D | **11/53: ARDS - 37A** | DARNALL - 39B | DARNALL - 39B | GORTON - 39A | COLWICK - 38A | MEXBOROUGH - 36B | MEXBOROUGH - 36B | **12/53: STAVE - 38D** |
| Aug-54 | STAVELEY - 38D | ARDSLEY - 37A | DARNALL - 39B | DARNALL - 39B | **6/54: COLW - 38A** | COLWICK - 38A | MEXBOROUGH - 36B | MEXBOROUGH - 36B | STAVELEY - 38D |
| Jan-55 | STAVELEY - 38D | ARDSLEY - 37A | DARNALL - 39B | DARNALL - 39B | COLWICK - 38A | COLWICK - 38A | MEXBOROUGH - 36B | MEXBOROUGH - 36B | STAVELEY - 38D |
| Aug-55 | STAVELEY - 38D | ARDSLEY - 37A | DARNALL - 39B | DARNALL - 39B | COLWICK - 38A | COLWICK - 38A | MEXBOROUGH - 36B | MEXBOROUGH - 36B | STAVELEY - 38D |
| Jan-56 | STAVELEY - 38D | ARDSLEY - 37A | DARNALL - 41A | DARNALL - 41A | **1/56: MEX - 36B** | **1/56: MEX - 36B** | MEXBOROUGH - 36B | MEXBOROUGH - 36B | STAVELEY - 38D |
| Aug-56 | STAVELEY - 38D | ARDSLEY - 56B | DARNALL - 41A | DARNALL - 41A | MEXBOROUGH - 36B | MEXBOROUGH - 36B | MEXBOROUGH - 36B | MEXBOROUGH - 36B | STAVELEY - 38D |
| Jan-57 | STAVELEY - 38D | ARDSLEY - 56B | DARNALL - 41A | DARNALL - 41A | MEXBOROUGH - 36B | MEXBOROUGH - 36B | MEXBOROUGH - 36B | MEXBOROUGH - 36B | STAVELEY - 38D |
| Aug-57 | STAVELEY - 38D | ARDSLEY - 56B | DARNALL - 41A | DARNALL - 41A | MEXBOROUGH - 36B | MEXBOROUGH - 36B | MEXBOROUGH - 36B | MEXBOROUGH - 36B | STAVELEY - 38D |
| Jan-58 | STAVELEY - 38D | ARDSLEY - 56B | DARNALL - 41A | DARNALL - 41A | MEXBOROUGH - 36B | MEXBOROUGH - 36B | MEXBOROUGH - 36B | MEXBOROUGH - 36B | STAVELEY - 38D |
| Aug-58 | STAVELEY (GC) - 41H | ARDSLEY - 56B | DARNALL - 41A | DARNALL - 41A | MEXBOROUGH - 41F | MEXBOROUGH - 41F | MEXBOROUGH - 41F | MEXBOROUGH - 41F | STAVELEY (GC) - 41H |
| Jan-59 | STAVELEY (GC) - 41H | ARDSLEY - 56B | DARNALL - 41A | DARNALL - 41A | MEXBOROUGH - 41F | MEXBOROUGH - 41F | MEXBOROUGH - 41F | MEXBOROUGH - 41F | STAVELEY (GC) - 41H |
| Aug-59 | STAVELEY (GC) - 41H | ARDSLEY - 56B | DARNALL - 41A | DARNALL - 41A | MEXBOROUGH - 41F | MEXBOROUGH - 41F | MEXBOROUGH - 41F | MEXBOROUGH - 41F | STAVELEY (GC) - 41H |
| Nov-59 | STAVELEY (GC) - 41H | ARDSLEY - 56B | DARNALL - 41A | **11/59: W/D** | MEXBOROUGH - 41F | MEXBOROUGH - 41F | MEXBOROUGH - 41F | MEXBOROUGH - 41F | STAVELEY (GC) - 41H |
| Jan-60 | **2/60: MEX - 41F** | ARDSLEY - 56B | DARNALL - 41A | | MEXBOROUGH - 41F | MEXBOROUGH - 41F | MEXBOROUGH - 41F | MEXBOROUGH - 41F | STAVELEY (GC) - 41H |
| Apr-60 | MEXBOROUGH - 41F | ARDSLEY - 56B | **3/60: W/D** | | MEXBOROUGH - 41F | MEXBOROUGH - 41F | MEXBOROUGH - 41F | MEXBOROUGH - 41F | STAVELEY (GC) - 41H |
| Aug-60 | MEXBOROUGH - 41F | ARDSLEY - 56B | | | MEXBOROUGH - 41F | **6/60: W/D** | MEXBOROUGH - 41F | MEXBOROUGH - 41F | STAVELEY (GC) - 41H |
| Nov-60 | MEXBOROUGH - 41F | ARDSLEY - 56B | | | MEXBOROUGH - 41F | | MEXBOROUGH - 41F | MEXBOROUGH - 41F | STAVELEY (GC) - 41H |

*If anything was calculated to raise the temperature at Manchester London Road, it was the presence of a Great Central freight coming from the Oxford Road direction and having to cross every line in the station approach without delaying any LNW traffic. Margins are calculated by the regulator as O4/3 2-8-0 63835 stands at the South Junction Platform waiting for a run across to GC metals with the 10.46 Ordsall Lane to Guide Bridge (Park) goods in May 1954. 63835 spent quite an interesting decade, starting the 1950's at Hull Dairycoates before being moved to Colwick in 1951. In the Spring of 1954 it was transferred to Gorton to a couple of months before returning to Colwick. Withdrawn in early 1959, its last three years were spent at Mexborough.*

*Ousted from the New England - Ferme Park services by Austerities and 9F 2-10-0's, the Great Northern O2 'Tango' 2-8-0's spent most of the 1950's working north of Peterborough; a respectable number being based at Grantham for the High Dyke - Frodingham iron ore trains. The class could also be seen on the GN&GE joint line on Doncaster - New England services; 63942 being seen between workings at New England in the summer of 1963.*

| | 63900 | 63902 | 63904 | 63905 | 63906 | 63907 | 63908 | 63911 | 63912 |
|---|---|---|---|---|---|---|---|---|---|
| Aug-50 | LANGWITH JCN - 40E | LANGWITH JCN - 40E | BARNSLEY - 36D | RETFORD - 36E | FRODINGHAM - 36C | RETFORD - 36E | RETFORD - 36E | FRODINGHAM - 36C | ANNESLEY - 38B |
| Jan-51 | LANGWITH JCN - 40E | LANGWITH JCN - 40E | BARNSLEY - 36D | RETFORD - 36E | FRODINGHAM - 36C | 3/51: BARN - 36D | 9/50: LANG JN - 40E | FRODINGHAM - 36C | 11/50: GORT - 39A |
| Aug-51 | LANGWITH JCN - 40E | LANGWITH JCN - 40E | BARNSLEY - 36D | RETFORD - 36E | FRODINGHAM - 36C | BARNSLEY - 36D | LANGWITH JCN - 40E | FRODINGHAM - 36C | GORTON - 39A |
| Jan-52 | 12/51: IMM - 40B | LANGWITH JCN - 40E | BARNSLEY - 36D | RETFORD - 36E | FRODINGHAM - 36C | BARNSLEY - 36D | 12/51: IMM - 40B | FRODINGHAM - 36C | GORTON - 39A |
| Aug-52 | IMMINGHAM - 40B | LANGWITH JCN - 40E | BARNSLEY - 36D | RETFORD - 36E | FRODINGHAM - 36C | BARNSLEY - 36D | IMMINGHAM - 40B | FRODINGHAM - 36C | 6/52: COLW - 38A |
| Jan-53 | IMMINGHAM - 40B | LANGWITH JCN - 40E | BARNSLEY - 36D | RETFORD - 36E | FRODINGHAM - 36C | BARNSLEY - 36D | IMMINGHAM - 40B | FRODINGHAM - 36C | COLWICK - 38A |
| Aug-53 | IMMINGHAM - 40B | LANGWITH JCN - 40E | BARNSLEY - 36D | RETFORD - 36E | FRODINGHAM - 36C | BARNSLEY - 36D | IMMINGHAM - 40B | FRODINGHAM - 36C | COLWICK - 38A |
| Jan-54 | IMMINGHAM - 40B | LANGWITH JCN - 40E | BARNSLEY - 36D | RETFORD - 36E | FRODINGHAM - 36C | BARNSLEY - 36D | 10/53: COLW - 38A | FRODINGHAM - 36C | COLWICK - 38A |
| Aug-54 | IMMINGHAM - 40B | LANGWITH JCN - 40E | BARNSLEY - 36D | RETFORD - 36E | FRODINGHAM - 36C | BARNSLEY - 36D | COLWICK - 38A | FRODINGHAM - 36C | 8/54: DARN - 39B |
| Jan-55 | IMMINGHAM - 40B | LANGWITH JCN - 40E | BARNSLEY - 36D | RETFORD - 36E | FRODINGHAM - 36C | BARNSLEY - 36D | COLWICK - 38A | FRODINGHAM - 36C | 1/55: IMM - 40B |
| Aug-55 | IMMINGHAM - 40B | LANGWITH JCN - 40E | BARNSLEY - 36D | RETFORD - 36E | FRODINGHAM - 36C | BARNSLEY - 36D | COLWICK - 38A | FRODINGHAM - 36C | IMMINGHAM - 40B |
| Jan-56 | IMMINGHAM - 40B | LANGWITH JCN - 40E | BARNSLEY - 36D | RETFORD - 36E | FRODINGHAM - 36C | BARNSLEY - 36D | 1/56: MEX - 36B | 11/55: BARN - 36D | IMMINGHAM - 40B |
| Aug-56 | IMMINGHAM - 40B | LANGWITH JCN - 40E | BARNSLEY - 36D | RETFORD - 36E | FRODINGHAM - 36C | BARNSLEY - 36D | MEXBOROUGH - 36B | BARNSLEY - 36D | IMMINGHAM - 40B |
| Jan-57 | IMMINGHAM - 40B | LANGWITH JCN - 40E | BARNSLEY - 36D | RETFORD - 36E | FRODINGHAM - 36C | BARNSLEY - 36D | MEXBOROUGH - 36B | BARNSLEY - 36D | IMMINGHAM - 40B |
| Aug-57 | IMMINGHAM - 40B | LANGWITH JCN - 40E | BARNSLEY - 36D | RETFORD - 36E | FRODINGHAM - 36C | BARNSLEY - 36D | MEXBOROUGH - 36B | BARNSLEY - 36D | IMMINGHAM - 40B |
| Jan-58 | IMMINGHAM - 40B | LANGWITH JCN - 40E | BARNSLEY - 36D | RETFORD - 36E | FRODINGHAM - 36C | BARNSLEY - 36D | MEXBOROUGH - 36B | BARNSLEY - 36D | IMMINGHAM - 40B |
| Aug-58 | IMMINGHAM - 40B | LANGWITH JCN - 40E | BARNSLEY - 41G | RETFORD - 36E | FRODINGHAM - 36C | BARNSLEY - 41G | MEXBOROUGH - 41F | BARNSLEY - 41G | IMMINGHAM - 40B |
| Jan-59 | IMMINGHAM - 40B | LANGWITH JCN - 40E | BARNSLEY - 41G | RETFORD - 36E | FRODINGHAM - 36C | BARNSLEY - 41G | MEXBOROUGH - 41F | BARNSLEY - 41G | 1/59: LANG JN - 41J |
| Aug-59 | IMMINGHAM - 40B | LANGWITH JCN - 40E | BARNSLEY - 41G | 4/59: W/D | FRODINGHAM - 36C | BARNSLEY - 41G | MEXBOROUGH - 41F | BARNSLEY - 41G | LANGWITH JCN - 41J |
| Nov-59 | IMMINGHAM - 40B | LANGWITH JCN - 40E | BARNSLEY - 41G | | FRODINGHAM - 36C | BARNSLEY - 41G | MEXBOROUGH - 41F | BARNSLEY - 41G | LANGWITH JCN - 41J |
| Jan-60 | IMMINGHAM - 40B | LANGWITH JCN - 40E | 1/60: MEX - 41F | | FRODINGHAM - 36C | 1/60: MEX - 41F | MEXBOROUGH - 41F | 1/60: MEX - 41F | LANGWITH JCN - 41J |
| Apr-60 | 5/60: COLW - 40E | LANGWITH JCN - 40E | MEXBOROUGH - 41F | | FRODINGHAM - 36C | MEXBOROUGH - 41F | MEXBOROUGH - 41F | MEXBOROUGH - 41F | LANGWITH JCN - 41J |
| Aug-60 | COLWICK - 40E | LANGWITH JCN - 40E | MEXBOROUGH - 41F | | FRODINGHAM - 36C | MEXBOROUGH - 41F | MEXBOROUGH - 41F | MEXBOROUGH - 41F | LANGWITH JCN - 41J |
| Nov-60 | COLWICK - 40E | LANGWITH JCN - 40E | MEXBOROUGH - 41F | | FRODINGHAM - 36C | MEXBOROUGH - 41F | MEXBOROUGH - 41F | MEXBOROUGH - 41F | LANGWITH JCN - 41J |

| | 63913 | 63915 | 63917 | 63920 | O2 2-8-0 (1921) 63922 | 63923 | 63924 | 63925 | 63926 |
|---|---|---|---|---|---|---|---|---|---|
| Aug-50 | BARNSLEY - 36D | GORTON - 39A | FRODINGHAM - 36C | FRODINGHAM - 36C | FRODINGHAM - 36C | NEW ENGLAND - 35A | MEXBOROUGH - 36B | DONCASTER - 36A | DONCASTER - 36A |
| Jan-51 | BARNSLEY - 36D | GORTON - 39A | FRODINGHAM - 36C | FRODINGHAM - 36C | FRODINGHAM - 36C | 3/51: GRAN - 35B | MEXBOROUGH - 36B | DONCASTER - 36A | DONCASTER - 36A |
| Aug-51 | BARNSLEY - 36D | GORTON - 39A | FRODINGHAM - 36C | FRODINGHAM - 36C | FRODINGHAM - 36C | GRANTHAM - 35B | MEXBOROUGH - 36B | DONCASTER - 36A | DONCASTER - 36A |
| Jan-52 | BARNSLEY - 36D | GORTON - 39A | FRODINGHAM - 36C | FRODINGHAM - 36C | FRODINGHAM - 36C | GRANTHAM - 35B | MEXBOROUGH - 36B | 3/53: RET - 36E | 3/53: RET - 36E |
| Aug-52 | BARNSLEY - 36D | 9/52: IMM - 40B | FRODINGHAM - 36C | 9/52: ARDS - 37A | FRODINGHAM - 36C | GRANTHAM - 35B | 9/52: RET - 36E | RETFORD - 36E | RETFORD - 36E |
| Jan-53 | BARNSLEY - 36D | IMMINGHAM - 40B | FRODINGHAM - 36C | ARDSLEY - 37A | FRODINGHAM - 36C | GRANTHAM - 35B | RETFORD - 36E | RETFORD - 36E | RETFORD - 36E |
| Aug-53 | BARNSLEY - 36D | IMMINGHAM - 40B | FRODINGHAM - 36C | ARDSLEY - 37A | FRODINGHAM - 36C | GRANTHAM - 35B | RETFORD - 36E | RETFORD - 36E | RETFORD - 36E |
| Jan-54 | BARNSLEY - 36D | 10/53: LANG JN - 40E | FRODINGHAM - 36C | 12/53: BRAD - 37C | FRODINGHAM - 36C | GRANTHAM - 35B | RETFORD - 36E | RETFORD - 36E | RETFORD - 36E |
| Aug-54 | BARNSLEY - 36D | LANGWITH JCN - 40E | FRODINGHAM - 36C | BRADFORD - 37C | 6/54: DCTR - 36A | GRANTHAM - 35B | RETFORD - 36E | RETFORD - 36E | RETFORD - 36E |
| Jan-55 | BARNSLEY - 36D | LANGWITH JCN - 40E | FRODINGHAM - 36C | BRADFORD - 37C | DONCASTER - 36A | GRANTHAM - 35B | RETFORD - 36E | RETFORD - 36E | RETFORD - 36E |
| Aug-55 | BARNSLEY - 36D | LANGWITH JCN - 40E | FRODINGHAM - 36C | BRADFORD - 37C | DONCASTER - 36A | GRANTHAM - 35B | RETFORD - 36E | RETFORD - 36E | RETFORD - 36E |
| Jan-56 | BARNSLEY - 36D | 1/56: GORT - 39A | FRODINGHAM - 36C | BRADFORD - 37C | DONCASTER - 36A | GRANTHAM - 35B | RETFORD - 36E | RETFORD - 36E | RETFORD - 36E |
| Aug-56 | BARNSLEY - 36D | GORTON - 39A | FRODINGHAM - 36C | BRADFORD - 56G | DONCASTER - 36A | GRANTHAM - 35B | RETFORD - 36E | RETFORD - 36E | RETFORD - 36E |
| Jan-57 | BARNSLEY - 36D | GORTON - 39A | FRODINGHAM - 36C | BRADFORD - 56G | DONCASTER - 36A | GRANTHAM - 35B | RETFORD - 36E | RETFORD - 36E | RETFORD - 36E |
| Aug-57 | BARNSLEY - 36D | GORTON - 39A | FRODINGHAM - 36C | BRADFORD - 56G | DONCASTER - 36A | GRANTHAM - 35B | RETFORD - 36E | RETFORD - 36E | RETFORD - 36E |
| Jan-58 | BARNSLEY - 36D | GORTON - 39A | FRODINGHAM - 36C | 2/58: ARDS - 56B | DONCASTER - 36A | GRANTHAM - 35B | RETFORD - 36E | RETFORD - 36E | RETFORD - 36E |
| Aug-58 | BARNSLEY - 41G | GORTON - 9G | FRODINGHAM - 36C | ARDSLEY - 56B | DONCASTER - 36A | GRANTHAM - 34F | RETFORD - 36E | RETFORD - 36E | RETFORD - 36E |
| Jan-59 | BARNSLEY - 41G | GORTON - 9G | FRODINGHAM - 36C | 1/59: WAKE - 56A | DONCASTER - 36A | GRANTHAM - 34F | RETFORD - 36E | RETFORD - 36E | RETFORD - 36E |
| Aug-59 | BARNSLEY - 41G | GORTON - 9G | FRODINGHAM - 36C | WAKEFIELD - 56A | DONCASTER - 36A | GRANTHAM - 34F | RETFORD - 36E | RETFORD - 36E | RETFORD - 36E |
| Nov-59 | BARNSLEY - 41G | GORTON - 9G | FRODINGHAM - 36C | WAKEFIELD - 56A | DONCASTER - 36A | GRANTHAM - 34F | RETFORD - 36E | RETFORD - 36E | RETFORD - 36E |
| Jan-60 | 1/60: MEX - 41F | GORTON - 9G | FRODINGHAM - 36C | WAKEFIELD - 56A | DONCASTER - 36A | GRANTHAM - 34F | RETFORD - 36E | RETFORD - 36E | RETFORD - 36E |
| Apr-60 | MEXBOROUGH - 41F | GORTON - 9G | FRODINGHAM - 36C | WAKEFIELD - 56A | DONCASTER - 36A | GRANTHAM - 34F | RETFORD - 36E | RETFORD - 36E | RETFORD - 36E |
| Aug-60 | MEXBOROUGH - 41F | GORTON - 9G | FRODINGHAM - 36C | WAKEFIELD - 56A | DONCASTER - 36A | GRANTHAM - 34F | RETFORD - 36E | RETFORD - 36E | RETFORD - 36E |
| Nov-60 | MEXBOROUGH - 41F | GORTON - 9G | FRODINGHAM - 36C | WAKEFIELD - 56A | DONCASTER - 36A | GRANTHAM - 34F | RETFORD - 36E | RETFORD - 36E | RETFORD - 36E |

| | 63927 | 63928 | 63929 | 63930 | 63931 | 63932 | 63933 | 63934 | 63935 |
|---|---|---|---|---|---|---|---|---|---|
| Aug-50 | MEXBOROUGH - 36B | DONCASTER - 36A | GRANTHAM - 35B | GRANTHAM - 35B | GRANTHAM - 35B | GRANTHAM - 35B | NEW ENGLAND - 35A | FRODINGHAM - 36C | NEW ENGLAND - 35A |
| Jan-51 | 2/51: DCTR - 36A | DONCASTER - 36A | GRANTHAM - 35B | GRANTHAM - 35B | GRANTHAM - 35B | GRANTHAM - 35B | 11/50: GRAN - 35B | FRODINGHAM - 36C | 11/50: GRAN - 35B |
| Aug-51 | DONCASTER - 36A | DONCASTER - 36A | GRANTHAM - 35B | GRANTHAM - 35B | GRANTHAM - 35B | GRANTHAM - 35B | 9/51: NEWE - 35A | FRODINGHAM - 36C | GRANTHAM - 35B |
| Jan-52 | 3/53: RET - 36E | DONCASTER - 36A | GRANTHAM - 35B | GRANTHAM - 35B | GRANTHAM - 35B | GRANTHAM - 35B | 10/51: GRAN - 35B | FRODINGHAM - 36C | 10/51: MEX - 36B |
| Aug-52 | RETFORD - 36E | DONCASTER - 36A | GRANTHAM - 35B | GRANTHAM - 35B | GRANTHAM - 35B | GRANTHAM - 35B | GRANTHAM - 35B | FRODINGHAM - 36C | MEXBOROUGH - 36B |
| Jan-53 | RETFORD - 36E | DONCASTER - 36A | GRANTHAM - 35B | GRANTHAM - 35B | GRANTHAM - 35B | GRANTHAM - 35B | GRANTHAM - 35B | FRODINGHAM - 36C | 11/52: DCTR - 36A |
| Aug-53 | RETFORD - 36E | DONCASTER - 36A | GRANTHAM - 35B | GRANTHAM - 35B | GRANTHAM - 35B | GRANTHAM - 35B | GRANTHAM - 35B | FRODINGHAM - 36C | DONCASTER - 36A |
| Jan-54 | RETFORD - 36E | DONCASTER - 36A | GRANTHAM - 35B | GRANTHAM - 35B | GRANTHAM - 35B | GRANTHAM - 35B | GRANTHAM - 35B | FRODINGHAM - 36C | DONCASTER - 36A |
| Aug-54 | RETFORD - 36E | DONCASTER - 36A | GRANTHAM - 35B | GRANTHAM - 35B | GRANTHAM - 35B | GRANTHAM - 35B | GRANTHAM - 35B | 6/54: DCTR - 36A | DONCASTER - 36A |
| Jan-55 | RETFORD - 36E | DONCASTER - 36A | GRANTHAM - 35B | GRANTHAM - 35B | GRANTHAM - 35B | GRANTHAM - 35B | GRANTHAM - 35B | DONCASTER - 36A | DONCASTER - 36A |
| Aug-55 | RETFORD - 36E | DONCASTER - 36A | GRANTHAM - 35B | GRANTHAM - 35B | GRANTHAM - 35B | GRANTHAM - 35B | GRANTHAM - 35B | DONCASTER - 36A | DONCASTER - 36A |
| Jan-56 | RETFORD - 36E | DONCASTER - 36A | GRANTHAM - 35B | GRANTHAM - 35B | GRANTHAM - 35B | GRANTHAM - 35B | GRANTHAM - 35B | DONCASTER - 36A | DONCASTER - 36A |
| Aug-56 | RETFORD - 36E | DONCASTER - 36A | GRANTHAM - 35B | GRANTHAM - 35B | GRANTHAM - 35B | GRANTHAM - 35B | GRANTHAM - 35B | DONCASTER - 36A | DONCASTER - 36A |
| Jan-57 | RETFORD - 36E | DONCASTER - 36A | GRANTHAM - 35B | GRANTHAM - 35B | GRANTHAM - 35B | GRANTHAM - 35B | GRANTHAM - 35B | DONCASTER - 36A | DONCASTER - 36A |
| Aug-57 | RETFORD - 36E | DONCASTER - 36A | GRANTHAM - 35B | GRANTHAM - 35B | GRANTHAM - 35B | GRANTHAM - 35B | GRANTHAM - 35B | DONCASTER - 36A | DONCASTER - 36A |
| Jan-58 | RETFORD - 36E | DONCASTER - 36A | GRANTHAM - 35B | GRANTHAM - 35B | GRANTHAM - 35B | GRANTHAM - 35B | GRANTHAM - 35B | DONCASTER - 36A | DONCASTER - 36A |
| Aug-58 | RETFORD - 36E | DONCASTER - 36A | GRANTHAM - 34F | GRANTHAM - 34F | GRANTHAM - 34F | GRANTHAM - 34F | GRANTHAM - 34F | DONCASTER - 36A | DONCASTER - 36A |
| Jan-59 | RETFORD - 36E | DONCASTER - 36A | GRANTHAM - 34F | GRANTHAM - 34F | GRANTHAM - 34F | GRANTHAM - 34F | GRANTHAM - 34F | DONCASTER - 36A | DONCASTER - 36A |
| Aug-59 | RETFORD - 36E | DONCASTER - 36A | GRANTHAM - 34F | GRANTHAM - 34F | GRANTHAM - 34F | GRANTHAM - 34F | GRANTHAM - 34F | DONCASTER - 36A | DONCASTER - 36A |
| Nov-59 | RETFORD - 36E | DONCASTER - 36A | GRANTHAM - 34F | GRANTHAM - 34F | GRANTHAM - 34F | GRANTHAM - 34F | GRANTHAM - 34F | DONCASTER - 36A | DONCASTER - 36A |
| Jan-60 | RETFORD - 36E | DONCASTER - 36A | GRANTHAM - 34F | GRANTHAM - 34F | GRANTHAM - 34F | GRANTHAM - 34F | GRANTHAM - 34F | DONCASTER - 36A | DONCASTER - 36A |
| Apr-60 | RETFORD - 36E | DONCASTER - 36A | GRANTHAM - 34F | GRANTHAM - 34F | GRANTHAM - 34F | GRANTHAM - 34F | GRANTHAM - 34F | DONCASTER - 36A | DONCASTER - 36A |
| Aug-60 | RETFORD - 36E | DONCASTER - 36A | GRANTHAM - 34F | GRANTHAM - 34F | GRANTHAM - 34F | GRANTHAM - 34F | GRANTHAM - 34F | DONCASTER - 36A | DONCASTER - 36A |
| Nov-60 | RETFORD - 36E | DONCASTER - 36A | GRANTHAM - 34F | GRANTHAM - 34F | GRANTHAM - 34F | GRANTHAM - 34F | GRANTHAM - 34F | 11/60: RET - 36E | DONCASTER - 36A |

| | 63936 | 63937 | 63938 | 63939 | 63940 | 63941 | 63942 | 63943 | 63944 |
|---|---|---|---|---|---|---|---|---|---|
| Aug-50 | GRANTHAM - 35B | FRODINGHAM - 36C | GRANTHAM - 35B | FRODINGHAM - 36C | GRANTHAM - 35B | DONCASTER - 36A | DONCASTER - 36A | DONCASTER - 36A | FRODINGHAM - 36C |
| Jan-51 | GRANTHAM - 35B | FRODINGHAM - 36C | GRANTHAM - 35B | FRODINGHAM - 36C | GRANTHAM - 35B | DONCASTER - 36A | DONCASTER - 36A | DONCASTER - 36A | FRODINGHAM - 36C |
| Aug-51 | GRANTHAM - 35B | FRODINGHAM - 36C | GRANTHAM - 35B | FRODINGHAM - 36C | GRANTHAM - 35B | DONCASTER - 36A | DONCASTER - 36A | DONCASTER - 36A | FRODINGHAM - 36C |
| Jan-52 | GRANTHAM - 35B | FRODINGHAM - 36C | GRANTHAM - 35B | FRODINGHAM - 36C | GRANTHAM - 35B | DONCASTER - 36A | DONCASTER - 36A | DONCASTER - 36A | FRODINGHAM - 36C |
| Aug-52 | GRANTHAM - 35B | FRODINGHAM - 36C | GRANTHAM - 35B | FRODINGHAM - 36C | GRANTHAM - 35B | DONCASTER - 36A | DONCASTER - 36A | DONCASTER - 36A | FRODINGHAM - 36C |
| Jan-53 | GRANTHAM - 35B | FRODINGHAM - 36C | GRANTHAM - 35B | FRODINGHAM - 36C | GRANTHAM - 35B | DONCASTER - 36A | DONCASTER - 36A | DONCASTER - 36A | FRODINGHAM - 36C |
| Aug-53 | GRANTHAM - 35B | FRODINGHAM - 36C | GRANTHAM - 35B | FRODINGHAM - 36C | GRANTHAM - 35B | DONCASTER - 36A | DONCASTER - 36A | DONCASTER - 36A | FRODINGHAM - 36C |
| Jan-54 | GRANTHAM - 35B | 11/53: RET - 36E | GRANTHAM - 35B | FRODINGHAM - 36C | GRANTHAM - 35B | DONCASTER - 36A | DONCASTER - 36A | DONCASTER - 36A | FRODINGHAM - 36C |
| Aug-54 | GRANTHAM - 35B | RETFORD - 36E | GRANTHAM - 35B | 8/54: DCTR - 36A | GRANTHAM - 35B | DONCASTER - 36A | DONCASTER - 36A | DONCASTER - 36A | 6/54: DCTR - 36A |
| Jan-55 | GRANTHAM - 35B | RETFORD - 36E | GRANTHAM - 35B | DONCASTER - 36A | GRANTHAM - 35B | DONCASTER - 36A | DONCASTER - 36A | DONCASTER - 36A | DONCASTER - 36A |
| Aug-55 | GRANTHAM - 35B | RETFORD - 36E | GRANTHAM - 35B | DONCASTER - 36A | GRANTHAM - 35B | DONCASTER - 36A | DONCASTER - 36A | DONCASTER - 36A | DONCASTER - 36A |
| Jan-56 | GRANTHAM - 35B | RETFORD - 36E | GRANTHAM - 35B | DONCASTER - 36A | GRANTHAM - 35B | DONCASTER - 36A | DONCASTER - 36A | DONCASTER - 36A | DONCASTER - 36A |
| Aug-56 | GRANTHAM - 35B | RETFORD - 36E | GRANTHAM - 35B | DONCASTER - 36A | GRANTHAM - 35B | DONCASTER - 36A | DONCASTER - 36A | DONCASTER - 36A | DONCASTER - 36A |
| Jan-57 | GRANTHAM - 35B | RETFORD - 36E | GRANTHAM - 35B | DONCASTER - 36A | GRANTHAM - 35B | DONCASTER - 36A | DONCASTER - 36A | DONCASTER - 36A | 2/57: RET - 36E |
| Aug-57 | GRANTHAM - 35B | RETFORD - 36E | GRANTHAM - 35B | DONCASTER - 36A | GRANTHAM - 35B | DONCASTER - 36A | DONCASTER - 36A | DONCASTER - 36A | RETFORD - 36E |
| Jan-58 | GRANTHAM - 35B | RETFORD - 36E | GRANTHAM - 35B | DONCASTER - 36A | GRANTHAM - 35B | DONCASTER - 36A | DONCASTER - 36A | DONCASTER - 36A | RETFORD - 36E |
| Aug-58 | GRANTHAM - 34F | RETFORD - 36E | GRANTHAM - 34F | DONCASTER - 36A | GRANTHAM - 34F | DONCASTER - 36A | DONCASTER - 36A | DONCASTER - 36A | RETFORD - 36E |
| Jan-59 | GRANTHAM - 34F | RETFORD - 36E | GRANTHAM - 34F | DONCASTER - 36A | GRANTHAM - 34F | DONCASTER - 36A | DONCASTER - 36A | DONCASTER - 36A | RETFORD - 36E |
| Aug-59 | GRANTHAM - 34F | RETFORD - 36E | GRANTHAM - 34F | DONCASTER - 36A | GRANTHAM - 34F | DONCASTER - 36A | DONCASTER - 36A | DONCASTER - 36A | RETFORD - 36E |
| Nov-59 | GRANTHAM - 34F | RETFORD - 36E | GRANTHAM - 34F | DONCASTER - 36A | GRANTHAM - 34F | DONCASTER - 36A | DONCASTER - 36A | DONCASTER - 36A | RETFORD - 36E |
| Jan-60 | GRANTHAM - 34F | RETFORD - 36E | GRANTHAM - 34F | 2/60: RET - 36E | GRANTHAM - 34F | DONCASTER - 36A | 2/60: RET - 36E | DONCASTER - 36A | RETFORD - 36E |
| Apr-60 | GRANTHAM - 34F | RETFORD - 36E | GRANTHAM - 34F | RETFORD - 36E | GRANTHAM - 34F | DONCASTER - 36A | RETFORD - 36E | DONCASTER - 36A | RETFORD - 36E |
| Aug-60 | GRANTHAM - 34F | RETFORD - 36E | GRANTHAM - 34F | RETFORD - 36E | GRANTHAM - 34F | DONCASTER - 36A | RETFORD - 36E | DONCASTER - 36A | RETFORD - 36E |
| Nov-60 | GRANTHAM - 34F | RETFORD - 36E | GRANTHAM - 34F | RETFORD - 36E | GRANTHAM - 34F | DONCASTER - 36A | RETFORD - 36E | DONCASTER - 36A | RETFORD - 36E |

| | 63945 | 63946 | 63947 | 63948 | 63949 | 63950 | 63951 | 63952 | 63953 |
|---|---|---|---|---|---|---|---|---|---|
| Aug-50 | DONCASTER - 36A | DONCASTER - 36A | DONCASTER - 36A | NEWENGLAND - 35A | GRANTHAM - 35B | GRANTHAM - 35B | DONCASTER - 36A | DONCASTER - 36A | DONCASTER - 36A |
| Jan-51 | DONCASTER - 36A | DONCASTER - 36A | DONCASTER - 36A | 1/51: GRAN - 35B | GRANTHAM - 35B | GRANTHAM - 35B | DONCASTER - 36A | DONCASTER - 36A | DONCASTER - 36A |
| Aug-51 | DONCASTER - 36A | DONCASTER - 36A | DONCASTER - 36A | GRANTHAM - 35B | 9/51: NEWE - 35A | 9/51: NEWE - 35A | DONCASTER - 36A | DONCASTER - 36A | DONCASTER - 36A |
| Jan-52 | DONCASTER - 36A | DONCASTER - 36A | DONCASTER - 36A | GRANTHAM - 35B | 10/51: MEX - 36B | 10/51: GRAN - 35B | DONCASTER - 36A | DONCASTER - 36A | DONCASTER - 36A |
| Aug-52 | DONCASTER - 36A | DONCASTER - 36A | DONCASTER - 36A | GRANTHAM - 35B | 9/52: RET - 36E | GRANTHAM - 35B | DONCASTER - 36A | DONCASTER - 36A | DONCASTER - 36A |
| Jan-53 | DONCASTER - 36A | DONCASTER - 36A | DONCASTER - 36A | GRANTHAM - 35B | RETFORD - 36E | GRANTHAM - 35B | DONCASTER - 36A | DONCASTER - 36A | DONCASTER - 36A |
| Aug-53 | 5/53: FROD - 36C | 5/53: GRAN - 35B | DONCASTER - 36A | GRANTHAM - 35B | RETFORD - 36E | GRANTHAM - 35B | DONCASTER - 36A | DONCASTER - 36A | DONCASTER - 36A |
| Jan-54 | 1/54: RET - 36E | GRANTHAM - 35B | DONCASTER - 36A | GRANTHAM - 35B | RETFORD - 36E | GRANTHAM - 35B | DONCASTER - 36A | DONCASTER - 36A | DONCASTER - 36A |
| Aug-54 | RETFORD - 36E | GRANTHAM - 35B | DONCASTER - 36A | GRANTHAM - 35B | RETFORD - 36E | GRANTHAM - 35B | DONCASTER - 36A | DONCASTER - 36A | DONCASTER - 36A |
| Jan-55 | RETFORD - 36E | GRANTHAM - 35B | DONCASTER - 36A | GRANTHAM - 35B | RETFORD - 36E | GRANTHAM - 35B | DONCASTER - 36A | DONCASTER - 36A | DONCASTER - 36A |
| Aug-55 | RETFORD - 36E | GRANTHAM - 35B | DONCASTER - 36A | GRANTHAM - 35B | RETFORD - 36E | GRANTHAM - 35B | DONCASTER - 36A | DONCASTER - 36A | DONCASTER - 36A |
| Jan-56 | RETFORD - 36E | GRANTHAM - 35B | DONCASTER - 36A | GRANTHAM - 35B | RETFORD - 36E | GRANTHAM - 35B | DONCASTER - 36A | DONCASTER - 36A | DONCASTER - 36A |
| Aug-56 | RETFORD - 36E | GRANTHAM - 35B | DONCASTER - 36A | GRANTHAM - 35B | RETFORD - 36E | GRANTHAM - 35B | DONCASTER - 36A | DONCASTER - 36A | DONCASTER - 36A |
| Jan-57 | RETFORD - 36E | GRANTHAM - 35B | DONCASTER - 36A | GRANTHAM - 35B | RETFORD - 36E | GRANTHAM - 35B | DONCASTER - 36A | DONCASTER - 36A | DONCASTER - 36A |
| Aug-57 | RETFORD - 36E | GRANTHAM - 35B | DONCASTER - 36A | GRANTHAM - 35B | RETFORD - 36E | GRANTHAM - 35B | DONCASTER - 36A | DONCASTER - 36A | DONCASTER - 36A |
| Jan-58 | RETFORD - 36E | GRANTHAM - 35B | 2/58: RET - 36E | GRANTHAM - 35B | RETFORD - 36E | GRANTHAM - 35B | DONCASTER - 36A | DONCASTER - 36A | DONCASTER - 36A |
| Aug-58 | RETFORD - 36E | GRANTHAM - 34F | RETFORD - 36E | GRANTHAM - 34F | RETFORD - 36E | GRANTHAM - 34F | DONCASTER - 36A | DONCASTER - 36A | DONCASTER - 36A |
| Jan-59 | RETFORD - 36E | GRANTHAM - 34F | RETFORD - 36E | GRANTHAM - 34F | RETFORD - 36E | GRANTHAM - 34F | DONCASTER - 36A | DONCASTER - 36A | DONCASTER - 36A |
| Aug-59 | RETFORD - 36E | GRANTHAM - 34F | RETFORD - 36E | GRANTHAM - 34F | RETFORD - 36E | GRANTHAM - 34F | DONCASTER - 36A | DONCASTER - 36A | DONCASTER - 36A |
| Nov-59 | RETFORD - 36E | GRANTHAM - 34F | RETFORD - 36E | GRANTHAM - 34F | RETFORD - 36E | GRANTHAM - 34F | DONCASTER - 36A | DONCASTER - 36A | DONCASTER - 36A |
| Jan-60 | RETFORD - 36E | GRANTHAM - 34F | RETFORD - 36E | GRANTHAM - 34F | RETFORD - 36E | GRANTHAM - 34F | DONCASTER - 36A | DONCASTER - 36A | DONCASTER - 36A |
| Apr-60 | RETFORD - 36E | GRANTHAM - 34F | RETFORD - 36E | GRANTHAM - 34F | RETFORD - 36E | GRANTHAM - 34F | DONCASTER - 36A | DONCASTER - 36A | DONCASTER - 36A |
| Aug-60 | RETFORD - 36E | GRANTHAM - 34F | RETFORD - 36E | GRANTHAM - 34F | RETFORD - 36E | GRANTHAM - 34F | DONCASTER - 36A | DONCASTER - 36A | DONCASTER - 36A |
| Nov-60 | RETFORD - 36E | GRANTHAM - 34F | RETFORD - 36E | GRANTHAM - 34F | RETFORD - 36E | 11/60: W/D | RETFORD - 36E | DONCASTER - 36A | 11/60: W/D |

| | 63954 | 63955 | 63956 | 63957 | 63958 | 63959 | 63960 | 63961 | 63962 |
|---|---|---|---|---|---|---|---|---|---|
| Aug-50 | DONCASTER - 36A | DONCASTER - 36A | DONCASTER - 36A | DONCASTER - 36A | DONCASTER - 36A | DONCASTER - 36A | GRANTHAM - 35B | DONCASTER - 36A | DONCASTER - 36A |
| Jan-51 | DONCASTER - 36A | DONCASTER - 36A | DONCASTER - 36A | DONCASTER - 36A | DONCASTER - 36A | DONCASTER - 36A | GRANTHAM - 35B | DONCASTER - 36A | DONCASTER - 36A |
| Aug-51 | DONCASTER - 36A | DONCASTER - 36A | DONCASTER - 36A | DONCASTER - 36A | DONCASTER - 36A | DONCASTER - 36A | GRANTHAM - 35B | DONCASTER - 36A | DONCASTER - 36A |
| Jan-52 | DONCASTER - 36A | DONCASTER - 36A | DONCASTER - 36A | DONCASTER - 36A | DONCASTER - 36A | DONCASTER - 36A | GRANTHAM - 35B | DONCASTER - 36A | DONCASTER - 36A |
| Aug-52 | DONCASTER - 36A | DONCASTER - 36A | DONCASTER - 36A | DONCASTER - 36A | DONCASTER - 36A | DONCASTER - 36A | GRANTHAM - 35B | DONCASTER - 36A | DONCASTER - 36A |
| Jan-53 | DONCASTER - 36A | DONCASTER - 36A | DONCASTER - 36A | DONCASTER - 36A | DONCASTER - 36A | DONCASTER - 36A | GRANTHAM - 35B | DONCASTER - 36A | DONCASTER - 36A |
| Aug-53 | DONCASTER - 36A | DONCASTER - 36A | DONCASTER - 36A | DONCASTER - 36A | DONCASTER - 36A | DONCASTER - 36A | GRANTHAM - 35B | 5/53: FROD - 36C | DONCASTER - 36A |
| Jan-54 | DONCASTER - 36A | DONCASTER - 36A | DONCASTER - 36A | DONCASTER - 36A | DONCASTER - 36A | DONCASTER - 36A | GRANTHAM - 35B | 1/54: RET - 36E | DONCASTER - 36A |
| Aug-54 | DONCASTER - 36A | DONCASTER - 36A | DONCASTER - 36A | DONCASTER - 36A | DONCASTER - 36A | DONCASTER - 36A | GRANTHAM - 35B | RETFORD - 36E | DONCASTER - 36A |
| Jan-55 | DONCASTER - 36A | DONCASTER - 36A | DONCASTER - 36A | DONCASTER - 36A | DONCASTER - 36A | DONCASTER - 36A | GRANTHAM - 35B | RETFORD - 36E | DONCASTER - 36A |
| Aug-55 | DONCASTER - 36A | DONCASTER - 36A | DONCASTER - 36A | DONCASTER - 36A | DONCASTER - 36A | DONCASTER - 36A | GRANTHAM - 35B | RETFORD - 36E | DONCASTER - 36A |
| Jan-56 | DONCASTER - 36A | DONCASTER - 36A | DONCASTER - 36A | DONCASTER - 36A | DONCASTER - 36A | DONCASTER - 36A | GRANTHAM - 35B | RETFORD - 36E | DONCASTER - 36A |
| Aug-56 | DONCASTER - 36A | DONCASTER - 36A | DONCASTER - 36A | DONCASTER - 36A | DONCASTER - 36A | DONCASTER - 36A | GRANTHAM - 35B | RETFORD - 36E | DONCASTER - 36A |
| Jan-57 | DONCASTER - 36A | DONCASTER - 36A | DONCASTER - 36A | DONCASTER - 36A | DONCASTER - 36A | DONCASTER - 36A | GRANTHAM - 35B | RETFORD - 36E | DONCASTER - 36A |
| Aug-57 | DONCASTER - 36A | DONCASTER - 36A | DONCASTER - 36A | DONCASTER - 36A | DONCASTER - 36A | DONCASTER - 36A | GRANTHAM - 35B | RETFORD - 36E | DONCASTER - 36A |
| Jan-58 | DONCASTER - 36A | DONCASTER - 36A | DONCASTER - 36A | DONCASTER - 36A | DONCASTER - 36A | 2/58: RET - 36E | GRANTHAM - 35B | RETFORD - 36E | DONCASTER - 36A |
| Aug-58 | DONCASTER - 36A | DONCASTER - 36A | DONCASTER - 36A | DONCASTER - 36A | DONCASTER - 36A | RETFORD - 36E | GRANTHAM - 34F | RETFORD - 36E | DONCASTER - 36A |
| Jan-59 | DONCASTER - 36A | DONCASTER - 36A | DONCASTER - 36A | DONCASTER - 36A | DONCASTER - 36A | RETFORD - 36E | GRANTHAM - 34F | RETFORD - 36E | DONCASTER - 36A |
| Aug-59 | DONCASTER - 36A | DONCASTER - 36A | DONCASTER - 36A | 6/59: GRAN - 34F | DONCASTER - 36A | RETFORD - 36E | GRANTHAM - 34F | RETFORD - 36E | DONCASTER - 36A |
| Nov-59 | DONCASTER - 36A | DONCASTER - 36A | DONCASTER - 36A | GRANTHAM - 34F | DONCASTER - 36A | RETFORD - 36E | GRANTHAM - 34F | RETFORD - 36E | DONCASTER - 36A |
| Jan-60 | 2/.60: RET - 36E | DONCASTER - 36A | DONCASTER - 36A | GRANTHAM - 34F | DONCASTER - 36A | RETFORD - 36E | GRANTHAM - 34F | RETFORD - 36E | DONCASTER - 36A |
| Apr-60 | RETFORD - 36E | DONCASTER - 36A | DONCASTER - 36A | GRANTHAM - 34F | DONCASTER - 36A | RETFORD - 36E | GRANTHAM - 34F | RETFORD - 36E | DONCASTER - 36A |
| Aug-60 | RETFORD - 36E | DONCASTER - 36A | DONCASTER - 36A | GRANTHAM - 34F | DONCASTER - 36A | RETFORD - 36E | GRANTHAM - 34F | RETFORD - 36E | DONCASTER - 36A |
| Nov-60 | RETFORD - 36E | 11/60: RET - 36E | DONCASTER - 36A | GRANTHAM - 34F | DONCASTER - 36A | 11/60: W/D | GRANTHAM - 34F | RETFORD - 36E | DONCASTER - 36A |

| | 63963 | 63964 | 63965 | 63966 | 63967 | 63968 | 63969 | 63970 | 63971 |
|---|---|---|---|---|---|---|---|---|---|
| Aug-50 | FRODINGHAM - 36C | DONCASTER - 36A | GRANTHAM - 35B | GRANTHAM - 35B | DONCASTER - 36A | DONCASTER - 36A | MEXBOROUGH - 36B | MEXBOROUGH - 36B | MEXBOROUGH - 36B |
| Jan-51 | FRODINGHAM - 36C | DONCASTER - 36A | GRANTHAM - 35B | GRANTHAM - 35B | DONCASTER - 36A | DONCASTER - 36A | 3/51: DCTR - 36A | MEXBOROUGH - 36B | 3/51: DCTR - 36A |
| Aug-51 | FRODINGHAM - 36C | DONCASTER - 36A | 10/51: MEX - 36B | GRANTHAM - 35B | DONCASTER - 36A | DONCASTER - 36A | DONCASTER - 36A | 8/51: RET - 36E | DONCASTER - 36A |
| Jan-52 | FRODINGHAM - 36C | DONCASTER - 36A | 3/52: RET - 36E | GRANTHAM - 35B | DONCASTER - 36A | DONCASTER - 36A | DONCASTER - 36A | RETFORD - 36E | DONCASTER - 36A |
| Aug-52 | FRODINGHAM - 36C | DONCASTER - 36A | RETFORD - 36E | GRANTHAM - 35B | DONCASTER - 36A | DONCASTER - 36A | DONCASTER - 36A | RETFORD - 36E | DONCASTER - 36A |
| Jan-53 | FRODINGHAM - 36C | DONCASTER - 36A | RETFORD - 36E | GRANTHAM - 35B | DONCASTER - 36A | DONCASTER - 36A | DONCASTER - 36A | RETFORD - 36E | DONCASTER - 36A |
| Aug-53 | FRODINGHAM - 36C | DONCASTER - 36A | RETFORD - 36E | GRANTHAM - 35B | DONCASTER - 36A | DONCASTER - 36A | DONCASTER - 36A | RETFORD - 36E | DONCASTER - 36A |
| Jan-54 | FRODINGHAM - 36C | DONCASTER - 36A | RETFORD - 36E | GRANTHAM - 35B | DONCASTER - 36A | DONCASTER - 36A | DONCASTER - 36A | RETFORD - 36E | DONCASTER - 36A |
| Aug-54 | 6/54: DCTR - 36A | DONCASTER - 36A | RETFORD - 36E | GRANTHAM - 35B | DONCASTER - 36A | DONCASTER - 36A | DONCASTER - 36A | RETFORD - 36E | DONCASTER - 36A |
| Jan-55 | DONCASTER - 36A | DONCASTER - 36A | RETFORD - 36E | GRANTHAM - 35B | DONCASTER - 36A | DONCASTER - 36A | DONCASTER - 36A | RETFORD - 36E | DONCASTER - 36A |
| Aug-55 | DONCASTER - 36A | DONCASTER - 36A | RETFORD - 36E | GRANTHAM - 35B | DONCASTER - 36A | DONCASTER - 36A | DONCASTER - 36A | RETFORD - 36E | DONCASTER - 36A |
| Jan-56 | DONCASTER - 36A | DONCASTER - 36A | RETFORD - 36E | GRANTHAM - 35B | DONCASTER - 36A | DONCASTER - 36A | DONCASTER - 36A | RETFORD - 36E | DONCASTER - 36A |
| Aug-56 | DONCASTER - 36A | DONCASTER - 36A | RETFORD - 36E | GRANTHAM - 35B | DONCASTER - 36A | DONCASTER - 36A | DONCASTER - 36A | RETFORD - 36E | DONCASTER - 36A |
| Jan-57 | DONCASTER - 36A | DONCASTER - 36A | RETFORD - 36E | GRANTHAM - 35B | DONCASTER - 36A | DONCASTER - 36A | DONCASTER - 36A | RETFORD - 36E | DONCASTER - 36A |
| Aug-57 | DONCASTER - 36A | DONCASTER - 36A | RETFORD - 36E | GRANTHAM - 35B | DONCASTER - 36A | DONCASTER - 36A | DONCASTER - 36A | RETFORD - 36E | DONCASTER - 36A |
| Jan-58 | DONCASTER - 36A | DONCASTER - 36A | RETFORD - 36E | GRANTHAM - 35B | DONCASTER - 36A | DONCASTER - 36A | DONCASTER - 36A | RETFORD - 36E | DONCASTER - 36A |
| Aug-58 | DONCASTER - 36A | DONCASTER - 36A | RETFORD - 36E | GRANTHAM - 34F | DONCASTER - 36A | DONCASTER - 36A | DONCASTER - 36A | RETFORD - 36E | 5/58: RET - 36E |
| Jan-59 | DONCASTER - 36A | DONCASTER - 36A | RETFORD - 36E | GRANTHAM - 34F | DONCASTER - 36A | DONCASTER - 36A | DONCASTER - 36A | RETFORD - 36E | RETFORD - 36E |
| Aug-59 | 6/59: GRAN - 34F | DONCASTER - 36A | RETFORD - 36E | GRANTHAM - 34F | DONCASTER - 36A | DONCASTER - 36A | DONCASTER - 36A | RETFORD - 36E | RETFORD - 36E |
| Nov-59 | GRANTHAM - 34F | DONCASTER - 36A | RETFORD - 36E | GRANTHAM - 34F | DONCASTER - 36A | DONCASTER - 36A | DONCASTER - 36A | RETFORD - 36E | RETFORD - 36E |
| Jan-60 | GRANTHAM - 34F | 2/60: RET - 36E | RETFORD - 36E | GRANTHAM - 34F | DONCASTER - 36A | DONCASTER - 36A | 2/60: RET - 36E | RETFORD - 36E | RETFORD - 36E |
| Apr-60 | GRANTHAM - 34F | RETFORD - 36E | RETFORD - 36E | GRANTHAM - 34F | DONCASTER - 36A | DONCASTER - 36A | RETFORD - 36E | 4/60: W/D | RETFORD - 36E |
| Aug-60 | GRANTHAM - 34F | RETFORD - 36E | RETFORD - 36E | GRANTHAM - 34F | DONCASTER - 36A | DONCASTER - 36A | RETFORD - 36E | | RETFORD - 36E |
| Nov-60 | GRANTHAM - 34F | RETFORD - 36E | RETFORD - 36E | GRANTHAM - 34F | DONCASTER - 36A | DONCASTER - 36A | RETFORD - 36E | | RETFORD - 36E |

| | 63972 | 63973 | 63974 | 63975 | 63976 | 63977 | 63978 | 63979 | 63980 |
|---|---|---|---|---|---|---|---|---|---|
| Aug-50 | MEXBOROUGH - 36B | DONCASTER - 36A | DONCASTER - 36A | MEXBOROUGH - 36B | MEXBOROUGH - 36B | MEXBOROUGH - 36B | MEXBOROUGH - 36B | MEXBOROUGH - 36B | MEXBOROUGH - 36B |
| Jan-51 | MEXBOROUGH - 36B | DONCASTER - 36A | DONCASTER - 36A | 3/51: DCTR - 36A | MEXBOROUGH - 36B | 3/51: DCTR - 36A | 3/51: DCTR - 36A | 3/51: DCTR - 36A | 2/51: DCTR - 36A |
| Aug-51 | 8/51: RET - 36E | DONCASTER - 36A | DONCASTER - 36A | DONCASTER - 36A | 8/51: RET - 36E | DONCASTER - 36A | DONCASTER - 36A | DONCASTER - 36A | DONCASTER - 36A |
| Jan-52 | RETFORD - 36E | DONCASTER - 36A | DONCASTER - 36A | DONCASTER - 36A | RETFORD - 36E | DONCASTER - 36A | DONCASTER - 36A | DONCASTER - 36A | DONCASTER - 36A |
| Aug-52 | RETFORD - 36E | DONCASTER - 36A | DONCASTER - 36A | DONCASTER - 36A | RETFORD - 36E | DONCASTER - 36A | DONCASTER - 36A | 9/52: RET - 36E | 9/52: RET - 36E |
| Jan-53 | RETFORD - 36E | DONCASTER - 36A | DONCASTER - 36A | DONCASTER - 36A | RETFORD - 36E | DONCASTER - 36A | DONCASTER - 36A | RETFORD - 36E | RETFORD - 36E |
| Aug-53 | RETFORD - 36E | DONCASTER - 36A | DONCASTER - 36A | DONCASTER - 36A | RETFORD - 36E | DONCASTER - 36A | DONCASTER - 36A | RETFORD - 36E | RETFORD - 36E |
| Jan-54 | RETFORD - 36E | DONCASTER - 36A | DONCASTER - 36A | DONCASTER - 36A | RETFORD - 36E | DONCASTER - 36A | DONCASTER - 36A | RETFORD - 36E | RETFORD - 36E |
| Aug-54 | RETFORD - 36E | DONCASTER - 36A | DONCASTER - 36A | DONCASTER - 36A | RETFORD - 36E | DONCASTER - 36A | DONCASTER - 36A | RETFORD - 36E | RETFORD - 36E |
| Jan-55 | RETFORD - 36E | DONCASTER - 36A | DONCASTER - 36A | DONCASTER - 36A | RETFORD - 36E | DONCASTER - 36A | DONCASTER - 36A | RETFORD - 36E | RETFORD - 36E |
| Aug-55 | RETFORD - 36E | DONCASTER - 36A | DONCASTER - 36A | DONCASTER - 36A | RETFORD - 36E | DONCASTER - 36A | DONCASTER - 36A | RETFORD - 36E | RETFORD - 36E |
| Jan-56 | RETFORD - 36E | DONCASTER - 36A | DONCASTER - 36A | DONCASTER - 36A | RETFORD - 36E | DONCASTER - 36A | DONCASTER - 36A | RETFORD - 36E | RETFORD - 36E |
| Aug-56 | RETFORD - 36E | DONCASTER - 36A | DONCASTER - 36A | DONCASTER - 36A | RETFORD - 36E | DONCASTER - 36A | DONCASTER - 36A | RETFORD - 36E | RETFORD - 36E |
| Jan-57 | RETFORD - 36E | DONCASTER - 36A | DONCASTER - 36A | DONCASTER - 36A | RETFORD - 36E | DONCASTER - 36A | DONCASTER - 36A | RETFORD - 36E | RETFORD - 36E |
| Aug-57 | RETFORD - 36E | DONCASTER - 36A | DONCASTER - 36A | DONCASTER - 36A | RETFORD - 36E | DONCASTER - 36A | DONCASTER - 36A | RETFORD - 36E | RETFORD - 36E |
| Jan-58 | RETFORD - 36E | DONCASTER - 36A | DONCASTER - 36A | DONCASTER - 36A | RETFORD - 36E | DONCASTER - 36A | DONCASTER - 36A | RETFORD - 36E | RETFORD - 36E |
| Aug-58 | RETFORD - 36E | DONCASTER - 36A | DONCASTER - 36A | DONCASTER - 36A | RETFORD - 36E | DONCASTER - 36A | DONCASTER - 36A | RETFORD - 36E | RETFORD - 36E |
| Jan-59 | RETFORD - 36E | DONCASTER - 36A | DONCASTER - 36A | DONCASTER - 36A | RETFORD - 36E | DONCASTER - 36A | DONCASTER - 36A | RETFORD - 36E | RETFORD - 36E |
| Aug-59 | RETFORD - 36E | DONCASTER - 36A | DONCASTER - 36A | DONCASTER - 36A | RETFORD - 36E | DONCASTER - 36A | DONCASTER - 36A | RETFORD - 36E | RETFORD - 36E |
| Nov-59 | RETFORD - 36E | DONCASTER - 36A | DONCASTER - 36A | DONCASTER - 36A | RETFORD - 36E | DONCASTER - 36A | DONCASTER - 36A | RETFORD - 36E | RETFORD - 36E |
| Jan-60 | RETFORD - 36E | DONCASTER - 36A | DONCASTER - 36A | DONCASTER - 36A | RETFORD - 36E | DONCASTER - 36A | DONCASTER - 36A | RETFORD - 36E | RETFORD - 36E |
| Apr-60 | RETFORD - 36E | DONCASTER - 36A | DONCASTER - 36A | DONCASTER - 36A | RETFORD - 36E | DONCASTER - 36A | DONCASTER - 36A | RETFORD - 36E | RETFORD - 36E |
| Aug-60 | RETFORD - 36E | DONCASTER - 36A | DONCASTER - 36A | DONCASTER - 36A | RETFORD - 36E | DONCASTER - 36A | DONCASTER - 36A | RETFORD - 36E | RETFORD - 36E |
| Nov-60 | RETFORD - 36E | 11/60: RET - 36E | DONCASTER - 36A | 11/60: RET - 36E | RETFORD - 36E | DONCASTER - 36A | DONCASTER - 36A | RETFORD - 36E | RETFORD - 36E |

**J3 0-6-0 (1912)** (above column 64105)

| | 63981 | 63982 | 63983 | 63984 | 63985 | 63986 | 63987 | 64105 | 64114 |
|---|---|---|---|---|---|---|---|---|---|
| Aug-50 | RETFORD-36E | MEXBOROUGH-36B | MEXBOROUGH-36B | MEXBOROUGH-36B | MEXBOROUGH-36B | DONCASTER-36A | DONCASTER-36A | HITCHIN-34D | HITCHIN-34D |
| Jan-51 | RETFORD-36E | MEXBOROUGH-36B | MEXBOROUGH-36B | MEXBOROUGH-36B | MEXBOROUGH-36B | DONCASTER-36A | DONCASTER-36A | HITCHIN-34D | HITCHIN-34D |
| Aug-51 | RETFORD-36E | 8/51: RET-36E | MEXBOROUGH-36B | MEXBOROUGH-36B | MEXBOROUGH-36B | DONCASTER-36A | DONCASTER-36A | 9/51: ARDS-37A | HITCHIN-34D |
| Jan-52 | RETFORD-36E | RETFORD-36E | MEXBOROUGH-36B | MEXBOROUGH-36B | MEXBOROUGH-36B | DONCASTER-36A | DONCASTER-36A | 1/52: W/D | HITCHIN-34D |
| Aug-52 | 9/52: DCTR-36A | RETFORD-36E | 9/52: FROD-36C | 9/52: FROD-36C | 9/52: FROD-36C | 9/52: RET-36E | 9/52: RET-36E | | 10/52: W/D |
| Jan-53 | DONCASTER-36A | RETFORD-36E | FRODINGHAM-36C | FRODINGHAM-36C | FRODINGHAM-36C | RETFORD-36E | RETFORD-36E | | |
| Aug-53 | DONCASTER-36A | RETFORD-36E | FRODINGHAM-36C | FRODINGHAM-36C | FRODINGHAM-36C | RETFORD-36E | RETFORD-36E | | |
| Jan-54 | DONCASTER-36A | RETFORD-36E | FRODINGHAM-36C | FRODINGHAM-36C | FRODINGHAM-36C | RETFORD-36E | RETFORD-36E | | |
| Aug-54 | DONCASTER-36A | RETFORD-36E | 6/54: DCTR-36A | 8/54: DCTR-36A | 6/54: DCTR-36A | RETFORD-36E | RETFORD-36E | | |
| Jan-55 | DONCASTER-36A | RETFORD-36E | DONCASTER-36A | DONCASTER-36A | DONCASTER-36A | RETFORD-36E | RETFORD-36E | | |
| Aug-55 | DONCASTER-36A | RETFORD-36E | DONCASTER-36A | DONCASTER-36A | DONCASTER-36A | RETFORD-36E | RETFORD-36E | | |
| Jan-56 | DONCASTER-36A | RETFORD-36E | DONCASTER-36A | DONCASTER-36A | DONCASTER-36A | RETFORD-36E | RETFORD-36E | | |
| Aug-56 | DONCASTER-36A | RETFORD-36E | DONCASTER-36A | DONCASTER-36A | DONCASTER-36A | RETFORD-36E | RETFORD-36E | | |
| Jan-57 | DONCASTER-36A | RETFORD-36E | DONCASTER-36A | DONCASTER-36A | DONCASTER-36A | RETFORD-36E | RETFORD-36E | | |
| Aug-57 | DONCASTER-36A | RETFORD-36E | DONCASTER-36A | DONCASTER-36A | DONCASTER-36A | RETFORD-36E | RETFORD-36E | | |
| Jan-58 | DONCASTER-36A | RETFORD-36E | DONCASTER-36A | DONCASTER-36A | DONCASTER-36A | RETFORD-36E | RETFORD-36E | | |
| Aug-58 | DONCASTER-36A | RETFORD-36E | DONCASTER-36A | DONCASTER-36A | DONCASTER-36A | RETFORD-36E | RETFORD-36E | | |
| Jan-59 | DONCASTER-36A | RETFORD-36E | DONCASTER-36A | DONCASTER-36A | DONCASTER-36A | RETFORD-36E | RETFORD-36E | | |
| Aug-59 | DONCASTER-36A | RETFORD-36E | DONCASTER-36A | DONCASTER-36A | DONCASTER-36A | RETFORD-36E | RETFORD-36E | | |
| Nov-59 | DONCASTER-36A | RETFORD-36E | DONCASTER-36A | DONCASTER-36A | DONCASTER-36A | RETFORD-36E | RETFORD-36E | | |
| Jan-60 | DONCASTER-36A | RETFORD-36E | DONCASTER-36A | DONCASTER-36A | DONCASTER-36A | RETFORD-36E | RETFORD-36E | | |
| Apr-60 | DONCASTER-36A | RETFORD-36E | DONCASTER-36A | DONCASTER-36A | DONCASTER-36A | RETFORD-36E | RETFORD-36E | | |
| Aug-60 | DONCASTER-36A | RETFORD-36E | DONCASTER-36A | DONCASTER-36A | DONCASTER-36A | RETFORD-36E | RETFORD-36E | | |
| Nov-60 | DONCASTER-36A | RETFORD-36E | 11/60: RET-36E | DONCASTER-36A | DONCASTER-36A | RETFORD-36E | RETFORD-36E | | |

| | 64115 | 64116 | 64117 | 64118 | 64119 | 64122 | 64123 | 64124 | 64125 |
|---|---|---|---|---|---|---|---|---|---|
| Aug-50 | BOSTON-40F | ARDSLEY-37A | HITCHIN-34D | NEWENGLAND-35A | ARDSLEY-37A | HITCHIN-34D | NEWENGLAND-35A | DONCASTER-36A | RETFORD-36E |
| Jan-51 | BOSTON-40F | ARDSLEY-37A | HITCHIN-34D | NEWENGLAND-35A | ARDSLEY-37A | HITCHIN-34D | NEWENGLAND-35A | DONCASTER-36A | RETFORD-36E |
| Aug-51 | 3/51: W/D | 5/51: NEWE-35A | HITCHIN-34D | NEWENGLAND-35A | 5/51: NEWE-35A | HITCHIN-34D | 5/51: W/D | DONCASTER-36A | RETFORD-36E |
| Jan-52 | | NEWENGLAND-35A | HITCHIN-34D | 3/52: ARDS-37A | NEWENGLAND-35A | HITCHIN-34D | | 9/51: W/D | RETFORD-36E |
| Aug-52 | | 6/52: W/D | 6/52: W/D | 6/52: W/D | NEWENGLAND-35A | HITCHIN-34D | | | RETFORD-36E |
| Jan-53 | | | | | NEWENGLAND-35A | HITCHIN-34D | | | RETFORD-36E |
| Aug-53 | | | | | NEWENGLAND-35A | 5/53: W/D | | | RETFORD-36E |
| Jan-54 | | | | | 12/53: W/D | | | | 12/53: W/D |

| | 64128 | 64129 | 64131 | 64132 | 64133 | 64135 | 64137 | 64140 | 64141 |
|---|---|---|---|---|---|---|---|---|---|
| Aug-50 | NEWENGLAND-35A | ARDSLEY-37A | NEWENGLAND-35A | BOSTON-40F | MEXBOROUGH-36B | NEWENGLAND-35A | BOSTON-40F | HITCHIN-34D | RETFORD-36E |
| Jan-51 | 11/50: W/D | ARDSLEY-37A | NEWENGLAND-35A | BOSTON-40F | MEXBOROUGH-36B | NEWENGLAND-35A | BOSTON-40F | HITCHIN-34D | RETFORD-36E |
| Aug-51 | | ARDSLEY-37A | NEWENGLAND-35A | BOSTON-40F | MEXBOROUGH-36B | 2/51: W/D | 2/51: W/D | HITCHIN-34D | RETFORD-36E |
| Jan-52 | | ARDSLEY-37A | NEWENGLAND-35A | BOSTON-40F | MEXBOROUGH-36B | | | HITCHIN-34D | RETFORD-36E |
| Aug-52 | | ARDSLEY-37A | NEWENGLAND-35A | BOSTON-40F | MEXBOROUGH-36B | | | 2/53: RET-36E | RETFORD-36E |
| Jan-53 | | 9/52: W/D | NEWENGLAND-35A | BOSTON-40F | 1/53: W/D | | | RETFORD-36E | RETFORD-36E |
| Aug-53 | | | NEWENGLAND-35A | BOSTON-40F | | | | RETFORD-36E | 9/53: W/D |
| Jan-54 | | | NEWENGLAND-35A | 11/53: RET-36E | | | | RETFORD-36E | |
| Aug-54 | | | 6/54: W/D | 6/54: W/D | | | | 12/54: W/D | |

**J4 0-6-0 (1896)** (above column 64112)

| | 64142 | 64148 | 64150 | 64151 | 64153 | 64158 | 64112 | 64120 | 64121 |
|---|---|---|---|---|---|---|---|---|---|
| Aug-50 | ARDSLEY-37A | RETFORD-36E | RETFORD-36E | NEWENGLAND-35A | HITCHIN-34D | NEWENGLAND-35A | NEWENGLAND-35A | NEWENGLAND-35A | NEWENGLAND-35A |
| Jan-51 | ARDSLEY-37A | RETFORD-36E | RETFORD-36E | NEWENGLAND-35A | HITCHIN-34D | NEWENGLAND-35A | NEWENGLAND-35A | 11/50: W/D | 11/50: W/D |
| Aug-51 | 8/51: W/D | 4/51: W/D | 6/51: W/D | 3/51: W/D | HITCHIN-34D | NEWENGLAND-35A | 12/51: W/D | | |
| Jan-52 | | | | | HITCHIN-34D | NEWENGLAND-35A | | | |
| Aug-52 | | | | | 5/52: W/D | NEWENGLAND-35A | | | |
| Jan-53 | | | | | | NEWENGLAND-35A | | | |
| Aug-53 | | | | | | NEWENGLAND-35A | | | |
| Jan-54 | | | | | | NEWENGLAND-35A | | | |
| Aug-54 | | | | | | NEWENGLAND-35A | | | |
| Jan-55 | | | | | | 12/54: W/D | | | |

| | 64160 | 64162 | J6 0-6-0 (1911) 64170 | 64171 | 64172 | 64173 | 64174 | 64175 | 64176 |
|---|---|---|---|---|---|---|---|---|---|
| Aug-50 | NEWENGLAND - 35A | NEWENGLAND - 35A | BRADFORD - 37C | NEWENGLAND - 35A | GRANTHAM - 35B | COPLEY HILL - 37B | ARDSLEY - 37A | HITCHIN - 34D | NEWENGLAND - 35A |
| Jan-51 | NEWENGLAND - 35A | NEWENGLAND - 35A | BRADFORD - 37C | NEWENGLAND - 35A | GRANTHAM - 35B | COPLEY HILL - 37B | ARDSLEY - 37A | HITCHIN - 34D | NEWENGLAND - 35A |
| Aug-51 | NEWENGLAND - 35A | NEWENGLAND - 35A | BRADFORD - 37C | NEWENGLAND - 35A | GRANTHAM - 35B | COPLEY HILL - 37B | ARDSLEY - 37A | HITCHIN - 34D | NEWENGLAND - 35A |
| Jan-52 | 12/51: W/D | 12/51: W/D | BRADFORD - 37C | NEWENGLAND - 35A | GRANTHAM - 35B | COPLEY HILL - 37B | ARDSLEY - 37A | HITCHIN - 34D | NEWENGLAND - 35A |
| Aug-52 | | | BRADFORD - 37C | NEWENGLAND - 35A | 6/52: NEWE - 35A | COPLEY HILL - 37B | ARDSLEY - 37A | HITCHIN - 34D | NEWENGLAND - 35A |
| Jan-53 | | | BRADFORD - 37C | NEWENGLAND - 35A | NEWENGLAND - 35A | COPLEY HILL - 37B | ARDSLEY - 37A | HITCHIN - 34D | NEWENGLAND - 35A |
| Aug-53 | | | BRADFORD - 37C | NEWENGLAND - 35A | NEWENGLAND - 35A | COPLEY HILL - 37B | ARDSLEY - 37A | HITCHIN - 34D | NEWENGLAND - 35A |
| Jan-54 | | | BRADFORD - 37C | NEWENGLAND - 35A | NEWENGLAND - 35A | COPLEY HILL - 37B | ARDSLEY - 37A | HITCHIN - 34D | NEWENGLAND - 35A |
| Aug-54 | | | BRADFORD - 37C | NEWENGLAND - 35A | NEWENGLAND - 35A | COPLEY HILL - 37B | ARDSLEY - 37A | HITCHIN - 34D | NEWENGLAND - 35A |
| Jan-55 | | | BRADFORD - 37C | NEWENGLAND - 35A | NEWENGLAND - 35A | COPLEY HILL - 37B | ARDSLEY - 37A | HITCHIN - 34D | NEWENGLAND - 35A |
| Aug-55 | | | BRADFORD - 37C | NEWENGLAND - 35A | NEWENGLAND - 35A | COPLEY HILL - 37B | ARDSLEY - 37A | HITCHIN - 34D | NEWENGLAND - 35A |
| Jan-56 | | | BRADFORD - 37C | NEWENGLAND - 35A | NEWENGLAND - 35A | COPLEY HILL - 37B | 12/55: RET - 36E | HITCHIN - 34D | NEWENGLAND - 35A |
| Aug-56 | | | BRADFORD - 56G | NEWENGLAND - 35A | NEWENGLAND - 35A | COPLEY HILL - 56C | RETFORD - 36E | HITCHIN - 34D | NEWENGLAND - 35A |
| Jan-57 | | | BRADFORD - 56G | NEWENGLAND - 35A | NEWENGLAND - 35A | COPLEY HILL - 56C | RETFORD - 36E | HITCHIN - 34D | NEWENGLAND - 35A |
| Aug-57 | | | BRADFORD - 56G | NEWENGLAND - 35A | NEWENGLAND - 35A | COPLEY HILL - 56C | RETFORD - 36E | HITCHIN - 34D | NEWENGLAND - 35A |
| Jan-58 | | | 1/58: LOWM - 56F | 12/57: BOST - 40F | 12/57: BOST - 40F | COPLEY HILL - 56C | RETFORD - 36E | HITCHIN - 34D | NEWENGLAND - 35A |
| Aug-58 | | | LOWMOOR - 56F | BOSTON - 40F | BOSTON - 40F | COPLEY HILL - 56C | RETFORD - 36E | HITCHIN - 34D | NEWENGLAND - 34E |
| Jan-59 | | | LOWMOOR - 56F | BOSTON - 40F | BOSTON - 40F | COPLEY HILL - 56C | RETFORD - 36E | HITCHIN - 34D | NEWENGLAND - 34E |
| Aug-59 | | | LOWMOOR - 56F | BOSTON - 40F | BOSTON - 40F | COPLEY HILL - 56C | RETFORD - 36E | HITCHIN - 34D | 3/59: W/D |
| Nov-59 | | | LOWMOOR - 56F | BOSTON - 40F | BOSTON - 40F | COPLEY HILL - 56C | RETFORD - 36E | HITCHIN - 34D | |
| Jan-60 | | | LOWMOOR - 56F | BOSTON - 40F | BOSTON - 40F | COPLEY HILL - 56C | RETFORD - 36E | HITCHIN - 34D | |
| Apr-60 | | | LOWMOOR - 56F | BOSTON - 40F | 3/60: W/D | COPLEY HILL - 56C | RETFORD - 36E | HITCHIN - 34D | |
| Aug-60 | | | LOWMOOR - 56F | BOSTON - 40F | | COPLEY HILL - 56C | RETFORD - 36E | 5/60: W/D | |
| Nov-60 | | | 10/60: ARDS - 56B | BOSTON - 40F | | 11/60: ARDS - 56B | RETFORD - 36E | | |

| | 64177 | 64178 | 64179 | 64180 | 64181 | 64182 | 64183 | 64184 | 64185 |
|---|---|---|---|---|---|---|---|---|---|
| Aug-50 | NEWENGLAND - 35A | GRANTHAM - 35B | DONCASTER - 36A | BOSTON - 40F | BOSTON - 40F | ARDSLEY - 37A | DONCASTER - 36A | NEWENGLAND - 35A | DONCASTER - 36A |
| Jan-51 | NEWENGLAND - 35A | GRANTHAM - 35B | DONCASTER - 36A | BOSTON - 40F | BOSTON - 40F | ARDSLEY - 37A | DONCASTER - 36A | NEWENGLAND - 35A | DONCASTER - 36A |
| Aug-51 | NEWENGLAND - 35A | GRANTHAM - 35B | DONCASTER - 36A | BOSTON - 40F | BOSTON - 40F | ARDSLEY - 37A | DONCASTER - 36A | NEWENGLAND - 35A | DONCASTER - 36A |
| Jan-52 | NEWENGLAND - 35A | GRANTHAM - 35B | DONCASTER - 36A | BOSTON - 40F | BOSTON - 40F | ARDSLEY - 37A | DONCASTER - 36A | NEWENGLAND - 35A | DONCASTER - 36A |
| Aug-52 | NEWENGLAND - 35A | GRANTHAM - 35B | DONCASTER - 36A | BOSTON - 40F | BOSTON - 40F | ARDSLEY - 37A | DONCASTER - 36A | NEWENGLAND - 35A | DONCASTER - 36A |
| Jan-53 | NEWENGLAND - 35A | GRANTHAM - 35B | DONCASTER - 36A | BOSTON - 40F | 3/53: NEWE - 35A | ARDSLEY - 37A | DONCASTER - 36A | NEWENGLAND - 35A | DONCASTER - 36A |
| Aug-53 | NEWENGLAND - 35A | GRANTHAM - 35B | DONCASTER - 36A | BOSTON - 40F | NEWENGLAND - 35A | ARDSLEY - 37A | DONCASTER - 36A | NEWENGLAND - 35A | DONCASTER - 36A |
| Jan-54 | NEWENGLAND - 35A | GRANTHAM - 35B | DONCASTER - 36A | BOSTON - 40F | NEWENGLAND - 35A | ARDSLEY - 37A | 12/53: COLW - 38A | NEWENGLAND - 35A | DONCASTER - 36A |
| Aug-54 | NEWENGLAND - 35A | GRANTHAM - 35B | DONCASTER - 36A | BOSTON - 40F | NEWENGLAND - 35A | ARDSLEY - 37A | COLWICK - 38A | NEWENGLAND - 35A | DONCASTER - 36A |
| Jan-55 | NEWENGLAND - 35A | GRANTHAM - 35B | DONCASTER - 36A | BOSTON - 40F | NEWENGLAND - 35A | ARDSLEY - 37A | COLWICK - 38A | NEWENGLAND - 35A | DONCASTER - 36A |
| Aug-55 | NEWENGLAND - 35A | GRANTHAM - 35B | DONCASTER - 36A | BOSTON - 40F | NEWENGLAND - 35A | ARDSLEY - 37A | COLWICK - 38A | NEWENGLAND - 35A | DONCASTER - 36A |
| Jan-56 | NEWENGLAND - 35A | GRANTHAM - 35B | DONCASTER - 36A | BOSTON - 40F | NEWENGLAND - 35A | ARDSLEY - 37A | COLWICK - 38A | NEWENGLAND - 35A | DONCASTER - 36A |
| Aug-56 | NEWENGLAND - 35A | GRANTHAM - 35B | DONCASTER - 36A | BOSTON - 40F | NEWENGLAND - 35A | ARDSLEY - 56B | COLWICK - 38A | NEWENGLAND - 35A | DONCASTER - 36A |
| Jan-57 | NEWENGLAND - 35A | GRANTHAM - 35B | DONCASTER - 36A | BOSTON - 40F | NEWENGLAND - 35A | ARDSLEY - 56B | COLWICK - 38A | NEWENGLAND - 35A | DONCASTER - 36A |
| Aug-57 | NEWENGLAND - 35A | GRANTHAM - 35B | DONCASTER - 36A | BOSTON - 40F | NEWENGLAND - 35A | ARDSLEY - 56B | COLWICK - 38A | NEWENGLAND - 35A | DONCASTER - 36A |
| Jan-58 | NEWENGLAND - 35A | GRANTHAM - 35B | DONCASTER - 36A | BOSTON - 40F | 1/58: GRAN - 35B | ARDSLEY - 56B | 11/57: LEIC - 38C | 2/58: HIT - 34D | DONCASTER - 36A |
| Aug-58 | NEWENGLAND - 34E | 7/58: RET - 36E | DONCASTER - 36A | BOSTON - 40F | GRANTHAM - 34F | ARDSLEY - 56B | LEICESTER (GC) - 15E | HITCHIN - 34D | DONCASTER - 36A |
| Jan-59 | NEWENGLAND - 34E | RETFORD - 36E | DONCASTER - 36A | BOSTON - 40F | GRANTHAM - 34F | ARDSLEY - 56B | 11/58: W/D | HITCHIN - 34D | DONCASTER - 36A |
| Aug-59 | NEWENGLAND - 34E | RETFORD - 36E | DONCASTER - 36A | 9/59: NEWE - 34E | 8/59: W/D | ARDSLEY - 56B | | HITCHIN - 34D | DONCASTER - 36A |
| Nov-59 | NEWENGLAND - 34E | RETFORD - 36E | DONCASTER - 36A | NEWENGLAND - 34E | | ARDSLEY - 56B | | 11/59: W/D | DONCASTER - 36A |
| Jan-60 | NEWENGLAND - 34E | RETFORD - 36E | DONCASTER - 36A | NEWENGLAND - 34E | | ARDSLEY - 56B | | | DONCASTER - 36A |
| Apr-60 | NEWENGLAND - 34E | 4/60: W/D | 4/60: W/D | 3/60: W/D | | ARDSLEY - 56B | | | DONCASTER - 36A |
| Aug-60 | NEWENGLAND - 34E | | | | | ARDSLEY - 56B | | | DONCASTER - 36A |
| Nov-60 | NEWENGLAND - 34E | | | | | ARDSLEY - 56B | | | DONCASTER - 36A |

| | 64186 | 64187 | 64188 | 64189 | 64190 | 64191 | 64192 | 64193 | 64194 |
|---|---|---|---|---|---|---|---|---|---|
| Aug-50 | NEWENGLAND - 35A | NEWENGLAND - 35A | HORNSEY - 34B | NEWENGLAND - 35A | BOSTON - 40F | NEWENGLAND - 35A | NEWENGLAND - 35A | DONCASTER - 36A | COLWICK - 38A |
| Jan-51 | 2/51: GRAN - 35B | 11/50: GRAM - 35B | 1/51: RET - 36E | NEWENGLAND - 35A | BOSTON - 40F | NEWENGLAND - 35A | NEWENGLAND - 35A | DONCASTER - 36A | COLWICK - 38A |
| Aug-51 | GRANTHAM - 35B | GRANTHAM - 35B | RETFORD - 36E | NEWENGLAND - 35A | BOSTON - 40F | NEWENGLAND - 35A | NEWENGLAND - 35A | DONCASTER - 36A | COLWICK - 38A |
| Jan-52 | GRANTHAM - 35B | GRANTHAM - 35B | RETFORD - 36E | NEWENGLAND - 35A | BOSTON - 40F | NEWENGLAND - 35A | NEWENGLAND - 35A | DONCASTER - 36A | COLWICK - 38A |
| Aug-52 | GRANTHAM - 35B | GRANTHAM - 35B | RETFORD - 36E | NEWENGLAND - 35A | BOSTON - 40F | NEWENGLAND - 35A | NEWENGLAND - 35A | DONCASTER - 36A | COLWICK - 38A |
| Jan-53 | 2/53: HIT - 34D | GRANTHAM - 35B | RETFORD - 36E | NEWENGLAND - 35A | BOSTON - 40F | NEWENGLAND - 35A | NEWENGLAND - 35A | DONCASTER - 36A | COLWICK - 38A |
| Aug-53 | HITCHIN - 34D | GRANTHAM - 35B | RETFORD - 36E | NEWENGLAND - 35A | BOSTON - 40F | NEWENGLAND - 35A | NEWENGLAND - 35A | DONCASTER - 36A | COLWICK - 38A |
| Jan-54 | HITCHIN - 34D | GRANTHAM - 35B | RETFORD - 36E | NEWENGLAND - 35A | BOSTON - 40F | NEWENGLAND - 35A | NEWENGLAND - 35A | DONCASTER - 36A | COLWICK - 38A |
| Aug-54 | HITCHIN - 34D | GRANTHAM - 35B | RETFORD - 36E | NEWENGLAND - 35A | BOSTON - 40F | NEWENGLAND - 35A | NEWENGLAND - 35A | DONCASTER - 36A | COLWICK - 38A |
| Jan-55 | HITCHIN - 34D | GRANTHAM - 35B | RETFORD - 36E | NEWENGLAND - 35A | BOSTON - 40F | NEWENGLAND - 35A | NEWENGLAND - 35A | DONCASTER - 36A | COLWICK - 38A |
| Aug-55 | HITCHIN - 34D | GRANTHAM - 35B | RETFORD - 36E | NEWENGLAND - 35A | BOSTON - 40F | NEWENGLAND - 35A | NEWENGLAND - 35A | DONCASTER - 36A | COLWICK - 38A |
| Jan-56 | HITCHIN - 34D | GRANTHAM - 35B | RETFORD - 36E | NEWENGLAND - 35A | BOSTON - 40F | NEWENGLAND - 35A | NEWENGLAND - 35A | DONCASTER - 36A | 11/55: W/D |
| Aug-56 | HITCHIN - 34D | GRANTHAM - 35B | RETFORD - 36E | NEWENGLAND - 35A | BOSTON - 40F | NEWENGLAND - 35A | NEWENGLAND - 35A | DONCASTER - 36A | |
| Jan-57 | HITCHIN - 34D | GRANTHAM - 35B | RETFORD - 36E | NEWENGLAND - 35A | BOSTON - 40F | NEWENGLAND - 35A | NEWENGLAND - 35A | DONCASTER - 36A | |
| Aug-57 | HITCHIN - 34D | GRANTHAM - 35B | RETFORD - 36E | NEWENGLAND - 35A | BOSTON - 40F | NEWENGLAND - 35A | NEWENGLAND - 35A | DONCASTER - 36A | |
| Jan-58 | 1/58: W/D | 1/58: W/D | RETFORD - 36E | NEWENGLAND - 35A | BOSTON - 40F | 12/57: BOST - 40F | 2/58: GRAN - 35B | 12/57: W/D | |
| Aug-58 | | | RETFORD - 36E | NEWENGLAND - 34E | BOSTON - 40F | BOSTON - 40F | 4/58: NEWE - 34E | | |
| Jan-59 | | | RETFORD - 36E | 10/58: W/D | BOSTON - 40F | BOSTON - 40F | NEWENGLAND - 34E | | |
| Aug-59 | | | RETFORD - 36E | | BOSTON - 40F | BOSTON - 40F | NEWENGLAND - 34E | | |
| Nov-59 | | | 10/59: W/D | | 9/59: W/D | BOSTON - 40F | NEWENGLAND - 34E | | |
| Jan-60 | | | | | | BOSTON - 40F | NEWENGLAND - 34E | | |
| Apr-60 | | | | | | BOSTON - 40F | 4/60: W/D | | |
| Aug-60 | | | | | | BOSTON - 40F | | | |
| Nov-60 | | | | | | BOSTON - 40F | | | |

| | 64195 | 64196 | 64197 | 64198 | 64199 | 64200 | 64201 | 64202 | 64203 |
|---|---|---|---|---|---|---|---|---|---|
| Aug-50 | DONCASTER - 36A | BOSTON - 40F | COLWICK - 38A | BOSTON - 40F | COLWICK - 38A | COLWICK - 38A | BOSTON - 40F | COLWICK - 38A | BRADFORD - 37C |
| Jan-51 | DONCASTER - 36A | BOSTON - 40F | COLWICK - 38A | BOSTON - 40F | COLWICK - 38A | COLWICK - 38A | BOSTON - 40F | COLWICK - 38A | BRADFORD - 37C |
| Aug-51 | DONCASTER - 36A | BOSTON - 40F | COLWICK - 38A | BOSTON - 40F | COLWICK - 38A | COLWICK - 38A | BOSTON - 40F | COLWICK - 38A | BRADFORD - 37C |
| Jan-52 | DONCASTER - 36A | BOSTON - 40F | COLWICK - 38A | BOSTON - 40F | COLWICK - 38A | COLWICK - 38A | BOSTON - 40F | COLWICK - 38A | BRADFORD - 37C |
| Aug-52 | DONCASTER - 36A | BOSTON - 40F | COLWICK - 38A | BOSTON - 40F | COLWICK - 38A | COLWICK - 38A | BOSTON - 40F | COLWICK - 38A | BRADFORD - 37C |
| Jan-53 | DONCASTER - 36A | BOSTON - 40F | 11/52: HIT - 34D | 3/53: NEWE - 35A | COLWICK - 38A | COLWICK - 38A | BOSTON - 40F | COLWICK - 38A | BRADFORD - 37C |
| Aug-53 | DONCASTER - 36A | BOSTON - 40F | HITCHIN - 34D | NEWENGLAND - 35A | COLWICK - 38A | COLWICK - 38A | BOSTON - 40F | COLWICK - 38A | BRADFORD - 37C |
| Jan-54 | DONCASTER - 36A | 11/53: HORN - 34B | HITCHIN - 34D | NEWENGLAND - 35A | COLWICK - 38A | COLWICK - 38A | BOSTON - 40F | COLWICK - 38A | BRADFORD - 37C |
| Aug-54 | DONCASTER - 36A | HORNSEY - 34B | HITCHIN - 34D | NEWENGLAND - 35A | COLWICK - 38A | COLWICK - 38A | BOSTON - 40F | COLWICK - 38A | BRADFORD - 37C |
| Jan-55 | DONCASTER - 36A | HORNSEY - 34B | HITCHIN - 34D | NEWENGLAND - 35A | COLWICK - 38A | COLWICK - 38A | BOSTON - 40F | COLWICK - 38A | BRADFORD - 37C |
| Aug-55 | DONCASTER - 36A | HORNSEY - 34B | HITCHIN - 34D | NEWENGLAND - 35A | COLWICK - 38A | COLWICK - 38A | BOSTON - 40F | COLWICK - 38A | BRADFORD - 37C |
| Jan-56 | 1/56: COLW - 38A | HORNSEY - 34B | HITCHIN - 34D | NEWENGLAND - 35A | COLWICK - 38A | COLWICK - 38A | BOSTON - 40F | COLWICK - 38A | 5/56: ARDS - 37A |
| Aug-56 | COLWICK - 38A | HORNSEY - 34B | HITCHIN - 34D | NEWENGLAND - 35A | COLWICK - 38A | COLWICK - 38A | BOSTON - 40F | COLWICK - 38A | 6/56: BRAD - 56G |
| Jan-57 | COLWICK - 38A | HORNSEY - 34B | HITCHIN - 34D | NEWENGLAND - 35A | COLWICK - 38A | COLWICK - 38A | BOSTON - 40F | COLWICK - 38A | BRADFORD - 56G |
| Aug-57 | COLWICK - 38A | HORNSEY - 34B | HITCHIN - 34D | NEWENGLAND - 35A | COLWICK - 38A | COLWICK - 38A | BOSTON - 40F | COLWICK - 38A | BRADFORD - 56G |
| Jan-58 | 1/58: W/D | HORNSEY - 34B | HITCHIN - 34D | 2/58: HIT - 34D | COLWICK - 38A | COLWICK - 38A | BOSTON - 40F | COLWICK - 38A | 2/58: LOWM - 56F |
| Aug-58 | | HORNSEY - 34B | HITCHIN - 34D | HITCHIN - 34D | 4/58: W/D | 2/58: W/D | BOSTON - 40F | COLWICK - 40E | 4/58: WAKE - 56A |
| Jan-59 | | HORNSEY - 34B | HITCHIN - 34D | HITCHIN - 34D | | | 11/58: W/D | 9/58: W/D | 6/58: LOWM - 56F |
| Aug-59 | | HORNSEY - 34B | HITCHIN - 34D | 3/59: W/D | | | | | LOWMOOR - 56F |
| Nov-59 | | HORNSEY - 34B | 10/59: W/D | | | | | | LOWMOOR - 56F |
| Jan-60 | | HORNSEY - 34B | | | | | | | LOWMOOR - 56F |
| Apr-60 | | 3/60: NEWE - 34E | | | | | | | LOWMOOR - 56F |
| Aug-60 | | NEWENGLAND - 34E | | | | | | | LOWMOOR - 56F |
| Nov-60 | | 9/60: W/D | | | | | | | 10/60: C.HILL - 56C |

| | 64204 | 64205 | 64206 | 64207 | 64208 | 64209 | 64210 | 64211 | 64212 |
|---|---|---|---|---|---|---|---|---|---|
| Aug-50 | BOSTON - 40F | BRADFORD - 37C | GRANTHAM - 35B | NEWENGLAND - 35A | ARDSLEY - 37A | DONCASTER - 36A | BOSTON - 40F | NEWENGLAND - 35A | COLWICK - 38A |
| Jan-51 | BOSTON - 40F | BRADFORD - 37C | GRANTHAM - 35B | NEWENGLAND - 35A | ARDSLEY - 37A | DONCASTER - 36A | BOSTON - 40F | NEWENGLAND - 35A | COLWICK - 38A |
| Aug-51 | BOSTON - 40F | BRADFORD - 37C | GRANTHAM - 35B | NEWENGLAND - 35A | ARDSLEY - 37A | DONCASTER - 36A | BOSTON - 40F | NEWENGLAND - 35A | COLWICK - 38A |
| Jan-52 | BOSTON - 40F | BRADFORD - 37C | GRANTHAM - 35B | NEWENGLAND - 35A | ARDSLEY - 37A | DONCASTER - 36A | BOSTON - 40F | NEWENGLAND - 35A | COLWICK - 38A |
| Aug-52 | BOSTON - 40F | BRADFORD - 37C | GRANTHAM - 35B | NEWENGLAND - 35A | ARDSLEY - 37A | DONCASTER - 36A | 9/52: NEWE - 35A | NEWENGLAND - 35A | COLWICK - 38A |
| Jan-53 | BOSTON - 40F | BRADFORD - 37C | 2/53: HIT - 34D | NEWENGLAND - 35A | ARDSLEY - 37A | DONCASTER - 36A | NEWENGLAND - 35A | NEWENGLAND - 35A | COLWICK - 38A |
| Aug-53 | BOSTON - 40F | BRADFORD - 37C | HITCHIN - 34D | NEWENGLAND - 35A | ARDSLEY - 37A | DONCASTER - 36A | NEWENGLAND - 35A | NEWENGLAND - 35A | COLWICK - 38A |
| Jan-54 | BOSTON - 40F | BRADFORD - 37C | HITCHIN - 34D | NEWENGLAND - 35A | ARDSLEY - 37A | DONCASTER - 36A | NEWENGLAND - 35A | NEWENGLAND - 35A | COLWICK - 38A |
| Aug-54 | BOSTON - 40F | BRADFORD - 37C | HITCHIN - 34D | NEWENGLAND - 35A | ARDSLEY - 37A | DONCASTER - 36A | NEWENGLAND - 35A | NEWENGLAND - 35A | COLWICK - 38A |
| Jan-55 | BOSTON - 40F | BRADFORD - 37C | HITCHIN - 34D | NEWENGLAND - 35A | ARDSLEY - 37A | DONCASTER - 36A | NEWENGLAND - 35A | NEWENGLAND - 35A | COLWICK - 38A |
| Aug-55 | BOSTON - 40F | BRADFORD - 37C | HITCHIN - 34D | NEWENGLAND - 35A | ARDSLEY - 37A | DONCASTER - 36A | NEWENGLAND - 35A | NEWENGLAND - 35A | COLWICK - 38A |
| Jan-56 | BOSTON - 40F | BRADFORD - 37C | HITCHIN - 34D | NEWENGLAND - 35A | ARDSLEY - 37A | DONCASTER - 36A | NEWENGLAND - 35A | NEWENGLAND - 35A | 12/55: W/D |
| Aug-56 | BOSTON - 40F | 6/56: ARDS - 37A | HITCHIN - 34D | NEWENGLAND - 35A | ARDSLEY - 56B | DONCASTER - 36A | NEWENGLAND - 35A | NEWENGLAND - 35A | |
| Jan-57 | BOSTON - 40F | ARDSLEY - 56B | HITCHIN - 34D | NEWENGLAND - 35A | ARDSLEY - 56B | DONCASTER - 36A | NEWENGLAND - 35A | NEWENGLAND - 35A | |
| Aug-57 | BOSTON - 40F | ARDSLEY - 56B | HITCHIN - 34D | NEWENGLAND - 35A | ARDSLEY - 56B | DONCASTER - 36A | NEWENGLAND - 35A | NEWENGLAND - 35A | |
| Jan-58 | 12/57: W/D | ARDSLEY - 56B | HITCHIN - 34D | 12/57: BOST - 40F | ARDSLEY - 56B | DONCASTER - 36A | NEWENGLAND - 35A | NEWENGLAND - 35A | |
| Aug-58 | | ARDSLEY - 56B | HITCHIN - 34D | BOSTON - 40F | ARDSLEY - 56B | DONCASTER - 36A | NEWENGLAND - 34E | 3/58: W/D | |
| Jan-59 | | 10/58: W/D | HITCHIN - 34D | BOSTON - 40F | ARDSLEY - 56B | DONCASTER - 36A | NEWENGLAND - 34E | | |
| Aug-59 | | | HITCHIN - 34D | 4/59: LINC - 40A | ARDSLEY - 56B | DONCASTER - 36A | 5/59: W/D | | |
| Nov-59 | | | HITCHIN - 34D | 10/59: W/D | ARDSLEY - 56B | DONCASTER - 36A | | | |
| Jan-60 | | | HITCHIN - 34D | | ARDSLEY - 56B | DONCASTER - 36A | | | |
| Apr-60 | | | HITCHIN - 34D | | ARDSLEY - 56B | DONCASTER - 36A | | | |
| Aug-60 | | | 6/60: NEWE - 34E | | ARDSLEY - 56B | DONCASTER - 36A | | | |
| Nov-60 | | | 10/60: W/D | | ARDSLEY - 56B | 9/60: W/D | | | |

| | 64213 | 64214 | 64215 | 64216 | 64217 | 64218 | 64219 | 64220 | 64221 |
|---|---|---|---|---|---|---|---|---|---|
| Aug-50 | COLWICK - 38A | ARDSLEY - 37A | COLWICK - 38A | NEWENGLAND - 35A | NEWENGLAND - 35A | DONCASTER - 36A | DONCASTER - 36A | NEWENGLAND - 35A | NEWENGLAND - 35A |
| Jan-51 | COLWICK - 38A | ARDSLEY - 37A | COLWICK - 38A | NEWENGLAND - 35A | NEWENGLAND - 35A | DONCASTER - 36A | DONCASTER - 36A | NEWENGLAND - 35A | NEWENGLAND - 35A |
| Aug-51 | COLWICK - 38A | 5/51: BOST - 40F | COLWICK - 38A | NEWENGLAND - 35A | NEWENGLAND - 35A | DONCASTER - 36A | DONCASTER - 36A | NEWENGLAND - 35A | NEWENGLAND - 35A |
| Jan-52 | COLWICK - 38A | BOSTON - 40F | COLWICK - 38A | NEWENGLAND - 35A | NEWENGLAND - 35A | DONCASTER - 36A | DONCASTER - 36A | NEWENGLAND - 35A | NEWENGLAND - 35A |
| Aug-52 | COLWICK - 38A | BOSTON - 40F | COLWICK - 38A | NEWENGLAND - 35A | NEWENGLAND - 35A | DONCASTER - 36A | 7/52: NEWE - 35A | NEWENGLAND - 35A | 9/52: HORN - 34B |
| Jan-53 | COLWICK - 38A | BOSTON - 40F | COLWICK - 38A | NEWENGLAND - 35A | NEWENGLAND - 35A | DONCASTER - 36A | NEWENGLAND - 35A | NEWENGLAND - 35A | HORNSEY - 34B |
| Aug-53 | COLWICK - 38A | BOSTON - 40F | COLWICK - 38A | NEWENGLAND - 35A | NEWENGLAND - 35A | DONCASTER - 36A | NEWENGLAND - 35A | NEWENGLAND - 35A | HORNSEY - 34B |
| Jan-54 | COLWICK - 38A | BOSTON - 40F | COLWICK - 38A | NEWENGLAND - 35A | NEWENGLAND - 35A | 12/53: COLW - 38A | NEWENGLAND - 35A | NEWENGLAND - 35A | HORNSEY - 34B |
| Aug-54 | COLWICK - 38A | BOSTON - 40F | COLWICK - 38A | NEWENGLAND - 35A | NEWENGLAND - 35A | COLWICK - 38A | NEWENGLAND - 35A | NEWENGLAND - 35A | HORNSEY - 34B |
| Jan-55 | COLWICK - 38A | BOSTON - 40F | COLWICK - 38A | NEWENGLAND - 35A | NEWENGLAND - 35A | COLWICK - 38A | NEWENGLAND - 35A | NEWENGLAND - 35A | HORNSEY - 34B |
| Aug-55 | COLWICK - 38A | BOSTON - 40F | COLWICK - 38A | NEWENGLAND - 35A | NEWENGLAND - 35A | COLWICK - 38A | NEWENGLAND - 35A | NEWENGLAND - 35A | HORNSEY - 34B |
| Jan-56 | COLWICK - 38A | BOSTON - 40F | COLWICK - 38A | NEWENGLAND - 35A | NEWENGLAND - 35A | COLWICK - 38A | NEWENGLAND - 35A | NEWENGLAND - 35A | 11/55: COLW - 38A |
| Aug-56 | COLWICK - 38A | BOSTON - 40F | COLWICK - 38A | NEWENGLAND - 35A | NEWENGLAND - 35A | COLWICK - 38A | NEWENGLAND - 35A | NEWENGLAND - 35A | COLWICK - 38A |
| Jan-57 | COLWICK - 38A | BOSTON - 40F | COLWICK - 38A | NEWENGLAND - 35A | NEWENGLAND - 35A | COLWICK - 38A | NEWENGLAND - 35A | NEWENGLAND - 35A | COLWICK - 38A |
| Aug-57 | COLWICK - 38A | BOSTON - 40F | COLWICK - 38A | NEWENGLAND - 35A | NEWENGLAND - 35A | COLWICK - 38A | NEWENGLAND - 35A | NEWENGLAND - 35A | COLWICK - 38A |
| Jan-58 | COLWICK - 38A | BOSTON - 40F | COLWICK - 38A | NEWENGLAND - 35A | NEWENGLAND - 35A | 2/58: LEIC - 38C | NEWENGLAND - 35A | NEWENGLAND - 35A | 1/58: W/D |
| Aug-58 | COLWICK - 40E | BOSTON - 40F | COLWICK - 40E | 4/58: LINC - 40A | NEWENGLAND - 34E | 6/58: COLW - 40E | 4/58: LINC - 40A | 6/58: W/D | |
| Jan-59 | COLWICK - 40E | BOSTON - 40F | COLWICK - 40E | 12/58: W/D | 1/59: W/D | 9/58: W/D | LINCOLN - 40A | | |
| Aug-59 | COLWICK - 40E | BOSTON - 40F | 3/59: W/D | | | | LINCOLN - 40A | | |
| Nov-59 | COLWICK - 40E | 10/59: W/D | | | | | LINCOLN - 40A | | |
| Jan-60 | COLWICK - 40E | | | | | | LINCOLN - 40A | | |
| Apr-60 | 3/60: W/D | | | | | | 3/60: COLW - 40E | | |
| Aug-60 | | | | | | | COLWICK - 40E | | |
| Nov-60 | | | | | | | COLWICK - 40E | | |

| | 64222 | 64223 | 64224 | 64225 | 64226 | 64227 | 64228 | 64229 | 64230 |
|---|---|---|---|---|---|---|---|---|---|
| Aug-50 | COLWICK - 38A | COLWICK - 38A | COLWICK - 38A | NEWENGLAND - 35A | BRADFORD - 37C | GRANTHAM - 35B | NEWENGLAND - 35A | BOSTON - 40F | COLWICK - 38A |
| Jan-51 | COLWICK - 38A | COLWICK - 38A | COLWICK - 38A | 2/51: COLW - 38A | BRADFORD - 37C | GRANTHAM - 35B | NEWENGLAND - 35A | BOSTON - 40F | COLWICK - 38A |
| Aug-51 | COLWICK - 38A | COLWICK - 38A | COLWICK - 38A | COLWICK - 38A | BRADFORD - 37C | GRANTHAM - 35B | NEWENGLAND - 35A | BOSTON - 40F | COLWICK - 38A |
| Jan-52 | COLWICK - 38A | COLWICK - 38A | COLWICK - 38A | COLWICK - 38A | BRADFORD - 37C | GRANTHAM - 35B | NEWENGLAND - 35A | BOSTON - 40F | COLWICK - 38A |
| Aug-52 | COLWICK - 38A | COLWICK - 38A | COLWICK - 38A | COLWICK - 38A | BRADFORD - 37C | GRANTHAM - 35B | NEWENGLAND - 35A | BOSTON - 40F | COLWICK - 38A |
| Jan-53 | COLWICK - 38A | COLWICK - 38A | 11/52: NEWE - 35A | COLWICK - 38A | BRADFORD - 37C | GRANTHAM - 35B | NEWENGLAND - 35A | BOSTON - 40F | COLWICK - 38A |
| Aug-53 | COLWICK - 38A | COLWICK - 38A | NEWENGLAND - 35A | COLWICK - 38A | BRADFORD - 37C | GRANTHAM - 35B | NEWENGLAND - 35A | BOSTON - 40F | COLWICK - 38A |
| Jan-54 | 11/53: HORN - 34B | 11/53: HORN - 34B | NEWENGLAND - 35A | COLWICK - 38A | BRADFORD - 37C | GRANTHAM - 35B | NEWENGLAND - 35A | BOSTON - 40F | COLWICK - 38A |
| Aug-54 | HORNSEY - 34B | HORNSEY - 34B | NEWENGLAND - 35A | COLWICK - 38A | BRADFORD - 37C | GRANTHAM - 35B | NEWENGLAND - 35A | BOSTON - 40F | COLWICK - 38A |
| Jan-55 | HORNSEY - 34B | HORNSEY - 34B | NEWENGLAND - 35A | COLWICK - 38A | BRADFORD - 37C | GRANTHAM - 35B | NEWENGLAND - 35A | BOSTON - 40F | COLWICK - 38A |
| Aug-55 | HORNSEY - 34B | HORNSEY - 34B | NEWENGLAND - 35A | COLWICK - 38A | BRADFORD - 37C | GRANTHAM - 35B | NEWENGLAND - 35A | BOSTON - 40F | COLWICK - 38A |
| Jan-56 | 3/56: ARDS - 37A | HORNSEY - 34B | NEWENGLAND - 35A | COLWICK - 38A | 5/56: ARDS - 37A | GRANTHAM - 35B | NEWENGLAND - 35A | BOSTON - 40F | COLWICK - 38A |
| Aug-56 | ARDSLEY - 56B | HORNSEY - 34B | NEWENGLAND - 35A | COLWICK - 38A | 6/56: BRAD - 37C | GRANTHAM - 35B | NEWENGLAND - 35A | BOSTON - 40F | COLWICK - 38A |
| Jan-57 | ARDSLEY - 56B | HORNSEY - 34B | NEWENGLAND - 35A | COLWICK - 38A | BRADFORD - 56G | GRANTHAM - 35B | NEWENGLAND - 35A | BOSTON - 40F | COLWICK - 38A |
| Aug-57 | ARDSLEY - 56B | HORNSEY - 34B | NEWENGLAND - 35A | COLWICK - 38A | BRADFORD - 56G | GRANTHAM - 35B | NEWENGLAND - 35A | BOSTON - 40F | COLWICK - 38A |
| Jan-58 | ARDSLEY - 56B | HORNSEY - 34B | NEWENGLAND - 35A | COLWICK - 38A | 2/58: LOWM - 56F | GRANTHAM - 35B | NEWENGLAND - 35A | BOSTON - 40F | 1/58: W/D |
| Aug-58 | ARDSLEY - 56B | HORNSEY - 34B | NEWENGLAND - 34E | 7/58: W/D | LOWMOOR - 56F | 7/58: W/D | NEWENGLAND - 34E | BOSTON - 40F | |
| Jan-59 | ARDSLEY - 56B | HORNSEY - 34B | NEWENGLAND - 34E | | LOWMOOR - 56F | | NEWENGLAND - 34E | BOSTON - 40F | |
| Aug-59 | ARDSLEY - 56B | HORNSEY - 34B | 5/59: W/D | | LOWMOOR - 56F | | 8/59: W/D | BOSTON - 40F | |
| Nov-59 | ARDSLEY - 56B | HORNSEY - 34B | | | LOWMOOR - 56F | | | 10/59: W/D | |
| Jan-60 | ARDSLEY - 56B | HORNSEY - 34B | | | LOWMOOR - 56F | | | | |
| Apr-60 | ARDSLEY - 56B | 3/60: NEWE - 34E | | | LOWMOOR - 56F | | | | |
| Aug-60 | ARDSLEY - 56B | NEWENGLAND - 34E | | | LOWMOOR - 56F | | | | |
| Nov-60 | ARDSLEY - 56B | NEWENGLAND - 34E | | | 10/60: ARDS - 56B | | | | |

| | 64231 | 64232 | 64233 | 64234 | 64235 | 64236 | 64237 | 64238 | 64239 |
|---|---|---|---|---|---|---|---|---|---|
| Aug-50 | COLWICK - 38A | DONCASTER - 36A | COLWICK - 38A | HORNSEY - 34B | NEWENGLAND - 35A | DONCASTER - 36A | GRANTHAM - 35B | NEWENGLAND - 35A | HORNSEY - 34B |
| Jan-51 | COLWICK - 38A | DONCASTER - 36A | COLWICK - 38A | 3/51: RET - 36E | 2/51: COLW - 38A | DONCASTER - 36A | GRANTHAM - 35B | 2/51: COLW - 38A | HORNSEY - 34B |
| Aug-51 | COLWICK - 38A | DONCASTER - 36A | COLWICK - 38A | RETFORD - 36E | COLWICK - 38A | DONCASTER - 36A | GRANTHAM - 35B | COLWICK - 38A | HORNSEY - 34B |
| Jan-52 | COLWICK - 38A | DONCASTER - 36A | COLWICK - 38A | RETFORD - 36E | COLWICK - 38A | DONCASTER - 36A | GRANTHAM - 35B | COLWICK - 38A | HORNSEY - 34B |
| Aug-52 | COLWICK - 38A | DONCASTER - 36A | COLWICK - 38A | RETFORD - 36E | COLWICK - 38A | DONCASTER - 36A | GRANTHAM - 35B | COLWICK - 38A | HORNSEY - 34B |
| Jan-53 | 3/53: NEWE - 35A | DONCASTER - 36A | COLWICK - 38A | RETFORD - 36E | COLWICK - 38A | DONCASTER - 36A | 2/53: HIT - 34D | COLWICK - 38A | HORNSEY - 34B |
| Aug-53 | NEWENGLAND - 35A | DONCASTER - 36A | COLWICK - 38A | RETFORD - 36E | COLWICK - 38A | DONCASTER - 36A | HITCHIN - 34D | COLWICK - 38A | HORNSEY - 34B |
| Jan-54 | NEWENGLAND - 35A | DONCASTER - 36A | 11/53: HORN - 34B | RETFORD - 36E | COLWICK - 38A | DONCASTER - 36A | HITCHIN - 34D | COLWICK - 38A | HORNSEY - 34B |
| Aug-54 | NEWENGLAND - 35A | DONCASTER - 36A | HORNSEY - 34B | RETFORD - 36E | COLWICK - 38A | DONCASTER - 36A | HITCHIN - 34D | COLWICK - 38A | HORNSEY - 34B |
| Jan-55 | NEWENGLAND - 35A | DONCASTER - 36A | HORNSEY - 34B | RETFORD - 36E | COLWICK - 38A | DONCASTER - 36A | HITCHIN - 34D | COLWICK - 38A | HORNSEY - 34B |
| Aug-55 | NEWENGLAND - 35A | DONCASTER - 36A | HORNSEY - 34B | RETFORD - 36E | COLWICK - 38A | DONCASTER - 36A | HITCHIN - 34D | COLWICK - 38A | HORNSEY - 34B |
| Jan-56 | NEWENGLAND - 35A | DONCASTER - 36A | HORNSEY - 34B | RETFORD - 36E | COLWICK - 38A | DONCASTER - 36A | HITCHIN - 34D | COLWICK - 38A | 11/55: COLW - 38A |
| Aug-56 | NEWENGLAND - 35A | DONCASTER - 36A | HORNSEY - 34B | RETFORD - 36E | COLWICK - 38A | DONCASTER - 36A | HITCHIN - 34D | COLWICK - 38A | COLWICK - 38A |
| Jan-57 | NEWENGLAND - 35A | DONCASTER - 36A | HORNSEY - 34B | RETFORD - 36E | COLWICK - 38A | 10/56: RET - 36E | HITCHIN - 34D | COLWICK - 38A | COLWICK - 38A |
| Aug-57 | NEWENGLAND - 35A | DONCASTER - 36A | HORNSEY - 34B | RETFORD - 36E | COLWICK - 38A | RETFORD - 36E | HITCHIN - 34D | COLWICK - 38A | COLWICK - 38A |
| Jan-58 | 12/57: BOST - 40F | DONCASTER - 36A | HORNSEY - 34B | RETFORD - 36E | COLWICK - 38A | RETFORD - 36E | HITCHIN - 34D | COLWICK - 38A | COLWICK - 38A |
| Aug-58 | BOSTON - 40F | DONCASTER - 36A | HORNSEY - 34B | RETFORD - 36E | COLWICK - 40E | RETFORD - 36E | HITCHIN - 34D | COLWICK - 40E | COLWICK - 40E |
| Jan-59 | BOSTON - 40F | DONCASTER - 36A | HORNSEY - 34B | RETFORD - 36E | COLWICK - 40E | RETFORD - 36E | HITCHIN - 34D | COLWICK - 40E | COLWICK - 40E |
| Aug-59 | BOSTON - 40F | DONCASTER - 36A | HORNSEY - 34B | RETFORD - 36E | COLWICK - 40E | RETFORD - 36E | HITCHIN - 34D | COLWICK - 40E | COLWICK - 40E |
| Nov-59 | BOSTON - 40F | DONCASTER - 36A | HORNSEY - 34B | RETFORD - 36E | 11/59: W/D | RETFORD - 36E | 11/59: W/D | 10/59: W/D | 10/59: W/D |
| Jan-60 | BOSTON - 40F | DONCASTER - 36A | 2/60: NEWE - 34E | 12/59: W/D | | RETFORD - 36E | | | |
| Apr-60 | BOSTON - 40F | DONCASTER - 36A | 2/60: W/D | | | RETFORD - 36E | | | |
| Aug-60 | BOSTON - 40F | DONCASTER - 36A | | | | RETFORD - 36E | | | |
| Nov-60 | BOSTON - 40F | DONCASTER - 36A | | | | RETFORD - 36E | | | |

| | 64240 | 64241 | 64242 | 64243 | 64244 | 64245 | 64246 | 64247 | 64248 |
|---|---|---|---|---|---|---|---|---|---|
| Aug-50 | HITCHIN - 34D | RETFORD - 36E | BOSTON - 40F | DONCASTER - 36A | BOSTON - 40F | NEWENGLAND - 35A | NEWENGLAND - 35A | BOSTON - 40F | BOSTON - 40F |
| Jan-51 | HITCHIN - 34D | RETFORD - 36E | BOSTON - 40F | DONCASTER - 36A | BOSTON - 40F | NEWENGLAND - 35A | NEWENGLAND - 35A | BOSTON - 40F | BOSTON - 40F |
| Aug-51 | HITCHIN - 34D | RETFORD - 36E | BOSTON - 40F | DONCASTER - 36A | BOSTON - 40F | 6/51: RET - 36E | NEWENGLAND - 35A | BOSTON - 40F | BOSTON - 40F |
| Jan-52 | HITCHIN - 34D | RETFORD - 36E | BOSTON - 40F | DONCASTER - 36A | BOSTON - 40F | RETFORD - 36E | NEWENGLAND - 35A | BOSTON - 40F | BOSTON - 40F |
| Aug-52 | HITCHIN - 34D | RETFORD - 36E | BOSTON - 40F | DONCASTER - 36A | BOSTON - 40F | RETFORD - 36E | NEWENGLAND - 35A | BOSTON - 40F | BOSTON - 40F |
| Jan-53 | HITCHIN - 34D | RETFORD - 36E | BOSTON - 40F | DONCASTER - 36A | BOSTON - 40F | RETFORD - 36E | NEWENGLAND - 35A | BOSTON - 40F | BOSTON - 40F |
| Aug-53 | HITCHIN - 34D | RETFORD - 36E | BOSTON - 40F | DONCASTER - 36A | BOSTON - 40F | RETFORD - 36E | NEWENGLAND - 35A | BOSTON - 40F | BOSTON - 40F |
| Jan-54 | HITCHIN - 34D | RETFORD - 36E | 11/53: HORN - 34B | DONCASTER - 36A | BOSTON - 40F | RETFORD - 36E | NEWENGLAND - 35A | BOSTON - 40F | BOSTON - 40F |
| Aug-54 | HITCHIN - 34D | RETFORD - 36E | HORNSEY - 34B | DONCASTER - 36A | BOSTON - 40F | RETFORD - 36E | NEWENGLAND - 35A | BOSTON - 40F | BOSTON - 40F |
| Jan-55 | HITCHIN - 34D | RETFORD - 36E | HORNSEY - 34B | DONCASTER - 36A | BOSTON - 40F | RETFORD - 36E | NEWENGLAND - 35A | BOSTON - 40F | BOSTON - 40F |
| Aug-55 | HITCHIN - 34D | RETFORD - 36E | 8/55: W/D | DONCASTER - 36A | BOSTON - 40F | RETFORD - 36E | NEWENGLAND - 35A | BOSTON - 40F | BOSTON - 40F |
| Jan-56 | HITCHIN - 34D | RETFORD - 36E | | DONCASTER - 36A | BOSTON - 40F | RETFORD - 36E | NEWENGLAND - 35A | BOSTON - 40F | 11/55: COLW - 38A |
| Aug-56 | HITCHIN - 34D | RETFORD - 36E | | DONCASTER - 36A | BOSTON - 40F | RETFORD - 36E | NEWENGLAND - 35A | BOSTON - 40F | COLWICK - 38A |
| Jan-57 | HITCHIN - 34D | RETFORD - 36E | | DONCASTER - 36A | BOSTON - 40F | RETFORD - 36E | NEWENGLAND - 35A | BOSTON - 40F | COLWICK - 38A |
| Aug-57 | HITCHIN - 34D | RETFORD - 36E | | DONCASTER - 36A | BOSTON - 40F | RETFORD - 36E | NEWENGLAND - 35A | BOSTON - 40F | COLWICK - 38A |
| Jan-58 | HITCHIN - 34D | RETFORD - 36E | | DONCASTER - 36A | BOSTON - 40F | RETFORD - 36E | 1/58: GRAN - 35B | BOSTON - 40F | COLWICK - 38A |
| Aug-58 | HITCHIN - 34D | RETFORD - 36E | | 6/58: W/D | 5/58: W/D | RETFORD - 36E | GRANTHAM - 34F | BOSTON - 40F | COLWICK - 40E |
| Jan-59 | HITCHIN - 34D | 10/58: DCTR - 36A | | | | RETFORD - 36E | GRANTHAM - 34F | BOSTON - 40F | COLWICK - 40E |
| Aug-59 | HITCHIN - 34D | DONCASTER - 36A | | | | RETFORD - 36E | 6/59: W/D | BOSTON - 40F | 3/59: W/D |
| Nov-59 | HITCHIN - 34D | 11/59: W/D | | | | RETFORD - 36E | | 10/59: W/D | |
| Jan-60 | HITCHIN - 34D | | | | | RETFORD - 36E | | | |
| Apr-60 | 5/60: NEWE - 34E | | | | | RETFORD - 36E | | | |
| Aug-60 | 8/60: W/D | | | | | RETFORD - 36E | | | |
| Nov-60 | | | | | | RETFORD - 36E | | | |

| | 64249 | 64250 | 64251 | 64252 | 64253 | 64254 | 64255 | 64256 | 64257 |
|---|---|---|---|---|---|---|---|---|---|
| Aug-50 | NEWENGLAND - 35A | COPLEY HILL - 37B | HORNSEY - 34B | NEWENGLAND - 35A | COLWICK - 38A | NEWENGLAND - 35A | DONCASTER - 36A | HORNSEY - 34B | NEWENGLAND - 35A |
| Jan-51 | 2/51: COLW - 38A | COPLEY HILL - 37B | HORNSEY - 34B | NEWENGLAND - 35A | COLWICK - 38A | NEWENGLAND - 35A | DONCASTER - 36A | HORNSEY - 34B | 2/51: COLW - 38A |
| Aug-51 | COLWICK - 38A | COPLEY HILL - 37B | HORNSEY - 34B | 6/51: RET - 36E | COLWICK - 38A | NEWENGLAND - 35A | DONCASTER - 36A | HORNSEY - 34B | COLWICK - 38A |
| Jan-52 | COLWICK - 38A | 3/52: BOST - 40F | HORNSEY - 34B | RETFORD - 36E | COLWICK - 38A | NEWENGLAND - 35A | DONCASTER - 36A | HORNSEY - 34B | COLWICK - 38A |
| Aug-52 | COLWICK - 38A | BOSTON - 40F | 5/52: NEAS - 34E | RETFORD - 36E | COLWICK - 38A | NEWENGLAND - 35A | DONCASTER - 36A | HORNSEY - 34B | COLWICK - 38A |
| Jan-53 | COLWICK - 38A | BOSTON - 40F | 1/53: HIT - 34D | RETFORD - 36E | COLWICK - 38A | NEWENGLAND - 35A | DONCASTER - 36A | HORNSEY - 34B | COLWICK - 38A |
| Aug-53 | COLWICK - 38A | BOSTON - 40F | HITCHIN - 34D | RETFORD - 36E | COLWICK - 38A | NEWENGLAND - 35A | DONCASTER - 36A | HORNSEY - 34B | COLWICK - 38A |
| Jan-54 | COLWICK - 38A | BOSTON - 40F | HITCHIN - 34D | RETFORD - 36E | 11/54: HORN - 34B | NEWENGLAND - 35A | DONCASTER - 36A | HORNSEY - 34B | COLWICK - 38A |
| Aug-54 | COLWICK - 38A | BOSTON - 40F | HITCHIN - 34D | RETFORD - 36E | HORNSEY - 34B | NEWENGLAND - 35A | DONCASTER - 36A | HORNSEY - 34B | COLWICK - 38A |
| Jan-55 | COLWICK - 38A | BOSTON - 40F | HITCHIN - 34D | RETFORD - 36E | HORNSEY - 34B | NEWENGLAND - 35A | 1/55: RET - 36E | HORNSEY - 34B | COLWICK - 38A |
| Aug-55 | COLWICK - 38A | BOSTON - 40F | HITCHIN - 34D | RETFORD - 36E | HORNSEY - 34B | NEWENGLAND - 35A | RETFORD - 36E | HORNSEY - 34B | COLWICK - 38A |
| Jan-56 | COLWICK - 38A | BOSTON - 40F | HITCHIN - 34D | RETFORD - 36E | HORNSEY - 34B | NEWENGLAND - 35A | RETFORD - 36E | 3/56: COLW - 38A | COLWICK - 38A |
| Aug-56 | COLWICK - 38A | BOSTON - 40F | HITCHIN - 34D | RETFORD - 36E | HORNSEY - 34B | NEWENGLAND - 35A | RETFORD - 36E | COLWICK - 38A | COLWICK - 38A |
| Jan-57 | COLWICK - 38A | BOSTON - 40F | HITCHIN - 34D | RETFORD - 36E | HORNSEY - 34B | NEWENGLAND - 35A | RETFORD - 36E | COLWICK - 38A | COLWICK - 38A |
| Aug-57 | COLWICK - 38A | BOSTON - 40F | HITCHIN - 34D | RETFORD - 36E | HORNSEY - 34B | NEWENGLAND - 35A | RETFORD - 36E | COLWICK - 38A | COLWICK - 38A |
| Jan-58 | COLWICK - 38A | BOSTON - 40F | HITCHIN - 34D | RETFORD - 36E | HORNSEY - 34B | 2/58: HIT - 34D | RETFORD - 36E | 11/57: LEIC - 38C | COLWICK - 38A |
| Aug-58 | COLWICK - 40E | BOSTON - 40F | HITCHIN - 34D | 7/58: W/D | HORNSEY - 34B | HITCHIN - 34D | 8/58: W/D | LEICESTER (GC) - 15E | COLWICK - 40E |
| Jan-59 | 10/58: W/D | BOSTON - 40F | HITCHIN - 34D | | HORNSEY - 34B | 12/58: NEWE - 34E | | LEICESTER (GC) - 15E | COLWICK - 40E |
| Aug-59 | | BOSTON - 40F | HITCHIN - 34D | | HORNSEY - 34B | NEWENGLAND - 34E | | GORTON - 9G | COLWICK - 40E |
| Nov-59 | | 10/59: W/D | HITCHIN - 34D | | HORNSEY - 34B | 10/59: W/D | | GORTON - 9G | COLWICK - 40E |
| Jan-60 | | | HITCHIN - 34D | | HORNSEY - 34B | | | GORTON - 9G | COLWICK - 40E |
| Apr-60 | | | 5/60: NEWE - 34E | | 3/60: NEWE - 34E | | | GORTON - 9G | COLWICK - 40E |
| Aug-60 | | | NEWENGLAND - 34E | | NEWENGLAND - 34E | | | 5/60: W/D | 6/60: W/D |
| Nov-60 | | | 10/60: W/D | | NEWENGLAND - 34E | | | | |

| | 64258 | 64259 | 64260 | 64261 | 64262 | 64263 | 64264 | 64265 | 64266 |
|---|---|---|---|---|---|---|---|---|---|
| Aug-50 | DONCASTER - 36A | DONCASTER - 36A | COPLEY HILL - 37B | DONCASTER - 36A | DONCASTER - 36A | DONCASTER - 36A | DONCASTER - 36A | NEWENGLAND - 35A | NEWENGLAND - 35A |
| Jan-51 | DONCASTER - 36A | DONCASTER - 36A | COPLEY HILL - 37B | DONCASTER - 36A | DONCASTER - 36A | DONCASTER - 36A | DONCASTER - 36A | NEWENGLAND - 35A | NEWENGLAND - 35A |
| Aug-51 | DONCASTER - 36A | DONCASTER - 36A | COPLEY HILL - 37B | DONCASTER - 36A | DONCASTER - 36A | DONCASTER - 36A | DONCASTER - 36A | NEWENGLAND - 35A | NEWENGLAND - 35A |
| Jan-52 | DONCASTER - 36A | DONCASTER - 36A | 3/52: BOST - 40F | DONCASTER - 36A | DONCASTER - 36A | DONCASTER - 36A | DONCASTER - 36A | NEWENGLAND - 35A | NEWENGLAND - 35A |
| Aug-52 | DONCASTER - 36A | 6/52: NEWE - 35A | BOSTON - 40F | DONCASTER - 36A | 9/52: ARDS - 37A | DONCASTER - 36A | DONCASTER - 36A | NEWENGLAND - 35A | 9/52: HORN - 34B |
| Jan-53 | DONCASTER - 36A | NEWENGLAND - 35A | BOSTON - 40F | DONCASTER - 36A | ARDSLEY - 37A | DONCASTER - 36A | DONCASTER - 36A | NEWENGLAND - 35A | HORNSEY - 34B |
| Aug-53 | DONCASTER - 36A | NEWENGLAND - 35A | BOSTON - 40F | DONCASTER - 36A | ARDSLEY - 37A | DONCASTER - 36A | DONCASTER - 36A | NEWENGLAND - 35A | HORNSEY - 34B |
| Jan-54 | DONCASTER - 36A | NEWENGLAND - 35A | BOSTON - 40F | DONCASTER - 36A | ARDSLEY - 37A | DONCASTER - 36A | DONCASTER - 36A | NEWENGLAND - 35A | HORNSEY - 34B |
| Aug-54 | DONCASTER - 36A | NEWENGLAND - 35A | BOSTON - 40F | DONCASTER - 36A | ARDSLEY - 37A | DONCASTER - 36A | DONCASTER - 36A | NEWENGLAND - 35A | HORNSEY - 34B |
| Jan-55 | DONCASTER - 36A | NEWENGLAND - 35A | BOSTON - 40F | DONCASTER - 36A | ARDSLEY - 37A | DONCASTER - 36A | DONCASTER - 36A | NEWENGLAND - 35A | HORNSEY - 34B |
| Aug-55 | DONCASTER - 36A | NEWENGLAND - 35A | BOSTON - 40F | DONCASTER - 36A | ARDSLEY - 37A | DONCASTER - 36A | DONCASTER - 36A | NEWENGLAND - 35A | HORNSEY - 34B |
| Jan-56 | DONCASTER - 36A | 12/55: RET - 36E | BOSTON - 40F | DONCASTER - 36A | 12/55: DCTR - 36A | DONCASTER - 36A | DONCASTER - 36A | NEWENGLAND - 35A | HORNSEY - 34B |
| Aug-56 | DONCASTER - 36A | RETFORD - 36E | BOSTON - 40F | DONCASTER - 36A | DONCASTER - 36A | DONCASTER - 36A | DONCASTER - 36A | NEWENGLAND - 35A | HORNSEY - 34B |
| Jan-57 | DONCASTER - 36A | RETFORD - 36E | BOSTON - 40F | DONCASTER - 36A | DONCASTER - 36A | DONCASTER - 36A | DONCASTER - 36A | NEWENGLAND - 35A | HORNSEY - 34B |
| Aug-57 | DONCASTER - 36A | RETFORD - 36E | BOSTON - 40F | DONCASTER - 36A | DONCASTER - 36A | DONCASTER - 36A | DONCASTER - 36A | NEWENGLAND - 35A | HORNSEY - 34B |
| Jan-58 | DONCASTER - 36A | RETFORD - 36E | BOSTON - 40F | DONCASTER - 36A | DONCASTER - 36A | DONCASTER - 36A | 1/58: W/D | NEWENGLAND - 35A | HORNSEY - 34B |
| Aug-58 | DONCASTER - 36A | RETFORD - 36E | BOSTON - 40F | DONCASTER - 36A | DONCASTER - 36A | 7/58: W/D | | NEWENGLAND - 34E | HORNSEY - 34B |
| Jan-59 | DONCASTER - 36A | 2/59: DCTR - 36A | BOSTON - 40F | DONCASTER - 36A | 2/59: W/D | | | NEWENGLAND - 34E | HORNSEY - 34B |
| Aug-59 | 5/59: W/D | 8/59: W/D | 9/59: HIT - 34D | 3/59: W/D | | | | NEWENGLAND - 34E | 4/59: W/D |
| Nov-59 | | | HITCHIN - 34D | | | | | NEWENGLAND - 34E | |
| Jan-60 | | | HITCHIN - 34D | | | | | NEWENGLAND - 34E | |
| Apr-60 | | | 4/60: KX - 34A | | | | | NEWENGLAND - 34E | |
| Aug-60 | | | KINGS CROSS - 34A | | | | | NEWENGLAND - 34E | |
| Nov-60 | | | KINGS CROSS - 34A | | | | | NEWENGLAND - 34E | |

| | 64267 | 64268 | 64269 | 64270 | 64271 | 64272 | 64273 | 64274 | 64275 |
|---|---|---|---|---|---|---|---|---|---|
| Aug-50 | ARDSLEY - 37A | BRADFORD - 37C | COLWICK - 38A | DONCASTER - 36A | BRADFORD - 37C | ARDSLEY - 37A | NEWENGLAND - 35A | BRADFORD - 37C | NEWENGLAND - 35A |
| Jan-51 | ARDSLEY - 37A | BRADFORD - 37C | COLWICK - 38A | DONCASTER - 36A | BRADFORD - 37C | ARDSLEY - 37A | 2/51: COLW - 38A | BRADFORD - 37C | NEWENGLAND - 35A |
| Aug-51 | ARDSLEY - 37A | BRADFORD - 37C | COLWICK - 38A | DONCASTER - 36A | BRADFORD - 37C | 5/51: BOS - 40F | COLWICK - 38A | BRADFORD - 37C | NEWENGLAND - 35A |
| Jan-52 | ARDSLEY - 37A | BRADFORD - 37C | COLWICK - 38A | DONCASTER - 36A | 3/52: ARDS - 37A | BOSTON - 40F | COLWICK - 38A | 3/52: ARDS - 37A | NEWENGLAND - 35A |
| Aug-52 | ARDSLEY - 37A | BRADFORD - 37C | COLWICK - 38A | DONCASTER - 36A | ARDSLEY - 37A | BOSTON - 40F | COLWICK - 38A | ARDSLEY - 37A | NEWENGLAND - 35A |
| Jan-53 | ARDSLEY - 37A | BRADFORD - 37C | COLWICK - 38A | DONCASTER - 36A | ARDSLEY - 37A | 3/53: NEWE - 35A | COLWICK - 38A | ARDSLEY - 37A | NEWENGLAND - 35A |
| Aug-53 | ARDSLEY - 37A | BRADFORD - 37C | COLWICK - 38A | DONCASTER - 36A | ARDSLEY - 37A | NEWENGLAND - 35A | COLWICK - 38A | ARDSLEY - 37A | NEWENGLAND - 35A |
| Jan-54 | ARDSLEY - 37A | BRADFORD - 37C | COLWICK - 38A | DONCASTER - 36A | ARDSLEY - 37A | NEWENGLAND - 35A | COLWICK - 38A | ARDSLEY - 37A | NEWENGLAND - 35A |
| Aug-54 | ARDSLEY - 37A | BRADFORD - 37C | COLWICK - 38A | DONCASTER - 36A | ARDSLEY - 37A | NEWENGLAND - 35A | COLWICK - 38A | ARDSLEY - 37A | NEWENGLAND - 35A |
| Jan-55 | ARDSLEY - 37A | BRADFORD - 37C | COLWICK - 38A | DONCASTER - 36A | ARDSLEY - 37A | NEWENGLAND - 35A | COLWICK - 38A | ARDSLEY - 37A | NEWENGLAND - 35A |
| Aug-55 | ARDSLEY - 37A | BRADFORD - 37C | COLWICK - 38A | DONCASTER - 36A | ARDSLEY - 37A | NEWENGLAND - 35A | COLWICK - 38A | ARDSLEY - 37A | NEWENGLAND - 35A |
| Jan-56 | 12/55: COLW - 38A | BRADFORD - 37C | COLWICK - 38A | DONCASTER - 36A | ARDSLEY - 37A | NEWENGLAND - 35A | COLWICK - 38A | ARDSLEY - 37A | NEWENGLAND - 35A |
| Aug-56 | COLWICK - 38A | 6/56: ARDS - 37A | COLWICK - 38A | DONCASTER - 36A | ARDSLEY - 56B | NEWENGLAND - 35A | COLWICK - 38A | ARDSLEY - 56B | NEWENGLAND - 35A |
| Jan-57 | COLWICK - 38A | ARDSLEY - 56B | COLWICK - 38A | DONCASTER - 36A | ARDSLEY - 56B | NEWENGLAND - 35A | COLWICK - 38A | ARDSLEY - 56B | NEWENGLAND - 35A |
| Aug-57 | COLWICK - 38A | ARDSLEY - 56B | COLWICK - 38A | DONCASTER - 36A | ARDSLEY - 56B | NEWENGLAND - 35A | COLWICK - 38A | ARDSLEY - 56B | NEWENGLAND - 35A |
| Jan-58 | COLWICK - 38A | ARDSLEY - 56B | COLWICK - 38A | DONCASTER - 36A | ARDSLEY - 56B | NEWENGLAND - 35A | COLWICK - 38A | ARDSLEY - 56B | NEWENGLAND - 35A |
| Aug-58 | 7/58: W/D | ARDSLEY - 56B | COLWICK - 40E | DONCASTER - 36A | ARDSLEY - 56B | NEWENGLAND - 34E | COLWICK - 40E | ARDSLEY - 56B | 8/58: W/D |
| Jan-59 | | ARDSLEY - 56B | COLWICK - 40E | DONCASTER - 36A | 10/58: W/D | NEWENGLAND - 34E | COLWICK - 40E | 12/58: W/D | |
| Aug-59 | | ARDSLEY - 56B | COLWICK - 40E | DONCASTER - 36A | | NEWENGLAND - 34E | COLWICK - 40E | | |
| Nov-59 | | 9/59: C.HILL - 56C | 10/59: W/D | DONCASTER - 36A | | 9/59: W/D | COLWICK - 40E | | |
| Jan-60 | | COPLEY HILL - 56C | | DONCASTER - 36A | | | 12/59: W/D | | |
| Apr-60 | | COPLEY HILL - 56C | | 4/60: W/D | | | | | |
| Aug-60 | | COPLEY HILL - 56C | | | | | | | |
| Nov-60 | | COPLEY HILL - 56C | | | | | | | |

| | 64276 | 64277 | 64278 | 64279 | 64280 | 64281 | 64282 | 64285 | 64286 |
|---|---|---|---|---|---|---|---|---|---|
| Aug-50 | BOSTON-40F | ARDSLEY-37A | NEWENGLAND-35A | DONCASTER-36A | RETFORD-36E | LANGWITHJCN-40E | RETFORD-36E | DONCASTER-36A | TUXFORD-40D |
| Jan-51 | BOSTON-40F | ARDSLEY-37A | NEWENGLAND-35A | DONCASTER-36A | RETFORD-36E | LANGWITHJCN-40E | RETFORD-36E | DONCASTER-36A | 9/50: LANG JN-40E |
| Aug-51 | BOSTON-40F | 5/51:BOST-40F | NEWENGLAND-35A | DONCASTER-36A | RETFORD-36E | LANGWITHJCN-40E | RETFORD-36E | DONCASTER-36A | 9/51: DARN-39B |
| Jan-52 | 3/52:C.HILL-37B | 3/52:C.HILL-37B | NEWENGLAND-35A | DONCASTER-36A | RETFORD-36E | LANGWITHJCN-40E | RETFORD-36E | DONCASTER-36A | DARNALL-39B |
| Aug-52 | COPLEYHILL-37B | COPLEYHILL-37B | NEWENGLAND-35A | DONCASTER-36A | RETFORD-36E | LANGWITHJCN-40E | RETFORD-36E | DONCASTER-36A | DARNALL-39B |
| Jan-53 | COPLEYHILL-37B | COPLEYHILL-37B | NEWENGLAND-35A | 3/53:NEWE-35A | RETFORD-36E | LANGWITHJCN-40E | RETFORD-36E | DONCASTER-36A | DARNALL-39B |
| Aug-53 | COPLEYHILL-37B | COPLEYHILL-37B | NEWENGLAND-35A | NEWENGLAND-35A | RETFORD-36E | LANGWITHJCN-40E | RETFORD-36E | DONCASTER-36A | DARNALL-39B |
| Jan-54 | COPLEYHILL-37B | COPLEYHILL-37B | NEWENGLAND-35A | NEWENGLAND-35A | RETFORD-36E | LANGWITHJCN-40E | RETFORD-36E | DONCASTER-36A | DARNALL-39B |
| Aug-54 | COPLEYHILL-37B | COPLEYHILL-37B | NEWENGLAND-35A | NEWENGLAND-35A | RETFORD-36E | LANGWITHJCN-40E | RETFORD-36E | DONCASTER-36A | DARNALL-39B |
| Jan-55 | COPLEYHILL-37B | COPLEYHILL-37B | NEWENGLAND-35A | NEWENGLAND-35A | RETFORD-36E | LANGWITHJCN-40E | RETFORD-36E | DONCASTER-36A | DARNALL-39B |
| Aug-55 | COPLEYHILL-37B | COPLEYHILL-37B | NEWENGLAND-35A | NEWENGLAND-35A | RETFORD-36E | LANGWITHJCN-40E | 4/55:W/D | DONCASTER-36A | DARNALL-39B |
| Jan-56 | COPLEYHILL-37B | COPLEYHILL-37B | NEWENGLAND-35A | NEWENGLAND-35A | RETFORD-36E | LANGWITHJCN-40E | | DONCASTER-36A | 10/55:W/D |
| Aug-56 | COPLEYHILL-56C | COPLEYHILL-56C | NEWENGLAND-35A | NEWENGLAND-35A | RETFORD-36E | LANGWITHJCN-40E | | DONCASTER-36A | |
| Jan-57 | COPLEYHILL-56C | COPLEYHILL-56C | NEWENGLAND-35A | NEWENGLAND-35A | RETFORD-36E | LANGWITHJCN-40E | | DONCASTER-36A | |
| Aug-57 | COPLEYHILL-56C | COPLEYHILL-56C | NEWENGLAND-35A | NEWENGLAND-35A | RETFORD-36E | LANGWITHJCN-40E | | 11/56:MEX-36B | |
| Jan-58 | COPLEYHILL-56C | COPLEYHILL-56C | 12/57:BOST-40F | NEWENGLAND-35A | RETFORD-36E | 2/58:GORT-9H | | MEXBOROUGH-36B | |
| Aug-58 | COPLEYHILL-56C | COPLEYHILL-56C | BOSTON-40F | NEWENGLAND-34E | RETFORD-36E | GORTON-9G | | MEXBOROUGH-36B | |
| Jan-59 | 10/58:W/D | COPLEYHILL-56C | BOSTON-40F | NEWENGLAND-34E | RETFORD-36E | 11/58:W/D | | 8/58:W/D | |
| Aug-59 | | COPLEYHILL-56C | 4/59:LINC-40A | 8/59:W/D | 6/59:W/D | | | | |
| Nov-59 | | COPLEYHILL-56C | LINCOLN-40A | | | | | | |
| Jan-60 | | COPLEYHILL-56C | LINCOLN-40A | | | | | | |
| Apr-60 | | COPLEYHILL-56C | LINCOLN-40A | | | | | | |
| Aug-60 | | COPLEYHILL-56C | LINCOLN-40A | | | | | | |
| Nov-60 | | COPLEYHILL-56C | LINCOLN-40A | | | | | | |

| | 64287 | 64288 | 64289 | 64290 | 64291 | 64292 | 64293 | 64294 | 64295 |
|---|---|---|---|---|---|---|---|---|---|
| Aug-50 | RETFORD-36E | MEXBOROUGH-36B | LANGWITHJCN-40E | BARNSLEY-36D | DARNALL-39B | ANNESLEY-38B | TUXFORD-40D | GORTON-39A | RETFORD-36E |
| Jan-51 | RETFORD-36E | MEXBOROUGH-36B | LANGWITHJCN-40E | BARNSLEY-36D | DARNALL-39B | ANNESLEY-38B | TUXFORD-40D | GORTON-39A | RETFORD-36E |
| Aug-51 | RETFORD-36E | MEXBOROUGH-36B | LANGWITHJCN-40E | BARNSLEY-36D | DARNALL-39B | ANNESLEY-38B | TUXFORD-40D | GORTON-39A | RETFORD-36E |
| Jan-52 | RETFORD-36E | 3/52:DCTR-36A | LANGWITHJCN-40E | BARNSLEY-36D | DARNALL-39B | ANNESLEY-38B | TUXFORD-40D | GORTON-39A | RETFORD-36E |
| Aug-52 | RETFORD-36E | 5/52:NORTH-9G | LANGWITHJCN-40E | BARNSLEY-36D | DARNALL-39B | ANNESLEY-38B | TUXFORD-40D | GORTON-39A | RETFORD-36E |
| Jan-53 | RETFORD-36E | 9/52:S.BGE-35C | LANGWITHJCN-40E | BARNSLEY-36D | DARNALL-39B | ANNESLEY-38B | 11/52:LANG JN;40E | GORTON-39A | RETFORD-36E |
| Aug-53 | RETFORD-36E | SPITAL BRIDGE-35C | LANGWITHJCN-40E | BARNSLEY-36D | DARNALL-39B | ANNESLEY-38B | LANGWITHJCN-40E | GORTON-39A | RETFORD-36E |
| Jan-54 | RETFORD-36E | SPITAL BRIDGE-35C | LANGWITHJCN-40E | BARNSLEY-36D | DARNALL-39B | ANNESLEY-38B | LANGWITHJCN-40E | GORTON-39A | RETFORD-36E |
| Aug-54 | RETFORD-36E | 9/54:COLW-38A | LANGWITHJCN-40E | BARNSLEY-36D | DARNALL-39B | ANNESLEY-38B | LANGWITHJCN-40E | GORTON-39A | RETFORD-36E |
| Jan-55 | RETFORD-36E | COLWICK-38A | LANGWITHJCN-40E | BARNSLEY-36D | DARNALL-39B | ANNESLEY-38B | LANGWITHJCN-40E | GORTON-39A | RETFORD-36E |
| Aug-55 | RETFORD-36E | COLWICK-38A | 6/55:W/D | BARNSLEY-36D | DARNALL-39B | 8/55:STAVE-38D | LANGWITHJCN-40E | GORTON-39A | RETFORD-36E |
| Jan-56 | RETFORD-36E | 12/55:GORT-39A | | BARNSLEY-36D | 11/55:W/D | STAVELEY-38D | LANGWITHJCN-40E | GORTON-39A | RETFORD-36E |
| Aug-56 | RETFORD-36E | GORTON-39A | | BARNSLEY-36D | | STAVELEY-38D | LANGWITHJCN-40E | GORTON-39A | RETFORD-36E |
| Jan-57 | RETFORD-36E | GORTON-39A | | BARNSLEY-36D | | STAVELEY-38D | LANGWITHJCN-40E | GORTON-39A | RETFORD-36E |
| Aug-57 | RETFORD-36E | GORTON-39A | | BARNSLEY-36D | | STAVELEY-38D | LANGWITHJCN-40E | GORTON-39A | RETFORD-36E |
| Jan-58 | RETFORD-36E | GORTON-39A | | BARNSLEY-36D | | STAVELEY-38D | 12/57:W/D | GORTON-39A | 9/57:W/D |
| Aug-58 | RETFORD-36E | GORTON-9G | | 5/58:W/D | | STAVELEY(GC)-41H | | GORTON-9G | |
| Jan-59 | RETFORD-36E | GORTON-9G | | | | STAVELEY(GC)-41H | | GORTON-9G | |
| Aug-59 | 5/59:W/D | GORTON-9G | | | | STAVELEY(GC)-41H | | 9/59:W/D | |
| Nov-59 | | GORTON-9G | | | | STAVELEY(GC)-41H | | | |
| Jan-60 | | GORTON-9G | | | | STAVELEY(GC)-41H | | | |
| Apr-60 | | GORTON-9G | | | | 5/60:DARN-41A | | | |
| Aug-60 | | GORTON-9G | | | | DARNALL-41A | | | |
| Nov-60 | | 11/60:W/D | | | | DARNALL-41A | | | |

| | 64296 | 64297 | 64298 | 64299 | 64300 | 64301 | 64302 | 64303 | 64305 |
|---|---|---|---|---|---|---|---|---|---|
| Aug-50 | MEXBOROUGH-36B | LANGWITHJCN-40E | GORTON-39A | TUXFORD-40D | ANNESLEY-38B | COLWICK-38A | MEXBOROUGH-36B | LINCOLN-40A | IMMINGHAM-40B |
| Jan-51 | MEXBOROUGH-36B | LANGWITHJCN-40E | GORTON-39A | TUXFORD-40D | ANNESLEY-38B | COLWICK-38A | MEXBOROUGH-36B | LINCOLN-40A | IMMINGHAM-40B |
| Aug-51 | MEXBOROUGH-36B | LANGWITHJCN-40E | GORTON-39A | TUXFORD-40D | ANNESLEY-38B | COLWICK-38A | MEXBOROUGH-36B | LINCOLN-40A | IMMINGHAM-40B |
| Jan-52 | 3/52:DCTR-36A | LANGWITHJCN-40E | GORTON-39A | TUXFORD-40D | ANNESLEY-38B | COLWICK-38A | MEXBOROUGH-36B | LINCOLN-40A | IMMINGHAM-40B |
| Aug-52 | DONCASTER-36A | LANGWITHJCN-40E | GORTON-39A | TUXFORD-40D | ANNESLEY-38B | COLWICK-38A | MEXBOROUGH-36B | LINCOLN-40A | IMMINGHAM-40B |
| Jan-53 | DONCASTER-36A | LANGWITHJCN-40E | GORTON-39A | TUXFORD-40D | ANNESLEY-38B | COLWICK-38A | MEXBOROUGH-36B | LINCOLN-40A | IMMINGHAM-40B |
| Aug-53 | DONCASTER-36A | LANGWITHJCN-40E | GORTON-39A | TUXFORD-40D | ANNESLEY-38B | COLWICK-38A | 7/53:BARN-36D | LINCOLN-40A | IMMINGHAM-40B |
| Jan-54 | DONCASTER-36A | LANGWITHJCN-40E | GORTON-39A | TUXFORD-40D | ANNESLEY-38B | COLWICK-38A | BARNSLEY-36D | LINCOLN-40A | IMMINGHAM-40B |
| Aug-54 | DONCASTER-36A | LANGWITHJCN-40E | GORTON-39A | TUXFORD-40D | ANNESLEY-38B | COLWICK-38A | BARNSLEY-36D | LINCOLN-40A | IMMINGHAM-40B |
| Jan-55 | DONCASTER-36A | LANGWITHJCN-40E | GORTON-39A | TUXFORD-40D | ANNESLEY-38B | COLWICK-38A | BARNSLEY-36D | LINCOLN-40A | IMMINGHAM-40B |
| Aug-55 | DONCASTER-36A | LANGWITHJCN-40E | GORTON-39A | TUXFORD-40D | 8/55:WOOD-38E | 5/55:W/D | BARNSLEY-36D | LINCOLN-40A | IMMINGHAM-40B |
| Jan-56 | DONCASTER-36A | LANGWITHJCN-40E | GORTON-39A | 11/55:W/D | WOODFORD HALSE-38E | | BARNSLEY-36D | LINCOLN-40A | IMMINGHAM-40B |
| Aug-56 | DONCASTER-36A | LANGWITHJCN-40E | GORTON-39A | | WOODFORD HALSE-38E | | BARNSLEY-36D | LINCOLN-40A | IMMINGHAM-40B |
| Jan-57 | 3/57:BARN-36D | LANGWITHJCN-40E | GORTON-39A | | WOODFORD HALSE-38E | | BARNSLEY-36D | 2/57:W/D | IMMINGHAM-40B |
| Aug-57 | BARNSLEY-36D | LANGWITHJCN-40E | GORTON-39A | | WOODFORD HALSE-38E | | BARNSLEY-36D | | IMMINGHAM-40B |
| Jan-58 | BARNSLEY-36D | 2/58:GORT-9H | GORTON-39A | | 9/57:W/D | | BARNSLEY-36D | | IMMINGHAM-40B |
| Aug-58 | 7/58:W/D | GORTON-9G | GORTON-9G | | | | BARNSLEY-41G | | IMMINGHAM-40B |
| Jan-59 | | GORTON-9G | GORTON-9G | | | | 9/58:W/D | | IMMINGHAM-40B |
| Aug-59 | | 6/59:W/D | GORTON-9G | | | | | | IMMINGHAM-40B |
| Nov-59 | | | GORTON-9G | | | | | | IMMINGHAM-40B |
| Jan-60 | | | 12/59:W/D | | | | | | IMMINGHAM-40B |
| Apr-60 | | | | | | | | | IMMINGHAM-40B |
| Aug-60 | | | | | | | | | IMMINGHAM-40B |
| Nov-60 | | | | | | | | | IMMINGHAM-40B |

| | 64306 | 64307 | 64308 | 64309 | 64310 | 64311 | 64312 | 64313 | 64315 |
|---|---|---|---|---|---|---|---|---|---|
| Aug-50 | RETFORD-36E | IMMINGHAM-40B | FRODINGHAM-36C | FRODINGHAM-36C | LANGWITHJCN-40E | GORTON-39A | IMMINGHAM-40B | NEASDEN-34E | LINCOLN-40A |
| Jan-51 | RETFORD-36E | IMMINGHAM-40B | FRODINGHAM-36C | FRODINGHAM-36C | LANGWITHJCN-40E | GORTON-39A | IMMINGHAM-40B | 1/51:WOOD-38E | LINCOLN-40A |
| Aug-51 | 6/51:GORT-39A | IMMINGHAM-40B | FRODINGHAM-36C | FRODINGHAM-36C | LANGWITHJCN-40E | GORTON-39A | IMMINGHAM-40B | WOODFORD HALSE-38E | LINCOLN-40A |
| Jan-52 | GORTON-39A | IMMINGHAM-40B | FRODINGHAM-36C | FRODINGHAM-36C | LANGWITHJCN-40E | GORTON-39A | IMMINGHAM-40B | WOODFORD HALSE-38E | LINCOLN-40A |
| Aug-52 | GORTON-39A | 10/52:TUX-40D | FRODINGHAM-36C | 9/52:DCTR-36A | LANGWITHJCN-40E | GORTON-39A | IMMINGHAM-40B | WOODFORD HALSE-38E | LINCOLN-40A |
| Jan-53 | GORTON-39A | 11/52:IMM-40B | FRODINGHAM-36C | DONCASTER-36A | LANGWITHJCN-40E | GORTON-39A | IMMINGHAM-40B | WOODFORD HALSE-38E | LINCOLN-40A |
| Aug-53 | GORTON-39A | IMMINGHAM-40B | FRODINGHAM-36C | DONCASTER-36A | LANGWITHJCN-40E | GORTON-39A | IMMINGHAM-40B | 12/53:STAVE-38D | LINCOLN-40A |
| Jan-54 | GORTON-39A | IMMINGHAM-40B | FRODINGHAM-36C | DONCASTER-36A | LANGWITHJCN-40E | GORTON-39A | IMMINGHAM-40B | STAVELEY-38D | LINCOLN-40A |
| Aug-54 | GORTON-39A | IMMINGHAM-40B | FRODINGHAM-36C | DONCASTER-36A | LANGWITHJCN-40E | GORTON-39A | IMMINGHAM-40B | STAVELEY-38D | LINCOLN-40A |
| Jan-55 | GORTON-39A | IMMINGHAM-40B | FRODINGHAM-36C | DONCASTER-36A | LANGWITHJCN-40E | GORTON-39A | IMMINGHAM-40B | STAVELEY-38D | LINCOLN-40A |
| Aug-55 | GORTON-39A | 7/55:W/D | FRODINGHAM-36C | DONCASTER-36A | LANGWITHJCN-40E | GORTON-39A | IMMINGHAM-40B | STAVELEY-38D | LINCOLN-40A |
| Jan-56 | GORTON-39A | | FRODINGHAM-36C | DONCASTER-36A | LANGWITHJCN-40E | GORTON-39A | IMMINGHAM-40B | STAVELEY-38D | LINCOLN-40A |
| Aug-56 | GORTON-39A | | FRODINGHAM-36C | 8/56:W/D | LANGWITHJCN-40E | GORTON-39A | IMMINGHAM-40B | STAVELEY-38D | LINCOLN-40A |
| Jan-57 | GORTON-39A | | FRODINGHAM-36C | | LANGWITHJCN-40E | GORTON-39A | 2/57:W/D | STAVELEY-38D | LINCOLN-40A |
| Aug-57 | GORTON-39A | | FRODINGHAM-36C | | LANGWITHJCN-40E | GORTON-39A | | STAVELEY-38D | LINCOLN-40A |
| Jan-58 | GORTON-39A | | FRODINGHAM-36C | | 2/58:GORT-9H | GORTON-39A | | STAVELEY-38D | 12/57:FROD-36C |
| Aug-58 | 8/58:W/D | | FRODINGHAM-36C | | GORTON-9G | GORTON-9G | | STAVELEY(GC)-41H | FRODINGHAM-36C |
| Jan-59 | | | FRODINGHAM-36C | | GORTON-9G | GORTON-9G | | STAVELEY(GC)-41H | FRODINGHAM-36C |
| Aug-59 | | | FRODINGHAM-36C | | GORTON-9G | GORTON-9G | | STAVELEY(GC)-41H | 8/59:RET-36E |
| Nov-59 | | | FRODINGHAM-36C | | GORTON-9G | GORTON-9G | | STAVELEY(GC)-41H | RETFORD-36E |
| Jan-60 | | | FRODINGHAM-36C | | GORTON-9G | GORTON-9G | | STAVELEY(GC)-41H | RETFORD-36E |
| Apr-60 | | | FRODINGHAM-36C | | GORTON-9G | GORTON-9G | | STAVELEY(GC)-41H | 4/60:W/D |
| Aug-60 | | | FRODINGHAM-36C | | GORTON-9G | GORTON-9G | | STAVELEY(GC)-41H | |
| Nov-60 | | | FRODINGHAM-36C | | GORTON-9G | GORTON-9G | | STAVELEY(GC)-41H | |

| | 64319 | 64320 | 64321 | 64322 | 64323 | 64325 | 64326 | 64327 | 64328 |
|---|---|---|---|---|---|---|---|---|---|
| Aug-50 | MEXBOROUGH-36B | LOUTH-40C | LANGWITH JCN-40E | GORTON-39A | IMMINGHAM-40B | IMMINGHAM-40B | GORTON-39A | WOODFORD HALSE-38E | LOUTH-40C |
| Jan-51 | MEXBOROUGH-36B | LOUTH-40C | LANGWITH JCN-40E | GORTON-39A | IMMINGHAM-40B | IMMINGHAM-40B | GORTON-39A | WOODFORD HALSE-38E | LOUTH-40C |
| Aug-51 | MEXBOROUGH-36B | LOUTH-40C | LANGWITH JCN-40E | GORTON-39A | IMMINGHAM-40B | IMMINGHAM-40B | GORTON-39A | WOODFORD HALSE-38E | LOUTH-40C |
| Jan-52 | MEXBOROUGH-36B | LOUTH-40C | LANGWITH JCN-40E | GORTON-39A | IMMINGHAM-40B | IMMINGHAM-40B | GORTON-39A | WOODFORD HALSE-38E | LOUTH-40C |
| Aug-52 | 9/52: DCTR - 36A, | LOUTH-40C | LANGWITH JCN-40E | GORTON-39A | IMMINGHAM-40B | IMMINGHAM-40B | GORTON-39A | WOODFORD HALSE-38E | LOUTH-40C |
| Jan-53 | DONCASTER-36A | LOUTH-40C | LANGWITH JCN-40E | GORTON-39A | IMMINGHAM-40B | IMMINGHAM-40B | GORTON-39A | WOODFORD HALSE-38E | LOUTH-40C |
| Aug-53 | DONCASTER-36A | LOUTH-40C | LANGWITH JCN-40E | GORTON-39A | IMMINGHAM-40B | IMMINGHAM-40B | GORTON-39A | WOODFORD HALSE-38E | LOUTH-40C |
| Jan-54 | DONCASTER-36A | LOUTH-40C | 6/54: RET - 36E | GORTON-39A | IMMINGHAM-40B | IMMINGHAM-40B | GORTON-39A | WOODFORD HALSE-38E | LOUTH-40C |
| Aug-54 | DONCASTER-36A | LOUTH-40C | RETFORD-36E | GORTON-39A | IMMINGHAM-40B | IMMINGHAM-40B | GORTON-39A | WOODFORD HALSE-38E | LOUTH-40C |
| Jan-55 | 11/54: FROD - 36C | LOUTH-40C | RETFORD-36E | GORTON-39A | IMMINGHAM-40B | IMMINGHAM-40B | GORTON-39A | WOODFORD HALSE-38E | LOUTH-40C |
| Aug-55 | FRODINGHAM-36C | LOUTH-40C | RETFORD-36E | GORTON-39A | IMMINGHAM-40B | IMMINGHAM-40B | 8/55: W/D | WOODFORD HALSE-38E | LOUTH-40C |
| Jan-56 | FRODINGHAM-36C | LOUTH-40C | RETFORD-36E | GORTON-39A | 10/55: W/D | IMMINGHAM-40B | | WOODFORD HALSE-38E | LOUTH-40C |
| Aug-56 | FRODINGHAM-36C | LOUTH-40C | RETFORD-36E | GORTON-39A | | IMMINGHAM-40B | | WOODFORD HALSE-38E | LOUTH-40C |
| Jan-57 | FRODINGHAM-36C | 12/56: IMM - 40B | RETFORD-36E | GORTON-39A | | IMMINGHAM-40B | | 2/57: W/D | LOUTH-40C |
| Aug-57 | FRODINGHAM-36C | IMMINGHAM-40B | RETFORD-36E | GORTON-39A | | IMMINGHAM-40B | | | LOUTH-40C |
| Jan-58 | FRODINGHAM-36C | 10/57: W/D | RETFORD-36E | 10/57: W/D | | IMMINGHAM-40B | | | LOUTH-40C |
| Aug-58 | FRODINGHAM-36C | | RETFORD-36E | | | IMMINGHAM-40B | | | LOUTH-40C |
| Jan-59 | FRODINGHAM-36C | | RETFORD-36E | | | IMMINGHAM-40B | | | LOUTH-40C |
| Aug-59 | 8/59: W/D | | 7/59: W/D | | | IMMINGHAM-40B | | | 3/59: W/D |
| Nov-59 | | | | | | IMMINGHAM-40B | | | |
| Jan-60 | | | | | | IMMINGHAM-40B | | | |
| Apr-60 | | | | | | IMMINGHAM-40B | | | |
| Aug-60 | | | | | | IMMINGHAM-40B | | | |
| Nov-60 | | | | | | 11/60: W/D | | | |

| | 64329 | 64330 | 64331 | 64334 | 64335 | 64336 | 64337 | 64338 | 64339 |
|---|---|---|---|---|---|---|---|---|---|
| Aug-50 | NEASDEN-34E | WOODFORD HALSE-38E | STAVELEY-38D | MEXBOROUGH-36B | RETFORD-36E | DARNALL-39B | TUXFORD-40D | WREXHAM-6E | FRODINGHAM-36C |
| Jan-51 | NEASDEN-34E | WOODFORD HALSE-38E | STAVELEY-38D | MEXBOROUGH-36B | RETFORD-36E | DARNALL-39B | TUXFORD-40D | WREXHAM-6E | FRODINGHAM-36C |
| Aug-51 | NEASDEN-34E | WOODFORD HALSE-38E | STAVELEY-38D | MEXBOROUGH-36B | RETFORD-36E | DARNALL-39B | TUXFORD-40D | WREXHAM-6E | FRODINGHAM-36C |
| Jan-52 | NEASDEN-34E | WOODFORD HALSE-38E | STAVELEY-38D | MEXBOROUGH-36B | RETFORD-36E | 12/51: STAVE - 38D | 12/51: LANG JN - 40E | WREXHAM-6E | FRODINGHAM-36C |
| Aug-52 | WOODFORD HALSE-38E | WOODFORD HALSE-38E | 9/52: WOOD - 38E | 9/52: DCTR - 36A | RETFORD-36E | STAVELEY-38D | LANGWITH JCN-40E | 9/52: S.BGE - 35C | FRODINGHAM-36C |
| Jan-53 | 3/53: DARN - 39B | WOODFORD HALSE-38E | WOODFORD HALSE-38E | DONCASTER-36A | RETFORD-36E | STAVELEY-38D | LANGWITH JCN-40E | SPITAL BRIDGE-35C | FRODINGHAM-36C |
| Aug-53 | DARNALL-39B | WOODFORD HALSE-38E | WOODFORD HALSE-38E | DONCASTER-36A | RETFORD-36E | STAVELEY-38D | LANGWITH JCN-40E | SPITAL BRIDGE-35C | FRODINGHAM-36C |
| Jan-54 | DARNALL-39B | WOODFORD HALSE-38E | WOODFORD HALSE-38E | DONCASTER-36A | RETFORD-36E | STAVELEY-38D | LANGWITH JCN-40E | SPITAL BRIDGE-35C | FRODINGHAM-36C |
| Aug-54 | DARNALL-39B | WOODFORD HALSE-38E | WOODFORD HALSE-38E | DONCASTER-36A | 9/54: W/D | STAVELEY-38D | LANGWITH JCN-40E | SPITAL BRIDGE-35C | FRODINGHAM-36C |
| Jan-55 | DARNALL-39B | WOODFORD HALSE-38E | WOODFORD HALSE-38E | DONCASTER-36A | | STAVELEY-38D | LANGWITH JCN-40E | 1/55: COLW-38A | 10/54: W/D |
| Aug-55 | DARNALL-39B | WOODFORD HALSE-38E | WOODFORD HALSE-38E | DONCASTER-36A | | STAVELEY-38D | LANGWITH JCN-40E | COLWICK-38A | |
| Jan-56 | DARNALL-41A | WOODFORD HALSE-38E | WOODFORD HALSE-38E | 11/55: W/D | | STAVELEY-38D | LANGWITH JCN-40E | 11/55: LEIC-38C | |
| Aug-56 | DARNALL-41A | WOODFORD HALSE-38E | WOODFORD HALSE-38E | | | STAVELEY-38D | LANGWITH JCN-40E | 9/56: COLW-38A | |
| Jan-57 | DARNALL-41A | 2/57: W/D | WOODFORD HALSE-38E | | | STAVELEY-38D | LANGWITH JCN-40E | COLWICK-38A | |
| Aug-57 | DARNALL-41A | | WOODFORD HALSE-38E | | | STAVELEY-38D | LANGWITH JCN-40E | COLWICK-38A | |
| Jan-58 | DARNALL-41A | | WOODFORD HALSE-38E | | | STAVELEY-38D | 2/58: GORT - 9H | COLWICK-38A | |
| Aug-58 | DARNALL-41A | | WOODFORD HALSE-2F | | | STAVELEY(GC)-41H | GORTON-9G | COLWICK-40E | |
| Jan-59 | DARNALL-41A | | 2/59: GORT - 9G | | | STAVELEY(GC)-41H | GORTON-9G | 10/58: W/D | |
| Aug-59 | DARNALL-41A | | GORTON-9G | | | 7/59: W/D | GORTON-9G | | |
| Nov-59 | DARNALL-41A | | GORTON-9G | | | | GORTON-9G | | |
| Jan-60 | DARNALL-41A | | GORTON-9G | | | | GORTON-9G | | |
| Apr-60 | DARNALL-41A | | 2/60: W/D | | | | GORTON-9G | | |
| Aug-60 | DARNALL-41A | | | | | | GORTON-9G | | |
| Nov-60 | DARNALL-41A | | | | | | GORTON-9G | | |

| | 64340 | 64341 | 64342 | 64343 | 64344 | 64345 | 64347 | 64348 | 64349 |
|---|---|---|---|---|---|---|---|---|---|
| Aug-50 | RETFORD-36E | RETFORD-36E | GORTON-39A | BARNSLEY-36D | TUXFORD-40D | STAVELEY-38D | RETFORD-36E | RETFORD-36E | DONCASTER-36A |
| Jan-51 | RETFORD-36E | RETFORD-36E | GORTON-39A | BARNSLEY-36D | TUXFORD-40D | STAVELEY-38D | RETFORD-36E | 3/51: MEX - 36B | DONCASTER-36A |
| Aug-51 | RETFORD-36E | RETFORD-36E | GORTON-39A | BARNSLEY-36D | TUXFORD-40D | STAVELEY-38D | RETFORD-36E | MEXBOROUGH-36B | DONCASTER-36A |
| Jan-52 | RETFORD-36E | RETFORD-36E | GORTON-39A | BARNSLEY-36D | TUXFORD-40D | STAVELEY-38D | RETFORD-36E | 3/52: DCTR - 36A | DONCASTER-36A |
| Aug-52 | RETFORD-36E | RETFORD-36E | GORTON-39A | BARNSLEY-36D | TUXFORD-40D | STAVELEY-38D | RETFORD-36E | DONCASTER-36A | DONCASTER-36A |
| Jan-53 | RETFORD-36E | RETFORD-36E | GORTON-39A | BARNSLEY-36D | TUXFORD-40D | STAVELEY-38D | RETFORD-36E | DONCASTER-36A | DONCASTER-36A |
| Aug-53 | RETFORD-36E | RETFORD-36E | GORTON-39A | BARNSLEY-36D | TUXFORD-40D | STAVELEY-38D | RETFORD-36E | DONCASTER-36A | DONCASTER-36A |
| Jan-54 | RETFORD-36E | RETFORD-36E | GORTON-39A | BARNSLEY-36D | TUXFORD-40D | STAVELEY-38D | RETFORD-36E | DONCASTER-36A | DONCASTER-36A |
| Aug-54 | RETFORD-36E | RETFORD-36E | GORTON-39A | BARNSLEY-36D | TUXFORD-40D | STAVELEY-38D | RETFORD-36E | DONCASTER-36A | DONCASTER-36A |
| Jan-55 | RETFORD-36E | RETFORD-36E | 3/55: W/D | BARNSLEY-36D | TUXFORD-40D | STAVELEY-38D | 3/55: W/D | DONCASTER-36A | DONCASTER-36A |
| Aug-55 | RETFORD-36E | RETFORD-36E | | BARNSLEY-36D | TUXFORD-40D | STAVELEY-38D | | DONCASTER-36A | 11/55: BARN - 36D |
| Jan-56 | RETFORD-36E | RETFORD-36E | | BARNSLEY-36D | TUXFORD-40D | STAVELEY-38D | | DONCASTER-36A | 12/55: GORT - 39A |
| Aug-56 | RETFORD-36E | RETFORD-36E | | BARNSLEY-36D | TUXFORD-40D | STAVELEY-38D | | DONCASTER-36A | GORTON-39A |
| Jan-57 | RETFORD-36E | RETFORD-36E | | BARNSLEY-36D | TUXFORD-40D | 11/56: COLW - 38A | | 2/57: RET - 36E | GORTON-39A |
| Aug-57 | RETFORD-36E | RETFORD-36E | | BARNSLEY-36D | TUXFORD-40D | COLWICK-38A | | RETFORD-36E | GORTON-39A |
| Jan-58 | RETFORD-36E | RETFORD-36E | | BARNSLEY-36D | 2/58: COLW - 40E | COLWICK-38A | | RETFORD-36E | 10/57: W/D |
| Aug-58 | 8/58: W/D | 3/58: GORT - 9H | | BARNSLEY-41G | 6/58: W/D | COLWICK-40E | | RETFORD-36E | |
| Jan-59 | | GORTON-9G | | 11/58: W/D | | 12/58: W/D | | 12/58: COLW - 40E | |
| Aug-59 | | GORTON-9G | | | | | | COLWICK-40E | |
| Nov-59 | | GORTON-9G | | | | | | COLWICK-40E | |
| Jan-60 | | GORTON-9G | | | | | | COLWICK-40E | |
| Apr-60 | | GORTON-9G | | | | | | 3/60: W/D | |
| Aug-60 | | GORTON-9G | | | | | | | |
| Nov-60 | | GORTON-9G | | | | | | | |

| | 64350 | 64351 | 64353 | 64355 | 64356 | 64357 | 64358 | 64360 | 64361 |
|---|---|---|---|---|---|---|---|---|---|
| Aug-50 | LINCOLN-40A | LINCOLN-40A | TUXFORD-40D | IMMINGHAM-40B | MEXBOROUGH-36B | GORTON-39A | LANGWITH JCN-40E | DARNALL-39B | ANNESLEY-38B |
| Jan-51 | LINCOLN-40A | LINCOLN-40A | TUXFORD-40D | IMMINGHAM-40B | MEXBOROUGH-36B | GORTON-39A | LANGWITH JCN-40E | DARNALL-39B | ANNESLEY-38B |
| Aug-51 | LINCOLN-40A | LINCOLN-40A | TUXFORD-40D | IMMINGHAM-40B | MEXBOROUGH-36B | GORTON-39A | LANGWITH JCN-40E | DARNALL-39B | ANNESLEY-38B |
| Jan-52 | LINCOLN-40A | LINCOLN-40A | TUXFORD-40D | IMMINGHAM-40B | MEXBOROUGH-36B | GORTON-39A | LANGWITH JCN-40E | DARNALL-39B | ANNESLEY-38B |
| Aug-52 | LINCOLN-40A | LINCOLN-40A | TUXFORD-40D | IMMINGHAM-40B | MEXBOROUGH-36B | GORTON-39A | LANGWITH JCN-40E | DARNALL-39B | ANNESLEY-38B |
| Jan-53 | LINCOLN-40A | LINCOLN-40A | TUXFORD-40D | IMMINGHAM-40B | MEXBOROUGH-36B | GORTON-39A | LANGWITH JCN-40E | DARNALL-39B | ANNESLEY-38B |
| Aug-53 | LINCOLN-40A | LINCOLN-40A | TUXFORD-40D | IMMINGHAM-40B | MEXBOROUGH-36B | GORTON-39A | LANGWITH JCN-40E | DARNALL-39B | ANNESLEY-38B |
| Jan-54 | LINCOLN-40A | LINCOLN-40A | TUXFORD-40D | IMMINGHAM-40B | MEXBOROUGH-36B | GORTON-39A | LANGWITH JCN-40E | DARNALL-39B | ANNESLEY-38B |
| Aug-54 | LINCOLN-40A | LINCOLN-40A | TUXFORD-40D | IMMINGHAM-40B | MEXBOROUGH-36B | GORTON-39A | LANGWITH JCN-40E | DARNALL-39B | ANNESLEY-38B |
| Jan-55 | LINCOLN-40A | LINCOLN-40A | TUXFORD-40D | IMMINGHAM-40B | MEXBOROUGH-36B | GORTON-39A | LANGWITH JCN-40E | DARNALL-39B | ANNESLEY-38B |
| Aug-55 | 8/55: W/D | LINCOLN-40A | TUXFORD-40D | IMMINGHAM-40B | 8/55: W/D | GORTON-39A | LANGWITH JCN-40E | 7/55: W/D | 8/55: STAVE - 38D |
| Jan-56 | | LINCOLN-40A | TUXFORD-40D | IMMINGHAM-40B | | GORTON-39A | 10/55: W/D | | STAVELEY-38D |
| Aug-56 | | LINCOLN-40A | TUXFORD-40D | IMMINGHAM-40B | | GORTON-39A | | | STAVELEY-38D |
| Jan-57 | | LINCOLN-40A | TUXFORD-40D | IMMINGHAM-40B | | GORTON-39A | | | STAVELEY-38D |
| Aug-57 | | LINCOLN-40A | TUXFORD-40D | IMMINGHAM-40B | | GORTON-39A | | | 4/57: COLW - 38A |
| Jan-58 | | 2/58: FROD - 36C | 1/58: GORT - 9H | IMMINGHAM-40B | | GORTON-39A | | | COLWICK-38A |
| Aug-58 | | FRODINGHAM-36C | 2/58: W/D | IMMINGHAM-40B | | GORTON-9G | | | COLWICK-40E |
| Jan-59 | | FRODINGHAM-36C | | IMMINGHAM-40B | | GORTON-9G | | | 3/59: W/D |
| Aug-59 | | FRODINGHAM-36C | | IMMINGHAM-40B | | GORTON-9G | | | |
| Nov-59 | | 10/59: W/D | | IMMINGHAM-40B | | GORTON-9G | | | |
| Jan-60 | | | | IMMINGHAM-40B | | GORTON-9G | | | |
| Apr-60 | | | | IMMINGHAM-40B | | 4/60: W/D | | | |
| Aug-60 | | | | IMMINGHAM-40B | | | | | |
| Nov-60 | | | | IMMINGHAM-40B | | | | | |

| | 64363 | 64365 | 64366 | 64367 | 64368 | 64369 | 64370 | 64371 | 64372 |
|---|---|---|---|---|---|---|---|---|---|
| Aug-50 | GORTON-39A | LINCOLN-40A | BARNSLEY-36D | NORTHWICH-9G | GORTON-39A | WOODFORDHALSE-38E | ANNESLEY-38B | LINCOLN-40A | IMMINGHAM-40B |
| Jan-51 | GORTON-39A | LINCOLN-40A | BARNSLEY-36D | NORTHWICH-9G | GORTON-39A | WOODFORDHALSE-38E | ANNESLEY-38B | LINCOLN-40A | IMMINGHAM-40B |
| Aug-51 | GORTON-39A | LINCOLN-40A | BARNSLEY-36D | NORTHWICH-9G | GORTON-39A | WOODFORDHALSE-38E | ANNESLEY-38B | LINCOLN-40A | IMMINGHAM-40B |
| Jan-52 | GORTON-39A | LINCOLN-40A | BARNSLEY-36D | NORTHWICH-9G | GORTON-39A | WOODFORDHALSE-38E | ANNESLEY-38B | LINCOLN-40A | IMMINGHAM-40B |
| Aug-52 | GORTON-39A | LINCOLN-40A | BARNSLEY-36D | 9/52: D CTR - 36A | GORTON-39A | WOODFORDHALSE-38E | ANNESLEY-38B | LINCOLN-40A | IMMINGHAM-40B |
| Jan-53 | GORTON-39A | LINCOLN-40A | BARNSLEY-36D | DONCASTER-36A | GORTON-39A | WOODFORDHALSE-38E | ANNESLEY-38B | LINCOLN-40A | IMMINGHAM-40B |
| Aug-53 | GORTON-39A | LINCOLN-40A | BARNSLEY-36D | DONCASTER-36A | GORTON-39A | WOODFORDHALSE-38E | ANNESLEY-38B | LINCOLN-40A | IMMINGHAM-40B |
| Jan-54 | GORTON-39A | LINCOLN-40A | BARNSLEY-36D | 1/54: W/D | GORTON-39A | 1/54: COLW - 38A | ANNESLEY-38B | LINCOLN-40A | IMMINGHAM-40B |
| Aug-54 | GORTON-39A | LINCOLN-40A | BARNSLEY-36D | | GORTON-39A | COLWICK-38A | ANNESLEY-38B | LINCOLN-40A | IMMINGHAM-40B |
| Aug-55 | GORTON-39A | LINCOLN-40A | BARNSLEY-36D | | GORTON-39A | COLWICK-38A | 6/55: W/D | LINCOLN-40A | IMMINGHAM-40B |
| Jan-56 | GORTON-39A | LINCOLN-40A | BARNSLEY-36D | | GORTON-39A | 10/55: W/D | | LINCOLN-40A | IMMINGHAM-40B |
| Aug-56 | GORTON-39A | LINCOLN-40A | BARNSLEY-36D | | GORTON-39A | | | LINCOLN-40A | IMMINGHAM-40B |
| Jan-57 | GORTON-39A | LINCOLN-40A | 12/56: W/D | | GORTON-39A | | | LINCOLN-40A | IMMINGHAM-40B |
| Aug-57 | GORTON-39A | 4/57: IMM - 40B | | | GORTON-39A | | | LINCOLN-40A | 10/57: W/D |
| Jan-58 | GORTON-39A | 12/57: FROD - 36C | | | GORTON-39A | | | LINCOLN-40A | |
| Aug-58 | GORTON-9G | FRODINGHAM-36C | | | GORTON-9G | | | LINCOLN-40A | |
| Jan-59 | GORTON-9G | FRODINGHAM-36C | | | GORTON-9G | | | LINCOLN-40A | |
| Aug-59 | GORTON-9G | 8/59: W/D | | | GORTON-9G | | | 6/59: LANG JN - 41J | |
| Nov-59 | GORTON-9G | | | | GORTON-9G | | | 9/59: FROD - 36C | |
| Jan-60 | GORTON-9G | | | | GORTON-9G | | | FRODINGHAM-36C | |
| Apr-60 | GORTON-9G | | | | GORTON-9G | | | FRODINGHAM-36C | |
| Aug-60 | GORTON-9G | | | | 6/60: W/D | | | FRODINGHAM-36C | |
| Nov-60 | GORTON-9G | | | | | | | FRODINGHAM-36C | |

| | 64374 | 64376 | 64377 | 64378 | 64380 | 64381 | 64382 | 64383 | 64384 |
|---|---|---|---|---|---|---|---|---|---|
| Aug-50 | MEXBOROUGH-36B | BRUNSWICK-8E | MEXBOROUGH-36B | LANGWITHJCN-40E | RETFORD-36E | WREXHAM-6E | GORTON-39A | GORTON-39A | STAVELEY-38D |
| Jan-51 | MEXBOROUGH-36B | BRUNSWICK-8E | MEXBOROUGH-36B | LANGWITHJCN-40E | RETFORD-36E | WREXHAM-6E | GORTON-39A | GORTON-39A | STAVELEY-38D |
| Aug-51 | MEXBOROUGH-36B | BRUNSWICK-8E | MEXBOROUGH-36B | LANGWITHJCN-40E | RETFORD-36E | WREXHAM-6E | GORTON-39A | GORTON-39A | STAVELEY-38D |
| Jan-52 | MEXBOROUGH-36B | BRUNSWICK-8E | MEXBOROUGH-36B | LANGWITHJCN-40E | RETFORD-36E | WREXHAM-6E | GORTON-39A | GORTON-39A | STAVELEY-38D |
| Aug-52 | MEXBOROUGH-36B | 9/52: D CTR - 36A | MEXBOROUGH-36B | LANGWITHJCN-40E | RETFORD-36E | 9/52: LINC - 40A | GORTON-39A | GORTON-39A | STAVELEY-38D |
| Jan-53 | MEXBOROUGH-36B | DONCASTER-36A | MEXBOROUGH-36B | LANGWITHJCN-40E | RETFORD-36E | LINCOLN-40A | GORTON-39A | GORTON-39A | STAVELEY-38D |
| Aug-53 | MEXBOROUGH-36B | DONCASTER-36A | MEXBOROUGH-36B | LANGWITHJCN-40E | RETFORD-36E | LINCOLN-40A | GORTON-39A | GORTON-39A | STAVELEY-38D |
| Jan-54 | MEXBOROUGH-36B | DONCASTER-36A | MEXBOROUGH-36B | 6/54: GORT - 39A | RETFORD-36E | LINCOLN-40A | GORTON-39A | GORTON-39A | STAVELEY-38D |
| Aug-54 | MEXBOROUGH-36B | DONCASTER-36A | MEXBOROUGH-36B | GORTON-39A | RETFORD-36E | LINCOLN-40A | GORTON-39A | GORTON-39A | STAVELEY-38D |
| Aug-55 | 7/55: W/D | DONCASTER-36A | MEXBOROUGH-36B | GORTON-39A | RETFORD-36E | LINCOLN-40A | GORTON-39A | GORTON-39A | STAVELEY-38D |
| Jan-56 | | DONCASTER-36A | MEXBOROUGH-36B | GORTON-39A | RETFORD-36E | LINCOLN-40A | GORTON-39A | GORTON-39A | STAVELEY-38D |
| Aug-56 | | DONCASTER-36A | MEXBOROUGH-36B | 12/56: W/D | 8/56: W/D | LINCOLN-40A | GORTON-39A | GORTON-39A | STAVELEY-38D |
| Jan-57 | | 3/57: BARN - 36D | MEXBOROUGH-36B | | | LINCOLN-40A | GORTON-39A | GORTON-39A | STAVELEY-38D |
| Aug-57 | | BARNSLEY-36D | MEXBOROUGH-36B | | | LINCOLN-40A | GORTON-39A | GORTON-39A | STAVELEY-38D |
| Jan-58 | | BARNSLEY-41G | MEXBOROUGH-41F | | | LINCOLN-40A | GORTON-9G | GORTON-9G | STAVELEY(GC)-41H |
| Aug-58 | | BARNSLEY-41G | MEXBOROUGH-41F | | | LINCOLN-40A | GORTON-9G | GORTON-9G | STAVELEY(GC)-41H |
| Jan-59 | | BARNSLEY-41G | MEXBOROUGH-41F | | | LINCOLN-40A | GORTON-9G | GORTON-9G | STAVELEY(GC)-41H |
| Aug-59 | | 11/59: W/D | MEXBOROUGH-41F | | | 3/59: W/D | 10/59: W/D | GORTON-9G | STAVELEY(GC)-41H |
| Nov-59 | | | MEXBOROUGH-41F | | | | | GORTON-9G | STAVELEY(GC)-41H |
| Jan-60 | | | MEXBOROUGH-41F | | | | | 3/60: W/D | STAVELEY(GC)-41H |
| Apr-60 | | | MEXBOROUGH-41F | | | | | | STAVELEY(GC)-41H |
| Aug-60 | | | MEXBOROUGH-41F | | | | | | STAVELEY(GC)-41H |
| Nov-60 | | | MEXBOROUGH-41F | | | | | | STAVELEY(GC)-41H |

| | 64385 | 64387 | 64388 | 64389 | 64390 | 64391 | 64392 | 64396 | 64397 |
|---|---|---|---|---|---|---|---|---|---|
| Aug-50 | RETFORD-36E | DARNALL-39B | WOODFORDHALSE-38E | LANGWITHJCN-40E | WOODFORDHALSE-38E | BARNSLEY-36D | TUXFORD-40D | STAVELEY-38D | SOUTHPORT-27E |
| Jan-51 | RETFORD-36E | DARNALL-39B | WOODFORDHALSE-38E | LANGWITHJCN-40E | WOODFORDHALSE-38E | BARNSLEY-36D | TUXFORD-40D | STAVELEY-38D | SOUTHPORT-27E |
| Aug-51 | RETFORD-36E | DARNALL-39B | WOODFORDHALSE-38E | LANGWITHJCN-40E | WOODFORDHALSE-38E | BARNSLEY-36D | TUXFORD-40D | STAVELEY-38D | SOUTHPORT-27E |
| Jan-52 | RETFORD-36E | DARNALL-39B | WOODFORDHALSE-38E | LANGWITHJCN-40E | WOODFORDHALSE-38E | BARNSLEY-36D | TUXFORD-40D | STAVELEY-38D | SOUTHPORT-27E |
| Aug-52 | RETFORD-36E | DARNALL-39B | WOODFORDHALSE-38E | LANGWITHJCN-40E | WOODFORDHALSE-38E | BARNSLEY-36D | TUXFORD-40D | STAVELEY-38D | SOUTHPORT-27E |
| Jan-53 | RETFORD-36E | DARNALL-39B | WOODFORDHALSE-38E | LANGWITHJCN-40E | WOODFORDHALSE-38E | BARNSLEY-36D | TUXFORD-40D | STAVELEY-38D | 2/53: S. BGE - 35C |
| Aug-53 | RETFORD-36E | DARNALL-39B | WOODFORDHALSE-38E | LANGWITHJCN-40E | WOODFORDHALSE-38E | BARNSLEY-36D | TUXFORD-40D | STAVELEY-38D | SPITAL BRIDGE - 35C |
| Jan-54 | RETFORD-36E | DARNALL-39B | WOODFORDHALSE-38E | LANGWITHJCN-40E | 1/54: COLW - 38A | BARNSLEY-36D | TUXFORD-40D | STAVELEY-38D | 3/54: NEW E - 35A |
| Aug-54 | RETFORD-36E | DARNALL-39B | WOODFORDHALSE-38E | LANGWITHJCN-40E | COLWICK-38A | BARNSLEY-36D | TUXFORD-40D | STAVELEY-38D | 8/54: COLW - 38A |
| Aug-55 | RETFORD-36E | DARNALL-39B | WOODFORDHALSE-38E | LANGWITHJCN-40E | 5/55: W/D | 1/55: W/D | TUXFORD-40D | STAVELEY-38D | COLWICK-38A |
| Jan-56 | RETFORD-36E | DARNALL-41A | WOODFORDHALSE-38E | LANGWITHJCN-40E | | | TUXFORD-40D | STAVELEY-38D | COLWICK-38A |
| Aug-56 | RETFORD-36E | DARNALL-41A | WOODFORDHALSE-38E | LANGWITHJCN-40E | | | TUXFORD-40D | STAVELEY-38D | COLWICK-38A |
| Jan-57 | RETFORD-36E | DARNALL-41A | 12/56: COLW - 38A | LANGWITHJCN-40E | | | TUXFORD-40D | STAVELEY-38D | COLWICK-38A |
| Aug-57 | RETFORD-36E | DARNALL-41A | COLWICK-38A | LANGWITHJCN-40E | | | TUXFORD-40D | STAVELEY-38D | COLWICK-38A |
| Jan-58 | RETFORD-36E | DARNALL-41A | 2/58: LANG JN - 41J | 2/58: GORT - 9H | | | 2/58: COLW - 40E | STAVELEY-38D | COLWICK-40E |
| Aug-58 | RETFORD-36E | DARNALL-41A | LANGWITHJCN-41J | GORTON-9G | | | COLWICK-40E | STAVELEY(GC)-41H | COLWICK-40E |
| Jan-59 | RETFORD-36E | DARNALL-41A | 3/59: W/D | GORTON-9G | | | 12/58: W/D | STAVELEY(GC)-41H | COLWICK-40E |
| Aug-59 | 8/59: FROD - 36C | DARNALL-41A | | GORTON-9G | | | | STAVELEY(GC)-41H | COLWICK-40E |
| Nov-59 | FRODINGHAM-36C | DARNALL-41A | | GORTON-9G | | | | STAVELEY(GC)-41H | COLWICK-40E |
| Jan-60 | FRODINGHAM-36C | DARNALL-41A | | 2/60: W/D | | | | 2/60: W/D | 3/60: LINC - 40A |
| Apr-60 | FRODINGHAM-36C | DARNALL-41A | | | | | | | 4/60: W/D |
| Aug-60 | FRODINGHAM-36C | 6/60: W/D | | | | | | | |
| Nov-60 | FRODINGHAM-36C | | | | | | | | |

| | 64398 | 64399 | 64400 | 64401 | 64403 | 64404 | 64405 | 64407 | 64408 |
|---|---|---|---|---|---|---|---|---|---|
| Aug-50 | BARNSLEY-36D | BARNSLEY-36D | MEXBOROUGH-36B | GORTON-39A | MEXBOROUGH-36B | MEXBOROUGH-36B | BRUNSWICK-8E | FRODINGHAM-36C | WOODFORDHALSE-38E |
| Jan-51 | BARNSLEY-36D | BARNSLEY-36D | MEXBOROUGH-36B | GORTON-39A | MEXBOROUGH-36B | MEXBOROUGH-36B | BRUNSWICK-8E | FRODINGHAM-36C | WOODFORDHALSE-38E |
| Aug-51 | BARNSLEY-36D | BARNSLEY-36D | MEXBOROUGH-36B | GORTON-39A | MEXBOROUGH-36B | MEXBOROUGH-36B | BRUNSWICK-8E | FRODINGHAM-36C | 6/51: DARN - 39B |
| Jan-52 | BARNSLEY-36D | BARNSLEY-36D | MEXBOROUGH-36B | GORTON-39A | MEXBOROUGH-36B | 3/52: D CTR - 36A | BRUNSWICK-8E | FRODINGHAM-36C | 9/51: LANG JN - 40E |
| Aug-52 | BARNSLEY-36D | BARNSLEY-36D | MEXBOROUGH-36B | GORTON-39A | 9/52: D CTR - 36A | DONCASTER-36A | 9/52: LINC - 40A | FRODINGHAM-36C | LANGWITHJCN-40E |
| Jan-53 | BARNSLEY-36D | BARNSLEY-36D | MEXBOROUGH-36B | GORTON-39A | DONCASTER-36A | DONCASTER-36A | LINCOLN-40A | FRODINGHAM-36C | LANGWITHJCN-40E |
| Aug-53 | BARNSLEY-36D | BARNSLEY-36D | MEXBOROUGH-36B | GORTON-39A | DONCASTER-36A | DONCASTER-36A | LINCOLN-40A | FRODINGHAM-36C | LANGWITHJCN-40E |
| Jan-54 | BARNSLEY-36D | BARNSLEY-36D | MEXBOROUGH-36B | GORTON-39A | DONCASTER-36A | DONCASTER-36A | LINCOLN-40A | FRODINGHAM-36C | LANGWITHJCN-40E |
| Aug-54 | BARNSLEY-36D | BARNSLEY-36D | MEXBOROUGH-36B | GORTON-39A | 10/54: RET - 36E | DONCASTER-36A | LINCOLN-40A | FRODINGHAM-36C | LANGWITHJCN-40E |
| Aug-55 | BARNSLEY-36D | BARNSLEY-36D | MEXBOROUGH-36B | GORTON-39A | RETFORD-36E | DONCASTER-36A | LINCOLN-40A | FRODINGHAM-36C | LANGWITHJCN-40E |
| Jan-56 | BARNSLEY-36D | BARNSLEY-36D | 11/55: W/D | GORTON-39A | RETFORD-36E | DONCASTER-36A | 3/56: TUX - 40D | FRODINGHAM-36C | LANGWITHJCN-40E |
| Aug-56 | BARNSLEY-36D | BARNSLEY-36D | | GORTON-39A | RETFORD-36E | DONCASTER-36A | TUXFORD-40D | FRODINGHAM-36C | 11/56: W/D |
| Jan-57 | 11/56: W/D | BARNSLEY-36D | | GORTON-39A | RETFORD-36E | 3/57: BARN - 36D | TUXFORD-40D | FRODINGHAM-36C | |
| Aug-57 | | BARNSLEY-36D | | GORTON-39A | RETFORD-36E | BARNSLEY-36D | TUXFORD-40D | FRODINGHAM-36C | |
| Jan-58 | | 10/57: W/D | | 10/57: W/D | 7/58: BARN - 41G | BARNSLEY-41G | 2/58: GORT - 9H | FRODINGHAM-36C | |
| Aug-58 | | | | | BARNSLEY-41G | BARNSLEY-41G | GORTON-9G | FRODINGHAM-36C | |
| Jan-59 | | | | | 4/59: MEX - 41F | 9/59: FROD - 36C | GORTON-9G | FRODINGHAM-36C | |
| Aug-59 | | | | | MEXBOROUGH-41F | FRODINGHAM-36C | GORTON-9G | FRODINGHAM-36C | |
| Nov-59 | | | | | MEXBOROUGH-41F | FRODINGHAM-36C | GORTON-9G | 12/59: W/D | |
| Jan-60 | | | | | MEXBOROUGH-41F | FRODINGHAM-36C | GORTON-9G | | |
| Apr-60 | | | | | 6/60: W/D | FRODINGHAM-36C | 4/60: W/D | | |
| Aug-60 | | | | | | FRODINGHAM-36C | | | |
| Nov-60 | | | | | | | | | |

| | 64409 | 64410 | 64411 | 64412 | 64413 | 64414 | 64415 | 64416 | 64419 |
|---|---|---|---|---|---|---|---|---|---|
| Aug-50 | GORTON-39A | DONCASTER-36A | IMMINGHAM-40B | DARNALL-39B | RETFORD-36E | LANGWITH JCN-40E | GORTON-39A | RETFORD-36E | DARNALL-39B |
| Jan-51 | GORTON-39A | DONCASTER-36A | IMMINGHAM-40B | DARNALL-39B | RETFORD-36E | LANGWITH JCN-40E | GORTON-39A | RETFORD-36E | DARNALL-39B |
| Aug-51 | GORTON-39A | DONCASTER-36A | IMMINGHAM-40B | DARNALL-39B | 6/51: GORT-39A | LANGWITH JCN-40E | GORTON-39A | RETFORD-36E | DARNALL-39B |
| Jan-52 | GORTON-39A | DONCASTER-36A | IMMINGHAM-40B | DARNALL-39B | GORTON-39A | LANGWITH JCN-40E | GORTON-39A | RETFORD-36E | DARNALL-39B |
| Aug-52 | GORTON-39A | DONCASTER-36A | IMMINGHAM-40B | DARNALL-39B | GORTON-39A | LANGWITH JCN-40E | GORTON-39A | RETFORD-36E | DARNALL-39B |
| Jan-53 | GORTON-39A | DONCASTER-36A | IMMINGHAM-40B | DARNALL-39B | GORTON-39A | LANGWITH JCN-40E | GORTON-39A | RETFORD-36E | DARNALL-39B |
| Aug-53 | GORTON-39A | DONCASTER-36A | IMMINGHAM-40B | DARNALL-39B | GORTON-39A | LANGWITH JCN-40E | GORTON-39A | RETFORD-36E | DARNALL-39B |
| Jan-54 | GORTON-39A | DONCASTER-36A | IMMINGHAM-40B | DARNALL-39B | GORTON-39A | LANGWITH JCN-40E | GORTON-39A | RETFORD-36E | DARNALL-39B |
| Aug-54 | GORTON-39A | DONCASTER-36A | IMMINGHAM-40B | DARNALL-39B | GORTON-39A | LANGWITH JCN-40E | GORTON-39A | RETFORD-36E | DARNALL-39B |
| Jan-55 | GORTON-39A | 11/54: FROD-36C | IMMINGHAM-40B | DARNALL-39B | GORTON-39A | LANGWITH JCN-40E | GORTON-39A | RETFORD-36E | DARNALL-39B |
| Aug-55 | GORTON-39A | FRODINGHAM-36C | IMMINGHAM-40B | DARNALL-39B | GORTON-39A | LANGWITH JCN-40E | GORTON-39A | RETFORD-36E | DARNALL-39B |
| Jan-56 | GORTON-39A | FRODINGHAM-36C | IMMINGHAM-40B | DARNALL-41A | 11/55: W/D | LANGWITH JCN-40E | 10/55: W/D | RETFORD-36E | DARNALL-41A |
| Aug-56 | GORTON-39A | FRODINGHAM-36C | IMMINGHAM-40B | DARNALL-41A | | LANGWITH JCN-40E | | RETFORD-36E | DARNALL-41A |
| Jan-57 | GORTON-39A | 12/56: W/D | IMMINGHAM-40B | DARNALL-41A | | LANGWITH JCN-40E | | RETFORD-36E | DARNALL-41A |
| Aug-57 | GORTON-39A | | IMMINGHAM-40B | DARNALL-41A | | 7/57: W/D | | RETFORD-36E | DARNALL-41A |
| Jan-58 | GORTON-39A | | 10/57: W/D | 10/57: W/D | | | | RETFORD-36E | DARNALL-41A |
| Aug-58 | GORTON-9G | | | | | | | RETFORD-36E | DARNALL-41A |
| Jan-59 | 12/58: W/D | | | | | | | 11/58: W/D | DARNALL-41A |
| Aug-59 | | | | | | | | | DARNALL-41A |
| Nov-59 | | | | | | | | | DARNALL-41A |
| Jan-60 | | | | | | | | | DARNALL-41A |
| Apr-60 | | | | | | | | | DARNALL-41A |
| Aug-60 | | | | | | | | | DARNALL-41A |
| Nov-60 | | | | | | | | | DARNALL-41A |

| | 64421 | 64422 | 64423 | 64424 | 64425 | 64426 | 64428 | 64429 | 64430 |
|---|---|---|---|---|---|---|---|---|---|
| Aug-50 | RETFORD-36E | RETFORD-36E | RETFORD-36E | TUXFORD-40D | BARNSLEY-36D | LANGWITH JCN-40E | STAVELEY-38D | FRODINGHAM-36C | LINCOLN-40A |
| Jan-51 | RETFORD-36E | RETFORD-36E | RETFORD-36E | TUXFORD-40D | BARNSLEY-36D | LANGWITH JCN-40E | STAVELEY-38D | FRODINGHAM-36C | LINCOLN-40A |
| Aug-51 | RETFORD-36E | RETFORD-36E | RETFORD-36E | TUXFORD-40D | BARNSLEY-36D | LANGWITH JCN-40E | STAVELEY-38D | FRODINGHAM-36C | LINCOLN-40A |
| Jan-52 | RETFORD-36E | RETFORD-36E | RETFORD-36E | TUXFORD-40D | BARNSLEY-36D | LANGWITH JCN-40E | 2/52: WOOD-38E | FRODINGHAM-36C | LINCOLN-40A |
| Aug-52 | RETFORD-36E | RETFORD-36E | RETFORD-36E | TUXFORD-40D | BARNSLEY-36D | LANGWITH JCN-40E | WOODFORD HALSE-38E | FRODINGHAM-36C | LINCOLN-40A |
| Jan-53 | RETFORD-36E | RETFORD-36E | RETFORD-36E | TUXFORD-40D | BARNSLEY-36D | LANGWITH JCN-40E | WOODFORD HALSE-38E | FRODINGHAM-36C | LINCOLN-40A |
| Aug-53 | RETFORD-36E | RETFORD-36E | RETFORD-36E | TUXFORD-40D | BARNSLEY-36D | LANGWITH JCN-40E | WOODFORD HALSE-38E | FRODINGHAM-36C | LINCOLN-40A |
| Jan-54 | RETFORD-36E | RETFORD-36E | RETFORD-36E | TUXFORD-40D | BARNSLEY-36D | LANGWITH JCN-40E | WOODFORD HALSE-38E | FRODINGHAM-36C | LINCOLN-40A |
| Aug-54 | RETFORD-36E | RETFORD-36E | RETFORD-36E | TUXFORD-40D | BARNSLEY-36D | 6/54: GORT-39A | WOODFORD HALSE-38E | FRODINGHAM-36C | LINCOLN-40A |
| Jan-55 | RETFORD-36E | RETFORD-36E | RETFORD-36E | TUXFORD-40D | BARNSLEY-36D | GORTON-39A | WOODFORD HALSE-38E | FRODINGHAM-36C | LINCOLN-40A |
| Aug-55 | RETFORD-36E | RETFORD-36E | RETFORD-36E | TUXFORD-40D | BARNSLEY-36D | GORTON-39A | WOODFORD HALSE-38E | FRODINGHAM-36C | LINCOLN-40A |
| Jan-56 | RETFORD-36E | RETFORD-36E | RETFORD-36E | TUXFORD-40D | BARNSLEY-36D | 1/56: W/D | WOODFORD HALSE-38E | FRODINGHAM-36C | LINCOLN-40A |
| Aug-56 | RETFORD-36E | RETFORD-36E | RETFORD-36E | TUXFORD-40D | BARNSLEY-36D | | WOODFORD HALSE-38E | FRODINGHAM-36C | LINCOLN-40A |
| Jan-57 | RETFORD-36E | RETFORD-36E | RETFORD-36E | TUXFORD-40D | BARNSLEY-36D | | WOODFORD HALSE-38E | FRODINGHAM-36C | LINCOLN-40A |
| Aug-57 | RETFORD-36E | RETFORD-36E | RETFORD-36E | TUXFORD-40D | BARNSLEY-36D | | WOODFORD HALSE-38E | FRODINGHAM-36C | LINCOLN-40A |
| Jan-58 | RETFORD-36E | RETFORD-36E | RETFORD-36E | 1/58: W/D | BARNSLEY-36D | | WOODFORD HALSE-38E | FRODINGHAM-36C | 12/57: FROD-36C |
| Aug-58 | RETFORD-36E | 8/58: W/D | RETFORD-36E | | BARNSLEY-41G | | WOODFORD HALSE-2F | FRODINGHAM-36C | 2/58: LINC-40A |
| Jan-59 | RETFORD-36E | | RETFORD-36E | | BARNSLEY-41G | | 2/59: GORT-9G | FRODINGHAM-36C | LINCOLN-40A |
| Aug-59 | 8/59: FROD-36C | | RETFORD-36E | | BARNSLEY-41G | | 4/59: W/D | FRODINGHAM-36C | 5/59: W/D |
| Nov-59 | FRODINGHAM-36C | | 11/59: FROD-36C | | BARNSLEY-41G | | | FRODINGHAM-36C | |
| Jan-60 | 12/59: W/D | | FRODINGHAM-36C | | 1/60: MEX-41F | | | 12/59: W/D | |
| Apr-60 | | | FRODINGHAM-36C | | MEXBOROUGH-41F | | | | |
| Aug-60 | | | FRODINGHAM-36C | | MEXBOROUGH-41F | | | | |
| Nov-60 | | | FRODINGHAM-36C | | 11/60: W/D | | | | |

| | 64431 | 64432 | 64433 | 64434 | 64435 | 64436 | 64437 | 64438 | 64440 |
|---|---|---|---|---|---|---|---|---|---|
| Aug-50 | ANNESLEY-38B | MEXBOROUGH-36B | STAVELEY-38D | GORTON-39A | GORTON-39A | BARNSLEY-36D | GORTON-39A | WOODFORD HALSE-38E | GORTON-39A |
| Jan-51 | ANNESLEY-38B | MEXBOROUGH-36B | STAVELEY-38D | GORTON-39A | GORTON-39A | BARNSLEY-36D | GORTON-39A | 1/51: NEAS-34E | GORTON-39A |
| Aug-51 | ANNESLEY-38B | MEXBOROUGH-36B | STAVELEY-38D | GORTON-39A | GORTON-39A | BARNSLEY-36D | GORTON-39A | NEASDEN-34E | GORTON-39A |
| Jan-52 | ANNESLEY-38B | MEXBOROUGH-36B | 12/51: WOOD-38E | GORTON-39A | GORTON-39A | BARNSLEY-36D | GORTON-39A | NEASDEN-34E | GORTON-39A |
| Aug-52 | ANNESLEY-38B | MEXBOROUGH-36B | 2/52: STAVE-38D | GORTON-39A | GORTON-39A | BARNSLEY-36D | GORTON-39A | NEASDEN-34E | GORTON-39A |
| Jan-53 | ANNESLEY-38B | MEXBOROUGH-36B | STAVELEY-38D | GORTON-39A | GORTON-39A | BARNSLEY-36D | GORTON-39A | 3/53: COLW-38A | GORTON-39A |
| Aug-53 | ANNESLEY-38B | MEXBOROUGH-36B | STAVELEY-38D | GORTON-39A | GORTON-39A | BARNSLEY-36D | GORTON-39A | COLWICK-38A | GORTON-39A |
| Jan-54 | ANNESLEY-38B | MEXBOROUGH-36B | STAVELEY-38D | GORTON-39A | GORTON-39A | BARNSLEY-36D | GORTON-39A | COLWICK-38A | GORTON-39A |
| Aug-54 | ANNESLEY-38B | MEXBOROUGH-36B | STAVELEY-38D | GORTON-39A | GORTON-39A | BARNSLEY-36D | GORTON-39A | 8/54: LEIC-38C | GORTON-39A |
| Jan-55 | ANNESLEY-38B | MEXBOROUGH-36B | STAVELEY-38D | GORTON-39A | GORTON-39A | BARNSLEY-36D | GORTON-39A | LEICESTER (GC)-38C | GORTON-39A |
| Aug-55 | 8/55: WOOD-38E | MEXBOROUGH-36B | STAVELEY-38D | GORTON-39A | GORTON-39A | BARNSLEY-36D | GORTON-39A | LEICESTER (GC)-38C | GORTON-39A |
| Jan-56 | WOODFORD HALSE-38E | MEXBOROUGH-36B | STAVELEY-38D | GORTON-39A | GORTON-39A | 11/55: W/D | GORTON-39A | 11/55: COLW-38A | GORTON-39A |
| Aug-56 | WOODFORD HALSE-38E | MEXBOROUGH-36B | STAVELEY-38D | GORTON-39A | GORTON-39A | | GORTON-39A | 11/56: WOOD-38E | GORTON-39A |
| Jan-57 | 9/56: W/D | 1/57: W/D | STAVELEY-38D | GORTON-39A | GORTON-39A | | GORTON-39A | 12/56: COLW-38A | GORTON-39A |
| Aug-57 | | | STAVELEY-38D | GORTON-39A | GORTON-39A | | GORTON-39A | COLWICK-38A | GORTON-39A |
| Jan-58 | | | STAVELEY-38D | GORTON-39A | GORTON-39A | | GORTON-39A | COLWICK-38A | GORTON-39A |
| Aug-58 | | | STAVELEY (GC)-41H | GORTON-9G | GORTON-9G | | GORTON-9G | COLWICK-40E | GORTON-9G |
| Jan-59 | | | STAVELEY (GC)-41H | GORTON-9G | GORTON-9G | | GORTON-9G | COLWICK-40E | GORTON-9G |
| Aug-59 | | | STAVELEY (GC)-41H | GORTON-9G | GORTON-9G | | GORTON-9G | COLWICK-40E | GORTON-9G |
| Nov-59 | | | STAVELEY (GC)-41H | GORTON-9G | GORTON-9G | | GORTON-9G | COLWICK-40E | GORTON-9G |
| Jan-60 | | | STAVELEY (GC)-41H | GORTON-9G | GORTON-9G | | GORTON-9G | 12/59: W/D | GORTON-9G |
| Apr-60 | | | 3/60: W/D | GORTON-9G | GORTON-9G | | GORTON-9G | | GORTON-9G |
| Aug-60 | | | | GORTON-9G | GORTON-9G | | GORTON-9G | | GORTON-9G |
| Nov-60 | | | | 10/60: W/D | GORTON-9G | | GORTON-9G | | GORTON-9G |

| | 64443 | 64444 | 64445 | 64446 | 64447 | 64448 | 64449 | 64451 | 64452 |
|---|---|---|---|---|---|---|---|---|---|
| Aug-50 | DARNALL-39B | STAVELEY-38D | DARNALL-39B | IMMINGHAM-40B | DARNALL-39B | BARNSLEY-36D | MEXBOROUGH-36B | RETFORD-36E | BARNSLEY-36D |
| Jan-51 | DARNALL-39B | STAVELEY-38D | DARNALL-39B | IMMINGHAM-40B | DARNALL-39B | BARNSLEY-36D | MEXBOROUGH-36B | RETFORD-36E | BARNSLEY-36D |
| Aug-51 | DARNALL-39B | STAVELEY-38D | 12/51: IMM-40B | IMMINGHAM-40B | DARNALL-39B | BARNSLEY-36D | MEXBOROUGH-36B | RETFORD-36E | BARNSLEY-36D |
| Jan-52 | DARNALL-39B | STAVELEY-38D | 2/52: DARN-39B | IMMINGHAM-40B | DARNALL-39B | BARNSLEY-36D | MEXBOROUGH-36B | RETFORD-36E | BARNSLEY-36D |
| Aug-52 | DARNALL-39B | STAVELEY-38D | DARNALL-39B | IMMINGHAM-40B | DARNALL-39B | BARNSLEY-36D | MEXBOROUGH-36B | RETFORD-36E | BARNSLEY-36D |
| Jan-53 | DARNALL-39B | STAVELEY-38D | DARNALL-39B | IMMINGHAM-40B | DARNALL-39B | BARNSLEY-36D | MEXBOROUGH-36B | RETFORD-36E | BARNSLEY-36D |
| Aug-53 | DARNALL-39B | STAVELEY-38D | DARNALL-39B | IMMINGHAM-40B | DARNALL-39B | BARNSLEY-36D | MEXBOROUGH-36B | RETFORD-36E | BARNSLEY-36D |
| Jan-54 | DARNALL-39B | STAVELEY-38D | DARNALL-39B | IMMINGHAM-40B | DARNALL-39B | BARNSLEY-36D | MEXBOROUGH-36B | RETFORD-36E | BARNSLEY-36D |
| Aug-54 | DARNALL-39B | STAVELEY-38D | DARNALL-39B | IMMINGHAM-40B | DARNALL-39B | BARNSLEY-36D | MEXBOROUGH-36B | RETFORD-36E | BARNSLEY-36D |
| Jan-55 | DARNALL-39B | STAVELEY-38D | DARNALL-39B | IMMINGHAM-40B | DARNALL-39B | BARNSLEY-36D | MEXBOROUGH-36B | RETFORD-36E | BARNSLEY-36D |
| Aug-55 | DARNALL-39B | STAVELEY-38D | DARNALL-39B | IMMINGHAM-40B | DARNALL-39B | BARNSLEY-36D | MEXBOROUGH-36B | RETFORD-36E | BARNSLEY-36D |
| Jan-56 | DARNALL-41A | STAVELEY-38D | DARNALL-41A | IMMINGHAM-40B | DARNALL-41A | BARNSLEY-36D | MEXBOROUGH-36B | RETFORD-36E | BARNSLEY-36D |
| Aug-56 | DARNALL-41A | STAVELEY-38D | DARNALL-41A | IMMINGHAM-40B | DARNALL-41A | BARNSLEY-36D | 9/56: W/D | RETFORD-36E | BARNSLEY-36D |
| Jan-57 | DARNALL-41A | STAVELEY-38D | DARNALL-41A | IMMINGHAM-40B | DARNALL-41A | 2/57: W/D | | RETFORD-36E | BARNSLEY-36D |
| Aug-57 | DARNALL-41A | STAVELEY-38D | DARNALL-41A | IMMINGHAM-40B | DARNALL-41A | | | RETFORD-36E | BARNSLEY-36D |
| Jan-58 | DARNALL-41A | STAVELEY-38D | DARNALL-41A | IMMINGHAM-40B | DARNALL-41A | | | RETFORD-36E | BARNSLEY-36D |
| Aug-58 | DARNALL-41A | STAVELEY (GC)-41H | DARNALL-41A | IMMINGHAM-40B | DARNALL-41A | | | RETFORD-36E | BARNSLEY-41G |
| Jan-59 | DARNALL-41A | STAVELEY (GC)-41H | DARNALL-41A | IMMINGHAM-40B | DARNALL-41A | | | RETFORD-36E | BARNSLEY-41G |
| Aug-59 | DARNALL-41A | STAVELEY (GC)-41H | DARNALL-41A | IMMINGHAM-40B | DARNALL-41A | | | RETFORD-36E | BARNSLEY-41G |
| Nov-59 | DARNALL-41A | STAVELEY (GC)-41H | DARNALL-41A | IMMINGHAM-40B | DARNALL-41A | | | RETFORD-36E | BARNSLEY-41G |
| Jan-60 | DARNALL-41A | STAVELEY (GC)-41H | DARNALL-41A | IMMINGHAM-40B | DARNALL-41A | | | 12/59: W/D | 1/60: MEX-41F |
| Apr-60 | DARNALL-41A | STAVELEY (GC)-41H | DARNALL-41A | IMMINGHAM-40B | DARNALL-41A | | | | MEXBOROUGH-41F |
| Aug-60 | DARNALL-41A | STAVELEY (GC)-41H | DARNALL-41A | IMMINGHAM-40B | DARNALL-41A | | | | 5/60: W/D |
| Nov-60 | DARNALL-41A | STAVELEY (GC)-41H | DARNALL-41A | IMMINGHAM-40B | DARNALL-41A | | | | |

| | | J11 0-6-0 (1942) | | | | | | | |
|---|---|---|---|---|---|---|---|---|---|
| | 64453 | 64283 | 64284 | 64304 | 64314 | 64316 | 64317 | 64318 | 64324 |
| Aug-50 | NORTHWICH - 9G | MEXBOROUGH - 36B | IMMINGHAM - 40B | BRUNSWICK - 8E | IMMINGHAM - 40B | GORTON - 39A | STAVELEY - 38D | ANNESLEY - 38B | WOODFORD HALSE - 38E |
| Jan-51 | NORTHWICH - 9G | MEXBOROUGH - 36B | IMMINGHAM - 40B | **11/50: GORT - 39A** | IMMINGHAM - 40B | GORTON - 39A | STAVELEY - 38D | ANNESLEY - 38B | WOODFORD HALSE - 38E |
| Aug-51 | NORTHWICH - 9G | MEXBOROUGH - 36B | IMMINGHAM - 40B | GORTON - 39A | IMMINGHAM - 40B | GORTON - 39A | STAVELEY - 38D | ANNESLEY - 38B | WOODFORD HALSE - 38E |
| Jan-52 | NORTHWICH - 9G | MEXBOROUGH - 36B | IMMINGHAM - 40B | GORTON - 39A | IMMINGHAM - 40B | GORTON - 39A | STAVELEY - 38D | ANNESLEY - 38B | WOODFORD HALSE - 38E |
| Aug-52 | **9/52: COLW - 38A** | MEXBOROUGH - 36B | IMMINGHAM - 40B | GORTON - 39A | IMMINGHAM - 40B | GORTON - 39A | STAVELEY - 38D | ANNESLEY - 38B | WOODFORD HALSE - 38E |
| Jan-53 | 1/53: NEAS - 34E | MEXBOROUGH - 36B | IMMINGHAM - 40B | GORTON - 39A | IMMINGHAM - 40B | GORTON - 39A | STAVELEY - 38D | ANNESLEY - 38B | WOODFORD HALSE - 38E |
| Aug-53 | **3/53: DCTR - 36A** | MEXBOROUGH - 36B | IMMINGHAM - 40B | GORTON - 39A | IMMINGHAM - 40B | GORTON - 39A | STAVELEY - 38D | ANNESLEY - 38B | WOODFORD HALSE - 38E |
| Jan-54 | DONCASTER - 36A | MEXBOROUGH - 36B | IMMINGHAM - 40B | GORTON - 39A | IMMINGHAM - 40B | GORTON - 39A | STAVELEY - 38D | ANNESLEY - 38B | WOODFORD HALSE - 38E |
| Aug-54 | **8/54: COLW - 38A** | MEXBOROUGH - 36B | IMMINGHAM - 40B | GORTON - 39A | IMMINGHAM - 40B | GORTON - 39A | STAVELEY - 38D | ANNESLEY - 38B | WOODFORD HALSE - 38E |
| Jan-55 | COLWICK - 38A | MEXBOROUGH - 36B | IMMINGHAM - 40B | GORTON - 39A | IMMINGHAM - 40B | GORTON - 39A | STAVELEY - 38D | ANNESLEY - 38B | WOODFORD HALSE - 38E |
| Aug-55 | COLWICK - 38A | **4/55: RET - 36E** | IMMINGHAM - 40B | GORTON - 39A | IMMINGHAM - 40B | GORTON - 39A | **8/55: ANN - 38B** | ANNESLEY - 38B | **8/55: ANN - 38B** |
| Jan-56 | COLWICK - 38A | RETFORD - 36E | IMMINGHAM - 40B | GORTON - 39A | IMMINGHAM - 40B | GORTON - 39A | **11/55: COLW - 38A** | ANNESLEY - 38B | ANNESLEY - 38B |
| Aug-56 | **9/56: LEIC - 38C** | RETFORD - 36E | IMMINGHAM - 40B | GORTON - 39A | IMMINGHAM - 40B | GORTON - 39A | **12/55: GORT - 39A** | ANNESLEY - 38B | ANNESLEY - 38B |
| Jan-57 | LEICESTER (GC) - 38C | RETFORD - 36E | IMMINGHAM - 40B | GORTON - 39A | **3/57: LANG JN - 40E** | GORTON - 39A | GORTON - 39A | ANNESLEY - 38B | ANNESLEY - 38B |
| Aug-57 | LEICESTER (GC) - 38C | RETFORD - 36E | IMMINGHAM - 40B | GORTON - 39A | LANGWITH JCN - 40E | GORTON - 39A | GORTON - 39A | **5/57: LINC - 40A** | ANNESLEY - 38B |
| Jan-58 | **10/57: W/D** | RETFORD - 36E | IMMINGHAM - 40B | GORTON - 39A | LANGWITH JCN - 40E | **2/58: LANG JN - 41J** | **2/58: LANG JN - 41J** | LINCOLN - 40A | **2/58: LANG JN - 41J** |
| Aug-58 | | RETFORD - 36E | IMMINGHAM - 40B | GORTON - 9G | LANGWITH JCN - 41J | LANGWITH JCN - 41J | LANGWITH JCN - 41J | LINCOLN - 40A | LANGWITH JCN - 41J |
| Jan-59 | | RETFORD - 36E | IMMINGHAM - 40B | GORTON - 9G | LANGWITH JCN - 41J | LANGWITH JCN - 41J | LANGWITH JCN - 41J | LINCOLN - 40A | LANGWITH JCN - 41J |
| Aug-59 | | **4/59: W/D** | IMMINGHAM - 40B | **4/59: W/D** | LANGWITH JCN - 41J | LANGWITH JCN - 41J | LANGWITH JCN - 41J | LINCOLN - 40A | LANGWITH JCN - 41J |
| Nov-59 | | | IMMINGHAM - 40B | | LANGWITH JCN - 41J | LANGWITH JCN - 41J | LANGWITH JCN - 41J | LINCOLN - 40A | LANGWITH JCN - 41J |
| Jan-60 | | | IMMINGHAM - 40B | | LANGWITH JCN - 41J | LANGWITH JCN - 41J | LANGWITH JCN - 41J | LINCOLN - 40A | LANGWITH JCN - 41J |
| Apr-60 | | | IMMINGHAM - 40B | | LANGWITH JCN - 41J | LANGWITH JCN - 41J | LANGWITH JCN - 41J | LINCOLN - 40A | LANGWITH JCN - 41J |
| Aug-60 | | | IMMINGHAM - 40B | | LANGWITH JCN - 41J | LANGWITH JCN - 41J | LANGWITH JCN - 41J | LINCOLN - 40A | LANGWITH JCN - 41J |
| Nov-60 | | | IMMINGHAM - 40B | | LANGWITH JCN - 41J | LANGWITH JCN - 41J | LANGWITH JCN - 41J | LINCOLN - 40A | LANGWITH JCN - 41J |

| | 64332 | 64333 | 64346 | 64352 | 64354 | 64359 | 64362 | 64364 | 64373 |
|---|---|---|---|---|---|---|---|---|---|
| Aug-50 | GORTON - 39A | GORTON - 39A | GORTON - 39A | MEXBOROUGH - 36B | ANNESLEY - 38B | LINCOLN - 40A | BARNSLEY - 36D | WOODFORD HALSE - 38E | DARNALL - 39B |
| Jan-51 | GORTON - 39A | GORTON - 39A | GORTON - 39A | MEXBOROUGH - 36B | ANNESLEY - 38B | LINCOLN - 40A | BARNSLEY - 36D | WOODFORD HALSE - 38E | DARNALL - 39B |
| Aug-51 | GORTON - 39A | GORTON - 39A | GORTON - 39A | MEXBOROUGH - 36B | ANNESLEY - 38B | LINCOLN - 40A | BARNSLEY - 36D | WOODFORD HALSE - 38E | DARNALL - 39B |
| Jan-52 | GORTON - 39A | GORTON - 39A | GORTON - 39A | MEXBOROUGH - 36B | ANNESLEY - 38B | LINCOLN - 40A | BARNSLEY - 36D | WOODFORD HALSE - 38E | DARNALL - 39B |
| Aug-52 | GORTON - 39A | GORTON - 39A | GORTON - 39A | MEXBOROUGH - 36B | ANNESLEY - 38B | LINCOLN - 40A | BARNSLEY - 36D | WOODFORD HALSE - 38E | DARNALL - 39B |
| Jan-53 | GORTON - 39A | GORTON - 39A | GORTON - 39A | MEXBOROUGH - 36B | ANNESLEY - 38B | LINCOLN - 40A | BARNSLEY - 36D | WOODFORD HALSE - 38E | DARNALL - 39B |
| Aug-53 | GORTON - 39A | GORTON - 39A | GORTON - 39A | MEXBOROUGH - 36B | ANNESLEY - 38B | LINCOLN - 40A | BARNSLEY - 36D | WOODFORD HALSE - 38E | DARNALL - 39B |
| Jan-54 | GORTON - 39A | GORTON - 39A | GORTON - 39A | MEXBOROUGH - 36B | ANNESLEY - 38B | LINCOLN - 40A | BARNSLEY - 36D | WOODFORD HALSE - 38E | DARNALL - 39B |
| Aug-54 | GORTON - 39A | GORTON - 39A | GORTON - 39A | MEXBOROUGH - 36B | ANNESLEY - 38B | LINCOLN - 40A | BARNSLEY - 36D | WOODFORD HALSE - 38E | DARNALL - 39B |
| Jan-55 | GORTON - 39A | GORTON - 39A | GORTON - 39A | MEXBOROUGH - 36B | ANNESLEY - 38B | LINCOLN - 40A | BARNSLEY - 36D | WOODFORD HALSE - 38E | DARNALL - 39B |
| Aug-55 | GORTON - 39A | GORTON - 39A | GORTON - 39A | MEXBOROUGH - 36B | ANNESLEY - 38B | LINCOLN - 40A | BARNSLEY - 36D | **8/55: ANN - 38B** | DARNALL - 39B |
| Jan-56 | GORTON - 39A | GORTON - 39A | GORTON - 39A | MEXBOROUGH - 36B | ANNESLEY - 38B | LINCOLN - 40A | BARNSLEY - 36D | ANNESLEY - 38B | DARNALL - 41A |
| Aug-56 | GORTON - 39A | GORTON - 39A | GORTON - 39A | MEXBOROUGH - 36B | ANNESLEY - 38B | LINCOLN - 40A | BARNSLEY - 36D | ANNESLEY - 38B | DARNALL - 41A |
| Jan-57 | GORTON - 39A | GORTON - 39A | GORTON - 39A | **5/57: ANN - 38B** | **5/57: COLW - 38A** | LINCOLN - 40A | BARNSLEY - 36D | ANNESLEY - 38B | DARNALL - 41A |
| Aug-57 | GORTON - 39A | GORTON - 39A | GORTON - 39A | **11/57: COLW - 38A** | COLWICK - 38A | **5/57: ANN - 38B** | BARNSLEY - 36D | **7/57: LEIC - 38C** | DARNALL - 41A |
| Jan-58 | **1/58: LANG JN - 41J** | **1/58: LANG JN - 41J** | **2/58: TUX - 41E** | **1/58: TUX - 41E** | **1/58: TUX - 41E** | ANNESLEY - 38B | BARNSLEY - 36D | **9/57: COLW - 38A** | DARNALL - 41A |
| Aug-58 | LANGWITH JCN - 41J | **2/58: TUX - 41E** | TUXFORD - 41K | **2/58: LANG JN - 41J** | TUXFORD - 41K | ANNESLEY - 16D | **7/58: LANG JN - 41J** | **2/58: TUX - 41K** | DARNALL - 41A |
| Jan-59 | LANGWITH JCN - 41J | **1/59: LANG JN - 41J** | **1/59: LANG JN - 41J** | LANGWITH JCN - 41J | **1/59: LANG JN - 41J** | **4/59: GORT - 9G** | LANGWITH JCN - 41J | **1/59: LANG JN - 41J** | DARNALL - 41A |
| Aug-59 | LANGWITH JCN - 41J | LANGWITH JCN - 41J | **6/59: LINC - 40A** | LANGWITH JCN - 41J | **6/59: STAVE - 41H** | GORTON - 9G | **6/59: LINC - 40A** | LANGWITH JCN - 41J | DARNALL - 41A |
| Nov-59 | LANGWITH JCN - 41J | LANGWITH JCN - 41J | LINCOLN - 40A | LANGWITH JCN - 41J | STAVELEY (GC) - 41H | GORTON - 9G | LINCOLN - 40A | LANGWITH JCN - 41J | DARNALL - 41A |
| Jan-60 | LANGWITH JCN - 41J | LANGWITH JCN - 41J | LINCOLN - 40A | LANGWITH JCN - 41J | STAVELEY (GC) - 41H | GORTON - 9G | LINCOLN - 40A | LANGWITH JCN - 41J | DARNALL - 41A |
| Apr-60 | LANGWITH JCN - 41J | LANGWITH JCN - 41J | LINCOLN - 40A | LANGWITH JCN - 41J | **4/60: RET - 36E** | GORTON - 9G | LINCOLN - 40A | LANGWITH JCN - 41J | DARNALL - 41A |
| Aug-60 | LANGWITH JCN - 41J | LANGWITH JCN - 41J | LINCOLN - 40A | LANGWITH JCN - 41J | RETFORD - 36E | GORTON - 9G | LINCOLN - 40A | LANGWITH JCN - 41J | DARNALL - 41A |
| Nov-60 | LANGWITH JCN - 41J | LANGWITH JCN - 41J | LINCOLN - 40A | LANGWITH JCN - 41J | RETFORD - 36E | GORTON - 9G | LINCOLN - 40A | LANGWITH JCN - 41J | DARNALL - 41A |

| | 64375 | 64379 | 64386 | 64393 | 64394 | 64395 | 64402 | 64406 | 64417 |
|---|---|---|---|---|---|---|---|---|---|
| Aug-50 | WOODFORD HALSE - 38E | LANGWITH JCN - 40E | STAVELEY - 38D | RETFORD - 36E | NEASDEN - 34E | FRODINGHAM - 36C | RETFORD - 36E | BRUNSWICK - 8E | BRUNSWICK - 8E |
| Jan-51 | **1/51: NEAS - 34E** | LANGWITH JCN - 40E | STAVELEY - 38D | RETFORD - 36E | 1/51: WOD - 38E | FRODINGHAM - 36C | RETFORD - 36E | **12/50: COLW - 38A** | **12/50: COLW - 38A** |
| Aug-51 | NEASDEN - 34E | LANGWITH JCN - 40E | STAVELEY - 38D | RETFORD - 36E | **6/51: DARN - 39B** | FRODINGHAM - 36C | RETFORD - 36E | **9/51: ANN - 38B** | **9/51: BARN - 36D** |
| Jan-52 | NEASDEN - 34E | LANGWITH JCN - 40E | STAVELEY - 38D | RETFORD - 36E | DARNALL - 39B | FRODINGHAM - 36C | RETFORD - 36E | ANNESLEY - 38B | BARNSLEY - 36D |
| Aug-52 | NEASDEN - 34E | LANGWITH JCN - 40E | STAVELEY - 38D | RETFORD - 36E | DARNALL - 39B | FRODINGHAM - 36C | RETFORD - 36E | ANNESLEY - 38B | BARNSLEY - 36D |
| Jan-53 | **3/53: COLW - 38A** | LANGWITH JCN - 40E | STAVELEY - 38D | RETFORD - 36E | DARNALL - 39B | FRODINGHAM - 36C | RETFORD - 36E | ANNESLEY - 38B | BARNSLEY - 36D |
| Aug-53 | COLWICK - 38A | LANGWITH JCN - 40E | STAVELEY - 38D | RETFORD - 36E | DARNALL - 39B | FRODINGHAM - 36C | RETFORD - 36E | ANNESLEY - 38B | BARNSLEY - 36D |
| Jan-54 | COLWICK - 38A | LANGWITH JCN - 40E | STAVELEY - 38D | RETFORD - 36E | DARNALL - 39B | FRODINGHAM - 36C | RETFORD - 36E | ANNESLEY - 38B | BARNSLEY - 36D |
| Aug-54 | **8/54: EIC - 38C** | LANGWITH JCN - 40E | STAVELEY - 38D | RETFORD - 36E | DARNALL - 39B | FRODINGHAM - 36C | RETFORD - 36E | ANNESLEY - 38B | BARNSLEY - 36D |
| Jan-55 | LEICESTER (GC) - 38C | LANGWITH JCN - 40E | STAVELEY - 38D | RETFORD - 36E | DARNALL - 39B | **4/55: RET - 36E** | RETFORD - 36E | ANNESLEY - 38B | BARNSLEY - 36D |
| Aug-55 | LEICESTER (GC) - 38C | LANGWITH JCN - 40E | **8/55: ANN - 38B** | RETFORD - 36E | DARNALL - 39B | RETFORD - 36E | RETFORD - 36E | ANNESLEY - 38B | BARNSLEY - 36D |
| Jan-56 | LEICESTER (GC) - 38C | LANGWITH JCN - 40E | ANNESLEY - 38B | **12/55: MEX - 36B** | DARNALL - 41A | RETFORD - 36E | **12/55: MEX - 36B** | ANNESLEY - 38B | BARNSLEY - 36D |
| Aug-56 | LEICESTER (GC) - 38C | LANGWITH JCN - 40E | ANNESLEY - 38B | MEXBOROUGH - 36B | DARNALL - 41A | RETFORD - 36E | MEXBOROUGH - 36B | ANNESLEY - 38B | BARNSLEY - 36D |
| Jan-57 | LEICESTER (GC) - 38C | LANGWITH JCN - 40E | ANNESLEY - 38B | MEXBOROUGH - 36B | DARNALL - 41A | RETFORD - 36E | MEXBOROUGH - 36B | ANNESLEY - 38B | BARNSLEY - 36D |
| Aug-57 | **7/57: ANN - 38B** | LANGWITH JCN - 40E | **5/57: IMM - 40B** | MEXBOROUGH - 36B | DARNALL - 41A | RETFORD - 36E | MEXBOROUGH - 36B | **5/57: MEX - 36B** | BARNSLEY - 36D |
| Jan-58 | ANNESLEY - 38B | LANGWITH JCN - 40E | IMMINGHAM - 40B | MEXBOROUGH - 36B | DARNALL - 41A | RETFORD - 36E | MEXBOROUGH - 36B | MEXBOROUGH - 36B | BARNSLEY - 36D |
| Aug-58 | ANNESLEY - 16D | LANGWITH JCN - 41J | IMMINGHAM - 40B | MEXBOROUGH - 41F | DARNALL - 41A | RETFORD - 36E | MEXBOROUGH - 41F | MEXBOROUGH - 41F | BARNSLEY - 41G |
| Jan-59 | ANNESLEY - 16D | LANGWITH JCN - 41J | IMMINGHAM - 40B | MEXBOROUGH - 41F | DARNALL - 41A | RETFORD - 36E | MEXBOROUGH - 41F | MEXBOROUGH - 41F | BARNSLEY - 41G |
| Aug-59 | ANNESLEY - 16D | LANGWITH JCN - 41J | IMMINGHAM - 40B | MEXBOROUGH - 41F | DARNALL - 41A | RETFORD - 36E | MEXBOROUGH - 41F | MEXBOROUGH - 41F | BARNSLEY - 41G |
| Nov-59 | ANNESLEY - 16D | LANGWITH JCN - 41J | IMMINGHAM - 40B | MEXBOROUGH - 41F | DARNALL - 41A | **11/59: FROD - 36C** | MEXBOROUGH - 41F | MEXBOROUGH - 41F | BARNSLEY - 41G |
| Jan-60 | ANNESLEY - 16D | LANGWITH JCN - 41J | IMMINGHAM - 40B | MEXBOROUGH - 41F | DARNALL - 41A | FRODINGHAM - 36C | MEXBOROUGH - 41F | MEXBOROUGH - 41F | **1/60: MEX - 41F** |
| Apr-60 | **5/60: GORT - 9G** | LANGWITH JCN - 41J | IMMINGHAM - 40B | MEXBOROUGH - 41F | DARNALL - 41A | FRODINGHAM - 36C | MEXBOROUGH - 41F | MEXBOROUGH - 41F | MEXBOROUGH - 41F |
| Aug-60 | GORTON - 9G | LANGWITH JCN - 41J | IMMINGHAM - 40B | MEXBOROUGH - 41F | DARNALL - 41A | FRODINGHAM - 36C | MEXBOROUGH - 41F | MEXBOROUGH - 41F | MEXBOROUGH - 41F |
| Nov-60 | GORTON - 9G | LANGWITH JCN - 41J | IMMINGHAM - 40B | MEXBOROUGH - 41F | DARNALL - 41A | **10/60: RET - 36E** | MEXBOROUGH - 41F | MEXBOROUGH - 41F | **10/60: STAVE - 41H** |

| | | | | | | | | J35 0-6-0 (1906) | |
|---|---|---|---|---|---|---|---|---|---|
| | 64418 | 64420 | 64427 | 64439 | 64441 | 64442 | 64450 | 64460 | 64461 |
| Aug-50 | LANGWITH JCN - 40E | BRUNSWICK - 8E | LANGWITH JCN - 40E | IMMINGHAM - 40B | DARNALL - 39B | MEXBOROUGH - 36B | GORTON - 39A | KIPPS - 65E | STIRLING - 63B |
| Jan-51 | LANGWITH JCN - 40E | BRUNSWICK - 8E | LANGWITH JCN - 40E | IMMINGHAM - 40B | DARNALL - 39B | MEXBOROUGH - 36B | GORTON - 39A | KIPPS - 65E | STIRLING - 63B |
| Aug-51 | LANGWITH JCN - 40E | BRUNSWICK - 8E | LANGWITH JCN - 40E | IMMINGHAM - 40B | DARNALL - 39B | MEXBOROUGH - 36B | GORTON - 39A | KIPPS - 65E | **11/51: CANAL - 68E** |
| Jan-52 | **12/51: STAVE - 38D** | BRUNSWICK - 8E | LANGWITH JCN - 40E | IMMINGHAM - 40B | DARNALL - 39B | MEXBOROUGH - 36B | GORTON - 39A | KIPPS - 65E | **1/52: PARK - 65C** |
| Aug-52 | STAVELEY - 38D | **9/52: COLW - 38A** | LANGWITH JCN - 40E | IMMINGHAM - 40B | DARNALL - 39B | MEXBOROUGH - 36B | GORTON - 39A | KIPPS - 65E | PARKHEAD - 65C |
| Jan-53 | STAVELEY - 38D | COLWICK - 38A | LANGWITH JCN - 40E | IMMINGHAM - 40B | DARNALL - 39B | MEXBOROUGH - 36B | GORTON - 39A | KIPPS - 65E | PARKHEAD - 65C |
| Aug-53 | **7/53: WOOD - 38E** | COLWICK - 38A | LANGWITH JCN - 40E | IMMINGHAM - 40B | DARNALL - 39B | MEXBOROUGH - 36B | GORTON - 39A | KIPPS - 65E | PARKHEAD - 65C |
| Jan-54 | WOODFORD HALSE - 38E | COLWICK - 38A | LANGWITH JCN - 40E | IMMINGHAM - 40B | DARNALL - 39B | **3/54: BARN - 36D** | GORTON - 39A | KIPPS - 65E | PARKHEAD - 65C |
| Aug-54 | WOODFORD HALSE - 38E | COLWICK - 38A | LANGWITH JCN - 40E | IMMINGHAM - 40B | DARNALL - 39B | BARNSLEY - 36D | GORTON - 39A | KIPPS - 65E | PARKHEAD - 65C |
| Jan-55 | WOODFORD HALSE - 38E | COLWICK - 38A | LANGWITH JCN - 40E | IMMINGHAM - 40B | DARNALL - 39B | BARNSLEY - 36D | GORTON - 39A | KIPPS - 65E | PARKHEAD - 65C |
| Aug-55 | WOODFORD HALSE - 38E | COLWICK - 38A | LANGWITH JCN - 40E | IMMINGHAM - 40B | DARNALL - 39B | BARNSLEY - 36D | GORTON - 39A | KIPPS - 65E | PARKHEAD - 65C |
| Jan-56 | WOODFORD HALSE - 38E | COLWICK - 38A | LANGWITH JCN - 40E | IMMINGHAM - 40B | DARNALL - 41A | BARNSLEY - 36D | GORTON - 39A | KIPPS - 65E | PARKHEAD - 65C |
| Aug-56 | WOODFORD HALSE - 38E | COLWICK - 38A | LANGWITH JCN - 40E | IMMINGHAM - 40B | DARNALL - 41A | BARNSLEY - 36D | GORTON - 39A | KIPPS - 65E | PARKHEAD - 65C |
| Jan-57 | WOODFORD HALSE - 38E | COLWICK - 38A | LANGWITH JCN - 40E | IMMINGHAM - 40B | DARNALL - 41A | BARNSLEY - 36D | GORTON - 39A | KIPPS - 65E | PARKHEAD - 65C |
| Aug-57 | WOODFORD HALSE - 38E | **5/57: ANN - 38B** | LANGWITH JCN - 40E | **5/57: ANN - 38B** | DARNALL - 41A | BARNSLEY - 36D | GORTON - 39A | KIPPS - 65E | PARKHEAD - 65C |
| Jan-58 | WOODFORD HALSE - 38E | ANNESLEY - 38B | LANGWITH JCN - 40E | ANNESLEY - 38B | DARNALL - 41A | BARNSLEY - 36D | **2/58: TUX - 41E** | KIPPS - 65E | PARKHEAD - 65C |
| Aug-58 | WOODFORD HALSE - 2F | ANNESLEY - 16D | LANGWITH JCN - 41J | ANNESLEY - 16D | DARNALL - 41A | BARNSLEY - 41G | TUXFORD - 41K | KIPPS - 65E | PARKHEAD - 65C |
| Jan-59 | **2/59: GORT - 9G** | ANNESLEY - 16D | LANGWITH JCN - 41J | ANNESLEY - 16D | DARNALL - 41A | BARNSLEY - 41G | **1/59: LANG JN - 41J** | KIPPS - 65E | PARKHEAD - 65C |
| Aug-59 | GORTON - 9G | ANNESLEY - 16D | LANGWITH JCN - 41J | **4/59: GORT - 9G** | DARNALL - 41A | BARNSLEY - 41G | **3/59: RET - 36E** | KIPPS - 65E | PARKHEAD - 65C |
| Nov-59 | GORTON - 9G | ANNESLEY - 16D | LANGWITH JCN - 41J | GORTON - 9G | DARNALL - 41A | BARNSLEY - 41G | RETFORD - 36E | **9/59: W/D** | PARKHEAD - 65C |
| Jan-60 | GORTON - 9G | ANNESLEY - 16D | LANGWITH JCN - 41J | GORTON - 9G | DARNALL - 41A | **1/60: MEX - 41F** | RETFORD - 36E | | PARKHEAD - 65C |
| Apr-60 | GORTON - 9G | **5/60: GORT - 9G** | LANGWITH JCN - 41J | GORTON - 9G | **5/60: RET - 36E** | MEXBOROUGH - 41F | RETFORD - 36E | | PARKHEAD - 65C |
| Aug-60 | GORTON - 9G | GORTON - 9G | LANGWITH JCN - 41J | GORTON - 9G | RETFORD - 36E | MEXBOROUGH - 41F | RETFORD - 36E | | PARKHEAD - 65C |
| Nov-60 | GORTON - 9G | GORTON - 9G | LANGWITH JCN - 41J | GORTON - 9G | RETFORD - 36E | MEXBOROUGH - 41F | RETFORD - 36E | | PARKHEAD - 65C |

| | 64462 | 64463 | 64464 | 64466 | 64468 | 64470 | 64471 | 64472 | 64473 |
|---|---|---|---|---|---|---|---|---|---|
| Aug-50 | EDINBURGH(SM) - 64A | HAWICK - 64G | THORNTONJCN - 62A | THORNTONJCN - 62A | BATHGATE - 64F | KIPPS - 65E | STIRLING - 63B | KIPPS - 65E | KIPPS - 65E |
| Jan-51 | EDINBURGH(SM) - 64A | HAWICK - 64G | THORNTONJCN - 62A | THORNTONJCN - 62A | BATHGATE - 64F | KIPPS - 65E | STIRLING - 63B | KIPPS - 65E | KIPPS - 65E |
| Aug-51 | EDINBURGH(SM) - 64A | HAWICK - 64G | THORNTONJCN - 62A | THORNTONJCN - 62A | BATHGATE - 64F | KIPPS - 65E | STIRLING - 63B | KIPPS - 65E | KIPPS - 65E |
| Jan-52 | EDINBURGH(SM) - 64A | HAWICK - 64G | THORNTONJCN - 62A | THORNTONJCN - 62A | BATHGATE - 64F | KIPPS - 65E | **11/51: CANAL - 68E** | KIPPS - 65E | KIPPS - 65E |
| Aug-52 | EDINBURGH(SM) - 64A | HAWICK - 64G | THORNTONJCN - 62A | THORNTONJCN - 62A | BATHGATE - 64F | KIPPS - 65E | CARLISE(CANAL) - 68E | KIPPS - 65E | KIPPS - 65E |
| Jan-53 | EDINBURGH(SM) - 64A | HAWICK - 64G | THORNTONJCN - 62A | THORNTONJCN - 62A | BATHGATE - 64F | KIPPS - 65E | CARLISE(CANAL) - 68E | KIPPS - 65E | KIPPS - 65E |
| Aug-53 | EDINBURGH(SM) - 64A | HAWICK - 64G | THORNTONJCN - 62A | THORNTONJCN - 62A | BATHGATE - 64F | KIPPS - 65E | CARLISE(CANAL) - 68E | KIPPS - 65E | KIPPS - 65E |
| Jan-54 | EDINBURGH(SM) - 64A | HAWICK - 64G | THORNTONJCN - 62A | THORNTONJCN - 62A | BATHGATE - 64F | KIPPS - 65E | CARLISE(CANAL) - 68E | KIPPS - 65E | KIPPS - 65E |
| Aug-54 | EDINBURGH(SM) - 64A | HAWICK - 64G | THORNTONJCN - 62A | THORNTONJCN - 62A | BATHGATE - 64F | KIPPS - 65E | CARLISE(CANAL) - 68E | KIPPS - 65E | KIPPS - 65E |
| Jan-55 | EDINBURGH(SM) - 64A | HAWICK - 64G | THORNTONJCN - 62A | THORNTONJCN - 62A | BATHGATE - 64F | KIPPS - 65E | **11/54: POL - 66A** | KIPPS - 65E | KIPPS - 65E |
| Aug-55 | EDINBURGH(SM) - 64A | HAWICK - 64G | THORNTONJCN - 62A | THORNTONJCN - 62A | BATHGATE - 64F | KIPPS - 65E | POLMADIE - 66A | KIPPS - 65E | KIPPS - 65E |
| Jan-56 | EDINBURGH(SM) - 64A | HAWICK - 64G | THORNTONJCN - 62A | THORNTONJCN - 62A | BATHGATE - 64F | KIPPS - 65E | POLMADIE - 66A | KIPPS - 65E | KIPPS - 65E |
| Aug-56 | EDINBURGH(SM) - 64A | HAWICK - 64G | THORNTONJCN - 62A | THORNTONJCN - 62A | BATHGATE - 64F | KIPPS - 65E | POLMADIE - 66A | KIPPS - 65E | KIPPS - 65E |
| Jan-57 | EDINBURGH(SM) - 64A | HAWICK - 64G | **1/57: POL - 66A** | THORNTONJCN - 62A | BATHGATE - 64F | KIPPS - 65E | POLMADIE - 66A | KIPPS - 65E | KIPPS - 65E |
| Aug-57 | EDINBURGH(SM) - 64A | HAWICK - 64G | POLMADIE - 66A | THORNTONJCN - 62A | BATHGATE - 64F | KIPPS - 65E | POLMADIE - 66A | KIPPS - 65E | KIPPS - 65E |
| Jan-58 | EDINBURGH(SM) - 64A | HAWICK - 64G | POLMADIE - 66A | THORNTONJCN - 62A | BATHGATE - 64F | KIPPS - 65E | POLMADIE - 66A | KIPPS - 65E | KIPPS - 65E |
| Aug-58 | EDINBURGH(SM) - 64A | HAWICK - 64G | **5/58: W/D** | THORNTONJCN - 62A | BATHGATE - 64F | KIPPS - 65E | POLMADIE - 66A | KIPPS - 65E | KIPPS - 65E |
| Jan-59 | EDINBURGH(SM) - 64A | HAWICK - 64G | | THORNTONJCN - 62A | BATHGATE - 64F | KIPPS - 65E | POLMADIE - 66A | KIPPS - 65E | KIPPS - 65E |
| Aug-59 | EDINBURGH(SM) - 64A | HAWICK - 64G | | **7/59: W/D** | BATHGATE - 64F | KIPPS - 65E | POLMADIE - 66A | KIPPS - 65E | KIPPS - 65E |
| Nov-59 | EDINBURGH(SM) - 64A | **11/59: ST M - 64A** | | | BATHGATE - 64F | KIPPS - 65E | POLMADIE - 66A | KIPPS - 65E | KIPPS - 65E |
| Jan-60 | EDINBURGH(SM) - 64A | EDINBURGH(SM) - 64A | | | BATHGATE - 64F | KIPPS - 65E | POLMADIE - 66A | KIPPS - 65E | **12/59: W/D** |
| Apr-60 | EDINBURGH(SM) - 64A | EDINBURGH(SM) - 64A | | | BATHGATE - 64F | KIPPS - 65E | POLMADIE - 66A | KIPPS - 65E | |
| Aug-60 | EDINBURGH(SM) - 64A | EDINBURGH(SM) - 64A | | | **6/60: W/D** | KIPPS - 65E | POLMADIE - 66A | KIPPS - 65E | |
| Nov-60 | EDINBURGH(SM) - 64A | **11/60: W/D** | | | | KIPPS - 65E | POLMADIE - 66A | KIPPS - 65E | |

| | 64474 | 64475 | 64476 | 64477 | 64478 | 64479 | 64480 | 64482 | 64483 |
|---|---|---|---|---|---|---|---|---|---|
| Aug-50 | THORNTONJCN - 62A | DUNFERMLINE - 62C | DUNFERMLINE - 62C | THORNTONJCN - 62A | CARLISLE(CANAL) - 12B | EDINBURGH(SM) - 64A | DUNFERMLINE - 62C | DUNDEE - 62B | DUNFERMLINE - 62C |
| Jan-51 | THORNTONJCN - 62A | DUNFERMLINE - 62C | DUNFERMLINE - 62C | THORNTONJCN - 62A | CARLISLE(CANAL) - 12B | EDINBURGH(SM) - 64A | DUNFERMLINE - 62C | DUNDEE - 62B | DUNFERMLINE - 62C |
| Aug-51 | THORNTONJCN - 62A | DUNFERMLINE - 62C | DUNFERMLINE - 62C | THORNTONJCN - 62A | CARLISE(CANAL) - 68E | EDINBURGH(SM) - 64A | DUNFERMLINE - 62C | DUNDEE - 62B | DUNFERMLINE - 62C |
| Jan-52 | THORNTONJCN - 62A | DUNFERMLINE - 62C | DUNFERMLINE - 62C | THORNTONJCN - 62A | CARLISE(CANAL) - 68E | EDINBURGH(SM) - 64A | DUNFERMLINE - 62C | **5/52: FERRY - 61B** | DUNFERMLINE - 62C |
| Aug-52 | THORNTONJCN - 62A | DUNFERMLINE - 62C | DUNFERMLINE - 62C | THORNTONJCN - 62A | CARLISE(CANAL) - 68E | EDINBURGH(SM) - 64A | DUNFERMLINE - 62C | **6/52: KITTY - 61A** | DUNFERMLINE - 62C |
| Jan-53 | THORNTONJCN - 62A | DUNFERMLINE - 62C | DUNFERMLINE - 62C | THORNTONJCN - 62A | CARLISE(CANAL) - 68E | EDINBURGH(SM) - 64A | DUNFERMLINE - 62C | KITTYBREWSTER - 61A | DUNFERMLINE - 62C |
| Aug-53 | THORNTONJCN - 62A | DUNFERMLINE - 62C | DUNFERMLINE - 62C | THORNTONJCN - 62A | CARLISE(CANAL) - 68E | EDINBURGH(SM) - 64A | DUNFERMLINE - 62C | KITTYBREWSTER - 61A | DUNFERMLINE - 62C |
| Jan-54 | THORNTONJCN - 62A | DUNFERMLINE - 62C | DUNFERMLINE - 62C | THORNTONJCN - 62A | CARLISE(CANAL) - 68E | EDINBURGH(SM) - 64A | DUNFERMLINE - 62C | KITTYBREWSTER - 61A | DUNFERMLINE - 62C |
| Aug-54 | THORNTONJCN - 62A | DUNFERMLINE - 62C | DUNFERMLINE - 62C | THORNTONJCN - 62A | CARLISE(CANAL) - 68E | EDINBURGH(SM) - 64A | DUNFERMLINE - 62C | KITTYBREWSTER - 61A | **7/54: FERRY - 61B** |
| Jan-55 | THORNTONJCN - 62A | DUNFERMLINE - 62C | DUNFERMLINE - 62C | THORNTONJCN - 62A | CARLISE(CANAL) - 68E | EDINBURGH(SM) - 64A | DUNFERMLINE - 62C | KITTYBREWSTER - 61A | FERRYHILL - 61B |
| Aug-55 | THORNTONJCN - 62A | DUNFERMLINE - 62C | DUNFERMLINE - 62C | THORNTONJCN - 62A | CARLISE(CANAL) - 68E | EDINBURGH(SM) - 64A | DUNFERMLINE - 62C | KITTYBREWSTER - 61A | FERRYHILL - 61B |
| Jan-56 | THORNTONJCN - 62A | DUNFERMLINE - 62C | DUNFERMLINE - 62C | THORNTONJCN - 62A | CARLISE(CANAL) - 68E | EDINBURGH(SM) - 64A | DUNFERMLINE - 62C | KITTYBREWSTER - 61A | FERRYHILL - 61B |
| Aug-56 | THORNTONJCN - 62A | DUNFERMLINE - 62C | DUNFERMLINE - 62C | THORNTONJCN - 62A | CARLISE(CANAL) - 68E | EDINBURGH(SM) - 64A | DUNFERMLINE - 62C | KITTYBREWSTER - 61A | FERRYHILL - 61B |
| Jan-57 | THORNTONJCN - 62A | DUNFERMLINE - 62C | DUNFERMLINE - 62C | **1/57: POL - 66A** | CARLISE(CANAL) - 68E | EDINBURGH(SM) - 64A | DUNFERMLINE - 62C | KITTYBREWSTER - 61A | FERRYHILL - 61B |
| Aug-57 | THORNTONJCN - 62A | DUNFERMLINE - 62C | DUNFERMLINE - 62C | POLMADIE - 66A | CARLISE(CANAL) - 68E | EDINBURGH(SM) - 64A | DUNFERMLINE - 62C | KITTYBREWSTER - 61A | FERRYHILL - 61B |
| Jan-58 | THORNTONJCN - 62A | DUNFERMLINE - 62C | DUNFERMLINE - 62C | POLMADIE - 66A | CARLISLECANAL - 68E | EDINBURGH(SM) - 64A | DUNFERMLINE - 62C | KITTYBREWSTER - 61A | FERRYHILL - 61B |
| Aug-58 | THORNTONJCN - 62A | DUNFERMLINE - 62C | DUNFERMLINE - 62C | POLMADIE - 66A | CARLISLECANAL - 12C | EDINBURGH(SM) - 64A | DUNFERMLINE - 62C | KITTYBREWSTER - 61A | FERRYHILL - 61B |
| Jan-59 | THORNTONJCN - 62A | DUNFERMLINE - 62C | DUNFERMLINE - 62C | POLMADIE - 66A | CARLISLECANAL - 12C | EDINBURGH(SM) - 64A | DUNFERMLINE - 62C | **2/59: ST M - 64A** | **2/59: ST M - 64A** |
| Aug-59 | THORNTONJCN - 62A | **4/59: W/D** | DUNFERMLINE - 62C | POLMADIE - 66A | CARLISLECANAL - 12C | EDINBURGH(SM) - 64A | DUNFERMLINE - 62C | EDINBURGH(SM) - 64A | EDINBURGH(SM) - 64A |
| Nov-59 | THORNTONJCN - 62A | | DUNFERMLINE - 62C | POLMADIE - 66A | CARLISLECANAL - 12C | EDINBURGH(SM) - 64A | DUNFERMLINE - 62C | EDINBURGH(SM) - 64A | EDINBURGH(SM) - 64A |
| Jan-60 | THORNTONJCN - 62A | | DUNFERMLINE - 62C | POLMADIE - 66A | CARLISLECANAL - 12C | EDINBURGH(SM) - 64A | DUNFERMLINE - 62C | EDINBURGH(SM) - 64A | EDINBURGH(SM) - 64A |
| Apr-60 | THORNTONJCN - 62A | | DUNFERMLINE - 62C | POLMADIE - 66A | CARLISLECANAL - 12C | EDINBURGH(SM) - 64A | DUNFERMLINE - 62C | EDINBURGH(SM) - 64A | EDINBURGH(SM) - 64A |
| Aug-60 | THORNTONJCN - 62A | | DUNFERMLINE - 62C | POLMADIE - 66A | CARLISLECANAL - 12C | EDINBURGH(SM) - 64A | DUNFERMLINE - 62C | EDINBURGH(SM) - 64A | **8/60: W/D** |
| Nov-60 | THORNTONJCN - 62A | | DUNFERMLINE - 62C | POLMADIE - 66A | CARLISLECANAL - 12C | EDINBURGH(SM) - 64A | DUNFERMLINE - 62C | EDINBURGH(SM) - 64A | |

| | 64484 | 64485 | 64486 | 64487 | 64488 | 64489 | 64490 | 64491 | 64492 |
|---|---|---|---|---|---|---|---|---|---|
| Aug-50 | POLMONT - 64E | DUNDEE - 62B | EDINBURGH(SM) - 64A | DUNFERMLINE - 62C | THORNTONJCN - 62A | EDINBURGH(SM) - 64A | POLMONT - 64E | BATHGATE - 64F | EDINBURGH(SM) - 64A |
| Jan-51 | POLMONT - 64E | DUNDEE - 62B | EDINBURGH(SM) - 64A | DUNFERMLINE - 62C | THORNTONJCN - 62A | EDINBURGH(SM) - 64A | POLMONT - 64E | BATHGATE - 64F | EDINBURGH(SM) - 64A |
| Aug-51 | POLMONT - 64E | DUNDEE - 62B | EDINBURGH(SM) - 64A | DUNFERMLINE - 62C | THORNTONJCN - 62A | EDINBURGH(SM) - 64A | POLMONT - 64E | BATHGATE - 64F | EDINBURGH(SM) - 64A |
| Jan-52 | **3/52: BATH - 64F** | DUNDEE - 62B | EDINBURGH(SM) - 64A | DUNFERMLINE - 62C | THORNTONJCN - 62A | EDINBURGH(SM) - 64A | POLMONT - 64E | BATHGATE - 64F | EDINBURGH(SM) - 64A |
| Aug-52 | BATHGATE - 64F | **5/52: FERRY - 61B** | EDINBURGH(SM) - 64A | DUNFERMLINE - 62C | THORNTONJCN - 62A | EDINBURGH(SM) - 64A | POLMONT - 64E | BATHGATE - 64F | EDINBURGH(SM) - 64A |
| Jan-53 | BATHGATE - 64F | FERRYHILL - 61B | EDINBURGH(SM) - 64A | DUNFERMLINE - 62C | THORNTONJCN - 62A | EDINBURGH(SM) - 64A | POLMONT - 64E | BATHGATE - 64F | EDINBURGH(SM) - 64A |
| Aug-53 | BATHGATE - 64F | FERRYHILL - 61B | EDINBURGH(SM) - 64A | DUNFERMLINE - 62C | THORNTONJCN - 62A | EDINBURGH(SM) - 64A | POLMONT - 64E | BATHGATE - 64F | EDINBURGH(SM) - 64A |
| Jan-54 | BATHGATE - 64F | FERRYHILL - 61B | EDINBURGH(SM) - 64A | DUNFERMLINE - 62C | THORNTONJCN - 62A | EDINBURGH(SM) - 64A | POLMONT - 64E | BATHGATE - 64F | EDINBURGH(SM) - 64A |
| Aug-54 | BATHGATE - 64F | FERRYHILL - 61B | EDINBURGH(SM) - 64A | DUNFERMLINE - 62C | THORNTONJCN - 62A | EDINBURGH(SM) - 64A | POLMONT - 64E | BATHGATE - 64F | EDINBURGH(SM) - 64A |
| Jan-55 | BATHGATE - 64F | FERRYHILL - 61B | EDINBURGH(SM) - 64A | DUNFERMLINE - 62C | THORNTONJCN - 62A | EDINBURGH(SM) - 64A | POLMONT - 64E | BATHGATE - 64F | EDINBURGH(SM) - 64A |
| Aug-55 | BATHGATE - 64F | FERRYHILL - 61B | EDINBURGH(SM) - 64A | DUNFERMLINE - 62C | THORNTONJCN - 62A | EDINBURGH(SM) - 64A | POLMONT - 64E | BATHGATE - 64F | EDINBURGH(SM) - 64A |
| Jan-56 | BATHGATE - 64F | FERRYHILL - 61B | EDINBURGH(SM) - 64A | DUNFERMLINE - 62C | THORNTONJCN - 62A | EDINBURGH(SM) - 64A | POLMONT - 64E | BATHGATE - 64F | EDINBURGH(SM) - 64A |
| Aug-56 | BATHGATE - 64F | FERRYHILL - 61B | EDINBURGH(SM) - 64A | DUNFERMLINE - 62C | THORNTONJCN - 62A | EDINBURGH(SM) - 64A | POLMONT - 64E | BATHGATE - 64F | EDINBURGH(SM) - 64A |
| Jan-57 | BATHGATE - 64F | FERRYHILL - 61B | EDINBURGH(SM) - 64A | DUNFERMLINE - 62C | THORNTONJCN - 62A | EDINBURGH(SM) - 64A | POLMONT - 64E | BATHGATE - 64F | EDINBURGH(SM) - 64A |
| Aug-57 | BATHGATE - 64F | FERRYHILL - 61B | EDINBURGH(SM) - 64A | DUNFERMLINE - 62C | THORNTONJCN - 62A | EDINBURGH(SM) - 64A | POLMONT - 64E | BATHGATE - 64F | EDINBURGH(SM) - 64A |
| Jan-58 | BATHGATE - 64F | FERRYHILL - 61B | EDINBURGH(SM) - 64A | DUNFERMLINE - 62C | THORNTONJCN - 62A | EDINBURGH(SM) - 64A | POLMONT - 64E | BATHGATE - 64F | EDINBURGH(SM) - 64A |
| Aug-58 | BATHGATE - 64F | FERRYHILL - 61B | **9/58: W/D** | DUNFERMLINE - 62C | THORNTONJCN - 62A | EDINBURGH(SM) - 64A | POLMONT - 64E | BATHGATE - 64F | EDINBURGH(SM) - 64A |
| Jan-59 | BATHGATE - 64F | FERRYHILL - 61B | | DUNFERMLINE - 62C | THORNTONJCN - 62A | EDINBURGH(SM) - 64A | POLMONT - 64E | BATHGATE - 64F | **2/59: W/D** |
| Aug-59 | BATHGATE - 64F | **3/59: W/D** | | DUNFERMLINE - 62C | THORNTONJCN - 62A | EDINBURGH(SM) - 64A | POLMONT - 64E | BATHGATE - 64F | |
| Nov-59 | **9/59: W/D** | | | DUNFERMLINE - 62C | THORNTONJCN - 62A | EDINBURGH(SM) - 64A | POLMONT - 64E | BATHGATE - 64F | |
| Jan-60 | | | | DUNFERMLINE - 62C | THORNTONJCN - 62A | EDINBURGH(SM) - 64A | **12/59: W/D** | BATHGATE - 64F | |
| Apr-60 | | | | DUNFERMLINE - 62C | THORNTONJCN - 62A | EDINBURGH(SM) - 64A | | BATHGATE - 64F | |
| Aug-60 | | | | **5/60: W/D** | THORNTONJCN - 62A | EDINBURGH(SM) - 64A | | BATHGATE - 64F | |
| Nov-60 | | | | | THORNTONJCN - 62A | EDINBURGH(SM) - 64A | | BATHGATE - 64F | |

| | 64493 | 64494 | 64495 | 64496 | 64497 | 64498 | 64499 | 64500 | 64501 |
|---|---|---|---|---|---|---|---|---|---|
| Aug-50 | DUNFERMLINE - 62C | HAWICK - 64G | THORNTONJCN - 62A | DUNFERMLINE - 62C | STIRLING - 63B | KIPPS - 65E | CARLISLE(CANAL) - 12B | THORNTONJCN - 62A | STIRLING - 63B |
| Jan-51 | DUNFERMLINE - 62C | HAWICK - 64G | THORNTONJCN - 62A | DUNFERMLINE - 62C | STIRLING - 63B | KIPPS - 65E | CARLISLE(CANAL) - 12B | THORNTONJCN - 62A | STIRLING - 63B |
| Aug-51 | DUNFERMLINE - 62C | HAWICK - 64G | THORNTONJCN - 62A | DUNFERMLINE - 62C | STIRLING - 63B | KIPPS - 65E | CARLISE(CANAL) - 68E | THORNTONJCN - 62A | STIRLING - 63B |
| Jan-52 | DUNFERMLINE - 62C | HAWICK - 64G | THORNTONJCN - 62A | DUNFERMLINE - 62C | STIRLING - 63B | KIPPS - 65E | CARLISE(CANAL) - 68E | THORNTONJCN - 62A | STIRLING - 63B |
| Aug-52 | DUNFERMLINE - 62C | HAWICK - 64G | THORNTONJCN - 62A | DUNFERMLINE - 62C | STIRLING - 63B | KIPPS - 65E | CARLISE(CANAL) - 68E | THORNTONJCN - 62A | STIRLING - 63B |
| Jan-53 | DUNFERMLINE - 62C | HAWICK - 64G | **12/52: DALRY - 64C** | DUNFERMLINE - 62C | STIRLING - 63B | KIPPS - 65E | CARLISE(CANAL) - 68E | **12/52: DALRY - 64C** | STIRLING - 63B |
| Aug-53 | DUNFERMLINE - 62C | HAWICK - 64G | DALRYRD - 64C | DUNFERMLINE - 62C | STIRLING - 63B | KIPPS - 65E | CARLISE(CANAL) - 68E | DALRYRD - 64C | STIRLING - 63B |
| Jan-54 | DUNFERMLINE - 62C | HAWICK - 64G | DALRYRD - 64C | DUNFERMLINE - 62C | STIRLING - 63B | KIPPS - 65E | CARLISE(CANAL) - 68E | DALRYRD - 64C | STIRLING - 63B |
| Aug-54 | DUNFERMLINE - 62C | HAWICK - 64G | DALRYRD - 64C | DUNFERMLINE - 62C | STIRLING - 63B | KIPPS - 65E | CARLISE(CANAL) - 68E | DALRYRD - 64C | STIRLING - 63B |
| Jan-55 | DUNFERMLINE - 62C | HAWICK - 64G | DALRYRD - 64C | DUNFERMLINE - 62C | STIRLING - 63B | KIPPS - 65E | CARLISE(CANAL) - 68E | DALRYRD - 64C | STIRLING - 63B |
| Aug-55 | DUNFERMLINE - 62C | HAWICK - 64G | DALRYRD - 64C | DUNFERMLINE - 62C | STIRLING - 63B | KIPPS - 65E | CARLISE(CANAL) - 68E | DALRYRD - 64C | STIRLING - 63B |
| Jan-56 | DUNFERMLINE - 62C | HAWICK - 64G | DALRYRD - 64C | DUNFERMLINE - 62C | STIRLING - 63B | KIPPS - 65E | CARLISE(CANAL) - 68E | DALRYRD - 64C | STIRLING - 63B |
| Aug-56 | DUNFERMLINE - 62C | HAWICK - 64G | DALRYRD - 64C | DUNFERMLINE - 62C | STIRLING - 63B | KIPPS - 65E | CARLISE(CANAL) - 68E | DALRYRD - 64C | STIRLING - 63B |
| Jan-57 | DUNFERMLINE - 62C | HAWICK - 64G | DALRYRD - 64C | DUNFERMLINE - 62C | STIRLING - 63B | KIPPS - 65E | CARLISE(CANAL) - 68E | DALRYRD - 64C | STIRLING - 63B |
| Aug-57 | DUNFERMLINE - 62C | HAWICK - 64G | DALRYRD - 64C | DUNFERMLINE - 62C | STIRLING - 63B | KIPPS - 65E | CARLISE(CANAL) - 68E | DALRYRD - 64C | STIRLING - 63B |
| Jan-58 | DUNFERMLINE - 62C | HAWICK - 64G | DALRYRD - 64C | DUNFERMLINE - 62C | STIRLING - 63B | KIPPS - 65E | CARLISLECANAL - 68E | DALRYRD - 64C | STIRLING - 63B |
| Aug-58 | DUNFERMLINE - 62C | HAWICK - 64G | **6/58: W/D** | DUNFERMLINE - 62C | STIRLING - 63B | KIPPS - 65E | CARLISLECANAL - 12C | DALRYRD - 64C | STIRLING - 63B |
| Jan-59 | DUNFERMLINE - 62C | HAWICK - 64G | | DUNFERMLINE - 62C | **3/59: DALRY - 64C** | KIPPS - 65E | CARLISLECANAL - 12C | DALRYRD - 64C | **3/59: DALRY - 64C** |
| Aug-59 | DUNFERMLINE - 62C | HAWICK - 64G | | DUNFERMLINE - 62C | DALRYRD - 64C | KIPPS - 65E | CARLISLECANAL - 12C | DALRYRD - 64C | **8/59: W/D** |
| Nov-59 | DUNFERMLINE - 62C | HAWICK - 64G | | **10/59: W/D** | DALRYRD - 64C | **9/59: W/D** | CARLISLECANAL - 12C | DALRYRD - 64C | |
| Jan-60 | DUNFERMLINE - 62C | HAWICK - 64G | | | DALRYRD - 64C | | CARLISLECANAL - 12C | DALRYRD - 64C | |
| Apr-60 | DUNFERMLINE - 62C | HAWICK - 64G | | | DALRYRD - 64C | | CARLISLECANAL - 12C | DALRYRD - 64C | |
| Aug-60 | DUNFERMLINE - 62C | HAWICK - 64G | | | DALRYRD - 64C | | CARLISLECANAL - 12C | DALRYRD - 64C | |
| Nov-60 | DUNFERMLINE - 62C | HAWICK - 64G | | | DALRYRD - 64C | | CARLISLECANAL - 12C | DALRYRD - 64C | |

| | 64502 | 64504 | 64505 | 64506 | 64507 | 64509 | 64510 | 64511 | 64512 |
|---|---|---|---|---|---|---|---|---|---|
| Aug-50 | POLMONT-64E | BATHGATE-64F | DUNFERMLINE-62C | EDINBURGH(SM)-64A | KIPPS-65E | HAWICK-64G | BATHGATE-64F | CARLISLE(C)-12B | EDINBURGH(SM)-64A |
| Jan-51 | POLMONT-64E | BATHGATE-64F | DUNFERMLINE-62C | EDINBURGH(SM)-64A | KIPPS-65E | HAWICK-64G | BATHGATE-64F | CARLISLE(C)-12B | 3/51: BATH-64F |
| Aug-51 | POLMONT-64E | BATHGATE-64F | DUNFERMLINE-62C | EDINBURGH(SM)-64A | KIPPS-65E | HAWICK-64G | BATHGATE-64F | CARLISLE(C)-68E | BATHGATE-64F |
| Jan-52 | POLMONT-64E | BATHGATE-64F | DUNFERMLINE-62C | EDINBURGH(SM)-64A | KIPPS-65E | HAWICK-64G | BATHGATE-64F | CARLISLE(C)-68E | BATHGATE-64F |
| Aug-52 | POLMONT-64E | BATHGATE-64F | DUNFERMLINE-62C | EDINBURGH(SM)-64A | KIPPS-65E | HAWICK-64G | BATHGATE-64F | CARLISLE(C)-68E | BATHGATE-64F |
| Jan-53 | POLMONT-64E | BATHGATE-64F | DUNFERMLINE-62C | EDINBURGH(SM)-64A | KIPPS-65E | HAWICK-64G | BATHGATE-64F | CARLISLE(C)-68E | BATHGATE-64F |
| Aug-53 | POLMONT-64E | BATHGATE-64F | DUNFERMLINE-62C | EDINBURGH(SM)-64A | KIPPS-65E | HAWICK-64G | BATHGATE-64F | CARLISLE(C)-68E | BATHGATE-64F |
| Jan-54 | POLMONT-64E | BATHGATE-64F | DUNFERMLINE-62C | EDINBURGH(SM)-64A | KIPPS-65E | HAWICK-64G | BATHGATE-64F | CARLISLE(C)-68E | BATHGATE-64F |
| Aug-54 | POLMONT-64E | BATHGATE-64F | DUNFERMLINE-62C | EDINBURGH(SM)-64A | KIPPS-65E | HAWICK-64G | BATHGATE-64F | CARLISLE(C)-68E | BATHGATE-64F |
| Jan-55 | POLMONT-64E | BATHGATE-64F | DUNFERMLINE-62C | EDINBURGH(SM)-64A | KIPPS-65E | HAWICK-64G | BATHGATE-64F | 2/55: POLM-66A | BATHGATE-64F |
| Aug-55 | POLMONT-64E | BATHGATE-64F | DUNFERMLINE-62C | EDINBURGH(SM)-64A | KIPPS-65E | HAWICK-64G | BATHGATE-64F | POLMADIE-66A | BATHGATE-64F |
| Jan-56 | POLMONT-64E | BATHGATE-64F | DUNFERMLINE-62C | EDINBURGH(SM)-64A | KIPPS-65E | HAWICK-64G | BATHGATE-64F | POLMADIE-66A | BATHGATE-64F |
| Aug-56 | POLMONT-64E | BATHGATE-64F | DUNFERMLINE-62C | EDINBURGH(SM)-64A | KIPPS-65E | HAWICK-64G | BATHGATE-64F | POLMADIE-66A | BATHGATE-64F |
| Jan-57 | POLMONT-64E | BATHGATE-64F | DUNFERMLINE-62C | EDINBURGH(SM)-64A | KIPPS-65E | HAWICK-64G | BATHGATE-64F | POLMADIE-66A | BATHGATE-64F |
| Aug-57 | POLMONT-64E | BATHGATE-64F | DUNFERMLINE-62C | EDINBURGH(SM)-64A | KIPPS-65E | HAWICK-64G | BATHGATE-64F | POLMADIE-66A | BATHGATE-64F |
| Jan-58 | POLMONT-64E | BATHGATE-64F | DUNFERMLINE-62C | EDINBURGH(SM)-64A | KIPPS-65E | HAWICK-64G | BATHGATE-64F | POLMADIE-66A | BATHGATE-64F |
| Aug-58 | POLMONT-64E | BATHGATE-64F | DUNFERMLINE-62C | EDINBURGH(SM)-64A | KIPPS-65E | HAWICK-64G | BATHGATE-64F | POLMADIE-66A | BATHGATE-64F |
| Jan-59 | POLMONT-64E | BATHGATE-64F | DUNFERMLINE-62C | EDINBURGH(SM)-64A | KIPPS-65E | HAWICK-64G | BATHGATE-64F | POLMADIE-66A | BATHGATE-64F |
| Aug-59 | POLMONT-64E | BATHGATE-64F | DUNFERMLINE-62C | EDINBURGH(SM)-64A | KIPPS-65E | HAWICK-64G | BATHGATE-64F | POLMADIE-66A | BATHGATE-64F |
| Nov-59 | POLMONT-64E | BATHGATE-64F | DUNFERMLINE-62C | EDINBURGH(SM)-64A | KIPPS-65E | 10/59: W/D | BATHGATE-64F | 10/59: W/D | BATHGATE-64F |
| Jan-60 | POLMONT-64E | BATHGATE-64F | DUNFERMLINE-62C | 12/59: W/D | KIPPS-65E | | BATHGATE-64F | | BATHGATE-64F |
| Apr-60 | POLMONT-65K | BATHGATE-64F | DUNFERMLINE-62C | | KIPPS-65E | | BATHGATE-64F | | BATHGATE-64F |
| Aug-60 | POLMONT-65K | BATHGATE-64F | DUNFERMLINE-62C | | KIPPS-65E | | BATHGATE-64F | | BATHGATE-64F |
| Nov-60 | 11/60: W/D | 11/60: W/D | DUNFERMLINE-62C | | KIPPS-65E | | BATHGATE-64F | | 11/60: W/D |

| | 64513 | 64514 | 64515 | 64516 | 64517 | 64518 | 64519 | 64520 | 64521 |
|---|---|---|---|---|---|---|---|---|---|
| Aug-50 | DUNFERMLINE-62C | THORNTONJCN-62A | EDINBURGH(SM)-64A | THORNTONJCN-62A | EDINBURGH(SM)-64A | EDINBURGH(SM)-64A | EDINBURGH(SM)-64A | STIRLING-63B | THORNTONJCN-62A |
| Jan-51 | DUNFERMLINE-62C | THORNTONJCN-62A | EDINBURGH(SM)-64A | THORNTONJCN-62A | EDINBURGH(SM)-64A | EDINBURGH(SM)-64A | EDINBURGH(SM)-64A | STIRLING-63B | THORNTONJCN-62A |
| Aug-51 | DUNFERMLINE-62C | THORNTONJCN-62A | EDINBURGH(SM)-64A | THORNTONJCN-62A | EDINBURGH(SM)-64A | EDINBURGH(SM)-64A | EDINBURGH(SM)-64A | STIRLING-63B | THORNTONJCN-62A |
| Jan-52 | DUNFERMLINE-62C | 1/52: PARK-65C | EDINBURGH(SM)-64A | THORNTONJCN-62A | EDINBURGH(SM)-64A | EDINBURGH(SM)-64A | EDINBURGH(SM)-64A | STIRLING-63B | THORNTONJCN-62A |
| Aug-52 | DUNFERMLINE-62C | PARKHEAD-65C | EDINBURGH(SM)-64A | THORNTONJCN-62A | EDINBURGH(SM)-64A | EDINBURGH(SM)-64A | EDINBURGH(SM)-64A | STIRLING-63B | THORNTONJCN-62A |
| Jan-53 | DUNFERMLINE-62C | PARKHEAD-65C | EDINBURGH(SM)-64A | THORNTONJCN-62A | EDINBURGH(SM)-64A | EDINBURGH(SM)-64A | EDINBURGH(SM)-64A | STIRLING-63B | THORNTONJCN-62A |
| Aug-53 | DUNFERMLINE-62C | PARKHEAD-65C | EDINBURGH(SM)-64A | THORNTONJCN-62A | EDINBURGH(SM)-64A | EDINBURGH(SM)-64A | EDINBURGH(SM)-64A | STIRLING-63B | THORNTONJCN-62A |
| Jan-54 | DUNFERMLINE-62C | PARKHEAD-65C | EDINBURGH(SM)-64A | THORNTONJCN-62A | EDINBURGH(SM)-64A | EDINBURGH(SM)-64A | EDINBURGH(SM)-64A | STIRLING-63B | THORNTONJCN-62A |
| Aug-54 | DUNFERMLINE-62C | PARKHEAD-65C | EDINBURGH(SM)-64A | THORNTONJCN-62A | 5/54: DALRY-64C | EDINBURGH(SM)-64A | EDINBURGH(SM)-64A | 4/54: DAWS-65D | THORNTONJCN-62A |
| Jan-55 | DUNFERMLINE-62C | PARKHEAD-65C | EDINBURGH(SM)-64A | THORNTONJCN-62A | DALRYRD-64C | EDINBURGH(SM)-64A | EDINBURGH(SM)-64A | DAWSHOLME-65D | THORNTONJCN-62A |
| Aug-55 | DUNFERMLINE-62C | PARKHEAD-65C | EDINBURGH(SM)-64A | THORNTONJCN-62A | DALRYRD-64C | EDINBURGH(SM)-64A | EDINBURGH(SM)-64A | DAWSHOLME-65D | THORNTONJCN-62A |
| Jan-56 | DUNFERMLINE-62C | PARKHEAD-65C | EDINBURGH(SM)-64A | THORNTONJCN-62A | DALRYRD-64C | EDINBURGH(SM)-64A | EDINBURGH(SM)-64A | DAWSHOLME-65D | THORNTONJCN-62A |
| Aug-56 | DUNFERMLINE-62C | PARKHEAD-65C | EDINBURGH(SM)-64A | THORNTONJCN-62A | DALRYRD-64C | EDINBURGH(SM)-64A | EDINBURGH(SM)-64A | DAWSHOLME-65D | THORNTONJCN-62A |
| Jan-57 | DUNFERMLINE-62C | PARKHEAD-65C | EDINBURGH(SM)-64A | 12/56: DUNF-62C | DALRYRD-64C | EDINBURGH(SM)-64A | EDINBURGH(SM)-64A | DAWSHOLME-65D | THORNTONJCN-62A |
| Aug-57 | DUNFERMLINE-62C | PARKHEAD-65C | EDINBURGH(SM)-64A | DUNFERMLINE-62C | DALRYRD-64C | EDINBURGH(SM)-64A | EDINBURGH(SM)-64A | PARKHEAD-65C | THORNTONJCN-62A |
| Jan-58 | DUNFERMLINE-62C | PARKHEAD-65C | EDINBURGH(SM)-64A | DUNFERMLINE-62C | DALRYRD-64C | EDINBURGH(SM)-64A | EDINBURGH(SM)-64A | PARKHEAD-65C | THORNTONJCN-62A |
| Aug-58 | DUNFERMLINE-62C | PARKHEAD-65C | EDINBURGH(SM)-64A | DUNFERMLINE-62C | DALRYRD-64C | EDINBURGH(SM)-64A | EDINBURGH(SM)-64A | PARKHEAD-65C | THORNTONJCN-62A |
| Jan-59 | DUNFERMLINE-62C | PARKHEAD-65C | EDINBURGH(SM)-64A | DUNFERMLINE-62C | 10/58: W/D | EDINBURGH(SM)-64A | EDINBURGH(SM)-64A | PARKHEAD-65C | THORNTONJCN-62A |
| Aug-59 | DUNFERMLINE-62C | PARKHEAD-65C | EDINBURGH(SM)-64A | 6/59: W/D | | EDINBURGH(SM)-64A | EDINBURGH(SM)-64A | PARKHEAD-65C | 4/59: W/D |
| Nov-59 | 9/59: W/D | PARKHEAD-65C | EDINBURGH(SM)-64A | | | EDINBURGH(SM)-64A | EDINBURGH(SM)-64A | 9/59: W/D | |
| Jan-60 | | PARKHEAD-65C | EDINBURGH(SM)-64A | | | EDINBURGH(SM)-64A | EDINBURGH(SM)-64A | | |
| Apr-60 | | PARKHEAD-65C | EDINBURGH(SM)-64A | | | EDINBURGH(SM)-64A | EDINBURGH(SM)-64A | | |
| Aug-60 | | PARKHEAD-65C | EDINBURGH(SM)-64A | | | EDINBURGH(SM)-64A | EDINBURGH(SM)-64A | | |
| Nov-60 | | PARKHEAD-65C | EDINBURGH(SM)-64A | | | EDINBURGH(SM)-64A | EDINBURGH(SM)-64A | | |

| | 64522 | 64523 | 64524 | 64525 | 64526 | 64527 | 64528 | 64529 | 64530 |
|---|---|---|---|---|---|---|---|---|---|
| Aug-50 | THORNTONJCN-62A | EDINBURGH(SM)-64A | EDINBURGH(SM)-64A | DUNFERMLINE-62C | CARLISLE(C)-12B | EDINBURGH(SM)-64A | POLMONT-64E | BATHGATE-64F | DUNDEE-62B |
| Jan-51 | THORNTONJCN-62A | EDINBURGH(SM)-64A | EDINBURGH(SM)-64A | DUNFERMLINE-62C | CARLISLE(C)-12B | EDINBURGH(SM)-64A | POLMONT-64E | BATHGATE-64F | DUNDEE-62B |
| Aug-51 | THORNTONJCN-62A | EDINBURGH(SM)-64A | EDINBURGH(SM)-64A | DUNFERMLINE-62C | CARLISLE(C)-68E | EDINBURGH(SM)-64A | POLMONT-64E | BATHGATE-64F | DUNDEE-62B |
| Jan-52 | THORNTONJCN-62A | EDINBURGH(SM)-64A | EDINBURGH(SM)-64A | DUNFERMLINE-62C | CARLISLE(C)-68E | EDINBURGH(SM)-64A | POLMONT-64E | BATHGATE-64F | DUNDEE-62B |
| Aug-52 | THORNTONJCN-62A | EDINBURGH(SM)-64A | EDINBURGH(SM)-64A | DUNFERMLINE-62C | CARLISLE(C)-68E | EDINBURGH(SM)-64A | POLMONT-64E | BATHGATE-64F | DUNDEE-62B |
| Jan-53 | THORNTONJCN-62A | EDINBURGH(SM)-64A | EDINBURGH(SM)-64A | DUNFERMLINE-62C | CARLISLE(C)-68E | EDINBURGH(SM)-64A | POLMONT-64E | BATHGATE-64F | DUNDEE-62B |
| Aug-53 | THORNTONJCN-62A | EDINBURGH(SM)-64A | EDINBURGH(SM)-64A | DUNFERMLINE-62C | CARLISLE(C)-68E | EDINBURGH(SM)-64A | POLMONT-64E | BATHGATE-64F | DUNDEE-62B |
| Jan-54 | THORNTONJCN-62A | EDINBURGH(SM)-64A | EDINBURGH(SM)-64A | DUNFERMLINE-62C | CARLISLE(C)-68E | EDINBURGH(SM)-64A | POLMONT-64E | BATHGATE-64F | DUNDEE-62B |
| Aug-54 | THORNTONJCN-62A | EDINBURGH(SM)-64A | EDINBURGH(SM)-64A | DUNFERMLINE-62C | CARLISLE(C)-68E | 4/54: DALRY-64C | POLMONT-64E | BATHGATE-64F | DUNDEE-62B |
| Jan-55 | THORNTONJCN-62A | EDINBURGH(SM)-64A | EDINBURGH(SM)-64A | DUNFERMLINE-62C | CARLISLE(C)-68E | DALRYRD-64C | 5/55: DALRY-64C | BATHGATE-64F | DUNDEE-62B |
| Aug-55 | THORNTONJCN-62A | EDINBURGH(SM)-64A | EDINBURGH(SM)-64A | DUNFERMLINE-62C | CARLISLE(C)-68E | DALRYRD-64C | 9/55: POLM-64E | BATHGATE-64F | DUNDEE-62B |
| Jan-56 | THORNTONJCN-62A | EDINBURGH(SM)-64A | EDINBURGH(SM)-64A | DUNFERMLINE-62C | CARLISLE(C)-68E | DALRYRD-64C | POLMONT-64E | BATHGATE-64F | DUNDEE-62B |
| Aug-56 | THORNTONJCN-62A | EDINBURGH(SM)-64A | EDINBURGH(SM)-64A | DUNFERMLINE-62C | CARLISLE(C)-68E | DALRYRD-64C | POLMONT-64E | BATHGATE-64F | DUNDEE-62B |
| Jan-57 | THORNTONJCN-62A | EDINBURGH(SM)-64A | EDINBURGH(SM)-64A | DUNFERMLINE-62C | CARLISLE(C)-68E | DALRYRD-64C | POLMONT-64E | BATHGATE-64F | DUNDEE-62B |
| Aug-57 | THORNTONJCN-62A | EDINBURGH(SM)-64A | EDINBURGH(SM)-64A | DUNFERMLINE-62C | CARLISLE(C)-68E | DALRYRD-64C | POLMONT-64E | BATHGATE-64F | DUNDEE-62B |
| Jan-58 | THORNTONJCN-62A | EDINBURGH(SM)-64A | EDINBURGH(SM)-64A | DUNFERMLINE-62C | CARLISLE(C)-68E | DALRYRD-64C | POLMONT-64E | BATHGATE-64F | DUNDEE-62B |
| Aug-58 | THORNTONJCN-62A | EDINBURGH(SM)-64A | EDINBURGH(SM)-64A | DUNFERMLINE-62C | 3/58: W/D | DALRYRD-64C | POLMONT-64E | BATHGATE-64F | DUNDEE-62B |
| Jan-59 | 1/59: W/D | EDINBURGH(SM)-64A | EDINBURGH(SM)-64A | DUNFERMLINE-62C | | DALRYRD-64C | | BATHGATE-64F | DUNDEE-62B |
| Aug-59 | | EDINBURGH(SM)-64A | EDINBURGH(SM)-64A | DUNFERMLINE-62C | | DALRYRD-64C | | BATHGATE-64F | DUNDEE-62B |
| Nov-59 | | 9/59: PARK-65C | EDINBURGH(SM)-64A | DUNFERMLINE-62C | | DALRYRD-64C | | BATHGATE-64F | 10/59: W/D |
| Jan-60 | | PARKHEAD-65C | EDINBURGH(SM)-64A | DUNFERMLINE-62C | | DALRYRD-64C | | BATHGATE-64F | |
| Apr-60 | | PARKHEAD-65C | EDINBURGH(SM)-64A | DUNFERMLINE-62C | | DALRYRD-64C | | BATHGATE-64F | |
| Aug-60 | | PARKHEAD-65C | EDINBURGH(SM)-64A | DUNFERMLINE-62C | | DALRYRD-64C | | BATHGATE-64F | |
| Nov-60 | | PARKHEAD-65C | EDINBURGH(SM)-64A | DUNFERMLINE-62C | | DALRYRD-64C | | 11/60: W/D | |

### J37 0-6-0 (1914)

| | 64531 | 64532 | 64533 | 64534 | 64535 | 64536 | 64537 | 64538 | 64539 |
|---|---|---|---|---|---|---|---|---|---|
| Aug-50 | KIPPS-65E | EDINBURGH(SM)-64A | EDINBURGH(SM)-64A | KIPPS-65E | EDINBURGH(SM)-64A | DALRYRD-64C | POLMONT-64E | EDINBURGH(SM)-64A | HAWICK-64G |
| Jan-51 | KIPPS-65E | EDINBURGH(SM)-64A | EDINBURGH(SM)-64A | KIPPS-65E | EDINBURGH(SM)-64A | DALRYRD-64C | POLMONT-64E | EDINBURGH(SM)-64A | HAWICK-64G |
| Aug-51 | KIPPS-65E | EDINBURGH(SM)-64A | EDINBURGH(SM)-64A | KIPPS-65E | EDINBURGH(SM)-64A | DALRYRD-64C | POLMONT-64E | EDINBURGH(SM)-64A | HAWICK-64G |
| Jan-52 | KIPPS-65E | EDINBURGH(SM)-64A | EDINBURGH(SM)-64A | KIPPS-65E | EDINBURGH(SM)-64A | DALRYRD-64C | POLMONT-64E | EDINBURGH(SM)-64A | HAWICK-64G |
| Aug-52 | KIPPS-65E | EDINBURGH(SM)-64A | EDINBURGH(SM)-64A | KIPPS-65E | EDINBURGH(SM)-64A | DALRYRD-64C | POLMONT-64E | EDINBURGH(SM)-64A | HAWICK-64G |
| Jan-53 | KIPPS-65E | EDINBURGH(SM)-64A | EDINBURGH(SM)-64A | KIPPS-65E | EDINBURGH(SM)-64A | DALRYRD-64C | POLMONT-64E | EDINBURGH(SM)-64A | HAWICK-64G |
| Aug-53 | KIPPS-65E | EDINBURGH(SM)-64A | EDINBURGH(SM)-64A | KIPPS-65E | EDINBURGH(SM)-64A | DALRYRD-64C | POLMONT-64E | EDINBURGH(SM)-64A | HAWICK-64G |
| Jan-54 | KIPPS-65E | EDINBURGH(SM)-64A | EDINBURGH(SM)-64A | KIPPS-65E | EDINBURGH(SM)-64A | DALRYRD-64C | POLMONT-64E | EDINBURGH(SM)-64A | HAWICK-64G |
| Aug-54 | KIPPS-65E | EDINBURGH(SM)-64A | EDINBURGH(SM)-64A | KIPPS-65E | EDINBURGH(SM)-64A | DALRYRD-64C | POLMONT-64E | EDINBURGH(SM)-64A | HAWICK-64G |
| Jan-55 | KIPPS-65E | EDINBURGH(SM)-64A | EDINBURGH(SM)-64A | KIPPS-65E | EDINBURGH(SM)-64A | DALRYRD-64C | POLMONT-64E | EDINBURGH(SM)-64A | HAWICK-64G |
| Aug-55 | KIPPS-65E | EDINBURGH(SM)-64A | EDINBURGH(SM)-64A | KIPPS-65E | EDINBURGH(SM)-64A | DALRYRD-64C | POLMONT-64E | EDINBURGH(SM)-64A | HAWICK-64G |
| Jan-56 | KIPPS-65E | EDINBURGH(SM)-64A | EDINBURGH(SM)-64A | KIPPS-65E | EDINBURGH(SM)-64A | DALRYRD-64C | POLMONT-64E | EDINBURGH(SM)-64A | HAWICK-64G |
| Aug-56 | KIPPS-65E | EDINBURGH(SM)-64A | EDINBURGH(SM)-64A | KIPPS-65E | EDINBURGH(SM)-64A | DALRYRD-64C | POLMONT-64E | EDINBURGH(SM)-64A | HAWICK-64G |
| Jan-57 | KIPPS-65E | EDINBURGH(SM)-64A | EDINBURGH(SM)-64A | KIPPS-65E | EDINBURGH(SM)-64A | DALRYRD-64C | POLMONT-64E | EDINBURGH(SM)-64A | HAWICK-64G |
| Aug-57 | KIPPS-65E | EDINBURGH(SM)-64A | EDINBURGH(SM)-64A | KIPPS-65E | EDINBURGH(SM)-64A | DALRYRD-64C | POLMONT-64E | EDINBURGH(SM)-64A | HAWICK-64G |
| Jan-58 | KIPPS-65E | EDINBURGH(SM)-64A | EDINBURGH(SM)-64A | KIPPS-65E | EDINBURGH(SM)-64A | DALRYRD-64C | POLMONT-64E | EDINBURGH(SM)-64A | HAWICK-64G |
| Aug-58 | KIPPS-65E | EDINBURGH(SM)-64A | EDINBURGH(SM)-64A | KIPPS-65E | EDINBURGH(SM)-64A | 9/58: ST.M-64A | POLMONT-64E | EDINBURGH(SM)-64A | HAWICK-64G |
| Jan-59 | KIPPS-65E | EDINBURGH(SM)-64A | EDINBURGH(SM)-64A | KIPPS-65E | EDINBURGH(SM)-64A | EDINBURGH(SM)-64A | POLMONT-64E | EDINBURGH(SM)-64A | HAWICK-64G |
| Aug-59 | KIPPS-65E | EDINBURGH(SM)-64A | EDINBURGH(SM)-64A | KIPPS-65E | EDINBURGH(SM)-64A | 5/59: W/D | POLMONT-64E | EDINBURGH(SM)-64A | HAWICK-64G |
| Nov-59 | KIPPS-65E | EDINBURGH(SM)-64A | EDINBURGH(SM)-64A | KIPPS-65E | EDINBURGH(SM)-64A | | POLMONT-64E | EDINBURGH(SM)-64A | 11/59: ST.M-64A |
| Jan-60 | KIPPS-65E | EDINBURGH(SM)-64A | EDINBURGH(SM)-64A | KIPPS-65E | EDINBURGH(SM)-64A | | POLMONT-64E | 12/59: W/D | EDINBURGH(SM)-64A |
| Apr-60 | KIPPS-65E | EDINBURGH(SM)-64A | EDINBURGH(SM)-64A | KIPPS-65E | EDINBURGH(SM)-64A | | POLMONT-64E | | EDINBURGH(SM)-64A |
| Aug-60 | KIPPS-65E | EDINBURGH(SM)-64A | EDINBURGH(SM)-64A | KIPPS-65E | EDINBURGH(SM)-64A | | POLMONT-64E | | EDINBURGH(SM)-64A |
| Nov-60 | KIPPS-65E | EDINBURGH(SM)-64A | EDINBURGH(SM)-64A | KIPPS-65E | EDINBURGH(SM)-64A | | POLMONT-64E | | EDINBURGH(SM)-64A |

| | 64540 | 64541 | 64542 | 64543 | 64544 | 64545 | 64546 | 64547 | 64548 |
|---|---|---|---|---|---|---|---|---|---|
| Aug-50 | EASTFIELD - 65A | EASTFIELD - 65A | STIRLING - 63B | EDINBURGH (SM) - 64A | STIRLING - 63B | DUNFERMLINE - 62C | THORNTON JCN - 62A | EDINBURGH (SM) - 64A | PARKHEAD - 65C |
| Jan-51 | EASTFIELD - 65A | EASTFIELD - 65A | STIRLING - 63B | EDINBURGH (SM) - 64A | STIRLING - 63B | DUNFERMLINE - 62C | THORNTON JCN - 62A | EDINBURGH (SM) - 64A | **2/51: KIPPS - 65E** |
| Aug-51 | EASTFIELD - 65A | EASTFIELD - 65A | STIRLING - 63B | EDINBURGH (SM) - 64A | STIRLING - 63B | DUNFERMLINE - 62C | THORNTON JCN - 62A | **5/51: DALRY - 64C** | KIPPS - 65E |
| Jan-52 | EASTFIELD - 65A | EASTFIELD - 65A | STIRLING - 63B | EDINBURGH (SM) - 64A | STIRLING - 63B | DUNFERMLINE - 62C | THORNTON JCN - 62A | DALRY RD - 64C | KIPPS - 65E |
| Aug-52 | EASTFIELD - 65A | EASTFIELD - 65A | STIRLING - 63B | EDINBURGH (SM) - 64A | STIRLING - 63B | DUNFERMLINE - 62C | THORNTON JCN - 62A | DALRY RD - 64C | KIPPS - 65E |
| Jan-53 | EASTFIELD - 65A | EASTFIELD - 65A | STIRLING - 63B | EDINBURGH (SM) - 64A | STIRLING - 63B | DUNFERMLINE - 62C | THORNTON JCN - 62A | **11/52: ST. M - 64A** | KIPPS - 65E |
| Aug-53 | EASTFIELD - 65A | EASTFIELD - 65A | STIRLING - 63B | EDINBURGH (SM) - 64A | STIRLING - 63B | DUNFERMLINE - 62C | THORNTON JCN - 62A | EDINBURGH (SM) - 64A | KIPPS - 65E |
| Jan-54 | EASTFIELD - 65A | EASTFIELD - 65A | STIRLING - 63B | EDINBURGH (SM) - 64A | STIRLING - 63B | DUNFERMLINE - 62C | THORNTON JCN - 62A | EDINBURGH (SM) - 64A | KIPPS - 65E |
| Aug-54 | EASTFIELD - 65A | EASTFIELD - 65A | STIRLING - 63B | EDINBURGH (SM) - 64A | STIRLING - 63B | DUNFERMLINE - 62C | THORNTON JCN - 62A | EDINBURGH (SM) - 64A | KIPPS - 65E |
| Jan-55 | EASTFIELD - 65A | EASTFIELD - 65A | STIRLING - 63B | EDINBURGH (SM) - 64A | STIRLING - 63B | DUNFERMLINE - 62C | THORNTON JCN - 62A | EDINBURGH (SM) - 64A | KIPPS - 65E |
| Aug-55 | EASTFIELD - 65A | EASTFIELD - 65A | STIRLING - 63B | EDINBURGH (SM) - 64A | STIRLING - 63B | DUNFERMLINE - 62C | THORNTON JCN - 62A | EDINBURGH (SM) - 64A | KIPPS - 65E |
| Jan-56 | EASTFIELD - 65A | EASTFIELD - 65A | STIRLING - 63B | EDINBURGH (SM) - 64A | STIRLING - 63B | DUNFERMLINE - 62C | THORNTON JCN - 62A | EDINBURGH (SM) - 64A | KIPPS - 65E |
| Aug-56 | EASTFIELD - 65A | EASTFIELD - 65A | STIRLING - 63B | EDINBURGH (SM) - 64A | STIRLING - 63B | DUNFERMLINE - 62C | THORNTON JCN - 62A | EDINBURGH (SM) - 64A | KIPPS - 65E |
| Jan-57 | EASTFIELD - 65A | EASTFIELD - 65A | STIRLING - 63B | EDINBURGH (SM) - 64A | STIRLING - 63B | **12/56: DUND - 62B** | THORNTON JCN - 62A | EDINBURGH (SM) - 64A | KIPPS - 65E |
| Aug-57 | EASTFIELD - 65A | EASTFIELD - 65A | DUNDEE - 62B | **5/57: DUNF - 62C** | **7/57: DUND - 62B** | DUNDEE - 62B | THORNTON JCN - 62A | EDINBURGH (SM) - 64A | **9/57: EAST - 65A** |
| Jan-58 | EASTFIELD - 65A | EASTFIELD - 65A | DUNDEE - 62B | DUNFERMLINE - 62C | DUNDEE - 62B | DUNDEE - 62B | THORNTON JCN - 62A | EDINBURGH (SM) - 64A | EASTFIELD - 65A |
| Aug-58 | EASTFIELD - 65A | EASTFIELD - 65A | DUNDEE - 62B | DUNFERMLINE - 62C | DUNDEE - 62B | DUNDEE - 62B | THORNTON JCN - 62A | EDINBURGH (SM) - 64A | EASTFIELD - 65A |
| Jan-59 | EASTFIELD - 65A | EASTFIELD - 65A | DUNDEE - 62B | DUNFERMLINE - 62C | DUNDEE - 62B | DUNDEE - 62B | THORNTON JCN - 62A | EDINBURGH (SM) - 64A | EASTFIELD - 65A |
| Aug-59 | EASTFIELD - 65A | EASTFIELD - 65A | DUNDEE - 62B | DUNFERMLINE - 62C | DUNDEE - 62B | DUNDEE - 62B | THORNTON JCN - 62A | EDINBURGH (SM) - 64A | EASTFIELD - 65A |
| Nov-59 | EASTFIELD - 65A | EASTFIELD - 65A | **11/59: KIPPS - 65E** | DUNFERMLINE - 62C | **11/59: KIPPS - 65E** | DUNDEE - 62B | THORNTON JCN - 62A | EDINBURGH (SM) - 64A | EASTFIELD - 65A |
| Jan-60 | EASTFIELD - 65A | EASTFIELD - 65A | KIPPS - 65E | DUNFERMLINE - 62C | KIPPS - 65E | **12/59: DUNF - 62C** | THORNTON JCN - 62A | EDINBURGH (SM) - 64A | EASTFIELD - 65A |
| Apr-60 | EASTFIELD - 65A | EASTFIELD - 65A | KIPPS - 65E | DUNFERMLINE - 62C | KIPPS - 65E | DUNFERMLINE - 62C | THORNTON JCN - 62A | EDINBURGH (SM) - 64A | EASTFIELD - 65A |
| Aug-60 | EASTFIELD - 65A | EASTFIELD - 65A | KIPPS - 65E | DUNFERMLINE - 62C | KIPPS - 65E | DUNFERMLINE - 62C | THORNTON JCN - 62A | EDINBURGH (SM) - 64A | EASTFIELD - 65A |
| Nov-60 | EASTFIELD - 65A | EASTFIELD - 65A | KIPPS - 65E | DUNFERMLINE - 62C | KIPPS - 65E | DUNFERMLINE - 62C | THORNTON JCN - 62A | EDINBURGH (SM) - 64A | EASTFIELD - 65A |

| | 64549 | 64550 | 64551 | 64552 | 64553 | 64554 | 64555 | 64556 | 64557 |
|---|---|---|---|---|---|---|---|---|---|
| Aug-50 | THORNTON JCN - 62A | THORNTON JCN - 62A | POLMONT - 64E | EDINBURGH (SM) - 64A | POLMONT - 64E | DUNFERMLINE - 62C | EDINBURGH (SM) - 64A | DUNFERMLINE - 62C | EDINBURGH (SM) - 64A |
| Jan-51 | THORNTON JCN - 62A | THORNTON JCN - 62A | POLMONT - 64E | EDINBURGH (SM) - 64A | POLMONT - 64E | DUNFERMLINE - 62C | EDINBURGH (SM) - 64A | DUNFERMLINE - 62C | EDINBURGH (SM) - 64A |
| Aug-51 | THORNTON JCN - 62A | THORNTON JCN - 62A | POLMONT - 64E | EDINBURGH (SM) - 64A | POLMONT - 64E | DUNFERMLINE - 62C | EDINBURGH (SM) - 64A | DUNFERMLINE - 62C | EDINBURGH (SM) - 64A |
| Jan-52 | THORNTON JCN - 62A | THORNTON JCN - 62A | POLMONT - 64E | EDINBURGH (SM) - 64A | **3/52: BATH - 64F** | DUNFERMLINE - 62C | EDINBURGH (SM) - 64A | DUNFERMLINE - 62C | EDINBURGH (SM) - 64A |
| Aug-52 | THORNTON JCN - 62A | THORNTON JCN - 62A | POLMONT - 64E | EDINBURGH (SM) - 64A | BATHGATE - 64F | DUNFERMLINE - 62C | EDINBURGH (SM) - 64A | DUNFERMLINE - 62C | EDINBURGH (SM) - 64A |
| Jan-53 | THORNTON JCN - 62A | THORNTON JCN - 62A | POLMONT - 64E | EDINBURGH (SM) - 64A | BATHGATE - 64F | DUNFERMLINE - 62C | EDINBURGH (SM) - 64A | DUNFERMLINE - 62C | EDINBURGH (SM) - 64A |
| Aug-53 | THORNTON JCN - 62A | THORNTON JCN - 62A | POLMONT - 64E | EDINBURGH (SM) - 64A | BATHGATE - 64F | DUNFERMLINE - 62C | EDINBURGH (SM) - 64A | DUNFERMLINE - 62C | EDINBURGH (SM) - 64A |
| Jan-54 | THORNTON JCN - 62A | THORNTON JCN - 62A | POLMONT - 64E | EDINBURGH (SM) - 64A | BATHGATE - 64F | DUNFERMLINE - 62C | EDINBURGH (SM) - 64A | DUNFERMLINE - 62C | EDINBURGH (SM) - 64A |
| Aug-54 | THORNTON JCN - 62A | THORNTON JCN - 62A | POLMONT - 64E | EDINBURGH (SM) - 64A | BATHGATE - 64F | DUNFERMLINE - 62C | EDINBURGH (SM) - 64A | DUNFERMLINE - 62C | EDINBURGH (SM) - 64A |
| Jan-55 | THORNTON JCN - 62A | THORNTON JCN - 62A | POLMONT - 64E | EDINBURGH (SM) - 64A | BATHGATE - 64F | DUNFERMLINE - 62C | EDINBURGH (SM) - 64A | DUNFERMLINE - 62C | EDINBURGH (SM) - 64A |
| Aug-55 | THORNTON JCN - 62A | THORNTON JCN - 62A | POLMONT - 64E | EDINBURGH (SM) - 64A | BATHGATE - 64F | DUNFERMLINE - 62C | EDINBURGH (SM) - 64A | DUNFERMLINE - 62C | EDINBURGH (SM) - 64A |
| Jan-56 | THORNTON JCN - 62A | THORNTON JCN - 62A | POLMONT - 64E | EDINBURGH (SM) - 64A | BATHGATE - 64F | DUNFERMLINE - 62C | EDINBURGH (SM) - 64A | DUNFERMLINE - 62C | EDINBURGH (SM) - 64A |
| Aug-56 | THORNTON JCN - 62A | THORNTON JCN - 62A | POLMONT - 64E | EDINBURGH (SM) - 64A | BATHGATE - 64F | **9/56: DALRY - 64C** | EDINBURGH (SM) - 64A | DUNFERMLINE - 62C | EDINBURGH (SM) - 64A |
| Jan-57 | THORNTON JCN - 62A | THORNTON JCN - 62A | POLMONT - 64E | EDINBURGH (SM) - 64A | BATHGATE - 64F | DALRY RD - 64C | EDINBURGH (SM) - 64A | **12/56: DUND - 62B** | EDINBURGH (SM) - 64A |
| Aug-57 | THORNTON JCN - 62A | THORNTON JCN - 62A | POLMONT - 64E | EDINBURGH (SM) - 64A | BATHGATE - 64F | DALRY RD - 64C | EDINBURGH (SM) - 64A | DUNDEE - 62B | EDINBURGH (SM) - 64A |
| Jan-58 | THORNTON JCN - 62A | THORNTON JCN - 62A | POLMONT - 64E | EDINBURGH (SM) - 64A | BATHGATE - 64F | DALRY RD - 64C | EDINBURGH (SM) - 64A | DUNDEE - 62B | EDINBURGH (SM) - 64A |
| Aug-58 | THORNTON JCN - 62A | THORNTON JCN - 62A | POLMONT - 64E | EDINBURGH (SM) - 64A | BATHGATE - 64F | DALRY RD - 64C | EDINBURGH (SM) - 64A | DUNDEE - 62B | EDINBURGH (SM) - 64A |
| Jan-59 | THORNTON JCN - 62A | THORNTON JCN - 62A | POLMONT - 64E | EDINBURGH (SM) - 64A | BATHGATE - 64F | DALRY RD - 64C | EDINBURGH (SM) - 64A | DUNDEE - 62B | EDINBURGH (SM) - 64A |
| Aug-59 | THORNTON JCN - 62A | THORNTON JCN - 62A | POLMONT - 64E | EDINBURGH (SM) - 64A | BATHGATE - 64F | DALRY RD - 64C | EDINBURGH (SM) - 64A | DUNDEE - 62B | EDINBURGH (SM) - 64A |
| Nov-59 | THORNTON JCN - 62A | THORNTON JCN - 62A | POLMONT - 64E | EDINBURGH (SM) - 64A | BATHGATE - 64F | DALRY RD - 64C | EDINBURGH (SM) - 64A | DUNDEE - 62B | EDINBURGH (SM) - 64A |
| Jan-60 | THORNTON JCN - 62A | THORNTON JCN - 62A | POLMONT - 64E | EDINBURGH (SM) - 64A | BATHGATE - 64F | DALRY RD - 64C | EDINBURGH (SM) - 64A | DUNDEE - 62B | EDINBURGH (SM) - 64A |
| Apr-60 | THORNTON JCN - 62A | THORNTON JCN - 62A | POLMONT - 65K | EDINBURGH (SM) - 64A | BATHGATE - 64F | DALRY RD - 64C | EDINBURGH (SM) - 64A | DUNDEE - 62B | EDINBURGH (SM) - 64A |
| Aug-60 | THORNTON JCN - 62A | THORNTON JCN - 62A | POLMONT - 65K | EDINBURGH (SM) - 64A | BATHGATE - 64F | DALRY RD - 64C | EDINBURGH (SM) - 64A | DUNDEE - 62B | EDINBURGH (SM) - 64A |
| Nov-60 | THORNTON JCN - 62A | THORNTON JCN - 62A | POLMONT - 65K | EDINBURGH (SM) - 64A | BATHGATE - 64F | DALRY RD - 64C | EDINBURGH (SM) - 64A | DUNDEE - 62B | EDINBURGH (SM) - 64A |

| | 64558 | 64559 | 64560 | 64561 | 64562 | 64563 | 64564 | 64565 | 64566 |
|---|---|---|---|---|---|---|---|---|---|
| Aug-50 | EASTFIELD - 65A | PARKHEAD - 65C | DUNFERMLINE - 62C | DUNFERMLINE - 62C | EDINBURGH (SM) - 64A | PARKHEAD - 65C | THORNTON JCN - 62A | THORNTON JCN - 62A | EDINBURGH (SM) - 64A |
| Jan-51 | EASTFIELD - 65A | PARKHEAD - 65C | DUNFERMLINE - 62C | DUNFERMLINE - 62C | EDINBURGH (SM) - 64A | PARKHEAD - 65C | THORNTON JCN - 62A | THORNTON JCN - 62A | EDINBURGH (SM) - 64A |
| Aug-51 | EASTFIELD - 65A | PARKHEAD - 65C | DUNFERMLINE - 62C | DUNFERMLINE - 62C | EDINBURGH (SM) - 64A | PARKHEAD - 65C | THORNTON JCN - 62A | THORNTON JCN - 62A | EDINBURGH (SM) - 64A |
| Jan-52 | EASTFIELD - 65A | PARKHEAD - 65C | DUNFERMLINE - 62C | DUNFERMLINE - 62C | EDINBURGH (SM) - 64A | PARKHEAD - 65C | THORNTON JCN - 62A | THORNTON JCN - 62A | EDINBURGH (SM) - 64A |
| Aug-52 | EASTFIELD - 65A | PARKHEAD - 65C | DUNFERMLINE - 62C | DUNFERMLINE - 62C | EDINBURGH (SM) - 64A | PARKHEAD - 65C | THORNTON JCN - 62A | THORNTON JCN - 62A | EDINBURGH (SM) - 64A |
| Jan-53 | EASTFIELD - 65A | PARKHEAD - 65C | DUNFERMLINE - 62C | DUNFERMLINE - 62C | EDINBURGH (SM) - 64A | PARKHEAD - 65C | THORNTON JCN - 62A | THORNTON JCN - 62A | EDINBURGH (SM) - 64A |
| Aug-53 | EASTFIELD - 65A | PARKHEAD - 65C | DUNFERMLINE - 62C | DUNFERMLINE - 62C | EDINBURGH (SM) - 64A | PARKHEAD - 65C | THORNTON JCN - 62A | THORNTON JCN - 62A | EDINBURGH (SM) - 64A |
| Jan-54 | EASTFIELD - 65A | PARKHEAD - 65C | DUNFERMLINE - 62C | DUNFERMLINE - 62C | EDINBURGH (SM) - 64A | PARKHEAD - 65C | THORNTON JCN - 62A | THORNTON JCN - 62A | EDINBURGH (SM) - 64A |
| Aug-54 | EASTFIELD - 65A | PARKHEAD - 65C | DUNFERMLINE - 62C | DUNFERMLINE - 62C | EDINBURGH (SM) - 64A | PARKHEAD - 65C | THORNTON JCN - 62A | THORNTON JCN - 62A | EDINBURGH (SM) - 64A |
| Jan-55 | EASTFIELD - 65A | PARKHEAD - 65C | DUNFERMLINE - 62C | DUNFERMLINE - 62C | EDINBURGH (SM) - 64A | PARKHEAD - 65C | THORNTON JCN - 62A | THORNTON JCN - 62A | EDINBURGH (SM) - 64A |
| Aug-55 | EASTFIELD - 65A | PARKHEAD - 65C | DUNFERMLINE - 62C | DUNFERMLINE - 62C | EDINBURGH (SM) - 64A | PARKHEAD - 65C | THORNTON JCN - 62A | THORNTON JCN - 62A | EDINBURGH (SM) - 64A |
| Jan-56 | EASTFIELD - 65A | PARKHEAD - 65C | DUNFERMLINE - 62C | DUNFERMLINE - 62C | EDINBURGH (SM) - 64A | PARKHEAD - 65C | THORNTON JCN - 62A | THORNTON JCN - 62A | EDINBURGH (SM) - 64A |
| Aug-56 | EASTFIELD - 65A | PARKHEAD - 65C | DUNFERMLINE - 62C | **9/56: DALRY - 64C** | EDINBURGH (SM) - 64A | PARKHEAD - 65C | THORNTON JCN - 62A | THORNTON JCN - 62A | EDINBURGH (SM) - 64A |
| Jan-57 | EASTFIELD - 65A | PARKHEAD - 65C | DUNFERMLINE - 62C | DALRY RD - 64C | EDINBURGH (SM) - 64A | PARKHEAD - 65C | THORNTON JCN - 62A | THORNTON JCN - 62A | EDINBURGH (SM) - 64A |
| Aug-57 | EASTFIELD - 65A | PARKHEAD - 65C | DUNFERMLINE - 62C | DALRY RD - 64C | EDINBURGH (SM) - 64A | PARKHEAD - 65C | THORNTON JCN - 62A | THORNTON JCN - 62A | EDINBURGH (SM) - 64A |
| Jan-58 | EASTFIELD - 65A | PARKHEAD - 65C | DUNFERMLINE - 62C | DALRY RD - 64C | EDINBURGH (SM) - 64A | PARKHEAD - 65C | THORNTON JCN - 62A | THORNTON JCN - 62A | EDINBURGH (SM) - 64A |
| Aug-58 | EASTFIELD - 65A | PARKHEAD - 65C | DUNFERMLINE - 62C | DALRY RD - 64C | EDINBURGH (SM) - 64A | PARKHEAD - 65C | THORNTON JCN - 62A | THORNTON JCN - 62A | EDINBURGH (SM) - 64A |
| Jan-59 | EASTFIELD - 65A | PARKHEAD - 65C | DUNFERMLINE - 62C | DALRY RD - 64C | EDINBURGH (SM) - 64A | PARKHEAD - 65C | THORNTON JCN - 62A | THORNTON JCN - 62A | EDINBURGH (SM) - 64A |
| Aug-59 | EASTFIELD - 65A | PARKHEAD - 65C | DUNFERMLINE - 62C | DALRY RD - 64C | EDINBURGH (SM) - 64A | PARKHEAD - 65C | THORNTON JCN - 62A | THORNTON JCN - 62A | EDINBURGH (SM) - 64A |
| Nov-59 | EASTFIELD - 65A | PARKHEAD - 65C | DUNFERMLINE - 62C | DALRY RD - 64C | EDINBURGH (SM) - 64A | PARKHEAD - 65C | THORNTON JCN - 62A | THORNTON JCN - 62A | EDINBURGH (SM) - 64A |
| Jan-60 | EASTFIELD - 65A | PARKHEAD - 65C | DUNFERMLINE - 62C | DALRY RD - 64C | EDINBURGH (SM) - 64A | PARKHEAD - 65C | THORNTON JCN - 62A | THORNTON JCN - 62A | EDINBURGH (SM) - 64A |
| Apr-60 | EASTFIELD - 65A | PARKHEAD - 65C | DUNFERMLINE - 62C | DALRY RD - 64C | EDINBURGH (SM) - 64A | PARKHEAD - 65C | THORNTON JCN - 62A | THORNTON JCN - 62A | EDINBURGH (SM) - 64A |
| Aug-60 | EASTFIELD - 65A | PARKHEAD - 65C | DUNFERMLINE - 62C | DALRY RD - 64C | EDINBURGH (SM) - 64A | PARKHEAD - 65C | THORNTON JCN - 62A | THORNTON JCN - 62A | EDINBURGH (SM) - 64A |
| Nov-60 | EASTFIELD - 65A | PARKHEAD - 65C | DUNFERMLINE - 62C | DALRY RD - 64C | EDINBURGH (SM) - 64A | PARKHEAD - 65C | THORNTON JCN - 62A | THORNTON JCN - 62A | EDINBURGH (SM) - 64A |

| | 64567 | 64568 | 64569 | 64570 | 64571 | 64572 | 64573 | 64574 | 64575 |
|---|---|---|---|---|---|---|---|---|---|
| Aug-50 | DUNFERMLINE - 62C | DUNFERMLINE - 62C | STIRLING - 63B | POLMONT - 64E | POLMONT - 64E | EDINBURGH (SM) - 64A | PARKHEAD - 65C | DUNFERMLINE - 62C | DUNDEE - 62B |
| Jan-51 | DUNFERMLINE - 62C | DUNFERMLINE - 62C | STIRLING - 63B | POLMONT - 64E | POLMONT - 64E | EDINBURGH (SM) - 64A | PARKHEAD - 65C | DUNFERMLINE - 62C | DUNDEE - 62B |
| Aug-51 | DUNFERMLINE - 62C | DUNFERMLINE - 62C | STIRLING - 63B | POLMONT - 64E | POLMONT - 64E | EDINBURGH (SM) - 64A | PARKHEAD - 65C | DUNFERMLINE - 62C | DUNDEE - 62B |
| Jan-52 | DUNFERMLINE - 62C | DUNFERMLINE - 62C | STIRLING - 63B | POLMONT - 64E | POLMONT - 64E | EDINBURGH (SM) - 64A | PARKHEAD - 65C | DUNFERMLINE - 62C | DUNDEE - 62B |
| Aug-52 | DUNFERMLINE - 62C | DUNFERMLINE - 62C | STIRLING - 63B | POLMONT - 64E | POLMONT - 64E | EDINBURGH (SM) - 64A | PARKHEAD - 65C | DUNFERMLINE - 62C | DUNDEE - 62B |
| Jan-53 | DUNFERMLINE - 62C | DUNFERMLINE - 62C | STIRLING - 63B | POLMONT - 64E | POLMONT - 64E | EDINBURGH (SM) - 64A | PARKHEAD - 65C | DUNFERMLINE - 62C | DUNDEE - 62B |
| Aug-53 | DUNFERMLINE - 62C | DUNFERMLINE - 62C | STIRLING - 63B | POLMONT - 64E | POLMONT - 64E | EDINBURGH (SM) - 64A | PARKHEAD - 65C | DUNFERMLINE - 62C | DUNDEE - 62B |
| Jan-54 | DUNFERMLINE - 62C | DUNFERMLINE - 62C | STIRLING - 63B | POLMONT - 64E | POLMONT - 64E | EDINBURGH (SM) - 64A | PARKHEAD - 65C | DUNFERMLINE - 62C | DUNDEE - 62B |
| Aug-54 | DUNFERMLINE - 62C | DUNFERMLINE - 62C | STIRLING - 63B | POLMONT - 64E | POLMONT - 64E | EDINBURGH (SM) - 64A | PARKHEAD - 65C | DUNFERMLINE - 62C | DUNDEE - 62B |
| Jan-55 | DUNFERMLINE - 62C | DUNFERMLINE - 62C | STIRLING - 63B | **5/55: GRANGE - 65F** | POLMONT - 64E | EDINBURGH (SM) - 64A | PARKHEAD - 65C | DUNFERMLINE - 62C | DUNDEE - 62B |
| Aug-55 | DUNFERMLINE - 62C | DUNFERMLINE - 62C | STIRLING - 63B | **7/55: POLM - 64E** | POLMONT - 64E | EDINBURGH (SM) - 64A | PARKHEAD - 65C | DUNFERMLINE - 62C | DUNDEE - 62B |
| Jan-56 | DUNFERMLINE - 62C | DUNFERMLINE - 62C | STIRLING - 63B | POLMONT - 64E | POLMONT - 64E | EDINBURGH (SM) - 64A | PARKHEAD - 65C | DUNFERMLINE - 62C | DUNDEE - 62B |
| Aug-56 | DUNFERMLINE - 62C | DUNFERMLINE - 62C | STIRLING - 63B | POLMONT - 64E | POLMONT - 64E | EDINBURGH (SM) - 64A | PARKHEAD - 65C | **9/56: DALRY - 64C** | DUNDEE - 62B |
| Jan-57 | DUNFERMLINE - 62C | DUNFERMLINE - 62C | STIRLING - 63B | POLMONT - 64E | POLMONT - 64E | EDINBURGH (SM) - 64A | PARKHEAD - 65C | DALRY RD - 64C | DUNDEE - 62B |
| Aug-57 | DUNFERMLINE - 62C | DUNFERMLINE - 62C | STIRLING - 63B | POLMONT - 64E | POLMONT - 64E | EDINBURGH (SM) - 64A | PARKHEAD - 65C | DALRY RD - 64C | DUNDEE - 62B |
| Jan-58 | DUNFERMLINE - 62C | DUNFERMLINE - 62C | STIRLING - 63B | POLMONT - 64E | POLMONT - 64E | EDINBURGH (SM) - 64A | PARKHEAD - 65C | DALRY RD - 64C | DUNDEE - 62B |
| Aug-58 | DUNFERMLINE - 62C | DUNFERMLINE - 62C | STIRLING - 63B | POLMONT - 64E | POLMONT - 64E | EDINBURGH (SM) - 64A | PARKHEAD - 65C | **9/58: ST. M - 64A** | DUNDEE - 62B |
| Jan-59 | DUNFERMLINE - 62C | DUNFERMLINE - 62C | **3/59: DALRY - 64C** | POLMONT - 64E | POLMONT - 64E | EDINBURGH (SM) - 64A | PARKHEAD - 65C | **1/59: KIPPS - 65E** | DUNDEE - 62B |
| Aug-59 | DUNFERMLINE - 62C | DUNFERMLINE - 62C | DALRY RD - 64C | POLMONT - 64E | POLMONT - 64E | EDINBURGH (SM) - 64A | PARKHEAD - 65C | KIPPS - 65E | DUNDEE - 62B |
| Nov-59 | DUNFERMLINE - 62C | DUNFERMLINE - 62C | DALRY RD - 64C | POLMONT - 64E | POLMONT - 64E | EDINBURGH (SM) - 64A | PARKHEAD - 65C | KIPPS - 65E | DUNDEE - 62B |
| Jan-60 | DUNFERMLINE - 62C | DUNFERMLINE - 62C | DALRY RD - 64C | POLMONT - 64E | POLMONT - 64E | EDINBURGH (SM) - 64A | PARKHEAD - 65C | KIPPS - 65E | DUNDEE - 62B |
| Apr-60 | **3/60: W/D** | DUNFERMLINE - 62C | DALRY RD - 64C | POLMONT - 65K | POLMONT - 65K | EDINBURGH (SM) - 64A | PARKHEAD - 65C | KIPPS - 65E | DUNDEE - 62B |
| Aug-60 | | DUNFERMLINE - 62C | DALRY RD - 64C | POLMONT - 65K | POLMONT - 65K | EDINBURGH (SM) - 64A | PARKHEAD - 65C | KIPPS - 65E | DUNDEE - 62B |
| Nov-60 | | DUNFERMLINE - 62C | DALRY RD - 64C | POLMONT - 65K | POLMONT - 65K | EDINBURGH (SM) - 64A | PARKHEAD - 65C | KIPPS - 65E | DUNDEE - 62B |

| | 64576 | 64577 | 64578 | 64579 | 64580 | 64581 | 64582 | 64583 | 64584 |
|---|---|---|---|---|---|---|---|---|---|
| Aug-50 | EDINBURGH(SM) - 64A | EDINBURGH(SM) - 64A | EASTFIELD - 65A | EASTFIELD - 65A | EASTFIELD - 65A | EASTFIELD - 65A | EDINBURGH(SM) - 64A | EASTFIELD - 65A | PARKHEAD - 65C |
| Jan-51 | EDINBURGH(SM) - 64A | EDINBURGH(SM) - 64A | EASTFIELD - 65A | EASTFIELD - 65A | EASTFIELD - 65A | EASTFIELD - 65A | EDINBURGH(SM) - 64A | EASTFIELD - 65A | PARKHEAD - 65C |
| Aug-51 | EDINBURGH(SM) - 64A | EDINBURGH(SM) - 64A | EASTFIELD - 65A | 4/51: KIPPS - 65E | EASTFIELD - 65A | EASTFIELD - 65A | EDINBURGH(SM) - 64A | 6/51: BATH - 64F | PARKHEAD - 65C |
| Jan-52 | EDINBURGH(SM) - 64A | EDINBURGH(SM) - 64A | EASTFIELD - 65A | KIPPS - 65E | EASTFIELD - 65A | EASTFIELD - 65A | EDINBURGH(SM) - 64A | BATHGATE - 64F | PARKHEAD - 65C |
| Aug-52 | EDINBURGH(SM) - 64A | EDINBURGH(SM) - 64A | EASTFIELD - 65A | KIPPS - 65E | EASTFIELD - 65A | EASTFIELD - 65A | EDINBURGH(SM) - 64A | BATHGATE - 64F | PARKHEAD - 65C |
| Jan-53 | EDINBURGH(SM) - 64A | EDINBURGH(SM) - 64A | EASTFIELD - 65A | KIPPS - 65E | EASTFIELD - 65A | EASTFIELD - 65A | EDINBURGH(SM) - 64A | BATHGATE - 64F | PARKHEAD - 65C |
| Aug-53 | EDINBURGH(SM) - 64A | EDINBURGH(SM) - 64A | EASTFIELD - 65A | KIPPS - 65E | EASTFIELD - 65A | EASTFIELD - 65A | EDINBURGH(SM) - 64A | BATHGATE - 64F | PARKHEAD - 65C |
| Jan-54 | EDINBURGH(SM) - 64A | EDINBURGH(SM) - 64A | EASTFIELD - 65A | KIPPS - 65E | EASTFIELD - 65A | EASTFIELD - 65A | EDINBURGH(SM) - 64A | BATHGATE - 64F | PARKHEAD - 65C |
| Aug-54 | EDINBURGH(SM) - 64A | EDINBURGH(SM) - 64A | EASTFIELD - 65A | KIPPS - 65E | EASTFIELD - 65A | EASTFIELD - 65A | EDINBURGH(SM) - 64A | BATHGATE - 64F | PARKHEAD - 65C |
| Jan-55 | EDINBURGH(SM) - 64A | EDINBURGH(SM) - 64A | EASTFIELD - 65A | KIPPS - 65E | EASTFIELD - 65A | EASTFIELD - 65A | EDINBURGH(SM) - 64A | BATHGATE - 64F | PARKHEAD - 65C |
| Aug-55 | EDINBURGH(SM) - 64A | EDINBURGH(SM) - 64A | EASTFIELD - 65A | KIPPS - 65E | EASTFIELD - 65A | EASTFIELD - 65A | EDINBURGH(SM) - 64A | BATHGATE - 64F | PARKHEAD - 65C |
| Jan-56 | EDINBURGH(SM) - 64A | EDINBURGH(SM) - 64A | EASTFIELD - 65A | KIPPS - 65E | EASTFIELD - 65A | EASTFIELD - 65A | EDINBURGH(SM) - 64A | BATHGATE - 64F | PARKHEAD - 65C |
| Aug-56 | EDINBURGH(SM) - 64A | EDINBURGH(SM) - 64A | EASTFIELD - 65A | KIPPS - 65E | EASTFIELD - 65A | EASTFIELD - 65A | EDINBURGH(SM) - 64A | BATHGATE - 64F | PARKHEAD - 65C |
| Jan-57 | EDINBURGH(SM) - 64A | EDINBURGH(SM) - 64A | EASTFIELD - 65A | KIPPS - 65E | EASTFIELD - 65A | EASTFIELD - 65A | EDINBURGH(SM) - 64A | BATHGATE - 64F | PARKHEAD - 65C |
| Aug-57 | EDINBURGH(SM) - 64A | EDINBURGH(SM) - 64A | EASTFIELD - 65A | KIPPS - 65E | EASTFIELD - 65A | EASTFIELD - 65A | EDINBURGH(SM) - 64A | BATHGATE - 64F | PARKHEAD - 65C |
| Jan-58 | EDINBURGH(SM) - 64A | EDINBURGH(SM) - 64A | EASTFIELD - 65A | KIPPS - 65E | EASTFIELD - 65A | EASTFIELD - 65A | EDINBURGH(SM) - 64A | BATHGATE - 64F | PARKHEAD - 65C |
| Aug-58 | EDINBURGH(SM) - 64A | EDINBURGH(SM) - 64A | EASTFIELD - 65A | KIPPS - 65E | EASTFIELD - 65A | EASTFIELD - 65A | EDINBURGH(SM) - 64A | BATHGATE - 64F | PARKHEAD - 65C |
| Jan-59 | EDINBURGH(SM) - 64A | EDINBURGH(SM) - 64A | EASTFIELD - 65A | KIPPS - 65E | EASTFIELD - 65A | EASTFIELD - 65A | EDINBURGH(SM) - 64A | BATHGATE - 64F | PARKHEAD - 65C |
| Aug-59 | EDINBURGH(SM) - 64A | EDINBURGH(SM) - 64A | EASTFIELD - 65A | KIPPS - 65E | EASTFIELD - 65A | EASTFIELD - 65A | EDINBURGH(SM) - 64A | BATHGATE - 64F | 7/59: W/D |
| Nov-59 | EDINBURGH(SM) - 64A | EDINBURGH(SM) - 64A | EASTFIELD - 65A | KIPPS - 65E | EASTFIELD - 65A | EASTFIELD - 65A | EDINBURGH(SM) - 64A | BATHGATE - 64F | |
| Jan-60 | EDINBURGH(SM) - 64A | EDINBURGH(SM) - 64A | EASTFIELD - 65A | KIPPS - 65E | EASTFIELD - 65A | EASTFIELD - 65A | EDINBURGH(SM) - 64A | BATHGATE - 64F | |
| Apr-60 | EDINBURGH(SM) - 64A | EDINBURGH(SM) - 64A | EASTFIELD - 65A | KIPPS - 65E | EASTFIELD - 65A | EASTFIELD - 65A | EDINBURGH(SM) - 64A | BATHGATE - 64F | |
| Aug-60 | EDINBURGH(SM) - 64A | EDINBURGH(SM) - 64A | EASTFIELD - 65A | KIPPS - 65E | EASTFIELD - 65A | EASTFIELD - 65A | EDINBURGH(SM) - 64A | BATHGATE - 64F | |
| Nov-60 | EDINBURGH(SM) - 64A | EDINBURGH(SM) - 64A | EASTFIELD - 65A | KIPPS - 65E | EASTFIELD - 65A | EASTFIELD - 65A | EDINBURGH(SM) - 64A | BATHGATE - 64F | |

| | 64585 | 64586 | 64587 | 64588 | 64589 | 64590 | 64591 | 64592 | 64593 |
|---|---|---|---|---|---|---|---|---|---|
| Aug-50 | STIRLING - 63B | EDINBURGH(SM) - 64A | DUNDEE - 62B | POLMONT - 64E | POLMONT - 64E | DUNFERMLINE - 62C | DALRYRD - 64C | POLMONT - 64E | POLMONT - 64E |
| Jan-51 | STIRLING - 63B | EDINBURGH(SM) - 64A | DUNDEE - 62B | POLMONT - 64E | POLMONT - 64E | DUNFERMLINE - 62C | DALRYRD - 64C | POLMONT - 64E | POLMONT - 64E |
| Aug-51 | STIRLING - 63B | EDINBURGH(SM) - 64A | DUNDEE - 62B | POLMONT - 64E | POLMONT - 64E | DUNFERMLINE - 62C | DALRYRD - 64C | POLMONT - 64E | POLMONT - 64E |
| Jan-52 | STIRLING - 63B | EDINBURGH(SM) - 64A | DUNDEE - 62B | POLMONT - 64E | POLMONT - 64E | DUNFERMLINE - 62C | DALRYRD - 64C | POLMONT - 64E | POLMONT - 64E |
| Aug-52 | STIRLING - 63B | EDINBURGH(SM) - 64A | DUNDEE - 62B | POLMONT - 64E | POLMONT - 64E | DUNFERMLINE - 62C | DALRYRD - 64C | POLMONT - 64E | POLMONT - 64E |
| Jan-53 | STIRLING - 63B | EDINBURGH(SM) - 64A | DUNDEE - 62B | POLMONT - 64E | POLMONT - 64E | 11/52: ST. M - 64A | DALRYRD - 64C | POLMONT - 64E | POLMONT - 64E |
| Aug-53 | STIRLING - 63B | EDINBURGH(SM) - 64A | DUNDEE - 62B | POLMONT - 64E | POLMONT - 64E | EDINBURGH(SM) - 64A | DALRYRD - 64C | POLMONT - 64E | POLMONT - 64E |
| Jan-54 | STIRLING - 63B | EDINBURGH(SM) - 64A | DUNDEE - 62B | POLMONT - 64E | POLMONT - 64E | EDINBURGH(SM) - 64A | DALRYRD - 64C | POLMONT - 64E | POLMONT - 64E |
| Aug-54 | STIRLING - 63B | EDINBURGH(SM) - 64A | DUNDEE - 62B | POLMONT - 64E | POLMONT - 64E | EDINBURGH(SM) - 64A | DALRYRD - 64C | POLMONT - 64E | POLMONT - 64E |
| Jan-55 | STIRLING - 63B | EDINBURGH(SM) - 64A | DUNDEE - 62B | POLMONT - 64E | POLMONT - 64E | EDINBURGH(SM) - 64A | DALRYRD - 64C | POLMONT - 64E | POLMONT - 64E |
| Aug-55 | STIRLING - 63B | EDINBURGH(SM) - 64A | DUNDEE - 62B | POLMONT - 64E | POLMONT - 64E | EDINBURGH(SM) - 64A | DALRYRD - 64C | POLMONT - 64E | POLMONT - 64E |
| Jan-56 | STIRLING - 63B | EDINBURGH(SM) - 64A | DUNDEE - 62B | POLMONT - 64E | POLMONT - 64E | EDINBURGH(SM) - 64A | DALRYRD - 64C | POLMONT - 64E | POLMONT - 64E |
| Aug-56 | STIRLING - 63B | EDINBURGH(SM) - 64A | DUNDEE - 62B | POLMONT - 64E | POLMONT - 64E | EDINBURGH(SM) - 64A | DALRYRD - 64C | POLMONT - 64E | POLMONT - 64E |
| Jan-57 | STIRLING - 63B | EDINBURGH(SM) - 64A | DUNDEE - 62B | POLMONT - 64E | POLMONT - 64E | EDINBURGH(SM) - 64A | DALRYRD - 64C | POLMONT - 64E | POLMONT - 64E |
| Aug-57 | 7/57: DUND - 62B | EDINBURGH(SM) - 64A | DUNDEE - 62B | POLMONT - 64E | POLMONT - 64E | EDINBURGH(SM) - 64A | DALRYRD - 64C | POLMONT - 64E | POLMONT - 64E |
| Jan-58 | DUNDEE - 62B | EDINBURGH(SM) - 64A | DUNDEE - 62B | POLMONT - 64E | POLMONT - 64E | EDINBURGH(SM) - 64A | DALRYRD - 64C | POLMONT - 64E | POLMONT - 64E |
| Aug-58 | DUNDEE - 62B | EDINBURGH(SM) - 64A | DUNDEE - 62B | POLMONT - 64E | POLMONT - 64E | EDINBURGH(SM) - 64A | 9/58: ST. M - 64A | POLMONT - 64E | POLMONT - 64E |
| Jan-59 | DUNDEE - 62B | EDINBURGH(SM) - 64A | DUNDEE - 62B | 1/59: GRANGE - 65F | 1/59: GRANGE - 65F | EDINBURGH(SM) - 64A | EDINBURGH(SM) - 64A | 1/59: GRANGE - 65F | 1/59: GRANGE - 65F |
| Aug-59 | DUNDEE - 62B | EDINBURGH(SM) - 64A | DUNDEE - 62B | 8/59: PARK - 65C | GRANGEMOUTH - 65F | EDINBURGH(SM) - 64A | EDINBURGH(SM) - 64A | GRANGEMOUTH - 65F | GRANGEMOUTH - 65F |
| Nov-59 | DUNDEE - 62B | EDINBURGH(SM) - 64A | DUNDEE - 62B | PARKHEAD - 65C | GRANGEMOUTH - 65F | EDINBURGH(SM) - 64A | EDINBURGH(SM) - 64A | GRANGEMOUTH - 65F | GRANGEMOUTH - 65F |
| Jan-60 | 1/60: DUNF - 62C | EDINBURGH(SM) - 64A | DUNDEE - 62B | PARKHEAD - 65C | GRANGEMOUTH - 65F | EDINBURGH(SM) - 64A | EDINBURGH(SM) - 64A | GRANGEMOUTH - 65F | GRANGEMOUTH - 65F |
| Apr-60 | DUNFERMLINE - 62C | EDINBURGH(SM) - 64A | DUNDEE - 62B | PARKHEAD - 65C | GRANGEMOUTH - 65F | EDINBURGH(SM) - 64A | EDINBURGH(SM) - 54A | GRANGEMOUTH - 65F | GRANGEMOUTH - 65F |
| Aug-60 | DUNFERMLINE - 62C | EDINBURGH(SM) - 64A | DUNDEE - 62B | PARKHEAD - 65C | GRANGEMOUTH - 65F | EDINBURGH(SM) - 64A | EDINBURGH(SM) - 64A | GRANGEMOUTH - 65F | GRANGEMOUTH - 65F |
| Nov-60 | DUNFERMLINE - 62C | EDINBURGH(SM) - 64A | DUNDEE - 62B | PARKHEAD - 65C | GRANGEMOUTH - 65F | EDINBURGH(SM) - 64A | EDINBURGH(SM) - 64A | GRANGEMOUTH - 65F | GRANGEMOUTH - 65F |

| | 64594 | 64595 | 64596 | 64597 | 64598 | 64599 | 64600 | 64601 | 64602 |
|---|---|---|---|---|---|---|---|---|---|
| Aug-50 | EDINBURGH(SM) - 64A | EDINBURGH(SM) - 64A | THORNTONJCN - 62A | THORNTONJCN - 62A | DUNDEE - 62B | EDINBURGH(SM) - 64A | THORNTONJCN - 62A | EASTFIELD - 65A | THORNTONJCN - 62A |
| Jan-51 | EDINBURGH(SM) - 64A | EDINBURGH(SM) - 64A | THORNTONJCN - 62A | THORNTONJCN - 62A | DUNDEE - 62B | EDINBURGH(SM) - 64A | THORNTONJCN - 62A | 3/51: BATH - 64F | THORNTONJCN - 62A |
| Aug-51 | EDINBURGH(SM) - 64A | EDINBURGH(SM) - 64A | THORNTONJCN - 62A | THORNTONJCN - 62A | DUNDEE - 62B | EDINBURGH(SM) - 64A | THORNTONJCN - 62A | BATHGATE - 64F | THORNTONJCN - 62A |
| Jan-52 | EDINBURGH(SM) - 64A | EDINBURGH(SM) - 64A | THORNTONJCN - 62A | THORNTONJCN - 62A | DUNDEE - 62B | EDINBURGH(SM) - 64A | THORNTONJCN - 62A | BATHGATE - 64F | THORNTONJCN - 62A |
| Aug-52 | EDINBURGH(SM) - 64A | EDINBURGH(SM) - 64A | THORNTONJCN - 62A | THORNTONJCN - 62A | DUNDEE - 62B | EDINBURGH(SM) - 64A | THORNTONJCN - 62A | BATHGATE - 64F | THORNTONJCN - 62A |
| Jan-53 | EDINBURGH(SM) - 64A | EDINBURGH(SM) - 64A | THORNTONJCN - 62A | 11/52: ST. M - 64A | DUNDEE - 62B | EDINBURGH(SM) - 64A | THORNTONJCN - 62A | BATHGATE - 64F | THORNTONJCN - 62A |
| Aug-53 | EDINBURGH(SM) - 64A | EDINBURGH(SM) - 64A | THORNTONJCN - 62A | EDINBURGH(SM) - 64A | DUNDEE - 62B | EDINBURGH(SM) - 64A | THORNTONJCN - 62A | 5/53: ST.M - 64A | THORNTONJCN - 62A |
| Jan-54 | EDINBURGH(SM) - 64A | EDINBURGH(SM) - 64A | THORNTONJCN - 62A | EDINBURGH(SM) - 64A | DUNDEE - 62B | EDINBURGH(SM) - 64A | THORNTONJCN - 62A | EDINBURGH(SM) - 64A | THORNTONJCN - 62A |
| Aug-54 | EDINBURGH(SM) - 64A | EDINBURGH(SM) - 64A | THORNTONJCN - 62A | EDINBURGH(SM) - 64A | DUNDEE - 62B | EDINBURGH(SM) - 64A | THORNTONJCN - 62A | EDINBURGH(SM) - 64A | THORNTONJCN - 62A |
| Jan-55 | EDINBURGH(SM) - 64A | EDINBURGH(SM) - 64A | THORNTONJCN - 62A | EDINBURGH(SM) - 64A | DUNDEE - 62B | EDINBURGH(SM) - 64A | THORNTONJCN - 62A | EDINBURGH(SM) - 64A | THORNTONJCN - 62A |
| Aug-55 | EDINBURGH(SM) - 64A | EDINBURGH(SM) - 64A | THORNTONJCN - 62A | EDINBURGH(SM) - 64A | DUNDEE - 62B | EDINBURGH(SM) - 64A | THORNTONJCN - 62A | EDINBURGH(SM) - 64A | THORNTONJCN - 62A |
| Jan-56 | EDINBURGH(SM) - 64A | EDINBURGH(SM) - 64A | THORNTONJCN - 62A | EDINBURGH(SM) - 64A | DUNDEE - 62B | EDINBURGH(SM) - 64A | THORNTONJCN - 62A | EDINBURGH(SM) - 64A | THORNTONJCN - 62A |
| Aug-56 | EDINBURGH(SM) - 64A | EDINBURGH(SM) - 64A | THORNTONJCN - 62A | EDINBURGH(SM) - 64A | DUNDEE - 62B | EDINBURGH(SM) - 64A | THORNTONJCN - 62A | EDINBURGH(SM) - 64A | THORNTONJCN - 62A |
| Jan-57 | EDINBURGH(SM) - 64A | EDINBURGH(SM) - 64A | THORNTONJCN - 62A | EDINBURGH(SM) - 64A | DUNDEE - 62B | EDINBURGH(SM) - 64A | THORNTONJCN - 62A | EDINBURGH(SM) - 64A | THORNTONJCN - 62A |
| Aug-57 | EDINBURGH(SM) - 64A | EDINBURGH(SM) - 64A | THORNTONJCN - 62A | 5/57: DUNF - 62C | DUNDEE - 62B | EDINBURGH(SM) - 64A | THORNTONJCN - 62A | EDINBURGH(SM) - 64A | THORNTONJCN - 62A |
| Jan-58 | EDINBURGH(SM) - 64A | EDINBURGH(SM) - 64A | THORNTONJCN - 62A | DUNFERMLINE - 62C | DUNDEE - 62B | EDINBURGH(SM) - 64A | THORNTONJCN - 62A | EDINBURGH(SM) - 64A | THORNTONJCN - 62A |
| Aug-58 | EDINBURGH(SM) - 64A | EDINBURGH(SM) - 64A | THORNTONJCN - 62A | DUNFERMLINE - 62C | DUNDEE - 62B | EDINBURGH(SM) - 64A | THORNTONJCN - 62A | EDINBURGH(SM) - 64A | THORNTONJCN - 62A |
| Jan-59 | EDINBURGH(SM) - 64A | EDINBURGH(SM) - 64A | THORNTONJCN - 62A | DUNFERMLINE - 62C | DUNDEE - 62B | EDINBURGH(SM) - 64A | THORNTONJCN - 62A | EDINBURGH(SM) - 64A | THORNTONJCN - 62A |
| Aug-59 | EDINBURGH(SM) - 64A | EDINBURGH(SM) - 64A | THORNTONJCN - 62A | DUNFERMLINE - 62C | DUNDEE - 62B | EDINBURGH(SM) - 64A | 8/59: DUND - 62B | EDINBURGH(SM) - 64A | 8/59: DUND - 62B |
| Nov-59 | EDINBURGH(SM) - 64A | EDINBURGH(SM) - 64A | THORNTONJCN - 62A | DUNFERMLINE - 62C | DUNDEE - 62B | EDINBURGH(SM) - 64A | DUNDEE - 62B | EDINBURGH(SM) - 64A | DUNDEE - 62B |
| Jan-60 | EDINBURGH(SM) - 64A | EDINBURGH(SM) - 64A | THORNTONJCN - 62A | DUNFERMLINE - 62C | DUNDEE - 62B | EDINBURGH(SM) - 64A | DUNDEE - 62B | EDINBURGH(SM) - 64A | DUNDEE - 62B |
| Apr-60 | EDINBURGH(SM) - 64A | EDINBURGH(SM) - 64A | THORNTONJCN - 62A | DUNFERMLINE - 62C | DUNDEE - 62B | EDINBURGH(SM) - 64A | DUNDEE - 62B | EDINBURGH(SM) - 64A | DUNDEE - 62B |
| Aug-60 | EDINBURGH(SM) - 64A | EDINBURGH(SM) - 64A | THORNTONJCN - 62A | DUNFERMLINE - 62C | DUNDEE - 62B | EDINBURGH(SM) - 64A | DUNDEE - 62B | EDINBURGH(SM) - 64A | DUNDEE - 62B |
| Nov-60 | EDINBURGH(SM) - 64A | EDINBURGH(SM) - 64A | THORNTONJCN - 62A | DUNFERMLINE - 62C | DUNDEE - 62B | EDINBURGH(SM) - 64A | DUNDEE - 62B | EDINBURGH(SM) - 64A | DUNDEE - 62B |

| | 64603 | 64604 | 64605 | 64606 | 64607 | 64608 | 64609 | 64610 | 64611 |
|---|---|---|---|---|---|---|---|---|---|
| Aug-50 | EDINBURGH(SM) - 64A | DUNFERMLINE - 62C | EDINBURGH(SM) - 64A | EDINBURGH(SM) - 64A | EDINBURGH(SM) - 64A | EDINBURGH(SM) - 64A | PARKHEAD - 65C | PARKHEAD - 65C | EASTFIELD - 65A |
| Jan-51 | EDINBURGH(SM) - 64A | DUNFERMLINE - 62C | EDINBURGH(SM) - 64A | EDINBURGH(SM) - 64A | EDINBURGH(SM) - 64A | EDINBURGH(SM) - 64A | PARKHEAD - 65C | PARKHEAD - 65C | EASTFIELD - 65A |
| Aug-51 | EDINBURGH(SM) - 64A | DUNFERMLINE - 62C | EDINBURGH(SM) - 64A | EDINBURGH(SM) - 64A | EDINBURGH(SM) - 64A | EDINBURGH(SM) - 64A | PARKHEAD - 65C | PARKHEAD - 65C | EASTFIELD - 65A |
| Jan-52 | EDINBURGH(SM) - 64A | DUNFERMLINE - 62C | EDINBURGH(SM) - 64A | EDINBURGH(SM) - 64A | EDINBURGH(SM) - 64A | EDINBURGH(SM) - 64A | PARKHEAD - 65C | PARKHEAD - 65C | EASTFIELD - 65A |
| Aug-52 | EDINBURGH(SM) - 64A | DUNFERMLINE - 62C | EDINBURGH(SM) - 64A | EDINBURGH(SM) - 64A | EDINBURGH(SM) - 64A | EDINBURGH(SM) - 64A | PARKHEAD - 65C | PARKHEAD - 65C | EASTFIELD - 65A |
| Jan-53 | EDINBURGH(SM) - 64A | DUNFERMLINE - 62C | EDINBURGH(SM) - 64A | EDINBURGH(SM) - 64A | EDINBURGH(SM) - 64A | EDINBURGH(SM) - 64A | PARKHEAD - 65C | PARKHEAD - 65C | EASTFIELD - 65A |
| Aug-53 | EDINBURGH(SM) - 64A | DUNFERMLINE - 62C | EDINBURGH(SM) - 64A | EDINBURGH(SM) - 64A | EDINBURGH(SM) - 64A | EDINBURGH(SM) - 64A | PARKHEAD - 65C | PARKHEAD - 65C | EASTFIELD - 65A |
| Jan-54 | EDINBURGH(SM) - 64A | DUNFERMLINE - 62C | EDINBURGH(SM) - 64A | EDINBURGH(SM) - 64A | EDINBURGH(SM) - 64A | EDINBURGH(SM) - 64A | PARKHEAD - 65C | PARKHEAD - 65C | EASTFIELD - 65A |
| Aug-54 | EDINBURGH(SM) - 64A | DUNFERMLINE - 62C | EDINBURGH(SM) - 64A | EDINBURGH(SM) - 64A | EDINBURGH(SM) - 64A | EDINBURGH(SM) - 64A | PARKHEAD - 65C | PARKHEAD - 65C | EASTFIELD - 65A |
| Jan-55 | EDINBURGH(SM) - 64A | DUNFERMLINE - 62C | EDINBURGH(SM) - 64A | EDINBURGH(SM) - 64A | EDINBURGH(SM) - 64A | EDINBURGH(SM) - 64A | PARKHEAD - 65C | PARKHEAD - 65C | EASTFIELD - 65A |
| Aug-55 | EDINBURGH(SM) - 64A | DUNFERMLINE - 62C | EDINBURGH(SM) - 64A | EDINBURGH(SM) - 64A | EDINBURGH(SM) - 64A | EDINBURGH(SM) - 64A | PARKHEAD - 65C | PARKHEAD - 65C | EASTFIELD - 65A |
| Jan-56 | EDINBURGH(SM) - 64A | DUNFERMLINE - 62C | EDINBURGH(SM) - 64A | EDINBURGH(SM) - 64A | EDINBURGH(SM) - 64A | EDINBURGH(SM) - 64A | PARKHEAD - 65C | PARKHEAD - 65C | EASTFIELD - 65A |
| Aug-56 | EDINBURGH(SM) - 64A | DUNFERMLINE - 62C | EDINBURGH(SM) - 64A | EDINBURGH(SM) - 64A | EDINBURGH(SM) - 64A | EDINBURGH(SM) - 64A | PARKHEAD - 65C | PARKHEAD - 65C | EASTFIELD - 65A |
| Jan-57 | EDINBURGH(SM) - 64A | DUNFERMLINE - 62C | EDINBURGH(SM) - 64A | EDINBURGH(SM) - 64A | EDINBURGH(SM) - 64A | EDINBURGH(SM) - 64A | PARKHEAD - 65C | PARKHEAD - 65C | EASTFIELD - 65A |
| Aug-57 | EDINBURGH(SM) - 64A | DUNFERMLINE - 62C | EDINBURGH(SM) - 64A | EDINBURGH(SM) - 64A | EDINBURGH(SM) - 64A | EDINBURGH(SM) - 64A | PARKHEAD - 65C | PARKHEAD - 65C | EASTFIELD - 65A |
| Jan-58 | EDINBURGH(SM) - 64A | DUNFERMLINE - 62C | EDINBURGH(SM) - 64A | EDINBURGH(SM) - 64A | EDINBURGH(SM) - 64A | EDINBURGH(SM) - 64A | PARKHEAD - 65C | PARKHEAD - 65C | EASTFIELD - 65A |
| Aug-58 | EDINBURGH(SM) - 64A | DUNFERMLINE - 62C | EDINBURGH(SM) - 64A | EDINBURGH(SM) - 64A | EDINBURGH(SM) - 64A | EDINBURGH(SM) - 64A | PARKHEAD - 65C | PARKHEAD - 65C | EASTFIELD - 65A |
| Jan-59 | EDINBURGH(SM) - 64A | DUNFERMLINE - 62C | EDINBURGH(SM) - 64A | EDINBURGH(SM) - 64A | EDINBURGH(SM) - 64A | EDINBURGH(SM) - 64A | PARKHEAD - 65C | PARKHEAD - 65C | EASTFIELD - 65A |
| Aug-59 | EDINBURGH(SM) - 64A | DUNFERMLINE - 62C | EDINBURGH(SM) - 64A | EDINBURGH(SM) - 64A | EDINBURGH(SM) - 64A | EDINBURGH(SM) - 64A | PARKHEAD - 65C | PARKHEAD - 65C | EASTFIELD - 65A |
| Nov-59 | EDINBURGH(SM) - 64A | DUNFERMLINE - 62C | EDINBURGH(SM) - 64A | EDINBURGH(SM) - 64A | EDINBURGH(SM) - 64A | EDINBURGH(SM) - 64A | PARKHEAD - 65C | PARKHEAD - 65C | EASTFIELD - 65A |
| Jan-60 | EDINBURGH(SM) - 64A | DUNFERMLINE - 62C | EDINBURGH(SM) - 64A | EDINBURGH(SM) - 64A | EDINBURGH(SM) - 64A | EDINBURGH(SM) - 64A | PARKHEAD - 65C | PARKHEAD - 65C | EASTFIELD - 65A |
| Apr-60 | EDINBURGH(SM) - 64A | DUNFERMLINE - 62C | EDINBURGH(SM) - 64A | EDINBURGH(SM) - 64A | EDINBURGH(SM) - 64A | EDINBURGH(SM) - 64A | PARKHEAD - 65C | PARKHEAD - 65C | EASTFIELD - 65A |
| Aug-60 | EDINBURGH(SM) - 64A | DUNFERMLINE - 62C | EDINBURGH(SM) - 64A | EDINBURGH(SM) - 64A | EDINBURGH(SM) - 64A | EDINBURGH(SM) - 64A | PARKHEAD - 65C | PARKHEAD - 65C | EASTFIELD - 65A |
| Nov-60 | EDINBURGH(SM) - 64A | DUNFERMLINE - 62C | EDINBURGH(SM) - 64A | EDINBURGH(SM) - 64A | EDINBURGH(SM) - 64A | EDINBURGH(SM) - 64A | PARKHEAD - 65C | PARKHEAD - 65C | EASTFIELD - 65A |

| | 64612 | 64613 | 64614 | 64615 | 64616 | 64617 | 64618 | 64619 | 64620 |
|---|---|---|---|---|---|---|---|---|---|
| Aug-50 | THORNTON JCN - 62A | POLMONT - 64E | EDINBURGH (SM) - 64A | DUNDEE - 62B | THORNTON JCN - 62A | DUNFERMLINE - 62C | THORNTON JCN - 62A | DUNDEE - 62B | DUNDEE - 62B |
| Jan-51 | THORNTON JCN - 62A | POLMONT - 64E | EDINBURGH (SM) - 64A | DUNDEE - 62B | THORNTON JCN - 62A | DUNFERMLINE - 62C | THORNTON JCN - 62A | DUNDEE - 62B | DUNDEE - 62B |
| Aug-51 | THORNTON JCN - 62A | POLMONT - 64E | EDINBURGH (SM) - 64A | DUNDEE - 62B | THORNTON JCN - 62A | DUNFERMLINE - 62C | THORNTON JCN - 62A | DUNDEE - 62B | DUNDEE - 62B |
| Jan-52 | THORNTON JCN - 62A | 11/51: ST. M - 64A | EDINBURGH (SM) - 64A | DUNDEE - 62B | THORNTON JCN - 62A | DUNFERMLINE - 62C | THORNTON JCN - 62A | DUNDEE - 62B | DUNDEE - 62B |
| Aug-52 | THORNTON JCN - 62A | EDINBURGH (SM) - 64A | EDINBURGH (SM) - 64A | DUNDEE - 62B | THORNTON JCN - 62A | DUNFERMLINE - 62C | THORNTON JCN - 62A | DUNDEE - 62B | DUNDEE - 62B |
| Jan-53 | THORNTON JCN - 62A | EDINBURGH (SM) - 64A | EDINBURGH (SM) - 64A | DUNDEE - 62B | THORNTON JCN - 62A | DUNFERMLINE - 62C | THORNTON JCN - 62A | DUNDEE - 62B | DUNDEE - 62B |
| Aug-53 | THORNTON JCN - 62A | EDINBURGH (SM) - 64A | EDINBURGH (SM) - 64A | DUNDEE - 62B | THORNTON JCN - 62A | DUNFERMLINE - 62C | THORNTON JCN - 62A | DUNDEE - 62B | DUNDEE - 62B |
| Jan-54 | THORNTON JCN - 62A | EDINBURGH (SM) - 64A | EDINBURGH (SM) - 64A | DUNDEE - 62B | THORNTON JCN - 62A | DUNFERMLINE - 62C | THORNTON JCN - 62A | DUNDEE - 62B | DUNDEE - 62B |
| Aug-54 | THORNTON JCN - 62A | EDINBURGH (SM) - 64A | EDINBURGH (SM) - 64A | DUNDEE - 62B | THORNTON JCN - 62A | DUNFERMLINE - 62C | THORNTON JCN - 62A | DUNDEE - 62B | DUNDEE - 62B |
| Jan-55 | THORNTON JCN - 62A | EDINBURGH (SM) - 64A | EDINBURGH (SM) - 64A | DUNDEE - 62B | THORNTON JCN - 62A | DUNFERMLINE - 62C | THORNTON JCN - 62A | DUNDEE - 62B | DUNDEE - 62B |
| Aug-55 | 9/55: CARS - 64D | EDINBURGH (SM) - 64A | EDINBURGH (SM) - 64A | DUNDEE - 62B | THORNTON JCN - 62A | DUNFERMLINE - 62C | THORNTON JCN - 62A | DUNDEE - 62B | DUNDEE - 62B |
| Jan-56 | CARSTAIRS - 64D | EDINBURGH (SM) - 64A | EDINBURGH (SM) - 64A | DUNDEE - 62B | THORNTON JCN - 62A | DUNFERMLINE - 62C | THORNTON JCN - 62A | DUNDEE - 62B | DUNDEE - 62B |
| Aug-56 | 4/56: DALRY - 64C | EDINBURGH (SM) - 64A | EDINBURGH (SM) - 64A | DUNDEE - 62B | THORNTON JCN - 62A | DUNFERMLINE - 62C | THORNTON JCN - 62A | DUNDEE - 62B | DUNDEE - 62B |
| Jan-57 | DALRY RD - 64C | EDINBURGH (SM) - 64A | EDINBURGH (SM) - 64A | DUNDEE - 62B | THORNTON JCN - 62A | DUNFERMLINE - 62C | THORNTON JCN - 62A | DUNDEE - 62B | DUNDEE - 62B |
| Aug-57 | DALRY RD - 64C | EDINBURGH (SM) - 64A | EDINBURGH (SM) - 64A | DUNDEE - 62B | THORNTON JCN - 62A | DUNFERMLINE - 62C | THORNTON JCN - 62A | DUNDEE - 62B | DUNDEE - 62B |
| Jan-58 | DALRY RD - 64C | EDINBURGH (SM) - 64A | EDINBURGH (SM) - 64A | DUNDEE - 62B | THORNTON JCN - 62A | DUNFERMLINE - 62C | THORNTON JCN - 62A | DUNDEE - 62B | DUNDEE - 62B |
| Aug-58 | 9/58: ST. M - 64A | EDINBURGH (SM) - 64A | EDINBURGH (SM) - 64A | DUNDEE - 62B | THORNTON JCN - 62A | DUNFERMLINE - 62C | THORNTON JCN - 62A | DUNDEE - 62B | DUNDEE - 62B |
| Jan-59 | EDINBURGH (SM) - 64A | EDINBURGH (SM) - 64A | EDINBURGH (SM) - 64A | DUNDEE - 62B | THORNTON JCN - 62A | DUNFERMLINE - 62C | THORNTON JCN - 62A | DUNDEE - 62B | DUNDEE - 62B |
| Aug-59 | EDINBURGH (SM) - 64A | EDINBURGH (SM) - 64A | EDINBURGH (SM) - 64A | DUNDEE - 62B | THORNTON JCN - 62A | DUNFERMLINE - 62C | THORNTON JCN - 62A | DUNDEE - 62B | DUNDEE - 62B |
| Nov-59 | EDINBURGH (SM) - 64A | EDINBURGH (SM) - 64A | EDINBURGH (SM) - 64A | DUNDEE - 62B | THORNTON JCN - 62A | DUNFERMLINE - 62C | THORNTON JCN - 62A | DUNDEE - 62B | DUNDEE - 62B |
| Jan-60 | EDINBURGH (SM) - 64A | EDINBURGH (SM) - 64A | EDINBURGH (SM) - 64A | DUNDEE - 62B | THORNTON JCN - 62A | DUNFERMLINE - 62C | THORNTON JCN - 62A | DUNDEE - 62B | DUNDEE - 62B |
| Apr-60 | EDINBURGH (SM) - 64A | EDINBURGH (SM) - 64A | EDINBURGH (SM) - 64A | DUNDEE - 62B | THORNTON JCN - 62A | DUNFERMLINE - 62C | THORNTON JCN - 62A | DUNDEE - 62B | DUNDEE - 62B |
| Aug-60 | EDINBURGH (SM) - 64A | EDINBURGH (SM) - 64A | EDINBURGH (SM) - 64A | DUNDEE - 62B | THORNTON JCN - 62A | DUNFERMLINE - 62C | THORNTON JCN - 62A | DUNDEE - 62B | DUNDEE - 62B |
| Nov-60 | EDINBURGH (SM) - 64A | EDINBURGH (SM) - 64A | EDINBURGH (SM) - 64A | DUNDEE - 62B | THORNTON JCN - 62A | DUNFERMLINE - 62C | THORNTON JCN - 62A | DUNDEE - 62B | DUNDEE - 62B |

| | 64621 | 64622 | 64623 | 64624 | 64625 | 64626 | 64627 | 64628 | 64629 |
|---|---|---|---|---|---|---|---|---|---|
| Aug-50 | PARKHEAD - 65C | EASTFIELD - 65A | EASTFIELD - 65A | EDINBURGH (SM) - 64A | EDINBURGH (SM) - 64A | PARKHEAD - 65C | DUNDEE - 62B | EASTFIELD - 65A | THORNTON JCN - 62A |
| Jan-51 | PARKHEAD - 65C | EASTFIELD - 65A | EASTFIELD - 65A | EDINBURGH (SM) - 64A | EDINBURGH (SM) - 64A | PARKHEAD - 65C | DUNDEE - 62B | EASTFIELD - 65A | THORNTON JCN - 62A |
| Aug-51 | PARKHEAD - 65C | EASTFIELD - 65A | EASTFIELD - 65A | EDINBURGH (SM) - 64A | EDINBURGH (SM) - 64A | PARKHEAD - 65C | DUNDEE - 62B | EASTFIELD - 65A | THORNTON JCN - 62A |
| Jan-52 | PARKHEAD - 65C | EASTFIELD - 65A | EASTFIELD - 65A | EDINBURGH (SM) - 64A | EDINBURGH (SM) - 64A | PARKHEAD - 65C | DUNDEE - 62B | EASTFIELD - 65A | THORNTON JCN - 62A |
| Aug-52 | PARKHEAD - 65C | EASTFIELD - 65A | EASTFIELD - 65A | EDINBURGH (SM) - 64A | EDINBURGH (SM) - 64A | PARKHEAD - 65C | DUNDEE - 62B | EASTFIELD - 65A | THORNTON JCN - 62A |
| Jan-53 | PARKHEAD - 65C | EASTFIELD - 65A | EASTFIELD - 65A | EDINBURGH (SM) - 64A | EDINBURGH (SM) - 64A | PARKHEAD - 65C | DUNDEE - 62B | EASTFIELD - 65A | THORNTON JCN - 62A |
| Aug-53 | PARKHEAD - 65C | EASTFIELD - 65A | EASTFIELD - 65A | EDINBURGH (SM) - 64A | EDINBURGH (SM) - 64A | PARKHEAD - 65C | DUNDEE - 62B | EASTFIELD - 65A | THORNTON JCN - 62A |
| Jan-54 | PARKHEAD - 65C | EASTFIELD - 65A | EASTFIELD - 65A | EDINBURGH (SM) - 64A | EDINBURGH (SM) - 64A | PARKHEAD - 65C | DUNDEE - 62B | EASTFIELD - 65A | THORNTON JCN - 62A |
| Aug-54 | PARKHEAD - 65C | EASTFIELD - 65A | EASTFIELD - 65A | EDINBURGH (SM) - 64A | EDINBURGH (SM) - 64A | PARKHEAD - 65C | DUNDEE - 62B | EASTFIELD - 65A | THORNTON JCN - 62A |
| Jan-55 | PARKHEAD - 65C | EASTFIELD - 65A | EASTFIELD - 65A | EDINBURGH (SM) - 64A | EDINBURGH (SM) - 64A | PARKHEAD - 65C | DUNDEE - 62B | EASTFIELD - 65A | THORNTON JCN - 62A |
| Aug-55 | PARKHEAD - 65C | EASTFIELD - 65A | EASTFIELD - 65A | EDINBURGH (SM) - 64A | EDINBURGH (SM) - 64A | PARKHEAD - 65C | DUNDEE - 62B | EASTFIELD - 65A | THORNTON JCN - 62A |
| Jan-56 | PARKHEAD - 65C | EASTFIELD - 65A | EASTFIELD - 65A | EDINBURGH (SM) - 64A | EDINBURGH (SM) - 64A | PARKHEAD - 65C | DUNDEE - 62B | EASTFIELD - 65A | THORNTON JCN - 62A |
| Aug-56 | PARKHEAD - 65C | EASTFIELD - 65A | EASTFIELD - 65A | EDINBURGH (SM) - 64A | EDINBURGH (SM) - 64A | PARKHEAD - 65C | DUNDEE - 62B | EASTFIELD - 65A | THORNTON JCN - 62A |
| Jan-57 | PARKHEAD - 65C | EASTFIELD - 65A | EASTFIELD - 65A | EDINBURGH (SM) - 64A | EDINBURGH (SM) - 64A | PARKHEAD - 65C | DUNDEE - 62B | EASTFIELD - 65A | THORNTON JCN - 62A |
| Aug-57 | PARKHEAD - 65C | EASTFIELD - 65A | EASTFIELD - 65A | EDINBURGH (SM) - 64A | EDINBURGH (SM) - 64A | PARKHEAD - 65C | DUNDEE - 62B | EASTFIELD - 65A | THORNTON JCN - 62A |
| Jan-58 | PARKHEAD - 65C | EASTFIELD - 65A | EASTFIELD - 65A | EDINBURGH (SM) - 64A | EDINBURGH (SM) - 64A | PARKHEAD - 65C | DUNDEE - 62B | 10/57: KIPPS - 65E | THORNTON JCN - 62A |
| Aug-58 | PARKHEAD - 65C | EASTFIELD - 65A | EASTFIELD - 65A | EDINBURGH (SM) - 64A | EDINBURGH (SM) - 64A | PARKHEAD - 65C | DUNDEE - 62B | KIPPS - 65E | THORNTON JCN - 62A |
| Jan-59 | PARKHEAD - 65C | EASTFIELD - 65A | EASTFIELD - 65A | EDINBURGH (SM) - 64A | EDINBURGH (SM) - 64A | PARKHEAD - 65C | DUNDEE - 62B | KIPPS - 65E | THORNTON JCN - 62A |
| Aug-59 | PARKHEAD - 65C | EASTFIELD - 65A | EASTFIELD - 65A | EDINBURGH (SM) - 64A | EDINBURGH (SM) - 64A | PARKHEAD - 65C | DUNDEE - 62B | KIPPS - 65E | THORNTON JCN - 62A |
| Nov-59 | PARKHEAD - 65C | EASTFIELD - 65A | EASTFIELD - 65A | EDINBURGH (SM) - 64A | EDINBURGH (SM) - 64A | PARKHEAD - 65C | DUNDEE - 62B | KIPPS - 65E | THORNTON JCN - 62A |
| Jan-60 | PARKHEAD - 65C | EASTFIELD - 65A | EASTFIELD - 65A | EDINBURGH (SM) - 64A | EDINBURGH (SM) - 64A | PARKHEAD - 65C | DUNDEE - 62B | KIPPS - 65E | THORNTON JCN - 62A |
| Apr-60 | PARKHEAD - 65C | EASTFIELD - 65A | EASTFIELD - 65A | EDINBURGH (SM) - 64A | EDINBURGH (SM) - 64A | PARKHEAD - 65C | DUNDEE - 62B | KIPPS - 65E | THORNTON JCN - 62A |
| Aug-60 | PARKHEAD - 65C | EASTFIELD - 65A | EASTFIELD - 65A | EDINBURGH (SM) - 64A | EDINBURGH (SM) - 64A | PARKHEAD - 65C | DUNDEE - 62B | KIPPS - 65E | THORNTON JCN - 62A |
| Nov-60 | PARKHEAD - 65C | EASTFIELD - 65A | EASTFIELD - 65A | EDINBURGH (SM) - 64A | EDINBURGH (SM) - 64A | PARKHEAD - 65C | DUNDEE - 62B | KIPPS - 65E | THORNTON JCN - 62A |

| | 64630 | 64631 | 64632 | 64633 | 64634 | 64635 | 64636 | 64637 | 64638 |
|---|---|---|---|---|---|---|---|---|---|
| Aug-50 | DUNFERMLINE - 62C | DUNDEE - 62B | EASTFIELD - 65A | EASTFIELD - 65A | DUNDEE - 62B | THORNTON JCN - 62A | EDINBURGH (SM) - 64A | EDINBURGH (SM) - 64A | EASTFIELD - 65A |
| Jan-51 | DUNFERMLINE - 62C | DUNDEE - 62B | EASTFIELD - 65A | EASTFIELD - 65A | DUNDEE - 62B | THORNTON JCN - 62A | EDINBURGH (SM) - 64A | EDINBURGH (SM) - 64A | EASTFIELD - 65A |
| Aug-51 | DUNFERMLINE - 62C | DUNDEE - 62B | EASTFIELD - 65A | EASTFIELD - 65A | DUNDEE - 62B | THORNTON JCN - 62A | EDINBURGH (SM) - 64A | EDINBURGH (SM) - 64A | EASTFIELD - 65A |
| Jan-52 | DUNFERMLINE - 62C | DUNDEE - 62B | EASTFIELD - 65A | EASTFIELD - 65A | DUNDEE - 62B | THORNTON JCN - 62A | 10/51: POLM - 64E | EDINBURGH (SM) - 64A | EASTFIELD - 65A |
| Aug-52 | DUNFERMLINE - 62C | DUNDEE - 62B | EASTFIELD - 65A | EASTFIELD - 65A | DUNDEE - 62B | THORNTON JCN - 62A | POLMONT - 64E | EDINBURGH (SM) - 64A | EASTFIELD - 65A |
| Jan-53 | DUNFERMLINE - 62C | DUNDEE - 62B | EASTFIELD - 65A | EASTFIELD - 65A | DUNDEE - 62B | THORNTON JCN - 62A | POLMONT - 64E | EDINBURGH (SM) - 64A | EASTFIELD - 65A |
| Aug-53 | DUNFERMLINE - 62C | DUNDEE - 62B | EASTFIELD - 65A | EASTFIELD - 65A | DUNDEE - 62B | THORNTON JCN - 62A | POLMONT - 64E | EDINBURGH (SM) - 64A | EASTFIELD - 65A |
| Jan-54 | DUNFERMLINE - 62C | DUNDEE - 62B | EASTFIELD - 65A | EASTFIELD - 65A | DUNDEE - 62B | THORNTON JCN - 62A | POLMONT - 64E | EDINBURGH (SM) - 64A | EASTFIELD - 65A |
| Aug-54 | DUNFERMLINE - 62C | DUNDEE - 62B | EASTFIELD - 65A | EASTFIELD - 65A | DUNDEE - 62B | THORNTON JCN - 62A | POLMONT - 64E | EDINBURGH (SM) - 64A | EASTFIELD - 65A |
| Jan-55 | DUNFERMLINE - 62C | DUNDEE - 62B | EASTFIELD - 65A | EASTFIELD - 65A | DUNDEE - 62B | THORNTON JCN - 62A | POLMONT - 64E | EDINBURGH (SM) - 64A | EASTFIELD - 65A |
| Aug-55 | DUNFERMLINE - 62C | DUNDEE - 62B | EASTFIELD - 65A | EASTFIELD - 65A | 9/55: CARS - 64D | THORNTON JCN - 62A | POLMONT - 64E | EDINBURGH (SM) - 64A | EASTFIELD - 65A |
| Jan-56 | DUNFERMLINE - 62C | DUNDEE - 62B | EASTFIELD - 65A | EASTFIELD - 65A | CARSTAIRS - 64D | THORNTON JCN - 62A | POLMONT - 64E | EDINBURGH (SM) - 64A | EASTFIELD - 65A |
| Aug-56 | DUNFERMLINE - 62C | DUNDEE - 62B | EASTFIELD - 65A | EASTFIELD - 65A | 4/56: BATH - 64F | THORNTON JCN - 62A | POLMONT - 64E | EDINBURGH (SM) - 64A | EASTFIELD - 65A |
| Jan-57 | DUNFERMLINE - 62C | DUNDEE - 62B | EASTFIELD - 65A | EASTFIELD - 65A | BATHGATE - 64F | THORNTON JCN - 62A | POLMONT - 64E | EDINBURGH (SM) - 64A | EASTFIELD - 65A |
| Aug-57 | DUNFERMLINE - 62C | DUNDEE - 62B | EASTFIELD - 65A | EASTFIELD - 65A | BATHGATE - 64F | THORNTON JCN - 62A | POLMONT - 64E | EDINBURGH (SM) - 64A | EASTFIELD - 65A |
| Jan-58 | DUNFERMLINE - 62C | DUNDEE - 62B | EASTFIELD - 65A | EASTFIELD - 65A | BATHGATE - 64F | THORNTON JCN - 62A | POLMONT - 64E | EDINBURGH (SM) - 64A | EASTFIELD - 65A |
| Aug-58 | DUNFERMLINE - 62C | DUNDEE - 62B | EASTFIELD - 65A | EASTFIELD - 65A | BATHGATE - 64F | THORNTON JCN - 62A | POLMONT - 64E | EDINBURGH (SM) - 64A | EASTFIELD - 65A |
| Jan-59 | DUNFERMLINE - 62C | DUNDEE - 62B | EASTFIELD - 65A | EASTFIELD - 65A | BATHGATE - 64F | THORNTON JCN - 62A | POLMONT - 64E | EDINBURGH (SM) - 64A | EASTFIELD - 65A |
| Aug-59 | DUNFERMLINE - 62C | DUNDEE - 62B | EASTFIELD - 65A | EASTFIELD - 65A | BATHGATE - 64F | THORNTON JCN - 62A | POLMONT - 64E | EDINBURGH (SM) - 64A | EASTFIELD - 65A |
| Nov-59 | DUNFERMLINE - 62C | DUNDEE - 62B | EASTFIELD - 65A | EASTFIELD - 65A | BATHGATE - 64F | THORNTON JCN - 62A | POLMONT - 64E | EDINBURGH (SM) - 64A | EASTFIELD - 65A |
| Jan-60 | DUNFERMLINE - 62C | DUNDEE - 62B | EASTFIELD - 65A | EASTFIELD - 65A | BATHGATE - 64F | THORNTON JCN - 62A | POLMONT - 64E | EDINBURGH (SM) - 64A | EASTFIELD - 65A |
| Apr-60 | DUNFERMLINE - 62C | DUNDEE - 62B | EASTFIELD - 65A | EASTFIELD - 65A | BATHGATE - 64F | THORNTON JCN - 62A | POLMONT - 65K | EDINBURGH (SM) - 64A | EASTFIELD - 65A |
| Aug-60 | DUNFERMLINE - 62C | DUNDEE - 62B | EASTFIELD - 65A | EASTFIELD - 65A | BATHGATE - 64F | THORNTON JCN - 62A | POLMONT - 65K | EDINBURGH (SM) - 64A | EASTFIELD - 65A |
| Nov-60 | DUNFERMLINE - 62C | DUNDEE - 62B | EASTFIELD - 65A | EASTFIELD - 65A | BATHGATE - 64F | THORNTON JCN - 62A | POLMONT - 65K | EDINBURGH (SM) - 64A | EASTFIELD - 65A |

| | | J19 0-6-0 (1912) | | | | | | | |
|---|---|---|---|---|---|---|---|---|---|
| | 64639 | 64640 | 64641 | 64642 | 64643 | 64644 | 64645 | 64646 | 64647 |
| Aug-50 | EASTFIELD - 65A | KINGS LYNN - 31C | MARCH - 31B | KINGS LYNN - 31C | MARCH - 31B | NORWICH - 32A | SOUTH LYNN - 31D | SOUTH LYNN - 31D | MARCH - 31B |
| Jan-51 | EASTFIELD - 65A | KINGS LYNN - 31C | MARCH - 31B | KINGS LYNN - 31C | MARCH - 31B | NORWICH - 32A | 1/51: CAMB - 31A | 1/51: CAMB - 31A | MARCH - 31B |
| Aug-51 | EASTFIELD - 65A | KINGS LYNN - 31C | MARCH - 31B | KINGS LYNN - 31C | MARCH - 31B | NORWICH - 32A | 9/51: COL - 30E | CAMBRIDGE - 31A | 5/51: CAMB - 31A |
| Jan-52 | EASTFIELD - 65A | 3/52: MARCH - 31B | MARCH - 31B | 3/52: MARCH - 31B | MARCH - 31B | NORWICH - 32A | COLCHESTER - 30E | CAMBRIDGE - 31A | 9/51: COL - 30E |
| Aug-52 | EASTFIELD - 65A | MARCH - 31B | MARCH - 31B | MARCH - 31B | MARCH - 31B | NORWICH - 32A | COLCHESTER - 30E | 7/52: S.LYNN - 31D | COLCHESTER - 30E |
| Jan-53 | EASTFIELD - 65A | MARCH - 31B | MARCH - 31B | MARCH - 31B | MARCH - 31B | NORWICH - 32A | COLCHESTER - 30E | SOUTH LYNN - 31D | COLCHESTER - 30E |
| Aug-53 | EASTFIELD - 65A | MARCH - 31B | MARCH - 31B | MARCH - 31B | MARCH - 31B | NORWICH - 32A | COLCHESTER - 30E | SOUTH LYNN - 31D | COLCHESTER - 30E |
| Jan-54 | EASTFIELD - 65A | MARCH - 31B | MARCH - 31B | MARCH - 31B | MARCH - 31B | NORWICH - 32A | COLCHESTER - 30E | SOUTH LYNN - 31D | COLCHESTER - 30E |
| Aug-54 | EASTFIELD - 65A | MARCH - 31B | MARCH - 31B | MARCH - 31B | MARCH - 31B | NORWICH - 32A | COLCHESTER - 30E | SOUTH LYNN - 31D | COLCHESTER - 30E |
| Jan-55 | EASTFIELD - 65A | MARCH - 31B | MARCH - 31B | MARCH - 31B | MARCH - 31B | NORWICH - 32A | COLCHESTER - 30E | 1/55: CAMB - 31A | COLCHESTER - 30E |
| Aug-55 | EASTFIELD - 65A | MARCH - 31B | MARCH - 31B | MARCH - 31B | MARCH - 31B | NORWICH - 32A | COLCHESTER - 30E | CAMBRIDGE - 31A | COLCHESTER - 30E |
| Jan-56 | EASTFIELD - 65A | MARCH - 31B | MARCH - 31B | MARCH - 31B | MARCH - 31B | NORWICH - 32A | COLCHESTER - 30E | CAMBRIDGE - 31A | COLCHESTER - 30E |
| Aug-56 | EASTFIELD - 65A | MARCH - 31B | MARCH - 31B | MARCH - 31B | MARCH - 31B | NORWICH - 32A | COLCHESTER - 30E | CAMBRIDGE - 31A | COLCHESTER - 30E |
| Jan-57 | EASTFIELD - 65A | 4/57: K.LYNN - 31C | MARCH - 31B | MARCH - 31B | MARCH - 31B | NORWICH - 32A | COLCHESTER - 30E | CAMBRIDGE - 31A | COLCHESTER - 30E |
| Aug-57 | EASTFIELD - 65A | KINGS LYNN - 31C | MARCH - 31B | MARCH - 31B | MARCH - 31B | NORWICH - 32A | COLCHESTER - 30E | CAMBRIDGE - 31A | COLCHESTER - 30E |
| Jan-58 | EASTFIELD - 65A | KINGS LYNN - 31C | MARCH - 31B | MARCH - 31B | MARCH - 31B | NORWICH - 32A | COLCHESTER - 30E | CAMBRIDGE - 31A | COLCHESTER - 30E |
| Aug-58 | EASTFIELD - 65A | KINGS LYNN - 31C | MARCH - 31B | MARCH - 31B | MARCH - 31B | NORWICH - 32A | COLCHESTER - 30E | CAMBRIDGE - 31A | COLCHESTER - 30E |
| Jan-59 | EASTFIELD - 65A | KINGS LYNN - 31C | 12/58: NOR - 32A | MARCH - 31B | 12/58: NOR - 32A | NORWICH - 32A | 12/58: W/D | CAMBRIDGE - 31A | 3/59: MARCH - 31B |
| Aug-59 | EASTFIELD - 65A | KINGS LYNN - 31C | 5/59: IPS - 32B | MARCH - 31B | NORWICH - 32A | 7/59: W/D | | CAMBRIDGE - 31A | 6/59: K.LYNN - 31C |
| Nov-59 | EASTFIELD - 65A | 11/59: W/D | 11/59: NOR - 32A | MARCH - 31B | NORWICH - 32A | | | CAMBRIDGE - 31A | KINGS LYNN - 31C |
| Jan-60 | EASTFIELD - 65A | | NORWICH - 32A | MARCH - 31B | NORWICH - 32A | | | CAMBRIDGE - 31A | 2/60: MARCH - 31B |
| Apr-60 | EASTFIELD - 65A | | 2/60: W/D | 3/60: W/D | NORWICH - 32A | | | CAMBRIDGE - 31A | 3/60: W/D |
| Aug-60 | EASTFIELD - 65A | | | | NORWICH - 32A | | | CAMBRIDGE - 31A | |
| Nov-60 | EASTFIELD - 65A | | | | NORWICH - 32A | | | CAMBRIDGE - 31A | |

| | 64648 | 64649 | 64650 | 64651 | 64652 | 64653 | 64654 | 64655 | 64656 |
|---|---|---|---|---|---|---|---|---|---|
| Aug-50 | MARCH - 31B | SOUTH LYNN - 31D | STRATFORD - 30A | STRATFORD - 30A | STRATFORD - 30A | SOUTH LYNN - 31D | KINGS LYNN - 31C | MARCH - 31B | MARCH - 31B |
| Jan-51 | MARCH - 31B | SOUTH LYNN - 31D | STRATFORD - 30A | STRATFORD - 30A | STRATFORD - 30A | **1/51: CAMB - 31A** | KINGS LYNN - 31C | MARCH - 31B | MARCH - 31B |
| Aug-51 | MARCH - 31B | **6/51: STRAT - 30A** | **9/51: COL - 30E** | **9/51: COL - 30E** | **9/51: COL - 30E** | **9/51: COL - 30E** | **8/51: CAMB - 31A** | MARCH - 31B | **6/51: STRAT - 30A** |
| Jan-52 | MARCH - 31B | **9/51: COL - 30E** | COLCHESTER - 30E | COLCHESTER - 30E | COLCHESTER - 30E | COLCHESTER - 30E | CAMBRIDGE - 31A | MARCH - 31B | STRATFORD - 30A |
| Aug-52 | MARCH - 31B | COLCHESTER - 30E | COLCHESTER - 30E | COLCHESTER - 30E | COLCHESTER - 30E | COLCHESTER - 30E | CAMBRIDGE - 31A | MARCH - 31B | STRATFORD - 30A |
| Jan-53 | MARCH - 31B | COLCHESTER - 30E | COLCHESTER - 30E | COLCHESTER - 30E | COLCHESTER - 30E | COLCHESTER - 30E | **1/53: BURY - 31E** | MARCH - 31B | STRATFORD - 30A |
| Aug-53 | MARCH - 31B | COLCHESTER - 30E | COLCHESTER - 30E | COLCHESTER - 30E | COLCHESTER - 30E | COLCHESTER - 30E | **2/53: CAMB - 31A** | MARCH - 31B | STRATFORD - 30A |
| Jan-54 | MARCH - 31B | COLCHESTER - 30E | COLCHESTER - 30E | COLCHESTER - 30E | COLCHESTER - 30E | COLCHESTER - 30E | CAMBRIDGE - 31A | MARCH - 31B | STRATFORD - 30A |
| Aug-54 | MARCH - 31B | COLCHESTER - 30E | COLCHESTER - 30E | COLCHESTER - 30E | COLCHESTER - 30E | COLCHESTER - 30E | CAMBRIDGE - 31A | MARCH - 31B | STRATFORD - 30A |
| Jan-55 | MARCH - 31B | COLCHESTER - 30E | COLCHESTER - 30E | COLCHESTER - 30E | COLCHESTER - 30E | COLCHESTER - 30E | CAMBRIDGE - 31A | MARCH - 31B | STRATFORD - 30A |
| Aug-55 | MARCH - 31B | COLCHESTER - 30E | COLCHESTER - 30E | COLCHESTER - 30E | COLCHESTER - 30E | COLCHESTER - 30E | CAMBRIDGE - 31A | MARCH - 31B | STRATFORD - 30A |
| Jan-56 | MARCH - 31B | COLCHESTER - 30E | COLCHESTER - 30E | COLCHESTER - 30E | COLCHESTER - 30E | COLCHESTER - 30E | CAMBRIDGE - 31A | MARCH - 31B | STRATFORD - 30A |
| Aug-56 | MARCH - 31B | COLCHESTER - 30E | COLCHESTER - 30E | COLCHESTER - 30E | COLCHESTER - 30E | COLCHESTER - 30E | CAMBRIDGE - 31A | MARCH - 31B | STRATFORD - 30A |
| Jan-57 | MARCH - 31B | COLCHESTER - 30E | COLCHESTER - 30E | COLCHESTER - 30E | COLCHESTER - 30E | COLCHESTER - 30E | CAMBRIDGE - 31A | MARCH - 31B | STRATFORD - 30A |
| Aug-57 | MARCH - 31B | COLCHESTER - 30E | COLCHESTER - 30E | COLCHESTER - 30E | COLCHESTER - 30E | COLCHESTER - 30E | CAMBRIDGE - 31A | MARCH - 31B | STRATFORD - 30A |
| Jan-58 | MARCH - 31B | COLCHESTER - 30E | COLCHESTER - 30E | COLCHESTER - 30E | COLCHESTER - 30E | COLCHESTER - 30E | CAMBRIDGE - 31A | **11/57: STRAT - 30A** | STRATFORD - 30A |
| Aug-58 | MARCH - 31B | COLCHESTER - 30E | COLCHESTER - 30E | COLCHESTER - 30E | COLCHESTER - 30E | COLCHESTER - 30E | CAMBRIDGE - 31A | STRATFORD - 30A | STRATFORD - 30A |
| Jan-59 | MARCH - 31B | **1/59: W/D** | COLCHESTER - 30E | **1/59: W/D** | **1/59: PARKS - 30F** | **3/59: STRAT - 30A** | CAMBRIDGE - 31A | **3/59: MARCH - 31B** | **3/59: MARCH - 31B** |
| Aug-59 | **8/59: W/D** | | COLCHESTER - 30E | | PARKESTON - 30F | STRATFORD - 30A | CAMBRIDGE - 31A | MARCH - 31B | MARCH - 31B |
| Nov-59 | | | COLCHESTER - 30E | | PARKESTON - 30F | STRATFORD - 30A | CAMBRIDGE - 31A | **11/59: K.LYNN - 31C** | MARCH - 31B |
| Jan-60 | | | **12/59: STRAT - 30A** | | PARKESTON - 30F | STRATFORD - 30A | CAMBRIDGE - 31A | KINGS LYNN - 31C | MARCH - 31B |
| Apr-60 | | | STRATFORD - 30A | | PARKESTON - 30F | STRATFORD - 30A | **2/60: W/D** | **3/60: W/D** | **4/60: W/D** |
| Aug-60 | | | STRATFORD - 30A | | PARKESTON - 30F | STRATFORD - 30A | | | |
| Nov-60 | | | **10/60: W/D** | | PARKESTON - 30F | STRATFORD - 30A | | | |

| | 64657 | 64658 | 64659 | 64660 | 64661 | 64662 | 64663 | 64664 | 64665 |
|---|---|---|---|---|---|---|---|---|---|
| Aug-50 | STRATFORD - 30A | SOUTH LYNN - 31D | MARCH - 31B | STRATFORD - 30A | MARCH - 31B | STRATFORD - 30A | STRATFORD - 30A | STRATFORD - 30A | STRATFORD - 30A |
| Jan-51 | STRATFORD - 30A | **1/51: CAMB - 31A** | MARCH - 31B | STRATFORD - 30A | MARCH - 31B | STRATFORD - 30A | STRATFORD - 30A | STRATFORD - 30A | STRATFORD - 30A |
| Aug-51 | STRATFORD - 30A | CAMBRIDGE - 31A | **9/51: COL - 30E** | STRATFORD - 30A | MARCH - 31B | STRATFORD - 30A | STRATFORD - 30A | STRATFORD - 30A | STRATFORD - 30A |
| Jan-52 | STRATFORD - 30A | CAMBRIDGE - 31A | COLCHESTER - 30E | STRATFORD - 30A | MARCH - 31B | STRATFORD - 30A | STRATFORD - 30A | STRATFORD - 30A | STRATFORD - 30A |
| Aug-52 | STRATFORD - 30A | CAMBRIDGE - 31A | COLCHESTER - 30E | STRATFORD - 30A | MARCH - 31B | STRATFORD - 30A | STRATFORD - 30A | STRATFORD - 30A | STRATFORD - 30A |
| Jan-53 | STRATFORD - 30A | CAMBRIDGE - 31A | COLCHESTER - 30E | STRATFORD - 30A | MARCH - 31B | STRATFORD - 30A | STRATFORD - 30A | STRATFORD - 30A | STRATFORD - 30A |
| Aug-53 | STRATFORD - 30A | CAMBRIDGE - 31A | COLCHESTER - 30E | STRATFORD - 30A | MARCH - 31B | STRATFORD - 30A | STRATFORD - 30A | STRATFORD - 30A | STRATFORD - 30A |
| Jan-54 | STRATFORD - 30A | CAMBRIDGE - 31A | COLCHESTER - 30E | **11/53: COL - 30E** | MARCH - 31B | STRATFORD - 30A | STRATFORD - 30A | STRATFORD - 30A | STRATFORD - 30A |
| Aug-54 | STRATFORD - 30A | CAMBRIDGE - 31A | COLCHESTER - 30E | COLCHESTER - 30E | MARCH - 31B | STRATFORD - 30A | STRATFORD - 30A | STRATFORD - 30A | STRATFORD - 30A |
| Jan-55 | STRATFORD - 30A | CAMBRIDGE - 31A | COLCHESTER - 30E | COLCHESTER - 30E | MARCH - 31B | STRATFORD - 30A | STRATFORD - 30A | STRATFORD - 30A | STRATFORD - 30A |
| Aug-55 | STRATFORD - 30A | CAMBRIDGE - 31A | COLCHESTER - 30E | COLCHESTER - 30E | MARCH - 31B | STRATFORD - 30A | STRATFORD - 30A | STRATFORD - 30A | STRATFORD - 30A |
| Jan-56 | STRATFORD - 30A | CAMBRIDGE - 31A | COLCHESTER - 30E | COLCHESTER - 30E | MARCH - 31B | STRATFORD - 30A | STRATFORD - 30A | STRATFORD - 30A | STRATFORD - 30A |
| Aug-56 | STRATFORD - 30A | CAMBRIDGE - 31A | COLCHESTER - 30E | COLCHESTER - 30E | MARCH - 31B | STRATFORD - 30A | STRATFORD - 30A | STRATFORD - 30A | STRATFORD - 30A |
| Jan-57 | STRATFORD - 30A | CAMBRIDGE - 31A | COLCHESTER - 30E | COLCHESTER - 30E | MARCH - 31B | STRATFORD - 30A | STRATFORD - 30A | STRATFORD - 30A | STRATFORD - 30A |
| Aug-57 | STRATFORD - 30A | CAMBRIDGE - 31A | COLCHESTER - 30E | COLCHESTER - 30E | MARCH - 31B | STRATFORD - 30A | STRATFORD - 30A | STRATFORD - 30A | STRATFORD - 30A |
| Jan-58 | STRATFORD - 30A | CAMBRIDGE - 31A | COLCHESTER - 30E | COLCHESTER - 30E | MARCH - 31B | STRATFORD - 30A | STRATFORD - 30A | STRATFORD - 30A | STRATFORD - 30A |
| Aug-58 | STRATFORD - 30A | CAMBRIDGE - 31A | COLCHESTER - 30E | COLCHESTER - 30E | MARCH - 31B | **10/58: NOR - 32A** | STRATFORD - 30A | STRATFORD - 30A | STRATFORD - 30A |
| Jan-59 | **3/59: COL - 30E** | CAMBRIDGE - 31A | **3/59: MARCH - 31B** | COLCHESTER - 30E | **10/58: CAMB - 31A** | **1/59: W/D** | STRATFORD - 30A | **3/59: COL - 30E** | **3/59: MARCH - 31B** |
| Aug-59 | COLCHESTER - 30E | **5/59: IPS - 32B** | **5/59: IPS - 32B** | COLCHESTER - 30E | **8/59: W/D** | | STRATFORD - 30A | COLCHESTER - 30E | **6/59: K.LYNN - 31C** |
| Nov-59 | COLCHESTER - 30E | **11/59: W/D** | IPSWICH - 32B | COLCHESTER - 30E | | | STRATFORD - 30A | **10/59: STRAT - 30A** | KINGS LYNN - 31C |
| Jan-60 | **12/59: STRAT - 30A** | | IPSWICH - 32B | **12/59: STRAT - 30A** | | | STRATFORD - 30A | STRATFORD - 30A | **12/59: W/D** |
| Apr-60 | STRATFORD - 30A | | **3/60: W/D** | STRATFORD - 30A | | | STRATFORD - 30A | STRATFORD - 30A | |
| Aug-60 | STRATFORD - 30A | | | **9/60: W/D** | | | STRATFORD - 30A | STRATFORD - 30A | |
| Nov-60 | STRATFORD - 30A | | | | | | **10/60: W/D** | STRATFORD - 30A | |

| | 64666 | 64667 | 64668 | 64669 | 64670 | 64671 | 64672 | 64673 | 64674 |
|---|---|---|---|---|---|---|---|---|---|
| Aug-50 | MARCH - 31B | MARCH - 31B | KINGS LYNN - 31C | MARCH - 31B | STRATFORD - 30A | MARCH - 31B | KINGS LYNN - 31C | SOUTH LYNN - 31D | NORWICH - 32A |
| Jan-51 | MARCH - 31B | MARCH - 31B | KINGS LYNN - 31C | MARCH - 31B | STRATFORD - 30A | MARCH - 31B | KINGS LYNN - 31C | **1/51: CAMB - 31A** | NORWICH - 32A |
| Aug-51 | **9/51: COL - 30E** | **9/51: COL - 30E** | KINGS LYNN - 31C | MARCH - 31B | STRATFORD - 30A | MARCH - 31B | KINGS LYNN - 31C | CAMBRIDGE - 31A | NORWICH - 32A |
| Jan-52 | COLCHESTER - 30E | COLCHESTER - 30E | **3/52: MARCH - 31B** | MARCH - 31B | STRATFORD - 30A | MARCH - 31B | **3/52: MARCH - 31B** | CAMBRIDGE - 31A | NORWICH - 32A |
| Aug-52 | COLCHESTER - 30E | COLCHESTER - 30E | MARCH - 31B | MARCH - 31B | STRATFORD - 30A | MARCH - 31B | MARCH - 31B | CAMBRIDGE - 31A | NORWICH - 32A |
| Jan-53 | COLCHESTER - 30E | COLCHESTER - 30E | MARCH - 31B | MARCH - 31B | STRATFORD - 30A | MARCH - 31B | MARCH - 31B | **1/53: BURY - 31E** | NORWICH - 32A |
| Aug-53 | COLCHESTER - 30E | COLCHESTER - 30E | MARCH - 31B | MARCH - 31B | STRATFORD - 30A | MARCH - 31B | MARCH - 31B | **2/53: CAMB - 31A** | NORWICH - 32A |
| Jan-54 | COLCHESTER - 30E | COLCHESTER - 30E | MARCH - 31B | MARCH - 31B | STRATFORD - 30A | MARCH - 31B | MARCH - 31B | CAMBRIDGE - 31A | NORWICH - 32A |
| Aug-54 | COLCHESTER - 30E | COLCHESTER - 30E | MARCH - 31B | MARCH - 31B | STRATFORD - 30A | MARCH - 31B | MARCH - 31B | CAMBRIDGE - 31A | NORWICH - 32A |
| Jan-55 | COLCHESTER - 30E | COLCHESTER - 30E | MARCH - 31B | MARCH - 31B | STRATFORD - 30A | MARCH - 31B | MARCH - 31B | CAMBRIDGE - 31A | NORWICH - 32A |
| Aug-55 | COLCHESTER - 30E | COLCHESTER - 30E | MARCH - 31B | MARCH - 31B | STRATFORD - 30A | MARCH - 31B | MARCH - 31B | CAMBRIDGE - 31A | NORWICH - 32A |
| Jan-56 | COLCHESTER - 30E | COLCHESTER - 30E | MARCH - 31B | MARCH - 31B | STRATFORD - 30A | MARCH - 31B | MARCH - 31B | CAMBRIDGE - 31A | NORWICH - 32A |
| Aug-56 | COLCHESTER - 30E | COLCHESTER - 30E | MARCH - 31B | MARCH - 31B | STRATFORD - 30A | MARCH - 31B | MARCH - 31B | CAMBRIDGE - 31A | NORWICH - 32A |
| Jan-57 | COLCHESTER - 30E | COLCHESTER - 30E | MARCH - 31B | MARCH - 31B | STRATFORD - 30A | MARCH - 31B | MARCH - 31B | CAMBRIDGE - 31A | NORWICH - 32A |
| Aug-57 | COLCHESTER - 30E | COLCHESTER - 30E | MARCH - 31B | MARCH - 31B | STRATFORD - 30A | MARCH - 31B | MARCH - 31B | CAMBRIDGE - 31A | NORWICH - 32A |
| Jan-58 | COLCHESTER - 30E | COLCHESTER - 30E | MARCH - 31B | MARCH - 31B | STRATFORD - 30A | MARCH - 31B | MARCH - 31B | CAMBRIDGE - 31A | NORWICH - 32A |
| Aug-58 | COLCHESTER - 30E | COLCHESTER - 30E | MARCH - 31B | MARCH - 31B | STRATFORD - 30A | MARCH - 31B | MARCH - 31B | CAMBRIDGE - 31A | NORWICH - 32A |
| Jan-59 | COLCHESTER - 30E | COLCHESTER - 30E | MARCH - 31B | MARCH - 31B | **3/59: MARCH - 31B** | MARCH - 31B | **1/59: W/D** | CAMBRIDGE - 31A | NORWICH - 32A |
| Aug-59 | COLCHESTER - 30E | COLCHESTER - 30E | MARCH - 31B | MARCH - 31B | MARCH - 31B | MARCH - 31B | | **6/59: K.LYNN - 31C** | NORWICH - 32A |
| Nov-59 | COLCHESTER - 30E | **10/59: STRAT - 30A** | MARCH - 31B | MARCH - 31B | **11/59: W/D** | MARCH - 31B | | KINGS LYNN - 31C | NORWICH - 32A |
| Jan-60 | **12/59: STRAT - 30A** | STRATFORD - 30A | **12/59: W/D** | MARCH - 31B | | MARCH - 31B | | KINGS LYNN - 31C | NORWICH - 32A |
| Apr-60 | STRATFORD - 30A | STRATFORD - 30A | | MARCH - 31B | | MARCH - 31B | | **3/60: CAMB - 31A** | NORWICH - 32A |
| Aug-60 | STRATFORD - 30A | STRATFORD - 30A | | MARCH - 31B | | MARCH - 31B | | CAMBRIDGE - 31A | NORWICH - 32A |
| Nov-60 | STRATFORD - 30A | STRATFORD - 30A | | MARCH - 31B | | MARCH - 31B | | CAMBRIDGE - 31A | NORWICH - 32A |

**J20 0-6-0 (1920)**

| | 64677 | 64678 | 64679 | 64680 | 64681 | 64682 | 64684 | 64685 | 64686 |
|---|---|---|---|---|---|---|---|---|---|
| Aug-50 | STRATFORD - 30A | CAMBRIDGE - 31A | CAMBRIDGE - 31A | STRATFORD - 30A | STRATFORD - 30A | STRATFORD - 30A | CAMBRIDGE - 31A | STRATFORD - 30A | STRATFORD - 30A |
| Jan-51 | STRATFORD - 30A | **2/51: HORN - 34B** | **2/51: HORN - 34B** | STRATFORD - 30A | STRATFORD - 30A | STRATFORD - 30A | **1/51: HORN - 34B** | STRATFORD - 30A | STRATFORD - 30A |
| Aug-51 | STRATFORD - 30A | HORNSEY - 34B | HORNSEY - 34B | STRATFORD - 30A | STRATFORD - 30A | STRATFORD - 30A | HORNSEY - 34B | STRATFORD - 30A | STRATFORD - 30A |
| Jan-52 | STRATFORD - 30A | HORNSEY - 34B | HORNSEY - 34B | STRATFORD - 30A | STRATFORD - 30A | STRATFORD - 30A | HORNSEY - 34B | STRATFORD - 30A | STRATFORD - 30A |
| Aug-52 | STRATFORD - 30A | HORNSEY - 34B | HORNSEY - 34B | STRATFORD - 30A | STRATFORD - 30A | STRATFORD - 30A | HORNSEY - 34B | STRATFORD - 30A | STRATFORD - 30A |
| Jan-53 | STRATFORD - 30A | HORNSEY - 34B | HORNSEY - 34B | STRATFORD - 30A | STRATFORD - 30A | STRATFORD - 30A | HORNSEY - 34B | STRATFORD - 30A | STRATFORD - 30A |
| Aug-53 | STRATFORD - 30A | HORNSEY - 34B | HORNSEY - 34B | STRATFORD - 30A | STRATFORD - 30A | STRATFORD - 30A | HORNSEY - 34B | STRATFORD - 30A | STRATFORD - 30A |
| Jan-54 | STRATFORD - 30A | **11/53: MARCH - 31B** | **11/53: MARCH - 31B** | STRATFORD - 30A | STRATFORD - 30A | STRATFORD - 30A | **11/53: MARCH - 31B** | STRATFORD - 30A | STRATFORD - 30A |
| Aug-54 | STRATFORD - 30A | MARCH - 31B | MARCH - 31B | STRATFORD - 30A | STRATFORD - 30A | STRATFORD - 30A | MARCH - 31B | STRATFORD - 30A | STRATFORD - 30A |
| Jan-55 | STRATFORD - 30A | MARCH - 31B | MARCH - 31B | STRATFORD - 30A | STRATFORD - 30A | STRATFORD - 30A | MARCH - 31B | STRATFORD - 30A | STRATFORD - 30A |
| Aug-55 | STRATFORD - 30A | MARCH - 31B | MARCH - 31B | STRATFORD - 30A | STRATFORD - 30A | STRATFORD - 30A | MARCH - 31B | STRATFORD - 30A | STRATFORD - 30A |
| Jan-56 | STRATFORD - 30A | MARCH - 31B | MARCH - 31B | STRATFORD - 30A | STRATFORD - 30A | STRATFORD - 30A | MARCH - 31B | STRATFORD - 30A | STRATFORD - 30A |
| Aug-56 | STRATFORD - 30A | MARCH - 31B | MARCH - 31B | STRATFORD - 30A | STRATFORD - 30A | STRATFORD - 30A | MARCH - 31B | STRATFORD - 30A | STRATFORD - 30A |
| Jan-57 | STRATFORD - 30A | MARCH - 31B | MARCH - 31B | STRATFORD - 30A | STRATFORD - 30A | STRATFORD - 30A | MARCH - 31B | STRATFORD - 30A | STRATFORD - 30A |
| Aug-57 | STRATFORD - 30A | MARCH - 31B | MARCH - 31B | STRATFORD - 30A | STRATFORD - 30A | STRATFORD - 30A | MARCH - 31B | STRATFORD - 30A | STRATFORD - 30A |
| Jan-58 | STRATFORD - 30A | MARCH - 31B | MARCH - 31B | STRATFORD - 30A | STRATFORD - 30A | STRATFORD - 30A | MARCH - 31B | STRATFORD - 30A | STRATFORD - 30A |
| Aug-58 | STRATFORD - 30A | MARCH - 31B | MARCH - 31B | STRATFORD - 30A | STRATFORD - 30A | STRATFORD - 30A | MARCH - 31B | STRATFORD - 30A | STRATFORD - 30A |
| Jan-59 | STRATFORD - 30A | MARCH - 31B | MARCH - 31B | STRATFORD - 30A | STRATFORD - 30A | STRATFORD - 30A | MARCH - 31B | STRATFORD - 30A | STRATFORD - 30A |
| Aug-59 | STRATFORD - 30A | **6/59: PARKS - 30F** | **6/59: PARKS - 30F** | STRATFORD - 30A | STRATFORD - 30A | STRATFORD - 30A | MARCH - 31B | STRATFORD - 30A | STRATFORD - 30A |
| Nov-59 | STRATFORD - 30A | PARKESTON - 30F | PARKESTON - 30F | STRATFORD - 30A | STRATFORD - 30A | STRATFORD - 30A | **11/59: CAMB - 31A** | STRATFORD - 30A | STRATFORD - 30A |
| Jan-60 | STRATFORD - 30A | PARKESTON - 30F | PARKESTON - 30F | STRATFORD - 30A | STRATFORD - 30A | STRATFORD - 30A | CAMBRIDGE - 31A | STRATFORD - 30A | STRATFORD - 30A |
| Apr-60 | STRATFORD - 30A | PARKESTON - 30F | PARKESTON - 30F | STRATFORD - 30A | STRATFORD - 30A | STRATFORD - 30A | CAMBRIDGE - 31A | STRATFORD - 30A | STRATFORD - 30A |
| Aug-60 | STRATFORD - 30A | **8/60: STRAT - 30A** | PARKESTON - 30F | **8/60: PARKS - 30F** | STRATFORD - 30A | STRATFORD - 30A | **6/60: W/D** | STRATFORD - 30A | STRATFORD - 30A |
| Nov-60 | STRATFORD - 30A | **10/60: W/D** | PARKESTON - 30F | PARKESTON - 30F | **11/60: W/D** | **10/60: W/D** | | **10/60: W/D** | **9/60: W/D** |

| | 64688 | 64691 | 64693 | 64694 | 64695 | 64697 | 64699 | J20 0-6-0 (1943)<br>64675 | 64676 |
|---|---|---|---|---|---|---|---|---|---|
| Aug-50 | MARCH - 31B | STRATFORD - 30A | MARCH - 31B | MARCH - 31B | STRATFORD - 30A | MARCH - 31B | MARCH - 31B | STRATFORD - 30A | STRATFORD - 30A |
| Jan-51 | MARCH - 31B | STRATFORD - 30A | MARCH - 31B | MARCH - 31B | STRATFORD - 30A | MARCH - 31B | MARCH - 31B | STRATFORD - 30A | STRATFORD - 30A |
| Aug-51 | **9/51: CAMB - 31A** | STRATFORD - 30A | MARCH - 31B | MARCH - 31B | STRATFORD - 30A | MARCH - 31B | **5/51: HORN - 34B** | STRATFORD - 30A | STRATFORD - 30A |
| Jan-52 | CAMBRIDGE - 31A | STRATFORD - 30A | MARCH - 31B | **3/52: CAMB - 31A** | STRATFORD - 30A | MARCH - 31B | HORNSEY - 34B | STRATFORD - 30A | STRATFORD - 30A |
| Aug-52 | CAMBRIDGE - 31A | STRATFORD - 30A | MARCH - 31B | **5/52: MARCH - 31B** | STRATFORD - 30A | MARCH - 31B | HORNSEY - 34B | STRATFORD - 30A | STRATFORD - 30A |
| Jan-53 | CAMBRIDGE - 31A | STRATFORD - 30A | MARCH - 31B | MARCH - 31B | STRATFORD - 30A | MARCH - 31B | HORNSEY - 34B | STRATFORD - 30A | STRATFORD - 30A |
| Aug-53 | CAMBRIDGE - 31A | STRATFORD - 30A | MARCH - 31B | MARCH - 31B | STRATFORD - 30A | MARCH - 31B | HORNSEY - 34B | STRATFORD - 30A | STRATFORD - 30A |
| Jan-54 | CAMBRIDGE - 31A | **1/54: MARCH - 31B** | MARCH - 31B | MARCH - 31B | **12/53: MARCH - 31B** | MARCH - 31B | **11/53: MARCH - 31B** | STRATFORD - 30A | STRATFORD - 30A |
| Aug-54 | CAMBRIDGE - 31A | MARCH - 31B | MARCH - 31B | MARCH - 31B | MARCH - 31B | MARCH - 31B | MARCH - 31B | STRATFORD - 30A | STRATFORD - 30A |
| Jan-55 | CAMBRIDGE - 31A | MARCH - 31B | **12/54: CAMB - 31A** | **12/54: CAMB - 31A** | MARCH - 31B | MARCH - 31B | MARCH - 31B | STRATFORD - 30A | STRATFORD - 30A |
| Aug-55 | CAMBRIDGE - 31A | MARCH - 31B | **5/55: STRAT - 30A** | **5/55: STRAT - 30A** | **6/55: CAMB - 31A** | MARCH - 31B | MARCH - 31B | STRATFORD - 30A | STRATFORD - 30A |
| Jan-56 | CAMBRIDGE - 31A | MARCH - 31B | STRATFORD - 30A | STRATFORD - 30A | CAMBRIDGE - 31A | MARCH - 31B | MARCH - 31B | STRATFORD - 30A | STRATFORD - 30A |
| Aug-56 | CAMBRIDGE - 31A | MARCH - 31B | STRATFORD - 30A | STRATFORD - 30A | CAMBRIDGE - 31A | MARCH - 31B | MARCH - 31B | STRATFORD - 30A | STRATFORD - 30A |
| Jan-57 | CAMBRIDGE - 31A | MARCH - 31B | STRATFORD - 30A | STRATFORD - 30A | CAMBRIDGE - 31A | MARCH - 31B | MARCH - 31B | STRATFORD - 30A | STRATFORD - 30A |
| Aug-57 | CAMBRIDGE - 31A | MARCH - 31B | STRATFORD - 30A | STRATFORD - 30A | CAMBRIDGE - 31A | MARCH - 31B | MARCH - 31B | STRATFORD - 30A | STRATFORD - 30A |
| Jan-58 | **11/57: STRAT - 30A** | MARCH - 31B | STRATFORD - 30A | STRATFORD - 30A | CAMBRIDGE - 31A | MARCH - 31B | MARCH - 31B | STRATFORD - 30A | STRATFORD - 30A |
| Aug-58 | STRATFORD - 30A | MARCH - 31B | STRATFORD - 30A | STRATFORD - 30A | CAMBRIDGE - 31A | MARCH - 31B | MARCH - 31B | STRATFORD - 30A | STRATFORD - 30A |
| Jan-59 | **1/59: W/D** | MARCH - 31B | STRATFORD - 30A | STRATFORD - 30A | CAMBRIDGE - 31A | MARCH - 31B | MARCH - 31B | STRATFORD - 30A | STRATFORD - 30A |
| Aug-59 | | MARCH - 31B | STRATFORD - 30A | STRATFORD - 30A | CAMBRIDGE - 31A | MARCH - 31B | MARCH - 31B | STRATFORD - 30A | STRATFORD - 30A |
| Nov-59 | | MARCH - 31B | STRATFORD - 30A | STRATFORD - 30A | CAMBRIDGE - 31A | MARCH - 31B | MARCH - 31B | STRATFORD - 30A | STRATFORD - 30A |
| Jan-60 | | MARCH - 31B | STRATFORD - 30A | **12/59: W/D** | **12/59: W/D** | MARCH - 31B | MARCH - 31B | **12/59: W/D** | STRATFORD - 30A |
| Apr-60 | | MARCH - 31B | STRATFORD - 30A | | | MARCH - 31B | MARCH - 31B | | STRATFORD - 30A |
| Aug-60 | | MARCH - 31B | STRATFORD - 30A | | | MARCH - 31B | MARCH - 31B | | STRATFORD - 30A |
| Nov-60 | | MARCH - 31B | **10/60: W/D** | | | MARCH - 31B | MARCH - 31B | | STRATFORD - 30A |

| | 64683 | 64687 | 64689 | 64690 | 64692 | 64696 | 64698 | J39 0-6-0 (1926)<br>64700 | 64701 |
|---|---|---|---|---|---|---|---|---|---|
| Aug-50 | CAMBRIDGE - 31A | CAMBRIDGE - 31A | MARCH - 31B | STRATFORD - 30A | MARCH - 31B | STRATFORD - 30A | MARCH - 31B | BLAYDON - 52C | GATES HEAD - 52A |
| Jan-51 | CAMBRIDGE - 31A | CAMBRIDGE - 31A | MARCH - 31B | STRATFORD - 30A | MARCH - 31B | STRATFORD - 30A | MARCH - 31B | BLAYDON - 52C | GATES HEAD - 52A |
| Aug-51 | **5/51: MARCH - 31B** | **5/51: MARCH - 31B** | **9/51: CAMB - 31A** | STRATFORD - 30A | MARCH - 31B | STRATFORD - 30A | MARCH - 31B | BLAYDON - 52C | GATES HEAD - 52A |
| Jan-52 | **9/51: CAMB - 31A** | MARCH - 31B | CAMBRIDGE - 31A | STRATFORD - 30A | MARCH - 31B | STRATFORD - 30A | MARCH - 31B | BLAYDON - 52C | GATES HEAD - 52A |
| Aug-52 | CAMBRIDGE - 31A | MARCH - 31B | CAMBRIDGE - 31A | STRATFORD - 30A | MARCH - 31B | STRATFORD - 30A | MARCH - 31B | BLAYDON - 52C | GATES HEAD - 52A |
| Jan-53 | CAMBRIDGE - 31A | MARCH - 31B | CAMBRIDGE - 31A | STRATFORD - 30A | MARCH - 31B | STRATFORD - 30A | MARCH - 31B | **1/53I B.GDNS - 54C** | GATES HEAD - 52A |
| Aug-53 | CAMBRIDGE - 31A | MARCH - 31B | CAMBRIDGE - 31A | STRATFORD - 30A | MARCH - 31B | STRATFORD - 30A | MARCH - 31B | BOR.GDNS - 54C | GATES HEAD - 52A |
| Jan-54 | CAMBRIDGE - 31A | MARCH - 31B | CAMBRIDGE - 31A | **1/54: MARCH - 31B** | MARCH - 31B | STRATFORD - 30A | MARCH - 31B | BOR.GDNS - 54C | GATES HEAD - 52A |
| Aug-54 | CAMBRIDGE - 31A | MARCH - 31B | CAMBRIDGE - 31A | MARCH - 31B | MARCH - 31B | **8/54: CAMB - 31A** | MARCH - 31B | BOR.GDNS - 54C | GATES HEAD - 52A |
| Jan-55 | CAMBRIDGE - 31A | MARCH - 31B | CAMBRIDGE - 31A | MARCH - 31B | MARCH - 31B | CAMBRIDGE - 31A | MARCH - 31B | BOR.GDNS - 54C | GATES HEAD - 52A |
| Aug-55 | CAMBRIDGE - 31A | MARCH - 31B | **5/55: STRAT - 30A** | MARCH - 31B | MARCH - 31B | CAMBRIDGE - 31A | MARCH - 31B | BOR.GDNS - 54C | GATES HEAD - 52A |
| Jan-56 | CAMBRIDGE - 31A | MARCH - 31B | STRATFORD - 30A | MARCH - 31B | MARCH - 31B | CAMBRIDGE - 31A | MARCH - 31B | BOR.GDNS - 54C | GATES HEAD - 52A |
| Aug-56 | CAMBRIDGE - 31A | MARCH - 31B | STRATFORD - 30A | MARCH - 31B | MARCH - 31B | CAMBRIDGE - 31A | MARCH - 31B | BOR.GDNS - 54C | GATES HEAD - 52A |
| Jan-57 | CAMBRIDGE - 31A | MARCH - 31B | STRATFORD - 30A | MARCH - 31B | MARCH - 31B | CAMBRIDGE - 31A | MARCH - 31B | BOR.GDNS - 54C | GATES HEAD - 52A |
| Aug-57 | CAMBRIDGE - 31A | MARCH - 31B | STRATFORD - 30A | MARCH - 31B | MARCH - 31B | CAMBRIDGE - 31A | MARCH - 31B | BOR.GDNS - 54C | **7/57: HTN - 52B** |
| Jan-58 | CAMBRIDGE - 31A | MARCH - 31B | STRATFORD - 30A | MARCH - 31B | MARCH - 31B | CAMBRIDGE - 31A | MARCH - 31B | BOR.GDNS - 54C | HEATON - 52B |
| Aug-58 | CAMBRIDGE - 31A | MARCH - 31B | STRATFORD - 30A | MARCH - 31B | MARCH - 31B | CAMBRIDGE - 31A | MARCH - 31B | BOR.GDNS - 54C | HEATON - 52B |
| Jan-59 | CAMBRIDGE - 31A | MARCH - 31B | STRATFORD - 30A | MARCH - 31B | MARCH - 31B | CAMBRIDGE - 31A | MARCH - 31B | BOR.GDNS - 52J | HEATON - 52B |
| Aug-59 | CAMBRIDGE - 31A | MARCH - 31B | STRATFORD - 30A | MARCH - 31B | MARCH - 31B | CAMBRIDGE - 31A | MARCH - 31B | **6/59: GHD - 52A** | HEATON - 52B |
| Nov-59 | **11/59: W/D** | MARCH - 31B | STRATFORD - 30A | MARCH - 31B | MARCH - 31B | CAMBRIDGE - 31A | **11/59: CAMB - 31A** | **10/59: SUND - 52G** | **12/59: SUND - 52G** |
| Jan-60 | | MARCH - 31B | STRATFORD - 30A | MARCH - 31B | MARCH - 31B | CAMBRIDGE - 31A | CAMBRIDGE - 31A | SUNDERLAND - 52G | SUNDERLAND - 52G |
| Apr-60 | | MARCH - 31B | STRATFORD - 30A | MARCH - 31B | MARCH - 31B | CAMBRIDGE - 31A | CAMBRIDGE - 31A | SUNDERLAND - 52G | SUNDERLAND - 52G |
| Aug-60 | | MARCH - 31B | STRATFORD - 30A | MARCH - 31B | MARCH - 31B | CAMBRIDGE - 31A | CAMBRIDGE - 31A | SUNDERLAND - 52G | SUNDERLAND - 52G |
| Nov-60 | | MARCH - 31B | STRATFORD - 30A | MARCH - 31B | MARCH - 31B | CAMBRIDGE - 31A | CAMBRIDGE - 31A | SUNDERLAND - 52G | SUNDERLAND - 52G |

| | 64702 | 64703 | 64704 | 64705 | 64706 | 64707 | 64708 | 64709 | 64710 |
|---|---|---|---|---|---|---|---|---|---|
| Aug-50 | LINCOLN - 40A | BLAYDON - 52C | GATES HEAD - 52A | BLAYDON - 52C | STARBECK - 50D | GATES HEAD - 52A | STRATFORD - 30A | HEATON - 52B | DARLINGTON - 51A |
| Jan-51 | LINCOLN - 40A | BLAYDON - 52C | GATES HEAD - 52A | BLAYDON - 52C | STARBECK - 50D | GATES HEAD - 52A | **9/50: IPS - 32B** | HEATON - 52B | **9/50: N.HILL - 50B** |
| Aug-51 | LINCOLN - 40A | BLAYDON - 52C | GATES HEAD - 52A | BLAYDON - 52C | STARBECK - 50D | GATES HEAD - 52A | **10/50: STRAT - 30A** | HEATON - 52B | **7/51: B.GDNS - 54C** |
| Jan-52 | LINCOLN - 40A | BLAYDON - 52C | GATES HEAD - 52A | BLAYDON - 52C | STARBECK - 50D | GATES HEAD - 52A | STRATFORD - 30A | **2/52: B.GDNS - 54C** | BOR.GDNS - 54C |
| Aug-52 | LINCOLN - 40A | **7/52: DAIRY - 53A** | GATES HEAD - 52A | BLAYDON - 52C | STARBECK - 50D | GATES HEAD - 52A | STRATFORD - 30A | BOR.GDNS - 54C | BOR.GDNS - 54C |
| Jan-53 | LINCOLN - 40A | **12/53: HTN - 52B** | GATES HEAD - 52A | BLAYDON - 52C | STARBECK - 50D | **1/53I B.GDNS - 54C** | STRATFORD - 30A | BOR.GDNS - 54C | BOR.GDNS - 54C |
| Aug-53 | LINCOLN - 40A | HEATON - 52B | GATES HEAD - 52A | BLAYDON - 52C | STARBECK - 50D | BOR.GDNS - 54C | STRATFORD - 30A | BOR.GDNS - 54C | BOR.GDNS - 54C |
| Jan-54 | LINCOLN - 40A | HEATON - 52B | GATES HEAD - 52A | BLAYDON - 52C | STARBECK - 50D | BOR.GDNS - 54C | STRATFORD - 30A | BOR.GDNS - 54C | BOR.GDNS - 54C |
| Aug-54 | LINCOLN - 40A | HEATON - 52B | GATES HEAD - 52A | BLAYDON - 52C | STARBECK - 50D | BOR.GDNS - 54C | STRATFORD - 30A | BOR.GDNS - 54C | BOR.GDNS - 54C |
| Jan-55 | LINCOLN - 40A | HEATON - 52B | GATES HEAD - 52A | BLAYDON - 52C | STARBECK - 50D | BOR.GDNS - 54C | STRATFORD - 30A | BOR.GDNS - 54C | BOR.GDNS - 54C |
| Aug-55 | LINCOLN - 40A | HEATON - 52B | GATES HEAD - 52A | BLAYDON - 52C | STARBECK - 50D | BOR.GDNS - 54C | STRATFORD - 30A | BOR.GDNS - 54C | BOR.GDNS - 54C |
| Jan-56 | LINCOLN - 40A | HEATON - 52B | GATES HEAD - 52A | BLAYDON - 52C | STARBECK - 50D | BOR.GDNS - 54C | STRATFORD - 30A | BOR.GDNS - 54C | BOR.GDNS - 54C |
| Aug-56 | LINCOLN - 40A | HEATON - 52B | GATES HEAD - 52A | BLAYDON - 52C | STARBECK - 50D | BOR.GDNS - 54C | STRATFORD - 30A | BOR.GDNS - 54C | BOR.GDNS - 54C |
| Jan-57 | LINCOLN - 40A | HEATON - 52B | GATES HEAD - 52A | BLAYDON - 52C | STARBECK - 50D | BOR.GDNS - 54C | STRATFORD - 30A | BOR.GDNS - 54C | BOR.GDNS - 54C |
| Aug-57 | LINCOLN - 40A | HEATON - 52B | GATES HEAD - 52A | **6/57: ALN - 52D** | STARBECK - 50D | BOR.GDNS - 54C | STRATFORD - 30A | BOR.GDNS - 54C | BOR.GDNS - 54C |
| Jan-58 | **11/57: STRAT - 30A** | HEATON - 52B | GATES HEAD - 52A | ALNMOUTH - 52D | STARBECK - 50D | BOR.GDNS - 54C | STRATFORD - 30A | BOR.GDNS - 54C | BOR.GDNS - 54C |
| Aug-58 | STRATFORD - 30A | HEATON - 52B | GATES HEAD - 52A | ALNMOUTH - 52D | STARBECK - 50D | BOR.GDNS - 54C | STRATFORD - 30A | BOR.GDNS - 54C | BOR.GDNS - 54C |
| Jan-59 | DARNALL - 41A | HEATON - 52B | GATES HEAD - 52A | **2/59: ARDS - 56B** | STARBECK - 50D | BOR.GDNS - 52J | STRATFORD - 30A | BOR.GDNS - 52J | BOR.GDNS - 52J |
| Aug-59 | DARNALL - 41A | HEATON - 52B | GATES HEAD - 52A | ARDSLEY - 56B | **9/59: YORK - 50A** | **6/59: GHD - 52A** | STRATFORD - 30A | BOR.GDNS - 52J | **6/59: GHD - 52A** |
| Nov-59 | **9/59: W/D** | HEATON - 52B | **10/59: SUND - 52G** | ARDSLEY - 56B | YORK - 50A | GATES HEAD - 52A | STRATFORD - 30A | BOR.GDNS - 52J | **10/59: SUND - 52G** |
| Jan-60 | | **12/59: SUND - 52G** | SUNDERLAND - 52G | ARDSLEY - 56B | YORK - 50A | GATES HEAD - 52A | STRATFORD - 30A | BOR.GDNS - 52J | SUNDERLAND - 52G |
| Apr-60 | | SUNDERLAND - 52G | SUNDERLAND - 52G | ARDSLEY - 56B | YORK - 50A | GATES HEAD - 52A | STRATFORD - 30A | BOR.GDNS - 52J | SUNDERLAND - 52G |
| Aug-60 | | SUNDERLAND - 52G | SUNDERLAND - 52G | **6/60: WAKE - 56A** | YORK - 50A | GATES HEAD - 52A | **8/60: W/D** | BOR.GDNS - 52J | SUNDERLAND - 52G |
| Nov-60 | | SUNDERLAND - 52G | SUNDERLAND - 52G | WAKEFIELD - 56A | YORK - 50A | GATES HEAD - 52A | | BOR.GDNS - 52J | SUNDERLAND - 52G |

| | 64711 | 64712 | 64713 | 64714 | 64715 | 64716 | 64717 | 64718 | 64719 |
|---|---|---|---|---|---|---|---|---|---|
| Aug-50 | TWEEDMOUTH - 52D | GORTON - 39A | DONCASTER - 36A | GORTON - 39A | LINCOLN - 40A | COLWICK - 38A | GORTON - 39A | GORTON - 39A | COLWICK - 38A |
| Jan-51 | TWEEDMOUTH - 52D | GORTON - 39A | DONCASTER - 36A | GORTON - 39A | LINCOLN - 40A | COLWICK - 38A | GORTON - 39A | GORTON - 39A | COLWICK - 38A |
| Aug-51 | TWEEDMOUTH - 52D | GORTON - 39A | **9/51: DAIRY - 53A** | GORTON - 39A | LINCOLN - 40A | COLWICK - 38A | GORTON - 39A | GORTON - 39A | COLWICK - 38A |
| Jan-52 | TWEEDMOUTH - 52D | GORTON - 39A | DAIRYCOATES - 53A | GORTON - 39A | LINCOLN - 40A | COLWICK - 38A | GORTON - 39A | GORTON - 39A | COLWICK - 38A |
| Aug-52 | TWEEDMOUTH - 52D | GORTON - 39A | **12/52: BLAY - 52C** | GORTON - 39A | LINCOLN - 40A | COLWICK - 38A | GORTON - 39A | GORTON - 39A | COLWICK - 38A |
| Jan-53 | TWEEDMOUTH - 52D | GORTON - 39A | **1/53: B.GDNS - 54C** | GORTON - 39A | LINCOLN - 40A | COLWICK - 38A | GORTON - 39A | GORTON - 39A | **10/52: S.BGE - 35C** |
| Aug-53 | TWEEDMOUTH - 52D | GORTON - 39A | BOR.GDNS - 54C | GORTON - 39A | LINCOLN - 40A | COLWICK - 38A | GORTON - 39A | GORTON - 39A | SPITAL BGE - 35C |
| Jan-54 | TWEEDMOUTH - 52D | **6/54: LINC - 40A** | BOR.GDNS - 54C | GORTON - 39A | LINCOLN - 40A | COLWICK - 38A | GORTON - 39A | GORTON - 39A | SPITAL BGE - 35C |
| Aug-54 | TWEEDMOUTH - 52D | **10/54: TUX - 40D** | BOR.GDNS - 54C | **6/54: LINC - 40A** | LINCOLN - 40A | COLWICK - 38A | GORTON - 39A | GORTON - 39A | SPITAL BGE - 35C |
| Jan-55 | TWEEDMOUTH - 52D | **1/55: LINC - 40A** | BOR.GDNS - 54C | LINCOLN - 40A | LINCOLN - 40A | COLWICK - 38A | GORTON - 39A | GORTON - 39A | SPITAL BGE - 35C |
| Aug-55 | TWEEDMOUTH - 52D | LINCOLN - 40A | BOR.GDNS - 54C | LINCOLN - 40A | **7/55: COLW - 38A** | COLWICK - 38A | GORTON - 39A | GORTON - 39A | SPITAL BGE - 35C |
| Jan-56 | TWEEDMOUTH - 52D | LINCOLN - 40A | BOR.GDNS - 54C | LINCOLN - 40A | COLWICK - 38A | COLWICK - 38A | GORTON - 39A | GORTON - 39A | SPITAL BGE - 35C |
| Aug-56 | TWEEDMOUTH - 52D | LINCOLN - 40A | BOR.GDNS - 54C | LINCOLN - 40A | COLWICK - 38A | COLWICK - 38A | GORTON - 39A | GORTON - 39A | SPITAL BGE - 35C |
| Jan-57 | TWEEDMOUTH - 52D | LINCOLN - 40A | BOR.GDNS - 54C | LINCOLN - 40A | COLWICK - 38A | COLWICK - 38A | GORTON - 39A | GORTON - 39A | SPITAL BGE - 35C |
| Aug-57 | TWEEDMOUTH - 52D | LINCOLN - 40A | **6/57: HTN - 52B** | LINCOLN - 40A | COLWICK - 38A | COLWICK - 38A | GORTON - 39A | GORTON - 39A | SPITAL BGE - 35C |
| Jan-58 | TWEEDMOUTH - 52D | LINCOLN - 40A | HEATON - 52B | LINCOLN - 40A | COLWICK - 38A | COLWICK - 38A | GORTON - 39A | GORTON - 39A | SPITAL BGE - 35C |
| Aug-58 | TWEEDMOUTH - 52D | **10/58: BOST - 40F** | HEATON - 52B | LINCOLN - 40A | COLWICK - 40E | **10/58: BOST - 40F** | GORTON - 9G | GORTON - 9G | SPITAL BGE - 31F |
| Jan-59 | TWEEDMOUTH - 52D | **3/59: COLW - 40E** | HEATON - 52B | **12/58: RET - 36E** | COLWICK - 40E | **3/59: DCTR - 36A** | GORTON - 9G | GORTON - 9G | **12/58: DARN - 41A** |
| Aug-59 | TWEEDMOUTH - 52D | COLWICK - 40E | **6/59: GHD - 52A** | **5/59: W/D** | **5/59: W/D** | DONCASTER - 36A | GORTON - 9G | GORTON - 9G | DARNALL - 41A |
| Nov-59 | TWEEDMOUTH - 52D | COLWICK - 40E | GATES HEAD - 52A | | | DONCASTER - 36A | GORTON - 9G | GORTON - 9G | DARNALL - 41A |
| Jan-60 | TWEEDMOUTH - 52D | COLWICK - 40E | GATES HEAD - 52A | | | DONCASTER - 36A | GORTON - 9G | GORTON - 9G | DARNALL - 41A |
| Apr-60 | TWEEDMOUTH - 52D | W/D | GATES HEAD - 52A | | | DONCASTER - 36A | GORTON - 9G | GORTON - 9G | DARNALL - 41A |
| Aug-60 | TWEEDMOUTH - 52D | **2/60: W/D** | GATES HEAD - 52A | | | DONCASTER - 36A | **9/60: W/D** | GORTON - 9G | **9/60: W.AUCK - 51F** |
| Nov-60 | TWEEDMOUTH - 52D | | GATES HEAD - 52A | | | DONCASTER - 36A | | GORTON - 9G | W.AUCKLAND - 51F |

| | 64720 | 64721 | 64722 | 64723 | 64724 | 64725 | 64726 | 64727 | 64728 |
|---|---|---|---|---|---|---|---|---|---|
| Aug-50 | COLWICK - 38A | DONCASTER - 36A | LINCOLN - 40A | TRAFFORD PARK - 9E | NORWICH - 32A | LINCOLN - 40A | NORWICH - 32A | HEATON MERSEY - 9F | LINCOLN - 40A |
| Jan-51 | COLWICK - 38A | DONCASTER - 36A | LINCOLN - 40A | **3/51: COLW - 38A** | NORWICH - 32A | LINCOLN - 40A | NORWICH - 32A | **1/51: CANAL - 12B** | LINCOLN - 40A |
| Aug-51 | **5/51: ARDS - 37A** | DONCASTER - 36A | LINCOLN - 40A | **8/51: H.MSY - 9F** | NORWICH - 32A | **9/51: DAIRY - 53A** | NORWICH - 32A | CARLISLE (CANAL) - 12B | LINCOLN - 40A |
| Jan-52 | ARDSLEY - 37A | DONCASTER - 36A | LINCOLN - 40A | HEATON MERSEY - 9F | NORWICH - 32A | DAIRYCOATES - 53A | NORWICH - 32A | CARLISLE (CANAL) - 12B | LINCOLN - 40A |
| Aug-52 | ARDSLEY - 37A | DONCASTER - 36A | LINCOLN - 40A | **9/52: S.BGE - 35C** | NORWICH - 32A | DAIRYCOATES - 53A | NORWICH - 32A | CARLISLE (CANAL) - 12B | LINCOLN - 40A |
| Jan-53 | ARDSLEY - 37A | DONCASTER - 36A | LINCOLN - 40A | SPITAL BRIDGE - 35C | NORWICH - 32A | DAIRYCOATES - 53A | NORWICH - 32A | CARLISLE (CANAL) - 12B | LINCOLN - 40A |
| Aug-53 | ARDSLEY - 37A | DONCASTER - 36A | LINCOLN - 40A | SPITAL BRIDGE - 35C | **11/53: LOW - 32C** | DAIRYCOATES - 53A | NORWICH - 32A | CARLISLE (CANAL) - 12B | LINCOLN - 40A |
| Jan-54 | ARDSLEY - 37A | DONCASTER - 36A | LINCOLN - 40A | SPITAL BRIDGE - 35C | **2/54: NOR - 32A** | DAIRYCOATES - 53A | NORWICH - 32A | CARLISLE (CANAL) - 12B | LINCOLN - 40A |
| Aug-54 | ARDSLEY - 37A | DONCASTER - 36A | LINCOLN - 40A | SPITAL BRIDGE - 35C | NORWICH - 32A | DAIRYCOATES - 53A | **5/54: IPS - 32B** | CARLISLE (CANAL) - 12B | LINCOLN - 40A |
| Jan-55 | ARDSLEY - 37A | DONCASTER - 36A | LINCOLN - 40A | SPITAL BRIDGE - 35C | NORWICH - 32A | **11/54: SELBY - 50C** | IPSWICH - 32B | CARLISLE (CANAL) - 12B | LINCOLN - 40A |
| Aug-55 | ARDSLEY - 37A | DONCASTER - 36A | LINCOLN - 40A | SPITAL BRIDGE - 35C | NORWICH - 32A | SELBY - 50C | IPSWICH - 32B | CARLISLE (CANAL) - 12B | LINCOLN - 40A |
| Jan-56 | ARDSLEY - 37A | DONCASTER - 36A | LINCOLN - 40A | SPITAL BRIDGE - 35C | **11/55: IPS - 32B** | SELBY - 50C | IPSWICH - 32B | CARLISLE (CANAL) - 12B | LINCOLN - 40A |
| Aug-56 | ARDSLEY - 56B | DONCASTER - 36A | LINCOLN - 40A | SPITAL BRIDGE - 35C | IPSWICH - 32B | SELBY - 50C | IPSWICH - 32B | CARLISLE (CANAL) - 12B | LINCOLN - 40A |
| Jan-57 | ARDSLEY - 56B | DONCASTER - 36A | LINCOLN - 40A | SPITAL BRIDGE - 35C | IPSWICH - 32B | SELBY - 50C | IPSWICH - 32B | CARLISLE (CANAL) - 12B | LINCOLN - 40A |
| Aug-57 | ARDSLEY - 56B | DONCASTER - 36A | LINCOLN - 40A | SPITAL BRIDGE - 35C | IPSWICH - 32B | **8/57: N.HILL - 50B** | IPSWICH - 32B | CARLISLE (CANAL) - 12B | LINCOLN - 40A |
| Jan-58 | ARDSLEY - 56B | DONCASTER - 36A | LINCOLN - 40A | SPITAL BRIDGE - 35C | IPSWICH - 32B | NEVILLE HILL - 50B | **7/58: M.CONS - 32G** | CARLISLE (CANAL) - 12B | LINCOLN - 40A |
| Aug-58 | ARDSLEY - 56B | DONCASTER - 36A | LINCOLN - 40A | SPITAL BRIDGE - 31F | IPSWICH - 32B | NEVILLE HILL - 50B | **10/58: LOW - 32C** | CARLISLE (CANAL) - 12B | **10/58: BOST - 40F** |
| Jan-59 | ARDSLEY - 56B | DONCASTER - 36A | **12/58: DCTR - 36A** | **12/58: INC - 40A** | IPSWICH - 32B | NEVILLE HILL - 50B | **12/58: LINC - 40A** | **12/58: GORT - 9G** | BOSTON - 40F |
| Aug-59 | ARDSLEY - 56B | DONCASTER - 36A | DONCASTER - 36A | **3/59: DCTR - 36A** | IPSWICH - 32B | **8/59: SELBY - 50C** | LINCOLN - 40A | GORTON - 9G | BOSTON - 40F |
| Nov-59 | ARDSLEY - 56B | DONCASTER - 36A | DONCASTER - 36A | DONCASTER - 36A | IPSWICH - 32B | **9/59: YORK - 50A** | LINCOLN - 40A | GORTON - 9G | BOSTON - 40F |
| Jan-60 | ARDSLEY - 56B | DONCASTER - 36A | DONCASTER - 36A | DONCASTER - 36A | IPSWICH - 32B | **12/59: TNBY - 51L** | LINCOLN - 40A | GORTON - 9G | BOSTON - 40F |
| Apr-60 | ARDSLEY - 56B | **3/60: W/D** | **3/60: W/D** | DONCASTER - 36A | **2/60: W/D** | THORNABY - 51L | LINCOLN - 40A | GORTON - 9G | **3/60: W/D** |
| Aug-60 | ARDSLEY - 56B | | | DONCASTER - 36A | | THORNABY - 51L | LINCOLN - 40A | GORTON - 9G | |
| Nov-60 | ARDSLEY - 56B | | | DONCASTER - 36A | | THORNABY - 51L | LINCOLN - 40A | GORTON - 9G | |

| | 64729 | 64730 | 64731 | 64732 | 64733 | 64734 | 64735 | 64736 | 64737 |
|---|---|---|---|---|---|---|---|---|---|
| Aug-50 | COLWICK - 38A | LINCOLN - 40A | NORWICH - 32A | CRICKLEWOOD - 14A | HEATON MERSEY - 9F | LINCOLN - 40A | COLWICK - 38A | LINCOLN - 40A | DONCASTER - 36A |
| Jan-51 | COLWICK - 38A | LINCOLN - 40A | NORWICH - 32A | **3/51: STRAT - 30A** | **1/51: CANAL - 12B** | LINCOLN - 40A | COLWICK - 38A | LINCOLN - 40A | DONCASTER - 36A |
| Aug-51 | **4/51: ARDS - 37A** | **9/51: DAIRY - 53A** | NORWICH - 32A | **4/51: CWD - 14A** | CARLISLE (CANAL) - 12B | LINCOLN - 40A | COLWICK - 38A | LINCOLN - 40A | DONCASTER - 36A |
| Jan-52 | ARDSLEY - 37A | **11/51: N.HILL - 50B** | NORWICH - 32A | CRICKLEWOOD - 14A | CARLISLE (CANAL) - 12B | LINCOLN - 40A | COLWICK - 38A | LINCOLN - 40A | DONCASTER - 36A |
| Aug-52 | ARDSLEY - 37A | NEVILLE HILL - 50B | NORWICH - 32A | **3/52: ARDS - 37A** | CARLISLE (CANAL) - 12B | LINCOLN - 40A | COLWICK - 38A | LINCOLN - 40A | DONCASTER - 36A |
| Jan-53 | ARDSLEY - 37A | NEVILLE HILL - 50B | NORWICH - 32A | ARDSLEY - 37A | CARLISLE (CANAL) - 12B | LINCOLN - 40A | COLWICK - 38A | LINCOLN - 40A | DONCASTER - 36A |
| Aug-53 | ARDSLEY - 37A | NEVILLE HILL - 50B | NORWICH - 32A | ARDSLEY - 37A | CARLISLE (CANAL) - 12B | LINCOLN - 40A | COLWICK - 38A | LINCOLN - 40A | DONCASTER - 36A |
| Jan-54 | **11/53: TUX - 40D** | NEVILLE HILL - 50B | NORWICH - 32A | ARDSLEY - 37A | CARLISLE (CANAL) - 12B | **12/53: TUX - 40D** | **11/53: TUX - 40D** | LINCOLN - 40A | DONCASTER - 36A |
| Aug-54 | TUXFORD - 40D | **10/54: SELBY - 50C** | NORWICH - 32A | ARDSLEY - 37A | CARLISLE (CANAL) - 12B | **3/54: LINC - 40A** | TUXFORD - 40D | LINCOLN - 40A | DONCASTER - 36A |
| Jan-55 | **1/55: STRAT - 30A** | SELBY - 50C | NORWICH - 32A | ARDSLEY - 37A | CARLISLE (CANAL) - 12B | LINCOLN - 40A | **1/55: COLW - 38A** | LINCOLN - 40A | DONCASTER - 36A |
| Aug-55 | **5/55: CAMB - 31A** | SELBY - 50C | NORWICH - 32A | ARDSLEY - 37A | CARLISLE (CANAL) - 12B | LINCOLN - 40A | COLWICK - 38A | **7/55: S.BGE - 35C** | DONCASTER - 36A |
| Jan-56 | CAMBRIDGE - 31A | SELBY - 50C | NORWICH - 32A | ARDSLEY - 37A | CARLISLE (CANAL) - 12B | LINCOLN - 40A | COLWICK - 38A | SPITAL BRIDGE - 35C | DONCASTER - 36A |
| Aug-56 | CAMBRIDGE - 31A | SELBY - 50C | NORWICH - 32A | ARDSLEY - 56B | CARLISLE (CANAL) - 12B | LINCOLN - 40A | COLWICK - 38A | SPITAL BRIDGE - 35C | DONCASTER - 36A |
| Jan-57 | CAMBRIDGE - 31A | SELBY - 50C | NORWICH - 32A | ARDSLEY - 56B | CARLISLE (CANAL) - 12B | LINCOLN - 40A | COLWICK - 38A | SPITAL BRIDGE - 35C | DONCASTER - 36A |
| Aug-57 | CAMBRIDGE - 31A | **9/57: N. HILL - 50B** | NORWICH - 32A | ARDSLEY - 56B | CARLISLE (CANAL) - 12B | LINCOLN - 40A | COLWICK - 38A | SPITAL BRIDGE - 35C | DONCASTER - 36A |
| Jan-58 | CAMBRIDGE - 31A | NEVILLE HILL - 50B | NORWICH - 32A | ARDSLEY - 56B | CARLISLE (CANAL) - 12B | LINCOLN - 40A | COLWICK - 38A | SPITAL BRIDGE - 35C | DONCASTER - 36A |
| Aug-58 | **10/58: MARCH - 31B** | NEVILLE HILL - 50B | NORWICH - 32A | ARDSLEY - 56B | CARLISLE (CANAL) - 12B | LINCOLN - 40A | COLWICK - 40E | SPITAL BRIDGE - 31F | DONCASTER - 36A |
| Jan-59 | **1/59: BOST - 40F** | NEVILLE HILL - 50B | NORWICH - 32A | ARDSLEY - 56B | CARLISLE (CANAL) - 12B | LINCOLN - 40A | COLWICK - 40E | **12/58: DARN - 41A** | DONCASTER - 36A |
| Aug-59 | BOSTON - 40F | NEVILLE HILL - 50B | **7/59: W/D** | ARDSLEY - 56B | CARLISLE (CANAL) - 12B | **5/59: W/D** | **8/59: W/D** | DARNALL - 41A | **8/59: W/D** |
| Nov-59 | **10/59: COLW - 40E** | **10/59: TNBY - 51L** | | ARDSLEY - 56B | CARLISLE (CANAL) - 12B | | | DARNALL - 41A | |
| Jan-60 | COLWICK - 40E | THORNABY - 51L | | ARDSLEY - 56B | CARLISLE (CANAL) - 12B | | | DARNALL - 41A | |
| Apr-60 | COLWICK - 40E | THORNABY - 51L | | ARDSLEY - 56B | CARLISLE (CANAL) - 12B | | | **3/60: COLW - 40E** | |
| Aug-60 | COLWICK - 40E | THORNABY - 51L | | ARDSLEY - 56B | CARLISLE (CANAL) - 12B | | | COLWICK - 40E | |
| Nov-60 | COLWICK - 40E | THORNABY - 51L | | ARDSLEY - 56B | CARLISLE (CANAL) - 12B | | | COLWICK - 40E | |

| | 64738 | 64739 | 64740 | 64741 | 64742 | 64743 | 64744 | 64745 | 64746 |
|---|---|---|---|---|---|---|---|---|---|
| Aug-50 | LINCOLN - 40A | COLWICK - 38A | GORTON - 39A | GORTON - 39A | GORTON - 39A | GORTON - 39A | GORTON - 39A | GORTON - 39A | DARNALL - 39B |
| Jan-51 | **3/51: GORT - 39A** | COLWICK - 38A | GORTON - 39A | GORTON - 39A | GORTON - 39A | GORTON - 39A | GORTON - 39A | GORTON - 39A | DARNALL - 39B |
| Aug-51 | GORTON - 39A | COLWICK - 38A | GORTON - 39A | GORTON - 39A | GORTON - 39A | GORTON - 39A | GORTON - 39A | GORTON - 39A | DARNALL - 39B |
| Jan-52 | GORTON - 39A | COLWICK - 38A | GORTON - 39A | GORTON - 39A | GORTON - 39A | GORTON - 39A | GORTON - 39A | GORTON - 39A | DARNALL - 39B |
| Aug-52 | GORTON - 39A | COLWICK - 38A | GORTON - 39A | GORTON - 39A | GORTON - 39A | GORTON - 39A | GORTON - 39A | GORTON - 39A | DARNALL - 39B |
| Jan-53 | **7/53: S. BGE - 35C** | COLWICK - 38A | GORTON - 39A | GORTON - 39A | GORTON - 39A | GORTON - 39A | GORTON - 39A | GORTON - 39A | DARNALL - 39B |
| Aug-53 | **10/53: NEWE - 35A** | COLWICK - 38A | GORTON - 39A | GORTON - 39A | GORTON - 39A | GORTON - 39A | GORTON - 39A | GORTON - 39A | DARNALL - 39B |
| Jan-54 | **11/53: GORT - 39A** | COLWICK - 38A | GORTON - 39A | GORTON - 39A | GORTON - 39A | GORTON - 39A | GORTON - 39A | GORTON - 39A | DARNALL - 39B |
| Aug-54 | **6/54: DARN - 39B** | COLWICK - 38A | GORTON - 39A | GORTON - 39A | GORTON - 39A | GORTON - 39A | **6/54: DARN - 39B** | GORTON - 39A | DARNALL - 39B |
| Jan-55 | DARNALL - 39B | COLWICK - 38A | GORTON - 39A | **10/54: LINC - 40A** | GORTON - 39A | GORTON - 39A | DARNALL - 39B | GORTON - 39A | DARNALL - 39B |
| Aug-55 | DARNALL - 39B | COLWICK - 38A | GORTON - 39A | **7/55: COLW - 38A** | GORTON - 39A | GORTON - 39A | DARNALL - 39B | GORTON - 39A | DARNALL - 39B |
| Jan-56 | DARNALL - 41A | COLWICK - 38A | GORTON - 39A | COLWICK - 38A | GORTON - 39A | GORTON - 39A | DARNALL - 41A | GORTON - 39A | DARNALL - 41A |
| Aug-56 | DARNALL - 41A | COLWICK - 38A | GORTON - 39A | COLWICK - 38A | GORTON - 39A | GORTON - 39A | DARNALL - 41A | GORTON - 39A | DARNALL - 41A |
| Jan-57 | DARNALL - 41A | COLWICK - 38A | GORTON - 39A | COLWICK - 38A | GORTON - 39A | GORTON - 39A | DARNALL - 41A | GORTON - 39A | DARNALL - 41A |
| Aug-57 | DARNALL - 41A | COLWICK - 38A | GORTON - 39A | COLWICK - 38A | GORTON - 39A | GORTON - 39A | DARNALL - 41A | GORTON - 39A | DARNALL - 41A |
| Jan-58 | **11/57: GORT - 39A** | **11/57: ANN - 38B** | GORTON - 39A | COLWICK - 38A | GORTON - 39A | GORTON - 39A | **11/57: GORT - 39A** | GORTON - 39A | DARNALL - 41A |
| Aug-58 | GORTON - 9G | ANNESLEY - 16D | GORTON - 9G | **10/58: BOST - 40F** | GORTON - 9G | GORTON - 9G | GORTON - 9G | GORTON - 9G | DARNALL - 41A |
| Jan-59 | GORTON - 9G | ANNESLEY - 16D | GORTON - 9G | **3/59: LINC - 40A** | GORTON - 9G | GORTON - 9G | GORTON - 9G | GORTON - 9G | DARNALL - 41A |
| Aug-59 | GORTON - 9G | ANNESLEY - 16D | GORTON - 9G | LINCOLN - 40A | GORTON - 9G | GORTON - 9G | GORTON - 9G | GORTON - 9G | DARNALL - 41A |
| Nov-59 | GORTON - 9G | ANNESLEY - 16D | GORTON - 9G | LINCOLN - 40A | GORTON - 9G | GORTON - 9G | GORTON - 9G | GORTON - 9G | DARNALL - 41A |
| Jan-60 | GORTON - 9G | ANNESLEY - 16D | GORTON - 9G | LINCOLN - 40A | GORTON - 9G | GORTON - 9G | GORTON - 9G | GORTON - 9G | DARNALL - 41A |
| Apr-60 | GORTON - 9G | ANNESLEY - 16D | GORTON - 9G | LINCOLN - 40A | GORTON - 9G | GORTON - 9G | GORTON - 9G | GORTON - 9G | **3/60: COLW - 40E** |
| Aug-60 | GORTON - 9G | ANNESLEY - 16D | GORTON - 9G | **6/60: W/D** | **6/60: WOOD - 2F** | GORTON - 9G | GORTON - 9G | GORTON - 9G | COLWICK - 40E |
| Nov-60 | **11/60: W/D** | ANNESLEY - 16D | GORTON - 9G | | WOODFORD HALSE - 2F | GORTON - 9G | GORTON - 9G | GORTON - 9G | COLWICK - 40E |

| | 64747 | 64748 | 64749 | 64750 | 64751 | 64752 | 64753 | 64754 | 64755 |
|---|---|---|---|---|---|---|---|---|---|
| Aug-50 | COLWICK - 38A | GORTON - 39A | ARDSLEY - 37A | COLWICK - 38A | ARDSLEY - 37A | IPSWICH - 32B | DARNALL - 39B | ARDSLEY - 37A | GORTON - 39A |
| Jan-51 | COLWICK - 38A | GORTON - 39A | ARDSLEY - 37A | COLWICK - 38A | ARDSLEY - 37A | IPSWICH - 32B | DARNALL - 39B | ARDSLEY - 37A | GORTON - 39A |
| Aug-51 | COLWICK - 38A | GORTON - 39A | ARDSLEY - 37A | COLWICK - 38A | ARDSLEY - 37A | IPSWICH - 32B | DARNALL - 39B | ARDSLEY - 37A | GORTON - 39A |
| Jan-52 | COLWICK - 38A | GORTON - 39A | ARDSLEY - 37A | COLWICK - 38A | ARDSLEY - 37A | IPSWICH - 32B | DARNALL - 39B | ARDSLEY - 37A | GORTON - 39A |
| Aug-52 | COLWICK - 38A | GORTON - 39A | ARDSLEY - 37A | COLWICK - 38A | ARDSLEY - 37A | IPSWICH - 32B | DARNALL - 39B | ARDSLEY - 37A | GORTON - 39A |
| Jan-53 | COLWICK - 38A | GORTON - 39A | ARDSLEY - 37A | COLWICK - 38A | ARDSLEY - 37A | IPSWICH - 32B | DARNALL - 39B | ARDSLEY - 37A | GORTON - 39A |
| Aug-53 | COLWICK - 38A | GORTON - 39A | ARDSLEY - 37A | COLWICK - 38A | ARDSLEY - 37A | IPSWICH - 32B | DARNALL - 39B | ARDSLEY - 37A | GORTON - 39A |
| Jan-54 | COLWICK - 38A | GORTON - 39A | ARDSLEY - 37A | **11/53: TUX - 40D** | **11/53: TUX - 40D** | IPSWICH - 32B | DARNALL - 39B | ARDSLEY - 37A | GORTON - 39A |
| Aug-54 | COLWICK - 38A | GORTON - 39A | ARDSLEY - 37A | TUXFORD - 40D | TUXFORD - 40D | IPSWICH - 32B | DARNALL - 39B | ARDSLEY - 37A | **6/54: LINC - 40A** |
| Jan-55 | COLWICK - 38A | GORTON - 39A | ARDSLEY - 37A | **1/55: STRAT - 30A** | **1/55: STRAT - 30A** | IPSWICH - 32B | DARNALL - 39B | ARDSLEY - 37A | LINCOLN - 40A |
| Aug-55 | COLWICK - 38A | GORTON - 39A | ARDSLEY - 37A | STRATFORD - 30A | **5/55: CAMB - 31A** | IPSWICH - 32B | DARNALL - 39B | ARDSLEY - 37A | LINCOLN - 40A |
| Jan-56 | COLWICK - 38A | GORTON - 39A | ARDSLEY - 37A | STRATFORD - 30A | CAMBRIDGE - 31A | IPSWICH - 32B | DARNALL - 41A | ARDSLEY - 37A | LINCOLN - 40A |
| Aug-56 | COLWICK - 38A | GORTON - 39A | ARDSLEY - 56B | STRATFORD - 30A | CAMBRIDGE - 31A | IPSWICH - 32B | DARNALL - 41A | ARDSLEY - 56B | LINCOLN - 40A |
| Jan-57 | COLWICK - 38A | GORTON - 39A | ARDSLEY - 56B | STRATFORD - 30A | CAMBRIDGE - 31A | IPSWICH - 32B | DARNALL - 41A | ARDSLEY - 56B | LINCOLN - 40A |
| Aug-57 | COLWICK - 38A | GORTON - 39A | ARDSLEY - 56B | STRATFORD - 30A | CAMBRIDGE - 31A | IPSWICH - 32B | DARNALL - 41A | ARDSLEY - 56B | LINCOLN - 40A |
| Jan-58 | **11/57: ANN - 38B** | GORTON - 39A | ARDSLEY - 56B | STRATFORD - 30A | CAMBRIDGE - 31A | IPSWICH - 32B | **11/57: GORT - 39A** | ARDSLEY - 56B | LINCOLN - 40A |
| Aug-58 | ANNESLEY - 16D | GORTON - 9G | ARDSLEY - 56B | STRATFORD - 30A | **10/58: MARCH - 31B** | IPSWICH - 32B | GORTON - 9G | ARDSLEY - 56B | **12/58: BOST - 40F** |
| Jan-59 | ANNESLEY - 16D | GORTON - 9G | ARDSLEY - 56B | STRATFORD - 30A | **12/58: LINC - 40A** | IPSWICH - 32B | GORTON - 9G | ARDSLEY - 56B | **3/59: LINC - 40A** |
| Aug-59 | **8/59: GORT - 9G** | GORTON - 9G | ARDSLEY - 56B | **10/59: TNBY - 51L** | LINCOLN - 40A | **6/59: W/D** | **8/59: W/D** | ARDSLEY - 56B | **8/59: W/D** |
| Nov-59 | GORTON - 9G | GORTON - 9G | ARDSLEY - 56B | **11/59: W/D** | LINCOLN - 40A | | | ARDSLEY - 56B | |
| Jan-60 | GORTON - 9G | GORTON - 9G | ARDSLEY - 56B | | **12/59: W/D** | | | ARDSLEY - 56B | |
| Apr-60 | GORTON - 9G | GORTON - 9G | ARDSLEY - 56B | | | | | ARDSLEY - 56B | |
| Aug-60 | **6/60: WOOD - 2F** | GORTON - 9G | ARDSLEY - 56B | | | | | ARDSLEY - 56B | |
| Nov-60 | WOODFORD HALSE - 2F | GORTON - 9G | ARDSLEY - 56B | | | | | ARDSLEY - 56B | |

| | 64756 | 64757 | 64758 | 64759 | 64760 | 64761 | 64762 | 64763 | 64764 |
|---|---|---|---|---|---|---|---|---|---|
| Aug-50 | W.AUCKLAND-51F | COLWICK-38A | DONCASTER-36A | RETFORD-36E | ARDSLEY-37A | NORWICH-32A | COLWICK-38A | COLWICK-38A | STRATFORD-30A |
| Jan-51 | W.AUCKLAND-51F | COLWICK-38A | DONCASTER-36A | RETFORD-36E | ARDSLEY-37A | NORWICH-32A | COLWICK-38A | COLWICK-38A | STRATFORD-30A |
| Aug-51 | W.AUCKLAND-51F | **5/51: ARDS - 37A** | **9/51: DARL - 51A** | RETFORD-36E | ARDSLEY-37A | NORWICH-32A | COLWICK-38A | **5/51: ARDS - 37A** | STRATFORD-30A |
| Jan-52 | W.AUCKLAND-51F | ARDSLEY-37A | DARLINGTON-51A | RETFORD-36E | ARDSLEY-37A | NORWICH-32A | COLWICK-38A | ARDSLEY-37A | STRATFORD-30A |
| Aug-52 | W.AUCKLAND-51F | ARDSLEY-37A | NEVILLE HILL-50B | RETFORD-36E | ARDSLEY-37A | NORWICH-32A | COLWICK-38A | ARDSLEY-37A | STRATFORD-30A |
| Jan-53 | W.AUCKLAND-51F | ARDSLEY-37A | NEVILLE HILL-50B | RETFORD-36E | ARDSLEY-37A | NORWICH-32A | COLWICK-38A | ARDSLEY-37A | STRATFORD-30A |
| Aug-53 | W.AUCKLAND-51F | ARDSLEY-37A | NEVILLE HILL-50B | RETFORD-36E | ARDSLEY-37A | NORWICH-32A | COLWICK-38A | ARDSLEY-37A | STRATFORD-30A |
| Jan-54 | W.AUCKLAND-51F | ARDSLEY-37A | NEVILLE HILL-50B | RETFORD-36E | ARDSLEY-37A | NORWICH-32A | COLWICK-38A | **11/53: TUX - 40D** | STRATFORD-30A |
| Aug-54 | W.AUCKLAND-51F | ARDSLEY-37A | NEVILLE HILL-50B | RETFORD-36E | ARDSLEY-37A | NORWICH-32A | COLWICK-38A | TUXFORD-40D | STRATFORD-30A |
| Jan-55 | **3/55: W.AUCK - 51F** | ARDSLEY-37A | NEVILLE HILL-50B | RETFORD-36E | ARDSLEY-37A | NORWICH-32A | COLWICK-38A | **1/55: COLW - 38A** | STRATFORD-30A |
| Aug-55 | **4/55: MBRO - 51D** | ARDSLEY-37A | NEVILLE HILL-50B | RETFORD-36E | ARDSLEY-37A | NORWICH-32A | COLWICK-38A | COLWICK-38A | STRATFORD-30A |
| Jan-56 | **6/55: W.AUCK - 51F** | ARDSLEY-37A | NEVILLE HILL-50B | RETFORD-36E | ARDSLEY-37A | NORWICH-32A | COLWICK-38A | COLWICK-38A | STRATFORD-30A |
| Aug-56 | W.AUCKLAND-51F | ARDSLEY-56B | NEVILLE HILL-50B | RETFORD-36E | ARDSLEY-56B | NORWICH-32A | COLWICK-38A | COLWICK-38A | STRATFORD-30A |
| Jan-57 | W.AUCKLAND-51F | ARDSLEY-56B | NEVILLE HILL-50B | RETFORD-36E | ARDSLEY-56B | NORWICH-32A | COLWICK-38A | COLWICK-38A | **11/56: PARKS - 30F** |
| Aug-57 | W.AUCKLAND-51F | ARDSLEY-56B | NEVILLE HILL-50B | RETFORD-36E | ARDSLEY-56B | NORWICH-32A | COLWICK-38A | COLWICK-38A | PARKESTON-30F |
| Jan-58 | W.AUCKLAND-51F | ARDSLEY-56B | NEVILLE HILL-50B | RETFORD-36E | ARDSLEY-56B | NORWICH-32A | COLWICK-38A | COLWICK-38A | **4/58: STRAT - 30A** |
| Aug-58 | W.AUCKLAND-51F | ARDSLEY-56B | NEVILLE HILL-50B | RETFORD-36E | ARDSLEY-56B | NORWICH-32A | COLWICK-40E | COLWICK-40E | **6/58: MARCH - 31B** |
| Jan-59 | W.AUCKLAND-51F | ARDSLEY-56B | NEVILLE HILL-50B | RETFORD-36E | ARDSLEY-56B | NORWICH-32A | COLWICK-40E | COLWICK-40E | MARCH-31B |
| Aug-59 | W.AUCKLAND-51F | ARDSLEY-56B | NEVILLE HILL-50B | RETFORD-36E | ARDSLEY-56B | NORWICH-32A | **6/59: W/D** | **6/59: W/D** | MARCH-31B |
| Nov-59 | W.AUCKLAND-51F | ARDSLEY-56B | NEVILLE HILL-50B | RETFORD-36E | ARDSLEY-56B | **11/59: W/D** | | | MARCH-31B |
| Jan-60 | W.AUCKLAND-51F | ARDSLEY-56B | NEVILLE HILL-50B | RETFORD-36E | ARDSLEY-56B | | | | MARCH-31B |
| Apr-60 | W.AUCKLAND-51F | ARDSLEY-56B | NEVILLE HILL-55H | **3/60: W/D** | ARDSLEY-56B | | | | MARCH-31B |
| Aug-60 | W.AUCKLAND-51F | ARDSLEY-56B | NEVILLE HILL-55H | | ARDSLEY-56B | | | | MARCH-31B |
| Nov-60 | W.AUCKLAND-51F | **11/60: TNBY - 51L** | NEVILLE HILL-55H | | ARDSLEY-56B | | | | **11/60: W/D** |

| | 64765 | 64766 | 64767 | 64768 | 64769 | 64770 | 64771 | 64772 | 64773 |
|---|---|---|---|---|---|---|---|---|---|
| Aug-50 | STRATFORD-30A | STRATFORD-30A | STRATFORD-30A | STRATFORD-30A | STRATFORD-30A | PARKESTON-30F | STRATFORD-30A | STRATFORD-30A | STRATFORD-30A |
| Jan-51 | STRATFORD-30A | STRATFORD-30A | **10/50: IPS - 32B** | STRATFORD-30A | STRATFORD-30A | PARKESTON-30F | **10/50: IPS - 32B** | STRATFORD-30A | **10/50: IPS - 32B** |
| Aug-51 | STRATFORD-30A | STRATFORD-30A | **1/51: STRAT - 30A** | STRATFORD-30A | **8/51: DUNF - 62C** | **6/51: STRAT - 30A** | **1/51: NOR - 32A** | STRATFORD-30A | **1/51: STRAT - 30A** |
| Jan-52 | STRATFORD-30A | STRATFORD-30A | STRATFORD-30A | STRATFORD-30A | DUNFERMLINE-62C | STRATFORD-30A | **4/51: STRAT - 30A** | STRATFORD-30A | **8/51: PARKS - 30F** |
| Aug-52 | STRATFORD-30A | STRATFORD-30A | STRATFORD-30A | STRATFORD-30A | DUNFERMLINE-62C | STRATFORD-30A | STRATFORD-30A | STRATFORD-30A | PARKESTON-30F |
| Jan-53 | STRATFORD-30A | STRATFORD-30A | STRATFORD-30A | STRATFORD-30A | DUNFERMLINE-62C | STRATFORD-30A | STRATFORD-30A | STRATFORD-30A | PARKESTON-30F |
| Aug-53 | **7/53: S.BGE - 35C** | STRATFORD-30A | STRATFORD-30A | STRATFORD-30A | DUNFERMLINE-62C | STRATFORD-30A | STRATFORD-30A | STRATFORD-30A | PARKESTON-30F |
| Jan-54 | **10/53: STRAT - 30A** | STRATFORD-30A | STRATFORD-30A | STRATFORD-30A | DUNFERMLINE-62C | STRATFORD-30A | STRATFORD-30A | STRATFORD-30A | PARKESTON-30F |
| Aug-54 | STRATFORD-30A | STRATFORD-30A | STRATFORD-30A | STRATFORD-30A | DUNFERMLINE-62C | STRATFORD-30A | STRATFORD-30A | STRATFORD-30A | PARKESTON-30F |
| Jan-55 | STRATFORD-30A | STRATFORD-30A | STRATFORD-30A | STRATFORD-30A | DUNFERMLINE-62C | STRATFORD-30A | STRATFORD-30A | STRATFORD-30A | PARKESTON-30F |
| Aug-55 | STRATFORD-30A | STRATFORD-30A | STRATFORD-30A | STRATFORD-30A | DUNFERMLINE-62C | STRATFORD-30A | STRATFORD-30A | STRATFORD-30A | PARKESTON-30F |
| Jan-56 | STRATFORD-30A | STRATFORD-30A | STRATFORD-30A | STRATFORD-30A | DUNFERMLINE-62C | STRATFORD-30A | STRATFORD-30A | STRATFORD-30A | PARKESTON-30F |
| Aug-56 | STRATFORD-30A | STRATFORD-30A | STRATFORD-30A | STRATFORD-30A | DUNFERMLINE-62C | STRATFORD-30A | STRATFORD-30A | STRATFORD-30A | PARKESTON-30F |
| Jan-57 | STRATFORD-30A | STRATFORD-30A | STRATFORD-30A | STRATFORD-30A | DUNFERMLINE-62C | STRATFORD-30A | **11/56: PARKS - 30F** | STRATFORD-30A | PARKESTON-30F |
| Aug-57 | STRATFORD-30A | STRATFORD-30A | STRATFORD-30A | STRATFORD-30A | DUNFERMLINE-62C | STRATFORD-30A | PARKESTON-30F | STRATFORD-30A | PARKESTON-30F |
| Jan-58 | STRATFORD-30A | STRATFORD-30A | STRATFORD-30A | STRATFORD-30A | **3/58: MARCH - 31B** | **3/58: MARCH - 31B** | PARKESTON-30F | **3/58: MARCH - 31B** | PARKESTON-30F |
| Aug-58 | STRATFORD-30A | STRATFORD-30A | STRATFORD-30A | STRATFORD-30A | MARCH-31B | MARCH-31B | **5/58: MARCH - 31B** | MARCH-31B | **4/58: STRAT - 30A** |
| Jan-59 | STRATFORD-30A | STRATFORD-30A | STRATFORD-30A | STRATFORD-30A | MARCH-31B | MARCH-31B | MARCH-31B | MARCH-31B | STRATFORD-30A |
| Aug-59 | STRATFORD-30A | STRATFORD-30A | STRATFORD-30A | **5/59: W/D** | MARCH-31B | MARCH-31B | MARCH-31B | MARCH-31B | **8/59: W/D** |
| Nov-59 | STRATFORD-30A | **9/59: W/D** | STRATFORD-30A | | MARCH-31B | MARCH-31B | MARCH-31B | MARCH-31B | |
| Jan-60 | STRATFORD-30A | | STRATFORD-30A | | MARCH-31B | MARCH-31B | MARCH-31B | MARCH-31B | |
| Apr-60 | STRATFORD-30A | | STRATFORD-30A | | **2/60: W/D** | MARCH-31B | W/D | MARCH-31B | |
| Aug-60 | **8/60: W/D** | | STRATFORD-30A | | | MARCH-31B | | MARCH-31B | |
| Nov-60 | | | STRATFORD-30A | | | **11/60: W/D** | | MARCH-31B | |

| | 64774 | 64775 | 64776 | 64777 | 64778 | 64779 | 64780 | 64781 | 64782 |
|---|---|---|---|---|---|---|---|---|---|
| Aug-50 | STRATFORD-30A | STRATFORD-30A | STRATFORD-30A | PARKESTON-30F | W.AUCKLAND-51F | PARKESTON-30F | STRATFORD-30A | STRATFORD-30A | STRATFORD-30A |
| Jan-51 | STRATFORD-30A | STRATFORD-30A | STRATFORD-30A | PARKESTON-30F | W.AUCKLAND-51F | PARKESTON-30F | STRATFORD-30A | **5/51: PARKS - 30F** | STRATFORD-30A |
| Aug-51 | STRATFORD-30A | STRATFORD-30A | STRATFORD-30A | PARKESTON-30F | W.AUCKLAND-51F | PARKESTON-30F | STRATFORD-30A | **6/51: STRAT - 30A** | STRATFORD-30A |
| Jan-52 | STRATFORD-30A | STRATFORD-30A | STRATFORD-30A | PARKESTON-30F | W.AUCKLAND-51F | PARKESTON-30F | STRATFORD-30A | STRATFORD-30A | STRATFORD-30A |
| Aug-52 | STRATFORD-30A | STRATFORD-30A | STRATFORD-30A | PARKESTON-30F | W.AUCKLAND-51F | PARKESTON-30F | STRATFORD-30A | STRATFORD-30A | STRATFORD-30A |
| Jan-53 | STRATFORD-30A | STRATFORD-30A | STRATFORD-30A | PARKESTON-30F | W.AUCKLAND-51F | PARKESTON-30F | STRATFORD-30A | STRATFORD-30A | STRATFORD-30A |
| Aug-53 | STRATFORD-30A | STRATFORD-30A | STRATFORD-30A | PARKESTON-30F | W.AUCKLAND-51F | PARKESTON-30F | STRATFORD-30A | STRATFORD-30A | STRATFORD-30A |
| Jan-54 | STRATFORD-30A | STRATFORD-30A | STRATFORD-30A | PARKESTON-30F | W.AUCKLAND-51F | PARKESTON-30F | STRATFORD-30A | STRATFORD-30A | STRATFORD-30A |
| Aug-54 | STRATFORD-30A | STRATFORD-30A | STRATFORD-30A | PARKESTON-30F | W.AUCKLAND-51F | PARKESTON-30F | STRATFORD-30A | STRATFORD-30A | STRATFORD-30A |
| Jan-55 | STRATFORD-30A | STRATFORD-30A | STRATFORD-30A | PARKESTON-30F | W.AUCKLAND-51F | PARKESTON-30F | STRATFORD-30A | STRATFORD-30A | STRATFORD-30A |
| Aug-55 | STRATFORD-30A | STRATFORD-30A | STRATFORD-30A | PARKESTON-30F | W.AUCKLAND-51F | PARKESTON-30F | STRATFORD-30A | STRATFORD-30A | STRATFORD-30A |
| Jan-56 | STRATFORD-30A | STRATFORD-30A | STRATFORD-30A | PARKESTON-30F | W.AUCKLAND-51F | PARKESTON-30F | STRATFORD-30A | STRATFORD-30A | STRATFORD-30A |
| Aug-56 | STRATFORD-30A | STRATFORD-30A | STRATFORD-30A | PARKESTON-30F | W.AUCKLAND-51F | PARKESTON-30F | STRATFORD-30A | STRATFORD-30A | STRATFORD-30A |
| Jan-57 | STRATFORD-30A | STRATFORD-30A | **11/56: PARKS - 30F** | PARKESTON-30F | W.AUCKLAND-51F | PARKESTON-30F | STRATFORD-30A | STRATFORD-30A | STRATFORD-30A |
| Aug-57 | STRATFORD-30A | STRATFORD-30A | PARKESTON-30F | PARKESTON-30F | W.AUCKLAND-51F | PARKESTON-30F | STRATFORD-30A | STRATFORD-30A | STRATFORD-30A |
| Jan-58 | **3/58: MARCH - 31B** | STRATFORD-30A | PARKESTON-30F | PARKESTON-30F | W.AUCKLAND-51F | PARKESTON-30F | STRATFORD-30A | STRATFORD-30A | STRATFORD-30A |
| Aug-58 | MARCH-31B | STRATFORD-30A | PARKESTON-30F | PARKESTON-30F | W.AUCKLAND-51F | **6/58: MARCH - 31B** | STRATFORD-30A | STRATFORD-30A | **5/58: MARCH - 31B** |
| Jan-59 | MARCH-31B | STRATFORD-30A | PARKESTON-30F | PARKESTON-30F | W.AUCKLAND-51F | MARCH-31B | STRATFORD-30A | STRATFORD-30A | MARCH-31B |
| Aug-59 | MARCH-31B | STRATFORD-30A | **8/59: W/D** | PARKESTON-30F | W.AUCKLAND-51F | MARCH-31B | STRATFORD-30A | STRATFORD-30A | MARCH-31B |
| Nov-59 | MARCH-31B | STRATFORD-30A | | **10/59: STRAT - 30A** | W.AUCKLAND-51F | MARCH-31B | STRATFORD-30A | STRATFORD-30A | MARCH-31B |
| Jan-60 | MARCH-31B | STRATFORD-30A | | **12/59: W/D** | W.AUCKLAND-51F | MARCH-31B | **12/59: W/D** | STRATFORD-30A | MARCH-31B |
| Apr-60 | **3/60: W/D** | STRATFORD-30A | | | W.AUCKLAND-51F | MARCH-31B | | **3/60: W/D** | **3/60: W/D** |
| Aug-60 | | STRATFORD-30A | | | W.AUCKLAND-51F | MARCH-31B | | | |
| Nov-60 | | **9/60: W/D** | | | **9/60: W/D** | MARCH-31B | | | |

| | 64783 | 64784 | 64785 | 64786 | 64787 | 64788 | 64789 | 64790 | 64791 |
|---|---|---|---|---|---|---|---|---|---|
| Aug-50 | STRATFORD-30A | NORWICH-32A | IPSWICH-32B | DUNDEE-62B | PARKESTON-30F | PARKESTON-30F | LINCOLN-40A | DUNDEE-62B | NEVILLE HILL-50B |
| Jan-51 | STRATFORD-30A | NORWICH-32A | IPSWICH-32B | DUNDEE-62B | **5/51: ARDS - 37A** | PARKESTON-30F | LINCOLN-40A | DUNDEE-62B | NEVILLE HILL-50B |
| Aug-51 | STRATFORD-30A | **9/51: STRAT - 30A** | IPSWICH-32B | DUNDEE-62B | **6/51: PARKS - 30F** | PARKESTON-30F | LINCOLN-40A | DUNDEE-62B | NEVILLE HILL-50B |
| Jan-52 | STRATFORD-30A | STRATFORD-30A | IPSWICH-32B | DUNDEE-62B | PARKESTON-30F | PARKESTON-30F | LINCOLN-40A | DUNDEE-62B | NEVILLE HILL-50B |
| Aug-52 | STRATFORD-30A | STRATFORD-30A | IPSWICH-32B | DUNDEE-62B | PARKESTON-30F | PARKESTON-30F | **10/52: S.BGE - 35C** | DUNDEE-62B | NEVILLE HILL-50B |
| Jan-53 | STRATFORD-30A | STRATFORD-30A | IPSWICH-32B | DUNDEE-62B | PARKESTON-30F | PARKESTON-30F | SPITAL BRIDGE-35C | DUNDEE-62B | NEVILLE HILL-50B |
| Aug-53 | STRATFORD-30A | STRATFORD-30A | IPSWICH-32B | DUNDEE-62B | PARKESTON-30F | PARKESTON-30F | SPITAL BRIDGE-35C | DUNDEE-62B | NEVILLE HILL-50B |
| Jan-54 | STRATFORD-30A | STRATFORD-30A | IPSWICH-32B | DUNDEE-62B | PARKESTON-30F | PARKESTON-30F | SPITAL BRIDGE-35C | DUNDEE-62B | NEVILLE HILL-50B |
| Aug-54 | STRATFORD-30A | STRATFORD-30A | IPSWICH-32B | DUNDEE-62B | PARKESTON-30F | PARKESTON-30F | SPITAL BRIDGE-35C | DUNDEE-62B | NEVILLE HILL-50B |
| Jan-55 | STRATFORD-30A | STRATFORD-30A | IPSWICH-32B | DUNDEE-62B | PARKESTON-30F | PARKESTON-30F | SPITAL BRIDGE-35C | DUNDEE-62B | NEVILLE HILL-50B |
| Aug-55 | **8/55: S.BGE - 35C** | STRATFORD-30A | IPSWICH-32B | DUNDEE-62B | PARKESTON-30F | PARKESTON-30F | SPITAL BRIDGE-35C | DUNDEE-62B | NEVILLE HILL-50B |
| Jan-56 | **9/55: STRAT - 30A** | STRATFORD-30A | IPSWICH-32B | DUNDEE-62B | PARKESTON-30F | PARKESTON-30F | SPITAL BRIDGE-35C | DUNDEE-62B | NEVILLE HILL-50B |
| Aug-56 | STRATFORD-30A | STRATFORD-30A | IPSWICH-32B | DUNDEE-62B | PARKESTON-30F | PARKESTON-30F | SPITAL BRIDGE-35C | DUNDEE-62B | NEVILLE HILL-50B |
| Jan-57 | STRATFORD-30A | STRATFORD-30A | IPSWICH-32B | DUNDEE-62B | PARKESTON-30F | PARKESTON-30F | SPITAL BRIDGE-35C | DUNDEE-62B | NEVILLE HILL-50B |
| Aug-57 | STRATFORD-30A | STRATFORD-30A | IPSWICH-32B | DUNDEE-62B | PARKESTON-30F | PARKESTON-30F | SPITAL BRIDGE-35C | DUNDEE-62B | **9/57: BRAD - 56G** |
| Jan-58 | STRATFORD-30A | STRATFORD-30A | IPSWICH-32B | DUNDEE-62B | **3/58: STRAT - 30A** | **3/58: STRAT - 30A** | SPITAL BRIDGE-35C | DUNDEE-62B | **2/58: LOW M - 56F** |
| Aug-58 | STRATFORD-30A | STRATFORD-30A | IPSWICH-32B | DUNDEE-62B | STRATFORD-30A | STRATFORD-30A | SPITAL BRIDGE-31F | DUNDEE-62B | LOWMOOR-56F |
| Jan-59 | STRATFORD-30A | STRATFORD-30A | IPSWICH-32B | DUNDEE-62B | STRATFORD-30A | STRATFORD-30A | SPITAL BRIDGE-31F | DUNDEE-62B | LOWMOOR-56F |
| Aug-59 | STRATFORD-30A | STRATFORD-30A | **6/59: W/D** | DUNDEE-62B | **6/59: W/D** | **6/59: W/D** | SPITAL BRIDGE-31F | **8/59: TH JN - 62A** | LOWMOOR-56F |
| Nov-59 | STRATFORD-30A | STRATFORD-30A | | DUNDEE-62B | | | SPITAL BRIDGE-31F | THORNTON JCN-62A | LOWMOOR-56F |
| Jan-60 | STRATFORD-30A | STRATFORD-30A | | DUNDEE-62B | | | **2/60: MARCH - 31B** | THORNTON JCN-62A | LOWMOOR-56F |
| Apr-60 | STRATFORD-30A | STRATFORD-30A | | DUNDEE-62B | | | MARCH-31B | THORNTON JCN-62A | LOWMOOR-56F |
| Aug-60 | STRATFORD-30A | **8/60: W/D** | | DUNDEE-62B | | | **6/60: W/D** | THORNTON JCN-62A | LOWMOOR-56F |
| Nov-60 | **11/60: W/D** | | | DUNDEE-62B | | | | THORNTON JCN-62A | LOWMOOR-56F |

| | 64792 | 64793 | 64794 | 64795 | 64796 | 64797 | 64798 | 64799 | 64800 |
|---|---|---|---|---|---|---|---|---|---|
| **Aug-50** | DUNDEE - 62B | IPSWICH - 32B | EDINBURGH (SM) - 64A | FERRYHILL - 61B | ARDSLEY - 37A | NORWICH - 32A | WOODFORD HALSE - 38E | ARDSLEY - 37A | IPSWICH - 32B |
| **Jan-51** | DUNDEE - 62B | IPSWICH - 32B | EDINBURGH (SM) - 64A | FERRYHILL - 61B | ARDSLEY - 37A | NORWICH - 32A | **9/50: ANN - 38B** | ARDSLEY - 37A | IPSWICH - 32B |
| **Aug-51** | DUNDEE - 62B | IPSWICH - 32B | EDINBURGH (SM) - 64A | FERRYHILL - 61B | ARDSLEY - 37A | **9/51: LOW - 32C** | **10/50: COLW - 38A** | ARDSLEY - 37A | IPSWICH - 32B |
| **Jan-52** | DUNDEE - 62B | IPSWICH - 32B | EDINBURGH (SM) - 64A | FERRYHILL - 61B | ARDSLEY - 37A | **3/52: NOR - 32A** | COLWICK - 38A | ARDSLEY - 37A | IPSWICH - 32B |
| **Aug-52** | DUNDEE - 62B | IPSWICH - 32B | EDINBURGH (SM) - 64A | FERRYHILL - 61B | ARDSLEY - 37A | **9/52: LOW - 32C** | COLWICK - 38A | ARDSLEY - 37A | IPSWICH - 32B |
| **Jan-53** | DUNDEE - 62B | IPSWICH - 32B | EDINBURGH (SM) - 64A | FERRYHILL - 61B | ARDSLEY - 37A | **1/53: NOR - 32A** | COLWICK - 38A | ARDSLEY - 37A | IPSWICH - 32B |
| **Aug-53** | DUNDEE - 62B | IPSWICH - 32B | **5/53: BATH - 64F** | FERRYHILL - 61B | ARDSLEY - 37A | NORWICH - 32A | COLWICK - 38A | ARDSLEY - 37A | IPSWICH - 32B |
| **Jan-54** | DUNDEE - 62B | IPSWICH - 32B | **3/54: ST. M - 64A** | FERRYHILL - 61B | ARDSLEY - 37A | NORWICH - 32A | COLWICK - 38A | **11/53: TUX - 40D** | IPSWICH - 32B |
| **Aug-54** | DUNDEE - 62B | IPSWICH - 32B | EDINBURGH (SM) - 64A | FERRYHILL - 61B | ARDSLEY - 37A | NORWICH - 32A | COLWICK - 38A | TUXFORD - 40D | IPSWICH - 32B |
| **Jan-55** | DUNDEE - 62B | IPSWICH - 32B | EDINBURGH (SM) - 64A | FERRYHILL - 61B | ARDSLEY - 37A | NORWICH - 32A | COLWICK - 38A | **1/55: STRAT - 30A** | IPSWICH - 32B |
| **Aug-55** | DUNDEE - 62B | IPSWICH - 32B | EDINBURGH (SM) - 64A | FERRYHILL - 61B | ARDSLEY - 37A | NORWICH - 32A | COLWICK - 38A | STRATFORD - 30A | IPSWICH - 32B |
| **Jan-56** | DUNDEE - 62B | IPSWICH - 32B | EDINBURGH (SM) - 64A | FERRYHILL - 61B | ARDSLEY - 37A | NORWICH - 32A | COLWICK - 38A | STRATFORD - 30A | IPSWICH - 32B |
| **Aug-56** | DUNDEE - 62B | IPSWICH - 32B | EDINBURGH (SM) - 64A | FERRYHILL - 61B | ARDSLEY - 56B | NORWICH - 32A | COLWICK - 38A | STRATFORD - 30A | IPSWICH - 32B |
| **Jan-57** | DUNDEE - 62B | IPSWICH - 32B | EDINBURGH (SM) - 64A | FERRYHILL - 61B | ARDSLEY - 56B | NORWICH - 32A | COLWICK - 38A | **11/56: NEW E - 35A** | IPSWICH - 32B |
| **Aug-57** | DUNDEE - 62B | IPSWICH - 32B | EDINBURGH (SM) - 64A | FERRYHILL - 61B | **6/57: BRAD - 56G** | **10/57: LOW - 32C** | COLWICK - 38A | **4/57: STRAT - 30A** | IPSWICH - 32B |
| **Jan-58** | DUNDEE - 62B | IPSWICH - 32B | EDINBURGH (SM) - 64A | FERRYHILL - 61B | **2/58: LOW M - 56F** | LOWESTOFT - 32C | **11/57: ANN - 38B** | STRATFORD - 30A | IPSWICH - 32B |
| **Aug-58** | DUNDEE - 62B | IPSWICH - 32B | **9/58: DALRY - 64C** | FERRYHILL - 61B | LOWMOOR - 56F | LOWESTOFT - 32C | ANNESLEY - 16D | STRATFORD - 30A | IPSWICH - 32B |
| **Jan-59** | DUNDEE - 62B | IPSWICH - 32B | DALRYRD - 64C | **2/59: ST.M - 64A** | LOWMOOR - 56F | LOWESTOFT - 32C | ANNESLEY - 16D | STRATFORD - 30A | IPSWICH - 32B |
| **Aug-59** | **8/59: TH JN - 62A** | IPSWICH - 32B | DALRYRD - 64C | EDINBURGH (SM) - 64A | **6/59: ARDS - 56B** | LOWESTOFT - 32C | ANNESLEY - 16D | **7/59: W/D** | IPSWICH - 32B |
| **Nov-59** | THORNTON JCN - 62A | **11/59: W/D** | DALRYRD - 64C | EDINBURGH (SM) - 64A | ARDSLEY - 56B | **9/59: W/D** | ANNESLEY - 16D | | **10/59: MARCH - 31B** |
| **Jan-60** | THORNTON JCN - 62A | | DALRYRD - 64C | EDINBURGH (SM) - 64A | ARDSLEY - 56B | | ANNESLEY - 16D | | MARCH - 31B |
| **Apr-60** | THORNTON JCN - 62A | | DALRYRD - 64C | EDINBURGH (SM) - 64A | ARDSLEY - 56B | | ANNESLEY - 16D | | **2/60: W/D** |
| **Aug-60** | THORNTON JCN - 62A | | DALRYRD - 64C | EDINBURGH (SM) - 64A | ARDSLEY - 56B | | ANNESLEY - 16D | | |
| **Nov-60** | THORNTON JCN - 62A | | DALRYRD - 64C | EDINBURGH (SM) - 64A | ARDSLEY - 56B | | ANNESLEY - 16D | | |

| | 64801 | 64802 | 64803 | 64804 | 64805 | 64806 | 64807 | 64808 | 64809 |
|---|---|---|---|---|---|---|---|---|---|
| **Aug-50** | ARDSLEY - 37A | NORWICH - 32A | IPSWICH - 32B | LINCOLN - 40A | COLWICK - 38A | ARDSLEY - 37A | COLWICK - 38A | DARNALL - 39B | DARNALL - 39B |
| **Jan-51** | ARDSLEY - 37A | NORWICH - 32A | IPSWICH - 32B | LINCOLN - 40A | COLWICK - 38A | ARDSLEY - 37A | COLWICK - 38A | DARNALL - 39B | DARNALL - 39B |
| **Aug-51** | ARDSLEY - 37A | NORWICH - 32A | **9/51: STRAT - 30A** | LINCOLN - 40A | COLWICK - 38A | ARDSLEY - 37A | COLWICK - 38A | DARNALL - 39B | DARNALL - 39B |
| **Jan-52** | ARDSLEY - 37A | NORWICH - 32A | STRATFORD - 30A | LINCOLN - 40A | COLWICK - 38A | ARDSLEY - 37A | COLWICK - 38A | DARNALL - 39B | DARNALL - 39B |
| **Aug-52** | ARDSLEY - 37A | NORWICH - 32A | STRATFORD - 30A | LINCOLN - 40A | COLWICK - 38A | ARDSLEY - 37A | COLWICK - 38A | DARNALL - 39B | DARNALL - 39B |
| **Jan-53** | ARDSLEY - 37A | NORWICH - 32A | STRATFORD - 30A | LINCOLN - 40A | COLWICK - 38A | ARDSLEY - 37A | COLWICK - 38A | DARNALL - 39B | DARNALL - 39B |
| **Aug-53** | ARDSLEY - 37A | NORWICH - 32A | STRATFORD - 30A | LINCOLN - 40A | COLWICK - 38A | ARDSLEY - 37A | COLWICK - 38A | DARNALL - 39B | DARNALL - 39B |
| **Jan-54** | ARDSLEY - 37A | NORWICH - 32A | STRATFORD - 30A | LINCOLN - 40A | **11/53: TUX - 40D** | ARDSLEY - 37A | **11/53: TUX - 40D** | DARNALL - 39B | DARNALL - 39B |
| **Aug-54** | ARDSLEY - 37A | NORWICH - 32A | STRATFORD - 30A | LINCOLN - 40A | TUXFORD - 40D | ARDSLEY - 37A | TUXFORD - 40D | DARNALL - 39B | DARNALL - 39B |
| **Jan-55** | ARDSLEY - 37A | NORWICH - 32A | STRATFORD - 30A | LINCOLN - 40A | **1/55: STRAT - 30A** | ARDSLEY - 37A | **1/55: STRAT - 30A** | DARNALL - 39B | DARNALL - 39B |
| **Aug-55** | ARDSLEY - 37A | NORWICH - 32A | **5/55: CAMB - 31A** | LINCOLN - 40A | STRATFORD - 30A | ARDSLEY - 37A | STRATFORD - 30A | DARNALL - 39B | DARNALL - 39B |
| **Jan-56** | ARDSLEY - 37A | **6/56: YAR (B) - 32F** | CAMBRIDGE - 31A | LINCOLN - 40A | STRATFORD - 30A | ARDSLEY - 37A | STRATFORD - 30A | DARNALL - 41A | DARNALL - 41A |
| **Aug-56** | **5/56: BRAD - 37C** | **8/56: NOR - 32A** | CAMBRIDGE - 31A | LINCOLN - 40A | STRATFORD - 30A | ARDSLEY - 56B | STRATFORD - 30A | DARNALL - 41A | DARNALL - 41A |
| **Jan-57** | BRADFORD - 56G | **2/57: M. CONS - 32G** | CAMBRIDGE - 31A | LINCOLN - 40A | **11/56: NEW E - 35A** | ARDSLEY - 56B | STRATFORD - 30A | DARNALL - 41A | DARNALL - 41A |
| **Aug-57** | BRADFORD - 56G | **10/57: NOR - 32A** | CAMBRIDGE - 31A | LINCOLN - 40A | **4/57: STRAT - 30A** | ARDSLEY - 56B | STRATFORD - 30A | DARNALL - 41A | DARNALL - 41A |
| **Jan-58** | **2/58: LOW M - 56F** | NORWICH - 32A | CAMBRIDGE - 31A | **11/57: STRAT - 30A** | STRATFORD - 30A | ARDSLEY - 56B | STRATFORD - 30A | DARNALL - 41A | **11/57: GORT - 39A** |
| **Aug-58** | LOWMOOR - 56F | **12/58: LINC - 40A** | CAMBRIDGE - 31A | **10/58: MARCH - 31B** | STRATFORD - 30A | ARDSLEY - 56B | STRATFORD - 30A | DARNALL - 41A | GORTON - 9G |
| **Jan-59** | LOWMOOR - 56F | **1/59: COLW - 40E** | CAMBRIDGE - 31A | **12/58: DARN - 41A** | STRATFORD - 30A | ARDSLEY - 56B | **12/58: DARN - 41A** | DARNALL - 41A | GORTON - 9G |
| **Aug-59** | LOWMOOR - 56F | COLWICK - 40E | CAMBRIDGE - 31A | DARNALL - 41A | STRATFORD - 30A | ARDSLEY - 56B | DARNALL - 41A | DARNALL - 41A | GORTON - 9G |
| **Nov-59** | LOWMOOR - 56F | COLWICK - 40E | **9/59: W/D** | DARNALL - 41A | **10/59: W/D** | **11/59: HTN - 52B** | DARNALL - 41A | DARNALL - 41A | GORTON - 9G |
| **Jan-60** | LOWMOOR - 56F | COLWICK - 40E | | DARNALL - 41A | | HEATON - 52B | DARNALL - 41A | DARNALL - 41A | GORTON - 9G |
| **Apr-60** | LOWMOOR - 56F | COLWICK - 40E | | **3/60: COLW - 40E** | | HEATON - 52B | **3/60: W/D** | DARNALL - 41A | GORTON - 9G |
| **Aug-60** | LOWMOOR - 56F | **8/60: W/D** | | COLWICK - 40E | | HEATON - 52B | | DARNALL - 41A | **6/60: WOOD - 2F** |
| **Nov-60** | LOWMOOR - 56F | | | COLWICK - 40E | | HEATON - 52B | | DARNALL - 41A | WOODFORD HALSE - 2F |

| | 64810 | 64811 | 64812 | 64813 | 64814 | 64815 | 64816 | 64817 | 64818 |
|---|---|---|---|---|---|---|---|---|---|
| **Aug-50** | GORTON - 39A | ARDSLEY - 37A | BLAYDON - 52C | TWEEDMOUTH - 52D | BLAYDON - 52C | ALNMOUTH - 52D | BLAYDON - 52C | HEATON - 52B | STARBECK - 50D |
| **Jan-51** | GORTON - 39A | ARDSLEY - 37A | BLAYDON - 52C | TWEEDMOUTH - 52D | BLAYDON - 52C | ALNMOUTH - 52D | BLAYDON - 52C | **11/50: DARL - 51A** | STARBECK - 50D |
| **Aug-51** | GORTON - 39A | ARDSLEY - 37A | BLAYDON - 52C | TWEEDMOUTH - 52D | BLAYDON - 52C | ALNMOUTH - 52D | BLAYDON - 52C | **1/51: MBRO - 51D** | STARBECK - 50D |
| **Jan-52** | GORTON - 39A | ARDSLEY - 37A | BLAYDON - 52C | TWEEDMOUTH - 52D | BLAYDON - 52C | ALNMOUTH - 52D | BLAYDON - 52C | MIDDLESBROUGH - 51D | STARBECK - 50D |
| **Aug-52** | GORTON - 39A | ARDSLEY - 37A | BLAYDON - 52C | TWEEDMOUTH - 52D | BLAYDON - 52C | ALNMOUTH - 52D | BLAYDON - 52C | MIDDLESBROUGH - 51D | STARBECK - 50D |
| **Jan-53** | GORTON - 39A | ARDSLEY - 37A | **1/53: ALS - 52C** | TWEEDMOUTH - 52D | BLAYDON - 52C | ALNMOUTH - 52D | BLAYDON - 52C | **10/52: W. HPL - 51C** | STARBECK - 50D |
| **Aug-53** | GORTON - 39A | ARDSLEY - 37A | **5/53: BLAY - 52C** | TWEEDMOUTH - 52D | BLAYDON - 52C | ALNMOUTH - 52D | BLAYDON - 52C | W. HARTLEPOOL - 51C | STARBECK - 50D |
| **Jan-54** | GORTON - 39A | ARDSLEY - 37A | BLAYDON - 52C | TWEEDMOUTH - 52D | BLAYDON - 52C | ALNMOUTH - 52D | BLAYDON - 52C | W. HARTLEPOOL - 51C | STARBECK - 50D |
| **Aug-54** | **8/54: DARN - 39B** | ARDSLEY - 37A | BLAYDON - 52C | TWEEDMOUTH - 52D | BLAYDON - 52C | ALNMOUTH - 52D | BLAYDON - 52C | **10/54: NORTH - 51J** | STARBECK - 50D |
| **Jan-55** | **11/54: STRAT - 30A** | ARDSLEY - 37A | BLAYDON - 52C | TWEEDMOUTH - 52D | BLAYDON - 52C | ALNMOUTH - 52D | BLAYDON - 52C | **3/55: W. AUCK - 51F** | STARBECK - 50D |
| **Aug-55** | **3/55: PARKS - 30F** | ARDSLEY - 37A | BLAYDON - 52C | TWEEDMOUTH - 52D | BLAYDON - 52C | ALNMOUTH - 52D | BLAYDON - 52C | **9/55: SUND - 54A** | STARBECK - 50D |
| **Jan-56** | **12/55: DCTR - 36A** | ARDSLEY - 37A | BLAYDON - 52C | TWEEDMOUTH - 52D | BLAYDON - 52C | ALNMOUTH - 52D | BLAYDON - 52C | SUNDERLAND - 54A | STARBECK - 50D |
| **Aug-56** | DONCASTER - 36A | ARDSLEY - 56B | BLAYDON - 52C | TWEEDMOUTH - 52D | BLAYDON - 52C | ALNMOUTH - 52D | BLAYDON - 52C | SUNDERLAND - 54A | STARBECK - 50D |
| **Jan-57** | DONCASTER - 36A | ARDSLEY - 56B | BLAYDON - 52C | TWEEDMOUTH - 52D | BLAYDON - 52C | **11/56: BLAY - 52C** | BLAYDON - 52C | SUNDERLAND - 54A | STARBECK - 50D |
| **Aug-57** | DONCASTER - 36A | ARDSLEY - 56B | BLAYDON - 52C | TWEEDMOUTH - 52D | BLAYDON - 52C | BLAYDON - 52C | BLAYDON - 52C | SUNDERLAND - 54A | STARBECK - 50D |
| **Jan-58** | DONCASTER - 36A | ARDSLEY - 56B | BLAYDON - 52C | TWEEDMOUTH - 52D | BLAYDON - 52C | BLAYDON - 52C | BLAYDON - 52C | SUNDERLAND - 54A | STARBECK - 50D |
| **Aug-58** | DONCASTER - 36A | ARDSLEY - 56B | BLAYDON - 52C | TWEEDMOUTH - 52D | BLAYDON - 52C | BLAYDON - 52C | BLAYDON - 52C | SUNDERLAND - 54A | STARBECK - 50D |
| **Jan-59** | DONCASTER - 36A | ARDSLEY - 56B | BLAYDON - 52C | TWEEDMOUTH - 52D | BLAYDON - 52C | BLAYDON - 52C | BLAYDON - 52C | **2/59: LOW M - 56F** | **6/59: SELBY - 50C** |
| **Aug-59** | DONCASTER - 36A | ARDSLEY - 56B | **6/59: GHD - 52A** | TWEEDMOUTH - 52D | **6/59: GHD - 52A** | BLAYDON - 52C | BLAYDON - 52C | LOWMOOR - 56F | **9/59: YORK - 50A** |
| **Nov-59** | DONCASTER - 36A | ARDSLEY - 56B | GATESHEAD - 52A | TWEEDMOUTH - 52D | GATESHEAD - 52A | BLAYDON - 52C | BLAYDON - 52C | LOWMOOR - 56F | **11/59: TNBY - 51L** |
| **Jan-60** | DONCASTER - 36A | ARDSLEY - 56B | GATESHEAD - 52A | TWEEDMOUTH - 52D | GATESHEAD - 52A | BLAYDON - 52C | BLAYDON - 52C | LOWMOOR - 56F | THORNABY - 51L |
| **Apr-60** | DONCASTER - 36A | ARDSLEY - 56B | GATESHEAD - 52A | TWEEDMOUTH - 52D | GATESHEAD - 52A | BLAYDON - 52C | BLAYDON - 52C | LOWMOOR - 56F | THORNABY - 51L |
| **Aug-60** | DONCASTER - 36A | ARDSLEY - 56B | GATESHEAD - 52A | TWEEDMOUTH - 52D | GATESHEAD - 52A | **10/60: W. HPL - 51C** | BLAYDON - 52C | LOWMOOR - 56F | THORNABY - 51L |
| **Nov-60** | **10/60: RET - 36E** | ARDSLEY - 56B | GATESHEAD - 52A | TWEEDMOUTH - 52D | GATESHEAD - 52A | W. HARTLEPOOL - 51C | BLAYDON - 52C | LOWMOOR - 56F | THORNABY - 51L |

| | 64819 | 64820 | 64821 | 64822 | 64823 | 64824 | 64825 | 64826 | 64827 |
|---|---|---|---|---|---|---|---|---|---|
| **Aug-50** | NEVILLE HILL - 50B | IPSWICH - 32B | MIDDLESBROUGH - 51D | DUNDEE - 62B | TRAFFORD PARK - 9E | GORTON - 39A | ARDSLEY - 37A | IPSWICH - 32B | COLWICK - 38A |
| **Jan-51** | NEVILLE HILL - 50B | **1/51: ARDS - 37A** | MIDDLESBROUGH - 51D | DUNDEE - 62B | **3/51: COLW - 38A** | GORTON - 39A | ARDSLEY - 37A | IPSWICH - 32B | COLWICK - 38A |
| **Aug-51** | NEVILLE HILL - 50B | ARDSLEY - 37A | MIDDLESBROUGH - 51D | DUNDEE - 62B | COLWICK - 38A | **4/51: DARN - 41A** | ARDSLEY - 37A | IPSWICH - 32B | COLWICK - 38A |
| **Jan-52** | NEVILLE HILL - 50B | ARDSLEY - 37A | MIDDLESBROUGH - 51D | DUNDEE - 62B | COLWICK - 38A | DARNALL - 39B | ARDSLEY - 37A | IPSWICH - 32B | COLWICK - 38A |
| **Aug-52** | NEVILLE HILL - 50B | ARDSLEY - 37A | MIDDLESBROUGH - 51D | DUNDEE - 62B | COLWICK - 38A | DARNALL - 39B | ARDSLEY - 37A | IPSWICH - 32B | COLWICK - 38A |
| **Jan-53** | NEVILLE HILL - 50B | ARDSLEY - 37A | MIDDLESBROUGH - 51D | DUNDEE - 62B | COLWICK - 38A | DARNALL - 39B | ARDSLEY - 37A | IPSWICH - 32B | COLWICK - 38A |
| **Aug-53** | NEVILLE HILL - 50B | ARDSLEY - 37A | **10/53: STAR - 50D** | DUNDEE - 62B | COLWICK - 38A | DARNALL - 39B | ARDSLEY - 37A | IPSWICH - 32B | COLWICK - 38A |
| **Jan-54** | NEVILLE HILL - 50B | ARDSLEY - 37A | STARBECK - 50D | DUNDEE - 62B | COLWICK - 38A | DARNALL - 39B | ARDSLEY - 37A | IPSWICH - 32B | COLWICK - 38A |
| **Aug-54** | **6/54: DAIRY - 53A** | ARDSLEY - 37A | STARBECK - 50D | DUNDEE - 62B | COLWICK - 38A | DARNALL - 39B | ARDSLEY - 37A | IPSWICH - 32B | COLWICK - 38A |
| **Jan-55** | DAIRYCOATES - 53A | ARDSLEY - 37A | STARBECK - 50D | DUNDEE - 62B | COLWICK - 38A | DARNALL - 39B | ARDSLEY - 37A | IPSWICH - 32B | COLWICK - 38A |
| **Aug-55** | DAIRYCOATES - 53A | ARDSLEY - 37A | STARBECK - 50D | DUNDEE - 62B | COLWICK - 38A | DARNALL - 39B | ARDSLEY - 37A | IPSWICH - 32B | COLWICK - 38A |
| **Jan-56** | DAIRYCOATES - 53A | ARDSLEY - 37A | STARBECK - 50D | DUNDEE - 62B | COLWICK - 38A | DARNALL - 41A | ARDSLEY - 37A | IPSWICH - 32B | COLWICK - 38A |
| **Aug-56** | DAIRYCOATES - 53A | ARDSLEY - 56B | STARBECK - 50D | DUNDEE - 62B | COLWICK - 38A | DARNALL - 41A | ARDSLEY - 56B | IPSWICH - 32B | COLWICK - 38A |
| **Jan-57** | DAIRYCOATES - 53A | ARDSLEY - 56B | STARBECK - 50D | DUNDEE - 62B | COLWICK - 38A | DARNALL - 41A | ARDSLEY - 56B | IPSWICH - 32B | COLWICK - 38A |
| **Aug-57** | DAIRYCOATES - 53A | ARDSLEY - 56B | STARBECK - 50D | DUNDEE - 62B | COLWICK - 38A | DARNALL - 41A | ARDSLEY - 56B | IPSWICH - 32B | COLWICK - 38A |
| **Jan-58** | DAIRYCOATES - 53A | ARDSLEY - 56B | STARBECK - 50D | DUNDEE - 62B | COLWICK - 38A | **11/57: GORT - 39A** | ARDSLEY - 56B | IPSWICH - 32B | COLWICK - 38A |
| **Aug-58** | DAIRYCOATES - 53A | ARDSLEY - 56B | STARBECK - 50D | DUNDEE - 62B | **10/58: BOST - 40F** | GORTON - 9G | ARDSLEY - 56B | IPSWICH - 32B | COLWICK - 40E |
| **Jan-59** | DAIRYCOATES - 53A | ARDSLEY - 56B | STARBECK - 50D | DUNDEE - 62B | BOSTON - 40F | GORTON - 9G | ARDSLEY - 56B | IPSWICH - 32B | **3/59: DCTR - 36A** |
| **Aug-59** | DAIRYCOATES - 53A | ARDSLEY - 56B | **9/59: YORK - 50A** | DUNDEE - 62B | BOSTON - 40F | GORTON - 9G | ARDSLEY - 56B | IPSWICH - 32B | DONCASTER - 36A |
| **Nov-59** | DAIRYCOATES - 53A | ARDSLEY - 56B | **12/59: TNBY - 51L** | DUNDEE - 62B | **10/59: COLW - 40E** | GORTON - 9G | ARDSLEY - 56B | **10/59: MARCH - 31B** | DONCASTER - 36A |
| **Jan-60** | DAIRYCOATES - 53A | ARDSLEY - 56B | THORNABY - 51L | DUNDEE - 62B | COLWICK - 40E | GORTON - 9G | **12/59: SUND - 52G** | MARCH - 31B | DONCASTER - 36A |
| **Apr-60** | DAIRYCOATES - 50B | ARDSLEY - 56B | THORNABY - 51L | DUNDEE - 62B | COLWICK - 40E | **4/60: W/D** | SUNDERLAND - 52G | **2/60: W/D** | **2/60: W/D** |
| **Aug-60** | DAIRYCOATES - 50B | ARDSLEY - 56B | THORNABY - 51L | DUNDEE - 62B | COLWICK - 40E | | SUNDERLAND - 52G | | |
| **Nov-60** | DAIRYCOATES - 50B | ARDSLEY - 56B | THORNABY - 51L | DUNDEE - 62B | COLWICK - 40E | | SUNDERLAND - 52G | | |

| | 64828 | 64829 | 64830 | 64831 | 64832 | 64833 | 64834 | 64835 | 64836 |
|---|---|---|---|---|---|---|---|---|---|
| Aug-50 | COLWICK-38A | IPSWICH-32B | RETFORD-36E | COLWICK-38A | COLWICK-38A | NORWICH-32A | IPSWICH-32B | DONCASTER-36A | ARDSLEY-37A |
| Jan-51 | COLWICK-38A | IPSWICH-32B | RETFORD-36E | **4/51: ARDS - 37A** | COLWICK-38A | **1/51: ARDS - 37A** | IPSWICH-32B | DONCASTER-36A | ARDSLEY-37A |
| Aug-51 | COLWICK-38A | IPSWICH-32B | RETFORD-36E | ARDSLEY-37A | COLWICK-38A | ARDSLEY-37A | IPSWICH-32B | **9/51: N. HILL - 50B** | ARDSLEY-37A |
| Jan-52 | COLWICK-38A | IPSWICH-32B | RETFORD-36E | ARDSLEY-37A | COLWICK-38A | ARDSLEY-37A | IPSWICH-32B | NEVILLE HILL-50B | ARDSLEY-37A |
| Aug-52 | COLWICK-38A | IPSWICH-32B | RETFORD-36E | ARDSLEY-37A | COLWICK-38A | ARDSLEY-37A | IPSWICH-32B | NEVILLE HILL-50B | ARDSLEY-37A |
| Jan-53 | COLWICK-38A | IPSWICH-32B | RETFORD-36E | ARDSLEY-37A | COLWICK-38A | **7/53: S. BGE - 35C** | IPSWICH-32B | NEVILLE HILL-50B | ARDSLEY-37A |
| Aug-53 | COLWICK-38A | IPSWICH-32B | RETFORD-36E | ARDSLEY-37A | COLWICK-38A | **10/53: NEWE - 35A** | IPSWICH-32B | NEVILLE HILL-50B | ARDSLEY-37A |
| Jan-54 | **11/53: TUX - 40D** | IPSWICH-32B | RETFORD-36E | ARDSLEY-37A | COLWICK-38A | **11/53: ARDS - 37A** | IPSWICH-32B | NEVILLE HILL-50B | ARDSLEY-37A |
| Aug-54 | TUXFORD-40D | IPSWICH-32B | RETFORD-36E | ARDSLEY-37A | COLWICK-38A | ARDSLEY-37A | IPSWICH-32B | NEVILLE HILL-50B | ARDSLEY-37A |
| Jan-55 | **1/55: STRAT - 30A** | IPSWICH-32B | RETFORD-36E | ARDSLEY-37A | COLWICK-38A | ARDSLEY-37A | IPSWICH-32B | NEVILLE HILL-50B | ARDSLEY-37A |
| Aug-55 | **3/55: DCTR - 36A** | IPSWICH-32B | RETFORD-36E | ARDSLEY-37A | COLWICK-38A | ARDSLEY-37A | IPSWICH-32B | NEVILLE HILL-50B | ARDSLEY-37A |
| Jan-56 | DONCASTER-36A | IPSWICH-32B | RETFORD-36E | ARDSLEY-37A | COLWICK-38A | ARDSLEY-37A | IPSWICH-32B | NEVILLE HILL-50B | ARDSLEY-37A |
| Aug-56 | DONCASTER-36A | IPSWICH-32B | RETFORD-36E | ARDSLEY-56B | COLWICK-38A | ARDSLEY-56B | IPSWICH-32B | NEVILLE HILL-50B | ARDSLEY-56B |
| Jan-57 | DONCASTER-36A | IPSWICH-32B | RETFORD-36E | ARDSLEY-56B | COLWICK-38A | ARDSLEY-56B | IPSWICH-32B | NEVILLE HILL-50B | ARDSLEY-56B |
| Aug-57 | **6/57: BARN - 36D** | IPSWICH-32B | RETFORD-36E | ARDSLEY-56B | COLWICK-38A | ARDSLEY-56B | IPSWICH-32B | NEVILLE HILL-50B | ARDSLEY-56B |
| Jan-58 | BARNSLEY-36D | IPSWICH-32B | RETFORD-36E | ARDSLEY-56B | COLWICK-38A | ARDSLEY-56B | IPSWICH-32B | NEVILLE HILL-50B | ARDSLEY-56B |
| Aug-58 | BARNSLEY-41G | IPSWICH-32B | RETFORD-36E | ARDSLEY-56B | COLWICK-40E | ARDSLEY-56B | IPSWICH-32B | NEVILLE HILL-50B | ARDSLEY-56B |
| Jan-59 | BARNSLEY-41G | IPSWICH-32B | RETFORD-36E | ARDSLEY-56B | COLWICK-40E | ARDSLEY-56B | IPSWICH-32B | NEVILLE HILL-50B | ARDSLEY-56B |
| Aug-59 | BARNSLEY-41G | **5/59: W/D** | RETFORD-36E | **5/59: DAIRY - 53A** | COLWICK-40E | **5/59: DAIRY - 53A** | IPSWICH-32B | NEVILLE HILL-50B | ARDSLEY-56B |
| Nov-59 | BARNSLEY-41G | | RETFORD-36E | DAIRYCOATES-53A | **9/59: W/D** | DAIRYCOATES-53A | **11/59: W/D** | NEVILLE HILL-50B | ARDSLEY-56B |
| Jan-60 | **1/60: MEX - 41F** | | RETFORD-36E | DAIRYCOATES-53A | | **12/59: SUND - 52G** | | **12/59: TNBY - 51L** | ARDSLEY-56B |
| Apr-60 | **3/60: W/D** | | **2/60: W/D** | DAIRYCOATES-50B | | SUNDERLAND-52G | | THORNABY-51L | ARDSLEY-56B |
| Aug-60 | | | | DAIRYCOATES-50B | | SUNDERLAND-52G | | **9/60: W.AUCK - 51F** | ARDSLEY-56B |
| Nov-60 | | | | DAIRYCOATES-50B | | SUNDERLAND-52G | | W.AUCKLAND-51F | ARDSLEY-56B |

| | 64837 | 64838 | 64839 | 64840 | 64841 | 64842 | 64843 | 64844 | 64845 |
|---|---|---|---|---|---|---|---|---|---|
| Aug-50 | COLWICK-38A | WOODFORD HALSE-38E | ARDSLEY-37A | ARDSLEY-37A | IPSWICH-32B | BLAYDON-52C | TWEEDMOUTH-52D | TWEEDMOUTH-52D | STARBECK-50D |
| Jan-51 | COLWICK-38A | **9/50: ANN - 38B** | ARDSLEY-37A | ARDSLEY-37A | IPSWICH-32B | BLAYDON-52C | TWEEDMOUTH-52D | TWEEDMOUTH-52D | STARBECK-50D |
| Aug-51 | **5/51: ARDS - 37A** | **10/50: COLW - 38A** | ARDSLEY-37A | ARDSLEY-37A | IPSWICH-32B | BLAYDON-52C | TWEEDMOUTH-52D | TWEEDMOUTH-52D | STARBECK-50D |
| Jan-52 | ARDSLEY-37A | COLWICK-38A | ARDSLEY-37A | ARDSLEY-37A | IPSWICH-32B | BLAYDON-52C | TWEEDMOUTH-52D | TWEEDMOUTH-52D | STARBECK-50D |
| Aug-52 | ARDSLEY-37A | COLWICK-38A | ARDSLEY-37A | ARDSLEY-37A | IPSWICH-32B | BLAYDON-52C | TWEEDMOUTH-52D | TWEEDMOUTH-52D | STARBECK-50D |
| Jan-53 | ARDSLEY-37A | COLWICK-38A | ARDSLEY-37A | ARDSLEY-37A | IPSWICH-32B | BLAYDON-52C | TWEEDMOUTH-52D | TWEEDMOUTH-52D | STARBECK-50D |
| Aug-53 | ARDSLEY-37A | COLWICK-38A | ARDSLEY-37A | ARDSLEY-37A | IPSWICH-32B | BLAYDON-52C | TWEEDMOUTH-52D | TWEEDMOUTH-52D | STARBECK-50D |
| Jan-54 | ARDSLEY-37A | **11/53: TUX - 40D** | ARDSLEY-37A | ARDSLEY-37A | IPSWICH-32B | BLAYDON-52C | TWEEDMOUTH-52D | TWEEDMOUTH-52D | STARBECK-50D |
| Aug-54 | ARDSLEY-37A | TUXFORD-40D | ARDSLEY-37A | ARDSLEY-37A | IPSWICH-32B | BLAYDON-52C | TWEEDMOUTH-52D | TWEEDMOUTH-52D | STARBECK-50D |
| Jan-55 | ARDSLEY-37A | **1/55: STRAT - 30A** | ARDSLEY-37A | ARDSLEY-37A | IPSWICH-32B | BLAYDON-52C | TWEEDMOUTH-52D | TWEEDMOUTH-52D | STARBECK-50D |
| Aug-55 | ARDSLEY-37A | **3/55: DCTR - 36A** | ARDSLEY-37A | ARDSLEY-37A | IPSWICH-32B | BLAYDON-52C | TWEEDMOUTH-52D | TWEEDMOUTH-52D | STARBECK-50D |
| Jan-56 | ARDSLEY-37A | DONCASTER-36A | ARDSLEY-37A | ARDSLEY-37A | IPSWICH-32B | BLAYDON-52C | TWEEDMOUTH-52D | TWEEDMOUTH-52D | STARBECK-50D |
| Aug-56 | ARDSLEY-56B | DONCASTER-36A | ARDSLEY-56B | ARDSLEY-56B | IPSWICH-32B | BLAYDON-52C | TWEEDMOUTH-52D | TWEEDMOUTH-52D | STARBECK-50D |
| Jan-57 | ARDSLEY-56B | DONCASTER-36A | ARDSLEY-56B | ARDSLEY-56B | IPSWICH-32B | BLAYDON-52C | TWEEDMOUTH-52D | TWEEDMOUTH-52D | STARBECK-50D |
| Aug-57 | ARDSLEY-56B | DONCASTER-36A | ARDSLEY-56B | ARDSLEY-56B | IPSWICH-32B | BLAYDON-52C | TWEEDMOUTH-52D | TWEEDMOUTH-52D | STARBECK-50D |
| Jan-58 | ARDSLEY-56B | DONCASTER-36A | ARDSLEY-56B | ARDSLEY-56B | IPSWICH-32B | BLAYDON-52C | TWEEDMOUTH-52D | TWEEDMOUTH-52D | STARBECK-50D |
| Aug-58 | ARDSLEY-56B | DONCASTER-36A | ARDSLEY-56B | ARDSLEY-56B | IPSWICH-32B | BLAYDON-52C | TWEEDMOUTH-52D | TWEEDMOUTH-52D | STARBECK-50D |
| Jan-59 | ARDSLEY-56B | DONCASTER-36A | ARDSLEY-56B | ARDSLEY-56B | IPSWICH-32B | BLAYDON-52C | TWEEDMOUTH-52D | TWEEDMOUTH-52D | STARBECK-50D |
| Aug-59 | ARDSLEY-56B | DONCASTER-36A | ARDSLEY-56B | ARDSLEY-56B | IPSWICH-32B | BLAYDON-52C | TWEEDMOUTH-52D | TWEEDMOUTH-52D | **9/59: YORK - 50A** |
| Nov-59 | ARDSLEY-56B | DONCASTER-36A | ARDSLEY-56B | ARDSLEY-56B | **10/59: W/D** | BLAYDON-52C | TWEEDMOUTH-52D | TWEEDMOUTH-52D | YORK-50A |
| Jan-60 | **12/59: HTN - 52B** | DONCASTER-36A | ARDSLEY-56B | ARDSLEY-56B | | BLAYDON-52C | TWEEDMOUTH-52D | TWEEDMOUTH-52D | **12/59: TNBY - 51L** |
| Apr-60 | HEATON-52B | **2/60: W/D** | ARDSLEY-56B | ARDSLEY-56B | | BLAYDON-52C | TWEEDMOUTH-52D | TWEEDMOUTH-52D | THORNABY-51L |
| Aug-60 | HEATON-52B | | ARDSLEY-56B | ARDSLEY-56B | | BLAYDON-52C | TWEEDMOUTH-52D | TWEEDMOUTH-52D | THORNABY-51L |
| Nov-60 | HEATON-52B | | ARDSLEY-56B | ARDSLEY-56B | | BLAYDON-52C | TWEEDMOUTH-52D | TWEEDMOUTH-52D | THORNABY-51L |

| | 64846 | 64847 | 64848 | 64849 | 64850 | 64851 | 64852 | 64853 | 64854 |
|---|---|---|---|---|---|---|---|---|---|
| Aug-50 | BOR.GDNS-54C | MIDDLESBROUGH-51D | W.AUCKLAND-51F | BLAYDON-52C | NEVILLE HILL-50B | ALSTON-52C | BLAYDON-52C | GATESHEAD-52A | TWEEDMOUTH-52D |
| Jan-51 | BOR.GDNS-54C | MIDDLESBROUGH-51D | W.AUCKLAND-51F | BLAYDON-52C | NEVILLE HILL-50B | ALSTON-52C | **3/51: GHD - 52A** | GATESHEAD-52A | TWEEDMOUTH-52D |
| Aug-51 | BOR.GDNS-54C | MIDDLESBROUGH-51D | W.AUCKLAND-51F | BLAYDON-52C | NEVILLE HILL-50B | ALSTON-52C | GATESHEAD-52A | GATESHEAD-52A | TWEEDMOUTH-52D |
| Jan-52 | BOR.GDNS-54C | MIDDLESBROUGH-51D | W.AUCKLAND-51F | BLAYDON-52C | NEVILLE HILL-50B | ALSTON-52C | GATESHEAD-52A | GATESHEAD-52A | TWEEDMOUTH-52D |
| Aug-52 | BOR.GDNS-54C | MIDDLESBROUGH-51D | W.AUCKLAND-51F | BLAYDON-52C | NEVILLE HILL-50B | ALSTON-52C | GATESHEAD-52A | GATESHEAD-52A | TWEEDMOUTH-52D |
| Jan-53 | BOR.GDNS-54C | MIDDLESBROUGH-51D | W.AUCKLAND-51F | BLAYDON-52C | NEVILLE HILL-50B | **1/53: B. GDNS - 54C** | GATESHEAD-52A | GATESHEAD-52A | **1/53: B. GDNS - 54C** |
| Aug-53 | BOR.GDNS-54C | MIDDLESBROUGH-51D | W.AUCKLAND-51F | BLAYDON-52C | NEVILLE HILL-50B | BOR.GDNS-54C | GATESHEAD-52A | **10/53: HTN - 52B** | BOR.GDNS-54C |
| Jan-54 | BOR.GDNS-54C | **10/53: STAR - 50D** | W.AUCKLAND-51F | BLAYDON-52C | NEVILLE HILL-50B | BOR.GDNS-54C | GATESHEAD-52A | HEATON-52B | BOR.GDNS-54C |
| Aug-54 | BOR.GDNS-54C | STARBECK-50D | **9/54: MBRO - 51D** | BLAYDON-52C | **10/54: SELBY - 50C** | BOR.GDNS-54C | GATESHEAD-52A | HEATON-52B | BOR.GDNS-54C |
| Jan-55 | BOR.GDNS-54C | STARBECK-50D | **3/55: W.AUCK - 51F** | BLAYDON-52C | SELBY-50C | BOR.GDNS-54C | GATESHEAD-52A | HEATON-52B | BOR.GDNS-54C |
| Aug-55 | BOR.GDNS-54C | STARBECK-50D | **4/55: MBRO - 51D** | BLAYDON-52C | **8/55: N. HILL - 50B** | BOR.GDNS-54C | GATESHEAD-52A | HEATON-52B | BOR.GDNS-54C |
| Jan-56 | BOR.GDNS-54C | STARBECK-50D | **6/55: W. AUCK - 51F** | BLAYDON-52C | NEVILLE HILL-50B | BOR.GDNS-54C | GATESHEAD-52A | HEATON-52B | BOR.GDNS-54C |
| Aug-56 | BOR.GDNS-54C | STARBECK-50D | W.AUCKLAND-51F | BLAYDON-52C | NEVILLE HILL-50B | BOR.GDNS-54C | GATESHEAD-52A | HEATON-52B | BOR.GDNS-54C |
| Jan-57 | BOR.GDNS-54C | STARBECK-50D | W.AUCKLAND-51F | BLAYDON-52C | NEVILLE HILL-50B | BOR.GDNS-54C | GATESHEAD-52A | HEATON-52B | BOR.GDNS-54C |
| Aug-57 | BOR.GDNS-54C | STARBECK-50D | W.AUCKLAND-51F | **7/57: HTN - 52B** | NEVILLE HILL-50B | BOR.GDNS-54C | GATESHEAD-52A | HEATON-52B | BOR.GDNS-54C |
| Jan-58 | BOR.GDNS-54C | STARBECK-50D | W.AUCKLAND-51F | **11/57: BLAY - 52C** | NEVILLE HILL-50B | BOR.GDNS-54C | GATESHEAD-52A | HEATON-52B | BOR.GDNS-54C |
| Aug-58 | BOR.GDNS-54C | STARBECK-50D | W.AUCKLAND-51F | BLAYDON-52C | NEVILLE HILL-50B | BOR.GDNS-54C | GATESHEAD-52A | HEATON-52B | BOR.GDNS-54C |
| Jan-59 | BOR.GDNS-52J | STARBECK-50D | W.AUCKLAND-51F | BLAYDON-52C | NEVILLE HILL-50B | BOR.GDNS-52J | GATESHEAD-52A | HEATON-52B | BOR.GDNS-52J |
| Aug-59 | **6/59: GHD - 52A** | **6/59: SELBY - 50C** | W.AUCKLAND-51F | BLAYDON-52C | NEVILLE HILL-50B | **6/59: GHD - 52A** | GATESHEAD-52A | HEATON-52B | **6/59: GHD - 52A** |
| Nov-59 | GATESHEAD-52A | **9/59: YORK - 50A** | W.AUCKLAND-51F | BLAYDON-52C | **10/59: TNBY - 51L** | GATESHEAD-52A | GATESHEAD-52A | HEATON-52B | GATESHEAD-52A |
| Jan-60 | GATESHEAD-52A | **11/59: SUND - 52G** | W.AUCKLAND-51F | BLAYDON-52C | THORNABY-51L | GATESHEAD-52A | GATESHEAD-52A | **12/59: SUND - 52G** | GATESHEAD-52A |
| Apr-60 | GATESHEAD-52A | SUNDERLAND-52G | W.AUCKLAND-51F | BLAYDON-52C | THORNABY-51L | GATESHEAD-52A | GATESHEAD-52A | SUNDERLAND-52G | GATESHEAD-52A |
| Aug-60 | GATESHEAD-52A | SUNDERLAND-52G | W.AUCKLAND-51F | **10/60: W.HPL - 51C** | THORNABY-51L | GATESHEAD-52A | GATESHEAD-52A | SUNDERLAND-52G | **9/60: SUND - 52G** |
| Nov-60 | GATESHEAD-52A | SUNDERLAND-52G | W.AUCKLAND-51F | W.HARTLEPOOL-51C | THORNABY-51L | GATESHEAD-52A | GATESHEAD-52A | SUNDERLAND-52G | SUNDERLAND-52G |

| | 64855 | 64856 | 64857 | 64858 | 64859 | 64860 | 64861 | 64862 | 64863 |
|---|---|---|---|---|---|---|---|---|---|
| Aug-50 | STARBECK-50D | HEATON-52B | STARBECK-50D | BLAYDON-52C | STARBECK-50D | STARBECK-50D | STARBECK-50D | W.HARTLEPOOL-51C | NEVILLE HILL-50B |
| Jan-51 | STARBECK-50D | HEATON-52B | STARBECK-50D | BLAYDON-52C | STARBECK-50D | STARBECK-50D | STARBECK-50D | **2/51: MBRO - 51D** | NEVILLE HILL-50B |
| Aug-51 | STARBECK-50D | HEATON-52B | STARBECK-50D | BLAYDON-52C | STARBECK-50D | STARBECK-50D | STARBECK-50D | MIDDLESBROUGH-51D | NEVILLE HILL-50B |
| Jan-52 | STARBECK-50D | HEATON-52B | STARBECK-50D | BLAYDON-52C | STARBECK-50D | STARBECK-50D | STARBECK-50D | MIDDLESBROUGH-51D | NEVILLE HILL-50B |
| Aug-52 | STARBECK-50D | HEATON-52B | STARBECK-50D | BLAYDON-52C | STARBECK-50D | STARBECK-50D | STARBECK-50D | **10/52: W.HPL - 51C** | NEVILLE HILL-50B |
| Jan-53 | STARBECK-50D | HEATON-52B | STARBECK-50D | BLAYDON-52C | STARBECK-50D | STARBECK-50D | STARBECK-50D | W.HARTLEPOOL-51C | NEVILLE HILL-50B |
| Aug-53 | STARBECK-50D | HEATON-52B | STARBECK-50D | BLAYDON-52C | STARBECK-50D | STARBECK-50D | STARBECK-50D | W.HARTLEPOOL-51C | NEVILLE HILL-50B |
| Jan-54 | STARBECK-50D | HEATON-52B | STARBECK-50D | BLAYDON-52C | STARBECK-50D | STARBECK-50D | STARBECK-50D | W.HARTLEPOOL-51C | NEVILLE HILL-50B |
| Aug-54 | STARBECK-50D | HEATON-52B | STARBECK-50D | BLAYDON-52C | STARBECK-50D | **6/54: N. HILL - 50B** | STARBECK-50D | W.HARTLEPOOL-51C | NEVILLE HILL-50B |
| Jan-55 | STARBECK-50D | HEATON-52B | STARBECK-50D | BLAYDON-52C | STARBECK-50D | NEVILLE HILL-50B | STARBECK-50D | **3/55: W. AUCK - 51F** | NEVILLE HILL-50B |
| Aug-55 | STARBECK-50D | HEATON-52B | STARBECK-50D | BLAYDON-52C | STARBECK-50D | **8/55: SELBY - 50C** | STARBECK-50D | W.AUCKLAND-51F | NEVILLE HILL-50B |
| Jan-56 | STARBECK-50D | HEATON-52B | STARBECK-50D | BLAYDON-52C | STARBECK-50D | SELBY-50C | STARBECK-50D | W.AUCKLAND-51F | NEVILLE HILL-50B |
| Aug-56 | STARBECK-50D | HEATON-52B | STARBECK-50D | BLAYDON-52C | STARBECK-50D | SELBY-50C | STARBECK-50D | W.AUCKLAND-51F | NEVILLE HILL-50B |
| Jan-57 | STARBECK-50D | HEATON-52B | STARBECK-50D | BLAYDON-52C | STARBECK-50D | SELBY-50C | STARBECK-50D | W.AUCKLAND-51F | NEVILLE HILL-50B |
| Aug-57 | STARBECK-50D | HEATON-52B | STARBECK-50D | BLAYDON-52C | STARBECK-50D | SELBY-50C | STARBECK-50D | W.AUCKLAND-51F | NEVILLE HILL-50B |
| Jan-58 | STARBECK-50D | HEATON-52B | STARBECK-50D | BLAYDON-52C | STARBECK-50D | SELBY-50C | STARBECK-50D | W.AUCKLAND-51F | NEVILLE HILL-50B |
| Aug-58 | STARBECK-50D | HEATON-52B | STARBECK-50D | BLAYDON-52C | STARBECK-50D | SELBY-50C | STARBECK-50D | W.AUCKLAND-51F | NEVILLE HILL-50B |
| Jan-59 | STARBECK-50D | HEATON-52B | STARBECK-50D | BLAYDON-52C | STARBECK-50D | SELBY-50C | STARBECK-50D | W.AUCKLAND-51F | NEVILLE HILL-50B |
| Aug-59 | **9/59: YORK - 50A** | HEATON-52B | **9/59: YORK - 50A** | BLAYDON-52C | **9/59: YORK - 50A** | **8/59: GHD - 52A** | **9/59: YORK - 50A** | W.AUCKLAND-51F | NEVILLE HILL-50B |
| Nov-59 | YORK-50A | HEATON-52B | **11/59: TNBY - 51L** | BLAYDON-52C | YORK-50A | GATESHEAD-52A | YORK-50A | W.AUCKLAND-51F | NEVILLE HILL-50B |
| Jan-60 | **12/59: TNBY - 51L** | HEATON-52B | THORNABY-51L | BLAYDON-52C | **12/59: TNBY - 51L** | GATESHEAD-52A | **12/59: TNBY - 51L** | W.AUCKLAND-51F | NEVILLE HILL-50B |
| Apr-60 | THORNABY-51L | HEATON-52B | THORNABY-51L | BLAYDON-52C | THORNABY-51L | GATESHEAD-52A | THORNABY-51L | W.AUCKLAND-51F | NEVILLE HILL-55H |
| Aug-60 | THORNABY-51L | HEATON-52B | THORNABY-51L | BLAYDON-52C | THORNABY-51L | GATESHEAD-52A | THORNABY-51L | W.AUCKLAND-51F | NEVILLE HILL-55H |
| Nov-60 | THORNABY-51L | HEATON-52B | THORNABY-51L | BLAYDON-52C | THORNABY-51L | GATESHEAD-52A | THORNABY-51L | W.AUCKLAND-51F | NEVILLE HILL-55H |

| | 64864 | 64865 | 64866 | 64867 | 64868 | 64869 | 64870 | 64871 | 64872 |
|---|---|---|---|---|---|---|---|---|---|
| Aug-50 | DAIRYCOATES - 53A | HEATON - 52B | STARBECK - 50D | DAIRYCOATES - 53A | ALNMOUTH - 52D | GATESHEAD - 52A | DAIRYCOATES - 53A | GATESHEAD - 52A | ARDSLEY - 37A |
| Jan-51 | 12/50: DAIRY - 53A | 3/51: GHD - 52A | STARBECK - 50D | 5/51: N.HILL - 50B | ALNMOUTH - 52D | GATESHEAD - 52A | 12/50: B. GDNS - 54C | GATESHEAD - 52A | ARDSLEY - 37A |
| Aug-51 | DAIRYCOATES - 53A | GATESHEAD - 52A | STARBECK - 50D | 6/51: MALT - 50F | ALNMOUTH - 52D | GATESHEAD - 52A | BOR. GDNS - 54C | GATESHEAD - 52A | ARDSLEY - 37A |
| Jan-52 | DAIRYCOATES - 53A | GATESHEAD - 52A | STARBECK - 50D | MALTON - 50F | ALNMOUTH - 52D | GATESHEAD - 52A | BOR. GDNS - 54C | GATESHEAD - 52A | ARDSLEY - 37A |
| Aug-52 | DAIRYCOATES - 53A | GATESHEAD - 52A | STARBECK - 50D | MALTON - 50F | ALNMOUTH - 52D | GATESHEAD - 52A | BOR. GDNS - 54C | GATESHEAD - 52A | ARDSLEY - 37A |
| Jan-53 | 1/53: BLAY - 52C | GATESHEAD - 52A | STARBECK - 50D | MALTON - 50F | ALNMOUTH - 52D | GATESHEAD - 52A | 1/53: BLAY - 52C | GATESHEAD - 52A | ARDSLEY - 37A |
| Aug-53 | BLAYDON - 52C | GATESHEAD - 52A | STARBECK - 50D | MALTON - 50F | ALNMOUTH - 52D | GATESHEAD - 52A | BLAYDON - 52C | GATESHEAD - 52A | ARDSLEY - 37A |
| Jan-54 | BLAYDON - 52C | GATESHEAD - 52A | STARBECK - 50D | MALTON - 50F | ALNMOUTH - 52D | GATESHEAD - 52A | BLAYDON - 52C | GATESHEAD - 52A | ARDSLEY - 37A |
| Aug-54 | 6/54: DAIRY - 53A | GATESHEAD - 52A | STARBECK - 50D | MALTON - 50F | ALNMOUTH - 52D | GATESHEAD - 52A | BLAYDON - 52C | GATESHEAD - 52A | ARDSLEY - 37A |
| Jan-55 | DAIRYCOATES - 53A | GATESHEAD - 52A | STARBECK - 50D | MALTON - 50F | ALNMOUTH - 52D | GATESHEAD - 52A | BLAYDON - 52C | GATESHEAD - 52A | ARDSLEY - 37A |
| Aug-55 | DAIRYCOATES - 53A | GATESHEAD - 52A | STARBECK - 50D | MALTON - 50F | ALNMOUTH - 52D | GATESHEAD - 52A | 6/55: N.HILL - 50B | GATESHEAD - 52A | ARDSLEY - 37A |
| Jan-56 | DAIRYCOATES - 53A | GATESHEAD - 52A | STARBECK - 50D | MALTON - 50F | ALNMOUTH - 52D | GATESHEAD - 52A | NEVILLE HILL - 50B | GATESHEAD - 52A | ARDSLEY - 37A |
| Aug-56 | DAIRYCOATES - 53A | GATESHEAD - 52A | STARBECK - 50D | MALTON - 50F | ALNMOUTH - 52D | GATESHEAD - 52A | NEVILLE HILL - 50B | GATESHEAD - 52A | ARDSLEY - 56B |
| Jan-57 | DAIRYCOATES - 53A | GATESHEAD - 52A | STARBECK - 50D | MALTON - 50F | ALNMOUTH - 52D | GATESHEAD - 52A | NEVILLE HILL - 50B | GATESHEAD - 52A | ARDSLEY - 56B |
| Aug-57 | 6/57: HTN - 52B | GATESHEAD - 52A | STARBECK - 50D | MALTON - 50F | ALNMOUTH - 52D | GATESHEAD - 52A | NEVILLE HILL - 50B | 7/57: HTN - 52B | 6/57: BRAD - 56G |
| Jan-58 | HEATON - 52B | GATESHEAD - 52A | STARBECK - 50D | MALTON - 50F | ALNMOUTH - 52D | GATESHEAD - 52A | NEVILLE HILL - 50B | HEATON - 52B | 2/58: LOWM - 56F |
| Aug-58 | HEATON - 52B | GATESHEAD - 52A | STARBECK - 50D | MALTON - 50F | ALNMOUTH - 52D | GATESHEAD - 52A | NEVILLE HILL - 50B | HEATON - 52B | LOWMOOR - 56F |
| Jan-59 | HEATON - 52B | GATESHEAD - 52A | STARBECK - 50D | MALTON - 50F | ALNMOUTH - 52D | GATESHEAD - 52A | NEVILLE HILL - 50B | HEATON - 52B | LOWMOOR - 56F |
| Aug-59 | HEATON - 52B | GATESHEAD - 52A | 9/59: YORK - 50A | MALTON - 50F | ALNMOUTH - 52D | GATESHEAD - 52A | NEVILLE HILL - 50B | HEATON - 52B | LOWMOOR - 56F |
| Nov-59 | HEATON - 52B | GATESHEAD - 52A | 11/59: SUND - 52G | MALTON - 50F | ALNMOUTH - 52D | GATESHEAD - 52A | NEVILLE HILL - 50B | HEATON - 52B | LOWMOOR - 56F |
| Jan-60 | HEATON - 52B | GATESHEAD - 52A | 12/59: HTN - 52B | MALTON - 50F | ALNMOUTH - 52D | GATESHEAD - 52A | 12/59: TNBY - 51L | HEATON - 52B | LOWMOOR - 56F |
| Apr-60 | HEATON - 52B | GATESHEAD - 52A | HEATON - 52B | MALTON - 50F | ALNMOUTH - 52D | GATESHEAD - 52A | THORNABY - 51L | HEATON - 52B | LOWMOOR - 56F |
| Aug-60 | HEATON - 52B | GATESHEAD - 52A | HEATON - 52B | MALTON - 50F | ALNMOUTH - 52D | GATESHEAD - 52A | THORNABY - 51L | HEATON - 52B | LOWMOOR - 56F |
| Nov-60 | HEATON - 52B | GATESHEAD - 52A | HEATON - 52B | MALTON - 50F | ALNMOUTH - 52D | GATESHEAD - 52A | THORNABY - 51L | HEATON - 52B | LOWMOOR - 56F |

| | 64873 | 64874 | 64875 | 64876 | 64877 | 64878 | 64879 | 64880 | 64881 |
|---|---|---|---|---|---|---|---|---|---|
| Aug-50 | PARKESTON - 30F | STRATFORD - 30A | CARLISLE(C) - 12B | STRATFORD - 30A | CARLISLE(C) - 12B | DARNALL - 39B | GORTON - 39A | CARLISLE(C) - 12B | LINCOLN - 40A |
| Jan-51 | PARKESTON - 30F | STRATFORD - 30A | CARLISLE(C) - 12B | STRATFORD - 30A | CARLISLE(C) - 12B | DARNALL - 39B | GORTON - 39A | CARLISLE(C) - 12B | LINCOLN - 40A |
| Aug-51 | PARKESTON - 30F | 6/51: PARKS - 30F | CARLISLE(C) - 68E | 6/51: ARDS - 37A | CARLISLE(C) - 68E | DARNALL - 39B | 4/51: DARN - 39B | CARLISLE(C) - 68E | LINCOLN - 40A |
| Jan-52 | PARKESTON - 30F | PARKESTON - 30F | CARLISLE(C) - 68E | ARDSLEY - 37A | CARLISLE(C) - 68E | DARNALL - 39B | 3/52: ARDS - 37A | CARLISLE(C) - 68E | LINCOLN - 40A |
| Aug-52 | PARKESTON - 30F | PARKESTON - 30F | CARLISLE(C) - 68E | 9/52: STRAT - 30A | CARLISLE(C) - 68E | DARNALL - 39B | ARDSLEY - 37A | CARLISLE(C) - 68E | LINCOLN - 40A |
| Jan-53 | PARKESTON - 30F | PARKESTON - 30F | CARLISLE(C) - 68E | STRATFORD - 30A | CARLISLE(C) - 68E | DARNALL - 39B | ARDSLEY - 37A | CARLISLE(C) - 68E | LINCOLN - 40A |
| Aug-53 | PARKESTON - 30F | PARKESTON - 30F | CARLISLE(C) - 68E | STRATFORD - 30A | CARLISLE(C) - 68E | DARNALL - 39B | ARDSLEY - 37A | CARLISLE(C) - 68E | LINCOLN - 40A |
| Jan-54 | PARKESTON - 30F | PARKESTON - 30F | CARLISLE(C) - 68E | STRATFORD - 30A | CARLISLE(C) - 68E | DARNALL - 39B | ARDSLEY - 37A | CARLISLE(C) - 68E | 12/53: TUX - 40D |
| Aug-54 | PARKESTON - 30F | PARKESTON - 30F | CARLISLE(C) - 68E | STRATFORD - 30A | CARLISLE(C) - 68E | DARNALL - 39B | ARDSLEY - 37A | CARLISLE(C) - 68E | 3/54: LINC - 40A |
| Jan-55 | PARKESTON - 30F | PARKESTON - 30F | CARLISLE(C) - 68E | STRATFORD - 30A | CARLISLE(C) - 68E | DARNALL - 39B | ARDSLEY - 37A | CARLISLE(C) - 68E | LINCOLN - 40A |
| Aug-55 | PARKESTON - 30F | PARKESTON - 30F | CARLISLE(C) - 68E | STRATFORD - 30A | CARLISLE(C) - 68E | DARNALL - 39B | ARDSLEY - 37A | CARLISLE(C) - 68E | LINCOLN - 40A |
| Jan-56 | PARKESTON - 30F | PARKESTON - 30F | CARLISLE(C) - 68E | 12/55: DCTR - 36A | CARLISLE(C) - 68E | DARNALL - 41A | ARDSLEY - 37A | CARLISLE(C) - 68E | LINCOLN - 40A |
| Aug-56 | PARKESTON - 30F | PARKESTON - 30F | CARLISLE(C) - 68E | DONCASTER - 36A | CARLISLE(C) - 68E | DARNALL - 41A | ARDSLEY - 56B | CARLISLE(C) - 68E | LINCOLN - 40A |
| Jan-57 | 11/56: NEWE - 35A | 11/56: NEWE - 35A | CARLISLE(C) - 68E | DONCASTER - 36A | CARLISLE(C) - 68E | DARNALL - 41A | ARDSLEY - 56B | CARLISLE(C) - 68E | LINCOLN - 40A |
| Aug-57 | 4/57: STRAT - 30A | 4/57: STRAT - 30A | CARLISLE(C) - 68E | DONCASTER - 36A | CARLISLE(C) - 68E | DARNALL - 41A | ARDSLEY - 56B | CARLISLE(C) - 68E | LINCOLN - 40A |
| Jan-58 | STRATFORD - 30A | STRATFORD - 30A | CARLISLE(C) - 68E | DONCASTER - 36A | CARLISLE(C) - 68E | DARNALL - 41A | ARDSLEY - 56B | CARLISLE(C) - 68E | LINCOLN - 40A |
| Aug-58 | STRATFORD - 30A | STRATFORD - 30A | CARLISLE(C) - 12C | DONCASTER - 36A | CARLISLE(C) - 12C | DARNALL - 41A | ARDSLEY - 56B | CARLISLE(C) - 12C | LINCOLN - 40A |
| Jan-59 | STRATFORD - 30A | 12/58: LINC - 40A | 11/58: GORT - 9G | DONCASTER - 36A | CARLISLE(C) - 12C | DARNALL - 41A | ARDSLEY - 56B | CARLISLE(C) - 12C | LINCOLN - 40A |
| Aug-59 | 5/59: W/D | 3/59: DCTR - 36A | GORTON - 9G | DONCASTER - 36A | CARLISLE(C) - 12C | DARNALL - 41A | ARDSLEY - 56B | CARLISLE(C) - 12C | LINCOLN - 40A |
| Nov-59 | | DONCASTER - 36A | GORTON - 9G | 9/59: W/D | CARLISLE(C) - 12C | DARNALL - 41A | ARDSLEY - 56B | CARLISLE(C) - 12C | 9/59: W/D |
| Jan-60 | | DONCASTER - 36A | GORTON - 9G | | CARLISLE(C) - 12C | DARNALL - 41A | ARDSLEY - 56B | CARLISLE(C) - 12C | |
| Apr-60 | | DONCASTER - 36A | GORTON - 9G | | CARLISLE(C) - 12C | DARNALL - 41A | ARDSLEY - 56B | CARLISLE(C) - 12C | |
| Aug-60 | | DONCASTER - 36A | GORTON - 9G | | CARLISLE(C) - 12C | DARNALL - 41A | ARDSLEY - 56B | CARLISLE(C) - 12C | |
| Nov-60 | | DONCASTER - 36A | GORTON - 9G | | CARLISLE(C) - 12C | DARNALL - 41A | ARDSLEY - 56B | CARLISLE(C) - 12C | |

| | 64882 | 64883 | 64884 | 64885 | 64886 | 64887 | 64888 | 64889 | 64890 |
|---|---|---|---|---|---|---|---|---|---|
| Aug-50 | NORWICH - 32A | LINCOLN - 40A | CARLISLE(C) - 12B | DONCASTER - 36A | LINCOLN - 40A | LINCOLN - 40A | CARLISLE(C) - 12B | NORWICH - 32A | DARNALL - 39B |
| Jan-51 | NORWICH - 32A | LINCOLN - 40A | CARLISLE(C) - 12B | DONCASTER - 36A | LINCOLN - 40A | LINCOLN - 40A | CARLISLE(C) - 12B | NORWICH - 32A | DARNALL - 39B |
| Aug-51 | NORWICH - 32A | LINCOLN - 40A | CARLISLE(C) - 68E | DONCASTER - 36A | 9/51: N. HILL - 50B | LINCOLN - 40A | CARLISLE(C) - 68E | NORWICH - 32A | DARNALL - 39B |
| Jan-52 | NORWICH - 32A | LINCOLN - 40A | CARLISLE(C) - 68E | DONCASTER - 36A | NEVILLE HILL - 50B | LINCOLN - 40A | CARLISLE(C) - 68E | NORWICH - 32A | DARNALL - 39B |
| Aug-52 | NORWICH - 32A | 10/52: S. BGE - 35C | CARLISLE(C) - 68E | DONCASTER - 36A | NEVILLE HILL - 50B | LINCOLN - 40A | CARLISLE(C) - 68E | NORWICH - 32A | DARNALL - 39B |
| Jan-53 | NORWICH - 32A | S. BGE - 35C | CARLISLE(C) - 68E | DONCASTER - 36A | NEVILLE HILL - 50B | LINCOLN - 40A | CARLISLE(C) - 68E | NORWICH - 32A | DARNALL - 39B |
| Aug-53 | 7/53: IPS - 32B | S. BGE - 35C | CARLISLE(C) - 68E | DONCASTER - 36A | NEVILLE HILL - 50B | LINCOLN - 40A | CARLISLE(C) - 68E | NORWICH - 32A | DARNALL - 39B |
| Jan-54 | 10/53: NOR - 32A | S. BGE - 35C | CARLISLE(C) - 68E | DONCASTER - 36A | NEVILLE HILL - 50B | LINCOLN - 40A | CARLISLE(C) - 68E | NORWICH - 32A | DARNALL - 39B |
| Aug-54 | NORWICH - 32A | S. BGE - 35C | CARLISLE(C) - 68E | DONCASTER - 36A | NEVILLE HILL - 50B | LINCOLN - 40A | CARLISLE(C) - 68E | NORWICH - 32A | DARNALL - 39B |
| Jan-55 | 2/55: IPS - 32B | S. BGE - 35C | CARLISLE(C) - 68E | DONCASTER - 36A | NEVILLE HILL - 50B | LINCOLN - 40A | CARLISLE(C) - 68E | NORWICH - 32A | 11/54: STRAT - 30A |
| Aug-55 | IPSWICH - 32B | S. BGE - 35C | CARLISLE(C) - 68E | DONCASTER - 36A | NEVILLE HILL - 50B | LINCOLN - 40A | CARLISLE(C) - 68E | NORWICH - 32A | 9/55: CAMB - 31A |
| Jan-56 | IPSWICH - 32B | S. BGE - 35C | CARLISLE(C) - 68E | DONCASTER - 36A | NEVILLE HILL - 50B | LINCOLN - 40A | CARLISLE(C) - 68E | NORWICH - 32A | CAMBRIDGE - 31A |
| Aug-56 | IPSWICH - 32B | S. BGE - 35C | CARLISLE(C) - 68E | DONCASTER - 36A | NEVILLE HILL - 50B | LINCOLN - 40A | CARLISLE(C) - 68E | NORWICH - 32A | CAMBRIDGE - 31A |
| Jan-57 | IPSWICH - 32B | 4/57: PLAIS - 33A | CARLISLE(C) - 68E | DONCASTER - 36A | NEVILLE HILL - 50B | LINCOLN - 40A | CARLISLE(C) - 68E | NORWICH - 32A | CAMBRIDGE - 31A |
| Aug-57 | IPSWICH - 32B | 6/57: DCTR - 36A | CARLISLE(C) - 68E | DONCASTER - 36A | 9/57: BRAD - 56G | LINCOLN - 40A | CARLISLE(C) - 68E | NORWICH - 32A | CAMBRIDGE - 31A |
| Jan-58 | 10/57: NOR - 32A | DONCASTER - 36A | CARLISLE(C) - 68E | DONCASTER - 36A | 2/58: LOWM - 56F | LINCOLN - 40A | CARLISLE(C) - 68E | NORWICH - 32A | CAMBRIDGE - 31A |
| Aug-58 | 12/58: LINC - 40A | DONCASTER - 36A | CARLISLE(C) - 12C | DONCASTER - 36A | LOWMOOR - 56F | 10/58: BOST - 40F | CARLISLE(C) - 12C | NORWICH - 32A | 10/58: MARCH - 31B |
| Jan-59 | 1/59: COLW - 40E | DONCASTER - 36A | CARLISLE(C) - 12C | DONCASTER - 36A | LOWMOOR - 56F | 3/59: COLW - 40E | CARLISLE(C) - 12C | 12/58: LINC - 40A | 12/58: LINC - 40A |
| Aug-59 | 3/59: RET - 36E | DONCASTER - 36A | CARLISLE(C) - 12C | DONCASTER - 36A | LOWMOOR - 56F | COLWICK - 40E | CARLISLE(C) - 12C | LINCOLN - 40A | LINCOLN - 40A |
| Nov-59 | RETFORD - 36E | DONCASTER - 36A | CARLISLE(C) - 12C | DONCASTER - 36A | LOWMOOR - 56F | COLWICK - 40E | CARLISLE(C) - 12C | 10/59: COLW - 40E | LINCOLN - 40A |
| Jan-60 | RETFORD - 36E | DONCASTER - 36A | CARLISLE(C) - 12C | DONCASTER - 36A | LOWMOOR - 56F | COLWICK - 40E | CARLISLE(C) - 12C | COLWICK - 40E | LINCOLN - 40A |
| Apr-60 | RETFORD - 36E | 3/60: W/D | CARLISLE(C) - 12C | DONCASTER - 36A | LOWMOOR - 56F | 2/60: W/D | CARLISLE(C) - 12C | COLWICK - 40E | 3/60: W/D |
| Aug-60 | RETFORD - 36E | | CARLISLE(C) - 12C | DONCASTER - 36A | LOWMOOR - 56F | | CARLISLE(C) - 12C | 8/60: W/D | |
| Nov-60 | RETFORD - 36E | | CARLISLE(C) - 12C | DONCASTER - 36A | LOWMOOR - 56F | | CARLISLE(C) - 12C | | |

| | 64891 | 64892 | 64893 | 64894 | 64895 | 64896 | 64897 | 64898 | 64899 |
|---|---|---|---|---|---|---|---|---|---|
| Aug-50 | DONCASTER - 36A | DUNDEE - 62B | DONCASTER - 36A | IPSWICH - 32B | CARLISLE(C) - 12B | ARDSLEY - 37A | DAIRYCOATES - 53A | RETFORD - 36E | CARLISLE(C) - 12B |
| Jan-51 | DONCASTER - 36A | DUNDEE - 62B | 3/51: RET - 36E | IPSWICH - 32B | CARLISLE(C) - 12B | ARDSLEY - 37A | 12/50: B. GDNS - 54C | RETFORD - 36E | CARLISLE(C) - 12B |
| Aug-51 | DONCASTER - 36A | DUNDEE - 62B | RETFORD - 36E | IPSWICH - 32B | CARLISLE(C) - 68E | ARDSLEY - 37A | BOR. GDNS - 54C | RETFORD - 36E | CARLISLE(C) - 68E |
| Jan-52 | DONCASTER - 36A | DUNDEE - 62B | RETFORD - 36E | IPSWICH - 32B | CARLISLE(C) - 68E | ARDSLEY - 37A | BOR. GDNS - 54C | RETFORD - 36E | CARLISLE(C) - 68E |
| Aug-52 | 6/52: COLW - 38A | DUNDEE - 62B | RETFORD - 36E | IPSWICH - 32B | CARLISLE(C) - 68E | ARDSLEY - 37A | BOR. GDNS - 54C | RETFORD - 36E | CARLISLE(C) - 68E |
| Jan-53 | COLWICK - 38A | DUNDEE - 62B | RETFORD - 36E | IPSWICH - 32B | CARLISLE(C) - 68E | 1/53: S. BGE - 35C | 1/53: BLAY - 52C | RETFORD - 36E | CARLISLE(C) - 68E |
| Aug-53 | 5/53: S. BGE - 35C | DUNDEE - 62B | RETFORD - 36E | IPSWICH - 32B | CARLISLE(C) - 68E | S. BGE - 35C | BLAYDON - 52C | RETFORD - 36E | CARLISLE(C) - 68E |
| Jan-54 | S. BGE - 35C | DUNDEE - 62B | RETFORD - 36E | IPSWICH - 32B | CARLISLE(C) - 68E | S. BGE - 35C | BLAYDON - 52C | RETFORD - 36E | CARLISLE(C) - 68E |
| Aug-54 | S. BGE - 35C | DUNDEE - 62B | RETFORD - 36E | IPSWICH - 32B | CARLISLE(C) - 68E | S. BGE - 35C | 4/57: ALN - 52D | RETFORD - 36E | CARLISLE(C) - 68E |
| Jan-55 | S. BGE - 35C | DUNDEE - 62B | RETFORD - 36E | IPSWICH - 32B | CARLISLE(C) - 68E | S. BGE - 35C | ALNMOUTH - 52D | RETFORD - 36E | CARLISLE(C) - 68E |
| Aug-55 | S. BGE - 35C | DUNDEE - 62B | RETFORD - 36E | IPSWICH - 32B | CARLISLE(C) - 68E | S. BGE - 35C | ALNMOUTH - 52D | RETFORD - 36E | CARLISLE(C) - 68E |
| Jan-56 | S. BGE - 35C | DUNDEE - 62B | RETFORD - 36E | IPSWICH - 32B | CARLISLE(C) - 68E | S. BGE - 35C | ALNMOUTH - 52D | RETFORD - 36E | CARLISLE(C) - 68E |
| Aug-56 | S. BGE - 35C | DUNDEE - 62B | RETFORD - 36E | IPSWICH - 32B | CARLISLE(C) - 68E | S. BGE - 35C | ALNMOUTH - 52D | RETFORD - 36E | CARLISLE(C) - 68E |
| Jan-57 | 4/57: PLAIS - 33A | DUNDEE - 62B | RETFORD - 36E | IPSWICH - 32B | CARLISLE(C) - 68E | 4/57: PLAIS - 33A | ALNMOUTH - 52D | RETFORD - 36E | CARLISLE(C) - 68E |
| Aug-57 | 6/57: IPS - 32B | DUNDEE - 62B | RETFORD - 36E | IPSWICH - 32B | CARLISLE(C) - 68E | 6/57: PARKS - 30F | ALNMOUTH - 52D | RETFORD - 36E | CARLISLE(C) - 68E |
| Jan-58 | IPSWICH - 32B | DUNDEE - 62B | RETFORD - 36E | IPSWICH - 32B | CARLISLE(C) - 68E | 3/58: STRAT - 30A | ALNMOUTH - 52D | RETFORD - 36E | CARLISLE(C) - 68E |
| Aug-58 | IPSWICH - 32B | DUNDEE - 62B | RETFORD - 36E | IPSWICH - 32B | CARLISLE(C) - 12C | STRATFORD - 30A | ALNMOUTH - 52D | RETFORD - 36E | CARLISLE(C) - 12C |
| Jan-59 | IPSWICH - 32B | DUNDEE - 62B | RETFORD - 36E | IPSWICH - 32B | CARLISLE(C) - 12C | 12/58: LINC - 40A | ALNMOUTH - 52D | RETFORD - 36E | CARLISLE(C) - 12C |
| Aug-59 | IPSWICH - 32B | DUNDEE - 62B | RETFORD - 36E | IPSWICH - 32B | CARLISLE(C) - 12C | LINCOLN - 40A | ALNMOUTH - 52D | RETFORD - 36E | CARLISLE(C) - 12C |
| Nov-59 | 10/59: MARCH - 31B | DUNDEE - 62B | RETFORD - 36E | 10/59: W/D | CARLISLE(C) - 12C | LINCOLN - 40A | ALNMOUTH - 52D | RETFORD - 36E | CARLISLE(C) - 12C |
| Jan-60 | MARCH - 31B | DUNDEE - 62B | RETFORD - 36E | | CARLISLE(C) - 12C | LINCOLN - 40A | ALNMOUTH - 52D | RETFORD - 36E | CARLISLE(C) - 12C |
| Apr-60 | 2/60: W/D | DUNDEE - 62B | RETFORD - 36E | | CARLISLE(C) - 12C | LINCOLN - 40A | ALNMOUTH - 52D | 3/60: W/D | CARLISLE(C) - 12C |
| Aug-60 | | DUNDEE - 62B | 6/60: W/D | | CARLISLE(C) - 12C | LINCOLN - 40A | ALNMOUTH - 52D | | CARLISLE(C) - 12C |
| Nov-60 | | DUNDEE - 62B | | | CARLISLE(C) - 12C | 9/60: W/D | ALNMOUTH - 52D | | CARLISLE(C) - 12C |

| | 64900 | 64901 | 64902 | 64903 | 64904 | 64905 | 64906 | 64907 | 64908 |
|---|---|---|---|---|---|---|---|---|---|
| Aug-50 | IPSWICH - 32B | TRAFFORD PARK - 9E | DONCASTER - 36A | DARNALL - 39B | LINCOLN - 40A | IPSWICH - 32B | RETFORD - 36E | ARDSLEY - 37A | RETFORD - 36E |
| Jan-51 | IPSWICH - 32B | TRAFFORD PARK - 9E | DONCASTER - 36A | DARNALL - 39B | LINCOLN - 40A | IPSWICH - 32B | RETFORD - 36E | ARDSLEY - 37A | RETFORD - 36E |
| Aug-51 | 6/51: NOR - 32A | 4/51: STOCK - 9B | DONCASTER - 36A | DARNALL - 39B | 9/51: DARL - 51A | IPSWICH - 32B | RETFORD - 36E | ARDSLEY - 37A | RETFORD - 36E |
| Jan-52 | NORWICH - 32A | STOCKPORT - 9B | DONCASTER - 36A | 12/51: ARDS - 37A | DARLINGTON - 51A | IPSWICH - 32B | RETFORD - 36E | 3/52: BRAD - 37C | RETFORD - 36E |
| Aug-52 | NORWICH - 32A | 9/52: S.BGE - 35C | 10/52: S.BGE - 35C | 3/52: BRAD - 37C | 7/52: DAIRY - 53A | IPSWICH - 32B | RETFORD - 36E | BRADFORD - 37C | RETFORD - 36E |
| Jan-53 | NORWICH - 32A | S.BGE - 35C | S.BGE - 35C | BRADFORD - 37C | 12/52: HTN - 52B | IPSWICH - 32B | RETFORD - 36E | BRADFORD - 37C | RETFORD - 36E |
| Aug-53 | NORWICH - 32A | S.BGE - 35C | S.BGE - 35C | BRADFORD - 37C | HEATON - 52B | IPSWICH - 32B | RETFORD - 36E | BRADFORD - 37C | RETFORD - 36E |
| Jan-54 | NORWICH - 32A | S.BGE - 35C | S.BGE - 35C | BRADFORD - 37C | HEATON - 52B | IPSWICH - 32B | RETFORD - 36E | BRADFORD - 37C | RETFORD - 36E |
| Aug-54 | 11/54: M.CONS - 32G | S.BGE - 35C | S.BGE - 35C | BRADFORD - 37C | 6/54: DAIRY - 53A | IPSWICH - 32B | RETFORD - 36E | BRADFORD - 37C | RETFORD - 36E |
| Jan-55 | MELTON.C - 32G | S.BGE - 35C | S.BGE - 35C | BRADFORD - 37C | 11/54: SELBY - 50C | IPSWICH - 32B | RETFORD - 36E | BRADFORD - 37C | RETFORD - 36E |
| Aug-55 | 3/55: NOR - 32A | S.BGE - 35C | S.BGE - 35C | BRADFORD - 37C | SELBY - 50C | IPSWICH - 32B | RETFORD - 36E | BRADFORD - 37C | RETFORD - 36E |
| Jan-56 | NORWICH - 32A | S.BGE - 35C | S.BGE - 35C | BRADFORD - 37C | SELBY - 50C | IPSWICH - 32B | RETFORD - 36E | BRADFORD - 37C | RETFORD - 36E |
| Aug-56 | NORWICH - 32A | S.BGE - 35C | S.BGE - 35C | BRADFORD - 56G | SELBY - 50C | IPSWICH - 32B | RETFORD - 36E | BRADFORD - 56G | RETFORD - 36E |
| Jan-57 | NORWICH - 32A | 4/57: PLAIS - 33A | 12/56: BARN - 36D | BRADFORD - 56G | SELBY - 50C | IPSWICH - 32B | RETFORD - 36E | BRADFORD - 56G | RETFORD - 36E |
| Aug-57 | NORWICH - 32A | 6/57: S.BGE - 35C | BARNSLEY - 36D | BRADFORD - 56G | SELBY - 50C | IPSWICH - 32B | RETFORD - 36E | BRADFORD - 56G | RETFORD - 36E |
| Jan-58 | NORWICH - 32A | S.BGE - 35C | BARNSLEY - 36D | 2/58: LOW M - 56F | SELBY - 50C | IPSWICH - 32B | RETFORD - 36E | 2/58: LOW M - 56F | RETFORD - 36E |
| Aug-58 | NORWICH - 32A | S.BGE - 31F | BARNSLEY - 41G | LOWMOOR - 56F | SELBY - 50C | IPSWICH - 32B | RETFORD - 36E | LOWMOOR - 56F | RETFORD - 36E |
| Jan-59 | NORWICH - 32A | S.BGE - 31F | BARNSLEY - 41G | LOWMOOR - 56F | SELBY - 50C | IPSWICH - 32B | RETFORD - 36E | LOWMOOR - 56F | RETFORD - 36E |
| Aug-59 | 7/59: W/D | S.BGE - 31F | BARNSLEY - 41G | LOWMOOR - 56F | 9/59: YORK - 50A | IPSWICH - 32B | RETFORD - 36E | LOWMOOR - 56F | RETFORD - 36E |
| Nov-59 | | S.BGE - 31F | BARNSLEY - 41G | LOWMOOR - 56F | 11/59: DAIRY - 53A | 9/59: W/D | RETFORD - 36E | LOWMOOR - 56F | RETFORD - 36E |
| Jan-60 | | 2/60: MARCH - 31B | 1/60: MEX - 41F | LOWMOOR - 56F | DAIRYCOATES - 53A | | RETFORD - 36E | LOWMOOR - 56F | RETFORD - 36E |
| Apr-60 | | MARCH - 31B | 3/60: W/D | LOWMOOR - 56F | DAIRYCOATES - 53A | | RETFORD - 36E | LOWMOOR - 56F | RETFORD - 36E |
| Aug-60 | | MARCH - 31B | | LOWMOOR - 56F | 9/60: SCAR - 50E | | RETFORD - 36E | LOWMOOR - 56F | RETFORD - 36E |
| Nov-60 | | MARCH - 31B | | LOWMOOR - 56F | 10/60: DAIRY - 50B | | RETFORD - 36E | LOWMOOR - 56F | RETFORD - 36E |

| | 64909 | 64910 | 64911 | 64912 | 64913 | 64914 | 64915 | 64916 | 64917 |
|---|---|---|---|---|---|---|---|---|---|
| Aug-50 | DONCASTER - 36A | DONCASTER - 36A | ARDSLEY - 37A | CARLISLE(C) - 12B | NORWICH - 32A | DAIRYCOATES - 53A | HEATON - 52B | W.HARTLEPOOL - 51C | TWEEDMOUTH - 52D |
| Jan-51 | DONCASTER - 36A | DONCASTER - 36A | ARDSLEY - 37A | CARLISLE(C) - 12B | NORWICH - 32A | DAIRYCOATES - 53A | HEATON - 52B | W.HARTLEPOOL - 51C | TWEEDMOUTH - 52D |
| Aug-51 | DONCASTER - 36A | 9/51: DAIRY - 53A | ARDSLEY - 37A | CARLISLE(C) - 68E | NORWICH - 32A | DAIRYCOATES - 53A | HEATON - 52B | W.HARTLEPOOL - 51C | TWEEDMOUTH - 52D |
| Jan-52 | DONCASTER - 36A | 11/51: MBRO - 51D | ARDSLEY - 37A | CARLISLE(C) - 68E | NORWICH - 32A | DAIRYCOATES - 53A | HEATON - 52B | W.HARTLEPOOL - 51C | TWEEDMOUTH - 52D |
| Aug-52 | DONCASTER - 36A | 10/52: W.HPL - 51C | ARDSLEY - 37A | CARLISLE(C) - 68E | NORWICH - 32A | DAIRYCOATES - 53A | HEATON - 52B | W.HARTLEPOOL - 51C | TWEEDMOUTH - 52D |
| Jan-53 | DONCASTER - 36A | W.HARTLEPOOL - 51C | ARDSLEY - 37A | CARLISLE(C) - 68E | NORWICH - 32A | DAIRYCOATES - 53A | HEATON - 52B | W.HARTLEPOOL - 51C | TWEEDMOUTH - 52D |
| Aug-53 | DONCASTER - 36A | W.HARTLEPOOL - 51C | ARDSLEY - 37A | CARLISLE(C) - 68E | NORWICH - 32A | DAIRYCOATES - 53A | HEATON - 52B | W.HARTLEPOOL - 51C | TWEEDMOUTH - 52D |
| Jan-54 | DONCASTER - 36A | W.HARTLEPOOL - 51C | ARDSLEY - 37A | CARLISLE(C) - 68E | NORWICH - 32A | DAIRYCOATES - 53A | HEATON - 52B | W.HARTLEPOOL - 51C | TWEEDMOUTH - 52D |
| Aug-54 | DONCASTER - 36A | 10/54: NORTH - 51J | 4/54: C.HILL - 37B | CARLISLE(C) - 68E | NORWICH - 32A | DAIRYCOATES - 53A | HEATON - 52B | W.HARTLEPOOL - 51C | TWEEDMOUTH - 52D |
| Jan-55 | DONCASTER - 36A | 3/55: W.AUCK - 51F | COPLEY HILL - 37B | CARLISLE(C) - 68E | NORWICH - 32A | DAIRYCOATES - 53A | HEATON - 52B | 10/54: HTN - 52B | TWEEDMOUTH - 52D |
| Aug-55 | DONCASTER - 36A | 9/55: SUND - 54A | COPLEY HILL - 37B | CARLISLE(C) - 68E | NORWICH - 32A | DAIRYCOATES - 53A | HEATON - 52B | 6/55: ALN - 52D | TWEEDMOUTH - 52D |
| Jan-56 | DONCASTER - 36A | SUNDERLAND - 54A | COPLEY HILL - 37B | CARLISLE(C) - 68E | 4/56: M.CONS - 32G | DAIRYCOATES - 53A | HEATON - 52B | ALNMOUTH - 52D | TWEEDMOUTH - 52D |
| Aug-56 | DONCASTER - 36A | 6/56: DAIRY - 53A | COPLEY HILL - 56C | CARLISLE(C) - 68E | 10/56: NOR - 32A | DAIRYCOATES - 53A | HEATON - 52B | ALNMOUTH - 52D | TWEEDMOUTH - 52D |
| Jan-57 | DONCASTER - 36A | DAIRYCOATES - 53A | COPLEY HILL - 56C | CARLISLE(C) - 68E | 1/57: M.CONS - 32G | DAIRYCOATES - 53A | HEATON - 52B | ALNMOUTH - 52D | TWEEDMOUTH - 52D |
| Aug-57 | DONCASTER - 36A | DAIRYCOATES - 53A | COPLEY HILL - 56C | CARLISLE(C) - 68E | 2/57: NOR - 32A | DAIRYCOATES - 53A | HEATON - 52B | ALNMOUTH - 52D | TWEEDMOUTH - 52D |
| Jan-58 | DONCASTER - 36A | DAIRYCOATES - 53A | 3/58: ARDS - 56B | CARLISLE(C) - 68E | NORWICH - 32A | DAIRYCOATES - 53A | HEATON - 52B | ALNMOUTH - 52D | TWEEDMOUTH - 52D |
| Aug-58 | DONCASTER - 36A | DAIRYCOATES - 53A | 9/58: C.HILL - 56C | CARLISLE(C) - 12C | NORWICH - 32A | DAIRYCOATES - 53A | HEATON - 52B | ALNMOUTH - 52D | TWEEDMOUTH - 52D |
| Jan-59 | DONCASTER - 36A | DAIRYCOATES - 53A | COPLEY HILL - 56C | CARLISLE(C) - 12C | NORWICH - 32A | DAIRYCOATES - 53A | HEATON - 52B | ALNMOUTH - 52D | TWEEDMOUTH - 52D |
| Aug-59 | DONCASTER - 36A | DAIRYCOATES - 53A | COPLEY HILL - 56C | CARLISLE(C) - 12C | NORWICH - 32A | DAIRYCOATES - 53A | HEATON - 52B | ALNMOUTH - 52D | TWEEDMOUTH - 52D |
| Nov-59 | DONCASTER - 36A | DAIRYCOATES - 53A | COPLEY HILL - 56C | 11/59: W/D | 10/59: W/D | DAIRYCOATES - 53A | HEATON - 52B | ALNMOUTH - 52D | TWEEDMOUTH - 52D |
| Jan-60 | DONCASTER - 36A | DAIRYCOATES - 53A | COPLEY HILL - 56C | | | DAIRYCOATES - 53A | HEATON - 52B | ALNMOUTH - 52D | TWEEDMOUTH - 52D |
| Apr-60 | DONCASTER - 36A | DAIRYCOATES - 50B | COPLEY HILL - 56C | | | DAIRYCOATES - 50B | HEATON - 52B | ALNMOUTH - 52D | TWEEDMOUTH - 52D |
| Aug-60 | DONCASTER - 36A | 9/60: N.HILL - 55H | COPLEY HILL - 56C | | | DAIRYCOATES - 50B | HEATON - 52B | ALNMOUTH - 52D | TWEEDMOUTH - 52D |
| Nov-60 | DONCASTER - 36A | NEVILLE HILL - 55H | 11/60: ARDS - 56B | | | DAIRYCOATES - 50B | HEATON - 52B | ALNMOUTH - 52D | TWEEDMOUTH - 52D |

| | 64918 | 64919 | 64920 | 64921 | 64922 | 64923 | 64924 | 64925 | 64926 |
|---|---|---|---|---|---|---|---|---|---|
| Aug-50 | CRICKLEWOOD - 14A | SCARBOROUGH - 50E | NEVILLE HILL - 50B | NEVILLE HILL - 50B | STARBECK - 50D | HEATON - 52B | ALNMOUTH - 52D | TWEEDMOUTH - 52D | DAIRYCOATES - 53A |
| Jan-51 | CRICKLEWOOD - 14A | 10/50: N.HILL - 50B | NEVILLE HILL - 50B | NEVILLE HILL - 50B | 10/50: N.HILL - 50B | HEATON - 52B | ALNMOUTH - 52D | TWEEDMOUTH - 52D | 2/51: B.GDNS - 54C |
| Aug-51 | CRICKLEWOOD - 14A | 7/51: B.GDNS - 54C | NEVILLE HILL - 50B | 7/51: B.GDNS - 54C | NEVILLE HILL - 50B | HEATON - 52B | ALNMOUTH - 52D | TWEEDMOUTH - 52D | BOR.GDNS - 54C |
| Jan-52 | 3/52: ARDS - 37A | BOR.GDNS - 54C | NEVILLE HILL - 50B | BOR.GDNS - 54C | NEVILLE HILL - 50B | HEATON - 52B | ALNMOUTH - 52D | TWEEDMOUTH - 52D | BOR.GDNS - 54C |
| Aug-52 | ARDSLEY - 37A | BOR.GDNS - 54C | NEVILLE HILL - 50B | BOR.GDNS - 54C | NEVILLE HILL - 50B | HEATON - 52B | ALNMOUTH - 52D | TWEEDMOUTH - 52D | BOR.GDNS - 54C |
| Jan-53 | ARDSLEY - 37A | 2/53: SUND - 54A | NEVILLE HILL - 50B | BOR.GDNS - 54C | NEVILLE HILL - 50B | HEATON - 52B | ALNMOUTH - 52D | TWEEDMOUTH - 52D | BOR.GDNS - 54C |
| Aug-53 | ARDSLEY - 37A | SUNDERLAND - 54A | NEVILLE HILL - 50B | BOR.GDNS - 54C | NEVILLE HILL - 50B | HEATON - 52B | ALNMOUTH - 52D | TWEEDMOUTH - 52D | BOR.GDNS - 54C |
| Jan-54 | ARDSLEY - 37A | SUNDERLAND - 54A | NEVILLE HILL - 50B | BOR.GDNS - 54C | NEVILLE HILL - 50B | HEATON - 52B | ALNMOUTH - 52D | TWEEDMOUTH - 52D | BOR.GDNS - 54C |
| Aug-54 | ARDSLEY - 37A | SUNDERLAND - 54A | NEVILLE HILL - 50B | BOR.GDNS - 54C | NEVILLE HILL - 50B | HEATON - 52B | ALNMOUTH - 52D | TWEEDMOUTH - 52D | BOR.GDNS - 54C |
| Jan-55 | ARDSLEY - 37A | SUNDERLAND - 54A | NEVILLE HILL - 50B | BOR.GDNS - 54C | 10/54: SELBY - 50C | HEATON - 52B | ALNMOUTH - 52D | TWEEDMOUTH - 52D | BOR.GDNS - 54C |
| Aug-55 | ARDSLEY - 37A | SUNDERLAND - 54A | NEVILLE HILL - 50B | BOR.GDNS - 54C | 6/55: N.HILL - 50B | HEATON - 52B | ALNMOUTH - 52D | TWEEDMOUTH - 52D | BOR.GDNS - 54C |
| Jan-56 | ARDSLEY - 37A | SUNDERLAND - 54A | NEVILLE HILL - 50B | BOR.GDNS - 54C | NEVILLE HILL - 50B | HEATON - 52B | ALNMOUTH - 52D | TWEEDMOUTH - 52D | BOR.GDNS - 54C |
| Aug-56 | ARDSLEY - 56B | SUNDERLAND - 54A | NEVILLE HILL - 50B | BOR.GDNS - 54C | NEVILLE HILL - 50B | HEATON - 52B | ALNMOUTH - 52D | TWEEDMOUTH - 52D | BOR.GDNS - 54C |
| Jan-57 | ARDSLEY - 56B | SUNDERLAND - 54A | NEVILLE HILL - 50B | BOR.GDNS - 54C | NEVILLE HILL - 50B | HEATON - 52B | ALNMOUTH - 52D | TWEEDMOUTH - 52D | BOR.GDNS - 54C |
| Aug-57 | ARDSLEY - 56B | SUNDERLAND - 54A | NEVILLE HILL - 50B | BOR.GDNS - 54C | NEVILLE HILL - 50B | HEATON - 52B | ALNMOUTH - 52D | TWEEDMOUTH - 52D | 6/57: HTN - 52B |
| Jan-58 | ARDSLEY - 56B | SUNDERLAND - 54A | NEVILLE HILL - 50B | BOR.GDNS - 54C | NEVILLE HILL - 50B | HEATON - 52B | ALNMOUTH - 52D | TWEEDMOUTH - 52D | HEATON - 52B |
| Aug-58 | ARDSLEY - 56B | SUNDERLAND - 54A | NEVILLE HILL - 50B | BOR.GDNS - 54C | NEVILLE HILL - 50B | HEATON - 52B | ALNMOUTH - 52D | TWEEDMOUTH - 52D | HEATON - 52B |
| Jan-59 | ARDSLEY - 56B | 2/59: LOW M - 56F | NEVILLE HILL - 50B | B.GDNS - 52J | NEVILLE HILL - 50B | HEATON - 52B | ALNMOUTH - 52D | TWEEDMOUTH - 52D | HEATON - 52B |
| Aug-59 | ARDSLEY - 56B | LOWMOOR - 56F | NEVILLE HILL - 50B | 6/59: GHD - 52A | NEVILLE HILL - 50B | HEATON - 52B | ALNMOUTH - 52D | TWEEDMOUTH - 52D | HEATON - 52B |
| Nov-59 | ARDSLEY - 56B | LOWMOOR - 56F | NEVILLE HILL - 50B | GATESHEAD - 52A | NEVILLE HILL - 50B | HEATON - 52B | ALNMOUTH - 52D | TWEEDMOUTH - 52D | HEATON - 52B |
| Jan-60 | ARDSLEY - 56B | LOWMOOR - 56F | NEVILLE HILL - 50B | GATESHEAD - 52A | NEVILLE HILL - 50B | HEATON - 52B | ALNMOUTH - 52D | TWEEDMOUTH - 52D | HEATON - 52B |
| Apr-60 | ARDSLEY - 56B | LOWMOOR - 56F | NEVILLE HILL - 55H | GATESHEAD - 52A | NEVILLE HILL - 55H | HEATON - 52B | ALNMOUTH - 52D | TWEEDMOUTH - 52D | HEATON - 52B |
| Aug-60 | ARDSLEY - 56B | LOWMOOR - 56F | NEVILLE HILL - 55H | GATESHEAD - 52A | NEVILLE HILL - 55H | HEATON - 52B | ALNMOUTH - 52D | TWEEDMOUTH - 52D | HEATON - 52B |
| Nov-60 | ARDSLEY - 56B | LOWMOOR - 56F | NEVILLE HILL - 55H | GATESHEAD - 52A | NEVILLE HILL - 55H | HEATON - 52B | ALNMOUTH - 52D | TWEEDMOUTH - 52D | HEATON - 52B |

| | 64927 | 64928 | 64929 | 64930 | 64931 | 64932 | 64933 | 64934 | 64935 |
|---|---|---|---|---|---|---|---|---|---|
| Aug-50 | DAIRYCOATES - 53A | DAIRYCOATES - 53A | BOR.GDNS - 54C | CARLISLE(C) - 12B | DAIRYCOATES - 53A | CARLISLE(C) - 12B | DARLINGTON - 51A | NEVILLE HILL - 50B | SCARBOROUGH - 50E |
| Jan-51 | 2/51: B.GDNS - 54C | DAIRYCOATES - 53A | BOR.GDNS - 54C | CARLISLE(C) - 12B | 12/50: B.GDNS - 54C | CARLISLE(C) - 12B | 9/50: N.HILL - 50B | NEVILLE HILL - 50B | 1/51: N.HILL - 50B |
| Aug-51 | BOR.GDNS - 54C | DAIRYCOATES - 53A | BOR.GDNS - 54C | CARLISLE(C) - 68E | BOR.GDNS - 54C | CARLISLE(C) - 68E | NEVILLE HILL - 50B | NEVILLE HILL - 50B | NEVILLE HILL - 50B |
| Jan-52 | BOR.GDNS - 54C | DAIRYCOATES - 53A | BOR.GDNS - 54C | CARLISLE(C) - 68E | BOR.GDNS - 54C | CARLISLE(C) - 68E | NEVILLE HILL - 50B | NEVILLE HILL - 50B | NEVILLE HILL - 50B |
| Aug-52 | BOR.GDNS - 54C | DAIRYCOATES - 53A | BOR.GDNS - 54C | CARLISLE(C) - 68E | BOR.GDNS - 54C | CARLISLE(C) - 68E | NEVILLE HILL - 50B | NEVILLE HILL - 50B | NEVILLE HILL - 50B |
| Jan-53 | BOR.GDNS - 54C | 11/52: MALT - 50F | 1/53: GHD - 52A | CARLISLE(C) - 68E | BOR.GDNS - 54C | CARLISLE(C) - 68E | NEVILLE HILL - 50B | NEVILLE HILL - 50B | NEVILLE HILL - 50B |
| Aug-53 | BOR.GDNS - 54C | MALTON - 50F | GATESHEAD - 52A | CARLISLE(C) - 68E | BOR.GDNS - 54C | CARLISLE(C) - 68E | NEVILLE HILL - 50B | NEVILLE HILL - 50B | NEVILLE HILL - 50B |
| Jan-54 | BOR.GDNS - 54C | MALTON - 50F | GATESHEAD - 52A | CARLISLE(C) - 68E | BOR.GDNS - 54C | CARLISLE(C) - 68E | NEVILLE HILL - 50B | NEVILLE HILL - 50B | NEVILLE HILL - 50B |
| Aug-54 | BOR.GDNS - 54C | MALTON - 50F | GATESHEAD - 52A | CARLISLE(C) - 68E | BOR.GDNS - 54C | CARLISLE(C) - 68E | NEVILLE HILL - 50B | NEVILLE HILL - 50B | NEVILLE HILL - 50B |
| Jan-55 | BOR.GDNS - 54C | MALTON - 50F | GATESHEAD - 52A | CARLISLE(C) - 68E | BOR.GDNS - 54C | CARLISLE(C) - 68E | NEVILLE HILL - 50B | NEVILLE HILL - 50B | NEVILLE HILL - 50B |
| Aug-55 | BOR.GDNS - 54C | MALTON - 50F | GATESHEAD - 52A | CARLISLE(C) - 68E | BOR.GDNS - 54C | CARLISLE(C) - 68E | NEVILLE HILL - 50B | NEVILLE HILL - 50B | NEVILLE HILL - 50B |
| Jan-56 | BOR.GDNS - 54C | MALTON - 50F | GATESHEAD - 52A | CARLISLE(C) - 68E | BOR.GDNS - 54C | CARLISLE(C) - 68E | NEVILLE HILL - 50B | NEVILLE HILL - 50B | NEVILLE HILL - 50B |
| Aug-56 | 6/56: W.AUCK - 51F | MALTON - 50F | GATESHEAD - 52A | CARLISLE(C) - 68E | BOR.GDNS - 54C | CARLISLE(C) - 68E | NEVILLE HILL - 50B | NEVILLE HILL - 50B | NEVILLE HILL - 50B |
| Jan-57 | W.AUCKLAND - 51F | MALTON - 50F | GATESHEAD - 52A | CARLISLE(C) - 68E | BOR.GDNS - 54C | CARLISLE(C) - 68E | NEVILLE HILL - 50B | NEVILLE HILL - 50B | NEVILLE HILL - 50B |
| Aug-57 | W.AUCKLAND - 51F | MALTON - 50F | 6/57: ALN - 52D | CARLISLE(C) - 68E | 6/57: HTN - 52B | CARLISLE(C) - 68E | NEVILLE HILL - 50B | NEVILLE HILL - 50B | NEVILLE HILL - 50B |
| Jan-58 | W.AUCKLAND - 51F | MALTON - 50F | ALNMOUTH - 52D | CARLISLE(C) - 68E | HEATON - 52B | CARLISLE(C) - 68E | NEVILLE HILL - 50B | NEVILLE HILL - 50B | NEVILLE HILL - 50B |
| Aug-58 | W.AUCKLAND - 51F | MALTON - 50F | ALNMOUTH - 52D | CARLISLE(C) - 12C | HEATON - 52B | CARLISLE(C) - 12C | NEVILLE HILL - 50B | NEVILLE HILL - 50B | NEVILLE HILL - 50B |
| Jan-59 | W.AUCKLAND - 51F | MALTON - 50F | ALNMOUTH - 52D | 11/58: GORT - 9G | HEATON - 52B | CARLISLE(C) - 12C | NEVILLE HILL - 50B | NEVILLE HILL - 50B | NEVILLE HILL - 50B |
| Aug-59 | W.AUCKLAND - 51F | MALTON - 50F | ALNMOUTH - 52D | GORTON - 9G | HEATON - 52B | CARLISLE(C) - 12C | NEVILLE HILL - 50B | NEVILLE HILL - 50B | NEVILLE HILL - 50B |
| Nov-59 | W.AUCKLAND - 51F | MALTON - 50F | ALNMOUTH - 52D | GORTON - 9G | HEATON - 52B | CARLISLE(C) - 12C | NEVILLE HILL - 50B | NEVILLE HILL - 50B | NEVILLE HILL - 50B |
| Jan-60 | W.AUCKLAND - 51F | MALTON - 50F | ALNMOUTH - 52D | GORTON - 9G | HEATON - 52B | CARLISLE(C) - 12C | NEVILLE HILL - 50B | NEVILLE HILL - 50B | NEVILLE HILL - 50B |
| Apr-60 | W.AUCKLAND - 51F | MALTON - 50F | ALNMOUTH - 52D | GORTON - 9G | HEATON - 52B | CARLISLE(C) - 12C | NEVILLE HILL - 55H | NEVILLE HILL - 55H | NEVILLE HILL - 55H |
| Aug-60 | W.AUCKLAND - 51F | MALTON - 50F | ALNMOUTH - 52D | GORTON - 9G | HEATON - 52B | CARLISLE(C) - 12C | NEVILLE HILL - 55H | NEVILLE HILL - 55H | NEVILLE HILL - 55H |
| Nov-60 | W.AUCKLAND - 51F | MALTON - 50F | ALNMOUTH - 52D | GORTON - 9G | HEATON - 52B | CARLISLE(C) - 12C | NEVILLE HILL - 55H | NEVILLE HILL - 55H | NEVILLE HILL - 55H |

| | 64936 | 64937 | 64938 | 64939 | 64940 | 64941 | 64942 | 64943 | 64944 |
|---|---|---|---|---|---|---|---|---|---|
| Aug-50 | BOR.GDNS-54C | LINCOLN-40A | STARBECK-50D | DAIRYCOATES-53A | BLAYDON-52C | DAIRYCOATES-53A | STARBECK-50D | NEVILLEHILL-50B | STARBECK-50D |
| Jan-51 | BOR.GDNS-54C | LINCOLN-40A | STARBECK-50D | **12/50: B.GDNS - 54C** | **11/50: DARL - 51A** | DAIRYCOATES-53A | STARBECK-50D | NEVILLEHILL-50B | STARBECK-50D |
| Aug-51 | BOR.GDNS-54C | LINCOLN-40A | STARBECK-50D | BOR.GDNS-54C | **1/51: MBRO - 51D** | **5/51: B.GDNS - 54C** | STARBECK-50D | NEVILLEHILL-50B | STARBECK-50D |
| Jan-52 | BOR.GDNS-54C | LINCOLN-40A | STARBECK-50D | BOR.GDNS-54C | MIDDLESBROUGH-51D | BOR.GDNS-54C | STARBECK-50D | NEVILLEHILL-50B | STARBECK-50D |
| Aug-52 | BOR.GDNS-54C | LINCOLN-40A | STARBECK-50D | BOR.GDNS-54C | **9/52: W.AUCK - 51F** | BOR.GDNS-54C | STARBECK-50D | NEVILLEHILL-50B | STARBECK-50D |
| Jan-53 | BOR.GDNS-54C | LINCOLN-40A | STARBECK-50D | **2/53: SUND - 54A** | W.AUCKLAND-51F | **1/53: TWEED - 52D** | STARBECK-50D | NEVILLEHILL-50B | STARBECK-50D |
| Aug-53 | BOR.GDNS-54C | LINCOLN-40A | STARBECK-50D | SUNDERLAND-54A | W.AUCKLAND-51F | TWEEDMOUTH-52D | STARBECK-50D | NEVILLEHILL-50B | STARBECK-50D |
| Jan-54 | BOR.GDNS-54C | LINCOLN-40A | STARBECK-50D | SUNDERLAND-54A | W.AUCKLAND-51F | TWEEDMOUTH-52D | STARBECK-50D | NEVILLEHILL-50B | STARBECK-50D |
| Aug-54 | BOR.GDNS-54C | LINCOLN-40A | **4/54: MALT - 50F** | SUNDERLAND-54A | W.AUCKLAND-51F | TWEEDMOUTH-52D | STARBECK-50D | NEVILLEHILL-50B | STARBECK-50D |
| Jan-55 | BOR.GDNS-54C | LINCOLN-40A | MALTON-50F | SUNDERLAND-54A | W.AUCKLAND-51F | TWEEDMOUTH-52D | STARBECK-50D | NEVILLEHILL-50B | STARBECK-50D |
| Aug-55 | BOR.GDNS-54C | LINCOLN-40A | MALTON-50F | SUNDERLAND-54A | **8/55: SUND - 54A** | TWEEDMOUTH-52D | STARBECK-50D | NEVILLEHILL-50B | STARBECK-50D |
| Jan-56 | BOR.GDNS-54C | LINCOLN-40A | MALTON-50F | SUNDERLAND-54A | SUNDERLAND-54A | TWEEDMOUTH-52D | STARBECK-50D | NEVILLEHILL-50B | STARBECK-50D |
| Aug-56 | BOR.GDNS-54C | LINCOLN-40A | MALTON-50F | **6/56: DAIRY - 53A** | **6/56: DAIRY - 53A** | TWEEDMOUTH-52D | STARBECK-50D | NEVILLEHILL-50B | STARBECK-50D |
| Jan-57 | BOR.GDNS-54C | LINCOLN-40A | MALTON-50F | DAIRYCOATES-53A | DAIRYCOATES-53A | TWEEDMOUTH-52D | STARBECK-50D | NEVILLEHILL-50B | STARBECK-50D |
| Aug-57 | BOR.GDNS-54C | LINCOLN-40A | MALTON-50F | **6/57: HTN - 52B** | DAIRYCOATES-53A | TWEEDMOUTH-52D | STARBECK-50D | NEVILLEHILL-50B | STARBECK-50D |
| Jan-58 | BOR.GDNS-54C | LINCOLN-40A | MALTON-50F | HEATON-52B | DAIRYCOATES-53A | TWEEDMOUTH-52D | STARBECK-50D | NEVILLEHILL-50B | STARBECK-50D |
| Aug-58 | BOR.GDNS-54C | LINCOLN-40A | MALTON-50F | HEATON-52B | DAIRYCOATES-53A | TWEEDMOUTH-52D | STARBECK-50D | NEVILLEHILL-50B | STARBECK-50D |
| Jan-59 | BOR.GDNS-52J | LINCOLN-40A | MALTON-50F | HEATON-52B | DAIRYCOATES-53A | TWEEDMOUTH-52D | STARBECK-50D | NEVILLEHILL-50B | STARBECK-50D |
| Aug-59 | **6/59: GHD - 52A** | LINCOLN-40A | **6/59: SELBY - 50C** | HEATON-52B | DAIRYCOATES-53A | TWEEDMOUTH-52D | **9/59: YORK - 50A** | NEVILLEHILL-50B | **9/59: YORK - 50A** |
| Nov-59 | GATESHEAD-52A | LINCOLN-40A | **8/59: GHD - 52A** | HEATON-52B | DAIRYCOATES-53A | TWEEDMOUTH-52D | YORK-50A | **11/59: DAIRY - 53A** | YORK-50A |
| Jan-60 | GATESHEAD-52A | LINCOLN-40A | GATESHEAD-52A | HEATON-52B | DAIRYCOATES-53A | TWEEDMOUTH-52D | YORK-50A | DAIRYCOATES-53A | **12/59: N.HILL - 55H** |
| Apr-60 | GATESHEAD-52A | **3/60: W/D** | GATESHEAD-52A | HEATON-52B | DAIRYCOATES-50B | TWEEDMOUTH-52D | **4/60: SUND - 52G** | DAIRYCOATES-50B | NEVILLEHILL-55H |
| Aug-60 | GATESHEAD-52A | | GATESHEAD-52A | HEATON-52B | DAIRYCOATES-50B | TWEEDMOUTH-52D | SUNDERLAND-52G | DAIRYCOATES-50B | NEVILLEHILL-55H |
| Nov-60 | GATESHEAD-52A | | GATESHEAD-52A | HEATON-52B | DAIRYCOATES-50B | TWEEDMOUTH-52D | SUNDERLAND-52G | DAIRYCOATES-50B | NEVILLEHILL-55H |

| | 64945 | 64946 | 64947 | 64948 | 64949 | 64950 | 64951 | 64952 | 64953 |
|---|---|---|---|---|---|---|---|---|---|
| Aug-50 | HEATON-52B | EDINBURGH(SM)-64A | HEATON-52B | CARLISLE(C)-12B | NEVILLEHILL-50B | DUNDEE-62B | DONCASTER-36A | DONCASTER-36A | PARKESTON-30F |
| Jan-51 | HEATON-52B | EDINBURGH(SM)-64A | HEATON-52B | CARLISLE(C)-12B | NEVILLEHILL-50B | DUNDEE-62B | DONCASTER-36A | DONCASTER-36A | PARKESTON-30F |
| Aug-51 | HEATON-52B | EDINBURGH(SM)-64A | HEATON-52B | CARLISLE(C)-68E | NEVILLEHILL-50B | DUNDEE-62B | DONCASTER-36A | DONCASTER-36A | PARKESTON-30F |
| Jan-52 | HEATON-52B | EDINBURGH(SM)-64A | **2/52: B.GDNS - 54C** | CARLISLE(C)-68E | NEVILLEHILL-50B | DUNDEE-62B | DONCASTER-36A | DONCASTER-36A | PARKESTON-30F |
| Aug-52 | HEATON-52B | EDINBURGH(SM)-64A | B.GDNS-54C | CARLISLE(C)-68E | NEVILLEHILL-50B | DUNDEE-62B | **10/52: S.BGE - 35C** | DONCASTER-36A | PARKESTON-30F |
| Jan-53 | HEATON-52B | EDINBURGH(SM)-64A | B.GDNS-54C | CARLISLE(C)-68E | NEVILLEHILL-50B | DUNDEE-62B | S.BGE-35C | DONCASTER-36A | PARKESTON-30F |
| Aug-53 | HEATON-52B | EDINBURGH(SM)-64A | B.GDNS-54C | CARLISLE(C)-68E | NEVILLEHILL-50B | DUNDEE-62B | S.BGE-35C | DONCASTER-36A | PARKESTON-30F |
| Jan-54 | HEATON-52B | EDINBURGH(SM)-64A | B.GDNS-54C | CARLISLE(C)-68E | NEVILLEHILL-50B | DUNDEE-62B | S.BGE-35C | DONCASTER-36A | PARKESTON-30F |
| Aug-54 | HEATON-52B | EDINBURGH(SM)-64A | **5/54: MALT - 50F** | CARLISLE(C)-68E | **6/54: DAIRY - 53A** | DUNDEE-62B | S.BGE-35C | DONCASTER-36A | PARKESTON-30F |
| Jan-55 | HEATON-52B | EDINBURGH(SM)-64A | MALTON-50F | CARLISLE(C)-68E | DAIRYCOATES-53A | DUNDEE-62B | S.BGE-35C | DONCASTER-36A | PARKESTON-30F |
| Aug-55 | HEATON-52B | EDINBURGH(SM)-64A | MALTON-50F | CARLISLE(C)-68E | DAIRYCOATES-53A | DUNDEE-62B | S.BGE-35C | DONCASTER-36A | PARKESTON-30F |
| Jan-56 | HEATON-52B | EDINBURGH(SM)-64A | MALTON-50F | CARLISLE(C)-68E | DAIRYCOATES-53A | DUNDEE-62B | S.BGE-35C | DONCASTER-36A | PARKESTON-30F |
| Aug-56 | HEATON-52B | EDINBURGH(SM)-64A | MALTON-50F | CARLISLE(C)-68E | DAIRYCOATES-53A | DUNDEE-62B | S.BGE-35C | DONCASTER-36A | PARKESTON-30F |
| Jan-57 | HEATON-52B | EDINBURGH(SM)-64A | MALTON-50F | CARLISLE(C)-68E | DAIRYCOATES-53A | DUNDEE-62B | S.BGE-35C | DONCASTER-36A | PARKESTON-30F |
| Aug-57 | HEATON-52B | EDINBURGH(SM)-64A | **9/57: BRAD - 56G** | CARLISLE(C)-68E | **6/57: HTN - 52B** | DUNDEE-62B | **4/57: PLAIS - 33A** | **6/57: PLAIS - 33A** | **6/57: PLAIS - 33A** |
| Jan-58 | HEATON-52B | EDINBURGH(SM)-64A | **2/58: LOW M - 56F** | CARLISLE(C)-68E | HEATON-52B | DUNDEE-62B | PLAISTOW-33A | PLAISTOW-33A | PLAISTOW-33A |
| Aug-58 | HEATON-52B | **9/58: DALRY - 64C** | **6/58: DAIRY - 53A** | CARLISLE(C)-12C | **6/58: ALN - 52D** | DUNDEE-62B | PLAISTOW-33A | PLAISTOW-33A | PLAISTOW-33A |
| Jan-59 | HEATON-52B | DALRYRD-64C | DAIRYCOATES-53A | CARLISLE(C)-12C | ALNMOUTH-52D | DUNDEE-62B | PLAISTOW-33A | PLAISTOW-33A | PLAISTOW-33A |
| Aug-59 | HEATON-52B | DALRYRD-64C | DAIRYCOATES-53A | CARLISLE(C)-12C | ALNMOUTH-52D | DUNDEE-62B | PLAISTOW-33A | PLAISTOW-33A | PLAISTOW-33A |
| Nov-59 | HEATON-52B | DALRYRD-64C | DAIRYCOATES-53A | CARLISLE(C)-12C | ALNMOUTH-52D | DUNDEE-62B | **10/59: TIL - 33B** | **10/59: TIL - 33B** | **10/59: TIL - 33B** |
| Jan-60 | HEATON-52B | DALRYRD-64C | DAIRYCOATES-53A | CARLISLE(C)-12C | ALNMOUTH-52D | DUNDEE-62B | TILBURY-33B | TILBURY-33B | TILBURY-33B |
| Apr-60 | HEATON-52B | DALRYRD-64C | DAIRYCOATES-50B | **4/60: W/D** | ALNMOUTH-52D | DUNDEE-62B | **3/60: W/D** | **3/60: W/D** | **3/60: W/D** |
| Aug-60 | HEATON-52B | DALRYRD-64C | **9/60: N.HILL - 55H** | | ALNMOUTH-52D | DUNDEE-62B | | | |
| Nov-60 | HEATON-52B | DALRYRD-64C | NEVILLEHILL-55H | | ALNMOUTH-52D | DUNDEE-62B | | | |

| | 64954 | 64955 | 64956 | 64957 | 64958 | 64959 | 64960 | 64961 | 64962 |
|---|---|---|---|---|---|---|---|---|---|
| Aug-50 | TRAFFORDPARK-9E | COLWICK-38A | RETFORD-36E | IPSWICH-32B | IPSWICH-32B | NORWICH-32A | DARNALL-39B | RETFORD-36E | GORTON-39A |
| Jan-51 | TRAFFORDPARK-9E | COLWICK-38A | RETFORD-36E | IPSWICH-32B | IPSWICH-32B | NORWICH-32A | DARNALL-39B | RETFORD-36E | GORTON-39A |
| Aug-51 | STOCKPORT-9B | COLWICK-38A | RETFORD-36E | IPSWICH-32B | **9/51: STRAT - 30A** | **9/51: STRAT - 30A** | DARNALL-39B | RETFORD-36E | **4/51: DARN - 39B** |
| Jan-52 | STOCKPORT-9B | COLWICK-38A | RETFORD-36E | IPSWICH-32B | STRATFORD-30A | STRATFORD-30A | DARNALL-39B | RETFORD-36E | DARNALL-39B |
| Aug-52 | STOCKPORT-9B | COLWICK-38A | **9/52: DCTR - 36A** | IPSWICH-32B | STRATFORD-30A | STRATFORD-30A | DARNALL-39B | RETFORD-36E | DARNALL-39B |
| Jan-53 | S.BGE-35C | COLWICK-38A | DONCASTER-36A | IPSWICH-32B | STRATFORD-30A | STRATFORD-30A | DARNALL-39B | RETFORD-36E | DARNALL-39B |
| Aug-53 | S.BGE-35C | COLWICK-38A | DONCASTER-36A | IPSWICH-32B | STRATFORD-30A | STRATFORD-30A | DARNALL-39B | RETFORD-36E | DARNALL-39B |
| Jan-54 | S.BGE-35C | COLWICK-38A | DONCASTER-36A | IPSWICH-32B | STRATFORD-30A | **12/53: LINC - 40A** | DARNALL-39B | RETFORD-36E | DARNALL-39B |
| Aug-54 | S.BGE-35C | COLWICK-38A | DONCASTER-36A | IPSWICH-32B | STRATFORD-30A | LINCOLN-40A | **8/54: LINC - 40A** | RETFORD-36E | DARNALL-39B |
| Jan-55 | S.BGE-35C | COLWICK-38A | DONCASTER-36A | IPSWICH-32B | STRATFORD-30A | LINCOLN-40A | LINCOLN-40A | RETFORD-36E | DARNALL-39B |
| Aug-55 | S.BGE-35C | COLWICK-38A | DONCASTER-36A | IPSWICH-32B | **9/55: CAMB - 31A** | LINCOLN-40A | LINCOLN-40A | RETFORD-36E | DARNALL-39B |
| Jan-56 | S.BGE-35C | COLWICK-38A | DONCASTER-36A | IPSWICH-32B | CAMBRIDGE-31A | LINCOLN-40A | LINCOLN-40A | RETFORD-36E | DARNALL-41A |
| Aug-56 | S.BGE-35C | COLWICK-38A | DONCASTER-36A | IPSWICH-32B | CAMBRIDGE-31A | LINCOLN-40A | LINCOLN-40A | RETFORD-36E | DARNALL-41A |
| Jan-57 | S.BGE-35C | COLWICK-38A | DONCASTER-36A | IPSWICH-32B | CAMBRIDGE-31A | LINCOLN-40A | LINCOLN-40A | RETFORD-36E | DARNALL-41A |
| Aug-57 | **6/57: PLAIS - 33A** | COLWICK-38A | **6/57: PLAIS - 33A** | **6/57: PLAIS - 33A** | CAMBRIDGE-31A | LINCOLN-40A | LINCOLN-40A | RETFORD-36E | **4/57: STRAT - 30A** |
| Jan-58 | PLAISTOW-33A | **11/57: ANN - 38B** | PLAISTOW-33A | PLAISTOW-33A | CAMBRIDGE-31A | LINCOLN-40A | LINCOLN-40A | RETFORD-36E | STRATFORD-30A |
| Aug-58 | PLAISTOW-33A | ANNESLEY-16D | PLAISTOW-33A | PLAISTOW-33A | **6/58: PLAIS - 33A** | LINCOLN-40A | **10/58: BOST - 40F** | RETFORD-36E | **6/58: PLAIS - 33A** |
| Jan-59 | PLAISTOW-33A | ANNESLEY-16D | PLAISTOW-33A | PLAISTOW-33A | PLAISTOW-33A | LINCOLN-40A | **12/58: LINC - 40A** | **12/58: LINC - 40A** | PLAISTOW-33A |
| Aug-59 | PLAISTOW-33A | ANNESLEY-16D | PLAISTOW-33A | PLAISTOW-33A | PLAISTOW-33A | LINCOLN-40A | LINCOLN-40A | LINCOLN-40A | PLAISTOW-33A |
| Nov-59 | **10/59: TIL - 33B** | ANNESLEY-16D | **10/59: TIL - 33B** | **10/59: TIL - 33B** | **10/59: TIL - 33B** | LINCOLN-40A | LINCOLN-40A | **10/59: W/D** | **10/59: TIL - 33B** |
| Jan-60 | TILBURY-33B | ANNESLEY-16D | TILBURY-33B | TILBURY-33B | TILBURY-33B | **12/59: W/D** | LINCOLN-40A | | TILBURY-33B |
| Apr-60 | **3/60: W/D** | ANNESLEY-16D | **3/60: W/D** | **3/60: W/D** | **3/60: W/D** | | **2/60: W/D** | | **3/60: W/D** |
| Aug-60 | | ANNESLEY-16D | | | | | | | |
| Nov-60 | | ANNESLEY-16D | | | | | | | |

| | 64963 | 64964 | 64965 | 64966 | 64967 | 64968 | 64969 | 64970 | 64971 |
|---|---|---|---|---|---|---|---|---|---|
| Aug-50 | EDINBURGH(SM)-64A | CARLISLE(C)-12B | COLWICK-38A | CRICKLEWOOD-14A | DONCASTER-36A | NORWICH-32A | DARNALL-39B | RETFORD-36E | LINCOLN-40A |
| Jan-51 | EDINBURGH(SM)-64A | CARLISLE(C)-12B | COLWICK-38A | **3/51: STRAT - 30A** | DONCASTER-36A | NORWICH-32A | DARNALL-39B | RETFORD-36E | LINCOLN-40A |
| Aug-51 | EDINBURGH(SM)-64A | CARLISLE(C)-68E | COLWICK-38A | **4/51: CWD - 14A** | DONCASTER-36A | NORWICH-32A | DARNALL-39B | RETFORD-36E | **9/51: HTN - 52B** |
| Jan-52 | EDINBURGH(SM)-64A | CARLISLE(C)-68E | COLWICK-38A | **3/52: ARDS - 37A** | DONCASTER-36A | NORWICH-32A | **3/52: ARDS - 37A** | RETFORD-36E | **2/52: B.GDNS - 54C** |
| Aug-52 | EDINBURGH(SM)-64A | CARLISLE(C)-68E | COLWICK-38A | ARDSLEY-37A | DONCASTER-36A | NORWICH-32A | ARDSLEY-37A | RETFORD-36E | B.GDNS-54C |
| Jan-53 | EDINBURGH(SM)-64A | CARLISLE(C)-68E | **10/52: S.BGE - 35C** | ARDSLEY-37A | DONCASTER-36A | NORWICH-32A | ARDSLEY-37A | RETFORD-36E | B.GDNS-54C |
| Aug-53 | EDINBURGH(SM)-64A | CARLISLE(C)-68E | S.BGE-35C | ARDSLEY-37A | DONCASTER-36A | **7/53: IPS - 32B** | ARDSLEY-37A | RETFORD-36E | B.GDNS-54C |
| Jan-54 | EDINBURGH(SM)-64A | CARLISLE(C)-68E | S.BGE-35C | ARDSLEY-37A | DONCASTER-36A | **11/53: NOR - 32A** | ARDSLEY-37A | RETFORD-36E | B.GDNS-54C |
| Aug-54 | EDINBURGH(SM)-64A | CARLISLE(C)-68E | S.BGE-35C | ARDSLEY-37A | DONCASTER-36A | NORWICH-32A | ARDSLEY-37A | RETFORD-36E | B.GDNS-54C |
| Jan-55 | EDINBURGH(SM)-64A | CARLISLE(C)-68E | S.BGE-35C | ARDSLEY-37A | DONCASTER-36A | NORWICH-32A | ARDSLEY-37A | RETFORD-36E | B.GDNS-54C |
| Aug-55 | EDINBURGH(SM)-64A | CARLISLE(C)-68E | S.BGE-35C | ARDSLEY-37A | DONCASTER-36A | NORWICH-32A | ARDSLEY-37A | RETFORD-36E | B.GDNS-54C |
| Jan-56 | EDINBURGH(SM)-64A | CARLISLE(C)-68E | S.BGE-35C | **1/56: DCTR - 36A** | DONCASTER-36A | NORWICH-32A | ARDSLEY-37A | RETFORD-36E | B.GDNS-54C |
| Aug-56 | EDINBURGH(SM)-64A | CARLISLE(C)-68E | S.BGE-35C | DONCASTER-36A | DONCASTER-36A | NORWICH-32A | ARDSLEY-56B | RETFORD-36E | B.GDNS-54C |
| Jan-57 | EDINBURGH(SM)-64A | CARLISLE(C)-68E | S.BGE-35C | DONCASTER-36A | DONCASTER-36A | **5/57: M.CONS - 32G** | ARDSLEY-56B | RETFORD-36E | B.GDNS-54C |
| Aug-57 | EDINBURGH(SM)-64A | CARLISLE(C)-68E | S.BGE-35C | DONCASTER-36A | DONCASTER-36A | **7/57: NOR - 32A** | ARDSLEY-56B | RETFORD-36E | B.GDNS-54C |
| Jan-58 | EDINBURGH(SM)-64A | CARLISLE(C)-68E | S.BGE-35C | DONCASTER-36A | DONCASTER-36A | NORWICH-32A | ARDSLEY-56B | RETFORD-36E | B.GDNS-54C |
| Aug-58 | **9/58: DALRY - 64C** | CARLISLE(C)-12C | **7/58: PLAIS - 33A** | DONCASTER-36A | DONCASTER-36A | **6/58: PLAIS - 33A** | ARDSLEY-56B | RETFORD-36E | B.GDNS-54C |
| Jan-59 | DALRYRD-64C | CARLISLE(C)-12C | PLAISTOW-33A | **12/58: LINC - 40A** | DONCASTER-36A | PLAISTOW-33A | ARDSLEY-56B | RETFORD-36E | B.GDNS-52J |
| Aug-59 | DALRYRD-64C | CARLISLE(C)-12C | PLAISTOW-33A | LINCOLN-40A | DONCASTER-36A | PLAISTOW-33A | ARDSLEY-56B | RETFORD-36E | B.GDNS-52J |
| Nov-59 | DALRYRD-64C | CARLISLE(C)-12C | **10/59: TIL - 33B** | LINCOLN-40A | DONCASTER-36A | **10/59: TIL - 33B** | ARDSLEY-56B | RETFORD-36E | B.GDNS-52J |
| Jan-60 | DALRYRD-64C | CARLISLE(C)-12C | TILBURY-33B | LINCOLN-40A | DONCASTER-36A | TILBURY-33B | ARDSLEY-56B | RETFORD-36E | B.GDNS-52J |
| Apr-60 | DALRYRD-64C | CARLISLE(C)-12C | **3/60: W/D** | LINCOLN-40A | **3/60: W/D** | **3/60: W/D** | ARDSLEY-56B | RETFORD-36E | B.GDNS-52J |
| Aug-60 | **7/60: DUNF - 62C** | CARLISLE(C)-12C | | **6/60: W/D** | | | ARDSLEY-56B | RETFORD-36E | B.GDNS-52J |
| Nov-60 | DUNFERMLINE-62C | CARLISLE(C)-12C | | | | | **11/60: W.AUCK - 51F** | RETFORD-36E | B.GDNS-52J |

## Block 1

| | 64972 | 64973 | 64974 | 64975 | 64976 | 64977 | 64978 | 64979 | 64980 |
|---|---|---|---|---|---|---|---|---|---|
| Aug-50 | GORTON-39A | DARNALL-39B | COLWICK-38A | FERRYHILL-61B | DONCASTER-36A | DONCASTER-36A | W.HARTLEPOOL-51C | ARDSLEY-37A | COLWICK-38A |
| Jan-51 | GORTON-39A | DARNALL-39B | COLWICK-38A | FERRYHILL-61B | DONCASTER-36A | DONCASTER-36A | W.HARTLEPOOL-51C | ARDSLEY-37A | COLWICK-38A |
| Aug-51 | GORTON-39A | DARNALL-39B | COLWICK-38A | FERRYHILL-61B | DONCASTER-36A | 9/51: LINC-40A | W.HARTLEPOOL-51C | ARDSLEY-37A | COLWICK-38A |
| Jan-52 | 12/51: ARDS-37A | DARNALL-39B | COLWICK-38A | FERRYHILL-61B | DONCASTER-36A | LINCOLN-40A | W.HARTLEPOOL-51C | ARDSLEY-37A | COLWICK-38A |
| Aug-52 | ARDSLEY-37A | DARNALL-39B | COLWICK-38A | FERRYHILL-61B | 6/52: COLW-38A | LINCOLN-40A | W.HARTLEPOOL-51C | ARDSLEY-37A | COLWICK-38A |
| Jan-53 | ARDSLEY-37A | DARNALL-39B | COLWICK-38A | FERRYHILL-61B | COLWICK-38A | LINCOLN-40A | W.HARTLEPOOL-51C | ARDSLEY-37A | COLWICK-38A |
| Aug-53 | ARDSLEY-37A | DARNALL-39B | COLWICK-38A | FERRYHILL-61B | COLWICK-38A | LINCOLN-40A | W.HARTLEPOOL-51C | ARDSLEY-37A | COLWICK-38A |
| Jan-54 | ARDSLEY-37A | DARNALL-39B | COLWICK-38A | FERRYHILL-61B | 11/53: TUX-40D | LINCOLN-40A | W.HARTLEPOOL-51C | ARDSLEY-37A | COLWICK-38A |
| Aug-54 | ARDSLEY-37A | DARNALL-39B | COLWICK-38A | FERRYHILL-61B | TUXFORD-40D | LINCOLN-40A | 10/54: NORTH-51J | ARDSLEY-37A | COLWICK-38A |
| Jan-55 | ARDSLEY-37A | 11/54: STRAT-30A | COLWICK-38A | FERRYHILL-61B | 1/55: COLW-38A | LINCOLN-40A | NORTHALLERTON-51J | ARDSLEY-37A | COLWICK-38A |
| Aug-55 | ARDSLEY-37A | STRATFORD-30A | COLWICK-38A | FERRYHILL-61B | COLWICK-38A | LINCOLN-40A | NORTHALLERTON-51J | ARDSLEY-37A | COLWICK-38A |
| Jan-56 | 1/56: DCTR-36A | STRATFORD-30A | COLWICK-38A | FERRYHILL-61B | COLWICK-38A | LINCOLN-40A | NORTHALLERTON-51J | ARDSLEY-37A | COLWICK-38A |
| Aug-56 | DONCASTER-36A | STRATFORD-30A | COLWICK-38A | FERRYHILL-61B | COLWICK-38A | LINCOLN-40A | NORTHALLERTON-51J | ARDSLEY-56B | COLWICK-38A |
| Jan-57 | DONCASTER-36A | STRATFORD-30A | COLWICK-38A | FERRYHILL-61B | COLWICK-38A | LINCOLN-40A | 11/56: W.AUCK-51F | ARDSLEY-56B | COLWICK-38A |
| Aug-57 | DONCASTER-36A | STRATFORD-30A | COLWICK-38A | FERRYHILL-61B | COLWICK-38A | LINCOLN-40A | W.AUCKLAND-51F | ARDSLEY-56B | COLWICK-38A |
| Jan-58 | DONCASTER-36A | STRATFORD-30A | COLWICK-38A | FERRYHILL-61B | COLWICK-38A | LINCOLN-40A | W.AUCKLAND-51F | ARDSLEY-56B | COLWICK-38A |
| Aug-58 | DONCASTER-36A | STRATFORD-30A | COLWICK-40E | FERRYHILL-61B | COLWICK-40E | LINCOLN-40A | W.AUCKLAND-51F | ARDSLEY-56B | COLWICK-40E |
| Jan-59 | DONCASTER-36A | STRATFORD-30A | COLWICK-40E | 2/59: ST.M-64A | COLWICK-40E | 12/58: COLW-40E | W.AUCKLAND-51F | ARDSLEY-56B | COLWICK-40E |
| Aug-59 | DONCASTER-36A | STRATFORD-30A | COLWICK-40E | EDINBURGH(SM)-64A | COLWICK-40E | COLWICK-40E | 8/59: GHD-52A | ARDSLEY-56B | COLWICK-40E |
| Nov-59 | DONCASTER-36A | 11/59: W/D | COLWICK-40E | EDINBURGH(SM)-64A | 11/59: W/D | COLWICK-40E | GATESHEAD-52A | ARDSLEY-56B | COLWICK-40E |
| Jan-60 | 12/59: W/D | | COLWICK-40E | EDINBURGH(SM)-64A | | COLWICK-40E | GATESHEAD-52A | ARDSLEY-56B | 12/59: W/D |
| Apr-60 | | | COLWICK-40E | EDINBURGH(SM)-64A | | 2/60: W/D | GATESHEAD-52A | ARDSLEY-56B | |
| Aug-60 | | | COLWICK-40E | 9/60: DAWS-65D | | | GATESHEAD-52A | ARDSLEY-56B | |
| Nov-60 | | | 9/60: W/D | DAWSHOLME-65D | | | GATESHEAD-52A | 11/60: W.AUCK-51F | |

## Block 2

| | 64981 | 64982 | 64983 | 64984 | 64985 | 64986 | 64987 | 64988 | J10-6-0 (1908) 65002 |
|---|---|---|---|---|---|---|---|---|---|
| Aug-50 | COLWICK-38A | TWEEDMOUTH-52D | COLWICK-38A | DONCASTER-36A | ARDSLEY-37A | EDINBURGH(SM)-64A | RETFORD-36E | COLWICK-38A | NEWENGLAND-35A |
| Jan-51 | COLWICK-38A | TWEEDMOUTH-52D | COLWICK-38A | 1/51: RET-36E | ARDSLEY-37A | EDINBURGH(SM)-64A | RETFORD-36E | COLWICK-38A | NEWENGLAND-35A |
| Aug-51 | 5/51: ARDS-37A | TWEEDMOUTH-52D | COLWICK-38A | 9/51: LINC-40A | ARDSLEY-37A | EDINBURGH(SM)-64A | RETFORD-36E | COLWICK-38A | NEWENGLAND-35A |
| Jan-52 | ARDSLEY-37A | TWEEDMOUTH-52D | COLWICK-38A | LINCOLN-40A | ARDSLEY-37A | EDINBURGH(SM)-64A | RETFORD-36E | COLWICK-38A | NEWENGLAND-35A |
| Aug-52 | 6/52: COLW-38A | 9/52: W.AUCK-51F | COLWICK-38A | LINCOLN-40A | 9/52: STRAT-30A | EDINBURGH(SM)-64A | 9/52: DCTR-36A | COLWICK-38A | NEWENGLAND-35A |
| Jan-53 | COLWICK-38A | W.AUCKLAND-51F | COLWICK-38A | LINCOLN-40A | STRATFORD-30A | EDINBURGH(SM)-64A | DONCASTER-36A | COLWICK-38A | 12/52: COLW-38A |
| Aug-53 | 5/53: S.BGE-35C | W.AUCKLAND-51F | COLWICK-38A | LINCOLN-40A | STRATFORD-30A | EDINBURGH(SM)-64A | DONCASTER-36A | COLWICK-38A | COLWICK-38A |
| Jan-54 | SPITALBRIDGE-35C | W.AUCKLAND-51F | COLWICK-38A | LINCOLN-40A | STRATFORD-30A | EDINBURGH(SM)-64A | DONCASTER-36A | COLWICK-38A | COLWICK-38A |
| Aug-54 | SPITALBRIDGE-35C | W.AUCKLAND-51F | COLWICK-38A | LINCOLN-40A | STRATFORD-30A | EDINBURGH(SM)-64A | DONCASTER-36A | COLWICK-38A | 8/54: W/D |
| Jan-55 | SPITALBRIDGE-35C | W.AUCKLAND-51F | COLWICK-38A | LINCOLN-40A | STRATFORD-30A | EDINBURGH(SM)-64A | DONCASTER-36A | COLWICK-38A | |
| Aug-55 | SPITALBRIDGE-35C | W.AUCKLAND-51F | COLWICK-38A | LINCOLN-40A | STRATFORD-30A | EDINBURGH(SM)-64A | DONCASTER-36A | COLWICK-38A | |
| Jan-56 | SPITALBRIDGE-35C | W.AUCKLAND-51F | COLWICK-38A | LINCOLN-40A | 12/55: PARKS-30F | EDINBURGH(SM)-64A | DONCASTER-36A | COLWICK-38A | |
| Aug-56 | SPITALBRIDGE-35C | W.AUCKLAND-51F | COLWICK-38A | LINCOLN-40A | PARKESTON-30F | EDINBURGH(SM)-64A | DONCASTER-36A | COLWICK-38A | |
| Jan-57 | 4/57: PLAIS-33A | W.AUCKLAND-51F | COLWICK-38A | LINCOLN-40A | 11/56: NEWE-35A | EDINBURGH(SM)-64A | DONCASTER-36A | COLWICK-38A | |
| Aug-57 | 6/57: DCTR-36A | W.AUCKLAND-51F | COLWICK-38A | LINCOLN-40A | 4/57: S.BGE-35C | EDINBURGH(SM)-64A | DONCASTER-36A | COLWICK-38A | |
| Jan-58 | DONCASTER-36A | W.AUCKLAND-51F | COLWICK-38A | LINCOLN-40A | SPITALBRIDGE-35C | EDINBURGH(SM)-64A | DONCASTER-36A | COLWICK-38A | |
| Aug-58 | DONCASTER-36A | W.AUCKLAND-51F | COLWICK-40E | LINCOLN-40A | 6/58: CAMB-31A | 9/58: DALRY-64C | DONCASTER-36A | COLWICK-40E | |
| Jan-59 | DONCASTER-36A | W.AUCKLAND-51F | COLWICK-40E | LINCOLN-40A | CAMBRIDGE-31A | DALRYRD-64C | DONCASTER-36A | COLWICK-40E | |
| Aug-59 | DONCASTER-36A | W.AUCKLAND-51F | COLWICK-40E | LINCOLN-40A | CAMBRIDGE-31A | DALRYRD-64C | DONCASTER-36A | COLWICK-40E | |
| Nov-59 | DONCASTER-36A | W.AUCKLAND-51F | 11/59: W/D | LINCOLN-40A | CAMBRIDGE-31A | DALRYRD-64C | DONCASTER-36A | COLWICK-40E | |
| Jan-60 | DONCASTER-36A | W.AUCKLAND-51F | | 12/59: W/D | 12/59: W/D | DALRYRD-64C | DONCASTER-36A | 12/59: W/D | |
| Apr-60 | 2/60: W/D | W.AUCKLAND-51F | | | | DALRYRD-64C | DONCASTER-36A | | |
| Aug-60 | | W.AUCKLAND-51F | | | | DALRYRD-64C | DONCASTER-36A | | |
| Nov-60 | | W.AUCKLAND-51F | | | | DALRYRD-64C | DONCASTER-36A | | |

## Block 3

| | 65003 | 65004 | 65005 | 65006 | 65007 | 65008 | 65009 | 65010 | 65013 |
|---|---|---|---|---|---|---|---|---|---|
| Aug-50 | HITCHIN-34D | NEWENGLAND-35A | NEWENGLAND-35A | NEWENGLAND-35A | COLWICK-38A | COLWICK-38A | COLWICK-38A | HITCHIN-34D | HITCHIN-34D |
| Jan-51 | HITCHIN-34D | NEWENGLAND-35A | NEWENGLAND-35A | NEWENGLAND-35A | COLWICK-38A | COLWICK-38A | COLWICK-38A | HITCHIN-34D | HITCHIN-34D |
| Aug-51 | HITCHIN-34D | NEWENGLAND-35A | NEWENGLAND-35A | NEWENGLAND-35A | COLWICK-38A | COLWICK-38A | COLWICK-38A | HITCHIN-34D | HITCHIN-34D |
| Jan-52 | HITCHIN-34D | NEWENGLAND-35A | NEWENGLAND-35A | NEWENGLAND-35A | COLWICK-38A | COLWICK-38A | COLWICK-38A | HITCHIN-34D | HITCHIN-34D |
| Aug-52 | HITCHIN-34D | 6/52: COLW-38A | 5/52: W/D | NEWENGLAND-35A | 2/52: W/D | 3/52: W/D | 3/52: W/D | HITCHIN-34D | HITCHIN-34D |
| Jan-53 | 1/53: W/D | 11/52: W/D | | 1/53: W/D | | | | 1/53: W/D | HITCHIN-34D |
| Aug-53 | | | | | | | | | HITCHIN-34D |
| Jan-54 | | | | | | | | | HITCHIN-34D |
| Aug-54 | | | | | | | | | HITCHIN-34D |
| Jan-55 | | | | | | | | | 11/54: W/D |

## Block 4

| | 65014 | J2 0-6-0 (1912) 65015 | 65016 | 65017 | 65018 | 65019 | 65020 | 65021 | 65022 |
|---|---|---|---|---|---|---|---|---|---|
| Aug-50 | COLWICK-38A | LEICESTER(GC)-38C | BOSTON-40F | BOSTON-40F | COLWICK-38A | COLWICK-38A | BOSTON-40F | LEICESTER(GC)-38C | COLWICK-38A |
| Jan-51 | COLWICK-38A | LEICESTER(GC)-38C | BOSTON-40F | BOSTON-40F | COLWICK-38A | COLWICK-38A | BOSTON-40F | 11/50: W/D | COLWICK-38A |
| Aug-51 | COLWICK-38A | 9/51: COLW-38A | BOSTON-40F | BOSTON-40F | COLWICK-38A | COLWICK-38A | BOSTON-40F | | COLWICK-38A |
| Jan-52 | COLWICK-38A | COLWICK-38A | BOSTON-40F | BOSTON-40F | COLWICK-38A | COLWICK-38A | BOSTON-40F | | COLWICK-38A |
| Aug-52 | COLWICK-38A | COLWICK-38A | BOSTON-40F | BOSTON-40F | COLWICK-38A | COLWICK-38A | BOSTON-40F | | COLWICK-38A |
| Jan-53 | COLWICK-38A | COLWICK-38A | BOSTON-40F | BOSTON-40F | COLWICK-38A | COLWICK-38A | BOSTON-40F | | COLWICK-38A |
| Aug-53 | 8/53: W/D | COLWICK-38A | BOSTON-40F | BOSTON-40F | COLWICK-38A | 3/53: W/D | BOSTON-40F | | COLWICK-38A |
| Jan-54 | | 12/53: W/D | 10/53: W/D | 1/54: W/D | 11/53: W/D | | BOSTON-40F | | 12/53: W/D |
| Aug-54 | | | | | | | 7/54: W/D | | |

104

**J21 0-6-0 (1886)**

| | 65023 | 65025 | 65028 | 65030 | 65033 | 65035 | 65038 | 65039 | 65040 |
|---|---|---|---|---|---|---|---|---|---|
| Aug-50 | COLWICK-38A | BLAYDON-52C | KIRKBYS.-51H | NORTHALLERTON-51J | DARLINGTON-51A | NORTH BLYTH-52F | DARLINGTON-51A | SELBY-50C | KIRKBYS.-51H |
| Jan-51 | COLWICK-38A | BLAYDON-52C | KIRKBYS.-51H | NORTHALLERTON-51J | DARLINGTON-51A | NORTH BLYTH-52F | DARLINGTON-51A | SELBY-50C | KIRKBYS.-51H |
| Aug-51 | COLWICK-38A | BLAYDON-52C | KIRKBYS.-51H | 4/51: W/D | DARLINGTON-51A | NORTH BLYTH-52F | DARLINGTON-51A | 4/51: BLAY-52C | KIRKBYS.-51H |
| Jan-52 | COLWICK-38A | 11/51: W/D | 9/51: W/D | | 11/51: REEDS-52C | NORTH BLYTH-52F | 12/51: NEWPT-51B | 12/52: DARL-51A | KIRKBYS.-51H |
| Aug-52 | COLWICK-38A | | | | REEDS MOUTH-52C | NORTH BLYTH-52F | 5/52: NORTH-51J | 1/53: HTN-52B | 9/52: W/D |
| Jan-53 | COLWICK-38A | | | | 10/52: S.BLYTH-52F | NORTH BLYTH-52F | NORTHALLERTON-51J | HEATON-52B | |
| Aug-53 | COLWICK-38A | | | | SOUTH BLYTH-52F | 10/52: HTN-52B | NORTHALLERTON-51J | HEATON-52B | |
| Jan-54 | 11/53: W/D | | | | SOUTH BLYTH-52F | HEATON-52B | NORTHALLERTON-51J | HEATON-52B | |
| Aug-54 | | | | | SOUTH BLYTH-52F | HEATON-52B | 11/54: W/D | HEATON-52B | |
| Jan-55 | | | | | SOUTH BLYTH-52F | HEATON-52B | | HEATON-52B | |
| Aug-55 | | | | | 12/55: HEX-52C | HEATON-52B | | 10/56: BLAY-52C | |
| Jan-56 | | | | | HEXHAM-52C | HEATON-52B | | 1/57: T.DCK-54B | |
| Aug-56 | | | | | HEXHAM-52C | 5/56: W/D | | TYNE DOCK-54B | |
| Jan-57 | | | | | HEXHAM-52C | | | TYNE DOCK-54B | |
| Aug-57 | | | | | HEXHAM-52C | | | TYNE DOCK-54B | |
| Jan-58 | | | | | 8/58: S.BLYTH-52F | | | 11/58: W/D | |
| Aug-58 | | | | | 12/58: BLAY-52C | | | | |
| Jan-59 | | | | | BLAYDON-52C | | | | |
| Aug-59 | | | | | BLAYDON-52C | | | | |
| Nov-59 | | | | | BLAYDON-52C | | | | |
| Jan-60 | | | | | 5/60: N.BLYTH-52F | | | | |
| Apr-60 | | | | | NORTH BLYTH-52F | | | | |
| Aug-60 | | | | | NORTH BLYTH-52F | | | | |
| Nov-60 | | | | | | | | | |

| | 65041 | 65042 | 65043 | 65047 | 65057 | 65061 | 65062 | 65064 | 65067 |
|---|---|---|---|---|---|---|---|---|---|
| Aug-50 | 8/50: NORTH-51J | SELBY-50C | YORK-50A | KIRKBYS.-51H | W.AUCKLAND-51F | W.AUCKLAND-51F | NEVILLE HILL-50B | W.AUCKLAND-51F | NEVILLE HILL-50B |
| Jan-51 | 9/50: N.HILL-50B | SELBY-50C | 1/51: W/D | KIRKBYS.-51H | 10/50: W/D | W.AUCKLAND-51F | 12/50: W.AUCK-51F | W.AUCKLAND-51F | 9/50: N BLYTH-52F |
| Aug-51 | 2/51: W/D | 4/51: REEDS-62C | | KIRKBYS.-51H | | W.AUCKLAND-51F | W.AUCKLAND-51F | W.AUCKLAND-51F | 3/51: HTN-52B |
| Jan-52 | | 1/52: BLAY-52C | | KIRKBYS.-51H | | W.AUCKLAND-51F | W.AUCKLAND-51F | W.AUCKLAND-51F | 11/51: W/D |
| Aug-52 | | BLAYDON-52C | | KIRKBYS.-51H | | W.AUCKLAND-51F | W.AUCKLAND-51F | W.AUCKLAND-51F | |
| Jan-53 | | BLAYDON-52C | | KIRKBYS.-51H | | W.AUCKLAND-51F | W.AUCKLAND-51F | W.AUCKLAND-51F | |
| Aug-53 | | BLAYDON-52C | | KIRKBYS.-51H | | W.AUCKLAND-51F | W.AUCKLAND-51F | W.AUCKLAND-51F | |
| Jan-54 | | 7/54: W/D | | KIRKBYS.-51H | | 4/54: DARL-51A | 12/54: W/D | 5/54: W.AUCK-51F | |
| Aug-54 | | | | 12/54: W/D | | DARLINGTON-51A | | 12/54: NORTH-51J | |
| Jan-55 | | | | | | 2/56: HTN-52B | | 3/55: DARL-51A | |
| Aug-55 | | | | | | HEATON-52B | | DARLINGTON-51A | |
| Jan-56 | | | | | | HEATON-52B | | DARLINGTON-51A | |
| Aug-56 | | | | | | HEATON-52B | | DARLINGTON-51A | |
| Jan-57 | | | | | | 11/57: TWEED-52D | | DARLINGTON-51A | |
| Aug-57 | | | | | | 5/58: W/D | | DARLINGTON-51A | |
| Jan-58 | | | | | | | | 9/58: W/D | |

| | 65068 | 65070 | 65075 | 65076 | 65077 | 65078 | 65080 | 65082 | 65088 |
|---|---|---|---|---|---|---|---|---|---|
| Aug-50 | DARLINGTON-51A | RETFORD-36E | YORK-50A | NEVILLE HILL-50B | W.AUCKLAND-51F | W.AUCKLAND-51F | SOUTH BLYTH-52F | BLAYDON-52C | W.AUCKLAND-51F |
| Jan-51 | DARLINGTON-51A | RETFORD-36E | 9/50: NORTH-51J | NEVILLE HILL-50B | W.AUCKLAND-51F | W.AUCKLAND-51F | SOUTH BLYTH-52F | BLAYDON-52C | W.AUCKLAND-51F |
| Aug-51 | DARLINGTON-51A | RETFORD-36E | NORTHALLERTON-51J | 6/51: W/D | W.AUCKLAND-51F | W.AUCKLAND-51F | SOUTH BLYTH-52F | BLAYDON-52C | W.AUCKLAND-51F |
| Jan-52 | DARLINGTON-51A | RETFORD-36E | 11/51: BLAY-52C | | W.AUCKLAND-51F | W.AUCKLAND-51F | 12/51: W/D | BLAYDON-52C | W.AUCKLAND-51F |
| Aug-52 | DARLINGTON-51A | RETFORD-36E | BLAYDON-52C | | W.AUCKLAND-51F | W.AUCKLAND-51F | | 3/52: TWEED-52D | W.AUCKLAND-51F |
| Jan-53 | DARLINGTON-51A | 11/52: DARL-51A | 1/53@ HTN-52B | | W.AUCKLAND-51F | W.AUCKLAND-51F | | TWEEDMOUTH-52D | W.AUCKLAND-51F |
| Aug-53 | DARLINGTON-51A | DARLINGTON-51A | HEATON-52B | | 8/53: W/D | W.AUCKLAND-51F | | TWEEDMOUTH-52D | W.AUCKLAND-51F |
| Jan-54 | 6/54: W/D | DARLINGTON-51A | HEATON-52B | | | W.AUCKLAND-51F | | TWEEDMOUTH-52D | W.AUCKLAND-51F |
| Aug-54 | | DARLINGTON-51A | 6/54: W/D | | | 4/54: DAR-51A | | 1/55: W/D | 11/54: HEX-52C |
| Jan-55 | | DARLINGTON-51A | | | | DARLINGTON-51A | | | HEXHAM-52C |
| Aug-55 | | 11/55: BLAY-52C | | | | 5/55: TWEED-52D | | | 11/55: W/D |
| Jan-56 | | BLAYDON-52C | | | | TWEEDMOUTH-52D | | | |
| Aug-56 | | BLAYDON-52C | | | | TWEEDMOUTH-52D | | | |
| Jan-57 | | 12/57: TWEED-52D | | | | TWEEDMOUTH-52D | | | |
| Aug-57 | | TWEEDMOUTH-52D | | | | 3/57: W/D | | | |
| Jan-58 | | TWEEDMOUTH-52D | | | | | | | |
| Aug-58 | | TWEEDMOUTH-52D | | | | | | | |
| Jan-59 | | 10/59: S.BLYTH-52F | | | | | | | |
| Aug-59 | | SOUTH BLYTH-52F | | | | | | | |
| Nov-59 | | SOUTH BLYTH-52F | | | | | | | |
| Jan-60 | | SOUTH BLYTH-52F | | | | | | | |
| Apr-60 | | 9/60: W/D | | | | | | | |

| | 65089 | 65090 | 65091 | 65092 | 65095 | 65097 | 65098 | 65099 | 65100 |
|---|---|---|---|---|---|---|---|---|---|
| Aug-50 | KIRKBYS.-51H | DARLINGTON-51A | W.AUCKLAND-51F | W.AUCKLAND-51F | DONCASTER-36A | W.AUCKLAND-51F | DARLINGTON-51A | BLAYDON-52C | KIRKBYS.-51H |
| Jan-51 | KIRKBYS.-51H | DARLINGTON-51A | W.AUCKLAND-51F | W.AUCKLAND-51F | DONCASTER-36A | W.AUCKLAND-51F | DARLINGTON-51A | BLAYDON-52C | KIRKBYS.-51H |
| Aug-51 | KIRKBYS.-51H | DARLINGTON-51A | W.AUCKLAND-51F | W.AUCKLAND-51F | 4/51: W/D | W.AUCKLAND-51F | DARLINGTON-51A | BLAYDON-52C | KIRKBYS.-51H |
| Jan-52 | 11/51: DARL-51A | 12/51: BLAY-52C | W.AUCKLAND-51F | W.AUCKLAND-51F | | W.AUCKLAND-51F | DARLINGTON-51A | 12/51: S BLYTH-52F | KIRKBYS.-51H |
| Aug-52 | DARLINGTON-51A | BLAYDON-52C | W.AUCKLAND-51F | W.AUCKLAND-51F | | W.AUCKLAND-51F | DARLINGTON-51A | S.BLYTH-52F | KIRKBYS.-51H |
| Jan-53 | DARLINGTON-51A | BLAYDON-52C | W.AUCKLAND-51F | W.AUCKLAND-51F | | W.AUCKLAND-51F | DARLINGTON-51A | S.BLYTH-52F | KIRKBYS.-51H |
| Aug-53 | DARLINGTON-51A | BLAYDON-52C | W.AUCKLAND-51F | W.AUCKLAND-51F | | W.AUCKLAND-51F | DARLINGTON-51A | S.BLYTH-52F | KIRKBYS.-51H |
| Jan-54 | DARLINGTON-51A | BLAYDON-52C | W.AUCKLAND-51F | 1/54: KYST-51H | | W.AUCKLAND-51F | DARLINGTON-51A | S.BLYTH-52F | KIRKBYS.-51H |
| Aug-54 | DARLINGTON-51A | BLAYDON-52C | W.AUCKLAND-51F | KIRKBYS.-51H | | 12/54: W/D | 12/54: W/D | S.BLYTH-52F | 12/54: W/D |
| Jan-55 | 12/54: W/D | BLAYDON-52C | 1/55: TWEED-52D | 12/54: W/D | | | | 3/55: TWEED-52D | |
| Aug-55 | | BLAYDON-52C | TWEEDMOUTH-52D | | | | | TWEEDMOUTH-52D | |
| Jan-56 | | 12/55: W/D | TWEEDMOUTH-52D | | | | | TWEEDMOUTH-52D | |
| Aug-56 | | | TWEEDMOUTH-52D | | | | | TWEEDMOUTH-52D | |
| Jan-57 | | | TWEEDMOUTH-52D | | | | | TWEEDMOUTH-52D | |
| Aug-57 | | | TWEEDMOUTH-52D | | | | | TWEEDMOUTH-52D | |
| Jan-58 | | | 10/57: W/D | | | | | 2/58: STOCK-51E | |
| Aug-58 | | | | | | | | STOCKTON-51E | |
| Jan-59 | | | | | | | | 12/58: T.DCK-52H | |
| Aug-59 | | | | | | | | TYNE DOCK-52H | |
| Nov-59 | | | | | | | | TYNE DOCK-52H | |
| Jan-60 | | | | | | | | TYNE DOCK-52H | |
| Apr-60 | | | | | | | | TYNE DOCK-52H | |
| Aug-60 | | | | | | | | TYNE DOCK-52H | |
| Nov-60 | | | | | | | | TYNE DOCK-52H | |

| | 65102 | 65103 | 65105 | 65110 | 65111 | 65117 | 65118 | 65119 | 65122 |
|---|---|---|---|---|---|---|---|---|---|
| Aug-50 | W.AUCKLAND-51F | KIRKBYS.-51H | SELBY-50C | DARLINGTON-51A | BLAYDON-52C | DONCASTER-36A | NEVILLE HILL-50B | DARLINGTON-51A | NEVILLE HILL-50B |
| Jan-51 | W.AUCKLAND-51F | KIRKBYS.-51H | 4/51:REEDS-62C | DARLINGTON-51A | BLAYDON-52C | DONCASTER-36A | 2/51:YORK-50A | DARLINGTON-51A | NEVILLE HILL-50B |
| Aug-51 | W.AUCKLAND-51F | KIRKBYS.-51H | REEDSMOUTH-62C | DARLINGTON-51A | 3/51:W/D | DONCASTER-36A | YORK-50A | DARLINGTON-51A | NEVILLE HILL-50B |
| Jan-52 | 11/51:W/D | 11/51:DARL-51A | 9/51:W/D | 12/51:HTN-52B | | DONCASTER-36A | 11/51:W/D | 12/51:REEDS-52C | 9/51:W/D |
| Aug-52 | | DARLINGTON-51A | | HEATON-52B | | DONCASTER-36A | | 10/52:HEX-52C | |
| Jan-53 | | DARLINGTON-51A | | HEATON-52B | | 11/52:DARL-51A | | HEXHAM-52C | |
| Aug-53 | | DARLINGTON-51A | | HEATON-52B | | DARLINGTON-51A | | HEXHAM-52C | |
| Jan-54 | | DARLINGTON-51A | | HEATON-52B | | DARLINGTON-51A | | HEXHAM-52C | |
| Aug-54 | | 10/54:BLAY-52C | | HEATON-52B | | DARLINGTON-51A | | HEXHAM-52C | |
| Jan-55 | | BLAYDON-52C | | HEATON-52B | | DARLINGTON-51A | | 12/54:W/D | |
| Aug-55 | | BLAYDON-52C | | HEATON-52B | | DARLINGTON-51A | | | |
| Jan-56 | | BLAYDON-52C | | HEATON-52B | | 2/56:BLAY-52C | | | |
| Aug-56 | | BLAYDON-52C | | HEATON-52B | | 3/56:HEX-52C | | | |
| Jan-57 | | BLAYDON-52C | | HEATON-52B | | HEXHAM-52C | | | |
| Aug-57 | | BLAYDON-52C | | HEATON-52B | | 12/57:HTN-52B | | | |
| Jan-58 | | BLAYDON-52C | | HEATON-52B | | 3/58:GHD-52A | | | |
| Aug-58 | | BLAYDON-52C | | HEATON-52B | | 4/58:T.DCK-54B | | | |
| Jan-59 | | 12/58:W/D | | HEATON-52B | | TYNE DOCK-52H | | | |
| Aug-59 | | | | HEATON-52B | | 2/59:W/D | | | |
| Nov-59 | | | | HEATON-52B | | | | | |
| Jan-60 | | | | HEATON-52B | | | | | |
| Apr-60 | | | | HEATON-52B | | | | | |
| Aug-60 | | | | HEATON-52B | | | | | |
| Nov-60 | | | | 8/60:W/D | | | | | |

### J10 0-6-0 (1892)

| | 65126 | 65128 | 65130 | 65131 | 65132 | 65133 | 65134 | 65135 | 65136 |
|---|---|---|---|---|---|---|---|---|---|
| Aug-50 | BRUNSWICK-8E | WIGAN-10F | SOUTHPORT-27E | NORTHWICH-9G | H.MERSEY-9F | SOUTHPORT-27E | NORTHWICH-9G | H.MERSEY-9F | BRUNSWICK-8E |
| Jan-51 | BRUNSWICK-8E | 10/50:W/D | SOUTHPORT-27E | 12/50:WIGAN-10F | H.MERSEY-9F | SOUTHPORT-27E | NORTHWICH-9G | 4/51:H.MSY-9F | BRUNSWICK-8E |
| Aug-51 | BRUNSWICK-8E | | SOUTHPORT-27E | 4/51:NWCH-9G | H.MERSEY-9F | SOUTHPORT-27E | NORTHWICH-9G | H.MERSEY-9F | BRUNSWICK-8E |
| Jan-52 | BRUNSWICK-8E | | SOUTHPORT-27E | NORTHWICH-9G | H.MERSEY-9F | SOUTHPORT-27E | NORTHWICH-9G | H.MERSEY-9F | BRUNSWICK-8E |
| Aug-52 | BRUNSWICK-8E | | 8/52:W/D | NORTHWICH-9G | H.MERSEY-9F | SOUTHPORT-27E | NORTHWICH-9G | H.MERSEY-9F | BRUNSWICK-8E |
| Jan-53 | 12/52:W/D | | | NORTHWICH-9G | H.MERSEY-9F | SOUTHPORT-27E | NORTHWICH-9G | H.MERSEY-9F | 2/53:W/D |
| Aug-53 | | | | NORTHWICH-9G | H.MERSEY-9F | SOUTHPORT-27E | NORTHWICH-9G | H.MERSEY-9F | |
| Jan-54 | | | | NORTHWICH-9G | H.MERSEY-9F | SOUTHPORT-27E | NORTHWICH-9G | H.MERSEY-9F | |
| Aug-54 | | | | NORTHWICH-9G | H.MERSEY-9F | SOUTHPORT-27E | NORTHWICH-9G | H.MERSEY-9F | |
| Jan-55 | | | | NORTHWICH-9G | H.MERSEY-9F | SOUTHPORT-27E | NORTHWICH-9G | H.MERSEY-9F | |
| Aug-55 | | | | NORTHWICH-9G | H.MERSEY-9F | SOUTHPORT-27E | NORTHWICH-9G | H.MERSEY-9F | |
| Jan-56 | | | | 3/56:S.BCH-10A | H.MERSEY-9F | SOUTHPORT-27E | NORTHWICH-9G | H.MERSEY-9F | |
| Aug-56 | | | | WIGAN(SB)-10A | H.MERSEY-9F | SOUTHPORT-27E | NORTHWICH-9G | H.MERSEY-9F | |
| Jan-57 | | | | WIGAN(SB)-10A | H.MERSEY-9F | SOUTHPORT-27E | NORTHWICH-9G | H.MERSEY-9F | |
| Aug-57 | | | | WIGAN(SB)-10A | H.MERSEY-9F | SOUTHPORT-27E | NORTHWICH-9G | H.MERSEY-9F | |
| Jan-58 | | | | WIGAN(SB)-8F | H.MERSEY-9F | SOUTHPORT-27E | NORTHWICH-9G | H.MERSEY-9F | |
| Aug-58 | | | | WIGAN(SB)-8F | 5/58:W/D | SOUTHPORT-27E | NORTHWICH-8E | 4/58:W/D | |
| Jan-59 | | | | 3/59:W/D | | SOUTHPORT-27E | NORTHWICH-8E | | |
| Aug-59 | | | | | | SOUTHPORT-27E | NORTHWICH-8E | | |
| Nov-59 | | | | | | SOUTHPORT-27E | NORTHWICH-8E | | |
| Jan-60 | | | | | | 12/59:W/D | 12/59:W/D | | |
| Apr-60 | | | | | | | | | |
| Aug-60 | | | | | | | | | |
| Nov-60 | | | | | | | | | |

| | 65137 | 65138 | 65139 | 65140 | 65141 | 65142 | 65143 | 65144 | 65145 |
|---|---|---|---|---|---|---|---|---|---|
| Aug-50 | T.PARK-9E | NORTHWICH-9G | NORTHWICH-9G | NORTHWICH-9G | T.PARK-9E | BRUNSWICK-8E | CHESTER(CLC)-6D | H.MERSEY-9F | H.MERSEY-9F |
| Jan-51 | T.PARK-9E | NORTHWICH-9G | NORTHWICH-9G | NORTHWICH-9G | T.PARK-9E | BRUNSWICK-8E | CHESTER(CLC)-6D | H.MERSEY-9F | H.MERSEY-9F |
| Aug-51 | T.PARK-9E | NORTHWICH-9G | NORTHWICH-9G | NORTHWICH-9G | T.PARK-9E | BRUNSWICK-8E | CHESTER(CLC)-6D | 4/51:WIGAN-10F | H.MERSEY-9F |
| Jan-52 | T.PARK-9E | NORTHWICH-9G | NORTHWICH-9G | NORTHWICH-9G | T.PARK-9E | BRUNSWICK-8E | CHESTER(CLC)-6D | WIGAN-10F | H.MERSEY-9F |
| Aug-52 | 5/52:W/D | NORTHWICH-9G | NORTHWICH-9G | NORTHWICH-9G | 9/52:W/D | BRUNSWICK-8E | CHESTER(CLC)-6D | WIGAN-10F | H.MERSEY-9F |
| Jan-53 | | 2/53:T.PK-9E | NORTHWICH-9G | 3/53:NGATE-6D | | BRUNSWICK-8E | CHESTER(CLC)-6D | WIGAN-10F | 1/53:BRUNS-8E |
| Aug-53 | | T.PARK-9E | NORTHWICH-9G | NORTHGATE-6D | | BRUNSWICK-8E | CHESTER(CLC)-6D | WIGAN-10F | BRUNSWICK-8E |
| Jan-54 | | T.PARK-9E | NORTHWICH-9G | NORTHGATE-6D | | BRUNSWICK-8E | CHESTER(CLC)-6D | WIGAN-10F | BRUNSWICK-8E |
| Aug-54 | | 6/54:WIDNES-8D | NORTHWICH-9G | NORTHGATE-6D | | BRUNSWICK-8E | CHESTER(CLC)-6D | WIGAN-10F | BRUNSWICK-8E |
| Jan-55 | | WIDNES-8D | NORTHWICH-9G | NORTHGATE-6D | | BRUNSWICK-8E | CHESTER(CLC)-6D | WIGAN-10F | BRUNSWICK-8E |
| Aug-55 | | WIDNES-8D | NORTHWICH-9G | NORTHGATE-6D | | BRUNSWICK-8E | CHESTER(CLC)-6D | WIGAN-10F | BRUNSWICK-8E |
| Jan-56 | | WIDNES-8D | NORTHWICH-9G | NORTHGATE-6D | | BRUNSWICK-8E | CHESTER(CLC)-6D | WIGAN-10F | BRUNSWICK-8E |
| Aug-56 | | WIDNES-8D | NORTHWICH-9G | NORTHGATE-6D | | BRUNSWICK-8E | 8/56:W/D | WIGAN-10F | BRUNSWICK-8E |
| Jan-57 | | 12/56:S.BCH-10A | 12/56:W/D | 12/56:S.BCH-10A | | BRUNSWICK-8E | | 12/56:S.BCH-10A | 12/56:S.BCH-10A |
| Aug-57 | | WIGAN(SB)-10A | | WIGAN(SB)-10A | | 7/57:GOOLE-53E | | WIGAN(SB)-10A | 7/57:GOOLE-53E |
| Jan-58 | | WIGAN(SB)-10A | | WIGAN(SB)-10A | | GOOLE-53E | | WIGAN(SB)-10A | GOOLE-53E |
| Aug-58 | | WIGAN(SB)-8F | | WIGAN(SB)-8F | | GOOLE-53E | | 4/58:W/D | GOOLE-53E |
| Jan-59 | | WIGAN(SB)-8F | | WIGAN(SB)-8F | | 10/58:W/D | | | 11/58:W/D |
| Aug-59 | | 8/59:W/D | | WIGAN(SB)-8F | | | | | |
| Nov-59 | | | | 11/59:W/D | | | | | |
| Jan-60 | | | | | | | | | |
| Apr-60 | | | | | | | | | |
| Aug-60 | | | | | | | | | |
| Nov-60 | | | | | | | | | |

| | 65146 | 65147 | 65148 | 65149 | 65151 | 65153 | 65154 | 65155 | 65156 |
|---|---|---|---|---|---|---|---|---|---|
| Aug-50 | H.MERSEY-9F | NORTHWICH-9G | H.MERSEY-9F | BRUNSWICK-8E | NORTHWICH-9G | BRUNSWICK-8E | T.PARK-9E | BRUNSWICK-8E | NORTHWICH-9G |
| Jan-51 | H.MERSEY-9F | NORTHWICH-9G | H.MERSEY-9F | BRUNSWICK-8E | NORTHWICH-9G | BRUNSWICK-8E | T.PARK-9E | BRUNSWICK-8E | NORTHWICH-9G |
| Aug-51 | H.MERSEY-9F | NORTHWICH-9G | H.MERSEY-9F | BRUNSWICK-8E | 4/51:WIGAN-10F | BRUNSWICK-8E | T.PARK-9E | BRUNSWICK-8E | NORTHWICH-9G |
| Jan-52 | H.MERSEY-9F | NORTHWICH-9G | H.MERSEY-9F | BRUNSWICK-8E | 4/52:S.BCH-10A | BRUNSWICK-8E | T.PARK-9E | BRUNSWICK-8E | NORTHWICH-9G |
| Aug-52 | H.MERSEY-9F | NORTHWICH-9G | H.MERSEY-9F | BRUNSWICK-8E | 5/52:W/D | 9/52:T.PARK-9E | T.PARK-9E | 6/52:W/D | NORTHWICH-9G |
| Jan-53 | H.MERSEY-9F | 3/53:BRUNS-8E | H.MERSEY-9F | 2/53:W/D | | T.PARK-9E | T.PARK-9E | | 3/53:T.PARK-9E |
| Aug-53 | 6/53:T.PARK-9E | BRUNSWICK-8E | H.MERSEY-9F | | | T.PARK-9E | 5/53:W/D | | T.PARK-9E |
| Jan-54 | T.PARK-9E | BRUNSWICK-8E | H.MERSEY-9F | | | T.PARK-9E | | | T.PARK-9E |
| Aug-54 | T.PARK-9E | BRUNSWICK-8E | H.MERSEY-9F | | | T.PARK-9E | | | T.PARK-9E |
| Jan-55 | T.PARK-9E | BRUNSWICK-8E | H.MERSEY-9F | | | T.PARK-9E | | | T.PARK-9E |
| Aug-55 | T.PARK-9E | BRUNSWICK-8E | H.MERSEY-9F | | | T.PARK-9E | | | T.PARK-9E |
| Jan-56 | 11/55:CHESTER-6D | BRUNSWICK-8E | H.MERSEY-9F | | | T.PARK-9E | | | 11/55:CHESTER-6D |
| Aug-56 | CHESTER(CLC)-6D | BRUNSWICK-8E | 11/56:DARL-51A | | | 11/56:DARL-51A | | | CHESTER(CLC)-6D |
| Jan-57 | 12/56:S.BCH-10A | BRUNSWICK-8E | 12/56:W/D | | | 12/56:W/D | | | 12/56:S.BCH-10A |
| Aug-57 | WIGAN(SB)-10A | 7/57:GOOLE-53E | | | | | | | WIGAN(SB)-10A |
| Jan-58 | WIGAN(SB)-10A | GOOLE-53E | | | | | | | 2/58:W/D |
| Aug-58 | WIGAN(SB)-8F | 3/58:W/D | | | | | | | |
| Jan-59 | WIGAN(SB)-8F | | | | | | | | |
| Aug-59 | WIGAN(SB)-8F | | | | | | | | |
| Nov-59 | 11/59:W/D | | | | | | | | |
| Jan-60 | | | | | | | | | |
| Apr-60 | | | | | | | | | |
| Aug-60 | | | | | | | | | |
| Nov-60 | | | | | | | | | |

| | 65157 | 65158 | 65159 | 65160 | 65161 | 65162 | 65163 | 65164 | 65165 |
|---|---|---|---|---|---|---|---|---|---|
| Aug-50 | H.MERSEY-9F | NORTHWICH-9G | WIGAN-10F | H.MERSEY-9F | T.PARK-9E | WIGAN-10F | BRUNSWICK-8E | WIGAN-10F | NORTHWICH-9G |
| Jan-51 | H.MERSEY-9F | NORTHWICH-9G | WIGAN-10F | H.MERSEY-9F | T.PARK-9E | WIGAN-10F | BRUNSWICK-8E | WIGAN-10F | NORTHWICH-9G |
| Aug-51 | H.MERSEY-9F | NORTHWICH-9G | WIGAN-10F | H.MERSEY-9F | T.PARK-9E | WIGAN-10F | BRUNSWICK-8E | WIGAN-10F | NORTHWICH-9G |
| Jan-52 | H.MERSEY-9F | NORTHWICH-9G | WIGAN-10F | H.MERSEY-9F | T.PARK-9E | WIGAN-10F | BRUNSWICK-8E | WIGAN-10F | NORTHWICH-9G |
| Aug-52 | H.MERSEY-9F | NORTHWICH-9G | WIGAN-10F | H.MERSEY-9F | 9/52: W/D | WIGAN-10F | BRUNSWICK-8E | WIGAN-10F | NORTHWICH-9G |
| Jan-53 | H.MERSEY-9F | NORTHWICH-9G | WIGAN-10F | H.MERSEY-9F | | WIGAN-10F | 12/52: W/D | 12/52: T PARK - 9E | NORTHWICH-9G |
| Aug-53 | 6/53: T PARK - 9E | NORTHWICH-9G | WIGAN-10F | H.MERSEY-9F | | WIGAN-10F | | 5/53: W/D | NORTHWICH-9G |
| Jan-54 | T.PARK-9E | NORTHWICH-9G | WIGAN-10F | H.MERSEY-9F | | WIGAN-10F | | | NORTHWICH-9G |
| Aug-54 | T.PARK-9E | NORTHWICH-9G | WIGAN-10F | H.MERSEY-9F | | WIGAN-10F | | | NORTHWICH-9G |
| Jan-55 | 3/55: WIDNES - 8D | NORTHWICH-9G | WIGAN-10F | H.MERSEY-9F | | WIGAN-10F | | | NORTHWICH-9G |
| Aug-55 | WIDNES-8D | NORTHWICH-9G | WIGAN-10F | H.MERSEY-9F | | WIGAN-10F | | | NORTHWICH-9G |
| Jan-56 | WIDNES-8D | NORTHWICH-9G | WIGAN-10F | H.MERSEY-9F | | WIGAN-10F | | | NORTHWICH-9G |
| Aug-56 | WIDNES-8D | NORTHWICH-9G | WIGAN-10F | H.MERSEY-9F | | 11/56: DARL - 51A | | | 8/56: W/D |
| Jan-57 | WIDNES-8D | NORTHWICH-9G | WIGAN-10F | H.MERSEY-9F | | 12/56: W/D | | | |
| Aug-57 | WIDNES-8D | NORTHWICH-9G | WIGAN-10F | H.MERSEY-9F | | | | | |
| Jan-58 | WIDNES-8D | 3/58: WOOD - 2F | 12/57: W/D | H.MERSEY-9F | | | | | |
| Aug-58 | WIDNES-8D | W.HALSE-2F | | 6/58: W/D | | | | | |
| Jan-59 | WIDNES-8D | W.HALSE-2F | | | | | | | |
| Aug-59 | WIDNES-8D | W.HALSE-2F | | | | | | | |
| Nov-59 | 11/59: S BCH - 8F | W.HALSE-2F | | | | | | | |
| Jan-60 | WIGAN (SB) - 8F | 12/59: W/D | | | | | | | |
| Apr-60 | WIGAN (SB) - 8F | | | | | | | | |
| Aug-60 | WIGAN (SB) - 8F | | | | | | | | |
| Nov-60 | WIGAN (SB) - 8F | | | | | | | | |

| | 65166 | 65167 | 65168 | 65169 | 65170 | 65171 | 65172 | 65173 | 65175 |
|---|---|---|---|---|---|---|---|---|---|
| Aug-50 | NORTHWICH-9G | CHESTER (CLC) - 6D | T.PARK-9E | NORTHWICH-9G | WIGAN-10F | NORTHWICH-9G | BRUNSWICK-8E | WIGAN-10F | WIGAN-10F |
| Jan-51 | NORTHWICH-9G | CHESTER (CLC) - 6D | T.PARK-9E | NORTHWICH-9G | WIGAN-10F | NORTHWICH-9G | BRUNSWICK-8E | WIGAN-10F | WIGAN-10F |
| Aug-51 | NORTHWICH-9G | CHESTER (CLC) - 6D | T.PARK-9E | NORTHWICH-9G | WIGAN-10F | NORTHWICH-9G | BRUNSWICK-8E | WIGAN-10F | WIGAN-10F |
| Jan-52 | NORTHWICH-9G | CHESTER (CLC) - 6D | T.PARK-9E | NORTHWICH-9G | WIGAN-10F | NORTHWICH-9G | BRUNSWICK-8E | WIGAN-10F | WIGAN-10F |
| Aug-52 | NORTHWICH-9G | CHESTER (CLC) - 6D | T.PARK-9E | NORTHWICH-9G | WIGAN-10F | NORTHWICH-9G | BRUNSWICK-8E | WIGAN-10F | WIGAN-10F |
| Jan-53 | 2/53: BRUNS - 8E | CHESTER (CLC) - 6D | 12/52: W/D | NORTHWICH-9G | T.PARK-9E | NORTHWICH-9G | BRUNSWICK-8E | WIGAN-10F | WIGAN-10F |
| Aug-53 | BRUNSWICK-8E | 5/53: T PARK - 9E | | NORTHWICH-9G | T.PARK-9E | NORTHWICH-9G | 2/53: W/D | WIGAN-10F | WIGAN-10F |
| Jan-54 | BRUNSWICK-8E | T.PARK-9E | | NORTHWICH-9G | T.PARK-9E | NORTHWICH-9G | | WIGAN-10F | WIGAN-10F |
| Aug-54 | BRUNSWICK-8E | 6/54: WIDNES - 9E | | NORTHWICH-9G | T.PARK-9E | NORTHWICH-9G | | WIGAN-10F | WIGAN-10F |
| Jan-55 | BRUNSWICK-8E | 9/54: T PARK - 9E | | NORTHWICH-9G | T.PARK-9E | NORTHWICH-9G | | WIGAN-10F | WIGAN-10F |
| Aug-55 | BRUNSWICK-8E | T.PARK-9E | | NORTHWICH-9G | T.PARK-9E | NORTHWICH-9G | | WIGAN-10F | WIGAN-10F |
| Jan-56 | BRUNSWICK-8E | T.PARK-9E | | NORTHWICH-9G | 11/55: CHTR - 6D | NORTHWICH-9G | | WIGAN-10F | WIGAN-10F |
| Aug-56 | BRUNSWICK-8E | T.PARK-9E | | NORTHWICH-9G | CHESTER (CLC) - 6D | NORTHWICH-9G | | 11/56: DARL - 51A | WIGAN-10F |
| Jan-57 | BRUNSWICK-8E | T.PARK-9E | | NORTHWICH-9G | 12/56: S. BCH - 10A | 10/56: W/D | | 12/56: W/D | WIGAN-10F |
| Aug-57 | BRUNSWICK-8E | T.PARK-9E | | NORTHWICH-9G | WIGAN (SB) - 10A | | | | WIGAN-10F |
| Jan-58 | BRUNSWICK-8E | T.PARK-9E | | NORTHWICH-9G | WIGAN (SB) - 10A | | | | 4/58: W/D |
| Aug-58 | 5/58: T. PARK - 9E | 9/58: W/D | | NORTHWICH-8E | 6/58: W/D | | | | |
| Jan-59 | T.PARK-9E | | | NORTHWICH-8E | | | | | |
| Aug-59 | T.PARK-9E | | | NORTHWICH-8E | | | | | |
| Nov-59 | T.PARK-9E | | | NORTHWICH-8E | | | | | |
| Jan-60 | 12/59: W/D | | | NORTHWICH-8E | | | | | |
| Apr-60 | | | | 3/60: W/D | | | | | |
| Aug-60 | | | | | | | | | |
| Nov-60 | | | | | | | | | |

| | 65176 | 65177 | 65178 | 65179 | 65180 | 65181 | 65182 | 65183 | 65184 |
|---|---|---|---|---|---|---|---|---|---|
| Aug-50 | WIGAN-10F | SOUTHPORT-27E | H.MERSEY-9F | T.PARK-9E | SOUTHPORT-27E | H.MERSEY-9F | BRUNSWICK-8E | T.PARK-9E | T.PARK-9E |
| Jan-51 | WIGAN-10F | SOUTHPORT-27E | H.MERSEY-9F | T.PARK-9E | SOUTHPORT-27E | H.MERSEY-9F | BRUNSWICK-8E | T.PARK-9E | T.PARK-9E |
| Aug-51 | WIGAN-10F | SOUTHPORT-27E | H.MERSEY-9F | T.PARK-9E | SOUTHPORT-27E | H.MERSEY-9F | BRUNSWICK-8E | T.PARK-9E | T.PARK-9E |
| Jan-52 | WIGAN-10F | SOUTHPORT-27E | H.MERSEY-9F | T.PARK-9E | SOUTHPORT-27E | H.MERSEY-9F | BRUNSWICK-8E | T.PARK-9E | T.PARK-9E |
| Aug-52 | WIGAN-10F | SOUTHPORT-27E | H.MERSEY-9F | T.PARK-9E | SOUTHPORT-27E | 9/52: T. PARK - 9E | BRUNSWICK-8E | 4/52: W/D | T.PARK-9E |
| Jan-53 | WIGAN-10F | SOUTHPORT-27E | H.MERSEY-9F | 11/52: W/D | SOUTHPORT-27E | T.PARK-9E | BRUNSWICK-8E | | T.PARK-9E |
| Aug-53 | WIGAN-10F | SOUTHPORT-27E | H.MERSEY-9F | | SOUTHPORT-27E | T.PARK-9E | BRUNSWICK-8E | | T.PARK-9E |
| Jan-54 | WIGAN-10F | SOUTHPORT-27E | H.MERSEY-9F | | SOUTHPORT-27E | T.PARK-9E | BRUNSWICK-8E | | T.PARK-9E |
| Aug-54 | WIGAN-10F | SOUTHPORT-27E | H.MERSEY-9F | | SOUTHPORT-27E | T.PARK-9E | BRUNSWICK-8E | | T.PARK-9E |
| Jan-55 | WIGAN-10F | SOUTHPORT-27E | H.MERSEY-9F | | SOUTHPORT-27E | T.PARK-9E | BRUNSWICK-8E | | T.PARK-9E |
| Aug-55 | WIGAN-10F | SOUTHPORT-27E | H.MERSEY-9F | | SOUTHPORT-27E | T.PARK-9E | BRUNSWICK-8E | | T.PARK-9E |
| Jan-56 | WIGAN-10F | SOUTHPORT-27E | H.MERSEY-9F | | SOUTHPORT-27E | 2/56: CHTR - 6D | BRUNSWICK-8E | | 12/55: WIDNES - 8D |
| Aug-56 | 11/56: DARL - 51A | SOUTHPORT-27E | H.MERSEY-9F | | SOUTHPORT-27E | 12/56: DARL - 51A | BRUNSWICK-8E | | WIDNES-8D |
| Jan-57 | 12/56: W/D | SOUTHPORT-27E | H.MERSEY-9F | | 12/56: W/D | 12/56: W/D | 11/56: W/D | | WIDNES-8D |
| Aug-57 | | SOUTHPORT-27E | H.MERSEY-9F | | | | | | WIDNES-8D |
| Jan-58 | | SOUTHPORT-27E | H.MERSEY-9F | | | | | | WIDNES-8D |
| Aug-58 | | SOUTHPORT-27E | H.MERSEY-9F | | | | | | WIDNES-8D |
| Jan-59 | | SOUTHPORT-27E | 10/58: W/D | | | | | | WIDNES-8D |
| Aug-59 | | 9/59: W/D | | | | | | | WIDNES-8D |
| Nov-59 | | | | | | | | | 9/59: W/D |
| Jan-60 | | | | | | | | | |
| Apr-60 | | | | | | | | | |
| Aug-60 | | | | | | | | | |
| Nov-60 | | | | | | | | | |

| | 65185 | 65186 | 65187 | 65188 | 65189 | 65190 | 65191 | 65192 | 65193 |
|---|---|---|---|---|---|---|---|---|---|
| Aug-50 | H.MERSEY-9F | T.PARK-9E | NORTHWICH-9G | H.MERSEY-9F | WIGAN-10F | NORTHWICH-9G | NORTHWICH-9G | SOUTHPORT-27E | H.MERSEY-9F |
| Jan-51 | H.MERSEY-9F | T.PARK-9E | NORTHWICH-9G | H.MERSEY-9F | WIGAN-10F | NORTHWICH-9G | NORTHWICH-9G | SOUTHPORT-27E | H.MERSEY-9F |
| Aug-51 | H.MERSEY-9F | T.PARK-9E | NORTHWICH-9G | H.MERSEY-9F | WIGAN-10F | NORTHWICH-9G | NORTHWICH-9G | SOUTHPORT-27E | H.MERSEY-9F |
| Jan-52 | H.MERSEY-9F | T.PARK-9E | NORTHWICH-9G | H.MERSEY-9F | WIGAN-10F | NORTHWICH-9G | NORTHWICH-9G | SOUTHPORT-27E | H.MERSEY-9F |
| Aug-52 | H.MERSEY-9F | T.PARK-9E | NORTHWICH-9G | 8/52: W/D | 9/52: W/D | NORTHWICH-9G | NORTHWICH-9G | SOUTHPORT-27E | 8/52: W/D |
| Jan-53 | H.MERSEY-9F | T.PARK-9E | NORTHWICH-9G | | | NORTHWICH-9G | NORTHWICH-9G | SOUTHPORT-27E | |
| Aug-53 | 5/53: BRUNS - 8E | T.PARK-9E | NORTHWICH-9G | | | 2/53: W/D | 5/53: T PARK - 9E | SOUTHPORT-27E | |
| Jan-54 | BRUNSWICK-8E | T.PARK-9E | NORTHWICH-9G | | | | T.PARK-9E | SOUTHPORT-27E | |
| Aug-54 | BRUNSWICK-8E | T.PARK-9E | NORTHWICH-9G | | | | T.PARK-9E | SOUTHPORT-27E | |
| Jan-55 | BRUNSWICK-8E | 3/55: WIDNES - 8D | NORTHWICH-9G | | | | T.PARK-9E | SOUTHPORT-27E | |
| Aug-55 | BRUNSWICK-8E | WIDNES-8D | NORTHWICH-9G | | | | T.PARK-9E | SOUTHPORT-27E | |
| Jan-56 | BRUNSWICK-8E | 12/55: T. PARK - 9E | NORTHWICH-9G | | | | T.PARK-9E | SOUTHPORT-27E | |
| Aug-56 | 12/56: DARL - 51A | T.PARK-9E | 5/56: H MSY - 9F | | | | T.PARK-9E | SOUTHPORT-27E | |
| Jan-57 | 12/56: W/D | T.PARK-9E | H.MERSEY-9F | | | | T.PARK-9E | SOUTHPORT-27E | |
| Aug-57 | | 8/57: W/D | H.MERSEY-9F | | | | T.PARK-9E | SOUTHPORT-27E | |
| Jan-58 | | | H.MERSEY-9F | | | | 1/58: W/D | SOUTHPORT-27E | |
| Aug-58 | | | H.MERSEY-9F | | | | | SOUTHPORT-27E | |
| Jan-59 | | | 2/59: W/D | | | | | SOUTHPORT-27E | |
| Aug-59 | | | | | | | | 8/59: S. BCH - 8F | |
| Nov-59 | | | | | | | | WIGAN (SB) - 8F | |
| Jan-60 | | | | | | | | WIGAN (SB) - 8F | |
| Apr-60 | | | | | | | | WIGAN (SB) - 8F | |
| Aug-60 | | | | | | | | 5/60: W/D | |
| Nov-60 | | | | | | | | | |

# L.N.E.R. (Southern Area.)

## ENGINE CASUALTY AND FAILURE CARD.

Engine No. ~~3211~~ 8910

District Stationed. { *West Riding* ~~WAKEFIELD~~

Load Class **4**

Works Class **J 50**

| Date. | C. or F. | Nature of Casualty or Failure. | Cause of Casualty or Failure. | Date of last General repair. | Miles run since last General repair. | Remarks. |
|---|---|---|---|---|---|---|
| 19.9.30 | C | Vac. release Valve casting cracked. | Probably caused by blow | 3.4.29 | | 1/Eng 2/2622 N.R. |
| 26.11.30 | C | Weigh Bar Shaft Peg thin | W & Tear | | | NR. 1/Eng/2/3162 |
| 4.5.33 | C | I.D. Spring broken | Defective | May 1932. | | NR. 1/Eng/2/3901 |
| 18.10.33 | C | I.D. flange joint | W & Tear | | | NR. 1/Eng 2/2275. |
| 26.5.41 | C | L.D. Spring broken. | Creeping fracture. Top Plate. | Feb. 1940. | | 1/Eng 2/2275 |
| 2.11.43 | - | Leak plug fused. | Insufficient water in boiler. | (Eng in loco - not case of failed) | | 1/Eng 2/3893 |
| 18.10.44 | F | Bridle rod coupling bolt lost out | No Trace | Sept 1942. | | 1/Eng 2/3320 . |
| 24.2.51 | F | L/arge end bolts/ strap fractured | Creeping fracture | 26.3.49 | 35,000 | 1/Eng 2/68910 |
| 5.6.59 | C | R.H. TRAILING COUPLED AXLE HOT. | OIL WAYS MADE UP WITH DIRT. | 18.6.58 | 17,339. | L.C. R.1 |
| 1.1.60 | | R.H. Trailing coupled axle hot | Trimmings out of position. | ✓ | 25,739 | Lc R1 |
| 24.2.61 | | L.T. Coupled Axle Hot | Spring Hanger Link broken. Causing unequal distribution of weight | 18.6.58 | 38,599 | |

The difference between shunting and main line work is clearly demonstrated by the two engine record cards shown here, the upper giving details of the last 30 years of J50 68910 and the lower V2 60861. The latter emerged from Darlington works on 6th June 1939 and was allocated to Doncaster after a brief spell at Gorton. No problems occurred until wartime maintenance neglect set in when, from February 1942 until the end of the war, when no less than 28 defects were reported which aggregated 708 minutes delay. Amongst the most spectacular was 100 minutes lost at Beaconsfield on 22 January 1944, due to a broken gauge glass, with J11 4355 (65197) eventually coming to the rescue. Six days later 92 minutes delay occurred at Neasden Junction because of leaking tubes whilst in July the same year 150 minutes were dropped at Ardsley with injector trouble. By comparison the section shown of 60861's history - 1951 to 1961 - shows a relatively trouble free decade. C and F distinguish between Casualties (usually a defect found on shed) and Failures where the engine caused an operational delay. Generally speaking casualties were the findings of a routine maintenance inspection whilst a failure was something that the traffic department might take an interest in with the possibility of an enquiry.

| Date | C. or F. | Nature of Casualty or Failure | Cause of Casualty or Failure | Date of last General repair | Miles run since last General repair | Remarks |
|---|---|---|---|---|---|---|
| 9/5 | F | m. Piston Gland blown out | Piston gland that works out of packing & lay between the packing & gland Rolling Ring Cones dirty | 23.4.51. | 2000 | Eng/60861/9.5.51 |
| 10/8 | F | R. Injector defective | | — | 15000 | 10.18/51 |
| 20.10.51 | C | Eng not steaming | | — | 7,000 | Eng 2/60861 |
| 23.1.52 | C | R.Tender Vac Piston not working | R. Piston Rod seized in bush | 26.4.51 | 34,000 | |
| ~~22.1.52~~ | ~~C~~ | ~~R~~ | | | | |
| 29.4.52 | C | Right Leading Pony box hot. | Grit down loose of wheel. | 26.4.51 | 45,000 | 1/Eng 2/60861 |
| 24.12.52 | F | Lubricator rod disconnected | Loss of lubrication rod pin | 26.4.51 | 75,000 | 1/Eng 2/60861 |
| 1.1.53 | F | R.H. Injector Steam Spindle stripped thread | Wear | 26.4.51 | 75,000 | 1/Eng 2/60861. |
| 19.4.53 | F | Right Driving axlebox hot. | Not apparent | 30.1.53 | 24,000 | |
| 6.8.54 | F | Right Driving box hot | Not apparent | 28.5.54 | 9,000 | |
| 28.1.55 | F | (1) Priming (2) middle Piston Gland blown out, packing scoured. | Lack of Lubrication caused by priming | 20.1.53 | 83,106 | |
| 12.11.55 | F | Burst intermediate heater pipe. Pipe fitted 10.9.55 | Deterioration of pipe | 15.4.55 | 23,288 | — |
| 5.5.56 | F | Left Hand leading axlebox hot | Metal flaked and cracked | 15.4.55 | 42,000 | — |
| 23.6.56 | F | Left leading axlebox hot | Not apparent oiling system in good order | 15.4.55 | 49,139 | — |
| 31.1.57 | F | R. Trailing Coupled Box hot. | Destroyed by Heating. | 15.4.55 | 71,000 | — |
| 5.1.58 | | { Middle Big End hot. { R.H. Regulator Gland Blowing | Oil Container Empty. Wear on Packing. | } 26.9.57 | 9,500 | L.C. 4/1A. |
| 26.6.58. | | Flange portion of R.Hand Leading side rod fractured and becoming detached. | Side rod cap fractured in radius where flange portion of cap is formed. | 9.57 | 28,600 | L.C. 152/1 |
| 25.9.58. | | Boiler unable to maintain full working pressure. | As several observed whilst last pipe top dirty. | Sept. 57. | 43,000 | L.C. |
| 9.9.59 | | L.T. Coupled Axlebox hot. | Overheating destroyed all evidence. | 26.9.57 | 71,000 | L.C. 252/1 |
| 9.7.60 | | R.H. Tender Axlebox hot. | All trace destroyed. | June 1960 | 690. | L.C. 171/1 |
| 2.5.61 | | Left trailing tender spring broken | P.M. New England, states, Fatigue fracture, top plate. | 16/6/60 | 34,500 | L.C 122/1 |

*Great Central J10 0-6-0 65186 of Trafford Park shunts stock at Manchester Central in 1954 when seventy-six of the original 124 engines remained in traffic. Their introduction predated the London extension of the Great Central and it may have been appropriate that they were only to be found on MS&L metals. After the electrification of the Sheffield - Manchester route they became even more isolated from the rest of the system, being confined to Manchester and the North West extremities of the Great Central. Half a dozen of the class survived into the 1960's.*

*Great Eastern J15 0-6-0 65460 at Beccles in September 1959. The engine was allocated to Lowestoft and ran light at 06.10 each morning to act as pilot at Halesworth, returning to Lowestoft with the 15.55 goods. The J15's had the widest availability of any LNER class; a feature that contributed to the longevity of the class; over a dozen surviving into 1961.*

## J36 0-6-0 (1888)

### Locomotives 65194–65203

| | 65194 | 65196 | 65197 | 65198 | 65199 | 65200 | 65201 | 65202 | 65203 |
|---|---|---|---|---|---|---|---|---|---|
| Aug-50 | H.MERSEY-9F | WIGAN-10F | H.MERSEY-9F | H.MERSEY-9F | WIGAN-10F | H.MERSEY-9F | STOCKPORT-9B | NORTHWICH-9G | WIGAN-10F |
| Jan-51 | H.MERSEY-9F | WIGAN-10F | H.MERSEY-9F | H.MERSEY-9F | WIGAN-10F | H.MERSEY-9F | STOCKPORT-9B | NORTHWICH-9G | WIGAN-10F |
| Aug-51 | H.MERSEY-9F | WIGAN-10F | H.MERSEY-9F | H.MERSEY-9F | WIGAN-10F | H.MERSEY-9F | STOCKPORT-9B | NORTHWICH-9G | WIGAN-10F |
| Jan-52 | H.MERSEY-9F | WIGAN-10F | H.MERSEY-9F | H.MERSEY-9F | WIGAN-10F | H.MERSEY-9F | STOCKPORT-9B | NORTHWICH-9G | WIGAN-10F |
| Aug-52 | H.MERSEY-9F | WIGAN-10F | H.MERSEY-9F | H.MERSEY-9F | WIGAN-10F | H.MERSEY-9F | STOCKPORT-9B | NORTHWICH-9G | WIGAN-10F |
| Jan-53 | H.MERSEY-9F | 2/53: BRUNS-8E | 6/53: T PARK-9E | 6/53: T PARK-9E | WIGAN-10F | H.MERSEY-9F | 3/53: W/D | NORTHWICH-9G | WIGAN-10F |
| Aug-53 | H.MERSEY-9F | BRUNSWICK-8E | T.PARK-9E | 1/54: WIDNES-8D | WIGAN-10F | H.MERSEY-9F | | NORTHWICH-9G | WIGAN-10F |
| Jan-54 | H.MERSEY-9F | BRUNSWICK-8E | T.PARK-9E | WIDNES-8D | WIGAN-10F | H.MERSEY-9F | | NORTHWICH-9G | WIGAN-10F |
| Aug-54 | H.MERSEY-9F | BRUNSWICK-8E | T.PARK-9E | WIDNES-8D | WIGAN-10F | H.MERSEY-9F | | NORTHWICH-9G | WIGAN-10F |
| Jan-55 | H.MERSEY-9F | BRUNSWICK-8E | T.PARK-9E | WIDNES-8D | WIGAN-10F | H.MERSEY-9F | | NORTHWICH-9G | WIGAN-10F |
| Aug-55 | H.MERSEY-9F | BRUNSWICK-8E | 5/56: W/D | WIDNES-8D | WIGAN-10F | H.MERSEY-9F | | NORTHWICH-9G | WIGAN-10F |
| Jan-56 | H.MERSEY-9F | BRUNSWICK-8E | | WIDNES-8D | WIGAN-10F | H.MERSEY-9F | | NORTHWICH-9G | WIGAN-10F |
| Aug-56 | H.MERSEY-9F | BRUNSWICK-8E | | WIDNES-8D | WIGAN-10F | H.MERSEY-9F | | NORTHWICH-9G | WIGAN-10F |
| Jan-57 | H.MERSEY-9F | BRUNSWICK-8E | | WIDNES-8D | WIGAN-10F | H.MERSEY-9F | | NORTHWICH-9G | 11/56: DARL-51A |
| Aug-57 | H.MERSEY-9F | 7/57: GOOLE-53E | | WIDNES-8D | WIGAN-10F | H.MERSEY-9F | | NORTHWICH-9G | 12/56: W/D |
| Jan-58 | H.MERSEY-9F | GOOLE-53E | | WIDNES-8D | WIGAN-10F | H.MERSEY-9F | | 3/58: W/D | |
| Aug-58 | H.MERSEY-9F | 6/58: W/D | | WIDNES-8D | WIGAN-10F | 4/58: W/D | | | |
| Jan-59 | H.MERSEY-9F | | | 8/59: S.BCH-8F | 12/58: W/D | | | | |
| Aug-59 | H.MERSEY-9F | | | WIGAN(SB)-8F | | | | | |
| Nov-59 | H.MERSEY-9F | | | WIGAN(SB)-8F | | | | | |
| Jan-60 | 12/59: W/D | | | WIGAN(SB)-8F | | | | | |
| Apr-60 | | | | WIGAN(SB)-8F | | | | | |
| Aug-60 | | | | | | | | | |
| Nov-60 | | | | | | | | | |

### Locomotives 65204–65216

| | 65204 | 65205 | 65208 | 65209 | 65210 | 65211 | 65213 | 65214 | 65216 |
|---|---|---|---|---|---|---|---|---|---|
| Aug-50 | STOCKPORT-9B | NORTHWICH-9G | NORTHWICH-9G | H.MERSEY-9F | KIPPS-65E | BATHGATE-64F | FERRYHILL-61B | KIPPS-65E | CARLISLE(C)-12B |
| Jan-51 | STOCKPORT-9B | NORTHWICH-9G | NORTHWICH-9G | H.MERSEY-9F | KIPPS-65E | BATHGATE-64F | FERRYHILL-61B | KIPPS-65E | CARLISLE(C)-12B |
| Aug-51 | STOCKPORT-9B | NORTHWICH-9G | NORTHWICH-9G | H.MERSEY-9F | KIPPS-65E | BATHGATE-64F | FERRYHILL-61B | KIPPS-65E | CARLISLE(C)-68E |
| Jan-52 | STOCKPORT-9B | NORTHWICH-9G | NORTHWICH-9G | H.MERSEY-9F | KIPPS-65E | BATHGATE-64F | FERRYHILL-61B | KIPPS-65E | CARLISLE(C)-68E |
| Aug-52 | STOCKPORT-9B | 5/52: T PARK-9E | NORTHWICH-9G | H.MERSEY-9F | KIPPS-65E | BATHGATE-64F | 12/52: KITTY-61A | KIPPS-65E | CARLISLE(C)-68E |
| Jan-53 | 11/52: W/D | T.PARK-9E | 3/53: NGATE-6D | 6/53: T PARK-9E | KIPPS-65E | BATHGATE-64F | KITTYBREWSTER-61A | KIPPS-65E | CARLISLE(C)-68E |
| Aug-53 | | T.PARK-9E | NORTHGATE-6D | T.PARK-9E | KIPPS-65E | BATHGATE-64F | KITTYBREWSTER-61A | KIPPS-65E | CARLISLE(C)-68E |
| Jan-54 | | T.PARK-9E | NORTHGATE-6D | 6/54: WIDNES-8D | KIPPS-65E | BATHGATE-64F | KITTYBREWSTER-61A | KIPPS-65E | CARLISLE(C)-68E |
| Aug-54 | | T.PARK-9E | NORTHGATE-6D | 9/54: T PARK-9E | KIPPS-65E | BATHGATE-64F | KITTYBREWSTER-61A | KIPPS-65E | CARLISLE(C)-68E |
| Jan-55 | | T.PARK-9E | NORTHGATE-6D | T.PARK-9E | KIPPS-65E | BATHGATE-64F | KITTYBREWSTER-61A | KIPPS-65E | CARLISLE(C)-68E |
| Aug-55 | | T.PARK-9E | NORTHGATE-6D | T.PARK-9E | KIPPS-65E | BATHGATE-64F | KITTYBREWSTER-61A | KIPPS-65E | CARLISLE(C)-68E |
| Jan-56 | | 7/56: W/D | NORTHGATE-6D | T.PARK-9E | KIPPS-65E | BATHGATE-64F | KITTYBREWSTER-61A | KIPPS-65E | CARLISLE(C)-68E |
| Aug-56 | | | NORTHGATE-6D | T.PARK-9E | KIPPS-65E | BATHGATE-64F | KITTYBREWSTER-61A | KIPPS-65E | 12/56: POLM-66A |
| Jan-57 | | | 12/56: T PARK-9E | T.PARK-9E | KIPPS-65E | 4/57: PARK-65C | KITTYBREWSTER-61A | KIPPS-65E | POLMADIE-66A |
| Aug-57 | | | T.PARK-9E | T.PARK-9E | KIPPS-65E | PARKHEAD-65C | 5/57: W/D | KIPPS-65E | POLMADIE-66A |
| Jan-58 | | | T.PARK-9E | T.PARK-9E | KIPPS-65E | PARKHEAD-65C | | KIPPS-65E | POLMADIE-66A |
| Aug-58 | | | T.PARK-9E | T.PARK-9E | KIPPS-65E | PARKHEAD-65C | | KIPPS-65E | POLMADIE-66A |
| Jan-59 | | | 12/58: W/D | 11/58: W/D | KIPPS-65E | PARKHEAD-65C | | KIPPS-65E | POLMADIE-66A |
| Aug-59 | | | | | KIPPS-65E | PARKHEAD-65C | | KIPPS-65E | POLMADIE-66A |
| Nov-59 | | | | | KIPPS-65E | PARKHEAD-65C | | KIPPS-65E | POLMADIE-66A |
| Jan-60 | | | | | KIPPS-65E | PARKHEAD-65C | | KIPPS-65E | 3/60: KIPPS-65E |
| Apr-60 | | | | | KIPPS-65E | PARKHEAD-65C | | KIPPS-65E | KIPPS-65E |
| Aug-60 | | | | | KIPPS-65E | PARKHEAD-65C | | KIPPS-65E | KIPPS-65E |
| Nov-60 | | | | | | | | | |

### Locomotives 65217–65228

| | 65217 | 65218 | 65221 | 65222 | 65224 | 65225 | 65226 | 65227 | 65228 |
|---|---|---|---|---|---|---|---|---|---|
| Aug-50 | KIPPS-65E | THORNTON JCN-62A | EASTFIELD-65A | POLMONT-64E | EDINBURGH(SM)-64A | BATHGATE-64F | KIPPS-65E | BALLOCH-65I | EASTFIELD-65A |
| Jan-51 | KIPPS-65E | THORNTON JCN-62A | EASTFIELD-65A | POLMONT-64E | EDINBURGH(SM)-64A | BATHGATE-64F | 3/51: BLAY-52C | BALLOCH-65I | EASTFIELD-65A |
| Aug-51 | KIPPS-65E | THORNTON JCN-62A | EASTFIELD-65A | POLMONT-64E | EDINBURGH(SM)-64A | BATHGATE-64F | 4/51: W/D | BALLOCH-65I | EASTFIELD-65A |
| Jan-52 | KIPPS-65E | THORNTON JCN-62A | EASTFIELD-65A | POLMONT-64E | EDINBURGH(SM)-64A | BATHGATE-64F | | BALLOCH-65I | EASTFIELD-65A |
| Aug-52 | KIPPS-65E | THORNTON JCN-62A | EASTFIELD-65A | POLMONT-64E | EDINBURGH(SM)-64A | BATHGATE-64F | | BALLOCH-65I | EASTFIELD-65A |
| Jan-53 | KIPPS-65E | THORNTON JCN-62A | EASTFIELD-65A | POLMONT-64E | EDINBURGH(SM)-64A | BATHGATE-64F | | BALLOCH-65I | EASTFIELD-65A |
| Aug-53 | KIPPS-65E | THORNTON JCN-62A | EASTFIELD-65A | POLMONT-64E | EDINBURGH(SM)-64A | BATHGATE-64F | | BALLOCH-65I | EASTFIELD-65A |
| Jan-54 | KIPPS-65E | THORNTON JCN-62A | EASTFIELD-65A | POLMONT-64E | EDINBURGH(SM)-64A | BATHGATE-64F | | BALLOCH-65I | EASTFIELD-65A |
| Aug-54 | KIPPS-65E | THORNTON JCN-62A | EASTFIELD-65A | POLMONT-64E | EDINBURGH(SM)-64A | BATHGATE-64F | | BALLOCH-65I | EASTFIELD-65A |
| Jan-55 | KIPPS-65E | THORNTON JCN-62A | EASTFIELD-65A | POLMONT-64E | EDINBURGH(SM)-64A | BATHGATE-64F | | BALLOCH-65I | EASTFIELD-65A |
| Aug-55 | KIPPS-65E | THORNTON JCN-62A | EASTFIELD-65A | POLMONT-64E | EDINBURGH(SM)-64A | BATHGATE-64F | | BALLOCH-65I | EASTFIELD-65A |
| Jan-56 | KIPPS-65E | THORNTON JCN-62A | EASTFIELD-65A | POLMONT-64E | EDINBURGH(SM)-64A | BATHGATE-64F | | BALLOCH-65I | EASTFIELD-65A |
| Aug-56 | KIPPS-65E | THORNTON JCN-62A | EASTFIELD-65A | POLMONT-64E | EDINBURGH(SM)-64A | BATHGATE-64F | | BALLOCH-65I | EASTFIELD-65A |
| Jan-57 | KIPPS-65E | THORNTON JCN-62A | EASTFIELD-65A | POLMONT-64E | EDINBURGH(SM)-64A | BATHGATE-64F | | BALLOCH-65I | EASTFIELD-65A |
| Aug-57 | KIPPS-65E | THORNTON JCN-62A | EASTFIELD-65A | POLMONT-64E | EDINBURGH(SM)-64A | 10/57: W/D | | BALLOCH-65I | EASTFIELD-65A |
| Jan-58 | KIPPS-65E | THORNTON JCN-62A | EASTFIELD-65A | POLMONT-64E | EDINBURGH(SM)-64A | | | BALLOCH-65I | EASTFIELD-65A |
| Aug-58 | KIPPS-65E | THORNTON JCN-62A | EASTFIELD-65A | POLMONT-64E | EDINBURGH(SM)-64A | | | BALLOCH-65I | EASTFIELD-65A |
| Jan-59 | KIPPS-65E | THORNTON JCN-62A | 2/59: KITTY-61A | POLMONT-64E | EDINBURGH(SM)-64A | | | 2/59: KITTY-61A | EASTFIELD-65A |
| Aug-59 | KIPPS-65E | THORNTON JCN-62A | 7/59: W/D | POLMONT-64E | EDINBURGH(SM)-64A | | | 8/59: KEITH-61C | EASTFIELD-65A |
| Nov-59 | KIPPS-65E | THORNTON JCN-62A | | POLMONT-64E | EDINBURGH(SM)-64A | | | 9/59: KITTY-61A | EASTFIELD-65A |
| Jan-60 | 2/60: GRANGE-65F | THORNTON JCN-62A | | POLMONT-64E | EDINBURGH(SM)-64A | | | KITTYBREWSTER-61A | EASTFIELD-65A |
| Apr-60 | GRANGEMOUTH-65F | THORNTON JCN-62A | | POLMONT-64E | EDINBURGH(SM)-64A | | | KITTYBREWSTER-61A | EASTFIELD-65A |
| Aug-60 | GRANGEMOUTH-65F | 7/60: EAST-65A | | POLMONT-64E | EDINBURGH(SM)-64A | | | KITTYBREWSTER-61A | EASTFIELD-65A |
| Nov-60 | GRANGEMOUTH-65F | EASTFIELD-65A | | POLMONT-64E | EDINBURGH(SM)-64A | | | | |

### Locomotives 65229–65237

| | 65229 | 65230 | 65231 | 65232 | 65233 | 65234 | 65235 | 65236 | 65237 |
|---|---|---|---|---|---|---|---|---|---|
| Aug-50 | BATHGATE-64F | BATHGATE-64F | BATHGATE-64F | HAWICK-64G | POLMONT-64E | BATHGATE-64F | BATHGATE-64F | KIPPS-65E | FORTWILLIAM-63D |
| Jan-51 | BATHGATE-64F | BATHGATE-64F | BATHGATE-64F | HAWICK-64G | POLMONT-64E | BATHGATE-64F | BATHGATE-64F | KIPPS-65E | FORTWILLIAM-63D |
| Aug-51 | BATHGATE-64F | BATHGATE-64F | BATHGATE-64F | HAWICK-64G | POLMONT-64E | BATHGATE-64F | BATHGATE-64F | KIPPS-65E | FORTWILLIAM-63D |
| Jan-52 | BATHGATE-64F | BATHGATE-64F | 4/52: W/D | HAWICK-64G | POLMONT-64E | BATHGATE-64F | 5/52: HMKT-64B | KIPPS-65E | FORTWILLIAM-63D |
| Aug-52 | BATHGATE-64F | BATHGATE-64F | | HAWICK-64G | POLMONT-64E | BATHGATE-64F | HAYMARKET-64B | KIPPS-65E | FORTWILLIAM-63D |
| Jan-53 | BATHGATE-64F | BATHGATE-64F | | HAWICK-64G | POLMONT-64E | BATHGATE-64F | HAYMARKET-64B | KIPPS-65E | FORTWILLIAM-63D |
| Aug-53 | BATHGATE-64F | BATHGATE-64F | | HAWICK-64G | POLMONT-64E | BATHGATE-64F | HAYMARKET-64B | KIPPS-65E | FORTWILLIAM-63D |
| Jan-54 | BATHGATE-64F | BATHGATE-64F | | HAWICK-64G | POLMONT-64E | BATHGATE-64F | HAYMARKET-64B | KIPPS-65E | FORTWILLIAM-63D |
| Aug-54 | BATHGATE-64F | BATHGATE-64F | | HAWICK-64G | POLMONT-64E | BATHGATE-64F | HAYMARKET-64B | KIPPS-65E | FORTWILLIAM-63D |
| Jan-55 | BATHGATE-64F | BATHGATE-64F | | HAWICK-64G | POLMONT-64E | BATHGATE-64F | HAYMARKET-64B | KIPPS-65E | FORTWILLIAM-63D |
| Aug-55 | BATHGATE-64F | BATHGATE-64F | | HAWICK-64G | POLMONT-64E | BATHGATE-64F | HAYMARKET-64B | KIPPS-65E | FORTWILLIAM-63D |
| Jan-56 | BATHGATE-64F | BATHGATE-64F | | HAWICK-64G | POLMONT-64E | BATHGATE-64F | HAYMARKET-64B | KIPPS-65E | FORTWILLIAM-63D |
| Aug-56 | BATHGATE-64F | BATHGATE-64F | | HAWICK-64G | POLMONT-64E | BATHGATE-64F | HAYMARKET-64B | 4/56: W/D | FORTWILLIAM-63D |
| Jan-57 | BATHGATE-64F | BATHGATE-64F | | 12/56: POLM-66A | POLMONT-64E | BATHGATE-64F | HAYMARKET-64B | | EASTFIELD-65A |
| Aug-57 | BATHGATE-64F | BATHGATE-64F | | POLMADIE-66A | POLMONT-64E | BATHGATE-64F | HAYMARKET-64B | | EASTFIELD-65A |
| Jan-58 | BATHGATE-64F | BATHGATE-64F | | POLMADIE-66A | POLMONT-64E | BATHGATE-64F | HAYMARKET-64B | | EASTFIELD-65A |
| Aug-58 | BATHGATE-64F | BATHGATE-64F | | POLMADIE-66A | POLMONT-64E | BATHGATE-64F | HAYMARKET-64B | | 1/59: CANAL-12C |
| Jan-59 | BATHGATE-64F | BATHGATE-64F | | 11/58: HWCK-64G | POLMONT-64E | BATHGATE-64F | BATHGATE-64F | | CARLISLE(C)-12C |
| Aug-59 | BATHGATE-64F | BATHGATE-64F | | HAWICK-64G | POLMONT-64E | BATHGATE-64F | BATHGATE-64F | | CARLISLE(C)-12C |
| Nov-59 | BATHGATE-64F | 9/59: PARK-65C | | 12/59: BATH-64F | POLMONT-64E | BATHGATE-64F | BATHGATE-64F | | CARLISLE(C)-12C |
| Jan-60 | BATHGATE-64F | PARKHEAD-65C | | BATHGATE-64F | BATHGATE-64F | BATHGATE-64F | BATHGATE-64F | | CARLISLE(C)-12C |
| Apr-60 | BATHGATE-64F | PARKHEAD-65C | | BATHGATE-64F | BATHGATE-64F | BATHGATE-64F | HAYMARKET-64B | | CARLISLE(C)-12C |
| Aug-60 | 5/59: W/D | PARKHEAD-65C | | BATHGATE-64F | BATHGATE-64F | BATHGATE-64F | HAYMARKET-64B | | CARLISLE(C)-12C |
| Nov-60 | | | | | | | | | |

## 65238 – 65246

| Date | 65238 | 65239 | 65240 | 65241 | 65242 | 65243 | 65244 | 65245 | 65246 |
|---|---|---|---|---|---|---|---|---|---|
| Aug-50 | KIPPS-65E | DUNFERMLINE-62C | HAYMARKET-64B | POLMONT-64E | HAWICK-64G | HAYMARKET-64B | POLMONT-64E | KIPPS-65E | POLMONT-64E |
| Jan-51 | KIPPS-65E | DUNFERMLINE-62C | HAYMARKET-64B | POLMONT-64E | HAWICK-64G | HAYMARKET-64B | POLMONT-64E | KIPPS-65E | POLMONT-64E |
| Aug-51 | 7/51: W/D | 9/51: ST. M-64A | HAYMARKET-64B | POLMONT-64E | HAWICK-64G | HAYMARKET-64B | POLMONT-64E | 6/51: W/D | POLMONT-64E |
| Jan-52 | | EDINBURGH(SM)-64A | HAYMARKET-64B | POLMONT-64E | HAWICK-64G | HAYMARKET-64B | POLMONT-64E | | POLMONT-64E |
| Aug-52 | | EDINBURGH(SM)-64A | 4/52: W/D | POLMONT-64E | HAWICK-64G | HAYMARKET-64B | POLMONT-64E | | POLMONT-64E |
| Jan-53 | | EDINBURGH(SM)-64A | | POLMONT-64E | HAWICK-64G | HAYMARKET-64B | POLMONT-64E | | POLMONT-64E |
| Aug-53 | | EDINBURGH(SM)-64A | | POLMONT-64E | HAWICK-64G | HAYMARKET-64B | POLMONT-64E | | POLMONT-64E |
| Jan-54 | | EDINBURGH(SM)-64A | | POLMONT-64E | 1/54: ST. M-64A | HAYMARKET-64B | POLMONT-64E | | POLMONT-64E |
| Aug-54 | | EDINBURGH(SM)-64A | | POLMONT-64E | EDINBURGH(SM)-64A | HAYMARKET-64B | POLMONT-64E | | POLMONT-64E |
| Jan-55 | | EDINBURGH(SM)-64A | | POLMONT-64E | EDINBURGH(SM)-64A | HAYMARKET-64B | POLMONT-64E | | POLMONT-64E |
| Aug-55 | | EDINBURGH(SM)-64A | | POLMONT-64E | 12/55: FERRY-61B | HAYMARKET-64B | POLMONT-64E | | POLMONT-64E |
| Jan-56 | | EDINBURGH(SM)-64A | | POLMONT-64E | FERRYHILL-61B | HAYMARKET-64B | POLMONT-64E | | POLMONT-64E |
| Aug-56 | | EDINBURGH(SM)-64A | | POLMONT-64E | FERRYHILL-61B | HAYMARKET-64B | POLMONT-64E | | POLMONT-64E |
| Jan-57 | | EDINBURGH(SM)-64A | | POLMONT-64E | 8/57: KITTY-61A | HAYMARKET-64B | POLMONT-64E | | POLMONT-64E |
| Aug-57 | | EDINBURGH(SM)-64A | | POLMONT-64E | 9/57: W/D | HAYMARKET-64B | 8/57: W/D | | POLMONT-64E |
| Jan-58 | | EDINBURGH(SM)-64A | | POLMONT-64E | | HAYMARKET-64B | | | POLMONT-64E |
| Aug-58 | | EDINBURGH(SM)-64A | | POLMONT-64E | | HAYMARKET-64B | | | POLMONT-64E |
| Jan-59 | | EDINBURGH(SM)-64A | | 1/59: GRANGE-65F | | HAYMARKET-64B | | | 1/59: GRANGE-65F |
| Aug-59 | | EDINBURGH(SM)-64A | | GRANGEMOUTH-65F | | HAYMARKET-64B | | | 9/59: PARK-65C |
| Nov-59 | | EDINBURGH(SM)-64A | | GRANGEMOUTH-65F | | HAYMARKET-64B | | | PARKHEAD-65C |
| Jan-60 | | EDINBURGH(SM)-64A | | 2/60: KIPPS-65E | | HAYMARKET-64B | | | PARKHEAD-65C |
| Apr-60 | | EDINBURGH(SM)-64A | | KIPPS-65E | | HAYMARKET-64B | | | PARKHEAD-65C |
| Aug-60 | | 6/60: PARK-65C | | KIPPS-65E | | HAYMARKET-64B | | | PARKHEAD-65C |
| Nov-60 | | PARKHEAD-65C | | KIPPS-65E | | HAYMARKET-64B | | | PARKHEAD-65C |

## 65247 – 65255

| Date | 65247 | 65248 | 65249 | 65250 | 65251 | 65252 | 65253 | 65254 | 65255 |
|---|---|---|---|---|---|---|---|---|---|
| Aug-50 | KITTYBREWSTER-61A | BATHGATE-64F | KIPPS-65E | BATHGATE-64F | EDINBURGH(SM)-64A | DUNFERMLINE-62C | DUNFERMLINE-62C | BATHGATE-64F | KIPPS-65E |
| Jan-51 | KITTYBREWSTER-61A | BATHGATE-64F | KIPPS-65E | BATHGATE-64F | EDINBURGH(SM)-64A | 1/51: TH JN-62A | DUNFERMLINE-62C | 3/51: BLAY-52C | KIPPS-65E |
| Aug-51 | KITTYBREWSTER-61A | BATHGATE-64F | KIPPS-65E | BATHGATE-64F | EDINBURGH(SM)-64A | THORNTON JCN-62A | DUNFERMLINE-62C | 4/51: W/D | 8/51: W/D |
| Jan-52 | KITTYBREWSTER-61A | BATHGATE-64F | KIPPS-65E | BATHGATE-64F | EDINBURGH(SM)-64A | THORNTON JCN-62A | DUNFERMLINE-62C | | |
| Aug-52 | KITTYBREWSTER-61A | BATHGATE-64F | KIPPS-65E | BATHGATE-64F | EDINBURGH(SM)-64A | THORNTON JCN-62A | DUNFERMLINE-62C | | |
| Jan-53 | 12/52: FERRY-61B | BATHGATE-64F | KIPPS-65E | BATHGATE-64F | EDINBURGH(SM)-64A | THORNTON JCN-62A | DUNFERMLINE-62C | | |
| Aug-53 | FERRYHILL-61B | BATHGATE-64F | KIPPS-65E | BATHGATE-64F | EDINBURGH(SM)-64A | THORNTON JCN-62A | DUNFERMLINE-62C | | |
| Jan-54 | FERRYHILL-61B | BATHGATE-64F | KIPPS-65E | BATHGATE-64F | EDINBURGH(SM)-64A | THORNTON JCN-62A | DUNFERMLINE-62C | | |
| Aug-54 | 7/54: KITTY-61A | BATHGATE-64F | KIPPS-65E | BATHGATE-64F | EDINBURGH(SM)-64A | THORNTON JCN-62A | DUNFERMLINE-62C | | |
| Jan-55 | KITTYBREWSTER-61A | BATHGATE-64F | KIPPS-65E | BATHGATE-64F | EDINBURGH(SM)-64A | THORNTON JCN-62A | DUNFERMLINE-62C | | |
| Aug-55 | KITTYBREWSTER-61A | BATHGATE-64F | KIPPS-65E | BATHGATE-64F | EDINBURGH(SM)-64A | THORNTON JCN-62A | DUNFERMLINE-62C | | |
| Jan-56 | KITTYBREWSTER-61A | BATHGATE-64F | KIPPS-65E | BATHGATE-64F | EDINBURGH(SM)-64A | THORNTON JCN-62A | DUNFERMLINE-62C | | |
| Aug-56 | KITTYBREWSTER-61A | 5/56: W/D | KIPPS-65E | BATHGATE-64F | EDINBURGH(SM)-64A | THORNTON JCN-62A | DUNFERMLINE-62C | | |
| Jan-57 | KITTYBREWSTER-61A | | KIPPS-65E | BATHGATE-64F | EDINBURGH(SM)-64A | THORNTON JCN-62A | DUNFERMLINE-62C | | |
| Aug-57 | 9/57: FERRY-61B | | 7/57: KIPPS-65E | 2/57: W/D | 5/57: KITTY-61A | THORNTON JCN-62A | DUNFERMLINE-62C | | |
| Jan-58 | 12/57: KITTY-61A | | KIPPS-65E | | KITTYBREWSTER-61A | THORNTON JCN-62A | DUNFERMLINE-62C | | |
| Aug-58 | KITTYBREWSTER-61A | | KIPPS-65E | | KITTYBREWSTER-61A | THORNTON JCN-62A | DUNFERMLINE-62C | | |
| Jan-59 | KITTYBREWSTER-61A | | KIPPS-65E | | KITTYBREWSTER-61A | THORNTON JCN-62A | DUNFERMLINE-62C | | |
| Aug-59 | 7/59: W/D | | KIPPS-65E | | KITTYBREWSTER-61A | THORNTON JCN-62A | DUNFERMLINE-62C | | |
| Nov-59 | | | KIPPS-65E | | KITTYBREWSTER-61A | THORNTON JCN-62A | DUNFERMLINE-62C | | |
| Jan-60 | | | KIPPS-65E | | KITTYBREWSTER-61A | THORNTON JCN-62A | DUNFERMLINE-62C | | |
| Apr-60 | | | KIPPS-65E | | KITTYBREWSTER-61A | THORNTON JCN-62A | DUNFERMLINE-62C | | |
| Aug-60 | | | KIPPS-65E | | KITTYBREWSTER-61A | 5/60: W/D | DUNFERMLINE-62C | | |
| Nov-60 | | | 11/60: W/D | | KITTYBREWSTER-61A | | DUNFERMLINE-62C | | |

## 65257 – 65267

| Date | 65257 | 65258 | 65259 | 65260 | 65261 | 65264 | 65265 | 65266 | 65267 |
|---|---|---|---|---|---|---|---|---|---|
| Aug-50 | POLMONT-64E | EDINBURGH(SM)-64A | HAWICK-64G | KIPPS-65E | BATHGATE-64F | KIPPS-65E | BATHGATE-64F | KIPPS-65E | EDINBURGH(SM)-64A |
| Jan-51 | POLMONT-64E | EDINBURGH(SM)-64A | HAWICK-64G | KIPPS-65E | BATHGATE-64F | KIPPS-65E | BATHGATE-64F | KIPPS-65E | EDINBURGH(SM)-64A |
| Aug-51 | POLMONT-64E | EDINBURGH(SM)-64A | HAWICK-64G | KIPPS-65E | BATHGATE-64F | KIPPS-65E | BATHGATE-64F | KIPPS-65E | EDINBURGH(SM)-64A |
| Jan-52 | POLMONT-64E | EDINBURGH(SM)-64A | HAWICK-64G | KIPPS-65E | BATHGATE-64F | KIPPS-65E | BATHGATE-64F | KIPPS-65E | EDINBURGH(SM)-64A |
| Aug-52 | POLMONT-64E | EDINBURGH(SM)-64A | HAWICK-64G | KIPPS-65E | BATHGATE-64F | 6/52: W/D | BATHGATE-64F | KIPPS-65E | EDINBURGH(SM)-64A |
| Jan-53 | POLMONT-64E | EDINBURGH(SM)-64A | HAWICK-64G | KIPPS-65E | BATHGATE-64F | | BATHGATE-64F | KIPPS-65E | EDINBURGH(SM)-64A |
| Aug-53 | POLMONT-64E | EDINBURGH(SM)-64A | HAWICK-64G | KIPPS-65E | BATHGATE-64F | | BATHGATE-64F | KIPPS-65E | EDINBURGH(SM)-64A |
| Jan-54 | POLMONT-64E | EDINBURGH(SM)-64A | HAWICK-64G | KIPPS-65E | BATHGATE-64F | | BATHGATE-64F | KIPPS-65E | EDINBURGH(SM)-64A |
| Aug-54 | POLMONT-64E | EDINBURGH(SM)-64A | HAWICK-64G | KIPPS-65E | BATHGATE-64F | | BATHGATE-64F | KIPPS-65E | EDINBURGH(SM)-64A |
| Jan-55 | POLMONT-64E | EDINBURGH(SM)-64A | HAWICK-64G | KIPPS-65E | BATHGATE-64F | | BATHGATE-64F | KIPPS-65E | EDINBURGH(SM)-64A |
| Aug-55 | POLMONT-64E | EDINBURGH(SM)-64A | HAWICK-64G | KIPPS-65E | BATHGATE-64F | | BATHGATE-64F | KIPPS-65E | EDINBURGH(SM)-64A |
| Jan-56 | POLMONT-64E | EDINBURGH(SM)-64A | 11/55: BATH-64F | KIPPS-65E | BATHGATE-64F | | BATHGATE-64F | KIPPS-65E | 11/55: FERRY-61B |
| Aug-56 | POLMONT-64E | EDINBURGH(SM)-64A | BATHGATE-64F | KIPPS-65E | BATHGATE-64F | | BATHGATE-64F | KIPPS-65E | 4/56: KEITH-61C |
| Jan-57 | POLMONT-64E | EDINBURGH(SM)-64A | BATHGATE-64F | KIPPS-65E | BATHGATE-64F | | BATHGATE-64F | KIPPS-65E | KEITH-61C |
| Aug-57 | POLMONT-64E | EDINBURGH(SM)-64A | BATHGATE-64F | KIPPS-65E | BATHGATE-64F | | BATHGATE-64F | KIPPS-65E | KEITH-61C |
| Jan-58 | POLMONT-64E | EDINBURGH(SM)-64A | BATHGATE-64F | KIPPS-65E | BATHGATE-64F | | BATHGATE-64F | KIPPS-65E | KEITH-61C |
| Aug-58 | POLMONT-64E | EDINBURGH(SM)-64A | BATHGATE-64F | KIPPS-65E | BATHGATE-64F | | BATHGATE-64F | KIPPS-65E | KEITH-61C |
| Jan-59 | POLMONT-64E | EDINBURGH(SM)-64A | BATHGATE-64F | KIPPS-65E | BATHGATE-64F | | BATHGATE-64F | KIPPS-65E | KEITH-61C |
| Aug-59 | POLMONT-64E | EDINBURGH(SM)-64A | 7/59: W/D | KIPPS-65E | BATHGATE-64F | | BATHGATE-64F | KIPPS-65E | KEITH-61C |
| Nov-59 | POLMONT-64E | EDINBURGH(SM)-64A | | KIPPS-65E | BATHGATE-64F | | BATHGATE-64F | KIPPS-65E | KEITH-61C |
| Jan-60 | POLMONT-64E | EDINBURGH(SM)-64A | | KIPPS-65E | BATHGATE-64F | | BATHGATE-64F | KIPPS-65E | KEITH-61C |
| Apr-60 | POLMONT-64E | EDINBURGH(SM)-64A | | KIPPS-65E | BATHGATE-64F | | BATHGATE-64F | KIPPS-65E | KEITH-61C |
| Aug-60 | POLMONT-64E | EDINBURGH(SM)-64A | | KIPPS-65E | BATHGATE-64F | | BATHGATE-64F | KIPPS-65E | KEITH-61C |
| Nov-60 | POLMONT-64E | EDINBURGH(SM)-64A | | KIPPS-65E | BATHGATE-64F | | BATHGATE-64F | KIPPS-65E | KEITH-61C |

## 65268 – 65278

| Date | 65268 | 65270 | 65271 | 75273 | 65274 | 65275 | 65276 | 65277 | 65278 |
|---|---|---|---|---|---|---|---|---|---|
| Aug-50 | POLMONT-64E | EASTFIELD-65A | DALRY RD-64C | EASTFIELD-65A | PARKHEAD-65C | POLMONT-64E | BATHGATE-64F | BATHGATE-64F | BATHGATE-64F |
| Jan-51 | POLMONT-64E | EASTFIELD-65A | DALRY RD-64C | EASTFIELD-65A | 12/50: W/D | POLMONT-64E | BATHGATE-64F | BATHGATE-64F | BATHGATE-64F |
| Aug-51 | POLMONT-64E | EASTFIELD-65A | DALRY RD-64C | EASTFIELD-65A | | POLMONT-64E | BATHGATE-64F | BATHGATE-64F | BATHGATE-64F |
| Jan-52 | 2/52: BATH-64F | EASTFIELD-65A | 8/52: W/D | EASTFIELD-65A | | POLMONT-64E | BATHGATE-64F | BATHGATE-64F | 1/52: W/D |
| Aug-52 | BATHGATE-64F | EASTFIELD-65A | | EASTFIELD-65A | | POLMONT-64E | BATHGATE-64F | BATHGATE-64F | |
| Jan-53 | BATHGATE-64F | EASTFIELD-65A | | EASTFIELD-65A | | POLMONT-64E | BATHGATE-64F | BATHGATE-64F | |
| Aug-53 | BATHGATE-64F | EASTFIELD-65A | | EASTFIELD-65A | | POLMONT-64E | BATHGATE-64F | BATHGATE-64F | |
| Jan-54 | BATHGATE-64F | EASTFIELD-65A | | EASTFIELD-65A | | POLMONT-64E | BATHGATE-64F | BATHGATE-64F | |
| Aug-54 | BATHGATE-64F | EASTFIELD-65A | | EASTFIELD-65A | | POLMONT-64E | BATHGATE-64F | BATHGATE-64F | |
| Jan-55 | BATHGATE-64F | EASTFIELD-65A | | EASTFIELD-65A | | POLMONT-64E | BATHGATE-64F | BATHGATE-64F | |
| Aug-55 | BATHGATE-64F | EASTFIELD-65A | | EASTFIELD-65A | | POLMONT-64E | BATHGATE-64F | BATHGATE-64F | |
| Jan-56 | BATHGATE-64F | EASTFIELD-65A | | EASTFIELD-65A | | POLMONT-64E | BATHGATE-64F | BATHGATE-64F | |
| Aug-56 | BATHGATE-64F | EASTFIELD-65A | | EASTFIELD-65A | | POLMONT-64E | BATHGATE-64F | BATHGATE-64F | |
| Jan-57 | BATHGATE-64F | EASTFIELD-65A | | EASTFIELD-65A | | POLMONT-64E | BATHGATE-64F | BATHGATE-64F | |
| Aug-57 | BATHGATE-64F | 7/57: PARK-65C | | EASTFIELD-65A | | POLMONT-64E | BATHGATE-64F | BATHGATE-64F | |
| Jan-58 | BATHGATE-64F | 2/58: W/D | | EASTFIELD-65A | | POLMONT-64E | BATHGATE-64F | BATHGATE-64F | |
| Aug-58 | BATHGATE-64F | | | 3/58: PARK-65C | | 8/58: HWCK-64G | BATHGATE-64F | BATHGATE-64F | |
| Jan-59 | BATHGATE-64F | | | PARKHEAD-65C | | HAWICK-64G | BATHGATE-64F | BATHGATE-64F | |
| Aug-59 | BATHGATE-64F | | | PARKHEAD-65C | | HAWICK-64G | BATHGATE-64F | BATHGATE-64F | |
| Nov-59 | BATHGATE-64F | | | PARKHEAD-65C | | HAWICK-64G | BATHGATE-64F | 9/59: KEITH-61C | |
| Jan-60 | BATHGATE-64F | | | PARKHEAD-65C | | HAWICK-64G | BATHGATE-64F | KEITH-61C | |
| Apr-60 | BATHGATE-64F | | | PARKHEAD-65C | | HAWICK-64G | BATHGATE-64F | KEITH-61C | |
| Aug-60 | BATHGATE-64F | | | PARKHEAD-65C | | HAWICK-64G | BATHGATE-64F | KEITH-61C | |
| Nov-60 | BATHGATE-64F | | | PARKHEAD-65C | | HAWICK-64G | BATHGATE-64F | KEITH-61C | |

| | 65279 | 65280 | 65281 | 65282 | 65283 | 65285 | 65286 | 65287 | 65288 |
|---|---|---|---|---|---|---|---|---|---|
| Aug-50 | HAWICK - 64G | BATHGATE - 64F | DUNFERMLINE - 62C | BATHGATE - 64F | PARKHEAD - 65C | KIPPS - 65E | EDINBURGH (SM) - 64A | KIPPS - 65E | EDINBURGH (SM) - 64A |
| Jan-51 | HAWICK - 64G | BATHGATE - 64F | DUNFERMLINE - 62C | BATHGATE - 64F | PARKHEAD - 65C | KIPPS - 65E | EDINBURGH (SM) - 64A | KIPPS - 65E | EDINBURGH (SM) - 64A |
| Aug-51 | 3/51: W/D | BATHGATE - 64F | DUNFERMLINE - 62C | BATHGATE - 64F | PARKHEAD - 65C | KIPPS - 65E | EDINBURGH (SM) - 64A | KIPPS - 65E | EDINBURGH (SM) - 64A |
| Jan-52 | | BATHGATE - 64F | DUNFERMLINE - 62C | BATHGATE - 64F | PARKHEAD - 65C | KIPPS - 65E | 2/52: W/D | KIPPS - 65E | EDINBURGH (SM) - 64A |
| Aug-52 | | BATHGATE - 64F | DUNFERMLINE - 62C | BATHGATE - 64F | PARKHEAD - 65C | KIPPS - 65E | | KIPPS - 65E | EDINBURGH (SM) - 64A |
| Jan-53 | | BATHGATE - 64F | DUNFERMLINE - 62C | BATHGATE - 64F | 12/52: W/D | KIPPS - 65E | | KIPPS - 65E | EDINBURGH (SM) - 64A |
| Aug-53 | | BATHGATE - 64F | DUNFERMLINE - 62C | BATHGATE - 64F | | KIPPS - 65E | | KIPPS - 65E | EDINBURGH (SM) - 64A |
| Jan-54 | | BATHGATE - 64F | DUNFERMLINE - 62C | BATHGATE - 64F | | KIPPS - 65E | | KIPPS - 65E | EDINBURGH (SM) - 64A |
| Aug-54 | | BATHGATE - 64F | DUNFERMLINE - 62C | BATHGATE - 64F | | KIPPS - 65E | | KIPPS - 65E | EDINBURGH (SM) - 64A |
| Jan-55 | | BATHGATE - 64F | DUNFERMLINE - 62C | BATHGATE - 64F | | KIPPS - 65E | | KIPPS - 65E | EDINBURGH (SM) - 64A |
| Aug-55 | | BATHGATE - 64F | DUNFERMLINE - 62C | BATHGATE - 64F | | KIPPS - 65E | | KIPPS - 65E | EDINBURGH (SM) - 64A |
| Jan-56 | | BATHGATE - 64F | DUNFERMLINE - 62C | BATHGATE - 64F | | KIPPS - 65E | | KIPPS - 65E | EDINBURGH (SM) - 64A |
| Aug-56 | | BATHGATE - 64F | DUNFERMLINE - 62C | BATHGATE - 64F | | KIPPS - 65E | | KIPPS - 65E | EDINBURGH (SM) - 64A |
| Jan-57 | | 12/56: POLM - 64E | DUNFERMLINE - 62C | BATHGATE - 64F | | KIPPS - 65E | | KIPPS - 65E | EDINBURGH (SM) - 64A |
| Aug-57 | | POLMONT - 64E | DUNFERMLINE - 62C | BATHGATE - 64F | | KIPPS - 65E | | KIPPS - 65E | EDINBURGH (SM) - 64A |
| Jan-58 | | POLMONT - 64E | DUNFERMLINE - 62C | BATHGATE - 64F | | KIPPS - 65E | | KIPPS - 65E | EDINBURGH (SM) - 64A |
| Aug-58 | | POLMONT - 64E | DUNFERMLINE - 62C | BATHGATE - 64F | | KIPPS - 65E | | KIPPS - 65E | EDINBURGH (SM) - 64A |
| Jan-59 | | POLMONT - 64E | DUNFERMLINE - 62C | BATHGATE - 64F | | KIPPS - 65E | | KIPPS - 65E | EDINBURGH (SM) - 64A |
| Aug-59 | | POLMONT - 64E | DUNFERMLINE - 62C | BATHGATE - 64F | | KIPPS - 65E | | KIPPS - 65E | EDINBURGH (SM) - 64A |
| Nov-59 | | POLMONT - 64E | DUNFERMLINE - 62C | BATHGATE - 64F | | KIPPS - 65E | | KIPPS - 65E | EDINBURGH (SM) - 64A |
| Jan-60 | | POLMONT - 64E | DUNFERMLINE - 62C | BATHGATE - 64F | | KIPPS - 65E | | KIPPS - 65E | EDINBURGH (SM) - 64A |
| Apr-60 | | POLMONT - 65K | DUNFERMLINE - 62C | BATHGATE - 64F | | KIPPS - 65E | | KIPPS - 65E | EDINBURGH (SM) - 64A |
| Aug-60 | | POLMONT - 65K | DUNFERMLINE - 62C | BATHGATE - 64F | | KIPPS - 65E | | KIPPS - 65E | EDINBURGH (SM) - 64A |
| Nov-60 | | POLMONT - 65K | 10/60: BATH - 64F | BATHGATE - 64F | | KIPPS - 65E | | KIPPS - 65E | EDINBURGH (SM) - 64A |

| | 65290 | 65291 | 65292 | 65293 | 65295 | 65296 | 65297 | 65298 | 65300 |
|---|---|---|---|---|---|---|---|---|---|
| Aug-50 | POLMONT - 64E | THORNTON JCN - 62A | EDINBURGH (SM) - 64A | CARLISLE (C) - 12B | BLAYDON - 52C | EASTFIELD - 65A | FERRYHILL - 61B | PARKHEAD - 65C | FORT WILLIAM - 63D |
| Jan-51 | POLMONT - 64E | 11/50: W/D | EDINBURGH (SM) - 64A | CARLISLE (C) - 12B | BLAYDON - 52C | EASTFIELD - 65A | FERRYHILL - 61B | 3/51: HEX - 52C | FORT WILLIAM - 63D |
| Aug-51 | POLMONT - 64E | | EDINBURGH (SM) - 64A | CARLISLE (C) - 68E | 3/51: PARK - 65C | EASTFIELD - 65A | FERRYHILL - 61B | 4/51: W/D | FORT WILLIAM - 63D |
| Jan-52 | POLMONT - 64E | | EDINBURGH (SM) - 64A | CARLISLE (C) - 68E | PARKHEAD - 65C | EASTFIELD - 65A | FERRYHILL - 61B | | FORT WILLIAM - 63D |
| Aug-52 | POLMONT - 64E | | EDINBURGH (SM) - 64A | CARLISLE (C) - 68E | PARKHEAD - 65C | EASTFIELD - 65A | FERRYHILL - 61B | | FORT WILLIAM - 63D |
| Jan-53 | POLMONT - 64E | | EDINBURGH (SM) - 64A | CARLISLE (C) - 68E | PARKHEAD - 65C | EASTFIELD - 65A | FERRYHILL - 61B | | FORT WILLIAM - 63D |
| Aug-53 | POLMONT - 64E | | EDINBURGH (SM) - 64A | CARLISLE (C) - 68E | PARKHEAD - 65C | EASTFIELD - 65A | FERRYHILL - 61B | | FORT WILLIAM - 63D |
| Jan-54 | POLMONT - 64E | | EDINBURGH (SM) - 64A | CARLISLE (C) - 68E | PARKHEAD - 65C | EASTFIELD - 65A | FERRYHILL - 61B | | FORT WILLIAM - 63D |
| Aug-54 | POLMONT - 64E | | EDINBURGH (SM) - 64A | CARLISLE (C) - 68E | PARKHEAD - 65C | EASTFIELD - 65A | FERRYHILL - 61B | | FORT WILLIAM - 63D |
| Jan-55 | POLMONT - 64E | | EDINBURGH (SM) - 64A | CARLISLE (C) - 68E | PARKHEAD - 65C | EASTFIELD - 65A | FERRYHILL - 61B | | FORT WILLIAM - 63D |
| Aug-55 | POLMONT - 64E | | EDINBURGH (SM) - 64A | CARLISLE (C) - 68E | PARKHEAD - 65C | EASTFIELD - 65A | FERRYHILL - 61B | | FORT WILLIAM - 63D |
| Jan-56 | POLMONT - 64E | | EDINBURGH (SM) - 64A | CARLISLE (C) - 68E | PARKHEAD - 65C | EASTFIELD - 65A | FERRYHILL - 61B | | FORT WILLIAM - 63D |
| Aug-56 | POLMONT - 64E | | EDINBURGH (SM) - 64A | CARLISLE (C) - 68E | PARKHEAD - 65C | EASTFIELD - 65A | 10/56: KEITH - 61C | | FORT WILLIAM - 63D |
| Jan-57 | 12/56: BATH - 64F | | EDINBURGH (SM) - 64A | CARLISLE (C) - 68E | PARKHEAD - 65C | EASTFIELD - 65A | KEITH - 61C | | FORT WILLIAM - 63D |
| Aug-57 | BATHGATE - 64F | | EDINBURGH (SM) - 64A | CARLISLE (C) - 68E | PARKHEAD - 65C | EASTFIELD - 65A | KEITH - 61C | | FORT WILLIAM - 63D |
| Jan-58 | BATHGATE - 64F | | EDINBURGH (SM) - 64A | CARLISLE (C) - 68E | PARKHEAD - 65C | EASTFIELD - 65A | KEITH - 61C | | FORT WILLIAM - 63D |
| Aug-58 | BATHGATE - 64F | | EDINBURGH (SM) - 64A | CARLISLE (C) - 12C | PARKHEAD - 65C | EASTFIELD - 65A | KEITH - 61C | | FORT WILLIAM - 63D |
| Jan-59 | BATHGATE - 64F | | EDINBURGH (SM) - 64A | CARLISLE (C) - 12C | PARKHEAD - 65C | EASTFIELD - 65A | 3/59: KITTY - 61A | | FORT WILLIAM - 63D |
| Aug-59 | BATHGATE - 64F | | EDINBURGH (SM) - 64A | CARLISLE (C) - 12C | PARKHEAD - 65C | EASTFIELD - 65A | KITTYBREWSTER - 61A | | FORT WILLIAM - 63D |
| Nov-59 | BATHGATE - 64F | | EDINBURGH (SM) - 64A | CARLISLE (C) - 12C | PARKHEAD - 65C | EASTFIELD - 65A | KITTYBREWSTER - 61A | | FORT WILLIAM - 63D |
| Jan-60 | BATHGATE - 64F | | EDINBURGH (SM) - 64A | CARLISLE (C) - 12C | PARKHEAD - 65C | EASTFIELD - 65A | KITTYBREWSTER - 61A | | FORT WILLIAM - 63D |
| Apr-60 | BATHGATE - 64F | | EDINBURGH (SM) - 64A | CARLISLE (C) - 12C | PARKHEAD - 65C | EASTFIELD - 65A | KITTYBREWSTER - 61A | | FORT WILLIAM - 63B |
| Aug-60 | BATHGATE - 64F | | EDINBURGH (SM) - 64A | CARLISLE (C) - 12C | PARKHEAD - 65C | EASTFIELD - 65A | KITTYBREWSTER - 61A | | FORT WILLIAM - 63B |
| Nov-60 | BATHGATE - 64F | | EDINBURGH (SM) - 64A | CARLISLE (C) - 12C | PARKHEAD - 65C | EASTFIELD - 65A | KITTYBREWSTER - 61A | | FORT WILLIAM - 63B |

| | 65303 | 65304 | 65305 | 65306 | 65307 | 65308 | 65309 | 65310 | 65311 |
|---|---|---|---|---|---|---|---|---|---|
| Aug-50 | BATHGATE - 64F | CARLISLE (C) - 12B | EDINBURGH (SM) - 64A | POLMONT - 64E | DUNFERMLINE - 62C | EASTFIELD - 65A | DUNDEE - 62B | EDINBURGH (SM) - 64A | EDINBURGH (SM) - 64A |
| Jan-51 | BATHGATE - 64F | CARLISLE (C) - 12B | EDINBURGH (SM) - 64A | POLMONT - 64E | DUNFERMLINE - 62C | EASTFIELD - 65A | DUNDEE - 62B | EDINBURGH (SM) - 64A | EDINBURGH (SM) - 64A |
| Aug-51 | BATHGATE - 64F | CARLISLE (C) - 68E | EDINBURGH (SM) - 64A | POLMONT - 64E | DUNFERMLINE - 62C | 6/51: EAST - 65A | DUNDEE - 62B | EDINBURGH (SM) - 64A | 5/51: DALRY - 64C |
| Jan-52 | BATHGATE - 64F | CARLISLE (C) - 68E | EDINBURGH (SM) - 64A | POLMONT - 64E | DUNFERMLINE - 62C | | DUNDEE - 62B | EDINBURGH (SM) - 64A | DALRY RD - 64C |
| Aug-52 | BATHGATE - 64F | CARLISLE (C) - 68E | EDINBURGH (SM) - 64A | POLMONT - 64E | DUNFERMLINE - 62C | | DUNDEE - 62B | EDINBURGH (SM) - 64A | DALRY RD - 64C |
| Jan-53 | BATHGATE - 64F | CARLISLE (C) - 68E | EDINBURGH (SM) - 64A | POLMONT - 64E | DUNFERMLINE - 62C | | DUNDEE - 62B | EDINBURGH (SM) - 64A | 11/52: STM - 64A |
| Aug-53 | BATHGATE - 64F | CARLISLE (C) - 68E | EDINBURGH (SM) - 64A | POLMONT - 64E | DUNFERMLINE - 62C | | DUNDEE - 62B | EDINBURGH (SM) - 64A | EDINBURGH (SM) - 64A |
| Jan-54 | BATHGATE - 64F | CARLISLE (C) - 68E | EDINBURGH (SM) - 64A | POLMONT - 64E | DUNFERMLINE - 62C | | DUNDEE - 62B | EDINBURGH (SM) - 64A | EDINBURGH (SM) - 64A |
| Aug-54 | BATHGATE - 64F | CARLISLE (C) - 68E | EDINBURGH (SM) - 64A | POLMONT - 64E | DUNFERMLINE - 62C | | DUNDEE - 62B | EDINBURGH (SM) - 64A | EDINBURGH (SM) - 64A |
| Jan-55 | BATHGATE - 64F | CARLISLE (C) - 68E | EDINBURGH (SM) - 64A | POLMONT - 64E | DUNFERMLINE - 62C | | DUNDEE - 62B | EDINBURGH (SM) - 64A | EDINBURGH (SM) - 64A |
| Aug-55 | BATHGATE - 64F | CARLISLE (C) - 68E | EDINBURGH (SM) - 64A | POLMONT - 64E | DUNFERMLINE - 62C | | DUNDEE - 62B | EDINBURGH (SM) - 64A | EDINBURGH (SM) - 64A |
| Jan-56 | BATHGATE - 64F | CARLISLE (C) - 68E | EDINBURGH (SM) - 64A | POLMONT - 64E | DUNFERMLINE - 62C | | DUNDEE - 62B | EDINBURGH (SM) - 64A | EDINBURGH (SM) - 64A |
| Aug-56 | 6/56: KITTY - 61A | 12/56: POLM - 66A | EDINBURGH (SM) - 64A | POLMONT - 64E | DUNFERMLINE - 62C | | DUNDEE - 62B | EDINBURGH (SM) - 64A | 6/56: POL - 64E |
| Jan-57 | KITTYBREWSTER - 61A | 3/57: KITTY - 61A | EDINBURGH (SM) - 64A | POLMONT - 64E | DUNFERMLINE - 62C | | DUNDEE - 62B | EDINBURGH (SM) - 64A | POLMONT - 64E |
| Aug-57 | KITTYBREWSTER - 61A | 4/57: KEITH - 61C | EDINBURGH (SM) - 64A | POLMONT - 64E | DUNFERMLINE - 62C | | DUNDEE - 62B | EDINBURGH (SM) - 64A | POLMONT - 64E |
| Jan-58 | KITTYBREWSTER - 61A | KEITH - 61C | EDINBURGH (SM) - 64A | POLMONT - 64E | DUNFERMLINE - 62C | | DUNDEE - 62B | EDINBURGH (SM) - 64A | POLMONT - 64E |
| Aug-58 | KITTYBREWSTER - 61A | KEITH - 61C | EDINBURGH (SM) - 64A | POLMONT - 64E | DUNFERMLINE - 62C | | DUNDEE - 62B | EDINBURGH (SM) - 64A | POLMONT - 64E |
| Jan-59 | KITTYBREWSTER - 61A | KEITH - 61C | 2/59: FERRY - 61B | POLMONT - 64E | DUNFERMLINE - 62C | | DUNDEE - 62B | 2/59: FERRY - 61B | POLMONT - 64E |
| Aug-59 | KITTYBREWSTER - 61A | KEITH - 61C | FERRYHILL - 61B | POLMONT - 64E | DUNFERMLINE - 62C | | DUNDEE - 62B | 4/59: KEITH - 61C | POLMONT - 64E |
| Nov-59 | KITTYBREWSTER - 61A | KEITH - 61C | FERRYHILL - 61B | POLMONT - 64E | DUNFERMLINE - 62C | | DUNDEE - 62B | KEITH - 61C | POLMONT - 64E |
| Jan-60 | KITTYBREWSTER - 61A | KEITH - 61C | FERRYHILL - 61B | POLMONT - 64E | DUNFERMLINE - 62C | | DUNDEE - 62B | KEITH - 61C | POLMONT - 64E |
| Apr-60 | KITTYBREWSTER - 61A | KEITH - 61C | 3/60: KEITH - 61C | POLMONT - 65K | DUNFERMLINE - 62C | | DUNDEE - 62B | KEITH - 61C | POLMONT - 65K |
| Aug-60 | KITTYBREWSTER - 61A | KEITH - 61C | KEITH - 61C | POLMONT - 65K | DUNFERMLINE - 62C | | DUNDEE - 62B | KEITH - 61C | POLMONT - 65K |
| Nov-60 | KITTYBREWSTER - 61A | KEITH - 61C | KEITH - 61C | POLMONT - 65K | DUNFERMLINE - 62C | | 10/60: BATH - 64F | KEITH - 61C | POLMONT - 65K |

| | 65312 | 65313 | 65314 | 65315 | 65316 | 65317 | 65318 | 65319 | 65320 |
|---|---|---|---|---|---|---|---|---|---|
| Aug-50 | CARLISLE (C) - 12B | FORT WILLIAM - 63D | BATHGATE - 64F | BALLOCH - 65I | EDINBURGH (SM) - 64A | HAWICK - 64G | BATHGATE - 64F | DUNDEE - 62B | DUNFERMLINE - 62C |
| Jan-51 | CARLISLE (C) - 12B | FORT WILLIAM - 63D | BATHGATE - 64F | BALLOCH - 65I | EDINBURGH (SM) - 64A | HAWICK - 64G | BATHGATE - 64F | DUNDEE - 62B | DUNFERMLINE - 62C |
| Aug-51 | CARLISLE (C) - 68E | FORT WILLIAM - 63D | BATHGATE - 64F | BALLOCH - 65I | 4/51: HWCK - 64G | HAWICK - 64G | BATHGATE - 64F | DUNDEE - 62B | DUNFERMLINE - 62C |
| Jan-52 | CARLISLE (C) - 68E | FORT WILLIAM - 63D | BATHGATE - 64F | BALLOCH - 65I | HAWICK - 64G | HAWICK - 64G | BATHGATE - 64F | DUNDEE - 62B | DUNFERMLINE - 62C |
| Aug-52 | CARLISLE (C) - 68E | FORT WILLIAM - 63D | BATHGATE - 64F | BALLOCH - 65I | HAWICK - 64G | HAWICK - 64G | BATHGATE - 64F | DUNDEE - 62B | DUNFERMLINE - 62C |
| Jan-53 | CARLISLE (C) - 68E | FORT WILLIAM - 63D | BATHGATE - 64F | BALLOCH - 65I | HAWICK - 64G | HAWICK - 64G | BATHGATE - 64F | DUNDEE - 62B | DUNFERMLINE - 62C |
| Aug-53 | CARLISLE (C) - 68E | FORT WILLIAM - 63D | BATHGATE - 64F | BALLOCH - 65I | HAWICK - 64G | HAWICK - 64G | BATHGATE - 64F | DUNDEE - 62B | DUNFERMLINE - 62C |
| Jan-54 | CARLISLE (C) - 68E | FORT WILLIAM - 63D | BATHGATE - 64F | BALLOCH - 65I | HAWICK - 64G | HAWICK - 64G | BATHGATE - 64F | DUNDEE - 62B | DUNFERMLINE - 62C |
| Aug-54 | CARLISLE (C) - 68E | FORT WILLIAM - 63D | BATHGATE - 64F | BALLOCH - 65I | HAWICK - 64G | HAWICK - 64G | BATHGATE - 64F | DUNDEE - 62B | DUNFERMLINE - 62C |
| Jan-55 | CARLISLE (C) - 68E | FORT WILLIAM - 63D | BATHGATE - 64F | BALLOCH - 65I | HAWICK - 64G | HAWICK - 64G | BATHGATE - 64F | DUNDEE - 62B | DUNFERMLINE - 62C |
| Aug-55 | CARLISLE (C) - 68E | FORT WILLIAM - 63D | 8/55: W/D | BALLOCH - 65I | HAWICK - 64G | HAWICK - 64G | BATHGATE - 64F | DUNDEE - 62B | DUNFERMLINE - 62C |
| Jan-56 | CARLISLE (C) - 68E | FORT WILLIAM - 63D | | BALLOCH - 65I | HAWICK - 64G | HAWICK - 64G | BATHGATE - 64F | DUNDEE - 62B | DUNFERMLINE - 62C |
| Aug-56 | CARLISLE (C) - 68E | FORT WILLIAM - 63D | | BALLOCH - 65I | HAWICK - 64G | HAWICK - 64G | BATHGATE - 64F | DUNDEE - 62B | DUNFERMLINE - 62C |
| Jan-57 | CARLISLE (C) - 68E | FORT WILLIAM - 63D | | BALLOCH - 65I | HAWICK - 64G | HAWICK - 64G | BATHGATE - 64F | DUNDEE - 62B | DUNFERMLINE - 62C |
| Aug-57 | CARLISLE (C) - 68E | FORT WILLIAM - 63D | | BALLOCH - 65I | HAWICK - 64G | HAWICK - 64G | BATHGATE - 64F | DUNDEE - 62B | DUNFERMLINE - 62C |
| Jan-58 | CARLISLE (C) - 68E | FORT WILLIAM - 63D | | BALLOCH - 65I | HAWICK - 64G | HAWICK - 64G | BATHGATE - 64F | DUNDEE - 62B | DUNFERMLINE - 62C |
| Aug-58 | CARLISLE (C) - 12C | FORT WILLIAM - 63D | | BALLOCH - 65I | 8/58: POLM - 64E | HAWICK - 64G | BATHGATE - 64F | DUNDEE - 62B | DUNFERMLINE - 62C |
| Jan-59 | CARLISLE (C) - 12C | FORT WILLIAM - 63D | | BALLOCH - 65I | POLMONT - 64E | HAWICK - 64G | BATHGATE - 64F | DUNDEE - 62B | DUNFERMLINE - 62C |
| Aug-59 | CARLISLE (C) - 12C | FORT WILLIAM - 63D | | BALLOCH - 65I | POLMONT - 64E | HAWICK - 64G | BATHGATE - 64F | DUNDEE - 62B | DUNFERMLINE - 62C |
| Nov-59 | CARLISLE (C) - 12C | FORT WILLIAM - 63D | | BALLOCH - 65I | POLMONT - 64E | HAWICK - 64G | BATHGATE - 64F | DUNDEE - 62B | DUNFERMLINE - 62C |
| Jan-60 | CARLISLE (C) - 12C | FORT WILLIAM - 63D | | BALLOCH - 65I | POLMONT - 64E | HAWICK - 64G | BATHGATE - 64F | DUNDEE - 62B | DUNFERMLINE - 62C |
| Apr-60 | CARLISLE (C) - 12C | FORT WILLIAM - 63B | | BALLOCH - 65I | POLMONT - 65K | HAWICK - 64G | BATHGATE - 64F | DUNDEE - 62B | DUNFERMLINE - 62C |
| Aug-60 | CARLISLE (C) - 12C | FORT WILLIAM - 63B | | BALLOCH - 65I | POLMONT - 65K | 8/60: W/D | BATHGATE - 64F | DUNDEE - 62B | 8/60: PARK - 65C |
| Nov-60 | CARLISLE (C) - 12C | FORT WILLIAM - 63B | | BALLOCH - 65I | POLMONT - 65K | | BATHGATE - 64F | DUNDEE - 62B | PARKHEAD - 65C |

|  | 65321 | 65322 | 65323 | 65324 | 65325 | 65327 | 65329 | 65330 | 65331 |
|---|---|---|---|---|---|---|---|---|---|
| Aug-50 | CARLISLE(C) - 12B | DUNFERMLINE - 62C | DUNFERMLINE - 62C | PARKHEAD - 65C | KIPPS - 65E | BATHGATE - 64F | CARSTAIRS - 64D | DUNDEE - 62B | BLAYDON - 52C |
| Jan-51 | CARLISLE(C) - 12B | DUNFERMLINE - 62C | DUNFERMLINE - 62C | PARKHEAD - 65C | KIPPS - 65E | BATHGATE - 64F | CARSTAIRS - 64D | DUNDEE - 62B | BLAYDON - 52C |
| Aug-51 | CARLISLE(C) - 68E | 8/51: W/D | DUNFERMLINE - 62C | PARKHEAD - 65C | KIPPS - 65E | 3/51: STM - 64A | CARSTAIRS - 64D | DUNDEE - 62B | BLAYDON - 52C |
| Jan-52 | CARLISLE(C) - 68E |  | DUNFERMLINE - 62C | PARKHEAD - 65C | KIPPS - 65E | EDINBURGH(SM) - 64A | CARSTAIRS - 64D | DUNDEE - 62B | 4/51: BATH - 64F |
| Aug-52 | CARLISLE(C) - 68E |  | DUNFERMLINE - 62C | PARKHEAD - 65C | KIPPS - 65E | EDINBURGH(SM) - 64A | CARSTAIRS - 64D | DUNDEE - 62B | BATHGATE - 64F |
| Jan-53 | CARLISLE(C) - 68E |  | DUNFERMLINE - 62C | PARKHEAD - 65C | KIPPS - 65E | EDINBURGH(SM) - 64A | CARSTAIRS - 64D | DUNDEE - 62B | 5/52: HWCK - 64G |
| Aug-53 | CARLISLE(C) - 68E |  | DUNFERMLINE - 62C | PARKHEAD - 65C | KIPPS - 65E | EDINBURGH(SM) - 64A | CARSTAIRS - 64D | DUNDEE - 62B | HAWCK - 64G |
| Jan-54 | CARLISLE(C) - 68E |  | DUNFERMLINE - 62C | PARKHEAD - 65C | KIPPS - 65E | EDINBURGH(SM) - 64A | CARSTAIRS - 64D | DUNDEE - 62B | HAWCK - 64G |
| Aug-54 | CARLISLE(C) - 68E |  | DUNFERMLINE - 62C | PARKHEAD - 65C | KIPPS - 65E | EDINBURGH(SM) - 64A | CARSTAIRS - 64D | DUNDEE - 62B | HAWCK - 64G |
| Jan-55 | CARLISLE(C) - 68E |  | DUNFERMLINE - 62C | PARKHEAD - 65C | KIPPS - 65E | EDINBURGH(SM) - 64A | CARSTAIRS - 64D | DUNDEE - 62B | HAWCK - 64G |
| Aug-55 | CARLISLE(C) - 68E |  | DUNFERMLINE - 62C | PARKHEAD - 65C | KIPPS - 65E | EDINBURGH(SM) - 64A | CARSTAIRS - 64D | DUNDEE - 62B | HAWCK - 64G |
| Jan-56 | CARLISLE(C) - 68E |  | DUNFERMLINE - 62C | PARKHEAD - 65C | KIPPS - 65E | EDINBURGH(SM) - 64A | CARSTAIRS - 64D | DUNDEE - 62B | HAWCK - 64G |
| Aug-56 | CARLISLE(C) - 68E |  | DUNFERMLINE - 62C | PARKHEAD - 65C | KIPPS - 65E | EDINBURGH(SM) - 64A | CARSTAIRS - 64D | DUNDEE - 62B | HAWCK - 64G |
| Jan-57 | CARLISLE(C) - 68E |  | DUNFERMLINE - 62C | 2/57: W/D | KIPPS - 65E | EDINBURGH(SM) - 64A | CARSTAIRS - 64D | DUNDEE - 62B | HAWCK - 64G |
| Aug-57 | CARLISLE(C) - 68E |  | DUNFERMLINE - 62C |  | KIPPS - 65E | EDINBURGH(SM) - 64A | CARSTAIRS - 64D | DUNDEE - 62B | HAWCK - 64G |
| Jan-58 | CARLISLE(C) - 68E |  | DUNFERMLINE - 62C |  | KIPPS - 65E | EDINBURGH(SM) - 64A | CARSTAIRS - 64D | DUNDEE - 62B | HAWCK - 64G |
| Aug-58 | CARLISLE(C) - 12C |  | DUNFERMLINE - 62C |  | KIPPS - 65E | EDINBURGH(SM) - 64A | CARSTAIRS - 64D | DUNDEE - 62B | HAWCK - 64G |
| Jan-59 | CARLISLE(C) - 12C |  | DUNFERMLINE - 62C |  | KIPPS - 65E | EDINBURGH(SM) - 64A | CARSTAIRS - 64D | DUNDEE - 62B | HAWCK - 64G |
| Aug-59 | CARLISLE(C) - 12C |  | DUNFERMLINE - 62C |  | KIPPS - 65E | EDINBURGH(SM) - 64A | CARSTAIRS - 64D | DUNDEE - 62B | HAWCK - 64G |
| Nov-59 | CARLISLE(C) - 12C |  | DUNFERMLINE - 62C |  | KIPPS - 65E | EDINBURGH(SM) - 64A | CARSTAIRS - 64D | DUNDEE - 62B | HAWCK - 64G |
| Jan-60 | CARLISLE(C) - 12C |  | DUNFERMLINE - 62C |  | KIPPS - 65E | EDINBURGH(SM) - 64A | CARSTAIRS - 64D | DUNDEE - 62B | HAWCK - 64G |
| Apr-60 | CARLISLE(C) - 12C |  | DUNFERMLINE - 62C |  | KIPPS - 65E | EDINBURGH(SM) - 64A | CARSTAIRS - 64D | DUNDEE - 62B | HAWCK - 64G |
| Aug-60 | CARLISLE(C) - 12C |  | DUNFERMLINE - 62C |  | KIPPS - 65E | EDINBURGH(SM) - 64A | CARSTAIRS - 66E | DUNDEE - 62B | HAWCK - 64G |
| Nov-60 | CARLISLE(C) - 12C |  | DUNFERMLINE - 62C |  | KIPPS - 65E | EDINBURGH(SM) - 64A | CARSTAIRS - 66E | 10/60: HWCK - 64G | HAWCK - 64G |

|  | 65333 | 65334 | 65335 | 65338 | 65339 | 65340 | 65341 | 65342 | 65343 |
|---|---|---|---|---|---|---|---|---|---|
| Aug-50 | DUNDEE - 62B | EDINBURGH(SM) - 64A | PARKHEAD - 65C | POLMONT - 64E | BALLOCH - 65I | HAWCK - 64G | BATHGATE - 64F | BATHGATE - 64F | BLAYDON - 52C |
| Jan-51 | DUNDEE - 62B | EDINBURGH(SM) - 64A | PARKHEAD - 65C | POLMONT - 64E | BALLOCH - 65I | HAWCK - 64G | BATHGATE - 64F | BATHGATE - 64F | BLAYDON - 52C |
| Aug-51 | DUNDEE - 62B | EDINBURGH(SM) - 64A | PARKHEAD - 65C | POLMONT - 64E | BALLOCH - 65I | HAWCK - 64G | BATHGATE - 64F | BATHGATE - 64F | BLAYDON - 52C |
| Jan-52 | DUNDEE - 62B | EDINBURGH(SM) - 64A | PARKHEAD - 65C | POLMONT - 64E | BALLOCH - 65I | 1/52: W/D | BATHGATE - 64F | BATHGATE - 64F | 4/51: KIPPS: 65E |
| Aug-52 | DUNDEE - 62B | EDINBURGH(SM) - 64A | PARKHEAD - 65C | POLMONT - 64E | BALLOCH - 65I |  | BATHGATE - 64F | BATHGATE - 64F | KIPPS - 65E |
| Jan-53 | DUNDEE - 62B | EDINBURGH(SM) - 64A | PARKHEAD - 65C | POLMONT - 64E | BALLOCH - 65I |  | BATHGATE - 64F | BATHGATE - 64F | KIPPS - 65E |
| Aug-53 | DUNDEE - 62B | EDINBURGH(SM) - 64A | PARKHEAD - 65C | POLMONT - 64E | BALLOCH - 65I |  | BATHGATE - 64F | BATHGATE - 64F | KIPPS - 65E |
| Jan-54 | DUNDEE - 62B | EDINBURGH(SM) - 64A | PARKHEAD - 65C | POLMONT - 64E | BALLOCH - 65I |  | BATHGATE - 64F | BATHGATE - 64F | KIPPS - 65E |
| Aug-54 | DUNDEE - 62B | EDINBURGH(SM) - 64A | PARKHEAD - 65C | POLMONT - 64E | BALLOCH - 65I |  | BATHGATE - 64F | BATHGATE - 64F | KIPPS - 65E |
| Jan-55 | DUNDEE - 62B | EDINBURGH(SM) - 64A | PARKHEAD - 65C | POLMONT - 64E | BALLOCH - 65I |  | BATHGATE - 64F | BATHGATE - 64F | KIPPS - 65E |
| Aug-55 | DUNDEE - 62B | EDINBURGH(SM) - 64A | PARKHEAD - 65C | POLMONT - 64E | BALLOCH - 65I |  | BATHGATE - 64F | BATHGATE - 64F | KIPPS - 65E |
| Jan-56 | DUNDEE - 62B | EDINBURGH(SM) - 64A | PARKHEAD - 65C | POLMONT - 64E | BALLOCH - 65I |  | BATHGATE - 64F | BATHGATE - 64F | KIPPS - 65E |
| Aug-56 | DUNDEE - 62B | EDINBURGH(SM) - 64A | PARKHEAD - 65C | 6/56: STM - 64A | BALLOCH - 65I |  | BATHGATE - 64F | BATHGATE - 64F | KIPPS - 65E |
| Jan-57 | DUNDEE - 62B | EDINBURGH(SM) - 64A | PARKHEAD - 65C | EDINBURGH(SM) - 64A | BALLOCH - 65I |  | BATHGATE - 64F | BATHGATE - 64F | KIPPS - 65E |
| Aug-57 | DUNDEE - 62B | EDINBURGH(SM) - 64A | PARKHEAD - 65C | EDINBURGH(SM) - 64A | BALLOCH - 65I |  | BATHGATE - 64F | BATHGATE - 64F | KIPPS - 65E |
| Jan-58 | DUNDEE - 62B | EDINBURGH(SM) - 64A | PARKHEAD - 65C | 10/57: KITTY - 61A | BALLOCH - 65I |  | BATHGATE - 64F | BATHGATE - 64F | KIPPS - 65E |
| Aug-58 | DUNDEE - 62B | EDINBURGH(SM) - 64A | PARKHEAD - 65C | KITTYBREWSTER - 61A | BALLOCH - 65I |  | BATHGATE - 64F | BATHGATE - 64F | KIPPS - 65E |
| Jan-59 | DUNDEE - 62B | EDINBURGH(SM) - 64A | PARKHEAD - 65C | 3/59: KEITH - 61C | BALLOCH - 65I |  | BATHGATE - 64F | BATHGATE - 64F | KIPPS - 65E |
| Aug-59 | DUNDEE - 62B | EDINBURGH(SM) - 64A | PARKHEAD - 65C | KEITH - 61C | BALLOCH - 65I |  | BATHGATE - 64F | BATHGATE - 64F | KIPPS - 65E |
| Nov-59 | 9/59: W.D | EDINBURGH(SM) - 64A | PARKHEAD - 65C | KEITH - 61C | BALLOCH - 65I |  | BATHGATE - 64F | BATHGATE - 64F | KIPPS - 65E |
| Jan-60 |  | EDINBURGH(SM) - 64A | PARKHEAD - 65C | KEITH - 61C | BALLOCH - 65I |  | BATHGATE - 64F | BATHGATE - 64F | KIPPS - 65E |
| Apr-60 |  | EDINBURGH(SM) - 64A | PARKHEAD - 65C | KEITH - 61C | 4/60: W/D |  | BATHGATE - 64F | 3/60: W/D | 3/60: W/D |
| Aug-60 |  | EDINBURGH(SM) - 64A | PARKHEAD - 65C | KEITH - 61C |  |  | BATHGATE - 64F |  |  |
| Nov-60 |  | EDINBURGH(SM) - 64A | PARKHEAD - 65C | KEITH - 61C |  |  | BATHGATE - 64F |  |  |

|  | 65344 | 65345 | 65346 | J15 0-6-0 (1883) 65350 | 65354 | 65355 | 65356 | 65359 | 65361 |
|---|---|---|---|---|---|---|---|---|---|
| Aug-50 | BATHGATE - 64F | THORNTONJCN - 62A | BATHGATE - 64F | CAMBRIDGE - 31A | PARKESTON - 30F | LOWESTOFT - 32C | CAMBRIDGE - 31A | KINGS LYNN - 31C | STRATFORD - 30A |
| Jan-51 | BATHGATE - 64F | THORNTONJCN - 62A | BATHGATE - 64F | CAMBRIDGE - 31A | PARKESTON - 30F | LOWESTOFT - 32C | CAMBRIDGE - 31A | KINGS LYNN - 31C | 10/50: COL - 30E |
| Aug-51 | BATHGATE - 64F | THORNTONJCN - 62A | BATHGATE - 64F | 2/51: W/D | 2/51: W/D | 4/51: W/D | CAMBRIDGE - 31A | KINGS LYNN - 31C | 11/50: IPS - 32B |
| Jan-52 | BATHGATE - 64F | THORNTONJCN - 62A | BATHGATE - 64F |  |  |  | 12/51: MARCH - 31B | KINGS LYNN - 31C | IPSWICH - 32B |
| Aug-52 | BATHGATE - 64F | THORNTONJCN - 62A | BATHGATE - 64F |  |  |  | MARCH - 31B | KINGS LYNN - 31C | IPSWICH - 32B |
| Jan-53 | BATHGATE - 64F | THORNTONJCN - 62A | BATHGATE - 64F |  |  |  | MARCH - 31B | KINGS LYNN - 31C | IPSWICH - 32B |
| Aug-53 | BATHGATE - 64F | THORNTONJCN - 62A | BATHGATE - 64F |  |  |  | MARCH - 31B | KINGS LYNN - 31C | IPSWICH - 32B |
| Jan-54 | BATHGATE - 64F | THORNTONJCN - 62A | BATHGATE - 64F |  |  |  | MARCH - 31B | KINGS LYNN - 31C | IPSWICH - 32B |
| Aug-54 | BATHGATE - 64F | THORNTONJCN - 62A | BATHGATE - 64F |  |  |  | MARCH - 31B | KINGS LYNN - 31C | IPSWICH - 32B |
| Jan-55 | BATHGATE - 64F | THORNTONJCN - 62A | BATHGATE - 64F |  |  |  | MARCH - 31B | KINGS LYNN - 31C | IPSWICH - 32B |
| Aug-55 | BATHGATE - 64F | THORNTONJCN - 62A | BATHGATE - 64F |  |  |  | MARCH - 31B | KINGS LYNN - 31C | IPSWICH - 32B |
| Jan-56 | BATHGATE - 64F | THORNTONJCN - 62A | BATHGATE - 64F |  |  |  | MARCH - 31B | 12/55: W/D | IPSWICH - 32B |
| Aug-56 | BATHGATE - 64F | THORNTONJCN - 62A | BATHGATE - 64F |  |  |  | MARCH - 31B |  | IPSWICH - 32B |
| Jan-57 | BATHGATE - 64F | THORNTONJCN - 62A | BATHGATE - 64F |  |  |  | MARCH - 31B |  | 2/57: STRAT - 30A |
| Aug-57 | BATHGATE - 64F | THORNTONJCN - 62A | BATHGATE - 64F |  |  |  | 4/57: W/D |  | STRATFORD - 30A |
| Jan-58 | BATHGATE - 64F | THORNTONJCN - 62A | BATHGATE - 64F |  |  |  |  |  | STRATFORD - 30A |
| Aug-58 | BATHGATE - 64F | THORNTONJCN - 62A | BATHGATE - 64F |  |  |  |  |  | STRATFORD - 30A |
| Jan-59 | BATHGATE - 64F | THORNTONJCN - 62A | BATHGATE - 64F |  |  |  |  |  | STRATFORD - 30A |
| Aug-59 | BATHGATE - 64F | THORNTONJCN - 62A | BATHGATE - 64F |  |  |  |  |  | STRATFORD - 30A |
| Nov-59 | BATHGATE - 64F | THORNTONJCN - 62A | BATHGATE - 64F |  |  |  |  |  | STRATFORD - 30A |
| Jan-60 | BATHGATE - 64F | THORNTONJCN - 62A | BATHGATE - 64F |  |  |  |  |  | STRATFORD - 30A |
| Apr-60 | BATHGATE - 64F | THORNTONJCN - 62A | BATHGATE - 64F |  |  |  |  |  | STRATFORD - 30A |
| Aug-60 | 9/60: STM - 64A | THORNTONJCN - 62A | BATHGATE - 64F |  |  |  |  |  | STRATFORD - 30A |
| Nov-60 | EDINBURGH(SM) - 64A | THORNTONJCN - 62A | BATHGATE - 64F |  |  |  |  |  | STRATFORD - 30A |

|  | 65362 | 65366 | 65369 | 65370 | 65373 | 65374 | 65377 | 65378 | 65382 |
|---|---|---|---|---|---|---|---|---|---|
| Aug-50 | BURY - 31E | MARCH - 31B | COLCHESTER - 30E | STRATFORD - 30A | NORWICH - 32A | LOWESTOFT - 32C | IPSWICH - 32B | KINGS LYNN - 31C | IPSWICH - 32B |
| Jan-51 | BURY - 31E | MARCH - 31B | COLCHESTER - 30E | STRATFORD - 30A | 10/50: W/D | 11/50: W/D | IPSWICH - 32B | KINGS LYNN - 31C | IPSWICH - 32B |
| Aug-51 | 7/51: W/D | MARCH - 31B | 2/51: W/D | STRATFORD - 30A |  |  | 2/51: W/D | 4/51: W/D | IPSWICH - 32B |
| Jan-52 |  | MARCH - 31B |  | STRATFORD - 30A |  |  |  |  | IPSWICH - 32B |
| Aug-52 |  | 6/52: W/D |  | STRATFORD - 30A |  |  |  |  | IPSWICH - 32B |
| Jan-53 |  |  |  | STRATFORD - 30A |  |  |  |  | 3/52: W/D |
| Aug-53 |  |  |  | STRATFORD - 30A |  |  |  |  |  |
| Jan-54 |  |  |  | STRATFORD - 30A |  |  |  |  |  |
| Aug-54 |  |  |  | STRATFORD - 30A |  |  |  |  |  |
| Jan-55 |  |  |  | STRATFORD - 30A |  |  |  |  |  |
| Aug-55 |  |  |  | STRATFORD - 30A |  |  |  |  |  |
| Jan-56 |  |  |  | STRATFORD - 30A |  |  |  |  |  |
| Aug-56 |  |  |  | 4/56: W/D |  |  |  |  |  |

## The
## North British Railway Study Group
# Journal

*The Waverley, Forth and Tay Bridges, P2 2-8-2's, heavy express, suburban and mineral traffic - there was plenty of life beyond No. 10 and one way to sample (and even contribute to) the LNER north of Berwick is to consider the NORTH BRITISH STUDY GROUP and its journal which brings the North British Railway back to life for the enthusiast and modeller alike.*

*Contact : Mr W. Lynn, 2 Brecken Court, Saltwell Road South, Low Fell, Gateshead, Tyne & Wear. NE9 6EY*

*(0191 - 4876936)*

| | 65384 | 65388 | 65389 | 65390 | 65391 | 65396 | 65398 | 65401 | 65402 |
|---|---|---|---|---|---|---|---|---|---|
| Aug-50 | STRATFORD-30A | STRATFORD-30A | LOWESTOFT-32C | NORWICH-32A | CAMBRIDGE-31A | IPSWICH-32B | NORWICH-32A | LOWESTOFT-32C | COLCHESTER-30E |
| Jan-51 | STRATFORD-30A | 11/50: NORW-32A | LOWESTOFT-32C | NORWICH-32A | CAMBRIDGE-31A | IPSWICH-32B | NORWICH-32A | LOWESTOFT-32C | 10/50: W/D |
| Aug-51 | STRATFORD-30A | NORWICH-32A | LOWESTOFT-32C | 5/51: CAMB-31A | CAMBRIDGE-31A | 3/51: W/D | NORWICH-32A | 9/51: W/D | |
| Jan-52 | STRATFORD-30A | 3/52: IPS-32B | LOWESTOFT-32C | CAMBRIDGE-31A | CAMBRIDGE-31A | | 2/52: W/D | | |
| Aug-52 | STRATFORD-30A | 9/52: NORW-32A | LOWESTOFT-32C | 6/52: MARCH-31B | 9/52: BURY-31E | | | | |
| Jan-53 | STRATFORD-30A | NORWICH-32A | LOWESTOFT-32C | 9/52: CAMB-31A | 10/52: CAMB-31A | | | | |
| Aug-53 | STRATFORD-30A | NORWICH-32A | LOWESTOFT-32C | CAMBRIDGE-31A | CAMBRIDGE-31A | | | | |
| Jan-54 | STRATFORD-30A | NORWICH-32A | LOWESTOFT-32C | CAMBRIDGE-31A | 11/53: BURY-31E | | | | |
| Aug-54 | STRATFORD-30A | NORWICH-32A | LOWESTOFT-32C | CAMBRIDGE-31A | BURY St.E-31E | | | | |
| Jan-55 | STRATFORD-30A | NORWICH-32A | LOWESTOFT-32C | CAMBRIDGE-31A | BURY St.E-31E | | | | |
| Aug-55 | 3/55: W/D | NORWICH-32A | LOWESTOFT-32C | CAMBRIDGE-31A | BURY St.E-31E | | | | |
| Jan-56 | | NORWICH-32A | LOWESTOFT-32C | CAMBRIDGE-31A | BURY St.E-31E | | | | |
| Aug-56 | | NORWICH-32A | LOWESTOFT-32C | CAMBRIDGE-31A | BURY St.E-31E | | | | |
| Jan-57 | | NORWICH-32A | 12/56: IPS-32B | 4/57: MARCH-31B | BURY St.E-31E | | | | |
| Aug-57 | | NORWICH-32A | IPSWICH-32B | 6/57: NEAS-34E | BURY St.E-31E | | | | |
| Jan-58 | | 2/58: IPS-32B | IPSWICH-32B | NEASDEN-34E | BURY St.E-31E | | | | |
| Aug-58 | | IPSWICH-32B | IPSWICH-32B | NEASDEN-14D | BURY St.E-31E | | | | |
| Jan-59 | | IPSWICH-32B | IPSWICH-32B | 12/58: W/D | 12/58: W/D | | | | |
| Aug-59 | | 5/59: W/D | IPSWICH-32B | | | | | | |
| Nov-59 | | | IPSWICH-32B | | | | | | |
| Jan-60 | | | IPSWICH-32B | | | | | | |
| Apr-60 | | | 3/60: PARKS-30F | | | | | | |
| Aug-60 | | | PARKESTON-30F | | | | | | |
| Nov-60 | | | PARKESTON-30F | | | | | | |

| | 65404 | 65405 | 65406 | 65407 | 65408 | 65413 | 65417 | 65420 | 65422 |
|---|---|---|---|---|---|---|---|---|---|
| Aug-50 | NORWICH-32A | CAMBRIDGE-31A | CAMBRIDGE-31A | IPSWICH-32B | IPSWICH-32B | CAMBRIDGE-31A | NORWICH-32A | BURY St.E-31E | NORWICH-32A |
| Jan-51 | NORWICH-32A | CAMBRIDGE-31A | CAMBRIDGE-31A | IPSWICH-32B | IPSWICH-32B | 11/51: W/D | NORWICH-32A | BURY St.E-31E | 3/51: IPS-32B |
| Aug-51 | NORWICH-32A | CAMBRIDGE-31A | 4/51: W/D | 4/51: W/D | IPSWICH-32B | | NORWICH-32A | BURY St.E-31E | IPSWICH-32B |
| Jan-52 | 11/51: IPS-32B | CAMBRIDGE-31A | | | 12/51: W/D | | NORWICH-32A | BURY St.E-31E | IPSWICH-32B |
| Aug-52 | IPSWICH-32B | 9/52: BURY-31E | | | | | NORWICH-32A | BURY St.E-31E | 9/52: MARCH-31B |
| Jan-53 | IPSWICH-32B | 10/52: CAMB-31A | | | | | NORWICH-32A | BURY St.E-31E | MARCH-31B |
| Aug-53 | IPSWICH-32B | CAMBRIDGE-31A | | | | | NORWICH-32A | BURY St.E-31E | MARCH-31B |
| Jan-54 | IPSWICH-32B | 11/53: BURY-31E | | | | | NORWICH-32A | BURY St.E-31E | MARCH-31B |
| Aug-54 | IPSWICH-32B | BURY St.E-31E | | | | | NORWICH-32A | BURY St.E-31E | MARCH-31B |
| Jan-55 | IPSWICH-32B | BURY St.E-31E | | | | | NORWICH-32A | BURY St.E-31E | MARCH-31B |
| Aug-55 | IPSWICH-32B | BURY St.E-31E | | | | | NORWICH-32A | BURY St.E-31E | 7/55: W/D |
| Jan-56 | IPSWICH-32B | BURY St.E-31E | | | | | NORWICH-32A | BURY St.E-31E | |
| Aug-56 | IPSWICH-32B | BURY St.E-31E | | | | | 8/56: W/D | BURY St.E-31E | |
| Jan-57 | 10/56: W/D | BURY St.E-31E | | | | | | BURY St.E-31E | |
| Aug-57 | | 6/57: NEAS-34E | | | | | | 6/57: MARCH-31B | |
| Jan-58 | | NEASDEN-34E | | | | | | MARCH-31B | |
| Aug-58 | | 9/58: W/D | | | | | | MARCH-31B | |
| Jan-59 | | | | | | | | MARCH-31B | |
| Aug-59 | | | | | | | | MARCH-31B | |
| Nov-59 | | | | | | | | MARCH-31B | |
| Jan-60 | | | | | | | | MARCH-31B | |
| Apr-60 | | | | | | | | MARCH-31B | |
| Aug-60 | | | | | | | | MARCH-31B | |
| Nov-60 | | | | | | | | MARCH-31B | |

| | 65423 | 65424 | 65425 | 65426 | 65427 | 65429 | 65430 | 65431 | 65432 |
|---|---|---|---|---|---|---|---|---|---|
| Aug-50 | IPSWICH-32B | COLCHESTER-30E | CAMBRIDGE-31A | NORWICH-32A | COLCHESTER-30E | IPSWICH-32B | IPSWICH-32B | COLCHESTER-30E | COLCHESTER-30E |
| Jan-51 | 11/50: W/D | COLCHESTER-30E | CAMBRIDGE-31A | NORWICH-32A | 10/50: W/D | 11/50: W/D | IPSWICH-32B | COLCHESTER-30E | COLCHESTER-30E |
| Aug-51 | | COLCHESTER-30E | CAMBRIDGE-31A | 5/51: W/D | | | IPSWICH-32B | 3/51: W/D | COLCHESTER-30E |
| Jan-52 | | COLCHESTER-30E | CAMBRIDGE-31A | | | | IPSWICH-32B | | COLCHESTER-30E |
| Aug-52 | | COLCHESTER-30E | CAMBRIDGE-31A | | | | IPSWICH-32B | | COLCHESTER-30E |
| Jan-53 | | COLCHESTER-30E | CAMBRIDGE-31A | | | | IPSWICH-32B | | COLCHESTER-30E |
| Aug-53 | | COLCHESTER-30E | CAMBRIDGE-31A | | | | IPSWICH-32B | | COLCHESTER-30E |
| Jan-54 | | COLCHESTER-30E | CAMBRIDGE-31A | | | | IPSWICH-32B | | COLCHESTER-30E |
| Aug-54 | | COLCHESTER-30E | CAMBRIDGE-31A | | | | IPSWICH-32B | | COLCHESTER-30E |
| Jan-55 | | COLCHESTER-30E | CAMBRIDGE-31A | | | | IPSWICH-32B | | COLCHESTER-30E |
| Aug-55 | | COLCHESTER-30E | CAMBRIDGE-31A | | | | IPSWICH-32B | | COLCHESTER-30E |
| Jan-56 | | COLCHESTER-30E | CAMBRIDGE-31A | | | | 1/56: W/D | | COLCHESTER-30E |
| Aug-56 | | COLCHESTER-30E | 9/56: W/D | | | | | | COLCHESTER-30E |
| Jan-57 | | COLCHESTER-30E | | | | | | | COLCHESTER-30E |
| Aug-57 | | COLCHESTER-30E | | | | | | | COLCHESTER-30E |
| Jan-58 | | COLCHESTER-30E | | | | | | | COLCHESTER-30E |
| Aug-58 | | COLCHESTER-30E | | | | | | | 3/58: W/D |
| Jan-59 | | COLCHESTER-30E | | | | | | | |
| Aug-59 | | COLCHESTER-30E | | | | | | | |
| Nov-59 | | COLCHESTER-30E | | | | | | | |
| Jan-60 | | 12/59: W/D | | | | | | | |
| Apr-60 | | | | | | | | | |
| Aug-60 | | | | | | | | | |
| Nov-60 | | | | | | | | | |

| | 65433 | 65434 | 65435 | 65437 | 65438 | 65439 | 65440 | 65441 | 65442 |
|---|---|---|---|---|---|---|---|---|---|
| Aug-50 | LOWESTOFT-32C | PARKESTON-30F | LOWESTOFT-32C | KINGS LYNN-31C | CAMBRIDGE-31A | MARCH-31B | STRATFORD-30A | COLCHESTER-30E | BURY St.E-31E |
| Jan-51 | LOWESTOFT-32C | PARKESTON-30F | LOWESTOFT-32C | 9/50: W/D | CAMBRIDGE-31A | MARCH-31B | 10/50: COL-30E | COLCHESTER-30E | BURY St.E-31E |
| Aug-51 | LOWESTOFT-32C | PARKESTON-30F | LOWESTOFT-32C | | CAMBRIDGE-31A | MARCH-31B | 11/50: STRAT-30A | COLCHESTER-30E | BURY St.E-31E |
| Jan-52 | LOWESTOFT-32C | PARKESTON-30F | LOWESTOFT-32C | | CAMBRIDGE-31A | 11/51: W/D | 3/51: COL-30E | COLCHESTER-30E | BURY St.E-31E |
| Aug-52 | LOWESTOFT-32C | PARKESTON-30F | LOWESTOFT-32C | | 9/52: BURY-31E | | COLCHESTER-30E | COLCHESTER-30E | 9/52: CAMB-31A |
| Jan-53 | LOWESTOFT-32C | PARKESTON-30F | LOWESTOFT-32C | | 10/52: CAMB-31A | | COLCHESTER-30E | COLCHESTER-30E | CAMBRIDGE-31A |
| Aug-53 | LOWESTOFT-32C | PARKESTON-30F | LOWESTOFT-32C | | CAMBRIDGE-31A | | COLCHESTER-30E | COLCHESTER-30E | CAMBRIDGE-31A |
| Jan-54 | LOWESTOFT-32C | PARKESTON-30F | LOWESTOFT-32C | | CAMBRIDGE-31A | | COLCHESTER-30E | COLCHESTER-30E | CAMBRIDGE-31A |
| Aug-54 | LOWESTOFT-32C | PARKESTON-30F | LOWESTOFT-32C | | CAMBRIDGE-31A | | COLCHESTER-30E | COLCHESTER-30E | CAMBRIDGE-31A |
| Jan-55 | LOWESTOFT-32C | PARKESTON-30F | LOWESTOFT-32C | | CAMBRIDGE-31A | | COLCHESTER-30E | COLCHESTER-30E | CAMBRIDGE-31A |
| Aug-55 | LOWESTOFT-32C | PARKESTON-30F | 8/55: IPS-32B | | CAMBRIDGE-31A | | COLCHESTER-30E | COLCHESTER-30E | CAMBRIDGE-31A |
| Jan-56 | LOWESTOFT-32C | PARKESTON-30F | IPSWICH-32B | | CAMBRIDGE-31A | | COLCHESTER-30E | COLCHESTER-30E | CAMBRIDGE-31A |
| Aug-56 | 3/56: IPS:32B | PARKESTON-30F | 9/56: W/D | | CAMBRIDGE-31A | | COLCHESTER-30E | COLCHESTER-30E | CAMBRIDGE-31A |
| Jan-57 | IPSWICH-32B | PARKESTON-30F | | | CAMBRIDGE-31A | | COLCHESTER-30E | COLCHESTER-30E | CAMBRIDGE-31A |
| Aug-57 | IPSWICH-32B | PARKESTON-30F | | | CAMBRIDGE-31A | | COLCHESTER-30E | COLCHESTER-30E | CAMBRIDGE-31A |
| Jan-58 | 1/58: W/D | PARKESTON-30F | | | CAMBRIDGE-31A | | COLCHESTER-30E | COLCHESTER-30E | CAMBRIDGE-31A |
| Aug-58 | | PARKESTON-30F | | | 6/58: W/D | | COLCHESTER-30E | COLCHESTER-30E | 5/58: W/D |
| Jan-59 | | PARKESTON-30F | | | | | COLCHESTER-30E | 10/58: W/D | |
| Aug-59 | | PARKESTON-30F | | | | | COLCHESTER-30E | | |
| Nov-59 | | 11/59: W/D | | | | | COLCHESTER-30E | | |
| Jan-60 | | | | | | | COLCHESTER-30E | | |
| Apr-60 | | | | | | | COLCHESTER-30E | | |
| Aug-60 | | | | | | | COLCHESTER-30E | | |
| Nov-60 | | | | | | | 10/60: W/D | | |

| | 65443 | 65444 | 65445 | 65446 | 65447 | 65448 | 65449 | 65450 | 65451 |
|---|---|---|---|---|---|---|---|---|---|
| Aug-50 | COLCHESTER - 30E | COLCHESTER - 30E | COLCHESTER - 30E | COLCHESTER - 30E | IPSWICH - 32B | COLCHESTER - 30E | STRATFORD - 30A | STRATFORD - 30A | CAMBRIDGE - 31A |
| Jan-51 | COLCHESTER - 30E | 10/50: STRAT - 30A | COLCHESTER - 30E | 10/50: STRAT - 30A | IPSWICH - 32B | COLCHESTER - 30E | STRATFORD - 30A | STRATFORD - 30A | CAMBRIDGE - 31A |
| Aug-51 | COLCHESTER - 30E | 6/51: COL - 30E | COLCHESTER - 30E | 2/51: PARK - 30F | IPSWICH - 32B | COLCHESTER - 30E | STRATFORD - 30A | STRATFORD - 30A | CAMBRIDGE - 31A |
| Jan-52 | COLCHESTER - 30E | COLCHESTER - 30E | COLCHESTER - 30E | PARKESTON - 30F | IPSWICH - 32B | COLCHESTER - 30E | STRATFORD - 30A | STRATFORD - 30A | CAMBRIDGE - 31A |
| Aug-52 | COLCHESTER - 30E | COLCHESTER - 30E | COLCHESTER - 30E | PARKESTON - 30F | IPSWICH - 32B | COLCHESTER - 30E | STRATFORD - 30A | STRATFORD - 30A | CAMBRIDGE - 31A |
| Jan-53 | 10/52: STRAT - 30A | COLCHESTER - 30E | COLCHESTER - 30E | PARKESTON - 30F | IPSWICH - 32B | COLCHESTER - 30E | STRATFORD - 30A | STRATFORD - 30A | CAMBRIDGE - 31A |
| Aug-53 | STRATFORD - 30A | COLCHESTER - 30E | COLCHESTER - 30E | PARKESTON - 30F | IPSWICH - 32B | COLCHESTER - 30E | STRATFORD - 30A | STRATFORD - 30A | CAMBRIDGE - 31A |
| Jan-54 | STRATFORD - 30A | COLCHESTER - 30E | COLCHESTER - 30E | PARKESTON - 30F | IPSWICH - 32B | COLCHESTER - 30E | STRATFORD - 30A | STRATFORD - 30A | CAMBRIDGE - 31A |
| Aug-54 | STRATFORD - 30A | COLCHESTER - 30E | COLCHESTER - 30E | PARKESTON - 30F | IPSWICH - 32B | COLCHESTER - 30E | STRATFORD - 30A | STRATFORD - 30A | CAMBRIDGE - 31A |
| Jan-55 | STRATFORD - 30A | COLCHESTER - 30E | COLCHESTER - 30E | PARKESTON - 30F | IPSWICH - 32B | COLCHESTER - 30E | STRATFORD - 30A | STRATFORD - 30A | CAMBRIDGE - 31A |
| Aug-55 | STRATFORD - 30A | COLCHESTER - 30E | COLCHESTER - 30E | PARKESTON - 30F | IPSWICH - 32B | COLCHESTER - 30E | STRATFORD - 30A | STRATFORD - 30A | CAMBRIDGE - 31A |
| Jan-56 | STRATFORD - 30A | COLCHESTER - 30E | COLCHESTER - 30E | PARKESTON - 30F | IPSWICH - 32B | COLCHESTER - 30E | STRATFORD - 30A | STRATFORD - 30A | CAMBRIDGE - 31A |
| Aug-56 | STRATFORD - 30A | COLCHESTER - 30E | COLCHESTER - 30E | PARKESTON - 30F | IPSWICH - 32B | COLCHESTER - 30E | STRATFORD - 30A | STRATFORD - 30A | CAMBRIDGE - 31A |
| Jan-57 | STRATFORD - 30A | COLCHESTER - 30E | COLCHESTER - 30E | PARKESTON - 30F | IPSWICH - 32B | COLCHESTER - 30E | STRATFORD - 30A | STRATFORD - 30A | CAMBRIDGE - 31A |
| Aug-57 | STRATFORD - 30A | COLCHESTER - 30E | COLCHESTER - 30E | PARKESTON - 30F | IPSWICH - 32B | COLCHESTER - 30E | STRATFORD - 30A | STRATFORD - 30A | CAMBRIDGE - 31A |
| Jan-58 | STRATFORD - 30A | COLCHESTER - 30E | COLCHESTER - 30E | PARKESTON - 30F | IPSWICH - 32B | COLCHESTER - 30E | STRATFORD - 30A | STRATFORD - 30A | CAMBRIDGE - 31A |
| Aug-58 | 9/58: COL - 30E | COLCHESTER - 30E | COLCHESTER - 30E | PARKESTON - 30F | IPSWICH - 32B | COLCHESTER - 30E | STRATFORD - 30A | 10/58: CAMB - 31A | CAMBRIDGE - 31A |
| Jan-59 | COLCHESTER - 30E | 10/58: W/D | COLCHESTER - 30E | 12/58: COL - 30E | IPSWICH - 32B | COLCHESTER - 30E | STRATFORD - 30A | CAMBRIDGE - 31A | CAMBRIDGE - 31A |
| Aug-59 | COLCHESTER - 30E | | COLCHESTER - 30E | COLCHESTER - 30E | 4/59: W/D | COLCHESTER - 30E | STRATFORD - 30A | CAMBRIDGE - 31A | CAMBRIDGE - 31A |
| Nov-59 | COLCHESTER - 30E | | 10/59: PARK - 30F | COLCHESTER - 30E | | 12/59: STRAT - 30A | STRATFORD - 30A | CAMBRIDGE - 31A | 9/59: W/D |
| Jan-60 | 12/59: W/D | | PARKESTON - 30F | 12/59: STRAT - 30A | | STRATFORD - 30A | 12/59: W/D | CAMBRIDGE - 31A | |
| Apr-60 | | | PARKESTON - 30F | STRATFORD - 30A | | 3/60: W/D | | CAMBRIDGE - 31A | |
| Aug-60 | | | PARKESTON - 30F | STRATFORD - 30A | | | | CAMBRIDGE - 31A | |
| Nov-60 | | | PARKESTON - 30F | STRATFORD - 30A | | | | CAMBRIDGE - 31A | |

| | 65452 | 65453 | 65454 | 65455 | 65456 | 65457 | 65458 | 65459 | 65460 |
|---|---|---|---|---|---|---|---|---|---|
| Aug-50 | STRATFORD - 30A | STRATFORD - 30A | COLCHESTER - 30E | STRATFORD - 30A | COLCHESTER - 30E | CAMBRIDGE - 31A | PARKESTON - 30F | IPSWICH - 32B | NORWICH - 32A |
| Jan-51 | STRATFORD - 30A | STRATFORD - 30A | 10/50: STRAT - 30A | STRATFORD - 30A | COLCHESTER - 30E | CAMBRIDGE - 31A | PARKESTON - 30F | IPSWICH - 32B | NORWICH - 32A |
| Aug-51 | STRATFORD - 30A | STRATFORD - 30A | STRATFORD - 30A | STRATFORD - 30A | COLCHESTER - 30E | CAMBRIDGE - 31A | PARKESTON - 30F | IPSWICH - 32B | NORWICH - 32A |
| Jan-52 | STRATFORD - 30A | STRATFORD - 30A | STRATFORD - 30A | STRATFORD - 30A | COLCHESTER - 30E | CAMBRIDGE - 31A | PARKESTON - 30F | IPSWICH - 32B | NORWICH - 32A |
| Aug-52 | STRATFORD - 30A | STRATFORD - 30A | STRATFORD - 30A | STRATFORD - 30A | COLCHESTER - 30E | CAMBRIDGE - 31A | PARKESTON - 30F | IPSWICH - 32B | NORWICH - 32A |
| Jan-53 | STRATFORD - 30A | STRATFORD - 30A | STRATFORD - 30A | STRATFORD - 30A | COLCHESTER - 30E | CAMBRIDGE - 31A | PARKESTON - 30F | IPSWICH - 32B | NORWICH - 32A |
| Aug-53 | STRATFORD - 30A | STRATFORD - 30A | STRATFORD - 30A | STRATFORD - 30A | COLCHESTER - 30E | CAMBRIDGE - 31A | PARKESTON - 30F | IPSWICH - 32B | NORWICH - 32A |
| Jan-54 | STRATFORD - 30A | STRATFORD - 30A | STRATFORD - 30A | STRATFORD - 30A | COLCHESTER - 30E | CAMBRIDGE - 31A | PARKESTON - 30F | IPSWICH - 32B | NORWICH - 32A |
| Aug-54 | STRATFORD - 30A | STRATFORD - 30A | STRATFORD - 30A | STRATFORD - 30A | COLCHESTER - 30E | CAMBRIDGE - 31A | PARKESTON - 30F | IPSWICH - 32B | NORWICH - 32A |
| Jan-55 | STRATFORD - 30A | STRATFORD - 30A | STRATFORD - 30A | STRATFORD - 30A | COLCHESTER - 30E | CAMBRIDGE - 31A | PARKESTON - 30F | IPSWICH - 32B | NORWICH - 32A |
| Aug-55 | STRATFORD - 30A | STRATFORD - 30A | STRATFORD - 30A | STRATFORD - 30A | COLCHESTER - 30E | CAMBRIDGE - 31A | PARKESTON - 30F | IPSWICH - 32B | 9/55: LOW - 32C |
| Jan-56 | STRATFORD - 30A | STRATFORD - 30A | STRATFORD - 30A | STRATFORD - 30A | COLCHESTER - 30E | CAMBRIDGE - 31A | PARKESTON - 30F | IPSWICH - 32B | LOWESTOFT - 32C |
| Aug-56 | STRATFORD - 30A | STRATFORD - 30A | STRATFORD - 30A | STRATFORD - 30A | COLCHESTER - 30E | CAMBRIDGE - 31A | PARKESTON - 30F | IPSWICH - 32B | LOWESTOFT - 32C |
| Jan-57 | STRATFORD - 30A | STRATFORD - 30A | STRATFORD - 30A | STRATFORD - 30A | COLCHESTER - 30E | CAMBRIDGE - 31A | PARKESTON - 30F | IPSWICH - 32B | LOWESTOFT - 32C |
| Aug-57 | STRATFORD - 30A | STRATFORD - 30A | STRATFORD - 30A | STRATFORD - 30A | COLCHESTER - 30E | CAMBRIDGE - 31A | PARKESTON - 30F | IPSWICH - 32B | LOWESTOFT - 32C |
| Jan-58 | STRATFORD - 30A | STRATFORD - 30A | STRATFORD - 30A | STRATFORD - 30A | COLCHESTER - 30E | CAMBRIDGE - 31A | PARKESTON - 30F | IPSWICH - 32B | LOWESTOFT - 32C |
| Aug-58 | STRATFORD - 30A | STRATFORD - 30A | 10/58: IPS - 32B | STRATFORD - 30A | 9/58: W/D | CAMBRIDGE - 31A | PARKESTON - 30F | IPSWICH - 32B | LOWESTOFT - 32C |
| Jan-59 | STRATFORD - 30A | STRATFORD - 30A | IPSWICH - 32B | STRATFORD - 30A | | CAMBRIDGE - 31A | PARKESTON - 30F | IPSWICH - 32B | LOWESTOFT - 32C |
| Aug-59 | STRATFORD - 30A | STRATFORD - 30A | 4/59: W/D | STRATFORD - 30A | | CAMBRIDGE - 31A | PARKESTON - 30F | IPSWICH - 32B | LOWESTOFT - 32C |
| Nov-59 | STRATFORD - 30A | STRATFORD - 30A | | STRATFORD - 30A | | CAMBRIDGE - 31A | PARKESTON - 30F | 12/59: STRAT - 30A | LOWESTOFT - 32C |
| Jan-60 | 12/59: W/D | STRATFORD - 30A | | STRATFORD - 30A | | CAMBRIDGE - 31A | PARKESTON - 30F | STRATFORD - 30A | LOWESTOFT - 32C |
| Apr-60 | | STRATFORD - 30A | | 3/60: W/D | | CAMBRIDGE - 31A | 3/60: MARCH - 31B | 2/60: W/D | LOWESTOFT - 32C |
| Aug-60 | | STRATFORD - 30A | | | | CAMBRIDGE - 31A | MARCH - 31B | | 9/60: NOR - 32A |
| Nov-60 | | STRATFORD - 30A | | | | CAMBRIDGE - 31A | MARCH - 31B | | NORWICH - 32A |

| | 65461 | 65462 | 65463 | 65464 | 65465 | 65466 | 65467 | 65468 | 65469 |
|---|---|---|---|---|---|---|---|---|---|
| Aug-50 | CAMBRIDGE - 31A | LOWESTOFT - 32C | STRATFORD - 30A | STRATFORD - 30A | COLCHESTER - 30E | STRATFORD - 30A | IPSWICH - 32B | COLCHESTER - 30E | NORWICH - 32A |
| Jan-51 | CAMBRIDGE - 31A | LOWESTOFT - 32C | STRATFORD - 30A | STRATFORD - 30A | COLCHESTER - 30E | STRATFORD - 30A | IPSWICH - 32B | COLCHESTER - 30E | NORWICH - 32A |
| Aug-51 | CAMBRIDGE - 31A | LOWESTOFT - 32C | STRATFORD - 30A | STRATFORD - 30A | COLCHESTER - 30E | STRATFORD - 30A | IPSWICH - 32B | COLCHESTER - 30E | NORWICH - 32A |
| Jan-52 | CAMBRIDGE - 31A | LOWESTOFT - 32C | STRATFORD - 30A | STRATFORD - 30A | COLCHESTER - 30E | STRATFORD - 30A | IPSWICH - 32B | COLCHESTER - 30E | NORWICH - 32A |
| Aug-52 | CAMBRIDGE - 31A | LOWESTOFT - 32C | STRATFORD - 30A | STRATFORD - 30A | COLCHESTER - 30E | STRATFORD - 30A | IPSWICH - 32B | COLCHESTER - 30E | NORWICH - 32A |
| Jan-53 | CAMBRIDGE - 31A | LOWESTOFT - 32C | STRATFORD - 30A | STRATFORD - 30A | COLCHESTER - 30E | STRATFORD - 30A | IPSWICH - 32B | COLCHESTER - 30E | NORWICH - 32A |
| Aug-53 | CAMBRIDGE - 31A | LOWESTOFT - 32C | STRATFORD - 30A | STRATFORD - 30A | COLCHESTER - 30E | 7/53: COL - 30E | IPSWICH - 32B | COLCHESTER - 30E | NORWICH - 32A |
| Jan-54 | CAMBRIDGE - 31A | LOWESTOFT - 32C | STRATFORD - 30A | STRATFORD - 30A | COLCHESTER - 30E | COLCHESTER - 30E | IPSWICH - 32B | COLCHESTER - 30E | NORWICH - 32A |
| Aug-54 | CAMBRIDGE - 31A | LOWESTOFT - 32C | STRATFORD - 30A | STRATFORD - 30A | COLCHESTER - 30E | COLCHESTER - 30E | IPSWICH - 32B | COLCHESTER - 30E | NORWICH - 32A |
| Jan-55 | CAMBRIDGE - 31A | LOWESTOFT - 32C | STRATFORD - 30A | STRATFORD - 30A | COLCHESTER - 30E | COLCHESTER - 30E | IPSWICH - 32B | COLCHESTER - 30E | NORWICH - 32A |
| Aug-55 | CAMBRIDGE - 31A | LOWESTOFT - 32C | STRATFORD - 30A | STRATFORD - 30A | COLCHESTER - 30E | COLCHESTER - 30E | IPSWICH - 32B | COLCHESTER - 30E | NORWICH - 32A |
| Jan-56 | CAMBRIDGE - 31A | LOWESTOFT - 32C | STRATFORD - 30A | STRATFORD - 30A | COLCHESTER - 30E | COLCHESTER - 30E | IPSWICH - 32B | COLCHESTER - 30E | NORWICH - 32A |
| Aug-56 | CAMBRIDGE - 31A | LOWESTOFT - 32C | STRATFORD - 30A | STRATFORD - 30A | COLCHESTER - 30E | COLCHESTER - 30E | IPSWICH - 32B | COLCHESTER - 30E | NORWICH - 32A |
| Jan-57 | CAMBRIDGE - 31A | LOWESTOFT - 32C | STRATFORD - 30A | STRATFORD - 30A | COLCHESTER - 30E | COLCHESTER - 30E | 2/57: STRAT - 30A | COLCHESTER - 30E | NORWICH - 32A |
| Aug-57 | CAMBRIDGE - 31A | LOWESTOFT - 32C | STRATFORD - 30A | STRATFORD - 30A | COLCHESTER - 30E | COLCHESTER - 30E | STRATFORD - 30A | COLCHESTER - 30E | 7/57: LOW - 32C |
| Jan-58 | CAMBRIDGE - 31A | LOWESTOFT - 32C | STRATFORD - 30A | STRATFORD - 30A | COLCHESTER - 30E | COLCHESTER - 30E | STRATFORD - 30A | COLCHESTER - 30E | 9/57: NOR - 32A |
| Aug-58 | CAMBRIDGE - 31A | LOWESTOFT - 32C | STRATFORD - 30A | STRATFORD - 30A | COLCHESTER - 30E | 7/58: W/D | STRATFORD - 30A | COLCHESTER - 30E | NORWICH - 32A |
| Jan-59 | CAMBRIDGE - 31A | LOWESTOFT - 32C | STRATFORD - 30A | STRATFORD - 30A | COLCHESTER - 30E | | 2/59: W/D | COLCHESTER - 30E | NORWICH - 32A |
| Aug-59 | CAMBRIDGE - 31A | LOWESTOFT - 32C | STRATFORD - 30A | STRATFORD - 30A | COLCHESTER - 30E | | | 9/59: W/D | NORWICH - 32A |
| Nov-59 | CAMBRIDGE - 31A | LOWESTOFT - 32C | 11/59: W/D | STRATFORD - 30A | 12/59: STRAT - 30A | | | | NORWICH - 32A |
| Jan-60 | CAMBRIDGE - 31A | LOWESTOFT - 32C | | STRATFORD - 30A | STRATFORD - 30A | | | | NORWICH - 32A |
| Apr-60 | 4/60: W/D | 6/60: NOR - 32A | | STRATFORD - 30A | STRATFORD - 30A | | | | NORWICH - 32A |
| Aug-60 | | NORWICH - 32A | | STRATFORD - 30A | STRATFORD - 30A | | | | NORWICH - 32A |
| Nov-60 | | NORWICH - 32A | | STRATFORD - 30A | STRATFORD - 30A | | | | NORWICH - 32A |

| | 65470 | 65471 | 65472 | 65473 | 65474 | 65475 | 65476 | 65477 | 65478 |
|---|---|---|---|---|---|---|---|---|---|
| Aug-50 | IPSWICH - 32B | NORWICH - 32A | NORWICH - 32A | COLCHESTER - 30E | CAMBRIDGE - 31A | CAMBRIDGE - 31A | STRATFORD - 30A | CAMBRIDGE - 31A | LOWESTOFT - 32C |
| Jan-51 | 11/50: COL - 30E | NORWICH - 32A | 5/51: CAMB - 31A | COLCHESTER - 30E | CAMBRIDGE - 31A | CAMBRIDGE - 31A | 2/51: COL - 30E | CAMBRIDGE - 31A | LOWESTOFT - 32C |
| Aug-51 | COLCHESTER - 30E | NORWICH - 32A | 6/51: NOR - 32A | COLCHESTER - 30E | CAMBRIDGE - 31A | CAMBRIDGE - 31A | 6/51: STRAT - 30A | CAMBRIDGE - 31A | LOWESTOFT - 32C |
| Jan-52 | COLCHESTER - 30E | NORWICH - 32A | NORWICH - 32A | COLCHESTER - 30E | CAMBRIDGE - 31A | CAMBRIDGE - 31A | STRATFORD - 30A | CAMBRIDGE - 31A | LOWESTOFT - 32C |
| Aug-52 | COLCHESTER - 30E | NORWICH - 32A | NORWICH - 32A | COLCHESTER - 30E | CAMBRIDGE - 31A | CAMBRIDGE - 31A | STRATFORD - 30A | CAMBRIDGE - 31A | LOWESTOFT - 32C |
| Jan-53 | COLCHESTER - 30E | NORWICH - 32A | NORWICH - 32A | COLCHESTER - 30E | CAMBRIDGE - 31A | CAMBRIDGE - 31A | STRATFORD - 30A | CAMBRIDGE - 31A | LOWESTOFT - 32C |
| Aug-53 | COLCHESTER - 30E | NORWICH - 32A | NORWICH - 32A | COLCHESTER - 30E | CAMBRIDGE - 31A | CAMBRIDGE - 31A | STRATFORD - 30A | CAMBRIDGE - 31A | LOWESTOFT - 32C |
| Jan-54 | COLCHESTER - 30E | NORWICH - 32A | NORWICH - 32A | COLCHESTER - 30E | CAMBRIDGE - 31A | CAMBRIDGE - 31A | STRATFORD - 30A | CAMBRIDGE - 31A | LOWESTOFT - 32C |
| Aug-54 | COLCHESTER - 30E | NORWICH - 32A | NORWICH - 32A | COLCHESTER - 30E | CAMBRIDGE - 31A | CAMBRIDGE - 31A | STRATFORD - 30A | CAMBRIDGE - 31A | LOWESTOFT - 32C |
| Jan-55 | COLCHESTER - 30E | NORWICH - 32A | NORWICH - 32A | COLCHESTER - 30E | CAMBRIDGE - 31A | CAMBRIDGE - 31A | STRATFORD - 30A | CAMBRIDGE - 31A | LOWESTOFT - 32C |
| Aug-55 | COLCHESTER - 30E | NORWICH - 32A | NORWICH - 32A | COLCHESTER - 30E | 6/55: MARCH - 31B | CAMBRIDGE - 31A | STRATFORD - 30A | CAMBRIDGE - 31A | LOWESTOFT - 32C |
| Jan-56 | COLCHESTER - 30E | NORWICH - 32A | 1/56: IPS - 32B | COLCHESTER - 30E | MARCH - 31B | CAMBRIDGE - 31A | STRATFORD - 30A | CAMBRIDGE - 31A | LOWESTOFT - 32C |
| Aug-56 | COLCHESTER - 30E | NORWICH - 32A | 3/56: NOR - 32A | COLCHESTER - 30E | MARCH - 31B | CAMBRIDGE - 31A | STRATFORD - 30A | CAMBRIDGE - 31A | LOWESTOFT - 32C |
| Jan-57 | COLCHESTER - 30E | NORWICH - 32A | NORWICH - 32A | COLCHESTER - 30E | MARCH - 31B | CAMBRIDGE - 31A | STRATFORD - 30A | CAMBRIDGE - 31A | LOWESTOFT - 32C |
| Aug-57 | COLCHESTER - 30E | NORWICH - 32A | 7/57: YAR(ST) - 32D | COLCHESTER - 30E | MARCH - 31B | CAMBRIDGE - 31A | STRATFORD - 30A | CAMBRIDGE - 31A | LOWESTOFT - 32C |
| Jan-58 | COLCHESTER - 30E | NORWICH - 32A | 9/57: NOR - 32A | COLCHESTER - 30E | MARCH - 31B | CAMBRIDGE - 31A | STRATFORD - 30A | CAMBRIDGE - 31A | LOWESTOFT - 32C |
| Aug-58 | COLCHESTER - 30E | NORWICH - 32A | 8/58: COL - 30E | COLCHESTER - 30E | MARCH - 31B | CAMBRIDGE - 31A | STRATFORD - 30A | CAMBRIDGE - 31A | LOWESTOFT - 32C |
| Jan-59 | COLCHESTER - 30E | NORWICH - 32A | COLCHESTER - 30E | COLCHESTER - 30E | MARCH - 31B | CAMBRIDGE - 31A | STRATFORD - 30A | CAMBRIDGE - 31A | 3/59: IPS - 32B |
| Aug-59 | COLCHESTER - 30E | NORWICH - 32A | COLCHESTER - 30E | COLCHESTER - 30E | MARCH - 31B | CAMBRIDGE - 31A | STRATFORD - 30A | CAMBRIDGE - 31A | IPSWICH - 32B |
| Nov-59 | COLCHESTER - 30E | NORWICH - 32A | 11/59: STRAT - 30A | COLCHESTER - 30E | MARCH - 31B | 9/59: W/D | STRATFORD - 30A | CAMBRIDGE - 31A | IPSWICH - 32B |
| Jan-60 | 12/59: W/D | NORWICH - 32A | 12/59: W/D | 12/59: STRAT - 30A | MARCH - 31B | | STRATFORD - 30A | CAMBRIDGE - 31A | IPSWICH - 32B |
| Apr-60 | | NORWICH - 32A | | 3/60: W/D | 2/60: W/D | | STRATFORD - 30A | 2/60: W/D | 3/60: CAMB - 31A |
| Aug-60 | | 6/60: W/D | | | | | STRATFORD - 30A | | CAMBRIDGE - 31A |
| Nov-60 | | | | | | | STRATFORD - 30A | | CAMBRIDGE - 31A |

**J5 0-6-0 (1909)** (column 65480)

| | 65479 | 65480 | 65481 | 65482 | 65483 | 65484 | 65485 | 65486 | 65487 |
|---|---|---|---|---|---|---|---|---|---|
| Aug-50 | NORWICH - 32A | COLWCK - 38A | COLWCK - 38A | COLWCK - 38A | COLWCK - 38A | COLWCK - 38A | COLWCK - 38A | COLWCK - 38A | COLWCK - 38A |
| Jan-51 | 11/50: COL - 30E | COLWCK - 38A | COLWCK - 38A | COLWCK - 38A | COLWCK - 38A | COLWCK - 38A | COLWCK - 38A | COLWCK - 38A | COLWCK - 38A |
| Aug-51 | COLCHESTER - 30E | COLWCK - 38A | COLWCK - 38A | COLWCK - 38A | COLWCK - 38A | COLWCK - 38A | 9/51: LEIC - 38C | COLWCK - 38A | COLWCK - 38A |
| Jan-52 | COLCHESTER - 30E | COLWCK - 38A | COLWCK - 38A | 7/52: HIT - 34D | COLWCK - 38A | COLWCK - 38A | LEICESTER (GC) - 38C | COLWCK - 38A | COLWCK - 38A |
| Aug-52 | COLCHESTER - 30E | COLWCK - 38A | COLWCK - 38A | 11/52: COLW - 38A | COLWCK - 38A | COLWCK - 38A | LEICESTER (GC) - 38C | COLWCK - 38A | COLWCK - 38A |
| Jan-53 | COLCHESTER - 30E | COLWCK - 38A | COLWCK - 38A | COLWCK - 38A | COLWCK - 38A | COLWCK - 38A | LEICESTER (GC) - 38C | COLWCK - 38A | COLWCK - 38A |
| Aug-53 | 7/53: HIT - 34D | COLWCK - 38A | COLWCK - 38A | COLWCK - 38A | COLWCK - 38A | 3/53: W/D | LEICESTER (GC) - 38C | COLWCK - 38A | 6/53: W/D |
| Jan-54 | HITCHIN - 34D | COLWCK - 38A | 10/53: W/D | 11/53: W/D | COLWCK - 38A | | LEICESTER (GC) - 38C | COLWCK - 38A | |
| Aug-54 | HITCHIN - 34D | COLWCK - 38A | | | COLWCK - 38A | | 8/54: COLW - 38A | COLWCK - 38A | |
| Jan-55 | HITCHIN - 34D | 10/54: W/D | | | COLWCK - 38A | | 12/54: W/D | 12/54: W/D | |
| Aug-55 | HITCHIN - 34D | | | | COLWCK - 38A | | | | |
| Jan-56 | HITCHIN - 34D | | | | 12/55: W/D | | | | |
| Aug-56 | HITCHIN - 34D | | | | | | | | |
| Jan-57 | HITCHIN - 34D | | | | | | | | |
| Aug-57 | HITCHIN - 34D | | | | | | | | |
| Jan-58 | HITCHIN - 34D | | | | | | | | |
| Aug-58 | HITCHIN - 34D | | | | | | | | |
| Jan-59 | HITCHIN - 34D | | | | | | | | |
| Aug-59 | HITCHIN - 34D | | | | | | | | |
| Nov-59 | HITCHIN - 34D | | | | | | | | |
| Jan-60 | HITCHIN - 34D | | | | | | | | |
| Apr-60 | HITCHIN - 34D | | | | | | | | |
| Aug-60 | 8/60: W/D | | | | | | | | |
| Nov-60 | | | | | | | | | |

| | 65488 | 65489 | 65490 | 65491 | 65492 | 65493 | 65494 | 65495 | 65496 |
|---|---|---|---|---|---|---|---|---|---|
| Aug-50 | COLWCK - 38A | COLWCK - 38A | COLWCK - 38A | COLWCK - 38A | COLWCK - 38A | COLWCK - 38A | ANNESLEY - 38B | LEICESTER (GC) - 38C | COLWCK - 38A |
| Jan-51 | COLWCK - 38A | COLWCK - 38A | COLWCK - 38A | COLWCK - 38A | COLWCK - 38A | COLWCK - 38A | ANNESLEY - 38B | LEICESTER (GC) - 38C | COLWCK - 38A |
| Aug-51 | COLWCK - 38A | COLWCK - 38A | COLWCK - 38A | COLWCK - 38A | COLWCK - 38A | COLWCK - 38A | ANNESLEY - 38B | LEICESTER (GC) - 38C | COLWCK - 38A |
| Jan-52 | COLWCK - 38A | COLWCK - 38A | COLWCK - 38A | COLWCK - 38A | COLWCK - 38A | COLWCK - 38A | 9/51: COLW - 38A | LEICESTER (GC) - 38C | COLWCK - 38A |
| Aug-52 | COLWCK - 38A | COLWCK - 38A | COLWCK - 38A | COLWCK - 38A | COLWCK - 38A | COLWCK - 38A | COLWCK - 38A | LEICESTER (GC) - 38C | COLWCK - 38A |
| Jan-53 | COLWCK - 38A | COLWCK - 38A | COLWCK - 38A | COLWCK - 38A | COLWCK - 38A | COLWCK - 38A | COLWCK - 38A | LEICESTER (GC) - 38C | COLWCK - 38A |
| Aug-53 | COLWCK - 38A | COLWCK - 38A | COLWCK - 38A | COLWCK - 38A | COLWCK - 38A | COLWCK - 38A | COLWCK - 38A | LEICESTER (GC) - 38C | COLWCK - 38A |
| Jan-54 | 10/53: W/D | 12/53: W/D | COLWCK - 38A | 10/53: W/D | 9/53: W/D | COLWCK - 38A | COLWCK - 38A | LEICESTER (GC) - 38C | 2/54: W.D |
| Aug-54 | | | COLWCK - 38A | | | COLWCK - 38A | COLWCK - 38A | 8/54: W/D | |
| Jan-55 | | | 10/54: W/D | | | 8/54: W/D | 1/55: W/D | 1/55: W/D | |
| Aug-55 | | | | | | | | | |
| Jan-56 | | | | | | | | | |
| Aug-56 | | | | | | | | | |
| Jan-57 | | | | | | | | | |
| Aug-57 | | | | | | | | | |
| Jan-58 | | | | | | | | | |
| Aug-58 | | | | | | | | | |
| Jan-59 | | | | | | | | | |
| Aug-59 | | | | | | | | | |
| Nov-59 | | | | | | | | | |
| Jan-60 | | | | | | | | | |
| Apr-60 | | | | | | | | | |
| Aug-60 | | | | | | | | | |
| Nov-60 | | | | | | | | | |

**J17 0-6-0 (1901)** (column 65500)

| | 65497 | 65498 | 65499 | 65500 | 65501 | 65502 | 65503 | 65504 | 65505 |
|---|---|---|---|---|---|---|---|---|---|
| Aug-50 | COLWCK - 38A | COLWCK - 38A | COLWCK - 38A | STRATFORD - 30A | CAMBRIDGE - 31A | CAMBRIDGE - 31A | CAMBRIDGE - 31A | SOUTH LYNN - 31D | MARCH - 31B |
| Jan-51 | COLWCK - 38A | COLWCK - 38A | COLWCK - 38A | STRATFORD - 30A | CAMBRIDGE - 31A | CAMBRIDGE - 31A | CAMBRIDGE - 31A | SOUTH LYNN - 31D | MARCH - 31B |
| Aug-51 | COLWCK - 38A | COLWCK - 38A | COLWCK - 38A | STRATFORD - 30A | CAMBRIDGE - 31A | CAMBRIDGE - 31A | CAMBRIDGE - 31A | 9/51: MARCH - 31B | 5/51: CAMB - 31A |
| Jan-52 | COLWCK - 38A | COLWCK - 38A | COLWCK - 38A | STRATFORD - 30A | 2/52: K.LYNN - 31C | CAMBRIDGE - 31A | CAMBRIDGE - 31A | 3/52: K.LYNN - 31C | CAMBRIDGE - 31A |
| Aug-52 | COLWCK - 38A | COLWCK - 38A | COLWCK - 38A | STRATFORD - 30A | KINGS LYNN - 31C | CAMBRIDGE - 31A | 5/52: MARCH - 31B | KINGS LYNN - 31C | CAMBRIDGE - 31A |
| Jan-53 | COLWCK - 38A | COLWCK - 38A | COLWCK - 38A | STRATFORD - 30A | KINGS LYNN - 31C | CAMBRIDGE - 31A | MARCH - 31B | MARCH - 31B | CAMBRIDGE - 31A |
| Aug-53 | COLWCK - 38A | COLWCK - 38A | 4/53: W/D | STRATFORD - 30A | KINGS LYNN - 31C | CAMBRIDGE - 31A | MARCH - 31B | 5/53: CAMB - 31A | CAMBRIDGE - 31A |
| Jan-54 | | COLWCK - 38A | | STRATFORD - 30A | KINGS LYNN - 31C | CAMBRIDGE - 31A | MARCH - 31B | CAMBRIDGE - 31A | CAMBRIDGE - 31A |
| Aug-54 | | COLWCK - 38A | | STRATFORD - 30A | KINGS LYNN - 31C | CAMBRIDGE - 31A | MARCH - 31B | CAMBRIDGE - 31A | CAMBRIDGE - 31A |
| Jan-55 | | COLWCK - 38A | | 2/55: CAMB - 31A | KINGS LYNN - 31C | CAMBRIDGE - 31A | MARCH - 31B | CAMBRIDGE - 31A | CAMBRIDGE - 31A |
| Aug-55 | | COLWCK - 38A | | CAMBRIDGE - 31A | KINGS LYNN - 31C | CAMBRIDGE - 31A | 5/55: S.LYNN : 31D | CAMBRIDGE - 31A | CAMBRIDGE - 31A |
| Jan-56 | | 12/55: W/D | | CAMBRIDGE - 31A | KINGS LYNN - 31C | CAMBRIDGE - 31A | 11/55: MARCH - 31B | CAMBRIDGE - 31A | CAMBRIDGE - 31A |
| Aug-56 | | | | CAMBRIDGE - 31A | KINGS LYNN - 31C | CAMBRIDGE - 31A | MARCH - 31B | CAMBRIDGE - 31A | CAMBRIDGE - 31A |
| Jan-57 | | | | CAMBRIDGE - 31A | 4/57: MARCH - 31B | CAMBRIDGE - 31A | MARCH - 31B | CAMBRIDGE - 31A | CAMBRIDGE - 31A |
| Aug-57 | | | | CAMBRIDGE - 31A | 10/57: CAMB - 31A | CAMBRIDGE - 31A | MARCH - 31B | CAMBRIDGE - 31A | CAMBRIDGE - 31A |
| Jan-58 | | | | CAMBRIDGE - 31A | 1/58: W/D | CAMBRIDGE - 31A | 7/58: S.LYNN - 31D | 3/58: STRAT - 30A | 3/58: STRAT - 30A |
| Aug-58 | | | | 3/58: W/D | | CAMBRIDGE - 31A | 10/58: MARCH - 31B | STRATFORD - 30A | STRATFORD - 30A |
| Jan-59 | | | | | | CAMBRIDGE - 31A | 12/58: COL - 30E | 10/58: W/D | 12/58: COL - 30E |
| Aug-59 | | | | | | CAMBRIDGE - 31A | COLCHESTER - 30E | | COLCHESTER - 30E |
| Nov-59 | | | | | | 9/59: W/D | 12/59: STRAT - 30A | | 11/59: W/D |
| Jan-60 | | | | | | | STRATFORD - 30A | | |
| Apr-60 | | | | | | | STRATFORD - 30A | | |
| Aug-60 | | | | | | | STRATFORD - 30A | | |
| Nov-60 | | | | | | | 9/60: W/D | | |

| | 65506 | 65507 | 65508 | 65509 | 65510 | 65511 | 65512 | 65513 | 65514 |
|---|---|---|---|---|---|---|---|---|---|
| Aug-50 | CAMBRIDGE - 31A | NORWCH - 32A | STRATFORD - 30A | MELTON C - 32G | IPSWICH - 32B | STRATFORD - 30A | NORWCH - 32A | NORWCH - 32A | NORWCH - 32A |
| Jan-51 | CAMBRIDGE - 31A | NORWCH - 32A | STRATFORD - 30A | MELTON C - 32G | 10/50: NOR - 32A | STRATFORD - 30A | 2/51: IPS - 32B | NORWCH - 32A | 4.51: LOW - 32C |
| Aug-51 | CAMBRIDGE - 31A | 5/51: LOW - 32C | STRATFORD - 30A | MELTON C - 32G | NORWCH - 32A | STRATFORD - 30A | 4/51: NOR - 32A | NORWCH - 32A | 5/51: NOR - 32A |
| Jan-52 | CAMBRIDGE - 31A | 9/51: NOR - 32A | STRATFORD - 30A | 3/52: YAR (B) - 32F | 12/51: IPS - 32B | STRATFORD - 30A | 3/52: CAMB - 31A | NORWCH - 32A | 3/52: LOW - 32C |
| Aug-52 | CAMBRIDGE - 31A | NORWCH - 32A | STRATFORD - 30A | YARMOUTH BEACH - 32F | IPSWICH - 32B | STRATFORD - 30A | CAMBRIDGE - 31A | NORWCH - 32A | LOWESTOFT - 32C |
| Jan-53 | CAMBRIDGE - 31A | 1/53: LOW - 32C | STRATFORD - 30A | YARMOUTH BEACH - 32F | IPSWICH - 32B | STRATFORD - 30A | CAMBRIDGE - 31A | NORWCH - 32A | 1/53: NOR - 32A |
| Aug-53 | CAMBRIDGE - 31A | LOWESTOFT - 32C | STRATFORD - 30A | 7/53: NOR - 32A | IPSWICH - 32B | STRATFORD - 30A | CAMBRIDGE - 31A | NORWCH - 32A | NORWCH - 32A |
| Jan-54 | CAMBRIDGE - 31A | LOWESTOFT - 32C | STRATFORD - 30A | 1/54: MELTON - 32G | IPSWICH - 32B | STRATFORD - 30A | CAMBRIDGE - 31A | 3/54: IPS - 32B | NORWCH - 32A |
| Aug-54 | CAMBRIDGE - 31A | LOWESTOFT - 32C | STRATFORD - 30A | MELTON C - 32G | IPSWICH - 32B | STRATFORD - 30A | CAMBRIDGE - 31A | IPSWICH - 32B | NORWCH - 32A |
| Jan-55 | 1/55: S.LYNN - 31D | LOWESTOFT - 32C | STRATFORD - 30A | MELTON C - 32G | IPSWICH - 32B | STRATFORD - 30A | 3/55: NOR - 32A | IPSWICH - 32B | NORWCH - 32A |
| Aug-55 | SOUTH LYNN - 31D | 6/55: NOR - 32A | STRATFORD - 30A | MELTON C - 32G | 3/55: W/D | STRATFORD - 30A | 8/55: IPS - 32B | IPSWICH - 32B | NORWCH - 32A |
| Jan-56 | SOUTH LYNN - 31D | 11/55: LOW - 32C | STRATFORD - 30A | MELTON C - 32G | | STRATFORD - 30A | IPSWICH - 32B | IPSWICH - 32B | 11/55: MELTON - 32G |
| Aug-56 | 5/56: CAMB - 31A | LOWESTOFT - 32C | STRATFORD - 30A | MELTON C - 32G | | STRATFORD - 30A | IPSWICH - 32B | IPSWICH - 32B | MELTON C - 32G |
| Jan-57 | 2/57: STRAT - 30A | LOWESTOFT - 32C | STRATFORD - 30A | MELTON C - 32G | | STRATFORD - 30A | IPSWICH - 32B | IPSWICH - 32B | 3/57: STRAT - 30A |
| Aug-57 | STRATFORD - 30A | LOWESTOFT - 32C | STRATFORD - 30A | 10/57: NOR - 32A | | STRATFORD - 30A | IPSWICH - 32B | IPSWICH - 32B | STRATFORD - 30A |
| Jan-58 | STRATFORD - 30A | LOWESTOFT - 32C | STRATFORD - 30A | 1/58: W/D | | STRATFORD - 30A | IPSWICH - 32B | IPSWICH - 32B | STRATFORD - 30A |
| Aug-58 | STRATFORD - 30A | LOWESTOFT - 32C | 6/58: W/D | | | STRATFORD - 30A | IPSWICH - 32B | IPSWICH - 32B | STRATFORD - 30A |
| Jan-59 | 12/58: COL - 30E | 12/58: COL - 30E | | | | 12/58: COL - 30E | IPSWICH - 32B | IPSWICH - 32B | 12/58: COL - 30E |
| Aug-59 | COLCHESTER - 30E | COLCHESTER - 30E | | | | COLCHESTER - 30E | IPSWICH - 32B | IPSWICH - 32B | COLCHESTER - 30E |
| Nov-59 | COLCHESTER - 30E | 10/59: STRAT - 30A | | | | COLCHESTER - 30E | IPSWICH - 32B | IPSWICH - 32B | 10/59: STRAT - 30A |
| Jan-60 | 12/59: STRAT - 30A | STRATFORD - 30A | | | | 12/59: STRAT - 30A | 12/59: W/D | IPSWICH - 32B | 12/59: W/D |
| Apr-60 | STRATFORD - 30A | STRATFORD - 30A | | | | STRATFORD - 30A | | 4/60: K.LYNN - 31C | |
| Aug-60 | STRATFORD - 30A | STRATFORD - 30A | | | | STRATFORD - 30A | | KINGS LYNN - 31C | |
| Nov-60 | 9/60: W/D | STRATFORD - 30A | | | | STRATFORD - 30A | | 9/60: CAMB - 31A | |

| | 65515 | 65516 | 65517 | 65518 | 65519 | 65520 | 65521 | 65522 | 65523 |
|---|---|---|---|---|---|---|---|---|---|
| Aug-50 | MARCH - 31B | MELTON C - 32G | CAMBRIDGE - 31A | MARCH - 31B | KINGS LYNN - 31C | CAMBRIDGE - 31A | MARCH - 31B | COLCHESTER - 30E | STRATFORD - 30A |
| Jan-51 | MARCH - 31B | MELTON C - 32G | CAMBRIDGE - 31A | MARCH - 31B | KINGS LYNN - 31C | CAMBRIDGE - 31A | MARCH - 31B | COLCHESTER - 30E | STRATFORD - 30A |
| Aug-51 | MARCH - 31B | MELTON C - 32G | 9/51: BURY - 31E | MARCH - 31B | KINGS LYNN - 31C | CAMBRIDGE - 31A | MARCH - 31B | COLCHESTER - 30E | STRATFORD - 30A |
| Jan-52 | MARCH - 31B | 3/52: NOR - 32A | 3/52: CAMB - 31A | 10/51: STRAT - 30A | KINGS LYNN - 31C | CAMBRIDGE - 31A | 3/52: K.LYNN - 31C | COLCHESTER - 30E | STRATFORD - 30A |
| Aug-52 | MARCH - 31B | NORWICH - 32A | CAMBRIDGE - 31A | 9/52: CAMB - 31A | KINGS LYNN - 31C | 9/52: BURY - 31E | KINGS LYNN - 31C | COLCHESTER - 30E | STRATFORD - 30A |
| Jan-53 | MARCH - 31B | NORWICH - 32A | CAMBRIDGE - 31A | CAMBRIDGE - 31A | KINGS LYNN - 31C | 1/53: CAMB - 31A | KINGS LYNN - 31C | COLCHESTER - 30E | STRATFORD - 30A |
| Aug-53 | MARCH - 31B | NORWICH - 32A | 7/53: S.LYNN - 31D | 5/53: K.LYNN - 31C | KINGS LYNN - 31C | 7/53: S.LYNN - 31D | KINGS LYNN - 31C | COLCHESTER - 30E | STRATFORD - 30A |
| Jan-54 | MARCH - 31B | NORWICH - 32A | SOUTH LYNN - 31D | KINGS LYNN - 31C | KINGS LYNN - 31C | 3/54: CAMB - 31A | KINGS LYNN - 31C | COLCHESTER - 30E | STRATFORD - 30A |
| Aug-54 | MARCH - 31B | NORWICH - 32A | SOUTH LYNN - 31D | KINGS LYNN - 31C | KINGS LYNN - 31C | CAMBRIDGE - 31A | KINGS LYNN - 31C | COLCHESTER - 30E | STRATFORD - 30A |
| Jan-55 | MARCH - 31B | NORWICH - 32A | SOUTH LYNN - 31D | KINGS LYNN - 31C | KINGS LYNN - 31C | CAMBRIDGE - 31A | KINGS LYNN - 31C | COLCHESTER - 30E | STRATFORD - 30A |
| Aug-55 | MARCH - 31B | 3/55: W/D | 5/55: W/D | KINGS LYNN - 31C | 9/55: NOR - 32A | CAMBRIDGE - 31A | KINGS LYNN - 31C | COLCHESTER - 30E | STRATFORD - 30A |
| Jan-56 | MARCH - 31B | | | KINGS LYNN - 31C | NORWICH - 32A | CAMBRIDGE - 31A | KINGS LYNN - 31C | COLCHESTER - 30E | STRATFORD - 30A |
| Aug-56 | MARCH - 31B | | | KINGS LYNN - 31C | NORWICH - 32A | CAMBRIDGE - 31A | KINGS LYNN - 31C | COLCHESTER - 30E | STRATFORD - 30A |
| Jan-57 | MARCH - 31B | | | KINGS LYNN - 31C | NORWICH - 32A | CAMBRIDGE - 31A | KINGS LYNN - 31C | COLCHESTER - 30E | STRATFORD - 30A |
| Aug-57 | MARCH - 31B | | | KINGS LYNN - 31C | NORWICH - 32A | CAMBRIDGE - 31A | KINGS LYNN - 31C | COLCHESTER - 30E | 5/57: W/D |
| Jan-58 | MARCH - 31B | | | KINGS LYNN - 31C | NORWICH - 32A | CAMBRIDGE - 31A | KINGS LYNN - 31C | COLCHESTER - 30E | |
| Aug-58 | 9/58: W/D | | | 9/58: W/D | NORWICH - 32A | CAMBRIDGE - 31A | KINGS LYNN - 31C | 9/58: W/D | |
| Jan-59 | | | | | NORWICH - 32A | CAMBRIDGE - 31A | KINGS LYNN - 31C | | |
| Aug-59 | | | | | NORWICH - 32A | CAMBRIDGE - 31A | KINGS LYNN - 31C | | |
| Nov-59 | | | | | NORWICH - 32A | CAMBRIDGE - 31A | KINGS LYNN - 31C | | |
| Jan-60 | | | | | NORWICH - 32A | CAMBRIDGE - 31A | KINGS LYNN - 31C | | |
| Apr-60 | | | | | 3/60: W/D | CAMBRIDGE - 31A | 3/60: MARCH - 31B | | |
| Aug-60 | | | | | | CAMBRIDGE - 31A | MARCH - 31B | | |
| Nov-60 | | | | | | CAMBRIDGE - 31A | MARCH - 31B | | |

| | 65524 | 65525 | 65526 | 65527 | 65528 | 65529 | 65530 | 65531 | 65532 |
|---|---|---|---|---|---|---|---|---|---|
| Aug-50 | NORWICH - 32A | CAMBRIDGE - 31A | SOUTH LYNN - 31D | KINGS LYNN - 31C | STRATFORD - 30A | CAMBRIDGE - 31A | KINGS LYNN - 31C | COLCHESTER - 30E | CAMBRIDGE - 31A |
| Jan-51 | NORWICH - 32A | CAMBRIDGE - 31A | SOUTH LYNN - 31D | KINGS LYNN - 31C | STRATFORD - 30A | CAMBRIDGE - 31A | KINGS LYNN - 31C | COLCHESTER - 30E | CAMBRIDGE - 31A |
| Aug-51 | NORWICH - 32A | CAMBRIDGE - 31A | 9/51: MARCH - 31B | KINGS LYNN - 31C | STRATFORD - 30A | CAMBRIDGE - 31A | KINGS LYNN - 31C | COLCHESTER - 30E | CAMBRIDGE - 31A |
| Jan-52 | NORWICH - 32A | 2/52: STRAT - 30A | 3/52: K.LYNN - 31C | KINGS LYNN - 31C | STRATFORD - 30A | CAMBRIDGE - 31A | KINGS LYNN - 31C | COLCHESTER - 30E | CAMBRIDGE - 31A |
| Aug-52 | NORWICH - 32A | STRATFORD - 30A | KINGS LYNN - 31C | KINGS LYNN - 31C | STRATFORD - 30A | CAMBRIDGE - 31A | KINGS LYNN - 31C | COLCHESTER - 30E | CAMBRIDGE - 31A |
| Jan-53 | NORWICH - 32A | STRATFORD - 30A | KINGS LYNN - 31C | KINGS LYNN - 31C | STRATFORD - 30A | 11/52: K.LYNN - 31C | KINGS LYNN - 31C | COLCHESTER - 30E | CAMBRIDGE - 31A |
| Aug-53 | NORWICH - 32A | STRATFORD - 30A | KINGS LYNN - 31C | KINGS LYNN - 31C | STRATFORD - 30A | KINGS LYNN - 31C | KINGS LYNN - 31C | COLCHESTER - 30E | CAMBRIDGE - 31A |
| Jan-54 | NORWICH - 32A | STRATFORD - 30A | KINGS LYNN - 31C | KINGS LYNN - 31C | STRATFORD - 30A | KINGS LYNN - 31C | KINGS LYNN - 31C | COLCHESTER - 30E | CAMBRIDGE - 31A |
| Aug-54 | NORWICH - 32A | STRATFORD - 30A | KINGS LYNN - 31C | KINGS LYNN - 31C | STRATFORD - 30A | 6/54: MARCH - 31B | KINGS LYNN - 31C | COLCHESTER - 30E | 10/54: BURY - 31E |
| Jan-55 | NORWICH - 32A | STRATFORD - 30A | KINGS LYNN - 31C | KINGS LYNN - 31C | STRATFORD - 30A | MARCH - 31B | KINGS LYNN - 31C | COLCHESTER - 30E | 1/55: CAMB - 31A |
| Aug-55 | 3/55: W/D | STRATFORD - 30A | KINGS LYNN - 31C | KINGS LYNN - 31C | STRATFORD - 30A | MARCH - 31B | KINGS LYNN - 31C | COLCHESTER - 30E | CAMBRIDGE - 31A |
| Jan-56 | | STRATFORD - 30A | KINGS LYNN - 31C | KINGS LYNN - 31C | STRATFORD - 30A | 12/55: K.LYNN - 31C | KINGS LYNN - 31C | COLCHESTER - 30E | CAMBRIDGE - 31A |
| Aug-56 | | STRATFORD - 30A | KINGS LYNN - 31C | KINGS LYNN - 31C | STRATFORD - 30A | KINGS LYNN - 31C | KINGS LYNN - 31C | COLCHESTER - 30E | CAMBRIDGE - 31A |
| Jan-57 | | STRATFORD - 30A | KINGS LYNN - 31C | KINGS LYNN - 31C | STRATFORD - 30A | KINGS LYNN - 31C | KINGS LYNN - 31C | COLCHESTER - 30E | CAMBRIDGE - 31A |
| Aug-57 | | STRATFORD - 30A | KINGS LYNN - 31C | KINGS LYNN - 31C | STRATFORD - 30A | KINGS LYNN - 31C | KINGS LYNN - 31C | COLCHESTER - 30E | CAMBRIDGE - 31A |
| Jan-58 | | STRATFORD - 30A | KINGS LYNN - 31C | KINGS LYNN - 31C | STRATFORD - 30A | KINGS LYNN - 31C | KINGS LYNN - 31C | COLCHESTER - 30E | CAMBRIDGE - 31A |
| Aug-58 | | STRATFORD - 30A | KINGS LYNN - 31C | KINGS LYNN - 31C | STRATFORD - 30A | 5/58: W/D | KINGS LYNN - 31C | COLCHESTER - 30E | CAMBRIDGE - 31A |
| Jan-59 | | STRATFORD - 30A | KINGS LYNN - 31C | KINGS LYNN - 31C | 1/59: CAMB - 31A | | KINGS LYNN - 31C | COLCHESTER - 30E | CAMBRIDGE - 31A |
| Aug-59 | | 4/59: W/D | 8/59: W/D | 4/59: W/D | CAMBRIDGE - 31A | | KINGS LYNN - 31C | 4/59: W/D | CAMBRIDGE - 31A |
| Nov-59 | | | | | CAMBRIDGE - 31A | | KINGS LYNN - 31C | | CAMBRIDGE - 31A |
| Jan-60 | | | | | CAMBRIDGE - 31A | | 12/59: W/D | | CAMBRIDGE - 31A |
| Apr-60 | | | | | CAMBRIDGE - 31A | | | | CAMBRIDGE - 31A |
| Aug-60 | | | | | CAMBRIDGE - 31A | | | | CAMBRIDGE - 31A |
| Nov-60 | | | | | CAMBRIDGE - 31A | | | | CAMBRIDGE - 31A |

| | 65533 | 65534 | 65535 | 65536 | 65537 | 65538 | 65539 | 65540 | 65541 |
|---|---|---|---|---|---|---|---|---|---|
| Aug-50 | SOUTH LYNN - 31D | NORWICH - 32A | CAMBRIDGE - 31A | STRATFORD - 30A | CAMBRIDGE - 31A | CAMBRIDGE - 31A | COLCHESTER - 30E | STRATFORD - 30A | STRATFORD - 30A |
| Jan-51 | SOUTH LYNN - 31D | NORWICH - 32A | CAMBRIDGE - 31A | STRATFORD - 30A | CAMBRIDGE - 31A | CAMBRIDGE - 31A | COLCHESTER - 30E | STRATFORD - 30A | STRATFORD - 30A |
| Aug-51 | 10/51: CAMB - 31A | NORWICH - 32A | CAMBRIDGE - 31A | STRATFORD - 30A | CAMBRIDGE - 31A | 9/51: MARCH - 31B | COLCHESTER - 30E | STRATFORD - 30A | STRATFORD - 30A |
| Jan-52 | 3/52: PLAIS - 33A | NORWICH - 32A | CAMBRIDGE - 31A | STRATFORD - 30A | CAMBRIDGE - 31A | 2/52: STRAT - 30A | COLCHESTER - 30E | STRATFORD - 30A | STRATFORD - 30A |
| Aug-52 | PLAISTOW - 33A | NORWICH - 32A | CAMBRIDGE - 31A | STRATFORD - 30A | CAMBRIDGE - 31A | STRATFORD - 30A | COLCHESTER - 30E | STRATFORD - 30A | 11/52: NOR - 32A |
| Jan-53 | PLAISTOW - 33A | 11/52: CAMB - 31A | CAMBRIDGE - 31A | STRATFORD - 30A | CAMBRIDGE - 31A | STRATFORD - 30A | COLCHESTER - 30E | STRATFORD - 30A | 1/53: STRAT - 30A |
| Aug-53 | PLAISTOW - 33A | CAMBRIDGE - 31A | CAMBRIDGE - 31A | STRATFORD - 30A | CAMBRIDGE - 31A | STRATFORD - 30A | COLCHESTER - 30E | STRATFORD - 30A | STRATFORD - 30A |
| Jan-54 | PLAISTOW - 33A | CAMBRIDGE - 31A | CAMBRIDGE - 31A | STRATFORD - 30A | CAMBRIDGE - 31A | 1/54: MARCH - 31B | COLCHESTER - 30E | STRATFORD - 30A | 12/53: MARCH - 31B |
| Aug-54 | PLAISTOW - 33A | CAMBRIDGE - 31A | CAMBRIDGE - 31A | STRATFORD - 30A | CAMBRIDGE - 31A | MARCH - 31B | COLCHESTER - 30E | STRATFORD - 30A | MARCH - 31B |
| Jan-55 | 5/55: NOR - 32A | CAMBRIDGE - 31A | 2/55: STRAT - 30A | STRATFORD - 30A | 3/55: NOW - 32A | MARCH - 31B | COLCHESTER - 30E | STRATFORD - 30A | MARCH - 31B |
| Aug-55 | 9/55: K.LYNN - 31C | CAMBRIDGE - 31A | STRATFORD - 30A | STRATFORD - 30A | 9/55: LOW - 32C | MARCH - 31B | COLCHESTER - 30E | STRATFORD - 30A | 4/55: CAMB - 31A |
| Jan-56 | KINGS LYNN - 31C | CAMBRIDGE - 31A | STRATFORD - 30A | STRATFORD - 30A | 11/55: NOR - 32A | MARCH - 31B | COLCHESTER - 30E | STRATFORD - 30A | CAMBRIDGE - 31A |
| Aug-56 | KINGS LYNN - 31C | CAMBRIDGE - 31A | STRATFORD - 30A | STRATFORD - 30A | NORWICH - 32A | MARCH - 31B | COLCHESTER - 30E | STRATFORD - 30A | CAMBRIDGE - 31A |
| Jan-57 | KINGS LYNN - 31C | CAMBRIDGE - 31A | STRATFORD - 30A | STRATFORD - 30A | 1/57: W/D | MARCH - 31B | COLCHESTER - 30E | STRATFORD - 30A | CAMBRIDGE - 31A |
| Aug-57 | KINGS LYNN - 31C | CAMBRIDGE - 31A | STRATFORD - 30A | STRATFORD - 30A | | MARCH - 31B | COLCHESTER - 30E | STRATFORD - 30A | CAMBRIDGE - 31A |
| Jan-58 | KINGS LYNN - 31C | CAMBRIDGE - 31A | STRATFORD - 30A | STRATFORD - 30A | | MARCH - 31B | COLCHESTER - 30E | STRATFORD - 30A | CAMBRIDGE - 31A |
| Aug-58 | KINGS LYNN - 31C | 5/58: W/D | 5/58: W/D | STRATFORD - 30A | | MARCH - 31B | COLCHESTER - 30E | STRATFORD - 30A | CAMBRIDGE - 31A |
| Jan-59 | KINGS LYNN - 31C | | | STRATFORD - 30A | | MARCH - 31B | COLCHESTER - 30E | 1/59: CAMB - 31A | CAMBRIDGE - 31A |
| Aug-59 | KINGS LYNN - 31C | | | STRATFORD - 30A | | 4/59: W/D | COLCHESTER - 30E | 4/59: W/D | CAMBRIDGE - 31A |
| Nov-59 | KINGS LYNN - 31C | | | STRATFORD - 30A | | | 10/59: STRAT - 30A | | CAMBRIDGE - 31A |
| Jan-60 | 12/59: W/D | | | STRATFORD - 30A | | | STRATFORD - 30A | | CAMBRIDGE - 31A |
| Apr-60 | | | | 3/60: W/D | | | STRATFORD - 30A | | CAMBRIDGE - 31A |
| Aug-60 | | | | | | | STRATFORD - 30A | | CAMBRIDGE - 31A |
| Nov-60 | | | | | | | 9/60: W/D | | 11/60: MARCH - 31B |

| | 65542 | 65543 | 65544 | 65545 | 65546 | 65547 | 65548 | 65549 | 65551 |
|---|---|---|---|---|---|---|---|---|---|
| Aug-50 | KINGS LYNN - 31C | STRATFORD - 30A | KINGS LYNN - 31C | SOUTH LYNN - 31D | CAMBRIDGE - 31A | CAMBRIDGE - 31A | KINGS LYNN - 31C | KINGS LYNN - 31C | MELTON C - 32G |
| Jan-51 | KINGS LYNN - 31C | STRATFORD - 30A | KINGS LYNN - 31C | 9/51: CAMB - 31A | CAMBRIDGE - 31A | CAMBRIDGE - 31A | 9/50: BURY : 31E | KINGS LYNN - 31C | MELTON C - 32G |
| Aug-51 | KINGS LYNN - 31C | STRATFORD - 30A | KINGS LYNN - 31C | 11/51: STRAT - 30A | CAMBRIDGE - 31A | 9/51: NOR - 32A | BURY ST EDMUNDS - 31E | KINGS LYNN - 31C | MELTON C - 32G |
| Jan-52 | KINGS LYNN - 31C | STRATFORD - 30A | KINGS LYNN - 31C | 3/52: PLAIS - 33A | 2/52: STRAT - 30A | 3/52: K.LYNN - 31C | BURY ST EDMUNDS - 31E | KINGS LYNN - 31C | 3/52: NOR - 32A |
| Aug-52 | 11/52: NOR - 32A | STRATFORD - 30A | KINGS LYNN - 31C | 5/52: SHOE - 33C | STRATFORD - 30A | KINGS LYNN - 31C | 9/52: CAMB - 31A | KINGS LYNN - 31C | NORWICH - 32A |
| Jan-53 | NORWICH - 32A | STRATFORD - 30A | KINGS LYNN - 31C | SHOEBURYNESS - 33C | STRATFORD - 30A | KINGS LYNN - 31C | CAMBRIDGE - 31A | KINGS LYNN - 31C | NORWICH - 32A |
| Aug-53 | NORWICH - 32A | STRATFORD - 30A | KINGS LYNN - 31C | SHOEBURYNESS - 33C | STRATFORD - 30A | 5/53: CAMB - 31A | CAMBRIDGE - 31A | KINGS LYNN - 31C | NORWICH - 32A |
| Jan-54 | NORWICH - 32A | STRATFORD - 30A | KINGS LYNN - 31C | 1/54: STRAT - 30A | STRATFORD - 30A | CAMBRIDGE - 31A | CAMBRIDGE - 31A | KINGS LYNN - 31C | NORWICH - 32A |
| Aug-54 | NORWICH - 32A | STRATFORD - 30A | KINGS LYNN - 31C | STRATFORD - 30A | STRATFORD - 30A | 9/54: W/D | CAMBRIDGE - 31A | KINGS LYNN - 31C | 5/54: MELTON - 32G |
| Jan-55 | NORWICH - 32A | STRATFORD - 30A | KINGS LYNN - 31C | STRATFORD - 30A | STRATFORD - 30A | | CAMBRIDGE - 31A | KINGS LYNN - 31C | MELTON C - 32G |
| Aug-55 | NORWICH - 32A | 5/55: W/D | KINGS LYNN - 31C | STRATFORD - 30A | STRATFORD - 30A | | CAMBRIDGE - 31A | KINGS LYNN - 31C | MELTON C - 32G |
| Jan-56 | NORWICH - 32A | | KINGS LYNN - 31C | STRATFORD - 30A | STRATFORD - 30A | | CAMBRIDGE - 31A | KINGS LYNN - 31C | MELTON C - 32G |
| Aug-56 | NORWICH - 32A | | KINGS LYNN - 31C | STRATFORD - 30A | STRATFORD - 30A | | CAMBRIDGE - 31A | KINGS LYNN - 31C | MELTON C - 32G |
| Jan-57 | NORWICH - 32A | | KINGS LYNN - 31C | STRATFORD - 30A | STRATFORD - 30A | | CAMBRIDGE - 31A | KINGS LYNN - 31C | MELTON C - 32G |
| Aug-57 | NORWICH - 32A | | KINGS LYNN - 31C | STRATFORD - 30A | STRATFORD - 30A | | CAMBRIDGE - 31A | KINGS LYNN - 31C | MELTON C - 32G |
| Jan-58 | NORWICH - 32A | | KINGS LYNN - 31C | STRATFORD - 30A | STRATFORD - 30A | | 3/58: STRAT - 30A | KINGS LYNN - 31C | MELTON C - 32G |
| Aug-58 | NORWICH - 32A | | KINGS LYNN - 31C | STRATFORD - 30A | STRATFORD - 30A | | STRATFORD - 30A | KINGS LYNN - 31C | MELTON C - 32G |
| Jan-59 | NORWICH - 32A | | KINGS LYNN - 31C | 12/58: COL - 30E | STRATFORD - 30A | | STRATFORD - 30A | KINGS LYNN - 31C | 3/59: NOR - 32A |
| Aug-59 | 5/59: W/D | | KINGS LYNN - 31C | COLCHESTER - 30E | STRATFORD - 30A | | STRATFORD - 30A | KINGS LYNN - 31C | NORWICH - 32A |
| Nov-59 | | | 11/59: W/D | 10/59: W/D | STRATFORD - 30A | | STRATFORD - 30A | KINGS LYNN - 31C | NORWICH - 32A |
| Jan-60 | | | | | 12/59: W/D | | STRATFORD - 30A | KINGS LYNN - 31C | NORWICH - 32A |
| Apr-60 | | | | | | | 3/60: W/D | KINGS LYNN - 31C | 2/60: W/D |
| Aug-60 | | | | | | | | KINGS LYNN - 31C | |
| Nov-60 | | | | | | | | KINGS LYNN - 31C | |

| | 65552 | 65553 | 65554 | 65555 | 65556 | 65557 | 65558 | 65559 | 65560 |
|---|---|---|---|---|---|---|---|---|---|
| Aug-50 | MELTON C - 32G | NORWICH - 32A | MARCH - 31B | MARCH - 31B | MARCH - 31B | MELTON C - 32G | YARMOUTH(B) - 32F | YARMOUTH(B) - 32F | IPSWICH - 32B |
| Jan-51 | MELTON C - 32G | NORWICH - 32A | MARCH - 31B | MARCH - 31B | MARCH - 31B | MELTON C - 32G | YARMOUTH(B) - 32F | YARMOUTH(B) - 32F | IPSWICH - 32B |
| Aug-51 | MELTON C - 32G | NORWICH - 32A | MARCH - 31B | MARCH - 31B | MARCH - 31B | MELTON C - 32G | **6/51: LOW - 32C** | **9/51: LOW - 32C** | IPSWICH - 32B |
| Jan-52 | **3/52: STRAT - 30A** | NORWICH - 32A | MARCH - 31B | **2/52: STRAT - 30A** | MARCH - 31B | MELTON C - 32G | LOWESTOFT - 32C | LOWESTOFT - 32C | IPSWICH - 32B |
| Aug-52 | **5/52: PLAIS - 33A** | NORWICH - 32A | MARCH - 31B | STRATFORD - 30A | MARCH - 31B | MELTON C - 32G | LOWESTOFT - 32C | LOWESTOFT - 32C | IPSWICH - 32B |
| Jan-53 | PLAISTOW - 33A | NORWICH - 32A | MARCH - 31B | STRATFORD - 30A | MARCH - 31B | MELTON C - 32G | LOWESTOFT - 32C | LOWESTOFT - 32C | IPSWICH - 32B |
| Aug-53 | PLAISTOW - 33A | NORWICH - 32A | MARCH - 31B | STRATFORD - 30A | MARCH - 31B | MELTON C - 32G | LOWESTOFT - 32C | LOWESTOFT - 32C | IPSWICH - 32B |
| Jan-54 | **1/54: STRAT - 30A** | NORWICH - 32A | MARCH - 31B | STRATFORD - 30A | MARCH - 31B | **1/54: NOR - 32A** | LOWESTOFT - 32C | LOWESTOFT - 32C | IPSWICH - 32B |
| Aug-54 | STRATFORD - 30A | NORWICH - 32A | MARCH - 31B | STRATFORD - 30A | MARCH - 31B | NORWICH - 32A | LOWESTOFT - 32C | LOWESTOFT - 32C | IPSWICH - 32B |
| Jan-55 | **1/55: W/D** | NORWICH - 32A | MARCH - 31B | STRATFORD - 30A | MARCH - 31B | NORWICH - 32A | LOWESTOFT - 32C | LOWESTOFT - 32C | IPSWICH - 32B |
| Aug-55 | | NORWICH - 32A | MARCH - 31B | STRATFORD - 30A | MARCH - 31B | NORWICH - 32A | LOWESTOFT - 32C | LOWESTOFT - 32C | IPSWICH - 32B |
| Jan-56 | | NORWICH - 32A | MARCH - 31B | STRATFORD - 30A | MARCH - 31B | **6/56: YAR (B) - 32F** | LOWESTOFT - 32C | LOWESTOFT - 32C | IPSWICH - 32B |
| Aug-56 | | NORWICH - 32A | MARCH - 31B | STRATFORD - 30A | MARCH - 31B | **10/56: MELTON - 32G** | LOWESTOFT - 32C | LOWESTOFT - 32C | IPSWICH - 32B |
| Jan-57 | | NORWICH - 32A | MARCH - 31B | STRATFORD - 30A | MARCH - 31B | **3/57: NOR - 32A** | LOWESTOFT - 32C | LOWESTOFT - 32C | IPSWICH - 32B |
| Aug-57 | | NORWICH - 32A | MARCH - 31B | STRATFORD - 30A | MARCH - 31B | NORWICH - 32A | LOWESTOFT - 32C | LOWESTOFT - 32C | IPSWICH - 32B |
| Jan-58 | | NORWICH - 32A | MARCH - 31B | STRATFORD - 30A | MARCH - 31B | NORWICH - 32A | LOWESTOFT - 32C | LOWESTOFT - 32C | IPSWICH - 32B |
| Aug-58 | | NORWICH - 32A | MARCH - 31B | STRATFORD - 30A | **4/58: STRAT - 30A** | NORWICH - 32A | LOWESTOFT - 32C | LOWESTOFT - 32C | IPSWICH - 32B |
| Jan-59 | | NORWICH - 32A | MARCH - 31B | STRATFORD - 30A | **1/59: CAMB - 31A** | NORWICH - 32A | LOWESTOFT - 32C | LOWESTOFT - 32C | IPSWICH - 32B |
| Aug-59 | | **4/59: W/D** | MARCH - 31B | STRATFORD - 30A | CAMBRIDGE - 31A | **4/59: W/D** | LOWESTOFT - 32C | LOWESTOFT - 32C | IPSWICH - 32B |
| Nov-59 | | | MARCH - 31B | STRATFORD - 30A | CAMBRIDGE - 31A | | LOWESTOFT - 32C | **11/59: W/D** | IPSWICH - 32B |
| Jan-60 | | | MARCH - 31B | STRATFORD - 30A | CAMBRIDGE - 31A | | **12/59: W/D** | | IPSWICH - 32B |
| Apr-60 | | | MARCH - 31B | **3/60: W/D** | CAMBRIDGE - 31A | | | | **4/60: K.LYNN - 31C** |
| Aug-60 | | | MARCH - 31B | | CAMBRIDGE - 31A | | | | **9/60: CAMB - 31A** |
| Nov-60 | | | MARCH - 31B | | CAMBRIDGE - 31A | | | | CAMBRIDGE - 31A |

| | 65561 | 65562 | 65563 | 65564 | 65565 | 65566 | 65567 | 65568 | 65569 |
|---|---|---|---|---|---|---|---|---|---|
| Aug-50 | CAMBRIDGE - 31A | SOUTH LYNN - 31D | CAMBRIDGE - 31A | COLCHESTER - 30E | CAMBRIDGE - 31A | LOWESTOFT - 32C | MELTON C - 32G | NORWICH - 32A | NORWICH - 32A |
| Jan-51 | CAMBRIDGE - 31A | SOUTH LYNN - 31D | CAMBRIDGE - 31A | COLCHESTER - 30E | CAMBRIDGE - 31A | LOWESTOFT - 32C | MELTON C - 32G | NORWICH - 32A | NORWICH - 32A |
| Aug-51 | CAMBRIDGE - 31A | **6/51: MARCH - 31B** | CAMBRIDGE - 31A | COLCHESTER - 30E | **9/51: BURY - 31E** | **4/51: YAR (B) - 32F** | MELTON C - 32G | NORWICH - 32A | NORWICH - 32A |
| Jan-52 | CAMBRIDGE - 31A | **9/51: CAMB - 31A** | **2/52: STRAT - 30A** | COLCHESTER - 30E | **3/52: CAMB - 31A** | **3/52: PLAIS - 33A** | **12/51: NOR - 32A** | NORWICH - 32A | NORWICH - 32A |
| Aug-52 | **9/52: BURY - 31E** | CAMBRIDGE - 31A | STRATFORD - 30A | COLCHESTER - 30E | CAMBRIDGE - 31A | PLAISTOW - 33A | NORWICH - 32A | NORWICH - 32A | NORWICH - 32A |
| Jan-53 | **1/53: CAMB - 31A** | **3/53: S.LYNN - 31D** | STRATFORD - 30A | COLCHESTER - 30E | CAMBRIDGE - 31A | PLAISTOW - 33A | NORWICH - 32A | **11/52: CAMB - 31A** | NORWICH - 32A |
| Aug-53 | CAMBRIDGE - 31A | SOUTH LYNN - 31D | STRATFORD - 30A | COLCHESTER - 30E | CAMBRIDGE - 31A | PLAISTOW - 33A | NORWICH - 32A | **5/52: K.LYNN - 31C** | NORWICH - 32A |
| Jan-54 | CAMBRIDGE - 31A | **3/54: MARCH - 31B** | STRATFORD - 30A | COLCHESTER - 30E | CAMBRIDGE - 31A | PLAISTOW - 33A | NORWICH - 32A | KINGS LYNN - 31C | NORWICH - 32A |
| Aug-54 | CAMBRIDGE - 31A | **6/54: K.LYNN - 32C** | STRATFORD - 30A | COLCHESTER - 30E | CAMBRIDGE - 31A | PLAISTOW - 33A | NORWICH - 32A | KINGS LYNN - 31C | NORWICH - 32A |
| Jan-55 | CAMBRIDGE - 31A | KINGS LYNN - 31C | STRATFORD - 30A | COLCHESTER - 30E | CAMBRIDGE - 31A | PLAISTOW - 33A | NORWICH - 32A | KINGS LYNN - 31C | **2/55: W/D** |
| Aug-55 | CAMBRIDGE - 31A | KINGS LYNN - 31C | STRATFORD - 30A | COLCHESTER - 30E | CAMBRIDGE - 31A | **6/55: NOR - 32A** | **9/55: MELTON - 32G** | KINGS LYNN - 31C | |
| Jan-56 | CAMBRIDGE - 31A | KINGS LYNN - 31C | STRATFORD - 30A | COLCHESTER - 30E | CAMBRIDGE - 31A | NORWICH - 32A | MELTON C - 32G | KINGS LYNN - 31C | |
| Aug-56 | CAMBRIDGE - 31A | KINGS LYNN - 31C | STRATFORD - 30A | COLCHESTER - 30E | CAMBRIDGE - 31A | NORWICH - 32A | MELTON C - 32G | KINGS LYNN - 31C | |
| Jan-57 | CAMBRIDGE - 31A | KINGS LYNN - 31C | STRATFORD - 30A | COLCHESTER - 30E | CAMBRIDGE - 31A | NORWICH - 32A | MELTON C - 32G | KINGS LYNN - 31C | |
| Aug-57 | CAMBRIDGE - 31A | **6/57: CAMB - 31A** | STRATFORD - 30A | COLCHESTER - 30E | CAMBRIDGE - 31A | NORWICH - 32A | MELTON C - 32G | KINGS LYNN - 31C | |
| Jan-58 | CAMBRIDGE - 31A | CAMBRIDGE - 31A | STRATFORD - 30A | COLCHESTER - 30E | CAMBRIDGE - 31A | NORWICH - 32A | MELTON C - 32G | KINGS LYNN - 31C | |
| Aug-58 | **6/58: IPS - 32B** | **8/58: W/D** | STRATFORD - 30A | COLCHESTER - 30E | CAMBRIDGE - 31A | NORWICH - 32A | **10/58: LOW - 32C** | **9/58: W/D** | |
| Jan-59 | IPSWICH - 32B | | STRATFORD - 30A | COLCHESTER - 30E | **12/58: K.LYNN - 31C** | NORWICH - 32A | LOWESTOFT - 32C | | |
| Aug-59 | IPSWICH - 32B | | STRATFORD - 30A | COLCHESTER - 30E | KINGS LYNN - 31C | NORWICH - 32A | LOWESTOFT - 32C | | |
| Nov-59 | IPSWICH - 32B | | STRATFORD - 30A | COLCHESTER - 30E | KINGS LYNN - 31C | NORWICH - 32A | LOWESTOFT - 32C | | |
| Jan-60 | **12/59: W/D** | | **12/59: W/D** | **12/59: STRAT - 30A** | KINGS LYNN - 31C | NORWICH - 32A | LOWESTOFT - 32C | | |
| Apr-60 | | | | STRATFORD - 30A | **3/60: W/D** | NORWICH - 32A | LOWESTOFT - 32C | | |
| Aug-60 | | | | **8/60: W/D** | | **6/60: W/D** | LOWESTOFT - 32C | | |
| Nov-60 | | | | | | | LOWESTOFT - 32C | | |

| | 65570 | 65571 | 65572 | 65573 | 65574 | 65575 | 65576 | 65577 | 65578 |
|---|---|---|---|---|---|---|---|---|---|
| Aug-50 | NORWICH - 32A | MARCH - 31B | KINGS LYNN - 31C | CAMBRIDGE - 31A | NORWICH - 32A | CAMBRIDGE - 31A | MARCH - 31B | MARCH - 31B | NORWICH - 32A |
| Jan-51 | **10/50: LOW - 32C** | MARCH - 31B | KINGS LYNN - 31C | CAMBRIDGE - 31A | NORWICH - 32A | CAMBRIDGE - 31A | MARCH - 31B | MARCH - 31B | **10/50: IPS - 32B** |
| Aug-51 | **2/51: NOR - 32A** | MARCH - 31B | **10/51: STRAT - 30A** | **10/51: MARCH - 31B** | **9/51: MELTON - 32G** | CAMBRIDGE - 31A | MARCH - 31B | MARCH - 31B | IPSWICH - 32B |
| Jan-52 | NORWICH - 32A | MARCH - 31B | STRATFORD - 30A | MARCH - 31B | **11/51: NOR - 32A** | CAMBRIDGE - 31A | MARCH - 31B | MARCH - 31B | IPSWICH - 32B |
| Aug-52 | NORWICH - 32A | MARCH - 31B | STRATFORD - 30A | MARCH - 31B | NORWICH - 32A | CAMBRIDGE - 31A | MARCH - 31B | MARCH - 31B | IPSWICH - 32B |
| Jan-53 | NORWICH - 32A | MARCH - 31B | STRATFORD - 30A | **11/52: NOR - 32A** | NORWICH - 32A | CAMBRIDGE - 31A | MARCH - 31B | MARCH - 31B | IPSWICH - 32B |
| Aug-53 | NORWICH - 32A | MARCH - 31B | STRATFORD - 30A | NORWICH - 32A | NORWICH - 32A | CAMBRIDGE - 31A | MARCH - 31B | MARCH - 31B | IPSWICH - 32B |
| Jan-54 | NORWICH - 32A | MARCH - 31B | **12/53: MARCH - 31B** | NORWICH - 32A | NORWICH - 32A | CAMBRIDGE - 31A | MARCH - 31B | MARCH - 31B | IPSWICH - 32B |
| Aug-54 | NORWICH - 32A | MARCH - 31B | MARCH - 31B | NORWICH - 32A | NORWICH - 32A | CAMBRIDGE - 31A | MARCH - 31B | MARCH - 31B | IPSWICH - 32B |
| Jan-55 | NORWICH - 32A | MARCH - 31B | MARCH - 31B | NORWICH - 32A | NORWICH - 32A | CAMBRIDGE - 31A | MARCH - 31B | MARCH - 31B | IPSWICH - 32B |
| Aug-55 | NORWICH - 32A | MARCH - 31B | MARCH - 31B | NORWICH - 32A | **4/55: W/D** | CAMBRIDGE - 31A | MARCH - 31B | MARCH - 31B | IPSWICH - 32B |
| Jan-56 | NORWICH - 32A | MARCH - 31B | MARCH - 31B | NORWICH - 32A | | CAMBRIDGE - 31A | MARCH - 31B | MARCH - 31B | IPSWICH - 32B |
| Aug-56 | NORWICH - 32A | MARCH - 31B | MARCH - 31B | NORWICH - 32A | | CAMBRIDGE - 31A | MARCH - 31B | MARCH - 31B | IPSWICH - 32B |
| Jan-57 | NORWICH - 32A | MARCH - 31B | MARCH - 31B | NORWICH - 32A | | CAMBRIDGE - 31A | MARCH - 31B | MARCH - 31B | IPSWICH - 32B |
| Aug-57 | NORWICH - 32A | MARCH - 31B | MARCH - 31B | NORWICH - 32A | | CAMBRIDGE - 31A | MARCH - 31B | MARCH - 31B | IPSWICH - 32B |
| Jan-58 | NORWICH - 32A | **2/58: W/D** | **12/57: W/D** | NORWICH - 32A | | **2/58: W/D** | MARCH - 31B | MARCH - 31B | IPSWICH - 32B |
| Aug-58 | NORWICH - 32A | | | NORWICH - 32A | | | MARCH - 31B | MARCH - 31B | IPSWICH - 32B |
| Jan-59 | NORWICH - 32A | | | **10/58: W/D** | | | MARCH - 31B | MARCH - 31B | IPSWICH - 32B |
| Aug-59 | NORWICH - 32A | | | | | | MARCH - 31B | **9/59: K.LYNN - 31C** | IPSWICH - 32B |
| Nov-59 | NORWICH - 32A | | | | | | MARCH - 31B | KINGS LYNN - 31C | IPSWICH - 32B |
| Jan-60 | NORWICH - 32A | | | | | | MARCH - 31B | KINGS LYNN - 31C | **12/59: CAMB - 31A** |
| Apr-60 | **4/60: W/D** | | | | | | MARCH - 31B | KINGS LYNN - 31C | CAMBRIDGE - 31A |
| Aug-60 | | | | | | | MARCH - 31B | KINGS LYNN - 31C | CAMBRIDGE - 31A |
| Nov-60 | | | | | | | MARCH - 31B | KINGS LYNN - 31C | CAMBRIDGE - 31A |

| | 65579 | 65580 | 65581 | 65582 | 65583 | 65584 | 65585 | 65586 | 65587 |
|---|---|---|---|---|---|---|---|---|---|
| Aug-50 | SOUTH LYNN - 31D | SOUTH LYNN - 31D | YARMOUTH(B) - 32F | SOUTH LYNN - 31D | MARCH - 31B | MARCH - 31B | CAMBRIDGE - 31A | MELTON C - 32G | CAMBRIDGE - 31A |
| Jan-51 | SOUTH LYNN - 31D | **1/51: CAMB - 31A** | YARMOUTH(B) - 32F | SOUTH LYNN - 31D | MARCH - 31B | MARCH - 31B | CAMBRIDGE - 31A | MELTON C - 32G | CAMBRIDGE - 31A |
| Aug-51 | **6/51: MARCH - 31B** | **9/51: IPS - 32B** | YARMOUTH(B) - 32F | **10/51: K.LYNN - 31C** | MARCH - 31B | MARCH - 31B | CAMBRIDGE - 31A | MELTON C - 32G | CAMBRIDGE - 31A |
| Jan-52 | MARCH - 31B | **3/52: MARCH - 31B** | YARMOUTH(B) - 32F | KINGS LYNN - 31C | MARCH - 31B | MARCH - 31B | CAMBRIDGE - 31A | **11/51: NOR - 32A** | CAMBRIDGE - 31A |
| Aug-52 | MARCH - 31B | MARCH - 31B | YARMOUTH(B) - 32F | KINGS LYNN - 31C | MARCH - 31B | **6/52: CAMB - 31A** | **6/52: K.LYNN - 31C** | **9/52: LOW - 32C** | **9/52: STRAT - 30A** |
| Jan-53 | **3/53: S.LYNN - 31D** | MARCH - 31B | YARMOUTH(B) - 32F | KINGS LYNN - 31C | MARCH - 31B | **11/52: MARCH - 31B** | KINGS LYNN - 31C | **1/53: NOR - 32A** | STRATFORD - 30A |
| Aug-53 | SOUTH LYNN - 31D | **11/53: BURY - 31E** | YARMOUTH(B) - 32F | KINGS LYNN - 31C | **11/53: BURY - 31E** | MARCH - 31B | KINGS LYNN - 31C | **7/53: YAR (B) - 32F** | STRATFORD - 30A |
| Jan-54 | SOUTH LYNN - 31D | **2/54: CAMB - 31A** | YARMOUTH(B) - 32F | KINGS LYNN - 31C | **2/54: MARCH - 31B** | MARCH - 31B | **11/53: CAMB - 31A** | YARMOUTH(B) - 32F | **1/54: CAMB - 31A** |
| Aug-54 | SOUTH LYNN - 31D | CAMBRIDGE - 31A | YARMOUTH(B) - 32F | KINGS LYNN - 31C | MARCH - 31B | MARCH - 31B | CAMBRIDGE - 31A | YARMOUTH(B) - 32F | CAMBRIDGE - 31A |
| Jan-55 | **11/54: W/D** | CAMBRIDGE - 31A | YARMOUTH(B) - 32F | KINGS LYNN - 31C | MARCH - 31B | MARCH - 31B | **11/54: W/D** | YARMOUTH(B) - 32F | CAMBRIDGE - 31A |
| Aug-55 | | CAMBRIDGE - 31A | YARMOUTH(B) - 32F | KINGS LYNN - 31C | MARCH - 31B | MARCH - 31B | | YARMOUTH(B) - 32F | CAMBRIDGE - 31A |
| Jan-56 | | CAMBRIDGE - 31A | YARMOUTH(B) - 32F | KINGS LYNN - 31C | MARCH - 31B | **11/55: S.LYNN - 31D** | | YARMOUTH(B) - 32F | CAMBRIDGE - 31A |
| Aug-56 | | CAMBRIDGE - 31A | YARMOUTH(B) - 32F | KINGS LYNN - 31C | MARCH - 31B | SOUTH LYNN - 31D | | YARMOUTH(B) - 32F | CAMBRIDGE - 31A |
| Jan-57 | | CAMBRIDGE - 31A | YARMOUTH(B) - 32F | KINGS LYNN - 31C | MARCH - 31B | SOUTH LYNN - 31D | | YARMOUTH(B) - 32F | CAMBRIDGE - 31A |
| Aug-57 | | CAMBRIDGE - 31A | YARMOUTH(B) - 32F | KINGS LYNN - 31C | MARCH - 31B | SOUTH LYNN - 31D | | YARMOUTH(B) - 32F | CAMBRIDGE - 31A |
| Jan-58 | | CAMBRIDGE - 31A | YARMOUTH(B) - 32F | KINGS LYNN - 31C | MARCH - 31B | SOUTH LYNN - 31D | | YARMOUTH(B) - 32F | CAMBRIDGE - 31A |
| Aug-58 | | CAMBRIDGE - 31A | YARMOUTH(B) - 32F | KINGS LYNN - 31C | MARCH - 31B | **10/58: MARCH - 31B** | | YARMOUTH(B) - 32F | CAMBRIDGE - 31A |
| Jan-59 | | CAMBRIDGE - 31A | **3/59: NOR - 32A** | KINGS LYNN - 31C | MARCH - 31B | MARCH - 31B | | **3/59: NOR - 32A** | **11/58: W/D** |
| Aug-59 | | CAMBRIDGE - 31A | NORWICH - 32A | KINGS LYNN - 31C | MARCH - 31B | MARCH - 31B | | NORWICH - 32A | |
| Nov-59 | | **11/59: W/D** | NORWICH - 32A | KINGS LYNN - 31C | MARCH - 31B | **11/59: K.LYNN - 31C** | | NORWICH - 32A | |
| Jan-60 | | | NORWICH - 32A | KINGS LYNN - 31C | MARCH - 31B | KINGS LYNN - 31C | | NORWICH - 32A | |
| Apr-60 | | | NORWICH - 32A | KINGS LYNN - 31C | MARCH - 31B | **2/60: W/D** | | NORWICH - 32A | |
| Aug-60 | | | NORWICH - 32A | **9/60: CAMB - 31A** | MARCH - 31B | | | NORWICH - 32A | |
| Nov-60 | | | NORWICH - 32A | CAMBRIDGE - 31A | MARCH - 31B | | | NORWICH - 32A | |

## J24 0-6-0 (1894)

| | 65588 | 65589 | 65600 | 65601 | 65604 | 65611 | 65614 | 65615 | 65617 |
|---|---|---|---|---|---|---|---|---|---|
| Aug-50 | SOUTHLYNN-31D | CAMBRIDGE-31A | MALTON-50F | NEWPORT-51B | NEWPORT-51B | BOROUGH GARDENS-54C | DUNDEE-62B | BOROUGH GARDENS-54C | EDINBURGH(SM)-64A |
| Jan-51 | 1/51:CAMB-31A | CAMBRIDGE-31A | 10/50:W/D | NEWPORT-51B | 12/50:W/D | 10/50:W/D | DUNDEE-62B | BOROUGH GARDENS-54C | EDINBURGH(SM)-64A |
| Aug-51 | 11/51:STRAT-30A | CAMBRIDGE-31A | | NEWPORT-51B | | | 5/51:W/D | BOROUGH GARDENS-54C | EDINBURGH(SM)-64A |
| Jan-52 | 3/52:PLAIS-33A | CAMBRIDGE-31A | | 12/51:W/D | | | | 11/51:W/D | 12/51:W/D |
| Aug-52 | PLAISTOW-33A | CAMBRIDGE-31A | | | | | | | |
| Jan-53 | PLAISTOW-33A | CAMBRIDGE-31A | | | | | | | |
| Aug-53 | PLAISTOW-33A | CAMBRIDGE-31A | | | | | | | |
| Jan-54 | PLAISTOW-33A | CAMBRIDGE-31A | | | | | | | |
| Aug-54 | PLAISTOW-33A | 10/54:BURY-31E | | | | | | | |
| Jan-55 | PLAISTOW-33A | 1/55:CAMB-31A | | | | | | | |
| Aug-55 | 6/55:NOR-32A | CAMBRIDGE-31A | | | | | | | |
| Jan-56 | NORWICH-32A | CAMBRIDGE-31A | | | | | | | |
| Aug-56 | NORWICH-32A | CAMBRIDGE-31A | | | | | | | |
| Jan-57 | 3/57:MELTON-32G | CAMBRIDGE-31A | | | | | | | |
| Aug-57 | MELTON C-32G | CAMBRIDGE-31A | | | | | | | |
| Jan-58 | MELTON C-32G | CAMBRIDGE-31A | | | | | | | |
| Aug-58 | 10/58:LOW-32C | CAMBRIDGE-31A | | | | | | | |
| Jan-59 | LOWESTOFT-32C | CAMBRIDGE-31A | | | | | | | |
| Aug-59 | LOWESTOFT-32C | CAMBRIDGE-31A | | | | | | | |
| Nov-59 | LOWESTOFT-32C | CAMBRIDGE-31A | | | | | | | |
| Jan-60 | LOWESTOFT-32C | CAMBRIDGE-31A | | | | | | | |
| Apr-60 | LOWESTOFT-32C | CAMBRIDGE-31A | | | | | | | |
| Aug-60 | 6/60:NOR-32A | CAMBRIDGE-31A | | | | | | | |
| Nov-60 | NORWICH-32A | CAMBRIDGE-31A | | | | | | | |

| | 65619 | 65621 | 65622 | 65623 | 65624 | 65627 | 65628 | 65631 | 65636 |
|---|---|---|---|---|---|---|---|---|---|
| Aug-50 | YORK-50A | WHITBY-50G | DUNDEE-62B | EDINBURGH(SM)-64A | WHITBY-50G | WHITBY-50G | WHITBY-50G | MALTON-50F | MALTON-50F |
| Jan-51 | YORK-50A | 9/50:W/D | DUNDEE-62B | EDINBURGH(SM)-64A | 9/50:W/D | 12/50:W/D | 11/50:W/D | 11/50:W/D | 12/50:W/D |
| Aug-51 | YORK-50A | | 2/51:W/D | 6/51:W/D | | | | | |
| Jan-52 | 11/51:W/D | | | | | | | | |

## J25 0-6-0 (1898)

| | 65640 | 65642 | 65644 | 65645 | 65647 | 65648 | 65650 | 65651 | 65653 |
|---|---|---|---|---|---|---|---|---|---|
| Aug-50 | MALTON-50F | MALTON-50F | MALTON-50F | NORTHALLERTON-51J | DAIRYCOATES-53A | DARLINGTON-51A | DARLINGTON-51A | DAIRYCOATES-53A | KIRKBYSTEPHEN-51H |
| Jan-51 | MALTON-50F | 11/50:W/D | MALTON-50F | NORTHALLERTON-51J | DAIRYCOATES-53A | DARLINGTON-51A | DARLINGTON-51A | 9/50:W/D | KIRKBYSTEPHEN-51H |
| Aug-51 | 4/51:W/D | | MALTON-50F | NORTHALLERTON-51J | 4/51:SELBY-50C | 9/51:MALT-50F | 9/51:YORK-50A | | 5/51:W/D |
| Jan-52 | | | 9/51:W/D | NORTHALLERTON-51J | SELBY-50C | MALTON-50F | YORK-50A | | |
| Aug-52 | | | | NORTHALLERTON-51J | 7/52:WHITBY-50G | MALTON-50F | YORK-50A | | |
| Jan-53 | | | | NORTHALLERTON-51J | WHITBY-50G | MALTON-50F | YORK-50A | | |
| Aug-53 | | | | 5/53:DARL-51A | WHITBY-50G | MALTON-50F | YORK-50A | | |
| Jan-54 | | | | 2/54:B.GDNS-54C | WHITBY-50G | MALTON-50F | YORK-50A | | |
| Aug-54 | | | | BOROUGH GARDENS-54C | WHITBY-50G | MALTON-50F | YORK-50A | | |
| Jan-55 | | | | BOROUGH GARDENS-54C | WHITBY-50G | 1/55:YORK-50A | YORK-50A | | |
| Aug-55 | | | | BOROUGH GARDENS-54C | 9/55:YORK-50A | YORK-50A | 5/55:N.HILL-50B | | |
| Jan-56 | | | | BOROUGH GARDENS-54C | YORK-50A | 1/56:N.HILL-50B | NEVILLE HILL-50B | | |
| Aug-56 | | | | BOROUGH GARDENS-54C | 4/56:W/D | NEVILLE HILL-50B | NEVILLE HILL-50B | | |
| Jan-57 | | | | BOROUGH GARDENS-54C | | NEVILLE HILL-50B | NEVILLE HILL-50B | | |
| Aug-57 | | | | 9/57:T.DCK-54B | | 6/57:WHITBY-50G | 9/57:W/D | | |
| Jan-58 | | | | TYNE DOCK-54B | | WHITBY-50G | | | |
| Aug-58 | | | | TYNE DOCK-54B | | 9/58:W/D | | | |
| Jan-59 | | | | TYNE DOCK-52H | | | | | |
| Aug-59 | | | | TYNE DOCK-52H | | | | | |
| Nov-59 | | | | TYNE DOCK-52H | | | | | |
| Jan-60 | | | | TYNE DOCK-52H | | | | | |
| Apr-60 | | | | TYNE DOCK-52H | | | | | |
| Aug-60 | | | | TYNE DOCK-52H | | | | | |
| Nov-60 | | | | 10/60:GHD-52A | | | | | |

| | 65654 | 65655 | 65656 | 65657 | 65659 | 65660 | 65661 | 65662 | 65663 |
|---|---|---|---|---|---|---|---|---|---|
| Aug-50 | DAIRYCOATES-53A | KIRKBYSTEPHEN-51H | YORK-50A | BOROUGH GARDENS-54C | W.AUCKLAND-51F | HAVERTONHILL-51G | BOROUGH GARDENS-54C | W.AUCKLAND-51F | DAIRYCOATES-53A |
| Jan-51 | 1/51:SUND-54A | KIRKBYSTEPHEN-51H | 10/50:MALT-50F | BOROUGH GARDENS-54C | W.AUCKLAND-51F | HAVERTONHILL-51G | BOROUGH GARDENS-54C | W.AUCKLAND-51F | DAIRYCOATES-53A |
| Aug-51 | 6/51:STOCK-51E | KIRKBYSTEPHEN-51H | MALTON-50F | BOROUGH GARDENS-54C | 2/51:W/D | HAVERTONHILL-51G | BOROUGH GARDENS-54C | W.AUCKLAND-51F | 4/51:SELB-50C |
| Jan-52 | STOCKTON-51E | KIRKBYSTEPHEN-51H | MALTON-50F | BOROUGH GARDENS-54C | | HAVERTONHILL-51G | BOROUGH GARDENS-54C | W.AUCKLAND-51F | SELBY-50C |
| Aug-52 | STOCKTON-51E | KIRKBYSTEPHEN-51H | MALTON-50F | BOROUGH GARDENS-54C | | HAVERTONHILL-51G | BOROUGH GARDENS-54C | W.AUCKLAND-51F | 7/52:WHITBY-50G |
| Jan-53 | STOCKTON-51E | KIRKBYSTEPHEN-51H | MALTON-50F | BOROUGH GARDENS-54C | | 1/53:W/D | BOROUGH GARDENS-54C | W.AUCKLAND-51F | WHITBY-50G |
| Aug-53 | STOCKTON-51E | KIRKBYSTEPHEN-51H | MALTON-50F | BOROUGH GARDENS-54C | | | BOROUGH GARDENS-54C | W.AUCKLAND-51F | WHITBY-50G |
| Jan-54 | 10/53:YORK-50A | KIRKBYSTEPHEN-51H | MALTON-50F | BOROUGH GARDENS-54C | | | BOROUGH GARDENS-54C | W.AUCKLAND-51F | WHITBY-50G |
| Aug-54 | YORK-50A | KIRKBYSTEPHEN-51H | MALTON-50F | BOROUGH GARDENS-54C | | | 10/54:W/D | W.AUCKLAND-51F | WHITBY-50G |
| Jan-55 | YORK-50A | 1/55:DARL-51A | 1/55:YORK-50A | BOROUGH GARDENS-54C | | | | W.AUCKLAND-51F | WHITBY-50G |
| Aug-55 | NEVILLE HILL-50B | 7/55:DAIRY-53A | 12/55:N.HILL-50B | BOROUGH GARDENS-54C | | | | W.AUCKLAND-51F | WHITBY-50G |
| Jan-56 | NEVILLE HILL-50B | DAIRYCOATES-53A | 2/56:HTN-52B | BOROUGH GARDENS-54C | | | | 12/55:DARL-51A | WHITBY-50G |
| Aug-56 | NEVILLE HILL-50B | DAIRYCOATES-53A | HEATON-52B | BOROUGH GARDENS-54C | | | | 7/56:SUND-51A | WHITBY-50G |
| Jan-57 | 6/57:YORK-50A | DAIRYCOATES-53A | HEATON-52B | BOROUGH GARDENS-54C | | | | SUNDERLAND-54A | WHITBY-50G |
| Aug-57 | 7/57:DAIRY-53A | DAIRYCOATES-53A | HEATON-52B | BOROUGH GARDENS-54C | | | | SUNDERLAND-54A | 6/57:DAIRY-53A |
| Jan-58 | DAIRYCOATES-53A | DAIRYCOATES-53A | HEATON-52B | BOROUGH GARDENS-54C | | | | SUNDERLAND-54A | 9/57:SPRING-53C |
| Aug-58 | 5/58:W/D | DAIRYCOATES-53A | HEATON-52B | BOROUGH GARDENS-54C | | | | SUNDERLAND-54A | 6/58:N.HILL-50B |
| Jan-59 | | 12/58:W/D | 2/59:GHD-52A | 11/58:W/D | | | | SUNDERLAND-52G | 2/59:SELBY-50C |
| Aug-59 | | | 8/59:W/D | | | | | SUNDERLAND-52G | 8/59:S.BLYTH-52F |
| Nov-59 | | | | | | | | SUNDERLAND-52G | SOUTHBLYTH-52F |
| Jan-60 | | | | | | | | SUNDERLAND-52G | SOUTHBLYTH-52F |
| Apr-60 | | | | | | | | SUNDERLAND-52G | SOUTHBLYTH-52F |
| Aug-60 | | | | | | | | 5/60:W/D | 5/60:BLAY-52C |
| Nov-60 | | | | | | | | | BLAYDON-52C |

| Date | 65664 | 65666 | 65667 | 65670 | 65671 | 65672 | 65673 | 65675 | 65676 |
|---|---|---|---|---|---|---|---|---|---|
| Aug-50 | DARLINGTON-51A | TYNEDOCK-54B | SPRINGHEAD-53C | TYNEDOCK-54B | W.AUCKLAND-51F | DARLINGTON-51A | K.STEPHEN-51H | W.AUCKLAND-51F | B.GARDENS-54C |
| Jan-51 | DARLINGTON-51A | TYNEDOCK-54B | 3/51: HEX-52C | TYNEDOCK-54B | 12/50: MALT-50F | DARLINGTON-51A | K.STEPHEN-51H | W.AUCKLAND-51F | B.GARDENS-54C |
| Aug-51 | DARLINGTON-51A | TYNEDOCK-54B | HEXHAM-52C | TYNEDOCK-54B | MALTON-50F | 5/51: W/D | K.STEPHEN-51H | W.AUCKLAND-51F | B.GARDENS-54C |
| Jan-52 | DARLINGTON-51A | TYNEDOCK-54B | HEXHAM-52C | TYNEDOCK-54B | MALTON-50F | | K.STEPHEN-51H | 10/51: YORK-50A | B.GARDENS-54C |
| Aug-52 | 9/52: W/D | TYNEDOCK-54B | HEXHAM-52C | TYNEDOCK-54B | MALTON-50F | | K.STEPHEN-51H | 5/52: SELBY-50C | B.GARDENS-54C |
| Jan-53 | | TYNEDOCK-54B | 10/52: N.BLYHTE: 52F | TYNEDOCK-54B | MALTON-50F | | K.STEPHEN-51H | SELBY-50C | B.GARDENS-54C |
| Aug-53 | | TYNEDOCK-54B | NORTHBLYTH-52F | TYNEDOCK-54B | MALTON-50F | | K.STEPHEN-51H | SELBY-50C | B.GARDENS-54C |
| Jan-54 | | TYNEDOCK-54B | NORTHBLYTH-52F | TYNEDOCK-54B | MALTON-50F | | K.STEPHEN-51H | SELBY-50C | 1/54: W/D |
| Aug-54 | | TYNEDOCK-54B | 9/54: W/D | TYNEDOCK-54B | 9/54: W/D | | K.STEPHEN-51H | 12/54: WHITBY-50G | |
| Jan-55 | | TYNEDOCK-54B | | TYNEDOCK-54B | | | 7/55: STAR-50D | 1/55: YORK-50A | |
| Aug-55 | | TYNEDOCK-54B | | TYNEDOCK-54B | | | STARBECK-50D | YORK-50A | |
| Jan-56 | | TYNEDOCK-54B | | TYNEDOCK-54B | | | STARBECK-50D | YORK-50A | |
| Aug-56 | | TYNEDOCK-54B | | TYNEDOCK-54B | | | STARBECK-50D | 6/56: HTN-52B | |
| Jan-57 | | TYNEDOCK-54B | | TYNEDOCK-54B | | | STARBECK-50D | 2/57: BLAY-52C | |
| Aug-57 | | TYNEDOCK-54B | | TYNEDOCK-54B | | | STARBECK-50D | BLAYDON-52C | |
| Jan-58 | | TYNEDOCK-54B | | TYNEDOCK-54B | | | 6/58: W/D | BLAYDON-52C | |
| Aug-58 | | 7/58:SUND-54A | | TYNEDOCK-54B | | | | BLAYDON-52C | |
| Jan-59 | | SUNDERLAND-52G | | TYNEDOCK-52H | | | | 12/58: GHD-52A | |
| Aug-59 | | SUNDERLAND-52G | | TYNEDOCK-52H | | | | 3/59: W/D | |
| Nov-59 | | SUNDERLAND-52G | | TYNEDOCK-52H | | | | | |
| Jan-60 | | SUNDERLAND-52G | | TYNEDOCK-52H | | | | | |
| Apr-60 | | SUNDERLAND-52G | | TYNEDOCK-52H | | | | | |
| Aug-60 | | 6/60:W/D | | TYNEDOCK-52H | | | | | |
| Nov-60 | | | | TYNEDOCK-52H | | | | | |

| Date | 65677 | 65679 | 65680 | 65683 | 65685 | 65686 | 65687 | 65688 | 65689 |
|---|---|---|---|---|---|---|---|---|---|
| Aug-50 | DARLINGTON-51A | YORK-50A | B.GARDENS-54C | W.AUCKLAND-51F | B.GARDENS-54C | B.GARDENS-54C | MIDDLESBROUGH-51D | DARLINGTON-51A | STOCKTON-51E |
| Jan-51 | DARLINGTON-51A | YORK-50A | B.GARDENS-54C | W.AUCKLAND-51F | B.GARDENS-54C | B.GARDENS-54C | 3/51: DARL-51A | DARLINGTON-51A | STOCKTON-51E |
| Aug-51 | DARLINGTON-51A | 5/51: W/D | B.GARDENS-54C | W.AUCKLAND-51F | B.GARDENS-54C | B.GARDENS-54C | DARLINGTON-51A | DARLINGTON-51A | STOCKTON-51E |
| Jan-52 | 12/51: YORK-50A | | B.GARDENS-54C | 10/51: YORK-50A | B.GARDENS-54C | B.GARDENS-54C | 12/51: YORK-50A | DARLINGTON-51A | STOCKTON-51E |
| Aug-52 | YORK-50A | | B.GARDENS-54C | 5/52: SELBY-50C | B.GARDENS-54C | B.GARDENS-54C | YORK-50A | DARLINGTON-51A | STOCKTON-51E |
| Jan-53 | YORK-50A | | B.GARDENS-54C | SELBY-50C | B.GARDENS-54C | B.GARDENS-54C | YORK-50A | DARLINGTON-51A | STOCKTON-51E |
| Aug-53 | YORK-50A | | B.GARDENS-54C | SELBY-50C | B.GARDENS-54C | B.GARDENS-54C | YORK-50A | DARLINGTON-51A | STOCKTON-51E |
| Jan-54 | YORK-50A | | B.GARDENS-54C | SELBY-50C | 10/53: MALT-50F | B.GARDENS-54C | YORK-50A | DARLINGTON-51A | STOCKTON-51E |
| Aug-54 | YORK-50A | | 6/54: T.DOCK-54B | SELBY-50C | MALTON-50F | B.GARDENS-54C | YORK-50A | 9/54: W/D | 5/54: W/D |
| Jan-55 | YORK-50A | | TYNEDOCK-54B | SELBY-50C | 1/55: WHIT-50G | 11/54: W/D | YORK-50A | | |
| Aug-55 | YORK-50A | | TYNEDOCK-54B | 7/55: N.HILL-50B | 9/55: YORK-50A | | YORK-50A | | |
| Jan-56 | 3/56:SPRING-53C | | TYNEDOCK-54B | NEVILLEHILL-50B | YORK-50A | | 11/55: WHIT-50G | | |
| Aug-56 | 4/56: DAIRY-53A | | TYNEDOCK-54B | NEVILLEHILL-50B | YORK-50A | | 6/56: HTN-52B | | |
| Jan-57 | DAIRYCOATES-53A | | TYNEDOCK-54B | NEVILLEHILL-50B | 6/57: DAIRY-53A | | 1/57: BLAY-52C | | |
| Aug-57 | DAIRYCOATES-53A | | 9/57: W/D | 6/57: YORK-50A | 9/57: SPRING-53C | | BLAYDON-52C | | |
| Jan-58 | DAIRYCOATES-53A | | | YORK-50A | 6/58: N.HILL-50B | | 11/57: GHD-52A | | |
| Aug-58 | DAIRYCOATES-53A | | | 6/58: W/D | 2/59: SELBY-50C | | GATESHEAD-52A | | |
| Jan-59 | 10/58: W/D | | | | SELBY-50C | | 12/58: S.BLYTH-52F | | |
| Aug-59 | | | | | 9/59: W/D | | 8/59: W/D | | |
| Nov-59 | | | | | | | | | |
| Jan-60 | | | | | | | | | |
| Apr-60 | | | | | | | | | |
| Aug-60 | | | | | | | | | |
| Nov-60 | | | | | | | | | |

| Date | 65690 | 65691 | 65692 | 65693 | 65694 | 65695 | 65696 | 65697 | 65698 |
|---|---|---|---|---|---|---|---|---|---|
| Aug-50 | DAIRYCOATES-53A | DARLINGTON-51A | DARLINGTON-51A | NORTHALLERTON-51J | TYNEDOCK-54B | K.STEPHEN-51H | DARLINGTON-51A | TWEEDMOUTH-52D | DAIRYCOATES-53A |
| Jan-51 | 1/51: WHIT-50G | 3/51: W.AUCK-51F | DARLINGTON-51A | NORTHALLERTON-51J | TYNEDOCK-54B | K.STEPHEN-51H | 11/50: W. HPL-51C | TWEEDMOUTH-52D | 10/50: CUD-53E |
| Aug-51 | WHITBY-50G | 9/51: YORK-50A | DARLINGTON-51A | NORTHALLERTON-51J | TYNEDOCK-54B | K.STEPHEN-51H | W.HARTLEPOOL-51C | TWEEDMOUTH-52D | 4/51: SELBY-50C |
| Jan-52 | WHITBY-50G | YORK-50A | DARLINGTON-51A | NORTHALLERTON-51J | TYNEDOCK-54B | K.STEPHEN-51H | W.HARTLEPOOL-51C | TWEEDMOUTH-52D | SELBY-50C |
| Aug-52 | WHITBY-50G | YORK-50A | DARLINGTON-51A | NORTHALLERTON-51J | TYNEDOCK-54B | K.STEPHEN-51H | W.HARTLEPOOL-51C | 7/52: HTN-52B | SELBY-50C |
| Jan-53 | WHITBY-50G | YORK-50A | DARLINGTON-51A | NORTHALLERTON-51J | TYNEDOCK-54B | K.STEPHEN-51H | W.HARTLEPOOL-51C | HEATON-52B | SELBY-50C |
| Aug-53 | WHITBY-50G | YORK-50A | DARLINGTON-51A | NORTHALLERTON-51J | TYNEDOCK-54B | K.STEPHEN-51H | 8/53: W.AUK-51F | 8/53: W.AUK-51F | SELBY-50C |
| Jan-54 | WHITBY-50G | YORK-50A | DARLINGTON-51A | NORTHALLERTON-51J | TYNEDOCK-54B | K.STEPHEN-51H | W.AUCKLAND-51F | W.AUCKLAND-51F | SELBY-50C |
| Aug-54 | WHITBY-50G | YORK-50A | 3/54: W/D | 4/54: DARL-51A | TYNEDOCK-54B | K.STEPHEN-51H | 11/54: B.GDNS-54C | W.AUCKLAND-51F | SELBY-50C |
| Jan-55 | WHITBY-50G | YORK-50A | | DARLINGTON-51A | 11/54: W/D | K.STEPHEN-51H | 12/54: DARL-51A | 12/54: B.GDNS-54C | SELBY-50C |
| Aug-55 | WHITBY-50G | YORK-50A | | 7/55: DAIRY-53A | | 7/55: DAIRY-53A | 7/55: B.GDNS-54C | B.GARDENS-54C | SELBY-50C |
| Jan-56 | WHITBY-50G | YORK-50A | | DAIRYCOATES-53A | | DAIRYCOATES-53A | 12/55: S.BLYTH-52F | B.GARDENS-54C | SELBY-50C |
| Aug-56 | WHITBY-50G | YORK-50A | | DAIRYCOATES-53A | | DAIRYCOATES-53A | S.BLYTH-52F | B.GARDENS-54C | SELBY-50C |
| Jan-57 | WHITBY-50G | YORK-50A | | DAIRYCOATES-53A | | DAIRYCOATES-53A | S.BLYTH-52F | B.GARDENS-54C | SELBY-50C |
| Aug-57 | WHITBY-50G | 6/57: DAIRY-53A | | DAIRYCOATES-53A | | 10/57: T.DCK-54B | S.BLYTH-52F | B.GARDENS-54C | SELBY-50C |
| Jan-58 | WHITBY-50G | DAIRYCOATES-53A | | DAIRYCOATES-53A | | TYNEDOCK-54B | S.BLYTH-52F | B.GARDENS-54C | SELBY-50C |
| Aug-58 | WHITBY-50G | DAIRYCOATES-53A | | DAIRYCOATES-53A | | TYNEDOCK-52H | S.BLYTH-52F | B.GARDENS-54C | 6/58: YORK-50A |
| Jan-59 | WHITBY-50G | DAIRYCOATES-53A | | DAIRYCOATES-53A | | TYNEDOCK-52H | 12/58: W/D | 12/58: W/D | YORK-50A |
| Aug-59 | WHITBY-50G | DAIRYCOATES-53A | | DAIRYCOATES-53A | | TYNEDOCK-52H | | | YORK-50A |
| Nov-59 | WHITBY-50G | DAIRYCOATES-53A | | DAIRYCOATES-53A | | TYNEDOCK-52H | | | 9/59: W/D |
| Jan-60 | WHITBY-50G | DAIRYCOATES-53A | | DAIRYCOATES-53A | | TYNEDOCK-52H | | | |
| Apr-60 | WHITBY-50G | DAIRYCOATES-50B | | DAIRYCOATES-50B | | TYNEDOCK-52H | | | |
| Aug-60 | WHITBY-50G | DAIRYCOATES-50B | | DAIRYCOATES-50B | | TYNEDOCK-52H | | | |
| Nov-60 | WHITBY-50G | DAIRYCOATES-50B | | DAIRYCOATES-50B | | TYNEDOCK-52H | | | |

| Date | 65699 | 65700 | 65702 | 65705 | 65706 | 65708 | 65710 | 65712 | 65713 |
|---|---|---|---|---|---|---|---|---|---|
| Aug-50 | DAIRYCOATES-53A | YORK-50A | DARLINGTON-51A | SPRINGHEAD-53C | W.AUCKLAND-51F | YORK-50A | MIDDLESBROUGH-51D | DAIRYCOATES-53A | DAIRYCOATES-53A |
| Jan-51 | 1/51: T.DCK-54B | YORK-50A | DARLINGTON-51A | 1/51: SUND-54A | W.AUCKLAND-51F | 10/50: MALT-50F | MIDDLESBROUGH-51D | 10/50: HTN-52B | 1/51: T.DCK-54B |
| Aug-51 | TYNEDOCK-54B | YORK-50A | DARLINGTON-51A | 6/51: B.GDNS-54C | W.AUCKLAND-51F | MALTON-50F | MIDDLESBROUGH-51D | 3/51: B.GDNS-54C | TYNEDOCK-54B |
| Jan-52 | TYNEDOCK-54B | YORK-50A | DARLINGTON-51A | B.GARDENS-54C | W.AUCKLAND-51F | MALTON-50F | 11/51: DARL-51A | 6/51: DARL-51A | TYNEDOCK-54B |
| Aug-52 | TYNEDOCK-54B | YORK-50A | DARLINGTON-51A | B.GARDENS-54C | W.AUCKLAND-51F | MALTON-50F | DARLINGTON-51A | DARLINGTON-51A | TYNEDOCK-54B |
| Jan-53 | TYNEDOCK-54B | YORK-50A | DARLINGTON-51A | B.GARDENS-54C | W.AUCKLAND-51F | 11/52: DARL-51A | DARLINGTON-51A | DARLINGTON-51A | TYNEDOCK-54B |
| Aug-53 | TYNEDOCK-54B | YORK-50A | DARLINGTON-51A | B.GARDENS-54C | W.AUCKLAND-51F | DARLINGTON-51A | DARLINGTON-51A | DARLINGTON-51A | TYNEDOCK-54B |
| Jan-54 | TYNEDOCK-54B | YORK-50A | DARLINGTON-51A | B.GARDENS-54C | 1/54: W.AUCK-51F | 1/54: W.AUCK-51F | 1/54: W.AUCK-51F | DARLINGTON-51A | TYNEDOCK-54B |
| Aug-54 | TYNEDOCK-54B | YORK-50A | 4/54: N'TON-51J | B.GARDENS-54C | W.AUCKLAND-51F | DARLINGTON-51A | W.AUCKLAND-51F | DARLINGTON-51A | TYNEDOCK-54B |
| Jan-55 | TYNEDOCK-54B | YORK-50A | 11/54: B.GDNS:54C | 10/54: W/D | 10/54: N.BLYTH-52F | 11/54: W/D | W.AUCKLAND-51F | 11/54: B.GDNS:54C | TYNEDOCK-54B |
| Aug-55 | TYNEDOCK-54B | YORK-50A | B.GARDENS-54C | | NORTHBLYTH-52F | | W.AUCKLAND-51F | B.GARDENS-54C | TYNEDOCK-54B |
| Jan-56 | TYNEDOCK-54B | 12/55: B.GDNS-54C | B.GARDENS-54C | | NORTHBLYTH-52F | | 11/55: SUND-54A | B.GARDENS-54C | TYNEDOCK-54B |
| Aug-56 | TYNEDOCK-54B | B.GARDENS-54C | B.GARDENS-54C | | NORTHBLYTH-52F | | 5/56: W/D | B.GARDENS-54C | TYNEDOCK-54B |
| Jan-57 | TYNEDOCK-54B | B.GARDENS-54C | B.GARDENS-54C | | NORTHBLYTH-52F | | | B.GARDENS-54C | TYNEDOCK-54B |
| Aug-57 | TYNEDOCK-54B | 9/57: W.HPL-51C | B.GARDENS-54C | | NORTHBLYTH-52F | | | B.GARDENS-54C | TYNEDOCK-54B |
| Jan-58 | TYNEDOCK-54B | W.HARTLEPOOL-51C | B.GARDENS-54C | | NORTHBLYTH-52F | | | B.GARDENS-54C | TYNEDOCK-54B |
| Aug-58 | 3/58: W/D | W.HARTLEPOOL-51C | B.GARDENS-54C | | NORTHBLYTH-52F | | | B.GARDENS-54C | TYNEDOCK-54B |
| Jan-59 | | 4/59: GHD-52A | B.GARDENS-52J | | SOUTHBLYTH-52F | | | B.GARDENS-52J | TYNEDOCK-52H |
| Aug-59 | | 8/59: W/D | 6/59: GHD-52A | | SOUTHBLYTH-52F | | | 6/59: GHD-52A | TYNEDOCK-52H |
| Nov-59 | | | 10/59: W/D | | SOUTHBLYTH-52F | | | GATESHEAD-52A | TYNEDOCK-52H |
| Jan-60 | | | | | 12/59: W/D | | | GATESHEAD-52A | TYNEDOCK-52H |
| Apr-60 | | | | | | | | GATESHEAD-52A | TYNEDOCK-52H |
| Aug-60 | | | | | | | | GATESHEAD-52A | TYNEDOCK-52H |
| Nov-60 | | | | | | | | 9/60: W/D | 8/60: W/D |

| | 65714 | 65716 | 65717 | 65718 | 65720 | 65723 | 65725 | 65726 | 65727 |
|---|---|---|---|---|---|---|---|---|---|
| Aug-50 | CUDWORTH-53E | TYNE DOCK-54B | KIRKBYSTEPHEN-51H | STOCKTON-51E | DARLINGTON-51A | YORK-50A | NORTHALLERTON-51J | MIDDLESBROUGH-51D | TWEEDMOUTH-52D |
| Jan-51 | 10/50: MALT-50F | TYNE DOCK-54B | KIRKBYSTEPHEN-51H | STOCKTON-51E | 1/51: N'TON-51J | YORK-50A | 10/50: W/D | 3/51: DARL-51A | TWEEDMOUTH-52D |
| Aug-51 | MALTON-50F | TYNE DOCK-54B | KIRKBYSTEPHEN-51H | 5/51: W/D | NORTHALLERTON-51J | 4/51: MALT-50F | | 10/51: N'TON-51J | TWEEDMOUTH-52D |
| Jan-52 | MALTON-50F | TYNE DOCK-54B | KIRKBYSTEPHEN-51H | | NORTHALLERTON-51J | MALTON-50F | | NORTHALLERTON-51J | TWEEDMOUTH-52D |
| Aug-52 | MALTON-50F | TYNE DOCK-54B | KIRKBYSTEPHEN-51H | | NORTHALLERTON-51J | MALTON-50F | | NORTHALLERTON-51J | TWEEDMOUTH-52D |
| Jan-53 | MALTON-50F | TYNE DOCK-54B | KIRKBYSTEPHEN-51H | | NORTHALLERTON-51J | MALTON-50F | | NORTHALLERTON-51J | TWEEDMOUTH-52D |
| Aug-53 | MALTON-50F | TYNE DOCK-54B | KIRKBYSTEPHEN-51H | | NORTHALLERTON-51J | MALTON-50F | | NORTHALLERTON-51J | TWEEDMOUTH-52D |
| Jan-54 | MALTON-50F | TYNE DOCK-54B | KIRKBYSTEPHEN-51H | | NORTHALLERTON-51J | MALTON-50F | | NORTHALLERTON-51J | TWEEDMOUTH-52D |
| Aug-54 | MALTON-50F | TYNE DOCK-54B | KIRKBYSTEPHEN-51H | | NORTHALLERTON-51J | MALTON-50F | | NORTHALLERTON-51J | TWEEDMOUTH-52D |
| Jan-55 | 1/55: YORK-50A | 4/54: W/D | 12.54: T. DCK-54B | | NORTHALLERTON-51J | 1/55: YORK-50A | | NORTHALLERTON-51J | 3/55: S.BLYTH-52F |
| Aug-55 | 7/55: N. HILL-50B | | TYNE DOCK-54B | | NORTHALLERTON-51J | 3/55: W/D | | 8/55: DAIRY-53A | S.BLYTH-52F |
| Jan-56 | 11/55: YORK-50A | | TYNE DOCK-54B | | 11/55: MBRO-51D | | | DAIRYCOATES-53A | S.BLYTH-52F |
| Aug-56 | YORK-50A | | TYNE DOCK-54B | | MIDDLESBROUGH-51D | | | DAIRYCOATES-53A | S.BLYTH-52F |
| Jan-57 | 6.57: DAIRY-53A | | TYNE DOCK-54B | | MIDDLESBROUGH-51D | | | DAIRYCOATES-53A | S.BLYTH-52F |
| Aug-57 | 7/57: YORK-50A | | TYNE DOCK-54B | | MIDDLESBROUGH-51D | | | DAIRYCOATES-53A | S.BLYTH-52F |
| Jan-58 | YORK-50A | | TYNE DOCK-54B | | MIDDLESBROUGH-51D | | | DAIRYCOATES-53A | S.BLYTH-52F |
| Aug-58 | YORK-50A | | TYNE DOCK-54B | | 6/58: TBY-51L | | | 6/58: N. HILL-50B | S.BLYTH-52F |
| Jan-59 | YORK-50A | | 10/58: W/D | | THORNABY-51L | | | NEVILLE HILL-50B | S.BLYTH-52F |
| Aug-59 | YORK-50A | | | | THORNABY-51L | | | 4/59: STAR-50D | S.BLYTH-52F |
| Nov-59 | YORK-50A | | | | THORNABY-51L | | | 9/59: SUND-52G | S.BLYTH-52F |
| Jan-60 | YORK-50A | | | | THORNABY-51L | | | SUNDERLAND-52G | S.BLYTH-52F |
| Apr-60 | YORK-50A | | | | THORNABY-51L | | | SUNDERLAND-52G | S.BLYTH-52F |
| Aug-60 | YORK-50A | | | | THORNABY-51L | | | SUNDERLAND-52G | S.BLYTH-52F |
| Nov-60 | YORK-50A | | | | THORNABY-51L | | | 10/60: GHD-52A | S.BLYTH-52F |

J260-6-0(1904)

| | 65728 | 65730 | 65731 | 65732 | 65733 | 65734 | 65735 | 65736 | 65737 |
|---|---|---|---|---|---|---|---|---|---|
| Aug-50 | SPRINGHEAD-53C | NEWPORT-51B | NEWPORT-51B | NEWPORT-51B | MIDDLESBROUGH-51D | NEWPORT-51B | NEWPORT-51B | NEWPORT-51B | NEWPORT-51B |
| Jan-51 | 3/51: B. GDNS-54C | NEWPORT-51B | NEWPORT-51B | NEWPORT-51B | MIDDLESBROUGH-51D | NEWPORT-51B | NEWPORT-51B | NEWPORT-51B | NEWPORT-51B |
| Aug-51 | B.GARDENS-54C | NEWPORT-51B | NEWPORT-51B | NEWPORT-51B | MIDDLESBROUGH-51D | NEWPORT-51B | NEWPORT-51B | NEWPORT-51B | NEWPORT-51B |
| Jan-52 | B.GARDENS-54C | NEWPORT-51B | NEWPORT-51B | NEWPORT-51B | 1/52: NPT-51B | NEWPORT-51B | NEWPORT-51B | NEWPORT-51B | 12/51: M'BRO-51D |
| Aug-52 | B.GARDENS-54C | NEWPORT-51B | NEWPORT-51B | NEWPORT-51B | NEWPORT-51B | NEWPORT-51B | NEWPORT-51B | NEWPORT-51B | MIDDLESBROUGH-51D |
| Jan-53 | B.GARDENS-54C | NEWPORT-51B | NEWPORT-51B | NEWPORT-51B | NEWPORT-51B | NEWPORT-51B | NEWPORT-51B | NEWPORT-51B | MIDDLESBROUGH-51D |
| Aug-53 | B.GARDENS-54C | NEWPORT-51B | NEWPORT-51B | NEWPORT-51B | NEWPORT-51B | NEWPORT-51B | NEWPORT-51B | NEWPORT-51B | MIDDLESBROUGH-51D |
| Jan-54 | B.GARDENS-54C | NEWPORT-51B | NEWPORT-51B | NEWPORT-51B | NEWPORT-51B | NEWPORT-51B | NEWPORT-51B | NEWPORT-51B | MIDDLESBROUGH-51D |
| Aug-54 | B.GARDENS-54C | NEWPORT-51B | NEWPORT-51B | NEWPORT-51B | NEWPORT-51B | NEWPORT-51B | NEWPORT-51B | NEWPORT-51B | MIDDLESBROUGH-51D |
| Jan-55 | B.GARDENS-54C | NEWPORT-51B | NEWPORT-51B | NEWPORT-51B | NEWPORT-51B | NEWPORT-51B | NEWPORT-51B | NEWPORT-51B | MIDDLESBROUGH-51D |
| Aug-55 | B.GARDENS-54C | NEWPORT-51B | 9/55: W.AUK-51F | NEWPORT-51B | 9/55: W.AUK-51F | NEWPORT-51B | 9/55: W.AUK-51F | NEWPORT-51B | MIDDLESBROUGH-51D |
| Jan-56 | B.GARDENS-54C | NEWPORT-51B | W.AUCKLAND-51F | NEWPORT-51B | W.AUCKLAND-51F | NEWPORT-51B | W.AUCKLAND-51F | NEWPORT-51B | MIDDLESBROUGH-51D |
| Aug-56 | B.GARDENS-54C | NEWPORT-51B | W.AUCKLAND-51F | NEWPORT-51B | W.AUCKLAND-51F | NEWPORT-51B | W.AUCKLAND-51F | NEWPORT-51B | MIDDLESBROUGH-51D |
| Jan-57 | B.GARDENS-54C | NEWPORT-51B | W.AUCKLAND-51F | NEWPORT-51B | W.AUCKLAND-51F | NEWPORT-51B | W.AUCKLAND-51F | NEWPORT-51B | MIDDLESBROUGH-51D |
| Aug-57 | B.GARDENS-54C | NEWPORT-51B | W.AUCKLAND-51F | NEWPORT-51B | W.AUCKLAND-51F | NEWPORT-51B | W.AUCKLAND-51F | NEWPORT-51B | MIDDLESBROUGH-51D |
| Jan-58 | B.GARDENS-54C | NEWPORT-51B | W.AUCKLAND-51F | NEWPORT-51B | W.AUCKLAND-51F | NEWPORT-51B | W.AUCKLAND-51F | NEWPORT-51B | MIDDLESBROUGH-51D |
| Aug-58 | B.GARDENS-54C | 6/58: TNBY-51L | W.AUCKLAND-51F | 6/58: TNBY-51L | W.AUCKLAND-51F | 6/58: TNBY-51L | W.AUCKLAND-51F | 6/58: TNBY-51L | 6/58: TNBY-51L |
| Jan-59 | B.GARDENS-52J | 1/59: W/D | W.AUCKLAND-51F | THORNABY-51L | 1/59: W/D | | W.AUCKLAND-51F | THORNABY-51L | THORNABY-51L |
| Aug-59 | 6/59: GHD-52A | | W.AUCKLAND-51F | THORNABY-51L | | | W.AUCKLAND-51F | THORNABY-51L | THORNABY-51L |
| Nov-59 | GATESHEAD-52A | | W.AUCKLAND-51F | 11/59: W/D | | | W.AUCKLAND-51F | THORNABY-51L | 10/59: W/D |
| Jan-60 | GATESHEAD-52A | | W.AUCKLAND-51F | | | | W.AUCKLAND-51F | THORNABY-51L | |
| Apr-60 | GATESHEAD-52A | | W.AUCKLAND-51F | | | | W.AUCKLAND-51F | THORNABY-51L | |
| Aug-60 | GATESHEAD-52A | | W.AUCKLAND-51F | | | | W.AUCKLAND-51F | THORNABY-51L | |
| Nov-60 | GATESHEAD-52A | | W.AUCKLAND-51F | | | | W.AUCKLAND-51F | THORNABY-51L | |

| | 65738 | 65739 | 65740 | 65741 | 65742 | 65743 | 65744 | 65745 | 65746 |
|---|---|---|---|---|---|---|---|---|---|
| Aug-50 | NEWPORT-51B | NEWPORT-51B | NEWPORT-51B | NEWPORT-51B | NEWPORT-51B | NEWPORT-51B | NEWPORT-51B | NEWPORT-51B | NEWPORT-51B |
| Jan-51 | NEWPORT-51B | 2/51: STOCK-51E | NEWPORT-51B | NEWPORT-51B | NEWPORT-51B | NEWPORT-51B | NEWPORT-51B | NEWPORT-51B | NEWPORT-51B |
| Aug-51 | NEWPORT-51B | STOCKTON-51E | NEWPORT-51B | NEWPORT-51B | NEWPORT-51B | NEWPORT-51B | NEWPORT-51B | NEWPORT-51B | NEWPORT-51B |
| Jan-52 | NEWPORT-51B | STOCKTON-51E | NEWPORT-51B | NEWPORT-51B | NEWPORT-51B | NEWPORT-51B | NEWPORT-51B | NEWPORT-51B | NEWPORT-51B |
| Aug-52 | NEWPORT-51B | STOCKTON-51E | NEWPORT-51B | NEWPORT-51B | NEWPORT-51B | NEWPORT-51B | NEWPORT-51B | NEWPORT-51B | NEWPORT-51B |
| Jan-53 | NEWPORT-51B | STOCKTON-51E | NEWPORT-51B | NEWPORT-51B | NEWPORT-51B | NEWPORT-51B | NEWPORT-51B | NEWPORT-51B | NEWPORT-51B |
| Aug-53 | NEWPORT-51B | STOCKTON-51E | NEWPORT-51B | NEWPORT-51B | NEWPORT-51B | NEWPORT-51B | NEWPORT-51B | NEWPORT-51B | NEWPORT-51B |
| Jan-54 | NEWPORT-51B | STOCKTON-51E | NEWPORT-51B | NEWPORT-51B | NEWPORT-51B | NEWPORT-51B | NEWPORT-51B | NEWPORT-51B | NEWPORT-51B |
| Aug-54 | NEWPORT-51B | STOCKTON-51E | NEWPORT-51B | NEWPORT-51B | NEWPORT-51B | NEWPORT-51B | NEWPORT-51B | NEWPORT-51B | NEWPORT-51B |
| Jan-55 | NEWPORT-51B | STOCKTON-51E | NEWPORT-51B | NEWPORT-51B | NEWPORT-51B | NEWPORT-51B | NEWPORT-51B | NEWPORT-51B | NEWPORT-51B |
| Aug-55 | NEWPORT-51B | STOCKTON-51E | NEWPORT-51B | NEWPORT-51B | NEWPORT-51B | NEWPORT-51B | NEWPORT-51B | NEWPORT-51B | NEWPORT-51B |
| Jan-56 | NEWPORT-51B | STOCKTON-51E | NEWPORT-51B | NEWPORT-51B | NEWPORT-51B | NEWPORT-51B | NEWPORT-51B | NEWPORT-51B | NEWPORT-51B |
| Aug-56 | NEWPORT-51B | STOCKTON-51E | NEWPORT-51B | NEWPORT-51B | NEWPORT-51B | NEWPORT-51B | NEWPORT-51B | NEWPORT-51B | NEWPORT-51B |
| Jan-57 | NEWPORT-51B | STOCKTON-51E | NEWPORT-51B | NEWPORT-51B | NEWPORT-51B | NEWPORT-51B | NEWPORT-51B | NEWPORT-51B | NEWPORT-51B |
| Aug-57 | NEWPORT-51B | STOCKTON-51E | NEWPORT-51B | NEWPORT-51B | NEWPORT-51B | NEWPORT-51B | NEWPORT-51B | NEWPORT-51B | NEWPORT-51B |
| Jan-58 | NEWPORT-51B | STOCKTON-51E | NEWPORT-51B | NEWPORT-51B | NEWPORT-51B | NEWPORT-51B | NEWPORT-51B | NEWPORT-51B | NEWPORT-51B |
| Aug-58 | 6/58: TNBY-51L | STOCKTON-51E | 6/58: TNBY-51L | 6/58: TNBY-51L | 6/58: TNBY-51L | 6/58: TNBY-51L | 6/58: TNBY-51L | 6/58: TNBY-51L | 5/58: W/D |
| Jan-59 | THORNABY-51L | STOCKTON-51E | 1/59: W/D | THORNABY-51L | THORNABY-51L | THORNABY-51L | THORNABY-51L | THORNABY-51L | |
| Aug-59 | 2/59: W/D | 2/59: W/D | | THORNABY-51L | 2/59: W/D | THORNABY-51L | 2/59: W/D | THORNABY-51L | |
| Nov-59 | | | | THORNABY-51L | | THORNABY-51L | | THORNABY-51L | |
| Jan-60 | | | | THORNABY-51L | | THORNABY-51L | | THORNABY-51L | |
| Apr-60 | | | | THORNABY-51L | | THORNABY-51L | | THORNABY-51L | |
| Aug-60 | | | | THORNABY-51L | | THORNABY-51L | | THORNABY-51L | |
| Nov-60 | | | | THORNABY-51L | | THORNABY-51L | | THORNABY-51L | |

| | 65747 | 65748 | 65749 | 65750 | 65751 | 65752 | 65753 | 65754 | 65755 |
|---|---|---|---|---|---|---|---|---|---|
| Aug-50 | W.HARTLEPOOL-51C | W.HARTLEPOOL-51C | NEWPORT-51B | NEWPORT-51B | NEWPORT-51B | NEWPORT-51B | NEWPORT-51B | NEWPORT-51B | NEWPORT-51B |
| Jan-51 | W.HARTLEPOOL-51C | W.HARTLEPOOL-51C | NEWPORT-51B | NEWPORT-51B | NEWPORT-51B | NEWPORT-51B | NEWPORT-51B | NEWPORT-51B | NEWPORT-51B |
| Aug-51 | W.HARTLEPOOL-51C | W.HARTLEPOOL-51C | NEWPORT-51B | NEWPORT-51B | NEWPORT-51B | NEWPORT-51B | NEWPORT-51B | NEWPORT-51B | NEWPORT-51B |
| Jan-52 | W.HARTLEPOOL-51C | W.HARTLEPOOL-51C | NEWPORT-51B | NEWPORT-51B | NEWPORT-51B | NEWPORT-51B | NEWPORT-51B | NEWPORT-51B | NEWPORT-51B |
| Aug-52 | W.HARTLEPOOL-51C | W.HARTLEPOOL-51C | NEWPORT-51B | NEWPORT-51B | NEWPORT-51B | NEWPORT-51B | NEWPORT-51B | NEWPORT-51B | NEWPORT-51B |
| Jan-53 | W.HARTLEPOOL-51C | W.HARTLEPOOL-51C | NEWPORT-51B | NEWPORT-51B | NEWPORT-51B | NEWPORT-51B | NEWPORT-51B | NEWPORT-51B | NEWPORT-51B |
| Aug-53 | W.HARTLEPOOL-51C | W.HARTLEPOOL-51C | NEWPORT-51B | NEWPORT-51B | NEWPORT-51B | NEWPORT-51B | NEWPORT-51B | NEWPORT-51B | NEWPORT-51B |
| Jan-54 | W.HARTLEPOOL-51C | W.HARTLEPOOL-51C | NEWPORT-51B | NEWPORT-51B | NEWPORT-51B | NEWPORT-51B | NEWPORT-51B | NEWPORT-51B | NEWPORT-51B |
| Aug-54 | W.HARTLEPOOL-51C | W.HARTLEPOOL-51C | NEWPORT-51B | NEWPORT-51B | NEWPORT-51B | NEWPORT-51B | NEWPORT-51B | NEWPORT-51B | NEWPORT-51B |
| Jan-55 | W.HARTLEPOOL-51C | W.HARTLEPOOL-51C | NEWPORT-51B | NEWPORT-51B | NEWPORT-51B | NEWPORT-51B | NEWPORT-51B | NEWPORT-51B | NEWPORT-51B |
| Aug-55 | W.HARTLEPOOL-51C | W.HARTLEPOOL-51C | NEWPORT-51B | NEWPORT-51B | NEWPORT-51B | NEWPORT-51B | NEWPORT-51B | NEWPORT-51B | NEWPORT-51B |
| Jan-56 | W.HARTLEPOOL-51C | W.HARTLEPOOL-51C | NEWPORT-51B | NEWPORT-51B | NEWPORT-51B | NEWPORT-51B | NEWPORT-51B | NEWPORT-51B | NEWPORT-51B |
| Aug-56 | W.HARTLEPOOL-51C | W.HARTLEPOOL-51C | NEWPORT-51B | NEWPORT-51B | NEWPORT-51B | NEWPORT-51B | NEWPORT-51B | NEWPORT-51B | NEWPORT-51B |
| Jan-57 | W.HARTLEPOOL-51C | W.HARTLEPOOL-51C | NEWPORT-51B | NEWPORT-51B | NEWPORT-51B | NEWPORT-51B | NEWPORT-51B | NEWPORT-51B | NEWPORT-51B |
| Aug-57 | W.HARTLEPOOL-51C | W.HARTLEPOOL-51C | NEWPORT-51B | NEWPORT-51B | NEWPORT-51B | NEWPORT-51B | NEWPORT-51B | NEWPORT-51B | NEWPORT-51B |
| Jan-58 | W.HARTLEPOOL-51C | W.HARTLEPOOL-51C | NEWPORT-51B | NEWPORT-51B | NEWPORT-51B | NEWPORT-51B | NEWPORT-51B | NEWPORT-51B | NEWPORT-51B |
| Aug-58 | W.HARTLEPOOL-51C | W.HARTLEPOOL-51C | 6/58: TNBY-51L | 6/58: TNBY-51L | 6/58: TNBY-51L | 6/58: W/D | 6/58: TNBY-51L | 6/58: W/D | 6/58: TNBY-51L |
| Jan-59 | 4/59: STOCK-51E | 1/59: W/D | THORNABY-51L | THORNABY-51L | THORNABY-51L | | THORNABY-51L | | THORNABY-51L |
| Aug-59 | 6/59: TNBY-51L | | 3/59: W/D | 2/59: W/D | THORNABY-51L | | THORNABY-51L | | THORNABY-51L |
| Nov-59 | THORNABY-51L | | | | THORNABY-51L | | THORNABY-51L | | THORNABY-51L |
| Jan-60 | THORNABY-51L | | | | THORNABY-51L | | THORNABY-51L | | THORNABY-51L |
| Apr-60 | THORNABY-51L | | | | THORNABY-51L | | THORNABY-51L | | THORNABY-51L |
| Aug-60 | THORNABY-51L | | | | THORNABY-51L | | THORNABY-51L | | THORNABY-51L |
| Nov-60 | THORNABY-51L | | | | THORNABY-51L | | THORNABY-51L | | THORNABY-51L |

| | 65756 | 65757 | 65758 | 65759 | 65760 | 65761 | 65762 | 65763 | 65764 |
|---|---|---|---|---|---|---|---|---|---|
| Aug-50 | NEWPORT-51B | NEWPORT-51B | NEWPORT-51B | NEWPORT-51B | NEWPORT-51B | NEWPORT-51B | NEWPORT-51B | NEWPORT-51B | MIDDLESBROUGH-51D |
| Jan-51 | NEWPORT-51B | NEWPORT-51B | NEWPORT-51B | NEWPORT-51B | NEWPORT-51B | NEWPORT-51B | NEWPORT-51B | NEWPORT-51B | MIDDLESBROUGH-51D |
| Aug-51 | NEWPORT-51B | NEWPORT-51B | NEWPORT-51B | NEWPORT-51B | NEWPORT-51B | NEWPORT-51B | NEWPORT-51B | NEWPORT-51B | MIDDLESBROUGH-51D |
| Jan-52 | NEWPORT-51B | NEWPORT-51B | NEWPORT-51B | NEWPORT-51B | NEWPORT-51B | NEWPORT-51B | NEWPORT-51B | NEWPORT-51B | MIDDLESBROUGH-51D |
| Aug-52 | NEWPORT-51B | NEWPORT-51B | NEWPORT-51B | NEWPORT-51B | NEWPORT-51B | NEWPORT-51B | NEWPORT-51B | NEWPORT-51B | **5/52: STOCK - 51E** |
| Jan-53 | NEWPORT-51B | NEWPORT-51B | NEWPORT-51B | NEWPORT-51B | NEWPORT-51B | NEWPORT-51B | NEWPORT-51B | NEWPORT-51B | STOCKTON-51E |
| Aug-53 | NEWPORT-51B | NEWPORT-51B | NEWPORT-51B | NEWPORT-51B | NEWPORT-51B | NEWPORT-51B | NEWPORT-51B | NEWPORT-51B | STOCKTON-51E |
| Jan-54 | NEWPORT-51B | NEWPORT-51B | NEWPORT-51B | NEWPORT-51B | NEWPORT-51B | NEWPORT-51B | NEWPORT-51B | NEWPORT-51B | STOCKTON-51E |
| Aug-54 | NEWPORT-51B | NEWPORT-51B | NEWPORT-51B | NEWPORT-51B | NEWPORT-51B | NEWPORT-51B | NEWPORT-51B | NEWPORT-51B | STOCKTON-51E |
| Jan-55 | NEWPORT-51B | NEWPORT-51B | NEWPORT-51B | NEWPORT-51B | NEWPORT-51B | NEWPORT-51B | NEWPORT-51B | NEWPORT-51B | STOCKTON-51E |
| Aug-55 | NEWPORT-51B | NEWPORT-51B | NEWPORT-51B | NEWPORT-51B | NEWPORT-51B | NEWPORT-51B | NEWPORT-51B | NEWPORT-51B | STOCKTON-51E |
| Jan-56 | NEWPORT-51B | NEWPORT-51B | NEWPORT-51B | NEWPORT-51B | NEWPORT-51B | NEWPORT-51B | NEWPORT-51B | NEWPORT-51B | STOCKTON-51E |
| Aug-56 | NEWPORT-51B | NEWPORT-51B | NEWPORT-51B | NEWPORT-51B | NEWPORT-51B | NEWPORT-51B | NEWPORT-51B | NEWPORT-51B | STOCKTON-51E |
| Jan-57 | NEWPORT-51B | NEWPORT-51B | NEWPORT-51B | NEWPORT-51B | NEWPORT-51B | NEWPORT-51B | NEWPORT-51B | NEWPORT-51B | STOCKTON-51E |
| Aug-57 | NEWPORT-51B | NEWPORT-51B | NEWPORT-51B | NEWPORT-51B | NEWPORT-51B | NEWPORT-51B | NEWPORT-51B | NEWPORT-51B | STOCKTON-51E |
| Jan-58 | NEWPORT-51B | NEWPORT-51B | NEWPORT-51B | NEWPORT-51B | NEWPORT-51B | NEWPORT-51B | NEWPORT-51B | NEWPORT-51B | STOCKTON-51E |
| Aug-58 | **6/58: TNBY - 51L** | **6/58: TNBY - 51L** | **6/58: TNBY - 51L** | **6/58: TNBY - 51L** | **6/58: TNBY - 51L** | **6/58: TNBY - 51L** | **6/58: TNBY - 51L** | **6/58: TNBY - 51L** | STOCKTON-51E |
| Jan-59 | THORNABY-51L | THORNABY-51L | **1/59: W/D** | **1/59: W/D** | THORNABY-51L | THORNABY-51L | THORNABY-51L | THORNABY-51L | STOCKTON-51E |
| Aug-59 | THORNABY-51L | THORNABY-51L | | | THORNABY-51L | THORNABY-51L | THORNABY-51L | THORNABY-51L | **3/59: W/D** |
| Nov-59 | THORNABY-51L | THORNABY-51L | | | THORNABY-51L | THORNABY-51L | THORNABY-51L | THORNABY-51L | |
| Jan-60 | THORNABY-51L | THORNABY-51L | | | THORNABY-51L | THORNABY-51L | THORNABY-51L | THORNABY-51L | |
| Apr-60 | THORNABY-51L | THORNABY-51L | | | THORNABY-51L | THORNABY-51L | THORNABY-51L | THORNABY-51L | |
| Aug-60 | THORNABY-51L | THORNABY-51L | | | THORNABY-51L | THORNABY-51L | THORNABY-51L | THORNABY-51L | |
| Nov-60 | THORNABY-51L | THORNABY-51L | | | THORNABY-51L | THORNABY-51L | THORNABY-51L | THORNABY-51L | |

| | 65765 | 65766 | 65767 | 65768 | 65769 | 65770 | 65771 | 65772 | 65773 |
|---|---|---|---|---|---|---|---|---|---|
| Aug-50 | NEWPORT-51B | NEWPORT-51B | NEWPORT-51B | NEWPORT-51B | NEWPORT-51B | NEWPORT-51B | MIDDLESBROUGH-51D | NEWPORT-51B | NEWPORT-51B |
| Jan-51 | NEWPORT-51B | NEWPORT-51B | NEWPORT-51B | NEWPORT-51B | NEWPORT-51B | NEWPORT-51B | MIDDLESBROUGH-51D | NEWPORT-51B | NEWPORT-51B |
| Aug-51 | NEWPORT-51B | NEWPORT-51B | NEWPORT-51B | NEWPORT-51B | NEWPORT-51B | NEWPORT-51B | MIDDLESBROUGH-51D | NEWPORT-51B | NEWPORT-51B |
| Jan-52 | NEWPORT-51B | NEWPORT-51B | NEWPORT-51B | NEWPORT-51B | NEWPORT-51B | NEWPORT-51B | MIDDLESBROUGH-51D | NEWPORT-51B | NEWPORT-51B |
| Aug-52 | NEWPORT-51B | NEWPORT-51B | NEWPORT-51B | NEWPORT-51B | NEWPORT-51B | NEWPORT-51B | **5/52: STOCK - 51E** | NEWPORT-51B | NEWPORT-51B |
| Jan-53 | NEWPORT-51B | NEWPORT-51B | NEWPORT-51B | NEWPORT-51B | NEWPORT-51B | NEWPORT-51B | STOCKTON-51E | NEWPORT-51B | NEWPORT-51B |
| Aug-53 | NEWPORT-51B | NEWPORT-51B | NEWPORT-51B | NEWPORT-51B | NEWPORT-51B | NEWPORT-51B | STOCKTON-51E | NEWPORT-51B | NEWPORT-51B |
| Jan-54 | NEWPORT-51B | NEWPORT-51B | NEWPORT-51B | NEWPORT-51B | NEWPORT-51B | NEWPORT-51B | STOCKTON-51E | NEWPORT-51B | NEWPORT-51B |
| Aug-54 | NEWPORT-51B | NEWPORT-51B | NEWPORT-51B | NEWPORT-51B | NEWPORT-51B | NEWPORT-51B | STOCKTON-51E | NEWPORT-51B | NEWPORT-51B |
| Jan-55 | NEWPORT-51B | NEWPORT-51B | NEWPORT-51B | NEWPORT-51B | NEWPORT-51B | NEWPORT-51B | STOCKTON-51E | NEWPORT-51B | NEWPORT-51B |
| Aug-55 | NEWPORT-51B | NEWPORT-51B | NEWPORT-51B | NEWPORT-51B | NEWPORT-51B | NEWPORT-51B | STOCKTON-51E | NEWPORT-51B | NEWPORT-51B |
| Jan-56 | NEWPORT-51B | NEWPORT-51B | NEWPORT-51B | NEWPORT-51B | NEWPORT-51B | NEWPORT-51B | STOCKTON-51E | NEWPORT-51B | NEWPORT-51B |
| Aug-56 | NEWPORT-51B | NEWPORT-51B | NEWPORT-51B | NEWPORT-51B | NEWPORT-51B | NEWPORT-51B | STOCKTON-51E | NEWPORT-51B | NEWPORT-51B |
| Jan-57 | NEWPORT-51B | NEWPORT-51B | NEWPORT-51B | NEWPORT-51B | NEWPORT-51B | NEWPORT-51B | STOCKTON-51E | NEWPORT-51B | NEWPORT-51B |
| Aug-57 | NEWPORT-51B | NEWPORT-51B | NEWPORT-51B | NEWPORT-51B | NEWPORT-51B | NEWPORT-51B | STOCKTON-51E | NEWPORT-51B | NEWPORT-51B |
| Jan-58 | NEWPORT-51B | NEWPORT-51B | NEWPORT-51B | NEWPORT-51B | NEWPORT-51B | NEWPORT-51B | STOCKTON-51E | NEWPORT-51B | NEWPORT-51B |
| Aug-58 | **6/58: W/D** | **6/58: TNBY - 51L** | **6/58: W/D** | **6/58: TNBY - 51L** | **6/58: TNBY - 51L** | **6/58: TNBY - 51L** | STOCKTON-51E | **6/58: TNBY - 51L** | **6/58: TNBY - 51L** |
| Jan-59 | | THORNABY-51L | | THORNABY-51L | THORNABY-51L | THORNABY-51L | **1/59: W/D** | THORNABY-51L | **2/59: STOCK - 51E** |
| Aug-59 | | **2/59: W/D** | | THORNABY-51L | THORNABY-51L | **2/59: W/D** | | THORNABY-51L | **6/59: TNBY - 51L** |
| Nov-59 | | | | THORNABY-51L | THORNABY-51L | | | THORNABY-51L | THORNABY-51L |
| Jan-60 | | | | THORNABY-51L | THORNABY-51L | | | THORNABY-51L | THORNABY-51L |
| Apr-60 | | | | THORNABY-51L | THORNABY-51L | | | THORNABY-51L | THORNABY-51L |
| Aug-60 | | | | THORNABY-51L | THORNABY-51L | | | THORNABY-51L | THORNABY-51L |
| Nov-60 | | | | THORNABY-51L | THORNABY-51L | | | THORNABY-51L | THORNABY-51L |

| | 65774 | 65775 | 65776 | 65777 | 65778 | 65779 | J27 0-6-0 (1906)<br>65780 | 65781 | 65782 |
|---|---|---|---|---|---|---|---|---|---|
| Aug-50 | NEWPORT-51B | MIDDLESBROUGH-51D | MIDDLESBROUGH-51D | NEWPORT-51B | NEWPORT-51B | MIDDLESBROUGH-51D | PERCYMAIN-52E | SOUTHBLYTH-52F | W.HARTLEPOOL-51C |
| Jan-51 | NEWPORT-51B | MIDDLESBROUGH-51D | MIDDLESBROUGH-51D | NEWPORT-51B | NEWPORT-51B | MIDDLESBROUGH-51D | PERCYMAIN-52E | SOUTHBLYTH-52F | W.HARTLEPOOL-51C |
| Aug-51 | NEWPORT-51B | MIDDLESBROUGH-51D | MIDDLESBROUGH-51D | NEWPORT-51B | NEWPORT-51B | MIDDLESBROUGH-51D | PERCYMAIN-52E | SOUTHBLYTH-52F | W.HARTLEPOOL-51C |
| Jan-52 | NEWPORT-51B | MIDDLESBROUGH-51D | MIDDLESBROUGH-51D | NEWPORT-51B | NEWPORT-51B | MIDDLESBROUGH-51D | PERCYMAIN-52E | SOUTHBLYTH-52F | W.HARTLEPOOL-51C |
| Aug-52 | NEWPORT-51B | MIDDLESBROUGH-51D | MIDDLESBROUGH-51D | NEWPORT-51B | NEWPORT-51B | MIDDLESBROUGH-51D | PERCYMAIN-52E | SOUTHBLYTH-52F | W.HARTLEPOOL-51C |
| Jan-53 | NEWPORT-51B | MIDDLESBROUGH-51D | MIDDLESBROUGH-51D | NEWPORT-51B | NEWPORT-51B | MIDDLESBROUGH-51D | PERCYMAIN-52E | SOUTHBLYTH-52F | W.HARTLEPOOL-51C |
| Aug-53 | NEWPORT-51B | MIDDLESBROUGH-51D | MIDDLESBROUGH-51D | NEWPORT-51B | NEWPORT-51B | MIDDLESBROUGH-51D | PERCYMAIN-52E | SOUTHBLYTH-52F | W.HARTLEPOOL-51C |
| Jan-54 | NEWPORT-51B | MIDDLESBROUGH-51D | MIDDLESBROUGH-51D | NEWPORT-51B | NEWPORT-51B | MIDDLESBROUGH-51D | PERCYMAIN-52E | SOUTHBLYTH-52F | W.HARTLEPOOL-51C |
| Aug-54 | NEWPORT-51B | MIDDLESBROUGH-51D | MIDDLESBROUGH-51D | NEWPORT-51B | NEWPORT-51B | MIDDLESBROUGH-51D | PERCYMAIN-52E | SOUTHBLYTH-52F | W.HARTLEPOOL-51C |
| Jan-55 | NEWPORT-51B | MIDDLESBROUGH-51D | MIDDLESBROUGH-51D | NEWPORT-51B | NEWPORT-51B | MIDDLESBROUGH-51D | PERCYMAIN-52E | SOUTHBLYTH-52F | W.HARTLEPOOL-51C |
| Aug-55 | NEWPORT-51B | MIDDLESBROUGH-51D | MIDDLESBROUGH-51D | NEWPORT-51B | NEWPORT-51B | MIDDLESBROUGH-51D | PERCYMAIN-52E | SOUTHBLYTH-52F | W.HARTLEPOOL-51C |
| Jan-56 | NEWPORT-51B | MIDDLESBROUGH-51D | MIDDLESBROUGH-51D | NEWPORT-51B | NEWPORT-51B | MIDDLESBROUGH-51D | PERCYMAIN-52E | SOUTHBLYTH-52F | W.HARTLEPOOL-51C |
| Aug-56 | NEWPORT-51B | MIDDLESBROUGH-51D | MIDDLESBROUGH-51D | NEWPORT-51B | NEWPORT-51B | MIDDLESBROUGH-51D | PERCYMAIN-52E | SOUTHBLYTH-52F | W.HARTLEPOOL-51C |
| Jan-57 | NEWPORT-51B | MIDDLESBROUGH-51D | MIDDLESBROUGH-51D | NEWPORT-51B | NEWPORT-51B | MIDDLESBROUGH-51D | PERCYMAIN-52E | SOUTHBLYTH-52F | W.HARTLEPOOL-51C |
| Aug-57 | NEWPORT-51B | MIDDLESBROUGH-51D | MIDDLESBROUGH-51D | NEWPORT-51B | NEWPORT-51B | MIDDLESBROUGH-51D | PERCYMAIN-52E | SOUTHBLYTH-52F | W.HARTLEPOOL-51C |
| Jan-58 | NEWPORT-51B | MIDDLESBROUGH-51D | MIDDLESBROUGH-51D | NEWPORT-51B | NEWPORT-51B | MIDDLESBROUGH-51D | PERCYMAIN-52E | SOUTHBLYTH-52F | W.HARTLEPOOL-51C |
| Aug-58 | **6/58: TNBY - 51L** | **6/58: TNBY - 51L** | **6/58: TNBY - 51L** | **6/58: TNBY - 51L** | **6/58: TNBY - 51L** | **6/58: TNBY - 51L** | PERCYMAIN-52E | SOUTHBLYTH-52F | W.HARTLEPOOL-51C |
| Jan-59 | THORNABY-51L | THORNABY-51L | THORNABY-51L | THORNABY-51L | THORNABY-51L | THORNABY-51L | PERCYMAIN-52E | SOUTHBLYTH-52F | W.HARTLEPOOL-51C |
| Aug-59 | THORNABY-51L | **2/59: W/D** | THORNABY-51L | THORNABY-51L | THORNABY-51L | THORNABY-51L | **4/59: W/D** | SOUTHBLYTH-52F | W.HARTLEPOOL-51C |
| Nov-59 | THORNABY-51L | | THORNABY-51L | THORNABY-51L | THORNABY-51L | THORNABY-51L | | **10/59: W/D** | W.HARTLEPOOL-51C |
| Jan-60 | THORNABY-51L | | THORNABY-51L | THORNABY-51L | THORNABY-51L | THORNABY-51L | | | W.HARTLEPOOL-51C |
| Apr-60 | THORNABY-51L | | THORNABY-51L | THORNABY-51L | THORNABY-51L | THORNABY-51L | | | W.HARTLEPOOL-51C |
| Aug-60 | THORNABY-51L | | THORNABY-51L | THORNABY-51L | THORNABY-51L | THORNABY-51L | | | W.HARTLEPOOL-51C |
| Nov-60 | THORNABY-51L | | THORNABY-51L | **9/60: W/D** | THORNABY-51L | THORNABY-51L | | | W.HARTLEPOOL-51C |

| | 65783 | 65784 | 65785 | 65786 | 65787 | 65788 | 65789 | 65790 | 65791 |
|---|---|---|---|---|---|---|---|---|---|
| Aug-50 | N.BLYTH-52F | PERCYMAIN-52E | SUNDERLAND-54A | N.BLYTH-52F | HAVERTONHILL-51G | HEATON-52B | N.BLYTH-52F | W.HARTLEPOOL-51C | PERCYMAIN-52E |
| Jan-51 | N.BLYTH-52F | PERCYMAIN-52E | SUNDERLAND-54A | N.BLYTH-52F | HAVERTONHILL-51G | **12/50: DARL - 51A** | N.BLYTH-52F | W.HARTLEPOOL-51C | PERCYMAIN-52E |
| Aug-51 | N.BLYTH-52F | PERCYMAIN-52E | SUNDERLAND-54A | N.BLYTH-52F | HAVERTONHILL-51G | **2/51: STOCK - 51E** | N.BLYTH-52F | W.HARTLEPOOL-51C | PERCYMAIN-52E |
| Jan-52 | N.BLYTH-52F | PERCYMAIN-52E | SUNDERLAND-54A | N.BLYTH-52F | HAVERTONHILL-51G | STOCKTON-51E | N.BLYTH-52F | W.HARTLEPOOL-51C | PERCYMAIN-52E |
| Aug-52 | N.BLYTH-52F | PERCYMAIN-52E | SUNDERLAND-54A | N.BLYTH-52F | HAVERTONHILL-51G | STOCKTON-51E | N.BLYTH-52F | W.HARTLEPOOL-51C | PERCYMAIN-52E |
| Jan-53 | N.BLYTH-52F | PERCYMAIN-52E | SUNDERLAND-54A | N.BLYTH-52F | HAVERTONHILL-51G | STOCKTON-51E | N.BLYTH-52F | W.HARTLEPOOL-51C | PERCYMAIN-52E |
| Aug-53 | N.BLYTH-52F | PERCYMAIN-52E | SUNDERLAND-54A | N.BLYTH-52F | HAVERTONHILL-51G | STOCKTON-51E | N.BLYTH-52F | W.HARTLEPOOL-51C | PERCYMAIN-52E |
| Jan-54 | N.BLYTH-52F | PERCYMAIN-52E | SUNDERLAND-54A | N.BLYTH-52F | HAVERTONHILL-51G | STOCKTON-51E | N.BLYTH-52F | **10/53: H. HILL - 51G** | PERCYMAIN-52E |
| Aug-54 | N.BLYTH-52F | PERCYMAIN-52E | SUNDERLAND-54A | N.BLYTH-52F | HAVERTONHILL-51G | STOCKTON-51E | N.BLYTH-52F | HAVERTONHILL-51G | PERCYMAIN-52E |
| Jan-55 | N.BLYTH-52F | PERCYMAIN-52E | SUNDERLAND-54A | N.BLYTH-52F | HAVERTONHILL-51G | STOCKTON-51E | N.BLYTH-52F | HAVERTONHILL-51G | PERCYMAIN-52E |
| Aug-55 | N.BLYTH-52F | PERCYMAIN-52E | SUNDERLAND-54A | N.BLYTH-52F | HAVERTONHILL-51G | STOCKTON-51E | N.BLYTH-52F | HAVERTONHILL-51G | PERCYMAIN-52E |
| Jan-56 | N.BLYTH-52F | PERCYMAIN-52E | SUNDERLAND-54A | N.BLYTH-52F | HAVERTONHILL-51G | STOCKTON-51E | N.BLYTH-52F | HAVERTONHILL-51G | PERCYMAIN-52E |
| Aug-56 | N.BLYTH-52F | PERCYMAIN-52E | SUNDERLAND-54A | N.BLYTH-52F | HAVERTONHILL-51G | STOCKTON-51E | N.BLYTH-52F | HAVERTONHILL-51G | PERCYMAIN-52E |
| Jan-57 | N.BLYTH-52F | PERCYMAIN-52E | **10/56: B. GDNS: 54C** | N.BLYTH-52F | HAVERTONHILL-51G | STOCKTON-51E | N.BLYTH-52F | HAVERTONHILL-51G | PERCYMAIN-52E |
| Aug-57 | N.BLYTH-52F | PERCYMAIN-52E | B.GDNS-54C | N.BLYTH-52F | HAVERTONHILL-51G | STOCKTON-51E | N.BLYTH-52F | HAVERTONHILL-51G | PERCYMAIN-52E |
| Jan-58 | N.BLYTH-52F | PERCYMAIN-52E | B.GDNS-54C | N.BLYTH-52F | HAVERTONHILL-51G | STOCKTON-51E | N.BLYTH-52F | HAVERTONHILL-51G | PERCYMAIN-52E |
| Aug-58 | N.BLYTH-52F | PERCYMAIN-52E | B.GDNS-54C | N.BLYTH-52F | HAVERTONHILL-51G | STOCKTON-51E | N.BLYTH-52F | HAVERTONHILL-51G | PERCYMAIN-52E |
| Jan-59 | N.BLYTH-52F | PERCYMAIN-52E | B.GDNS-52J | N.BLYTH-52F | **10/58: STOCK - 51E** | STOCKTON-51E | N.BLYTH-52F | **2/59: TBY - 51L** | PERCYMAIN-52E |
| Aug-59 | **6/59: W/D** | **8/59: W/D** | **6/59: W/D** | N.BLYTH-52F | **6/59: TBY - 51L** | **6/59: TBY - 51L** | N.BLYTH-52F | THORNABY-51L | PERCYMAIN-52E |
| Nov-59 | | | | N.BLYTH-52F | THORNABY-51L | THORNABY-51L | N.BLYTH-52F | THORNABY-51L | PERCYMAIN-52E |
| Jan-60 | | | | N.BLYTH-52F | THORNABY-51L | THORNABY-51L | N.BLYTH-52F | THORNABY-51L | PERCYMAIN-52E |
| Apr-60 | | | | N.BLYTH-52F | THORNABY-51L | THORNABY-51L | N.BLYTH-52F | THORNABY-51L | PERCYMAIN-52E |
| Aug-60 | | | | N.BLYTH-52F | THORNABY-51L | THORNABY-51L | N.BLYTH-52F | THORNABY-51L | PERCYMAIN-52E |
| Nov-60 | | | | N.BLYTH-52F | THORNABY-51L | THORNABY-51L | N.BLYTH-52F | THORNABY-51L | PERCYMAIN-52E |

| | 65792 | 65793 | 65794 | 65795 | 65796 | 65797 | 65798 | 65799 | 65800 |
|---|---|---|---|---|---|---|---|---|---|
| Aug-50 | PERCY MAIN-52E | SELBY-50C | PERCY MAIN-52E | PERCY MAIN-52E | PERCY MAIN-52E | N.BLYTH-52F | SUNDERLAND-54A | N.BLYTH-52F | HEATON-52B |
| Jan-51 | **11/50: N. BLYTH - 52F** | SELBY-50C | N.BLYTH-52F | PERCY MAIN-52E | PERCY MAIN-52E | N.BLYTH-52F | SUNDERLAND-54A | N.BLYTH-52F | HEATON-52B |
| Aug-51 | N.BLYTH-52F | SELBY-50C | N.BLYTH-52F | PERCY MAIN-52E | PERCY MAIN-52E | N.BLYTH-52F | SUNDERLAND-54A | N.BLYTH-52F | N.BLYTH-52F |
| Jan-52 | N.BLYTH-52F | SELBY-50C | N.BLYTH-52F | PERCY MAIN-52E | PERCY MAIN-52E | N.BLYTH-52F | SUNDERLAND-54A | N.BLYTH-52F | N.BLYTH-52F |
| Aug-52 | N.BLYTH-52F | SELBY-50C | N.BLYTH-52F | PERCY MAIN-52E | PERCY MAIN-52E | N.BLYTH-52F | SUNDERLAND-54A | PERCY MAIN-52E | N.BLYTH-52F |
| Jan-53 | N.BLYTH-52F | SELBY-50C | N.BLYTH-52F | PERCY MAIN-52E | PERCY MAIN-52E | N.BLYTH-52F | SUNDERLAND-54A | PERCY MAIN-52E | N.BLYTH-52F |
| Aug-53 | N.BLYTH-52F | SELBY-50C | N.BLYTH-52F | PERCY MAIN-52E | PERCY MAIN-52E | N.BLYTH-52F | SUNDERLAND-54A | PERCY MAIN-52E | N.BLYTH-52F |
| Jan-54 | N.BLYTH-52F | SELBY-50C | N.BLYTH-52F | PERCY MAIN-52E | PERCY MAIN-52E | N.BLYTH-52F | SUNDERLAND-54A | PERCY MAIN-52E | N.BLYTH-52F |
| Aug-54 | N.BLYTH-52F | SELBY-50C | N.BLYTH-52F | PERCY MAIN-52E | PERCY MAIN-52E | N.BLYTH-52F | SUNDERLAND-54A | PERCY MAIN-52E | N.BLYTH-52F |
| Jan-55 | N.BLYTH-52F | YORK-50A | N.BLYTH-52F | PERCY MAIN-52E | PERCY MAIN-52E | N.BLYTH-52F | SUNDERLAND-54A | PERCY MAIN-52E | N.BLYTH-52F |
| Aug-55 | N.BLYTH-52F | YORK-50A | N.BLYTH-52F | PERCY MAIN-52E | PERCY MAIN-52E | N.BLYTH-52F | SUNDERLAND-54A | PERCY MAIN-52E | N.BLYTH-52F |
| Jan-56 | N.BLYTH-52F | YORK-50A | N.BLYTH-52F | PERCY MAIN-52E | PERCY MAIN-52E | N.BLYTH-52F | SUNDERLAND-54A | PERCY MAIN-52E | N.BLYTH-52F |
| Aug-56 | N.BLYTH-52F | YORK-50A | N.BLYTH-52F | PERCY MAIN-52E | PERCY MAIN-52E | N.BLYTH-52F | SUNDERLAND-54A | PERCY MAIN-52E | N.BLYTH-52F |
| Jan-57 | N.BLYTH-52F | YORK-50A | N.BLYTH-52F | PERCY MAIN-52E | PERCY MAIN-52E | N.BLYTH-52F | SUNDERLAND-54A | PERCY MAIN-52E | N.BLYTH-52F |
| Aug-57 | N.BLYTH-52F | YORK-50A | N.BLYTH-52F | PERCY MAIN-52E | PERCY MAIN-52E | N.BLYTH-52F | SUNDERLAND-54A | PERCY MAIN-52E | N.BLYTH-52F |
| Jan-58 | N.BLYTH-52F | SELBY-50C | N.BLYTH-52F | PERCY MAIN-52E | PERCY MAIN-52E | N.BLYTH-52F | SUNDERLAND-54A | PERCY MAIN-52E | N.BLYTH-52F |
| Aug-58 | N.BLYTH-52F | SELBY-50C | N.BLYTH-52F | PERCY MAIN-52E | PERCY MAIN-52E | N.BLYTH-52F | SUNDERLAND-54A | PERCY MAIN-52E | N.BLYTH-52F |
| Jan-59 | N.BLYTH-52F | SELBY-50C | N.BLYTH-52F | PERCY MAIN-52E | PERCY MAIN-52E | N.BLYTH-52F | SUNDERLAND-52G | PERCY MAIN-52E | N.BLYTH-52F |
| Aug-59 | N.BLYTH-52F | W/D | N.BLYTH-52F | PERCY MAIN-52E | PERCY MAIN-52E | N.BLYTH-52F | | S.BLYTH-52F | N.BLYTH-52F |
| Nov-59 | N.BLYTH-52F | W/D | N.BLYTH-52F | PERCY MAIN-52E | PERCY MAIN-52E | N.BLYTH-52F | | S.BLYTH-52F | N.BLYTH-52F |
| Jan-60 | N.BLYTH-52F | W/D | N.BLYTH-52F | PERCY MAIN-52E | PERCY MAIN-52E | N.BLYTH-52F | | S.BLYTH-52F | N.BLYTH-52F |
| Apr-60 | N.BLYTH-52F | W/D | N.BLYTH-52F | PERCY MAIN-52E | PERCY MAIN-52E | N.BLYTH-52F | | S.BLYTH-52F | N.BLYTH-52F |
| Aug-60 | N.BLYTH-52F | W/D | N.BLYTH-52F | PERCY MAIN-52E | PERCY MAIN-52E | N.BLYTH-52F | | S.BLYTH-52F | N.BLYTH-52F |
| Nov-60 | N.BLYTH-52F | W/D | N.BLYTH-52F | PERCY MAIN-52E | PERCY MAIN-52E | N.BLYTH-52F | | S.BLYTH-52F | N.BLYTH-52F |

| | 65801 | 65802 | 65803 | 65804 | 65805 | 65806 | 65807 | 65808 | 65809 |
|---|---|---|---|---|---|---|---|---|---|
| Aug-50 | N.BLYTH-52F | PERCY MAIN-52E | W.HARTLEPOOL-51C | N.BLYTH-52F | HAVERTON HILL-51G | PERCY MAIN-52E | HEATON-52B | S.BLYTH-52F | PERCY MAIN-52E |
| Jan-51 | N.BLYTH-52F | PERCY MAIN-52E | W.HARTLEPOOL-51C | N.BLYTH-52F | HAVERTON HILL-51G | PERCY MAIN-52E | HEATON-52B | S.BLYTH-52F | PERCY MAIN-52E |
| Aug-51 | N.BLYTH-52F | PERCY MAIN-52E | W.HARTLEPOOL-51C | N.BLYTH-52F | HAVERTON HILL-51G | PERCY MAIN-52E | HEATON-52B | S.BLYTH-52F | PERCY MAIN-52E |
| Jan-52 | N.BLYTH-52F | PERCY MAIN-52E | W.HARTLEPOOL-51C | N.BLYTH-52F | HAVERTON HILL-51G | PERCY MAIN-52E | HEATON-52B | S.BLYTH-52F | PERCY MAIN-52E |
| Aug-52 | N.BLYTH-52F | PERCY MAIN-52E | W.HARTLEPOOL-51C | N.BLYTH-52F | HAVERTON HILL-51G | PERCY MAIN-52E | **7/52: PCYM - 52E** | S.BLYTH-52F | PERCY MAIN-52E |
| Jan-53 | N.BLYTH-52F | PERCY MAIN-52E | W.HARTLEPOOL-51C | N.BLYTH-52F | HAVERTON HILL-51G | PERCY MAIN-52E | PERCY MAIN-52E | S.BLYTH-52F | PERCY MAIN-52E |
| Aug-53 | N.BLYTH-52F | PERCY MAIN-52E | W.HARTLEPOOL-51C | N.BLYTH-52F | HAVERTON HILL-51G | PERCY MAIN-52E | PERCY MAIN-52E | S.BLYTH-52F | PERCY MAIN-52E |
| Jan-54 | N.BLYTH-52F | PERCY MAIN-52E | W.HARTLEPOOL-51C | N.BLYTH-52F | HAVERTON HILL-51G | PERCY MAIN-52E | PERCY MAIN-52E | S.BLYTH-52F | PERCY MAIN-52E |
| Aug-54 | N.BLYTH-52F | PERCY MAIN-52E | W.HARTLEPOOL-51C | N.BLYTH-52F | HAVERTON HILL-51G | PERCY MAIN-52E | PERCY MAIN-52E | S.BLYTH-52F | PERCY MAIN-52E |
| Jan-55 | N.BLYTH-52F | PERCY MAIN-52E | W.HARTLEPOOL-51C | N.BLYTH-52F | HAVERTON HILL-51G | PERCY MAIN-52E | PERCY MAIN-52E | S.BLYTH-52F | PERCY MAIN-52E |
| Aug-55 | N.BLYTH-52F | PERCY MAIN-52E | W.HARTLEPOOL-51C | N.BLYTH-52F | HAVERTON HILL-51G | PERCY MAIN-52E | PERCY MAIN-52E | S.BLYTH-52F | PERCY MAIN-52E |
| Jan-56 | N.BLYTH-52F | PERCY MAIN-52E | W.HARTLEPOOL-51C | N.BLYTH-52F | HAVERTON HILL-51G | PERCY MAIN-52E | PERCY MAIN-52E | S.BLYTH-52F | PERCY MAIN-52E |
| Aug-56 | N.BLYTH-52F | HEATON-52B | W.HARTLEPOOL-51C | N.BLYTH-52F | HAVERTON HILL-51G | PERCY MAIN-52E | PERCY MAIN-52E | S.BLYTH-52F | PERCY MAIN-52E |
| Jan-57 | N.BLYTH-52F | PERCY MAIN-52E | W.HARTLEPOOL-51C | N.BLYTH-52F | HAVERTON HILL-51G | PERCY MAIN-52E | PERCY MAIN-52E | S.BLYTH-52F | PERCY MAIN-52E |
| Aug-57 | N.BLYTH-52F | PERCY MAIN-52E | W.HARTLEPOOL-51C | N.BLYTH-52F | HAVERTON HILL-51G | PERCY MAIN-52E | PERCY MAIN-52E | S.BLYTH-52F | PERCY MAIN-52E |
| Jan-58 | N.BLYTH-52F | PERCY MAIN-52E | W.HARTLEPOOL-51C | N.BLYTH-52F | HAVERTON HILL-51G | **10/57: N.BLYTH - 52F** | PERCY MAIN-52E | S.BLYTH-52F | PERCY MAIN-52E |
| Aug-58 | N.BLYTH-52F | PERCY MAIN-52E | W.HARTLEPOOL-51C | N.BLYTH-52F | HAVERTON HILL-51G | N.BLYTH-52F | PERCY MAIN-52E | S.BLYTH-52F | PERCY MAIN-52E |
| Jan-59 | N.BLYTH-52F | PERCY MAIN-52E | W.HARTLEPOOL-51C | N.BLYTH-52F | W.HARTLEPOOL-51C | N.BLYTH-52F | PERCY MAIN-52E | S.BLYTH-52F | PERCY MAIN-52E |
| Aug-59 | N.BLYTH-52F | PERCY MAIN-52E | **4/59: W/D** | N.BLYTH-52F | W.HARTLEPOOL-51C | **7/59: W/D** | PERCY MAIN-52E | S.BLYTH-52F | PERCY MAIN-52E |
| Nov-59 | N.BLYTH-52F | PERCY MAIN-52E | | N.BLYTH-52F | W.HARTLEPOOL-51C | | PERCY MAIN-52E | S.BLYTH-52F | PERCY MAIN-52E |
| Jan-60 | N.BLYTH-52F | PERCY MAIN-52E | | N.BLYTH-52F | W.HARTLEPOOL-51C | | PERCY MAIN-52E | S.BLYTH-52F | PERCY MAIN-52E |
| Apr-60 | N.BLYTH-52F | PERCY MAIN-52E | | N.BLYTH-52F | W.HARTLEPOOL-51C | | PERCY MAIN-52E | S.BLYTH-52F | PERCY MAIN-52E |
| Aug-60 | N.BLYTH-52F | PERCY MAIN-52E | | N.BLYTH-52F | W.HARTLEPOOL-51C | | PERCY MAIN-52E | S.BLYTH-52F | PERCY MAIN-52E |
| Nov-60 | N.BLYTH-52F | PERCY MAIN-52E | | N.BLYTH-52F | W.HARTLEPOOL-51C | | PERCY MAIN-52E | S.BLYTH-52F | PERCY MAIN-52E |

| | 65810 | 65811 | 65812 | 65813 | 65814 | 65815 | 65816 | 65817 | 65818 |
|---|---|---|---|---|---|---|---|---|---|
| Aug-50 | S.BLYTH-52F | N.BLYTH-52F | PERCY MAIN-52E | PERCY MAIN-52E | PERCY MAIN-52E | PERCY MAIN-52E | W.HARTLEPOOL-51C | SUNDERLAND-54A | W.HARTLEPOOL-51C |
| Jan-51 | S.BLYTH-52F | N.BLYTH-52F | PERCY MAIN-52E | PERCY MAIN-52E | PERCY MAIN-52E | PERCY MAIN-52E | W.HARTLEPOOL-51C | SUNDERLAND-54A | W.HARTLEPOOL-51C |
| Aug-51 | S.BLYTH-52F | N.BLYTH-52F | PERCY MAIN-52E | PERCY MAIN-52E | PERCY MAIN-52E | PERCY MAIN-52E | W.HARTLEPOOL-51C | SUNDERLAND-54A | W.HARTLEPOOL-51C |
| Jan-52 | S.BLYTH-52F | N.BLYTH-52F | PERCY MAIN-52E | PERCY MAIN-52E | PERCY MAIN-52E | PERCY MAIN-52E | W.HARTLEPOOL-51C | SUNDERLAND-54A | W.HARTLEPOOL-51C |
| Aug-52 | S.BLYTH-52F | N.BLYTH-52F | PERCY MAIN-52E | PERCY MAIN-52E | PERCY MAIN-52E | PERCY MAIN-52E | W.HARTLEPOOL-51C | SUNDERLAND-54A | W.HARTLEPOOL-51C |
| Jan-53 | S.BLYTH-52F | N.BLYTH-52F | PERCY MAIN-52E | PERCY MAIN-52E | PERCY MAIN-52E | PERCY MAIN-52E | W.HARTLEPOOL-51C | SUNDERLAND-54A | W.HARTLEPOOL-51C |
| Aug-53 | S.BLYTH-52F | N.BLYTH-52F | PERCY MAIN-52E | PERCY MAIN-52E | PERCY MAIN-52E | PERCY MAIN-52E | W.HARTLEPOOL-51C | SUNDERLAND-54A | W.HARTLEPOOL-51C |
| Jan-54 | S.BLYTH-52F | N.BLYTH-52F | PERCY MAIN-52E | PERCY MAIN-52E | PERCY MAIN-52E | **11/53: N.BLYTH - 52F** | W.HARTLEPOOL-51C | SUNDERLAND-54A | W.HARTLEPOOL-51C |
| Aug-54 | S.BLYTH-52F | N.BLYTH-52F | PERCY MAIN-52E | PERCY MAIN-52E | PERCY MAIN-52E | N.BLYTH-52F | W.HARTLEPOOL-51C | SUNDERLAND-54A | W.HARTLEPOOL-51C |
| Jan-55 | S.BLYTH-52F | N.BLYTH-52F | PERCY MAIN-52E | PERCY MAIN-52E | PERCY MAIN-52E | N.BLYTH-52F | W.HARTLEPOOL-51C | SUNDERLAND-54A | W.HARTLEPOOL-51C |
| Aug-55 | S.BLYTH-52F | N.BLYTH-52F | PERCY MAIN-52E | PERCY MAIN-52E | PERCY MAIN-52E | N.BLYTH-52F | W.HARTLEPOOL-51C | SUNDERLAND-54A | W.HARTLEPOOL-51C |
| Jan-56 | S.BLYTH-52F | N.BLYTH-52F | PERCY MAIN-52E | PERCY MAIN-52E | PERCY MAIN-52E | N.BLYTH-52F | W.HARTLEPOOL-51C | SUNDERLAND-54A | W.HARTLEPOOL-51C |
| Aug-56 | S.BLYTH-52F | N.BLYTH-52F | PERCY MAIN-52E | PERCY MAIN-52E | PERCY MAIN-52E | N.BLYTH-52F | W.HARTLEPOOL-51C | SUNDERLAND-54A | W.HARTLEPOOL-51C |
| Jan-57 | S.BLYTH-52F | N.BLYTH-52F | PERCY MAIN-52E | PERCY MAIN-52E | PERCY MAIN-52E | N.BLYTH-52F | W.HARTLEPOOL-51C | SUNDERLAND-54A | W.HARTLEPOOL-51C |
| Aug-57 | S.BLYTH-52F | N.BLYTH-52F | PERCY MAIN-52E | PERCY MAIN-52E | PERCY MAIN-52E | N.BLYTH-52F | W.HARTLEPOOL-51C | SUNDERLAND-54A | W.HARTLEPOOL-51C |
| Jan-58 | S.BLYTH-52F | N.BLYTH-52F | PERCY MAIN-52E | PERCY MAIN-52E | PERCY MAIN-52E | N.BLYTH-52F | W.HARTLEPOOL-51C | SUNDERLAND-54A | W.HARTLEPOOL-51C |
| Aug-58 | S.BLYTH-52F | N.BLYTH-52F | PERCY MAIN-52E | PERCY MAIN-52E | PERCY MAIN-52E | N.BLYTH-52F | W.HARTLEPOOL-51C | SUNDERLAND-54A | W.HARTLEPOOL-51C |
| Jan-59 | S.BLYTH-52F | N.BLYTH-52F | PERCY MAIN-52E | PERCY MAIN-52E | PERCY MAIN-52E | N.BLYTH-52F | W.HARTLEPOOL-51C | SUNDERLAND-52G | W.HARTLEPOOL-51C |
| Aug-59 | S.BLYTH-52F | N.BLYTH-52F | PERCY MAIN-52E | PERCY MAIN-52E | PERCY MAIN-52E | N.BLYTH-52F | W.HARTLEPOOL-51C | SUNDERLAND-52G | W.HARTLEPOOL-51C |
| Nov-59 | S.BLYTH-52F | N.BLYTH-52F | PERCY MAIN-52E | PERCY MAIN-52E | PERCY MAIN-52E | N.BLYTH-52F | **10/59: W/D** | SUNDERLAND-52G | W.HARTLEPOOL-51C |
| Jan-60 | S.BLYTH-52F | N.BLYTH-52F | PERCY MAIN-52E | PERCY MAIN-52E | PERCY MAIN-52E | N.BLYTH-52F | | SUNDERLAND-52G | W.HARTLEPOOL-51C |
| Apr-60 | S.BLYTH-52F | N.BLYTH-52F | PERCY MAIN-52E | PERCY MAIN-52E | PERCY MAIN-52E | N.BLYTH-52F | | SUNDERLAND-52G | W.HARTLEPOOL-51C |
| Aug-60 | S.BLYTH-52F | N.BLYTH-52F | PERCY MAIN-52E | PERCY MAIN-52E | PERCY MAIN-52E | N.BLYTH-52F | | SUNDERLAND-52G | W.HARTLEPOOL-51C |
| Nov-60 | S.BLYTH-52F | N.BLYTH-52F | PERCY MAIN-52E | PERCY MAIN-52E | PERCY MAIN-52E | N.BLYTH-52F | | SUNDERLAND-52G | W.HARTLEPOOL-51C |

| | 65819 | 65820 | 65821 | 65822 | 65823 | 65824 | 65825 | 65826 | 65827 |
|---|---|---|---|---|---|---|---|---|---|
| Aug-50 | N.BLYTH-52F | W.HARTLEPOOL-51C | PERCY MAIN-52E | PERCY MAIN-52E | SUNDERLAND-54A | S.BLYTH-52F | PERCY MAIN-52E | PERCY MAIN-52E | SELBY-50C |
| Jan-51 | N.BLYTH-52F | W.HARTLEPOOL-51C | PERCY MAIN-52E | PERCY MAIN-52E | SUNDERLAND-54A | S.BLYTH-52F | PERCY MAIN-52E | PERCY MAIN-52E | SELBY-50C |
| Aug-51 | N.BLYTH-52F | W.HARTLEPOOL-51C | PERCY MAIN-52E | PERCY MAIN-52E | SUNDERLAND-54A | S.BLYTH-52F | PERCY MAIN-52E | PERCY MAIN-52E | SELBY-50C |
| Jan-52 | N.BLYTH-52F | W.HARTLEPOOL-51C | PERCY MAIN-52E | PERCY MAIN-52E | SUNDERLAND-54A | S.BLYTH-52F | PERCY MAIN-52E | PERCY MAIN-52E | **10/51: YORK - 50A** |
| Aug-52 | N.BLYTH-52F | W.HARTLEPOOL-51C | PERCY MAIN-52E | PERCY MAIN-52E | SUNDERLAND-54A | S.BLYTH-52F | PERCY MAIN-52E | PERCY MAIN-52E | YORK-50A |
| Jan-53 | N.BLYTH-52F | W.HARTLEPOOL-51C | PERCY MAIN-52E | PERCY MAIN-52E | SUNDERLAND-54A | S.BLYTH-52F | PERCY MAIN-52E | PERCY MAIN-52E | YORK-50A |
| Aug-53 | N.BLYTH-52F | W.HARTLEPOOL-51C | PERCY MAIN-52E | PERCY MAIN-52E | SUNDERLAND-54A | S.BLYTH-52F | PERCY MAIN-52E | PERCY MAIN-52E | YORK-50A |
| Jan-54 | N.BLYTH-52F | W.HARTLEPOOL-51C | PERCY MAIN-52E | PERCY MAIN-52E | SUNDERLAND-54A | S.BLYTH-52F | PERCY MAIN-52E | PERCY MAIN-52E | YORK-50A |
| Aug-54 | N.BLYTH-52F | W.HARTLEPOOL-51C | PERCY MAIN-52E | PERCY MAIN-52E | SUNDERLAND-54A | S.BLYTH-52F | PERCY MAIN-52E | PERCY MAIN-52E | YORK-50A |
| Jan-55 | N.BLYTH-52F | W.HARTLEPOOL-51C | PERCY MAIN-52E | PERCY MAIN-52E | SUNDERLAND-54A | S.BLYTH-52F | PERCY MAIN-52E | PERCY MAIN-52E | **1/55: MALT - 50F** |
| Aug-55 | N.BLYTH-52F | W.HARTLEPOOL-51C | PERCY MAIN-52E | PERCY MAIN-52E | SUNDERLAND-54A | S.BLYTH-52F | PERCY MAIN-52E | PERCY MAIN-52E | MALTON-50F |
| Jan-56 | N.BLYTH-52F | W.HARTLEPOOL-51C | PERCY MAIN-52E | PERCY MAIN-52E | SUNDERLAND-54A | S.BLYTH-52F | PERCY MAIN-52E | PERCY MAIN-52E | MALTON-50F |
| Aug-56 | N.BLYTH-52F | W.HARTLEPOOL-51C | PERCY MAIN-52E | PERCY MAIN-52E | SUNDERLAND-54A | S.BLYTH-52F | PERCY MAIN-52E | PERCY MAIN-52E | MALTON-50F |
| Jan-57 | N.BLYTH-52F | W.HARTLEPOOL-51C | PERCY MAIN-52E | PERCY MAIN-52E | **10/56: B. GDNS - 54C** | S.BLYTH-52F | PERCY MAIN-52E | PERCY MAIN-52E | MALTON-50F |
| Aug-57 | N.BLYTH-52F | W.HARTLEPOOL-51C | PERCY MAIN-52E | PERCY MAIN-52E | BOROUGH GARDENS-54C | S.BLYTH-52F | PERCY MAIN-52E | PERCY MAIN-52E | MALTON-50F |
| Jan-58 | N.BLYTH-52F | W.HARTLEPOOL-51C | PERCY MAIN-52E | PERCY MAIN-52E | BOROUGH GARDENS-54C | S.BLYTH-52F | PERCY MAIN-52E | PERCY MAIN-52E | MALTON-50F |
| Aug-58 | N.BLYTH-52F | W.HARTLEPOOL-51C | PERCY MAIN-52E | PERCY MAIN-52E | BOROUGH GARDENS-54C | S.BLYTH-52F | PERCY MAIN-52E | PERCY MAIN-52E | MALTON-50F |
| Jan-59 | N.BLYTH-52F | W.HARTLEPOOL-51C | PERCY MAIN-52E | PERCY MAIN-52E | BOROUGH GARDENS-52J | S.BLYTH-52F | PERCY MAIN-52E | **5/59: SUND - 52G** | MALTON-50F |
| Aug-59 | N.BLYTH-52F | W.HARTLEPOOL-51C | PERCY MAIN-52E | PERCY MAIN-52E | **6/59: SUND - 52G** | S.BLYTH-52F | PERCY MAIN-52E | **8/59: W/D** | **7/59: W/D** |
| Nov-59 | N.BLYTH-52F | W.HARTLEPOOL-51C | PERCY MAIN-52E | PERCY MAIN-52E | SUNDERLAND-52G | S.BLYTH-52F | PERCY MAIN-52E | | |
| Jan-60 | N.BLYTH-52F | W.HARTLEPOOL-51C | PERCY MAIN-52E | PERCY MAIN-52E | SUNDERLAND-52G | **12/59: W/D** | PERCY MAIN-52E | | |
| Apr-60 | N.BLYTH-52F | W.HARTLEPOOL-51C | PERCY MAIN-52E | PERCY MAIN-52E | SUNDERLAND-52G | | PERCY MAIN-52E | | |
| Aug-60 | N.BLYTH-52F | W.HARTLEPOOL-51C | PERCY MAIN-52E | PERCY MAIN-52E | SUNDERLAND-52G | | PERCY MAIN-52E | | |
| Nov-60 | N.BLYTH-52F | W.HARTLEPOOL-51C | PERCY MAIN-52E | PERCY MAIN-52E | SUNDERLAND-52G | | PERCY MAIN-52E | | |

|  | 65828 | 65829 | 65830 | 65831 | 65832 | 65833 | 65834 | 65835 | 65836 |
|---|---|---|---|---|---|---|---|---|---|
| Aug-50 | N. BLYTH - 52F | S. BLYTH - 52F | HAVERTON HILL - 51G | PERCY MAIN - 52E | SUNDERLAND - 54A | SUNDERLAND - 54A | S. BLYTH - 52F | SUNDERLAND - 54A | SUNDERLAND - 54A |
| Jan-51 | N. BLYTH - 52F | S. BLYTH - 52F | HAVERTON HILL - 51G | PERCY MAIN - 52E | SUNDERLAND - 54A | SUNDERLAND - 54A | S. BLYTH - 52F | SUNDERLAND - 54A | SUNDERLAND - 54A |
| Aug-51 | N. BLYTH - 52F | S. BLYTH - 52F | HAVERTON HILL - 51G | PERCY MAIN - 52E | SUNDERLAND - 54A | SUNDERLAND - 54A | S. BLYTH - 52F | SUNDERLAND - 54A | SUNDERLAND - 54A |
| Jan-52 | N. BLYTH - 52F | S. BLYTH - 52F | HAVERTON HILL - 51G | PERCY MAIN - 52E | SUNDERLAND - 54A | SUNDERLAND - 54A | S. BLYTH - 52F | SUNDERLAND - 54A | SUNDERLAND - 54A |
| Aug-52 | N. BLYTH - 52F | S. BLYTH - 52F | HAVERTON HILL - 51G | PERCY MAIN - 52E | SUNDERLAND - 54A | SUNDERLAND - 54A | S. BLYTH - 52F | SUNDERLAND - 54A | SUNDERLAND - 54A |
| Jan-53 | N. BLYTH - 52F | S. BLYTH - 52F | HAVERTON HILL - 51G | PERCY MAIN - 52E | SUNDERLAND - 54A | SUNDERLAND - 54A | S. BLYTH - 52F | SUNDERLAND - 54A | SUNDERLAND - 54A |
| Aug-53 | N. BLYTH - 52F | S. BLYTH - 52F | HAVERTON HILL - 51G | PERCY MAIN - 52E | SUNDERLAND - 54A | SUNDERLAND - 54A | S. BLYTH - 52F | SUNDERLAND - 54A | SUNDERLAND - 54A |
| Jan-54 | N. BLYTH - 52F | S. BLYTH - 52F | HAVERTON HILL - 51G | PERCY MAIN - 52E | SUNDERLAND - 54A | SUNDERLAND - 54A | S. BLYTH - 52F | SUNDERLAND - 54A | SUNDERLAND - 54A |
| Aug-54 | N. BLYTH - 52F | S. BLYTH - 52F | HAVERTON HILL - 51G | PERCY MAIN - 52E | SUNDERLAND - 54A | SUNDERLAND - 54A | S. BLYTH - 52F | SUNDERLAND - 54A | SUNDERLAND - 54A |
| Jan-55 | N. BLYTH - 52F | S. BLYTH - 52F | HAVERTON HILL - 51G | PERCY MAIN - 52E | SUNDERLAND - 54A | SUNDERLAND - 54A | S. BLYTH - 52F | SUNDERLAND - 54A | SUNDERLAND - 54A |
| Aug-55 | N. BLYTH - 52F | S. BLYTH - 52F | HAVERTON HILL - 51G | PERCY MAIN - 52E | SUNDERLAND - 54A | SUNDERLAND - 54A | S. BLYTH - 52F | SUNDERLAND - 54A | SUNDERLAND - 54A |
| Jan-56 | N. BLYTH - 52F | S. BLYTH - 52F | HAVERTON HILL - 51G | PERCY MAIN - 52E | SUNDERLAND - 54A | SUNDERLAND - 54A | S. BLYTH - 52F | SUNDERLAND - 54A | SUNDERLAND - 54A |
| Aug-56 | N. BLYTH - 52F | S. BLYTH - 52F | HAVERTON HILL - 51G | PERCY MAIN - 52E | SUNDERLAND - 54A | SUNDERLAND - 54A | S. BLYTH - 52F | SUNDERLAND - 54A | SUNDERLAND - 54A |
| Jan-57 | N. BLYTH - 52F | S. BLYTH - 52F | HAVERTON HILL - 51G | PERCY MAIN - 52E | SUNDERLAND - 54A | SUNDERLAND - 54A | S. BLYTH - 52F | SUNDERLAND - 54A | SUNDERLAND - 54A |
| Aug-57 | N. BLYTH - 52F | S. BLYTH - 52F | HAVERTON HILL - 51G | PERCY MAIN - 52E | SUNDERLAND - 54A | SUNDERLAND - 54A | S. BLYTH - 52F | SUNDERLAND - 54A | SUNDERLAND - 54A |
| Jan-58 | N. BLYTH - 52F | S. BLYTH - 52F | HAVERTON HILL - 51G | PERCY MAIN - 52E | SUNDERLAND - 54A | SUNDERLAND - 54A | S. BLYTH - 52F | SUNDERLAND - 54A | SUNDERLAND - 54A |
| Aug-58 | N. BLYTH - 52F | S. BLYTH - 52F | **6/58: W. HART - 51C** | PERCY MAIN - 52E | SUNDERLAND - 54A | SUNDERLAND - 54A | S. BLYTH - 52F | SUNDERLAND - 54A | SUNDERLAND - 54A |
| Jan-59 | N. BLYTH - 52F | S. BLYTH - 52F | W. HARTLEPOOL - 51C | PERCY MAIN - 52E | SUNDERLAND - 52G | SUNDERLAND - 52G | S. BLYTH - 52F | SUNDERLAND - 52G | SUNDERLAND - 52G |
| Aug-59 | N. BLYTH - 52F | **3/59: W/D** | W. HARTLEPOOL - 51C | PERCY MAIN - 52E | SUNDERLAND - 52G | SUNDERLAND - 52G | S. BLYTH - 52F | SUNDERLAND - 52G | **4/59: W/D** |
| Nov-59 | N. BLYTH - 52F |  | W. HARTLEPOOL - 51C | PERCY MAIN - 52E | SUNDERLAND - 52G | SUNDERLAND - 52G | S. BLYTH - 52F | SUNDERLAND - 52G |  |
| Jan-60 | N. BLYTH - 52F |  | W. HARTLEPOOL - 51C | PERCY MAIN - 52E | SUNDERLAND - 52G | SUNDERLAND - 52G | S. BLYTH - 52F | SUNDERLAND - 52G |  |
| Apr-60 | N. BLYTH - 52F |  | W. HARTLEPOOL - 51C | PERCY MAIN - 52E | SUNDERLAND - 52G | SUNDERLAND - 52G | S. BLYTH - 52F | SUNDERLAND - 52G |  |
| Aug-60 | N. BLYTH - 52F |  | W. HARTLEPOOL - 51C | PERCY MAIN - 52E | SUNDERLAND - 52G | SUNDERLAND - 52G | S. BLYTH - 52F | SUNDERLAND - 52G |  |
| Nov-60 | N. BLYTH - 52F |  | W. HARTLEPOOL - 51C | PERCY MAIN - 52E | SUNDERLAND - 52G | SUNDERLAND - 52G | S. BLYTH - 52F | SUNDERLAND - 52G |  |

|  | 65837 | 65838 | 65839 | 65840 | 65841 | 65842 | 65843 | 65844 | 65845 |
|---|---|---|---|---|---|---|---|---|---|
| Aug-50 | PERCY MAIN - 52E | PERCY MAIN - 52E | PERCY MAIN - 52E | SUNDERLAND - 54A | SUNDERLAND - 54A | HEATON - 52B | SUNDERLAND - 54A | SELBY - 50C | YORK - 50A |
| Jan-51 | PERCY MAIN - 52E | PERCY MAIN - 52E | PERCY MAIN - 52E | SUNDERLAND - 54A | SUNDERLAND - 54A | HEATON - 52B | SUNDERLAND - 54A | SELBY - 50C | YORK - 50A |
| Aug-51 | PERCY MAIN - 52E | PERCY MAIN - 52E | PERCY MAIN - 52E | SUNDERLAND - 54A | SUNDERLAND - 54A | HEATON - 52B | SUNDERLAND - 54A | SELBY - 50C | YORK - 50A |
| Jan-52 | PERCY MAIN - 52E | PERCY MAIN - 52E | PERCY MAIN - 52E | SUNDERLAND - 54A | SUNDERLAND - 54A | HEATON - 52B | SUNDERLAND - 54A | **10/51: YORK - 50A** | YORK - 50A |
| Aug-52 | PERCY MAIN - 52E | PERCY MAIN - 52E | PERCY MAIN - 52E | SUNDERLAND - 54A | SUNDERLAND - 54A | **7/52: PCYM - 52E** | SUNDERLAND - 54A | YORK - 50A | YORK - 50A |
| Jan-53 | PERCY MAIN - 52E | PERCY MAIN - 52E | PERCY MAIN - 52E | SUNDERLAND - 54A | SUNDERLAND - 54A | PERCY MAIN - 52E | SUNDERLAND - 54A | YORK - 50A | YORK - 50A |
| Aug-53 | PERCY MAIN - 52E | **11/53: N.BLYTH - 52F** | PERCY MAIN - 52E | SUNDERLAND - 54A | SUNDERLAND - 54A | PERCY MAIN - 52E | SUNDERLAND - 54A | YORK - 50A | YORK - 50A |
| Jan-54 | PERCY MAIN - 52E | **12/53: S.BLYTH - 52F** | PERCY MAIN - 52E | SUNDERLAND - 54A | SUNDERLAND - 54A | PERCY MAIN - 52E | SUNDERLAND - 54A | YORK - 50A | YORK - 50A |
| Aug-54 | PERCY MAIN - 52E | S. BLYTH - 52F | PERCY MAIN - 52E | SUNDERLAND - 54A | SUNDERLAND - 54A | PERCY MAIN - 52E | SUNDERLAND - 54A | YORK - 50A | YORK - 50A |
| Jan-55 | PERCY MAIN - 52E | S. BLYTH - 52F | PERCY MAIN - 52E | SUNDERLAND - 54A | SUNDERLAND - 54A | PERCY MAIN - 52E | SUNDERLAND - 54A | **1/55: MALT - 50F** | YORK - 50A |
| Aug-55 | PERCY MAIN - 52E | S. BLYTH - 52F | PERCY MAIN - 52E | SUNDERLAND - 54A | SUNDERLAND - 54A | PERCY MAIN - 52E | SUNDERLAND - 54A | MALTON - 50F | YORK - 50A |
| Jan-56 | PERCY MAIN - 52E | S. BLYTH - 52F | PERCY MAIN - 52E | SUNDERLAND - 54A | SUNDERLAND - 54A | PERCY MAIN - 52E | SUNDERLAND - 54A | MALTON - 50F | YORK - 50A |
| Aug-56 | PERCY MAIN - 52E | S. BLYTH - 52F | PERCY MAIN - 52E | SUNDERLAND - 54A | SUNDERLAND - 54A | PERCY MAIN - 52E | SUNDERLAND - 54A | MALTON - 50F | YORK - 50A |
| Jan-57 | PERCY MAIN - 52E | S. BLYTH - 52F | PERCY MAIN - 52E | SUNDERLAND - 54A | SUNDERLAND - 54A | PERCY MAIN - 52E | SUNDERLAND - 54A | MALTON - 50F | YORK - 50A |
| Aug-57 | PERCY MAIN - 52E | S. BLYTH - 52F | PERCY MAIN - 52E | SUNDERLAND - 54A | SUNDERLAND - 54A | PERCY MAIN - 52E | SUNDERLAND - 54A | MALTON - 50F | YORK - 50A |
| Jan-58 | PERCY MAIN - 52E | S. BLYTH - 52F | PERCY MAIN - 52E | SUNDERLAND - 54A | SUNDERLAND - 54A | PERCY MAIN - 52E | SUNDERLAND - 54A | MALTON - 50F | YORK - 50A |
| Aug-58 | PERCY MAIN - 52E | S. BLYTH - 52F | PERCY MAIN - 52E | SUNDERLAND - 54A | SUNDERLAND - 54A | PERCY MAIN - 52E | SUNDERLAND - 54A | MALTON - 50F | YORK - 50A |
| Jan-59 | PERCY MAIN - 52E | S. BLYTH - 52F | PERCY MAIN - 52E | SUNDERLAND - 52G | SUNDERLAND - 52G | PERCY MAIN - 52E | SUNDERLAND - 52G | MALTON - 50F | YORK - 50A |
| Aug-59 | PERCY MAIN - 52E | S. BLYTH - 52F | PERCY MAIN - 52E | **5/59: W/D** | SUNDERLAND - 52G | PERCY MAIN - 52E | **4/59: W/D** | MALTON - 50F | YORK - 50A |
| Nov-59 | PERCY MAIN - 52E | S. BLYTH - 52F | PERCY MAIN - 52E |  | SUNDERLAND - 52G | PERCY MAIN - 52E |  | MALTON - 50F | YORK - 50A |
| Jan-60 | PERCY MAIN - 52E | S. BLYTH - 52F | PERCY MAIN - 52E |  | SUNDERLAND - 52G | PERCY MAIN - 52E |  | MALTON - 50F | YORK - 50A |
| Apr-60 | PERCY MAIN - 52E | S. BLYTH - 52F | PERCY MAIN - 52E |  | SUNDERLAND - 52G | PERCY MAIN - 52E |  | MALTON - 50F | YORK - 50A |
| Aug-60 | PERCY MAIN - 52E | S. BLYTH - 52F | PERCY MAIN - 52E |  | SUNDERLAND - 52G | PERCY MAIN - 52E |  | MALTON - 50F | YORK - 50A |
| Nov-60 | PERCY MAIN - 52E | S. BLYTH - 52F | PERCY MAIN - 52E |  | SUNDERLAND - 52G | PERCY MAIN - 52E |  | MALTON - 50F | YORK - 50A |

|  | 65846 | 65847 | 65848 | 65849 | 65850 | 65851 | 65852 | 65853 | 65854 |
|---|---|---|---|---|---|---|---|---|---|
| Aug-50 | W. HARTLEPOOL - 51C | SUNDERLAND - 54A | SELBY - 50C | YORK - 50A | SUNDERLAND - 54A | N. BLYTH - 52F | PERCY MAIN - 52E | HAVERTON HILL - 51G | SUNDERLAND - 54A |
| Jan-51 | W. HARTLEPOOL - 51C | SUNDERLAND - 54A | SELBY - 50C | YORK - 50A | SUNDERLAND - 54A | N. BLYTH - 52F | PERCY MAIN - 52E | HAVERTON HILL - 51G | SUNDERLAND - 54A |
| Aug-51 | W. HARTLEPOOL - 51C | SUNDERLAND - 54A | SELBY - 50C | YORK - 50A | SUNDERLAND - 54A | N. BLYTH - 52F | PERCY MAIN - 52E | HAVERTON HILL - 51G | SUNDERLAND - 54A |
| Jan-52 | W. HARTLEPOOL - 51C | SUNDERLAND - 54A | **10/51: YORK - 50A** | YORK - 50A | SUNDERLAND - 54A | N. BLYTH - 52F | PERCY MAIN - 52E | HAVERTON HILL - 51G | SUNDERLAND - 54A |
| Aug-52 | W. HARTLEPOOL - 51C | SUNDERLAND - 54A | YORK - 50A | YORK - 50A | SUNDERLAND - 54A | N. BLYTH - 52F | PERCY MAIN - 52E | HAVERTON HILL - 51G | SUNDERLAND - 54A |
| Jan-53 | W. HARTLEPOOL - 51C | SUNDERLAND - 54A | YORK - 50A | YORK - 50A | SUNDERLAND - 54A | N. BLYTH - 52F | PERCY MAIN - 52E | HAVERTON HILL - 51G | SUNDERLAND - 54A |
| Aug-53 | W. HARTLEPOOL - 51C | SUNDERLAND - 54A | YORK - 50A | YORK - 50A | SUNDERLAND - 54A | N. BLYTH - 52F | PERCY MAIN - 52E | HAVERTON HILL - 51G | SUNDERLAND - 54A |
| Jan-54 | W. HARTLEPOOL - 51C | SUNDERLAND - 54A | YORK - 50A | YORK - 50A | SUNDERLAND - 54A | N. BLYTH - 52F | PERCY MAIN - 52E | HAVERTON HILL - 51G | SUNDERLAND - 54A |
| Aug-54 | W. HARTLEPOOL - 51C | SUNDERLAND - 54A | YORK - 50A | YORK - 50A | SUNDERLAND - 54A | N. BLYTH - 52F | PERCY MAIN - 52E | HAVERTON HILL - 51G | SUNDERLAND - 54A |
| Jan-55 | W. HARTLEPOOL - 51C | SUNDERLAND - 54A | **1/55: MALT - 50F** | **1/55: MALT - 50F** | SUNDERLAND - 54A | N. BLYTH - 52F | PERCY MAIN - 52E | HAVERTON HILL - 51G | SUNDERLAND - 54A |
| Aug-55 | W. HARTLEPOOL - 51C | SUNDERLAND - 54A | MALTON - 50F | MALTON - 50F | SUNDERLAND - 54A | N. BLYTH - 52F | PERCY MAIN - 52E | HAVERTON HILL - 51G | SUNDERLAND - 54A |
| Jan-56 | W. HARTLEPOOL - 51C | SUNDERLAND - 54A | MALTON - 50F | MALTON - 50F | SUNDERLAND - 54A | N. BLYTH - 52F | PERCY MAIN - 52E | HAVERTON HILL - 51G | SUNDERLAND - 54A |
| Aug-56 | W. HARTLEPOOL - 51C | SUNDERLAND - 54A | MALTON - 50F | MALTON - 50F | SUNDERLAND - 54A | N. BLYTH - 52F | PERCY MAIN - 52E | HAVERTON HILL - 51G | SUNDERLAND - 54A |
| Jan-57 | W. HARTLEPOOL - 51C | SUNDERLAND - 54A | MALTON - 50F | MALTON - 50F | SUNDERLAND - 54A | N. BLYTH - 52F | PERCY MAIN - 52E | HAVERTON HILL - 51G | SUNDERLAND - 54A |
| Aug-57 | W. HARTLEPOOL - 51C | SUNDERLAND - 54A | MALTON - 50F | MALTON - 50F | SUNDERLAND - 54A | N. BLYTH - 52F | PERCY MAIN - 52E | HAVERTON HILL - 51G | SUNDERLAND - 54A |
| Jan-58 | W. HARTLEPOOL - 51C | SUNDERLAND - 54A | MALTON - 50F | MALTON - 50F | SUNDERLAND - 54A | N. BLYTH - 52F | PERCY MAIN - 52E | HAVERTON HILL - 51G | SUNDERLAND - 54A |
| Aug-58 | W. HARTLEPOOL - 51C | **6/58: B.GDNS - 54C** | MALTON - 50F | MALTON - 50F | SUNDERLAND - 54A | N. BLYTH - 52F | PERCY MAIN - 52E | HAVERTON HILL - 51G | SUNDERLAND - 54A |
| Jan-59 | W. HARTLEPOOL - 51C | BOROUGH GARDENS - 52J | MALTON - 50F | MALTON - 50F | SUNDERLAND - 52G | N. BLYTH - 52F | PERCY MAIN - 52E | **10/58: STOCK - 51E** | SUNDERLAND - 52G |
| Aug-59 | W. HARTLEPOOL - 51C | **6/59: S.BLYTH - 52F** | MALTON - 50F | MALTON - 50F | SUNDERLAND - 52G | N. BLYTH - 52F | PERCY MAIN - 52E | **6/59: TBY - 51L** | SUNDERLAND - 52G |
| Nov-59 | W. HARTLEPOOL - 51C | S. BLYTH - 52F | **9/59: W/D** | MALTON - 50F | SUNDERLAND - 52G | N. BLYTH - 52F | PERCY MAIN - 52E | THORNABY - 51L | SUNDERLAND - 52G |
| Jan-60 | W. HARTLEPOOL - 51C | S. BLYTH - 52F |  | MALTON - 50F | SUNDERLAND - 52G | N. BLYTH - 52F | PERCY MAIN - 52E | THORNABY - 51L | SUNDERLAND - 52G |
| Apr-60 | W. HARTLEPOOL - 51C | **2/60: W/D** |  | MALTON - 50F | SUNDERLAND - 52G | N. BLYTH - 52F | PERCY MAIN - 52E | THORNABY - 51L | SUNDERLAND - 52G |
| Aug-60 | W. HARTLEPOOL - 51C |  |  | MALTON - 50F | SUNDERLAND - 52G | N. BLYTH - 52F | PERCY MAIN - 52E | THORNABY - 51L | SUNDERLAND - 52G |
| Nov-60 | W. HARTLEPOOL - 51C |  |  | MALTON - 50F | SUNDERLAND - 52G | N. BLYTH - 52F | PERCY MAIN - 52E | THORNABY - 51L | SUNDERLAND - 52G |

|  | 65855 | 65856 | 65857 | 65858 | 65859 | 65860 | 65861 | 65862 | 65863 |
|---|---|---|---|---|---|---|---|---|---|
| Aug-50 | HAVERTON HILL - 51G | SUNDERLAND - 54A | SALTBURN - 51K | PERCY MAIN - 52E | HAVERTON HILL - 51G | STOCKTON - 51E | YORK - 50A | HEATON - 52B | HEATON - 52B |
| Jan-51 | HAVERTON HILL - 51G | SUNDERLAND - 54A | **1/51: WHITBY - 50G** | PERCY MAIN - 52E | HAVERTON HILL - 51G | STOCKTON - 51E | YORK - 50A | HEATON - 52B | HEATON - 52B |
| Aug-51 | HAVERTON HILL - 51G | SUNDERLAND - 54A | WHITBY - 50G | PERCY MAIN - 52E | HAVERTON HILL - 51G | STOCKTON - 51E | YORK - 50A | HEATON - 52B | HEATON - 52B |
| Jan-52 | HAVERTON HILL - 51G | SUNDERLAND - 54A | WHITBY - 50G | PERCY MAIN - 52E | HAVERTON HILL - 51G | STOCKTON - 51E | YORK - 50A | HEATON - 52B | HEATON - 52B |
| Aug-52 | HAVERTON HILL - 51G | SUNDERLAND - 54A | **7/52: SELBY - 50C** | PERCY MAIN - 52E | HAVERTON HILL - 51G | STOCKTON - 51E | YORK - 50A | HEATON - 52B | HEATON - 52B |
| Jan-53 | HAVERTON HILL - 51G | SUNDERLAND - 54A | SELBY - 50C | PERCY MAIN - 52E | HAVERTON HILL - 51G | STOCKTON - 51E | YORK - 50A | HEATON - 52B | **12/52: N.BLYTH - 52F** |
| Aug-53 | HAVERTON HILL - 51G | SUNDERLAND - 54A | SELBY - 50C | PERCY MAIN - 52E | HAVERTON HILL - 51G | STOCKTON - 51E | YORK - 50A | HEATON - 52B | N. BLYTH - 52F |
| Jan-54 | HAVERTON HILL - 51G | SUNDERLAND - 54A | SELBY - 50C | PERCY MAIN - 52E | HAVERTON HILL - 51G | STOCKTON - 51E | YORK - 50A | HEATON - 52B | N. BLYTH - 52F |
| Aug-54 | HAVERTON HILL - 51G | SUNDERLAND - 54A | SELBY - 50C | PERCY MAIN - 52E | HAVERTON HILL - 51G | STOCKTON - 51E | **6/54: SELBY - 50C** | HEATON - 52B | N. BLYTH - 52F |
| Jan-55 | HAVERTON HILL - 51G | SUNDERLAND - 54A | **11/54: YORK - 50A** | PERCY MAIN - 52E | HAVERTON HILL - 51G | STOCKTON - 51E | SELBY - 50C | HEATON - 52B | N. BLYTH - 52F |
| Aug-55 | HAVERTON HILL - 51G | SUNDERLAND - 54A | YORK - 50A | PERCY MAIN - 52E | HAVERTON HILL - 51G | STOCKTON - 51E | SELBY - 50C | HEATON - 52B | N. BLYTH - 52F |
| Jan-56 | HAVERTON HILL - 51G | SUNDERLAND - 54A | YORK - 50A | PERCY MAIN - 52E | HAVERTON HILL - 51G | STOCKTON - 51E | SELBY - 50C | HEATON - 52B | N. BLYTH - 52F |
| Aug-56 | HAVERTON HILL - 51G | SUNDERLAND - 54A | YORK - 50A | PERCY MAIN - 52E | HAVERTON HILL - 51G | STOCKTON - 51E | SELBY - 50C | HEATON - 52B | N. BLYTH - 52F |
| Jan-57 | HAVERTON HILL - 51G | SUNDERLAND - 54A | YORK - 50A | PERCY MAIN - 52E | HAVERTON HILL - 51G | **10/56: DARL - 51A** | SELBY - 50C | HEATON - 52B | N. BLYTH - 52F |
| Aug-57 | HAVERTON HILL - 51G | SUNDERLAND - 54A | YORK - 50A | PERCY MAIN - 52E | HAVERTON HILL - 51G | DARLINGTON - 51A | SELBY - 50C | HEATON - 52B | N. BLYTH - 52F |
| Jan-58 | HAVERTON HILL - 51G | SUNDERLAND - 54A | **10/57: N.BLYTH - 52F** | PERCY MAIN - 52E | HAVERTON HILL - 51G | DARLINGTON - 51A | SELBY - 50C | HEATON - 52B | N. BLYTH - 52F |
| Aug-58 | HAVERTON HILL - 51G | SUNDERLAND - 54A | N. BLYTH - 52F | PERCY MAIN - 52E | HAVERTON HILL - 51G | DARLINGTON - 51A | SELBY - 50C | HEATON - 52B | N. BLYTH - 52F |
| Jan-59 | **2/59: TBY - 51L** | SUNDERLAND - 52G | N. BLYTH - 52F | PERCY MAIN - 52E | **2/59: TBY - 51L** | DARLINGTON - 51A | SELBY - 50C | HEATON - 52B | N. BLYTH - 52F |
| Aug-59 | THORNABY - 51L | **8/59: W/D** | N. BLYTH - 52F | PERCY MAIN - 52E | THORNABY - 51L | DARLINGTON - 51A | **9/59: S.BLYTH - 52F** | HEATON - 52B | N. BLYTH - 52F |
| Nov-59 | THORNABY - 51L |  | N. BLYTH - 52F | PERCY MAIN - 52E | THORNABY - 51L | DARLINGTON - 51A | S. BLYTH - 52F | HEATON - 52B | N. BLYTH - 52F |
| Jan-60 | THORNABY - 51L |  | N. BLYTH - 52F | PERCY MAIN - 52E | THORNABY - 51L | DARLINGTON - 51A | S. BLYTH - 52F | HEATON - 52B | N. BLYTH - 52F |
| Apr-60 | THORNABY - 51L |  | N. BLYTH - 52F | PERCY MAIN - 52E | THORNABY - 51L | DARLINGTON - 51A | S. BLYTH - 52F | HEATON - 52B | N. BLYTH - 52F |
| Aug-60 | THORNABY - 51L |  | N. BLYTH - 52F | PERCY MAIN - 52E | THORNABY - 51L | DARLINGTON - 51A | S. BLYTH - 52F | HEATON - 52B | N. BLYTH - 52F |
| Nov-60 | THORNABY - 51L |  | N. BLYTH - 52F | PERCY MAIN - 52E | THORNABY - 51L | DARLINGTON - 51A | S. BLYTH - 52F | HEATON - 52B | N. BLYTH - 52F |

*The J27 was the standard NER goods 0-6-0, not much less powerful than a Q6 but with a much wider route availability. The class was scattered over most parts of the North Eastern although the majority were to be found in the Tyne area where, since most local trains were limited to a maximum of 50 wagons, there was often nothing to be gained from using a larger engine. 65863 stands at North Blyth shed in July 1959.*

## DISTRIBUTION OF 0-6-0 GOODS ENGINES : 1957

| Shed | J6 | J10 | J11 | J15 | J17 | J19 | J20 | J21 | J25 | J26 | J27 | J35 | J36 | J37 | J38 | J39 | Total |
|---|---|---|---|---|---|---|---|---|---|---|---|---|---|---|---|---|---|
| St Margarets | | | | | | | | | | | | 14 | 11 | 29 | 12 | 4 | 70 |
| Stratford | | | | 10 | 12 | 7 | 11 | | | | | | | | | | 57 |
| Colwick | 21 | 6 | | | | | | | | | | | | | | 18 | 45 |
| Newport | | | | | | | | | | | 38 | | | | | | 38 |
| Cambridge | | | | 8 | 16 | 4 | 4 | | | | | | | | | 5 | 37 |
| Thornton Jcn | | | | | | | | | | | | 7 | 3 | 12 | 15 | | 37 |
| March | | | | 2 | 10 | 11 | 10 | | | | | | | | | | 33 |
| New England | 27 | | | | | | | | | | | | | | | 5 | 32 |
| Gorton | | | 25 | | | | | | | | | | | | | 7 | 32 |
| Retford | 9 | 15 | | | | | | | | | | | | | | 8 | 32 |
| Doncaster | 12 | 4 | | | | | | | | | | | | | | 14 | 30 |
| Ardsley | 7 | | | | | | | | | | | | | | | 22 | 29 |
| Bathgate | | | | | | | | | | | | 7 | 19 | 3 | | | 29 |
| Colchester | | | | 13 | 4 | 11 | | | | | | | | | | | 28 |
| Dunfermline | | | | | | | | | | | | 10 | 5 | 6 | 6 | 1 | 28 |
| N. Blyth | | | | | | | | | 1 | | 24 | | | | | | 25 |
| Ipswich | | | | 6 | 4 | | | | | | | | | | | 14 | 24 |
| Lincoln | | 8 | | | | | | | | | | | | | | 15 | 23 |
| Borough Gdns | | | | | | | | 7 | | | 3 | | | | | 13 | 23 |
| P. Main | | | | | | | | | | 23 | | | | | | | 23 |
| Sunderland | | | | | | | | | 1 | | 18 | | | | | 2 | 21 |
| Dundee | | | | | | | | | | | | | 4 | 10 | | 6 | 20 |
| Norwich | | | | 4 | 7 | 2 | | | | | | | | | | 7 | 20 |
| Carlisle (C) | | | | | | | | | | | | 3 | 3 | | | 14 | 20 |
| Polmont | | | | | | | | | | | | 3 | 6 | 9 | 2 | | 20 |
| Darnall | | | 10 | | | | | | | | | | | | | 9 | 19 |
| Eastfield | | | | | | | | | | | | 5 | | 14 | | | 19 |
| Heaton | | | | | | | | | 2 | 2 | 7 | | | | | 6 | 17 |
| Neville Hill | | | | | | | | | 4 | | | | | | | 13 | 17 |
| K. Lynn | | | | 13 | | | | | | | | | | | | | 13 |
| Starbeck | | | | | | | | | 1 | | | | | | | 12 | 13 |
| Parkhead | | | | | | | | | | | | 2 | 3 | 8 | | | 13 |
| Parkeston | | | | 3 | | | | | | | | | | | | 9 | 12 |
| Spital Bge | | | | | | | | | | | | | | | | 12 | 12 |
| Dairycoates | | | | | | | | | | 5 | | | | | | 7 | 12 |
| Kipps | | | | | | | | | | | | 8 | 2 | 2 | | | 12 |
| Barnsley | | 10 | | | | | | | | | | | | | | 1 | 11 |
| Immingham | | 11 | | | | | | | | | | | | | | | 11 |
| Blaydon | | | | | | | | 2 | 1 | | | | | | | 8 | 11 |
| Selby | | | | | | | | | 1 | | 6 | | | | | 4 | 11 |
| York | | | | | | | | | 3 | 8 | | | | | | | 11 |
| Boston | 10 | | | | | | | | | | | | | | | | 10 |
| Wigan | | 10 | | | | | | | | | | | | | | | 10 |
| Tweedmouth | | | | | | | | | 3 | | | | | | | 7 | 10 |
| W. Auckland | | | | | | | | | 3 | | | | | | | 7 | 10 |
| W. Hartlepool | | | | | | | | | 2 | 8 | | | | | | | 10 |
| Dalry Rd | | | | | | | | | | | | 4 | | 6 | | | 10 |
| Langwith Jcn | | | 9 | | | | | | | | | | | | | | 9 |

| Shed | J6 | J10 | J11 | J15 | J17 | J21 | J25 | J26 | J27 | J35 | J36 | J37 | J39 | Total |
|---|---|---|---|---|---|---|---|---|---|---|---|---|---|---|
| Hitchin | 7 | | | 1 | | | | | | | | | | 8 |
| Staveley | | | 8 | | | | | | | | | | | 8 |
| Malton | | | | | | | | | | | | 4 | 4 | 8 |
| H. Mersey | | 7 | | | | | | | | | | | | 7 |
| Tyne Dock | | | | | | | | 1 | 6 | | | | | 7 |
| H. Hill | | | | | | | | | 7 | | | | | 7 |
| Gateshead | | | | | | | | | | | | | 7 | 7 |
| St Rollox | | | | | | | | | | | 7 | | | 7 |
| Hawick | | | | | | | | | | 3 | 3 | 1 | | 7 |
| Bradford | 3 | | | | | | | | | | | | 3 | 6 |
| Annesley | | | 6 | | | | | | | | | | | 6 |
| Woodford | | | 6 | | | | | | | | | | | 6 |
| Lowestoft | | | | 3 | 3 | | | | | | | | | 6 |
| Melton C | | | | | 5 | | | | | | | | 1 | 6 |
| Middlesbrough | | | | | | | 1 | 4 | 1 | | | | | 6 |
| Stockton | | | | | | | | 3 | 3 | | | | | 6 |
| Haymarket | | | | | | | | | | | | 6 | | 6 |
| Stirling | | | | | | | | | | 2 | | 4 | | 6 |
| Hornsey | 5 | | | | | | | | | | | | | 5 |
| Mexborough | | | 5 | | | | | | | | | | | 5 |
| Brunswick | | 5 | | | | | | | | | | | | 5 |
| Northwich | | 5 | | | | | | | | | | | | 5 |
| T. Park | | 5 | | | | | | | | | | | | 5 |
| Tuxford | | | 5 | | | | | | | | | | | 5 |
| Ferryhill | | | | | | | | | | 2 | 1 | | 2 | 5 |
| Polmadie | | | | | | | | | | 2 | 3 | | | 5 |
| Copley Hill | 3 | | | | | | | | | | | 1 | | 4 |
| Frodingham | | | 4 | | | | | | | | | | | 4 |
| S. Blyth | | | | | | | | 2 | 2 | | | | | 4 |
| Alnmouth | | | | | | | | | | | | | 4 | 4 |
| Kittybrewster | | | | | | | | | | 1 | 3 | | | 4 |
| Grantham | 3 | | | | | | | | | | | | | 3 |
| Widnes | | 3 | | | | | | | | | | | | 3 |
| Bury St.E | | | | | 3 | | | | | | | | | 3 |
| Balloch | | | | | | | | | | | 3 | | | 3 |
| Fort William | | | | | | | | | | | 3 | | | 3 |
| Leicester | | | 2 | | | | | | | | | | | 2 |
| Southport | 2 | | | | | | | | | | | | | 2 |
| Yarmouth (B) | | | | | 2 | | | | | | | | | 2 |
| Darlington | | | | | | | | 1 | 1 | | | | | 2 |
| Hexham | | | | | | | 2 | | | | | | | 2 |
| Whitby | | | | | | | | | 2 | | | | | 2 |
| Keith | | | | | | | | | | | | 2 | | 2 |
| Louth | | 1 | | | | | | | | | | | | 2 |
| Aintree | 1 | | | | | | | | | | | | | 1 |
| S. Lynn | | | | | 1 | | | | | | | | | 1 |
| Dawsholme | | | | | | | | | | | 1 | | | 1 |
| Carstairs | | | | | | | | | | | | 1 | | 1 |

GN : 196, GE : 214, NE : 307, GC : 186, NB : 329

| | 65864 | 65865 | 65866 | 65867 | 65868 | 65869 | 65870 | 65871 | 65872 |
|---|---|---|---|---|---|---|---|---|---|
| Aug-50 | HEATON - 52B | HAVERTON HILL - 51G | W.HARTLEPOOL - 51C | N.BLYTH - 52F | STOCKTON - 51E | HEATON - 52B | N.BLYTH - 52F | SUNDERLAND - 54A | SUNDERLAND - 54A |
| Jan-51 | HEATON - 52B | HAVERTON HILL - 51G | W.HARTLEPOOL - 51C | N.BLYTH - 52F | STOCKTON - 51E | HEATON - 52B | N.BLYTH - 52F | SUNDERLAND - 54A | SUNDERLAND - 54A |
| Aug-51 | HEATON - 52B | HAVERTON HILL - 51G | W.HARTLEPOOL - 51C | N.BLYTH - 52F | STOCKTON - 51E | HEATON - 52B | N.BLYTH - 52F | SUNDERLAND - 54A | SUNDERLAND - 54A |
| Jan-52 | HEATON - 52B | HAVERTON HILL - 51G | W.HARTLEPOOL - 51C | N.BLYTH - 52F | STOCKTON - 51E | HEATON - 52B | N.BLYTH - 52F | SUNDERLAND - 54A | SUNDERLAND - 54A |
| Aug-52 | HEATON - 52B | HAVERTON HILL - 51G | W.HARTLEPOOL - 51C | N.BLYTH - 52F | STOCKTON - 51E | HEATON - 52B | N.BLYTH - 52F | SUNDERLAND - 54A | SUNDERLAND - 54A |
| Jan-53 | **12/52: N.BLYTH - 52F** | HAVERTON HILL - 51G | W.HARTLEPOOL - 51C | N.BLYTH - 52F | STOCKTON - 51E | HEATON - 52B | N.BLYTH - 52F | SUNDERLAND - 54A | SUNDERLAND - 54A |
| Aug-53 | N.BLYTH - 52F | HAVERTON HILL - 51G | W.HARTLEPOOL - 51C | N.BLYTH - 52F | STOCKTON - 51E | HEATON - 52B | N.BLYTH - 52F | SUNDERLAND - 54A | SUNDERLAND - 54A |
| Jan-54 | N.BLYTH - 52F | **10/53: W.HPL - 51C** | W.HARTLEPOOL - 51C | N.BLYTH - 52F | STOCKTON - 51E | HEATON - 52B | N.BLYTH - 52F | SUNDERLAND - 54A | SUNDERLAND - 54A |
| Aug-54 | N.BLYTH - 52F | W.HARTLEPOOL - 51C | W.HARTLEPOOL - 51C | N.BLYTH - 52F | STOCKTON - 51E | HEATON - 52B | N.BLYTH - 52F | SUNDERLAND - 54A | SUNDERLAND - 54A |
| Jan-55 | N.BLYTH - 52F | W.HARTLEPOOL - 51C | W.HARTLEPOOL - 51C | N.BLYTH - 52F | **3/55: MBRO - 51D** | HEATON - 52B | N.BLYTH - 52F | SUNDERLAND - 54A | SUNDERLAND - 54A |
| Aug-55 | N.BLYTH - 52F | W.HARTLEPOOL - 51C | W.HARTLEPOOL - 51C | N.BLYTH - 52F | **8/55: STOCK - 51E** | HEATON - 52B | N.BLYTH - 52F | SUNDERLAND - 54A | SUNDERLAND - 54A |
| Jan-56 | N.BLYTH - 52F | W.HARTLEPOOL - 51C | W.HARTLEPOOL - 51C | N.BLYTH - 52F | STOCKTON - 51E | HEATON - 52B | N.BLYTH - 52F | SUNDERLAND - 54A | SUNDERLAND - 54A |
| Aug-56 | **8/56: P.MAIN - 52E** | W.HARTLEPOOL - 51C | W.HARTLEPOOL - 51C | N.BLYTH - 52F | STOCKTON - 51E | HEATON - 52B | **8/56: MBRO - 51D** | SUNDERLAND - 54A | SUNDERLAND - 54A |
| Jan-57 | **10/56: HTN - 52B** | W.HARTLEPOOL - 51C | W.HARTLEPOOL - 51C | N.BLYTH - 52F | STOCKTON - 51E | HEATON - 52B | **2/57: SALT - 51K** | SUNDERLAND - 54A | SUNDERLAND - 54A |
| Aug-57 | HEATON - 52B | W.HARTLEPOOL - 51C | W.HARTLEPOOL - 51C | N.BLYTH - 52F | STOCKTON - 51E | HEATON - 52B | **3/57: MBRO - 51D** | SUNDERLAND - 54A | SUNDERLAND - 54A |
| Jan-58 | HEATON - 52B | W.HARTLEPOOL - 51C | W.HARTLEPOOL - 51C | N.BLYTH - 52F | STOCKTON - 51E | HEATON - 52B | MIDDLESBROUGH - 51D | SUNDERLAND - 54A | SUNDERLAND - 54A |
| Aug-58 | HEATON - 52B | W.HARTLEPOOL - 51C | W.HARTLEPOOL - 51C | N.BLYTH - 52F | STOCKTON - 51E | HEATON - 52B | **6/58: TBY - 51L** | SUNDERLAND - 54A | SUNDERLAND - 54A |
| Jan-59 | HEATON - 52B | **2/59: TBY - 51L** | W.HARTLEPOOL - 51C | N.BLYTH - 52F | **2/59: TBY - 51L** | HEATON - 52B | THORNABY - 51L | SUNDERLAND - 52G | SUNDERLAND - 52G |
| Aug-59 | HEATON - 52B | THORNABY - 51L | **6/59: W/D** | N.BLYTH - 52F | THORNABY - 51L | HEATON - 52B | THORNABY - 51L | SUNDERLAND - 52G | SUNDERLAND - 52G |
| Nov-59 | HEATON - 52B | THORNABY - 51L | | N.BLYTH - 52F | THORNABY - 51L | HEATON - 52B | THORNABY - 51L | SUNDERLAND - 52G | SUNDERLAND - 52G |
| Jan-60 | HEATON - 52B | THORNABY - 51L | | N.BLYTH - 52F | THORNABY - 51L | HEATON - 52B | THORNABY - 51L | SUNDERLAND - 52G | SUNDERLAND - 52G |
| Apr-60 | HEATON - 52B | THORNABY - 51L | | N.BLYTH - 52F | THORNABY - 51L | HEATON - 52B | THORNABY - 51L | SUNDERLAND - 52G | SUNDERLAND - 52G |
| Aug-60 | HEATON - 52B | THORNABY - 51L | | N.BLYTH - 52F | THORNABY - 51L | HEATON - 52B | THORNABY - 51L | SUNDERLAND - 52G | SUNDERLAND - 52G |
| Nov-60 | HEATON - 52B | THORNABY - 51L | | N.BLYTH - 52F | THORNABY - 51L | HEATON - 52B | THORNABY - 51L | SUNDERLAND - 52G | SUNDERLAND - 52G |

| | 65873 | 65874 | 65875 | 65876 | 65877 | 65878 | 65879 | 65880 | 65881 |
|---|---|---|---|---|---|---|---|---|---|
| Aug-50 | HEATON - 52B | SELBY - 50C | SELBY - 50C | N.BLYTH - 52F | N.BLYTH - 52F | SUNDERLAND - 54A | N.BLYTH - 52F | N.BLYTH - 52F | SELBY - 50C |
| Jan-51 | HEATON - 52B | **2/51: YORK - 50A** | SELBY - 50C | N.BLYTH - 52F | N.BLYTH - 52F | SUNDERLAND - 54A | N.BLYTH - 52F | N.BLYTH - 52F | SELBY - 50C |
| Aug-51 | HEATON - 52B | YORK - 50A | SELBY - 50C | N.BLYTH - 52F | N.BLYTH - 52F | SUNDERLAND - 54A | N.BLYTH - 52F | N.BLYTH - 52F | SELBY - 50C |
| Jan-52 | HEATON - 52B | YORK - 50A | SELBY - 50C | N.BLYTH - 52F | N.BLYTH - 52F | SUNDERLAND - 54A | N.BLYTH - 52F | N.BLYTH - 52F | SELBY - 50C |
| Aug-52 | HEATON - 52B | YORK - 50A | SELBY - 50C | N.BLYTH - 52F | N.BLYTH - 52F | SUNDERLAND - 54A | N.BLYTH - 52F | N.BLYTH - 52F | SELBY - 50C |
| Jan-53 | HEATON - 52B | YORK - 50A | SELBY - 50C | N.BLYTH - 52F | N.BLYTH - 52F | SUNDERLAND - 54A | N.BLYTH - 52F | N.BLYTH - 52F | SELBY - 50C |
| Aug-53 | HEATON - 52B | YORK - 50A | SELBY - 50C | N.BLYTH - 52F | N.BLYTH - 52F | SUNDERLAND - 54A | N.BLYTH - 52F | N.BLYTH - 52F | SELBY - 50C |
| Jan-54 | HEATON - 52B | YORK - 50A | SELBY - 50C | N.BLYTH - 52F | N.BLYTH - 52F | SUNDERLAND - 54A | N.BLYTH - 52F | N.BLYTH - 52F | SELBY - 50C |
| Aug-54 | HEATON - 52B | YORK - 50A | SELBY - 50C | N.BLYTH - 52F | N.BLYTH - 52F | SUNDERLAND - 54A | N.BLYTH - 52F | N.BLYTH - 52F | SELBY - 50C |
| Jan-55 | HEATON - 52B | YORK - 50A | SELBY - 50C | N.BLYTH - 52F | N.BLYTH - 52F | SUNDERLAND - 54A | N.BLYTH - 52F | N.BLYTH - 52F | SELBY - 50C |
| Aug-55 | HEATON - 52B | YORK - 50A | SELBY - 50C | N.BLYTH - 52F | N.BLYTH - 52F | SUNDERLAND - 54A | N.BLYTH - 52F | N.BLYTH - 52F | SELBY - 50C |
| Jan-56 | HEATON - 52B | YORK - 50A | SELBY - 50C | N.BLYTH - 52F | N.BLYTH - 52F | SUNDERLAND - 54A | N.BLYTH - 52F | N.BLYTH - 52F | SELBY - 50C |
| Aug-56 | **6/56: SUND - 54A** | YORK - 50A | SELBY - 50C | **6/56: HTN - 52B** | **8/56: S.BLYTH - 52F** | SUNDERLAND - 54A | **9/56: HTN - 52B** | N.BLYTH - 52F | SELBY - 50C |
| Jan-57 | **10/56: B.GDNS - 54C** | YORK - 50A | SELBY - 50C | HEATON - 52B | S.BLYTH - 52F | SUNDERLAND - 54A | HEATON - 52B | N.BLYTH - 52F | SELBY - 50C |
| Aug-57 | BOR.GDNS - 54C | YORK - 50A | **10/57: N.BLYTH - 52F** | HEATON - 52B | **7/57: HTN - 52B** | SUNDERLAND - 54A | HEATON - 52B | N.BLYTH - 52F | SELBY - 50C |
| Jan-58 | BOR.GDNS - 54C | YORK - 50A | N.BLYTH - 52F | HEATON - 52B | HEATON - 52B | SUNDERLAND - 54A | **10/57: N.BLYTH - 52F** | N.BLYTH - 52F | SELBY - 50C |
| Aug-58 | BOR.GDNS - 54C | YORK - 50A | N.BLYTH - 52F | HEATON - 52B | HEATON - 52B | SUNDERLAND - 54A | N.BLYTH - 52F | N.BLYTH - 52F | SELBY - 50C |
| Jan-59 | BOR.GDNS - 52J | YORK - 50A | N.BLYTH - 52F | HEATON - 52B | HEATON - 52B | SUNDERLAND - 52G | N.BLYTH - 52F | N.BLYTH - 52F | SELBY - 50C |
| Aug-59 | **5/59: SUND - 52G** | YORK - 50A | N.BLYTH - 52F | HEATON - 52B | HEATON - 52B | SUNDERLAND - 52G | N.BLYTH - 52F | N.BLYTH - 52F | SELBY - 50C |
| Nov-59 | SUNDERLAND - 52G | YORK - 50A | N.BLYTH - 52F | HEATON - 52B | **11/59: N.BLYTH - 52F** | SUNDERLAND - 52G | N.BLYTH - 52F | N.BLYTH - 52F | **9/59: N.BLYTH - 52F** |
| Jan-60 | SUNDERLAND - 52G | YORK - 50A | N.BLYTH - 52F | HEATON - 52B | N.BLYTH - 52F | SUNDERLAND - 52G | N.BLYTH - 52F | N.BLYTH - 52F | N.BLYTH - 52F |
| Apr-60 | SUNDERLAND - 52G | YORK - 50A | N.BLYTH - 52F | HEATON - 52B | N.BLYTH - 52F | SUNDERLAND - 52G | N.BLYTH - 52F | N.BLYTH - 52F | N.BLYTH - 52F |
| Aug-60 | SUNDERLAND - 52G | YORK - 50A | N.BLYTH - 52F | HEATON - 52B | N.BLYTH - 52F | SUNDERLAND - 52G | N.BLYTH - 52F | N.BLYTH - 52F | N.BLYTH - 52F |
| Nov-60 | SUNDERLAND - 52G | YORK - 50A | N.BLYTH - 52F | HEATON - 52B | N.BLYTH - 52F | SUNDERLAND - 52G | N.BLYTH - 52F | N.BLYTH - 52F | N.BLYTH - 52F |

| | 65882 | 65883 | 65884 | 65885 | 65886 | 65887 | 65888 | 65889 | 65890 |
|---|---|---|---|---|---|---|---|---|---|
| Aug-50 | SELBY - 50C | YORK - 50A | SUNDERLAND - 54A | YORK - 50A | HEATON - 52B | STOCKTON - 51E | YORK - 50A | HEATON - 52B | YORK - 50A |
| Jan-51 | SELBY - 50C | YORK - 50A | **12/50: SALT - 51K** | YORK - 50A | HEATON - 52B | **12/50: WHITBY - 50G** | YORK - 50A | HEATON - 52B | YORK - 50A |
| Aug-51 | SELBY - 50C | **8/51: WHITBY - 50G** | SALTBURN - 51K | YORK - 50A | HEATON - 52B | **8/51: YORK - 50A** | **8/51: WHITBY - 50G** | HEATON - 52B | YORK - 50A |
| Jan-52 | SELBY - 50C | **9/51: YORK - 50A** | SALTBURN - 51K | YORK - 50A | HEATON - 52B | YORK - 50A | WHITBY - 50G | HEATON - 52B | YORK - 50A |
| Aug-52 | SELBY - 50C | YORK - 50A | SALTBURN - 51K | YORK - 50A | **7/52: N.BLYTH - 52F** | YORK - 50A | **7/52: SELBY - 50C** | **7/52: N.BLYTH - 52F** | YORK - 50A |
| Jan-53 | SELBY - 50C | YORK - 50A | SALTBURN - 51K | YORK - 50A | N.BLYTH - 52F | YORK - 50A | SELBY - 50C | N.BLYTH - 52F | YORK - 50A |
| Aug-53 | SELBY - 50C | YORK - 50A | SALTBURN - 51K | YORK - 50A | N.BLYTH - 52F | YORK - 50A | SELBY - 50C | N.BLYTH - 52F | YORK - 50A |
| Jan-54 | SELBY - 50C | YORK - 50A | SALTBURN - 51K | YORK - 50A | N.BLYTH - 52F | YORK - 50A | SELBY - 50C | N.BLYTH - 52F | YORK - 50A |
| Aug-54 | **5/54: HTN - 52B** | YORK - 50A | **8/54: M'BRO - 51D** | **6/54: SELBY - 50C** | N.BLYTH - 52F | YORK - 50A | SELBY - 50C | N.BLYTH - 52F | YORK - 50A |
| Jan-55 | HEATON - 52B | YORK - 50A | MIDDLESBROUGH - 51D | SELBY - 50C | N.BLYTH - 52F | YORK - 50A | SELBY - 50C | N.BLYTH - 52F | YORK - 50A |
| Aug-55 | HEATON - 52B | YORK - 50A | **8/55: STOCK - 51E** | SELBY - 50C | N.BLYTH - 52F | YORK - 50A | SELBY - 50C | N.BLYTH - 52F | YORK - 50A |
| Jan-56 | HEATON - 52B | YORK - 50A | STOCKTON - 51E | SELBY - 50C | N.BLYTH - 52F | YORK - 50A | SELBY - 50C | N.BLYTH - 52F | YORK - 50A |
| Aug-56 | HEATON - 52B | YORK - 50A | STOCKTON - 51E | SELBY - 50C | **9/56: HTN - 52B** | YORK - 50A | SELBY - 50C | N.BLYTH - 52F | YORK - 50A |
| Jan-57 | HEATON - 52B | YORK - 50A | STOCKTON - 51E | SELBY - 50C | HEATON - 52B | YORK - 50A | SELBY - 50C | N.BLYTH - 52F | YORK - 50A |
| Aug-57 | HEATON - 52B | YORK - 50A | STOCKTON - 51E | SELBY - 50C | HEATON - 52B | YORK - 50A | SELBY - 50C | N.BLYTH - 52F | YORK - 50A |
| Jan-58 | HEATON - 52B | YORK - 50A | STOCKTON - 51E | SELBY - 50C | HEATON - 52B | YORK - 50A | SELBY - 50C | N.BLYTH - 52F | YORK - 50A |
| Aug-58 | HEATON - 52B | YORK - 50A | STOCKTON - 51E | SELBY - 50C | HEATON - 52B | YORK - 50A | SELBY - 50C | N.BLYTH - 52F | YORK - 50A |
| Jan-59 | HEATON - 52B | YORK - 50A | STOCKTON - 51E | SELBY - 50C | HEATON - 52B | YORK - 50A | SELBY - 50C | N.BLYTH - 52F | YORK - 50A |
| Aug-59 | **6/59: N.BLYTH - 52F** | YORK - 50A | **6/59: TBY - 51L** | **8/59: MALTON - 50F** | **8/59: W/D** | YORK - 50A | **9/59: MALTON - 50F** | N.BLYTH - 52F | YORK - 50A |
| Nov-59 | N.BLYTH - 52F | YORK - 50A | THORNABY - 51L | MALTON - 50F | | YORK - 50A | MALTON - 50F | N.BLYTH - 52F | YORK - 50A |
| Jan-60 | N.BLYTH - 52F | YORK - 50A | THORNABY - 51L | MALTON - 50F | | YORK - 50A | MALTON - 50F | N.BLYTH - 52F | YORK - 50A |
| Apr-60 | N.BLYTH - 52F | YORK - 50A | THORNABY - 51L | MALTON - 50F | | YORK - 50A | MALTON - 50F | N.BLYTH - 52F | YORK - 50A |
| Aug-60 | N.BLYTH - 52F | YORK - 50A | THORNABY - 51L | **9/60: YORK - 50A** | | YORK - 50A | MALTON - 50F | N.BLYTH - 52F | YORK - 50A |
| Nov-60 | N.BLYTH - 52F | YORK - 50A | THORNABY - 51L | YORK - 50A | | YORK - 50A | MALTON - 50F | N.BLYTH - 52F | YORK - 50A |

| | | | | | J38 0-6-0 (1926) | | | | |
|---|---|---|---|---|---|---|---|---|---|
| | 65891 | 65892 | 65893 | 65894 | 65900 | 65901 | 65902 | 65903 | 65904 |
| Aug-50 | SELBY - 50C | N.BLYTH - 52F | HEATON - 52B | YORK - 50A | DUNFERMLINE - 62C | THORNTON JCN - 62A | THORNTON JCN - 62A | THORNTON JCN - 62A | THORNTON JCN - 62A |
| Jan-51 | SELBY - 50C | N.BLYTH - 52F | HEATON - 52B | YORK - 50A | DUNFERMLINE - 62C | THORNTON JCN - 62A | THORNTON JCN - 62A | THORNTON JCN - 62A | THORNTON JCN - 62A |
| Aug-51 | SELBY - 50C | N.BLYTH - 52F | HEATON - 52B | YORK - 50A | DUNFERMLINE - 62C | THORNTON JCN - 62A | THORNTON JCN - 62A | THORNTON JCN - 62A | THORNTON JCN - 62A |
| Jan-52 | SELBY - 50C | N.BLYTH - 52F | HEATON - 52B | YORK - 50A | DUNFERMLINE - 62C | THORNTON JCN - 62A | THORNTON JCN - 62A | THORNTON JCN - 62A | THORNTON JCN - 62A |
| Aug-52 | SELBY - 50C | N.BLYTH - 52F | HEATON - 52B | YORK - 50A | DUNFERMLINE - 62C | THORNTON JCN - 62A | THORNTON JCN - 62A | THORNTON JCN - 62A | THORNTON JCN - 62A |
| Jan-53 | SELBY - 50C | N.BLYTH - 52F | HEATON - 52B | YORK - 50A | DUNFERMLINE - 62C | THORNTON JCN - 62A | THORNTON JCN - 62A | THORNTON JCN - 62A | THORNTON JCN - 62A |
| Aug-53 | SELBY - 50C | N.BLYTH - 52F | HEATON - 52B | YORK - 50A | DUNFERMLINE - 62C | THORNTON JCN - 62A | THORNTON JCN - 62A | THORNTON JCN - 62A | THORNTON JCN - 62A |
| Jan-54 | SELBY - 50C | N.BLYTH - 52F | HEATON - 52B | YORK - 50A | DUNFERMLINE - 62C | THORNTON JCN - 62A | THORNTON JCN - 62A | THORNTON JCN - 62A | THORNTON JCN - 62A |
| Aug-54 | SELBY - 50C | N.BLYTH - 52F | HEATON - 52B | YORK - 50A | DUNFERMLINE - 62C | THORNTON JCN - 62A | THORNTON JCN - 62A | THORNTON JCN - 62A | THORNTON JCN - 62A |
| Jan-55 | SELBY - 50C | **10/54: HTN - 52B** | HEATON - 52B | YORK - 50A | DUNFERMLINE - 62C | THORNTON JCN - 62A | THORNTON JCN - 62A | THORNTON JCN - 62A | THORNTON JCN - 62A |
| Aug-55 | SELBY - 50C | HEATON - 52B | HEATON - 52B | YORK - 50A | DUNFERMLINE - 62C | THORNTON JCN - 62A | THORNTON JCN - 62A | THORNTON JCN - 62A | THORNTON JCN - 62A |
| Jan-56 | SELBY - 50C | HEATON - 52B | HEATON - 52B | YORK - 50A | DUNFERMLINE - 62C | THORNTON JCN - 62A | THORNTON JCN - 62A | THORNTON JCN - 62A | THORNTON JCN - 62A |
| Aug-56 | SELBY - 50C | **6/56: SUND - 54A** | **6/56: SUND - 54A** | YORK - 50A | DUNFERMLINE - 62C | THORNTON JCN - 62A | THORNTON JCN - 62A | THORNTON JCN - 62A | THORNTON JCN - 62A |
| Jan-57 | SELBY - 50C | SUNDERLAND - 54A | SUNDERLAND - 54A | YORK - 50A | **12/56: TH.JN - 62A** | THORNTON JCN - 62A | THORNTON JCN - 62A | THORNTON JCN - 62A | THORNTON JCN - 62A |
| Aug-57 | SELBY - 50C | SUNDERLAND - 54A | SUNDERLAND - 54A | YORK - 50A | THORNTON JCN - 62A | THORNTON JCN - 62A | THORNTON JCN - 62A | THORNTON JCN - 62A | THORNTON JCN - 62A |
| Jan-58 | SELBY - 50C | SUNDERLAND - 54A | SUNDERLAND - 54A | YORK - 50A | THORNTON JCN - 62A | THORNTON JCN - 62A | THORNTON JCN - 62A | THORNTON JCN - 62A | THORNTON JCN - 62A |
| Aug-58 | SELBY - 50C | SUNDERLAND - 54A | **6/58: B.GDNS - 54C** | YORK - 50A | THORNTON JCN - 62A | THORNTON JCN - 62A | THORNTON JCN - 62A | THORNTON JCN - 62A | THORNTON JCN - 62A |
| Jan-59 | SELBY - 50C | SUNDERLAND - 52G | BOR.GDNS - 52J | YORK - 50A | THORNTON JCN - 62A | THORNTON JCN - 62A | THORNTON JCN - 62A | THORNTON JCN - 62A | THORNTON JCN - 62A |
| Aug-59 | **9/59: SUND - 52G** | SUNDERLAND - 52G | **6/59: N.BLYTH - 52F** | YORK - 50A | THORNTON JCN - 62A | THORNTON JCN - 62A | THORNTON JCN - 62A | THORNTON JCN - 62A | THORNTON JCN - 62A |
| Nov-59 | **11/59: S.BLYTH - 52F** | SUNDERLAND - 52G | N.BLYTH - 52F | YORK - 50A | THORNTON JCN - 62A | THORNTON JCN - 62A | THORNTON JCN - 62A | THORNTON JCN - 62A | THORNTON JCN - 62A |
| Jan-60 | S.BLYTH - 52F | SUNDERLAND - 52G | N.BLYTH - 52F | YORK - 50A | THORNTON JCN - 62A | THORNTON JCN - 62A | THORNTON JCN - 62A | THORNTON JCN - 62A | THORNTON JCN - 62A |
| Apr-60 | S.BLYTH - 52F | SUNDERLAND - 52G | N.BLYTH - 52F | YORK - 50A | THORNTON JCN - 62A | THORNTON JCN - 62A | THORNTON JCN - 62A | THORNTON JCN - 62A | THORNTON JCN - 62A |
| Aug-60 | S.BLYTH - 52F | SUNDERLAND - 52G | N.BLYTH - 52F | YORK - 50A | THORNTON JCN - 62A | THORNTON JCN - 62A | THORNTON JCN - 62A | THORNTON JCN - 62A | THORNTON JCN - 62A |
| Nov-60 | S.BLYTH - 52F | SUNDERLAND - 52G | N.BLYTH - 52F | YORK - 50A | THORNTON JCN - 62A | THORNTON JCN - 62A | THORNTON JCN - 62A | THORNTON JCN - 62A | THORNTON JCN - 62A |

| | 65905 | 65906 | 65907 | 65908 | 65909 | 65910 | 65911 | 65912 | 65913 |
|---|---|---|---|---|---|---|---|---|---|
| Aug-50 | DUNFERMLINE - 62C | EDINBURGH (SM) - 64A | THORNTON JCN - 62A | THORNTON JCN - 62A | POLMONT - 64E | THORNTON JCN - 62A | THORNTON JCN - 62A | EDINBURGH (SM) - 64A | THORNTON JCN - 62A |
| Jan-51 | DUNFERMLINE - 62C | EDINBURGH (SM) - 64A | THORNTON JCN - 62A | THORNTON JCN - 62A | POLMONT - 64E | THORNTON JCN - 62A | THORNTON JCN - 62A | EDINBURGH (SM) - 64A | THORNTON JCN - 62A |
| Aug-51 | DUNFERMLINE - 62C | EDINBURGH (SM) - 64A | THORNTON JCN - 62A | THORNTON JCN - 62A | POLMONT - 64E | THORNTON JCN - 62A | THORNTON JCN - 62A | EDINBURGH (SM) - 64A | THORNTON JCN - 62A |
| Jan-52 | DUNFERMLINE - 62C | EDINBURGH (SM) - 64A | THORNTON JCN - 62A | THORNTON JCN - 62A | POLMONT - 64E | THORNTON JCN - 62A | THORNTON JCN - 62A | EDINBURGH (SM) - 64A | THORNTON JCN - 62A |
| Aug-52 | DUNFERMLINE - 62C | EDINBURGH (SM) - 64A | THORNTON JCN - 62A | THORNTON JCN - 62A | POLMONT - 64E | THORNTON JCN - 62A | THORNTON JCN - 62A | EDINBURGH (SM) - 64A | THORNTON JCN - 62A |
| Jan-53 | DUNFERMLINE - 62C | EDINBURGH (SM) - 64A | THORNTON JCN - 62A | THORNTON JCN - 62A | POLMONT - 64E | THORNTON JCN - 62A | THORNTON JCN - 62A | EDINBURGH (SM) - 64A | THORNTON JCN - 62A |
| Aug-53 | DUNFERMLINE - 62C | EDINBURGH (SM) - 64A | THORNTON JCN - 62A | THORNTON JCN - 62A | POLMONT - 64E | THORNTON JCN - 62A | THORNTON JCN - 62A | EDINBURGH (SM) - 64A | THORNTON JCN - 62A |
| Jan-54 | DUNFERMLINE - 62C | EDINBURGH (SM) - 64A | THORNTON JCN - 62A | THORNTON JCN - 62A | POLMONT - 64E | THORNTON JCN - 62A | THORNTON JCN - 62A | EDINBURGH (SM) - 64A | THORNTON JCN - 62A |
| Aug-54 | DUNFERMLINE - 62C | EDINBURGH (SM) - 64A | THORNTON JCN - 62A | THORNTON JCN - 62A | POLMONT - 64E | THORNTON JCN - 62A | THORNTON JCN - 62A | EDINBURGH (SM) - 64A | THORNTON JCN - 62A |
| Jan-55 | DUNFERMLINE - 62C | EDINBURGH (SM) - 64A | THORNTON JCN - 62A | THORNTON JCN - 62A | POLMONT - 64E | THORNTON JCN - 62A | THORNTON JCN - 62A | EDINBURGH (SM) - 64A | THORNTON JCN - 62A |
| Aug-55 | DUNFERMLINE - 62C | EDINBURGH (SM) - 64A | THORNTON JCN - 62A | THORNTON JCN - 62A | POLMONT - 64E | THORNTON JCN - 62A | THORNTON JCN - 62A | EDINBURGH (SM) - 64A | THORNTON JCN - 62A |
| Jan-56 | DUNFERMLINE - 62C | EDINBURGH (SM) - 64A | THORNTON JCN - 62A | THORNTON JCN - 62A | POLMONT - 64E | THORNTON JCN - 62A | THORNTON JCN - 62A | EDINBURGH (SM) - 64A | THORNTON JCN - 62A |
| Aug-56 | DUNFERMLINE - 62C | EDINBURGH (SM) - 64A | THORNTON JCN - 62A | THORNTON JCN - 62A | POLMONT - 64E | THORNTON JCN - 62A | THORNTON JCN - 62A | EDINBURGH (SM) - 64A | THORNTON JCN - 62A |
| Jan-57 | 12/56: TH.JN - 62A | EDINBURGH (SM) - 64A | THORNTON JCN - 62A | THORNTON JCN - 62A | POLMONT - 64E | THORNTON JCN - 62A | THORNTON JCN - 62A | EDINBURGH (SM) - 64A | THORNTON JCN - 62A |
| Aug-57 | THORNTON JCN - 62A | EDINBURGH (SM) - 64A | THORNTON JCN - 62A | THORNTON JCN - 62A | POLMONT - 64E | THORNTON JCN - 62A | THORNTON JCN - 62A | EDINBURGH (SM) - 64A | THORNTON JCN - 62A |
| Jan-58 | THORNTON JCN - 62A | EDINBURGH (SM) - 64A | THORNTON JCN - 62A | THORNTON JCN - 62A | POLMONT - 64E | THORNTON JCN - 62A | THORNTON JCN - 62A | EDINBURGH (SM) - 64A | THORNTON JCN - 62A |
| Aug-58 | THORNTON JCN - 62A | EDINBURGH (SM) - 64A | THORNTON JCN - 62A | THORNTON JCN - 62A | POLMONT - 64E | THORNTON JCN - 62A | THORNTON JCN - 62A | EDINBURGH (SM) - 64A | THORNTON JCN - 62A |
| Jan-59 | THORNTON JCN - 62A | EDINBURGH (SM) - 64A | THORNTON JCN - 62A | THORNTON JCN - 62A | POLMONT - 64E | THORNTON JCN - 62A | THORNTON JCN - 62A | EDINBURGH (SM) - 64A | THORNTON JCN - 62A |
| Aug-59 | THORNTON JCN - 62A | EDINBURGH (SM) - 64A | THORNTON JCN - 62A | THORNTON JCN - 62A | POLMONT - 64E | THORNTON JCN - 62A | THORNTON JCN - 62A | EDINBURGH (SM) - 64A | THORNTON JCN - 62A |
| Nov-59 | THORNTON JCN - 62A | EDINBURGH (SM) - 64A | THORNTON JCN - 62A | THORNTON JCN - 62A | POLMONT - 64E | THORNTON JCN - 62A | THORNTON JCN - 62A | EDINBURGH (SM) - 64A | THORNTON JCN - 62A |
| Jan-60 | THORNTON JCN - 62A | EDINBURGH (SM) - 64A | THORNTON JCN - 62A | THORNTON JCN - 62A | POLMONT - 64E | THORNTON JCN - 62A | THORNTON JCN - 62A | EDINBURGH (SM) - 64A | THORNTON JCN - 62A |
| Apr-60 | THORNTON JCN - 62A | EDINBURGH (SM) - 64A | THORNTON JCN - 62A | THORNTON JCN - 62A | POLMONT - 64E | THORNTON JCN - 62A | THORNTON JCN - 62A | EDINBURGH (SM) - 64A | THORNTON JCN - 62A |
| Aug-60 | THORNTON JCN - 62A | EDINBURGH (SM) - 64A | THORNTON JCN - 62A | THORNTON JCN - 62A | POLMONT - 65K | THORNTON JCN - 62A | THORNTON JCN - 62A | EDINBURGH (SM) - 64A | THORNTON JCN - 62A |
| Nov-60 | THORNTON JCN - 62A | EDINBURGH (SM) - 64A | THORNTON JCN - 62A | THORNTON JCN - 62A | POLMONT - 65K | THORNTON JCN - 62A | THORNTON JCN - 62A | EDINBURGH (SM) - 64A | THORNTON JCN - 62A |

| | 65914 | 65915 | 65916 | 65917 | 65918 | 65919 | 65920 | 65921 | 65922 |
|---|---|---|---|---|---|---|---|---|---|
| Aug-50 | EDINBURGH (SM) - 64A | EDINBURGH (SM) - 64A | DUNFERMLINE - 62C | POLMONT - 64E | EDINBURGH (SM) - 64A | EDINBURGH (SM) - 64A | EDINBURGH (SM) - 64A | THORNTON JCN - 62A | DUNFERMLINE - 62C |
| Jan-51 | EDINBURGH (SM) - 64A | EDINBURGH (SM) - 64A | DUNFERMLINE - 62C | POLMONT - 64E | EDINBURGH (SM) - 64A | EDINBURGH (SM) - 64A | EDINBURGH (SM) - 64A | THORNTON JCN - 62A | DUNFERMLINE - 62C |
| Aug-51 | EDINBURGH (SM) - 64A | EDINBURGH (SM) - 64A | DUNFERMLINE - 62C | POLMONT - 64E | EDINBURGH (SM) - 64A | EDINBURGH (SM) - 64A | EDINBURGH (SM) - 64A | THORNTON JCN - 62A | DUNFERMLINE - 62C |
| Jan-52 | EDINBURGH (SM) - 64A | EDINBURGH (SM) - 64A | DUNFERMLINE - 62C | POLMONT - 64E | EDINBURGH (SM) - 64A | EDINBURGH (SM) - 64A | EDINBURGH (SM) - 64A | THORNTON JCN - 62A | DUNFERMLINE - 62C |
| Aug-52 | EDINBURGH (SM) - 64A | EDINBURGH (SM) - 64A | DUNFERMLINE - 62C | POLMONT - 64E | EDINBURGH (SM) - 64A | EDINBURGH (SM) - 64A | EDINBURGH (SM) - 64A | THORNTON JCN - 62A | DUNFERMLINE - 62C |
| Jan-53 | EDINBURGH (SM) - 64A | EDINBURGH (SM) - 64A | DUNFERMLINE - 62C | POLMONT - 64E | EDINBURGH (SM) - 64A | EDINBURGH (SM) - 64A | EDINBURGH (SM) - 64A | THORNTON JCN - 62A | DUNFERMLINE - 62C |
| Aug-53 | EDINBURGH (SM) - 64A | EDINBURGH (SM) - 64A | DUNFERMLINE - 62C | POLMONT - 64E | EDINBURGH (SM) - 64A | EDINBURGH (SM) - 64A | EDINBURGH (SM) - 64A | THORNTON JCN - 62A | DUNFERMLINE - 62C |
| Jan-54 | EDINBURGH (SM) - 64A | EDINBURGH (SM) - 64A | DUNFERMLINE - 62C | POLMONT - 64E | EDINBURGH (SM) - 64A | EDINBURGH (SM) - 64A | EDINBURGH (SM) - 64A | THORNTON JCN - 62A | DUNFERMLINE - 62C |
| Aug-54 | EDINBURGH (SM) - 64A | EDINBURGH (SM) - 64A | DUNFERMLINE - 62C | POLMONT - 64E | EDINBURGH (SM) - 64A | EDINBURGH (SM) - 64A | EDINBURGH (SM) - 64A | THORNTON JCN - 62A | DUNFERMLINE - 62C |
| Jan-55 | EDINBURGH (SM) - 64A | EDINBURGH (SM) - 64A | 11/54: ST.M - 64A | POLMONT - 64E | EDINBURGH (SM) - 64A | EDINBURGH (SM) - 64A | EDINBURGH (SM) - 64A | THORNTON JCN - 62A | DUNFERMLINE - 62C |
| Aug-55 | EDINBURGH (SM) - 64A | EDINBURGH (SM) - 64A | EDINBURGH (SM) - 64A | POLMONT - 64E | EDINBURGH (SM) - 64A | EDINBURGH (SM) - 64A | EDINBURGH (SM) - 64A | THORNTON JCN - 62A | 11/54: ST.M - 64A |
| Jan-56 | EDINBURGH (SM) - 64A | EDINBURGH (SM) - 64A | EDINBURGH (SM) - 64A | POLMONT - 64E | EDINBURGH (SM) - 64A | EDINBURGH (SM) - 64A | EDINBURGH (SM) - 64A | THORNTON JCN - 62A | EDINBURGH (SM) - 64A |
| Aug-56 | EDINBURGH (SM) - 64A | EDINBURGH (SM) - 64A | EDINBURGH (SM) - 64A | POLMONT - 64E | EDINBURGH (SM) - 64A | EDINBURGH (SM) - 64A | EDINBURGH (SM) - 64A | THORNTON JCN - 62A | EDINBURGH (SM) - 64A |
| Jan-57 | EDINBURGH (SM) - 64A | EDINBURGH (SM) - 64A | EDINBURGH (SM) - 64A | POLMONT - 64E | EDINBURGH (SM) - 64A | EDINBURGH (SM) - 64A | EDINBURGH (SM) - 64A | THORNTON JCN - 62A | EDINBURGH (SM) - 64A |
| Aug-57 | EDINBURGH (SM) - 64A | EDINBURGH (SM) - 64A | EDINBURGH (SM) - 64A | POLMONT - 64E | EDINBURGH (SM) - 64A | EDINBURGH (SM) - 64A | EDINBURGH (SM) - 64A | THORNTON JCN - 62A | EDINBURGH (SM) - 64A |
| Jan-58 | EDINBURGH (SM) - 64A | EDINBURGH (SM) - 64A | EDINBURGH (SM) - 64A | POLMONT - 64E | EDINBURGH (SM) - 64A | EDINBURGH (SM) - 64A | EDINBURGH (SM) - 64A | THORNTON JCN - 62A | EDINBURGH (SM) - 64A |
| Aug-58 | EDINBURGH (SM) - 64A | EDINBURGH (SM) - 64A | EDINBURGH (SM) - 64A | POLMONT - 64E | EDINBURGH (SM) - 64A | EDINBURGH (SM) - 64A | EDINBURGH (SM) - 64A | THORNTON JCN - 62A | EDINBURGH (SM) - 64A |
| Jan-59 | EDINBURGH (SM) - 64A | EDINBURGH (SM) - 64A | EDINBURGH (SM) - 64A | POLMONT - 64E | EDINBURGH (SM) - 64A | EDINBURGH (SM) - 64A | EDINBURGH (SM) - 64A | THORNTON JCN - 62A | EDINBURGH (SM) - 64A |
| Aug-59 | EDINBURGH (SM) - 64A | EDINBURGH (SM) - 64A | EDINBURGH (SM) - 64A | POLMONT - 64E | EDINBURGH (SM) - 64A | EDINBURGH (SM) - 64A | EDINBURGH (SM) - 64A | THORNTON JCN - 62A | EDINBURGH (SM) - 64A |
| Nov-59 | EDINBURGH (SM) - 64A | EDINBURGH (SM) - 64A | EDINBURGH (SM) - 64A | POLMONT - 64E | EDINBURGH (SM) - 64A | EDINBURGH (SM) - 64A | EDINBURGH (SM) - 64A | THORNTON JCN - 62A | EDINBURGH (SM) - 64A |
| Jan-60 | EDINBURGH (SM) - 64A | EDINBURGH (SM) - 64A | EDINBURGH (SM) - 64A | POLMONT - 64E | EDINBURGH (SM) - 64A | EDINBURGH (SM) - 64A | EDINBURGH (SM) - 64A | THORNTON JCN - 62A | EDINBURGH (SM) - 64A |
| Apr-60 | EDINBURGH (SM) - 64A | EDINBURGH (SM) - 64A | EDINBURGH (SM) - 64A | POLMONT - 65K | EDINBURGH (SM) - 64A | EDINBURGH (SM) - 64A | EDINBURGH (SM) - 64A | THORNTON JCN - 62A | EDINBURGH (SM) - 64A |
| Aug-60 | EDINBURGH (SM) - 64A | EDINBURGH (SM) - 64A | EDINBURGH (SM) - 64A | POLMONT - 65K | EDINBURGH (SM) - 64A | EDINBURGH (SM) - 64A | EDINBURGH (SM) - 64A | THORNTON JCN - 62A | EDINBURGH (SM) - 64A |
| Nov-60 | EDINBURGH (SM) - 64A | EDINBURGH (SM) - 64A | EDINBURGH (SM) - 64A | POLMONT - 65K | EDINBURGH (SM) - 64A | EDINBURGH (SM) - 64A | EDINBURGH (SM) - 64A | THORNTON JCN - 62A | EDINBURGH (SM) - 64A |

| | 65923 | 65924 | 65925 | 65926 | 65927 | 65928 | 65929 | 65930 | 65931 |
|---|---|---|---|---|---|---|---|---|---|
| Aug-50 | DUNFERMLINE - 62C | DUNFERMLINE - 62C | THORNTON JCN - 62A | DUNFERMLINE - 62C | EDINBURGH (SM) - 64A | DUNFERMLINE - 62C | EDINBURGH (SM) - 64A | DUNFERMLINE - 62C | THORNTON JCN - 62A |
| Jan-51 | DUNFERMLINE - 62C | DUNFERMLINE - 62C | THORNTON JCN - 62A | DUNFERMLINE - 62C | EDINBURGH (SM) - 64A | DUNFERMLINE - 62C | EDINBURGH (SM) - 64A | DUNFERMLINE - 62C | THORNTON JCN - 62A |
| Aug-51 | DUNFERMLINE - 62C | DUNFERMLINE - 62C | THORNTON JCN - 62A | DUNFERMLINE - 62C | EDINBURGH (SM) - 64A | DUNFERMLINE - 62C | EDINBURGH (SM) - 64A | DUNFERMLINE - 62C | THORNTON JCN - 62A |
| Jan-52 | DUNFERMLINE - 62C | DUNFERMLINE - 62C | THORNTON JCN - 62A | DUNFERMLINE - 62C | EDINBURGH (SM) - 64A | DUNFERMLINE - 62C | EDINBURGH (SM) - 64A | DUNFERMLINE - 62C | THORNTON JCN - 62A |
| Aug-52 | DUNFERMLINE - 62C | DUNFERMLINE - 62C | THORNTON JCN - 62A | DUNFERMLINE - 62C | EDINBURGH (SM) - 64A | DUNFERMLINE - 62C | EDINBURGH (SM) - 64A | DUNFERMLINE - 62C | THORNTON JCN - 62A |
| Jan-53 | DUNFERMLINE - 62C | DUNFERMLINE - 62C | THORNTON JCN - 62A | DUNFERMLINE - 62C | EDINBURGH (SM) - 64A | DUNFERMLINE - 62C | EDINBURGH (SM) - 64A | DUNFERMLINE - 62C | THORNTON JCN - 62A |
| Aug-53 | DUNFERMLINE - 62C | DUNFERMLINE - 62C | THORNTON JCN - 62A | DUNFERMLINE - 62C | EDINBURGH (SM) - 64A | DUNFERMLINE - 62C | EDINBURGH (SM) - 64A | DUNFERMLINE - 62C | THORNTON JCN - 62A |
| Jan-54 | DUNFERMLINE - 62C | DUNFERMLINE - 62C | THORNTON JCN - 62A | DUNFERMLINE - 62C | EDINBURGH (SM) - 64A | DUNFERMLINE - 62C | EDINBURGH (SM) - 64A | DUNFERMLINE - 62C | THORNTON JCN - 62A |
| Aug-54 | DUNFERMLINE - 62C | DUNFERMLINE - 62C | THORNTON JCN - 62A | DUNFERMLINE - 62C | EDINBURGH (SM) - 64A | DUNFERMLINE - 62C | EDINBURGH (SM) - 64A | DUNFERMLINE - 62C | THORNTON JCN - 62A |
| Jan-55 | DUNFERMLINE - 62C | DUNFERMLINE - 62C | THORNTON JCN - 62A | DUNFERMLINE - 62C | EDINBURGH (SM) - 64A | DUNFERMLINE - 62C | EDINBURGH (SM) - 64A | DUNFERMLINE - 62C | THORNTON JCN - 62A |
| Aug-55 | DUNFERMLINE - 62C | DUNFERMLINE - 62C | THORNTON JCN - 62A | DUNFERMLINE - 62C | EDINBURGH (SM) - 64A | DUNFERMLINE - 62C | EDINBURGH (SM) - 64A | DUNFERMLINE - 62C | THORNTON JCN - 62A |
| Jan-56 | DUNFERMLINE - 62C | DUNFERMLINE - 62C | THORNTON JCN - 62A | DUNFERMLINE - 62C | EDINBURGH (SM) - 64A | DUNFERMLINE - 62C | EDINBURGH (SM) - 64A | DUNFERMLINE - 62C | THORNTON JCN - 62A |
| Aug-56 | DUNFERMLINE - 62C | DUNFERMLINE - 62C | THORNTON JCN - 62A | DUNFERMLINE - 62C | EDINBURGH (SM) - 64A | DUNFERMLINE - 62C | EDINBURGH (SM) - 64A | DUNFERMLINE - 62C | THORNTON JCN - 62A |
| Jan-57 | DUNFERMLINE - 62C | DUNFERMLINE - 62C | THORNTON JCN - 62A | DUNFERMLINE - 62C | EDINBURGH (SM) - 64A | DUNFERMLINE - 62C | EDINBURGH (SM) - 64A | DUNFERMLINE - 62C | THORNTON JCN - 62A |
| Aug-57 | DUNFERMLINE - 62C | DUNFERMLINE - 62C | THORNTON JCN - 62A | DUNFERMLINE - 62C | EDINBURGH (SM) - 64A | DUNFERMLINE - 62C | EDINBURGH (SM) - 64A | DUNFERMLINE - 62C | THORNTON JCN - 62A |
| Jan-58 | DUNFERMLINE - 62C | DUNFERMLINE - 62C | THORNTON JCN - 62A | DUNFERMLINE - 62C | EDINBURGH (SM) - 64A | DUNFERMLINE - 62C | EDINBURGH (SM) - 64A | DUNFERMLINE - 62C | THORNTON JCN - 62A |
| Aug-58 | DUNFERMLINE - 62C | DUNFERMLINE - 62C | THORNTON JCN - 62A | DUNFERMLINE - 62C | EDINBURGH (SM) - 64A | DUNFERMLINE - 62C | EDINBURGH (SM) - 64A | DUNFERMLINE - 62C | THORNTON JCN - 62A |
| Jan-59 | DUNFERMLINE - 62C | DUNFERMLINE - 62C | THORNTON JCN - 62A | DUNFERMLINE - 62C | EDINBURGH (SM) - 64A | DUNFERMLINE - 62C | EDINBURGH (SM) - 64A | DUNFERMLINE - 62C | THORNTON JCN - 62A |
| Aug-59 | DUNFERMLINE - 62C | DUNFERMLINE - 62C | THORNTON JCN - 62A | DUNFERMLINE - 62C | EDINBURGH (SM) - 64A | DUNFERMLINE - 62C | EDINBURGH (SM) - 64A | DUNFERMLINE - 62C | THORNTON JCN - 62A |
| Nov-59 | DUNFERMLINE - 62C | DUNFERMLINE - 62C | THORNTON JCN - 62A | DUNFERMLINE - 62C | EDINBURGH (SM) - 64A | DUNFERMLINE - 62C | EDINBURGH (SM) - 64A | DUNFERMLINE - 62C | THORNTON JCN - 62A |
| Jan-60 | DUNFERMLINE - 62C | DUNFERMLINE - 62C | THORNTON JCN - 62A | DUNFERMLINE - 62C | EDINBURGH (SM) - 64A | DUNFERMLINE - 62C | EDINBURGH (SM) - 64A | DUNFERMLINE - 62C | THORNTON JCN - 62A |
| Apr-60 | DUNFERMLINE - 62C | DUNFERMLINE - 62C | THORNTON JCN - 62A | DUNFERMLINE - 62C | EDINBURGH (SM) - 64A | DUNFERMLINE - 62C | EDINBURGH (SM) - 64A | DUNFERMLINE - 62C | THORNTON JCN - 62A |
| Aug-60 | DUNFERMLINE - 62C | DUNFERMLINE - 62C | THORNTON JCN - 62A | DUNFERMLINE - 62C | EDINBURGH (SM) - 64A | DUNFERMLINE - 62C | EDINBURGH (SM) - 64A | DUNFERMLINE - 62C | THORNTON JCN - 62A |
| Nov-60 | DUNFERMLINE - 62C | DUNFERMLINE - 62C | THORNTON JCN - 62A | DUNFERMLINE - 62C | EDINBURGH (SM) - 64A | DUNFERMLINE - 62C | EDINBURGH (SM) - 64A | DUNFERMLINE - 62C | THORNTON JCN - 62A |

| | | | | F2 2-4-2T (1898) | F3 2-4-2T (1893) | | | F4 2-4-2T (1884) | |
|---|---|---|---|---|---|---|---|---|---|
| | 65932 | 65933 | 65934 | 67111 | 67127 | 67128 | 67139 | 67151 | 67152 |
| Aug-50 | THORNTON JCN - 62A | DUNFERMLINE - 62C | DUNFERMLINE - 62C | KINGS CROSS - 34A | LOWESTOFT - 32C | IPSWICH - 32B | NORWICH - 32A | KITTYBREWSTER - 61A | MELTON CONSTABLE - 32G |
| Jan-51 | THORNTON JCN - 62A | DUNFERMLINE - 62C | DUNFERMLINE - 62C | 12/50: W/D | LOWESTOFT - 32C | 12/50: W/D | 12/50: W/D | KITTYBREWSTER - 61A | MELTON CONSTABLE - 32G |
| Aug-51 | THORNTON JCN - 62A | DUNFERMLINE - 62C | DUNFERMLINE - 62C | | LOWESTOFT - 32C | | | 8/51: W/D | MELTON CONSTABLE - 32G |
| Jan-52 | THORNTON JCN - 62A | DUNFERMLINE - 62C | DUNFERMLINE - 62C | | LOWESTOFT - 32C | | | | MELTON CONSTABLE - 32G |
| Aug-52 | THORNTON JCN - 62A | DUNFERMLINE - 62C | DUNFERMLINE - 62C | | LOWESTOFT - 32C | | | | 2/52: W/D |
| Jan-53 | THORNTON JCN - 62A | DUNFERMLINE - 62C | DUNFERMLINE - 62C | | 1/53: IPS - 32B | | | | |
| Aug-53 | THORNTON JCN - 62A | DUNFERMLINE - 62C | DUNFERMLINE - 62C | | 3/53: W/D | | | | |
| Jan-54 | THORNTON JCN - 62A | DUNFERMLINE - 62C | DUNFERMLINE - 62C | | | | | | |
| Aug-54 | THORNTON JCN - 62A | DUNFERMLINE - 62C | DUNFERMLINE - 62C | | | | | | |
| Jan-55 | THORNTON JCN - 62A | DUNFERMLINE - 62C | 11/54: ST.M - 64A | | | | | | |
| Aug-55 | THORNTON JCN - 62A | DUNFERMLINE - 62C | EDINBURGH (SM) - 64A | | | | | | |
| Jan-56 | THORNTON JCN - 62A | DUNFERMLINE - 62C | EDINBURGH (SM) - 64A | | | | | | |
| Aug-56 | THORNTON JCN - 62A | DUNFERMLINE - 62C | EDINBURGH (SM) - 64A | | | | | | |
| Jan-57 | THORNTON JCN - 62A | DUNFERMLINE - 62C | EDINBURGH (SM) - 64A | | | | | | |
| Aug-57 | THORNTON JCN - 62A | DUNFERMLINE - 62C | EDINBURGH (SM) - 64A | | | | | | |
| Jan-58 | THORNTON JCN - 62A | DUNFERMLINE - 62C | EDINBURGH (SM) - 64A | | | | | | |
| Aug-58 | THORNTON JCN - 62A | DUNFERMLINE - 62C | EDINBURGH (SM) - 64A | | | | | | |
| Jan-59 | THORNTON JCN - 62A | DUNFERMLINE - 62C | EDINBURGH (SM) - 64A | | | | | | |
| Aug-59 | THORNTON JCN - 62A | DUNFERMLINE - 62C | EDINBURGH (SM) - 64A | | | | | | |
| Nov-59 | THORNTON JCN - 62A | DUNFERMLINE - 62C | EDINBURGH (SM) - 64A | | | | | | |
| Jan-60 | THORNTON JCN - 62A | DUNFERMLINE - 62C | EDINBURGH (SM) - 64A | | | | | | |
| Apr-60 | THORNTON JCN - 62A | DUNFERMLINE - 62C | EDINBURGH (SM) - 64A | | | | | | |
| Aug-60 | THORNTON JCN - 62A | DUNFERMLINE - 62C | EDINBURGH (SM) - 64A | | | | | | |
| Nov-60 | THORNTON JCN - 62A | DUNFERMLINE - 62C | EDINBURGH (SM) - 64A | | | | | | |

## Block 1

| | 67153 | 67154 | 67155 | 67156 | 67157 | 67158 | 67162 | 67163 | 67164 |
|---|---|---|---|---|---|---|---|---|---|
| Aug-50 | MARCH-31B | YARMOUTH (ST)-32D | MALTON-50F | LOWESTOFT-32C | KITTYBREWSTER-61A | LOWESTOFT-32C | MELTON CONSTABLE-32G | LOWESTOFT-32C | KITTYBREWSTER-61A |
| Jan-51 | MARCH-31B | YARMOUTH (ST)-32D | MALTON-50F | 11/50: W/D | KITTYBREWSTER-61A | LOWESTOFT-32C | MELTON CONSTABLE-32G | LOWESTOFT-32C | KITTYBREWSTER-61A |
| Aug-51 | 8/51: W/D | YARMOUTH (ST)-32D | 8/51: W/D | | KITTYBREWSTER-61A | LOWESTOFT-32C | MELTON CONSTABLE-32G | 12/51: W/D | 8/51: W/D |
| Jan-52 | | 9/51: W/D | | | KITTYBREWSTER-61A | LOWESTOFT-32C | 9/51: YAR (V)-32E | | |
| Aug-52 | | | | | KITTYBREWSTER-61A | LOWESTOFT-32C | YARMOUTH (VAUX)-32E | | |
| Jan-53 | | | | | KITTYBREWSTER-61A | 1/53: W/D | YARMOUTH (VAUX)-32E | | |
| Aug-53 | | | | | KITTYBREWSTER-61A | | YARMOUTH (VAUX)-32E | | |
| Jan-54 | | | | | KITTYBREWSTER-61A | | YARMOUTH (VAUX)-32E | | |
| Aug-54 | | | | | KITTYBREWSTER-61A | | YARMOUTH (VAUX)-32E | | |
| Jan-55 | | | | | KITTYBREWSTER-61A | | YARMOUTH (VAUX)-32E | | |
| Aug-55 | | | | | KITTYBREWSTER-61A | | 8/55: W/D | | |
| Jan-56 | | | | | KITTYBREWSTER-61A | | | | |
| Aug-56 | | | | | 6/56: W/D | | | | |
| Jan-57 | | | | | | | | | |
| Aug-57 | | | | | | | | | |
| Jan-58 | | | | | | | | | |
| Aug-58 | | | | | | | | | |
| Jan-59 | | | | | | | | | |
| Aug-59 | | | | | | | | | |
| Nov-59 | | | | | | | | | |
| Jan-60 | | | | | | | | | |
| Apr-60 | | | | | | | | | |
| Aug-60 | | | | | | | | | |
| Nov-60 | | | | | | | | | |

## Block 2

| | 67165 | 67166 | 67167 | 67171 | 67174 | 67175 | 67176 | 67177 | 67178 |
|---|---|---|---|---|---|---|---|---|---|
| Aug-50 | LOWESTOFT-32C | LOWESTOFT-32C | LOWESTOFT-32C | DAIRYCOATES-53A | LOWESTOFT-32C | DAIRYCOATES-53A | NORWICH-32A | LOWESTOFT-32C | NORWICH-32A |
| Jan-51 | 1/51: W/D | LOWESTOFT-32C | LOWESTOFT-32C | DAIRYCOATES-53A | LOWESTOFT-32C | DAIRYCOATES-53A | NORWICH-32A | LOWESTOFT-32C | NORWICH-32A |
| Aug-51 | | 4/51: W/D | LOWESTOFT-32C | 8/51: W/D | LOWESTOFT-32C | 8/51: W/D | 6/51: LOW-32C | 3/51: W/D | 6/51: LOW-32C |
| Jan-52 | | | LOWESTOFT-32C | | LOWESTOFT-32C | | LOWESTOFT-32C | | LOWESTOFT-32C |
| Aug-52 | | | 9/52: W/D | | LOWESTOFT-32C | | LOWESTOFT-32C | | 8/52: W/D |
| Jan-53 | | | | | LOWESTOFT-32C | | LOWESTOFT-32C | | |
| Aug-53 | | | | | LOWESTOFT-32C | | 7/53: W/D | | |
| Jan-54 | | | | | LOWESTOFT-32C | | | | |
| Aug-54 | | | | | 12/54: W/D | | | | |
| Jan-55 | | | | | | | | | |
| Aug-55 | | | | | | | | | |
| Jan-56 | | | | | | | | | |
| Aug-56 | | | | | | | | | |
| Jan-57 | | | | | | | | | |
| Aug-57 | | | | | | | | | |
| Jan-58 | | | | | | | | | |
| Aug-58 | | | | | | | | | |
| Jan-59 | | | | | | | | | |
| Aug-59 | | | | | | | | | |
| Nov-59 | | | | | | | | | |
| Jan-60 | | | | | | | | | |
| Apr-60 | | | | | | | | | |
| Aug-60 | | | | | | | | | |
| Nov-60 | | | | | | | | | |

## Block 3

F5 2-4-2T (1911)  *(class heading above columns 67188–67192)*

| | 67182 | 67184 | 67186 | 67187 | 67188 | 67189 | 67190 | 67191 | 67192 |
|---|---|---|---|---|---|---|---|---|---|
| Aug-50 | LOWESTOFT-32C | LOWESTOFT-32C | LOWESTOFT-32C | MARCH-31B | COLCHESTER-30E | COLCHESTER-30E | COLCHESTER-30E | COLCHESTER-30E | STRATFORD-30A |
| Jan-51 | LOWESTOFT-32C | LOWESTOFT-32C | LOWESTOFT-32C | MARCH-31B | COLCHESTER-30E | COLCHESTER-30E | COLCHESTER-30E | COLCHESTER-30E | STRATFORD-30A |
| Aug-51 | LOWESTOFT-32C | LOWESTOFT-32C | LOWESTOFT-32C | MARCH-31B | COLCHESTER-30E | COLCHESTER-30E | COLCHESTER-30E | COLCHESTER-30E | STRATFORD-30A |
| Jan-52 | LOWESTOFT-32C | LOWESTOFT-32C | LOWESTOFT-32C | 2/52: LOW-32C | STRATFORD-30A | COLCHESTER-30E | COLCHESTER-30E | COLCHESTER-30E | STRATFORD-30A |
| Aug-52 | 5/52: IPS-32B | LOWESTOFT-32C | LOWESTOFT-32C | LOWESTOFT-32C | STRATFORD-30A | COLCHESTER-30E | 9/52: LOW-32C | COLCHESTER-30E | STRATFORD-30A |
| Jan-53 | 1/53: W/D | 12/52: W/D | LOWESTOFT-32C | LOWESTOFT-32C | 5/53: COL-30E | COLCHESTER-30E | LOWESTOFT-32C | COLCHESTER-30E | STRATFORD-30A |
| Aug-53 | | | 7/53: W/D | LOWESTOFT-32C | 12/53: STRAT-30A | COLCHESTER-30E | LOWESTOFT-32C | COLCHESTER-30E | STRATFORD-30A |
| Jan-54 | | | | LOWESTOFT-32C | STRATFORD-30A | COLCHESTER-30E | LOWESTOFT-32C | COLCHESTER-30E | STRATFORD-30A |
| Aug-54 | | | | LOWESTOFT-32C | STRATFORD-30A | COLCHESTER-30E | LOWESTOFT-32C | COLCHESTER-30E | STRATFORD-30A |
| Jan-55 | | | | LOWESTOFT-32C | 11/55: COL-30E | COLCHESTER-30E | LOWESTOFT-32C | COLCHESTER-30E | STRATFORD-30A |
| Aug-55 | | | | 8/55: W/D | 12/55: W/D | COLCHESTER-30E | 12/55: W/D | 12/55: W/D | 12/55: COL-30E |
| Jan-56 | | | | | | COLCHESTER-30E | | | COLCHESTER-30E |
| Aug-56 | | | | | | 12/56: W/D | | | COLCHESTER-30E |
| Jan-57 | | | | | | | | | COLCHESTER-30E |
| Aug-57 | | | | | | | | | COLCHESTER-30E |
| Jan-58 | | | | | | | | | 4/58: W/D |
| Aug-58 | | | | | | | | | |
| Jan-59 | | | | | | | | | |
| Aug-59 | | | | | | | | | |
| Nov-59 | | | | | | | | | |
| Jan-60 | | | | | | | | | |
| Apr-60 | | | | | | | | | |
| Aug-60 | | | | | | | | | |
| Nov-60 | | | | | | | | | |

## Block 4

| | 67193 | 67194 | 67195 | 67196 | 67197 | 67198 | 67199 | 67200 | 67201 |
|---|---|---|---|---|---|---|---|---|---|
| Aug-50 | STRATFORD-30A | COLCHESTER-30E | COLCHESTER-30E | COLCHESTER-30E | STRATFORD-30A | STRATFORD-30A | YARMOUTH (ST)-32D | STRATFORD-30A | LOWESTOFT-32C |
| Jan-51 | STRATFORD-30A | COLCHESTER-30E | COLCHESTER-30E | COLCHESTER-30E | STRATFORD-30A | STRATFORD-30A | YARMOUTH (ST)-32D | STRATFORD-30A | LOWESTOFT-32C |
| Aug-51 | STRATFORD-30A | COLCHESTER-30E | COLCHESTER-30E | COLCHESTER-30E | STRATFORD-30A | STRATFORD-30A | YARMOUTH (ST)-32D | STRATFORD-30A | LOWESTOFT-32C |
| Jan-52 | STRATFORD-30A | COLCHESTER-30E | 3/52: STRAT-30A | COLCHESTER-30E | STRATFORD-30A | STRATFORD-30A | YARMOUTH (ST)-32D | STRATFORD-30A | LOWESTOFT-32C |
| Aug-52 | STRATFORD-30A | COLCHESTER-30E | STRATFORD-30A | COLCHESTER-30E | STRATFORD-30A | STRATFORD-30A | YARMOUTH (ST)-32D | STRATFORD-30A | LOWESTOFT-32C |
| Jan-53 | STRATFORD-30A | COLCHESTER-30E | 10/52: LOW-32C | COLCHESTER-30E | STRATFORD-30A | STRATFORD-30A | YARMOUTH (ST)-32D | STRATFORD-30A | LOWESTOFT-32C |
| Aug-53 | STRATFORD-30A | 5/53: STRAT-30A | LOWESTOFT-32C | COLCHESTER-30E | STRATFORD-30A | STRATFORD-30A | YARMOUTH (ST)-32D | STRATFORD-30A | LOWESTOFT-32C |
| Jan-54 | STRATFORD-30A | STRATFORD-30A | LOWESTOFT-32C | COLCHESTER-30E | STRATFORD-30A | STRATFORD-30A | YARMOUTH (ST)-32D | STRATFORD-30A | LOWESTOFT-32C |
| Aug-54 | STRATFORD-30A | STRATFORD-30A | 10/54: YAR (ST)-32D | COLCHESTER-30E | STRATFORD-30A | STRATFORD-30A | 10/54: STRAT-30A | STRATFORD-30A | LOWESTOFT-32C |
| Jan-55 | STRATFORD-30A | 3/55: COL-30E | 12/54: LOW-32C | 3/55: W/D | 3/55: W/D | STRATFORD-30A | 11/54: YAR (ST)-32D | STRATFORD-30A | LOWESTOFT-32C |
| Aug-55 | STRATFORD-30A | COLCHESTER-30E | LOWESTOFT-32C | | | 8/55: W/D | 6/55: LOW-32C | STRATFORD-30A | LOWESTOFT-32C |
| Jan-56 | STRATFORD-30A | 3/56: STRAT-30A | LOWESTOFT-32C | | | | 9/55: YAR (ST)-32D | STRATFORD-30A | LOWESTOFT-32C |
| Aug-56 | STRATFORD-30A | STRATFORD-30A | 11/56: STRAT-30A | | | | YARMOUTH (ST)-32D | STRATFORD-30A | 12/56: W/D |
| Jan-57 | STRATFORD-30A | 10/56: W/D | STRATFORD-30A | | | | 1/57: STRAT-30A | STRATFORD-30A | |
| Aug-57 | STRATFORD-30A | | STRATFORD-30A | | | | 2/57: W/D | STRATFORD-30A | |
| Jan-58 | 11/57: W/D | | 5/58: W/D | | | | | 12/57: W/D | |
| Aug-58 | | | | | | | | | |
| Jan-59 | | | | | | | | | |
| Aug-59 | | | | | | | | | |
| Nov-59 | | | | | | | | | |
| Jan-60 | | | | | | | | | |
| Apr-60 | | | | | | | | | |
| Aug-60 | | | | | | | | | |
| Nov-60 | | | | | | | | | |

## 67202 – 67210

| | 67202 | 67203 | 67204 | 67205 | 67206 | 67207 | 67208 | 67209 | 67210 |
|---|---|---|---|---|---|---|---|---|---|
| Aug-50 | STRATFORD-30A | STRATFORD-30A | COLCHESTER-30E | STRATFORD-30A | STRATFORD-30A | STRATFORD-30A | STRATFORD-30A | STRATFORD-30A | STRATFORD-30A |
| Jan-51 | STRATFORD-30A | STRATFORD-30A | COLCHESTER-30E | STRATFORD-30A | STRATFORD-30A | STRATFORD-30A | STRATFORD-30A | STRATFORD-30A | STRATFORD-30A |
| Aug-51 | STRATFORD-30A | STRATFORD-30A | COLCHESTER-30E | STRATFORD-30A | STRATFORD-30A | STRATFORD-30A | STRATFORD-30A | STRATFORD-30A | STRATFORD-30A |
| Jan-52 | STRATFORD-30A | STRATFORD-30A | 11/51: STRAT-30A | STRATFORD-30A | STRATFORD-30A | STRATFORD-30A | STRATFORD-30A | STRATFORD-30A | STRATFORD-30A |
| Aug-52 | STRATFORD-30A | STRATFORD-30A | STRATFORD-30A | STRATFORD-30A | STRATFORD-30A | STRATFORD-30A | STRATFORD-30A | STRATFORD-30A | STRATFORD-30A |
| Jan-53 | STRATFORD-30A | STRATFORD-30A | STRATFORD-30A | STRATFORD-30A | STRATFORD-30A | STRATFORD-30A | STRATFORD-30A | STRATFORD-30A | STRATFORD-30A |
| Aug-53 | STRATFORD-30A | STRATFORD-30A | 5/53: LOW-32C | STRATFORD-30A | 2/53: LOW-32C | 2/53: LOW-32C | STRATFORD-30A | STRATFORD-30A | STRATFORD-30A |
| Jan-54 | STRATFORD-30A | STRATFORD-30A | LOWESTOFT-32C | STRATFORD-30A | LOWESTOFT-32C | LOWESTOFT-32C | STRATFORD-30A | STRATFORD-30A | STRATFORD-30A |
| Aug-54 | STRATFORD-30A | STRATFORD-30A | LOWESTOFT-32C | STRATFORD-30A | LOWESTOFT-32C | LOWESTOFT-32C | STRATFORD-30A | STRATFORD-30A | STRATFORD-30A |
| Jan-55 | STRATFORD-30A | STRATFORD-30A | LOWESTOFT-32C | STRATFORD-30A | LOWESTOFT-32C | LOWESTOFT-32C | STRATFORD-30A | STRATFORD-30A | STRATFORD-30A |
| Aug-55 | STRATFORD-30A | STRATFORD-30A | LOWESTOFT-32C | STRATFORD-30A | LOWESTOFT-32C | LOWESTOFT-32C | STRATFORD-30A | STRATFORD-30A | 7/55: W/D |
| Jan-56 | STRATFORD-30A | STRATFORD-30A | 9/55: W/D | 11/55: W/D | 9/55: W/D | 12/55: W/D | STRATFORD-30A | STRATFORD-30A | |
| Aug-56 | STRATFORD-30A | STRATFORD-30A | | | | | STRATFORD-30A | STRATFORD-30A | |
| Jan-57 | STRATFORD-30A | STRATFORD-30A | | | | | 1/57: W/D | STRATFORD-30A | |
| Aug-57 | STRATFORD-30A | STRATFORD-30A | | | | | | 2/57: W/D | |
| Jan-58 | 12/57: W/D | 12/57: W/D | | | | | | | |
| Aug-58 | | | | | | | | | |
| Jan-59 | | | | | | | | | |
| Aug-59 | | | | | | | | | |
| Nov-59 | | | | | | | | | |
| Jan-60 | | | | | | | | | |
| Apr-60 | | | | | | | | | |
| Aug-60 | | | | | | | | | |
| Nov-60 | | | | | | | | | |

## 67211 – 67219   (67218: F6 2-4-2T (1911))

| | 67211 | 67212 | 67213 | 67214 | 67215 | 67216 | 67217 | 67218 | 67219 |
|---|---|---|---|---|---|---|---|---|---|
| Aug-50 | STRATFORD-30A | STRATFORD-30A | STRATFORD-30A | STRATFORD-30A | COLCHESTER-30E | LOWESTOFT-32C | COLCHESTER-30E | YARMOUTH(ST)-32D | COLCHESTER-30E |
| Jan-51 | STRATFORD-30A | STRATFORD-30A | STRATFORD-30A | STRATFORD-30A | COLCHESTER-30E | LOWESTOFT-32C | COLCHESTER-30E | YARMOUTH(ST)-32D | COLCHESTER-30E |
| Aug-51 | STRATFORD-30A | STRATFORD-30A | STRATFORD-30A | STRATFORD-30A | COLCHESTER-30E | LOWESTOFT-32C | COLCHESTER-30E | YARMOUTH(ST)-32D | COLCHESTER-30E |
| Jan-52 | STRATFORD-30A | STRATFORD-30A | STRATFORD-30A | STRATFORD-30A | 11/51: STRAT-30A | LOWESTOFT-32C | 11/51: STRAT-30A | YARMOUTH(ST)-32D | 3/52: STRAT-30A |
| Aug-52 | STRATFORD-30A | STRATFORD-30A | STRATFORD-30A | STRATFORD-30A | STRATFORD-30A | LOWESTOFT-32C | 9/52: COL-30E | YARMOUTH(ST)-32D | STRATFORD-30A |
| Jan-53 | STRATFORD-30A | STRATFORD-30A | STRATFORD-30A | LOWESTOFT-32C | STRATFORD-30A | LOWESTOFT-32C | COLCHESTER-30E | YARMOUTH(ST)-32D | STRATFORD-30A |
| Aug-53 | STRATFORD-30A | STRATFORD-30A | STRATFORD-30A | LOWESTOFT-32C | STRATFORD-30A | LOWESTOFT-32C | COLCHESTER-30E | YARMOUTH(ST)-32D | STRATFORD-30A |
| Jan-54 | STRATFORD-30A | STRATFORD-30A | STRATFORD-30A | LOWESTOFT-32C | STRATFORD-30A | LOWESTOFT-32C | COLCHESTER-30E | YARMOUTH(ST)-32D | STRATFORD-30A |
| Aug-54 | STRATFORD-30A | STRATFORD-30A | STRATFORD-30A | 10/54: YAR(ST)-32D | STRATFORD-30A | LOWESTOFT-32C | COLCHESTER-30E | 10/54: YAR(ST)-32D | STRATFORD-30A |
| Jan-55 | STRATFORD-30A | STRATFORD-30A | STRATFORD-30A | 11/54: LOW-32C | STRATFORD-30A | LOWESTOFT-32C | COLCHESTER-30E | 11/54: YAR(ST)-32D | STRATFORD-30A |
| Aug-55 | STRATFORD-30A | STRATFORD-30A | 2/55: W/D | LOWESTOFT-32C | STRATFORD-30A | LOWESTOFT-32C | COLCHESTER-30E | 4/55: STRAT-30A | STRATFORD-30A |
| Jan-56 | STRATFORD-30A | STRATFORD-30A | | LOWESTOFT-32C | 9/55: W/D | LOWESTOFT-32C | 11/55: W/D | STRATFORD-30A | STRATFORD-30A |
| Aug-56 | STRATFORD-30A | STRATFORD-30A | | LOWESTOFT-32C | | LOWESTOFT-32C | | STRATFORD-30A | STRATFORD-30A |
| Jan-57 | 10/56: W/D | STRATFORD-30A | | 11/56: STRAT-30A | | 12/56: W/D | | STRATFORD-30A | 11/56: W/D |
| Aug-57 | | STRATFORD-30A | | STRATFORD-30A | | | | STRATFORD-30A | |
| Jan-58 | | STRATFORD-30A | | STRATFORD-30A | | | | STRATFORD-30A | |
| Aug-58 | | 5/58: W/D | | 5/58: W/D | | | | 3/58: W/D | |
| Jan-59 | | | | | | | | | |
| Aug-59 | | | | | | | | | |
| Nov-59 | | | | | | | | | |
| Jan-60 | | | | | | | | | |
| Apr-60 | | | | | | | | | |
| Aug-60 | | | | | | | | | |
| Nov-60 | | | | | | | | | |

## 67220 – 67228

| | 67220 | 67221 | 67222 | 67223 | 67224 | 67225 | 67226 | 67227 | 67228 |
|---|---|---|---|---|---|---|---|---|---|
| Aug-50 | IPSWICH-32B | KINGS LYNN-31C | CAMBRIDGE-31A | YARMOUTH(B)-32F | MELTON.C-32G | MELTON.C-32G | YARMOUTH(B)-32F | KINGS LYNN-31C | MELTON.C-32G |
| Jan-51 | IPSWICH-32B | 12/50: BURY-31E | CAMBRIDGE-31A | YARMOUTH(B)-32F | 9/50: NOR-32A | MELTON.C-32G | YARMOUTH(B)-32F | 11/50: S.LYNN-31D | MELTON.C-32G |
| Aug-51 | IPSWICH-32B | BURYSt.E-31E | CAMBRIDGE-31A | YARMOUTH(B)-32F | 9/51: MELTON-32G | MELTON.C-32G | YARMOUTH(B)-32F | SOUTH LYNN-31D | MELTON.C-32G |
| Jan-52 | IPSWICH-32B | BURYSt.E-31E | CAMBRIDGE-31A | YARMOUTH(B)-32F | MELTON.C-32G | MELTON.C-32G | YARMOUTH(B)-32F | 2/52: CAMB-31A | MELTON.C-32G |
| Aug-52 | IPSWICH-32B | BURYSt.E-31E | 9/52: BURY-31E | YARMOUTH(B)-32F | MELTON.C-32G | MELTON.C-32G | YARMOUTH(B)-32F | CAMBRIDGE-31A | MELTON.C-32G |
| Jan-53 | IPSWICH-32B | 11/52: CAMB-31A | BURYSt.E-31E | YARMOUTH(B)-32F | MELTON.C-32G | MELTON.C-32G | YARMOUTH(B)-32F | CAMBRIDGE-31A | MELTON.C-32G |
| Aug-53 | IPSWICH-32B | CAMBRIDGE-31A | BURYSt.E-31E | YARMOUTH(B)-32F | MELTON.C-32G | MELTON.C-32G | YARMOUTH(B)-32F | CAMBRIDGE-31A | MELTON.C-32G |
| Jan-54 | IPSWICH-32B | CAMBRIDGE-31A | BURYSt.E-31E | 11/53: LOW-32C | MELTON.C-32G | MELTON.C-32G | 11/53: LOW-32C | 10/54: K.LYNN-31C | MELTON.C-32G |
| Aug-54 | IPSWICH-32B | 10/54: K.LYNN-31C | BURYSt.E-31E | LOWESTOFT-32C | MELTON.C-32G | MELTON.C-32G | LOWESTOFT-32C | 1/55: CAMB-31A | MELTON.C-32G |
| Jan-55 | IPSWICH-32B | 1/55: CAMB-31A | BURYSt.E-31E | LOWESTOFT-32C | MELTON.C-32G | MELTON.C-32G | LOWESTOFT-32C | CAMBRIDGE-31A | MELTON.C-32G |
| Aug-55 | 7/55: W/D | CAMBRIDGE-31A | 8/55: W/D | LOWESTOFT-32C | MELTON.C-32G | 11/55: STRAT-30A | LOWESTOFT-32C | 12/55: STRAT-30A | STRATFORD-30A |
| Jan-56 | | 12/55: STRAT-30A | | 12/55: W/D | 12/55: LOW-32C | 12/55: COL-30E | 11/55: W/D | 6/56: COL-30E | STRATFORD-30A |
| Aug-56 | | STRATFORD-30A | | | LOWESTOFT-32C | 5/56: W/D | | COLCHESTER-30E | 3/56: COL-30E |
| Jan-57 | | STRATFORD-30A | | | 11/56: W/D | | | COLCHESTER-30E | COLCHESTER-30E |
| Aug-57 | | STRATFORD-30A | | | | | | COLCHESTER-30E | COLCHESTER-30E |
| Jan-58 | | 10/57: W/D | | | | | | COLCHESTER-30E | 12/57: STRAT-30A |
| Aug-58 | | | | | | | | 5/58: W/D | 4/58: W/D |
| Jan-59 | | | | | | | | | |
| Aug-59 | | | | | | | | | |
| Nov-59 | | | | | | | | | |
| Jan-60 | | | | | | | | | |
| Apr-60 | | | | | | | | | |
| Aug-60 | | | | | | | | | |
| Nov-60 | | | | | | | | | |

## 67229 – 67237

| | 67229 | 67230 | 67231 | 67232 | 67233 | 67234 | 67235 | 67236 | 67237 |
|---|---|---|---|---|---|---|---|---|---|
| Aug-50 | NORWICH-32A | IPSWICH-32B | LOWESTOFT-32C | NORWICH-32A | YARMOUTH(B)-32F | YARMOUTH(B)-32F | YARMOUTH(B)-32F | BURYSt.E-31E | BURYSt.E-31E |
| Jan-51 | NORWICH-32A | IPSWICH-32B | LOWESTOFT-32C | NORWICH-32A | YARMOUTH(B)-32F | YARMOUTH(B)-32F | YARMOUTH(B)-32F | BURYSt.E-31E | BURYSt.E-31E |
| Aug-51 | NORWICH-32A | IPSWICH-32B | 5/51: LOW-32C | NORWICH-32A | YARMOUTH(B)-32F | YARMOUTH(B)-32F | YARMOUTH(B)-32F | BURYSt.E-31E | BURYSt.E-31E |
| Jan-52 | NORWICH-32A | IPSWICH-32B | LOWESTOFT-32C | LOWESTOFT-32C | YARMOUTH(B)-32F | YARMOUTH(B)-32F | YARMOUTH(B)-32F | 2/52: MARCH-31B | BURYSt.E-31E |
| Aug-52 | 8/52: MELTON-32G | IPSWICH-32B | LOWESTOFT-32C | LOWESTOFT-32C | YARMOUTH(B)-32F | YARMOUTH(B)-32F | YARMOUTH(B)-32F | MARCH-31B | BURYSt.E-31E |
| Jan-53 | MELTON.C-32G | IPSWICH-32B | LOWESTOFT-32C | LOWESTOFT-32C | YARMOUTH(B)-32F | YARMOUTH(B)-32F | YARMOUTH(B)-32F | 1/53: BURY-31E | 11/52: CAMB-31A |
| Aug-53 | 7/53: LOW-32C | IPSWICH-32B | LOWESTOFT-32C | LOWESTOFT-32C | YARMOUTH(B)-32F | YARMOUTH(B)-32F | YARMOUTH(B)-32F | BURYSt.E-31E | 5/53: BURY-31E |
| Jan-54 | LOWESTOFT-32C | IPSWICH-32B | LOWESTOFT-32C | LOWESTOFT-32C | 10/53: LOW-32C | 11/53: LOW-32C | YARMOUTH(B)-32F | BURYSt.E-31E | BURYSt.E-31E |
| Aug-54 | 10/54: YAR(ST)-32D | IPSWICH-32B | LOWESTOFT-32C | LOWESTOFT-32C | LOWESTOFT-32C | LOWESTOFT-32C | 10/53: YAR(ST)-32D | BURYSt.E-31E | BURYSt.E-31E |
| Jan-55 | 11/54: LOW-32C | IPSWICH-32B | LOWESTOFT-32C | LOWESTOFT-32C | LOWESTOFT-32C | LOWESTOFT-32C | YARMOUTH(ST)-32D | BURYSt.E-31E | BURYSt.E-31E |
| Aug-55 | LOWESTOFT-32C | IPSWICH-32B | LOWESTOFT-32C | LOWESTOFT-32C | LOWESTOFT-32C | LOWESTOFT-32C | 12/55: STRAT-30A | 8/55: W/D | 8/55: W/D |
| Jan-56 | LOWESTOFT-32C | IPSWICH-32B | LOWESTOFT-32C | 11/55: W/D | 12/55: W/D | LOWESTOFT-32C | 1/56: W/D | | |
| Aug-56 | LOWESTOFT-32C | IPSWICH-32B | LOWESTOFT-32C | | | 8/56: W/D | | | |
| Jan-57 | LOWESTOFT-32C | 11/56: STRAT-30A | LOWESTOFT-32C | | | | | | |
| Aug-57 | LOWESTOFT-32C | STRATFORD-30A | LOWESTOFT-32C | | | | | | |
| Jan-58 | LOWESTOFT-32C | STRATFORD-30A | LOWESTOFT-32C | | | | | | |
| Aug-58 | 3/58: W/D | 5/58: W/D | 3/58: W/D | | | | | | |
| Jan-59 | | | | | | | | | |
| Aug-59 | | | | | | | | | |
| Nov-59 | | | | | | | | | |
| Jan-60 | | | | | | | | | |
| Apr-60 | | | | | | | | | |
| Aug-60 | | | | | | | | | |
| Nov-60 | | | | | | | | | |

G5 0-4-4T (1894)

| Date | 67238 | 67239 | 67240 | 67241 | 67242 | 67243 | 67244 | 67245 | 67246 |
|---|---|---|---|---|---|---|---|---|---|
| Aug-50 | BURY St.E- 31E | IPSWICH- 32B | NEVILLE HILL- 50B | BLAYDON- 52C | STOCKTON- 51E | SUNDERLAND- 54A | S.BLYTH- 52F | HEXHAM- 52C | S.BLYTH- 52F |
| Jan-51 | BURY St.E- 31E | IPSWICH- 32B | NEVILLE HILL- 50B | BLAYDON- 52C | STOCKTON- 51E | SUNDERLAND- 54A | S.BLYTH- 52F | HEXHAM- 52C | S.BLYTH- 52F |
| Aug-51 | BURY St.E- 31E | IPSWICH- 32B | NEVILLE HILL- 50B | BLAYDON- 52C | 6/51: W.AUCK - 51F | SUNDERLAND- 54A | 7/51: GHD - 52A | 6/51: W/D | S.BLYTH- 52F |
| Jan-52 | BURY St.E- 31E | IPSWICH- 32B | NEVILLE HILL- 50B | BLAYDON- 52C | 1/52: STOCK - 51E | SUNDERLAND- 54A | GATESHEAD- 52A | | S.BLYTH- 52F |
| Aug-52 | BURY St.E- 31E | IPSWICH- 32B | NEVILLE HILL- 50B | BLAYDON- 52C | STOCKTON- 51E | SUNDERLAND- 54A | GATESHEAD- 52A | | S.BLYTH- 52F |
| Jan-53 | BURY St.E- 31E | IPSWICH- 32B | NEVILLE HILL- 50B | BLAYDON- 52C | STOCKTON- 51E | SUNDERLAND- 54A | 11/52: W/D | | S.BLYTH- 52F |
| Aug-53 | 5/53: CAMB - 31A | IPSWICH- 32B | 7/53: WHITBY - 50G | BLAYDON- 52C | 2/53: W/D | SUNDERLAND- 54A | | | S.BLYTH- 52F |
| Jan-54 | CAMBRIDGE- 31A | IPSWICH- 32B | WHITBY- 50G | BLAYDON- 52C | | SUNDERLAND- 54A | | | S.BLYTH- 52F |
| Aug-54 | CAMBRIDGE- 31A | IPSWICH- 32B | WHITBY- 50G | BLAYDON- 52C | | SUNDERLAND- 54A | | | S.BLYTH- 52F |
| Jan-55 | CAMBRIDGE- 31A | IPSWICH- 32B | WHITBY- 50G | 3/55: W/D | | SUNDERLAND- 54A | | | S.BLYTH- 52F |
| Aug-55 | CAMBRIDGE- 31A | 11/55: STRAT - 30A | WHITBY- 50G | | | 9/55: W/D | | | 11/55: BLAY - 52C |
| Jan-56 | 11/55: W/D | 1/56: W/D | 11/55: MALT - 50F | | | | | | 12/56: COP H - 56C |
| Aug-56 | | | 4/56: W/D | | | | | | COPLEY HILL- 56C |
| Jan-57 | | | | | | | | | 2/57: SUND - 54A |
| Aug-57 | | | | | | | | | SUNDERLAND- 54A |
| Jan-58 | | | | | | | | | SUNDERLAND- 54A |
| Aug-58 | | | | | | | | | 11/58: W/D |
| Jan-59 | | | | | | | | | |
| Aug-59 | | | | | | | | | |
| Nov-59 | | | | | | | | | |
| Jan-60 | | | | | | | | | |
| Apr-60 | | | | | | | | | |
| Aug-60 | | | | | | | | | |
| Nov-60 | | | | | | | | | |

| Date | 67247 | 67248 | 67249 | 67250 | 67251 | 67252 | 67253 | 67254 | 67255 |
|---|---|---|---|---|---|---|---|---|---|
| Aug-50 | SUNDERLAND- 54A | TWEEDMOUTH- 52D | HEXHAM- 52C | SELBY- 50C | SUNDERLAND- 54A | SUNDERLAND- 54A | STARBECK- 50D | BOT. GDNS - 53B | BLAYDON- 52C |
| Jan-51 | SUNDERLAND- 54A | TWEEDMOUTH- 52D | HEXHAM- 52C | SELBY- 50C | SUNDERLAND- 54A | SUNDERLAND- 54A | STARBECK- 50D | BOT. GDNS - 53B | BLAYDON- 52C |
| Aug-51 | SUNDERLAND- 54A | TWEEDMOUTH- 52D | HEXHAM- 52C | SELBY- 50C | 7/51: HTN - 52B | | 4/51: B. GDNS - 53B | BOT. GDNS - 53B | 5/51: W/D |
| Jan-52 | SUNDERLAND- 54A | TWEEDMOUTH- 52D | HEXHAM- 52C | SELBY- 50C | 5/52: GHD - 52A | | BOT. GDNS - 53B | BOT. GDNS - 53B | |
| Aug-52 | SUNDERLAND- 54A | 7/52: BLAY - 52C | HEXHAM- 52C | SELBY- 50C | 7/52: BLAY - 52C | 11/52: W/D | BOT. GDNS - 53B | BOT. GDNS - 53B | |
| Jan-53 | SUNDERLAND- 54A | BLAYDON- 52C | HEXHAM- 52C | SELBY- 50C | SUNDERLAND- 54A | | BOT. GDNS - 53B | 2/53: BRID - 53D | |
| Aug-53 | SUNDERLAND- 54A | BLAYDON- 52C | HEXHAM- 52C | SELBY- 50C | SUNDERLAND- 54A | | BOT. GDNS - 53B | 5/53: B. GDNS - 53B | |
| Jan-54 | SUNDERLAND- 54A | BLAYDON- 52C | HEXHAM- 52C | SELBY- 50C | SUNDERLAND- 54A | | BOT. GDNS - 53B | BOT. GDNS - 53B | |
| Aug-54 | SUNDERLAND- 54A | BLAYDON- 52C | HEXHAM- 52C | SELBY- 50C | SUNDERLAND- 54A | | BOT. GDNS - 53B | BOT. GDNS - 53B | |
| Jan-55 | 12/54: W/D | BLAYDON- 52C | HEXHAM- 52C | SELBY- 50C | SUNDERLAND- 54A | | BOT. GDNS - 53B | BOT. GDNS - 53B | |
| Aug-55 | | BLAYDON- 52C | 3/55: W/D | SELBY- 50C | SUNDERLAND- 54A | | BOT. GDNS - 53B | 9/55: SUND - 54A | |
| Jan-56 | | BLAYDON- 52C | | SELBY- 50C | 3/56: W/D | | BOT. GDNS - 53B | SUNDERLAND- 54A | |
| Aug-56 | | BLAYDON- 52C | | SELBY- 50C | | | BOT. GDNS - 53B | SUNDERLAND- 54A | |
| Jan-57 | | DURHAM- 54A | | SELBY- 50C | | | 5/57: S. BLYTH - 52F | SUNDERLAND- 54A | |
| Aug-57 | | DURHAM- 54A | | SELBY- 50C | | | 7/57: SUND - 54A | 12/57: W/D | |
| Jan-58 | | 12/57: MALT - 50F | | 9/57: W/D | | | SUNDERLAND- 54A | | |
| Aug-58 | | MALTON- 50F | | | | | SUNDERLAND- 54A | | |
| Jan-59 | | 12/58: W/D | | | | | 10/58: W/D | | |
| Aug-59 | | | | | | | | | |
| Nov-59 | | | | | | | | | |
| Jan-60 | | | | | | | | | |
| Apr-60 | | | | | | | | | |
| Aug-60 | | | | | | | | | |
| Nov-60 | | | | | | | | | |

| Date | 67256 | 67257 | 67258 | 67259 | 67260 | 67261 | 67262 | 67263 | 67264 |
|---|---|---|---|---|---|---|---|---|---|
| Aug-50 | BOT. GDNS - 53B | SUNDERLAND- 54A | DURHAM- 54A | BLAYDON- 52C | SUNDERLAND- 54A | S.BLYTH- 52F | NEVILLE HILL- 50B | DURHAM- 54A | SUNDERLAND- 54A |
| Jan-51 | BOT. GDNS - 53B | SUNDERLAND- 54A | DURHAM- 54A | BLAYDON- 52C | SUNDERLAND- 54A | S.BLYTH- 52F | NEVILLE HILL- 50B | DURHAM- 54A | SUNDERLAND- 54A |
| Aug-51 | BOT. GDNS - 53B | SUNDERLAND- 54A | DURHAM- 54A | BLAYDON- 52C | SUNDERLAND- 54A | S.BLYTH- 52F | NEVILLE HILL- 50B | DURHAM- 54A | 7/51: W/D |
| Jan-52 | BOT. GDNS - 53B | SUNDERLAND- 54A | DURHAM- 54A | BLAYDON- 52C | SUNDERLAND- 54A | S.BLYTH- 52F | NEVILLE HILL- 50B | DURHAM- 54A | |
| Aug-52 | BOT. GDNS - 53B | SUNDERLAND- 54A | DURHAM- 54A | BLAYDON- 52C | SUNDERLAND- 54A | S.BLYTH- 52F | NEVILLE HILL- 50B | DURHAM- 54A | |
| Jan-53 | BOT. GDNS - 53B | SUNDERLAND- 54A | DURHAM- 54A | BLAYDON- 52C | 11/52: W/D | S.BLYTH- 52F | NEVILLE HILL- 50B | DURHAM- 54A | |
| Aug-53 | BOT. GDNS - 53B | SUNDERLAND- 54A | DURHAM- 54A | BLAYDON- 52C | | S.BLYTH- 52F | NEVILLE HILL- 50B | DURHAM- 54A | |
| Jan-54 | BOT. GDNS - 53B | SUNDERLAND- 54A | DURHAM- 54A | BLAYDON- 52C | | S.BLYTH- 52F | NEVILLE HILL- 50B | DURHAM- 54A | |
| Aug-54 | BOT. GDNS - 53B | 4/54: W/D | 4/54: GHD - 52A | 4/54: GHD - 52A | | S.BLYTH- 52F | NEVILLE HILL- 50B | DURHAM- 54A | |
| Jan-55 | BOT. GDNS - 53B | | DURHAM- 54A | 1/55: BLAY - 52C | | 12/54: B. GDNS - 53B | NEVILLE HILL- 50B | DURHAM- 54A | |
| Aug-55 | BOT. GDNS - 53B | | DURHAM- 54A | BLAYDON- 52C | | BOT. GDNS - 53B | NEVILLE HILL- 50B | DURHAM- 54A | |
| Jan-56 | BOT. GDNS - 53B | | DURHAM- 54A | 12/55: SUND - 54A | | BOT. GDNS - 53B | NEVILLE HILL- 50B | 4/56: S. BLYTH - 52F | |
| Aug-56 | BOT. GDNS - 53B | | DURHAM- 54A | SUNDERLAND- 54A | | BOT. GDNS - 53B | NEVILLE HILL- 50B | S. BLYTH- 52F | |
| Jan-57 | 12/56: BRID - 53D | | DURHAM- 54A | SUNDERLAND- 54A | | BOT. GDNS - 53B | NEVILLE HILL- 50B | 6/57: B. GDNS - 53B | |
| Aug-57 | 4/57: W/D | | DURHAM- 54A | 12/57: W/D | | 7/57: S. BLYTH - 52F | NEVILLE HILL- 50B | BOT. GDNS - 53B | |
| Jan-58 | | | 10/57: W/D | | | S.BLYTH- 52F | NEVILLE HILL- 50B | BOT. GDNS - 53B | |
| Aug-58 | | | | | | 10/58: SUND - 52G | NEVILLE HILL- 50B | 10/58: W/D | |
| Jan-59 | | | | | | 12/58: W/D | 12/58: W/D | | |
| Aug-59 | | | | | | | | | |
| Nov-59 | | | | | | | | | |
| Jan-60 | | | | | | | | | |
| Apr-60 | | | | | | | | | |
| Aug-60 | | | | | | | | | |
| Nov-60 | | | | | | | | | |

| Date | 67265 | 67266 | 67267 | 67268 | 67269 | 67270 | 67271 | 67272 | 67273 |
|---|---|---|---|---|---|---|---|---|---|
| Aug-50 | HEXHAM- 52C | NEVILLE HILL- 50B | SUNDERLAND- 54A | HEXHAM- 52C | STRATFORD- 30A | SUNDERLAND- 54A | W. HARTLEPOOL- 51C | DARLINGTON- 51A | MALTON- 50F |
| Jan-51 | HEXHAM- 52C | NEVILLE HILL- 50B | SUNDERLAND- 54A | HEXHAM- 52C | STRATFORD- 30A | SUNDERLAND- 54A | 10/50: W. HPL - 51C | W. HARTLEPOOL- 51C | 10/50: DARL - 51A |
| Aug-51 | HEXHAM- 52C | NEVILLE HILL- 50B | SUNDERLAND- 54A | HEXHAM- 52C | STRATFORD- 30A | 7/51: HTN - 52B | W. HARTLEPOOL- 51C | W. HARTLEPOOL- 51C | DARLINGTON- 51A |
| Jan-52 | HEXHAM- 52C | NEVILLE HILL- 50B | SUNDERLAND- 54A | HEXHAM- 52C | STRATFORD- 30A | 5/52: GHD - 52A | W. HARTLEPOOL- 51C | W. HARTLEPOOL- 51C | DARLINGTON- 51A |
| Aug-52 | HEXHAM- 52C | NEVILLE HILL- 50B | SUNDERLAND- 54A | HEXHAM- 52C | STRATFORD- 30A | 7/52: HTN - 52B | W. HARTLEPOOL- 51C | W. HARTLEPOOL- 51C | 11/52: W.AUCK - 51F |
| Jan-53 | HEXHAM- 52C | NEVILLE HILL- 50B | SUNDERLAND- 54A | HEXHAM- 52C | STRATFORD- 30A | 2/53: TWEED - 52D | W. HARTLEPOOL- 51C | W. HARTLEPOOL- 51C | 2/53: B. GDNS - 53B |
| Aug-53 | HEXHAM- 52C | NEVILLE HILL- 50B | SUNDERLAND- 54A | HEXHAM- 52C | STRATFORD- 30A | TWEEDMOUTH- 52D | W. HARTLEPOOL- 51C | W. HARTLEPOOL- 51C | BOT. GDNS - 53B |
| Jan-54 | HEXHAM- 52C | NEVILLE HILL- 50B | SUNDERLAND- 54A | 2/54: BLAY - 52C | STRATFORD- 30A | TWEEDMOUTH- 52D | W. HARTLEPOOL- 51C | W. HARTLEPOOL- 51C | BOT. GDNS - 53B |
| Aug-54 | 10/54: GHD - 52A | NEVILLE HILL- 50B | 6/54: W/D | 5/54: TWEED - 52D | STRATFORD- 30A | 5/54: HEX - 52C | 8/54: STOCK - 51E | 8/54: N'TON - 51J | BOT. GDNS - 53B |
| Jan-55 | 3/55: HEX - 52C | NEVILLE HILL- 50B | | TWEEDMOUTH- 52D | STRATFORD- 30A | HEXHAM- 52C | 2/54: W/D | 11/54: W/D | 9/55: SELBY - 50C |
| Aug-55 | HEXHAM- 52C | NEVILLE HILL- 50B | | 4/55: W/D | STRATFORD- 30A | HEXHAM- 52C | | | SELBY- 50C |
| Jan-56 | HEXHAM- 52C | 12/55: W/D | | | STRATFORD- 30A | 3/56: SUND - 54A | | | SELBY- 50C |
| Aug-56 | HEXHAM- 52C | | | | 9/56: W/D | SUNDERLAND- 54A | | | SELBY- 50C |
| Jan-57 | 1/57: SUND - 54A | | | | | SUNDERLAND- 54A | | | 5/57: W/D |
| Aug-57 | SUNDERLAND- 54A | | | | | SUNDERLAND- 54A | | | |
| Jan-58 | SUNDERLAND- 54A | | | | | 1/58: W/D | | | |
| Aug-58 | 2/58: W/D | | | | | | | | |
| Jan-59 | | | | | | | | | |
| Aug-59 | | | | | | | | | |
| Nov-59 | | | | | | | | | |
| Jan-60 | | | | | | | | | |
| Apr-60 | | | | | | | | | |
| Aug-60 | | | | | | | | | |
| Nov-60 | | | | | | | | | |

The development of suburban tanks under the LNER and its successor makes an interesting study since the former, influenced by the Great Wester[n] and the LMS who had both produced large modern tanks engines for suburban works, brought out a class of excellent 2-6-2T's which, although tried wit[h] success on services from both Liverpool Street and Kings Cross, were relegated to Scotland and the North East, leaving the Great Northern suburba[n] workings in the hands of 0-6-2 tanks whilst outer suburban services to Hitchin and the Cambridge branch survived with elderly 4-4-0's made redundant b[y] Atlantics and Pacifics. The position at Liverpool Street was even more extreme where almost the whole of the Jazz service relied upon 0-6-2T and 2-[4-]2T engines.

Postwar years saw large numbers of standard 2-6-4T's appear but the few which found their way onto LNER metals were allocated to the nor[th] leaving N1 and N2 tanks to pound their way up the hill from Kings Cross to Potters Bar and Hatfield. The only leavening came with the L1 2-6-4T's, [a] poor performer compared with the V1 2-6-2T, which replaced the 4-4-0's on the Hitchin workings. A couple of LMS 2-6-4T's were tried out by King[s]

| | L1 | LM4 | BR4 | BR3 | V1 | A5 | A8 | N1 | N2 | N15 | N5 | N7 | C12 | C13 | C14 | C15 | C16 | F5 | F6 | G5 | Total |
|---|---|---|---|---|---|---|---|---|---|---|---|---|---|---|---|---|---|---|---|---|---|
| **DISTRIBUTION OF PASSENGER TANKS : 1957** | | | | | | | | | | | | | | | | | | | | | |
| Stratford | 21 | | | | | | | | | | | 94 | | | | | | 9 | 3 | | 127 |
| Kings Cross | 12 | | | | | | | | 66 | | | | | | | | | | | | 78 |
| Parkhead | | | | | 19 | | 8 | 16 | | | | | | | 3 | | | | | | 46 |
| Neasden | 20 | 12 | 8 | | | | | | | | | | | 3 | | | | | | | 43 |
| Shoeburyness | | 42 | | | | | | | | | | | | | | | | | | | 42 |
| St Margarets | | | | | 13 | | | | | 21 | | | | | | | 2 | | | | 36 |
| Eastfield | | | | | 6 | | | | | 19 | | | | | | 2 | 1 | | | | 28 |
| Plaistow | | 11 | 16 | | | | | | | | | | | | | | | | | | 27 |
| Hatfield | | | | | | | | 9 | | | | 15 | | | | | | | | | 24 |
| Gorton | | | | | | 8 | | | | | | | 4 | 9 | | | | | | | 21 |
| Bot Gdns | | | | | 7 | 5 | 6 | | | | | | | | | | | | | 3 | 21 |
| Hornsey | | | | | | | | 2 | 14 | | | 4 | | | | | | | | | 20 |
| Tilbury | | | 12 | | | | | | | | | 4 | 1 | | | | | | | | 17 |
| Sunderland | | | | | 5 | | | | | | | | | | | | | | | 11 | 16 |
| Darlington | 3 | | | | 8 | | 2 | | | | | | | | | | | | | 1 | 14 |
| Darnall | | | | | | | | | | 12 | | | | 1 | | | | | | | 13 |
| Middlesbrough | 5 | | | | | | 6 | | | | | | | | | | | | | 2 | 13 |
| Colwick | 5 | | | | 7 | | | | | | | | | | | | | | | | 12 |
| Ipswich | 12 | | | | | | | | | | | | | | | | | | | | 12 |
| Kittybrewster | | 10 | | | 2 | | | | | | | | | | | | | | | | 12 |
| Heaton | | | | | | | 11 | | | | | | | | | | | | | | 11 |
| Dunfermline | | | | | 2 | | | | 9 | | | | | | | | | | | | 11 |
| Kipps | | | | | 5 | | | 2 | 4 | | | | | | | | | | | | 11 |
| Hitchin | 8 | | | | | | | 2 | | | | | | | | | | | | | 10 |
| Barnsley | | | | | | | | | | 8 | | | | 2 | | | | | | | 10 |
| Whitby | 2 | | 5 | | 3 | | | | | | | | | | | | | | | | 10 |
| Saltburn | | | | | 9 | | | | | | | | | | | | | | | | 9 |
| Dawsholme | | | | | | | 3 | 6 | | | | | | | | | | | | | 9 |
| Copley Hill | | | | | | 2 | | | | | | | | 2 | | | | | | 4 | 8 |
| Lowestoft | 2 | | | | 3 | | | | | | | 1 | | | | | 2 | | | | 8 |
| Yarmouth (ST) | 3 | | | | | | | | | | | 3 | 1 | | | | | | | | 7 |
| Blaydon | | | | | 6 | | | | | | | | | | | | | | | 1 | 7 |
| W. Auckland | | | | | | | 6 | | | | | | | | | | | | | 1 | 7 |
| Dundee | | 2 | | | | | | | | | | | | | | 5 | | | | | 7 |
| Thornton Jcn | | | | | | | | 7 | | | | | | | | | | | | | 7 |
| Grantham | 2 | | | | 2 | | | | | | | 2 | | | | | | | | | 6 |
| New England | | | | | | | | | | | | 6 | | | | | | | | | 6 |
| Ardsley | | | | | | 5 | | | | | | | | 1 | | | | | | | 6 |
| Cambridge | | | | | | | | | | 3 | 3 | | | | | | | | | | 6 |
| Colchester | | | | | | | | | | 3 | | | | | | 1 | 2 | | | | 6 |
| S. Blyth | | | | | | | | | | | | | | | | | | | | 6 | 6 |
| Helensburgh | | | | | 6 | | | | | | | | | | | | | | | | 6 |
| Annesley | | | | | | 4 | | | | | | 1 | | | | | | | | | 5 |
| Parkeston | | | | | | | | | | | | 5 | | | | | | | | | 5 |
| Norwich | 3 | | | | | | | | | | | 2 | | | | | | | | | 5 |
| Malton | | | | | | | 1 | | | | | | | | | | | | | 4 | 5 |
| Hexham | | | | | | 5 | | | | | | | | | | | | | | | 5 |
| Bathgate | | | | | | | | | | 5 | | | | | | | | | | | 5 |
| Haymarket | | | | | | 3 | | | | 2 | | | | | | | | | | | 5 |
| Bradford | | | | | 4 | | | | | | | 7 | | | | | | | | | 11 |
| Kirkby Stephen | | | | 4 | | | | | | | | | | | | | | | | | 4 |
| Neville Hill | | | | | | 2 | | | | | | | | | | | | | | 2 | 4 |
| Ferryhill | | | | | | | | | | 3 | | | | | | 1 | | | | | 4 |
| Polmont | | | | | | | | | | 2 | | | | | | 2 | | | | | 4 |
| Carlisle (C) | | | | | | | | | | 4 | | | | | | | | | | | 4 |
| Wrexham | | | | | | | | | | | | | | 1 | 2 | | | | | | 3 |
| W. Hartlepool | | | | | | 3 | | | | | | | | | | | | | | | 3 |
| Gateshead | | | | | 3 | | | | | | | | | | | | | | | | 3 |
| Keith | | 2 | | | | | | | | | | | | | | 1 | | | | | 3 |
| Boston | | | | | | | | 1 | | | 1 | | | | | | | | | | 2 |
| Lincoln | | | | | 2 | | | | | | | | | | | | | | | | 2 |
| Brunswick | | | | | | | | | | | 2 | | | | | | | | | | 2 |
| Woodford | 2 | | | | | | | | | | | | | | | | | | | | 2 |
| Chester | | | | | | | | | | | 1 | 1 | | | | | | | | | 2 |
| Stockton | | | | | 2 | | | | | | | | | | | | | | | | 2 |
| Durham | | | | | | | | | | | | | | | | | | | | 2 | 2 |
| Selby | | | | | | | | | | | | | | | | | | | | 2 | 2 |
| Hawick | | | | | | 1 | | | | | | | | | | 1 | | | | | 2 |
| Stirling | | | | | | 2 | | | | | | | | | | | | | | | 2 |
| Staveley | | | | | 1 | | | | | | | | | | | | | | | | 1 |
| Immingham | | | | | | | | | | | | 1 | | | | | | | | | 1 |
| K. Lynn | | | | | | | | | | | | 1 | | | | | | | | | 1 |
| S. Lynn | | | | | | | | | | | | 1 | | | | | | | | | 1 |
| Spital Bge | | | | | | | | | | | | 1 | | | | | | | | | 1 |
| Bridlington | | | | | | | | | | | | | | | | | | | | 1 | 1 |
| York | | | | | 1 | | | | | | | | | | | | | | | | 1 |
| Scarborough | | | | | 1 | | | | | | | | | | | | | | | | 1 |
| Dalry Rd | | | | | 1 | | | | | | | | | | | | | | | | 1 |
| Balloch | | | | | 1 | | | | | | | | | | | | | | | | 1 |

*Dating from 1895 the North Eastern G5 0-4-4T's survived in spite of six-coupled engines and the electrification of Tyneside and until the arrival of multiple units in the late 1950's they were to be found in respectable numbers, especially around Sunderland working the frequent local services to South Shields and Newcastle. Some of the Sunderland duties were outbased to Durham, where 67258 was found on 23rd September 1956, and included the banking of main line services up the bank to Relly Mill. Most of the class remained on their home metals but three were could be found working from Kittybrewster and Keith on the GNoS whilst another trio operated from Stratford on the Palace Gates branch.*

| | 67274 | 67275 | 67276 | 67277 | 67278 | 67279 | 67280 | 67281 | 67282 |
|---|---|---|---|---|---|---|---|---|---|
| Aug-50 | NEVILLE HILL-50B | MALTON-50F | SUNDERLAND-54A | BLAYDON-52C | STOCKTON-51E | STRATFORD-30A | BOTANIC GARDENS-53B | MIDDLESBROUGH-51D | BOTANIC GARDENS-53 |
| Jan-51 | NEVILLE HILL-50B | MALTON-50F | SUNDERLAND-54A | BLAYDON-52C | STOCKTON-51E | STRATFORD-30A | BOTANIC GARDENS-53B | MIDDLESBROUGH-51D | BOTANIC GARDENS-53 |
| Aug-51 | NEVILLE HILL-50B | MALTON-50F | SUNDERLAND-54A | BLAYDON-52C | STOCKTON-51E | STRATFORD-30A | BOTANIC GARDENS-53B | MIDDLESBROUGH-51D | BOTANIC GARDENS-53 |
| Jan-52 | NEVILLE HILL-50B | MALTON-50F | SUNDERLAND-54A | BLAYDON-52C | 1/52: W.AUCK-51F | STRATFORD-30A | BOTANIC GARDENS-53B | MIDDLESBROUGH-51D | BOTANIC GARDENS-53 |
| Aug-52 | NEVILLE HILL-50B | MALTON-50F | SUNDERLAND-54A | BLAYDON-52C | W.AUCKLAND-51F | STRATFORD-30A | BOTANIC GARDENS-53B | MIDDLESBROUGH-51D | BOTANIC GARDENS-53 |
| Jan-53 | NEVILLE HILL-50B | 9/52: W/D | 10/52: W/D | BLAYDON-52C | 11/52: STOCK-51E | STRATFORD-30A | BOTANIC GARDENS-53B | MIDDLESBROUGH-51D | BOTANIC GARDENS-53 |
| Aug-53 | NEVILLE HILL-50B | | | BLAYDON-52C | STOCKTON-51E | STRATFORD-30A | BOTANIC GARDENS-53B | MIDDLESBROUGH-51D | BOTANIC GARDENS-53 |
| Jan-54 | NEVILLE HILL-50B | | | BLAYDON-52C | STOCKTON-51E | STRATFORD-30A | BOTANIC GARDENS-53B | MIDDLESBROUGH-51D | BOTANIC GARDENS-53 |
| Aug-54 | NEVILLE HILL-50B | | | BLAYDON-52C | 8/54: W.HPL-51C | STRATFORD-30A | BOTANIC GARDENS-53B | MIDDLESBROUGH-51D | BOTANIC GARDENS-53 |
| Jan-55 | NEVILLE HILL-50B | | | 12/54: S.BLYTH-52F | 12/54: N'TON-51J | STRATFORD-30A | BOTANIC GARDENS-53B | 10/54: STOCK-51E | BOTANIC GARDENS-53 |
| Aug-55 | NEVILLE HILL-50B | | | SOUTHBLYTH-52F | NORTHALLERTON-51J | STRATFORD-30A | BOTANIC GARDENS-53B | 4/55: S.BLYTH-52F | BOTANIC GARDENS-53 |
| Jan-56 | NEVILLE HILL-50B | | | SOUTHBLYTH-52F | NORTHALLERTON-51J | STRATFORD-30A | BOTANIC GARDENS-53B | S.BLYTH-52F | BOTANIC GARDENS-53 |
| Aug-56 | NEVILLE HILL-50B | | | SOUTHBLYTH-52F | 3/56: SUND-54A | STRATFORD-30A | BOTANIC GARDENS-53B | S.BLYTH-52F | BOTANIC GARDENS-53 |
| Jan-57 | NEVILLE HILL-50B | | | SOUTHBLYTH-52F | SUNDERLAND-54A | 11/56: W/D | 10/56: C.HILL-56C | S.BLYTH-52F | BOTANIC GARDENS-53 |
| Aug-57 | 6/57: B.GDNS-53B | | | SOUTHBLYTH-52F | 7/57: W/D | | 3/57: B.GDNS-53B | S.BLYTH-52F | 5/57: W/D |
| Jan-58 | BOTANIC GARDENS-53B | | | 10/57: W/D | | | 4/57: BRID-53D | S.BLYTH-52F | |
| Aug-58 | BOTANIC GARDENS-53B | | | | | | BRIDLINGTON-53D | S.BLYTH-52F | |
| Jan-59 | 12/58: W/D | | | | | | 6/58: DAIRY-53A | 12/58: W/D | |
| Aug-59 | | | | | | | 12/58: W/D | | |
| Nov-59 | | | | | | | | | |
| Jan-60 | | | | | | | | | |
| Apr-60 | | | | | | | | | |
| Aug-60 | | | | | | | | | |
| Nov-60 | | | | | | | | | |

| | 67283 | 67284 | 67285 | 67286 | 67287 | 67288 | 67289 | 67290 | 67291 | 67292 |
|---|---|---|---|---|---|---|---|---|---|---|
| Aug-50 | SUNDERLAND-54A | STARBECK-50D | SELBY-50C | KITTYBREWSTER-61A | TYNE DOCK-54B | STARBECK-50D | NEVILLE HILL-50B | NEVILLE HILL-50B | W.HARTLEPOOL-51C | KEITH-61C |
| Jan-51 | SUNDERLAND-54A | 10/50: B.GDNS-53B | SELBY-50C | KITTYBREWSTER-61A | TYNE DOCK-54B | STARBECK-50D | NEVILLE HILL-50B | NEVILLE HILL-50B | 10/50: W.AUCK-51F | KEITH-61C |
| Aug-51 | SUNDERLAND-54A | 12/50: DARL-51A | SELBY-50C | KITTYBREWSTER-61A | 11/51: HTN-52B | 8/51: N.HILL-50B | NEVILLE HILL-50B | NEVILLE HILL-50B | 6/51: N'TON-51J | KEITH-61C |
| Jan-52 | SUNDERLAND-54A | DARLINGTON-51A | SELBY-50C | KITTYBREWSTER-61A | 2/52: B.GDNS-54C | NEVILLE HILL-50B | NEVILLE HILL-50B | NEVILLE HILL-50B | NORTHALLERTON-51J | 8/52: W/D |
| Aug-52 | SUNDERLAND-54A | DARLINGTON-51A | SELBY-50C | KITTYBREWSTER-61A | 3/52: STOCK-51E | NEVILLE HILL-50B | NEVILLE HILL-50B | NEVILLE HILL-50B | NORTHALLERTON-51J | |
| Jan-53 | SUNDERLAND-54A | DARLINGTON-51A | SELBY-50C | 3/53: W/D | STOCKTON-51E | NEVILLE HILL-50B | NEVILLE HILL-50B | NEVILLE HILL-50B | 2/53: W/D | |
| Aug-53 | SUNDERLAND-54A | DARLINGTON-51A | SELBY-50C | | STOCKTON-51E | NEVILLE HILL-50B | NEVILLE HILL-50B | NEVILLE HILL-50B | | |
| Jan-54 | SUNDERLAND-54A | DARLINGTON-51A | SELBY-50C | | 6/54: W/D | NEVILLE HILL-50B | NEVILLE HILL-50B | NEVILLE HILL-50B | | |
| Aug-54 | 8/54: W/D | DARLINGTON-51A | SELBY-50C | | | 6/54: MALT-50F | 6/54: W/D | NEVILLE HILL-50B | | |
| Jan-55 | | DARLINGTON-51A | SELBY-50C | | | MALTON-50F | | NEVILLE HILL-50B | | |
| Aug-55 | | DARLINGTON-51A | SELBY-50C | | | MALTON-50F | | NEVILLE HILL-50B | | |
| Jan-56 | | DARLINGTON-51A | SELBY-50C | | | MALTON-50F | | NEVILLE HILL-50B | | |
| Aug-56 | | DARLINGTON-51A | SELBY-50C | | | MALTON-50F | | 3/56: W/D | | |
| Jan-57 | | 10/56: W/D | 10/56: W/D | | | 12/56: W/D | | | | |
| Aug-57 | | | | | | | | | | |
| Jan-58 | | | | | | | | | | |
| Aug-58 | | | | | | | | | | |
| Jan-59 | | | | | | | | | | |
| Aug-59 | | | | | | | | | | |
| Nov-59 | | | | | | | | | | |
| Jan-60 | | | | | | | | | | |
| Apr-60 | | | | | | | | | | |
| Aug-60 | | | | | | | | | | |
| Nov-60 | | | | | | | | | | |

| | 67293 | 67294 | 67295 | 67296 | 67297 | 67298 | 67300 | 67301 | 67302 |
|---|---|---|---|---|---|---|---|---|---|
| Aug-50 | NEVILLE HILL-50B | W.AUCKLAND-51F | SOUTHBLYTH-52F | NORTHBLYTH-52F | SUNDERLAND-54A | DURHAM-54A | SUNDERLAND-54A | BOTANIC GARDENS-53B | WHITBY-50G |
| Jan-51 | NEVILLE HILL-50B | 10/50: W.HPL-51C | SOUTHBLYTH-52F | NORTHBLYTH-52F | SUNDERLAND-54A | DURHAM-54A | SUNDERLAND-54A | BOTANIC GARDENS-53B | WHITBY-50G |
| Aug-51 | 7/51: SELBY-50C | W.HARTLEPOOL-51C | SOUTHBLYTH-52F | NORTHBLYTH-52F | SUNDERLAND-54A | DURHAM-54A | SUNDERLAND-54A | BOTANIC GARDENS-53B | WHITBY-50G |
| Jan-52 | SELBY-50C | W.HARTLEPOOL-51C | SOUTHBLYTH-52F | NORTHBLYTH-52F | SUNDERLAND-54A | DURHAM-54A | SUNDERLAND-54A | BOTANIC GARDENS-53B | WHITBY-50G |
| Aug-52 | SELBY-50C | W.HARTLEPOOL-51C | SOUTHBLYTH-52F | NORTHBLYTH-52F | SUNDERLAND-54A | DURHAM-54A | SUNDERLAND-54A | BOTANIC GARDENS-53B | WHITBY-50G |
| Jan-53 | SELBY-50C | W.HARTLEPOOL-51C | SOUTHBLYTH-52F | 10/52: GHD-52A | SUNDERLAND-54A | DURHAM-54A | SUNDERLAND-54A | BOTANIC GARDENS-53B | WHITBY-50G |
| Aug-53 | SELBY-50C | W.HARTLEPOOL-51C | SOUTHBLYTH-52F | GATESHEAD-52A | SUNDERLAND-54A | DURHAM-54A | SUNDERLAND-54A | BOTANIC GARDENS-53B | WHITBY-50G |
| Jan-54 | 3/54: N.HILL-50B | W.HARTLEPOOL-51C | 3/54: W/D | GATESHEAD-52A | SUNDERLAND-54A | DURHAM-54A | SUNDERLAND-54A | BOTANIC GARDENS-53B | WHITBY-50G |
| Aug-54 | 5/54: MALT-50F | 9/54: SUND-54A | | 3/54: S.BLYTH-52F | SUNDERLAND-54A | DURHAM-54A | SUNDERLAND-54A | BOTANIC GARDENS-53B | WHITBY-50G |
| Jan-55 | MALTON-50F | SUNDERLAND-54A | | SOUTHBLYTH-52F | SUNDERLAND-54A | DURHAM-54A | SUNDERLAND-54A | 3/55: W/D | WHITBY-50G |
| Aug-55 | 4/55: W/D | 7/55: S.BLYTH-52F | | 3/55: W/D | SUNDERLAND-54A | DURHAM-54A | 11/55: W/D | | WHITBY-50G |
| Jan-56 | | S.BLYTH-52F | | | SUNDERLAND-54A | DURHAM-54A | | | WHITBY-50G |
| Aug-56 | | 4/56: D'HAM-54A | | | SUNDERLAND-54A | DURHAM-54A | | | 4/56: W/D |
| Jan-57 | | 1/57: W/D | | | SUNDERLAND-54A | 12/56: W/D | | | |
| Aug-57 | | | | | SUNDERLAND-54A | | | | |
| Jan-58 | | | | | SUNDERLAND-54A | | | | |
| Aug-58 | | | | | SUNDERLAND-54A | | | | |
| Jan-59 | | | | | 9/58: W/D | | | | |
| Aug-59 | | | | | | | | | |
| Nov-59 | | | | | | | | | |
| Jan-60 | | | | | | | | | |
| Apr-60 | | | | | | | | | |
| Aug-60 | | | | | | | | | |
| Nov-60 | | | | | | | | | |

| | 67303 | 67304 | 67305 | 67307 | 67308 | 67309 | 67310 | 67311 | 67312 |
|---|---|---|---|---|---|---|---|---|---|
| Aug-50 | TWEEDMOUTH-52D | TWEEDMOUTH-52D | STOCKTON-51E | DURHAM-54A | NEVILLE HILL-50B | GATESHEAD-52A | SUNDERLAND-54A | BOTANIC GARDENS-53B | W.AUCKLAND-51F |
| Jan-51 | TWEEDMOUTH-52D | TWEEDMOUTH-52D | STOCKTON-51E | DURHAM-54A | NEVILLE HILL-50B | GATESHEAD-52A | SUNDERLAND-54A | BOTANIC GARDENS-53B | W.AUCKLAND-51F |
| Aug-51 | TWEEDMOUTH-52D | TWEEDMOUTH-52D | STOCKTON-51E | DURHAM-54A | NEVILLE HILL-50B | 9/51: HEX-52C | 7/51: HTN-52B | BOTANIC GARDENS-53B | W.AUCKLAND-51F |
| Jan-52 | TWEEDMOUTH-52D | TWEEDMOUTH-52D | STOCKTON-51E | DURHAM-54A | NEVILLE HILL-50B | HEXHAM-52C | 11/51: SUND-54A | BOTANIC GARDENS-53B | W.AUCKLAND-51F |
| Aug-52 | TWEEDMOUTH-52D | 7/52: HTN-52B | STOCKTON-51E | DURHAM-54A | NEVILLE HILL-50B | HEXHAM-52C | SUNDERLAND-54A | BOTANIC GARDENS-53B | W.AUCKLAND-51F |
| Jan-53 | TWEEDMOUTH-52D | 12/52: BLAY-52C | 11/52: DARL-51A | DURHAM-54A | 2/53: PICK-50F | HEXHAM-52C | SUNDERLAND-54A | BOTANIC GARDENS-53B | 12/52: N'TON-51J |
| Aug-53 | 2/53: W/D | BLAYDON-52C | DARLINGTON-51A | DURHAM-54A | PICKERING-50F | HEXHAM-52C | SUNDERLAND-54A | BOTANIC GARDENS-53B | NORTHALLERTON-51J |
| Jan-54 | | BLAYDON-52C | DARLINGTON-51A | DURHAM-54A | PICKERING-50F | HEXHAM-52C | SUNDERLAND-54A | BOTANIC GARDENS-53B | NORTHALLERTON-51J |
| Aug-54 | | BLAYDON-52C | DARLINGTON-51A | DURHAM-54A | PICKERING-50F | HEXHAM-52C | SUNDERLAND-54A | BOTANIC GARDENS-53B | 3/54: DARL-51A |
| Jan-55 | | 2/55: W/D | DARLINGTON-51A | DURHAM-54A | PICKERING-50F | HEXHAM-52C | SUNDERLAND-54A | BOTANIC GARDENS-53B | 2/55: STOCK-51E |
| Aug-55 | | | DARLINGTON-51A | 5/55: W/D | 11/55: W/D | 3/55: W/D | 9/55: W/D | BOTANIC GARDENS-53B | STOCKTON-51E |
| Jan-56 | | | DARLINGTON-51A | | | | | BOTANIC GARDENS-53B | STOCKTON-51E |
| Aug-56 | | | DARLINGTON-51A | | | | | BOTANIC GARDENS-53B | 4/56: W/D |
| Jan-57 | | | DARLINGTON-51A | | | | | 10/56: C.HILL-56C | |
| Aug-57 | | | DARLINGTON-51A | | | | | 3/57: B.GDNS-53B | |
| Jan-58 | | | 10/57: S.BLYTH-52F | | | | | 4/57: SELBY-50C | |
| Aug-58 | | | S.BLYTH-52F | | | | | 9/57: MALT-50F | |
| Jan-59 | | | 12/58: W/D | | | | | 3/58: S.BLYTH-52F | |
| Aug-59 | | | | | | | | 12/58: W/D | |
| Nov-59 | | | | | | | | | |
| Jan-60 | | | | | | | | | |
| Apr-60 | | | | | | | | | |
| Aug-60 | | | | | | | | | |
| Nov-60 | | | | | | | | | |

Cross and Hitchin but with interest at the time focused on modernisation plans – not to mention the expectation of imminent electrification - the 0-6-2T remained in situ until replaced by diesels although it has to be said that even had an imported 2-6-4 been received with open arms, the problems of the Moorgate line which was limited to N1's, N2's and N7's, would have been very difficult to overcome.

The number of engines involved was extraordinary. The Kings Cross and Liverpool Street districts had just over one hundred and thirty suburban engines each whilst Glasgow – where the LNER served only a proportion of the city's needs – had eighty. The Great Central was very much smaller with only forty engines although much of the inner suburban needs were taken care of by London Transport whilst the North Eastern's commuting trade, Tyneside having been electrified, was largely confined to the Hull area although the very sprightly service of trains between Darlington and Saltburn was operated with all the discipline of a suburban system.

For the most part suburban services were operated with a mix of old and new engines – not that the former were in any way decrepit – and the one system that was fully up to date in any sense of the expression was the Tilbury section which, although coming within the orbit of Liverpool Street after nationalisation, remained visibly L.M.S. with BR or Stanier 2-6-4T's handling almost every trains in and out of Fenchurch Street.

## Block 1 — 67313–67321

| | 67313 | 67314 | 67315 | 67316 | 67317 | 67318 | 67319 | 67320 | 67321 |
|---|---|---|---|---|---|---|---|---|---|
| Aug-50 | HEXHAM-52C | W.HARTLEPOOL-51C | BLAYDON-52C | W.HARTLEPOOL-51C | STOCKTON-51E | STOCKTON-51E | NEVILLEHILL-50B | GATESHEAD-52A | BOT.GDNS-53B |
| Jan-51 | HEXHAM-52C | W.HARTLEPOOL-51C | BLAYDON-52C | 10/50: DARL-51A | STOCKTON-51E | STOCKTON-51E | NEVILLEHILL-50B | GATESHEAD-52A | BOT.GDNS-53B |
| Aug-51 | 8/51: W/D | W.HARTLEPOOL-51C | BLAYDON-52C | 6/51: W.HPL-51C | STOCKTON-51E | STOCKTON-51E | NEVILLEHILL-50B | GATESHEAD-52A | BOT.GDNS-53B |
| Jan-52 | | W.HARTLEPOOL-51C | BLAYDON-52C | 7/51: BLAY-52C | STOCKTON-51E | STOCKTON-51E | NEVILLEHILL-50B | GATESHEAD-52A | BOT.GDNS-53B |
| Aug-52 | | W.HARTLEPOOL-51C | BLAYDON-52C | BLAYDON-52C | 9/51: W/D | 3/52: W.AUCK-51F | NEVILLEHILL-50B | GATESHEAD-52A | BOT.GDNS-53B |
| Jan-53 | | W.HARTLEPOOL-51C | BLAYDON-52C | BLAYDON-52C | | 2/53: N'TON-51J | NEVILLEHILL-50B | GATESHEAD-52A | 5/53: BRID-53D |
| Aug-53 | | 6/53: DARL-51A | 2/54: HEX-52C | BLAYDON-52C | | NORTHALLERTON-51J | NEVILLEHILL-50B | GATESHEAD-52A | 12/53: B.GDNS-53B |
| Jan-54 | | 3/54: N'TON-51J | 4/54: GHD-52A | BLAYDON-52C | | NORTHALLERTON-51J | NEVILLEHILL-50B | GATESHEAD-52A | BOT.GDNS-53B |
| Aug-54 | | 8/54: W.HPL-51C | 7/54: SUND-54A | BLAYDON-52C | | 3/54: DARL-51A | 4/55: MALT-50F | 4/54: BLAY-52C | BOT.GDNS-53B |
| Jan-55 | | W.HARTLEPOOL-51C | SUNDERLAND-54A | BLAYDON-52C | | DARLINGTON-51A | MALTON-50F | 1/55: GHD-52A | 12/55: SUND-54A |
| Aug-55 | | W.HARTLEPOOL-51C | 7/55: S.BLYTH-52F | 6/55: SUND-54A | | DARLINGTON-51A | MALTON-50F | 3/55: BLAY-52C | SUNDERLAND-54A |
| Jan-56 | | 12/55: W/D | S.BLYTH-52F | 12/55: W/D | | 9/55: SUND-54A | MALTON-50F | 11/55: S.BLYTH-52F | 1/57: W/D |
| Aug-56 | | | 4/56: MALT-50F | | | SUNDERLAND-54A | MALTON-50F | S.BLYTH-52F | |
| Jan-57 | | | MALTON-50F | | | SUNDERLAND-54A | 12/57: W/D | 1/57: D'HAM-54A | |
| Aug-57 | | | MALTON-50F | | | 3/57: W/D | | DURHAM-54A | |
| Jan-58 | | | MALTON-50F | | | | | DURHAM-54A | |
| Aug-58 | | | MALTON-50F | | | | | DURHAM-54A | |
| Jan-59 | | | 12/58: W/D | | | | | DURHAM-54A | |
| Aug-59 | | | | | | | | 11/58: W/D | |
| Nov-59 | | | | | | | | | |
| Jan-60 | | | | | | | | | |
| Apr-60 | | | | | | | | | |
| Aug-60 | | | | | | | | | |
| Nov-60 | | | | | | | | | |

## Block 2 — 67322–67330

| | 67322 | 67323 | 67324 | 67325 | 67326 | 67327 | 67328 | 67329 | 67330 |
|---|---|---|---|---|---|---|---|---|---|
| Aug-50 | STRATFORD-30A | BLAYDON-52C | NORTHALLERTON-51J | GATESHEAD-52A | S.BLYTH-52F | KITTYBREWSTER-61A | SUNDERLAND-54A | GATESHEAD-52A | MALTON-50F |
| Jan-51 | STRATFORD-30A | BLAYDON-52C | NORTHALLERTON-51J | 5/51: BLAY-52C | S.BLYTH-52F | KITTYBREWSTER-61A | SUNDERLAND-54A | GATESHEAD-52A | MALTON-50F |
| Aug-51 | STRATFORD-30A | BLAYDON-52C | 6/51: W.AUCK-51F | BLAYDON-52C | S.BLYTH-52F | KITTYBREWSTER-61A | SUNDERLAND-54A | GATESHEAD-52A | MALTON-50F |
| Jan-52 | STRATFORD-30A | BLAYDON-52C | 1/52: W.HPL-51C | BLAYDON-52C | S.BLYTH-52F | KITTYBREWSTER-61A | SUNDERLAND-54A | GATESHEAD-52A | MALTON-50F |
| Aug-52 | STRATFORD-30A | BLAYDON-52C | 9/52: DARL-51A | BLAYDON-52C | S.BLYTH-52F | KITTYBREWSTER-61A | SUNDERLAND-54A | GATESHEAD-52A | MALTON-50F |
| Jan-53 | STRATFORD-30A | BLAYDON-52C | DARLINGTON-51A | BLAYDON-52C | S.BLYTH-52F | 9/52: KEITH-61C | SUNDERLAND-54A | GATESHEAD-52A | 12/52: W/D |
| Aug-53 | STRATFORD-30A | BLAYDON-52C | 6/53: W.HPL-51C | BLAYDON-52C | S.BLYTH-52F | KEITH-61C | SUNDERLAND-54A | GATESHEAD-52A | |
| Jan-54 | STRATFORD-30A | BLAYDON-52C | W.HARTLEPOOL-51C | BLAYDON-52C | S.BLYTH-52F | KEITH-61C | SUNDERLAND-54A | 4/54: HEX-52C | |
| Aug-54 | STRATFORD-30A | 11/54: S.BLYTH-52F | W.HARTLEPOOL-51C | BLAYDON-52C | S.BLYTH-52F | 7/54: KITTY-61A | SUNDERLAND-54A | HEXHAM-52C | |
| Jan-55 | STRATFORD-30A | S.BLYTH-52F | W.HARTLEPOOL-51C | BLAYDON-52C | S.BLYTH-52F | KITTYBREWSTER-61A | SUNDERLAND-54A | HEXHAM-52C | |
| Aug-55 | STRATFORD-30A | S.BLYTH-52F | W.HARTLEPOOL-51C | 4/56: MALT-50F | 11/55: BLAY-52C | 2/55: W/D | 11/55: W/D | HEXHAM-52C | |
| Jan-56 | STRATFORD-30A | 12/56: M'BRO-51D | W.HARTLEPOOL-51C | MALTON-50F | BLAYDON-52C | | | HEXHAM-52C | |
| Aug-56 | STRATFORD-30A | 3/57: S.BLYTH-52F | W.HARTLEPOOL-51C | 6/57: N.HILL-50B | 5/57: BRID-53D | | | 2/57: SUND-54A | |
| Jan-57 | 11/56: W/D | S.BLYTH-52F | 11/57: W/D | NEVILLEHILL-50B | 10/57: W/D | | | SUNDERLAND-54A | |
| Aug-57 | | S.BLYTH-52F | | NEVILLEHILL-50B | | | | SUNDERLAND-54A | |
| Jan-58 | | 12/58: W/D | | 10/58: W/D | | | | SUNDERLAND-54A | |
| Aug-58 | | | | | | | | 11/58: W/D | |
| Jan-59 | | | | | | | | | |
| Aug-59 | | | | | | | | | |
| Nov-59 | | | | | | | | | |
| Jan-60 | | | | | | | | | |
| Apr-60 | | | | | | | | | |
| Aug-60 | | | | | | | | | |
| Nov-60 | | | | | | | | | |

## Block 3 — 67331–67339

| | 67331 | 67332 | 67333 | 67334 | 67335 | 67336 | 67337 | 67338 | 67339 |
|---|---|---|---|---|---|---|---|---|---|
| Aug-50 | W.HARTLEPOOL-51C | MALTON-50F | DARLINGTON-51A | S.BLYTH-52F | WHITBY-50G | SUNDERLAND-54A | NEVILLEHILL-50B | MIDDLESBROUGH-51D | BLAYDON-52C |
| Jan-51 | W.HARTLEPOOL-51C | MALTON-50F | DARLINGTON-51A | S.BLYTH-52F | WHITBY-50G | SUNDERLAND-54A | 2/51: STAR-50D | MIDDLESBROUGH-51D | BLAYDON-52C |
| Aug-51 | 6/51: DARL-51A | MALTON-50F | 6/51: N'TON-51J | S.BLYTH-52F | WHITBY-50G | SUNDERLAND-54A | 4/51: B.GDNS-53B | MIDDLESBROUGH-51D | BLAYDON-52C |
| Jan-52 | 1/52: N'TON-51J | MALTON-50F | 1/52: DARL-51A | S.BLYTH-52F | WHITBY-50G | SUNDERLAND-54A | BOT.GDNS-53B | MIDDLESBROUGH-51D | BLAYDON-52C |
| Aug-52 | NORTHALLERTON-51J | MALTON-50F | DARLINGTON-51A | S.BLYTH-52F | WHITBY-50G | SUNDERLAND-54A | BOT.GDNS-53B | MIDDLESBROUGH-51D | BLAYDON-52C |
| Jan-53 | 12/52: W.AUCK-51F | MALTON-50F | 9/52: W.HPL-51C | S.BLYTH-52F | WHITBY-50G | SUNDERLAND-54A | BOT.GDNS-53B | MIDDLESBROUGH-51D | BLAYDON-52C |
| Aug-53 | 1/53: W/D | MALTON-50F | W.HARTLEPOOL-51C | S.BLYTH-52F | 8/53: W/D | SUNDERLAND-54A | BOT.GDNS-53B | MIDDLESBROUGH-51D | BLAYDON-52C |
| Jan-54 | | MALTON-50F | W.HARTLEPOOL-51C | S.BLYTH-52F | | SUNDERLAND-54A | BOT.GDNS-53B | MIDDLESBROUGH-51D | BLAYDON-52C |
| Aug-54 | | MALTON-50F | W.HARTLEPOOL-51C | S.BLYTH-52F | | SUNDERLAND-54A | BOT.GDNS-53B | 10/54: W.HPL-51C | 11/54: S.BLYTH-52F |
| Jan-55 | | MALTON-50F | 7/55: SUND-54A | 7/55: SUND-54A | | 3/55: W/D | BOT.GDNS-53B | W.HARTLEPOOL-51C | S.BLYTH-52F |
| Aug-55 | | MALTON-50F | SUNDERLAND-54A | SUNDERLAND-54A | | | BOT.GDNS-53B | 12/55: SUND-54A | S.BLYTH-52F |
| Jan-56 | | 4/56: W/D | 3/56: SUND-54A | 3/56: W/D | | | BOT.GDNS-53B | SUNDERLAND-54A | S.BLYTH-52F |
| Aug-56 | | | 10/56: W/D | | | | 12/56: M'BRO-51D | SUNDERLAND-54A | S.BLYTH-52F |
| Jan-57 | | | | | | | 3/57: W/D | 8/57: W/D | 3/57: W/D |
| Aug-57 | | | | | | | | | |
| Jan-58 | | | | | | | | | |
| Aug-58 | | | | | | | | | |
| Jan-59 | | | | | | | | | |
| Aug-59 | | | | | | | | | |
| Nov-59 | | | | | | | | | |
| Jan-60 | | | | | | | | | |
| Apr-60 | | | | | | | | | |
| Aug-60 | | | | | | | | | |
| Nov-60 | | | | | | | | | |

## Block 4 — 67340–67348

| | 67340 | 67341 | 67342 | 67343 | 67344 | 67345 | 67346 | 67347 | 67348 |
|---|---|---|---|---|---|---|---|---|---|
| Aug-50 | BOT.GDNS-53B | S.BLYTH-52F | DARLINGTON-51A | W.HARTLEPOOL-51C | NORTHALLERTON-51J | W.AUCKLAND-51F | NORTHALLERTON-51J | S.BLYTH-52F | SUNDERLAND-54A |
| Jan-51 | BOT.GDNS-53B | S.BLYTH-52F | DARLINGTON-51A | W.HARTLEPOOL-51C | NORTHALLERTON-51J | W.AUCKLAND-51F | NORTHALLERTON-51J | S.BLYTH-52F | SUNDERLAND-54A |
| Aug-51 | BOT.GDNS-53B | S.BLYTH-52F | 7/51: W.HPL-51C | W.HARTLEPOOL-51C | 6/51: DARL-51A | 6/51: DARL-51A | 6/51: DARL-51A | S.BLYTH-52F | SUNDERLAND-54A |
| Jan-52 | BOT.GDNS-53B | S.BLYTH-52F | 1/52: W.AUCK-51F | W.HARTLEPOOL-51C | 1/52: N'TON-51J | 6/51: STOCK-51E | 1/52: DARL-51A | S.BLYTH-52F | SUNDERLAND-54A |
| Aug-52 | BOT.GDNS-53B | S.BLYTH-52F | 9/52: DARL-51A | 9/52: DARL-51A | NORTHALLERTON-51J | STOCKTON-51E | 9/52: W.HPL-51C | S.BLYTH-52F | SUNDERLAND-54A |
| Jan-53 | BOT.GDNS-53B | S.BLYTH-52F | 11/52: N'TON-51J | DARLINGTON-51A | 11/52: W.AUCK-51F | STOCKTON-51E | W.HARTLEPOOL-51C | S.BLYTH-52F | 1/53: W/D |
| Aug-53 | BOT.GDNS-53B | S.BLYTH-52F | NORTHALLERTON-51J | 6/53: STOCK-51E | 2/53: SUND-54A | 6/53: DARL-51A | 6/53: DARL-51A | S.BLYTH-52F | |
| Jan-54 | BOT.GDNS-53B | S.BLYTH-52F | NORTHALLERTON-51J | STOCKTON-51E | SUNDERLAND-54A | 3/54: N'TON-51J | 3/54: N'TON-51J | S.BLYTH-52F | |
| Aug-54 | 12/54: S.BLYTH-52F | 4/55: BLAY-52C | NORTHALLERTON-51J | 8/54: W.HPL-51C | SUNDERLAND-54A | 3/54: SUND-54A | 3/54: SUND-54A | S.BLYTH-52F | |
| Jan-55 | S.BLYTH-52F | 11/55: S.BLYTH-52F | NORTHALLERTON-51J | W.HARTLEPOOL-51C | SUNDERLAND-54A | SUNDERLAND-54A | 8/54: STOCK-51E | 7/55: SUND-54A | |
| Aug-55 | S.BLYTH-52F | S.BLYTH-52F | NORTHALLERTON-51J | W.HARTLEPOOL-51C | SUNDERLAND-54A | SUNDERLAND-54A | STOCKTON-51E | SUNDERLAND-54A | |
| Jan-56 | S.BLYTH-52F | S.BLYTH-52F | 12/55: SUND-54A | 2/56: SUND-54A | 2/56: W/D | 12/55: W/D | STOCKTON-51E | 3/56: W/D | |
| Aug-56 | S.BLYTH-52F | 7/57: B.GDNS-53B | SUNDERLAND-54A | SUNDERLAND-54A | | | STOCKTON-51E | | |
| Jan-57 | S.BLYTH-52F | 10/57: BRID-53D | SUNDERLAND-54A | SUNDERLAND-54A | | | 12/56: MALT-50F | | |
| Aug-57 | S.BLYTH-52F | 6/58: DAIRY-53A | SUNDERLAND-54A | 11/57: W/D | | | 2/57: W/D | | |
| Jan-58 | 4/58: W/D | 11/58: W/D | SUNDERLAND-54A | | | | | | |
| Aug-58 | | | 3/58: MALT-50F | | | | | | |
| Jan-59 | | | 12/58: W/D | | | | | | |
| Aug-59 | | | | | | | | | |
| Nov-59 | | | | | | | | | |
| Jan-60 | | | | | | | | | |
| Apr-60 | | | | | | | | | |
| Aug-60 | | | | | | | | | |
| Nov-60 | | | | | | | | | |

**67350**: C12 4-4-2T (1898)

| | 67349 | 67350 | 67352 | 67353 | 67354 | 67356 | 67357 | 67360 | 67361 |
|---|---|---|---|---|---|---|---|---|---|
| Aug-50 | MALTON-50F | BOSTON-40F | LOUTH-40C | COPLEYHILL-37B | BOTANIC GARDENS-53B | KINGS CROSS-34A | NEWENGLAND-35A | CAMBRIDGE-31A | NEWENGLAND-35A |
| Jan-51 | MALTON-50F | BOSTON-40F | LOUTH-40C | COPLEYHILL-37B | BOTANIC GARDENS-53B | KINGS CROSS-34A | NEWENGLAND-35A | CAMBRIDGE-31A | NEWENGLAND-35A |
| Aug-51 | MALTON-50F | BOSTON-40F | LOUTH-40C | 4/51: ARDS-37A | BOTANIC GARDENS-53B | 6/51: S.LYNN-31D | NEWENGLAND-35A | CAMBRIDGE-31A | NEWENGLAND-35A |
| Jan-52 | MALTON-50F | BOSTON-40F | LOUTH-40C | 12/51: C.HILL-37B | BOTANIC GARDENS-53B | 10/51: W/D | NEWENGLAND-35A | CAMBRIDGE-31A | NEWENGLAND-35A |
| Aug-52 | MALTON-50F | BOSTON-40F | LOUTH-40C | COPLEYHILL-37B | BOTANIC GARDENS-53B | | NEWENGLAND-35A | CAMBRIDGE-31A | NEWENGLAND-35A |
| Jan-53 | MALTON-50F | BOSTON-40F | LOUTH-40C | 11/52: ARDS-37A | BOTANIC GARDENS-53B | | NEWENGLAND-35A | 10/52: BURY-31E | NEWENGLAND-35A |
| Aug-53 | MALTON-50F | 7/53: NEWE-35A | 7/53: B.GDNS-53B | 7/53: B.GDNS-53B | | | NEWENGLAND-35A | 7/53: CAMB-31A | NEWENGLAND-35A |
| Jan-54 | MALTON-50F | NEWENGLAND-35A | BOTANIC GARDENS-53B | BOTANIC GARDENS-53B | | | NEWENGLAND-35A | 11/53: K.LYNN-31C | NEWENGLAND-35A |
| Aug-54 | 4/54: W/D | NEWENGLAND-35A | BOTANIC GARDENS-53B | BOTANIC GARDENS-53B | | | NEWENGLAND-35A | KINGS LYNN-31C | NEWENGLAND-35A |
| Jan-55 | | 3/55: B.GDNS-53B | BOTANIC GARDENS-53B | BOTANIC GARDENS-53B | | | NEWENGLAND-35A | 1/55: W/D | 3/55: B.GDNS-53B |
| Aug-55 | | 4/55: W/D | 4/55: NEWE-35A | 4/55: W/D | | | NEWENGLAND-35A | | 4/55: W/D |
| Jan-56 | | | 11/55: S.BGE-35C | | | | NEWENGLAND-35A | | |
| Aug-56 | | | SPITAL BRIDGE-35C | | | | NEWENGLAND-35A | | |
| Jan-57 | | | SPITAL BRIDGE-35C | | | | NEWENGLAND-35A | | |
| Aug-57 | | | 7/57: GRAN-35B | | | | NEWENGLAND-35A | | |
| Jan-58 | | | GRANTHAM-35B | | | | NEWENGLAND-35A | | |
| Aug-58 | | | GRANTHAM-34F | | | | 5/58: W/D | | |
| Jan-59 | | | 11/58: W/D | | | | | | |
| Aug-59 | | | | | | | | | |
| Nov-59 | | | | | | | | | |
| Jan-60 | | | | | | | | | |
| Apr-60 | | | | | | | | | |
| Aug-60 | | | | | | | | | |
| Nov-60 | | | | | | | | | |

| | 67362 | 67363 | 67364 | 67365 | 67366 | 67367 | 67368 | 67369 | 67371 |
|---|---|---|---|---|---|---|---|---|---|
| Aug-50 | SPITAL BRIDGE-35C | ANNESLEY-38B | LOUTH-40C | NEWENGLAND-35A | TRAFFORD PARK-9E | CAMBRIDGE-31A | NEWENGLAND-35A | TRAFFORD PARK-9E | BOTANIC GARDENS-53B |
| Jan-51 | SPITAL BRIDGE-35C | ANNESLEY-38B | LOUTH-40C | NEWENGLAND-35A | TRAFFORD PARK-9E | CAMBRIDGE-31A | NEWENGLAND-35A | TRAFFORD PARK-9E | BOTANIC GARDENS-53B |
| Aug-51 | SPITAL BRIDGE-35C | ANNESLEY-38B | LOUTH-40C | NEWENGLAND-35A | TRAFFORD PARK-9E | CAMBRIDGE-31A | NEWENGLAND-35A | TRAFFORD PARK-9E | BOTANIC GARDENS-53B |
| Jan-52 | SPITAL BRIDGE-35C | ANNESLEY-38B | LOUTH-40C | NEWENGLAND-35A | TRAFFORD PARK-9E | CAMBRIDGE-31A | NEWENGLAND-35A | TRAFFORD PARK-9E | BOTANIC GARDENS-53B |
| Aug-52 | SPITAL BRIDGE-35C | ANNESLEY-38B | LOUTH-40C | NEWENGLAND-35A | TRAFFORD PARK-9E | CAMBRIDGE-31A | NEWENGLAND-35A | TRAFFORD PARK-9E | BOTANIC GARDENS-53B |
| Jan-53 | SPITAL BRIDGE-35C | 7/53: STRAT-30A | LOUTH-40C | NEWENGLAND-35A | 2/53: S.BGE-35C | 10/52: BURY-31E | NEWENGLAND-35A | 2/53: NEWE-35A | BOTANIC GARDENS-53B |
| Aug-53 | SPITAL BRIDGE-35C | 8/53: ANNES-38B | LOUTH-40C | NEWENGLAND-35A | SPITAL BRIDGE-35C | 7/53: CAMB-31A | 5/53: S.BGE-35C | NEWENGLAND-35A | BOTANIC GARDENS-53B |
| Jan-54 | SPITAL BRIDGE-35C | ANNESLEY-38B | LOUTH-40C | NEWENGLAND-35A | SPITAL BRIDGE-35C | 12/53: K.LYNN-31C | SPITAL BRIDGE-35C | NEWENGLAND-35A | BOTANIC GARDENS-53B |
| Aug-54 | 5/54: GRAN-35B | ANNESLEY-38B | LOUTH-40C | NEWENGLAND-35A | SPITAL BRIDGE-35C | KINGS LYNN-31C | SPITAL BRIDGE-35C | 7/54: W/D | BOTANIC GARDENS-53B |
| Jan-55 | GRANTHAM-35B | ANNESLEY-38B | LOUTH-40C | NEWENGLAND-35A | 1/55: NEWE-35A | KINGS LYNN-31C | SPITAL BRIDGE-35C | | BOTANIC GARDENS-53B |
| Aug-55 | GRANTHAM-35B | ANNESLEY-38B | LOUTH-40C | NEWENGLAND-35A | 4/55: YAR(ST)-32D | KINGS LYNN-31C | SPITAL BRIDGE-35C | | 4/55: W/D |
| Jan-56 | GRANTHAM-35B | ANNESLEY-38B | LOUTH-40C | NEWENGLAND-35A | YARMOUTH(ST)-32D | 11/55: CAMB-31A | 10/55: W/D | | |
| Aug-56 | GRANTHAM-35B | ANNESLEY-38B | 5/56: W/D | NEWENGLAND-35A | YARMOUTH(ST)-32D | CAMBRIDGE-31A | | | |
| Jan-57 | GRANTHAM-35B | 10/56: TIL-33B | | NEWENGLAND-35A | YARMOUTH(ST)-32D | 4/57: S.BGE-35C | | | |
| Aug-57 | GRANTHAM-35B | TILBURY-33B | | NEWENGLAND-35A | YARMOUTH(ST)-32D | 7/57: GRAN-35B | | | |
| Jan-58 | 1/58: W/D | TILBURY-33B | | NEWENGLAND-35A | YARMOUTH(ST)-32D | GRANTHAM-35B | | | |
| Aug-58 | | 9/58: NEWE-34E | | 5/58: W/D | 4/58: W/D | 8/58: W/D | | | |
| Jan-59 | | 11/58: W/D | | | | | | | |
| Aug-59 | | | | | | | | | |
| Nov-59 | | | | | | | | | |
| Jan-60 | | | | | | | | | |
| Apr-60 | | | | | | | | | |
| Aug-60 | | | | | | | | | |
| Nov-60 | | | | | | | | | |

| | 67372 | 67373 | 67374 | 67375 | 67376 | 67379 | 67380 | 67381 | 67382 |
|---|---|---|---|---|---|---|---|---|---|
| Aug-50 | COPLEYHILL-37B | NEWENGLAND-35A | KINGS CROSS-34A | CAMBRIDGE-31A | HORNSEY-34B | LOUTH-40C | GRANTHAM-35B | LOUTH-40C | GRANTHAM-35B |
| Jan-51 | COPLEYHILL-37B | NEWENGLAND-35A | KINGS CROSS-34A | CAMBRIDGE-31A | 1/51: NEWE-35A | LOUTH-40C | GRANTHAM-35B | LOUTH-40C | GRANTHAM-35B |
| Aug-51 | COPLEYHILL-37B | 3/51: W/D | 6/51: S.LYNN-31D | CAMBRIDGE-31A | NEWENGLAND-35A | LOUTH-40C | GRANTHAM-35B | LOUTH-40C | GRANTHAM-35B |
| Jan-52 | COPLEYHILL-37B | | SOUTHLYNN-31D | CAMBRIDGE-31A | NEWENGLAND-35A | LOUTH-40C | GRANTHAM-35B | 1/52: W/D | GRANTHAM-35B |
| Aug-52 | COPLEYHILL-37B | | SOUTHLYNN-31D | 5/52: MARCH-31B | NEWENGLAND-35A | LOUTH-40C | GRANTHAM-35B | | GRANTHAM-35B |
| Jan-53 | COPLEYHILL-37B | | SOUTHLYNN-31D | 10/52: BURY-31E | NEWENGLAND-35A | LOUTH-40C | GRANTHAM-35B | | GRANTHAM-35B |
| Aug-53 | 5/53: W/D | | SOUTHLYNN-31D | BURY-STEDMUNDS-31E | NEWENGLAND-35A | LOUTH-40C | GRANTHAM-35B | | GRANTHAM-35B |
| Jan-54 | | | SOUTHLYNN-31D | BURY-STEDMUNDS-31E | NEWENGLAND-35A | LOUTH-40C | GRANTHAM-35B | | GRANTHAM-35B |
| Aug-54 | | | SOUTHLYNN-31D | BURY-STEDMUNDS-31E | NEWENGLAND-35A | LOUTH-40C | 5/54: S.BGE-35C | | GRANTHAM-35B |
| Jan-55 | | | SOUTHLYNN-31D | 3/55: B.GDNS-53B | NEWENGLAND-35A | LOUTH-40C | SPITAL BRIDGE-35C | | 3/55: B.GDNS_53B |
| Aug-55 | | | SOUTHLYNN-31D | 4/55: W/D | NEWENGLAND-35A | 10/55: S.BGE-35C | SPITAL BRIDGE-35C | | 4/55: W/D |
| Jan-56 | | | SOUTHLYNN-31D | | NEWENGLAND-35A | 11/55: NEWE-35A | SPITAL BRIDGE-35C | | |
| Aug-56 | | | SOUTHLYNN-31D | | NEWENGLAND-35A | NEWENGLAND-35A | SPITAL BRIDGE-35C | | |
| Jan-57 | | | SOUTHLYNN-31D | | NEWENGLAND-35A | NEWENGLAND-35A | 11/56: NEW.E-35A | | |
| Aug-57 | | | SOUTHLYNN-31D | | NEWENGLAND-35A | NEWENGLAND-35A | NEWENGLAND-35A | | |
| Jan-58 | | | SOUTHLYNN-31D | | NEWENGLAND-35A | NEWENGLAND-35A | NEWENGLAND-35A | | |
| Aug-58 | | | 4/58: W/D | | 5/58: W/D | 6/58: W/D | 5/58: W/D | | |
| Jan-59 | | | | | | | | | |
| Aug-59 | | | | | | | | | |
| Nov-59 | | | | | | | | | |
| Jan-60 | | | | | | | | | |
| Apr-60 | | | | | | | | | |
| Aug-60 | | | | | | | | | |
| Nov-60 | | | | | | | | | |

| | 67383 | 67384 | 67385 | 67386 | 67387 | 67389 | 67390 | 67391 | 67392 |
|---|---|---|---|---|---|---|---|---|---|
| Aug-50 | LOUTH-40C | LOUTH-40C | CAMBRIDGE-31A | ARDSLEY-37A | ANNESLEY-38B | LINCOLN-40A | NEWENGLAND-35A | BOTANIC GARDENS-53B | BOTANIC GARDENS-53B |
| Jan-51 | LOUTH-40C | LOUTH-40C | CAMBRIDGE-31A | ARDSLEY-37A | ANNESLEY-38B | 12/50: CAMB-31A | NEWENGLAND-35A | BOTANIC GARDENS-53B | BOTANIC GARDENS-53B |
| Aug-51 | LOUTH-40C | LOUTH-40C | CAMBRIDGE-31A | 9/51: K.LYNN-31C | ANNESLEY-38B | 4/51: NEWE-35A | NEWENGLAND-35A | BOTANIC GARDENS-53B | BOTANIC GARDENS-53B |
| Jan-52 | LOUTH-40C | LOUTH-40C | CAMBRIDGE-31A | KINGS LYNN-31C | 12/51: YAR(ST)-32D | NEWENGLAND-35A | NEWENGLAND-35A | BOTANIC GARDENS-53B | BOTANIC GARDENS-53B |
| Aug-52 | LOUTH-40C | LOUTH-40C | 9/52: MARCH-31B | KINGS LYNN-31C | YARMOUTH(ST)-32D | NEWENGLAND-35A | NEWENGLAND-35A | BOTANIC GARDENS-53B | BOTANIC GARDENS-53B |
| Jan-53 | LOUTH-40C | LOUTH-40C | 10/52: BURY-31E | KINGS LYNN-31C | YARMOUTH(ST)-32D | NEWENGLAND-35A | NEWENGLAND-35A | BOTANIC GARDENS-53B | BOTANIC GARDENS-53B |
| Aug-53 | LOUTH-40C | LOUTH-40C | BURY-STEDMUNDS-31E | KINGS LYNN-31C | YARMOUTH(ST)-32D | NEWENGLAND-35A | 6/53: W/D | BOTANIC GARDENS-53B | BOTANIC GARDENS-53B |
| Jan-54 | LOUTH-40C | LOUTH-40C | BURY-STEDMUNDS-31E | KINGS LYNN-31C | 8/54: LOW-32C | NEWENGLAND-35A | | BOTANIC GARDENS-53B | BOTANIC GARDENS-53B |
| Aug-54 | LOUTH-40C | LOUTH-40C | BURY-STEDMUNDS-31E | 10/54: STRAT-30A | 10/54: STRAT-30A | NEWENGLAND-35A | | BOTANIC GARDENS-53B | BOTANIC GARDENS-53B |
| Jan-55 | 1/55: W/D | LOUTH-40C | 3/55: B.GDNS_53B | 12/54: K.LYNN-31C | 11/54: YAR(ST)-32D | 3/55: B.GDNS_53B | | BOTANIC GARDENS-53B | BOTANIC GARDENS-53B |
| Aug-55 | | LOUTH-40C | 4/55: W/D | KINGS LYNN-31C | 2/55: W/D | 4/55: W/D | | 4/55: GRAN-35B | 4/55: NEW.E-35A |
| Jan-56 | | LOUTH-40C | | KINGS LYNN-31C | | | | GRANTHAM-35B | NEWENGLAND-35A |
| Aug-56 | | 5/56: W/D | | KINGS LYNN-31C | | | | GRANTHAM-35B | NEWENGLAND-35A |
| Jan-57 | | | | KINGS LYNN-31C | | | | GRANTHAM-35B | 9/56: W/D |
| Aug-57 | | | | KINGS LYNN-31C | | | | GRANTHAM-35B | |
| Jan-58 | | | | KINGS LYNN-31C | | | | 1/58: W/D | |
| Aug-58 | | | | 4/58: W/D | | | | | |
| Jan-59 | | | | | | | | | |
| Aug-59 | | | | | | | | | |
| Nov-59 | | | | | | | | | |
| Jan-60 | | | | | | | | | |
| Apr-60 | | | | | | | | | |
| Aug-60 | | | | | | | | | |
| Nov-60 | | | | | | | | | |

**C13 4-4-2T (1903)**

| | 67393 | 67394 | 67395 | 67397 | 67398 | 67400 | 67401 | 67402 | 67403 |
|---|---|---|---|---|---|---|---|---|---|
| Aug-50 | BOTANIC GARDENS - 53B | BOTANIC GARDENS - 53B | BOTANIC GARDENS - 53B | BOTANIC GARDENS - 53B | LOUTH - 40C | CHESTER (CLC) - 6D | GORTON - 39A | GORTON - 39A | GORTON - 39A |
| Jan-51 | BOTANIC GARDENS - 53B | BOTANIC GARDENS - 53B | BOTANIC GARDENS - 53B | BOTANIC GARDENS - 53B | LOUTH - 40C | CHESTER (CLC) - 6D | GORTON - 39A | GORTON - 39A | GORTON - 39A |
| Aug-51 | BOTANIC GARDENS - 53B | BOTANIC GARDENS - 53B | BOTANIC GARDENS - 53B | BOTANIC GARDENS - 53B | LOUTH - 40C | CHESTER (CLC) - 6D | GORTON - 39A | GORTON - 39A | GORTON - 39A |
| Jan-52 | BOTANIC GARDENS - 53B | BOTANIC GARDENS - 53B | BOTANIC GARDENS - 53B | BOTANIC GARDENS - 53B | LOUTH - 40C | CHESTER (CLC) - 6D | GORTON - 39A | GORTON - 39A | GORTON - 39A |
| Aug-52 | BOTANIC GARDENS - 53B | BOTANIC GARDENS - 53B | BOTANIC GARDENS - 53B | BOTANIC GARDENS - 53B | LOUTH - 40C | CHESTER (CLC) - 6D | GORTON - 39A | GORTON - 39A | GORTON - 39A |
| Jan-53 | BOTANIC GARDENS - 53B | BOTANIC GARDENS - 53B | BOTANIC GARDENS - 53B | BOTANIC GARDENS - 53B | LOUTH - 40C | CHESTER (CLC) - 6D | GORTON - 39A | GORTON - 39A | GORTON - 39A |
| Aug-53 | 5/53: W/D | BOTANIC GARDENS - 53B | BOTANIC GARDENS - 53B | BOTANIC GARDENS - 53B | LOUTH - 40C | CHESTER (CLC) - 6D | GORTON - 39A | GORTON - 39A | GORTON - 39A |
| Jan-54 | | BOTANIC GARDENS - 53B | BOTANIC GARDENS - 53B | BOTANIC GARDENS - 53B | LOUTH - 40C | CHESTER (CLC) - 6D | GORTON - 39A | GORTON - 39A | GORTON - 39A |
| Aug-54 | | BOTANIC GARDENS - 53B | BOTANIC GARDENS - 53B | BOTANIC GARDENS - 53B | LOUTH - 40C | CHESTER (CLC) - 6D | GORTON - 39A | GORTON - 39A | GORTON - 39A |
| Jan-55 | | BOTANIC GARDENS - 53B | BOTANIC GARDENS - 53B | BOTANIC GARDENS - 53B | LOUTH - 40C | CHESTER (CLC) - 6D | GORTON - 39A | 8/54: W/D | GORTON - 39A |
| Aug-55 | | 4/55: NEW.E - 35A | 4/55: BURY - 31E | 4/55: BURY - 31E | LOUTH - 40C | CHESTER (CLC) - 6D | GORTON - 39A | | 4/55: W/D |
| Jan-56 | | NEWENGLAND - 35A | 1/56: CAMB - 31A | 1/56: CAMB - 31A | LOUTH - 40C | 11/55: WREX - 6E | 11/55: W/D | | |
| Aug-56 | | NEWENGLAND - 35A | CAMBRIDGE - 31A | CAMBRIDGE - 31A | 12/56: IMM - 40B | WREXHAM - 6E | | | |
| Jan-57 | | NEWENGLAND - 35A | CAMBRIDGE - 31A | 4/57: S. BGE - 35C | 2/57: NEW.E - 35A | 12/56: W/D | | | |
| Aug-57 | | NEWENGLAND - 35A | 3/57: W/D | 7/57: GRAN - 35B | NEWENGLAND - 35A | | | | |
| Jan-58 | | NEWENGLAND - 35A | | GRANTHAM - 35B | NEWENGLAND - 34E | | | | |
| Aug-58 | | 6/58: W/D | | GRANTHAM - 34F | 11/58: W/D | | | | |
| Jan-59 | | | | 12/58: W/D | | | | | |
| Aug-59 | | | | | | | | | |
| Nov-59 | | | | | | | | | |
| Jan-60 | | | | | | | | | |
| Apr-60 | | | | | | | | | |
| Aug-60 | | | | | | | | | |
| Nov-60 | | | | | | | | | |

| | 67404 | 67405 | 67406 | 67407 | 67408 | 67409 | 67410 | 67411 | 67412 |
|---|---|---|---|---|---|---|---|---|---|
| Aug-50 | DARNALL - 39B | GORTON - 39A | DARNALL - 39B | GORTON - 39A | GORTON - 39A | BARNSLEY - 36D | GORTON - 39A | BARNSLEY - 36D | GORTON - 39A |
| Jan-51 | DARNALL - 39B | GORTON - 39A | DARNALL - 39B | GORTON - 39A | GORTON - 39A | BARNSLEY - 36D | GORTON - 39A | BARNSLEY - 36D | GORTON - 39A |
| Aug-51 | DARNALL - 39B | GORTON - 39A | DARNALL - 39B | GORTON - 39A | GORTON - 39A | BARNSLEY - 36D | GORTON - 39A | BARNSLEY - 36D | GORTON - 39A |
| Jan-52 | DARNALL - 39B | GORTON - 39A | DARNALL - 39B | GORTON - 39A | 2/52: W. HALSE - 38E | BARNSLEY - 36D | 12/51: STAVE - 38D | BARNSLEY - 36D | GORTON - 39A |
| Aug-52 | DARNALL - 39B | GORTON - 39A | DARNALL - 39B | GORTON - 39A | WOODFORD HALSE - 38E | BARNSLEY - 36D | STAVELEY - 38D | BARNSLEY - 36D | GORTON - 39A |
| Jan-53 | DARNALL - 39B | GORTON - 39A | DARNALL - 39B | GORTON - 39A | 2/53: ANN - 38B | BARNSLEY - 36D | STAVELEY - 38D | BARNSLEY - 36D | GORTON - 39A |
| Aug-53 | 2/53: W/D | GORTON - 39A | 3/53: W/D | GORTON - 39A | 5/53: STAVE - 38D | BARNSLEY - 36D | 3/53: W/D | BARNSLEY - 36D | 11/52: WREX - 6E |
| Jan-54 | | GORTON - 39A | | GORTON - 39A | STAVELEY - 38D | BARNSLEY - 36D | | BARNSLEY - 36D | WREXHAM - 6E |
| Aug-54 | | GORTON - 39A | | GORTON - 39A | 5/54: W/D | BARNSLEY - 36D | | BARNSLEY - 36D | 6/54: W/D |
| Jan-55 | | GORTON - 39A | | GORTON - 39A | | BARNSLEY - 36D | | BARNSLEY - 36D | |
| Aug-55 | | 5/55: W/D | | GORTON - 39A | | BARNSLEY - 36D | | 5/55: BARN - 36D | |
| Jan-56 | | | | GORTON - 39A | | BARNSLEY - 36D | | | |
| Aug-56 | | | | GORTON - 39A | | BARNSLEY - 36D | | | |
| Jan-57 | | | | 9/56: W/D | | 12/56: W/D | | | |
| Aug-57 | | | | | | | | | |
| Jan-58 | | | | | | | | | |
| Aug-58 | | | | | | | | | |
| Jan-59 | | | | | | | | | |
| Aug-59 | | | | | | | | | |
| Nov-59 | | | | | | | | | |
| Jan-60 | | | | | | | | | |
| Apr-60 | | | | | | | | | |
| Aug-60 | | | | | | | | | |
| Nov-60 | | | | | | | | | |

| | 67413 | 67414 | 67415 | 67416 | 67417 | 67418 | 67419 | 67420 | 67421 |
|---|---|---|---|---|---|---|---|---|---|
| Aug-50 | CHESTER (CLC) - 6D | CHESTER (CLC) - 6D | GORTON - 39A | GORTON - 39A | GORTON - 39A | NEASDEN - 34E | GORTON - 39A | NEASDEN - 34E | GORTON - 39A |
| Jan-51 | CHESTER (CLC) - 6D | CHESTER (CLC) - 6D | GORTON - 39A | 11/50: KX - 34A | GORTON - 39A | NEASDEN - 34E | GORTON - 39A | NEASDEN - 34E | GORTON - 39A |
| Aug-51 | CHESTER (CLC) - 6D | CHESTER (CLC) - 6D | GORTON - 39A | 3/51: NEAS - 34E | GORTON - 39A | NEASDEN - 34E | GORTON - 39A | NEASDEN - 34E | GORTON - 39A |
| Jan-52 | CHESTER (CLC) - 6D | CHESTER (CLC) - 6D | GORTON - 39A | NEASDEN - 34E | GORTON - 39A | NEASDEN - 34E | 12/51: STAVE - 38D | NEASDEN - 34E | GORTON - 39A |
| Aug-52 | CHESTER (CLC) - 6D | CHESTER (CLC) - 6D | GORTON - 39A | NEASDEN - 34E | GORTON - 39A | NEASDEN - 34E | STAVELEY - 38D | NEASDEN - 34E | GORTON - 39A |
| Jan-53 | CHESTER (CLC) - 6D | CHESTER (CLC) - 6D | GORTON - 39A | NEASDEN - 34E | GORTON - 39A | NEASDEN - 34E | STAVELEY - 38D | NEASDEN - 34E | GORTON - 39A |
| Aug-53 | CHESTER (CLC) - 6D | CHESTER (CLC) - 6D | GORTON - 39A | NEASDEN - 34E | GORTON - 39A | NEASDEN - 34E | STAVELEY - 38D | NEASDEN - 34E | GORTON - 39A |
| Jan-54 | CHESTER (CLC) - 6D | CHESTER (CLC) - 6D | GORTON - 39A | NEASDEN - 34E | GORTON - 39A | NEASDEN - 34E | STAVELEY - 38D | NEASDEN - 34E | GORTON - 39A |
| Aug-54 | CHESTER (CLC) - 6D | 6/54: WREX - 6E | GORTON - 39A | NEASDEN - 34E | GORTON - 39A | NEASDEN - 34E | STAVELEY - 38D | NEASDEN - 34E | GORTON - 39A |
| Jan-55 | CHESTER (CLC) - 6D | WREXHAM - 6E | GORTON - 39A | NEASDEN - 34E | GORTON - 39A | NEASDEN - 34E | STAVELEY - 38D | NEASDEN - 34E | GORTON - 39A |
| Aug-55 | CHESTER (CLC) - 6D | 6/55: W/D | GORTON - 39A | NEASDEN - 34E | GORTON - 39A | NEASDEN - 34E | STAVELEY - 38D | NEASDEN - 34E | GORTON - 39A |
| Jan-56 | CHESTER (CLC) - 6D | | 2/56: W/D | NEASDEN - 34E | GORTON - 39A | NEASDEN - 34E | STAVELEY - 38D | NEASDEN - 34E | GORTON - 39A |
| Aug-56 | CHESTER (CLC) - 6D | | | NEASDEN - 34E | GORTON - 39A | NEASDEN - 34E | 11/56: GORT - 39A | NEASDEN - 34E | GORTON - 39A |
| Jan-57 | CHESTER (CLC) - 6D | | | NEASDEN - 34E | GORTON - 39A | NEASDEN - 34E | 6/57: W/D | NEASDEN - 34E | GORTON - 39A |
| Aug-57 | CHESTER (CLC) - 6D | | | NEASDEN - 34E | GORTON - 39A | NEASDEN - 34E | | NEASDEN - 34E | GORTON - 39A |
| Jan-58 | 12/57: W/D | | | NEASDEN - 34E | GORTON - 39A | NEASDEN - 34E | | NEASDEN - 34E | GORTON - 39A |
| Aug-58 | | | | NEASDEN - 14D | GORTON - 9G | NEASDEN - 14D | | NEASDEN - 14D | GORTON - 9G |
| Jan-59 | | | | 12/58: W/D | GORTON - 9G | 11/58: W/D | | 12/58: W/D | 12/58: W/D |
| Aug-59 | | | | | GORTON - 9G | | | | |
| Nov-59 | | | | | GORTON - 9G | | | | |
| Jan-60 | | | | | GORTON - 9G | | | | |
| Apr-60 | | | | | 2/60: W/D | | | | |
| Aug-60 | | | | | | | | | |
| Nov-60 | | | | | | | | | |

| | 67422 | 67423 | 67424 | 67425 | 67426 | 67427 | 67428 | 67429 | 67430 |
|---|---|---|---|---|---|---|---|---|---|
| Aug-50 | GORTON - 39A | GORTON - 39A | GORTON - 39A | GORTON - 39A | GORTON - 39A | GORTON - 39A | WREXHAM - 6E | WREXHAM - 6E | WREXHAM - 6E |
| Jan-51 | GORTON - 39A | GORTON - 39A | GORTON - 39A | GORTON - 39A | GORTON - 39A | GORTON - 39A | WREXHAM - 6E | WREXHAM - 6E | WREXHAM - 6E |
| Aug-51 | GORTON - 39A | GORTON - 39A | GORTON - 39A | GORTON - 39A | GORTON - 39A | GORTON - 39A | WREXHAM - 6E | WREXHAM - 6E | WREXHAM - 6E |
| Jan-52 | GORTON - 39A | GORTON - 39A | GORTON - 39A | GORTON - 39A | GORTON - 39A | GORTON - 39A | WREXHAM - 6E | WREXHAM - 6E | WREXHAM - 6E |
| Aug-52 | GORTON - 39A | GORTON - 39A | GORTON - 39A | GORTON - 39A | GORTON - 39A | GORTON - 39A | WREXHAM - 6E | WREXHAM - 6E | WREXHAM - 6E |
| Jan-53 | GORTON - 39A | GORTON - 39A | 3/53: ANN - 38B | GORTON - 39A | GORTON - 39A | GORTON - 39A | WREXHAM - 6E | WREXHAM - 6E | WREXHAM - 6E |
| Aug-53 | GORTON - 39A | GORTON - 39A | ANNESLEY - 38B | GORTON - 39A | GORTON - 39A | GORTON - 39A | WREXHAM - 6E | WREXHAM - 6E | WREXHAM - 6E |
| Jan-54 | GORTON - 39A | GORTON - 39A | ANNESLEY - 38B | GORTON - 39A | GORTON - 39A | GORTON - 39A | WREXHAM - 6E | WREXHAM - 6E | WREXHAM - 6E |
| Aug-54 | GORTON - 39A | GORTON - 39A | ANNESLEY - 38B | GORTON - 39A | GORTON - 39A | GORTON - 39A | WREXHAM - 6E | WREXHAM - 6E | WREXHAM - 6E |
| Jan-55 | 9/54: W/D | GORTON - 39A | ANNESLEY - 38B | GORTON - 39A | 12/54: W/D | 11/54: L. JCN - 40E | WREXHAM - 6E | 12/54: W/D | WREXHAM - 6E |
| Aug-55 | | GORTON - 39A | ANNESLEY - 38B | GORTON - 39A | | 5/55: ARDS - 37A | WREXHAM - 6E | | WREXHAM - 6E |
| Jan-56 | | GORTON - 39A | ANNESLEY - 38B | GORTON - 39A | | ARDSLEY - 56B | WREXHAM - 6E | | WREXHAM - 6E |
| Aug-56 | | GORTON - 39A | ANNESLEY - 38B | 8/56: W/D | | ARDSLEY - 56B | WREXHAM - 6E | | 4/56: W/D |
| Jan-57 | | 12/56: BARN - 36D | ANNESLEY - 38B | | | ARDSLEY - 56B | WREXHAM - 6E | | |
| Aug-57 | | BARNSLEY - 36D | ANNESLEY - 38B | | | ARDSLEY - 56B | WREXHAM - 6E | | |
| Jan-58 | | 10/57: W/D | ANNESLEY - 38B | | | 1/58: W/D | 11/57: W/D | | |
| Aug-58 | | | ANNESLEY - 16D | | | | | | |
| Jan-59 | | | 11/58: W/D | | | | | | |
| Aug-59 | | | | | | | | | |
| Nov-59 | | | | | | | | | |
| Jan-60 | | | | | | | | | |
| Apr-60 | | | | | | | | | |
| Aug-60 | | | | | | | | | |
| Nov-60 | | | | | | | | | |

*Two generations of Great Central suburban motive power. Above, C14 4-4-2T 67448 prepares to leave Sheffield Victoria for Barnsley in 1959 and, below, A5 4-6-2T is turned in the loco sidings at Manchester Central in 1954. Both classes were designed for the London suburban workings of the Great Central, the C14's lasting only from 1907 until 1911 when they were superseded by the A5's which remained on the workings until being displaced by L1 2-6-4T's in 1954. In common with several GC classes the LNER seemed uncertain what to do with them and C14's and A5's both spent some years on the Great Eastern, the C14's working over the Felixstowe branch with the A5's operating from Norwich and, until early 1957, Lowestoft. Fourteen years after being introduced an additional thirteen A5's were built by the LNER and used chiefly on the Darlington - Saltburn line until being replaced by multiple units in 1958. The earlier engines survived the LNER batch by several years, their final years being spent between no less than nine different sheds. At the time of the photograph 69802 was a rarity in Manchester and was being used on a Guide Bridge - Manchester Central diagram before being returned to Hull after a works visit to Gorton.*

| | 67431 | 67432 | 67433 | 67434 | 67435 | 67436 | 67437 | 67438 | 67439 |
|---|---|---|---|---|---|---|---|---|---|
| Aug-50 | GORTON - 39A | WREXHAM - 6E | CHESTER (CLC) - 6D | BARNSLEY - 36D | WREXHAM - 6E | CHESTER (CLC) - 6D | GORTON - 39A | GORTON - 39A | GORTON - 39A |
| Jan-51 | GORTON - 39A | WREXHAM - 6E | CHESTER (CLC) - 6D | BARNSLEY - 36D | WREXHAM - 6E | CHESTER (CLC) - 6D | GORTON - 39A | GORTON - 39A | GORTON - 39A |
| Aug-51 | GORTON - 39A | WREXHAM - 6E | CHESTER (CLC) - 6D | BARNSLEY - 36D | WREXHAM - 6E | CHESTER (CLC) - 6D | GORTON - 39A | GORTON - 39A | GORTON - 39A |
| Jan-52 | GORTON - 39A | WREXHAM - 6E | CHESTER (CLC) - 6D | BARNSLEY - 36D | WREXHAM - 6E | CHESTER (CLC) - 6D | GORTON - 39A | GORTON - 39A | GORTON - 39A |
| Aug-52 | GORTON - 39A | WREXHAM - 6E | CHESTER (CLC) - 6D | BARNSLEY - 36D | WREXHAM - 6E | CHESTER (CLC) - 6D | GORTON - 39A | GORTON - 39A | GORTON - 39A |
| Jan-53 | GORTON - 39A | WREXHAM - 6E | CHESTER (CLC) - 6D | BARNSLEY - 36D | 12/52: W/D | CHESTER (CLC) - 6D | GORTON - 39A | GORTON - 39A | 5/53: DARN - 39B |
| Aug-53 | GORTON - 39A | WREXHAM - 6E | CHESTER (CLC) - 6D | BARNSLEY - 36D | | CHESTER (CLC) - 6D | GORTON - 39A | GORTON - 39A | DARNALL - 39B |
| Jan-54 | GORTON - 39A | WREXHAM - 6E | CHESTER (CLC) - 6D | BARNSLEY - 36D | | CHESTER (CLC) - 6D | GORTON - 39A | GORTON - 39A | DARNALL - 39B |
| Aug-54 | GORTON - 39A | WREXHAM - 6E | CHESTER (CLC) - 6D | BARNSLEY - 36D | | CHESTER (CLC) - 6D | 11/54: L. JCN - 40E | 11/54: C. HILL - 37B | DARNALL - 39B |
| Jan-55 | GORTON - 39A | 12/54: W/D | CHESTER (CLC) - 6D | BARNSLEY - 36D | | CHESTER (CLC) - 6D | 5/55: ARDS - 37A | COPLEYHILL - 37B | DARNALL - 41A |
| Aug-55 | GORTON - 39A | | 11/55: RET - 36E | BARNSLEY - 36D | | CHESTER (CLC) - 6D | 1/56: GORT - 39A | COPLEYHILL - 37B | DARNALL - 41A |
| Jan-56 | GORTON - 39A | | 12/55: ARDS - 37A | BARNSLEY - 36D | | 2/56: W/D | GORTON - 39A | COPLEYHILL - 56C | DARNALL - 41A |
| Aug-56 | GORTON - 39A | | 1/56: C. HILL - 37B | BARNSLEY - 36D | | | GORTON - 39A | COPLEYHILL - 56C | DARNALL - 41A |
| Jan-57 | 9/56: W/D | | COPLEYHILL - 56C | BARNSLEY - 36D | | | 8/57: W/D | 3/57: ARDS - 56B | DARNALL - 41A |
| Aug-57 | | | 3/57: ARDS - 56B | 10/57: W/D | | | | 1/58: W/D | DARNALL - 41A |
| Jan-58 | | | 1/58: W/D | | | | | | 11/58: W/D |
| Aug-58 | | | | | | | | | |
| Jan-59 | | | | | | | | | |
| Aug-59 | | | | | | | | | |
| Nov-59 | | | | | | | | | |
| Jan-60 | | | | | | | | | |
| Apr-60 | | | | | | | | | |
| Aug-60 | | | | | | | | | |
| Nov-60 | | | | | | | | | |

## C14 4-4-2T (1907)

| | 67440 | 67441 | 67442 | 67443 | 67444 | 67445 | 67446 | 67447 | 67448 |
|---|---|---|---|---|---|---|---|---|---|
| Aug-50 | ARDSLEY - 37A | ARDSLEY - 37A | WREXHAM - 6E | ARDSLEY - 37A | ARDSLEY - 37A | ARDSLEY - 37A | ARDSLEY - 37A | BRADFORD - 37C | BRADFORD - 37C |
| Jan-51 | 3/51: C. HILL - 37B | ARDSLEY - 37A | WREXHAM - 6E | ARDSLEY - 37A | ARDSLEY - 37A | ARDSLEY - 37A | ARDSLEY - 37A | BRADFORD - 37C | BRADFORD - 37C |
| Aug-51 | 6/51: ARDS - 37A | 6/51: GORT - 39A | WREXHAM - 6E | ARDSLEY - 37A | ARDSLEY - 37A | ARDSLEY - 37A | ARDSLEY - 37A | 6/51: GORT - 39A | 6/51: GORT - 39A |
| Jan-52 | ARDSLEY - 37A | GORTON - 39A | WREXHAM - 6E | ARDSLEY - 37A | ARDSLEY - 37A | ARDSLEY - 37A | ARDSLEY - 37A | GORTON - 39A | GORTON - 39A |
| Aug-52 | ARDSLEY - 37A | GORTON - 39A | WREXHAM - 6E | ARDSLEY - 37A | ARDSLEY - 37A | ARDSLEY - 37A | ARDSLEY - 37A | GORTON - 39A | GORTON - 39A |
| Jan-53 | ARDSLEY - 37A | GORTON - 39A | WREXHAM - 6E | ARDSLEY - 37A | 3/53: GORT - 39A | 1/53: GORT - 39A | ARDSLEY - 37A | GORTON - 39A | GORTON - 39A |
| Aug-53 | 5/53: GORT - 39A | GORTON - 39A | WREXHAM - 6E | ARDSLEY - 37A | GORTON - 39A | GORTON - 39A | ARDSLEY - 37A | GORTON - 39A | GORTON - 39A |
| Jan-54 | GORTON - 39A | GORTON - 39A | WREXHAM - 6E | ARDSLEY - 37A | GORTON - 39A | GORTON - 39A | ARDSLEY - 37A | GORTON - 39A | GORTON - 39A |
| Aug-54 | GORTON - 39A | GORTON - 39A | WREXHAM - 6E | ARDSLEY - 37A | GORTON - 39A | GORTON - 39A | ARDSLEY - 37A | GORTON - 39A | GORTON - 39A |
| Jan-55 | GORTON - 39A | GORTON - 39A | WREXHAM - 6E | ARDSLEY - 37A | GORTON - 39A | GORTON - 39A | ARDSLEY - 37A | GORTON - 39A | GORTON - 39A |
| Aug-55 | GORTON - 39A | GORTON - 39A | WREXHAM - 6E | 5/55: GORT - 39A | GORTON - 39A | GORTON - 39A | 5/55: GORT - 39A | GORTON - 39A | GORTON - 39A |
| Jan-56 | GORTON - 39A | GORTON - 39A | WREXHAM - 6E | GORTON - 39A | GORTON - 39A | GORTON - 39A | GORTON - 39A | GORTON - 39A | GORTON - 39A |
| Aug-56 | GORTON - 39A | GORTON - 39A | WREXHAM - 6E | GORTON - 39A | GORTON - 39A | GORTON - 39A | GORTON - 39A | GORTON - 39A | GORTON - 39A |
| Jan-57 | GORTON - 39A | GORTON - 39A | WREXHAM - 6E | GORTON - 39A | GORTON - 39A | GORTON - 39A | 5/57: W/D | GORTON - 39A | GORTON - 39A |
| Aug-57 | 6/57: W/D | 8/57: W/D | WREXHAM - 6E | 6/57: W/D | 6/57: W/D | 7/57: BARN - 36D | | 11/57: BARN - 41G | 7/57: BARN - 36D |
| Jan-58 | | | 11/57: W/D | | | BARNSLEY - 36D | | BARNSLEY - 41G | BARNSLEY - 36D |
| Aug-58 | | | | | | BARNSLEY - 41G | | 11/58: W/D | BARNSLEY - 41G |
| Jan-59 | | | | | | BARNSLEY - 41G | | | 6/59: W/D |
| Aug-59 | | | | | | BARNSLEY - 41G | | | |
| Nov-59 | | | | | | 12/59: W/D | | | |
| Jan-60 | | | | | | | | | |
| Apr-60 | | | | | | | | | |
| Aug-60 | | | | | | | | | |
| Nov-60 | | | | | | | | | |

| | 67449 | 67450 | 67451 | | 67452 | 67453 | 67454 | 67455 | 67456 | 67457 |
|---|---|---|---|---|---|---|---|---|---|---|
| Aug-50 | WREXHAM - 6E | BRADFORD - 37C | ARDSLEY - 37A | | THORNTON JCN - 62A | DUNFERMLINE - 62C | PARKHEAD - 65C | FERRYHILL - 61B | EASTFIELD - 65A | HAWICK - 64G |
| Jan-51 | WREXHAM - 6E | BRADFORD - 37C | ARDSLEY - 37A | | THORNTON JCN - 62A | DUNFERMLINE - 62C | PARKHEAD - 65C | FERRYHILL - 61B | EASTFIELD - 65A | HAWICK - 64G |
| Aug-51 | WREXHAM - 6E | 6/51: GORT - 39A | 6/51: GORT - 39A | | THORNTON JCN - 62A | 8/51: Burntisland (Dept) | PARKHEAD - 65C | FERRYHILL - 61B | EASTFIELD - 65A | HAWICK - 64G |
| Jan-52 | WREXHAM - 6E | GORTON - 39A | GORTON - 39A | | THORNTON JCN - 62A | Burntisland (Dept) | 11/51: EFLD - 65A | FERRYHILL - 61B | EASTFIELD - 65A | HAWICK - 64G |
| Aug-52 | WREXHAM - 6E | GORTON - 39A | GORTON - 39A | | THORNTON JCN - 62A | Burntisland (Dept) | EASTFIELD - 65A | 9/52: KITTY - 61A | EASTFIELD - 65A | HAWICK - 64G |
| Jan-53 | WREXHAM - 6E | GORTON - 39A | GORTON - 39A | | THORNTON JCN - 62A | Burntisland (Dept) | 12/52: STLG - 63B | KITTYBREWSTER - 61A | 12/52: GMTH - 65F | HAWICK - 64G |
| Aug-53 | WREXHAM - 6E | GORTON - 39A | GORTON - 39A | | THORNTON JCN - 62A | 1/54: W/D | 2/53: EFLD - 65A | KITTYBREWSTER - 61A | GRANGEMOUTH - 65F | HAWICK - 64G |
| Jan-54 | WREXHAM - 6E | GORTON - 39A | GORTON - 39A | | THORNTON JCN - 62A | | EASTFIELD - 65A | KITTYBREWSTER - 61A | GRANGEMOUTH - 65F | HAWICK - 64G |
| Aug-54 | WREXHAM - 6E | GORTON - 39A | GORTON - 39A | | THORNTON JCN - 62A | | 6/54: W/D | KITTYBREWSTER - 61A | GRANGEMOUTH - 65F | HAWICK - 64G |
| Jan-55 | WREXHAM - 6E | GORTON - 39A | GORTON - 39A | | THORNTON JCN - 62A | | | KITTYBREWSTER - 61A | 9/54: W/D | HAWICK - 64G |
| Aug-55 | WREXHAM - 6E | GORTON - 39A | GORTON - 39A | | THORNTON JCN - 62A | | | 2/55: W/D | | HAWICK - 64G |
| Jan-56 | WREXHAM - 6E | GORTON - 39A | GORTON - 39A | | 2/56: W/D | | | | | HAWICK - 64G |
| Aug-56 | WREXHAM - 6E | GORTON - 39A | GORTON - 39A | | | | | | | HAWICK - 64G |
| Jan-57 | WREXHAM - 6E | GORTON - 39A | 1/57: W/D | | | | | | | 6/55: W/D |
| Aug-57 | WREXHAM - 6E | GORTON - 39A | | | | | | | | |
| Jan-58 | 12/57: W/D | GORTON - 39A | | | | | | | | |
| Aug-58 | | GORTON - 9G | | | | | | | | |
| Jan-59 | | GORTON - 9G | | | | | | | | |
| Aug-59 | | GORTON - 9G | | | | | | | | |
| Nov-59 | | GORTON - 9G | | | | | | | | |
| Jan-60 | | GORTON - 9G | | | | | | | | |
| Apr-60 | | 2/60: W/D | | | | | | | | |
| Aug-60 | | | | | | | | | | |
| Nov-60 | | | | | | | | | | |

*C15 4-4-2T (1911)* — columns 67452–67457 above.

| | 67458 | 67459 | 67460 | 67461 | 67462 | 67463 | 67464 | 67465 | 67466 |
|---|---|---|---|---|---|---|---|---|---|
| Aug-50 | CARLISLE (C) - 12B | HAWICK - 64G | EASTFIELD - 65A | DUNDEE - 62B | STIRLING - 63B | POLMONT - 64E | POLMONT - 64E | HAWICK - 64G | DUNFERMLINE - 62C |
| Jan-51 | CARLISLE (C) - 12B | HAWICK - 64G | EASTFIELD - 65A | DUNDEE - 62B | STIRLING - 63B | POLMONT - 64E | POLMONT - 64E | HAWICK - 64G | DUNFERMLINE - 62C |
| Aug-51 | CARLISLE (C) - 68E | HAWICK - 64G | EASTFIELD - 65A | DUNDEE - 62B | STIRLING - 63B | POLMONT - 64E | POLMONT - 64E | HAWICK - 64G | 7/51: DUN - 62B |
| Jan-52 | CARLISLE (C) - 68E | HAWICK - 64G | EASTFIELD - 65A | DUNDEE - 62B | 9/51: POL - 64E | POLMONT - 64E | POLMONT - 64E | HAWICK - 64G | DUNDEE - 62B |
| Aug-52 | CARLISLE (C) - 68E | HAWICK - 64G | EASTFIELD - 65A | DUNDEE - 62B | POLMONT - 64E | POLMONT - 64E | POLMONT - 64E | HAWICK - 64G | DUNDEE - 62B |
| Jan-53 | CARLISLE (C) - 68E | HAWICK - 64G | EASTFIELD - 65A | 9/52: T. JCN : 62A | POLMONT - 64E | POLMONT - 64E | POLMONT - 64E | HAWICK - 64G | DUNDEE - 62B |
| Aug-53 | CARLISLE (C) - 68E | HAWICK - 64G | EASTFIELD - 65A | THORNTON JCN - 62A | POLMONT - 64E | POLMONT - 64E | 8/53: W/D | HAWICK - 64G | DUNDEE - 62B |
| Jan-54 | CARLISLE (C) - 68E | 1/54: POL - 64E | EASTFIELD - 65A | THORNTON JCN - 62A | POLMONT - 64E | POLMONT - 64E | | HAWICK - 64G | 2/54: DUNF - 62C |
| Aug-54 | CARLISLE (C) - 68E | POLMONT - 64E | EASTFIELD - 65A | THORNTON JCN - 62A | 6/54: W/D | POLMONT - 64E | | HAWICK - 64G | DUNFERMLINE - 62C |
| Jan-55 | CARLISLE (C) - 68E | POLMONT - 64E | EASTFIELD - 65A | 12/54: W/D | | POLMONT - 64E | | 11/54: W/D | DUNFERMLINE - 62C |
| Aug-55 | CARLISLE (C) - 68E | 10/55: W/D | EASTFIELD - 65A | | | POLMONT - 64E | | | DUNFERMLINE - 62C |
| Jan-56 | 3/56: W/D | | EASTFIELD - 65A | | | 9/55: W/D | | | DUNFERMLINE - 62C |
| Aug-56 | | | EASTFIELD - 65A | | | | | | 4/56: W/D |
| Jan-57 | | | EASTFIELD - 65A | | | | | | |
| Aug-57 | | | EASTFIELD - 65A | | | | | | |
| Jan-58 | | | EASTFIELD - 65A | | | | | | |
| Aug-58 | | | EASTFIELD - 65A | | | | | | |
| Jan-59 | | | EASTFIELD - 65A | | | | | | |
| Aug-59 | | | EASTFIELD - 65A | | | | | | |
| Nov-59 | | | EASTFIELD - 65A | | | | | | |
| Jan-60 | | | EASTFIELD - 65A | | | | | | |
| Apr-60 | | | 4/60: W/D | | | | | | |
| Aug-60 | | | | | | | | | |
| Nov-60 | | | | | | | | | |

# C15 / C16 4-4-2T locomotives — shed allocations

**Nos. 67467–67475**

| | 67467 | 67468 | 67469 | 67470 | 67471 | 67472 | 67473 | 67474 | 67475 |
|---|---|---|---|---|---|---|---|---|---|
| Aug-50 | EASTFIELD-65A | POLMONT-64E | DUNFERMLINE-62C | PARKHEAD-65C | DUNDEE-62B | HAWCK-64G | POLMONT-64E | CARLISLE(C)-12B | KIPPS-65E |
| Jan-51 | 11/50: KIPPS-65E | POLMONT-64E | DUNFERMLINE-62C | PARKHEAD-65C | DUNDEE-62B | HAWCK-64G | POLMONT-64E | CARLISLE(C)-12B | 11/50: EFLD-65A |
| Aug-51 | KIPPS-65E | POLMONT-64E | DUNFERMLINE-62C | PARKHEAD-65C | DUNDEE-62B | HAWCK-64G | POLMONT-64E | CARLISLE(C)-68E | EASTFIELD-65A |
| Jan-52 | KIPPS-65E | POLMONT-64E | DUNFERMLINE-62C | PARKHEAD-65C | 9/52: T.JCN-62A | HAWCK-64G | POLMONT-64E | CARLISLE(C)-68E | EASTFIELD-65A |
| Aug-52 | KIPPS-65E | POLMONT-64E | 7/52: Burntisland (Dept) | PARKHEAD-65C | 12/52: W/D | HAWCK-64G | POLMONT-64E | CARLISLE(C)-68E | EASTFIELD-65A |
| Jan-53 | KIPPS-65E | POLMONT-64E | Burntisland (Dept) | PARKHEAD-65C | | HAWCK-64G | POLMONT-64E | CARLISLE(C)-68E | EASTFIELD-65A |
| Aug-53 | KIPPS-65E | POLMONT-64E | Burntisland (Dept) | PARKHEAD-65C | | HAWCK-64G | POLMONT-64E | CARLISLE(C)-68E | EASTFIELD-65A |
| Jan-54 | KIPPS-65E | 10/53: W/D | Burntisland (Dept) | PARKHEAD-65C | | HAWCK-64G | POLMONT-64E | CARLISLE(C)-68E | EASTFIELD-65A |
| Aug-54 | KIPPS-65E | | Burntisland (Dept) | PARKHEAD-65C | | HAWCK-64G | POLMONT-64E | CARLISLE(C)-68E | 4/54: W/D |
| Jan-55 | KIPPS-65E | | 9/54: W/D | 11/54: W/D | | HAWCK-64G | 12/54: W/D | 9/54: EFLD-65A | |
| Aug-55 | 3/55: W/D | | | | | HAWCK-64G | | EASTFIELD-65A | |
| Jan-56 | | | | | | 11/55: POL-64E | | EASTFIELD-65A | |
| Aug-56 | | | | | | 4/56: W/D | | EASTFIELD-65A | |
| Jan-57 | | | | | | | | EASTFIELD-65A | |
| Aug-57 | | | | | | | | EASTFIELD-65A | |
| Jan-58 | | | | | | | | EASTFIELD-65A | |
| Aug-58 | | | | | | | | EASTFIELD-65A | |
| Jan-59 | | | | | | | | EASTFIELD-65A | |
| Aug-59 | | | | | | | | EASTFIELD-65A | |
| Nov-59 | | | | | | | | EASTFIELD-65A | |
| Jan-60 | | | | | | | | EASTFIELD-65A | |
| Apr-60 | | | | | | | | 4/60: W/D | |
| Aug-60 | | | | | | | | | |
| Nov-60 | | | | | | | | | |

**Nos. 67476–67484** — (67482 onward: C16 4-4-2T (1915))

| | 67476 | 67477 | 67478 | 67479 | 67480 | 67481 | 67482 | 67483 | 67484 |
|---|---|---|---|---|---|---|---|---|---|
| Aug-50 | THORNTON JCN-62A | HAWCK-64G | FERRYHILL-61B | PARKHEAD-65C | PARKHEAD-65C | CARLISLE(C)-12B | EASTFIELD-65A | DUNDEE-62B | DUNDEE-62B |
| Jan-51 | THORNTON JCN-62A | HAWCK-64G | FERRYHILL-61B | PARKHEAD-65C | PARKHEAD-65C | CARLISLE(C)-12B | EASTFIELD-65A | DUNDEE-62B | DUNDEE-62B |
| Aug-51 | THORNTON JCN-62A | HAWCK-64G | FERRYHILL-61B | PARKHEAD-65C | PARKHEAD-65C | CARLISLE(C)-68E | EASTFIELD-65A | DUNDEE-62B | DUNDEE-62B |
| Jan-52 | THORNTON JCN-62A | HAWCK-64G | FERRYHILL-61B | PARKHEAD-65C | 11/51: EFLD-65A | CARLISLE(C)-68E | 11/51: PKHD-65C | DUNDEE-62B | DUNDEE-62B |
| Aug-52 | THORNTON JCN-62A | HAWCK-64G | FERRYHILL-61B | PARKHEAD-65C | EASTFIELD-65A | CARLISLE(C)-68E | PARKHEAD-65C | DUNDEE-62B | DUNDEE-62B |
| Jan-53 | THORNTON JCN-62A | HAWCK-64G | FERRYHILL-61B | PARKHEAD-65C | EASTFIELD-65A | CARLISLE(C)-68E | PARKHEAD-65C | DUNDEE-62B | DUNDEE-62B |
| Aug-53 | THORNTON JCN-62A | HAWCK-64G | FERRYHILL-61B | PARKHEAD-65C | EASTFIELD-65A | CARLISLE(C)-68E | PARKHEAD-65C | DUNDEE-62B | DUNDEE-62B |
| Jan-54 | THORNTON JCN-62A | HAWCK-64G | 6/54: KITTY-61A | 1/54: W/D | EASTFIELD-65A | CARLISLE(C)-68E | PARKHEAD-65C | DUNDEE-62B | DUNDEE-62B |
| Aug-54 | THORNTON JCN-62A | HAWCK-64G | 7/54: KEITH-61C | | EASTFIELD-65A | CARLISLE(C)-68E | PARKHEAD-65C | DUNDEE-62B | DUNDEE-62B |
| Jan-55 | 9/54: W/D | 9/54: W/D | KEITH-61C | | EASTFIELD-65A | CARLISLE(C)-68E | PARKHEAD-65C | DUNDEE-62B | DUNDEE-62B |
| Aug-55 | | | KEITH-61C | | EASTFIELD-65A | CARLISLE(C)-68E | PARKHEAD-65C | DUNDEE-62B | DUNDEE-62B |
| Jan-56 | | | KEITH-61C | | EASTFIELD-65A | CARLISLE(C)-68E | PARKHEAD-65C | DUNDEE-62B | DUNDEE-62B |
| Aug-56 | | | 2/56: W/D | | 2/56: W/D | 2/56: W/D | PARKHEAD-65C | 4/56: W/D | DUNDEE-62B |
| Jan-57 | | | | | | | PARKHEAD-65C | | DUNDEE-62B |
| Aug-57 | | | | | | | PARKHEAD-65C | | DUNDEE-62B |
| Jan-58 | | | | | | | PARKHEAD-65C | | DUNDEE-62B |
| Aug-58 | | | | | | | PARKHEAD-65C | | DUNDEE-62B |
| Jan-59 | | | | | | | PARKHEAD-65C | | DUNDEE-62B |
| Aug-59 | | | | | | | PARKHEAD-65C | | DUNDEE-62B |
| Nov-59 | | | | | | | 10/59: W/D | | DUNDEE-62B |
| Jan-60 | | | | | | | | | DUNDEE-62B |
| Apr-60 | | | | | | | | | DUNDEE-62B |
| Aug-60 | | | | | | | | | 5/60: W/D |
| Nov-60 | | | | | | | | | |

**Nos. 67485–67493**

| | 67485 | 67486 | 67487 | 67488 | 67489 | 67490 | 67491 | 67492 | 67493 |
|---|---|---|---|---|---|---|---|---|---|
| Aug-50 | EASTFIELD-65A | DUNDEE-62B | PARKHEAD-65C | EASTFIELD-65A | DUNDEE-62B | DUNDEE-62B | DUNDEE-62B | EDINBURGH(SM)-64A | DUNDEE-62B |
| Jan-51 | EASTFIELD-65A | DUNDEE-62B | PARKHEAD-65C | EASTFIELD-65A | DUNDEE-62B | DUNDEE-62B | DUNDEE-62B | EDINBURGH(SM)-64A | DUNDEE-62B |
| Aug-51 | EASTFIELD-65A | DUNDEE-62B | PARKHEAD-65C | EASTFIELD-65A | DUNDEE-62B | DUNDEE-62B | DUNDEE-62B | EDINBURGH(SM)-64A | DUNDEE-62B |
| Jan-52 | EASTFIELD-65A | DUNDEE-62B | PARKHEAD-65C | 10/51: STRX-65B | DUNDEE-62B | DUNDEE-62B | DUNDEE-62B | EDINBURGH(SM)-64A | DUNDEE-62B |
| Aug-52 | EASTFIELD-65A | DUNDEE-62B | PARKHEAD-65C | 7/52: EFLD-65A | DUNDEE-62B | DUNDEE-62B | DUNDEE-62B | EDINBURGH(SM)-64A | DUNDEE-62B |
| Jan-53 | EASTFIELD-65A | DUNDEE-62B | 12/52: FOR-63C | EASTFIELD-65A | DUNDEE-62B | DUNDEE-62B | DUNDEE-62B | EDINBURGH(SM)-64A | DUNDEE-62B |
| Aug-53 | EASTFIELD-65A | DUNDEE-62B | 3/53: PKHD-65C | EASTFIELD-65A | DUNDEE-62B | DUNDEE-62B | DUNDEE-62B | EDINBURGH(SM)-64A | DUNDEE-62B |
| Jan-54 | EASTFIELD-65A | DUNDEE-62B | PARKHEAD-65C | EASTFIELD-65A | DUNDEE-62B | DUNDEE-62B | DUNDEE-62B | EDINBURGH(SM)-64A | DUNDEE-62B |
| Aug-54 | EASTFIELD-65A | DUNDEE-62B | PARKHEAD-65C | EASTFIELD-65A | DUNDEE-62B | DUNDEE-62B | DUNDEE-62B | EDINBURGH(SM)-64A | DUNDEE-62B |
| Jan-55 | EASTFIELD-65A | DUNDEE-62B | PARKHEAD-65C | EASTFIELD-65A | DUNDEE-62B | DUNDEE-62B | DUNDEE-62B | EDINBURGH(SM)-64A | 1/55: TH JN-62A |
| Aug-55 | EASTFIELD-65A | DUNDEE-62B | PARKHEAD-65C | EASTFIELD-65A | DUNDEE-62B | DUNDEE-62B | DUNDEE-62B | EDINBURGH(SM)-64A | THORNTON JCN-62A |
| Jan-56 | EASTFIELD-65A | DUNDEE-62B | PARKHEAD-65C | 10/55: POL-64E | 9/55: HWCK-64G | DUNDEE-62B | DUNDEE-62B | EDINBURGH(SM)-64A | THORNTON JCN-62A |
| Aug-56 | EASTFIELD-65A | DUNDEE-62B | PARKHEAD-65C | POLMONT-64E | HAWCK-64G | DUNDEE-62B | DUNDEE-62B | EDINBURGH(SM)-64A | 4/56: W/D |
| Jan-57 | EASTFIELD-65A | DUNDEE-62B | PARKHEAD-65C | POLMONT-64E | HAWCK-64G | DUNDEE-62B | DUNDEE-62B | EDINBURGH(SM)-64A | |
| Aug-57 | EASTFIELD-65A | DUNDEE-62B | PARKHEAD-65C | POLMONT-64E | HAWCK-64G | DUNDEE-62B | DUNDEE-62B | EDINBURGH(SM)-64A | |
| Jan-58 | EASTFIELD-65A | DUNDEE-62B | PARKHEAD-65C | POLMONT-64E | HAWCK-64G | DUNDEE-62B | DUNDEE-62B | EDINBURGH(SM)-64A | |
| Aug-58 | EASTFIELD-65A | DUNDEE-62B | PARKHEAD-65C | POLMONT-64E | HAWCK-64G | DUNDEE-62B | DUNDEE-62B | EDINBURGH(SM)-64A | |
| Jan-59 | EASTFIELD-65A | DUNDEE-62B | PARKHEAD-65C | POLMONT-64E | HAWCK-64G | DUNDEE-62B | DUNDEE-62B | EDINBURGH(SM)-64A | |
| Aug-59 | EASTFIELD-65A | DUNDEE-62B | PARKHEAD-65C | POLMONT-64E | HAWCK-64G | DUNDEE-62B | DUNDEE-62B | EDINBURGH(SM)-64A | |
| Nov-59 | EASTFIELD-65A | DUNDEE-62B | 10/59: W/D | 10/59: W/D | HAWCK-64G | DUNDEE-62B | DUNDEE-62B | EDINBURGH(SM)-64A | |
| Jan-60 | EASTFIELD-65A | DUNDEE-62B | | | HAWCK-64G | DUNDEE-62B | DUNDEE-62B | EDINBURGH(SM)-64A | |
| Apr-60 | EASTFIELD-65A | DUNDEE-62B | | | HAWCK-64G | DUNDEE-62B | 3/60: W/D | 3/60: W/D | |
| Aug-60 | EASTFIELD-65A | 5/60: W/D | | | HAWCK-64G | DUNDEE-62B | | | |
| Nov-60 | EASTFIELD-65A | | | | HAWCK-64G | DUNDEE-62B | | | |

**Nos. 67494–67502**

| | 67494 | 67495 | 67496 | 67497 | 67498 | 67499 | 67500 | 67501 | 67502 |
|---|---|---|---|---|---|---|---|---|---|
| Aug-50 | EDINBURGH(SM)-64A | EDINBURGH(SM)-64A | EDINBURGH(SM)-64A | EDINBURGH(SM)-64A | DUNDEE-62B | DUNDEE-62B | EASTFIELD-65A | EASTFIELD-65A | DUNDEE-62B |
| Jan-51 | EDINBURGH(SM)-64A | EDINBURGH(SM)-64A | EDINBURGH(SM)-64A | EDINBURGH(SM)-64A | DUNDEE-62B | DUNDEE-62B | EASTFIELD-65A | EASTFIELD-65A | DUNDEE-62B |
| Aug-51 | EDINBURGH(SM)-64A | EDINBURGH(SM)-64A | EDINBURGH(SM)-64A | EDINBURGH(SM)-64A | DUNDEE-62B | DUNDEE-62B | EASTFIELD-65A | EASTFIELD-65A | DUNDEE-62B |
| Jan-52 | EDINBURGH(SM)-64A | EDINBURGH(SM)-64A | 11/51: FYHILL-61B | EDINBURGH(SM)-64A | DUNDEE-62B | DUNDEE-62B | 11/51: PKHD-65C | 10/51: FYHLL-61B | DUNDEE-62B |
| Aug-52 | EDINBURGH(SM)-64A | EDINBURGH(SM)-64A | FERRYHILL-61B | EDINBURGH(SM)-64A | DUNDEE-62B | DUNDEE-62B | PARKHEAD-65C | FERRYHILL-61B | DUNDEE-62B |
| Jan-53 | EDINBURGH(SM)-64A | EDINBURGH(SM)-64A | FERRYHILL-61B | EDINBURGH(SM)-64A | DUNDEE-62B | DUNDEE-62B | PARKHEAD-65C | FERRYHILL-61B | DUNDEE-62B |
| Aug-53 | EDINBURGH(SM)-64A | EDINBURGH(SM)-64A | FERRYHILL-61B | EDINBURGH(SM)-64A | DUNDEE-62B | DUNDEE-62B | PARKHEAD-65C | FERRYHILL-61B | DUNDEE-62B |
| Jan-54 | 9/53: POL-64E | EDINBURGH(SM)-64A | FERRYHILL-61B | EDINBURGH(SM)-64A | DUNDEE-62B | DUNDEE-62B | PARKHEAD-65C | FERRYHILL-61B | DUNDEE-62B |
| Aug-54 | POLMONT-64E | EDINBURGH(SM)-64A | FERRYHILL-61B | EDINBURGH(SM)-64A | DUNDEE-62B | DUNDEE-62B | PARKHEAD-65C | FERRYHILL-61B | DUNDEE-62B |
| Jan-55 | POLMONT-64E | 1/55: POL-64E | FERRYHILL-61B | EDINBURGH(SM)-64A | DUNDEE-62B | DUNDEE-62B | PARKHEAD-65C | FERRYHILL-61B | DUNDEE-62B |
| Aug-55 | POLMONT-64E | 5/55: HWCK-64G | FERRYHILL-61B | EDINBURGH(SM)-64A | 7/55: W/D | DUNDEE-62B | PARKHEAD-65C | FERRYHILL-61B | DUNDEE-62B |
| Jan-56 | POLMONT-64E | HAWCK-64G | FERRYHILL-61B | EDINBURGH(SM)-64A | | 11/55: W/D | PARKHEAD-65C | FERRYHILL-61B | DUNDEE-62B |
| Aug-56 | POLMONT-64E | 5/56: W/D | FERRYHILL-61B | EDINBURGH(SM)-64A | | | PARKHEAD-65C | FERRYHILL-61B | DUNDEE-62B |
| Jan-57 | POLMONT-64E | | 10/56: KEITH-61C | EDINBURGH(SM)-64A | | | PARKHEAD-65C | FERRYHILL-61B | DUNDEE-62B |
| Aug-57 | POLMONT-64E | | KEITH-61C | EDINBURGH(SM)-64A | | | PARKHEAD-65C | 4/57: KEITH-61C | DUNDEE-62B |
| Jan-58 | POLMONT-64E | | 1/58: DUN-62B | EDINBURGH(SM)-64A | | | PARKHEAD-65C | 12/57: DUN-62B | DUNDEE-62B |
| Aug-58 | POLMONT-64E | | DUNDEE-62B | EDINBURGH(SM)-64A | | | PARKHEAD-65C | DUNDEE-62B | DUNDEE-62B |
| Jan-59 | POLMONT-64E | | DUNDEE-62B | EDINBURGH(SM)-64A | | | PARKHEAD-65C | DUNDEE-62B | DUNDEE-62B |
| Aug-59 | POLMONT-64E | | DUNDEE-62B | EDINBURGH(SM)-64A | | | PARKHEAD-65C | DUNDEE-62B | DUNDEE-62B |
| Nov-59 | POLMONT-64E | | DUNDEE-62B | 10/59: W/D | | | 10/59: W/D | DUNDEE-62B | DUNDEE-62B |
| Jan-60 | POLMONT-64E | | DUNDEE-62B | | | | | DUNDEE-62B | DUNDEE-62B |
| Apr-60 | POLMONT-65K | | 3/60: W/D | | | | | DUNDEE-62B | DUNDEE-62B |
| Aug-60 | POLMONT-65K | | | | | | | 5/60: W/D | 5/60: W/D |
| Nov-60 | POLMONT-65K | | | | | | | | |

V1/V3 2-6-2T (1930)

| | 67600 | 67601 | 67602 | 67603 | 67604 | 67605 | 67606 | 67607 | 67608 |
|---|---|---|---|---|---|---|---|---|---|
| Aug-50 | EASTFIELD - 65A | BALLOCH - 65I | EASTFIELD - 65A | EASTFIELD - 65A | PARKHEAD - 65C | EDINBURGH (SM) - 64A | EDINBURGH (SM) - 64A | EDINBURGH (SM) - 64A | EDINBURGH (SM) - 64A |
| Jan-51 | EASTFIELD - 65A | BALLOCH - 65I | EASTFIELD - 65A | EASTFIELD - 65A | PARKHEAD - 65C | EDINBURGH (SM) - 64A | EDINBURGH (SM) - 64A | EDINBURGH (SM) - 64A | EDINBURGH (SM) - 64A |
| Aug-51 | EASTFIELD - 65A | BALLOCH - 65I | EASTFIELD - 65A | EASTFIELD - 65A | PARKHEAD - 65C | EDINBURGH (SM) - 64A | EDINBURGH (SM) - 64A | EDINBURGH (SM) - 64A | EDINBURGH (SM) - 64A |
| Jan-52 | EASTFIELD - 65A | BALLOCH - 65I | EASTFIELD - 65A | EASTFIELD - 65A | PARKHEAD - 65C | EDINBURGH (SM) - 64A | EDINBURGH (SM) - 64A | EDINBURGH (SM) - 64A | EDINBURGH (SM) - 64A |
| Aug-52 | EASTFIELD - 65A | BALLOCH - 65I | EASTFIELD - 65A | EASTFIELD - 65A | PARKHEAD - 65C | EDINBURGH (SM) - 64A | EDINBURGH (SM) - 64A | EDINBURGH (SM) - 64A | EDINBURGH (SM) - 64A |
| Jan-53 | EASTFIELD - 65A | BALLOCH - 65I | EASTFIELD - 65A | EASTFIELD - 65A | PARKHEAD - 65C | EDINBURGH (SM) - 64A | EDINBURGH (SM) - 64A | EDINBURGH (SM) - 64A | EDINBURGH (SM) - 64A |
| Aug-53 | EASTFIELD - 65A | BALLOCH - 65I | EASTFIELD - 65A | EASTFIELD - 65A | PARKHEAD - 65C | EDINBURGH (SM) - 64A | EDINBURGH (SM) - 64A | EDINBURGH (SM) - 64A | EDINBURGH (SM) - 64A |
| Jan-54 | EASTFIELD - 65A | BALLOCH - 65I | EASTFIELD - 65A | EASTFIELD - 65A | PARKHEAD - 65C | EDINBURGH (SM) - 64A | EDINBURGH (SM) - 64A | EDINBURGH (SM) - 64A | EDINBURGH (SM) - 64A |
| Aug-54 | EASTFIELD - 65A | BALLOCH - 65I | EASTFIELD - 65A | EASTFIELD - 65A | PARKHEAD - 65C | EDINBURGH (SM) - 64A | EDINBURGH (SM) - 64A | EDINBURGH (SM) - 64A | EDINBURGH (SM) - 64A |
| Jan-55 | EASTFIELD - 65A | BALLOCH - 65I | EASTFIELD - 65A | EASTFIELD - 65A | PARKHEAD - 65C | EDINBURGH (SM) - 64A | EDINBURGH (SM) - 64A | EDINBURGH (SM) - 64A | EDINBURGH (SM) - 64A |
| Aug-55 | EASTFIELD - 65A | BALLOCH - 65I | EASTFIELD - 65A | EASTFIELD - 65A | PARKHEAD - 65C | EDINBURGH (SM) - 64A | EDINBURGH (SM) - 64A | EDINBURGH (SM) - 64A | EDINBURGH (SM) - 64A |
| Jan-56 | EASTFIELD - 65A | BALLOCH - 65I | EASTFIELD - 65A | 1/56: KIPPS - 65E | PARKHEAD - 65C | EDINBURGH (SM) - 64A | EDINBURGH (SM) - 64A | EDINBURGH (SM) - 64A | EDINBURGH (SM) - 64A |
| Aug-56 | EASTFIELD - 65A | BALLOCH - 65I | EASTFIELD - 65A | 3/56: EFLD - 65A | PARKHEAD - 65C | EDINBURGH (SM) - 64A | 4/56: HWCK - 64G | EDINBURGH (SM) - 64A | EDINBURGH (SM) - 64A |
| Jan-57 | EASTFIELD - 65A | BALLOCH - 65I | EASTFIELD - 65A | EASTFIELD - 65A | PARKHEAD - 65C | EDINBURGH (SM) - 64A | HAWICK - 64G | EDINBURGH (SM) - 64A | EDINBURGH (SM) - 64A |
| Aug-57 | EASTFIELD - 65A | BALLOCH - 65I | EASTFIELD - 65A | EASTFIELD - 65A | PARKHEAD - 65C | EDINBURGH (SM) - 64A | HAWICK - 64G | EDINBURGH (SM) - 64A | EDINBURGH (SM) - 64A |
| Jan-58 | EASTFIELD - 65A | BALLOCH - 65I | EASTFIELD - 65A | EASTFIELD - 65A | PARKHEAD - 65C | EDINBURGH (SM) - 64A | HAWICK - 64G | EDINBURGH (SM) - 64A | EDINBURGH (SM) - 64A |
| Aug-58 | EASTFIELD - 65A | BALLOCH - 65I | EASTFIELD - 65A | EASTFIELD - 65A | PARKHEAD - 65C | 8/58: KIPPS - 65E | HAWICK - 64G | 8/58: PARK - 65C | 7/58: PARK - 65C |
| Jan-59 | EASTFIELD - 65A | BALLOCH - 65I | EASTFIELD - 65A | EASTFIELD - 65A | PARKHEAD - 65C | KIPPS - 65E | HAWICK - 64G | PARKHEAD - 65C | PARKHEAD - 65C |
| Aug-59 | EASTFIELD - 65A | BALLOCH - 65I | EASTFIELD - 65A | EASTFIELD - 65A | PARKHEAD - 65C | KIPPS - 65E | 6/59: EBRO (SM) - 64A | PARKHEAD - 65C | PARKHEAD - 65C |
| Nov-59 | EASTFIELD - 65A | BALLOCH - 65I | EASTFIELD - 65A | EASTFIELD - 65A | PARKHEAD - 65C | KIPPS - 65E | EDINBURGH (SM) - 64A | PARKHEAD - 65C | PARKHEAD - 65C |
| Jan-60 | EASTFIELD - 65A | BALLOCH - 65I | EASTFIELD - 65A | EASTFIELD - 65A | PARKHEAD - 65C | KIPPS - 65E | EDINBURGH (SM) - 64A | PARKHEAD - 65C | PARKHEAD - 65C |
| Apr-60 | EASTFIELD - 65A | BALLOCH - 65I | EASTFIELD - 65A | EASTFIELD - 65A | PARKHEAD - 65C | KIPPS - 65E | EDINBURGH (SM) - 64A | PARKHEAD - 65C | PARKHEAD - 65C |
| Aug-60 | EASTFIELD - 65A | BALLOCH - 65I | EASTFIELD - 65A | EASTFIELD - 65A | 8/60: DAWS - 65D | KIPPS - 65E | EDINBURGH (SM) - 64A | PARKHEAD - 65C | PARKHEAD - 65C |
| Nov-60 | EASTFIELD - 65A | BALLOCH - 65I | EASTFIELD - 65A | EASTFIELD - 65A | DAWSHOLME - 65D | KIPPS - 65E | EDINBURGH (SM) - 64A | PARKHEAD - 65C | PARKHEAD - 65C |

| | 67609 | 67610 | 67611 | 67612 | 67613 | 67614 | 67615 | 67616 | 67617 |
|---|---|---|---|---|---|---|---|---|---|
| Aug-50 | EDINBURGH (SM) - 64A | HAYMARKET - 64B | PARKHEAD - 65C | PARKHEAD - 65C | HELENSBURGH - 65H | HELENSBURGH - 65H | HAYMARKET - 64B | HELENSBURGH - 65H | EDINBURGH (SM) - 64A |
| Jan-51 | EDINBURGH (SM) - 64A | HAYMARKET - 64B | PARKHEAD - 65C | PARKHEAD - 65C | HELENSBURGH - 65H | HELENSBURGH - 65H | HAYMARKET - 64B | HELENSBURGH - 65H | EDINBURGH (SM) - 64A |
| Aug-51 | EDINBURGH (SM) - 64A | HAYMARKET - 64B | PARKHEAD - 65C | PARKHEAD - 65C | HELENSBURGH - 65H | HELENSBURGH - 65H | HAYMARKET - 64B | HELENSBURGH - 65H | EDINBURGH (SM) - 64A |
| Jan-52 | EDINBURGH (SM) - 64A | HAYMARKET - 64B | PARKHEAD - 65C | PARKHEAD - 65C | HELENSBURGH - 65H | HELENSBURGH - 65H | HAYMARKET - 64B | HELENSBURGH - 65H | EDINBURGH (SM) - 64A |
| Aug-52 | EDINBURGH (SM) - 64A | HAYMARKET - 64B | PARKHEAD - 65C | PARKHEAD - 65C | HELENSBURGH - 65H | HELENSBURGH - 65H | HAYMARKET - 64B | HELENSBURGH - 65H | EDINBURGH (SM) - 64A |
| Jan-53 | EDINBURGH (SM) - 64A | HAYMARKET - 64B | PARKHEAD - 65C | PARKHEAD - 65C | HELENSBURGH - 65H | HELENSBURGH - 65H | HAYMARKET - 64B | HELENSBURGH - 65H | EDINBURGH (SM) - 64A |
| Aug-53 | EDINBURGH (SM) - 64A | HAYMARKET - 64B | PARKHEAD - 65C | PARKHEAD - 65C | HELENSBURGH - 65H | HELENSBURGH - 65H | HAYMARKET - 64B | HELENSBURGH - 65H | EDINBURGH (SM) - 64A |
| Jan-54 | EDINBURGH (SM) - 64A | HAYMARKET - 64B | PARKHEAD - 65C | PARKHEAD - 65C | HELENSBURGH - 65H | HELENSBURGH - 65H | HAYMARKET - 64B | HELENSBURGH - 65H | EDINBURGH (SM) - 64A |
| Aug-54 | EDINBURGH (SM) - 64A | HAYMARKET - 64B | PARKHEAD - 65C | PARKHEAD - 65C | HELENSBURGH - 65H | HELENSBURGH - 65H | HAYMARKET - 64B | HELENSBURGH - 65H | EDINBURGH (SM) - 64A |
| Jan-55 | EDINBURGH (SM) - 64A | HAYMARKET - 64B | PARKHEAD - 65C | PARKHEAD - 65C | HELENSBURGH - 65H | HELENSBURGH - 65H | HAYMARKET - 64B | HELENSBURGH - 65H | EDINBURGH (SM) - 64A |
| Aug-55 | EDINBURGH (SM) - 64A | HAYMARKET - 64B | PARKHEAD - 65C | PARKHEAD - 65C | HELENSBURGH - 65H | HELENSBURGH - 65H | HAYMARKET - 64B | HELENSBURGH - 65H | EDINBURGH (SM) - 64A |
| Jan-56 | EDINBURGH (SM) - 64A | HAYMARKET - 64B | PARKHEAD - 65C | PARKHEAD - 65C | HELENSBURGH - 65H | HELENSBURGH - 65H | HAYMARKET - 64B | HELENSBURGH - 65H | EDINBURGH (SM) - 64A |
| Aug-56 | EDINBURGH (SM) - 64A | HAYMARKET - 64B | PARKHEAD - 65C | PARKHEAD - 65C | HELENSBURGH - 65H | HELENSBURGH - 65H | HAYMARKET - 64B | HELENSBURGH - 65H | EDINBURGH (SM) - 64A |
| Jan-57 | EDINBURGH (SM) - 64A | HAYMARKET - 64B | PARKHEAD - 65C | PARKHEAD - 65C | HELENSBURGH - 65H | HELENSBURGH - 65H | HAYMARKET - 64B | HELENSBURGH - 65H | EDINBURGH (SM) - 64A |
| Aug-57 | EDINBURGH (SM) - 64A | HAYMARKET - 64B | PARKHEAD - 65C | PARKHEAD - 65C | HELENSBURGH - 65H | HELENSBURGH - 65H | HAYMARKET - 64B | HELENSBURGH - 65H | EDINBURGH (SM) - 64A |
| Jan-58 | EDINBURGH (SM) - 64A | HAYMARKET - 64B | PARKHEAD - 65C | PARKHEAD - 65C | HELENSBURGH - 65H | HELENSBURGH - 65H | HAYMARKET - 64B | HELENSBURGH - 65H | EDINBURGH (SM) - 64A |
| Aug-58 | 7/58: KIPPS - 65E | HAYMARKET - 64B | PARKHEAD - 65C | PARKHEAD - 65C | HELENSBURGH - 65H | HELENSBURGH - 65H | HAYMARKET - 64B | HELENSBURGH - 65H | EDINBURGH (SM) - 64A |
| Jan-59 | KIPPS - 65E | HAYMARKET - 64B | PARKHEAD - 65C | PARKHEAD - 65C | HELENSBURGH - 65H | HELENSBURGH - 65H | HAYMARKET - 64B | HELENSBURGH - 65H | EDINBURGH (SM) - 64A |
| Aug-59 | KIPPS - 65E | HAYMARKET - 64B | PARKHEAD - 65C | PARKHEAD - 65C | HELENSBURGH - 65H | HELENSBURGH - 65H | HAYMARKET - 64B | HELENSBURGH - 65H | EDINBURGH (SM) - 64A |
| Nov-59 | KIPPS - 65E | HAYMARKET - 64B | PARKHEAD - 65C | PARKHEAD - 65C | HELENSBURGH - 65H | HELENSBURGH - 65H | HAYMARKET - 64B | HELENSBURGH - 65H | EDINBURGH (SM) - 64A |
| Jan-60 | KIPPS - 65E | HAYMARKET - 64B | PARKHEAD - 65C | PARKHEAD - 65C | HELENSBURGH - 65H | HELENSBURGH - 65H | HAYMARKET - 64B | HELENSBURGH - 65H | EDINBURGH (SM) - 64A |
| Apr-60 | KIPPS - 65E | HAYMARKET - 64B | PARKHEAD - 65C | PARKHEAD - 65C | HELENSBURGH - 65H | HELENSBURGH - 65H | HAYMARKET - 64B | HELENSBURGH - 65H | EDINBURGH (SM) - 64A |
| Aug-60 | KIPPS - 65E | HAYMARKET - 64B | PARKHEAD - 65C | PARKHEAD - 65C | HELENSBURGH - 65H | HELENSBURGH - 65H | HAYMARKET - 64B | HELENSBURGH - 65H | EDINBURGH (SM) - 64A |
| Nov-60 | KIPPS - 65E | HAYMARKET - 64B | PARKHEAD - 65C | PARKHEAD - 65C | HELENSBURGH - 65H | HELENSBURGH - 65H | HAYMARKET - 64B | HELENSBURGH - 65H | EDINBURGH (SM) - 64A |

| | 67618 | 67619 | 67620 | 67621 | 67622 | 67623 | 67624 | 67625 | 67626 |
|---|---|---|---|---|---|---|---|---|---|
| Aug-50 | EASTFIELD - 65A | PARKHEAD - 65C | HAYMARKET - 64B | PARKHEAD - 65C | PARKHEAD - 65C | PARKHEAD - 65C | EDINBURGH (SM) - 64A | HELENSBURGH - 65H | PARKHEAD - 65C |
| Jan-51 | 11/50: KIPPS - 65E | PARKHEAD - 65C | HAYMARKET - 64B | PARKHEAD - 65C | PARKHEAD - 65C | PARKHEAD - 65C | EDINBURGH (SM) - 64A | HELENSBURGH - 65H | PARKHEAD - 65C |
| Aug-51 | KIPPS - 65E | PARKHEAD - 65C | HAYMARKET - 64B | PARKHEAD - 65C | PARKHEAD - 65C | PARKHEAD - 65C | EDINBURGH (SM) - 64A | HELENSBURGH - 65H | PARKHEAD - 65C |
| Jan-52 | KIPPS - 65E | PARKHEAD - 65C | HAYMARKET - 64B | PARKHEAD - 65C | PARKHEAD - 65C | PARKHEAD - 65C | EDINBURGH (SM) - 64A | HELENSBURGH - 65H | PARKHEAD - 65C |
| Aug-52 | KIPPS - 65E | PARKHEAD - 65C | HAYMARKET - 64B | PARKHEAD - 65C | PARKHEAD - 65C | PARKHEAD - 65C | EDINBURGH (SM) - 64A | HELENSBURGH - 65H | PARKHEAD - 65C |
| Jan-53 | KIPPS - 65E | PARKHEAD - 65C | HAYMARKET - 64B | PARKHEAD - 65C | PARKHEAD - 65C | PARKHEAD - 65C | EDINBURGH (SM) - 64A | HELENSBURGH - 65H | PARKHEAD - 65C |
| Aug-53 | KIPPS - 65E | PARKHEAD - 65C | HAYMARKET - 64B | PARKHEAD - 65C | PARKHEAD - 65C | PARKHEAD - 65C | EDINBURGH (SM) - 64A | HELENSBURGH - 65H | PARKHEAD - 65C |
| Jan-54 | KIPPS - 65E | PARKHEAD - 65C | HAYMARKET - 64B | PARKHEAD - 65C | PARKHEAD - 65C | PARKHEAD - 65C | EDINBURGH (SM) - 64A | HELENSBURGH - 65H | PARKHEAD - 65C |
| Aug-54 | KIPPS - 65E | PARKHEAD - 65C | HAYMARKET - 64B | PARKHEAD - 65C | PARKHEAD - 65C | PARKHEAD - 65C | EDINBURGH (SM) - 64A | HELENSBURGH - 65H | PARKHEAD - 65C |
| Jan-55 | KIPPS - 65E | PARKHEAD - 65C | HAYMARKET - 64B | PARKHEAD - 65C | PARKHEAD - 65C | PARKHEAD - 65C | EDINBURGH (SM) - 64A | HELENSBURGH - 65H | PARKHEAD - 65C |
| Aug-55 | KIPPS - 65E | PARKHEAD - 65C | HAYMARKET - 64B | PARKHEAD - 65C | PARKHEAD - 65C | PARKHEAD - 65C | EDINBURGH (SM) - 64A | HELENSBURGH - 65H | PARKHEAD - 65C |
| Jan-56 | KIPPS - 65E | PARKHEAD - 65C | HAYMARKET - 64B | PARKHEAD - 65C | PARKHEAD - 65C | PARKHEAD - 65C | EDINBURGH (SM) - 64A | HELENSBURGH - 65H | PARKHEAD - 65C |
| Aug-56 | KIPPS - 65E | PARKHEAD - 65C | HAYMARKET - 64B | PARKHEAD - 65C | PARKHEAD - 65C | PARKHEAD - 65C | EDINBURGH (SM) - 64A | HELENSBURGH - 65H | PARKHEAD - 65C |
| Jan-57 | KIPPS - 65E | PARKHEAD - 65C | HAYMARKET - 64B | PARKHEAD - 65C | PARKHEAD - 65C | PARKHEAD - 65C | EDINBURGH (SM) - 64A | HELENSBURGH - 65H | PARKHEAD - 65C |
| Aug-57 | KIPPS - 65E | PARKHEAD - 65C | HAYMARKET - 64B | PARKHEAD - 65C | PARKHEAD - 65C | PARKHEAD - 65C | EDINBURGH (SM) - 64A | HELENSBURGH - 65H | PARKHEAD - 65C |
| Jan-58 | KIPPS - 65E | PARKHEAD - 65C | HAYMARKET - 64B | PARKHEAD - 65C | PARKHEAD - 65C | PARKHEAD - 65C | EDINBURGH (SM) - 64A | HELENSBURGH - 65H | PARKHEAD - 65C |
| Aug-58 | KIPPS - 65E | PARKHEAD - 65C | HAYMARKET - 64B | PARKHEAD - 65C | PARKHEAD - 65C | PARKHEAD - 65C | EDINBURGH (SM) - 64A | HELENSBURGH - 65H | PARKHEAD - 65C |
| Jan-59 | KIPPS - 65E | PARKHEAD - 65C | HAYMARKET - 64B | PARKHEAD - 65C | PARKHEAD - 65C | PARKHEAD - 65C | EDINBURGH (SM) - 64A | HELENSBURGH - 65H | PARKHEAD - 65C |
| Aug-59 | KIPPS - 65E | PARKHEAD - 65C | HAYMARKET - 64B | PARKHEAD - 65C | PARKHEAD - 65C | PARKHEAD - 65C | EDINBURGH (SM) - 64A | HELENSBURGH - 65H | PARKHEAD - 65C |
| Nov-59 | KIPPS - 65E | PARKHEAD - 65C | HAYMARKET - 64B | PARKHEAD - 65C | PARKHEAD - 65C | PARKHEAD - 65C | EDINBURGH (SM) - 64A | HELENSBURGH - 65H | PARKHEAD - 65C |
| Jan-60 | KIPPS - 65E | PARKHEAD - 65C | HAYMARKET - 64B | PARKHEAD - 65C | PARKHEAD - 65C | PARKHEAD - 65C | EDINBURGH (SM) - 64A | HELENSBURGH - 65H | PARKHEAD - 65C |
| Apr-60 | KIPPS - 65E | PARKHEAD - 65C | HAYMARKET - 64B | PARKHEAD - 65C | PARKHEAD - 65C | PARKHEAD - 65C | EDINBURGH (SM) - 64A | HELENSBURGH - 65H | PARKHEAD - 65C |
| Aug-60 | KIPPS - 65E | PARKHEAD - 65C | HAYMARKET - 64B | PARKHEAD - 65C | PARKHEAD - 65C | PARKHEAD - 65C | EDINBURGH (SM) - 64A | HELENSBURGH - 65H | PARKHEAD - 65C |
| Nov-60 | KIPPS - 65E | PARKHEAD - 65C | HAYMARKET - 64B | PARKHEAD - 65C | PARKHEAD - 65C | PARKHEAD - 65C | 11/60: W/D | HELENSBURGH - 65H | PARKHEAD - 65C |

| | 67627 | 67628 | 67629 | 67630 | 67631 | 67632 | 67633 | 67634 | 67635 |
|---|---|---|---|---|---|---|---|---|---|
| Aug-50 | KIPPS - 65E | PARKHEAD - 65C | EDINBURGH (SM) - 64A | EDINBURGH (SM) - 64A | HELENSBURGH - 65H | HELENSBURGH - 65H | PARKHEAD - 65C | GATESHEAD - 52A | HEATON - 52B |
| Jan-51 | KIPPS - 65E | PARKHEAD - 65C | EDINBURGH (SM) - 64A | EDINBURGH (SM) - 64A | HELENSBURGH - 65H | HELENSBURGH - 65H | PARKHEAD - 65C | GATESHEAD - 52A | HEATON - 52B |
| Aug-51 | KIPPS - 65E | PARKHEAD - 65C | EDINBURGH (SM) - 64A | EDINBURGH (SM) - 64A | HELENSBURGH - 65H | HELENSBURGH - 65H | PARKHEAD - 65C | GATESHEAD - 52A | HEATON - 52B |
| Jan-52 | KIPPS - 65E | PARKHEAD - 65C | EDINBURGH (SM) - 64A | EDINBURGH (SM) - 64A | HELENSBURGH - 65H | HELENSBURGH - 65H | PARKHEAD - 65C | GATESHEAD - 52A | HEATON - 52B |
| Aug-52 | KIPPS - 65E | PARKHEAD - 65C | EDINBURGH (SM) - 64A | EDINBURGH (SM) - 64A | HELENSBURGH - 65H | HELENSBURGH - 65H | PARKHEAD - 65C | GATESHEAD - 52A | HEATON - 52B |
| Jan-53 | KIPPS - 65E | PARKHEAD - 65C | EDINBURGH (SM) - 64A | EDINBURGH (SM) - 64A | HELENSBURGH - 65H | HELENSBURGH - 65H | PARKHEAD - 65C | GATESHEAD - 52A | HEATON - 52B |
| Aug-53 | KIPPS - 65E | PARKHEAD - 65C | EDINBURGH (SM) - 64A | EDINBURGH (SM) - 64A | HELENSBURGH - 65H | HELENSBURGH - 65H | PARKHEAD - 65C | GATESHEAD - 52A | HEATON - 52B |
| Jan-54 | KIPPS - 65E | PARKHEAD - 65C | EDINBURGH (SM) - 64A | EDINBURGH (SM) - 64A | HELENSBURGH - 65H | HELENSBURGH - 65H | PARKHEAD - 65C | GATESHEAD - 52A | HEATON - 52B |
| Aug-54 | KIPPS - 65E | PARKHEAD - 65C | EDINBURGH (SM) - 64A | EDINBURGH (SM) - 64A | HELENSBURGH - 65H | HELENSBURGH - 65H | PARKHEAD - 65C | GATESHEAD - 52A | HEATON - 52B |
| Jan-55 | KIPPS - 65E | PARKHEAD - 65C | EDINBURGH (SM) - 64A | EDINBURGH (SM) - 64A | HELENSBURGH - 65H | HELENSBURGH - 65H | PARKHEAD - 65C | GATESHEAD - 52A | HEATON - 52B |
| Aug-55 | KIPPS - 65E | PARKHEAD - 65C | EDINBURGH (SM) - 64A | EDINBURGH (SM) - 64A | HELENSBURGH - 65H | HELENSBURGH - 65H | PARKHEAD - 65C | GATESHEAD - 52A | HEATON - 52B |
| Jan-56 | KIPPS - 65E | PARKHEAD - 65C | EDINBURGH (SM) - 64A | 2/56: HWCK - 64G | HELENSBURGH - 65H | HELENSBURGH - 65H | PARKHEAD - 65C | 12/55: BLAY - 52C | HEATON - 52B |
| Aug-56 | KIPPS - 65E | PARKHEAD - 65C | EDINBURGH (SM) - 64A | 4/56: EBRO (SM) - 64A | HELENSBURGH - 65H | HELENSBURGH - 65H | PARKHEAD - 65C | BLAYDON - 52C | HEATON - 52B |
| Jan-57 | KIPPS - 65E | PARKHEAD - 65C | EDINBURGH (SM) - 64A | EDINBURGH (SM) - 64A | HELENSBURGH - 65H | HELENSBURGH - 65H | PARKHEAD - 65C | BLAYDON - 52C | HEATON - 52B |
| Aug-57 | KIPPS - 65E | PARKHEAD - 65C | EDINBURGH (SM) - 64A | EDINBURGH (SM) - 64A | HELENSBURGH - 65H | HELENSBURGH - 65H | PARKHEAD - 65C | BLAYDON - 52C | HEATON - 52B |
| Jan-58 | KIPPS - 65E | PARKHEAD - 65C | EDINBURGH (SM) - 64A | EDINBURGH (SM) - 64A | HELENSBURGH - 65H | HELENSBURGH - 65H | PARKHEAD - 65C | BLAYDON - 52C | HEATON - 52B |
| Aug-58 | KIPPS - 65E | PARKHEAD - 65C | EDINBURGH (SM) - 64A | EDINBURGH (SM) - 64A | HELENSBURGH - 65H | HELENSBURGH - 65H | PARKHEAD - 65C | BLAYDON - 52C | HEATON - 52B |
| Jan-59 | KIPPS - 65E | PARKHEAD - 65C | 1/59: PARK - 65C | 1/59: PARK - 65C | HELENSBURGH - 65H | HELENSBURGH - 65H | PARKHEAD - 65C | BLAYDON - 52C | 2/59: B.GDNS - 53B |
| Aug-59 | KIPPS - 65E | PARKHEAD - 65C | PARKHEAD - 65C | PARKHEAD - 65C | HELENSBURGH - 65H | HELENSBURGH - 65H | PARKHEAD - 65C | BLAYDON - 52C | 6/59: DAIRY - 53A |
| Nov-59 | KIPPS - 65E | PARKHEAD - 65C | PARKHEAD - 65C | PARKHEAD - 65C | HELENSBURGH - 65H | HELENSBURGH - 65H | PARKHEAD - 65C | BLAYDON - 52C | DAIRYCOATES - 53A |
| Jan-60 | KIPPS - 65E | PARKHEAD - 65C | PARKHEAD - 65C | PARKHEAD - 65C | HELENSBURGH - 65H | HELENSBURGH - 65H | PARKHEAD - 65C | BLAYDON - 52C | DAIRYCOATES - 53A |
| Apr-60 | KIPPS - 65E | PARKHEAD - 65C | PARKHEAD - 65C | PARKHEAD - 65C | HELENSBURGH - 65H | HELENSBURGH - 65H | PARKHEAD - 65C | BLAYDON - 52C | DAIRYCOATES - 50B |
| Aug-60 | KIPPS - 65E | PARKHEAD - 65C | PARKHEAD - 65C | PARKHEAD - 65C | HELENSBURGH - 65H | HELENSBURGH - 65H | PARKHEAD - 65C | BLAYDON - 52C | DAIRYCOATES - 50B |
| Nov-60 | KIPPS - 65E | PARKHEAD - 65C | PARKHEAD - 65C | PARKHEAD - 65C | HELENSBURGH - 65H | HELENSBURGH - 65H | PARKHEAD - 65C | BLAYDON - 52C | DAIRYCOATES - 50B |

| | 67636 | 67637 | 67638 | 67639 | 67640 | 67641 | 67642 | 67643 | 67644 |
|---|---|---|---|---|---|---|---|---|---|
| Aug-50 | BLAYDON - 52C | HEATON - 52B | MIDDLESBROUGH - 51D | MIDDLESBROUGH - 51D | HEATON - 52B | HEATON - 52B | HEATON - 52B | PARKHEAD - 65C | EASTFIELD - 65A |
| Jan-51 | BLAYDON - 52C | HEATON - 52B | MIDDLESBROUGH - 51D | MIDDLESBROUGH - 51D | HEATON - 52B | HEATON - 52B | HEATON - 52B | PARKHEAD - 65C | EASTFIELD - 65A |
| Aug-51 | BLAYDON - 52C | HEATON - 52B | MIDDLESBROUGH - 51D | MIDDLESBROUGH - 51D | HEATON - 52B | HEATON - 52B | HEATON - 52B | PARKHEAD - 65C | EASTFIELD - 65A |
| Jan-52 | BLAYDON - 52C | HEATON - 52B | MIDDLESBROUGH - 51D | MIDDLESBROUGH - 51D | HEATON - 52B | HEATON - 52B | HEATON - 52B | PARKHEAD - 65C | EASTFIELD - 65A |
| Aug-52 | BLAYDON - 52C | HEATON - 52B | MIDDLESBROUGH - 51D | MIDDLESBROUGH - 51D | HEATON - 52B | HEATON - 52B | HEATON - 52B | PARKHEAD - 65C | EASTFIELD - 65A |
| Jan-53 | BLAYDON - 52C | HEATON - 52B | MIDDLESBROUGH - 51D | **10/52: HTN - 52B** | HEATON - 52B | HEATON - 52B | HEATON - 52B | PARKHEAD - 65C | EASTFIELD - 65A |
| Aug-53 | BLAYDON - 52C | HEATON - 52B | MIDDLESBROUGH - 51D | **5/53: MBRO - 51D** | HEATON - 52B | HEATON - 52B | HEATON - 52B | PARKHEAD - 65C | EASTFIELD - 65A |
| Jan-54 | BLAYDON - 52C | HEATON - 52B | MIDDLESBROUGH - 51D | MIDDLESBROUGH - 51D | HEATON - 52B | HEATON - 52B | HEATON - 52B | PARKHEAD - 65C | EASTFIELD - 65A |
| Aug-54 | BLAYDON - 52C | HEATON - 52B | MIDDLESBROUGH - 51D | MIDDLESBROUGH - 51D | HEATON - 52B | HEATON - 52B | HEATON - 52B | PARKHEAD - 65C | EASTFIELD - 65A |
| Jan-55 | BLAYDON - 52C | HEATON - 52B | MIDDLESBROUGH - 51D | **10/54: BLAY - 52C** | HEATON - 52B | HEATON - 52B | HEATON - 52B | PARKHEAD - 65C | EASTFIELD - 65A |
| Aug-55 | BLAYDON - 52C | HEATON - 52B | MIDDLESBROUGH - 51D | BLAYDON - 52C | HEATON - 52B | HEATON - 52B | HEATON - 52B | PARKHEAD - 65C | EASTFIELD - 65A |
| Jan-56 | BLAYDON - 52C | HEATON - 52B | MIDDLESBROUGH - 51D | **12/55: HEX - 52C** | HEATON - 52B | HEATON - 52B | HEATON - 52B | PARKHEAD - 65C | EASTFIELD - 65A |
| Aug-56 | BLAYDON - 52C | HEATON - 52B | **6/56: B.GDNS - 53B** | HEXHAM - 52C | HEATON - 52B | HEATON - 52B | HEATON - 52B | PARKHEAD - 65C | EASTFIELD - 65A |
| Jan-57 | BLAYDON - 52C | HEATON - 52B | BOTANIC GARDENS - 53B | HEXHAM - 52C | HEATON - 52B | HEATON - 52B | HEATON - 52B | PARKHEAD - 65C | EASTFIELD - 65A |
| Aug-57 | BLAYDON - 52C | HEATON - 52B | BOTANIC GARDENS - 53B | **4/57: GHD - 52A** | HEATON - 52B | HEATON - 52B | HEATON - 52B | PARKHEAD - 65C | EASTFIELD - 65A |
| Jan-58 | BLAYDON - 52C | HEATON - 52B | BOTANIC GARDENS - 53B | GATESHEAD - 52A | HEATON - 52B | **11/57: ALN - 52D** | **11/57: ALN - 52D** | PARKHEAD - 65C | EASTFIELD - 65A |
| Aug-58 | BLAYDON - 52C | **9/58: SUND - 54A** | BOTANIC GARDENS - 53B | GATESHEAD - 52A | **9/58: B.GDNS - 53B** | **6/58: HTN - 52B** | **6/58: HTN - 52B** | PARKHEAD - 65C | EASTFIELD - 65A |
| Jan-59 | BLAYDON - 52C | **2/59: GHD - 52A** | BOTANIC GARDENS - 53B | GATESHEAD - 52A | BOTANIC GARDENS - 53B | HEATON - 52B | HEATON - 52B | PARKHEAD - 65C | EASTFIELD - 65A |
| Aug-59 | BLAYDON - 52C | GATESHEAD - 52A | **6/59: DAIRY - 53A** | GATESHEAD - 52A | **6/59: DAIRY - 53A** | HEATON - 52B | HEATON - 52B | PARKHEAD - 65C | EASTFIELD - 65A |
| Nov-59 | BLAYDON - 52C | GATESHEAD - 52A | DAIRYCOATES - 53A | GATESHEAD - 52A | DAIRYCOATES - 53A | HEATON - 52B | HEATON - 52B | PARKHEAD - 65C | EASTFIELD - 65A |
| Jan-60 | BLAYDON - 52C | GATESHEAD - 52A | DAIRYCOATES - 53A | GATESHEAD - 52A | DAIRYCOATES - 53A | HEATON - 52B | HEATON - 52B | PARKHEAD - 65C | EASTFIELD - 65A |
| Apr-60 | BLAYDON - 52C | GATESHEAD - 52A | DAIRYCOATES - 50B | GATESHEAD - 52A | DAIRYCOATES - 50B | HEATON - 52B | HEATON - 52B | PARKHEAD - 65C | EASTFIELD - 65A |
| Aug-60 | BLAYDON - 52C | GATESHEAD - 52A | DAIRYCOATES - 50B | GATESHEAD - 52A | DAIRYCOATES - 50B | HEATON - 52B | HEATON - 52B | PARKHEAD - 65C | EASTFIELD - 65A |
| Nov-60 | BLAYDON - 52C | GATESHEAD - 52A | DAIRYCOATES - 50B | GATESHEAD - 52A | DAIRYCOATES - 50B | HEATON - 52B | HEATON - 52B | PARKHEAD - 65C | EASTFIELD - 65A |

| | 67645 | 67646 | 67647 | 67648 | 67649 | 67650 | 67651 | 67652 | 67653 |
|---|---|---|---|---|---|---|---|---|---|
| Aug-50 | HEATON - 52B | HEATON - 52B | MIDDLESBROUGH - 51D | PARKHEAD - 65C | EDINBURGH (SM) - 64A | STIRLING - 63B | HEATON - 52B | HEATON - 52B | BLAYDON - 52C |
| Jan-51 | HEATON - 52B | HEATON - 52B | **10/50: GHD - 52A** | PARKHEAD - 65C | EDINBURGH (SM) - 64A | STIRLING - 63B | HEATON - 52B | HEATON - 52B | BLAYDON - 52C |
| Aug-51 | HEATON - 52B | HEATON - 52B | **7/51: STOCK - 51E** | PARKHEAD - 65C | EDINBURGH (SM) - 64A | STIRLING - 63B | HEATON - 52B | HEATON - 52B | BLAYDON - 52C |
| Jan-52 | HEATON - 52B | HEATON - 52B | **9/51: GHD - 52A** | PARKHEAD - 65C | EDINBURGH (SM) - 64A | STIRLING - 63B | HEATON - 52B | HEATON - 52B | BLAYDON - 52C |
| Aug-52 | HEATON - 52B | HEATON - 52B | **7/52: HTN - 52B** | PARKHEAD - 65C | EDINBURGH (SM) - 64A | STIRLING - 63B | HEATON - 52B | HEATON - 52B | BLAYDON - 52C |
| Jan-53 | HEATON - 52B | HEATON - 52B | HEATON - 52B | PARKHEAD - 65C | EDINBURGH (SM) - 64A | STIRLING - 63B | HEATON - 52B | HEATON - 52B | BLAYDON - 52C |
| Aug-53 | HEATON - 52B | HEATON - 52B | HEATON - 52B | PARKHEAD - 65C | EDINBURGH (SM) - 64A | STIRLING - 63B | HEATON - 52B | HEATON - 52B | BLAYDON - 52C |
| Jan-54 | HEATON - 52B | HEATON - 52B | HEATON - 52B | PARKHEAD - 65C | EDINBURGH (SM) - 64A | STIRLING - 63B | HEATON - 52B | HEATON - 52B | BLAYDON - 52C |
| Aug-54 | HEATON - 52B | HEATON - 52B | HEATON - 52B | PARKHEAD - 65C | EDINBURGH (SM) - 64A | STIRLING - 63B | HEATON - 52B | HEATON - 52B | BLAYDON - 52C |
| Jan-55 | HEATON - 52B | HEATON - 52B | HEATON - 52B | PARKHEAD - 65C | EDINBURGH (SM) - 64A | STIRLING - 63B | HEATON - 52B | HEATON - 52B | BLAYDON - 52C |
| Aug-55 | HEATON - 52B | HEATON - 52B | HEATON - 52B | PARKHEAD - 65C | EDINBURGH (SM) - 64A | STIRLING - 63B | HEATON - 52B | HEATON - 52B | BLAYDON - 52C |
| Jan-56 | HEATON - 52B | HEATON - 52B | HEATON - 52B | PARKHEAD - 65C | EDINBURGH (SM) - 64A | STIRLING - 63B | HEATON - 52B | HEATON - 52B | BLAYDON - 52C |
| Aug-56 | HEATON - 52B | HEATON - 52B | HEATON - 52B | PARKHEAD - 65C | EDINBURGH (SM) - 64A | STIRLING - 63B | HEATON - 52B | HEATON - 52B | BLAYDON - 52C |
| Jan-57 | HEATON - 52B | HEATON - 52B | HEATON - 52B | PARKHEAD - 65C | EDINBURGH (SM) - 64A | STIRLING - 63B | HEATON - 52B | HEATON - 52B | BLAYDON - 52C |
| Aug-57 | HEATON - 52B | HEATON - 52B | HEATON - 52B | PARKHEAD - 65C | EDINBURGH (SM) - 64A | STIRLING - 63B | HEATON - 52B | HEATON - 52B | BLAYDON - 52C |
| Jan-58 | **11/57: GHD - 52A** | HEATON - 52B | **11/57: ALN - 52D** | PARKHEAD - 65C | EDINBURGH (SM) - 64A | STIRLING - 63B | HEATON - 52B | HEATON - 52B | BLAYDON - 52C |
| Aug-58 | **9/58: SUND - 54A** | HEATON - 52B | **6/58: HTN - 52B** | PARKHEAD - 65C | EDINBURGH (SM) - 64A | STIRLING - 63B | HEATON - 52B | HEATON - 52B | BLAYDON - 52C |
| Jan-59 | SUNDERLAND - 52G | HEATON - 52B | HEATON - 52B | PARKHEAD - 65C | EDINBURGH (SM) - 64A | **2/59: PARK - 65C** | HEATON - 52B | HEATON - 52B | BLAYDON - 52C |
| Aug-59 | **6/59: HTN - 52B** | HEATON - 52B | HEATON - 52B | PARKHEAD - 65C | EDINBURGH (SM) - 64A | PARKHEAD - 65C | HEATON - 52B | HEATON - 52B | BLAYDON - 52C |
| Nov-59 | **9/59: SUND - 52G** | HEATON - 52B | HEATON - 52B | PARKHEAD - 65C | EDINBURGH (SM) - 64A | PARKHEAD - 65C | HEATON - 52B | HEATON - 52B | BLAYDON - 52C |
| Jan-60 | SUNDERLAND - 52G | HEATON - 52B | HEATON - 52B | PARKHEAD - 65C | EDINBURGH (SM) - 64A | PARKHEAD - 65C | HEATON - 52B | HEATON - 52B | BLAYDON - 52C |
| Apr-60 | SUNDERLAND - 52G | HEATON - 52B | HEATON - 52B | PARKHEAD - 65C | EDINBURGH (SM) - 64A | PARKHEAD - 65C | HEATON - 52B | HEATON - 52B | BLAYDON - 52C |
| Aug-60 | SUNDERLAND - 52G | HEATON - 52B | HEATON - 52B | PARKHEAD - 65C | EDINBURGH (SM) - 64A | PARKHEAD - 65C | HEATON - 52B | HEATON - 52B | BLAYDON - 52C |
| Nov-60 | SUNDERLAND - 52G | HEATON - 52B | HEATON - 52B | PARKHEAD - 65C | EDINBURGH (SM) - 64A | PARKHEAD - 65C | HEATON - 52B | HEATON - 52B | BLAYDON - 52C |

| | 67654 | 67655 | 67656 | 67657 | 67658 | 67659 | 67660 | 67661 | 67662 |
|---|---|---|---|---|---|---|---|---|---|
| Aug-50 | HEATON - 52B | PARKHEAD - 65C | BLAYDON - 52C | BLAYDON - 52C | BLAYDON - 52C | EDINBURGH (SM) - 64A | KIPPS - 65E | PARKHEAD - 65C | PARKHEAD - 65C |
| Jan-51 | HEATON - 52B | PARKHEAD - 65C | BLAYDON - 52C | BLAYDON - 52C | BLAYDON - 52C | EDINBURGH (SM) - 64A | KIPPS - 65E | PARKHEAD - 65C | PARKHEAD - 65C |
| Aug-51 | HEATON - 52B | PARKHEAD - 65C | BLAYDON - 52C | BLAYDON - 52C | BLAYDON - 52C | EDINBURGH (SM) - 64A | KIPPS - 65E | PARKHEAD - 65C | PARKHEAD - 65C |
| Jan-52 | HEATON - 52B | PARKHEAD - 65C | BLAYDON - 52C | BLAYDON - 52C | BLAYDON - 52C | EDINBURGH (SM) - 64A | KIPPS - 65E | PARKHEAD - 65C | PARKHEAD - 65C |
| Aug-52 | HEATON - 52B | PARKHEAD - 65C | BLAYDON - 52C | BLAYDON - 52C | BLAYDON - 52C | EDINBURGH (SM) - 64A | KIPPS - 65E | PARKHEAD - 65C | PARKHEAD - 65C |
| Jan-53 | HEATON - 52B | PARKHEAD - 65C | BLAYDON - 52C | BLAYDON - 52C | BLAYDON - 52C | EDINBURGH (SM) - 64A | KIPPS - 65E | PARKHEAD - 65C | PARKHEAD - 65C |
| Aug-53 | HEATON - 52B | PARKHEAD - 65C | BLAYDON - 52C | BLAYDON - 52C | BLAYDON - 52C | EDINBURGH (SM) - 64A | KIPPS - 65E | PARKHEAD - 65C | PARKHEAD - 65C |
| Jan-54 | HEATON - 52B | PARKHEAD - 65C | BLAYDON - 52C | BLAYDON - 52C | BLAYDON - 52C | EDINBURGH (SM) - 64A | KIPPS - 65E | PARKHEAD - 65C | PARKHEAD - 65C |
| Aug-54 | HEATON - 52B | PARKHEAD - 65C | BLAYDON - 52C | BLAYDON - 52C | BLAYDON - 52C | EDINBURGH (SM) - 64A | KIPPS - 65E | PARKHEAD - 65C | PARKHEAD - 65C |
| Jan-55 | HEATON - 52B | PARKHEAD - 65C | BLAYDON - 52C | BLAYDON - 52C | BLAYDON - 52C | EDINBURGH (SM) - 64A | KIPPS - 65E | PARKHEAD - 65C | PARKHEAD - 65C |
| Aug-55 | HEATON - 52B | PARKHEAD - 65C | BLAYDON - 52C | BLAYDON - 52C | BLAYDON - 52C | EDINBURGH (SM) - 64A | KIPPS - 65E | PARKHEAD - 65C | PARKHEAD - 65C |
| Jan-56 | HEATON - 52B | PARKHEAD - 65C | BLAYDON - 52C | **12/55: HEX - 52C** | **12/55: HEX - 52C** | EDINBURGH (SM) - 64A | KIPPS - 65E | PARKHEAD - 65C | PARKHEAD - 65C |
| Aug-56 | HEATON - 52B | PARKHEAD - 65C | BLAYDON - 52C | HEXHAM - 52C | HEXHAM - 52C | EDINBURGH (SM) - 64A | KIPPS - 65E | PARKHEAD - 65C | PARKHEAD - 65C |
| Jan-57 | HEATON - 52B | PARKHEAD - 65C | **5/57: ALN - 52C** | **4/57: GHD - 52A** | HEXHAM - 52C | EDINBURGH (SM) - 64A | KIPPS - 65E | PARKHEAD - 65C | PARKHEAD - 65C |
| Aug-57 | HEATON - 52B | PARKHEAD - 65C | **6/57: HTN - 52B** | GATESHEAD - 52A | **6/57: HTN - 52B** | EDINBURGH (SM) - 64A | KIPPS - 65E | PARKHEAD - 65C | PARKHEAD - 65C |
| Jan-58 | HEATON - 52B | PARKHEAD - 65C | HEATON - 52B | GATESHEAD - 52A | HEATON - 52B | EDINBURGH (SM) - 64A | KIPPS - 65E | PARKHEAD - 65C | PARKHEAD - 65C |
| Aug-58 | HEATON - 52B | PARKHEAD - 65C | HEATON - 52B | GATESHEAD - 52A | HEATON - 52B | EDINBURGH (SM) - 64A | KIPPS - 65E | PARKHEAD - 65C | PARKHEAD - 65C |
| Jan-59 | HEATON - 52B | PARKHEAD - 65C | HEATON - 52B | GATESHEAD - 52A | HEATON - 52B | EDINBURGH (SM) - 64A | KIPPS - 65E | PARKHEAD - 65C | PARKHEAD - 65C |
| Aug-59 | HEATON - 52B | PARKHEAD - 65C | HEATON - 52B | GATESHEAD - 52A | HEATON - 52B | EDINBURGH (SM) - 64A | KIPPS - 65E | PARKHEAD - 65C | PARKHEAD - 65C |
| Nov-59 | HEATON - 52B | PARKHEAD - 65C | HEATON - 52B | GATESHEAD - 52A | HEATON - 52B | EDINBURGH (SM) - 64A | KIPPS - 65E | PARKHEAD - 65C | PARKHEAD - 65C |
| Jan-60 | HEATON - 52B | PARKHEAD - 65C | HEATON - 52B | GATESHEAD - 52A | HEATON - 52B | EDINBURGH (SM) - 64A | KIPPS - 65E | PARKHEAD - 65C | PARKHEAD - 65C |
| Apr-60 | HEATON - 52B | PARKHEAD - 65C | HEATON - 52B | GATESHEAD - 52A | HEATON - 52B | EDINBURGH (SM) - 64A | KIPPS - 65E | PARKHEAD - 65C | PARKHEAD - 65C |
| Aug-60 | HEATON - 52B | PARKHEAD - 65C | HEATON - 52B | GATESHEAD - 52A | HEATON - 52B | EDINBURGH (SM) - 64A | KIPPS - 65E | PARKHEAD - 65C | PARKHEAD - 65C |
| Nov-60 | HEATON - 52B | PARKHEAD - 65C | HEATON - 52B | GATESHEAD - 52A | HEATON - 52B | EDINBURGH (SM) - 64A | KIPPS - 65E | PARKHEAD - 65C | PARKHEAD - 65C |

| | 67663 | 67664 | 67665 | 67666 | 67667 | 67668 | 67669 | 67670 | 67671 |
|---|---|---|---|---|---|---|---|---|---|
| Aug-50 | NORWICH - 32A | NORWICH - 32A | KIPPS - 65E | EDINBURGH (SM) - 64A | KITTYBREWSTER - 61A | EDINBURGH (SM) - 64A | DUNFERMLINE - 62C | EDINBURGH (SM) - 64A | KITTYBREWSTER - 61A |
| Jan-51 | **2/51: MBRO - 51D** | NORWICH - 32A | KIPPS - 65E | EDINBURGH (SM) - 64A | KITTYBREWSTER - 61A | EDINBURGH (SM) - 64A | DUNFERMLINE - 62C | EDINBURGH (SM) - 64A | KITTYBREWSTER - 61A |
| Aug-51 | MIDDLESBROUGH - 51D | NORWICH - 32A | KIPPS - 65E | EDINBURGH (SM) - 64A | KITTYBREWSTER - 61A | EDINBURGH (SM) - 64A | DUNFERMLINE - 62C | EDINBURGH (SM) - 64A | KITTYBREWSTER - 61A |
| Jan-52 | MIDDLESBROUGH - 51D | NORWICH - 32A | KIPPS - 65E | EDINBURGH (SM) - 64A | KITTYBREWSTER - 61A | EDINBURGH (SM) - 64A | DUNFERMLINE - 62C | EDINBURGH (SM) - 64A | KITTYBREWSTER - 61A |
| Aug-52 | MIDDLESBROUGH - 51D | **6/52: EAST - 65A** | KIPPS - 65E | EDINBURGH (SM) - 64A | KITTYBREWSTER - 61A | EDINBURGH (SM) - 64A | DUNFERMLINE - 62C | EDINBURGH (SM) - 64A | KITTYBREWSTER - 61A |
| Jan-53 | MIDDLESBROUGH - 51D | EASTFIELD - 65A | KIPPS - 65E | EDINBURGH (SM) - 64A | KITTYBREWSTER - 61A | EDINBURGH (SM) - 64A | DUNFERMLINE - 62C | EDINBURGH (SM) - 64A | KITTYBREWSTER - 61A |
| Aug-53 | MIDDLESBROUGH - 51D | EASTFIELD - 65A | KIPPS - 65E | EDINBURGH (SM) - 64A | KITTYBREWSTER - 61A | EDINBURGH (SM) - 64A | DUNFERMLINE - 62C | EDINBURGH (SM) - 64A | KITTYBREWSTER - 61A |
| Jan-54 | MIDDLESBROUGH - 51D | EASTFIELD - 65A | KIPPS - 65E | EDINBURGH (SM) - 64A | KITTYBREWSTER - 61A | EDINBURGH (SM) - 64A | DUNFERMLINE - 62C | EDINBURGH (SM) - 64A | KITTYBREWSTER - 61A |
| Aug-54 | MIDDLESBROUGH - 51D | EASTFIELD - 65A | KIPPS - 65E | EDINBURGH (SM) - 64A | KITTYBREWSTER - 61A | EDINBURGH (SM) - 64A | DUNFERMLINE - 62C | EDINBURGH (SM) - 64A | KITTYBREWSTER - 61A |
| Jan-55 | MIDDLESBROUGH - 51D | EASTFIELD - 65A | KIPPS - 65E | EDINBURGH (SM) - 64A | KITTYBREWSTER - 61A | EDINBURGH (SM) - 64A | DUNFERMLINE - 62C | EDINBURGH (SM) - 64A | KITTYBREWSTER - 61A |
| Aug-55 | MIDDLESBROUGH - 51D | EASTFIELD - 65A | KIPPS - 65E | EDINBURGH (SM) - 64A | KITTYBREWSTER - 61A | EDINBURGH (SM) - 64A | DUNFERMLINE - 62C | EDINBURGH (SM) - 64A | KITTYBREWSTER - 61A |
| Jan-56 | MIDDLESBROUGH - 51D | EASTFIELD - 65A | KIPPS - 65E | EDINBURGH (SM) - 64A | KITTYBREWSTER - 61A | EDINBURGH (SM) - 64A | DUNFERMLINE - 62C | EDINBURGH (SM) - 64A | KITTYBREWSTER - 61A |
| Aug-56 | **5/56: B.GDNS - 53B** | EASTFIELD - 65A | KIPPS - 65E | EDINBURGH (SM) - 64A | KITTYBREWSTER - 61A | EDINBURGH (SM) - 64A | DUNFERMLINE - 62C | EDINBURGH (SM) - 64A | KITTYBREWSTER - 61A |
| Jan-57 | BOTANIC GARDENS - 53B | EASTFIELD - 65A | KIPPS - 65E | EDINBURGH (SM) - 64A | KITTYBREWSTER - 61A | EDINBURGH (SM) - 64A | DUNFERMLINE - 62C | EDINBURGH (SM) - 64A | KITTYBREWSTER - 61A |
| Aug-57 | **7/57: MBRO - 51D** | EASTFIELD - 65A | KIPPS - 65E | EDINBURGH (SM) - 64A | KITTYBREWSTER - 61A | EDINBURGH (SM) - 64A | DUNFERMLINE - 62C | EDINBURGH (SM) - 64A | KITTYBREWSTER - 61A |
| Jan-58 | **9/57: HTN - 52B** | EASTFIELD - 65A | KIPPS - 65E | EDINBURGH (SM) - 64A | KITTYBREWSTER - 61A | EDINBURGH (SM) - 64A | DUNFERMLINE - 62C | EDINBURGH (SM) - 64A | KITTYBREWSTER - 61A |
| Aug-58 | HEATON - 52B | EASTFIELD - 65A | KIPPS - 65E | EDINBURGH (SM) - 64A | KITTYBREWSTER - 61A | EDINBURGH (SM) - 64A | DUNFERMLINE - 62C | EDINBURGH (SM) - 64A | KITTYBREWSTER - 61A |
| Jan-59 | HEATON - 52B | EASTFIELD - 65A | KIPPS - 65E | EDINBURGH (SM) - 64A | KITTYBREWSTER - 61A | EDINBURGH (SM) - 64A | DUNFERMLINE - 62C | EDINBURGH (SM) - 64A | KITTYBREWSTER - 61A |
| Aug-59 | **6/59: DAIRY - 53A** | EASTFIELD - 65A | KIPPS - 65E | EDINBURGH (SM) - 64A | KITTYBREWSTER - 61A | **7/59: DY RD - 64C** | DUNFERMLINE - 62C | EDINBURGH (SM) - 64A | KITTYBREWSTER - 61A |
| Nov-59 | DAIRYCOATES - 53A | EASTFIELD - 65A | KIPPS - 65E | EDINBURGH (SM) - 64A | KITTYBREWSTER - 61A | DALRY ROAD - 64C | DUNFERMLINE - 62C | EDINBURGH (SM) - 64A | KITTYBREWSTER - 61A |
| Jan-60 | DAIRYCOATES - 53A | EASTFIELD - 65A | KIPPS - 65E | EDINBURGH (SM) - 64A | KITTYBREWSTER - 61A | DALRY ROAD - 64C | DUNFERMLINE - 62C | EDINBURGH (SM) - 64A | KITTYBREWSTER - 61A |
| Apr-60 | DAIRYCOATES - 50B | EASTFIELD - 65A | KIPPS - 65E | EDINBURGH (SM) - 64A | KITTYBREWSTER - 61A | DALRY ROAD - 64C | DUNFERMLINE - 62C | EDINBURGH (SM) - 64A | KITTYBREWSTER - 61A |
| Aug-60 | DAIRYCOATES - 50B | EASTFIELD - 65A | KIPPS - 65E | EDINBURGH (SM) - 64A | KITTYBREWSTER - 61A | DALRY ROAD - 64C | **6/60: KIPPS - 65E** | EDINBURGH (SM) - 64A | **8/60: W/D** |
| Nov-60 | DAIRYCOATES - 50B | EASTFIELD - 65A | KIPPS - 65E | EDINBURGH (SM) - 64A | KITTYBREWSTER - 61A | DALRY ROAD - 64C | KIPPS - 65E | EDINBURGH (SM) - 64A | |

| | 67672 | 67673 | 67674 | 67675 | 67676 | 67677 | 67678 | 67679 | 67680 |
|---|---|---|---|---|---|---|---|---|---|
| Aug-50 | DUNFERMLINE - 62C | MIDDLESBROUGH - 51D | KIPPS - 65E | STIRLING - 63B | PARKHEAD - 65C | NORWICH - 32A | PARKHEAD - 65C | NORWICH - 32A | EASTFIELD - 65A |
| Jan-51 | DUNFERMLINE - 62C | **11/50: HTN - 52B** | KIPPS - 65E | STIRLING - 63B | PARKHEAD - 65C | **2/51: MBRO - 51D** | PARKHEAD - 65C | NORWICH - 32A | EASTFIELD - 65A |
| Aug-51 | DUNFERMLINE - 62C | **7/51: MBRO - 51D** | KIPPS - 65E | STIRLING - 63B | PARKHEAD - 65C | MIDDLESBROUGH - 51D | PARKHEAD - 65C | NORWICH - 32A | EASTFIELD - 65A |
| Jan-52 | DUNFERMLINE - 62C | **9/51: HTN - 52B** | KIPPS - 65E | STIRLING - 63B | PARKHEAD - 65C | MIDDLESBROUGH - 51D | PARKHEAD - 65C | NORWICH - 32A | EASTFIELD - 65A |
| Aug-52 | DUNFERMLINE - 62C | HEATON - 52B | KIPPS - 65E | STIRLING - 63B | PARKHEAD - 65C | MIDDLESBROUGH - 51D | PARKHEAD - 65C | **6/52: PARK - 65C** | EASTFIELD - 65A |
| Jan-53 | DUNFERMLINE - 62C | HEATON - 52B | KIPPS - 65E | STIRLING - 63B | PARKHEAD - 65C | **10/52: HTN - 52B** | PARKHEAD - 65C | PARKHEAD - 65C | EASTFIELD - 65A |
| Aug-53 | DUNFERMLINE - 62C | HEATON - 52B | KIPPS - 65E | STIRLING - 63B | PARKHEAD - 65C | **5/53: MBRO - 51D** | PARKHEAD - 65C | PARKHEAD - 65C | EASTFIELD - 65A |
| Jan-54 | DUNFERMLINE - 62C | HEATON - 52B | KIPPS - 65E | STIRLING - 63B | PARKHEAD - 65C | MIDDLESBROUGH - 51D | PARKHEAD - 65C | PARKHEAD - 65C | EASTFIELD - 65A |
| Aug-54 | DUNFERMLINE - 62C | HEATON - 52B | KIPPS - 65E | STIRLING - 63B | PARKHEAD - 65C | MIDDLESBROUGH - 51D | PARKHEAD - 65C | PARKHEAD - 65C | EASTFIELD - 65A |
| Jan-55 | DUNFERMLINE - 62C | HEATON - 52B | KIPPS - 65E | STIRLING - 63B | PARKHEAD - 65C | MIDDLESBROUGH - 51D | PARKHEAD - 65C | PARKHEAD - 65C | EASTFIELD - 65A |
| Aug-55 | DUNFERMLINE - 62C | HEATON - 52B | KIPPS - 65E | STIRLING - 63B | PARKHEAD - 65C | MIDDLESBROUGH - 51D | PARKHEAD - 65C | PARKHEAD - 65C | EASTFIELD - 65A |
| Jan-56 | DUNFERMLINE - 62C | HEATON - 52B | KIPPS - 65E | STIRLING - 63B | PARKHEAD - 65C | MIDDLESBROUGH - 51D | PARKHEAD - 65C | PARKHEAD - 65C | EASTFIELD - 65A |
| Aug-56 | DUNFERMLINE - 62C | HEATON - 52B | KIPPS - 65E | STIRLING - 63B | PARKHEAD - 65C | **5/56: B.GDNS - 53B** | PARKHEAD - 65C | PARKHEAD - 65C | EASTFIELD - 65A |
| Jan-57 | DUNFERMLINE - 62C | **11/56: BLAY - 52C** | KIPPS - 65E | STIRLING - 63B | PARKHEAD - 65C | BOTANIC GARDENS - 53B | PARKHEAD - 65C | PARKHEAD - 65C | EASTFIELD - 65A |
| Aug-57 | DUNFERMLINE - 62C | **4/57: GHD - 52A** | KIPPS - 65E | STIRLING - 63B | PARKHEAD - 65C | **7/57: MBRO - 51D** | PARKHEAD - 65C | PARKHEAD - 65C | EASTFIELD - 65A |
| Jan-58 | DUNFERMLINE - 62C | GATESHEAD - 52A | KIPPS - 65E | STIRLING - 63B | PARKHEAD - 65C | **9/57: HTN - 52B** | PARKHEAD - 65C | PARKHEAD - 65C | EASTFIELD - 65A |
| Aug-58 | DUNFERMLINE - 62C | **9/58: SUND - 54A** | KIPPS - 65E | STIRLING - 63B | PARKHEAD - 65C | HEATON - 52B | PARKHEAD - 65C | PARKHEAD - 65C | EASTFIELD - 65A |
| Jan-59 | DUNFERMLINE - 62C | SUNDERLAND - 52G | KIPPS - 65E | **2/59: PARK - 65C** | PARKHEAD - 65C | HEATON - 52B | PARKHEAD - 65C | PARKHEAD - 65C | EASTFIELD - 65A |
| Aug-59 | DUNFERMLINE - 62C | **6/59: HTN - 52B** | KIPPS - 65E | PARKHEAD - 65C | PARKHEAD - 65C | **6/59: DAIRY - 53A** | PARKHEAD - 65C | PARKHEAD - 65C | EASTFIELD - 65A |
| Nov-59 | DUNFERMLINE - 62C | **9/59: SUND - 52G** | KIPPS - 65E | PARKHEAD - 65C | PARKHEAD - 65C | DAIRYCOATES - 53A | PARKHEAD - 65C | PARKHEAD - 65C | EASTFIELD - 65A |
| Jan-60 | DUNFERMLINE - 62C | SUNDERLAND - 52G | KIPPS - 65E | PARKHEAD - 65C | PARKHEAD - 65C | DAIRYCOATES - 53A | PARKHEAD - 65C | PARKHEAD - 65C | EASTFIELD - 65A |
| Apr-60 | DUNFERMLINE - 62C | SUNDERLAND - 52G | KIPPS - 65E | PARKHEAD - 65C | PARKHEAD - 65C | DAIRYCOATES - 50B | PARKHEAD - 65C | PARKHEAD - 65C | EASTFIELD - 65A |
| Aug-60 | DUNFERMLINE - 62C | SUNDERLAND - 52G | KIPPS - 65E | PARKHEAD - 65C | PARKHEAD - 65C | DAIRYCOATES - 50B | PARKHEAD - 65C | PARKHEAD - 65C | EASTFIELD - 65A |
| Nov-60 | DUNFERMLINE - 62C | SUNDERLAND - 52G | KIPPS - 65E | PARKHEAD - 65C | PARKHEAD - 65C | DAIRYCOATES - 50B | PARKHEAD - 65C | PARKHEAD - 65C | EASTFIELD - 65A |

| | 67681 | 67682 | 67683 | 67684 | 67685 | 67686 | 67687 | 67688 | 67689 |
|---|---|---|---|---|---|---|---|---|---|
| Aug-50 | PARKHEAD - 65C | STOCKTON - 51E | GATESHEAD - 52A | MIDDLESBROUGH - 51D | MIDDLESBROUGH - 51D | MIDDLESBROUGH - 51D | GATESHEAD - 52A | GATESHEAD - 52A | GATESHEAD - 52A |
| Jan-51 | PARKHEAD - 65C | **10/50: GHD - 52A** | GATESHEAD - 52A | MIDDLESBROUGH - 51D | MIDDLESBROUGH - 51D | MIDDLESBROUGH - 51D | GATESHEAD - 52A | GATESHEAD - 52A | GATESHEAD - 52A |
| Aug-51 | PARKHEAD - 65C | GATESHEAD - 52A | GATESHEAD - 52A | MIDDLESBROUGH - 51D | MIDDLESBROUGH - 51D | MIDDLESBROUGH - 51D | GATESHEAD - 52A | GATESHEAD - 52A | GATESHEAD - 52A |
| Jan-52 | PARKHEAD - 65C | GATESHEAD - 52A | GATESHEAD - 52A | MIDDLESBROUGH - 51D | MIDDLESBROUGH - 51D | MIDDLESBROUGH - 51D | GATESHEAD - 52A | GATESHEAD - 52A | GATESHEAD - 52A |
| Aug-52 | PARKHEAD - 65C | GATESHEAD - 52A | GATESHEAD - 52A | MIDDLESBROUGH - 51D | MIDDLESBROUGH - 51D | MIDDLESBROUGH - 51D | GATESHEAD - 52A | GATESHEAD - 52A | GATESHEAD - 52A |
| Jan-53 | PARKHEAD - 65C | GATESHEAD - 52A | GATESHEAD - 52A | MIDDLESBROUGH - 51D | MIDDLESBROUGH - 51D | MIDDLESBROUGH - 51D | GATESHEAD - 52A | GATESHEAD - 52A | GATESHEAD - 52A |
| Aug-53 | PARKHEAD - 65C | GATESHEAD - 52A | GATESHEAD - 52A | MIDDLESBROUGH - 51D | MIDDLESBROUGH - 51D | MIDDLESBROUGH - 51D | GATESHEAD - 52A | GATESHEAD - 52A | GATESHEAD - 52A |
| Jan-54 | PARKHEAD - 65C | GATESHEAD - 52A | GATESHEAD - 52A | MIDDLESBROUGH - 51D | MIDDLESBROUGH - 51D | MIDDLESBROUGH - 51D | GATESHEAD - 52A | GATESHEAD - 52A | GATESHEAD - 52A |
| Aug-54 | PARKHEAD - 65C | GATESHEAD - 52A | GATESHEAD - 52A | MIDDLESBROUGH - 51D | MIDDLESBROUGH - 51D | MIDDLESBROUGH - 51D | GATESHEAD - 52A | GATESHEAD - 52A | GATESHEAD - 52A |
| Jan-55 | PARKHEAD - 65C | **1/55: HEX - 52C** | GATESHEAD - 52A | MIDDLESBROUGH - 51D | MIDDLESBROUGH - 51D | MIDDLESBROUGH - 51D | **1/55: HEX - 52C** | GATESHEAD - 52A | GATESHEAD - 52A |
| Aug-55 | PARKHEAD - 65C | HEXHAM - 52C | GATESHEAD - 52A | MIDDLESBROUGH - 51D | MIDDLESBROUGH - 51D | MIDDLESBROUGH - 51D | HEXHAM - 52C | GATESHEAD - 52A | GATESHEAD - 52A |
| Jan-56 | PARKHEAD - 65C | HEXHAM - 52C | **12/55: BLAY - 52C** | MIDDLESBROUGH - 51D | MIDDLESBROUGH - 51D | MIDDLESBROUGH - 51D | HEXHAM - 52C | GATESHEAD - 52A | GATESHEAD - 52A |
| Aug-56 | PARKHEAD - 65C | HEXHAM - 52C | BLAYDON - 52C | **5/56: B.GDNS - 53B** | **6/56: B.GDNS - 53B** | **6/56: B.GDNS - 53B** | HEXHAM - 52C | GATESHEAD - 52A | GATESHEAD - 52A |
| Jan-57 | PARKHEAD - 65C | HEXHAM - 52C | **5/57: ALN - 52D** | BOTANIC GARDENS - 53B | BOTANIC GARDENS - 53B | BOTANIC GARDENS - 53B | **4/57: GHD - 52A** | GATESHEAD - 52A | GATESHEAD - 52A |
| Aug-57 | PARKHEAD - 65C | HEXHAM - 52C | **6/57: HTN - 52B** | **7/57: MBRO - 51D** | **7/57: HTN - 52B** | BOTANIC GARDENS - 53B | GATESHEAD - 52A | GATESHEAD - 52A | GATESHEAD - 52A |
| Jan-58 | PARKHEAD - 65C | HEXHAM - 52C | HEATON - 52B | **9/57: HTN - 52B** | HEATON - 52B | BOTANIC GARDENS - 53B | GATESHEAD - 52A | GATESHEAD - 52A | GATESHEAD - 52A |
| Aug-58 | PARKHEAD - 65C | HEXHAM - 52C | HEATON - 52B | HEATON - 52B | HEATON - 52B | BOTANIC GARDENS - 53B | GATESHEAD - 52A | GATESHEAD - 52A | GATESHEAD - 52A |
| Jan-59 | PARKHEAD - 65C | **2/59: B. GDNS - 53B** | HEATON - 52B | HEATON - 52B | HEATON - 52B | BOTANIC GARDENS - 53B | GATESHEAD - 52A | GATESHEAD - 52A | GATESHEAD - 52A |
| Aug-59 | PARKHEAD - 65C | **6/59: DAIRY - 53A** | HEATON - 52B | **6/59: DAIRY - 53A** | HEATON - 52B | **6/59: DAIRY - 53A** | GATESHEAD - 52A | GATESHEAD - 52A | GATESHEAD - 52A |
| Nov-59 | PARKHEAD - 65C | DAIRYCOATES - 53A | HEATON - 52B | DAIRYCOATES - 53A | HEATON - 52B | DAIRYCOATES - 53A | GATESHEAD - 52A | GATESHEAD - 52A | GATESHEAD - 52A |
| Jan-60 | PARKHEAD - 65C | DAIRYCOATES - 53A | HEATON - 52B | DAIRYCOATES - 53A | HEATON - 52B | DAIRYCOATES - 53A | GATESHEAD - 52A | GATESHEAD - 52A | GATESHEAD - 52A |
| Apr-60 | PARKHEAD - 65C | DAIRYCOATES - 50B | HEATON - 52B | DAIRYCOATES - 50B | HEATON - 52B | DAIRYCOATES - 50B | GATESHEAD - 52A | GATESHEAD - 52A | GATESHEAD - 52A |
| Aug-60 | PARKHEAD - 65C | DAIRYCOATES - 50B | HEATON - 52B | DAIRYCOATES - 50B | HEATON - 52B | DAIRYCOATES - 50B | GATESHEAD - 52A | GATESHEAD - 52A | GATESHEAD - 52A |
| Nov-60 | PARKHEAD - 65C | DAIRYCOATES - 50B | HEATON - 52B | DAIRYCOATES - 50B | HEATON - 52B | DAIRYCOATES - 50B | GATESHEAD - 52A | GATESHEAD - 52A | GATESHEAD - 52A |

| | 67690 | 67691 | L1 2-6-4T (1945)<br>67701 | 67702 | 67703 | 67704 | 67705 | 67706 | 67707 |
|---|---|---|---|---|---|---|---|---|---|
| Aug-50 | GATESHEAD - 52A | MIDDLESBROUGH - 51D | STRATFORD - 30A | IPSWICH - 32B | IPSWICH - 32B | IPSWICH - 32B | IPSWICH - 32B | IPSWICH - 32B | NEASDEN - 34E |
| Jan-51 | GATESHEAD - 52A | MIDDLESBROUGH - 51D | **4/51: DARL - 51A** | IPSWICH - 32B | IPSWICH - 32B | IPSWICH - 32B | IPSWICH - 32B | IPSWICH - 32B | **12/50: HSEY - 34B** |
| Aug-51 | GATESHEAD - 52A | MIDDLESBROUGH - 51D | **5/51: STRAT - 30A** | IPSWICH - 32B | IPSWICH - 32B | **9/51: LOW - 32C** | IPSWICH - 32B | IPSWICH - 32B | HORNSEY - 34B |
| Jan-52 | GATESHEAD - 52A | MIDDLESBROUGH - 51D | STRATFORD - 30A | IPSWICH - 32B | IPSWICH - 32B | **10/51: NOR - 32A** | IPSWICH - 32B | IPSWICH - 32B | **12/51: NEAS - 34E** |
| Aug-52 | GATESHEAD - 52A | MIDDLESBROUGH - 51D | STRATFORD - 30A | IPSWICH - 32B | IPSWICH - 32B | **6/52: IPS - 32B** | IPSWICH - 32B | IPSWICH - 32B | NEASDEN - 34E |
| Jan-53 | GATESHEAD - 52A | MIDDLESBROUGH - 51D | STRATFORD - 30A | IPSWICH - 32B | IPSWICH - 32B | **9/52: LOW - 32C** | IPSWICH - 32B | IPSWICH - 32B | **2/52: NOR - 32A** |
| Aug-53 | GATESHEAD - 52A | MIDDLESBROUGH - 51D | STRATFORD - 30A | IPSWICH - 32B | IPSWICH - 32B | LOWESTOFT - 32C | IPSWICH - 32B | IPSWICH - 32B | NORWICH - 32A |
| Jan-54 | GATESHEAD - 52A | MIDDLESBROUGH - 51D | STRATFORD - 30A | IPSWICH - 32B | IPSWICH - 32B | **2/54: YAR(ST) - 32D** | IPSWICH - 32B | IPSWICH - 32B | **2/54: YAR(ST) - 32D** |
| Aug-54 | GATESHEAD - 52A | MIDDLESBROUGH - 51D | STRATFORD - 30A | IPSWICH - 32B | IPSWICH - 32B | **6/54: IPS - 32B** | IPSWICH - 32B | IPSWICH - 32B | **4/54: NOR - 32A** |
| Jan-55 | GATESHEAD - 52A | MIDDLESBROUGH - 51D | STRATFORD - 30A | IPSWICH - 32B | IPSWICH - 32B | **10/54: LOW - 32C** | IPSWICH - 32B | IPSWICH - 32B | NORWICH - 32A |
| Aug-55 | GATESHEAD - 52A | MIDDLESBROUGH - 51D | STRATFORD - 30A | IPSWICH - 32B | IPSWICH - 32B | LOWESTOFT - 32C | **11/55: YAR(ST) - 32D** | IPSWICH - 32B | **11/55: YAR(ST) - 32D** |
| Jan-56 | GATESHEAD - 52A | MIDDLESBROUGH - 51D | STRATFORD - 30A | IPSWICH - 32B | IPSWICH - 32B | LOWESTOFT - 32C | **1/56: IPS - 32B** | IPSWICH - 32B | **1/56: NOR - 32A** |
| Aug-56 | GATESHEAD - 52A | **5/56: B.GDNS - 53B** | STRATFORD - 30A | IPSWICH - 32B | IPSWICH - 32B | LOWESTOFT - 32C | IPSWICH - 32B | IPSWICH - 32B | NORWICH - 32A |
| Jan-57 | GATESHEAD - 52A | BOTANIC GARDENS - 53B | STRATFORD - 30A | **2/57: YAR(ST) - 32D** | IPSWICH - 32B | LOWESTOFT - 32C | IPSWICH - 32B | **2/57: YAR(ST) - 32D** | NORWICH - 32A |
| Aug-57 | GATESHEAD - 52A | **7/57: HTN - 52B** | STRATFORD - 30A | **6/57: IPS - 32B** | IPSWICH - 32B | LOWESTOFT - 32C | IPSWICH - 32B | **6/57: IPS - 32B** | NORWICH - 32A |
| Jan-58 | GATESHEAD - 52A | HEATON - 52B | STRATFORD - 30A | IPSWICH - 32B | IPSWICH - 32B | LOWESTOFT - 32C | IPSWICH - 32B | IPSWICH - 32B | NORWICH - 32A |
| Aug-58 | GATESHEAD - 52A | HEATON - 52B | STRATFORD - 30A | IPSWICH - 32B | IPSWICH - 32B | LOWESTOFT - 32C | IPSWICH - 32B | IPSWICH - 32B | **9/58: LOW - 32C** |
| Jan-59 | GATESHEAD - 52A | HEATON - 52B | **1/59: CAMB - 30A** | **12/58: STRAT - 30A** | **12/58: STRAT - 30A** | **12/58: STRAT - 30A** | IPSWICH - 32B | **12/58: STRAT - 30A** | LOWESTOFT - 32C |
| Aug-59 | GATESHEAD - 52A | HEATON - 52B | **9/59: LOW - 32C** | STRATFORD - 30A | STRATFORD - 30A | STRATFORD - 30A | IPSWICH - 32B | STRATFORD - 30A | LOWESTOFT - 32C |
| Nov-59 | GATESHEAD - 52A | HEATON - 52B | LOWESTOFT - 32C | STRATFORD - 30A | STRATFORD - 30A | STRATFORD - 30A | **10/59: STRAT - 30A** | STRATFORD - 30A | LOWESTOFT - 32C |
| Jan-60 | GATESHEAD - 52A | HEATON - 52B | **12/59: STRAT - 30A** | STRATFORD - 30A | STRATFORD - 30A | STRATFORD - 30A | STRATFORD - 30A | STRATFORD - 30A | **2/60: COLW - 40E** |
| Apr-60 | GATESHEAD - 52A | HEATON - 52B | STRATFORD - 30A | STRATFORD - 30A | STRATFORD - 30A | STRATFORD - 30A | STRATFORD - 30A | STRATFORD - 30A | COLWICK - 40E |
| Aug-60 | GATESHEAD - 52A | HEATON - 52B | STRATFORD - 30A | STRATFORD - 30A | STRATFORD - 30A | STRATFORD - 30A | STRATFORD - 30A | STRATFORD - 30A | COLWICK - 40E |
| Nov-60 | GATESHEAD - 52A | HEATON - 52B | STRATFORD - 30A | **11/60: W/D** | STRATFORD - 30A | STRATFORD - 30A | STRATFORD - 30A | STRATFORD - 30A | COLWICK - 40E |

| | 67708 | 67709 | 67710 | 67711 | 67712 | 67713 | 67714 | 67715 | 67716 |
|---|---|---|---|---|---|---|---|---|---|
| Aug-50 | IPSWICH - 32B | IPSWICH - 32B | IPSWICH - 32B | IPSWICH - 32B | STRATFORD - 30A | STRATFORD - 30A | NEASDEN - 34E | NEASDEN - 34E | IPSWICH - 32B |
| Jan-51 | IPSWICH - 32B | IPSWICH - 32B | **4/51: DARL - 51A** | IPSWICH - 32B | STRATFORD - 30A | STRATFORD - 30A | NEASDEN - 34E | NEASDEN - 34E | IPSWICH - 32B |
| Aug-51 | IPSWICH - 32B | IPSWICH - 32B | **6/51: IPS - 32B** | IPSWICH - 32B | STRATFORD - 30A | STRATFORD - 30A | NEASDEN - 34E | NEASDEN - 34E | IPSWICH - 32B |
| Jan-52 | **10/51: NOR - 32A** | IPSWICH - 32B | IPSWICH - 32B | IPSWICH - 32B | STRATFORD - 30A | STRATFORD - 30A | NEASDEN - 34E | NEASDEN - 34E | IPSWICH - 32B |
| Aug-52 | **6/52: IPS - 32B** | IPSWICH - 32B | IPSWICH - 32B | IPSWICH - 32B | STRATFORD - 30A | STRATFORD - 30A | NEASDEN - 34E | NEASDEN - 34E | IPSWICH - 32B |
| Jan-53 | IPSWICH - 32B | IPSWICH - 32B | IPSWICH - 32B | IPSWICH - 32B | STRATFORD - 30A | STRATFORD - 30A | **2/53: NOR - 32A** | **2/53: LOW - 32C** | IPSWICH - 32B |
| Aug-53 | IPSWICH - 32B | IPSWICH - 32B | IPSWICH - 32B | IPSWICH - 32B | STRATFORD - 30A | STRATFORD - 30A | **7/53: LOW - 32C** | **7/53: IPS - 32B** | IPSWICH - 32B |
| Jan-54 | IPSWICH - 32B | **2/54: YAR(ST) - 32D** | **2/54: YAR(ST) - 32D** | IPSWICH - 32B | STRATFORD - 30A | STRATFORD - 30A | LOWESTOFT - 32C | IPSWICH - 32B | IPSWICH - 32B |
| Aug-54 | IPSWICH - 32B | **4/54: IPS - 32B** | **4/54: IPS - 32B** | IPSWICH - 32B | STRATFORD - 30A | STRATFORD - 30A | LOWESTOFT - 32C | IPSWICH - 32B | IPSWICH - 32B |
| Jan-55 | IPSWICH - 32B | IPSWICH - 32B | IPSWICH - 32B | IPSWICH - 32B | STRATFORD - 30A | STRATFORD - 30A | LOWESTOFT - 32C | IPSWICH - 32B | IPSWICH - 32B |
| Aug-55 | IPSWICH - 32B | IPSWICH - 32B | IPSWICH - 32B | IPSWICH - 32B | STRATFORD - 30A | STRATFORD - 30A | LOWESTOFT - 32C | IPSWICH - 32B | IPSWICH - 32B |
| Jan-56 | IPSWICH - 32B | IPSWICH - 32B | IPSWICH - 32B | IPSWICH - 32B | STRATFORD - 30A | STRATFORD - 30A | **3/56: NOR - 32A** | IPSWICH - 32B | IPSWICH - 32B |
| Aug-56 | IPSWICH - 32B | IPSWICH - 32B | IPSWICH - 32B | IPSWICH - 32B | STRATFORD - 30A | STRATFORD - 30A | NORWICH - 32A | IPSWICH - 32B | IPSWICH - 32B |
| Jan-57 | IPSWICH - 32B | IPSWICH - 32B | **2/57: LOW - 32C** | IPSWICH - 32B | STRATFORD - 30A | STRATFORD - 30A | NORWICH - 32A | IPSWICH - 32B | IPSWICH - 32B |
| Aug-57 | IPSWICH - 32B | **9/57: LOW - 32C** | **6/57: IPS - 32B** | **9/57: LOW - 32C** | STRATFORD - 30A | STRATFORD - 30A | NORWICH - 32A | IPSWICH - 32B | IPSWICH - 32B |
| Jan-58 | IPSWICH - 32B | LOWESTOFT - 32C | **9/57: LOW - 32C** | LOWESTOFT - 32C | STRATFORD - 30A | STRATFORD - 30A | NORWICH - 32A | IPSWICH - 32B | IPSWICH - 32B |
| Aug-58 | **10/58: LOW - 32C** | LOWESTOFT - 32C | **6/58: IPS - 32B** | **6/58: IPS - 32B** | STRATFORD - 30A | STRATFORD - 30A | NORWICH - 32A | IPSWICH - 32B | IPSWICH - 32B |
| Jan-59 | **12/58: STRAT - 30A** | **12/58: STRAT - 30A** | IPSWICH - 32B | IPSWICH - 32B | **1/59: CAMB - 31A** | STRATFORD - 30A | NORWICH - 32A | **12/58: STRAT - 30A** | **12/58: STRAT - 30A** |
| Aug-59 | STRATFORD - 30A | STRATFORD - 30A | **6/59: LOW - 32C** | IPSWICH - 32B | CAMBRIDGE - 31A | **4/59: CAMB - 31A** | NORWICH - 32A | STRATFORD - 30A | STRATFORD - 30A |
| Nov-59 | STRATFORD - 30A | STRATFORD - 30A | LOWESTOFT - 32C | **10/59: STRAT - 30A** | CAMBRIDGE - 31A | CAMBRIDGE - 31A | **12/59: STRAT - 30A** | STRATFORD - 30A | STRATFORD - 30A |
| Jan-60 | STRATFORD - 30A | STRATFORD - 30A | **2/60: KX - 34A** | STRATFORD - 30A | CAMBRIDGE - 31A | CAMBRIDGE - 31A | STRATFORD - 30A | STRATFORD - 30A | STRATFORD - 30A |
| Apr-60 | STRATFORD - 30A | STRATFORD - 30A | **3/60: COLW - 40E** | STRATFORD - 30A | CAMBRIDGE - 31A | CAMBRIDGE - 31A | STRATFORD - 30A | STRATFORD - 30A | STRATFORD - 30A |
| Aug-60 | STRATFORD - 30A | STRATFORD - 30A | COLWICK - 40E | STRATFORD - 30A | CAMBRIDGE - 31A | CAMBRIDGE - 31A | STRATFORD - 30A | STRATFORD - 30A | STRATFORD - 30A |
| Nov-60 | STRATFORD - 30A | STRATFORD - 30A | COLWICK - 40E | STRATFORD - 30A | CAMBRIDGE - 31A | CAMBRIDGE - 31A | STRATFORD - 30A | STRATFORD - 30A | STRATFORD - 30A |

| | 67717 | 67718 | 67719 | 67720 | 67721 | 67722 | 67723 | 67724 | 67725 |
|---|---|---|---|---|---|---|---|---|---|
| Aug-50 | NEASDEN - 34E | NEASDEN - 34E | IPSWICH - 32B | NEASDEN - 34E | STRATFORD - 30A | STRATFORD - 30A | STRATFORD - 30A | STRATFORD - 30A | STRATFORD - 30A |
| Jan-51 | NEASDEN - 34E | NEASDEN - 34E | IPSWICH - 32B | NEASDEN - 34E | STRATFORD - 30A | STRATFORD - 30A | STRATFORD - 30A | STRATFORD - 30A | STRATFORD - 30A |
| Aug-51 | NEASDEN - 34E | NEASDEN - 34E | **9/51: LOW - 32C** | NEASDEN - 34E | STRATFORD - 30A | STRATFORD - 30A | STRATFORD - 30A | STRATFORD - 30A | STRATFORD - 30A |
| Jan-52 | NEASDEN - 34E | NEASDEN - 34E | LOWESTOFT - 32C | NEASDEN - 34E | STRATFORD - 30A | STRATFORD - 30A | STRATFORD - 30A | STRATFORD - 30A | STRATFORD - 30A |
| Aug-52 | NEASDEN - 34E | NEASDEN - 34E | **7/52: IPS - 32B** | NEASDEN - 34E | STRATFORD - 30A | STRATFORD - 30A | STRATFORD - 30A | STRATFORD - 30A | STRATFORD - 30A |
| Jan-53 | **2/53: LOW - 32C** | **2/53: NOR - 32A** | **9/52: LOW - 32C** | **2/53: IPS - 32B** | STRATFORD - 30A | STRATFORD - 30A | STRATFORD - 30A | **3/53: HIT - 34D** | STRATFORD - 30A |
| Aug-53 | LOWESTOFT - 32C | **5/53: KX - 34A** | **5/53: IPS - 32B** | **5/53: KX - 34A** | STRATFORD - 30A | STRATFORD - 30A | STRATFORD - 30A | **5/53: STRAT - 30A** | STRATFORD - 30A |
| Jan-54 | LOWESTOFT - 32C | KINGS CROSS - 34A | IPSWICH - 32B | KINGS CROSS - 34A | STRATFORD - 30A | STRATFORD - 30A | STRATFORD - 30A | STRATFORD - 30A | STRATFORD - 30A |
| Aug-54 | LOWESTOFT - 32C | KINGS CROSS - 34A | IPSWICH - 32B | KINGS CROSS - 34A | STRATFORD - 30A | STRATFORD - 30A | STRATFORD - 30A | STRATFORD - 30A | STRATFORD - 30A |
| Jan-55 | **6/55: IPS - 32B** | **1/55: HIT - 34D** | IPSWICH - 32B | **3/55: STRAT - 30A** | STRATFORD - 30A | STRATFORD - 30A | STRATFORD - 30A | STRATFORD - 30A | STRATFORD - 30A |
| Aug-55 | **9/55: LOW - 32C** | **3/55: STRAT - 30A** | IPSWICH - 32B | STRATFORD - 30A | STRATFORD - 30A | STRATFORD - 30A | STRATFORD - 30A | STRATFORD - 30A | STRATFORD - 30A |
| Jan-56 | **1/56: NOR - 32A** | STRATFORD - 30A | IPSWICH - 32B | STRATFORD - 30A | STRATFORD - 30A | STRATFORD - 30A | STRATFORD - 30A | STRATFORD - 30A | STRATFORD - 30A |
| Aug-56 | NORWICH - 32A | STRATFORD - 30A | IPSWICH - 32B | STRATFORD - 30A | STRATFORD - 30A | STRATFORD - 30A | STRATFORD - 30A | STRATFORD - 30A | STRATFORD - 30A |
| Jan-57 | NORWICH - 32A | STRATFORD - 30A | IPSWICH - 32B | STRATFORD - 30A | STRATFORD - 30A | STRATFORD - 30A | STRATFORD - 30A | STRATFORD - 30A | STRATFORD - 30A |
| Aug-57 | NORWICH - 32A | STRATFORD - 30A | IPSWICH - 32B | STRATFORD - 30A | STRATFORD - 30A | STRATFORD - 30A | STRATFORD - 30A | STRATFORD - 30A | STRATFORD - 30A |
| Jan-58 | NORWICH - 32A | STRATFORD - 30A | IPSWICH - 32B | STRATFORD - 30A | STRATFORD - 30A | STRATFORD - 30A | STRATFORD - 30A | STRATFORD - 30A | STRATFORD - 30A |
| Aug-58 | NORWICH - 32A | STRATFORD - 30A | IPSWICH - 32B | STRATFORD - 30A | STRATFORD - 30A | STRATFORD - 30A | STRATFORD - 30A | STRATFORD - 30A | STRATFORD - 30A |
| Jan-59 | NORWICH - 32A | **1/59: CAMB - 31A** | IPSWICH - 32B | **1/59: CAMB - 31A** | **1/59: CAMB - 31A** | **1/59: CAMB - 31A** | **1/59: CAMB - 31A** | STRATFORD - 30A | STRATFORD - 30A |
| Aug-59 | NORWICH - 32A | CAMBRIDGE - 31A | IPSWICH - 32B | CAMBRIDGE - 31A | CAMBRIDGE - 31A | CAMBRIDGE - 31A | CAMBRIDGE - 31A | STRATFORD - 30A | STRATFORD - 30A |
| Nov-59 | NORWICH - 32A | CAMBRIDGE - 31A | IPSWICH - 32B | CAMBRIDGE - 31A | CAMBRIDGE - 31A | CAMBRIDGE - 31A | CAMBRIDGE - 31A | STRATFORD - 30A | STRATFORD - 30A |
| Jan-60 | NORWICH - 32A | CAMBRIDGE - 31A | **2/60: KX - 34A** | CAMBRIDGE - 31A | CAMBRIDGE - 31A | CAMBRIDGE - 31A | CAMBRIDGE - 31A | STRATFORD - 30A | STRATFORD - 30A |
| Apr-60 | NORWICH - 32A | CAMBRIDGE - 31A | KINGS CROSS - 34A | CAMBRIDGE - 31A | CAMBRIDGE - 31A | CAMBRIDGE - 31A | CAMBRIDGE - 31A | STRATFORD - 30A | STRATFORD - 30A |
| Aug-60 | NORWICH - 32A | CAMBRIDGE - 31A | KINGS CROSS - 34A | CAMBRIDGE - 31A | CAMBRIDGE - 31A | CAMBRIDGE - 31A | CAMBRIDGE - 31A | STRATFORD - 30A | STRATFORD - 30A |
| Nov-60 | NORWICH - 32A | CAMBRIDGE - 31A | **11/60: COLW - 40E** | CAMBRIDGE - 31A | CAMBRIDGE - 31A | CAMBRIDGE - 31A | CAMBRIDGE - 31A | STRATFORD - 30A | STRATFORD - 30A |

| | 67726 | 67727 | 67728 | 67729 | 67730 | 67731 | 67732 | 67733 | 67734 |
|---|---|---|---|---|---|---|---|---|---|
| Aug-50 | STRATFORD - 30A | STRATFORD - 30A | STRATFORD - 30A | STRATFORD - 30A | STRATFORD - 30A | STRATFORD - 30A | STRATFORD - 30A | STRATFORD - 30A | STRATFORD - 30A |
| Jan-51 | STRATFORD - 30A | **4/51: DARL - 51A** | STRATFORD - 30A | STRATFORD - 30A | STRATFORD - 30A | STRATFORD - 30A | STRATFORD - 30A | STRATFORD - 30A | STRATFORD - 30A |
| Aug-51 | STRATFORD - 30A | **5/51: STRAT - 30A** | STRATFORD - 30A | STRATFORD - 30A | STRATFORD - 30A | STRATFORD - 30A | STRATFORD - 30A | STRATFORD - 30A | STRATFORD - 30A |
| Jan-52 | STRATFORD - 30A | STRATFORD - 30A | STRATFORD - 30A | STRATFORD - 30A | STRATFORD - 30A | STRATFORD - 30A | STRATFORD - 30A | STRATFORD - 30A | STRATFORD - 30A |
| Aug-52 | STRATFORD - 30A | STRATFORD - 30A | STRATFORD - 30A | STRATFORD - 30A | STRATFORD - 30A | STRATFORD - 30A | STRATFORD - 30A | STRATFORD - 30A | STRATFORD - 30A |
| Jan-53 | STRATFORD - 30A | STRATFORD - 30A | STRATFORD - 30A | STRATFORD - 30A | STRATFORD - 30A | STRATFORD - 30A | STRATFORD - 30A | STRATFORD - 30A | STRATFORD - 30A |
| Aug-53 | STRATFORD - 30A | STRATFORD - 30A | STRATFORD - 30A | **9/53: TOTON - 18A** | STRATFORD - 30A | STRATFORD - 30A | STRATFORD - 30A | STRATFORD - 30A | STRATFORD - 30A |
| Jan-54 | STRATFORD - 30A | STRATFORD - 30A | STRATFORD - 30A | **10/53: STRAT - 30A** | STRATFORD - 30A | STRATFORD - 30A | STRATFORD - 30A | STRATFORD - 30A | STRATFORD - 30A |
| Aug-54 | STRATFORD - 30A | STRATFORD - 30A | STRATFORD - 30A | STRATFORD - 30A | STRATFORD - 30A | STRATFORD - 30A | STRATFORD - 30A | STRATFORD - 30A | STRATFORD - 30A |
| Jan-55 | STRATFORD - 30A | STRATFORD - 30A | STRATFORD - 30A | STRATFORD - 30A | STRATFORD - 30A | STRATFORD - 30A | STRATFORD - 30A | STRATFORD - 30A | STRATFORD - 30A |
| Aug-55 | STRATFORD - 30A | STRATFORD - 30A | STRATFORD - 30A | STRATFORD - 30A | STRATFORD - 30A | STRATFORD - 30A | STRATFORD - 30A | STRATFORD - 30A | STRATFORD - 30A |
| Jan-56 | STRATFORD - 30A | STRATFORD - 30A | STRATFORD - 30A | STRATFORD - 30A | STRATFORD - 30A | STRATFORD - 30A | STRATFORD - 30A | STRATFORD - 30A | STRATFORD - 30A |
| Aug-56 | STRATFORD - 30A | STRATFORD - 30A | STRATFORD - 30A | STRATFORD - 30A | STRATFORD - 30A | STRATFORD - 30A | STRATFORD - 30A | STRATFORD - 30A | STRATFORD - 30A |
| Jan-57 | STRATFORD - 30A | STRATFORD - 30A | **11/56: YAR(ST) - 32D** | STRATFORD - 30A | STRATFORD - 30A | STRATFORD - 30A | STRATFORD - 30A | STRATFORD - 30A | STRATFORD - 30A |
| Aug-57 | STRATFORD - 30A | STRATFORD - 30A | YARMOUTH (ST) - 32D | STRATFORD - 30A | STRATFORD - 30A | STRATFORD - 30A | STRATFORD - 30A | STRATFORD - 30A | STRATFORD - 30A |
| Jan-58 | STRATFORD - 30A | STRATFORD - 30A | YARMOUTH (ST) - 32D | STRATFORD - 30A | STRATFORD - 30A | STRATFORD - 30A | STRATFORD - 30A | STRATFORD - 30A | STRATFORD - 30A |
| Aug-58 | STRATFORD - 30A | STRATFORD - 30A | YARMOUTH (ST) - 32D | STRATFORD - 30A | STRATFORD - 30A | STRATFORD - 30A | STRATFORD - 30A | STRATFORD - 30A | STRATFORD - 30A |
| Jan-59 | STRATFORD - 30A | STRATFORD - 30A | **12/58: STRAT - 30A** | STRATFORD - 30A | STRATFORD - 30A | STRATFORD - 30A | STRATFORD - 30A | **1/59: CAMB - 31A** | **1/59: CAMB - 31A** |
| Aug-59 | STRATFORD - 30A | STRATFORD - 30A | STRATFORD - 30A | STRATFORD - 30A | STRATFORD - 30A | STRATFORD - 30A | STRATFORD - 30A | **6/59: NOR - 32A** | CAMBRIDGE - 31A |
| Nov-59 | STRATFORD - 30A | STRATFORD - 30A | STRATFORD - 30A | STRATFORD - 30A | STRATFORD - 30A | STRATFORD - 30A | STRATFORD - 30A | NORWICH - 32A | CAMBRIDGE - 31A |
| Jan-60 | STRATFORD - 30A | STRATFORD - 30A | STRATFORD - 30A | STRATFORD - 30A | STRATFORD - 30A | STRATFORD - 30A | STRATFORD - 30A | **1/60: KX - 34A** | CAMBRIDGE - 31A |
| Apr-60 | STRATFORD - 30A | **3/60: COLW - 40E** | STRATFORD - 30A | STRATFORD - 30A | STRATFORD - 30A | STRATFORD - 30A | STRATFORD - 30A | KINGS CROSS - 34A | CAMBRIDGE - 31A |
| Aug-60 | STRATFORD - 30A | COLWICK - 40E | STRATFORD - 30A | STRATFORD - 30A | STRATFORD - 30A | STRATFORD - 30A | STRATFORD - 30A | KINGS CROSS - 34A | CAMBRIDGE - 31A |
| Nov-60 | STRATFORD - 30A | COLWICK - 40E | STRATFORD - 30A | STRATFORD - 30A | STRATFORD - 30A | STRATFORD - 30A | STRATFORD - 30A | KINGS CROSS - 34A | CAMBRIDGE - 31A |

| | 67735 | 67736 | 67737 | 67738 | 67739 | 67740 | 67741 | 67742 | 67743 |
|---|---|---|---|---|---|---|---|---|---|
| Aug-50 | STRATFORD - 30A | STRATFORD - 30A | STRATFORD - 30A | STRATFORD - 30A | STRATFORD - 30A | HITCHIN - 34D | HITCHIN - 34D | DARLINGTON - 51A | HITCHIN - 34D |
| Jan-51 | STRATFORD - 30A | STRATFORD - 30A | STRATFORD - 30A | STRATFORD - 30A | **4/51: DARL - 51A** | HITCHIN - 34D | HITCHIN - 34D | DARLINGTON - 51A | HITCHIN - 34D |
| Aug-51 | STRATFORD - 30A | STRATFORD - 30A | STRATFORD - 30A | STRATFORD - 30A | **5/51: STRAT - 30A** | HITCHIN - 34D | HITCHIN - 34D | DARLINGTON - 51A | HITCHIN - 34D |
| Jan-52 | STRATFORD - 30A | STRATFORD - 30A | STRATFORD - 30A | STRATFORD - 30A | STRATFORD - 30A | HITCHIN - 34D | HITCHIN - 34D | DARLINGTON - 51A | HITCHIN - 34D |
| Aug-52 | STRATFORD - 30A | STRATFORD - 30A | STRATFORD - 30A | STRATFORD - 30A | STRATFORD - 30A | HITCHIN - 34D | HITCHIN - 34D | DARLINGTON - 51A | HITCHIN - 34D |
| Jan-53 | STRATFORD - 30A | **3/53: HIT - 34D** | STRATFORD - 30A | STRATFORD - 30A | **5/53: KX - 34A** | HITCHIN - 34D | HITCHIN - 34D | DARLINGTON - 51A | HITCHIN - 34D |
| Aug-53 | STRATFORD - 30A | **5/53: STRAT - 30A** | **9/53: TOTON - 18A** | STRATFORD - 30A | **7/53: IPS - 32B** | **7/53: NEAS - 34E** | HITCHIN - 34D | DARLINGTON - 51A | HITCHIN - 34D |
| Jan-54 | STRATFORD - 30A | STRATFORD - 30A | **10/53: STRAT - 30A** | STRATFORD - 30A | **10/53: NOR - 32A** | NEASDEN - 34E | HITCHIN - 34D | DARLINGTON - 51A | HITCHIN - 34D |
| Aug-54 | STRATFORD - 30A | STRATFORD - 30A | STRATFORD - 30A | STRATFORD - 30A | NORWICH - 32A | NEASDEN - 34E | HITCHIN - 34D | DARLINGTON - 51A | HITCHIN - 34D |
| Jan-55 | STRATFORD - 30A | STRATFORD - 30A | STRATFORD - 30A | STRATFORD - 30A | NORWICH - 32A | NEASDEN - 34E | HITCHIN - 34D | DARLINGTON - 51A | HITCHIN - 34D |
| Aug-55 | STRATFORD - 30A | STRATFORD - 30A | STRATFORD - 30A | STRATFORD - 30A | **8/55: IPS - 32B** | NEASDEN - 34E | HITCHIN - 34D | DARLINGTON - 51A | HITCHIN - 34D |
| Jan-56 | STRATFORD - 30A | STRATFORD - 30A | STRATFORD - 30A | STRATFORD - 30A | **9/55: NOR - 32A** | NEASDEN - 34E | HITCHIN - 34D | DARLINGTON - 51A | HITCHIN - 34D |
| Aug-56 | STRATFORD - 30A | STRATFORD - 30A | STRATFORD - 30A | STRATFORD - 30A | **1/56: IPS - 32B** | NEASDEN - 34E | HITCHIN - 34D | DARLINGTON - 51A | **7/56: NEAS - 34E** |
| Jan-57 | STRATFORD - 30A | **11/56: YAR(ST) - 32D** | STRATFORD - 30A | STRATFORD - 30A | IPSWICH - 32B | NEASDEN - 34E | HITCHIN - 34D | DARLINGTON - 51A | NEASDEN - 34E |
| Aug-57 | STRATFORD - 30A | YARMOUTH (ST) - 32D | STRATFORD - 30A | **7/57: LOW - 32C** | IPSWICH - 32B | NEASDEN - 34E | HITCHIN - 34D | DARLINGTON - 51A | NEASDEN - 34E |
| Jan-58 | STRATFORD - 30A | YARMOUTH (ST) - 32D | STRATFORD - 30A | LOWESTOFT - 32C | IPSWICH - 32B | NEASDEN - 34E | HITCHIN - 34D | DARLINGTON - 51A | NEASDEN - 34E |
| Aug-58 | STRATFORD - 30A | YARMOUTH (ST) - 32D | STRATFORD - 30A | LOWESTOFT - 32C | IPSWICH - 32B | **6/58: WILL - 1A** | HITCHIN - 34D | DARLINGTON - 51A | NEASDEN - 14D |
| Jan-59 | STRATFORD - 30A | **12/58: STRAT - 30A** | STRATFORD - 30A | LOWESTOFT - 32C | **12/58: STRAT - 30A** | **9/58: W. HSE - 2F** | HITCHIN - 34D | DARLINGTON - 51A | **10/58: GORT - 9G** |
| Aug-59 | STRATFORD - 30A | STRATFORD - 30A | STRATFORD - 30A | LOWESTOFT - 32C | STRATFORD - 30A | WOODFORD HALSE - 2F | **6/59: COLW - 40E** | DARLINGTON - 51A | GORTON - 9G |
| Nov-59 | STRATFORD - 30A | STRATFORD - 30A | STRATFORD - 30A | LOWESTOFT - 32C | STRATFORD - 30A | WOODFORD HALSE - 2F | COLWICK - 40E | DARLINGTON - 51A | GORTON - 9G |
| Jan-60 | STRATFORD - 30A | STRATFORD - 30A | STRATFORD - 30A | LOWESTOFT - 32C | STRATFORD - 30A | WOODFORD HALSE - 2F | COLWICK - 40E | DARLINGTON - 51A | GORTON - 9G |
| Apr-60 | STRATFORD - 30A | STRATFORD - 30A | STRATFORD - 30A | LOWESTOFT - 32C | STRATFORD - 30A | WOODFORD HALSE - 2F | COLWICK - 40E | DARLINGTON - 51A | **3/60: W. HSE - 2F** |
| Aug-60 | STRATFORD - 30A | STRATFORD - 30A | STRATFORD - 30A | LOWESTOFT - 32C | **8/60: NEAS - 14D** | WOODFORD HALSE - 2F | COLWICK - 40E | DARLINGTON - 51A | WOODFORD HALSE - 2F |
| Nov-60 | STRATFORD - 30A | STRATFORD - 30A | STRATFORD - 30A | **10/60: NOR - 32A** | NEASDEN - 14D | WOODFORD HALSE - 2F | COLWICK - 40E | DARLINGTON - 51A | **11/60: GORT - 9G** |

| | 67744 | 67745 | 67746 | 67747 | 67748 | 67749 | 67750 | 67751 | 67752 |
|---|---|---|---|---|---|---|---|---|---|
| Aug-50 | HITCHIN - 34D | HITCHIN - 34D | HITCHIN - 34D | NEASDEN - 34E | NEASDEN - 34E | NEASDEN - 34E | DARLINGTON - 51A | NEASDEN - 34E | NEASDEN - 34E |
| Jan-51 | HITCHIN - 34D | HITCHIN - 34D | HITCHIN - 34D | NEASDEN - 34E | NEASDEN - 34E | NEASDEN - 34E | DARLINGTON - 51A | NEASDEN - 34E | NEASDEN - 34E |
| Aug-51 | HITCHIN - 34D | HITCHIN - 34D | HITCHIN - 34D | NEASDEN - 34E | NEASDEN - 34E | NEASDEN - 34E | DARLINGTON - 51A | NEASDEN - 34E | NEASDEN - 34E |
| Jan-52 | HITCHIN - 34D | HITCHIN - 34D | HITCHIN - 34D | NEASDEN - 34E | NEASDEN - 34E | **12/51: HSEY - 34B** | DARLINGTON - 51A | NEASDEN - 34E | NEASDEN - 34E |
| Aug-52 | HITCHIN - 34D | HITCHIN - 34D | HITCHIN - 34D | NEASDEN - 34E | NEASDEN - 34E | **3/52: NEAS - 34E** | DARLINGTON - 51A | NEASDEN - 34E | NEASDEN - 34E |
| Jan-53 | HITCHIN - 34D | HITCHIN - 34D | HITCHIN - 34D | NEASDEN - 34E | NEASDEN - 34E | NEASDEN - 34E | DARLINGTON - 51A | NEASDEN - 34E | NEASDEN - 34E |
| Aug-53 | HITCHIN - 34D | HITCHIN - 34D | HITCHIN - 34D | NEASDEN - 34E | NEASDEN - 34E | NEASDEN - 34E | DARLINGTON - 51A | NEASDEN - 34E | NEASDEN - 34E |
| Jan-54 | HITCHIN - 34D | HITCHIN - 34D | HITCHIN - 34D | NEASDEN - 34E | NEASDEN - 34E | NEASDEN - 34E | DARLINGTON - 51A | NEASDEN - 34E | NEASDEN - 34E |
| Aug-54 | HITCHIN - 34D | HITCHIN - 34D | HITCHIN - 34D | NEASDEN - 34E | NEASDEN - 34E | NEASDEN - 34E | DARLINGTON - 51A | NEASDEN - 34E | NEASDEN - 34E |
| Jan-55 | HITCHIN - 34D | HITCHIN - 34D | HITCHIN - 34D | NEASDEN - 34E | NEASDEN - 34E | NEASDEN - 34E | DARLINGTON - 51A | **11/54: KX - 34A** | NEASDEN - 34E |
| Aug-55 | HITCHIN - 34D | HITCHIN - 34D | HITCHIN - 34D | NEASDEN - 34E | NEASDEN - 34E | NEASDEN - 34E | DARLINGTON - 51A | KINGS CROSS - 34A | NEASDEN - 34E |
| Jan-56 | HITCHIN - 34D | HITCHIN - 34D | HITCHIN - 34D | NEASDEN - 34E | NEASDEN - 34E | NEASDEN - 34E | DARLINGTON - 51A | KINGS CROSS - 34A | NEASDEN - 34E |
| Aug-56 | HITCHIN - 34D | HITCHIN - 34D | HITCHIN - 34D | NEASDEN - 34E | KINGS CROSS - 34A | **6/56: KX - 34A** | DARLINGTON - 51A | KINGS CROSS - 34A | NEASDEN - 34E |
| Jan-57 | HITCHIN - 34D | HITCHIN - 34D | HITCHIN - 34D | NEASDEN - 34E | NEASDEN - 34E | KINGS CROSS - 34A | DARLINGTON - 51A | **11/56: COLW - 38A** | NEASDEN - 34E |
| Aug-57 | HITCHIN - 34D | HITCHIN - 34D | HITCHIN - 34D | NEASDEN - 34E | NEASDEN - 34E | **6/57: HIT - 34D** | DARLINGTON - 51A | **5/57: GORT - 39A** | NEASDEN - 34E |
| Jan-58 | HITCHIN - 34D | HITCHIN - 34D | HITCHIN - 34D | NEASDEN - 34E | NEASDEN - 34E | HITCHIN - 34D | DARLINGTON - 51A | GORTON - 39A | NEASDEN - 34E |
| Aug-58 | HITCHIN - 34D | HITCHIN - 34D | HITCHIN - 34D | **6/58: WILL - 1A** | NEASDEN - 14D | HITCHIN - 34D | DARLINGTON - 51A | GORTON - 9G | NEASDEN - 14D |
| Jan-59 | HITCHIN - 34D | HITCHIN - 34D | HITCHIN - 34D | **9/58: GORT - 9G** | GORTON - 9G | HITCHIN - 34D | DARLINGTON - 51A | GORTON - 9G | **1/59: STRAT - 30A** |
| Aug-59 | HITCHIN - 34D | HITCHIN - 34D | HITCHIN - 34D | GORTON - 9G | GORTON - 9G | HITCHIN - 34D | DARLINGTON - 51A | GORTON - 9G | STRATFORD - 30A |
| Nov-59 | HITCHIN - 34D | HITCHIN - 34D | HITCHIN - 34D | GORTON - 9G | GORTON - 9G | HITCHIN - 34D | DARLINGTON - 51A | GORTON - 9G | STRATFORD - 30A |
| Jan-60 | HITCHIN - 34D | HITCHIN - 34D | HITCHIN - 34D | GORTON - 9G | GORTON - 9G | **1/60: KX - 34A** | DARLINGTON - 51A | GORTON - 9G | STRATFORD - 30A |
| Apr-60 | HITCHIN - 34D | HITCHIN - 34D | HITCHIN - 34D | GORTON - 9G | GORTON - 9G | KINGS CROSS - 34A | DARLINGTON - 51A | GORTON - 9G | **3/60: KX - 34A** |
| Aug-60 | HITCHIN - 34D | HITCHIN - 34D | HITCHIN - 34D | GORTON - 9G | GORTON - 9G | KINGS CROSS - 34A | DARLINGTON - 51A | GORTON - 9G | KINGS CROSS - 34A |
| Nov-60 | HITCHIN - 34D | **10/60: KX - 34A** | **10/60: KX - 34A** | GORTON - 9G | GORTON - 9G | KINGS CROSS - 34A | DARLINGTON - 51A | GORTON - 9G | KINGS CROSS - 34A |

| | 67753 | 67754 | 67755 | 67756 | 67757 | 67758 | 67759 | 67760 | 67761 |
|---|---|---|---|---|---|---|---|---|---|
| Aug-50 | NEASDEN - 34E | DARLINGTON - 51A | MIDDLESBROUGH - 51D | NEASDEN - 34E | NEASDEN - 34E | NEASDEN - 34E | MIDDLESBROUGH - 51D | NEASDEN - 34E | NEASDEN - 34E |
| Jan-51 | NEASDEN - 34E | DARLINGTON - 51A | **11/50: B.GDNS - 53B** | **12/50: HSEY - 34B** | **12/50: HSEY - 34B** | **4/51: DARL - 51A** | **11/50: B.GDNS - 53B** | NEASDEN - 34E | **12/50: HSEY - 34B** |
| Aug-51 | NEASDEN - 34E | DARLINGTON - 51A | BOTGDNS - 53B | **6/51: NEAS - 34E** | HORNSEY - 34B | **5/51: NEAS - 34E** | BOTGDNS - 53B | NEASDEN - 34E | **3/51: NEAS - 34E** |
| Jan-52 | NEASDEN - 34E | DARLINGTON - 51A | BOTGDNS - 53B | **11/51: HSEY - 34B** | HORNSEY - 34B | NEASDEN - 34E | BOTGDNS - 53B | NEASDEN - 34E | NEASDEN - 34E |
| Aug-52 | NEASDEN - 34E | DARLINGTON - 51A | BOTGDNS - 53B | HORNSEY - 34B | HORNSEY - 34B | NEASDEN - 34E | BOTGDNS - 53B | NEASDEN - 34E | NEASDEN - 34E |
| Jan-53 | NEASDEN - 34E | DARLINGTON - 51A | BOTGDNS - 53B | **10/52: KX - 34A** | **10/52: KX - 34A** | NEASDEN - 34E | BOTGDNS - 53B | NEASDEN - 34E | NEASDEN - 34E |
| Aug-53 | NEASDEN - 34E | DARLINGTON - 51A | BOTGDNS - 53B | KINGS CROSS - 34A | KINGS CROSS - 34A | NEASDEN - 34E | BOTGDNS - 53B | NEASDEN - 34E | NEASDEN - 34E |
| Jan-54 | NEASDEN - 34E | DARLINGTON - 51A | BOTGDNS - 53B | KINGS CROSS - 34A | KINGS CROSS - 34A | NEASDEN - 34E | BOTGDNS - 53B | NEASDEN - 34E | NEASDEN - 34E |
| Aug-54 | NEASDEN - 34E | **6/54: B.GDNS - 53B** | BOTGDNS - 53B | KINGS CROSS - 34A | KINGS CROSS - 34A | NEASDEN - 34E | BOTGDNS - 53B | NEASDEN - 34E | NEASDEN - 34E |
| Jan-55 | NEASDEN - 34E | BOTGDNS - 53B | **1/55: BRID - 53D** | KINGS CROSS - 34A | KINGS CROSS - 34A | **3/55: KX - 34A** | BOTGDNS - 53B | NEASDEN - 34E | NEASDEN - 34E |
| Aug-55 | NEASDEN - 34E | BOTGDNS - 53B | **6/55: B.GDNS - 53B** | KINGS CROSS - 34A | KINGS CROSS - 34A | KINGS CROSS - 34A | BOTGDNS - 53B | NEASDEN - 34E | NEASDEN - 34E |
| Jan-56 | NEASDEN - 34E | BOTGDNS - 53B | BOTGDNS - 53B | KINGS CROSS - 34A | KINGS CROSS - 34A | **12/55: NEAS - 34E** | BOTGDNS - 53B | **3/56: COLW - 38A** | NEASDEN - 34E |
| Aug-56 | NEASDEN - 34E | **5/56: MBRO - 51D** | **5/56: MBRO - 51D** | **7/56: NSDN - 34E** | KINGS CROSS - 34A | NEASDEN - 34E | **6/56: MBRO - 51D** | COLWICK - 38A | **9/56: KX - 34A** |
| Jan-57 | NEASDEN - 34E | MIDDLESBROUGH - 51D | MIDDLESBROUGH - 51D | NEASDEN - 34E | KINGS CROSS - 34A | NEASDEN - 34E | MIDDLESBROUGH - 51D | COLWICK - 38A | **2/57: HIT - 34D** |
| Aug-57 | NEASDEN - 34E | MIDDLESBROUGH - 51D | **9/57: DARL - 51A** | NEASDEN - 34E | KINGS CROSS - 34A | NEASDEN - 34E | MIDDLESBROUGH - 51D | COLWICK - 38A | HITCHIN - 34D |
| Jan-58 | NEASDEN - 34E | MIDDLESBROUGH - 51D | DARLINGTON - 51A | NEASDEN - 34E | KINGS CROSS - 34A | NEASDEN - 34E | MIDDLESBROUGH - 51D | COLWICK - 38A | HITCHIN - 34D |
| Aug-58 | NEASDEN - 14D | **7/58: STOCK - 51E** | DARLINGTON - 51A | NEASDEN - 14D | KINGS CROSS - 34A | NEASDEN - 14D | **9/58: W.HPL - 51C** | COLWICK - 40E | HITCHIN - 34D |
| Jan-59 | **10/58: COLW - 40E** | STOCKTON - 51E | DARLINGTON - 51A | **10/58: GORT - 9G** | KINGS CROSS - 34A | **10/58: COLW - 40E** | **12/58: TBY - 51L** | COLWICK - 40E | HITCHIN - 34D |
| Aug-59 | COLWICK - 40E | **6/59: TBY - 51L** | DARLINGTON - 51A | GORTON - 9G | KINGS CROSS - 34A | COLWICK - 40E | THORNABY - 51L | COLWICK - 40E | HITCHIN - 34D |
| Nov-59 | COLWICK - 40E | THORNABY - 51L | DARLINGTON - 51A | GORTON - 9G | KINGS CROSS - 34A | COLWICK - 40E | THORNABY - 51L | COLWICK - 40E | **10/59: GRAN - 34F** |
| Jan-60 | COLWICK - 40E | THORNABY - 51L | DARLINGTON - 51A | GORTON - 9G | KINGS CROSS - 34A | COLWICK - 40E | THORNABY - 51L | COLWICK - 40E | GRANTHAM - 34F |
| Apr-60 | COLWICK - 40E | THORNABY - 51L | DARLINGTON - 51A | GORTON - 9G | KINGS CROSS - 34A | COLWICK - 40E | THORNABY - 51L | COLWICK - 40E | GRANTHAM - 34F |
| Aug-60 | COLWICK - 40E | THORNABY - 51L | DARLINGTON - 51A | GORTON - 9G | KINGS CROSS - 34A | COLWICK - 40E | THORNABY - 51L | COLWICK - 40E | GRANTHAM - 34F |
| Nov-60 | COLWICK - 40E | THORNABY - 51L | DARLINGTON - 51A | GORTON - 9G | KINGS CROSS - 34A | COLWICK - 40E | THORNABY - 51L | COLWICK - 40E | GRANTHAM - 34F |

| | 67762 | 67763 | 67764 | 67765 | 67766 | 67767 | 67768 | 67769 | 67770 |
|---|---|---|---|---|---|---|---|---|---|
| Aug-50 | NEASDEN - 34E | MIDDLESBROUGH - 51D | MIDDLESBROUGH - 51D | MIDDLESBROUGH - 51D | MIDDLESBROUGH - 51D | NEASDEN - 34E | NEASDEN - 34E | NEASDEN - 34E | NEASDEN - 34E |
| Jan-51 | NEASDEN - 34E | **11/50: B.GDNS - 53B** | **11/50: B.GDNS - 53B** | **11/50: B.GDNS - 53B** | **11/50: B.GDNS - 53B** | NEASDEN - 34E | NEASDEN - 34E | NEASDEN - 34E | NEASDEN - 34E |
| Aug-51 | NEASDEN - 34E | BOTGDNS - 53B | BOTGDNS - 53B | BOTGDNS - 53B | BOTGDNS - 53B | NEASDEN - 34E | NEASDEN - 34E | NEASDEN - 34E | NEASDEN - 34E |
| Jan-52 | NEASDEN - 34E | BOTGDNS - 53B | BOTGDNS - 53B | BOTGDNS - 53B | BOTGDNS - 53B | NEASDEN - 34E | NEASDEN - 34E | NEASDEN - 34E | NEASDEN - 34E |
| Aug-52 | NEASDEN - 34E | BOTGDNS - 53B | BOTGDNS - 53B | BOTGDNS - 53B | BOTGDNS - 53B | NEASDEN - 34E | NEASDEN - 34E | NEASDEN - 34E | NEASDEN - 34E |
| Jan-53 | NEASDEN - 34E | BOTGDNS - 53B | BOTGDNS - 53B | BOTGDNS - 53B | BOTGDNS - 53B | NEASDEN - 34E | NEASDEN - 34E | NEASDEN - 34E | NEASDEN - 34E |
| Aug-53 | NEASDEN - 34E | BOTGDNS - 53B | BOTGDNS - 53B | BOTGDNS - 53B | BOTGDNS - 53B | NEASDEN - 34E | NEASDEN - 34E | NEASDEN - 34E | NEASDEN - 34E |
| Jan-54 | NEASDEN - 34E | BOTGDNS - 53B | BOTGDNS - 53B | BOTGDNS - 53B | BOTGDNS - 53B | NEASDEN - 34E | NEASDEN - 34E | NEASDEN - 34E | NEASDEN - 34E |
| Aug-54 | NEASDEN - 34E | BOTGDNS - 53B | BOTGDNS - 53B | BOTGDNS - 53B | BOTGDNS - 53B | NEASDEN - 34E | NEASDEN - 34E | NEASDEN - 34E | NEASDEN - 34E |
| Jan-55 | NEASDEN - 34E | BOTGDNS - 53B | **1/55: BRID - 53D** | BOTGDNS - 53B | BOTGDNS - 53B | NEASDEN - 34E | NEASDEN - 34E | NEASDEN - 34E | **3/55: KX - 34A** |
| Aug-55 | NEASDEN - 34E | BOTGDNS - 53B | **6/55: B.GDNS - 53B** | BOTGDNS - 53B | BOTGDNS - 53B | NEASDEN - 34E | NEASDEN - 34E | **4/55: COLW - 38A** | **6/55: IPS - 32B** |
| Jan-56 | NEASDEN - 34E | BOTGDNS - 53B | BOTGDNS - 53B | BOTGDNS - 53B | BOTGDNS - 53B | NEASDEN - 34E | NEASDEN - 34E | **1/56: NEAS - 34E** | **12/55: LOW - 32C** |
| Aug-56 | NEASDEN - 34E | **6/56: MBRO - 51D** | **6/56: MBRO - 51D** | **5/56: MBRO - 51D** | **5/56: MBRO - 51D** | NEASDEN - 34E | **7/56: KX - 34A** | NEASDEN - 34E | LOWESTOFT - 32C |
| Jan-57 | NEASDEN - 34E | **1/57: WHITBY - 50G** | MIDDLESBROUGH - 51D | **1/57: WHITBY - 50G** | MIDDLESBROUGH - 51D | NEASDEN - 34E | KINGS CROSS - 34A | NEASDEN - 34E | LOWESTOFT - 32C |
| Aug-57 | NEASDEN - 34E | **3/57: MBRO - 51D** | MIDDLESBROUGH - 51D | **3/57: MBRO - 51D** | MIDDLESBROUGH - 51D | NEASDEN - 34E | KINGS CROSS - 34A | NEASDEN - 34E | **7/57: KX - 34A** |
| Jan-58 | NEASDEN - 34E | **9/57: DARL - 51A** | MIDDLESBROUGH - 51D | MIDDLESBROUGH - 51D | MIDDLESBROUGH - 51D | NEASDEN - 34E | KINGS CROSS - 34A | NEASDEN - 34E | KINGS CROSS - 34A |
| Aug-58 | NEASDEN - 14D | DARLINGTON - 51A | **6/58: TBY - 51L** | **6/58: TBY - 51L** | **7/58: STOCK - 51E** | **9/58: KX - 34A** | KINGS CROSS - 34A | NEASDEN - 14D | KINGS CROSS - 34A |
| Jan-59 | **10/58: GORT - 9G** | DARLINGTON - 51A | THORNABY - 51L | **9/58: W.HPL - 51C** | STOCKTON - 51E | KINGS CROSS - 34A | KINGS CROSS - 34A | **10/58: COLW - 40E** | KINGS CROSS - 34A |
| Aug-59 | GORTON - 9G | DARLINGTON - 51A | THORNABY - 51L | **6/59: DARL - 51A** | **6/59: TBY - 51L** | KINGS CROSS - 34A | KINGS CROSS - 34A | COLWICK - 40E | KINGS CROSS - 34A |
| Nov-59 | GORTON - 9G | DARLINGTON - 51A | THORNABY - 51L | DARLINGTON - 51A | THORNABY - 51L | KINGS CROSS - 34A | KINGS CROSS - 34A | COLWICK - 40E | KINGS CROSS - 34A |
| Jan-60 | GORTON - 9G | DARLINGTON - 51A | THORNABY - 51L | DARLINGTON - 51A | THORNABY - 51L | KINGS CROSS - 34A | KINGS CROSS - 34A | COLWICK - 40E | KINGS CROSS - 34A |
| Apr-60 | GORTON - 9G | DARLINGTON - 51A | THORNABY - 51L | DARLINGTON - 51A | THORNABY - 51L | KINGS CROSS - 34A | KINGS CROSS - 34A | COLWICK - 40E | KINGS CROSS - 34A |
| Aug-60 | GORTON - 9G | DARLINGTON - 51A | THORNABY - 51L | DARLINGTON - 51A | THORNABY - 51L | KINGS CROSS - 34A | KINGS CROSS - 34A | COLWICK - 40E | KINGS CROSS - 34A |
| Nov-60 | GORTON - 9G | DARLINGTON - 51A | THORNABY - 51L | DARLINGTON - 51A | THORNABY - 51L | KINGS CROSS - 34A | **11/60: GRAN - 34F** | COLWICK - 40E | KINGS CROSS - 34A |

| | 67771 | 67772 | 67773 | 67774 | 67775 | 67776 | 67777 | 67778 | 67779 |
|---|---|---|---|---|---|---|---|---|---|
| Aug-50 | NEASDEN - 34E | NEASDEN - 34E | NEASDEN - 34E | NEASDEN - 34E | NEASDEN - 34E | NEASDEN - 34E | DARLINGTON - 51A | NEASDEN - 34E | NEASDEN - 34E |
| Jan-51 | NEASDEN - 34E | NEASDEN - 34E | NEASDEN - 34E | NEASDEN - 34E | NEASDEN - 34E | NEASDEN - 34E | DARLINGTON - 51A | NEASDEN - 34E | NEASDEN - 34E |
| Aug-51 | **4/51: HSEY - 34B** | NEASDEN - 34E | NEASDEN - 34E | **7/51: HSEY - 34B** | NEASDEN - 34E | NEASDEN - 34E | DARLINGTON - 51A | NEASDEN - 34E | NEASDEN - 34E |
| Jan-52 | **9/51: NEAS - 34E** | NEASDEN - 34E | NEASDEN - 34E | **11/51: NEAS - 34E** | **3/52: HSEY - 34B** | NEASDEN - 34E | DARLINGTON - 51A | NEASDEN - 34E | NEASDEN - 34E |
| Aug-52 | NEASDEN - 34E | NEASDEN - 34E | NEASDEN - 34E | NEASDEN - 34E | HORNSEY - 34B | NEASDEN - 34E | DARLINGTON - 51A | NEASDEN - 34E | NEASDEN - 34E |
| Jan-53 | NEASDEN - 34E | NEASDEN - 34E | NEASDEN - 34E | NEASDEN - 34E | **10/52: KX - 34A** | NEASDEN - 34E | DARLINGTON - 51A | NEASDEN - 34E | NEASDEN - 34E |
| Aug-53 | NEASDEN - 34E | NEASDEN - 34E | NEASDEN - 34E | NEASDEN - 34E | KINGS CROSS - 34A | NEASDEN - 34E | DARLINGTON - 51A | NEASDEN - 34E | NEASDEN - 34E |
| Jan-54 | NEASDEN - 34E | **3/54: GRAN - 35B** | NEASDEN - 34E | NEASDEN - 34E | **2/54: NEAS - 34E** | NEASDEN - 34E | DARLINGTON - 51A | NEASDEN - 34E | NEASDEN - 34E |
| Aug-54 | NEASDEN - 34E | **5/54: NEAS - 34E** | NEASDEN - 34E | NEASDEN - 34E | **5/54: KX - 34A** | NEASDEN - 34E | DARLINGTON - 51A | NEASDEN - 34E | NEASDEN - 34E |
| Jan-55 | NEASDEN - 34E | NEASDEN - 34E | NEASDEN - 34E | NEASDEN - 34E | **5/55: NEAS - 34E** | **1/55: KX - 34A** | DARLINGTON - 51A | **1/55: KX - 34A** | **1/55: KX - 34A** |
| Aug-55 | NEASDEN - 34E | NEASDEN - 34E | NEASDEN - 34E | NEASDEN - 34E | **6/55: IPS - 32B** | KINGS CROSS - 34A | DARLINGTON - 51A | **4/55: NEAS - 34E** | KINGS CROSS - 34A |
| Jan-56 | 1/56:COLW - 38A | NEASDEN - 34E | NEASDEN - 34E | NEASDEN - 34E | IPSWICH - 32B | KINGS CROSS - 34A | DARLINGTON - 51A | NEASDEN - 34E | KINGS CROSS - 34A |
| Aug-56 | COLWICK - 38A | NEASDEN - 34E | **9/56: KX - 34A** | NEASDEN - 34E | IPSWICH - 32B | KINGS CROSS - 34A | DARLINGTON - 51A | NEASDEN - 34E | KINGS CROSS - 34A |
| Jan-57 | **12/56: W.HSE - 38E** | **10/56: KX - 34A** | KINGS CROSS - 34A | **10/56: KX - 34A** | IPSWICH - 32B | **10/56: GRAN - 35B** | DARLINGTON - 51A | NEASDEN - 34E | KINGS CROSS - 34A |
| Aug-57 | W.HALSE - 38E | KINGS CROSS - 34A | KINGS CROSS - 34A | KINGS CROSS - 34A | IPSWICH - 32B | GRANTHAM - 35B | DARLINGTON - 51A | NEASDEN - 34E | KINGS CROSS - 34A |
| Jan-58 | W.HALSE - 38E | **10/57: HSEY - 34B** | KINGS CROSS - 34A | KINGS CROSS - 34A | IPSWICH - 32B | GRANTHAM - 35B | DARLINGTON - 51A | NEASDEN - 34E | KINGS CROSS - 34A |
| Aug-58 | W.HALSE - 2F | HORNSEY - 34B | KINGS CROSS - 34A | KINGS CROSS - 34A | IPSWICH - 32B | **4/58: KX - 34A** | DARLINGTON - 51A | NEASDEN - 14D | KINGS CROSS - 34A |
| Jan-59 | W.HALSE - 2F | **10/58: KX - 34A** | KINGS CROSS - 34A | KINGS CROSS - 34A | IPSWICH - 32B | KINGS CROSS - 34A | DARLINGTON - 51A | **1/59: STRAT - 30A** | KINGS CROSS - 34A |
| Aug-59 | W.HALSE - 2F | KINGS CROSS - 34A | KINGS CROSS - 34A | KINGS CROSS - 34A | IPSWICH - 32B | KINGS CROSS - 34A | DARLINGTON - 51A | STRATFORD - 30A | KINGS CROSS - 34A |
| Nov-59 | W.HALSE - 2F | KINGS CROSS - 34A | KINGS CROSS - 34A | KINGS CROSS - 34A | IPSWICH - 32B | KINGS CROSS - 34A | DARLINGTON - 51A | STRATFORD - 30A | KINGS CROSS - 34A |
| Jan-60 | W.HALSE - 2F | KINGS CROSS - 34A | KINGS CROSS - 34A | KINGS CROSS - 34A | IPSWICH - 32B | KINGS CROSS - 34A | DARLINGTON - 51A | STRATFORD - 30A | KINGS CROSS - 34A |
| Apr-60 | W.HALSE - 2F | KINGS CROSS - 34A | KINGS CROSS - 34A | KINGS CROSS - 34A | **3/60: COLW - 40E** | KINGS CROSS - 34A | DARLINGTON - 51A | STRATFORD - 30A | KINGS CROSS - 34A |
| Aug-60 | W.HALSE - 2F | KINGS CROSS - 34A | KINGS CROSS - 34A | KINGS CROSS - 34A | COLWICK - 40E | KINGS CROSS - 34A | DARLINGTON - 51A | **8/60: NEAS - 14D** | KINGS CROSS - 34A |
| Nov-60 | W.HALSE - 2F | KINGS CROSS - 34A | KINGS CROSS - 34A | KINGS CROSS - 34A | COLWICK - 40E | **11/60: GRAN - 34F** | DARLINGTON - 51A | NEASDEN - 14D | KINGS CROSS - 34A |

| | 67780 | 67781 | 67782 | 67783 | 67784 | 67785 | 67786 | 67787 | 67788 |
|---|---|---|---|---|---|---|---|---|---|
| Aug-50 | NEASDEN - 34E | NEASDEN - 34E | NEASDEN - 34E | NEASDEN - 34E | NEASDEN - 34E | NEASDEN - 34E | NEASDEN - 34E | IPSWICH - 32B | NORWICH - 32A |
| Jan-51 | **3/51: HSEY - 34B** | NEASDEN - 34E | NEASDEN - 34E | NEASDEN - 34E | **3/51: HSEY - 34B** | NEASDEN - 34E | NEASDEN - 34E | IPSWICH - 32B | NORWICH - 32A |
| Aug-51 | **4/51: NEAS - 34E** | NEASDEN - 34E | NEASDEN - 34E | NEASDEN - 34E | **4/51: NEAS - 34E** | NEASDEN - 34E | NEASDEN - 34E | IPSWICH - 32B | NORWICH - 32A |
| Jan-52 | NEASDEN - 34E | NEASDEN - 34E | NEASDEN - 34E | NEASDEN - 34E | NEASDEN - 34E | NEASDEN - 34E | NEASDEN - 34E | IPSWICH - 32B | NORWICH - 32A |
| Aug-52 | NEASDEN - 34E | NEASDEN - 34E | NEASDEN - 34E | NEASDEN - 34E | NEASDEN - 34E | NEASDEN - 34E | NEASDEN - 34E | IPSWICH - 32B | NORWICH - 32A |
| Jan-53 | NEASDEN - 34E | NEASDEN - 34E | NEASDEN - 34E | NEASDEN - 34E | NEASDEN - 34E | NEASDEN - 34E | NEASDEN - 34E | **2/53: NEAS - 34E** | **2/53: NEAS - 34E** |
| Aug-53 | NEASDEN - 34E | NEASDEN - 34E | NEASDEN - 34E | NEASDEN - 34E | NEASDEN - 34E | **7/53: HIT - 34D** | NEASDEN - 34E | NEASDEN - 34E | NEASDEN - 34E |
| Jan-54 | NEASDEN - 34E | NEASDEN - 34E | **5/54: KX - 34A** | NEASDEN - 34E | NEASDEN - 34E | HITCHIN - 34D | NEASDEN - 34E | **5/54: KX - 34A** | NEASDEN - 34E |
| Aug-54 | NEASDEN - 34E | **5/54: KX - 34A** | **6/54: NEAS - 34E** | NEASDEN - 34E | NEASDEN - 34E | HITCHIN - 34D | NEASDEN - 34E | **6/54: NEAS - 34E** | NEASDEN - 34E |
| Jan-55 | NEASDEN - 34E | **1/55: NEAS - 34E** | NEASDEN - 34E | NEASDEN - 34E | **1/55: KX - 34A** | HITCHIN - 34D | NEASDEN - 34E | NEASDEN - 34E | NEASDEN - 34E |
| Aug-55 | NEASDEN - 34E | NEASDEN - 34E | NEASDEN - 34E | NEASDEN - 34E | KINGS CROSS - 34A | HITCHIN - 34D | NEASDEN - 34E | NEASDEN - 34E | NEASDEN - 34E |
| Jan-56 | NEASDEN - 34E | NEASDEN - 34E | NEASDEN - 34E | NEASDEN - 34E | KINGS CROSS - 34A | HITCHIN - 34D | NEASDEN - 34E | NEASDEN - 34E | NEASDEN - 34E |
| Aug-56 | **7/56: KX - 34A** | NEASDEN - 34E | NEASDEN - 34E | NEASDEN - 34E | KINGS CROSS - 34A | HITCHIN - 34D | **7/56: HIT - 34D** | NEASDEN - 34E | NEASDEN - 34E |
| Jan-57 | KINGS CROSS - 34A | NEASDEN - 34E | NEASDEN - 34E | NEASDEN - 34E | KINGS CROSS - 34A | HITCHIN - 34D | **2/57: COLW - 38A** | NEASDEN - 34E | **10/56: COLW - 38A** |
| Aug-57 | KINGS CROSS - 34A | **6/57: GORT - 39A** | **6/57: GORT - 39A** | NEASDEN - 34E | KINGS CROSS - 34A | HITCHIN - 34D | **9/57: LTR(GC) - 38C** | NEASDEN - 34E | COLWICK - 38A |
| Jan-58 | **10/57: HSEY - 34B** | GORTON - 39A | GORTON - 39A | NEASDEN - 34E | KINGS CROSS - 34A | HITCHIN - 34D | **10/57: YAR(ST) - 32D** | NEASDEN - 34E | COLWICK - 38A |
| Aug-58 | **8/58: KX - 34A** | GORTON - 9G | GORTON - 9G | **9/58: KX - 34A** | KINGS CROSS - 34A | HITCHIN - 34D | YARMOUTH (ST) - 32D | **9/58: KX - 34A** | COLWICK - 40E |
| Jan-59 | KINGS CROSS - 34A | GORTON - 9G | GORTON - 9G | KINGS CROSS - 34A | KINGS CROSS - 34A | HITCHIN - 34D | **12/58: NOR - 32A** | KINGS CROSS - 34A | COLWICK - 40E |
| Aug-59 | KINGS CROSS - 34A | GORTON - 9G | GORTON - 9G | KINGS CROSS - 34A | KINGS CROSS - 34A | HITCHIN - 34D | NORWICH - 32A | KINGS CROSS - 34A | COLWICK - 40E |
| Nov-59 | KINGS CROSS - 34A | GORTON - 9G | GORTON - 9G | KINGS CROSS - 34A | KINGS CROSS - 34A | **10/59: GRAN - 34F** | NORWICH - 32A | KINGS CROSS - 34A | COLWICK - 40E |
| Jan-60 | KINGS CROSS - 34A | GORTON - 9G | GORTON - 9G | KINGS CROSS - 34A | KINGS CROSS - 34A | GRANTHAM - 34F | **2/60: KX - 34A** | KINGS CROSS - 34A | COLWICK - 40E |
| Apr-60 | KINGS CROSS - 34A | **4/60: LTR(GC) - 15E** | **4/60: LTR(GC) - 15E** | KINGS CROSS - 34A | KINGS CROSS - 34A | GRANTHAM - 34F | KINGS CROSS - 34A | KINGS CROSS - 34A | COLWICK - 40E |
| Aug-60 | KINGS CROSS - 34A | LEICESTER (GC) - 15E | LEICESTER (GC) - 15E | KINGS CROSS - 34A | KINGS CROSS - 34A | GRANTHAM - 34F | KINGS CROSS - 34A | KINGS CROSS - 34A | COLWICK - 40E |
| Nov-60 | **10/60: DCTR - 36A** | LEICESTER (GC) - 15E | LEICESTER (GC) - 15E | KINGS CROSS - 34A | **10/60: DCTR - 36A** | GRANTHAM - 34F | KINGS CROSS - 34A | **10/60: DCTR - 36A** | COLWICK - 40E |

*Apart from a handful of engines in the North East and East Anglia, the L1 2-6-4T's had always been associated with the London area, working the GN, GC and part of the GE outer-suburban service. With very little passenger work Annesley, where former GN 67746 was discovered on 23 April 1961, was the last place 2-6-4T's were likely to be found yet immediately after dieselisation, the class being too new for withdrawal, many were exported to the Nottingham division where they suffered a rather tenuous existence until being withdrawn between 1960 and 1962.*

*The seventy-five J94 Austerity 0-6-0T's were a north country feature - most of the class were spread across the NER - and until the arrival of diesel shunters in large numbers the most southerly shed to have an allocation was Immingham which was a stronghold of the class. 68074, a former Immingham engine, moved to Colwick, where it is seen above, in the summer of 1960 after being displaced by a 350hp diesel.*

| | 67789 | 67790 | 67791 | 67792 | 67793 | 67794 | 67795 | 67796 | 67797 |
|---|---|---|---|---|---|---|---|---|---|
| Aug-50 | NORWICH-32A | HITCHIN-34D | HITCHIN-34D | KINGS CROSS-34A | KINGS CROSS-34A | NORWICH-32A | NORWICH-32A | KINGS CROSS-34A | KINGS CROSS-34A |
| Jan-51 | NORWICH-32A | HITCHIN-34D | HITCHIN-34D | **4/51: DARL - 51A** | KINGS CROSS-34A | **10/50: LOW - 32C** | NORWICH-32A | KINGS CROSS-34A | KINGS CROSS-34A |
| Aug-51 | NORWICH-32A | HITCHIN-34D | HITCHIN-34D | **5/51: KX - 34A** | KINGS CROSS-34A | LOWESTOFT-32C | **4/51: LOW - 32C** | KINGS CROSS-34A | KINGS CROSS-34A |
| Jan-52 | NORWICH-32A | HITCHIN-34D | HITCHIN-34D | KINGS CROSS-34A | KINGS CROSS-34A | LOWESTOFT-32C | LOWESTOFT-32C | KINGS CROSS-34A | KINGS CROSS-34A |
| Aug-52 | NORWICH-32A | HITCHIN-34D | HITCHIN-34D | **8/52: NEAS - 34E** | KINGS CROSS-34A | LOWESTOFT-32C | LOWESTOFT-32C | **9/52: NEAS - 34E** | KINGS CROSS-34A |
| Jan-53 | **2/53: NEAS - 34E** | HITCHIN-34D | HITCHIN-34D | NEASDEN-34E | KINGS CROSS-34A | **2/53: NEAS - 34E** | **2/53: NEAS - 34E** | NEASDEN-34E | KINGS CROSS-34A |
| Aug-53 | NEASDEN-34E | HITCHIN-34D | HITCHIN-34D | NEASDEN-34E | KINGS CROSS-34A | NEASDEN-34E | NEASDEN-34E | NEASDEN-34E | KINGS CROSS-34A |
| Jan-54 | NEASDEN-34E | HITCHIN-34D | HITCHIN-34D | NEASDEN-34E | KINGS CROSS-34A | NEASDEN-34E | NEASDEN-34E | NEASDEN-34E | KINGS CROSS-34A |
| Aug-54 | NEASDEN-34E | HITCHIN-34D | HITCHIN-34D | NEASDEN-34E | KINGS CROSS-34A | NEASDEN-34E | **12/54: KX - 34A** | NEASDEN-34E | KINGS CROSS-34A |
| Jan-55 | **4/55: W.HSE - 38E** | HITCHIN-34D | HITCHIN-34D | **12/54: KX - 34A** | KINGS CROSS-34A | NEASDEN-34E | **1/55: NEAS - 34E** | NEASDEN-34E | **4/55: NEAS - 34E** |
| Aug-55 | W.HALSE-38E | HITCHIN-34D | HITCHIN-34D | **5/55: NEAS - 34E** | KINGS CROSS-34A | NEASDEN-34E | NEASDEN-34E | **4/55: COLW - 38A** | **5/55: KX - 34A** |
| Jan-56 | W.HALSE-38E | HITCHIN-34D | HITCHIN-34D | NEASDEN-34E | KINGS CROSS-34A | NEASDEN-34E | NEASDEN-34E | **3/56: NEAS - 34E** | KINGS CROSS-34A |
| Aug-56 | W.HALSE-38E | HITCHIN-34D | HITCHIN-34D | NEASDEN-34E | KINGS CROSS-34A | NEASDEN-34E | NEASDEN-34E | NEASDEN-34E | KINGS CROSS-34A |
| Jan-57 | W.HALSE-38E | HITCHIN-34D | HITCHIN-34D | NEASDEN-34E | KINGS CROSS-34A | NEASDEN-34E | NEASDEN-34E | NEASDEN-34E | KINGS CROSS-34A |
| Aug-57 | W.HALSE-38E | HITCHIN-34D | HITCHIN-34D | NEASDEN-34E | KINGS CROSS-34A | **7/57: KX - 34A** | NEASDEN-34E | NEASDEN-34E | KINGS CROSS-34A |
| Jan-58 | W.HALSE-38E | HITCHIN-34D | HITCHIN-34D | NEASDEN-34E | KINGS CROSS-34A | KINGS CROSS-34A | NEASDEN-34E | NEASDEN-34E | KINGS CROSS-34A |
| Aug-58 | W.HALSE-2F | HITCHIN-34D | HITCHIN-34D | **8/58: KX - 34A** | KINGS CROSS-34A | **9/58: GRAN - 34F** | NEASDEN-14D | NEASDEN-14D | KINGS CROSS-34A |
| Jan-59 | W.HALSE-2F | HITCHIN-34D | HITCHIN-34D | KINGS CROSS-34A | KINGS CROSS-34A | GRANTHAM-34F | GORTON-9G | GORTON-9G | KINGS CROSS-34A |
| Aug-59 | W.HALSE-2F | **6/59: COLW - 40E** | **6/59: GRAN - 34F** | KINGS CROSS-34A | KINGS CROSS-34A | GRANTHAM-34F | GORTON-9G | GORTON-9G | KINGS CROSS-34A |
| Nov-59 | W.HALSE-2F | COLWICK-40E | GRANTHAM-34F | KINGS CROSS-34A | KINGS CROSS-34A | **11/59: KX - 34A** | GORTON-9G | GORTON-9G | KINGS CROSS-34A |
| Jan-60 | W.HALSE-2F | COLWICK-40E | GRANTHAM-34F | KINGS CROSS-34A | KINGS CROSS-34A | KINGS CROSS-34A | GORTON-9G | GORTON-9G | KINGS CROSS-34A |
| Apr-60 | W.HALSE-2F | COLWICK-40E | GRANTHAM-34F | KINGS CROSS-34A | KINGS CROSS-34A | KINGS CROSS-34A | GORTON-9G | GORTON-9G | KINGS CROSS-34A |
| Aug-60 | W.HALSE-2F | COLWICK-40E | GRANTHAM-34F | KINGS CROSS-34A | KINGS CROSS-34A | KINGS CROSS-34A | GORTON-9G | GORTON-9G | KINGS CROSS-34A |
| Nov-60 | W.HALSE-2F | COLWICK-40E | GRANTHAM-34F | KINGS CROSS-34A | KINGS CROSS-34A | KINGS CROSS-34A | GORTON-9G | GORTON-9G | KINGS CROSS-34A |

| | | | | J94 0-6-0T (1943) | | | | | |
|---|---|---|---|---|---|---|---|---|---|
| | 67798 | 67799 | 67800 | 68006 | 68007 | 68008 | 68009 | 68010 | 68011 |
| Aug-50 | NORWICH-32A | | | BIDSTON-6F | NEWPORT-51B | DARLINGTON-51A | IMMINGHAM-40B | BLAYDON-52C | NEWPORT-51B |
| Jan-51 | NORWICH-32A | **9/50: KX - 34A** | **9/50: KX - 34A** | BIDSTON-6F | NEWPORT-51B | DARLINGTON-51A | IMMINGHAM-40B | BLAYDON-52C | NEWPORT-51B |
| Aug-51 | NORWICH-32A | KINGS CROSS-34A | KINGS CROSS-34A | BIDSTON-6F | NEWPORT-51B | DARLINGTON-51A | IMMINGHAM-40B | BLAYDON-52C | NEWPORT-51B |
| Jan-52 | NORWICH-32A | KINGS CROSS-34A | KINGS CROSS-34A | BIDSTON-6F | NEWPORT-51B | DARLINGTON-51A | IMMINGHAM-40B | BLAYDON-52C | NEWPORT-51B |
| Aug-52 | NORWICH-32A | KINGS CROSS-34A | KINGS CROSS-34A | BIDSTON-6F | NEWPORT-51B | DARLINGTON-51A | IMMINGHAM-40B | BLAYDON-52C | NEWPORT-51B |
| Jan-53 | **2/53: NEAS - 34E** | KINGS CROSS-34A | KINGS CROSS-34A | BIDSTON-6F | NEWPORT-51B | DARLINGTON-51A | IMMINGHAM-40B | BLAYDON-52C | NEWPORT-51B |
| Aug-53 | NEASDEN-34E | KINGS CROSS-34A | KINGS CROSS-34A | BIDSTON-6F | NEWPORT-51B | DARLINGTON-51A | IMMINGHAM-40B | BLAYDON-52C | NEWPORT-51B |
| Jan-54 | NEASDEN-34E | KINGS CROSS-34A | KINGS CROSS-34A | BIDSTON-6F | NEWPORT-51B | DARLINGTON-51A | IMMINGHAM-40B | BLAYDON-52C | NEWPORT-51B |
| Aug-54 | NEASDEN-34E | KINGS CROSS-34A | KINGS CROSS-34A | BIDSTON-6F | NEWPORT-51B | DARLINGTON-51A | IMMINGHAM-40B | BLAYDON-52C | NEWPORT-51B |
| Jan-55 | NEASDEN-34E | **3/55: COLW - 38A** | KINGS CROSS-34A | BIDSTON-6F | NEWPORT-51B | DARLINGTON-51A | IMMINGHAM-40B | BLAYDON-52C | NEWPORT-51B |
| Aug-55 | NEASDEN-34E | COLWICK-38A | KINGS CROSS-34A | BIDSTON-6F | NEWPORT-51B | DARLINGTON-51A | IMMINGHAM-40B | BLAYDON-52C | NEWPORT-51B |
| Jan-56 | NEASDEN-34E | COLWICK-38A | KINGS CROSS-34A | BIDSTON-6F | NEWPORT-51B | DARLINGTON-51A | IMMINGHAM-40B | BLAYDON-52C | NEWPORT-51B |
| Aug-56 | NEASDEN-34E | COLWICK-38A | KINGS CROSS-34A | **8/56: ROWS - 17D** | NEWPORT-51B | DARLINGTON-51A | IMMINGHAM-40B | BLAYDON-52C | NEWPORT-51B |
| Jan-57 | **10/56: COLW - 38A** | COLWICK-38A | **10/56: GRAN - 35B** | ROWSLEY-17D | **10/56: DARL - 51A** | DARLINGTON-51A | IMMINGHAM-40B | BLAYDON-52C | NEWPORT-51B |
| Aug-57 | **5/57: GORT - 39A** | COLWICK-38A | GRANTHAM-35B | ROWSLEY-17D | DARLINGTON-51A | DARLINGTON-51A | IMMINGHAM-40B | BLAYDON-52C | NEWPORT-51B |
| Jan-58 | GORTON-39A | COLWICK-38A | GRANTHAM-35B | ROWSLEY-17D | DARLINGTON-51A | DARLINGTON-51A | IMMINGHAM-40B | BLAYDON-52C | NEWPORT-51B |
| Aug-58 | GORTON-9G | COLWICK-40E | **9/58 : KX - 34A** | ROWSLEY-17C | DARLINGTON-51A | DARLINGTON-51A | IMMINGHAM-40B | BLAYDON-52C | **9/58: DAIRY - 53A** |
| Jan-59 | GORTON-9G | COLWICK-40E | KINGS CROSS-34A | ROWSLEY-17C | DARLINGTON-51A | DARLINGTON-51A | IMMINGHAM-40B | BLAYDON-52C | DAIRYCOATES-53A |
| Aug-59 | GORTON-9G | COLWICK-40E | KINGS CROSS-34A | ROWSLEY-17C | DARLINGTON-51A | DARLINGTON-51A | IMMINGHAM-40B | BLAYDON-52C | DAIRYCOATES-53A |
| Nov-59 | GORTON-9G | COLWICK-40E | KINGS CROSS-34A | ROWSLEY-17C | DARLINGTON-51A | DARLINGTON-51A | IMMINGHAM-40B | BLAYDON-52C | DAIRYCOATES-53A |
| Jan-60 | GORTON-9G | COLWICK-40E | KINGS CROSS-34A | ROWSLEY-17C | DARLINGTON-51A | DARLINGTON-51A | IMMINGHAM-40B | BLAYDON-52C | DAIRYCOATES-53A |
| Apr-60 | GORTON-9G | COLWICK-40E | KINGS CROSS-34A | ROWSLEY-17C | DARLINGTON-51A | DARLINGTON-51A | **3/60: COLW - 40E** | BLAYDON-52C | DAIRYCOATES-50B |
| Aug-60 | GORTON-9G | COLWICK-40E | KINGS CROSS-34A | ROWSLEY-17C | DARLINGTON-51A | DARLINGTON-51A | COLWICK-40E | BLAYDON-52C | DAIRYCOATES-50B |
| Nov-60 | GORTON-9G | COLWICK-40E | KINGS CROSS-34A | ROWSLEY-17C | DARLINGTON-51A | DARLINGTON-51A | COLWICK-40E | BLAYDON-52C | DAIRYCOATES-50B |

| | 68012 | 68013 | 68014 | 68015 | 68016 | 68017 | 68018 | 68019 | 68020 |
|---|---|---|---|---|---|---|---|---|---|
| Aug-50 | GORTON-39A | IMMINGHAM-40B | HEATON-52B | DARLINGTON-51A | SUNDERLAND-54A | YORK-50A | IMMINGHAM-40B | BLAYDON-52C | IMMINGHAM-40B |
| Jan-51 | GORTON-39A | IMMINGHAM-40B | HEATON-52B | DARLINGTON-51A | SUNDERLAND-54A | **12/50: CONS - 54D** | IMMINGHAM-40B | **12/50: CONS - 54D** | IMMINGHAM-40B |
| Aug-51 | GORTON-39A | IMMINGHAM-40B | HEATON-52B | DARLINGTON-51A | SUNDERLAND-54A | **2/51: SUND - 54A** | IMMINGHAM-40B | CONSETT-54D | IMMINGHAM-40B |
| Jan-52 | GORTON-39A | **12/51: BIRK - 6C** | HEATON-52B | DARLINGTON-51A | SUNDERLAND-54A | SUNDERLAND-54A | IMMINGHAM-40B | CONSETT-54D | IMMINGHAM-40B |
| Aug-52 | GORTON-39A | **7/52: BIDS - 6F** | HEATON-52B | DARLINGTON-51A | SUNDERLAND-54A | SUNDERLAND-54A | IMMINGHAM-40B | CONSETT-54D | IMMINGHAM-40B |
| Jan-53 | GORTON-39A | BIDSTON-6F | HEATON-52B | DARLINGTON-51A | SUNDERLAND-54A | SUNDERLAND-54A | IMMINGHAM-40B | CONSETT-54D | IMMINGHAM-40B |
| Aug-53 | GORTON-39A | BIDSTON-6F | HEATON-52B | DARLINGTON-51A | SUNDERLAND-54A | SUNDERLAND-54A | IMMINGHAM-40B | CONSETT-54D | IMMINGHAM-40B |
| Jan-54 | GORTON-39A | BIDSTON-6F | HEATON-52B | DARLINGTON-51A | SUNDERLAND-54A | SUNDERLAND-54A | IMMINGHAM-40B | CONSETT-54D | IMMINGHAM-40B |
| Aug-54 | GORTON-39A | BIDSTON-6F | HEATON-52B | DARLINGTON-51A | SUNDERLAND-54A | SUNDERLAND-54A | IMMINGHAM-40B | CONSETT-54D | IMMINGHAM-40B |
| Jan-55 | GORTON-39A | BIDSTON-6F | HEATON-52B | DARLINGTON-51A | SUNDERLAND-54A | SUNDERLAND-54A | IMMINGHAM-40B | CONSETT-54D | IMMINGHAM-40B |
| Aug-55 | GORTON-39A | BIDSTON-6F | HEATON-52B | DARLINGTON-51A | SUNDERLAND-54A | SUNDERLAND-54A | IMMINGHAM-40B | CONSETT-54D | IMMINGHAM-40B |
| Jan-56 | GORTON-39A | BIDSTON-6F | HEATON-52B | DARLINGTON-51A | SUNDERLAND-54A | SUNDERLAND-54A | IMMINGHAM-40B | CONSETT-54D | **11/56: DCTR - 36A** |
| Aug-56 | GORTON-39A | **8/56: ROWS - 17D** | HEATON-52B | DARLINGTON-51A | SUNDERLAND-54A | SUNDERLAND-54A | IMMINGHAM-40B | CONSETT-54D | DONCASTER-36A |
| Jan-57 | GORTON-39A | ROWSLEY-17D | HEATON-52B | DARLINGTON-51A | SUNDERLAND-54A | SUNDERLAND-54A | IMMINGHAM-40B | CONSETT-54D | DONCASTER-36A |
| Aug-57 | GORTON-39A | ROWSLEY-17D | HEATON-52B | DARLINGTON-51A | SUNDERLAND-54A | SUNDERLAND-54A | IMMINGHAM-40B | CONSETT-54D | DONCASTER-36A |
| Jan-58 | GORTON-39A | ROWSLEY-17D | HEATON-52B | DARLINGTON-51A | SUNDERLAND-54A | SUNDERLAND-54A | IMMINGHAM-40B | CONSETT-54D | DONCASTER-36A |
| Aug-58 | GORTON-9G | ROWSLEY-17C | HEATON-52B | DARLINGTON-51A | SUNDERLAND-54A | SUNDERLAND-54A | IMMINGHAM-40B | CONSETT-54D | DONCASTER-36A |
| Jan-59 | GORTON-9G | ROWSLEY-17C | HEATON-52B | DARLINGTON-51A | SUNDERLAND-52G | **12/58: DARL - 51A** | IMMINGHAM-40B | CONSETT-52K | DONCASTER-36A |
| Aug-59 | **9/59: ROWS - 17C** | ROWSLEY-17C | **5/59: BLAY - 52C** | DARLINGTON-51A | SUNDERLAND-52G | DARLINGTON-51A | IMMINGHAM-40B | **5/59: TYNE D - 52H** | DONCASTER-36A |
| Nov-59 | ROWSLEY-17C | ROWSLEY-17C | BLAYDON-52C | DARLINGTON-51A | SUNDERLAND-52G | DARLINGTON-51A | IMMINGHAM-40B | TYNE DOCK-52H | DONCASTER-36A |
| Jan-60 | ROWSLEY-17C | ROWSLEY-17C | BLAYDON-52C | DARLINGTON-51A | SUNDERLAND-52G | DARLINGTON-51A | IMMINGHAM-40B | TYNE DOCK-52H | DONCASTER-36A |
| Apr-60 | ROWSLEY-17C | ROWSLEY-17C | BLAYDON-52C | DARLINGTON-51A | SUNDERLAND-52G | DARLINGTON-51A | IMMINGHAM-40B | TYNE DOCK-52H | DONCASTER-36A |
| Aug-60 | ROWSLEY-17C | ROWSLEY-17C | BLAYDON-52C | DARLINGTON-51A | SUNDERLAND-52G | DARLINGTON-51A | IMMINGHAM-40B | TYNE DOCK-52H | DONCASTER-36A |
| Nov-60 | **10/60: GORT - 9G** | ROWSLEY-17C | BLAYDON-52C | DARLINGTON-51A | SUNDERLAND-52G | DARLINGTON-51A | IMMINGHAM-40B | TYNE DOCK-52H | DONCASTER-36A |

| | 68021 | 68022 | 68023 | 68024 | 68025 | 68026 | 68027 | 68028 | 68029 |
|---|---|---|---|---|---|---|---|---|---|
| Aug-50 | BLAYDON-52C | IMMINGHAM-40B | NEWPORT-51B | BLAYDON-52C | DARLINGTON-51A | IMMINGHAM-40B | DARLINGTON-51A | IMMINGHAM-40B | BLAYDON-52C |
| Jan-51 | BLAYDON-52C | IMMINGHAM-40B | NEWPORT-51B | BLAYDON-52C | DARLINGTON-51A | IMMINGHAM-40B | DARLINGTON-51A | IMMINGHAM-40B | BLAYDON-52C |
| Aug-51 | **5/51: HTN - 52B** | IMMINGHAM-40B | NEWPORT-51B | BLAYDON-52C | DARLINGTON-51A | IMMINGHAM-40B | DARLINGTON-51A | IMMINGHAM-40B | **5/51: YORK - 50A** |
| Jan-52 | HEATON-52B | IMMINGHAM-40B | NEWPORT-51B | **11/51: SUND - 54A** | DARLINGTON-51A | IMMINGHAM-40B | DARLINGTON-51A | IMMINGHAM-40B | YORK-50A |
| Aug-52 | HEATON-52B | IMMINGHAM-40B | NEWPORT-51B | SUNDERLAND-54A | DARLINGTON-51A | IMMINGHAM-40B | DARLINGTON-51A | IMMINGHAM-40B | YORK-50A |
| Jan-53 | HEATON-52B | IMMINGHAM-40B | NEWPORT-51B | SUNDERLAND-54A | DARLINGTON-51A | IMMINGHAM-40B | DARLINGTON-51A | IMMINGHAM-40B | YORK-50A |
| Aug-53 | HEATON-52B | IMMINGHAM-40B | NEWPORT-51B | SUNDERLAND-54A | DARLINGTON-51A | IMMINGHAM-40B | DARLINGTON-51A | IMMINGHAM-40B | YORK-50A |
| Jan-54 | HEATON-52B | IMMINGHAM-40B | NEWPORT-51B | SUNDERLAND-54A | DARLINGTON-51A | IMMINGHAM-40B | DARLINGTON-51A | IMMINGHAM-40B | YORK-50A |
| Aug-54 | HEATON-52B | IMMINGHAM-40B | NEWPORT-51B | SUNDERLAND-54A | DARLINGTON-51A | IMMINGHAM-40B | DARLINGTON-51A | IMMINGHAM-40B | YORK-50A |
| Jan-55 | HEATON-52B | IMMINGHAM-40B | NEWPORT-51B | SUNDERLAND-54A | DARLINGTON-51A | IMMINGHAM-40B | DARLINGTON-51A | IMMINGHAM-40B | YORK-50A |
| Aug-55 | **9/55: W.HPL - 51C** | IMMINGHAM-40B | NEWPORT-51B | SUNDERLAND-54A | DARLINGTON-51A | IMMINGHAM-40B | DARLINGTON-51A | IMMINGHAM-40B | YORK-50A |
| Jan-56 | W.HARTLEPOOL-51C | **11/56: DCTR - 36A** | NEWPORT-51B | SUNDERLAND-54A | DARLINGTON-51A | IMMINGHAM-40B | DARLINGTON-51A | IMMINGHAM-40B | YORK-50A |
| Aug-56 | W.HARTLEPOOL-51C | DONCASTER-36A | NEWPORT-51B | SUNDERLAND-54A | DARLINGTON-51A | IMMINGHAM-40B | DARLINGTON-51A | IMMINGHAM-40B | YORK-50A |
| Jan-57 | W.HARTLEPOOL-51C | DONCASTER-36A | NEWPORT-51B | SUNDERLAND-54A | DARLINGTON-51A | IMMINGHAM-40B | DARLINGTON-51A | IMMINGHAM-40B | YORK-50A |
| Aug-57 | W.HARTLEPOOL-51C | DONCASTER-36A | NEWPORT-51B | SUNDERLAND-54A | DARLINGTON-51A | IMMINGHAM-40B | DARLINGTON-51A | IMMINGHAM-40B | **9/57: TYNE D - 54B** |
| Jan-58 | W.HARTLEPOOL-51C | DONCASTER-36A | NEWPORT-51B | SUNDERLAND-54A | DARLINGTON-51A | IMMINGHAM-40B | DARLINGTON-51A | IMMINGHAM-40B | TYNE DOCK-54B |
| Aug-58 | W.HARTLEPOOL-51C | DONCASTER-36A | **6/58: TBY - 51L** | SUNDERLAND-54A | DARLINGTON-51A | **7/58: LANG JN - 41J** | DARLINGTON-51A | IMMINGHAM-40B | TYNE DOCK-54B |
| Jan-59 | W.HARTLEPOOL-51C | DONCASTER-36A | THORNABY-51L | **12/58: DARL - 51A** | DARLINGTON-51A | LANGWITH JCN-41J | DARLINGTON-51A | **12/58: COLW - 40E** | TYNE DOCK-52H |
| Aug-59 | W.HARTLEPOOL-51C | DONCASTER-36A | THORNABY-51L | DARLINGTON-51A | DARLINGTON-51A | LANGWITH JCN-41J | DARLINGTON-51A | COLWICK-40E | TYNE DOCK-52H |
| Nov-59 | W.HARTLEPOOL-51C | DONCASTER-36A | THORNABY-51L | DARLINGTON-51A | DARLINGTON-51A | LANGWITH JCN-41J | DARLINGTON-51A | COLWICK-40E | TYNE DOCK-52H |
| Jan-60 | W.HARTLEPOOL-51C | DONCASTER-36A | THORNABY-51L | DARLINGTON-51A | DARLINGTON-51A | LANGWITH JCN-41J | DARLINGTON-51A | COLWICK-40E | TYNE DOCK-52H |
| Apr-60 | W.HARTLEPOOL-51C | DONCASTER-36A | THORNABY-51L | DARLINGTON-51A | DARLINGTON-51A | LANGWITH JCN-41J | DARLINGTON-51A | COLWICK-40E | TYNE DOCK-52H |
| Aug-60 | W.HARTLEPOOL-51C | **9/60: W/D** | THORNABY-51L | DARLINGTON-51A | DARLINGTON-51A | LANGWITH JCN-41J | DARLINGTON-51A | **9/60: W/D** | TYNE DOCK-52H |
| Nov-60 | W.HARTLEPOOL-51C | | THORNABY-51L | DARLINGTON-51A | DARLINGTON-51A | LANGWITH JCN-41J | DARLINGTON-51A | | TYNE DOCK-52H |

| | 68030 | 68031 | 68032 | 68033 | 68034 | 68035 | 68036 | 68037 | 68038 |
|---|---|---|---|---|---|---|---|---|---|
| Aug-50 | IMMINGHAM-40B | YORK-50A | YORK-50A | IMMINGHAM-40B | IMMINGHAM-40B | BLAYDON-52C | BLAYDON-52C | NEWPORT-51B | BLAYDON-52C |
| Jan-51 | IMMINGHAM-40B | YORK-50A | YORK-50A | IMMINGHAM-40B | IMMINGHAM-40B | BLAYDON-52C | BLAYDON-52C | NEWPORT-51B | BLAYDON-52C |
| Aug-51 | IMMINGHAM-40B | YORK-50A | YORK-50A | IMMINGHAM-40B | IMMINGHAM-40B | BLAYDON-52C | BLAYDON-52C | NEWPORT-51B | BLAYDON-52C |
| Jan-52 | **12/51: BIRK - 6C** | YORK-50A | YORK-50A | IMMINGHAM-40B | **12/51: BIRK - 6C** | BLAYDON-52C | BLAYDON-52C | NEWPORT-51B | BLAYDON-52C |
| Aug-52 | **7/52: BIDS - 6F** | YORK-50A | YORK-50A | IMMINGHAM-40B | **7/52: BIDS - 6F** | BLAYDON-52C | BLAYDON-52C | NEWPORT-51B | BLAYDON-52C |
| Jan-53 | BIDSTON-6F | YORK-50A | YORK-50A | IMMINGHAM-40B | BIDSTON-6F | BLAYDON-52C | BLAYDON-52C | NEWPORT-51B | BLAYDON-52C |
| Aug-53 | BIDSTON-6F | YORK-50A | YORK-50A | IMMINGHAM-40B | BIDSTON-6F | BLAYDON-52C | BLAYDON-52C | NEWPORT-51B | BLAYDON-52C |
| Jan-54 | BIDSTON-6F | YORK-50A | YORK-50A | IMMINGHAM-40B | BIDSTON-6F | BLAYDON-52C | BLAYDON-52C | NEWPORT-51B | BLAYDON-52C |
| Aug-54 | BIDSTON-6F | YORK-50A | YORK-50A | IMMINGHAM-40B | BIDSTON-6F | BLAYDON-52C | BLAYDON-52C | NEWPORT-51B | BLAYDON-52C |
| Jan-55 | BIDSTON-6F | YORK-50A | YORK-50A | IMMINGHAM-40B | BIDSTON-6F | BLAYDON-52C | BLAYDON-52C | NEWPORT-51B | BLAYDON-52C |
| Aug-55 | BIDSTON-6F | YORK-50A | YORK-50A | IMMINGHAM-40B | BIDSTON-6F | BLAYDON-52C | BLAYDON-52C | NEWPORT-51B | BLAYDON-52C |
| Jan-56 | BIDSTON-6F | YORK-50A | YORK-50A | IMMINGHAM-40B | BIDSTON-6F | BLAYDON-52C | BLAYDON-52C | NEWPORT-51B | BLAYDON-52C |
| Aug-56 | **8/56: ROWS - 17D** | YORK-50A | YORK-50A | IMMINGHAM-40B | BIDSTON-6F | BLAYDON-52C | BLAYDON-52C | **7/56: DARL - 51A** | BLAYDON-52C |
| Jan-57 | ROWSLEY-17D | YORK-50A | YORK-50A | IMMINGHAM-40B | BIDSTON-6F | BLAYDON-52C | BLAYDON-52C | DARLINGTON-51A | BLAYDON-52C |
| Aug-57 | ROWSLEY-17D | **6/57: TYNE D - 54B** | YORK-50A | IMMINGHAM-40B | **8/57: ROWS - 17D** | BLAYDON-52C | BLAYDON-52C | DARLINGTON-51A | BLAYDON-52C |
| Jan-58 | ROWSLEY-17D | TYNE DOCK-54B | YORK-50A | **2/58: COLW - 40E** | ROWSLEY-17D | BLAYDON-52C | BLAYDON-52C | DARLINGTON-51A | BLAYDON-52C |
| Aug-58 | ROWSLEY-17C | TYNE DOCK-54B | YORK-50A | **10/58: IMM - 40B** | ROWSLEY-17C | BLAYDON-52C | BLAYDON-52C | DARLINGTON-51A | BLAYDON-52C |
| Jan-59 | ROWSLEY-17C | TYNE DOCK-52H | YORK-50A | **1/59: KX - 34A** | ROWSLEY-17C | BLAYDON-52C | BLAYDON-52C | DARLINGTON-51A | BLAYDON-52C |
| Aug-59 | ROWSLEY-17C | TYNE DOCK-52H | **6/59: DARL - 51A** | **3/59: HSEY - 34B** | ROWSLEY-17C | BLAYDON-52C | BLAYDON-52C | DARLINGTON-51A | **5/59: TYNE D - 52H** |
| Nov-59 | ROWSLEY-17C | TYNE DOCK-52H | DARLINGTON-51A | HORNSEY-34B | ROWSLEY-17C | BLAYDON-52C | BLAYDON-52C | DARLINGTON-51A | TYNE DOCK-52H |
| Jan-60 | ROWSLEY-17C | TYNE DOCK-52H | DARLINGTON-51A | HORNSEY-34B | ROWSLEY-17C | BLAYDON-52C | BLAYDON-52C | DARLINGTON-51A | TYNE DOCK-52H |
| Apr-60 | ROWSLEY-17C | TYNE DOCK-52H | DARLINGTON-51A | **3/60: COLW - 40E** | ROWSLEY-17C | BLAYDON-52C | BLAYDON-52C | DARLINGTON-51A | TYNE DOCK-52H |
| Aug-60 | ROWSLEY-17C | TYNE DOCK-52H | **9/60: W.HPL - 51C** | COLWICK-40E | ROWSLEY-17C | BLAYDON-52C | BLAYDON-52C | DARLINGTON-51A | TYNE DOCK-52H |
| Nov-60 | ROWSLEY-17C | TYNE DOCK-52H | W.HARTLEPOOL-51C | **11/60: W/D** | ROWSLEY-17C | BLAYDON-52C | **10/60: TYNE D - 52H** | DARLINGTON-51A | TYNE DOCK-52H |

| | 68039 | 68040 | 68041 | 68042 | 68043 | 68044 | 68045 | 68046 | 68047 |
|---|---|---|---|---|---|---|---|---|---|
| Aug-50 | DARLINGTON-51A | YORK-50A | BLAYDON-52C | W.HARTLEPOOL-51C | DARLINGTON-51A | YORK-50A | DARLINGTON-51A | YORK-50A | DARLINGTON-51A |
| Jan-51 | DARLINGTON-51A | YORK-50A | BLAYDON-52C | **3/51: YORK - 50A** | DARLINGTON-51A | YORK-50A | DARLINGTON-51A | YORK-50A | DARLINGTON-51A |
| Aug-51 | DARLINGTON-51A | YORK-50A | **6/51: SUND - 54A** | YORK-50A | DARLINGTON-51A | YORK-50A | DARLINGTON-51A | YORK-50A | DARLINGTON-51A |
| Jan-52 | DARLINGTON-51A | YORK-50A | SUNDERLAND-54A | YORK-50A | DARLINGTON-51A | YORK-50A | DARLINGTON-51A | YORK-50A | DARLINGTON-51A |
| Aug-52 | DARLINGTON-51A | YORK-50A | SUNDERLAND-54A | YORK-50A | DARLINGTON-51A | YORK-50A | DARLINGTON-51A | YORK-50A | DARLINGTON-51A |
| Jan-53 | DARLINGTON-51A | YORK-50A | SUNDERLAND-54A | YORK-50A | DARLINGTON-51A | YORK-50A | DARLINGTON-51A | YORK-50A | DARLINGTON-51A |
| Aug-53 | DARLINGTON-51A | YORK-50A | SUNDERLAND-54A | YORK-50A | DARLINGTON-51A | YORK-50A | DARLINGTON-51A | YORK-50A | DARLINGTON-51A |
| Jan-54 | DARLINGTON-51A | YORK-50A | SUNDERLAND-54A | YORK-50A | DARLINGTON-51A | YORK-50A | DARLINGTON-51A | YORK-50A | DARLINGTON-51A |
| Aug-54 | DARLINGTON-51A | YORK-50A | SUNDERLAND-54A | YORK-50A | DARLINGTON-51A | YORK-50A | DARLINGTON-51A | YORK-50A | DARLINGTON-51A |
| Jan-55 | DARLINGTON-51A | YORK-50A | SUNDERLAND-54A | YORK-50A | DARLINGTON-51A | YORK-50A | DARLINGTON-51A | YORK-50A | DARLINGTON-51A |
| Aug-55 | DARLINGTON-51A | YORK-50A | SUNDERLAND-54A | YORK-50A | DARLINGTON-51A | YORK-50A | DARLINGTON-51A | YORK-50A | DARLINGTON-51A |
| Jan-56 | DARLINGTON-51A | YORK-50A | SUNDERLAND-54A | YORK-50A | DARLINGTON-51A | YORK-50A | DARLINGTON-51A | YORK-50A | DARLINGTON-51A |
| Aug-56 | DARLINGTON-51A | YORK-50A | SUNDERLAND-54A | YORK-50A | DARLINGTON-51A | YORK-50A | DARLINGTON-51A | YORK-50A | DARLINGTON-51A |
| Jan-57 | DARLINGTON-51A | YORK-50A | SUNDERLAND-54A | YORK-50A | DARLINGTON-51A | YORK-50A | DARLINGTON-51A | YORK-50A | DARLINGTON-51A |
| Aug-57 | DARLINGTON-51A | YORK-50A | SUNDERLAND-54A | **7/57: DAIRY - 53A** | DARLINGTON-51A | **9/57: SUND - 54A** | DARLINGTON-51A | YORK-50A | DARLINGTON-51A |
| Jan-58 | DARLINGTON-51A | YORK-50A | SUNDERLAND-54A | DAIRYCOATES-53A | DARLINGTON-51A | SUNDERLAND-54A | DARLINGTON-51A | YORK-50A | DARLINGTON-51A |
| Aug-58 | DARLINGTON-51A | YORK-50A | SUNDERLAND-54A | DAIRYCOATES-53A | DARLINGTON-51A | SUNDERLAND-54A | DARLINGTON-51A | YORK-50A | DARLINGTON-51A |
| Jan-59 | DARLINGTON-51A | YORK-50A | SUNDERLAND-52G | DAIRYCOATES-53A | DARLINGTON-51A | SUNDERLAND-52G | DARLINGTON-51A | YORK-50A | DARLINGTON-51A |
| Aug-59 | DARLINGTON-51A | **6/59: DARL - 51A** | SUNDERLAND-52G | DAIRYCOATES-53A | DARLINGTON-51A | SUNDERLAND-52G | DARLINGTON-51A | YORK-50A | DARLINGTON-51A |
| Nov-59 | DARLINGTON-51A | DARLINGTON-51A | SUNDERLAND-52G | DAIRYCOATES-53A | DARLINGTON-51A | SUNDERLAND-52G | DARLINGTON-51A | YORK-50A | DARLINGTON-51A |
| Jan-60 | DARLINGTON-51A | DARLINGTON-51A | SUNDERLAND-52G | DAIRYCOATES-53A | DARLINGTON-51A | SUNDERLAND-52G | DARLINGTON-51A | YORK-50A | DARLINGTON-51A |
| Apr-60 | DARLINGTON-51A | DARLINGTON-51A | SUNDERLAND-52G | DAIRYCOATES-50B | DARLINGTON-51A | SUNDERLAND-52G | DARLINGTON-51A | YORK-50A | DARLINGTON-51A |
| Aug-60 | **9/60: TBY - 51L** | DARLINGTON-51A | SUNDERLAND-52G | DAIRYCOATES-50B | DARLINGTON-51A | SUNDERLAND-52G | DARLINGTON-51A | YORK-50A | DARLINGTON-51A |
| Nov-60 | THORNABY-51L | DARLINGTON-51A | SUNDERLAND-52G | DAIRYCOATES-50B | DARLINGTON-51A | SUNDERLAND-52G | DARLINGTON-51A | YORK-50A | DARLINGTON-51A |

| | 68048 | 68049 | 68050 | 68051 | 68052 | 68053 | 68054 | 68055 | 68056 |
|---|---|---|---|---|---|---|---|---|---|
| Aug-50 | BLAYDON-52C | NEWPORT-51B | DARLINGTON-51A | DARLINGTON-51A | DARLINGTON-51A | W.HARTLEPOOL-51C | W.HARTLEPOOL-51C | W.HARTLEPOOL-51C | W.HARTLEPOOL-51C |
| Jan-51 | BLAYDON-52C | NEWPORT-51B | DARLINGTON-51A | DARLINGTON-51A | DARLINGTON-51A | W.HARTLEPOOL-51C | W.HARTLEPOOL-51C | W.HARTLEPOOL-51C | W.HARTLEPOOL-51C |
| Aug-51 | BLAYDON-52C | NEWPORT-51B | DARLINGTON-51A | **4/51: YORK - 50A** | DARLINGTON-51A | W.HARTLEPOOL-51C | W.HARTLEPOOL-51C | W.HARTLEPOOL-51C | W.HARTLEPOOL-51C |
| Jan-52 | **11/51: SUND - 54A** | NEWPORT-51B | DARLINGTON-51A | YORK-50A | DARLINGTON-51A | W.HARTLEPOOL-51C | W.HARTLEPOOL-51C | W.HARTLEPOOL-51C | W.HARTLEPOOL-51C |
| Aug-52 | SUNDERLAND-54A | NEWPORT-51B | DARLINGTON-51A | YORK-50A | DARLINGTON-51A | W.HARTLEPOOL-51C | W.HARTLEPOOL-51C | W.HARTLEPOOL-51C | W.HARTLEPOOL-51C |
| Jan-53 | SUNDERLAND-54A | NEWPORT-51B | DARLINGTON-51A | YORK-50A | DARLINGTON-51A | W.HARTLEPOOL-51C | W.HARTLEPOOL-51C | W.HARTLEPOOL-51C | W.HARTLEPOOL-51C |
| Aug-53 | SUNDERLAND-54A | NEWPORT-51B | DARLINGTON-51A | YORK-50A | DARLINGTON-51A | W.HARTLEPOOL-51C | W.HARTLEPOOL-51C | W.HARTLEPOOL-51C | W.HARTLEPOOL-51C |
| Jan-54 | SUNDERLAND-54A | NEWPORT-51B | DARLINGTON-51A | YORK-50A | DARLINGTON-51A | W.HARTLEPOOL-51C | W.HARTLEPOOL-51C | W.HARTLEPOOL-51C | W.HARTLEPOOL-51C |
| Aug-54 | SUNDERLAND-54A | NEWPORT-51B | DARLINGTON-51A | YORK-50A | DARLINGTON-51A | W.HARTLEPOOL-51C | W.HARTLEPOOL-51C | W.HARTLEPOOL-51C | W.HARTLEPOOL-51C |
| Jan-55 | SUNDERLAND-54A | NEWPORT-51B | DARLINGTON-51A | YORK-50A | DARLINGTON-51A | W.HARTLEPOOL-51C | W.HARTLEPOOL-51C | W.HARTLEPOOL-51C | W.HARTLEPOOL-51C |
| Aug-55 | SUNDERLAND-54A | NEWPORT-51B | DARLINGTON-51A | **9/55: W.HPL - 51C** | DARLINGTON-51A | W.HARTLEPOOL-51C | W.HARTLEPOOL-51C | W.HARTLEPOOL-51C | W.HARTLEPOOL-51C |
| Jan-56 | SUNDERLAND-54A | NEWPORT-51B | DARLINGTON-51A | W.HARTLEPOOL-51C | DARLINGTON-51A | W.HARTLEPOOL-51C | W.HARTLEPOOL-51C | W.HARTLEPOOL-51C | W.HARTLEPOOL-51C |
| Aug-56 | SUNDERLAND-54A | NEWPORT-51B | DARLINGTON-51A | W.HARTLEPOOL-51C | DARLINGTON-51A | W.HARTLEPOOL-51C | W.HARTLEPOOL-51C | W.HARTLEPOOL-51C | W.HARTLEPOOL-51C |
| Jan-57 | SUNDERLAND-54A | NEWPORT-51B | DARLINGTON-51A | W.HARTLEPOOL-51C | DARLINGTON-51A | W.HARTLEPOOL-51C | W.HARTLEPOOL-51C | W.HARTLEPOOL-51C | W.HARTLEPOOL-51C |
| Aug-57 | SUNDERLAND-54A | NEWPORT-51B | DARLINGTON-51A | W.HARTLEPOOL-51C | DARLINGTON-51A | W.HARTLEPOOL-51C | W.HARTLEPOOL-51C | W.HARTLEPOOL-51C | W.HARTLEPOOL-51C |
| Jan-58 | SUNDERLAND-54A | NEWPORT-51B | DARLINGTON-51A | W.HARTLEPOOL-51C | DARLINGTON-51A | W.HARTLEPOOL-51C | W.HARTLEPOOL-51C | W.HARTLEPOOL-51C | W.HARTLEPOOL-51C |
| Aug-58 | SUNDERLAND-54A | **10/58: STOCK - 51E** | DARLINGTON-51A | W.HARTLEPOOL-51C | DARLINGTON-51A | W.HARTLEPOOL-51C | W.HARTLEPOOL-51C | W.HARTLEPOOL-51C | W.HARTLEPOOL-51C |
| Jan-59 | SUNDERLAND-52G | STOCKTON-51E | DARLINGTON-51A | W.HARTLEPOOL-51C | DARLINGTON-51A | W.HARTLEPOOL-51C | W.HARTLEPOOL-51C | W.HARTLEPOOL-51C | W.HARTLEPOOL-51C |
| Aug-59 | SUNDERLAND-52G | **6/59: TBY - 51L** | DARLINGTON-51A | W.HARTLEPOOL-51C | DARLINGTON-51A | W.HARTLEPOOL-51C | W.HARTLEPOOL-51C | W.HARTLEPOOL-51C | W.HARTLEPOOL-51C |
| Nov-59 | SUNDERLAND-52G | THORNABY-51L | DARLINGTON-51A | W.HARTLEPOOL-51C | DARLINGTON-51A | W.HARTLEPOOL-51C | W.HARTLEPOOL-51C | W.HARTLEPOOL-51C | W.HARTLEPOOL-51C |
| Jan-60 | SUNDERLAND-52G | THORNABY-51L | DARLINGTON-51A | W.HARTLEPOOL-51C | DARLINGTON-51A | W.HARTLEPOOL-51C | W.HARTLEPOOL-51C | W.HARTLEPOOL-51C | W.HARTLEPOOL-51C |
| Apr-60 | SUNDERLAND-52G | THORNABY-51L | DARLINGTON-51A | W.HARTLEPOOL-51C | DARLINGTON-51A | W.HARTLEPOOL-51C | W.HARTLEPOOL-51C | W.HARTLEPOOL-51C | W.HARTLEPOOL-51C |
| Aug-60 | SUNDERLAND-52G | THORNABY-51L | DARLINGTON-51A | W.HARTLEPOOL-51C | DARLINGTON-51A | W.HARTLEPOOL-51C | W.HARTLEPOOL-51C | W.HARTLEPOOL-51C | W.HARTLEPOOL-51C |
| Nov-60 | SUNDERLAND-52G | THORNABY-51L | DARLINGTON-51A | W.HARTLEPOOL-51C | DARLINGTON-51A | W.HARTLEPOOL-51C | W.HARTLEPOOL-51C | W.HARTLEPOOL-51C | W.HARTLEPOOL-51C |

| | 68057 | 68058 | 68059 | 68060 | 68061 | 68062 | 68063 | 68064 | 68065 |
|---|---|---|---|---|---|---|---|---|---|
| Aug-50 | W.HARTLEPOOL-51C | BLAYDON-52C | BLAYDON-52C | NEWPORT-51B | YORK-50A | NEWPORT-51B | WREXHAM-6E | TRAFFORD PARK-9E | BIDSTON-6F |
| Jan-51 | W.HARTLEPOOL-51C | BLAYDON-52C | BLAYDON-52C | NEWPORT-51B | YORK-50A | NEWPORT-51B | **12/50: BIDS - 6F** | **9/50: GORT - 39A** | BIDSTON-6F |
| Aug-51 | W.HARTLEPOOL-51C | **6/51: SUND - 51A** | BLAYDON-52C | NEWPORT-51B | YORK-50A | NEWPORT-51B | BIDSTON-6F | **3/51: T.PARK - 9E** | BIDSTON-6F |
| Jan-52 | W.HARTLEPOOL-51C | SUNDERLAND-54A | BLAYDON-52C | NEWPORT-51B | YORK-50A | NEWPORT-51B | BIDSTON-6F | **5/51: GORT - 39A** | BIDSTON-6F |
| Aug-52 | W.HARTLEPOOL-51C | SUNDERLAND-54A | BLAYDON-52C | NEWPORT-51B | YORK-50A | NEWPORT-51B | BIDSTON-6F | GORTON-39A | BIDSTON-6F |
| Jan-53 | W.HARTLEPOOL-51C | SUNDERLAND-54A | BLAYDON-52C | NEWPORT-51B | YORK-50A | NEWPORT-51B | BIDSTON-6F | GORTON-39A | BIDSTON-6F |
| Aug-53 | W.HARTLEPOOL-51C | SUNDERLAND-54A | BLAYDON-52C | NEWPORT-51B | YORK-50A | NEWPORT-51B | BIDSTON-6F | GORTON-39A | **9/53: T.PARK - 9E** |
| Jan-54 | W.HARTLEPOOL-51C | SUNDERLAND-54A | BLAYDON-52C | NEWPORT-51B | YORK-50A | NEWPORT-51B | BIDSTON-6F | GORTON-39A | **10/53: BIDS - 6F** |
| Aug-54 | W.HARTLEPOOL-51C | SUNDERLAND-54A | BLAYDON-52C | NEWPORT-51B | YORK-50A | NEWPORT-51B | BIDSTON-6F | GORTON-39A | BIDSTON-6F |
| Jan-55 | W.HARTLEPOOL-51C | SUNDERLAND-54A | BLAYDON-52C | NEWPORT-51B | YORK-50A | NEWPORT-51B | BIDSTON-6F | GORTON-39A | BIDSTON-6F |
| Aug-55 | W.HARTLEPOOL-51C | SUNDERLAND-54A | BLAYDON-52C | NEWPORT-51B | YORK-50A | NEWPORT-51B | BIDSTON-6F | GORTON-39A | BIDSTON-6F |
| Jan-56 | W.HARTLEPOOL-51C | SUNDERLAND-54A | BLAYDON-52C | NEWPORT-51B | YORK-50A | NEWPORT-51B | BIDSTON-6F | GORTON-39A | BIDSTON-6F |
| Aug-56 | W.HARTLEPOOL-51C | SUNDERLAND-54A | BLAYDON-52C | NEWPORT-51B | YORK-50A | NEWPORT-51B | BIDSTON-6F | GORTON-39A | BIDSTON-6F |
| Jan-57 | W.HARTLEPOOL-51C | SUNDERLAND-54A | BLAYDON-52C | NEWPORT-51B | YORK-50A | NEWPORT-51B | BIDSTON-6F | GORTON-39A | BIDSTON-6F |
| Aug-57 | W.HARTLEPOOL-51C | SUNDERLAND-54A | **6/57: TYNE D - 54B** | NEWPORT-51B | YORK-50A | NEWPORT-51B | BIDSTON-6F | GORTON-39A | BIDSTON-6F |
| Jan-58 | W.HARTLEPOOL-51C | SUNDERLAND-54A | TYNE DOCK-54B | NEWPORT-51B | YORK-50A | NEWPORT-51B | BIDSTON-6F | GORTON-39A | BIDSTON-6F |
| Aug-58 | W.HARTLEPOOL-51C | SUNDERLAND-54A | TYNE DOCK-54B | **6/58: TBY - 51L** | YORK-50A | **6/58: TBY - 51L** | BIDSTON-6F | GORTON-9G | BIDSTON-6F |
| Jan-59 | W.HARTLEPOOL-51C | SUNDERLAND-52G | TYNE DOCK-52H | THORNABY-51L | YORK-50A | THORNABY-51L | BIDSTON-6F | GORTON-9G | BIDSTON-6F |
| Aug-59 | W.HARTLEPOOL-51C | SUNDERLAND-52G | TYNE DOCK-52H | THORNABY-51L | YORK-50A | THORNABY-51L | BIDSTON-6F | GORTON-9G | BIDSTON-6F |
| Nov-59 | W.HARTLEPOOL-51C | SUNDERLAND-52G | TYNE DOCK-52H | THORNABY-51L | YORK-50A | THORNABY-51L | BIDSTON-6F | GORTON-9G | BIDSTON-6F |
| Jan-60 | W.HARTLEPOOL-51C | SUNDERLAND-52G | TYNE DOCK-52H | **1/60: DARL - 51A** | YORK-50A | THORNABY-51L | BIDSTON-6F | GORTON-9G | BIDSTON-6F |
| Apr-60 | W.HARTLEPOOL-51C | SUNDERLAND-52G | TYNE DOCK-52H | DARLINGTON-51A | YORK-50A | THORNABY-51L | BIDSTON-6F | GORTON-9G | BIDSTON-6F |
| Aug-60 | W.HARTLEPOOL-51C | SUNDERLAND-52G | TYNE DOCK-52H | DARLINGTON-51A | YORK-50A | THORNABY-51L | BIDSTON-6F | GORTON-9G | BIDSTON-6F |
| Nov-60 | W.HARTLEPOOL-51C | SUNDERLAND-52G | TYNE DOCK-52H | DARLINGTON-51A | YORK-50A | THORNABY-51L | BIDSTON-6F | GORTON-9G | BIDSTON-6F |

## 68066 – 68074

| | 68066 | 68067 | 68068 | 68069 | 68070 | 68071 | 68072 | 68073 | 68074 |
|---|---|---|---|---|---|---|---|---|---|
| Aug-50 | BIDSTON-6F | GORTON-39A | IMMINGHAM-40B | IMMINGHAM-40B | IMMINGHAM-40B | GORTON-39A | IMMINGHAM-40B | IMMINGHAM-40B | IMMINGHAM-40B |
| Jan-51 | BIDSTON-6F | 10/50:T.PARK-9E | IMMINGHAM-40B | IMMINGHAM-40B | IMMINGHAM-40B | 12/50:BRUNS-8E | IMMINGHAM-40B | IMMINGHAM-40B | IMMINGHAM-40B |
| Aug-51 | BIDSTON-6F | TRAFFORD PARK-9E | IMMINGHAM-40B | IMMINGHAM-40B | IMMINGHAM-40B | 2/51:GORT-39A | IMMINGHAM-40B | IMMINGHAM-40B | IMMINGHAM-40B |
| Jan-52 | BIDSTON-6F | TRAFFORD PARK-9E | IMMINGHAM-40B | IMMINGHAM-40B | IMMINGHAM-40B | GORTON-39A | IMMINGHAM-40B | IMMINGHAM-40B | IMMINGHAM-40B |
| Aug-52 | BIDSTON-6F | TRAFFORD PARK-9E | IMMINGHAM-40B | IMMINGHAM-40B | IMMINGHAM-40B | GORTON-39A | IMMINGHAM-40B | IMMINGHAM-40B | IMMINGHAM-40B |
| Jan-53 | BIDSTON-6F | TRAFFORD PARK-9E | IMMINGHAM-40B | IMMINGHAM-40B | IMMINGHAM-40B | GORTON-39A | IMMINGHAM-40B | IMMINGHAM-40B | IMMINGHAM-40B |
| Aug-53 | BIDSTON-6F | TRAFFORD PARK-9E | IMMINGHAM-40B | IMMINGHAM-40B | IMMINGHAM-40B | GORTON-39A | IMMINGHAM-40B | IMMINGHAM-40B | IMMINGHAM-40B |
| Jan-54 | BIDSTON-6F | 3/54:IMM-40B | IMMINGHAM-40B | IMMINGHAM-40B | IMMINGHAM-40B | 3/54:IMM-40B | IMMINGHAM-40B | IMMINGHAM-40B | IMMINGHAM-40B |
| Aug-54 | BIDSTON-6F | IMMINGHAM-40B | IMMINGHAM-40B | IMMINGHAM-40B | IMMINGHAM-40B | IMMINGHAM-40B | IMMINGHAM-40B | IMMINGHAM-40B | IMMINGHAM-40B |
| Aug-55 | BIDSTON-6F | IMMINGHAM-40B | IMMINGHAM-40B | IMMINGHAM-40B | IMMINGHAM-40B | IMMINGHAM-40B | IMMINGHAM-40B | IMMINGHAM-40B | IMMINGHAM-40B |
| Jan-56 | BIDSTON-6F | IMMINGHAM-40B | IMMINGHAM-40B | IMMINGHAM-40B | IMMINGHAM-40B | IMMINGHAM-40B | IMMINGHAM-40B | IMMINGHAM-40B | IMMINGHAM-40B |
| Aug-56 | BIDSTON-6F | IMMINGHAM-40B | IMMINGHAM-40B | IMMINGHAM-40B | IMMINGHAM-40B | IMMINGHAM-40B | IMMINGHAM-40B | IMMINGHAM-40B | IMMINGHAM-40B |
| Jan-57 | BIDSTON-6F | IMMINGHAM-40B | IMMINGHAM-40B | IMMINGHAM-40B | IMMINGHAM-40B | IMMINGHAM-40B | IMMINGHAM-40B | IMMINGHAM-40B | IMMINGHAM-40B |
| Aug-57 | BIDSTON-6F | IMMINGHAM-40B | 5/57:GORT-39A | IMMINGHAM-40B | IMMINGHAM-40B | 5/57:DCTR-36A | IMMINGHAM-40B | IMMINGHAM-40B | IMMINGHAM-40B |
| Jan-58 | BIDSTON-6F | IMMINGHAM-40B | GORTON-39A | 2/58:DCTR-36A | IMMINGHAM-40B | DONCASTER-36A | IMMINGHAM-40B | IMMINGHAM-40B | IMMINGHAM-40B |
| Aug-58 | BIDSTON-6F | IMMINGHAM-40B | GORTON-9G | DONCASTER-36A | IMMINGHAM-40B | DONCASTER-36A | IMMINGHAM-40B | IMMINGHAM-40B | IMMINGHAM-40B |
| Jan-59 | BIDSTON-6F | 12/58:HSEY-34B | GORTON-9G | DONCASTER-36A | IMMINGHAM-40B | DONCASTER-36A | 12/58:COLW-40E | 1/59:HSEY-34B | IMMINGHAM-40B |
| Aug-59 | BIDSTON-6F | HORNSEY-34B | GORTON-9G | DONCASTER-36A | IMMINGHAM-40B | DONCASTER-36A | COLWICK-40E | HORNSEY-34B | IMMINGHAM-40B |
| Nov-59 | BIDSTON-6F | HORNSEY-34B | GORTON-9G | DONCASTER-36A | IMMINGHAM-40B | DONCASTER-36A | COLWICK-40E | HORNSEY-34B | IMMINGHAM-40B |
| Jan-60 | BIDSTON-6F | HORNSEY-34B | GORTON-9G | DONCASTER-36A | IMMINGHAM-40B | DONCASTER-36A | COLWICK-40E | HORNSEY-34B | IMMINGHAM-40B |
| Apr-60 | BIDSTON-6F | HORNSEY-34B | GORTON-9G | DONCASTER-36A | IMMINGHAM-40B | DONCASTER-36A | COLWICK-40E | HORNSEY-34B | IMMINGHAM-40B |
| Aug-60 | BIDSTON-6F | HORNSEY-34B | GORTON-9G | DONCASTER-36A | 8/60:COLW-40E | DONCASTER-36A | 9/60:W/D | HORNSEY-34B | 8/60:COLW-40E |
| Nov-60 | BIDSTON-6F | HORNSEY-34B | GORTON-9G | DONCASTER-36A | COLWICK-40E | DONCASTER-36A | | HORNSEY-34B | COLWICK-40E |

## 68075 – 68088

68082 / 68083: Y6 0-4-0T (1883)    68088: Y7 0-4-0T (1923)

| | 68075 | 68076 | 68077 | 68078 | 68079 | 68080 | 68082 | 68083 | 68088 |
|---|---|---|---|---|---|---|---|---|---|
| Aug-50 | IMMINGHAM-40B | IMMINGHAM-40B | IMMINGHAM-40B | IMMINGHAM-40B | GORTON-39A | IMMINGHAM-40B | KINGS LYNN-31C | KINGS LYNN-31C | STRATFORD-30A |
| Jan-51 | IMMINGHAM-40B | IMMINGHAM-40B | IMMINGHAM-40B | IMMINGHAM-40B | GORTON-39A | IMMINGHAM-40B | KINGS LYNN-31C | KINGS LYNN-31C | STRATFORD-30A |
| Aug-51 | IMMINGHAM-40B | IMMINGHAM-40B | IMMINGHAM-40B | IMMINGHAM-40B | GORTON-39A | IMMINGHAM-40B | 5/51:W/D | KINGS LYNN-31C | STRATFORD-30A |
| Jan-52 | IMMINGHAM-40B | IMMINGHAM-40B | IMMINGHAM-40B | IMMINGHAM-40B | GORTON-39A | IMMINGHAM-40B | | KINGS LYNN-31C | STRATFORD-30A |
| Aug-52 | IMMINGHAM-40B | IMMINGHAM-40B | IMMINGHAM-40B | IMMINGHAM-40B | GORTON-39A | IMMINGHAM-40B | | 9/52:MARCH-31B | STRATFORD-30A |
| Jan-53 | IMMINGHAM-40B | IMMINGHAM-40B | IMMINGHAM-40B | IMMINGHAM-40B | GORTON-39A | IMMINGHAM-40B | | 11/52:W/D | 12/52:W/D |
| Aug-53 | IMMINGHAM-40B | IMMINGHAM-40B | IMMINGHAM-40B | IMMINGHAM-40B | GORTON-39A | IMMINGHAM-40B | | | |
| Jan-54 | IMMINGHAM-40B | IMMINGHAM-40B | IMMINGHAM-40B | IMMINGHAM-40B | GORTON-39A | IMMINGHAM-40B | | | |
| Aug-54 | IMMINGHAM-40B | IMMINGHAM-40B | IMMINGHAM-40B | IMMINGHAM-40B | GORTON-39A | IMMINGHAM-40B | | | |
| Aug-55 | IMMINGHAM-40B | IMMINGHAM-40B | IMMINGHAM-40B | IMMINGHAM-40B | GORTON-39A | IMMINGHAM-40B | | | |
| Jan-56 | IMMINGHAM-40B | IMMINGHAM-40B | IMMINGHAM-40B | IMMINGHAM-40B | GORTON-39A | IMMINGHAM-40B | | | |
| Aug-56 | IMMINGHAM-40B | IMMINGHAM-40B | IMMINGHAM-40B | IMMINGHAM-40B | GORTON-39A | IMMINGHAM-40B | | | |
| Jan-57 | IMMINGHAM-40B | IMMINGHAM-40B | IMMINGHAM-40B | IMMINGHAM-40B | GORTON-39A | IMMINGHAM-40B | | | |
| Aug-57 | IMMINGHAM-40B | IMMINGHAM-40B | IMMINGHAM-40B | IMMINGHAM-40B | GORTON-39A | IMMINGHAM-40B | | | |
| Aug-58 | IMMINGHAM-40B | IMMINGHAM-40B | IMMINGHAM-40B | IMMINGHAM-40B | GORTON-9G | 7/58:LANG JN-41J | | | |
| Jan-59 | 1/59:HSEY-34B | 12/58:COLW-40E | 1/59:HSEY-34B | IMMINGHAM-40B | GORTON-9G | LANGWITH JCN-41J | | | |
| Aug-59 | HORNSEY-34B | COLWICK-40E | HORNSEY-34B | IMMINGHAM-40B | GORTON-9G | LANGWITH JCN-41J | | | |
| Nov-59 | HORNSEY-34B | COLWICK-40E | HORNSEY-34B | IMMINGHAM-40B | GORTON-9G | LANGWITH JCN-41J | | | |
| Jan-60 | HORNSEY-34B | COLWICK-40E | HORNSEY-34B | IMMINGHAM-40B | GORTON-9G | LANGWITH JCN-41J | | | |
| Apr-60 | HORNSEY-34B | COLWICK-40E | HORNSEY-34B | IMMINGHAM-40B | GORTON-9G | LANGWITH JCN-41J | | | |
| Aug-60 | HORNSEY-34B | 9/60:W/D | HORNSEY-34B | IMMINGHAM-40B | GORTON-9G | LANGWITH JCN-41J | | | |
| Nov-60 | HORNSEY-34B | | HORNSEY-34B | IMMINGHAM-40B | GORTON-9G | LANGWITH JCN-41J | | | |

## 68089 – 68098

68091: Y8 0-4-0T (1890)    68092: Y9 0-4-0ST (1882)

| | 68089 | 68091 | 68092 | 68093 | 68094 | 68095 | 68096 | 68097 | 68098 |
|---|---|---|---|---|---|---|---|---|---|
| Aug-50 | TWEEDMOUTH-52D | YORK-50A | EDINBURGH(SM)-64A | EDINBURGH(SM)-64A | KIPPS-65E | EDINBURGH(SM)-64A | EDINBURGH(SM)-64A | EDINBURGH(SM)-64A | EDINBURGH(SM)-64A |
| Jan-51 | TWEEDMOUTH-52D | YORK-50A | EDINBURGH(SM)-64A | EDINBURGH(SM)-64A | KIPPS-65E | EDINBURGH(SM)-64A | EDINBURGH(SM)-64A | EDINBURGH(SM)-64A | EDINBURGH(SM)-64A |
| Aug-51 | TWEEDMOUTH-52D | YORK-50A | EDINBURGH(SM)-64A | EDINBURGH(SM)-64A | KIPPS-65E | EDINBURGH(SM)-64A | EDINBURGH(SM)-64A | EDINBURGH(SM)-64A | EDINBURGH(SM)-64A |
| Jan-52 | 1/52:W/D | YORK-50A | EDINBURGH(SM)-64A | EDINBURGH(SM)-64A | KIPPS-65E | EDINBURGH(SM)-64A | EDINBURGH(SM)-64A | EDINBURGH(SM)-64A | EDINBURGH(SM)-64A |
| Aug-52 | | YORK-50A | EDINBURGH(SM)-64A | EDINBURGH(SM)-64A | KIPPS-65E | EDINBURGH(SM)-64A | EDINBURGH(SM)-64A | EDINBURGH(SM)-64A | EDINBURGH(SM)-64A |
| Jan-53 | | YORK-50A | EDINBURGH(SM)-64A | EDINBURGH(SM)-64A | KIPPS-65E | EDINBURGH(SM)-64A | EDINBURGH(SM)-64A | EDINBURGH(SM)-64A | EDINBURGH(SM)-64A |
| Aug-53 | | YORK-50A | 3/53:W/D | EDINBURGH(SM)-64A | KIPPS-65E | EDINBURGH(SM)-64A | EDINBURGH(SM)-64A | EDINBURGH(SM)-64A | EDINBURGH(SM)-64A |
| Jan-54 | | YORK-50A | | EDINBURGH(SM)-64A | KIPPS-65E | EDINBURGH(SM)-64A | EDINBURGH(SM)-64A | EDINBURGH(SM)-64A | EDINBURGH(SM)-64A |
| Aug-54 | | YORK-50A | | EDINBURGH(SM)-64A | KIPPS-65E | EDINBURGH(SM)-64A | 5/54:W/D | EDINBURGH(SM)-64A | EDINBURGH(SM)-64A |
| Jan-55 | | YORK-50A | | EDINBURGH(SM)-64A | KIPPS-65E | EDINBURGH(SM)-64A | | EDINBURGH(SM)-64A | 12/54:W/D |
| Aug-55 | | YORK-50A | | 5/55:W/D | 4/55:W/D | EDINBURGH(SM)-64A | | EDINBURGH(SM)-64A | |
| Jan-56 | | YORK-50A | | | | EDINBURGH(SM)-64A | | EDINBURGH(SM)-64A | |
| Aug-56 | | YORK-50A | | | | EDINBURGH(SM)-64A | | EDINBURGH(SM)-64A | |
| Jan-57 | | 11/56:W/D | | | | EDINBURGH(SM)-64A | | EDINBURGH(SM)-64A | |
| Aug-57 | | | | | | EDINBURGH(SM)-64A | | EDINBURGH(SM)-64A | |
| Jan-58 | | | | | | EDINBURGH(SM)-64A | | EDINBURGH(SM)-64A | |
| Aug-58 | | | | | | EDINBURGH(SM)-64A | | EDINBURGH(SM)-64A | |
| Jan-59 | | | | | | EDINBURGH(SM)-64A | | 10/58:W/D | |
| Aug-59 | | | | | | EDINBURGH(SM)-64A | | | |
| Nov-59 | | | | | | EDINBURGH(SM)-64A | | | |
| Jan-60 | | | | | | EDINBURGH(SM)-64A | | | |
| Apr-60 | | | | | | EDINBURGH(SM)-64A | | | |
| Aug-60 | | | | | | EDINBURGH(SM)-64A | | | |
| Nov-60 | | | | | | EDINBURGH(SM)-64A | | | |

## 68099 – 68107

| | 68099 | 68100 | 68101 | 68102 | 68103 | 68104 | 68105 | 68106 | 68107 |
|---|---|---|---|---|---|---|---|---|---|
| Aug-50 | EDINBURGH(SM)-64A | DUNDEE-62B | DUNFERMLINE-62C | EDINBURGH(SM)-64A | EASTFIELD-65A | POLMONT-64E | EDINBURGH(SM)-64A | KIPPS-65E | DUNDEE-62B |
| Jan-51 | EDINBURGH(SM)-64A | DUNDEE-62B | DUNFERMLINE-62C | EDINBURGH(SM)-64A | EASTFIELD-65A | POLMONT-64E | EDINBURGH(SM)-64A | KIPPS-65E | DUNDEE-62B |
| Aug-51 | EDINBURGH(SM)-64A | DUNDEE-62B | DUNFERMLINE-62C | EDINBURGH(SM)-64A | EASTFIELD-65A | POLMONT-64E | EDINBURGH(SM)-64A | KIPPS-65E | DUNDEE-62B |
| Jan-52 | EDINBURGH(SM)-64A | DUNDEE-62B | DUNFERMLINE-62C | EDINBURGH(SM)-64A | EASTFIELD-65A | POLMONT-64E | EDINBURGH(SM)-64A | KIPPS-65E | DUNDEE-62B |
| Aug-52 | EDINBURGH(SM)-64A | DUNDEE-62B | DUNFERMLINE-62C | EDINBURGH(SM)-64A | EASTFIELD-65A | POLMONT-64E | EDINBURGH(SM)-64A | KIPPS-65E | DUNDEE-62B |
| Jan-53 | EDINBURGH(SM)-64A | DUNDEE-62B | DUNFERMLINE-62C | EDINBURGH(SM)-64A | EASTFIELD-65A | POLMONT-64E | EDINBURGH(SM)-64A | KIPPS-65E | DUNDEE-62B |
| Aug-53 | EDINBURGH(SM)-64A | DUNDEE-62B | DUNFERMLINE-62C | EDINBURGH(SM)-64A | 8/53:EBRO(SM)-64A | POLMONT-64E | EDINBURGH(SM)-64A | KIPPS-65E | DUNDEE-62B |
| Jan-54 | EDINBURGH(SM)-64A | DUNDEE-62B | DUNFERMLINE-62C | EDINBURGH(SM)-64A | 1/54:DUN-62B | POLMONT-64E | EDINBURGH(SM)-64A | KIPPS-65E | 12/53:W/D |
| Aug-54 | EDINBURGH(SM)-64A | DUNDEE-62B | DUNFERMLINE-62C | EDINBURGH(SM)-64A | 6/54:W/D | POLMONT-64E | EDINBURGH(SM)-64A | KIPPS-65E | |
| Jan-55 | EDINBURGH(SM)-64A | DUNDEE-62B | DUNFERMLINE-62C | EDINBURGH(SM)-64A | | POLMONT-64E | EDINBURGH(SM)-64A | KIPPS-65E | |
| Aug-55 | EDINBURGH(SM)-64A | DUNDEE-62B | DUNFERMLINE-62C | EDINBURGH(SM)-64A | | POLMONT-64E | 4/55:W/D | KIPPS-65E | |
| Jan-56 | EDINBURGH(SM)-64A | DUNDEE-62B | DUNFERMLINE-62C | 2/56:POL-64E | | POLMONT-64E | | KIPPS-65E | |
| Aug-56 | EDINBURGH(SM)-64A | DUNDEE-62B | DUNFERMLINE-62C | 4/56:EBRO(SM)-64A | | POLMONT-64E | | KIPPS-65E | |
| Jan-57 | 11/56:W/D | DUNDEE-62B | DUNFERMLINE-62C | EDINBURGH(SM)-64A | | POLMONT-64E | | KIPPS-65E | |
| Aug-57 | | 9/57:KIPPS-65E | DUNFERMLINE-62C | EDINBURGH(SM)-64A | | POLMONT-64E | | 8/57:W/D | |
| Jan-58 | | KIPPS-65E | DUNFERMLINE-62C | EDINBURGH(SM)-64A | | POLMONT-64E | | | |
| Aug-58 | | KIPPS-65E | DUNFERMLINE-62C | EDINBURGH(SM)-64A | | POLMONT-64E | | | |
| Jan-59 | | KIPPS-65E | DUNFERMLINE-62C | 12/58:W/D | | POLMONT-64E | | | |
| Aug-59 | | KIPPS-65E | DUNFERMLINE-62C | | | POLMONT-64E | | | |
| Nov-59 | | KIPPS-65E | DUNFERMLINE-62C | | | POLMONT-64E | | | |
| Jan-60 | | KIPPS-65E | DUNFERMLINE-62C | | | POLMONT-64E | | | |
| Apr-60 | | 5/60:W/D | DUNFERMLINE-62C | | | POLMONT-64E | | | |
| Aug-60 | | | DUNFERMLINE-62C | | | POLMONT-65K | | | |
| Nov-60 | | | DUNFERMLINE-62C | | | POLMONT-65K | | | |

## 68108 – 68116

| | 68108 | 68109 | 68110 | 68111 | 68112 | 68113 | 68114 | 68115 | 68116 |
|---|---|---|---|---|---|---|---|---|---|
| Aug-50 | INVERNESS-60A | EASTFIELD-65A | DUNDEE-62B | EDINBURGH(SM)-64A | YOKER-65G | POLMONT-64E | DUNDEE-62B | EDINBURGH(SM)-64A | KIPPS-65E |
| Jan-51 | 10/50: DUN - 62B | EASTFIELD-65A | DUNDEE-62B | EDINBURGH(SM)-64A | YOKER-65G | POLMONT-64E | DUNDEE-62B | EDINBURGH(SM)-64A | KIPPS-65E |
| Aug-51 | DUNDEE-62B | EASTFIELD-65A | DUNDEE-62B | EDINBURGH(SM)-64A | YOKER-65G | POLMONT-64E | DUNDEE-62B | EDINBURGH(SM)-64A | KIPPS-65E |
| Jan-52 | DUNDEE-62B | EASTFIELD-65A | DUNDEE-62B | EDINBURGH(SM)-64A | YOKER-65G | POLMONT-64E | DUNDEE-62B | EDINBURGH(SM)-64A | KIPPS-65E |
| Aug-52 | DUNDEE-62B | EASTFIELD-65A | DUNDEE-62B | EDINBURGH(SM)-64A | YOKER-65G | POLMONT-64E | DUNDEE-62B | EDINBURGH(SM)-64A | KIPPS-65E |
| Jan-53 | DUNDEE-62B | EASTFIELD-65A | DUNDEE-62B | 3/53: W/D | YOKER-65G | POLMONT-64E | DUNDEE-62B | EDINBURGH(SM)-64A | KIPPS-65E |
| Aug-53 | DUNDEE-62B | EASTFIELD-65A | DUNDEE-62B | | YOKER-65G | POLMONT-64E | DUNDEE-62B | EDINBURGH(SM)-64A | KIPPS-65E |
| Jan-54 | DUNDEE-62B | EASTFIELD-65A | DUNDEE-62B | | YOKER-65G | POLMONT-64E | DUNDEE-62B | EDINBURGH(SM)-64A | KIPPS-65E |
| Aug-54 | DUNDEE-62B | 4/54: W/D | DUNDEE-62B | | YOKER-65G | POLMONT-64E | DUNDEE-62B | EDINBURGH(SM)-64A | KIPPS-65E |
| Jan-55 | DUNDEE-62B | | DUNDEE-62B | | 1/55: W/D | POLMONT-64E | DUNDEE-62B | EDINBURGH(SM)-64A | KIPPS-65E |
| Aug-55 | 6/55: EBRO(SM) - 64A | | DUNDEE-62B | | | POLMONT-64E | DUNDEE-62B | EDINBURGH(SM)-64A | KIPPS-65E |
| Jan-56 | 9/55: DUN - 62B | | 2/56: EFLD - 65A | | | POLMONT-64E | DUNDEE-62B | EDINBURGH(SM)-64A | KIPPS-65E |
| Aug-56 | DUNDEE-62B | | 3/56: KIPPS - 65E | | | POLMONT-64E | DUNDEE-62B | EDINBURGH(SM)-64A | KIPPS-65E |
| Jan-57 | DUNDEE-62B | | KIPPS-65E | | | POLMONT-64E | DUNDEE-62B | EDINBURGH(SM)-64A | KIPPS-65E |
| Aug-57 | DUNDEE-62B | | KIPPS-65E | | | POLMONT-64E | DUNDEE-62B | 7/57: W/D | KIPPS-65E |
| Jan-58 | 12/57: KIPPS - 65E | | KIPPS-65E | | | 1/58: W/D | 4/58: DAWS - 65D | | 2/58: W/D |
| Aug-58 | KIPPS-65E | | KIPPS-65E | | | | DAWSHOLME-65D | | |
| Jan-59 | KIPPS-65E | | KIPPS-65E | | | | DAWSHOLME-65D | | |
| Aug-59 | KIPPS-65E | | 9/59: AYR - 67C | | | | 5/59: KIPPS - 65E | | |
| Nov-59 | 11/59: W/D | | 12/59: KIPPS - 65E | | | | KIPPS-65E | | |
| Jan-60 | | | KIPPS-65E | | | | KIPPS-65E | | |
| Apr-60 | | | KIPPS-65E | | | | KIPPS-65E | | |
| Aug-60 | | | KIPPS-65E | | | | 9/60: W/D | | |
| Nov-60 | | | KIPPS-65E | | | | | | |

## 68117 – 68125 (Y4 0-4-0T (1913) over 68125)

| | 68117 | 68118 | 68119 | 68120 | 68121 | 68122 | 68123 | 68124 | 68125 |
|---|---|---|---|---|---|---|---|---|---|
| Aug-50 | KIPPS-65E | EASTFIELD-65A | EDINBURGH(SM)-64A | KIPPS-65E | KIPPS-65E | EDINBURGH(SM)-64A | DUNDEE-62B | EASTFIELD-65A | STRATFORD-30A |
| Jan-51 | KIPPS-65E | 3/51: AYR - 67C | EDINBURGH(SM)-64A | KIPPS-65E | KIPPS-65E | EDINBURGH(SM)-64A | DUNDEE-62B | EASTFIELD-65A | STRATFORD-30A |
| Aug-51 | KIPPS-65E | 5/51: EAST - 65A | EDINBURGH(SM)-64A | KIPPS-65E | KIPPS-65E | EDINBURGH(SM)-64A | DUNDEE-62B | EASTFIELD-65A | STRATFORD-30A |
| Jan-52 | KIPPS-65E | EASTFIELD-65A | EDINBURGH(SM)-64A | KIPPS-65E | KIPPS-65E | EDINBURGH(SM)-64A | DUNDEE-62B | EASTFIELD-65A | STRATFORD-30A |
| Aug-52 | KIPPS-65E | 7/52: YOKER - 65G | EDINBURGH(SM)-64A | KIPPS-65E | KIPPS-65E | EDINBURGH(SM)-64A | DUNDEE-62B | EASTFIELD-65A | STRATFORD-30A |
| Jan-53 | KIPPS-65E | YOKER-65G | EDINBURGH(SM)-64A | KIPPS-65E | KIPPS-65E | EDINBURGH(SM)-64A | DUNDEE-62B | EASTFIELD-65A | STRATFORD-30A |
| Aug-53 | KIPPS-65E | YOKER-65G | EDINBURGH(SM)-64A | KIPPS-65E | KIPPS-65E | EDINBURGH(SM)-64A | DUNDEE-62B | EASTFIELD-65A | STRATFORD-30A |
| Jan-54 | KIPPS-65E | YOKER-65G | EDINBURGH(SM)-64A | KIPPS-65E | KIPPS-65E | EDINBURGH(SM)-64A | DUNDEE-62B | EASTFIELD-65A | STRATFORD-30A |
| Aug-54 | KIPPS-65E | YOKER-65G | EDINBURGH(SM)-64A | KIPPS-65E | KIPPS-65E | EDINBURGH(SM)-64A | DUNDEE-62B | EASTFIELD-65A | STRATFORD-30A |
| Jan-55 | KIPPS-65E | 2/55: EDINBURGH(SM) - 64A | EDINBURGH(SM)-64A | KIPPS-65E | KIPPS-65E | EDINBURGH(SM)-64A | DUNDEE-62B | EASTFIELD-65A | STRATFORD-30A |
| Aug-55 | KIPPS-65E | EDINBURGH(SM)-64A | EDINBURGH(SM)-64A | 8/55: W/D | 7/55: W/D | 8/55: W/D | DUNDEE-62B | 7/55: KIPPS - 65E | 9/55: W/D |
| Jan-56 | KIPPS-65E | 12/55: AYR - 67C | EDINBURGH(SM)-64A | | | | DUNDEE-62B | KIPPS-65E | |
| Aug-56 | KIPPS-65E | AYR-67C | EDINBURGH(SM)-64A | | | | DUNDEE-62B | KIPPS-65E | |
| Jan-57 | KIPPS-65E | AYR-67C | EDINBURGH(SM)-64A | | | | DUNDEE-62B | KIPPS-65E | |
| Aug-57 | KIPPS-65E | 8/57: EBRO(SM) - 64A | EDINBURGH(SM)-64A | | | | DUNDEE-62B | KIPPS-65E | |
| Jan-58 | KIPPS-65E | EDINBURGH(SM)-64A | EDINBURGH(SM)-64A | | | | 12/57: KIPPE - 65E | Calder:Hire | |
| Aug-58 | KIPPS-65E | EDINBURGH(SM)-64A | EDINBURGH(SM)-64A | | | | KIPPS-65E | 12/58: AYR - 67C | |
| Jan-59 | KIPPS-65E | 10/58: W/D | EDINBURGH(SM)-64A | | | | KIPPS-65E | AYR-67C | |
| Aug-59 | KIPPS-65E | | EDINBURGH(SM)-64A | | | | KIPPS-65E | 9/59: W/D | |
| Nov-59 | KIPPS-65E | | EDINBURGH(SM)-64A | | | | KIPPS-65E | | |
| Jan-60 | KIPPS-65E | | EDINBURGH(SM)-64A | | | | KIPPS-65E | | |
| Apr-60 | KIPPS-65E | | EDINBURGH(SM)-64A | | | | KIPPS-65E | | |
| Aug-60 | KIPPS-65E | | EDINBURGH(SM)-64A | | | | 9/60: W/D | | |
| Nov-60 | KIPPS-65E | | EDINBURGH(SM)-64A | | | | | | |

## 68126 – 68136 (Y1 0-4-0T (1925) over 68130)

| | 68126 | 68127 | 68128 | 68129 | 68130 | 68131 | 68132 | 68133 | 68136 |
|---|---|---|---|---|---|---|---|---|---|
| Aug-50 | STRATFORD-30A | STRATFORD-30A | STRATFORD-30A | STRATFORD-30A | LOWESTOFT-32C | LOWESTOFT-32C | DONCASTER-36A | NEWENGLAND-35A | DARLINGTON-51A |
| Jan-51 | STRATFORD-30A | STRATFORD-30A | STRATFORD-30A | STRATFORD-30A | LOWESTOFT-32C | LOWESTOFT-32C | DONCASTER-36A | NEWENGLAND-35A | DARLINGTON-51A |
| Aug-51 | STRATFORD-30A | STRATFORD-30A | STRATFORD-30A | STRATFORD-30A | LOWESTOFT-32C | LOWESTOFT-32C | DONCASTER-36A | NEWENGLAND-35A | DARLINGTON-51A |
| Jan-52 | STRATFORD-30A | STRATFORD-30A | STRATFORD-30A | STRATFORD-30A | LOWESTOFT-32C | LOWESTOFT-32C | DONCASTER-36A | NEWENGLAND-35A | DARLINGTON-51A |
| Aug-52 | STRATFORD-30A | STRATFORD-30A | STRATFORD-30A | 9/52: 30A (Dept) | LOWESTOFT-32C | LOWESTOFT-32C | DONCASTER-36A | NEWENGLAND-35A | DARLINGTON-51A |
| Jan-53 | STRATFORD-30A | STRATFORD-30A | STRATFORD-30A | Stratford(Dept) | LOWESTOFT-32C | LOWESTOFT-32C | DONCASTER-36A | NEWENGLAND-35A | DARLINGTON-51A |
| Aug-53 | STRATFORD-30A | STRATFORD-30A | STRATFORD-30A | Stratford(Dept) | LOWESTOFT-32C | LOWESTOFT-32C | DONCASTER-36A | NEWENGLAND-35A | DARLINGTON-51A |
| Jan-54 | STRATFORD-30A | STRATFORD-30A | STRATFORD-30A | Stratford(Dept) | LOWESTOFT-32C | LOWESTOFT-32C | DONCASTER-36A | NEWENGLAND-35A | DARLINGTON-51A |
| Aug-54 | STRATFORD-30A | STRATFORD-30A | STRATFORD-30A | Stratford(Dept) | LOWESTOFT-32C | LOWESTOFT-32C | DONCASTER-36A | NEWENGLAND-35A | DARLINGTON-51A |
| Jan-55 | STRATFORD-30A | STRATFORD-30A | STRATFORD-30A | Stratford(Dept) | LOWESTOFT-32C | LOWESTOFT-32C | DONCASTER-36A | NEWENGLAND-35A | DARLINGTON-51A |
| Aug-55 | STRATFORD-30A | STRATFORD-30A | STRATFORD-30A | Stratford(Dept) | LOWESTOFT-32C | LOWESTOFT-32C | DONCASTER-36A | NEWENGLAND-35A | DARLINGTON-51A |
| Jan-56 | STRATFORD-30A | STRATFORD-30A | STRATFORD-30A | Stratford(Dept) | LOWESTOFT-32C | LOWESTOFT-32C | DONCASTER-36A | 11/55: W/D | DARLINGTON-51A |
| Aug-56 | STRATFORD-30A | 4/56: W/D | 9/56: W/D | Stratford(Dept) | 4/56: W/D | LOWESTOFT-32C | DONCASTER-36A | | DARLINGTON-51A |
| Jan-57 | STRATFORD-30A | | | Stratford(Dept) | | LOWESTOFT-32C | DONCASTER-36A | | 11/56: W/D |
| Aug-57 | STRATFORD-30A | | | Stratford(Dept) | | LOWESTOFT-32C | DONCASTER-36A | | |
| Jan-58 | 10/57: W/D | | | Stratford(Dept) | | LOWESTOFT-32C | DONCASTER-36A | | |
| Aug-58 | | | | Stratford(Dept) | | LOWESTOFT-32C | DONCASTER-36A | | |
| Jan-59 | | | | Stratford(Dept) | | LOWESTOFT-32C | DONCASTER-36A | | |
| Aug-59 | | | | Stratford(Dept) | | LOWESTOFT-32C | 8/59: W/D | | |
| Nov-59 | | | | Stratford(Dept) | | LOWESTOFT-32C | | | |
| Jan-60 | | | | Stratford(Dept) | | LOWESTOFT-32C | | | |
| Apr-60 | | | | Stratford(Dept) | | LOWESTOFT-32C | | | |
| Aug-60 | | | | Stratford(Dept) | | LOWESTOFT-32C | | | |
| Nov-60 | | | | Stratford(Dept) | | LOWESTOFT-32C | | | |

## 68137 – 68145

| | 68137 | 68138 | 68139 | 68140 | 68141 | 68142 | 68143 | 68144 | 68145 |
|---|---|---|---|---|---|---|---|---|---|
| Aug-50 | DAIRYCOATES-53A | HAWICK-64G | DAIRYCOATES-53A | DAIRYCOATES-53A | GATESHEAD-52A | W.AUCKLAND-51F | SELBY-50C | STOCKTON-51E | W.AUCKLAND-51F |
| Jan-51 | DAIRYCOATES-53A | HAWICK-64G | DAIRYCOATES-53A | DAIRYCOATES-53A | GATESHEAD-52A | W.AUCKLAND-51F | SELBY-50C | STOCKTON-51E | W.AUCKLAND-51F |
| Aug-51 | DAIRYCOATES-53A | HAWICK-64G | DAIRYCOATES-53A | DAIRYCOATES-53A | GATESHEAD-52A | W.AUCKLAND-51F | SELBY-50C | STOCKTON-51E | W.AUCKLAND-51F |
| Jan-52 | DAIRYCOATES-53A | HAWICK-64G | 9/51: W/D | DAIRYCOATES-53A | GATESHEAD-52A | 11/51: DARL - 51A | SELBY-50C | STOCKTON-51E | W.AUCKLAND-51F |
| Aug-52 | DAIRYCOATES-53A | HAWICK-64G | | DAIRYCOATES-53A | 2/52: W/D | DARLINGTON-51A | SELBY-50C | STOCKTON-51E | W.AUCKLAND-51F |
| Jan-53 | DAIRYCOATES-53A | HAWICK-64G | | DAIRYCOATES-53A | | DARLINGTON-51A | SELBY-50C | STOCKTON-51E | W.AUCKLAND-51F |
| Aug-53 | DAIRYCOATES-53A | HAWICK-64G | | DAIRYCOATES-53A | | DARLINGTON-51A | SELBY-50C | STOCKTON-51E | W.AUCKLAND-51F |
| Jan-54 | 12/53: W/D | HAWICK-64G | | DAIRYCOATES-53A | | DARLINGTON-51A | SELBY-50C | STOCKTON-51E | W.AUCKLAND-51F |
| Aug-54 | | HAWICK-64G | | 5/54: W/D | | DARLINGTON-51A | 5/54: W/D | STOCKTON-51E | W.AUCKLAND-51F |
| Jan-55 | | HAWICK-64G | | | | 1/55: W.AUCK - 51F | | 11/54: W/D | W.AUCKLAND-51F |
| Aug-55 | | 8/55: AYR - 67C | | | | W.AUCKLAND-51F | | | 8/55: DAIRY - 53A |
| Jan-56 | | AYR-67C | | | | W.AUCKLAND-51F | | | DAIRYCOATES-53A |
| Aug-56 | | AYR-67C | | | | W.AUCKLAND-51F | | | 4/56: BRID - 53D |
| Jan-57 | | AYR-67C | | | | W.AUCKLAND-51F | | | 1/57: W/D |
| Aug-57 | | AYR-67C | | | | 5/57: W/D | | | |
| Jan-58 | | AYR-67C | | | | | | | |
| Aug-58 | | AYR-67C | | | | | | | |
| Jan-59 | | 1/59: W/D | | | | | | | |

148

**Y3 0-4-0T (1927)** — (heading above column 68154)

| | 68146 | 68147 | 68148 | 68149 | 68150 | 68151 | 68152 | 68153 | 68154 |
|---|---|---|---|---|---|---|---|---|---|
| Aug-50 | GATESHEAD-52A | MALTON-50F | BRIDLINGTON-53D | W.AUCKLAND-51F | MALTON-50F | BOTANIC GARDENS-53B | YORK-50A | DARLINGTON-51A | GATESHEAD-52A |
| Jan-51 | GATESHEAD-52A | MALTON-50F | BRIDLINGTON-53D | W.AUCKLAND-51F | MALTON-50F | BOTANIC GARDENS-53B | YORK-50A | DARLINGTON-51A | GATESHEAD-52A |
| Aug-51 | GATESHEAD-52A | MALTON-50F | BRIDLINGTON-53D | W.AUCKLAND-51F | MALTON-50F | BOTANIC GARDENS-53B | YORK-50A | DARLINGTON-51A | GATESHEAD-52A |
| Jan-52 | GATESHEAD-52A | 2/52: W/D | BRIDLINGTON-53D | W.AUCKLAND-51F | MALTON-50F | BOTANIC GARDENS-53B | YORK-50A | DARLINGTON-51A | GATESHEAD-52A |
| Aug-52 | GATESHEAD-52A | | BRIDLINGTON-53D | W.AUCKLAND-51F | MALTON-50F | BOTANIC GARDENS-53B | YORK-50A | DARLINGTON-51A | GATESHEAD-52A |
| Jan-53 | GATESHEAD-52A | | BRIDLINGTON-53D | W.AUCKLAND-51F | MALTON-50F | BOTANIC GARDENS-53B | YORK-50A | DARLINGTON-51A | GATESHEAD-52A |
| Aug-53 | GATESHEAD-52A | | BRIDLINGTON-53D | W.AUCKLAND-51F | MALTON-50F | BOTANIC GARDENS-53B | YORK-50A | DARLINGTON-51A | GATESHEAD-52A |
| Jan-54 | GATESHEAD-52A | | 1/54: DAIRY-53A | W.AUCKLAND-51F | MALTON-50F | BOTANIC GARDENS-53B | YORK-50A | DARLINGTON-51A | 10/53: W/D |
| Aug-54 | 4/54: W/D | | DAIRYCOATES-53A | W.AUCKLAND-51F | 6/54: SELBY-50C | 10/54: DAIRY-53A | YORK-50A | DARLINGTON-51A | |
| Jan-55 | | | DAIRYCOATES-53A | W.AUCKLAND-51F | SELBY-50C | 11/54: W/D | YORK-50A | DARLINGTON-51A | |
| Aug-55 | | | DAIRYCOATES-53A | W.AUCKLAND-51F | SELBY-50C | | YORK-50A | DARLINGTON-51A | |
| Jan-56 | | | 12/55: W/D | W.AUCKLAND-51F | SELBY-50C | | YORK-50A | DARLINGTON-51A | |
| Aug-56 | | | | W.AUCKLAND-51F | SELBY-50C | | YORK-50A | DARLINGTON-51A | |
| Jan-57 | | | | W.AUCKLAND-51F | SELBY-50C | | YORK-50A | DARLINGTON-51A | |
| Aug-57 | | | | W.AUCKLAND-51F | SELBY-50C | | YORK-50A | DARLINGTON-51A | |
| Jan-58 | | | | 1/58: W/D | SELBY-50C | | YORK-50A | DARLINGTON-51A | |
| Aug-58 | | | | | SELBY-50C | | YORK-50A | DARLINGTON-51A | |
| Jan-59 | | | | | SELBY-50C | | YORK-50A | DARLINGTON-51A | |
| Aug-59 | | | | | 5/59: W/D | | 3/59: W/D | DARLINGTON-51A | |
| Nov-59 | | | | | | | | DARLINGTON-51A | |
| Jan-60 | | | | | | | | DARLINGTON-51A | |
| Apr-60 | | | | | | | | DARLINGTON-51A | |
| Aug-60 | | | | | | | | DARLINGTON-51A | |
| Nov-60 | | | | | | | | DARLINGTON-51A | |

| | 68155 | 68156 | 68157 | 68158 | 68159 | 68160 | 68161 | 68162 | 68163 |
|---|---|---|---|---|---|---|---|---|---|
| Aug-50 | BRIDLINGTON-53D | SELBY-50C | MALTON-50F | SELBY-50C | NORTHALLERTON-51J | GATESHEAD-52A | SELBY-50C | IMMINGHAM-40B | WREXHAM-6E |
| Jan-51 | BRIDLINGTON-53D | SELBY-50C | MALTON-50F | SELBY-50C | NORTHALLERTON-51J | GATESHEAD-52A | SELBY-50C | IMMINGHAM-40B | WREXHAM-6E |
| Aug-51 | BRIDLINGTON-53D | SELBY-50C | MALTON-50F | SELBY-50C | NORTHALLERTON-51J | GATESHEAD-52A | SELBY-50C | 7/51: WREX-6E | 5/51: W/D |
| Jan-52 | BRIDLINGTON-53D | SELBY-50C | MALTON-50F | SELBY-50C | NORTHALLERTON-51J | GATESHEAD-52A | 3/52: MALT-50F | WREXHAM-6E | |
| Aug-52 | BRIDLINGTON-53D | SELBY-50C | MALTON-50F | SELBY-50C | NORTHALLERTON-51J | GATESHEAD-52A | MALTON-50F | WREXHAM-6E | |
| Jan-53 | BRIDLINGTON-53D | SELBY-50C | 12/52: W/D | SELBY-50C | NORTHALLERTON-51J | GATESHEAD-52A | MALTON-50F | WREXHAM-6E | |
| Aug-53 | BRIDLINGTON-53D | SELBY-50C | | SELBY-50C | NORTHALLERTON-51J | GATESHEAD-52A | 8/53: W/D | WREXHAM-6E | |
| Jan-54 | BRIDLINGTON-53D | SELBY-50C | | SELBY-50C | NORTHALLERTON-51J | GATESHEAD-52A | | WREXHAM-6E | |
| Aug-54 | BRIDLINGTON-53D | 6/54: W/D | | SELBY-50C | 5/54: GHD-52A | GATESHEAD-52A | | WREXHAM-6E | |
| Jan-55 | BRIDLINGTON-53D | | | SELBY-50C | GATESHEAD-52A | GATESHEAD-52A | | WREXHAM-6E | |
| Aug-55 | 8/55: W/D | | | 9/55: W/D | GATESHEAD-52A | DAIRYCOATES-53A | | WREXHAM-6E | |
| Jan-56 | | | | | GATESHEAD-52A | DAIRYCOATES-53A | | 1/56: W/D | |
| Aug-56 | | | | | GATESHEAD-52A | 11/56: DARL-51A | | | |
| Jan-57 | | | | | 3/57: W/D | DARLINGTON-51A | | | |
| Aug-57 | | | | | | DARLINGTON-51A | | | |
| Jan-58 | | | | | | DARLINGTON-51A | | | |
| Aug-58 | | | | | | DARLINGTON-51A | | | |
| Jan-59 | | | | | | DARLINGTON-51A | | | |
| Aug-59 | | | | | | DARLINGTON-51A | | | |
| Nov-59 | | | | | | DARLINGTON-51A | | | |
| Jan-60 | | | | | | DARLINGTON-51A | | | |
| Apr-60 | | | | | | DARLINGTON-51A | | | |
| Aug-60 | | | | | | DARLINGTON-51A | | | |
| Nov-60 | | | | | | DARLINGTON-51A | | | |

| | 68164 | 68165 | 68166 | 68168 | 68169 | 68171 | 68172 | 68173 | 68174 |
|---|---|---|---|---|---|---|---|---|---|
| Aug-50 | WREXHAM-6E | DONCASTER-36A | BOSTON-40F | LOWESTOFT-32C | GORTON-39A | BOSTON-40F | NEASDEN-34E | LOWESTOFT-32C | STRATFORD-30A |
| Jan-51 | WREXHAM-6E | DONCASTER-36A | BOSTON-40F | LOWESTOFT-32C | GORTON-39A | 12/50: IMM-40B | NEASDEN-34E | LOWESTOFT-32C | STRATFORD-30A |
| Aug-51 | WREXHAM-6E | DONCASTER-36A | BOSTON-40F | LOWESTOFT-32C | GORTON-39A | 4/51: BOST-40F | NEASDEN-34E | LOWESTOFT-32C | STRATFORD-30A |
| Jan-52 | WREXHAM-6E | DONCASTER-36A | BOSTON-40F | LOWESTOFT-32C | GORTON-39A | 11/51: W/D | 12/51: W/D | LOWESTOFT-32C | 3/51: IMM-40B |
| Aug-52 | WREXHAM-6E | DONCASTER-36A | BOSTON-40F | LOWESTOFT-32C | GORTON-39A | | | LOWESTOFT-32C | IMMINGHAM-40B |
| Jan-53 | WREXHAM-6E | DONCASTER-36A | BOSTON-40F | LOWESTOFT-32C | GORTON-39A | | | LOWESTOFT-32C | IMMINGHAM-40B |
| Aug-53 | WREXHAM-6E | DONCASTER-36A | BOSTON-40F | LOWESTOFT-32C | GORTON-39A | | | LOWESTOFT-32C | 3/53: W/D |
| Jan-54 | WREXHAM-6E | DONCASTER-36A | BOSTON-40F | LOWESTOFT-32C | GORTON-39A | | | LOWESTOFT-32C | |
| Aug-54 | WREXHAM-6E | DONCASTER-36A | BOSTON-40F | LOWESTOFT-32C | GORTON-39A | | | LOWESTOFT-32C | |
| Jan-55 | WREXHAM-6E | DONCASTER-36A | BOSTON-40F | LOWESTOFT-32C | 3/55: IMM-40B | | | LOWESTOFT-32C | |
| Aug-55 | WREXHAM-6E | DONCASTER-36A | BOSTON-40F | LOWESTOFT-32C | 7/55: W/D | | | LOWESTOFT-32C | |
| Jan-56 | WREXHAM-6E | DONCASTER-36A | BOSTON-40F | LOWESTOFT-32C | | | | LOWESTOFT-32C | |
| Aug-56 | WREXHAM-6E | DONCASTER-36A | BOSTON-40F | LOWESTOFT-32C | | | | LOWESTOFT-32C | |
| Jan-57 | 11/56: SHBY-84G | DONCASTER-36A | BOSTON-40F | LOWESTOFT-32C | | | | LOWESTOFT-32C | |
| Aug-57 | 8/57: WREX-6E | DONCASTER-36A | BOSTON-40F | LOWESTOFT-32C | | | | LOWESTOFT-32C | |
| Jan-58 | 9/57: W/D | DONCASTER-36A | BOSTON-40F | LOWESTOFT-32C | | | | LOWESTOFT-32C | |
| Aug-58 | | DONCASTER-36A | BOSTON-40F | LOWESTOFT-32C | | | | LOWESTOFT-32C | |
| Jan-59 | | 11/58: W/D | BOSTON-40F | LOWESTOFT-32C | | | | LOWESTOFT-32C | |
| Aug-59 | | | BOSTON-40F | 3/59: W/D | | | | LOWESTOFT-32C | |
| Nov-59 | | | BOSTON-40F | | | | | LOWESTOFT-32C | |
| Jan-60 | | | BOSTON-40F | | | | | LOWESTOFT-32C | |
| Apr-60 | | | BOSTON-40F | | | | | LOWESTOFT-32C | |
| Aug-60 | | | BOSTON-40F | | | | | LOWESTOFT-32C | |
| Nov-60 | | | BOSTON-40F | | | | | LOWESTOFT-32C | |

| | 68175 | 68176 | 68177 | 68178 | 68179 | 68180 | 68181 | 68182 | 68183 |
|---|---|---|---|---|---|---|---|---|---|
| Aug-50 | HITCHIN-34D | DARNALL-39B | LOWESTOFT-32C | LOWESTOFT-32C | IMMINGHAM-40B | GATESHEAD-52A | TYNEDOCK-54B | W.AUCKLAND-51F | TYNEDOCK-54B |
| Jan-51 | HITCHIN-34D | 1/51: GORT-39A | LOWESTOFT-32C | LOWESTOFT-32C | IMMINGHAM-40B | GATESHEAD-52A | TYNEDOCK-54B | W.AUCKLAND-51F | TYNEDOCK-54B |
| Aug-51 | 8/51: W/D | 4/51: DARN-39B | LOWESTOFT-32C | LOWESTOFT-32C | IMMINGHAM-40B | GATESHEAD-52A | 8/51: Ranskill | W.AUCKLAND-51F | TYNEDOCK-54B |
| Jan-52 | | 11/51: GORT-39A | LOWESTOFT-32C | LOWESTOFT-32C | 12/52: W/D | GATESHEAD-52A | Ranskill Works | 11/51: DARL-51A | 10/51: DAIRY-53A |
| Aug-52 | | 2/52: DARN-39B | LOWESTOFT-32C | LOWESTOFT-32C | | GATESHEAD-52A | Ranskill Works | DARLINGTON-51A | DAIRYCOATES-53A |
| Jan-53 | | DARNALL-39B | LOWESTOFT-32C | LOWESTOFT-32C | | GATESHEAD-52A | Ranskill Works | DARLINGTON-51A | DAIRYCOATES-53A |
| Aug-53 | | 8/53: W/D | LOWESTOFT-32C | LOWESTOFT-32C | | GATESHEAD-52A | Ranskill Works | DARLINGTON-51A | DAIRYCOATES-53A |
| Jan-54 | | | LOWESTOFT-32C | LOWESTOFT-32C | | GATESHEAD-52A | Ranskill Works | DARLINGTON-51A | DAIRYCOATES-53A |
| Aug-54 | | | LOWESTOFT-32C | LOWESTOFT-32C | | 7/54: SELBY-50C | Ranskill Works | 7/54: DAIRY-53A | DAIRYCOATES-53A |
| Jan-55 | | | LOWESTOFT-32C | LOWESTOFT-32C | | SELBY-50C | Ranskill Works | DAIRYCOATES-53A | DAIRYCOATES-53A |
| Aug-55 | | | LOWESTOFT-32C | LOWESTOFT-32C | | SELBY-50C | Ranskill Works | DAIRYCOATES-53A | DAIRYCOATES-53A |
| Jan-56 | | | LOWESTOFT-32C | LOWESTOFT-32C | | SELBY-50C | Ranskill Works | DAIRYCOATES-53A | DAIRYCOATES-53A |
| Aug-56 | | | LOWESTOFT-32C | LOWESTOFT-32C | | 5/56: W/D | Ranskill Works | 6/56: SELBY-50C | DAIRYCOATES-53A |
| Jan-57 | | | LOWESTOFT-32C | LOWESTOFT-32C | | | Ranskill Works | SELBY-50C | DAIRYCOATES-53A |
| Aug-57 | | | LOWESTOFT-32C | LOWESTOFT-32C | | | Ranskill Works | SELBY-50C | DAIRYCOATES-53A |
| Jan-58 | | | LOWESTOFT-32C | LOWESTOFT-32C | | | Ranskill Works | 1/58: W/D | DAIRYCOATES-53A |
| Aug-58 | | | LOWESTOFT-32C | LOWESTOFT-32C | | | Ranskill Works | | DAIRYCOATES-53A |
| Jan-59 | | | LOWESTOFT-32C | LOWESTOFT-32C | | | Ranskill Works | | 1/59: W/D |
| Aug-59 | | | LOWESTOFT-32C | LOWESTOFT-32C | | | Ranskill Works | | |
| Nov-59 | | | LOWESTOFT-32C | LOWESTOFT-32C | | | 11/59: W/D | | |
| Jan-60 | | | LOWESTOFT-32C | LOWESTOFT-32C | | | | | |
| Apr-60 | | | LOWESTOFT-32C | LOWESTOFT-32C | | | | | |
| Aug-60 | | | LOWESTOFT-32C | 7/60: W/D | | | | | |
| Nov-60 | | | LOWESTOFT-32C | | | | | | |

## Block 1

Classes: Y10 0-4-0T (1930) — 68186; Z4 0-4-2T (1915) — 68190, 68191; Z5 0-4-0T (1915) — 68192, 68193; J62 0-6-0ST (1897) — 68200; J63 0-6-0T (1906) — 68204

| | 68184 | 68185 | 68186 | 68190 | 68191 | 68192 | 68193 | 68200 | 68204 |
|---|---|---|---|---|---|---|---|---|---|
| Aug-50 | DARNALL-39B | NEWENGLAND-35A | YARMOUTH(ST)-32D | KITTYBREWSTER-61A | KITTYBREWSTER-61A | KITTYBREWSTER-61A | KITTYBREWSTER-61A | WREXHAM-6E | IMMINGHAM-40B |
| Jan-51 | DARNALL-39B | NEWENGLAND-35A | YARMOUTH(ST)-32D | KITTYBREWSTER-61A | KITTYBREWSTER-61A | KITTYBREWSTER-61A | KITTYBREWSTER-61A | WREXHAM-6E | IMMINGHAM-40B |
| Aug-51 | DARNALL-39B | NEWENGLAND-35A | YARMOUTH(ST)-32D | KITTYBREWSTER-61A | KITTYBREWSTER-61A | KITTYBREWSTER-61A | KITTYBREWSTER-61A | WREXHAM-6E | IMMINGHAM-40B |
| Jan-52 | DARNALL-39B | NEWENGLAND-35A | 2/52: W/D | KITTYBREWSTER-61A | KITTYBREWSTER-61A | KITTYBREWSTER-61A | KITTYBREWSTER-61A | 11/51: W/D | IMMINGHAM-40B |
| Aug-52 | 8/52: GORT-39A | NEWENGLAND-35A | | KITTYBREWSTER-61A | KITTYBREWSTER-61A | 12/52: Elgin (Hire) | KITTYBREWSTER-61A | | IMMINGHAM-40B |
| Jan-53 | 1/53: DARN-39B | NEWENGLAND-35A | | KITTYBREWSTER-61A | KITTYBREWSTER-61A | 2/53: KITTY-61A | KITTYBREWSTER-61A | | IMMINGHAM-40B |
| Aug-53 | 3/53: GORT-39A | 5/53: IMM-40B | | KITTYBREWSTER-61A | KITTYBREWSTER-61A | KITTYBREWSTER-61A | KITTYBREWSTER-61A | | IMMINGHAM-40B |
| Jan-54 | 5/53: DARN-39B | IMMINGHAM-40B | | KITTYBREWSTER-61A | KITTYBREWSTER-61A | KITTYBREWSTER-61A | KITTYBREWSTER-61A | | IMMINGHAM-40B |
| Aug-54 | DARNALL-39B | IMMINGHAM-40B | | KITTYBREWSTER-61A | KITTYBREWSTER-61A | KITTYBREWSTER-61A | KITTYBREWSTER-61A | | IMMINGHAM-40B |
| Jan-55 | 11/54: W/D | IMMINGHAM-40B | | KITTYBREWSTER-61A | KITTYBREWSTER-61A | KITTYBREWSTER-61A | KITTYBREWSTER-61A | | IMMINGHAM-40B |
| Aug-55 | | 4/55: W/D | | KITTYBREWSTER-61A | KITTYBREWSTER-61A | KITTYBREWSTER-61A | KITTYBREWSTER-61A | | IMMINGHAM-40B |
| Jan-56 | | | | KITTYBREWSTER-61A | KITTYBREWSTER-61A | KITTYBREWSTER-61A | 4/56: W/D | | IMMINGHAM-40B |
| Aug-56 | | | | KITTYBREWSTER-61A | KITTYBREWSTER-61A | KITTYBREWSTER-61A | | | 4/56: W/D |
| Jan-57 | | | | KITTYBREWSTER-61A | KITTYBREWSTER-61A | KITTYBREWSTER-61A | | | |
| Aug-57 | | | | KITTYBREWSTER-61A | KITTYBREWSTER-61A | KITTYBREWSTER-61A | | | |
| Jan-58 | | | | KITTYBREWSTER-61A | KITTYBREWSTER-61A | KITTYBREWSTER-61A | | | |
| Aug-58 | | | | KITTYBREWSTER-61A | KITTYBREWSTER-61A | KITTYBREWSTER-61A | | | |
| Jan-59 | | | | KITTYBREWSTER-61A | KITTYBREWSTER-61A | KITTYBREWSTER-61A | | | |
| Aug-59 | | | | KITTYBREWSTER-61A | 3/59: W/D | KITTYBREWSTER-61A | | | |
| Nov-59 | | | | KITTYBREWSTER-61A | | KITTYBREWSTER-61A | | | |
| Jan-60 | | | | KITTYBREWSTER-61A | | KITTYBREWSTER-61A | | | |
| Apr-60 | | | | KITTYBREWSTER-61A | | KITTYBREWSTER-61A | | | |
| Aug-60 | | | | 5/60: W/D | | 5/60: W/D | | | |
| Nov-60 | | | | | | | | | |

## Block 2

Classes: J65 0-6-0T (1889) — 68211; 68214; J70 0-6-0T (1903) — 68216

| | 68205 | 68206 | 68207 | 68208 | 68209 | 68210 | 68211 | 68214 | 68216 |
|---|---|---|---|---|---|---|---|---|---|
| Aug-50 | IMMINGHAM-40B | IMMINGHAM-40B | IMMINGHAM-40B | IMMINGHAM-40B | IMMINGHAM-40B | IMMINGHAM-40B | IPSWICH-32B | YARMOUTH BEACH-32F | IPSWICH-32B |
| Jan-51 | IMMINGHAM-40B | IMMINGHAM-40B | IMMINGHAM-40B | IMMINGHAM-40B | IMMINGHAM-40B | IMMINGHAM-40B | IPSWICH-32B | YARMOUTH BEACH-32F | IPSWICH-32B |
| Aug-51 | IMMINGHAM-40B | IMMINGHAM-40B | IMMINGHAM-40B | IMMINGHAM-40B | IMMINGHAM-40B | IMMINGHAM-40B | IPSWICH-32B | YARMOUTH BEACH-32F | IPSWICH-32B |
| Jan-52 | IMMINGHAM-40B | IMMINGHAM-40B | IMMINGHAM-40B | IMMINGHAM-40B | 12/51: WREX-6E | IMMINGHAM-40B | IPSWICH-32B | YARMOUTH BEACH-32F | IPSWICH-32B |
| Aug-52 | IMMINGHAM-40B | IMMINGHAM-40B | IMMINGHAM-40B | IMMINGHAM-40B | WREXHAM-6E | IMMINGHAM-40B | IPSWICH-32B | YARMOUTH BEACH-32F | IPSWICH-32B |
| Jan-53 | IMMINGHAM-40B | IMMINGHAM-40B | IMMINGHAM-40B | IMMINGHAM-40B | WREXHAM-6E | IMMINGHAM-40B | IPSWICH-32B | YARMOUTH BEACH-32F | IPSWICH-32B |
| Aug-53 | IMMINGHAM-40B | IMMINGHAM-40B | IMMINGHAM-40B | 9/53: W/D | WREXHAM-6E | IMMINGHAM-40B | IPSWICH-32B | YARMOUTH BEACH-32F | IPSWICH-32B |
| Jan-54 | IMMINGHAM-40B | IMMINGHAM-40B | IMMINGHAM-40B | | WREXHAM-6E | IMMINGHAM-40B | 11/53: W/D | YARMOUTH BEACH-32F | 11/53: W/D |
| Aug-54 | IMMINGHAM-40B | IMMINGHAM-40B | IMMINGHAM-40B | | WREXHAM-6E | IMMINGHAM-40B | | 11/54: M.CONS-32G | |
| Jan-55 | IMMINGHAM-40B | IMMINGHAM-40B | IMMINGHAM-40B | | 1/55: W/D | IMMINGHAM-40B | | 1/55: YAR(B)-32F | |
| Aug-55 | IMMINGHAM-40B | 3/55: W/D | IMMINGHAM-40B | | | IMMINGHAM-40B | | YARMOUTH BEACH-32F | |
| Jan-56 | IMMINGHAM-40B | | IMMINGHAM-40B | | | IMMINGHAM-40B | | YARMOUTH BEACH-32F | |
| Aug-56 | 4/56: W/D | | 4/56: W/D | | | IMMINGHAM-40B | | 8/56: W/D | |
| Jan-57 | | | | | | 2/57: W/D | | | |
| Aug-57 | | | | | | | | | |
| Jan-58 | | | | | | | | | |
| Aug-58 | | | | | | | | | |
| Jan-59 | | | | | | | | | |
| Aug-59 | | | | | | | | | |
| Nov-59 | | | | | | | | | |
| Jan-60 | | | | | | | | | |
| Apr-60 | | | | | | | | | |
| Aug-60 | | | | | | | | | |
| Nov-60 | | | | | | | | | |

## Block 3

| | 68217 | 68219 | 68220 | 68221 | 68222 | 68223 | 68224 | 68225 | 68226 |
|---|---|---|---|---|---|---|---|---|---|
| Aug-50 | KINGS LYNN-31C | YARMOUTH(ST)-32D | KINGS LYNN-31C | IPSWICH-32B | KINGS LYNN-31C | KINGS LYNN-31C | IPSWICH-32B | KINGS LYNN-31C | COLCHESTER-30E |
| Jan-51 | KINGS LYNN-31C | YARMOUTH(ST)-32D | KINGS LYNN-31C | IPSWICH-32B | KINGS LYNN-31C | KINGS LYNN-31C | IPSWICH-32B | KINGS LYNN-31C | COLCHESTER-30E |
| Aug-51 | KINGS LYNN-31C | YARMOUTH(ST)-32D | 2/51: YAR(ST)-32D | 5/51: W/D | KINGS LYNN-31C | KINGS LYNN-31C | IPSWICH-32B | 9/51: COL-30E | COLCHESTER-30E |
| Jan-52 | KINGS LYNN-31C | YARMOUTH(ST)-32D | 7/51: K.LYNN-31C | | KINGS LYNN-31C | KINGS LYNN-31C | IPSWICH-32B | 12/51: K.LYNN-31C | COLCHESTER-30E |
| Aug-52 | 9/52: MARCH-31B | YARMOUTH(ST)-32D | 9/51: IPS-32B | | 9/52: MARCH-31B | 9/52: MARCH-31B | 3/52: W/D | 9/52: MARCH-31B | COLCHESTER-30E |
| Jan-53 | MARCH-31B | 2/53: IPS-32B | IPSWICH-32B | | MARCH-31B | MARCH-31B | | MARCH-31B | COLCHESTER-30E |
| Aug-53 | 3/53: W/D | 8/53: W/D | 2/53: W/D | | 8/53: COL-30E | MARCH-31B | | 8/53: IPS-32B | COLCHESTER-30E |
| Jan-54 | | | | | 12/53: IPS-32B | 12/53: YAR(V)-32E | | IPSWICH-32B | COLCHESTER-30E |
| Aug-54 | | | | | IPSWICH-32B | YARMOUTH(V)-32E | | IPSWICH-32B | COLCHESTER-30E |
| Jan-55 | | | | | 1/55: W/D | YARMOUTH(V)-32E | | IPSWICH-32B | COLCHESTER-30E |
| Aug-55 | | | | | | 7/55: W/D | | 3/55: W/D | 8/55: W/D |
| Jan-56 | | | | | | | | | |
| Aug-56 | | | | | | | | | |
| Jan-57 | | | | | | | | | |
| Aug-57 | | | | | | | | | |
| Jan-58 | | | | | | | | | |
| Aug-58 | | | | | | | | | |
| Jan-59 | | | | | | | | | |
| Aug-59 | | | | | | | | | |
| Nov-59 | | | | | | | | | |
| Jan-60 | | | | | | | | | |
| Apr-60 | | | | | | | | | |
| Aug-60 | | | | | | | | | |
| Nov-60 | | | | | | | | | |

## Block 4

Class: J71 0-6-0T (1886)

| | 68230 | 68231 | 68232 | 68233 | 68234 | 68235 | 68236 | 68238 | 68239 |
|---|---|---|---|---|---|---|---|---|---|
| Aug-50 | YORK-50A | DARLINGTON-51A | DAIRYCOATES-53A | W.HARTLEPOOL-51C | HEATON-52B | DARLINGTON-51A | DARLINGTON-51A | YORK-50A | DARLINGTON-51A |
| Jan-51 | YORK-50A | DARLINGTON-51A | DAIRYCOATES-53A | W.HARTLEPOOL-51C | HEATON-52B | DARLINGTON-51A | DARLINGTON-51A | YORK-50A | DARLINGTON-51A |
| Aug-51 | YORK-50A | 7/51: W/D | DAIRYCOATES-53A | W.HARTLEPOOL-51C | HEATON-52B | DARLINGTON-51A | DARLINGTON-51A | YORK-50A | DARLINGTON-51A |
| Jan-52 | YORK-50A | | DAIRYCOATES-53A | W.HARTLEPOOL-51C | HEATON-52B | DARLINGTON-51A | DARLINGTON-51A | 12/51: NOR'N-20D | DARLINGTON-51A |
| Aug-52 | YORK-50A | | DAIRYCOATES-53A | W.HARTLEPOOL-51C | HEATON-52B | DARLINGTON-51A | DARLINGTON-51A | NORMANTON-20D | DARLINGTON-51A |
| Jan-53 | YORK-50A | | DAIRYCOATES-53A | W.HARTLEPOOL-51C | HEATON-52B | DARLINGTON-51A | DARLINGTON-51A | NORMANTON-20D | DARLINGTON-51A |
| Aug-53 | YORK-50A | | DAIRYCOATES-53A | W.HARTLEPOOL-51C | HEATON-52B | DARLINGTON-51A | DARLINGTON-51A | NORMANTON-20D | DARLINGTON-51A |
| Jan-54 | YORK-50A | | DAIRYCOATES-53A | W.HARTLEPOOL-51C | HEATON-52B | DARLINGTON-51A | DARLINGTON-51A | NORMANTON-20D | DARLINGTON-51A |
| Aug-54 | YORK-50A | | DAIRYCOATES-53A | W.HARTLEPOOL-51C | 8/54: W/D | DARLINGTON-51A | DARLINGTON-51A | NORMANTON-20D | DARLINGTON-51A |
| Jan-55 | YORK-50A | | DAIRYCOATES-53A | W.HARTLEPOOL-51C | | DARLINGTON-51A | DARLINGTON-51A | NORMANTON-20D | DARLINGTON-51A |
| Aug-55 | 9/55: DAIRY-53A | | DAIRYCOATES-53A | W.HARTLEPOOL-51C | | DARLINGTON-51A | DARLINGTON-51A | 9/55: W/D | DARLINGTON-51A |
| Jan-56 | DAIRYCOATES-53A | | DAIRYCOATES-53A | W.HARTLEPOOL-51C | | DARLINGTON-51A | 11/55: W/D | | DARLINGTON-51A |
| Aug-56 | DAIRYCOATES-53A | | DAIRYCOATES-53A | W.HARTLEPOOL-51C | | DARLINGTON-51A | | | DARLINGTON-51A |
| Jan-57 | DAIRYCOATES-53A | | DAIRYCOATES-53A | W.HARTLEPOOL-51C | | DARLINGTON-51A | | | 11/56: W/D |
| Aug-57 | DAIRYCOATES-53A | | 2/57: W/D | W.HARTLEPOOL-51C | | DARLINGTON-51A | | | |
| Jan-58 | DAIRYCOATES-53A | | | W.HARTLEPOOL-51C | | DARLINGTON-51A | | | |
| Aug-58 | DAIRYCOATES-53A | | | W.HARTLEPOOL-51C | | 6/58: W.AUCK-51F | | | |
| Jan-59 | DAIRYCOATES-53A | | | W.HARTLEPOOL-51C | | W.AUCKLAND-51F | | | |
| Aug-59 | DAIRYCOATES-53A | | | W.HARTLEPOOL-51C | | W.AUCKLAND-51F | | | |
| Nov-59 | DAIRYCOATES-53A | | | W.HARTLEPOOL-51C | | W.AUCKLAND-51F | | | |
| Jan-60 | DAIRYCOATES-53A | | | W.HARTLEPOOL-51C | | W.AUCKLAND-51F | | | |
| Apr-60 | 2/60: W/D | | | W.HARTLEPOOL-51C | | W.AUCKLAND-51F | | | |
| Aug-60 | | | | W.HARTLEPOOL-51C | | W.AUCKLAND-51F | | | |
| Nov-60 | | | | W.HARTLEPOOL-51C | | 11/60: W/D | | | |

**Table — Block 1**

| | 68240 | 68242 | 68244 | 68245 | 68246 | 68247 | 68248 | 68249 | 68250 |
|---|---|---|---|---|---|---|---|---|---|
| Aug-50 | YORK-50A | DAIRYCOATES-53A | W.HARTLEPOOL-51C | HEATON-52B | YORK-50A | HEATON-52B | W.HARTLEPOOL-51C | W.AUCKLAND-51F | YORK-50A |
| Jan-51 | YORK-50A | DAIRYCOATES-53A | W.HARTLEPOOL-51C | HEATON-52B | YORK-50A | HEATON-52B | W.HARTLEPOOL-51C | W.AUCKLAND-51F | YORK-50A |
| Aug-51 | YORK-50A | DAIRYCOATES-53A | W.HARTLEPOOL-51C | HEATON-52B | YORK-50A | 8/51: W/D | 6/51: W/D | W.AUCKLAND-51F | YORK-50A |
| Jan-52 | YORK-50A | DAIRYCOATES-53A | W.HARTLEPOOL-51C | HEATON-52B | YORK-50A | | | W.AUCKLAND-51F | YORK-50A |
| Aug-52 | YORK-50A | DAIRYCOATES-53A | W.HARTLEPOOL-51C | HEATON-52B | YORK-50A | | | W.AUCKLAND-51F | YORK-50A |
| Jan-53 | YORK-50A | DAIRYCOATES-53A | W.HARTLEPOOL-51C | HEATON-52B | YORK-50A | | | 1/53: W/D | YORK-50A |
| Aug-53 | YORK-50A | DAIRYCOATES-53A | W.HARTLEPOOL-51C | HEATON-52B | YORK-50A | | | | YORK-50A |
| Jan-54 | YORK-50A | DAIRYCOATES-53A | W.HARTLEPOOL-51C | HEATON-52B | YORK-50A | | | | YORK-50A |
| Aug-54 | YORK-50A | DAIRYCOATES-53A | W.HARTLEPOOL-51C | HEATON-52B | YORK-50A | | | | YORK-50A |
| Jan-55 | YORK-50A | 4/55: STOCK-51E | W.HARTLEPOOL-51C | HEATON-52B | YORK-50A | | | | YORK-50A |
| Aug-55 | YORK-50A | 6/55: W.AUCK-51F | W.HARTLEPOOL-51C | 5/55: M'BRO-51D | YORK-50A | | | | YORK-50A |
| Jan-56 | YORK-50A | W.AUCKLAND-51F | W.HARTLEPOOL-51C | MIDDLESBROUGH-51D | YORK-50A | | | | YORK-50A |
| Aug-56 | 9/56: W/D | W.AUCKLAND-51F | W.HARTLEPOOL-51C | MIDDLESBROUGH-51D | YORK-50A | | | | YORK-50A |
| Jan-57 | | W.AUCKLAND-51F | W.HARTLEPOOL-51C | MIDDLESBROUGH-51D | YORK-50A | | | | YORK-50A |
| Aug-57 | | W.AUCKLAND-51F | W.HARTLEPOOL-51C | MIDDLESBROUGH-51D | YORK-50A | | | | YORK-50A |
| Jan-58 | | W.AUCKLAND-51F | W.HARTLEPOOL-51C | MIDDLESBROUGH-51D | YORK-50A | | | | YORK-50A |
| Aug-58 | | 8/58: W/D | 4/58: W/D | 6/58: TBY-51L | YORK-50A | | | | YORK-50A |
| Jan-59 | | | | THORNABY-51L | 11/58: W/D | | | | YORK-50A |
| Aug-59 | | | | 4/59: W/D | | | | | 4/59: W/D |
| Nov-59 | | | | | | | | | |
| Jan-60 | | | | | | | | | |
| Apr-60 | | | | | | | | | |
| Aug-60 | | | | | | | | | |
| Nov-60 | | | | | | | | | |

**Table — Block 2**

| | 68251 | 68252 | 68253 | 68254 | 68255 | 68256 | 68258 | 68259 | 68260 |
|---|---|---|---|---|---|---|---|---|---|
| Aug-50 | GATESHEAD-52A | DAIRYCOATES-53A | YORK-50A | W.AUCKLAND-51F | W.AUCKLAND-51F | HEATON-52B | W.HARTLEPOOL-51C | DARLINGTON-51A | MIDDLESBROUGH-51D |
| Jan-51 | GATESHEAD-52A | DAIRYCOATES-53A | YORK-50A | W.AUCKLAND-51F | W.AUCKLAND-51F | HEATON-52B | W.HARTLEPOOL-51C | DARLINGTON-51A | MIDDLESBROUGH-51D |
| Aug-51 | GATESHEAD-52A | DAIRYCOATES-53A | YORK-50A | W.AUCKLAND-51F | W.AUCKLAND-51F | HEATON-52B | W.HARTLEPOOL-51C | DARLINGTON-51A | MIDDLESBROUGH-51D |
| Jan-52 | GATESHEAD-52A | DAIRYCOATES-53A | YORK-50A | W.AUCKLAND-51F | W.AUCKLAND-51F | HEATON-52B | W.HARTLEPOOL-51C | DARLINGTON-51A | MIDDLESBROUGH-51D |
| Aug-52 | GATESHEAD-52A | DAIRYCOATES-53A | YORK-50A | W.AUCKLAND-51F | 8/52: W/D | HEATON-52B | W.HARTLEPOOL-51C | DARLINGTON-51A | MIDDLESBROUGH-51D |
| Jan-53 | GATESHEAD-52A | DAIRYCOATES-53A | YORK-50A | W.AUCKLAND-51F | | HEATON-52B | W.HARTLEPOOL-51C | DARLINGTON-51A | MIDDLESBROUGH-51D |
| Aug-53 | GATESHEAD-52A | DAIRYCOATES-53A | YORK-50A | W.AUCKLAND-51F | | HEATON-52B | W.HARTLEPOOL-51C | DARLINGTON-51A | MIDDLESBROUGH-51D |
| Jan-54 | 12/53: HTN-53B | DAIRYCOATES-53A | YORK-50A | W.AUCKLAND-51F | | HEATON-52B | W.HARTLEPOOL-51C | DARLINGTON-51A | MIDDLESBROUGH-51D |
| Aug-54 | HEATON-52B | DAIRYCOATES-53A | YORK-50A | W.AUCKLAND-51F | | 7/54: W/D | W.HARTLEPOOL-51C | DARLINGTON-51A | MIDDLESBROUGH-51D |
| Jan-55 | HEATON-52B | DAIRYCOATES-53A | YORK-50A | W.AUCKLAND-51F | | | 11/54: W/D | DARLINGTON-51A | MIDDLESBROUGH-51D |
| Aug-55 | HEATON-52B | DAIRYCOATES-53A | YORK-50A | W.AUCKLAND-51F | | | | 9/55: W/D | MIDDLESBROUGH-51D |
| Jan-56 | HEATON-52B | DAIRYCOATES-53A | YORK-50A | W.AUCKLAND-51F | | | | | MIDDLESBROUGH-51D |
| Aug-56 | HEATON-52B | DAIRYCOATES-53A | YORK-50A | W.AUCKLAND-51F | | | | | MIDDLESBROUGH-51D |
| Jan-57 | 4/57: DAIRY-53A | DAIRYCOATES-53A | 12/56: NOR'N-20D | W.AUCKLAND-51F | | | | | MIDDLESBROUGH-51D |
| Aug-57 | 7/57: B.GDNS-53B | 4/57: W/D | 9/57: W/D | W.AUCKLAND-51F | | | | | MIDDLESBROUGH-51D |
| Jan-58 | 10/57: DAIRY-53A | | | W.AUCKLAND-51F | | | | | MIDDLESBROUGH-51D |
| Aug-58 | DAIRYCOATES-53A | | | W.AUCKLAND-51F | | | | | 6/58: TBY-51L |
| Jan-59 | 1/59: W/D | | | W.AUCKLAND-51F | | | | | 12/58: STOCK-51E |
| Aug-59 | | | | W.AUCKLAND-51F | | | | | 6/59: TBY-51L |
| Nov-59 | | | | W.AUCKLAND-51F | | | | | THORNABY-51L |
| Jan-60 | | | | W.AUCKLAND-51F | | | | | THORNABY-51L |
| Apr-60 | | | | W.AUCKLAND-51F | | | | | 3/60: W/D |
| Aug-60 | | | | W.AUCKLAND-51F | | | | | |
| Nov-60 | | | | W.AUCKLAND-51F | | | | | |

**Table — Block 3**

| | 68262 | 68263 | 68264 | 68265 | 68266 | 68267 | 68268 | 68269 | 68270 |
|---|---|---|---|---|---|---|---|---|---|
| Aug-50 | HEATON-52B | W.HARTLEPOOL-51C | HEATON-52B | BLAYDON-52C | TYNE DOCK-54B | HEATON-52B | SELBY-50C | W.AUCKLAND-51F | GATESHEAD-52A |
| Jan-51 | HEATON-52B | W.HARTLEPOOL-51C | HEATON-52B | BLAYDON-52C | TYNE DOCK-54B | HEATON-52B | SELBY-50C | W.AUCKLAND-51F | GATESHEAD-52A |
| Aug-51 | HEATON-52B | W.HARTLEPOOL-51C | 5/51: HTN-52B | BLAYDON-52C | TYNE DOCK-54B | 6/51: BLAY-52C | SELBY-50C | W.AUCKLAND-51F | GATESHEAD-52A |
| Jan-52 | HEATON-52B | W.HARTLEPOOL-51C | HEATON-52B | HEATON-52B | TYNE DOCK-54B | BLAYDON-52C | SELBY-50C | W.AUCKLAND-51F | GATESHEAD-52A |
| Aug-52 | HEATON-52B | W.HARTLEPOOL-51C | HEATON-52B | HEATON-52B | TYNE DOCK-54B | BLAYDON-52C | 5/52: W/D | W.AUCKLAND-51F | GATESHEAD-52A |
| Jan-53 | HEATON-52B | W.HARTLEPOOL-51C | 1/53: T.DCK-54B | 1/53: T.DCK-54B | TYNE DOCK-54B | BLAYDON-52C | | W.AUCKLAND-51F | GATESHEAD-52A |
| Aug-53 | HEATON-52B | W.HARTLEPOOL-51C | TYNE DOCK-54B | TYNE DOCK-54B | TYNE DOCK-54B | BLAYDON-52C | | W.AUCKLAND-51F | GATESHEAD-52A |
| Jan-54 | HEATON-52B | W.HARTLEPOOL-51C | TYNE DOCK-54B | TYNE DOCK-54B | TYNE DOCK-54B | BLAYDON-52C | | W.AUCKLAND-51F | GATESHEAD-52A |
| Aug-54 | HEATON-52B | 9/54: HTN-52B | HEATON-52B | TYNE DOCK-54B | TYNE DOCK-54B | BLAYDON-52C | | W.AUCKLAND-51F | GATESHEAD-52A |
| Jan-55 | HEATON-52B | HEATON-52B | HEATON-52B | TYNE DOCK-54B | TYNE DOCK-54B | BLAYDON-52C | | W.AUCKLAND-51F | GATESHEAD-52A |
| Aug-55 | HEATON-52B | HEATON-52B | HEATON-52B | TYNE DOCK-54B | TYNE DOCK-54B | BLAYDON-52C | | W.AUCKLAND-51F | 11/55: W/D |
| Jan-56 | HEATON-52B | HEATON-52B | HEATON-52B | TYNE DOCK-54B | TYNE DOCK-54B | 11/55: GHD-52A | | W.AUCKLAND-51F | |
| Aug-56 | HEATON-52B | HEATON-52B | HEATON-52B | TYNE DOCK-54B | TYNE DOCK-54B | GATESHEAD-52A | | W.AUCKLAND-51F | |
| Jan-57 | 3/57: T.DOCK-54B | HEATON-52B | HEATON-52B | TYNE DOCK-54B | 2/57: W/D | GATESHEAD-52A | | W.AUCKLAND-51F | |
| Aug-57 | TYNE DOCK-54B | HEATON-52B | 5/57: DAIRY-53A | TYNE DOCK-54B | | GATESHEAD-52A | | W.AUCKLAND-51F | |
| Jan-58 | TYNE DOCK-54B | 3/58: GHD-52A | DAIRYCOATES-53A | TYNE DOCK-54B | | 11/57: W/D | | W.AUCKLAND-51F | |
| Aug-58 | TYNE DOCK-54B | GATESHEAD-52A | DAIRYCOATES-53A | TYNE DOCK-54B | | | | W.AUCKLAND-51F | |
| Jan-59 | TYNE DOCK-52H | 5/59: HTN-52B | DAIRYCOATES-53A | TYNE DOCK-52H | | | | W.AUCKLAND-51F | |
| Aug-59 | TYNE DOCK-52H | 6/59: W/D | DAIRYCOATES-53A | 8/59: W/D | | | | W.AUCKLAND-51F | |
| Nov-59 | TYNE DOCK-52H | | DAIRYCOATES-53A | | | | | W.AUCKLAND-51F | |
| Jan-60 | 2/60: W/D | | 2/60: W/D | | | | | W.AUCKLAND-51F | |
| Apr-60 | | | | | | | | W.AUCKLAND-51F | |
| Aug-60 | | | | | | | | W.AUCKLAND-51F | |
| Nov-60 | | | | | | | | 10/60: W/D | |

**Table — Block 4**

| | 68271 | 68272 | 68273 | 68275 | 68276 | 68277 | 68278 | 68279 | 68280 |
|---|---|---|---|---|---|---|---|---|---|
| Aug-50 | HEATON-52B | TYNE DOCK-54B | HEATON-52B | YORK-50A | W.HARTLEPOOL-51C | DAIRYCOATES-53A | HEATON-52B | DARLINGTON-51A | YORK-50A |
| Jan-51 | HEATON-52B | TYNE DOCK-54B | HEATON-52B | YORK-50A | W.HARTLEPOOL-51C | 11/50: W/D | HEATON-52B | DARLINGTON-51A | YORK-50A |
| Aug-51 | HEATON-52B | TYNE DOCK-54B | 6/51: BLAY-52C | YORK-50A | W.HARTLEPOOL-51C | | HEATON-52B | DARLINGTON-51A | YORK-50A |
| Jan-52 | HEATON-52B | TYNE DOCK-54B | BLAYDON-52C | YORK-50A | W.HARTLEPOOL-51C | | 11/51: BLAY-52C | DARLINGTON-51A | YORK-50A |
| Aug-52 | HEATON-52B | TYNE DOCK-54B | BLAYDON-52C | YORK-50A | W.HARTLEPOOL-51C | | BLAYDON-52C | DARLINGTON-51A | YORK-50A |
| Jan-53 | HEATON-52B | 1/53: HTN-52B | BLAYDON-52C | YORK-50A | W.HARTLEPOOL-51C | | 11/52: HEX-52C | DARLINGTON-51A | YORK-50A |
| Aug-53 | HEATON-52B | HEATON-52B | BLAYDON-52C | YORK-50A | W.HARTLEPOOL-51C | | HEXHAM-52C | DARLINGTON-51A | YORK-50A |
| Jan-54 | HEATON-52B | 12/53: GHD-52A | BLAYDON-52C | YORK-50A | W.HARTLEPOOL-51C | | HEXHAM-52C | DARLINGTON-51A | YORK-50A |
| Aug-54 | 5/54: W/D | GATESHEAD-52A | BLAYDON-52C | YORK-50A | W.HARTLEPOOL-51C | | 5/54: BLAY-52C | DARLINGTON-51A | YORK-50A |
| Jan-55 | | GATESHEAD-52A | BLAYDON-52C | YORK-50A | W.HARTLEPOOL-51C | | 9/54: HTN-52B | DARLINGTON-51A | YORK-50A |
| Aug-55 | | GATESHEAD-52A | BLAYDON-52C | YORK-50A | W.HARTLEPOOL-51C | | HEATON-52B | DARLINGTON-51A | YORK-50A |
| Jan-56 | | GATESHEAD-52A | 2/56: SELBY-50C | YORK-50A | W.HARTLEPOOL-51C | | HEATON-52B | DARLINGTON-51A | YORK-50A |
| Aug-56 | | GATESHEAD-52A | SELBY-50C | SELBY-50C | W.HARTLEPOOL-51C | | HEATON-52B | DARLINGTON-51A | YORK-50A |
| Jan-57 | | GATESHEAD-52A | SELBY-50C | SELBY-50C | 11/56: W/D | | 12/56: B.GDNS-54C | DARLINGTON-51A | YORK-50A |
| Aug-57 | | GATESHEAD-52A | 7/57: YORK-50A | SELBY-50C | | | BOROUGH GARDENS-54C | 6/57: W/D | 5/57: W/D |
| Jan-58 | | GATESHEAD-52A | 11/57: W/D | SELBY-50C | | | BOROUGH GARDENS-54C | | |
| Aug-58 | | GATESHEAD-52A | | SELBY-50C | | | BOROUGH GARDENS-54C | | |
| Jan-59 | | 2/59: TBY-51L | | SELBY-50C | | | BOROUGH GARDENS-52J | | |
| Aug-59 | | THORNABY-51L | | 9/59: NOR'N-55E | | | 6/59: TBY-51L | | |
| Nov-59 | | THORNABY-51L | | NORMANTON-55E | | | THORNABY-51L | | |
| Jan-60 | | THORNABY-51L | | NORMANTON-55E | | | THORNABY-51L | | |
| Apr-60 | | THORNABY-51L | | NORMANTON-55E | | | THORNABY-51L | | |
| Aug-60 | | THORNABY-51L | | NORMANTON-55E | | | THORNABY-51L | | |
| Nov-60 | | THORNABY-51L | | NORMANTON-55E | | | | | |

J88 allocation tables — locomotive history records.

| | 68281 | 68282 | 68283 | 68284 | 68286 | 68287 | 68288 | 68289 | 68290 |
|---|---|---|---|---|---|---|---|---|---|
| Aug-50 | DARLINGTON - 51A | YORK - 50A | GATESHEAD - 52A | TWEEDMOUTH - 52D | YORK - 50A | B. GARDENS - 54C | DAIRYCOATES - 53A | B. GARDENS - 54C | W. HARTLEPOOL - 51C |
| Jan-51 | DARLINGTON - 51A | YORK - 50A | GATESHEAD - 52A | TWEEDMOUTH - 52D | YORK - 50A | B. GARDENS - 54C | 11/50: W/D | B. GARDENS - 54C | W. HARTLEPOOL - 51C |
| Aug-51 | 9/51: W.HPL - 51C | YORK - 50A | GATESHEAD - 52A | TWEEDMOUTH - 52D | YORK - 50A | B. GARDENS - 54C | | B. GARDENS - 54C | W. HARTLEPOOL - 51C |
| Jan-52 | W. HARTLEPOOL - 51C | YORK - 50A | GATESHEAD - 52A | TWEEDMOUTH - 52D | YORK - 50A | B. GARDENS - 54C | | B. GARDENS - 54C | W. HARTLEPOOL - 51C |
| Aug-52 | W. HARTLEPOOL - 51C | YORK - 50A | GATESHEAD - 52A | TWEEDMOUTH - 52D | 6/52: W/D | B. GARDENS - 54C | | B. GARDENS - 54C | W. HARTLEPOOL - 51C |
| Jan-53 | W. HARTLEPOOL - 51C | YORK - 50A | GATESHEAD - 52A | TWEEDMOUTH - 52D | | B. GARDENS - 54C | | B. GARDENS - 54C | W. HARTLEPOOL - 51C |
| Aug-53 | 5/53: DAIRY - 53A | YORK - 50A | GATESHEAD - 52A | 9/53: DAIRY - 53A | | B. GARDENS - 54C | | B. GARDENS - 54C | W. HARTLEPOOL - 51C |
| Jan-54 | 11/53: W/D | 10/53: W/D | GATESHEAD - 52A | 10/53: S'HEAD - 53C | | B. GARDENS - 54C | | B. GARDENS - 54C | W. HARTLEPOOL - 51C |
| Aug-54 | | | GATESHEAD - 52A | 2/54: DAIRY - 53A | | B. GARDENS - 54C | | B. GARDENS - 54C | W. HARTLEPOOL - 51C |
| Jan-55 | | | GATESHEAD - 52A | DAIRYCOATES - 53A | | B. GARDENS - 54C | | B. GARDENS - 54C | W. HARTLEPOOL - 51C |
| Aug-55 | | | GATESHEAD - 52A | DAIRYCOATES - 53A | | B. GARDENS - 54C | | 6/55: W/D | 9/55: M'BRO - 51D |
| Jan-56 | | | GATESHEAD - 52A | 10/55: W/D | | B. GARDENS - 54C | | | MIDDLESBROUGH - 51D |
| Aug-56 | | | GATESHEAD - 52A | | | B. GARDENS - 54C | | | MIDDLESBROUGH - 51D |
| Jan-57 | | | GATESHEAD - 52A | | | 11/56: W/D | | | MIDDLESBROUGH - 51D |
| Aug-57 | | | GATESHEAD - 52A | | | | | | MIDDLESBROUGH - 51D |
| Jan-58 | | | GATESHEAD - 52A | | | | | | MIDDLESBROUGH - 51D |
| Aug-58 | | | GATESHEAD - 52A | | | | | | 6/58: TBY - 51L |
| Jan-59 | | | GATESHEAD - 52A | | | | | | 1/59: W/D |
| Aug-59 | | | 7/59: W/D | | | | | | |
| Nov-59 | | | | | | | | | |
| Jan-60 | | | | | | | | | |
| Apr-60 | | | | | | | | | |
| Aug-60 | | | | | | | | | |
| Nov-60 | | | | | | | | | |

| | 68291 | 68292 | 68293 | 68294 | 68295 | 68296 | 68297 | 68298 | 68299 |
|---|---|---|---|---|---|---|---|---|---|
| Aug-50 | W. HARTLEPOOL - 51C | YORK - 50A | YORK - 50A | YORK - 50A | W. HARTLEPOOL - 51C | DAIRYCOATES - 53A | YORK - 50A | DAIRYCOATES - 53A | B. GARDENS - 54C |
| Jan-51 | W. HARTLEPOOL - 51C | YORK - 50A | YORK - 50A | YORK - 50A | W. HARTLEPOOL - 51C | DAIRYCOATES - 53A | YORK - 50A | DAIRYCOATES - 53A | B. GARDENS - 54C |
| Aug-51 | W. HARTLEPOOL - 51C | YORK - 50A | YORK - 50A | YORK - 50A | W. HARTLEPOOL - 51C | DAIRYCOATES - 53A | YORK - 50A | DAIRYCOATES - 53A | B. GARDENS - 54C |
| Jan-52 | W. HARTLEPOOL - 51C | 12/51: NOR'N - 20D | YORK - 50A | 12/51: NOR'N - 20D | W. HARTLEPOOL - 51C | DAIRYCOATES - 53A | YORK - 50A | DAIRYCOATES - 53A | B. GARDENS - 54C |
| Aug-52 | W. HARTLEPOOL - 51C | NORMANTON - 20D | YORK - 50A | NORMANTON - 20D | W. HARTLEPOOL - 51C | DAIRYCOATES - 53A | YORK - 50A | DAIRYCOATES - 53A | B. GARDENS - 54C |
| Jan-53 | W. HARTLEPOOL - 51C | NORMANTON - 20D | YORK - 50A | NORMANTON - 20D | W. HARTLEPOOL - 51C | DAIRYCOATES - 53A | YORK - 50A | DAIRYCOATES - 53A | 12/52: W/D |
| Aug-53 | W. HARTLEPOOL - 51C | NORMANTON - 20D | YORK - 50A | NORMANTON - 20D | W. HARTLEPOOL - 51C | DAIRYCOATES - 53A | YORK - 50A | DAIRYCOATES - 53A | |
| Jan-54 | W. HARTLEPOOL - 51C | NORMANTON - 20D | YORK - 50A | NORMANTON - 20D | W. HARTLEPOOL - 51C | DAIRYCOATES - 53A | YORK - 50A | DAIRYCOATES - 53A | |
| Aug-54 | W. HARTLEPOOL - 51C | NORMANTON - 20D | YORK - 50A | NORMANTON - 20D | W. HARTLEPOOL - 51C | DAIRYCOATES - 53A | YORK - 50A | DAIRYCOATES - 53A | |
| Jan-55 | W. HARTLEPOOL - 51C | 10/54: W/D | YORK - 50A | NORMANTON - 20D | W. HARTLEPOOL - 51C | DAIRYCOATES - 53A | YORK - 50A | DAIRYCOATES - 53A | |
| Aug-55 | W. HARTLEPOOL - 51C | | YORK - 50A | NORMANTON - 20D | W. HARTLEPOOL - 51C | DAIRYCOATES - 53A | YORK - 50A | DAIRYCOATES - 53A | |
| Jan-56 | W. HARTLEPOOL - 51C | | YORK - 50A | NORMANTON - 20D | W. HARTLEPOOL - 51C | DAIRYCOATES - 53A | YORK - 50A | DAIRYCOATES - 53A | |
| Aug-56 | 4/56: W/D | | 9/56: W/D | NORMANTON - 20D | W. HARTLEPOOL - 51C | DAIRYCOATES - 53A | 5/56: W/D | DAIRYCOATES - 53A | |
| Jan-57 | | | | 11/56: W/D | W. HARTLEPOOL - 51C | DAIRYCOATES - 53A | | DAIRYCOATES - 53A | |
| Aug-57 | | | | | 6/57: W.AUCK - 51F | DAIRYCOATES - 53A | | 3/57: W/D | |
| Jan-58 | | | | | W. AUCKLAND - 51F | DAIRYCOATES - 53A | | | |
| Aug-58 | | | | | W. AUCKLAND - 51F | 6/58: W/D | | | |
| Jan-59 | | | | | 2/59: W/D | | | | |
| Aug-59 | | | | | | | | | |
| Nov-59 | | | | | | | | | |
| Jan-60 | | | | | | | | | |
| Apr-60 | | | | | | | | | |
| Aug-60 | | | | | | | | | |
| Nov-60 | | | | | | | | | |

| | 68300 | 68301 | 68302 | 68303 | 68304 | 68305 | 68306 | 68307 | 68308 |
|---|---|---|---|---|---|---|---|---|---|
| Aug-50 | DARLINGTON - 51A | W. HARTLEPOOL - 51C | W. HARTLEPOOL - 51C | MIDDLESBROUGH - 51D | DAIRYCOATES - 53A | STOCKTON - 51E | W. HARTLEPOOL - 51C | MIDDLESBROUGH - 51D | DARLINGTON - 51A |
| Jan-51 | DARLINGTON - 51A | W. HARTLEPOOL - 51C | W. HARTLEPOOL - 51C | MIDDLESBROUGH - 51D | DAIRYCOATES - 53A | STOCKTON - 51E | W. HARTLEPOOL - 51C | MIDDLESBROUGH - 51D | DARLINGTON - 51A |
| Aug-51 | DARLINGTON - 51A | W. HARTLEPOOL - 51C | 9/51: W/D | MIDDLESBROUGH - 51D | DAIRYCOATES - 53A | STOCKTON - 51E | W. HARTLEPOOL - 51C | MIDDLESBROUGH - 51D | DARLINGTON - 51A |
| Jan-52 | DARLINGTON - 51A | W. HARTLEPOOL - 51C | | MIDDLESBROUGH - 51D | DAIRYCOATES - 53A | STOCKTON - 51E | W. HARTLEPOOL - 51C | MIDDLESBROUGH - 51D | DARLINGTON - 51A |
| Aug-52 | DARLINGTON - 51A | W. HARTLEPOOL - 51C | | MIDDLESBROUGH - 51D | DAIRYCOATES - 53A | STOCKTON - 51E | W. HARTLEPOOL - 51C | MIDDLESBROUGH - 51D | DARLINGTON - 51A |
| Jan-53 | DARLINGTON - 51A | W. HARTLEPOOL - 51C | | MIDDLESBROUGH - 51D | DAIRYCOATES - 53A | STOCKTON - 51E | W. HARTLEPOOL - 51C | MIDDLESBROUGH - 51D | DARLINGTON - 51A |
| Aug-53 | DARLINGTON - 51A | W. HARTLEPOOL - 51C | | MIDDLESBROUGH - 51D | DAIRYCOATES - 53A | STOCKTON - 51E | W. HARTLEPOOL - 51C | MIDDLESBROUGH - 51D | DARLINGTON - 51A |
| Jan-54 | DARLINGTON - 51A | W. HARTLEPOOL - 51C | | MIDDLESBROUGH - 51D | DAIRYCOATES - 53A | STOCKTON - 51E | W. HARTLEPOOL - 51C | MIDDLESBROUGH - 51D | DARLINGTON - 51A |
| Aug-54 | DARLINGTON - 51A | W. HARTLEPOOL - 51C | | MIDDLESBROUGH - 51D | DAIRYCOATES - 53A | STOCKTON - 51E | W. HARTLEPOOL - 51C | MIDDLESBROUGH - 51D | DARLINGTON - 51A |
| Jan-55 | DARLINGTON - 51A | W. HARTLEPOOL - 51C | | MIDDLESBROUGH - 51D | 10/54: W/D | STOCKTON - 51E | W. HARTLEPOOL - 51C | MIDDLESBROUGH - 51D | DARLINGTON - 51A |
| Aug-55 | 3/55: W/D | W. HARTLEPOOL - 51C | | 6/55: W/D | | STOCKTON - 51E | W. HARTLEPOOL - 51C | 6/55: W/D | DARLINGTON - 51A |
| Jan-56 | | W. HARTLEPOOL - 51C | | | | STOCKTON - 51E | W. HARTLEPOOL - 51C | | DARLINGTON - 51A |
| Aug-56 | | W. HARTLEPOOL - 51C | | | | STOCKTON - 51E | W. HARTLEPOOL - 51C | | DARLINGTON - 51A |
| Jan-57 | | 11/56: W/D | | | | STOCKTON - 51E | W. HARTLEPOOL - 51C | | DARLINGTON - 51A |
| Aug-57 | | | | | | STOCKTON - 51E | W. HARTLEPOOL - 51C | | DARLINGTON - 51A |
| Jan-58 | | | | | | STOCKTON - 51E | W. HARTLEPOOL - 51C | | DARLINGTON - 51A |
| Aug-58 | | | | | | STOCKTON - 51E | 7/58: W/D | | 4/58: W/D |
| Jan-59 | | | | | | 11/58: W/D | | | |
| Aug-59 | | | | | | | | | |
| Nov-59 | | | | | | | | | |
| Jan-60 | | | | | | | | | |
| Apr-60 | | | | | | | | | |
| Aug-60 | | | | | | | | | |
| Nov-60 | | | | | | | | | |

| | 68309 | 68310 | 68311 | 68312 | 68313 | 68314 | 68316 | J88 0-6-0T (1904) 68320 | 68321 |
|---|---|---|---|---|---|---|---|---|---|
| Aug-50 | GATESHEAD - 52A | YORK - 50A | DAIRYCOATES - 53A | MIDDLESBROUGH - 51D | YORK - 50A | GATESHEAD - 52A | DAIRYCOATES - 53A | EDINBURGH (SM) - 64A | THORNTON JCN - 62A |
| Jan-51 | GATESHEAD - 52A | 11/50: W/D | DAIRYCOATES - 53A | MIDDLESBROUGH - 51D | YORK - 50A | GATESHEAD - 52A | DAIRYCOATES - 53A | EDINBURGH (SM) - 64A | THORNTON JCN - 62A |
| Aug-51 | GATESHEAD - 52A | | 8/51: W/D | MIDDLESBROUGH - 51D | YORK - 50A | GATESHEAD - 52A | DAIRYCOATES - 53A | EDINBURGH (SM) - 64A | THORNTON JCN - 62A |
| Jan-52 | GATESHEAD - 52A | | | MIDDLESBROUGH - 51D | YORK - 50A | GATESHEAD - 52A | DAIRYCOATES - 53A | EDINBURGH (SM) - 64A | THORNTON JCN - 62A |
| Aug-52 | GATESHEAD - 52A | | | MIDDLESBROUGH - 51D | YORK - 50A | GATESHEAD - 52A | DAIRYCOATES - 53A | EDINBURGH (SM) - 64A | THORNTON JCN - 62A |
| Jan-53 | GATESHEAD - 52A | | | MIDDLESBROUGH - 51D | YORK - 50A | GATESHEAD - 52A | 2/53: B. GDNS - 54C | EDINBURGH (SM) - 64A | THORNTON JCN - 62A |
| Aug-53 | GATESHEAD - 52A | | | MIDDLESBROUGH - 51D | YORK - 50A | GATESHEAD - 52A | B. GARDENS - 54C | EDINBURGH (SM) - 64A | THORNTON JCN - 62A |
| Jan-54 | GATESHEAD - 52A | | | MIDDLESBROUGH - 51D | YORK - 50A | GATESHEAD - 52A | B. GARDENS - 54C | EDINBURGH (SM) - 64A | THORNTON JCN - 62A |
| Aug-54 | GATESHEAD - 52A | | | MIDDLESBROUGH - 51D | YORK - 50A | GATESHEAD - 52A | B. GARDENS - 54C | EDINBURGH (SM) - 64A | THORNTON JCN - 62A |
| Jan-55 | GATESHEAD - 52A | | | MIDDLESBROUGH - 51D | YORK - 50A | GATESHEAD - 52A | B. GARDENS - 54C | EDINBURGH (SM) - 64A | THORNTON JCN - 62A |
| Aug-55 | GATESHEAD - 52A | | | MIDDLESBROUGH - 51D | YORK - 50A | GATESHEAD - 52A | B. GARDENS - 54C | EDINBURGH (SM) - 64A | THORNTON JCN - 62A |
| Jan-56 | GATESHEAD - 52A | | | MIDDLESBROUGH - 51D | YORK - 50A | GATESHEAD - 52A | B. GARDENS - 54C | EDINBURGH (SM) - 64A | THORNTON JCN - 62A |
| Aug-56 | GATESHEAD - 52A | | | MIDDLESBROUGH - 51D | 9/56: W/D | GATESHEAD - 52A | B. GARDENS - 54C | EDINBURGH (SM) - 64A | THORNTON JCN - 62A |
| Jan-57 | GATESHEAD - 52A | | | MIDDLESBROUGH - 51D | | GATESHEAD - 52A | B. GARDENS - 54C | EDINBURGH (SM) - 64A | THORNTON JCN - 62A |
| Aug-57 | GATESHEAD - 52A | | | MIDDLESBROUGH - 51D | | GATESHEAD - 52A | B. GARDENS - 54C | EDINBURGH (SM) - 64A | THORNTON JCN - 62A |
| Jan-58 | GATESHEAD - 52A | | | MIDDLESBROUGH - 51D | | GATESHEAD - 52A | B. GARDENS - 54C | EDINBURGH (SM) - 64A | THORNTON JCN - 62A |
| Aug-58 | GATESHEAD - 52A | | | 6/58: TBY - 51L | | GATESHEAD - 52A | B. GARDENS - 54C | EDINBURGH (SM) - 64A | 6/58: W/D |
| Jan-59 | GATESHEAD - 52A | | | 2/59: W/D | | GATESHEAD - 52A | B. GARDENS - 52J | EDINBURGH (SM) - 64A | |
| Aug-59 | 4/59: YORK - 50A | | | | | GATESHEAD - 52A | 6/59: W.HPL - 51C | EDINBURGH (SM) - 64A | |
| Nov-59 | YORK - 50A | | | | | GATESHEAD - 52A | W. HARTLEPOOL - 51C | EDINBURGH (SM) - 64A | |
| Jan-60 | YORK - 50A | | | | | 2/60: TWEED - 52D | W. HARTLEPOOL - 51C | EDINBURGH (SM) - 64A | |
| Apr-60 | 4/60: W/D | | | | | 4/60: W/D | W. HARTLEPOOL - 51C | EDINBURGH (SM) - 64A | |
| Aug-60 | | | | | | | W. HARTLEPOOL - 51C | 8/60: W/D | |
| Nov-60 | | | | | | | 10/60: W/D | | |

| | 68322 | 68323 | 68324 | 68325 | 68326 | 68327 | 68328 | 68329 | 68330 |
|---|---|---|---|---|---|---|---|---|---|
| Aug-50 | THORNTONJCN-62A | THORNTONJCN-62A | POLMONT-64E | EDINBURGH (SM)-64A | EASTFIELD-65A | EASTFIELD-65A | HAYMARKET-64B | KIPPS-65E | EASTFIELD-65A |
| Jan-51 | THORNTONJCN-62A | THORNTONJCN-62A | POLMONT-64E | EDINBURGH (SM)-64A | EASTFIELD-65A | EASTFIELD-65A | HAYMARKET-64B | KIPPS-65E | EASTFIELD-65A |
| Aug-51 | THORNTONJCN-62A | THORNTONJCN-62A | POLMONT-64E | EDINBURGH (SM)-64A | EASTFIELD-65A | EASTFIELD-65A | HAYMARKET-64B | KIPPS-65E | EASTFIELD-65A |
| Jan-52 | THORNTONJCN-62A | THORNTONJCN-62A | POLMONT-64E | EDINBURGH (SM)-64A | EASTFIELD-65A | EASTFIELD-65A | HAYMARKET-64B | KIPPS-65E | EASTFIELD-65A |
| Aug-52 | THORNTONJCN-62A | THORNTONJCN-62A | POLMONT-64E | EDINBURGH (SM)-64A | EASTFIELD-65A | EASTFIELD-65A | HAYMARKET-64B | KIPPS-65E | EASTFIELD-65A |
| Jan-53 | THORNTONJCN-62A | THORNTONJCN-62A | POLMONT-64E | EDINBURGH (SM)-64A | EASTFIELD-65A | EASTFIELD-65A | HAYMARKET-64B | KIPPS-65E | EASTFIELD-65A |
| Aug-53 | THORNTONJCN-62A | THORNTONJCN-62A | POLMONT-64E | EDINBURGH (SM)-64A | EASTFIELD-65A | EASTFIELD-65A | HAYMARKET-64B | KIPPS-65E | EASTFIELD-65A |
| Jan-54 | THORNTONJCN-62A | THORNTONJCN-62A | POLMONT-64E | EDINBURGH (SM)-64A | EASTFIELD-65A | EASTFIELD-65A | HAYMARKET-64B | KIPPS-65E | EASTFIELD-65A |
| Aug-54 | THORNTONJCN-62A | THORNTONJCN-62A | POLMONT-64E | EDINBURGH (SM)-64A | EASTFIELD-65A | EASTFIELD-65A | HAYMARKET-64B | KIPPS-65E | EASTFIELD-65A |
| Jan-55 | THORNTONJCN-62A | THORNTONJCN-62A | POLMONT-64E | EDINBURGH (SM)-64A | EASTFIELD-65A | EASTFIELD-65A | HAYMARKET-64B | KIPPS-65E | EASTFIELD-65A |
| Aug-55 | THORNTONJCN-62A | THORNTONJCN-62A | POLMONT-64E | EDINBURGH (SM)-64A | 9/55: G'MTH - 65F | EASTFIELD-65A | HAYMARKET-64B | KIPPS-65E | EASTFIELD-65A |
| Jan-56 | THORNTONJCN-62A | THORNTONJCN-62A | POLMONT-64E | EDINBURGH (SM)-64A | GRANGEMOUTH-65F | EASTFIELD-65A | HAYMARKET-64B | KIPPS-65E | EASTFIELD-65A |
| Aug-56 | THORNTONJCN-62A | THORNTONJCN-62A | POLMONT-64E | EDINBURGH (SM)-64A | GRANGEMOUTH-65F | EASTFIELD-65A | HAYMARKET-64B | KIPPS-65E | EASTFIELD-65A |
| Jan-57 | THORNTONJCN-62A | 10/56: W/D | POLMONT-64E | EDINBURGH (SM)-64A | GRANGEMOUTH-65F | EASTFIELD-65A | HAYMARKET-64B | KIPPS-65E | EASTFIELD-65A |
| Aug-57 | THORNTONJCN-62A | | POLMONT-64E | EDINBURGH (SM)-64A | GRANGEMOUTH-65F | EASTFIELD-65A | HAYMARKET-64B | KIPPS-65E | EASTFIELD-65A |
| Jan-58 | THORNTONJCN-62A | | POLMONT-64E | EDINBURGH (SM)-64A | GRANGEMOUTH-65F | EASTFIELD-65A | HAYMARKET-64B | KIPPS-65E | EASTFIELD-65A |
| Aug-58 | THORNTONJCN-62A | | 7/58: W/D | EDINBURGH (SM)-64A | GRANGEMOUTH-65F | 7/58: W/D | 3/58: W/D | KIPPS-65E | 8/58: W/D |
| Jan-59 | 12/58: W/D | | | EDINBURGH (SM)-64A | GRANGEMOUTH-65F | | | 2/59: W/D | |
| Aug-59 | | | | 4/59: EFLD - 65A | GRANGEMOUTH-65F | | | | |
| Nov-59 | | | | EASTFIELD-65A | 10/59: W/D | | | | |
| Jan-60 | | | | EASTFIELD-65A | | | | | |
| Apr-60 | | | | EASTFIELD-65A | | | | | |
| Aug-60 | | | | 9/60: STRX - 65B | | | | | |
| Nov-60 | | | | STROLLOX-65B | | | | | |

| | 68331 | 68332 | 68333 | 68334 | 68335 | 68336 | 68337 | 68338 | 68339 |
|---|---|---|---|---|---|---|---|---|---|
| Aug-50 | KIPPS-65E | THORNTONJCN-62A | EASTFIELD-65A | EDINBURGH (SM)-64A | THORNTONJCN-62A | EASTFIELD-65A | THORNTONJCN-62A | EDINBURGH (SM)-64A | HAYMARKET-64B |
| Jan-51 | KIPPS-65E | THORNTONJCN-62A | 11/50: DAWS - 65D | EDINBURGH (SM)-64A | THORNTONJCN-62A | EASTFIELD-65A | THORNTONJCN-62A | EDINBURGH (SM)-64A | HAYMARKET-64B |
| Aug-51 | KIPPS-65E | THORNTONJCN-62A | DAWSHOLME-65D | EDINBURGH (SM)-64A | THORNTONJCN-62A | EASTFIELD-65A | THORNTONJCN-62A | EDINBURGH (SM)-64A | HAYMARKET-64B |
| Jan-52 | KIPPS-65E | THORNTONJCN-62A | DAWSHOLME-65D | EDINBURGH (SM)-64A | THORNTONJCN-62A | 5/52: M'WELL - 66B | THORNTONJCN-62A | EDINBURGH (SM)-64A | HAYMARKET-64B |
| Aug-52 | KIPPS-65E | THORNTONJCN-62A | DAWSHOLME-65D | EDINBURGH (SM)-64A | THORNTONJCN-62A | 6/52: EFLD - 65A | THORNTONJCN-62A | EDINBURGH (SM)-64A | HAYMARKET-64B |
| Jan-53 | KIPPS-65E | THORNTONJCN-62A | DAWSHOLME-65D | EDINBURGH (SM)-64A | THORNTONJCN-62A | EASTFIELD-65A | THORNTONJCN-62A | EDINBURGH (SM)-64A | HAYMARKET-64B |
| Aug-53 | KIPPS-65E | THORNTONJCN-62A | DAWSHOLME-65D | EDINBURGH (SM)-64A | THORNTONJCN-62A | EASTFIELD-65A | THORNTONJCN-62A | EDINBURGH (SM)-64A | HAYMARKET-64B |
| Jan-54 | KIPPS-65E | THORNTONJCN-62A | DAWSHOLME-65D | EDINBURGH (SM)-64A | THORNTONJCN-62A | EASTFIELD-65A | THORNTONJCN-62A | EDINBURGH (SM)-64A | HAYMARKET-64B |
| Aug-54 | KIPPS-65E | THORNTONJCN-62A | DAWSHOLME-65D | EDINBURGH (SM)-64A | THORNTONJCN-62A | 4/54: KIPPS - 65E | THORNTONJCN-62A | EDINBURGH (SM)-64A | HAYMARKET-64B |
| Jan-55 | 1/55: DAWS - 65D | THORNTONJCN-62A | DAWSHOLME-65D | 12/54: TH JN - 62A | THORNTONJCN-62A | KIPPS-65E | THORNTONJCN-62A | EDINBURGH (SM)-64A | HAYMARKET-64B |
| Aug-55 | 2/55: KIPPS - 65E | THORNTONJCN-62A | DAWSHOLME-65D | THORNTONJCN-62A | THORNTONJCN-62A | KIPPS-65E | THORNTONJCN-62A | EDINBURGH (SM)-64A | HAYMARKET-64B |
| Jan-56 | KIPPS-65E | THORNTONJCN-62A | DAWSHOLME-65D | THORNTONJCN-62A | THORNTONJCN-62A | KIPPS-65E | 11/55: W/D | EDINBURGH (SM)-64A | HAYMARKET-64B |
| Aug-56 | KIPPS-65E | THORNTONJCN-62A | DAWSHOLME-65D | THORNTONJCN-62A | THORNTONJCN-62A | KIPPS-65E | | EDINBURGH (SM)-64A | HAYMARKET-64B |
| Jan-57 | 12/56: TH JN - 62A | THORNTONJCN-62A | DAWSHOLME-65D | THORNTONJCN-62A | THORNTONJCN-62A | KIPPS-65E | | EDINBURGH (SM)-64A | HAYMARKET-64B |
| Aug-57 | THORNTONJCN-62A | THORNTONJCN-62A | DAWSHOLME-65D | THORNTONJCN-62A | THORNTONJCN-62A | KIPPS-65E | | EDINBURGH (SM)-64A | HAYMARKET-64B |
| Jan-58 | THORNTONJCN-62A | THORNTONJCN-62A | DAWSHOLME-65D | THORNTONJCN-62A | THORNTONJCN-62A | KIPPS-65E | | EDINBURGH (SM)-64A | HAYMARKET-64B |
| Aug-58 | THORNTONJCN-62A | THORNTONJCN-62A | 3/58: W/D | THORNTONJCN-62A | THORNTONJCN-62A | KIPPS-65E | | EDINBURGH (SM)-64A | HAYMARKET-64B |
| Jan-59 | THORNTONJCN-62A | THORNTONJCN-62A | | THORNTONJCN-62A | THORNTONJCN-62A | KIPPS-65E | | EDINBURGH (SM)-64A | 10/58: W/D |
| Aug-59 | 3/59: W/D | THORNTONJCN-62A | | 6/59: W/D | THORNTONJCN-62A | KIPPS-65E | | EDINBURGH (SM)-64A | |
| Nov-59 | | THORNTONJCN-62A | | | 12/59: HMKT - 64B | KIPPS-65E | | EDINBURGH (SM)-64A | |
| Jan-60 | | THORNTONJCN-62A | | | HAYMARKET-64B | KIPPS-65E | | EDINBURGH (SM)-64A | |
| Apr-60 | | THORNTONJCN-62A | | | HAYMARKET-64B | KIPPS-65E | | EDINBURGH (SM)-64A | |
| Aug-60 | | 9/60: W/D | | | HAYMARKET-64B | KIPPS-65E | | EDINBURGH (SM)-64A | |
| Nov-60 | | | | | HAYMARKET-64B | 10/60: DAWS - 65D | | EDINBURGH (SM)-64A | |

| | 68340 | 68341 | 68342 | 68343 | 68344 | 68345 | 68346 | 68347 | 68348 |
|---|---|---|---|---|---|---|---|---|---|
| Aug-50 | EDINBURGH (SM)-64A | THORNTONJCN-62A | EDINBURGH (SM)-64A | KIPPS-65E | KIPPS-65E | DUNFERMLINE-62C | DUNFERMLINE-62C | EASTFIELD-65A | EDINBURGH (SM)-64A |
| Jan-51 | EDINBURGH (SM)-64A | THORNTONJCN-62A | EDINBURGH (SM)-64A | KIPPS-65E | KIPPS-65E | DUNFERMLINE-62C | DUNFERMLINE-62C | EASTFIELD-65A | EDINBURGH (SM)-64A |
| Aug-51 | EDINBURGH (SM)-64A | THORNTONJCN-62A | EDINBURGH (SM)-64A | KIPPS-65E | KIPPS-65E | DUNFERMLINE-62C | DUNFERMLINE-62C | EASTFIELD-65A | EDINBURGH (SM)-64A |
| Jan-52 | EDINBURGH (SM)-64A | THORNTONJCN-62A | EDINBURGH (SM)-64A | KIPPS-65E | 1/52: M'WELL - 66B | DUNFERMLINE-62C | DUNFERMLINE-62C | EASTFIELD-65A | EDINBURGH (SM)-64A |
| Aug-52 | EDINBURGH (SM)-64A | THORNTONJCN-62A | EDINBURGH (SM)-64A | KIPPS-65E | MOTHERWELL-66B | DUNFERMLINE-62C | DUNFERMLINE-62C | EASTFIELD-65A | EDINBURGH (SM)-64A |
| Jan-53 | EDINBURGH (SM)-64A | THORNTONJCN-62A | EDINBURGH (SM)-64A | KIPPS-65E | MOTHERWELL-66B | DUNFERMLINE-62C | DUNFERMLINE-62C | EASTFIELD-65A | EDINBURGH (SM)-64A |
| Aug-53 | EDINBURGH (SM)-64A | THORNTONJCN-62A | EDINBURGH (SM)-64A | KIPPS-65E | MOTHERWELL-66B | DUNFERMLINE-62C | DUNFERMLINE-62C | EASTFIELD-65A | EDINBURGH (SM)-64A |
| Jan-54 | EDINBURGH (SM)-64A | THORNTONJCN-62A | EDINBURGH (SM)-64A | KIPPS-65E | MOTHERWELL-66B | DUNFERMLINE-62C | DUNFERMLINE-62C | EASTFIELD-65A | EDINBURGH (SM)-64A |
| Aug-54 | EDINBURGH (SM)-64A | THORNTONJCN-62A | EDINBURGH (SM)-64A | KIPPS-65E | MOTHERWELL-66B | DUNFERMLINE-62C | DUNFERMLINE-62C | EASTFIELD-65A | EDINBURGH (SM)-64A |
| Jan-55 | EDINBURGH (SM)-64A | 11/54: W/D | EDINBURGH (SM)-64A | KIPPS-65E | MOTHERWELL-66B | DUNFERMLINE-62C | DUNFERMLINE-62C | EASTFIELD-65A | EDINBURGH (SM)-64A |
| Aug-55 | EDINBURGH (SM)-64A | | EDINBURGH (SM)-64A | KIPPS-65E | MOTHERWELL-66B | DUNFERMLINE-62C | DUNFERMLINE-62C | EASTFIELD-65A | EDINBURGH (SM)-64A |
| Jan-56 | EDINBURGH (SM)-64A | | EDINBURGH (SM)-64A | KIPPS-65E | 12/55: DAWS - 65D | DUNFERMLINE-62C | DUNFERMLINE-62C | EASTFIELD-65A | EDINBURGH (SM)-64A |
| Aug-56 | EDINBURGH (SM)-64A | | EDINBURGH (SM)-64A | KIPPS-65E | 4/56: KIPPS - 65E | DUNFERMLINE-62C | DUNFERMLINE-62C | EASTFIELD-65A | EDINBURGH (SM)-64A |
| Jan-57 | EDINBURGH (SM)-64A | | EDINBURGH (SM)-64A | KIPPS-65E | KIPPS-65E | DUNFERMLINE-62C | DUNFERMLINE-62C | EASTFIELD-65A | EDINBURGH (SM)-64A |
| Aug-57 | EDINBURGH (SM)-64A | | EDINBURGH (SM)-64A | KIPPS-65E | KIPPS-65E | 9/57: DFLN - 62C | DUNFERMLINE-62C | EASTFIELD-65A | EDINBURGH (SM)-64A |
| Jan-58 | 2/58: W/D | | EDINBURGH (SM)-64A | KIPPS-65E | KIPPS-65E | DUNFERMLINE-62C | DUNFERMLINE-62C | EASTFIELD-65A | EDINBURGH (SM)-64A |
| Aug-58 | | | EDINBURGH (SM)-64A | KIPPS-65E | 4/58: DAWS - 65D | 9/58: EFLD - 65A | DUNFERMLINE-62C | 8/58: W/D | 8/58: W/D |
| Jan-59 | | | EDINBURGH (SM)-64A | KIPPS-65E | DAWSHOLME-65D | EASTFIELD-65A | DUNFERMLINE-62C | | |
| Aug-59 | | | EDINBURGH (SM)-64A | KIPPS-65E | DAWSHOLME-65D | EASTFIELD-65A | DUNFERMLINE-62C | | |
| Nov-59 | | | EDINBURGH (SM)-64A | KIPPS-65E | DAWSHOLME-65D | EASTFIELD-65A | DUNFERMLINE-62C | | |
| Jan-60 | | | EDINBURGH (SM)-64A | KIPPS-65E | DAWSHOLME-65D | EASTFIELD-65A | DUNFERMLINE-62C | | |
| Apr-60 | | | EDINBURGH (SM)-64A | KIPPS-65E | DAWSHOLME-65D | EASTFIELD-65A | DUNFERMLINE-62C | | |
| Aug-60 | | | EDINBURGH (SM)-64A | KIPPS-65E | DAWSHOLME-65D | 9/60: STRX - 65B | DUNFERMLINE-62C | | |
| Nov-60 | | | EDINBURGH (SM)-64A | 11/60: W/D | 10/60: G'MTH - 65F | STROLLOX-65B | DUNFERMLINE-62C | | |

| | | | | | | | J73 0-6-0T (1891) | | |
|---|---|---|---|---|---|---|---|---|---|
| | 68349 | 68350 | 68351 | 68352 | 68353 | 68354 | 68355 | 68356 | 68357 |
| Aug-50 | EASTFIELD-65A | POLMONT-64E | DUNFERMLINE-62C | EDINBURGH (SM)-64A | THORNTONJCN-62A | POLMONT-64E | W.HARTLEPOOL-51C | SELBY-50C | SELBY-50C |
| Jan-51 | EASTFIELD-65A | POLMONT-64E | DUNFERMLINE-62C | EDINBURGH (SM)-64A | THORNTONJCN-62A | POLMONT-64E | W.HARTLEPOOL-51C | SELBY-50C | SELBY-50C |
| Aug-51 | EASTFIELD-65A | POLMONT-64E | DUNFERMLINE-62C | EDINBURGH (SM)-64A | THORNTONJCN-62A | POLMONT-64E | W.HARTLEPOOL-51C | SELBY-50C | SELBY-50C |
| Jan-52 | EASTFIELD-65A | POLMONT-64E | DUNFERMLINE-62C | EDINBURGH (SM)-64A | THORNTONJCN-62A | POLMONT-64E | W.HARTLEPOOL-51C | SELBY-50C | SELBY-50C |
| Aug-52 | EASTFIELD-65A | POLMONT-64E | DUNFERMLINE-62C | EDINBURGH (SM)-64A | THORNTONJCN-62A | POLMONT-64E | W.HARTLEPOOL-51C | SELBY-50C | SELBY-50C |
| Jan-53 | EASTFIELD-65A | POLMONT-64E | DUNFERMLINE-62C | EDINBURGH (SM)-64A | THORNTONJCN-62A | POLMONT-64E | W.HARTLEPOOL-51C | SELBY-50C | SELBY-50C |
| Aug-53 | EASTFIELD-65A | POLMONT-64E | DUNFERMLINE-62C | EDINBURGH (SM)-64A | THORNTONJCN-62A | POLMONT-64E | W.HARTLEPOOL-51C | SELBY-50C | SELBY-50C |
| Jan-54 | EASTFIELD-65A | POLMONT-64E | DUNFERMLINE-62C | EDINBURGH (SM)-64A | THORNTONJCN-62A | POLMONT-64E | W.HARTLEPOOL-51C | SELBY-50C | SELBY-50C |
| Aug-54 | EASTFIELD-65A | POLMONT-64E | DUNFERMLINE-62C | EDINBURGH (SM)-64A | THORNTONJCN-62A | POLMONT-64E | W.HARTLEPOOL-51C | SELBY-50C | SELBY-50C |
| Jan-55 | EASTFIELD-65A | POLMONT-64E | DUNFERMLINE-62C | EDINBURGH (SM)-64A | THORNTONJCN-62A | POLMONT-64E | W.HARTLEPOOL-51C | SELBY-50C | SELBY-50C |
| Aug-55 | EASTFIELD-65A | POLMONT-64E | DUNFERMLINE-62C | EDINBURGH (SM)-64A | THORNTONJCN-62A | POLMONT-64E | W.HARTLEPOOL-51C | SELBY-50C | SELBY-50C |
| Jan-56 | EASTFIELD-65A | POLMONT-64E | DUNFERMLINE-62C | EDINBURGH (SM)-64A | THORNTONJCN-62A | POLMONT-64E | W.HARTLEPOOL-51C | SELBY-50C | SELBY-50C |
| Aug-56 | EASTFIELD-65A | POLMONT-64E | DUNFERMLINE-62C | EDINBURGH (SM)-64A | THORNTONJCN-62A | POLMONT-64E | W.HARTLEPOOL-51C | SELBY-50C | SELBY-50C |
| Jan-57 | EASTFIELD-65A | 2/57: DFLN - 62C | 1/57: W/D | EDINBURGH (SM)-64A | THORNTONJCN-62A | POLMONT-64E | W.HARTLEPOOL-51C | SELBY-50C | SELBY-50C |
| Aug-57 | EASTFIELD-65A | DUNFERMLINE-62C | | EDINBURGH (SM)-64A | THORNTONJCN-62A | 11/57: KIPPS - 65E | W.HARTLEPOOL-51C | SELBY-50C | SELBY-50C |
| Jan-58 | 3/58: STRX - 65B | DUNFERMLINE-62C | | EDINBURGH (SM)-64A | THORNTONJCN-62A | 1/58: POL - 64E | W.HARTLEPOOL-51C | SELBY-50C | 1/58: W/D |
| Aug-58 | STROLLOX-65B | DUNFERMLINE-62C | | EDINBURGH (SM)-64A | THORNTONJCN-62A | POLMONT-64E | W.HARTLEPOOL-51C | 8/58: W/D | |
| Jan-59 | STROLLOX-65B | DUNFERMLINE-62C | | EDINBURGH (SM)-64A | THORNTONJCN-62A | POLMONT-64E | 12/58: W/D | | |
| Aug-59 | STROLLOX-65B | DUNFERMLINE-62C | | 4/59: EFLD - 65A | THORNTONJCN-62A | POLMONT-64E | | | |
| Nov-59 | 11/59: G'MTH - 65F | DUNFERMLINE-62C | | EASTFIELD-65A | THORNTONJCN-62A | POLMONT-64E | | | |
| Jan-60 | GRANGEMOUTH-65F | 2/60: POL - 64E | | EASTFIELD-65A | THORNTONJCN-62A | 2/60: KIPPS - 65E | | | |
| Apr-60 | GRANGEMOUTH-65F | POLMONT-65K | | EASTFIELD-65A | THORNTONJCN-62A | KIPPS-65E | | | |
| Aug-60 | 9/60: W/D | POLMONT-65K | | 8/60: W/D | THORNTONJCN-62A | KIPPS-65E | | | |
| Nov-60 | | POLMONT-65K | | | THORNTONJCN-62A | 11/60: W/D | | | |

*In spite of having an allocation two and a half times as large, St Margarets, Edinburgh, was much less well known than its neighbour, Haymarket. The division of work between the two sheds was complex but, broadly, Haymarket worked the express traffic leaving goods and suburban duties to St Margarets. Although its allocation included a good number of V2 and K3's, it was the J88 0-6-0T's that provided the main attraction of St Margarets: small outside cylinder shunting engines, some still with valves on the dome, fitted with dumbbell buffers to avoid becoming buffer-locked on the curved sidings in the Leith yards. 68320, 68352 and 68348 stand on the turntable roads at St Margarets in June 1952.*

*One had to peer carefully at the numbers of J72 0-6-0T's to determine whether the specimen was a museum piece or a brand new engine. Probably setting a world record in production terms, the first of the class appeared in 1898 whilst the last took to the rails as late as May 1951. Established by the time of the grouping as the standard N.E.R. shunting engine, the LNER added to the class and had some examples transferred to the North British and Great Central lines. 68736 saw regular use as one of the York station pilots and was distinguished by bearing full North Eastern Railway livery plus BR totem. Above, in rather more dusty condition, 68691 of West Auckland and several others wait to enter Darlington works in September 1956.*

**J66 0-6-0T (1886): 68370, 68371**

| Date | 68358 | 68359 | 68360 | 68361 | 68362 | 68363 | 68364 | 68370 | 68371 |
|---|---|---|---|---|---|---|---|---|---|
| Aug-50 | W.HARTLEPOOL-51C | W.HARTLEPOOL-51C | SPRINGHEAD-53C | SPRINGHEAD-53C | SELBY-50C | SPRINGHEAD-53C | W.HARTLEPOOL-51C | Stratford (Dept) | STAVELEY-38D |
| Jan-51 | W.HARTLEPOOL-51C | 1/51: N'TON-51J | SPRINGHEAD-53C | SPRINGHEAD-53C | SELBY-50C | SPRINGHEAD-53C | W.HARTLEPOOL-51C | Stratford (Dept) | STAVELEY-38D |
| Aug-51 | W.HARTLEPOOL-51C | NORTHALLERTON-51J | SPRINGHEAD-53C | SPRINGHEAD-53C | SELBY-50C | SPRINGHEAD-53C | W.HARTLEPOOL-51C | Stratford (Dept) | STAVELEY-38D |
| Jan-52 | W.HARTLEPOOL-51C | NORTHALLERTON-51J | SPRINGHEAD-53C | SPRINGHEAD-53C | SELBY-50C | SPRINGHEAD-53C | W.HARTLEPOOL-51C | Stratford (Dept) | STAVELEY-38D |
| Aug-52 | W.HARTLEPOOL-51C | NORTHALLERTON-51J | SPRINGHEAD-53C | SPRINGHEAD-53C | SELBY-50C | SPRINGHEAD-53C | W.HARTLEPOOL-51C | Stratford (Dept) | STAVELEY-38D |
| Jan-53 | W.HARTLEPOOL-51C | NORTHALLERTON-51J | SPRINGHEAD-53C | SPRINGHEAD-53C | SELBY-50C | SPRINGHEAD-53C | W.HARTLEPOOL-51C | Stratford (Dept) | STAVELEY-38D |
| Aug-53 | W.HARTLEPOOL-51C | NORTHALLERTON-51J | SPRINGHEAD-53C | SPRINGHEAD-53C | SELBY-50C | SPRINGHEAD-53C | W.HARTLEPOOL-51C | Stratford (Dept) | STAVELEY-38D |
| Jan-54 | W.HARTLEPOOL-51C | NORTHALLERTON-51J | SPRINGHEAD-53C | SPRINGHEAD-53C | SELBY-50C | 1/54: B.GDNS-53B | W.HARTLEPOOL-51C | Stratford (Dept) | STAVELEY-38D |
| Aug-54 | W.HARTLEPOOL-51C | NORTHALLERTON-51J | SPRINGHEAD-53C | SPRINGHEAD-53C | SELBY-50C | BOTANIC GARDENS-53B | W.HARTLEPOOL-51C | Stratford (Dept) | 4/54: W/D |
| Jan-55 | W.HARTLEPOOL-51C | NORTHALLERTON-51J | SPRINGHEAD-53C | SPRINGHEAD-53C | SELBY-50C | BOTANIC GARDENS-53B | W.HARTLEPOOL-51C | Stratford (Dept) | |
| Aug-55 | 3/55: W/D | 3/55: W.HPL-51C | SPRINGHEAD-53C | SPRINGHEAD-53C | SELBY-50C | BOTANIC GARDENS-53B | W.HARTLEPOOL-51C | Stratford (Dept) | |
| Jan-56 | | W.HARTLEPOOL-51C | SPRINGHEAD-53C | SPRINGHEAD-53C | SELBY-50C | BOTANIC GARDENS-53B | W.HARTLEPOOL-51C | Stratford (Dept) | |
| Aug-56 | | W.HARTLEPOOL-51C | SPRINGHEAD-53C | SPRINGHEAD-53C | SELBY-50C | BOTANIC GARDENS-53B | W.HARTLEPOOL-51C | Stratford (Dept) | |
| Jan-57 | | W.HARTLEPOOL-51C | SPRINGHEAD-53C | SPRINGHEAD-53C | SELBY-50C | BOTANIC GARDENS-53B | W.HARTLEPOOL-51C | Stratford (Dept) | |
| Aug-57 | | W.HARTLEPOOL-51C | SPRINGHEAD-53C | SPRINGHEAD-53C | SELBY-50C | BOTANIC GARDENS-53B | W.HARTLEPOOL-51C | Stratford (Dept) | |
| Jan-58 | | W.HARTLEPOOL-51C | SPRINGHEAD-53C | SPRINGHEAD-53C | 9/57: W/D | BOTANIC GARDENS-53B | W.HARTLEPOOL-51C | Stratford (Dept) | |
| Aug-58 | | W.HARTLEPOOL-51C | SPRINGHEAD-53C | SPRINGHEAD-53C | | BOTANIC GARDENS-53B | W.HARTLEPOOL-51C | Stratford (Dept) | |
| Jan-59 | | W.HARTLEPOOL-51C | 12/58: DAIRY-53A | 12/58: DAIRY-53A | | BOTANIC GARDENS-53B | W.HARTLEPOOL-51C | Stratford (Dept) | |
| Aug-59 | | W.HARTLEPOOL-51C | DAIRYCOATES-53A | DAIRYCOATES-53A | | 6/59: DAIRY-53A | W.HARTLEPOOL-51C | Stratford (Dept) | |
| Nov-59 | | 12/59: W/D | DAIRYCOATES-53A | DAIRYCOATES-53A | | 10/59: W/D | W.HARTLEPOOL-51C | Stratford (Dept) | |
| Jan-60 | | | 2/60: W/D | DAIRYCOATES-53A | | | W.HARTLEPOOL-51C | Stratford (Dept) | |
| Apr-60 | | | | DAIRYCOATES-50B | | | 4/60: W/D | Stratford (Dept) | |
| Aug-60 | | | | DAIRYCOATES-50B | | | | Stratford (Dept) | |
| Nov-60 | | | | 11/60: W/D | | | | Stratford (Dept) | |

| Date | 68372 | 68373 | 68374 | 68375 | 68376 | 68377 | 68378 | 68379 | 68380 |
|---|---|---|---|---|---|---|---|---|---|
| Aug-50 | CAMBRIDGE-31A | IPSWICH-32B | IPSWICH-32B | IPSWICH-32B | LINCOLN-40A | MELTON CONSTABLE-32G | SOUTH LYNN-31D | STAVELEY-38D | STRATFORD-30A |
| Jan-51 | 2/51: W/D | IPSWICH-32B | IPSWICH-32B | IPSWICH-32B | LINCOLN-40A | MELTON CONSTABLE-32G | SOUTH LYNN-31D | 10/50: W/D | STRATFORD-30A |
| Aug-51 | | IPSWICH-32B | IPSWICH-32B | IPSWICH-32B | 7/51: W/D | 5/51: W/D | SOUTH LYNN-31D | | STRATFORD-30A |
| Jan-52 | | 1/52: W/D | IPSWICH-32B | IPSWICH-32B | | | SOUTH LYNN-31D | | STRATFORD-30A |
| Aug-52 | | | IPSWICH-32B | IPSWICH-32B | | | 8/52: Strat(dept) | | 3/52: W/D |
| Jan-53 | | | IPSWICH-32B | 11/52: W/D | | | Stratford (Dept) | | |
| Aug-53 | | | 7/53: STAVE-38D | | | | Stratford (Dept) | | |
| Jan-54 | | | STAVELEY-38D | | | | Stratford (Dept) | | |
| Aug-54 | | | 6/54: W/D | | | | Stratford (Dept) | | |
| Jan-55 | | | | | | | Stratford (Dept) | | |
| Aug-55 | | | | | | | Stratford (Dept) | | |
| Jan-56 | | | | | | | Stratford (Dept) | | |
| Aug-56 | | | | | | | Stratford (Dept) | | |
| Jan-57 | | | | | | | Stratford (Dept) | | |
| Aug-57 | | | | | | | Stratford (Dept) | | |
| Jan-58 | | | | | | | Stratford (Dept) | | |
| Aug-58 | | | | | | | Stratford (Dept) | | |
| Jan-59 | | | | | | | 1/59: W/D | | |
| Aug-59 | | | | | | | | | |
| Nov-59 | | | | | | | | | |
| Jan-60 | | | | | | | | | |
| Apr-60 | | | | | | | | | |
| Aug-60 | | | | | | | | | |
| Nov-60 | | | | | | | | | |

**J77 0-6-0T (1899): 68391, 68392, 68393**

| Date | 68381 | 68382 | 68383 | 68385 | 68387 | 68388 | 68391 | 68392 | 68393 |
|---|---|---|---|---|---|---|---|---|---|
| Aug-50 | NORWICH-32A | STAVELEY-38D | CAMBRIDGE-31A | LINCOLN-40A | NEWENGLAND-35A | NORWICH-32A | W.AUCKLAND-51F | STARBECK-50D | STARBECK-50D |
| Jan-51 | 10/50: W/D | STAVELEY-38D | CAMBRIDGE-31A | LINCOLN-40A | 1/51: STRAT-30A | NORWICH-32A | W.AUCKLAND-51F | STARBECK-50D | STARBECK-50D |
| Aug-51 | | STAVELEY-38D | CAMBRIDGE-31A | 6/51: W/D | 2/51: W/D | 5/51: M.CONS-32G | W.AUCKLAND-51F | STARBECK-50D | STARBECK-50D |
| Jan-52 | | STAVELEY-38D | CAMBRIDGE-31A | | | MELTON CONSTABLE-32G | W.AUCKLAND-51F | STARBECK-50D | STARBECK-50D |
| Aug-52 | | 6/52: Strat(dept) | CAMBRIDGE-31A | | | 4/52: W/D | W.AUCKLAND-51F | STARBECK-50D | STARBECK-50D |
| Jan-53 | | Stratford (Dept) | CAMBRIDGE-31A | | | | W.AUCKLAND-51F | STARBECK-50D | STARBECK-50D |
| Aug-53 | | Stratford (Dept) | 7/53: STAVE-38D | | | | W.AUCKLAND-51F | STARBECK-50D | STARBECK-50D |
| Jan-54 | | Stratford (Dept) | STAVELEY-38D | | | | W.AUCKLAND-51F | STARBECK-50D | STARBECK-50D |
| Aug-54 | | Stratford (Dept) | STAVELEY-38D | | | | W.AUCKLAND-51F | STARBECK-50D | STARBECK-50D |
| Jan-55 | | Stratford (Dept) | STAVELEY-38D | | | | W.AUCKLAND-51F | STARBECK-50D | STARBECK-50D |
| Aug-55 | | Stratford (Dept) | STAVELEY-38D | | | | W.AUCKLAND-51F | STARBECK-50D | 7/55: W/D |
| Jan-56 | | Stratford (Dept) | 10/55: W/D | | | | W.AUCKLAND-51F | STARBECK-50D | |
| Aug-56 | | Stratford (Dept) | | | | | W.AUCKLAND-51F | STARBECK-50D | |
| Jan-57 | | Stratford (Dept) | | | | | W.AUCKLAND-51F | STARBECK-50D | |
| Aug-57 | | Stratford (Dept) | | | | | 7/57: W/D | 12/57: N.BLYTH-52F | |
| Jan-58 | | Stratford (Dept) | | | | | | N.BLYTH-52F | |
| Aug-58 | | Stratford (Dept) | | | | | | 1/59: YORK-50A | |
| Jan-59 | | Stratford (Dept) | | | | | | YORK-50A | |
| Aug-59 | | Stratford (Dept) | | | | | | YORK-50A | |
| Nov-59 | | Stratford (Dept) | | | | | | 5/60: W/D | |
| Jan-60 | | Stratford (Dept) | | | | | | | |
| Apr-60 | | Stratford (Dept) | | | | | | | |
| Aug-60 | | Stratford (Dept) | | | | | | | |
| Nov-60 | | Stratford (Dept) | | | | | | | |

| Date | 68395 | 68397 | 68398 | 68399 | 68401 | 68402 | 68404 | 68405 | 68406 |
|---|---|---|---|---|---|---|---|---|---|
| Aug-50 | NEVILLE HILL-50B | N.BLYTH-52F | N.BLYTH-52F | SELBY-50C | BOTANIC GARDENS-53B | SPRINGHEAD-53C | STARBECK-50D | N.BLYTH-52F | NEVILLE HILL-50B |
| Jan-51 | NEVILLE HILL-50B | N.BLYTH-52F | N.BLYTH-52F | SELBY-50C | BOTANIC GARDENS-53B | SPRINGHEAD-53C | STARBECK-50D | N.BLYTH-52F | NEVILLE HILL-50B |
| Aug-51 | NEVILLE HILL-50B | N.BLYTH-52F | N.BLYTH-52F | SELBY-50C | BOTANIC GARDENS-53B | SPRINGHEAD-53C | 4/51: W/D | N.BLYTH-52F | 6/51: SELBY-50C |
| Jan-52 | NEVILLE HILL-50B | N.BLYTH-52F | N.BLYTH-52F | 11/51: N.BLYTH-52F | BOTANIC GARDENS-53B | SPRINGHEAD-53C | | N.BLYTH-52F | SELBY-50C |
| Aug-52 | NEVILLE HILL-50B | N.BLYTH-52F | N.BLYTH-52F | N.BLYTH-52F | BOTANIC GARDENS-53B | SPRINGHEAD-53C | | N.BLYTH-52F | SELBY-50C |
| Jan-53 | NEVILLE HILL-50B | N.BLYTH-52F | 1/53: W/D | N.BLYTH-52F | BOTANIC GARDENS-53B | 2/53: DAIRY-53A | | N.BLYTH-52F | SELBY-50C |
| Aug-53 | NEVILLE HILL-50B | N.BLYTH-52F | | N.BLYTH-52F | BOTANIC GARDENS-53B | DAIRYCOATES-53A | | N.BLYTH-52F | SELBY-50C |
| Jan-54 | NEVILLE HILL-50B | N.BLYTH-52F | | N.BLYTH-52F | 1/54: YORK-50A | DAIRYCOATES-53A | | N.BLYTH-52F | SELBY-50C |
| Aug-54 | NEVILLE HILL-50B | N.BLYTH-52F | | N.BLYTH-52F | 7/54: W/D | 5/54: TWEED-52D | | N.BLYTH-52F | SELBY-50C |
| Jan-55 | NEVILLE HILL-50B | N.BLYTH-52F | | N.BLYTH-52F | | TWEEDMOUTH-52D | | N.BLYTH-52F | SELBY-50C |
| Aug-55 | NEVILLE HILL-50B | N.BLYTH-52F | | N.BLYTH-52F | | TWEEDMOUTH-52D | | N.BLYTH-52F | SELBY-50C |
| Jan-56 | NEVILLE HILL-50B | N.BLYTH-52F | | N.BLYTH-52F | | TWEEDMOUTH-52D | | N.BLYTH-52F | SELBY-50C |
| Aug-56 | 6/56: W/D | N.BLYTH-52F | | N.BLYTH-52F | | 7/56: N.BLYTH-52F# | | N.BLYTH-52F | SELBY-50C |
| Jan-57 | | N.BLYTH-52F | | N.BLYTH-52F | | N.BLYTH-52F | | N.BLYTH-52F | SELBY-50C |
| Aug-57 | | N.BLYTH-52F | | N.BLYTH-52F | | N.BLYTH-52F | | N.BLYTH-52F | SELBY-50C |
| Jan-58 | | 1/58: W/D | | N.BLYTH-52F | | N.BLYTH-52F | | N.BLYTH-52F | 5/58: N.BLYTH-52F |
| Aug-58 | | | | 4/58: W/D | | 5/58: W/D | | N.BLYTH-52F | 12/58: TBY-51L |
| Jan-59 | | | | | | | | 12/58: W/D | THORNABY-51L |
| Aug-59 | | | | | | | | | 11/59: W/D |
| Nov-59 | | | | | | | | | |
| Jan-60 | | | | | | | | | |
| Apr-60 | | | | | | | | | |
| Aug-60 | | | | | | | | | |
| Nov-60 | | | | | | | | | |

| | 68407 | 68408 | 68409 | 68410 | 68412 | 68413 | 68414 | 68417 | 68420 |
|---|---|---|---|---|---|---|---|---|---|
| Aug-50 | STOCKTON-51E | DARLINGTON-51A | MIDDLESBROUGH-51D | DARLINGTON-51A | STOCKTON-51E | SPRINGHEAD-53C | MIDDLESBROUGH-51D | N.BLYTH-52F | STOCKTON-51E |
| Jan-51 | STOCKTON-51E | DARLINGTON-51A | MIDDLESBROUGH-51D | DARLINGTON-51A | STOCKTON-51E | SPRINGHEAD-53C | MIDDLESBROUGH-51D | N.BLYTH-52F | STOCKTON-51E |
| Aug-51 | STOCKTON-51E | DARLINGTON-51A | MIDDLESBROUGH-51D | DARLINGTON-51A | STOCKTON-51E | SPRINGHEAD-53C | MIDDLESBROUGH-51D | N.BLYTH-52F | STOCKTON-51E |
| Jan-52 | STOCKTON-51E | DARLINGTON-51A | MIDDLESBROUGH-51D | DARLINGTON-51A | STOCKTON-51E | SPRINGHEAD-53C | MIDDLESBROUGH-51D | N.BLYTH-52F | STOCKTON-51E |
| Aug-52 | STOCKTON-51E | DARLINGTON-51A | MIDDLESBROUGH-51D | DARLINGTON-51A | STOCKTON-51E | SPRINGHEAD-53C | MIDDLESBROUGH-51D | N.BLYTH-52F | STOCKTON-51E |
| Jan-53 | STOCKTON-51E | DARLINGTON-51A | MIDDLESBROUGH-51D | DARLINGTON-51A | STOCKTON-51E | 2/53: DAIRY-53A | MIDDLESBROUGH-51D | N.BLYTH-52F | STOCKTON-51E |
| Aug-53 | STOCKTON-51E | DARLINGTON-51A | MIDDLESBROUGH-51D | DARLINGTON-51A | STOCKTON-51E | DAIRYCOATES-53A | MIDDLESBROUGH-51D | N.BLYTH-52F | STOCKTON-51E |
| Jan-54 | STOCKTON-51E | DARLINGTON-51A | MIDDLESBROUGH-51D | DARLINGTON-51A | STOCKTON-51E | 12/53: W/D | MIDDLESBROUGH-51D | N.BLYTH-52F | STOCKTON-51E |
| Aug-54 | STOCKTON-51E | DARLINGTON-51A | MIDDLESBROUGH-51D | DARLINGTON-51A | STOCKTON-51E | 5/54: W/D | MIDDLESBROUGH-51D | N.BLYTH-52F | STOCKTON-51E |
| Jan-55 | STOCKTON-51E | DARLINGTON-51A | MIDDLESBROUGH-51D | DARLINGTON-51A | STOCKTON-51E | | MIDDLESBROUGH-51D | N.BLYTH-52F | 4/55: W/D |
| Aug-55 | STOCKTON-51E | DARLINGTON-51A | MIDDLESBROUGH-51D | DARLINGTON-51A | STOCKTON-51E | | MIDDLESBROUGH-51D | N.BLYTH-52F | |
| Jan-56 | 2/56: W/D | DARLINGTON-51A | MIDDLESBROUGH-51D | DARLINGTON-51A | STOCKTON-51E | | MIDDLESBROUGH-51D | N.BLYTH-52F | |
| Aug-56 | | 7/56: S.BLYTH-52F | MIDDLESBROUGH-51D | DARLINGTON-51A | STOCKTON-51E | | MIDDLESBROUGH-51D | 9/56: W/D | |
| Jan-57 | | S.BLYTH-52F | MIDDLESBROUGH-51D | DARLINGTON-51A | 2/57: W/D | | MIDDLESBROUGH-51D | | |
| Aug-57 | | S.BLYTH-52F | MIDDLESBROUGH-51D | DARLINGTON-51A | | | MIDDLESBROUGH-51D | | |
| Jan-58 | | S.BLYTH-52F | 5/58: N.BLYTH-52F | 3/58: STOCK-51E | | | 5/58: N.BLYTH-52F | | |
| Aug-58 | | S.BLYTH-52F | 7/58: DAIRY-53A | 5/58: S.BLYTH-52F | | | 9/58: DAIRY-53A | | |
| Jan-59 | | S.BLYTH-52F | DAIRYCOATES-53A | 1/59: W.HPL-51C | | | 12/58: W/D | | |
| Aug-59 | | S.BLYTH-52F | DAIRYCOATES-53A | W.HARTLEPOOL-51C | | | | | |
| Nov-59 | | S.BLYTH-52F | 11/59: W/D | W.HARTLEPOOL-51C | | | | | |
| Jan-60 | | S.BLYTH-52F | | W.HARTLEPOOL-51C | | | | | |
| Apr-60 | | S.BLYTH-52F | | W.HARTLEPOOL-51C | | | | | |
| Aug-60 | | S.BLYTH-52F | | 11/60: W/D | | | | | |
| Nov-60 | | S.BLYTH-52F | | | | | | | |

| | 68421 | 68422 | 68423 | 68424 | 68425 | 68426 | 68427 | 68428 | 68429 |
|---|---|---|---|---|---|---|---|---|---|
| Aug-50 | TWEEDMOUTH-52D | MIDDLESBROUGH-51D | DARLINGTON-51A | N.BLYTH-52F | MIDDLESBROUGH-51D | N.BLYTH-52F | N.BLYTH-52F | N.BLYTH-52F | SPRINGHEAD-53C |
| Jan-51 | TWEEDMOUTH-52D | MIDDLESBROUGH-51D | DARLINGTON-51A | N.BLYTH-52F | MIDDLESBROUGH-51D | N.BLYTH-52F | N.BLYTH-52F | N.BLYTH-52F | SPRINGHEAD-53C |
| Aug-51 | TWEEDMOUTH-52D | MIDDLESBROUGH-51D | DARLINGTON-51A | N.BLYTH-52F | MIDDLESBROUGH-51D | N.BLYTH-52F | N.BLYTH-52F | N.BLYTH-52F | SPRINGHEAD-53C |
| Jan-52 | TWEEDMOUTH-52D | MIDDLESBROUGH-51D | DARLINGTON-51A | N.BLYTH-52F | MIDDLESBROUGH-51D | N.BLYTH-52F | N.BLYTH-52F | N.BLYTH-52F | SPRINGHEAD-53C |
| Aug-52 | TWEEDMOUTH-52D | MIDDLESBROUGH-51D | DARLINGTON-51A | N.BLYTH-52F | MIDDLESBROUGH-51D | N.BLYTH-52F | N.BLYTH-52F | N.BLYTH-52F | SPRINGHEAD-53C |
| Jan-53 | TWEEDMOUTH-52D | MIDDLESBROUGH-51D | DARLINGTON-51A | N.BLYTH-52F | MIDDLESBROUGH-51D | N.BLYTH-52F | N.BLYTH-52F | N.BLYTH-52F | SPRINGHEAD-53C |
| Aug-53 | TWEEDMOUTH-52D | MIDDLESBROUGH-51D | DARLINGTON-51A | N.BLYTH-52F | MIDDLESBROUGH-51D | N.BLYTH-52F | N.BLYTH-52F | N.BLYTH-52F | SPRINGHEAD-53C |
| Jan-54 | TWEEDMOUTH-52D | MIDDLESBROUGH-51D | DARLINGTON-51A | N.BLYTH-52F | MIDDLESBROUGH-51D | N.BLYTH-52F | N.BLYTH-52F | 12/53: HTN-52B | 2/54: DAIRY-53A |
| Aug-54 | 5/54: W/D | 6/54: W/D | DARLINGTON-51A | N.BLYTH-52F | MIDDLESBROUGH-51D | N.BLYTH-52F | N.BLYTH-52F | HEATON-52B | DAIRYCOATES-53A |
| Jan-55 | | | DARLINGTON-51A | N.BLYTH-52F | MIDDLESBROUGH-51D | N.BLYTH-52F | N.BLYTH-52F | 2/55: W/D | 10/54: SELBY-50C |
| Aug-55 | | | DARLINGTON-51A | N.BLYTH-52F | MIDDLESBROUGH-51D | N.BLYTH-52F | N.BLYTH-52F | | SELBY-50C |
| Jan-56 | | | DARLINGTON-51A | N.BLYTH-52F | MIDDLESBROUGH-51D | N.BLYTH-52F | N.BLYTH-52F | | 1/56: W/D |
| Aug-56 | | | 10/56: H.HILL-51G | N.BLYTH-52F | 7/56: DARL-51A | N.BLYTH-52F | N.BLYTH-52F | | |
| Jan-57 | | | HAVERTONHILL-51G | N.BLYTH-52F | DARLINGTON-51A | N.BLYTH-52F | N.BLYTH-52F | | |
| Aug-57 | | | 11/57: W/D | N.BLYTH-52F | DARLINGTON-51A | 8/57: W/D | N.BLYTH-52F | | |
| Jan-58 | | | | N.BLYTH-52F | 2/58: N.BLYTH-52F | | 1/58: W/D | | |
| Aug-58 | | | | 6/58: W/D | 7/58: DAIRY-53A | | | | |
| Jan-59 | | | | | DAIRYCOATES-53A | | | | |
| Aug-59 | | | | | DAIRYCOATES-53A | | | | |
| Nov-59 | | | | | 12/59: W/D | | | | |
| Jan-60 | | | | | | | | | |
| Apr-60 | | | | | | | | | |
| Aug-60 | | | | | | | | | |
| Nov-60 | | | | | | | | | |

| | 68430 | 68431 | 68432 | 68433 | 68434 | 68435 | 68436 | 68437 | 68438 |
|---|---|---|---|---|---|---|---|---|---|
| Aug-50 | HEATON-52B | N.BLYTH-52F | DARLINGTON-51A | SELBY-50C | STARBECK-50D | SPRINGHEAD-53C | YORK-50A | TWEEDMOUTH-52D | STARBECK-50D |
| Jan-51 | HEATON-52B | N.BLYTH-52F | DARLINGTON-51A | SELBY-50C | STARBECK-50D | SPRINGHEAD-53C | YORK-50A | TWEEDMOUTH-52D | STARBECK-50D |
| Aug-51 | HEATON-52B | N.BLYTH-52F | DARLINGTON-51A | 5/51: W/D | STARBECK-50D | SPRINGHEAD-53C | 6/51: N.HILL-50B | TWEEDMOUTH-52D | STARBECK-50D |
| Jan-52 | HEATON-52B | N.BLYTH-52F | DARLINGTON-51A | | STARBECK-50D | SPRINGHEAD-53C | NEVILLEHILL-50B | TWEEDMOUTH-52D | STARBECK-50D |
| Aug-52 | HEATON-52B | N.BLYTH-52F | DARLINGTON-51A | | STARBECK-50D | SPRINGHEAD-53C | NEVILLEHILL-50B | TWEEDMOUTH-52D | STARBECK-50D |
| Jan-53 | HEATON-52B | N.BLYTH-52F | DARLINGTON-51A | | STARBECK-50D | SPRINGHEAD-53C | NEVILLEHILL-50B | TWEEDMOUTH-52D | 12/52: SELBY-50C |
| Aug-53 | HEATON-52B | N.BLYTH-52F | DARLINGTON-51A | | STARBECK-50D | SPRINGHEAD-53C | 10/53: TWEED-52D | TWEEDMOUTH-52D | SELBY-50C |
| Jan-54 | 12/53: S.BLYTH-52F | N.BLYTH-52F | DARLINGTON-51A | | STARBECK-50D | 1/54: YORK-50A | TWEEDMOUTH-52D | TWEEDMOUTH-52D | SELBY-50C |
| Aug-54 | SOUTHBLYTH-52F | N.BLYTH-52F | DARLINGTON-51A | | STARBECK-50D | YORK-50A | TWEEDMOUTH-52D | TWEEDMOUTH-52D | SELBY-50C |
| Jan-55 | SOUTHBLYTH-52F | N.BLYTH-52F | DARLINGTON-51A | | STARBECK-50D | YORK-50A | TWEEDMOUTH-52D | TWEEDMOUTH-52D | 6/55: DARL-51A |
| Aug-55 | SOUTHBLYTH-52F | N.BLYTH-52F | 5/55: W/D | | STARBECK-50D | YORK-50A | TWEEDMOUTH-52D | TWEEDMOUTH-52D | 2/56: W.AUCK-51F |
| Jan-56 | SOUTHBLYTH-52F | N.BLYTH-52F | | | STARBECK-50D | YORK-50A | 6/56: W/D | 1/56: W/D | W.AUCKLAND-51F |
| Aug-56 | 6/56: W/D | N.BLYTH-52F | | | STARBECK-50D | YORK-50A | | | W.AUCKLAND-51F |
| Jan-57 | | N.BLYTH-52F | | | 1/57: W/D | YORK-50A | | | 2/58: W/D |
| Aug-57 | | N.BLYTH-52F | | | | YORK-50A | | | |
| Jan-58 | | N.BLYTH-52F | | | | 11/57: N.BLYTH-52F | | | |
| Aug-58 | | N.BLYTH-52F | | | | 8/58: STOCK-51E | | | |
| Jan-59 | | 2/59: YORK-50A | | | | 10/58: W/D | | | |
| Aug-59 | | YORK-50A | | | | | | | |
| Nov-59 | | YORK-50A | | | | | | | |
| Jan-60 | | YORK-50A | | | | | | | |
| Apr-60 | | 3/60: W/D | | | | | | | |
| Aug-60 | | | | | | | | | |
| Nov-60 | | | | | | | | | |

J83 0-6-0T (1900)

| | 68440 | 68442 | 68443 | 68444 | 68445 | 68446 | 68447 | 68448 | 68449 |
|---|---|---|---|---|---|---|---|---|---|
| Aug-50 | SPRINGHEAD-53C | KIPPS-65E | KIPPS-65E | KIPPS-65E | KIPPS-65E | DUNDEE-62B | EASTFIELD-65A | EDINBURGH(SM)-64A | EDINBURGH(SM)-64A |
| Jan-51 | 6/51: BLAY-52C | KIPPS-65E | KIPPS-65E | KIPPS-65E | KIPPS-65E | DUNDEE-62B | EASTFIELD-65A | EDINBURGH(SM)-64A | EDINBURGH(SM)-64A |
| Aug-51 | 7/51: P.MAIN-52E | KIPPS-65E | KIPPS-65E | KIPPS-65E | KIPPS-65E | DUNDEE-62B | EASTFIELD-65A | EDINBURGH(SM)-64A | EDINBURGH(SM)-64A |
| Jan-52 | PERCYMAIN-52E | KIPPS-65E | KIPPS-65E | KIPPS-65E | KIPPS-65E | DUNDEE-62B | EASTFIELD-65A | EDINBURGH(SM)-64A | EDINBURGH(SM)-64A |
| Aug-52 | 7/52: HTN-52B | KIPPS-65E | KIPPS-65E | KIPPS-65E | KIPPS-65E | DUNDEE-62B | EASTFIELD-65A | EDINBURGH(SM)-64A | EDINBURGH(SM)-64A |
| Jan-53 | HEATON-52B | KIPPS-65E | KIPPS-65E | KIPPS-65E | KIPPS-65E | DUNDEE-62B | EASTFIELD-65A | EDINBURGH(SM)-64A | EDINBURGH(SM)-64A |
| Aug-53 | HEATON-52B | KIPPS-65E | KIPPS-65E | KIPPS-65E | KIPPS-65E | DUNDEE-62B | EASTFIELD-65A | EDINBURGH(SM)-64A | EDINBURGH(SM)-64A |
| Jan-54 | HEATON-52B | KIPPS-65E | KIPPS-65E | KIPPS-65E | KIPPS-65E | DUNDEE-62B | EASTFIELD-65A | EDINBURGH(SM)-64A | EDINBURGH(SM)-64A |
| Aug-54 | 8/54: W/D | KIPPS-65E | KIPPS-65E | KIPPS-65E | KIPPS-65E | DUNDEE-62B | EASTFIELD-65A | EDINBURGH(SM)-64A | EDINBURGH(SM)-64A |
| Jan-55 | | KIPPS-65E | KIPPS-65E | KIPPS-65E | KIPPS-65E | DUNDEE-62B | EASTFIELD-65A | EDINBURGH(SM)-64A | EDINBURGH(SM)-64A |
| Aug-55 | | KIPPS-65E | KIPPS-65E | KIPPS-65E | KIPPS-65E | DUNDEE-62B | EASTFIELD-65A | EDINBURGH(SM)-64A | EDINBURGH(SM)-64A |
| Jan-56 | | KIPPS-65E | KIPPS-65E | KIPPS-65E | KIPPS-65E | 3/56: W/D | EASTFIELD-65A | EDINBURGH(SM)-64A | EDINBURGH(SM)-64A |
| Aug-56 | | KIPPS-65E | KIPPS-65E | KIPPS-65E | KIPPS-65E | | EASTFIELD-65A | EDINBURGH(SM)-64A | EDINBURGH(SM)-64A |
| Jan-57 | | KIPPS-65E | KIPPS-65E | KIPPS-65E | KIPPS-65E | | EASTFIELD-65A | EDINBURGH(SM)-64A | EDINBURGH(SM)-64A |
| Aug-57 | | KIPPS-65E | KIPPS-65E | KIPPS-65E | KIPPS-65E | | EASTFIELD-65A | EDINBURGH(SM)-64A | EDINBURGH(SM)-64A |
| Jan-58 | | KIPPS-65E | KIPPS-65E | KIPPS-65E | KIPPS-65E | | EASTFIELD-65A | EDINBURGH(SM)-64A | EDINBURGH(SM)-64A |
| Aug-58 | | KIPPS-65E | KIPPS-65E | KIPPS-65E | KIPPS-65E | | EASTFIELD-65A | EDINBURGH(SM)-64A | 9/58: W/D |
| Jan-59 | | KIPPS-65E | KIPPS-65E | KIPPS-65E | KIPPS-65E | | EASTFIELD-65A | EDINBURGH(SM)-64A | |
| Aug-59 | | KIPPS-65E | KIPPS-65E | KIPPS-65E | KIPPS-65E | | EASTFIELD-65A | EDINBURGH(SM)-64A | |
| Nov-59 | | KIPPS-65E | KIPPS-65E | KIPPS-65E | KIPPS-65E | | EASTFIELD-65A | EDINBURGH(SM)-64A | |
| Jan-60 | | KIPPS-65E | KIPPS-65E | KIPPS-65E | KIPPS-65E | | EASTFIELD-65A | EDINBURGH(SM)-64A | |
| Apr-60 | | KIPPS-65E | KIPPS-65E | 2/60: W/D | KIPPS-65E | | EASTFIELD-65A | EDINBURGH(SM)-64A | |
| Aug-60 | | KIPPS-65E | KIPPS-65E | | KIPPS-65E | | EASTFIELD-65A | EDINBURGH(SM)-64A | |
| Nov-60 | | KIPPS-65E | KIPPS-65E | | KIPPS-65E | | EASTFIELD-65A | EDINBURGH(SM)-64A | |

| | 68450 | 68451 | 68452 | 68453 | 68454 | 68455 | 68456 | 68457 | 68458 |
|---|---|---|---|---|---|---|---|---|---|
| Aug-50 | EDINBURGH(SM)-64A | THORNTONJCN-62A | DUNDEE-62B | THORNTONJCN-62A | EDINBURGH(SM)-64A | DUNDEE-62B | THORNTONJCN-62A | HAYMARKET-64B | THORNTONJCN-62A |
| Jan-51 | EDINBURGH(SM)-64A | THORNTONJCN-62A | DUNDEE-62B | THORNTONJCN-62A | EDINBURGH(SM)-64A | DUNDEE-62B | THORNTONJCN-62A | HAYMARKET-64B | THORNTONJCN-62A |
| Aug-51 | EDINBURGH(SM)-64A | THORNTONJCN-62A | DUNDEE-62B | THORNTONJCN-62A | EDINBURGH(SM)-64A | DUNDEE-62B | THORNTONJCN-62A | HAYMARKET-64B | THORNTONJCN-62A |
| Jan-52 | EDINBURGH(SM)-64A | THORNTONJCN-62A | DUNDEE-62B | THORNTONJCN-62A | EDINBURGH(SM)-64A | DUNDEE-62B | THORNTONJCN-62A | HAYMARKET-64B | THORNTONJCN-62A |
| Aug-52 | EDINBURGH(SM)-64A | THORNTONJCN-62A | DUNDEE-62B | THORNTONJCN-62A | EDINBURGH(SM)-64A | DUNDEE-62B | THORNTONJCN-62A | HAYMARKET-64B | THORNTONJCN-62A |
| Jan-53 | EDINBURGH(SM)-64A | THORNTONJCN-62A | DUNDEE-62B | THORNTONJCN-62A | EDINBURGH(SM)-64A | DUNDEE-62B | THORNTONJCN-62A | HAYMARKET-64B | THORNTONJCN-62A |
| Aug-53 | EDINBURGH(SM)-64A | THORNTONJCN-62A | DUNDEE-62B | THORNTONJCN-62A | EDINBURGH(SM)-64A | DUNDEE-62B | THORNTONJCN-62A | HAYMARKET-64B | THORNTONJCN-62A |
| Jan-54 | EDINBURGH(SM)-64A | THORNTONJCN-62A | DUNDEE-62B | THORNTONJCN-62A | EDINBURGH(SM)-64A | DUNDEE-62B | THORNTONJCN-62A | HAYMARKET-64B | THORNTONJCN-62A |
| Aug-54 | EDINBURGH(SM)-64A | THORNTONJCN-62A | DUNDEE-62B | THORNTONJCN-62A | EDINBURGH(SM)-64A | DUNDEE-62B | THORNTONJCN-62A | HAYMARKET-64B | THORNTONJCN-62A |
| Jan-55 | EDINBURGH(SM)-64A | THORNTONJCN-62A | DUNDEE-62B | THORNTONJCN-62A | EDINBURGH(SM)-64A | DUNDEE-62B | THORNTONJCN-62A | HAYMARKET-64B | THORNTONJCN-62A |
| Aug-55 | EDINBURGH(SM)-64A | THORNTONJCN-62A | DUNDEE-62B | THORNTONJCN-62A | EDINBURGH(SM)-64A | DUNDEE-62B | THORNTONJCN-62A | HAYMARKET-64B | THORNTONJCN-62A |
| Jan-56 | EDINBURGH(SM)-64A | THORNTONJCN-62A | DUNDEE-62B | THORNTONJCN-62A | EDINBURGH(SM)-64A | DUNDEE-62B | THORNTONJCN-62A | HAYMARKET-64B | THORNTONJCN-62A |
| Aug-56 | EDINBURGH(SM)-64A | THORNTONJCN-62A | DUNDEE-62B | THORNTONJCN-62A | EDINBURGH(SM)-64A | 5/56: W/D | THORNTONJCN-62A | HAYMARKET-64B | THORNTONJCN-62A |
| Jan-57 | EDINBURGH(SM)-64A | THORNTONJCN-62A | DUNDEE-62B | THORNTONJCN-62A | EDINBURGH(SM)-64A | | THORNTONJCN-62A | HAYMARKET-64B | THORNTONJCN-62A |
| Aug-57 | EDINBURGH(SM)-64A | THORNTONJCN-62A | DUNDEE-62B | THORNTONJCN-62A | EDINBURGH(SM)-64A | | THORNTONJCN-62A | HAYMARKET-64B | THORNTONJCN-62A |
| Jan-58 | 12/57: W/D | 2/58: W/D | DUNDEE-62B | THORNTONJCN-62A | EDINBURGH(SM)-64A | | THORNTONJCN-62A | HAYMARKET-64B | THORNTONJCN-62A |
| Aug-58 | | | 6/58: W/D | THORNTONJCN-62A | EDINBURGH(SM)-64A | | THORNTONJCN-62A | HAYMARKET-64B | THORNTONJCN-62A |
| Jan-59 | | | | THORNTONJCN-62A | EDINBURGH(SM)-64A | | THORNTONJCN-62A | HAYMARKET-64B | THORNTONJCN-62A |
| Aug-59 | | | | 8/59: EBRO(SM) - 64A | EDINBURGH(SM)-64A | | 8/59:POL-64E | HAYMARKET-64B | THORNTONJCN-62A |
| Nov-59 | | | | EDINBURGH(SM)-64A | EDINBURGH(SM)-64A | | POLMONT-64E | HAYMARKET-64B | THORNTONJCN-62A |
| Jan-60 | | | | EDINBURGH(SM)-64A | EDINBURGH(SM)-64A | | POLMONT-64E | HAYMARKET-64B | 2/60: C'HILL - 67A |
| Apr-60 | | | | EDINBURGH(SM)-64A | EDINBURGH(SM)-64A | | POLMONT-65K | 3/60: W/D | CORKERHILL-67A |
| Aug-60 | | | | EDINBURGH(SM)-64A | EDINBURGH(SM)-64A | | POLMONT-65K | | CORKERHILL-67A |
| Nov-60 | | | | EDINBURGH(SM)-64A | EDINBURGH(SM)-64A | | POLMONT-65K | | CORKERHILL-67A |

| | 68459 | 68460 | 68461 | 68463 | 68464 | 68465 | 68466 | 68467 | 68468 |
|---|---|---|---|---|---|---|---|---|---|
| Aug-50 | THORNTONJCN-62A | HAYMARKET-64B | KIPPS-65E | EDINBURGH(SM)-64A | EDINBURGH(SM)-64A | DUNFERMLINE-62C | DUNDEE-62B | THORNTONJCN-62A | EASTFIELD-65A |
| Jan-51 | THORNTONJCN-62A | HAYMARKET-64B | KIPPS-65E | EDINBURGH(SM)-64A | EDINBURGH(SM)-64A | DUNFERMLINE-62C | DUNDEE-62B | THORNTONJCN-62A | EASTFIELD-65A |
| Aug-51 | THORNTONJCN-62A | HAYMARKET-64B | KIPPS-65E | EDINBURGH(SM)-64A | EDINBURGH(SM)-64A | 4/51: DUN - 62B | DUNDEE-62B | THORNTONJCN-62A | EASTFIELD-65A |
| Jan-52 | THORNTONJCN-62A | HAYMARKET-64B | KIPPS-65E | EDINBURGH(SM)-64A | EDINBURGH(SM)-64A | DUNDEE-62B | DUNDEE-62B | THORNTONJCN-62A | EASTFIELD-65A |
| Aug-52 | THORNTONJCN-62A | HAYMARKET-64B | KIPPS-65E | EDINBURGH(SM)-64A | EDINBURGH(SM)-64A | DUNDEE-62B | DUNDEE-62B | THORNTONJCN-62A | EASTFIELD-65A |
| Jan-53 | THORNTONJCN-62A | HAYMARKET-64B | KIPPS-65E | EDINBURGH(SM)-64A | EDINBURGH(SM)-64A | DUNDEE-62B | DUNDEE-62B | THORNTONJCN-62A | EASTFIELD-65A |
| Aug-53 | THORNTONJCN-62A | HAYMARKET-64B | KIPPS-65E | EDINBURGH(SM)-64A | EDINBURGH(SM)-64A | DUNDEE-62B | DUNDEE-62B | THORNTONJCN-62A | EASTFIELD-65A |
| Jan-54 | THORNTONJCN-62A | HAYMARKET-64B | KIPPS-65E | EDINBURGH(SM)-64A | EDINBURGH(SM)-64A | DUNDEE-62B | DUNDEE-62B | THORNTONJCN-62A | EASTFIELD-65A |
| Aug-54 | THORNTONJCN-62A | HAYMARKET-64B | KIPPS-65E | EDINBURGH(SM)-64A | EDINBURGH(SM)-64A | DUNDEE-62B | DUNDEE-62B | THORNTONJCN-62A | EASTFIELD-65A |
| Jan-55 | THORNTONJCN-62A | HAYMARKET-64B | KIPPS-65E | EDINBURGH(SM)-64A | EDINBURGH(SM)-64A | DUNDEE-62B | DUNDEE-62B | THORNTONJCN-62A | EASTFIELD-65A |
| Aug-55 | THORNTONJCN-62A | HAYMARKET-64B | KIPPS-65E | EDINBURGH(SM)-64A | EDINBURGH(SM)-64A | DUNDEE-62B | DUNDEE-62B | THORNTONJCN-62A | EASTFIELD-65A |
| Jan-56 | THORNTONJCN-62A | HAYMARKET-64B | KIPPS-65E | EDINBURGH(SM)-64A | EDINBURGH(SM)-64A | DUNDEE-62B | DUNDEE-62B | THORNTONJCN-62A | EASTFIELD-65A |
| Aug-56 | THORNTONJCN-62A | HAYMARKET-64B | KIPPS-65E | EDINBURGH(SM)-64A | EDINBURGH(SM)-64A | DUNDEE-62B | DUNDEE-62B | 9/56: POL - 64E | EASTFIELD-65A |
| Jan-57 | THORNTONJCN-62A | HAYMARKET-64B | KIPPS-65E | EDINBURGH(SM)-64A | EDINBURGH(SM)-64A | DUNDEE-62B | DUNDEE-62B | POLMONT-64E | EASTFIELD-65A |
| Aug-57 | THORNTONJCN-62A | HAYMARKET-64B | KIPPS-65E | EDINBURGH(SM)-64A | EDINBURGH(SM)-64A | 8/57: W/D | DUNDEE-62B | POLMONT-64E | EASTFIELD-65A |
| Jan-58 | THORNTONJCN-62A | HAYMARKET-64B | KIPPS-65E | EDINBURGH(SM)-64A | EDINBURGH(SM)-64A | | DUNDEE-62B | POLMONT-64E | EASTFIELD-65A |
| Aug-58 | THORNTONJCN-62A | HAYMARKET-64B | 6/58: W/D | EDINBURGH(SM)-64A | 3/58: W/D | | 5/58: EBRO(SM) - 64A | POLMONT-64E | EASTFIELD-65A |
| Jan-59 | THORNTONJCN-62A | 11/58: W/D | | 11/58: W/D | | | 12/58: W/D | POLMONT-64E | EASTFIELD-65A |
| Aug-59 | THORNTONJCN-62A | | | | | | | POLMONT-64E | 6/59:W/D |
| Nov-59 | THORNTONJCN-62A | | | | | | | 9/59: W/D | |
| Jan-60 | THORNTONJCN-62A | | | | | | | | |
| Apr-60 | THORNTONJCN-62A | | | | | | | | |
| Aug-60 | THORNTONJCN-62A | | | | | | | | |
| Nov-60 | THORNTONJCN-62A | | | | | | | | |

| | 68469 | 68470 | 68471 | 68472 | 68473 | 68474 | 68475 | 68476 | 68477 |
|---|---|---|---|---|---|---|---|---|---|
| Aug-50 | EDINBURGH(SM)-64A | DUNDEE-62B | POLMONT-64E | EDINBURGH(SM)-64A | HAYMARKET-64B | EDINBURGH(SM)-64A | EASTFIELD-65A | EASTFIELD-65A | EDINBURGH(SM)-64A |
| Jan-51 | EDINBURGH(SM)-64A | DUNDEE-62B | POLMONT-64E | EDINBURGH(SM)-64A | HAYMARKET-64B | EDINBURGH(SM)-64A | EASTFIELD-65A | EASTFIELD-65A | EDINBURGH(SM)-64A |
| Aug-51 | EDINBURGH(SM)-64A | DUNDEE-62B | POLMONT-64E | EDINBURGH(SM)-64A | HAYMARKET-64B | EDINBURGH(SM)-64A | EASTFIELD-65A | EASTFIELD-65A | EDINBURGH(SM)-64A |
| Jan-52 | EDINBURGH(SM)-64A | DUNDEE-62B | POLMONT-64E | EDINBURGH(SM)-64A | HAYMARKET-64B | EDINBURGH(SM)-64A | EASTFIELD-65A | EASTFIELD-65A | EDINBURGH(SM)-64A |
| Aug-52 | EDINBURGH(SM)-64A | DUNDEE-62B | POLMONT-64E | EDINBURGH(SM)-64A | HAYMARKET-64B | EDINBURGH(SM)-64A | EASTFIELD-65A | EASTFIELD-65A | EDINBURGH(SM)-64A |
| Jan-53 | EDINBURGH(SM)-64A | DUNDEE-62B | POLMONT-64E | EDINBURGH(SM)-64A | HAYMARKET-64B | EDINBURGH(SM)-64A | EASTFIELD-65A | EASTFIELD-65A | EDINBURGH(SM)-64A |
| Aug-53 | EDINBURGH(SM)-64A | DUNDEE-62B | POLMONT-64E | EDINBURGH(SM)-64A | HAYMARKET-64B | EDINBURGH(SM)-64A | EASTFIELD-65A | EASTFIELD-65A | EDINBURGH(SM)-64A |
| Jan-54 | EDINBURGH(SM)-64A | DUNDEE-62B | POLMONT-64E | EDINBURGH(SM)-64A | HAYMARKET-64B | EDINBURGH(SM)-64A | EASTFIELD-65A | EASTFIELD-65A | EDINBURGH(SM)-64A |
| Aug-54 | EDINBURGH(SM)-64A | DUNDEE-62B | POLMONT-64E | EDINBURGH(SM)-64A | HAYMARKET-64B | EDINBURGH(SM)-64A | EASTFIELD-65A | EASTFIELD-65A | EDINBURGH(SM)-64A |
| Jan-55 | EDINBURGH(SM)-64A | DUNDEE-62B | POLMONT-64E | EDINBURGH(SM)-64A | HAYMARKET-64B | EDINBURGH(SM)-64A | EASTFIELD-65A | EASTFIELD-65A | EDINBURGH(SM)-64A |
| Aug-55 | EDINBURGH(SM)-64A | DUNDEE-62B | POLMONT-64E | EDINBURGH(SM)-64A | HAYMARKET-64B | EDINBURGH(SM)-64A | EASTFIELD-65A | EASTFIELD-65A | EDINBURGH(SM)-64A |
| Jan-56 | EDINBURGH(SM)-64A | DUNDEE-62B | POLMONT-64E | EDINBURGH(SM)-64A | HAYMARKET-64B | EDINBURGH(SM)-64A | EASTFIELD-65A | 3/56: W/D | EDINBURGH(SM)-64A |
| Aug-56 | EDINBURGH(SM)-64A | DUNDEE-62B | POLMONT-64E | EDINBURGH(SM)-64A | 5/56: W/D | EDINBURGH(SM)-64A | EASTFIELD-65A | | EDINBURGH(SM)-64A |
| Jan-57 | 10/56: W/D | DUNDEE-62B | POLMONT-64E | EDINBURGH(SM)-64A | | EDINBURGH(SM)-64A | EASTFIELD-65A | | EDINBURGH(SM)-64A |
| Aug-57 | | DUNDEE-62B | POLMONT-64E | EDINBURGH(SM)-64A | | EDINBURGH(SM)-64A | EASTFIELD-65A | | EDINBURGH(SM)-64A |
| Jan-58 | | DUNDEE-62B | POLMONT-64E | EDINBURGH(SM)-64A | | EDINBURGH(SM)-64A | EASTFIELD-65A | | EDINBURGH(SM)-64A |
| Aug-58 | | 4/58: EBRO(SM) - 64A | POLMONT-64E | EDINBURGH(SM)-64A | | 4/58: W/D | 3/58: W/D | | EDINBURGH(SM)-64A |
| Jan-59 | | EDINBURGH(SM)-64A | POLMONT-64E | EDINBURGH(SM)-64A | | | | | EDINBURGH(SM)-64A |
| Aug-59 | | EDINBURGH(SM)-64A | POLMONT-64E | EDINBURGH(SM)-64A | | | | | EDINBURGH(SM)-64A |
| Nov-59 | | EDINBURGH(SM)-64A | POLMONT-64E | EDINBURGH(SM)-64A | | | | | EDINBURGH(SM)-64A |
| Jan-60 | | EDINBURGH(SM)-64A | POLMONT-64E | EDINBURGH(SM)-64A | | | | | EDINBURGH(SM)-64A |
| Apr-60 | | EDINBURGH(SM)-64A | POLMONT-64E | EDINBURGH(SM)-64A | | | | | EDINBURGH(SM)-64A |
| Aug-60 | | EDINBURGH(SM)-64A | POLMONT-64E | EDINBURGH(SM)-64A | | | | | EDINBURGH(SM)-64A |
| Nov-60 | | EDINBURGH(SM)-64A | POLMONT-64E | EDINBURGH(SM)-64A | | | | | EDINBURGH(SM)-64A |

| | | | | | J67 0-6-0T (1890) | | | | |
|---|---|---|---|---|---|---|---|---|---|
| | 68478 | 68479 | 68480 | 68481 | 68490 | 68492 | 68493 | 68496 | 68498 |
| Aug-50 | HAYMARKET-64B | EASTFIELD-65A | EASTFIELD-65A | HAYMARKET-64B | | EDINBURGH(SM)-64A | KINGS LYNN-31C | STRATFORD-30A | IPSWCH-32B |
| Jan-51 | HAYMARKET-64B | EASTFIELD-65A | EASTFIELD-65A | HAYMARKET-64B | KINGS LYNN-31C | EDINBURGH(SM)-64A | KINGS LYNN-31C | STRATFORD-30A | IPSWCH-32B |
| Aug-51 | HAYMARKET-64B | EASTFIELD-65A | EASTFIELD-65A | HAYMARKET-64B | KINGS LYNN-31C | EDINBURGH(SM)-64A | KINGS LYNN-31C | STRATFORD-30A | IPSWCH-32B |
| Jan-52 | HAYMARKET-64B | EASTFIELD-65A | EASTFIELD-65A | HAYMARKET-64B | KINGS LYNN-31C | EDINBURGH(SM)-64A | KINGS LYNN-31C | STRATFORD-30A | IPSWCH-32B |
| Aug-52 | HAYMARKET-64B | EASTFIELD-65A | EASTFIELD-65A | HAYMARKET-64B | KINGS LYNN-31C | EDINBURGH(SM)-64A | KINGS LYNN-31C | STRATFORD-30A | IPSWCH-32B |
| Jan-53 | HAYMARKET-64B | EASTFIELD-65A | EASTFIELD-65A | HAYMARKET-64B | KINGS LYNN-31C | EDINBURGH(SM)-64A | KINGS LYNN-31C | STRATFORD-30A | IPSWCH-32B |
| Aug-53 | HAYMARKET-64B | EASTFIELD-65A | EASTFIELD-65A | HAYMARKET-64B | KINGS LYNN-31C | EDINBURGH(SM)-64A | 7/53: IPS - 32B | STRATFORD-30A | 7/53: K.LYNN - 31C |
| Jan-54 | HAYMARKET-64B | EASTFIELD-65A | EASTFIELD-65A | HAYMARKET-64B | KINGS LYNN-31C | EDINBURGH(SM)-64A | IPSWCH-32B | STRATFORD-30A | KINGS LYNN-31C |
| Aug-54 | HAYMARKET-64B | EASTFIELD-65A | EASTFIELD-65A | HAYMARKET-64B | KINGS LYNN-31C | EDINBURGH(SM)-64A | IPSWCH-32B | 5/54: HIT - 34D | KINGS LYNN-31C |
| Jan-55 | HAYMARKET-64B | EASTFIELD-65A | EASTFIELD-65A | HAYMARKET-64B | KINGS LYNN-31C | EDINBURGH(SM)-64A | 10/54: W/D | 10/54: NEW.E - 35A | KINGS LYNN-31C |
| Aug-55 | HAYMARKET-64B | EASTFIELD-65A | EASTFIELD-65A | HAYMARKET-64B | KINGS LYNN-31C | EDINBURGH(SM)-64A | | 2/55: HIT - 34D | KINGS LYNN-31C |
| Jan-56 | HAYMARKET-64B | EASTFIELD-65A | EASTFIELD-65A | HAYMARKET-64B | KINGS LYNN-31C | EDINBURGH(SM)-64A | | HITCHIN-34D | KINGS LYNN-31C |
| Aug-56 | HAYMARKET-64B | EASTFIELD-65A | EASTFIELD-65A | HAYMARKET-64B | KINGS LYNN-31C | 5/56: W/D | | 5/56: W/D | KINGS LYNN-31C |
| Jan-57 | HAYMARKET-64B | EASTFIELD-65A | EASTFIELD-65A | HAYMARKET-64B | KINGS LYNN-31C | | | | KINGS LYNN-31C |
| Aug-57 | HAYMARKET-64B | EASTFIELD-65A | EASTFIELD-65A | HAYMARKET-64B | KINGS LYNN-31C | | | | KINGS LYNN-31C |
| Jan-58 | HAYMARKET-64B | EASTFIELD-65A | EASTFIELD-65A | HAYMARKET-64B | KINGS LYNN-31C | | | | KINGS LYNN-31C |
| Aug-58 | HAYMARKET-64B | EASTFIELD-65A | EASTFIELD-65A | HAYMARKET-64B | 5/58: W/D | | | | 8/58: RET - 36E |
| Jan-59 | 11/58: W/D | EASTFIELD-65A | EASTFIELD-65A | HAYMARKET-64B | | | | | 10/58: DCTR - 36A |
| Aug-59 | | EASTFIELD-65A | 3/59: W/D | HAYMARKET-64B | | | | | 8/59: W/D |
| Nov-59 | | EASTFIELD-65A | | HAYMARKET-64B | | | | | |
| Jan-60 | | EASTFIELD-65A | | HAYMARKET-64B | | | | | |
| Apr-60 | | EASTFIELD-65A | | HAYMARKET-64B | | | | | |
| Aug-60 | | EASTFIELD-65A | | HAYMARKET-64B | | | | | |
| Nov-60 | | EASTFIELD-65A | | HAYMARKET-64B | | | | | |

### Block 1

| | 68509 | 68510 | 68511 | 68512 | 68513 | 68514 | 68515 | 68516 | 68517 |
|---|---|---|---|---|---|---|---|---|---|
| Aug-50 | CAMBRIDGE-31A | STRATFORD-30A | EDINBURGH(SM)-64A | HITCHIN-34D | STRATFORD-30A | KINGS LYNN-31C | KINGS LYNN-31C | CAMBRIDGE-31A | STRATFORD-30A |
| Jan-51 | CAMBRIDGE-31A | STRATFORD-30A | EDINBURGH(SM)-64A | HITCHIN-34D | STRATFORD-30A | KINGS LYNN-31C | KINGS LYNN-31C | CAMBRIDGE-31A | STRATFORD-30A |
| Aug-51 | CAMBRIDGE-31A | STRATFORD-30A | EDINBURGH(SM)-64A | HITCHIN-34D | STRATFORD-30A | KINGS LYNN-31C | KINGS LYNN-31C | CAMBRIDGE-31A | STRATFORD-30A |
| Jan-52 | CAMBRIDGE-31A | STRATFORD-30A | EDINBURGH(SM)-64A | 10/52: HIT-34D | STRATFORD-30A | KINGS LYNN-31C | 9/52: S.LYNN-31D | CAMBRIDGE-31A | STRATFORD-30A |
| Aug-52 | CAMBRIDGE-31A | STRATFORD-30A | EDINBURGH(SM)-64A | HITCHIN-34D | STRATFORD-30A | KINGS LYNN-31C | SOUTH LYNN-31D | CAMBRIDGE-31A | STRATFORD-30A |
| Jan-53 | CAMBRIDGE-31A | STRATFORD-30A | EDINBURGH(SM)-64A | 7/53: LINC-40A | STRATFORD-30A | KINGS LYNN-31C | 7/53: M.CONS-32G | 7/53: NOR-32A | STRATFORD-30A |
| Aug-53 | 7/53: IPS-32B | STRATFORD-30A | EDINBURGH(SM)-64A | 8/54: STAVE-38D | STRATFORD-30A | 7/53: NOR-32A | MELTON.C-32G | NORWICH-32A | STRATFORD-30A |
| Jan-54 | IPSWICH-32B | STRATFORD-30A | EDINBURGH(SM)-64A | 9/54: LINC-40A | STRATFORD-30A | NORWICH-32A | MELTON.C-32G | NORWICH-32A | STRATFORD-30A |
| Aug-54 | 3/54: W/D | STRATFORD-30A | EDINBURGH(SM)-64A | 4/55: STAVE-38D | STRATFORD-30A | NORWICH-32A | MELTON.C-32G | NORWICH-32A | 3/56: W/D |
| Jan-55 | | STRATFORD-30A | EDINBURGH(SM)-64A | STAVELEY-38D | STRATFORD-30A | 7/55: W/D | MELTON.C-32G | NORWICH-32A | |
| Aug-55 | | STRATFORD-30A | EDINBURGH(SM)-64A | STAVELEY-38D | STRATFORD-30A | | MELTON.C-32G | NORWICH-32A | |
| Jan-56 | | STRATFORD-30A | EDINBURGH(SM)-64A | STAVELEY-38D | STRATFORD-30A | | 1/57: W/D | NORWICH-32A | |
| Aug-56 | | STRATFORD-30A | 12/56: W/D | 4/57: W/D | STRATFORD-30A | | | 12/56: STRAT-30A | |
| Jan-57 | | STRATFORD-30A | | | STRATFORD-30A | | | 5/57: W/D | |
| Aug-57 | | STRATFORD-30A | | | STRATFORD-30A | | | | |
| Jan-58 | | 6/58: LINC-40A | | | STRATFORD-30A | | | | |
| Aug-58 | | LINCOLN-40A | | | STRATFORD-30A | | | | |
| Jan-59 | | 9/59: W/D | | | STRATFORD-30A | | | | |
| Aug-59 | | | | | STRATFORD-30A | | | | |
| Nov-59 | | | | | STRATFORD-30A | | | | |
| Jan-60 | | | | | STRATFORD-30A | | | | |
| Apr-60 | | | | | STRATFORD-30A | | | | |
| Aug-60 | | | | | STRATFORD-30A | | | | |
| Nov-60 | | | | | 11/60: W/D | | | | |

### Block 2

| | 68518 | 68519 | 68520 | 68521 | 68522 | 68523 | 68529 | 68531 | 68536 |
|---|---|---|---|---|---|---|---|---|---|
| Aug-50 | IPSWICH-32B | STRATFORD-30A | STRATFORD-30A | STRATFORD-30A | COLCHESTER-30E | STRATFORD-30A | LINCOLN-40A | WREXHAM-6E | MELTON.C-32G |
| Jan-51 | IPSWICH-32B | STRATFORD-30A | STRATFORD-30A | STRATFORD-30A | COLCHESTER-30E | STRATFORD-30A | LINCOLN-40A | WREXHAM-6E | MELTON.C-32G |
| Aug-51 | IPSWICH-32B | STRATFORD-30A | STRATFORD-30A | STRATFORD-30A | COLCHESTER-30E | STRATFORD-30A | LINCOLN-40A | WREXHAM-6E | MELTON.C-32G |
| Jan-52 | IPSWICH-32B | STRATFORD-30A | STRATFORD-30A | STRATFORD-30A | COLCHESTER-30E | STRATFORD-30A | LINCOLN-40A | WREXHAM-6E | MELTON.C-32G |
| Aug-52 | IPSWICH-32B | STRATFORD-30A | STRATFORD-30A | STRATFORD-30A | COLCHESTER-30E | STRATFORD-30A | LINCOLN-40A | WREXHAM-6E | MELTON.C-32G |
| Jan-53 | IPSWICH-32B | STRATFORD-30A | STRATFORD-30A | STRATFORD-30A | COLCHESTER-30E | 2/53: STAVE-38D | 7/53: HIT-34D | WREXHAM-6E | MELTON.C-32G |
| Aug-53 | IPSWICH-32B | STRATFORD-30A | STRATFORD-30A | STRATFORD-30A | COLCHESTER-30E | 8/53: IPS-32B | HITCHIN-34D | WREXHAM-6E | MELTON.C-32G |
| Jan-54 | IPSWICH-32B | STRATFORD-30A | 4/54: MEX-36B | LINCOLN-40A | COLCHESTER-30E | 10/53: NOR-32A | 5/54: STRAT-30A | WREXHAM-6E | MELTON.C-32G |
| Aug-54 | IPSWICH-32B | STRATFORD-30A | MEXBOROUGH-36B | 4/54: IPS-32B | COLCHESTER-30E | NORWICH-32A | STRATFORD-30A | WREXHAM-6E | MELTON.C-32G |
| Jan-55 | IPSWICH-32B | 11/55: NEW.E-35A | 11/55: DCTR-36A | IPSWICH-32B | COLCHESTER-30E | NORWICH-32A | 9/55: K.LYNN-31C | WREXHAM-6E | MELTON.C-32G |
| Aug-55 | IPSWICH-32B | 12/55: RET-36E | 12/55: RET-36E | IPSWICH-32B | COLCHESTER-30E | 12/55: W/D | 11/55: CAMB-31A | 10/55: W/D | MELTON.C-32G |
| Jan-56 | IPSWICH-32B | RETFORD-36E | RETFORD-36E | 8/56: W/D | COLCHESTER-30E | | 2/56: STRAT-30A | | MELTON.C-32G |
| Aug-56 | IPSWICH-32B | RETFORD-36E | 2/57: DCTR-36A | | COLCHESTER-30E | | STRATFORD-30A | | MELTON.C-32G |
| Jan-57 | IPSWICH-32B | RETFORD-36E | DONCASTER-36A | | COLCHESTER-30E | | STRATFORD-30A | | MELTON.C-32G |
| Aug-57 | IPSWICH-32B | RETFORD-36E | DONCASTER-36A | | 6/58: STRAT-30A | | STRATFORD-30A | | 2/58: W/D |
| Jan-58 | 2/58: W/D | 8/58: W/D | DONCASTER-36A | | 8/58: COLW-40E | | 8/58: W/D | | |
| Aug-58 | | | DONCASTER-36A | | COLWICK-40E | | | | |
| Jan-59 | | | 8/59: W/D | | 10/59: BOST-40F | | | | |
| Aug-59 | | | | | BOSTON-40F | | | | |
| Nov-59 | | | | | BOSTON-40F | | | | |
| Jan-60 | | | | | BOSTON-40F | | | | |
| Apr-60 | | | | | BOSTON-40F | | | | |

### Block 3

| | 68540 | 68547 | 68572 | 68583 | 68584 | 68586 | 68588 | 68589 | 68590 |
|---|---|---|---|---|---|---|---|---|---|
| Aug-50 | TRAFFORD PARK-9E | WIDNES-8D | HATFIELD-34C | TRAFFORD PARK-9E | SOUTHPORT-27E | NORWICH-32A | STRATFORD-30A | STRATFORD-30A | STRATFORD-30A |
| Jan-51 | TRAFFORD PARK-9E | 12/50: BRUNS-8E | HATFIELD-34C | TRAFFORD PARK-9E | SOUTHPORT-27E | NORWICH-32A | STRATFORD-30A | STRATFORD-30A | STRATFORD-30A |
| Aug-51 | TRAFFORD PARK-9E | BRUNSWICK-8E | HATFIELD-34C | TRAFFORD PARK-9E | 10/51: WREX-6E | NORWICH-32A | STRATFORD-30A | STRATFORD-30A | STRATFORD-30A |
| Jan-52 | TRAFFORD PARK-9E | BRUNSWICK-8E | 3/52: IPS-32B | TRAFFORD PARK-9E | WREXHAM-6E | 3/52: IPS-32B | STRATFORD-30A | STRATFORD-30A | STRATFORD-30A |
| Aug-52 | TRAFFORD PARK-9E | BRUNSWICK-8E | IPSWICH-32B | TRAFFORD PARK-9E | WREXHAM-6E | 6/52: NOR-32A | STRATFORD-30A | STRATFORD-30A | STRATFORD-30A |
| Jan-53 | 2/53: LINC-40A | BRUNSWICK-8E | IPSWICH-32B | TRAFFORD PARK-9E | WREXHAM-6E | NORWICH-32A | STRATFORD-30A | STRATFORD-30A | STRATFORD-30A |
| Aug-53 | 7/53: HIT-34D | 8/53: WREX-6E | IPSWICH-32B | TRAFFORD PARK-9E | WREXHAM-6E | 10/53: IPS-32B | STRATFORD-30A | STRATFORD-30A | STRATFORD-30A |
| Jan-54 | HITCHIN-34D | 10/53: BRUNS-8E | IPSWICH-32B | TRAFFORD PARK-9E | WREXHAM-6E | IPSWICH-32B | STRATFORD-30A | 5/54: STAVE-38D | 12/54: STAVE-38D |
| Aug-54 | HITCHIN-34D | BRUNSWICK-8E | 11/54: W/D | TRAFFORD PARK-9E | WREXHAM-6E | IPSWICH-32B | STRATFORD-30A | STAVELEY-38D | 1/55: STRAT-30A |
| Jan-55 | HITCHIN-34D | BRUNSWICK-8E | | TRAFFORD PARK-9E | 8/55: W/D | IPSWICH-32B | STRATFORD-30A | 1/56: W/D | 9/55: W/D |
| Aug-55 | HITCHIN-34D | BRUNSWICK-8E | | TRAFFORD PARK-9E | | IPSWICH-32B | STRATFORD-30A | | |
| Jan-56 | 1/56: W/D | BRUNSWICK-8E | | TRAFFORD PARK-9E | | 5/56: W/D | STRATFORD-30A | | |
| Aug-56 | | 4/56: W/D | | 3/57: BIDS-6F | | | STRATFORD-30A | | |
| Jan-57 | | | | BIDSTON-6F | | | STRATFORD-30A | | |
| Aug-57 | | | | BIDSTON-6F | | | STRATFORD-30A | | |
| Jan-58 | | | | 4/58: W/D | | | 5/58: W/D | | |

### Block 4

| | 68591 | 68592 | 68593 | 68594 | 68595 | 68597 | 68606 | 68608 | 68609 |
|---|---|---|---|---|---|---|---|---|---|
| Aug-50 | STRATFORD-30A | STRATFORD-30A | IPSWICH-32B | STRATFORD-30A | TRAFFORD PARK-9E | SOUTH LYNN-31D | STRATFORD-30A | STRATFORD-30A | CAMBRIDGE-31A |
| Jan-51 | STRATFORD-30A | STRATFORD-30A | IPSWICH-32B | STRATFORD-30A | TRAFFORD PARK-9E | SOUTH LYNN-31D | STRATFORD-30A | 9/50: COL-30E | CAMBRIDGE-31A |
| Aug-51 | STRATFORD-30A | STRATFORD-30A | IPSWICH-32B | STRATFORD-30A | TRAFFORD PARK-9E | SOUTH LYNN-31D | STRATFORD-30A | COLCHESTER-30E | CAMBRIDGE-31A |
| Jan-52 | STRATFORD-30A | STRATFORD-30A | IPSWICH-32B | STRATFORD-30A | TRAFFORD PARK-9E | SOUTH LYNN-31D | STRATFORD-30A | 2/52: STRAT-30A | CAMBRIDGE-31A |
| Aug-52 | STRATFORD-30A | 9/52: STAVE-38D | IPSWICH-32B | STRATFORD-30A | TRAFFORD PARK-9E | SOUTH LYNN-31D | STRATFORD-30A | STRATFORD-30A | 10/52: BURY-31E |
| Jan-53 | STRATFORD-30A | STAVELEY-38D | IPSWICH-32B | STRATFORD-30A | TRAFFORD PARK-9E | 7/53: NOR-32A | 7/53: IPS-32B | STRATFORD-30A | 1/53: CAMB-31A |
| Aug-53 | STRATFORD-30A | 7/53: NOR-32A | IPSWICH-32B | STRATFORD-30A | TRAFFORD PARK-9E | NORWICH-32A | IPSWICH-32B | 7/53: NOR-32A | 7/53: NOR-32A |
| Jan-54 | STRATFORD-30A | NORWICH-32A | IPSWICH-32B | STRATFORD-30A | 8/54: WREX-6E | NORWICH-32A | IPSWICH-32B | NORWICH-32A | CAMBRIDGE-31A |
| Aug-54 | STRATFORD-30A | NORWICH-32A | IPSWICH-32B | 11/54: IPS-32B | WREXHAM-6E | NORWICH-32A | 3/55: W/D | NORWICH-32A | CAMBRIDGE-31A |
| Jan-55 | STRATFORD-30A | NORWICH-32A | IPSWICH-32B | IPSWICH-32B | WREXHAM-6E | 10/55: W/D | | NORWICH-32A | CAMBRIDGE-31A |
| Aug-55 | STRATFORD-30A | 7/55: W/D | IPSWICH-32B | 11/55: W/D | WREXHAM-6E | | | 3/56: STAVE-38D | CAMBRIDGE-31A |
| Jan-56 | STRATFORD-30A | | IPSWICH-32B | | 1/57: W/D | | | STAVELEY-38D | CAMBRIDGE-31A |
| Aug-56 | STRATFORD-30A | | IPSWICH-32B | | | | | STAVELEY-38D | CAMBRIDGE-31A |
| Jan-57 | STRATFORD-30A | | IPSWICH-32B | | | | | STAVELEY-38D | CAMBRIDGE-31A |
| Aug-57 | STRATFORD-30A | | IPSWICH-32B | | | | | STAVELEY(GC)-41H | CAMBRIDGE-31A |
| Jan-58 | STRATFORD-30A | | 1/58: W/D | | | | | 10/58: W/D | CAMBRIDGE-31A |
| Aug-58 | 6/58: STAVE-41H | | | | | | | | CAMBRIDGE-31A |
| Jan-59 | STAVELEY(GC)-41H | | | | | | | | CAMBRIDGE-31A |
| Aug-59 | 9/59: L.JN-41J | | | | | | | | 10/59: STRAT-30A |
| Nov-59 | LANGWITH JCN-41J | | | | | | | | STRATFORD-30A |
| Jan-60 | 12/59: W/D | | | | | | | | STRATFORD-30A |
| Apr-60 | | | | | | | | | STRATFORD-30A |
| Aug-60 | | | | | | | | | STRATFORD-30A |

| Date | 68610 | 68611 | 68616 | 68628 | J69 0-6-0T (1902) 68491 | 68494 | 68495 | 68497 | 68499 |
|---|---|---|---|---|---|---|---|---|---|
| Aug-50 | LINCOLN - 40A | LOWESTOFT - 32C | COLCHESTER - 30E | YARMOUTH (ST) - 32D | STRATFORD - 30A | KINGS LYNN - 31C | NORWICH - 32A | BURY St.E - 31E | CARLISLE (CANAL) - 12B |
| Jan-51 | LINCOLN - 40A | LOWESTOFT - 32C | COLCHESTER - 30E | YARMOUTH (ST) - 32D | STRATFORD - 30A | KINGS LYNN - 31C | NORWICH - 32A | BURY St.E - 31E | **3/51: BRUNS - 8E** |
| Aug-51 | LINCOLN - 40A | LOWESTOFT - 32C | COLCHESTER - 30E | YARMOUTH (ST) - 32D | STRATFORD - 30A | KINGS LYNN - 31C | NORWICH - 32A | BURY St.E - 31E | BRUNSWICK - 8E |
| Jan-52 | LINCOLN - 40A | LOWESTOFT - 32C | **2/52: STRAT - 30A** | YARMOUTH (ST) - 32D | STRATFORD - 30A | KINGS LYNN - 31C | NORWICH - 32A | BURY St.E - 31E | BRUNSWICK - 8E |
| Aug-52 | LINCOLN - 40A | LOWESTOFT - 32C | STRATFORD - 30A | YARMOUTH (ST) - 32D | STRATFORD - 30A | **6/52: NOR - 32A** | NORWICH - 32A | BURY St.E - 31E | BRUNSWICK - 8E |
| Jan-53 | LINCOLN - 40A | LOWESTOFT - 32C | STRATFORD - 30A | YARMOUTH (ST) - 32D | STRATFORD - 30A | NORWICH - 32A | NORWICH - 32A | BURY St.E - 31E | **2/53: LINC - 40A** |
| Aug-53 | **7/53: HIT - 34D** | LOWESTOFT - 32C | **7/53: NOR - 32A** | YARMOUTH (ST) - 32D | **7/53: CAMB - 31A** | **7/53: S.LYNN - 31D** | **7/55: K.LYNN - 31C** | BURY St.E - 31E | **7/53: BOST - 40F** |
| Jan-54 | HITCHIN - 34D | LOWESTOFT - 32C | NORWICH - 32A | YARMOUTH (ST) - 32D | CAMBRIDGE - 31A | SOUTH LYNN - 31D | KINGS LYNN - 31C | BURY St.E - 31E | BOSTON - 40F |
| Aug-54 | HITCHIN - 34D | LOWESTOFT - 32C | NORWICH - 32A | YARMOUTH (ST) - 32D | CAMBRIDGE - 31A | SOUTH LYNN - 31D | KINGS LYNN - 31C | BURY St.E - 31E | BOSTON - 40F |
| Jan-55 | HITCHIN - 34D | LOWESTOFT - 32C | NORWICH - 32A | YARMOUTH (ST) - 32D | CAMBRIDGE - 31A | SOUTH LYNN - 31D | KINGS LYNN - 31C | BURY St.E - 31E | **4/55: STRAT - 30A** |
| Aug-55 | HITCHIN - 34D | **7/55: W/D** | NORWICH - 32A | YARMOUTH (ST) - 32D | CAMBRIDGE - 31A | SOUTH LYNN - 31D | KINGS LYNN - 31C | BURY St.E - 31E | **9/55: K.LYNN - 31C** |
| Jan-56 | HITCHIN - 34D | | **11/55: STAVE - 38D** | YARMOUTH (ST) - 32D | **3/56: NEW.E - 35A** | SOUTH LYNN - 31D | KINGS LYNN - 31C | BURY St.E - 31E | KINGS LYNN - 31C |
| Aug-56 | HITCHIN - 34D | | STAVELEY - 38D | YARMOUTH (ST) - 32D | NEW ENGLAND - 35A | SOUTH LYNN - 31D | KINGS LYNN - 31C | BURY St.E - 31E | KINGS LYNN - 31C |
| Jan-57 | **1/57: W/D** | | STAVELEY - 38D | **3/57: LOW - 32D** | NEW ENGLAND - 35A | SOUTH LYNN - 31D | KINGS LYNN - 31C | BURY St.E - 31E | KINGS LYNN - 31C |
| Aug-57 | | | STAVELEY - 38D | LOWESTOFT - 32C | NEW ENGLAND - 35A | SOUTH LYNN - 31D | KINGS LYNN - 31C | BURY St.E - 31E | KINGS LYNN - 31C |
| Jan-58 | | | STAVELEY - 38D | **2/58: W/D** | NEW ENGLAND - 35A | SOUTH LYNN - 31D | KINGS LYNN - 31C | **2/58: DARN - 41A** | **5/58: S.LYNN - 31D** |
| Aug-58 | | | STAVELEY (GC) - 41H | | **6/58: W/D** | **4/58: W/D** | **5/58: W/D** | **3/58: MEX - 41F** | 8/58: K.LYNN - 31C |
| Jan-59 | | | **11/58: W/D** | | | | | MEXBOROUGH - 41F | KINGS LYNN - 31C |
| Aug-59 | | | | | | | | MEXBOROUGH - 41F | KINGS LYNN - 31C |
| Nov-59 | | | | | | | | MEXBOROUGH - 41F | KINGS LYNN - 31C |
| Jan-60 | | | | | | | | MEXBOROUGH - 41F | KINGS LYNN - 31C |
| Apr-60 | | | | | | | | **3/58: SH (MR) - 41B** | KINGS LYNN - 31C |
| Aug-60 | | | | | | | | SHEFFIELD (MR) - 41B | KINGS LYNN - 31C |
| Nov-60 | | | | | | | | **10/60: W/D** | KINGS LYNN - 31C |

| Date | 68500 | 68501 | 68502 | 68503 | 68504 | 68505 | 68507 | 68508 | 68524 |
|---|---|---|---|---|---|---|---|---|---|
| Aug-50 | STRATFORD - 30A | NORWICH - 32A | KINGS LYNN - 31C | PARKHEAD - 65C | THORNTON JCN - 62A | EDINBURGH (SM) - 64A | STRATFORD - 30A | STRATFORD - 30A | POLMONT - 64E |
| Jan-51 | STRATFORD - 30A | NORWICH - 32A | KINGS LYNN - 31C | PARKHEAD - 65C | THORNTON JCN - 62A | EDINBURGH (SM) - 64A | STRATFORD - 30A | STRATFORD - 30A | POLMONT - 64E |
| Aug-51 | **4/51: PARK - 30F** | NORWICH - 32A | KINGS LYNN - 31C | PARKHEAD - 65C | THORNTON JCN - 62A | EDINBURGH (SM) - 64A | STRATFORD - 30A | STRATFORD - 30A | POLMONT - 64E |
| Jan-52 | PARKSTON - 30F | NORWICH - 32A | KINGS LYNN - 31C | PARKHEAD - 65C | THORNTON JCN - 62A | EDINBURGH (SM) - 64A | STRATFORD - 30A | STRATFORD - 30A | POLMONT - 64E |
| Aug-52 | PARKSTON - 30F | NORWICH - 32A | KINGS LYNN - 31C | PARKHEAD - 65C | THORNTON JCN - 62A | **7/52: DFRS _ 68B** | STRATFORD - 30A | STRATFORD - 30A | POLMONT - 64E |
| Jan-53 | PARKSTON - 30F | NORWICH - 32A | KINGS LYNN - 31C | PARKHEAD - 65C | THORNTON JCN - 62A | DUMFRIES - 68B | STRATFORD - 30A | STRATFORD - 30A | POLMONT - 64E |
| Aug-53 | PARKSTON - 30F | **7/53: BOST - 40F** | KINGS LYNN - 31C | PARKHEAD - 65C | THORNTON JCN - 62A | DUMFRIES - 68B | STRATFORD - 30A | STRATFORD - 30A | POLMONT - 64E |
| Jan-54 | PARKSTON - 30F | BOSTON - 40F | KINGS LYNN - 31C | PARKHEAD - 65C | THORNTON JCN - 62A | **11/53: W/D** | STRATFORD - 30A | **12/53: COL - 30E** | POLMONT - 64E |
| Aug-54 | PARKSTON - 30F | BOSTON - 40F | KINGS LYNN - 31C | PARKHEAD - 65C | THORNTON JCN - 62A | | STRATFORD - 30A | COLCHESTER - 30E | POLMONT - 64E |
| Jan-55 | **2/55: STRAT - 30A** | BOSTON - 40F | KINGS LYNN - 31C | PARKHEAD - 65C | THORNTON JCN - 62A | | STRATFORD - 30A | COLCHESTER - 30E | POLMONT - 64E |
| Aug-55 | STRATFORD - 30A | BOSTON - 40F | KINGS LYNN - 31C | PARKHEAD - 65C | THORNTON JCN - 62A | | **11/55: NEW.E - 35A** | COLCHESTER - 30E | POLMONT - 64E |
| Jan-56 | STRATFORD - 30A | BOSTON - 40F | KINGS LYNN - 31C | PARKHEAD - 65C | **1/56: W/D** | | **12/55: DCTR - 36A** | 1/56: STRAT - 30A | POLMONT - 64E |
| Aug-56 | STRATFORD - 30A | BOSTON - 40F | KINGS LYNN - 31C | PARKHEAD - 65C | | | DONCASTER - 36A | **10/56: RET - 36E** | POLMONT - 64E |
| Jan-57 | STRATFORD - 30A | BOSTON - 40F | KINGS LYNN - 31C | **1/57: W/D** | | | DONCASTER - 36A | RETFORD - 36E | POLMONT - 64E |
| Aug-57 | STRATFORD - 30A | **6/57: LINC - 40A** | KINGS LYNN - 31C | | | | DONCASTER - 36A | RETFORD - 36E | POLMONT - 64E |
| Jan-58 | STRATFORD - 30A | LINCOLN - 40A | KINGS LYNN - 31C | | | | DONCASTER - 36A | RETFORD - 36E | POLMONT - 64E |
| Aug-58 | STRATFORD - 30A | LINCOLN - 40A | **6/58: RET - 36E** | | | | DONCASTER - 36A | **10/58: DCTR - 36A** | POLMONT - 64E |
| Jan-59 | STRATFORD - 30A | LINCOLN - 40A | **10/58: DCTR - 36A** | | | | DONCASTER - 36A | DONCASTER - 36A | POLMONT - 64E |
| Aug-59 | STRATFORD - 30A | LINCOLN - 40A | **6/59: RET - 36E** | | | | DONCASTER - 36A | DONCASTER - 36A | **6/59: W/D** |
| Nov-59 | STRATFORD - 30A | LINCOLN - 40A | RETFORD - 36E | | | | DONCASTER - 36A | DONCASTER - 36A | |
| Jan-60 | STRATFORD - 30A | LINCOLN - 40A | RETFORD - 36E | | | | DONCASTER - 36A | DONCASTER - 36A | |
| Apr-60 | STRATFORD - 30A | LINCOLN - 40A | RETFORD - 36E | | | | **5/60: W/D** | DONCASTER - 36A | |
| Aug-60 | STRATFORD - 30A | **8/60: W/D** | RETFORD - 36E | | | | | DONCASTER - 36A | |
| Nov-60 | STRATFORD - 30A | | RETFORD - 36E | | | | | DONCASTER - 36A | |

| Date | 68525 | 68526 | 68527 | 68528 | 68530 | 68532 | 68533 | 68534 | 68535 |
|---|---|---|---|---|---|---|---|---|---|
| Aug-50 | EDINBURGH (SM) - 64A | STRATFORD - 30A | STRATFORD - 30A | BOSTON - 40F | CAMBRIDGE - 31A | STRATFORD - 30A | POLMONT - 64E | STRATFORD - 30A | THORNTON JCN - 62A |
| Jan-51 | **3/51: KITTY - 61A** | STRATFORD - 30A | **9/50: PARKS - 30F** | BOSTON - 40F | CAMBRIDGE - 31A | STRATFORD - 30A | POLMONT - 64E | STRATFORD - 30A | THORNTON JCN - 62A |
| Aug-51 | KITTYBREWSTER - 61A | STRATFORD - 30A | **2/51: STRAT - 30A** | **9/51: LINC - 40A** | CAMBRIDGE - 31A | STRATFORD - 30A | POLMONT - 64E | STRATFORD - 30A | THORNTON JCN - 62A |
| Jan-52 | **1/52: LINC - 40A** | STRATFORD - 30A | STRATFORD - 30A | LINCOLN - 40A | CAMBRIDGE - 31A | STRATFORD - 30A | **5/52: DFRS - 68B** | STRATFORD - 30A | THORNTON JCN - 62A |
| Aug-52 | LINCOLN - 40A | STRATFORD - 30A | STRATFORD - 30A | LINCOLN - 40A | CAMBRIDGE - 31A | STRATFORD - 30A | **7/52: EBRO (SM) - 64A** | STRATFORD - 30A | THORNTON JCN - 62A |
| Jan-53 | LINCOLN - 40A | STRATFORD - 30A | STRATFORD - 30A | LINCOLN - 40A | CAMBRIDGE - 31A | STRATFORD - 30A | **11/52: Bathgate (Dept)** | STRATFORD - 30A | THORNTON JCN - 62A |
| Aug-53 | LINCOLN - 40A | STRATFORD - 30A | STRATFORD - 30A | LINCOLN - 40A | CAMBRIDGE - 31A | STRATFORD - 30A | **7/53: W/D** | STRATFORD - 30A | THORNTON JCN - 62A |
| Jan-54 | **12/53: W/D** | STRATFORD - 30A | STRATFORD - 30A | LINCOLN - 40A | CAMBRIDGE - 31A | STRATFORD - 30A | | STRATFORD - 30A | THORNTON JCN - 62A |
| Aug-54 | | STRATFORD - 30A | STRATFORD - 30A | LINCOLN - 40A | CAMBRIDGE - 31A | STRATFORD - 30A | | **8/54: W/D** | **8/54: DUN - 62B** |
| Jan-55 | | STRATFORD - 30A | STRATFORD - 30A | LINCOLN - 40A | CAMBRIDGE - 31A | STRATFORD - 30A | | | DUNDEE - 62B |
| Aug-55 | | STRATFORD - 30A | **11/55: NEW.E - 35A** | LINCOLN - 40A | CAMBRIDGE - 31A | STRATFORD - 30A | | | DUNDEE - 62B |
| Jan-56 | | STRATFORD - 30A | **1/56: RET - 36E** | LINCOLN - 40A | CAMBRIDGE - 31A | STRATFORD - 30A | | | DUNDEE - 62B |
| Aug-56 | | STRATFORD - 30A | RETFORD - 36E | LINCOLN - 40A | CAMBRIDGE - 31A | STRATFORD - 30A | | | DUNDEE - 62B |
| Jan-57 | | STRATFORD - 30A | RETFORD - 36E | LINCOLN - 40A | CAMBRIDGE - 31A | STRATFORD - 30A | | | DUNDEE - 62B |
| Aug-57 | | STRATFORD - 30A | RETFORD - 36E | LINCOLN - 40A | CAMBRIDGE - 31A | STRATFORD - 30A | | | DUNDEE - 62B |
| Jan-58 | | STRATFORD - 30A | RETFORD - 36E | LINCOLN - 40A | **2/58: DARN - 41A** | STRATFORD - 30A | | | DUNDEE - 62B |
| Aug-58 | | STRATFORD - 30A | **6/58: W/D** | LINCOLN - 40A | **5/58: RET - 36E** | STRATFORD - 30A | | | DUNDEE - 62B |
| Jan-59 | | STRATFORD - 30A | | LINCOLN - 40A | **10/58: DCTR - 36A** | **12/58: W/D** | | | DUNDEE - 62B |
| Aug-59 | | STRATFORD - 30A | | LINCOLN - 40A | **6/59: RET - 36E** | | | | **8/59: W/D** |
| Nov-59 | | **10/59: PARKS - 30F** | | **10/59: W/D** | RETFORD - 36E | | | | |
| Jan-60 | | **2/60: STRAT - 30A** | | | RETFORD - 36E | | | | |
| Apr-60 | | STRATFORD - 30A | | | RETFORD - 36E | | | | |
| Aug-60 | | STRATFORD - 30A | | | RETFORD - 36E | | | | |
| Nov-60 | | **10/60: W/D** | | | RETFORD - 36E | | | | |

| Date | 68537 | 68538 | 68541 | 68542 | 68543 | 68544 | 68545 | 68546 | 68548 |
|---|---|---|---|---|---|---|---|---|---|
| Aug-50 | LINCOLN - 40A | STRATFORD - 30A | HITCHIN - 34D | SOUTH LYNN - 31D | BOSTON - 40F | POLMONT - 64E | KINGS LYNN - 31C | STRATFORD - 30A | STRATFORD - 30A |
| Jan-51 | LINCOLN - 40A | STRATFORD - 30A | HITCHIN - 34D | SOUTH LYNN - 31D | BOSTON - 40F | POLMONT - 64E | KINGS LYNN - 31C | STRATFORD - 30A | STRATFORD - 30A |
| Aug-51 | LINCOLN - 40A | STRATFORD - 30A | HITCHIN - 34D | SOUTH LYNN - 31D | BOSTON - 40F | POLMONT - 64E | KINGS LYNN - 31C | STRATFORD - 30A | STRATFORD - 30A |
| Jan-52 | LINCOLN - 40A | STRATFORD - 30A | HITCHIN - 34D | SOUTH LYNN - 31D | BOSTON - 40F | POLMONT - 64E | KINGS LYNN - 31C | STRATFORD - 30A | STRATFORD - 30A |
| Aug-52 | LINCOLN - 40A | STRATFORD - 30A | HITCHIN - 34D | SOUTH LYNN - 31D | BOSTON - 40F | POLMONT - 64E | KINGS LYNN - 31C | STRATFORD - 30A | STRATFORD - 30A |
| Jan-53 | LINCOLN - 40A | STRATFORD - 30A | HITCHIN - 34D | SOUTH LYNN - 31D | BOSTON - 40F | POLMONT - 64E | KINGS LYNN - 31C | STRATFORD - 30A | STRATFORD - 30A |
| Aug-53 | LINCOLN - 40A | STRATFORD - 30A | **7/53: LINC - 40A** | SOUTH LYNN - 31D | BOSTON - 40F | POLMONT - 64E | KINGS LYNN - 31C | STRATFORD - 30A | STRATFORD - 30A |
| Jan-54 | LINCOLN - 40A | STRATFORD - 30A | LINCOLN - 40A | SOUTH LYNN - 31D | BOSTON - 40F | POLMONT - 64E | KINGS LYNN - 31C | STRATFORD - 30A | **11/53: W/D** |
| Aug-54 | LINCOLN - 40A | STRATFORD - 30A | LINCOLN - 40A | SOUTH LYNN - 31D | BOSTON - 40F | POLMONT - 64E | KINGS LYNN - 31C | STRATFORD - 30A | |
| Jan-55 | LINCOLN - 40A | STRATFORD - 30A | LINCOLN - 40A | SOUTH LYNN - 31D | BOSTON - 40F | **2/55: W/D** | KINGS LYNN - 31C | STRATFORD - 30A | |
| Aug-55 | LINCOLN - 40A | STRATFORD - 30A | LINCOLN - 40A | SOUTH LYNN - 31D | BOSTON - 40F | | KINGS LYNN - 31C | STRATFORD - 30A | |
| Jan-56 | LINCOLN - 40A | STRATFORD - 30A | LINCOLN - 40A | SOUTH LYNN - 31D | BOSTON - 40F | | KINGS LYNN - 31C | STRATFORD - 30A | |
| Aug-56 | LINCOLN - 40A | STRATFORD - 30A | LINCOLN - 40A | SOUTH LYNN - 31D | BOSTON - 40F | | KINGS LYNN - 31C | STRATFORD - 30A | |
| Jan-57 | LINCOLN - 40A | STRATFORD - 30A | LINCOLN - 40A | SOUTH LYNN - 31D | BOSTON - 40F | | KINGS LYNN - 31C | STRATFORD - 30A | |
| Aug-57 | LINCOLN - 40A | STRATFORD - 30A | LINCOLN - 40A | SOUTH LYNN - 31D | **6/57: STRAT - 30A** | | KINGS LYNN - 31C | STRATFORD - 30A | |
| Jan-58 | LINCOLN - 40A | STRATFORD - 30A | LINCOLN - 40A | SOUTH LYNN - 31D | STRATFORD - 30A | | KINGS LYNN - 31C | STRATFORD - 30A | |
| Aug-58 | **6/58: W/D** | STRATFORD - 30A | **8/58: W/D** | **8/58: K.LYNN - 31C** | **6/58: LINC - 40A** | | **8/58: LINC - 40A** | **5/58: W/D** | |
| Jan-59 | | STRATFORD - 30A | | KINGS LYNN - 31C | LINCOLN - 40A | | **1/59: COLW - 40E** | | |
| Aug-59 | | STRATFORD - 30A | | KINGS LYNN - 31C | LINCOLN - 40A | | COLWICK - 40E | | |
| Nov-59 | | STRATFORD - 30A | | KINGS LYNN - 31C | **11/59: W/D** | | COLWICK - 40E | | |
| Jan-60 | | STRATFORD - 30A | | KINGS LYNN - 31C | | | COLWICK - 40E | | |
| Apr-60 | | STRATFORD - 30A | | KINGS LYNN - 31C | | | COLWICK - 40E | | |
| Aug-60 | | STRATFORD - 30A | | **8/60: STRAT - 30A** | | | COLWICK - 40E | | |
| Nov-60 | | STRATFORD - 30A | | STRATFORD - 30A | | | COLWICK - 40E | | |

| | 68549 | 68550 | 68551 | 68552 | 68553 | 68554 | 68555 | 68556 | 68557 |
|---|---|---|---|---|---|---|---|---|---|
| Aug-50 | STRATFORD - 30A | THORNTONJCN - 62A | EASTFIELD - 65A | EASTFIELD - 65A | LINCOLN - 40A | STRATFORD - 30A | THORNTONJCN - 62A | PARKESTON - 30F | PARKESTON - 30F |
| Jan-51 | STRATFORD - 30A | THORNTONJCN - 62A | EASTFIELD - 65A | **4/51: KITTY - 61A** | LINCOLN - 40A | STRATFORD - 30A | THORNTONJCN - 62A | PARKESTON - 30F | STRATFORD - 30A |
| Aug-51 | STRATFORD - 30A | THORNTONJCN - 62A | **4/51: YOKER - 65G** | **6/51: EBRO(SM) - 64A** | LINCOLN - 40A | STRATFORD - 30A | THORNTONJCN - 62A | **4/51: STRAT - 30A** | STRATFORD - 30A |
| Jan-52 | STRATFORD - 30A | **2/52: STRAT - 30A** | **11/51: DAWS - 65D** | **2/52: STRAT - 30A** | LINCOLN - 40A | STRATFORD - 30A | **2/52: IPS - 32B** | STRATFORD - 30A | STRATFORD - 30A |
| Aug-52 | STRATFORD - 30A | STRATFORD - 30A | DAWSHOLME - 65D | STRATFORD - 30A | LINCOLN - 40A | STRATFORD - 30A | IPSWICH - 32B | STRATFORD - 30A | **11/52: NOR - 32A** |
| Jan-53 | STRATFORD - 30A | STRATFORD - 30A | DAWSHOLME - 65D | STRATFORD - 30A | LINCOLN - 40A | STRATFORD - 30A | IPSWICH - 32B | STRATFORD - 30A | **1/53: IPS - 32B** |
| Aug-53 | STRATFORD - 30A | STRATFORD - 30A | DAWSHOLME - 65D | STRATFORD - 30A | **12/53: STAVE - 38D** | STRATFORD - 30A | **7/53: CAMB - 31A** | STRATFORD - 30A | **7/53: BOST - 40F** |
| Jan-54 | STRATFORD - 30A | STRATFORD - 30A | DAWSHOLME - 65D | STRATFORD - 30A | **1/54: LINC - 40A** | STRATFORD - 30A | **11/53: BURY - 31E** | STRATFORD - 30A | BOSTON - 40F |
| Aug-54 | STRATFORD - 30A | STRATFORD - 30A | **4/54: DUND - 62B** | STRATFORD - 30A | LINCOLN - 40A | STRATFORD - 30A | **2/54: CAMB - 31A** | STRATFORD - 30A | BOSTON - 40F |
| Jan-55 | STRATFORD - 30A | STRATFORD - 30A | DUNDEE - 62B | STRATFORD - 30A | LINCOLN - 40A | **2/55: PARK - 30F** | **10/54: S.LYNN - 31D** | STRATFORD - 30A | BOSTON - 40F |
| Aug-55 | STRATFORD - 30A | STRATFORD - 30A | DUNDEE - 62B | STRATFORD - 30A | LINCOLN - 40A | PARKESTON - 30F | **3/55: CAMB - 31A** | **9/55: K.LYNN - 31C** | BOSTON - 40F |
| Jan-56 | STRATFORD - 30A | **12/55: COLW - 38A** | DUNDEE - 62B | **3/56: COL - 30E** | LINCOLN - 40A | PARKESTON - 30F | **3/56: NOR - 32A** | KINGS LYNN - 31C | BOSTON - 40F |
| Aug-56 | STRATFORD - 30A | COLWICK - 38A | DUNDEE - 62B | COLCHESTER - 30E | LINCOLN - 40A | PARKESTON - 30F | NORWICH - 32A | KINGS LYNN - 31C | BOSTON - 40F |
| Jan-57 | STRATFORD - 30A | COLWICK - 38A | DUNDEE - 62B | COLCHESTER - 30E | LINCOLN - 40A | **10/56: CAMB - 31A** | NORWICH - 32A | KINGS LYNN - 31C | BOSTON - 40F |
| Aug-57 | STRATFORD - 30A | COLWICK - 38A | **6/57: W/D** | COLCHESTER - 30E | **4/57: WREX - 6E** | CAMBRIDGE - 31A | NORWICH - 32A | KINGS LYNN - 31C | BOSTON - 40F |
| Jan-58 | STRATFORD - 30A | COLWICK - 38A | | COLCHESTER - 30E | WREXHAM - 6E | **2/58: COLW - 40E** | **2/58: IPS - 32B** | **5/58: S.LYNN - 31D** | BOSTON - 40F |
| Aug-58 | STRATFORD - 30A | COLWICK - 40E | | COLCHESTER - 30E | **10/58: BIDS - 6E** | COLWICK - 40E | **4/58: W/D** | **7/58: DCTR - 36A** | BOSTON - 40F |
| Jan-59 | STRATFORD - 30A | COLWICK - 40E | | COLCHESTER - 30E | **12/58: W/D** | COLWICK - 40E | | DONCASTER - 36A | BOSTON - 40F |
| Aug-59 | STRATFORD - 30A | COLWICK - 40E | | COLCHESTER - 30E | | COLWICK - 40E | | DONCASTER - 36A | BOSTON - 40F |
| Nov-59 | STRATFORD - 30A | COLWICK - 40E | | **10/59: PARK - 30F** | | **10/59: LINC - 40A** | | DONCASTER - 36A | **10/59: W/D** |
| Jan-60 | STRATFORD - 30A | COLWICK - 40E | | PARKESTON - 30F | | LINCOLN - 40A | | DONCASTER - 36A | |
| Apr-60 | STRATFORD - 30A | **3/60: BOST - 40F** | | **3/60: STRAT - 30A** | | LINCOLN - 40A | | **4/60: L.JCN - 41J** | |
| Aug-60 | STRATFORD - 30A | BOSTON - 40F | | STRATFORD - 30A | | LINCOLN - 40A | | LANGWITHJCN - 41J | |
| Nov-60 | STRATFORD - 30A | BOSTON - 40F | | STRATFORD - 30A | | LINCOLN - 40A | | LANGWITHJCN - 41J | |

| | 68558 | 68559 | 68560 | 68561 | 68562 | 68563 | 68565 | 68566 | 68567 |
|---|---|---|---|---|---|---|---|---|---|
| Aug-50 | LINCOLN - 40A | BRUNSWICK - 8E | BOSTON - 40F | PARKESTON - 30F | EDINBURGH(SM) - 64A | STRATFORD - 30A | HATFIELD - 34C | SOUTHLYNN - 31D | PARKHEAD - 65C |
| Jan-51 | LINCOLN - 40A | BRUNSWICK - 8E | BOSTON - 40F | PARKESTON - 30F | **1/51: DFRS - 68B** | STRATFORD - 30A | HATFIELD - 34C | SOUTHLYNN - 31D | PARKHEAD - 65C |
| Aug-51 | LINCOLN - 40A | **10/51: WREX - 6E** | BOSTON - 40F | PARKESTON - 30F | **7/51: N.BLYTH - 52F** | STRATFORD - 30A | **6/51: STRAT - 30A** | SOUTHLYNN - 31D | PARKHEAD - 65C |
| Jan-52 | LINCOLN - 40A | **3/52: BRUNS - 6E** | BOSTON - 40F | PARKESTON - 30F | NORTHBLYTHE - 52F | STRATFORD - 30A | STRATFORD - 30A | SOUTHLYNN - 31D | **2/52: NOR - 32A** |
| Aug-52 | LINCOLN - 40A | BRUNSWICK - 8E | BOSTON - 40F | PARKESTON - 30F | NORTHBLYTHE - 52F | STRATFORD - 30A | STRATFORD - 30A | SOUTHLYNN - 31D | NORWICH - 32A |
| Jan-53 | **5/53: STAVE - 38D** | **5/53: T.PARK - 9E** | BOSTON - 40F | **3/53: STRAT - 30A** | NORTHBLYTHE - 52F | STRATFORD - 30A | STRATFORD - 30A | SOUTHLYNN - 31D | NORWICH - 32A |
| Aug-53 | **7/53: LINC - 40A** | **8/53: BRUNS - 8E** | BOSTON - 40F | STRATFORD - 30A | NORTHBLYTHE - 52F | STRATFORD - 30A | STRATFORD - 30A | SOUTHLYNN - 31D | **7/53: CAMB - 31A** |
| Jan-54 | LINCOLN - 40A | BRUNSWICK - 8E | BOSTON - 40F | STRATFORD - 30A | NORTHBLYTHE - 52F | STRATFORD - 30A | STRATFORD - 30A | SOUTHLYNN - 31D | **11/53: S.LYNN - 31B** |
| Aug-54 | LINCOLN - 40A | **12/54: WREX - 6E** | BOSTON - 40F | STRATFORD - 30A | NORTHBLYTHE - 52F | STRATFORD - 30A | STRATFORD - 30A | SOUTHLYNN - 31D | **2/54: CAMB - 31A** |
| Jan-55 | LINCOLN - 40A | **1/55: BRUNS - 8E** | BOSTON - 40F | **2/55: COL - 30E** | **3/55: POL - 64E** | STRATFORD - 30A | STRATFORD - 30A | SOUTHLYNN - 31D | CAMBRIDGE - 31A |
| Aug-55 | LINCOLN - 40A | **5/55: BIRK - 6C** | BOSTON - 40F | COLCHESTER - 30E | POLMONT - 64E | STRATFORD - 30A | STRATFORD - 30A | SOUTHLYNN - 31D | **9/55: S.LYNN - 31D** |
| Jan-56 | LINCOLN - 40A | **3/56: WREX - 6E** | BOSTON - 40F | COLCHESTER - 30E | POLMONT - 64E | STRATFORD - 30A | **12/55: YAR(ST) - 32D** | SOUTHLYNN - 31D | **1/56: CAMB - 31A** |
| Aug-56 | LINCOLN - 40A | **4/56: W/D** | BOSTON - 40F | COLCHESTER - 30E | **8/56: W/D** | STRATFORD - 30A | **3/56: LOW - 32C** | SOUTHLYNN - 31D | CAMBRIDGE - 31A |
| Jan-57 | LINCOLN - 40A | | BOSTON - 40F | **10/56: RET - 36E** | | STRATFORD - 30A | LOWESTOFT - 32C | SOUTHLYNN - 31D | CAMBRIDGE - 31A |
| Aug-57 | **4/57: DCTR - 36A** | | BOSTON - 40F | RETFORD - 36E | | STRATFORD - 30A | LOWESTOFT - 32C | SOUTHLYNN - 31D | **8/57: W/D** |
| Jan-58 | DONCASTER - 36A | | BOSTON - 40F | RETFORD - 36E | | STRATFORD - 30A | LOWESTOFT - 32C | SOUTHLYNN - 31D | |
| Aug-58 | DONCASTER - 36A | | BOSTON - 40F | **7/58: W/D** | | STRATFORD - 30A | LOWESTOFT - 32C | SOUTHLYNN - 31D | |
| Jan-59 | DONCASTER - 36A | | **3/59: LINC - 40A** | | | STRATFORD - 30A | LOWESTOFT - 32C | **3/59: CAMB - 31A** | |
| Aug-59 | DONCASTER - 36A | | LINCOLN - 40A | | | STRATFORD - 30A | LOWESTOFT - 32C | **6/59:K.LYNN - 31C** | |
| Nov-59 | DONCASTER - 36A | | LINCOLN - 40A | | | **10/59: PARK - 30F** | **10/59: STRAT - 30A** | KINGS LYNN - 31C | |
| Jan-60 | DONCASTER - 36A | | LINCOLN - 40A | | | PARKESTON - 30F | STRATFORD - 30A | KINGS LYNN - 31C | |
| Apr-60 | DONCASTER - 36A | | LINCOLN - 40A | | | **3/60: STRAT - 30A** | STRATFORD - 30A | KINGS LYNN - 31C | |
| Aug-60 | **6/60: COLW - 40E** | | LINCOLN - 40A | | | STRATFORD - 30A | STRATFORD - 30A | **8/60: STRAT - 30A** | |
| Nov-60 | COLWICK - 40E | | LINCOLN - 40A | | | **10/60: W/D** | STRATFORD - 30A | STRATFORD - 30A | |

| | 68568 | 68569 | 68570 | 68571 | 68573 | 68574 | 68575 | 68576 | 68577 |
|---|---|---|---|---|---|---|---|---|---|
| Aug-50 | FERRYHILL - 61B | STRATFORD - 30A | NORWICH - 32A | STRATFORD - 30A | STRATFORD - 30A | STRATFORD - 30A | STRATFORD - 30A | STRATFORD - 30A | STRATFORD - 30A |
| Jan-51 | **3/51: KITTY - 61A** | STRATFORD - 30A | NORWICH - 32A | STRATFORD - 30A | STRATFORD - 30A | STRATFORD - 30A | STRATFORD - 30A | STRATFORD - 30A | STRATFORD - 30A |
| Aug-51 | KITTYBREWSTER - 61A | STRATFORD - 30A | NORWICH - 32A | STRATFORD - 30A | STRATFORD - 30A | STRATFORD - 30A | STRATFORD - 30A | STRATFORD - 30A | STRATFORD - 30A |
| Jan-52 | **2/52: LINC - 40A** | STRATFORD - 30A | NORWICH - 32A | STRATFORD - 30A | STRATFORD - 30A | STRATFORD - 30A | STRATFORD - 30A | STRATFORD - 30A | STRATFORD - 30A |
| Aug-52 | **6/52: PLAIS - 33A** | STRATFORD - 30A | NORWICH - 32A | STRATFORD - 30A | STRATFORD - 30A | STRATFORD - 30A | STRATFORD - 30A | STRATFORD - 30A | STRATFORD - 30A |
| Jan-53 | PLAISTOW - 33A | STRATFORD - 30A | NORWICH - 32A | STRATFORD - 30A | STRATFORD - 30A | STRATFORD - 30A | STRATFORD - 30A | STRATFORD - 30A | STRATFORD - 30A |
| Aug-53 | **7/53: STRAT - 30A** | STRATFORD - 30A | **7/53: BOST - 40F** | STRATFORD - 30A | STRATFORD - 30A | STRATFORD - 30A | STRATFORD - 30A | STRATFORD - 30A | STRATFORD - 30A |
| Jan-54 | STRATFORD - 30A | **1/54: LINC - 40A** | BOSTON - 40F | STRATFORD - 30A | STRATFORD - 30A | STRATFORD - 30A | STRATFORD - 30A | STRATFORD - 30A | STRATFORD - 30A |
| Aug-54 | STRATFORD - 30A | LINCOLN - 40A | BOSTON - 40F | STRATFORD - 30A | STRATFORD - 30A | STRATFORD - 30A | STRATFORD - 30A | STRATFORD - 30A | STRATFORD - 30A |
| Jan-55 | STRATFORD - 30A | LINCOLN - 40A | BOSTON - 40F | STRATFORD - 30A | STRATFORD - 30A | STRATFORD - 30A | STRATFORD - 30A | STRATFORD - 30A | STRATFORD - 30A |
| Aug-55 | STRATFORD - 30A | LINCOLN - 40A | BOSTON - 40F | STRATFORD - 30A | STRATFORD - 30A | STRATFORD - 30A | STRATFORD - 30A | STRATFORD - 30A | STRATFORD - 30A |
| Jan-56 | STRATFORD - 30A | LINCOLN - 40A | BOSTON - 40F | STRATFORD - 30A | STRATFORD - 30A | STRATFORD - 30A | STRATFORD - 30A | STRATFORD - 30A | STRATFORD - 30A |
| Aug-56 | STRATFORD - 30A | **11/56: BOST - 40F** | BOSTON - 40F | STRATFORD - 30A | STRATFORD - 30A | STRATFORD - 30A | STRATFORD - 30A | STRATFORD - 30A | STRATFORD - 30A |
| Jan-57 | STRATFORD - 30A | **12/56: LINC - 40A** | BOSTON - 40F | STRATFORD - 30A | STRATFORD - 30A | STRATFORD - 30A | STRATFORD - 30A | STRATFORD - 30A | STRATFORD - 30A |
| Aug-57 | STRATFORD - 30A | **6/57: DCTR - 36A** | BOSTON - 40F | STRATFORD - 30A | STRATFORD - 30A | STRATFORD - 30A | STRATFORD - 30A | STRATFORD - 30A | STRATFORD - 30A |
| Jan-58 | STRATFORD - 30A | DONCASTER - 36A | BOSTON - 40F | STRATFORD - 30A | STRATFORD - 30A | STRATFORD - 30A | STRATFORD - 30A | STRATFORD - 30A | STRATFORD - 30A |
| Aug-58 | **5/58: W/D** | DONCASTER - 36A | BOSTON - 40F | STRATFORD - 30A | **5/58: COL - 30E** | STRATFORD - 30A | STRATFORD - 30A | **3/58: W/D** | STRATFORD - 30A |
| Jan-59 | | DONCASTER - 36A | BOSTON - 40F | STRATFORD - 30A | COLCHESTER - 30E | **1/59: W/D** | STRATFORD - 30A | | STRATFORD - 30A |
| Aug-59 | | DONCASTER - 36A | BOSTON - 40F | STRATFORD - 30A | COLCHESTER - 30E | | STRATFORD - 30A | | STRATFORD - 30A |
| Nov-59 | | **11/59: L.JCN - 41J** | BOSTON - 40F | STRATFORD - 30A | **10/59: PARK - 30F** | | STRATFORD - 30A | | STRATFORD - 30A |
| Jan-60 | | LANGWITHJCN - 41J | BOSTON - 40F | STRATFORD - 30A | PARKESTON - 30F | | STRATFORD - 30A | | STRATFORD - 30A |
| Apr-60 | | LANGWITHJCN - 41J | **3/60: COLW - 40E** | STRATFORD - 30A | PARKESTON - 30F | | STRATFORD - 30A | | **3/60: PARK - 30F** |
| Aug-60 | | **5/60: W/D** | COLWICK - 40E | STRATFORD - 30A | **8/60: W/D** | | STRATFORD - 30A | | PARKESTON - 30F |
| Nov-60 | | | COLWICK - 40E | STRATFORD - 30A | | | **10/60: W/D** | | **11/60: W/D** |

| | 68578 | 68579 | 68581 | 68585 | 68587 | 68596 | 68598 | 68599 | 68600 |
|---|---|---|---|---|---|---|---|---|---|
| Aug-50 | COLCHESTER - 30E | CAMBRIDGE - 31A | BOSTON - 40F | SOUTHPORT - 27E | LINCOLN - 40A | PARKESTON - 30F | TRAFFORD PARK - 9E | LINCOLN - 40A | SOUTHLYNN - 31D |
| Jan-51 | COLCHESTER - 30E | CAMBRIDGE - 31A | BOSTON - 40F | SOUTHPORT - 27E | LINCOLN - 40A | **1/51: STRAT - 30A** | TRAFFORD PARK - 9E | LINCOLN - 40A | SOUTHLYNN - 31D |
| Aug-51 | COLCHESTER - 30E | CAMBRIDGE - 31A | BOSTON - 40F | SOUTHPORT - 27E | LINCOLN - 40A | STRATFORD - 30A | TRAFFORD PARK - 9E | LINCOLN - 40A | SOUTHLYNN - 31D |
| Jan-52 | COLCHESTER - 30E | CAMBRIDGE - 31A | BOSTON - 40F | SOUTHPORT - 27E | LINCOLN - 40A | STRATFORD - 30A | TRAFFORD PARK - 9E | LINCOLN - 40A | **2/52: K.LYNN - 31C** |
| Aug-52 | COLCHESTER - 30E | **9/52: STRAT - 30A** | BOSTON - 40F | SOUTHPORT - 27E | LINCOLN - 40A | STRATFORD - 30A | TRAFFORD PARK - 9E | LINCOLN - 40A | KINGS LYNN - 31C |
| Jan-53 | COLCHESTER - 30E | STRATFORD - 30A | BOSTON - 40F | SOUTHPORT - 27E | LINCOLN - 40A | STRATFORD - 30A | TRAFFORD PARK - 9E | LINCOLN - 40A | KINGS LYNN - 31C |
| Aug-53 | COLCHESTER - 30E | STRATFORD - 30A | BOSTON - 40F | SOUTHPORT - 27E | LINCOLN - 40A | STRATFORD - 30A | TRAFFORD PARK - 9E | LINCOLN - 40A | **7/53: CAMB - 31A** |
| Jan-54 | COLCHESTER - 30E | STRATFORD - 30A | BOSTON - 40F | SOUTHPORT - 27E | LINCOLN - 40A | STRATFORD - 30A | TRAFFORD PARK - 9E | LINCOLN - 40A | CAMBRIDGE - 31A |
| Aug-54 | COLCHESTER - 30E | STRATFORD - 30A | BOSTON - 40F | SOUTHPORT - 27E | LINCOLN - 40A | STRATFORD - 30A | TRAFFORD PARK - 9E | LINCOLN - 40A | CAMBRIDGE - 31A |
| Jan-55 | **2/55: STRAT - 30A** | STRATFORD - 30A | BOSTON - 40F | SOUTHPORT - 27E | LINCOLN - 40A | STRATFORD - 30A | **12/54: BRUNS - 8E** | LINCOLN - 40A | CAMBRIDGE - 31A |
| Aug-55 | STRATFORD - 30A | STRATFORD - 30A | BOSTON - 40F | SOUTHPORT - 27E | LINCOLN - 40A | STRATFORD - 30A | BRUNSWICK - 8E | LINCOLN - 40A | CAMBRIDGE - 31A |
| Jan-56 | STRATFORD - 30A | STRATFORD - 30A | BOSTON - 40F | SOUTHPORT - 27E | LINCOLN - 40A | STRATFORD - 30A | BRUNSWICK - 8E | LINCOLN - 40A | CAMBRIDGE - 31A |
| Aug-56 | STRATFORD - 30A | STRATFORD - 30A | BOSTON - 40F | **5/56: WREX - 6E** | LINCOLN - 40A | STRATFORD - 30A | BRUNSWICK - 8E | LINCOLN - 40A | CAMBRIDGE - 31A |
| Jan-57 | STRATFORD - 30A | STRATFORD - 30A | BOSTON - 40F | WREXHAM - 6E | LINCOLN - 40A | STRATFORD - 30A | **1/57: WREX - 6E** | LINCOLN - 40A | CAMBRIDGE - 31A |
| Aug-57 | STRATFORD - 30A | STRATFORD - 30A | BOSTON - 40F | WREXHAM - 6E | **4/57: DCTR - 36A** | STRATFORD - 30A | **5/57: W/D** | LINCOLN - 40A | CAMBRIDGE - 31A |
| Jan-58 | STRATFORD - 30A | STRATFORD - 30A | **3/58: LINC - 40A** | WREXHAM - 6E | DONCASTER - 36A | STRATFORD - 30A | | LINCOLN - 40A | CAMBRIDGE - 31A |
| Aug-58 | STRATFORD - 30A | **5/58: COL - 30E** | LINCOLN - 40A | **6/58: W/D** | DONCASTER - 36A | STRATFORD - 30A | | LINCOLN - 40A | CAMBRIDGE - 31A |
| Jan-59 | STRATFORD - 30A | COLCHESTER - 30E | LINCOLN - 40A | | DONCASTER - 36A | STRATFORD - 30A | | LINCOLN - 40A | **1/59: STRAT - 30A** |
| Aug-59 | STRATFORD - 30A | COLCHESTER - 30E | LINCOLN - 40A | | DONCASTER - 36A | STRATFORD - 30A | | LINCOLN - 40A | STRATFORD - 30A |
| Nov-59 | STRATFORD - 30A | **10/59: STRAT - 30A** | **9/59: W/D** | | **10/59: W/D** | **11/59: W/D** | | **11/59: W/D** | STRATFORD - 30A |
| Jan-60 | STRATFORD - 30A | STRATFORD - 30A | | | | | | | STRATFORD - 30A |
| Apr-60 | STRATFORD - 30A | **2/60: W/D** | | | | | | | STRATFORD - 30A |
| Aug-60 | STRATFORD - 30A | | | | | | | | STRATFORD - 30A |
| Nov-60 | STRATFORD - 30A | | | | | | | | STRATFORD - 30A |

| | 68601 | 68602 | 68603 | 68605 | 68607 | 68612 | 68613 | 68617 | 68618 |
|---|---|---|---|---|---|---|---|---|---|
| Aug-50 | STRATFORD-30A | NORWICH-32A | NORWICH-32A | HITCHIN-34D | STRATFORD-30A | STRATFORD-30A | STRATFORD-30A | STRATFORD-30A | LINCOLN-40A |
| Jan-51 | 2/51: PARK - 30F | NORWICH-32A | NORWICH-32A | HITCHIN-34D | STRATFORD-30A | STRATFORD-30A | STRATFORD-30A | STRATFORD-30A | LINCOLN-40A |
| Aug-51 | PARKESTON-30F | NORWICH-32A | NORWICH-32A | HITCHIN-34D | STRATFORD-30A | STRATFORD-30A | STRATFORD-30A | STRATFORD-30A | LINCOLN-40A |
| Jan-52 | PARKESTON-30F | NORWICH-32A | NORWICH-32A | HITCHIN-34D | STRATFORD-30A | STRATFORD-30A | STRATFORD-30A | STRATFORD-30A | 3/52: STAVE - 38D |
| Aug-52 | PARKESTON-30F | NORWICH-32A | NORWICH-32A | HITCHIN-34D | STRATFORD-30A | STRATFORD-30A | STRATFORD-30A | STRATFORD-30A | 9/52: DARN - 39B |
| Jan-53 | 3/53: STRAT - 30A | NORWICH-32A | NORWICH-32A | HITCHIN-34D | STRATFORD-30A | STRATFORD-30A | STRATFORD-30A | STRATFORD-30A | 3/53: LINC - 40A |
| Aug-53 | STRATFORD-30A | 7/53: BOST - 40F | 7/53: MARCH - 31B | 7/53: LINC - 40A | STRATFORD-30A | STRATFORD-30A | STRATFORD-30A | STRATFORD-30A | LINCOLN-40A |
| Jan-54 | STRATFORD-30A | BOSTON-40F | MARCH-31B | LINCOLN-40A | STRATFORD-30A | STRATFORD-30A | STRATFORD-30A | STRATFORD-30A | LINCOLN-40A |
| Aug-54 | STRATFORD-30A | BOSTON-40F | MARCH-31B | LINCOLN-40A | STRATFORD-30A | STRATFORD-30A | STRATFORD-30A | STRATFORD-30A | LINCOLN-40A |
| Jan-55 | 3/55: COL - 30E | BOSTON-40F | MARCH-31B | LINCOLN-40A | STRATFORD-30A | STRATFORD-30A | STRATFORD-30A | STRATFORD-30A | LINCOLN-40A |
| Aug-55 | COLCHESTER-30E | BOSTON-40F | MARCH-31B | LINCOLN-40A | STRATFORD-30A | STRATFORD-30A | STRATFORD-30A | STRATFORD-30A | LINCOLN-40A |
| Jan-56 | 3/56: COLW - 38A | BOSTON-40F | MARCH-31B | LINCOLN-40A | STRATFORD-30A | STRATFORD-30A | STRATFORD-30A | 1/56: STAVE - 38D | LINCOLN-40A |
| Aug-56 | COLWICK-38A | BOSTON-40F | MARCH-31B | LINCOLN-40A | STRATFORD-30A | STRATFORD-30A | STRATFORD-30A | STAVELEY-38D | LINCOLN-40A |
| Jan-57 | COLWICK-38A | BOSTON-40F | MARCH-31B | LINCOLN-40A | STRATFORD-30A | STRATFORD-30A | STRATFORD-30A | STAVELEY-38D | LINCOLN-40A |
| Aug-57 | COLWICK-38A | BOSTON-40F | MARCH-31B | LINCOLN-40A | STRATFORD-30A | STRATFORD-30A | STRATFORD-30A | STAVELEY-38D | LINCOLN-40A |
| Jan-58 | COLWICK-38A | BOSTON-40F | 3/58: W/D | LINCOLN-40A | STRATFORD-30A | STRATFORD-30A | STRATFORD-30A | STAVELEY-38D | 3/58: BOST - 40F |
| Aug-58 | COLWICK-40E | BOSTON-40F | | 7/58: W/D | 5/58: W/D | STRATFORD-30A | STRATFORD-30A | 7/58: W/D | 7/58: COLW - 40E |
| Jan-59 | COLWICK-40E | BOSTON-40F | | | | STRATFORD-30A | STRATFORD-30A | | 9/58: W/D |
| Aug-59 | COLWICK-40E | BOSTON-40F | | | | STRATFORD-30A | STRATFORD-30A | | |
| Nov-59 | 10/59: W/D | 10/59: W/D | | | | STRATFORD-30A | STRATFORD-30A | | |
| Jan-60 | | | | | | STRATFORD-30A | STRATFORD-30A | | |
| Apr-60 | | | | | | STRATFORD-30A | STRATFORD-30A | | |
| Aug-60 | | | | | | STRATFORD-30A | STRATFORD-30A | | |
| Nov-60 | | | | | | STRATFORD-30A | STRATFORD-30A | | |

| | 68619 | 68621 | 68623 | 68625 | 68626 | 68629 | 68630 | 68631 | 68632 |
|---|---|---|---|---|---|---|---|---|---|
| Aug-50 | STRATFORD-30A | STRATFORD-30A | EDINBURGH (SM)-64A | YARMOUTH (ST)-32D | STRATFORD-30A | COLCHESTER-30E | COLCHESTER-30E | STRATFORD-30A | NEW ENGLAND-35A |
| Jan-51 | STRATFORD-30A | STRATFORD-30A | EDINBURGH (SM)-64A | YARMOUTH (ST)-32D | STRATFORD-30A | 10/50: STRAT - 30A | 12/50: STRAT - 30A | STRATFORD-30A | NEW ENGLAND-35A |
| Aug-51 | STRATFORD-30A | STRATFORD-30A | 7/51: NOR - 32A | YARMOUTH (ST)-32D | STRATFORD-30A | STRATFORD-30A | STRATFORD-30A | STRATFORD-30A | 3/51: STRAT - 30A |
| Jan-52 | STRATFORD-30A | STRATFORD-30A | NORWICH-32A | YARMOUTH (ST)-32D | STRATFORD-30A | STRATFORD-30A | STRATFORD-30A | STRATFORD-30A | STRATFORD-30A |
| Aug-52 | STRATFORD-30A | STRATFORD-30A | 6/52: M.CONS - 32G | YARMOUTH (ST)-32D | STRATFORD-30A | STRATFORD-30A | STRATFORD-30A | STRATFORD-30A | 11/52: STAVE - 38D |
| Jan-53 | STRATFORD-30A | STRATFORD-30A | MELTON CONSTABLE-32G | YARMOUTH (ST)-32D | STRATFORD-30A | STRATFORD-30A | STRATFORD-30A | STRATFORD-30A | 1/53: STRAT - 30A |
| Aug-53 | STRATFORD-30A | STRATFORD-30A | 7/53: S.LYNN - 31D | 7/53: CAMB - 31A | STRATFORD-30A | STRATFORD-30A | STRATFORD-30A | STRATFORD-30A | STRATFORD-30A |
| Jan-54 | STRATFORD-30A | STRATFORD-30A | SOUTH LYNN-31D | CAMBRIDGE-31A | STRATFORD-30A | STRATFORD-30A | STRATFORD-30A | STRATFORD-30A | STRATFORD-30A |
| Aug-54 | STRATFORD-30A | STRATFORD-30A | SOUTH LYNN-31D | 10/54: BURY - 31E | STRATFORD-30A | STRATFORD-30A | STRATFORD-30A | STRATFORD-30A | STRATFORD-30A |
| Jan-55 | STRATFORD-30A | STRATFORD-30A | SOUTH LYNN-31D | 1/55: CAMB - 31A | STRATFORD-30A | STRATFORD-30A | STRATFORD-30A | STRATFORD-30A | STRATFORD-30A |
| Aug-55 | STRATFORD-30A | STRATFORD-30A | SOUTH LYNN-31D | CAMBRIDGE-31A | STRATFORD-30A | STRATFORD-30A | STRATFORD-30A | STRATFORD-30A | STRATFORD-30A |
| Jan-56 | STRATFORD-30A | DONCASTER-36A | SOUTH LYNN-31D | 12/55: M.CONS - 32G | 11/55: NEWE - 35A | 12/55: COLW - 38A | STRATFORD-30A | STRATFORD-30A | STRATFORD-30A |
| Aug-56 | STRATFORD-30A | DONCASTER-36A | SOUTH LYNN-31D | MELTON CONSTABLE-32G | NEW ENGLAND-35A | COLWICK-38A | STRATFORD-30A | STRATFORD-30A | STRATFORD-30A |
| Jan-57 | STRATFORD-30A | DONCASTER-36A | SOUTH LYNN-31D | MELTON CONSTABLE-32G | NEW ENGLAND-35A | COLWICK-38A | STRATFORD-30A | STRATFORD-30A | STRATFORD-30A |
| Aug-57 | STRATFORD-30A | DONCASTER-36A | SOUTH LYNN-31D | MELTON CONSTABLE-32G | NEW ENGLAND-35A | COLWICK-38A | STRATFORD-30A | STRATFORD-30A | STRATFORD-30A |
| Jan-58 | STRATFORD-30A | DONCASTER-36A | 6/58: B.HILL - 41E | MELTON CONSTABLE-32G | NEW ENGLAND-35A | COLWICK-38A | STRATFORD-30A | STRATFORD-30A | STRATFORD-30A |
| Aug-58 | STRATFORD-30A | DONCASTER-36A | 7/58: MEX - 41F | 7/58: YAR(ST) - 32B | 4/58: GRAN - 34F | COLWICK-40E | STRATFORD-30A | 7/58: W/D | 4/58: W/D |
| Jan-59 | STRATFORD-30A | DONCASTER-36A | MEXBOROUGH-41F | 1/59: W/D | GRANTHAM-34F | COLWICK-40E | 1/59: W/D | | |
| Aug-59 | STRATFORD-30A | DONCASTER-36A | MEXBOROUGH-41F | | GRANTHAM-34F | COLWICK-40E | | | |
| Nov-59 | STRATFORD-30A | 12/59: RET - 36E | MEXBOROUGH-41F | | GRANTHAM-34F | 11/59: W/D | | | |
| Jan-60 | STRATFORD-30A | 3/60: DCTR - 36A | 2/60: L.JCN - 41J | | GRANTHAM-34F | | | | |
| Apr-60 | STRATFORD-30A | 4/60: L.JN - 41J | LANGWITH JCN-41J | | GRANTHAM-34F | | | | |
| Aug-60 | STRATFORD-30A | 8/60: CANK - 41D | LANGWITH JCN-41J | | 5/60: W/D | | | | |
| Nov-60 | STRATFORD-30A | CANKLOW-41D | LANGWITH JCN-41J | | | | | | |

| | 68633 | 68635 | 68636 | J68 0-6-0T (1912) 68638 | 68639 | 68640 | 68641 | 68642 | 68643 |
|---|---|---|---|---|---|---|---|---|---|
| Aug-50 | STRATFORD-30A | DUNFERMLINE-62C | STRATFORD-30A | STRATFORD-30A | STRATFORD-30A | LOWESTOFT-32C | NORWICH-32A | STRATFORD-30A | PARKESTON-30F |
| Jan-51 | STRATFORD-30A | DUNFERMLINE-62C | 12/50: COL - 30E | 10/50: COL - 30E | STRATFORD-30A | LOWESTOFT-32C | NORWICH-32A | STRATFORD-30A | PARKESTON-30F |
| Aug-51 | STRATFORD-30A | 6/51: DCTR - 36A | COLCHESTER-30E | COLCHESTER-30E | STRATFORD-30A | LOWESTOFT-32C | NORWICH-32A | STRATFORD-30A | PARKESTON-30F |
| Jan-52 | STRATFORD-30A | 9/51: NOR - 32A | COLCHESTER-30E | COLCHESTER-30E | STRATFORD-30A | LOWESTOFT-32C | NORWICH-32A | STRATFORD-30A | PARKESTON-30F |
| Aug-52 | STRATFORD-30A | NORWICH-32A | COLCHESTER-30E | COLCHESTER-30E | STRATFORD-30A | LOWESTOFT-32C | NORWICH-32A | STRATFORD-30A | PARKESTON-30F |
| Jan-53 | STRATFORD-30A | NORWICH-32A | COLCHESTER-30E | COLCHESTER-30E | STRATFORD-30A | LOWESTOFT-32C | NORWICH-32A | STRATFORD-30A | PARKESTON-30F |
| Aug-53 | STRATFORD-30A | 7/53: K.LYNN - 31C | COLCHESTER-30E | COLCHESTER-30E | STRATFORD-30A | LOWESTOFT-32C | NORWICH-32A | STRATFORD-30A | PARKESTON-30F |
| Jan-54 | STRATFORD-30A | KINGS LYNN-31C | COLCHESTER-30E | COLCHESTER-30E | STRATFORD-30A | LOWESTOFT-32C | NORWICH-32A | STRATFORD-30A | PARKESTON-30F |
| Aug-54 | STRATFORD-30A | KINGS LYNN-31C | COLCHESTER-30E | COLCHESTER-30E | STRATFORD-30A | LOWESTOFT-32C | NORWICH-32A | STRATFORD-30A | PARKESTON-30F |
| Jan-55 | STRATFORD-30A | KINGS LYNN-31C | 2/55: STRAT - 30A | COLCHESTER-30E | STRATFORD-30A | LOWESTOFT-32C | NORWICH-32A | STRATFORD-30A | PARKESTON-30F |
| Aug-55 | STRATFORD-30A | KINGS LYNN-31C | STRATFORD-30A | COLCHESTER-30E | STRATFORD-30A | LOWESTOFT-32C | NORWICH-32A | 8/55: NOR - 32A | PARKESTON-30F |
| Jan-56 | STRATFORD-30A | 3/56: NEW.E - 35A | STRATFORD-30A | 2/56: STRAT - 30A | STRATFORD-30A | 11/55: NOR - 32A | NORWICH-32A | NORWICH-32A | PARKESTON-30F |
| Aug-56 | STRATFORD-30A | NEW ENGLAND-35A | STRATFORD-30A | 6/56: HIT - 34D | STRATFORD-30A | NORWICH-32A | NORWICH-32A | NORWICH-32A | PARKESTON-30F |
| Jan-57 | STRATFORD-30A | NEW ENGLAND-35A | STRATFORD-30A | HITCHIN-34D | STRATFORD-30A | NORWICH-32A | NORWICH-32A | NORWICH-32A | PARKESTON-30F |
| Aug-57 | STRATFORD-30A | NEW ENGLAND-35A | STRATFORD-30A | HITCHIN-34D | STRATFORD-30A | NORWICH-32A | NORWICH-32A | NORWICH-32A | PARKESTON-30F |
| Jan-58 | STRATFORD-30A | NEW ENGLAND-35A | STRATFORD-30A | HITCHIN-34D | STRATFORD-30A | NORWICH-32A | NORWICH-32A | NORWICH-32A | PARKESTON-30F |
| Aug-58 | STRATFORD-30A | NEW ENGLAND-34E | STRATFORD-30A | 4/58: GRAN - 34F | STRATFORD-30A | NORWICH-32A | NORWICH-32A | 8/58: LOW - 32C | PARKESTON-30F |
| Jan-59 | STRATFORD-30A | 1/59: GRAN - 34F | 1/59: W/D | 2/59: W/D | STRATFORD-30A | NORWICH-32A | NORWICH-32A | LOWESTOFT-32C | PARKESTON-30F |
| Aug-59 | STRATFORD-30A | GRANTHAM-34F | | | 4/59: W/D | 4/59: W/D | NORWICH-32A | LOWESTOFT-32C | PARKESTON-30F |
| Nov-59 | STRATFORD-30A | GRANTHAM-34F | | | | | 11/59: W/D | 10/59: STRAT - 30A | 11/59: W/D |
| Jan-60 | STRATFORD-30A | GRANTHAM-34F | | | | | | STRATFORD-30A | |
| Apr-60 | STRATFORD-30A | 5/60: COLW - 40E | | | | | | STRATFORD-30A | |
| Aug-60 | 8/60: PARK - 30F | COLWICK-40E | | | | | | STRATFORD-30A | |
| Nov-60 | PARKESTON-30F | COLWICK-40E | | | | | | STRATFORD-30A | |

| | 68644 | 68645 | 68646 | 68647 | 68648 | 68649 | 68650 | 68651 | 68652 |
|---|---|---|---|---|---|---|---|---|---|
| Aug-50 | STRATFORD-30A | CAMBRIDGE-31A | STRATFORD-30A | STRATFORD-30A | STRATFORD-30A | STRATFORD-30A | STRATFORD-30A | YARMOUTH (B)-32F | STRATFORD-30A |
| Jan-51 | STRATFORD-30A | CAMBRIDGE-31A | STRATFORD-30A | STRATFORD-30A | STRATFORD-30A | 1/51: PARK - 30F | STRATFORD-30A | YARMOUTH (B)-32F | STRATFORD-30A |
| Aug-51 | STRATFORD-30A | CAMBRIDGE-31A | STRATFORD-30A | STRATFORD-30A | STRATFORD-30A | PARKESTON-30F | STRATFORD-30A | YARMOUTH (B)-32F | STRATFORD-30A |
| Jan-52 | STRATFORD-30A | CAMBRIDGE-31A | STRATFORD-30A | STRATFORD-30A | STRATFORD-30A | PARKESTON-30F | STRATFORD-30A | YARMOUTH (B)-32F | STRATFORD-30A |
| Aug-52 | STRATFORD-30A | CAMBRIDGE-31A | STRATFORD-30A | STRATFORD-30A | 6/52: PLAIS - 33A | PARKESTON-30F | STRATFORD-30A | YARMOUTH (B)-32F | STRATFORD-30A |
| Jan-53 | STRATFORD-30A | CAMBRIDGE-31A | STRATFORD-30A | STRATFORD-30A | PLAISTOW-33A | 3/53: STRAT - 30A | STRATFORD-30A | YARMOUTH (B)-32F | STRATFORD-30A |
| Aug-53 | STRATFORD-30A | 7/53: NOR - 32A | STRATFORD-30A | STRATFORD-30A | 5/53: STRAT - 30A | STRATFORD-30A | STRATFORD-30A | YARMOUTH (B)-32F | STRATFORD-30A |
| Jan-54 | STRATFORD-30A | NORWICH-32A | STRATFORD-30A | STRATFORD-30A | STRATFORD-30A | STRATFORD-30A | STRATFORD-30A | YARMOUTH (B)-32F | STRATFORD-30A |
| Aug-54 | STRATFORD-30A | NORWICH-32A | STRATFORD-30A | STRATFORD-30A | STRATFORD-30A | STRATFORD-30A | STRATFORD-30A | YARMOUTH (B)-32F | STRATFORD-30A |
| Jan-55 | STRATFORD-30A | NORWICH-32A | STRATFORD-30A | STRATFORD-30A | STRATFORD-30A | STRATFORD-30A | STRATFORD-30A | YARMOUTH (B)-32F | STRATFORD-30A |
| Aug-55 | STRATFORD-30A | NORWICH-32A | STRATFORD-30A | STRATFORD-30A | STRATFORD-30A | STRATFORD-30A | STRATFORD-30A | YARMOUTH (B)-32F | STRATFORD-30A |
| Jan-56 | STRATFORD-30A | NORWICH-32A | STRATFORD-30A | STRATFORD-30A | STRATFORD-30A | STRATFORD-30A | STRATFORD-30A | YARMOUTH (B)-32F | STRATFORD-30A |
| Aug-56 | STRATFORD-30A | NORWICH-32A | STRATFORD-30A | STRATFORD-30A | STRATFORD-30A | STRATFORD-30A | STRATFORD-30A | YARMOUTH (B)-32F | STRATFORD-30A |
| Jan-57 | STRATFORD-30A | NORWICH-32A | STRATFORD-30A | STRATFORD-30A | STRATFORD-30A | STRATFORD-30A | STRATFORD-30A | YARMOUTH (B)-32F | STRATFORD-30A |
| Aug-57 | STRATFORD-30A | NORWICH-32A | STRATFORD-30A | STRATFORD-30A | STRATFORD-30A | STRATFORD-30A | STRATFORD-30A | YARMOUTH (B)-32F | STRATFORD-30A |
| Jan-58 | STRATFORD-30A | NORWICH-32A | STRATFORD-30A | STRATFORD-30A | STRATFORD-30A | STRATFORD-30A | STRATFORD-30A | YARMOUTH (B)-32F | STRATFORD-30A |
| Aug-58 | STRATFORD-30A | 8/58: LOW - 32C | STRATFORD-30A | STRATFORD-30A | STRATFORD-30A | STRATFORD-30A | STRATFORD-30A | 5/58: W/D | STRATFORD-30A |
| Jan-59 | STRATFORD-30A | 11/58: NOR - 32A | STRATFORD-30A | STRATFORD-30A | STRATFORD-30A | STRATFORD-30A | STRATFORD-30A | | STRATFORD-30A |
| Aug-59 | STRATFORD-30A | NORWICH-32A | STRATFORD-30A | STRATFORD-30A | 8/59: W/D | STRATFORD-30A | STRATFORD-30A | | STRATFORD-30A |
| Nov-59 | STRATFORD-30A | 11/59: W/D | STRATFORD-30A | STRATFORD-30A | | STRATFORD-30A | STRATFORD-30A | | 9/59: W/D |
| Jan-60 | STRATFORD-30A | | STRATFORD-30A | STRATFORD-30A | | STRATFORD-30A | STRATFORD-30A | | |
| Apr-60 | STRATFORD-30A | | STRATFORD-30A | STRATFORD-30A | | STRATFORD-30A | STRATFORD-30A | | |
| Aug-60 | STRATFORD-30A | | STRATFORD-30A | STRATFORD-30A | | STRATFORD-30A | STRATFORD-30A | | |
| Nov-60 | STRATFORD-30A | | STRATFORD-30A | STRATFORD-30A | | STRATFORD-30A | 10/60: W/D | | |

| | 68653 | 68654 | 68655 | 68656 | 68657 | 68658 | 68659 | 68660 | 68661 |
|---|---|---|---|---|---|---|---|---|---|
| Aug-50 | PARKESTON - 30F | MARCH - 31B | BOSTON - 40F | KINGS LYNN - 31C | BOSTON - 40F | BOSTON - 40F | BOSTON - 40F | STRATFORD - 30A | STRATFORD - 30A |
| Jan-51 | PARKESTON - 30F | 2/51: STRAT - 30A | BOSTON - 40F | KINGS LYNN - 31C | BOSTON - 40F | BOSTON - 40F | BOSTON - 40F | STRATFORD - 30A | STRATFORD - 30A |
| Aug-51 | 6/51: STRAT - 30A | STRATFORD - 30A | BOSTON - 40F | KINGS LYNN - 31C | BOSTON - 40F | BOSTON - 40F | BOSTON - 40F | STRATFORD - 30A | 6/51: PARK - 30F |
| Jan-52 | STRATFORD - 30A | STRATFORD - 30A | BOSTON - 40F | KINGS LYNN - 31C | BOSTON - 40F | BOSTON - 40F | BOSTON - 40F | STRATFORD - 30A | PARKESTON - 30F |
| Aug-52 | STRATFORD - 30A | STRATFORD - 30A | BOSTON - 40F | KINGS LYNN - 31C | BOSTON - 40F | BOSTON - 40F | BOSTON - 40F | STRATFORD - 30A | PARKESTON - 30F |
| Jan-53 | STRATFORD - 30A | STRATFORD - 30A | BOSTON - 40F | KINGS LYNN - 31C | BOSTON - 40F | BOSTON - 40F | BOSTON - 40F | STRATFORD - 30A | 3/53: STRAT - 30A |
| Aug-53 | STRATFORD - 30A | STRATFORD - 30A | 7/53: STRAT - 30A | 7/53: YAR(ST) - 32D | 7/53: STRAT - 30A | 7/53: STRAT - 30A | 7/53: STRAT - 30A | STRATFORD - 30A | STRATFORD - 30A |
| Jan-54 | STRATFORD - 30A | STRATFORD - 30A | STRATFORD - 30A | YARMOUTH (ST) - 32D | STRATFORD - 30A | STRATFORD - 30A | STRATFORD - 30A | STRATFORD - 30A | STRATFORD - 30A |
| Aug-54 | STRATFORD - 30A | STRATFORD - 30A | STRATFORD - 30A | YARMOUTH (ST) - 32D | STRATFORD - 30A | STRATFORD - 30A | STRATFORD - 30A | STRATFORD - 30A | STRATFORD - 30A |
| Jan-55 | STRATFORD - 30A | STRATFORD - 30A | STRATFORD - 30A | YARMOUTH (ST) - 32D | STRATFORD - 30A | STRATFORD - 30A | STRATFORD - 30A | STRATFORD - 30A | STRATFORD - 30A |
| Aug-55 | STRATFORD - 30A | STRATFORD - 30A | STRATFORD - 30A | YARMOUTH (ST) - 32D | STRATFORD - 30A | STRATFORD - 30A | STRATFORD - 30A | STRATFORD - 30A | STRATFORD - 30A |
| Jan-56 | STRATFORD - 30A | STRATFORD - 30A | STRATFORD - 30A | YARMOUTH (ST) - 32D | STRATFORD - 30A | STRATFORD - 30A | STRATFORD - 30A | STRATFORD - 30A | 2/56: HIT - 34D |
| Aug-56 | STRATFORD - 30A | STRATFORD - 30A | STRATFORD - 30A | YARMOUTH (ST) - 32D | STRATFORD - 30A | STRATFORD - 30A | STRATFORD - 30A | STRATFORD - 30A | HITCHIN - 34D |
| Jan-57 | STRATFORD - 30A | 12/56: HIT - 34D | STRATFORD - 30A | YARMOUTH (ST) - 32D | STRATFORD - 30A | STRATFORD - 30A | STRATFORD - 30A | STRATFORD - 30A | HITCHIN - 34D |
| Aug-57 | STRATFORD - 30A | HITCHIN - 34D | STRATFORD - 30A | YARMOUTH (ST) - 32D | STRATFORD - 30A | STRATFORD - 30A | STRATFORD - 30A | STRATFORD - 30A | HITCHIN - 34D |
| Jan-58 | STRATFORD - 30A | HITCHIN - 34D | STRATFORD - 30A | YARMOUTH (ST) - 32D | STRATFORD - 30A | STRATFORD - 30A | STRATFORD - 30A | STRATFORD - 30A | HITCHIN - 34D |
| Aug-58 | 6/58: W/D | 7/58: DCTR - 36A | STRATFORD - 30A | YARMOUTH (ST) - 32D | 8/58: W/D | STRATFORD - 30A | 8/58: W/D | STRATFORD - 30A | HITCHIN - 34D |
| Jan-59 | | DONCASTER - 36A | STRATFORD - 30A | YARMOUTH (ST) - 32D | | STRATFORD - 30A | | STRATFORD - 30A | HITCHIN - 34D |
| Aug-59 | | DONCASTER - 36A | STRATFORD - 30A | YARMOUTH (ST) - 32D | | 4/59: W/D | | STRATFORD - 30A | HITCHIN - 34D |
| Nov-59 | | DONCASTER - 36A | 11/59: W/D | 10/59: LOW - 32C | | | | STRATFORD - 30A | 12/59: W/D |
| Jan-60 | | DONCASTER - 36A | | LOWESTOFT - 32C | | | | STRATFORD - 30A | |
| Apr-60 | | 3/60: W/D | | 3/60: W/D | | | | STRATFORD - 30A | |
| Aug-60 | | | | | | | | STRATFORD - 30A | |
| Nov-60 | | | | | | | | STRATFORD - 30A | |

| | | | | | | J92 0-6-0T ( 1891 ) | | | J72 0-6-0T ( 1898 ) |
|---|---|---|---|---|---|---|---|---|---|
| | 68662 | 68663 | 68664 | 68665 | 68666 | 68667 | 68668 | 68669 | 68670 |
| Aug-50 | STRATFORD - 30A | STRATFORD - 30A | MARCH - 31B | STRATFORD - 30A | STRATFORD - 30A | STRATFORD - 30A | STRATFORD - 30A | STRATFORD - 30A | SPRINGHEAD - 53C |
| Jan-51 | STRATFORD - 30A | STRATFORD - 30A | MARCH - 31B | STRATFORD - 30A | STRATFORD - 30A | STRATFORD - 30A | STRATFORD - 30A | STRATFORD - 30A | SPRINGHEAD - 53C |
| Aug-51 | STRATFORD - 30A | STRATFORD - 30A | MARCH - 31B | STRATFORD - 30A | STRATFORD - 30A | STRATFORD - 30A | STRATFORD - 30A | STRATFORD - 30A | SPRINGHEAD - 53C |
| Jan-52 | STRATFORD - 30A | STRATFORD - 30A | MARCH - 31B | STRATFORD - 30A | STRATFORD - 30A | STRATFORD - 30A | STRATFORD - 30A | STRATFORD - 30A | SPRINGHEAD - 53C |
| Aug-52 | STRATFORD - 30A | STRATFORD - 30A | MARCH - 31B | STRATFORD - 30A | STRATFORD - 30A | 5/52: W/D | STRATFORD - 30A | STRATFORD - 30A | SPRINGHEAD - 53C |
| Jan-53 | STRATFORD - 30A | STRATFORD - 30A | MARCH - 31B | STRATFORD - 30A | STRATFORD - 30A | | 10/52: W/D | 10/52: W/D | SPRINGHEAD - 53C |
| Aug-53 | STRATFORD - 30A | STRATFORD - 30A | 7/53: NOR - 32A | STRATFORD - 30A | STRATFORD - 30A | | | | SPRINGHEAD - 53C |
| Jan-54 | STRATFORD - 30A | STRATFORD - 30A | NORWICH - 32A | STRATFORD - 30A | STRATFORD - 30A | | | | SPRINGHEAD - 53C |
| Aug-54 | STRATFORD - 30A | STRATFORD - 30A | NORWICH - 32A | STRATFORD - 30A | STRATFORD - 30A | | | | 5/54: DAIRY - 53A |
| Jan-55 | STRATFORD - 30A | STRATFORD - 30A | NORWICH - 32A | STRATFORD - 30A | STRATFORD - 30A | | | | DAIRYCOATES - 53A |
| Aug-55 | STRATFORD - 30A | STRATFORD - 30A | NORWICH - 32A | STRATFORD - 30A | STRATFORD - 30A | | | | DAIRYCOATES - 53A |
| Jan-56 | 2/56: COL - 30E | STRATFORD - 30A | 11/55: LOW - 32C | STRATFORD - 30A | 1/56: COL - 30E | | | | DAIRYCOATES - 53A |
| Aug-56 | COLCHESTER - 30E | STRATFORD - 30A | LOWESTOFT - 32C | STRATFORD - 30A | COLCHESTER - 30E | | | | DAIRYCOATES - 53A |
| Jan-57 | COLCHESTER - 30E | STRATFORD - 30A | LOWESTOFT - 32C | STRATFORD - 30A | COLCHESTER - 30E | | | | DAIRYCOATES - 53A |
| Aug-57 | COLCHESTER - 30E | STRATFORD - 30A | LOWESTOFT - 32C | STRATFORD - 30A | COLCHESTER - 30E | | | | DAIRYCOATES - 53A |
| Jan-58 | COLCHESTER - 30E | STRATFORD - 30A | LOWESTOFT - 32C | STRATFORD - 30A | 5/58: STRAT - 30A | | | | DAIRYCOATES - 53A |
| Aug-58 | 5/58: STRAT - 30A | STRATFORD - 30A | LOWESTOFT - 32C | STRATFORD - 30A | 8/58: W/D | | | | DAIRYCOATES - 53A |
| Jan-59 | 9/58: W/D | STRATFORD - 30A | 9/58: W/D | STRATFORD - 30A | | | | | DAIRYCOATES - 53A |
| Aug-59 | | STRATFORD - 30A | | STRATFORD - 30A | | | | | DAIRYCOATES - 53A |
| Nov-59 | | STRATFORD - 30A | | STRATFORD - 30A | | | | | DAIRYCOATES - 53A |
| Jan-60 | | STRATFORD - 30A | | 12/59: W/D | | | | | DAIRYCOATES - 53A |
| Apr-60 | | STRATFORD - 30A | | | | | | | 2/60: W/D |
| Aug-60 | | STRATFORD - 30A | | | | | | | |
| Nov-60 | | 10/60: W/D | | | | | | | |

| | 68671 | 68672 | 68673 | 68674 | 68675 | 68676 | 68677 | 68678 | 68679 |
|---|---|---|---|---|---|---|---|---|---|
| Aug-50 | BIDSTON - 6F | NEVILLE HILL - 50B | SPRINGHEAD - 53C | GATESHEAD - 52A | GATESHEAD - 52A | SPRINGHEAD - 53C | NEVILLE HILL - 50B | SUNDERLAND - 54A | DARLINGTON - 51A |
| Jan-51 | 12/50: WREX - 6E | NEVILLE HILL - 50B | 2/51: DAIRY - 53A | GATESHEAD - 52A | GATESHEAD - 52A | SPRINGHEAD - 53C | 10/50: YORK - 50A | SUNDERLAND - 54A | DARLINGTON - 51A |
| Aug-51 | WREXHAM - 6E | NEVILLE HILL - 50B | 7/51: ALEX.D - 53C | GATESHEAD - 52A | GATESHEAD - 52A | SPRINGHEAD - 53C | YORK - 50A | SUNDERLAND - 54A | DARLINGTON - 51A |
| Jan-52 | WREXHAM - 6E | NEVILLE HILL - 50B | ALEXDOCK - 53C | GATESHEAD - 52A | GATESHEAD - 52A | SPRINGHEAD - 53C | YORK - 50A | SUNDERLAND - 54A | DARLINGTON - 51A |
| Aug-52 | WREXHAM - 6E | NEVILLE HILL - 50B | ALEXDOCK - 53C | GATESHEAD - 52A | GATESHEAD - 52A | SPRINGHEAD - 53C | YORK - 50A | SUNDERLAND - 54A | DARLINGTON - 51A |
| Jan-53 | WREXHAM - 6E | NEVILLE HILL - 50B | ALEXDOCK - 53C | GATESHEAD - 52A | GATESHEAD - 52A | SPRINGHEAD - 53C | YORK - 50A | SUNDERLAND - 54A | DARLINGTON - 51A |
| Aug-53 | WREXHAM - 6E | NEVILLE HILL - 50B | ALEXDOCK - 53C | GATESHEAD - 52A | GATESHEAD - 52A | SPRINGHEAD - 53C | YORK - 50A | SUNDERLAND - 54A | DARLINGTON - 51A |
| Jan-54 | WREXHAM - 6E | NEVILLE HILL - 50B | ALEXDOCK - 53C | GATESHEAD - 52A | GATESHEAD - 52A | SPRINGHEAD - 53C | YORK - 50A | SUNDERLAND - 54A | DARLINGTON - 51A |
| Aug-54 | WREXHAM - 6E | NEVILLE HILL - 50B | ALEXDOCK - 53C | GATESHEAD - 52A | GATESHEAD - 52A | SPRINGHEAD - 53C | YORK - 50A | SUNDERLAND - 54A | DARLINGTON - 51A |
| Jan-55 | WREXHAM - 6E | NEVILLE HILL - 50B | ALEXDOCK - 53C | GATESHEAD - 52A | GATESHEAD - 52A | SPRINGHEAD - 53C | YORK - 50A | SUNDERLAND - 54A | DARLINGTON - 51A |
| Aug-55 | WREXHAM - 6E | NEVILLE HILL - 50B | ALEXDOCK - 53C | GATESHEAD - 52A | GATESHEAD - 52A | SPRINGHEAD - 53C | YORK - 50A | SUNDERLAND - 54A | DARLINGTON - 51A |
| Jan-56 | WREXHAM - 6E | NEVILLE HILL - 50B | ALEXDOCK - 53C | GATESHEAD - 52A | GATESHEAD - 52A | SPRINGHEAD - 53C | YORK - 50A | SUNDERLAND - 54A | DARLINGTON - 51A |
| Aug-56 | WREXHAM - 6E | NEVILLE HILL - 50B | ALEXDOCK - 53C | GATESHEAD - 52A | GATESHEAD - 52A | SPRINGHEAD - 53C | YORK - 50A | SUNDERLAND - 54A | DARLINGTON - 51A |
| Jan-57 | WREXHAM - 6E | 4/57: DAIRY - 53A | ALEXDOCK - 53C | GATESHEAD - 52A | GATESHEAD - 52A | SPRINGHEAD - 53C | YORK - 50A | SUNDERLAND - 54A | DARLINGTON - 51A |
| Aug-57 | WREXHAM - 6E | 7/57: ALEX.D - 53C | ALEXDOCK - 53C | GATESHEAD - 52A | GATESHEAD - 52A | SPRINGHEAD - 53C | YORK - 50A | SUNDERLAND - 54A | DARLINGTON - 51A |
| Jan-58 | WREXHAM - 6E | ALEXDOCK - 53C | ALEXDOCK - 53C | GATESHEAD - 52A | GATESHEAD - 52A | SPRINGHEAD - 53C | YORK - 50A | SUNDERLAND - 54A | DARLINGTON - 51A |
| Aug-58 | 10/58: BIDS - 6F | ALEXDOCK - 53C | ALEXDOCK - 53C | GATESHEAD - 52A | GATESHEAD - 52A | SPRINGHEAD - 53C | YORK - 50A | SUNDERLAND - 54A | DARLINGTON - 51A |
| Jan-59 | BIDSTON - 6F | 2/59: DAIRY - 53A | ALEXDOCK - 53C | GATESHEAD - 52A | GATESHEAD - 52A | SPRINGHEAD - 53C | YORK - 50A | SUNDERLAND - 52G | DARLINGTON - 51A |
| Aug-59 | BIDSTON - 6F | DAIRYCOATES - 53A | ALEXDOCK - 53C | GATESHEAD - 52A | GATESHEAD - 52A | SPRINGHEAD - 53C | YORK - 50A | SUNDERLAND - 52G | DARLINGTON - 51A |
| Nov-59 | BIDSTON - 6F | DAIRYCOATES - 53A | ALEXDOCK - 53C | GATESHEAD - 52A | GATESHEAD - 52A | SPRINGHEAD - 53C | YORK - 50A | SUNDERLAND - 52G | DARLINGTON - 51A |
| Jan-60 | BIDSTON - 6F | DAIRYCOATES - 53A | ALEXDOCK - 53C | GATESHEAD - 52A | GATESHEAD - 52A | SPRINGHEAD - 53C | YORK - 50A | SUNDERLAND - 52G | DARLINGTON - 51A |
| Apr-60 | 3/60: W/D | DAIRYCOATES - 50B | ALEXDOCK - 53C | GATESHEAD - 52A | GATESHEAD - 52A | SPRINGHEAD - 53C | YORK - 50A | SUNDERLAND - 52G | DARLINGTON - 51A |
| Aug-60 | | DAIRYCOATES - 50B | ALEXDOCK - 53C | GATESHEAD - 52A | 9/60: W.AUCK - 51F | 9/60: W/D | YORK - 50A | SUNDERLAND - 52G | 6/60: W/D |
| Nov-60 | | DAIRYCOATES - 50B | ALEXDOCK - 53C | GATESHEAD - 52A | W.AUCKLAND - 51F | | YORK - 50A | SUNDERLAND - 52G | |

| | 68680 | 68681 | 68682 | 68683 | 68684 | 68685 | 68686 | 68687 | 68688 |
|---|---|---|---|---|---|---|---|---|---|
| Aug-50 | GATESHEAD - 52A | NEVILLE HILL - 50B | HEATON - 52B | W.HARTLEPOOL - 51C | W.HARTLEPOOL - 51C | W.HARTLEPOOL - 51C | SPRINGHEAD - 53C | HEATON - 52B | MIDDLESBROUGH - 51D |
| Jan-51 | GATESHEAD - 52A | NEVILLE HILL - 50B | HEATON - 52B | W.HARTLEPOOL - 51C | W.HARTLEPOOL - 51C | W.HARTLEPOOL - 51C | SPRINGHEAD - 53C | HEATON - 52B | MIDDLESBROUGH - 51D |
| Aug-51 | GATESHEAD - 52A | NEVILLE HILL - 50B | HEATON - 52B | W.HARTLEPOOL - 51C | W.HARTLEPOOL - 51C | W.HARTLEPOOL - 51C | SPRINGHEAD - 53C | HEATON - 52B | MIDDLESBROUGH - 51D |
| Jan-52 | GATESHEAD - 52A | NEVILLE HILL - 50B | HEATON - 52B | W.HARTLEPOOL - 51C | W.HARTLEPOOL - 51C | W.HARTLEPOOL - 51C | SPRINGHEAD - 53C | HEATON - 52B | MIDDLESBROUGH - 51D |
| Aug-52 | GATESHEAD - 52A | NEVILLE HILL - 50B | HEATON - 52B | W.HARTLEPOOL - 51C | W.HARTLEPOOL - 51C | W.HARTLEPOOL - 51C | SPRINGHEAD - 53C | 9/52: BLAY - 52C | MIDDLESBROUGH - 51D |
| Jan-53 | GATESHEAD - 52A | NEVILLE HILL - 50B | HEATON - 52B | W.HARTLEPOOL - 51C | W.HARTLEPOOL - 51C | W.HARTLEPOOL - 51C | SPRINGHEAD - 53C | 10/52: T.DCK - 54B | MIDDLESBROUGH - 51D |
| Aug-53 | GATESHEAD - 52A | NEVILLE HILL - 50B | HEATON - 52B | W.HARTLEPOOL - 51C | W.HARTLEPOOL - 51C | W.HARTLEPOOL - 51C | SPRINGHEAD - 53C | TYNE DOCK - 54B | MIDDLESBROUGH - 51D |
| Jan-54 | GATESHEAD - 52A | NEVILLE HILL - 50B | HEATON - 52B | W.HARTLEPOOL - 51C | W.HARTLEPOOL - 51C | W.HARTLEPOOL - 51C | SPRINGHEAD - 53C | TYNE DOCK - 54B | MIDDLESBROUGH - 51D |
| Aug-54 | GATESHEAD - 52A | NEVILLE HILL - 50B | HEATON - 52B | W.HARTLEPOOL - 51C | W.HARTLEPOOL - 51C | W.HARTLEPOOL - 51C | SPRINGHEAD - 53C | TYNE DOCK - 54B | MIDDLESBROUGH - 51D |
| Jan-55 | GATESHEAD - 52A | NEVILLE HILL - 50B | HEATON - 52B | W.HARTLEPOOL - 51C | W.HARTLEPOOL - 51C | W.HARTLEPOOL - 51C | 11/54: YORK - 50A | TYNE DOCK - 54B | MIDDLESBROUGH - 51D |
| Aug-55 | GATESHEAD - 52A | NEVILLE HILL - 50B | HEATON - 52B | W.HARTLEPOOL - 51C | 9/55: MBRO - 51D | W.HARTLEPOOL - 51C | YORK - 50A | TYNE DOCK - 54B | MIDDLESBROUGH - 51D |
| Jan-56 | GATESHEAD - 52A | YORK - 50A | HEATON - 52B | W.HARTLEPOOL - 51C | MIDDLESBROUGH - 51D | W.HARTLEPOOL - 51C | YORK - 50A | TYNE DOCK - 54B | MIDDLESBROUGH - 51D |
| Aug-56 | GATESHEAD - 52A | YORK - 50A | 7/56: TWEED - 52D | W.HARTLEPOOL - 51C | MIDDLESBROUGH - 51D | 5/56: W.AUCK - 51F | YORK - 50A | TYNE DOCK - 54B | MIDDLESBROUGH - 51D |
| Jan-57 | GATESHEAD - 52A | 11/56: N'TON - 20D | TWEEDMOUTH - 52D | W.HARTLEPOOL - 51C | MIDDLESBROUGH - 51D | W.AUCKLAND - 51F | YORK - 50A | TYNE DOCK - 54B | MIDDLESBROUGH - 51D |
| Aug-57 | GATESHEAD - 52A | NORMANTON - 20D | TWEEDMOUTH - 52D | W.HARTLEPOOL - 51C | MIDDLESBROUGH - 51D | W.AUCKLAND - 51F | YORK - 50A | 6/57: YORK - 50A | MIDDLESBROUGH - 51D |
| Jan-58 | GATESHEAD - 52A | NORMANTON - 20D | TWEEDMOUTH - 52D | W.HARTLEPOOL - 51C | MIDDLESBROUGH - 51D | W.AUCKLAND - 51F | YORK - 50A | YORK - 50A | MIDDLESBROUGH - 51D |
| Aug-58 | GATESHEAD - 52A | NORMANTON - 20D | TWEEDMOUTH - 52D | W.HARTLEPOOL - 51C | 6/58: TBY - 51L | W.AUCKLAND - 51F | 5/58: SELBY - 50C | YORK - 50A | 6/58: MBRO - 5 |
| Jan-59 | GATESHEAD - 52A | NORMANTON - 20D | TWEEDMOUTH - 52D | W.HARTLEPOOL - 51C | THORNABY - 51L | W.AUCKLAND - 51F | SELBY - 50C | YORK - 50A | THORNABY - 51L |
| Aug-59 | GATESHEAD - 52A | NORMANTON - 20D | TWEEDMOUTH - 52D | W.HARTLEPOOL - 51C | THORNABY - 51L | W.AUCKLAND - 51F | 9/59: YORK - 50A | YORK - 50A | THORNABY - 51L |
| Nov-59 | GATESHEAD - 52A | NORMANTON - 20D | TWEEDMOUTH - 52D | W.HARTLEPOOL - 51C | THORNABY - 51L | W.AUCKLAND - 51F | YORK - 50A | YORK - 50A | THORNABY - 51L |
| Jan-60 | GATESHEAD - 52A | NORMANTON - 20D | 12/59: W/D | W.HARTLEPOOL - 51C | THORNABY - 51L | W.AUCKLAND - 51F | YORK - 50A | YORK - 50A | THORNABY - 51L |
| Apr-60 | GATESHEAD - 52A | NORMANTON - 20D | | W.HARTLEPOOL - 51C | THORNABY - 51L | W.AUCKLAND - 51F | YORK - 50A | YORK - 50A | THORNABY - 51L |
| Aug-60 | GATESHEAD - 52A | NORMANTON - 20D | | W.HARTLEPOOL - 51C | THORNABY - 51L | W.AUCKLAND - 51F | YORK - 50A | YORK - 50A | THORNABY - 51L |
| Nov-60 | GATESHEAD - 52A | NORMANTON - 20D | | W.HARTLEPOOL - 51C | THORNABY - 51L | 10/60: W/D | YORK - 50A | YORK - 50A | W.AUCKLAND - 51F |

| | 68689 | 68690 | 68691 | 68692 | 68693 | 68694 | 68695 | 68696 | 68697 |
|---|---|---|---|---|---|---|---|---|---|
| Aug-50 | MIDDLESBROUGH - 51D | MIDDLESBROUGH - 51D | W.AUCKLAND - 51F | W.HARTLEPOOL - 51C | GATESHEAD - 52A | W.HARTLEPOOL - 51C | YORK - 50A | W.AUCKLAND - 51F | W.HARTLEPOOL - 51C |
| Jan-51 | MIDDLESBROUGH - 51D | MIDDLESBROUGH - 51D | W.AUCKLAND - 51F | W.HARTLEPOOL - 51C | GATESHEAD - 52A | W.HARTLEPOOL - 51C | YORK - 50A | W.AUCKLAND - 51F | W.HARTLEPOOL - 51C |
| Aug-51 | MIDDLESBROUGH - 51D | MIDDLESBROUGH - 51D | W.AUCKLAND - 51F | W.HARTLEPOOL - 51C | GATESHEAD - 52A | W.HARTLEPOOL - 51C | YORK - 50A | W.AUCKLAND - 51F | W.HARTLEPOOL - 51C |
| Jan-52 | MIDDLESBROUGH - 51D | MIDDLESBROUGH - 51D | W.AUCKLAND - 51F | W.HARTLEPOOL - 51C | GATESHEAD - 52A | W.HARTLEPOOL - 51C | YORK - 50A | W.AUCKLAND - 51F | W.HARTLEPOOL - 51C |
| Aug-52 | MIDDLESBROUGH - 51D | MIDDLESBROUGH - 51D | W.AUCKLAND - 51F | W.HARTLEPOOL - 51C | GATESHEAD - 52A | W.HARTLEPOOL - 51C | YORK - 50A | W.AUCKLAND - 51F | W.HARTLEPOOL - 51C |
| Jan-53 | MIDDLESBROUGH - 51D | MIDDLESBROUGH - 51D | W.AUCKLAND - 51F | W.HARTLEPOOL - 51C | GATESHEAD - 52A | W.HARTLEPOOL - 51C | YORK - 50A | W.AUCKLAND - 51F | W.HARTLEPOOL - 51C |
| Aug-53 | MIDDLESBROUGH - 51D | MIDDLESBROUGH - 51D | W.AUCKLAND - 51F | W.AUCKLAND - 51F | GATESHEAD - 52A | W.HARTLEPOOL - 51C | YORK - 50A | W.AUCKLAND - 51F | W.HARTLEPOOL - 51C |
| Jan-54 | MIDDLESBROUGH - 51D | MIDDLESBROUGH - 51D | W.AUCKLAND - 51F | W.AUCKLAND - 51F | GATESHEAD - 52A | W.HARTLEPOOL - 51C | YORK - 50A | W.AUCKLAND - 51F | **2/54: B.GDNS - 54C** |
| Aug-54 | MIDDLESBROUGH - 51D | MIDDLESBROUGH - 51D | W.AUCKLAND - 51F | W.AUCKLAND - 51F | GATESHEAD - 52A | **4/54: B.GDNS - 54C** | YORK - 50A | W.AUCKLAND - 51F | B.GARDENS - 54C |
| Jan-55 | MIDDLESBROUGH - 51D | MIDDLESBROUGH - 51D | W.AUCKLAND - 51F | W.AUCKLAND - 51F | GATESHEAD - 52A | B.GARDENS - 54C | YORK - 50A | W.AUCKLAND - 51F | B.GARDENS - 54C |
| Aug-55 | MIDDLESBROUGH - 51D | MIDDLESBROUGH - 51D | W.AUCKLAND - 51F | W.AUCKLAND - 51F | GATESHEAD - 52A | B.GARDENS - 54C | YORK - 50A | **6/55: STOCK - 51E** | B.GARDENS - 54C |
| Jan-56 | MIDDLESBROUGH - 51D | MIDDLESBROUGH - 51D | W.AUCKLAND - 51F | W.AUCKLAND - 51F | GATESHEAD - 52A | B.GARDENS - 54C | YORK - 50A | STOCKTON - 51E | B.GARDENS - 54C |
| Aug-56 | MIDDLESBROUGH - 51D | MIDDLESBROUGH - 51D | W.AUCKLAND - 51F | W.AUCKLAND - 51F | GATESHEAD - 52A | B.GARDENS - 54C | YORK - 50A | STOCKTON - 51E | B.GARDENS - 54C |
| Jan-57 | MIDDLESBROUGH - 51D | MIDDLESBROUGH - 51D | W.AUCKLAND - 51F | W.AUCKLAND - 51F | GATESHEAD - 52A | B.GARDENS - 54C | **1/57: B.GDNS - 54C** | STOCKTON - 51E | B.GARDENS - 54C |
| Aug-57 | MIDDLESBROUGH - 51D | MIDDLESBROUGH - 51D | W.AUCKLAND - 51F | W.AUCKLAND - 51F | GATESHEAD - 52A | B.GARDENS - 54C | B.GARDENS - 54C | STOCKTON - 51E | B.GARDENS - 54C |
| Jan-58 | MIDDLESBROUGH - 51D | MIDDLESBROUGH - 51D | W.AUCKLAND - 51F | W.AUCKLAND - 51F | GATESHEAD - 52A | B.GARDENS - 54C | B.GARDENS - 54C | STOCKTON - 51E | B.GARDENS - 54C |
| Aug-58 | **6/58: TBY - 51L** | **6/58: TBY - 51L** | W.AUCKLAND - 51F | W.AUCKLAND - 51F | GATESHEAD - 52A | B.GARDENS - 54C | B.GARDENS - 54C | STOCKTON - 51E | B.GARDENS - 54C |
| Jan-59 | THORNABY - 51L | THORNABY - 51L | W.AUCKLAND - 51F | W.AUCKLAND - 51F | GATESHEAD - 52A | B.GARDENS - 52J | B.GARDENS - 52J | STOCKTON - 51E | B.GARDENS - 52J |
| Aug-59 | THORNABY - 51L | THORNABY - 51L | W.AUCKLAND - 51F | W.AUCKLAND - 51F | GATESHEAD - 52A | **6/59: GHD - 52A** | **6/59: GHD - 52A** | **6/59: TBY - 51L** | **6/59: GHD - 52A** |
| Nov-59 | THORNABY - 51L | THORNABY - 51L | W.AUCKLAND - 51F | W.AUCKLAND - 51F | GATESHEAD - 52A | **11/59: W/D** | GATESHEAD - 52A | THORNABY - 51L | GATESHEAD - 52A |
| Jan-60 | THORNABY - 51L | THORNABY - 51L | W.AUCKLAND - 51F | W.AUCKLAND - 51F | GATESHEAD - 52A | | GATESHEAD - 52A | THORNABY - 51L | GATESHEAD - 52A |
| Apr-60 | THORNABY - 51L | THORNABY - 51L | W.AUCKLAND - 51F | W.AUCKLAND - 51F | GATESHEAD - 52A | | GATESHEAD - 52A | THORNABY - 51L | **2/60: W/D** |
| Aug-60 | THORNABY - 51L | THORNABY - 51L | W.AUCKLAND - 51F | W.AUCKLAND - 51F | GATESHEAD - 52A | | GATESHEAD - 52A | THORNABY - 51L | |
| Nov-60 | THORNABY - 51L | THORNABY - 51L | W.AUCKLAND - 51F | W.AUCKLAND - 51F | GATESHEAD - 52A | | GATESHEAD - 52A | THORNABY - 51L | |

| | 68698 | 68699 | 68700 | 68701 | 68702 | 68703 | 68704 | 68705 | 68706 |
|---|---|---|---|---|---|---|---|---|---|
| Aug-50 | SUNDERLAND - 54A | YORK - 50A | KITTYBREWSTER - 61A | BIDSTON - 6F | GATESHEAD - 52A | W.HARTLEPOOL - 51C | SUNDERLAND - 54A | B.GARDENS - 54C | TYNEDOCK - 54B |
| Jan-51 | SUNDERLAND - 54A | YORK - 50A | KITTYBREWSTER - 61A | BIDSTON - 6F | **12/50: BLAY - 52C** | W.HARTLEPOOL - 51C | SUNDERLAND - 54A | B.GARDENS - 54C | TYNEDOCK - 54B |
| Aug-51 | SUNDERLAND - 54A | YORK - 50A | KITTYBREWSTER - 61A | BIDSTON - 6F | **5/51: HTN - 52B** | W.HARTLEPOOL - 51C | SUNDERLAND - 54A | B.GARDENS - 54C | TYNEDOCK - 54B |
| Jan-52 | SUNDERLAND - 54A | YORK - 50A | KITTYBREWSTER - 61A | BIDSTON - 6F | HEATON - 52B | W.HARTLEPOOL - 51C | SUNDERLAND - 54A | B.GARDENS - 54C | TYNEDOCK - 54B |
| Aug-52 | SUNDERLAND - 54A | YORK - 50A | KITTYBREWSTER - 61A | BIDSTON - 6F | HEATON - 52B | W.HARTLEPOOL - 51C | SUNDERLAND - 54A | B.GARDENS - 54C | TYNEDOCK - 54B |
| Jan-53 | SUNDERLAND - 54A | YORK - 50A | KITTYBREWSTER - 61A | BIDSTON - 6F | HEATON - 52B | W.HARTLEPOOL - 51C | SUNDERLAND - 54A | B.GARDENS - 54C | TYNEDOCK - 54B |
| Aug-53 | SUNDERLAND - 54A | YORK - 50A | KITTYBREWSTER - 61A | BIDSTON - 6F | HEATON - 52B | W.HARTLEPOOL - 51C | SUNDERLAND - 54A | B.GARDENS - 54C | TYNEDOCK - 54B |
| Jan-54 | SUNDERLAND - 54A | YORK - 50A | KITTYBREWSTER - 61A | BIDSTON - 6F | HEATON - 52B | W.HARTLEPOOL - 51C | SUNDERLAND - 54A | B.GARDENS - 54C | TYNEDOCK - 54B |
| Aug-54 | SUNDERLAND - 54A | YORK - 50A | KITTYBREWSTER - 61A | BIDSTON - 6F | HEATON - 52B | W.HARTLEPOOL - 51C | SUNDERLAND - 54A | B.GARDENS - 54C | TYNEDOCK - 54B |
| Jan-55 | SUNDERLAND - 54A | YORK - 50A | KITTYBREWSTER - 61A | **11/54: N'TON - 20D** | HEATON - 52B | W.HARTLEPOOL - 51C | SUNDERLAND - 54A | B.GARDENS - 54C | TYNEDOCK - 54B |
| Aug-55 | SUNDERLAND - 54A | YORK - 50A | KITTYBREWSTER - 61A | NORMANTON - 20D | HEATON - 52B | W.HARTLEPOOL - 51C | SUNDERLAND - 54A | B.GARDENS - 54C | TYNEDOCK - 54B |
| Jan-56 | SUNDERLAND - 54A | YORK - 50A | **2/56: KEITH - 61C** | NORMANTON - 20D | HEATON - 52B | W.HARTLEPOOL - 51C | SUNDERLAND - 54A | B.GARDENS - 54C | TYNEDOCK - 54B |
| Aug-56 | SUNDERLAND - 54A | **6/56: B.GDNS - 54C** | KEITH - 61C | NORMANTON - 20D | HEATON - 52B | W.HARTLEPOOL - 51C | SUNDERLAND - 54A | B.GARDENS - 54C | TYNEDOCK - 54B |
| Jan-57 | SUNDERLAND - 54A | B.GARDENS - 54C | KEITH - 61C | NORMANTON - 20D | HEATON - 52B | W.HARTLEPOOL - 51C | SUNDERLAND - 54A | B.GARDENS - 54C | TYNEDOCK - 54B |
| Aug-57 | **9/57: YORK - 50A** | B.GARDENS - 54C | KEITH - 61C | NORMANTON - 20D | HEATON - 52B | W.HARTLEPOOL - 51C | SUNDERLAND - 54A | B.GARDENS - 54C | TYNEDOCK - 54B |
| Jan-58 | YORK - 50A | B.GARDENS - 54C | KEITH - 61C | NORMANTON - 20D | HEATON - 52B | W.HARTLEPOOL - 51C | SUNDERLAND - 54A | B.GARDENS - 54C | TYNEDOCK - 54B |
| Aug-58 | **7/58: W.HPL - 51C** | B.GARDENS - 54C | KEITH - 61C | NORMANTON - 20D | HEATON - 52B | W.HARTLEPOOL - 51C | SUNDERLAND - 54A | B.GARDENS - 54C | TYNEDOCK - 54B |
| Jan-59 | W.HARTLEPOOL - 51C | **12/58: W/D** | **12/58: W/D** | NORMANTON - 20D | HEATON - 52B | W.HARTLEPOOL - 51C | SUNDERLAND - 52G | **6/59: GHD - 52A** | TYNEDOCK - 52H |
| Aug-59 | W.HARTLEPOOL - 51C | | | NORMANTON - 20D | HEATON - 52B | W.HARTLEPOOL - 51C | SUNDERLAND - 52G | 8/59: GOOLE - 53E | TYNEDOCK - 52H |
| Nov-59 | W.HARTLEPOOL - 51C | | | NORMANTON - 20D | HEATON - 52B | W.HARTLEPOOL - 51C | SUNDERLAND - 52G | **11/59: DAIRY - 53A** | TYNEDOCK - 52H |
| Jan-60 | W.HARTLEPOOL - 51C | | | NORMANTON - 20D | HEATON - 52B | W.HARTLEPOOL - 51C | SUNDERLAND - 52G | DAIRYCOATES - 53A | TYNEDOCK - 52H |
| Apr-60 | W.HARTLEPOOL - 51C | | | NORMANTON - 20D | HEATON - 52B | W.HARTLEPOOL - 51C | SUNDERLAND - 52G | DAIRYCOATES - 50B | TYNEDOCK - 52H |
| Aug-60 | W.HARTLEPOOL - 51C | | | NORMANTON - 20D | HEATON - 52B | W.HARTLEPOOL - 51C | **6/60: T.DCK - 52H** | DAIRYCOATES - 50B | TYNEDOCK - 52H |
| Nov-60 | W.HARTLEPOOL - 51C | | | **10/60: W/D** | HEATON - 52B | W.HARTLEPOOL - 51C | TYNEDOCK - 52H | **11/60: W/D** | **11/60: W/D** |

| | 68707 | 68708 | 68709 | 68710 | 68711 | 68712 | 68713 | 68714 | 68715 |
|---|---|---|---|---|---|---|---|---|---|
| Aug-50 | DARLINGTON - 51A | B.GARDENS - 54C | EASTFIELD - 65A | KITTYBREWSTER - 61A | W.HARTLEPOOL - 51C | MIDDLESBROUGH - 51D | MIDDLESBROUGH - 51D | BIDSTON - 6F | YORK - 50A |
| Jan-51 | DARLINGTON - 51A | B.GARDENS - 54C | EASTFIELD - 65A | KITTYBREWSTER - 61A | W.HARTLEPOOL - 51C | MIDDLESBROUGH - 51D | MIDDLESBROUGH - 51D | BIDSTON - 6F | **3/51: W.HPL - 51C** |
| Aug-51 | DARLINGTON - 51A | B.GARDENS - 54C | EASTFIELD - 65A | KITTYBREWSTER - 61A | W.HARTLEPOOL - 51C | MIDDLESBROUGH - 51D | MIDDLESBROUGH - 51D | BIDSTON - 6F | W.HARTLEPOOL - 51C |
| Jan-52 | DARLINGTON - 51A | B.GARDENS - 54C | EASTFIELD - 65A | KITTYBREWSTER - 61A | W.HARTLEPOOL - 51C | MIDDLESBROUGH - 51D | MIDDLESBROUGH - 51D | BIDSTON - 6F | W.HARTLEPOOL - 51C |
| Aug-52 | DARLINGTON - 51A | B.GARDENS - 54C | EASTFIELD - 65A | KITTYBREWSTER - 61A | W.HARTLEPOOL - 51C | MIDDLESBROUGH - 51D | MIDDLESBROUGH - 51D | **7/52: BIRK - 6C** | W.HARTLEPOOL - 51C |
| Jan-53 | **10/52: W.AUCK - 51F** | B.GARDENS - 54C | EASTFIELD - 65A | KITTYBREWSTER - 61A | W.HARTLEPOOL - 51C | MIDDLESBROUGH - 51D | MIDDLESBROUGH - 51D | BIRKENHEAD - 6C | W.HARTLEPOOL - 51C |
| Aug-53 | W.AUCKLAND - 51F | B.GARDENS - 54C | EASTFIELD - 65A | KITTYBREWSTER - 61A | W.HARTLEPOOL - 51C | MIDDLESBROUGH - 51D | MIDDLESBROUGH - 51D | BIRKENHEAD - 6C | W.HARTLEPOOL - 51C |
| Jan-54 | W.AUCKLAND - 51F | **2/54: HTN - 52B** | EASTFIELD - 65A | KITTYBREWSTER - 61A | W.HARTLEPOOL - 51C | MIDDLESBROUGH - 51D | MIDDLESBROUGH - 51D | BIRKENHEAD - 6C | W.HARTLEPOOL - 51C |
| Aug-54 | W.AUCKLAND - 51F | HEATON - 52B | EASTFIELD - 65A | KITTYBREWSTER - 61A | W.HARTLEPOOL - 51C | MIDDLESBROUGH - 51D | MIDDLESBROUGH - 51D | BIRKENHEAD - 6C | W.HARTLEPOOL - 51C |
| Jan-55 | W.AUCKLAND - 51F | HEATON - 52B | EASTFIELD - 65A | KITTYBREWSTER - 61A | W.HARTLEPOOL - 51C | MIDDLESBROUGH - 51D | MIDDLESBROUGH - 51D | BIRKENHEAD - 6C | W.HARTLEPOOL - 51C |
| Aug-55 | W.AUCKLAND - 51F | HEATON - 52B | EASTFIELD - 65A | KITTYBREWSTER - 61A | W.HARTLEPOOL - 51C | MIDDLESBROUGH - 51D | **5/55: HTN - 52B** | BIRKENHEAD - 6C | W.HARTLEPOOL - 51C |
| Jan-56 | W.AUCKLAND - 51F | HEATON - 52B | EASTFIELD - 65A | KITTYBREWSTER - 61A | W.HARTLEPOOL - 51C | MIDDLESBROUGH - 51D | HEATON - 52B | BIRKENHEAD - 6C | W.HARTLEPOOL - 51C |
| Aug-56 | **5/56: W.HPL - 51C** | HEATON - 52B | EASTFIELD - 65A | KITTYBREWSTER - 61A | W.HARTLEPOOL - 51C | MIDDLESBROUGH - 51D | HEATON - 52B | BIRKENHEAD - 6C | W.HARTLEPOOL - 51C |
| Jan-57 | W.HARTLEPOOL - 51C | HEATON - 52B | EASTFIELD - 65A | KITTYBREWSTER - 61A | W.HARTLEPOOL - 51C | MIDDLESBROUGH - 51D | HEATON - 52B | **2/57: WREX - 6E** | W.HARTLEPOOL - 51C |
| Aug-57 | W.HARTLEPOOL - 51C | HEATON - 52B | EASTFIELD - 65A | KITTYBREWSTER - 61A | W.HARTLEPOOL - 51C | MIDDLESBROUGH - 51D | HEATON - 52B | WREXHAM - 6E | W.HARTLEPOOL - 51C |
| Jan-58 | W.HARTLEPOOL - 51C | HEATON - 52B | **1/58: KIPPS - 65E** | KITTYBREWSTER - 61A | W.HARTLEPOOL - 51C | MIDDLESBROUGH - 51D | HEATON - 52B | WREXHAM - 6E | W.HARTLEPOOL - 51C |
| Aug-58 | W.HARTLEPOOL - 51C | HEATON - 52B | KIPPS - 65E | KITTYBREWSTER - 61A | W.HARTLEPOOL - 51C | **6/58: TBY - 51L** | HEATON - 52B | **10/58: BIDS - 6F** | W.HARTLEPOOL - 51C |
| Jan-59 | W.HARTLEPOOL - 51C | HEATON - 52B | KIPPS - 65E | KITTYBREWSTER - 61A | W.HARTLEPOOL - 51C | **1/59: W/D** | HEATON - 52B | BIDSTON - 6F | W.HARTLEPOOL - 51C |
| Aug-59 | W.HARTLEPOOL - 51C | HEATON - 52B | KIPPS - 65E | **3/59: W/D** | W.HARTLEPOOL - 51C | | HEATON - 52B | BIDSTON - 6F | W.HARTLEPOOL - 51C |
| Nov-59 | W.HARTLEPOOL - 51C | HEATON - 52B | KIPPS - 65E | | W.HARTLEPOOL - 51C | | HEATON - 52B | BIDSTON - 6F | W.HARTLEPOOL - 51C |
| Jan-60 | W.HARTLEPOOL - 51C | HEATON - 52B | KIPPS - 65E | | W.HARTLEPOOL - 51C | | HEATON - 52B | BIDSTON - 6F | W.HARTLEPOOL - 51C |
| Apr-60 | W.HARTLEPOOL - 51C | HEATON - 52B | KIPPS - 65E | | W.HARTLEPOOL - 51C | | HEATON - 52B | **4/60: W/D** | W.HARTLEPOOL - 51C |
| Aug-60 | W.HARTLEPOOL - 51C | **9/60: W.AUCK - 51F** | KIPPS - 65E | | W.HARTLEPOOL - 51C | | HEATON - 52B | | W.HARTLEPOOL - 51C |
| Nov-60 | W.HARTLEPOOL - 51C | W.AUCKLAND - 51F | KIPPS - 65E | | W.HARTLEPOOL - 51C | | HEATON - 52B | | W.HARTLEPOOL - 51C |

| | 68716 | 68717 | 68718 | 68719 | 68720 | 68721 | 68722 | 68723 | 68724 |
|---|---|---|---|---|---|---|---|---|---|
| Aug-50 | W.HARTLEPOOL - 51C | KITTYBREWSTER - 61A | SUNDERLAND - 54A | KITTYBREWSTER - 61A | GATESHEAD - 52A | MIDDLESBROUGH - 51D | YORK - 50A | GATESHEAD - 52A | SPRINGHEAD - 53C |
| Jan-51 | W.HARTLEPOOL - 51C | KITTYBREWSTER - 61A | SUNDERLAND - 54A | KITTYBREWSTER - 61A | GATESHEAD - 52A | MIDDLESBROUGH - 51D | YORK - 50A | GATESHEAD - 52A | SPRINGHEAD - 53C |
| Aug-51 | W.HARTLEPOOL - 51C | KITTYBREWSTER - 61A | SUNDERLAND - 54A | KITTYBREWSTER - 61A | GATESHEAD - 52A | MIDDLESBROUGH - 51D | YORK - 50A | GATESHEAD - 52A | SPRINGHEAD - 53C |
| Jan-52 | W.HARTLEPOOL - 51C | KITTYBREWSTER - 61A | SUNDERLAND - 54A | KITTYBREWSTER - 61A | GATESHEAD - 52A | MIDDLESBROUGH - 51D | YORK - 50A | GATESHEAD - 52A | SPRINGHEAD - 53C |
| Aug-52 | W.HARTLEPOOL - 51C | KITTYBREWSTER - 61A | **9/52: S'HEAD - 53C** | KITTYBREWSTER - 61A | GATESHEAD - 52A | MIDDLESBROUGH - 51D | YORK - 50A | GATESHEAD - 52A | SPRINGHEAD - 53C |
| Jan-53 | W.HARTLEPOOL - 51C | KITTYBREWSTER - 61A | SPRINGHEAD - 53C | KITTYBREWSTER - 61A | GATESHEAD - 52A | MIDDLESBROUGH - 51D | YORK - 50A | GATESHEAD - 52A | SPRINGHEAD - 53C |
| Aug-53 | W.HARTLEPOOL - 51C | KITTYBREWSTER - 61A | SPRINGHEAD - 53C | KITTYBREWSTER - 61A | GATESHEAD - 52A | MIDDLESBROUGH - 51D | YORK - 50A | GATESHEAD - 52A | SPRINGHEAD - 53C |
| Jan-54 | W.HARTLEPOOL - 51C | KITTYBREWSTER - 61A | SPRINGHEAD - 53C | KITTYBREWSTER - 61A | GATESHEAD - 52A | MIDDLESBROUGH - 51D | YORK - 50A | GATESHEAD - 52A | **10/53: YORK - 50A** |
| Aug-54 | W.HARTLEPOOL - 51C | KITTYBREWSTER - 61A | **5/54: DAIRY - 53A** | KITTYBREWSTER - 61A | GATESHEAD - 52A | MIDDLESBROUGH - 51D | YORK - 50A | GATESHEAD - 52A | YORK - 50A |
| Jan-55 | W.HARTLEPOOL - 51C | KITTYBREWSTER - 61A | DAIRYCOATES - 53A | KITTYBREWSTER - 61A | GATESHEAD - 52A | MIDDLESBROUGH - 51D | YORK - 50A | GATESHEAD - 52A | YORK - 50A |
| Aug-55 | W.HARTLEPOOL - 51C | KITTYBREWSTER - 61A | DAIRYCOATES - 53A | KITTYBREWSTER - 61A | GATESHEAD - 52A | MIDDLESBROUGH - 51D | YORK - 50A | GATESHEAD - 52A | YORK - 50A |
| Jan-56 | W.HARTLEPOOL - 51C | KITTYBREWSTER - 61A | DAIRYCOATES - 53A | KITTYBREWSTER - 61A | GATESHEAD - 52A | MIDDLESBROUGH - 51D | YORK - 50A | GATESHEAD - 52A | YORK - 50A |
| Aug-56 | **5/56: HTN - 52B** | KITTYBREWSTER - 61A | DAIRYCOATES - 53A | KITTYBREWSTER - 61A | GATESHEAD - 52A | MIDDLESBROUGH - 51D | YORK - 50A | GATESHEAD - 52A | YORK - 50A |
| Jan-57 | HEATON - 52B | KITTYBREWSTER - 61A | DAIRYCOATES - 53A | KITTYBREWSTER - 61A | GATESHEAD - 52A | MIDDLESBROUGH - 51D | YORK - 50A | GATESHEAD - 52A | YORK - 50A |
| Aug-57 | HEATON - 52B | KITTYBREWSTER - 61A | DAIRYCOATES - 53A | KITTYBREWSTER - 61A | GATESHEAD - 52A | MIDDLESBROUGH - 51D | YORK - 50A | GATESHEAD - 52A | YORK - 50A |
| Jan-58 | HEATON - 52B | KITTYBREWSTER - 61A | DAIRYCOATES - 53A | KITTYBREWSTER - 61A | GATESHEAD - 52A | MIDDLESBROUGH - 51D | YORK - 50A | GATESHEAD - 52A | YORK - 50A |
| Aug-58 | HEATON - 52B | KITTYBREWSTER - 61A | **6/58: W/D** | KITTYBREWSTER - 61A | GATESHEAD - 52A | **6/58: TBY - 51L** | **7/58: H.HILL - 51G** | GATESHEAD - 52A | **7/58: W.AUCK - 51F** |
| Jan-59 | **2/59: DARL - 51A** | KITTYBREWSTER - 61A | | KITTYBREWSTER - 61A | GATESHEAD - 52A | THORNABY - 51L | **9/58: W.HPL - 51C** | GATESHEAD - 52A | W.AUCKLAND - 51F |
| Aug-59 | DARLINGTON - 51A | KITTYBREWSTER - 61A | | KITTYBREWSTER - 61A | GATESHEAD - 52A | THORNABY - 51L | W.HARTLEPOOL - 51C | GATESHEAD - 52A | W.AUCKLAND - 51F |
| Nov-59 | DARLINGTON - 51A | KITTYBREWSTER - 61A | | KITTYBREWSTER - 61A | GATESHEAD - 52A | THORNABY - 51L | W.HARTLEPOOL - 51C | GATESHEAD - 52A | W.AUCKLAND - 51F |
| Jan-60 | **1/60: DAIRY - 53A** | KITTYBREWSTER - 61A | | KITTYBREWSTER - 61A | GATESHEAD - 52A | THORNABY - 51L | W.HARTLEPOOL - 51C | GATESHEAD - 52A | W.AUCKLAND - 51F |
| Apr-60 | DAIRYCOATES - 50B | KITTYBREWSTER - 61A | | KITTYBREWSTER - 61A | **5/60: TWEED - 52D** | THORNABY - 51L | **3/60: W/D** | GATESHEAD - 52A | W.AUCKLAND - 51F |
| Aug-60 | DAIRYCOATES - 50B | KITTYBREWSTER - 61A | | KITTYBREWSTER - 61A | TWEEDMOUTH - 52D | THORNABY - 51L | | GATESHEAD - 52A | W.AUCKLAND - 51F |
| Nov-60 | DAIRYCOATES - 50B | KITTYBREWSTER - 61A | | KITTYBREWSTER - 61A | TWEEDMOUTH - 52D | THORNABY - 51L | | GATESHEAD - 52A | W.AUCKLAND - 51F |

*Ex works J50 0-6-0T 68922 waits at Doncaster in July 1956 to return to Bradford to join the other sixteen of the class based at that shed. For many years the J50 had had an association with the Leeds district of the GN where in 1950 forty nine of the class had been shared between Bradford, Ardsley and Bradford: an affinity earning them the soubriquet 'Ardsley Tanks'. The most interesting point in their careers came in 1952 when twenty-seven of the class were moved south to Hornsey to take over from the J50 0-6-0T's the Widened Lines workings between Ferme Park and the SR.*

## DISTRIBUTION OF GOODS TANKS : 1957

| | J50 | J52 | J63 | J67 | J68 | Y1 | Y3 | Dsl | Total |
|---|---|---|---|---|---|---|---|---|---|
| Hornsey | 32 | 6 | | | | | | 4 | 42 |
| Doncaster | 4 | 14 | | 2 | | 1 | 1 | 1 | 23 |
| Kings Cross | | 6 | | | | | 17 | | 23 |
| Ardsley | 18 | 3 | | | | | | | 21 |
| Colwick | 5 | 10 | | 4 | 1 | | | | 20 |
| New England | | 5 | | 3 | | | 10 | | 18 |
| Bradford | 17 | | | | | | | | 17 |
| Lincoln | | | 10 | | | | 6 | | 16 |
| Boston | | | 7 | | | | 1 | 1 | 9 |
| Copley Hill | 7 | | | | | | | | 7 |
| Hitchin | | | | 3 | | | | | 3 |
| Hatfield | | 1 | | | | | | | 1 |

| | J50 | J67 | J68 | Y1 | Y3 | Y4 | Dsl | Total |
|---|---|---|---|---|---|---|---|---|
| Stratford | | 31 | 15 | | | 1 | 47 | 94 |
| Norwich | 3 | 1 | 4 | | | | 4 | 12 |
| Ipswich | | 2 | | | | | 9 | 11 |
| March | | 1 | | | | | 9 | 10 |
| Lowestoft | | 1 | 1 | 1 | 4 | | 1 | 8 |
| K. Lynn | | 7 | | | | | | 7 |
| Cambridge | | 5 | | | | | | 5 |
| Parkeston | | | 1 | | 4 | | | 5 |
| S. Lynn | | 4 | | | | | | 4 |
| Colchester | | 1 | 2 | | | | | 3 |
| Melton C. | | 2 | | | | | | 2 |
| Yarmouth (ST) | | 1 | 1 | | | | | 2 |
| Bury St.E | | 1 | | | | | | 1 |
| Yarmouth (B) | | | 1 | | | | | 1 |
| Yarmouth (V) | | | | | | | 1 | 1 |

| | J50 | J52 | J63 | J67 | J72 | J94 | Dsl | Total |
|---|---|---|---|---|---|---|---|---|
| Immingham | 1 | | 1 | | | 18 | 14 | 34 |
| Mexborough | | 2 | | | | | 9 | 11 |
| Frodingham | 6 | | | | | | | 6 |
| Neasden | | | | | | 5 | | 5 |
| Woodford Halse | | | | | | 5 | | 5 |
| Retford | | | | 5 | | | | 5 |
| Darnall | | | | | | | 5 | 5 |
| Bidston | | | | | 4 | | | 4 |
| Wrexham | | | | 2 | 2 | | | 4 |
| Staveley | | | | 4 | | | | 4 |
| Gorton | | | | | 3 | | | 3 |
| Annesley | 2 | | | | | | | 2 |
| Birkenhead | | | | 1 | | | | 1 |
| T. Park | | | | 1 | | | | 1 |
| Leicester | | 1 | | | | | | 1 |

| | J67 | J71 | J72 | J73 | J77 | J94 | A7 | T1 | N10 | Y1 | Y3 | Dsl | Total |
|---|---|---|---|---|---|---|---|---|---|---|---|---|---|
| Darlington | | 3 | 6 | | 2 | 12 | 1 | 1 | | | | 18 | 43 |
| York | | 3 | 8 | 1 | 8 | 3 | | | 1 | | | 10 | 34 |
| Dairycoats | | 5 | 5 | | | | | | 6 | | 1 | 15 | 32 |
| W. Hartlepool | | 4 | 6 | 3 | 7 | | | | | | | 9 | 29 |
| Springhead | | | 8 | 2 | | 3 | | | | | | 15 | 28 |
| Gateshead | | 5 | 9 | | | | | | 4 | | 1 | | 19 |
| Heaton | 4 | 10 | | | 1 | | | | | | | | 15 |
| Middlesbrough | 4 | 9 | | 2 | | | | | | | | | 15 |
| Percy Main | | | | | | | | | | | | 13 | 13 |
| Tyne Dock | | 2 | 5 | | | | | 1 | 4 | | | | 12 |
| Sunderland | | | 5 | | 6 | | | 1 | | | | | 12 |
| Blaydon | 1 | | 5 | | 5 | | | | | | | | 11 |
| Borough Gdns | 2 | | 9 | | | | | | | | | | 11 |
| W. Auckland | 3 | 4 | | 2 | | | | | 2 | | | | 11 |
| N. Blyth | 1 | | 8 | | | | | | | | | | 9 |
| Selby | | 1 | | 3 | 1 | | 1 | | | 1 | 1 | | 8 |
| Neville Hill | | 1 | 1 | | | | | | 1 | | | 5 | 7 |
| Newport | | | | | | 5 | 2 | | | | | | 7 |
| Stockton | 1 | 1 | | | 1 | | | | 2 | | | | 5 |
| Normanton | 1 | 2 | | | | | | | | | | | 3 |
| Starbeck | | | 1 | | 1 | | | | | | | | 2 |
| Tweedmouth | | | 2 | | | | | | | | | | 2 |
| Consett | | | | | | 1 | | | 1 | | | | 2 |
| Stourton | | | | | | | | | | | 2 | | 2 |
| Alex Dock | | | 1 | | | | | | | | | | 1 |
| Scarborough | | | 1 | | | | | | | | | | 1 |
| Botanic Gdns | | | | 1 | | | | | | | | | 1 |
| Haverton Hill | | | | | 1 | | | | | | | | 1 |
| S. Blyth | | | 1 | | | | | | | | | | 1 |

| | J50 | J67 | J72 | J83 | J88 | Y9 | Z4 | Z5 | Dsl | Total |
|---|---|---|---|---|---|---|---|---|---|---|
| St Margarets | | | 1 | 9 | 7 | 5 | | | 3 | 25 |
| Eastfield | 7 | | 2 | 6 | 4 | | | | 4 | 23 |
| Thornton Jcn | | | 2 | 5 | 7 | | | | 3 | 17 |
| Kipps | | | | 5 | 4 | 5 | | | | 14 |
| Dundee | | 2 | | 4 | 4 | | | | 1 | 11 |
| Polmont | | 1 | | 1 | 3 | 2 | | | 1 | 8 |
| Kittybrewster | | | 5 | | | | 2 | 1 | | 8 |
| Haymarket | | | | 5 | 2 | | | | | 7 |
| Parkhead | | | 1 | | | | 4 | | | 5 |
| St Rollox | | | | | | | 5 | | | 5 |
| Dunfermline | | | | | 2 | 1 | | | | 3 |
| Ayr | | | | | | 1 | | | | 1 |
| Keith | | 1 | | | | | | | | 1 |
| Dawsholme | | | | | 1 | | | | | 1 |
| Grangemouth | | | | | 1 | | | | | 1 |

| | 68725 | 68726 | 68727 | 68728 | 68729 | 68730 | 68731 | 68732 | 68733 |
|---|---|---|---|---|---|---|---|---|---|
| Aug-50 | HEATON-52B | YORK-50A | BIDSTON-6F | B.GARDENS-54C | TYNEDOCK-54B | B.GARDENS-54C | TYNEDOCK-54B | GATESHEAD-52A | EASTFIELD-65A |
| Jan-51 | HEATON-52B | YORK-50A | BIDSTON-6F | B.GARDENS-54C | TYNEDOCK-54B | B.GARDENS-54C | TYNEDOCK-54B | GATESHEAD-52A | EASTFIELD-65A |
| Aug-51 | HEATON-52B | YORK-50A | BIDSTON-6F | B.GARDENS-54C | TYNEDOCK-54B | B.GARDENS-54C | TYNEDOCK-54B | GATESHEAD-52A | EASTFIELD-65A |
| Jan-52 | HEATON-52B | YORK-50A | BIDSTON-6F | B.GARDENS-54C | TYNEDOCK-54B | B.GARDENS-54C | TYNEDOCK-54B | GATESHEAD-52A | EASTFIELD-65A |
| Aug-52 | HEATON-52B | YORK-50A | BIDSTON-6F | B.GARDENS-54C | TYNEDOCK-54B | B.GARDENS-54C | TYNEDOCK-54B | GATESHEAD-52A | EASTFIELD-65A |
| Jan-53 | HEATON-52B | YORK-50A | BIDSTON-6F | B.GARDENS-54C | TYNEDOCK-54B | B.GARDENS-54C | 10/52: BLAY - 52C | GATESHEAD-52A | EASTFIELD-65A |
| Aug-53 | HEATON-52B | YORK-50A | BIDSTON-6F | B.GARDENS-54C | TYNEDOCK-54B | B.GARDENS-54C | BLAYDON-52C | GATESHEAD-52A | EASTFIELD-65A |
| Jan-54 | HEATON-52B | YORK-50A | BIDSTON-6F | B.GARDENS-54C | TYNEDOCK-54B | B.GARDENS-54C | BLAYDON-52C | GATESHEAD-52A | EASTFIELD-65A |
| Aug-54 | HEATON-52B | YORK-50A | 6/54: WREX - 6E | B.GARDENS-54C | TYNEDOCK-54B | B.GARDENS-54C | BLAYDON-52C | GATESHEAD-52A | EASTFIELD-65A |
| Jan-55 | HEATON-52B | YORK-50A | WREXHAM-6E | B.GARDENS-54C | TYNEDOCK-54B | B.GARDENS-54C | BLAYDON-52C | GATESHEAD-52A | EASTFIELD-65A |
| Aug-55 | HEATON-52B | YORK-50A | WREXHAM-6E | B.GARDENS-54C | TYNEDOCK-54B | B.GARDENS-54C | BLAYDON-52C | GATESHEAD-52A | EASTFIELD-65A |
| Jan-56 | HEATON-52B | YORK-50A | WREXHAM-6E | B.GARDENS-54C | TYNEDOCK-54B | B.GARDENS-54C | BLAYDON-52C | GATESHEAD-52A | EASTFIELD-65A |
| Aug-56 | 7/56: TWEED - 52D | YORK-50A | WREXHAM-6E | B.GARDENS-54C | TYNEDOCK-54B | B.GARDENS-54C | BLAYDON-52C | GATESHEAD-52A | EASTFIELD-65A |
| Jan-57 | TWEEDMOUTH-52D | YORK-50A | WREXHAM-6E | B.GARDENS-54C | TYNEDOCK-54B | B.GARDENS-54C | 2/57: GHD - 52A | GATESHEAD-52A | EASTFIELD-65A |
| Aug-57 | TWEEDMOUTH-52D | YORK-50A | WREXHAM-6E | B.GARDENS-54C | 9/57: YORK - 50A | B.GARDENS-54C | GATESHEAD-52A | GATESHEAD-52A | EASTFIELD-65A |
| Jan-58 | TWEEDMOUTH-52D | 1/58: N'TON - 20D | WREXHAM-6E | B.GARDENS-54C | YORK-50A | B.GARDENS-54C | GATESHEAD-52A | GATESHEAD-52A | 1/58: KIPPS - 65E |
| Aug-58 | TWEEDMOUTH-52D | NORMANTON-20D | 10/58: BIDS - 6F | B.GARDENS-54C | 6/58: ARDS - 56B | B.GARDENS-54C | GATESHEAD-52A | GATESHEAD-52A | KIPPS-65E |
| Jan-59 | TWEEDMOUTH-52D | NORMANTON-20D | BIDSTON-6F | B.GARDENS-52J | 2/59: TBY - 51L | 6/59: GHD - 52A | GATESHEAD-52A | 2/59: BLAY - 52C | KIPPS-65E |
| Aug-59 | TWEEDMOUTH-52D | NORMANTON-20D | BIDSTON-6F | 6/59: GHD - 52A | THORNABY-51L | 8/59: T.DCK - 52H | 8/59: T.DCK - 52H | 10/59: HTN - 52B | KIPPS-65E |
| Nov-59 | TWEEDMOUTH-52D | NORMANTON-20D | BIDSTON-6F | GATESHEAD-52A | THORNABY-51L | TYNEDOCK-52H | TYNEDOCK-52H | HEATON-52B | KIPPS-65E |
| Jan-60 | TWEEDMOUTH-52D | NORMANTON-20D | BIDSTON-6F | GATESHEAD-52A | THORNABY-51L | TYNEDOCK-52H | TYNEDOCK-52H | HEATON-52B | KIPPS-65E |
| Apr-60 | 4/60: W/D | NORMANTON-20D | 3/60: W/D | GATESHEAD-52A | THORNABY-51L | TYNEDOCK-52H | 4/60: W/D | HEATON-52B | KIPPS-65E |
| Aug-60 | | NORMANTON-20D | | GATESHEAD-52A | THORNABY-51L | TYNEDOCK-52H | | HEATON-52B | KIPPS-65E |
| Nov-60 | | NORMANTON-20D | | GATESHEAD-52A | THORNABY-51L | 11/60: W/D | | HEATON-52B | KIPPS-65E |

| | 68734 | 68735 | 68736 | 68737 | 68738 | 68739 | 68740 | 68741 | 68742 |
|---|---|---|---|---|---|---|---|---|---|
| Aug-50 | W.HARTLEPOOL-51C | YORK-50A | B.GARDENS-54C | B.GARDENS-54C | HEATON-52B | YORK-50A | MIDDLESBROUGH-51D | YORK-50A | HEATON-52B |
| Jan-51 | W.HARTLEPOOL-51C | YORK-50A | B.GARDENS-54C | B.GARDENS-54C | HEATON-52B | YORK-50A | MIDDLESBROUGH-51D | YORK-50A | HEATON-52B |
| Aug-51 | W.HARTLEPOOL-51C | YORK-50A | B.GARDENS-54C | B.GARDENS-54C | HEATON-52B | YORK-50A | MIDDLESBROUGH-51D | YORK-50A | HEATON-52B |
| Jan-52 | W.HARTLEPOOL-51C | YORK-50A | B.GARDENS-54C | B.GARDENS-54C | HEATON-52B | YORK-50A | MIDDLESBROUGH-51D | YORK-50A | HEATON-52B |
| Aug-52 | W.HARTLEPOOL-51C | YORK-50A | B.GARDENS-54C | B.GARDENS-54C | HEATON-52B | YORK-50A | MIDDLESBROUGH-51D | YORK-50A | HEATON-52B |
| Jan-53 | W.HARTLEPOOL-51C | YORK-50A | B.GARDENS-54C | B.GARDENS-54C | HEATON-52B | YORK-50A | MIDDLESBROUGH-51D | YORK-50A | HEATON-52B |
| Aug-53 | W.HARTLEPOOL-51C | YORK-50A | B.GARDENS-54C | B.GARDENS-54C | HEATON-52B | YORK-50A | MIDDLESBROUGH-51D | 10/53: S'HEAD - 53C | HEATON-52B |
| Jan-54 | W.HARTLEPOOL-51C | YORK-50A | B.GARDENS-54C | B.GARDENS-54C | HEATON-52B | YORK-50A | MIDDLESBROUGH-51D | SPRINGHEAD-53C | HEATON-52B |
| Aug-54 | W.HARTLEPOOL-51C | YORK-50A | B.GARDENS-54C | B.GARDENS-54C | HEATON-52B | YORK-50A | MIDDLESBROUGH-51D | 5/54: DAIRY - 53A | HEATON-52B |
| Jan-55 | W.HARTLEPOOL-51C | YORK-50A | B.GARDENS-54C | B.GARDENS-54C | HEATON-52B | YORK-50A | MIDDLESBROUGH-51D | DAIRYCOATES-53A | HEATON-52B |
| Aug-55 | W.HARTLEPOOL-51C | YORK-50A | B.GARDENS-54C | B.GARDENS-54C | HEATON-52B | YORK-50A | MIDDLESBROUGH-51D | DAIRYCOATES-53A | HEATON-52B |
| Jan-56 | W.HARTLEPOOL-51C | YORK-50A | B.GARDENS-54C | B.GARDENS-54C | HEATON-52B | YORK-50A | MIDDLESBROUGH-51D | DAIRYCOATES-53A | HEATON-52B |
| Aug-56 | W.HARTLEPOOL-51C | YORK-50A | B.GARDENS-54C | B.GARDENS-54C | HEATON-52B | YORK-50A | MIDDLESBROUGH-51D | DAIRYCOATES-53A | HEATON-52B |
| Jan-57 | W.HARTLEPOOL-51C | YORK-50A | 1/57: STAR - 50D | B.GARDENS-54C | HEATON-52B | YORK-50A | MIDDLESBROUGH-51D | DAIRYCOATES-53A | HEATON-52B |
| Aug-57 | W.HARTLEPOOL-51C | YORK-50A | STARBECK-50D | B.GARDENS-54C | HEATON-52B | YORK-50A | MIDDLESBROUGH-51D | 7/57: A.DCK - 53C | HEATON-52B |
| Jan-58 | W.HARTLEPOOL-51C | YORK-50A | STARBECK-50D | B.GARDENS-54C | HEATON-52B | YORK-50A | MIDDLESBROUGH-51D | ALEXDOCK-53C | HEATON-52B |
| Aug-58 | W.HARTLEPOOL-51C | YORK-50A | STARBECK-50D | B.GARDENS-54C | HEATON-52B | YORK-50A | 6/58: TBY - 51L | ALEXDOCK-53C | HEATON-52B |
| Jan-59 | W.HARTLEPOOL-51C | 10/58: W/D | 12/58: YORK - 50A | B.GARDENS-52J | HEATON-52B | 12/58: SCAR - 50E | THORNABY-51L | 2/59: DAIRY - 53A | HEATON-52B |
| Aug-59 | W.HARTLEPOOL-51C | | YORK-50A | 6/59: GHD - 52A | HEATON-52B | 8/59: W/D | THORNABY-51L | 6/59: W/D | HEATON-52B |
| Nov-59 | W.HARTLEPOOL-51C | | YORK-50A | GATESHEAD-52A | HEATON-52B | | THORNABY-51L | | HEATON-52B |
| Jan-60 | W.HARTLEPOOL-51C | | YORK-50A | GATESHEAD-52A | HEATON-52B | | THORNABY-51L | | HEATON-52B |
| Apr-60 | W.HARTLEPOOL-51C | | YORK-50A | GATESHEAD-52A | HEATON-52B | | THORNABY-51L | | HEATON-52B |
| Aug-60 | W.HARTLEPOOL-51C | | YORK-50A | 9/60: W.HPL - 51C | HEATON-52B | | THORNABY-51L | | HEATON-52B |
| Nov-60 | W.HARTLEPOOL-51C | | YORK-50A | W.HARTLEPOOL-51C | HEATON-52B | | THORNABY-51L | | HEATON-52B |

| | 68743 | 68744 | 68745 | 68746 | 68747 | 68748 | 68749 | 68750 | 68751 |
|---|---|---|---|---|---|---|---|---|---|
| Aug-50 | SPRINGHEAD-53C | GATESHEAD-52A | YORK-50A | SPRINGHEAD-53C | SPRINGHEAD-53C | DAIRYCOATES-53A | KITTYBREWSTER-61A | KITTYBREWSTER-61A | SPRINGHEAD-53C |
| Jan-51 | SPRINGHEAD-53C | GATESHEAD-52A | YORK-50A | SPRINGHEAD-53C | SPRINGHEAD-53C | 1/51: DARL - 51A | KITTYBREWSTER-61A | KITTYBREWSTER-61A | SPRINGHEAD-53C |
| Aug-51 | SPRINGHEAD-53C | GATESHEAD-52A | YORK-50A | SPRINGHEAD-53C | SPRINGHEAD-53C | DARLINGTON-51A | KITTYBREWSTER-61A | KITTYBREWSTER-61A | SPRINGHEAD-53C |
| Jan-52 | SPRINGHEAD-53C | GATESHEAD-52A | YORK-50A | SPRINGHEAD-53C | SPRINGHEAD-53C | DARLINGTON-51A | KITTYBREWSTER-61A | KITTYBREWSTER-61A | SPRINGHEAD-53C |
| Aug-52 | SPRINGHEAD-53C | GATESHEAD-52A | YORK-50A | SPRINGHEAD-53C | SPRINGHEAD-53C | DARLINGTON-51A | KITTYBREWSTER-61A | KITTYBREWSTER-61A | SPRINGHEAD-53C |
| Jan-53 | SPRINGHEAD-53C | GATESHEAD-52A | YORK-50A | SPRINGHEAD-53C | SPRINGHEAD-53C | DARLINGTON-51A | KITTYBREWSTER-61A | KITTYBREWSTER-61A | SPRINGHEAD-53C |
| Aug-53 | SPRINGHEAD-53C | GATESHEAD-52A | YORK-50A | SPRINGHEAD-53C | 12/53: DAIRY - 53A | DARLINGTON-51A | KITTYBREWSTER-61A | KITTYBREWSTER-61A | SPRINGHEAD-53C |
| Jan-54 | 12/53: DAIRY - 53A | GATESHEAD-52A | YORK-50A | SPRINGHEAD-53C | 2/54: S'HEAD - 53C | DARLINGTON-51A | KITTYBREWSTER-61A | KITTYBREWSTER-61A | 3/54: DAIRY - 53A |
| Aug-54 | 6/54: T.DCK - 54B | GATESHEAD-52A | YORK-50A | 7/54: SPRING - 53C | 9/54: HTN - 52B | DARLINGTON-51A | KITTYBREWSTER-61A | KITTYBREWSTER-61A | DAIRYCOATES-53A |
| Jan-55 | TYNEDOCK-54B | GATESHEAD-52A | 11/54: SPRING - 53C | SPRINGHEAD-53C | HEATON-52B | DARLINGTON-51A | KITTYBREWSTER-61A | KITTYBREWSTER-61A | DAIRYCOATES-53A |
| Aug-55 | TYNEDOCK-54B | GATESHEAD-52A | SPRINGHEAD-53C | SPRINGHEAD-53C | HEATON-52B | DARLINGTON-51A | KITTYBREWSTER-61A | KITTYBREWSTER-61A | DAIRYCOATES-53A |
| Jan-56 | TYNEDOCK-54B | GATESHEAD-52A | SPRINGHEAD-53C | SPRINGHEAD-53C | HEATON-52B | DARLINGTON-51A | KITTYBREWSTER-61A | KITTYBREWSTER-61A | DAIRYCOATES-53A |
| Aug-56 | TYNEDOCK-54B | GATESHEAD-52A | SPRINGHEAD-53C | SPRINGHEAD-53C | HEATON-52B | DARLINGTON-51A | KITTYBREWSTER-61A | KITTYBREWSTER-61A | DAIRYCOATES-53A |
| Jan-57 | TYNEDOCK-54B | GATESHEAD-52A | SPRINGHEAD-53C | SPRINGHEAD-53C | HEATON-52B | DARLINGTON-51A | KITTYBREWSTER-61A | KITTYBREWSTER-61A | DAIRYCOATES-53A |
| Aug-57 | TYNEDOCK-54B | GATESHEAD-52A | SPRINGHEAD-53C | 7/57: DAIRY - 53A | HEATON-52B | DARLINGTON-51A | KITTYBREWSTER-61A | KITTYBREWSTER-61A | DAIRYCOATES-53A |
| Jan-58 | TYNEDOCK-54B | GATESHEAD-52A | SPRINGHEAD-53C | DAIRYCOATES-53A | HEATON-52B | DARLINGTON-51A | KITTYBREWSTER-61A | KITTYBREWSTER-61A | DAIRYCOATES-53A |
| Aug-58 | TYNEDOCK-54B | GATESHEAD-52A | SPRINGHEAD-53C | DAIRYCOATES-53A | HEATON-52B | DARLINGTON-51A | KITTYBREWSTER-61A | KITTYBREWSTER-61A | DAIRYCOATES-53A |
| Jan-59 | TYNEDOCK-52H | 6/59: W.HPL - 51C | SPRINGHEAD-53C | 12/58: W/D | HEATON-52B | 1/59: W/D | KITTYBREWSTER-61A | KITTYBREWSTER-61A | DAIRYCOATES-53A |
| Aug-59 | TYNEDOCK-52H | 8/59: DARL - 51A | SPRINGHEAD-53C | | HEATON-52B | | KITTYBREWSTER-61A | KITTYBREWSTER-61A | 5/59: W/D |
| Nov-59 | TYNEDOCK-52H | DARLINGTON-51A | SPRINGHEAD-53C | | HEATON-52B | | KITTYBREWSTER-61A | KITTYBREWSTER-61A | |
| Jan-60 | TYNEDOCK-52H | DARLINGTON-51A | SPRINGHEAD-53C | | HEATON-52B | | KITTYBREWSTER-61A | KITTYBREWSTER-61A | |
| Apr-60 | TYNEDOCK-52H | DARLINGTON-51A | SPRINGHEAD-53C | | HEATON-52B | | KITTYBREWSTER-61A | KITTYBREWSTER-61A | |
| Aug-60 | TYNEDOCK-52H | DARLINGTON-51A | SPRINGHEAD-53C | | HEATON-52B | | 9/60: W/D | KITTYBREWSTER-61A | |
| Nov-60 | TYNEDOCK-52H | DARLINGTON-51A | SPRINGHEAD-53C | | 11/60: T.DCK - 52H | | | KITTYBREWSTER-61A | |

| | 68752 | 68753 | 68754 | J52 0-6-0ST (1897) 68757 | 68758 | 68759 | 68760 | 68761 | 68762 |
|---|---|---|---|---|---|---|---|---|---|
| Aug-50 | SPRINGHEAD-53C | SPRINGHEAD-53C | MIDDLESBROUGH-51D | HORNSEY-34B | HORNSEY-34B | HORNSEY-34B | HORNSEY-34B | HORNSEY-34B | COLWICK-38A |
| Jan-51 | SPRINGHEAD-53C | SPRINGHEAD-53C | MIDDLESBROUGH-51D | HORNSEY-34B | HORNSEY-34B | HORNSEY-34B | HORNSEY-34B | HORNSEY-34B | COLWICK-38A |
| Aug-51 | SPRINGHEAD-53C | SPRINGHEAD-53C | MIDDLESBROUGH-51D | HORNSEY-34B | HORNSEY-34B | HORNSEY-34B | HORNSEY-34B | HORNSEY-34B | 8/51: W/D |
| Jan-52 | SPRINGHEAD-53C | SPRINGHEAD-53C | MIDDLESBROUGH-51D | 11/51: KX - 34A | HORNSEY-34B | HORNSEY-34B | HORNSEY-34B | HORNSEY-34B | |
| Aug-52 | SPRINGHEAD-53C | SPRINGHEAD-53C | MIDDLESBROUGH-51D | KINGS CROSS-34A | 9/52: COLW - 38A | 9/52: DCTR - 36A | 9/52: NEW.E - 35A | 10/52: DCTR - 36A | |
| Jan-53 | SPRINGHEAD-53C | SPRINGHEAD-53C | MIDDLESBROUGH-51D | KINGS CROSS-34A | COLWICK-38A | 2/53: S.BGE - 35C | NEWENGLAND-35A | DONCASTER-36A | |
| Aug-53 | SPRINGHEAD-53C | SPRINGHEAD-53C | MIDDLESBROUGH-51D | KINGS CROSS-34A | COLWICK-38A | SPITALBRIDGE-35C | NEWENGLAND-35A | DONCASTER-36A | |
| Jan-54 | SPRINGHEAD-53C | SPRINGHEAD-53C | MIDDLESBROUGH-51D | KINGS CROSS-34A | COLWICK-38A | SPITALBRIDGE-35C | NEWENGLAND-35A | DONCASTER-36A | |
| Aug-54 | SPRINGHEAD-53C | 5/54: DAIRY - 53A | MIDDLESBROUGH-51D | KINGS CROSS-34A | COLWICK-38A | SPITALBRIDGE-35C | NEWENGLAND-35A | DONCASTER-36A | |
| Jan-55 | SPRINGHEAD-53C | DAIRYCOATES-53A | MIDDLESBROUGH-51D | 11/54: W/D | COLWICK-38A | 1/55: NEW.E - 35A | 11/54: W/D | DONCASTER-36A | |
| Aug-55 | SPRINGHEAD-53C | DAIRYCOATES-53A | MIDDLESBROUGH-51D | | COLWICK-38A | NEWENGLAND-35A | | DONCASTER-36A | |
| Jan-56 | SPRINGHEAD-53C | DAIRYCOATES-53A | MIDDLESBROUGH-51D | | 11/55: W/D | 11/55: COLW - 38A | | DONCASTER-36A | |
| Aug-56 | SPRINGHEAD-53C | DAIRYCOATES-53A | 8/56: DARL - 51A | | | 7/56: W/D | | DONCASTER-36A | |
| Jan-57 | SPRINGHEAD-53C | DAIRYCOATES-53A | DARLINGTON-51A | | | | | DONCASTER-36A | |
| Aug-57 | 7/57: DAIRY - 53A | DAIRYCOATES-53A | DARLINGTON-51A | | | | | 5/57: W/D | |
| Jan-58 | DAIRYCOATES-53A | DAIRYCOATES-53A | DARLINGTON-51A | | | | | | |
| Aug-58 | DAIRYCOATES-53A | DAIRYCOATES-53A | DARLINGTON-51A | | | | | | |
| Jan-59 | DAIRYCOATES-53A | DAIRYCOATES-53A | DARLINGTON-51A | | | | | | |
| Aug-59 | DAIRYCOATES-53A | DAIRYCOATES-53A | DARLINGTON-51A | | | | | | |
| Nov-59 | DAIRYCOATES-53A | DAIRYCOATES-53A | DARLINGTON-51A | | | | | | |
| Jan-60 | 2/60: W/D | DAIRYCOATES-53A | DARLINGTON-51A | | | | | | |
| Apr-60 | | DAIRYCOATES-50B | DARLINGTON-51A | | | | | | |
| Aug-60 | | 8/60: W/D | DARLINGTON-51A | | | | | | |
| Nov-60 | | | DARLINGTON-51A | | | | | | |

With express freight handled by 2-6-0's or 2-6-2's and mineral trains worked by 2-8-0's, one might justifiably wonder why the 0-6-0 tender engine remained hard at work in large numbers well into the final days of steam. The answer lies in the restrictions placed upon axle loadings and the fact that most steam engines were a compromise between power and weight. Generally the more powerful the engine, the greater its weight and the more restricted its movements became. In addition there were many cases where the additional power of an eight coupled engine could not be utilised: in Scotland (NBR) the maximum number of vehicles a goods train could convey was sixty vehicles and since the capacity of a 5F 0-6-0 locomotive was in excess of this figure, there was very little point in providing anything larger.

## 68763 – 68771

| | 68763 | 68764 | 68765 | 68766 | 68767 | 68768 | 68769 | 68770 | 68771 |
|---|---|---|---|---|---|---|---|---|---|
| Aug-50 | DONCASTER - 36A | KINGS CROSS - 34A | NEWENGLAND - 35A | RETFORD - 36E | COLWCK - 38A | COLWCK - 38A | DONCASTER - 36A | KINGS CROSS - 34A | KINGS CROSS - 34A |
| Jan-51 | 10/50: W/D | KINGS CROSS - 34A | NEWENGLAND - 35A | 3/51: DCTR - 36A | 11/50: W/D | COLWCK - 38A | DONCASTER - 36A | KINGS CROSS - 34A | KINGS CROSS - 34A |
| Aug-51 | | KINGS CROSS - 34A | NEWENGLAND - 35A | DONCASTER - 36A | | COLWCK - 38A | DONCASTER - 36A | KINGS CROSS - 34A | KINGS CROSS - 34A |
| Jan-52 | | KINGS CROSS - 34A | NEWENGLAND - 35A | 1/52: W/D | | COLWCK - 38A | DONCASTER - 36A | 11/51: HSEY - 34B | KINGS CROSS - 34A |
| Aug-52 | | KINGS CROSS - 34A | NEWENGLAND - 35A | | | COLWCK - 38A | DONCASTER - 36A | 10/52: DARN - 39B | KINGS CROSS - 34A |
| Jan-53 | | KINGS CROSS - 34A | NEWENGLAND - 35A | | | COLWCK - 38A | DONCASTER - 36A | 2/53: ARDS - 37A | KINGS CROSS - 34A |
| Aug-53 | | KINGS CROSS - 34A | NEWENGLAND - 35A | | | COLWCK - 38A | DONCASTER - 36A | 8/53: W/D | KINGS CROSS - 34A |
| Jan-54 | | KINGS CROSS - 34A | NEWENGLAND - 35A | | | COLWCK - 38A | DONCASTER - 36A | | 10/53: NEW.E - 35A |
| Aug-54 | | KINGS CROSS - 34A | NEWENGLAND - 35A | | | COLWCK - 38A | DONCASTER - 36A | | NEWENGLAND - 35A |
| Jan-55 | | 11/54: W/D | 1/55: COLW - 38A | | | COLWCK - 38A | DONCASTER - 36A | | NEWENGLAND - 35A |
| Aug-55 | | | COLWCK - 38A | | | COLWCK - 38A | 9/55: W/D | | 10/55: W/D |
| Jan-56 | | | 12/55: W/D | | | COLWCK - 38A | | | |
| Aug-56 | | | | | | COLWCK - 38A | | | |
| Jan-57 | | | | | | COLWCK - 38A | | | |
| Aug-57 | | | | | | 10/57: W/D | | | |
| Jan-58 | | | | | | | | | |
| Aug-58 | | | | | | | | | |
| Jan-59 | | | | | | | | | |
| Aug-59 | | | | | | | | | |
| Nov-59 | | | | | | | | | |
| Jan-60 | | | | | | | | | |
| Apr-60 | | | | | | | | | |
| Aug-60 | | | | | | | | | |
| Nov-60 | | | | | | | | | |

## 68772 – 68780

| | 68772 | 68773 | 68774 | 68775 | 68776 | 68777 | 68778 | 68779 | 68780 |
|---|---|---|---|---|---|---|---|---|---|
| Aug-50 | KINGS CROSS - 34A | HORNSEY - 34B | HORNSEY - 34B | DONCASTER - 36A | HORNSEY - 34B | HORNSEY - 34B | HORNSEY - 34B | COLWCK - 38A | KINGS CROSS - 34A |
| Jan-51 | KINGS CROSS - 34A | HORNSEY - 34B | HORNSEY - 34B | DONCASTER - 36A | HORNSEY - 34B | HORNSEY - 34B | HORNSEY - 34B | COLWCK - 38A | KINGS CROSS - 34A |
| Aug-51 | KINGS CROSS - 34A | HORNSEY - 34B | HORNSEY - 34B | DONCASTER - 36A | HORNSEY - 34B | HORNSEY - 34B | HORNSEY - 34B | COLWCK - 38A | KINGS CROSS - 34A |
| Jan-52 | KINGS CROSS - 34A | HORNSEY - 34B | HORNSEY - 34B | DONCASTER - 36A | HORNSEY - 34B | HORNSEY - 34B | HORNSEY - 34B | COLWCK - 38A | KINGS CROSS - 34A |
| Aug-52 | KINGS CROSS - 34A | 9/52: COLW - 38A | 10/52: ARDS - 37A | 6/52: W/D | 10/52: ARDS - 37A | 10/52: COLW - 38A | 9/52: DCTR - 36A | 4/53: W/D | KINGS CROSS - 34A |
| Jan-53 | KINGS CROSS - 34A | COLWCK - 38A | 11/52: DCTR - 36A | | 11/52: DCTR - 36A | COLWCK - 38A | DONCASTER - 36A | | KINGS CROSS - 34A |
| Aug-53 | KINGS CROSS - 34A | 4/53: W/D | 7/53: W/D | | DONCASTER - 36A | COLWCK - 38A | DONCASTER - 36A | | 1/54: W/D |
| Jan-54 | KINGS CROSS - 34A | | | | 10/53: W/D | COLWCK - 38A | DONCASTER - 36A | | |
| Aug-54 | 9/54: W/D | | | | | 11/54: W/D | DONCASTER - 36A | | |
| Jan-55 | | | | | | | DONCASTER - 36A | | |
| Aug-55 | | | | | | | DONCASTER - 36A | | |
| Jan-56 | | | | | | | DONCASTER - 36A | | |
| Aug-56 | | | | | | | DONCASTER - 36A | | |
| Jan-57 | | | | | | | 7/57: W/D | | |
| Aug-57 | | | | | | | | | |
| Jan-58 | | | | | | | | | |
| Aug-58 | | | | | | | | | |
| Jan-59 | | | | | | | | | |
| Aug-59 | | | | | | | | | |
| Nov-59 | | | | | | | | | |
| Jan-60 | | | | | | | | | |
| Apr-60 | | | | | | | | | |
| Aug-60 | | | | | | | | | |
| Nov-60 | | | | | | | | | |

## 68781 – 68790

| | 68781 | 68783 | 68784 | 68785 | 68786 | 68787 | 68788 | 68789 | 68790 |
|---|---|---|---|---|---|---|---|---|---|
| Aug-50 | HORNSEY - 34B | HORNSEY - 34B | HORNSEY - 34B | HORNSEY - 34B | DONCASTER - 36A | HORNSEY - 34B | HORNSEY - 34B | NEWENGLAND - 35A | ARDSLEY - 37A |
| Jan-51 | HORNSEY - 34B | HORNSEY - 34B | HORNSEY - 34B | HORNSEY - 34B | 1/51: NEW.E - 35A | HORNSEY - 34B | HORNSEY - 34B | NEWENGLAND - 35A | ARDSLEY - 37A |
| Aug-51 | HORNSEY - 34B | HORNSEY - 34B | HORNSEY - 34B | HORNSEY - 34B | NEWENGLAND - 35A | HORNSEY - 34B | HORNSEY - 34B | NEWENGLAND - 35A | ARDSLEY - 37A |
| Jan-52 | HORNSEY - 34B | HORNSEY - 34B | HORNSEY - 34B | HORNSEY - 34B | NEWENGLAND - 35A | HORNSEY - 34B | HORNSEY - 34B | NEWENGLAND - 35A | ARDSLEY - 37A |
| Aug-52 | 9/52: COLW - 38A | 10/52: DARN - 39B | 9/52: DCTR - 36A | 9/52: DCTR - 36A | NEWENGLAND - 35A | 9/52: COLW - 38A | 9/52: COLW - 38A | 4/52: W/D | ARDSLEY - 37A |
| Jan-53 | COLWCK - 38A | 2/53: S.BGE - 35C | DONCASTER - 36A | DONCASTER - 36A | NEWENGLAND - 35A | COLWCK - 38A | COLWCK - 38A | | ARDSLEY - 37A |
| Aug-53 | COLWCK - 38A | SPITAL BRIDGE - 35C | DONCASTER - 36A | DONCASTER - 36A | 11/53: W/D | COLWCK - 38A | COLWCK - 38A | | ARDSLEY - 37A |
| Jan-54 | COLWCK - 38A | SPITAL BRIDGE - 35C | DONCASTER - 36A | DONCASTER - 36A | | COLWCK - 38A | 12/54: W/D | | ARDSLEY - 37A |
| Aug-54 | COLWCK - 38A | SPITAL BRIDGE - 35C | DONCASTER - 36A | DONCASTER - 36A | | COLWCK - 38A | | | ARDSLEY - 37A |
| Jan-55 | 12/54: W/D | 1/55: NEW.E - 35A | DONCASTER - 36A | DONCASTER - 36A | | COLWCK - 38A | | | ARDSLEY - 37A |
| Aug-55 | | NEWENGLAND - 35A | DONCASTER - 36A | 11/55: COLW - 38A | | 10/55: W/D | | | 7/55: W/D |
| Jan-56 | | 1/56: W/D | DONCASTER - 36A | COLWCK - 38A | | | | | |
| Aug-56 | | | DONCASTER - 36A | COLWCK - 38A | | | | | |
| Jan-57 | | | DONCASTER - 36A | 1/58: W/D | | | | | |
| Aug-57 | | | 11/57: W/D | | | | | | |
| Jan-58 | | | | | | | | | |
| Aug-58 | | | | | | | | | |
| Jan-59 | | | | | | | | | |
| Aug-59 | | | | | | | | | |
| Nov-59 | | | | | | | | | |
| Jan-60 | | | | | | | | | |
| Apr-60 | | | | | | | | | |
| Aug-60 | | | | | | | | | |
| Nov-60 | | | | | | | | | |

## 68791 – 68799

| | 68791 | 68792 | 68793 | 68794 | 68795 | 68796 | 68797 | 68798 | 68799 |
|---|---|---|---|---|---|---|---|---|---|
| Aug-50 | HORNSEY - 34B | COLWCK - 38A | HORNSEY - 34B | HORNSEY - 34B | HORNSEY - 34B | HORNSEY - 34B | KINGS CROSS - 34A | NEWENGLAND - 35A | KINGS CROSS - 34A |
| Jan-51 | HORNSEY - 34B | COLWCK - 38A | HORNSEY - 34B | HORNSEY - 34B | HORNSEY - 34B | HORNSEY - 34B | KINGS CROSS - 34A | 12/50: GRAN - 35B | KINGS CROSS - 34A |
| Aug-51 | HORNSEY - 34B | COLWCK - 38A | HORNSEY - 34B | HORNSEY - 34B | HORNSEY - 34B | HORNSEY - 34B | KINGS CROSS - 34A | GRANTHAM - 35B | KINGS CROSS - 34A |
| Jan-52 | HORNSEY - 34B | COLWCK - 38A | HORNSEY - 34B | HORNSEY - 34B | HORNSEY - 34B | HORNSEY - 34B | KINGS CROSS - 34A | GRANTHAM - 35B | KINGS CROSS - 34A |
| Aug-52 | 10/52: COLW - 38A | 6/52: W/D | 10/52: FROD - 36C | 9/52: DCTR - 36A | 10/52: DCTR - 36A | 10/52: DCTR - 36A | KINGS CROSS - 34A | 1/53: FROD - 36C | KINGS CROSS - 34A |
| Jan-53 | COLWCK - 38A | | 7/53: DCTR - 36A | DONCASTER - 36A | DONCASTER - 36A | DONCASTER - 36A | 2/53: S.BGE - 35C | 5/53: COLW - 38A | KINGS CROSS - 34A |
| Aug-53 | COLWCK - 38A | | 8/53: NEW.E - 35A | DONCASTER - 36A | DONCASTER - 36A | DONCASTER - 36A | SPITAL BRIDGE - 35C | COLWCK - 38A | KINGS CROSS - 34A |
| Jan-54 | COLWCK - 38A | | NEWENGLAND - 35A | 12/53: W/D | DONCASTER - 36A | DONCASTER - 36A | SPITAL BRIDGE - 35C | COLWCK - 38A | KINGS CROSS - 34A |
| Aug-54 | COLWCK - 38A | | NEWENGLAND - 35A | | DONCASTER - 36A | DONCASTER - 36A | SPITAL BRIDGE - 35C | 11/54: W/D | KINGS CROSS - 34A |
| Jan-55 | 11/54: W/D | | NEWENGLAND - 35A | | DONCASTER - 36A | DONCASTER - 36A | SPITAL BRIDGE - 35C | | 10/54: W/D |
| Aug-55 | | | NEWENGLAND - 35A | | 11/55: W/D | 11/55: W/D | 11/55: W/D | | |
| Jan-56 | | | 5/56: W/D | | | | | | |
| Aug-56 | | | | | | | | | |
| Jan-57 | | | | | | | | | |
| Aug-57 | | | | | | | | | |
| Jan-58 | | | | | | | | | |
| Aug-58 | | | | | | | | | |
| Jan-59 | | | | | | | | | |
| Aug-59 | | | | | | | | | |
| Nov-59 | | | | | | | | | |
| Jan-60 | | | | | | | | | |
| Apr-60 | | | | | | | | | |
| Aug-60 | | | | | | | | | |
| Nov-60 | | | | | | | | | |

As a rule of thumb, on level track the vehicles (loaded goods) for each category of locomotive was: 1F – 46 wagons, 2F – 50, 3F – 53, 4F – 58, 5F – 62, 6F – 66, 7F – 72 and 8F – 80 vehicles. For loaded mineral trains the limits were about 55% less whilst trains of empties could take about 12% more. Thus an eight coupled engine was only necessary if the capacity of the line could accept a train which approached the maximum the 2-8-0 could haul or there were gradients of such severity that loads for an 0-6-0 became absurdly small. On lines which had a length limit of 60 vehicles and were more or less level, it can be seen that the a 5F engine such as a J39 0-6-0 could haul more than the line could handle. The length of trains was influenced by the capacity of loop lines rather than the power of locomotives and on double line sections such as Whitemoor to Temple Mills goods trains tended to be shuffled from

## 68800 – 68808

| | 68800 | 68801 | 68802 | 68803 | 68804 | 68805 | 68806 | 68807 | 68808 |
|---|---|---|---|---|---|---|---|---|---|
| Aug-50 | DONCASTER - 36A | GRANTHAM - 35B | | KINGS CROSS - 34A | DONCASTER - 36A | KINGS CROSS - 34A | DONCASTER - 36A | COLWICK - 38A | HORNSEY - 34B |
| Jan-51 | DONCASTER - 36A | 11/50: W/D | | KINGS CROSS - 34A | DONCASTER - 36A | KINGS CROSS - 34A | DONCASTER - 36A | COLWICK - 38A | HORNSEY - 34B |
| Aug-51 | DONCASTER - 36A | | KINGS CROSS - 34A | KINGS CROSS - 34A | DONCASTER - 36A | KINGS CROSS - 34A | DONCASTER - 36A | COLWICK - 38A | HORNSEY - 34B |
| Jan-52 | DONCASTER - 36A | | KINGS CROSS - 34A | KINGS CROSS - 34A | DONCASTER - 36A | KINGS CROSS - 34A | DONCASTER - 36A | COLWICK - 38A | HORNSEY - 34B |
| Aug-52 | DONCASTER - 36A | | KINGS CROSS - 34A | KINGS CROSS - 34A | DONCASTER - 36A | KINGS CROSS - 34A | DONCASTER - 36A | COLWICK - 38A | HORNSEY - 34B |
| Jan-53 | DONCASTER - 36A | | KINGS CROSS - 34A | KINGS CROSS - 34A | DONCASTER - 36A | KINGS CROSS - 34A | DONCASTER - 36A | COLWICK - 38A | 10/52: ARDS - 37A |
| Aug-53 | DONCASTER - 36A | | KINGS CROSS - 34A | 8/53: W/D | DONCASTER - 36A | KINGS CROSS - 34A | DONCASTER - 36A | COLWICK - 38A | 11/52: HSEY - 34B |
| Jan-54 | DONCASTER - 36A | | KINGS CROSS - 34A | | DONCASTER - 36A | KINGS CROSS - 34A | DONCASTER - 36A | COLWICK - 38A | HORNSEY - 34B |
| Aug-54 | DONCASTER - 36A | | KINGS CROSS - 34A | | DONCASTER - 36A | KINGS CROSS - 34A | DONCASTER - 36A | COLWICK - 38A | HORNSEY - 34B |
| Jan-55 | DONCASTER - 36A | | 11/54: W/D | | DONCASTER - 36A | KINGS CROSS - 34A | DONCASTER - 36A | COLWICK - 38A | HORNSEY - 34B |
| Aug-55 | DONCASTER - 36A | | | | DONCASTER - 36A | KINGS CROSS - 34A | DONCASTER - 36A | COLWICK - 38A | HORNSEY - 34B |
| Jan-56 | DONCASTER - 36A | | | | 10/55: W/D | 10/55: W/D | 11/55: W/D | 9/55: W/D | HORNSEY - 34B |
| Aug-56 | DONCASTER - 36A | | | | | | | | HORNSEY - 34B |
| Jan-57 | DONCASTER - 36A | | | | | | | | HORNSEY - 34B |
| Aug-57 | DONCASTER - 36A | | | | | | | | 4/57: W/D |
| Jan-58 | DONCASTER - 36A | | | | | | | | |
| Aug-58 | 7/58: W/D | | | | | | | | |
| Jan-59 | | | | | | | | | |
| Aug-59 | | | | | | | | | |
| Nov-59 | | | | | | | | | |
| Jan-60 | | | | | | | | | |
| Apr-60 | | | | | | | | | |
| Aug-60 | | | | | | | | | |
| Nov-60 | | | | | | | | | |

## 68809 – 68818

| | 68809 | 68810 | 68811 | 68812 | 68813 | 68814 | 68815 | 68817 | 68818 |
|---|---|---|---|---|---|---|---|---|---|
| Aug-50 | KINGS CROSS - 34A | COLWICK - 38A | HORNSEY - 34B | COLWICK - 38A | DONCASTER - 36A | COLWICK - 38A | HORNSEY - 34B | NEWENGLAND - 35A | KINGS CROSS - 34A |
| Jan-51 | KINGS CROSS - 34A | COLWICK - 38A | HORNSEY - 34B | COLWICK - 38A | DONCASTER - 36A | COLWICK - 38A | HORNSEY - 34B | NEWENGLAND - 35A | KINGS CROSS - 34A |
| Aug-51 | KINGS CROSS - 34A | COLWICK - 38A | HORNSEY - 34B | COLWICK - 38A | DONCASTER - 36A | COLWICK - 38A | HORNSEY - 34B | NEWENGLAND - 35A | KINGS CROSS - 34A |
| Jan-52 | KINGS CROSS - 34A | COLWICK - 38A | HORNSEY - 34B | COLWICK - 38A | DONCASTER - 36A | COLWICK - 38A | HORNSEY - 34B | NEWENGLAND - 35A | KINGS CROSS - 34A |
| Aug-52 | KINGS CROSS - 34A | COLWICK - 38A | 10/52: DARN - 39B | COLWICK - 38A | DONCASTER - 36A | COLWICK - 38A | 10/52: FROD - 36C | NEWENGLAND - 35A | KINGS CROSS - 34A |
| Jan-53 | 2/53: S.BGE - 35C | COLWICK - 38A | 2/53: DCTR - 36A | COLWICK - 38A | DONCASTER - 36A | COLWICK - 38A | 1/53: GRAN - 35B | NEWENGLAND - 35A | KINGS CROSS - 34A |
| Aug-53 | SPITAL BRIDGE - 35C | COLWICK - 38A | DONCASTER - 36A | COLWICK - 38A | DONCASTER - 36A | COLWICK - 38A | GRANTHAM - 35B | NEWENGLAND - 35A | KINGS CROSS - 34A |
| Jan-54 | SPITAL BRIDGE - 35C | COLWICK - 38A | DONCASTER - 36A | COLWICK - 38A | DONCASTER - 36A | COLWICK - 38A | GRANTHAM - 35B | NEWENGLAND - 35A | KINGS CROSS - 34A |
| Aug-54 | SPITAL BRIDGE - 35C | COLWICK - 38A | DONCASTER - 36A | COLWICK - 38A | DONCASTER - 36A | COLWICK - 38A | GRANTHAM - 35B | NEWENGLAND - 35A | KINGS CROSS - 34A |
| Jan-55 | SPITAL BRIDGE - 35C | COLWICK - 38A | DONCASTER - 36A | COLWICK - 38A | DONCASTER - 36A | COLWICK - 38A | GRANTHAM - 35B | 5/55: S.BGE - 35C | KINGS CROSS - 34A |
| Aug-55 | SPITAL BRIDGE - 35C | COLWICK - 38A | DONCASTER - 36A | 9/55: W/D | DONCASTER - 36A | COLWICK - 38A | GRANTHAM - 35B | 10/55: NEW.E - 35A | KINGS CROSS - 34A |
| Jan-56 | 12/55: NEW.E - 35A | 11/55: W/D | DONCASTER - 36A | | DONCASTER - 36A | 11/55: W/D | NEWENGLAND - 35A | NEWENGLAND - 35A | 11/55: W/D |
| Aug-56 | 9/56: W/D | | DONCASTER - 36A | | 9/56: W/D | | NEWENGLAND - 35A | 4/56: DCTR - 36A | |
| Jan-57 | | | 6/57: W/D | | | | 12/57: DCTR - 36A | DONCASTER - 36A | |
| Aug-57 | | | | | | | 5/58: W/D | DONCASTER - 36A | |
| Jan-58 | | | | | | | | 4/58: W/D | |
| Aug-58 | | | | | | | | | |
| Jan-59 | | | | | | | | | |
| Aug-59 | | | | | | | | | |
| Nov-59 | | | | | | | | | |
| Jan-60 | | | | | | | | | |
| Apr-60 | | | | | | | | | |
| Aug-60 | | | | | | | | | |
| Nov-60 | | | | | | | | | |

## 68819 – 68827

| | 68819 | 68820 | 68821 | 68822 | 68823 | 68824 | 68825 | 68826 | 68827 |
|---|---|---|---|---|---|---|---|---|---|
| Aug-50 | NEWENGLAND - 35A | NEWENGLAND - 35A | NEWENGLAND - 35A | KINGS CROSS - 34A | NEWENGLAND - 35A | NEWENGLAND - 35A | HORNSEY - 34B | HORNSEY - 34B | HORNSEY - 34B |
| Jan-51 | NEWENGLAND - 35A | NEWENGLAND - 35A | NEWENGLAND - 35A | KINGS CROSS - 34A | NEWENGLAND - 35A | NEWENGLAND - 35A | HORNSEY - 34B | HORNSEY - 34B | HORNSEY - 34B |
| Aug-51 | NEWENGLAND - 35A | NEWENGLAND - 35A | NEWENGLAND - 35A | KINGS CROSS - 34A | NEWENGLAND - 35A | NEWENGLAND - 35A | HORNSEY - 34B | HORNSEY - 34B | HORNSEY - 34B |
| Jan-52 | NEWENGLAND - 35A | NEWENGLAND - 35A | NEWENGLAND - 35A | KINGS CROSS - 34A | NEWENGLAND - 35A | NEWENGLAND - 35A | HORNSEY - 34B | HORNSEY - 34B | 11/51: KX - 34A |
| Aug-52 | NEWENGLAND - 35A | NEWENGLAND - 35A | NEWENGLAND - 35A | KINGS CROSS - 34A | NEWENGLAND - 35A | 10/52: ANNES - 38B | 10/52: ANNES - 38B | 9/52: NEW.E - 35A | KINGS CROSS - 34A |
| Jan-53 | NEWENGLAND - 35A | NEWENGLAND - 35A | NEWENGLAND - 35A | KINGS CROSS - 34A | NEWENGLAND - 35A | 11/52: HSEY - 34B | 11/52: HSEY - 34B | NEWENGLAND - 35A | KINGS CROSS - 34A |
| Aug-53 | NEWENGLAND - 35A | NEWENGLAND - 35A | NEWENGLAND - 35A | KINGS CROSS - 34A | NEWENGLAND - 35A | 10/53: HSEY - 34B | 8/53: W/D | NEWENGLAND - 35A | KINGS CROSS - 34A |
| Jan-54 | 10/54: HIT - 34D | NEWENGLAND - 35A | NEWENGLAND - 35A | KINGS CROSS - 34A | NEWENGLAND - 35A | HORNSEY - 34B | | NEWENGLAND - 35A | KINGS CROSS - 34A |
| Aug-54 | 2/55: NEW.E - 35A | NEWENGLAND - 35A | 11/54: COLW - 38A | KINGS CROSS - 34A | NEWENGLAND - 35A | HORNSEY - 34B | | NEWENGLAND - 35A | KINGS CROSS - 34A |
| Jan-55 | NEWENGLAND - 35A | NEWENGLAND - 35A | COLWICK - 38A | KINGS CROSS - 34A | NEWENGLAND - 35A | HORNSEY - 34B | | 1/55: COLW - 38A | KINGS CROSS - 34A |
| Aug-55 | 11/55: COLW - 38A | NEWENGLAND - 35A | 3/56: W/D | KINGS CROSS - 34A | NEWENGLAND - 35A | HORNSEY - 34B | | COLWICK - 38A | 1/56: W/D |
| Jan-56 | 6/56: W/D | 12/55: W/D | | KINGS CROSS - 34A | NEWENGLAND - 35A | HORNSEY - 34B | | COLWICK - 38A | |
| Aug-56 | | | | 9/56: W/D | NEWENGLAND - 35A | HORNSEY - 34B | | 3/57: W/D | |
| Jan-57 | | | | | 4/57: DCTR - 36A | HORNSEY - 34B | | | |
| Aug-57 | | | | | 6/57: W/D | HORNSEY - 34B | | | |
| Jan-58 | | | | | | HORNSEY - 34B | | | |
| Aug-58 | | | | | | HORNSEY - 34B | | | |
| Jan-59 | | | | | | 4/59: ARDS - 56B | | | |
| Aug-59 | | | | | | 5/59: W/D | | | |
| Nov-59 | | | | | | | | | |
| Jan-60 | | | | | | | | | |
| Apr-60 | | | | | | | | | |
| Aug-60 | | | | | | | | | |
| Nov-60 | | | | | | | | | |

## 68828 – 68836

| | 68828 | 68829 | 68830 | 68831 | 68832 | 68833 | 68834 | 68835 | 68836 |
|---|---|---|---|---|---|---|---|---|---|
| Aug-50 | KINGS CROSS - 34A | HORNSEY - 34B | KINGS CROSS - 34A | KINGS CROSS - 34A | KINGS CROSS - 34A | HORNSEY - 34B | HORNSEY - 34B | DONCASTER - 36A | DONCASTER - 36A |
| Jan-51 | KINGS CROSS - 34A | HORNSEY - 34B | KINGS CROSS - 34A | KINGS CROSS - 34A | KINGS CROSS - 34A | HORNSEY - 34B | HORNSEY - 34B | DONCASTER - 36A | DONCASTER - 36A |
| Aug-51 | KINGS CROSS - 34A | HORNSEY - 34B | KINGS CROSS - 34A | KINGS CROSS - 34A | KINGS CROSS - 34A | HORNSEY - 34B | HORNSEY - 34B | DONCASTER - 36A | DONCASTER - 36A |
| Jan-52 | KINGS CROSS - 34A | 11/51: KX - 34A | KINGS CROSS - 34A | KINGS CROSS - 34A | KINGS CROSS - 34A | HORNSEY - 34B | HORNSEY - 34B | DONCASTER - 36A | DONCASTER - 36A |
| Aug-52 | KINGS CROSS - 34A | KINGS CROSS - 34A | KINGS CROSS - 34A | KINGS CROSS - 34A | KINGS CROSS - 34A | 10/52: DCTR - 36A | 10/52: ANNES - 38B | DONCASTER - 36A | DONCASTER - 36A |
| Jan-53 | 2/53: NEW.E - 35A | KINGS CROSS - 34A | KINGS CROSS - 34A | 2/53: S.BGE - 35C | KINGS CROSS - 34A | DONCASTER - 36A | 11/52: HSEY - 34B | DONCASTER - 36A | DONCASTER - 36A |
| Aug-53 | NEWENGLAND - 35A | KINGS CROSS - 34A | KINGS CROSS - 34A | SPITAL BRIDGE - 35C | KINGS CROSS - 34A | DONCASTER - 36A | HORNSEY - 34B | DONCASTER - 36A | DONCASTER - 36A |
| Jan-54 | NEWENGLAND - 35A | KINGS CROSS - 34A | KINGS CROSS - 34A | 3/54: GRAN - 35B | KINGS CROSS - 34A | DONCASTER - 36A | HORNSEY - 34B | DONCASTER - 36A | DONCASTER - 36A |
| Aug-54 | NEWENGLAND - 35A | KINGS CROSS - 34A | KINGS CROSS - 34A | GRANTHAM - 35B | KINGS CROSS - 34A | 5/54: MEX - 36B | HORNSEY - 34B | DONCASTER - 36A | DONCASTER - 36A |
| Jan-55 | NEWENGLAND - 35A | KINGS CROSS - 34A | KINGS CROSS - 34A | GRANTHAM - 35B | KINGS CROSS - 34A | MEXBOROUGH - 36B | HORNSEY - 34B | DONCASTER - 36A | DONCASTER - 36A |
| Aug-55 | NEWENGLAND - 35A | KINGS CROSS - 34A | KINGS CROSS - 34A | GRANTHAM - 35B | KINGS CROSS - 34A | MEXBOROUGH - 36B | HORNSEY - 34B | DONCASTER - 36A | DONCASTER - 36A |
| Jan-56 | NEWENGLAND - 35A | KINGS CROSS - 34A | KINGS CROSS - 34A | 5/56: NEW.E - 35A | KINGS CROSS - 34A | 2/56: W/D | HORNSEY - 34B | DONCASTER - 36A | DONCASTER - 36A |
| Aug-56 | NEWENGLAND - 35A | 8/56: COLW - 38A | 7/56: W/D | NEWENGLAND - 35A | KINGS CROSS - 34A | | HORNSEY - 34B | DONCASTER - 36A | 9/56: W/D |
| Jan-57 | NEWENGLAND - 35A | COLWICK - 38A | | 4/57: KX - 34A | KINGS CROSS - 34A | | HORNSEY - 34B | DONCASTER - 36A | |
| Aug-57 | NEWENGLAND - 35A | COLWICK - 38A | | KINGS CROSS - 34A | 10/57: W/D | | HORNSEY - 34B | DONCASTER - 36A | |
| Jan-58 | 12/57: DCTR - 36A | 2/58: W/D | | KINGS CROSS - 34A | | | HORNSEY - 34B | 2/58: W/D | |
| Aug-58 | 2/58: W/D | | | KINGS CROSS - 34A | | | HORNSEY - 34B | | |
| Jan-59 | | | | 1/59: W/D | | | 2/59: ARDS - 56B | | |
| Aug-59 | | | | | | | ARDSLEY - 56B | | |
| Nov-59 | | | | | | | ARDSLEY - 56B | | |
| Jan-60 | | | | | | | ARDSLEY - 56B | | |
| Apr-60 | | | | | | | 3/60: W/D | | |
| Aug-60 | | | | | | | | | |
| Nov-60 | | | | | | | | | |

one loop to the next. Occasionally goods trains would be run with a load greater than the usual maximum but they had to be regulated with the greatest care to ensure they were not refuged in a loop that was too short.

At the other extreme there were instances where an eight coupled engine had an unassailable advantage over an 0-6-0; a good example being the Manchester – Sheffield (GCR) route where the route permitted trains of up to 100 wagons. On the steepest section of the line, as far as Dunford, a J39 was limited to sixty empty wagons whilst an O2 2-8-0 could take eighty-six.

| | 68837 | 68838 | 68839 | 68840 | 68841 | 68842 | 68843 | 68844 | 68846 |
|---|---|---|---|---|---|---|---|---|---|
| Aug-50 | DONCASTER-36A | KINGS CROSS-34A | COLWICK-38A | NEWENGLAND-35A | DONCASTER-36A | DONCASTER-36A | DONCASTER-36A | NEWENGLAND-35A | NEWENGLAND-35A |
| Jan-51 | DONCASTER-36A | KINGS CROSS-34A | COLWICK-38A | NEWENGLAND-35A | DONCASTER-36A | DONCASTER-36A | DONCASTER-36A | NEWENGLAND-35A | NEWENGLAND-35A |
| Aug-51 | DONCASTER-36A | KINGS CROSS-34A | COLWICK-38A | NEWENGLAND-35A | DONCASTER-36A | DONCASTER-36A | DONCASTER-36A | NEWENGLAND-35A | NEWENGLAND-35A |
| Jan-52 | DONCASTER-36A | KINGS CROSS-34A | COLWICK-38A | NEWENGLAND-35A | DONCASTER-36A | DONCASTER-36A | DONCASTER-36A | NEWENGLAND-35A | NEWENGLAND-35A |
| Aug-52 | DONCASTER-36A | KINGS CROSS-34A | 9/52: LTR(GC)-38C | NEWENGLAND-35A | DONCASTER-36A | DONCASTER-36A | DONCASTER-36A | NEWENGLAND-35A | NEWENGLAND-35A |
| Jan-53 | 11/52: ARDS-37A | KINGS CROSS-34A | LEICESTER(GC)-38C | NEWENGLAND-35A | DONCASTER-36A | DONCASTER-36A | DONCASTER-36A | NEWENGLAND-35A | NEWENGLAND-35A |
| Aug-53 | ARDSLEY-37A | KINGS CROSS-34A | LEICESTER(GC)-38C | NEWENGLAND-35A | DONCASTER-36A | DONCASTER-36A | DONCASTER-36A | NEWENGLAND-35A | NEWENGLAND-35A |
| Jan-54 | ARDSLEY-37A | KINGS CROSS-34A | LEICESTER(GC)-38C | NEWENGLAND-35A | DONCASTER-36A | DONCASTER-36A | DONCASTER-36A | NEWENGLAND-35A | NEWENGLAND-35A |
| Aug-54 | ARDSLEY-37A | KINGS CROSS-34A | LEICESTER(GC)-38C | NEWENGLAND-35A | DONCASTER-36A | DONCASTER-36A | DONCASTER-36A | 10/54: W/D | NEWENGLAND-35A |
| Jan-55 | ARDSLEY-37A | KINGS CROSS-34A | LEICESTER(GC)-38C | NEWENGLAND-35A | DONCASTER-36A | 9/55: RET-36E | DONCASTER-36A | | NEWENGLAND-35A |
| Aug-55 | ARDSLEY-37A | KINGS CROSS-34A | LEICESTER(GC)-38C | NEWENGLAND-35A | DONCASTER-36A | 11/55: DCTR-36A | DONCASTER-36A | | 3/56: HSEY-34B |
| Jan-56 | ARDSLEY-56B | KINGS CROSS-34A | LEICESTER(GC)-38C | NEWENGLAND-35A | DONCASTER-36A | DONCASTER-36A | DONCASTER-36A | | HORNSEY-34B |
| Aug-56 | ARDSLEY-56B | 8/56: W/D | LEICESTER(GC)-38C | NEWENGLAND-35A | DONCASTER-36A | DONCASTER-36A | 4/57: W/D | | HORNSEY-34B |
| Jan-57 | ARDSLEY-56B | | LEICESTER(GC)-38C | NEWENGLAND-35A | 4/57: W/D | DONCASTER-36A | | | HORNSEY-34B |
| Aug-57 | ARDSLEY-56B | | LEICESTER(GC)-38C | 4/57: DCTR-36A | | DONCASTER-36A | | | HORNSEY-34B |
| Jan-58 | ARDSLEY-56B | | 4/58: W/D | 1/58: D'Ter Works | | 7/58: W/D | | | HORNSEY-34B |
| Aug-58 | ARDSLEY-56B | | | *Doncaster Works* | | | | | 3/59: KX-34A |
| Jan-59 | 2/59: W/D | | | *Doncaster Works* | | | | | 5/59: W/D |
| Aug-59 | | | | *Doncaster Works* | | | | | |
| Nov-59 | | | | *Doncaster Works* | | | | | |
| Jan-60 | | | | *Doncaster Works* | | | | | |
| Apr-60 | | | | *Doncaster Works* | | | | | |
| Aug-60 | | | | *Doncaster Works* | | | | | |
| Nov-60 | | | | *Doncaster Works* | | | | | |

| | 68847 | 68848 | 68849 | 68850 | 68851 | 68852 | 68853 | 68854 | 68855 |
|---|---|---|---|---|---|---|---|---|---|
| Aug-50 | DONCASTER-36A | ARDSLEY-37A | DONCASTER-36A | NEWENGLAND-35A | HORNSEY-34B | NEWENGLAND-35A | HORNSEY-34B | KINGS CROSS-34A | KINGS CROSS-34A |
| Jan-51 | DONCASTER-36A | ARDSLEY-37A | DONCASTER-36A | NEWENGLAND-35A | HORNSEY-34B | NEWENGLAND-35A | HORNSEY-34B | KINGS CROSS-34A | KINGS CROSS-34A |
| Aug-51 | DONCASTER-36A | ARDSLEY-37A | DONCASTER-36A | NEWENGLAND-35A | HORNSEY-34B | NEWENGLAND-35A | HORNSEY-34B | KINGS CROSS-34A | KINGS CROSS-34A |
| Jan-52 | DONCASTER-36A | ARDSLEY-37A | DONCASTER-36A | NEWENGLAND-35A | HORNSEY-34B | NEWENGLAND-35A | HORNSEY-34B | KINGS CROSS-34A | KINGS CROSS-34A |
| Aug-52 | DONCASTER-36A | ARDSLEY-37A | DONCASTER-36A | NEWENGLAND-35A | 10/52: ANNES-38B | NEWENGLAND-35A | 10/52: DCTR-36A | KINGS CROSS-34A | KINGS CROSS-34A |
| Jan-53 | DONCASTER-36A | ARDSLEY-37A | DONCASTER-36A | NEWENGLAND-35A | 1/53: COLW-38A | NEWENGLAND-35A | DONCASTER-36A | KINGS CROSS-34A | KINGS CROSS-34A |
| Aug-53 | DONCASTER-36A | ARDSLEY-37A | DONCASTER-36A | NEWENGLAND-35A | COLWICK-38A | NEWENGLAND-35A | DONCASTER-36A | KINGS CROSS-34A | KINGS CROSS-34A |
| Jan-54 | DONCASTER-36A | ARDSLEY-37A | DONCASTER-36A | NEWENGLAND-35A | COLWICK-38A | NEWENGLAND-35A | DONCASTER-36A | 7/54: W/D | KINGS CROSS-34A |
| Aug-54 | DONCASTER-36A | ARDSLEY-37A | DONCASTER-36A | 10/54: W/D | COLWICK-38A | NEWENGLAND-35A | DONCASTER-36A | | KINGS CROSS-34A |
| Jan-55 | DONCASTER-36A | ARDSLEY-37A | DONCASTER-36A | | COLWICK-38A | 1/55: COLW-38A | DONCASTER-36A | | KINGS CROSS-34A |
| Aug-55 | DONCASTER-36A | ARDSLEY-37A | DONCASTER-36A | | COLWICK-38A | COLWICK-38A | DONCASTER-36A | | KINGS CROSS-34A |
| Jan-56 | 11/55: MEX-36B | ARDSLEY-37A | DONCASTER-36A | | COLWICK-38A | 12/55: W/D | 7/56: W/D | | KINGS CROSS-34A |
| Aug-56 | MEXBOROUGH-36B | ARDSLEY-56B | DONCASTER-36A | | COLWICK-38A | | | | KINGS CROSS-34A |
| Jan-57 | MEXBOROUGH-36B | ARDSLEY-56B | DONCASTER-36A | | 5/57: W/D | | | | KINGS CROSS-34A |
| Aug-57 | MEXBOROUGH-36B | ARDSLEY-56B | DONCASTER-36A | | | | | | 11/56: W/D |
| Jan-58 | MEXBOROUGH-36B | ARDSLEY-56B | 12/57: W/D | | | | | | |
| Aug-58 | 8/58: W/D | 7/58: W/D | | | | | | | |

| | 68856 | 68857 | 68858 | 68859 | 68860 | 68861 | 68862 | 68863 | 68864 |
|---|---|---|---|---|---|---|---|---|---|
| Aug-50 | HORNSEY-34B | DONCASTER-36A | DONCASTER-36A | COLWICK-38A | DONCASTER-36A | KINGS CROSS-34A | KINGS CROSS-34A | COLWICK-38A | KINGS CROSS-34A |
| Jan-51 | HORNSEY-34B | DONCASTER-36A | DONCASTER-36A | COLWICK-38A | DONCASTER-36A | KINGS CROSS-34A | KINGS CROSS-34A | COLWICK-38A | KINGS CROSS-34A |
| Aug-51 | HORNSEY-34B | DONCASTER-36A | DONCASTER-36A | COLWICK-38A | DONCASTER-36A | KINGS CROSS-34A | KINGS CROSS-34A | COLWICK-38A | KINGS CROSS-34A |
| Jan-52 | HORNSEY-34B | DONCASTER-36A | DONCASTER-36A | COLWICK-38A | DONCASTER-36A | KINGS CROSS-34A | KINGS CROSS-34A | COLWICK-38A | KINGS CROSS-34A |
| Aug-52 | 10/52: DCTR-36A | DONCASTER-36A | DONCASTER-36A | COLWICK-38A | DONCASTER-36A | KINGS CROSS-34A | KINGS CROSS-34A | COLWICK-38A | KINGS CROSS-34A |
| Jan-53 | DONCASTER-36A | 11/52: ARDS-37A | DONCASTER-36A | COLWICK-38A | DONCASTER-36A | KINGS CROSS-34A | KINGS CROSS-34A | COLWICK-38A | KINGS CROSS-34A |
| Aug-53 | DONCASTER-36A | ARDSLEY-37A | DONCASTER-36A | COLWICK-38A | DONCASTER-36A | KINGS CROSS-34A | KINGS CROSS-34A | COLWICK-38A | KINGS CROSS-34A |
| Jan-54 | DONCASTER-36A | ARDSLEY-37A | DONCASTER-36A | 8/54: W/D | DONCASTER-36A | KINGS CROSS-34A | KINGS CROSS-34A | COLWICK-38A | KINGS CROSS-34A |
| Aug-54 | DONCASTER-36A | ARDSLEY-37A | DONCASTER-36A | | DONCASTER-36A | KINGS CROSS-34A | KINGS CROSS-34A | COLWICK-38A | KINGS CROSS-34A |
| Jan-55 | DONCASTER-36A | ARDSLEY-37A | DONCASTER-36A | | DONCASTER-36A | KINGS CROSS-34A | KINGS CROSS-34A | COLWICK-38A | KINGS CROSS-34A |
| Aug-55 | DONCASTER-36A | ARDSLEY-37A | DONCASTER-36A | | 11/55: COLW-38A | 10/55: W/D | KINGS CROSS-34A | COLWICK-38A | 1/56: W/D |
| Jan-56 | 11/55: W/D | ARDSLEY-37A | 11/55: W/D | | COLWICK-38A | | KINGS CROSS-34A | COLWICK-38A | |
| Aug-56 | | ARDSLEY-56B | | | COLWICK-38A | | KINGS CROSS-34A | COLWICK-38A | |
| Jan-57 | | ARDSLEY-56B | | | COLWICK-38A | | KINGS CROSS-34A | COLWICK-38A | |
| Aug-57 | | ARDSLEY-56B | | | 12/57: W/D | | KINGS CROSS-34A | 5/58: W/D | |
| Jan-58 | | 4/58: W/D | | | | | 9/58: DCTR-36A | | |
| Aug-58 | | | | | | | 10/58: W/D | | |

| | 68865 | 68866 | 68867 | 68868 | 68869 | 68870 | 68871 | 68872 | 68873 |
|---|---|---|---|---|---|---|---|---|---|
| Aug-50 | DONCASTER-36A | NEWENGLAND-35A | DONCASTER-36A | NEWENGLAND-35A | DONCASTER-36A | DONCASTER-36A | ARDSLEY-37A | ARDSLEY-37A | KINGS CROSS-34A |
| Jan-51 | DONCASTER-36A | NEWENGLAND-35A | DONCASTER-36A | NEWENGLAND-35A | DONCASTER-36A | DONCASTER-36A | ARDSLEY-37A | ARDSLEY-37A | KINGS CROSS-34A |
| Aug-51 | DONCASTER-36A | NEWENGLAND-35A | DONCASTER-36A | NEWENGLAND-35A | DONCASTER-36A | DONCASTER-36A | ARDSLEY-37A | ARDSLEY-37A | 11/51: HSEY-34B |
| Jan-52 | DONCASTER-36A | NEWENGLAND-35A | 3/52: HAT-34C | NEWENGLAND-35A | DONCASTER-36A | DONCASTER-36A | ARDSLEY-37A | ARDSLEY-37A | 9/52: COLW-38A |
| Aug-52 | DONCASTER-36A | NEWENGLAND-35A | HATFIELD-34C | NEWENGLAND-35A | DONCASTER-36A | DONCASTER-36A | ARDSLEY-37A | ARDSLEY-37A | COLWICK-38A |
| Jan-53 | DONCASTER-36A | NEWENGLAND-35A | HATFIELD-34C | NEWENGLAND-35A | DONCASTER-36A | DONCASTER-36A | ARDSLEY-37A | ARDSLEY-37A | COLWICK-38A |
| Aug-53 | DONCASTER-36A | NEWENGLAND-35A | HATFIELD-34C | 8/53: ARDS-37A | DONCASTER-36A | DONCASTER-36A | ARDSLEY-37A | ARDSLEY-37A | COLWICK-38A |
| Jan-54 | DONCASTER-36A | 10/53: HSEY-34B | 6/54: KX-34A | ARDSLEY-37A | DONCASTER-36A | DONCASTER-36A | ARDSLEY-37A | ARDSLEY-37A | COLWICK-38A |
| Aug-54 | DONCASTER-36A | HORNSEY-34B | 8/54: HAT-34C | ARDSLEY-37A | DONCASTER-36A | DONCASTER-36A | ARDSLEY-37A | ARDSLEY-37A | COLWICK-38A |
| Jan-55 | DONCASTER-36A | HORNSEY-34B | HATFIELD-34C | ARDSLEY-37A | DONCASTER-36A | DONCASTER-36A | ARDSLEY-37A | ARDSLEY-37A | 9/55: W/D |
| Aug-55 | DONCASTER-36A | HORNSEY-34B | HATFIELD-34C | 10/55: W/D | DONCASTER-36A | 11/55: MEX-36B | 12/55: COLW-38A | ARDSLEY-37A | |
| Jan-56 | 10/55: W/D | HORNSEY-34B | HATFIELD-34C | | DONCASTER-36A | MEXBOROUGH-36B | COLWICK-38A | 8/56: W/D | |
| Aug-56 | | HORNSEY-34B | HATFIELD-34C | | DONCASTER-36A | MEXBOROUGH-36B | COLWICK-38A | | |
| Jan-57 | | HORNSEY-34B | HATFIELD-34C | | DONCASTER-36A | MEXBOROUGH-36B | COLWICK-38A | | |
| Aug-57 | | HORNSEY-34B | HATFIELD-34C | | DONCASTER-36A | 3/58: W/D | 2/58: W/D | | |
| Jan-58 | | HORNSEY-34B | 2/58: W/D | | DONCASTER-36A | | | | |
| Aug-58 | | 9/58: W/D | | | 9/58: HSEY-34B | | | | |
| Jan-59 | | | | | HORNSEY-34B | | | | |
| Aug-59 | | | | | 4/59: ARDS-56B | | | | |
| Nov-59 | | | | | ARDSLEY-56B | | | | |
| Jan-60 | | | | | ARDSLEY-56B | | | | |
| Apr-60 | | | | | ARDSLEY-56B | | | | |
| Aug-60 | | | | | ARDSLEY-56B | | | | |
| Nov-60 | | | | | | | | | |

A further problem that increased the utility of 0-6-0 engines was the fluid nature of mineral workings which varied according to daily demand, a situation that was especially acute in Scotland where many of the workings (100 daily) had no timings other than the time they were due off shed, the details of the workings being calculated by the district controller only an hour or two before the crew signed on.  The North British main lines could accommodate the largest locomotives in the LNER fleet but many of the branches and colliery yards were a different kettle of fish and special authority had had to be given to sanction the use of even J37 and J38 0-6-0's.  To have supplied Thornton Junction or Dunfermline with 2-8-0's en masse would simply have

| | 68874 | 68875 | 68876 | 68877 | 68878 | 68879 | 68880 | 68881 | 68882 |
|---|---|---|---|---|---|---|---|---|---|
| Aug-50 | KINGS CROSS - 34A | COLWICK - 38A | NEWENGLAND - 35A | GRANTHAM - 35B | KINGS CROSS - 34A | NEWENGLAND - 35A | NEWENGLAND - 35A | KINGS CROSS - 34A | COLWICK - 38A |
| Jan-51 | KINGS CROSS - 34A | COLWICK - 38A | NEWENGLAND - 35A | GRANTHAM - 35B | KINGS CROSS - 34A | NEWENGLAND - 35A | NEWENGLAND - 35A | KINGS CROSS - 34A | COLWICK - 38A |
| Aug-51 | KINGS CROSS - 34A | COLWICK - 38A | NEWENGLAND - 35A | GRANTHAM - 35B | KINGS CROSS - 34A | NEWENGLAND - 35A | NEWENGLAND - 35A | KINGS CROSS - 34A | COLWICK - 38A |
| Jan-52 | KINGS CROSS - 34A | COLWICK - 38A | NEWENGLAND - 35A | GRANTHAM - 35B | KINGS CROSS - 34A | NEWENGLAND - 35A | NEWENGLAND - 35A | KINGS CROSS - 34A | COLWICK - 38A |
| Aug-52 | KINGS CROSS - 34A | COLWICK - 38A | NEWENGLAND - 35A | GRANTHAM - 35B | KINGS CROSS - 34A | NEWENGLAND - 35A | NEWENGLAND - 35A | KINGS CROSS - 34A | COLWICK - 38A |
| Jan-53 | KINGS CROSS - 34A | 1/53: ARDS - 37A | NEWENGLAND - 35A | GRANTHAM - 35B | KINGS CROSS - 34A | NEWENGLAND - 35A | NEWENGLAND - 35A | KINGS CROSS - 34A | COLWICK - 38A |
| Aug-53 | KINGS CROSS - 34A | ARDSLEY - 37A | NEWENGLAND - 35A | GRANTHAM - 35B | KINGS CROSS - 34A | NEWENGLAND - 35A | NEWENGLAND - 35A | KINGS CROSS - 34A | COLWICK - 38A |
| Jan-54 | KINGS CROSS - 34A | ARDSLEY - 37A | NEWENGLAND - 35A | GRANTHAM - 35B | KINGS CROSS - 34A | NEWENGLAND - 35A | NEWENGLAND - 35A | KINGS CROSS - 34A | COLWICK - 38A |
| Aug-54 | KINGS CROSS - 34A | ARDSLEY - 37A | NEWENGLAND - 35A | GRANTHAM - 35B | KINGS CROSS - 34A | NEWENGLAND - 35A | 9/54: COLW - 38A | KINGS CROSS - 34A | COLWICK - 38A |
| Jan-55 | KINGS CROSS - 34A | ARDSLEY - 37A | 11/54: COLW - 38A | GRANTHAM - 35B | KINGS CROSS - 34A | NEWENGLAND - 35A | COLWICK - 38A | KINGS CROSS - 34A | COLWICK - 38A |
| Aug-55 | KINGS CROSS - 34A | ARDSLEY - 37A | COLWICK - 38A | GRANTHAM - 35B | KINGS CROSS - 34A | 9/55: W/D | COLWICK - 38A | KINGS CROSS - 34A | COLWICK - 38A |
| Jan-56 | KINGS CROSS - 34A | 12/55: COLW - 38A | 3/56: W/D | GRANTHAM - 35B | KINGS CROSS - 34A | | COLWICK - 38A | 11/55: W/D | COLWICK - 38A |
| Aug-56 | KINGS CROSS - 34A | 3/56: HSEY - 34B | | 4/56: COLW - 38A | 5/56: W/D | | 8/56: W/D | | COLWICK - 38A |
| Jan-57 | KINGS CROSS - 34A | HORNSEY - 34B | | 11/56: W/D | | | | | COLWICK - 38A |
| Aug-57 | KINGS CROSS - 34A | HORNSEY - 34B | | | | | | | COLWICK - 38A |
| Jan-58 | 10/57: W/D | HORNSEY - 34B | | | | | | | 1/58: W/D |
| Aug-58 | | HORNSEY - 34B | | | | | | | |
| Jan-59 | | HORNSEY - 34B | | | | | | | |
| Aug-59 | | ARDSLEY - 56B | | | | | | | |
| Nov-59 | | ARDSLEY - 56B | | | | | | | |
| Jan-60 | | ARDSLEY - 56B | | | | | | | |
| Apr-60 | | ARDSLEY - 56B | | | | | | | |
| Aug-60 | | ARDSLEY - 56B | | | | | | | |
| Nov-60 | | ARDSLEY - 56B | | | | | | | |

| | 68883 | 68884 | 68885 | 68886 | 68887 | 68888 | 68889 | J50 0-6-0T (1922) 68890 | 68891 |
|---|---|---|---|---|---|---|---|---|---|
| Aug-50 | HORNSEY - 34B | KINGS CROSS - 34A | DONCASTER - 36A | DONCASTER - 36A | COLWICK - 38A | KINGS CROSS - 34A | KINGS CROSS - 34A | MEXBOROUGH - 36B | COLWICK - 38A |
| Jan-51 | HORNSEY - 34B | KINGS CROSS - 34A | DONCASTER - 36A | DONCASTER - 36A | COLWICK - 38A | KINGS CROSS - 34A | KINGS CROSS - 34A | 10/50: DCTR - 36A | COLWICK - 38A |
| Aug-51 | HORNSEY - 34B | KINGS CROSS - 34A | DONCASTER - 36A | DONCASTER - 36A | COLWICK - 38A | KINGS CROSS - 34A | KINGS CROSS - 34A | DONCASTER - 36A | COLWICK - 38A |
| Jan-52 | HORNSEY - 34B | KINGS CROSS - 34A | 12/51: HAT - 35C | DONCASTER - 36A | COLWICK - 38A | KINGS CROSS - 34A | KINGS CROSS - 34A | DONCASTER - 36A | COLWICK - 38A |
| Aug-52 | 10/52: ANNES - 38B | KINGS CROSS - 34A | HATFIELD - 34C | DONCASTER - 36A | COLWICK - 38A | KINGS CROSS - 34A | KINGS CROSS - 34A | 10/52: HSEY - 34B | 9/52: HSEY - 34B |
| Jan-53 | 11/52: HSEY - 34B | KINGS CROSS - 34A | HATFIELD - 34C | DONCASTER - 36A | COLWICK - 38A | KINGS CROSS - 34A | 2/53: S.BGE - 35C | 11/52I ARDS - 37A | HORNSEY - 34B |
| Aug-53 | HORNSEY - 34B | KINGS CROSS - 34A | HATFIELD - 34C | DONCASTER - 36A | COLWICK - 38A | KINGS CROSS - 34A | SPITAL BRIDGE - 35C | ARDSLEY - 37A | HORNSEY - 34B |
| Jan-54 | HORNSEY - 34B | 10/53: NEW.E - 35A | HATFIELD - 34C | DONCASTER - 36A | COLWICK - 38A | KINGS CROSS - 34A | SPITAL BRIDGE - 35C | ARDSLEY - 37A | HORNSEY - 34B |
| Aug-54 | HORNSEY - 34B | NEWENGLAND - 35A | HATFIELD - 34C | DONCASTER - 36A | COLWICK - 38A | KINGS CROSS - 34A | SPITAL BRIDGE - 35C | ARDSLEY - 37A | HORNSEY - 34B |
| Jan-55 | HORNSEY - 34B | NEWENGLAND - 35A | 2/55: KX - 34A | DONCASTER - 36A | COLWICK - 38A | KINGS CROSS - 34A | SPITAL BRIDGE - 35C | ARDSLEY - 37A | HORNSEY - 34B |
| Aug-55 | 9/55: W/D | 9/55: W/D | KINGS CROSS - 34A | 11/55: RET - 36E | COLWICK - 38A | KINGS CROSS - 34A | 5/55: W/D | ARDSLEY - 37A | HORNSEY - 34B |
| Jan-56 | | | KINGS CROSS - 34A | 12/55: DCTR - 36A | COLWICK - 38A | KINGS CROSS - 34A | | ARDSLEY - 37A | HORNSEY - 34B |
| Aug-56 | | | 9/56: W/D | DONCASTER - 36A | COLWICK - 38A | KINGS CROSS - 34A | | ARDSLEY - 56B | HORNSEY - 34B |
| Jan-57 | | | | DONCASTER - 36A | COLWICK - 38A | KINGS CROSS - 34A | | ARDSLEY - 56B | HORNSEY - 34B |
| Aug-57 | | | | DONCASTER - 36A | 9/57: W/D | KINGS CROSS - 34A | | ARDSLEY - 56B | HORNSEY - 34B |
| Jan-58 | | | | 11/57: W/D | | 10/57: W/D | | ARDSLEY - 56B | HORNSEY - 34B |
| Aug-58 | | | | | | | | ARDSLEY - 56B | HORNSEY - 34B |
| Jan-59 | | | | | | | | ARDSLEY - 56B | HORNSEY - 34B |
| Aug-59 | | | | | | | | ARDSLEY - 56B | HORNSEY - 34B |
| Nov-59 | | | | | | | | ARDSLEY - 56B | HORNSEY - 34B |
| Jan-60 | | | | | | | | ARDSLEY - 56B | HORNSEY - 34B |
| Apr-60 | | | | | | | | ARDSLEY - 56B | HORNSEY - 34B |
| Aug-60 | | | | | | | | ARDSLEY - 56B | HORNSEY - 34B |
| Nov-60 | | | | | | | | ARDSLEY - 56B | HORNSEY - 34B |

| | 68892 | 68893 | 68894 | 68895 | 68896 | 68897 | 68898 | 68899 | 68900 |
|---|---|---|---|---|---|---|---|---|---|
| Aug-50 | BRADFORD - 37C | DONCASTER - 36A | COLWICK - 38A | BRADFORD - 37C | ARDSLEY - 37A | BRADFORD - 37C | BRADFORD - 37C | NORWICH - 32A | ARDSLEY - 37A |
| Jan-51 | BRADFORD - 37C | DONCASTER - 36A | COLWICK - 38A | BRADFORD - 37C | ARDSLEY - 37A | BRADFORD - 37C | BRADFORD - 37C | NORWICH - 32A | ARDSLEY - 37A |
| Aug-51 | BRADFORD - 37C | DONCASTER - 36A | COLWICK - 38A | BRADFORD - 37C | ARDSLEY - 37A | BRADFORD - 37C | BRADFORD - 37C | NORWICH - 32A | ARDSLEY - 37A |
| Jan-52 | BRADFORD - 37C | DONCASTER - 36A | COLWICK - 38A | BRADFORD - 37C | ARDSLEY - 37A | BRADFORD - 37C | BRADFORD - 37C | NORWICH - 32A | ARDSLEY - 37A |
| Aug-52 | BRADFORD - 37C | 6/52: IMM - 40B | 9/52: HSEY - 34B | BRADFORD - 37C | ARDSLEY - 37A | BRADFORD - 37C | BRADFORD - 37C | NORWICH - 32A | ARDSLEY - 37A |
| Jan-53 | BRADFORD - 37C | IMMINGHAM - 40B | HORNSEY - 34B | BRADFORD - 37C | 1/53: ANNES - 38B | BRADFORD - 37C | BRADFORD - 37C | NORWICH - 32A | ARDSLEY - 37A |
| Aug-53 | BRADFORD - 37C | IMMINGHAM - 40B | HORNSEY - 34B | BRADFORD - 37C | ANNESLEY - 38B | BRADFORD - 37C | BRADFORD - 37C | NORWICH - 32A | ARDSLEY - 37A |
| Jan-54 | BRADFORD - 37C | IMMINGHAM - 40B | HORNSEY - 34B | BRADFORD - 37C | ANNESLEY - 38B | BRADFORD - 37C | BRADFORD - 37C | NORWICH - 32A | ARDSLEY - 37A |
| Aug-54 | BRADFORD - 37C | IMMINGHAM - 40B | HORNSEY - 34B | BRADFORD - 37C | ANNESLEY - 38B | BRADFORD - 37C | BRADFORD - 37C | NORWICH - 32A | ARDSLEY - 37A |
| Jan-55 | BRADFORD - 37C | 3/55: STRAT - 30A | HORNSEY - 34B | BRADFORD - 37C | ANNESLEY - 38B | BRADFORD - 37C | BRADFORD - 37C | NORWICH - 32A | ARDSLEY - 37A |
| Aug-55 | BRADFORD - 37C | STRATFORD - 30A | HORNSEY - 34B | BRADFORD - 37C | ANNESLEY - 38B | BRADFORD - 37C | BRADFORD - 37C | NORWICH - 32A | ARDSLEY - 37A |
| Jan-56 | BRADFORD - 37C | 1/56: COLW - 38A | HORNSEY - 34B | BRADFORD - 37C | ANNESLEY - 38B | BRADFORD - 37C | BRADFORD - 37C | NORWICH - 32A | ARDSLEY - 37A |
| Aug-56 | BRADFORD - 56G | COLWICK - 38A | HORNSEY - 34B | BRADFORD - 56G | ANNESLEY - 38B | BRADFORD - 56G | BRADFORD - 56G | NORWICH - 32A | ARDSLEY - 56B |
| Jan-57 | BRADFORD - 56G | COLWICK - 38A | HORNSEY - 34B | BRADFORD - 56G | ANNESLEY - 38B | BRADFORD - 56G | BRADFORD - 56G | NORWICH - 32A | ARDSLEY - 56B |
| Aug-57 | BRADFORD - 56G | COLWICK - 38A | HORNSEY - 34B | BRADFORD - 56G | ANNESLEY - 38B | BRADFORD - 56G | 9/57: ARDS - 56B | NORWICH - 32A | ARDSLEY - 56B |
| Jan-58 | 2/58: L.MOOR - 56F | COLWICK - 38A | HORNSEY - 34B | 2/58: L.MOOR - 56F | ANNESLEY - 38B | 2/58: DARL - 51A | ARDSLEY - 56B | NORWICH - 32A | ARDSLEY - 56B |
| Aug-58 | 5/58: STOCK - 51E | COLWICK - 40E | HORNSEY - 34B | LOWMOOR - 56F | ANNESLEY - 16D | DARLINGTON - 51A | 6/58: DARL - 51A | NORWICH - 32A | ARDSLEY - 56B |
| Jan-59 | STOCKTON - 51E | COLWICK - 40E | HORNSEY - 34B | LOWMOOR - 56F | 12/58: NEW. E - 34E | DARLINGTON - 51A | DARLINGTON - 51A | NORWICH - 32A | ARDSLEY - 56B |
| Aug-59 | 6/59: SELBY - 50C | COLWICK - 40E | HORNSEY - 34B | LOWMOOR - 56F | NEWENGLAND - 34E | 6/59: WAKE - 56A | 6/59: WAKE - 56A | NORWICH - 32A | ARDSLEY - 56B |
| Nov-59 | 9/59: ARDS - 56B | 10/59: W/D | HORNSEY - 34B | LOWMOOR - 56F | NEWENGLAND - 34E | WAKEFIELD - 56A | WAKEFIELD - 56A | NORWICH - 32A | ARDSLEY - 56B |
| Jan-60 | ARDSLEY - 56B | | HORNSEY - 34B | LOWMOOR - 56F | 2/60: HSEY - 34B | WAKEFIELD - 56A | 1/60: W/D | NORWICH - 32A | ARDSLEY - 56B |
| Apr-60 | ARDSLEY - 56B | | HORNSEY - 34B | 3/60: W/D | HORNSEY - 34B | WAKEFIELD - 56A | | 4/60: STRAT - 30A | ARDSLEY - 56B |
| Aug-60 | 6/60: C.HILL - 56C | | HORNSEY - 34B | | HORNSEY - 34B | WAKEFIELD - 56A | | STRATFORD - 30A | ARDSLEY - 56B |
| Nov-60 | COPLEYHILL - 56C | | HORNSEY - 34B | | HORNSEY - 34B | 11/60: W/D | | STRATFORD - 30A | ARDSLEY - 56B |

| | 68901 | 68902 | 68903 | 68904 | 68905 | 68906 | 68907 | 68908 | 68909 |
|---|---|---|---|---|---|---|---|---|---|
| Aug-50 | ARDSLEY - 37A | BRADFORD - 37C | ARDSLEY - 37A | ARDSLEY - 37A | NORWICH - 32A | BRADFORD - 37C | ARDSLEY - 37A | BRADFORD - 37C | ARDSLEY - 37A |
| Jan-51 | ARDSLEY - 37A | BRADFORD - 37C | ARDSLEY - 37A | ARDSLEY - 37A | NORWICH - 32A | BRADFORD - 37C | ARDSLEY - 37A | BRADFORD - 37C | ARDSLEY - 37A |
| Aug-51 | ARDSLEY - 37A | BRADFORD - 37C | ARDSLEY - 37A | ARDSLEY - 37A | NORWICH - 32A | BRADFORD - 37C | ARDSLEY - 37A | BRADFORD - 37C | ARDSLEY - 37A |
| Jan-52 | ARDSLEY - 37A | BRADFORD - 37C | ARDSLEY - 37A | ARDSLEY - 37A | NORWICH - 32A | BRADFORD - 37C | ARDSLEY - 37A | BRADFORD - 37C | ARDSLEY - 37A |
| Aug-52 | ARDSLEY - 37A | BRADFORD - 37C | ARDSLEY - 37A | ARDSLEY - 37A | NORWICH - 32A | BRADFORD - 37C | ARDSLEY - 37A | BRADFORD - 37C | ARDSLEY - 37A |
| Jan-53 | ARDSLEY - 37A | 2/53: ARDS - 37A | 10/52: HSEY - 34B | ARDSLEY - 37A | NORWICH - 32A | 2/53: HSEY - 34B | 2/53: HSEY - 34B | BRADFORD - 37C | ARDSLEY - 37A |
| Aug-53 | ARDSLEY - 37A | ARDSLEY - 37A | HORNSEY - 34B | ARDSLEY - 37A | NORWICH - 32A | HORNSEY - 34B | HORNSEY - 34B | BRADFORD - 37C | ARDSLEY - 37A |
| Jan-54 | ARDSLEY - 37A | ARDSLEY - 37A | HORNSEY - 34B | ARDSLEY - 37A | NORWICH - 32A | HORNSEY - 34B | HORNSEY - 34B | BRADFORD - 37C | ARDSLEY - 37A |
| Aug-54 | ARDSLEY - 37A | ARDSLEY - 37A | HORNSEY - 34B | ARDSLEY - 37A | NORWICH - 32A | HORNSEY - 34B | HORNSEY - 34B | BRADFORD - 37C | ARDSLEY - 37A |
| Jan-55 | ARDSLEY - 37A | ARDSLEY - 37A | HORNSEY - 34B | ARDSLEY - 37A | NORWICH - 32A | HORNSEY - 34B | HORNSEY - 34B | BRADFORD - 37C | ARDSLEY - 37A |
| Aug-55 | ARDSLEY - 37A | ARDSLEY - 37A | HORNSEY - 34B | ARDSLEY - 37A | NORWICH - 32A | HORNSEY - 34B | HORNSEY - 34B | BRADFORD - 37C | ARDSLEY - 37A |
| Jan-56 | ARDSLEY - 37A | ARDSLEY - 37A | HORNSEY - 34B | ARDSLEY - 37A | NORWICH - 32A | HORNSEY - 34B | HORNSEY - 34B | BRADFORD - 37C | ARDSLEY - 37A |
| Aug-56 | ARDSLEY - 56B | ARDSLEY - 56B | HORNSEY - 34B | ARDSLEY - 56B | NORWICH - 32A | HORNSEY - 34B | HORNSEY - 34B | BRADFORD - 56G | ARDSLEY - 56B |
| Jan-57 | ARDSLEY - 56B | ARDSLEY - 56B | HORNSEY - 34B | ARDSLEY - 56B | NORWICH - 32A | HORNSEY - 34B | HORNSEY - 34B | BRADFORD - 56G | ARDSLEY - 56B |
| Aug-57 | ARDSLEY - 56B | ARDSLEY - 56B | HORNSEY - 34B | ARDSLEY - 56B | NORWICH - 32A | HORNSEY - 34B | HORNSEY - 34B | BRADFORD - 56G | ARDSLEY - 56B |
| Jan-58 | ARDSLEY - 56B | ARDSLEY - 56B | HORNSEY - 34B | ARDSLEY - 56B | NORWICH - 32A | HORNSEY - 34B | HORNSEY - 34B | 2/58: L.MOOR - 56F | ARDSLEY - 56B |
| Aug-58 | ARDSLEY - 56B | ARDSLEY - 56B | HORNSEY - 34B | ARDSLEY - 56B | NORWICH - 32A | HORNSEY - 34B | HORNSEY - 34B | 6/58: TBY - 51L | 6/58: STOCK - 51E |
| Jan-59 | ARDSLEY - 56B | ARDSLEY - 56B | HORNSEY - 34B | 2/59: WAKE - 56A | NORWICH - 32A | HORNSEY - 34B | HORNSEY - 34B | 2/59: L. MOOR - 56F | 9/58: DARL - 51A |
| Aug-59 | ARDSLEY - 56B | ARDSLEY - 56B | HORNSEY - 34B | WAKEFIELD - 56A | NORWICH - 32A | 5/59: W/D | HORNSEY - 34B | LOWMOOR - 56F | 6/59: WAKE - 56A |
| Nov-59 | ARDSLEY - 56B | ARDSLEY - 56B | HORNSEY - 34B | WAKEFIELD - 56A | NORWICH - 32A | | HORNSEY - 34B | LOWMOOR - 56F | WAKEFIELD - 56A |
| Jan-60 | ARDSLEY - 56B | ARDSLEY - 56B | HORNSEY - 34B | WAKEFIELD - 56A | NORWICH - 32A | | HORNSEY - 34B | LOWMOOR - 56F | WAKEFIELD - 56A |
| Apr-60 | ARDSLEY - 56B | ARDSLEY - 56B | HORNSEY - 34B | WAKEFIELD - 56A | 4/60: STRAT - 30A | | HORNSEY - 34B | LOWMOOR - 56F | 4/60: W/D |
| Aug-60 | ARDSLEY - 56B | ARDSLEY - 56B | HORNSEY - 34B | WAKEFIELD - 56A | STRATFORD - 30A | | HORNSEY - 34B | LOWMOOR - 56F | |
| Nov-60 | 10/60: W/D | 10/60: W/D | HORNSEY - 34B | WAKEFIELD - 56A | STRATFORD - 30A | | HORNSEY - 34B | LOWMOOR - 56F | |

resulted in trains being cancelled whilst engines stood idle on shed since there were even sections of line over which an 0-6-0 was prohibited, a circumstance which saw Y9 0-4-0 68101 being retained at Dunfermline for the daily 08.30 trip to Netherton and back.

| | 68910 | 68911 | 68912 | 68913 | 68914 | 68915 | 68916 | 68917 | 68918 |
|---|---|---|---|---|---|---|---|---|---|
| Aug-50 | ARDSLEY - 37A | COPLEYHILL - 37B | BRADFORD - 37C | COPLEYHILL - 37B | ARDSLEY - 37A | ARDSLEY - 37A | ARDSLEY - 37A | DONCASTER - 36A | DONCASTER - 36A |
| Jan-51 | ARDSLEY - 37A | COPLEYHILL - 37B | BRADFORD - 37C | COPLEYHILL - 37B | ARDSLEY - 37A | ARDSLEY - 37A | ARDSLEY - 37A | DONCASTER - 36A | DONCASTER - 36A |
| Aug-51 | ARDSLEY - 37A | COPLEYHILL - 37B | BRADFORD - 37C | COPLEYHILL - 37B | ARDSLEY - 37A | ARDSLEY - 37A | ARDSLEY - 37A | DONCASTER - 36A | DONCASTER - 36A |
| Jan-52 | ARDSLEY - 37A | COPLEYHILL - 37B | BRADFORD - 37C | COPLEYHILL - 37B | ARDSLEY - 37A | ARDSLEY - 37A | ARDSLEY - 37A | DONCASTER - 36A | DONCASTER - 36A |
| Aug-52 | ARDSLEY - 37A | COPLEYHILL - 37B | BRADFORD - 37C | COPLEYHILL - 37B | ARDSLEY - 37A | ARDSLEY - 37A | ARDSLEY - 37A | DONCASTER - 36A | **9/52: HSEY - 34B** |
| Jan-53 | ARDSLEY - 37A | COPLEYHILL - 37B | BRADFORD - 37C | COPLEYHILL - 37B | ARDSLEY - 37A | ARDSLEY - 37A | ARDSLEY - 37A | **10/52: HSEY - 34B** | HORNSEY - 34B |
| Aug-53 | ARDSLEY - 37A | COPLEYHILL - 37B | BRADFORD - 37C | COPLEYHILL - 37B | ARDSLEY - 37A | ARDSLEY - 37A | ARDSLEY - 37A | HORNSEY - 34B | HORNSEY - 34B |
| Jan-54 | ARDSLEY - 37A | COPLEYHILL - 37B | BRADFORD - 37C | COPLEYHILL - 37B | ARDSLEY - 37A | ARDSLEY - 37A | ARDSLEY - 37A | HORNSEY - 34B | HORNSEY - 34B |
| Aug-54 | ARDSLEY - 37A | COPLEYHILL - 37B | BRADFORD - 37C | COPLEYHILL - 37B | ARDSLEY - 37A | ARDSLEY - 37A | ARDSLEY - 37A | HORNSEY - 34B | HORNSEY - 34B |
| Jan-55 | ARDSLEY - 37A | COPLEYHILL - 37B | BRADFORD - 37C | COPLEYHILL - 37B | ARDSLEY - 37A | ARDSLEY - 37A | ARDSLEY - 37A | HORNSEY - 34B | HORNSEY - 34B |
| Aug-55 | ARDSLEY - 37A | COPLEYHILL - 37B | BRADFORD - 37C | COPLEYHILL - 37B | ARDSLEY - 37A | ARDSLEY - 37A | ARDSLEY - 37A | HORNSEY - 34B | HORNSEY - 34B |
| Jan-56 | ARDSLEY - 37A | COPLEYHILL - 37B | BRADFORD - 37C | COPLEYHILL - 37B | ARDSLEY - 37A | ARDSLEY - 37A | ARDSLEY - 37A | HORNSEY - 34B | HORNSEY - 34B |
| Aug-56 | ARDSLEY - 56B | COPLEYHILL - 56C | BRADFORD - 56G | COPLEYHILL - 56C | ARDSLEY - 56B | ARDSLEY - 56B | ARDSLEY - 56B | HORNSEY - 34B | HORNSEY - 34B |
| Jan-57 | ARDSLEY - 56B | COPLEYHILL - 56C | BRADFORD - 56G | COPLEYHILL - 56C | ARDSLEY - 56B | ARDSLEY - 56B | ARDSLEY - 56B | HORNSEY - 34B | HORNSEY - 34B |
| Aug-57 | ARDSLEY - 56B | COPLEYHILL - 56C | BRADFORD - 56G | COPLEYHILL - 56C | ARDSLEY - 56B | ARDSLEY - 56B | ARDSLEY - 56B | HORNSEY - 34B | HORNSEY - 34B |
| Jan-58 | ARDSLEY - 56B | COPLEYHILL - 56C | **2/58: DAIRY - 53A** | COPLEYHILL - 56C | ARDSLEY - 56B | ARDSLEY - 56B | ARDSLEY - 56B | HORNSEY - 34B | HORNSEY - 34B |
| Aug-58 | ARDSLEY - 56B | COPLEYHILL - 56C | **6/58: GOOLE - 53E** | COPLEYHILL - 56C | ARDSLEY - 56B | ARDSLEY - 56B | ARDSLEY - 56B | HORNSEY - 34B | HORNSEY - 34B |
| Jan-59 | **2/59: WAKE - 56A** | COPLEYHILL - 56C | **2/59: L. MOOR - 56F** | COPLEYHILL - 56C | ARDSLEY - 56B | ARDSLEY - 56B | ARDSLEY - 56B | HORNSEY - 34B | HORNSEY - 34B |
| Aug-59 | WAKEFIELD - 56A | COPLEYHILL - 56C | LOWMOOR - 56F | COPLEYHILL - 56C | ARDSLEY - 56B | ARDSLEY - 56B | ARDSLEY - 56B | HORNSEY - 34B | HORNSEY - 34B |
| Nov-59 | WAKEFIELD - 56A | COPLEYHILL - 56C | **9/59: W/D** | COPLEYHILL - 56C | ARDSLEY - 56B | ARDSLEY - 56B | ARDSLEY - 56B | HORNSEY - 34B | HORNSEY - 34B |
| Jan-60 | WAKEFIELD - 56A | COPLEYHILL - 56C | | COPLEYHILL - 56C | ARDSLEY - 56B | ARDSLEY - 56B | ARDSLEY - 56B | HORNSEY - 34B | HORNSEY - 34B |
| Apr-60 | WAKEFIELD - 56A | COPLEYHILL - 56C | | COPLEYHILL - 56C | ARDSLEY - 56B | ARDSLEY - 56B | ARDSLEY - 56B | HORNSEY - 34B | HORNSEY - 34B |
| Aug-60 | WAKEFIELD - 56A | COPLEYHILL - 56C | | **9/60: W/D** | ARDSLEY - 56B | ARDSLEY - 56B | ARDSLEY - 56B | HORNSEY - 34B | HORNSEY - 34B |
| Nov-60 | WAKEFIELD - 56A | COPLEYHILL - 56C | | | | | ARDSLEY - 56B | HORNSEY - 34B | HORNSEY - 34B |

| | 68919 | 68920 | 68921 | 68922 | 68923 | 68924 | 68925 | 68926 | 68927 |
|---|---|---|---|---|---|---|---|---|---|
| Aug-50 | ARDSLEY - 37A | COLWICK - 38A | ARDSLEY - 37A | BRADFORD - 37C | BRADFORD - 37C | NORWICH - 32A | COPLEYHILL - 37B | DONCASTER - 36A | ANNESLEY - 38B |
| Jan-51 | ARDSLEY - 37A | COLWICK - 38A | ARDSLEY - 37A | BRADFORD - 37C | BRADFORD - 37C | NORWICH - 32A | COPLEYHILL - 37B | DONCASTER - 36A | ANNESLEY - 38B |
| Aug-51 | ARDSLEY - 37A | COLWICK - 38A | ARDSLEY - 37A | BRADFORD - 37C | BRADFORD - 37C | NORWICH - 32A | COPLEYHILL - 37B | DONCASTER - 36A | ANNESLEY - 38B |
| Jan-52 | ARDSLEY - 37A | COLWICK - 38A | ARDSLEY - 37A | BRADFORD - 37C | BRADFORD - 37C | NORWICH - 32A | COPLEYHILL - 37B | DONCASTER - 36A | ANNESLEY - 38B |
| Aug-52 | ARDSLEY - 37A | **9/52: HSEY - 34B** | ARDSLEY - 37A | BRADFORD - 37C | BRADFORD - 37C | NORWICH - 32A | COPLEYHILL - 37B | **6/52: IMM - 40B** | ANNESLEY - 38B |
| Jan-53 | ARDSLEY - 37A | HORNSEY - 34B | **10/52: HSEY - 34B** | BRADFORD - 37C | BRADFORD - 37C | NORWICH - 32A | COPLEYHILL - 37B | IMMINGHAM - 40B | ANNESLEY - 38B |
| Aug-53 | ARDSLEY - 37A | HORNSEY - 34B | HORNSEY - 34B | BRADFORD - 37C | BRADFORD - 37C | NORWICH - 32A | COPLEYHILL - 37B | IMMINGHAM - 40B | ANNESLEY - 38B |
| Jan-54 | ARDSLEY - 37A | HORNSEY - 34B | HORNSEY - 34B | BRADFORD - 37C | BRADFORD - 37C | NORWICH - 32A | COPLEYHILL - 37B | IMMINGHAM - 40B | ANNESLEY - 38B |
| Aug-54 | ARDSLEY - 37A | HORNSEY - 34B | HORNSEY - 34B | BRADFORD - 37C | BRADFORD - 37C | NORWICH - 32A | COPLEYHILL - 37B | IMMINGHAM - 40B | ANNESLEY - 38B |
| Jan-55 | ARDSLEY - 37A | HORNSEY - 34B | HORNSEY - 34B | BRADFORD - 37C | BRADFORD - 37C | NORWICH - 32A | COPLEYHILL - 37B | IMMINGHAM - 40B | ANNESLEY - 38B |
| Aug-55 | ARDSLEY - 37A | HORNSEY - 34B | HORNSEY - 34B | BRADFORD - 37C | BRADFORD - 37C | NORWICH - 32A | COPLEYHILL - 37B | IMMINGHAM - 40B | ANNESLEY - 38B |
| Jan-56 | ARDSLEY - 37A | HORNSEY - 34B | HORNSEY - 34B | BRADFORD - 37C | BRADFORD - 37C | NORWICH - 32A | COPLEYHILL - 37B | **11/55: DCTR - 36A** | **2/56: COLW - 38A** |
| Aug-56 | ARDSLEY - 56B | HORNSEY - 34B | HORNSEY - 34B | BRADFORD - 56G | BRADFORD - 56G | NORWICH - 32A | COPLEYHILL - 56C | DONCASTER - 36A | COLWICK - 38A |
| Jan-57 | ARDSLEY - 56B | HORNSEY - 34B | HORNSEY - 34B | BRADFORD - 56G | BRADFORD - 56G | NORWICH - 32A | COPLEYHILL - 56C | DONCASTER - 36A | COLWICK - 38A |
| Aug-57 | ARDSLEY - 56B | HORNSEY - 34B | HORNSEY - 34B | BRADFORD - 56G | BRADFORD - 56G | NORWICH - 32A | COPLEYHILL - 56C | DONCASTER - 36A | COLWICK - 38A |
| Jan-58 | ARDSLEY - 56B | HORNSEY - 34B | HORNSEY - 34B | **2/58: L.MOOR - 56F** | **2/58: L.MOOR - 56F** | NORWICH - 32A | COPLEYHILL - 56C | DONCASTER - 36A | COLWICK - 38A |
| Aug-58 | ARDSLEY - 56B | HORNSEY - 34B | HORNSEY - 34B | LOWMOOR - 56F | LOWMOOR - 56F | NORWICH - 32A | COPLEYHILL - 56C | DONCASTER - 36A | COLWICK - 40E |
| Jan-59 | ARDSLEY - 56B | HORNSEY - 34B | HORNSEY - 34B | LOWMOOR - 56F | LOWMOOR - 56F | NORWICH - 32A | COPLEYHILL - 56C | **10/58: HSEY - 34B** | COLWICK - 40E |
| Aug-59 | ARDSLEY - 56B | HORNSEY - 34B | HORNSEY - 34B | LOWMOOR - 56F | LOWMOOR - 56F | NORWICH - 32A | COPLEYHILL - 56C | HORNSEY - 34B | COLWICK - 40E |
| Nov-59 | **9/59: W/D** | HORNSEY - 34B | HORNSEY - 34B | LOWMOOR - 56F | LOWMOOR - 56F | NORWICH - 32A | COPLEYHILL - 56C | HORNSEY - 34B | COLWICK - 40E |
| Jan-60 | | HORNSEY - 34B | HORNSEY - 34B | LOWMOOR - 56F | LOWMOOR - 56F | NORWICH - 32A | COPLEYHILL - 56C | HORNSEY - 34B | COLWICK - 40E |
| Apr-60 | | HORNSEY - 34B | HORNSEY - 34B | LOWMOOR - 56F | LOWMOOR - 56F | **4/60: STRAT - 30A** | COPLEYHILL - 56C | HORNSEY - 34B | COLWICK - 40E |
| Aug-60 | | HORNSEY - 34B | HORNSEY - 34B | LOWMOOR - 56F | LOWMOOR - 56F | STRATFORD - 30A | COPLEYHILL - 56C | HORNSEY - 34B | COLWICK - 40E |
| Nov-60 | | HORNSEY - 34B | HORNSEY - 34B | LOWMOOR - 56F | LOWMOOR - 56F | STRATFORD - 30A | COPLEYHILL - 56C | HORNSEY - 34B | COLWICK - 40E |

| | 68928 | 68929 | 68930 | 68931 | 68932 | 68933 | 68934 | 68935 | 68936 |
|---|---|---|---|---|---|---|---|---|---|
| Aug-50 | DARNALL - 39B | ANNESLEY - 38B | ARDSLEY - 37A | ARDSLEY - 37A | BRADFORD - 37C | BRADFORD - 37C | BRADFORD - 37C | COLWICK - 38A | DONCASTER - 36A |
| Jan-51 | DARNALL - 39B | ANNESLEY - 38B | ARDSLEY - 37A | ARDSLEY - 37A | BRADFORD - 37C | BRADFORD - 37C | BRADFORD - 37C | COLWICK - 38A | DONCASTER - 36A |
| Aug-51 | DARNALL - 39B | ANNESLEY - 38B | ARDSLEY - 37A | ARDSLEY - 37A | BRADFORD - 37C | BRADFORD - 37C | BRADFORD - 37C | COLWICK - 38A | DONCASTER - 36A |
| Jan-52 | DARNALL - 39B | ANNESLEY - 38B | ARDSLEY - 37A | ARDSLEY - 37A | BRADFORD - 37C | BRADFORD - 37C | BRADFORD - 37C | COLWICK - 38A | DONCASTER - 36A |
| Aug-52 | DARNALL - 39B | ANNESLEY - 38B | ARDSLEY - 37A | **8/52: HSEY - 34B** | BRADFORD - 37C | BRADFORD - 37C | BRADFORD - 37C | **9/52: ARDS - 37A** | **9/52: HSEY - 34B** |
| Jan-53 | **10/52: HSEY - 34B** | **10/52: HSEY - 34B** | **10/52: HSEY - 34B** | HORNSEY - 34B | BRADFORD - 37C | BRADFORD - 37C | BRADFORD - 37C | ARDSLEY - 37A | HORNSEY - 34B |
| Aug-53 | HORNSEY - 34B | HORNSEY - 34B | HORNSEY - 34B | HORNSEY - 34B | BRADFORD - 37C | BRADFORD - 37C | BRADFORD - 37C | ARDSLEY - 37A | HORNSEY - 34B |
| Jan-54 | HORNSEY - 34B | HORNSEY - 34B | HORNSEY - 34B | HORNSEY - 34B | BRADFORD - 37C | BRADFORD - 37C | BRADFORD - 37C | ARDSLEY - 37A | HORNSEY - 34B |
| Aug-54 | HORNSEY - 34B | HORNSEY - 34B | HORNSEY - 34B | HORNSEY - 34B | BRADFORD - 37C | BRADFORD - 37C | BRADFORD - 37C | ARDSLEY - 37A | HORNSEY - 34B |
| Jan-55 | HORNSEY - 34B | HORNSEY - 34B | HORNSEY - 34B | HORNSEY - 34B | BRADFORD - 37C | BRADFORD - 37C | BRADFORD - 37C | ARDSLEY - 37A | HORNSEY - 34B |
| Aug-55 | HORNSEY - 34B | HORNSEY - 34B | HORNSEY - 34B | HORNSEY - 34B | BRADFORD - 37C | BRADFORD - 37C | BRADFORD - 37C | ARDSLEY - 37A | HORNSEY - 34B |
| Jan-56 | HORNSEY - 34B | HORNSEY - 34B | HORNSEY - 34B | HORNSEY - 34B | BRADFORD - 37C | BRADFORD - 37C | BRADFORD - 37C | ARDSLEY - 37A | HORNSEY - 34B |
| Aug-56 | HORNSEY - 34B | HORNSEY - 34B | HORNSEY - 34B | HORNSEY - 34B | BRADFORD - 56G | BRADFORD - 56G | BRADFORD - 56G | ARDSLEY - 56B | HORNSEY - 34B |
| Jan-57 | HORNSEY - 34B | HORNSEY - 34B | HORNSEY - 34B | HORNSEY - 34B | BRADFORD - 56G | BRADFORD - 56G | BRADFORD - 56G | ARDSLEY - 56B | HORNSEY - 34B |
| Aug-57 | HORNSEY - 34B | HORNSEY - 34B | HORNSEY - 34B | HORNSEY - 34B | BRADFORD - 56G | BRADFORD - 56G | BRADFORD - 56G | ARDSLEY - 56B | HORNSEY - 34B |
| Jan-58 | HORNSEY - 34B | HORNSEY - 34B | HORNSEY - 34B | HORNSEY - 34B | **2/58: L.MOOR - 56F** | **2/58: L.MOOR - 56F** | **2/58: L.MOOR - 56F** | ARDSLEY - 56B | HORNSEY - 34B |
| Aug-58 | HORNSEY - 34B | HORNSEY - 34B | HORNSEY - 34B | HORNSEY - 34B | LOWMOOR - 56F | LOWMOOR - 56F | **3/58: DARL - 51A** | ARDSLEY - 56B | HORNSEY - 34B |
| Jan-59 | HORNSEY - 34B | HORNSEY - 34B | HORNSEY - 34B | HORNSEY - 34B | LOWMOOR - 56F | LOWMOOR - 56F | DARLINGTON - 51A | ARDSLEY - 56B | HORNSEY - 34B |
| Aug-59 | HORNSEY - 34B | HORNSEY - 34B | HORNSEY - 34B | HORNSEY - 34B | LOWMOOR - 56F | LOWMOOR - 56F | **8/59: ARDS - 56B** | ARDSLEY - 56B | HORNSEY - 34B |
| Nov-59 | HORNSEY - 34B | HORNSEY - 34B | HORNSEY - 34B | HORNSEY - 34B | LOWMOOR - 56F | LOWMOOR - 56F | ARDSLEY - 56B | ARDSLEY - 56B | HORNSEY - 34B |
| Jan-60 | HORNSEY - 34B | HORNSEY - 34B | HORNSEY - 34B | HORNSEY - 34B | LOWMOOR - 56F | LOWMOOR - 56F | ARDSLEY - 56B | ARDSLEY - 56B | HORNSEY - 34B |
| Apr-60 | HORNSEY - 34B | HORNSEY - 34B | HORNSEY - 34B | HORNSEY - 34B | LOWMOOR - 56F | **5/60: WAKE - 56A** | ARDSLEY - 56B | ARDSLEY - 56B | HORNSEY - 34B |
| Aug-60 | HORNSEY - 34B | HORNSEY - 34B | HORNSEY - 34B | HORNSEY - 34B | LOWMOOR - 56F | WAKEFIELD - 56A | ARDSLEY - 56B | ARDSLEY - 56B | HORNSEY - 34B |
| Nov-60 | HORNSEY - 34B | HORNSEY - 34B | HORNSEY - 34B | HORNSEY - 34B | LOWMOOR - 56F | WAKEFIELD - 56A | ARDSLEY - 56B | ARDSLEY - 56B | HORNSEY - 34B |

| | 68937 | 68938 | 68939 | 68940 | 68941 | 68942 | 68943 | 68944 | 68945 |
|---|---|---|---|---|---|---|---|---|---|
| Aug-50 | COPLEYHILL - 37B | ARDSLEY - 37A | ARDSLEY - 37A | BRADFORD - 37C | BRADFORD - 37C | BRADFORD - 37C | BRADFORD - 37C | BRADFORD - 37C | DONCASTER - 36A |
| Jan-51 | COPLEYHILL - 37B | ARDSLEY - 37A | ARDSLEY - 37A | BRADFORD - 37C | BRADFORD - 37C | BRADFORD - 37C | BRADFORD - 37C | BRADFORD - 37C | DONCASTER - 36A |
| Aug-51 | COPLEYHILL - 37B | ARDSLEY - 37A | ARDSLEY - 37A | BRADFORD - 37C | BRADFORD - 37C | BRADFORD - 37C | BRADFORD - 37C | BRADFORD - 37C | DONCASTER - 36A |
| Jan-52 | COPLEYHILL - 37B | ARDSLEY - 37A | ARDSLEY - 37A | BRADFORD - 37C | BRADFORD - 37C | BRADFORD - 37C | BRADFORD - 37C | BRADFORD - 37C | DONCASTER - 36A |
| Aug-52 | COPLEYHILL - 37B | ARDSLEY - 37A | ARDSLEY - 37A | BRADFORD - 37C | BRADFORD - 37C | BRADFORD - 37C | BRADFORD - 37C | BRADFORD - 37C | **9/52: HSEY - 34B** |
| Jan-53 | COPLEYHILL - 37B | ARDSLEY - 37A | ARDSLEY - 37A | BRADFORD - 37C | BRADFORD - 37C | BRADFORD - 37C | BRADFORD - 37C | BRADFORD - 37C | HORNSEY - 34B |
| Aug-53 | COPLEYHILL - 37B | ARDSLEY - 37A | ARDSLEY - 37A | BRADFORD - 37C | **5/53: ARDS - 37A** | BRADFORD - 37C | BRADFORD - 37C | BRADFORD - 37C | HORNSEY - 34B |
| Jan-54 | COPLEYHILL - 37B | ARDSLEY - 37A | ARDSLEY - 37A | BRADFORD - 37C | ARDSLEY - 37A | BRADFORD - 37C | BRADFORD - 37C | BRADFORD - 37C | HORNSEY - 34B |
| Aug-54 | COPLEYHILL - 37B | ARDSLEY - 37A | ARDSLEY - 37A | BRADFORD - 37C | ARDSLEY - 37A | BRADFORD - 37C | BRADFORD - 37C | BRADFORD - 37C | HORNSEY - 34B |
| Jan-55 | COPLEYHILL - 37B | ARDSLEY - 37A | ARDSLEY - 37A | BRADFORD - 37C | ARDSLEY - 37A | BRADFORD - 37C | BRADFORD - 37C | BRADFORD - 37C | HORNSEY - 34B |
| Aug-55 | COPLEYHILL - 37B | ARDSLEY - 37A | ARDSLEY - 37A | BRADFORD - 37C | ARDSLEY - 37A | BRADFORD - 37C | BRADFORD - 37C | BRADFORD - 37C | HORNSEY - 34B |
| Jan-56 | COPLEYHILL - 37B | ARDSLEY - 37A | ARDSLEY - 37A | BRADFORD - 37C | ARDSLEY - 37A | BRADFORD - 37C | BRADFORD - 37C | BRADFORD - 37C | HORNSEY - 34B |
| Aug-56 | COPLEYHILL - 56C | ARDSLEY - 56B | ARDSLEY - 56B | BRADFORD - 56G | ARDSLEY - 56B | BRADFORD - 56G | BRADFORD - 56G | BRADFORD - 56G | HORNSEY - 34B |
| Jan-57 | COPLEYHILL - 56C | ARDSLEY - 56B | ARDSLEY - 56B | BRADFORD - 56G | ARDSLEY - 56B | BRADFORD - 56G | BRADFORD - 56G | BRADFORD - 56G | HORNSEY - 34B |
| Aug-57 | **8/57: ARDS - 56B** | ARDSLEY - 56B | ARDSLEY - 56B | BRADFORD - 56G | ARDSLEY - 56B | BRADFORD - 56G | BRADFORD - 56G | BRADFORD - 56G | HORNSEY - 34B |
| Jan-58 | ARDSLEY - 56B | ARDSLEY - 56B | ARDSLEY - 56B | **2/58: L.MOOR - 56F** | ARDSLEY - 56B | **2/58: L.MOOR - 56F** | **2/58: L.MOOR - 56F** | **2/58: L.MOOR - 56F** | HORNSEY - 34B |
| Aug-58 | ARDSLEY - 56B | ARDSLEY - 56B | ARDSLEY - 56B | **9/58: W/D** | **6/58: W.HPL - 51C** | **6/58: TBY - 51L** | LOWMOOR - 56F | LOWMOOR - 56F | HORNSEY - 34B |
| Jan-59 | ARDSLEY - 56B | ARDSLEY - 56B | **2/59: WAKE - 56A** | | W.HARTLEPOOL - 51C | **9/58: W/D** | LOWMOOR - 56F | LOWMOOR - 56F | HORNSEY - 34B |
| Aug-59 | ARDSLEY - 56B | ARDSLEY - 56B | WAKEFIELD - 56A | | **6/59: SELBY - 50C** | | LOWMOOR - 56F | LOWMOOR - 56F | HORNSEY - 34B |
| Nov-59 | ARDSLEY - 56B | **10/59: W/D** | WAKEFIELD - 56A | | **9/59: ARDS - 56B** | | LOWMOOR - 56F | LOWMOOR - 56F | HORNSEY - 34B |
| Jan-60 | ARDSLEY - 56B | | WAKEFIELD - 56A | | ARDSLEY - 56B | | LOWMOOR - 56F | LOWMOOR - 56F | HORNSEY - 34B |
| Apr-60 | ARDSLEY - 56B | | WAKEFIELD - 56A | | ARDSLEY - 56B | | LOWMOOR - 56F | LOWMOOR - 56F | HORNSEY - 34B |
| Aug-60 | ARDSLEY - 56B | | WAKEFIELD - 56A | | ARDSLEY - 56B | | LOWMOOR - 56F | LOWMOOR - 56F | HORNSEY - 34B |
| Nov-60 | ARDSLEY - 56B | | WAKEFIELD - 56A | | ARDSLEY - 56B | | LOWMOOR - 56F | **9/60: W/D** | HORNSEY - 34B |

| | 68946 | 68947 | 68948 | 68949 | 68950 | 68951 | 68952 | 68953 | 68954 |
|---|---|---|---|---|---|---|---|---|---|
| Aug-50 | MEXBOROUGH - 36B | ARDSLEY - 37A | ARDSLEY - 37A | ARDSLEY - 37A | STRATFORD - 30A | ARDSLEY - 37A | EDINBURGH (SM) - 64A | EASTFIELD - 65A | EASTFIELD - 65A |
| Jan-51 | MEXBOROUGH - 36B | ARDSLEY - 37A | ARDSLEY - 37A | ARDSLEY - 37A | STRATFORD - 30A | ARDSLEY - 37A | EDINBURGH (SM) - 64A | EASTFIELD - 65A | EASTFIELD - 65A |
| Aug-51 | MEXBOROUGH - 36B | ARDSLEY - 37A | ARDSLEY - 37A | 5/51: NEAS - 34E | STRATFORD - 30A | ARDSLEY - 37A | EDINBURGH (SM) - 64A | EASTFIELD - 65A | EASTFIELD - 65A |
| Jan-52 | MEXBOROUGH - 36B | ARDSLEY - 37A | ARDSLEY - 37A | 3/52: HSEY - 34B | STRATFORD - 30A | ARDSLEY - 37A | 1/52: EAST - 65A | EASTFIELD - 65A | EASTFIELD - 65A |
| Aug-52 | MEXBOROUGH - 36B | ARDSLEY - 37A | ARDSLEY - 37A | HORNSEY - 34B | STRATFORD - 30A | ARDSLEY - 37A | EASTFIELD - 65A | EASTFIELD - 65A | EASTFIELD - 65A |
| Jan-53 | MEXBOROUGH - 36B | ARDSLEY - 37A | ARDSLEY - 37A | HORNSEY - 34B | STRATFORD - 30A | ARDSLEY - 37A | EASTFIELD - 65A | EASTFIELD - 65A | EASTFIELD - 65A |
| Aug-53 | 7/53: IMM - 40B | ARDSLEY - 37A | ARDSLEY - 37A | HORNSEY - 34B | STRATFORD - 30A | ARDSLEY - 37A | EASTFIELD - 65A | EASTFIELD - 65A | EASTFIELD - 65A |
| Jan-54 | IMMINGHAM - 40B | ARDSLEY - 37A | ARDSLEY - 37A | HORNSEY - 34B | STRATFORD - 30A | ARDSLEY - 37A | EASTFIELD - 65A | EASTFIELD - 65A | EASTFIELD - 65A |
| Aug-54 | IMMINGHAM - 40B | ARDSLEY - 37A | ARDSLEY - 37A | HORNSEY - 34B | STRATFORD - 30A | ARDSLEY - 37A | EASTFIELD - 65A | EASTFIELD - 65A | EASTFIELD - 65A |
| Jan-55 | IMMINGHAM - 40B | ARDSLEY - 37A | ARDSLEY - 37A | HORNSEY - 34B | STRATFORD - 30A | ARDSLEY - 37A | EASTFIELD - 65A | EASTFIELD - 65A | EASTFIELD - 65A |
| Aug-55 | 4/55: HSEY - 34B | ARDSLEY - 37A | ARDSLEY - 37A | HORNSEY - 34B | STRATFORD - 30A | ARDSLEY - 37A | EASTFIELD - 65A | EASTFIELD - 65A | EASTFIELD - 65A |
| Jan-56 | HORNSEY - 34B | ARDSLEY - 37A | ARDSLEY - 37A | HORNSEY - 34B | 1/56: IMM - 40B | ARDSLEY - 37A | EASTFIELD - 65A | EASTFIELD - 65A | EASTFIELD - 65A |
| Aug-56 | HORNSEY - 34B | ARDSLEY - 56B | ARDSLEY - 56B | HORNSEY - 34B | 7/56: COLW - 38A | ARDSLEY - 56B | EASTFIELD - 65A | EASTFIELD - 65A | EASTFIELD - 65A |
| Jan-57 | HORNSEY - 34B | ARDSLEY - 56B | ARDSLEY - 56B | HORNSEY - 34B | COLWICK - 38A | ARDSLEY - 56B | EASTFIELD - 65A | EASTFIELD - 65A | EASTFIELD - 65A |
| Aug-57 | HORNSEY - 34B | ARDSLEY - 56B | ARDSLEY - 56B | HORNSEY - 34B | COLWICK - 38A | ARDSLEY - 56B | EASTFIELD - 65A | 5/57: POLM - 66A | EASTFIELD - 65A |
| Jan-58 | HORNSEY - 34B | ARDSLEY - 56B | ARDSLEY - 56B | HORNSEY - 34B | COLWICK - 38A | ARDSLEY - 56B | EASTFIELD - 65A | POLMADIE - 66A | EASTFIELD - 65A |
| Aug-58 | HORNSEY - 34B | ARDSLEY - 56B | 6/58: TBY - 51L | HORNSEY - 34B | COLWICK - 40E | 6/58: W.HPL - 51C | EASTFIELD - 65A | POLMADIE - 66A | EASTFIELD - 65A |
| Jan-59 | HORNSEY - 34B | ARDSLEY - 56B | 12/58: SELBY - 50C | HORNSEY - 34B | COLWICK - 40E | W.HARTLEPOOL - 51C | EASTFIELD - 65A | POLMADIE - 66A | EASTFIELD - 65A |
| Aug-59 | HORNSEY - 34B | ARDSLEY - 56B | 9/59: L.MOOR - 56F | 4/59: W/D | COLWICK - 40E | W.HARTLEPOOL - 51C | EASTFIELD - 65A | 7/59: W/D | EASTFIELD - 65A |
| Nov-59 | HORNSEY - 34B | ARDSLEY - 56B | LOWMOOR - 56F | | COLWICK - 40E | W.HARTLEPOOL - 51C | EASTFIELD - 65A | | EASTFIELD - 65A |
| Jan-60 | HORNSEY - 34B | ARDSLEY - 56B | LOWMOOR - 56F | | COLWICK - 40E | W.HARTLEPOOL - 51C | EASTFIELD - 65A | | EASTFIELD - 65A |
| Apr-60 | HORNSEY - 34B | ARDSLEY - 56B | LOWMOOR - 56F | | 3/60: HSEY - 34B | W.HARTLEPOOL - 51C | EASTFIELD - 65A | | EASTFIELD - 65A |
| Aug-60 | HORNSEY - 34B | ARDSLEY - 56B | LOWMOOR - 56F | | HORNSEY - 34B | W.HARTLEPOOL - 51C | 9/60: W/D | | 9/60: W/D |
| Nov-60 | HORNSEY - 34B | ARDSLEY - 56B | LOWMOOR - 56F | | HORNSEY - 34B | W.HARTLEPOOL - 51C | | | |

| | 68955 | 68956 | 68957 | 68958 | 68959 | 68960 | 68961 | 68962 | 68963 |
|---|---|---|---|---|---|---|---|---|---|
| Aug-50 | EASTFIELD - 65A | EASTFIELD - 65A | EASTFIELD - 65A | EASTFIELD - 65A | BRADFORD - 37C | MEXBOROUGH - 36B | DONCASTER - 36A | FRODINGHAM - 36C | STRATFORD - 30A |
| Jan-51 | EASTFIELD - 65A | EASTFIELD - 65A | EASTFIELD - 65A | EASTFIELD - 65A | BRADFORD - 37C | 10/50: DCTR - 36A | DONCASTER - 36A | FRODINGHAM - 36C | STRATFORD - 30A |
| Aug-51 | EASTFIELD - 65A | EASTFIELD - 65A | EASTFIELD - 65A | EASTFIELD - 65A | BRADFORD - 37C | 4/51: FROD - 36C | DONCASTER - 36A | FRODINGHAM - 36C | STRATFORD - 30A |
| Jan-52 | EASTFIELD - 65A | EASTFIELD - 65A | EASTFIELD - 65A | EASTFIELD - 65A | BRADFORD - 37C | FRODINGHAM - 36C | DONCASTER - 36A | FRODINGHAM - 36C | STRATFORD - 30A |
| Aug-52 | EASTFIELD - 65A | EASTFIELD - 65A | EASTFIELD - 65A | EASTFIELD - 65A | BRADFORD - 37C | FRODINGHAM - 36C | 9/52: HSEY - 34B | FRODINGHAM - 36C | STRATFORD - 30A |
| Jan-53 | EASTFIELD - 65A | EASTFIELD - 65A | EASTFIELD - 65A | EASTFIELD - 65A | BRADFORD - 37C | FRODINGHAM - 36C | HORNSEY - 34B | FRODINGHAM - 36C | STRATFORD - 30A |
| Aug-53 | EASTFIELD - 65A | EASTFIELD - 65A | EASTFIELD - 65A | EASTFIELD - 65A | BRADFORD - 37C | FRODINGHAM - 36C | HORNSEY - 34B | FRODINGHAM - 36C | STRATFORD - 30A |
| Jan-54 | EASTFIELD - 65A | EASTFIELD - 65A | EASTFIELD - 65A | EASTFIELD - 65A | BRADFORD - 37C | FRODINGHAM - 36C | HORNSEY - 34B | FRODINGHAM - 36C | STRATFORD - 30A |
| Aug-54 | EASTFIELD - 65A | EASTFIELD - 65A | EASTFIELD - 65A | EASTFIELD - 65A | BRADFORD - 37C | FRODINGHAM - 36C | HORNSEY - 34B | FRODINGHAM - 36C | STRATFORD - 30A |
| Jan-55 | EASTFIELD - 65A | EASTFIELD - 65A | EASTFIELD - 65A | EASTFIELD - 65A | BRADFORD - 37C | FRODINGHAM - 36C | HORNSEY - 34B | FRODINGHAM - 36C | STRATFORD - 30A |
| Aug-55 | EASTFIELD - 65A | EASTFIELD - 65A | EASTFIELD - 65A | EASTFIELD - 65A | BRADFORD - 37C | FRODINGHAM - 36C | HORNSEY - 34B | FRODINGHAM - 36C | STRATFORD - 30A |
| Jan-56 | EASTFIELD - 65A | EASTFIELD - 65A | EASTFIELD - 65A | EASTFIELD - 65A | BRADFORD - 37C | FRODINGHAM - 36C | HORNSEY - 34B | FRODINGHAM - 36C | 1/56: IMM - 40B |
| Aug-56 | EASTFIELD - 65A | EASTFIELD - 65A | EASTFIELD - 65A | EASTFIELD - 65A | BRADFORD - 56G | FRODINGHAM - 36C | HORNSEY - 34B | FRODINGHAM - 36C | 8/56: DCTR - 36A |
| Jan-57 | EASTFIELD - 65A | EASTFIELD - 65A | EASTFIELD - 65A | EASTFIELD - 65A | BRADFORD - 56G | FRODINGHAM - 36C | HORNSEY - 34B | FRODINGHAM - 36C | 2/57: FROD - 36C |
| Aug-57 | EASTFIELD - 65A | EASTFIELD - 65A | EASTFIELD - 65A | 5/57: POLM - 66A | BRADFORD - 56G | FRODINGHAM - 36C | HORNSEY - 34B | FRODINGHAM - 36C | FRODINGHAM - 36C |
| Jan-58 | EASTFIELD - 65A | EASTFIELD - 65A | EASTFIELD - 65A | POLMADIE - 66A | 10/57: ARDS - 56B | FRODINGHAM - 36C | HORNSEY - 34B | FRODINGHAM - 36C | FRODINGHAM - 36C |
| Aug-58 | EASTFIELD - 65A | EASTFIELD - 65A | EASTFIELD - 65A | POLMADIE - 66A | 6/58: W.AUCK - 51F | 7/58: DCTR - 36A | HORNSEY - 34B | FRODINGHAM - 36C | FRODINGHAM - 36C |
| Jan-59 | EASTFIELD - 65A | EASTFIELD - 65A | EASTFIELD - 65A | POLMADIE - 66A | 1/59: DARL - 51A | 10/58: HSEY - 34B | HORNSEY - 34B | 1/59: DCTR - 36A | FRODINGHAM - 36C |
| Aug-59 | EASTFIELD - 65A | EASTFIELD - 65A | EASTFIELD - 65A | POLMADIE - 66A | 8/59: WAKE - 56A | HORNSEY - 34B | HORNSEY - 34B | DONCASTER - 36A | 5/59: DCTR - 36A |
| Nov-59 | EASTFIELD - 65A | EASTFIELD - 65A | EASTFIELD - 65A | POLMADIE - 66A | WAKEFIELD - 56A | HORNSEY - 34B | HORNSEY - 34B | DONCASTER - 36A | DONCASTER - 36A |
| Jan-60 | 12/59: W/D | EASTFIELD - 65A | EASTFIELD - 65A | POLMADIE - 66A | WAKEFIELD - 56A | HORNSEY - 34B | HORNSEY - 34B | DONCASTER - 36A | DONCASTER - 36A |
| Apr-60 | | EASTFIELD - 65A | EASTFIELD - 65A | 4/60: W/D | 5/60: L.MOOR - 56F | HORNSEY - 34B | HORNSEY - 34B | DONCASTER - 36A | DONCASTER - 36A |
| Aug-60 | | 9/60: W/D | 9/60: W/D | | LOWMOOR - 56F | HORNSEY - 34B | HORNSEY - 34B | DONCASTER - 36A | DONCASTER - 36A |
| Nov-60 | | | | | LOWMOOR - 56F | HORNSEY - 34B | HORNSEY - 34B | DONCASTER - 36A | DONCASTER - 36A |

| | 68964 | 68965 | 68966 | 68967 | 68968 | 68969 | 68970 | 68971 | 68972 |
|---|---|---|---|---|---|---|---|---|---|
| Aug-50 | FRODINGHAM - 36C | STRATFORD - 30A | ARDSLEY - 37A | STRATFORD - 30A | FRODINGHAM - 36C | BRADFORD - 37C | FRODINGHAM - 36C | FRODINGHAM - 36C | COLWICK - 38A |
| Jan-51 | FRODINGHAM - 36C | STRATFORD - 30A | ARDSLEY - 37A | STRATFORD - 30A | FRODINGHAM - 36C | BRADFORD - 37C | FRODINGHAM - 36C | FRODINGHAM - 36C | COLWICK - 38A |
| Aug-51 | FRODINGHAM - 36C | STRATFORD - 30A | ARDSLEY - 37A | STRATFORD - 30A | FRODINGHAM - 36C | BRADFORD - 37C | FRODINGHAM - 36C | FRODINGHAM - 36C | COLWICK - 38A |
| Jan-52 | FRODINGHAM - 36C | STRATFORD - 30A | ARDSLEY - 37A | STRATFORD - 30A | FRODINGHAM - 36C | BRADFORD - 37C | FRODINGHAM - 36C | FRODINGHAM - 36C | COLWICK - 38A |
| Aug-52 | FRODINGHAM - 36C | STRATFORD - 30A | ARDSLEY - 37A | STRATFORD - 30A | FRODINGHAM - 36C | BRADFORD - 37C | FRODINGHAM - 36C | FRODINGHAM - 36C | 9/52: HSEY - 34B |
| Jan-53 | FRODINGHAM - 36C | STRATFORD - 30A | ARDSLEY - 37A | STRATFORD - 30A | 10/52 : HSEY - 34B | BRADFORD - 37C | FRODINGHAM - 36C | 10/52: HSEY - 34B | HORNSEY - 34B |
| Aug-53 | FRODINGHAM - 36C | STRATFORD - 30A | ARDSLEY - 37A | STRATFORD - 30A | HORNSEY - 34B | BRADFORD - 37C | FRODINGHAM - 36C | HORNSEY - 34B | HORNSEY - 34B |
| Jan-54 | FRODINGHAM - 36C | STRATFORD - 30A | ARDSLEY - 37A | STRATFORD - 30A | HORNSEY - 34B | BRADFORD - 37C | FRODINGHAM - 36C | HORNSEY - 34B | HORNSEY - 34B |
| Aug-54 | FRODINGHAM - 36C | STRATFORD - 30A | ARDSLEY - 37A | STRATFORD - 30A | HORNSEY - 34B | BRADFORD - 37C | FRODINGHAM - 36C | HORNSEY - 34B | HORNSEY - 34B |
| Jan-55 | FRODINGHAM - 36C | STRATFORD - 30A | ARDSLEY - 37A | STRATFORD - 30A | HORNSEY - 34B | BRADFORD - 37C | FRODINGHAM - 36C | HORNSEY - 34B | HORNSEY - 34B |
| Aug-55 | FRODINGHAM - 36C | STRATFORD - 30A | ARDSLEY - 37A | STRATFORD - 30A | HORNSEY - 34B | BRADFORD - 37C | FRODINGHAM - 36C | HORNSEY - 34B | HORNSEY - 34B |
| Jan-56 | FRODINGHAM - 36C | 1/56: IMM - 40B | 3/56: HSEY - 34B | 1/56: IMM - 40B | HORNSEY - 34B | BRADFORD - 37C | FRODINGHAM - 36C | HORNSEY - 34B | HORNSEY - 34B |
| Aug-56 | FRODINGHAM - 36C | IMMINGHAM - 40B | HORNSEY - 34B | 9/56: COLW - 38A | HORNSEY - 34B | BRADFORD - 56G | FRODINGHAM - 36C | HORNSEY - 34B | HORNSEY - 34B |
| Jan-57 | FRODINGHAM - 36C | 12/56: FROD - 36C | HORNSEY - 34B | COLWICK - 38A | HORNSEY - 34B | BRADFORD - 56G | FRODINGHAM - 36C | HORNSEY - 34B | HORNSEY - 34B |
| Aug-57 | FRODINGHAM - 36C | FRODINGHAM - 36C | HORNSEY - 34B | COLWICK - 38A | HORNSEY - 34B | BRADFORD - 56G | FRODINGHAM - 36C | HORNSEY - 34B | HORNSEY - 34B |
| Jan-58 | FRODINGHAM - 36C | FRODINGHAM - 36C | HORNSEY - 34B | COLWICK - 38A | HORNSEY - 34B | 2/58: L.MOOR - 56F | FRODINGHAM - 36C | HORNSEY - 34B | HORNSEY - 34B |
| Aug-58 | FRODINGHAM - 36C | FRODINGHAM - 36C | HORNSEY - 34B | COLWICK - 40E | HORNSEY - 34B | LOWMOOR - 56F | 7/58: DCTR - 36A | HORNSEY - 34B | HORNSEY - 34B |
| Jan-59 | 1/59: DCTR - 36A | 1/59: DCTR - 36A | HORNSEY - 34B | COLWICK - 40E | HORNSEY - 34B | LOWMOOR - 56F | 10/58: HSEY - 34B | HORNSEY - 34B | HORNSEY - 34B |
| Aug-59 | DONCASTER - 36A | DONCASTER - 36A | HORNSEY - 34B | 6/59: W/D | HORNSEY - 34B | LOWMOOR - 56F | HORNSEY - 34B | HORNSEY - 34B | HORNSEY - 34B |
| Nov-59 | DONCASTER - 36A | DONCASTER - 36A | HORNSEY - 34B | | HORNSEY - 34B | LOWMOOR - 56F | HORNSEY - 34B | HORNSEY - 34B | HORNSEY - 34B |
| Jan-60 | DONCASTER - 36A | DONCASTER - 36A | HORNSEY - 34B | | HORNSEY - 34B | LOWMOOR - 56F | HORNSEY - 34B | HORNSEY - 34B | HORNSEY - 34B |
| Apr-60 | DONCASTER - 36A | DONCASTER - 36A | HORNSEY - 34B | | HORNSEY - 34B | 3/60: W/D | HORNSEY - 34B | HORNSEY - 34B | HORNSEY - 34B |
| Aug-60 | DONCASTER - 36A | DONCASTER - 36A | HORNSEY - 34B | | HORNSEY - 34B | | HORNSEY - 34B | HORNSEY - 34B | HORNSEY - 34B |
| Nov-60 | DONCASTER - 36A | DONCASTER - 36A | HORNSEY - 34B | | HORNSEY - 34B | | HORNSEY - 34B | HORNSEY - 34B | HORNSEY - 34B |

| | 68973 | 68974 | 68975 | 68976 | 68977 | 68978 | 68979 | 68980 | 68981 |
|---|---|---|---|---|---|---|---|---|---|
| Aug-50 | FRODINGHAM - 36C | MEXBOROUGH - 36B | ANNESLEY - 38B | ANNESLEY - 38B | STRATFORD - 30A | COPLEYHILL - 37B | FRODINGHAM - 36C | DONCASTER - 36A | LEICESTER (GC) - 38C |
| Jan-51 | FRODINGHAM - 36C | 10/50: FROD - 36C | ANNESLEY - 38B | ANNESLEY - 38B | STRATFORD - 30A | COPLEYHILL - 37B | 10/50: MEX - 36B | DONCASTER - 36A | LEICESTER (GC) - 38C |
| Aug-51 | FRODINGHAM - 36C | FRODINGHAM - 36C | ANNESLEY - 38B | ANNESLEY - 38B | STRATFORD - 30A | COPLEYHILL - 37B | MEXBOROUGH - 36B | DONCASTER - 36A | LEICESTER (GC) - 38C |
| Jan-52 | FRODINGHAM - 36C | FRODINGHAM - 36C | ANNESLEY - 38B | ANNESLEY - 38B | STRATFORD - 30A | COPLEYHILL - 37B | MEXBOROUGH - 36B | 11/51: MEX - 36B | LEICESTER (GC) - 38C |
| Aug-52 | FRODINGHAM - 36C | FRODINGHAM - 36C | ANNESLEY - 38B | ANNESLEY - 38B | STRATFORD - 30A | COPLEYHILL - 37B | MEXBOROUGH - 36B | MEXBOROUGH - 36B | 9/52: COLW - 38A |
| Jan-53 | FRODINGHAM - 36C | FRODINGHAM - 36C | ANNESLEY - 38B | ANNESLEY - 38B | STRATFORD - 30A | COPLEYHILL - 37B | MEXBOROUGH - 36B | MEXBOROUGH - 36B | 10/52: HSEY - 34B |
| Aug-53 | 7/53: DCTR - 36A | 7/53: DCTR - 36A | ANNESLEY - 38B | ANNESLEY - 38B | STRATFORD - 30A | COPLEYHILL - 37B | 7/53: IMM - 40B | 5/53: FROD - 36C | HORNSEY - 34B |
| Jan-54 | DONCASTER - 36A | DONCASTER - 36A | ANNESLEY - 38B | ANNESLEY - 38B | STRATFORD - 30A | COPLEYHILL - 37B | IMMINGHAM - 40B | FRODINGHAM - 36C | HORNSEY - 34B |
| Aug-54 | 6/54: FROD - 36C | DONCASTER - 36A | ANNESLEY - 38B | ANNESLEY - 38B | STRATFORD - 30A | COPLEYHILL - 37B | IMMINGHAM - 40B | FRODINGHAM - 36C | HORNSEY - 34B |
| Jan-55 | FRODINGHAM - 36C | DONCASTER - 36A | ANNESLEY - 38B | ANNESLEY - 38B | STRATFORD - 30A | COPLEYHILL - 37B | 3/55: HSEY - 40B | FRODINGHAM - 36C | HORNSEY - 34B |
| Aug-55 | FRODINGHAM - 36C | DONCASTER - 36A | ANNESLEY - 38B | ANNESLEY - 38B | STRATFORD - 30A | COPLEYHILL - 37B | HORNSEY - 34B | FRODINGHAM - 36C | HORNSEY - 34B |
| Jan-56 | FRODINGHAM - 36C | DONCASTER - 36A | 11/55: COLW - 38A | ANNESLEY - 38B | 1/56: IMM - 40B | COPLEYHILL - 37B | HORNSEY - 34B | FRODINGHAM - 36C | HORNSEY - 34B |
| Aug-56 | FRODINGHAM - 36C | DONCASTER - 36A | COLWICK - 38A | ANNESLEY - 38B | IMMINGHAM - 40B | COPLEYHILL - 56C | HORNSEY - 34B | 5/56: DCTR - 36A | HORNSEY - 34B |
| Jan-57 | FRODINGHAM - 36C | DONCASTER - 36A | COLWICK - 38A | ANNESLEY - 38B | 2/57: FROD - 36C | COPLEYHILL - 56C | HORNSEY - 34B | DONCASTER - 36A | HORNSEY - 34B |
| Aug-57 | FRODINGHAM - 36C | DONCASTER - 36A | COLWICK - 38A | ANNESLEY - 38B | FRODINGHAM - 36C | COPLEYHILL - 56C | HORNSEY - 34B | DONCASTER - 36A | HORNSEY - 34B |
| Jan-58 | FRODINGHAM - 36C | 2/58: COLW - 40E | COLWICK - 38A | ANNESLEY - 38B | FRODINGHAM - 36C | COPLEYHILL - 56C | HORNSEY - 34B | DONCASTER - 36A | HORNSEY - 34B |
| Aug-58 | FRODINGHAM - 36C | COLWICK - 40E | COLWICK - 40E | ANNESLEY - 16D | FRODINGHAM - 36C | COPLEYHILL - 56C | HORNSEY - 34B | DONCASTER - 36A | HORNSEY - 34B |
| Jan-59 | 1/59: DCTR - 36A | COLWICK - 40E | COLWICK - 40E | 12/58: NEW.E - 34E | FRODINGHAM - 36C | 11/58: W/D | HORNSEY - 34B | 10/58: HSEY - 34B | HORNSEY - 34B |
| Aug-59 | 7/59: W/D | 8/59: W/D | COLWICK - 40E | NEWENGLAND - 34E | 5/59: DCTR - 36A | | HORNSEY - 34B | HORNSEY - 34B | HORNSEY - 34B |
| Nov-59 | | | COLWICK - 40E | NEWENGLAND - 34E | DONCASTER - 36A | | HORNSEY - 34B | HORNSEY - 34B | HORNSEY - 34B |
| Jan-60 | | | COLWICK - 40E | 2/60: HSEY - 34B | DONCASTER - 36A | | HORNSEY - 34B | HORNSEY - 34B | HORNSEY - 34B |
| Apr-60 | | | COLWICK - 40E | HORNSEY - 34B | DONCASTER - 36A | | HORNSEY - 34B | 3/60: W/D | HORNSEY - 34B |
| Aug-60 | | | COLWICK - 40E | HORNSEY - 34B | DONCASTER - 36A | | HORNSEY - 34B | | HORNSEY - 34B |
| Nov-60 | | | COLWICK - 40E | HORNSEY - 34B | DONCASTER - 36A | | HORNSEY - 34B | | HORNSEY - 34B |

| | 68982 | 68983 | 68984 | 68985 | 68966 | 68987 | 68988 | 68989 | 68990 |
|---|---|---|---|---|---|---|---|---|---|
| Aug-50 | COLWICK - 38A | DARNALL - 39B | COPLEYHILL - 37B | DONCASTER - 36A | DONCASTER - 36A | DONCASTER - 36A | COPLEYHILL - 37B | DONCASTER - 36A | DARNALL - 39B |
| Jan-51 | COLWICK - 38A | DARNALL - 39B | COPLEYHILL - 37B | DONCASTER - 36A | DONCASTER - 36A | DONCASTER - 36A | COPLEYHILL - 37B | DONCASTER - 36A | DARNALL - 39B |
| Aug-51 | COLWICK - 38A | DARNALL - 39B | COPLEYHILL - 37B | DONCASTER - 36A | DONCASTER - 36A | DONCASTER - 36A | COPLEYHILL - 37B | DONCASTER - 36A | DARNALL - 39B |
| Jan-52 | COLWICK - 38A | DARNALL - 39B | COPLEYHILL - 37B | DONCASTER - 36A | DONCASTER - 36A | DONCASTER - 36A | COPLEYHILL - 37B | DONCASTER - 36A | DARNALL - 39B |
| Aug-52 | COLWICK - 38A | DARNALL - 39B | COPLEYHILL - 37B | DONCASTER - 36A | DONCASTER - 36A | DONCASTER - 36A | COPLEYHILL - 37B | DONCASTER - 36A | DARNALL - 39B |
| Jan-53 | **10/52: HSEY - 34B** | **10/52: HSEY - 34B** | COPLEYHILL - 37B | **10/52: HSEY - 34B** | **10/52: HSEY - 34B** | **10/52: HSEY - 34B** | COPLEYHILL - 37B | **10/52: HSEY - 34B** | **10/52: HSEY - 34B** |
| Aug-53 | HORNSEY - 34B | HORNSEY - 34B | COPLEYHILL - 37B | HORNSEY - 34B | HORNSEY - 34B | HORNSEY - 34B | COPLEYHILL - 37B | HORNSEY - 34B | HORNSEY - 34B |
| Jan-54 | HORNSEY - 34B | HORNSEY - 34B | COPLEYHILL - 37B | HORNSEY - 34B | HORNSEY - 34B | HORNSEY - 34B | COPLEYHILL - 37B | HORNSEY - 34B | HORNSEY - 34B |
| Aug-54 | HORNSEY - 34B | HORNSEY - 34B | COPLEYHILL - 37B | HORNSEY - 34B | HORNSEY - 34B | HORNSEY - 34B | COPLEYHILL - 37B | HORNSEY - 34B | HORNSEY - 34B |
| Jan-55 | HORNSEY - 34B | HORNSEY - 34B | COPLEYHILL - 37B | HORNSEY - 34B | HORNSEY - 34B | HORNSEY - 34B | COPLEYHILL - 37B | HORNSEY - 34B | HORNSEY - 34B |
| Aug-55 | HORNSEY - 34B | HORNSEY - 34B | COPLEYHILL - 37B | HORNSEY - 34B | HORNSEY - 34B | HORNSEY - 34B | COPLEYHILL - 37B | HORNSEY - 34B | HORNSEY - 34B |
| Jan-56 | HORNSEY - 34B | HORNSEY - 34B | COPLEYHILL - 37B | HORNSEY - 34B | HORNSEY - 34B | HORNSEY - 34B | COPLEYHILL - 37B | HORNSEY - 34B | HORNSEY - 34B |
| Aug-56 | HORNSEY - 34B | HORNSEY - 34B | COPLEYHILL - 56C | HORNSEY - 34B | HORNSEY - 34B | HORNSEY - 34B | COPLEYHILL - 56C | HORNSEY - 34B | HORNSEY - 34B |
| Jan-57 | HORNSEY - 34B | HORNSEY - 34B | COPLEYHILL - 56C | HORNSEY - 34B | HORNSEY - 34B | HORNSEY - 34B | COPLEYHILL - 56C | HORNSEY - 34B | HORNSEY - 34B |
| Aug-57 | HORNSEY - 34B | HORNSEY - 34B | COPLEYHILL - 56C | HORNSEY - 34B | HORNSEY - 34B | HORNSEY - 34B | COPLEYHILL - 56C | HORNSEY - 34B | HORNSEY - 34B |
| Jan-58 | HORNSEY - 34B | HORNSEY - 34B | COPLEYHILL - 56C | HORNSEY - 34B | HORNSEY - 34B | HORNSEY - 34B | COPLEYHILL - 56C | HORNSEY - 34B | HORNSEY - 34B |
| Aug-58 | HORNSEY - 34B | HORNSEY - 34B | COPLEYHILL - 56C | HORNSEY - 34B | HORNSEY - 34B | HORNSEY - 34B | COPLEYHILL - 56C | HORNSEY - 34B | HORNSEY - 34B |
| Jan-59 | HORNSEY - 34B | HORNSEY - 34B | COPLEYHILL - 56C | HORNSEY - 34B | HORNSEY - 34B | HORNSEY - 34B | COPLEYHILL - 56C | HORNSEY - 34B | HORNSEY - 34B |
| Aug-59 | HORNSEY - 34B | HORNSEY - 34B | COPLEYHILL - 56C | HORNSEY - 34B | HORNSEY - 34B | HORNSEY - 34B | COPLEYHILL - 56C | HORNSEY - 34B | HORNSEY - 34B |
| Nov-59 | HORNSEY - 34B | HORNSEY - 34B | COPLEYHILL - 56C | **11/59: W/D** | HORNSEY - 34B | HORNSEY - 34B | COPLEYHILL - 56C | HORNSEY - 34B | HORNSEY - 34B |
| Jan-60 | HORNSEY - 34B | HORNSEY - 34B | COPLEYHILL - 56C | | HORNSEY - 34B | HORNSEY - 34B | COPLEYHILL - 56C | HORNSEY - 34B | HORNSEY - 34B |
| Apr-60 | HORNSEY - 34B | HORNSEY - 34B | COPLEYHILL - 56C | | HORNSEY - 34B | HORNSEY - 34B | COPLEYHILL - 56C | HORNSEY - 34B | HORNSEY - 34B |
| Aug-60 | HORNSEY - 34B | HORNSEY - 34B | COPLEYHILL - 56C | | HORNSEY - 34B | HORNSEY - 34B | COPLEYHILL - 56C | HORNSEY - 34B | HORNSEY - 34B |
| Nov-60 | HORNSEY - 34B | HORNSEY - 34B | COPLEYHILL - 56C | | HORNSEY - 34B | HORNSEY - 34B | COPLEYHILL - 56C | HORNSEY - 34B | HORNSEY - 34B |

| | | J72 0-6-0T (1949) | | | | | | | |
|---|---|---|---|---|---|---|---|---|---|
| | 68991 | 69001 | 69002 | 69003 | 69004 | 69005 | 69006 | 69007 | 69008 |
| Aug-50 | DONCASTER - 36A | SPRINGHEAD - 53C | SPRINGHEAD - 53C | SPRINGHEAD - 53C | DARLINGTON - 51A | GATESHEAD - 52A | MIDDLESBROUGH - 51D | W.AUCKLAND - 51F | TYNEDOCK - 54B |
| Jan-51 | DONCASTER - 36A | SPRINGHEAD - 53C | SPRINGHEAD - 53C | SPRINGHEAD - 53C | DARLINGTON - 51A | GATESHEAD - 52A | MIDDLESBROUGH - 51D | W.AUCKLAND - 51F | TYNEDOCK - 54B |
| Aug-51 | DONCASTER - 36A | SPRINGHEAD - 53C | SPRINGHEAD - 53C | SPRINGHEAD - 53C | DARLINGTON - 51A | GATESHEAD - 52A | MIDDLESBROUGH - 51D | W.AUCKLAND - 51F | TYNEDOCK - 54B |
| Jan-52 | DONCASTER - 36A | SPRINGHEAD - 53C | SPRINGHEAD - 53C | SPRINGHEAD - 53C | DARLINGTON - 51A | GATESHEAD - 52A | MIDDLESBROUGH - 51D | W.AUCKLAND - 51F | TYNEDOCK - 54B |
| Aug-52 | **9/52: HSEY - 34B** | SPRINGHEAD - 53C | **9/52: SUND - 54A** | SPRINGHEAD - 53C | DARLINGTON - 51A | GATESHEAD - 52A | MIDDLESBROUGH - 51D | **9/52: SUND - 54A** | TYNEDOCK - 54B |
| Jan-53 | HORNSEY - 34B | SPRINGHEAD - 53C | SUNDERLAND - 54A | SPRINGHEAD - 53C | DARLINGTON - 51A | GATESHEAD - 52A | MIDDLESBROUGH - 51D | SUNDERLAND - 54A | TYNEDOCK - 54B |
| Aug-53 | HORNSEY - 34B | SPRINGHEAD - 53C | SUNDERLAND - 54A | SPRINGHEAD - 53C | DARLINGTON - 51A | GATESHEAD - 52A | MIDDLESBROUGH - 51D | SUNDERLAND - 54A | TYNEDOCK - 54B |
| Jan-54 | HORNSEY - 34B | SPRINGHEAD - 53C | SUNDERLAND - 54A | SPRINGHEAD - 53C | DARLINGTON - 51A | GATESHEAD - 52A | MIDDLESBROUGH - 51D | SUNDERLAND - 54A | TYNEDOCK - 54B |
| Aug-54 | HORNSEY - 34B | SPRINGHEAD - 53C | SUNDERLAND - 54A | SPRINGHEAD - 53C | DARLINGTON - 51A | GATESHEAD - 52A | MIDDLESBROUGH - 51D | SUNDERLAND - 54A | TYNEDOCK - 54B |
| Jan-55 | HORNSEY - 34B | SPRINGHEAD - 53C | SUNDERLAND - 54A | SPRINGHEAD - 53C | DARLINGTON - 51A | GATESHEAD - 52A | MIDDLESBROUGH - 51D | SUNDERLAND - 54A | TYNEDOCK - 54B |
| Aug-55 | HORNSEY - 34B | **6/55: HTN - 52B** | SUNDERLAND - 54A | SPRINGHEAD - 53C | DARLINGTON - 51A | GATESHEAD - 52A | MIDDLESBROUGH - 51D | SUNDERLAND - 54A | TYNEDOCK - 54B |
| Jan-56 | HORNSEY - 34B | HEATON - 52B | SUNDERLAND - 54A | SPRINGHEAD - 53C | DARLINGTON - 51A | GATESHEAD - 52A | MIDDLESBROUGH - 51D | SUNDERLAND - 54A | TYNEDOCK - 54B |
| Aug-56 | HORNSEY - 34B | HEATON - 52B | SUNDERLAND - 54A | SPRINGHEAD - 53C | DARLINGTON - 51A | GATESHEAD - 52A | MIDDLESBROUGH - 51D | SUNDERLAND - 54A | TYNEDOCK - 54B |
| Jan-57 | HORNSEY - 34B | HEATON - 52B | SUNDERLAND - 54A | SPRINGHEAD - 53C | DARLINGTON - 51A | GATESHEAD - 52A | MIDDLESBROUGH - 51D | SUNDERLAND - 54A | TYNEDOCK - 54B |
| Aug-57 | HORNSEY - 34B | **6/57: BLAY - 52C** | SUNDERLAND - 54A | SPRINGHEAD - 53C | DARLINGTON - 51A | GATESHEAD - 52A | MIDDLESBROUGH - 51D | SUNDERLAND - 54A | **6/57: GOOLE - 53E** |
| Jan-58 | HORNSEY - 34B | BLAYDON - 52C | SUNDERLAND - 54A | SPRINGHEAD - 53C | DARLINGTON - 51A | GATESHEAD - 52A | MIDDLESBROUGH - 51D | SUNDERLAND - 54A | GOOLE - 53E |
| Aug-58 | HORNSEY - 34B | BLAYDON - 52C | SUNDERLAND - 54A | SPRINGHEAD - 53C | DARLINGTON - 51A | GATESHEAD - 52A | **6/58: TBY - 51L** | SUNDERLAND - 54A | GOOLE - 53E |
| Jan-59 | HORNSEY - 34B | **2/59: GHD - 52A** | SUNDERLAND - 52G | SPRINGHEAD - 53C | DARLINGTON - 51A | GATESHEAD - 52A | THORNABY - 51L | **2/59: W.AUCK - 51F** | **12/58: DAIRY - 53A** |
| Aug-59 | HORNSEY - 34B | GATESHEAD - 52A | SUNDERLAND - 52G | SPRINGHEAD - 53C | DARLINGTON - 51A | GATESHEAD - 52A | THORNABY - 51L | W.AUCKLAND - 51F | DAIRYCOATES - 53A |
| Nov-59 | HORNSEY - 34B | GATESHEAD - 52A | SUNDERLAND - 52G | SPRINGHEAD - 53C | DARLINGTON - 51A | GATESHEAD - 52A | THORNABY - 51L | W.AUCKLAND - 51F | DAIRYCOATES - 53A |
| Jan-60 | HORNSEY - 34B | GATESHEAD - 52A | SUNDERLAND - 52G | SPRINGHEAD - 53C | DARLINGTON - 51A | GATESHEAD - 52A | THORNABY - 51L | W.AUCKLAND - 51F | DAIRYCOATES - 53A |
| Apr-60 | HORNSEY - 34B | GATESHEAD - 52A | SUNDERLAND - 52G | **3/60: YORK - 50A** | DARLINGTON - 51A | GATESHEAD - 52A | THORNABY - 51L | W.AUCKLAND - 51F | **3/60: YORK - 50A** |
| Aug-60 | HORNSEY - 34B | GATESHEAD - 52A | **9/60: W.AUCK - 51F** | YORK - 50A | DARLINGTON - 51A | GATESHEAD - 52A | THORNABY - 51L | W.AUCKLAND - 51F | YORK - 50A |
| Nov-60 | HORNSEY - 34B | GATESHEAD - 52A | W.AUCKLAND - 51F | YORK - 50A | DARLINGTON - 51A | GATESHEAD - 52A | THORNABY - 51L | W.AUCKLAND - 51F | YORK - 50A |

| | 69009 | 69010 | 69011 | 69012 | 69013 | 69014 | 69015 | 69016 | 69017 |
|---|---|---|---|---|---|---|---|---|---|
| Aug-50 | SPRINGHEAD - 53C | DAIRYCOATES - 53A | DAIRYCOATES - 53A | IPSWICH - 32B | IPSWICH - 32B | DONCASTER - 36A | DARNALL - 39B | SCARBOROUGH - 50E | B.GARDENS - 54C |
| Jan-51 | SPRINGHEAD - 53C | DAIRYCOATES - 53A | DAIRYCOATES - 53A | IPSWICH - 32B | IPSWICH - 32B | DONCASTER - 36A | **9/50: DCTR - 36A** | SCARBOROUGH - 50E | B.GARDENS - 54C |
| Aug-51 | SPRINGHEAD - 53C | DAIRYCOATES - 53A | DAIRYCOATES - 53A | IPSWICH - 32B | IPSWICH - 32B | DONCASTER - 36A | DONCASTER - 36A | SCARBOROUGH - 50E | B.GARDENS - 54C |
| Jan-52 | SPRINGHEAD - 53C | DAIRYCOATES - 53A | DAIRYCOATES - 53A | **2/52: TH JN - 62A** | **2/52: TH JN - 62A** | **2/52: EBRO(SM) -64A** | **2/52: P'HEAD - 65C** | SCARBOROUGH - 50E | B.GARDENS - 54C |
| Aug-52 | SPRINGHEAD - 53C | DAIRYCOATES - 53A | DAIRYCOATES - 53A | THORNTONJCN - 62A | THORNTONJCN - 62A | EDINBURGH(SM) - 64A | PARKHEAD - 65C | SCARBOROUGH - 50E | B.GARDENS - 54C |
| Jan-53 | SPRINGHEAD - 53C | **2/53: S'HEAD - 53C** | **2/53: S'HEAD - 53C** | THORNTONJCN - 62A | THORNTONJCN - 62A | EDINBURGH(SM) - 64A | PARKHEAD - 65C | SCARBOROUGH - 50E | B.GARDENS - 54C |
| Aug-53 | SPRINGHEAD - 53C | SPRINGHEAD - 53C | SPRINGHEAD - 53C | THORNTONJCN - 62A | THORNTONJCN - 62A | EDINBURGH(SM) - 64A | PARKHEAD - 65C | SCARBOROUGH - 50E | B.GARDENS - 54C |
| Jan-54 | SPRINGHEAD - 53C | SPRINGHEAD - 53C | SPRINGHEAD - 53C | THORNTONJCN - 62A | THORNTONJCN - 62A | EDINBURGH(SM) - 64A | PARKHEAD - 65C | SCARBOROUGH - 50E | B.GARDENS - 54C |
| Aug-54 | SPRINGHEAD - 53C | SPRINGHEAD - 53C | SPRINGHEAD - 53C | THORNTONJCN - 62A | THORNTONJCN - 62A | EDINBURGH(SM) - 64A | PARKHEAD - 65C | SCARBOROUGH - 50E | B.GARDENS - 54C |
| Jan-55 | SPRINGHEAD - 53C | SPRINGHEAD - 53C | SPRINGHEAD - 53C | THORNTONJCN - 62A | THORNTONJCN - 62A | EDINBURGH(SM) - 64A | PARKHEAD - 65C | SCARBOROUGH - 50E | B.GARDENS - 54C |
| Aug-55 | SPRINGHEAD - 53C | SPRINGHEAD - 53C | SPRINGHEAD - 53C | THORNTONJCN - 62A | THORNTONJCN - 62A | EDINBURGH(SM) - 64A | PARKHEAD - 65C | SCARBOROUGH - 50E | B.GARDENS - 54C |
| Jan-56 | SPRINGHEAD - 53C | SPRINGHEAD - 53C | SPRINGHEAD - 53C | THORNTONJCN - 62A | THORNTONJCN - 62A | EDINBURGH(SM) - 64A | PARKHEAD - 65C | SCARBOROUGH - 50E | B.GARDENS - 54C |
| Aug-56 | SPRINGHEAD - 53C | SPRINGHEAD - 53C | SPRINGHEAD - 53C | THORNTONJCN - 62A | THORNTONJCN - 62A | EDINBURGH(SM) - 64A | PARKHEAD - 65C | SCARBOROUGH - 50E | B.GARDENS - 54C |
| Jan-57 | SPRINGHEAD - 53C | SPRINGHEAD - 53C | SPRINGHEAD - 53C | THORNTONJCN - 62A | THORNTONJCN - 62A | EDINBURGH(SM) - 64A | PARKHEAD - 65C | SCARBOROUGH - 50E | B.GARDENS - 54C |
| Aug-57 | SPRINGHEAD - 53C | SPRINGHEAD - 53C | SPRINGHEAD - 53C | THORNTONJCN - 62A | THORNTONJCN - 62A | EDINBURGH(SM) - 64A | PARKHEAD - 65C | SCARBOROUGH - 50E | B.GARDENS - 54C |
| Jan-58 | SPRINGHEAD - 53C | SPRINGHEAD - 53C | SPRINGHEAD - 53C | THORNTONJCN - 62A | **12/57: EBRO(SM) - 64A** | EDINBURGH(SM) - 64A | PARKHEAD - 65C | SCARBOROUGH - 50E | B.GARDENS - 54C |
| Aug-58 | SPRINGHEAD - 53C | SPRINGHEAD - 53C | SPRINGHEAD - 53C | THORNTONJCN - 62A | EDINBURGH(SM) - 64A | EDINBURGH(SM) - 64A | PARKHEAD - 65C | SCARBOROUGH - 50E | B.GARDENS - 54C |
| Jan-59 | SPRINGHEAD - 53C | SPRINGHEAD - 53C | SPRINGHEAD - 53C | THORNTONJCN - 62A | EDINBURGH(SM) - 64A | EDINBURGH(SM) - 64A | PARKHEAD - 65C | **12/58: YORK - 50A** | **6/59: W.HPL - 51C** |
| Aug-59 | SPRINGHEAD - 53C | SPRINGHEAD - 53C | SPRINGHEAD - 53C | THORNTONJCN - 62A | EDINBURGH(SM) - 64A | EDINBURGH(SM) - 64A | PARKHEAD - 65C | YORK - 50A | **8/59: DARL - 51A** |
| Nov-59 | SPRINGHEAD - 53C | SPRINGHEAD - 53C | SPRINGHEAD - 53C | THORNTONJCN - 62A | EDINBURGH(SM) - 64A | EDINBURGH(SM) - 64A | PARKHEAD - 65C | YORK - 50A | DARLINGTON - 51A |
| Jan-60 | SPRINGHEAD - 53C | SPRINGHEAD - 53C | SPRINGHEAD - 53C | THORNTONJCN - 62A | EDINBURGH(SM) - 64A | EDINBURGH(SM) - 64A | PARKHEAD - 65C | YORK - 50A | DARLINGTON - 51A |
| Apr-60 | SPRINGHEAD - 53C | SPRINGHEAD - 53C | SPRINGHEAD - 53C | THORNTONJCN - 62A | EDINBURGH(SM) - 64A | EDINBURGH(SM) - 64A | PARKHEAD - 65C | YORK - 50A | DARLINGTON - 51A |
| Aug-60 | SPRINGHEAD - 53C | SPRINGHEAD - 53C | SPRINGHEAD - 53C | THORNTONJCN - 62A | EDINBURGH(SM) - 64A | EDINBURGH(SM) - 64A | PARKHEAD - 65C | YORK - 50A | DARLINGTON - 51A |
| Nov-60 | SPRINGHEAD - 53C | SPRINGHEAD - 53C | SPRINGHEAD - 53C | THORNTONJCN - 62A | EDINBURGH(SM) - 64A | EDINBURGH(SM) - 64A | PARKHEAD - 65C | YORK - 50A | DARLINGTON - 51A |

| | 69018 | 69019 | 69020 | 69021 | 69022 | 69023 | 69024 | 69025 | 69026 |
|---|---|---|---|---|---|---|---|---|---|
| Aug-50 | SUNDERLAND - 54A | MIDDLESBROUGH - 51D | YORK - 50A | | | | | | |
| Jan-51 | SUNDERLAND - 54A | MIDDLESBROUGH - 51D | YORK - 50A | | | | | | |
| Aug-51 | SUNDERLAND - 54A | MIDDLESBROUGH - 51D | YORK - 50A | **4/51: DARL - 51A** | **4/51: DARL - 51A** | **4/51: BLAY - 52C** | **4/51: BLAY - 52C** | **4/51: BLAY - 52C** | **5/51: HEX - 52C** |
| Jan-52 | SUNDERLAND - 54A | MIDDLESBROUGH - 51D | YORK - 50A | DARLINGTON - 51A | DARLINGTON - 51A | BLAYDON - 52C | BLAYDON - 52C | BLAYDON - 52C | HEXHAM - 52C |
| Aug-52 | **9/52: W.AUCK - 51F** | MIDDLESBROUGH - 51D | YORK - 50A | DARLINGTON - 51A | DARLINGTON - 51A | BLAYDON - 52C | BLAYDON - 52C | BLAYDON - 52C | HEXHAM - 52C |
| Jan-53 | W.AUCKLAND - 51F | MIDDLESBROUGH - 51D | YORK - 50A | DARLINGTON - 51A | DARLINGTON - 51A | BLAYDON - 52C | BLAYDON - 52C | BLAYDON - 52C | **11/52: BLAY - 52C** |
| Aug-53 | W.AUCKLAND - 51F | MIDDLESBROUGH - 51D | YORK - 50A | DARLINGTON - 51A | DARLINGTON - 51A | BLAYDON - 52C | BLAYDON - 52C | BLAYDON - 52C | BLAYDON - 52C |
| Jan-54 | W.AUCKLAND - 51F | MIDDLESBROUGH - 51D | YORK - 50A | DARLINGTON - 51A | DARLINGTON - 51A | BLAYDON - 52C | BLAYDON - 52C | BLAYDON - 52C | BLAYDON - 52C |
| Aug-54 | W.AUCKLAND - 51F | MIDDLESBROUGH - 51D | YORK - 50A | DARLINGTON - 51A | DARLINGTON - 51A | BLAYDON - 52C | BLAYDON - 52C | BLAYDON - 52C | BLAYDON - 52C |
| Jan-55 | W.AUCKLAND - 51F | MIDDLESBROUGH - 51D | YORK - 50A | DARLINGTON - 51A | DARLINGTON - 51A | BLAYDON - 52C | BLAYDON - 52C | BLAYDON - 52C | BLAYDON - 52C |
| Aug-55 | W.AUCKLAND - 51F | MIDDLESBROUGH - 51D | YORK - 50A | DARLINGTON - 51A | DARLINGTON - 51A | BLAYDON - 52C | BLAYDON - 52C | BLAYDON - 52C | BLAYDON - 52C |
| Jan-56 | W.AUCKLAND - 51F | MIDDLESBROUGH - 51D | YORK - 50A | DARLINGTON - 51A | DARLINGTON - 51A | BLAYDON - 52C | BLAYDON - 52C | BLAYDON - 52C | BLAYDON - 52C |
| Aug-56 | W.AUCKLAND - 51F | MIDDLESBROUGH - 51D | YORK - 50A | DARLINGTON - 51A | DARLINGTON - 51A | BLAYDON - 52C | BLAYDON - 52C | BLAYDON - 52C | BLAYDON - 52C |
| Jan-57 | W.AUCKLAND - 51F | MIDDLESBROUGH - 51D | YORK - 50A | DARLINGTON - 51A | DARLINGTON - 51A | BLAYDON - 52C | BLAYDON - 52C | BLAYDON - 52C | BLAYDON - 52C |
| Aug-57 | W.AUCKLAND - 51F | MIDDLESBROUGH - 51D | YORK - 50A | DARLINGTON - 51A | DARLINGTON - 51A | BLAYDON - 52C | BLAYDON - 52C | BLAYDON - 52C | BLAYDON - 52C |
| Jan-58 | W.AUCKLAND - 51F | MIDDLESBROUGH - 51D | YORK - 50A | DARLINGTON - 51A | DARLINGTON - 51A | BLAYDON - 52C | BLAYDON - 52C | BLAYDON - 52C | BLAYDON - 52C |
| Aug-58 | W.AUCKLAND - 51F | **6/58: TBY - 51L** | YORK - 50A | DARLINGTON - 51A | DARLINGTON - 51A | BLAYDON - 52C | BLAYDON - 52C | BLAYDON - 52C | BLAYDON - 52C |
| Jan-59 | W.AUCKLAND - 51F | THORNABY - 51L | YORK - 50A | DARLINGTON - 51A | DARLINGTON - 51A | BLAYDON - 52C | BLAYDON - 52C | BLAYDON - 52C | BLAYDON - 52C |
| Aug-59 | W.AUCKLAND - 51F | THORNABY - 51L | YORK - 50A | DARLINGTON - 51A | DARLINGTON - 51A | BLAYDON - 52C | BLAYDON - 52C | BLAYDON - 52C | BLAYDON - 52C |
| Nov-59 | W.AUCKLAND - 51F | THORNABY - 51L | YORK - 50A | DARLINGTON - 51A | DARLINGTON - 51A | BLAYDON - 52C | BLAYDON - 52C | BLAYDON - 52C | BLAYDON - 52C |
| Jan-60 | W.AUCKLAND - 51F | THORNABY - 51L | YORK - 50A | DARLINGTON - 51A | DARLINGTON - 51A | BLAYDON - 52C | BLAYDON - 52C | BLAYDON - 52C | BLAYDON - 52C |
| Apr-60 | W.AUCKLAND - 51F | THORNABY - 51L | **3/60: DAIRY - 53A** | DARLINGTON - 51A | DARLINGTON - 51A | BLAYDON - 52C | BLAYDON - 52C | BLAYDON - 52C | BLAYDON - 52C |
| Aug-60 | W.AUCKLAND - 51F | THORNABY - 51L | DAIRYCOATES - 50B | DARLINGTON - 51A | DARLINGTON - 51A | BLAYDON - 52C | BLAYDON - 52C | BLAYDON - 52C | BLAYDON - 52C |
| Nov-60 | W.AUCKLAND - 51F | THORNABY - 51L | DAIRYCOATES - 50B | DARLINGTON - 51A | DARLINGTON - 51A | BLAYDON - 52C | BLAYDON - 52C | BLAYDON - 52C | BLAYDON - 52C |

**L3 2-6-4T (1914)** (column 69050)

| | 69027 | 69028 | 69050 | 69051 | 69052 | 69055 | 69056 | 69060 | 69061 |
|---|---|---|---|---|---|---|---|---|---|
| Aug-50 | | | W.HALSE-38E | FRODINGHAM-36C | NORTHWCH-9G | NEASDEN-34E | NEASDEN-34E | NEASDEN-34E | NEASDEN-34E |
| Jan-51 | | | W.HALSE-38E | FRODINGHAM-36C | NORTHWCH-9G | NEASDEN-34E | 1/51: W/D | NEASDEN-34E | NEASDEN-34E |
| Aug-51 | 5/51: HTN - 52B | 5/51: HTN - 52B | W.HALSE-38E | 5/51: W/D | NORTHWCH-9G | 7/51: W/D | | NEASDEN-34E | NEASDEN-34E |
| Jan-52 | HEATON-52B | HEATON-52B | W.HALSE-38E | | NORTHWCH-9G | | | NEASDEN-34E | NEASDEN-34E |
| Aug-52 | HEATON-52B | HEATON-52B | W.HALSE-38E | | NORTHWCH-9G | | | NEASDEN-34E | NEASDEN-34E |
| Jan-53 | HEATON-52B | HEATON-52B | W.HALSE-38E | | NORTHWCH-9G | | | NEASDEN-34E | 2/53: W/D |
| Aug-53 | HEATON-52B | HEATON-52B | W.HALSE-38E | | NORTHWCH-9G | | | NEASDEN-34E | |
| Jan-54 | HEATON-52B | HEATON-52B | W.HALSE-38E | | 8/54: W/D | | | 7/53: FROD - 36C | |
| Aug-54 | HEATON-52B | HEATON-52B | W.HALSE-38E | | | | | FRODINGHAM-36C | |
| Jan-55 | HEATON-52B | HEATON-52B | W.HALSE-38E | | | | | 6/54: W/D | |
| Aug-55 | HEATON-52B | HEATON-52B | 3/55: W/D | | | | | | |
| Jan-56 | HEATON-52B | HEATON-52B | | | | | | | |
| Aug-56 | HEATON-52B | HEATON-52B | | | | | | | |
| Jan-57 | HEATON-52B | HEATON-52B | | | | | | | |
| Aug-57 | HEATON-52B | HEATON-52B | | | | | | | |
| Jan-58 | HEATON-52B | HEATON-52B | | | | | | | |
| Aug-58 | HEATON-52B | HEATON-52B | | | | | | | |
| Jan-59 | 2/59: GHD - 52A | HEATON-52B | | | | | | | |
| Aug-59 | GATESHEAD-52A | HEATON-52B | | | | | | | |
| Nov-59 | GATESHEAD-52A | HEATON-52B | | | | | | | |
| Jan-60 | GATESHEAD-52A | HEATON-52B | | | | | | | |
| Apr-60 | GATESHEAD-52A | HEATON-52B | | | | | | | |
| Aug-60 | GATESHEAD-52A | HEATON-52B | | | | | | | |
| Nov-60 | GATESHEAD-52A | HEATON-52B | | | | | | | |

**N10 0-6-2T (1902)** (columns 69090–69093)

| | 69062 | 69064 | 69065 | 69067 | 69069 | 69090 | 69091 | 69092 | 69093 |
|---|---|---|---|---|---|---|---|---|---|
| Aug-50 | NORTHWCH-9G | NEWENGLAND-35A | NEASDEN-34E | NEASDEN-34E | W.HALSE-38E | GATESHEAD-52A | GATESHEAD-52A | GATESHEAD-52A | DAIRYCOATES-53A |
| Jan-51 | NORTHWCH-9G | 1/51: NEAS - 34E | NEASDEN-34E | 2/51: W/D | W.HALSE-38E | GATESHEAD-52A | GATESHEAD-52A | GATESHEAD-52A | DAIRYCOATES-53A |
| Aug-51 | 5/51: W/D | NEASDEN-34E | NEASDEN-34E | | W.HALSE-38E | GATESHEAD-52A | GATESHEAD-52A | GATESHEAD-52A | DAIRYCOATES-53A |
| Jan-52 | | NEASDEN-34E | NEASDEN-34E | | W.HALSE-38E | GATESHEAD-52A | GATESHEAD-52A | GATESHEAD-52A | DAIRYCOATES-53A |
| Aug-52 | | NEASDEN-34E | NEASDEN-34E | | W.HALSE-38E | GATESHEAD-52A | GATESHEAD-52A | GATESHEAD-52A | DAIRYCOATES-53A |
| Jan-53 | | NEASDEN-34E | NEASDEN-34E | | W.HALSE-38E | GATESHEAD-52A | GATESHEAD-52A | GATESHEAD-52A | DAIRYCOATES-53A |
| Aug-53 | | 7/53: FROD - 36C | 7/53: FROD - 36C | | W.HALSE-38E | GATESHEAD-52A | GATESHEAD-52A | GATESHEAD-52A | DAIRYCOATES-53A |
| Jan-54 | | FRODINGHAM-36C | FRODINGHAM-36C | | W.HALSE-38E | GATESHEAD-52A | GATESHEAD-52A | GATESHEAD-52A | DAIRYCOATES-53A |
| Aug-54 | | FRODINGHAM-36C | 5/54: W/D | | W.HALSE-38E | GATESHEAD-52A | GATESHEAD-52A | GATESHEAD-52A | DAIRYCOATES-53A |
| Jan-55 | | 1/55: W/D | | | W.HALSE-38E | GATESHEAD-52A | GATESHEAD-52A | GATESHEAD-52A | DAIRYCOATES-53A |
| Aug-55 | | | | | 7/55: W/D | GATESHEAD-52A | GATESHEAD-52A | GATESHEAD-52A | 7/55: T.DCK - 54B |
| Jan-56 | | | | | | GATESHEAD-52A | GATESHEAD-52A | GATESHEAD-52A | TYNEDOCK-54B |
| Aug-56 | | | | | | GATESHEAD-52A | GATESHEAD-52A | GATESHEAD-52A | TYNEDOCK-54B |
| Jan-57 | | | | | | 11/56: W/D | 11/56: W/D | GATESHEAD-52A | TYNEDOCK-54B |
| Aug-57 | | | | | | | | GATESHEAD-52A | |
| Jan-58 | | | | | | | | GATESHEAD-52A | |
| Aug-58 | | | | | | | | GATESHEAD-52A | |
| Jan-59 | | | | | | | | GATESHEAD-52A | |
| Aug-59 | | | | | | | | 4/59: W/D | |
| Nov-59 | | | | | | | | | |
| Jan-60 | | | | | | | | | |
| Apr-60 | | | | | | | | | |
| Aug-60 | | | | | | | | | |
| Nov-60 | | | | | | | | | |

| | 69094 | 69095 | 69096 | 69097 | 69098 | 69099 | 69100 | 69101 | 69102 |
|---|---|---|---|---|---|---|---|---|---|
| Aug-50 | DAIRYCOATES-53A | BLAYDON-52C | DAIRYCOATES-53A | GATESHEAD-52A | DAIRYCOATES-53A | DAIRYCOATES-53A | GATESHEAD-52A | NORTHALLERTON-51J | DAIRYCOATES-53A |
| Jan-51 | DAIRYCOATES-53A | BLAYDON-52C | DAIRYCOATES-53A | GATESHEAD-52A | DAIRYCOATES-53A | DAIRYCOATES-53A | GATESHEAD-52A | 1/51: SUND - 54A | DAIRYCOATES-53A |
| Aug-51 | DAIRYCOATES-53A | BLAYDON-52C | DAIRYCOATES-53A | GATESHEAD-52A | DAIRYCOATES-53A | DAIRYCOATES-53A | GATESHEAD-52A | SUNDERLAND-54A | DAIRYCOATES-53A |
| Jan-52 | DAIRYCOATES-53A | BLAYDON-52C | DAIRYCOATES-53A | GATESHEAD-52A | DAIRYCOATES-53A | DAIRYCOATES-53A | GATESHEAD-52A | SUNDERLAND-54A | DAIRYCOATES-53A |
| Aug-52 | DAIRYCOATES-53A | 7/52: GHD - 52A | DAIRYCOATES-53A | GATESHEAD-52A | DAIRYCOATES-53A | DAIRYCOATES-53A | GATESHEAD-52A | SUNDERLAND-54A | DAIRYCOATES-53A |
| Jan-53 | DAIRYCOATES-53A | GATESHEAD-52A | DAIRYCOATES-53A | GATESHEAD-52A | DAIRYCOATES-53A | DAIRYCOATES-53A | GATESHEAD-52A | SUNDERLAND-54A | DAIRYCOATES-53A |
| Aug-53 | DAIRYCOATES-53A | GATESHEAD-52A | DAIRYCOATES-53A | GATESHEAD-52A | DAIRYCOATES-53A | DAIRYCOATES-53A | GATESHEAD-52A | SUNDERLAND-54A | DAIRYCOATES-53A |
| Jan-54 | DAIRYCOATES-53A | GATESHEAD-52A | DAIRYCOATES-53A | GATESHEAD-52A | DAIRYCOATES-53A | DAIRYCOATES-53A | GATESHEAD-52A | SUNDERLAND-54A | DAIRYCOATES-53A |
| Aug-54 | DAIRYCOATES-53A | GATESHEAD-52A | DAIRYCOATES-53A | GATESHEAD-52A | DAIRYCOATES-53A | DAIRYCOATES-53A | GATESHEAD-52A | SUNDERLAND-54A | DAIRYCOATES-53A |
| Jan-55 | DAIRYCOATES-53A | GATESHEAD-52A | DAIRYCOATES-53A | GATESHEAD-52A | 1/55: N.HILL - 50B | DAIRYCOATES-53A | GATESHEAD-52A | SUNDERLAND-54A | DAIRYCOATES-53A |
| Aug-55 | DAIRYCOATES-53A | 10/55: W/D | DAIRYCOATES-53A | GATESHEAD-52A | NEVILLEHILL-50B | DAIRYCOATES-53A | GATESHEAD-52A | SUNDERLAND-54A | 7/55: T.DCK - 54B |
| Jan-56 | DAIRYCOATES-53A | | DAIRYCOATES-53A | GATESHEAD-52A | NEVILLEHILL-50B | DAIRYCOATES-53A | GATESHEAD-52A | SUNDERLAND-54A | TYNEDOCK-54B |
| Aug-56 | DAIRYCOATES-53A | | DAIRYCOATES-53A | GATESHEAD-52A | NEVILLEHILL-50B | DAIRYCOATES-53A | GATESHEAD-52A | SUNDERLAND-54A | TYNEDOCK-54B |
| Jan-57 | DAIRYCOATES-53A | | DAIRYCOATES-53A | GATESHEAD-52A | NEVILLEHILL-50B | DAIRYCOATES-53A | GATESHEAD-52A | SUNDERLAND-54A | TYNEDOCK-54B |
| Aug-57 | 7/57: W/D | | DAIRYCOATES-53A | GATESHEAD-52A | 9/57: W/D | DAIRYCOATES-53A | GATESHEAD-52A | SUNDERLAND-54A | |
| Jan-58 | | | 12/57: W/D | GATESHEAD-52A | | 2/58: W/D | 11/57: W/D | SUNDERLAND-54A | 11/57: GHD - 52A |
| Aug-58 | | | | GATESHEAD-52A | | | | 7/58: T.DCK - 54B | GATESHEAD-52A |
| Jan-59 | | | | GATESHEAD-52A | | | | TYNEDOCK-52H | 2/59: W/D |
| Aug-59 | | | | GATESHEAD-52A | | | | 5/59: GHD - 52A | |
| Nov-59 | | | | GATESHEAD-52A | | | | GATESHEAD-52A | |
| Jan-60 | | | | GATESHEAD-52A | | | | GATESHEAD-52A | |
| Apr-60 | | | | GATESHEAD-52A | | | | GATESHEAD-52A | |
| Aug-60 | | | | GATESHEAD-52A | | | | GATESHEAD-52A | |
| Nov-60 | | | | GATESHEAD-52A | | | | | |

**N13 0-6-2T (1913)** (columns 69111–69113)

| | 69104 | 69105 | 69106 | 69107 | 69108 | 69109 | 69111 | 69112 | 69113 |
|---|---|---|---|---|---|---|---|---|---|
| Aug-50 | DAIRYCOATES-53A | DAIRYCOATES-53A | DAIRYCOATES-53A | DAIRYCOATES-53A | DAIRYCOATES-53A | GATESHEAD-52A | HULL (AD) - 53C | SPRINGHEAD-53C | SPRINGHEAD-53C |
| Jan-51 | DAIRYCOATES-53A | 12/50: T.DOCK - 54B | DAIRYCOATES-53A | DAIRYCOATES-53A | DAIRYCOATES-53A | GATESHEAD-52A | 11/50: S'HEAD - 53C | SPRINGHEAD-53C | SPRINGHEAD-53C |
| Aug-51 | DAIRYCOATES-53A | TYNEDOCK-54B | DAIRYCOATES-53A | DAIRYCOATES-53A | DAIRYCOATES-53A | GATESHEAD-52A | SPRINGHEAD-53C | SPRINGHEAD-53C | SPRINGHEAD-53C |
| Jan-52 | DAIRYCOATES-53A | TYNEDOCK-54B | DAIRYCOATES-53A | DAIRYCOATES-53A | DAIRYCOATES-53A | GATESHEAD-52A | SPRINGHEAD-53C | SPRINGHEAD-53C | SPRINGHEAD-53C |
| Aug-52 | DAIRYCOATES-53A | TYNEDOCK-54B | DAIRYCOATES-53A | DAIRYCOATES-53A | DAIRYCOATES-53A | GATESHEAD-52A | 8/52: W/D | SPRINGHEAD-53C | SPRINGHEAD-53C |
| Jan-53 | DAIRYCOATES-53A | TYNEDOCK-54B | DAIRYCOATES-53A | DAIRYCOATES-53A | DAIRYCOATES-53A | GATESHEAD-52A | | 11/52: W/D | 1/53: N.HILL - 50B |
| Aug-53 | DAIRYCOATES-53A | TYNEDOCK-54B | DAIRYCOATES-53A | DAIRYCOATES-53A | DAIRYCOATES-53A | GATESHEAD-52A | | | 5/53: W/D |
| Jan-54 | DAIRYCOATES-53A | TYNEDOCK-54B | DAIRYCOATES-53A | DAIRYCOATES-53A | DAIRYCOATES-53A | GATESHEAD-52A | | | |
| Aug-54 | DAIRYCOATES-53A | TYNEDOCK-54B | DAIRYCOATES-53A | DAIRYCOATES-53A | DAIRYCOATES-53A | GATESHEAD-52A | | | |
| Jan-55 | DAIRYCOATES-53A | TYNEDOCK-54B | DAIRYCOATES-53A | DAIRYCOATES-53A | DAIRYCOATES-53A | GATESHEAD-52A | | | |
| Aug-55 | DAIRYCOATES-53A | TYNEDOCK-54B | 7/55: T.DCK - 54B | DAIRYCOATES-53A | DAIRYCOATES-53A | GATESHEAD-52A | | | |
| Jan-56 | DAIRYCOATES-53A | TYNEDOCK-54B | TYNEDOCK-54B | DAIRYCOATES-53A | DAIRYCOATES-53A | GATESHEAD-52A | | | |
| Aug-56 | DAIRYCOATES-53A | TYNEDOCK-54B | TYNEDOCK-54B | DAIRYCOATES-53A | DAIRYCOATES-53A | GATESHEAD-52A | | | |
| Jan-57 | DAIRYCOATES-53A | TYNEDOCK-54B | TYNEDOCK-54B | DAIRYCOATES-53A | DAIRYCOATES-53A | GATESHEAD-52A | | | |
| Aug-57 | DAIRYCOATES-53A | TYNEDOCK-54B | TYNEDOCK-54B | DAIRYCOATES-53A | 7/57: W/D | GATESHEAD-52A | | | |
| Jan-58 | 3/58: W/D | TYNEDOCK-54B | 3/58: W/D | 11/57: W/D | | GATESHEAD-52A | | | |
| Aug-58 | | TYNEDOCK-54B | | | | GATESHEAD-52A | | | |
| Jan-59 | | TYNEDOCK-52H | | | | GATESHEAD-52A | | | |
| Aug-59 | | 5/59: GHD - 52A | | | | GATESHEAD-52A | | | |
| Nov-59 | | GATESHEAD-52A | | | | GATESHEAD-52A | | | |
| Jan-60 | | GATESHEAD-52A | | | | GATESHEAD-52A | | | |
| Apr-60 | | GATESHEAD-52A | | | | GATESHEAD-52A | | | |
| Aug-60 | | GATESHEAD-52A | | | | GATESHEAD-52A | | | |
| Nov-60 | | | | | | GATESHEAD-52A | | | |

As a change from the big stuff on the East Coast there were worse places to explore than Hull Springhead on a Sunday when most of the shunters were on shed. Above can be seen 69001, the first of the BR-built J72 0-6-0T's, three years old at the time of the photograph with no concessions made to half a century's development since the first of the class appeared. Normally 69001 was to be found at Alexandra Dock where it was a regular pilot in the dock sidings. In the adjacent road lies the unmistakable bulk of a NER A7 4-6-2. Below, Hull and Barnsley N13 0-6-2T 69119 waits to take up Target 77 duty - a weeks continuous shunting in Springhead Yard - on 24th August 1952.

| | 69114 | 69115 | 69116 | 69117 | 69118 | 69119 | N14 0-6-2T (1909) 69120 | 69124 | 69125 |
|---|---|---|---|---|---|---|---|---|---|
| Aug-50 | NEVILLEHILL - 50B | NEVILLEHILL - 50B | SPRINGHEAD - 53C | NEVILLEHILL - 50B | NEVILLEHILL - 50B | SPRINGHEAD - 53C | EASTFIELD - 65A | EASTFIELD - 65A | KITTYBREWSTER - 61A |
| Jan-51 | NEVILLEHILL - 50B | NEVILLEHILL - 50B | SPRINGHEAD - 53C | NEVILLEHILL - 50B | NEVILLEHILL - 50B | SPRINGHEAD - 53C | EASTFIELD - 65A | 11/51: W/D | 12/50: F'HILL - 61B |
| Aug-51 | NEVILLEHILL - 50B | NEVILLEHILL - 50B | SPRINGHEAD - 53C | NEVILLEHILL - 50B | NEVILLEHILL - 50B | SPRINGHEAD - 53C | EASTFIELD - 65A | | FERRYHILL - 61B |
| Jan-52 | NEVILLEHILL - 50B | NEVILLEHILL - 50B | SPRINGHEAD - 53C | NEVILLEHILL - 50B | NEVILLEHILL - 50B | SPRINGHEAD - 53C | EASTFIELD - 65A | | FERRYHILL - 61B |
| Aug-52 | NEVILLEHILL - 50B | NEVILLEHILL - 50B | SPRINGHEAD - 53C | NEVILLEHILL - 50B | 5/52: W/D | SPRINGHEAD - 53C | EASTFIELD - 65A | | FERRYHILL - 61B |
| Jan-53 | NEVILLEHILL - 50B | NEVILLEHILL - 50B | 4/53: N.HILL - 50B | NEVILLEHILL - 50B | | SPRINGHEAD - 53C | EASTFIELD - 65A | | FERRYHILL - 61B |
| Aug-53 | NEVILLEHILL - 50B | NEVILLEHILL - 50B | NEVILLEHILL - 50B | NEVILLEHILL - 50B | | SPRINGHEAD - 53C | EASTFIELD - 65A | | FERRYHILL - 61B |
| Jan-54 | NEVILLEHILL - 50B | NEVILLEHILL - 50B | NEVILLEHILL - 50B | NEVILLEHILL - 50B | | 10/53: N.HILL - 50B | 3/54: W/D | | 3/54: W/D |
| Aug-54 | NEVILLEHILL - 50B | NEVILLEHILL - 50B | NEVILLEHILL - 50B | NEVILLEHILL - 50B | | NEVILLEHILL - 50B | | | |
| Jan-55 | NEVILLEHILL - 50B | NEVILLEHILL - 50B | 12/55: W/D | NEVILLEHILL - 50B | | NEVILLEHILL - 50B | | | |
| Aug-55 | NEVILLEHILL - 50B | 5/55: W/D | | 7/55: W/D | | 6/55: W/D | | | |
| Jan-56 | NEVILLEHILL - 50B | | | | | | | | |
| Aug-56 | 10/56: W/D | | | | | | | | |
| Jan-57 | | | | | | | | | |
| Aug-57 | | | | | | | | | |
| Jan-58 | | | | | | | | | |
| Aug-58 | | | | | | | | | |
| Jan-59 | | | | | | | | | |
| Aug-59 | | | | | | | | | |
| Nov-59 | | | | | | | | | |
| Jan-60 | | | | | | | | | |
| Apr-60 | | | | | | | | | |
| Aug-60 | | | | | | | | | |
| Nov-60 | | | | | | | | | |

| | N15 0-6-2T (1910) 69126 | 69127 | 69128 | 69129 | 69130 | 69131 | 69132 | 69133 | 69134 |
|---|---|---|---|---|---|---|---|---|---|
| Aug-50 | EASTFIELD - 65A | EASTFIELD - 65A | FERRYHILL - 61B | FERRYHILL - 61B | EDINBURGH(SM) - 64A | EASTFIELD - 65A | THORNTONJCN - 62A | EDINBURGH(SM) - 64A | EDINBURGH(SM) - 64A |
| Jan-51 | EASTFIELD - 65A | EASTFIELD - 65A | FERRYHILL - 61B | FERRYHILL - 61B | EDINBURGH(SM) - 64A | EASTFIELD - 65A | THORNTONJCN - 62A | EDINBURGH(SM) - 64A | EDINBURGH(SM) - 64A |
| Aug-51 | EASTFIELD - 65A | EASTFIELD - 65A | FERRYHILL - 61B | FERRYHILL - 61B | EDINBURGH(SM) - 64A | EASTFIELD - 65A | THORNTONJCN - 62A | EDINBURGH(SM) - 64A | EDINBURGH(SM) - 64A |
| Jan-52 | EASTFIELD - 65A | EASTFIELD - 65A | FERRYHILL - 61B | FERRYHILL - 61B | EDINBURGH(SM) - 64A | EASTFIELD - 65A | THORNTONJCN - 62A | EDINBURGH(SM) - 64A | EDINBURGH(SM) - 64A |
| Aug-52 | EASTFIELD - 65A | EASTFIELD - 65A | FERRYHILL - 61B | FERRYHILL - 61B | EDINBURGH(SM) - 64A | EASTFIELD - 65A | THORNTONJCN - 62A | EDINBURGH(SM) - 64A | EDINBURGH(SM) - 64A |
| Jan-53 | EASTFIELD - 65A | EASTFIELD - 65A | FERRYHILL - 61B | FERRYHILL - 61B | EDINBURGH(SM) - 64A | EASTFIELD - 65A | THORNTONJCN - 62A | EDINBURGH(SM) - 64A | EDINBURGH(SM) - 64A |
| Aug-53 | EASTFIELD - 65A | EASTFIELD - 65A | FERRYHILL - 61B | FERRYHILL - 61B | EDINBURGH(SM) - 64A | EASTFIELD - 65A | THORNTONJCN - 62A | EDINBURGH(SM) - 64A | EDINBURGH(SM) - 64A |
| Jan-54 | EASTFIELD - 65A | EASTFIELD - 65A | FERRYHILL - 61B | FERRYHILL - 61B | EDINBURGH(SM) - 64A | EASTFIELD - 65A | THORNTONJCN - 62A | EDINBURGH(SM) - 64A | EDINBURGH(SM) - 64A |
| Aug-54 | EASTFIELD - 65A | EASTFIELD - 65A | FERRYHILL - 61B | FERRYHILL - 61B | EDINBURGH(SM) - 64A | EASTFIELD - 65A | THORNTONJCN - 62A | EDINBURGH(SM) - 64A | EDINBURGH(SM) - 64A |
| Jan-55 | EASTFIELD - 65A | EASTFIELD - 65A | FERRYHILL - 61B | FERRYHILL - 61B | EDINBURGH(SM) - 64A | EASTFIELD - 65A | THORNTONJCN - 62A | EDINBURGH(SM) - 64A | EDINBURGH(SM) - 64A |
| Aug-55 | EASTFIELD - 65A | EASTFIELD - 65A | FERRYHILL - 61B | FERRYHILL - 61B | EDINBURGH(SM) - 64A | EASTFIELD - 65A | THORNTONJCN - 62A | EDINBURGH(SM) - 64A | EDINBURGH(SM) - 64A |
| Jan-56 | EASTFIELD - 65A | EASTFIELD - 65A | FERRYHILL - 61B | FERRYHILL - 61B | EDINBURGH(SM) - 64A | EASTFIELD - 65A | THORNTONJCN - 62A | EDINBURGH(SM) - 64A | EDINBURGH(SM) - 64A |
| Aug-56 | EASTFIELD - 65A | EASTFIELD - 65A | FERRYHILL - 61B | FERRYHILL - 61B | EDINBURGH(SM) - 64A | EASTFIELD - 65A | THORNTONJCN - 62A | EDINBURGH(SM) - 64A | EDINBURGH(SM) - 64A |
| Jan-57 | EASTFIELD - 65A | EASTFIELD - 65A | FERRYHILL - 61B | FERRYHILL - 61B | EDINBURGH(SM) - 64A | EASTFIELD - 65A | THORNTONJCN - 62A | EDINBURGH(SM) - 64A | EDINBURGH(SM) - 64A |
| Aug-57 | 9/57: ST RX - 65B | 9/57: ST RX - 65B | FERRYHILL - 61B | FERRYHILL - 61B | EDINBURGH(SM) - 64A | EASTFIELD - 65A | THORNTONJCN - 62A | EDINBURGH(SM) - 64A | EDINBURGH(SM) - 64A |
| Jan-58 | 1/58: DAWS - 65D | STROLLOX - 65B | FERRYHILL - 61B | FERRYHILL - 61B | 12/57: W/D | EASTFIELD - 65A | THORNTONJCN - 62A | EDINBURGH(SM) - 64A | EDINBURGH(SM) - 64A |
| Aug-58 | DAWSHOLME - 65D | 5/58: F'HILL - 61B | FERRYHILL - 61B | FERRYHILL - 61B | | EASTFIELD - 65A | THORNTONJCN - 62A | EDINBURGH(SM) - 64A | EDINBURGH(SM) - 64A |
| Jan-59 | DAWSHOLME - 65D | FERRYHILL - 61B | FERRYHILL - 61B | 12/58: W/D | | EASTFIELD - 65A | THORNTONJCN - 62A | EDINBURGH(SM) - 64A | EDINBURGH(SM) - 64A |
| Aug-59 | DAWSHOLME - 65D | 6/59: W/D | FERRYHILL - 61B | | | EASTFIELD - 65A | THORNTONJCN - 62A | EDINBURGH(SM) - 64A | EDINBURGH(SM) - 64A |
| Nov-59 | DAWSHOLME - 65D | | FERRYHILL - 61B | | | EASTFIELD - 65A | 12/59: M'WELL - 66B | EDINBURGH(SM) - 64A | EDINBURGH(SM) - 64A |
| Jan-60 | DAWSHOLME - 65D | | FERRYHILL - 61B | | | EASTFIELD - 65A | MOTHERWELL - 66B | EDINBURGH(SM) - 64A | EDINBURGH(SM) - 64A |
| Apr-60 | DAWSHOLME - 65D | | FERRYHILL - 61B | | | EASTFIELD - 65A | MOTHERWELL - 66B | EDINBURGH(SM) - 64A | EDINBURGH(SM) - 64A |
| Aug-60 | DAWSHOLME - 65D | | FERRYHILL - 61B | | | EASTFIELD - 65A | MOTHERWELL - 66B | 9/60: W/D | EDINBURGH(SM) - 64A |
| Nov-60 | DAWSHOLME - 65D | | FERRYHILL - 61B | | | EASTFIELD - 65A | MOTHERWELL - 66B | | EDINBURGH(SM) - 64A |

| | 69135 | 69136 | 69137 | 69138 | 69139 | 69140 | 69141 | 69142 | 69143 |
|---|---|---|---|---|---|---|---|---|---|
| Aug-50 | DUNFERMLINE - 62C | DUNFERMLINE - 62C | POLMONT - 64E | EASTFIELD - 65A | CARLISLE(CANAL) - 12B | EDINBURGH(SM) - 64A | EDINBURGH(SM) - 64A | BATHGATE - 64F | PARKHEAD - 65C |
| Jan-51 | DUNFERMLINE - 62C | DUNFERMLINE - 62C | POLMONT - 64E | EASTFIELD - 65A | CARLISLE(CANAL) - 12B | EDINBURGH(SM) - 64A | EDINBURGH(SM) - 64A | BATHGATE - 64F | PARKHEAD - 65C |
| Aug-51 | DUNFERMLINE - 62C | DUNFERMLINE - 62C | POLMONT - 64E | EASTFIELD - 65A | CARLISLE(CANAL) - 68E | EDINBURGH(SM) - 64A | EDINBURGH(SM) - 64A | BATHGATE - 64F | PARKHEAD - 65C |
| Jan-52 | DUNFERMLINE - 62C | DUNFERMLINE - 62C | POLMONT - 64E | EASTFIELD - 65A | CARLISLE(CANAL) - 68E | EDINBURGH(SM) - 64A | EDINBURGH(SM) - 64A | BATHGATE - 64F | 1/52: TH JN - 62A |
| Aug-52 | DUNFERMLINE - 62C | DUNFERMLINE - 62C | POLMONT - 64E | EASTFIELD - 65A | CARLISLE(CANAL) - 68E | EDINBURGH(SM) - 64A | EDINBURGH(SM) - 64A | BATHGATE - 64F | THORNTONJCN - 62A |
| Jan-53 | DUNFERMLINE - 62C | DUNFERMLINE - 62C | POLMONT - 64E | EASTFIELD - 65A | CARLISLE(CANAL) - 68E | EDINBURGH(SM) - 64A | EDINBURGH(SM) - 64A | BATHGATE - 64F | THORNTONJCN - 62A |
| Aug-53 | DUNFERMLINE - 62C | DUNFERMLINE - 62C | POLMONT - 64E | EASTFIELD - 65A | CARLISLE(CANAL) - 68E | EDINBURGH(SM) - 64A | EDINBURGH(SM) - 64A | BATHGATE - 64F | THORNTONJCN - 62A |
| Jan-54 | DUNFERMLINE - 62C | DUNFERMLINE - 62C | POLMONT - 64E | EASTFIELD - 65A | CARLISLE(CANAL) - 68E | EDINBURGH(SM) - 64A | EDINBURGH(SM) - 64A | BATHGATE - 64F | THORNTONJCN - 62A |
| Aug-54 | DUNFERMLINE - 62C | DUNFERMLINE - 62C | POLMONT - 64E | EASTFIELD - 65A | CARLISLE(CANAL) - 68E | EDINBURGH(SM) - 64A | EDINBURGH(SM) - 64A | BATHGATE - 64F | THORNTONJCN - 62A |
| Jan-55 | DUNFERMLINE - 62C | DUNFERMLINE - 62C | POLMONT - 64E | EASTFIELD - 65A | CARLISLE(CANAL) - 68E | EDINBURGH(SM) - 64A | EDINBURGH(SM) - 64A | BATHGATE - 64F | THORNTONJCN - 62A |
| Aug-55 | DUNFERMLINE - 62C | DUNFERMLINE - 62C | POLMONT - 64E | EASTFIELD - 65A | CARLISLE(CANAL) - 68E | EDINBURGH(SM) - 64A | EDINBURGH(SM) - 64A | BATHGATE - 64F | THORNTONJCN - 62A |
| Jan-56 | DUNFERMLINE - 62C | DUNFERMLINE - 62C | POLMONT - 64E | EASTFIELD - 65A | CARLISLE(CANAL) - 68E | EDINBURGH(SM) - 64A | EDINBURGH(SM) - 64A | BATHGATE - 64F | THORNTONJCN - 62A |
| Aug-56 | DUNFERMLINE - 62C | DUNFERMLINE - 62C | POLMONT - 64E | EASTFIELD - 65A | CARLISLE(CANAL) - 68E | EDINBURGH(SM) - 64A | EDINBURGH(SM) - 64A | BATHGATE - 64F | THORNTONJCN - 62A |
| Jan-57 | DUNFERMLINE - 62C | DUNFERMLINE - 62C | POLMONT - 64E | EASTFIELD - 65A | CARLISLE(CANAL) - 68E | EDINBURGH(SM) - 64A | EDINBURGH(SM) - 64A | BATHGATE - 64F | THORNTONJCN - 62A |
| Aug-57 | 9/57: DUN - 62B | 8/57: DUN - 62B | POLMONT - 64E | 7/57: ST RX - 65B | CARLISLE(CANAL) - 68E | EDINBURGH(SM) - 64A | EDINBURGH(SM) - 64A | BATHGATE - 64F | THORNTONJCN - 62A |
| Jan-58 | DUNDEE - 62B | DUNDEE - 62B | POLMONT - 64E | 9/57: F'HILL - 61B | CARLISLECANAL - 68E | EDINBURGH(SM) - 64A | EDINBURGH(SM) - 64A | 1/58: W/D | THORNTONJCN - 62A |
| Aug-58 | 5/58: EBRO(SM) - 64A | DUNDEE - 62B | POLMONT - 64E | FERRYHILL - 61B | 4/58: W/D | 6/58: W/D | EDINBURGH(SM) - 64A | | THORNTONJCN - 62A |
| Jan-59 | EDINBURGH(SM) - 64A | DUNDEE - 62B | POLMONT - 64E | FERRYHILL - 61B | | | EDINBURGH(SM) - 64A | | THORNTONJCN - 62A |
| Aug-59 | EDINBURGH(SM) - 64A | DUNDEE - 62B | POLMONT - 64E | FERRYHILL - 61B | | | EDINBURGH(SM) - 64A | | THORNTONJCN - 62A |
| Nov-59 | EDINBURGH(SM) - 64A | 12/59: TH JN - 62A | POLMONT - 64E | FERRYHILL - 61B | | | EDINBURGH(SM) - 64A | | 12/59: M'WELL - 66B |
| Jan-60 | EDINBURGH(SM) - 64A | THORNTONJCN - 62A | POLMONT - 64E | FERRYHILL - 61B | | | EDINBURGH(SM) - 64A | | MOTHERWELL - 66B |
| Apr-60 | EDINBURGH(SM) - 64A | THORNTONJCN - 62A | POLMONT - 64E | FERRYHILL - 61B | | | EDINBURGH(SM) - 64A | | MOTHERWELL - 66B |
| Aug-60 | EDINBURGH(SM) - 64A | THORNTONJCN - 62A | POLMONT - 64E | FERRYHILL - 61B | | | EDINBURGH(SM) - 64A | | MOTHERWELL - 66B |
| Nov-60 | EDINBURGH(SM) - 64A | THORNTONJCN - 62A | POLMONT - 64E | FERRYHILL - 61B | | | | | |

| | 69144 | 69145 | 69146 | 69147 | 69148 | 69149 | 69150 | 69151 | 69152 |
|---|---|---|---|---|---|---|---|---|---|
| Aug-50 | EDINBURGH(SM) - 64A | KIPPS - 65E | EDINBURGH(SM) - 64A | EDINBURGH(SM) - 64A | EDINBURGH(SM) - 64A | EDINBURGH(SM) - 64A | THORNTONJCN - 62A | PARKHEAD - 65C | EDINBURGH(SM) - 64A |
| Jan-51 | EDINBURGH(SM) - 64A | KIPPS - 65E | EDINBURGH(SM) - 64A | EDINBURGH(SM) - 64A | EDINBURGH(SM) - 64A | EDINBURGH(SM) - 64A | THORNTONJCN - 62A | PARKHEAD - 65C | EDINBURGH(SM) - 64A |
| Aug-51 | EDINBURGH(SM) - 64A | KIPPS - 65E | EDINBURGH(SM) - 64A | EDINBURGH(SM) - 64A | EDINBURGH(SM) - 64A | EDINBURGH(SM) - 64A | THORNTONJCN - 62A | PARKHEAD - 65C | EDINBURGH(SM) - 64A |
| Jan-52 | EDINBURGH(SM) - 64A | KIPPS - 65E | EDINBURGH(SM) - 64A | EDINBURGH(SM) - 64A | EDINBURGH(SM) - 64A | EDINBURGH(SM) - 64A | THORNTONJCN - 62A | PARKHEAD - 65C | EDINBURGH(SM) - 64A |
| Aug-52 | EDINBURGH(SM) - 64A | KIPPS - 65E | EDINBURGH(SM) - 64A | EDINBURGH(SM) - 64A | EDINBURGH(SM) - 64A | EDINBURGH(SM) - 64A | THORNTONJCN - 62A | PARKHEAD - 65C | EDINBURGH(SM) - 64A |
| Jan-53 | EDINBURGH(SM) - 64A | KIPPS - 65E | EDINBURGH(SM) - 64A | EDINBURGH(SM) - 64A | EDINBURGH(SM) - 64A | EDINBURGH(SM) - 64A | THORNTONJCN - 62A | PARKHEAD - 65C | EDINBURGH(SM) - 64A |
| Aug-53 | EDINBURGH(SM) - 64A | KIPPS - 65E | EDINBURGH(SM) - 64A | EDINBURGH(SM) - 64A | EDINBURGH(SM) - 64A | EDINBURGH(SM) - 64A | THORNTONJCN - 62A | PARKHEAD - 65C | EDINBURGH(SM) - 64A |
| Jan-54 | EDINBURGH(SM) - 64A | KIPPS - 65E | EDINBURGH(SM) - 64A | EDINBURGH(SM) - 64A | EDINBURGH(SM) - 64A | EDINBURGH(SM) - 64A | THORNTONJCN - 62A | PARKHEAD - 65C | EDINBURGH(SM) - 64A |
| Aug-54 | EDINBURGH(SM) - 64A | KIPPS - 65E | EDINBURGH(SM) - 64A | EDINBURGH(SM) - 64A | EDINBURGH(SM) - 64A | EDINBURGH(SM) - 64A | THORNTONJCN - 62A | PARKHEAD - 65C | EDINBURGH(SM) - 64A |
| Jan-55 | EDINBURGH(SM) - 64A | KIPPS - 65E | EDINBURGH(SM) - 64A | EDINBURGH(SM) - 64A | EDINBURGH(SM) - 64A | EDINBURGH(SM) - 64A | THORNTONJCN - 62A | PARKHEAD - 65C | EDINBURGH(SM) - 64A |
| Aug-55 | EDINBURGH(SM) - 64A | KIPPS - 65E | EDINBURGH(SM) - 64A | EDINBURGH(SM) - 64A | EDINBURGH(SM) - 64A | EDINBURGH(SM) - 64A | THORNTONJCN - 62A | PARKHEAD - 65C | EDINBURGH(SM) - 64A |
| Jan-56 | EDINBURGH(SM) - 64A | KIPPS - 65E | EDINBURGH(SM) - 64A | EDINBURGH(SM) - 64A | EDINBURGH(SM) - 64A | EDINBURGH(SM) - 64A | THORNTONJCN - 62A | PARKHEAD - 65C | EDINBURGH(SM) - 64A |
| Aug-56 | EDINBURGH(SM) - 64A | KIPPS - 65E | EDINBURGH(SM) - 64A | EDINBURGH(SM) - 64A | EDINBURGH(SM) - 64A | EDINBURGH(SM) - 64A | THORNTONJCN - 62A | PARKHEAD - 65C | EDINBURGH(SM) - 64A |
| Jan-57 | EDINBURGH(SM) - 64A | KIPPS - 65E | EDINBURGH(SM) - 64A | EDINBURGH(SM) - 64A | EDINBURGH(SM) - 64A | EDINBURGH(SM) - 64A | THORNTONJCN - 62A | PARKHEAD - 65C | EDINBURGH(SM) - 64A |
| Aug-57 | EDINBURGH(SM) - 64A | KIPPS - 65E | EDINBURGH(SM) - 64A | EDINBURGH(SM) - 64A | EDINBURGH(SM) - 64A | EDINBURGH(SM) - 64A | 9/57: DUN - 62B | PARKHEAD - 65C | EDINBURGH(SM) - 64A |
| Jan-58 | EDINBURGH(SM) - 64A | KIPPS - 65E | EDINBURGH(SM) - 64A | EDINBURGH(SM) - 64A | EDINBURGH(SM) - 64A | EDINBURGH(SM) - 64A | DUNDEE - 62B | PARKHEAD - 65C | EDINBURGH(SM) - 64A |
| Aug-58 | EDINBURGH(SM) - 64A | KIPPS - 65E | EDINBURGH(SM) - 64A | 6/58: W/D | 6/58: W/D | EDINBURGH(SM) - 64A | 5/58: EBRO(SM) - 64A | PARKHEAD - 65C | EDINBURGH(SM) - 64A |
| Jan-59 | EDINBURGH(SM) - 64A | KIPPS - 65E | EDINBURGH(SM) - 64A | | | EDINBURGH(SM) - 64A | EDINBURGH(SM) - 64A | 2/59: W/D | 12/58: W/D |
| Aug-59 | EDINBURGH(SM) - 64A | KIPPS - 65E | 7/59: W/D | | | EDINBURGH(SM) - 64A | EDINBURGH(SM) - 64A | | |
| Nov-59 | EDINBURGH(SM) - 64A | 12/59: POLM - 66A | | | | EDINBURGH(SM) - 64A | EDINBURGH(SM) - 64A | | |
| Jan-60 | EDINBURGH(SM) - 64A | POLMADIE - 66A | | | | EDINBURGH(SM) - 64A | EDINBURGH(SM) - 64A | | |
| Apr-60 | 3/60: W/D | 3/60: W/D | | | | 4/60: W/D | EDINBURGH(SM) - 64A | | |
| Aug-60 | | | | | | | EDINBURGH(SM) - 64A | | |
| Nov-60 | | | | | | | EDINBURGH(SM) - 64A | | |

| | 69153 | 69154 | 69155 | 69156 | 69157 | 69158 | 69159 | 69160 | 69161 |
|---|---|---|---|---|---|---|---|---|---|
| Aug-50 | THORNTONJCN - 62A | DUNFERMLINE - 62C | CARLISLE(CANAL) - 12B | BATHGATE - 64F | PARKHEAD - 65C | BATHGATE - 64F | BATHGATE - 64F | DUNFERMLINE - 62C | PARKHEAD - 65C |
| Jan-51 | THORNTONJCN - 62A | DUNFERMLINE - 62C | CARLISLE(CANAL) - 12B | BATHGATE - 64F | PARKHEAD - 65C | BATHGATE - 64F | BATHGATE - 64F | DUNFERMLINE - 62C | PARKHEAD - 65C |
| Aug-51 | THORNTONJCN - 62A | DUNFERMLINE - 62C | CARLISLE(CANAL) - 68E | BATHGATE - 64F | PARKHEAD - 65C | BATHGATE - 64F | BATHGATE - 64F | DUNFERMLINE - 62C | PARKHEAD - 65C |
| Jan-52 | THORNTONJCN - 62A | DUNFERMLINE - 62C | CARLISLE(CANAL) - 68E | BATHGATE - 64F | PARKHEAD - 65C | BATHGATE - 64F | BATHGATE - 64F | DUNFERMLINE - 62C | PARKHEAD - 65C |
| Aug-52 | THORNTONJCN - 62A | DUNFERMLINE - 62C | CARLISLE(CANAL) - 68E | BATHGATE - 64F | PARKHEAD - 65C | BATHGATE - 64F | BATHGATE - 64F | DUNFERMLINE - 62C | PARKHEAD - 65C |
| Jan-53 | THORNTONJCN - 62A | DUNFERMLINE - 62C | CARLISLE(CANAL) - 68E | BATHGATE - 64F | PARKHEAD - 65C | BATHGATE - 64F | BATHGATE - 64F | DUNFERMLINE - 62C | PARKHEAD - 65C |
| Aug-53 | THORNTONJCN - 62A | DUNFERMLINE - 62C | CARLISLE(CANAL) - 68E | BATHGATE - 64F | PARKHEAD - 65C | BATHGATE - 64F | BATHGATE - 64F | DUNFERMLINE - 62C | PARKHEAD - 65C |
| Jan-54 | THORNTONJCN - 62A | DUNFERMLINE - 62C | CARLISLE(CANAL) - 68E | BATHGATE - 64F | PARKHEAD - 65C | BATHGATE - 64F | BATHGATE - 64F | DUNFERMLINE - 62C | PARKHEAD - 65C |
| Aug-54 | THORNTONJCN - 62A | DUNFERMLINE - 62C | CARLISLE(CANAL) - 68E | BATHGATE - 64F | PARKHEAD - 65C | BATHGATE - 64F | BATHGATE - 64F | DUNFERMLINE - 62C | PARKHEAD - 65C |
| Jan-55 | THORNTONJCN - 62A | DUNFERMLINE - 62C | CARLISLE(CANAL) - 68E | BATHGATE - 64F | PARKHEAD - 65C | BATHGATE - 64F | BATHGATE - 64F | DUNFERMLINE - 62C | PARKHEAD - 65C |
| Aug-55 | THORNTONJCN - 62A | DUNFERMLINE - 62C | CARLISLE(CANAL) - 68E | BATHGATE - 64F | PARKHEAD - 65C | BATHGATE - 64F | BATHGATE - 64F | DUNFERMLINE - 62C | PARKHEAD - 65C |
| Jan-56 | THORNTONJCN - 62A | DUNFERMLINE - 62C | CARLISLE(CANAL) - 68E | BATHGATE - 64F | PARKHEAD - 65C | BATHGATE - 64F | BATHGATE - 64F | DUNFERMLINE - 62C | PARKHEAD - 65C |
| Aug-56 | THORNTONJCN - 62A | DUNFERMLINE - 62C | CARLISLE(CANAL) - 68E | BATHGATE - 64F | PARKHEAD - 65C | BATHGATE - 64F | BATHGATE - 64F | DUNFERMLINE - 62C | PARKHEAD - 65C |
| Jan-57 | THORNTONJCN - 62A | DUNFERMLINE - 62C | CARLISLE(CANAL) - 68E | BATHGATE - 64F | PARKHEAD - 65C | BATHGATE - 64F | BATHGATE - 64F | DUNFERMLINE - 62C | PARKHEAD - 65C |
| Aug-57 | THORNTONJCN - 62A | **9/57: DUN - 62B** | CARLISLE(CANAL) - 68E | BATHGATE - 64F | PARKHEAD - 65C | BATHGATE - 64F | BATHGATE - 64F | DUNFERMLINE - 62C | PARKHEAD - 65C |
| Jan-58 | THORNTONJCN - 62A | DUNDEE - 62B | CARLISLECANAL - 68E | BATHGATE - 64F | PARKHEAD - 65C | BATHGATE - 64F | BATHGATE - 64F | **4/58: EBRO(SM) - 64A** | PARKHEAD - 65C |
| Aug-58 | **9/58: W/D** | **5/58: EBRO(SM) - 64A** | CARLISLE(CANAL) - 12D | BATHGATE - 64F | **4/58: W/D** | **5/58: W/D** | BATHGATE - 64F | **8/58: W/D** | PARKHEAD - 65C |
| Jan-59 | | EDINBURGH(SM) - 64A | CARLISLE(CANAL) - 12D | BATHGATE - 64F | | | BATHGATE - 64F | | PARKHEAD - 65C |
| Aug-59 | | EDINBURGH(SM) - 64A | CARLISLE(CANAL) - 12D | BATHGATE - 64F | | | BATHGATE - 64F | | PARKHEAD - 65C |
| Nov-59 | | **11/59: W/D** | CARLISLE(CANAL) - 12D | BATHGATE - 64F | | | BATHGATE - 64F | | PARKHEAD - 65C |
| Jan-60 | | | CARLISLE(CANAL) - 12D | BATHGATE - 64F | | | BATHGATE - 64F | | PARKHEAD - 65C |
| Apr-60 | | | CARLISLE(CANAL) - 12D | BATHGATE - 64F | | | BATHGATE - 64F | | PARKHEAD - 65C |
| Aug-60 | | | CARLISLE(CANAL) - 12D | BATHGATE - 64F | | | BATHGATE - 64F | | PARKHEAD - 65C |
| Nov-60 | | | CARLISLE(CANAL) - 12D | BATHGATE - 64F | | | BATHGATE - 64F | | **9/60: W/D** |

| | 69162 | 69163 | 69164 | 69165 | 69166 | 69167 | 69168 | 69169 | 69170 |
|---|---|---|---|---|---|---|---|---|---|
| Aug-50 | POLMONT - 64E | EASTFIELD - 65A | DUNFERMLINE - 62C | EASTFIELD - 65A | EASTFIELD - 65A | EDINBURGH(SM) - 64A | EDINBURGH(SM) - 64A | HAYMARKET - 64B | EASTFIELD - 65A |
| Jan-51 | POLMONT - 64E | **11/50: DAWS - 65D** | DUNFERMLINE - 62C | **11/50: P'HEAD - 65C** | **11/50: P'HEAD - 65C** | EDINBURGH(SM) - 64A | EDINBURGH(SM) - 64A | HAYMARKET - 64B | EASTFIELD - 65A |
| Aug-51 | POLMONT - 64E | DAWSHOLME - 65D | DUNFERMLINE - 62C | PARKHEAD - 65C | PARKHEAD - 65C | EDINBURGH(SM) - 64A | EDINBURGH(SM) - 64A | HAYMARKET - 64B | EASTFIELD - 65A |
| Jan-52 | POLMONT - 64E | DAWSHOLME - 65D | DUNFERMLINE - 62C | PARKHEAD - 65C | PARKHEAD - 65C | EDINBURGH(SM) - 64A | EDINBURGH(SM) - 64A | HAYMARKET - 64B | EASTFIELD - 65A |
| Aug-52 | POLMONT - 64E | DAWSHOLME - 65D | DUNFERMLINE - 62C | PARKHEAD - 65C | PARKHEAD - 65C | EDINBURGH(SM) - 64A | EDINBURGH(SM) - 64A | HAYMARKET - 64B | EASTFIELD - 65A |
| Jan-53 | POLMONT - 64E | DAWSHOLME - 65D | DUNFERMLINE - 62C | PARKHEAD - 65C | PARKHEAD - 65C | EDINBURGH(SM) - 64A | EDINBURGH(SM) - 64A | HAYMARKET - 64B | EASTFIELD - 65A |
| Aug-53 | POLMONT - 64E | DAWSHOLME - 65D | DUNFERMLINE - 62C | PARKHEAD - 65C | PARKHEAD - 65C | EDINBURGH(SM) - 64A | EDINBURGH(SM) - 64A | HAYMARKET - 64B | EASTFIELD - 65A |
| Jan-54 | POLMONT - 64E | DAWSHOLME - 65D | DUNFERMLINE - 62C | PARKHEAD - 65C | PARKHEAD - 65C | EDINBURGH(SM) - 64A | EDINBURGH(SM) - 64A | HAYMARKET - 64B | EASTFIELD - 65A |
| Aug-54 | POLMONT - 64E | **6/54: EFLD - 65A** | DUNFERMLINE - 62C | PARKHEAD - 65C | PARKHEAD - 65C | EDINBURGH(SM) - 64A | EDINBURGH(SM) - 64A | HAYMARKET - 64B | EASTFIELD - 65A |
| Jan-55 | POLMONT - 64E | EASTFIELD - 65A | DUNFERMLINE - 62C | PARKHEAD - 65C | PARKHEAD - 65C | EDINBURGH(SM) - 64A | EDINBURGH(SM) - 64A | HAYMARKET - 64B | EASTFIELD - 65A |
| Aug-55 | POLMONT - 64E | EASTFIELD - 65A | DUNFERMLINE - 62C | PARKHEAD - 65C | PARKHEAD - 65C | EDINBURGH(SM) - 64A | EDINBURGH(SM) - 64A | HAYMARKET - 64B | EASTFIELD - 65A |
| Jan-56 | POLMONT - 64E | EASTFIELD - 65A | DUNFERMLINE - 62C | PARKHEAD - 65C | PARKHEAD - 65C | EDINBURGH(SM) - 64A | EDINBURGH(SM) - 64A | HAYMARKET - 64B | EASTFIELD - 65A |
| Aug-56 | POLMONT - 64E | EASTFIELD - 65A | DUNFERMLINE - 62C | PARKHEAD - 65C | PARKHEAD - 65C | EDINBURGH(SM) - 64A | EDINBURGH(SM) - 64A | HAYMARKET - 64B | EASTFIELD - 65A |
| Jan-57 | POLMONT - 64E | EASTFIELD - 65A | DUNFERMLINE - 62C | PARKHEAD - 65C | PARKHEAD - 65C | EDINBURGH(SM) - 64A | EDINBURGH(SM) - 64A | HAYMARKET - 64B | EASTFIELD - 65A |
| Aug-57 | POLMONT - 64E | **7/57: STRX - 65B** | DUNFERMLINE - 62C | PARKHEAD - 65C | PARKHEAD - 65C | EDINBURGH(SM) - 64A | EDINBURGH(SM) - 64A | HAYMARKET - 64B | EASTFIELD - 65A |
| Jan-58 | POLMONT - 64E | **9/57: EFLD - 65A** | DUNFERMLINE - 62C | PARKHEAD - 65C | PARKHEAD - 65C | **12/57: W/D** | EDINBURGH(SM) - 64A | HAYMARKET - 64B | EASTFIELD - 65A |
| Aug-58 | POLMONT - 64E | EASTFIELD - 65A | **8/58: DUN - 62B** | PARKHEAD - 65C | PARKHEAD - 65C | | EDINBURGH(SM) - 64A | HAYMARKET - 64B | EASTFIELD - 65A |
| Jan-59 | **3/59: W/D** | EASTFIELD - 65A | DUNDEE - 62B | PARKHEAD - 65C | PARKHEAD - 65C | | EDINBURGH(SM) - 64A | **2/59: W/D** | EASTFIELD - 65A |
| Aug-59 | | EASTFIELD - 65A | **4/59: W/D** | PARKHEAD - 65C | PARKHEAD - 65C | | EDINBURGH(SM) - 64A | | EASTFIELD - 65A |
| Nov-59 | | EASTFIELD - 65A | | PARKHEAD - 65C | **12/59: W/D** | | EDINBURGH(SM) - 64A | | EASTFIELD - 65A |
| Jan-60 | | EASTFIELD - 65A | | PARKHEAD - 65C | | | EDINBURGH(SM) - 64A | | EASTFIELD - 65A |
| Apr-60 | | EASTFIELD - 65A | | PARKHEAD - 65C | | | **3/60: W/D** | | **2/60: W/D** |
| Aug-60 | | EASTFIELD - 65A | | **6/60: W/D** | | | | | |
| Nov-60 | | EASTFIELD - 65A | | | | | | | |

| | 69171 | 69172 | 69173 | 69174 | 69175 | 69176 | 69177 | 69178 | 69179 |
|---|---|---|---|---|---|---|---|---|---|
| Aug-50 | PARKHEAD - 65C | EDINBURGH(SM) - 64A | EDINBURGH(SM) - 64A | CARLISLE(CANAL) - 12B | EDINBURGH(SM) - 64A | EASTFIELD - 65A | EASTFIELD - 65A | EASTFIELD - 65A | EASTFIELD - 65A |
| Jan-51 | PARKHEAD - 65C | EDINBURGH(SM) - 64A | EDINBURGH(SM) - 64A | CARLISLE(CANAL) - 12B | EDINBURGH(SM) - 64A | **11/50: DAWS - 65D** | **11/50: DAWS - 65D** | EASTFIELD - 65A | EASTFIELD - 65A |
| Aug-51 | PARKHEAD - 65C | EDINBURGH(SM) - 64A | EDINBURGH(SM) - 64A | CARLISLE(CANAL) - 68E | EDINBURGH(SM) - 64A | DAWSHOLME - 65D | DAWSHOLME - 65D | EASTFIELD - 65A | EASTFIELD - 65A |
| Jan-52 | **3/52: EFLD - 65A** | EDINBURGH(SM) - 64A | EDINBURGH(SM) - 64A | CARLISLE(CANAL) - 68E | EDINBURGH(SM) - 64A | DAWSHOLME - 65D | DAWSHOLME - 65D | EASTFIELD - 65A | EASTFIELD - 65A |
| Aug-52 | EASTFIELD - 65A | EDINBURGH(SM) - 64A | EDINBURGH(SM) - 64A | CARLISLE(CANAL) - 68E | EDINBURGH(SM) - 64A | DAWSHOLME - 65D | DAWSHOLME - 65D | EASTFIELD - 65A | EASTFIELD - 65A |
| Jan-53 | EASTFIELD - 65A | EDINBURGH(SM) - 64A | EDINBURGH(SM) - 64A | CARLISLE(CANAL) - 68E | EDINBURGH(SM) - 64A | DAWSHOLME - 65D | DAWSHOLME - 65D | EASTFIELD - 65A | EASTFIELD - 65A |
| Aug-53 | EASTFIELD - 65A | EDINBURGH(SM) - 64A | EDINBURGH(SM) - 64A | CARLISLE(CANAL) - 68E | EDINBURGH(SM) - 64A | DAWSHOLME - 65D | DAWSHOLME - 65D | EASTFIELD - 65A | EASTFIELD - 65A |
| Jan-54 | EASTFIELD - 65A | EDINBURGH(SM) - 64A | EDINBURGH(SM) - 64A | CARLISLE(CANAL) - 68E | EDINBURGH(SM) - 64A | DAWSHOLME - 65D | DAWSHOLME - 65D | EASTFIELD - 65A | EASTFIELD - 65A |
| Aug-54 | EASTFIELD - 65A | EDINBURGH(SM) - 64A | EDINBURGH(SM) - 64A | CARLISLE(CANAL) - 68E | EDINBURGH(SM) - 64A | DAWSHOLME - 65D | DAWSHOLME - 65D | EASTFIELD - 65A | EASTFIELD - 65A |
| Jan-55 | EASTFIELD - 65A | EDINBURGH(SM) - 64A | **5/55: HAY - 64B** | CARLISLE(CANAL) - 68E | EDINBURGH(SM) - 64A | DAWSHOLME - 65D | DAWSHOLME - 65D | EASTFIELD - 65A | EASTFIELD - 65A |
| Aug-55 | EASTFIELD - 65A | EDINBURGH(SM) - 64A | **7/55: EBRO(SM) - 64A** | CARLISLE(CANAL) - 68E | EDINBURGH(SM) - 64A | DAWSHOLME - 65D | DAWSHOLME - 65D | EASTFIELD - 65A | EASTFIELD - 65A |
| Jan-56 | EASTFIELD - 65A | EDINBURGH(SM) - 64A | EDINBURGH(SM) - 64A | CARLISLE(CANAL) - 68E | EDINBURGH(SM) - 64A | DAWSHOLME - 65D | DAWSHOLME - 65D | EASTFIELD - 65A | EASTFIELD - 65A |
| Aug-56 | EASTFIELD - 65A | EDINBURGH(SM) - 64A | EDINBURGH(SM) - 64A | CARLISLE(CANAL) - 68E | EDINBURGH(SM) - 64A | DAWSHOLME - 65D | DAWSHOLME - 65D | EASTFIELD - 65A | EASTFIELD - 65A |
| Jan-57 | EASTFIELD - 65A | EDINBURGH(SM) - 64A | EDINBURGH(SM) - 64A | CARLISLE(CANAL) - 68E | EDINBURGH(SM) - 64A | DAWSHOLME - 65D | DAWSHOLME - 65D | EASTFIELD - 65A | EASTFIELD - 65A |
| Aug-57 | EASTFIELD - 65A | EDINBURGH(SM) - 64A | EDINBURGH(SM) - 64A | CARLISLE(CANAL) - 68E | EDINBURGH(SM) - 64A | DAWSHOLME - 65D | DAWSHOLME - 65D | EASTFIELD - 65A | EASTFIELD - 65A |
| Jan-58 | EASTFIELD - 65A | EDINBURGH(SM) - 64A | EDINBURGH(SM) - 64A | CARLISLECANAL - 68E | EDINBURGH(SM) - 64A | DAWSHOLME - 65D | DAWSHOLME - 65D | EASTFIELD - 65A | EASTFIELD - 65A |
| Aug-58 | EASTFIELD - 65A | EDINBURGH(SM) - 64A | EDINBURGH(SM) - 64A | CARLISLECANAL - 12C | EDINBURGH(SM) - 64A | DAWSHOLME - 65D | DAWSHOLME - 65D | EASTFIELD - 65A | EASTFIELD - 65A |
| Jan-59 | EASTFIELD - 65A | **11/58: W/D** | EDINBURGH(SM) - 64A | **11/58: W/D** | **10/58: W/D** | DAWSHOLME - 65D | DAWSHOLME - 65D | EASTFIELD - 65A | EASTFIELD - 65A |
| Aug-59 | EASTFIELD - 65A | | EDINBURGH(SM) - 64A | | | **8/59: W/D** | DAWSHOLME - 65D | EASTFIELD - 65A | EASTFIELD - 65A |
| Nov-59 | EASTFIELD - 65A | | EDINBURGH(SM) - 64A | | | | DAWSHOLME - 65D | EASTFIELD - 65A | EASTFIELD - 65A |
| Jan-60 | EASTFIELD - 65A | | EDINBURGH(SM) - 64A | | | | DAWSHOLME - 65D | EASTFIELD - 65A | EASTFIELD - 65A |
| Apr-60 | EASTFIELD - 65A | | EDINBURGH(SM) - 64A | | | | DAWSHOLME - 65D | EASTFIELD - 65A | EASTFIELD - 65A |
| Aug-60 | **8/60: W/D** | | EDINBURGH(SM) - 64A | | | | **9/60: W/D** | EASTFIELD - 65A | EASTFIELD - 65A |
| Nov-60 | | | EDINBURGH(SM) - 64A | | | | | EASTFIELD - 65A | **11/60: W/D** |

| | 69180 | 69181 | 69182 | 69183 | 69184 | 69185 | 69186 | 69187 | 69188 |
|---|---|---|---|---|---|---|---|---|---|
| Aug-50 | EASTFIELD - 65A | EASTFIELD - 65A | EASTFIELD - 65A | EASTFIELD - 65A | EASTFIELD - 65A | CARLISLE(CANAL) - 12B | EDINBURGH(SM) - 64A | DALRYRD - 64C | EASTFIELD - 65A |
| Jan-51 | EASTFIELD - 65A | EASTFIELD - 65A | EASTFIELD - 65A | EASTFIELD - 65A | **11/50: DAWS - 65D** | CARLISLE(CANAL) - 12B | EDINBURGH(SM) - 64A | DALRYRD - 64C | EASTFIELD - 65A |
| Aug-51 | EASTFIELD - 65A | EASTFIELD - 65A | EASTFIELD - 65A | EASTFIELD - 65A | DAWSHOLME - 65D | **8/51: EFLD - 65A** | EDINBURGH(SM) - 64A | DALRYRD - 64C | EASTFIELD - 65A |
| Jan-52 | EASTFIELD - 65A | EASTFIELD - 65A | EASTFIELD - 65A | EASTFIELD - 65A | DAWSHOLME - 65D | **1/52: EBRO(SM) - 64A** | EDINBURGH(SM) - 64A | DALRYRD - 64C | EASTFIELD - 65A |
| Aug-52 | EASTFIELD - 65A | EASTFIELD - 65A | EASTFIELD - 65A | EASTFIELD - 65A | DAWSHOLME - 65D | EDINBURGH(SM) - 64A | EDINBURGH(SM) - 64A | DALRYRD - 64C | EASTFIELD - 65A |
| Jan-53 | EASTFIELD - 65A | EASTFIELD - 65A | EASTFIELD - 65A | EASTFIELD - 65A | DAWSHOLME - 65D | EDINBURGH(SM) - 64A | EDINBURGH(SM) - 64A | DALRYRD - 64C | EASTFIELD - 65A |
| Aug-53 | EASTFIELD - 65A | EASTFIELD - 65A | EASTFIELD - 65A | EASTFIELD - 65A | DAWSHOLME - 65D | EDINBURGH(SM) - 64A | EDINBURGH(SM) - 64A | DALRYRD - 64C | EASTFIELD - 65A |
| Jan-54 | EASTFIELD - 65A | EASTFIELD - 65A | EASTFIELD - 65A | EASTFIELD - 65A | DAWSHOLME - 65D | EDINBURGH(SM) - 64A | EDINBURGH(SM) - 64A | DALRYRD - 64C | EASTFIELD - 65A |
| Aug-54 | EASTFIELD - 65A | EASTFIELD - 65A | EASTFIELD - 65A | EASTFIELD - 65A | DAWSHOLME - 65D | EDINBURGH(SM) - 64A | EDINBURGH(SM) - 64A | DALRYRD - 64C | EASTFIELD - 65A |
| Jan-55 | EASTFIELD - 65A | EASTFIELD - 65A | EASTFIELD - 65A | EASTFIELD - 65A | DAWSHOLME - 65D | EDINBURGH(SM) - 64A | EDINBURGH(SM) - 64A | DALRYRD - 64C | EASTFIELD - 65A |
| Aug-55 | EASTFIELD - 65A | EASTFIELD - 65A | EASTFIELD - 65A | EASTFIELD - 65A | DAWSHOLME - 65D | EDINBURGH(SM) - 64A | EDINBURGH(SM) - 64A | DALRYRD - 64C | EASTFIELD - 65A |
| Jan-56 | EASTFIELD - 65A | EASTFIELD - 65A | EASTFIELD - 65A | EASTFIELD - 65A | DAWSHOLME - 65D | EDINBURGH(SM) - 64A | EDINBURGH(SM) - 64A | DALRYRD - 64C | EASTFIELD - 65A |
| Aug-56 | EASTFIELD - 65A | EASTFIELD - 65A | EASTFIELD - 65A | EASTFIELD - 65A | DAWSHOLME - 65D | EDINBURGH(SM) - 64A | EDINBURGH(SM) - 64A | DALRYRD - 64C | EASTFIELD - 65A |
| Jan-57 | EASTFIELD - 65A | EASTFIELD - 65A | EASTFIELD - 65A | EASTFIELD - 65A | DAWSHOLME - 65D | EDINBURGH(SM) - 64A | EDINBURGH(SM) - 64A | DALRYRD - 64C | EASTFIELD - 65A |
| Aug-57 | **9/57: STRX - 65B** | EASTFIELD - 65A | EASTFIELD - 65A | EASTFIELD - 65A | DAWSHOLME - 65D | EDINBURGH(SM) - 64A | EDINBURGH(SM) - 64A | DALRYRD - 64C | EASTFIELD - 65A |
| Jan-58 | STROLLOX - 65B | EASTFIELD - 65A | EASTFIELD - 65A | EASTFIELD - 65A | DAWSHOLME - 65D | EDINBURGH(SM) - 64A | EDINBURGH(SM) - 64A | DALRYRD - 64C | EASTFIELD - 65A |
| Aug-58 | **7/58: EFLD - 65A** | EASTFIELD - 65A | EASTFIELD - 65A | EASTFIELD - 65A | DAWSHOLME - 65D | EDINBURGH(SM) - 64A | EDINBURGH(SM) - 64A | DALRYRD - 64C | EASTFIELD - 65A |
| Jan-59 | EASTFIELD - 65A | EASTFIELD - 65A | EASTFIELD - 65A | EASTFIELD - 65A | DAWSHOLME - 65D | EDINBURGH(SM) - 64A | EDINBURGH(SM) - 64A | DALRYRD - 64C | EASTFIELD - 65A |
| Aug-59 | **4/59: KITTY - 61A** | EASTFIELD - 65A | **9/59: W/D** | EASTFIELD - 65A | DAWSHOLME - 65D | **7/59: W/D** | **7/59: W/D** | DALRYRD - 64C | EASTFIELD - 65A |
| Nov-59 | KITTYBREWSTER - 61A | EASTFIELD - 65A | | EASTFIELD - 65A | DAWSHOLME - 65D | | | **12/59: W/D** | EASTFIELD - 65A |
| Jan-60 | KITTYBREWSTER - 61A | EASTFIELD - 65A | | EASTFIELD - 65A | DAWSHOLME - 65D | | | | EASTFIELD - 65A |
| Apr-60 | KITTYBREWSTER - 61A | EASTFIELD - 65A | | EASTFIELD - 65A | DAWSHOLME - 65D | | | | EASTFIELD - 65A |
| Aug-60 | KITTYBREWSTER - 61A | EASTFIELD - 65A | | EASTFIELD - 65A | DAWSHOLME - 65D | | | | EASTFIELD - 65A |
| Nov-60 | KITTYBREWSTER - 61A | EASTFIELD - 65A | | EASTFIELD - 65A | DAWSHOLME - 65D | | | | EASTFIELD - 65A |

| | 69189 | 69190 | 69191 | 69192 | 69193 | 69194 | 69195 | 69196 | 69197 |
|---|---|---|---|---|---|---|---|---|---|
| Aug-50 | EASTFIELD - 65A | PARKHEAD - 65C | EASTFIELD - 65A | DUNFERMLINE - 62C | PARKHEAD - 65C | PARKHEAD - 65C | PARKHEAD - 65C | KIPPS - 65E | CARLISLE(C) - 12B |
| Jan-51 | EASTFIELD - 65A | PARKHEAD - 65C | EASTFIELD - 65A | DUNFERMLINE - 62C | PARKHEAD - 65C | PARKHEAD - 65C | PARKHEAD - 65C | KIPPS - 65E | CARLISLE(C) - 12B |
| Aug-51 | EASTFIELD - 65A | PARKHEAD - 65C | EASTFIELD - 65A | DUNFERMLINE - 62C | PARKHEAD - 65C | PARKHEAD - 65C | PARKHEAD - 65C | KIPPS - 65E | **8/51: EFLD - 65A** |
| Jan-52 | EASTFIELD - 65A | PARKHEAD - 65C | EASTFIELD - 65A | DUNFERMLINE - 62C | PARKHEAD - 65C | PARKHEAD - 65C | PARKHEAD - 65C | KIPPS - 65E | EASTFIELD - 65A |
| Aug-52 | EASTFIELD - 65A | PARKHEAD - 65C | EASTFIELD - 65A | DUNFERMLINE - 62C | PARKHEAD - 65C | PARKHEAD - 65C | PARKHEAD - 65C | KIPPS - 65E | EASTFIELD - 65A |
| Jan-53 | EASTFIELD - 65A | PARKHEAD - 65C | EASTFIELD - 65A | DUNFERMLINE - 62C | PARKHEAD - 65C | PARKHEAD - 65C | PARKHEAD - 65C | KIPPS - 65E | EASTFIELD - 65A |
| Aug-53 | EASTFIELD - 65A | PARKHEAD - 65C | EASTFIELD - 65A | DUNFERMLINE - 62C | PARKHEAD - 65C | PARKHEAD - 65C | PARKHEAD - 65C | KIPPS - 65E | EASTFIELD - 65A |
| Jan-54 | EASTFIELD - 65A | PARKHEAD - 65C | EASTFIELD - 65A | DUNFERMLINE - 62C | PARKHEAD - 65C | PARKHEAD - 65C | PARKHEAD - 65C | KIPPS - 65E | EASTFIELD - 65A |
| Aug-54 | EASTFIELD - 65A | PARKHEAD - 65C | EASTFIELD - 65A | DUNFERMLINE - 62C | PARKHEAD - 65C | PARKHEAD - 65C | PARKHEAD - 65C | KIPPS - 65E | EASTFIELD - 65A |
| Jan-55 | EASTFIELD - 65A | PARKHEAD - 65C | EASTFIELD - 65A | DUNFERMLINE - 62C | PARKHEAD - 65C | PARKHEAD - 65C | PARKHEAD - 65C | KIPPS - 65E | EASTFIELD - 65A |
| Aug-55 | EASTFIELD - 65A | PARKHEAD - 65C | EASTFIELD - 65A | DUNFERMLINE - 62C | PARKHEAD - 65C | PARKHEAD - 65C | PARKHEAD - 65C | KIPPS - 65E | EASTFIELD - 65A |
| Jan-56 | EASTFIELD - 65A | PARKHEAD - 65C | EASTFIELD - 65A | DUNFERMLINE - 62C | PARKHEAD - 65C | PARKHEAD - 65C | PARKHEAD - 65C | KIPPS - 65E | EASTFIELD - 65A |
| Aug-56 | EASTFIELD - 65A | PARKHEAD - 65C | EASTFIELD - 65A | DUNFERMLINE - 62C | PARKHEAD - 65C | PARKHEAD - 65C | PARKHEAD - 65C | KIPPS - 65E | EASTFIELD - 65A |
| Jan-57 | EASTFIELD - 65A | PARKHEAD - 65C | EASTFIELD - 65A | DUNFERMLINE - 62C | PARKHEAD - 65C | PARKHEAD - 65C | PARKHEAD - 65C | KIPPS - 65E | EASTFIELD - 65A |
| Aug-57 | **7/57: STRX - 65B** | PARKHEAD - 65C | EASTFIELD - 65A | DUNFERMLINE - 62C | PARKHEAD - 65C | PARKHEAD - 65C | PARKHEAD - 65C | KIPPS - 65E | EASTFIELD - 65A |
| Jan-58 | **9/57: F'HILL - 61B** | PARKHEAD - 65C | EASTFIELD - 65A | DUNFERMLINE - 62C | PARKHEAD - 65C | PARKHEAD - 65C | **3/58: W/D** | KIPPS - 65E | EASTFIELD - 65A |
| Aug-58 | **4/58: W/D** | PARKHEAD - 65C | EASTFIELD - 65A | DUNFERMLINE - 62C | **8/58: W/D** | PARKHEAD - 65C | | KIPPS - 65E | EASTFIELD - 65A |
| Jan-59 | | PARKHEAD - 65C | EASTFIELD - 65A | **3/59: W/D** | | PARKHEAD - 65C | | KIPPS - 65E | EASTFIELD - 65A |
| Aug-59 | | PARKHEAD - 65C | EASTFIELD - 65A | | | PARKHEAD - 65C | | KIPPS - 65E | EASTFIELD - 65A |
| Nov-59 | | PARKHEAD - 65C | EASTFIELD - 65A | | | PARKHEAD - 65C | | **12/59: HAM - 66C** | **12/59: W/D** |
| Jan-60 | | PARKHEAD - 65C | EASTFIELD - 65A | | | PARKHEAD - 65C | | HAMILTON - 66C | |
| Apr-60 | | PARKHEAD - 65C | EASTFIELD - 65A | | | PARKHEAD - 65C | | HAMILTON - 66C | |
| Aug-60 | | **9/60: W/D** | EASTFIELD - 65A | | | PARKHEAD - 65C | | HAMILTON - 66C | |
| Nov-60 | | | EASTFIELD - 65A | | | **11/60: W/D** | | HAMILTON - 66C | |

| | 69198 | 69199 | 69200 | 69201 | 69202 | 69203 | 69204 | 69205 | 69206 |
|---|---|---|---|---|---|---|---|---|---|
| Aug-50 | PARKHEAD - 65C | PARKHEAD - 65C | POLMONT - 64E | FERRYHILL - 61B | DUNFERMLINE - 62C | EASTFIELD - 65A | DUNFERMLINE - 62C | EASTFIELD - 65A | KIPPS - 65E |
| Jan-51 | PARKHEAD - 65C | PARKHEAD - 65C | POLMONT - 64E | FERRYHILL - 61B | DUNFERMLINE - 62C | **11/50: DAWS - 65D** | DUNFERMLINE - 62C | **11/50: DAWS - 65D** | KIPPS - 65E |
| Aug-51 | PARKHEAD - 65C | PARKHEAD - 65C | POLMONT - 64E | FERRYHILL - 61B | DUNFERMLINE - 62C | DAWSHOLME - 65D | DUNFERMLINE - 62C | DAWSHOLME - 65D | KIPPS - 65E |
| Jan-52 | PARKHEAD - 65C | PARKHEAD - 65C | POLMONT - 64E | FERRYHILL - 61B | DUNFERMLINE - 62C | DAWSHOLME - 65D | DUNFERMLINE - 62C | DAWSHOLME - 65D | KIPPS - 65E |
| Aug-52 | PARKHEAD - 65C | PARKHEAD - 65C | POLMONT - 64E | FERRYHILL - 61B | DUNFERMLINE - 62C | DAWSHOLME - 65D | DUNFERMLINE - 62C | DAWSHOLME - 65D | KIPPS - 65E |
| Jan-53 | PARKHEAD - 65C | PARKHEAD - 65C | POLMONT - 64E | FERRYHILL - 61B | DUNFERMLINE - 62C | DAWSHOLME - 65D | DUNFERMLINE - 62C | DAWSHOLME - 65D | KIPPS - 65E |
| Aug-53 | PARKHEAD - 65C | PARKHEAD - 65C | POLMONT - 64E | FERRYHILL - 61B | DUNFERMLINE - 62C | DAWSHOLME - 65D | DUNFERMLINE - 62C | DAWSHOLME - 65D | KIPPS - 65E |
| Jan-54 | PARKHEAD - 65C | PARKHEAD - 65C | POLMONT - 64E | FERRYHILL - 61B | DUNFERMLINE - 62C | DAWSHOLME - 65D | DUNFERMLINE - 62C | DAWSHOLME - 65D | KIPPS - 65E |
| Aug-54 | PARKHEAD - 65C | PARKHEAD - 65C | POLMONT - 64E | FERRYHILL - 61B | DUNFERMLINE - 62C | DAWSHOLME - 65D | DUNFERMLINE - 62C | DAWSHOLME - 65D | KIPPS - 65E |
| Jan-55 | PARKHEAD - 65C | PARKHEAD - 65C | POLMONT - 64E | FERRYHILL - 61B | DUNFERMLINE - 62C | DAWSHOLME - 65D | DUNFERMLINE - 62C | DAWSHOLME - 65D | KIPPS - 65E |
| Aug-55 | PARKHEAD - 65C | PARKHEAD - 65C | POLMONT - 64E | FERRYHILL - 61B | DUNFERMLINE - 62C | DAWSHOLME - 65D | DUNFERMLINE - 62C | DAWSHOLME - 65D | KIPPS - 65E |
| Jan-56 | PARKHEAD - 65C | PARKHEAD - 65C | POLMONT - 64E | FERRYHILL - 61B | DUNFERMLINE - 62C | DAWSHOLME - 65D | DUNFERMLINE - 62C | DAWSHOLME - 65D | KIPPS - 65E |
| Aug-56 | PARKHEAD - 65C | PARKHEAD - 65C | POLMONT - 64E | FERRYHILL - 61B | DUNFERMLINE - 62C | DAWSHOLME - 65D | DUNFERMLINE - 62C | DAWSHOLME - 65D | KIPPS - 65E |
| Jan-57 | PARKHEAD - 65C | PARKHEAD - 65C | POLMONT - 64E | FERRYHILL - 61B | DUNFERMLINE - 62C | DAWSHOLME - 65D | DUNFERMLINE - 62C | DAWSHOLME - 65D | KIPPS - 65E |
| Aug-57 | PARKHEAD - 65C | PARKHEAD - 65C | POLMONT - 64E | **12/57: KTH - 61C** | DUNFERMLINE - 62C | DAWSHOLME - 65D | **8/57: DUN - 62B** | DAWSHOLME - 65D | KIPPS - 65E |
| Jan-58 | PARKHEAD - 65C | PARKHEAD - 65C | POLMONT - 64E | **1/58: W/D** | DUNFERMLINE - 62C | DAWSHOLME - 65D | DUNDEE - 62B | DAWSHOLME - 65D | KIPPS - 65E |
| Aug-58 | PARKHEAD - 65C | PARKHEAD - 65C | **6/58: W/D** | | DUNFERMLINE - 62C | **6/58: W/D** | DUNDEE - 62B | DAWSHOLME - 65D | KIPPS - 65E |
| Jan-59 | PARKHEAD - 65C | PARKHEAD - 65C | | | DUNFERMLINE - 62C | | DUNDEE - 62B | DAWSHOLME - 65D | KIPPS - 65E |
| Aug-59 | PARKHEAD - 65C | PARKHEAD - 65C | | | DUNFERMLINE - 62C | | DUNDEE - 62B | DAWSHOLME - 65D | KIPPS - 65E |
| Nov-59 | PARKHEAD - 65C | PARKHEAD - 65C | | | DUNFERMLINE - 62C | | **12/59: TH JN - 62A** | DAWSHOLME - 65D | KIPPS - 65E |
| Jan-60 | PARKHEAD - 65C | PARKHEAD - 65C | | | DUNFERMLINE - 62C | | THORNTON JCN - 62A | DAWSHOLME - 65D | KIPPS - 65E |
| Apr-60 | PARKHEAD - 65C | PARKHEAD - 65C | | | DUNFERMLINE - 62C | | THORNTON JCN - 62A | **3/60: W/D** | KIPPS - 65E |
| Aug-60 | **8/60: W/D** | PARKHEAD - 65C | | | **6/60: W/D** | | THORNTON JCN - 62A | | **6/60 : W/D** |
| Nov-60 | | PARKHEAD - 65C | | | | | THORNTON JCN - 62A | | |

| | 69207 | 69208 | 69209 | 69210 | 69211 | 69212 | 69213 | 69214 | 69215 |
|---|---|---|---|---|---|---|---|---|---|
| Aug-50 | KIPPS - 65E | EASTFIELD - 65A | PARKHEAD - 65C | PARKHEAD - 65C | THORNTON JCN - 62A | PARKHEAD - 65C | PARKHEAD - 65C | PARKHEAD - 65C | CARLISLE(C) - 12B |
| Jan-51 | KIPPS - 65E | **11/50: DAWS - 65D** | PARKHEAD - 65C | PARKHEAD - 65C | THORNTON JCN - 62A | PARKHEAD - 65C | PARKHEAD - 65C | PARKHEAD - 65C | CARLISLE(C) - 12B |
| Aug-51 | KIPPS - 65E | DAWSHOLME - 65D | PARKHEAD - 65C | PARKHEAD - 65C | THORNTON JCN - 62A | PARKHEAD - 65C | PARKHEAD - 65C | PARKHEAD - 65C | CARLISLE(C) - 68E |
| Jan-52 | KIPPS - 65E | DAWSHOLME - 65D | PARKHEAD - 65C | PARKHEAD - 65C | THORNTON JCN - 62A | PARKHEAD - 65C | PARKHEAD - 65C | **3/52: EFLD - 65A** | CARLISLE(C) - 68E |
| Aug-52 | KIPPS - 65E | DAWSHOLME - 65D | PARKHEAD - 65C | PARKHEAD - 65C | THORNTON JCN - 62A | PARKHEAD - 65C | PARKHEAD - 65C | EASTFIELD - 65A | CARLISLE(C) - 68E |
| Jan-53 | KIPPS - 65E | DAWSHOLME - 65D | PARKHEAD - 65C | PARKHEAD - 65C | THORNTON JCN - 62A | PARKHEAD - 65C | PARKHEAD - 65C | EASTFIELD - 65A | CARLISLE(C) - 68E |
| Aug-53 | KIPPS - 65E | DAWSHOLME - 65D | PARKHEAD - 65C | PARKHEAD - 65C | THORNTON JCN - 62A | PARKHEAD - 65C | PARKHEAD - 65C | EASTFIELD - 65A | CARLISLE(C) - 68E |
| Jan-54 | KIPPS - 65E | DAWSHOLME - 65D | PARKHEAD - 65C | PARKHEAD - 65C | THORNTON JCN - 62A | PARKHEAD - 65C | PARKHEAD - 65C | EASTFIELD - 65A | CARLISLE(C) - 68E |
| Aug-54 | KIPPS - 65E | DAWSHOLME - 65D | PARKHEAD - 65C | PARKHEAD - 65C | THORNTON JCN - 62A | PARKHEAD - 65C | PARKHEAD - 65C | EASTFIELD - 65A | CARLISLE(C) - 68E |
| Jan-55 | KIPPS - 65E | DAWSHOLME - 65D | PARKHEAD - 65C | PARKHEAD - 65C | THORNTON JCN - 62A | PARKHEAD - 65C | PARKHEAD - 65C | EASTFIELD - 65A | CARLISLE(C) - 68E |
| Aug-55 | KIPPS - 65E | DAWSHOLME - 65D | PARKHEAD - 65C | PARKHEAD - 65C | THORNTON JCN - 62A | PARKHEAD - 65C | PARKHEAD - 65C | EASTFIELD - 65A | CARLISLE(C) - 68E |
| Jan-56 | KIPPS - 65E | DAWSHOLME - 65D | PARKHEAD - 65C | PARKHEAD - 65C | THORNTON JCN - 62A | PARKHEAD - 65C | PARKHEAD - 65C | EASTFIELD - 65A | CARLISLE(C) - 68E |
| Aug-56 | KIPPS - 65E | DAWSHOLME - 65D | PARKHEAD - 65C | PARKHEAD - 65C | THORNTON JCN - 62A | PARKHEAD - 65C | PARKHEAD - 65C | EASTFIELD - 65A | CARLISLE(C) - 68E |
| Jan-57 | KIPPS - 65E | DAWSHOLME - 65D | PARKHEAD - 65C | PARKHEAD - 65C | THORNTON JCN - 62A | PARKHEAD - 65C | PARKHEAD - 65C | EASTFIELD - 65A | CARLISLE(C) - 68E |
| Aug-57 | KIPPS - 65E | DAWSHOLME - 65D | PARKHEAD - 65C | **10/57: W/D** | THORNTON JCN - 62A | **7/57: EFLD - 65A** | PARKHEAD - 65C | EASTFIELD - 65A | CARLISLE(C) - 68E |
| Jan-58 | KIPPS - 65E | DAWSHOLME - 65D | PARKHEAD - 65C | | THORNTON JCN - 62A | EASTFIELD - 65A | PARKHEAD - 65C | EASTFIELD - 65A | CARLISLE CANAL - 68E |
| Aug-58 | KIPPS - 65E | DAWSHOLME - 65D | PARKHEAD - 65C | | THORNTON JCN - 62A | EASTFIELD - 65A | PARKHEAD - 65C | EASTFIELD - 65A | CARLISLE CANAL - 12C |
| Jan-59 | KIPPS - 65E | DAWSHOLME - 65D | PARKHEAD - 65C | | **2/59: HAY - 64B** | EASTFIELD - 65A | PARKHEAD - 65C | EASTFIELD - 65A | CARLISLE CANAL - 12C |
| Aug-59 | KIPPS - 65E | DAWSHOLME - 65D | PARKHEAD - 65C | | HAYMARKET - 64B | EASTFIELD - 65A | PARKHEAD - 65C | **5/59: W/D** | CARLISLE CANAL - 12C |
| Nov-59 | **12/59: POLM - 66A** | **12/59: W/D** | PARKHEAD - 65C | | HAYMARKET - 64B | EASTFIELD - 65A | **10/59: W/D** | | **11/59: W/D** |
| Jan-60 | POLMADIE - 66A | | PARKHEAD - 65C | | HAYMARKET - 64B | EASTFIELD - 65A | | | |
| Apr-60 | **3/60: W/D** | | PARKHEAD - 65C | | HAYMARKET - 64B | EASTFIELD - 65A | | | |
| Aug-60 | | | PARKHEAD - 65C | | HAYMARKET - 64B | EASTFIELD - 65A | | | |
| Nov-60 | | | **11/60: W/D** | | HAYMARKET - 64B | EASTFIELD - 65A | | | |

| | 69216 | 69217 | 69218 | 69219 | 69220 | 69221 | 69222 | 69223 | 69224 |
|---|---|---|---|---|---|---|---|---|---|
| Aug-50 | BATHGATE - 64F | PARKHEAD - 65C | CARLISLE(C) - 12B | EDINBURGH (SM) - 64A | HAYMARKET - 64B | DUNFERMLINE - 62C | EASTFIELD - 65A | THORNTON JCN - 62A | THORNTON JCN - 62A |
| Jan-51 | BATHGATE - 64F | PARKHEAD - 65C | CARLISLE(C) - 12B | EDINBURGH (SM) - 64A | HAYMARKET - 64B | DUNFERMLINE - 62C | EASTFIELD - 65A | THORNTON JCN - 62A | THORNTON JCN - 62A |
| Aug-51 | BATHGATE - 64F | PARKHEAD - 65C | **8/51: EFLD - 65A** | EDINBURGH (SM) - 64A | HAYMARKET - 64B | DUNFERMLINE - 62C | EASTFIELD - 65A | THORNTON JCN - 62A | THORNTON JCN - 62A |
| Jan-52 | BATHGATE - 64F | PARKHEAD - 65C | EASTFIELD - 65A | EDINBURGH (SM) - 64A | HAYMARKET - 64B | DUNFERMLINE - 62C | EASTFIELD - 65A | THORNTON JCN - 62A | THORNTON JCN - 62A |
| Aug-52 | BATHGATE - 64F | PARKHEAD - 65C | EASTFIELD - 65A | EDINBURGH (SM) - 64A | HAYMARKET - 64B | DUNFERMLINE - 62C | **7/52: EBRO(SM) - 64A** | THORNTON JCN - 62A | THORNTON JCN - 62A |
| Jan-53 | BATHGATE - 64F | PARKHEAD - 65C | EASTFIELD - 65A | EDINBURGH (SM) - 64A | HAYMARKET - 64B | DUNFERMLINE - 62C | EDINBURGH (SM) - 64A | THORNTON JCN - 62A | THORNTON JCN - 62A |
| Aug-53 | BATHGATE - 64F | PARKHEAD - 65C | EASTFIELD - 65A | EDINBURGH (SM) - 64A | HAYMARKET - 64B | DUNFERMLINE - 62C | EDINBURGH (SM) - 64A | THORNTON JCN - 62A | THORNTON JCN - 62A |
| Jan-54 | BATHGATE - 64F | PARKHEAD - 65C | EASTFIELD - 65A | EDINBURGH (SM) - 64A | HAYMARKET - 64B | DUNFERMLINE - 62C | EDINBURGH (SM) - 64A | THORNTON JCN - 62A | THORNTON JCN - 62A |
| Aug-54 | BATHGATE - 64F | PARKHEAD - 65C | EASTFIELD - 65A | EDINBURGH (SM) - 64A | HAYMARKET - 64B | DUNFERMLINE - 62C | EDINBURGH (SM) - 64A | THORNTON JCN - 62A | THORNTON JCN - 62A |
| Jan-55 | BATHGATE - 64F | PARKHEAD - 65C | EASTFIELD - 65A | EDINBURGH (SM) - 64A | HAYMARKET - 64B | DUNFERMLINE - 62C | EDINBURGH (SM) - 64A | THORNTON JCN - 62A | THORNTON JCN - 62A |
| Aug-55 | BATHGATE - 64F | PARKHEAD - 65C | EASTFIELD - 65A | EDINBURGH (SM) - 64A | HAYMARKET - 64B | DUNFERMLINE - 62C | EDINBURGH (SM) - 64A | THORNTON JCN - 62A | THORNTON JCN - 62A |
| Jan-56 | BATHGATE - 64F | PARKHEAD - 65C | EASTFIELD - 65A | EDINBURGH (SM) - 64A | HAYMARKET - 64B | DUNFERMLINE - 62C | EDINBURGH (SM) - 64A | THORNTON JCN - 62A | THORNTON JCN - 62A |
| Aug-56 | BATHGATE - 64F | PARKHEAD - 65C | EASTFIELD - 65A | EDINBURGH (SM) - 64A | HAYMARKET - 64B | DUNFERMLINE - 62C | EDINBURGH (SM) - 64A | THORNTON JCN - 62A | THORNTON JCN - 62A |
| Jan-57 | BATHGATE - 64F | PARKHEAD - 65C | EASTFIELD - 65A | EDINBURGH (SM) - 64A | HAYMARKET - 64B | DUNFERMLINE - 62C | EDINBURGH (SM) - 64A | THORNTON JCN - 62A | THORNTON JCN - 62A |
| Aug-57 | BATHGATE - 64F | **7/57: DAWS - 65D** | EASTFIELD - 65A | EDINBURGH (SM) - 64A | HAYMARKET - 64B | DUNFERMLINE - 62C | EDINBURGH (SM) - 64A | THORNTON JCN - 62A | **9/57: DUN - 62B** |
| Jan-58 | BATHGATE - 64F | DAWSHOLME - 65D | EASTFIELD - 65A | EDINBURGH (SM) - 64A | HAYMARKET - 64B | DUNFERMLINE - 62C | EDINBURGH (SM) - 64A | THORNTON JCN - 62A | **3/58: KEITH - 61C** |
| Aug-58 | BATHGATE - 64F | DAWSHOLME - 65D | EASTFIELD - 65A | EDINBURGH (SM) - 64A | HAYMARKET - 64B | DUNFERMLINE - 62C | EDINBURGH (SM) - 64A | THORNTON JCN - 62A | KEITH - 61C |
| Jan-59 | BATHGATE - 64F | DAWSHOLME - 65D | EASTFIELD - 65A | EDINBURGH (SM) - 64A | **11/58: W/D** | DUNFERMLINE - 62C | EDINBURGH (SM) - 64A | THORNTON JCN - 62A | **3/59: F'HILL - 61B** |
| Aug-59 | BATHGATE - 64F | DAWSHOLME - 65D | EASTFIELD - 65A | EDINBURGH (SM) - 64A | | DUNFERMLINE - 62C | **5/59: W/D** | THORNTON JCN - 62A | FERRYHILL - 61B |
| Nov-59 | BATHGATE - 64F | **10/59: W/D** | EASTFIELD - 65A | EDINBURGH (SM) - 64A | | DUNFERMLINE - 62C | | **12/59: M'WELL - 66B** | FERRYHILL - 61B |
| Jan-60 | BATHGATE - 64F | | EASTFIELD - 65A | EDINBURGH (SM) - 64A | | DUNFERMLINE - 62C | | MOTHERWELL - 66B | FERRYHILL - 61B |
| Apr-60 | BATHGATE - 64F | | EASTFIELD - 65A | EDINBURGH (SM) - 64A | | DUNFERMLINE - 62C | | MOTHERWELL - 66B | FERRYHILL - 61B |
| Aug-60 | BATHGATE - 64F | | EASTFIELD - 65A | EDINBURGH (SM) - 64A | | DUNFERMLINE - 62C | | **9/60: W/D** | FERRYHILL - 61B |
| Nov-60 | BATHGATE - 64F | | EASTFIELD - 65A | EDINBURGH (SM) - 64A | | DUNFERMLINE - 62C | | | FERRYHILL - 61B |

| | 69225 | 69227 | 69228 | 69229 | 69230 | 69231 | 69232 | 69233 | 69234 |
|---|---|---|---|---|---|---|---|---|---|
| Aug-50 | DARNALL-39B | DARNALL-39B | DARNALL-39B | DARNALL-39B | DARNALL-39B | DARNALL-39B | DARNALL-39B | DARNALL-39B | DARNALL-39B |
| Jan-51 | DARNALL-39B | DARNALL-39B | DARNALL-39B | DARNALL-39B | DARNALL-39B | DARNALL-39B | DARNALL-39B | DARNALL-39B | DARNALL-39B |
| Aug-51 | DARNALL-39B | DARNALL-39B | DARNALL-39B | DARNALL-39B | DARNALL-39B | DARNALL-39B | DARNALL-39B | DARNALL-39B | DARNALL-39B |
| Jan-52 | DARNALL-39B | DARNALL-39B | DARNALL-39B | DARNALL-39B | DARNALL-39B | DARNALL-39B | DARNALL-39B | DARNALL-39B | DARNALL-39B |
| Aug-52 | DARNALL-39B | DARNALL-39B | DARNALL-39B | 6/52: W/D | DARNALL-39B | DARNALL-39B | DARNALL-39B | DARNALL-39B | 1/53: W/D |
| Jan-53 | DARNALL-39B | DARNALL-39B | DARNALL-39B | | DARNALL-39B | DARNALL-39B | DARNALL-39B | DARNALL-39B | |
| Aug-53 | DARNALL-39B | DARNALL-39B | DARNALL-39B | | DARNALL-39B | DARNALL-39B | DARNALL-39B | DARNALL-39B | |
| Jan-54 | DARNALL-39B | 11/53: W/D | DARNALL-39B | | DARNALL-39B | DARNALL-39B | DARNALL-39B | DARNALL-39B | |
| Aug-54 | DARNALL-39B | | DARNALL-39B | | 12/54: W/D | 10/54: W/D | 12/54: W/D | 11/54: W/D | |
| Jan-55 | 12/54: W/D | | 12/54: W/D | | | | | | |
| Aug-55 | | | | | | | | | |
| Jan-56 | | | | | | | | | |
| Aug-56 | | | | | | | | | |
| Jan-57 | | | | | | | | | |
| Aug-57 | | | | | | | | | |
| Jan-58 | | | | | | | | | |
| Aug-58 | | | | | | | | | |
| Jan-59 | | | | | | | | | |
| Aug-59 | | | | | | | | | |
| Nov-59 | | | | | | | | | |
| Jan-60 | | | | | | | | | |
| Apr-60 | | | | | | | | | |
| Aug-60 | | | | | | | | | |
| Nov-60 | | | | | | | | | |

| | 69235 | 69236 | 69239 | 69240 | 69242 | 69244 | 69245 | 69246 | 69250 |
|---|---|---|---|---|---|---|---|---|---|
| Aug-50 | DARNALL-39B | DARNALL-39B | DARNALL-39B | DARNALL-39B | DARNALL-39B | DARNALL-39B | 10/50: W/D | DARNALL-39B | GORTON-39A |
| Jan-51 | DARNALL-39B | DARNALL-39B | DARNALL-39B | DARNALL-39B | DARNALL-39B | DARNALL-39B | | DARNALL-39B | GORTON-39A |
| Aug-51 | DARNALL-39B | DARNALL-39B | DARNALL-39B | DARNALL-39B | DARNALL-39B | DARNALL-39B | | DARNALL-39B | GORTON-39A |
| Jan-52 | DARNALL-39B | DARNALL-39B | DARNALL-39B | DARNALL-39B | ?/52: W/D | 2/52: W/D | | 4/52: W/D | GORTON-39A |
| Aug-52 | DARNALL-39B | DARNALL-39B | DARNALL-39B | DARNALL-39B | | | | | GORTON-39A |
| Jan-53 | DARNALL-39B | DARNALL-39B | DARNALL-39B | 11/52: W/D | | | | | GORTON-39A |
| Aug-53 | DARNALL-39B | DARNALL-39B | DARNALL-39B | | | | | | GORTON-39A |
| Jan-54 | DARNALL-39B | DARNALL-39B | 3/54: W/D | | | | | | GORTON-39A |
| Aug-54 | 8/54: W/D | DARNALL-39B | | | | | | | GORTON-39A |
| Jan-55 | | 11/54: W/D | | | | | | | GORTON-39A |
| Aug-55 | | | | | | | | | GORTON-39A |
| Jan-56 | | | | | | | | | GORTON-39A |
| Aug-56 | | | | | | | | | 8/56: W/D |
| Jan-57 | | | | | | | | | |
| Aug-57 | | | | | | | | | |
| Jan-58 | | | | | | | | | |
| Aug-58 | | | | | | | | | |
| Jan-59 | | | | | | | | | |
| Aug-59 | | | | | | | | | |
| Nov-59 | | | | | | | | | |
| Jan-60 | | | | | | | | | |
| Apr-60 | | | | | | | | | |
| Aug-60 | | | | | | | | | |
| Nov-60 | | | | | | | | | |

| | 69252 | 69253 | 69254 | 69255 | 69256 | 69257 | 69258 | 69259 | 69260 |
|---|---|---|---|---|---|---|---|---|---|
| Aug-50 | T.PARK-9E | LINCOLN-40A | BRUNSWCK-8E | T.PARK-9E | BOSTON-40F | NEASDEN-34E | BRUNSWCK-8E | NEASDEN-34E | GORTON-39A |
| Jan-51 | T.PARK-9E | LINCOLN-40A | BRUNSWCK-8E | T.PARK-9E | BOSTON-40F | 3/51: KX-34A | BRUNSWCK-8E | NEASDEN-34E | GORTON-39A |
| Aug-51 | 8/51: W/D | LINCOLN-40A | BRUNSWCK-8E | T.PARK-9E | BOSTON-40F | 9/51: NEAS-34E | BRUNSWCK-8E | NEASDEN-34E | GORTON-39A |
| Jan-52 | | LINCOLN-40A | BRUNSWCK-8E | T.PARK-9E | BOSTON-40F | NEASDEN-34E | BRUNSWCK-8E | NEASDEN-34E | GORTON-39A |
| Aug-52 | | LINCOLN-40A | BRUNSWCK-8E | T.PARK-9E | BOSTON-40F | NEASDEN-34E | BRUNSWCK-8E | NEASDEN-34E | GORTON-39A |
| Jan-53 | | LINCOLN-40A | BRUNSWCK-8E | T.PARK-9E | BOSTON-40F | 8/53: ANNES-38B | BRUNSWCK-8E | NEASDEN-34E | GORTON-39A |
| Aug-53 | | LINCOLN-40A | BRUNSWCK-8E | T.PARK-9E | BOSTON-40F | 10/53: NEAS-34E | BRUNSWCK-8E | NEASDEN-34E | GORTON-39A |
| Jan-54 | | LINCOLN-40A | BRUNSWCK-8E | T.PARK-9E | BOSTON-40F | 10/54: STRAT-30A | BRUNSWCK-8E | NEASDEN-34E | GORTON-39A |
| Aug-54 | | 4/54: DARN-39B | BRUNSWCK-8E | T.PARK-9E | BOSTON-40F | 11/54: NEAS-34E | BRUNSWCK-8E | 1/55: DARN-39B | GORTON-39A |
| Jan-55 | | DARNALL-39B | BRUNSWCK-8E | 4/55: NWCH-9G | BOSTON-40F | NEASDEN-34E | BRUNSWCK-8E | DARNALL-39B | 8/55: RET-36E |
| Aug-55 | | DARNALL-39B | BRUNSWCK-8E | 7/55: T.PARK-9E | BOSTON-40F | NEASDEN-34E | BRUNSWCK-8E | DARNALL-41A | RETFORD-36E |
| Jan-56 | | 11/55: W/D | 11/55: WREX-6E | T.PARK-9E | 11/55: W/D | NEASDEN-34E | BRUNSWCK-8E | DARNALL-41A | 7/56: W/D |
| Aug-56 | | | 3/56: W/D | 6/56: W/D | | NEASDEN-34E | BRUNSWCK-8E | DARNALL-41A | |
| Jan-57 | | | | | | NEASDEN-34E | BRUNSWCK-8E | DARNALL-41A | |
| Aug-57 | | | | | | NEASDEN-34E | BRUNSWCK-8E | DARNALL-41A | |
| Jan-58 | | | | | | NEASDEN-34E | 5/58: NEW.E.-34E | DARNALL-41A | |
| Aug-58 | | | | | | NEASDEN-14D | DARNALL-41A | 11/58: W/D | |
| Jan-59 | | | | | | NEASDEN-14D | DARNALL-41A | | |
| Aug-59 | | | | | | 12/59: W/D | DARNALL-41A | | |
| Nov-59 | | | | | | | DARNALL-41A | | |
| Jan-60 | | | | | | | DARNALL-41A | | |
| Apr-60 | | | | | | | DARNALL-41A | | |
| Aug-60 | | | | | | | 9/60: W/D | | |
| Nov-60 | | | | | | | | | |

| | 69261 | 69262 | 69263 | 69264 | 69265 | 69266 | 69267 | 69268 | 69269 |
|---|---|---|---|---|---|---|---|---|---|
| Aug-50 | BOSTON-40F | NORTHWCH-9G | W.HALSE-38E | MEXBOROUGH-36B | SOUTHPORT-27E | COPLEY HILL-37B | WREXHAM-6E | BARNSLEY-36D | W.HALSE-38E |
| Jan-51 | BOSTON-40F | NORTHWCH-9G | W.HALSE-38E | MEXBOROUGH-36B | SOUTHPORT-27E | COPLEY HILL-37B | WREXHAM-6E | BARNSLEY-36D | W.HALSE-38E |
| Aug-51 | BOSTON-40F | NORTHWCH-9G | W.HALSE-38E | MEXBOROUGH-36B | SOUTHPORT-27E | COPLEY HILL-37B | WREXHAM-6E | BARNSLEY-36D | W.HALSE-38E |
| Jan-52 | BOSTON-40F | NORTHWCH-9G | W.HALSE-38E | MEXBOROUGH-36B | SOUTHPORT-27E | COPLEY HILL-37B | WREXHAM-6E | BARNSLEY-36D | W.HALSE-38E |
| Aug-52 | BOSTON-40F | NORTHWCH-9G | W.HALSE-38E | MEXBOROUGH-36B | SOUTHPORT-27E | 9/52: ARDS-37A | WREXHAM-6E | BARNSLEY-36D | 3/53: STAVE-38D |
| Jan-53 | BOSTON-40F | 11/52: H.MSY-9F | W.HALSE-38E | MEXBOROUGH-36B | SOUTHPORT-27E | 2/53: DARN-39B | WREXHAM-6E | BARNSLEY-36D | STAVELEY-38D |
| Aug-53 | BOSTON-40F | H.MERSEY-9F | W.HALSE-38E | MEXBOROUGH-36B | SOUTHPORT-27E | DARNALL-39B | WREXHAM-6E | BARNSLEY-36D | STAVELEY-38D |
| Jan-54 | BOSTON-40F | H.MERSEY-9F | 12/53: COLW-38A | MEXBOROUGH-36B | SOUTHPORT-27E | DARNALL-39B | WREXHAM-6E | BARNSLEY-36D | STAVELEY-38D |
| Aug-54 | BOSTON-40F | H.MERSEY-9F | COLWICK-38A | MEXBOROUGH-36B | SOUTHPORT-27E | DARNALL-39B | WREXHAM-6E | BARNSLEY-36D | STAVELEY-38D |
| Jan-55 | BOSTON-40F | H.MERSEY-9F | 11/54: STAVE-38D | 2/55: W/D | SOUTHPORT-27E | DARNALL-39B | WREXHAM-6E | BARNSLEY-36D | 11/55: IMM-40B |
| Aug-55 | BOSTON-40F | H.MERSEY-9F | STAVELEY-38D | | SOUTHPORT-27E | DARNALL-39B | WREXHAM-6E | BARNSLEY-36D | 3/56: BOST-40F |
| Jan-56 | 11/55: IMM-40B | H.MERSEY-9F | STAVELEY-38D | | SOUTHPORT-27E | DARNALL-41A | WREXHAM-6E | BARNSLEY-36D | 7/56: STAVE-38D |
| Aug-56 | IMMINGHAM-40B | H.MERSEY-9F | STAVELEY-38D | | SOUTHPORT-27E | DARNALL-41A | WREXHAM-6E | BARNSLEY-36D | STAVELEY-38D |
| Jan-57 | 2/57: L.JCN-40E | H.MERSEY-9F | STAVELEY-38D | | SOUTHPORT-27E | DARNALL-41A | WREXHAM-6E | BARNSLEY-36D | STAVELEY-38D |
| Aug-57 | LANGWTHJCN-40E | H.MERSEY-9F | STAVELEY-38D | | SOUTHPORT-27E | DARNALL-41A | 8/57: T.DCK-54B | BARNSLEY-36D | STAVELEY-38D |
| Jan-58 | 12/57: W/D | H.MERSEY-9F | STAVELEY-38D | | SOUTHPORT-27E | DARNALL-41A | TYNEDOCK-54B | BARNSLEY-36D | STAVELEY-38D |
| Aug-58 | | 5/58: NEW.E.-34E | STAVELEY(GC)-41H | | SOUTHPORT-27E | DARNALL-41A | 7/58: N.ENG-34E | BARNSLEY-41G | STAVELEY(GC)-41H |
| Jan-59 | | NEWENGLAND-34E | STAVELEY(GC)-41H | | SOUTHPORT-27E | 12/58: NEW.E.-34E | NEWENGLAND-34E | BARNSLEY-41G | 10/58: W/D |
| Aug-59 | | NEWENGLAND-34E | STAVELEY(GC)-41H | | SOUTHPORT-27E | 8/59: HAT-34C | NEWENGLAND-34E | BARNSLEY-41G | |
| Nov-59 | | NEWENGLAND-34E | 10/59: L.JCN-41J | | SOUTHPORT-27E | 10/59: NEW.E.-34E | 2/60: W/D | 10/59: L.JCN-41J | |
| Jan-60 | | 12/59: W/D | LANGWTHJCN-41J | | 12/59: W/D | NEWENGLAND-34E | | 2/60: W/D | |
| Apr-60 | | | LANGWTHJCN-41J | | | NEWENGLAND-34E | | | |
| Aug-60 | | | LANGWTHJCN-41J | | | NEWENGLAND-34E | | | |
| Nov-60 | | | LANGWTHJCN-41J | | | NEWENGLAND-34E | | | |

### 69270 – 69278

| | 69270 | 69271 | 69272 | 69273 | 69274 | 69275 | 69276 | 69277 | 69278 |
|---|---|---|---|---|---|---|---|---|---|
| Aug-50 | GORTON - 39A | COPLEY HILL - 37B | BRUNSWICK - 8E | RETFORD - 36E | CHESTER (CLC) - 6D | LINCOLN - 40A | HEATON MERSEY - 9F | RETFORD - 36E | BARNSLEY - 36D |
| Jan-51 | GORTON - 39A | 2/51: ARDS - 37A | BRUNSWICK - 8E | RETFORD - 36E | CHESTER (CLC) - 6D | LINCOLN - 40A | HEATON MERSEY - 9F | RETFORD - 36E | BARNSLEY - 36D |
| Aug-51 | GORTON - 39A | ARDSLEY - 37A | BRUNSWICK - 8E | RETFORD - 36E | CHESTER (CLC) - 6D | LINCOLN - 40A | HEATON MERSEY - 9F | RETFORD - 36E | BARNSLEY - 36D |
| Jan-52 | GORTON - 39A | ARDSLEY - 37A | BRUNSWICK - 8E | RETFORD - 36E | CHESTER (CLC) - 6D | LINCOLN - 40A | HEATON MERSEY - 9F | RETFORD - 36E | BARNSLEY - 36D |
| Aug-52 | GORTON - 39A | ARDSLEY - 37A | BRUNSWICK - 8E | RETFORD - 36E | CHESTER (CLC) - 6D | LINCOLN - 40A | HEATON MERSEY - 9F | RETFORD - 36E | BARNSLEY - 36D |
| Jan-53 | GORTON - 39A | ARDSLEY - 37A | BRUNSWICK - 8E | 1/53: NEAS - 34E | CHESTER (CLC) - 6D | LINCOLN - 40A | HEATON MERSEY - 9F | RETFORD - 36E | BARNSLEY - 36D |
| Aug-53 | GORTON - 39A | 5/53: COLW - 38A | BRUNSWICK - 8E | NEASDEN - 34E | CHESTER (CLC) - 6D | LINCOLN - 40A | HEATON MERSEY - 9F | RETFORD - 36E | BARNSLEY - 36D |
| Jan-54 | GORTON - 39A | COLWICK - 38A | BRUNSWICK - 8E | NEASDEN - 34E | CHESTER (CLC) - 6D | LINCOLN - 40A | HEATON MERSEY - 9F | RETFORD - 36E | BARNSLEY - 36D |
| Aug-54 | GORTON - 39A | COLWICK - 38A | BRUNSWICK - 8E | NEASDEN - 34E | CHESTER (CLC) - 6D | LINCOLN - 40A | HEATON MERSEY - 9F | RETFORD - 36E | BARNSLEY - 36D |
| Jan-55 | GORTON - 39A | COLWICK - 38A | BRUNSWICK - 8E | 6/55: W/D | CHESTER (CLC) - 6D | LINCOLN - 40A | HEATON MERSEY - 9F | RETFORD - 36E | BARNSLEY - 36D |
| Aug-55 | GORTON - 39A | COLWICK - 38A | BRUNSWICK - 8E | | CHESTER (CLC) - 6D | LINCOLN - 40A | HEATON MERSEY - 9F | RETFORD - 36E | BARNSLEY - 36D |
| Jan-56 | GORTON - 39A | 12/55: DARN - 41A | BRUNSWICK - 8E | | CHESTER (CLC) - 6D | 11/55: W/D | HEATON MERSEY - 9F | RETFORD - 36E | 11/55: W/D |
| Aug-56 | GORTON - 39A | DARNALL - 41A | 4/56: W/D | | CHESTER (CLC) - 6D | | HEATON MERSEY - 9F | RETFORD - 36E | |
| Jan-57 | 10/56: W/D | DARNALL - 41A | | | CHESTER (CLC) - 6D | | HEATON MERSEY - 9F | 11/56: W/D | |
| Aug-57 | | DARNALL - 41A | | | CHESTER (CLC) - 6D | | HEATON MERSEY - 9F | | |
| Jan-58 | | 3/58: DARN - 41A | | | CHESTER (CLC) - 6D | | HEATON MERSEY - 9F | | |
| Aug-58 | | | | | 5/58: NEW.E. - 34E | | 5/58: NEW.E. - 34E | | |
| Jan-59 | | | | | NEW ENGLAND - 34E | | NEW ENGLAND - 34E | | |
| Aug-59 | | | | | NEW ENGLAND - 34E | | NEW ENGLAND - 34E | | |
| Nov-59 | | | | | NEW ENGLAND - 34E | | 12/59: W/D | | |
| Jan-60 | | | | | NEW ENGLAND - 34E | | | | |
| Apr-60 | | | | | NEW ENGLAND - 34E | | | | |
| Aug-60 | | | | | NEW ENGLAND - 34E | | | | |
| Nov-60 | | | | | NEW ENGLAND - 34E | | | | |

### 69279 – 69287

| | 69279 | 69280 | 69281 | 69282 | 69283 | 69284 | 69285 | 69286 | 69287 |
|---|---|---|---|---|---|---|---|---|---|
| Aug-50 | STAVELEY - 38D | BOSTON - 40F | CHESTER (CLC) - 6D | RETFORD - 36E | NEASDEN - 34E | LANGWITH JCN - 40E | BARNSLEY - 36D | W.HALSE - 38E | LINCOLN - 40A |
| Jan-51 | STAVELEY - 38D | 11/50: LOUTH - 40C | CHESTER (CLC) - 6D | RETFORD - 36E | NEASDEN - 34E | LANGWITH JCN - 40E | BARNSLEY - 36D | W.HALSE - 38E | LINCOLN - 40A |
| Aug-51 | STAVELEY - 38D | LOUTH - 40C | CHESTER (CLC) - 6D | RETFORD - 36E | NEASDEN - 34E | LANGWITH JCN - 40E | 9/51: DCTR - 36A | W.HALSE - 38E | LINCOLN - 40A |
| Jan-52 | STAVELEY - 38D | LOUTH - 40C | CHESTER (CLC) - 6D | RETFORD - 36E | NEASDEN - 34E | LANGWITH JCN - 40E | 5/52: RET - 36E | W.HALSE - 38E | 2/52: IMM - 40B |
| Aug-52 | STAVELEY - 38D | LOUTH - 40C | CHESTER (CLC) - 6D | RETFORD - 36E | NEASDEN - 34E | LANGWITH JCN - 40E | 6/52: DCTR - 36A | W.HALSE - 38E | 7/52: LINC - 40A |
| Jan-53 | STAVELEY - 38D | LOUTH - 40C | CHESTER (CLC) - 6D | 1/53: RET - 36E | 1/53: RET - 36E | LANGWITH JCN - 40E | 2/53: DARN - 39B | W.HALSE - 38E | LINCOLN - 40A |
| Aug-53 | STAVELEY - 38D | 7/53: MEX - 36B | CHESTER (CLC) - 6D | RETFORD - 36E | RETFORD - 36E | LANGWITH JCN - 40E | DARNALL - 39B | W.HALSE - 38E | LINCOLN - 40A |
| Jan-54 | STAVELEY - 38D | MEXBOROUGH - 36B | CHESTER (CLC) - 6D | RETFORD - 36E | RETFORD - 36E | LANGWITH JCN - 40E | DARNALL - 39B | 12/53: COLW - 38A | 12/53: DARN - 39B |
| Aug-54 | STAVELEY - 38D | MEXBOROUGH - 36B | CHESTER (CLC) - 6D | RETFORD - 36E | RETFORD - 36E | LANGWITH JCN - 40E | DARNALL - 39B | COLWICK - 38A | DARNALL - 39B |
| Jan-55 | STAVELEY - 38D | MEXBOROUGH - 36B | CHESTER (CLC) - 6D | 7/55: W/D | RETFORD - 36E | LANGWITH JCN - 40E | DARNALL - 39B | COLWICK - 38A | DARNALL - 39B |
| Aug-55 | 6/55: W/D | MEXBOROUGH - 36B | 7/55: WREX - 6E | | RETFORD - 36E | LANGWITH JCN - 40E | DARNALL - 39B | COLWICK - 38A | 7/55: W/D |
| Jan-56 | | 11/55: W/D | WREXHAM - 6E | | RETFORD - 36E | LANGWITH JCN - 40E | 11/55: W/D | 12/55: DARN - 41A | |
| Aug-56 | | | WREXHAM - 6E | | RETFORD - 36E | LANGWITH JCN - 40E | | DARNALL - 41A | |
| Jan-57 | | | WREXHAM - 6E | | RETFORD - 36E | 7/56: BOST - 40F | | DARNALL - 41A | |
| Aug-57 | | | WREXHAM - 6E | | RETFORD - 36E | 2/57: L.JCN - 40E | | DARNALL - 41A | |
| Jan-58 | | | WREXHAM - 6E | | RETFORD - 36E | LANGWITH JCN - 40E | | DARNALL - 41A | |
| Aug-58 | | | WREXHAM - 6E | | 6/58: W/D | 2/58: W/D | | DARNALL - 41A | |
| Jan-59 | | | WREXHAM - 6E | | | | | DARNALL - 41A | |
| Aug-59 | | | WREXHAM - 6E | | | | | DARNALL - 41A | |
| Nov-59 | | | WREXHAM - 6E | | | | | 4/59: L.JCN - 41J | |
| Jan-60 | | | WREXHAM - 6E | | | | | LANGWITH JCN - 41J | |
| Apr-60 | | | WREXHAM - 6E | | | | | LANGWITH JCN - 41J | |
| Aug-60 | | | WREXHAM - 6E | | | | | LANGWITH JCN - 41J | |
| Nov-60 | | | WREXHAM - 6E | | | | | LANGWITH JCN - 41J | |

### 69288 – 69296

| | 69288 | 69289 | 69290 | 69291 | 69292 | 69293 | 69294 | 69295 | 69296 |
|---|---|---|---|---|---|---|---|---|---|
| Aug-50 | BRUNSWICK - 8E | BIDSTON - 6F | WREXHAM - 6E | BARNSLEY - 36D | STAVELEY - 38D | NORTHWCH - 9G | RETFORD - 36E | STAVELEY - 38D | GORTON - 39A |
| Jan-51 | BRUNSWICK - 8E | BIDSTON - 6F | WREXHAM - 6E | BARNSLEY - 36D | STAVELEY - 38D | NORTHGATE - 6D | RETFORD - 36E | STAVELEY - 38D | GORTON - 39A |
| Aug-51 | BRUNSWICK - 8E | BIDSTON - 6F | WREXHAM - 6E | BARNSLEY - 36D | STAVELEY - 38D | NORTHGATE - 6D | RETFORD - 36E | STAVELEY - 38D | GORTON - 39A |
| Jan-52 | BRUNSWICK - 8E | BIDSTON - 6F | WREXHAM - 6E | BARNSLEY - 36D | STAVELEY - 38D | NORTHGATE - 6D | RETFORD - 36E | STAVELEY - 38D | GORTON - 39A |
| Aug-52 | BRUNSWICK - 8E | BIDSTON - 6F | WREXHAM - 6E | BARNSLEY - 36D | STAVELEY - 38D | NORTHGATE - 6D | 6/52: DCTR - 36A | STAVELEY - 38D | GORTON - 39A |
| Jan-53 | BRUNSWICK - 8E | WREXHAM - 6E | WREXHAM - 6E | BARNSLEY - 36D | 3/53: DARN - 39B | NORTHGATE - 6D | 2/53: DARN - 39B | STAVELEY - 38D | GORTON - 39A |
| Aug-53 | BRUNSWICK - 8E | WREXHAM - 6E | WREXHAM - 6E | BARNSLEY - 36D | DARNALL - 39B | NORTHGATE - 6D | DARNALL - 39B | 3/53: DARN - 39B | GORTON - 39A |
| Jan-54 | BRUNSWICK - 8E | 1/54: W/D | WREXHAM - 6E | BARNSLEY - 36D | DARNALL - 39B | NORTHGATE - 6D | DARNALL - 39B | DARNALL - 39B | GORTON - 39A |
| Aug-54 | BRUNSWICK - 8E | | WREXHAM - 6E | BARNSLEY - 36D | DARNALL - 39B | NORTHGATE - 6D | DARNALL - 39B | DARNALL - 39B | GORTON - 39A |
| Jan-55 | BRUNSWICK - 8E | | WREXHAM - 6E | BARNSLEY - 36D | DARNALL - 39B | NORTHGATE - 6D | DARNALL - 39B | DARNALL - 39B | GORTON - 39A |
| Aug-55 | 4/55: W/D | | WREXHAM - 6E | BARNSLEY - 36D | DARNALL - 39B | NORTHGATE - 6D | DARNALL - 39B | DARNALL - 39B | 1/55: DARN - 39B |
| Jan-56 | | | WREXHAM - 6E | 11/55: W/D | DARNALL - 41A | NORTHGATE - 6D | DARNALL - 41A | DARNALL - 41A | DARNALL - 39B |
| Aug-56 | | | WREXHAM - 6E | | DARNALL - 41A | NORTHGATE - 6D | DARNALL - 41A | DARNALL - 41A | DARNALL - 41A |
| Jan-57 | | | WREXHAM - 6E | | DARNALL - 41A | NORTHGATE - 6D | DARNALL - 41A | DARNALL - 41A | DARNALL - 41A |
| Aug-57 | | | 8/57: T.DCK - 54B | | DARNALL - 41A | NORTHGATE - 6D | DARNALL - 41A | DARNALL - 41A | DARNALL - 41A |
| Jan-58 | | | TYNE DOCK - 54B | | DARNALL - 41A | NORTHGATE - 6D | DARNALL - 41A | 3/58: W/D | DARNALL - 41A |
| Aug-58 | | | 7/58: NEW.E. - 34E | | DARNALL - 41A | NORTHGATE - 6D | DARNALL - 41A | | DARNALL - 41A |
| Jan-59 | | | 12/58: DARN - 41A | | 12/58: NEW.E - 34E | 5/58: NEW.E - 34E | DARNALL - 41A | | DARNALL - 41A |
| Aug-59 | | | DARNALL - 41A | | NEW ENGLAND - 34E | NEW ENGLAND - 34E | DARNALL - 41A | | DARNALL - 41A |
| Nov-59 | | | 10/59: W/D | | NEW ENGLAND - 34E | NEW ENGLAND - 34E | 10/59: W/D | | DARNALL - 41A |
| Jan-60 | | | | | 2/60: W/D | NEW ENGLAND - 34E | | | DARNALL - 41A |
| Apr-60 | | | | | | NEW ENGLAND - 34E | | | DARNALL - 41A |
| Aug-60 | | | | | | NEW ENGLAND - 34E | | | DARNALL - 41A |
| Nov-60 | | | | | | NEW ENGLAND - 34E | | | DARNALL - 41A |

### 69297 – 69305

| | 69297 | 69298 | 69299 | 69300 | 69301 | 69302 | 69303 | 69304 | 69305 |
|---|---|---|---|---|---|---|---|---|---|
| Aug-50 | MEXBOROUGH - 36B | SOUTHPORT - 27E | GORTON - 39A | NEASDEN - 34E | STAVELEY - 38D | NEASDEN - 34E | BARNSLEY - 36D | TRAFFORD PARK - 9E | IMMINGHAM - 40B |
| Jan-51 | MEXBOROUGH - 36B | SOUTHPORT - 27E | GORTON - 39A | NEASDEN - 34E | STAVELEY - 38D | NEASDEN - 34E | BARNSLEY - 36D | TRAFFORD PARK - 9E | IMMINGHAM - 40B |
| Aug-51 | MEXBOROUGH - 36B | SOUTHPORT - 27E | GORTON - 39A | NEASDEN - 34E | STAVELEY - 38D | NEASDEN - 34E | BARNSLEY - 36D | TRAFFORD PARK - 9E | IMMINGHAM - 40B |
| Jan-52 | MEXBOROUGH - 36B | SOUTHPORT - 27E | GORTON - 39A | NEASDEN - 34E | STAVELEY - 38D | NEASDEN - 34E | BARNSLEY - 36D | TRAFFORD PARK - 9E | IMMINGHAM - 40B |
| Aug-52 | MEXBOROUGH - 36B | SOUTHPORT - 27E | 9/52: H.MSY - 9F | NEASDEN - 34E | STAVELEY - 38D | NEASDEN - 34E | BARNSLEY - 36D | TRAFFORD PARK - 9E | IMMINGHAM - 40B |
| Jan-53 | MEXBOROUGH - 36B | SOUTHPORT - 27E | HEATON MERSEY - 9F | 1/53: RET - 36E | STAVELEY - 38D | NEASDEN - 34E | BARNSLEY - 36D | TRAFFORD PARK - 9E | IMMINGHAM - 40B |
| Aug-53 | MEXBOROUGH - 36B | SOUTHPORT - 27E | HEATON MERSEY - 9F | RETFORD - 36E | STAVELEY - 38D | NEASDEN - 34E | BARNSLEY - 36D | TRAFFORD PARK - 9E | IMMINGHAM - 40B |
| Jan-54 | MEXBOROUGH - 36B | SOUTHPORT - 27E | HEATON MERSEY - 9F | RETFORD - 36E | STAVELEY - 38D | NEASDEN - 34E | BARNSLEY - 36D | TRAFFORD PARK - 9E | IMMINGHAM - 40B |
| Aug-54 | MEXBOROUGH - 36B | SOUTHPORT - 27E | HEATON MERSEY - 9F | RETFORD - 36E | STAVELEY - 38D | NEASDEN - 34E | BARNSLEY - 36D | TRAFFORD PARK - 9E | IMMINGHAM - 40B |
| Jan-55 | MEXBOROUGH - 36B | SOUTHPORT - 27E | HEATON MERSEY - 9F | RETFORD - 36E | STAVELEY - 38D | 1/55: DARN - 39B | BARNSLEY - 36D | 2/55: W/D | IMMINGHAM - 40B |
| Aug-55 | MEXBOROUGH - 36B | SOUTHPORT - 27E | HEATON MERSEY - 9F | RETFORD - 36E | STAVELEY - 38D | DARNALL - 39B | BARNSLEY - 36D | | IMMINGHAM - 40B |
| Jan-56 | 11/55: IMM - 40B | SOUTHPORT - 27E | HEATON MERSEY - 9F | BARNSLEY - 36D | 12/55: W/D | DARNALL - 39B | BARNSLEY - 36D | | IMMINGHAM - 40B |
| Aug-56 | 7/56: BARN - 36D | SOUTHPORT - 27E | HEATON MERSEY - 9F | BARNSLEY - 36D | | DARNALL - 41A | 11/55: W/D | | 11/55: MEX - 36B |
| Jan-57 | BARNSLEY - 36D | SOUTHPORT - 27E | HEATON MERSEY - 9F | BARNSLEY - 36D | | DARNALL - 41A | | | MEXBOROUGH - 36B |
| Aug-57 | BARNSLEY - 36D | SOUTHPORT - 27E | HEATON MERSEY - 9F | BARNSLEY - 36D | | DARNALL - 41A | | | MEXBOROUGH - 36B |
| Jan-58 | BARNSLEY - 36D | SOUTHPORT - 27E | 6/58: DARN - 41A | 2/58: W/D | | 12/57: W/D | | | MEXBOROUGH - 36B |
| Aug-58 | 8/58: W/D | SOUTHPORT - 27E | 7/58: L.JCN - 41J | | | | | | 2/58: W/D |
| Jan-59 | | SOUTHPORT - 27E | LANGWITH JCN - 41J | | | | | | |
| Aug-59 | | SOUTHPORT - 27E | LANGWITH JCN - 41J | | | | | | |
| Nov-59 | | 12/59: W/D | 2/60: W/D | | | | | | |
| Jan-60 | | | | | | | | | |
| Apr-60 | | | | | | | | | |
| Aug-60 | | | | | | | | | |
| Nov-60 | | | | | | | | | |

Locomotive numbers 69306 – 69314

| | 69306 | 69307 | 69308 | 69309 | 69310 | 69311 | 69312 | 69313 | 69314 |
|---|---|---|---|---|---|---|---|---|---|
| Aug-50 | LOUTH-40C | GORTON-39A | GORTON-39A | IMMINGHAM-40B | W.HALSE-38E | LINCOLN-40A | COLWICK-38A | RETFORD-36E | MEXBOROUGH-36B |
| Jan-51 | LOUTH-40C | GORTON-39A | GORTON-39A | IMMINGHAM-40B | W.HALSE-38E | LINCOLN-40A | COLWICK-38A | RETFORD-36E | 3/51:RET-36E |
| Aug-51 | LOUTH-40C | GORTON-39A | GORTON-39A | IMMINGHAM-40B | W.HALSE-38E | LINCOLN-40A | 6/51:DARN-39B | RETFORD-36E | RETFORD-36E |
| Jan-52 | LOUTH-40C | GORTON-39A | GORTON-39A | IMMINGHAM-40B | W.HALSE-38E | 2/52:W/D | DARNALL-39B | RETFORD-36E | RETFORD-36E |
| Aug-52 | LOUTH-40C | GORTON-39A | GORTON-39A | IMMINGHAM-40B | W.HALSE-38E | | DARNALL-39B | RETFORD-36E | RETFORD-36E |
| Jan-53 | LOUTH-40C | GORTON-39A | GORTON-39A | IMMINGHAM-40B | W.HALSE-38E | | DARNALL-39B | RETFORD-36E | RETFORD-36E |
| Aug-53 | 7/53:MEX-36B | GORTON-39A | GORTON-39A | 7/53:LOUTH-40C | W.HALSE-38E | | DARNALL-39B | RETFORD-36E | RETFORD-36E |
| Jan-54 | MEXBOROUGH-36B | GORTON-39A | GORTON-39A | LOUTH-40C | 12/53:COLW-38A | | DARNALL-39B | RETFORD-36E | RETFORD-36E |
| Aug-54 | MEXBOROUGH-36B | GORTON-39A | GORTON-39A | LOUTH-40C | COLWICK-38A | | DARNALL-39B | RETFORD-36E | RETFORD-36E |
| Jan-55 | MEXBOROUGH-36B | GORTON-39A | GORTON-39A | LOUTH-40C | COLWICK-38A | | DARNALL-39B | 3/55:W/D | RETFORD-36E |
| Aug-55 | MEXBOROUGH-36B | GORTON-39A | 4/55:RET-36E | LOUTH-40C | 11/55:W/D | | DARNALL-39B | | RETFORD-36E |
| Jan-56 | 10/55:W/D | GORTON-39A | 12/55:MEX-36B | STAVELEY-38D | | | DARNALL-41A | | RETFORD-36E |
| Aug-56 | | GORTON-39A | MEXBOROUGH-36B | STAVELEY-38D | | | DARNALL-41A | | RETFORD-36E |
| Jan-57 | | GORTON-39A | MEXBOROUGH-36B | STAVELEY-38D | | | DARNALL-41A | | RETFORD-36E |
| Aug-57 | | GORTON-39A | MEXBOROUGH-36B | STAVELEY-38D | | | 10/57:W/D | | RETFORD-36E |
| Jan-58 | | GORTON-39A | MEXBOROUGH-36B | STAVELEY-38D | | | | | RETFORD-36E |
| Aug-58 | | GORTON-9G | MEXBOROUGH-41F | STAVELEY(GC)-41H | | | | | 10/58:NEW.E-34E |
| Jan-59 | | GORTON-9G | MEXBOROUGH-41F | STAVELEY(GC)-41H | | | | | 12/58:DARN-41A |
| Aug-59 | | GORTON-9G | MEXBOROUGH-41F | STAVELEY(GC)-41H | | | | | DARNALL-41A |
| Nov-59 | | GORTON-9G | MEXBOROUGH-41F | STAVELEY(GC)-41H | | | | | DARNALL-41A |
| Jan-60 | | GORTON-9G | MEXBOROUGH-41F | STAVELEY(GC)-41H | | | | | 2/60:W/D |
| Apr-60 | | GORTON-9G | 3/60:W/D | STAVELEY(GC)-41H | | | | | |
| Aug-60 | | GORTON-9G | | STAVELEY(GC)-41H | | | | | |
| Nov-60 | | GORTON-9G | | STAVELEY(GC)-41H | | | | | |

Locomotive numbers 69315 – 69323

| | 69315 | 69316 | 69317 | 69318 | 69319 | 69320 | 69321 | 69322 | 69323 |
|---|---|---|---|---|---|---|---|---|---|
| Aug-50 | NEASDEN-34E | MEXBOROUGH-36B | H.MERSEY-9F | NEASDEN-34E | LANGWITHJCN-40E | BARNSLEY-36D | RETFORD-36E | IMMINGHAM-40B | LANGWITHJCN-40E |
| Jan-51 | NEASDEN-34E | MEXBOROUGH-36B | H.MERSEY-9F | NEASDEN-34E | LANGWITHJCN-40E | BARNSLEY-36D | RETFORD-36E | IMMINGHAM-40B | LANGWITHJCN-40E |
| Aug-51 | NEASDEN-34E | MEXBOROUGH-36B | H.MERSEY-9F | NEASDEN-34E | LANGWITHJCN-40E | BARNSLEY-36D | RETFORD-36E | IMMINGHAM-40B | LANGWITHJCN-40E |
| Jan-52 | NEASDEN-34E | MEXBOROUGH-36B | H.MERSEY-9F | NEASDEN-34E | LANGWITHJCN-40E | BARNSLEY-36D | RETFORD-36E | IMMINGHAM-40B | LANGWITHJCN-40E |
| Aug-52 | NEASDEN-34E | MEXBOROUGH-36B | H.MERSEY-9F | NEASDEN-34E | LANGWITHJCN-40E | BARNSLEY-36D | RETFORD-36E | IMMINGHAM-40B | LANGWITHJCN-40E |
| Jan-53 | NEASDEN-34E | MEXBOROUGH-36B | H.MERSEY-9F | NEASDEN-34E | LANGWITHJCN-40E | BARNSLEY-36D | RETFORD-36E | IMMINGHAM-40B | LANGWITHJCN-40E |
| Aug-53 | NEASDEN-34E | MEXBOROUGH-36B | H.MERSEY-9F | NEASDEN-34E | LANGWITHJCN-40E | BARNSLEY-36D | RETFORD-36E | 7/53:LOUTH-40C | LANGWITHJCN-40E |
| Jan-54 | NEASDEN-34E | MEXBOROUGH-36B | H.MERSEY-9F | NEASDEN-34E | LANGWITHJCN-40E | BARNSLEY-36D | RETFORD-36E | LOUTH-40C | LANGWITHJCN-40E |
| Aug-54 | NEASDEN-34E | MEXBOROUGH-36B | H.MERSEY-9F | NEASDEN-34E | LANGWITHJCN-40E | BARNSLEY-36D | RETFORD-36E | LOUTH-40C | 8/54:DARN-39B |
| Jan-55 | NEASDEN-34E | 12/54:DARN-39B | H.MERSEY-9F | NEASDEN-34E | LANGWITHJCN-40E | BARNSLEY-36D | RETFORD-36E | LOUTH-40C | DARNALL-39B |
| Aug-55 | NEASDEN-34E | DARNALL-39B | H.MERSEY-9F | NEASDEN-34E | LANGWITHJCN-40E | BARNSLEY-36D | RETFORD-36E | LOUTH-40C | DARNALL-39B |
| Jan-56 | NEASDEN-34E | DARNALL-41A | 2/56:W/D | NEASDEN-34E | LANGWITHJCN-40E | BARNSLEY-36D | RETFORD-36E | LOUTH-40C | DARNALL-41A |
| Aug-56 | NEASDEN-34E | DARNALL-41A | | NEASDEN-34E | LANGWITHJCN-40E | BARNSLEY-36D | 9/56:W/D | 10/56:L.JCN-40E | DARNALL-41A |
| Jan-57 | 11/56:BARN-36D | 3/57:W/D | | 11/56:W/D | 2/57:NEAS-34E | BARNSLEY-36D | | 2/57:RET-36E | 11/56:W/D |
| Aug-57 | BARNSLEY-36D | | | | NEASDEN-34E | BARNSLEY-36D | | RETFORD-36E | |
| Jan-58 | BARNSLEY-36D | | | | NEASDEN-34E | BARNSLEY-36D | | RETFORD-36E | |
| Aug-58 | 6/58:W/D | | | | NEASDEN-14D | BARNSLEY-41G | | 10/58:NEW.E-34E | |
| Jan-59 | | | | | NEASDEN-14D | BARNSLEY-41G | | NEWENGLAND-34E | |
| Aug-59 | | | | | NEASDEN-14D | BARNSLEY-41G | | 6/59:W/D | |
| Nov-59 | | | | | 12/59:W/D | 10/59:W/D | | | |
| Jan-60 | | | | | | | | | |
| Apr-60 | | | | | | | | | |
| Aug-60 | | | | | | | | | |
| Nov-60 | | | | | | | | | |

Locomotive numbers 69324 – 69332

| | 69324 | 69325 | 69326 | 69327 | 69328 | 69329 | 69330 | 69331 | 69332 |
|---|---|---|---|---|---|---|---|---|---|
| Aug-50 | COLWICK-38A | BARNSLEY-36D | T.PARK-9E | LANGWITHJCN-40E | H.MERSEY-9F | WREXHAM-6E | WREXHAM-6E | H.MERSEY-9F | H.MERSEY-9F |
| Jan-51 | COLWICK-38A | BARNSLEY-36D | T.PARK-9E | LANGWITHJCN-40E | H.MERSEY-9F | WREXHAM-6E | WREXHAM-6E | H.MERSEY-9F | H.MERSEY-9F |
| Aug-51 | 6/51:DARN-39B | BARNSLEY-36D | T.PARK-9E | LANGWITHJCN-40E | H.MERSEY-9F | WREXHAM-6E | WREXHAM-6E | H.MERSEY-9F | H.MERSEY-9F |
| Jan-52 | DARNALL-39B | BARNSLEY-36D | T.PARK-9E | 3/52:LINC-40A | H.MERSEY-9F | WREXHAM-6E | WREXHAM-6E | H.MERSEY-9F | H.MERSEY-9F |
| Aug-52 | DARNALL-39B | BARNSLEY-36D | T.PARK-9E | LINCOLN-40A | 9/52:GORT-39A | WREXHAM-6E | WREXHAM-6E | H.MERSEY-9F | H.MERSEY-9F |
| Jan-53 | DARNALL-39B | BARNSLEY-36D | T.PARK-9E | LINCOLN-40A | GORTON-39A | WREXHAM-6E | WREXHAM-6E | H.MERSEY-9F | 3/53:N'GATE-6D |
| Aug-53 | DARNALL-39B | BARNSLEY-36D | T.PARK-9E | 7/53:LOUTH-40C | GORTON-39A | WREXHAM-6E | WREXHAM-6E | H.MERSEY-9F | NORTHGATE-6D |
| Jan-54 | DARNALL-39B | BARNSLEY-36D | T.PARK-9E | LOUTH-40C | GORTON-39A | WREXHAM-6E | WREXHAM-6E | H.MERSEY-9F | NORTHGATE-6D |
| Aug-54 | DARNALL-39B | BARNSLEY-36D | T.PARK-9E | LOUTH-40C | GORTON-39A | WREXHAM-6E | WREXHAM-6E | H.MERSEY-9F | NORTHGATE-6D |
| Jan-55 | 11/54:W/D | BARNSLEY-36D | T.PARK-9E | LOUTH-40C | GORTON-39A | WREXHAM-6E | 2/55:W/D | H.MERSEY-9F | NORTHGATE-6D |
| Aug-55 | | BARNSLEY-36D | T.PARK-9E | LOUTH-40C | GORTON-39A | WREXHAM-6E | | H.MERSEY-9F | NORTHGATE-6D |
| Jan-56 | | BARNSLEY-36D | T.PARK-9E | 11/55:DARN-41A | GORTON-39A | WREXHAM-6E | | H.MERSEY-9F | NORTHGATE-6D |
| Aug-56 | | 9/56:W/D | T.PARK-9E | DARNALL-41A | GORTON-39A | WREXHAM-6E | | H.MERSEY-9F | NORTHGATE-6D |
| Jan-57 | | | 10/56:W/D | DARNALL-41A | 1/57:W/D | WREXHAM-6E | | 1/57:W/D | NORTHGATE-6D |
| Aug-57 | | | | DARNALL-41A | | 9/57:W/D | | | NORTHGATE-6D |
| Jan-58 | | | | DARNALL-41A | | | | | 5/58:DARN-41A |
| Aug-58 | | | | 12/58:NEW.E.-34E | | | | | 7/58:BARN-41G |
| Jan-59 | | | | NEWENGLAND-34E | | | | | 2/59:W/D |
| Aug-59 | | | | 9/59:W/D | | | | | |
| Nov-59 | | | | | | | | | |
| Jan-60 | | | | | | | | | |
| Apr-60 | | | | | | | | | |
| Aug-60 | | | | | | | | | |
| Nov-60 | | | | | | | | | |

Locomotive numbers 69333 – 69341

| | 69333 | 69334 | 69335 | 69336 | 69337 | 69338 | 69339 | 69340 | 69341 |
|---|---|---|---|---|---|---|---|---|---|
| Aug-50 | GORTON-39A | BARNSLEY-36D | NORTHWICH-9G | T.PARK-9E | NEWENGLAND-35A | GORTON-39A | BRUNSWICK-8E | WREXHAM-6E | NEASDEN-34E |
| Jan-51 | GORTON-39A | BARNSLEY-36D | NORTHWICH-9G | T.PARK-9E | 9/50:ARDS-37A | GORTON-39A | BRUNSWICK-8E | WREXHAM-6E | NEASDEN-34E |
| Aug-51 | GORTON-39A | BARNSLEY-36D | NORTHWICH-9G | T.PARK-9E | ARDSLEY-37A | GORTON-39A | BRUNSWICK-8E | WREXHAM-6E | NEASDEN-34E |
| Jan-52 | GORTON-39A | BARNSLEY-36D | NORTHWICH-9G | T.PARK-9E | ARDSLEY-37A | GORTON-39A | BRUNSWICK-8E | WREXHAM-6E | NEASDEN-34E |
| Aug-52 | GORTON-39A | BARNSLEY-36D | NORTHWICH-9G | T.PARK-9E | ARDSLEY-37A | GORTON-39A | BRUNSWICK-8E | WREXHAM-6E | NEASDEN-34E |
| Jan-53 | GORTON-39A | BARNSLEY-36D | NORTHWICH-9G | T.PARK-9E | ARDSLEY-37A | GORTON-39A | BRUNSWICK-8E | WREXHAM-6E | NEASDEN-34E |
| Aug-53 | GORTON-39A | BARNSLEY-36D | NORTHWICH-9G | T.PARK-9E | 5/53:MEX-36B | GORTON-39A | BRUNSWICK-8E | WREXHAM-6E | NEASDEN-34E |
| Jan-54 | GORTON-39A | BARNSLEY-36D | NORTHWICH-9G | T.PARK-9E | MEXBOROUGH-36B | GORTON-39A | BRUNSWICK-8E | WREXHAM-6E | NEASDEN-34E |
| Aug-54 | GORTON-39A | BARNSLEY-36D | NORTHWICH-9G | T.PARK-9E | MEXBOROUGH-36B | GORTON-39A | BRUNSWICK-8E | WREXHAM-6E | NEASDEN-34E |
| Jan-55 | GORTON-39A | BARNSLEY-36D | NORTHWICH-9G | 12/54:W/D | 12/54:DARN-39B | 3/55:W/D | BRUNSWICK-8E | WREXHAM-6E | NEASDEN-34E |
| Aug-55 | GORTON-39A | BARNSLEY-36D | 6/55:WREX-6E | | DARNALL-39B | | BRUNSWICK-8E | WREXHAM-6E | NEASDEN-34E |
| Jan-56 | 1/56:W/D | BARNSLEY-36D | WREXHAM-6E | | DARNALL-41A | | BRUNSWICK-8E | WREXHAM-6E | NEASDEN-34E |
| Aug-56 | | 7/56:W/D | WREXHAM-6E | | 8/56:W/D | | 3/56:W/D | 5/56:W/D | NEASDEN-34E |
| Jan-57 | | | WREXHAM-6E | | | | | | NEASDEN-34E |
| Aug-57 | | | 9/57:W/D | | | | | | NEASDEN-34E |
| Jan-58 | | | | | | | | | NEASDEN-34E |
| Aug-58 | | | | | | | | | NEASDEN-14D |
| Jan-59 | | | | | | | | | NEASDEN-14D |
| Aug-59 | | | | | | | | | NEASDEN-14D |
| Nov-59 | | | | | | | | | NEASDEN-14D |
| Jan-60 | | | | | | | | | 12/59:W/D |
| Apr-60 | | | | | | | | | |
| Aug-60 | | | | | | | | | |
| Nov-60 | | | | | | | | | |

## 69342 – 69350

| | 69342 | 69343 | 69344 | 69345 | 69346 | 69347 | 69348 | 69349 | 69350 |
|---|---|---|---|---|---|---|---|---|---|
| Aug-50 | BRUNSWICK-8E | T.PARK-9E | SOUTHPORT-27E | BARNSLEY-36D | WREXHAM-6E | GORTON-39A | BARNSLEY-36D | WREXHAM-6E | NEASDEN-34E |
| Jan-51 | BRUNSWICK-8E | T.PARK-9E | SOUTHPORT-27E | BARNSLEY-36D | WREXHAM-6E | 9/50: T.PARK-9E | BARNSLEY-36D | WREXHAM-6E | NEASDEN-34E |
| Aug-51 | BRUNSWICK-8E | T.PARK-9E | SOUTHPORT-27E | BARNSLEY-36D | WREXHAM-6E | T.PARK-9E | BARNSLEY-36D | WREXHAM-6E | NEASDEN-34E |
| Jan-52 | BRUNSWICK-8E | T.PARK-9E | SOUTHPORT-27E | BARNSLEY-36D | WREXHAM-6E | T.PARK-9E | BARNSLEY-36D | WREXHAM-6E | NEASDEN-34E |
| Aug-52 | BRUNSWICK-8E | T.PARK-9E | SOUTHPORT-27E | BARNSLEY-36D | WREXHAM-6E | T.PARK-9E | BARNSLEY-36D | WREXHAM-6E | NEASDEN-34E |
| Jan-53 | BRUNSWICK-8E | T.PARK-9E | SOUTHPORT-27E | BARNSLEY-36D | WREXHAM-6E | T.PARK-9E | BARNSLEY-36D | WREXHAM-6E | NEASDEN-34E |
| Aug-53 | BRUNSWICK-8E | T.PARK-9E | SOUTHPORT-27E | BARNSLEY-36D | WREXHAM-6E | T.PARK-9E | BARNSLEY-36D | WREXHAM-6E | NEASDEN-34E |
| Jan-54 | BRUNSWICK-8E | T.PARK-9E | SOUTHPORT-27E | BARNSLEY-36D | WREXHAM-6E | T.PARK-9E | 6/54: DCTR-36A | WREXHAM-6E | NEASDEN-34E |
| Aug-54 | BRUNSWICK-8E | T.PARK-9E | SOUTHPORT-27E | BARNSLEY-36D | WREXHAM-6E | T.PARK-9E | 11/54: DARN-39B | WREXHAM-6E | NEASDEN-34E |
| Jan-55 | BRUNSWICK-8E | T.PARK-9E | SOUTHPORT-27E | BARNSLEY-36D | WREXHAM-6E | T.PARK-9E | DARNALL-39B | WREXHAM-6E | NEASDEN-34E |
| Aug-55 | BRUNSWICK-8E | T.PARK-9E | SOUTHPORT-27E | BARNSLEY-36D | WREXHAM-6E | T.PARK-9E | DARNALL-41A | WREXHAM-6E | NEASDEN-34E |
| Jan-56 | BRUNSWICK-8E | 11/55: WREX-6E | SOUTHPORT-27E | BARNSLEY-36D | WREXHAM-6E | T.PARK-9E | DARNALL-41A | WREXHAM-6E | NEASDEN-34E |
| Aug-56 | BRUNSWICK-8E | WREXHAM-6E | SOUTHPORT-27E | 9/56: W/D | WREXHAM-6E | T.PARK-9E | 1/57: W/D | WREXHAM-6E | NEASDEN-34E |
| Jan-57 | BRUNSWICK-8E | 11/56: T.PARK-9E | SOUTHPORT-27E | | WREXHAM-6E | T.PARK-9E | | WREXHAM-6E | 1/57: W/D |
| Aug-57 | BRUNSWICK-8E | | SOUTHPORT-27E | | WREXHAM-6E | T.PARK-9E | | WREXHAM-6E | |
| Jan-58 | 5/58: DARN-41A | 5/58: DARN-41A | SOUTHPORT-27E | | 9/57: W/D | 10/57: W/D | | WREXHAM-6E | |
| Aug-58 | 7/58: BARN-41G | 7/58: BARN-41G | SOUTHPORT-27E | | | | | WREXHAM-6E | |
| Jan-59 | BARNSLEY-41G | BARNSLEY-41G | SOUTHPORT-27E | | | | | WREXHAM-6E | |
| Aug-59 | 8/59: W/D | BARNSLEY-41G | SOUTHPORT-27E | | | | | WREXHAM-6E | |
| Nov-59 | | BARNSLEY-41G | SOUTHPORT-27E | | | | | WREXHAM-6E | |
| Jan-60 | | 12/59: W/D | 12/59: W/D | | | | | WREXHAM-6E | |
| Apr-60 | | | | | | | | WREXHAM-6E | |
| Aug-60 | | | | | | | | WREXHAM-6E | |
| Nov-60 | | | | | | | | WREXHAM-6E | |

## 69351 – 69359

| | 69351 | 69352 | 69353 | 69354 | 69355 | 69356 | 69357 | 69358 | 69359 |
|---|---|---|---|---|---|---|---|---|---|
| Aug-50 | STAVELEY-38D | WREXHAM-6E | GORTON-39A | RETFORD-36E | BARNSLEY-36D | SOUTHPORT-27E | BARNSLEY-36D | NEASDEN-34E | H.MERSEY-9F |
| Jan-51 | STAVELEY-38D | WREXHAM-6E | GORTON-39A | RETFORD-36E | BARNSLEY-36D | SOUTHPORT-27E | BARNSLEY-36D | NEASDEN-34E | H.MERSEY-9F |
| Aug-51 | STAVELEY-38D | WREXHAM-6E | GORTON-39A | RETFORD-36E | BARNSLEY-36D | SOUTHPORT-27E | BARNSLEY-36D | 9/51: T.PARK-9E | H.MERSEY-9F |
| Aug-52 | STAVELEY-38D | WREXHAM-6E | GORTON-39A | RETFORD-36E | BARNSLEY-36D | SOUTHPORT-27E | BARNSLEY-36D | T.PARK-9E | H.MERSEY-9F |
| Aug-52 | STAVELEY-38D | WREXHAM-6E | GORTON-39A | RETFORD-36E | BARNSLEY-36D | SOUTHPORT-27E | BARNSLEY-36D | T.PARK-9E | H.MERSEY-9F |
| Jan-53 | STAVELEY-38D | WREXHAM-6E | GORTON-39A | 1/53: NEAS-34E | BARNSLEY-36D | SOUTHPORT-27E | BARNSLEY-36D | T.PARK-9E | H.MERSEY-9F |
| Aug-53 | STAVELEY-38D | WREXHAM-6E | GORTON-39A | NEASDEN-34E | BARNSLEY-36D | SOUTHPORT-27E | BARNSLEY-36D | T.PARK-9E | H.MERSEY-9F |
| Jan-54 | STAVELEY-38D | WREXHAM-6E | GORTON-39A | NEASDEN-34E | BARNSLEY-36D | SOUTHPORT-27E | 3/54: MEX-36B | T.PARK-9E | H.MERSEY-9F |
| Aug-54 | STAVELEY-38D | WREXHAM-6E | GORTON-39A | NEASDEN-34E | BARNSLEY-36D | SOUTHPORT-27E | MEXBOROUGH-36B | T.PARK-9E | H.MERSEY-9F |
| Jan-55 | STAVELEY-38D | WREXHAM-6E | GORTON-39A | NEASDEN-34E | BARNSLEY-36D | SOUTHPORT-27E | MEXBOROUGH-36B | T.PARK-9E | H.MERSEY-9F |
| Aug-55 | STAVELEY-38D | 6/55: W/D | 11/55: W/D | NEASDEN-34E | BARNSLEY-36D | SOUTHPORT-27E | 11/55: W/D | T.PARK-9E | H.MERSEY-9F |
| Jan-56 | 12/55: GORT-39A | | | NEASDEN-34E | BARNSLEY-36D | SOUTHPORT-27E | | T.PARK-9E | 4/56: W/D |
| Aug-56 | 9/56: W/D | | | 10/56: BARN-36D | BARNSLEY-36D | SOUTHPORT-27E | | 11/56: W/D | |
| Jan-57 | | | | BARNSLEY-36D | BARNSLEY-36D | 2/57: W/D | | | |
| Aug-57 | | | | BARNSLEY-36D | BARNSLEY-36D | | | | |
| Jan-58 | | | | BARNSLEY-36D | BARNSLEY-36D | | | | |
| Aug-58 | | | | BARNSLEY-41G | 4/58: W/D | | | | |
| Jan-59 | | | | BARNSLEY-41G | | | | | |
| Aug-59 | | | | BARNSLEY-41G | | | | | |
| Nov-59 | | | | BARNSLEY-41G | | | | | |
| Jan-60 | | | | 1/60: MEX-41F | | | | | |
| Apr-60 | | | | 2/60: W/D | | | | | |

## 69360 – 69368

| | 69360 | 69361 | 69362 | 69363 | 69364 | 69365 | 69366 | 69367 | 69368 |
|---|---|---|---|---|---|---|---|---|---|
| Aug-50 | W.HALSE-38E | T.PARK-9E | WREXHAM-6E | STAVELEY-38D | T.PARK-9E | BARNSLEY-36D | WREXHAM-6E | BARNSLEY-36D | BARNSLEY-36D |
| Jan-51 | W.HALSE-38E | T.PARK-9E | WREXHAM-6E | STAVELEY-38D | T.PARK-9E | BARNSLEY-36D | WREXHAM-6E | BARNSLEY-36D | BARNSLEY-36D |
| Aug-51 | W.HALSE-38E | T.PARK-9E | WREXHAM-6E | STAVELEY-38D | T.PARK-9E | BARNSLEY-36D | WREXHAM-6E | BARNSLEY-36D | BARNSLEY-36D |
| Jan-52 | W.HALSE-38E | T.PARK-9E | WREXHAM-6E | STAVELEY-38D | T.PARK-9E | BARNSLEY-36D | WREXHAM-6E | BARNSLEY-36D | BARNSLEY-36D |
| Aug-52 | W.HALSE-38E | T.PARK-9E | WREXHAM-6E | STAVELEY-38D | T.PARK-9E | BARNSLEY-36D | WREXHAM-6E | BARNSLEY-36D | BARNSLEY-36D |
| Jan-53 | W.HALSE-38E | T.PARK-9E | WREXHAM-6E | STAVELEY-38D | T.PARK-9E | BARNSLEY-36D | WREXHAM-6E | BARNSLEY-36D | BARNSLEY-36D |
| Aug-53 | W.HALSE-38E | T.PARK-9E | WREXHAM-6E | STAVELEY-38D | T.PARK-9E | BARNSLEY-36D | WREXHAM-6E | BARNSLEY-36D | BARNSLEY-36D |
| Jan-54 | 12/53: COLW-38A | T.PARK-9E | WREXHAM-6E | STAVELEY-38D | T.PARK-9E | BARNSLEY-36D | WREXHAM-6E | BARNSLEY-36D | BARNSLEY-36D |
| Aug-54 | COLWICK-38A | T.PARK-9E | WREXHAM-6E | STAVELEY-38D | T.PARK-9E | BARNSLEY-36D | WREXHAM-6E | BARNSLEY-36D | BARNSLEY-36D |
| Jan-55 | COLWICK-38A | T.PARK-9E | WREXHAM-6E | STAVELEY-38D | T.PARK-9E | BARNSLEY-36D | WREXHAM-6E | BARNSLEY-36D | BARNSLEY-36D |
| Aug-55 | COLWICK-38A | T.PARK-9E | WREXHAM-6E | STAVELEY-38D | T.PARK-9E | BARNSLEY-36D | WREXHAM-6E | BARNSLEY-36D | 5/55: W/D |
| Jan-56 | 12/55: GORT-39A | T.PARK-9E | WREXHAM-6E | STAVELEY-38D | 8/55: W/D | BARNSLEY-36D | WREXHAM-6E | 11/55: W/D | |
| Aug-56 | GORTON-39A | T.PARK-9E | WREXHAM-6E | 7/56: W/D | | BARNSLEY-36D | 8/56: W/D | | |
| Jan-57 | GORTON-39A | T.PARK-9E | WREXHAM-6E | | | 2/57: W/D | | | |
| Aug-57 | GORTON-39A | T.PARK-9E | WREXHAM-6E | | | | | | |
| Jan-58 | GORTON-39A | T.PARK-9E | WREXHAM-6E | | | | | | |
| Aug-58 | GORTON-9G | 5/58: DARN-41A | WREXHAM-6E | | | | | | |
| Jan-59 | GORTON-9G | DARNALL-41A | WREXHAM-6E | | | | | | |
| Aug-59 | GORTON-9G | 6/59: W/D | WREXHAM-6E | | | | | | |
| Nov-59 | GORTON-9G | | WREXHAM-6E | | | | | | |
| Jan-60 | GORTON-9G | | WREXHAM-6E | | | | | | |
| Apr-60 | 3/60: W/D | | WREXHAM-6E | | | | | | |
| Aug-60 | | | WREXHAM-6E | | | | | | |
| Nov-60 | | | WREXHAM-6E | | | | | | |

## 69369 – 69381

N8 0-6-2T (1886) — columns 69371 onwards

| | 69369 | 69370 | 69371 | 69372 | 69377 | 69378 | 69379 | 69380 | 69381 |
|---|---|---|---|---|---|---|---|---|---|
| Aug-50 | NEASDEN-34E | T.PARK-9E | HEATON-52B | HEATON-52B | DAIRYCOATES-53A | TYNE DOCK-54B | DAIRYCOATES-53A | HEATON-52B | DAIRYCOATES-53A |
| Jan-51 | NEASDEN-34E | T.PARK-9E | HEATON-52B | 11/50: W/D | DAIRYCOATES-53A | TYNE DOCK-54B | DAIRYCOATES-53A | 11/50: W/D | DAIRYCOATES-53A |
| Aug-51 | NEASDEN-34E | T.PARK-9E | HEATON-52B | | DAIRYCOATES-53A | TYNE DOCK-54B | DAIRYCOATES-53A | | DAIRYCOATES-53A |
| Jan-52 | NEASDEN-34E | T.PARK-9E | HEATON-52B | | DAIRYCOATES-53A | 11/51: HTN-52B | DAIRYCOATES-53A | | DAIRYCOATES-53A |
| Aug-52 | NEASDEN-34E | T.PARK-9E | 3/52: W/D | | DAIRYCOATES-53A | HEATON-52B | DAIRYCOATES-53A | | DAIRYCOATES-53A |
| Jan-53 | NEASDEN-34E | T.PARK-9E | | | 2/53: HTN-52B | 10/53: SPRING-53C | 10/52: W/D | | DAIRYCOATES-53A |
| Aug-53 | NEASDEN-34E | T.PARK-9E | | | HEATON-52B | 12/53: BRID-53D | | | DAIRYCOATES-53A |
| Jan-54 | NEASDEN-34E | T.PARK-9E | | | HEATON-52B | BRIDLINGTON-53D | | | DAIRYCOATES-53A |
| Aug-54 | NEASDEN-34E | T.PARK-9E | | | HEATON-52B | BRIDLINGTON-53D | | | DAIRYCOATES-53A |
| Jan-55 | 1/55: DARN-39B | T.PARK-9E | | | HEATON-52B | 9/55: W/D | | | DAIRYCOATES-53A |
| Aug-55 | 11/55: BOST-40F | T.PARK-9E | | | 6/55: W/D | | | | 6/55: W/D |
| Jan-56 | 0 | T.PARK-9E | | | | | | | |
| Aug-56 | 3/56: IMM-40B | T.PARK-9E | | | | | | | |
| Jan-57 | 2/57: W/D | T.PARK-9E | | | | | | | |
| Aug-57 | | T.PARK-9E | | | | | | | |
| Jan-58 | | 5/58: DARN-41A | | | | | | | |
| Aug-58 | | 7/58: BARN-41G | | | | | | | |
| Jan-59 | | BARNSLEY-41G | | | | | | | |
| Aug-59 | | BARNSLEY-41G | | | | | | | |
| Nov-59 | | BARNSLEY-41G | | | | | | | |
| Jan-60 | | 1/60: MEX-41F | | | | | | | |
| Apr-60 | | MEXBOROUGH-41F | | | | | | | |
| Aug-60 | | 9/60: W/D | | | | | | | |
| Nov-60 | | | | | | | | | |

| Date | 69382 | 69385 | 69386 | 69387 | 69389 | 69390 | 69391 | 69392 | 69393 |
|---|---|---|---|---|---|---|---|---|---|
| Aug-50 | DAIRYCOATES-53A | DAIRYCOATES-53A | DAIRYCOATES-53A | HEATON-52B | DAIRYCOATES-53A | HEATON-52B | BOROUGH GARDENS-54C | DAIRYCOATES-53A | DAIRYCOATES-53A |
| Jan-51 | DAIRYCOATES-53A | DAIRYCOATES-53A | DAIRYCOATES-53A | HEATON-52B | DAIRYCOATES-53A | HEATON-52B | 12/50: HTN - 52B | DAIRYCOATES-53A | DAIRYCOATES-53A |
| Aug-51 | DAIRYCOATES-53A | DAIRYCOATES-53A | DAIRYCOATES-53A | HEATON-52B | DAIRYCOATES-53A | HEATON-52B | HEATON-52B | DAIRYCOATES-53A | DAIRYCOATES-53A |
| Jan-52 | DAIRYCOATES-53A | DAIRYCOATES-53A | DAIRYCOATES-53A | HEATON-52B | DAIRYCOATES-53A | HEATON-52B | HEATON-52B | DAIRYCOATES-53A | DAIRYCOATES-53A |
| Aug-52 | 7/52: W/D | DAIRYCOATES-53A | DAIRYCOATES-53A | 7/52: W/D | 7/52: W/D | HEATON-52B | HEATON-52B | DAIRYCOATES-53A | 10/52: W/D |
| Jan-53 | | DAIRYCOATES-53A | DAIRYCOATES-53A | | | 10/52: CON - 54D | 2/53: W/D | 2/53: SUND - 54A | |
| Aug-53 | | DAIRYCOATES-53A | DAIRYCOATES-53A | | | CONSETT-54D | | SUNDERLAND-54A | |
| Jan-54 | | DAIRYCOATES-53A | DAIRYCOATES-53A | | | 2/54: SUND - 54A | | SUNDERLAND-54A | |
| Aug-54 | | DAIRYCOATES-53A | DAIRYCOATES-53A | | | SUNDERLAND-54A | | SUNDERLAND-54A | |
| Jan-55 | | 10/54: W/D | 2/55: W/D | | | SUNDERLAND-54A | | 5/55: W/D | |
| Aug-55 | | | | | | SUNDERLAND-54A | | | |
| Jan-56 | | | | | | 11/55: T.DCK - 54B | | | |
| Aug-56 | | | | | | 9/56: W/D | | | |

N9 0-6-2T (1893) — applies to 69410, 69413, 69418, 69423

| Date | 69394 | 69395 | 69398 | 69400 | 69401 | 69410 | 69413 | 69418 | 69423 |
|---|---|---|---|---|---|---|---|---|---|
| Aug-50 | CONSETT-54D | CONSETT-54D | DAIRYCOATES-53A | TYNE DOCK-54B | DAIRYCOATES-53A | TYNE DOCK-54B | SUNDERLAND-54A | SUNDERLAND-54A | SUNDERLAND-54A |
| Jan-51 | CONSETT-54D | CONSETT-54D | DAIRYCOATES-53A | TYNE DOCK-54B | DAIRYCOATES-53A | 10/50: W/D | 11/50: W/D | 1/51: W/D | SUNDERLAND-54A |
| Aug-51 | CONSETT-54D | CONSETT-54D | DAIRYCOATES-53A | TYNE DOCK-54B | 9/51: W/D | | | | 7/51: W/D |
| Jan-52 | CONSETT-54D | CONSETT-54D | 10/51: W/D | 10/51: W/D | | | | | |
| Aug-52 | CONSETT-54D | 8/52: W/D | | | | | | | |
| Jan-53 | CONSETT-54D | | | | | | | | |
| Aug-53 | CONSETT-54D | | | | | | | | |
| Jan-54 | 2/54: T.DCK - 54B | | | | | | | | |
| Aug-54 | TYNE DOCK-54B | | | | | | | | |
| Jan-55 | TYNE DOCK-54B | | | | | | | | |
| Aug-55 | TYNE DOCK-54B | | | | | | | | |
| Jan-56 | 10/55: W/D | | | | | | | | |

N10 0-6-2T (1907) — applies to 69430, 69431, 69432, 69433

| Date | 69424 | 69425 | 69426 | 69427 | 69429 | 69430 | 69431 | 69432 | 69433 |
|---|---|---|---|---|---|---|---|---|---|
| Aug-50 | SUNDERLAND-54A | SUNDERLAND-54A | DARLINGTON-51A | SUNDERLAND-54A | TYNE DOCK-54B | COPLEY HILL-37B | HORNSEY-34B | HORNSEY-34B | HORNSEY-34B |
| Jan-51 | SUNDERLAND-54A | 11/50: W/D | 2/51: SUND - 54A | SUNDERLAND-54A | TYNE DOCK-54B | COPLEY HILL-37B | HORNSEY-34B | HORNSEY-34B | HORNSEY-34B |
| Aug-51 | SUNDERLAND-54A | | SUNDERLAND-54A | SUNDERLAND-54A | TYNE DOCK-54B | COPLEY HILL-37B | HORNSEY-34B | 6/51: BRAD - 37C | HORNSEY-34B |
| Jan-52 | 11/51: T.DCK - 54B | | 11/51: T.DCK - 54B | SUNDERLAND-54A | TYNE DOCK-54B | COPLEY HILL-37B | HORNSEY-34B | BRADFORD-37C | HORNSEY-34B |
| Aug-52 | TYNE DOCK-54B | | TYNE DOCK-54B | SUNDERLAND-54A | TYNE DOCK-54B | COPLEY HILL-37B | HORNSEY-34B | BRADFORD-37C | HORNSEY-34B |
| Jan-53 | TYNE DOCK-54B | | 2/53: W/D | 2/53: T/DCK - 54B | TYNE DOCK-54B | COPLEY HILL-37B | 3/53: ARDS - 37A | BRADFORD-37C | 2/53: BRAD - 37C |
| Aug-53 | TYNE DOCK-54B | | | TYNE DOCK-54B | TYNE DOCK-54B | COPLEY HILL-37B | ARDSLEY-37A | BRADFORD-37C | BRADFORD-37C |
| Jan-54 | TYNE DOCK-54B | | | TYNE DOCK-54B | TYNE DOCK-54B | COPLEY HILL-37B | ARDSLEY-37A | BRADFORD-37C | BRADFORD-37C |
| Aug-54 | TYNE DOCK-54B | | | TYNE DOCK-54B | TYNE DOCK-54B | COPLEY HILL-37B | ARDSLEY-37A | BRADFORD-37C | BRADFORD-37C |
| Jan-55 | TYNE DOCK-54B | | | TYNE DOCK-54B | TYNE DOCK-54B | COPLEY HILL-37B | 3/55: W/D | 11/54: W/D | 12/54: W/D |
| Aug-55 | 6/55: W/D | | | 6/55: W/D | 7/55: W/D | COPLEY HILL-37B | | | |
| Jan-56 | | | | | | COPLEY HILL-37B | | | |
| Aug-56 | | | | | | COPLEY HILL-56C | | | |
| Jan-57 | | | | | | 12/56: W/D | | | |

| Date | 69434 | 69435 | 69436 | 69437 | 69439 | 69440 | 69441 | 69442 | 69443 |
|---|---|---|---|---|---|---|---|---|---|
| Aug-50 | HORNSEY-34B | HORNSEY-34B | COPLEY HILL-37B | COPLEY HILL-37B | HORNSEY-34B | COPLEY HILL-37B | HORNSEY-34B | HORNSEY-34B | BRADFORD-37C |
| Jan-51 | HORNSEY-34B | HORNSEY-34B | COPLEY HILL-37B | COPLEY HILL-37B | HORNSEY-34B | COPLEY HILL-37B | HORNSEY-34B | HORNSEY-34B | BRADFORD-37C |
| Aug-51 | 6/51: BRAD - 37C | HORNSEY-34B | COPLEY HILL-37B | COPLEY HILL-37B | 6/51: BRAD - 37C | COPLEY HILL-37B | HORNSEY-34B | HORNSEY-34B | BRADFORD-37C |
| Jan-52 | BRADFORD-37C | HORNSEY-34B | COPLEY HILL-37B | COPLEY HILL-37B | BRADFORD-37C | COPLEY HILL-37B | HORNSEY-34B | HORNSEY-34B | BRADFORD-37C |
| Aug-52 | BRADFORD-37C | HORNSEY-34B | COPLEY HILL-37B | COPLEY HILL-37B | BRADFORD-37C | COPLEY HILL-37B | HORNSEY-34B | HORNSEY-34B | BRADFORD-37C |
| Jan-53 | BRADFORD-37C | HORNSEY-34B | COPLEY HILL-37B | COPLEY HILL-37B | BRADFORD-37C | COPLEY HILL-37B | HORNSEY-34B | 1/53: BRAD - 37C | BRADFORD-37C |
| Aug-53 | BRADFORD-37C | HORNSEY-34B | COPLEY HILL-37B | COPLEY HILL-37B | BRADFORD-37C | COPLEY HILL-37B | HORNSEY-34B | 9/53: W/D | BRADFORD-37C |
| Jan-54 | BRADFORD-37C | HORNSEY-34B | COPLEY HILL-37B | COPLEY HILL-37B | BRADFORD-37C | COPLEY HILL-37B | HORNSEY-34B | | BRADFORD-37C |
| Aug-54 | BRADFORD-37C | HORNSEY-34B | 8/54: BRAD - 37C | 6/54: W/D | BRADFORD-37C | COPLEY HILL-37B | 4/54: COLW - 38A | | BRADFORD-37C |
| Jan-55 | BRADFORD-37C | 3/55: W/D | BRADFORD-37C | | BRADFORD-37C | 12/54: ARDS - 37A | 4/55: BRAD - 37C | | BRADFORD-37C |
| Aug-55 | BRADFORD-37C | | 7/55: W/D | | 11/55: W/D | ARDSLEY-37A | 5/55: W/D | | BRADFORD-37C |
| Jan-56 | BRADFORD-37C | | | | | ARDSLEY-37A | | | BRADFORD-37C |
| Aug-56 | BRADFORD-56G | | | | | ARDSLEY-56B | | | BRADFORD-56G |
| Jan-57 | 1/57: C.HILL - 56C | | | | | 3/57: W/D | | | BRADFORD-56G |
| Aug-57 | COPLEY HILL-56C | | | | | | | | BRADFORD-56G |
| Jan-58 | COPLEY HILL-56C | | | | | | | | 11/57: ARDS - 56B |
| Aug-58 | COPLEY HILL-56C | | | | | | | | ARDSLEY-56B |
| Jan-59 | 3/59: W/D | | | | | | | | 3/59: W/D |

Table 1 — Locomotives 69444–69452

| Date | 69444 | 69445 | 69446 | 69447 | 69448 | 69449 | 69450 | 69451 | 69452 |
|---|---|---|---|---|---|---|---|---|---|
| Aug-50 | COPLEY HILL - 37B | HORNSEY - 34B | COPLEY HILL - 37B | BRADFORD - 37C | BRADFORD - 37C | BRADFORD - 37C | HORNSEY - 34B | HORNSEY - 34B | ARDSLEY - 37A |
| Jan-51 | COPLEY HILL - 37B | HORNSEY - 34B | COPLEY HILL - 37B | BRADFORD - 37C | BRADFORD - 37C | BRADFORD - 37C | HORNSEY - 34B | HORNSEY - 34B | ARDSLEY - 37A |
| Aug-51 | COPLEY HILL - 37B | HORNSEY - 34B | COPLEY HILL - 37B | BRADFORD - 37C | BRADFORD - 37C | BRADFORD - 37C | 6/51: C.HILL - 37A | HORNSEY - 34B | ARDSLEY - 37A |
| Jan-52 | COPLEY HILL - 37B | HORNSEY - 34B | COPLEY HILL - 37B | BRADFORD - 37C | BRADFORD - 37C | BRADFORD - 37C | COPLEY HILL - 37B | HORNSEY - 34B | ARDSLEY - 37A |
| Aug-52 | COPLEY HILL - 37B | HORNSEY - 34B | COPLEY HILL - 37B | BRADFORD - 37C | BRADFORD - 37C | BRADFORD - 37C | COPLEY HILL - 37B | HORNSEY - 34B | ARDSLEY - 37A |
| Jan-53 | COPLEY HILL - 37B | HORNSEY - 34B | COPLEY HILL - 37B | BRADFORD - 37C | 1/53: W/D | BRADFORD - 37C | COPLEY HILL - 37B | HORNSEY - 34B | ARDSLEY - 37A |
| Aug-53 | COPLEY HILL - 37B | HORNSEY - 34B | 6/53: W/D | BRADFORD - 37C | | BRADFORD - 37C | COPLEY HILL - 37B | HORNSEY - 34B | ARDSLEY - 37A |
| Jan-54 | COPLEY HILL - 37B | HORNSEY - 34B | | BRADFORD - 37C | | BRADFORD - 37C | COPLEY HILL - 37B | 1/54: COLW - 38A | ARDSLEY - 37A |
| Aug-54 | COPLEY HILL - 37B | HORNSEY - 34B | | BRADFORD - 37C | | BRADFORD - 37C | COPLEY HILL - 37B | COLWICK - 38A | ARDSLEY - 37A |
| Jan-55 | COPLEY HILL - 37B | 1/55: W/D | | BRADFORD - 37C | | 4/55: W/D | COPLEY HILL - 37B | 4/55: BRAD - 37C | ARDSLEY - 37A |
| Aug-55 | COPLEY HILL - 37B | | | BRADFORD - 37C | | | COPLEY HILL - 37B | 10/55: W/D | ARDSLEY - 37A |
| Jan-56 | COPLEY HILL - 37B | | | BRADFORD - 37C | | | COPLEY HILL - 56C | | ARDSLEY - 56B |
| Aug-56 | COPLEY HILL - 56C | | | BRADFORD - 56G | | | COPLEY HILL - 56C | | ARDSLEY - 56B |
| Jan-57 | 10/56: W/D | | | 10/56: W/D | | | COPLEY HILL - 56C | | ARDSLEY - 56B |
| Aug-57 | | | | | | | COPLEY HILL - 56C | | ARDSLEY - 56B |
| Jan-58 | | | | | | | COPLEY HILL - 56C | | ARDSLEY - 56B |
| Aug-58 | | | | | | | 3/59: W/D | | 3/59: W/D |
| Jan-59 | | | | | | | | | |
| Aug-59 | | | | | | | | | |
| Nov-59 | | | | | | | | | |
| Jan-60 | | | | | | | | | |
| Apr-60 | | | | | | | | | |
| Aug-60 | | | | | | | | | |
| Nov-60 | | | | | | | | | |

Table 2 — Locomotives 69453–69461

| Date | 69453 | 69454 | 69455 | 69456 | 69457 | 69458 | 69459 | 69460 | 69461 |
|---|---|---|---|---|---|---|---|---|---|
| Aug-50 | HORNSEY - 34B | BRADFORD - 37C | HORNSEY - 34B | HORNSEY - 34B | HORNSEY - 34B | HORNSEY - 34B | BRADFORD - 37C | HORNSEY - 34B | ARDSLEY - 37A |
| Jan-51 | HORNSEY - 34B | BRADFORD - 37C | HORNSEY - 34B | HORNSEY - 34B | HORNSEY - 34B | HORNSEY - 34B | BRADFORD - 37C | HORNSEY - 34B | ARDSLEY - 37A |
| Aug-51 | HORNSEY - 34B | BRADFORD - 37C | HORNSEY - 34B | HORNSEY - 34B | HORNSEY - 34B | HORNSEY - 34B | BRADFORD - 37C | HORNSEY - 34B | ARDSLEY - 37A |
| Jan-52 | HORNSEY - 34B | BRADFORD - 37C | HORNSEY - 34B | HORNSEY - 34B | HORNSEY - 34B | HORNSEY - 34B | BRADFORD - 37C | HORNSEY - 34B | ARDSLEY - 37A |
| Aug-52 | HORNSEY - 34B | BRADFORD - 37C | HORNSEY - 34B | HORNSEY - 34B | HORNSEY - 34B | HORNSEY - 34B | BRADFORD - 37C | HORNSEY - 34B | ARDSLEY - 37A |
| Jan-53 | HORNSEY - 34B | BRADFORD - 37C | HORNSEY - 34B | HORNSEY - 34B | HORNSEY - 34B | HORNSEY - 34B | BRADFORD - 37C | HORNSEY - 34B | ARDSLEY - 37A |
| Aug-53 | HORNSEY - 34B | BRADFORD - 37C | HORNSEY - 34B | 5/53: ARDS - 37A | HORNSEY - 34B | HORNSEY - 34B | BRADFORD - 37C | HORNSEY - 34B | ARDSLEY - 37A |
| Jan-54 | HORNSEY - 34B | BRADFORD - 37C | 4/54: COLW - 38A | ARDSLEY - 37A | 2/54: COLW - 38A | HORNSEY - 34B | BRADFORD - 37C | HORNSEY - 34B | ARDSLEY - 37A |
| Aug-54 | 5/54: COLW - 38A | BRADFORD - 37C | 5/54: HSEY - 34B | ARDSLEY - 37A | COLWICK - 38A | HORNSEY - 34B | BRADFORD - 37C | HORNSEY - 34B | 6/54: W/D |
| Jan-55 | 3/55: ARDS - 37A | 2/55: W/D | 3/55: BRAD - 37C | 11/54: W/D | COLWICK - 38A | HORNSEY - 34B | 3/55: W/D | HORNSEY - 34B | |
| Aug-55 | ARDSLEY - 37A | | 5/55: W/D | | COLWICK - 38A | HORNSEY - 34B | | 8/55: W/D | |
| Jan-56 | ARDSLEY - 37A | | | | 11/55: ARDS - 37A | 11/55: W/D | | | |
| Aug-56 | ARDSLEY - 56B | | | | 4/56: BRAD - 37C | | | | |
| Jan-57 | ARDSLEY - 56B | | | | 3/57: C.HILL - 37A | | | | |
| Aug-57 | ARDSLEY - 56B | | | | 4/57: W/D | | | | |
| Jan-58 | 4/58: W/D | | | | | | | | |
| Aug-58 | | | | | | | | | |
| Jan-59 | | | | | | | | | |
| Aug-59 | | | | | | | | | |
| Nov-59 | | | | | | | | | |
| Jan-60 | | | | | | | | | |
| Apr-60 | | | | | | | | | |
| Aug-60 | | | | | | | | | |
| Nov-60 | | | | | | | | | |

Table 3 — Locomotives 69462–69470

| Date | 69462 | 69463 | 69464 | 69465 | 69466 | 69467 | 69468 | 69469 | 69470 |
|---|---|---|---|---|---|---|---|---|---|
| Aug-50 | HORNSEY - 34B | HORNSEY - 34B | BRADFORD - 37C | HORNSEY - 34B | HORNSEY - 34B | HORNSEY - 34B | HORNSEY - 34B | HORNSEY - 34B | HORNSEY - 34B |
| Jan-51 | HORNSEY - 34B | HORNSEY - 34B | BRADFORD - 37C | HORNSEY - 34B | HORNSEY - 34B | HORNSEY - 34B | HORNSEY - 34B | HORNSEY - 34B | HORNSEY - 34B |
| Aug-51 | HORNSEY - 34B | 6/51: ARDS - 37A | BRADFORD - 37C | HORNSEY - 34B | HORNSEY - 34B | HORNSEY - 34B | HORNSEY - 34B | HORNSEY - 34B | HORNSEY - 34B |
| Jan-52 | HORNSEY - 34B | ARDSLEY - 37A | BRADFORD - 37C | HORNSEY - 34B | HORNSEY - 34B | HORNSEY - 34B | HORNSEY - 34B | HORNSEY - 34B | HORNSEY - 34B |
| Aug-52 | HORNSEY - 34B | ARDSLEY - 37A | BRADFORD - 37C | HORNSEY - 34B | HORNSEY - 34B | HORNSEY - 34B | HORNSEY - 34B | HORNSEY - 34B | HORNSEY - 34B |
| Jan-53 | HORNSEY - 34B | ARDSLEY - 37A | BRADFORD - 37C | HORNSEY - 34B | HORNSEY - 34B | HORNSEY - 34B | HORNSEY - 34B | HORNSEY - 34B | HORNSEY - 34B |
| Aug-53 | 7/53: C.HILL - 37B | ARDSLEY - 37A | BRADFORD - 37C | HORNSEY - 34B | HORNSEY - 34B | HORNSEY - 34B | 7/53: C.HILL - 37B | HORNSEY - 34B | HORNSEY - 34B |
| Jan-54 | COPLEY HILL - 37B | ARDSLEY - 37A | BRADFORD - 37C | HORNSEY - 34B | HORNSEY - 34B | HORNSEY - 34B | 3/54: W/D | 2/54: COLW - 38A | HORNSEY - 34B |
| Aug-54 | 8/54: KX - 34A | ARDSLEY - 37A | BRADFORD - 37C | HORNSEY - 34B | HORNSEY - 34B | 4/54: COLW - 38A | | 4/54: STAVE - 38D | HORNSEY - 34B |
| Jan-55 | 10/54: HAT - 34C | ARDSLEY - 37A | BRADFORD - 37C | HORNSEY - 34B | HORNSEY - 34B | COLWICK - 38A | | 11/54: COLW - 38A | HORNSEY - 34B |
| Aug-55 | 5/55: HSEY - 34B | ARDSLEY - 37A | 8/55: W/D | HORNSEY - 34B | 7/55: W/D | 4/55: BRAD - 37C | | COLWICK - 38A | HORNSEY - 34B |
| Jan-56 | HORNSEY - 34B | 10/55: W/D | | 12/55: W/D | | BRADFORD - 37C | | 11/55: ARDS - 37A | HORNSEY - 34B |
| Aug-56 | HORNSEY - 34B | | | | | 7/56: W/D | | ARDSLEY - 56B | 8/56: W/D |
| Jan-57 | HORNSEY - 34B | | | | | | | 11/56: C.HILL - 56C | |
| Aug-57 | 6/57: C.HILL - 56C | | | | | | | 4/57: W/D | |
| Jan-58 | COPLEY HILL - 56C | | | | | | | | |
| Aug-58 | COPLEY HILL - 56C | | | | | | | | |
| Jan-59 | COPLEY HILL - 56C | | | | | | | | |
| Aug-59 | 4/59: W/D | | | | | | | | |
| Nov-59 | | | | | | | | | |
| Jan-60 | | | | | | | | | |
| Apr-60 | | | | | | | | | |
| Aug-60 | | | | | | | | | |
| Nov-60 | | | | | | | | | |

Table 4 — Locomotives 69471–69479

| Date | 69471 | 69472 | 69473 | 69474 | 69475 | 69476 | 69477 | 69478 | 69479 |
|---|---|---|---|---|---|---|---|---|---|
| Aug-50 | COPLEY HILL - 37B | COPLEY HILL - 37B | COPLEY HILL - 37B | BRADFORD - 37C | HORNSEY - 34B | HORNSEY - 34B | HORNSEY - 34B | BRADFORD - 37C | BRADFORD - 37C |
| Jan-51 | COPLEY HILL - 37B | 3/51: ARDS - 37A | COPLEY HILL - 37B | BRADFORD - 37C | HORNSEY - 34B | HORNSEY - 34B | HORNSEY - 34B | BRADFORD - 37C | BRADFORD - 37C |
| Aug-51 | COPLEY HILL - 37B | ARDSLEY - 37A | COPLEY HILL - 37B | BRADFORD - 37C | HORNSEY - 34B | HORNSEY - 34B | HORNSEY - 34B | BRADFORD - 37C | BRADFORD - 37C |
| Jan-52 | COPLEY HILL - 37B | ARDSLEY - 37A | COPLEY HILL - 37B | BRADFORD - 37C | HORNSEY - 34B | HORNSEY - 34B | HORNSEY - 34B | BRADFORD - 37C | BRADFORD - 37C |
| Aug-52 | COPLEY HILL - 37B | ARDSLEY - 37A | 9/52: W/D | BRADFORD - 37C | HORNSEY - 34B | HORNSEY - 34B | 9/52: C.HILL - 37B | BRADFORD - 37C | 10/52: W/D |
| Jan-53 | COPLEY HILL - 37B | ARDSLEY - 37A | | BRADFORD - 37C | 2/53: BRAD - 37C | HORNSEY - 34B | COPLEY HILL - 37B | BRADFORD - 37C | |
| Aug-53 | COPLEY HILL - 37B | ARDSLEY - 37A | | BRADFORD - 37C | BRADFORD - 37C | HORNSEY - 34B | COPLEY HILL - 37B | BRADFORD - 37C | |
| Jan-54 | COPLEY HILL - 37B | ARDSLEY - 37A | | BRADFORD - 37C | 8/54: KX - 34A | HORNSEY - 34B | 8/54: KX - 34A | BRADFORD - 37C | |
| Aug-54 | 8/54: BRAD - 37C | ARDSLEY - 37A | | BRADFORD - 37C | 10/54: HAT - 34C | 4/54: COLW - 38A | 10/54: HAT - 34C | BRADFORD - 37C | |
| Jan-55 | BRADFORD - 37C | ARDSLEY - 37A | | BRADFORD - 37C | 2/55: C.HILL - 37B | COLWICK - 38A | 2/55: HSEY - 34B | BRADFORD - 37C | |
| Aug-55 | BRADFORD - 37C | ARDSLEY - 37A | | BRADFORD - 37C | 3/55: BRAD - 37C | 3/55: W/D | HORNSEY - 34B | BRADFORD - 37C | |
| Jan-56 | 1/56: W/D | ARDSLEY - 37A | | BRADFORD - 37C | 4/55: W/D | | HORNSEY - 34B | BRADFORD - 37C | |
| Aug-56 | | ARDSLEY - 56B | | BRADFORD - 56G | | | 6/57: C.HILL - 56C | BRADFORD - 56G | |
| Jan-57 | | ARDSLEY - 56B | | BRADFORD - 56G | | | COPLEY HILL - 56C | 12/56: W/D | |
| Aug-57 | | ARDSLEY - 56B | | 10/57: ARDS - 56B | | | COPLEY HILL - 56C | | |
| Jan-58 | | ARDSLEY - 56B | | ARDSLEY - 56B | | | COPLEY HILL - 56C | | |
| Aug-58 | | 8/58: W/D | | ARDSLEY - 56B | | | 4/59: W/D | | |
| Jan-59 | | | | 3/59: W/D | | | | | |
| Aug-59 | | | | | | | | | |
| Nov-59 | | | | | | | | | |
| Jan-60 | | | | | | | | | |
| Apr-60 | | | | | | | | | |
| Aug-60 | | | | | | | | | |
| Nov-60 | | | | | | | | | |

N2 0-6-2T (1925)

| | 69480 | 69481 | 69482 | 69483 | 69484 | 69485 | 69490 | 69491 | 69492 |
|---|---|---|---|---|---|---|---|---|---|
| Aug-50 | HORNSEY-34B | HORNSEY-34B | BRADFORD-37C | BRADFORD-37C | HATFIELD-34C | BRADFORD-37C | KINGS CROSS-34A | KINGS CROSS-34A | KINGS CROSS-34A |
| Jan-51 | HORNSEY-34B | HORNSEY-34B | BRADFORD-37C | 2/51: C.HILL - 37B | HATFIELD-34C | BRADFORD-37C | KINGS CROSS-34A | KINGS CROSS-34A | KINGS CROSS-34A |
| Aug-51 | 6/51: W/D | HORNSEY-34B | BRADFORD-37C | COPLEYHILL-37B | 9/51: ARDS - 37A | BRADFORD-37C | KINGS CROSS-34A | KINGS CROSS-34A | KINGS CROSS-34A |
| Jan-52 | | HORNSEY-34B | BRADFORD-37C | COPLEYHILL-37B | ARDSLEY-37A | BRADFORD-37C | KINGS CROSS-34A | KINGS CROSS-34A | KINGS CROSS-34A |
| Aug-52 | | HORNSEY-34B | BRADFORD-37C | COPLEYHILL-37B | ARDSLEY-37A | BRADFORD-37C | KINGS CROSS-34A | KINGS CROSS-34A | KINGS CROSS-34A |
| Jan-53 | | HORNSEY-34B | BRADFORD-37C | COPLEYHILL-37B | ARDSLEY-37A | BRADFORD-37C | KINGS CROSS-34A | KINGS CROSS-34A | KINGS CROSS-34A |
| Aug-53 | | HORNSEY-34B | BRADFORD-37C | COPLEYHILL-37B | ARDSLEY-37A | BRADFORD-37C | KINGS CROSS-34A | KINGS CROSS-34A | KINGS CROSS-34A |
| Jan-54 | | 1/54: COLW - 38A | BRADFORD-37C | COPLEYHILL-37B | ARDSLEY-37A | BRADFORD-37C | KINGS CROSS-34A | KINGS CROSS-34A | KINGS CROSS-34A |
| Aug-54 | | COLWICK-38A | 8/54: W/D | COPLEYHILL-37B | ARDSLEY-37A | BRADFORD-37C | KINGS CROSS-34A | KINGS CROSS-34A | KINGS CROSS-34A |
| Jan-55 | | COLWICK-38A | | 3/55: W/D | ARDSLEY-37A | 11/54: W/D | KINGS CROSS-34A | KINGS CROSS-34A | KINGS CROSS-34A |
| Aug-55 | | COLWICK-38A | | | ARDSLEY-37A | | KINGS CROSS-34A | KINGS CROSS-34A | KINGS CROSS-34A |
| Jan-56 | | 11/55: ARDS - 37A | | | ARDSLEY-37A | | KINGS CROSS-34A | KINGS CROSS-34A | KINGS CROSS-34A |
| Aug-56 | | 5/56: W/D | | | ARDSLEY-56B | | KINGS CROSS-34A | KINGS CROSS-34A | KINGS CROSS-34A |
| Jan-57 | | | | | ARDSLEY-56B | | KINGS CROSS-34A | KINGS CROSS-34A | KINGS CROSS-34A |
| Aug-57 | | | | | 9/57: W/D | | KINGS CROSS-34A | KINGS CROSS-34A | KINGS CROSS-34A |
| Jan-58 | | | | | | | KINGS CROSS-34A | KINGS CROSS-34A | KINGS CROSS-34A |
| Aug-58 | | | | | | | KINGS CROSS-34A | KINGS CROSS-34A | KINGS CROSS-34A |
| Jan-59 | | | | | | | KINGS CROSS-34A | 1/59: W/D | KINGS CROSS-34A |
| Aug-59 | | | | | | | 7/59: W/D | | KINGS CROSS-34A |
| Nov-59 | | | | | | | | | KINGS CROSS-34A |
| Jan-60 | | | | | | | | | KINGS CROSS-34A |
| Apr-60 | | | | | | | | | 3/60: W/D |
| Aug-60 | | | | | | | | | |
| Nov-60 | | | | | | | | | |

| | 69493 | 69494 | 69495 | 69496 | 69497 | 69498 | 69499 | 69500 | 69501 |
|---|---|---|---|---|---|---|---|---|---|
| Aug-50 | HATFIELD-34C | HATFIELD-34C | KINGS CROSS-34A | KINGS CROSS-34A | KINGS CROSS-34A | KINGS CROSS-34A | KINGS CROSS-34A | PARKHEAD-65C | COLWICK-38A |
| Jan-51 | HATFIELD-34C | HATFIELD-34C | KINGS CROSS-34A | KINGS CROSS-34A | KINGS CROSS-34A | KINGS CROSS-34A | KINGS CROSS-34A | PARKHEAD-65C | COLWICK-38A |
| Aug-51 | HATFIELD-34C | 9/51: KX - 34A | KINGS CROSS-34A | KINGS CROSS-34A | KINGS CROSS-34A | KINGS CROSS-34A | KINGS CROSS-34A | PARKHEAD-65C | 5/51: HAT - 34C |
| Jan-52 | KINGS CROSS-34A | 12/51: HAT - 34C | KINGS CROSS-34A | KINGS CROSS-34A | KINGS CROSS-34A | KINGS CROSS-34A | KINGS CROSS-34A | PARKHEAD-65C | HATFIELD-34C |
| Aug-52 | KINGS CROSS-34A | HATFIELD-34C | KINGS CROSS-34A | KINGS CROSS-34A | KINGS CROSS-34A | KINGS CROSS-34A | KINGS CROSS-34A | PARKHEAD-65C | HATFIELD-34C |
| Jan-53 | KINGS CROSS-34A | HATFIELD-34C | KINGS CROSS-34A | KINGS CROSS-34A | KINGS CROSS-34A | KINGS CROSS-34A | KINGS CROSS-34A | PARKHEAD-65C | HATFIELD-34C |
| Aug-53 | KINGS CROSS-34A | HATFIELD-34C | KINGS CROSS-34A | KINGS CROSS-34A | KINGS CROSS-34A | KINGS CROSS-34A | KINGS CROSS-34A | PARKHEAD-65C | HATFIELD-34C |
| Jan-54 | KINGS CROSS-34A | HATFIELD-34C | KINGS CROSS-34A | KINGS CROSS-34A | KINGS CROSS-34A | KINGS CROSS-34A | KINGS CROSS-34A | PARKHEAD-65C | 11/53: KX - 34A |
| Aug-54 | KINGS CROSS-34A | 8/54: KX - 34A | KINGS CROSS-34A | KINGS CROSS-34A | KINGS CROSS-34A | KINGS CROSS-34A | KINGS CROSS-34A | PARKHEAD-65C | 3/54: HSEY - 34B |
| Jan-55 | KINGS CROSS-34A | 10/54: HAT - 34C | KINGS CROSS-34A | KINGS CROSS-34A | KINGS CROSS-34A | KINGS CROSS-34A | KINGS CROSS-34A | PARKHEAD-65C | HORNSEY-34B |
| Aug-55 | KINGS CROSS-34A | HATFIELD-34C | KINGS CROSS-34A | KINGS CROSS-34A | KINGS CROSS-34A | KINGS CROSS-34A | KINGS CROSS-34A | PARKHEAD-65C | HORNSEY-34B |
| Jan-56 | KINGS CROSS-34A | HATFIELD-34C | KINGS CROSS-34A | KINGS CROSS-34A | KINGS CROSS-34A | KINGS CROSS-34A | KINGS CROSS-34A | PARKHEAD-65C | HORNSEY-34B |
| Aug-56 | KINGS CROSS-34A | HATFIELD-34C | KINGS CROSS-34A | KINGS CROSS-34A | KINGS CROSS-34A | KINGS CROSS-34A | KINGS CROSS-34A | PARKHEAD-65C | HORNSEY-34B |
| Jan-57 | KINGS CROSS-34A | HATFIELD-34C | KINGS CROSS-34A | KINGS CROSS-34A | KINGS CROSS-34A | KINGS CROSS-34A | KINGS CROSS-34A | PARKHEAD-65C | HORNSEY-34B |
| Aug-57 | KINGS CROSS-34A | HATFIELD-34C | KINGS CROSS-34A | 10/57: HSEY - 34B | KINGS CROSS-34A | KINGS CROSS-34A | KINGS CROSS-34A | 8/57: W/D | HORNSEY-34B |
| Jan-58 | KINGS CROSS-34A | 1/58: W/D | KINGS CROSS-34A | 11/57: KX - 34A | 3/58: W/D | KINGS CROSS-34A | KINGS CROSS-34A | | 11/57: W/D |
| Aug-58 | KINGS CROSS-34A | | 9/58: W/D | 4/58: W/D | | KINGS CROSS-34A | 9/58: W/D | | |
| Jan-59 | | | | | | KINGS CROSS-34A | | | |
| Aug-59 | | | | | | KINGS CROSS-34A | | | |
| Nov-59 | | | | | | KINGS CROSS-34A | | | |
| Jan-60 | | | | | | KINGS CROSS-34A | | | |
| Apr-60 | | | | | | KINGS CROSS-34A | | | |
| Aug-60 | | | | | | KINGS CROSS-34A | | | |
| Nov-60 | | | | | | 10/60: HSEY - 34B | | | |

| | 69502 | 69503 | 69504 | 69505 | 69506 | 69507 | 69508 | 69509 | 69510 |
|---|---|---|---|---|---|---|---|---|---|
| Aug-50 | KINGS CROSS-34A | KIPPS-65E | HATFIELD-34C | HORNSEY-34B | KINGS CROSS-34A | PARKHEAD-65C | KIPPS-65E | KIPPS-65E | PARKHEAD-65C |
| Jan-51 | KINGS CROSS-34A | KIPPS-65E | HATFIELD-34C | HORNSEY-34B | KINGS CROSS-34A | PARKHEAD-65C | KIPPS-65E | KIPPS-65E | PARKHEAD-65C |
| Aug-51 | KINGS CROSS-34A | KIPPS-65E | HATFIELD-34C | HORNSEY-34B | KINGS CROSS-34A | 10/51: KIPPS - 65E | 10/51: P'HEAD - 65C | 10/51: P'HEAD - 65C | 10/51: KIPPS - 65E |
| Jan-52 | KINGS CROSS-34A | KIPPS-65E | HATFIELD-34C | HORNSEY-34B | KINGS CROSS-34A | KIPPS-65E | PARKHEAD-65C | PARKHEAD-65C | KIPPS-65E |
| Aug-52 | 9/52: PARKS - 30F | KIPPS-65E | HATFIELD-34C | HORNSEY-34B | KINGS CROSS-34A | 4/52: P'HEAD - 65C | PARKHEAD-65C | 5/52: DAWS - 65D | 4/52: P'HEAD - 65C |
| Jan-53 | PARKESTON-30F | KIPPS-65E | HATFIELD-34C | HORNSEY-34B | KINGS CROSS-34A | PARKHEAD-65C | PARKHEAD-65C | DAWSHOLME-65D | PARKHEAD-65C |
| Aug-53 | PARKESTON-30F | KIPPS-65E | 7/53: KX - 34A | HORNSEY-34B | KINGS CROSS-34A | PARKHEAD-65C | PARKHEAD-65C | DAWSHOLME-65D | PARKHEAD-65C |
| Jan-54 | PARKESTON-30F | KIPPS-65E | 11/53: HAT - 34C | HORNSEY-34B | KINGS CROSS-34A | PARKHEAD-65C | PARKHEAD-65C | DAWSHOLME-65D | PARKHEAD-65C |
| Aug-54 | PARKESTON-30F | 6/54: F'HILL - 61B | 5/54: KX - 34A | HORNSEY-34B | KINGS CROSS-34A | PARKHEAD-65C | PARKHEAD-65C | DAWSHOLME-65D | PARKHEAD-65C |
| Jan-55 | PARKESTON-30F | FERRYHILL-61B | 8/54: HAT - 34C | HORNSEY-34B | KINGS CROSS-34A | PARKHEAD-65C | PARKHEAD-65C | DAWSHOLME-65D | PARKHEAD-65C |
| Aug-55 | PARKESTON-30F | FERRYHILL-61B | HATFIELD-34C | HORNSEY-34B | KINGS CROSS-34A | PARKHEAD-65C | PARKHEAD-65C | DAWSHOLME-65D | PARKHEAD-65C |
| Jan-56 | PARKESTON-30F | FERRYHILL-61B | HATFIELD-34C | HORNSEY-34B | KINGS CROSS-34A | PARKHEAD-65C | PARKHEAD-65C | DAWSHOLME-65D | PARKHEAD-65C |
| Aug-56 | PARKESTON-30F | FERRYHILL-61B | HATFIELD-34C | HORNSEY-34B | KINGS CROSS-34A | PARKHEAD-65C | PARKHEAD-65C | DAWSHOLME-65D | PARKHEAD-65C |
| Jan-57 | 11/56: KX - 34A | 1/57: W/D | HATFIELD-34C | HORNSEY-34B | KINGS CROSS-34A | PARKHEAD-65C | PARKHEAD-65C | DAWSHOLME-65D | 2/57: HWCK - 64G |
| Aug-57 | 4/57: HSEY - 34B | | HATFIELD-34C | HORNSEY-34B | KINGS CROSS-34A | PARKHEAD-65C | PARKHEAD-65C | 9/57: P'HEAD - 65C | HAWICK-64G |
| Jan-58 | HORNSEY-34B | | HATFIELD-34C | HORNSEY-34B | KINGS CROSS-34A | PARKHEAD-65C | PARKHEAD-65C | PARKHEAD-65C | HAWICK-64G |
| Aug-58 | 5/58: W/D | | 6/58: KX - 34A | HORNSEY-34B | KINGS CROSS-34A | PARKHEAD-65C | PARKHEAD-65C | PARKHEAD-65C | HAWICK-64G |
| Jan-59 | | | KINGS CROSS-34A | HORNSEY-34B | KINGS CROSS-34A | PARKHEAD-65C | PARKHEAD-65C | PARKHEAD-65C | HAWICK-64G |
| Aug-59 | | | KINGS CROSS-34A | 6/59: GRAN - 34F | KINGS CROSS-34A | PARKHEAD-65C | PARKHEAD-65C | PARKHEAD-65C | HAWICK-64G |
| Nov-59 | | | 11/59: HSEY - 34B | GRANTHAM-34F | KINGS CROSS-34A | PARKHEAD-65C | 12/59: W/D | PARKHEAD-65C | 11/59: W/D |
| Jan-60 | | | HORNSEY-34B | GRANTHAM-34F | 2/60: NEW.E - 34E | PARKHEAD-65C | | PARKHEAD-65C | |
| Apr-60 | | | HORNSEY-34B | GRANTHAM-34F | NEWENGLAND-34E | 5/60: W/D | | PARKHEAD-65C | |
| Aug-60 | | | HORNSEY-34B | GRANTHAM-34F | NEWENGLAND-34E | | | PARKHEAD-65C | |
| Nov-60 | | | HORNSEY-34B | 11/60: W/D | NEWENGLAND-34E | | | 11/60: W/D | |

| | 69511 | 69512 | 69513 | 69514 | 69515 | 69516 | 69517 | 69518 | 69519 |
|---|---|---|---|---|---|---|---|---|---|
| Aug-50 | PARKHEAD-65C | KINGS CROSS-34A | HORNSEY-34B | PARKHEAD-65C | HITCHIN-34D | HORNSEY-34B | KINGS CROSS-34A | KIPPS-65E | KINGS CROSS-34A |
| Jan-51 | PARKHEAD-65C | KINGS CROSS-34A | HORNSEY-34B | PARKHEAD-65C | HITCHIN-34D | HORNSEY-34B | KINGS CROSS-34A | KIPPS-65E | KINGS CROSS-34A |
| Aug-51 | PARKHEAD-65C | KINGS CROSS-34A | HORNSEY-34B | PARKHEAD-65C | HITCHIN-34D | 9/51: KX - 34A | KINGS CROSS-34A | KIPPS-65E | KINGS CROSS-34A |
| Jan-52 | PARKHEAD-65C | KINGS CROSS-34A | HORNSEY-34B | PARKHEAD-65C | HITCHIN-34D | KINGS CROSS-34A | KINGS CROSS-34A | KIPPS-65E | KINGS CROSS-34A |
| Aug-52 | 4/52: DAWS - 65D | KINGS CROSS-34A | HORNSEY-34B | PARKHEAD-65C | HITCHIN-34D | 6/52: HAT - 34C | KINGS CROSS-34A | KIPPS-65E | KINGS CROSS-34A |
| Jan-53 | DAWSHOLME-65D | KINGS CROSS-34A | HORNSEY-34B | PARKHEAD-65C | HITCHIN-34D | HATFIELD-34C | KINGS CROSS-34A | KIPPS-65E | KINGS CROSS-34A |
| Aug-53 | DAWSHOLME-65D | KINGS CROSS-34A | HORNSEY-34B | PARKHEAD-65C | HITCHIN-34D | 7/53: KX - 34A | KINGS CROSS-34A | KIPPS-65E | KINGS CROSS-34A |
| Jan-54 | DAWSHOLME-65D | KINGS CROSS-34A | HORNSEY-34B | PARKHEAD-65C | HITCHIN-34D | 12/53: HAT - 34C | KINGS CROSS-34A | KIPPS-65E | KINGS CROSS-34A |
| Aug-54 | DAWSHOLME-65D | KINGS CROSS-34A | HORNSEY-34B | PARKHEAD-65C | HITCHIN-34D | 6/54: KX - 34A | KINGS CROSS-34A | KIPPS-65E | KINGS CROSS-34A |
| Jan-55 | DAWSHOLME-65D | KINGS CROSS-34A | HORNSEY-34B | PARKHEAD-65C | HITCHIN-34D | 8/54: HAT - 34C | KINGS CROSS-34A | KIPPS-65E | KINGS CROSS-34A |
| Aug-55 | DAWSHOLME-65D | KINGS CROSS-34A | HORNSEY-34B | 9/55: W/D | HITCHIN-34D | HATFIELD-34C | KINGS CROSS-34A | KIPPS-65E | KINGS CROSS-34A |
| Jan-56 | DAWSHOLME-65D | KINGS CROSS-34A | HORNSEY-34B | | HITCHIN-34D | HATFIELD-34C | KINGS CROSS-34A | KIPPS-65E | KINGS CROSS-34A |
| Aug-56 | DAWSHOLME-65D | KINGS CROSS-34A | HORNSEY-34B | | HITCHIN-34D | HATFIELD-34C | KINGS CROSS-34A | KIPPS-65E | KINGS CROSS-34A |
| Jan-57 | DAWSHOLME-65D | KINGS CROSS-34A | HORNSEY-34B | | HITCHIN-34D | HATFIELD-34C | KINGS CROSS-34A | KIPPS-65E | KINGS CROSS-34A |
| Aug-57 | DAWSHOLME-65D | KINGS CROSS-34A | HORNSEY-34B | | HITCHIN-34D | HATFIELD-34C | KINGS CROSS-34A | KIPPS-65E | KINGS CROSS-34A |
| Jan-58 | DAWSHOLME-65D | KINGS CROSS-34A | HORNSEY-34B | | HITCHIN-34D | 3/58: KX - 34A | KINGS CROSS-34A | KIPPS-65E | 10/57: W/D |
| Aug-58 | DAWSHOLME-65D | KINGS CROSS-34A | HORNSEY-34B | | HITCHIN-34D | KINGS CROSS-34A | 6/58: HSEY - 34B | KIPPS-65E | |
| Jan-59 | DAWSHOLME-65D | KINGS CROSS-34A | HORNSEY-34B | | HITCHIN-34D | 11/58: GRAN - 34F | HORNSEY-34B | KIPPS-65E | |
| Aug-59 | DAWSHOLME-65D | KINGS CROSS-34A | 6/59: NEW.E - 34E | | 7/59: W/D | GRANTHAM-34F | 8/59: W/D | KIPPS-65E | |
| Nov-59 | DAWSHOLME-65D | KINGS CROSS-34A | NEWENGLAND-34E | | | GRANTHAM-34F | | KIPPS-65E | |
| Jan-60 | DAWSHOLME-65D | KINGS CROSS-34A | NEWENGLAND-34E | | | GRANTHAM-34F | | KIPPS-65E | |
| Apr-60 | DAWSHOLME-65D | KINGS CROSS-34A | NEWENGLAND-34E | | | GRANTHAM-34F | | KIPPS-65E | |
| Aug-60 | DAWSHOLME-65D | KINGS CROSS-34A | NEWENGLAND-34E | | | GRANTHAM-34F | | KIPPS-65E | |
| Nov-60 | DAWSHOLME-65D | 10/60: HSEY - 34B | NEWENGLAND-34E | | | GRANTHAM-34F | | KIPPS-65E | |

| | 69520 | 69521 | 69522 | 69523 | 69524 | 69525 | 69526 | 69527 | 69528 |
|---|---|---|---|---|---|---|---|---|---|
| Aug-50 | KINGS CROSS - 34A | KINGS CROSS - 34A | HORNSEY - 34B | KINGS CROSS - 34A | KINGS CROSS - 34A | KINGS CROSS - 34A | KINGS CROSS - 34A | KINGS CROSS - 34A | KINGS CROSS - 34A |
| Jan-51 | KINGS CROSS - 34A | KINGS CROSS - 34A | HORNSEY - 34B | KINGS CROSS - 34A | KINGS CROSS - 34A | KINGS CROSS - 34A | KINGS CROSS - 34A | KINGS CROSS - 34A | KINGS CROSS - 34A |
| Aug-51 | KINGS CROSS - 34A | KINGS CROSS - 34A | 9/51: KX - 34A | KINGS CROSS - 34A | KINGS CROSS - 34A | KINGS CROSS - 34A | KINGS CROSS - 34A | KINGS CROSS - 34A | KINGS CROSS - 34A |
| Jan-52 | KINGS CROSS - 34A | KINGS CROSS - 34A | KINGS CROSS - 34A | KINGS CROSS - 34A | KINGS CROSS - 34A | KINGS CROSS - 34A | KINGS CROSS - 34A | KINGS CROSS - 34A | KINGS CROSS - 34A |
| Aug-52 | KINGS CROSS - 34A | KINGS CROSS - 34A | KINGS CROSS - 34A | KINGS CROSS - 34A | KINGS CROSS - 34A | KINGS CROSS - 34A | KINGS CROSS - 34A | KINGS CROSS - 34A | KINGS CROSS - 34A |
| Jan-53 | KINGS CROSS - 34A | KINGS CROSS - 34A | 10/52: HSEY - 34B | KINGS CROSS - 34A | KINGS CROSS - 34A | KINGS CROSS - 34A | KINGS CROSS - 34A | KINGS CROSS - 34A | KINGS CROSS - 34A |
| Aug-53 | KINGS CROSS - 34A | KINGS CROSS - 34A | HORNSEY - 34B | KINGS CROSS - 34A | KINGS CROSS - 34A | KINGS CROSS - 34A | KINGS CROSS - 34A | KINGS CROSS - 34A | KINGS CROSS - 34A |
| Jan-54 | KINGS CROSS - 34A | KINGS CROSS - 34A | HORNSEY - 34B | KINGS CROSS - 34A | KINGS CROSS - 34A | KINGS CROSS - 34A | KINGS CROSS - 34A | KINGS CROSS - 34A | KINGS CROSS - 34A |
| Aug-54 | KINGS CROSS - 34A | KINGS CROSS - 34A | HORNSEY - 34B | KINGS CROSS - 34A | KINGS CROSS - 34A | KINGS CROSS - 34A | KINGS CROSS - 34A | KINGS CROSS - 34A | KINGS CROSS - 34A |
| Jan-55 | KINGS CROSS - 34A | KINGS CROSS - 34A | HORNSEY - 34B | KINGS CROSS - 34A | KINGS CROSS - 34A | KINGS CROSS - 34A | KINGS CROSS - 34A | KINGS CROSS - 34A | KINGS CROSS - 34A |
| Aug-55 | KINGS CROSS - 34A | KINGS CROSS - 34A | HORNSEY - 34B | KINGS CROSS - 34A | KINGS CROSS - 34A | KINGS CROSS - 34A | KINGS CROSS - 34A | KINGS CROSS - 34A | KINGS CROSS - 34A |
| Jan-56 | KINGS CROSS - 34A | KINGS CROSS - 34A | HORNSEY - 34B | KINGS CROSS - 34A | KINGS CROSS - 34A | KINGS CROSS - 34A | KINGS CROSS - 34A | KINGS CROSS - 34A | KINGS CROSS - 34A |
| Aug-56 | KINGS CROSS - 34A | KINGS CROSS - 34A | HORNSEY - 34B | KINGS CROSS - 34A | KINGS CROSS - 34A | KINGS CROSS - 34A | KINGS CROSS - 34A | KINGS CROSS - 34A | KINGS CROSS - 34A |
| Jan-57 | KINGS CROSS - 34A | KINGS CROSS - 34A | HORNSEY - 34B | KINGS CROSS - 34A | KINGS CROSS - 34A | KINGS CROSS - 34A | KINGS CROSS - 34A | KINGS CROSS - 34A | KINGS CROSS - 34A |
| Aug-57 | KINGS CROSS - 34A | KINGS CROSS - 34A | HORNSEY - 34B | KINGS CROSS - 34A | KINGS CROSS - 34A | KINGS CROSS - 34A | KINGS CROSS - 34A | KINGS CROSS - 34A | KINGS CROSS - 34A |
| Jan-58 | KINGS CROSS - 34A | KINGS CROSS - 34A | HORNSEY - 34B | KINGS CROSS - 34A | KINGS CROSS - 34A | 10/57: HSEY - 34B | KINGS CROSS - 34A | KINGS CROSS - 34A | KINGS CROSS - 34A |
| Aug-58 | KINGS CROSS - 34A | KINGS CROSS - 34A | HORNSEY - 34B | KINGS CROSS - 34A | KINGS CROSS - 34A | 8/58: KX - 34A | KINGS CROSS - 34A | 6/58: W/D | KINGS CROSS - 34A |
| Jan-59 | KINGS CROSS - 34A | KINGS CROSS - 34A | HORNSEY - 34B | KINGS CROSS - 34A | KINGS CROSS - 34A | 3/59: W/D | KINGS CROSS - 34A | | KINGS CROSS - 34A |
| Aug-59 | KINGS CROSS - 34A | 8/59: NEW.E - 34E | 6/59: HIT - 34D | KINGS CROSS - 34A | KINGS CROSS - 34A | | 8/59: W/D | | KINGS CROSS - 34A |
| Nov-59 | 11/59: HSEY - 34B | NEWENGLAND - 34E | HITCHIN - 34D | KINGS CROSS - 34A | 11/59: W/D | | | | KINGS CROSS - 34A |
| Jan-60 | HORNSEY - 34B | NEWENGLAND - 34E | HITCHIN - 34D | KINGS CROSS - 34A | | | | | KINGS CROSS - 34A |
| Apr-60 | HORNSEY - 34B | NEWENGLAND - 34E | 3/60: W/D | KINGS CROSS - 34A | | | | | 3/60: W/D |
| Aug-60 | HORNSEY - 34B | NEWENGLAND - 34E | | KINGS CROSS - 34A | | | | | |
| Nov-60 | HORNSEY - 34B | NEWENGLAND - 34E | | KINGS CROSS - 34A | | | | | |

| | 69529 | 69530 | 69531 | 69532 | 69533 | 69534 | 69535 | 69536 | 69537 |
|---|---|---|---|---|---|---|---|---|---|
| Aug-50 | KINGS CROSS - 34A | HORNSEY - 34B | HORNSEY - 34B | KINGS CROSS - 34A | HORNSEY - 34B | HATFIELD - 34C | KINGS CROSS - 34A | KINGS CROSS - 34A | HATFIELD - 34C |
| Jan-51 | KINGS CROSS - 34A | HORNSEY - 34B | HORNSEY - 34B | KINGS CROSS - 34A | HORNSEY - 34B | HATFIELD - 34C | KINGS CROSS - 34A | KINGS CROSS - 34A | HATFIELD - 34C |
| Aug-51 | KINGS CROSS - 34A | HORNSEY - 34B | HORNSEY - 34B | KINGS CROSS - 34A | HORNSEY - 34B | HATFIELD - 34C | KINGS CROSS - 34A | KINGS CROSS - 34A | HATFIELD - 34C |
| Jan-52 | KINGS CROSS - 34A | HORNSEY - 34B | HORNSEY - 34B | KINGS CROSS - 34A | HORNSEY - 34B | HATFIELD - 34C | KINGS CROSS - 34A | KINGS CROSS - 34A | HATFIELD - 34C |
| Aug-52 | KINGS CROSS - 34A | HORNSEY - 34B | HORNSEY - 34B | KINGS CROSS - 34A | HORNSEY - 34B | HATFIELD - 34C | KINGS CROSS - 34A | KINGS CROSS - 34A | HATFIELD - 34C |
| Jan-53 | KINGS CROSS - 34A | HORNSEY - 34B | HORNSEY - 34B | KINGS CROSS - 34A | HORNSEY - 34B | HATFIELD - 34C | KINGS CROSS - 34A | KINGS CROSS - 34A | HATFIELD - 34C |
| Aug-53 | KINGS CROSS - 34A | HORNSEY - 34B | HORNSEY - 34B | KINGS CROSS - 34A | HORNSEY - 34B | HATFIELD - 34C | KINGS CROSS - 34A | KINGS CROSS - 34A | HATFIELD - 34C |
| Jan-54 | KINGS CROSS - 34A | HORNSEY - 34B | HORNSEY - 34B | KINGS CROSS - 34A | HORNSEY - 34B | HATFIELD - 34C | KINGS CROSS - 34A | KINGS CROSS - 34A | HATFIELD - 34C |
| Aug-54 | KINGS CROSS - 34A | HORNSEY - 34B | HORNSEY - 34B | KINGS CROSS - 34A | HORNSEY - 34B | 1/54: KX - 34A | KINGS CROSS - 34A | KINGS CROSS - 34A | 1/54: HSEY - 34B |
| Jan-55 | KINGS CROSS - 34A | HORNSEY - 34B | HORNSEY - 34B | KINGS CROSS - 34A | HORNSEY - 34B | 3/54: HAT - 34C | KINGS CROSS - 34A | KINGS CROSS - 34A | HORNSEY - 34B |
| Aug-55 | KINGS CROSS - 34A | HORNSEY - 34B | HORNSEY - 34B | KINGS CROSS - 34A | HORNSEY - 34B | HATFIELD - 34C | KINGS CROSS - 34A | KINGS CROSS - 34A | HORNSEY - 34B |
| Jan-56 | KINGS CROSS - 34A | HORNSEY - 34B | HORNSEY - 34B | KINGS CROSS - 34A | HORNSEY - 34B | HATFIELD - 34C | KINGS CROSS - 34A | KINGS CROSS - 34A | HORNSEY - 34B |
| Aug-56 | KINGS CROSS - 34A | HORNSEY - 34B | HORNSEY - 34B | KINGS CROSS - 34A | HORNSEY - 34B | HATFIELD - 34C | KINGS CROSS - 34A | KINGS CROSS - 34A | HORNSEY - 34B |
| Jan-57 | KINGS CROSS - 34A | HORNSEY - 34B | HORNSEY - 34B | KINGS CROSS - 34A | HORNSEY - 34B | HATFIELD - 34C | KINGS CROSS - 34A | KINGS CROSS - 34A | HORNSEY - 34B |
| Aug-57 | KINGS CROSS - 34A | HORNSEY - 34B | HORNSEY - 34B | KINGS CROSS - 34A | HORNSEY - 34B | HATFIELD - 34C | KINGS CROSS - 34A | KINGS CROSS - 34A | HORNSEY - 34B |
| Jan-58 | KINGS CROSS - 34A | HORNSEY - 34B | HORNSEY - 34B | KINGS CROSS - 34A | HORNSEY - 34B | HATFIELD - 34C | KINGS CROSS - 34A | KINGS CROSS - 34A | HORNSEY - 34B |
| Aug-58 | KINGS CROSS - 34A | HORNSEY - 34B | HORNSEY - 34B | KINGS CROSS - 34A | HORNSEY - 34B | HATFIELD - 34C | KINGS CROSS - 34A | KINGS CROSS - 34A | HORNSEY - 34B |
| Jan-59 | KINGS CROSS - 34A | HORNSEY - 34B | 1/59: HIT - 34D | KINGS CROSS - 34A | HORNSEY - 34B | 6/58: HSEY - 34B | KINGS CROSS - 34A | KINGS CROSS - 34A | HORNSEY - 34B |
| Aug-59 | KINGS CROSS - 34A | HORNSEY - 34B | 4/59: HAT - 34C | 6/59: W/D | HORNSEY - 34B | 2/59: W/D | KINGS CROSS - 34A | 1/59: HIT - 34D | HORNSEY - 34B |
| Nov-59 | KINGS CROSS - 34A | HORNSEY - 34B | HATFIELD - 34C | | 11/59: KX - 34A | | KINGS CROSS - 34A | | 4/59: W/D |
| Jan-60 | KINGS CROSS - 34A | 1/60: KX - 34A | HATFIELD - 34C | | KINGS CROSS - 34A | | KINGS CROSS - 34A | | |
| Apr-60 | KINGS CROSS - 34A | KINGS CROSS - 34A | HATFIELD - 34C | | KINGS CROSS - 34A | | KINGS CROSS - 34A | | |
| Aug-60 | KINGS CROSS - 34A | KINGS CROSS - 34A | 6/60 : GRAN - 34F | | KINGS CROSS - 34A | | KINGS CROSS - 34A | | |
| Nov-60 | KINGS CROSS - 34A | KINGS CROSS - 34A | GRANTHAM - 34F | | KINGS CROSS - 34A | | KINGS CROSS - 34A | | |

| | 69538 | 69539 | 69540 | 69541 | 69542 | 69543 | 69544 | 69545 | 69546 |
|---|---|---|---|---|---|---|---|---|---|
| Aug-50 | KINGS CROSS - 34A | KINGS CROSS - 34A | KINGS CROSS - 34A | KINGS CROSS - 34A | KINGS CROSS - 34A | KINGS CROSS - 34A | KINGS CROSS - 34A | KINGS CROSS - 34A | KINGS CROSS - 34A |
| Jan-51 | KINGS CROSS - 34A | KINGS CROSS - 34A | KINGS CROSS - 34A | KINGS CROSS - 34A | KINGS CROSS - 34A | KINGS CROSS - 34A | KINGS CROSS - 34A | KINGS CROSS - 34A | KINGS CROSS - 34A |
| Aug-51 | KINGS CROSS - 34A | KINGS CROSS - 34A | KINGS CROSS - 34A | KINGS CROSS - 34A | KINGS CROSS - 34A | KINGS CROSS - 34A | KINGS CROSS - 34A | KINGS CROSS - 34A | KINGS CROSS - 34A |
| Jan-52 | KINGS CROSS - 34A | KINGS CROSS - 34A | KINGS CROSS - 34A | KINGS CROSS - 34A | KINGS CROSS - 34A | KINGS CROSS - 34A | KINGS CROSS - 34A | KINGS CROSS - 34A | KINGS CROSS - 34A |
| Aug-52 | KINGS CROSS - 34A | KINGS CROSS - 34A | KINGS CROSS - 34A | KINGS CROSS - 34A | KINGS CROSS - 34A | KINGS CROSS - 34A | KINGS CROSS - 34A | KINGS CROSS - 34A | KINGS CROSS - 34A |
| Jan-53 | KINGS CROSS - 34A | KINGS CROSS - 34A | KINGS CROSS - 34A | KINGS CROSS - 34A | KINGS CROSS - 34A | KINGS CROSS - 34A | KINGS CROSS - 34A | KINGS CROSS - 34A | KINGS CROSS - 34A |
| Aug-53 | KINGS CROSS - 34A | KINGS CROSS - 34A | KINGS CROSS - 34A | KINGS CROSS - 34A | KINGS CROSS - 34A | KINGS CROSS - 34A | KINGS CROSS - 34A | KINGS CROSS - 34A | KINGS CROSS - 34A |
| Jan-54 | KINGS CROSS - 34A | KINGS CROSS - 34A | KINGS CROSS - 34A | KINGS CROSS - 34A | KINGS CROSS - 34A | KINGS CROSS - 34A | KINGS CROSS - 34A | KINGS CROSS - 34A | KINGS CROSS - 34A |
| Aug-54 | KINGS CROSS - 34A | KINGS CROSS - 34A | KINGS CROSS - 34A | KINGS CROSS - 34A | KINGS CROSS - 34A | KINGS CROSS - 34A | KINGS CROSS - 34A | KINGS CROSS - 34A | KINGS CROSS - 34A |
| Jan-55 | KINGS CROSS - 34A | KINGS CROSS - 34A | KINGS CROSS - 34A | KINGS CROSS - 34A | KINGS CROSS - 34A | KINGS CROSS - 34A | KINGS CROSS - 34A | KINGS CROSS - 34A | KINGS CROSS - 34A |
| Aug-55 | KINGS CROSS - 34A | KINGS CROSS - 34A | KINGS CROSS - 34A | KINGS CROSS - 34A | KINGS CROSS - 34A | KINGS CROSS - 34A | KINGS CROSS - 34A | KINGS CROSS - 34A | KINGS CROSS - 34A |
| Jan-56 | KINGS CROSS - 34A | KINGS CROSS - 34A | KINGS CROSS - 34A | KINGS CROSS - 34A | KINGS CROSS - 34A | KINGS CROSS - 34A | KINGS CROSS - 34A | KINGS CROSS - 34A | KINGS CROSS - 34A |
| Aug-56 | KINGS CROSS - 34A | KINGS CROSS - 34A | KINGS CROSS - 34A | KINGS CROSS - 34A | KINGS CROSS - 34A | KINGS CROSS - 34A | KINGS CROSS - 34A | KINGS CROSS - 34A | KINGS CROSS - 34A |
| Jan-57 | KINGS CROSS - 34A | KINGS CROSS - 34A | KINGS CROSS - 34A | KINGS CROSS - 34A | KINGS CROSS - 34A | KINGS CROSS - 34A | KINGS CROSS - 34A | KINGS CROSS - 34A | KINGS CROSS - 34A |
| Aug-57 | KINGS CROSS - 34A | KINGS CROSS - 34A | KINGS CROSS - 34A | 10/57: HSEY - 34B | KINGS CROSS - 34A | KINGS CROSS - 34A | KINGS CROSS - 34A | KINGS CROSS - 34A | KINGS CROSS - 34A |
| Jan-58 | KINGS CROSS - 34A | KINGS CROSS - 34A | KINGS CROSS - 34A | 11/57 : KX - 34A | KINGS CROSS - 34A | KINGS CROSS - 34A | KINGS CROSS - 34A | KINGS CROSS - 34A | KINGS CROSS - 34A |
| Aug-58 | KINGS CROSS - 34A | KINGS CROSS - 34A | KINGS CROSS - 34A | KINGS CROSS - 34A | KINGS CROSS - 34A | KINGS CROSS - 34A | KINGS CROSS - 34A | KINGS CROSS - 34A | KINGS CROSS - 34A |
| Jan-59 | KINGS CROSS - 34A | KINGS CROSS - 34A | 1/59: HIT - 34D | KINGS CROSS - 34A | KINGS CROSS - 34A | KINGS CROSS - 34A | 12/58: W/D | KINGS CROSS - 34A | KINGS CROSS - 34A |
| Aug-59 | KINGS CROSS - 34A | 7/59: W/D | 6/59: NEW.E - 34E | 8/59: W/D | 4/59: W/D | KINGS CROSS - 34A | | 7/59: W/D | KINGS CROSS - 34A |
| Nov-59 | KINGS CROSS - 34A | | NEWENGLAND - 34E | | | KINGS CROSS - 34A | | | KINGS CROSS - 34A |
| Jan-60 | KINGS CROSS - 34A | | NEWENGLAND - 34E | | | KINGS CROSS - 34A | | | KINGS CROSS - 34A |
| Apr-60 | KINGS CROSS - 34A | | NEWENGLAND - 34E | | | KINGS CROSS - 34A | | | KINGS CROSS - 34A |
| Aug-60 | KINGS CROSS - 34A | | 8/60: W/D | | | KINGS CROSS - 34A | | | KINGS CROSS - 34A |
| Nov-60 | KINGS CROSS - 34A | | | | | 10/60: HSEY - 34B | | | KINGS CROSS - 34A |

| | 69547 | 69548 | 69549 | 69550 | 69551 | 69552 | 69553 | 69554 | 69555 |
|---|---|---|---|---|---|---|---|---|---|
| Aug-50 | HORNSEY - 34B | KINGS CROSS - 34A | KINGS CROSS - 34A | COLWICK - 38A | HATFIELD - 34C | COLWICK - 38A | PARKHEAD - 65C | HATFIELD - 34C | COLWICK - 38A |
| Jan-51 | HORNSEY - 34B | KINGS CROSS - 34A | KINGS CROSS - 34A | 4/51: KX - 34A | HATFIELD - 34C | COLWICK - 38A | PARKHEAD - 65C | HATFIELD - 34C | 4/51: KX - 34A |
| Aug-51 | HORNSEY - 34B | KINGS CROSS - 34A | KINGS CROSS - 34A | 5/51: HAT - 34C | HATFIELD - 34C | 5/51: HAT - 34C | 10/51: KIPPS - 65C | HATFIELD - 34C | 5/51: HAT - 34C |
| Jan-52 | HORNSEY - 34B | KINGS CROSS - 34A | KINGS CROSS - 34A | HATFIELD - 34C | HATFIELD - 34C | 6/52: KX - 34A | 4/52: P'HEAD - 65C | HATFIELD - 34C | HATFIELD - 34C |
| Aug-52 | HORNSEY - 34B | KINGS CROSS - 34A | KINGS CROSS - 34A | 9/52: COL - 30E | 9/52: PARKS - 30F | 9/52: PARKS - 30F | 5/52: DAWS - 65D | HATFIELD - 34C | 9/52: COL - 30E |
| Jan-53 | HORNSEY - 34B | KINGS CROSS - 34A | KINGS CROSS - 34A | 3/53: STRAT - 30A | PARKESTON - 30F | PARKESTON - 30F | DAWSHOLME - 65D | HATFIELD - 34C | COLCHESTER - 30E |
| Aug-53 | HORNSEY - 34B | KINGS CROSS - 34A | KINGS CROSS - 34A | STRATFORD - 30A | PARKESTON - 30F | PARKESTON - 30F | DAWSHOLME - 65D | 7/53: KX - 34A | COLCHESTER - 30E |
| Jan-54 | HORNSEY - 34B | KINGS CROSS - 34A | KINGS CROSS - 34A | STRATFORD - 30A | PARKESTON - 30F | PARKESTON - 30F | DAWSHOLME - 65D | 2/54: HAT - 34C | COLCHESTER - 30E |
| Aug-54 | HORNSEY - 34B | KINGS CROSS - 34A | KINGS CROSS - 34A | STRATFORD - 30A | PARKESTON - 30F | PARKESTON - 30F | DAWSHOLME - 65D | HATFIELD - 34C | COLCHESTER - 30E |
| Jan-55 | HORNSEY - 34B | KINGS CROSS - 34A | KINGS CROSS - 34A | STRATFORD - 30A | PARKESTON - 30F | PARKESTON - 30F | DAWSHOLME - 65D | HATFIELD - 34C | COLCHESTER - 30E |
| Aug-55 | HORNSEY - 34B | KINGS CROSS - 34A | KINGS CROSS - 34A | STRATFORD - 30A | PARKESTON - 30F | PARKESTON - 30F | DAWSHOLME - 65D | HATFIELD - 34C | 11/55: HSEY - 34B |
| Jan-56 | 11/55: HAT - 34C | KINGS CROSS - 34A | KINGS CROSS - 34A | STRATFORD - 30A | PARKESTON - 30F | PARKESTON - 30F | DAWSHOLME - 65D | 11/55: HSEY - 34B | 12/55: COL - 30E |
| Aug-56 | HATFIELD - 34C | KINGS CROSS - 34A | KINGS CROSS - 34A | 10/56: KX - 34A | PARKESTON - 30F | PARKESTON - 30F | DAWSHOLME - 65D | HORNSEY - 34B | 10/56: KX - 34A |
| Jan-57 | HATFIELD - 34C | KINGS CROSS - 34A | KINGS CROSS - 34A | KINGS CROSS - 34A | 11/56: K.X. - 34A | 11/56: K.X. - 34A | DAWSHOLME - 65D | HORNSEY - 34B | KINGS CROSS - 34A |
| Aug-57 | HATFIELD - 34C | 10/57: HSEY - 34B | KINGS CROSS - 34A | 7/57: HSEY - 34B | 6/57: HSEY - 34B | 6/57: HSEY - 34B | DAWSHOLME - 65D | HORNSEY - 34B | 4/57: HSEY - 34B |
| Jan-58 | HATFIELD - 34C | 11/57 : KX - 34A | KINGS CROSS - 34A | HORNSEY - 34B | HORNSEY - 34B | HORNSEY - 34B | DAWSHOLME - 65D | HORNSEY - 34B | HORNSEY - 34B |
| Aug-58 | HATFIELD - 34C | 12/58: NEW.E - 34E | KINGS CROSS - 34A | 9/58: W/D | HORNSEY - 34B | HORNSEY - 34B | DAWSHOLME - 65D | 6/58: W/D | HORNSEY - 34B |
| Jan-59 | HATFIELD - 34C | 1/59: HIT - 34D | KINGS CROSS - 34A | | 12/58: W/D | 11/58: GRAN - 34F | DAWSHOLME - 65D | | HORNSEY - 34B |
| Aug-59 | 6/59: W/D | 7/59: W/D | KINGS CROSS - 34A | | | GRANTHAM - 34F | DAWSHOLME - 65D | | 4/59: W/D |
| Nov-59 | | | KINGS CROSS - 34A | | | GRANTHAM - 34F | 12/59: W/D | | |
| Jan-60 | | | KINGS CROSS - 34A | | | GRANTHAM - 34F | | | |
| Apr-60 | | | KINGS CROSS - 34A | | | GRANTHAM - 34F | | | |
| Aug-60 | | | 6/60: GRAN - 34F | | | GRANTHAM - 34F | | | |
| Nov-60 | | | GRANTHAM - 34F | | | GRANTHAM - 34F | | | |

*Whilst the N2 0-6-2T Met Tanks dominated the GN inner-suburban service, local workings from Kings Cross to Hitchin and beyond tended to be worked by L1 2-6-4T's or B1 4-6-0's although Hitchin had a pair of N2's on its books for a daily passenger trip to and from Sandy each day. 69561 and 69552, behind, had been allocated to Parkeston for working the Harwich - Manningtree locals but were replaced by N7's in 1956 and recalled to the Great Northern when withdrawals threatened the number of engines available for the suburban services. Neither engine had condensing gear and 69561 went to Hitchin in mid-1957 whilst 69552 was sent to Hornsey for ECS workings to and from Kings Cross. The two engines, which are seen above at Hitchin in 1957, were reunited late in the decade when they were transferred to Grantham following dieselisation of the Kings Cross division.*

*Apart from the A5 engines built for the North East in 1925, the NER. operated two classes of 4-6-2 passenger tanks both of which had been rebuilt from other wheel arrangements. The earlier of the two were the ten-strong A6 locomotives which had been introduced as 4-6-0T's in 1907 but rebuilt as 4-6-2T's in 1914 to increase their coal capacity. The more numerous (45) A8 4-6-2T's appeared in 1913 as 4-4-4T's and were converted from 1931 largely as a measure to improve their stability. Both classes (together with the A5's) tended to operate on the severely graded secondary routes of the NER which were posing a strain on the G5 0-4-4T's. A8 69888 waits to leave Hartlepool with the 17.48 empty stock to West Hartlepool in 1954. Regular services had been withdrawn between the two Hartlepool stations in 1947 although unadvertised school and workmens trains continued to run until 1964.*

| | 69556 | 69557 | 69558 | 69559 | 69560 | 69561 | 69562 | 69563 | 69564 |
|---|---|---|---|---|---|---|---|---|---|
| Aug-50 | HORNSEY - 34B | HITCHIN - 34D | HATFIELD - 34C | HATFIELD - 34C | W.HALSE - 38E | KINGS CROSS - 34A | PARKHEAD - 65C | KIPPS - 65E | PARKHEAD - 65C |
| Jan-51 | HORNSEY - 34B | HITCHIN - 34D | HATFIELD - 34C | HATFIELD - 34C | W.HALSE - 38E | KINGS CROSS - 34A | PARKHEAD - 65C | 10/50: EBRO(SM) - 64A | PARKHEAD - 65C |
| Aug-51 | HORNSEY - 34B | HITCHIN - 34D | HATFIELD - 34C | HATFIELD - 34C | 4/51: HAT - 34C | 8/51: PARKS - 30F | PARKHEAD - 65C | 11/50: KIPPS - 65E | PARKHEAD - 65C |
| Jan-52 | HORNSEY - 34B | HITCHIN - 34D | HATFIELD - 34C | HATFIELD - 34C | 9/51: KX - 34A | PARKESTON - 30F | PARKHEAD - 65C | KIPPS - 65E | PARKHEAD - 65C |
| Aug-52 | HORNSEY - 34B | HITCHIN - 34D | 9/52: COL - 30E | 9/52: STRAT - 30A | KINGS CROSS - 34A | PARKESTON - 30F | PARKHEAD - 65C | KIPPS - 65E | PARKHEAD - 65C |
| Jan-53 | HORNSEY - 34B | HITCHIN - 34D | COLCHESTER - 30E | STRATFORD - 30A | 10/52: HSEY - 34B | PARKESTON - 30F | PARKHEAD - 65C | 12/52: P'HEAD - 65C | PARKHEAD - 65C |
| Aug-53 | HORNSEY - 34B | HITCHIN - 34D | COLCHESTER - 30E | STRATFORD - 30A | HORNSEY - 34B | PARKESTON - 30F | PARKHEAD - 65C | PARKHEAD - 65C | PARKHEAD - 65C |
| Jan-54 | HORNSEY - 34B | HITCHIN - 34D | COLCHESTER - 30E | STRATFORD - 30A | HORNSEY - 34B | PARKESTON - 30F | PARKHEAD - 65C | PARKHEAD - 65C | PARKHEAD - 65C |
| Aug-54 | HORNSEY - 34B | HITCHIN - 34D | COLCHESTER - 30E | STRATFORD - 30A | HORNSEY - 34B | PARKESTON - 30F | PARKHEAD - 65C | PARKHEAD - 65C | PARKHEAD - 65C |
| Jan-55 | HORNSEY - 34B | HITCHIN - 34D | COLCHESTER - 30E | STRATFORD - 30A | HORNSEY - 34B | PARKESTON - 30F | PARKHEAD - 65C | PARKHEAD - 65C | PARKHEAD - 65C |
| Aug-55 | HORNSEY - 34B | HITCHIN - 34D | COLCHESTER - 30E | STRATFORD - 30A | HORNSEY - 34B | PARKESTON - 30F | PARKHEAD - 65C | PARKHEAD - 65C | PARKHEAD - 65C |
| Jan-56 | HORNSEY - 34B | HITCHIN - 34D | COLCHESTER - 30E | STRATFORD - 30A | HORNSEY - 34B | PARKESTON - 30F | 1/56: W/D | PARKHEAD - 65C | PARKHEAD - 65C |
| Aug-56 | HORNSEY - 34B | HITCHIN - 34D | 8/56: KX - 34A | 8/56: KX - 34A | HORNSEY - 34B | PARKESTON - 30F | | PARKHEAD - 65C | PARKHEAD - 65C |
| Jan-57 | HORNSEY - 34B | HITCHIN - 34D | KINGS CROSS - 34A | KINGS CROSS - 34A | HORNSEY - 34B | 11/56: KX - 34A | | PARKHEAD - 65C | PARKHEAD - 65C |
| Aug-57 | HORNSEY - 34B | 5/57: W/D | 5/57: W/D | 6/57: W/D | HORNSEY - 34B | 6/57: HIT - 34D | | PARKHEAD - 65C | 9/57: CANAL - 68E |
| Jan-58 | HORNSEY - 34B | | | | HORNSEY - 34B | HITCHIN - 34D | | PARKHEAD - 65C | CARLISLE(C) - 68E |
| Aug-58 | HORNSEY - 34B | | | | HORNSEY - 34B | 8/58: HSEY - 34B | | PARKHEAD - 65C | CARLISLE(C) - 12C |
| Jan-59 | HORNSEY - 34B | | | | HORNSEY - 34B | HORNSEY - 34B | | PARKHEAD - 65C | CARLISLE(C) - 12C |
| Aug-59 | HORNSEY - 34B | | | | 6/59: GRAN - 34F | 6/59: GRAN - 34F | | PARKHEAD - 65C | CARLISLE(C) - 12C |
| Nov-59 | 12/59: W/D | | | | GRANTHAM - 34F | GRANTHAM - 34F | | PARKHEAD - 65C | CARLISLE(C) - 12C |
| Jan-60 | | | | | GRANTHAM - 34F | GRANTHAM - 34F | | PARKHEAD - 65C | CARLISLE(C) - 12C |
| Apr-60 | | | | | GRANTHAM - 34F | GRANTHAM - 34F | | 5/60: W/D | CARLISLE(C) - 12C |
| Aug-60 | | | | | GRANTHAM - 34F | GRANTHAM - 34F | | | CARLISLE(C) - 12C |
| Nov-60 | | | | | 11/60: W/D | GRANTHAM - 34F | | | CARLISLE(C) - 12C |

| | 69565 | 69566 | 69567 | 69568 | 69569 | 69570 | 69571 | 69572 | 69573 |
|---|---|---|---|---|---|---|---|---|---|
| Aug-50 | PARKHEAD - 65C | HORNSEY - 34B | HORNSEY - 34B | KINGS CROSS - 34A | KINGS CROSS - 34A | KINGS CROSS - 34A | KINGS CROSS - 34A | KINGS CROSS - 34A | KINGS CROSS - 34A |
| Jan-51 | PARKHEAD - 65C | HORNSEY - 34B | HORNSEY - 34B | KINGS CROSS - 34A | KINGS CROSS - 34A | KINGS CROSS - 34A | KINGS CROSS - 34A | KINGS CROSS - 34A | KINGS CROSS - 34A |
| Aug-51 | PARKHEAD - 65C | 8/51: PARKS - 30F | 9/51: KX - 34A | KINGS CROSS - 34A | KINGS CROSS - 34A | KINGS CROSS - 34A | KINGS CROSS - 34A | KINGS CROSS - 34A | KINGS CROSS - 34A |
| Jan-52 | PARKHEAD - 65C | PARKESTON - 30F | KINGS CROSS - 34A | KINGS CROSS - 34A | KINGS CROSS - 34A | KINGS CROSS - 34A | KINGS CROSS - 34A | KINGS CROSS - 34A | KINGS CROSS - 34A |
| Aug-52 | PARKHEAD - 65C | PARKESTON - 30F | KINGS CROSS - 34A | KINGS CROSS - 34A | KINGS CROSS - 34A | KINGS CROSS - 34A | KINGS CROSS - 34A | KINGS CROSS - 34A | KINGS CROSS - 34A |
| Jan-53 | PARKHEAD - 65C | PARKESTON - 30F | KINGS CROSS - 34A | KINGS CROSS - 34A | KINGS CROSS - 34A | KINGS CROSS - 34A | KINGS CROSS - 34A | KINGS CROSS - 34A | KINGS CROSS - 34A |
| Aug-53 | PARKHEAD - 65C | PARKESTON - 30F | 5/53: HSEY - 34B | KINGS CROSS - 34A | KINGS CROSS - 34A | KINGS CROSS - 34A | KINGS CROSS - 34A | KINGS CROSS - 34A | KINGS CROSS - 34A |
| Jan-54 | PARKHEAD - 65C | PARKESTON - 30F | HORNSEY - 34B | KINGS CROSS - 34A | KINGS CROSS - 34A | KINGS CROSS - 34A | KINGS CROSS - 34A | KINGS CROSS - 34A | KINGS CROSS - 34A |
| Aug-54 | PARKHEAD - 65C | PARKESTON - 30F | HORNSEY - 34B | KINGS CROSS - 34A | KINGS CROSS - 34A | KINGS CROSS - 34A | KINGS CROSS - 34A | KINGS CROSS - 34A | KINGS CROSS - 34A |
| Jan-55 | PARKHEAD - 65C | PARKESTON - 30F | HORNSEY - 34B | KINGS CROSS - 34A | KINGS CROSS - 34A | KINGS CROSS - 34A | KINGS CROSS - 34A | KINGS CROSS - 34A | KINGS CROSS - 34A |
| Aug-55 | PARKHEAD - 65C | PARKESTON - 30F | HORNSEY - 34B | KINGS CROSS - 34A | KINGS CROSS - 34A | KINGS CROSS - 34A | KINGS CROSS - 34A | KINGS CROSS - 34A | KINGS CROSS - 34A |
| Jan-56 | PARKHEAD - 65C | PARKESTON - 30F | HORNSEY - 34B | KINGS CROSS - 34A | KINGS CROSS - 34A | KINGS CROSS - 34A | KINGS CROSS - 34A | KINGS CROSS - 34A | KINGS CROSS - 34A |
| Aug-56 | PARKHEAD - 65C | PARKESTON - 30F | HORNSEY - 34B | KINGS CROSS - 34A | KINGS CROSS - 34A | KINGS CROSS - 34A | KINGS CROSS - 34A | KINGS CROSS - 34A | KINGS CROSS - 34A |
| Jan-57 | PARKHEAD - 65C | 11/56: KX - 34A | HORNSEY - 34B | KINGS CROSS - 34A | KINGS CROSS - 34A | KINGS CROSS - 34A | KINGS CROSS - 34A | KINGS CROSS - 34A | KINGS CROSS - 34A |
| Aug-57 | PARKHEAD - 65C | 6/57: W/D | HORNSEY - 34B | 10/57: HSEY - 34B | KINGS CROSS - 34A | KINGS CROSS - 34A | KINGS CROSS - 34A | 10/57: HSEY - 34B | KINGS CROSS - 34A |
| Jan-58 | PARKHEAD - 65C | | HORNSEY - 34B | 11/57: KX - 34A | KINGS CROSS - 34A | KINGS CROSS - 34A | KINGS CROSS - 34A | HORNSEY - 34B | KINGS CROSS - 34A |
| Aug-58 | 4/58: W/D | | HORNSEY - 34B | KINGS CROSS - 34A | KINGS CROSS - 34A | KINGS CROSS - 34A | KINGS CROSS - 34A | HORNSEY - 34B | KINGS CROSS - 34A |
| Jan-59 | | | HORNSEY - 34B | KINGS CROSS - 34A | 3/59: W/D | KINGS CROSS - 34A | 4/59: HAT - 34C | HORNSEY - 34B | 11/58: W/D |
| Aug-59 | | | 4/59: W/D | KINGS CROSS - 34A | | KINGS CROSS - 34A | 6/59: NEW.E - 34E | HORNSEY - 34B | |
| Nov-59 | | | | KINGS CROSS - 34A | | 12/59: W/D | NEWENGLAND - 34E | 11/59: KX - 34A | |
| Jan-60 | | | | KINGS CROSS - 34A | | | NEWENGLAND - 34E | KINGS CROSS - 34A | |
| Apr-60 | | | | KINGS CROSS - 34A | | | NEWENGLAND - 34E | KINGS CROSS - 34A | |
| Aug-60 | | | | KINGS CROSS - 34A | | | NEWENGLAND - 34E | KINGS CROSS - 34A | |
| Nov-60 | | | | KINGS CROSS - 34A | | | NEWENGLAND - 34E | KINGS CROSS - 34A | |

| | 69574 | 69575 | 69576 | 69577 | 69578 | 69579 | 69580 | 69581 | 69582 |
|---|---|---|---|---|---|---|---|---|---|
| Aug-50 | KINGS CROSS - 34A | KINGS CROSS - 34A | KINGS CROSS - 34A | KINGS CROSS - 34A | KINGS CROSS - 34A | KINGS CROSS - 34A | HATFIELD - 34C | KINGS CROSS - 34A | HATFIELD - 34C |
| Jan-51 | KINGS CROSS - 34A | KINGS CROSS - 34A | KINGS CROSS - 34A | KINGS CROSS - 34A | KINGS CROSS - 34A | KINGS CROSS - 34A | HATFIELD - 34C | KINGS CROSS - 34A | HATFIELD - 34C |
| Aug-51 | KINGS CROSS - 34A | KINGS CROSS - 34A | KINGS CROSS - 34A | KINGS CROSS - 34A | KINGS CROSS - 34A | KINGS CROSS - 34A | HATFIELD - 34C | KINGS CROSS - 34A | HATFIELD - 34C |
| Jan-52 | KINGS CROSS - 34A | KINGS CROSS - 34A | KINGS CROSS - 34A | KINGS CROSS - 34A | KINGS CROSS - 34A | KINGS CROSS - 34A | HATFIELD - 34C | KINGS CROSS - 34A | HATFIELD - 34C |
| Aug-52 | KINGS CROSS - 34A | KINGS CROSS - 34A | KINGS CROSS - 34A | KINGS CROSS - 34A | KINGS CROSS - 34A | KINGS CROSS - 34A | HATFIELD - 34C | KINGS CROSS - 34A | HATFIELD - 34C |
| Jan-53 | KINGS CROSS - 34A | KINGS CROSS - 34A | KINGS CROSS - 34A | KINGS CROSS - 34A | KINGS CROSS - 34A | KINGS CROSS - 34A | HATFIELD - 34C | KINGS CROSS - 34A | HATFIELD - 34C |
| Aug-53 | KINGS CROSS - 34A | KINGS CROSS - 34A | KINGS CROSS - 34A | KINGS CROSS - 34A | KINGS CROSS - 34A | KINGS CROSS - 34A | 12/53: KX - 34A | KINGS CROSS - 34A | HATFIELD - 34C |
| Jan-54 | KINGS CROSS - 34A | KINGS CROSS - 34A | KINGS CROSS - 34A | KINGS CROSS - 34A | KINGS CROSS - 34A | KINGS CROSS - 34A | 1/54: HAT - 34C | KINGS CROSS - 34A | HATFIELD - 34C |
| Aug-54 | KINGS CROSS - 34A | KINGS CROSS - 34A | KINGS CROSS - 34A | KINGS CROSS - 34A | KINGS CROSS - 34A | KINGS CROSS - 34A | 6/54: KX - 34A | KINGS CROSS - 34A | HATFIELD - 34C |
| Jan-55 | KINGS CROSS - 34A | KINGS CROSS - 34A | KINGS CROSS - 34A | KINGS CROSS - 34A | KINGS CROSS - 34A | KINGS CROSS - 34A | 8/54: HAT - 34C | KINGS CROSS - 34A | HATFIELD - 34C |
| Aug-55 | KINGS CROSS - 34A | KINGS CROSS - 34A | KINGS CROSS - 34A | KINGS CROSS - 34A | KINGS CROSS - 34A | KINGS CROSS - 34A | HATFIELD - 34C | KINGS CROSS - 34A | HATFIELD - 34C |
| Jan-56 | KINGS CROSS - 34A | KINGS CROSS - 34A | KINGS CROSS - 34A | KINGS CROSS - 34A | KINGS CROSS - 34A | KINGS CROSS - 34A | HATFIELD - 34C | KINGS CROSS - 34A | HATFIELD - 34C |
| Aug-56 | KINGS CROSS - 34A | KINGS CROSS - 34A | KINGS CROSS - 34A | KINGS CROSS - 34A | KINGS CROSS - 34A | KINGS CROSS - 34A | HATFIELD - 34C | KINGS CROSS - 34A | HATFIELD - 34C |
| Jan-57 | KINGS CROSS - 34A | KINGS CROSS - 34A | KINGS CROSS - 34A | KINGS CROSS - 34A | KINGS CROSS - 34A | KINGS CROSS - 34A | HATFIELD - 34C | KINGS CROSS - 34A | HATFIELD - 34C |
| Aug-57 | KINGS CROSS - 34A | KINGS CROSS - 34A | KINGS CROSS - 34A | KINGS CROSS - 34A | KINGS CROSS - 34A | KINGS CROSS - 34A | HATFIELD - 34C | KINGS CROSS - 34A | HATFIELD - 34C |
| Jan-58 | KINGS CROSS - 34A | KINGS CROSS - 34A | KINGS CROSS - 34A | KINGS CROSS - 34A | KINGS CROSS - 34A | KINGS CROSS - 34A | 3/58: KX - 34A | KINGS CROSS - 34A | HATFIELD - 34C |
| Aug-58 | KINGS CROSS - 34A | KINGS CROSS - 34A | KINGS CROSS - 34A | KINGS CROSS - 34A | KINGS CROSS - 34A | KINGS CROSS - 34A | KINGS CROSS - 34A | KINGS CROSS - 34A | HATFIELD - 34C |
| Jan-59 | KINGS CROSS - 34A | KINGS CROSS - 34A | KINGS CROSS - 34A | 1/59: HAT - 34A | KINGS CROSS - 34A | KINGS CROSS - 34A | KINGS CROSS - 34A | KINGS CROSS - 34A | HATFIELD - 34C |
| Aug-59 | KINGS CROSS - 34A | KINGS CROSS - 34A | 7/59: W/D | 5/59: W/D | KINGS CROSS - 34A | KINGS CROSS - 34A | 8/59: HAT - 34C | KINGS CROSS - 34A | 6/59: NEW.E. - 34E |
| Nov-59 | KINGS CROSS - 34A | KINGS CROSS - 34A | | | KINGS CROSS - 34A | KINGS CROSS - 34A | HATFIELD - 34C | KINGS CROSS - 34A | NEWENGLAND - 34E |
| Jan-60 | KINGS CROSS - 34A | KINGS CROSS - 34A | | | KINGS CROSS - 34A | KINGS CROSS - 34A | HATFIELD - 34C | KINGS CROSS - 34A | NEWENGLAND - 34E |
| Apr-60 | KINGS CROSS - 34A | KINGS CROSS - 34A | | | 3/60: W/D | KINGS CROSS - 34A | HATFIELD - 34C | KINGS CROSS - 34A | NEWENGLAND - 34E |
| Aug-60 | KINGS CROSS - 34A | KINGS CROSS - 34A | | | | 8/60: HSEY - 34B | 6/60: GRAN - 34F | KINGS CROSS - 34A | NEWENGLAND - 34E |
| Nov-60 | KINGS CROSS - 34A | KINGS CROSS - 34A | | | | HORNSEY - 34B | GRANTHAM - 34F | KINGS CROSS - 34A | 10/60: W/D |

| | 69583 | 69584 | 69585 | 69586 | 69587 | 69588 | 69589 | 69590 | 69591 |
|---|---|---|---|---|---|---|---|---|---|
| Aug-50 | KINGS CROSS - 34A | KINGS CROSS - 34A | KINGS CROSS - 34A | HATFIELD - 34C | HATFIELD - 34C | HATFIELD - 34C | KINGS CROSS - 34A | KINGS CROSS - 34A | KINGS CROSS - 34A |
| Jan-51 | KINGS CROSS - 34A | KINGS CROSS - 34A | KINGS CROSS - 34A | HATFIELD - 34C | HATFIELD - 34C | HATFIELD - 34C | KINGS CROSS - 34A | KINGS CROSS - 34A | KINGS CROSS - 34A |
| Aug-51 | KINGS CROSS - 34A | KINGS CROSS - 34A | KINGS CROSS - 34A | HATFIELD - 34C | HATFIELD - 34C | HATFIELD - 34C | KINGS CROSS - 34A | KINGS CROSS - 34A | KINGS CROSS - 34A |
| Jan-52 | KINGS CROSS - 34A | KINGS CROSS - 34A | KINGS CROSS - 34A | HATFIELD - 34C | HATFIELD - 34C | HATFIELD - 34C | KINGS CROSS - 34A | KINGS CROSS - 34A | KINGS CROSS - 34A |
| Aug-52 | KINGS CROSS - 34A | KINGS CROSS - 34A | KINGS CROSS - 34A | HATFIELD - 34C | HATFIELD - 34C | HATFIELD - 34C | KINGS CROSS - 34A | 10/52: HSEY - 34B | KINGS CROSS - 34A |
| Jan-53 | KINGS CROSS - 34A | KINGS CROSS - 34A | KINGS CROSS - 34A | HATFIELD - 34C | HATFIELD - 34C | HATFIELD - 34C | KINGS CROSS - 34A | HORNSEY - 34B | KINGS CROSS - 34A |
| Aug-53 | KINGS CROSS - 34A | KINGS CROSS - 34A | KINGS CROSS - 34A | 7/53: KX - 34A | 11/53: KX - 34A | HATFIELD - 34C | KINGS CROSS - 34A | 5/53: KX - 34A | KINGS CROSS - 34A |
| Jan-54 | KINGS CROSS - 34A | KINGS CROSS - 34A | KINGS CROSS - 34A | 11/53: HAT - 34C | 1/54: HSEY - 34B | 2/54: KX - 34A | KINGS CROSS - 34A | KINGS CROSS - 34A | KINGS CROSS - 34A |
| Aug-54 | KINGS CROSS - 34A | KINGS CROSS - 34A | KINGS CROSS - 34A | HATFIELD - 34C | HORNSEY - 34B | 6/54: HAT - 34C | KINGS CROSS - 34A | KINGS CROSS - 34A | KINGS CROSS - 34A |
| Jan-55 | KINGS CROSS - 34A | KINGS CROSS - 34A | KINGS CROSS - 34A | HATFIELD - 34C | HORNSEY - 34B | HATFIELD - 34C | KINGS CROSS - 34A | KINGS CROSS - 34A | KINGS CROSS - 34A |
| Aug-55 | KINGS CROSS - 34A | KINGS CROSS - 34A | KINGS CROSS - 34A | HATFIELD - 34C | HORNSEY - 34B | HATFIELD - 34C | KINGS CROSS - 34A | KINGS CROSS - 34A | KINGS CROSS - 34A |
| Jan-56 | KINGS CROSS - 34A | KINGS CROSS - 34A | KINGS CROSS - 34A | HATFIELD - 34C | HORNSEY - 34B | HATFIELD - 34C | KINGS CROSS - 34A | KINGS CROSS - 34A | KINGS CROSS - 34A |
| Aug-56 | KINGS CROSS - 34A | KINGS CROSS - 34A | KINGS CROSS - 34A | HATFIELD - 34C | HORNSEY - 34B | HATFIELD - 34C | KINGS CROSS - 34A | KINGS CROSS - 34A | KINGS CROSS - 34A |
| Jan-57 | KINGS CROSS - 34A | KINGS CROSS - 34A | KINGS CROSS - 34A | HATFIELD - 34C | HORNSEY - 34B | HATFIELD - 34C | KINGS CROSS - 34A | KINGS CROSS - 34A | KINGS CROSS - 34A |
| Aug-57 | KINGS CROSS - 34A | KINGS CROSS - 34A | KINGS CROSS - 34A | HATFIELD - 34C | HORNSEY - 34B | HATFIELD - 34C | KINGS CROSS - 34A | 6/57: W/D | KINGS CROSS - 34A |
| Jan-58 | KINGS CROSS - 34A | KINGS CROSS - 34A | KINGS CROSS - 34A | HATFIELD - 34C | HORNSEY - 34B | HATFIELD - 34C | KINGS CROSS - 34A | | KINGS CROSS - 34A |
| Aug-58 | KINGS CROSS - 34A | KINGS CROSS - 34A | KINGS CROSS - 34A | HATFIELD - 34C | HORNSEY - 34B | HATFIELD - 34C | KINGS CROSS - 34A | | KINGS CROSS - 34A |
| Jan-59 | KINGS CROSS - 34A | KINGS CROSS - 34A | KINGS CROSS - 34A | HATFIELD - 34C | HORNSEY - 34B | HATFIELD - 34C | KINGS CROSS - 34A | | 1/59: HAT - 34C |
| Aug-59 | KINGS CROSS - 34A | 7/59: W/D | KINGS CROSS - 34A | HATFIELD - 34C | HORNSEY - 34B | HATFIELD - 34C | KINGS CROSS - 34A | | 8/59: W/D |
| Nov-59 | KINGS CROSS - 34A | | KINGS CROSS - 34A | HATFIELD - 34C | HORNSEY - 34B | HATFIELD - 34C | KINGS CROSS - 34A | | |
| Jan-60 | KINGS CROSS - 34A | | KINGS CROSS - 34A | HATFIELD - 34C | HORNSEY - 34B | HATFIELD - 34C | KINGS CROSS - 34A | | |
| Apr-60 | KINGS CROSS - 34A | | KINGS CROSS - 34A | 4/60: KX - 34A | HORNSEY - 34B | 3/60: W/D | 3/60: W/D | | |
| Aug-60 | KINGS CROSS - 34A | | KINGS CROSS - 34A | KINGS CROSS - 34A | 6/60: W/D | | | | |
| Nov-60 | KINGS CROSS - 34A | | KINGS CROSS - 34A | KINGS CROSS - 34A | | | | | |

| | 69592 | 69593 | 69594 | 69595 | 69596 | N7 0-6-2T (1914) 69600 | 69601 | 69602 | 69603 |
|---|---|---|---|---|---|---|---|---|---|
| Aug-50 | KINGS CROSS - 34A | KINGS CROSS - 34A | HATFIELD - 34C | PARKHEAD - 65C | KIPPS - 65E | STRATFORD - 30A | STRATFORD - 30A | STRATFORD - 30A | STRATFORD - 30A |
| Jan-51 | KINGS CROSS - 34A | KINGS CROSS - 34A | HATFIELD - 34C | PARKHEAD - 65C | KIPPS - 65E | STRATFORD - 30A | STRATFORD - 30A | STRATFORD - 30A | STRATFORD - 30A |
| Aug-51 | KINGS CROSS - 34A | KINGS CROSS - 34A | HATFIELD - 34C | PARKHEAD - 65C | KIPPS - 65E | STRATFORD - 30A | STRATFORD - 30A | STRATFORD - 30A | STRATFORD - 30A |
| Jan-52 | KINGS CROSS - 34A | KINGS CROSS - 34A | HATFIELD - 34C | PARKHEAD - 65C | KIPPS - 65E | STRATFORD - 30A | STRATFORD - 30A | STRATFORD - 30A | STRATFORD - 30A |
| Aug-52 | KINGS CROSS - 34A | KINGS CROSS - 34A | HATFIELD - 34C | PARKHEAD - 65C | KIPPS - 65E | STRATFORD - 30A | STRATFORD - 30A | STRATFORD - 30A | STRATFORD - 30A |
| Jan-53 | KINGS CROSS - 34A | KINGS CROSS - 34A | HATFIELD - 34C | PARKHEAD - 65C | KIPPS - 65E | STRATFORD - 30A | STRATFORD - 30A | STRATFORD - 30A | STRATFORD - 30A |
| Aug-53 | KINGS CROSS - 34A | KINGS CROSS - 34A | HATFIELD - 34C | PARKHEAD - 65C | KIPPS - 65E | STRATFORD - 30A | STRATFORD - 30A | STRATFORD - 30A | STRATFORD - 30A |
| Jan-54 | KINGS CROSS - 34A | KINGS CROSS - 34A | HATFIELD - 34C | PARKHEAD - 65C | KIPPS - 65E | STRATFORD - 30A | STRATFORD - 30A | STRATFORD - 30A | STRATFORD - 30A |
| Aug-54 | KINGS CROSS - 34A | KINGS CROSS - 34A | 4/54: HSEY - 34B | PARKHEAD - 65C | KIPPS - 65E | STRATFORD - 30A | STRATFORD - 30A | STRATFORD - 30A | STRATFORD - 30A |
| Jan-55 | KINGS CROSS - 34A | KINGS CROSS - 34A | HORNSEY - 34B | PARKHEAD - 65C | KIPPS - 65E | STRATFORD - 30A | STRATFORD - 30A | STRATFORD - 30A | STRATFORD - 30A |
| Aug-55 | KINGS CROSS - 34A | KINGS CROSS - 34A | HORNSEY - 34B | PARKHEAD - 65C | KIPPS - 65E | STRATFORD - 30A | STRATFORD - 30A | STRATFORD - 30A | STRATFORD - 30A |
| Jan-56 | KINGS CROSS - 34A | KINGS CROSS - 34A | HORNSEY - 34B | PARKHEAD - 65C | KIPPS - 65E | STRATFORD - 30A | STRATFORD - 30A | STRATFORD - 30A | STRATFORD - 30A |
| Aug-56 | KINGS CROSS - 34A | KINGS CROSS - 34A | HORNSEY - 34B | PARKHEAD - 65C | KIPPS - 65E | STRATFORD - 30A | STRATFORD - 30A | STRATFORD - 30A | STRATFORD - 30A |
| Jan-57 | KINGS CROSS - 34A | KINGS CROSS - 34A | HORNSEY - 34B | PARKHEAD - 65C | KIPPS - 65E | STRATFORD - 30A | STRATFORD - 30A | STRATFORD - 30A | STRATFORD - 30A |
| Aug-57 | KINGS CROSS - 34A | KINGS CROSS - 34A | HORNSEY - 34B | PARKHEAD - 65C | KIPPS - 65E | STRATFORD - 30A | STRATFORD - 30A | STRATFORD - 30A | STRATFORD - 30A |
| Jan-58 | KINGS CROSS - 34A | KINGS CROSS - 34A | HORNSEY - 34B | 10/57: W/D | KIPPS - 65E | STRATFORD - 30A | STRATFORD - 30A | STRATFORD - 30A | STRATFORD - 30A |
| Aug-58 | KINGS CROSS - 34A | KINGS CROSS - 34A | HORNSEY - 34B | | KIPPS - 65E | STRATFORD - 30A | 5/58: W/D | STRATFORD - 30A | STRATFORD - 30A |
| Jan-59 | KINGS CROSS - 34A | KINGS CROSS - 34A | HORNSEY - 34B | | KIPPS - 65E | 2/59: W/D | | STRATFORD - 30A | STRATFORD - 30A |
| Aug-59 | KINGS CROSS - 34A | KINGS CROSS - 34A | 6/59: HIT - 34D | | KIPPS - 65E | | | 7/59: W/D | 7/59: W/D |
| Nov-59 | KINGS CROSS - 34A | KINGS CROSS - 34A | HITCHIN - 34D | | KIPPS - 65E | | | | |
| Jan-60 | KINGS CROSS - 34A | KINGS CROSS - 34A | 12/59: W/D | | KIPPS - 65E | | | | |
| Apr-60 | KINGS CROSS - 34A | KINGS CROSS - 34A | | | KIPPS - 65E | | | | |
| Aug-60 | KINGS CROSS - 34A | KINGS CROSS - 34A | | | KIPPS - 65E | | | | |
| Nov-60 | KINGS CROSS - 34A | KINGS CROSS - 34A | | | | | | | |

| | 69604 | 69605 | 69606 | 69607 | 69608 | 69609 | 69610 | 69611 | 69612 |
|---|---|---|---|---|---|---|---|---|---|
| Aug-50 | STRATFORD - 30A | STRATFORD - 30A | STRATFORD - 30A | STRATFORD - 30A | STRATFORD - 30A | STRATFORD - 30A | STRATFORD - 30A | STRATFORD - 30A | PARKESTON - 30F |
| Jan-51 | STRATFORD - 30A | STRATFORD - 30A | STRATFORD - 30A | STRATFORD - 30A | STRATFORD - 30A | STRATFORD - 30A | STRATFORD - 30A | STRATFORD - 30A | PARKESTON - 30F |
| Aug-51 | STRATFORD - 30A | STRATFORD - 30A | STRATFORD - 30A | STRATFORD - 30A | STRATFORD - 30A | STRATFORD - 30A | STRATFORD - 30A | STRATFORD - 30A | PARKESTON - 30F |
| Jan-52 | STRATFORD - 30A | STRATFORD - 30A | STRATFORD - 30A | STRATFORD - 30A | STRATFORD - 30A | STRATFORD - 30A | STRATFORD - 30A | STRATFORD - 30A | PARKESTON - 30F |
| Aug-52 | STRATFORD - 30A | STRATFORD - 30A | STRATFORD - 30A | STRATFORD - 30A | STRATFORD - 30A | STRATFORD - 30A | STRATFORD - 30A | STRATFORD - 30A | 9/52: STRAT - 30A |
| Jan-53 | STRATFORD - 30A | STRATFORD - 30A | STRATFORD - 30A | STRATFORD - 30A | STRATFORD - 30A | STRATFORD - 30A | STRATFORD - 30A | STRATFORD - 30A | STRATFORD - 30A |
| Aug-53 | STRATFORD - 30A | STRATFORD - 30A | STRATFORD - 30A | STRATFORD - 30A | STRATFORD - 30A | STRATFORD - 30A | STRATFORD - 30A | STRATFORD - 30A | STRATFORD - 30A |
| Jan-54 | STRATFORD - 30A | STRATFORD - 30A | STRATFORD - 30A | STRATFORD - 30A | STRATFORD - 30A | STRATFORD - 30A | STRATFORD - 30A | STRATFORD - 30A | STRATFORD - 30A |
| Aug-54 | STRATFORD - 30A | STRATFORD - 30A | STRATFORD - 30A | STRATFORD - 30A | STRATFORD - 30A | STRATFORD - 30A | STRATFORD - 30A | STRATFORD - 30A | STRATFORD - 30A |
| Jan-55 | STRATFORD - 30A | STRATFORD - 30A | STRATFORD - 30A | STRATFORD - 30A | STRATFORD - 30A | STRATFORD - 30A | STRATFORD - 30A | STRATFORD - 30A | STRATFORD - 30A |
| Aug-55 | STRATFORD - 30A | STRATFORD - 30A | STRATFORD - 30A | STRATFORD - 30A | STRATFORD - 30A | STRATFORD - 30A | STRATFORD - 30A | STRATFORD - 30A | STRATFORD - 30A |
| Jan-56 | STRATFORD - 30A | STRATFORD - 30A | STRATFORD - 30A | STRATFORD - 30A | STRATFORD - 30A | STRATFORD - 30A | STRATFORD - 30A | STRATFORD - 30A | STRATFORD - 30A |
| Aug-56 | STRATFORD - 30A | STRATFORD - 30A | STRATFORD - 30A | STRATFORD - 30A | STRATFORD - 30A | STRATFORD - 30A | STRATFORD - 30A | STRATFORD - 30A | 6/56: HSEY - 34B |
| Jan-57 | STRATFORD - 30A | STRATFORD - 30A | STRATFORD - 30A | STRATFORD - 30A | STRATFORD - 30A | STRATFORD - 30A | STRATFORD - 30A | STRATFORD - 30A | HORNSEY - 34B |
| Aug-57 | STRATFORD - 30A | STRATFORD - 30A | STRATFORD - 30A | STRATFORD - 30A | STRATFORD - 30A | STRATFORD - 30A | STRATFORD - 30A | STRATFORD - 30A | 7/57: COL - 30E |
| Jan-58 | STRATFORD - 30A | STRATFORD - 30A | STRATFORD - 30A | STRATFORD - 30A | STRATFORD - 30A | STRATFORD - 30A | STRATFORD - 30A | STRATFORD - 30A | COLCHESTER - 30E |
| Aug-58 | STRATFORD - 30A | STRATFORD - 30A | 8/58: W/D | 7/58: W/D | 8/58: W/D | 4/58: W/D | STRATFORD - 30A | STRATFORD - 30A | COLCHESTER - 30E |
| Jan-59 | STRATFORD - 30A | 10/58: W/D | | | | | 1/59: W/D | STRATFORD - 30A | COLCHESTER - 30E |
| Aug-59 | 8/59: W/D | | | | | | | STRATFORD - 30A | 8/59: W/D |
| Nov-59 | | | | | | | | STRATFORD - 30A | |
| Jan-60 | | | | | | | | STRATFORD - 30A | |
| Apr-60 | | | | | | | | STRATFORD - 30A | |
| Aug-60 | | | | | | | | STRATFORD - 30A | |
| Nov-60 | | | | | | | | STRATFORD - 30A | |

| | 69613 | 69614 | 69615 | 69616 | 69617 | 69618 | 69619 | 69620 | 69621 |
|---|---|---|---|---|---|---|---|---|---|
| Aug-50 | HATFIELD - 34C | PARKESTON - 30F | HATFIELD - 34C | STRATFORD - 30A | STRATFORD - 30A | STRATFORD - 30A | STRATFORD - 30A | HATFIELD - 34C | PARKESTON - 30F |
| Jan-51 | HATFIELD - 34C | PARKESTCN - 30F | HATFIELD - 34C | STRATFORD - 30A | STRATFORD - 30A | STRATFORD - 30A | STRATFORD - 30A | HATFIELD - 34C | PARKESTON - 30F |
| Aug-51 | 4/51: COLW - 38A | 8/51: STRAT - 30A | 4/51: COLW - 38A | STRATFORD - 30A | STRATFORD - 30A | STRATFORD - 30A | STRATFORD - 30A | 4/51: COLW - 38A | 8/51: STRAT - 30A |
| Jan-52 | 11/51: HAT - 34C | STRATFORD - 30A | COLWICK - 38A | STRATFORD - 30A | STRATFORD - 30A | STRATFORD - 30A | STRATFORD - 30A | COLWICK - 38A | STRATFORD - 30A |
| Aug-52 | HATFIELD - 34C | STRATFORD - 30A | COLWICK - 38A | STRATFORD - 30A | STRATFORD - 30A | STRATFORD - 30A | STRATFORD - 30A | COLWICK - 38A | 7/52: COLW - 38A |
| Jan-53 | HATFIELD - 34C | STRATFORD - 30A | COLWICK - 38A | STRATFORD - 30A | 10/52: HAT - 34C | STRATFORD - 30A | STRATFORD - 30A | COLWICK - 38A | 2/53: W.HALSE - 38E |
| Aug-53 | HATFIELD - 34C | STRATFORD - 30A | COLWICK - 38A | STRATFORD - 30A | HATFIELD - 34C | STRATFORD - 30A | STRATFORD - 30A | COLWICK - 38A | 7/53: COLW - 38A |
| Jan-54 | 12/53: STRAT - 30A | STRATFORD - 30A | COLWICK - 38A | STRATFORD - 30A | 12/53: STRAT - 30A | STRATFORD - 30A | STRATFORD - 30A | COLWICK - 38A | COLWICK - 38A |
| Aug-54 | STRATFORD - 30A | STRATFORD - 30A | 4/54: STRAT - 30A | STRATFORD - 30A | STRATFORD - 30A | STRATFORD - 30A | STRATFORD - 30A | 4/54: STRAT - 30A | 4/54: STRAT - 30A |
| Jan-55 | STRATFORD - 30A | STRATFORD - 30A | STRATFORD - 30A | STRATFORD - 30A | STRATFORD - 30A | STRATFORD - 30A | STRATFORD - 30A | STRATFORD - 30A | STRATFORD - 30A |
| Aug-55 | STRATFORD - 30A | STRATFORD - 30A | STRATFORD - 30A | STRATFORD - 30A | STRATFORD - 30A | STRATFORD - 30A | STRATFORD - 30A | STRATFORD - 30A | STRATFORD - 30A |
| Jan-56 | STRATFORD - 30A | STRATFORD - 30A | STRATFORD - 30A | STRATFORD - 30A | STRATFORD - 30A | 11/55: HSEY - 34B | 11/55: COL - 30E | STRATFORD - 30A | STRATFORD - 30A |
| Aug-56 | STRATFORD - 30A | STRATFORD - 30A | 6/56: HSEY - 34B | STRATFORD - 30A | STRATFORD - 30A | HORNSEY - 34B | 3/56: STRAT - 30A | STRATFORD - 30A | STRATFORD - 30A |
| Jan-57 | STRATFORD - 30A | STRATFORD - 30A | HORNSEY - 34B | 2/57: CAMB - 31A | 2/57: CAMB - 31A | HORNSEY - 34B | 1/57: CAMB - 31A | 1/57: CAMB - 31A | 3/57: LOW - 32C |
| Aug-57 | STRATFORD - 30A | STRATFORD - 30A | 6/57: LOW - 32C | 5/57: BURY - 31E | CAMBRIDGE - 31A | HORNSEY - 34B | CAMBRIDGE - 31A | 5/57: BURY - 31E | LOWESTOFT - 32C |
| Jan-58 | 10/57: COL - 30E | STRATFORD - 30A | LOWESTOFT - 32C | BURYSTEDMUNDS - 31E | 3/58: K.LYNN - 31C | HORNSEY - 34B | CAMBRIDGE - 31A | BURYSTEDMUNDS - 31E | LOWESTOFT - 32C |
| Aug-58 | COLCHESTER - 30E | STRATFORD - 30A | LOWESTOFT - 32C | BURYSTEDMUNDS - 31E | 12/58: STRAT - 30A | HORNSEY - 34B | 6/58: K.LYNN - 31C | 6/58: K.LYNN - 31C | LOWESTOFT - 32C |
| Jan-59 | COLCHESTER - 30E | STRATFORD - 30A | 12/58: STRAT - 30A | 1/59: W/D | 1/59: COL - 30E | 1/59: HAT - 34C | 12/58: STRAT - 30A | 3/59: STRAT - 30A | 9/59: STRAT - 30A |
| Aug-59 | 10/59: PARKS - 30F | STRATFORD - 30A | STRATFORD - 30A | | COLCHESTER - 30E | HATFIELD - 34C | 2/59: W/D | STRATFORD - 30A | STRATFORD - 30A |
| Nov-59 | 11/59: W/D | STRATFORD - 30A | STRATFORD - 30A | | 12/59: STRAT - 30A | HATFIELD - 34C | | STRATFORD - 30A | STRATFORD - 30A |
| Jan-60 | | STRATFORD - 30A | STRATFORD - 30A | | STRATFORD - 30A | HATFIELD - 34C | | STRATFORD - 30A | STRATFORD - 30A |
| Apr-60 | | STRATFORD - 30A | STRATFORD - 30A | | STRATFORD - 30A | HATFIELD - 34C | | STRATFORD - 30A | STRATFORD - 30A |
| Aug-60 | | STRATFORD - 30A | 9/60: W/D | | 6/60: W/D | HATFIELD - 34C | | STRATFORD - 30A | STRATFORD - 30A |
| Nov-60 | | STRATFORD - 30A | | | | HATFIELD - 34C | | STRATFORD - 30A | STRATFORD - 30A |

| | 69622 | 69623 | 69624 | 69625 | 69626 | 69627 | 69628 | 69629 | 69630 |
|---|---|---|---|---|---|---|---|---|---|
| Aug-50 | STRATFORD - 30A | STRATFORD - 30A | STRATFORD - 30A | STRATFORD - 30A | STRATFORD - 30A | STRATFORD - 30A | STRATFORD - 30A | STRATFORD - 30A | STRATFORD - 30A |
| Jan-51 | STRATFORD - 30A | STRATFORD - 30A | STRATFORD - 30A | STRATFORD - 30A | STRATFORD - 30A | STRATFORD - 30A | STRATFORD - 30A | STRATFORD - 30A | STRATFORD - 30A |
| Aug-51 | STRATFORD - 30A | STRATFORD - 30A | STRATFORD - 30A | STRATFORD - 30A | STRATFORD - 30A | STRATFORD - 30A | STRATFORD - 30A | STRATFORD - 30A | STRATFORD - 30A |
| Jan-52 | STRATFORD - 30A | STRATFORD - 30A | STRATFORD - 30A | STRATFORD - 30A | STRATFORD - 30A | STRATFORD - 30A | STRATFORD - 30A | STRATFORD - 30A | STRATFORD - 30A |
| Aug-52 | STRATFORD - 30A | STRATFORD - 30A | STRATFORD - 30A | STRATFORD - 30A | STRATFORD - 30A | STRATFORD - 30A | STRATFORD - 30A | STRATFORD - 30A | STRATFORD - 30A |
| Jan-53 | STRATFORD - 30A | STRATFORD - 30A | STRATFORD - 30A | STRATFORD - 30A | STRATFORD - 30A | STRATFORD - 30A | STRATFORD - 30A | STRATFORD - 30A | STRATFORD - 30A |
| Aug-53 | STRATFORD - 30A | STRATFORD - 30A | STRATFORD - 30A | STRATFORD - 30A | STRATFORD - 30A | STRATFORD - 30A | STRATFORD - 30A | STRATFORD - 30A | STRATFORD - 30A |
| Jan-54 | STRATFORD - 30A | STRATFORD - 30A | STRATFORD - 30A | STRATFORD - 30A | STRATFORD - 30A | STRATFORD - 30A | STRATFORD - 30A | STRATFORD - 30A | STRATFORD - 30A |
| Aug-54 | STRATFORD - 30A | STRATFORD - 30A | STRATFORD - 30A | STRATFORD - 30A | STRATFORD - 30A | STRATFORD - 30A | STRATFORD - 30A | STRATFORD - 30A | STRATFORD - 30A |
| Jan-55 | STRATFORD - 30A | STRATFORD - 30A | STRATFORD - 30A | STRATFORD - 30A | STRATFORD - 30A | STRATFORD - 30A | STRATFORD - 30A | STRATFORD - 30A | STRATFORD - 30A |
| Aug-55 | STRATFORD - 30A | STRATFORD - 30A | STRATFORD - 30A | STRATFORD - 30A | STRATFORD - 30A | STRATFORD - 30A | STRATFORD - 30A | STRATFORD - 30A | STRATFORD - 30A |
| Jan-56 | STRATFORD - 30A | STRATFORD - 30A | STRATFORD - 30A | STRATFORD - 30A | STRATFORD - 30A | STRATFORD - 30A | STRATFORD - 30A | 12/55: HSEY - 34B | STRATFORD - 30A |
| Aug-56 | STRATFORD - 30A | STRATFORD - 30A | STRATFORD - 30A | STRATFORD - 30A | STRATFORD - 30A | STRATFORD - 30A | STRATFORD - 30A | HORNSEY - 34B | STRATFORD - 30A |
| Jan-57 | STRATFORD - 30A | STRATFORD - 30A | STRATFORD - 30A | STRATFORD - 30A | STRATFORD - 30A | STRATFORD - 30A | STRATFORD - 30A | HORNSEY - 34B | STRATFORD - 30A |
| Aug-57 | STRATFORD - 30A | STRATFORD - 30A | STRATFORD - 30A | STRATFORD - 30A | STRATFORD - 30A | STRATFORD - 30A | STRATFORD - 30A | HORNSEY - 34B | STRATFORD - 30A |
| Jan-58 | STRATFORD - 30A | STRATFORD - 30A | STRATFORD - 30A | STRATFORD - 30A | STRATFORD - 30A | STRATFORD - 30A | STRATFORD - 30A | HORNSEY - 34B | STRATFORD - 30A |
| Aug-58 | STRATFORD - 30A | STRATFORD - 30A | STRATFORD - 30A | STRATFORD - 30A | STRATFORD - 30A | STRATFORD - 30A | STRATFORD - 30A | HORNSEY - 34B | STRATFORD - 30A |
| Jan-59 | STRATFORD - 30A | 2/59: W/D | 12/58: W/D | 4/59: W/D | STRATFORD - 30A | 3/59: W/D | 12/58:W/D | 3/59: HAT - 34C | STRATFORD - 30A |
| Aug-59 | STRATFORD - 30A | | | | 6/59: W/D | | | HATFIELD - 34C | STRATFORD - 30A |
| Nov-59 | STRATFORD - 30A | | | | | | | HATFIELD - 34C | STRATFORD - 30A |
| Jan-60 | STRATFORD - 30A | | | | | | | HATFIELD - 34C | STRATFORD - 30A |
| Apr-60 | 3/60: W/D | | | | | | | HATFIELD - 34C | STRATFORD - 30A |
| Aug-60 | | | | | | | | 9/60: W/D | STRATFORD - 30A |
| Nov-60 | | | | | | | | | STRATFORD - 30A |

| | 69631 | 69632 | 69633 | 69634 | 69635 | 69636 | 69637 | 69638 | 69639 |
|---|---|---|---|---|---|---|---|---|---|
| Aug-50 | STRATFORD - 30A | HATFIELD - 34C | STRATFORD - 30A | STRATFORD - 30A | PARKESTON - 30F | STRATFORD - 30A | STRATFORD - 30A | STRATFORD - 30A | HATFIELD - 34C |
| Jan-51 | STRATFORD - 30A | HATFIELD - 34C | STRATFORD - 30A | STRATFORD - 30A | PARKESTON - 30F | STRATFORD - 30A | STRATFORD - 30A | 4/51: COLW - 38A | HATFIELD - 34C |
| Aug-51 | STRATFORD - 30A | HATFIELD - 34C | STRATFORD - 30A | STRATFORD - 30A | PARKESTON - 30F | STRATFORD - 30A | STRATFORD - 30A | COLWICK - 38A | HATFIELD - 34C |
| Jan-52 | STRATFORD - 30A | HATFIELD - 34C | STRATFORD - 30A | STRATFORD - 30A | PARKESTON - 30F | STRATFORD - 30A | STRATFORD - 30A | 11/51: HAT - 34C | HATFIELD - 34C |
| Aug-52 | STRATFORD - 30A | HATFIELD - 34C | STRATFORD - 30A | STRATFORD - 30A | 9/52: STRAT - 30A | STRATFORD - 30A | STRATFORD - 30A | HATFIELD - 34C | HATFIELD - 34C |
| Jan-53 | STRATFORD - 30A | HATFIELD - 34C | STRATFORD - 30A | STRATFORD - 30A | STRATFORD - 30A | STRATFORD - 30A | STRATFORD - 30A | HATFIELD - 34C | HATFIELD - 34C |
| Aug-53 | STRATFORD - 30A | HATFIELD - 34C | STRATFORD - 30A | STRATFORD - 30A | STRATFORD - 30A | STRATFORD - 30A | STRATFORD - 30A | HATFIELD - 34C | HATFIELD - 34C |
| Jan-54 | 4/54: HAT - 34C | HATFIELD - 34C | STRATFORD - 30A | STRATFORD - 30A | 12/53: HAT - 34C | STRATFORD - 30A | 4/54: HAT - 34C | HATFIELD - 34C | HATFIELD - 34C |
| Aug-54 | HATFIELD - 34C | 8/54: KX - 34A | STRATFORD - 30A | STRATFORD - 30A | HATFIELD - 34C | STRATFORD - 30A | HATFIELD - 34C | 8/54: KX - 34A | HATFIELD - 34C |
| Jan-55 | HATFIELD - 34C | 9/54: HAT - 34C | STRATFORD - 30A | STRATFORD - 30A | HATFIELD - 34C | STRATFORD - 30A | HATFIELD - 34C | 9/54: HAT - 34C | HATFIELD - 34C |
| Aug-55 | HATFIELD - 34C | HATFIELD - 34C | STRATFORD - 30A | STRATFORD - 30A | HATFIELD - 34C | STRATFORD - 30A | HATFIELD - 34C | HATFIELD - 34C | HATFIELD - 34C |
| Jan-56 | HATFIELD - 34C | HATFIELD - 34C | STRATFORD - 30A | STRATFORD - 30A | HATFIELD - 34C | STRATFORD - 30A | HATFIELD - 34C | HATFIELD - 34C | HATFIELD - 34C |
| Aug-56 | HATFIELD - 34C | HATFIELD - 34C | STRATFORD - 30A | STRATFORD - 30A | HATFIELD - 34C | STRATFORD - 30A | HATFIELD - 34C | HATFIELD - 34C | HATFIELD - 34C |
| Jan-57 | HATFIELD - 34C | HATFIELD - 34C | STRATFORD - 30A | STRATFORD - 30A | HATFIELD - 34C | STRATFORD - 30A | HATFIELD - 34C | HATFIELD - 34C | HATFIELD - 34C |
| Aug-57 | HATFIELD - 34C | HATFIELD - 34C | STRATFORD - 30A | STRATFORD - 30A | HATFIELD - 34C | STRATFORD - 30A | HATFIELD - 34C | HATFIELD - 34C | HATFIELD - 34C |
| Jan-58 | HATFIELD - 34C | HATFIELD - 34C | STRATFORD - 30A | STRATFORD - 30A | HATFIELD - 34C | STRATFORD - 30A | HATFIELD - 34C | HATFIELD - 34C | HATFIELD - 34C |
| Aug-58 | HATFIELD - 34C | HATFIELD - 34C | STRATFORD - 30A | STRATFORD - 30A | HATFIELD - 34C | STRATFORD - 30A | HATFIELD - 34C | HATFIELD - 34C | HATFIELD - 34C |
| Jan-59 | HATFIELD - 34C | HATFIELD - 34C | STRATFORD - 30A | 1/59: W/D | 3/59: W/D | STRATFORD - 30A | 3/59: W/D | HATFIELD - 34C | 1/59: W/D |
| Aug-59 | HATFIELD - 34C | HATFIELD - 34C | 8/59: W/D | | | STRATFORD - 30A | | 5/59: W/D | |
| Nov-59 | HATFIELD - 34C | HATFIELD - 34C | | | | STRATFORD - 30A | | | |
| Jan-60 | HATFIELD - 34C | HATFIELD - 34C | | | | STRATFORD - 30A | | | |
| Apr-60 | HATFIELD - 34C | HATFIELD - 34C | | | | STRATFORD - 30A | | | |
| Aug-60 | HATFIELD - 34C | HATFIELD - 34C | | | | STRATFORD - 30A | | | |
| Nov-60 | HATFIELD - 34C | HATFIELD - 34C | | | | STRATFORD - 30A | | | |

| | 69640 | 69641 | 69642 | 69643 | 69644 | 69645 | 69646 | 69647 | 69648 |
|---|---|---|---|---|---|---|---|---|---|
| Aug-50 | HATFIELD - 34C | STRATFORD - 30A | STRATFORD - 30A | STRATFORD - 30A | HATFIELD - 34C | STRATFORD - 30A | STRATFORD - 30A | STRATFORD - 30A | STRATFORD - 30A |
| Jan-51 | HATFIELD - 34C | STRATFORD - 30A | 10/50: K.LYNN - 31C | STRATFORD - 30A | HATFIELD - 34C | STRATFORD - 30A | STRATFORD - 30A | STRATFORD - 30A | STRATFORD - 30A |
| Aug-51 | HATFIELD - 34C | STRATFORD - 30A | 11/50: STRAT - 30A | STRATFORD - 30A | HATFIELD - 34C | STRATFORD - 30A | STRATFORD - 30A | STRATFORD - 30A | STRATFORD - 30A |
| Jan-52 | HATFIELD - 34C | STRATFORD - 30A | STRATFORD - 30A | STRATFORD - 30A | HATFIELD - 34C | STRATFORD - 30A | STRATFORD - 30A | STRATFORD - 30A | STRATFORD - 30A |
| Aug-52 | HATFIELD - 34C | STRATFORD - 30A | STRATFORD - 30A | STRATFORD - 30A | HATFIELD - 34C | STRATFORD - 30A | STRATFORD - 30A | STRATFORD - 30A | 9/52: HAT - 34C |
| Jan-53 | HATFIELD - 34C | STRATFORD - 30A | STRATFORD - 30A | STRATFORD - 30A | HATFIELD - 34C | STRATFORD - 30A | STRATFORD - 30A | STRATFORD - 30A | HATFIELD - 34C |
| Aug-53 | HATFIELD - 34C | STRATFORD - 30A | STRATFORD - 30A | STRATFORD - 30A | HATFIELD - 34C | STRATFORD - 30A | STRATFORD - 30A | STRATFORD - 30A | HATFIELD - 34C |
| Jan-54 | HATFIELD - 34C | STRATFORD - 30A | STRATFORD - 30A | STRATFORD - 30A | HATFIELD - 34C | STRATFORD - 30A | STRATFORD - 30A | STRATFORD - 30A | HATFIELD - 34C |
| Aug-54 | HATFIELD - 34C | STRATFORD - 30A | STRATFORD - 30A | STRATFORD - 30A | HATFIELD - 34C | STRATFORD - 30A | STRATFORD - 30A | STRATFORD - 30A | HATFIELD - 34C |
| Jan-55 | HATFIELD - 34C | STRATFORD - 30A | STRATFORD - 30A | STRATFORD - 30A | HATFIELD - 34C | STRATFORD - 30A | STRATFORD - 30A | STRATFORD - 30A | HATFIELD - 34C |
| Aug-55 | HATFIELD - 34C | STRATFORD - 30A | STRATFORD - 30A | STRATFORD - 30A | HATFIELD - 34C | STRATFORD - 30A | STRATFORD - 30A | STRATFORD - 30A | HATFIELD - 34C |
| Jan-56 | HATFIELD - 34C | STRATFORD - 30A | STRATFORD - 30A | STRATFORD - 30A | HATFIELD - 34C | STRATFORD - 30A | STRATFORD - 30A | STRATFORD - 30A | HATFIELD - 34C |
| Aug-56 | HATFIELD - 34C | STRATFORD - 30A | STRATFORD - 30A | STRATFORD - 30A | HATFIELD - 34C | STRATFORD - 30A | STRATFORD - 30A | STRATFORD - 30A | HATFIELD - 34C |
| Jan-57 | HATFIELD - 34C | STRATFORD - 30A | STRATFORD - 30A | STRATFORD - 30A | HATFIELD - 34C | STRATFORD - 30A | STRATFORD - 30A | STRATFORD - 30A | HATFIELD - 34C |
| Aug-57 | HATFIELD - 34C | STRATFORD - 30A | STRATFORD - 30A | STRATFORD - 30A | HATFIELD - 34C | STRATFORD - 30A | STRATFORD - 30A | STRATFORD - 30A | HATFIELD - 34C |
| Jan-58 | HATFIELD - 34C | STRATFORD - 30A | STRATFORD - 30A | STRATFORD - 30A | HATFIELD - 34C | STRATFORD - 30A | STRATFORD - 30A | STRATFORD - 30A | HATFIELD - 34C |
| Aug-58 | HATFIELD - 34C | STRATFORD - 30A | STRATFORD - 30A | 5/58: W/D | HATFIELD - 34C | STRATFORD - 30A | STRATFORD - 30A | STRATFORD - 30A | HATFIELD - 34C |
| Jan-59 | HATFIELD - 34C | 12/58: W/D | STRATFORD - 30A | | 1/59: W/D | STRATFORD - 30A | STRATFORD - 30A | STRATFORD - 30A | HATFIELD - 34C |
| Aug-59 | HATFIELD - 34C | | STRATFORD - 30A | | | STRATFORD - 30A | STRATFORD - 30A | STRATFORD - 30A | HATFIELD - 34C |
| Nov-59 | HATFIELD - 34C | | STRATFORD - 30A | | | STRATFORD - 30A | STRATFORD - 30A | STRATFORD - 30A | HATFIELD - 34C |
| Jan-60 | HATFIELD - 34C | | STRATFORD - 30A | | | STRATFORD - 30A | STRATFORD - 30A | STRATFORD - 30A | HATFIELD - 34C |
| Apr-60 | HATFIELD - 34C | | STRATFORD - 30A | | | STRATFORD - 30A | STRATFORD - 30A | STRATFORD - 30A | HATFIELD - 34C |
| Aug-60 | HATFIELD - 34C | | STRATFORD - 30A | | | STRATFORD - 30A | STRATFORD - 30A | STRATFORD - 30A | 9/60: W/D |
| Nov-60 | HATFIELD - 34C | | STRATFORD - 30A | | | 11/60: W/D | STRATFORD - 30A | STRATFORD - 30A | |

| | 69649 | 69650 | 69651 | 69652 | 69653 | 69654 | 69655 | 69656 | 69657 |
|---|---|---|---|---|---|---|---|---|---|
| Aug-50 | STRATFORD - 30A | STRATFORD - 30A | STRATFORD - 30A | STRATFORD - 30A | STRATFORD - 30A | STRATFORD - 30A | STRATFORD - 30A | STRATFORD - 30A | STRATFORD - 30A |
| Jan-51 | STRATFORD - 30A | STRATFORD - 30A | 4/51: COLW - 38A | STRATFORD - 30A | STRATFORD - 30A | STRATFORD - 30A | STRATFORD - 30A | STRATFORD - 30A | STRATFORD - 30A |
| Aug-51 | STRATFORD - 30A | STRATFORD - 30A | COLWICK - 38A | STRATFORD - 30A | STRATFORD - 30A | STRATFORD - 30A | STRATFORD - 30A | STRATFORD - 30A | STRATFORD - 30A |
| Jan-52 | STRATFORD - 30A | STRATFORD - 30A | 12/51: ANNES - 38B | STRATFORD - 30A | STRATFORD - 30A | STRATFORD - 30A | STRATFORD - 30A | STRATFORD - 30A | STRATFORD - 30A |
| Aug-52 | STRATFORD - 30A | STRATFORD - 30A | ANNESLEY - 38B | STRATFORD - 30A | STRATFORD - 30A | 7/52: COLW - 38A | STRATFORD - 30A | STRATFORD - 30A | STRATFORD - 30A |
| Jan-53 | STRATFORD - 30A | STRATFORD - 30A | ANNESLEY - 38B | STRATFORD - 30A | STRATFORD - 30A | COLWICK - 38A | STRATFORD - 30A | STRATFORD - 30A | STRATFORD - 30A |
| Aug-53 | STRATFORD - 30A | STRATFORD - 30A | ANNESLEY - 38B | STRATFORD - 30A | STRATFORD - 30A | COLWICK - 38A | STRATFORD - 30A | STRATFORD - 30A | STRATFORD - 30A |
| Jan-54 | 12/53: HAT - 34C | 4/54: HAT - 34C | ANNESLEY - 38B | STRATFORD - 30A | STRATFORD - 30A | 4/54: HAT - 34C | STRATFORD - 30A | STRATFORD - 30A | STRATFORD - 30A |
| Aug-54 | HATFIELD - 34C | HATFIELD - 34C | ANNESLEY - 38B | STRATFORD - 30A | STRATFORD - 30A | HATFIELD - 34C | STRATFORD - 30A | STRATFORD - 30A | STRATFORD - 30A |
| Jan-55 | HATFIELD - 34C | HATFIELD - 34C | ANNESLEY - 38B | STRATFORD - 30A | STRATFORD - 30A | HATFIELD - 34C | STRATFORD - 30A | STRATFORD - 30A | STRATFORD - 30A |
| Aug-55 | HATFIELD - 34C | HATFIELD - 34C | ANNESLEY - 38B | STRATFORD - 30A | STRATFORD - 30A | HATFIELD - 34C | STRATFORD - 30A | STRATFORD - 30A | STRATFORD - 30A |
| Jan-56 | HATFIELD - 34C | HATFIELD - 34C | ANNESLEY - 38B | STRATFORD - 30A | STRATFORD - 30A | HATFIELD - 34C | STRATFORD - 30A | STRATFORD - 30A | STRATFORD - 30A |
| Aug-56 | HATFIELD - 34C | HATFIELD - 34C | 10/56: CAMB - 31A | STRATFORD - 30A | STRATFORD - 30A | HATFIELD - 34C | STRATFORD - 30A | STRATFORD - 30A | STRATFORD - 30A |
| Jan-57 | HATFIELD - 34C | HATFIELD - 34C | CAMBRIDGE - 31A | STRATFORD - 30A | STRATFORD - 30A | HATFIELD - 34C | STRATFORD - 30A | STRATFORD - 30A | STRATFORD - 30A |
| Aug-57 | HATFIELD - 34C | HATFIELD - 34C | CAMBRIDGE - 31A | STRATFORD - 30A | STRATFORD - 30A | HATFIELD - 34C | STRATFORD - 30A | STRATFORD - 30A | STRATFORD - 30A |
| Jan-58 | HATFIELD - 34C | HATFIELD - 34C | CAMBRIDGE - 31A | STRATFORD - 30A | STRATFORD - 30A | HATFIELD - 34C | STRATFORD - 30A | STRATFORD - 30A | STRATFORD - 30A |
| Aug-58 | HATFIELD - 34C | HATFIELD - 34C | 8/58: STRAT - 30A | STRATFORD - 30A | STRATFORD - 30A | HATFIELD - 34C | STRATFORD - 30A | STRATFORD - 30A | STRATFORD - 30A |
| Jan-59 | HATFIELD - 34C | HATFIELD - 34C | STRATFORD - 30A | 1/59: COL - 30E | STRATFORD - 30A | HATFIELD - 34C | STRATFORD - 30A | STRATFORD - 30A | STRATFORD - 30A |
| Aug-59 | 6/59: W/D | 5/59: W/D | 8/59: K.LYNN - 31C | COLCHESTER - 30E | STRATFORD - 30A | HATFIELD - 34C | 8/59: W/D | STRATFORD - 30A | 6/59: W/D |
| Nov-59 | | | 9/59: STRAT - 30A | 12/59: STRAT - 30A | STRATFORD - 30A | HATFIELD - 34C | | STRATFORD - 30A | |
| Jan-60 | | | 1/60: PARKS - 30F | STRATFORD - 30A | STRATFORD - 30A | 2/60: STRAT - 30A | | STRATFORD - 30A | |
| Apr-60 | | | PARKESTON - 30F | STRATFORD - 30A | STRATFORD - 30A | STRATFORD - 30A | | STRATFORD - 30A | |
| Aug-60 | | | 8/60: STRAT - 30A | STRATFORD - 30A | STRATFORD - 30A | STRATFORD - 30A | | STRATFORD - 30A | |
| Nov-60 | | | 11/60: PARKS - 30F | STRATFORD - 30A | STRATFORD - 30A | STRATFORD - 30A | | STRATFORD - 30A | |

| | 69658 | 69659 | 69660 | 69661 | 69662 | 69663 | 69664 | 69665 | 69666 |
|---|---|---|---|---|---|---|---|---|---|
| Aug-50 | STRATFORD - 30A | STRATFORD - 30A | STRATFORD - 30A | STRATFORD - 30A | STRATFORD - 30A | STRATFORD - 30A | STRATFORD - 30A | STRATFORD - 30A | STRATFORD - 30A |
| Jan-51 | STRATFORD - 30A | STRATFORD - 30A | STRATFORD - 30A | STRATFORD - 30A | STRATFORD - 30A | STRATFORD - 30A | STRATFORD - 30A | STRATFORD - 30A | STRATFORD - 30A |
| Aug-51 | STRATFORD - 30A | STRATFORD - 30A | STRATFORD - 30A | STRATFORD - 30A | STRATFORD - 30A | STRATFORD - 30A | STRATFORD - 30A | STRATFORD - 30A | STRATFORD - 30A |
| Jan-52 | STRATFORD - 30A | STRATFORD - 30A | STRATFORD - 30A | STRATFORD - 30A | STRATFORD - 30A | STRATFORD - 30A | STRATFORD - 30A | STRATFORD - 30A | STRATFORD - 30A |
| Aug-52 | STRATFORD - 30A | STRATFORD - 30A | STRATFORD - 30A | STRATFORD - 30A | STRATFORD - 30A | STRATFORD - 30A | STRATFORD - 30A | STRATFORD - 30A | STRATFORD - 30A |
| Jan-53 | STRATFORD - 30A | STRATFORD - 30A | STRATFORD - 30A | STRATFORD - 30A | STRATFORD - 30A | STRATFORD - 30A | STRATFORD - 30A | STRATFORD - 30A | STRATFORD - 30A |
| Aug-53 | STRATFORD - 30A | STRATFORD - 30A | STRATFORD - 30A | STRATFORD - 30A | STRATFORD - 30A | STRATFORD - 30A | STRATFORD - 30A | STRATFORD - 30A | STRATFORD - 30A |
| Jan-54 | STRATFORD - 30A | STRATFORD - 30A | STRATFORD - 30A | STRATFORD - 30A | STRATFORD - 30A | STRATFORD - 30A | STRATFORD - 30A | STRATFORD - 30A | STRATFORD - 30A |
| Aug-54 | STRATFORD - 30A | STRATFORD - 30A | STRATFORD - 30A | STRATFORD - 30A | STRATFORD - 30A | STRATFORD - 30A | STRATFORD - 30A | STRATFORD - 30A | STRATFORD - 30A |
| Jan-55 | STRATFORD - 30A | STRATFORD - 30A | STRATFORD - 30A | STRATFORD - 30A | STRATFORD - 30A | STRATFORD - 30A | STRATFORD - 30A | STRATFORD - 30A | STRATFORD - 30A |
| Aug-55 | STRATFORD - 30A | STRATFORD - 30A | STRATFORD - 30A | STRATFORD - 30A | STRATFORD - 30A | STRATFORD - 30A | STRATFORD - 30A | STRATFORD - 30A | STRATFORD - 30A |
| Jan-56 | STRATFORD - 30A | STRATFORD - 30A | STRATFORD - 30A | STRATFORD - 30A | STRATFORD - 30A | STRATFORD - 30A | STRATFORD - 30A | STRATFORD - 30A | STRATFORD - 30A |
| Aug-56 | STRATFORD - 30A | STRATFORD - 30A | STRATFORD - 30A | STRATFORD - 30A | STRATFORD - 30A | STRATFORD - 30A | STRATFORD - 30A | STRATFORD - 30A | STRATFORD - 30A |
| Jan-57 | STRATFORD - 30A | STRATFORD - 30A | STRATFORD - 30A | STRATFORD - 30A | STRATFORD - 30A | STRATFORD - 30A | STRATFORD - 30A | STRATFORD - 30A | STRATFORD - 30A |
| Aug-57 | STRATFORD - 30A | STRATFORD - 30A | STRATFORD - 30A | STRATFORD - 30A | STRATFORD - 30A | STRATFORD - 30A | STRATFORD - 30A | STRATFORD - 30A | STRATFORD - 30A |
| Jan-58 | STRATFORD - 30A | STRATFORD - 30A | STRATFORD - 30A | STRATFORD - 30A | STRATFORD - 30A | STRATFORD - 30A | STRATFORD - 30A | STRATFORD - 30A | STRATFORD - 30A |
| Aug-58 | STRATFORD - 30A | STRATFORD - 30A | STRATFORD - 30A | STRATFORD - 30A | STRATFORD - 30A | STRATFORD - 30A | STRATFORD - 30A | STRATFORD - 30A | STRATFORD - 30A |
| Jan-59 | STRATFORD - 30A | 1/59: W/D | STRATFORD - 30A | STRATFORD - 30A | STRATFORD - 30A | STRATFORD - 30A | STRATFORD - 30A | STRATFORD - 30A | 3/59: W/D |
| Aug-59 | STRATFORD - 30A | | 4/59: W/D | STRATFORD - 30A | 5/59: W/D | STRATFORD - 30A | STRATFORD - 30A | STRATFORD - 30A | |
| Nov-59 | STRATFORD - 30A | | | 10/59: W/D | | STRATFORD - 30A | STRATFORD - 30A | STRATFORD - 30A | |
| Jan-60 | STRATFORD - 30A | | | | | STRATFORD - 30A | STRATFORD - 30A | STRATFORD - 30A | |
| Apr-60 | STRATFORD - 30A | | | | | STRATFORD - 30A | STRATFORD - 30A | 3/60: W/D | |
| Aug-60 | STRATFORD - 30A | | | | | STRATFORD - 30A | STRATFORD - 30A | | |
| Nov-60 | STRATFORD - 30A | | | | | 11/60: W/D | STRATFORD - 30A | | |

| | 69667 | 69668 | 69669 | 69670 | 69671 | 69672 | 69673 | 69674 | 69675 |
|---|---|---|---|---|---|---|---|---|---|
| Aug-50 | STRATFORD - 30A | STRATFORD - 30A | STRATFORD - 30A | STRATFORD - 30A | STRATFORD - 30A | STRATFORD - 30A | STRATFORD - 30A | STRATFORD - 30A | STRATFORD - 30A |
| Jan-51 | STRATFORD - 30A | STRATFORD - 30A | STRATFORD - 30A | STRATFORD - 30A | STRATFORD - 30A | STRATFORD - 30A | STRATFORD - 30A | STRATFORD - 30A | STRATFORD - 30A |
| Aug-51 | STRATFORD - 30A | STRATFORD - 30A | STRATFORD - 30A | STRATFORD - 30A | STRATFORD - 30A | STRATFORD - 30A | STRATFORD - 30A | STRATFORD - 30A | STRATFORD - 30A |
| Jan-52 | STRATFORD - 30A | STRATFORD - 30A | STRATFORD - 30A | STRATFORD - 30A | STRATFORD - 30A | **11/51: COL - 30E** | STRATFORD - 30A | STRATFORD - 30A | STRATFORD - 30A |
| Aug-52 | STRATFORD - 30A | STRATFORD - 30A | STRATFORD - 30A | STRATFORD - 30A | STRATFORD - 30A | **8/52: STRAT - 30A** | STRATFORD - 30A | STRATFORD - 30A | STRATFORD - 30A |
| Jan-53 | STRATFORD - 30A | STRATFORD - 30A | STRATFORD - 30A | STRATFORD - 30A | STRATFORD - 30A | **10/52: COL - 30E** | **3/53: COL - 30E** | STRATFORD - 30A | STRATFORD - 30A |
| Aug-53 | STRATFORD - 30A | STRATFORD - 30A | STRATFORD - 30A | STRATFORD - 30A | STRATFORD - 30A | COLCHESTER - 30E | COLCHESTER - 30E | STRATFORD - 30A | STRATFORD - 30A |
| Jan-54 | STRATFORD - 30A | STRATFORD - 30A | STRATFORD - 30A | STRATFORD - 30A | STRATFORD - 30A | COLCHESTER - 30E | COLCHESTER - 30E | STRATFORD - 30A | STRATFORD - 30A |
| Aug-54 | STRATFORD - 30A | STRATFORD - 30A | STRATFORD - 30A | STRATFORD - 30A | STRATFORD - 30A | COLCHESTER - 30E | COLCHESTER - 30E | STRATFORD - 30A | STRATFORD - 30A |
| Jan-55 | STRATFORD - 30A | STRATFORD - 30A | STRATFORD - 30A | STRATFORD - 30A | STRATFORD - 30A | COLCHESTER - 30E | COLCHESTER - 30E | STRATFORD - 30A | STRATFORD - 30A |
| Aug-55 | STRATFORD - 30A | STRATFORD - 30A | STRATFORD - 30A | STRATFORD - 30A | STRATFORD - 30A | COLCHESTER - 30E | COLCHESTER - 30E | STRATFORD - 30A | STRATFORD - 30A |
| Jan-56 | STRATFORD - 30A | STRATFORD - 30A | STRATFORD - 30A | STRATFORD - 30A | STRATFORD - 30A | **3/56: STRAT - 30A** | COLCHESTER - 30E | STRATFORD - 30A | STRATFORD - 30A |
| Aug-56 | STRATFORD - 30A | STRATFORD - 30A | STRATFORD - 30A | STRATFORD - 30A | STRATFORD - 30A | STRATFORD - 30A | COLCHESTER - 30E | STRATFORD - 30A | STRATFORD - 30A |
| Jan-57 | STRATFORD - 30A | STRATFORD - 30A | STRATFORD - 30A | STRATFORD - 30A | STRATFORD - 30A | **11/56: PARKS - 30F** | COLCHESTER - 30E | STRATFORD - 30A | **11/56: PARKS - 30F** |
| Aug-57 | STRATFORD - 30A | STRATFORD - 30A | STRATFORD - 30A | STRATFORD - 30A | STRATFORD - 30A | PARKESTON - 30F | COLCHESTER - 30E | STRATFORD - 30A | PARKESTON - 30F |
| Jan-58 | STRATFORD - 30A | STRATFORD - 30A | STRATFORD - 30A | STRATFORD - 30A | STRATFORD - 30A | PARKESTON - 30F | COLCHESTER - 30E | STRATFORD - 30A | PARKESTON - 30F |
| Aug-58 | STRATFORD - 30A | STRATFORD - 30A | STRATFORD - 30A | STRATFORD - 30A | STRATFORD - 30A | PARKESTON - 30F | COLCHESTER - 30E | STRATFORD - 30A | PARKESTON - 30F |
| Jan-59 | **2/59: W/D** | STRATFORD - 30A | STRATFORD - 30A | STRATFORD - 30A | STRATFORD - 30A | PARKESTON - 30F | COLCHESTER - 30E | STRATFORD - 30A | PARKESTON - 30F |
| Aug-59 | | STRATFORD - 30A | **4/59: W/D** | STRATFORD - 30A | STRATFORD - 30A | PARKESTON - 30F | COLCHESTER - 30E | STRATFORD - 30A | PARKESTON - 30F |
| Nov-59 | | STRATFORD - 30A | | STRATFORD - 30A | STRATFORD - 30A | **10/59: W/D** | **10/59: PARKS - 30F** | STRATFORD - 30A | PARKESTON - 30F |
| Jan-60 | | STRATFORD - 30A | | STRATFORD - 30A | STRATFORD - 30A | | **2/60: STRAT - 30A** | STRATFORD - 30A | **2/60: STRAT - 30A** |
| Apr-60 | | STRATFORD - 30A | | STRATFORD - 30A | STRATFORD - 30A | | STRATFORD - 30A | STRATFORD - 30A | STRATFORD - 30A |
| Aug-60 | | STRATFORD - 30A | | STRATFORD - 30A | STRATFORD - 30A | | STRATFORD - 30A | STRATFORD - 30A | STRATFORD - 30A |
| Nov-60 | | STRATFORD - 30A | | STRATFORD - 30A | STRATFORD - 30A | | STRATFORD - 30A | STRATFORD - 30A | STRATFORD - 30A |

| | 69676 | 69677 | 69678 | 69679 | 69680 | 69681 | 69682 | 69683 | 69684 |
|---|---|---|---|---|---|---|---|---|---|
| Aug-50 | STRATFORD - 30A | PARKESTON - 30F | STRATFORD - 30A | MELTON CONSTABLE - 32G | STRATFORD - 30A | STRATFORD - 30A | STRATFORD - 30A | STRATFORD - 30A | STRATFORD - 30A |
| Jan-51 | STRATFORD - 30A | PARKESTON - 30F | STRATFORD - 30A | **9/50: NOR - 32A** | STRATFORD - 30A | STRATFORD - 30A | STRATFORD - 30A | STRATFORD - 30A | STRATFORD - 30A |
| Aug-51 | STRATFORD - 30A | PARKESTON - 30F | STRATFORD - 30A | NORWICH - 32A | STRATFORD - 30A | STRATFORD - 30A | STRATFORD - 30A | STRATFORD - 30A | STRATFORD - 30A |
| Jan-52 | STRATFORD - 30A | PARKESTON - 30F | **11/51: COL - 30E** | NORWICH - 32A | STRATFORD - 30A | STRATFORD - 30A | STRATFORD - 30A | STRATFORD - 30A | STRATFORD - 30A |
| Aug-52 | STRATFORD - 30A | **9/52: STRAT - 30A** | **9/52: HAT - 34C** | NORWICH - 32A | STRATFORD - 30A | STRATFORD - 30A | STRATFORD - 30A | STRATFORD - 30A | STRATFORD - 30A |
| Jan-53 | STRATFORD - 30A | STRATFORD - 30A | HATFIELD - 34C | NORWICH - 32A | STRATFORD - 30A | STRATFORD - 30A | STRATFORD - 30A | STRATFORD - 30A | STRATFORD - 30A |
| Aug-53 | STRATFORD - 30A | STRATFORD - 30A | HATFIELD - 34C | NORWICH - 32A | STRATFORD - 30A | STRATFORD - 30A | STRATFORD - 30A | STRATFORD - 30A | STRATFORD - 30A |
| Jan-54 | STRATFORD - 30A | STRATFORD - 30A | HATFIELD - 34C | NORWICH - 32A | STRATFORD - 30A | STRATFORD - 30A | STRATFORD - 30A | STRATFORD - 30A | STRATFORD - 30A |
| Aug-54 | STRATFORD - 30A | STRATFORD - 30A | HATFIELD - 34C | NORWICH - 32A | STRATFORD - 30A | STRATFORD - 30A | STRATFORD - 30A | STRATFORD - 30A | STRATFORD - 30A |
| Jan-55 | STRATFORD - 30A | STRATFORD - 30A | HATFIELD - 34C | NORWICH - 32A | STRATFORD - 30A | STRATFORD - 30A | STRATFORD - 30A | STRATFORD - 30A | STRATFORD - 30A |
| Aug-55 | STRATFORD - 30A | STRATFORD - 30A | HATFIELD - 34C | NORWICH - 32A | STRATFORD - 30A | STRATFORD - 30A | STRATFORD - 30A | STRATFORD - 30A | STRATFORD - 30A |
| Jan-56 | STRATFORD - 30A | STRATFORD - 30A | HATFIELD - 34C | NORWICH - 32A | STRATFORD - 30A | STRATFORD - 30A | STRATFORD - 30A | STRATFORD - 30A | STRATFORD - 30A |
| Aug-56 | STRATFORD - 30A | STRATFORD - 30A | HATFIELD - 34C | **7/56: LOW - 32C** | STRATFORD - 30A | STRATFORD - 30A | STRATFORD - 30A | STRATFORD - 30A | STRATFORD - 30A |
| Jan-57 | STRATFORD - 30A | STRATFORD - 30A | HATFIELD - 34C | **5/57: YAR(ST) - 32D** | STRATFORD - 30A | STRATFORD - 30A | STRATFORD - 30A | STRATFORD - 30A | STRATFORD - 30A |
| Aug-57 | STRATFORD - 30A | STRATFORD - 30A | HATFIELD - 34C | **10/57: STRAT - 30A** | STRATFORD - 30A | STRATFORD - 30A | STRATFORD - 30A | STRATFORD - 30A | STRATFORD - 30A |
| Jan-58 | STRATFORD - 30A | STRATFORD - 30A | HATFIELD - 34C | **11/57: TIL - 33B** | STRATFORD - 30A | STRATFORD - 30A | STRATFORD - 30A | STRATFORD - 30A | STRATFORD - 30A |
| Aug-58 | STRATFORD - 30A | STRATFORD - 30A | HATFIELD - 34C | **3/58: YAR(ST) - 32D** | STRATFORD - 30A | STRATFORD - 30A | STRATFORD - 30A | STRATFORD - 30A | STRATFORD - 30A |
| Jan-59 | **2/59: W/D** | STRATFORD - 30A | HATFIELD - 34C | **1/59: STRAT - 30A** | STRATFORD - 30A | STRATFORD - 30A | STRATFORD - 30A | STRATFORD - 30A | STRATFORD - 30A |
| Aug-59 | | STRATFORD - 30A | HATFIELD - 34C | STRATFORD - 30A | STRATFORD - 30A | STRATFORD - 30A | STRATFORD - 30A | STRATFORD - 30A | STRATFORD - 30A |
| Nov-59 | | STRATFORD - 30A | HATFIELD - 34C | STRATFORD - 30A | STRATFORD - 30A | STRATFORD - 30A | STRATFORD - 30A | STRATFORD - 30A | STRATFORD - 30A |
| Jan-60 | | STRATFORD - 30A | HATFIELD - 34C | STRATFORD - 30A | STRATFORD - 30A | STRATFORD - 30A | STRATFORD - 30A | STRATFORD - 30A | STRATFORD - 30A |
| Apr-60 | | STRATFORD - 30A | HATFIELD - 34C | STRATFORD - 30A | STRATFORD - 30A | STRATFORD - 30A | STRATFORD - 30A | **3/60: W/D** | STRATFORD - 30A |
| Aug-60 | | STRATFORD - 30A | **9/60: STRAT - 30A** | STRATFORD - 30A | STRATFORD - 30A | STRATFORD - 30A | STRATFORD - 30A | | **9/60: W/D** |
| Nov-60 | | STRATFORD - 30A | STRATFORD - 30A | STRATFORD - 30A | STRATFORD - 30A | STRATFORD - 30A | STRATFORD - 30A | | |

| | 69685 | 69686 | 69687 | 69688 | 69689 | 69690 | 69691 | 69692 | 69693 |
|---|---|---|---|---|---|---|---|---|---|
| Aug-50 | STRATFORD - 30A | STRATFORD - 30A | STRATFORD - 30A | STRATFORD - 30A | NEASDEN - 34E | NEASDEN - 34E | HATFIELD - 34C | NEASDEN - 34E | STRATFORD - 30A |
| Jan-51 | STRATFORD - 30A | STRATFORD - 30A | STRATFORD - 30A | STRATFORD - 30A | NEASDEN - 34E | NEASDEN - 34E | HATFIELD - 34C | NEASDEN - 34E | STRATFORD - 30A |
| Aug-51 | STRATFORD - 30A | STRATFORD - 30A | STRATFORD - 30A | STRATFORD - 30A | **7/51: KX - 34A** | **9/51: KX - 34A** | HATFIELD - 34C | NEASDEN - 34E | STRATFORD - 30A |
| Jan-52 | STRATFORD - 30A | STRATFORD - 30A | STRATFORD - 30A | STRATFORD - 30A | KINGS CROSS - 34A | KINGS CROSS - 34A | **11/51: ANNES - 38B** | NEASDEN - 34E | STRATFORD - 30A |
| Aug-52 | STRATFORD - 30A | STRATFORD - 30A | STRATFORD - 30A | STRATFORD - 30A | KINGS CROSS - 34A | KINGS CROSS - 34A | ANNESLEY - 38B | NEASDEN - 34E | STRATFORD - 30A |
| Jan-53 | STRATFORD - 30A | STRATFORD - 30A | STRATFORD - 30A | STRATFORD - 30A | KINGS CROSS - 34A | **3/53: NOR - 32A** | ANNESLEY - 38B | NEASDEN - 34E | STRATFORD - 30A |
| Aug-53 | STRATFORD - 30A | STRATFORD - 30A | STRATFORD - 30A | STRATFORD - 30A | KINGS CROSS - 34A | NORWICH - 32A | ANNESLEY - 38B | NEASDEN - 34E | STRATFORD - 30A |
| Jan-54 | STRATFORD - 30A | STRATFORD - 30A | STRATFORD - 30A | STRATFORD - 30A | KINGS CROSS - 34A | NORWICH - 32A | ANNESLEY - 38B | **5/54: ANNES - 38B** | STRATFORD - 30A |
| Aug-54 | STRATFORD - 30A | STRATFORD - 30A | STRATFORD - 30A | STRATFORD - 30A | **5/54: ANNES - 38B** | NORWICH - 32A | **5/54: ARDS - 37A** | **11/54: STRAT - 30A** | STRATFORD - 30A |
| Jan-55 | STRATFORD - 30A | STRATFORD - 30A | STRATFORD - 30A | STRATFORD - 30A | **3/55: YAR(ST) - 32D** | NORWICH - 32A | **10/54: C.HILL - 37B** | **12/54: ANNES - 38B** | STRATFORD - 30A |
| Aug-55 | STRATFORD - 30A | STRATFORD - 30A | STRATFORD - 30A | STRATFORD - 30A | YARMOUTH(ST) - 32D | NORWICH - 32A | COPLEYHILL - 37B | ANNESLEY - 38B | STRATFORD - 30A |
| Jan-56 | STRATFORD - 30A | STRATFORD - 30A | STRATFORD - 30A | STRATFORD - 30A | YARMOUTH(ST) - 32D | NORWICH - 32A | **12/55: PLAIS - 33A** | ANNESLEY - 38B | STRATFORD - 30A |
| Aug-56 | STRATFORD - 30A | STRATFORD - 30A | STRATFORD - 30A | STRATFORD - 30A | YARMOUTH(ST) - 32D | **6/56: LOW - 32C** | PLAISTOW - 33A | **10/56: CAMB - 31A** | STRATFORD - 30A |
| Jan-57 | STRATFORD - 30A | STRATFORD - 30A | STRATFORD - 30A | STRATFORD - 30A | **3/57: W/D** | **10/56: CAMB - 31A** | **10/56: TIL - 33B** | CAMBRIDGE - 31A | STRATFORD - 30A |
| Aug-57 | STRATFORD - 30A | STRATFORD - 30A | STRATFORD - 30A | STRATFORD - 30A | | CAMBRIDGE - 31A | TILBURY - 33B | CAMBRIDGE - 31A | STRATFORD - 30A |
| Jan-58 | STRATFORD - 30A | STRATFORD - 30A | STRATFORD - 30A | STRATFORD - 30A | | CAMBRIDGE - 31A | **11/57: STRAT - 30A** | CAMBRIDGE - 31A | STRATFORD - 30A |
| Aug-58 | STRATFORD - 30A | STRATFORD - 30A | STRATFORD - 30A | STRATFORD - 30A | | **7/58: LOW - 32C** | STRATFORD - 30A | **8/58: STRAT - 30A** | STRATFORD - 30A |
| Jan-59 | STRATFORD - 30A | **1/59: COL - 30E** | STRATFORD - 30A | STRATFORD - 30A | | **4/59: STRAT - 30A** | STRATFORD - 30A | **4/59: HAT - 34C** | STRATFORD - 30A |
| Aug-59 | STRATFORD - 30A | **5/59: STRAT - 30A** | STRATFORD - 30A | STRATFORD - 30A | | STRATFORD - 30A | STRATFORD - 30A | HATFIELD - 34C | STRATFORD - 30A |
| Nov-59 | STRATFORD - 30A | STRATFORD - 30A | STRATFORD - 30A | STRATFORD - 30A | | STRATFORD - 30A | STRATFORD - 30A | HATFIELD - 34C | STRATFORD - 30A |
| Jan-60 | STRATFORD - 30A | STRATFORD - 30A | STRATFORD - 30A | STRATFORD - 30A | | **2/60: PARKS - 30F** | **2/60: PARKS - 30F** | HATFIELD - 34C | STRATFORD - 30A |
| Apr-60 | STRATFORD - 30A | STRATFORD - 30A | STRATFORD - 30A | STRATFORD - 30A | | PARKESTON - 30F | PARKESTON - 30F | HATFIELD - 34C | STRATFORD - 30A |
| Aug-60 | STRATFORD - 30A | **8/60: PARKS - 30F** | STRATFORD - 30A | STRATFORD - 30A | | PARKESTON - 30F | **8/60: STRAT - 30A** | HATFIELD - 34C | STRATFORD - 30A |
| Nov-60 | STRATFORD - 30A | **11/60: STRAT - 30A** | STRATFORD - 30A | STRATFORD - 30A | | PARKESTON - 30F | STRATFORD - 30A | HATFIELD - 34C | STRATFORD - 30A |

| | 69694 | 69695 | 69696 | 69697 | 69698 | 69699 | 69700 | 69701 | 69702 |
|---|---|---|---|---|---|---|---|---|---|
| Aug-50 | NEASDEN - 34E | HATFIELD - 34C | HATFIELD - 34C | STRATFORD - 30A | NEASDEN - 34E | STRATFORD - 30A | STRATFORD - 30A | COLCHESTER - 30E | STRATFORD - 30A |
| Jan-51 | NEASDEN - 34E | HATFIELD - 34C | HATFIELD - 34C | STRATFORD - 30A | NEASDEN - 34E | STRATFORD - 30A | STRATFORD - 30A | COLCHESTER - 30E | STRATFORD - 30A |
| Aug-51 | NEASDEN - 34E | HATFIELD - 34C | HATFIELD - 34C | STRATFORD - 30A | **9/51: KX - 34A** | STRATFORD - 30A | STRATFORD - 30A | COLCHESTER - 30E | STRATFORD - 30A |
| Jan-52 | NEASDEN - 34E | **11/51: ANNES - 38B** | HATFIELD - 34C | STRATFORD - 30A | KINGS CROSS - 34A | STRATFORD - 30A | STRATFORD - 30A | COLCHESTER - 30E | STRATFORD - 30A |
| Aug-52 | NEASDEN - 34E | ANNESLEY - 38B | HATFIELD - 34C | STRATFORD - 30A | KINGS CROSS - 34A | STRATFORD - 30A | STRATFORD - 30A | COLCHESTER - 30E | STRATFORD - 30A |
| Jan-53 | NEASDEN - 34E | ANNESLEY - 38B | **3/53: NOR - 32A** | STRATFORD - 30A | KINGS CROSS - 34A | STRATFORD - 30A | STRATFORD - 30A | COLCHESTER - 30E | STRATFORD - 30A |
| Aug-53 | NEASDEN - 34E | ANNESLEY - 38B | NORWICH - 32A | STRATFORD - 30A | KINGS CROSS - 34A | STRATFORD - 30A | STRATFORD - 30A | COLCHESTER - 30E | STRATFORD - 30A |
| Jan-54 | NEASDEN - 34E | ANNESLEY - 38B | NORWICH - 32A | STRATFORD - 30A | KINGS CROSS - 34A | STRATFORD - 30A | STRATFORD - 30A | COLCHESTER - 30E | STRATFORD - 30A |
| Aug-54 | **5/54: ARDS - 37A** | **5/54: ARDS - 37A** | **5/54: ARDS - 37A** | STRATFORD - 30A | **6/54: NOR - 32A** | STRATFORD - 30A | STRATFORD - 30A | COLCHESTER - 30E | STRATFORD - 30A |
| Jan-55 | **10/54: C.HILL - 37B** | **10/54: C.HILL - 37B** | **10/54: C.HILL - 37B** | STRATFORD - 30A | NORWICH - 32A | STRATFORD - 30A | STRATFORD - 30A | COLCHESTER - 30E | STRATFORD - 30A |
| Aug-55 | COPLEYHILL - 37B | COPLEYHILL - 37B | **7/55: BRAD - 37C** | STRATFORD - 30A | NORWICH - 32A | STRATFORD - 30A | STRATFORD - 30A | COLCHESTER - 30E | STRATFORD - 30A |
| Jan-56 | COPLEYHILL - 37B | **12/55: PLAIS - 33A** | **4/56: C.HILL - 37B** | STRATFORD - 30A | NORWICH - 32A | STRATFORD - 30A | STRATFORD - 30A | COLCHESTER - 30E | STRATFORD - 30A |
| Aug-56 | COPLEYHILL - 56C | PLAISTOW - 33A | COPLEYHILL - 56C | STRATFORD - 30A | **7/56: YAR(ST) - 32D** | STRATFORD - 30A | STRATFORD - 30A | COLCHESTER - 30E | STRATFORD - 30A |
| Jan-57 | **11/56: TIL - 33B** | **10/56: TIL - 33B** | **11/56: YAR(ST) - 32D** | STRATFORD - 30A | **10/56: TIL - 33B** | STRATFORD - 30A | STRATFORD - 30A | COLCHESTER - 30E | STRATFORD - 30A |
| Aug-57 | TILBURY - 33B | TILBURY - 33B | **10/57: STRAT - 30A** | STRATFORD - 30A | TILBURY - 33B | STRATFORD - 30A | STRATFORD - 30A | COLCHESTER - 30E | STRATFORD - 30A |
| Jan-58 | **3/58: K.LYNN - 31C** | TILBURY - 33B | STRATFORD - 30A | STRATFORD - 30A | **3/58: K.LYNN - 31C** | STRATFORD - 30A | STRATFORD - 30A | COLCHESTER - 30E | STRATFORD - 30A |
| Aug-58 | KINGS LYNN - 31C | **8/58: STRAT - 30A** | **8/58: STRAT - 30A** | STRATFORD - 30A | KINGS LYNN - 31C | STRATFORD - 30A | STRATFORD - 30A | COLCHESTER - 30E | STRATFORD - 30A |
| Jan-59 | KINGS LYNN - 31C | **12/58: W/D** | STRATFORD - 30A | STRATFORD - 30A | **3/59: HAT - 34C** | STRATFORD - 30A | STRATFORD - 30A | COLCHESTER - 30E | STRATFORD - 30A |
| Aug-59 | KINGS LYNN - 31C | | STRATFORD - 30A | STRATFORD - 30A | HATFIELD - 34C | STRATFORD - 30A | STRATFORD - 30A | COLCHESTER - 30E | STRATFORD - 30A |
| Nov-59 | KINGS LYNN - 31C | | **10/59: HAT - 34C** | STRATFORD - 30A | HATFIELD - 34C | STRATFORD - 30A | STRATFORD - 30A | COLCHESTER - 30E | STRATFORD - 30A |
| Jan-60 | KINGS LYNN - 31C | | HATFIELD - 34C | STRATFORD - 30A | HATFIELD - 34C | STRATFORD - 30A | STRATFORD - 30A | COLCHESTER - 30E | STRATFORD - 30A |
| Apr-60 | KINGS LYNN - 31C | | HATFIELD - 34C | STRATFORD - 30A | HATFIELD - 34C | STRATFORD - 30A | STRATFORD - 30A | COLCHESTER - 30E | STRATFORD - 30A |
| Aug-60 | **8/60: STRAT - 30A** | | HATFIELD - 34C | STRATFORD - 30A | HATFIELD - 34C | STRATFORD - 30A | STRATFORD - 30A | COLCHESTER - 30E | STRATFORD - 30A |
| Nov-60 | **11/60: PARKS - 30F** | | HATFIELD - 34C | STRATFORD - 30A | HATFIELD - 34C | STRATFORD - 30A | STRATFORD - 30A | COLCHESTER - 30E | STRATFORD - 30A |

| | 69703 | 69704 | 69705 | 69706 | 69707 | 69708 | 69709 | 69710 | 69711 |
|---|---|---|---|---|---|---|---|---|---|
| Aug-50 | IPSWICH - 32B | STRATFORD - 30A | STRATFORD - 30A | NORWICH - 32A | NORWICH - 32A | NORWICH - 32A | NORWICH - 32A | STRATFORD - 30A | IPSWICH - 32B |
| Jan-51 | 1/51: STRAT - 30A | STRATFORD - 30A | STRATFORD - 30A | NORWICH - 32A | NORWICH - 32A | 12/50: M.CONS - 32G | NORWICH - 32A | STRATFORD - 30A | 9/50: STRAT - 30A |
| Aug-51 | STRATFORD - 30A | STRATFORD - 30A | STRATFORD - 30A | NORWICH - 32A | NORWICH - 32A | 9/51: NOR - 32A | NORWICH - 32A | STRATFORD - 30A | 10/50: K.LYNN - 31C |
| Jan-52 | STRATFORD - 30A | STRATFORD - 30A | STRATFORD - 30A | NORWICH - 32A | NORWICH - 32A | NORWICH - 32A | NORWICH - 32A | STRATFORD - 30A | 11/50: STRAT - 30A |
| Aug-52 | STRATFORD - 30A | 9/52: HAT - 34C | STRATFORD - 30A | NORWICH - 32A | NORWICH - 32A | NORWICH - 32A | NORWICH - 32A | STRATFORD - 30A | STRATFORD - 30A |
| Jan-53 | STRATFORD - 30A | HATFIELD - 34C | STRATFORD - 30A | NORWICH - 32A | NORWICH - 32A | NORWICH - 32A | NORWICH - 32A | STRATFORD - 30A | STRATFORD - 30A |
| Aug-53 | STRATFORD - 30A | HATFIELD - 34C | STRATFORD - 30A | NORWICH - 32A | NORWICH - 32A | NORWICH - 32A | 5/53: HAT - 34C | STRATFORD - 30A | STRATFORD - 30A |
| Jan-54 | STRATFORD - 30A | HATFIELD - 34C | STRATFORD - 30A | NORWICH - 32A | NORWICH - 32A | 4/54: YAR(ST) - 32D | HATFIELD - 34C | STRATFORD - 30A | STRATFORD - 30A |
| Aug-54 | STRATFORD - 30A | HATFIELD - 34C | STRATFORD - 30A | NORWICH - 32A | NORWICH - 32A | 10/54: STRAT - 30A | HATFIELD - 34C | STRATFORD - 30A | STRATFORD - 30A |
| Jan-55 | STRATFORD - 30A | HATFIELD - 34C | STRATFORD - 30A | NORWICH - 32A | NORWICH - 32A | 12/54: YAR(ST) - 32D | HATFIELD - 34C | STRATFORD - 30A | STRATFORD - 30A |
| Aug-55 | STRATFORD - 30A | HATFIELD - 34C | STRATFORD - 30A | NORWICH - 32A | NORWICH - 32A | YARMOUTH(ST) - 32D | HATFIELD - 34C | STRATFORD - 30A | STRATFORD - 30A |
| Jan-56 | STRATFORD - 30A | HATFIELD - 34C | STRATFORD - 30A | NORWICH - 32A | NORWICH - 32A | YARMOUTH(ST) - 32D | HATFIELD - 34C | STRATFORD - 30A | STRATFORD - 30A |
| Aug-56 | STRATFORD - 30A | HATFIELD - 34C | STRATFORD - 30A | 7/56: LOW - 32C | NORWICH - 32A | YARMOUTH(ST) - 32D | HATFIELD - 34C | STRATFORD - 30A | STRATFORD - 30A |
| Jan-57 | STRATFORD - 30A | HATFIELD - 34C | STRATFORD - 30A | 10/56: NOR - 32A | NORWICH - 32A | YARMOUTH(ST) - 32D | HATFIELD - 34C | STRATFORD - 30A | STRATFORD - 30A |
| Aug-57 | STRATFORD - 30A | HATFIELD - 34C | STRATFORD - 30A | 6/57: LOW - 32C | NORWICH - 32A | 7/57: LOW - 32C | 8/57: COL - 30E | STRATFORD - 30A | STRATFORD - 30A |
| Jan-58 | STRATFORD - 30A | HATFIELD - 34C | STRATFORD - 30A | LOWESTOFT - 32C | NORWICH - 32A | 10/57: YAR(ST) - 32D | 10/57: STRAT - 30A | STRATFORD - 30A | STRATFORD - 30A |
| Aug-58 | STRATFORD - 30A | HATFIELD - 34C | STRATFORD - 30A | LOWESTOFT - 32C | NORWICH - 32A | YARMOUTH(ST) - 32D | STRATFORD - 30A | STRATFORD - 30A | STRATFORD - 30A |
| Jan-59 | 1/59: W/D | HATFIELD - 34C | STRATFORD - 30A | LOWESTOFT - 32C | NORWICH - 32A | 1/59: STRAT - 30A | STRATFORD - 30A | STRATFORD - 30A | STRATFORD - 30A |
| Aug-59 | | HATFIELD - 34C | 6/59: W/D | 9/59: STRAT - 30A | 9/59: STRAT - 30A | STRATFORD - 30A | STRATFORD - 30A | STRATFORD - 30A | STRATFORD - 30A |
| Nov-59 | | HATFIELD - 34C | | STRATFORD - 30A | STRATFORD - 30A | STRATFORD - 30A | STRATFORD - 30A | STRATFORD - 30A | STRATFORD - 30A |
| Jan-60 | | 1/60: STRAT - 30A | | STRATFORD - 30A | STRATFORD - 30A | 2/60: PARKS - 30F | STRATFORD - 30A | STRATFORD - 30A | STRATFORD - 30A |
| Apr-60 | | STRATFORD - 30A | | STRATFORD - 30A | STRATFORD - 30A | PARKESTON - 30F | STRATFORD - 30A | STRATFORD - 30A | 3/60: W/D |
| Aug-60 | | STRATFORD - 30A | | STRATFORD - 30A | STRATFORD - 30A | PARKESTON - 30F | STRATFORD - 30A | STRATFORD - 30A | |
| Nov-60 | | 11/60: W/D | | STRATFORD - 30A | STRATFORD - 30A | PARKESTON - 30F | 11/60: W/D | STRATFORD - 30A | |

| | 69712 | 69713 | 69714 | 69715 | 69716 | 69717 | 69718 | 69719 | 69720 |
|---|---|---|---|---|---|---|---|---|---|
| Aug-50 | STRATFORD - 30A | STRATFORD - 30A | STRATFORD - 30A | STRATFORD - 30A | STRATFORD - 30A | STRATFORD - 30A | STRATFORD - 30A | STRATFORD - 30A | STRATFORD - 30A |
| Jan-51 | 10/50: K.LYNN - 31C | STRATFORD - 30A | STRATFORD - 30A | STRATFORD - 30A | 10/50: K.LYNN - 31C | STRATFORD - 30A | STRATFORD - 30A | STRATFORD - 30A | STRATFORD - 30A |
| Aug-51 | 11/50: STRAT - 30A | STRATFORD - 30A | STRATFORD - 30A | STRATFORD - 30A | 11/50: STRAT - 30A | 7/51: COL - 30E | STRATFORD - 30A | STRATFORD - 30A | STRATFORD - 30A |
| Jan-52 | STRATFORD - 30A | STRATFORD - 30A | STRATFORD - 30A | STRATFORD - 30A | STRATFORD - 30A | 9/51: STRAT - 30A | STRATFORD - 30A | STRATFORD - 30A | STRATFORD - 30A |
| Aug-52 | STRATFORD - 30A | STRATFORD - 30A | STRATFORD - 30A | STRATFORD - 30A | 7/52: COL - 30E | 11/51: COL - 30E | STRATFORD - 30A | 7/52: COL - 30E | STRATFORD - 30A |
| Jan-53 | STRATFORD - 30A | STRATFORD - 30A | STRATFORD - 30A | STRATFORD - 30A | 9/52: STRAT - 30A | 9/52: STRAT - 30A | STRATFORD - 30A | 9/52: STRAT - 30A | STRATFORD - 30A |
| Aug-53 | STRATFORD - 30A | STRATFORD - 30A | STRATFORD - 30A | STRATFORD - 30A | STRATFORD - 30A | STRATFORD - 30A | STRATFORD - 30A | 10/52: COL - 30E | STRATFORD - 30A |
| Jan-54 | STRATFORD - 30A | STRATFORD - 30A | STRATFORD - 30A | STRATFORD - 30A | STRATFORD - 30A | STRATFORD - 30A | STRATFORD - 30A | 12/53: STRAT - 30A | STRATFORD - 30A |
| Aug-54 | STRATFORD - 30A | STRATFORD - 30A | STRATFORD - 30A | STRATFORD - 30A | STRATFORD - 30A | STRATFORD - 30A | STRATFORD - 30A | STRATFORD - 30A | STRATFORD - 30A |
| Jan-55 | STRATFORD - 30A | STRATFORD - 30A | STRATFORD - 30A | STRATFORD - 30A | STRATFORD - 30A | STRATFORD - 30A | STRATFORD - 30A | STRATFORD - 30A | STRATFORD - 30A |
| Aug-55 | STRATFORD - 30A | STRATFORD - 30A | STRATFORD - 30A | STRATFORD - 30A | STRATFORD - 30A | STRATFORD - 30A | STRATFORD - 30A | STRATFORD - 30A | 4/55: COL - 30E |
| Jan-56 | STRATFORD - 30A | STRATFORD - 30A | STRATFORD - 30A | STRATFORD - 30A | STRATFORD - 30A | STRATFORD - 30A | STRATFORD - 30A | STRATFORD - 30A | COLCHESTER - 30E |
| Aug-56 | STRATFORD - 30A | STRATFORD - 30A | STRATFORD - 30A | STRATFORD - 30A | STRATFORD - 30A | STRATFORD - 30A | STRATFORD - 30A | STRATFORD - 30A | 10/56: STRAT - 30A |
| Jan-57 | STRATFORD - 30A | STRATFORD - 30A | STRATFORD - 30A | STRATFORD - 30A | STRATFORD - 30A | STRATFORD - 30A | STRATFORD - 30A | STRATFORD - 30A | STRATFORD - 30A |
| Aug-57 | STRATFORD - 30A | STRATFORD - 30A | STRATFORD - 30A | STRATFORD - 30A | STRATFORD - 30A | STRATFORD - 30A | STRATFORD - 30A | STRATFORD - 30A | STRATFORD - 30A |
| Jan-58 | STRATFORD - 30A | STRATFORD - 30A | STRATFORD - 30A | STRATFORD - 30A | STRATFORD - 30A | STRATFORD - 30A | STRATFORD - 30A | STRATFORD - 30A | STRATFORD - 30A |
| Aug-58 | STRATFORD - 30A | STRATFORD - 30A | STRATFORD - 30A | STRATFORD - 30A | STRATFORD - 30A | STRATFORD - 30A | STRATFORD - 30A | STRATFORD - 30A | STRATFORD - 30A |
| Jan-59 | STRATFORD - 30A | STRATFORD - 30A | STRATFORD - 30A | STRATFORD - 30A | 2/59: W/D | 1/59: W/D | STRATFORD - 30A | STRATFORD - 30A | STRATFORD - 30A |
| Aug-59 | STRATFORD - 30A | STRATFORD - 30A | STRATFORD - 30A | STRATFORD - 30A | | | STRATFORD - 30A | STRATFORD - 30A | STRATFORD - 30A |
| Nov-59 | STRATFORD - 30A | STRATFORD - 30A | STRATFORD - 30A | STRATFORD - 30A | | | STRATFORD - 30A | STRATFORD - 30A | STRATFORD - 30A |
| Jan-60 | STRATFORD - 30A | STRATFORD - 30A | STRATFORD - 30A | STRATFORD - 30A | | | STRATFORD - 30A | STRATFORD - 30A | STRATFORD - 30A |
| Apr-60 | STRATFORD - 30A | STRATFORD - 30A | STRATFORD - 30A | STRATFORD - 30A | | | STRATFORD - 30A | STRATFORD - 30A | STRATFORD - 30A |
| Aug-60 | STRATFORD - 30A | STRATFORD - 30A | STRATFORD - 30A | STRATFORD - 30A | | | STRATFORD - 30A | STRATFORD - 30A | STRATFORD - 30A |
| Nov-60 | STRATFORD - 30A | STRATFORD - 30A | STRATFORD - 30A | STRATFORD - 30A | | | STRATFORD - 30A | STRATFORD - 30A | 11/60: W/D |

| | 69721 | 69722 | 69723 | 69724 | 69725 | 69726 | 69727 | 69728 | 69729 |
|---|---|---|---|---|---|---|---|---|---|
| Aug-50 | STRATFORD - 30A | STRATFORD - 30A | STRATFORD - 30A | STRATFORD - 30A | STRATFORD - 30A | COLCHESTER - 30E | STRATFORD - 30A | STRATFORD - 30A | STRATFORD - 30A |
| Jan-51 | STRATFORD - 30A | STRATFORD - 30A | STRATFORD - 30A | STRATFORD - 30A | STRATFORD - 30A | 3/51: STRAT - 30A | STRATFORD - 30A | STRATFORD - 30A | STRATFORD - 30A |
| Aug-51 | STRATFORD - 30A | STRATFORD - 30A | STRATFORD - 30A | STRATFORD - 30A | STRATFORD - 30A | STRATFORD - 30A | STRATFORD - 30A | STRATFORD - 30A | STRATFORD - 30A |
| Jan-52 | STRATFORD - 30A | STRATFORD - 30A | STRATFORD - 30A | STRATFORD - 30A | STRATFORD - 30A | STRATFORD - 30A | STRATFORD - 30A | STRATFORD - 30A | STRATFORD - 30A |
| Aug-52 | STRATFORD - 30A | STRATFORD - 30A | STRATFORD - 30A | STRATFORD - 30A | STRATFORD - 30A | STRATFORD - 30A | STRATFORD - 30A | STRATFORD - 30A | STRATFORD - 30A |
| Jan-53 | STRATFORD - 30A | STRATFORD - 30A | STRATFORD - 30A | STRATFORD - 30A | STRATFORD - 30A | STRATFORD - 30A | STRATFORD - 30A | STRATFORD - 30A | STRATFORD - 30A |
| Aug-53 | STRATFORD - 30A | STRATFORD - 30A | STRATFORD - 30A | STRATFORD - 30A | STRATFORD - 30A | STRATFORD - 30A | STRATFORD - 30A | STRATFORD - 30A | STRATFORD - 30A |
| Jan-54 | STRATFORD - 30A | STRATFORD - 30A | STRATFORD - 30A | STRATFORD - 30A | STRATFORD - 30A | STRATFORD - 30A | STRATFORD - 30A | STRATFORD - 30A | STRATFORD - 30A |
| Aug-54 | STRATFORD - 30A | STRATFORD - 30A | STRATFORD - 30A | STRATFORD - 30A | STRATFORD - 30A | STRATFORD - 30A | STRATFORD - 30A | STRATFORD - 30A | STRATFORD - 30A |
| Jan-55 | STRATFORD - 30A | STRATFORD - 30A | STRATFORD - 30A | STRATFORD - 30A | STRATFORD - 30A | STRATFORD - 30A | STRATFORD - 30A | STRATFORD - 30A | STRATFORD - 30A |
| Aug-55 | STRATFORD - 30A | STRATFORD - 30A | STRATFORD - 30A | STRATFORD - 30A | STRATFORD - 30A | STRATFORD - 30A | STRATFORD - 30A | STRATFORD - 30A | STRATFORD - 30A |
| Jan-56 | STRATFORD - 30A | STRATFORD - 30A | STRATFORD - 30A | STRATFORD - 30A | STRATFORD - 30A | STRATFORD - 30A | STRATFORD - 30A | STRATFORD - 30A | STRATFORD - 30A |
| Aug-56 | 11/56: PARKS - 30F | STRATFORD - 30A | STRATFORD - 30A | STRATFORD - 30A | STRATFORD - 30A | STRATFORD - 30A | 11/56: PARKS - 30F | STRATFORD - 30A | STRATFORD - 30A |
| Jan-57 | 2/57: COL - 30E | STRATFORD - 30A | STRATFORD - 30A | STRATFORD - 30A | STRATFORD - 30A | STRATFORD - 30A | 2/57: COL - 30E | STRATFORD - 30A | STRATFORD - 30A |
| Aug-57 | 10/57: STRAT - 30A | STRATFORD - 30A | STRATFORD - 30A | STRATFORD - 30A | STRATFORD - 30A | STRATFORD - 30A | COLCHESTER - 30E | STRATFORD - 30A | STRATFORD - 30A |
| Jan-58 | STRATFORD - 30A | STRATFORD - 30A | STRATFORD - 30A | STRATFORD - 30A | STRATFORD - 30A | STRATFORD - 30A | COLCHESTER - 30E | STRATFORD - 30A | STRATFORD - 30A |
| Aug-58 | STRATFORD - 30A | STRATFORD - 30A | STRATFORD - 30A | STRATFORD - 30A | STRATFORD - 30A | STRATFORD - 30A | COLCHESTER - 30E | STRATFORD - 30A | STRATFORD - 30A |
| Jan-59 | STRATFORD - 30A | STRATFORD - 30A | STRATFORD - 30A | STRATFORD - 30A | STRATFORD - 30A | STRATFORD - 30A | COLCHESTER - 30E | STRATFORD - 30A | STRATFORD - 30A |
| Aug-59 | STRATFORD - 30A | STRATFORD - 30A | STRATFORD - 30A | STRATFORD - 30A | STRATFORD - 30A | STRATFORD - 30A | 5/59: STRAT - 30A | STRATFORD - 30A | STRATFORD - 30A |
| Nov-59 | STRATFORD - 30A | STRATFORD - 30A | STRATFORD - 30A | STRATFORD - 30A | STRATFORD - 30A | STRATFORD - 30A | STRATFORD - 30A | STRATFORD - 30A | STRATFORD - 30A |
| Jan-60 | STRATFORD - 30A | STRATFORD - 30A | STRATFORD - 30A | STRATFORD - 30A | STRATFORD - 30A | STRATFORD - 30A | STRATFORD - 30A | STRATFORD - 30A | STRATFORD - 30A |
| Apr-60 | STRATFORD - 30A | STRATFORD - 30A | STRATFORD - 30A | STRATFORD - 30A | STRATFORD - 30A | STRATFORD - 30A | STRATFORD - 30A | STRATFORD - 30A | STRATFORD - 30A |
| Aug-60 | STRATFORD - 30A | STRATFORD - 30A | STRATFORD - 30A | STRATFORD - 30A | STRATFORD - 30A | STRATFORD - 30A | STRATFORD - 30A | STRATFORD - 30A | STRATFORD - 30A |
| Nov-60 | STRATFORD - 30A | STRATFORD - 30A | STRATFORD - 30A | STRATFORD - 30A | STRATFORD - 30A | STRATFORD - 30A | STRATFORD - 30A | STRATFORD - 30A | STRATFORD - 30A |

| | 69730 | 69731 | 69732 | 69733 |
|---|---|---|---|---|
| Aug-50 | STRATFORD - 30A | STRATFORD - 30A | STRATFORD - 30A | STRATFORD - 30A |
| Jan-51 | STRATFORD - 30A | STRATFORD - 30A | STRATFORD - 30A | STRATFORD - 30A |
| Aug-51 | STRATFORD - 30A | STRATFORD - 30A | STRATFORD - 30A | STRATFORD - 30A |
| Jan-52 | STRATFORD - 30A | STRATFORD - 30A | STRATFORD - 30A | STRATFORD - 30A |
| Aug-52 | STRATFORD - 30A | STRATFORD - 30A | STRATFORD - 30A | STRATFORD - 30A |
| Jan-53 | STRATFORD - 30A | STRATFORD - 30A | STRATFORD - 30A | STRATFORD - 30A |
| Aug-53 | STRATFORD - 30A | STRATFORD - 30A | STRATFORD - 30A | STRATFORD - 30A |
| Jan-54 | STRATFORD - 30A | STRATFORD - 30A | 12/53: COL - 30E | STRATFORD - 30A |
| Aug-54 | STRATFORD - 30A | STRATFORD - 30A | COLCHESTER - 30E | STRATFORD - 30A |
| Jan-55 | STRATFORD - 30A | STRATFORD - 30A | COLCHESTER - 30E | STRATFORD - 30A |
| Aug-55 | STRATFORD - 30A | STRATFORD - 30A | COLCHESTER - 30E | STRATFORD - 30A |
| Jan-56 | STRATFORD - 30A | STRATFORD - 30A | COLCHESTER - 30E | STRATFORD - 30A |
| Aug-56 | STRATFORD - 30A | STRATFORD - 30A | COLCHESTER - 30E | 11/56: PARKS - 30F |
| Jan-57 | STRATFORD - 30A | STRATFORD - 30A | COLCHESTER - 30E | 2/57: COL - 30E |
| Aug-57 | STRATFORD - 30A | STRATFORD - 30A | COLCHESTER - 30E | COLCHESTER - 30E |
| Jan-58 | STRATFORD - 30A | STRATFORD - 30A | COLCHESTER - 30E | COLCHESTER - 30E |
| Aug-58 | STRATFORD - 30A | STRATFORD - 30A | COLCHESTER - 30E | COLCHESTER - 30E |
| Jan-59 | STRATFORD - 30A | 2/59: W/D | COLCHESTER - 30E | COLCHESTER - 30E |
| Aug-59 | STRATFORD - 30A | | COLCHESTER - 30E | COLCHESTER - 30E |
| Nov-59 | 11/59: PARKS - 30F | | 10/59: PARKS - 30F | 11/59: STRAT - 30A |
| Jan-60 | 2/60: STRAT - 30A | | 2/60: STRAT - 30A | STRATFORD - 30A |
| Apr-60 | STRATFORD - 30A | | STRATFORD - 30A | STRATFORD - 30A |
| Aug-60 | 8/60: PARKS - 30F | | STRATFORD - 30A | STRATFORD - 30A |
| Nov-60 | 11/60: STRAT - 30A | | STRATFORD - 30A | 11/60: W/D |

A7 4-6-2T (1910)

| | 69770 | 69771 | 69772 | 69773 | 69774 |
|---|---|---|---|---|---|
| Aug-50 | DAIRYCOATES - 53A | DAIRYCOATES - 53A | DAIRYCOATES - 53A | DAIRYCOATES - 53A | SPRINGHEAD - 53C |
| Jan-51 | DAIRYCOATES - 53A | DAIRYCOATES - 53A | DAIRYCOATES - 53A | DAIRYCOATES - 53A | SPRINGHEAD - 53C |
| Aug-51 | DAIRYCOATES - 53A | DAIRYCOATES - 53A | DAIRYCOATES - 53A | DAIRYCOATES - 53A | SPRINGHEAD - 53C |
| Jan-52 | DAIRYCOATES - 53A | DAIRYCOATES - 53A | DAIRYCOATES - 53A | DAIRYCOATES - 53A | SPRINGHEAD - 53C |
| Aug-52 | DAIRYCOATES - 53A | DAIRYCOATES - 53A | DAIRYCOATES - 53A | DAIRYCOATES - 53A | SPRINGHEAD - 53C |
| Jan-53 | DAIRYCOATES - 53A | DAIRYCOATES - 53A | DAIRYCOATES - 53A | DAIRYCOATES - 53A | SPRINGHEAD - 53C |
| Aug-53 | DAIRYCOATES - 53A | DAIRYCOATES - 53A | DAIRYCOATES - 53A | DAIRYCOATES - 53A | SPRINGHEAD - 53C |
| Jan-54 | DAIRYCOATES - 53A | DAIRYCOATES - 53A | DAIRYCOATES - 53A | DAIRYCOATES - 53A | SPRINGHEAD - 53C |
| Aug-54 | 10/54: W/D | 10/54: S'HEAD - 53C | DAIRYCOATES - 53A | DAIRYCOATES - 53A | 8/54: W/D |
| Jan-55 | | 11/54: W/D | DAIRYCOATES - 53A | 3/55: W/D | |
| Aug-55 | | | DAIRYCOATES - 53A | | |
| Jan-56 | | | SPRINGHEAD - 53C | | |
| Aug-56 | | | SPRINGHEAD - 53C | | |
| Jan-57 | | | SPRINGHEAD - 53C | | |
| Aug-57 | | | SPRINGHEAD - 53C | | |
| Jan-58 | | | 12/57: W/D | | |

### Group 1 — 69775–69783

| | 69775 | 69776 | 69777 | 69778 | 69779 | 69780 | 69781 | 69782 | 69783 |
|---|---|---|---|---|---|---|---|---|---|
| Aug-50 | DAIRYCOATES-53A | SPRINGHEAD-53C | DAIRYCOATES-53A | DAIRYCOATES-53A | DAIRYCOATES-53A | DAIRYCOATES-53A | STOCKTON-51E | DAIRYCOATES-53A | DAIRYCOATES-53A |
| Jan-51 | DAIRYCOATES-53A | SPRINGHEAD-53C | DAIRYCOATES-53A | DAIRYCOATES-53A | DAIRYCOATES-53A | 6/51: S'HEAD-53C | STOCKTON-51E | DAIRYCOATES-53A | DAIRYCOATES-53A |
| Aug-51 | DAIRYCOATES-53A | SPRINGHEAD-53C | DAIRYCOATES-53A | DAIRYCOATES-53A | DAIRYCOATES-53A | SPRINGHEAD-53C | STOCKTON-51E | DAIRYCOATES-53A | DAIRYCOATES-53A |
| Jan-52 | DAIRYCOATES-53A | SPRINGHEAD-53C | DAIRYCOATES-53A | DAIRYCOATES-53A | DAIRYCOATES-53A | SPRINGHEAD-53C | STOCKTON-51E | DAIRYCOATES-53A | DAIRYCOATES-53A |
| Aug-52 | 4/52: W/D | SPRINGHEAD-53C | 5/52: W/D | DAIRYCOATES-53A | DAIRYCOATES-53A | SPRINGHEAD-53C | 2/53: DAIRY-53A | DAIRYCOATES-53A | 10/52: S'HEAD-53C |
| Jan-53 | | SPRINGHEAD-53C | | DAIRYCOATES-53A | DAIRYCOATES-53A | SPRINGHEAD-53C | DAIRYCOATES-53A | DAIRYCOATES-53A | SPRINGHEAD-53C |
| Aug-53 | | SPRINGHEAD-53C | | DAIRYCOATES-53A | DAIRYCOATES-53A | SPRINGHEAD-53C | DAIRYCOATES-53A | DAIRYCOATES-53A | SPRINGHEAD-53C |
| Jan-54 | | 3/54: DAIRY-53A | | 10/54: S'HEAD-53C | DAIRYCOATES-53A | 11/54: W/D | 10/54: S'HEAD-53C | DAIRYCOATES-53A | SPRINGHEAD-53C |
| Aug-54 | | 5/54: S'HEAD-53C | | SPRINGHEAD-53C | 11/54: W/D | | SPRINGHEAD-53C | DAIRYCOATES-53A | SPRINGHEAD-53C |
| Jan-55 | | 6/54: W/D | | 5/55: W/D | | | SPRINGHEAD-53C | 3/55: T.DCK-54B | SPRINGHEAD-53C |
| Aug-55 | | | | | | | SPRINGHEAD-53C | TYNE DOCK-54B | SPRINGHEAD-53C |
| Jan-56 | | | | | | | SPRINGHEAD-53C | TYNE DOCK-54B | SPRINGHEAD-53C |
| Aug-56 | | | | | | | 11/56: W/D | 12/56: S'HEAD-53C | 12/56: W/D |
| Jan-57 | | | | | | | | SPRINGHEAD-53C | |
| Aug-57 | | | | | | | | 12/57: W/D | |
| Jan-58 | | | | | | | | | |
| Aug-58 | | | | | | | | | |
| Jan-59 | | | | | | | | | |
| Aug-59 | | | | | | | | | |
| Nov-59 | | | | | | | | | |
| Jan-60 | | | | | | | | | |
| Apr-60 | | | | | | | | | |
| Aug-60 | | | | | | | | | |
| Nov-60 | | | | | | | | | |

### Group 2 — 69784–69789, and A6 4-6-2T (1915) 69791, 69793, 69794

| | 69784 | 69785 | 69786 | 69787 | 69788 | 69789 | 69791 | 69793 | 69794 |
|---|---|---|---|---|---|---|---|---|---|
| Aug-50 | DAIRYCOATES-53A | SPRINGHEAD-53C | DAIRYCOATES-53A | STOCKTON-51E | DAIRYCOATES-53A | SPRINGHEAD-53C | STARBECK-50D | STARBECK-50D | STARBECK-50D |
| Jan-51 | DAIRYCOATES-53A | SPRINGHEAD-53C | DAIRYCOATES-53A | STOCKTON-51E | DAIRYCOATES-53A | SPRINGHEAD-53C | 2/51: B.GDNS-53B | 2/51: B.GDNS-53B | STARBECK-50D |
| Aug-51 | 9/51: S'HEAD-53C | SPRINGHEAD-53C | DAIRYCOATES-53A | STOCKTON-51E | DAIRYCOATES-53A | 5/51: W/D | 8/51: W/D | 4/51: W/D | 8/51: W/D |
| Jan-52 | SPRINGHEAD-53C | SPRINGHEAD-53C | DAIRYCOATES-53A | STOCKTON-51E | DAIRYCOATES-53A | | | | |
| Aug-52 | SPRINGHEAD-53C | SPRINGHEAD-53C | DAIRYCOATES-53A | STOCKTON-51E | DAIRYCOATES-53A | | | | |
| Jan-53 | SPRINGHEAD-53C | SPRINGHEAD-53C | DAIRYCOATES-53A | 2/53: DAIRY-53A | DAIRYCOATES-53A | | | | |
| Aug-53 | SPRINGHEAD-53C | SPRINGHEAD-53C | DAIRYCOATES-53A | 4/53: S'HEAD-53C | DAIRYCOATES-53A | | | | |
| Jan-54 | SPRINGHEAD-53C | SPRINGHEAD-53C | DAIRYCOATES-53A | SPRINGHEAD-53C | DAIRYCOATES-53A | | | | |
| Aug-54 | SPRINGHEAD-53C | SPRINGHEAD-53C | DAIRYCOATES-53A | 8/54: W/D | DAIRYCOATES-53A | | | | |
| Jan-55 | SPRINGHEAD-53C | SPRINGHEAD-53C | DAIRYCOATES-53A | | DAIRYCOATES-53A | | | | |
| Aug-55 | SPRINGHEAD-53C | SPRINGHEAD-53C | DAIRYCOATES-53A | | 10/55: S'HEAD-53C | | | | |
| Jan-56 | 3/56: W/D | 11/55: W/D | 3/56: S'HEAD-53C | | 11/55: W/D | | | | |
| Aug-56 | | | SPRINGHEAD-53C | | | | | | |
| Jan-57 | | | SPRINGHEAD-53C | | | | | | |
| Aug-57 | | | SPRINGHEAD-53C | | | | | | |
| Jan-58 | | | 12/57: W/D | | | | | | |
| Aug-58 | | | | | | | | | |
| Jan-59 | | | | | | | | | |
| Aug-59 | | | | | | | | | |
| Nov-59 | | | | | | | | | |
| Jan-60 | | | | | | | | | |
| Apr-60 | | | | | | | | | |
| Aug-60 | | | | | | | | | |
| Nov-60 | | | | | | | | | |

### Group 3 — 69796–69798, and A5 4-6-2T (1911) 69800–69805

| | 69796 | 69797 | 69798 | 69800 | 69801 | 69802 | 69803 | 69804 | 69805 |
|---|---|---|---|---|---|---|---|---|---|
| Aug-50 | B.GARDENS-53B | STARBECK-50D | B.GARDENS-53B | IMMINGHAM-40B | COLWICK-38A | SALTBURN-51K | GRANTHAM-35B | LINCOLN-40A | NEASDEN-34E |
| Jan-51 | B.GARDENS-53B | STARBECK-50D | 2/51: W/D | IMMINGHAM-40B | 2/51: DARL-51A | SALTBURN-51K | 11/50: BOST-40F | LINCOLN-40A | NEASDEN-34E |
| Aug-51 | B.GARDENS-53B | 8/51: W/D | | IMMINGHAM-40B | 7/51: COLW-38A | 8/51: B.GDNS-53B | BOSTON-40F | LINCOLN-40A | NEASDEN-34E |
| Jan-52 | B.GARDENS-53B | | | IMMINGHAM-40B | COLWICK-38A | B.GARDENS-53B | BOSTON-40F | LINCOLN-40A | NEASDEN-34E |
| Aug-52 | B.GARDENS-53B | | | IMMINGHAM-40B | COLWICK-38A | B.GARDENS-53B | BOSTON-40F | LINCOLN-40A | NEASDEN-34E |
| Jan-53 | 3/53: W/D | | | IMMINGHAM-40B | COLWICK-38A | B.GARDENS-53B | BOSTON-40F | LINCOLN-40A | NEASDEN-34E |
| Aug-53 | | | | IMMINGHAM-40B | COLWICK-38A | B.GARDENS-53B | BOSTON-40F | LINCOLN-40A | 6/54: GORT-39A |
| Jan-54 | | | | IMMINGHAM-40B | COLWICK-38A | 1/55: BRID-53D | BOSTON-40F | 2/55: IMM-40B | GORTON-39A |
| Aug-54 | | | | IMMINGHAM-40B | 1/55: BRID-53D | 6/55: B.GDNS-53B | 9/55: IMM-40B | 4/55: BOST-40F | GORTON-39A |
| Jan-55 | | | | 11/55: COL-38A | 6/55: B.GDNS-53B | IMMINGHAM-40B | IMMINGHAM-40B | 5/55: L.JCN-40E | GORTON-39A |
| Aug-55 | | | | COLWICK-38A | 10/56: GORT-39A | B.GARDENS-53B | 6/56: L.JCN-40E | 11/55: COLW-38A | GORTON-39A |
| Jan-56 | | | | COLWICK-38A | GORTON-39A | B.GARDENS-53B | 11/56: STAVE-38D | COLWICK-38A | GORTON-39A |
| Aug-56 | | | | 10/57: LTR(GC)-38C | GORTON-39A | B.GARDENS-53B | STAVELEY-38D | COLWICK-38A | 5/57: COLW-38A |
| Jan-57 | | | | 2/58: STAVE-41H | GORTON-9G | B.GARDENS-53B | 4/58: DARN-41A | COLWICK-38A | COLWICK-38A |
| Aug-57 | | | | 6/58: LTR(GC)-15E | GORTON-9G | 12/58: W/D | 6/58: LINC-40A | 4/58: W/D | COLWICK-38A |
| Jan-58 | | | | COLWICK-40E | GORTON-9G | | LINCOLN-40A | | COLWICK-40E |
| Aug-58 | | | | 8/59: W/D | GORTON-9G | | 6/59: W/D | | 9/59: W/D |
| Jan-59 | | | | | GORTON-9G | | | | |
| Aug-59 | | | | | 3/60: W/D | | | | |
| Nov-59 | | | | | | | | | |
| Jan-60 | | | | | | | | | |
| Apr-60 | | | | | | | | | |
| Aug-60 | | | | | | | | | |
| Nov-60 | | | | | | | | | |

### Group 4 — 69806–69814

| | 69806 | 69807 | 69808 | 69809 | 69810 | 69811 | 69812 | 69813 | 69814 |
|---|---|---|---|---|---|---|---|---|---|
| Aug-50 | COLWICK-38A | COLWICK-38A | BOSTON-40F | COLWICK-38A | COLWICK-38A | SALTBURN-51K | LANGWTH JCN-40E | LINCOLN-40A | COLWICK-38A |
| Jan-51 | COLWICK-38A | COLWICK-38A | BOSTON-40F | COLWICK-38A | 2/51: DARL-51A | SALTBURN-51K | LANGWTH JCN-40E | LINCOLN-40A | COLWICK-38A |
| Aug-51 | COLWICK-38A | COLWICK-38A | BOSTON-40F | COLWICK-38A | 7/51: COLW-38A | 8/51: B.GDNS-53B | LANGWTH JCN-40E | LINCOLN-40A | 4/51: NEAS-34E |
| Jan-52 | COLWICK-38A | COLWICK-38A | BOSTON-40F | COLWICK-38A | COLWICK-38A | B.GARDENS-53B | LANGWTH JCN-40E | LINCOLN-40A | NEASDEN-34E |
| Aug-52 | COLWICK-38A | COLWICK-38A | BOSTON-40F | COLWICK-38A | COLWICK-38A | B.GARDENS-53B | LANGWTH JCN-40E | LINCOLN-40A | NEASDEN-34E |
| Jan-53 | COLWICK-38A | COLWICK-38A | BOSTON-40F | COLWICK-38A | COLWICK-38A | B.GARDENS-53B | LANGWTH JCN-40E | LINCOLN-40A | NEASDEN-34E |
| Aug-53 | COLWICK-38A | COLWICK-38A | BOSTON-40F | COLWICK-38A | COLWICK-38A | B.GARDENS-53B | LANGWTH JCN-40E | LINCOLN-40A | NEASDEN-34E |
| Jan-54 | COLWICK-38A | COLWICK-38A | BOSTON-40F | COLWICK-38A | COLWICK-38A | B.GARDENS-53B | LANGWTH JCN-40E | LINCOLN-40A | 5/54: GRAN-35B |
| Aug-54 | 6/54: GORT-39A | COLWICK-38A | BOSTON-40F | COLWICK-38A | COLWICK-38A | B.GARDENS-53B | 11/54: LINC-40A | 10/54: IMM-40B | GRANTHAM-35B |
| Jan-55 | GORTON-39A | COLWICK-38A | BOSTON-40F | COLWICK-38A | COLWICK-38A | B.GARDENS-53B | 2/55: IMM-40B | IMMINGHAM-40B | GRANTHAM-35B |
| Aug-55 | GORTON-39A | COLWICK-38A | 2/56: IMM-40B | COLWICK-38A | COLWICK-38A | B.GARDENS-53B | 3/56: BOST-40F | 2/56: RET-36E | GRANTHAM-35B |
| Jan-56 | GORTON-39A | COLWICK-38A | 3/56: BOST-40F | COLWICK-38A | COLWICK-38A | B.GARDENS-53B | 8/56: COLW-38A | 3/56: IMM-40B | GRANTHAM-35B |
| Aug-56 | GORTON-39A | COLWICK-38A | BOSTON-40F | 10/56: ANNES-38B | 10/56: ANNES-38B | B.GARDENS-53B | COLWICK-38A | 11/56: LIONC-40A | GRANTHAM-35B |
| Jan-57 | GORTON-39A | COLWICK-38A | BOSTON-40F | ANNESLEY-38B | COLWICK-38A | B.GARDENS-53B | COLWICK-38A | 12/56: GORT-39A | GRANTHAM-35B |
| Aug-57 | GORTON-39A | COLWICK-38A | BOSTON-40F | ANNESLEY-38B | COLWICK-38A | B.GARDENS-53B | COLWICK-40E | GORTON-39A | GRANTHAM-34F |
| Jan-58 | GORTON-39A | 7/58: W/D | BOSTON-40F | ANNESLEY-38B | COLWICK-38A | B.GARDENS-53B | COLWICK-40E | GORTON-9G | GRANTHAM-34F |
| Aug-58 | GORTON-9G | | 3/59: LINC-40A | 12/58: COLW-40E | COLWICK-40E | 10/58: W/D | 7/59: W/D | GORTON-9G | GRANTHAM-34F |
| Jan-59 | GORTON-9G | | LINCOLN-40A | 5/59: W/D | 10/58: W/D | | | GORTON-9G | 1/60: KX-34A |
| Aug-59 | GORTON-9G | | LINCOLN-40A | | | | | GORTON-9G | 5/60: LINC-40A |
| Nov-59 | GORTON-9G | | LINCOLN-40A | | | | | 3/60: W/D | 6/60: COLW-40E |
| Jan-60 | GORTON-9G | | LINCOLN-40A | | | | | | COLWICK-40E |
| Apr-60 | 3/60: W/D | | LINCOLN-40A | | | | | | |
| Aug-60 | | | | | | | | | |
| Nov-60 | | | | | | | | | |

| | 69815 | 69816 | 69817 | 69818 | 69819 | 69820 | 69821 | 69822 | 69823 |
|---|---|---|---|---|---|---|---|---|---|
| Aug-50 | LANGWTHJCN-40E | GRANTHAM-35B | COLWICK-38A | LANGWTHJCN-40E | BOSTON-40F | LINCOLN-40A | COLWICK-38A | NEASDEN-34E | COLWICK-38A |
| Jan-51 | LANGWTHJCN-40E | 10/50: LINC - 40A | COLWICK-38A | 1/51: DARL - 51A | BOSTON-40F | LINCOLN-40A | 2/51: L.JCN - 40E | NEASDEN-34E | COLWICK-38A |
| Aug-51 | LANGWTHJCN-40E | 11/50: BOST - 40F | COLWICK-38A | 7/51: COLW - 38A | BOSTON-40F | LINCOLN-40A | LANGWTHJCN-40E | NEASDEN-34E | COLWICK-38A |
| Jan-52 | LANGWTHJCN-40E | BOSTON-40F | COLWICK-38A | COLWICK-38A | BOSTON-40F | 3/52: IMM - 40B | 3/52: BOST - 40F | NEASDEN-34E | COLWICK-38A |
| Aug-52 | LANGWTHJCN-40E | BOSTON-40F | COLWICK-38A | COLWICK-38A | BOSTON-40F | IMMINGHAM-40B | 6/52: L.JCN - 40E | NEASDEN-34E | COLWICK-38A |
| Jan-53 | LANGWTHJCN-40E | BOSTON-40F | COLWICK-38A | COLWICK-38A | BOSTON-40F | IMMINGHAM-40B | LANGWTHJCN-40E | 1/53: COLW - 38A | COLWICK-38A |
| Aug-53 | LANGWTHJCN-40E | BOSTON-40F | COLWICK-38A | COLWICK-38A | BOSTON-40F | IMMINGHAM-40B | LANGWTHJCN-40E | COLWICK-38A | COLWICK-38A |
| Jan-54 | LANGWTHJCN-40E | BOSTON-40F | COLWICK-38A | COLWICK-38A | BOSTON-40F | IMMINGHAM-40B | LANGWTHJCN-40E | COLWICK-38A | COLWICK-38A |
| Aug-54 | LANGWTHJCN-40E | BOSTON-40F | 6/54: GORT - 39A | COLWICK-38A | BOSTON-40F | IMMINGHAM-40B | 11/54: LINC - 40A | COLWICK-38A | 6/54: GORT - 39A |
| Jan-55 | 11/54: IMM - 40B | BOSTON-40F | GORTON-39A | COLWICK-38A | BOSTON-40F | IMMINGHAM-40B | 2/55: IMM - 40B | COLWICK-38A | GORTON-39A |
| Aug-55 | 9/55: GORT - 39A | BOSTON-40F | GORTON-39A | COLWICK-38A | BOSTON-40F | IMMINGHAM-40B | 7/55: L.JCN - 40E | COLWICK-38A | GORTON-39A |
| Jan-56 | GORTON-39A | 3/56: IMM - 40B | GORTON-39A | COLWICK-38A | BOSTON-40F | IMMINGHAM-40B | 11/55: COLW - 38A | COLWICK-38A | GORTON-39A |
| Aug-56 | GORTON-39A | IMMINGHAM-40B | GORTON-39A | 10/56: ANNES - 38B | BOSTON-40F | IMMINGHAM-40B | COLWICK-38A | COLWICK-38A | GORTON-39A |
| Jan-57 | GORTON-39A | 12/56: LINC - 40A | GORTON-39A | ANNESLEY-38B | 12/56: ANNES - 38B | 12/56: LINC - 40A | 2/57: IMM - 40B | 2/57: GORT - 39A | GORTON-39A |
| Aug-57 | 7/57: W/D | LINCOLN-40A | GORTON-39A | ANNESLEY-38B | ANNESLEY-38B | LINCOLN-40A | 6/57: LINC - 40A | GORTON-39A | GORTON-39A |
| Jan-58 | | LINCOLN-40A | GORTON-39A | ANNESLEY-38B | 3/58: W/D | LINCOLN-40A | LINCOLN-40A | GORTON-39A | GORTON-39A |
| Aug-58 | | LINCOLN-40A | GORTON-9G | ANNESLEY-16D | | LINCOLN-40A | LINCOLN-40A | GORTON-9G | GORTON-9G |
| Jan-59 | | 1/59: W/D | GORTON-9G | 12/58: W/D | | LINCOLN-40A | LINCOLN-40A | 11/58: W/D | GORTON-9G |
| Aug-59 | | | GORTON-9G | | | LINCOLN-40A | LINCOLN-40A | | GORTON-9G |
| Nov-59 | | | GORTON-9G | | | LINCOLN-40A | LINCOLN-40A | | GORTON-9G |
| Jan-60 | | | GORTON-9G | | | LINCOLN-40A | LINCOLN-40A | | GORTON-9G |
| Apr-60 | | | 4/60: W/D | | | LINCOLN-40A | 5/60: W/D | | 4/60: W/D |
| Aug-60 | | | | | | 7/60: IMM - 40B | | | |
| Nov-60 | | | | | | IMMINGHAM-40B | | | |

| | 69824 | 69825 | 69826 | 69827 | 69828 | 69829 | A5 4-6-2T (1925) 69830 | 69831 | 69832 |
|---|---|---|---|---|---|---|---|---|---|
| Aug-50 | GRANTHAM-35B | COLWICK-38A | COLWICK-38A | NEASDEN-34E | NEASDEN-34E | NEASDEN-34E | DARLINGTON-51A | SALTBURN-51K | DARLINGTON-51A |
| Jan-51 | 10/50: BOST - 40F | COLWICK-38A | 2/51: DARL - 51A | NEASDEN-34E | NEASDEN-34E | NEASDEN-34E | 4/51: STRAT - 30A | SALTBURN-51K | 4/51: STRAT - 30A |
| Aug-51 | 5/51: LINC - 40A | COLWICK-38A | 9/51: COLW - 38A | NEASDEN-34E | NEASDEN-34E | NEASDEN-34E | 5/51: DARL - 51A | SALTBURN-51K | 5/51: DARL - 51A |
| Jan-52 | LINCOLN-40A | COLWICK-38A | COLWICK-38A | NEASDEN-34E | NEASDEN-34E | NEASDEN-34E | DARLINGTON-51A | SALTBURN-51K | DARLINGTON-51A |
| Aug-52 | 6/52: NOR - 32A | COLWICK-38A | 6/52: NOR - 32A | NEASDEN-34E | 7/52: LINC - 40A | NEASDEN-34E | DARLINGTON-51A | SALTBURN-51K | DARLINGTON-51A |
| Jan-53 | NORWICH-32A | COLWICK-38A | NORWICH-32A | NEASDEN-34E | LINCOLN-40A | NEASDEN-34E | DARLINGTON-51A | SALTBURN-51K | DARLINGTON-51A |
| Aug-53 | NORWICH-32A | COLWICK-38A | NORWICH-32A | NEASDEN-34E | 10/53: L.JCN - 40E | NEASDEN-34E | DARLINGTON-51A | SALTBURN-51K | DARLINGTON-51A |
| Jan-54 | NORWICH-32A | COLWICK-38A | NORWICH-32A | NEASDEN-34E | 11/53: LINC - 40A | NEASDEN-34E | DARLINGTON-51A | SALTBURN-51K | DARLINGTON-51A |
| Aug-54 | NORWICH-32A | COLWICK-38A | NORWICH-32A | 5/54: GRAN - 35B | LINCOLN-40A | 6/54: GORT - 39A | 6/54: STOCK - 51E | 6/54: DARL - 51A | DARLINGTON-51A |
| Jan-55 | NORWICH-32A | COLWICK-38A | NORWICH-32A | GRANTHAM-35B | LINCOLN-40A | GORTON-39A | 10/54: DARL - 51A | 2/55: STOCK - 51E | DARLINGTON-51A |
| Aug-55 | NORWICH-32A | COLWICK-38A | NORWICH-32A | GRANTHAM-35B | 5/55: L.JCN - 40E | 9/55: NOR - 32A | DARLINGTON-51A | 9/55: DARL - 51A | DARLINGTON-51A |
| Jan-56 | 11/55: LOW - 32C | COLWICK-38A | 1/56: LOW - 32C | GRANTHAM-35B | 12/55: TUX - 40D | 1/56: LOW - 32C | DARLINGTON-51A | DARLINGTON-51A | DARLINGTON-51A |
| Aug-56 | LOWESTOFT-32C | 10/56: ANNES - 38B | LOWESTOFT-32C | GRANTHAM-35B | 8/56: COLW - 38A | LOWESTOFT-32C | DARLINGTON-51A | DARLINGTON-51A | DARLINGTON-51A |
| Jan-57 | 2/57: IMM - 40B | ANNESLEY-38B | 2/57: IMM - 40B | GRANTHAM-35B | 10/56: GORT - 39A | 2/57: IMM - 40B | 9/57: W.HPL - 51C | 9/57: W.HPL - 51C | DARLINGTON-51A |
| Aug-57 | IMMINGHAM-40B | ANNESLEY-38B | IMMINGHAM-40B | GRANTHAM-35B | 5/57: COLW - 38A | IMMINGHAM-40B | 11/57: SALT - 51K | 11/57: SALT - 51K | 9/57: B.GDNS - 53B |
| Jan-58 | 4/58: GRAN - 34F | ANNESLEY-38B | IMMINGHAM-40B | GRANTHAM-35B | COLWICK-38A | IMMINGHAM-40B | 2/58: MBRO - 51D | 2/58: MBRO - 51D | B.GARDENS-53B |
| Aug-58 | 6/58: LINC - 40A | ANNESLEY-16D | 6/58: W/D | GRANTHAM-34F | COLWICK-40E | IMMINGHAM-40B | 6/58: TBY - 51L | 6/58: TBY - 51L | B.GARDENS-53B |
| Jan-59 | 12/58: W/D | 12/58: COLW - 40E | | GRANTHAM-34F | 11/58: W/D | IMMINGHAM-40B | 11/58: W/D | 11/58: W/D | 10/58: W/D |
| Aug-59 | | COLWICK-40E | | GRANTHAM-34F | | IMMINGHAM-40B | | | |
| Nov-59 | | 11/59: W/D | | 11/59: W/D | | IMMINGHAM-40B | | | |
| Jan-60 | | | | | | IMMINGHAM-40B | | | |
| Apr-60 | | | | | | 5/60: W/D | | | |
| Aug-60 | | | | | | | | | |
| Nov-60 | | | | | | | | | |

| | 69833 | 69834 | 69835 | 69836 | 69837 | 69838 | 69839 | 69840 | 69841 |
|---|---|---|---|---|---|---|---|---|---|
| Aug-50 | DARLINGTON-51A | SALTBURN-51K | DARLINGTON-51A | DARLINGTON-51A | DARLINGTON-51A | DARLINGTON-51A | DARLINGTON-51A | DARLINGTON-51A | DARLINGTON-51A |
| Jan-51 | 4/51: STRAT - 30A | SALTBURN-51K | 1/51: NOR - 32A | 2/51: NOR - 32A | 2/51: NOR - 32A | 4/51: STRAT - 30A | 4/51: STRAT - 30A | 2/51: NOR - 32A | 4/51: STRAT - 30A |
| Aug-51 | 5/51: DARL - 51A | SALTBURN-51K | 4/51: STRAT - 30A | 8/51: DARL - 51A | 4/51: STRAT - 30A | 5/51: DARL - 51A | 5/51: DARL - 51A | 4/51: STRAT - 30A | 7/51: DARL - 51A |
| Jan-52 | DARLINGTON-51A | SALTBURN-51K | 5/51: NOR - 32A | DARLINGTON-51A | 5/51: NOR - 32A | DARLINGTON-51A | DARLINGTON-51A | 5/51: NOR - 32A | DARLINGTON-51A |
| Aug-52 | DARLINGTON-51A | SALTBURN-51K | 8/51: DARL - 51A | 7/52: B.GDNS - 53B | 8/51: DARL - 51A | DARLINGTON-51A | DARLINGTON-51A | 6/51: DARL - 51A | DARLINGTON-51A |
| Jan-53 | DARLINGTON-51A | SALTBURN-51K | DARLINGTON-51A | B.GARDENS-53B | 8/52: B.GDNS - 53B | DARLINGTON-51A | DARLINGTON-51A | DARLINGTON-51A | DARLINGTON-51A |
| Aug-53 | DARLINGTON-51A | SALTBURN-51K | DARLINGTON-51A | B.GARDENS-53B | B.GARDENS-53B | DARLINGTON-51A | DARLINGTON-51A | DARLINGTON-51A | DARLINGTON-51A |
| Jan-54 | DARLINGTON-51A | SALTBURN-51K | DARLINGTON-51A | B.GARDENS-53B | B.GARDENS-53B | DARLINGTON-51A | DARLINGTON-51A | DARLINGTON-51A | DARLINGTON-51A |
| Aug-54 | DARLINGTON-51A | 6/54: STOCK - 51E | 6/54: B.GDNS - 53B | B.GARDENS-53B | B.GARDENS-53B | DARLINGTON-51A | 6/54: STOCK - 51E | DARLINGTON-51A | 6/54: STOCK - 51E |
| Jan-55 | DARLINGTON-51A | 10/54: DARL - 51A | B.GARDENS-53B | B.GARDENS-53B | B.GARDENS-53B | DARLINGTON-51A | 10/54: DARL - 51A | DARLINGTON-51A | 10/54: DARL - 51A |
| Aug-55 | DARLINGTON-51A | 2/55: STOCK - 51E | B.GARDENS-53B | B.GARDENS-53B | B.GARDENS-53B | 6/55: STOCK - 51E | DARLINGTON-51A | DARLINGTON-51A | DARLINGTON-51A |
| Jan-56 | DARLINGTON-51A | 9/55: DARL - 51A | B.GARDENS-53B | B.GARDENS-53B | B.GARDENS-53B | STOCKTON-51E | DARLINGTON-51A | DARLINGTON-51A | DARLINGTON-51A |
| Aug-56 | DARLINGTON-51A | DARLINGTON-51A | B.GARDENS-53B | B.GARDENS-53B | B.GARDENS-53B | STOCKTON-51E | DARLINGTON-51A | DARLINGTON-51A | DARLINGTON-51A |
| Jan-57 | DARLINGTON-51A | 8/57: W.HPL - 51C | B.GARDENS-53B | B.GARDENS-53B | B.GARDENS-53B | STOCKTON-51E | DARLINGTON-51A | DARLINGTON-51A | DARLINGTON-51A |
| Aug-57 | 4/57: W/D | 11/57: SALT - 51K | 6/57: STOCK - 51C | 6/57: DARL - 51A | B.GARDENS-53B | STOCKTON-51E | DARLINGTON-51A | DARLINGTON-51A | DARLINGTON-51A |
| Jan-58 | | 2/58: MBRO - 51D | STOCKTON-51E | 9/57: B.GDNS - 53B | B.GARDENS-53B | STOCKTON-51E | DARLINGTON-51A | DARLINGTON-51A | DARLINGTON-51A |
| Aug-58 | | 6/58: TBY - 51L | STOCKTON-51E | 8/58: W/D | B.GARDENS-53B | STOCKTON-51E | 9/58: W/D | 9/58: W/D | 9/58: W/D |
| Jan-59 | | 10/58: W/D | 11/58: W/D | | 12/58: W/D | 11/58: W/D | | | |
| Aug-59 | | | | | | | | | |
| Nov-59 | | | | | | | | | |
| Jan-60 | | | | | | | | | |
| Apr-60 | | | | | | | | | |
| Aug-60 | | | | | | | | | |
| Nov-60 | | | | | | | | | |

| | 69842 | A8 4-6-2T (1931) 69850 | 69851 | 69852 | 69853 | 69854 | 69855 | 69856 | 69857 |
|---|---|---|---|---|---|---|---|---|---|
| Aug-50 | SALTBURN-51K | SUNDERLAND-54A | W.AUCKLAND-51F | W.HARTLEPOOL-51C | SUNDERLAND-54A | B.GARDENS-53B | B.GARDENS-53B | W.AUCKLAND-51F | SUNDERLAND-54A |
| Jan-51 | 2/51: NOR - 32A | SUNDERLAND-54A | W.AUCKLAND-51F | W.HARTLEPOOL-51C | SUNDERLAND-54A | 11/50: MBRO - 51D | B.GARDENS-53B | W.AUCKLAND-51F | SUNDERLAND-54A |
| Aug-51 | 3/51: NEAS - 34E | SUNDERLAND-54A | W.AUCKLAND-51F | W.HARTLEPOOL-51C | SUNDERLAND-54A | MIDDLESBROUGH-51D | 8/51: SALT - 51K | W.AUCKLAND-51F | SUNDERLAND-54A |
| Jan-52 | 4/51: STRAT - 30A | SUNDERLAND-54A | W.AUCKLAND-51F | W.HARTLEPOOL-51C | SUNDERLAND-54A | MIDDLESBROUGH-51D | SALTBURN-51K | W.AUCKLAND-51F | SUNDERLAND-54A |
| Aug-52 | 5/51: NEAS - 34E | SUNDERLAND-54A | W.AUCKLAND-51F | 7/52: STOCK - 51E | SUNDERLAND-54A | MIDDLESBROUGH-51D | SALTBURN-51K | W.AUCKLAND-51F | SUNDERLAND-54A |
| Jan-53 | 7/51: DARL - 51A | SUNDERLAND-54A | W.AUCKLAND-51F | 11/52: MBRO - 51D | SUNDERLAND-54A | MIDDLESBROUGH-51D | SALTBURN-51K | W.AUCKLAND-51F | SUNDERLAND-54A |
| Aug-53 | DARLINGTON-51A | SUNDERLAND-54A | W.AUCKLAND-51F | MIDDLESBROUGH-51D | SUNDERLAND-54A | MIDDLESBROUGH-51D | SALTBURN-51K | W.AUCKLAND-51F | SUNDERLAND-54A |
| Jan-54 | DARLINGTON-51A | SUNDERLAND-54A | W.AUCKLAND-51F | MIDDLESBROUGH-51D | SUNDERLAND-54A | MIDDLESBROUGH-51D | SALTBURN-51K | W.AUCKLAND-51F | SUNDERLAND-54A |
| Aug-54 | DARLINGTON-51A | SUNDERLAND-54A | W.AUCKLAND-51F | MIDDLESBROUGH-51D | SUNDERLAND-54A | MIDDLESBROUGH-51D | SALTBURN-51K | W.AUCKLAND-51F | SUNDERLAND-54A |
| Jan-55 | DARLINGTON-51A | SUNDERLAND-54A | W.AUCKLAND-51F | 10/54: SALT - 51K | SUNDERLAND-54A | MIDDLESBROUGH-51D | SALTBURN-51K | W.AUCKLAND-51F | SUNDERLAND-54A |
| Aug-55 | 6/55: STOCK - 51E | SUNDERLAND-54A | W.AUCKLAND-51F | SALTBURN-51K | SUNDERLAND-54A | MIDDLESBROUGH-51D | SALTBURN-51K | W.AUCKLAND-51F | SUNDERLAND-54A |
| Jan-56 | STOCKTON-51E | SUNDERLAND-54A | W.AUCKLAND-51F | SALTBURN-51K | SUNDERLAND-54A | MIDDLESBROUGH-51D | SALTBURN-51K | W.AUCKLAND-51F | SUNDERLAND-54A |
| Aug-56 | STOCKTON-51E | SUNDERLAND-54A | W.AUCKLAND-51F | SALTBURN-51K | SUNDERLAND-54A | MIDDLESBROUGH-51D | SALTBURN-51K | W.AUCKLAND-51F | SUNDERLAND-54A |
| Jan-57 | 9/57: W.HPL - 51C | SUNDERLAND-54A | W.AUCKLAND-51F | SALTBURN-51K | SUNDERLAND-54A | MIDDLESBROUGH-51D | SALTBURN-51K | W.AUCKLAND-51F | SUNDERLAND-54A |
| Aug-57 | 11/57: SALT - 51E | SUNDERLAND-54A | W.AUCKLAND-51F | 9/57: SUND - 54A | SUNDERLAND-54A | 9/57: SUND - 54A | 9/57: SUND - 54A | W.AUCKLAND-51F | SUNDERLAND-54A |
| Jan-58 | 2/58: MBRO - 51D | SUNDERLAND-54A | W.AUCKLAND-51F | SUNDERLAND-54A | SUNDERLAND-54A | SUNDERLAND-54A | SUNDERLAND-54A | W.AUCKLAND-51F | SUNDERLAND-54A |
| Aug-58 | 6/58: TBY - 51L | SUNDERLAND-54A | W.AUCKLAND-51F | SUNDERLAND-54A | SUNDERLAND-54A | SUNDERLAND-54A | SUNDERLAND-54A | W.AUCKLAND-51F | SUNDERLAND-54A |
| Jan-59 | 10/58: W/D | SUNDERLAND-52G | 11/58: W/D | SUNDERLAND-52G | SUNDERLAND-52G | SUNDERLAND-52G | SUNDERLAND-52G | W.AUCKLAND-51F | SUNDERLAND-52G |
| Aug-59 | | SUNDERLAND-52G | | SUNDERLAND-52G | SUNDERLAND-52G | SUNDERLAND-52G | SUNDERLAND-52G | W.AUCKLAND-51F | SUNDERLAND-52G |
| Nov-59 | | SUNDERLAND-52G | | 11/59: W/D | SUNDERLAND-52G | SUNDERLAND-52G | SUNDERLAND-52G | 11/59: W/D | SUNDERLAND-52G |
| Jan-60 | | SUNDERLAND-52G | | | SUNDERLAND-52G | SUNDERLAND-52G | SUNDERLAND-52G | | SUNDERLAND-52G |
| Apr-60 | | SUNDERLAND-52G | | | 2/60: W/D | 4/60: W/D | 2/60: W/D | | 2/60: W/D |
| Aug-60 | | 6/60: W/D | | | | | | | |
| Nov-60 | | | | | | | | | |

The Ex-LNER did not make much use of the post-nationalisation standard engines and apart from the introduction of 9F 2-10-0's at New England, Doncaster and Tyne Dock the only concentration of standards was on the Great Eastern where a batch of Britannia Pacifics dominated the Liverpool Street - Norwich workings. After only six years the Pacifics started to give way to the English Electric 2000hp diesels with the result that they spent some time on services to Clacton and Yarmouth. 70034 'Thomas Hardy' prepares to leave Yarmouth South Town with an express for Liverpool Street on 9th September 1959.

By the time the last ER 9F 2-10-0's had been delivered, 95 of the class were at work from six locations: Annesley (30), Frodingham (7), and Immingham (5) on the Great Central, New England (27) and Doncaster (16) on the Great Northern and 10 at Tyne Dock on the North Eastern. In spite of being only five months old when it was photographed at Doncaster on 12 July 1956, 92073 was showing signs of being well used having spent much of its time working Doncaster - Whitemoor mineral services on which the 9F's could haul a load nine vehicles (loaded 16t minerals) greater than an O4 2-8-0. The New England allocation worked the last regular steam workings on the ex-LNER, difficulties with the 2750hp Brush-Sulzer diesels keeping the 9F's on the New England - Colwick services until 1965.

| | 69858 | 69859 | 69860 | 69861 | 69862 | 69863 | 69864 | 69865 | 69866 |
|---|---|---|---|---|---|---|---|---|---|
| Aug-50 | WHITBY-50G | BOTANIC GARDENS-53B | WHITBY-50G | WHITBY-50G | W.HARTLEPOOL-51C | W.HARTLEPOOL-51C | WHITBY-50G | WHITBY-50G | BOTANIC GARDENS-53B |
| Jan-51 | WHITBY-50G | **11/50: MBRO - 51D** | WHITBY-50G | WHITBY-50G | W.HARTLEPOOL-51C | W.HARTLEPOOL-51C | WHITBY-50G | WHITBY-50G | **11/50: MBRO - 51D** |
| Aug-51 | WHITBY-50G | MIDDLESBROUGH-51D | WHITBY-50G | WHITBY-50G | W.HARTLEPOOL-51C | W.HARTLEPOOL-51C | WHITBY-50G | WHITBY-50G | MIDDLESBROUGH-51D |
| Jan-52 | WHITBY-50G | MIDDLESBROUGH-51D | WHITBY-50G | **10/51: SELBY - 50C** | W.HARTLEPOOL-51C | W.HARTLEPOOL-51C | WHITBY-50G | WHITBY-50G | MIDDLESBROUGH-51D |
| Aug-52 | WHITBY-50G | MIDDLESBROUGH-51D | WHITBY-50G | **5/52: WHITBY - 50G** | **7/52: STOCK - 51E** | **7/52: SUND - 54A** | WHITBY-50G | WHITBY-50G | MIDDLESBROUGH-51D |
| Jan-53 | WHITBY-50G | MIDDLESBROUGH-51D | WHITBY-50G | WHITBY-50G | **11/52: M'BRO - 51D** | SUNDERLAND-54A | WHITBY-50G | WHITBY-50G | MIDDLESBROUGH-51D |
| Aug-53 | WHITBY-50G | **6/53: STOCK - 51E** | WHITBY-50G | WHITBY-50G | **6/53: STOCK - 51E** | SUNDERLAND-54A | WHITBY-50G | WHITBY-50G | MIDDLESBROUGH-51D |
| Jan-54 | WHITBY-50G | **10/53: MBRO - 51D** | WHITBY-50G | WHITBY-50G | **10/53: M'BRO - 51D** | SUNDERLAND-54A | WHITBY-50G | WHITBY-50G | MIDDLESBROUGH-51D |
| Aug-54 | WHITBY-50G | **6/54: SALT - 51K** | WHITBY-50G | WHITBY-50G | MIDDLESBROUGH-51D | SUNDERLAND-54A | WHITBY-50G | WHITBY-50G | MIDDLESBROUGH-51D |
| Jan-55 | **10/54: N.HILL - 50B** | SALTBURN-51K | WHITBY-50G | WHITBY-50G | MIDDLESBROUGH-51D | SUNDERLAND-54A | WHITBY-50G | WHITBY-50G | **10/54: SALT - 51K** |
| Aug-55 | NEVILLE HILL-50B | SALTBURN-51K | **9/55: B.GDNS - 53B** | WHITBY-50G | MIDDLESBROUGH-51D | SUNDERLAND-54A | WHITBY-50G | WHITBY-50G | SALTBURN-51K |
| Jan-56 | NEVILLE HILL-50B | SALTBURN-51K | BOTANIC GARDENS-53B | WHITBY-50G | MIDDLESBROUGH-51D | SUNDERLAND-54A | WHITBY-50G | WHITBY-50G | SALTBURN-51K |
| Aug-56 | **6/56: B.GDNS - 53B** | SALTBURN-51K | BOTANIC GARDENS-53B | **6/56: MALT - 50F** | MIDDLESBROUGH-51D | SUNDERLAND-54A | WHITBY-50G | WHITBY-50G | SALTBURN-51K |
| Jan-57 | BOTANIC GARDENS-53B | SALTBURN-51K | BOTANIC GARDENS-53B | MALTON-50F | MIDDLESBROUGH-51D | SUNDERLAND-54A | WHITBY-50G | WHITBY-50G | SALTBURN-51K |
| Aug-57 | **6/57: M'BRO - 51D** | **9/57: SUND - 54A** | **6/57: MBRO - 51D** | MALTON-50F | **9/57: SUND - 54A** | SUNDERLAND-54A | WHITBY-50G | WHITBY-50G | SALTBURN-51K |
| Jan-58 | **9/57: SUND - 54A** | SUNDERLAND-54A | MIDDLESBROUGH-51D | MALTON-50F | SUNDERLAND-54A | SUNDERLAND-54A | WHITBY-50G | WHITBY-50G | **2/58: MBRO - 51D** |
| Aug-58 | SUNDERLAND-54A | SUNDERLAND-54A | **6/58: TBY - 51L** | MALTON-50F | **7/58: W/D** | SUNDERLAND-54A | WHITBY-50G | **4/58: W/D** | **6/58: TBY - 51L** |
| Jan-59 | SUNDERLAND-52G | SUNDERLAND-52G | THORNABY-51L | MALTON-50F | | **11/58: W/D** | **10/58: W/D** | | **11/58: W/D** |
| Aug-59 | SUNDERLAND-52G | SUNDERLAND-52G | THORNABY-51L | MALTON-50F | | | | | |
| Nov-59 | SUNDERLAND-52G | SUNDERLAND-52G | THORNABY-51L | MALTON-50F | | | | | |
| Jan-60 | SUNDERLAND-52G | SUNDERLAND-52G | THORNABY-51L | MALTON-50F | | | | | |
| Apr-60 | **4/60: W/D** | **2/60: W/D** | **5/60: W/D** | MALTON-50F | | | | | |
| Aug-60 | | | | **6/60: W/D** | | | | | |
| Nov-60 | | | | | | | | | |

| | 69867 | 69868 | 69869 | 69870 | 69871 | 69872 | 69873 | 69874 | 69875 |
|---|---|---|---|---|---|---|---|---|---|
| Aug-50 | SELBY-50C | W.AUCKLAND-51F | SALTBURN-51K | W.AUCKLAND-51F | W.HARTLEPOOL-51C | W.AUCKLAND-51F | BOTANIC GARDENS-53B | SUNDERLAND-54A | W.AUCKLAND-51F |
| Jan-51 | SELBY-50C | W.AUCKLAND-51F | SALTBURN-51K | W.AUCKLAND-51F | W.HARTLEPOOL-51C | W.AUCKLAND-51F | **11/50: M'BRO - 51D** | SUNDERLAND-54A | W.AUCKLAND-51F |
| Aug-51 | **7/51: SCAR - 50E** | W.AUCKLAND-51F | SALTBURN-51K | W.AUCKLAND-51F | W.HARTLEPOOL-51C | W.AUCKLAND-51F | MIDDLESBROUGH-51D | SUNDERLAND-54A | W.AUCKLAND-51F |
| Jan-52 | **10/51: SELBY - 50C** | W.AUCKLAND-51F | SALTBURN-51K | W.AUCKLAND-51F | W.HARTLEPOOL-51C | W.AUCKLAND-51F | MIDDLESBROUGH-51D | SUNDERLAND-54A | W.AUCKLAND-51F |
| Aug-52 | **4/52: SCAR - 50E** | W.AUCKLAND-51F | SALTBURN-51K | W.AUCKLAND-51F | W.HARTLEPOOL-51C | W.AUCKLAND-51F | MIDDLESBROUGH-51D | SUNDERLAND-54A | W.AUCKLAND-51F |
| Jan-53 | SCARBOROUGH-50E | W.AUCKLAND-51F | SALTBURN-51K | W.AUCKLAND-51F | W.HARTLEPOOL-51C | W.AUCKLAND-51F | MIDDLESBROUGH-51D | SUNDERLAND-54A | W.AUCKLAND-51F |
| Aug-53 | SCARBOROUGH-50E | W.AUCKLAND-51F | SALTBURN-51K | W.AUCKLAND-51F | W.HARTLEPOOL-51C | W.AUCKLAND-51F | MIDDLESBROUGH-51D | SUNDERLAND-54A | W.AUCKLAND-51F |
| Jan-54 | SCARBOROUGH-50E | W.AUCKLAND-51F | SALTBURN-51K | W.AUCKLAND-51F | W.HARTLEPOOL-51C | W.AUCKLAND-51F | MIDDLESBROUGH-51D | SUNDERLAND-54A | W.AUCKLAND-51F |
| Aug-54 | SCARBOROUGH-50E | W.AUCKLAND-51F | SALTBURN-51K | W.AUCKLAND-51F | W.HARTLEPOOL-51C | W.AUCKLAND-51F | MIDDLESBROUGH-51D | SUNDERLAND-54A | W.AUCKLAND-51F |
| Jan-55 | **1/55: B.GDNS - 53B** | W.AUCKLAND-51F | SALTBURN-51K | W.AUCKLAND-51F | W.HARTLEPOOL-51C | W.AUCKLAND-51F | MIDDLESBROUGH-51D | SUNDERLAND-54A | W.AUCKLAND-51F |
| Aug-55 | **6/55: SCAR - 50E** | W.AUCKLAND-51F | SALTBURN-51K | W.AUCKLAND-51F | W.HARTLEPOOL-51C | W.AUCKLAND-51F | **7/55: W.HPL - 51C** | SUNDERLAND-54A | W.AUCKLAND-51F |
| Jan-56 | SCARBOROUGH-50E | W.AUCKLAND-51F | SALTBURN-51K | W.AUCKLAND-51F | **11/55: DARL - 51A** | W.AUCKLAND-51F | W.HARTLEPOOL-51C | SUNDERLAND-54A | W.AUCKLAND-51F |
| Aug-56 | SCARBOROUGH-50E | W.AUCKLAND-51F | SALTBURN-51K | W.AUCKLAND-51F | DARLINGTON-51A | W.AUCKLAND-51F | W.HARTLEPOOL-51C | SUNDERLAND-54A | W.AUCKLAND-51F |
| Jan-57 | SCARBOROUGH-50E | W.AUCKLAND-51F | SALTBURN-51K | W.AUCKLAND-51F | DARLINGTON-51A | W.AUCKLAND-51F | W.HARTLEPOOL-51C | SUNDERLAND-54A | W.AUCKLAND-51F |
| Aug-57 | SCARBOROUGH-50E | W.AUCKLAND-51F | SALTBURN-51K | W.AUCKLAND-51F | DARLINGTON-51A | **9/57: SUND - 54A** | **9/57: DUR - 54A** | SUNDERLAND-54A | W.AUCKLAND-51F |
| Jan-58 | SCARBOROUGH-50E | **11/57: W/D** | **2/58: M'BRO - 51D** | W.AUCKLAND-51F | DARLINGTON-51A | SUNDERLAND-54A | DURHAM-54A | SUNDERLAND-54A | W.AUCKLAND-51F |
| Aug-58 | SCARBOROUGH-50E | | **6/58: TBY - 51L** | **7/58: SUND - 54A** | DARLINGTON-51A | SUNDERLAND-54A | DURHAM-54A | SUNDERLAND-54A | **7/58: SUND - 54A** |
| Jan-59 | SCARBOROUGH-50E | | THORNABY-51L | SUNDERLAND-52G | **11/58: W/D** | **10/58: W/D** | **12/58: SUND - 54A** | SUNDERLAND-52G | SUNDERLAND-52G |
| Aug-59 | SCARBOROUGH-50E | | THORNABY-51L | SUNDERLAND-52G | | | SUNDERLAND-52G | SUNDERLAND-52G | SUNDERLAND-52G |
| Nov-59 | SCARBOROUGH-50E | | THORNABY-51L | SUNDERLAND-52G | | | SUNDERLAND-52G | SUNDERLAND-52G | SUNDERLAND-52G |
| Jan-60 | **12/59: W/D** | | THORNABY-51L | SUNDERLAND-52G | | | **2/60: W/D** | SUNDERLAND-52G | SUNDERLAND-52G |
| Apr-60 | | | THORNABY-51L | SUNDERLAND-52G | | | | **5/60: W/D** | **5/60: W/D** |
| Aug-60 | | | | **6/60: W/D** | | | | | |
| Nov-60 | | | | | | | | | |

| | 69876 | 69877 | 69878 | 69879 | 69880 | 69881 | 69882 | 69883 | 69884 |
|---|---|---|---|---|---|---|---|---|---|
| Aug-50 | BOTANIC GARDENS-53B | SCARBOROUGH-50E | BOTANIC GARDENS-53B | SELBY-50C | BOTANIC GARDENS-53B | SCARBOROUGH-50E | SCARBOROUGH-50E | STOCKTON-51E | SALTBURN-51K |
| Jan-51 | **11/50: M'BRO - 51D** | **11/50: SELBY - 50C** | **11/50: M'BRO - 51D** | SELBY-50C | **11/50: M'BRO - 51D** | SCARBOROUGH-50E | **10/50: WHITBY - 50G** | STOCKTON-51E | SALTBURN-51K |
| Aug-51 | MIDDLESBROUGH-51D | **7/51: N.HILL - 50B** | MIDDLESBROUGH-51D | **7/51: SCAR - 50E** | MIDDLESBROUGH-51D | SCARBOROUGH-50E | **11/50: N.HILL - 50B** | STOCKTON-51E | SALTBURN-51K |
| Jan-52 | MIDDLESBROUGH-51D | **10/51: SELBY - 50C** | MIDDLESBROUGH-51D | SCARBOROUGH-50E | MIDDLESBROUGH-51D | SCARBOROUGH-50E | NEVILLE HILL-50B | STOCKTON-51E | SALTBURN-51K |
| Aug-52 | MIDDLESBROUGH-51D | **5/52: N.HILL - 50B** | MIDDLESBROUGH-51D | SCARBOROUGH-50E | MIDDLESBROUGH-51D | SCARBOROUGH-50E | NEVILLE HILL-50B | **10/52: M'BRO - 51D** | SALTBURN-51K |
| Jan-53 | MIDDLESBROUGH-51D | NEVILLE HILL-50B | MIDDLESBROUGH-51D | SCARBOROUGH-50E | MIDDLESBROUGH-51D | SCARBOROUGH-50E | NEVILLE HILL-50B | **11/52: N'TON - 51J** | SALTBURN-51K |
| Aug-53 | MIDDLESBROUGH-51D | **5/53: MALT - 50F** | MIDDLESBROUGH-51D | SCARBOROUGH-50E | MIDDLESBROUGH-51D | SCARBOROUGH-50E | **7/53: WHITBY - 50G** | **2/53: M'BRO - 51D** | SALTBURN-51K |
| Jan-54 | MIDDLESBROUGH-51D | MALTON-50F | MIDDLESBROUGH-51D | SCARBOROUGH-50E | MIDDLESBROUGH-51D | SCARBOROUGH-50E | **10/53: N.HILL - 50B** | **5/53: STOCK - 51E** | SALTBURN-51K |
| Aug-54 | MIDDLESBROUGH-51D | MALTON-50F | MIDDLESBROUGH-51D | SCARBOROUGH-50E | **6/54: SALT - 51K** | SCARBOROUGH-50E | **6/54: WHITBY - 50G** | **9/53: M'BRO - 51D** | SALTBURN-51K |
| Jan-55 | MIDDLESBROUGH-51D | MALTON-50F | MIDDLESBROUGH-51D | SCARBOROUGH-50E | SALTBURN-51K | **1/55: B.GDNS - 53B** | **10/54: N.HILL - 50B** | **2/54: W.HPL - 51C** | SALTBURN-51K |
| Aug-55 | MIDDLESBROUGH-51D | MALTON-50F | MIDDLESBROUGH-51D | **9/55: B.GDNS - 53B** | SALTBURN-51K | **6/55: SCAR - 50E** | NEVILLE HILL-50B | W.HARTLEPOOL-51C | SALTBURN-51K |
| Jan-56 | MIDDLESBROUGH-51D | MALTON-50F | MIDDLESBROUGH-51D | BOTANIC GARDENS-53B | SALTBURN-51K | SCARBOROUGH-50E | NEVILLE HILL-50B | W.HARTLEPOOL-51C | SALTBURN-51K |
| Aug-56 | MIDDLESBROUGH-51D | **10/56: YORK - 50A** | MIDDLESBROUGH-51D | BOTANIC GARDENS-53B | SALTBURN-51K | SCARBOROUGH-50E | **6/56: B.GDNS - 53B** | W.HARTLEPOOL-51C | SALTBURN-51K |
| Jan-57 | MIDDLESBROUGH-51D | **3/57: MALT - 50F** | MIDDLESBROUGH-51D | BOTANIC GARDENS-53B | SALTBURN-51K | **12/56: N.HILL - 50B** | BOTANIC GARDENS-53B | W.HARTLEPOOL-51C | SALTBURN-51K |
| Aug-57 | MIDDLESBROUGH-51D | **9/57: N.HILL - 50B** | **9/57: SUND - 54A** | BOTANIC GARDENS-53B | SALTBURN-51K | **6/57: SCAR - 50E** | **7/57: M'BRO - 51D** | **9/57: D'HAM - 54A** | SALTBURN-51K |
| Jan-58 | **10/57: W/D** | NEVILLE HILL-50B | SUNDERLAND-54A | BOTANIC GARDENS-53B | **11/57: W.HPL - 51C** | SCARBOROUGH-50E | MIDDLESBROUGH-51D | DURHAM-54A | **11/57: W.HPL - 51C** |
| Aug-58 | | **6/58: SCAR - 50E** | SUNDERLAND-54A | BOTANIC GARDENS-53B | W.HARTLEPOOL-51C | **7/58: W/D** | **6/58: TBY - 51L** | DURHAM-54A | W.HARTLEPOOL-51C |
| Jan-59 | | SCARBOROUGH-50E | SUNDERLAND-52G | **11/58: W/D** | W.HARTLEPOOL-51C | | **11/58: W/D** | **12/58: SUND - 54A** | **11/58: W/D** |
| Aug-59 | | SCARBOROUGH-50E | SUNDERLAND-52G | | W.HARTLEPOOL-51C | | | SUNDERLAND-52G | |
| Nov-59 | | SCARBOROUGH-50E | SUNDERLAND-52G | | W.HARTLEPOOL-51C | | | SUNDERLAND-52G | |
| Jan-60 | | **12/59: W/D** | SUNDERLAND-52G | | W.HARTLEPOOL-51C | | | SUNDERLAND-52G | |
| Apr-60 | | | SUNDERLAND-52G | | W.HARTLEPOOL-51C | | | **5/60: W/D** | |
| Aug-60 | | | **6/60: W/D** | | **6/60: W/D** | | | | |
| Nov-60 | | | | | | | | | |

| | 69885 | 69886 | 69887 | 69888 | 69889 | 69890 | 69891 | 69892 | 69893 |
|---|---|---|---|---|---|---|---|---|---|
| Aug-50 | SCARBOROUGH-50E | SCARBOROUGH-50E | SUNDERLAND-54A | WHITBY-50G | SALTBURN-51K | WHITBY-50G | SALTBURN-51K | SALTBURN-51K | W.HARTLEPOOL-51C |
| Jan-51 | SCARBOROUGH-50E | SCARBOROUGH-50E | SUNDERLAND-54A | WHITBY-50G | SALTBURN-51K | WHITBY-50G | SALTBURN-51K | SALTBURN-51K | W.HARTLEPOOL-51C |
| Aug-51 | **10/51: SELBY - 50C** | SCARBOROUGH-50E | SUNDERLAND-54A | WHITBY-50G | SALTBURN-51K | WHITBY-50G | SALTBURN-51K | SALTBURN-51K | W.HARTLEPOOL-51C |
| Jan-52 | SELBY-50C | SCARBOROUGH-50E | SUNDERLAND-54A | WHITBY-50G | SALTBURN-51K | WHITBY-50G | SALTBURN-51K | SALTBURN-51K | W.HARTLEPOOL-51C |
| Aug-52 | **5/52: SCAR - 50E** | SCARBOROUGH-50E | SUNDERLAND-54A | WHITBY-50G | SALTBURN-51K | WHITBY-50G | SALTBURN-51K | SALTBURN-51K | W.HARTLEPOOL-51C |
| Jan-53 | SCARBOROUGH-50E | SCARBOROUGH-50E | SUNDERLAND-54A | WHITBY-50G | SALTBURN-51K | WHITBY-50G | SALTBURN-51K | SALTBURN-51K | W.HARTLEPOOL-51C |
| Aug-53 | SCARBOROUGH-50E | SCARBOROUGH-50E | SUNDERLAND-54A | WHITBY-50G | SALTBURN-51K | WHITBY-50G | SALTBURN-51K | SALTBURN-51K | W.HARTLEPOOL-51C |
| Jan-54 | SCARBOROUGH-50E | SCARBOROUGH-50E | SUNDERLAND-54A | WHITBY-50G | SALTBURN-51K | WHITBY-50G | SALTBURN-51K | SALTBURN-51K | W.HARTLEPOOL-51C |
| Aug-54 | SCARBOROUGH-50E | SCARBOROUGH-50E | SUNDERLAND-54A | WHITBY-50G | SALTBURN-51K | WHITBY-50G | SALTBURN-51K | SALTBURN-51K | W.HARTLEPOOL-51C |
| Jan-55 | SCARBOROUGH-50E | SCARBOROUGH-50E | SUNDERLAND-54A | WHITBY-50G | **10/54: MBRO - 51D** | WHITBY-50G | **10/54: MBRO - 51D** | SALTBURN-51K | W.HARTLEPOOL-51C |
| Aug-55 | SCARBOROUGH-50E | **8/55: B.GDNS - 53B** | SUNDERLAND-54A | **8/55: B.GDNS - 53B** | MIDDLESBROUGH-51D | WHITBY-50G | MIDDLESBROUGH-51D | SALTBURN-51K | W.HARTLEPOOL-51C |
| Jan-56 | SCARBOROUGH-50E | BOTANIC GARDENS-53B | SUNDERLAND-54A | BOTANIC GARDENS-53B | MIDDLESBROUGH-51D | **2/56: YORK - 50A** | MIDDLESBROUGH-51D | SALTBURN-51K | W.HARTLEPOOL-51C |
| Aug-56 | SCARBOROUGH-50E | BOTANIC GARDENS-53B | **6/56: DARL - 51A** | BOTANIC GARDENS-53B | MIDDLESBROUGH-51D | **6/56: WHITBY - 50G** | MIDDLESBROUGH-51D | SALTBURN-51K | W.HARTLEPOOL-51C |
| Jan-57 | **12/56: N.HILL - 50B** | BOTANIC GARDENS-53B | DARLINGTON-51A | BOTANIC GARDENS-53B | MIDDLESBROUGH-51D | WHITBY-50G | MIDDLESBROUGH-51D | SALTBURN-51K | W.HARTLEPOOL-51C |
| Aug-57 | **6/57: SCAR - 50E** | BOTANIC GARDENS-53B | DARLINGTON-51A | BOTANIC GARDENS-53B | **9/57: SUND - 54A** | **7/57: MALT - 50F** | MIDDLESBROUGH-51D | SALTBURN-51K | **9/57: D'HAM - 54A** |
| Jan-58 | **9/57: N.HILL - 50B** | **2/58: MALT - 50F** | DARLINGTON-51A | BOTANIC GARDENS-53B | SUNDERLAND-54A | **1/58: W/D** | MIDDLESBROUGH-51D | **11/57: W.HPL - 51C** | DURHAM-54A |
| Aug-58 | **6/58: SCAR - 50E** | MALTON-50F | DARLINGTON-51A | BOTANIC GARDENS-53B | SUNDERLAND-54A | | **6/56: TBY - 51L** | W.HARTLEPOOL-51C | DURHAM-54A |
| Jan-59 | SCARBOROUGH-50E | MALTON-50F | DARLINGTON-51A | **10/58: W/D** | SUNDERLAND-52G | | **9/58: W/D** | **11/58: W/D** | **11/58: W/D** |
| Aug-59 | SCARBOROUGH-50E | MALTON-50F | DARLINGTON-51A | | SUNDERLAND-52G | | | | |
| Nov-59 | SCARBOROUGH-50E | MALTON-50F | **12/59: W/D** | | SUNDERLAND-52G | | | | |
| Jan-60 | SCARBOROUGH-50E | MALTON-50F | | | SUNDERLAND-52G | | | | |
| Apr-60 | SCARBOROUGH-50E | MALTON-50F | | | **5/60: W/D** | | | | |
| Aug-60 | **6/60: W/D** | **6/60: W/D** | | | | | | | |
| Nov-60 | | | | | | | | | |

Locomotive allocation tables. Class headings as printed: 69900 = **S 1 0-8-4T (1907)**; 69910 = **T1 4-8-0T (1909)**; 69925 = **Q1 0-8-0T (1902)**; 69999 = **U1 2-8-8-2 (1925)**.

| Date | 69894 | 69900 | 69901 | 69902 | 69903 | 69904 | 69905 | 69910 | 69911 |
|---|---|---|---|---|---|---|---|---|---|
| Aug-50 | BOTANIC GARDENS - 53B | MEXBOROUGH - 36B | MEXBOROUGH - 36B | FRODINGHAM - 36C | FRODINGHAM - 36C | MEXBOROUGH - 36B | MEXBOROUGH - 36B | NEWPORT - 51B | NEWPORT - 51B |
| Jan-51 | BOTANIC GARDENS - 53B | MEXBOROUGH - 36B | MEXBOROUGH - 36B | 1/51: MEX - 36B | 12/50: MEX - 36B | MEXBOROUGH - 36B | MEXBOROUGH - 36B | NEWPORT - 51B | NEWPORT - 51B |
| Aug-51 | 8/51: SALT - 51K | MEXBOROUGH - 36B | MEXBOROUGH - 36B | MEXBOROUGH - 36B | MEXBOROUGH - 36B | MEXBOROUGH - 36B | MEXBOROUGH - 36B | NEWPORT - 51B | NEWPORT - 51B |
| Jan-52 | SALTBURN - 51K | MEXBOROUGH - 36B | MEXBOROUGH - 36B | MEXBOROUGH - 36B | MEXBOROUGH - 36B | MEXBOROUGH - 36B | MEXBOROUGH - 36B | NEWPORT - 51B | NEWPORT - 51B |
| Aug-52 | SALTBURN - 51K | MEXBOROUGH - 36B | MEXBOROUGH - 36B | MEXBOROUGH - 36B | MEXBOROUGH - 36B | MEXBOROUGH - 36B | MEXBOROUGH - 36B | NEWPORT - 51B | NEWPORT - 51B |
| Jan-53 | SALTBURN - 51K | MEXBOROUGH - 36B | MEXBOROUGH - 36B | MEXBOROUGH - 36B | MEXBOROUGH - 36B | MEXBOROUGH - 36B | MEXBOROUGH - 36B | NEWPORT - 51B | NEWPORT - 51B |
| Aug-53 | SALTBURN - 51K | 12/53: DARN - 39B | MEXBOROUGH - 36B | MEXBOROUGH - 36B | MEXBOROUGH - 36B | MEXBOROUGH - 36B | MEXBOROUGH - 36B | NEWPORT - 51B | NEWPORT - 51B |
| Jan-54 | SALTBURN - 51K | 1/54: DCTR - 36A | 1/54: DCTR - 36A | 1/54: DCTR - 36A | 12/53: IMM - 40B | 1/54: IMM - 40B | 1/54: DCTR - 36A | NEWPORT - 51B | NEWPORT - 51B |
| Aug-54 | SALTBURN - 51K | DONCASTER - 36A | DONCASTER - 36A | DONCASTER - 36A | 3/54: W/D | 4/54: DCTR - 36A | DONCASTER - 36A | NEWPORT - 51B | NEWPORT - 51B |
| Jan-55 | SALTBURN - 51K | DONCASTER - 36A | 4/55: FROD - 36C | DONCASTER - 36A |  | DONCASTER - 36A | 4/55: FROD - 36C | NEWPORT - 51B | NEWPORT - 51B |
| Aug-55 | SALTBURN - 51K | DONCASTER - 36A | FRODINGHAM - 36C | DONCASTER - 36A |  | DONCASTER - 36A | FRODINGHAM - 36C | 9/55: YORK - 50A | NEWPORT - 51B |
| Jan-56 | SALTBURN - 51K | 1/56: W/D | FRODINGHAM - 36C | 1/56: W/D |  | 1/56: W/D | FRODINGHAM - 36C | YORK - 50A | NEWPORT - 51B |
| Aug-56 | SALTBURN - 51K |  | FRODINGHAM - 36C |  |  |  | FRODINGHAM - 36C | YORK - 50A | NEWPORT - 51B |
| Jan-57 | SALTBURN - 51K |  | 1/57: W/D |  |  |  | 1/57: W/D | YORK - 50A | 3/57: W/D |
| Aug-57 | SALTBURN - 51K |  |  |  |  |  |  | YORK - 50A |  |
| Jan-58 | 11/57: W.HPL - 51C |  |  |  |  |  |  | YORK - 50A |  |
| Aug-58 | W. HARTLEPOOL - 51C |  |  |  |  |  |  | YORK - 50A |  |
| Jan-59 | W.HARTLEPOOL - 51C |  |  |  |  |  |  | 11/58: SELBY - 50C |  |
| Aug-59 | W.HARTLEPOOL - 51C |  |  |  |  |  |  | 9/59: YORK - 50A |  |
| Nov-59 | W.HARTLEPOOL - 51C |  |  |  |  |  |  | 10/59: W/D |  |
| Jan-60 | W.HARTLEPOOL - 51C |  |  |  |  |  |  |  |  |
| Apr-60 | W.HARTLEPOOL - 51C |  |  |  |  |  |  |  |  |
| Aug-60 | 6/60: W/D |  |  |  |  |  |  |  |  |
| Nov-60 |  |  |  |  |  |  |  |  |  |

| Date | 69912 | 69913 | 69914 | 69915 | 69916 | 69917 | 69918 | 69919 | 69920 |
|---|---|---|---|---|---|---|---|---|---|
| Aug-50 | DAIRYCOATES - 53A | NEWPORT - 51B | DAIRYCOATES - 53A | DAIRYCOATES - 53A | NEWPORT - 51B | NEWPORT - 51B | STOCKTON - 51E | NEWPORT - 51B | DAIRYCOATES - 53A |
| Jan-51 | DAIRYCOATES - 53A | NEWPORT - 51B | DAIRYCOATES - 53A | DAIRYCOATES - 53A | NEWPORT - 51B | NEWPORT - 51B | STOCKTON - 51E | NEWPORT - 51B | 11/50: T.DCK - 54B |
| Aug-51 | DAIRYCOATES - 53A | NEWPORT - 51B | DAIRYCOATES - 53A | 7/51: N'PORT - 51B | NEWPORT - 51B | NEWPORT - 51B | STOCKTON - 51E | 7/51: DAIRY - 53A | TYNEDOCK - 54B |
| Jan-52 | DAIRYCOATES - 53A | NEWPORT - 51B | DAIRYCOATES - 53A | NEWPORT - 51B | NEWPORT - 51B | NEWPORT - 51B | STOCKTON - 51E | DAIRYCOATES - 53A | TYNEDOCK - 54B |
| Aug-52 | DAIRYCOATES - 53A | NEWPORT - 51B | DAIRYCOATES - 53A | NEWPORT - 51B | NEWPORT - 51B | NEWPORT - 51B | STOCKTON - 51E | DAIRYCOATES - 53A | TYNEDOCK - 54B |
| Jan-53 | 10/52: STOCK - 51E | NEWPORT - 51B | 10/52: T.DCK - 54B | NEWPORT - 51B | NEWPORT - 51B | NEWPORT - 51B | STOCKTON - 51E | 10/52: STOCK - 51E | TYNEDOCK - 54B |
| Aug-53 | STOCKTON - 51E | NEWPORT - 51B | TYNEDOCK - 54B | NEWPORT - 51B | NEWPORT - 51B | NEWPORT - 51B | STOCKTON - 51E | STOCKTON - 51E | TYNEDOCK - 54B |
| Jan-54 | STOCKTON - 51E | NEWPORT - 51B | TYNEDOCK - 54B | NEWPORT - 51B | NEWPORT - 51B | NEWPORT - 51B | STOCKTON - 51E | STOCKTON - 51E | TYNEDOCK - 54B |
| Aug-54 | STOCKTON - 51E | NEWPORT - 51B | TYNEDOCK - 54B | NEWPORT - 51B | NEWPORT - 51B | NEWPORT - 51B | STOCKTON - 51E | STOCKTON - 51E | TYNEDOCK - 54B |
| Jan-55 | STOCKTON - 51E | NEWPORT - 51B | 3/55: STOCK - 51E | NEWPORT - 51B | NEWPORT - 51B | NEWPORT - 51B | STOCKTON - 51E | 2/55: W/D | TYNEDOCK - 54B |
| Aug-55 | STOCKTON - 51E | NEWPORT - 51B | 8/55: W/D | 9/55: YORK - 50A | 9/55: YORK - 50A | NEWPORT - 51B | STOCKTON - 51E |  | TYNEDOCK - 54B |
| Jan-56 | STOCKTON - 51E | NEWPORT - 51B |  | YORK - 50A | YORK - 50A | 6/56: CON - 54D | STOCKTON - 51E |  | TYNEDOCK - 54B |
| Aug-56 | STOCKTON - 51E | 10/56: YORK - 50A |  | 7/56: SELBY - 50C | YORK - 50A | CONSETT - 54D | STOCKTON - 51E |  | TYNEDOCK - 54B |
| Jan-57 | STOCKTON - 51E | YORK - 50A |  | SELBY - 50C | YORK - 50A | CONSETT - 54D | 6/57: DAIRY - 53A |  | TYNEDOCK - 54B |
| Aug-57 | 4/57: SELBY - 50C | 12/57: W/D |  | SELBY - 50C | 8/57: W/D | CONSETT - 54D | 7/57: GOOLE - 53E |  | TYNEDOCK - 54B |
| Jan-58 | SELBY - 50C |  |  | SELBY - 50C |  | CONSETT - 54D | GOOLE - 53E |  | TYNEDOCK - 54B |
| Aug-58 | SELBY - 50C |  |  | SELBY - 50C |  | CONSETT - 54D | GOOLE - 53E |  | TYNEDOCK - 54B |
| Jan-59 | SELBY - 50C |  |  | 3/59: W/D |  | 2/59: T.DCK - 52H | 10/58: W/D |  | 1/59: W/D |
| Aug-59 | 9/59: YORK - 50A |  |  |  |  | TYNEDOCK - 52H |  |  |  |
| Nov-59 | 10/59: W/D |  |  |  |  | 11/59: W/D |  |  |  |

| Date | 69921 | 69922 | 69925 | 69926 | 69927 | 69928 | 69929 | 69930 | 69931 |
|---|---|---|---|---|---|---|---|---|---|
| Aug-50 | NEWPORT - 51B | DAIRYCOATES - 53A | EASTFIELD - 65A | MARCH - 31B | EASTFIELD - 65A | LANGWITH JCN - 40E | LANGWITH JCN - 40E | FRODINGHAM - 36C | SELBY - 50C |
| Jan-51 | NEWPORT - 51B | DAIRYCOATES - 53A | EASTFIELD - 65A | MARCH - 31B | EASTFIELD - 65A | LANGWITH JCN - 40E | LANGWITH JCN - 40E | FRODINGHAM - 36C | SELBY - 50C |
| Aug-51 | NEWPORT - 51B | DAIRYCOATES - 53A | EASTFIELD - 65A | 4/51: FROD - 36C | EASTFIELD - 65A | LANGWITH JCN - 40E | LANGWITH JCN - 40E | FRODINGHAM - 36C | SELBY - 50C |
| Jan-52 | NEWPORT - 51B | DAIRYCOATES - 53A | EASTFIELD - 65A | FRODINGHAM - 36C | EASTFIELD - 65A | LANGWITH JCN - 40E | LANGWITH JCN - 40E | FRODINGHAM - 36C | SELBY - 50C |
| Aug-52 | NEWPORT - 51B | DAIRYCOATES - 53A | EASTFIELD - 65A | FRODINGHAM - 36C | EASTFIELD - 65A | LANGWITH JCN - 40E | LANGWITH JCN - 40E | FRODINGHAM - 36C | SELBY - 50C |
| Jan-53 | NEWPORT - 51B | 10/52: N'PORT - 51B | EASTFIELD - 65A | FRODINGHAM - 36C | EASTFIELD - 65A | LANGWITH JCN - 40E | LANGWITH JCN - 40E | FRODINGHAM - 36C | SELBY - 50C |
| Aug-53 | NEWPORT - 51B | NEWPORT - 51B | EASTFIELD - 65A | FRODINGHAM - 36C | EASTFIELD - 65A | LANGWITH JCN - 40E | LANGWITH JCN - 40E | FRODINGHAM - 36C | SELBY - 50C |
| Jan-54 | NEWPORT - 51B | NEWPORT - 51B | EASTFIELD - 65A | FRODINGHAM - 36C | EASTFIELD - 65A | LANGWITH JCN - 40E | LANGWITH JCN - 40E | FRODINGHAM - 36C | SELBY - 50C |
| Aug-54 | NEWPORT - 51B | NEWPORT - 51B | 8/54: W/D | FRODINGHAM - 36C | EASTFIELD - 65A | LANGWITH JCN - 40E | LANGWITH JCN - 40E | FRODINGHAM - 36C | SELBY - 50C |
| Jan-55 | NEWPORT - 51B | NEWPORT - 51B |  | FRODINGHAM - 36C | EASTFIELD - 65A | LANGWITH JCN - 40E | LANGWITH JCN - 40E | FRODINGHAM - 36C | SELBY - 50C |
| Aug-55 | 9/55: STOCK - 51E | 9/55: YORK - 50A |  | FRODINGHAM - 36C | EASTFIELD - 65A | LANGWITH JCN - 40E | LANGWITH JCN - 40E | FRODINGHAM - 36C | SELBY - 50C |
| Jan-56 | STOCKTON - 51E | YORK - 50A |  | FRODINGHAM - 36C | 4/56: W/D | LANGWITH JCN - 40E | LANGWITH JCN - 40E | FRODINGHAM - 36C | SELBY - 50C |
| Aug-56 | STOCKTON - 51E | YORK - 50A |  | FRODINGHAM - 36C |  | LANGWITH JCN - 40E | LANGWITH JCN - 40E | FRODINGHAM - 36C | SELBY - 50C |
| Jan-57 | 6/57: DAIRY - 53A | 10/56: W/D |  | FRODINGHAM - 36C |  | LANGWITH JCN - 40E | LANGWITH JCN - 40E | FRODINGHAM - 36C | SELBY - 50C |
| Aug-57 | 7/57: GOOLE - 53E |  |  | FRODINGHAM - 36C |  | LANGWITH JCN - 40E | LANGWITH JCN - 40E | FRODINGHAM - 36C | SELBY - 50C |
| Jan-58 | GOOLE - 53E |  |  | 2/58: W/D |  | 7/58: FROD - 36C | 7/58: FROD - 36C | FRODINGHAM - 36C | SELBY - 50C |
| Aug-58 | GOOLE - 53E |  |  |  |  | FRODINGHAM - 36C | FRODINGHAM - 36C | 10/58: W/D | 11/58: W/D |
| Jan-59 | 2/59: SELBY - 50C |  |  |  |  | 8/59: W/D | 8/59: W/D |  |  |
| Aug-59 | 9/59: T.DCK - 52H |  |  |  |  |  |  |  |  |
| Nov-59 | TYNEDOCK - 52H |  |  |  |  |  |  |  |  |
| Jan-60 | TYNEDOCK - 52H |  |  |  |  |  |  |  |  |
| Apr-60 | TYNEDOCK - 52H |  |  |  |  |  |  |  |  |
| Aug-60 | TYNEDOCK - 52H |  |  |  |  |  |  |  |  |
| Nov-60 | TYNEDOCK - 52H |  |  |  |  |  |  |  |  |

| Date | 69932 | 69933 | 69934 | 69935 | 69936 | 69937 | 69999 |
|---|---|---|---|---|---|---|---|
| Aug-50 | FRODINGHAM - 36C | SELBY - 50C | FRODINGHAM - 36C | FRODINGHAM - 36C | FRODINGHAM - 36C | FRODINGHAM - 36C | BROMSGROVE - 21C |
| Jan-51 | FRODINGHAM - 36C | SELBY - 50C | FRODINGHAM - 36C | FRODINGHAM - 36C | FRODINGHAM - 36C | FRODINGHAM - 36C | 11/50: MEX - 36B |
| Aug-51 | FRODINGHAM - 36C | SELBY - 50C | FRODINGHAM - 36C | FRODINGHAM - 36C | FRODINGHAM - 36C | FRODINGHAM - 36C | MEXBOROUGH - 36C |
| Jan-52 | FRODINGHAM - 36C | SELBY - 50C | FRODINGHAM - 36C | FRODINGHAM - 36C | FRODINGHAM - 36C | FRODINGHAM - 36C | MEXBOROUGH - 36C |
| Aug-52 | FRODINGHAM - 36C | SELBY - 50C | FRODINGHAM - 36C | FRODINGHAM - 36C | FRODINGHAM - 36C | FRODINGHAM - 36C | MEXBOROUGH - 36C |
| Jan-53 | FRODINGHAM - 36C | SELBY - 50C | FRODINGHAM - 36C | FRODINGHAM - 36C | FRODINGHAM - 36C | FRODINGHAM - 36C | MEXBOROUGH - 36C |
| Aug-53 | FRODINGHAM - 36C | SELBY - 50C | FRODINGHAM - 36C | FRODINGHAM - 36C | FRODINGHAM - 36C | FRODINGHAM - 36C | MEXBOROUGH - 36C |
| Jan-54 | FRODINGHAM - 36C | SELBY - 50C | FRODINGHAM - 36C | FRODINGHAM - 36C | FRODINGHAM - 36C | FRODINGHAM - 36C | MEXBOROUGH - 36C |
| Aug-54 | FRODINGHAM - 36C | SELBY - 50C | FRODINGHAM - 36C | FRODINGHAM - 36C | FRODINGHAM - 36C | FRODINGHAM - 36C | 7/55: BROMS - 21C |
| Jan-55 | FRODINGHAM - 36C | SELBY - 50C | FRODINGHAM - 36C | FRODINGHAM - 36C | FRODINGHAM - 36C | FRODINGHAM - 36C | 9/55: BURTON - 17B |
| Aug-55 | FRODINGHAM - 36C | SELBY - 50C | FRODINGHAM - 36C | FRODINGHAM - 36C | FRODINGHAM - 36C | FRODINGHAM - 36C | 10/55: GORT - 39A |
| Jan-56 | FRODINGHAM - 36C | SELBY - 50C | FRODINGHAM - 36C | FRODINGHAM - 36C | FRODINGHAM - 36C | FRODINGHAM - 36C | 12/55: W/D |
| Aug-56 | FRODINGHAM - 36C | SELBY - 50C | FRODINGHAM - 36C | FRODINGHAM - 36C | FRODINGHAM - 36C | FRODINGHAM - 36C |  |
| Jan-57 | FRODINGHAM - 36C | SELBY - 50C | FRODINGHAM - 36C | FRODINGHAM - 36C | FRODINGHAM - 36C | 11/56: W/D |  |
| Aug-57 | FRODINGHAM - 36C | SELBY - 50C | FRODINGHAM - 36C | FRODINGHAM - 36C | FRODINGHAM - 36C |  |  |
| Jan-58 | FRODINGHAM - 36C | SELBY - 50C | FRODINGHAM - 36C | FRODINGHAM - 36C | FRODINGHAM - 36C |  |  |
| Aug-58 | FRODINGHAM - 36C | SELBY - 50C | FRODINGHAM - 36C | FRODINGHAM - 36C | FRODINGHAM - 36C |  |  |
| Jan-59 | 11/58: W/D | 12/58: W/D | FRODINGHAM - 36C | FRODINGHAM - 36C | FRODINGHAM - 36C |  |  |
| Aug-59 |  |  | 8/59: W/D | 9/59: W/D | 9/59: W/D |  |  |

196

**LMS Designed locomotives added to L.N.E.R. stock.**

**4MT 2-6-0 (1947)**

| LOCO | 43050 | 43051 | 43052 | 43053 | 43054 | 43055 | 43056 | 43057 | 43058 |
|---|---|---|---|---|---|---|---|---|---|
| Aug-50 | DARLINGTON-51A | DARLINGTON-51A | SCARBOROUGH-50E | HULL (D) - 53A | DARLINGTON-51A | DARLINGTON-51A | | | NEWENGLAND-35A |
| Jan-51 | **11/50: MBRO - 51D** | **11/50: MBRO - 51D** | SCARBOROUGH-50E | HULL (D) - 53A | **11/50: MBRO - 51D** | DARLINGTON-51A | **9/50: DARL - 51A** | **9/50: DARL - 51A** | NEWENGLAND-35A |
| Aug-51 | MIDDLESBROUGH-51D | MIDDLESBROUGH-51D | **8/51: N. HILL - 50B** | HULL (D) - 53A | MIDDLESBROUGH-51D | DARLINGTON-51A | DARLINGTON-51A | DARLINGTON-51A | NEWENGLAND-35A |
| Jan-52 | MIDDLESBROUGH-51D | MIDDLESBROUGH-51D | NEVILLEHILL-50B | HULL (D) - 53A | MIDDLESBROUGH-51D | **1/52: W. HPL - 51C** | DARLINGTON-51A | DARLINGTON-51A | NEWENGLAND-35A |
| Aug-52 | MIDDLESBROUGH-51D | MIDDLESBROUGH-51D | NEVILLEHILL-50B | HULL (D) - 53A | MIDDLESBROUGH-51D | W.HARTLEPOOL-51C | DARLINGTON-51A | DARLINGTON-51A | NEWENGLAND-35A |
| Jan-53 | MIDDLESBROUGH-51D | MIDDLESBROUGH-51D | NEVILLEHILL-50B | HULL (D) - 53A | MIDDLESBROUGH-51D | W.HARTLEPOOL-51C | DARLINGTON-51A | DARLINGTON-51A | **11/52: GRAN - 35B** |
| Aug-53 | MIDDLESBROUGH-51D | MIDDLESBROUGH-51D | NEVILLEHILL-50B | HULL (D) - 53A | MIDDLESBROUGH-51D | W.HARTLEPOOL-51C | DARLINGTON-51A | DARLINGTON-51A | GRANTHAM-35B |
| Jan-54 | MIDDLESBROUGH-51D | MIDDLESBROUGH-51D | NEVILLEHILL-50B | HULL (D) - 53A | MIDDLESBROUGH-51D | W.HARTLEPOOL-51C | DARLINGTON-51A | DARLINGTON-51A | **5/54: NEW.E - 35A** |
| Aug-54 | MIDDLESBROUGH-51D | MIDDLESBROUGH-51D | NEVILLEHILL-50B | HULL (D) - 53A | **8/54: SALT - 51K** | W.HARTLEPOOL-51C | DARLINGTON-51A | DARLINGTON-51A | NEWENGLAND-35A |
| Jan-55 | MIDDLESBROUGH-51D | MIDDLESBROUGH-51D | NEVILLEHILL-50B | HULL (D) - 53A | SALTBURN-51K | W.HARTLEPOOL-51C | DARLINGTON-51A | DARLINGTON-51A | NEWENGLAND-35A |
| Aug-55 | MIDDLESBROUGH-51D | MIDDLESBROUGH-51D | NEVILLEHILL-50B | HULL (D) - 53A | SALTBURN-51K | **5/55: KBY.S - 51H** | **5/55: W.AUCK - 51F** | **5/55: W.AUCK - 51F** | NEWENGLAND-35A |
| Jan-56 | **4/56: H. HILL - 51G** | MIDDLESBROUGH-51D | NEVILLEHILL-50B | HULL (D) - 53A | SALTBURN-51K | KIRKBYSTEPHEN-51H | W.AUCKLAND-51F | W.AUCKLAND-51F | NEWENGLAND-35A |
| Aug-56 | **10/56: DARL - 51A** | MIDDLESBROUGH-51D | NEVILLEHILL-50B | HULL (D) - 53A | SALTBURN-51K | **5/56: GHD - 52A** | **5/56: BLAY - 52C** | **5/56: BLAY - 52C** | NEWENGLAND-35A |
| Jan-57 | DARLINGTON-51A | MIDDLESBROUGH-51D | NEVILLEHILL-50B | HULL (D) - 53A | **1/57: MBRO - 51D** | **11/56: HTN - 52B** | **9/56: HTN - 52B** | **10/56: TWEED - 52D** | NEWENGLAND-35A |
| Aug-57 | DARLINGTON-51A | **8/57: S'TON - 55B** | NEVILLEHILL-50B | HULL (D) - 53A | **2/57: SALT - 51K** | **6/57: HOLB - 55A** | **6/57: HOLB - 55A** | **6/57: MBRO - 51D** | NEWENGLAND-35A |
| Jan-58 | DARLINGTON-51A | STOURTON-55B | NEVILLEHILL-50B | HULL (D) - 53A | **9/57: MBRO - 51D** | HOLBECK-55A | HOLBECK-55A | MIDDLESBROUGH-51D | NEWENGLAND-35A |
| Aug-58 | DARLINGTON-51A | **8/58: SELBY - 50C** | NEVILLEHILL-50B | HULL (D) - 53A | **5/58: TBY - 51L** | HOLBECK-55A | HOLBECK-55A | **5/58: TBY - 51L** | **5/58: BOST - 40F** |
| Jan-59 | DARLINGTON-51A | **2/59: N. HILL - 50B** | NEVILLEHILL-50B | HULL (D) - 53A | **11/58: SELBY - 50C** | HOLBECK-55A | HOLBECK-55A | **11/58: SELBY - 50C** | BOSTON-40F |
| Aug-59 | DARLINGTON-51A | **4/59: SELBY - 50C** | **5/59: To LM** | **6/59: LOW. M - 56F** | **2/59: N. HILL - 50B** | HOLBECK-55A | HOLBECK-55A | SELBY-50C | BOSTON-40F |
| Nov-59 | DARLINGTON-51A | **5/59: N. HILL - 50B** | | **11/59: W. HPL - 51C** | **4/59: SELBY - 50C** | **11/59: YORK - 50A** | **11/59: YORK - 50A** | **10/59: N. HILL - 50B** | BOSTON-40F |
| Jan-60 | DARLINGTON-51A | NEVILLEHILL-50B | | W.HARTLEPOOL-51C | **5/59: N. HILL - 50B** | YORK-50A | YORK-50A | NEVILLEHILL-50B | BOSTON-40F |
| Apr-60 | DARLINGTON-51A | NEVILLEHILL-55H | | W.HARTLEPOOL-51C | NEVILLEHILL-55H | YORK-50A | YORK-50A | NEVILLEHILL-55H | BOSTON-40F |
| Aug-60 | DARLINGTON-51A | NEVILLEHILL-55H | | W.HARTLEPOOL-51C | NEVILLEHILL-55H | YORK-50A | YORK-50A | NEVILLEHILL-55H | BOSTON-40F |
| Nov-60 | DARLINGTON-51A | NEVILLEHILL-55H | | W.HARTLEPOOL-51C | NEVILLEHILL-55H | YORK-50A | YORK-50A | NEVILLEHILL-55H | BOSTON-40F |

| LOCO | 43059 | 43060 | 43061 | 43062 | 43063 | 43064 | 43065 | 43066 | 43067 |
|---|---|---|---|---|---|---|---|---|---|
| Aug-50 | | | | | | | | | |
| Jan-51 | **10/50: NEW.E - 35A** | **10/50: NEW.E - 35A** | **10/50: NEW.E - 35A** | **10/50: NEW.E - 35A** | **11/50: NEW.E - 35A** | **11/50: S.BGE - 35C** | **11/50: NEW.E - 35A** | **12/50: NEW.E - 35A** | **12/50: NEW.E - 35A** |
| Aug-51 | NEWENGLAND-35A | NEWENGLAND-35A | NEWENGLAND-35A | NEWENGLAND-35A | NEWENGLAND-35A | S.BGE-35C | NEWENGLAND-35A | NEWENGLAND-35A | NEWENGLAND-35A |
| Jan-52 | NEWENGLAND-35A | NEWENGLAND-35A | NEWENGLAND-35A | NEWENGLAND-35A | NEWENGLAND-35A | S.BGE-35C | NEWENGLAND-35A | NEWENGLAND-35A | NEWENGLAND-35A |
| Aug-52 | NEWENGLAND-35A | NEWENGLAND-35A | NEWENGLAND-35A | NEWENGLAND-35A | NEWENGLAND-35A | S.BGE-35C | NEWENGLAND-35A | NEWENGLAND-35A | NEWENGLAND-35A |
| Jan-53 | NEWENGLAND-35A | NEWENGLAND-35A | NEWENGLAND-35A | NEWENGLAND-35A | NEWENGLAND-35A | S.BGE-35C | **2/53: NEAS - 34E** | **1/53: NEAS - 34E** | **2/53: NEAS - 34E** |
| Aug-53 | NEWENGLAND-35A | NEWENGLAND-35A | NEWENGLAND-35A | NEWENGLAND-35A | NEWENGLAND-35A | S.BGE-35C | NEASDEN-34E | NEASDEN-34E | NEASDEN-34E |
| Jan-54 | NEWENGLAND-35A | NEWENGLAND-35A | NEWENGLAND-35A | NEWENGLAND-35A | NEWENGLAND-35A | **3/53: NEW.E - 35A** | NEASDEN-34E | NEASDEN-34E | NEASDEN-34E |
| Aug-54 | NEWENGLAND-35A | NEWENGLAND-35A | NEWENGLAND-35A | NEWENGLAND-35A | NEWENGLAND-35A | NEWENGLAND-35A | **8/54: NEW.E - 35A** | **8/54: NEW.E - 35A** | **8/54: NEW.E - 35A** |
| Jan-55 | NEWENGLAND-35A | NEWENGLAND-35A | NEWENGLAND-35A | NEWENGLAND-35A | NEWENGLAND-35A | NEWENGLAND-35A | NEWENGLAND-35A | NEWENGLAND-35A | NEWENGLAND-35A |
| Aug-55 | NEWENGLAND-35A | NEWENGLAND-35A | NEWENGLAND-35A | NEWENGLAND-35A | NEWENGLAND-35A | NEWENGLAND-35A | NEWENGLAND-35A | NEWENGLAND-35A | NEWENGLAND-35A |
| Jan-56 | NEWENGLAND-35A | NEWENGLAND-35A | NEWENGLAND-35A | NEWENGLAND-35A | NEWENGLAND-35A | NEWENGLAND-35A | NEWENGLAND-35A | NEWENGLAND-35A | NEWENGLAND-35A |
| Aug-56 | NEWENGLAND-35A | NEWENGLAND-35A | NEWENGLAND-35A | NEWENGLAND-35A | **5/56: W. HALSE - 38E** | NEWENGLAND-35A | NEWENGLAND-35A | NEWENGLAND-35A | NEWENGLAND-35A |
| Jan-57 | NEWENGLAND-35A | NEWENGLAND-35A | NEWENGLAND-35A | NEWENGLAND-35A | W. HALSE-38E | NEWENGLAND-35A | NEWENGLAND-35A | NEWENGLAND-35A | NEWENGLAND-35A |
| Aug-57 | NEWENGLAND-35A | NEWENGLAND-35A | NEWENGLAND-35A | NEWENGLAND-35A | W. HALSE-38E | NEWENGLAND-35A | NEWENGLAND-35A | NEWENGLAND-35A | NEWENGLAND-35A |
| Jan-58 | **12/57: BOST - 40F** | NEWENGLAND-35A | **12/57: BOST - 40F** | **12/57: BOST - 40F** | W. HALSE-38E | **12/57: BOST - 40F** | **12/57: BOST - 40F** | NEWENGLAND-35A | NEWENGLAND-35A |
| Aug-58 | BOSTON-40F | **5/58: BOST - 40F** | BOSTON-40F | BOSTON-40F | W. HALSE-2F | BOSTON-40F | BOSTON-40F | **5/58: BOST - 40F** | NEWENGLAND-34E |
| Jan-59 | BOSTON-40F | BOSTON-40F | BOSTON-40F | BOSTON-40F | W. HALSE-2F | BOSTON-40F | BOSTON-40F | BOSTON-40F | NEWENGLAND-34E |
| Aug-59 | BOSTON-40F | **8/59: COLW - 40E** | BOSTON-40F | BOSTON-40F | W. HALSE-2F | BOSTON-40F | BOSTON-40F | BOSTON-40F | NEWENGLAND-34E |
| Nov-59 | BOSTON-40F | **10/59: LINC - 40A** | BOSTON-40F | BOSTON-40F | W. HALSE-2F | BOSTON-40F | BOSTON-40F | BOSTON-40F | NEWENGLAND-34E |
| Jan-60 | BOSTON-40F | LINCOLN-40A | BOSTON-40F | BOSTON-40F | W. HALSE-2F | BOSTON-40F | BOSTON-40F | BOSTON-40F | NEWENGLAND-34E |
| Apr-60 | BOSTON-40F | LINCOLN-40A | BOSTON-40F | BOSTON-40F | W. HALSE-2F | BOSTON-40F | BOSTON-40F | BOSTON-40F | NEWENGLAND-34E |
| Aug-60 | BOSTON-40F | LINCOLN-40A | BOSTON-40F | BOSTON-40F | W. HALSE-2F | BOSTON-40F | BOSTON-40F | BOSTON-40F | NEWENGLAND-34E |
| Nov-60 | BOSTON-40F | LINCOLN-40A | BOSTON-40F | BOSTON-40F | W. HALSE-2F | BOSTON-40F | BOSTON-40F | BOSTON-40F | NEWENGLAND-34E |

| LOCO | 43068 | 43069 | 43070 | 43071 | 43072 | 43073 | 43074 | 43075 | 43076 |
|---|---|---|---|---|---|---|---|---|---|
| Aug-50 | | | HEATON-52B | DARLINGTON-51A | DARLINGTON-51A | **9/50: DARL - 51A** | **9/50: DARL - 51A** | **9/50: DARL - 51A** | **10/50: HULL(D) - 53A** |
| Jan-51 | **12/50: NEW.E - 35A** | **12/50: NEW.E - 35A** | HEATON-52B | DARLINGTON-51A | **3/51: MBRO - 51D** | **3/51: MBRO - 51D** | **3/51: MBRO - 51D** | DARLINGTON-51A | HULL (D) - 53A |
| Aug-51 | NEWENGLAND-35A | **4/51: NEAS - 34E** | HEATON-52B | DARLINGTON-51A | MIDDLESBROUGH-51D | MIDDLESBROUGH-51D | MIDDLESBROUGH-51D | DARLINGTON-51A | HULL (D) - 53A |
| Jan-52 | NEWENGLAND-35A | **4/52: DAIRY - 53A** | HEATON-52B | DARLINGTON-51A | MIDDLESBROUGH-51D | MIDDLESBROUGH-51D | MIDDLESBROUGH-51D | DARLINGTON-51A | HULL (D) - 53A |
| Aug-52 | NEWENGLAND-35A | HULL (D) - 53A | HEATON-52B | DARLINGTON-51A | MIDDLESBROUGH-51D | MIDDLESBROUGH-51D | MIDDLESBROUGH-51D | DARLINGTON-51A | HULL (D) - 53A |
| Jan-53 | **2/53: NEAS - 34E** | HULL (D) - 53A | HEATON-52B | DARLINGTON-51A | MIDDLESBROUGH-51D | MIDDLESBROUGH-51D | MIDDLESBROUGH-51D | DARLINGTON-51A | HULL (D) - 53A |
| Aug-53 | NEASDEN-34E | HULL (D) - 53A | HEATON-52B | DARLINGTON-51A | MIDDLESBROUGH-51D | MIDDLESBROUGH-51D | MIDDLESBROUGH-51D | DARLINGTON-51A | HULL (D) - 53A |
| Jan-54 | NEASDEN-34E | HULL (D) - 53A | HEATON-52B | DARLINGTON-51A | MIDDLESBROUGH-51D | MIDDLESBROUGH-51D | MIDDLESBROUGH-51D | DARLINGTON-51A | HULL (D) - 53A |
| Aug-54 | **7/54: S.LYNN - 31D** | HULL (D) - 53A | HEATON-52B | DARLINGTON-51A | MIDDLESBROUGH-51D | MIDDLESBROUGH-51D | MIDDLESBROUGH-51D | DARLINGTON-51A | HULL (D) - 53A |
| Jan-55 | SOUTHLYNN-31D | HULL (D) - 53A | HEATON-52B | DARLINGTON-51A | MIDDLESBROUGH-51D | MIDDLESBROUGH-51D | MIDDLESBROUGH-51D | DARLINGTON-51A | HULL (D) - 53A |
| Aug-55 | SOUTHLYNN-31D | HULL (D) - 53A | HEATON-52B | **5/55: W. AUCK - 51F** | MIDDLESBROUGH-51D | MIDDLESBROUGH-51D | MIDDLESBROUGH-51D | **5/55: W. AUCK - 51F** | HULL (D) - 53A |
| Jan-56 | SOUTHLYNN-31D | HULL (D) - 53A | HEATON-52B | W.AUCKLAND-51F | MIDDLESBROUGH-51D | MIDDLESBROUGH-51D | MIDDLESBROUGH-51D | **5/56: GHD - 52A** | HULL (D) - 53A |
| Aug-56 | SOUTHLYNN-31D | HULL (D) - 53A | HEATON-52B | **5/56: BLAY - 52D** | MIDDLESBROUGH-51D | MIDDLESBROUGH-51D | MIDDLESBROUGH-51D | GATESHEAD-52A | HULL (D) - 53A |
| Jan-57 | SOUTHLYNN-31D | HULL (D) - 53A | HEATON-52B | **10/56: TWEED - 52D** | MIDDLESBROUGH-51D | MIDDLESBROUGH-51D | MIDDLESBROUGH-51D | **11/56: HTN - 52B** | HULL (D) - 53A |
| Aug-57 | SOUTHLYNN-31D | HULL (D) - 53A | **6/57: HOLB - 55A** | **6/57: MBRO - 51D** | MIDDLESBROUGH-51D | MIDDLESBROUGH-51D | **8/57: NORM - 55E** | **6/57: ARDS - 56B** | HULL (D) - 53A |
| Jan-58 | SOUTHLYNN-31D | HULL (D) - 53A | HOLBECK-55A | MIDDLESBROUGH-51D | MIDDLESBROUGH-51D | MIDDLESBROUGH-51D | NORMANTON-55E | **8/57: WAKE - 56A** | HULL (D) - 53A |
| Aug-58 | SOUTHLYNN-31D | HULL (D) - 53A | HOLBECK-55A | **5/58: TBY - 51L** | **5/58: TBY - 51L** | **5/58: TBY - 51L** | NORMANTON-55E | **5/58: ARDS - 56B** | HULL (D) - 53A |
| Jan-59 | **2/59: BOST - 40F** | HULL (D) - 53A | **1/59: MANN - 56F** | **11/58: SELBY - 50C** | THORNABY-51L | THORNABY-51L | NORMANTON-55E | ARDSLEY-56B | HULL (D) - 53A |
| Aug-59 | BOSTON-40F | HULL (D) - 53A | MANNINGHAM-55F | **10/59: N. HILL - 50B** | THORNABY-51L | **5/59: HTN.M - 9F** | NORMANTON-55E | **6/59: WAKE - 56A** | HULL (D) - 53A |
| Nov-59 | BOSTON-40F | HULL (D) - 53A | **11/59: YORK - 50A** | **11/59: YORK - 50A** | THORNABY-51L | **9/59 : To LM** | NORMANTON-55E | WAKEFIELD-56A | HULL (D) - 53A |
| Jan-60 | BOSTON-40F | HULL (D) - 53A | YORK-50A | YORK-50A | THORNABY-51L | | NORMANTON-55E | WAKEFIELD-56A | HULL (D) - 53A |
| Apr-60 | BOSTON-40F | HULL (D) - 50B | YORK-50A | YORK-50A | THORNABY-51L | | NORMANTON-55E | WAKEFIELD-56A | HULL (D) - 50B |
| Aug-60 | BOSTON-40F | HULL (D) - 50B | YORK-50A | YORK-50A | **9/60: DARL - 51A** | | NORMANTON-55E | WAKEFIELD-56A | HULL (D) - 50B |
| Nov-60 | BOSTON-40F | HULL (D) - 50B | YORK-50A | YORK-50A | DARLINGTON-51A | | NORMANTON-55E | WAKEFIELD-56A | HULL (D) - 50B |

| LOCO | 43077 | 43078 | 43079 | 43080 | 43081 | 43082 | 43083 | 43084 | 43085 |
|---|---|---|---|---|---|---|---|---|---|
| Aug-50 | **10/50: HULL(D) - 53A** | **10/50: HULL(D) - 53A** | **10/50: HULL(D) - 53A** | **10/50: NEW.E - 35A** | **10/50: NEW.E - 35A** | **10/50: NEW.E - 35A** | **11/50: NEW.E - 35A** | **11/50: NEW.E - 35A** | **11/50: NEW.E - 35A** |
| Jan-51 | HULL (D) - 53A | HULL (D) - 53A | HULL (D) - 53A | NEWENGLAND-35A | NEWENGLAND-35A | NEWENGLAND-35A | NEWENGLAND-35A | NEWENGLAND-35A | NEWENGLAND-35A |
| Aug-51 | HULL (D) - 53A | HULL (D) - 53A | HULL (D) - 53A | NEWENGLAND-35A | NEWENGLAND-35A | NEWENGLAND-35A | NEWENGLAND-35A | NEWENGLAND-35A | NEWENGLAND-35A |
| Jan-52 | HULL (D) - 53A | HULL (D) - 53A | HULL (D) - 53A | NEWENGLAND-35A | NEWENGLAND-35A | NEWENGLAND-35A | NEWENGLAND-35A | NEWENGLAND-35A | NEWENGLAND-35A |
| Aug-52 | HULL (D) - 53A | HULL (D) - 53A | HULL (D) - 53A | NEWENGLAND-35A | NEWENGLAND-35A | NEWENGLAND-35A | NEWENGLAND-35A | GRANTHAM-35B | NEWENGLAND-35A |
| Jan-53 | HULL (D) - 53A | HULL (D) - 53A | HULL (D) - 53A | NEWENGLAND-35A | NEWENGLAND-35A | NEWENGLAND-35A | NEWENGLAND-35A | NEWENGLAND-35A | NEWENGLAND-35A |
| Aug-53 | HULL (D) - 53A | HULL (D) - 53A | HULL (D) - 53A | NEWENGLAND-35A | NEWENGLAND-35A | NEWENGLAND-35A | NEWENGLAND-35A | NEWENGLAND-35A | NEWENGLAND-35A |
| Jan-54 | HULL (D) - 53A | HULL (D) - 53A | HULL (D) - 53A | **3/54: S.BGE - 35C** | NEWENGLAND-35A | NEWENGLAND-35A | NEWENGLAND-35A | NEWENGLAND-35A | NEWENGLAND-35A |
| Aug-54 | HULL (D) - 53A | HULL (D) - 53A | HULL (D) - 53A | **8/54: NEW.E - 35A** | NEWENGLAND-35A | NEWENGLAND-35A | NEWENGLAND-35A | NEWENGLAND-35A | NEWENGLAND-35A |
| Jan-55 | HULL (D) - 53A | HULL (D) - 53A | HULL (D) - 53A | NEWENGLAND-35A | NEWENGLAND-35A | NEWENGLAND-35A | NEWENGLAND-35A | NEWENGLAND-35A | NEWENGLAND-35A |
| Aug-55 | HULL (D) - 53A | HULL (D) - 53A | HULL (D) - 53A | NEWENGLAND-35A | NEWENGLAND-35A | NEWENGLAND-35A | NEWENGLAND-35A | NEWENGLAND-35A | NEWENGLAND-35A |
| Jan-56 | HULL (D) - 53A | HULL (D) - 53A | HULL (D) - 53A | NEWENGLAND-35A | NEWENGLAND-35A | NEWENGLAND-35A | NEWENGLAND-35A | NEWENGLAND-35A | NEWENGLAND-35A |
| Aug-56 | HULL (D) - 53A | HULL (D) - 53A | HULL (D) - 53A | NEWENGLAND-35A | NEWENGLAND-35A | NEWENGLAND-35A | NEWENGLAND-35A | NEWENGLAND-35A | NEWENGLAND-35A |
| Jan-57 | HULL (D) - 53A | HULL (D) - 53A | HULL (D) - 53A | NEWENGLAND-35A | NEWENGLAND-35A | NEWENGLAND-35A | NEWENGLAND-35A | NEWENGLAND-35A | NEWENGLAND-35A |
| Aug-57 | HULL (D) - 53A | HULL (D) - 53A | HULL (D) - 53A | NEWENGLAND-35A | NEWENGLAND-35A | NEWENGLAND-35A | NEWENGLAND-35A | NEWENGLAND-35A | NEWENGLAND-35A |
| Jan-58 | HULL (D) - 53A | HULL (D) - 53A | HULL (D) - 53A | **12/57: BOST - 40F** | NEWENGLAND-35A | NEWENGLAND-35A | **12/57: BOST - 40F** | NEWENGLAND-35A | **12/57: BOST - 40F** |
| Aug-58 | HULL (D) - 53A | HULL (D) - 53A | HULL (D) - 53A | BOSTON-40F | NEWENGLAND-34E | NEWENGLAND-34E | BOSTON-40F | NEWENGLAND-34E | BOSTON-40F |
| Jan-59 | HULL (D) - 53A | HULL (D) - 53A | HULL (D) - 53A | BOSTON-40F | NEWENGLAND-34E | NEWENGLAND-34E | BOSTON-40F | NEWENGLAND-34E | BOSTON-40F |
| Aug-59 | HULL (D) - 53A | HULL (D) - 53A | HULL (D) - 53A | BOSTON-40F | NEWENGLAND-34E | NEWENGLAND-34E | BOSTON-40F | NEWENGLAND-34E | BOSTON-40F |
| Nov-59 | HULL (D) - 53A | HULL (D) - 53A | HULL (D) - 53A | BOSTON-40F | NEWENGLAND-34E | NEWENGLAND-34E | BOSTON-40F | NEWENGLAND-34E | BOSTON-40F |
| Jan-60 | HULL (D) - 53A | HULL (D) - 53A | HULL (D) - 53A | BOSTON-40F | NEWENGLAND-34E | NEWENGLAND-34E | BOSTON-40F | NEWENGLAND-34E | BOSTON-40F |
| Apr-60 | HULL (D) - 50B | HULL (D) - 50B | HULL (D) - 50B | BOSTON-40F | NEWENGLAND-34E | NEWENGLAND-34E | BOSTON-40F | NEWENGLAND-34E | BOSTON-40F |
| Aug-60 | HULL (D) - 50B | HULL (D) - 50B | HULL (D) - 50B | BOSTON-40F | NEWENGLAND-34E | NEWENGLAND-34E | BOSTON-40F | NEWENGLAND-34E | BOSTON-40F |
| Nov-60 | HULL (D) - 50B | HULL (D) - 50B | HULL (D) - 50B | BOSTON-40F | NEWENGLAND-34E | NEWENGLAND-34E | BOSTON-40F | NEWENGLAND-34E | BOSTON-40F |

## 43086 – 43094

| | 43086 | 43087 | 43088 | 43089 | 43090 | 43091 | 43092 | 43093 | 43094 |
|---|---|---|---|---|---|---|---|---|---|
| Aug-50 | 11/50: NEW.E - 35A | 11/50: NEW.E - 35A | | | | | | | |
| Jan-51 | NEWENGLAND-35A | NEWENGLAND-35A | 12/50: NEW.E - 35A | 12/50: NEW.E - 35A | 12/50: S.LYNN - 31D | 12/50: S.LYNN - 31D | 12/50: S.LYNN - 31D | 12/50: S.LYNN - 31D | 12/50: S.LYNN - 31D |
| Aug-51 | NEWENGLAND-35A | NEWENGLAND-35A | NEWENGLAND-35A | 4/51: NEAS - 34E | S.LYNN-31D | S.LYNN-31D | S.LYNN-31D | S.LYNN-31D | 5/51: Swindon Test |
| Jan-52 | NEWENGLAND-35A | NEWENGLAND-35A | NEWENGLAND-35A | NEASDEN-34E | S.LYNN-31D | S.LYNN-31D | S.LYNN-31D | S.LYNN-31D | 11/51: S.BGE - 35C |
| Aug-52 | NEWENGLAND-35A | NEWENGLAND-35A | NEWENGLAND-35A | NEASDEN-34E | S.LYNN-31D | S.LYNN-31D | S.LYNN-31D | S.LYNN-31D | S.BGE - 35C |
| Jan-53 | NEWENGLAND-35A | NEWENGLAND-35A | NEWENGLAND-35A | NEASDEN-34E | S.LYNN-31D | S.LYNN-31D | S.LYNN-31D | S.LYNN-31D | 10/52: S.LYNN - 31D |
| Aug-53 | NEWENGLAND-35A | NEWENGLAND-35A | NEWENGLAND-35A | NEASDEN-34E | S.LYNN-31D | S.LYNN-31D | S.LYNN-31D | S.LYNN-31D | S.LYNN-31D |
| Jan-54 | NEWENGLAND-35A | NEWENGLAND-35A | NEWENGLAND-35A | NEASDEN-34E | S.LYNN-31D | S.LYNN-31D | S.LYNN-31D | S.LYNN-31D | S.LYNN-31D |
| Aug-54 | NEWENGLAND-35A | NEWENGLAND-35A | NEWENGLAND-35A | 8/54: S.BGE - 35C | S.LYNN-31D | S.LYNN-31D | S.LYNN-31D | S.LYNN-31D | S.LYNN-31D |
| Jan-55 | NEWENGLAND-35A | NEWENGLAND-35A | NEWENGLAND-35A | S.BGE - 35C | S.LYNN-31D | S.LYNN-31D | S.LYNN-31D | S.LYNN-31D | S.LYNN-31D |
| Aug-55 | NEWENGLAND-35A | NEWENGLAND-35A | NEWENGLAND-35A | S.BGE - 35C | S.LYNN-31D | S.LYNN-31D | S.LYNN-31D | S.LYNN-31D | S.LYNN-31D |
| Jan-56 | NEWENGLAND-35A | NEWENGLAND-35A | NEWENGLAND-35A | S.BGE - 35C | S.LYNN-31D | S.LYNN-31D | S.LYNN-31D | S.LYNN-31D | S.LYNN-31D |
| Aug-56 | NEWENGLAND-35A | NEWENGLAND-35A | NEWENGLAND-35A | S.BGE - 35C | S.LYNN-31D | S.LYNN-31D | S.LYNN-31D | S.LYNN-31D | S.LYNN-31D |
| Jan-57 | NEWENGLAND-35A | NEWENGLAND-35A | NEWENGLAND-35A | S.BGE - 35C | S.LYNN-31D | S.LYNN-31D | S.LYNN-31D | S.LYNN-31D | S.LYNN-31D |
| Aug-57 | 6/57: MELTON.C - 32G | 6/57: CAMB - 31A | NEWENGLAND-35A | 6/57: MELTON.C - 32G | S.LYNN-31D | S.LYNN-31D | S.LYNN-31D | S.LYNN-31D | S.LYNN-31D |
| Jan-58 | 9/57: NEW.E - 35A | CAMBRIDGE-31A | NEWENGLAND-35A | 9/57: CAMB - 31A | S.LYNN-31D | S.LYNN-31D | S.LYNN-31D | S.LYNN-31D | S.LYNN-31D |
| Aug-58 | NEWENGLAND-34E | CAMBRIDGE-31A | NEWENGLAND-34E | 11/57: K.LYNN - 31C | S.LYNN-31D | S.LYNN-31D | S.LYNN-31D | S.LYNN-31D | S.LYNN-31D |
| Jan-59 | NEWENGLAND-34E | CAMBRIDGE-31A | NEWENGLAND-34E | KINGS LYNN - 31C | 2/59: K.LYNN - 31C | 2/59: K.LYNN - 31C | 2/59: BOST - 40F | 2/59: BOST - 40F | 2/59: K.LYNN - 31C |
| Aug-59 | NEWENGLAND-34E | 6/59: K.LYNN - 31C | NEWENGLAND-34E | KINGS LYNN - 31C | KINGS LYNN - 31C | KINGS LYNN - 31C | BOSTON - 40F | BOSTON - 40F | KINGS LYNN - 31C |
| Nov-59 | NEWENGLAND-34E | KINGS LYNN - 31C | NEWENGLAND-34E | KINGS LYNN - 31C | KINGS LYNN - 31C | KINGS LYNN - 31C | BOSTON - 40F | BOSTON - 40F | KINGS LYNN - 31C |
| Jan-60 | NEWENGLAND-34E | KINGS LYNN - 31C | NEWENGLAND-34E | KINGS LYNN - 31C | KINGS LYNN - 31C | KINGS LYNN - 31C | BOSTON - 40F | BOSTON - 40F | KINGS LYNN - 31C |
| Apr-60 | NEWENGLAND-34E | 3/60: STAVE - 41H | NEWENGLAND-34E | KINGS LYNN - 31C | KINGS LYNN - 31C | KINGS LYNN - 31C | BOSTON - 40F | BOSTON - 40F | KINGS LYNN - 31C |
| Aug-60 | NEWENGLAND-34E | STAVELEY(GC) - 41H | NEWENGLAND-34E | KINGS LYNN - 31C | KINGS LYNN - 31C | KINGS LYNN - 31C | BOSTON - 40F | BOSTON - 40F | 9/60: LINC - 40A |
| Nov-60 | NEWENGLAND-34E | STAVELEY(GC) - 41H | NEWENGLAND-34E | KINGS LYNN - 31C | KINGS LYNN - 31C | KINGS LYNN - 31C | BOSTON - 40F | BOSTON - 40F | LINCOLN - 40A |

## 43095 – 43103

| | 43095 | 43096 | 43097 | 43098 | 43099 | 43100 | 43101 | 43102 | 43103 |
|---|---|---|---|---|---|---|---|---|---|
| Aug-50 | | | | | | | | | |
| Jan-51 | 12/50: S.LYNN - 31D | 12/50: SELBY - 50C | 1/51: SELBY - 50C | 2/51: SELBY - 50C | 2/51: SELBY - 50C | 2/51: SELBY - 50C | 2/51: SELBY - 50C | 3/51: HULL(D) - 53A | 3/51: HULL(D) - 53A |
| Aug-51 | S.LYNN-31D | SELBY-50C | SELBY-50C | SELBY-50C | SELBY-50C | SELBY-50C | SELBY-50C | HULL(D) - 53A | HULL(D) - 53A |
| Jan-52 | S.LYNN-31D | SELBY-50C | SELBY-50C | SELBY-50C | SELBY-50C | SELBY-50C | SELBY-50C | HULL(D) - 53A | HULL(D) - 53A |
| Aug-52 | S.LYNN-31D | SELBY-50C | SELBY-50C | SELBY-50C | SELBY-50C | SELBY-50C | SELBY-50C | HULL(D) - 53A | HULL(D) - 53A |
| Jan-53 | S.LYNN-31D | SELBY-50C | SELBY-50C | SELBY-50C | SELBY-50C | SELBY-50C | SELBY-50C | HULL(D) - 53A | HULL(D) - 53A |
| Aug-53 | S.LYNN-31D | SELBY-50C | SELBY-50C | SELBY-50C | SELBY-50C | SELBY-50C | SELBY-50C | HULL(D) - 53A | HULL(D) - 53A |
| Jan-54 | S.LYNN-31D | SELBY-50C | SELBY-50C | SELBY-50C | SELBY-50C | SELBY-50C | SELBY-50C | HULL(D) - 53A | HULL(D) - 53A |
| Aug-54 | S.LYNN-31D | SELBY-50C | SELBY-50C | SELBY-50C | SELBY-50C | SELBY-50C | SELBY-50C | HULL(D) - 53A | HULL(D) - 53A |
| Jan-55 | S.LYNN-31D | SELBY-50C | SELBY-50C | SELBY-50C | SELBY-50C | SELBY-50C | SELBY-50C | HULL(D) - 53A | HULL(D) - 53A |
| Aug-55 | S.LYNN-31D | SELBY-50C | SELBY-50C | SELBY-50C | SELBY-50C | SELBY-50C | 11/55: KIRKBY.S - 51H | HULL(D) - 53A | HULL(D) - 53A |
| Jan-56 | S.LYNN-31D | SELBY-50C | SELBY-50C | SELBY-50C | SELBY-50C | SELBY-50C | 5/56: GHD - 52A | HULL(D) - 53A | HULL(D) - 53A |
| Aug-56 | S.LYNN-31D | SELBY-50C | SELBY-50C | SELBY-50C | SELBY-50C | SELBY-50C | 11/56: HTN - 52B | HULL(D) - 53A | HULL(D) - 53A |
| Jan-57 | S.LYNN-31D | SELBY-50C | SELBY-50C | SELBY-50C | SELBY-50C | SELBY-50C | 6/57: ARDS - 56B | HULL(D) - 53A | HULL(D) - 53A |
| Aug-57 | S.LYNN-31D | 6/57: N.HILL - 50B | SELBY-50C | SELBY-50C | SELBY-50C | SELBY-50C | 8/57: LOW.M - 56F | HULL(D) - 53A | HULL(D) - 53A |
| Jan-58 | S.LYNN-31D | 8/57: SELBY - 50C | SELBY-50C | SELBY-50C | SELBY-50C | SELBY-50C | 5/58: ARDS - 56B | 5/58: TBY - 51L | HULL(D) - 53A |
| Aug-58 | S.LYNN-31D | SELBY-50C | SELBY-50C | SELBY-50C | SELBY-50C | SELBY-50C | ARDSLEY-56B | THORNABY-51L | HULL(D) - 53A |
| Jan-59 | 2/59: BOST - 40F | SELBY-50C | SELBY-50C | SELBY-50C | 6/59: C.HILL - 56C | 6/59: C.HILL - 56C | 6/59: WAKE - 56A | THORNABY-51L | 5/59: To LM |
| Aug-59 | 9/59: LIONC - 40A | 10/59: N.HILL - 50B | SELBY-50C | SELBY-50C | 10/59: ARDS - 56B | 10/59: ARDS - 56B | WAKEFIELD-56A | THORNABY-51L | SALTLEY - 21A |
| Nov-59 | LINCOLN - 40A | 11/59: YORK - 50A | 10/59: GOOLE - 53E | 10/59: GOOLE - 53E | 11/59: DARL - 51A | 11/59: W.HPL - 51C | WAKEFIELD-56A | THORNABY-51L | SALTLEY - 21A |
| Jan-60 | LINCOLN - 40A | YORK - 50A | GOOLE (L&Y) - 53E | GOOLE (L&Y) - 50D | DARLINGTON - 51A | W.HARTLEPOOL - 51C | WAKEFIELD-56A | THORNABY-51L | SALTLEY - 21A |
| Apr-60 | LINCOLN - 40A | YORK - 50A | GOOLE (L&Y) - 50D | GOOLE (L&Y) - 50D | DARLINGTON - 51A | W.HARTLEPOOL - 51C | WAKEFIELD-56A | 4/60: KIRKBY.S - 12D | |
| Aug-60 | LINCOLN - 40A | YORK - 50A | GOOLE (L&Y) - 50D | GOOLE (L&Y) - 50D | DARLINGTON - 51A | W.HARTLEPOOL - 51C | WAKEFIELD-56A | 7/60: To LM | |
| Nov-60 | LINCOLN - 40A | YORK - 50A | GOOLE (L&Y) - 50D | GOOLE (L&Y) - 50D | DARLINGTON - 51A | W.HARTLEPOOL - 51C | WAKEFIELD-56A | | |

## 43104 – 43122

| | 43104 | 43105 | 43106 | 43107 | 43108 | 43109 | 43110 | 43111 | 43122 |
|---|---|---|---|---|---|---|---|---|---|
| Aug-50 | | | | | | | | | |
| Jan-51 | 3/51: S.LYNN - 31D | 3/51: S.LYNN - 31D | 4/51: S.LYNN - 31D | 5/51: NEW.E - 35A | 5/51: NEW.E - 35A | 6/51: S.LYNN - 31D | 7/51: S.LYNN - 31D | 7/51: S.LYNN - 31D | 8/51: HULL(D) - 53A |
| Aug-51 | S.LYNN-31D | S.LYNN-31D | S.LYNN-31D | NEWENGLAND-35A | NEWENGLAND-35A | S.LYNN-31D | S.LYNN-31D | S.LYNN-31D | HULL(D) - 53A |
| Jan-52 | S.LYNN-31D | S.LYNN-31D | S.LYNN-31D | NEWENGLAND-35A | NEWENGLAND-35A | S.LYNN-31D | S.LYNN-31D | S.LYNN-31D | HULL(D) - 53A |
| Aug-52 | S.LYNN-31D | S.LYNN-31D | S.LYNN-31D | NEWENGLAND-35A | NEWENGLAND-35A | S.LYNN-31D | S.LYNN-31D | S.LYNN-31D | HULL(D) - 53A |
| Jan-53 | S.LYNN-31D | S.LYNN-31D | S.LYNN-31D | 2/53: NEAS - 34E | NEWENGLAND-35A | S.LYNN-31D | S.LYNN-31D | S.LYNN-31D | HULL(D) - 53A |
| Aug-53 | S.LYNN-31D | S.LYNN-31D | S.LYNN-31D | NEASDEN-34E | NEWENGLAND-35A | S.LYNN-31D | S.LYNN-31D | S.LYNN-31D | HULL(D) - 53A |
| Jan-54 | S.LYNN-31D | S.LYNN-31D | S.LYNN-31D | NEASDEN-34E | NEWENGLAND-35A | S.LYNN-31D | S.LYNN-31D | S.LYNN-31D | HULL(D) - 53A |
| Aug-54 | S.LYNN-31D | S.LYNN-31D | S.LYNN-31D | 7/54: S.LYNN - 31D | NEWENGLAND-35A | S.LYNN-31D | S.LYNN-31D | S.LYNN-31D | HULL(D) - 53A |
| Jan-55 | S.LYNN-31D | S.LYNN-31D | S.LYNN-31D | S.LYNN-31D | NEWENGLAND-35A | S.LYNN-31D | S.LYNN-31D | S.LYNN-31D | HULL(D) - 53A |
| Aug-55 | S.LYNN-31D | S.LYNN-31D | S.LYNN-31D | S.LYNN-31D | NEWENGLAND-35A | S.LYNN-31D | S.LYNN-31D | S.LYNN-31D | 5/55: KIRKBY.S - 51H |
| Jan-56 | S.LYNN-31D | S.LYNN-31D | S.LYNN-31D | S.LYNN-31D | NEWENGLAND-35A | S.LYNN-31D | S.LYNN-31D | S.LYNN-31D | KIRKBY STEPHEN - 51H |
| Aug-56 | S.LYNN-31D | S.LYNN-31D | 6/56: W.HALSE - 38E | S.LYNN-31D | NEWENGLAND-35A | S.LYNN-31D | S.LYNN-31D | S.LYNN-31D | 5/56: HULL(D) - 53A |
| Jan-57 | S.LYNN-31D | S.LYNN-31D | W.HALSE-38E | S.LYNN-31D | NEWENGLAND-35A | S.LYNN-31D | S.LYNN-31D | S.LYNN-31D | HULL(D) - 53A |
| Aug-57 | S.LYNN-31D | S.LYNN-31D | W.HALSE-38E | S.LYNN-31D | NEWENGLAND-35A | S.LYNN-31D | 6/57: K.LYNN - 31C | S.LYNN-31D | HULL(D) - 53A |
| Jan-58 | S.LYNN-31D | S.LYNN-31D | W.HALSE-38E | S.LYNN-31D | NEWENGLAND-34E | S.LYNN-31D | 8/57: S.LYNN - 31D | S.LYNN-31D | HULL(D) - 53A |
| Aug-58 | S.LYNN-31D | S.LYNN-31D | W.HALSE - 2F | S.LYNN-31D | NEWENGLAND-34E | S.LYNN-31D | S.LYNN-31D | S.LYNN-31D | HULL(D) - 53A |
| Jan-59 | 2/59: BOST - 40F | 2/59: STRAT - 30A | W.HALSE - 2F | 2/59: BOST - 40F | 2/59: BOST - 40F | 2/59: BOST - 40F | 2/59: BOST - 40F | 2/59: BOST - 40F | 5/59: To LM |
| Aug-59 | 9/59: LINC - 40A | STRATFORD - 30A | W.HALSE - 2F | BOSTON - 40F | 8/59: COLW - 40E | BOSTON - 40F | BOSTON - 40F | 8/59: COLW - 40E | |
| Nov-59 | LINCOLN - 40A | STRATFORD - 30A | W.HALSE - 2F | BOSTON - 40F | COLWICK - 40E | BOSTON - 40F | BOSTON - 40F | 10/59: SHEFF - 41B | |
| Jan-60 | LINCOLN - 40A | STRATFORD - 30A | W.HALSE - 2F | BOSTON - 40F | COLWICK - 40E | BOSTON - 40F | BOSTON - 40F | SHEFFIELD - 41B | |
| Apr-60 | LINCOLN - 40A | STRATFORD - 30A | W.HALSE - 2F | BOSTON - 40F | COLWICK - 40E | BOSTON - 40F | BOSTON - 40F | SHEFFIELD - 41B | |
| Aug-60 | LINCOLN - 40A | STRATFORD - 30A | W.HALSE - 2F | BOSTON - 40F | COLWICK - 40E | BOSTON - 40F | BOSTON - 40F | SHEFFIELD - 41B | |
| Nov-60 | LINCOLN - 40A | STRATFORD - 30A | W.HALSE - 2F | BOSTON - 40F | COLWICK - 40E | BOSTON - 40F | BOSTON - 40F | SHEFFIELD - 41B | |

## 43123 – 43131

| | 43123 | 43124 | 43125 | 43126 | 43127 | 43128 | 43129 | 43130 | 43131 |
|---|---|---|---|---|---|---|---|---|---|
| Aug-50 | | | | | | | | | |
| Jan-51 | | | | | | | | | |
| Aug-51 | 8/51: SELBY - 50C | 9/51: HULL(D) - 53A | 9/51: HULL(D) - 53A | 9/51: HULL(D) - 53A | 9/51: HULL(D) - 53A | 10/51: HTN - 53B | 10/51: HTN - 53B | 10/51: HULL(D) - 53A | 10/51: HULL(D) - 53A |
| Jan-52 | SELBY-50C | HULL(D) - 53A | 10/51: HTN - 53B | 10/51: HTN - 53B | 4/52: NEAS - 34E | HEATON - 52B | HEATON - 52B | HULL(D) - 53A | HULL(D) - 53A |
| Aug-52 | SELBY-50C | HULL(D) - 53A | HEATON - 52B | HEATON - 52B | NEASDEN-34E | HEATON - 52B | HEATON - 52B | HULL(D) - 53A | HULL(D) - 53A |
| Jan-53 | SELBY-50C | HULL(D) - 53A | HEATON - 52B | HEATON - 52B | NEASDEN-34E | HEATON - 52B | HEATON - 52B | HULL(D) - 53A | HULL(D) - 53A |
| Aug-53 | SELBY-50C | HULL(D) - 53A | HEATON - 52B | 6/53: ALSTON - 52C | NEASDEN-34E | 6/53: ALSTON - 52C | HEATON - 52B | HULL(D) - 53A | HULL(D) - 53A |
| Jan-54 | SELBY-50C | HULL(D) - 53A | HEATON - 52B | ALSTON - 52C | 7/54: NEW.E - 35A | ALSTON - 52C | HEATON - 52B | HULL(D) - 53A | HULL(D) - 53A |
| Aug-54 | SELBY-50C | HULL(D) - 53A | 5/54: SELBY - 50C | ALSTON - 52C | 8/54: S.BGE - 35C | ALSTON - 52C | HEATON - 52B | HULL(D) - 53A | HULL(D) - 53A |
| Jan-55 | SELBY-50C | HULL(D) - 53A | SELBY-50C | ALSTON - 52C | S.BGE - 35C | ALSTON - 52C | HEATON - 52B | HULL(D) - 53A | HULL(D) - 53A |
| Aug-55 | SELBY-50C | 5/55: KIRKBY.S - 51H | 5/55: W.AUCK - 51F | 6/55: HTN - 52B | S.BGE - 35C | 5/55: KIRKBY.S - 51H | HEATON - 52B | 5/55: KIRKBY.S - 51H | HULL(D) - 53A |
| Jan-56 | SELBY-50C | KIRKBY STEPHEN - 51H | W.AUCKLAND - 51F | HEATON - 52B | S.BGE - 35C | KIRKBY STEPHEN - 51H | HEATON - 52B | KIRKBY STEPHEN - 51H | HULL(D) - 53A |
| Aug-56 | SELBY-50C | 6/56: DARL - 51A | 5/56: SELBY - 50C | HEATON - 52B | S.BGE - 35C | 6/56: W.HPL - 51C | HEATON - 52B | 9/56: DARL - 51A | HULL(D) - 53A |
| Jan-57 | SELBY-50C | DARLINGTON - 51A | SELBY-50C | HEATON - 52B | S.BGE - 35C | W.HARTLEPOOL - 51C | 6/57: DARL - 51A | DARLINGTON - 51A | HULL(D) - 53A |
| Aug-57 | SELBY-50C | 8/57: HOLB - 55A | SELBY-50C | 6/57: ARDS - 56B | S.BGE - 35C | W.HARTLEPOOL - 51C | DARLINGTON - 51A | 8/57: HOLB - 55A | HULL(D) - 53A |
| Jan-58 | SELBY-50C | HOLBECK - 55A | SELBY-50C | 8/57: SOW.B - 56E | S.BGE - 31F | W.HARTLEPOOL - 51C | DARLINGTON - 51A | HOLBECK - 55A | HULL(D) - 53A |
| Aug-58 | SELBY-50C | HOLBECK - 55A | SELBY-50C | SOWBGE - 56E | S.BGE - 31F | W.HARTLEPOOL - 51C | DARLINGTON - 51A | HOLBECK - 55A | HULL(D) - 53A |
| Jan-59 | SELBY-50C | HOLBECK - 55A | SELBY-50C | SOWBGE - 56E | S.BGE - 31F | W.HARTLEPOOL - 51C | DARLINGTON - 51A | HOLBECK - 55A | HULL(D) - 53A |
| Aug-59 | SELBY-50C | HOLBECK - 55A | SELBY-50C | 7/59: HTN - 52B | S.BGE - 31F | W.HARTLEPOOL - 51C | DARLINGTON - 51A | HOLBECK - 55A | HULL(D) - 53A |
| Nov-59 | 10/59: HULL(D) - 53A | HOLBECK - 55A | 10/59: GOOLE - 53E | HEATON - 52B | S.BGE - 31F | W.HARTLEPOOL - 51C | DARLINGTON - 51A | HOLBECK - 55A | HULL(D) - 53A |
| Jan-60 | HULL(D) - 53A | HOLBECK - 55A | GOOLE (L&Y) - 53E | HEATON - 52B | 1/60: NEW.E - 35A | W.HARTLEPOOL - 51C | DARLINGTON - 51A | HOLBECK - 55A | HULL(D) - 53A |
| Apr-60 | HULL(D) - 50B | HOLBECK - 55A | GOOLE (L&Y) - 50D | 5/60: GHD - 52A | NEWENGLAND - 34E | W.HARTLEPOOL - 51C | DARLINGTON - 51A | HOLBECK - 55A | HULL(D) - 50B |
| Aug-60 | HULL(D) - 50B | HOLBECK - 55A | GOOLE (L&Y) - 50D | 9/60: SUND - 52G | NEWENGLAND - 34E | W.HARTLEPOOL - 51C | DARLINGTON - 51A | HOLBECK - 55A | HULL(D) - 50B |
| Nov-60 | HULL(D) - 50B | HOLBECK - 55A | GOOLE (L&Y) - 50D | SUNDERLAND - 52G | NEWENGLAND - 34E | W.HARTLEPOOL - 51C | DARLINGTON - 51A | HOLBECK - 55A | HULL(D) - 50B |

| | 43132 | 43133 | 43134 | 43135 | 43136 | 43137 | 43138 | 43139 | 43140 |
|---|---|---|---|---|---|---|---|---|---|
| Aug-50 | | | | | | | | | |
| Jan-51 | | | | | | | | | |
| Aug-51 | | | | | | 7/51: S.LYNN - 31D | 8/51: EFLD - 65A | 8/51: CAR (C) - 68E | 8/51: POL - 64E |
| Jan-52 | 10/51: EFLD - 65A | 12/51: EFLD - 65A | 12/51: EFLD - 65A | 12/51: EFLD - 65A | 1/52: EFLD - 65A | S.LYNN - 31D | EASTFIELD - 65A | CARLISLE (C) - 68E | POLMONT - 64E |
| Aug-52 | EASTFIELD - 65A | EASTFIELD - 65A | EASTFIELD - 65A | EASTFIELD - 65A | EASTFIELD - 65A | S.LYNN - 31D | EASTFIELD - 65A | CARLISLE (C) - 68E | POLMONT - 64E |
| Jan-53 | 6/53: FORT.W - 63D | 6/53: FORT.W - 63D | EASTFIELD - 65A | 6/53: FT.W - 63D | EASTFIELD - 65A | 6/53: FT.W - 63D | EASTFIELD - 65A | CARLISLE (C) - 68E | POLMONT - 64E |
| Aug-53 | 7/53: EFLD - 65A | 7/53: EFLD - 65A | EASTFIELD - 65A | 7/53: EFLD - 65A | EASTFIELD - 65A | 7/53: EFLD - 65A | EASTFIELD - 65A | CARLISLE (C) - 68E | POLMONT - 64E |
| Jan-54 | EASTFIELD - 65A | EASTFIELD - 65A | EASTFIELD - 65A | EASTFIELD - 65A | EASTFIELD - 65A | EASTFIELD - 65A | 4/54: BATH - 64F | CARLISLE (C) - 68E | POLMONT - 64E |
| Aug-54 | EASTFIELD - 65A | EASTFIELD - 65A | EASTFIELD - 65A | EASTFIELD - 65A | EASTFIELD - 65A | EASTFIELD - 65A | BATHGATE - 64F | CARLISLE (C) - 68E | POLMONT - 64E |
| Jan-55 | EASTFIELD - 65A | EASTFIELD - 65A | EASTFIELD - 65A | EASTFIELD - 65A | 4/55: PTH - 63A | EASTFIELD - 65A | BATHGATE - 64F | CARLISLE (C) - 68E | POLMONT - 64E |
| Aug-55 | EASTFIELD - 65A | EASTFIELD - 65A | EASTFIELD - 65A | EASTFIELD - 65A | 5/55: EFLD - 65A | EASTFIELD - 65A | BATHGATE - 64F | CARLISLE (C) - 68E | POLMONT - 64E |
| Jan-56 | 3/56: KIPPS - 65E | EASTFIELD - 65A | 3/56: KIPPS - 65E | EASTFIELD - 65A | EASTFIELD - 65A | EASTFIELD - 65A | BATHGATE - 64F | CARLISLE (C) - 68E | POLMONT - 64E |
| Aug-56 | KIPPS - 65E | EASTFIELD - 65A | KIPPS - 65E | EASTFIELD - 65A | EASTFIELD - 65A | EASTFIELD - 65A | BATHGATE - 64F | CARLISLE (C) - 68E | POLMONT - 64E |
| Jan-57 | KIPPS - 65E | 12/56: KIPPS - 65E | KIPPS - 65E | EASTFIELD - 65A | EASTFIELD - 65A | EASTFIELD - 65A | BATHGATE - 64F | CARLISLE (C) - 68E | POLMONT - 64E |
| Aug-57 | KIPPS - 65E | KIPPS - 65E | KIPPS - 65E | EASTFIELD - 65A | EASTFIELD - 65A | EASTFIELD - 65A | BATHGATE - 64F | CARLISLE (C) - 68E | POLMONT - 64E |
| Jan-58 | KIPPS - 65E | KIPPS - 65E | KIPPS - 65E | EASTFIELD - 65A | EASTFIELD - 65A | EASTFIELD - 65A | BATHGATE - 64F | CARLISLE (C) - 68E | POLMONT - 64E |
| Aug-58 | KIPPS - 65E | KIPPS - 65E | KIPPS - 65E | EASTFIELD - 65A | EASTFIELD - 65A | EASTFIELD - 65A | BATHGATE - 64F | CARLISLE (C) - 12C | POLMONT - 64E |
| Jan-59 | KIPPS - 65E | KIPPS - 65E | KIPPS - 65E | EASTFIELD - 65A | EASTFIELD - 65A | EASTFIELD - 65A | BATHGATE - 64F | CARLISLE (C) - 12C | 3/59: G'MTH - 65F |
| Aug-59 | KIPPS - 65E | KIPPS - 65E | KIPPS - 65E | EASTFIELD - 65A | EASTFIELD - 65A | EASTFIELD - 65A | BATHGATE - 64F | CARLISLE (C) - 12C | 4/59: STR - 65B |
| Nov-59 | KIPPS - 65E | KIPPS - 65E | KIPPS - 65E | EASTFIELD - 65A | EASTFIELD - 65A | EASTFIELD - 65A | BATHGATE - 64F | CARLISLE (C) - 12C | STROLLOX - 65B |
| Jan-60 | KIPPS - 65E | KIPPS - 65E | KIPPS - 65E | EASTFIELD - 65A | EASTFIELD - 65A | EASTFIELD - 65A | BATHGATE - 64F | CARLISLE (C) - 12C | STROLLOX - 65B |
| Apr-60 | KIPPS - 65E | KIPPS - 65E | KIPPS - 65E | EASTFIELD - 65A | EASTFIELD - 65A | EASTFIELD - 65A | BATHGATE - 64F | CARLISLE (C) - 12C | STROLLOX - 65B |
| Aug-60 | KIPPS - 65E | KIPPS - 65E | KIPPS - 65E | 7/60: PARK - 65C | 7/60: PARK - 65C | EASTFIELD - 65A | 7/60: PARK - 65C | CARLISLE (C) - 12C | 7/60: PARK - 65C |
| Nov-60 | KIPPS - 65E | KIPPS - 65E | KIPPS - 65E | PARKHEAD - 65C | PARKHEAD - 65C | EASTFIELD - 65A | PARKHEAD - 65C | CARLISLE (C) - 12C | PARKHEAD - 65C |

| | 43141 | 43142 | 43143 | 43144 | 43145 | 43146 | 43147 | 43148 | 43149 |
|---|---|---|---|---|---|---|---|---|---|
| Aug-50 | | | | | | | | | |
| Jan-51 | | | | | | | | | |
| Aug-51 | 9/51: POL - 64E | 8/51: S.LYNN - 31D | 9/51: S.LYNN - 31D | 9/51: S.LYNN - 31D | 9/51: S.LYNN - 31D | 9/51: M. CONS - 32G | 10/51: M. CONS - 32G | 10/51: M. CONS - 32G | 10/51: M. CONS - 32G |
| Jan-52 | POLMONT - 64E | S.LYNN - 31D | S.LYNN - 31D | S.LYNN - 31D | 10/51: YAR(B) - 32F | MELTON C. - 32G | MELTON C. - 32G | MELTON C. - 32G | MELTON C. - 32G |
| Aug-52 | POLMONT - 64E | S.LYNN - 31D | S.LYNN - 31D | S.LYNN - 31D | 2/52: M. CONS - 32G | MELTON C. - 32G | MELTON C. - 32G | MELTON C. - 32G | MELTON C. - 32G |
| Jan-53 | POLMONT - 64E | S.LYNN - 31D | S.LYNN - 31D | 2/53: NEAS - 34E | MELTON C. - 32G | MELTON C. - 32G | MELTON C. - 32G | MELTON C. - 32G | MELTON C. - 32G |
| Aug-53 | POLMONT - 64E | S.LYNN - 31D | S.LYNN - 31D | NEASDEN - 34E | MELTON C. - 32G | MELTON C. - 32G | MELTON C. - 32G | MELTON C. - 32G | MELTON C. - 32G |
| Jan-54 | POLMONT - 64E | S.LYNN - 31D | S.LYNN - 31D | NEASDEN - 34E | MELTON C. - 32G | MELTON C. - 32G | MELTON C. - 32G | MELTON C. - 32G | MELTON C. - 32G |
| Aug-54 | POLMONT - 64E | S.LYNN - 31D | S.LYNN - 31D | 7/54: S.LYNN - 31D | MELTON C. - 32G | MELTON C. - 32G | MELTON C. - 32G | MELTON C. - 32G | MELTON C. - 32G |
| Jan-55 | POLMONT - 64E | S.LYNN - 31D | S.LYNN - 31D | S.LYNN - 31D | MELTON C. - 32G | MELTON C. - 32G | MELTON C. - 32G | MELTON C. - 32G | MELTON C. - 32G |
| Aug-55 | POLMONT - 64E | S.LYNN - 31D | S.LYNN - 31D | S.LYNN - 31D | MELTON C. - 32G | MELTON C. - 32G | MELTON C. - 32G | MELTON C. - 32G | MELTON C. - 32G |
| Jan-56 | POLMONT - 64E | S.LYNN - 31D | S.LYNN - 31D | S.LYNN - 31D | MELTON C. - 32G | MELTON C. - 32G | MELTON C. - 32G | MELTON C. - 32G | MELTON C. - 32G |
| Aug-56 | POLMONT - 64E | S.LYNN - 31D | S.LYNN - 31D | S.LYNN - 31D | MELTON C. - 32G | MELTON C. - 32G | MELTON C. - 32G | MELTON C. - 32G | MELTON C. - 32G |
| Jan-57 | POLMONT - 64E | S.LYNN - 31D | S.LYNN - 31D | S.LYNN - 31D | MELTON C. - 32G | MELTON C. - 32G | MELTON C. - 32G | MELTON C. - 32G | MELTON C. - 32G |
| Aug-57 | POLMONT - 64E | S.LYNN - 31D | S.LYNN - 31D | S.LYNN - 31D | MELTON C. - 32G | MELTON C. - 32G | MELTON C. - 32G | MELTON C. - 32G | MELTON C. - 32G |
| Jan-58 | POLMONT - 64E | S.LYNN - 31D | S.LYNN - 31D | S.LYNN - 31D | MELTON C. - 32G | MELTON C. - 32G | MELTON C. - 32G | MELTON C. - 32G | MELTON C. - 32G |
| Aug-58 | 7/58: HWCK - 64G | S.LYNN - 31D | S.LYNN - 31D | S.LYNN - 31D | MELTON C. - 32G | MELTON C. - 32G | MELTON C. - 32G | MELTON C. - 32G | MELTON C. - 32G |
| Jan-59 | HAWICK - 64G | 2/59: BOST - 40F | 2/59: BOST - 40F | 2/59: STRAT - 30A | 2/59: NOR - 32A | 2/59: NOR - 32A | 2/59: BOST - 40F | 2/59: STRAT - 30A | 2/59: STRAT - 30A |
| Aug-59 | HAWICK - 64G | BOSTON - 40F | BOSTON - 40F | STRATFORD - 30A | NORWICH - 32A | NORWICH - 32A | BOSTON - 40F | STRATFORD - 30A | STRATFORD - 30A |
| Nov-59 | HAWICK - 64G | BOSTON - 40F | BOSTON - 40F | STRATFORD - 30A | NORWICH - 32A | NORWICH - 32A | BOSTON - 40F | STRATFORD - 30A | STRATFORD - 30A |
| Jan-60 | HAWICK - 64G | BOSTON - 40F | BOSTON - 40F | STRATFORD - 30A | NORWICH - 32A | 1/60: SHEFF - 41B | BOSTON - 40F | 2/60: COLW - 40E | STRATFORD - 30A |
| Apr-60 | HAWICK - 64G | BOSTON - 40F | BOSTON - 40F | STRATFORD - 30A | 3/60: STAVE - 41H | SHEFFIELD - 41B | BOSTON - 40F | COLWICK - 40E | STRATFORD - 30A |
| Aug-60 | 7/60: PARK - 65C | BOSTON - 40F | BOSTON - 40F | STRATFORD - 30A | STAVELEY(GC) - 41H | SHEFFIELD - 41B | BOSTON - 40F | COLWICK - 40E | STRATFORD - 30A |
| Nov-60 | PARKHEAD - 65C | BOSTON - 40F | BOSTON - 40F | STRATFORD - 30A | STAVELEY(GC) - 41H | SHEFFIELD - 41B | BOSTON - 40F | COLWICK - 40E | STRATFORD - 30A |

| | 43150 | 43151 | 43152 | 43153 | 43154 | 43155 | 43156 | 43157 | 43158 |
|---|---|---|---|---|---|---|---|---|---|
| Aug-50 | | | | | | | | | |
| Jan-51 | | | | | | | | | |
| Aug-51 | 10/51: M. CONS - 32G | 10/51: M. CONS - 32G | 10/51: M. CONS - 32G | 12/51: M. CONS - 32G | 12/51: M. CONS - 32G | 12/51: M. CONS - 32G | | | |
| Jan-52 | MELTON C. - 32G | MELTON C. - 32G | MELTON C. - 32G | MELTON C. - 32G | MELTON C. - 32G | MELTON C. - 32G | 1/52: M. CONS - 32G | | |
| Aug-52 | MELTON C. - 32G | MELTON C. - 32G | MELTON C. - 32G | MELTON C. - 32G | MELTON C. - 32G | MELTON C. - 32G | 2/52: YAR(B) - 32F | 7/52: YAR(B) - 32F | 7/52: YAR(B) - 32F |
| Jan-53 | MELTON C. - 32G | MELTON C. - 32G | MELTON C. - 32G | MELTON C. - 32G | MELTON C. - 32G | MELTON C. - 32G | YARMOUTH(B) - 32F | YARMOUTH(B) - 32F | YARMOUTH(B) - 32F |
| Aug-53 | MELTON C. - 32G | MELTON C. - 32G | MELTON C. - 32G | MELTON C. - 32G | MELTON C. - 32G | MELTON C. - 32G | YARMOUTH(B) - 32F | YARMOUTH(B) - 32F | YARMOUTH(B) - 32F |
| Jan-54 | MELTON C. - 32G | MELTON C. - 32G | MELTON C. - 32G | MELTON C. - 32G | MELTON C. - 32G | MELTON C. - 32G | YARMOUTH(B) - 32F | YARMOUTH(B) - 32F | YARMOUTH(B) - 32F |
| Aug-54 | MELTON C. - 32G | MELTON C. - 32G | MELTON C. - 32G | MELTON C. - 32G | MELTON C. - 32G | MELTON C. - 32G | YARMOUTH(B) - 32F | YARMOUTH(B) - 32F | YARMOUTH(B) - 32F |
| Jan-55 | MELTON C. - 32G | MELTON C. - 32G | MELTON C. - 32G | MELTON C. - 32G | MELTON C. - 32G | MELTON C. - 32G | YARMOUTH(B) - 32F | YARMOUTH(B) - 32F | YARMOUTH(B) - 32F |
| Aug-55 | MELTON C. - 32G | MELTON C. - 32G | MELTON C. - 32G | MELTON C. - 32G | MELTON C. - 32G | MELTON C. - 32G | YARMOUTH(B) - 32F | YARMOUTH(B) - 32F | YARMOUTH(B) - 32F |
| Jan-56 | MELTON C. - 32G | MELTON C. - 32G | MELTON C. - 32G | MELTON C. - 32G | MELTON C. - 32G | MELTON C. - 32G | YARMOUTH(B) - 32F | YARMOUTH(B) - 32F | YARMOUTH(B) - 32F |
| Aug-56 | MELTON C. - 32G | MELTON C. - 32G | MELTON C. - 32G | MELTON C. - 32G | MELTON C. - 32G | MELTON C. - 32G | YARMOUTH(B) - 32F | YARMOUTH(B) - 32F | YARMOUTH(B) - 32F |
| Jan-57 | MELTON C. - 32G | MELTON C. - 32G | MELTON C. - 32G | MELTON C. - 32G | MELTON C. - 32G | MELTON C. - 32G | YARMOUTH(B) - 32F | YARMOUTH(B) - 32F | YARMOUTH(B) - 32F |
| Aug-57 | MELTON C. - 32G | MELTON C. - 32G | MELTON C. - 32G | MELTON C. - 32G | MELTON C. - 32G | MELTON C. - 32G | YARMOUTH(B) - 32F | YARMOUTH(B) - 32F | YARMOUTH(B) - 32F |
| Jan-58 | MELTON C. - 32G | MELTON C. - 32G | MELTON C. - 32G | MELTON C. - 32G | MELTON C. - 32G | MELTON C. - 32G | YARMOUTH(B) - 32F | YARMOUTH(B) - 32F | YARMOUTH(B) - 32F |
| Aug-58 | MELTON C. - 32G | MELTON C. - 32G | MELTON C. - 32G | MELTON C. - 32G | MELTON C. - 32G | MELTON C. - 32G | YARMOUTH(B) - 32F | YARMOUTH(B) - 32F | YARMOUTH(B) - 32F |
| Jan-59 | 2/59: STRAT - 30A | 2/59: STRAT - 30A | 2/59: COL - 30E | 2/59: COL - 30E | 2/59: BOST - 40F | 2/59: BOST - 40F | 2/59: NOR - 32A | 2/59: NOR - 32A | 2/59: BOST - 40F |
| Aug-59 | STRATFORD - 30A | STRATFORD - 30A | COLCHESTER - 30E | COLCHESTER - 30E | 3/59: COLW - 40E | 3/59: COLW - 40E | NORWICH - 32A | 4/59: BOST - 40F | 3/59: COLW - 40E |
| Nov-59 | STRATFORD - 30A | STRATFORD - 30A | 12/59: STRAT - 30A | 12/59: STRAT - 30A | 10/59: LINC - 40A | COLWICK - 40E | NORWICH - 32A | BOSTON - 40F | 10/59: LINC - 40A |
| Jan-60 | 1/60: NEW.E - 34E | STRATFORD - 30A | 2/60: COLW - 40E | STRATFORD - 30A | LINCOLN - 40A | COLWICK - 40E | 2/60: COLW - 40E | BOSTON - 40F | LINCOLN - 40A |
| Apr-60 | NEWENGLAND - 34E | 3/60: NEW.E - 34E | COLWICK - 40E | STRATFORD - 30A | LINCOLN - 40A | COLWICK - 40E | COLWICK - 40E | BOSTON - 40F | LINCOLN - 40A |
| Aug-60 | NEWENGLAND - 34E | NEWENGLAND - 34E | COLWICK - 40E | 9/60: LINC - 40A | LINCOLN - 40A | COLWICK - 40E | COLWICK - 40E | BOSTON - 40F | LINCOLN - 40A |
| Nov-60 | NEWENGLAND - 34E | NEWENGLAND - 34E | COLWICK - 40E | LINCOLN - 40A | LINCOLN - 40A | COLWICK - 40E | COLWICK - 40E | BOSTON - 40F | LINCOLN - 40A |

| | 43159 | 43160 | 43161 | 2MT 2-6-0 (1946)<br>46460 | 46461 | 46462 | 46463 | 46464 | 46465 |
|---|---|---|---|---|---|---|---|---|---|
| Aug-50 | | | | EDINBURGH(SM) - 64A | EDINBURGH(SM) - 64A | EDINBURGH(SM) - 64A | DUNDEE - 62B | DUNDEE - 62B | |
| Jan-51 | | | | EDINBURGH(SM) - 64A | EDINBURGH(SM) - 64A | EDINBURGH(SM) - 64A | DUNDEE - 62B | 12/50: EBRO(SM) - 64A | |
| Aug-51 | | | | EDINBURGH(SM) - 64A | EDINBURGH(SM) - 64A | EDINBURGH(SM) - 64A | DUNDEE - 62B | EDINBURGH(SM) - 64A | 6/51: CAMB - 31A |
| Jan-52 | | | | 1/52: KITTY - 61A | EDINBURGH(SM) - 64A | EDINBURGH(SM) - 64A | DUNDEE - 62B | EDINBURGH(SM) - 64A | CAMBRIDGE - 31A |
| Aug-52 | 8/52: YAR(B) - 32F | 8/52: YAR(B) - 32F | 9/52: YAR(B) - 32F | KITTYBREWSTER - 61A | EDINBURGH(SM) - 64A | EDINBURGH(SM) - 64A | DUNDEE - 62B | EDINBURGH(SM) - 64A | CAMBRIDGE - 31A |
| Jan-53 | YARMOUTH(B) - 32F | YARMOUTH(B) - 32F | 2/53: NEAS - 34E | KITTYBREWSTER - 61A | EDINBURGH(SM) - 64A | EDINBURGH(SM) - 64A | DUNDEE - 62B | EDINBURGH(SM) - 64A | CAMBRIDGE - 31A |
| Aug-53 | YARMOUTH(B) - 32F | YARMOUTH(B) - 32F | NEASDEN - 34E | KITTYBREWSTER - 61A | EDINBURGH(SM) - 64A | EDINBURGH(SM) - 64A | DUNDEE - 62B | EDINBURGH(SM) - 64A | CAMBRIDGE - 31A |
| Jan-54 | YARMOUTH(B) - 32F | YARMOUTH(B) - 32F | NEASDEN - 34E | KITTYBREWSTER - 61A | EDINBURGH(SM) - 64A | EDINBURGH(SM) - 64A | DUNDEE - 62B | EDINBURGH(SM) - 64A | CAMBRIDGE - 31A |
| Aug-54 | YARMOUTH(B) - 32F | YARMOUTH(B) - 32F | 8/54: YAR(B) - 32F | KITTYBREWSTER - 61A | EDINBURGH(SM) - 64A | EDINBURGH(SM) - 64A | DUNDEE - 62B | EDINBURGH(SM) - 64A | CAMBRIDGE - 31A |
| Jan-55 | YARMOUTH(B) - 32F | YARMOUTH(B) - 32F | YARMOUTH(B) - 32F | KITTYBREWSTER - 61A | EDINBURGH(SM) - 64A | EDINBURGH(SM) - 64A | DUNDEE - 62B | EDINBURGH(SM) - 64A | CAMBRIDGE - 31A |
| Aug-55 | YARMOUTH(B) - 32F | YARMOUTH(B) - 32F | YARMOUTH(B) - 32F | KITTYBREWSTER - 61A | EDINBURGH(SM) - 64A | EDINBURGH(SM) - 64A | DUNDEE - 62B | 5/55: KITTY - 61A | CAMBRIDGE - 31A |
| Jan-56 | YARMOUTH(B) - 32F | YARMOUTH(B) - 32F | YARMOUTH(B) - 32F | KITTYBREWSTER - 61A | EDINBURGH(SM) - 64A | EDINBURGH(SM) - 64A | DUNDEE - 62B | 12/55: DUND - 62B | CAMBRIDGE - 31A |
| Aug-56 | YARMOUTH(B) - 32F | YARMOUTH(B) - 32F | YARMOUTH(B) - 32F | KITTYBREWSTER - 61A | EDINBURGH(SM) - 64A | EDINBURGH(SM) - 64A | DUNDEE - 62B | DUNDEE - 62B | CAMBRIDGE - 31A |
| Jan-57 | YARMOUTH(B) - 32F | YARMOUTH(B) - 32F | YARMOUTH(B) - 32F | KITTYBREWSTER - 61A | EDINBURGH(SM) - 64A | EDINBURGH(SM) - 64A | DUNDEE - 62B | DUNDEE - 62B | CAMBRIDGE - 31A |
| Aug-57 | YARMOUTH(B) - 32F | YARMOUTH(B) - 32F | YARMOUTH(B) - 32F | KITTYBREWSTER - 61A | EDINBURGH(SM) - 64A | EDINBURGH(SM) - 64A | DUNDEE - 62B | 8/57: KITTY - 61A | CAMBRIDGE - 31A |
| Jan-58 | YARMOUTH(B) - 32F | YARMOUTH(B) - 32F | YARMOUTH(B) - 32F | KITTYBREWSTER - 61A | EDINBURGH(SM) - 64A | EDINBURGH(SM) - 64A | DUNDEE - 62B | 11/57: DUND - 62B | CAMBRIDGE - 31A |
| Aug-58 | YARMOUTH(B) - 32F | YARMOUTH(B) - 32F | YARMOUTH(B) - 32F | KITTYBREWSTER - 61A | EDINBURGH(SM) - 64A | EDINBURGH(SM) - 64A | DUNDEE - 62B | DUNDEE - 62B | CAMBRIDGE - 31A |
| Jan-59 | 2/59: NOR - 32A | 2/59: NOR - 32A | 2/59: NOR - 32A | KITTYBREWSTER - 61A | EDINBURGH(SM) - 64A | EDINBURGH(SM) - 64A | DUNDEE - 62B | DUNDEE - 62B | CAMBRIDGE - 31A |
| Aug-59 | 4/59: BOST - 40F | NORWICH - 32A | NORWICH - 32A | KITTYBREWSTER - 61A | EDINBURGH(SM) - 64A | EDINBURGH(SM) - 64A | DUNDEE - 62B | DUNDEE - 62B | CAMBRIDGE - 31A |
| Nov-59 | 8/59: COLW - 40E | NORWICH - 32A | NORWICH - 32A | KITTYBREWSTER - 61A | EDINBURGH(SM) - 64A | EDINBURGH(SM) - 64A | DUNDEE - 62B | DUNDEE - 62B | CAMBRIDGE - 31A |
| Jan-60 | 10/59: SHEFF - 41B | NORWICH - 32A | NORWICH - 32A | KITTYBREWSTER - 61A | 2/60: KEITH - 61C | EDINBURGH(SM) - 64A | DUNDEE - 62B | DUNDEE - 62B | CAMBRIDGE - 31A |
| Apr-60 | SHEFFIELD - 41B | NORWICH - 32A | NORWICH - 32A | 5/60: KEITH - 61C | 5/60: EBRO(SM) - 64A | EDINBURGH(SM) - 64A | DUNDEE - 62B | DUNDEE - 62B | CAMBRIDGE - 31A |
| Aug-60 | SHEFFIELD - 41B | NORWICH - 32A | NORWICH - 32A | KEITH - 61C | EDINBURGH(SM) - 64A | EDINBURGH(SM) - 64A | DUNDEE - 62B | DUNDEE - 62B | CAMBRIDGE - 31A |
| Nov-60 | SHEFFIELD - 41B | NORWICH - 32A | NORWICH - 32A | KEITH - 61C | EDINBURGH(SM) - 64A | EDINBURGH(SM) - 64A | DUNDEE - 62B | DUNDEE - 62B | CAMBRIDGE - 31A |

| Date | 46466 | 46467 | 46468 | 46469 | 46470 | 46471 | 46472 | 46473 | 46474 |
|---|---|---|---|---|---|---|---|---|---|
| Aug-50 | | | | | | | | | |
| Jan-51 | | | | | | | | | |
| Aug-51 | 7/51: CAMB - 31A | 7/51: CAMB - 31A | 7/51: COL - 30E | 7/51: COL - 30E | 8/51: W.AUCK - 51F | 8/51: KY.S - 51H | 8/51: DARL - 51A | 8/51: W.AUCK - 51F | 8/51: KY.S - 51H |
| Jan-52 | CAMBRIDGE - 31A | CAMBRIDGE - 31A | COLCHESTER - 30E | COLCHESTER - 30E | W.AUCKLAND - 51F | KIRKBYS. - 51H | DARLINGTON - 51A | W.AUCKLAND - 51F | KIRKBYS. - 51H |
| Aug-52 | CAMBRIDGE - 31A | CAMBRIDGE - 31A | COLCHESTER - 30E | COLCHESTER - 30E | W.AUCKLAND - 51F | KIRKBYS. - 51H | DARLINGTON - 51A | W.AUCKLAND - 51F | KIRKBYS. - 51H |
| Jan-53 | CAMBRIDGE - 31A | CAMBRIDGE - 31A | COLCHESTER - 30E | COLCHESTER - 30E | W.AUCKLAND - 51F | KIRKBYS. - 51H | DARLINGTON - 51A | W.AUCKLAND - 51F | KIRKBYS. - 51H |
| Aug-53 | CAMBRIDGE - 31A | CAMBRIDGE - 31A | COLCHESTER - 30E | COLCHESTER - 30E | W.AUCKLAND - 51F | KIRKBYS. - 51H | DARLINGTON - 51A | W.AUCKLAND - 51F | KIRKBYS. - 51H |
| Jan-54 | CAMBRIDGE - 31A | CAMBRIDGE - 31A | COLCHESTER - 30E | COLCHESTER - 30E | W.AUCKLAND - 51F | KIRKBYS. - 51H | DARLINGTON - 51A | W.AUCKLAND - 51F | KIRKBYS. - 51H |
| Aug-54 | CAMBRIDGE - 31A | CAMBRIDGE - 31A | COLCHESTER - 30E | COLCHESTER - 30E | W.AUCKLAND - 51F | KIRKBYS. - 51H | DARLINGTON - 51A | W.AUCKLAND - 51F | KIRKBYS. - 51H |
| Jan-55 | CAMBRIDGE - 31A | CAMBRIDGE - 31A | COLCHESTER - 30E | COLCHESTER - 30E | 12/54: KIRKBY.S - 51H | 12/54: W.AUCK - 51F | 12/54: KIRKBY.S - 51H | 12/54: KIRKBY.S - 51H | KIRKBYS. - 51H |
| Aug-55 | CAMBRIDGE - 31A | CAMBRIDGE - 31A | COLCHESTER - 30E | COLCHESTER - 30E | KIRKBYS. - 51H | 6/55: DARL - 51A | KIRKBYS. - 51H | 6/55: DARL - 51A | 6/55: DARL - 51A |
| Jan-56 | CAMBRIDGE - 31A | CAMBRIDGE - 31A | COLCHESTER - 30E | COLCHESTER - 30E | KIRKBYS. - 51H | 11/55: W. AUCK - 51F | KIRKBYS. - 51H | DARLINGTON - 51A | DARLINGTON - 51A |
| Aug-56 | CAMBRIDGE - 31A | CAMBRIDGE - 31A | COLCHESTER - 30E | COLCHESTER - 30E | KIRKBYS. - 51H | W.AUCKLAND - 51F | KIRKBYS. - 51H | DARLINGTON - 51A | DARLINGTON - 51A |
| Jan-57 | CAMBRIDGE - 31A | CAMBRIDGE - 31A | COLCHESTER - 30E | COLCHESTER - 30E | KIRKBYS. - 51H | W.AUCKLAND - 51F | KIRKBYS. - 51H | DARLINGTON - 51A | DARLINGTON - 51A |
| Aug-57 | CAMBRIDGE - 31A | CAMBRIDGE - 31A | COLCHESTER - 30E | COLCHESTER - 30E | KIRKBYS. - 51H | W.AUCKLAND - 51F | KIRKBYS. - 51H | DARLINGTON - 51A | DARLINGTON - 51A |
| Jan-58 | CAMBRIDGE - 31A | CAMBRIDGE - 31A | COLCHESTER - 30E | COLCHESTER - 30E | KIRKBYS. - 12D | 3/58: N'TON - 51J | KIRKBYS. - 12D | DARLINGTON - 51A | DARLINGTON - 51A |
| Aug-58 | CAMBRIDGE - 31A | CAMBRIDGE - 31A | COLCHESTER - 30E | COLCHESTER - 30E | KIRKBYS. - 12D | NORTHALLERTON - 51J | KIRKBYS. - 12D | DARLINGTON - 51A | DARLINGTON - 51A |
| Jan-59 | CAMBRIDGE - 31A | CAMBRIDGE - 31A | COLCHESTER - 30E | COLCHESTER - 30E | KIRKBYS. - 12D | NORTHALLERTON - 51J | 12/58: To LM | DARLINGTON - 51A | DARLINGTON - 51A |
| Aug-59 | CAMBRIDGE - 31A | CAMBRIDGE - 31A | COLCHESTER - 30E | COLCHESTER - 30E | KIRKBYS. - 12D | NORTHALLERTON - 51J | | DARLINGTON - 51A | DARLINGTON - 51A |
| Nov-59 | CAMBRIDGE - 31A | CAMBRIDGE - 31A | 10/59: PARK - 30F | 10/59: PARK - 30F | KIRKBYS. - 12D | NORTHALLERTON - 51J | | DARLINGTON - 51A | DARLINGTON - 51A |
| Jan-60 | CAMBRIDGE - 31A | CAMBRIDGE - 31A | PARKESTON - 30F | PARKESTON - 30F | KIRKBYS. - 12D | NORTHALLERTON - 51J | | DARLINGTON - 51A | DARLINGTON - 51A |
| Apr-60 | CAMBRIDGE - 31A | CAMBRIDGE - 31A | PARKESTON - 30F | PARKESTON - 30F | 9?60: To LM | 3/60: W.AUCK - 51F | | 9/60: BLYTH - 52F | 9/60: BLYTH - 52F |
| Aug-60 | CAMBRIDGE - 31A | CAMBRIDGE - 31A | PARKESTON - 30F | PARKESTON - 30F | | 9/60: BLYTH - 52F | | BLYTH - 52F | BLYTH - 52F |
| Nov-60 | CAMBRIDGE - 31A | CAMBRIDGE - 31A | PARKESTON - 30F | PARKESTON - 30F | | BLYTH - 52F | | BLYTH - 52F | BLYTH - 52F |

| Date | 46475 | 46476 | 46477 | 46478 | 46479 | 46480 | 46481 | 46482 |
|---|---|---|---|---|---|---|---|---|
| Aug-50 | | | | | | | | |
| Jan-51 | | | | | | | | |
| Aug-51 | 8/51: DARL - 51A | 9/51: KY.S - 51H | 9/51: DARL - 51A | 9/51: KY.S - 51H | 9/51: W.AUCK - 51F | DARLINGTON - 51A | 9/51: KY.S - 51H | 9/51: W.AUCK - 51F |
| Jan-52 | DARLINGTON - 51A | KIRKBYS. - 51H | DARLINGTON - 51A | KIRKBYS. - 51H | W.AUCKLAND - 51F | DARLINGTON - 51A | KIRKBYS. - 51H | W.AUCKLAND - 51F |
| Aug-52 | DARLINGTON - 51A | KIRKBYS. - 51H | DARLINGTON - 51A | KIRKBYS. - 51H | W.AUCKLAND - 51F | DARLINGTON - 51A | KIRKBYS. - 51H | W.AUCKLAND - 51F |
| Jan-53 | DARLINGTON - 51A | KIRKBYS. - 51H | 3/53: KIRKBY.S - 51H | KIRKBYS. - 51H | W.AUCKLAND - 51F | 2/53: KIRKBY.S - 51H | KIRKBYS. - 51H | W.AUCKLAND - 51F |
| Aug-53 | DARLINGTON - 51A | KIRKBYS. - 51H | KIRKBYS. - 51H | KIRKBYS. - 51H | W.AUCKLAND - 51F | KIRKBYS. - 51H | KIRKBYS. - 51H | W.AUCKLAND - 51F |
| Jan-54 | DARLINGTON - 51A | KIRKBYS. - 51H | KIRKBYS. - 51H | KIRKBYS. - 51H | W.AUCKLAND - 51F | KIRKBYS. - 51H | KIRKBYS. - 51H | W.AUCKLAND - 51F |
| Aug-54 | DARLINGTON - 51A | KIRKBYS. - 51H | KIRKBYS. - 51H | KIRKBYS. - 51H | 11/54: DARL - 51A | KIRKBYS. - 51H | KIRKBYS. - 51H | W.AUCKLAND - 51F |
| Jan-55 | DARLINGTON - 51A | 4/55: W.AUCK - 51F | KIRKBYS. - 51H | KIRKBYS. - 51H | DARLINGTON - 51A | 12/54: W.AUCK - 51F | 4/55: W.AUCK - 51F | W.AUCKLAND - 51F |
| Aug-55 | DARLINGTON - 51A | 6/55: DARL - 51A | 6/55: DARL - 51A | 6/55: DARL - 51A | DARLINGTON - 51A | W.AUCKLAND - 51F | W.AUCKLAND - 51F | W.AUCKLAND - 51F |
| Jan-56 | DARLINGTON - 51A | DARLINGTON - 51A | DARLINGTON - 51A | DARLINGTON - 51A | DARLINGTON - 51A | W.AUCKLAND - 51F | W.AUCKLAND - 51F | W.AUCKLAND - 51F |
| Aug-56 | DARLINGTON - 51A | DARLINGTON - 51A | DARLINGTON - 51A | DARLINGTON - 51A | DARLINGTON - 51A | W.AUCKLAND - 51F | W.AUCKLAND - 51F | W.AUCKLAND - 51F |
| Jan-57 | DARLINGTON - 51A | DARLINGTON - 51A | DARLINGTON - 51A | 3/57: STOCK - 51E | DARLINGTON - 51A | W.AUCKLAND - 51F | W.AUCKLAND - 51F | W.AUCKLAND - 51F |
| Aug-57 | DARLINGTON - 51A | DARLINGTON - 51A | DARLINGTON - 51A | STOCKTON - 51E | DARLINGTON - 51A | W.AUCKLAND - 51F | W.AUCKLAND - 51F | W.AUCKLAND - 51F |
| Jan-58 | DARLINGTON - 51A | 1/58: TWEED - 52D | DARLINGTON - 51A | STOCKTON - 51E | DARLINGTON - 51A | W.AUCKLAND - 51F | W.AUCKLAND - 51F | W.AUCKLAND - 51F |
| Aug-58 | DARLINGTON - 51A | TWEEDMOUTH - 52D | DARLINGTON - 51A | STOCKTON - 51E | DARLINGTON - 51A | 7/58: YORK - 50A | 7/58: YORK - 50A | W.AUCKLAND - 51F |
| Jan-59 | DARLINGTON - 51A | TWEEDMOUTH - 52D | DARLINGTON - 51A | STOCKTON - 51E | DARLINGTON - 51A | YORK - 50A | YORK - 50A | W.AUCKLAND - 51F |
| Aug-59 | DARLINGTON - 51A | TWEEDMOUTH - 52D | DARLINGTON - 51A | 6/59: TBY - 51L | DARLINGTON - 51A | YORK - 50A | YORK - 50A | 10/59: TWEED - 52D |
| Nov-59 | DARLINGTON - 51A | TWEEDMOUTH - 52D | DARLINGTON - 51A | THORNABY - 51L | DARLINGTON - 51A | YORK - 50A | YORK - 50A | TWEEDMOUTH - 52D |
| Jan-60 | DARLINGTON - 51A | TWEEDMOUTH - 52D | DARLINGTON - 51A | THORNABY - 51L | DARLINGTON - 51A | YORK - 50A | YORK - 50A | TWEEDMOUTH - 52D |
| Apr-60 | DARLINGTON - 51A | TWEEDMOUTH - 52D | DARLINGTON - 51A | 3/60: GOOLE - 50D | DARLINGTON - 51A | YORK - 50A | YORK - 50A | TWEEDMOUTH - 52D |
| Aug-60 | DARLINGTON - 51A | TWEEDMOUTH - 52D | DARLINGTON - 51A | GOOLE (L&Y) - 50D | 9/60: BLYTH - 52F | YORK - 50A | YORK - 50A | TWEEDMOUTH - 52D |
| Nov-60 | DARLINGTON - 51A | TWEEDMOUTH - 52D | DARLINGTON - 51A | GOOLE (L&Y) - 50D | BLYTH - 52F | YORK - 50A | YORK - 50A | TWEEDMOUTH - 52D |

Coming under LNER control in 1936, the Midland & Great Northern had to wait until the war and its aftermath was settled before attention could be given to the modernisation of its locomotive fleet which by 1950 was showing signs of wear and tear.

The problem was not easy to solve since the nine-mile section of line between Sutton Bridge and South Lynn could take nothing larger than a D16 or K2 - both classes being cleared under special arrangement - which were candidates ready for replacement. In the past the question of M&GN power had been addressed by the import of redundant locomotives from elsewhere on the system - from 1939 until 1946 Great Central D9 4-4-0's had been allocated to a number of M&GN sheds - but by the late 1940's there was little that was fit for transfer and could be accommodated on the line. Standard BR designs lay some time in the future and the only class available with the durability for the long M&GN runs - Peterborough to Yarmouth was a four and a half hour, 110 mile trip - and the axleweight to satisfy the limitations of the route was the LMS 1947 Ivatt 2-6-0 which started to appear in large numbers on the line during 1950 and 1951.

It should not be thought that the M&GN was an especially easy system to operate. Traffic was heavy - On a winter weekday there were fifty-three services booked through South Lynn whilst about half the route between Yarmouth and Peterborough was single tracked and during the summer and autumn months holiday specials and sugar-beet trains left very little spare capacity.

The LM 4MT 2-6-0's changed not only the appearance of the line but its performance too and by the mid-1950's punctuality - even on a busy Saturday - was quite different to what it had been half a decade earlier with much of the credit going to a fleet of modern locomotives - probably the only new engines the system had ever had - which were both dependable and powerful. Altogether no less than fifty of the class were allocated to the line with nineteen being shedded at New England, fourteen at South Lynn, eleven at Melton Constable and six at Yarmouth Beach.

In appearance the Ivatt 4MT's were rather ungainly looking machines - rather too American for most tastes - but it was by no means inappropriate that a route whose origins included the Midland Railway should become an oasis of LMS power in the midst of the Eastern desert. Had the M&GN soldiered on unassisted for a few years longer it is probable that it would have been worked by one of the BR 4MT standard classes, both the 4-6-0 and 2-6-0 cleared for the route.

Although they had nothing like the impact of the 4MT's, the small LMS 2MT 2-6-0's offered an exceptional power to weight ratio - they possessed the same route availability as a Y9 0-4-0 - and twenty-three were imported to take over from ageing 2-4-0 and 0-6-0's on routes such as the Darlington - Kirkby Stephen, Cambridge - Kettering and Colchester - Cambridge.

## BR 7 4-6-2 (1951)

| Date | 70000 | 70001 | 70002 | 70003 | 70004 | 70005 | 70006 | 70007 | 70008 |
|---|---|---|---|---|---|---|---|---|---|
| Aug-50 | | | | | | | | | |
| Jan-51 | 1/51: STRAT - 30A | 2/51: STRAT - 30A | 3/51: STRAT - 30A | 3/51: STRAT - 30A | 3/51: STRAT - 30A | 5/51: Rygby Test | | | |
| Aug-51 | STRATFORD-30A | STRATFORD-30A | STRATFORD-30A | STRATFORD-30A | 9/51: To SR | 4/51: STRAT - 30A | 4/51: STRAT - 30A | 4/51: STRAT - 30A | 4/51: NOR - 32A |
| Jan-52 | STRATFORD-30A | STRATFORD-30A | STRATFORD-30A | STRATFORD-30A | | 12/51: Rugby Test | NORWICH-32A | 5/51: NOR - 32A | NORWICH-32A |
| Aug-52 | STRATFORD-30A | STRATFORD-30A | STRATFORD-30A | STRATFORD-30A | | 3/52: STRAT - 30A | NORWICH-32A | NORWICH-32A | NORWICH-32A |
| Jan-53 | STRATFORD-30A | STRATFORD-30A | STRATFORD-30A | STRATFORD-30A | | STRATFORD-30A | NORWICH-32A | NORWICH-32A | NORWICH-32A |
| Aug-53 | STRATFORD-30A | STRATFORD-30A | STRATFORD-30A | STRATFORD-30A | | STRATFORD-30A | NORWICH-32A | NORWICH-32A | NORWICH-32A |
| Jan-54 | STRATFORD-30A | STRATFORD-30A | STRATFORD-30A | STRATFORD-30A | | STRATFORD-30A | NORWICH-32A | NORWICH-32A | NORWICH-32A |
| Aug-54 | STRATFORD-30A | STRATFORD-30A | STRATFORD-30A | STRATFORD-30A | | STRATFORD-30A | NORWICH-32A | NORWICH-32A | NORWICH-32A |
| Jan-55 | STRATFORD-30A | STRATFORD-30A | STRATFORD-30A | STRATFORD-30A | | STRATFORD-30A | NORWICH-32A | NORWICH-32A | NORWICH-32A |
| Aug-55 | STRATFORD-30A | STRATFORD-30A | STRATFORD-30A | STRATFORD-30A | | STRATFORD-30A | NORWICH-32A | NORWICH-32A | NORWICH-32A |
| Jan-56 | STRATFORD-30A | STRATFORD-30A | STRATFORD-30A | STRATFORD-30A | | STRATFORD-30A | NORWICH-32A | NORWICH-32A | NORWICH-32A |
| Aug-56 | STRATFORD-30A | STRATFORD-30A | STRATFORD-30A | STRATFORD-30A | | STRATFORD-30A | NORWICH-32A | NORWICH-32A | NORWICH-32A |
| Jan-57 | STRATFORD-30A | STRATFORD-30A | STRATFORD-30A | STRATFORD-30A | | STRATFORD-30A | NORWICH-32A | NORWICH-32A | NORWICH-32A |
| Aug-57 | STRATFORD-30A | STRATFORD-30A | STRATFORD-30A | STRATFORD-30A | | STRATFORD-30A | NORWICH-32A | NORWICH-32A | NORWICH-32A |
| Jan-58 | STRATFORD-30A | STRATFORD-30A | STRATFORD-30A | STRATFORD-30A | | STRATFORD-30A | NORWICH-32A | NORWICH-32A | NORWICH-32A |
| Aug-58 | STRATFORD-30A | STRATFORD-30A | 12/58: YAR(ST) - 32D | STRATFORD-30A | | STRATFORD-30A | NORWICH-32A | NORWICH-32A | NORWICH-32A |
| Jan-59 | 1/59: NOR - 32A | 1/59: NOR - 32A | 1/59: NOR - 32A | 1/59: NOR - 32A | | 1/59: NOR - 32A | NORWICH-32A | NORWICH-32A | NORWICH-32A |
| Aug-59 | NORWICH-32A | NORWICH-32A | NORWICH-32A | NORWICH-32A | | NORWICH-32A | NORWICH-32A | NORWICH-32A | NORWICH-32A |
| Nov-59 | NORWICH-32A | NORWICH-32A | NORWICH-32A | NORWICH-32A | | NORWICH-32A | NORWICH-32A | NORWICH-32A | NORWICH-32A |
| Jan-60 | NORWICH-32A | NORWICH-32A | NORWICH-32A | NORWICH-32A | | NORWICH-32A | NORWICH-32A | NORWICH-32A | NORWICH-32A |
| Apr-60 | NORWICH-32A | NORWICH-32A | NORWICH-32A | NORWICH-32A | | NORWICH-32A | NORWICH-32A | NORWICH-32A | NORWICH-32A |
| Aug-60 | NORWICH-32A | NORWICH-32A | NORWICH-32A | NORWICH-32A | | NORWICH-32A | NORWICH-32A | NORWICH-32A | NORWICH-32A |
| Nov-60 | NORWICH-32A | NORWICH-32A | NORWICH-32A | NORWICH-32A | | NORWICH-32A | NORWICH-32A | NORWICH-32A | NORWICH-32A |

| Date | 70009 | 70010 | 70011 | 70012 | 70013 | 70014 | 70015 | 70016 | 70030 |
|---|---|---|---|---|---|---|---|---|---|
| Aug-50 | | | | | | | | | |
| Jan-51 | 4/51: NOR - 32A | 5/51: NOR - 32A | 5/51: NOR - 32A | 5/51: NOR - 32A | 5/51: NOR - 32A | 5/51: NOR - 32A | | | |
| Aug-51 | 6/51: To SR | NORWICH-32A | NORWICH-32A | NORWICH-32A | NORWICH-32A | 6/51: To SR | | | |
| Jan-52 | 9/51: NOR : 32A | NORWICH-32A | NORWICH-32A | NORWICH-32A | NORWICH-32A | | | | |
| Aug-52 | NORWICH-32A | NORWICH-32A | NORWICH-32A | NORWICH-32A | NORWICH-32A | | 3/52: STRAT - 30A | 3/52: STRAT - 30A | |
| Jan-53 | NORWICH-32A | NORWICH-32A | NORWICH-32A | NORWICH-32A | NORWICH-32A | | STRATFORD-30A | STRATFORD-30A | |
| Aug-53 | NORWICH-32A | NORWICH-32A | NORWICH-32A | NORWICH-32A | NORWICH-32A | | STRATFORD-30A | STRATFORD-30A | |
| Jan-54 | NORWICH-32A | NORWICH-32A | NORWICH-32A | NORWICH-32A | NORWICH-32A | | 5/53: To WR | 5/53: To WR | 7/53: NOR - 32A |
| Aug-54 | NORWICH-32A | NORWICH-32A | NORWICH-32A | NORWICH-32A | NORWICH-32A | | | | NORWICH-32A |
| Jan-55 | NORWICH-32A | NORWICH-32A | NORWICH-32A | NORWICH-32A | NORWICH-32A | | | | NORWICH-32A |
| Aug-55 | NORWICH-32A | NORWICH-32A | NORWICH-32A | NORWICH-32A | NORWICH-32A | | | | NORWICH-32A |
| Jan-56 | NORWICH-32A | NORWICH-32A | NORWICH-32A | NORWICH-32A | NORWICH-32A | | | | NORWICH-32A |
| Aug-56 | NORWICH-32A | NORWICH-32A | NORWICH-32A | NORWICH-32A | NORWICH-32A | | | | NORWICH-32A |
| Jan-57 | NORWICH-32A | NORWICH-32A | NORWICH-32A | NORWICH-32A | NORWICH-32A | | | | NORWICH-32A |
| Aug-57 | NORWICH-32A | NORWICH-32A | NORWICH-32A | NORWICH-32A | NORWICH-32A | | | | NORWICH-32A |
| Jan-58 | NORWICH-32A | NORWICH-32A | NORWICH-32A | NORWICH-32A | NORWICH-32A | | | | NORWICH-32A |
| Aug-58 | NORWICH-32A | NORWICH-32A | NORWICH-32A | 10/58: STRAT - 30A | 9/58: IPS - 32B | | | | NORWICH-32A |
| Jan-59 | NORWICH-32A | NORWICH-32A | NORWICH-32A | 12/58: YAR(ST) - 32D | 12/58: NOR - 32A | | | | 9/58: YAR(ST) - 32D |
| Aug-59 | NORWICH-32A | NORWICH-32A | NORWICH-32A | 1/59: NOR - 32A | NORWICH-32A | | | | 1/59: NOR - 32A |
| Nov-59 | NORWICH-32A | NORWICH-32A | NORWICH-32A | NORWICH-32A | NORWICH-32A | | | | NORWICH-32A |
| Jan-60 | NORWICH-32A | NORWICH-32A | NORWICH-32A | NORWICH-32A | NORWICH-32A | | | | NORWICH-32A |
| Apr-60 | NORWICH-32A | NORWICH-32A | NORWICH-32A | NORWICH-32A | NORWICH-32A | | | | NORWICH-32A |
| Aug-60 | NORWICH-32A | NORWICH-32A | NORWICH-32A | NORWICH-32A | NORWICH-32A | | | | NORWICH-32A |
| Nov-60 | NORWICH-32A | NORWICH-32A | NORWICH-32A | NORWICH-32A | NORWICH-32A | | | | NORWICH-32A |

| Date | 70034 | 70035 | 70036 | 70037 | 70038 | 70039 | 70040 | 70041 | 70042 |
|---|---|---|---|---|---|---|---|---|---|
| Aug-50 | | | | | | | | | |
| Jan-51 | | | | | | | | | |
| Aug-51 | | | | | | | | | |
| Jan-52 | | | | | | | | | |
| Aug-52 | | | | | | | | | |
| Jan-53 | | | | | | | | | |
| Aug-53 | 7/53: NOR - 32A | 7/53: NOR - 32A | 1/53: STRAT - 30A | 1/53: STRAT - 30A | 1/53: STRAT - 30A | 2/53: NOR - 32A | 3/53: NOR - 32A | 3/53: STRAT - 30A | 4/53: STRAT - 30A |
| Jan-54 | NORWICH-32A | NORWICH-32A | STRATFORD-30A | STRATFORD-30A | STRATFORD-30A | NORWICH-32A | NORWICH-32A | STRATFORD-30A | STRATFORD-30A |
| Aug-54 | NORWICH-32A | NORWICH-32A | STRATFORD-30A | STRATFORD-30A | STRATFORD-30A | NORWICH-32A | NORWICH-32A | STRATFORD-30A | STRATFORD-30A |
| Jan-55 | NORWICH-32A | NORWICH-32A | STRATFORD-30A | STRATFORD-30A | STRATFORD-30A | NORWICH-32A | NORWICH-32A | STRATFORD-30A | STRATFORD-30A |
| Aug-55 | NORWICH-32A | NORWICH-32A | STRATFORD-30A | STRATFORD-30A | STRATFORD-30A | NORWICH-32A | NORWICH-32A | STRATFORD-30A | STRATFORD-30A |
| Jan-56 | NORWICH-32A | NORWICH-32A | STRATFORD-30A | STRATFORD-30A | STRATFORD-30A | NORWICH-32A | NORWICH-32A | STRATFORD-30A | STRATFORD-30A |
| Aug-56 | NORWICH-32A | NORWICH-32A | STRATFORD-30A | STRATFORD-30A | STRATFORD-30A | NORWICH-32A | NORWICH-32A | STRATFORD-30A | STRATFORD-30A |
| Jan-57 | NORWICH-32A | NORWICH-32A | STRATFORD-30A | STRATFORD-30A | STRATFORD-30A | NORWICH-32A | NORWICH-32A | STRATFORD-30A | STRATFORD-30A |
| Aug-57 | NORWICH-32A | NORWICH-32A | STRATFORD-30A | STRATFORD-30A | STRATFORD-30A | NORWICH-32A | NORWICH-32A | STRATFORD-30A | STRATFORD-30A |
| Jan-58 | 1/58: STRAT - 30A | NORWICH-32A | STRATFORD-30A | STRATFORD-30A | STRATFORD-30A | NORWICH-32A | NORWICH-32A | STRATFORD-30A | STRATFORD-30A |
| Aug-58 | STRATFORD-30A | 6/58: MARCH - 31B | STRATFORD-30A | STRATFORD-30A | STRATFORD-30A | NORWICH-32A | NORWICH-32A | STRATFORD-30A | STRATFORD-30A |
| Jan-59 | 1/59: NOR - 32A | 1/59: NOR - 32A | STRATFORD-30A | STRATFORD-30A | 1/59: NOR - 32A | NORWICH-32A | NORWICH-32A | STRATFORD-30A | 6/58: To LM |
| Aug-59 | NORWICH-32A | NORWICH-32A | STRATFORD-30A | STRATFORD-30A | NORWICH-32A | NORWICH-32A | NORWICH-32A | 1/59: NOR - 32A | |
| Nov-59 | NORWICH-32A | NORWICH-32A | STRATFORD-30A | STRATFORD-30A | NORWICH-32A | NORWICH-32A | NORWICH-32A | NORWICH-32A | |
| Jan-60 | NORWICH-32A | NORWICH-32A | STRATFORD-30A | STRATFORD-30A | NORWICH-32A | NORWICH-32A | NORWICH-32A | NORWICH-32A | |
| Apr-60 | NORWICH-32A | NORWICH-32A | STRATFORD-30A | STRATFORD-30A | NORWICH-32A | NORWICH-32A | NORWICH-32A | NORWICH-32A | |
| Aug-60 | NORWICH-32A | NORWICH-32A | STRATFORD-30A | STRATFORD-30A | NORWICH-32A | NORWICH-32A | NORWICH-32A | NORWICH-32A | |
| Nov-60 | NORWICH-32A | NORWICH-32A | STRATFORD-30A | STRATFORD-30A | NORWICH-32A | NORWICH-32A | NORWICH-32A | NORWICH-32A | |

## BR 6 4-6-2 (1952)

| Date | 70044 | 70053 | 70054 | 72000 | 72001 | 72002 | 72003 | 72004 | 72005 |
|---|---|---|---|---|---|---|---|---|---|
| Aug-50 | | | | | | | | | |
| Jan-51 | | | | | | | | | |
| Aug-51 | | | | | | | | | |
| Jan-52 | | | | | | | | | |
| Aug-52 | | | | | | | | | |
| Jan-53 | | | | | | | | | |
| Aug-53 | | | | | | | | | |
| Jan-54 | | | | | | | | | |
| Aug-54 | | | | | | | | | |
| Jan-55 | | | | | | | | | |
| Aug-55 | | | | | | | | | |
| Jan-56 | | | | | | | | | |
| Aug-56 | | | | | | | | | |
| Jan-57 | | | | | | | | | |
| Aug-57 | | | | | | | | | |
| Jan-58 | | | | *Ex Polmadie* | | | | | *Ex Carlisle* |
| Aug-58 | | | | 11/57: HAY - 64B | | | 11/57: HAY - 64B | | 11/57: HAY - 64B |
| Jan-59 | 12/58: HOLB - 55A | 11/58: HOLB - 55A | 11/58: HOLB - 55A | 3/58: To 66A | | | 3/58: To 66A | | 3/58: To 66A |
| Aug-59 | HOLBECK-55A | HOLBECK-55A | HOLBECK-55A | | | | | | |
| Nov-59 | HOLBECK-55A | HOLBECK-55A | HOLBECK-55A | *Ex Polmadie* | 12/59: HAY - 64B | 12/59: HAY - 64B | 12/59: EBRO(SM) - 64A | 12/59: EBRO(SM) - 64A | |
| Jan-60 | HOLBECK-55A | HOLBECK-55A | HOLBECK-55A | 12/59: EBRO(SM) - 64A | HAYMARKET-64B | HAYMARKET-64B | EDINBURGH(SM)-64A | EDINBURGH(SM)-64A | |
| Apr-60 | HOLBECK-55A | HOLBECK-55A | HOLBECK-55A | 4/60: To 66A | 4/60: To 66A | 4/60: To 66A | 4/60: To 66A | 4/60: To 66A | |
| Aug-60 | HOLBECK-55A | HOLBECK-55A | HOLBECK-55A | | | | | | |
| Nov-60 | HOLBECK-55A | HOLBECK-55A | HOLBECK-55A | | | | | | |

## BR5 4-6-0 (1951) and related

| Date | 72006 | 72009 | 73000 | 73002 | 73071 | 73074 | 73077 | 73078 | 73105 |
|---|---|---|---|---|---|---|---|---|---|
| Aug-50 | | | | | | | | | |
| Jan-51 | | | | | | | | | |
| Aug-51 | | | 11/51: STRAT - 30A | 11/51: STRAT - 30A | | | | | |
| Jan-52 | | | STRATFORD - 30A | 1/52: To LM | | | | | |
| Aug-52 | | | 3/52: To LM | | | | | | |
| Jan-53 | | | | | | | | | |
| Aug-53 | | | | | | | | | |
| Jan-54 | | | | | | | | | |
| Aug-54 | | | | | | | | | |
| Jan-55 | | | | | | | | | |
| Aug-55 | | | | | | | 5/55: EFLD - 65A | 5/55: EFLD - 65A | |
| Jan-56 | | | | | 1/56: KX - 34A | | EASTFIELD - 65A | EASTFIELD - 65A | 12/55: EFLD - 65A |
| Aug-56 | | | | | KINGS CROSS - 34A | | EASTFIELD - 65A | EASTFIELD - 65A | EASTFIELD - 65A |
| Jan-57 | | | | | KINGS CROSS - 34A | | EASTFIELD - 65A | EASTFIELD - 65A | EASTFIELD - 65A |
| Aug-57 | *Ex Carlisle* | *Ex Carlisle* | | | 5/57: To LM | | EASTFIELD - 65A | EASTFIELD - 65A | EASTFIELD - 65A |
| Jan-58 | 11/57: HAY - 64B | | | | | | EASTFIELD - 65A | EASTFIELD - 65A | EASTFIELD - 65A |
| Aug-58 | 3/58: To 66A | 9/58: STRAT - 30A | 5/58: SHEFF(LM) - 41B | 5/58: CANK - 41D | | 12/58: SHEFF(LM) - 41B | EASTFIELD - 65A | EASTFIELD - 65A | EASTFIELD - 65A |
| Jan-59 | | 10/58: To LM | SHEFFIELD (MR) - 41B | CANKLOW - 41D | | SHEFFIELD (MR) - 41B | EASTFIELD - 65A | EASTFIELD - 65A | EASTFIELD - 65A |
| Aug-59 | | | SHEFFIELD (MR) - 41B | CANKLOW - 41D | | SHEFFIELD (MR) - 41B | EASTFIELD - 65A | EASTFIELD - 65A | EASTFIELD - 65A |
| Nov-59 | | | SHEFFIELD (MR) - 41B | CANKLOW - 41D | | SHEFFIELD (MR) - 41B | EASTFIELD - 65A | EASTFIELD - 65A | EASTFIELD - 65A |
| Jan-60 | | | SHEFFIELD (MR) - 41B | 1/60: MILL - 41C | | SHEFFIELD (MR) - 41B | EASTFIELD - 65A | EASTFIELD - 65A | EASTFIELD - 65A |
| Apr-60 | | | SHEFFIELD (MR) - 41B | MILLHOUSES - 41C | | SHEFFIELD (MR) - 41B | EASTFIELD - 65A | EASTFIELD - 65A | EASTFIELD - 65A |
| Aug-60 | | | SHEFFIELD (MR) - 41B | MILLHOUSES - 41C | | | EASTFIELD - 65A | EASTFIELD - 65A | EASTFIELD - 65A |
| Nov-60 | | | SHEFFIELD (MR) - 41B | MILLHOUSES - 41C | | | | | |

| Date | 73106 | 73107 | 73108 | 73109 | 73153 | 73154 | 73155 | 73156 | 73157 |
|---|---|---|---|---|---|---|---|---|---|
| Aug-50 | | | | | | | | | |
| Jan-51 | | | | | | | | | |
| Aug-51 | | | | | | | | | |
| Jan-52 | | | | | | | | | |
| Aug-52 | | | | | | | | | |
| Jan-53 | | | | | | | | | |
| Aug-53 | | | | | | | | | |
| Jan-54 | | | | | | | | | |
| Aug-54 | | | | | | | | | |
| Jan-55 | | | | | | | | | |
| Aug-55 | | | | | | | | | |
| Jan-56 | 12/55: EFLD - 65A | 12/55: EFLD - 65A | 12/55: EFLD - 65A | 1/56: EFLD - 65A | | | | | |
| Aug-56 | EASTFIELD - 65A | EASTFIELD - 65A | EASTFIELD - 65A | EASTFIELD - 65A | | | 12/56: NEAS - 34E | 12/56: NEAS - 34E | 12/56: NEAS - 34E |
| Jan-57 | EASTFIELD - 65A | EASTFIELD - 65A | EASTFIELD - 65A | EASTFIELD - 65A | | | NEASDEN - 34E | NEASDEN - 34E | 10/57: KX - 34A |
| Aug-57 | 7/57: To INV (60A) | 7/57: To INV (60A) | EASTFIELD - 65A | EASTFIELD - 65A | 5/57: EFLD - 65A | 6/57: EFLD - 65A | NEASDEN - 34E | NEASDEN - 34E | KINGS CROSS - 34A |
| Jan-58 | | | EASTFIELD - 65A | EASTFIELD - 65A | EASTFIELD - 65A | EASTFIELD - 65A | NEASDEN - 34E | NEASDEN - 14D | 10/58: DARN - 41A |
| Aug-58 | | | EASTFIELD - 65A | EASTFIELD - 65A | EASTFIELD - 65A | EASTFIELD - 65A | NEASDEN - 14D | 12/58: SHEFF(LM) - 41B | 12/58: To LM |
| Jan-59 | | | EASTFIELD - 65A | EASTFIELD - 65A | EASTFIELD - 65A | EASTFIELD - 65A | NEASDEN - 14D | SHEFFIELD (MR) - 41B | |
| Aug-59 | | | EASTFIELD - 65A | EASTFIELD - 65A | EASTFIELD - 65A | EASTFIELD - 65A | NEASDEN - 14D | SHEFFIELD (MR) - 41B | |
| Nov-59 | | | EASTFIELD - 65A | EASTFIELD - 65A | EASTFIELD - 65A | EASTFIELD - 65A | NEASDEN - 14D | SHEFFIELD (MR) - 41B | |
| Jan-60 | | | EASTFIELD - 65A | EASTFIELD - 65A | EASTFIELD - 65A | EASTFIELD - 65A | NEASDEN - 14D | 9/60: To LM | |
| Apr-60 | | | EASTFIELD - 65A | EASTFIELD - 65A | EASTFIELD - 65A | EASTFIELD - 65A | NEASDEN - 14D | | |
| Aug-60 | | | EASTFIELD - 65A | EASTFIELD - 65A | EASTFIELD - 65A | EASTFIELD - 65A | NEASDEN - 14D | | |
| Nov-60 | | | EASTFIELD - 65A | EASTFIELD - 65A | EASTFIELD - 65A | EASTFIELD - 65A | | | |

| Date | 73158 | 73159 | 73160 | 73161 | 73162 | 73163 | 73164 | 73165 | 73166 |
|---|---|---|---|---|---|---|---|---|---|
| Aug-50 | | | | | | | | | |
| Jan-51 | | | | | | | | | |
| Aug-51 | | | | | | | | | |
| Jan-52 | | | | | | | | | |
| Aug-52 | | | | | | | | | |
| Jan-53 | | | | | | | | | |
| Aug-53 | | | | | | | | | |
| Jan-54 | | | | | | | | | |
| Aug-54 | | | | | | | | | |
| Jan-55 | | | | | | | | | |
| Aug-55 | | | | | | | | | |
| Jan-56 | | | | | | | | | |
| Jan-57 | 12/56: NEAS - 34E | 1/57: NEAS - 34E | 1/57: BLAY - 52C | | | | | | |
| Aug-57 | 10/57: KX - 34A | 10/57: KX - 34A | 2/57: GHD - 52A | 2/57: GHD - 52A | 2/57: YORK - 50A | 2/57: YORK - 50A | 3/57: YORK - 50A | 3/57: YORK - 50A | 3/57: YORK - 50A |
| Jan-58 | KINGS CROSS - 34A | KINGS CROSS - 34A | 9/57: N'TON - 55E | GATESHEAD - 52A | YORK - 50A | YORK - 50A | YORK - 50A | YORK - 50A | YORK - 50A |
| Aug-58 | 10/58: DARN - 41A | 10/58: DARN - 41A | NORMANTON - 55E | NORMANTON - 55E | YORK - 50A | YORK - 50A | YORK - 50A | YORK - 50A | YORK - 50A |
| Jan-59 | 12/58: To LM | 12/58: To LM | NORMANTON - 55E | NORMANTON - 55E | 10/58: HUDD - 55G | 10/58: HUDD - 55G | 10/58: HUDD - 55G | 10/58: HUDD - 55G | 10/58: HUDD - 55G |
| Aug-59 | | | NORMANTON - 55E | NORMANTON - 55E | HUDDERSFIELD - 55G | HUDDERSFIELD - 55G | HUDDERSFIELD - 55G | HUDDERSFIELD - 55G | HUDDERSFIELD - 55G |
| Nov-59 | | | NORMANTON - 55E | NORMANTON - 55E | HUDDERSFIELD - 55G | HUDDERSFIELD - 55G | HUDDERSFIELD - 55G | HUDDERSFIELD - 55G | HUDDERSFIELD - 55G |
| Jan-60 | | | NORMANTON - 55E | NORMANTON - 55E | HUDDERSFIELD - 55G | HUDDERSFIELD - 55G | HUDDERSFIELD - 55G | HUDDERSFIELD - 55G | HUDDERSFIELD - 55G |
| Apr-60 | | | NORMANTON - 55E | NORMANTON - 55E | HUDDERSFIELD - 55G | HUDDERSFIELD - 55G | HUDDERSFIELD - 55G | HUDDERSFIELD - 55G | HUDDERSFIELD - 55G |
| Aug-60 | | | NORMANTON - 55E | NORMANTON - 55E | HUDDERSFIELD - 55G | HUDDERSFIELD - 55G | HUDDERSFIELD - 55G | HUDDERSFIELD - 55G | HUDDERSFIELD - 55G |
| Nov-60 | | | NORMANTON - 55E | NORMANTON - 55E | HUDDERSFIELD - 55G | HUDDERSFIELD - 55G | | | |

## BR4 2-6-0 (1952) and related

| Date | 73167 | 73168 | 73169 | 73170 | 73171 | 76020 | 76021 | 76022 | 76023 |
|---|---|---|---|---|---|---|---|---|---|
| Aug-50 | | | | | | | | | |
| Jan-51 | | | | | | | | | |
| Aug-51 | | | | | | | | | |
| Jan-52 | | | | | | | | | |
| Aug-52 | | | | | | 12/52: DARL - 51A | 12/52: YORK - 50A | 12/52: DAIRY - 53A | |
| Jan-53 | | | | | | DARLINGTON - 51A | 2/53: N.HILL - 50B | DAIRYCOATES - 53A | |
| Aug-53 | | | | | | DARLINGTON - 51A | 3/53: SELBY - 50C | DAIRYCOATES - 53A | |
| Jan-54 | | | | | | DARLINGTON - 51A | 5/53: MALT - 50F | DAIRYCOATES - 53A | 12/53: SUND - 54A |
| Aug-54 | | | | | | DARLINGTON - 51A | 9/53: N.HILL - 50B | DAIRYCOATES - 53A | SUNDERLAND - 54A |
| Jan-55 | | | | | | DARLINGTON - 51A | 1/54: SELBY - 50C | DAIRYCOATES - 53A | SUNDERLAND - 54A |
| Aug-55 | | | | | | DARLINGTON - 51A | SELBY - 50C | DAIRYCOATES - 53A | SUNDERLAND - 54A |
| Jan-56 | | | | | | 6/56: W.AUCK - 51F | 6/56: W.AUCK - 51F | 6/56: KY ST - 51H | 5/55: W.HPL - 51C |
| Aug-56 | | | | | | K.STEPHEN - 51H | W.AUCKLAND - 51F | K.STEPHEN - 51H | W.HARTLEPOOL - 51C |
| Jan-57 | 4/57: YORK - 50A | 4/57: YORK - 50A | 4/57: YORK - 50A | 5/57: YORK - 50A | 5/57: YORK - 50A | K.STEPHEN - 51H | W.AUCKLAND - 51F | K.STEPHEN - 51H | 7/56: KY ST - 51H |
| Aug-57 | YORK - 50A | YORK - 50A | YORK - 50A | YORK - 50A | YORK - 50A | K.STEPHEN - 51H | W.AUCKLAND - 51F | K.STEPHEN - 51H | K.STEPHEN - 51H |
| Jan-58 | YORK - 50A | YORK - 50A | YORK - 50A | YORK - 50A | YORK - 50A | K.STEPHEN - 12D | W.AUCKLAND - 51F | K.STEPHEN - 12D | K.STEPHEN - 51H |
| Aug-58 | YORK - 50A | YORK - 50A | YORK - 50A | YORK - 50A | HOLBECK - 55A | K.STEPHEN - 12D | W.AUCKLAND - 51F | K.STEPHEN - 12D | K.STEPHEN - 51H |
| Jan-59 | 1/59: SCAR - 50E | 1/59: SCAR - 50E | 1/59: SCAR - 50E | 1/59: SCAR - 50E | HOLBECK - 55A | 6/59: To LM | W.AUCKLAND - 51F | K.STEPHEN - 12D | K.STEPHEN - 12D |
| Aug-59 | 6/59: N'TON - 55E | 6/59: HOL - 55A | 6/59: HOL - 55A | 6/59: HOL - 55A | HOLBECK - 55A | | W.AUCKLAND - 51F | K.STEPHEN - 12D | K.STEPHEN - 12D |
| Nov-59 | NORMANTON - 55E | HOLBECK - 55A | HOLBECK - 55A | HOLBECK - 55A | HOLBECK - 55A | | W.AUCKLAND - 51F | K.STEPHEN - 12D | K.STEPHEN - 12D |
| Jan-60 | NORMANTON - 55E | HOLBECK - 55A | HOLBECK - 55A | HOLBECK - 55A | HOLBECK - 55A | | W.AUCKLAND - 51F | K.STEPHEN - 12D | K.STEPHEN - 12D |
| Apr-60 | NORMANTON - 55E | HOLBECK - 55A | HOLBECK - 55A | HOLBECK - 55A | HOLBECK - 55A | | W.AUCKLAND - 51F | K.STEPHEN - 12D | K.STEPHEN - 12D |
| Aug-60 | NORMANTON - 55E | HOLBECK - 55A | HOLBECK - 55A | HOLBECK - 55A | HOLBECK - 55A | | W.AUCKLAND - 51F | K.STEPHEN - 12D | 9/60: To LM |
| Nov-60 | NORMANTON - 55E | HOLBECK - 55A | HOLBECK - 55A | HOLBECK - 55A | HOLBECK - 55A | | W.AUCKLAND - 51F | K.STEPHEN - 12D | |

# Block 1

| | 76024 | 76030 | 76031 | 76032 | 76033 | 76034 | 76035 | 76036 | 76037 |
|---|---|---|---|---|---|---|---|---|---|
| Aug-50 | | | | | | | | | |
| Jan-51 | | | | | | | | | |
| Aug-51 | | | | | | | | | |
| Jan-52 | | | | | | | | | |
| Aug-52 | | | | | | | | | |
| Jan-53 | 1/53: GHD - 52A | | | | | | | | |
| Aug-53 | 2/53: BLAY - 52C | | | | | | | | |
| Jan-54 | 3/53: CUD - 52E | | | | | | | | |
| Aug-54 | 4/54: ALSTON - 52C | 11/53: STRAT - 30A | 11/53: STRAT - 30A | 12/53: STRAT - 30A | 12/53: STRAT - 30A | 12/53: STRAT - 30A | | | |
| Jan-55 | ALSTON - 52C | STRATFORD - 30A | STRATFORD - 30A | STRATFORD - 30A | STRATFORD - 30A | STRATFORD - 30A | 5/54: NEAS - 34E | 6/54: NEAS - 34E | 6/54: NEAS - 34E |
| Aug-55 | ALSTON - 52C | STRATFORD - 30A | STRATFORD - 30A | STRATFORD - 30A | STRATFORD - 30A | STRATFORD - 30A | 3/55: HIT - 34D | NEASDEN - 34E | NEASDEN - 34E |
| Jan-56 | 12/55: BLAY - 52C | STRATFORD - 30A | STRATFORD - 30A | STRATFORD - 30A | STRATFORD - 30A | STRATFORD - 30A | 6/55: W.HSE - 38E | NEASDEN - 34E | NEASDEN - 34E |
| Aug-56 | 6/56: W.AUCK - 51F | STRATFORD - 30A | STRATFORD - 30A | STRATFORD - 30A | STRATFORD - 30A | STRATFORD - 30A | WOODFORD HALSE - 38E | NEASDEN - 34E | NEASDEN - 34E |
| Jan-57 | W.AUCKLAND - 51F | STRATFORD - 30A | STRATFORD - 30A | STRATFORD - 30A | STRATFORD - 30A | STRATFORD - 30A | 7/56: NEAS - 34E | NEASDEN - 34E | NEASDEN - 34E |
| Aug-57 | W.AUCKLAND - 51F | STRATFORD - 30A | STRATFORD - 30A | STRATFORD - 30A | STRATFORD - 30A | STRATFORD - 30A | NEASDEN - 34E | NEASDEN - 34E | NEASDEN - 34E |
| Jan-58 | W.AUCKLAND - 51F | STRATFORD - 30A | STRATFORD - 30A | STRATFORD - 30A | STRATFORD - 30A | STRATFORD - 30A | NEASDEN - 34E | NEASDEN - 34E | NEASDEN - 34E |
| Aug-58 | W.AUCKLAND - 51F | STRATFORD - 30A | STRATFORD - 30A | STRATFORD - 30A | STRATFORD - 30A | STRATFORD - 30A | NEASDEN - 34E | NEASDEN - 34E | NEASDEN - 34E |
| Jan-59 | W.AUCKLAND - 51F | STRATFORD - 30A | STRATFORD - 30A | STRATFORD - 30A | STRATFORD - 30A | STRATFORD - 30A | NEASDEN - 14D | NEASDEN - 14D | NEASDEN - 14D |
| Aug-59 | 6/59: GHD - 52A | STRATFORD - 30A | STRATFORD - 30A | STRATFORD - 30A | STRATFORD - 30A | STRATFORD - 30A | NEASDEN - 14D | NEASDEN - 14D | NEASDEN - 14D |
| Nov-59 | 11/59: HTN - 52B | STRATFORD - 30A | STRATFORD - 30A | STRATFORD - 30A | STRATFORD - 30A | STRATFORD - 30A | NEASDEN - 14D | NEASDEN - 14D | NEASDEN - 14D |
| Jan-60 | HEATON - 52B | STRATFORD - 30A | STRATFORD - 30A | STRATFORD - 30A | STRATFORD - 30A | STRATFORD - 30A | NEASDEN - 14D | NEASDEN - 14D | NEASDEN - 14D |
| Apr-60 | HEATON - 52B | STRATFORD - 30A | STRATFORD - 30A | STRATFORD - 30A | STRATFORD - 30A | STRATFORD - 30A | NEASDEN - 14D | NEASDEN - 14D | NEASDEN - 14D |
| Aug-60 | 7/60: SUND - 52G | STRATFORD - 30A | STRATFORD - 30A | 6/60: CAMB - 31A | 6/60: CAMB - 31A | STRATFORD - 30A | NEASDEN - 14D | NEASDEN - 14D | NEASDEN - 14D |
| Nov-60 | SUNDERLAND - 52G | 9/60: MARCH - 31B | STRATFORD - 30A | 9/60: MARCH - 31B | 9/60: MARCH - 31B | STRATFORD - 30A | NEASDEN - 14D | NEASDEN - 14D | NEASDEN - 14D |

# Block 2

| | 76038 | 76039 | 76040 | 76041 | 76042 | 76043 | 76044 | 76045 | 76046 |
|---|---|---|---|---|---|---|---|---|---|
| Aug-50 | | | | | | | | | |
| Jan-51 | | | | | | | | | |
| Aug-51 | | | | | | | | | |
| Jan-52 | | | | | | | | | |
| Aug-52 | | | | | | | | | |
| Jan-53 | | | | | | | | | |
| Aug-53 | | | | | | | | | |
| Jan-54 | | | | | | | | | |
| Aug-54 | 7/54: NEAS - 34E | 7/54: NEAS - 34E | 7/54: NEAS - 34E | 7/54: NEAS - 34E | 8/54: NEAS - 34E | 8/54: NEAS - 34E | 8/54: NEAS - 34E | | |
| Jan-55 | NEASDEN - 34E | NEASDEN - 34E | NEASDEN - 34E | NEASDEN - 34E | NEASDEN - 34E | NEASDEN - 34E | NEASDEN - 34E | | |
| Aug-55 | NEASDEN - 34E | NEASDEN - 34E | NEASDEN - 34E | NEASDEN - 34E | NEASDEN - 34E | NEASDEN - 34E | NEASDEN - 34E | 3/55: GHD - 52A | 3/55: GHD - 52A |
| Jan-56 | NEASDEN - 34E | NEASDEN - 34E | NEASDEN - 34E | NEASDEN - 34E | NEASDEN - 34E | NEASDEN - 34E | NEASDEN - 34E | 9/55: BLAY - 52C | BLAYDON - 52C |
| Aug-56 | NEASDEN - 34E | NEASDEN - 34E | NEASDEN - 34E | NEASDEN - 34E | NEASDEN - 34E | NEASDEN - 34E | NEASDEN - 34E | 12/55: GHD - 52A | 6/56: W.AUCK - 51F |
| Jan-57 | NEASDEN - 34E | NEASDEN - 34E | NEASDEN - 34E | NEASDEN - 34E | NEASDEN - 34E | NEASDEN - 34E | NEASDEN - 34E | 6/56: W.AUCK - 51F | W.AUCKLAND - 51F |
| Aug-57 | NEASDEN - 34E | NEASDEN - 34E | NEASDEN - 34E | NEASDEN - 34E | NEASDEN - 34E | NEASDEN - 34E | NEASDEN - 34E | W.AUCKLAND - 51F | W.AUCKLAND - 51F |
| Jan-58 | NEASDEN - 34E | NEASDEN - 34E | NEASDEN - 34E | NEASDEN - 34E | NEASDEN - 34E | NEASDEN - 34E | NEASDEN - 34E | W.AUCKLAND - 51F | W.AUCKLAND - 51F |
| Aug-58 | NEASDEN - 34E | NEASDEN - 34E | NEASDEN - 34E | NEASDEN - 34E | NEASDEN - 34E | NEASDEN - 34E | NEASDEN - 34E | W.AUCKLAND - 51F | W.AUCKLAND - 51F |
| Jan-59 | NEASDEN - 14D | NEASDEN - 14D | NEASDEN - 14D | NEASDEN - 14D | NEASDEN - 14D | NEASDEN - 14D | NEASDEN - 14D | W.AUCKLAND - 51F | W.AUCKLAND - 51F |
| Aug-59 | NEASDEN - 14D | NEASDEN - 14D | NEASDEN - 14D | NEASDEN - 14D | NEASDEN - 14D | NEASDEN - 14D | NEASDEN - 14D | W.AUCKLAND - 51F | W.AUCKLAND - 51F |
| Nov-59 | NEASDEN - 14D | NEASDEN - 14D | NEASDEN - 14D | NEASDEN - 14D | NEASDEN - 14D | NEASDEN - 14D | NEASDEN - 14D | W.AUCKLAND - 51F | W.AUCKLAND - 51F |
| Jan-60 | NEASDEN - 14D | NEASDEN - 14D | NEASDEN - 14D | NEASDEN - 14D | NEASDEN - 14D | NEASDEN - 14D | NEASDEN - 14D | W.AUCKLAND - 51F | W.AUCKLAND - 51F |
| Apr-60 | NEASDEN - 14D | NEASDEN - 14D | NEASDEN - 14D | NEASDEN - 14D | NEASDEN - 14D | NEASDEN - 14D | NEASDEN - 14D | W.AUCKLAND - 51F | W.AUCKLAND - 51F |
| Aug-60 | NEASDEN - 14D | NEASDEN - 14D | NEASDEN - 14D | NEASDEN - 14D | NEASDEN - 14D | NEASDEN - 14D | NEASDEN - 14D | W.AUCKLAND - 51F | W.AUCKLAND - 51F |
| Nov-60 | NEASDEN - 14D | NEASDEN - 14D | NEASDEN - 14D | NEASDEN - 14D | NEASDEN - 14D | NEASDEN - 14D | NEASDEN - 14D | W.AUCKLAND - 51F | W.AUCKLAND - 51F |

# Block 3

| | 76047 | 76048 | 76049 | 76050 | 76051 | 76052 | 76074 | 76100 | 76101 |
|---|---|---|---|---|---|---|---|---|---|
| Aug-50 | | | | | | | | | |
| Jan-51 | | | | | | | | | |
| Aug-51 | | | | | | | | | |
| Jan-52 | | | | | | | | | |
| Aug-52 | | | | | | | | | |
| Jan-53 | | | | | | | | | |
| Jan-54 | | | | | | | | | |
| Aug-54 | | | | | | | | | |
| Jan-55 | 3/55: GHD - 52A | 3/55: GHD - 52A | 4/55: GHD - 52A | | | | | | |
| Aug-55 | 9/55: BLAY - 52C | 9/55: BLAY - 52C | 5/55: BLAY - 52C | | | | | | |
| Jan-56 | BLAYDON - 52C | BLAYDON - 52C | 1/56: GHD - 52A | | | | | | |
| Aug-56 | 6/56: KY ST - 51H | 6/56: KY ST - 51H | 6/56: W.AUCK - 51F | 8/56: DARL - 51A | 8/56: YORK - 50A | 9/56: YORK - 50A | | | |
| Jan-57 | K.STEPHEN - 51H | K.STEPHEN - 51H | W.AUCKLAND - 51F | 10/56: W.AUCK - 51F | 10/56: KY ST - 51H | 10/56: KY ST - 51H | 11/56: EFLD - 65A | | |
| Aug-57 | K.STEPHEN - 51H | K.STEPHEN - 51H | W.AUCKLAND - 51F | W.AUCKLAND - 51F | K.STEPHEN - 51H | K.STEPHEN - 51H | EASTFIELD - 65A | 5/57: DAWS - 65D | 6/57: DAWS - 65D |
| Jan-58 | K.STEPHEN - 51H | K.STEPHEN - 51H | W.AUCKLAND - 51F | W.AUCKLAND - 51F | K.STEPHEN - 51H | K.STEPHEN - 51H | EASTFIELD - 65A | DAWS HOLME - 65D | DAWS HOLME - 65D |
| Aug-58 | K.STEPHEN - 12D | K.STEPHEN - 12D | W.AUCKLAND - 51F | W.AUCKLAND - 51F | K.STEPHEN - 12D | K.STEPHEN - 12D | EASTFIELD - 65A | DAWS HOLME - 65D | DAWS HOLME - 65D |
| Jan-59 | K.STEPHEN - 12D | K.STEPHEN - 12D | W.AUCKLAND - 51F | W.AUCKLAND - 51F | K.STEPHEN - 12D | K.STEPHEN - 12D | EASTFIELD - 65A | DAWS HOLME - 65D | DAWS HOLME - 65D |
| Aug-59 | K.STEPHEN - 12D | 6/59: To LM | W.AUCKLAND - 51F | W.AUCKLAND - 51F | K.STEPHEN - 12D | K.STEPHEN - 12D | EASTFIELD - 65A | DAWS HOLME - 65D | DAWS HOLME - 65D |
| Nov-59 | K.STEPHEN - 12D | | W.AUCKLAND - 51F | W.AUCKLAND - 51F | K.STEPHEN - 12D | K.STEPHEN - 12D | EASTFIELD - 65A | DAWS HOLME - 65D | DAWS HOLME - 65D |
| Jan-60 | K.STEPHEN - 12D | | W.AUCKLAND - 51F | W.AUCKLAND - 51F | K.STEPHEN - 12D | K.STEPHEN - 12D | EASTFIELD - 65A | DAWS HOLME - 65D | DAWS HOLME - 65D |
| Apr-60 | K.STEPHEN - 12D | | W.AUCKLAND - 51F | W.AUCKLAND - 51F | K.STEPHEN - 12D | K.STEPHEN - 12D | EASTFIELD - 65A | DAWS HOLME - 65D | DAWS HOLME - 65D |
| Aug-60 | 8/60: To LM | | W.AUCKLAND - 51F | W.AUCKLAND - 51F | K.STEPHEN - 12D | 5/60: To LM | EASTFIELD - 65A | 8/60: PARK - 65C | DAWS HOLME - 65D |
| Nov-60 | | | W.AUCKLAND - 51F | W.AUCKLAND - 51F | K.STEPHEN - 12D | | EASTFIELD - 65A | PARKHEAD - 65C | DAWS HOLME - 65D |

# Block 4

| | 76102 | 76103 | 76104 | 76105 | 76106 | 76107 | 76108 | 76109 | 76110 |
|---|---|---|---|---|---|---|---|---|---|
| Aug-50 | | | | | | | | | |
| Jan-51 | | | | | | | | | |
| Jan-52 | | | | | | | | | |
| Aug-52 | | | | | | | | | |
| Jan-53 | | | | | | | | | |
| Aug-53 | | | | | | | | | |
| Jan-54 | | | | | | | | | |
| Aug-54 | | | | | | | | | |
| Jan-55 | | | | | | | | | |
| Aug-55 | | | | | | | | | |
| Jan-56 | | | | | | | | | |
| Aug-56 | | | | | | | | | |
| Jan-57 | | | | | | | | | |
| Aug-57 | 6/57: DAWS - 65D | 6/57: DAWS - 65D | 7/57: KITTY - 61A | 7/57: KITTY - 61A | 7/57: KITTY - 61A | 8/57: KITTY - 61A | 8/57: KITTY - 61A | 8/57: TH JN - 62A | 8/57: TH JN - 62A |
| Jan-58 | 7/57: PARK - 65C | 7/57: PARK - 65C | KITTYBREWSTER - 61A | KITTYBREWSTER - 61A | KITTYBREWSTER - 61A | KITTYBREWSTER - 61A | KITTYBREWSTER - 61A | THORNTONJCN - 62A | THORNTONJCN - 62A |
| Aug-58 | PARKHEAD - 65C | PARKHEAD - 65C | KITTYBREWSTER - 61A | KITTYBREWSTER - 61A | KITTYBREWSTER - 61A | KITTYBREWSTER - 61A | KITTYBREWSTER - 61A | THORNTONJCN - 62A | THORNTONJCN - 62A |
| Jan-59 | 3/59: STRX - 65B | 3/59: STRX - 65B | KITTYBREWSTER - 61A | KITTYBREWSTER - 61A | KITTYBREWSTER - 61A | KITTYBREWSTER - 61A | KITTYBREWSTER - 61A | THORNTONJCN - 62A | THORNTONJCN - 62A |
| Aug-59 | STROLLOX - 65B | STROLLOX - 65B | KITTYBREWSTER - 61A | KITTYBREWSTER - 61A | KITTYBREWSTER - 61A | KITTYBREWSTER - 61A | KITTYBREWSTER - 61A | THORNTONJCN - 62A | THORNTONJCN - 62A |
| Nov-59 | STROLLOX - 65B | STROLLOX - 65B | KITTYBREWSTER - 61A | KITTYBREWSTER - 61A | KITTYBREWSTER - 61A | KITTYBREWSTER - 61A | KITTYBREWSTER - 61A | THORNTONJCN - 62A | THORNTONJCN - 62A |
| Jan-60 | STROLLOX - 65B | STROLLOX - 65B | KITTYBREWSTER - 61A | KITTYBREWSTER - 61A | KITTYBREWSTER - 61A | KITTYBREWSTER - 61A | KITTYBREWSTER - 61A | 1/60: DUNF - 62C | THORNTONJCN - 62A |
| Apr-60 | STROLLOX - 65B | STROLLOX - 65B | KITTYBREWSTER - 61A | KITTYBREWSTER - 61A | KITTYBREWSTER - 61A | KITTYBREWSTER - 61A | KITTYBREWSTER - 61A | DUNFERMLINE - 62C | THORNTONJCN - 62A |
| Aug-60 | 8/60: PARK - 65C | 8/60: PARK - 65C | KITTYBREWSTER - 61A | KITTYBREWSTER - 61A | 6/60: KEITH - 61C | 6/60: KEITH - 61C | KITTYBREWSTER - 61A | DUNFERMLINE - 62C | 6/60: DUNF - 62C |
| Nov-60 | PARKHEAD - 65C | PARKHEAD - 65C | KITTYBREWSTER - 61A | KITTYBREWSTER - 61A | KEITH - 61C | KEITH - 61C | KITTYBREWSTER - 61A | DUNFERMLINE - 62C | DUNFERMLINE - 62C |

| | 76111 | 76113 | 76114 | BR3 2-6-0 (1953) 77000 | 77001 | 77002 | 77003 | 77004 | 77010 |
|---|---|---|---|---|---|---|---|---|---|
| Aug-50 | | | | | | | | | |
| Jan-51 | | | | | | | | | |
| Aug-51 | | | | | | | | | |
| Jan-52 | | | | | | | | | |
| Aug-52 | | | | | | | | | |
| Jan-53 | | | | | | | | | |
| Aug-53 | | | | | | | | | |
| Jan-54 | | | | 2/54: DARL - 51A | 2/54: DARL - 51A | 2/54: DARL - 51A | 3/54: DARL - 51A | 3/54: DARL - 51A | 6/54: DARL - 51A |
| Aug-54 | | | | 8/54: W.AUCK - 51F | 8/54: W.AUCK - 51F | 8/54: W.AUCK - 51F | 8/54: W.AUCK - 51F | 8/54: W.AUCK - 51F | 8/54: W.AUCK - 51F |
| Jan-55 | | | | W.AUCKLAND - 51F | W.AUCKLAND - 51F | W.AUCKLAND - 51F | W.AUCKLAND - 51F | 1/55: DARL - 51A | W.AUCKLAND - 51F |
| Aug-55 | | | | 6/55: DAIRY - 53A | 6/55: DAIRY - 53A | W.AUCKLAND - 51F | W.AUCKLAND - 51F | 9/55: WHITBY - 50G | 6/55: DAIRY - 53A |
| Jan-56 | | | | 9/55: B.GDNS - 53B | 9/55: B.GDNS - 53B | W.AUCKLAND - 51F | W.AUCKLAND - 51F | 11/55: W.AUCK - 51F | 9/55: B.GDNS - 53B |
| Aug-56 | | | | B.GARDENS - 53B | B.GARDENS - 53B | W.AUCKLAND - 51F | W.AUCKLAND - 51F | W.AUCKLAND - 51F | B.GARDENS - 53B |
| Jan-57 | | | | B.GARDENS - 53B | B.GARDENS - 53B | W.AUCKLAND - 51F | W.AUCKLAND - 51F | W.AUCKLAND - 51F | B.GARDENS - 53B |
| Aug-57 | 8/57: TH JN - 62A | 12/57: STRX - 65B | 12/57: STRX - 65B | B.GARDENS - 53B | B.GARDENS - 53B | W.AUCKLAND - 51F | W.AUCKLAND - 51F | W.AUCKLAND - 51F | B.GARDENS - 53B |
| Jan-58 | THORNTON JCN - 62A | STROLLOX - 65B | STROLLOX - 65B | 12/57: S'HEAD - 53C | B.GARDENS - 53B | W.AUCKLAND - 51F | W.AUCKLAND - 51F | W.AUCKLAND - 51F | B.GARDENS - 53B |
| Aug-58 | THORNTON JCN - 62A | STROLLOX - 65B | STROLLOX - 65B | SPRINGHEAD - 53C | B.GARDENS - 53B | W.AUCKLAND - 51F | W.AUCKLAND - 51F | 8/58: YORK - 50A | 10/58: S'HEAD - 53C |
| Jan-59 | THORNTON JCN - 62A | STROLLOX - 65B | STROLLOX - 65B | 12/58: DAIRY - 53A | B.GARDENS - 53B | W.AUCKLAND - 51F | W.AUCKLAND - 51F | 10/58: WHITBY - 50G | 12/58: DAIRY - 53A |
| Aug-59 | THORNTON JCN - 62A | STROLLOX - 65B | STROLLOX - 65B | DAIRYCOATES - 53A | 6/59: DAIRY - 53A | W.AUCKLAND - 51F | W.AUCKLAND - 51F | 4/59: N.HILL - 50B | DAIRYCOATES - 53A |
| Nov-59 | THORNTON JCN - 62A | STROLLOX - 65B | STROLLOX - 65B | DAIRYCOATES - 53A | DAIRYCOATES - 53A | W.AUCKLAND - 51F | W.AUCKLAND - 51F | 5/59: SELBY - 50C | DAIRYCOATES - 53A |
| Jan-60 | THORNTON JCN - 62A | STROLLOX - 65B | STROLLOX - 65B | DAIRYCOATES - 53A | DAIRYCOATES - 53A | W.AUCKLAND - 51F | W.AUCKLAND - 51F | 9/59: YORK - 50A | DAIRYCOATES - 53A |
| Apr-60 | THORNTON JCN - 62A | STROLLOX - 65B | STROLLOX - 65B | DAIRYCOATES - 50B | DAIRYCOATES - 50B | W.AUCKLAND - 51F | W.AUCKLAND - 51F | 11/59: SCAR - 50E | DAIRYCOATES - 50B |
| Aug-60 | 6/60: DUNF - 62C | STROLLOX - 65B | 8/60: PARK - 65C | DAIRYCOATES - 50B | DAIRYCOATES - 50B | W.AUCKLAND - 51F | W.AUCKLAND - 51F | SCARBOROUGH - 50E | DAIRYCOATES - 50B |
| Nov-60 | DUNFERMLINE - 62C | STROLLOX - 65B | PARKHEAD - 65C | DAIRYCOATES - 50B | DAIRYCOATES - 50B | W.AUCKLAND - 51F | W.AUCKLAND - 51F | SCARBOROUGH - 50E | DAIRYCOATES - 50B |

| | 77011 | 77012 | 77013 | 77014 | BR2 2-6-0 (1953) 78010 | 78011 | 78012 | 78013 | 78014 |
|---|---|---|---|---|---|---|---|---|---|
| Aug-50 | | | | | | | | | |
| Jan-51 | | | | | | | | | |
| Aug-51 | | | | | | | | | |
| Jan-52 | | | | | | | | | |
| Aug-52 | | | | | | | | | |
| Jan-53 | | | | | | | | | |
| Aug-53 | | | | | | | | | |
| Jan-54 | 6/54: DARL - 51A | 6/54: DARL - 51A | | | 12/53: W.AUCK - 51F | 12/53: W.AUCK - 51F | 1/54: W.AUCK - 51F | 1/54: W.AUCK - 51F | 2/54: W.AUCK - 51F |
| Aug-54 | 8/54: W.AUCK - 51F | DARLINGTON - 51A | 7/54: DARL - 51A | 7/54: DARL - 51A | W.AUCKLAND - 51F | W.AUCKLAND - 51F | W.AUCKLAND - 51F | W.AUCKLAND - 51F | W.AUCKLAND - 51F |
| Jan-55 | W.AUCKLAND - 51F | 1/55: W.AUCK - 51F | DARLINGTON - 51A | DARLINGTON - 51A | 3/55: N'TON - 51J | 3/55: N'TON - 51J | 3/55: N'TON - 51J | 3/55: N'TON - 51J | 3/55: N'TON - 51J |
| Aug-55 | 6/55: BLAY - 52C | W.AUCKLAND - 51F | 9/55: WHITBY - 50G | 9/55: WHITBY - 50G | NORTHALLERTON - 51J | NORTHALLERTON - 51J | NORTHALLERTON - 51J | NORTHALLERTON - 51J | NORTHALLERTON - 51J |
| Jan-56 | 12/55: ALS - 52C | W.AUCKLAND - 51F | WHITBY - 50G | WHITBY - 50G | NORTHALLERTON - 51J | NORTHALLERTON - 51J | 11/55: WHITBY - 50G | NORTHALLERTON - 51J | NORTHALLERTON - 51J |
| Aug-56 | ALSTON - 52C | W.AUCKLAND - 51F | WHITBY - 50G | 6/56: BLAY - 52C | NORTHALLERTON - 51J | NORTHALLERTON - 51J | WHITBY - 50G | NORTHALLERTON - 51J | NORTHALLERTON - 51J |
| Jan-57 | ALSTON - 52C | W.AUCKLAND - 51F | WHITBY - 50G | BLAYDON - 52C | NORTHALLERTON - 51J | NORTHALLERTON - 51J | WHITBY - 50G | NORTHALLERTON - 51J | NORTHALLERTON - 51J |
| Aug-57 | ALSTON - 52C | W.AUCKLAND - 51F | WHITBY - 50G | BLAYDON - 52C | NORTHALLERTON - 51J | NORTHALLERTON - 51J | WHITBY - 50G | NORTHALLERTON - 51J | NORTHALLERTON - 51J |
| Jan-58 | ALSTON - 52C | W.AUCKLAND - 51F | WHITBY - 50G | BLAYDON - 52C | NORTHALLERTON - 51J | NORTHALLERTON - 51J | WHITBY - 50G | 2/58: KYST - 12D | NORTHALLERTON - 51J |
| Aug-58 | ALSTON - 52C | W.AUCKLAND - 51F | WHITBY - 50G | BLAYDON - 52C | NORTHALLERTON - 51J | NORTHALLERTON - 51J | WHITBY - 50G | K.STEPHEN - 12D | NORTHALLERTON - 51J |
| Jan-59 | ALSTON - 52C | 12/58: YORK - 50A | WHITBY - 50G | BLAYDON - 52C | NORTHALLERTON - 51J | NORTHALLERTON - 51J | WHITBY - 50G | 4/59: N.HILL - 50B | NORTHALLERTON - 51J |
| Aug-59 | 9/59: GHD - 52A | YORK - 50A | 9/59: YORK - 50A | 9/59: GHD - 52A | NORTHALLERTON - 51J | NORTHALLERTON - 51J | WHITBY - 50G | 5/59: SELBY - 50C | NORTHALLERTON - 51J |
| Nov-59 | GATESHEAD - 52A | YORK - 50A | YORK - 50A | GATESHEAD - 52A | NORTHALLERTON - 51J | NORTHALLERTON - 51J | WHITBY - 50G | SELBY - 50C | NORTHALLERTON - 51J |
| Jan-60 | GATESHEAD - 52A | YORK - 50A | YORK - 50A | GATESHEAD - 52A | NORTHALLERTON - 51J | NORTHALLERTON - 51J | WHITBY - 50G | SELBY - 50C | NORTHALLERTON - 51J |
| Apr-60 | GATESHEAD - 52A | YORK - 50A | YORK - 50A | GATESHEAD - 52A | NORTHALLERTON - 51J | NORTHALLERTON - 51J | WHITBY - 50G | SELBY - 50C | NORTHALLERTON - 51J |
| Aug-60 | 9/60: T.DCK - 52H | YORK - 50A | 10/60: SCAR - 50E | 9/60: T.DCK - 52H | NORTHALLERTON - 51J | NORTHALLERTON - 51J | WHITBY - 50G | 6/60: To LM | NORTHALLERTON - 51J |
| Nov-60 | TYNEDOCK - 52H | YORK - 50A | SCARBOROUGH - 50E | TYNEDOCK - 52H | NORTHALLERTON - 51J | NORTHALLERTON - 51J | WHITBY - 50G | | NORTHALLERTON - 51J |

| | 78015 | 78016 | 78017 | 78018 | 78019 | 78045 | 78046 | 78047 | 78048 |
|---|---|---|---|---|---|---|---|---|---|
| Aug-50 | | | | | | | | | |
| Jan-51 | | | | | | | | | |
| Aug-51 | | | | | | | | | |
| Jan-52 | | | | | | | | | |
| Aug-52 | | | | | | | | | |
| Jan-53 | | | | | | | | | |
| Aug-53 | | | | | | | | | |
| Jan-54 | 2/54: W.AUCK - 51F | 3/54: KYST - 51H | 3/54: KYST - 51H | 3/54: KYST - 51H | 3/54: KYST - 51H | | | | |
| Aug-54 | W.AUCKLAND - 51F | K.STEPHEN - 51H | K.STEPHEN - 51H | K.STEPHEN - 51H | K.STEPHEN - 51H | | | | |
| Jan-55 | W.AUCKLAND - 51F | K.STEPHEN - 51H | K.STEPHEN - 51H | K.STEPHEN - 51H | K.STEPHEN - 51H | | | | |
| Aug-55 | W.AUCKLAND - 51F | K.STEPHEN - 51H | K.STEPHEN - 51H | K.STEPHEN - 51H | K.STEPHEN - 51H | 10/55: KITTY - 61A | 10/55: HWCK - 64G | 10/55: HWCK - 64G | 10/55: EBRO(SM) - 64A |
| Jan-56 | W.AUCKLAND - 51F | K.STEPHEN - 51H | K.STEPHEN - 51H | K.STEPHEN - 51H | K.STEPHEN - 51H | KITTYBREWSTER - 61A | HAWICK - 64G | HAWICK - 64G | EDINBURGH(SM) - 64A |
| Aug-56 | W.AUCKLAND - 51F | K.STEPHEN - 51H | K.STEPHEN - 51H | K.STEPHEN - 51H | K.STEPHEN - 51H | KITTYBREWSTER - 61A | HAWICK - 64G | HAWICK - 64G | EDINBURGH(SM) - 64A |
| Jan-57 | 11/56: N'TON - 51J | K.STEPHEN - 51H | K.STEPHEN - 51H | K.STEPHEN - 51H | K.STEPHEN - 51H | KITTYBREWSTER - 61A | HAWICK - 64G | HAWICK - 64G | EDINBURGH(SM) - 64A |
| Aug-57 | NORTHALLERTON - 51J | K.STEPHEN - 51H | K.STEPHEN - 51H | K.STEPHEN - 51H | K.STEPHEN - 51H | KITTYBREWSTER - 61A | HAWICK - 64G | HAWICK - 64G | EDINBURGH(SM) - 64A |
| Jan-58 | NORTHALLERTON - 51J | 2/58: N'TON - 51J | K.STEPHEN - 51H | K.STEPHEN - 51H | K.STEPHEN - 51H | KITTYBREWSTER - 61A | HAWICK - 64G | HAWICK - 64G | EDINBURGH(SM) - 64A |
| Aug-58 | NORTHALLERTON - 51J | 4/58: W.AUCK - 51F | K.STEPHEN - 12D | K.STEPHEN - 12D | K.STEPHEN - 12D | KITTYBREWSTER - 61A | HAWICK - 64G | HAWICK - 64G | EDINBURGH(SM) - 64A |
| Jan-59 | NORTHALLERTON - 51J | W.AUCKLAND - 51F | K.STEPHEN - 12D | K.STEPHEN - 12D | K.STEPHEN - 12D | KITTYBREWSTER - 61A | HAWICK - 64G | HAWICK - 64G | EDINBURGH(SM) - 64A |
| Aug-59 | NORTHALLERTON - 51J | W.AUCKLAND - 51F | K.STEPHEN - 12D | K.STEPHEN - 12D | K.STEPHEN - 12D | KITTYBREWSTER - 61A | HAWICK - 64G | HAWICK - 64G | EDINBURGH(SM) - 64A |
| Nov-59 | NORTHALLERTON - 51J | W.AUCKLAND - 51F | K.STEPHEN - 12D | K.STEPHEN - 12D | K.STEPHEN - 12D | KITTYBREWSTER - 61A | HAWICK - 64G | HAWICK - 64G | EDINBURGH(SM) - 64A |
| Jan-60 | NORTHALLERTON - 51J | W.AUCKLAND - 51F | K.STEPHEN - 12D | K.STEPHEN - 12D | K.STEPHEN - 12D | KITTYBREWSTER - 61A | HAWICK - 64G | HAWICK - 64G | EDINBURGH(SM) - 64A |
| Apr-60 | NORTHALLERTON - 51J | W.AUCKLAND - 51F | 5/60: To LM | 5/60: To LM | 5/60: To LM | KITTYBREWSTER - 61A | HAWICK - 64G | HAWICK - 64G | EDINBURGH(SM) - 64A |
| Aug-60 | NORTHALLERTON - 51J | W.AUCKLAND - 51F | | | | 7/60: KEITH - 61C | HAWICK - 64G | HAWICK - 64G | 8/60: HWCK - 64G |
| Nov-60 | NORTHALLERTON - 51J | W.AUCKLAND - 51F | | | | KEITH - 61C | HAWICK - 64G | HAWICK - 64G | HAWICK - 64G |

| | 78049 | 78052 | 78053 | 78054 | BR4 2-6-4T (1951) 80004 | 80005 | 80007 | 80021 | 80028 |
|---|---|---|---|---|---|---|---|---|---|
| Aug-50 | | | | | | | | | |
| Jan-51 | | | | | | | | | |
| Aug-51 | | | | | | | | | |
| Jan-52 | | | | | | | | 11/51: KITTY - 61A | 1/52: KITTY - 61A |
| Aug-52 | | | | | | | | KITTYBREWSTER - 61A | KITTYBREWSTER - 61A |
| Jan-53 | | | | | 12/52: KITTY - 61A | 12/52: KITTY - 61A | | KITTYBREWSTER - 61A | KITTYBREWSTER - 61A |
| Aug-53 | | | | | KITTYBREWSTER - 61A | KITTYBREWSTER - 61A | | KITTYBREWSTER - 61A | KITTYBREWSTER - 61A |
| Jan-54 | | | | | KITTYBREWSTER - 61A | KITTYBREWSTER - 61A | | KITTYBREWSTER - 61A | KITTYBREWSTER - 61A |
| Aug-54 | | | | | KITTYBREWSTER - 61A | KITTYBREWSTER - 61A | Ex CR | KITTYBREWSTER - 61A | KITTYBREWSTER - 61A |
| Jan-55 | | | | | KITTYBREWSTER - 61A | KITTYBREWSTER - 61A | 3/55: HWCK - 64G | KITTYBREWSTER - 61A | KITTYBREWSTER - 61A |
| Aug-55 | 11/55: EBRO(SM) - 64A | | | | KITTYBREWSTER - 61A | KITTYBREWSTER - 61A | 5/55: To CR | KITTYBREWSTER - 61A | KITTYBREWSTER - 61A |
| Jan-56 | EDINBURGH(SM) - 64A | | | | KITTYBREWSTER - 61A | KITTYBREWSTER - 61A | | KITTYBREWSTER - 61A | KITTYBREWSTER - 61A |
| Aug-56 | EDINBURGH(SM) - 64A | | 10/56: F'HILL - 61B | 10/56: F'HILL - 61B | KITTYBREWSTER - 61A | KITTYBREWSTER - 61A | | KITTYBREWSTER - 61A | KITTYBREWSTER - 61A |
| Jan-57 | EDINBURGH(SM) - 64A | | 11/56: KEITH - 61C | 11/56: KEITH - 61C | KITTYBREWSTER - 61A | KITTYBREWSTER - 61A | | KITTYBREWSTER - 61A | KITTYBREWSTER - 61A |
| Aug-57 | EDINBURGH(SM) - 64A | | KEITH - 61C | KEITH - 61C | KITTYBREWSTER - 61A | KITTYBREWSTER - 61A | | KITTYBREWSTER - 61A | KITTYBREWSTER - 61A |
| Jan-58 | EDINBURGH(SM) - 64A | Ex HR | KEITH - 61C | KEITH - 61C | KITTYBREWSTER - 61A | KITTYBREWSTER - 61A | | KITTYBREWSTER - 61A | KITTYBREWSTER - 61A |
| Aug-58 | EDINBURGH(SM) - 64A | 9/58: EBRO(SM) - 64A | KEITH - 61C | KEITH - 61C | KITTYBREWSTER - 61A | KITTYBREWSTER - 61A | | KITTYBREWSTER - 61A | KITTYBREWSTER - 61A |
| Jan-59 | EDINBURGH(SM) - 64A | 11/58: AVIE - 60B | KEITH - 61C | KEITH - 61C | KITTYBREWSTER - 61A | KITTYBREWSTER - 61A | | KITTYBREWSTER - 61A | KITTYBREWSTER - 61A |
| Aug-59 | 6/59: HWCK - 64G | AVIEMORE - 60B | KEITH - 61C | KEITH - 61C | KITTYBREWSTER - 61A | 7/59: To GSWR | | KITTYBREWSTER - 61A | KITTYBREWSTER - 61A |
| Nov-59 | HAWICK - 64G | AVIEMORE - 60B | KEITH - 61C | KEITH - 61C | KITTYBREWSTER - 61A | | | KITTYBREWSTER - 61A | KITTYBREWSTER - 61A |
| Jan-60 | HAWICK - 64G | AVIEMORE - 60B | KEITH - 61C | KEITH - 61C | KITTYBREWSTER - 61A | | | KITTYBREWSTER - 61A | KITTYBREWSTER - 61A |
| Apr-60 | HAWICK - 64G | AVIEMORE - 60B | KEITH - 61C | KEITH - 61C | KITTYBREWSTER - 61A | | | KITTYBREWSTER - 61A | KITTYBREWSTER - 61A |
| Aug-60 | HAWICK - 64G | AVIEMORE - 60B | KEITH - 61C | KEITH - 61C | KITTYBREWSTER - 61A | | | KITTYBREWSTER - 61A | KITTYBREWSTER - 61A |
| Nov-60 | HAWICK - 64G | AVIEMORE - 60B | KEITH - 61C | KEITH - 61C | KITTYBREWSTER - 61A | | | KITTYBREWSTER - 61A | KITTYBREWSTER - 61A |

| | 80029 | 80069 | 80070 | 80071 | 80072 | 80073 | 80074 | 80075 | 80076 |
|---|---|---|---|---|---|---|---|---|---|
| Aug-50 | | | | | | | | | |
| Jan-51 | | | | | | | | | |
| Aug-51 | | | | | | | | | |
| Jan-52 | 1/52: KITTY - 61A | | | | | | | | |
| Aug-52 | KITTYBREWSTER - 61A | | | | | | | | |
| Jan-53 | KITTYBREWSTER - 61A | | | | | | | | |
| Aug-53 | KITTYBREWSTER - 61A | 9/53: PLAIS - 33A | 10/53: PLAIS - 33A | 10/53: PLAIS - 33A | | | | | |
| Jan-54 | KITTYBREWSTER - 61A | 1/54: TIL - 33B | 1/54: TIL - 33B | 1/54: TIL - 33B | 1/54: TIL - 33B | 1/54: TIL - 33B | 11/53: PLAIS - 33A | 12/53: PLAIS - 33A | 12/53: PLAIS - 33A |
| Aug-54 | KITTYBREWSTER - 61A | TILBURY-33B | TILBURY-33B | TILBURY-33B | TILBURY-33B | TILBURY-33B | PLAISTOW-33A | PLAISTOW-33A | PLAISTOW-33A |
| Jan-55 | KITTYBREWSTER - 61A | TILBURY-33B | TILBURY-33B | TILBURY-33B | TILBURY-33B | TILBURY-33B | PLAISTOW-33A | PLAISTOW-33A | PLAISTOW-33A |
| Aug-55 | KITTYBREWSTER - 61A | TILBURY-33B | TILBURY-33B | TILBURY-33B | TILBURY-33B | TILBURY-33B | PLAISTOW-33A | PLAISTOW-33A | PLAISTOW-33A |
| Jan-56 | KITTYBREWSTER - 61A | TILBURY-33B | TILBURY-33B | TILBURY-33B | TILBURY-33B | TILBURY-33B | PLAISTOW-33A | PLAISTOW-33A | PLAISTOW-33A |
| Aug-56 | KITTYBREWSTER - 61A | TILBURY-33B | TILBURY-33B | TILBURY-33B | TILBURY-33B | TILBURY-33B | PLAISTOW-33A | PLAISTOW-33A | PLAISTOW-33A |
| Jan-57 | KITTYBREWSTER - 61A | TILBURY-33B | TILBURY-33B | TILBURY-33B | TILBURY-33B | TILBURY-33B | PLAISTOW-33A | PLAISTOW-33A | PLAISTOW-33A |
| Aug-57 | KITTYBREWSTER - 61A | TILBURY-33B | TILBURY-33B | TILBURY-33B | TILBURY-33B | TILBURY-33B | 11/56: TIL - 33B | 11/56: TIL - 33B | 11/56: TIL - 33B |
| Jan-58 | KITTYBREWSTER - 61A | TILBURY-33B | TILBURY-33B | TILBURY-33B | TILBURY-33B | TILBURY-33B | TILBURY-33B | TILBURY-33B | TILBURY-33B |
| Aug-58 | KITTYBREWSTER - 61A | TILBURY-33B | TILBURY-33B | TILBURY-33B | TILBURY-33B | TILBURY-33B | TILBURY-33B | TILBURY-33B | TILBURY-33B |
| Jan-59 | KITTYBREWSTER - 61A | TILBURY-33B | TILBURY-33B | TILBURY-33B | TILBURY-33B | TILBURY-33B | TILBURY-33B | TILBURY-33B | TILBURY-33B |
| Aug-59 | KITTYBREWSTER - 61A | TILBURY-33B | TILBURY-33B | TILBURY-33B | TILBURY-33B | TILBURY-33B | TILBURY-33B | TILBURY-33B | TILBURY-33B |
| Nov-59 | KITTYBREWSTER - 61A | TILBURY-33B | TILBURY-33B | TILBURY-33B | TILBURY-33B | TILBURY-33B | TILBURY-33B | TILBURY-33B | TILBURY-33B |
| Jan-60 | KITTYBREWSTER - 61A | TILBURY-33B | TILBURY-33B | TILBURY-33B | TILBURY-33B | TILBURY-33B | TILBURY-33B | TILBURY-33B | TILBURY-33B |
| Apr-60 | KITTYBREWSTER - 61A | TILBURY-33B | TILBURY-33B | TILBURY-33B | TILBURY-33B | TILBURY-33B | TILBURY-33B | TILBURY-33B | TILBURY-33B |
| Aug-60 | KITTYBREWSTER - 61A | TILBURY-33B | TILBURY-33B | TILBURY-33B | TILBURY-33B | TILBURY-33B | TILBURY-33B | TILBURY-33B | TILBURY-33B |
| Nov-60 | KITTYBREWSTER - 61A | TILBURY-33B | TILBURY-33B | TILBURY-33B | TILBURY-33B | TILBURY-33B | TILBURY-33B | TILBURY-33B | TILBURY-33B |

| | 80077 | 80078 | 80079 | 80080 | 80090 | 80096 | 80097 | 80098 | 80099 |
|---|---|---|---|---|---|---|---|---|---|
| Aug-50 | | | | | | | | | |
| Jan-51 | | | | | | | | | |
| Aug-51 | | | | | | | | | |
| Jan-52 | | | | | | | | | |
| Aug-52 | | | | | | | | | |
| Jan-53 | | | | | | | | | |
| Aug-53 | | | | | | | | | |
| Jan-54 | 1/54: PLAIS - 33A | 1/54: PLAIS - 33A | 3/54: PLAIS - 33A | 3/54: PLAIS - 33A | | | | | |
| Aug-54 | PLAISTOW-33A | PLAISTOW-33A | 4/54: TIL - 33B | 4/54: TIL - 33B | | | | | |
| Jan-55 | PLAISTOW-33A | PLAISTOW-33A | TILBURY-33B | TILBURY-33B | | 11/54: PLAIS - 33A | 12/54: PLAIS - 33A | 12/54: PLAIS - 33A | 1/55: PLAIS - 33A |
| Aug-55 | PLAISTOW-33A | PLAISTOW-33A | TILBURY-33B | TILBURY-33B | | PLAISTOW-33A | PLAISTOW-33A | PLAISTOW-33A | PLAISTOW-33A |
| Jan-56 | PLAISTOW-33A | PLAISTOW-33A | TILBURY-33B | TILBURY-33B | | PLAISTOW-33A | PLAISTOW-33A | PLAISTOW-33A | PLAISTOW-33A |
| Aug-56 | PLAISTOW-33A | PLAISTOW-33A | TILBURY-33B | TILBURY-33B | | PLAISTOW-33A | PLAISTOW-33A | PLAISTOW-33A | PLAISTOW-33A |
| Jan-57 | 11/56: TIL - 33B | 11/56: TIL - 33B | TILBURY-33B | TILBURY-33B | | PLAISTOW-33A | PLAISTOW-33A | PLAISTOW-33A | PLAISTOW-33A |
| Aug-57 | TILBURY-33B | TILBURY-33B | TILBURY-33B | TILBURY-33B | | PLAISTOW-33A | PLAISTOW-33A | PLAISTOW-33A | PLAISTOW-33A |
| Jan-58 | TILBURY-33B | TILBURY-33B | TILBURY-33B | TILBURY-33B | | PLAISTOW-33A | PLAISTOW-33A | PLAISTOW-33A | PLAISTOW-33A |
| Aug-58 | TILBURY-33B | TILBURY-33B | TILBURY-33B | TILBURY-33B | | PLAISTOW-33A | PLAISTOW-33A | PLAISTOW-33A | PLAISTOW-33A |
| Jan-59 | TILBURY-33B | TILBURY-33B | TILBURY-33B | TILBURY-33B | | PLAISTOW-33A | PLAISTOW-33A | PLAISTOW-33A | PLAISTOW-33A |
| Aug-59 | TILBURY-33B | TILBURY-33B | TILBURY-33B | TILBURY-33B | | PLAISTOW-33A | PLAISTOW-33A | PLAISTOW-33A | PLAISTOW-33A |
| Nov-59 | TILBURY-33B | TILBURY-33B | TILBURY-33B | TILBURY-33B | | 10/59: TIL - 33B | 10/59: TIL - 33B | 10/59: TIL - 33B | 10/59: TIL - 33B |
| Jan-60 | TILBURY-33B | TILBURY-33B | TILBURY-33B | TILBURY-33B | Ex LM | TILBURY-33B | TILBURY-33B | TILBURY-33B | TILBURY-33B |
| Apr-60 | TILBURY-33B | TILBURY-33B | TILBURY-33B | TILBURY-33B | 2/60: DUN - 62B | TILBURY-33B | TILBURY-33B | TILBURY-33B | TILBURY-33B |
| Aug-60 | TILBURY-33B | TILBURY-33B | TILBURY-33B | TILBURY-33B | DUNDEE - 62B | TILBURY-33B | TILBURY-33B | TILBURY-33B | TILBURY-33B |
| Nov-60 | TILBURY-33B | TILBURY-33B | TILBURY-33B | TILBURY-33B | DUNDEE - 62B | TILBURY-33B | TILBURY-33B | TILBURY-33B | TILBURY-33B |

| | 80100 | 80101 | 80102 | 80103 | 80104 | 80105 | 80106 | 80107 | 80108 |
|---|---|---|---|---|---|---|---|---|---|
| Aug-50 | | | | | | | | | |
| Jan-51 | | | | | | | | | |
| Aug-51 | | | | | | | | | |
| Jan-52 | | | | | | | | | |
| Aug-52 | | | | | | | | | |
| Jan-53 | | | | | | | | | |
| Aug-53 | | | | | | | | | |
| Jan-54 | | | | | | | | | |
| Aug-54 | | | | | | | 10/54: KITTY - 61A | 10/54: KITTY - 61A | |
| Jan-55 | 1/55: PLAIS - 33A | 2/55: PLAIS - 33A | 3/55: PLAIS - 33A | 3/55: PLAIS - 33A | 3/55: PLAIS - 33A | 4/55: PLAISD - 33A | KITTYBREWSTER - 61A | KITTYBREWSTER - 61A | 11/54: KITTY - 61A |
| Aug-55 | PLAISTOW-33A | PLAISTOW-33A | PLAISTOW-33A | PLAISTOW-33A | PLAISTOW-33A | PLAISTOW-33A | KITTYBREWSTER - 61A | KITTYBREWSTER - 61A | KITTYBREWSTER - 61A |
| Jan-56 | PLAISTOW-33A | PLAISTOW-33A | PLAISTOW-33A | PLAISTOW-33A | PLAISTOW-33A | PLAISTOW-33A | KITTYBREWSTER - 61A | KITTYBREWSTER - 61A | KITTYBREWSTER - 61A |
| Aug-56 | PLAISTOW-33A | PLAISTOW-33A | PLAISTOW-33A | PLAISTOW-33A | PLAISTOW-33A | PLAISTOW-33A | KITTYBREWSTER - 61A | KITTYBREWSTER - 61A | KITTYBREWSTER - 61A |
| Jan-57 | PLAISTOW-33A | PLAISTOW-33A | PLAISTOW-33A | PLAISTOW-33A | PLAISTOW-33A | PLAISTOW-33A | KITTYBREWSTER - 61A | KITTYBREWSTER - 61A | KITTYBREWSTER - 61A |
| Aug-57 | PLAISTOW-33A | PLAISTOW-33A | PLAISTOW-33A | PLAISTOW-33A | PLAISTOW-33A | PLAISTOW-33A | 5/57: To CR | 5/57: To CR | 5/57: To CR |
| Jan-58 | PLAISTOW-33A | PLAISTOW-33A | PLAISTOW-33A | PLAISTOW-33A | PLAISTOW-33A | PLAISTOW-33A | | | |
| Aug-58 | PLAISTOW-33A | PLAISTOW-33A | PLAISTOW-33A | PLAISTOW-33A | PLAISTOW-33A | PLAISTOW-33A | | | |
| Jan-59 | PLAISTOW-33A | PLAISTOW-33A | PLAISTOW-33A | PLAISTOW-33A | PLAISTOW-33A | PLAISTOW-33A | | | |
| Aug-59 | PLAISTOW-33A | PLAISTOW-33A | PLAISTOW-33A | PLAISTOW-33A | PLAISTOW-33A | PLAISTOW-33A | | | |
| Nov-59 | 10/59: TIL - 33B | 10/59: TIL - 33B | 10/59: TIL - 33B | 10/59: TIL - 33B | 10/59: TIL - 33B | 10/59: TIL - 33B | | | |
| Jan-60 | TILBURY-33B | TILBURY-33B | TILBURY-33B | TILBURY-33B | TILBURY-33B | TILBURY-33B | | | |
| Apr-60 | TILBURY-33B | TILBURY-33B | TILBURY-33B | TILBURY-33B | TILBURY-33B | TILBURY-33B | | | |
| Aug-60 | TILBURY-33B | TILBURY-33B | TILBURY-33B | TILBURY-33B | TILBURY-33B | TILBURY-33B | | | |
| Nov-60 | TILBURY-33B | TILBURY-33B | TILBURY-33B | TILBURY-33B | TILBURY-33B | TILBURY-33B | | | |

| | 80109 | 80110 | 80111 | 80112 | 80113 | 80114 | 80115 | 80116 | 80117 |
|---|---|---|---|---|---|---|---|---|---|
| Aug-50 | | | | | | | | | |
| Jan-51 | | | | | | | | | |
| Aug-51 | | | | | | | | | |
| Jan-52 | | | | | | | | | |
| Aug-52 | | | | | | | | | |
| Jan-53 | | | | | | | | | |
| Jan-54 | | | | | | | | | |
| Aug-54 | | | | | | | | | |
| Jan-55 | 11/54: KITTY - 61A | 11/54: KITTY - 61A | | | | | | | |
| Aug-55 | KITTYBREWSTER - 61A | KITTYBREWSTER - 61A | | | | | | 5/55: WHITBY - 50G | 5/55: WHITBY - 50G |
| Jan-56 | KITTYBREWSTER - 61A | KITTYBREWSTER - 61A | | | | | | 2/56: SCAR - 50E | WHITBY - 50G |
| Aug-56 | KITTYBREWSTER - 61A | KITTYBREWSTER - 61A | | | | | | 5/56: WHITBY - 50G | WHITBY - 50G |
| Jan-57 | KITTYBREWSTER - 61A | KITTYBREWSTER - 61A | | | | | | WHITBY - 50G | WHITBY - 50G |
| Aug-57 | 5/57: To CR | 6/57: To CR | Ex CR | Ex CR | Ex CR | Ex CR | | WHITBY - 50G | WHITBY - 50G |
| Jan-58 | | | 5/57: KITTY - 61A | 5/57: KITTY - 61A | 5/57: KITTY - 61A | 5/57: KITTY - 61A | | WHITBY - 50G | WHITBY - 50G |
| Aug-58 | | | KITTYBREWSTER - 61A | KITTYBREWSTER - 61A | KITTYBREWSTER - 61A | KITTYBREWSTER - 61A | | 6/58: N.HILL - 50B | 6/58: N.HILL - 50B |
| Jan-59 | | | KITTYBREWSTER - 61A | KITTYBREWSTER - 61A | KITTYBREWSTER - 61A | KITTYBREWSTER - 61A | | NEVILLE HILL - 50B | NEVILLE HILL - 50B |
| Aug-59 | | | KITTYBREWSTER - 61A | KITTYBREWSTER - 61A | KITTYBREWSTER - 61A | KITTYBREWSTER - 61A | | NEVILLE HILL - 50B | NEVILLE HILL - 50B |
| Nov-59 | | | KITTYBREWSTER - 61A | KITTYBREWSTER - 61A | KITTYBREWSTER - 61A | KITTYBREWSTER - 61A | | NEVILLE HILL - 50B | NEVILLE HILL - 50B |
| Jan-60 | | | KITTYBREWSTER - 61A | KITTYBREWSTER - 61A | KITTYBREWSTER - 61A | KITTYBREWSTER - 61A | | NEVILLE HILL - 50B | NEVILLE HILL - 50B |
| Apr-60 | | | KITTYBREWSTER - 61A | KITTYBREWSTER - 61A | KITTYBREWSTER - 61A | KITTYBREWSTER - 61A | | NEVILLE HILL - 55H | NEVILLE HILL - 55H |
| Aug-60 | | | KITTYBREWSTER - 61A | KITTYBREWSTER - 61A | 7/60: KEITH - 61C | KITTYBREWSTER - 61A | ExCR | NEVILLE HILL - 55H | NEVILLE HILL - 55H |
| Nov-60 | | | KITTYBREWSTER - 61A | KITTYBREWSTER - 61A | KEITH-61C | 10/60: KEITH - 61C | 10/60: KEITH - 61C | NEVILLE HILL - 55H | NEVILLE HILL - 55H |

Locomotive class: BR 4 2-6-4T

| | 80118 | 80119 | 80120 | 80121 | 80122 | 80123 | 80124 | 80131 | 80132 |
|---|---|---|---|---|---|---|---|---|---|
| Aug-50 | | | | | | | | | |
| Jan-51 | | | | | | | | | |
| Aug-51 | | | | | | | | | |
| Jan-52 | | | | | | | | | |
| Aug-52 | | | | | | | | | |
| Jan-53 | | | | | | | | | |
| Aug-53 | | | | | | | | | |
| Jan-54 | | | | | | | | | |
| Aug-54 | | | | | | | | | |
| Jan-55 | | | | | | | | | |
| Aug-55 | 6/55: WHITBY - 50G | 6/55: WHITBY - 50G | 7/55: WHITBY - 50G | 7/55: KITTY - 61A | 8/55: KITTY - 61A | 9/55: DUN - 62B | 9/55: DUN - 62B | | |
| Jan-56 | WHITBY- 50G | 2/56: SCAR - 50E | WHITBY- 50G | 11/55: KEITH - 61C | 11/55: KEITH - 61C | DUNDEE- 62B | DUNDEE- 62B | 3/56: PLAIS - 33A | 3/56: PLAIS - 33A |
| Aug-56 | WHITBY- 50G | 5/56: WHITBY - 50G | WHITBY- 50G | KEITH- 61C | KEITH- 61C | DUNDEE- 62B | DUNDEE- 62B | PLAISTOW- 33A | PLAISTOW- 33A |
| Jan-57 | WHITBY- 50G | WHITBY- 50G | WHITBY- 50G | KEITH- 61C | KEITH- 61C | DUNDEE- 62B | DUNDEE- 62B | PLAISTOW- 33A | PLAISTOW- 33A |
| Aug-57 | WHITBY- 50G | WHITBY- 50G | WHITBY- 50G | KEITH- 61C | KEITH- 61C | DUNDEE- 62B | DUNDEE- 62B | PLAISTOW- 33A | PLAISTOW- 33A |
| Jan-58 | WHITBY- 50G | WHITBY- 50G | WHITBY- 50G | KEITH- 61C | KEITH- 61C | DUNDEE- 62B | DUNDEE- 62B | PLAISTOW- 33A | PLAISTOW- 33A |
| Aug-58 | 6/58: N.HILL - 50B | 6/58: N.HILL - 50B | 6/58: N.HILL - 50B | KEITH- 61C | KEITH- 61C | DUNDEE- 62B | DUNDEE- 62B | PLAISTOW- 33A | PLAISTOW- 33A |
| Jan-59 | NEVILLEHILL- 50B | NEVILLEHILL- 50B | NEVILLEHILL- 50B | KEITH- 61C | KEITH- 61C | DUNDEE- 62B | DUNDEE- 62B | PLAISTOW- 33A | PLAISTOW- 33A |
| Aug-59 | NEVILLEHILL- 50B | NEVILLEHILL- 50B | NEVILLEHILL- 50B | KEITH- 61C | KEITH- 61C | DUNDEE- 62B | DUNDEE- 62B | 10/59: TIL - 33B | 10/59: TIL - 33B |
| Nov-59 | NEVILLEHILL- 50B | NEVILLEHILL- 50B | NEVILLEHILL- 50B | KEITH- 61C | KEITH- 61C | DUNDEE- 62B | DUNDEE- 62B | TILBURY- 33B | TILBURY- 33B |
| Jan-60 | NEVILLEHILL- 50B | NEVILLEHILL- 50B | NEVILLEHILL- 50B | KEITH- 61C | KEITH- 61C | DUNDEE- 62B | DUNDEE- 62B | TILBURY- 33B | TILBURY- 33B |
| Apr-60 | NEVILLEHILL- 55H | NEVILLEHILL- 55H | NEVILLEHILL- 55H | KEITH- 61C | KEITH- 61C | DUNDEE- 62B | DUNDEE- 62B | TILBURY- 33B | TILBURY- 33B |
| Aug-60 | NEVILLEHILL- 55H | NEVILLEHILL- 55H | NEVILLEHILL- 55H | KEITH- 61C | KEITH- 61C | DUNDEE- 62B | DUNDEE- 62B | TILBURY- 33B | TILBURY- 33B |
| Nov-60 | NEVILLEHILL- 55H | NEVILLEHILL- 55H | NEVILLEHILL- 55H | KEITH- 61C | KEITH- 61C | DUNDEE- 62B | DUNDEE- 62B | TILBURY- 33B | TILBURY- 33B |

| | 80133 | 80134 | 80135 | 80136 | 80137 | 80138 | 80139 | 80140 | 80141 |
|---|---|---|---|---|---|---|---|---|---|
| Aug-50 | | | | | | | | | |
| Jan-51 | | | | | | | | | |
| Aug-51 | | | | | | | | | |
| Jan-52 | | | | | | | | | |
| Aug-52 | | | | | | | | | |
| Jan-53 | | | | | | | | | |
| Aug-53 | | | | | | | | | |
| Jan-54 | | | | | | | | | |
| Jan-55 | | | | | | | | | |
| Aug-55 | | | | | | | | | |
| Jan-56 | 3/56: PLAIS - 33A | 4/56: PLAIS - 33A | 4/56: PLAIS - 33A | | | | | | |
| Aug-56 | PLAISTOW- 33A | PLAISTOW- 33A | PLAISTOW- 33A | 5/56: PLAIS - 33A | 5/56: NEAS - 34E | 6/56: NEAS - 34E | 6/56: NEAS - 34E | 7/56: NEAS - 34E | 7/56: NEAS - 34E |
| Jan-57 | PLAISTOW- 33A | PLAISTOW- 33A | PLAISTOW- 33A | PLAISTOW- 33A | NEASDEN- 34E | NEASDEN- 34E | NEASDEN- 34E | NEASDEN- 34E | NEASDEN- 34E |
| Aug-57 | PLAISTOW- 33A | PLAISTOW- 33A | PLAISTOW- 33A | PLAISTOW- 33A | NEASDEN- 34E | NEASDEN- 34E | NEASDEN- 34E | NEASDEN- 34E | NEASDEN- 34E |
| Jan-58 | PLAISTOW- 33A | PLAISTOW- 33A | PLAISTOW- 33A | PLAISTOW- 33A | NEASDEN- 34E | NEASDEN- 14D | NEASDEN- 14D | NEASDEN- 14D | NEASDEN- 14D |
| Aug-58 | PLAISTOW- 33A | PLAISTOW- 33A | PLAISTOW- 33A | PLAISTOW- 33A | NEASDEN- 14D | NEASDEN- 14D | NEASDEN- 14D | NEASDEN- 14D | NEASDEN- 14D |
| Aug-59 | PLAISTOW- 33A | PLAISTOW- 33A | PLAISTOW- 33A | PLAISTOW- 33A | NEASDEN- 14D | NEASDEN- 14D | NEASDEN- 14D | NEASDEN- 14D | NEASDEN- 14D |
| Nov-59 | 10/59: SHOE - 33C | 10/59: TIL - 33B | 10/59: TIL - 33B | 10/59: TIL - 33B | NEASDEN- 14D | NEASDEN- 14D | NEASDEN- 14D | NEASDEN- 14D | NEASDEN- 14D |
| Jan-60 | SHOEBURYNESS- 33C | TILBURY- 33B | TILBURY- 33B | TILBURY- 33B | NEASDEN- 14D | NEASDEN- 14D | NEASDEN- 14D | NEASDEN- 14D | NEASDEN- 14D |
| Apr-60 | SHOEBURYNESS- 33C | TILBURY- 33B | TILBURY- 33B | TILBURY- 33B | NEASDEN- 14D | NEASDEN- 14D | NEASDEN- 14D | NEASDEN- 14D | NEASDEN- 14D |
| Aug-60 | SHOEBURYNESS- 33C | TILBURY- 33B | TILBURY- 33B | TILBURY- 33B | NEASDEN- 14D | NEASDEN- 14D | NEASDEN- 14D | NEASDEN- 14D | NEASDEN- 14D |
| Nov-60 | SHOEBURYNESS- 33C | TILBURY- 33B | TILBURY- 33B | TILBURY- 33B | NEASDEN- 14D | NEASDEN- 14D | NEASDEN- 14D | NEASDEN- 14D | NEASDEN- 14D |

Class labels: 80142–80144 (BR 4 2-6-4T); 82026–82029 BR 3 2-6-2T (1952); 84009 BR 2 2-6-2T (1954); 90000 WD 2-8-0 (1943)

| | 80142 | 80143 | 80144 | 82026 | 82027 | 82028 | 82029 | 84009 | 90000 |
|---|---|---|---|---|---|---|---|---|---|
| Aug-50 | | | | | | | | | COLWICK- 38A |
| Jan-51 | | | | | | | | | COLWICK- 38A |
| Aug-51 | | | | | | | | | COLWICK- 38A |
| Jan-52 | | | | | | | | | COLWICK- 38A |
| Aug-52 | | | | | | | | | COLWICK- 38A |
| Jan-53 | | | | | | | | | COLWICK- 38A |
| Aug-53 | | | | | | | | | COLWICK- 38A |
| Jan-54 | | | | | | | | | COLWICK- 38A |
| Aug-54 | | | | | | | | | COLWICK- 38A |
| Jan-55 | | | | 11/54: KYST - 51H | 11/54: KYST - 51H | 11/54: DARL - 51A | 11/54: DARL - 51A | | COLWICK- 38A |
| Aug-55 | | | | K.STEPHEN- 51H | K.STEPHEN- 51H | DARLINGTON- 51A | DARLINGTON- 51A | | COLWICK- 38A |
| Jan-56 | | | | K.STEPHEN- 51H | K.STEPHEN- 51H | DARLINGTON- 51A | DARLINGTON- 51A | | COLWICK- 38A |
| Aug-56 | 8/56: NEAS - 34E | 9/56: NEAS - 34E | 10/56: NEAS - 34E | K.STEPHEN- 51H | K.STEPHEN- 51H | DARLINGTON- 51A | DARLINGTON- 51A | | COLWICK- 38A |
| Jan-57 | NEASDEN- 34E | NEASDEN- 34E | NEASDEN- 34E | K.STEPHEN- 51H | K.STEPHEN- 51H | DARLINGTON- 51A | DARLINGTON- 51A | | COLWICK- 38A |
| Aug-57 | NEASDEN- 34E | NEASDEN- 34E | NEASDEN- 34E | K.STEPHEN- 51H | K.STEPHEN- 51H | DARLINGTON- 51A | DARLINGTON- 51A | | COLWICK- 38A |
| Jan-58 | NEASDEN- 34E | NEASDEN- 34E | NEASDEN- 34E | K.STEPHEN- 51H | 2/58: W.HPL - 51C | DARLINGTON- 51A | 2/58: W.HPL - 50F | | COLWICK- 38A |
| Aug-58 | NEASDEN- 14D | NEASDEN- 14D | NEASDEN- 14D | 9/58: SCAR - 50E | 9/58: MALT - 50F | 9/58: SCAR - 50E | 9/58: MALT - 50F | | COLWICK- 40E |
| Jan-59 | NEASDEN- 14D | NEASDEN- 14D | NEASDEN- 14D | SCARBOROUGH- 50E | MALTON- 50F | SCARBOROUGH- 50E | MALTON- 50F | | 2/59: NEW E. - 34E |
| Aug-59 | NEASDEN- 14D | NEASDEN- 14D | NEASDEN- 14D | SCARBOROUGH- 50E | MALTON- 50F | SCARBOROUGH- 50E | MALTON- 50F | 6/59: DAIRY - 53A | NEWENGLAND- 34E |
| Nov-59 | NEASDEN- 14D | NEASDEN- 14D | NEASDEN- 14D | SCARBOROUGH- 50E | MALTON- 50F | SCARBOROUGH- 50E | MALTON- 50F | DAIRYCOATES- 53A | NEWENGLAND- 34E |
| Jan-60 | NEASDEN- 14D | NEASDEN- 14D | NEASDEN- 14D | SCARBOROUGH- 50E | MALTON- 50F | SCARBOROUGH- 50E | MALTON- 50F | DAIRYCOATES- 53A | NEWENGLAND- 34E |
| Apr-60 | NEASDEN- 14D | NEASDEN- 14D | NEASDEN- 14D | SCARBOROUGH- 50E | 6/60: SCAR - 50E | SCARBOROUGH- 50E | 6/60: SCAR - 50E | DAIRYCOATES- 53A | NEWENGLAND- 34E |
| Aug-60 | NEASDEN- 14D | NEASDEN- 14D | NEASDEN- 14D | SCARBOROUGH- 50E | SCARBOROUGH- 50E | SCARBOROUGH- 50E | SCARBOROUGH- 50E | DAIRYCOATES- 53A | NEWENGLAND- 34E |
| Nov-60 | NEASDEN- 14D | NEASDEN- 14D | NEASDEN- 14D | SCARBOROUGH- 50E | SCARBOROUGH- 50E | SCARBOROUGH- 50E | SCARBOROUGH- 50E | DAIRYCOATES- 53A | NEWENGLAND- 34E |

| | 90001 | 90002 | 90003 | 90004 | 90005 | 90006 | 90007 | 90008 | 90009 |
|---|---|---|---|---|---|---|---|---|---|
| Aug-50 | TWEEDMOUTH- 52D | COLWICK- 38A | MARCH- 31B | THORNTONJCN- 62A | MARCH- 31B | DAIRYCOATES- 53A | SPRINGHEAD- 53C | DAIRYCOATES- 53A | DAIRYCOATES- 53A |
| Jan-51 | 1/51: DAIRY - 53A | 1/51: STAVE - 38D | MARCH- 31B | THORNTONJCN- 62A | MARCH- 31B | DAIRYCOATES- 53A | 9/50: DAIRY - 53A | 12/50: TWEED - 52D | DAIRYCOATES- 53A |
| Aug-51 | 4/51: ANNES - 38B | 9/51: COLW - 38A | | THORNTONJCN- 62A | MARCH- 31B | DAIRYCOATES- 53A | DAIRYCOATES- 53A | 5/51: DAIRY - 53A | DAIRYCOATES- 53A |
| Jan-52 | 9/51: IMM - 40B | COLWICK- 38A | MARCH- 31B | THORNTONJCN- 62A | MARCH- 31B | DAIRYCOATES- 53A | 1/52: To LM | DAIRYCOATES- 53A | DAIRYCOATES- 53A |
| Aug-52 | 12/51: COLW - 38A | COLWICK- 38A | MARCH- 31B | THORNTONJCN- 62A | MARCH- 31B | DAIRYCOATES- 53A | 6/52 : COLW - 38A | DAIRYCOATES- 53A | DAIRYCOATES- 53A |
| Jan-53 | COLWICK- 38A | COLWICK- 38A | MARCH- 31B | THORNTONJCN- 62A | MARCH- 31B | DAIRYCOATES- 53A | COLWICK- 38A | DAIRYCOATES- 53A | DAIRYCOATES- 53A |
| Aug-53 | COLWICK- 38A | COLWICK- 38A | MARCH- 31B | THORNTONJCN- 62A | MARCH- 31B | DAIRYCOATES- 53A | COLWICK- 38A | DAIRYCOATES- 53A | DAIRYCOATES- 53A |
| Jan-54 | COLWICK- 38A | COLWICK- 38A | 10/53: IMM - 40B | THORNTONJCN- 62A | 11/53: DCTR - 36A | DAIRYCOATES- 53A | COLWICK- 38A | DAIRYCOATES- 53A | DAIRYCOATES- 53A |
| Aug-54 | COLWICK- 38A | COLWICK- 38A | IMMINGHAM- 40B | THORNTONJCN- 62A | 6/54: MEX - 36B | DAIRYCOATES- 53A | COLWICK- 38A | DAIRYCOATES- 53A | DAIRYCOATES- 53A |
| Jan-55 | COLWICK- 38A | COLWICK- 38A | IMMINGHAM- 40B | THORNTONJCN- 62A | MEXBOROUGH- 36B | DAIRYCOATES- 53A | COLWICK- 38A | DAIRYCOATES- 53A | DAIRYCOATES- 53A |
| Aug-55 | COLWICK- 38A | COLWICK- 38A | IMMINGHAM- 40B | THORNTONJCN- 62A | MEXBOROUGH- 36B | DAIRYCOATES- 53A | COLWICK- 38A | DAIRYCOATES- 53A | DAIRYCOATES- 53A |
| Jan-56 | COLWICK- 38A | COLWICK- 38A | IMMINGHAM- 40B | THORNTONJCN- 62A | 1/56: COLW - 38A | DAIRYCOATES- 53A | 1/56: STAVE - 38D | DAIRYCOATES- 53A | DAIRYCOATES- 53A |
| Aug-56 | COLWICK- 38A | COLWICK- 38A | IMMINGHAM- 40B | THORNTONJCN- 62A | COLWICK- 38A | DAIRYCOATES- 53A | STAVELEY- 38D | DAIRYCOATES- 53A | DAIRYCOATES- 53A |
| Jan-57 | COLWICK- 38A | COLWICK- 38A | IMMINGHAM- 40B | THORNTONJCN- 62A | COLWICK- 38A | DAIRYCOATES- 53A | STAVELEY- 38D | DAIRYCOATES- 53A | DAIRYCOATES- 53A |
| Aug-57 | 8/57: MARCH - 31B | COLWICK- 38A | IMMINGHAM- 40B | THORNTONJCN- 62A | COLWICK- 38A | DAIRYCOATES- 53A | STAVELEY- 38D | DAIRYCOATES- 53A | DAIRYCOATES- 53A |
| Jan-58 | MARCH- 31B | COLWICK- 38A | IMMINGHAM- 40B | THORNTONJCN- 62A | COLWICK- 40E | DAIRYCOATES- 53A | STAVELEY(GC) - 41H | DAIRYCOATES- 53A | DAIRYCOATES- 53A |
| Aug-58 | MARCH- 31B | COLWICK- 40E | IMMINGHAM- 40B | THORNTONJCN- 62A | COLWICK- 40E | DAIRYCOATES- 53A | STAVELEY(GC) - 41H | DAIRYCOATES- 53A | DAIRYCOATES- 53A |
| Jan-59 | MARCH- 31B | COLWICK- 40E | IMMINGHAM- 40B | THORNTONJCN- 62A | COLWICK- 40E | DAIRYCOATES- 53A | STAVELEY(GC) - 41H | DAIRYCOATES- 53A | DAIRYCOATES- 53A |
| Aug-59 | MARCH- 31B | COLWICK- 40E | IMMINGHAM- 40B | THORNTONJCN- 62A | COLWICK- 40E | DAIRYCOATES- 53A | STAVELEY(GC) - 41H | DAIRYCOATES- 53A | DAIRYCOATES- 53A |
| Nov-59 | MARCH- 31B | COLWICK- 40E | IMMINGHAM- 40B | THORNTONJCN- 62A | COLWICK- 40E | DAIRYCOATES- 53A | 2/60: FROD - 36C | DAIRYCOATES- 53A | DAIRYCOATES- 53A |
| Jan-60 | MARCH- 31B | COLWICK- 40E | IMMINGHAM- 40B | THORNTONJCN- 62A | COLWICK- 40E | DAIRYCOATES- 53A | FRODINGHAM- 36C | DAIRYCOATES- 53A | DAIRYCOATES- 53A |
| Apr-60 | MARCH- 31B | COLWICK- 40E | IMMINGHAM- 40B | THORNTONJCN- 62A | COLWICK- 40E | DAIRYCOATES- 50B | FRODINGHAM- 36C | DAIRYCOATES- 50B | DAIRYCOATES- 50B |
| Aug-60 | MARCH- 31B | COLWICK- 40E | IMMINGHAM- 40B | 6/60: POL - 66A | COLWICK- 40E | DAIRYCOATES- 50B | FRODINGHAM- 36C | DAIRYCOATES- 50B | DAIRYCOATES- 50B |
| Nov-60 | 10/60: DCTR - 36A | COLWICK- 40E | IMMINGHAM- 40B | POLMADIE- 66A | COLWICK- 40E | DAIRYCOATES- 50B | FRODINGHAM- 36C | DAIRYCOATES- 50B | DAIRYCOATES- 50B |

| | 90010 | 90011 | 90012 | 90013 | 90014 | 90015 | 90016 | 90017 | 90018 |
|---|---|---|---|---|---|---|---|---|---|
| Aug-50 | SPRINGHEAD-53C | SPRINGHEAD-53C | STOCKTON-51E | MARCH-31B | NEWPORT-51B | MARCH-31B | NEWPORT-51B | DUNDEE-62B | MARCH-31B |
| Jan-51 | SPRINGHEAD-53C | SPRINGHEAD-53C | STOCKTON-51E | 3/51: FROD - 36C | NEWPORT-51B | MARCH-31B | NEWPORT-51B | DUNDEE-62B | MARCH-31B |
| Aug-51 | 9/51: IMM - 40B | SPRINGHEAD-53C | STOCKTON-51E | FRODINGHAM-36C | NEWPORT-51B | MARCH-31B | NEWPORT-51B | DUNDEE-62B | MARCH-31B |
| Jan-52 | 11/51: To WR | SPRINGHEAD-53C | STOCKTON-51E | FRODINGHAM-36C | NEWPORT-51B | MARCH-31B | NEWPORT-51B | 10/51: DUNF - 62C | MARCH-31B |
| Aug-52 | | SPRINGHEAD-53C | STOCKTON-51E | FRODINGHAM-36C | NEWPORT-51B | MARCH-31B | NEWPORT-51B | DUNFERMLINE-62C | MARCH-31B |
| Jan-53 | | SPRINGHEAD-53C | STOCKTON-51E | FRODINGHAM-36C | NEWPORT-51B | 1/53: MEX - 36B | NEWPORT-51B | DUNFERMLINE-62C | MARCH-31B |
| Aug-53 | | SPRINGHEAD-53C | STOCKTON-51E | FRODINGHAM-36C | NEWPORT-51B | MEXBOROUGH-36B | NEWPORT-51B | DUNFERMLINE-62C | MARCH-31B |
| Jan-54 | | SPRINGHEAD-53C | STOCKTON-51E | FRODINGHAM-36C | NEWPORT-51B | MEXBOROUGH-36B | NEWPORT-51B | DUNFERMLINE-62C | MARCH-31B |
| Aug-54 | | SPRINGHEAD-53C | STOCKTON-51E | FRODINGHAM-36C | NEWPORT-51B | MEXBOROUGH-36B | NEWPORT-51B | DUNFERMLINE-62C | MARCH-31B |
| Jan-55 | | SPRINGHEAD-53C | STOCKTON-51E | FRODINGHAM-36C | NEWPORT-51B | MEXBOROUGH-36B | NEWPORT-51B | DUNFERMLINE-62C | MARCH-31B |
| Aug-55 | | SPRINGHEAD-53C | 8/55: W.HPL - 51C | FRODINGHAM-36C | NEWPORT-51B | MEXBOROUGH-36B | NEWPORT-51B | DUNFERMLINE-62C | MARCH-31B |
| Jan-56 | | SPRINGHEAD-53C | W.HARTLEPOOL-51C | FRODINGHAM-36C | NEWPORT-51B | 1/56: COLW - 38A | NEWPORT-51B | DUNFERMLINE-62C | MARCH-31B |
| Aug-56 | | SPRINGHEAD-53C | W.HARTLEPOOL-51C | FRODINGHAM-36C | NEWPORT-51B | COLWICK-38A | NEWPORT-51B | DUNFERMLINE-62C | MARCH-31B |
| Jan-57 | | SPRINGHEAD-53C | W.HARTLEPOOL-51C | FRODINGHAM-36C | NEWPORT-51B | COLWICK-38A | NEWPORT-51B | DUNFERMLINE-62C | MARCH-31B |
| Aug-57 | | SPRINGHEAD-53C | 6/57: YORK - 50A | FRODINGHAM-36C | NEWPORT-51B | COLWICK-38A | NEWPORT-51B | DUNFERMLINE-62C | MARCH-31B |
| Jan-58 | | SPRINGHEAD-53C | 9/57: N'TON - 55E | FRODINGHAM-36C | NEWPORT-51B | COLWICK-38A | NEWPORT-51B | DUNFERMLINE-62C | MARCH-31B |
| Aug-58 | | SPRINGHEAD-53C | NORMANTON-55E | FRODINGHAM-36C | THORNABY-51L | COLWICK-40E | THORNABY-51L | DUNFERMLINE-62C | MARCH-31B |
| Jan-59 | | 12/58: DAIRY - 53A | NORMANTON-55E | FRODINGHAM-36C | THORNABY-51L | 2/59: NEW.E - 34E | THORNABY-51L | DUNFERMLINE-62C | MARCH-31B |
| Aug-59 | | 6/59: DARL - 51A | NORMANTON-55E | FRODINGHAM-36C | THORNABY-51L | NEWENGLAND-34E | 5/59: WAKE - 56A | DUNFERMLINE-62C | MARCH-31B |
| Nov-59 | | DARLINGTON-51A | NORMANTON-55E | FRODINGHAM-36C | THORNABY-51L | NEWENGLAND-34E | WAKEFIELD-56A | DUNFERMLINE-62C | MARCH-31B |
| Jan-60 | | DARLINGTON-51A | NORMANTON-55E | FRODINGHAM-36C | THORNABY-51L | NEWENGLAND-34E | WAKEFIELD-56A | DUNFERMLINE-62C | MARCH-31B |
| Apr-60 | | DARLINGTON-51A | NORMANTON-55E | FRODINGHAM-36C | THORNABY-51L | NEWENGLAND-34E | WAKEFIELD-56A | DUNFERMLINE-62C | MARCH-31B |
| Aug-60 | | DARLINGTON-51A | NORMANTON-55E | FRODINGHAM-36C | 6/60: DARL - 51A | NEWENGLAND-34E | 6/60: DARL - 51A | DUNFERMLINE-62C | MARCH-31B |
| Nov-60 | | DARLINGTON-51A | NORMANTON-55E | FRODINGHAM-36C | DARLINGTON-51A | NEWENGLAND-34E | DARLINGTON-51A | DUNFERMLINE-62C | MARCH-31B |

| | 90019 | 90020 | 90021 | 90022 | 90023 | 90024 | 90025 | 90026 | 90027 |
|---|---|---|---|---|---|---|---|---|---|
| Aug-50 | THORNTONJCN-62A | EASTFIELD-65A | DAIRYCOATES-53A | DAIRYCOATES-53A | MARCH-31B | MARCH-31B | COLWICK-38A | TYNEDOCK-54B | NEWPORT-51B |
| Jan-51 | THORNTONJCN-62A | EASTFIELD-65A | DAIRYCOATES-53A | 1/51: DARL - 51A | MARCH-31B | MARCH-31B | 1/51: ANNES - 38B | TYNEDOCK-54B | NEWPORT-51B |
| Aug-51 | THORNTONJCN-62A | EASTFIELD-65A | DAIRYCOATES-53A | 9/51: DAIRY - 53A | MARCH-31B | MARCH-31B | 9/51: IMM - 40B | TYNEDOCK-54B | NEWPORT-51B |
| Jan-52 | THORNTONJCN-62A | 2/52: F'HILL - 61B | DAIRYCOATES-53A | DAIRYCOATES-53A | MARCH-31B | MARCH-31B | IMMINGHAM-40B | TYNEDOCK-54B | NEWPORT-51B |
| Aug-52 | THORNTONJCN-62A | FERRYHILL-61B | DAIRYCOATES-53A | DAIRYCOATES-53A | MARCH-31B | MARCH-31B | IMMINGHAM-40B | TYNEDOCK-54B | NEWPORT-51B |
| Jan-53 | THORNTONJCN-62A | FERRYHILL-61B | DAIRYCOATES-53A | DAIRYCOATES-53A | MARCH-31B | MARCH-31B | IMMINGHAM-40B | TYNEDOCK-54B | NEWPORT-51B |
| Aug-53 | THORNTONJCN-62A | 5/53: TH JN - 62A | DAIRYCOATES-53A | DAIRYCOATES-53A | MARCH-31B | MARCH-31B | 7/53 : COLW - 38A | TYNEDOCK-54B | NEWPORT-51B |
| Jan-54 | THORNTONJCN-62A | THORNTONJCN-62A | DAIRYCOATES-53A | DAIRYCOATES-53A | MARCH-31B | 11/53: DCTR - 36A | COLWICK-38A | TYNEDOCK-54B | NEWPORT-51B |
| Aug-54 | THORNTONJCN-62A | THORNTONJCN-62A | DAIRYCOATES-53A | DAIRYCOATES-53A | MARCH-31B | DONCASTER-36A | COLWICK-38A | TYNEDOCK-54B | NEWPORT-51B |
| Jan-55 | THORNTONJCN-62A | THORNTONJCN-62A | DAIRYCOATES-53A | DAIRYCOATES-53A | MARCH-31B | DONCASTER-36A | COLWICK-38A | TYNEDOCK-54B | NEWPORT-51B |
| Aug-55 | THORNTONJCN-62A | THORNTONJCN-62A | DAIRYCOATES-53A | DAIRYCOATES-53A | MARCH-31B | 5/55: MEX - 36B | COLWICK-38A | TYNEDOCK-54B | NEWPORT-51B |
| Jan-56 | THORNTONJCN-62A | THORNTONJCN-62A | 11/55: YORK - 50A | DAIRYCOATES-53A | MARCH-31B | 1/56: COLW - 38A | COLWICK-38A | TYNEDOCK-54B | NEWPORT-51B |
| Aug-56 | THORNTONJCN-62A | THORNTONJCN-62A | 6/56: DARL - 51A | DAIRYCOATES-53A | MARCH-31B | COLWICK-38A | COLWICK-38A | TYNEDOCK-54B | NEWPORT-51B |
| Jan-57 | THORNTONJCN-62A | THORNTONJCN-62A | DARLINGTON-51A | DAIRYCOATES-53A | MARCH-31B | COLWICK-38A | COLWICK-38A | TYNEDOCK-54B | NEWPORT-51B |
| Aug-57 | THORNTONJCN-62A | THORNTONJCN-62A | 6/57: YORK - 50A | DAIRYCOATES-53A | MARCH-31B | COLWICK-38A | COLWICK-38A | 6/57: N.HILL - 50B | NEWPORT-51B |
| Jan-58 | THORNTONJCN-62A | THORNTONJCN-62A | 9/57: N'TON - 55E | DAIRYCOATES-53A | MARCH-31B | COLWICK-38A | COLWICK-38A | NEVILLEHILL-50B | NEWPORT-51B |
| Aug-58 | THORNTONJCN-62A | THORNTONJCN-62A | NORMANTON-55E | DAIRYCOATES-53A | MARCH-31B | COLWICK-40E | COLWICK-40E | NEVILLEHILL-50B | 6/58 : TBY - 51L |
| Jan-59 | THORNTONJCN-62A | THORNTONJCN-62A | NORMANTON-55E | DAIRYCOATES-53A | MARCH-31B | COLWICK-40E | COLWICK-40E | NEVILLEHILL-50B | THORNABY-51L |
| Aug-59 | THORNTONJCN-62A | THORNTONJCN-62A | NORMANTON-55E | DAIRYCOATES-53A | MARCH-31B | COLWICK-40E | COLWICK-40E | NEVILLEHILL-50B | THORNABY-51L |
| Nov-59 | THORNTONJCN-62A | THORNTONJCN-62A | NORMANTON-55E | DAIRYCOATES-53A | 12/59: S.BGE - 31F | COLWICK-40E | COLWICK-40E | 12/59: YORK - 50A | THORNABY-51L |
| Jan-60 | THORNTONJCN-62A | THORNTONJCN-62A | NORMANTON-55E | 2/60: TBY - 51L | SPITALBRIDGE-31F | COLWICK-40E | COLWICK-40E | YORK-50A | THORNABY-51L |
| Apr-60 | THORNTONJCN-62A | THORNTONJCN-62A | NORMANTON-55E | THORNABY-51L | 2/60: TIL - 33B | 3/60: NEW.E - 34E | COLWICK-40E | YORK-50A | THORNABY-51L |
| Aug-60 | THORNTONJCN-62A | THORNTONJCN-62A | NORMANTON-55E | THORNABY-51L | TILBURY-33B | NEWENGLAND-34E | COLWICK-40E | YORK-50A | THORNABY-51L |
| Nov-60 | THORNTONJCN-62A | THORNTONJCN-62A | NORMANTON-55E | THORNABY-51L | TILBURY-33B | NEWENGLAND-34E | 11/60: FROD - 36C | YORK-50A | THORNABY-51L |

| | 90028 | 90029 | 90030 | 90031 | 90032 | 90033 | 90034 | 90035 | 90036 |
|---|---|---|---|---|---|---|---|---|---|
| Aug-50 | NEWENGLAND-35A | COLCHESTER-30E | TWEEDMOUTH-52D | NEWENGLAND-35A | IMMINGHAM-40B | W.HALSE-38E | NEWENGLAND-35A | MARCH-31B | COLWICK-38A |
| Jan-51 | NEWENGLAND-35A | COLCHESTER-30E | TWEEDMOUTH-52D | NEWENGLAND-35A | 10/50: MARCH - 31B | W.HALSE-38E | NEWENGLAND-35A | MARCH-31B | 1/51: STAVE - 38D |
| Aug-51 | NEWENGLAND-35A | 9/51: MARCH - 31B | 5/51: DAIRY - 53A | 7/51: FROD - 36C | 3/51: FROD - 36C | W.HALSE-38E | NEWENGLAND-35A | MARCH-31B | 3/51: COLW - 38A |
| Jan-52 | NEWENGLAND-35A | MARCH-31B | DAIRYCOATES-53A | FRODINGHAM-36C | FRODINGHAM-36C | W.HALSE-38E | NEWENGLAND-35A | MARCH-31B | COLWICK-38A |
| Aug-52 | NEWENGLAND-35A | MARCH-31B | DAIRYCOATES-53A | FRODINGHAM-36C | FRODINGHAM-36C | W.HALSE-38E | NEWENGLAND-35A | MARCH-31B | COLWICK-38A |
| Jan-53 | NEWENGLAND-35A | MARCH-31B | DAIRYCOATES-53A | FRODINGHAM-36C | FRODINGHAM-36C | W.HALSE-38E | NEWENGLAND-35A | MARCH-31B | COLWICK-38A |
| Aug-53 | NEWENGLAND-35A | MARCH-31B | DAIRYCOATES-53A | FRODINGHAM-36C | FRODINGHAM-36C | W.HALSE-38E | NEWENGLAND-35A | MARCH-31B | COLWICK-38A |
| Jan-54 | NEWENGLAND-35A | 10/53: IMM - 40B | DAIRYCOATES-53A | FRODINGHAM-36C | FRODINGHAM-36C | W.HALSE-38E | NEWENGLAND-35A | 10/53: IMM - 40B | COLWICK-38A |
| Aug-54 | NEWENGLAND-35A | IMMINGHAM-40B | DAIRYCOATES-53A | FRODINGHAM-36C | FRODINGHAM-36C | W.HALSE-38E | NEWENGLAND-35A | IMMINGHAM-40B | COLWICK-38A |
| Jan-55 | NEWENGLAND-35A | IMMINGHAM-40B | DAIRYCOATES-53A | FRODINGHAM-36C | FRODINGHAM-36C | W.HALSE-38E | NEWENGLAND-35A | IMMINGHAM-40B | COLWICK-38A |
| Aug-55 | NEWENGLAND-35A | IMMINGHAM-40B | DAIRYCOATES-53A | FRODINGHAM-36C | FRODINGHAM-36C | W.HALSE-38E | NEWENGLAND-35A | IMMINGHAM-40B | COLWICK-38A |
| Jan-56 | NEWENGLAND-35A | IMMINGHAM-40B | DAIRYCOATES-53A | FRODINGHAM-36C | FRODINGHAM-36C | W.HALSE-38E | NEWENGLAND-35A | IMMINGHAM-40B | COLWICK-38A |
| Aug-56 | NEWENGLAND-35A | IMMINGHAM-40B | DAIRYCOATES-53A | FRODINGHAM-36C | FRODINGHAM-36C | W.HALSE-38E | NEWENGLAND-35A | IMMINGHAM-40B | COLWICK-38A |
| Jan-57 | NEWENGLAND-35A | IMMINGHAM-40B | DAIRYCOATES-53A | FRODINGHAM-36C | FRODINGHAM-36C | W.HALSE-38E | NEWENGLAND-35A | IMMINGHAM-40B | COLWICK-38A |
| Aug-57 | NEWENGLAND-35A | IMMINGHAM-40B | DAIRYCOATES-53A | FRODINGHAM-36C | FRODINGHAM-36C | W.HALSE-38E | NEWENGLAND-35A | IMMINGHAM-40B | COLWICK-38A |
| Jan-58 | 10/57: MARCH - 31B | IMMINGHAM-40B | DAIRYCOATES-53A | FRODINGHAM-36C | FRODINGHAM-36C | W.HALSE-38E | NEWENGLAND-35A | IMMINGHAM-40B | COLWICK-38A |
| Aug-58 | MARCH-31B | IMMINGHAM-40B | DAIRYCOATES-53A | FRODINGHAM-36C | FRODINGHAM-36C | W.HALSE-2F | 5/58: TIL - 33B | IMMINGHAM-40B | 9/58: IMM - 40B |
| Jan-59 | MARCH-31B | IMMINGHAM-40B | DAIRYCOATES-53A | FRODINGHAM-36C | FRODINGHAM-36C | W.HALSE-2F | TILBURY-33B | IMMINGHAM-40B | IMMINGHAM-40B |
| Aug-59 | 5/59: STRAT - 30A | IMMINGHAM-40B | DAIRYCOATES-53A | FRODINGHAM-36C | FRODINGHAM-36C | W.HALSE-2F | TILBURY-33B | IMMINGHAM-40B | IMMINGHAM-40B |
| Nov-59 | STRATFORD-30A | IMMINGHAM-40B | DAIRYCOATES-53A | FRODINGHAM-36C | FRODINGHAM-36C | W.HALSE-2F | TILBURY-33B | IMMINGHAM-40B | IMMINGHAM-40B |
| Jan-60 | STRATFORD-30A | IMMINGHAM-40B | DAIRYCOATES-53A | FRODINGHAM-36C | FRODINGHAM-36C | W.HALSE-2F | TILBURY-33B | IMMINGHAM-40B | IMMINGHAM-40B |
| Apr-60 | 5/60: MEX - 41F | IMMINGHAM-40B | DAIRYCOATES-50B | FRODINGHAM-36C | FRODINGHAM-36C | W.HALSE-2F | TILBURY-33B | IMMINGHAM-40B | IMMINGHAM-40B |
| Aug-60 | MEXBOROUGH-41F | IMMINGHAM-40B | DAIRYCOATES-50B | FRODINGHAM-36C | FRODINGHAM-36C | W.HALSE-2F | TILBURY-33B | IMMINGHAM-40B | IMMINGHAM-40B |
| Nov-60 | MEXBOROUGH-41F | IMMINGHAM-40B | DAIRYCOATES-50B | FRODINGHAM-36C | FRODINGHAM-36C | W.HALSE-2F | TILBURY-33B | IMMINGHAM-40B | 11/60: COLW - 40E |

| | 90037 | 90038 | 90039 | 90040 | 90041 | 90042 | 90043 | 90044 | 90045 |
|---|---|---|---|---|---|---|---|---|---|
| Aug-50 | MARCH-31B | EDINBURGH(SM)-64A | W.HALSE-38E | W.HALSE-38E | FERRYHILL-61B | MARCH-31B | COLWICK-38A | ExCR | NEWPORT-51B |
| Jan-51 | MARCH-31B | EDINBURGH(SM)-64A | W.HALSE-38E | W.HALSE-38E | FERRYHILL-61B | MARCH-31B | COLWICK-38A | 9/50: NEWPT - 51b | NEWPORT-51B |
| Aug-51 | MARCH-31B | EDINBURGH(SM)-64A | W.HALSE-38E | W.HALSE-38E | FERRYHILL-61B | MARCH-31B | 9/51: WFRD.H - 38E | NEWPORT-51B | NEWPORT-51B |
| Jan-52 | MARCH-31B | EDINBURGH(SM)-64A | W.HALSE-38E | W.HALSE-38E | FERRYHILL-61B | MARCH-31B | W.HALSE-38E | NEWPORT-51B | NEWPORT-51B |
| Aug-52 | MARCH-31B | EDINBURGH(SM)-64A | W.HALSE-38E | W.HALSE-38E | FERRYHILL-61B | MARCH-31B | 6/52: COLW - 38A | NEWPORT-51B | NEWPORT-51B |
| Jan-53 | MARCH-31B | EDINBURGH(SM)-64A | W.HALSE-38E | W.HALSE-38E | FERRYHILL-61B | MARCH-31B | COLWICK-38A | NEWPORT-51B | 3/53: CON - 54D |
| Aug-53 | MARCH-31B | EDINBURGH(SM)-64A | W.HALSE-38E | W.HALSE-38E | FERRYHILL-61B | MARCH-31B | COLWICK-38A | NEWPORT-51B | CONSETT-54D |
| Jan-54 | 11/53: DCTR - 36A | 10/53: COLW - 38A | W.HALSE-38E | W.HALSE-38E | FERRYHILL-61B | 11/53: DCTR - 36A | COLWICK-38A | NEWPORT-51B | CONSETT-54D |
| Aug-54 | DONCASTER-36A | COLWICK-38A | W.HALSE-38E | W.HALSE-38E | FERRYHILL-61B | DONCASTER-36A | 6/54: L.JCN - 40E | 8/54: YORK - 50A | CONSETT-54D |
| Jan-55 | DONCASTER-36A | COLWICK-38A | W.HALSE-38E | W.HALSE-38E | FERRYHILL-61B | DONCASTER-36A | LANGWTHJCN-40E | YORK-50A | 2/55: T.DCK - 54B |
| Aug-55 | DONCASTER-36A | COLWICK-38A | W.HALSE-38E | W.HALSE-38E | FERRYHILL-61B | DONCASTER-36A | LANGWTHJCN-40E | YORK-50A | TYNEDOCK-54B |
| Jan-56 | 1/56: COLW - 38A | COLWICK-38A | W.HALSE-38E | W.HALSE-38E | FERRYHILL-61B | DONCASTER-36A | LANGWTHJCN-40E | 11/55: STAR - 50D | TYNEDOCK-54B |
| Aug-56 | COLWICK-38A | COLWICK-38A | W.HALSE-38E | W.HALSE-38E | FERRYHILL-61B | DONCASTER-36A | LANGWTHJCN-40E | STARBECK-50D | TYNEDOCK-54B |
| Jan-57 | COLWICK-38A | COLWICK-38A | 3/57: DAWS - 65D | W.HALSE-38E | FERRYHILL-61B | 10/56: MARCH - 31B | LANGWTHJCN-40E | STARBECK-50D | TYNEDOCK-54B |
| Aug-57 | COLWICK-38A | COLWICK-38A | 5/57: G'MTH - 65F | W.HALSE-38E | FERRYHILL-61B | MARCH-31B | LANGWTHJCN-40E | STARBECK-50D | 6/57: N.HILL - 50B |
| Jan-58 | COLWICK-38A | COLWICK-38A | 4/58: DAWS - 65D | W.HALSE-38E | FERRYHILL-61B | MARCH-31B | LANGWTHJCN-40E | STARBECK-50D | NEVILLEHILL-50B |
| Aug-58 | COLWICK-40E | COLWICK-40E | 8/58: POLM - 66A | W.HALSE-2F | FERRYHILL-61B | MARCH-31B | LANGWTHJCN-41J | STARBECK-50D | NEVILLEHILL-50B |
| Jan-59 | COLWICK-40E | COLWICK-40E | POLMADIE-66A | W.HALSE-2F | FERRYHILL-61B | MARCH-31B | LANGWTHJCN-41J | STARBECK-50D | NEVILLEHILL-50B |
| Aug-59 | COLWICK-40E | COLWICK-40E | POLMADIE-66A | W.HALSE-2F | FERRYHILL-61B | MARCH-31B | LANGWTHJCN-41J | 9/59: GOOLE - 53E | NEVILLEHILL-50B |
| Nov-59 | COLWICK-40E | COLWICK-40E | POLMADIE-66A | W.HALSE-2F | FERRYHILL-61B | MARCH-31B | LANGWTHJCN-41J | GOOLE-53E | 12/59: YORK - 50A |
| Jan-60 | COLWICK-40E | COLWICK-40E | POLMADIE-66A | W.HALSE-2F | FERRYHILL-61B | 2/60: TIL - 33B | LANGWTHJCN-41J | GOOLE-53E | YORK-50A |
| Apr-60 | COLWICK-40E | COLWICK-40E | POLMADIE-66A | W.HALSE-2F | FERRYHILL-61B | TILBURY-33B | LANGWTHJCN-41J | GOOLE-50D | YORK-50A |
| Aug-60 | COLWICK-40E | COLWICK-40E | POLMADIE-66A | W.HALSE-2F | FERRYHILL-61B | TILBURY-33B | LANGWTHJCN-41J | GOOLE-50D | YORK-50A |
| Nov-60 | COLWICK-40E | COLWICK-40E | POLMADIE-66A | W.HALSE-2F | FERRYHILL-61B | TILBURY-33B | LANGWTHJCN-41J | GOOLE-50D | YORK-50A |

| | 90046 | 90047 | 90048 | 90049 | 90050 | 90051 | 90052 | 90053 | 90054 |
|---|---|---|---|---|---|---|---|---|---|
| **Aug-50** | W.HALSE-38E | SPRINGHEAD-53C | STOCKTON-51E | THORNTONJCN-62A | COLWICK-38A | W.HALSE-38E | SPRINGHEAD-53C | MARCH-31B | NEWPORT-51B |
| **Jan-51** | W.HALSE-38E | **11/50: DAIRY - =53A** | STOCKTON-51E | **11/50: EBRO(SM) -64A** | COLWICK-38A | **10/50: COLW - 38A** | **4/51: ANNES - 38B** | MARCH-31B | NEWPORT-51B |
| **Aug-51** | W.HALSE-38E | DAIRYCOATES-53A | STOCKTON-51E | EDINBURGH(SM)-64A | COLWICK-38A | COLWICK-38A | **9/51: IMM - 40B** | MARCH-31B | NEWPORT-51B |
| **Jan-52** | W.HALSE-38E | DAIRYCOATES-53A | STOCKTON-51E | EDINBURGH(SM)-64A | COLWICK-38A | COLWICK-38A | **12/51: STAVE - 38D** | MARCH-31B | NEWPORT-51B |
| **Aug-52** | W.HALSE-38E | DAIRYCOATES-53A | STOCKTON-51E | EDINBURGH(SM)-64A | **10/52: MARCH - 31B** | COLWICK-38A | **2/52: COLW - 38A** | MARCH-31B | NEWPORT-51B |
| **Jan-53** | W.HALSE-38E | DAIRYCOATES-53A | STOCKTON-51E | EDINBURGH(SM)-64A | **1/53: MEX - 36B** | COLWICK-38A | COLWICK-38A | MARCH-31B | **3/53: CON - 54D** |
| **Aug-53** | W.HALSE-38E | **5/53: YORK - 50A** | STOCKTON-51E | EDINBURGH(SM)-64A | **2/53: COLW - 38A** | COLWICK-38A | COLWICK-38A | MARCH-31B | CONSETT-54D |
| **Jan-54** | W.HALSE-38E | YORK-50A | STOCKTON-51E | EDINBURGH(SM)-64A | COLWICK-38A | COLWICK-38A | COLWICK-38A | **11/53: DCTR - 36A** | CONSETT-54D |
| **Aug-54** | W.HALSE-38E | YORK-50A | STOCKTON-51E | **To CR** | COLWICK-38A | **6/54: L. JCN - 40E** | COLWICK-38A | **6/54: MEX - 36B** | CONSETT-54D |
| **Jan-55** | W.HALSE-38E | YORK-50A | STOCKTON-51E | **11/54: EFLD - 65A** | COLWICK-38A | LANGWITHJCN-40E | COLWICK-38A | MEXBOROUGH-36B | **2/55: T.DCK - 54B** |
| **Aug-55** | W.HALSE-38E | YORK-50A | STOCKTON-51E | EASTFIELD-65A | COLWICK-38A | LANGWITHJCN-40E | COLWICK-38A | MEXBOROUGH-36B | TYNEDOCK-54B |
| **Jan-56** | W.HALSE-38E | YORK-50A | **11/55: W.HPL - 51C** | EASTFIELD-65A | COLWICK-38A | LANGWITHJCN-40E | COLWICK-38A | **1/56: COLW - 38A** | TYNEDOCK-54B |
| **Aug-56** | W.HALSE-38E | **6/56: DARL - 51A** | W.HARTLEPOOL-51C | EASTFIELD-65A | COLWICK-38A | LANGWITHJCN-40E | COLWICK-38A | COLWICK-38A | TYNEDOCK-54B |
| **Jan-57** | W.HALSE-38E | DARLINGTON-51A | W.HARTLEPOOL-51C | EASTFIELD-65A | COLWICK-38A | LANGWITHJCN-40E | COLWICK-38A | COLWICK-38A | TYNEDOCK-54B |
| **Aug-57** | W.HALSE-38E | DARLINGTON-51A | W.HARTLEPOOL-51C | EASTFIELD-65A | COLWICK-38A | LANGWITHJCN-40E | COLWICK-38A | COLWICK-38A | **6/57: STAR - 50D** |
| **Jan-58** | W.HALSE-38E | DARLINGTON-51A | W.HARTLEPOOL-51C | EASTFIELD-65A | COLWICK-38A | LANGWITHJCN-40E | COLWICK-38A | COLWICK-38A | STARBECK-50D |
| **Aug-58** | W.HALSE-2F | **9/58: WAKE - 56A** | W.HARTLEPOOL-51C | EASTFIELD-65A | COLWICK-40E | LANGWITHJCN-41J | COLWICK-40E | COLWICK-40E | STARBECK-50D |
| **Jan-59** | W.HALSE-2F | WAKEFIELD-56A | W.HARTLEPOOL-51C | EASTFIELD-65A | COLWICK-40E | LANGWITHJCN-41J | **5/59: BARN - 41G** | COLWICK-40E | STARBECK-50D |
| **Aug-59** | W.HALSE-2F | WAKEFIELD-56A | **8/59: TBY - 51L** | EASTFIELD-65A | COLWICK-40E | **6/59: CANK - 41D** | **6/59: MEX - 41F** | COLWICK-40E | **9/59: WAKE - 56A** |
| **Nov-59** | W.HALSE-2F | WAKEFIELD-56A | THORNABY-51L | EASTFIELD-65A | COLWICK-40E | **9/59: COLW - 40E** | MEXBOROUGH-41F | COLWICK-40E | WAKEFIELD-56A |
| **Jan-60** | W.HALSE-2F | WAKEFIELD-56A | THORNABY-51L | EASTFIELD-65A | COLWICK-40E | COLWICK-40E | MEXBOROUGH-41F | COLWICK-40E | WAKEFIELD-56A |
| **Apr-60** | W.HALSE-2F | WAKEFIELD-56A | THORNABY-51L | EASTFIELD-65A | **3/60: NEW.E. - 34E** | COLWICK-40E | MEXBOROUGH-41F | **5/60: IMM - 40B** | WAKEFIELD-56A |
| **Aug-60** | W.HALSE-2F | WAKEFIELD-56A | THORNABY-51L | EASTFIELD-65A | NEWENGLAND-34E | COLWICK-40E | MEXBOROUGH-41F | IMMINGHAM-40B | WAKEFIELD-56A |
| **Nov-60** | | WAKEFIELD-56A | THORNABY-51L | EASTFIELD-65A | NEWENGLAND-34E | COLWICK-40E | MEXBOROUGH-41F | **10/60: FROD - 36C** | WAKEFIELD-56A |

| | 90055 | 90056 | 90057 | 90058 | 90059 | 90060 | 90061 | 90062 | 90063 |
|---|---|---|---|---|---|---|---|---|---|
| **Aug-50** | MARCH-31B | YORK-50A | DAIRYCOATES-53A | THORNTONJCN-62A | NEWENGLAND-35A | MARCH-31B | DARLINGTON-51A | NEWENGLAND-35A | NEWENGLAND-35A |
| **Jan-51** | MARCH-31B | YORK-50A | DAIRYCOATES-53A | THORNTONJCN-62A | NEWENGLAND-35A | MARCH-31B | DARLINGTON-51A | NEWENGLAND-35A | NEWENGLAND-35A |
| **Aug-51** | MARCH-31B | YORK-50A | DAIRYCOATES-53A | THORNTONJCN-62A | NEWENGLAND-35A | MARCH-31B | **8/51: DAIRY - 53A** | NEWENGLAND-35A | NEWENGLAND-35A |
| **Jan-52** | MARCH-31B | YORK-50A | DAIRYCOATES-53A | THORNTONJCN-62A | **1/52: DCTR - 36A** | MARCH-31B | DAIRYCOATES-53A | NEWENGLAND-35A | NEWENGLAND-35A |
| **Aug-52** | MARCH-31B | YORK-50A | DAIRYCOATES-53A | THORNTONJCN-62A | **3/52: FROD - 36C** | MARCH-31B | DAIRYCOATES-53A | NEWENGLAND-35A | NEWENGLAND-35A |
| **Jan-53** | MARCH-31B | YORK-50A | DAIRYCOATES-53A | THORNTONJCN-62A | FRODINGHAM-36C | MARCH-31B | DAIRYCOATES-53A | NEWENGLAND-35A | NEWENGLAND-35A |
| **Aug-53** | MARCH-31B | YORK-50A | DAIRYCOATES-53A | THORNTONJCN-62A | FRODINGHAM-36C | MARCH-31B | DAIRYCOATES-53A | NEWENGLAND-35A | NEWENGLAND-35A |
| **Jan-54** | **10/53: IMM - 40B** | YORK-50A | DAIRYCOATES-53A | THORNTONJCN-62A | FRODINGHAM-36C | **11/53: DCTR - 36A** | **3/54: S'HEAD - 53C** | NEWENGLAND-35A | NEWENGLAND-35A |
| **Aug-54** | IMMINGHAM-40B | YORK-50A | DAIRYCOATES-53A | THORNTONJCN-62A | FRODINGHAM-36C | DONCASTER-36A | SPRINGHEAD-53C | NEWENGLAND-35A | NEWENGLAND-35A |
| **Jan-55** | IMMINGHAM-40B | YORK-50A | DAIRYCOATES-53A | THORNTONJCN-62A | FRODINGHAM-36C | DONCASTER-36A | SPRINGHEAD-53C | **2/55: STRAT - 30A** | NEWENGLAND-35A |
| **Aug-55** | **8/55: L. JCN - 40E** | YORK-50A | DAIRYCOATES-53A | THORNTONJCN-62A | FRODINGHAM-36C | DONCASTER-36A | SPRINGHEAD-53C | STRATFORD-30A | NEWENGLAND-35A |
| **Jan-56** | LANGWITHJCN-40E | YORK-50A | DAIRYCOATES-53A | THORNTONJCN-62A | FRODINGHAM-36C | DONCASTER-36A | SPRINGHEAD-53C | STRATFORD-30A | NEWENGLAND-35A |
| **Aug-56** | LANGWITHJCN-40E | **6/56: DARL - 51A** | DAIRYCOATES-53A | THORNTONJCN-62A | FRODINGHAM-36C | **10/56: MARCH - 31B** | SPRINGHEAD-53C | STRATFORD-30A | NEWENGLAND-35A |
| **Jan-57** | LANGWITHJCN-40E | DARLINGTON-51A | DAIRYCOATES-53A | THORNTONJCN-62A | FRODINGHAM-36C | **3/57: POL - 66A** | SPRINGHEAD-53C | STRATFORD-30A | NEWENGLAND-35A |
| **Aug-57** | LANGWITHJCN-40E | DARLINGTON-51A | DAIRYCOATES-53A | THORNTONJCN-62A | FRODINGHAM-36C | **7/57: DAWS - 65D** | SPRINGHEAD-53C | STRATFORD-30A | NEWENGLAND-35A |
| **Jan-58** | LANGWITHJCN-40E | DARLINGTON-51A | DAIRYCOATES-53A | THORNTONJCN-62A | FRODINGHAM-36C | **2/58: POL - 66A** | SPRINGHEAD-53C | STRATFORD-30A | NEWENGLAND-35A |
| **Aug-58** | **7/58: STAVE - 41H** | **9/58: WAKE - 56A** | DAIRYCOATES-53A | THORNTONJCN-62A | FRODINGHAM-36C | POLMADIE-66A | **6/58: DARL - 51A** | STRATFORD-30A | NEWENGLAND-34E |
| **Jan-59** | STAVELEY(GC)-41H | WAKEFIELD-56A | DAIRYCOATES-53A | THORNTONJCN-62A | FRODINGHAM-36C | POLMADIE-66A | **9/58: WAKE - 56A** | STRATFORD-30A | NEWENGLAND-34E |
| **Aug-59** | STAVELEY(GC)-41H | WAKEFIELD-56A | **6/59: DARL - 51A** | THORNTONJCN-62A | FRODINGHAM-36C | POLMADIE-66A | WAKEFIELD-56A | STRATFORD-30A | NEWENGLAND-34E |
| **Nov-59** | STAVELEY(GC)-41H | WAKEFIELD-56A | DARLINGTON-51A | THORNTONJCN-62A | FRODINGHAM-36C | POLMADIE-66A | WAKEFIELD-56A | STRATFORD-30A | NEWENGLAND-34E |
| **Jan-60** | STAVELEY(GC)-41H | WAKEFIELD-56A | DARLINGTON-51A | THORNTONJCN-62A | FRODINGHAM-36C | POLMADIE-66A | WAKEFIELD-56A | **12/59: W/D** | **2/60: MARCH - 31B** |
| **Apr-60** | LANGWITHJCN-41J | WAKEFIELD-56A | DARLINGTON-51A | THORNTONJCN-62A | FRODINGHAM-36C | POLMADIE-66A | WAKEFIELD-56A | | MARCH-31B |
| **Aug-60** | **5/60: NEW.E - 34E** | WAKEFIELD-56A | DARLINGTON-51A | THORNTONJCN-62A | FRODINGHAM-36C | POLMADIE-66A | WAKEFIELD-56A | | MARCH-31B |
| **Nov-60** | NEWENGLAND-34E | WAKEFIELD-56A | DARLINGTON-51A | THORNTONJCN-62A | FRODINGHAM-36C | POLMADIE-66A | WAKEFIELD-56A | | **10/60: DCTR - 36A** |

| | 90064 | 90065 | 90066 | 90067 | 90068 | 90069 | 90070 | 90071 | 90072 |
|---|---|---|---|---|---|---|---|---|---|
| **Aug-50** | MARCH-31B | W.HALSE-38E | MARCH-31B | STOCKTON-51E | NEWPORT-51B | YORK-50A | NEWENGLAND-35A | DUNDEE-62B | TWEEDMOUTH-52D |
| **Jan-51** | MARCH-31B | W.HALSE-38E | MARCH-31B | STOCKTON-51E | NEWPORT-51B | YORK-50A | **10/50: MARCH - 31B** | **11/50: EBRO(SM) - 64A** | **1/51: DAIRY - 53A** |
| **Aug-51** | MARCH-31B | W.HALSE-38E | MARCH-31B | STOCKTON-51E | NEWPORT-51B | **9/51: IMM - 40B** | **3/51: FROD - 36C** | **3/51: To CR** | DAIRYCOATES-53A |
| **Jan-52** | MARCH-31B | W.HALSE-38E | MARCH-31B | STOCKTON-51E | NEWPORT-51B | IMMINGHAM-40B | FRODINGHAM-36C | | DAIRYCOATES-53A |
| **Aug-52** | MARCH-31B | W.HALSE-38E | MARCH-31B | STOCKTON-51E | NEWPORT-51B | IMMINGHAM-40B | FRODINGHAM-36C | | DAIRYCOATES-53A |
| **Jan-53** | MARCH-31B | W.HALSE-38E | MARCH-31B | STOCKTON-51E | NEWPORT-51B | IMMINGHAM-40B | FRODINGHAM-36C | | DAIRYCOATES-53A |
| **Aug-53** | MARCH-31B | W.HALSE-38E | MARCH-31B | STOCKTON-51E | NEWPORT-51B | IMMINGHAM-40B | FRODINGHAM-36C | | DAIRYCOATES-53A |
| **Jan-54** | **11/53: DCTR - 36A** | W.HALSE-38E | **11/53: DCTR - 36A** | STOCKTON-51E | NEWPORT-51B | IMMINGHAM-40B | FRODINGHAM-36C | | DAIRYCOATES-53A |
| **Aug-54** | DONCASTER-36A | W.HALSE-38E | **6/54: MEX - 36B** | STOCKTON-51E | NEWPORT-51B | IMMINGHAM-40B | FRODINGHAM-36C | | DAIRYCOATES-53A |
| **Jan-55** | DONCASTER-36A | W.HALSE-38E | MEXBOROUGH-36B | STOCKTON-51E | NEWPORT-51B | IMMINGHAM-40B | FRODINGHAM-36C | | DAIRYCOATES-53A |
| **Aug-55** | DONCASTER-36A | W.HALSE-38E | MEXBOROUGH-36B | **8/55: W.HPL - 51C** | NEWPORT-51B | IMMINGHAM-40B | FRODINGHAM-36C | | DAIRYCOATES-53A |
| **Jan-56** | **1/56: COLW - 38A** | W.HALSE-38E | **1/56: COLW - 38A** | W.HARTLEPOOL-51C | NEWPORT-51B | IMMINGHAM-40B | FRODINGHAM-36C | | DAIRYCOATES-53A |
| **Aug-56** | COLWICK-38A | W.HALSE-38E | COLWICK-38A | W.HARTLEPOOL-51C | NEWPORT-51B | IMMINGHAM-40B | FRODINGHAM-36C | | DAIRYCOATES-53A |
| **Jan-57** | COLWICK-38A | W.HALSE-38E | **2/57: WFD.H - 38E** | W.HARTLEPOOL-51C | NEWPORT-51B | IMMINGHAM-40B | FRODINGHAM-36C | | DAIRYCOATES-53A |
| **Aug-57** | COLWICK-38A | W.HALSE-38E | W.HALSE-38E | W.HARTLEPOOL-51C | **6/57: YORK - 50A** | IMMINGHAM-40B | FRODINGHAM-36C | | DAIRYCOATES-53A |
| **Jan-58** | COLWICK-38A | W.HALSE-38E | W.HALSE-38E | W.HARTLEPOOL-51C | YORK-50A | IMMINGHAM-40B | FRODINGHAM-36C | | DAIRYCOATES-53A |
| **Aug-58** | COLWICK-40E | W.HALSE-2F | W.HALSE-2F | W.HARTLEPOOL-51C | YORK-50A | IMMINGHAM-40B | FRODINGHAM-36C | | DAIRYCOATES-53A |
| **Jan-59** | **5/59: BARN - 41G** | W.HALSE-2F | W.HALSE-2F | W.HARTLEPOOL-51C | YORK-50A | IMMINGHAM-40B | FRODINGHAM-36C | | DAIRYCOATES-53A |
| **Aug-59** | **6/59: MEX - 41F** | W.HALSE-2F | W.HALSE-2F | W.HARTLEPOOL-51C | **10/59: WAKE - 56A** | IMMINGHAM-40B | FRODINGHAM-36C | | DAIRYCOATES-53A |
| **Nov-59** | MEXBOROUGH-41F | W.HALSE-2F | W.HALSE-2F | W.HARTLEPOOL-51C | **11/59: LOW M - 56F** | IMMINGHAM-40B | FRODINGHAM-36C | | DAIRYCOATES-53A |
| **Jan-60** | MEXBOROUGH-41F | W.HALSE-2F | W.HALSE-2F | W.HARTLEPOOL-51C | LOWMOOR-56F | IMMINGHAM-40B | FRODINGHAM-36C | | **2/60: TBY - 51L** |
| **Apr-60** | MEXBOROUGH-41F | W.HALSE-2F | W.HALSE-2F | W.HARTLEPOOL-51C | LOWMOOR-56F | IMMINGHAM-40B | FRODINGHAM-36C | | THORNABY-51L |
| **Aug-60** | MEXBOROUGH-41F | W.HALSE-2F | W.HALSE-2F | W.HARTLEPOOL-51C | LOWMOOR-56F | IMMINGHAM-40B | FRODINGHAM-36C | | THORNABY-51L |
| **Nov-60** | MEXBOROUGH-41F | W.HALSE-2F | W.HALSE-2F | W.HARTLEPOOL-51C | LOWMOOR-56F | IMMINGHAM-40B | FRODINGHAM-36C | | THORNABY-51L |

| | 90073 | 90074 | 90075 | 90076 | 90077 | 90078 | 90079 | 90080 | 90081 |
|---|---|---|---|---|---|---|---|---|---|
| **Aug-50** | COLWICK-38A | NEWPORT-51B | IMMINGHAM-40B | NEWPORT-51B | DUNDEE-62B | DARLINGTON-51A | NEWENGLAND-35A | W.HALSE-38E | NEWPORT-51B |
| **Jan-51** | COLWICK-38A | NEWPORT-51B | **10/50: MARCH - 31B** | NEWPORT-51B | DUNDEE-62B | DARLINGTON-51A | NEWENGLAND-35A | W.HALSE-38E | NEWPORT-51B |
| **Aug-51** | COLWICK-38A | NEWPORT-51B | MARCH-31B | NEWPORT-51B | DUNDEE-62B | **9/51: DAIRY - 53A** | NEWENGLAND-35A | W.HALSE-38E | NEWPORT-51B |
| **Jan-52** | COLWICK-38A | NEWPORT-51B | MARCH-31B | NEWPORT-51B | DUNDEE-62B | DAIRYCOATES-53A | NEWENGLAND-35A | W.HALSE-38E | NEWPORT-51B |
| **Aug-52** | COLWICK-38A | NEWPORT-51B | MARCH-31B | NEWPORT-51B | DUNDEE-62B | DAIRYCOATES-53A | NEWENGLAND-35A | W.HALSE-38E | NEWPORT-51B |
| **Jan-53** | COLWICK-38A | NEWPORT-51B | MARCH-31B | NEWPORT-51B | DUNDEE-62B | DAIRYCOATES-53A | NEWENGLAND-35A | W.HALSE-38E | NEWPORT-51B |
| **Aug-53** | COLWICK-38A | NEWPORT-51B | **10/53: COLW - 38A** | NEWPORT-51B | DUNDEE-62B | DAIRYCOATES-53A | NEWENGLAND-35A | W.HALSE-38E | NEWPORT-51B |
| **Jan-54** | COLWICK-38A | NEWPORT-51B | COLWICK-38A | NEWPORT-51B | DUNDEE-62B | DAIRYCOATES-53A | **1/54: MARCH - 31B** | W.HALSE-38E | NEWPORT-51B |
| **Aug-54** | COLWICK-38A | NEWPORT-51B | COLWICK-38A | NEWPORT-51B | DUNDEE-62B | DAIRYCOATES-53A | MARCH-31B | W.HALSE-38E | NEWPORT-51B |
| **Jan-55** | COLWICK-38A | NEWPORT-51B | COLWICK-38A | NEWPORT-51B | DUNDEE-62B | DAIRYCOATES-53A | MARCH-31B | W.HALSE-38E | NEWPORT-51B |
| **Aug-55** | COLWICK-38A | NEWPORT-51B | COLWICK-38A | NEWPORT-51B | DUNDEE-62B | DAIRYCOATES-53A | MARCH-31B | W.HALSE-38E | NEWPORT-51B |
| **Jan-56** | COLWICK-38A | NEWPORT-51B | COLWICK-38A | NEWPORT-51B | DUNDEE-62B | DAIRYCOATES-53A | MARCH-31B | W.HALSE-38E | NEWPORT-51B |
| **Aug-56** | COLWICK-38A | NEWPORT-51B | COLWICK-38A | NEWPORT-51B | DUNDEE-62B | DAIRYCOATES-53A | MARCH-31B | W.HALSE-38E | NEWPORT-51B |
| **Jan-57** | COLWICK-38A | NEWPORT-51B | COLWICK-38A | NEWPORT-51B | DUNDEE-62B | DAIRYCOATES-53A | MARCH-31B | W.HALSE-38E | NEWPORT-51B |
| **Aug-57** | COLWICK-38A | NEWPORT-51B | COLWICK-38A | NEWPORT-51B | **8/57: DAWS - 65D** | DAIRYCOATES-53A | MARCH-31B | W.HALSE-38E | NEWPORT-51B |
| **Jan-58** | COLWICK-38A | NEWPORT-51B | COLWICK-38A | NEWPORT-51B | DAWSHOLME-65D | DAIRYCOATES-53A | MARCH-31B | W.HALSE-38E | NEWPORT-51B |
| **Aug-58** | COLWICK-40E | **6/58: TBY - 51L** | COLWICK-40E | **6/58: TBY - 51L** | **8/58: POL - 66A** | DAIRYCOATES-53A | MARCH-31B | W.HALSE-2F | **6/58: TBY - 51L** |
| **Jan-59** | COLWICK-40E | THORNABY-51L | COLWICK-40E | **4/59: WAKE - 56A** | POLMADIE-66A | DAIRYCOATES-53A | MARCH-31B | W.HALSE-2F | THORNABY-51L |
| **Aug-59** | COLWICK-40E | THORNABY-51L | COLWICK-40E | WAKEFIELD-56A | POLMADIE-66A | DAIRYCOATES-53A | MARCH-31B | W.HALSE-2F | THORNABY-51L |
| **Nov-59** | **12/59: NEW.E - 34E** | THORNABY-51L | COLWICK-40E | WAKEFIELD-56A | POLMADIE-66A | DAIRYCOATES-53A | MARCH-31B | W.HALSE-2F | THORNABY-51L |
| **Jan-60** | NEWENGLAND-34E | THORNABY-51L | COLWICK-40E | WAKEFIELD-56A | POLMADIE-66A | DAIRYCOATES-53A | MARCH-31B | W.HALSE-2F | THORNABY-51L |
| **Apr-60** | NEWENGLAND-34E | THORNABY-51L | **3/60: NEW.E - 34E** | WAKEFIELD-56A | POLMADIE-66A | DAIRYCOATES-50B | MARCH-31B | W.HALSE-2F | THORNABY-51L |
| **Aug-60** | NEWENGLAND-34E | THORNABY-51L | NEWENGLAND-34E | WAKEFIELD-56A | POLMADIE-66A | DAIRYCOATES-50B | MARCH-31B | W.HALSE-2F | THORNABY-51L |
| **Nov-60** | NEWENGLAND-34E | THORNABY-51L | NEWENGLAND-34E | WAKEFIELD-56A | POLMADIE-66A | DAIRYCOATES-50B | **10/60: DCTR - 36A** | W.HALSE-2F | THORNABY-51L |

## 90082–90090

| | 90082 | 90083 | 90084 | 90085 | 90086 | 90087 | 90088 | 90089 | 90090 |
|---|---|---|---|---|---|---|---|---|---|
| Aug-50 | STOCKTON-51E | MARCH-31B | COLWICK-38A | COLCHESTER-30E | STOCKTON-51E | MARCH-31B | NEWENGLAND-35A | NEWPORT-51B | NEWPORT-51B |
| Jan-51 | STOCKTON-51E | MARCH-31B | COLWICK-38A | COLCHESTER-30E | STOCKTON-51E | MARCH-31B | NEWENGLAND-35A | NEWPORT-51B | NEWPORT-51B |
| Aug-51 | STOCKTON-51E | MARCH-31B | COLWICK-38A | 9/51: MARCH-31B | STOCKTON-51E | MARCH-31B | NEWENGLAND-35A | 9/51: DAIRY-53A | NEWPORT-51B |
| Jan-52 | STOCKTON-51E | MARCH-31B | COLWICK-38A | MARCH-31B | STOCKTON-51E | MARCH-31B | NEWENGLAND-35A | DAIRYCOATES-53A | NEWPORT-51B |
| Aug-52 | 5/52: S'HEAD-53C | MARCH-31B | COLWICK-38A | MARCH-31B | STOCKTON-51E | MARCH-31B | NEWENGLAND-35A | DAIRYCOATES-53A | NEWPORT-51B |
| Jan-53 | SPRINGHEAD-53C | MARCH-31B | COLWICK-38A | 2/53: MEX-36B | STOCKTON-51E | MARCH-31B | NEWENGLAND-35A | DAIRYCOATES-53A | NEWPORT-51B |
| Aug-53 | SPRINGHEAD-53C | MARCH-31B | COLWICK-38A | MEXBOROUGH-36B | STOCKTON-51E | MARCH-31B | NEWENGLAND-35A | DAIRYCOATES-53A | NEWPORT-51B |
| Jan-54 | SPRINGHEAD-53C | 11/53: IMM-40B | COLWICK-38A | MEXBOROUGH-36B | STOCKTON-51E | MARCH-31B | NEWENGLAND-35A | DAIRYCOATES-53A | NEWPORT-51B |
| Aug-54 | SPRINGHEAD-53C | IMMINGHAM-40B | COLWICK-38A | MEXBOROUGH-36B | STOCKTON-51E | 10/53: IMM-40B | NEWENGLAND-35A | DAIRYCOATES-53A | NEWPORT-51B |
| Jan-55 | SPRINGHEAD-53C | IMMINGHAM-40B | COLWICK-38A | MEXBOROUGH-36B | STOCKTON-51E | IMMINGHAM-40B | NEWENGLAND-35A | DAIRYCOATES-53A | NEWPORT-51B |
| Aug-55 | 9/55: N.HILL-50B | IMMINGHAM-40B | COLWICK-38A | MEXBOROUGH-36B | STOCKTON-51E | 3/55: L.JCN-40E | NEWENGLAND-35A | DAIRYCOATES-53A | NEWPORT-51B |
| Jan-56 | NEVILLEHILL-50B | IMMINGHAM-40B | COLWICK-38A | 1/56: COLW-38A | STOCKTON-51E | LANGWITH JCN-40E | NEWENGLAND-35A | DAIRYCOATES-53A | NEWPORT-51B |
| Aug-56 | NEVILLEHILL-50B | 10/56: MARCH-31B | COLWICK-38A | COLWICK-38A | STOCKTON-51E | LANGWITH JCN-40E | NEWENGLAND-35A | DAIRYCOATES-53A | NEWPORT-51B |
| Jan-57 | NEVILLEHILL-50B | MARCH-31B | COLWICK-38A | 11/56: STAVE-38D | STOCKTON-51E | LANGWITH JCN-40E | NEWENGLAND-35A | DAIRYCOATES-53A | NEWPORT-51B |
| Aug-57 | NEVILLEHILL-50B | MARCH-31B | COLWICK-38A | STAVELEY-38D | STOCKTON-51E | LANGWITH JCN-40E | NEWENGLAND-35A | DAIRYCOATES-53A | NEWPORT-51B |
| Jan-58 | 11/57: STOCK-51E | MARCH-31B | COLWICK-38A | STAVELEY-38D | STOCKTON-51E | LANGWITH JCN-40E | 9/57: IMM-40B | 9/57: WAKE-56A | NEWPORT-51B |
| Aug-58 | STOCKTON-51E | MARCH-31B | COLWICK-40E | STAVELEY(GC)-41H | 8/58: H.HILL-51G | 7/58: STAVE-41H | WAKEFIELD-56A | WAKEFIELD-56A | 6/58: TBY-51L |
| Jan-59 | STOCKTON-51E | MARCH-31B | COLWICK-40E | STAVELEY(GC)-41H | HAVERTON HILL-51G | STAVELEY(GC)-41H | WAKEFIELD-56A | WAKEFIELD-56A | THORNABY-51L |
| Aug-59 | 6/59: DARL-51A | MARCH-31B | COLWICK-40E | STAVELEY(GC)-41H | 6/59: TBY-51L | STAVELEY(GC)-41H | WAKEFIELD-56A | WAKEFIELD-56A | THORNABY-51L |
| Nov-59 | DARLINGTON-51A | MARCH-31B | COLWICK-40E | STAVELEY(GC)-41H | THORNABY-51L | STAVELEY(GC)-41H | WAKEFIELD-56A | WAKEFIELD-56A | THORNABY-51L |
| Jan-60 | DARLINGTON-51A | 12/59: W/D | COLWICK-40E | 3/60: L.JCN-41J | THORNABY-51L | 2/60: FROD-36C | LANGWITH JCN-41J | WAKEFIELD-56A | THORNABY-51L |
| Apr-60 | DARLINGTON-51A | | COLWICK-40E | 4/60: CANK-41D | THORNABY-51L | FRODINGHAM-36C | LANGWITH JCN-41J | WAKEFIELD-56A | THORNABY-51L |
| Aug-60 | DARLINGTON-51A | | COLWICK-40E | CANKLOW-41D | THORNABY-51L | FRODINGHAM-36C | LANGWITH JCN-41J | WAKEFIELD-56A | THORNABY-51L |
| Nov-60 | DARLINGTON-51A | | COLWICK-40E | CANKLOW-41D | THORNABY-51L | FRODINGHAM-36C | LANGWITH JCN-41J | WAKEFIELD-56A | THORNABY-51L |

## 90091–90099

| | 90091 | 90092 | 90093 | 90094 | 90095 | 90096 | 90097 | 90098 | 90099 |
|---|---|---|---|---|---|---|---|---|---|
| Aug-50 | NEWPORT-51B | STOCKTON-51E | NEWENGLAND-35A | SPRINGHEAD-53C | WOODFORDHALSE-38E | NEWENGLAND-35A | FERRYHILL-61B | NEWPORT-51B | YORK-50A |
| Jan-51 | NEWPORT-51B | STOCKTON-51E | NEWENGLAND-35A | SPRINGHEAD-53C | WOODFORDHALSE-38E | NEWENGLAND-35A | FERRYHILL-61B | NEWPORT-51B | YORK-50A |
| Aug-51 | NEWPORT-51B | STOCKTON-51E | NEWENGLAND-35A | SPRINGHEAD-53C | WOODFORDHALSE-38E | NEWENGLAND-35A | FERRYHILL-61B | NEWPORT-51B | 9/51: DAIRY-53A |
| Jan-52 | NEWPORT-51B | STOCKTON-51E | NEWENGLAND-35A | SPRINGHEAD-53C | WOODFORDHALSE-38E | NEWENGLAND-35A | FERRYHILL-61B | NEWPORT-51B | DAIRYCOATES-53A |
| Aug-52 | NEWPORT-51B | STOCKTON-51E | NEWENGLAND-35A | SPRINGHEAD-53C | WOODFORDHALSE-38E | NEWENGLAND-35A | FERRYHILL-61B | NEWPORT-51B | DAIRYCOATES-53A |
| Jan-53 | NEWPORT-51B | STOCKTON-51E | NEWENGLAND-35A | SPRINGHEAD-53C | WOODFORDHALSE-38E | NEWENGLAND-35A | FERRYHILL-61B | NEWPORT-51B | DAIRYCOATES-53A |
| Aug-53 | NEWPORT-51B | STOCKTON-51E | NEWENGLAND-35A | SPRINGHEAD-53C | WOODFORDHALSE-38E | NEWENGLAND-35A | FERRYHILL-61B | NEWPORT-51B | DAIRYCOATES-53A |
| Jan-54 | NEWPORT-51B | STOCKTON-51E | NEWENGLAND-35A | SPRINGHEAD-53C | WOODFORDHALSE-38E | NEWENGLAND-35A | FERRYHILL-61B | NEWPORT-51B | DAIRYCOATES-53A |
| Aug-54 | NEWPORT-51B | STOCKTON-51E | NEWENGLAND-35A | SPRINGHEAD-53C | WOODFORDHALSE-38E | NEWENGLAND-35A | FERRYHILL-61B | NEWPORT-51B | DAIRYCOATES-53A |
| Jan-55 | NEWPORT-51B | STOCKTON-51E | NEWENGLAND-35A | SPRINGHEAD-53C | WOODFORDHALSE-38E | NEWENGLAND-35A | FERRYHILL-61B | NEWPORT-51B | DAIRYCOATES-53A |
| Aug-55 | NEWPORT-51B | 8/55: W.HPL-51C | NEWENGLAND-35A | SPRINGHEAD-53C | WOODFORDHALSE-38E | NEWENGLAND-35A | FERRYHILL-61B | NEWPORT-51B | DAIRYCOATES-53A |
| Jan-56 | NEWPORT-51B | W.HARTLEPOOL-51C | NEWENGLAND-35A | SPRINGHEAD-53C | WOODFORDHALSE-38E | NEWENGLAND-35A | FERRYHILL-61B | NEWPORT-51B | DAIRYCOATES-53A |
| Aug-56 | NEWPORT-51B | W.HARTLEPOOL-51C | NEWENGLAND-35A | SPRINGHEAD-53C | WOODFORDHALSE-38E | NEWENGLAND-35A | FERRYHILL-61B | NEWPORT-51B | DAIRYCOATES-53A |
| Jan-57 | NEWPORT-51B | W.HARTLEPOOL-51C | NEWENGLAND-35A | SPRINGHEAD-53C | WOODFORDHALSE-38E | NEWENGLAND-35A | FERRYHILL-61B | NEWPORT-51B | DAIRYCOATES-53A |
| Aug-57 | NEWPORT-51B | W.HARTLEPOOL-51C | NEWENGLAND-35A | SPRINGHEAD-53C | WOODFORDHALSE-38E | NEWENGLAND-35A | FERRYHILL-61B | NEWPORT-51B | DAIRYCOATES-53A |
| Jan-58 | NEWPORT-51B | W.HARTLEPOOL-51C | NEWENGLAND-35A | SPRINGHEAD-53C | WOODFORDHALSE-38E | NEWENGLAND-35A | FERRYHILL-61B | NEWPORT-51B | DAIRYCOATES-53A |
| Aug-58 | 6/58: TBY-51L | W.HARTLEPOOL-51C | 5/58: TIL-33B | 10/58: GOOLE-53E | WOODFORDHALSE-2F | NEWENGLAND-35A | FERRYHILL-61B | 6/58: TBY-51L | DAIRYCOATES-53A |
| Jan-59 | THORNABY-51L | W.HARTLEPOOL-51C | TILBURY-33B | GOOLE-53E | WOODFORDHALSE-2F | NEWENGLAND-34E | FERRYHILL-61B | THORNABY-51L | DAIRYCOATES-53A |
| Aug-59 | THORNABY-51L | W.HARTLEPOOL-51C | 6/59: MARCH-31B | GOOLE-53E | WOODFORDHALSE-2F | NEWENGLAND-34E | FERRYHILL-61B | THORNABY-51L | DAIRYCOATES-53A |
| Nov-59 | THORNABY-51L | W.HARTLEPOOL-51C | 9/59: PLAIS-33A | GOOLE-53E | WOODFORDHALSE-2F | NEWENGLAND-34E | FERRYHILL-61B | THORNABY-51L | DAIRYCOATES-53A |
| Jan-60 | THORNABY-51L | W.HARTLEPOOL-51C | 10/59: TIL-33B | GOOLE-53E | WOODFORDHALSE-2F | NEWENGLAND-34E | FERRYHILL-61B | THORNABY-51L | DAIRYCOATES-53A |
| Apr-60 | THORNABY-51L | W.HARTLEPOOL-51C | TILBURY-33B | GOOLE-50D | WOODFORDHALSE-2F | NEWENGLAND-34E | FERRYHILL-61B | THORNABY-51L | DAIRYCOATES-50B |
| Aug-60 | THORNABY-51L | W.HARTLEPOOL-51C | TILBURY-33B | GOOLE-50D | WOODFORDHALSE-2F | NEWENGLAND-34E | FERRYHILL-61B | THORNABY-51L | DAIRYCOATES-50B |
| Nov-60 | THORNABY-51L | W.HARTLEPOOL-51C | TILBURY-33B | GOOLE-50D | WOODFORDHALSE-2F | NEWENGLAND-34E | FERRYHILL-61B | THORNABY-51L | DAIRYCOATES-50B |

## 90100–90114

| | 90100 | 90103 | 90104 | 90106 | 90108 | 90111 | 90112 | 90113 | 90114 |
|---|---|---|---|---|---|---|---|---|---|
| Aug-50 | YORK-50A | COLWICK-38A | MEXBOROUGH-36B | NEWENGLAND-35A | MEXBOROUGH-36B | COLWICK-38A | | | |
| Jan-51 | YORK-50A | COLWICK-38A | MEXBOROUGH-36B | NEWENGLAND-35A | MEXBOROUGH-36B | 10/50: MARCH-31B | | | EDINBURGH(SM)-64A |
| Aug-51 | YORK-50A | COLWICK-38A | MEXBOROUGH-36B | NEWENGLAND-35A | 5/51: DCTR-36A | 3/51: FROD-36C | | | EDINBURGH(SM)-64A |
| Jan-52 | YORK-50A | COLWICK-38A | 10/51: MARCH-31B | NEWENGLAND-35A | 3/52: NEW.E-35A | FRODINGHAM-36C | | | 3/51: To CR |
| Aug-52 | YORK-50A | COLWICK-38A | MARCH-31B | NEWENGLAND-35A | 5/52: To CR | FRODINGHAM-36C | | | |
| Jan-53 | YORK-50A | COLWICK-38A | 2/53: MEX-36B | NEWENGLAND-35A | 11/52: DCTR-36A | FRODINGHAM-36C | | | |
| Aug-53 | YORK-50A | COLWICK-38A | MEXBOROUGH-36B | NEWENGLAND-35A | DONCASTER-36A | FRODINGHAM-36C | | | |
| Jan-54 | YORK-50A | COLWICK-38A | MEXBOROUGH-36B | NEWENGLAND-35A | DONCASTER-36A | FRODINGHAM-36C | | | |
| Aug-54 | YORK-50A | COLWICK-38A | MEXBOROUGH-36B | NEWENGLAND-35A | DONCASTER-36A | FRODINGHAM-36C | | | |
| Jan-55 | YORK-50A | COLWICK-38A | MEXBOROUGH-36B | NEWENGLAND-35A | DONCASTER-36A | FRODINGHAM-36C | | | |
| Aug-55 | YORK-50A | COLWICK-38A | MEXBOROUGH-36B | NEWENGLAND-35A | DONCASTER-36A | FRODINGHAM-36C | | | |
| Jan-56 | YORK-50A | COLWICK-38A | 1/56: COLW-38A | NEWENGLAND-35A | DONCASTER-36A | FRODINGHAM-36C | | | |
| Aug-56 | 10/56: DAIRY-53A | COLWICK-38A | COLWICK-38A | NEWENGLAND-35A | 10/56: MARCH-31B | 10/56: MARCH-31B | | | |
| Jan-57 | DAIRYCOATES-53A | COLWICK-38A | COLWICK-38A | NEWENGLAND-35A | 2/57: DCTR-36A | FRODINGHAM-36C | | | |
| Aug-57 | 9/57: WAKE-56A | COLWICK-38A | COLWICK-38A | NEWENGLAND-35A | DONCASTER-36A | FRODINGHAM-36C | | | |
| Jan-58 | WAKEFIELD-56A | COLWICK-38A | COLWICK-38A | 3/58: COLW-33B | DONCASTER-36A | FRODINGHAM-36C | Ex LM | Ex LM | |
| Aug-58 | WAKEFIELD-56A | COLWICK-40E | COLWICK-40E | TILBURY-33B | DONCASTER-36A | FRODINGHAM-36C | 6/58: WAKE-56A | 12/57: SOW.B-56E | |
| Jan-59 | WAKEFIELD-56A | COLWICK-40E | COLWICK-40E | TILBURY-33B | DONCASTER-36A | FRODINGHAM-36C | WAKEFIELD-56A | SOWERBYBRIDGE-56E | |
| Aug-59 | WAKEFIELD-56A | COLWICK-40E | COLWICK-40E | 6/59: MARCH-31B | DONCASTER-36A | FRODINGHAM-36C | WAKEFIELD-56A | SOWERBYBRIDGE-56E | |
| Nov-59 | WAKEFIELD-56A | COLWICK-40E | COLWICK-40E | 9/59: PLAIS-33A | DONCASTER-36A | FRODINGHAM-36C | WAKEFIELD-56A | SOWERBYBRIDGE-56E | |
| Jan-60 | WAKEFIELD-56A | COLWICK-40E | COLWICK-40E | 10/59: TIL-33B | 2/60: RET-36A | FRODINGHAM-36C | WAKEFIELD-56A | SOWERBYBRIDGE-56E | |
| Apr-60 | WAKEFIELD-56A | COLWICK-40E | COLWICK-40E | TILBURY-33B | RETFORD-36E | FRODINGHAM-36C | WAKEFIELD-56A | SOWERBYBRIDGE-56E | |
| Aug-60 | WAKEFIELD-56A | COLWICK-40E | COLWICK-40E | TILBURY-33B | RETFORD-36E | FRODINGHAM-36C | WAKEFIELD-56A | SOWERBYBRIDGE-56E | |
| Nov-60 | WAKEFIELD-56A | COLWICK-40E | COLWICK-40E | TILBURY-33B | 11/60: FROD-36C | FRODINGHAM-36C | WAKEFIELD-56A | SOWERBYBRIDGE-56E | |

## 90115–90124

| | 90115 | 90116 | 90117 | 90118 | 90119 | 90120 | 90121 | 90122 | 90124 |
|---|---|---|---|---|---|---|---|---|---|
| Aug-50 | STAVELEY-38D | SPRINGHEAD-53C | DUNFERMLINE-62C | MARCH-31B | MARCH-31B | MEXBOROUGH-36B | FERRYHILL-61B | Ex LM | |
| Jan-51 | STAVELEY-38D | SPRINGHEAD-53C | DUNFERMLINE-62C | 3/51: MEX-36B | 3/51: MEX-36B | MEXBOROUGH-36B | FERRYHILL-61B | 11/50: COLW-38A | |
| Aug-51 | STAVELEY-38D | SPRINGHEAD-53C | DUNFERMLINE-62C | MEXBOROUGH-36B | MEXBOROUGH-36B | MEXBOROUGH-36B | 8/51: To LM | 9/51: To LM | |
| Jan-52 | STAVELEY-38D | SPRINGHEAD-53C | DUNFERMLINE-62C | MEXBOROUGH-36B | MEXBOROUGH-36B | MEXBOROUGH-36B | | | |
| Aug-52 | STAVELEY-38D | SPRINGHEAD-53C | DUNFERMLINE-62C | MEXBOROUGH-36B | MEXBOROUGH-36B | MEXBOROUGH-36B | | | |
| Jan-53 | STAVELEY-38D | SPRINGHEAD-53C | DUNFERMLINE-62C | MEXBOROUGH-36B | MEXBOROUGH-36B | MEXBOROUGH-36B | | | |
| Aug-53 | STAVELEY-38D | SPRINGHEAD-53C | DUNFERMLINE-62C | MEXBOROUGH-36B | MEXBOROUGH-36B | MEXBOROUGH-36B | | | |
| Jan-54 | STAVELEY-38D | SPRINGHEAD-53C | DUNFERMLINE-62C | MEXBOROUGH-36B | MEXBOROUGH-36B | MEXBOROUGH-36B | | | |
| Aug-54 | STAVELEY-38D | SPRINGHEAD-53C | DUNFERMLINE-62C | MEXBOROUGH-36B | MEXBOROUGH-36B | MEXBOROUGH-36B | | | |
| Jan-55 | STAVELEY-38D | SPRINGHEAD-53C | DUNFERMLINE-62C | MEXBOROUGH-36B | MEXBOROUGH-36B | MEXBOROUGH-36B | | | |
| Aug-55 | 7/55: COLW-38A | SPRINGHEAD-53C | DUNFERMLINE-62C | MEXBOROUGH-36B | MEXBOROUGH-36B | MEXBOROUGH-36B | | | |
| Jan-56 | COLWICK-38A | SPRINGHEAD-53C | DUNFERMLINE-62C | 1/56: COLW-38A | 1/56: COLW-38A | 1/56: COLW-38A | | | |
| Aug-56 | COLWICK-38A | SPRINGHEAD-53C | DUNFERMLINE-62C | COLWICK-38A | 3/56: MARCH-31B | COLWICK-38A | | | |
| Jan-57 | COLWICK-38A | SPRINGHEAD-53C | 12/56: TH JN-62A | COLWICK-38A | 3/57: DCTR-36A | COLWICK-38A | | | |
| Aug-57 | COLWICK-38A | SPRINGHEAD-53C | THORNTONJCN-62A | COLWICK-38A | DONCASTER-36A | COLWICK-38A | | | |
| Jan-58 | COLWICK-40E | 5/58: GOOLE-53E | THORNTONJCN-62A | COLWICK-38A | DONCASTER-36A | COLWICK-38A | | | Ex LM |
| Aug-58 | COLWICK-40E | 6/58: DARL-51A | THORNTONJCN-62A | COLWICK-40E | 7/58: MEX-41F | COLWICK-40E | | | 6/58: WAKE-56A |
| Jan-59 | COLWICK-40E | 9/58: WAKE-56A | THORNTONJCN-62A | COLWICK-40E | MEXBOROUGH-41F | COLWICK-40E | | | WAKEFIELD-56A |
| Aug-59 | COLWICK-40E | WAKEFIELD-56A | THORNTONJCN-62A | COLWICK-40E | MEXBOROUGH-41F | COLWICK-40E | | | WAKEFIELD-56A |
| Nov-59 | COLWICK-40E | WAKEFIELD-56A | THORNTONJCN-62A | COLWICK-40E | MEXBOROUGH-41F | COLWICK-40E | | | WAKEFIELD-56A |
| Jan-60 | COLWICK-40E | WAKEFIELD-56A | THORNTONJCN-62A | COLWICK-40E | MEXBOROUGH-41F | COLWICK-40E | | | WAKEFIELD-56A |
| Apr-60 | COLWICK-40E | WAKEFIELD-56A | THORNTONJCN-62A | COLWICK-40E | MEXBOROUGH-41F | COLWICK-40E | | | WAKEFIELD-56A |
| Aug-60 | COLWICK-40E | WAKEFIELD-56A | THORNTONJCN-62A | COLWICK-40E | MEXBOROUGH-41F | COLWICK-40E | | | WAKEFIELD-56A |
| Nov-60 | 11/60: FROD-36C | WAKEFIELD-56A | THORNTONJCN-62A | COLWICK-40E | MEXBOROUGH-41F | 11/60: FROD-36C | | | WAKEFIELD-56A |

| | 90126 | 90128 | 90129 | 90130 | 90131 | 90132 | 90133 | 90135 | 90136 |
|---|---|---|---|---|---|---|---|---|---|
| Aug-50 | Ex LM | THORNTONJCN-62A | COLWICK-38A | NEWENGLAND-35A | MARCH-31B | NEWPORT-51B | IMMINGHAM-40B | | COLWICK-38A |
| Jan-51 | 11/50: COLW - 38A | THORNTONJCN-62A | COLWICK-38A | NEWENGLAND-35A | MARCH-31B | NEWPORT-51B | IMMINGHAM-40B | | COLWICK-38A |
| Aug-51 | 9/51: To LM | THORNTONJCN-62A | COLWICK-38A | NEWENGLAND-35A | MARCH-31B | NEWPORT-51B | 5/51: FROD - 36C | | COLWICK-38A |
| Jan-52 | | THORNTONJCN-62A | COLWICK-38A | 11/51: MEX - 36B | MARCH-31B | NEWPORT-51B | FRODINGHAM-36C | | COLWICK-38A |
| Aug-52 | | THORNTONJCN-62A | COLWICK-38A | MEXBOROUGH-36B | MARCH-31B | NEWPORT-51B | FRODINGHAM-36C | | COLWICK-38A |
| Jan-53 | | THORNTONJCN-62A | COLWICK-38A | MEXBOROUGH-36B | MARCH-31B | NEWPORT-51B | FRODINGHAM-36C | | COLWICK-38A |
| Aug-53 | | THORNTONJCN-62A | COLWICK-38A | MEXBOROUGH-36B | MARCH-31B | NEWPORT-51B | FRODINGHAM-36C | | COLWICK-38A |
| Jan-54 | | THORNTONJCN-62A | 1/54: MARCH - 31B | MEXBOROUGH-36B | 10/53: IMM - 40B | NEWPORT-51B | FRODINGHAM-36C | | COLWICK-38A |
| Aug-54 | | THORNTONJCN-62A | MARCH-31B | MEXBOROUGH-36B | IMMINGHAM-40B | NEWPORT-51B | FRODINGHAM-36C | | COLWICK-38A |
| Jan-55 | | THORNTONJCN-62A | MARCH-31B | MEXBOROUGH-36B | IMMINGHAM-40B | NEWPORT-51B | FRODINGHAM-36C | | COLWICK-38A |
| Aug-55 | | THORNTONJCN-62A | MARCH-31B | MEXBOROUGH-36B | IMMINGHAM-40B | NEWPORT-51B | FRODINGHAM-36C | | COLWICK-38A |
| Jan-56 | | THORNTONJCN-62A | MARCH-31B | 1/56: COLW - 38A | IMMINGHAM-40B | NEWPORT-51B | FRODINGHAM-36C | | COLWICK-38A |
| Aug-56 | | THORNTONJCN-62A | MARCH-31B | COLWICK-38A | IMMINGHAM-40B | NEWPORT-51B | FRODINGHAM-36C | | COLWICK-38A |
| Jan-57 | | THORNTONJCN-62A | MARCH-31B | COLWICK-38A | IMMINGHAM-40B | NEWPORT-51B | FRODINGHAM-36C | | COLWICK-38A |
| Aug-57 | | THORNTONJCN-62A | MARCH-31B | COLWICK-38A | IMMINGHAM-40B | NEWPORT-51B | FRODINGHAM-36C | | COLWICK-38A |
| Jan-58 | | THORNTONJCN-62A | MARCH-31B | COLWICK-38A | IMMINGHAM-40B | 6/58: TBY - 51L | FRODINGHAM-36C | Ex LM | COLWICK-38A |
| Aug-58 | | THORNTONJCN-62A | MARCH-31B | COLWICK-40E | IMMINGHAM-40B | THORNABY-51L | FRODINGHAM-36C | 6/58: DARL - 51A | 7/58: MEX - 41F |
| Jan-59 | | THORNTONJCN-62A | MARCH-31B | COLWICK-40E | IMMINGHAM-40B | THORNABY-51L | FRODINGHAM-36C | DARLINGTON-51A | MEXBOROUGH-41F |
| Aug-59 | | 6/59: EFLD - 65A | 4/59: STRAT - 30A | COLWICK-40E | IMMINGHAM-40B | THORNABY-51L | FRODINGHAM-36C | DARLINGTON-51A | MEXBOROUGH-41F |
| Nov-59 | | EASTFIELD-65A | STRATFORD-30A | COLWICK-40E | IMMINGHAM-40B | THORNABY-51L | FRODINGHAM-36C | 10/59: MIR - 56D | MEXBOROUGH-41F |
| Jan-60 | | EASTFIELD-65A | STRATFORD-30A | COLWICK-40E | IMMINGHAM-40B | THORNABY-51L | FRODINGHAM-36C | MIRFIELD-56D | MEXBOROUGH-41F |
| Apr-60 | | EASTFIELD-65A | 5/60: HSEY - 34B | 5/60: NEW.E - 34E | IMMINGHAM-40B | THORNABY-51L | FRODINGHAM-36C | MIRFIELD-56D | MEXBOROUGH-41F |
| Aug-60 | | EASTFIELD-65A | HORNSEY-34B | NEWENGLAND-34E | IMMINGHAM-40B | THORNABY-51L | FRODINGHAM-36C | MIRFIELD-56D | MEXBOROUGH-41F |
| Nov-60 | | EASTFIELD-65A | HORNSEY-34B | NEWENGLAND-34E | IMMINGHAM-40B | THORNABY-51L | FRODINGHAM-36C | MIRFIELD-56D | MEXBOROUGH-41F |

| | 90137 | 90139 | 90140 | 90144 | 90145 | 90146 | 90147 | 90149 | 90150 |
|---|---|---|---|---|---|---|---|---|---|
| Aug-50 | W.HALSE-38E | COLWICK-38A | Ex LM | MEXBOROUGH-36B | THORNTONJCN-62A | MEXBOROUGH-36B | EASTFIELD-65A | EASTFIELD-65A | MEXBOROUGH-36B |
| Jan-51 | W.HALSE-38E | COLWICK-38A | 11/50: COLW - 38A | MEXBOROUGH-36B | THORNTONJCN-62A | MEXBOROUGH-36B | 11/50: COLW - 38A | EASTFIELD-65A | MEXBOROUGH-36B |
| Aug-51 | W.HALSE-38E | COLWICK-38A | 9/51: To LM | MEXBOROUGH-36B | THORNTONJCN-62A | MEXBOROUGH-36B | COLWICK-38A | EASTFIELD-65A | MEXBOROUGH-36B |
| Jan-52 | W.HALSE-38E | COLWICK-38A | | MEXBOROUGH-36B | 3/52: MARCH - 31B | MEXBOROUGH-36B | COLWICK-38A | | MEXBOROUGH-36B |
| Aug-52 | W.HALSE-38E | COLWICK-38A | | MEXBOROUGH-36B | MARCH-31B | MEXBOROUGH-36B | 5/52: To LM | | MEXBOROUGH-36B |
| Jan-53 | W.HALSE-38E | COLWICK-38A | | MEXBOROUGH-36B | MARCH-31B | MEXBOROUGH-36B | | | MEXBOROUGH-36B |
| Aug-53 | W.HALSE-38E | COLWICK-38A | | MEXBOROUGH-36B | 10/53: IMM - 40B | MEXBOROUGH-36B | | | MEXBOROUGH-36B |
| Jan-54 | W.HALSE-38E | COLWICK-38A | | MEXBOROUGH-36B | IMMINGHAM-40B | MEXBOROUGH-36B | | | MEXBOROUGH-36B |
| Aug-54 | W.HALSE-38E | COLWICK-38A | | MEXBOROUGH-36B | IMMINGHAM-40B | MEXBOROUGH-36B | | | MEXBOROUGH-36B |
| Jan-55 | W.HALSE-38E | COLWICK-38A | | MEXBOROUGH-36B | IMMINGHAM-40B | MEXBOROUGH-36B | | | MEXBOROUGH-36B |
| Aug-55 | W.HALSE-38E | COLWICK-38A | | MEXBOROUGH-36B | IMMINGHAM-40B | MEXBOROUGH-36B | | | MEXBOROUGH-36B |
| Jan-56 | W.HALSE-38E | COLWICK-38A | | 1/56: COLW - 38A | IMMINGHAM-40B | 1/56: COLW - 38A | | | 1/56: COLW - 38A |
| Aug-56 | W.HALSE-38E | COLWICK-38A | | 3/56: MARCH - 31B | IMMINGHAM-40B | COLWICK-38A | | | 3/56: MARCH - 31B |
| Jan-57 | W.HALSE-38E | COLWICK-38A | | 3/57: DCTR - 36A | IMMINGHAM-40B | COLWICK-38A | | | MARCH-31B |
| Aug-57 | W.HALSE-38E | COLWICK-38A | | DONCASTER-36A | IMMINGHAM-40B | COLWICK-38A | | | MARCH-31B |
| Jan-58 | W.HALSE-38E | COLWICK-38A | | DONCASTER-36A | IMMINGHAM-40B | COLWICK-38A | | | MARCH-31B |
| Aug-58 | W.HALSE-2F | 7/58: MEX - 41F | | DONCASTER-36A | IMMINGHAM-40B | COLWICK-40E | | | MARCH-31B |
| Jan-59 | W.HALSE-2F | MEXBOROUGH-41F | | DONCASTER-36A | IMMINGHAM-40B | COLWICK-40E | | | MARCH-31B |
| Aug-59 | W.HALSE-2F | MEXBOROUGH-41F | | DONCASTER-36A | 9/59: CANK - 41D | COLWICK-40E | | | MARCH-31B |
| Nov-59 | W.HALSE-2F | MEXBOROUGH-41F | | DONCASTER-36A | CANKLOW-41D | COLWICK-40E | | | MARCH-31B |
| Jan-60 | W.HALSE-2F | MEXBOROUGH-41F | | DONCASTER-36A | CANKLOW-41D | COLWICK-40E | | | MARCH-31B |
| Apr-60 | W.HALSE-2F | MEXBOROUGH-41F | | DONCASTER-36A | CANKLOW-41D | COLWICK-40E | | | MARCH-31B |
| Aug-60 | W.HALSE-2F | MEXBOROUGH-41F | | DONCASTER-36A | CANKLOW-41D | NEWENGLAND-34E | | | MARCH-31B |
| Nov-60 | W.HALSE-2F | MEXBOROUGH-41F | | DONCASTER-36A | CANKLOW-41D | NEWENGLAND-34E | | | MARCH-31B |

| | 90151 | 90153 | 90154 | 90155 | 90156 | 90157 | 90158 | 90160 | 90161 |
|---|---|---|---|---|---|---|---|---|---|
| Aug-50 | NEWENGLAND-35A | MEXBOROUGH-36B | MEXBOROUGH-36B | STOCKTON-51E | NEWENGLAND-35A | Ex LM | NEWENGLAND-35A | SPRINGHEAD-53C | MEXBOROUGH-36B |
| Jan-51 | NEWENGLAND-35A | MEXBOROUGH-36B | MEXBOROUGH-36B | STOCKTON-51E | NEWENGLAND-35A | 11/50: COLW - 38A | NEWENGLAND-35A | 11/50: DAIRY - 53A | MEXBOROUGH-36B |
| Aug-51 | NEWENGLAND-35A | MEXBOROUGH-36B | MEXBOROUGH-36B | STOCKTON-51E | NEWENGLAND-35A | 2/51: STAVE - 38D | NEWENGLAND-35A | DAIRYCOATES-53A | MEXBOROUGH-36B |
| Jan-52 | NEWENGLAND-35A | MEXBOROUGH-36B | MEXBOROUGH-36B | STOCKTON-51E | NEWENGLAND-35A | STAVELEY-38D | NEWENGLAND-35A | DAIRYCOATES-53A | MEXBOROUGH-36B |
| Aug-52 | NEWENGLAND-35A | MEXBOROUGH-36B | 6/52 : COLW - 38A | STOCKTON-51E | NEWENGLAND-35A | 4/52: To LM | NEWENGLAND-35A | DAIRYCOATES-53A | 4/52: To WR |
| Jan-53 | NEWENGLAND-35A | MEXBOROUGH-36B | COLWICK-38A | STOCKTON-51E | NEWENGLAND-35A | | NEWENGLAND-35A | DAIRYCOATES-53A | |
| Aug-53 | NEWENGLAND-35A | MEXBOROUGH-36B | COLWICK-38A | STOCKTON-51E | NEWENGLAND-35A | | NEWENGLAND-35A | DAIRYCOATES-53A | |
| Jan-54 | NEWENGLAND-35A | MEXBOROUGH-36B | COLWICK-38A | STOCKTON-51E | 1/54: S.BGE - 35C | | NEWENGLAND-35A | DAIRYCOATES-53A | |
| Aug-54 | NEWENGLAND-35A | MEXBOROUGH-36B | COLWICK-38A | STOCKTON-51E | SPITAL BRIDGE-35C | | NEWENGLAND-35A | DAIRYCOATES-53A | |
| Jan-55 | NEWENGLAND-35A | MEXBOROUGH-36B | COLWICK-38A | STOCKTON-51E | SPITAL BRIDGE-35C | | NEWENGLAND-35A | DAIRYCOATES-53A | |
| Aug-55 | NEWENGLAND-35A | MEXBOROUGH-36B | COLWICK-38A | STOCKTON-51E | SPITAL BRIDGE-35C | | NEWENGLAND-35A | DAIRYCOATES-53A | |
| Jan-56 | NEWENGLAND-35A | 1/56: COLW - 38A | COLWICK-38A | STOCKTON-51E | 3/56: MARCH - 31B | | NEWENGLAND-35A | DAIRYCOATES-53A | 1/56: COLW - 38A |
| Aug-56 | NEWENGLAND-35A | COLWICK-38A | COLWICK-38A | STOCKTON-51E | MARCH-31B | | NEWENGLAND-35A | DAIRYCOATES-53A | COLWICK-38A |
| Jan-57 | NEWENGLAND-35A | COLWICK-38A | COLWICK-38A | STOCKTON-51E | MARCH-31B | | NEWENGLAND-35A | DAIRYCOATES-53A | COLWICK-38A |
| Aug-57 | NEWENGLAND-35A | COLWICK-38A | COLWICK-38A | STOCKTON-51E | MARCH-31B | | NEWENGLAND-35A | DAIRYCOATES-53A | COLWICK-38A |
| Jan-58 | NEWENGLAND-35A | COLWICK-38A | COLWICK-38A | STOCKTON-51E | MARCH-31B | | NEWENGLAND-35A | DAIRYCOATES-53A | COLWICK-38A |
| Aug-58 | NEWENGLAND-34E | 7/58: MEX - 41F | COLWICK-40E | STOCKTON-51E | MARCH-31B | | NEWENGLAND-34E | DAIRYCOATES-53A | COLWICK-40E |
| Jan-59 | NEWENGLAND-34E | MEXBOROUGH-41F | COLWICK-40E | STOCKTON-51E | 4/59: STRAT - 30A | | NEWENGLAND-34E | DAIRYCOATES-53A | COLWICK-40E |
| Aug-59 | NEWENGLAND-34E | MEXBOROUGH-41F | COLWICK-40E | 6/59: DARL - 51A | STRATFORD-30A | | NEWENGLAND-34E | DAIRYCOATES-53A | COLWICK-40E |
| Nov-59 | NEWENGLAND-34E | MEXBOROUGH-41F | 12/59: NEW.E - 34E | DARLINGTON-51A | STRATFORD-30A | | NEWENGLAND-34E | DAIRYCOATES-53A | COLWICK-40E |
| Jan-60 | NEWENGLAND-34E | MEXBOROUGH-41F | NEWENGLAND-34E | DARLINGTON-51A | STRATFORD-30A | | NEWENGLAND-34E | 2/60: GOOLE - 50D | COLWICK-40E |
| Apr-60 | NEWENGLAND-34E | MEXBOROUGH-41F | NEWENGLAND-34E | DARLINGTON-51A | 5/60: HSEY - 34B | | NEWENGLAND-34E | GOOLE-50D | 5/60: IMM - 40B |
| Aug-60 | NEWENGLAND-34E | MEXBOROUGH-41F | NEWENGLAND-34E | DARLINGTON-51A | HORNSEY-34B | | NEWENGLAND-34E | GOOLE-50D | IMMINGHAM-40B |
| Nov-60 | NEWENGLAND-34E | MEXBOROUGH-41F | NEWENGLAND-34E | DARLINGTON-51A | HORNSEY-34B | | NEWENGLAND-34E | GOOLE-50D | 10/60: FROD - 36C |

| | 90162 | 90163 | 90165 | 90166 | 90168 | 90169 | 90170 | 90172 | 90174 |
|---|---|---|---|---|---|---|---|---|---|
| Aug-50 | IMMINGHAM-40B | Ex LM | NEWENGLAND-35A | MEXBOROUGH-36B | THORNTONJCN-62A | NEWENGLAND-35A | THORNTONJCN-62A | STOCKTON-51E | EASTFIELD-65A |
| Jan-51 | 3/51: NEW.E - 35A | 11/50: COLW - 38A | NEWENGLAND-35A | MEXBOROUGH-36B | THORNTONJCN-62A | NEWENGLAND-35A | THORNTONJCN-62A | STOCKTON-51E | EASTFIELD-65A |
| Aug-51 | NEWENGLAND-35A | 9/51: To LM | NEWENGLAND-35A | MEXBOROUGH-36B | THORNTONJCN-62A | NEWENGLAND-35A | THORNTONJCN-62A | STOCKTON-51E | EASTFIELD-65A |
| Jan-52 | NEWENGLAND-35A | | NEWENGLAND-35A | MEXBOROUGH-36B | THORNTONJCN-62A | NEWENGLAND-35A | THORNTONJCN-62A | STOCKTON-51E | 10/51: To WR |
| Aug-52 | NEWENGLAND-35A | | NEWENGLAND-35A | MEXBOROUGH-36B | THORNTONJCN-62A | NEWENGLAND-35A | THORNTONJCN-62A | STOCKTON-51E | |
| Jan-53 | NEWENGLAND-35A | | NEWENGLAND-35A | MEXBOROUGH-36B | THORNTONJCN-62A | NEWENGLAND-35A | THORNTONJCN-62A | STOCKTON-51E | |
| Aug-53 | NEWENGLAND-35A | | NEWENGLAND-35A | MEXBOROUGH-36B | THORNTONJCN-62A | NEWENGLAND-35A | THORNTONJCN-62A | STOCKTON-51E | |
| Jan-54 | NEWENGLAND-35A | | NEWENGLAND-35A | MEXBOROUGH-36B | THORNTONJCN-62A | NEWENGLAND-35A | THORNTONJCN-62A | STOCKTON-51E | |
| Aug-54 | NEWENGLAND-35A | | NEWENGLAND-35A | MEXBOROUGH-36B | THORNTONJCN-62A | NEWENGLAND-35A | 6/54: To CR | STOCKTON-51E | |
| Jan-55 | 1/55: L. JCN - 40E | | NEWENGLAND-35A | MEXBOROUGH-36B | THORNTONJCN-62A | NEWENGLAND-35A | | STOCKTON-51E | |
| Aug-55 | LANGWITHJCN-40E | | NEWENGLAND-35A | MEXBOROUGH-36B | THORNTONJCN-62A | NEWENGLAND-35A | | STOCKTON-51E | |
| Jan-56 | LANGWITHJCN-40E | | NEWENGLAND-35A | 1/56: COLW - 38A | THORNTONJCN-62A | NEWENGLAND-35A | | STOCKTON-51E | |
| Aug-56 | LANGWITHJCN-40E | | NEWENGLAND-35A | COLWICK-38A | THORNTONJCN-62A | NEWENGLAND-35A | | STOCKTON-51E | |
| Jan-57 | LANGWITHJCN-40E | | NEWENGLAND-35A | COLWICK-38A | THORNTONJCN-62A | NEWENGLAND-35A | | STOCKTON-51E | |
| Aug-57 | LANGWITHJCN-40E | | NEWENGLAND-35A | COLWICK-38A | THORNTONJCN-62A | NEWENGLAND-35A | | STOCKTON-51E | |
| Jan-58 | LANGWITHJCN-40E | | NEWENGLAND-35A | COLWICK-38A | THORNTONJCN-62A | NEWENGLAND-35A | | STOCKTON-51E | |
| Aug-58 | LANGWITHJCN-41J | | NEWENGLAND-34E | COLWICK-40E | THORNTONJCN-62A | NEWENGLAND-34E | | STOCKTON-51E | |
| Jan-59 | LANGWITHJCN-41J | | NEWENGLAND-34E | COLWICK-40E | THORNTONJCN-62A | NEWENGLAND-34E | | STOCKTON-51E | |
| Aug-59 | 6/59: CANK - 40B | | NEWENGLAND-34E | COLWICK-40E | THORNTONJCN-62A | NEWENGLAND-34E | | 6/59: DARL - 51A | |
| Nov-59 | 9/59: IMM - 40B | | NEWENGLAND-34E | COLWICK-40E | THORNTONJCN-62A | NEWENGLAND-34E | | DARLINGTON-51A | |
| Jan-60 | 1/60: CANK - 41D | | NEWENGLAND-34E | COLWICK-40E | THORNTONJCN-62A | NEWENGLAND-34E | | DARLINGTON-51A | |
| Apr-60 | CANKLOW-41D | | NEWENGLAND-34E | 5/60: IMM - 40B | THORNTONJCN-62A | NEWENGLAND-34E | | DARLINGTON-51A | |
| Aug-60 | CANKLOW-41D | | NEWENGLAND-34E | IMMINGHAM-40B | THORNTONJCN-62A | NEWENGLAND-34E | | DARLINGTON-51A | |
| Nov-60 | CANKLOW-41D | | NEWENGLAND-34E | 10/60: FROD - 36C | THORNTONJCN-62A | NEWENGLAND-34E | | DARLINGTON-51A | |

| | 90175 | 90177 | 90178 | 90180 | 90182 | 90184 | 90185 | 90187 | 90189 |
|---|---|---|---|---|---|---|---|---|---|
| Aug-50 | MARCH-31B | THORNTON JCN-62A | Ex LM | NEWENGLAND-35A | THORNTON JCN-62A | STOCKTON-51E | W.HALSE-38E | Ex LM | MEXBOROUGH-36B |
| Jan-51 | MARCH-31B | THORNTON JCN-62A | 11/50: COLW - 38A | NEWENGLAND-35A | THORNTON JCN-62A | STOCKTON-51E | 10/50: COLW - 38A | 11/50: COLW - 38A | MEXBOROUGH-36B |
| Aug-51 | MARCH-31B | THORNTON JCN-62A | COLWICK-38A | NEWENGLAND-35A | THORNTON JCN-62A | STOCKTON-51E | COLWICK-38A | 9/51: WFD.H - 38E | MEXBOROUGH-36B |
| Jan-52 | MARCH-31B | THORNTON JCN-62A | COLWICK-38A | NEWENGLAND-35A | THORNTON JCN-62A | STOCKTON-51E | COLWICK-38A | 10/51: COLW - 38A | MEXBOROUGH-36B |
| Aug-52 | MARCH-31B | THORNTON JCN-62A | 5/52: To LM | NEWENGLAND-35A | THORNTON JCN-62A | STOCKTON-51E | COLWICK-38A | 5/52: To LM | MEXBOROUGH-36B |
| Jan-53 | MARCH-31B | THORNTON JCN-62A | | NEWENGLAND-35A | THORNTON JCN-62A | STOCKTON-51E | COLWICK-38A | | MEXBOROUGH-36B |
| Aug-53 | MARCH-31B | THORNTON JCN-62A | | NEWENGLAND-35A | THORNTON JCN-62A | STOCKTON-51E | COLWICK-38A | | MEXBOROUGH-36B |
| Jan-54 | 11/53: IMM - 40B | THORNTON JCN-62A | | NEWENGLAND-35A | THORNTON JCN-62A | STOCKTON-51E | COLWICK-38A | | MEXBOROUGH-36B |
| Aug-54 | IMMINGHAM-40B | THORNTON JCN-62A | | NEWENGLAND-35A | THORNTON JCN-62A | STOCKTON-51E | COLWICK-38A | | MEXBOROUGH-36B |
| Jan-55 | IMMINGHAM-40B | 11/54: DUNF - 62C | | NEWENGLAND-35A | THORNTON JCN-62A | STOCKTON-51E | COLWICK-38A | | MEXBOROUGH-36B |
| Aug-55 | IMMINGHAM-40B | DUNFERMLINE-62C | | NEWENGLAND-35A | THORNTON JCN-62A | STOCKTON-51E | COLWICK-38A | | MEXBOROUGH-36B |
| Jan-56 | IMMINGHAM-40B | DUNFERMLINE-62C | | NEWENGLAND-35A | THORNTON JCN-62A | STOCKTON-51E | COLWICK-38A | | 1/56: COLW - 38A |
| Aug-56 | IMMINGHAM-40B | DUNFERMLINE-62C | | NEWENGLAND-35A | THORNTON JCN-62A | STOCKTON-51E | COLWICK-38A | | COLWICK-38A |
| Jan-57 | IMMINGHAM-40B | DUNFERMLINE-62C | | NEWENGLAND-35A | THORNTON JCN-62A | STOCKTON-51E | COLWICK-38A | | COLWICK-38A |
| Aug-57 | IMMINGHAM-40B | DUNFERMLINE-62C | | NEWENGLAND-35A | THORNTON JCN-62A | STOCKTON-51E | COLWICK-38A | | COLWICK-38A |
| Jan-58 | IMMINGHAM-40B | DUNFERMLINE-62C | | NEWENGLAND-35A | THORNTON JCN-62A | STOCKTON-51E | COLWICK-38A | | COLWICK-38A |
| Aug-58 | IMMINGHAM-40B | DUNFERMLINE-62C | | NEWENGLAND-34E | THORNTON JCN-62A | STOCKTON-51E | COLWICK-40E | | COLWICK-40E |
| Jan-59 | IMMINGHAM-40B | DUNFERMLINE-62C | | NEWENGLAND-34E | THORNTON JCN-62A | STOCKTON-51E | COLWICK-40E | | COLWICK-40E |
| Aug-59 | IMMINGHAM-40B | DUNFERMLINE-62C | | NEWENGLAND-34E | THORNTON JCN-62A | STOCKTON-51E | COLWICK-40E | | COLWICK-40E |
| Nov-59 | IMMINGHAM-40B | DUNFERMLINE-62C | | NEWENGLAND-34E | THORNTON JCN-62A | 6/59: DARL - 51A | COLWICK-40E | | COLWICK-40E |
| Jan-60 | IMMINGHAM-40B | DUNFERMLINE-62C | | NEWENGLAND-34E | THORNTON JCN-62A | 10/59: MIOR - 56D | COLWICK-40E | | COLWICK-40E |
| Apr-60 | IMMINGHAM-40B | DUNFERMLINE-62C | | NEWENGLAND-34E | THORNTON JCN-62A | MIRFIELD-56D | 5/60: NEW.E - 35A | | 3/60: To LM |
| Aug-60 | IMMINGHAM-40B | DUNFERMLINE-62C | | NEWENGLAND-34E | THORNTON JCN-62A | MIRFIELD-56D | NEWENGLAND-34E | | |
| Nov-60 | IMMINGHAM-40B | DUNFERMLINE-62C | | NEWENGLAND-34E | THORNTON JCN-62A | MIRFIELD-56D | NEWENGLAND-34E | | |

| | 90190 | 90191 | 90192 | 90193 | 90195 | 90196 | 90197 | 90198 | 90199 |
|---|---|---|---|---|---|---|---|---|---|
| Aug-50 | MEXBOROUGH-36B | NEWENGLAND-35A | EASTFIELD-65A | EASTFIELD-65A | MEXBOROUGH-36B | MEXBOROUGH-36B | Ex LM | DUNDEE-62B | DUNFERMLINE-62C |
| Jan-51 | MEXBOROUGH-36B | NEWENGLAND-35A | EASTFIELD-65A | EASTFIELD-65A | MEXBOROUGH-36B | MEXBOROUGH-36B | 11/50: COLW - 38A | DUNDEE-62B | DUNFERMLINE-62C |
| Aug-51 | MEXBOROUGH-36B | NEWENGLAND-35A | EASTFIELD-65A | 7/51: DAWS - 64D | MEXBOROUGH-36B | MEXBOROUGH-36B | 9/51: To LM | DUNDEE-62B | DUNFERMLINE-62C |
| Jan-52 | MEXBOROUGH-36B | NEWENGLAND-35A | 12/51: To WR | DAWSHOLME-64D | MEXBOROUGH-36B | MEXBOROUGH-36B | | DUNDEE-62B | DUNFERMLINE-62C |
| Aug-52 | MEXBOROUGH-36B | NEWENGLAND-35A | | DAWSHOLME-64D | MEXBOROUGH-36B | MEXBOROUGH-36B | | DUNDEE-62B | DUNFERMLINE-62C |
| Jan-53 | MEXBOROUGH-36B | NEWENGLAND-35A | | DAWSHOLME-64D | MEXBOROUGH-36B | MEXBOROUGH-36B | | DUNDEE-62B | DUNFERMLINE-62C |
| Aug-53 | MEXBOROUGH-36B | NEWENGLAND-35A | | DAWSHOLME-64D | MEXBOROUGH-36B | MEXBOROUGH-36B | | DUNDEE-62B | DUNFERMLINE-62C |
| Jan-54 | MEXBOROUGH-36B | NEWENGLAND-35A | | DAWSHOLME-64D | MEXBOROUGH-36B | MEXBOROUGH-36B | | DUNDEE-62B | DUNFERMLINE-62C |
| Aug-54 | MEXBOROUGH-36B | NEWENGLAND-35A | | DAWSHOLME-64D | MEXBOROUGH-36B | MEXBOROUGH-36B | | DUNDEE-62B | 8/54: TH JN - 62A |
| Jan-55 | MEXBOROUGH-36B | NEWENGLAND-35A | | DAWSHOLME-64D | MEXBOROUGH-36B | MEXBOROUGH-36B | | DUNDEE-62B | THORNTON JCN-62A |
| Aug-55 | MEXBOROUGH-36B | NEWENGLAND-35A | | DAWSHOLME-64D | MEXBOROUGH-36B | 5/55: PLAIS - 33A | | DUNDEE-62B | THORNTON JCN-62A |
| Jan-56 | MEXBOROUGH-36B | NEWENGLAND-35A | | DAWSHOLME-64D | MEXBOROUGH-36B | PLAISTOW-33A | | DUNDEE-62B | 10/55: G'MTH - 65F |
| Aug-56 | MEXBOROUGH-36B | NEWENGLAND-35A | | DAWSHOLME-64D | MEXBOROUGH-36B | PLAISTOW-33A | | DUNDEE-62B | GRANGEMOUTH-65F |
| Jan-57 | MEXBOROUGH-36B | NEWENGLAND-35A | | DAWSHOLME-64D | MEXBOROUGH-36B | PLAISTOW-33A | | DUNDEE-62B | GRANGEMOUTH-65F |
| Aug-57 | MEXBOROUGH-36B | NEWENGLAND-35A | | DAWSHOLME-64D | MEXBOROUGH-36B | PLAISTOW-33A | | 8/57: DAWS - 65D | GRANGEMOUTH-65F |
| Jan-58 | MEXBOROUGH-36B | 11/57: MARCH - 31B | | DAWSHOLME-64D | MEXBOROUGH-36B | PLAISTOW-33A | | DAWSHOLME-65D | GRANGEMOUTH-65F |
| Aug-58 | MEXBOROUGH-41F | MARCH-31B | | DAWSHOLME-64D | MEXBOROUGH-41F | PLAISTOW-33A | | 8/58: POL - 66A | 8/58: POL - 66A |
| Jan-59 | MEXBOROUGH-41F | MARCH-31B | | DAWSHOLME-64D | MEXBOROUGH-41F | PLAISTOW-33A | | POLMADIE-66A | POLMADIE-66A |
| Aug-59 | MEXBOROUGH-41F | MARCH-31B | | DAWSHOLME-64D | MEXBOROUGH-41F | PLAISTOW-33A | | POLMADIE-66A | POLMADIE-66A |
| Nov-59 | MEXBOROUGH-41F | MARCH-31B | | DAWSHOLME-64D | MEXBOROUGH-41F | 10/59: TIL - 33B | | POLMADIE-66A | POLMADIE-66A |
| Jan-60 | MEXBOROUGH-41F | 2/60: W/D | | DAWSHOLME-64D | MEXBOROUGH-41F | TILBURY-33B | | POLMADIE-66A | POLMADIE-66A |
| Apr-60 | MEXBOROUGH-41F | | | DAWSHOLME-64D | MEXBOROUGH-41F | TILBURY-33B | | POLMADIE-66A | POLMADIE-66A |
| Aug-60 | MEXBOROUGH-41F | | | DAWSHOLME-64D | MEXBOROUGH-41F | TILBURY-33B | | POLMADIE-66A | POLMADIE-66A |
| Nov-60 | MEXBOROUGH-41F | | | DAWSHOLME-64D | MEXBOROUGH-41F | TILBURY-33B | | POLMADIE-66A | POLMADIE-66A |

| | 90200 | 90202 | 90203 | 90204 | 90208 | 90209 | 90210 | 90211 | |
|---|---|---|---|---|---|---|---|---|---|
| Aug-50 | YORK-50A | COLWICK-38A | FERRYHILL-61B | Ex LM | NEWENGLAND-35A | MEXBOROUGH-36B | TYNE DOCK-54B | MEXBOROUGH-36B | Ex LM |
| Jan-51 | YORK-50A | COLWICK-38A | FERRYHILL-61B | 11/50: COLW - 38A | NEWENGLAND-35A | MEXBOROUGH-36B | 1/51: DAIRY - 53A | MEXBOROUGH-36B | 11/50: COLW - 38A |
| Aug-51 | YORK-50A | COLWICK-38A | FERRYHILL-61B | 9/51: To LM | NEWENGLAND-35A | MEXBOROUGH-36B | DAIRYCOATES-53A | MEXBOROUGH-36B | COLWICK-38A |
| Jan-52 | YORK-50A | COLWICK-38A | 3/52: MARCH - 31B | | NEWENGLAND-35A | MEXBOROUGH-36B | DAIRYCOATES-53A | MEXBOROUGH-36B | COLWICK-38A |
| Aug-52 | YORK-50A | COLWICK-38A | MARCH-31B | | NEWENGLAND-35A | MEXBOROUGH-36B | DAIRYCOATES-53A | MEXBOROUGH-36B | |
| Jan-53 | YORK-50A | COLWICK-38A | MARCH-31B | | NEWENGLAND-35A | MEXBOROUGH-36B | DAIRYCOATES-53A | MEXBOROUGH-36B | |
| Aug-53 | YORK-50A | COLWICK-38A | MARCH-31B | | NEWENGLAND-35A | MEXBOROUGH-36B | DAIRYCOATES-53A | MEXBOROUGH-36B | |
| Jan-54 | YORK-50A | COLWICK-38A | 11/53: IMM - 40B | | NEWENGLAND-35A | MEXBOROUGH-36B | DAIRYCOATES-53A | MEXBOROUGH-36B | |
| Aug-54 | YORK-50A | COLWICK-38A | IMMINGHAM-40B | | 4/54: COLW - 38A | MEXBOROUGH-36B | DAIRYCOATES-53A | MEXBOROUGH-36B | |
| Jan-55 | YORK-50A | COLWICK-38A | IMMINGHAM-40B | | COLWICK-38A | MEXBOROUGH-36B | DAIRYCOATES-53A | MEXBOROUGH-36B | |
| Aug-55 | YORK-50A | COLWICK-38A | IMMINGHAM-40B | | COLWICK-38A | MEXBOROUGH-36B | DAIRYCOATES-53A | MEXBOROUGH-36B | |
| Jan-56 | YORK-50A | COLWICK-38A | IMMINGHAM-40B | | 1/56: WFD.H - 38E | MEXBOROUGH-36B | 11/55: YORK - 50A | MEXBOROUGH-36B | |
| Aug-56 | 6/56: DARL - 51A | COLWICK-38A | 10/56: MARCH - 31B | | W.HALSE-38E | MEXBOROUGH-36B | 6/56: DARL - 51A | MEXBOROUGH-36B | |
| Jan-57 | DARLINGTON-51A | COLWICK-38A | 3/57: DCTR - 36A | | 10/56: MARCH - 31B | MEXBOROUGH-36B | DARLINGTON-51A | MEXBOROUGH-36B | |
| Aug-57 | DARLINGTON-51A | COLWICK-38A | DONCASTER-36A | | MARCH-31B | MEXBOROUGH-36B | DARLINGTON-51A | MEXBOROUGH-36B | |
| Jan-58 | DARLINGTON-51A | COLWICK-38A | DONCASTER-36A | | MARCH-31B | MEXBOROUGH-36B | DARLINGTON-51A | MEXBOROUGH-36B | |
| Aug-58 | DARLINGTON-51A | COLWICK-40E | 7/58: MEX - 41F | | MARCH-31B | MEXBOROUGH-41F | 9/58: SOW.B - 56E | MEXBOROUGH-41F | |
| Jan-59 | 2/59: YORK - 50A | COLWICK-40E | MEXBOROUGH-41F | | MARCH-31B | MEXBOROUGH-41F | SOWERBY BRIDGE-56E | MEXBOROUGH-41F | |
| Aug-59 | 10/59: WAKE - 56A | COLWICK-40E | MEXBOROUGH-41F | | MARCH-31B | MEXBOROUGH-41F | SOWERBY BRIDGE-56E | MEXBOROUGH-41F | |
| Nov-59 | 11/59: LOWM - 56F | COLWICK-40E | MEXBOROUGH-41F | | MARCH-31B | MEXBOROUGH-41F | SOWERBY BRIDGE-56E | MEXBOROUGH-41F | |
| Jan-60 | LOWMOOR-56F | COLWICK-40E | MEXBOROUGH-41F | | MARCH-31B | MEXBOROUGH-41F | SOWERBY BRIDGE-56E | MEXBOROUGH-41F | |
| Apr-60 | LOWMOOR-56F | 3/60: CANK - 41D | MEXBOROUGH-41F | | MARCH-31B | MEXBOROUGH-41F | SOWERBY BRIDGE-56E | MEXBOROUGH-41F | |
| Aug-60 | LOWMOOR-56F | CANKLOW-41D | MEXBOROUGH-41F | | MARCH-31B | MEXBOROUGH-41F | SOWERBY BRIDGE-56E | MEXBOROUGH-41F | |
| Nov-60 | LOWMOOR-56F | CANKLOW-41D | MEXBOROUGH-41F | | MARCH-31B | MEXBOROUGH-41F | SOWERBY BRIDGE-56E | MEXBOROUGH-41F | |

| | 90215 | 90217 | 90218 | 90220 | 90221 | | 90223 | 90224 | 90229 |
|---|---|---|---|---|---|---|---|---|---|
| Aug-50 | COLWICK-38A | SPRINGHEAD-53C | W.HALSE-38E | MEXBOROUGH-36B | MARCH-31B | EASTFIELD-65A | MEXBOROUGH-36B | MARCH-31B | MEXBOROUGH-36B |
| Jan-51 | COLWICK-38A | SPRINGHEAD-53C | W.HALSE-38E | MEXBOROUGH-36B | MARCH-31B | EASTFIELD-65A | MEXBOROUGH-36B | MARCH-31B | MEXBOROUGH-36B |
| Aug-51 | COLWICK-38A | SPRINGHEAD-53C | W.HALSE-38E | 10/51: DCTR - 36A | MARCH-31B | 8/51: To LM | MEXBOROUGH-36B | MARCH-31B | MEXBOROUGH-36B |
| Jan-52 | COLWICK-38A | SPRINGHEAD-53C | W.HALSE-38E | 3/52: NEW.E - 35A | MARCH-31B | | 12/51: LINC - 40A | MARCH-31B | MEXBOROUGH-36B |
| Aug-52 | COLWICK-38A | SPRINGHEAD-53C | W.HALSE-38E | 5/52: DCTR - 36A | MARCH-31B | | LINCOLN-40A | MARCH-31B | MEXBOROUGH-36B |
| Jan-53 | COLWICK-38A | SPRINGHEAD-53C | W.HALSE-38E | DONCASTER-36A | MARCH-31B | | LINCOLN-40A | MARCH-31B | MEXBOROUGH-36B |
| Aug-53 | COLWICK-38A | SPRINGHEAD-53C | W.HALSE-38E | DONCASTER-36A | MARCH-31B | | 5/53: IMM - 40B | MARCH-31B | MEXBOROUGH-36B |
| Jan-54 | COLWICK-38A | SPRINGHEAD-53C | W.HALSE-38E | DONCASTER-36A | 11/53: IMM - 40B | | IMMINGHAM-40B | 10/53: IMM - 40B | MEXBOROUGH-36B |
| Aug-54 | COLWICK-38A | SPRINGHEAD-53C | W.HALSE-38E | 6/54: MEX - 36B | IMMINGHAM-40B | | IMMINGHAM-40B | IMMINGHAM-40B | MEXBOROUGH-36B |
| Jan-55 | COLWICK-38A | SPRINGHEAD-53C | W.HALSE-38E | MEXBOROUGH-36B | IMMINGHAM-40B | | IMMINGHAM-40B | IMMINGHAM-40B | MEXBOROUGH-36B |
| Aug-55 | COLWICK-38A | SPRINGHEAD-53C | W.HALSE-38E | MEXBOROUGH-36B | IMMINGHAM-40B | | IMMINGHAM-40B | IMMINGHAM-40B | MEXBOROUGH-36B |
| Jan-56 | COLWICK-38A | SPRINGHEAD-53C | W.HALSE-38E | MEXBOROUGH-36B | IMMINGHAM-40B | | IMMINGHAM-40B | IMMINGHAM-40B | MEXBOROUGH-36B |
| Aug-56 | COLWICK-38A | SPRINGHEAD-53C | W.HALSE-38E | MEXBOROUGH-36B | IMMINGHAM-40B | | IMMINGHAM-40B | IMMINGHAM-40B | MEXBOROUGH-36B |
| Jan-57 | COLWICK-38A | SPRINGHEAD-53C | W.HALSE-38E | MEXBOROUGH-36B | IMMINGHAM-40B | | IMMINGHAM-40B | IMMINGHAM-40B | 3/57: POL - 66A |
| Aug-57 | COLWICK-38A | SPRINGHEAD-53C | W.HALSE-38E | MEXBOROUGH-36B | IMMINGHAM-40B | | IMMINGHAM-40B | IMMINGHAM-40B | POLMADIE-66A |
| Jan-58 | COLWICK-38A | SPRINGHEAD-53C | W.HALSE-38E | MEXBOROUGH-36B | IMMINGHAM-40B | | IMMINGHAM-40B | IMMINGHAM-40B | POLMADIE-66A |
| Aug-58 | COLWICK-40E | SPRINGHEAD-53C | W.HALSE-2F | MEXBOROUGH-41F | IMMINGHAM-40B | | IMMINGHAM-40B | IMMINGHAM-40B | POLMADIE-66A |
| Jan-59 | COLWICK-40E | 10/58: DAIRY - 53A | W.HALSE-2F | MEXBOROUGH-41F | IMMINGHAM-40B | | 2/59: NEW.E - 35A | IMMINGHAM-40B | POLMADIE-66A |
| Aug-59 | COLWICK-40E | DAIRYCOATES-53A | W.HALSE-2F | MEXBOROUGH-41F | IMMINGHAM-40B | | NEWENGLAND-34E | IMMINGHAM-40B | POLMADIE-66A |
| Nov-59 | COLWICK-40E | DAIRYCOATES-53A | W.HALSE-2F | MEXBOROUGH-41F | IMMINGHAM-40B | | NEWENGLAND-34E | IMMINGHAM-40B | POLMADIE-66A |
| Jan-60 | COLWICK-40E | DAIRYCOATES-53A | W.HALSE-2F | MEXBOROUGH-41F | IMMINGHAM-40B | | NEWENGLAND-34E | IMMINGHAM-40B | POLMADIE-66A |
| Apr-60 | 5/60: NEW.E - 35A | DAIRYCOATES-50B | W.HALSE-2F | MEXBOROUGH-41F | IMMINGHAM-40B | | NEWENGLAND-34E | IMMINGHAM-40B | POLMADIE-66A |
| Aug-60 | NEWENGLAND-34E | DAIRYCOATES-50B | W.HALSE-2F | MEXBOROUGH-41F | IMMINGHAM-40B | | NEWENGLAND-34E | IMMINGHAM-40B | POLMADIE-66A |
| Nov-60 | NEWENGLAND-34E | DAIRYCOATES-50B | W.HALSE-2F | MEXBOROUGH-41F | IMMINGHAM-40B | | NEWENGLAND-34E | IMMINGHAM-40B | POLMADIE-66A |

| | 90230 | 90232 | 90233 | 90235 | 90236 | 90239 | 90240 | 90242 | 90243 |
|---|---|---|---|---|---|---|---|---|---|
| Aug-50 | NEWPORT-51B | MEXBOROUGH-36B | SPRINGHEAD-53C | YORK-50A | | NEWENGLAND-35A | STOCKTON-51E | Ex LM | |
| Jan-51 | NEWPORT-51B | MEXBOROUGH-36B | SPRINGHEAD-53C | YORK-50A | | NEWENGLAND-35A | STOCKTON-51E | 11/50: COLW - 38A | |
| Aug-51 | NEWPORT-51B | MEXBOROUGH-36B | MEXBOROUGH-36B | 10/51: DAIRY - 53A | | NEWENGLAND-35A | STOCKTON-51E | COLWICK-38A | |
| Jan-52 | NEWPORT-51B | MEXBOROUGH-36B | 10/51: S'HEAD - 53C | 1:51: To LM | | NEWENGLAND-35A | STOCKTON-51E | COLWICK-38A | |
| Aug-52 | NEWPORT-51B | MEXBOROUGH-36B | SPRINGHEAD-53C | 6/52: COLW - 38A | | NEWENGLAND-35A | STOCKTON-51E | 4/52: To LM | |
| Jan-53 | NEWPORT-51B | MEXBOROUGH-36B | SPRINGHEAD-53C | COLWICK-38A | | NEWENGLAND-35A | STOCKTON-51E | | |
| Aug-53 | NEWPORT-51B | 5/53: FROD - 36C | SPRINGHEAD-53C | COLWICK-38A | | NEWENGLAND-35A | STOCKTON-51E | | |
| Jan-54 | NEWPORT-51B | FRODINGHAM-36C | SPRINGHEAD-53C | COLWICK-38A | | NEWENGLAND-35A | STOCKTON-51E | | |
| Aug-54 | NEWPORT-51B | FRODINGHAM-36C | SPRINGHEAD-53C | COLWICK-38A | | NEWENGLAND-35A | STOCKTON-51E | | |
| Jan-55 | NEWPORT-51B | FRODINGHAM-36C | SPRINGHEAD-53C | COLWICK-38A | | NEWENGLAND-35A | STOCKTON-51E | | |
| Aug-55 | NEWPORT-51B | FRODINGHAM-36C | SPRINGHEAD-53C | COLWICK-38A | | NEWENGLAND-35A | STOCKTON-51E | | |
| Jan-56 | NEWPORT-51B | FRODINGHAM-36C | SPRINGHEAD-53C | COLWICK-38A | | NEWENGLAND-35A | STOCKTON-51E | | |
| Aug-56 | NEWPORT-51B | FRODINGHAM-36C | SPRINGHEAD-53C | COLWICK-38A | | NEWENGLAND-35A | STOCKTON-51E | | |
| Jan-57 | NEWPORT-51B | FRODINGHAM-36C | SPRINGHEAD-53C | COLWICK-38A | | NEWENGLAND-35A | STOCKTON-51E | | |
| Aug-57 | NEWPORT-51B | FRODINGHAM-36C | SPRINGHEAD-53C | COLWICK-38A | | NEWENGLAND-35A | STOCKTON-51E | | |
| Jan-58 | 11/57: N.HILL - 50B | FRODINGHAM-36C | SPRINGHEAD-53C | COLWICK-38A | Ex LM | NEWENGLAND-35A | 11/57: NEWPT - 51B | | |
| Aug-58 | 6/58: YORK - 50A | FRODINGHAM-36C | SPRINGHEAD-53C | COLWICK-40E | 6/58: YORK - 50A | NEWENGLAND-34E | 6/58: TBY - 51L | | |
| Jan-59 | YORK-50A | FRODINGHAM-36C | 12/58: DAIRY - 53A | COLWICK-40E | YORK-50A | NEWENGLAND-34E | THORNABY-51L | | Ex LM |
| Aug-59 | YORK-50A | FRODINGHAM-36C | 6/59: DARL - 51A | COLWICK-40E | 10/59: WAKE - 56A | NEWENGLAND-34E | THORNABY-51L | | 6/59: ROY - 55D |
| Nov-59 | 10/59: WAKE - 56A | FRODINGHAM-36C | 9/59: TBY - 51L | COLWICK-40E | 11/59: LOW. M - 56F | NEWENGLAND-34E | THORNABY-51L | | ROYSTON-55D |
| Jan-60 | WAKEFIELD-56A | FRODINGHAM-36C | 10/59: MIR - 56D | COLWICK-40E | LOWMOOR-56F | NEWENGLAND-34E | THORNABY-51L | | ROYSTON-55D |
| Apr-60 | WAKEFIELD-56A | FRODINGHAM-36C | MIRFIELD-56D | COLWICK-40E | LOWMOOR-56F | NEWENGLAND-34E | THORNABY-51L | | ROYSTON-55D |
| Aug-60 | WAKEFIELD-56A | FRODINGHAM-36C | 6/60: SOW.B - 56E | COLWICK-40E | LOWMOOR-56F | NEWENGLAND-34E | THORNABY-51L | | ROYSTON-55D |
| Nov-60 | WAKEFIELD-56A | FRODINGHAM-36C | SOWERBYBRIDGE-56E | 11/60: DCTR - 36A | LOWMOOR-56F | NEWENGLAND-34E | THORNABY-51L | | ROYSTON-55D |

| | 90244 | 90246 | 90247 | 90248 | 90249 | 90250 | 90251 | 90252 | 90253 |
|---|---|---|---|---|---|---|---|---|---|
| Aug-50 | NEWENGLAND-35A | MEXBOROUGH-36B | | EDINBURGH(SM)-64A | | MEXBOROUGH-36B | COLWICK-38A | MEXBOROUGH-36B | NEWENGLAND-35A |
| Jan-51 | NEWENGLAND-35A | MEXBOROUGH-36B | | EDINBURGH(SM)-64A | | MEXBOROUGH-36B | COLWICK-38A | MEXBOROUGH-36B | NEWENGLAND-35A |
| Aug-51 | NEWENGLAND-35A | MEXBOROUGH-36B | | 8/51: To LM | | MEXBOROUGH-36B | COLWICK-38A | MEXBOROUGH-36B | NEWENGLAND-35A |
| Jan-52 | NEWENGLAND-35A | 10/51: NEW.E - 35A | | | | MEXBOROUGH-36B | 10/51: To WR | MEXBOROUGH-36B | NEWENGLAND-35A |
| Aug-52 | NEWENGLAND-35A | NEWENGLAND-35A | | | | MEXBOROUGH-36B | | MEXBOROUGH-36B | NEWENGLAND-35A |
| Jan-53 | NEWENGLAND-35A | NEWENGLAND-35A | | | | MEXBOROUGH-36B | | MEXBOROUGH-36B | NEWENGLAND-35A |
| Aug-53 | NEWENGLAND-35A | NEWENGLAND-35A | | | | MEXBOROUGH-36B | | MEXBOROUGH-36B | NEWENGLAND-35A |
| Jan-54 | NEWENGLAND-35A | NEWENGLAND-35A | | | | MEXBOROUGH-36B | | MEXBOROUGH-36B | NEWENGLAND-35A |
| Aug-54 | NEWENGLAND-35A | NEWENGLAND-35A | | | | MEXBOROUGH-36B | | MEXBOROUGH-36B | NEWENGLAND-35A |
| Jan-55 | NEWENGLAND-35A | NEWENGLAND-35A | | | | MEXBOROUGH-36B | | MEXBOROUGH-36B | NEWENGLAND-35A |
| Aug-55 | NEWENGLAND-35A | NEWENGLAND-35A | | | | MEXBOROUGH-36B | | MEXBOROUGH-36B | NEWENGLAND-35A |
| Jan-56 | 1/56: COLW - 38A | NEWENGLAND-35A | | | | MEXBOROUGH-36B | | MEXBOROUGH-36B | NEWENGLAND-35A |
| Aug-56 | 2/56: NEW.E - 35A | NEWENGLAND-35A | | | | MEXBOROUGH-36B | | MEXBOROUGH-36B | NEWENGLAND-35A |
| Jan-57 | NEWENGLAND-35A | NEWENGLAND-35A | Ex L&Y | | | MEXBOROUGH-36B | | MEXBOROUGH-36B | NEWENGLAND-35A |
| Aug-57 | NEWENGLAND-35A | NEWENGLAND-35A | | | | MEXBOROUGH-36B | | MEXBOROUGH-36B | NEWENGLAND-35A |
| Jan-58 | NEWENGLAND-35A | NEWENGLAND-35A | 10/57: NORM - 55E | | | MEXBOROUGH-36B | | MEXBOROUGH-36B | NEWENGLAND-35A |
| Aug-58 | 5/58: PLAIS - 33A | NEWENGLAND-34E | NORMANTON-55E | | | MEXBOROUGH-41F | | MEXBOROUGH-41F | NEWENGLAND-34E |
| Jan-59 | PLAISTOW-33A | NEWENGLAND-34E | NORMANTON-55E | | Ex LM | MEXBOROUGH-41F | | MEXBOROUGH-41F | NEWENGLAND-34E |
| Aug-59 | 6/59: MARCH - 31B | NEWENGLAND-34E | NORMANTON-55E | | | MEXBOROUGH-41F | | MEXBOROUGH-41F | NEWENGLAND-34E |
| Nov-59 | 9/59: PLAIS - 33A | NEWENGLAND-34E | NORMANTON-55E | | 10/5(: NOR - 55E | MEXBOROUGH-41F | | MEXBOROUGH-41F | NEWENGLAND-34E |
| Jan-60 | 10/59: TIL - 33B | NEWENGLAND-34E | NORMANTON-55E | | NORMANTON-55E | MEXBOROUGH-41F | | MEXBOROUGH-41F | NEWENGLAND-34E |
| Apr-60 | TILBURY-33B | NEWENGLAND-34E | NORMANTON-55E | | NORMANTON-55E | MEXBOROUGH-41F | | MEXBOROUGH-41F | NEWENGLAND-34E |
| Aug-60 | TILBURY-33B | NEWENGLAND-34E | NORMANTON-55E | | NORMANTON-55E | MEXBOROUGH-41F | | MEXBOROUGH-41F | NEWENGLAND-34E |
| Nov-60 | TILBURY-33B | NEWENGLAND-34E | NORMANTON-55E | | NORMANTON-55E | MEXBOROUGH-41F | | MEXBOROUGH-41F | NEWENGLAND-34E |

| | 90254 | 90255 | 90256 | 90259 | 90260 | 90263 | 90265 | 90269 | 90270 |
|---|---|---|---|---|---|---|---|---|---|
| Aug-50 | | MEXBOROUGH-36B | NEWENGLAND-35A | NEWENGLAND-35A | FERRYHILL-61B | WOODFORD HALSE-38E | EASTFIELD-65A | STAVELEY-38D | MEXBOROUGH-36B |
| Jan-51 | | MEXBOROUGH-36B | NEWENGLAND-35A | NEWENGLAND-35A | FERRYHILL-61B | WOODFORD HALSE-38E | EASTFIELD-65A | STAVELEY-38D | MEXBOROUGH-36B |
| Aug-51 | | MEXBOROUGH-36B | NEWENGLAND-35A | NEWENGLAND-35A | 8/51: To LM | WOODFORD HALSE-38E | 8/51: To LM | STAVELEY-38D | 5/51: DCTR - 36A |
| Jan-52 | | MEXBOROUGH-36B | 10/51: To LM | NEWENGLAND-35A | | WOODFORD HALSE-38E | | STAVELEY-38D | DONCASTER-36A |
| Aug-52 | | MEXBOROUGH-36B | | NEWENGLAND-35A | | 11/52: STAVE - 38D | | STAVELEY-38D | DONCASTER-36A |
| Jan-53 | | MEXBOROUGH-36B | | NEWENGLAND-35A | | 1/53: WFD.H - 38E | | STAVELEY-38D | DONCASTER-36A |
| Aug-53 | | MEXBOROUGH-36B | | NEWENGLAND-35A | | 5/53: COLW - 38A | | STAVELEY-38D | DONCASTER-36A |
| Jan-54 | | MEXBOROUGH-36B | | NEWENGLAND-35A | | COLWICK-38A | | STAVELEY-38D | DONCASTER-36A |
| Aug-54 | | MEXBOROUGH-36B | | NEWENGLAND-35A | | COLWICK-38A | | 6/54: COLW - 38A | DONCASTER-36A |
| Jan-55 | | MEXBOROUGH-36B | | 1/55: L. JCN - 40E | | COLWICK-38A | | COLWICK-38A | DONCASTER-36A |
| Aug-55 | | MEXBOROUGH-36B | 6/55: PLAIS - 33A | LANGWITHJCN-40E | | COLWICK-38A | | COLWICK-38A | 5/55: MEX - 36B |
| Jan-56 | | MEXBOROUGH-36B | PLAISTOW-33A | LANGWITHJCN-40E | | COLWICK-38A | | COLWICK-38A | MEXBOROUGH-36B |
| Aug-56 | | MEXBOROUGH-36B | PLAISTOW-33A | LANGWITHJCN-40E | | COLWICK-38A | | COLWICK-38A | MEXBOROUGH-36B |
| Jan-57 | | 10/56: MARCH - 31B | PLAISTOW-33A | LANGWITHJCN-40E | | COLWICK-38A | | COLWICK-38A | MEXBOROUGH-36B |
| Aug-57 | | 3/57: DCTR - 36A | PLAISTOW-33A | LANGWITHJCN-40E | | COLWICK-38A | Ex LM | COLWICK-38A | MEXBOROUGH-36B |
| Jan-58 | | DONCASTER-36A | PLAISTOW-33A | LANGWITHJCN-40E | | COLWICK-38A | 3/58: S'HEAD - 53C | COLWICK-38A | MEXBOROUGH-36B |
| Aug-58 | | DONCASTER-36A | PLAISTOW-33A | LANGWITHJCN-41J | | COLWICK-40E | 6/58: GOOLE - 53E | COLWICK-40E | MEXBOROUGH-41F |
| Jan-59 | | DONCASTER-36A | PLAISTOW-33A | LANGWITHJCN-41J | | 12/58: IMM - 40B | GOOLE-53E | 1/59: NEW.E - 35A | MEXBOROUGH-41F |
| Aug-59 | | DONCASTER-36A | PLAISTOW-33A | LANGWITHJCN-41J | | 8/59: COLW - 40E | GOOLE-53E | NEWENGLAND-34E | MEXBOROUGH-41F |
| Nov-59 | NORMANTON-55E | DONCASTER-36A | 10/59: TIL - 33B | LANGWITHJCN-41J | | COLWICK-40E | GOOLE-53E | NEWENGLAND-34E | MEXBOROUGH-41F |
| Jan-60 | NORMANTON-55E | DONCASTER-36A | TILBURY-33B | LANGWITHJCN-41J | | COLWICK-40E | GOOLE-53E | NEWENGLAND-34E | MEXBOROUGH-41F |
| Apr-60 | NORMANTON-55E | DONCASTER-36A | TILBURY-33B | 5/60: COLW - 40E | | COLWICK-40E | GOOLE-50D | NEWENGLAND-34E | MEXBOROUGH-41F |
| Aug-60 | NORMANTON-55E | DONCASTER-36A | TILBURY-33B | COLWICK-40E | | COLWICK-40E | GOOLE-50D | NEWENGLAND-34E | MEXBOROUGH-41F |
| Nov-60 | NORMANTON-55E | DONCASTER-36A | TILBURY-33B | COLWICK-40E | | COLWICK-40E | GOOLE-50D | NEWENGLAND-34E | MEXBOROUGH-41F |

| | 90272 | 90273 | 90275 | 90276 | 90278 | 90279 | 90280 | 90281 | 90282 |
|---|---|---|---|---|---|---|---|---|---|
| Aug-50 | TYNE DOCK-54B | NEWPORT-51B | MARCH-31B | STAVELEY-38D | DUNFERMLINE-62C | NEWENGLAND-35A | MEXBOROUGH-36B | | THORNTON JCN-62A |
| Jan-51 | 2/51: DAIRY - 53A | NEWPORT-51B | MARCH-31B | STAVELEY-38D | DUNFERMLINE-62C | NEWENGLAND-35A | MEXBOROUGH-36B | | THORNTON JCN-62A |
| Aug-51 | DAIRYCOATES-53A | NEWPORT-51B | MARCH-31B | STAVELEY-38D | 8/51: To LM | NEWENGLAND-35A | 5/51: MARCH - 31B | | 8/51: To LM |
| Jan-52 | DAIRYCOATES-53A | NEWPORT-51B | MARCH-31B | STAVELEY-38D | | NEWENGLAND-35A | MARCH-31B | | |
| Aug-52 | DAIRYCOATES-53A | NEWPORT-51B | MARCH-31B | STAVELEY-38D | | NEWENGLAND-35A | MARCH-31B | | |
| Jan-53 | DAIRYCOATES-53A | NEWPORT-51B | MARCH-31B | STAVELEY-38D | | NEWENGLAND-35A | MARCH-31B | | |
| Aug-53 | DAIRYCOATES-53A | NEWPORT-51B | MARCH-31B | STAVELEY-38D | | NEWENGLAND-35A | MARCH-31B | | |
| Jan-54 | DAIRYCOATES-53A | NEWPORT-51B | 11/53: IMM - 40B | STAVELEY-38D | | NEWENGLAND-35A | 10/53: IMM - 40B | | |
| Aug-54 | DAIRYCOATES-53A | NEWPORT-51B | IMMINGHAM-40B | 6/54: COLW - 38A | | NEWENGLAND-35A | IMMINGHAM-40B | | |
| Jan-55 | DAIRYCOATES-53A | NEWPORT-51B | IMMINGHAM-40B | COLWICK-38A | | NEWENGLAND-35A | IMMINGHAM-40B | | |
| Aug-55 | DAIRYCOATES-53A | NEWPORT-51B | 8/55: L. JN - 40E | COLWICK-38A | | NEWENGLAND-35A | IMMINGHAM-40B | | |
| Jan-56 | DAIRYCOATES-53A | NEWPORT-51B | LANGWITHJCN-40E | 1/56: STAVE - 38D | | NEWENGLAND-35A | IMMINGHAM-40B | | |
| Aug-56 | DAIRYCOATES-53A | NEWPORT-51B | LANGWITHJCN-40E | STAVELEY-38D | | NEWENGLAND-35A | IMMINGHAM-40B | | |
| Jan-57 | DAIRYCOATES-53A | NEWPORT-51B | LANGWITHJCN-40E | STAVELEY-38D | | NEWENGLAND-35A | IMMINGHAM-40B | | |
| Aug-57 | DAIRYCOATES-53A | NEWPORT-51B | LANGWITHJCN-40E | STAVELEY-38D | | NEWENGLAND-35A | IMMINGHAM-40B | | |
| Jan-58 | DAIRYCOATES-53A | NEWPORT-51B | LANGWITHJCN-40E | STAVELEY-38D | | 11/57: MARCH - 31B | IMMINGHAM-40B | | |
| Aug-58 | DAIRYCOATES-53A | 6/58: TBY - 51L | LANGWITHJCN-41J | STAVELEY(GC)-41H | | MARCH-31B | IMMINGHAM-40B | | |
| Jan-59 | DAIRYCOATES-53A | THORNABY-51L | LANGWITHJCN-41J | STAVELEY(GC)-41H | | MARCH-31B | IMMINGHAM-40B | Ex LM | |
| Aug-59 | DAIRYCOATES-53A | THORNABY-51L | LANGWITHJCN-41J | STAVELEY(GC)-41H | | MARCH-31B | IMMINGHAM-40B | 6/59: MIR - 56D | |
| Nov-59 | DAIRYCOATES-53A | THORNABY-51L | LANGWITHJCN-41J | STAVELEY(GC)-41H | | MARCH-31B | IMMINGHAM-40B | MIRFIELD-56D | |
| Jan-60 | DAIRYCOATES-53A | THORNABY-51L | LANGWITHJCN-41J | 3/60: L. JCN - 41H | | MARCH-31B | IMMINGHAM-40B | MIRFIELD-56D | |
| Apr-60 | DAIRYCOATES-50B | THORNABY-51L | LANGWITHJCN-41J | 4/60: CANK - 41D | | MARCH-31B | IMMINGHAM-40B | MIRFIELD-56D | |
| Aug-60 | DAIRYCOATES-50B | THORNABY-51L | LANGWITHJCN-41J | CANKLOW-41D | | MARCH-31B | IMMINGHAM-40B | 6/60: SOW.B - 56E | |
| Nov-60 | DAIRYCOATES-50B | THORNABY-51L | LANGWITHJCN-41J | CANKLOW-41D | | MARCH-31B | IMMINGHAM-40B | SOWERBYBRIDGE-56E | |

## 90285 – 90294

| | 90285 | 90286 | 90287 | 90288 | 90289 | 90290 | 90291 | 90293 | 90294 |
|---|---|---|---|---|---|---|---|---|---|
| Aug-50 | MEXBOROUGH-36B | MEXBOROUGH-36B | NEW ENGLAND-35A | NEW ENGLAND-35A | EDINBURGH(SM)-64A | MEXBOROUGH-36B | EDINBURGH(SM)-64A | DUNFERMLINE-62C | MARCH-31B |
| Jan-51 | MEXBOROUGH-36B | MEXBOROUGH-36B | NEW ENGLAND-35A | NEW ENGLAND-35A | EDINBURGH(SM)-64A | MEXBOROUGH-36B | EDINBURGH(SM)-64A | DUNFERMLINE-62C | MARCH-31B |
| Aug-51 | MEXBOROUGH-36B | MEXBOROUGH-36B | NEW ENGLAND-35A | NEW ENGLAND-35A | 8/51: To LM | 10/51: MARCH - 31B | 8/51: To LM | DUNFERMLINE-62C | MARCH-31B |
| Jan-52 | 12/51: IMM - 40B | MEXBOROUGH-36B | 11/51: COLW - 38A | NEW ENGLAND-35A | | 2/52: DCTR - 36A | | DUNFERMLINE-62C | MARCH-31B |
| Aug-52 | IMMINGHAM-40B | MEXBOROUGH-36B | COLWICK-38A | NEW ENGLAND-35A | | 3/52: NEW.E - 35A | | 3/52: MARCH - 31B | MARCH-31B |
| Jan-53 | IMMINGHAM-40B | MEXBOROUGH-36B | COLWICK-38A | NEW ENGLAND-35A | | 5/52: DCTR - 36A | | MARCH-31B | MARCH-31B |
| Aug-53 | IMMINGHAM-40B | MEXBOROUGH-36B | COLWICK-38A | 7/53: COLW - 38A | | DONCASTER-36A | | MARCH-31B | MARCH-31B |
| Jan-54 | IMMINGHAM-40B | MEXBOROUGH-36B | COLWICK-38A | COLWICK-38A | | DONCASTER-36A | | MARCH-31B | 11/53: IMM - 40B |
| Aug-54 | IMMINGHAM-40B | MEXBOROUGH-36B | 6/54: L. JCN - 40E | COLWICK-38A | | 6/54: MEX - 36B | | MARCH-31B | IMMINGHAM-40B |
| Jan-55 | IMMINGHAM-40B | MEXBOROUGH-36B | LANGWITH JCN-40E | COLWICK-38A | | MEXBOROUGH-36B | | MARCH-31B | IMMINGHAM-40B |
| Aug-55 | IMMINGHAM-40B | MEXBOROUGH-36B | LANGWITH JCN-40E | COLWICK-38A | | MEXBOROUGH-36B | | MARCH-31B | IMMINGHAM-40B |
| Jan-56 | IMMINGHAM-40B | MEXBOROUGH-36B | LANGWITH JCN-40E | COLWICK-38A | | MEXBOROUGH-36B | | MARCH-31B | IMMINGHAM-40B |
| Aug-56 | IMMINGHAM-40B | MEXBOROUGH-36B | LANGWITH JCN-40E | COLWICK-38A | | MEXBOROUGH-36B | | MARCH-31B | IMMINGHAM-40B |
| Jan-57 | IMMINGHAM-40B | MEXBOROUGH-36B | LANGWITH JCN-40E | COLWICK-38A | | MEXBOROUGH-36B | | MARCH-31B | IMMINGHAM-40B |
| Aug-57 | IMMINGHAM-40B | MEXBOROUGH-36B | LANGWITH JCN-40E | COLWICK-38A | | MEXBOROUGH-36B | | MARCH-31B | IMMINGHAM-40B |
| Jan-58 | IMMINGHAM-40B | MEXBOROUGH-36B | LANGWITH JCN-41F | COLWICK-40E | | MEXBOROUGH-41F | | MARCH-31B | IMMINGHAM-40B |
| Aug-58 | IMMINGHAM-40B | MEXBOROUGH-36B | LANGWITH JCN-41J | COLWICK-40E | | MEXBOROUGH-41F | | MARCH-31B | IMMINGHAM-40B |
| Jan-59 | IMMINGHAM-40B | MEXBOROUGH-41F | LANGWITH JCN-41J | COLWICK-40E | | MEXBOROUGH-41F | | MARCH-31B | IMMINGHAM-40B |
| Aug-59 | IMMINGHAM-40B | MEXBOROUGH-41F | LANGWITH JCN-41J | COLWICK-40E | | MEXBOROUGH-41F | | MARCH-31B | IMMINGHAM-40B |
| Nov-59 | IMMINGHAM-40B | MEXBOROUGH-41F | LANGWITH JCN-41J | COLWICK-40E | | MEXBOROUGH-41F | | MARCH-31B | IMMINGHAM-40B |
| Jan-60 | IMMINGHAM-40B | MEXBOROUGH-41F | 5/60: COLW - 40E | 5/60: IMM - 40B | | MEXBOROUGH-41F | | MARCH-31B | IMMINGHAM-40B |
| Apr-60 | IMMINGHAM-40B | MEXBOROUGH-41F | COLWICK-40E | 8/60: COLW - 40E | | MEXBOROUGH-41F | | MARCH-31B | IMMINGHAM-40B |
| Aug-60 | IMMINGHAM-40B | MEXBOROUGH-41F | COLWICK-40E | 10/60: FROD - 36C | | 5/60: MEX - 41J | | MARCH-31B | IMMINGHAM-40B |
| Nov-60 | IMMINGHAM-40B | MEXBOROUGH-41F | COLWICK-40E | | | 8/60: CANK - 41D | | MARCH-31B | IMMINGHAM-40B |
| | | | | | | CANKLOW-41J | | | |

## 90296 – 90305

| | 90296 | 90298 | 90299 | 90300 | 90301 | 90302 | 90303 | 90304 | 90305 |
|---|---|---|---|---|---|---|---|---|---|
| Aug-50 | MEXBOROUGH-36B | EASTFIELD-65A | STAVELEY-38D | THORNTON JCN-62A | MEXBOROUGH-36B | MARCH-31B | COLWICK-38A | COLCHESTER-30E | NEW ENGLAND-35A |
| Jan-51 | MEXBOROUGH-36B | EASTFIELD-65A | STAVELEY-38D | 9/50: To LM | MEXBOROUGH-36B | MARCH-31B | COLWICK-38A | COLCHESTER-30E | NEW ENGLAND-35A |
| Aug-51 | 5/51: MARCH - 31B | EASTFIELD-65A | STAVELEY-38D | | 5/51: DCTR - 36A | MARCH-31B | COLWICK-38A | 9/51: MARCH - 31B | NEW ENGLAND-35A |
| Jan-52 | MARCH-31B | | STAVELEY-38D | | DONCASTER-36A | MARCH-31B | COLWICK-38A | MARCH-31B | 2/52: DCTR - 36A |
| Aug-52 | MARCH-31B | 3/52: MARCH - 31B | STAVELEY-38D | | DONCASTER-36A | MARCH-31B | COLWICK-38A | MARCH-31B | DONCASTER-36A |
| Jan-53 | MARCH-31B | MARCH-31B | STAVELEY-38D | | DONCASTER-36A | MARCH-31B | COLWICK-38A | 1/53: MEX - 31B | DONCASTER-36A |
| Aug-53 | MARCH-31B | MARCH-31B | STAVELEY-38D | | DONCASTER-36A | 11/53: IMM - 40B | COLWICK-38A | MEXBOROUGH-36B | DONCASTER-36A |
| Jan-54 | 10/53: COLW - 38A | 11/53: IMM - 40B | STAVELEY-38D | | DONCASTER-36A | IMMINGHAM-40B | COLWICK-38A | MEXBOROUGH-36B | DONCASTER-36A |
| Aug-54 | COLWICK-38A | IMMINGHAM-40B | STAVELEY-38D | | DONCASTER-36A | IMMINGHAM-40B | COLWICK-38A | MEXBOROUGH-36B | DONCASTER-36A |
| Jan-55 | COLWICK-38A | IMMINGHAM-40B | 1/55: WFD.H - 38E | | DONCASTER-36A | 8/55: L. JCN - 40E | COLWICK-38A | MEXBOROUGH-36B | DONCASTER-36A |
| Aug-55 | COLWICK-38A | IMMINGHAM-40B | W.HALSE-38E | | DONCASTER-36A | LANGWITH JCN-40E | COLWICK-38A | MEXBOROUGH-36B | DONCASTER-36A |
| Jan-56 | COLWICK-38A | IMMINGHAM-40B | W.HALSE-38E | | DONCASTER-36A | LANGWITH JCN-40E | COLWICK-38A | MEXBOROUGH-36B | DONCASTER-36A |
| Aug-56 | COLWICK-38A | 10/56: MARCH - 31B | W.HALSE-38E | | DONCASTER-36A | LANGWITH JCN-40E | COLWICK-38A | MEXBOROUGH-36B | 10/56: MARCH - 31B |
| Jan-57 | COLWICK-38A | 2/57: STRAT - 30A | W.HALSE-38E | | DONCASTER-36A | LANGWITH JCN-40E | COLWICK-38A | MEXBOROUGH-36B | MARCH-31B |
| Aug-57 | COLWICK-38A | STRATFORD-30A | W.HALSE-38E | | DONCASTER-36A | LANGWITH JCN-40E | COLWICK-38A | MEXBOROUGH-36B | MARCH-31B |
| Jan-58 | COLWICK-40E | STRATFORD-30A | W.HALSE-38E | | 7/58: MEX - 36B | LANGWITH JCN-41J | COLWICK-38A | MEXBOROUGH-41F | MARCH-31B |
| Aug-58 | COLWICK-40E | 10/58: MARCH - 31B | W.HALSE-2F | | MEXBOROUGH-41F | LANGWITH JCN-41J | COLWICK-38A | MEXBOROUGH-41F | MARCH-31B |
| Jan-59 | COLWICK-40E | FRODINGHAM-36C | W.HALSE-2F | Ex LM | MEXBOROUGH-41F | LANGWITH JCN-41J | COLWICK-40E | MEXBOROUGH-41F | MARCH-31B |
| Aug-59 | COLWICK-40E | FRODINGHAM-36C | W.HALSE-2F | 6/59: MIR - 56D | MEXBOROUGH-41F | LANGWITH JCN-41J | COLWICK-40E | MEXBOROUGH-41F | MARCH-31B |
| Nov-59 | COLWICK-40E | FRODINGHAM-36C | W.HALSE-2F | MIRFIELD-56D | MEXBOROUGH-41F | LANGWITH JCN-41J | COLWICK-40E | MEXBOROUGH-41F | MARCH-31B |
| Jan-60 | COLWICK-40E | 2/60: TIL - 33B | W.HALSE-2F | MIRFIELD-56D | 5/60: L. JCN - 41J | LANGWITH JCN-41J | COLWICK-40E | MEXBOROUGH-41F | MARCH-31B |
| Apr-60 | COLWICK-40E | TILBURY-33B | W.HALSE-2F | MIRFIELD-56D | LANGWITH JCN-41J | LANGWITH JCN-41J | COLWICK-40E | MEXBOROUGH-41F | MARCH-31B |
| Aug-60 | COLWICK-40E | TILBURY-33B | W.HALSE-2F | MIRFIELD-56D | LANGWITH JCN-41J | LANGWITH JCN-41J | COLWICK-40E | MEXBOROUGH-41F | MARCH-31B |
| Nov-60 | 11/60: DCTR - 36A | TILBURY-33B | W.HALSE-2F | MIRFIELD-56D | LANGWITH JCN-41J | LANGWITH JCN-41J | COLWICK-40E | MEXBOROUGH-41F | MARCH-31B |

## 90306 – 90322

| | 90306 | 90309 | 90311 | 90313 | 90318 | 90319 | 90320 | 90321 | 90322 |
|---|---|---|---|---|---|---|---|---|---|
| Aug-50 | DUNFERMLINE-62C | TYNE DOCK-54B | MEXBOROUGH-36B | EASTFIELD-65A | | THORNTON JCN-62A | | | |
| Jan-51 | 11/50: EBRO(SM) - 64A | TYNE DOCK-54B | MEXBOROUGH-36B | 7/51: DAWS - 64D | | THORNTON JCN-62A | | | |
| Aug-51 | 8/51: To LM | TYNE DOCK-54B | MEXBOROUGH-36B | 8/51: E'FLD - 65A | | THORNTON JCN-62A | | | |
| Jan-52 | | TYNE DOCK-54B | MEXBOROUGH-36B | 12/51: To WR | | THORNTON JCN-62A | | | |
| Aug-52 | | TYNE DOCK-54B | MEXBOROUGH-36B | | | THORNTON JCN-62A | | | |
| Jan-53 | | TYNE DOCK-54B | MEXBOROUGH-36B | | | THORNTON JCN-62A | | | |
| Aug-53 | | TYNE DOCK-54B | MEXBOROUGH-36B | | | THORNTON JCN-62A | | | |
| Jan-54 | | TYNE DOCK-54B | MEXBOROUGH-36B | | | THORNTON JCN-62A | | | |
| Aug-54 | | TYNE DOCK-54B | MEXBOROUGH-36B | | | THORNTON JCN-62A | | | |
| Jan-55 | | TYNE DOCK-54B | MEXBOROUGH-36B | | | THORNTON JCN-62A | | | |
| Aug-55 | | TYNE DOCK-54B | MEXBOROUGH-36B | | | THORNTON JCN-62A | | | |
| Jan-56 | | TYNE DOCK-54B | MEXBOROUGH-36B | | | THORNTON JCN-62A | | | |
| Aug-56 | | TYNE DOCK-54B | MEXBOROUGH-36B | | | THORNTON JCN-62A | | | |
| Jan-57 | | TYNE DOCK-54B | MEXBOROUGH-36B | | | THORNTON JCN-62A | | | |
| Aug-57 | | 9/57: NOR - 55E | MEXBOROUGH-36B | | | THORNTON JCN-62A | Ex CR | Ex LM | Ex LM |
| Jan-58 | | NORMANTON-55E | MEXBOROUGH-36B | | | THORNTON JCN-62A | 7/57: DAWS - 65D | 6/58: WAKE - 56A | |
| Aug-58 | | NORMANTON-55E | MEXBOROUGH-36B | | | THORNTON JCN-62A | DAWSHOLME-65D | WAKEFIELD-56A | |
| Jan-59 | | NORMANTON-55E | MEXBOROUGH-41F | | | THORNTON JCN-62A | 4/58: POL - 66A | WAKEFIELD-56A | |
| Aug-59 | | NORMANTON-55E | MEXBOROUGH-41F | | Ex LM | THORNTON JCN-62A | POLMADIE-66A | WAKEFIELD-56A | |
| Nov-59 | | NORMANTON-55E | MEXBOROUGH-41F | | 10/59: N'TON - 55E | THORNTON JCN-62A | POLMADIE-66A | WAKEFIELD-56A | |
| Jan-60 | | NORMANTON-55E | MEXBOROUGH-41F | | NORMANTON-55E | THORNTON JCN-62A | POLMADIE-66A | WAKEFIELD-56A | |
| Apr-60 | | NORMANTON-55E | MEXBOROUGH-41F | | NORMANTON-55E | THORNTON JCN-62A | POLMADIE-66A | WAKEFIELD-56A | 2/60: LOW M - 56F |
| Aug-60 | | NORMANTON-55E | MEXBOROUGH-41F | | NORMANTON-55E | THORNTON JCN-62A | POLMADIE-66A | WAKEFIELD-56A | LOW MOOR-56F |
| Nov-60 | | NORMANTON-55E | MEXBOROUGH-41F | | NORMANTON-55E | THORNTON JCN-62A | POLMADIE-66A | WAKEFIELD-56A | LOW MOOR-56F |

## 90323 – 90344

| | 90323 | 90326 | 90330 | 90333 | 90334 | 90336 | 90337 | 90340 | 90344 |
|---|---|---|---|---|---|---|---|---|---|
| Aug-50 | COLWICK-38A | | COLWICK-38A | | | | | MEXBOROUGH-36B | STOCKTON-51E |
| Jan-51 | COLWICK-38A | | 11/50: STAVE - 38D | | | | | MEXBOROUGH-36B | STOCKTON-51E |
| Aug-51 | 9/51: To WR | | 7/51: COLW - 38A | | | | | MEXBOROUGH-36B | STOCKTON-51E |
| Jan-52 | | | COLWICK-38A | | | | | MEXBOROUGH-36B | STOCKTON-51E |
| Aug-52 | | | COLWICK-38A | | | | | MEXBOROUGH-36B | STOCKTON-51E |
| Jan-53 | | | 2/53: MEX - 36B | | | | | MEXBOROUGH-36B | STOCKTON-51E |
| Aug-53 | | | MEXBOROUGH-36B | | | | | MEXBOROUGH-36B | STOCKTON-51E |
| Jan-54 | | | MEXBOROUGH-36B | | | | | MEXBOROUGH-36B | STOCKTON-51E |
| Aug-54 | | | MEXBOROUGH-36B | | | | | MEXBOROUGH-36B | STOCKTON-51E |
| Jan-55 | | | MEXBOROUGH-36B | | | | | MEXBOROUGH-36B | STOCKTON-51E |
| Aug-55 | | | MEXBOROUGH-36B | | | | | MEXBOROUGH-36B | STOCKTON-51E |
| Jan-56 | | | MEXBOROUGH-36B | | | | | MEXBOROUGH-36B | 11/55: W.HPL - 51C |
| Aug-56 | | | MEXBOROUGH-36B | | | | | MEXBOROUGH-36B | W.HARTLEPOOL-51C |
| Jan-57 | | | MEXBOROUGH-36B | | Ex L&Y | | Ex L&Y | 10/56: MARCH - 31B | W.HARTLEPOOL-51C |
| Aug-57 | | | MEXBOROUGH-36B | | 6/57: N'TON - 55E | | 6/57: N'TON - 55E | MARCH-31B | W.HARTLEPOOL-51C |
| Jan-58 | | Ex LM | MEXBOROUGH-36B | Ex LM | NORMANTON-55E | | NORMANTON-55E | MARCH-31B | W.HARTLEPOOL-51C |
| Aug-58 | | 6/58: WAKE - 56A | MEXBOROUGH-36B | 10/58: LOW.M - 56F | NORMANTON-55E | Ex LM | NORMANTON-55E | MARCH-31B | W.HARTLEPOOL-51C |
| Jan-59 | | WAKEFIELD-56A | MEXBOROUGH-41F | LOW MOOR-56F | 1/59: FY JN - 55C | | NORMANTON-55E | MARCH-31B | W.HARTLEPOOL-51C |
| Aug-59 | | WAKEFIELD-56A | MEXBOROUGH-41F | LOW MOOR-56F | FARNLEY JCN-55C | 6/59: ROY - 55D | NORMANTON-55E | MARCH-31B | W.HARTLEPOOL-51C |
| Nov-59 | | WAKEFIELD-56A | MEXBOROUGH-41F | LOW MOOR-56F | FARNLEY JCN-55C | ROYSTON-55D | NORMANTON-55E | MARCH-31B | W.HARTLEPOOL-51C |
| Jan-60 | | WAKEFIELD-56A | MEXBOROUGH-41F | LOW MOOR-56F | FARNLEY JCN-55C | ROYSTON-55D | NORMANTON-55E | MARCH-31B | W.HARTLEPOOL-51C |
| Apr-60 | | WAKEFIELD-56A | MEXBOROUGH-41F | LOW MOOR-56F | FARNLEY JCN-55C | ROYSTON-55D | NORMANTON-55E | MARCH-31B | W.HARTLEPOOL-51C |
| Aug-60 | | WAKEFIELD-56A | MEXBOROUGH-41F | LOW MOOR-56F | FARNLEY JCN-55C | ROYSTON-55D | NORMANTON-55E | MARCH-31B | W.HARTLEPOOL-51C |
| Nov-60 | | WAKEFIELD-56A | MEXBOROUGH-41F | LOW MOOR-56F | FARNLEY JCN-55C | ROYSTON-55D | NORMANTON-55E | MARCH-31B | W.HARTLEPOOL-51C |

| | 90346 | 90348 | 90349 | 90350 | 90351 | 90352 | 90357 | 90358 | 90361 |
|---|---|---|---|---|---|---|---|---|---|
| Aug-50 | NEWENGLAND - 35A | | NEWENGLAND - 35A | THORNTONJCN - 62A | | TYNEDOCK - 54B | | COLWICK - 38A | |
| Jan-51 | NEWENGLAND - 35A | | NEWENGLAND - 35A | THORNTONJCN - 62A | | TYNEDOCK - 54B | | 11/50: STAVE - 38D | |
| Aug-51 | 9/51: IMM - 40B | | NEWENGLAND - 35A | THORNTONJCN - 62A | | 9/51: DAIRY - 53A | | 3/51: COLW - 38A | |
| Jan-52 | 12/51: STAVE - 38D | | NEWENGLAND - 35A | THORNTONJCN - 62A | | DAIRYCOATES - 53A | | COLWICK - 38A | |
| Aug-52 | 6/52: COLW - 38A | | NEWENGLAND - 35A | THORNTONJCN - 62A | | DAIRYCOATES - 53A | | COLWICK - 38A | |
| Jan-53 | COLWICK - 38A | | NEWENGLAND - 35A | THORNTONJCN - 62A | | DAIRYCOATES - 53A | | 2/53: MEX - 36B | |
| Aug-53 | COLWICK - 38A | | NEWENGLAND - 35A | THORNTONJCN - 62A | | DAIRYCOATES - 53A | | MEXBOROUGH - 36B | |
| Jan-54 | COLWICK - 38A | | NEWENGLAND - 35A | THORNTONJCN - 62A | | DAIRYCOATES - 53A | | MEXBOROUGH - 36B | |
| Aug-54 | COLWICK - 38A | | NEWENGLAND - 35A | THORNTONJCN - 62A | | DAIRYCOATES - 53A | | MEXBOROUGH - 36B | |
| Jan-55 | COLWICK - 38A | | NEWENGLAND - 35A | THORNTONJCN - 62A | | DAIRYCOATES - 53A | | MEXBOROUGH - 36B | |
| Aug-55 | COLWICK - 38A | | NEWENGLAND - 35A | THORNTONJCN - 62A | | DAIRYCOATES - 53A | | MEXBOROUGH - 36B | |
| Jan-56 | COLWICK - 38A | | NEWENGLAND - 35A | THORNTONJCN - 62A | | 11/55: S'HEAD - 53C | | MEXBOROUGH - 36B | |
| Aug-56 | COLWICK - 38A | | NEWENGLAND - 35A | THORNTONJCN - 62A | | SPRINGHEAD - 53C | | MEXBOROUGH - 36B | |
| Jan-57 | 11/56: WFD.H - 38E | | NEWENGLAND - 35A | THORNTONJCN - 62A | | SPRINGHEAD - 53C | Ex L&Y | MEXBOROUGH - 36B | |
| Aug-57 | W.HALSE - 38E | | NEWENGLAND - 35A | THORNTONJCN - 62A | | SPRINGHEAD - 53C | 6/57: NOR - 55E | MEXBOROUGH - 36B | |
| Jan-58 | W.HALSE - 38E | Ex LM | NEWENGLAND - 35A | THORNTONJCN - 62A | | SPRINGHEAD - 53C | NORMANTON - 55E | MEXBOROUGH - 36B | |
| Aug-58 | W.HALSE - 2F | 6/58: WAKE - 56A | NEWENGLAND - 34E | THORNTONJCN - 62A | | SPRINGHEAD - 53C | NORMANTON - 55E | MEXBOROUGH - 41F | |
| Jan-59 | W.HALSE - 2F | WAKEFIELD - 56A | NEWENGLAND - 34E | THORNTONJCN - 62A | Ex LM | 12/58: DAIRY - 53A | NORMANTON - 55E | MEXBOROUGH - 41F | |
| Aug-59 | W.HALSE - 2F | WAKEFIELD - 56A | NEWENGLAND - 34E | THORNTONJCN - 62A | 6/59: MIR - 56D | DAIRYCOATES - 53A | NORMANTON - 55E | MEXBOROUGH - 41F | |
| Nov-59 | W.HALSE - 2F | WAKEFIELD - 56A | NEWENGLAND - 34E | THORNTONJCN - 62A | MIRFIELD - 56D | DAIRYCOATES - 53A | NORMANTON - 55E | MEXBOROUGH - 41F | |
| Jan-60 | W.HALSE - 2F | WAKEFIELD - 56A | NEWENGLAND - 34E | THORNTONJCN - 62A | 2/60: LOW.M - 56F | DAIRYCOATES - 53A | NORMANTON - 55E | MEXBOROUGH - 41F | |
| Apr-60 | W.HALSE - 2F | WAKEFIELD - 56A | NEWENGLAND - 34E | THORNTONJCN - 62A | LOWMOOR - 56F | DAIRYCOATES - 50B | NORMANTON - 55E | MEXBOROUGH - 41F | Ex LM |
| Aug-60 | W.HALSE - 2F | WAKEFIELD - 56A | NEWENGLAND - 34E | THORNTONJCN - 62A | LOWMOOR - 56F | DAIRYCOATES - 50B | NORMANTON - 55E | MEXBOROUGH - 41F | 6/60: ARDS - 56B |
| Nov-60 | W.HALSE - 2F | WAKEFIELD - 56A | NEWENGLAND - 34E | THORNTONJCN - 62A | LOWMOOR - 56F | DAIRYCOATES - 50B | NORMANTON - 55E | MEXBOROUGH - 41F | ARDSLEY - 56B |

| | 90362 | 90363 | 90365 | 90368 | 90369 | 90373 | 90376 | 90377 | 90378 |
|---|---|---|---|---|---|---|---|---|---|
| Aug-50 | | | W.HALSE - 38E | COLWICK - 38A | COLWICK - 38A | NEWPORT - 51B | EDINBURGH(SM) - 64A | STOCKTON - 51E | SPRINGHEAD - 53C |
| Jan-51 | | | W.HALSE - 38E | COLWICK - 38A | COLWICK - 38A | NEWPORT - 51B | EDINBURGH(SM) - 64A | STOCKTON - 51E | 9/50: DAIRY - 53A |
| Aug-51 | | | W.HALSE - 38E | COLWICK - 38A | COLWICK - 38A | NEWPORT - 51B | 8/51: To LM | STOCKTON - 51E | DAIRYCOATES - 53A |
| Jan-52 | | | W.HALSE - 38E | COLWICK - 38A | COLWICK - 38A | NEWPORT - 51B | | STOCKTON - 51E | DAIRYCOATES - 53A |
| Aug-52 | | | W.HALSE - 38E | COLWICK - 38A | 7/52: WFD.H - 38E | NEWPORT - 51B | | STOCKTON - 51E | DAIRYCOATES - 53A |
| Jan-53 | | | W.HALSE - 38E | COLWICK - 38A | 9/52: COLW - 38A | NEWPORT - 51B | | STOCKTON - 51E | DAIRYCOATES - 53A |
| Aug-53 | | | W.HALSE - 38E | COLWICK - 38A | COLWICK - 38A | NEWPORT - 51B | | STOCKTON - 51E | DAIRYCOATES - 53A |
| Jan-54 | | | W.HALSE - 38E | COLWICK - 38A | COLWICK - 38A | NEWPORT - 51B | | STOCKTON - 51E | DAIRYCOATES - 53A |
| Aug-54 | | | W.HALSE - 38E | COLWICK - 38A | 3/54: To LM | NEWPORT - 51B | | STOCKTON - 51E | DAIRYCOATES - 53A |
| Jan-55 | | | W.HALSE - 38E | COLWICK - 38A | | NEWPORT - 51B | | STOCKTON - 51E | DAIRYCOATES - 53A |
| Aug-55 | | | W.HALSE - 38E | COLWICK - 38A | | NEWPORT - 51B | | STOCKTON - 51E | DAIRYCOATES - 53A |
| Jan-56 | | | W.HALSE - 38E | COLWICK - 38A | | NEWPORT - 51B | | STOCKTON - 51E | DAIRYCOATES - 53A |
| Aug-56 | | | W.HALSE - 38E | COLWICK - 38A | | NEWPORT - 51B | | STOCKTON - 51E | DAIRYCOATES - 53A |
| Jan-57 | Ex L&Y | Ex L&Y | W.HALSE - 38E | COLWICK - 38A | | NEWPORT - 51B | | STOCKTON - 51E | 12/56: S'HEAD - 53C |
| Aug-57 | 6/57: NOR - 55E | 6/57: NOR - 55E | W.HALSE - 38E | COLWICK - 38A | | NEWPORT - 51B | | STOCKTON - 51E | SPRINGHEAD - 53C |
| Jan-58 | NORMANTON - 55E | 2/58: WAKE - 56A | W.HALSE - 38E | COLWICK - 38A | | NEWPORT - 51B | | STOCKTON - 51E | 2/58: DAIRY - 53A |
| Aug-58 | NORMANTON - 55E | WAKEFIELD - 56A | W.HALSE - 2F | COLWICK - 40E | | 6/58: TBY - 51L | | 6/58: TBY - 51L | 5/58: S'HEAD - 53C |
| Jan-59 | NORMANTON - 55E | WAKEFIELD - 56A | W.HALSE - 2F | COLWICK - 40E | | THORNABY - 51L | | THORNABY - 51L | 12/58: DAIRY - 53A |
| Aug-59 | NORMANTON - 55E | WAKEFIELD - 56A | W.HALSE - 2F | 9/59: CANK - 41D | | THORNABY - 51L | | 6/59: DARL - 51A | DAIRYCOATES - 53A |
| Nov-59 | NORMANTON - 55E | WAKEFIELD - 56A | W.HALSE - 2F | CANKLOW - 41D | | THORNABY - 51L | | 9/59: TBY - 51L | DAIRYCOATES - 53A |
| Jan-60 | NORMANTON - 55E | WAKEFIELD - 56A | W.HALSE - 2F | CANKLOW - 41D | | THORNABY - 51L | | THORNABY - 51L | DAIRYCOATES - 53A |
| Apr-60 | NORMANTON - 55E | WAKEFIELD - 56A | W.HALSE - 2F | CANKLOW - 41D | | THORNABY - 51L | | THORNABY - 51L | DAIRYCOATES - 50B |
| Aug-60 | NORMANTON - 55E | WAKEFIELD - 56A | W.HALSE - 2F | CANKLOW - 41D | | 6/60: DARL - 51A | | THORNABY - 51L | DAIRYCOATES - 50B |
| Nov-60 | NORMANTON - 55E | WAKEFIELD - 56A | W.HALSE - 2F | CANKLOW - 41D | | DARLINGTON - 51A | | THORNABY - 51L | DAIRYCOATES - 50B |

| | 90382 | 90383 | 90384 | 90391 | 90392 | 90393 | 90394 | 90395 | 90397 |
|---|---|---|---|---|---|---|---|---|---|
| Aug-50 | DAIRYCOATES - 53A | MEXBOROUGH - 36B | MARCH - 31B | COLWICK - 38A | MARCH - 31B | MARCH - 31B | STAVELEY - 38D | | |
| Jan-51 | 9/50: H.HILL - 51G | 9/50: MARCH - 31B | MARCH - 31B | COLWICK - 38A | MARCH - 31B | MARCH - 31B | STAVELEY - 38D | | |
| Aug-51 | 9/51: DAIRY - 53A | 2/51: MEX - 36B | MARCH - 31B | COLWICK - 38A | MARCH - 31B | MARCH - 31B | STAVELEY - 38D | | |
| Jan-52 | DAIRYCOATES - 53A | 5/51: DCTR - 36A | MARCH - 31B | COLWICK - 38A | MARCH - 31B | MARCH - 31B | STAVELEY - 38D | | |
| Aug-52 | DAIRYCOATES - 53A | DONCASTER - 36A | MARCH - 31B | COLWICK - 38A | MARCH - 31B | MARCH - 31B | STAVELEY - 38D | | |
| Jan-53 | DAIRYCOATES - 53A | DONCASTER - 36A | MARCH - 31B | COLWICK - 38A | MARCH - 31B | MARCH - 31B | STAVELEY - 38D | | |
| Aug-53 | DAIRYCOATES - 53A | DONCASTER - 36A | MARCH - 31B | COLWICK - 38A | MARCH - 31B | MARCH - 31B | STAVELEY - 38D | | |
| Jan-54 | DAIRYCOATES - 53A | DONCASTER - 36A | 10/53: COLW - 38A | COLWICK - 38A | 11/53: COLW - 38A | 10/53: IMM - 40B | STAVELEY - 38D | | |
| Aug-54 | DAIRYCOATES - 53A | DONCASTER - 36A | COLWICK - 38A | COLWICK - 38A | 3/54: To LM | IMMINGHAM - 40B | STAVELEY - 38D | | |
| Jan-55 | DAIRYCOATES - 53A | DONCASTER - 36A | COLWICK - 38A | COLWICK - 38A | | IMMINGHAM - 40B | STAVELEY - 38D | | |
| Aug-55 | DAIRYCOATES - 53A | DONCASTER - 36A | COLWICK - 38A | COLWICK - 38A | | IMMINGHAM - 40B | 7/55: COLW - 38A | | |
| Jan-56 | DAIRYCOATES - 53A | DONCASTER - 36A | COLWICK - 38A | 1/56: STAVE - 38D | | IMMINGHAM - 40B | COLWICK - 38A | | |
| Aug-56 | DAIRYCOATES - 53A | DONCASTER - 36A | COLWICK - 38A | STAVELEY - 38D | | IMMINGHAM - 40B | COLWICK - 38A | | |
| Jan-57 | DAIRYCOATES - 53A | 2/57: IMM - 40B | COLWICK - 38A | STAVELEY - 38D | | IMMINGHAM - 40B | COLWICK - 38A | | |
| Aug-57 | 9/57: WAKE - 56A | IMMINGHAM - 40B | COLWICK - 38A | STAVELEY - 38D | | IMMINGHAM - 40B | COLWICK - 38A | | |
| Jan-58 | WAKEFIELD - 56A | IMMINGHAM - 40B | COLWICK - 38A | STAVELEY - 38D | | IMMINGHAM - 40B | COLWICK - 38A | | Ex LM |
| Aug-58 | WAKEFIELD - 56A | IMMINGHAM - 40B | 7/58: MEX - 41F | STAVELEY(GC) - 41H | | IMMINGHAM - 40B | COLWICK - 40E | | 6/58: DARL - 51A |
| Jan-59 | WAKEFIELD - 56A | IMMINGHAM - 40B | MEXBOROUGH - 41F | STAVELEY(GC) - 41H | | IMMINGHAM - 40B | COLWICK - 40E | | 10/58: H.HILL - 51G |
| Aug-59 | WAKEFIELD - 56A | IMMINGHAM - 40B | MEXBOROUGH - 41F | STAVELEY(GC) - 41H | | IMMINGHAM - 40B | COLWICK - 40E | | 6/59: TBY - 51L |
| Nov-59 | WAKEFIELD - 56A | IMMINGHAM - 40B | MEXBOROUGH - 41F | 12/59: CANK - 41D | | IMMINGHAM - 40B | COLWICK - 40E | | 10/59: MIR - 56D |
| Jan-60 | WAKEFIELD - 56A | IMMINGHAM - 40B | MEXBOROUGH - 41F | CANKLOW - 41D | | IMMINGHAM - 40B | COLWICK - 40E | 2/60: ROY - 55D | 2/60: LOW.M - 56F |
| Apr-60 | WAKEFIELD - 56A | IMMINGHAM - 40B | MEXBOROUGH - 41F | CANKLOW - 41D | | IMMINGHAM - 40B | 5/60: IMM - 40B | ROYSTON - 55D | LOWMOOR - 56F |
| Aug-60 | WAKEFIELD - 56A | IMMINGHAM - 40B | MEXBOROUGH - 41F | CANKLOW - 41D | | IMMINGHAM - 40B | IMMINGHAM - 40B | ROYSTON - 55D | LOWMOOR - 56F |
| Nov-60 | WAKEFIELD - 56A | 11/60: COLW - 40E | MEXBOROUGH - 41F | CANKLOW - 41D | | 11/60: COLW - 40E | IMMINGHAM - 40B | ROYSTON - 55D | LOWMOOR - 56F |

| | 90400 | 90401 | 90403 | 90405 | 90406 | 90409 | 90410 | 90411 | 90414 |
|---|---|---|---|---|---|---|---|---|---|
| Aug-50 | MEXBOROUGH - 36B | MEXBOROUGH - 36B | STAVELEY - 38D | STOCKTON - 51E | | DAIRYCOATES - 53A | MEXBOROUGH - 36B | COLWICK - 38A | |
| Jan-51 | MEXBOROUGH - 36B | MEXBOROUGH - 36B | STAVELEY - 38D | STOCKTON - 51E | | DAIRYCOATES - 53A | MEXBOROUGH - 36B | 1/51: ANNES - 38B | |
| Aug-51 | MEXBOROUGH - 36B | MEXBOROUGH - 36B | STAVELEY - 38D | STOCKTON - 51E | | DAIRYCOATES - 53A | MEXBOROUGH - 36B | 6/51: COLW - 38A | |
| Jan-52 | MEXBOROUGH - 36B | MEXBOROUGH - 36B | STAVELEY - 38D | STOCKTON - 51E | | DAIRYCOATES - 53A | MEXBOROUGH - 36B | 9/51: WFD.H - 38E | |
| Aug-52 | MEXBOROUGH - 36B | MEXBOROUGH - 36B | STAVELEY - 38D | STOCKTON - 51E | | DAIRYCOATES - 53A | MEXBOROUGH - 36B | 5/52: COLW - 38A | |
| Jan-53 | MEXBOROUGH - 36B | MEXBOROUGH - 36B | STAVELEY - 38D | STOCKTON - 51E | | DAIRYCOATES - 53A | MEXBOROUGH - 36B | COLWICK - 38A | |
| Aug-53 | MEXBOROUGH - 36B | MEXBOROUGH - 36B | STAVELEY - 38D | STOCKTON - 51E | | DAIRYCOATES - 53A | MEXBOROUGH - 36B | COLWICK - 38A | |
| Jan-54 | MEXBOROUGH - 36B | MEXBOROUGH - 36B | STAVELEY - 38D | STOCKTON - 51E | | DAIRYCOATES - 53A | MEXBOROUGH - 36B | 1/54: MARCH - 31B | |
| Aug-54 | MEXBOROUGH - 36B | MEXBOROUGH - 36B | STAVELEY - 38D | STOCKTON - 51E | | DAIRYCOATES - 53A | MEXBOROUGH - 36B | 4/54: COLW - 38A | |
| Jan-55 | MEXBOROUGH - 36B | MEXBOROUGH - 36B | 1/55: WFD.H - 38E | STOCKTON - 51E | | DAIRYCOATES - 53A | MEXBOROUGH - 36B | 6/54: L.JCN - 40E | |
| Aug-55 | MEXBOROUGH - 36B | MEXBOROUGH - 36B | W.HALSE - 38E | STOCKTON - 51E | | DAIRYCOATES - 53A | MEXBOROUGH - 36B | LANGWITH JCN - 40E | |
| Jan-56 | MEXBOROUGH - 36B | MEXBOROUGH - 36B | W.HALSE - 38E | STOCKTON - 51E | | 11/55: YORK - 50A | MEXBOROUGH - 36B | LANGWITH JCN - 40E | |
| Aug-56 | MEXBOROUGH - 36B | MEXBOROUGH - 36B | W.HALSE - 38E | STOCKTON - 51E | | 6/56: NEWPT - 51B | MEXBOROUGH - 36B | LANGWITH JCN - 40E | |
| Jan-57 | MEXBOROUGH - 36B | MEXBOROUGH - 36B | W.HALSE - 38E | STOCKTON - 51E | | NEWPORT - 51B | MEXBOROUGH - 36B | LANGWITH JCN - 40E | |
| Aug-57 | MEXBOROUGH - 36B | MEXBOROUGH - 36B | W.HALSE - 38E | 6/57: YORK - 50A | | NEWPORT - 51B | MEXBOROUGH - 36B | LANGWITH JCN - 40E | |
| Jan-58 | MEXBOROUGH - 36B | MEXBOROUGH - 36B | W.HALSE - 38E | YORK - 50A | Ex LM | NEWPORT - 51B | MEXBOROUGH - 36B | LANGWITH JCN - 40E | |
| Aug-58 | MEXBOROUGH - 41F | MEXBOROUGH - 41F | W.HALSE - 2F | YORK - 50A | 6/58: DARL - 51A | 6/56: TBY - 51L | MEXBOROUGH - 41F | LANGWITH JCN - 41J | |
| Jan-59 | MEXBOROUGH - 41F | MEXBOROUGH - 41F | W.HALSE - 2F | YORK - 50A | DARLINGTON - 56A | THORNABY - 51L | MEXBOROUGH - 41F | LANGWITH JCN - 41J | Ex L&Y |
| Aug-59 | MEXBOROUGH - 41F | MEXBOROUGH - 41F | W.HALSE - 2F | YORK - 50A | 9/59: TBY - 51L | THORNABY - 51L | MEXBOROUGH - 41F | 6/59: CANK - 41D | 9/59: CANK - 41D |
| Nov-59 | MEXBOROUGH - 41F | MEXBOROUGH - 41F | W.HALSE - 2F | 10/59: WAKE - 56A | THORNABY - 51L | THORNABY - 51L | MEXBOROUGH - 41F | 9/59: IMM - 40B | CANKLOW - 41D |
| Jan-60 | MEXBOROUGH - 41F | MEXBOROUGH - 41F | W.HALSE - 2F | WAKEFIELD - 56A | THORNABY - 51L | THORNABY - 51L | MEXBOROUGH - 41F | 1/60: CANK - 41D | CANKLOW - 41D |
| Apr-60 | MEXBOROUGH - 41F | MEXBOROUGH - 41F | W.HALSE - 2F | WAKEFIELD - 56A | THORNABY - 51L | THORNABY - 51L | MEXBOROUGH - 41F | CANKLOW - 41D | CANKLOW - 41D |
| Aug-60 | MEXBOROUGH - 41F | MEXBOROUGH - 41F | W.HALSE - 2F | 6/60: DARL - 51A | THORNABY - 51L | THORNABY - 51L | MEXBOROUGH - 41F | 8/60: L.JCN - 41J | CANKLOW - 41D |
| Nov-60 | MEXBOROUGH - 41F | MEXBOROUGH - 41F | W.HALSE - 2F | DARLINGTON - 51A | THORNABY - 51L | THORNABY - 51L | MEXBOROUGH - 41F | LANGWITH JCN - 41J | CANKLOW - 41D |

| | 90418 | 90421 | 90422 | 90423 | 90424 | 90425 | 90426 | 90427 | 90428 |
|---|---|---|---|---|---|---|---|---|---|
| Aug-50 | STAVELEY-38D | MEXBOROUGH-36B | MARCH-31B | DARLINGTON-51A | YORK-50A | MARCH-31B | NEWPORT-51B | TWEEDMOUTH-52D | NEWENGLAND-35A |
| Jan-51 | STAVELEY-38D | MEXBOROUGH-36B | 3/51: FROD - 38C | DARLINGTON-51A | YORK-50A | 3/51: FROD - 36C | NEWPORT-51B | 5/51: DAIRY - 53A | NEWENGLAND-35A |
| Aug-51 | STAVELEY-38D | MEXBOROUGH-36B | FRODINGHAM-36C | 9/51: DAIRY - 53A | YORK-50A | FRODINGHAM-36C | NEWPORT-51B | 7/51: S'HEAD - 53C | NEWENGLAND-35A |
| Jan-52 | STAVELEY-38D | MEXBOROUGH-36B | FRODINGHAM-36C | 1/52: To LM | YORK-50A | FRODINGHAM-36C | NEWPORT-51B | SPRINGHEAD-53C | NEWENGLAND-35A |
| Aug-52 | STAVELEY-38D | MEXBOROUGH-36B | FRODINGHAM-36C | 6/52: COLW - 38A | YORK-50A | FRODINGHAM-36C | NEWPORT-51B | SPRINGHEAD-53C | NEWENGLAND-35A |
| Jan-53 | STAVELEY-38D | MEXBOROUGH-36B | FRODINGHAM-36C | COLWICK-38A | YORK-50A | FRODINGHAM-36C | NEWPORT-51B | SPRINGHEAD-53C | NEWENGLAND-35A |
| Aug-53 | STAVELEY-38D | MEXBOROUGH-36B | FRODINGHAM-36C | COLWICK-38A | SELBY-50C | FRODINGHAM-36C | NEWPORT-51B | SPRINGHEAD-53C | NEWENGLAND-35A |
| Jan-54 | STAVELEY-38D | MEXBOROUGH-36B | FRODINGHAM-36C | 3/54: To LM | SELBY-50C | FRODINGHAM-36C | NEWPORT-51B | SPRINGHEAD-53C | NEWENGLAND-35A |
| Aug-54 | STAVELEY-38D | MEXBOROUGH-36B | FRODINGHAM-36C | | YORK-50A | FRODINGHAM-36C | NEWPORT-51B | SPRINGHEAD-53C | NEWENGLAND-35A |
| Jan-55 | STAVELEY-38D | MEXBOROUGH-36B | FRODINGHAM-36C | | YORK-50A | FRODINGHAM-36C | NEWPORT-51B | SPRINGHEAD-53C | NEWENGLAND-35A |
| Aug-55 | 7/55: COLW - 38A | MEXBOROUGH-36B | FRODINGHAM-36C | | YORK-50A | FRODINGHAM-36C | NEWPORT-51B | SPRINGHEAD-53C | NEWENGLAND-35A |
| Jan-56 | 1/56: STAVE - 38D | MEXBOROUGH-36B | FRODINGHAM-36C | | YORK-50A | FRODINGHAM-36C | NEWPORT-51B | SPRINGHEAD-53C | NEWENGLAND-35A |
| Aug-56 | STAVELEY-38D | MEXBOROUGH-36B | FRODINGHAM-36C | | 6/56: NEWPT - 51B | FRODINGHAM-36C | NEWPORT-51B | SPRINGHEAD-53C | NEWENGLAND-35A |
| Jan-57 | STAVELEY-38D | MEXBOROUGH-36B | FRODINGHAM-36C | | NEWPORT-51B | FRODINGHAM-36C | NEWPORT-51B | SPRINGHEAD-53C | NEWENGLAND-35A |
| Aug-57 | STAVELEY-38D | MEXBOROUGH-36B | FRODINGHAM-36C | | 6/57: YORK - 50A | FRODINGHAM-36C | NEWPORT-51B | SPRINGHEAD-53C | NEWENGLAND-35A |
| Jan-58 | STAVELEY-38D | MEXBOROUGH-36B | FRODINGHAM-36C | | YORK-50A | FRODINGHAM-36C | NEWPORT-51B | SPRINGHEAD-53C | NEWENGLAND-35A |
| Aug-58 | STAVELEY(GC)-41H | MEXBOROUGH-41F | FRODINGHAM-36C | | YORK-50A | FRODINGHAM-36C | 6/58: TBY - 51L | SPRINGHEAD-53C | NEWENGLAND-34E |
| Jan-59 | STAVELEY(GC)-41H | MEXBOROUGH-41F | FRODINGHAM-36C | | YORK-50A | FRODINGHAM-36C | THORNABY-51L | 12/58: DAIRY - 53A | NEWENGLAND-34E |
| Aug-59 | STAVELEY(GC)-41H | MEXBOROUGH-41F | FRODINGHAM-36C | | YORK-50A | FRODINGHAM-36C | THORNABY-51L | DAIRYCOATES-53A | NEWENGLAND-34E |
| Nov-59 | STAVELEY(GC)-41H | MEXBOROUGH-41F | FRODINGHAM-36C | | YORK-50A | FRODINGHAM-36C | THORNABY-51L | DAIRYCOATES-53A | NEWENGLAND-34E |
| Jan-60 | STAVELEY(GC)-41H | MEXBOROUGH-41F | FRODINGHAM-36C | | YORK-50A | FRODINGHAM-36C | THORNABY-51L | DAIRYCOATES-53A | NEWENGLAND-34E |
| Apr-60 | 3/60: L.JCN - 41J | MEXBOROUGH-41F | FRODINGHAM-36C | | YORK-50A | FRODINGHAM-36C | THORNABY-51L | DAIRYCOATES-50B | NEWENGLAND-34E |
| Aug-60 | 5/60: SHEFF(MR) - 41B | MEXBOROUGH-41F | FRODINGHAM-36C | | YORK-50A | FRODINGHAM-36C | THORNABY-51L | DAIRYCOATES-50B | NEWENGLAND-34E |
| Nov-60 | SHEFFIELD(MR)-41B | MEXBOROUGH-41F | FRODINGHAM-36C | | YORK-50A | FRODINGHAM-36C | THORNABY-51L | DAIRYCOATES-50B | NEWENGLAND-34E |

| | 90429 | 90430 | 90431 | 90432 | 90433 | 90434 | 90435 | 90436 | 90437 |
|---|---|---|---|---|---|---|---|---|---|
| Aug-50 | SPRINGHEAD-53C | TYNEDOCK-54B | COLCHESTER-30E | YORK-50A | MARCH-31B | NEWPORT-51B | TWEEDMOUTH-52D | EDINBURGH(SM)-64A | COLWICK-38A |
| Jan-51 | SPRINGHEAD-53C | TYNEDOCK-54B | COLCHESTER-30E | YORK-50A | MARCH-31B | NEWPORT-51B | 11/50: DAIRY - 53A | EDINBURGH(SM)-64A | COLWICK-38A |
| Aug-51 | SPRINGHEAD-53C | 9/51: DAIRY - 53A | 9/51: MARCH - 31B | 10/51: DAIRY - 53A | MARCH-31B | NEWPORT-51B | DAIRYCOATES-53A | EDINBURGH(SM)-64A | COLWICK-38A |
| Jan-52 | SPRINGHEAD-53C | DAIRYCOATES-53A | MARCH-31B | 1/52: To LM | MARCH-31B | NEWPORT-51B | DAIRYCOATES-53A | EDINBURGH(SM)-64A | COLWICK-38A |
| Aug-52 | SPRINGHEAD-53C | DAIRYCOATES-53A | MARCH-31B | 6/52: COLW - 38A | MARCH-31B | NEWPORT-51B | DAIRYCOATES-53A | EDINBURGH(SM)-64A | COLWICK-38A |
| Jan-53 | SPRINGHEAD-53C | DAIRYCOATES-53A | MARCH-31B | COLWICK-38A | MARCH-31B | NEWPORT-51B | 11/52: NEWPT - 51B | 11/52: DAWS - 65D | COLWICK-38A |
| Aug-53 | SPRINGHEAD-53C | DAIRYCOATES-53A | MARCH-31B | COLWICK-38A | MARCH-31B | NEWPORT-51B | NEWPORT-51B | DAWSHOLME-65D | COLWICK-38A |
| Jan-54 | SPRINGHEAD-53C | DAIRYCOATES-53A | 10/53: IMM - 40B | COLWICK-38A | 10/53: COLW - 38A | NEWPORT-51B | NEWPORT-51B | DAWSHOLME-65D | COLWICK-38A |
| Aug-54 | SPRINGHEAD-53C | DAIRYCOATES-53A | IMMINGHAM-40B | COLWICK-38A | COLWICK-38A | NEWPORT-51B | NEWPORT-51B | DAWSHOLME-65D | COLWICK-38A |
| Jan-55 | SPRINGHEAD-53C | DAIRYCOATES-53A | IMMINGHAM-40B | COLWICK-38A | COLWICK-38A | NEWPORT-51B | NEWPORT-51B | DAWSHOLME-65D | COLWICK-38A |
| Aug-55 | SPRINGHEAD-53C | DAIRYCOATES-53A | 8/55: L.JCN - 40E | COLWICK-38A | COLWICK-38A | NEWPORT-51B | NEWPORT-51B | DAWSHOLME-65D | COLWICK-38A |
| Jan-56 | SPRINGHEAD-53C | DAIRYCOATES-53A | LANGWITHJCN-40E | COLWICK-38A | 2/56: WFD.H - 38E | NEWPORT-51B | NEWPORT-51B | DAWSHOLME-65D | COLWICK-38A |
| Aug-56 | SPRINGHEAD-53C | DAIRYCOATES-53A | LANGWITHJCN-40E | COLWICK-38A | W.HALSE-38E | NEWPORT-51B | NEWPORT-51B | DAWSHOLME-65D | COLWICK-38A |
| Jan-57 | SPRINGHEAD-53C | DAIRYCOATES-53A | LANGWITHJCN-40E | COLWICK-38A | W.HALSE-38E | NEWPORT-51B | NEWPORT-51B | DAWSHOLME-65D | COLWICK-38A |
| Aug-57 | 9/57: WAKE - 56A | DAIRYCOATES-53A | LANGWITHJCN-40E | COLWICK-38A | W.HALSE-38E | NEWPORT-51B | NEWPORT-51B | DAWSHOLME-65D | COLWICK-38A |
| Jan-58 | WAKEFIELD-56A | 5/58: GOOLE - 53E | LANGWITHJCN-40E | COLWICK-38A | W.HALSE-38E | NEWPORT-51B | NEWPORT-51B | DAWSHOLME-65D | COLWICK-38A |
| Aug-58 | WAKEFIELD-56A | 6/58: STOCK - 51E | LANGWITHJCN-41J | COLWICK-40E | W.HALSE-2F | 6/58: TBY - 51L | 6/58: TBY - 51L | DAWSHOLME-65D | COLWICK-40E |
| Jan-59 | WAKEFIELD-56A | STOCKTON-51E | LANGWITHJCN-41J | COLWICK-40E | W.HALSE-2F | THORNABY-51L | THORNABY-51L | DAWSHOLME-65D | COLWICK-40E |
| Aug-59 | WAKEFIELD-56A | 6/59: DARL - 51A | LANGWITHJCN-41J | COLWICK-40E | W.HALSE-2F | THORNABY-51L | THORNABY-51L | DAWSHOLME-65D | COLWICK-40E |
| Nov-59 | WAKEFIELD-56A | DARLINGTON-56A | LANGWITHJCN-41J | COLWICK-40E | W.HALSE-2F | THORNABY-51L | THORNABY-51L | DAWSHOLME-65D | COLWICK-40E |
| Jan-60 | WAKEFIELD-56A | DARLINGTON-56A | LANGWITHJCN-41J | COLWICK-40E | W.HALSE-2F | THORNABY-51L | THORNABY-51L | DAWSHOLME-65D | COLWICK-40E |
| Apr-60 | WAKEFIELD-56A | DARLINGTON-56A | LANGWITHJCN-41J | COLWICK-40E | W.HALSE-2F | THORNABY-51L | THORNABY-51L | DAWSHOLME-65D | COLWICK-40E |
| Aug-60 | WAKEFIELD-56A | DARLINGTON-56A | LANGWITHJCN-41J | COLWICK-40E | W.HALSE-2F | THORNABY-51L | THORNABY-51L | DAWSHOLME-65D | COLWICK-40E |
| Nov-60 | WAKEFIELD-56A | DARLINGTON-56A | LANGWITHJCN-41J | COLWICK-40E | W.HALSE-2F | THORNABY-51L | THORNABY-51L | DAWSHOLME-65D | COLWICK-40E |

| | 90438 | 90439 | 90441 | 90442 | 90443 | 90444 | 90445 | 90446 | 90447 |
|---|---|---|---|---|---|---|---|---|---|
| Aug-50 | NEWENGLAND-35A | NEWENGLAND-35A | EASTFIELD-65A | MARCH-31B | COLCHESTER-30E | DUNDEE-62B | TYNEDOCK-54B | NEWPORT-51B | NEWENGLAND-35A |
| Jan-51 | NEWENGLAND-35A | NEWENGLAND-35A | EASTFIELD-65A | MARCH-31B | COLCHESTER-30E | DUNDEE-62B | TYNEDOCK-54B | NEWPORT-51B | NEWENGLAND-35A |
| Aug-51 | NEWENGLAND-35A | NEWENGLAND-35A | EASTFIELD-65A | MARCH-31B | 9/51: MARCH - 31B | DUNDEE-62B | TYNEDOCK-54B | NEWPORT-51B | NEWENGLAND-35A |
| Jan-52 | NEWENGLAND-35A | NEWENGLAND-35A | 2/52: TH JN - 62A | MARCH-31B | MARCH-31B | DUNDEE-62B | TYNEDOCK-54B | NEWPORT-51B | NEWENGLAND-35A |
| Aug-52 | NEWENGLAND-35A | NEWENGLAND-35A | THORNTONJCN-62A | MARCH-31B | MARCH-31B | DUNDEE-62B | TYNEDOCK-54B | NEWPORT-51B | NEWENGLAND-35A |
| Jan-53 | NEWENGLAND-35A | NEWENGLAND-35A | THORNTONJCN-62A | MARCH-31B | MARCH-31B | DUNDEE-62B | TYNEDOCK-54B | NEWPORT-51B | NEWENGLAND-35A |
| Aug-53 | NEWENGLAND-35A | NEWENGLAND-35A | THORNTONJCN-62A | MARCH-31B | MARCH-31B | DUNDEE-62B | TYNEDOCK-54B | NEWPORT-51B | NEWENGLAND-35A |
| Jan-54 | NEWENGLAND-35A | NEWENGLAND-35A | THORNTONJCN-62A | 10/53: IMM - 40B | MARCH-31B | DUNDEE-62B | TYNEDOCK-54B | NEWPORT-51B | NEWENGLAND-35A |
| Aug-54 | NEWENGLAND-35A | NEWENGLAND-35A | THORNTONJCN-62A | IMMINGHAM-40B | MARCH-31B | DUNDEE-62B | TYNEDOCK-54B | NEWPORT-51B | NEWENGLAND-35A |
| Jan-55 | NEWENGLAND-35A | NEWENGLAND-35A | THORNTONJCN-62A | IMMINGHAM-40B | 2/55: STRAT - 30A | DUNDEE-62B | TYNEDOCK-54B | NEWPORT-51B | NEWENGLAND-35A |
| Aug-55 | NEWENGLAND-35A | NEWENGLAND-35A | THORNTONJCN-62A | 5/55: PLAIS - 33A | 3/55: PLAIS - 33A | DUNDEE-62B | TYNEDOCK-54B | NEWPORT-51B | NEWENGLAND-35A |
| Jan-56 | NEWENGLAND-35A | NEWENGLAND-35A | THORNTONJCN-62A | PLAISTOW-33A | 5/55: IMM - 40B | DUNDEE-62B | TYNEDOCK-54B | NEWPORT-51B | NEWENGLAND-35A |
| Aug-56 | NEWENGLAND-35A | NEWENGLAND-35A | THORNTONJCN-62A | PLAISTOW-33A | IMMINGHAM-40B | DUNDEE-62B | TYNEDOCK-54B | NEWPORT-51B | NEWENGLAND-35A |
| Jan-57 | NEWENGLAND-35A | NEWENGLAND-35A | THORNTONJCN-62A | PLAISTOW-33A | IMMINGHAM-40B | DUNDEE-62B | TYNEDOCK-54B | NEWPORT-51B | NEWENGLAND-35A |
| Aug-57 | 9/57: IMM - 40B | NEWENGLAND-35A | THORNTONJCN-62A | PLAISTOW-33A | IMMINGHAM-40B | DUNDEE-62B | 6/57: YORK - 50A | NEWPORT-51B | NEWENGLAND-35A |
| Jan-58 | 10/57: L.JCN - 40E | NEWENGLAND-35A | THORNTONJCN-62A | PLAISTOW-33A | IMMINGHAM-40B | DUNDEE-62B | YORK-50A | NEWPORT-51B | NEWENGLAND-35A |
| Aug-58 | LANGWITHJCN-41J | NEWENGLAND-34E | THORNTONJCN-62A | PLAISTOW-33A | IMMINGHAM-40B | DUNDEE-62B | YORK-50A | 6/58: TBY - 51L | NEWENGLAND-34E |
| Jan-59 | LANGWITHJCN-41J | NEWENGLAND-34E | THORNTONJCN-62A | 10/58: TIL - 33A | IMMINGHAM-40B | DUNDEE-62B | YORK-50A | THORNABY-51L | NEWENGLAND-34E |
| Aug-59 | LANGWITHJCN-41J | NEWENGLAND-34E | THORNTONJCN-62A | TILBURY-33B | IMMINGHAM-40B | DUNDEE-62B | YORK-50A | THORNABY-51L | NEWENGLAND-34E |
| Nov-59 | LANGWITHJCN-41J | NEWENGLAND-34E | THORNTONJCN-62A | TILBURY-33B | IMMINGHAM-40B | DUNDEE-62B | 10/59: WAKE - 56A | THORNABY-51L | NEWENGLAND-34E |
| Jan-60 | LANGWITHJCN-41J | NEWENGLAND-34E | THORNTONJCN-62A | TILBURY-33B | IMMINGHAM-40B | DUNDEE-62B | WAKEFIELD-56A | THORNABY-51L | 2/60: MARCH - 31B |
| Apr-60 | 5/60: COLW - 40E | NEWENGLAND-34E | THORNTONJCN-62A | TILBURY-33B | IMMINGHAM-40B | DUNDEE-62B | WAKEFIELD-56A | THORNABY-51L | MARCH-31B |
| Aug-60 | COLWICK-40E | NEWENGLAND-34E | THORNTONJCN-62A | TILBURY-33B | IMMINGHAM-40B | DUNDEE-62B | 6/60: DARL - 51A | THORNABY-51L | MARCH-31B |
| Nov-60 | COLWICK-40E | NEWENGLAND-34E | THORNTONJCN-62A | TILBURY-33B | IMMINGHAM-40B | DUNDEE-62B | DARLINGTON-51A | THORNABY-51L | MARCH-31B |

| | 90448 | 90449 | 90450 | 90451 | 90452 | 90453 | 90454 | 90455 | 90456 |
|---|---|---|---|---|---|---|---|---|---|
| Aug-50 | COLWICK-38A | DARLINGTON-51A | DAIRYCOATES-53A | NEWPORT-51B | NEWPORT-51B | MARCH-31B | NEWENGLAND-35A | FERRYHILL-61B | IMMINGHAM-40B |
| Jan-51 | COLWICK-38A | DARLINGTON-51A | 1/51: DARL - 51A | NEWPORT-51B | NEWPORT-51B | MARCH-31B | NEWENGLAND-35A | FERRYHILL-61B | IMMINGHAM-40B |
| Aug-51 | 6/51: WFD.H - 38E | 9/51: DAIRY - 53A | 8/51: DAIRY - 53A | NEWPORT-51B | NEWPORT-51B | MARCH-31B | NEWENGLAND-35A | FERRYHILL-61B | 5/51: FROD - 36C |
| Jan-52 | W.HALSE-38E | 1/52: To LM | DAIRYCOATES-53A | NEWPORT-51B | NEWPORT-51B | MARCH-31B | NEWENGLAND-35A | FERRYHILL-61B | FRODINGHAM-36C |
| Aug-52 | W.HALSE-38E | 6/52: COLW - 38A | DAIRYCOATES-53A | NEWPORT-51B | NEWPORT-51B | MARCH-31B | NEWENGLAND-35A | FERRYHILL-61B | FRODINGHAM-36C |
| Jan-53 | W.HALSE-38E | COLWICK-38A | DAIRYCOATES-53A | NEWPORT-51B | NEWPORT-51B | MARCH-31B | NEWENGLAND-35A | FERRYHILL-61B | FRODINGHAM-36C |
| Aug-53 | W.HALSE-38E | COLWICK-38A | DAIRYCOATES-53A | NEWPORT-51B | NEWPORT-51B | MARCH-31B | NEWENGLAND-35A | FERRYHILL-61B | FRODINGHAM-36C |
| Jan-54 | W.HALSE-38E | COLWICK-38A | DAIRYCOATES-53A | NEWPORT-51B | NEWPORT-51B | 10/53: IMM - 40B | NEWENGLAND-35A | FERRYHILL-61B | FRODINGHAM-36C |
| Aug-54 | W.HALSE-38E | 6/54: L.JCN - 40E | DAIRYCOATES-53A | NEWPORT-51B | NEWPORT-51B | IMMINGHAM-40B | NEWENGLAND-35A | FERRYHILL-61B | FRODINGHAM-36C |
| Jan-55 | W.HALSE-38E | LANGWITHJCN-40E | DAIRYCOATES-53A | NEWPORT-51B | NEWPORT-51B | IMMINGHAM-40B | NEWENGLAND-35A | FERRYHILL-61B | FRODINGHAM-36C |
| Aug-55 | W.HALSE-38E | LANGWITHJCN-40E | DAIRYCOATES-53A | NEWPORT-51B | NEWPORT-51B | IMMINGHAM-40B | NEWENGLAND-35A | FERRYHILL-61B | FRODINGHAM-36C |
| Jan-56 | W.HALSE-38E | LANGWITHJCN-40E | DAIRYCOATES-53A | NEWPORT-51B | NEWPORT-51B | IMMINGHAM-40B | NEWENGLAND-35A | FERRYHILL-61B | FRODINGHAM-36C |
| Aug-56 | W.HALSE-38E | LANGWITHJCN-40E | DAIRYCOATES-53A | NEWPORT-51B | NEWPORT-51B | 10/56: MARCH - 31B | NEWENGLAND-35A | FERRYHILL-61B | FRODINGHAM-36C |
| Jan-57 | W.HALSE-38E | LANGWITHJCN-40E | DAIRYCOATES-53A | NEWPORT-51B | NEWPORT-51B | 3/57: DCTR - 36A | NEWENGLAND-35A | FERRYHILL-61B | FRODINGHAM-36C |
| Aug-57 | W.HALSE-38E | LANGWITHJCN-40E | DAIRYCOATES-53A | NEWPORT-51B | NEWPORT-51B | DONCASTER-36A | NEWENGLAND-35A | FERRYHILL-61B | FRODINGHAM-36C |
| Jan-58 | W.HALSE-38E | LANGWITHJCN-40E | DAIRYCOATES-53A | NEWPORT-51B | NEWPORT-51B | DONCASTER-36A | NEWENGLAND-35A | FERRYHILL-61B | FRODINGHAM-36C |
| Aug-58 | W.HALSE-2F | LANGWITHJCN-41J | DAIRYCOATES-53A | 6/58: TBY - 51L | 6/58: TBY - 51L | DONCASTER-36A | NEWENGLAND-34E | FERRYHILL-61B | FRODINGHAM-36C |
| Jan-59 | W.HALSE-2F | LANGWITHJCN-41J | DAIRYCOATES-53A | THORNABY-51L | THORNABY-51L | DONCASTER-36A | NEWENGLAND-34E | FERRYHILL-61B | FRODINGHAM-36C |
| Aug-59 | W.HALSE-2F | LANGWITHJCN-41J | DAIRYCOATES-53A | THORNABY-51L | THORNABY-51L | DONCASTER-36A | NEWENGLAND-34E | FERRYHILL-61B | FRODINGHAM-36C |
| Nov-59 | W.HALSE-2F | LANGWITHJCN-41J | DAIRYCOATES-53A | THORNABY-51L | THORNABY-51L | DONCASTER-36A | NEWENGLAND-34E | FERRYHILL-61B | FRODINGHAM-36C |
| Jan-60 | W.HALSE-2F | LANGWITHJCN-41J | DAIRYCOATES-53A | THORNABY-51L | THORNABY-51L | DONCASTER-36A | NEWENGLAND-34E | FERRYHILL-61B | FRODINGHAM-36C |
| Apr-60 | W.HALSE-2F | LANGWITHJCN-41J | DAIRYCOATES-50B | THORNABY-51L | THORNABY-51L | DONCASTER-36A | NEWENGLAND-34E | FERRYHILL-61B | FRODINGHAM-36C |
| Aug-60 | W.HALSE-2F | LANGWITHJCN-41J | DAIRYCOATES-50B | THORNABY-51L | THORNABY-51L | DONCASTER-36A | NEWENGLAND-34E | FERRYHILL-61B | FRODINGHAM-36C |
| Nov-60 | W.HALSE-2F | LANGWITHJCN-41J | DAIRYCOATES-50B | THORNABY-51L | THORNABY-51L | DONCASTER-36A | NEWENGLAND-34E | FERRYHILL-61B | FRODINGHAM-36C |

| | 90457 | 90458 | 90459 | 90460 | 90461 | 90462 | 90463 | 90464 | 90465 |
|---|---|---|---|---|---|---|---|---|---|
| Aug-50 | NEWPORT-51B | TYNE DOCK-54B | NEWPORT-51B | IMMINGHAM-40B | NEWPORT-51B | NEWPORT-51B | DUNDEE-62B | | NEWPORT-51B |
| Jan-51 | NEWPORT-51B | TYNE DOCK-54B | NEWPORT-51B | **3/51: NEW.E-35A** | NEWPORT-51B | NEWPORT-51B | DUNDEE-62B | | NEWPORT-51B |
| Aug-51 | NEWPORT-51B | **9/51: DAIRY - 53A** | NEWPORT-51B | **9/51: IMM - 40B** | NEWPORT-51B | NEWPORT-51B | DUNDEE-62B | | NEWPORT-51B |
| Jan-52 | NEWPORT-51B | DAIRYCOATES-53A | NEWPORT-51B | STAVELEY-38D | NEWPORT-51B | NEWPORT-51B | DUNDEE-62B | | NEWPORT-51B |
| Aug-52 | NEWPORT-51B | DAIRYCOATES-53A | NEWPORT-51B | STAVELEY-38D | NEWPORT-51B | NEWPORT-51B | DUNDEE-62B | | NEWPORT-51B |
| Jan-53 | NEWPORT-51B | DAIRYCOATES-53A | NEWPORT-51B | STAVELEY-38D | NEWPORT-51B | NEWPORT-51B | DUNDEE-62B | Ex CR | NEWPORT-51B |
| Aug-53 | NEWPORT-51B | DAIRYCOATES-53A | NEWPORT-51B | STAVELEY-38D | NEWPORT-51B | NEWPORT-51B | DUNDEE-62B | **10/53: EBRO(SM) - 64A** | NEWPORT-51B |
| Jan-54 | NEWPORT-51B | DAIRYCOATES-53A | NEWPORT-51B | STAVELEY-38D | NEWPORT-51B | NEWPORT-51B | DUNDEE-62B | EDINBURGH(SM)-64A | NEWPORT-51B |
| Aug-54 | NEWPORT-51B | DAIRYCOATES-53A | NEWPORT-51B | STAVELEY-38D | NEWPORT-51B | NEWPORT-51B | DUNDEE-62B | **6/54: To CR** | NEWPORT-51B |
| Jan-55 | NEWPORT-51B | DAIRYCOATES-53A | NEWPORT-51B | STAVELEY-38D | NEWPORT-51B | NEWPORT-51B | DUNDEE-62B | | NEWPORT-51B |
| Aug-55 | NEWPORT-51B | DAIRYCOATES-53A | NEWPORT-51B | **7/55: COLW - 38A** | NEWPORT-51B | NEWPORT-51B | DUNDEE-62B | | NEWPORT-51B |
| Jan-56 | NEWPORT-51B | DAIRYCOATES-53A | NEWPORT-51B | COLWICK-38A | NEWPORT-51B | NEWPORT-51B | DUNDEE-62B | | NEWPORT-51B |
| Aug-56 | NEWPORT-51B | DAIRYCOATES-53A | NEWPORT-51B | COLWICK-38A | NEWPORT-51B | NEWPORT-51B | DUNDEE-62B | | NEWPORT-51B |
| Jan-57 | **2/57: STAR - 50D** | DAIRYCOATES-53A | NEWPORT-51B | COLWICK-38A | NEWPORT-51B | NEWPORT-51B | DUNDEE-62B | | NEWPORT-51B |
| Aug-57 | STARBECK-50D | DAIRYCOATES-53A | NEWPORT-51B | COLWICK-38A | NEWPORT-51B | NEWPORT-51B | DUNDEE-62B | | NEWPORT-51B |
| Jan-58 | STARBECK-50D | DAIRYCOATES-53A | NEWPORT-51B | COLWICK-38A | NEWPORT-51B | NEWPORT-51B | DUNDEE-62B | | NEWPORT-51B |
| Aug-58 | STARBECK-50D | DAIRYCOATES-53A | **6/58: TBY - 51L** | **9/58: IMM - 40B** | **6/58: TBY - 51L** | **6/58: TBY - 51L** | DUNDEE-62B | | **6/58: TBY - 51L** |
| Jan-59 | STARBECK-50D | DAIRYCOATES-53A | THORNABY-51L | IMMINGHAM-40B | THORNABY-51L | THORNABY-51L | **10/58: AYR - 67C** | | THORNABY-51L |
| Aug-59 | STARBECK-50D | DAIRYCOATES-53A | THORNABY-51L | IMMINGHAM-40B | THORNABY-51L | THORNABY-51L | AYR-67C | | THORNABY-51L |
| Nov-59 | **9/59: MIR - 56D** | DAIRYCOATES-53A | THORNABY-51L | IMMINGHAM-40B | THORNABY-51L | THORNABY-51L | AYR-67C | | THORNABY-51L |
| Jan-60 | MIRFIELD-56D | DAIRYCOATES-53A | THORNABY-51L | IMMINGHAM-40B | THORNABY-51L | THORNABY-51L | AYR-67C | | THORNABY-51L |
| Apr-60 | MIRFIELD-56D | DAIRYCOATES-50B | THORNABY-51L | IMMINGHAM-40B | THORNABY-51L | THORNABY-51L | AYR-67C | | THORNABY-51L |
| Aug-60 | MIRFIELD-56D | DAIRYCOATES-50B | THORNABY-51L | IMMINGHAM-40B | THORNABY-51L | THORNABY-51L | AYR-67C | | THORNABY-51L |
| Nov-60 | MIRFIELD-56D | DAIRYCOATES-50B | THORNABY-51L | IMMINGHAM-40B | THORNABY-51L | THORNABY-51L | AYR-67C | | THORNABY-51L |

| | 90466 | 90467 | 90468 | 90469 | 90470 | 90471 | 90472 | 90473 | 90474 |
|---|---|---|---|---|---|---|---|---|---|
| Aug-50 | COLWICK-38A | DARLINGTON-51A | EDINBURGH(SM)-64A | EDINBURGH(SM)-64A | SPRINGHEAD-53C | COLCHESTER-30E | THORNTON JCN-62A | MARCH-31B | MARCH-31B |
| Jan-51 | COLWICK-38A | DARLINGTON-51A | EDINBURGH(SM)-64A | EDINBURGH(SM)-64A | SPRINGHEAD-53C | COLCHESTER-30E | THORNTON JCN-62A | MARCH-31B | MARCH-31B |
| Aug-51 | **9/51: To WR** | **9/51: S'HEAD - 53C** | **T6/51: To CR** | EDINBURGH(SM)-64A | SPRINGHEAD-53C | **9/51: MARCH - 31B** | THORNTON JCN-62A | MARCH-31B | MARCH-31B |
| Jan-52 | | SPRINGHEAD-53C | | EDINBURGH(SM)-64A | SPRINGHEAD-53C | MARCH-31B | THORNTON JCN-62A | MARCH-31B | MARCH-31B |
| Aug-52 | | SPRINGHEAD-53C | | EDINBURGH(SM)-64A | SPRINGHEAD-53C | MARCH-31B | THORNTON JCN-62A | MARCH-31B | MARCH-31B |
| Jan-53 | | SPRINGHEAD-53C | | EDINBURGH(SM)-64A | SPRINGHEAD-53C | MARCH-31B | THORNTON JCN-62A | MARCH-31B | MARCH-31B |
| Aug-53 | | SPRINGHEAD-53C | | EDINBURGH(SM)-64A | SPRINGHEAD-53C | MARCH-31B | THORNTON JCN-62A | MARCH-31B | MARCH-31B |
| Jan-54 | | SPRINGHEAD-53C | | **10/53: DCTR - 36A** | SPRINGHEAD-53C | **10/53: IMM - 40B** | THORNTON JCN-62A | **11/53: COLW - 38A** | **11/53: WFD.H - 38E** |
| Aug-54 | | SPRINGHEAD-53C | | DONCASTER-36A | SPRINGHEAD-53C | IMMINGHAM-40B | THORNTON JCN-62A | COLWICK-38A | W.HALSE-38E |
| Jan-55 | | SPRINGHEAD-53C | | DONCASTER-36A | SPRINGHEAD-53C | IMMINGHAM-40B | THORNTON JCN-62A | COLWICK-38A | W.HALSE-38E |
| Aug-55 | | **9/55: N.HILL - 50B** | | DONCASTER-36A | SPRINGHEAD-53C | IMMINGHAM-40B | THORNTON JCN-62A | COLWICK-38A | W.HALSE-38E |
| Jan-56 | | NEVILLE HILL-50B | | DONCASTER-36A | SPRINGHEAD-53C | IMMINGHAM-40B | THORNTON JCN-62A | COLWICK-38A | W.HALSE-38E |
| Aug-56 | | NEVILLE HILL-50B | | **10/56: MARCH - 31B** | SPRINGHEAD-53C | IMMINGHAM-40B | THORNTON JCN-62A | COLWICK-38A | W.HALSE-38E |
| Jan-57 | | NEVILLE HILL-50B | | **2/57: DCTR - 36A** | SPRINGHEAD-53C | IMMINGHAM-40B | THORNTON JCN-62A | COLWICK-38A | W.HALSE-38E |
| Aug-57 | | NEVILLE HILL-50B | | DONCASTER-36A | **9/57: WAKE - 56A** | IMMINGHAM-40B | THORNTON JCN-62A | COLWICK-38A | W.HALSE-38E |
| Jan-58 | | NEVILLE HILL-50B | | DONCASTER-36A | WAKEFIELD-56A | IMMINGHAM-40B | THORNTON JCN-62A | COLWICK-38A | W.HALSE-38E |
| Aug-58 | | NEVILLE HILL-50B | | **7/58: FROD - 36C** | WAKEFIELD-56A | IMMINGHAM-40B | THORNTON JCN-62A | COLWICK-40E | W.HALSE-2F |
| Jan-59 | | NEVILLE HILL-50B | | FRODINGHAM-36C | **2/59: SOW.B - 56E** | IMMINGHAM-40B | THORNTON JCN-62A | COLWICK-40E | W.HALSE-2F |
| Aug-59 | | **6/59: YORK - 50A** | | FRODINGHAM-36C | SOWERBYBRIDGE-56E | **9/59: CANK - 41D** | THORNTON JCN-62A | COLWICK-40E | W.HALSE-2F |
| Nov-59 | | YORK-50A | | FRODINGHAM-36C | SOWERBYBRIDGE-56E | CANKLOW-41D | THORNTON JCN-62A | COLWICK-40E | W.HALSE-2F |
| Jan-60 | | YORK-50A | | FRODINGHAM-36C | SOWERBYBRIDGE-56E | CANKLOW-41D | THORNTON JCN-62A | COLWICK-40E | W.HALSE-2F |
| Apr-60 | | YORK-50A | | FRODINGHAM-36C | SOWERBYBRIDGE-56E | CANKLOW-41D | THORNTON JCN-62A | COLWICK-40E | W.HALSE-2F |
| Aug-60 | | YORK-50A | | FRODINGHAM-36C | SOWERBYBRIDGE-56E | CANKLOW-41D | THORNTON JCN-62A | COLWICK-40E | W.HALSE-2F |
| Nov-60 | | YORK-50A | | FRODINGHAM-36C | SOWERBYBRIDGE-56E | CANKLOW-41D | THORNTON JCN-62A | COLWICK-40E | W.HALSE-2F |

| | 90475 | 90476 | 90477 | 90478 | 90479 | 90480 | 90481 | 90482 | 90483 |
|---|---|---|---|---|---|---|---|---|---|
| Aug-50 | NEWPORT-51B | MARCH-31B | COLCHESTER-30E | SPRINGHEAD-53C | TWEEDMOUTH-52D | MARCH-31B | NEWPORT-51B | TYNE DOCK-54B | DAIRYCOATES-53A |
| Jan-51 | NEWPORT-51B | MARCH-31B | COLCHESTER-30E | SPRINGHEAD-53C | TWEEDMOUTH-52D | MARCH-31B | NEWPORT-51B | TYNE DOCK-54B | DAIRYCOATES-53A |
| Aug-51 | NEWPORT-51B | MARCH-31B | **9/51: MARCH - 31B** | SPRINGHEAD-53C | **5/51: DAIRY - 53A** | MARCH-31B | NEWPORT-51B | **9/51: DAIRY - 53A** | **9/51: IMM - 40B** |
| Jan-52 | NEWPORT-51B | MARCH-31B | MARCH-31B | SPRINGHEAD-53C | DAIRYCOATES-53A | MARCH-31B | NEWPORT-51B | DAIRYCOATES-53A | **11/51: To WR** |
| Aug-52 | NEWPORT-51B | MARCH-31B | MARCH-31B | SPRINGHEAD-53C | DAIRYCOATES-53A | MARCH-31B | NEWPORT-51B | DAIRYCOATES-53A | |
| Jan-53 | NEWPORT-51B | MARCH-31B | MARCH-31B | SPRINGHEAD-53C | DAIRYCOATES-53A | MARCH-31B | NEWPORT-51B | DAIRYCOATES-53A | |
| Aug-53 | NEWPORT-51B | **7/53: COLW - 38A** | MARCH-31B | SPRINGHEAD-53C | DAIRYCOATES-53A | MARCH-31B | NEWPORT-51B | DAIRYCOATES-53A | |
| Jan-54 | NEWPORT-51B | COLWICK-38A | **10/53: IMM - 40B** | SPRINGHEAD-53C | DAIRYCOATES-53A | MARCH-31B | NEWPORT-51B | DAIRYCOATES-53A | |
| Aug-54 | NEWPORT-51B | COLWICK-38A | IMMINGHAM-40B | SPRINGHEAD-53C | DAIRYCOATES-53A | MARCH-31B | NEWPORT-51B | DAIRYCOATES-53A | |
| Jan-55 | **5/55: DARL - 51A** | COLWICK-38A | IMMINGHAM-40B | SPRINGHEAD-53C | DAIRYCOATES-53A | MARCH-31B | NEWPORT-51B | DAIRYCOATES-53A | |
| Aug-55 | **7/55: NEWPT - 51B** | COLWICK-38A | IMMINGHAM-40B | SPRINGHEAD-53C | DAIRYCOATES-53A | MARCH-31B | NEWPORT-51B | DAIRYCOATES-53A | |
| Jan-56 | NEWPORT-51B | COLWICK-38A | IMMINGHAM-40B | SPRINGHEAD-53C | DAIRYCOATES-53A | MARCH-31B | NEWPORT-51B | DAIRYCOATES-53A | |
| Aug-56 | NEWPORT-51B | COLWICK-38A | **10/56: MARCH - 31B** | SPRINGHEAD-53C | DAIRYCOATES-53A | MARCH-31B | NEWPORT-51B | DAIRYCOATES-53A | |
| Jan-57 | NEWPORT-51B | COLWICK-38A | MARCH-31B | SPRINGHEAD-53C | DAIRYCOATES-53A | MARCH-31B | NEWPORT-51B | **12/56: S'HEAD - 53C** | |
| Aug-57 | **6/57: YORK - 50A** | COLWICK-38A | MARCH-31B | SPRINGHEAD-53C | DAIRYCOATES-53A | MARCH-31B | NEWPORT-51B | SPRINGHEAD-53C | |
| Jan-58 | YORK-50A | COLWICK-38A | MARCH-31B | SPRINGHEAD-53C | **5/58: GOOLE - 53E** | MARCH-31B | NEWPORT-51B | SPRINGHEAD-53C | |
| Aug-58 | YORK-50A | COLWICK-40E | MARCH-31B | SPRINGHEAD-53C | **6/58: H.HILL - 51G** | MARCH-31B | **6/58: TBY - 51L** | SPRINGHEAD-53C | |
| Jan-59 | YORK-50A | COLWICK-40E | MARCH-31B | **11/58: GOOLE - 53E** | HAVERTON HILL-51G | **4/59: STRAT - 30A** | THORNABY-51L | **12/58: DAIRY - 53A** | |
| Aug-59 | YORK-50A | COLWICK-40E | MARCH-31B | GOOLE-53E | **6/59: TBY - 51L** | STRATFORD-30A | THORNABY-51L | DAIRYCOATES-53A | |
| Nov-59 | YORK-50A | COLWICK-40E | MARCH-31B | GOOLE-53E | THORNABY-51L | STRATFORD-30A | THORNABY-51L | DAIRYCOATES-53A | |
| Jan-60 | YORK-50A | COLWICK-40E | MARCH-31B | GOOLE-53E | THORNABY-51L | STRATFORD-30A | THORNABY-51L | DAIRYCOATES-53A | |
| Apr-60 | YORK-50A | COLWICK-40E | MARCH-31B | GOOLE-50D | THORNABY-51L | **4/60: HSEY - 34B** | THORNABY-51L | DAIRYCOATES-50B | |
| Aug-60 | **6/60: GOOLE - 50D** | COLWICK-40E | MARCH-31B | GOOLE-50D | THORNABY-51L | HORNSEY-34B | THORNABY-51L | DAIRYCOATES-50B | |
| Nov-60 | GOOLE-50D | **11/60: DCTR - 40E** | MARCH-31B | GOOLE-50D | THORNABY-51L | HORNSEY-34B | THORNABY-51L | DAIRYCOATES-50B | |

| | 90484 | 90485 | 90486 | 90487 | 90488 | 90489 | 90490 | 90491 | 90492 |
|---|---|---|---|---|---|---|---|---|---|
| Aug-50 | COLWICK-38A | TYNE DOCK-54B | W.HALSE-38E | NEWPORT-51B | NEWPORT-51B | THORNTON JCN-62A | NEW ENGLAND-35A | COLWICK-38A | COLWICK-38A |
| Jan-51 | COLWICK-38A | **2/51: MALT - 50F** | W.HALSE-38E | NEWPORT-51B | NEWPORT-51B | THORNTON JCN-62A | NEW ENGLAND-35A | COLWICK-38A | **1/51: ANNES - 38B** |
| Aug-51 | **6/51: WFD.H - 38E** | **6/51: YORK - 50A** | W.HALSE-38E | NEWPORT-51B | NEWPORT-51B | THORNTON JCN-62A | **7/51: FROD - 36C** | COLWICK-38A | **9/51: IMM - 40B** |
| Jan-52 | W.HALSE-38E | **9/51: IMM - 40B** | W.HALSE-38E | NEWPORT-51B | NEWPORT-51B | THORNTON JCN-62A | FRODINGHAM-36C | COLWICK-38A | IMMINGHAM-40B |
| Aug-52 | W.HALSE-38E | IMMINGHAM-40B | **11/52: STAVE - 38D** | NEWPORT-51B | NEWPORT-51B | THORNTON JCN-62A | FRODINGHAM-36C | COLWICK-38A | IMMINGHAM-40B |
| Jan-53 | W.HALSE-38E | IMMINGHAM-40B | **1/53: WFD.H - 38E** | NEWPORT-51B | NEWPORT-51B | THORNTON JCN-62A | FRODINGHAM-36C | COLWICK-38A | IMMINGHAM-40B |
| Aug-53 | W.HALSE-38E | IMMINGHAM-40B | W.HALSE-38E | NEWPORT-51B | NEWPORT-51B | THORNTON JCN-62A | FRODINGHAM-36C | COLWICK-38A | IMMINGHAM-40B |
| Jan-54 | W.HALSE-38E | IMMINGHAM-40B | W.HALSE-38E | NEWPORT-51B | NEWPORT-51B | THORNTON JCN-62A | FRODINGHAM-36C | COLWICK-38A | IMMINGHAM-40B |
| Aug-54 | W.HALSE-38E | IMMINGHAM-40B | W.HALSE-38E | NEWPORT-51B | NEWPORT-51B | THORNTON JCN-62A | FRODINGHAM-36C | COLWICK-38A | IMMINGHAM-40B |
| Jan-55 | W.HALSE-38E | IMMINGHAM-40B | W.HALSE-38E | NEWPORT-51B | NEWPORT-51B | **11/54: EFLD - 65A** | FRODINGHAM-36C | COLWICK-38A | **3/55: IMM - 40E** |
| Aug-55 | W.HALSE-38E | IMMINGHAM-40B | W.HALSE-38E | NEWPORT-51B | NEWPORT-51B | EASTFIELD-65A | FRODINGHAM-36C | COLWICK-38A | LANGWITH JCN-40E |
| Jan-56 | W.HALSE-38E | IMMINGHAM-40B | W.HALSE-38E | NEWPORT-51B | NEWPORT-51B | EASTFIELD-65A | FRODINGHAM-36C | **2/56@ WFD.H - 38E** | LANGWITH JCN-40E |
| Aug-56 | W.HALSE-38E | IMMINGHAM-40B | W.HALSE-38E | NEWPORT-51B | NEWPORT-51B | EASTFIELD-65A | FRODINGHAM-36C | **10/56: MARCH - 31B** | LANGWITH JCN-40E |
| Jan-57 | **10/56: MARCH - 31B** | IMMINGHAM-40B | W.HALSE-38E | NEWPORT-51B | NEWPORT-51B | EASTFIELD-65A | FRODINGHAM-36C | **3/57: DCTR - 36A** | LANGWITH JCN-40E |
| Aug-57 | MARCH-31B | IMMINGHAM-40B | W.HALSE-38E | **6/57: YORK - 50A** | NEWPORT-51B | EASTFIELD-65A | FRODINGHAM-36C | DONCASTER-36A | LANGWITH JCN-40E |
| Jan-58 | MARCH-31B | IMMINGHAM-40B | W.HALSE-38E | **9/57: NOR - 55E** | NEWPORT-51B | EASTFIELD-65A | FRODINGHAM-36C | DONCASTER-36A | LANGWITH JCN-40E |
| Aug-58 | MARCH-31B | IMMINGHAM-40B | W.HALSE-2F | NORMANTON-55E | **6/58: TBY - 51L** | EASTFIELD-65A | FRODINGHAM-36C | **7/58: MEX - 41F** | LANGWITH JCN-41J |
| Jan-59 | MARCH-31B | IMMINGHAM-40B | W.HALSE-2F | NORMANTON-55E | THORNABY-51L | EASTFIELD-65A | FRODINGHAM-36C | MEXBOROUGH-41F | LANGWITH JCN-41J |
| Aug-59 | MARCH-31B | IMMINGHAM-40B | W.HALSE-2F | NORMANTON-55E | **4/59: ROY - 55D** | EASTFIELD-65A | FRODINGHAM-36C | MEXBOROUGH-41F | LANGWITH JCN-41J |
| Nov-59 | MARCH-31B | IMMINGHAM-40B | W.HALSE-2F | NORMANTON-55E | ROYSTON-55D | EASTFIELD-65A | FRODINGHAM-36C | MEXBOROUGH-41F | LANGWITH JCN-41J |
| Jan-60 | MARCH-31B | IMMINGHAM-40B | W.HALSE-2F | NORMANTON-55E | ROYSTON-55D | EASTFIELD-65A | FRODINGHAM-36C | MEXBOROUGH-41F | LANGWITH JCN-41J |
| Apr-60 | MARCH-31B | IMMINGHAM-40B | W.HALSE-2F | NORMANTON-55E | ROYSTON-55D | EASTFIELD-65A | FRODINGHAM-36C | MEXBOROUGH-41F | **5/60: COLW - 40E** |
| Aug-60 | MARCH-31B | IMMINGHAM-40B | W.HALSE-2F | NORMANTON-55E | ROYSTON-55D | EASTFIELD-65A | FRODINGHAM-36C | MEXBOROUGH-41F | COLWICK-40E |
| Nov-60 | MARCH-31B | IMMINGHAM-40B | W.HALSE-2F | NORMANTON-55E | ROYSTON-55D | EASTFIELD-65A | FRODINGHAM-36C | MEXBOROUGH-41F | COLWICK-40E |

| | 90493 | 90494 | 90495 | 90496 | 90497 | 90498 | 90499 | 90500 | 90501 |
|---|---|---|---|---|---|---|---|---|---|
| Aug-50 | EDINBURGH(SM) - 64A | NEWENGLAND - 35A | NEWENGLAND - 35A | EDINBURGH(SM) - 64A | SPRINGHEAD - 53C | THORNTONJCN - 62A | COLWICK - 38A | NEWPORT - 51B | NEWENGLAND - 35A |
| Jan-51 | EDINBURGH(SM) - 64A | NEWENGLAND - 35A | NEWENGLAND - 35A | EDINBURGH(SM) - 64A | SPRINGHEAD - 53C | THORNTONJCN - 62A | COLWICK - 38A | NEWPORT - 51B | NEWENGLAND - 35A |
| Aug-51 | **7/51: To CR** | NEWENGLAND - 35A | NEWENGLAND - 35A | EDINBURGH(SM) - 64A | SPRINGHEAD - 53C | THORNTONJCN - 62A | **9/51: WFD.H - 38E** | NEWPORT - 51B | NEWENGLAND - 35A |
| Jan-52 | **12/51: DAWS - 65D** | NEWENGLAND - 35A | **11/51: MEX - 36B** | EDINBURGH(SM) - 64A | SPRINGHEAD - 53C | THORNTONJCN - 62A | **11/51: COLW - 38A** | NEWPORT - 51B | NEWENGLAND - 35A |
| Aug-52 | DAWSHOLME - 65D | NEWENGLAND - 35A | MEXBOROUGH - 36B | EDINBURGH(SM) - 64A | SPRINGHEAD - 53C | **9/52: EBRO(SM) - 64A** | COLWICK - 38A | NEWPORT - 51B | NEWENGLAND - 35A |
| Jan-53 | DAWSHOLME - 65D | NEWENGLAND - 35A | MEXBOROUGH - 36B | EDINBURGH(SM) - 64A | SPRINGHEAD - 53C | EDINBURGH(SM) - 64A | COLWICK - 38A | NEWPORT - 51B | NEWENGLAND - 35A |
| Aug-53 | DAWSHOLME - 65D | NEWENGLAND - 35A | MEXBOROUGH - 36B | EDINBURGH(SM) - 64A | SPRINGHEAD - 53C | EDINBURGH(SM) - 64A | COLWICK - 38A | **5/53: YORK - 50A** | NEWENGLAND - 35A |
| Jan-54 | DAWSHOLME - 65D | NEWENGLAND - 35A | MEXBOROUGH - 36B | **10/53: COLW - 38A** | SPRINGHEAD - 53C | **10/53: DCTR - 36A** | COLWICK - 38A | YORK - 50A | NEWENGLAND - 35A |
| Aug-54 | DAWSHOLME - 65D | NEWENGLAND - 35A | MEXBOROUGH - 36B | COLWICK - 38A | SPRINGHEAD - 53C | **6/54: MEX - 36B** | COLWICK - 38A | YORK - 50A | NEWENGLAND - 35A |
| Jan-55 | DAWSHOLME - 65D | NEWENGLAND - 35A | MEXBOROUGH - 36B | COLWICK - 38A | SPRINGHEAD - 53C | MEXBOROUGH - 36B | COLWICK - 38A | YORK - 50A | NEWENGLAND - 35A |
| Aug-55 | DAWSHOLME - 65D | NEWENGLAND - 35A | MEXBOROUGH - 36B | COLWICK - 38A | SPRINGHEAD - 53C | MEXBOROUGH - 36B | COLWICK - 38A | YORK - 50A | NEWENGLAND - 35A |
| Jan-56 | DAWSHOLME - 65D | NEWENGLAND - 35A | MEXBOROUGH - 36B | COLWICK - 38A | SPRINGHEAD - 53C | MEXBOROUGH - 36B | COLWICK - 38A | YORK - 50A | NEWENGLAND - 35A |
| Aug-56 | DAWSHOLME - 65D | NEWENGLAND - 35A | MEXBOROUGH - 36B | COLWICK - 38A | SPRINGHEAD - 53C | **10/56: MARCH - 31B** | COLWICK - 38A | **6/56: NEWPT - 51B** | NEWENGLAND - 35A |
| Jan-57 | DAWSHOLME - 65D | NEWENGLAND - 35A | MEXBOROUGH - 36B | COLWICK - 38A | SPRINGHEAD - 53C | **2/57: STRAT - 30A** | COLWICK - 38A | NEWPORT - 51B | NEWENGLAND - 35A |
| Aug-57 | DAWSHOLME - 65D | NEWENGLAND - 35A | MEXBOROUGH - 36B | COLWICK - 38A | SPRINGHEAD - 53C | STRATFORD - 30A | COLWICK - 38A | NEWPORT - 51B | NEWENGLAND - 35A |
| Jan-58 | DAWSHOLME - 65D | **3/58: TIL - 33B** | MEXBOROUGH - 36B | COLWICK - 38A | **11/57: WAKE - 56A** | STRATFORD - 30A | COLWICK - 38A | NEWPORT - 51B | NEWENGLAND - 35A |
| Aug-58 | DAWSHOLME - 65D | TILBURY - 33B | MEXBOROUGH - 41F | COLWICK - 40E | WAKEFIELD - 56A | **10/58: MARCH - 31B** | **7/58: MEX - 41F** | **6/58: TBY - 51L** | NEWENGLAND - 34E |
| Jan-59 | DAWSHOLME - 65D | TILBURY - 33B | MEXBOROUGH - 41F | COLWICK - 40E | WAKEFIELD - 56A | **12/58: FROD - 36C** | MEXBOROUGH - 41F | THORNABY - 51L | NEWENGLAND - 34E |
| Aug-59 | DAWSHOLME - 65D | TILBURY - 33B | MEXBOROUGH - 41F | COLWICK - 40E | WAKEFIELD - 56A | FRODINGHAM - 36C | MEXBOROUGH - 41F | THORNABY - 51L | NEWENGLAND - 34E |
| Nov-59 | DAWSHOLME - 65D | TILBURY - 33B | MEXBOROUGH - 41F | COLWICK - 40E | WAKEFIELD - 56A | FRODINGHAM - 36C | MEXBOROUGH - 41F | THORNABY - 51L | NEWENGLAND - 34E |
| Jan-60 | DAWSHOLME - 65D | TILBURY - 33B | MEXBOROUGH - 41F | COLWICK - 40E | WAKEFIELD - 56A | FRODINGHAM - 36C | MEXBOROUGH - 41F | THORNABY - 51L | **2/60: MARCH - 31B** |
| Apr-60 | DAWSHOLME - 65D | TILBURY - 33B | MEXBOROUGH - 41F | COLWICK - 40E | WAKEFIELD - 56A | FRODINGHAM - 36C | MEXBOROUGH - 41F | THORNABY - 51L | MARCH - 31B |
| Aug-60 | DAWSHOLME - 65D | TILBURY - 33B | MEXBOROUGH - 41F | COLWICK - 40E | WAKEFIELD - 56A | FRODINGHAM - 36C | MEXBOROUGH - 41F | THORNABY - 51L | MARCH - 31B |
| Nov-60 | DAWSHOLME - 65D | TILBURY - 33B | MEXBOROUGH - 41F | **11/60: DCTR - 36A** | WAKEFIELD - 56A | **11/60: DCTR - 36A** | MEXBOROUGH - 41F | THORNABY - 51L | MARCH - 31B |

| | 90502 | 90503 | 90504 | 90506 | 90507 | 90508 | 90509 | 90510 | 90511 |
|---|---|---|---|---|---|---|---|---|---|
| Aug-50 | MARCH - 31B | NEWPORT - 51B | W.HALSE - 38E | MARCH - 31B | W.HALSE - 38E | COLCHESTER - 30E | W.HALSE - 38E | MARCH - 31B | YORK - 50A |
| Jan-51 | **3/51: MEX - 36B** | NEWPORT - 51B | W.HALSE - 38E | MARCH - 31B | W.HALSE - 38E | COLCHESTER - 30E | W.HALSE - 38E | MARCH - 31B | YORK - 50A |
| Aug-51 | MEXBOROUGH - 36B | NEWPORT - 51B | W.HALSE - 38E | MARCH - 31B | W.HALSE - 38E | **8/51: MARCH - 31B** | W.HALSE - 38E | MARCH - 31B | YORK - 50A |
| Jan-52 | **10/51: NEW.E - 35A** | NEWPORT - 51B | W.HALSE - 38E | MARCH - 31B | W.HALSE - 38E | MARCH - 31B | W.HALSE - 38E | MARCH - 31B | YORK - 50A |
| Aug-52 | NEWENGLAND - 35A | NEWPORT - 51B | W.HALSE - 38E | MARCH - 31B | W.HALSE - 38E | MARCH - 31B | W.HALSE - 38E | MARCH - 31B | YORK - 50A |
| Jan-53 | NEWENGLAND - 35A | NEWPORT - 51B | W.HALSE - 38E | MARCH - 31B | W.HALSE - 38E | MARCH - 31B | W.HALSE - 38E | MARCH - 31B | **3/53: S'HEAD - 53C** |
| Aug-53 | NEWENGLAND - 35A | NEWPORT - 51B | W.HALSE - 38E | MARCH - 31B | W.HALSE - 38E | MARCH - 31B | W.HALSE - 38E | MARCH - 31B | SPRINGHEAD - 53C |
| Jan-54 | NEWENGLAND - 35A | NEWPORT - 51B | W.HALSE - 38E | **11/53: DCTR - 36A** | W.HALSE - 38E | **10/53: IMM - 40B** | W.HALSE - 38E | **10/53: IMM - 40B** | SPRINGHEAD - 53C |
| Aug-54 | NEWENGLAND - 35A | NEWPORT - 51B | W.HALSE - 38E | **6/54: MEX - 36B** | W.HALSE - 38E | IMMINGHAM - 40B | W.HALSE - 38E | IMMINGHAM - 40B | SPRINGHEAD - 53C |
| Jan-55 | **1/55: L.JCN - 40E** | NEWPORT - 51B | W.HALSE - 38E | MEXBOROUGH - 36B | W.HALSE - 38E | **3/55: L.JCN - 40E** | W.HALSE - 38E | IMMINGHAM - 40B | SPRINGHEAD - 53C |
| Aug-55 | LANGWITHJCN - 40E | NEWPORT - 51B | W.HALSE - 38E | MEXBOROUGH - 36B | W.HALSE - 38E | LANGWITHJCN - 40E | W.HALSE - 38E | IMMINGHAM - 40B | SPRINGHEAD - 53C |
| Jan-56 | LANGWITHJCN - 40E | NEWPORT - 51B | W.HALSE - 38E | MEXBOROUGH - 36B | W.HALSE - 38E | **11/55: STRAT - 30A** | W.HALSE - 38E | IMMINGHAM - 40B | SPRINGHEAD - 53C |
| Aug-56 | LANGWITHJCN - 40E | NEWPORT - 51B | W.HALSE - 38E | MEXBOROUGH - 36B | W.HALSE - 38E | STRATFORD - 30A | W.HALSE - 38E | IMMINGHAM - 40B | SPRINGHEAD - 53C |
| Jan-57 | LANGWITHJCN - 40E | **6/57: YORK - 50A** | W.HALSE - 38E | MEXBOROUGH - 36B | W.HALSE - 38E | STRATFORD - 30A | W.HALSE - 38E | IMMINGHAM - 40B | SPRINGHEAD - 53C |
| Aug-57 | LANGWITHJCN - 40E | **9/57: WAKE - 56A** | W.HALSE - 38E | MEXBOROUGH - 36B | W.HALSE - 38E | STRATFORD - 30A | W.HALSE - 38E | IMMINGHAM - 40B | SPRINGHEAD - 53C |
| Jan-58 | LANGWITHJCN - 40E | **11/57: S'HEAD - 53C** | W.HALSE - 38E | MEXBOROUGH - 36B | W.HALSE - 38E | STRATFORD - 30A | W.HALSE - 38E | IMMINGHAM - 40B | SPRINGHEAD - 53C |
| Aug-58 | **7/58: STAVE - 41H** | SPRINGHEAD - 53C | W.HALSE - 2F | MEXBOROUGH - 41F | W.HALSE - 2F | STRATFORD - 30A | W.HALSE - 2F | IMMINGHAM - 40B | SPRINGHEAD - 53C |
| Jan-59 | STAVELEY(GC) - 41H | **12/58: DAIRY - 53A** | W.HALSE - 2F | MEXBOROUGH - 41F | **2/59: To LM** | STRATFORD - 30A | **2/59: To LM** | IMMINGHAM - 40B | **1/59: DAIRY - 53A** |
| Aug-59 | STAVELEY(GC) - 41H | DAIRYCOATES - 53A | W.HALSE - 2F | MEXBOROUGH - 41F | | STRATFORD - 30A | | IMMINGHAM - 40B | DAIRYCOATES - 53A |
| Nov-59 | STAVELEY(GC) - 41H | DAIRYCOATES - 53A | W.HALSE - 2F | MEXBOROUGH - 41F | | STRATFORD - 30A | | IMMINGHAM - 40B | DAIRYCOATES - 53A |
| Jan-60 | **1/60: HSEY - 34B** | **2/60: TBY - 51L** | W.HALSE - 2F | MEXBOROUGH - 41F | | STRATFORD - 30A | | IMMINGHAM - 40B | **2/60: TBY - 51L** |
| Apr-60 | **2/60: NEW.E - 34E** | THORNABY - 51L | W.HALSE - 2F | MEXBOROUGH - 41F | | **5/60: MEX - 41F** | | IMMINGHAM - 40B | THORNABY - 51L |
| Aug-60 | NEWENGLAND - 34E | THORNABY - 51L | W.HALSE - 2F | MEXBOROUGH - 41F | | MEXBOROUGH - 41F | | IMMINGHAM - 40B | THORNABY - 51L |
| Nov-60 | NEWENGLAND - 34E | THORNABY - 51L | W.HALSE - 2F | MEXBOROUGH - 41F | | MEXBOROUGH - 41F | | **11/60: COLW - 40E** | THORNABY - 51L |

| | 90512 | 90513 | 90514 | 90515 | 90516 | 90517 | 90518 | 90519 | 90520 |
|---|---|---|---|---|---|---|---|---|---|
| Aug-50 | NEWENGLAND - 35A | DUNFERMLINE - 62C | NEWENGLAND - 35A | DUNDEE - 62B | W.HALSE - 38E | NEWPORT - 51B | YORK - 50A | MARCH - 31B | W.HALSE - 38E |
| Jan-51 | NEWENGLAND - 35A | DUNFERMLINE - 62C | NEWENGLAND - 35A | DUNDEE - 62B | W.HALSE - 38E | NEWPORT - 51B | YORK - 50A | MARCH - 31B | W.HALSE - 38E |
| Aug-51 | NEWENGLAND - 35A | DUNFERMLINE - 62C | NEWENGLAND - 35A | DUNDEE - 62B | W.HALSE - 38E | NEWPORT - 51B | YORK - 50A | MARCH - 31B | W.HALSE - 38E |
| Jan-52 | NEWENGLAND - 35A | DUNFERMLINE - 62C | NEWENGLAND - 35A | DUNDEE - 62B | W.HALSE - 38E | NEWPORT - 51B | YORK - 50A | MARCH - 31B | W.HALSE - 38E |
| Aug-52 | NEWENGLAND - 35A | DUNFERMLINE - 62C | NEWENGLAND - 35A | DUNDEE - 62B | W.HALSE - 38E | NEWPORT - 51B | YORK - 50A | MARCH - 31B | W.HALSE - 38E |
| Jan-53 | NEWENGLAND - 35A | DUNFERMLINE - 62C | NEWENGLAND - 35A | DUNDEE - 62B | W.HALSE - 38E | NEWPORT - 51B | YORK - 50A | MARCH - 31B | W.HALSE - 38E |
| Aug-53 | NEWENGLAND - 35A | DUNFERMLINE - 62C | NEWENGLAND - 35A | DUNDEE - 62B | W.HALSE - 38E | NEWPORT - 51B | YORK - 50A | MARCH - 31B | W.HALSE - 38E |
| Jan-54 | **10/53: FROD - 36C** | DUNFERMLINE - 62C | NEWENGLAND - 35A | DUNDEE - 62B | W.HALSE - 38E | NEWPORT - 51B | YORK - 50A | MARCH - 31B | W.HALSE - 38E |
| Aug-54 | FRODINGHAM - 36C | DUNFERMLINE - 62C | NEWENGLAND - 35A | DUNDEE - 62B | W.HALSE - 38E | **8/54: YORK - 50A** | YORK - 50A | **4/54: COLW - 38A** | W.HALSE - 38E |
| Jan-55 | FRODINGHAM - 36C | DUNFERMLINE - 62C | NEWENGLAND - 35A | DUNDEE - 62B | W.HALSE - 38E | YORK - 50A | YORK - 50A | COLWICK - 38A | W.HALSE - 38E |
| Aug-55 | FRODINGHAM - 36C | DUNFERMLINE - 62C | NEWENGLAND - 35A | DUNDEE - 62B | W.HALSE - 38E | YORK - 50A | YORK - 50A | COLWICK - 38A | W.HALSE - 38E |
| Jan-56 | FRODINGHAM - 36C | **1/56: TH JN - 62A** | NEWENGLAND - 35A | DUNDEE - 62B | W.HALSE - 38E | YORK - 50A | **11/55 : STAR - 50D** | COLWICK - 38A | W.HALSE - 38E |
| Aug-56 | FRODINGHAM - 36C | THORNTONJCN - 62A | NEWENGLAND - 35A | DUNDEE - 62B | W.HALSE - 38E | **6/56: NEWP'T - 51B** | STARBECK - 50D | COLWICK - 38A | W.HALSE - 38E |
| Jan-57 | FRODINGHAM - 36C | THORNTONJCN - 62A | NEWENGLAND - 35A | DUNDEE - 62B | W.HALSE - 38E | NEWPORT - 51B | STARBECK - 50D | COLWICK - 38A | W.HALSE - 38E |
| Aug-57 | FRODINGHAM - 36C | THORNTONJCN - 62A | NEWENGLAND - 35A | DUNDEE - 62B | W.HALSE - 38E | NEWPORT - 51B | STARBECK - 50D | COLWICK - 38A | W.HALSE - 38E |
| Jan-58 | FRODINGHAM - 36C | THORNTONJCN - 62A | NEWENGLAND - 35A | DUNDEE - 62B | W.HALSE - 38E | NEWPORT - 51B | STARBECK - 50D | COLWICK - 38A | W.HALSE - 38E |
| Aug-58 | FRODINGHAM - 36C | THORNTONJCN - 62A | **5/58: PLAIS - 33A** | DUNDEE - 62B | W.HALSE - 2F | **6/58: TBY - 51L** | STARBECK - 50D | COLWICK - 40E | W.HALSE - 2F |
| Jan-59 | FRODINGHAM - 36C | THORNTONJCN - 62A | PLAISTOW - 33A | DUNDEE - 62B | W.HALSE - 2F | THORNABY - 51L | STARBECK - 50D | **5/59: BARN - 41G** | W.HALSE - 2F |
| Aug-59 | FRODINGHAM - 36C | THORNTONJCN - 62A | **6/59: MARCH - 31B** | DUNDEE - 62B | W.HALSE - 2F | THORNABY - 51L | **9/59: YORK - 50A** | **6/59: MEX - 41F** | W.HALSE - 2F |
| Nov-59 | FRODINGHAM - 36C | THORNTONJCN - 62A | **9/59: PLAIS - 33A** | DUNDEE - 62B | W.HALSE - 2F | THORNABY - 51L | YORK - 50A | MEXBOROUGH - 41F | W.HALSE - 2F |
| Jan-60 | FRODINGHAM - 36C | THORNTONJCN - 62A | **10/59: TIL - 33B** | DUNDEE - 62B | W.HALSE - 2F | THORNABY - 51L | YORK - 50A | MEXBOROUGH - 41F | W.HALSE - 2F |
| Apr-60 | FRODINGHAM - 36C | THORNTONJCN - 62A | TILBURY - 33B | DUNDEE - 62B | W.HALSE - 2F | THORNABY - 51L | YORK - 50A | MEXBOROUGH - 41F | W.HALSE - 2F |
| Aug-60 | FRODINGHAM - 36C | THORNTONJCN - 62A | TILBURY - 33B | DUNDEE - 62B | W.HALSE - 2F | THORNABY - 51L | YORK - 50A | MEXBOROUGH - 41F | W.HALSE - 2F |
| Nov-60 | FRODINGHAM - 36C | THORNTONJCN - 62A | TILBURY - 33B | DUNDEE - 62B | W.HALSE - 2F | THORNABY - 51L | YORK - 50A | MEXBOROUGH - 41F | W.HALSE - 2F |

| | 90521 | 90522 | 90526 | 90528 | 90532 | 90534 | 90537 | 90538 | 90539 |
|---|---|---|---|---|---|---|---|---|---|
| Aug-50 | MEXBOROUGH - 36B | COLCHESTER - 30E | STAVELEY - 38D | NEWENGLAND - 35A | COLWICK - 38A | THORNTONJCN - 62A | MEXBOROUGH - 36B | MEXBOROUGH - 36B | THORNTONJCN - 62A |
| Jan-51 | MEXBOROUGH - 36B | COLCHESTER - 30E | STAVELEY - 38D | NEWENGLAND - 35A | COLWICK - 38A | THORNTONJCN - 62A | MEXBOROUGH - 36B | MEXBOROUGH - 36B | THORNTONJCN - 62A |
| Aug-51 | MEXBOROUGH - 36B | **9/51: MARCH - 31B** | STAVELEY - 38D | NEWENGLAND - 35A | **9/51: WFD.H - 38E** | THORNTONJCN - 62A | **10/51: DCTR - 36A** | **5/51: DCTR - 36A** | THORNTONJCN - 62A |
| Jan-52 | MEXBOROUGH - 36B | MARCH - 31B | **3/52: NEW.E - 35A** | NEWENGLAND - 35A | W.HALSE - 38E | THORNTONJCN - 62A | DONCASTER - 36A | DONCASTER - 36A | THORNTONJCN - 62A |
| Aug-52 | MEXBOROUGH - 36B | MARCH - 31B | NEWENGLAND - 35A | NEWENGLAND - 35A | **6/52: STAVE - 38D** | THORNTONJCN - 62A | DONCASTER - 36A | DONCASTER - 36A | THORNTONJCN - 62A |
| Jan-53 | MEXBOROUGH - 36B | MARCH - 31B | NEWENGLAND - 35A | NEWENGLAND - 35A | **9/52: COLW - 38A** | THORNTONJCN - 62A | DONCASTER - 36A | DONCASTER - 36A | THORNTONJCN - 62A |
| Aug-53 | MEXBOROUGH - 36B | MARCH - 31B | NEWENGLAND - 35A | NEWENGLAND - 35A | COLWICK - 38A | THORNTONJCN - 62A | DONCASTER - 36A | DONCASTER - 36A | THORNTONJCN - 62A |
| Jan-54 | MEXBOROUGH - 36B | MARCH - 31B | NEWENGLAND - 35A | NEWENGLAND - 35A | **3/54: To LM** | THORNTONJCN - 62A | DONCASTER - 36A | DONCASTER - 36A | THORNTONJCN - 62A |
| Aug-54 | MEXBOROUGH - 36B | MARCH - 31B | NEWENGLAND - 35A | NEWENGLAND - 35A | | THORNTONJCN - 62A | DONCASTER - 36A | DONCASTER - 36A | THORNTONJCN - 62A |
| Jan-55 | MEXBOROUGH - 36B | MARCH - 31B | **2/55: STRAT - 30A** | NEWENGLAND - 35A | | THORNTONJCN - 62A | DONCASTER - 36A | DONCASTER - 36A | THORNTONJCN - 62A |
| Aug-55 | MEXBOROUGH - 36B | MARCH - 31B | **3/55: PLAIS - 33A** | NEWENGLAND - 35A | | THORNTONJCN - 62A | DONCASTER - 36A | DONCASTER - 36A | THORNTONJCN - 62A |
| Jan-56 | MEXBOROUGH - 36B | MARCH - 31B | **5/55: MEX - 36B** | **1/56: COLW - 38A** | | THORNTONJCN - 62A | DONCASTER - 36A | DONCASTER - 36A | THORNTONJCN - 62A |
| Aug-56 | MEXBOROUGH - 36B | MARCH - 31B | MEXBOROUGH - 36B | **2/56: NEW.E - 35A** | | THORNTONJCN - 62A | **10/56: MARCH - 31B** | **10/56: MARCH - 31B** | THORNTONJCN - 62A |
| Jan-57 | MEXBOROUGH - 36B | MARCH - 31B | MEXBOROUGH - 36B | NEWENGLAND - 35A | | THORNTONJCN - 62A | **2/57: DCTR - 36A** | **2/57: DCTR - 36A** | THORNTONJCN - 62A |
| Aug-57 | MEXBOROUGH - 36B | MARCH - 31B | MEXBOROUGH - 36B | NEWENGLAND - 35A | | THORNTONJCN - 62A | DONCASTER - 36A | DONCASTER - 36A | THORNTONJCN - 62A |
| Jan-58 | MEXBOROUGH - 36B | MARCH - 31B | MEXBOROUGH - 36B | **10/57: S.BGE - 35C** | | THORNTONJCN - 62A | DONCASTER - 36A | DONCASTER - 36A | THORNTONJCN - 62A |
| Aug-58 | MEXBOROUGH - 41F | MARCH - 31B | MEXBOROUGH - 41F | SPITALBRIDGE - 31F | | THORNTONJCN - 62A | DONCASTER - 36A | DONCASTER - 36A | THORNTONJCN - 62A |
| Jan-59 | MEXBOROUGH - 41F | MARCH - 31B | MEXBOROUGH - 41F | SPITALBRIDGE - 31F | | THORNTONJCN - 62A | DONCASTER - 36A | DONCASTER - 36A | THORNTONJCN - 62A |
| Aug-59 | MEXBOROUGH - 41F | MARCH - 31B | MEXBOROUGH - 41F | SPITALBRIDGE - 31F | | THORNTONJCN - 62A | DONCASTER - 36A | DONCASTER - 36A | THORNTONJCN - 62A |
| Nov-59 | MEXBOROUGH - 41F | MARCH - 31B | MEXBOROUGH - 41F | SPITALBRIDGE - 31F | | THORNTONJCN - 62A | DONCASTER - 36A | DONCASTER - 36A | THORNTONJCN - 62A |
| Jan-60 | MEXBOROUGH - 41F | MARCH - 31B | MEXBOROUGH - 41F | **2/60: MARCH - 31B** | | THORNTONJCN - 62A | DONCASTER - 36A | DONCASTER - 36A | **12/59: G'MTH - 65F** |
| Apr-60 | MEXBOROUGH - 41F | MARCH - 31B | MEXBOROUGH - 41F | MARCH - 31B | | THORNTONJCN - 62A | DONCASTER - 36A | DONCASTER - 36A | GRANGEMOUTH - 65F |
| Aug-60 | MEXBOROUGH - 41F | MARCH - 31B | MEXBOROUGH - 41F | MARCH - 31B | | THORNTONJCN - 62A | DONCASTER - 36A | DONCASTER - 36A | GRANGEMOUTH - 65F |
| Nov-60 | MEXBOROUGH - 41F | MARCH - 31B | MEXBOROUGH - 41F | MARCH - 31B | | THORNTONJCN - 62A | DONCASTER - 36A | DONCASTER - 36A | GRANGEMOUTH - 65F |

| | 90540 | 90542 | 90543 | 90544 | 90545 | 90547 | 90550 | 90551 | 90553 |
|---|---|---|---|---|---|---|---|---|---|
| Aug-50 | MARCH-31B | DUNFERMLINE-62C | | COLWICK-38A | EASTFIELD-65A | THORNTONJCN-62A | MEXBOROUGH-36B | COLWICK-38A | DUNFERMLINE-62C |
| Jan-51 | **3/51: FROD - 36C** | DUNFERMLINE-62C | | COLWICK-38A | EASTFIELD-65A | THORNTONJCN-62A | MEXBOROUGH-36B | COLWICK-38A | DUNFERMLINE-62C |
| Aug-51 | FRODINGHAM-36C | DUNFERMLINE-62C | | **9/51: To WR** | EASTFIELD-65A | THORNTONJCN-62A | **10/51: MARCH - 31B** | **9/51: STAVE - 38D** | DUNFERMLINE-62C |
| Jan-52 | FRODINGHAM-36C | DUNFERMLINE-62C | | | **2/52: EBRO(SM) -64A** | THORNTONJCN-62A | MARCH-31B | **3/52: NEW.E - 35A** | DUNFERMLINE-62C |
| Aug-52 | FRODINGHAM-36C | DUNFERMLINE-62C | | | EDINBURGH(SM)-64A | **9/52: EBRO(SM) - 64A** | MARCH-31B | NEWENGLAND-35A | DUNFERMLINE-62C |
| Jan-53 | FRODINGHAM-36C | DUNFERMLINE-62C | | | EDINBURGH(SM)-64A | EDINBURGH(SM)-64A | MARCH-31B | NEWENGLAND-35A | DUNFERMLINE-62C |
| Aug-53 | FRODINGHAM-36C | DUNFERMLINE-62C | | | **10/53: COLW - 38A** | EDINBURGH(SM)-64A | MARCH-31B | NEWENGLAND-35A | DUNFERMLINE-62C |
| Jan-54 | FRODINGHAM-36C | DUNFERMLINE-62C | | | COLWICK-38A | EDINBURGH(SM)-64A | MARCH-31B | NEWENGLAND-35A | DUNFERMLINE-62C |
| Aug-54 | FRODINGHAM-36C | DUNFERMLINE-62C | | | **6/54: L.JCN - 40E** | EDINBURGH(SM)-64A | MARCH-31B | NEWENGLAND-35A | DUNFERMLINE-62C |
| Jan-55 | FRODINGHAM-36C | DUNFERMLINE-62C | | | LANGWITHJCN-40E | **12/54: DUNF - 62C** | MARCH-31B | **2/55: STRAT - 30A** | DUNFERMLINE-62C |
| Aug-55 | FRODINGHAM-36C | DUNFERMLINE-62C | | | LANGWITHJCN-40E | DUNFERMLINE-62C | MARCH-31B | STRATFORD-30A | DUNFERMLINE-62C |
| Jan-56 | FRODINGHAM-36C | DUNFERMLINE-62C | | | LANGWITHJCN-40E | DUNFERMLINE-62C | MARCH-31B | STRATFORD-30A | DUNFERMLINE-62C |
| Aug-56 | FRODINGHAM-36C | DUNFERMLINE-62C | | | LANGWITHJCN-40E | DUNFERMLINE-62C | MARCH-31B | STRATFORD-30A | DUNFERMLINE-62C |
| Jan-57 | FRODINGHAM-36C | DUNFERMLINE-62C | | | LANGWITHJCN-40E | DUNFERMLINE-62C | **3/57: DCTR - 36A** | STRATFORD-30A | DUNFERMLINE-62C |
| Aug-57 | FRODINGHAM-36C | DUNFERMLINE-62C | | | LANGWITHJCN-40E | DUNFERMLINE-62C | DONCASTER-36A | STRATFORD-30A | DUNFERMLINE-62C |
| Jan-58 | FRODINGHAM-36C | DUNFERMLINE-62C | Ex LM | | LANGWITHJCN-40E | DUNFERMLINE-62C | DONCASTER-36A | STRATFORD-30A | DUNFERMLINE-62C |
| Aug-58 | FRODINGHAM-36C | DUNFERMLINE-62C | **6/58: YORK - 50A** | | LANGWITHJCN-41J | DUNFERMLINE-62C | DONCASTER-36A | STRATFORD-30A | DUNFERMLINE-62C |
| Jan-59 | FRODINGHAM-36C | DUNFERMLINE-62C | YORK-50A | | LANGWITHJCN-41J | DUNFERMLINE-62C | DONCASTER-36A | STRATFORD-30A | DUNFERMLINE-62C |
| Aug-59 | FRODINGHAM-36C | DUNFERMLINE-62C | YORK-50A | | LANGWITHJCN-41J | DUNFERMLINE-62C | DONCASTER-36A | STRATFORD-30A | DUNFERMLINE-62C |
| Nov-59 | FRODINGHAM-36C | DUNFERMLINE-62C | **10/59: WAKE - 56A** | | LANGWITHJCN-41J | DUNFERMLINE-62C | DONCASTER-36A | STRATFORD-30A | DUNFERMLINE-62C |
| Jan-60 | FRODINGHAM-36C | DUNFERMLINE-62C | WAKEFIELD-56A | | LANGWITHJCN-41J | DUNFERMLINE-62C | **2/60: FROD - 36C** | STRATFORD-30A | DUNFERMLINE-62C |
| Apr-60 | FRODINGHAM-36C | DUNFERMLINE-62C | WAKEFIELD-56A | | **5/60: COLW - 40E** | DUNFERMLINE-62C | FRODINGHAM-36C | STRATFORD-30A | DUNFERMLINE-62C |
| Aug-60 | FRODINGHAM-36C | DUNFERMLINE-62C | WAKEFIELD-56A | | COLWICK-40E | DUNFERMLINE-62C | FRODINGHAM-36C | STRATFORD-30A | DUNFERMLINE-62C |
| Nov-60 | FRODINGHAM-36C | DUNFERMLINE-62C | WAKEFIELD-56A | | COLWICK-40E | DUNFERMLINE-62C | FRODINGHAM-36C | **11/60: DCTR - 36A** | DUNFERMLINE-62C |

| | 90554 | 90555 | 90559 | 90560 | 90567 | 90569 | 90571 | 90574 | 90575 |
|---|---|---|---|---|---|---|---|---|---|
| Aug-50 | NEWENGLAND-35A | EDINBURGH(SM)-64A | NEWENGLAND-35A | DUNFERMLINE-62C | DAIRYCOATES-53A | DUNFERMLINE-62C | SPRINGHEAD-53C | COLWICK-38A | DUNFERMLINE-62C |
| Jan-51 | NEWENGLAND-35A | EDINBURGH(SM)-64A | NEWENGLAND-35A | DUNFERMLINE-62C | DAIRYCOATES-53A | **11/50: EBRO(SM) - 64A** | SPRINGHEAD-53C | COLWICK-38A | DUNFERMLINE-62C |
| Aug-51 | NEWENGLAND-35A | **8/51: To LM** | NEWENGLAND-35A | DUNFERMLINE-62C | DAIRYCOATES-53A | EDINBURGH(SM)-64A | SPRINGHEAD-53C | **6/51: WFD.H - 38E** | DUNFERMLINE-62C |
| Jan-52 | NEWENGLAND-35A | | NEWENGLAND-35A | DUNFERMLINE-62C | **1/52: To LM** | **3/52: MARCH - 31B** | SPRINGHEAD-53C | W.HALSE-38E | DUNFERMLINE-62C |
| Aug-52 | NEWENGLAND-35A | | NEWENGLAND-35A | **9/52: EBRO(SM) - 64A** | **6/52 : COLW - 38A** | MARCH-31B | SPRINGHEAD-53C | W.HALSE-38E | DUNFERMLINE-62C |
| Jan-53 | NEWENGLAND-35A | | NEWENGLAND-35A | EDINBURGH(SM)-64A | COLWICK-38A | MARCH-31B | SPRINGHEAD-53C | W.HALSE-38E | DUNFERMLINE-62C |
| Aug-53 | NEWENGLAND-35A | | NEWENGLAND-35A | EDINBURGH(SM)-64A | COLWICK-38A | MARCH-31B | SPRINGHEAD-53C | W.HALSE-38E | DUNFERMLINE-62C |
| Jan-54 | NEWENGLAND-35A | | NEWENGLAND-35A | EDINBURGH(SM)-64A | COLWICK-38A | MARCH-31B | SPRINGHEAD-53C | W.HALSE-38E | DUNFERMLINE-62C |
| Aug-54 | NEWENGLAND-35A | | NEWENGLAND-35A | EDINBURGH(SM)-64A | **6/54: L.JCN - 40E** | MARCH-31B | SPRINGHEAD-53C | W.HALSE-38E | DUNFERMLINE-62C |
| Jan-55 | **1/55: L.JCN - 40E** | | NEWENGLAND-35A | **11/54: DUNF - 62C** | LANGWITHJCN-40E | MARCH-31B | SPRINGHEAD-53C | W.HALSE-38E | DUNFERMLINE-62C |
| Aug-55 | LANGWITHJCN-40E | | NEWENGLAND-35A | DUNFERMLINE-62C | LANGWITHJCN-40E | MARCH-31B | SPRINGHEAD-53C | W.HALSE-38E | DUNFERMLINE-62C |
| Jan-56 | LANGWITHJCN-40E | | NEWENGLAND-35A | DUNFERMLINE-62C | LANGWITHJCN-40E | MARCH-31B | SPRINGHEAD-53C | W.HALSE-38E | DUNFERMLINE-62C |
| Aug-56 | LANGWITHJCN-40E | | NEWENGLAND-35A | DUNFERMLINE-62C | **7/56: MARCH - 31B** | MARCH-31B | SPRINGHEAD-53C | W.HALSE-38E | DUNFERMLINE-62C |
| Jan-57 | LANGWITHJCN-40E | | NEWENGLAND-35A | DUNFERMLINE-62C | **3/57: DCTR - 36A** | **3/57: DCTR - 36A** | SPRINGHEAD-53C | W.HALSE-38E | DUNFERMLINE-62C |
| Aug-57 | LANGWITHJCN-40E | | **10/57: MARCH - 31B** | DUNFERMLINE-62C | DONCASTER-36A | DONCASTER-36A | SPRINGHEAD-53C | W.HALSE-38E | DUNFERMLINE-62C |
| Jan-58 | LANGWITHJCN-40E | | MARCH-31B | DUNFERMLINE-62C | DONCASTER-36A | DONCASTER-36A | SPRINGHEAD-53C | W.HALSE-38E | DUNFERMLINE-62C |
| Aug-58 | LANGWITHJCN-41J | | MARCH-31B | DUNFERMLINE-62C | **7/58: MEX - 41F** | DONCASTER-36A | **10/58: DAIRY - 53A** | W.HALSE-2F | DUNFERMLINE-62C |
| Jan-59 | LANGWITHJCN-41J | | **4/59: NOR - 32A** | DUNFERMLINE-62C | MEXBOROUGH-41F | DONCASTER-36A | DAIRYCOATES-53A | **2/59: WIGAN - 8F** | DUNFERMLINE-62C |
| Aug-59 | LANGWITHJCN-41J | | NORWICH-32A | DUNFERMLINE-62C | MEXBOROUGH-41F | DONCASTER-36A | DAIRYCOATES-53A | WIGAN(SB)-8F | DUNFERMLINE-62C |
| Nov-59 | LANGWITHJCN-41J | | NORWICH-32A | DUNFERMLINE-62C | MEXBOROUGH-41F | DONCASTER-36A | DAIRYCOATES-53A | WIGAN(SB)-8F | DUNFERMLINE-62C |
| Jan-60 | LANGWITHJCN-41J | | **2/60: MARCH - 31B** | DUNFERMLINE-62C | MEXBOROUGH-41F | DONCASTER-36A | DAIRYCOATES-53A | WIGAN(SB)-8F | DUNFERMLINE-62C |
| Apr-60 | **5/60: COLW - 40E** | | MARCH-31B | DUNFERMLINE-62C | MEXBOROUGH-41F | DONCASTER-36A | DAIRYCOATES-50B | WIGAN(SB)-8F | DUNFERMLINE-62C |
| Aug-60 | COLWICK-40E | | MARCH-31B | DUNFERMLINE-62C | MEXBOROUGH-41F | DONCASTER-36A | DAIRYCOATES-50B | WIGAN(SB)-8F | DUNFERMLINE-62C |
| Nov-60 | COLWICK-40E | | MARCH-31B | DUNFERMLINE-62C | MEXBOROUGH-41F | DONCASTER-36A | DAIRYCOATES-50B | WIGAN(SB)-8F | DUNFERMLINE-62C |

| | 90577 | 90578 | 90580 | 90581 | 90582 | 90583 | 90586 | 90587 | 90590 |
|---|---|---|---|---|---|---|---|---|---|
| Aug-50 | NEWENGLAND-35A | | MARCH-31B | | MARCH-31B | MEXBOROUGH-36B | SPRINGHEAD-53C | MEXBOROUGH-36B | MEXBOROUGH-36B |
| Jan-51 | NEWENGLAND-35A | | MARCH-31B | **3/51: MEX - 36B** | MARCH-31B | MEXBOROUGH-36B | SPRINGHEAD-53C | MEXBOROUGH-36B | MEXBOROUGH-36B |
| Aug-51 | NEWENGLAND-35A | | MARCH-31B | MEXBOROUGH-36B | **5/51: DCTR - 36A** | MEXBOROUGH-36B | SPRINGHEAD-53C | MEXBOROUGH-36B | MEXBOROUGH-36B |
| Jan-52 | NEWENGLAND-35A | | MARCH-31B | MEXBOROUGH-36B | DONCASTER-36A | **12/51: IMM - 40B** | SPRINGHEAD-53C | MEXBOROUGH-36B | MEXBOROUGH-36B |
| Aug-52 | NEWENGLAND-35A | | MARCH-31B | MEXBOROUGH-36B | **9/52: MEX - 36B** | IMMINGHAM-40B | SPRINGHEAD-53C | MEXBOROUGH-36B | MEXBOROUGH-36B |
| Jan-53 | NEWENGLAND-35A | | **2/53: MEX - 36B** | **2/53: To LM** | MEXBOROUGH-36B | IMMINGHAM-40B | SPRINGHEAD-53C | MEXBOROUGH-36B | MEXBOROUGH-36B |
| Aug-53 | NEWENGLAND-35A | | MEXBOROUGH-36B | | MEXBOROUGH-36B | IMMINGHAM-40B | SPRINGHEAD-53C | MEXBOROUGH-36B | MEXBOROUGH-36B |
| Jan-54 | NEWENGLAND-35A | | MEXBOROUGH-36B | | MEXBOROUGH-36B | IMMINGHAM-40B | SPRINGHEAD-53C | MEXBOROUGH-36B | MEXBOROUGH-36B |
| Aug-54 | NEWENGLAND-35A | | MEXBOROUGH-36B | | MEXBOROUGH-36B | IMMINGHAM-40B | SPRINGHEAD-53C | MEXBOROUGH-36B | MEXBOROUGH-36B |
| Jan-55 | **1/55: L.JCN - 40E** | | MEXBOROUGH-36B | | MEXBOROUGH-36B | IMMINGHAM-40B | SPRINGHEAD-53C | MEXBOROUGH-36B | MEXBOROUGH-36B |
| Aug-55 | LANGWITHJCN-40E | | MEXBOROUGH-36B | | MEXBOROUGH-36B | IMMINGHAM-40B | SPRINGHEAD-53C | MEXBOROUGH-36B | MEXBOROUGH-36B |
| Jan-56 | LANGWITHJCN-40E | | MEXBOROUGH-36B | | MEXBOROUGH-36B | IMMINGHAM-40B | SPRINGHEAD-53C | MEXBOROUGH-36B | MEXBOROUGH-36B |
| Aug-56 | LANGWITHJCN-40E | | MEXBOROUGH-36B | | MEXBOROUGH-36B | IMMINGHAM-40B | SPRINGHEAD-53C | MEXBOROUGH-36B | MEXBOROUGH-36B |
| Jan-57 | LANGWITHJCN-40E | | MEXBOROUGH-36B | | MEXBOROUGH-36B | IMMINGHAM-40B | SPRINGHEAD-53C | MEXBOROUGH-36B | MEXBOROUGH-36B |
| Aug-57 | LANGWITHJCN-40E | | MEXBOROUGH-36B | | MEXBOROUGH-36B | IMMINGHAM-40B | SPRINGHEAD-53C | MEXBOROUGH-36B | MEXBOROUGH-36B |
| Jan-58 | LANGWITHJCN-40E | Ex LM | MEXBOROUGH-36B | | MEXBOROUGH-36B | IMMINGHAM-40B | SPRINGHEAD-53C | MEXBOROUGH-36B | MEXBOROUGH-36B |
| Aug-58 | LANGWITHJCN-41J | **6/58: YORK - 50A** | MEXBOROUGH-41F | | MEXBOROUGH-41F | IMMINGHAM-40B | SPRINGHEAD-53C | MEXBOROUGH-41F | MEXBOROUGH-41F |
| Jan-59 | LANGWITHJCN-41J | YORK-50A | MEXBOROUGH-41F | | MEXBOROUGH-41F | IMMINGHAM-40B | **12/58: DAIRY - 53A** | MEXBOROUGH-41F | MEXBOROUGH-41F |
| Aug-59 | LANGWITHJCN-41J | YORK-50A | MEXBOROUGH-41F | | MEXBOROUGH-41F | IMMINGHAM-40B | DAIRYCOATES-53A | MEXBOROUGH-41F | MEXBOROUGH-41F |
| Nov-59 | LANGWITHJCN-41J | YORK-50A | MEXBOROUGH-41F | | MEXBOROUGH-41F | IMMINGHAM-40B | DAIRYCOATES-53A | MEXBOROUGH-41F | MEXBOROUGH-41F |
| Jan-60 | LANGWITHJCN-41J | YORK-50A | MEXBOROUGH-41F | | MEXBOROUGH-41F | IMMINGHAM-40B | DAIRYCOATES-53A | MEXBOROUGH-41F | MEXBOROUGH-41F |
| Apr-60 | **5/60: COLW - 40E** | YORK-50A | MEXBOROUGH-41F | | MEXBOROUGH-41F | IMMINGHAM-40B | DAIRYCOATES-50B | MEXBOROUGH-41F | MEXBOROUGH-41F |
| Aug-60 | COLWICK-40E | YORK-50A | MEXBOROUGH-41F | | MEXBOROUGH-41F | IMMINGHAM-40B | DAIRYCOATES-50B | MEXBOROUGH-41F | MEXBOROUGH-41F |
| Nov-60 | COLWICK-40E | YORK-50A | MEXBOROUGH-41F | | MEXBOROUGH-41F | IMMINGHAM-40B | DAIRYCOATES-50B | MEXBOROUGH-41F | MEXBOROUGH-41F |

| | 90593 | 90594 | 90596 | 90597 | 90598 | 90600 | 90601 | 90602 | 90603 |
|---|---|---|---|---|---|---|---|---|---|
| Aug-50 | | MEXBOROUGH-36B | MEXBOROUGH-36B | MEXBOROUGH-36B | MEXBOROUGH-36B | DUNDEE-62B | MARCH-31B | MARCH-31B | STOCKTON-51E |
| Jan-51 | | MEXBOROUGH-36B | MEXBOROUGH-36B | MEXBOROUGH-36B | MEXBOROUGH-36B | DUNDEE-62B | MARCH-31B | MARCH-31B | STOCKTON-51E |
| Aug-51 | | MEXBOROUGH-36B | MEXBOROUGH-36B | MEXBOROUGH-36B | MEXBOROUGH-36B | DUNDEE-62B | MARCH-31B | MARCH-31B | STOCKTON-51E |
| Jan-52 | | **12/51: IMM - 40B** | MEXBOROUGH-36B | MEXBOROUGH-36B | MEXBOROUGH-36B | DUNDEE-62B | MARCH-31B | MARCH-31B | STOCKTON-51E |
| Aug-52 | | IMMINGHAM-40B | MEXBOROUGH-36B | MEXBOROUGH-36B | MEXBOROUGH-36B | DUNDEE-62B | MARCH-31B | MARCH-31B | STOCKTON-51E |
| Jan-53 | | IMMINGHAM-40B | MEXBOROUGH-36B | MEXBOROUGH-36B | MEXBOROUGH-36B | DUNDEE-62B | MARCH-31B | MARCH-31B | STOCKTON-51E |
| Aug-53 | | IMMINGHAM-40B | **5/53: FROD - 36C** | MEXBOROUGH-36B | MEXBOROUGH-36B | DUNDEE-62B | MARCH-31B | MARCH-31B | STOCKTON-51E |
| Jan-54 | | IMMINGHAM-40B | FRODINGHAM-36C | MEXBOROUGH-36B | MEXBOROUGH-36B | DUNDEE-62B | MARCH-31B | MARCH-31B | STOCKTON-51E |
| Aug-54 | | IMMINGHAM-40B | FRODINGHAM-36C | MEXBOROUGH-36B | MEXBOROUGH-36B | DUNDEE-62B | MARCH-31B | MARCH-31B | **8/54: YORK - 50A** |
| Jan-55 | | IMMINGHAM-40B | FRODINGHAM-36C | MEXBOROUGH-36B | MEXBOROUGH-36B | DUNDEE-62B | **1/55: DCTR - 36A** | MARCH-31B | YORK-50A |
| Aug-55 | | **8/55: L.JCN - 40E** | FRODINGHAM-36C | MEXBOROUGH-36B | MEXBOROUGH-36B | DUNDEE-62B | **2/55: FROD - 36C** | MARCH-31B | YORK-50A |
| Jan-56 | | LANGWITHJCN-40E | FRODINGHAM-36C | **11/55: FROD - 36C** | **11/55: FROD - 36C** | DUNDEE-62B | FRODINGHAM-36C | MARCH-31B | YORK-50A |
| Aug-56 | | LANGWITHJCN-40E | FRODINGHAM-36C | FRODINGHAM-36C | FRODINGHAM-36C | DUNDEE-62B | FRODINGHAM-36C | MARCH-31B | **6/56: TBY - 51L** |
| Jan-57 | | LANGWITHJCN-40E | **3/57: DAWS - 65D** | FRODINGHAM-36C | FRODINGHAM-36C | **4/57: DUNF - 62C** | FRODINGHAM-36C | **3/57: DCTR - 36A** | NEWPORT-51B |
| Aug-57 | | LANGWITHJCN-40E | DAWSHOLME-65D | FRODINGHAM-36C | FRODINGHAM-36C | DUNFERMLINE-62C | FRODINGHAM-36C | DONCASTER-36A | NEWPORT-51B |
| Jan-58 | Ex LM | LANGWITHJCN-40E | **4/58: POL - 66A** | FRODINGHAM-36C | FRODINGHAM-36C | DUNFERMLINE-62C | FRODINGHAM-36C | DONCASTER-36A | NEWPORT-51B |
| Aug-58 | **6/58: DARL - 51A** | LANGWITHJCN-41J | POLMADIE-66A | FRODINGHAM-36C | FRODINGHAM-36C | DUNFERMLINE-62C | FRODINGHAM-36C | DONCASTER-36A | **6/58: TBY - 51L** |
| Jan-59 | DARLINGTON-51A | LANGWITHJCN-41J | POLMADIE-66A | FRODINGHAM-36C | FRODINGHAM-36C | DUNFERMLINE-62C | FRODINGHAM-36C | DONCASTER-36A | THORNABY-51L |
| Aug-59 | **9/59: TBY - 51L** | LANGWITHJCN-41J | POLMADIE-66A | FRODINGHAM-36C | FRODINGHAM-36C | DUNFERMLINE-62C | FRODINGHAM-36C | DONCASTER-36A | THORNABY-51L |
| Nov-59 | THORNABY-51L | LANGWITHJCN-41J | POLMADIE-66A | FRODINGHAM-36C | FRODINGHAM-36C | DUNFERMLINE-62C | FRODINGHAM-36C | DONCASTER-36A | THORNABY-51L |
| Jan-60 | THORNABY-51L | LANGWITHJCN-41J | POLMADIE-66A | FRODINGHAM-36C | FRODINGHAM-36C | DUNFERMLINE-62C | FRODINGHAM-36C | DONCASTER-36A | THORNABY-51L |
| Apr-60 | THORNABY-51L | **5/60: COLW - 40E** | POLMADIE-66A | FRODINGHAM-36C | FRODINGHAM-36C | DUNFERMLINE-62C | FRODINGHAM-36C | DONCASTER-36A | THORNABY-51L |
| Aug-60 | THORNABY-51L | COLWICK-40E | POLMADIE-66A | FRODINGHAM-36C | FRODINGHAM-36C | DUNFERMLINE-62C | FRODINGHAM-36C | DONCASTER-36A | THORNABY-51L |
| Nov-60 | THORNABY-51L | COLWICK-40E | POLMADIE-66A | FRODINGHAM-36C | FRODINGHAM-36C | DUNFERMLINE-62C | FRODINGHAM-36C | DONCASTER-36A | THORNABY-51L |

| | 90605 | 90606 | 90607 | 90608 | 90609 | 90610 | 90611 | 90612 | 90613 |
|---|---|---|---|---|---|---|---|---|---|
| Aug-50 | NEWPORT-51B | STAVELEY-38D | | MARCH-31B | YORK-50A | | TYNE DOCK-54B | MEXBOROUGH-36B | NEWENGLAND-35A |
| Jan-51 | NEWPORT-51B | STAVELEY-38D | | MARCH-31B | YORK-50A | | TYNE DOCK-54B | MEXBOROUGH-36B | NEWENGLAND-35A |
| Aug-51 | NEWPORT-51B | **4/51: COLW - 38A** | | MARCH-31B | **9/51: DAIRY - 53A** | | TYNE DOCK-54B | MEXBOROUGH-36B | NEWENGLAND-35A |
| Jan-52 | NEWPORT-51B | COLWICK-38A | | MARCH-31B | DAIRYCOATES-53A | | TYNE DOCK-54B | MEXBOROUGH-36B | NEWENGLAND-35A |
| Aug-52 | NEWPORT-51B | **5/52: To LM** | | MARCH-31B | DAIRYCOATES-53A | | TYNE DOCK-54B | MEXBOROUGH-36B | NEWENGLAND-35A |
| Jan-53 | NEWPORT-51B | | | MARCH-31B | DAIRYCOATES-53A | | TYNE DOCK-54B | MEXBOROUGH-36B | NEWENGLAND-35A |
| Aug-53 | NEWPORT-51B | | | MARCH-31B | DAIRYCOATES-53A | | TYNE DOCK-54B | MEXBOROUGH-36B | NEWENGLAND-35A |
| Jan-54 | NEWPORT-51B | | | MARCH-31B | DAIRYCOATES-53A | | TYNE DOCK-54B | MEXBOROUGH-36B | NEWENGLAND-35A |
| Aug-54 | NEWPORT-51B | | | MARCH-31B | DAIRYCOATES-53A | | TYNE DOCK-54B | MEXBOROUGH-36B | NEWENGLAND-35A |
| Jan-55 | NEWPORT-51B | | | MARCH-31B | DAIRYCOATES-53A | | TYNE DOCK-54B | MEXBOROUGH-36B | NEWENGLAND-35A |
| Aug-55 | NEWPORT-51B | | | MARCH-31B | DAIRYCOATES-53A | | TYNE DOCK-54B | MEXBOROUGH-36B | NEWENGLAND-35A |
| Jan-56 | NEWPORT-51B | | | MARCH-31B | DAIRYCOATES-53A | | TYNE DOCK-54B | MEXBOROUGH-36B | NEWENGLAND-35A |
| Aug-56 | NEWPORT-51B | | | MARCH-31B | DAIRYCOATES-53A | | TYNE DOCK-54B | MEXBOROUGH-36B | NEWENGLAND-35A |
| Jan-57 | NEWPORT-51B | | Ex L&Y | **3/57: DCTR - 36A** | DAIRYCOATES-53A | Ex L&Y | TYNE DOCK-54B | MEXBOROUGH-36B | NEWENGLAND-35A |
| Aug-57 | NEWPORT-51B | | **6/57: N'TON - 55E** | DONCASTER-36A | DAIRYCOATES-53A | **6/57: N'TON - 55E** | **6/57: YORK - 50A** | MEXBOROUGH-36B | NEWENGLAND-35A |
| Jan-58 | NEWPORT-51B | | **10/57: WAKE - 56A** | DONCASTER-36A | DAIRYCOATES-53A | NORMANTON-55E | YORK-50A | MEXBOROUGH-36B | NEWENGLAND-35A |
| Aug-58 | **6/58: TBY - 51L** | | WAKEFIELD-56A | **7/58: MEX - 41F** | DAIRYCOATES-53A | NORMANTON-55E | YORK-50A | MEXBOROUGH-41F | NEWENGLAND-34E |
| Jan-59 | THORNABY-51L | | WAKEFIELD-56A | MEXBOROUGH-41F | DAIRYCOATES-53A | NORMANTON-55E | **4/59: ROY - 55D** | MEXBOROUGH-41F | NEWENGLAND-34E |
| Aug-59 | **6/59: ROY - 55D** | | WAKEFIELD-56A | MEXBOROUGH-41F | DAIRYCOATES-53A | NORMANTON-55E | ROYSTON-55D | MEXBOROUGH-41F | NEWENGLAND-34E |
| Nov-59 | ROYSTON-55D | | WAKEFIELD-56A | MEXBOROUGH-41F | DAIRYCOATES-53A | NORMANTON-55E | ROYSTON-55D | MEXBOROUGH-41F | NEWENGLAND-34E |
| Jan-60 | ROYSTON-55D | | WAKEFIELD-56A | MEXBOROUGH-41F | DAIRYCOATES-53A | NORMANTON-55E | ROYSTON-55D | MEXBOROUGH-41F | NEWENGLAND-34E |
| Apr-60 | ROYSTON-55D | | WAKEFIELD-56A | MEXBOROUGH-41F | DAIRYCOATES-50B | NORMANTON-55E | ROYSTON-55D | MEXBOROUGH-41F | NEWENGLAND-34E |
| Aug-60 | ROYSTON-55D | | WAKEFIELD-56A | MEXBOROUGH-41F | DAIRYCOATES-50B | NORMANTON-55E | ROYSTON-55D | MEXBOROUGH-41F | NEWENGLAND-34E |
| Nov-60 | ROYSTON-55D | | WAKEFIELD-56A | MEXBOROUGH-41F | DAIRYCOATES-50B | NORMANTON-55E | ROYSTON-55D | MEXBOROUGH-41F | NEWENGLAND-34E |

| | 90614 | 90617 | 90618 | 90623 | 90625 | 90627 | 90629 | 90634 | 90636 |
|---|---|---|---|---|---|---|---|---|---|
| Aug-50 | THORNTONJCN-62A | | MEXBOROUGH-36B | STOCKTON-51E | NEWPORT-51B | TYNE DOCK-54B | COLWICK-38A | STAVELEY-38D | COLWICK-38A |
| Jan-51 | THORNTONJCN-62A | | MEXBOROUGH-36B | STOCKTON-51E | NEWPORT-51B | TYNE DOCK-54B | COLWICK-38A | STAVELEY-38D | COLWICK-38A |
| Aug-51 | THORNTONJCN-62A | | MEXBOROUGH-36B | STOCKTON-51E | NEWPORT-51B | **9/51: DAIRY - 53A** | COLWICK-38A | **6/51: COLW - 38A** | **8/51: To WR** |
| Jan-52 | THORNTONJCN-62A | | MEXBOROUGH-36B | STOCKTON-51E | NEWPORT-51B | DAIRYCOATES-53A | COLWICK-38A | **11/51: STAVE - 38D** | **10/51: COLW - 38A** |
| Aug-52 | THORNTONJCN-62A | | **6/52: COLW - 38A** | **5/52: S'HEAD - 53C** | NEWPORT-51B | DAIRYCOATES-53A | COLWICK-38A | **12/51: COLW - 38A** | COLWICK-38A |
| Jan-53 | THORNTONJCN-62A | | COLWICK-38A | SPRINGHEAD-53C | NEWPORT-51B | DAIRYCOATES-53A | COLWICK-38A | COLWICK-38A | COLWICK-38A |
| Aug-53 | THORNTONJCN-62A | | COLWICK-38A | SPRINGHEAD-53C | NEWPORT-51B | DAIRYCOATES-53A | COLWICK-38A | COLWICK-38A | COLWICK-38A |
| Jan-54 | THORNTONJCN-62A | | COLWICK-38A | SPRINGHEAD-53C | NEWPORT-51B | DAIRYCOATES-53A | COLWICK-38A | COLWICK-38A | COLWICK-38A |
| Aug-54 | THORNTONJCN-62A | | COLWICK-38A | SPRINGHEAD-53C | NEWPORT-51B | DAIRYCOATES-53A | COLWICK-38A | COLWICK-38A | COLWICK-38A |
| Jan-55 | THORNTONJCN-62A | | COLWICK-38A | SPRINGHEAD-53C | NEWPORT-51B | DAIRYCOATES-53A | COLWICK-38A | COLWICK-38A | **11/54: DCTR - 36A** |
| Aug-55 | THORNTONJCN-62A | | COLWICK-38A | SPRINGHEAD-53C | NEWPORT-51B | DAIRYCOATES-53A | COLWICK-38A | COLWICK-38A | DONCASTER-36A |
| Jan-56 | THORNTONJCN-62A | | COLWICK-38A | SPRINGHEAD-53C | NEWPORT-51B | DAIRYCOATES-53A | COLWICK-38A | COLWICK-38A | DONCASTER-36A |
| Aug-56 | THORNTONJCN-62A | | COLWICK-38A | SPRINGHEAD-53C | NEWPORT-51B | DAIRYCOATES-53A | COLWICK-38A | COLWICK-38A | **10/56: MARCH - 31B** |
| Jan-57 | THORNTONJCN-62A | Ex L&Y | COLWICK-38A | SPRINGHEAD-53C | NEWPORT-51B | DAIRYCOATES-53A | COLWICK-38A | COLWICK-38A | **2/57: DCTR - 36A** |
| Aug-57 | THORNTONJCN-62A | **6/57: N'TON - 55E** | COLWICK-38A | SPRINGHEAD-53C | **6/57: YORK - 50A** | DAIRYCOATES-53A | COLWICK-38A | COLWICK-38A | DONCASTER-36A |
| Jan-58 | THORNTONJCN-62A | NORMANTON-55E | COLWICK-38A | SPRINGHEAD-53C | **9/57: WAKE - 56A** | DAIRYCOATES-53A | COLWICK-38A | COLWICK-38A | DONCASTER-36A |
| Aug-58 | THORNTONJCN-62A | NORMANTON-55E | COLWICK-40E | SPRINGHEAD-53C | WAKEFIELD-56A | DAIRYCOATES-53A | COLWICK-40E | COLWICK-40E | DONCASTER-36A |
| Jan-59 | THORNTONJCN-62A | NORMANTON-55E | COLWICK-40E | **12/58: DAIRY - 53A** | WAKEFIELD-56A | DAIRYCOATES-53A | COLWICK-40E | COLWICK-40E | DONCASTER-36A |
| Aug-59 | THORNTONJCN-62A | NORMANTON-55E | COLWICK-40E | DAIRYCOATES-53A | WAKEFIELD-56A | DAIRYCOATES-53A | COLWICK-40E | COLWICK-40E | DONCASTER-36A |
| Nov-59 | THORNTONJCN-62A | NORMANTON-55E | COLWICK-40E | DAIRYCOATES-53A | WAKEFIELD-56A | DAIRYCOATES-53A | COLWICK-40E | COLWICK-40E | DONCASTER-36A |
| Jan-60 | THORNTONJCN-62A | NORMANTON-55E | COLWICK-40E | DAIRYCOATES-53A | WAKEFIELD-56A | DAIRYCOATES-53A | COLWICK-40E | COLWICK-40E | DONCASTER-36A |
| Apr-60 | THORNTONJCN-62A | NORMANTON-55E | **5/60: NEW.E - 34E** | DAIRYCOATES-50B | WAKEFIELD-56A | DAIRYCOATES-50B | COLWICK-40E | COLWICK-40E | DONCASTER-36A |
| Aug-60 | THORNTONJCN-62A | NORMANTON-55E | NEWENGLAND-34E | DAIRYCOATES-50B | WAKEFIELD-56A | DAIRYCOATES-50B | COLWICK-40E | COLWICK-40E | DONCASTER-36A |
| Nov-60 | THORNTONJCN-62A | NORMANTON-55E | NEWENGLAND-34E | DAIRYCOATES-50B | WAKEFIELD-56A | DAIRYCOATES-50B | COLWICK-40E | COLWICK-40E | DONCASTER-36A |

| | 90637 | 90638 | 90640 | 90644 | 90646 | 90647 | 90648 | 90649 | 90650 |
|---|---|---|---|---|---|---|---|---|---|
| Aug-50 | | W.HALSE-38E | | | IMMINGHAM-40B | IMMINGHAM-40B | COLWICK-38A | | |
| Jan-51 | | **10/50: COLW - 38A** | | | IMMINGHAM-40B | **3/51: NEW.E - 35A** | **3/51: WFD.H - 38E** | | |
| Aug-51 | | **3/51: WFD.H - 38E** | | | **5/51: FROD - 36C** | **7/51: FROD - 36C** | W.HALSE-38E | | |
| Jan-52 | | W.HALSE-38E | | | FRODINGHAM-36C | FRODINGHAM-36C | W.HALSE-38E | | |
| Aug-52 | | W.HALSE-38E | | | FRODINGHAM-36C | FRODINGHAM-36C | W.HALSE-38E | | |
| Jan-53 | | W.HALSE-38E | | | FRODINGHAM-36C | FRODINGHAM-36C | W.HALSE-38E | | |
| Aug-53 | | W.HALSE-38E | | | FRODINGHAM-36C | FRODINGHAM-36C | **5/53: COLW - 38A** | | |
| Jan-54 | | W.HALSE-38E | | | FRODINGHAM-36C | FRODINGHAM-36C | COLWICK-38A | | |
| Aug-54 | | W.HALSE-38E | | | FRODINGHAM-36C | FRODINGHAM-36C | COLWICK-38A | | |
| Jan-55 | | W.HALSE-38E | | | FRODINGHAM-36C | FRODINGHAM-36C | COLWICK-38A | | |
| Aug-55 | | W.HALSE-38E | | | FRODINGHAM-36C | FRODINGHAM-36C | COLWICK-38A | | |
| Jan-56 | | W.HALSE-38E | | | FRODINGHAM-36C | FRODINGHAM-36C | COLWICK-38A | | |
| Aug-56 | | W.HALSE-38E | | | FRODINGHAM-36C | FRODINGHAM-36C | COLWICK-38A | | |
| Jan-57 | Ex L&Y | W.HALSE-38E | Ex CR | | FRODINGHAM-36C | FRODINGHAM-36C | COLWICK-38A | | |
| Aug-57 | **8/57: N'TON - 55E** | W.HALSE-38E | **7/57: DAWS - 65D** | | FRODINGHAM-36C | FRODINGHAM-36C | COLWICK-38A | | |
| Jan-58 | NORMANTON-55E | W.HALSE-38E | DAWSHOLME-65D | | FRODINGHAM-36C | FRODINGHAM-36C | COLWICK-38A | | |
| Aug-58 | NORMANTON-55E | W.HALSE-2F | DAWSHOLME-65D | | FRODINGHAM-36C | FRODINGHAM-36C | **9/58: IMM - 40B** | | |
| Jan-59 | NORMANTON-55E | W.HALSE-2F | DAWSHOLME-65D | | FRODINGHAM-36C | FRODINGHAM-36C | IMMINGHAM-40B | Ex LM | |
| Aug-59 | NORMANTON-55E | W.HALSE-2F | DAWSHOLME-65D | | FRODINGHAM-36C | FRODINGHAM-36C | **8/59: COLW - 40E** | **6/59: HUDD - 55G** | |
| Nov-59 | NORMANTON-55E | W.HALSE-2F | DAWSHOLME-65D | | FRODINGHAM-36C | FRODINGHAM-36C | COLWICK-40E | HUDDERSFIELD-55G | |
| Jan-60 | NORMANTON-55E | W.HALSE-2F | DAWSHOLME-65D | Ex LM | FRODINGHAM-36C | FRODINGHAM-36C | COLWICK-40E | HUDDERSFIELD-55G | Ex LM |
| Apr-60 | NORMANTON-55E | W.HALSE-2F | DAWSHOLME-65D | | FRODINGHAM-36C | FRODINGHAM-36C | COLWICK-40E | HUDDERSFIELD-55G | |
| Aug-60 | NORMANTON-55E | W.HALSE-2F | DAWSHOLME-65D | **6/60: ARDS - 56B** | FRODINGHAM-36C | FRODINGHAM-36C | **8/60: IMM - 40B** | HUDDERSFIELD-55G | |
| Nov-60 | NORMANTON-55E | W.HALSE-2F | DAWSHOLME-65D | ARDSLEY-56B | FRODINGHAM-36C | FRODINGHAM-36C | **10/60: FROD - 36C** | HUDDERSFIELD-55G | **11/60: ROY - 55D** |

| | 90652 | 90653 | 90657 | 90659 | 90660 | 90661 | 90662 | 90663 | 90664 |
|---|---|---|---|---|---|---|---|---|---|
| Aug-50 | | MEXBOROUGH-36B | NEWENGLAND-35A | NEWENGLAND-35A | MARCH-31B | SPRINGHEAD-53C | COLWICK-38A | DAIRYCOATES-53A | |
| Jan-51 | | **9/50: MARCH - 31B** | NEWENGLAND-35A | NEWENGLAND-35A | MARCH-31B | SPRINGHEAD-53C | COLWICK-38A | DAIRYCOATES-53A | |
| Aug-51 | | **2/51: MEX - 36B** | NEWENGLAND-35A | NEWENGLAND-35A | MARCH-31B | SPRINGHEAD-53C | COLWICK-38A | **7/51: S'HEAD - 53C** | |
| Jan-52 | | MEXBOROUGH-36B | NEWENGLAND-35A | NEWENGLAND-35A | MARCH-31B | SPRINGHEAD-53C | COLWICK-38A | SPRINGHEAD-53C | |
| Aug-52 | | MEXBOROUGH-36B | NEWENGLAND-35A | NEWENGLAND-35A | MARCH-31B | SPRINGHEAD-53C | COLWICK-38A | SPRINGHEAD-53C | |
| Jan-53 | | MEXBOROUGH-36B | NEWENGLAND-35A | NEWENGLAND-35A | MARCH-31B | SPRINGHEAD-53C | COLWICK-38A | SPRINGHEAD-53C | |
| Aug-53 | | MEXBOROUGH-36B | NEWENGLAND-35A | NEWENGLAND-35A | MARCH-31B | SPRINGHEAD-53C | COLWICK-38A | SPRINGHEAD-53C | |
| Jan-54 | | MEXBOROUGH-36B | NEWENGLAND-35A | NEWENGLAND-35A | **10/53: IMM - 40B** | SPRINGHEAD-53C | COLWICK-38A | SPRINGHEAD-53C | |
| Aug-54 | | MEXBOROUGH-36B | NEWENGLAND-35A | NEWENGLAND-35A | IMMINGHAM-40B | SPRINGHEAD-53C | COLWICK-38A | SPRINGHEAD-53C | |
| Jan-55 | | MEXBOROUGH-36B | NEWENGLAND-35A | NEWENGLAND-35A | IMMINGHAM-40B | SPRINGHEAD-53C | COLWICK-38A | SPRINGHEAD-53C | |
| Aug-55 | | **5/55: PLAIS - 33A** | NEWENGLAND-35A | **12/55: COLW - 38A** | **8/55: L. JCN - 40E** | SPRINGHEAD-53C | COLWICK-38A | **9/55: N.HILL - 50B** | |
| Jan-56 | | PLAISTOW-33A | NEWENGLAND-35A | **1/56: NEW.E - 35A** | **11/55: STRAT - 30A** | SPRINGHEAD-53C | COLWICK-38A | NEVILLE HILL-50B | |
| Aug-56 | | PLAISTOW-33A | NEWENGLAND-35A | NEWENGLAND-35A | STRATFORD-30A | SPRINGHEAD-53C | COLWICK-38A | NEVILLE HILL-50B | |
| Jan-57 | Ex L&Y | PLAISTOW-33A | NEWENGLAND-35A | NEWENGLAND-35A | STRATFORD-30A | SPRINGHEAD-53C | COLWICK-38A | NEVILLE HILL-50B | |
| Aug-57 | **6/57: N'TON - 55E** | PLAISTOW-33A | **9/57: IMM - 40B** | NEWENGLAND-35A | STRATFORD-30A | SPRINGHEAD-53C | COLWICK-38A | NEVILLE HILL-50B | |
| Jan-58 | NORMANTON-55E | PLAISTOW-33A | **10/57: L. JCN - 40E** | NEWENGLAND-35A | STRATFORD-30A | SPRINGHEAD-53C | COLWICK-38A | NEVILLE HILL-50B | |
| Aug-58 | NORMANTON-55E | PLAISTOW-33A | LANGWITH JCN-41J | NEWENGLAND-34E | STRATFORD-30A | **6/58: H.HILL - 51G** | COLWICK-40E | NEVILLE HILL-50B | |
| Jan-59 | NORMANTON-55E | PLAISTOW-33A | LANGWITH JCN-41J | NEWENGLAND-34E | STRATFORD-30A | HAVERTON HILL-51G | COLWICK-40E | NEVILLE HILL-50B | Ex LM |
| Aug-59 | NORMANTON-55E | PLAISTOW-33A | LANGWITH JCN-41J | NEWENGLAND-34E | STRATFORD-30A | **4/59: ROY - 55D** | COLWICK-40E | **6/59: YORK - 50A** | **6/59: ROY - 55D** |
| Nov-59 | NORMANTON-55E | **10/59: TIL - 33B** | LANGWITH JCN-41J | NEWENGLAND-34E | STRATFORD-30A | **10/59: N'TON - 55E** | COLWICK-40E | YORK-50A | **10/59: N'TON - 55E** |
| Jan-60 | NORMANTON-55E | TILBURY-33B | LANGWITH JCN-41J | NEWENGLAND-34E | STRATFORD-30A | NORMANTON-55E | COLWICK-40E | YORK-50A | NORMANTON-55E |
| Apr-60 | NORMANTON-55E | TILBURY-33B | LANGWITH JCN-41J | NEWENGLAND-34E | **5/60: HSEY - 34B** | NORMANTON-55E | **5/60: NEW.E - 34E** | YORK-50A | NORMANTON-55E |
| Aug-60 | NORMANTON-55E | TILBURY-33B | LANGWITH JCN-41J | NEWENGLAND-34E | HORNSEY-34B | NORMANTON-55E | NEWENGLAND-34E | YORK-50A | NORMANTON-55E |
| Nov-60 | NORMANTON-55E | TILBURY-33B | LANGWITH JCN-41J | NEWENGLAND-34E | HORNSEY-34B | NORMANTON-55E | NEWENGLAND-34E | YORK-50A | NORMANTON-55E |

| | 90665 | 90666 | 90668 | 90670 | 90672 | 90673 | 90674 | 90676 | 90677 |
|---|---|---|---|---|---|---|---|---|---|
| Aug-50 | NEWENGLAND - 35A | | MARCH - 31B | YORK - 50A | COLWICK - 38A | | TWEEDMOUTH - 52D | COLWICK - 38A | SPRINGHEAD - 53C |
| Jan-51 | NEWENGLAND - 35A | | MARCH - 31B | YORK - 50A | COLWICK - 38A | | TWEEDMOUTH - 52D | COLWICK - 38A | SPRINGHEAD - 53C |
| Aug-51 | NEWENGLAND - 35A | | MARCH - 31B | YORK - 50A | COLWICK - 38A | | **5/51: DAIRY - 53A** | COLWICK - 38A | SPRINGHEAD - 53C |
| Jan-52 | NEWENGLAND - 35A | | MARCH - 31B | YORK - 50A | COLWICK - 38A | | **1/52: To LM** | **10/51: To WR** | SPRINGHEAD - 53C |
| Aug-52 | NEWENGLAND - 35A | | MARCH - 31B | YORK - 50A | COLWICK - 38A | | **6/52: COLW - 38A** | | SPRINGHEAD - 53C |
| Jan-53 | NEWENGLAND - 35A | | MARCH - 31B | YORK - 50A | COLWICK - 38A | | COLWICK - 38A | | SPRINGHEAD - 53C |
| Aug-53 | NEWENGLAND - 35A | | MARCH - 31B | YORK - 50A | COLWICK - 38A | | COLWICK - 38A | | SPRINGHEAD - 53C |
| Jan-54 | NEWENGLAND - 35A | | MARCH - 31B | YORK - 50A | COLWICK - 38A | | COLWICK - 38A | | SPRINGHEAD - 53C |
| Aug-54 | NEWENGLAND - 35A | | MARCH - 31B | **5/54: SELBY - 50C** | COLWICK - 38A | | COLWICK - 38A | | SPRINGHEAD - 53C |
| Jan-55 | NEWENGLAND - 35A | | **2/55: STRAT - 30A** | SELBY - 50C | COLWICK - 38A | | **11/54: DCTR - 36A** | | SPRINGHEAD - 53C |
| Aug-55 | NEWENGLAND - 35A | | **3/55: PLAIS - 33A** | SELBY - 50C | COLWICK - 38A | | DONCASTER - 36A | | SPRINGHEAD - 53C |
| Jan-56 | NEWENGLAND - 35A | | **5/55: MEX - 36B** | SELBY - 50C | COLWICK - 38A | | **1/56: COLW - 38A** | | SPRINGHEAD - 53C |
| Aug-56 | NEWENGLAND - 35A | | MEXBOROUGH - 36B | **10/56: DAIRY - 53A** | COLWICK - 38A | | **2/56: DCTR - 36A** | | SPRINGHEAD - 53C |
| Jan-57 | NEWENGLAND - 35A | | MEXBOROUGH - 36B | DAIRYCOATES - 53A | COLWICK - 38A | Ex L&Y | **2/57: IMM - 40B** | | SPRINGHEAD - 53C |
| Aug-57 | NEWENGLAND - 35A | | MEXBOROUGH - 36B | DAIRYCOATES - 53A | COLWICK - 38A | **6/57: N'TON - 55E** | IMMINGHAM - 40B | | SPRINGHEAD - 53C |
| Jan-58 | NEWENGLAND - 35A | | MEXBOROUGH - 36B | DAIRYCOATES - 53A | COLWICK - 38A | NORMANTON - 55E | IMMINGHAM - 40B | | **2/58: DAIRY - 53A** |
| Aug-58 | NEWENGLAND - 34E | | MEXBOROUGH - 41F | DAIRYCOATES - 53A | COLWICK - 40E | NORMANTON - 55E | IMMINGHAM - 40B | | **5/58: S'HEAD - 53C** |
| Jan-59 | NEWENGLAND - 34E | Ex LM | MEXBOROUGH - 41F | DAIRYCOATES - 53A | COLWICK - 40E | NORMANTON - 55E | IMMINGHAM - 40B | | **12/58: DAIRY - 53A** |
| Aug-59 | NEWENGLAND - 34E | **6/59: HUDD - 55G** | MEXBOROUGH - 41F | DAIRYCOATES - 53A | COLWICK - 40E | NORMANTON - 55E | IMMINGHAM - 40B | | DAIRYCOATES - 53A |
| Nov-59 | NEWENGLAND - 34E | HUDDERSFIELD - 55G | MEXBOROUGH - 41F | DAIRYCOATES - 53A | COLWICK - 40E | NORMANTON - 55E | IMMINGHAM - 40B | | DAIRYCOATES - 53A |
| Jan-60 | NEWENGLAND - 34E | HUDDERSFIELD - 55G | MEXBOROUGH - 41F | DAIRYCOATES - 53A | COLWICK - 40E | NORMANTON - 55E | IMMINGHAM - 40B | | DAIRYCOATES - 53A |
| Apr-60 | NEWENGLAND - 34E | HUDDERSFIELD - 55G | MEXBOROUGH - 41F | DAIRYCOATES - 50B | COLWICK - 40E | NORMANTON - 55E | IMMINGHAM - 40B | | DAIRYCOATES - 50B |
| Aug-60 | NEWENGLAND - 34E | HUDDERSFIELD - 55G | MEXBOROUGH - 41F | DAIRYCOATES - 50B | COLWICK - 40E | NORMANTON - 55E | IMMINGHAM - 40B | | DAIRYCOATES - 50B |
| Nov-60 | NEWENGLAND - 34E | HUDDERSFIELD - 55G | MEXBOROUGH - 41F | DAIRYCOATES - 50B | COLWICK - 40E | NORMANTON - 55E | **11/60: COLW - 40E** | | DAIRYCOATES - 50B |

| | 90682 | 90683 | 90688 | 90690 | 90692 | 90695 | 90696 | 90697 | 90698 |
|---|---|---|---|---|---|---|---|---|---|
| Aug-50 | | NEWENGLAND - 35A | SPRINGHEAD - 53C | THORNTONJCN - 62A | | DAIRYCOATES - 53A | MEXBOROUGH - 36B | COLWICK - 38A | |
| Jan-51 | | NEWENGLAND - 35A | SPRINGHEAD - 53C | THORNTONJCN - 62A | | **9/50: H.HILL - 51G** | MEXBOROUGH - 36B | COLWICK - 38A | |
| Aug-51 | | NEWENGLAND - 35A | SPRINGHEAD - 53C | THORNTONJCN - 62A | | **9/51: DAIRY - 53A** | **10/51: MARCH - 31B** | **9/51: WFD.H - 38E** | |
| Jan-52 | | NEWENGLAND - 35A | SPRINGHEAD - 53C | THORNTONJCN - 62A | | DAIRYCOATES - 53A | **2/52: DCTR - 36A** | W.HALSE - 38E | |
| Aug-52 | | NEWENGLAND - 35A | SPRINGHEAD - 53C | THORNTONJCN - 62A | | DAIRYCOATES - 53A | **10/52: MARCH - 31B** | W.HALSE - 38E | |
| Jan-53 | | NEWENGLAND - 35A | SPRINGHEAD - 53C | THORNTONJCN - 62A | | DAIRYCOATES - 53A | **11/52: DCTR - 36A** | W.HALSE - 38E | |
| Aug-53 | | NEWENGLAND - 35A | SPRINGHEAD - 53C | THORNTONJCN - 62A | | DAIRYCOATES - 53A | DONCASTER - 36A | W.HALSE - 38E | |
| Jan-54 | | NEWENGLAND - 35A | SPRINGHEAD - 53C | THORNTONJCN - 62A | | DAIRYCOATES - 53A | DONCASTER - 36A | W.HALSE - 38E | |
| Aug-54 | | NEWENGLAND - 35A | SPRINGHEAD - 53C | THORNTONJCN - 62A | | DAIRYCOATES - 53A | DONCASTER - 36A | W.HALSE - 38E | |
| Jan-55 | | NEWENGLAND - 35A | SPRINGHEAD - 53C | THORNTONJCN - 62A | | DAIRYCOATES - 53A | DONCASTER - 36A | W.HALSE - 38E | |
| Aug-55 | | NEWENGLAND - 35A | SPRINGHEAD - 53C | THORNTONJCN - 62A | | DAIRYCOATES - 53A | DONCASTER - 36A | W.HALSE - 38E | |
| Jan-56 | | NEWENGLAND - 35A | SPRINGHEAD - 53C | THORNTONJCN - 62A | | DAIRYCOATES - 53A | DONCASTER - 36A | W.HALSE - 38E | |
| Aug-56 | | NEWENGLAND - 35A | SPRINGHEAD - 53C | THORNTONJCN - 62A | | DAIRYCOATES - 53A | **10/56: MARCH - 31B** | W.HALSE - 38E | |
| Jan-57 | Ex LM | NEWENGLAND - 35A | SPRINGHEAD - 53C | THORNTONJCN - 62A | | DAIRYCOATES - 53A | **2/57: DCTR - 36A** | W.HALSE - 38E | Ex LM |
| Aug-57 | | NEWENGLAND - 35A | SPRINGHEAD - 53C | THORNTONJCN - 62A | | DAIRYCOATES - 53A | DONCASTER - 36A | W.HALSE - 38E | **10/57: ARDS - 56B** |
| Jan-58 | **2/58: N'TON - 55E** | **11/57: MARCH - 31B** | SPRINGHEAD - 53C | THORNTONJCN - 62A | | DAIRYCOATES - 53A | DONCASTER - 36A | W.HALSE - 38E | **2/58: LOW.M - 56F** |
| Aug-58 | NORMANTON - 55E | MARCH - 31B | SPRINGHEAD - 53C | THORNTONJCN - 62A | | DAIRYCOATES - 53A | DONCASTER - 36A | W.HALSE - 2F | **6/58: DARL - 51A** |
| Jan-59 | NORMANTON - 55E | MARCH - 31B | **12/58: DAIRY - 53A** | THORNTONJCN - 62A | | DAIRYCOATES - 53A | DONCASTER - 36A | W.HALSE - 2F | DARLINGTON - 51A |
| Aug-59 | NORMANTON - 55E | MARCH - 31B | DAIRYCOATES - 53A | THORNTONJCN - 62A | | DAIRYCOATES - 53A | DONCASTER - 36A | W.HALSE - 2F | **8/59: TBY - 51L** |
| Nov-59 | NORMANTON - 55E | MARCH - 31B | DAIRYCOATES - 53A | THORNTONJCN - 62A | | DAIRYCOATES - 53A | DONCASTER - 36A | W.HALSE - 2F | **10/59: MIR - 56D** |
| Jan-60 | NORMANTON - 55E | MARCH - 31B | DAIRYCOATES - 53A | THORNTONJCN - 62A | Ex LM | DAIRYCOATES - 53A | **2/60: FROD - 36C** | W.HALSE - 2F | MIRFIELD - 56D |
| Apr-60 | NORMANTON - 55E | MARCH - 31B | DAIRYCOATES - 50B | THORNTONJCN - 62A | | DAIRYCOATES - 50B | FRODINGHAM - 36C | W.HALSE - 2F | MIRFIELD - 56D |
| Aug-60 | NORMANTON - 55E | MARCH - 31B | DAIRYCOATES - 50B | THORNTONJCN - 62A | | DAIRYCOATES - 50B | FRODINGHAM - 36C | W.HALSE - 2F | MIRFIELD - 56D |
| Nov-60 | NORMANTON - 55E | MARCH - 31B | DAIRYCOATES - 50B | THORNTONJCN - 62A | **11/60: ARDS - 56B** | DAIRYCOATES - 50B | FRODINGHAM - 36C | W.HALSE - 2F | MIRFIELD - 56D |

| | 90700 | 90703 | 90704 | 90705 | 90709 | 90711 | 90714 | 90717 | 90719 |
|---|---|---|---|---|---|---|---|---|---|
| Aug-50 | MEXBOROUGH - 36B | COLWICK - 38A | TWEEDMOUTH - 52D | DUNFERMLINE - 62C | MEXBOROUGH - 36B | | MEXBOROUGH - 36B | COLWICK - 38A | |
| Jan-51 | MEXBOROUGH - 36B | COLWICK - 38A | **11/50: DAIRY - 53A** | DUNFERMLINE - 62C | **9/50: MARCH - 31B** | | MEXBOROUGH - 36B | COLWICK - 38A | |
| Aug-51 | MEXBOROUGH - 36B | COLWICK - 38A | **10/51: S'HEAD - 53C** | DUNFERMLINE - 62C | **2/51: MEX - 36B** | | **10/51: DCTR - 36A** | COLWICK - 38A | |
| Jan-52 | MEXBOROUGH - 36B | COLWICK - 38A | **11/51: DAIRY - 53A** | DUNFERMLINE - 62C | **10/51: NEW.E - 35A** | | **3/52: FROD - 36C** | COLWICK - 38A | |
| Aug-52 | MEXBOROUGH - 36B | COLWICK - 38A | DAIRYCOATES - 53A | DUNFERMLINE - 62C | NEWENGLAND - 35A | | FRODINGHAM - 36C | COLWICK - 38A | |
| Jan-53 | MEXBOROUGH - 36B | COLWICK - 38A | DAIRYCOATES - 53A | DUNFERMLINE - 62C | NEWENGLAND - 35A | | FRODINGHAM - 36C | COLWICK - 38A | |
| Aug-53 | MEXBOROUGH - 36B | COLWICK - 38A | DAIRYCOATES - 53A | DUNFERMLINE - 62C | NEWENGLAND - 35A | | FRODINGHAM - 36C | COLWICK - 38A | |
| Jan-54 | MEXBOROUGH - 36B | COLWICK - 38A | DAIRYCOATES - 53A | DUNFERMLINE - 62C | NEWENGLAND - 35A | | FRODINGHAM - 36C | COLWICK - 38A | |
| Aug-54 | MEXBOROUGH - 36B | COLWICK - 38A | DAIRYCOATES - 53A | DUNFERMLINE - 62C | NEWENGLAND - 35A | | FRODINGHAM - 36C | COLWICK - 38A | |
| Jan-55 | MEXBOROUGH - 36B | COLWICK - 38A | DAIRYCOATES - 53A | DUNFERMLINE - 62C | **3/55: PLAIS - 33A** | | FRODINGHAM - 36C | COLWICK - 38A | |
| Aug-55 | MEXBOROUGH - 36B | COLWICK - 38A | DAIRYCOATES - 53A | DUNFERMLINE - 62C | **6/55: NEW.E - 35A** | | FRODINGHAM - 36C | COLWICK - 38A | |
| Jan-56 | MEXBOROUGH - 36B | COLWICK - 38A | DAIRYCOATES - 53A | DUNFERMLINE - 62C | NEWENGLAND - 35A | | FRODINGHAM - 36C | COLWICK - 38A | |
| Aug-56 | MEXBOROUGH - 36B | COLWICK - 38A | DAIRYCOATES - 53A | DUNFERMLINE - 62C | NEWENGLAND - 35A | | FRODINGHAM - 36C | COLWICK - 38A | |
| Jan-57 | MEXBOROUGH - 36B | COLWICK - 38A | DAIRYCOATES - 53A | **12/56: TH JN - 62A** | NEWENGLAND - 35A | Ex LM | FRODINGHAM - 36C | COLWICK - 38A | |
| Aug-57 | MEXBOROUGH - 36B | COLWICK - 38A | DAIRYCOATES - 53A | THORNTONJCN - 62A | NEWENGLAND - 35A | **10/57: ARDS - 56B** | FRODINGHAM - 36C | COLWICK - 38A | |
| Jan-58 | MEXBOROUGH - 36B | COLWICK - 38A | DAIRYCOATES - 53A | THORNTONJCN - 62A | **10/57: MARCH - 31B** | ARDSLEY - 56B | FRODINGHAM - 36C | COLWICK - 38A | |
| Aug-58 | MEXBOROUGH - 41F | COLWICK - 40E | DAIRYCOATES - 53A | THORNTONJCN - 62A | MARCH - 31B | **6/58: LOW.M - 56F** | FRODINGHAM - 36C | COLWICK - 40E | |
| Jan-59 | MEXBOROUGH - 41F | COLWICK - 40E | DAIRYCOATES - 53A | THORNTONJCN - 62A | MARCH - 31B | LOWMOOR - 56F | FRODINGHAM - 36C | COLWICK - 40E | Ex LM |
| Aug-59 | MEXBOROUGH - 41F | COLWICK - 40E | DAIRYCOATES - 53A | THORNTONJCN - 62A | MARCH - 31B | LOWMOOR - 56F | FRODINGHAM - 36C | COLWICK - 40E | **9/59: CANK - 41D** |
| Nov-59 | MEXBOROUGH - 41F | COLWICK - 40E | **10/59: GOOLE - 53E** | THORNTONJCN - 62A | MARCH - 31B | LOWMOOR - 56F | FRODINGHAM - 36C | COLWICK - 40E | CANKLOW - 41D |
| Jan-60 | MEXBOROUGH - 41F | COLWICK - 40E | GOOLE - 53E | THORNTONJCN - 62A | MARCH - 31B | LOWMOOR - 56F | FRODINGHAM - 36C | COLWICK - 40E | CANKLOW - 41D |
| Apr-60 | MEXBOROUGH - 41F | **5/60: NEW.E - 35A** | GOOLE - 50D | THORNTONJCN - 62A | MARCH - 31B | LOWMOOR - 56F | FRODINGHAM - 36C | **5/60: NEW.E - 35A** | CANKLOW - 41D |
| Aug-60 | MEXBOROUGH - 41F | NEWENGLAND - 34E | GOOLE - 50D | THORNTONJCN - 62A | MARCH - 31B | LOWMOOR - 56F | FRODINGHAM - 36C | NEWENGLAND - 34E | CANKLOW - 41D |
| Nov-60 | MEXBOROUGH - 41F | NEWENGLAND - 34E | GOOLE - 50D | THORNTONJCN - 62A | MARCH - 31B | LOWMOOR - 56F | FRODINGHAM - 36C | NEWENGLAND - 34E | CANKLOW - 41D |

| | 90722 | 90727 | 90730 | 90732 | WD 2-10-0 (1943) 90763 | BR 9F 2-10-0 (1954) 92010 | 92011 | 92012 | 92013 |
|---|---|---|---|---|---|---|---|---|---|
| Aug-50 | | DUNDEE - 62B | NEWENGLAND - 35A | COLCHESTER - 30E | | | | | |
| Jan-51 | | DUNDEE - 62B | NEWENGLAND - 35A | COLCHESTER - 30E | | | | | |
| Aug-51 | | DUNDEE - 62B | NEWENGLAND - 35A | **9/51: MARCH - 31B** | Ex CR | | | | |
| Jan-52 | | DUNDEE - 62B | NEWENGLAND - 35A | MARCH - 31B | **6/52: DCTR - 36A** | | | | |
| Aug-52 | | **9/52: EBRO(SM) - 64A** | NEWENGLAND - 35A | MARCH - 31B | **9/52: To CR** | | | | |
| Jan-53 | | EDINBURGH(SM) - 64A | NEWENGLAND - 35A | MARCH - 31B | | | | | |
| Aug-53 | | EDINBURGH(SM) - 64A | NEWENGLAND - 35A | MARCH - 31B | | | | | |
| Jan-54 | | EDINBURGH(SM) - 64A | NEWENGLAND - 35A | MARCH - 31B | | **4/54: MARCH - 31B** | **5/54: MARCH - 31B** | **5/54: MARCH - 31B** | |
| Aug-54 | | EDINBURGH(SM) - 64A | NEWENGLAND - 35A | MARCH - 31B | | MARCH - 31B | MARCH - 31B | MARCH - 31B | |
| Jan-55 | | **11/54: DUNF - 62C** | NEWENGLAND - 35A | MARCH - 31B | | MARCH - 31B | MARCH - 31B | MARCH - 31B | **11/54: MARCH - 31B** |
| Aug-55 | | DUNFERMLINE - 62C | NEWENGLAND - 35A | MARCH - 31B | | MARCH - 31B | **9/55: NEW.E - 35A** | **9/55: NEW.E - 35A** | MARCH - 31B |
| Jan-56 | | DUNFERMLINE - 62C | NEWENGLAND - 35A | MARCH - 31B | | MARCH - 31B | NEWENGLAND - 35A | NEWENGLAND - 35A | MARCH - 31B |
| Aug-56 | | DUNFERMLINE - 62C | NEWENGLAND - 35A | MARCH - 31B | | MARCH - 31B | NEWENGLAND - 35A | NEWENGLAND - 35A | MARCH - 31B |
| Jan-57 | Ex L&Y | DUNFERMLINE - 62C | NEWENGLAND - 35A | **3/57: DCTR - 36A** | | **2/57: ANNES - 38B** | NEWENGLAND - 35A | NEWENGLAND - 35A | **2/57: ANNES - 38B** |
| Aug-57 | **6/57: N'TON - 55E** | DUNFERMLINE - 62C | NEWENGLAND - 35A | DONCASTER - 36A | | ANNESLEY - 38B | **5/57: ANNES - 38B** | **6/57: ANNES - 38B** | ANNESLEY - 38B |
| Jan-58 | NORMANTON - 55E | DUNFERMLINE - 62C | NEWENGLAND - 35A | DONCASTER - 36A | | ANNESLEY - 38B | ANNESLEY - 38B | ANNESLEY - 38B | ANNESLEY - 38B |
| Aug-58 | NORMANTON - 55E | DUNFERMLINE - 62C | NEWENGLAND - 34E | DONCASTER - 36A | | ANNESLEY - 16D | ANNESLEY - 16D | ANNESLEY - 16D | ANNESLEY - 16D |
| Jan-59 | NORMANTON - 55E | DUNFERMLINE - 62C | NEWENGLAND - 34E | DONCASTER - 36A | | ANNESLEY - 16D | ANNESLEY - 16D | ANNESLEY - 16D | ANNESLEY - 16D |
| Aug-59 | NORMANTON - 55E | DUNFERMLINE - 62C | NEWENGLAND - 34E | DONCASTER - 36A | | ANNESLEY - 16D | ANNESLEY - 16D | ANNESLEY - 16D | **9/59: WFD.H - 38E** |
| Nov-59 | NORMANTON - 55E | DUNFERMLINE - 62C | NEWENGLAND - 34E | DONCASTER - 36A | | ANNESLEY - 16D | ANNESLEY - 16D | ANNESLEY - 16D | W.HALSE - 2F |
| Jan-60 | NORMANTON - 55E | DUNFERMLINE - 62C | NEWENGLAND - 34E | **2/60: FROD - 36C** | | ANNESLEY - 16D | ANNESLEY - 16D | ANNESLEY - 16D | W.HALSE - 2F |
| Apr-60 | NORMANTON - 55E | DUNFERMLINE - 62C | NEWENGLAND - 34E | FRODINGHAM - 36C | | ANNESLEY - 16D | ANNESLEY - 16D | ANNESLEY - 16D | W.HALSE - 2F |
| Aug-60 | NORMANTON - 55E | DUNFERMLINE - 62C | NEWENGLAND - 34E | FRODINGHAM - 36C | | ANNESLEY - 16D | ANNESLEY - 16D | ANNESLEY - 16D | W.HALSE - 2F |
| Nov-60 | NORMANTON - 55E | DUNFERMLINE - 62C | NEWENGLAND - 34E | FRODINGHAM - 36C | | ANNESLEY - 16D | ANNESLEY - 16D | ANNESLEY - 16D | W.HALSE - 2F |

| | 92014 | 92030 | 92031 | 92032 | 92033 | 92034 | 92035 | 92036 | 92037 |
|---|---|---|---|---|---|---|---|---|---|
| Aug-50 | | | | | | | | | |
| Jan-51 | | | | | | | | | |
| Aug-51 | | | | | | | | | |
| Jan-52 | | | | | | | | | |
| Aug-52 | | | | | | | | | |
| Jan-53 | | | | | | | | | |
| Aug-53 | | | | | | | | | |
| Jan-54 | 5/54: MARCH - 31B | | | | | | | | |
| Aug-54 | 8/54: STRAT - 30A | | | | | | | | |
| Jan-55 | STRATFORD-30A | 11/54: NEW.E - 35A | 11/54: MARCH - 31B | 11/54: NEW.E - 35A | 11/54: NEW.E - 35A | 12/54: NEW.E - 35A | 12/54: NEW.E - 35A | 12/54: NEW.E - 35A | 12/54: NEW.E - 35A |
| Aug-55 | STRATFORD-30A | NEWENGLAND-35A | 3/55: NEW.E - 35A | NEWENGLAND-35A | NEWENGLAND-35A | NEWENGLAND-35A | NEWENGLAND-35A | NEWENGLAND-35A | NEWENGLAND-35A |
| Jan-56 | 1/56: MARCH - 31B | NEWENGLAND-35A | NEWENGLAND-35A | NEWENGLAND-35A | NEWENGLAND-35A | NEWENGLAND-35A | NEWENGLAND-35A | NEWENGLAND-35A | NEWENGLAND-35A |
| Aug-56 | MARCH-31B | NEWENGLAND-35A | NEWENGLAND-35A | NEWENGLAND-35A | NEWENGLAND-35A | NEWENGLAND-35A | NEWENGLAND-35A | NEWENGLAND-35A | NEWENGLAND-35A |
| Jan-57 | 2/57: ANNES - 38B | NEWENGLAND-35A | NEWENGLAND-35A | NEWENGLAND-35A | NEWENGLAND-35A | NEWENGLAND-35A | NEWENGLAND-35A | NEWENGLAND-35A | NEWENGLAND-35A |
| Aug-57 | ANNESLEY-38B | 6/57: ANNES - 38B | 5/57: ANNES - 38B | 6/57: ANNES - 38B | 6/57: ANNES - 38B | NEWENGLAND-35A | NEWENGLAND-35A | NEWENGLAND-35A | NEWENGLAND-35A |
| Jan-58 | ANNESLEY-38B | ANNESLEY-38B | ANNESLEY-38B | ANNESLEY-38B | ANNESLEY-38B | NEWENGLAND-35A | NEWENGLAND-35A | NEWENGLAND-35A | NEWENGLAND-35A |
| Aug-58 | ANNESLEY-16D | ANNESLEY-16D | ANNESLEY-16D | ANNESLEY-16D | ANNESLEY-16D | NEWENGLAND-34E | NEWENGLAND-34E | NEWENGLAND-34E | NEWENGLAND-34E |
| Jan-59 | ANNESLEY-16D | ANNESLEY-16D | ANNESLEY-16D | ANNESLEY-16D | ANNESLEY-16D | 12/58: FROD - 36C | 12/58: FROD - 36C | NEWENGLAND-34E | NEWENGLAND-34E |
| Nov-59 | ANNESLEY-16D | ANNESLEY-16D | ANNESLEY-16D | ANNESLEY-16D | ANNESLEY-16D | 4/59: NEW.E - 34E | 4/59: NEW.E - 34E | NEWENGLAND-34E | NEWENGLAND-34E |
| Jan-60 | ANNESLEY-16D | ANNESLEY-16D | ANNESLEY-16D | ANNESLEY-16D | ANNESLEY-16D | NEWENGLAND-34E | NEWENGLAND-34E | NEWENGLAND-34E | NEWENGLAND-34E |
| Apr-60 | ANNESLEY-16D | ANNESLEY-16D | ANNESLEY-16D | ANNESLEY-16D | ANNESLEY-16D | NEWENGLAND-34E | NEWENGLAND-34E | NEWENGLAND-34E | NEWENGLAND-34E |
| Aug-60 | ANNESLEY-16D | ANNESLEY-16D | ANNESLEY-16D | ANNESLEY-16D | ANNESLEY-16D | NEWENGLAND-34E | NEWENGLAND-34E | NEWENGLAND-34E | NEWENGLAND-34E |
| Nov-60 | ANNESLEY-16D | ANNESLEY-16D | ANNESLEY-16D | ANNESLEY-16D | ANNESLEY-16D | NEWENGLAND-34E | NEWENGLAND-34E | NEWENGLAND-34E | NEWENGLAND-34E |

| | 92038 | 92039 | 92040 | 92041 | 92042 | 92043 | 92044 | 92060 | 92061 |
|---|---|---|---|---|---|---|---|---|---|
| Aug-50 | | | | | | | | | |
| Jan-51 | | | | | | | | | |
| Aug-51 | | | | | | | | | |
| Jan-52 | | | | | | | | | |
| Aug-52 | | | | | | | | | |
| Jan-53 | | | | | | | | | |
| Aug-53 | | | | | | | | | |
| Jan-54 | | | | | | | | | |
| Aug-54 | | | | | | | | | |
| Jan-55 | 12/54: NEW.E - 35A | 12/54: NEW.E - 35A | 12/54: NEW.E - 35A | 12/54: NEW.E - 35A | 1/55: NEW.E - 35A | 1/55: MARCH - 31B | 1/55: MARCH - 31B | | |
| Aug-55 | NEWENGLAND-35A | NEWENGLAND-35A | NEWENGLAND-35A | NEWENGLAND-35A | NEWENGLAND-35A | MARCH-31B | MARCH-31B | 8/55: T.DCK - 54B | 8/55: T.DCK - 54B |
| Jan-56 | NEWENGLAND-35A | NEWENGLAND-35A | NEWENGLAND-35A | NEWENGLAND-35A | NEWENGLAND-35A | MARCH-31B | MARCH-31B | 12/55: To LM | 12/55: To LM |
| Aug-56 | NEWENGLAND-35A | NEWENGLAND-35A | NEWENGLAND-35A | NEWENGLAND-35A | NEWENGLAND-35A | MARCH-31B | MARCH-31B | 3/56: T. DCK - 54B | 4/56: T. DCK - 54B |
| Jan-57 | NEWENGLAND-35A | NEWENGLAND-35A | NEWENGLAND-35A | NEWENGLAND-35A | NEWENGLAND-35A | 2/57: ANNES - 38B | MARCH-31B | TYNEDOCK-54B | TYNEDOCK-54B |
| Aug-57 | NEWENGLAND-35A | NEWENGLAND-35A | NEWENGLAND-35A | NEWENGLAND-35A | NEWENGLAND-35A | ANNESLEY-38B | 6/57: NEW.E - 35A | TYNEDOCK-54B | TYNEDOCK-54B |
| Jan-58 | NEWENGLAND-35A | NEWENGLAND-35A | NEWENGLAND-35A | NEWENGLAND-35A | NEWENGLAND-35A | ANNESLEY-38B | NEWENGLAND-35A | TYNEDOCK-54B | TYNEDOCK-54B |
| Aug-58 | NEWENGLAND-34E | NEWENGLAND-34E | NEWENGLAND-34E | NEWENGLAND-34E | NEWENGLAND-34E | ANNESLEY-16D | NEWENGLAND-34E | TYNEDOCK-54B | TYNEDOCK-54B |
| Jan-59 | NEWENGLAND-34E | 1/59: IMM - 40B | NEWENGLAND-34E | NEWENGLAND-34E | NEWENGLAND-34E | ANNESLEY-16D | NEWENGLAND-34E | TYNEDOCK-52H | TYNEDOCK-52H |
| Nov-59 | NEWENGLAND-34E | IMMINGHAM-40B | NEWENGLAND-34E | NEWENGLAND-34E | NEWENGLAND-34E | ANNESLEY-16D | NEWENGLAND-34E | TYNEDOCK-52H | TYNEDOCK-52H |
| Jan-60 | NEWENGLAND-34E | IMMINGHAM-40B | NEWENGLAND-34E | NEWENGLAND-34E | NEWENGLAND-34E | ANNESLEY-16D | NEWENGLAND-34E | TYNEDOCK-52H | TYNEDOCK-52H |
| Apr-60 | NEWENGLAND-34E | IMMINGHAM-40B | NEWENGLAND-34E | NEWENGLAND-34E | NEWENGLAND-34E | ANNESLEY-16D | NEWENGLAND-34E | TYNEDOCK-52H | TYNEDOCK-52H |
| Aug-60 | NEWENGLAND-34E | IMMINGHAM-40B | NEWENGLAND-34E | NEWENGLAND-34E | NEWENGLAND-34E | ANNESLEY-16D | NEWENGLAND-34E | TYNEDOCK-52H | TYNEDOCK-52H |
| Nov-60 | NEWENGLAND-34E | IMMINGHAM-40B | NEWENGLAND-34E | NEWENGLAND-34E | NEWENGLAND-34E | ANNESLEY-16D | NEWENGLAND-34E | TYNEDOCK-52H | TYNEDOCK-52H |

| | 92062 | 92063 | 92064 | 92065 | 92066 | 92067 | 92068 | 92069 | 92070 |
|---|---|---|---|---|---|---|---|---|---|
| Aug-50 | | | | | | | | | |
| Jan-51 | | | | | | | | | |
| Aug-51 | | | | | | | | | |
| Jan-52 | | | | | | | | | |
| Aug-52 | | | | | | | | | |
| Jan-53 | | | | | | | | | |
| Aug-53 | | | | | | | | | |
| Jan-54 | | | | | | | | | |
| Aug-54 | | | | | | | | | |
| Jan-55 | | | | | | | | | |
| Aug-55 | 8/55: T.DCK - 54B | 8/55: T.DCK - 54B | | | | | | | |
| Jan-56 | 12/55: To LM | 12/55: To LM | To LMR | To LMR | To LMR | 12/55: DCTR - 36A | 12/55: DCTR - 36A | 12/55: DCTR - 36A | 1/56: DCTR - 36A |
| Aug-56 | 4/56: T. DCK - 54B | 5/56: T.DCK - 54B | 5/56: T.DCK - 54B | 5/56: T.DCK - 54B | 5/56: T.DCK - 54B | DONCASTER-36A | DONCASTER-36A | DONCASTER-36A | DONCASTER-36A |
| Jan-57 | TYNEDOCK-54B | TYNEDOCK-54B | TYNEDOCK-54B | TYNEDOCK-54B | TYNEDOCK-54B | 2/57: ANNES - 38B | 2/57: ANNES - 38B | 2/57: ANNES - 38B | 2/57: ANNES - 38B |
| Aug-57 | TYNEDOCK-54B | TYNEDOCK-54B | TYNEDOCK-54B | TYNEDOCK-54B | TYNEDOCK-54B | ANNESLEY-38B | ANNESLEY-38B | ANNESLEY-38B | ANNESLEY-38B |
| Jan-58 | TYNEDOCK-54B | TYNEDOCK-54B | TYNEDOCK-54B | TYNEDOCK-54B | TYNEDOCK-54B | ANNESLEY-16D | ANNESLEY-38B | ANNESLEY-38B | ANNESLEY-38B |
| Aug-58 | TYNEDOCK-54B | TYNEDOCK-54B | TYNEDOCK-54B | TYNEDOCK-54B | TYNEDOCK-54B | ANNESLEY-16D | ANNESLEY-16D | ANNESLEY-16D | ANNESLEY-16D |
| Jan-59 | TYNEDOCK-52H | TYNEDOCK-52H | TYNEDOCK-52H | TYNEDOCK-52H | TYNEDOCK-52H | ANNESLEY-16D | ANNESLEY-16D | ANNESLEY-16D | ANNESLEY-16D |
| Nov-59 | TYNEDOCK-52H | TYNEDOCK-52H | TYNEDOCK-52H | TYNEDOCK-52H | TYNEDOCK-52H | ANNESLEY-16D | ANNESLEY-16D | ANNESLEY-16D | ANNESLEY-16D |
| Jan-60 | TYNEDOCK-52H | TYNEDOCK-52H | TYNEDOCK-52H | TYNEDOCK-52H | TYNEDOCK-52H | ANNESLEY-16D | ANNESLEY-16D | ANNESLEY-16D | ANNESLEY-16D |
| Apr-60 | TYNEDOCK-52H | TYNEDOCK-52H | TYNEDOCK-52H | TYNEDOCK-52H | TYNEDOCK-52H | ANNESLEY-16D | ANNESLEY-16D | ANNESLEY-16D | ANNESLEY-16D |
| Aug-60 | TYNEDOCK-52H | TYNEDOCK-52H | TYNEDOCK-52H | TYNEDOCK-52H | TYNEDOCK-52H | ANNESLEY-16D | ANNESLEY-16D | ANNESLEY-16D | ANNESLEY-16D |
| Nov-60 | TYNEDOCK-52H | TYNEDOCK-52H | TYNEDOCK-52H | TYNEDOCK-52H | TYNEDOCK-52H | ANNESLEY-16D | ANNESLEY-16D | ANNESLEY-16D | ANNESLEY-16D |

| | 92071 | 92072 | 92073 | 92074 | 92075 | 92076 | 92087 | 92088 | 92089 |
|---|---|---|---|---|---|---|---|---|---|
| Aug-50 | | | | | | | | | |
| Jan-51 | | | | | | | | | |
| Aug-51 | | | | | | | | | |
| Jan-52 | | | | | | | | | |
| Aug-52 | | | | | | | | | |
| Jan-53 | | | | | | | | | |
| Aug-53 | | | | | | | | | |
| Jan-54 | | | | | | | | | |
| Aug-54 | | | | | | | | | |
| Jan-55 | | | | | | | | | |
| Aug-55 | | | | | | | | | |
| Jan-56 | 1/56: DCTR - 36A | 2/56: DCTR - 36A | 2/56: DCTR - 36A | 2/56: DCTR - 36A | 3/56: DCTR - 36A | 3/56: DCTR - 36A | | | |
| Aug-56 | DONCASTER-36A | DONCASTER-36A | DONCASTER-36A | DONCASTER-36A | DONCASTER-36A | DONCASTER-36A | 8/56: DCTR - 36A | 9/56: DCTR - 36A | 9/56: DCTR - 36A |
| Jan-57 | 2/57: ANNES - 38B | 2/57: ANNES - 38B | 3/57: ANNES - 38B | 3/57: ANNES - 38B | 3/57: ANNES - 38B | 3/57: ANNES - 38B | 3/57: ANNES - 38B | 3/57: ANNES - 38B | 3/57: ANNES - 38B |
| Aug-57 | ANNESLEY-38B | ANNESLEY-38B | ANNESLEY-38B | ANNESLEY-38B | ANNESLEY-38B | ANNESLEY-38B | ANNESLEY-38B | ANNESLEY-38B | ANNESLEY-38B |
| Jan-58 | ANNESLEY-38B | ANNESLEY-38B | ANNESLEY-38B | ANNESLEY-38B | ANNESLEY-38B | ANNESLEY-38B | ANNESLEY-38B | ANNESLEY-38B | ANNESLEY-38B |
| Aug-58 | ANNESLEY-16D | ANNESLEY-16D | ANNESLEY-16D | ANNESLEY-16D | ANNESLEY-16D | ANNESLEY-16D | ANNESLEY-16D | ANNESLEY-16D | ANNESLEY-16D |
| Jan-59 | ANNESLEY-16D | ANNESLEY-16D | ANNESLEY-16D | ANNESLEY-16D | ANNESLEY-16D | ANNESLEY-16D | ANNESLEY-16D | ANNESLEY-16D | ANNESLEY-16D |
| Nov-59 | ANNESLEY-16D | ANNESLEY-16D | ANNESLEY-16D | ANNESLEY-16D | ANNESLEY-16D | ANNESLEY-16D | ANNESLEY-16D | ANNESLEY-16D | ANNESLEY-16D |
| Jan-60 | ANNESLEY-16D | ANNESLEY-16D | ANNESLEY-16D | ANNESLEY-16D | ANNESLEY-16D | ANNESLEY-16D | ANNESLEY-16D | ANNESLEY-16D | ANNESLEY-16D |
| Apr-60 | ANNESLEY-16D | ANNESLEY-16D | ANNESLEY-16D | ANNESLEY-16D | ANNESLEY-16D | ANNESLEY-16D | ANNESLEY-16D | ANNESLEY-16D | ANNESLEY-16D |
| Aug-60 | ANNESLEY-16D | ANNESLEY-16D | ANNESLEY-16D | ANNESLEY-16D | ANNESLEY-16D | ANNESLEY-16D | ANNESLEY-16D | ANNESLEY-16D | ANNESLEY-16D |
| Nov-60 | ANNESLEY-16D | ANNESLEY-16D | ANNESLEY-16D | ANNESLEY-16D | ANNESLEY-16D | ANNESLEY-16D | ANNESLEY-16D | ANNESLEY-16D | ANNESLEY-16D |

## Block 1

| | 92090 | 92091 | 92092 | 92093 | 92094 | 92095 | 92096 | 92097 | 92098 |
|---|---|---|---|---|---|---|---|---|---|
| Aug-50 | | | | | | | | | |
| Jan-51 | | | | | | | | | |
| Aug-51 | | | | | | | | | |
| Jan-52 | | | | | | | | | |
| Aug-52 | | | | | | | | | |
| Jan-53 | | | | | | | | | |
| Aug-53 | | | | | | | | | |
| Jan-54 | | | | | | | | | |
| Aug-54 | | | | | | | | | |
| Jan-55 | | | | | | | | | |
| Aug-55 | | | | | | | | | |
| Jan-56 | | | | | | | | | |
| Aug-56 | | | | | | | | 6/56: T.DCK - 54B | 7/57: T.DCK - 54B |
| Jan-57 | 11/56: DCTR - 36A | 11/56: DCTR - 36A | 12/56: DCTR - 36A | 1/57: DCTR - 36A | | 3/57: ANNES - 38B | 4/57: ANNES - 38B | TYNEDOCK-54B | TYNEDOCK-54B |
| Aug-57 | 3/57: ANNES - 38B | 3/57: ANNES - 38B | 3/57: ANNES - 38B | 3/57: ANNES - 38B | ANNESLEY-38B | ANNESLEY-38B | ANNESLEY-38B | TYNEDOCK-54B | TYNEDOCK-54B |
| Jan-58 | ANNESLEY-38B | ANNESLEY-38B | ANNESLEY-38B | ANNESLEY-38B | ANNESLEY-38B | ANNESLEY-38B | ANNESLEY-38B | TYNEDOCK-54B | TYNEDOCK-54B |
| Aug-58 | ANNESLEY-16D | ANNESLEY-16D | ANNESLEY-16D | ANNESLEY-16D | ANNESLEY-16D | ANNESLEY-16D | ANNESLEY-16D | TYNEDOCK-52H | TYNEDOCK-52H |
| Jan-59 | ANNESLEY-16D | ANNESLEY-16D | ANNESLEY-16D | ANNESLEY-16D | ANNESLEY-16D | ANNESLEY-16D | ANNESLEY-16D | TYNEDOCK-52H | TYNEDOCK-52H |
| Aug-59 | ANNESLEY-16D | ANNESLEY-16D | ANNESLEY-16D | ANNESLEY-16D | ToLM | ANNESLEY-16D | ANNESLEY-16D | TYNEDOCK-52H | TYNEDOCK-52H |
| Nov-59 | ANNESLEY-16D | ANNESLEY-16D | ANNESLEY-16D | ANNESLEY-16D | ToLM | ANNESLEY-16D | ANNESLEY-16D | TYNEDOCK-52H | TYNEDOCK-52H |
| Jan-60 | ANNESLEY-16D | ANNESLEY-16D | ANNESLEY-16D | ANNESLEY-16D | ToLM | ANNESLEY-16D | ANNESLEY-16D | TYNEDOCK-52H | TYNEDOCK-52H |
| Apr-60 | ANNESLEY-16D | ANNESLEY-16D | ANNESLEY-16D | ANNESLEY-16D | ToLM | ANNESLEY-16D | ANNESLEY-16D | TYNEDOCK-52H | TYNEDOCK-52H |
| Aug-60 | ANNESLEY-16D | ANNESLEY-16D | ANNESLEY-16D | ANNESLEY-16D | ToLM | ANNESLEY-16D | ANNESLEY-16D | TYNEDOCK-52H | TYNEDOCK-52H |
| Nov-60 | ANNESLEY-16D | ANNESLEY-16D | ANNESLEY-16D | ANNESLEY-16D | ToLM | ANNESLEY-16D | ANNESLEY-16D | TYNEDOCK-52H | TYNEDOCK-52H |

## Block 2

| | 92099 | 92140 | 92141 | 92142 | 92143 | 92144 | 92145 | 92146 | 92147 |
|---|---|---|---|---|---|---|---|---|---|
| Aug-50 | | | | | | | | | |
| Jan-51 | | | | | | | | | |
| Aug-51 | | | | | | | | | |
| Jan-52 | | | | | | | | | |
| Aug-52 | | | | | | | | | |
| Jan-53 | | | | | | | | | |
| Aug-53 | | | | | | | | | |
| Jan-54 | | | | | | | | | |
| Aug-54 | | | | | | | | | |
| Jan-55 | | | | | | | | | |
| Aug-55 | | | | | | | | | |
| Jan-56 | | | | | | | | | |
| Aug-56 | 7/57: T.DCK - 54B | | | | | | | | |
| Jan-57 | TYNEDOCK-54B | | | | | | | | |
| Aug-57 | TYNEDOCK-54B | 7/57: NEW.E - 35A | 7/57: NEW.E - 35A | 7/57: NEW.E - 35A | 8/57: NEW.E - 35A | 8/57: NEW.E - 35A | 8/57: NEW.E - 35A | 9/57: NEW.E - 35A | 9/57: NEW.E - 35A |
| Jan-58 | TYNEDOCK-54B | NEWENGLAND-35A | NEWENGLAND-35A | NEWENGLAND-35A | NEWENGLAND-35A | NEWENGLAND-35A | NEWENGLAND-35A | NEWENGLAND-35A | NEWENGLAND-35A |
| Aug-58 | TYNEDOCK-54B | NEWENGLAND-34E | NEWENGLAND-34E | NEWENGLAND-34E | NEWENGLAND-34E | NEWENGLAND-34E | NEWENGLAND-34E | NEWENGLAND-34E | NEWENGLAND-34E |
| Jan-59 | TYNEDOCK-52H | NEWENGLAND-34E | NEWENGLAND-34E | NEWENGLAND-34E | NEWENGLAND-34E | NEWENGLAND-34E | NEWENGLAND-34E | NEWENGLAND-34E | NEWENGLAND-34E |
| Aug-59 | TYNEDOCK-52H | NEWENGLAND-34E | NEWENGLAND-34E | NEWENGLAND-34E | NEWENGLAND-34E | NEWENGLAND-34E | NEWENGLAND-34E | NEWENGLAND-34E | NEWENGLAND-34E |
| Nov-59 | TYNEDOCK-52H | NEWENGLAND-34E | NEWENGLAND-34E | NEWENGLAND-34E | NEWENGLAND-34E | NEWENGLAND-34E | NEWENGLAND-34E | NEWENGLAND-34E | NEWENGLAND-34E |
| Jan-60 | TYNEDOCK-52H | NEWENGLAND-34E | NEWENGLAND-34E | NEWENGLAND-34E | NEWENGLAND-34E | NEWENGLAND-34E | NEWENGLAND-34E | NEWENGLAND-34E | NEWENGLAND-34E |
| Apr-60 | TYNEDOCK-52H | NEWENGLAND-34E | NEWENGLAND-34E | NEWENGLAND-34E | NEWENGLAND-34E | NEWENGLAND-34E | NEWENGLAND-34E | NEWENGLAND-34E | NEWENGLAND-34E |
| Aug-60 | TYNEDOCK-52H | NEWENGLAND-34E | NEWENGLAND-34E | NEWENGLAND-34E | NEWENGLAND-34E | NEWENGLAND-34E | NEWENGLAND-34E | NEWENGLAND-34E | NEWENGLAND-34E |
| Nov-60 | TYNEDOCK-52H | NEWENGLAND-34E | NEWENGLAND-34E | NEWENGLAND-34E | NEWENGLAND-34E | NEWENGLAND-34E | NEWENGLAND-34E | NEWENGLAND-34E | NEWENGLAND-34E |

## Block 3

| | 92148 | 92149 | 92168 | 92169 | 92170 | 92171 | 92172 | 92173 | 92174 |
|---|---|---|---|---|---|---|---|---|---|
| Aug-50 | | | | | | | | | |
| Jan-51 | | | | | | | | | |
| Aug-51 | | | | | | | | | |
| Jan-52 | | | | | | | | | |
| Aug-52 | | | | | | | | | |
| Jan-53 | | | | | | | | | |
| Aug-53 | | | | | | | | | |
| Jan-54 | | | | | | | | | |
| Aug-54 | | | | | | | | | |
| Jan-55 | | | | | | | | | |
| Aug-55 | | | | | | | | | |
| Jan-56 | | | | | | | | | |
| Aug-56 | | | | | | | | | |
| Jan-57 | | | | | | | | | |
| Aug-57 | 9/57: NEW.E - 35A | 10/57: NEW.E - 35A | | | | | | | |
| Jan-58 | NEWENGLAND-35A | NEWENGLAND-35A | 12/57: DCTR - 36A | 12/57: DCTR - 36A | 12/57: DCTR - 36A | 2/58: DCTR - 36A | 1/58: DCTR - 36A | 2/58: DCTR - 36A | 2/58: DCTR - 36A |
| Aug-58 | NEWENGLAND-34E | NEWENGLAND-34E | DONCASTER-36A | DONCASTER-36A | DONCASTER-36A | DONCASTER-36A | DONCASTER-36A | DONCASTER-36A | DONCASTER-36A |
| Jan-59 | NEWENGLAND-34E | NEWENGLAND-34E | DONCASTER-36A | DONCASTER-36A | DONCASTER-36A | DONCASTER-36A | DONCASTER-36A | DONCASTER-36A | DONCASTER-36A |
| Aug-59 | NEWENGLAND-34E | NEWENGLAND-34E | DONCASTER-36A | DONCASTER-36A | DONCASTER-36A | DONCASTER-36A | DONCASTER-36A | DONCASTER-36A | DONCASTER-36A |
| Nov-59 | NEWENGLAND-34E | NEWENGLAND-34E | DONCASTER-36A | DONCASTER-36A | DONCASTER-36A | DONCASTER-36A | DONCASTER-36A | DONCASTER-36A | DONCASTER-36A |
| Jan-60 | NEWENGLAND-34E | NEWENGLAND-34E | DONCASTER-36A | DONCASTER-36A | DONCASTER-36A | DONCASTER-36A | DONCASTER-36A | DONCASTER-36A | DONCASTER-36A |
| Apr-60 | NEWENGLAND-34E | NEWENGLAND-34E | DONCASTER-36A | DONCASTER-36A | DONCASTER-36A | DONCASTER-36A | DONCASTER-36A | DONCASTER-36A | DONCASTER-36A |
| Aug-60 | 6/60 : IMM - 40B | NEWENGLAND-34E | DONCASTER-36A | DONCASTER-36A | DONCASTER-36A | DONCASTER-36A | DONCASTER-36A | DONCASTER-36A | DONCASTER-36A |
| Nov-60 | IMMINGHAM-40B | NEWENGLAND-34E | DONCASTER-36A | DONCASTER-36A | DONCASTER-36A | DONCASTER-36A | DONCASTER-36A | DONCASTER-36A | DONCASTER-36A |

## Block 4

| | 92175 | 92176 | 92177 | 92178 | 92179 | 92180 | 92181 | 92182 | 92183 |
|---|---|---|---|---|---|---|---|---|---|
| Aug-50 | | | | | | | | | |
| Jan-51 | | | | | | | | | |
| Aug-51 | | | | | | | | | |
| Jan-52 | | | | | | | | | |
| Aug-52 | | | | | | | | | |
| Jan-53 | | | | | | | | | |
| Aug-53 | | | | | | | | | |
| Jan-54 | | | | | | | | | |
| Aug-54 | | | | | | | | | |
| Jan-55 | | | | | | | | | |
| Aug-55 | | | | | | | | | |
| Jan-56 | | | | | | | | | |
| Aug-56 | | | | | | | | | |
| Jan-57 | | | | | | | | | |
| Aug-57 | | | | 9/57: NEW.E - 35A | | | | | |
| Jan-58 | 2/58: DCTR - 36A | 3/58: DCTR - 36A | 3/58: DCTR - 36A | 12/57: Swindon Test | 10/57: NEW.E - 35A | 11/57: NEW.E - 35A | 11/57: NEW.E - 35A | 12/57: NEW.E - 35A | 12/57: NEW.E - 35/ |
| Aug-58 | DONCASTER-36A | DONCASTER-36A | DONCASTER-36A | 3/58: NEW.E - 35A | NEWENGLAND-34E | NEWENGLAND-34E | NEWENGLAND-34E | NEWENGLAND-34E | NEWENGLAND-34E |
| Jan-59 | DONCASTER-36A | DONCASTER-36A | DONCASTER-36A | NEWENGLAND-34E | NEWENGLAND-34E | NEWENGLAND-34E | NEWENGLAND-34E | NEWENGLAND-34E | NEWENGLAND-34E |
| Aug-59 | DONCASTER-36A | DONCASTER-36A | DONCASTER-36A | NEWENGLAND-34E | NEWENGLAND-34E | NEWENGLAND-34E | NEWENGLAND-34E | NEWENGLAND-34E | NEWENGLAND-34E |
| Nov-59 | DONCASTER-36A | DONCASTER-36A | DONCASTER-36A | NEWENGLAND-34E | NEWENGLAND-34E | NEWENGLAND-34E | NEWENGLAND-34E | NEWENGLAND-34E | NEWENGLAND-34E |
| Jan-60 | DONCASTER-36A | DONCASTER-36A | DONCASTER-36A | NEWENGLAND-34E | NEWENGLAND-34E | NEWENGLAND-34E | NEWENGLAND-34E | NEWENGLAND-34E | NEWENGLAND-34E |
| Apr-60 | DONCASTER-36A | DONCASTER-36A | DONCASTER-36A | NEWENGLAND-34E | NEWENGLAND-34E | NEWENGLAND-34E | NEWENGLAND-34E | NEWENGLAND-34E | NEWENGLAND-34E |
| Aug-60 | DONCASTER-36A | DONCASTER-36A | DONCASTER-36A | NEWENGLAND-34E | NEWENGLAND-34E | NEWENGLAND-34E | NEWENGLAND-34E | NEWENGLAND-34E | NEWENGLAND-34E |
| Nov-60 | DONCASTER-36A | DONCASTER-36A | DONCASTER-36A | NEWENGLAND-34E | NEWENGLAND-34E | NEWENGLAND-34E | NEWENGLAND-34E | NEWENGLAND-34E | NEWENGLAND-34E |

## 92184 – 92192

| Date | 92184 | 92185 | 92186 | 92187 | 92188 | 92189 | 92190 | 92191 | 92192 |
|---|---|---|---|---|---|---|---|---|---|
| Aug-50 | | | | | | | | | |
| Jan-51 | | | | | | | | | |
| Aug-51 | | | | | | | | | |
| Jan-52 | | | | | | | | | |
| Aug-52 | | | | | | | | | |
| Jan-53 | | | | | | | | | |
| Aug-53 | | | | | | | | | |
| Jan-54 | | | | | | | | | |
| Aug-54 | | | | | | | | | |
| Jan-55 | | | | | | | | | |
| Aug-55 | | | | | | | | | |
| Jan-56 | | | | | | | | | |
| Aug-56 | | | | | | | | | |
| Jan-57 | | | | | | | | | |
| Aug-57 | | | | | | | | | |
| Jan-58 | 1/58: NEW.E - 35A | 1/58: NEW.E - 35A | 1/58: NEW.E - 35A | 2/58: NEW.E - 35A | 2/58: NEW.E - 35A | 3/58: MEX - 41F | 3/58: MEX - 41F | 4/58: DARN - 41A | |
| Aug-58 | NEWENGLAND-34E | NEWENGLAND-34E | NEWENGLAND-34E | 6/58: GRAN - 34F | 6/58: GRAN - 34F | 4/58: DARN - 41A | 4/58: DARN - 41A | 5/58: DCTR - 36A | 5/58: DCTR - 36A |
| Jan-59 | 12/58: FROD - 36C | NEWENGLAND-34E | NEWENGLAND-34E | 9/58: NEW.E - 34E | 9/58: NEW.E - 34E | 5/58: DCTR - 36A | 5/58: DCTR - 36A | DONCASTER - 36A | DONCASTER - 36A |
| Aug-59 | 6/59: NEW.E - 34E | NEWENGLAND-34E | NEWENGLAND-34E | NEWENGLAND-34E | NEWENGLAND-34E | 4/59: DCTR - 36A | DONCASTER - 36A | DONCASTER - 36A | DONCASTER - 36A |
| Nov-59 | NEWENGLAND-34E | NEWENGLAND-34E | NEWENGLAND-34E | NEWENGLAND-34E | NEWENGLAND-34E | DONCASTER - 36A | DONCASTER - 36A | DONCASTER - 36A | DONCASTER - 36A |
| Jan-60 | NEWENGLAND-34E | NEWENGLAND-34E | NEWENGLAND-34E | NEWENGLAND-34E | NEWENGLAND-34E | DONCASTER - 36A | DONCASTER - 36A | DONCASTER - 36A | DONCASTER - 36A |
| Apr-60 | NEWENGLAND-34E | NEWENGLAND-34E | NEWENGLAND-34E | NEWENGLAND-34E | NEWENGLAND-34E | DONCASTER - 36A | DONCASTER - 36A | DONCASTER - 36A | DONCASTER - 36A |
| Aug-60 | NEWENGLAND-34E | NEWENGLAND-34E | NEWENGLAND-34E | NEWENGLAND-34E | NEWENGLAND-34E | DONCASTER - 36A | DONCASTER - 36A | DONCASTER - 36A | DONCASTER - 36A |
| Nov-60 | NEWENGLAND-34E | NEWENGLAND-34E | NEWENGLAND-34E | NEWENGLAND-34E | NEWENGLAND-34E | DONCASTER - 36A | DONCASTER - 36A | DONCASTER - 36A | DONCASTER - 36A |

## 92193 – 92201

| Date | 92193 | 92194 | 92195 | 92196 | 92197 | 92198 | 92199 | 92200 | 92201 |
|---|---|---|---|---|---|---|---|---|---|
| Aug-50 | | | | | | | | | |
| Jan-51 | | | | | | | | | |
| Aug-51 | | | | | | | | | |
| Jan-52 | | | | | | | | | |
| Aug-52 | | | | | | | | | |
| Jan-53 | | | | | | | | | |
| Aug-53 | | | | | | | | | |
| Jan-54 | | | | | | | | | |
| Aug-54 | | | | | | | | | |
| Jan-55 | | | | | | | | | |
| Aug-55 | | | | | | | | | |
| Jan-56 | | | | | | | | | |
| Aug-56 | | | | | | | | | |
| Jan-57 | | | | | | | | | |
| Aug-57 | | | | | | | | | |
| Jan-58 | | | | | | | | | |
| Aug-58 | 5/58: DCTR - 36A | 6/58: DCTR - 36A | 6/58: DCTR - 36A | 8/58: DCTR - 36A | 8/58: DCTR - 36A | 10/58: DCTR - 36A | 10/58: DCTR - 36A | | |
| Jan-59 | 1/59: IMM - 40B | 1/59: IMM - 40B | 1/59: IMM - 40B | 1/59: IMM - 40B | 1/59: FROD - 36C | 1/59: FROD - 36C | DONCASTER - 36A | 11/58: DCTR - 36A | 12/58: DCTR - 36A |
| Aug-59 | IMMINGHAM-40B | IMMINGHAM-40B | IMMINGHAM-40B | IMMINGHAM-40B | 5/59: DCTR - 36A | 6/59: DCTR - 36A | DONCASTER - 36A | DONCASTER - 36A | DONCASTER - 36A |
| Nov-59 | IMMINGHAM-40B | IMMINGHAM-40B | IMMINGHAM-40B | IMMINGHAM-40B | DONCASTER - 36A | DONCASTER - 36A | DONCASTER - 36A | DONCASTER - 36A | DONCASTER - 36A |
| Jan-60 | IMMINGHAM-40B | IMMINGHAM-40B | IMMINGHAM-40B | IMMINGHAM-40B | DONCASTER - 36A | DONCASTER - 36A | DONCASTER - 36A | DONCASTER - 36A | DONCASTER - 36A |
| Apr-60 | IMMINGHAM-40B | IMMINGHAM-40B | IMMINGHAM-40B | IMMINGHAM-40B | DONCASTER - 36A | DONCASTER - 36A | DONCASTER - 36A | DONCASTER - 36A | DONCASTER - 36A |
| Aug-60 | IMMINGHAM-40B | IMMINGHAM-40B | IMMINGHAM-40B | IMMINGHAM-40B | 9/60: IMM - 40B | DONCASTER - 36A | DONCASTER - 36A | DONCASTER - 36A | DONCASTER - 36A |
| Nov-60 | IMMINGHAM-40B | IMMINGHAM-40B | IMMINGHAM-40B | IMMINGHAM-40B | IMMINGHAM-40B | DONCASTER - 36A | DONCASTER - 36A | DONCASTER - 36A | DONCASTER - 36A |

## 92202

| Date | 92202 |
|---|---|
| Aug-50 | |
| Jan-51 | |
| Aug-51 | |
| Jan-52 | |
| Aug-52 | |
| Jan-53 | |
| Aug-53 | |
| Jan-54 | |
| Aug-54 | |
| Jan-55 | |
| Aug-55 | |
| Jan-56 | |
| Aug-56 | |
| Jan-57 | |
| Aug-57 | |
| Jan-58 | |
| Aug-58 | |
| Jan-59 | 12/58: DCTR - 36A |
| Aug-59 | 4/59: IMM - 40B |
| Nov-59 | IMMINGHAM-40B |
| Jan-60 | IMMINGHAM-40B |
| Apr-60 | IMMINGHAM-40B |
| Aug-60 | IMMINGHAM-40B |
| Nov-60 | IMMINGHAM-40B |

### DISTRIBUTION OF MAIN LINE DIESEL & ELECTRIC LOCOMOTIVES 1961/2

| | D200 | D5000 | D5300 | D5500 | D5907 | D6100 | D8000 | D8200 | D8400 | EM1 | EM2 | Total |
|---|---|---|---|---|---|---|---|---|---|---|---|---|
| Clarence Yard | 6 | | 2 | 46 | 10 | | 13 | | | | | 77 |
| Stratford | 5 | 16 | | 33 | | | | 10 | 10 | | | 74 |
| Ipswich | | 15 | | 44 | | | | 8 | | | | 67 |
| Reddish | | | | | | | | | | 58 | 7 | 65 |
| March | | 17 | | 27 | | | | 10 | | | | 54 |
| Gateshead | 26 | 12 | | | | | | | | | | 38 |
| Eastfield | | | | | | 36 | | | | | | 36 |
| Haymarket | 7 | | 24 | | | | | | | | | 31 |
| Norwich | | | | 17 | | | | 8 | | | | 25 |
| Kittybrewster | | | | | | 18 | 4 | | | | | 22 |
| Inverness | | | 18 | | | | | | | | | 18 |
| York | 12 | | | | | | | | | | | 12 |
| St Margarets | | | 3 | | | | | | | | | 3 |
| Heaton | | 2 | | | | | | | | | | 2 |
| Thornton Jcn | | | | | | 1 | | | | | | 1 |
| Darnall | | | | 1 | | | | | | | | 1 |
| Total | 56 | 62 | 47 | 168 | 10 | 55 | 17 | 36 | 10 | 58 | 7 | 526 |

**GN : 77, GE : 220, GC : 66 (65 Electrics), NE : 52, NB/GNoS : 111 (End 1960)**

Unlike the other regions which had experimented with the early BR diesels, the first contact the Eastern Region had came in late 1957 on the Great Eastern with a small initial delivery of Mirlees diesels, followed by a trio of 2000hp Type 4's which arrived at Stratford in March 1958 as replacements for Britannia Pacifics on the Liverpool Street - Norwich workings. Within a few weeks a small number of Type 4's were delivered to Hornsey, their first working being the newly introduced 'Master Culter' Pullman between Kings Cross and Sheffield, each diesel performing two round trips each day.

Although considerably more simple to drive than a steam locomotive the diesel was perceived to be a more complex piece of equipment and a decision was taken to 'train' each driver on each type of locomotive: an expensive process which imposed a considerable delay in their beng placed in regular service.

One of the first objects had been the dieselisation of the self-contained Great Eastern and much of the energies of the very late 1950's were directed to this goal which included the building of maintenance depots at Stratford, March, Ipswich and Norwich. At the same time many rural passenger services were taken over by diesel multiple units based upon Coldham Lane (Cambridge) and Lincoln. (Multiple units took to the rails rather earlier than locomotives and the first section to be effected was the GN between Leeds Central and Bradford Exchange in 1954).

The focus of diesel operation on the Great Northern was the suburban service when North British and English Electric 1100hp locomotives started to take over from the L1 and N2's in mid-1959. Almost immediately a suburban system that had worked well for years fell apart in the wake of diesel failures that reached epidemic proportions. Adding to the problems were the Type 4 locomotives which seemed incapable of performing a round trip to Newcastle without running into trouble. In the case of the latter matters were rectified by substituting newly modified A3 Pacifics which cheerfully managed the 536 round trip without incident. Fortunately the number of main line diesel locomotives available was so small that steam operations continued with very little dilution.

Matters were a little better on the Great Eastern since the suburban service was (or was becoming) electrified, leaving diesel locomotives to operate long distance services, the majority of which involved goods workings from Whitemoor to Temple Mills, Norwich and Ipswich as well as the passenger services from Liverpool Street to Norwich and Kings Lynn.

The problems at Kings Cross were eventually resolved by replacing the earlier classes of locomotives with 1450hp Brush Type 2's which proved robust and trouble-free; the Baby Deltic's being withdrawn for several years whilst the North British Type 2's were transferred to Scotland. Dieselisation of main line services on the Great Northern remained patchy until the arrival of the Brush Type 4 2750 locomotives and 3300hp Deltics in 1962.

## ES 1 Electric (1905) / EB 1 Electric (1914) / EM 1 Electric

| | ES 1 Electric (1905) | | EB 1 Electric (1914) | EM 1 Electric | | | | | |
|---|---|---|---|---|---|---|---|---|---|
| | 26500 | 26501 | 26510 | 26000 | 26001 | 26002 | 26003 | 26004 | 26005 |
| Aug-50 | HEATON-52B | HEATON-52B | STRATFORD-30A | Holland | | | | | |
| Jan-51 | HEATON-52B | HEATON-52B | STRATFORD-30A | Holland | 10/50: GORT-39A | 10/50: GORT-39A | 11/50: GORT-39A | 2/51: GORT-39A | 1/51: GORT-39A |
| Aug-51 | HEATON-52B | HEATON-52B | STRATFORD-30A | Holland | GORTON-39A | GORTON-39A | GORTON-39A | GORTON-39A | GORTON-39A |
| Jan-52 | HEATON-52B | HEATON-52B | STRATFORD-30A | 3/52: ILFORD | GORTON-39A | GORTON-39A | GORTON-39A | GORTON-39A | GORTON-39A |
| Aug-52 | HEATON-52B | HEATON-52B | STRATFORD-30A | ILFORD-30A | 5/52: ILFORD | 5/52: WATH-36B | 5/52: ILFORD | 5/52: ILFORD | 5/52: ILFORD |
| Jan-53 | HEATON-52B | HEATON-52B | STRATFORD-30A | 3/53: GORT-39A | 3/53: GORT-39A | 3/53: GORT-39A | 9/52: WATH-36B | 9/52: WATH-36B | 9/52: WATH-36B |
| Aug-53 | HEATON-52B | HEATON-52B | STRATFORD-30A | GORTON-39A | GORTON-39A | 5/53: MEX-36B | 3/53: GORT-39A | 3/53: GORT-39A | 3/53: GORT-39A |
| Jan-54 | HEATON-52B | HEATON-52B | STRATFORD-30A | GORTON-39A | GORTON-39A | 1/54: GORT-39A | 4/54: MEX-36B | GORTON-39A | 3/54: MEX-36B |
| Aug-54 | HEATON-52B | HEATON-52B | STRATFORD-30A | 6/54: REDDISH | 6/54: REDDISH | 6/54: REDDISH | 6/54: REDDISH | 6/54: REDDISH | 6/54: REDDISH |
| Jan-55 | HEATON-52B | HEATON-52B | STRATFORD-30A | REDDISH | REDDISH | REDDISH | REDDISH | REDDISH | REDDISH |
| Aug-55 | HEATON-52B | HEATON-52B | STRATFORD-30A | REDDISH | REDDISH | REDDISH | REDDISH | REDDISH | REDDISH |
| Jan-56 | HEATON-52B | HEATON-52B | STRATFORD-30A | REDDISH | REDDISH | REDDISH | REDDISH | REDDISH | REDDISH |
| Aug-56 | HEATON-52B | HEATON-52B | STRATFORD-30A | REDDISH | REDDISH | REDDISH | REDDISH | REDDISH | REDDISH |
| Jan-57 | HEATON-52B | HEATON-52B | STRATFORD-30A | REDDISH | REDDISH | REDDISH | REDDISH | REDDISH | REDDISH |
| Aug-57 | HEATON-52B | HEATON-52B | STRATFORD-30A | REDDISH | REDDISH | REDDISH | REDDISH | REDDISH | REDDISH |
| Jan-58 | HEATON-52B | HEATON-52B | STRATFORD-30A | REDDISH | REDDISH | REDDISH | REDDISH | REDDISH | REDDISH |
| Aug-58 | HEATON-52B | HEATON-52B | STRATFORD-30A | REDDISH | REDDISH | REDDISH | REDDISH | REDDISH | REDDISH |
| Jan-59 | HEATON-52B | HEATON-52B | 1/59: W/D | REDDISH | REDDISH | REDDISH | REDDISH | REDDISH | REDDISH |
| Aug-59 | HEATON-52B | HEATON-52B | | REDDISH | REDDISH | REDDISH | REDDISH | REDDISH | REDDISH |
| Nov-59 | HEATON-52B | HEATON-52B | | REDDISH | REDDISH | REDDISH | REDDISH | REDDISH | REDDISH |
| Jan-60 | HEATON-52B | HEATON-52B | | REDDISH | REDDISH | REDDISH | REDDISH | REDDISH | REDDISH |
| Apr-60 | HEATON-52B | HEATON-52B | | REDDISH | REDDISH | REDDISH | REDDISH | REDDISH | REDDISH |
| Aug-60 | HEATON-52B | HEATON-52B | | REDDISH | REDDISH | REDDISH | REDDISH | REDDISH | REDDISH |
| Nov-60 | HEATON-52B | HEATON-52B | | REDDISH | REDDISH | REDDISH | REDDISH | REDDISH | REDDISH |

| | 26006 | 26007 | 26008 | 26009 | 26010 | 26011 | 26012 | 26013 | 26014 |
|---|---|---|---|---|---|---|---|---|---|
| Aug-50 | | | | | | | | | |
| Jan-51 | 1/51: GORT-39A | 2/51: GORT-39A | 3/51: GORT-39A | 3/51: GORT-39A | 3/51: GORT-39A | 5/51: GORT-39A | 5/51: GORT-39A | 5/51: GORT-39A | 5/51: GORT-39A |
| Aug-51 | GORTON-39A | GORTON-39A | GORTON-39A | GORTON-39A | GORTON-39A | GORTON-39A | GORTON-39A | GORTON-39A | GORTON-39A |
| Jan-52 | GORTON-39A | GORTON-39A | GORTON-39A | GORTON-39A | GORTON-39A | GORTON-39A | GORTON-39A | GORTON-39A | GORTON-39A |
| Aug-52 | 5/52: ILFORD | 5/52: ILFORD | 5/52: ILFORD | 5/52: ILFORD | 5/52: ILFORD | 5/52: ILFORD | 5/52: WATH-36B | 5/52: WATH-36B | 5/52: WATH-36B |
| Jan-53 | 9/52: WATH-36B | ILFORD-30A | ILFORD-30A | ILFORD-30A | ILFORD-30A | 3/53: GORT-39A | WATH-36B | 7/53: GORT-39A | 3/53: GORT-39A |
| Aug-53 | 3/53: GORT-39A | 3/53: GORT-39A | 3/53: GORT-39A | 3/53: GORT-39A | 3/53: GORT-39A | 5/53: MEX-36B | WATH-36B | 10/53: MEX-36B | 5/53: MEX-36B |
| Jan-54 | GORTON-39A | GORTON-39A | GORTON-39A | GORTON-39A | GORTON-39A | 4/54: GORT-39A | 12/53: GORT-39A | 3/54: GORT-39A | 3/54: GORT-39A |
| Aug-54 | 6/54: REDDISH | 6/54: REDDISH | 6/54: REDDISH | 6/54: REDDISH | 6/54: REDDISH | 6/54: REDDISH | 6/54: REDDISH | 6/54: REDDISH | 6/54: REDDISH |
| Jan-55 | REDDISH | REDDISH | REDDISH | REDDISH | REDDISH | REDDISH | REDDISH | REDDISH | REDDISH |
| Aug-55 | REDDISH | REDDISH | REDDISH | REDDISH | REDDISH | REDDISH | REDDISH | REDDISH | REDDISH |
| Jan-56 | REDDISH | REDDISH | REDDISH | REDDISH | REDDISH | REDDISH | REDDISH | REDDISH | REDDISH |
| Aug-56 | REDDISH | REDDISH | REDDISH | REDDISH | REDDISH | REDDISH | REDDISH | REDDISH | REDDISH |
| Jan-57 | REDDISH | REDDISH | REDDISH | REDDISH | REDDISH | REDDISH | REDDISH | REDDISH | REDDISH |
| Aug-57 | REDDISH | REDDISH | REDDISH | REDDISH | REDDISH | REDDISH | REDDISH | REDDISH | REDDISH |
| Jan-58 | REDDISH | REDDISH | REDDISH | REDDISH | REDDISH | REDDISH | REDDISH | REDDISH | REDDISH |
| Aug-58 | REDDISH | REDDISH | REDDISH | REDDISH | REDDISH | REDDISH | REDDISH | REDDISH | REDDISH |
| Jan-59 | REDDISH | REDDISH | REDDISH | REDDISH | REDDISH | REDDISH | REDDISH | REDDISH | REDDISH |
| Aug-59 | REDDISH | REDDISH | REDDISH | REDDISH | REDDISH | REDDISH | REDDISH | REDDISH | REDDISH |
| Nov-59 | REDDISH | REDDISH | REDDISH | REDDISH | REDDISH | REDDISH | REDDISH | REDDISH | REDDISH |
| Jan-60 | REDDISH | REDDISH | REDDISH | REDDISH | REDDISH | REDDISH | REDDISH | REDDISH | REDDISH |
| Apr-60 | REDDISH | REDDISH | REDDISH | REDDISH | REDDISH | REDDISH | REDDISH | REDDISH | REDDISH |
| Aug-60 | REDDISH | REDDISH | REDDISH | REDDISH | REDDISH | REDDISH | REDDISH | REDDISH | REDDISH |
| Nov-60 | REDDISH | REDDISH | REDDISH | REDDISH | REDDISH | REDDISH | REDDISH | REDDISH | REDDISH |

| | 26015 | 26016 | 26017 | 26018 | 26019 | 26020 | 26021 | 26022 | 26023 |
|---|---|---|---|---|---|---|---|---|---|
| Aug-50 | | | | | | | | | |
| Jan-51 | | | | | | | 2/51: GORT-39A | | |
| Aug-51 | 6/51: GORT-39A | 6/51: GORT-39A | 6/51: GORT-39A | 9/51: GORT-39A | 9/51: GORT-39A | GORTON-39A | 10/51: GORT-39A | 9/51: GORT-39A | 9/51: GORT-39A |
| Jan-52 | GORTON-39A | GORTON-39A | GORTON-39A | GORTON-39A | GORTON-39A | GORTON-39A | GORTON-39A | GORTON-39A | GORTON-39A |
| Aug-52 | 5/52: WATH-36B | 5/52: WATH-36B | 5/52: WATH-36B | 5/52: WATH-36B | 5/52: WATH-36B | 5/52: WATH-36B | 5/52: WATH-36B | 5/52: WATH-36B | 5/52: WATH-36B |
| Jan-53 | WATH-36B | WATH-36B | WATH-36B | 3/53: GORT-39A | 3/53: GORT-39A | WATH-36B | WATH-36B | 3/53: GORT-39A | WATH-36B |
| Aug-53 | 11/53: GORT-39A | 1/54: MEX-36B | 1/54: MEX-36B | 5/53: MEX-36B | GORTON-39A | 4/54: DARN-39B | 5/53: GORT-39A | GORTON-39A | 10/53: GORT-39A |
| Jan-54 | 1/54: MEX-36B | 3/54: GORT-39A | 5/54: GORT-39A | 3/54: GORT-39A | GORTON-39A | 5/54: GORT-39A | 10/53: MEX-36B | GORTON-39A | 11/53: MEX-36B |
| Aug-54 | 6/54: REDDISH | 6/54: REDDISH | 6/54: REDDISH | 6/54: REDDISH | 6/54: REDDISH | 6/54: REDDISH | 6/54: REDDISH | 6/54: REDDISH | 6/54: REDDISH |
| Jan-55 | REDDISH | REDDISH | REDDISH | REDDISH | REDDISH | REDDISH | REDDISH | REDDISH | REDDISH |
| Aug-55 | REDDISH | REDDISH | REDDISH | REDDISH | REDDISH | REDDISH | REDDISH | REDDISH | REDDISH |
| Jan-56 | REDDISH | REDDISH | REDDISH | REDDISH | REDDISH | REDDISH | REDDISH | REDDISH | REDDISH |
| Aug-56 | REDDISH | REDDISH | REDDISH | REDDISH | REDDISH | REDDISH | REDDISH | REDDISH | REDDISH |
| Jan-57 | REDDISH | REDDISH | REDDISH | REDDISH | REDDISH | REDDISH | REDDISH | REDDISH | REDDISH |
| Aug-57 | REDDISH | REDDISH | REDDISH | REDDISH | REDDISH | REDDISH | REDDISH | REDDISH | REDDISH |
| Jan-58 | REDDISH | REDDISH | REDDISH | REDDISH | REDDISH | REDDISH | REDDISH | REDDISH | REDDISH |
| Aug-58 | REDDISH | REDDISH | REDDISH | REDDISH | REDDISH | REDDISH | REDDISH | REDDISH | REDDISH |
| Jan-59 | REDDISH | REDDISH | REDDISH | REDDISH | REDDISH | REDDISH | REDDISH | REDDISH | REDDISH |
| Aug-59 | REDDISH | REDDISH | REDDISH | REDDISH | REDDISH | REDDISH | REDDISH | REDDISH | REDDISH |
| Nov-59 | REDDISH | REDDISH | REDDISH | REDDISH | REDDISH | REDDISH | REDDISH | REDDISH | REDDISH |
| Jan-60 | REDDISH | REDDISH | REDDISH | REDDISH | REDDISH | REDDISH | REDDISH | REDDISH | REDDISH |
| Apr-60 | REDDISH | REDDISH | REDDISH | REDDISH | REDDISH | REDDISH | REDDISH | REDDISH | REDDISH |
| Aug-60 | REDDISH | REDDISH | REDDISH | REDDISH | REDDISH | REDDISH | REDDISH | REDDISH | REDDISH |
| Nov-60 | REDDISH | REDDISH | REDDISH | REDDISH | REDDISH | REDDISH | REDDISH | REDDISH | REDDISH |

| | 26024 | 26025 | 26026 | 26027 | 26028 | 26029 | 26030 | 26031 | 26032 |
|---|---|---|---|---|---|---|---|---|---|
| Aug-50 | | | | | | | | | |
| Jan-51 | | | | | | | | | |
| Aug-51 | 9/51: GORT-39A | | | | | | | | |
| Jan-52 | GORTON-39A | 1/52: GORT-39A | 1/52: GORT-39A | 1/52: GORT-39A | 1/52: GORT-39A | 1/52: GORT-39A | 1/52: GORT-39A | 1/52: GORT-39A | 1/52: GORT-39A |
| Aug-52 | 5/52: WATH-36B | 5/52: WATH-36B | 5/52: WATH-36B | 5/52: WATH-36B | 5/52: WATH-36B | 5/52: WATH-36B | 5/52: WATH-36B | 5/52: WATH-36B | 5/52: WATH-36B |
| Jan-53 | WATH-36B | WATH-36B | WATH-36B | WATH-36B | WATH-36B | WATH-36B | 3/53: GORT-39A | WATH-36B | WATH-36B |
| Aug-53 | WATH-36B | 1/54: MEX-36B | WATH-36B | 1/54: MEX-36B | 1/54: MEX-36B | 7/53: GORT-39A | 7/53: MEX-36B | 7/53: GORT-39A | 7/53: GORT-39A |
| Jan-54 | 12/53: GORT-39A | 5/54: GORT-39A | 1/54: GORT-39A | 4/54: GORT-39A | 4/54: GORT-39A | GORTON-39A | MEXBOROUGH-36B | 12/53: MEX-36B | 11/53: MEX-36B |
| Aug-54 | 6/54: REDDISH | 6/54: REDDISH | 6/54: REDDISH | 6/54: REDDISH | 6/54: REDDISH | 6/54: REDDISH | 6/54: REDDISH | 6/54: REDDISH | 6/54: REDDISH |
| Jan-55 | REDDISH | REDDISH | REDDISH | REDDISH | REDDISH | REDDISH | REDDISH | REDDISH | REDDISH |
| Aug-55 | REDDISH | REDDISH | REDDISH | REDDISH | REDDISH | REDDISH | REDDISH | REDDISH | REDDISH |
| Jan-56 | REDDISH | REDDISH | REDDISH | REDDISH | REDDISH | REDDISH | REDDISH | REDDISH | REDDISH |
| Aug-56 | REDDISH | REDDISH | REDDISH | REDDISH | REDDISH | REDDISH | REDDISH | REDDISH | REDDISH |
| Jan-57 | REDDISH | REDDISH | REDDISH | REDDISH | REDDISH | REDDISH | REDDISH | REDDISH | REDDISH |
| Aug-57 | REDDISH | REDDISH | REDDISH | REDDISH | REDDISH | REDDISH | REDDISH | REDDISH | REDDISH |
| Jan-58 | REDDISH | REDDISH | REDDISH | REDDISH | REDDISH | REDDISH | REDDISH | REDDISH | REDDISH |
| Aug-58 | REDDISH | REDDISH | REDDISH | REDDISH | REDDISH | REDDISH | REDDISH | REDDISH | REDDISH |
| Jan-59 | REDDISH | REDDISH | REDDISH | REDDISH | REDDISH | REDDISH | REDDISH | REDDISH | REDDISH |
| Aug-59 | REDDISH | REDDISH | REDDISH | REDDISH | REDDISH | REDDISH | REDDISH | REDDISH | REDDISH |
| Nov-59 | REDDISH | REDDISH | REDDISH | REDDISH | REDDISH | REDDISH | REDDISH | REDDISH | REDDISH |
| Jan-60 | REDDISH | REDDISH | REDDISH | REDDISH | REDDISH | REDDISH | REDDISH | REDDISH | REDDISH |
| Apr-60 | REDDISH | REDDISH | REDDISH | REDDISH | REDDISH | REDDISH | REDDISH | REDDISH | REDDISH |
| Aug-60 | REDDISH | REDDISH | REDDISH | REDDISH | REDDISH | REDDISH | REDDISH | REDDISH | REDDISH |
| Nov-60 | REDDISH | REDDISH | REDDISH | REDDISH | REDDISH | REDDISH | REDDISH | REDDISH | REDDISH |

The largest project undertaken during the first decade of the BTC was the electrification of the Great Central line between Sheffield/Wath and Manchester: :the first main line electrification in the country and the first main line to be closed.  Initially the project raised hopes of a renaissance of Great Central fortunes with Marylebone becoming 'the' station for Manchester but in the event the pattern of passenger services hardly changed.  The maximum speed between Manchester and Sheffield remained at 60 mph whilst the hourly train service from London Road consisted in the main of five coach formations (plus occasional parcels vehicles) aimed at Cleethorpes and Hull rather than London.  The mineral service, on the other hand, saw some acceleration and although the loads hauled did not increase, running times from Wath to Mottram were reduced from three and a half to two hours.  Two classes of locomotive were provided, the four -axle EM1 goods engines and the six-axle EM2, the latter intended for passenger work.  Above EM1 26055 'Prometheus' and, below, EM2 27002 'Aurora' run round their trains at Sheffield Victoria in 1960.

## 26033 – 26041

| | 26033 | 26034 | 26035 | 26036 | 26037 | 26038 | 26039 | 26040 | 26041 |
|---|---|---|---|---|---|---|---|---|---|
| Aug-50 | | | | | | | | | |
| Jan-51 | | | | | | | | | |
| Aug-51 | | | | | | | | | |
| Jan-52 | 1/52: GORT - 39A | 1/52: GORT - 39A | 1/52: GORT - 39A | 2/52: GORT - 39A | 2/52: GORT - 39A | 4/52: GORT - 39A | 4/52: GORT - 39A | 4/52: MEX - 36B | 4/52: MEX - 36B |
| Aug-52 | 5/52: WATH - 36B | 5/52: WATH - 36B | 5/52: WATH - 36B | 5/52: WATH - 36B | 5/52: WATH - 36B | GORTON - 39A | GORTON - 39A | MEXBOROUGH - 36B | MEXBOROUGH - 36B |
| Jan-53 | WATH - 36B | 3/53: MEX - 36B | 3/53: MEX - 36B | WATH - 36B | WATH - 36B | WATH - 36B | GORTON - 39A | MEXBOROUGH - 36B | MEXBOROUGH - 36B |
| Aug-53 | WATH - 36B | MEXBOROUGH - 36B | 7/53: MEX - 36B | 7/53: MEX - 36B | WATH - 36B | 7/53: MEX - 36B | GORTON - 39A | MEXBOROUGH - 36B | MEXBOROUGH - 36B |
| Jan-54 | 12/53: GORT - 39A | MEXBOROUGH - 36B | 5/54: GORT - 39A | 12/53: GORT - 39A | 3/54: MEX - 36B | 3/54: GORT - 39A | GORTON - 39A | 10/53: GORT - 39A | 11/53: GORT - 39A |
| Aug-54 | 6/54: REDDISH | 6/54: REDDISH | 6/54: REDDISH | 6/54: REDDISH | 6/54: REDDISH | 6/54: REDDISH | 6/54: REDDISH | 6/54: REDDISH | 6/54: REDDISH |
| Jan-55 | REDDISH | REDDISH | REDDISH | REDDISH | REDDISH | REDDISH | REDDISH | REDDISH | REDDISH |
| Aug-55 | REDDISH | REDDISH | REDDISH | REDDISH | REDDISH | REDDISH | REDDISH | REDDISH | REDDISH |
| Jan-56 | REDDISH | REDDISH | REDDISH | REDDISH | REDDISH | REDDISH | REDDISH | REDDISH | REDDISH |
| Aug-56 | REDDISH | REDDISH | REDDISH | REDDISH | REDDISH | REDDISH | REDDISH | REDDISH | REDDISH |
| Jan-57 | REDDISH | REDDISH | REDDISH | REDDISH | REDDISH | REDDISH | REDDISH | REDDISH | REDDISH |
| Aug-57 | REDDISH | REDDISH | REDDISH | REDDISH | REDDISH | REDDISH | REDDISH | REDDISH | REDDISH |
| Jan-58 | REDDISH | REDDISH | REDDISH | REDDISH | REDDISH | REDDISH | REDDISH | REDDISH | REDDISH |
| Aug-58 | REDDISH | REDDISH | REDDISH | REDDISH | REDDISH | REDDISH | REDDISH | REDDISH | REDDISH |
| Jan-59 | REDDISH | REDDISH | REDDISH | REDDISH | REDDISH | REDDISH | REDDISH | REDDISH | REDDISH |
| Aug-59 | REDDISH | REDDISH | REDDISH | REDDISH | REDDISH | REDDISH | REDDISH | REDDISH | REDDISH |
| Nov-59 | REDDISH | REDDISH | REDDISH | REDDISH | REDDISH | REDDISH | REDDISH | REDDISH | REDDISH |
| Jan-60 | REDDISH | REDDISH | REDDISH | REDDISH | REDDISH | REDDISH | REDDISH | REDDISH | REDDISH |
| Apr-60 | REDDISH | REDDISH | REDDISH | REDDISH | REDDISH | REDDISH | REDDISH | REDDISH | REDDISH |
| Aug-60 | REDDISH | REDDISH | REDDISH | REDDISH | REDDISH | REDDISH | REDDISH | REDDISH | REDDISH |
| Nov-60 | REDDISH | REDDISH | REDDISH | REDDISH | REDDISH | REDDISH | REDDISH | REDDISH | REDDISH |

## 26042 – 26050

| | 26042 | 26043 | 26044 | 26045 | 26046 | 26047 | 26048 | 26049 | 26050 |
|---|---|---|---|---|---|---|---|---|---|
| Aug-50 | | | | | | | | | |
| Jan-51 | | | | | | | | | |
| Aug-51 | | | | | | | | | |
| Jan-52 | | | | | | | | | |
| Aug-52 | 5/52: MEX - 36B | 5/52: MEX - 36B | 5/52: MEX - 36B | 6/52: MEX - 36B | 8/52: MEX - 36B | 8/52: MEX - 36B | 9/52: MEX - 36B | 9/52: MEX - 36B | 11/52: MEX - 36B |
| Jan-53 | 3/53: GORT - 39A | 3/53: GORT - 39A | 3/53: GORT - 39A | 3/53: GORT - 39A | 3/53: GORT - 39A | 3/53: GORT - 39A | 3/53: GORT - 39A | 3/53: GORT - 39A | 3/53: GORT - 39A |
| Aug-53 | GORTON - 39A | GORTON - 39A | GORTON - 39A | GORTON - 39A | GORTON - 39A | GORTON - 39A | GORTON - 39A | GORTON - 39A | GORTON - 39A |
| Jan-54 | 3/54: MEX - 36B | 3/54: MEX - 36B | 12/53: MEX - 36B | 12/53: MEX - 36B | 12/53: MEX - 36B | 1/54: MEX - 36B | 1/54: MEX - 36B | 1/54: MEX - 36B | 3/54: MEX - 36B |
| Aug-54 | 6/54: REDDISH | 6/54: REDDISH | 6/54: REDDISH | 6/54: REDDISH | 6/54: REDDISH | 6/54: REDDISH | 6/54: REDDISH | 6/54: REDDISH | 6/54: REDDISH |
| Jan-55 | REDDISH | REDDISH | REDDISH | REDDISH | REDDISH | REDDISH | REDDISH | REDDISH | REDDISH |
| Aug-55 | REDDISH | REDDISH | REDDISH | REDDISH | REDDISH | REDDISH | REDDISH | REDDISH | REDDISH |
| Jan-56 | REDDISH | REDDISH | REDDISH | REDDISH | REDDISH | REDDISH | REDDISH | REDDISH | REDDISH |
| Aug-56 | REDDISH | REDDISH | REDDISH | REDDISH | REDDISH | REDDISH | REDDISH | REDDISH | REDDISH |
| Jan-57 | REDDISH | REDDISH | REDDISH | REDDISH | REDDISH | REDDISH | REDDISH | REDDISH | REDDISH |
| Aug-57 | REDDISH | REDDISH | REDDISH | REDDISH | REDDISH | REDDISH | REDDISH | REDDISH | REDDISH |
| Jan-58 | REDDISH | REDDISH | REDDISH | REDDISH | REDDISH | REDDISH | REDDISH | REDDISH | REDDISH |
| Aug-58 | REDDISH | REDDISH | REDDISH | REDDISH | REDDISH | REDDISH | REDDISH | REDDISH | REDDISH |
| Jan-59 | REDDISH | REDDISH | REDDISH | REDDISH | REDDISH | REDDISH | REDDISH | REDDISH | REDDISH |
| Aug-59 | REDDISH | REDDISH | REDDISH | REDDISH | REDDISH | REDDISH | REDDISH | REDDISH | REDDISH |
| Nov-59 | REDDISH | REDDISH | REDDISH | REDDISH | REDDISH | REDDISH | REDDISH | REDDISH | REDDISH |
| Jan-60 | REDDISH | REDDISH | REDDISH | REDDISH | REDDISH | REDDISH | REDDISH | REDDISH | REDDISH |
| Apr-60 | REDDISH | REDDISH | REDDISH | REDDISH | REDDISH | REDDISH | REDDISH | REDDISH | REDDISH |
| Aug-60 | REDDISH | REDDISH | REDDISH | REDDISH | REDDISH | REDDISH | REDDISH | REDDISH | REDDISH |
| Nov-60 | REDDISH | REDDISH | REDDISH | REDDISH | REDDISH | REDDISH | REDDISH | REDDISH | REDDISH |

## 26051 – 26057, EM2 (1953) 27000 – 27001

| | 26051 | 26052 | 26053 | 26054 | 26055 | 26056 | 26057 | 27000 | 27001 |
|---|---|---|---|---|---|---|---|---|---|
| | | | | | | | | EM2 (1953) | |
| Aug-50 | | | | | | | | | |
| Jan-51 | | | | | | | | | |
| Aug-51 | | | | | | | | | |
| Jan-52 | | | | | | | | | |
| Aug-52 | 12/52: MEX - 36B | | | | | | | | |
| Jan-53 | 3/53: GORT - 39A | 1/53: GORT - 39A | 3/53: GORT - 39A | 4/53: GORT - 39A | | | | | |
| Aug-53 | GORTON - 39A | GORTON - 39A | GORTON - 39A | GORTON - 39A | 6/53: GORT - 39A | 7/53: GORT - 39A | 8/53: GORT - 39A | | |
| Jan-54 | 4/54: MEX - 36B | 4/54: MEX - 36B | 4/54: MEX - 36B | GORTON - 39A | GORTON - 39A | GORTON - 39A | GORTON - 39A | 12/53: MEX - 36B | 3/54: MEX - 36B |
| Aug-54 | 6/54: REDDISH | 6/54: REDDISH | 6/54: REDDISH | 6/54: REDDISH | 6/54: REDDISH | 6/54: REDDISH | 6/54: REDDISH | 6/54: REDDISH | 6/54: REDDISH |
| Jan-55 | REDDISH | REDDISH | REDDISH | REDDISH | REDDISH | REDDISH | REDDISH | REDDISH | REDDISH |
| Aug-55 | REDDISH | REDDISH | REDDISH | REDDISH | REDDISH | REDDISH | REDDISH | REDDISH | REDDISH |
| Jan-56 | REDDISH | REDDISH | REDDISH | REDDISH | REDDISH | REDDISH | REDDISH | REDDISH | REDDISH |
| Aug-56 | REDDISH | REDDISH | REDDISH | REDDISH | REDDISH | REDDISH | REDDISH | REDDISH | REDDISH |
| Jan-57 | REDDISH | REDDISH | REDDISH | REDDISH | REDDISH | REDDISH | REDDISH | REDDISH | REDDISH |
| Aug-57 | REDDISH | REDDISH | REDDISH | REDDISH | REDDISH | REDDISH | REDDISH | REDDISH | REDDISH |
| Jan-58 | REDDISH | REDDISH | REDDISH | REDDISH | REDDISH | REDDISH | REDDISH | REDDISH | REDDISH |
| Aug-58 | REDDISH | REDDISH | REDDISH | REDDISH | REDDISH | REDDISH | REDDISH | REDDISH | REDDISH |
| Jan-59 | REDDISH | REDDISH | REDDISH | REDDISH | REDDISH | REDDISH | REDDISH | REDDISH | REDDISH |
| Aug-59 | REDDISH | REDDISH | REDDISH | REDDISH | REDDISH | REDDISH | REDDISH | REDDISH | REDDISH |
| Nov-59 | REDDISH | REDDISH | REDDISH | REDDISH | REDDISH | REDDISH | REDDISH | REDDISH | REDDISH |
| Jan-60 | REDDISH | REDDISH | REDDISH | REDDISH | REDDISH | REDDISH | REDDISH | REDDISH | REDDISH |
| Apr-60 | REDDISH | REDDISH | REDDISH | REDDISH | REDDISH | REDDISH | REDDISH | REDDISH | REDDISH |
| Aug-60 | REDDISH | REDDISH | REDDISH | REDDISH | REDDISH | REDDISH | REDDISH | REDDISH | REDDISH |
| Nov-60 | REDDISH | REDDISH | REDDISH | REDDISH | REDDISH | REDDISH | REDDISH | REDDISH | REDDISH |

## 27002 – 27006, 2000hp Diesel D200 – D203

| | 27002 | 27003 | 27004 | 27005 | 27006 | D200 | D201 | D202 | D203 |
|---|---|---|---|---|---|---|---|---|---|
| | | | | | | 2000hp Diesel | | | |
| Aug-50 | | | | | | | | | |
| Jan-51 | | | | | | | | | |
| Aug-51 | | | | | | | | | |
| Jan-52 | | | | | | | | | |
| Aug-52 | | | | | | | | | |
| Jan-53 | | | | | | | | | |
| Aug-53 | | | | | | | | | |
| Jan-54 | 5/54: MEX _ 36B | | | | | | | | |
| Aug-54 | 6/54: REDDISH | 6/54: REDDISH | 6/54: REDDISH | | | | | | |
| Jan-55 | REDDISH | REDDISH | REDDISH | 12/54: REDDISH | 12/54: REDDISH | | | | |
| Aug-55 | REDDISH | REDDISH | REDDISH | REDDISH | REDDISH | | | | |
| Jan-56 | REDDISH | REDDISH | REDDISH | REDDISH | REDDISH | | | | |
| Aug-56 | REDDISH | REDDISH | REDDISH | REDDISH | REDDISH | | | | |
| Jan-57 | REDDISH | REDDISH | REDDISH | REDDISH | REDDISH | | | | |
| Aug-57 | REDDISH | REDDISH | REDDISH | REDDISH | REDDISH | | | | |
| Jan-58 | REDDISH | REDDISH | REDDISH | REDDISH | REDDISH | 3/58: STRAT - 30A | 4/58: STRAT - 30A | 4/58: STRAT - 30A | |
| Aug-58 | REDDISH | REDDISH | REDDISH | REDDISH | REDDISH | STRATFORD - 30A | 5/58: HSEY - 34B | STRATFORD - 30A | 5/58: STRAT - 30A |
| Jan-59 | REDDISH | REDDISH | REDDISH | REDDISH | REDDISH | STRATFORD - 30A | HORNSEY - 34B | STRATFORD - 30A | STRATFORD - 30A |
| Aug-59 | REDDISH | REDDISH | REDDISH | REDDISH | REDDISH | 6/59: NOR - 32A | HORNSEY - 34B | 6/59: NOR - 32A | 6/59: NOR - 32A |
| Nov-59 | REDDISH | REDDISH | REDDISH | REDDISH | REDDISH | 10/59: STRAT - 30A | HORNSEY - 34B | 10/59: STRAT - 30A | 10/59: STRAT - 30A |
| Jan-60 | REDDISH | REDDISH | REDDISH | REDDISH | REDDISH | STRATFORD - 30A | HORNSEY - 34B | STRATFORD - 30A | STRATFORD - 30A |
| Apr-60 | REDDISH | REDDISH | REDDISH | REDDISH | REDDISH | STRATFORD - 30A | 5/60: C. YARD - 34G | STRATFORD - 30A | STRATFORD - 30A |
| Aug-60 | REDDISH | REDDISH | REDDISH | REDDISH | REDDISH | STRATFORD - 30A | CLARENCE YARD - 34G | STRATFORD - 30A | STRATFORD - 30A |
| Nov-60 | REDDISH | REDDISH | REDDISH | REDDISH | REDDISH | STRATFORD - 30A | CLARENCE YARD - 34G | STRATFORD - 30A | STRATFORD - 30A |

| Date | D204 | D205 | D206 | D207 | D208 | D209 | D237 | D238 | D239 |
|---|---|---|---|---|---|---|---|---|---|
| Jan-58 | | | | | | | | | |
| Aug-58 | 5/58: STRAT - 30A | 6/58: STRAT - 30A | 7/58: HSEY - 34B | 7/58: HSEY - 34B | 8/58: HSEY - 34B | 9/58: HSEY - 34B | | | |
| Jan-59 | STRATFORD-30A | STRATFORD-30A | HORNSEY-34B | HORNSEY-34B | HORNSEY-34B | HORNSEY-34B | | | |
| Aug-59 | 6/59: NOR - 32A | 6/59: NOR - 32A | HORNSEY-34B | HORNSEY-34B | HORNSEY-34B | HORNSEY-34B | | | |
| Nov-59 | 10/59: STRAT - 30A | 10/59: STRAT - 30A | HORNSEY-34B | HORNSEY-34B | HORNSEY-34B | HORNSEY-34B | 10/59: GHD - 52A | 10/59: GHD - 52A | 10/59: GHD - 52A |
| Jan-60 | STRATFORD-30A | STRATFORD-30A | HORNSEY-34B | HORNSEY-34B | HORNSEY-34B | HORNSEY-34B | GATESHEAD-52A | GATESHEAD-52A | GATESHEAD-52A |
| Apr-60 | STRATFORD-30A | STRATFORD-30A | 5/60: C. YARD - 34G | 5/60: C. YARD - 34G | HORNSEY-34B | 5/60: C. YARD - 34G | GATESHEAD-52A | GATESHEAD-52A | GATESHEAD-52A |
| Aug-60 | STRATFORD-30A | STRATFORD-30A | CLARENCE YARD-34G | CLARENCE YARD-34G | CLARENCE YARD-34G | CLARENCE YARD-34G | GATESHEAD-52A | GATESHEAD-52A | GATESHEAD-52A |
| Nov-60 | STRATFORD-30A | STRATFORD-30A | CLARENCE YARD-34G | CLARENCE YARD-34G | CLARENCE YARD-34G | CLARENCE YARD-34G | GATESHEAD-52A | GATESHEAD-52A | GATESHEAD-52A |

| Date | D240 | D241 | D242 | D243 | D244 | D245 | D246 | D247 | D248 |
|---|---|---|---|---|---|---|---|---|---|
| Jan-59 | | | | | | | | | |
| Aug-59 | | | | | | | | | |
| Nov-59 | 10/59: GHD - 52A | 10/59: GHD - 52A | 11/59: GHD - 52A | 11/59: GHD - 52A | 11/59: GHD - 52A | 11/59: GHD - 52A | 11/59: GHD - 52A | 11/59: GHD - 52A | 11/59: GHD - 52A |
| Jan-60 | GATESHEAD-52A | GATESHEAD-52A | GATESHEAD-52A | GATESHEAD-52A | GATESHEAD-52A | GATESHEAD-52A | GATESHEAD-52A | GATESHEAD-52A | 12/59: HSEY - 34B |
| Apr-60 | GATESHEAD-52A | GATESHEAD-52A | GATESHEAD-52A | GATESHEAD-52A | GATESHEAD-52A | GATESHEAD-52A | GATESHEAD-52A | GATESHEAD-52A | 5/60: C. YARD - 34G |
| Aug-60 | GATESHEAD-52A | GATESHEAD-52A | GATESHEAD-52A | GATESHEAD-52A | GATESHEAD-52A | GATESHEAD-52A | GATESHEAD-52A | GATESHEAD-52A | CLARENCE YARD-34G |
| Nov-60 | GATESHEAD-52A | GATESHEAD-52A | GATESHEAD-52A | GATESHEAD-52A | GATESHEAD-52A | GATESHEAD-52A | GATESHEAD-52A | GATESHEAD-52A | CLARENCE YARD-34G |

| Date | D249 | D250 | D251 | D252 | D253 | D254 | D256 | D257 | D258 |
|---|---|---|---|---|---|---|---|---|---|
| Jan-59 | | | | | | | | | |
| Aug-59 | | | | | | | | | |
| Nov-59 | 11/59: GHD - 52A | 11/59: GHD - 52A | 11/59: YORK - 50A | 11/59: YORK - 50A | 11/59: YORK - 50A | 11/59: YORK - 50A | 1/60: YORK - 50A | 1/60: YORK - 50A | 1/60: YORK - 50A |
| Jan-60 | GATESHEAD-52A | 2/60: YORK - 50A | YORK-50A | YORK-50A | 2/60: LEITH - 64H | 2/60: LEITH - 64H | 2/60: HAY - 64B | 2/60: HAY - 64B | 2/60: HAY - 64B |
| Apr-60 | GATESHEAD-52A | YORK-50A | YORK-50A | YORK-50A | 3/60: YORK - 50A | 4/50: YORK - 50A | 4/60: GHD - 52A | 3/60: YORK - 50A | 3/60: YORK - 50A |
| Aug-60 | GATESHEAD-52A | YORK-50A | YORK-50A | YORK-50A | YORK-50A | YORK-50A | GATESHEAD-52A | GATESHEAD-52A | YORK-50A |
| Nov-60 | GATESHEAD-52A | 10/60: GHD - 52A | 10/60: GHD - 52A | YORK-50A | YORK-50A | YORK-50A | | | YORK-50A |

| Date | D259 | D260 | D261 | D262 | D263 | D264 | D265 | D266 | D270 |
|---|---|---|---|---|---|---|---|---|---|
| Jan-59 | | | | | | | | | |
| Aug-59 | | | | | | | | | |
| Nov-59 | 1/60: YORK - 50A | | | | | | | | |
| Jan-60 | 2/60: HAY - 64B | 2/60: HAY - 64B | 2/60: HAY - 64B | 2/60: HAY - 64B | 2/60: HAY - 64B | 2/60: HAY - 64B | 4/60: HAY - 64B | 4/60: HAY - 64B | 4/60: GHD - 52A |
| Apr-60 | 3/60: YORK - 50A | HAYMARKET-64B | HAYMARKET-64B | HAYMARKET-64B | HAYMARKET-64B | HAYMARKET-64B | HAYMARKET-64B | HAYMARKET-64B | GATESHEAD-52A |
| Aug-60 | YORK - 50A | HAYMARKET-64B | HAYMARKET-64B | HAYMARKET-64B | HAYMARKET-64B | HAYMARKET-64B | HAYMARKET-64B | HAYMARKET-64B | GATESHEAD-52A |
| Nov-60 | YORK-50A | HAYMARKET-64B | HAYMARKET-64B | HAYMARKET-64B | HAYMARKET-64B | HAYMARKET-64B | HAYMARKET-64B | HAYMARKET-64B | GATESHEAD-52A |

| Date | D271 | D272 | D273 | D274 | D275 | D276 | D277 | D278 | D279 |
|---|---|---|---|---|---|---|---|---|---|
| Jan-60 | | | | | | | | | |
| Apr-60 | 4/60: GHD - 52A | 4/60: GHD - 52A | 4/60: GHD - 52A | 4/60: GHD - 52A | 5/60: YORK - 50A | 5/60: YORK - 50A | 5/60: YORK - 50A | 5/60: GHD - 52A | 5/60: GHD - 52A |
| Aug-60 | GATESHEAD-52A | GATESHEAD-52A | GATESHEAD-52A | GATESHEAD-52A | YORK - 50A | YORK - 50A | 7/60: GHD - 52A | GATESHEAD-52A | GATESHEAD-52A |
| Nov-60 | GATESHEAD-52A | GATESHEAD-52A | GATESHEAD-52A | GATESHEAD-52A | YORK - 50A | YORK - 50A | GATESHEAD-52A | GATESHEAD-52A | GATESHEAD-52A |

| Date | D280 | D281 | D282 | D283 | D284 | D285 | D286 |
|---|---|---|---|---|---|---|---|
| Jan-60 | | | | | | | |
| Apr-60 | 5/60: GHD - 52A | 6/60: YORK - 50A | 6/60: YORK - 50A | 6/60: YORK - 50A | 6/60: YORK - 50A | | |
| Aug-60 | GATESHEAD-52A | YORK - 50A | YORK - 50A | YORK - 50A | YORK - 50A | 7/60: YORK - 50A | 7/60: GHD - 52A |
| Nov-60 | GATESHEAD-52A | YORK - 50A | YORK - 50A | YORK - 50A | YORK - 50A | YORK - 50A | GATESHEAD-52A |

### 1160hp Diesel

| Date | D5020 | D5021 | D5022 | D5023 | D5024 | D5025 | D5026 | D5027 | D5028 |
|---|---|---|---|---|---|---|---|---|---|
| Aug-59 | 8/59: IPS - 32B | 8/59: IPS - 32B | 9/59: NOR - 32A | 9/59: NOR - 32A | | | | | |
| Nov-59 | IPSWICH-32B | IPSWICH-32B | 10/59: IPS - 32B | 9/59: IPS - 32B | 10/59: IPS - 32B | 10/59: IPS - 32B | 10/59: IPS - 32B | 10/59: IPS - 32B | 11/59: IPS - 32B |
| Jan-60 | IPSWICH-32B | IPSWICH-32B | IPSWICH-32B | IPSWICH-32B | IPSWICH-32B | IPSWICH-32B | IPSWICH-32B | IPSWICH-32B | IPSWICH-32B |
| Apr-60 | IPSWICH-32B | IPSWICH-32B | IPSWICH-32B | IPSWICH-32B | IPSWICH-32B | IPSWICH-32B | IPSWICH-32B | IPSWICH-32B | IPSWICH-32B |
| Aug-60 | IPSWICH-32B | IPSWICH-32B | IPSWICH-32B | IPSWICH-32B | IPSWICH-32B | IPSWICH-32B | 9/60: STRAT - 30A | 9/60: STRAT - 30A | 9/60: STRAT - 30A |
| Nov-60 | IPSWICH-32B | IPSWICH-32B | IPSWICH-32B | IPSWICH-32B | IPSWICH-32B | IPSWICH-32B | STRATFORD-30A | STRATFORD-30A | STRATFORD-30A |

| Date | D5029 | D5030 | D5031 | D5032 | D5033 | D5034 | D5035 | D5036 | D5037 |
|---|---|---|---|---|---|---|---|---|---|
| Aug-59 | | 6/59: MARCH - 31B | 6/59: MARCH - 31B | 7/59: MARCH - 31B | 7/59: MARCH - 31B | 9/59: MARCH - 31B | 8/59: MARCH - 31B | 9/59: MARCH - 31B | 9/59: MARCH - 31B |
| Nov-59 | 11/59: IPS - 32B | MARCH-31B | 8/59: STRAT - 30A | MARCH-31B | 10/59: STRAT - 30A | MARCH-31B | MARCH-31B | MARCH-31B | MARCH-31B |
| Jan-60 | IPSWICH-32B | 1/60: STRAT - 30A | STRATFORD-30A | 1/60: STRAT - 30A | STRATFORD-30A | MARCH-31B | MARCH-31B | MARCH-31B | MARCH-31B |
| Apr-60 | IPSWICH-32B | STRATFORD-30A | STRATFORD-30A | STRATFORD-30A | STRATFORD-30A | 3/60: STRAT - 30A | 3/60: STRAT - 30A | 5/60: IPS - 32B | 5/60: IPS - 32B |
| Aug-60 | 9/60: STRAT - 30A | STRATFORD-30A | STRATFORD-30A | STRATFORD-30A | STRATFORD-30A | STRATFORD-30A | STRATFORD-30A | IPSWICH-32B | IPSWICH-32B |
| Nov-60 | STRATFORD-30A | STRATFORD-30A | STRATFORD-30A | STRATFORD-30A | STRATFORD-30A | STRATFORD-30A | STRATFORD-30A | IPSWICH-32B | IPSWICH-32B |

| Date | D5038 | D5039 | D5040 | D5041 | D5042 | D5043 | D5044 | D5045 | D5046 |
|---|---|---|---|---|---|---|---|---|---|
| Aug-59 | 9/59: IPS - 32B | 9/59: IPS - 32B | 10/59: IPS - 32B | 9/59: IPS - 32B | 10/59: IPS - 32B | 10/59: IPS - 32B | 10/59: IPS - 32B | | |
| Nov-59 | IPSWICH-32B | 11/59: MARCH - 31B | 11/59: MARCH - 31B | 11/59: MARCH - 31B | 11/59: MARCH - 31B | 11/59: MARCH - 31B | 11/59: MARCH - 31B | 11/59: MARCH - 31B | 11/59: MARCH - 31B |
| Jan-60 | 1/60: MARCH - 31B | MARCH-31B | MARCH-31B | MARCH-31B | MARCH-31B | MARCH-31B | MARCH-31B | MARCH-31B | MARCH-31B |
| Apr-60 | MARCH-31B | MARCH-31B | MARCH-31B | MARCH-31B | 6/60: IPS - 32B | MARCH-31B | MARCH-31B | MARCH-31B | MARCH-31B |
| Aug-60 | 6/60: IPS - 32B | 6/60: IPS - 32B | 6/60: IPS - 32B | 6/60: IPS - 32B | IPSWICH-32B | 8/60: IPS - 32B | 8/60: IPS - 32B | 9/60: STRAT - 30A | 9/60: STRAT - 30A |
| Nov-60 | IPSWICH-32B | IPSWICH-32B | IPSWICH-32B | IPSWICH-32B | IPSWICH-32B | IPSWICH-32B | IPSWICH-32B | STRATFORD-30A | STRATFORD-30A |

| Date | D5047 | D5048 | D5049 | D5050 | D5051 | D5052 | D5053 | D5054 | D5055 |
|---|---|---|---|---|---|---|---|---|---|
| Aug-59 | | | | | | | | | |
| Nov-59 | 11/59: MARCH - 31B | 11/59: MARCH - 31B | | 11/59: MARCH - 31B | 11/59: MARCH - 31B | 11/59: MARCH - 31B | 11/59: MARCH - 31B | | |
| Jan-60 | MARCH-31B | MARCH-31B | | MARCH-31B | MARCH-31B | MARCH-31B | MARCH-31B | 12/59: MARCH - 31B | 12/59: MARCH - 31B |
| Apr-60 | MARCH-31B | MARCH-31B | 3/60: MARCH - 31B | MARCH-31B | MARCH-31B | MARCH-31B | MARCH-31B | MARCH-31B | MARCH-31B |
| Aug-60 | 9/60: STRAT - 30A | 9/60: STRAT - 30A | 9/60: STRAT - 30A | 9/60: STRAT - 30A | MARCH-31B | MARCH-31B | MARCH-31B | MARCH-31B | MARCH-31B |
| Nov-60 | STRATFORD-30A | STRATFORD-30A | STRATFORD-30A | STRATFORD-30A | MARCH-31B | MARCH-31B | MARCH-31B | MARCH-31B | MARCH-31B |

| Date | D5056 | D5057 | D5058 | D5059 | D5060 | D5061 | D5062 | D5063 | D5064 |
|---|---|---|---|---|---|---|---|---|---|
| Jan-60 | 12/59: MARCH - 31B | 12/59: MARCH - 31B | | 12/59: MARCH - 31B | 12/59: MARCH - 31B | 12/59: MARCH - 31B | 2/60: MARCH - 31B | | 2/60: MARCH - 31B |
| Apr-60 | MARCH-31B | MARCH-31B | 12/59: MARCH - 31B | MARCH-31B | MARCH-31B | MARCH-31B | MARCH-31B | 2/60: MARCH - 31B | MARCH-31B |
| Aug-60 | MARCH-31B | MARCH-31B | MARCH-31B | MARCH-31B | MARCH-31B | MARCH-31B | MARCH-31B | MARCH-31B | MARCH-31B |
| Nov-60 | MARCH-31B | MARCH-31B | MARCH-31B | 11/60: To LM | 11/60: To LM | 11/60: To LM | MARCH-31B | 11/60: To LM | 11/60: To LM |

| Date | D5065 | D5066 | D5067 | D5068 | D5069 | D5070 | D5071 | D5072 | D5073 |
|---|---|---|---|---|---|---|---|---|---|
| Jan-60 | 2/60: MARCH - 31B | 12/59: MARCH - 31B | 12/59: MARCH - 31B | 12/59: MARCH - 31B | 12/59: MARCH - 31B | 2/60: MARCH - 31B | 2/60: MARCH - 31B | 2/60: MARCH - 31B | 2/60: MARCH - 31B |
| Apr-60 | MARCH-31B | MARCH-31B | MARCH-31B | MARCH-31B | MARCH-31B | MARCH-31B | MARCH-31B | 4/60: To LM | 4/60: To LM |
| Aug-60 | MARCH-31B | MARCH-31B | MARCH-31B | MARCH-31B | MARCH-31B | MARCH-31B | MARCH-31B | | |
| Nov-60 | 11/60: To LM | MARCH-31B | MARCH-31B | MARCH-31B | MARCH-31B | MARCH-31B | MARCH-31B | | |

| Date | D5074 | D5076 | D5077 | D5078 | D5079 | D5080 | D5094 | D5095 | D5096 |
|---|---|---|---|---|---|---|---|---|---|
| Jan-60 | 2/60: MARCH - 31B | 2/60: MARCH - 31B | 2/60: MARCH - 31B | 2/60: MARCH - 31B | 2/60: MARCH - 31B | 2/60: MARCH - 31B | 2/60: MARCH - 31B | | |
| Apr-60 | 4/60: To LM | MARCH-31B | MARCH-31B | MARCH-31B | 4/60: To LM | 4/60: To LM | MARCH-31B | 3/60: MARCH - 31B | 4/60: GHD - 52A |
| Aug-60 | | 8/60: To LM | 8/60: To LM | | | | MARCH-31B | MARCH-31B | GATESHEAD-52A |
| Nov-60 | | | | | | | MARCH-31B | MARCH-31B | GATESHEAD-52A |

| Date | D5097 | D5098 | D5099 | D5100 | D5101 | D5102 | D5103 | D5104 | D5105 |
|---|---|---|---|---|---|---|---|---|---|
| Jan-60 | | | | | | | | | |
| Apr-60 | 4/60: GHD - 52A | 5/60: HTN - 52B | 5/60: HTN - 52B | 6/60: GHD - 52A | 6/60: GHD - 52A | 6/60: GHD - 52A | | | |
| Aug-60 | GATESHEAD-52A | HEATON-52B | HEATON-52B | GATESHEAD-52A | GATESHEAD-52A | GATESHEAD-52A | 8/60: GHD - 52A | 9/60: GHD - 52A | 9/60: GHD - 52A |
| Nov-60 | GATESHEAD-52A | HEATON-52B | HEATON-52B | GATESHEAD-52A | GATESHEAD-52A | GATESHEAD-52A | GATESHEAD-52A | GATESHEAD-52A | GATESHEAD-52A |

| Date | D5106 | D5107 | D5108 | D5109 |
|---|---|---|---|---|
| Aug-60 | | | | |
| Nov-60 | 10/60: GHD - 52A | 10/60: GHD - 52A | 11/60: GHD - 52A | 11/60: GHD - 52A |

| | 1160hp Diesel D5300 | D5301 | D5302 | D5303 | D5304 | D5305 | D5306 | D5307 | D5308 |
|---|---|---|---|---|---|---|---|---|---|
| Jan-58 | | | | | | | | | |
| Aug-58 | 7/58: HSEY - 34B | 9/58: HSEY - 34B | 10/58: HSEY - 34B | 10/58: HSEY - 34B | 10/58: HSEY - 34B | 10/58: HSEY - 34B | | | |
| Jan-59 | HORNSEY-34B | HORNSEY-34B | HORNSEY-34B | HORNSEY-34B | HORNSEY-34B | HORNSEY-34B | 11/58: HSEY - 34B | 12/58: HSEY - 34B | 12/58: HSEY - 34B |
| Aug-59 | HORNSEY-34B | HORNSEY-34B | HORNSEY-34B | HORNSEY-34B | HORNSEY-34B | HORNSEY-34B | HORNSEY-34B | HORNSEY-34B | HORNSEY-34B |
| Nov-59 | HORNSEY-34B | HORNSEY-34B | HORNSEY-34B | HORNSEY-34B | HORNSEY-34B | HORNSEY-34B | HORNSEY-34B | HORNSEY-34B | HORNSEY-34B |
| Jan-60 | HORNSEY-34B | HORNSEY-34B | HORNSEY-34B | HORNSEY-34B | HORNSEY-34B | HORNSEY-34B | HORNSEY-34B | HORNSEY-34B | HORNSEY-34B |
| Apr-60 | 5/60: HAY - 64B | 5/60: HAY - 64B | 5/60: HAY - 64B | 5/60: HAY - 64B | 5/60: HAY - 64B | 5/60: HAY - 64B | 5/60: C.YARD - 34G | 5/60: HAY - 64B | 5/60: HAY - 64B |
| Aug-60 | HAYMARKET-64B | HAYMARKET-64B | HAYMARKET-64B | HAYMARKET-64B | HAYMARKET-64B | HAYMARKET-64B | CLARENCE YARD-34G | HAYMARKET-64B | HAYMARKET-64B |
| Nov-60 | HAYMARKET-64B | HAYMARKET-64B | HAYMARKET-64B | HAYMARKET-64B | HAYMARKET-64B | HAYMARKET-64B | CLARENCE YARD-34G | HAYMARKET-64B | HAYMARKET-64B |

| | D5309 | D5310 | D5311 | D5312 | D5313 | D5314 | D5315 | D5316 | D5317 |
|---|---|---|---|---|---|---|---|---|---|
| Jan-58 | | | | | | | | | |
| Aug-58 | | | | | | | | | |
| Jan-59 | 12/58: HSEY - 34B | 1/59: HSEY - 34B | 1/59: HSEY - 34B | 1/59: HSEY - 34B | 1/59: HSEY - 34B | 1/59: HSEY - 34B | 1/59: HSEY - 34B | 1/59: HSEY - 34B | 2/59: HSEY - 34B |
| Aug-59 | HORNSEY-34B | HORNSEY-34B | HORNSEY-34B | HORNSEY-34B | HORNSEY-34B | HORNSEY-34B | HORNSEY-34B | HORNSEY-34B | HORNSEY-34B |
| Nov-59 | HORNSEY-34B | HORNSEY-34B | HORNSEY-34B | HORNSEY-34B | HORNSEY-34B | HORNSEY-34B | HORNSEY-34B | HORNSEY-34B | HORNSEY-34B |
| Jan-60 | HORNSEY-34B | HORNSEY-34B | HORNSEY-34B | HORNSEY-34B | HORNSEY-34B | HORNSEY-34B | HORNSEY-34B | HORNSEY-34B | HORNSEY-34B |
| Apr-60 | 5/60: HAY - 64B | 5/60: C.YARD - 34G | 5/60: C.YARD - 34G | 5/60: C.YARD - 34G | 5/60: C.YARD - 34G | 5/60: C.YARD - 34G | 5/60: C.YARD - 34G | 5/60: C.YARD - 34G | 5/60: C.YARD - 34G |
| Aug-60 | HAYMARKET-64B | CLARENCE YARD-34G | CLARENCE YARD-34G | HAYMARKET-64B | HAYMARKET-64B | HAYMARKET-64B | HAYMARKET-64B | HAYMARKET-64B | HAYMARKET-64B |
| Nov-60 | HAYMARKET-64B | CLARENCE YARD-34G | 10/60: HAY - 64B | HAYMARKET-64B | HAYMARKET-64B | HAYMARKET-64B | HAYMARKET-64B | HAYMARKET-64B | HAYMARKET-64B |

| | D5318 | D5319 | D5320 | D5321 | D5322 | D5323 | D5324 | D5325 | D5326 |
|---|---|---|---|---|---|---|---|---|---|
| Jan-58 | | | | | | | | | |
| Aug-58 | | | | | | | | | |
| Jan-59 | 3/59: HSEY - 34B | 3/59: HSEY - 34B | 4/59: HAY - 64B | 4/59: HAY - 64B | 4/59: HAY - 64B | 5/59: HAY - 64B | 5/59: HAY - 64B | 5/59: HAY - 64B | 5/59: HAY - 64B |
| Aug-59 | HORNSEY-34B | HORNSEY-34B | HAYMARKET-64B | HAYMARKET-64B | HAYMARKET-64B | HAYMARKET-64B | HAYMARKET-64B | HAYMARKET-64B | HAYMARKET-64B |
| Nov-59 | HORNSEY-34B | HORNSEY-34B | HAYMARKET-64B | HAYMARKET-64B | HAYMARKET-64B | HAYMARKET-64B | HAYMARKET-64B | HAYMARKET-64B | HAYMARKET-64B |
| Jan-60 | HORNSEY-34B | HORNSEY-34B | HAYMARKET-64B | HAYMARKET-64B | HAYMARKET-64B | HAYMARKET-64B | HAYMARKET-64B | HAYMARKET-64B | HAYMARKET-64B |
| Apr-60 | 5/60: C.YARD - 34G | 5/60: C.YARD - 34G | HAYMARKET-64B | HAYMARKET-64B | HAYMARKET-64B | HAYMARKET-64B | HAYMARKET-64B | HAYMARKET-64B | HAYMARKET-64B |
| Aug-60 | CLARENCE YARD-34G | CLARENCE YARD-34G | 7/60: INV - 60A | 7/60: INV - 60A | 7/60: INV - 60A | 7/60: INV - 60A | 7/60: INV - 60A | 7/60: INV - 60A | HAYMARKET-64B |
| Nov-60 | 10/60: HAY - 64B | 10/60: HAY - 64B | INVERNESS-60A | INVERNESS-60A | INVERNESS-60A | INVERNESS-60A | INVERNESS-60A | INVERNESS-60A | HAYMARKET-64B |

| | D5327 | D5328 | D5329 | D5330 | D5331 | D5332 | D5333 | D5334 | D5335 |
|---|---|---|---|---|---|---|---|---|---|
| Jan-58 | | | | | | | | | |
| Aug-58 | | | | | | | | | |
| Jan-59 | 6/59: HAY - 64B | 6/59: HAY - 64B | 6/59: HAY - 64B | 7/59: HAY - 64B | 7/59: HAY - 64B | 7/59: HAY - 64B | 7/59: HAY - 64B | 7/59: HAY - 64B | 7/59: HAY - 64B |
| Aug-59 | HAYMARKET-64B | HAYMARKET-64B | HAYMARKET-64B | 8/59: HSEY - 34B | 8/59: HSEY - 34B | 8/59: HSEY - 34B | 8/59: HSEY - 34B | 8/59: HSEY - 34B | 8/59: HSEY - 34B |
| Nov-59 | HAYMARKET-64B | HAYMARKET-64B | HAYMARKET-64B | 10/59: HAY - 64B | 10/59: HAY - 64B | 10/59: HAY - 64B | 10/59: HAY - 64B | 10/59: HAY - 64B | 10/59: HAY - 64B |
| Jan-60 | HAYMARKET-64B | HAYMARKET-64B | HAYMARKET-64B | HAYMARKET-64B | HAYMARKET-64B | HAYMARKET-64B | HAYMARKET-64B | HAYMARKET-64B | HAYMARKET-64B |
| Apr-60 | HAYMARKET-64B | HAYMARKET-64B | HAYMARKET-64B | HAYMARKET-64B | HAYMARKET-64B | HAYMARKET-64B | HAYMARKET-64B | HAYMARKET-64B | HAYMARKET-64B |
| Aug-60 | HAYMARKET-64B | 7/60: INV - 60A | HAYMARKET-64B | 8/60: EBRO(SM) - 64A | 8/60: EBRO(SM) - 64A | HAYMARKET-64B | 7/60: INV - 60A | 8/60: EBRO(SM) - 64A | 7/60: INV - 60A |
| Nov-60 | HAYMARKET-64B | INVERNESS-60A | HAYMARKET-64B | EDINBURGH (SM) - 64A | EDINBURGH (SM) - 64A | HAYMARKET-64B | INVERNESS-60A | EDINBURGH (SM) - 64A | INVERNESS-60A |

| | D5336 | D5337 | D5338 | D5339 | D5340 | D5341 | D5342 | D5343 | D5344 |
|---|---|---|---|---|---|---|---|---|---|
| Jan-58 | | | | | | | | | |
| Aug-58 | | | | | | | | | |
| Jan-59 | | | | | | | | | |
| Aug-59 | 8/59: HAY - 64B | 8/59: HAY - 64B | 8/59: HAY - 64B | 9/59: HAY - 64B | | | | | |
| Nov-59 | HAYMARKET-64B | HAYMARKET-64B | HAYMARKET-64B | HAYMARKET-64B | 10/59: HAY - 64B | 10/59: HAY - 64B | 10/59: HAY - 64B | 10/59: HAY - 64B | 10/59: HAY - 64B |
| Jan-60 | HAYMARKET-64B | HAYMARKET-64B | 3/60: INV - 60A | 3/60: INV - 60A | 3/60: INV - 60A | 3/60: INV - 60A | 3/60: INV - 60A | 3/60: INV - 60A | 3/60: INV - 60A |
| Apr-60 | HAYMARKET-64B | HAYMARKET-64B | INVERNESS-60A | INVERNESS-60A | 4/60: KITTY - 61A | 4/60: KITTY - 61A | 4/60: DUN - 62B | 4/60: DUN - 62B | 4/60: HAY - 64B |
| Aug-60 | HAYMARKET-64B | 7/60: INV - 60A | INVERNESS-60A | INVERNESS-60A | 7/60: INV - 60A | 7/60: INV - 60A | 7/60: INV - 60A | 7/60: INV - 60A | 7/60: INV - 60A |
| Nov-60 | HAYMARKET-64B | INVERNESS-60A | INVERNESS-60A | INVERNESS-60A | INVERNESS-60A | INVERNESS-60A | INVERNESS-60A | INVERNESS-60A | INVERNESS-60A |

| | D5345 | D5346 | 1250hp Diesel D5500 | D5501 | D5502 | D5503 | D5504 | D5505 | D5506 |
|---|---|---|---|---|---|---|---|---|---|
| Jan-57 | | | | | | | | | |
| Aug-57 | | | 10/57: STRAT - 30A | 11/57: STRAT - 30A | | | | | |
| Jan-58 | | | STRATFORD-30A | STRATFORD-30A | 12/57: STRAT - 30A | 1/58: STRAT - 30A | 1/58: STRAT - 30A | 2/58: STRAT - 30A | 3/58: STRAT - 30A |
| Aug-58 | | | STRATFORD-30A | STRATFORD-30A | STRATFORD-30A | STRATFORD-30A | STRATFORD-30A | STRATFORD-30A | STRATFORD-30A |
| Jan-59 | | | STRATFORD-30A | STRATFORD-30A | 3/59: IPS - 32B | STRATFORD-30A | STRATFORD-30A | STRATFORD-30A | STRATFORD-30A |
| Aug-59 | | | 6/59: IPS - 32B | STRATFORD-30A | IPSWICH-32B | 5/59: MARCH - 31B | 6/59: MARCH - 31B | STRATFORD-30A | STRATFORD-30A |
| Nov-59 | 10/59: HAY - 64B | 10/59: HAY - 64B | IPSWICH-32B | STRATFORD-30A | 10/59: STRAT - 30A | 11/59: STRAT - 30A | 11/59: STRAT - 30A | STRATFORD-30A | STRATFORD-30A |
| Jan-60 | 3/60: INV - 60A | HAYMARKET-64B | IPSWICH-32B | STRATFORD-30A | STRATFORD-30A | STRATFORD-30A | STRATFORD-30A | STRATFORD-30A | STRATFORD-30A |
| Apr-60 | 4/60: HAY - 64B | HAYMARKET-64B | IPSWICH-32B | STRATFORD-30A | STRATFORD-30A | STRATFORD-30A | STRATFORD-30A | STRATFORD-30A | STRATFORD-30A |
| Aug-60 | 7/60: INV - 60A | HAYMARKET-64B | IPSWICH-32B | STRATFORD-30A | STRATFORD-30A | STRATFORD-30A | STRATFORD-30A | STRATFORD-30A | STRATFORD-30A |
| Nov-60 | INVERNESS-60A | HAYMARKET-64B | IPSWICH-32B | STRATFORD-30A | STRATFORD-30A | STRATFORD-30A | STRATFORD-30A | STRATFORD-30A | STRATFORD-30A |

| | D5507 | D5508 | D5509 | D5510 | D5511 | D5512 | D5513 | D5514 | D5515 |
|---|---|---|---|---|---|---|---|---|---|
| Jan-58 | 4/58: STRAT - 30A | 4/58: STRAT - 30A | 5/58: STRAT - 30A | 5/58: STRAT - 30A | 6/58: STRAT - 30A | 6/58: STRAT - 30A | | | |
| Aug-58 | STRATFORD-30A | STRATFORD-30A | STRATFORD-30A | STRATFORD-30A | 6/58: Sc.R trials | STRATFORD-30A | 7/58: STRAT - 30A | 7/58: STRAT - 30A | 7/58: STRAT - 30A |
| Jan-59 | 3/59: MARCH - 31B | 3/59: MARCH - 31B | STRATFORD-30A | 3/59: MARCH - 31B | 9/58: STRAT - 30A | STRATFORD-30A | STRATFORD-30A | STRATFORD-30A | 3/59: MARCH - 31B |
| Aug-59 | MARCH-31B | MARCH-31B | STRATFORD-30A | MARCH-31B | STRATFORD-30A | STRATFORD-30A | STRATFORD-30A | STRATFORD-30A | MARCH-31B |
| Nov-59 | 11/59: STRAT - 30A | 11/59: STRAT - 30A | STRATFORD-30A | MARCH-31B | STRATFORD-30A | STRATFORD-30A | STRATFORD-30A | STRATFORD-30A | MARCH-31B |
| Jan-60 | STRATFORD-30A | STRATFORD-30A | STRATFORD-30A | 1/60: STRAT - 30A | STRATFORD-30A | STRATFORD-30A | STRATFORD-30A | STRATFORD-30A | 3/60: NOR - 32A |
| Apr-60 | STRATFORD-30A | STRATFORD-30A | STRATFORD-30A | STRATFORD-30A | STRATFORD-30A | STRATFORD-30A | STRATFORD-30A | STRATFORD-30A | 4/60: IPS - 32B |
| Aug-60 | 9/60: IPS - 32B | 9/60: IPS - 32B | STRATFORD-30A | STRATFORD-30A | STRATFORD-30A | STRATFORD-30A | STRATFORD-30A | STRATFORD-30A | 9/60: STRAT - 30A |
| Nov-60 | IPSWICH-32B | MARCH-31B | STRATFORD-30A | STRATFORD-30A | STRATFORD-30A | STRATFORD-30A | STRATFORD-30A | STRATFORD-30A | STRATFORD-30A |

| | D5516 | D5517 | D5518 | D5519 | D5520 | D5521 | D5522 | D5523 | D5524 |
|---|---|---|---|---|---|---|---|---|---|
| Jan-58 | | | | | | | | | |
| Aug-58 | 9/58: STRAT - 30A | 9/58: STRAT - 30A | 10/58: STRAT - 30A | 12/58: STRAT - 30A | | | | | |
| Jan-59 | STRATFORD-30A | STRATFORD-30A | 3/59: MARCH - 31B | 3/59: MARCH - 31B | 2/59: STRAT - 30A | 3/59: IPS - 32B | 3/59: STRAT - 30A | 3/59: STRAT - 30A | 3/59: NOR - 32A |
| Aug-59 | STRATFORD-30A | STRATFORD-30A | MARCH-31B | MARCH-31B | STRATFORD-30A | IPSWICH-32B | STRATFORD-30A | STRATFORD-30A | 6/59: MARCH - 31B |
| Nov-59 | STRATFORD-30A | STRATFORD-30A | MARCH-31B | MARCH-31B | 10/59: IPS - 32B | IPSWICH-32B | 10/59: IPS - 32B | 10/59: IPS - 32B | 11/59: STRAT - 30A |
| Jan-60 | STRATFORD-30A | STRATFORD-30A | MARCH-31B | MARCH-31B | IPSWICH-32B | IPSWICH-32B | IPSWICH-32B | IPSWICH-32B | STRATFORD-30A |
| Apr-60 | STRATFORD-30A | STRATFORD-30A | MARCH-31B | MARCH-31B | IPSWICH-32B | IPSWICH-32B | IPSWICH-32B | IPSWICH-32B | STRATFORD-30A |
| Aug-60 | STRATFORD-30A | STRATFORD-30A | 9/60: STRAT - 30A | MARCH-31B | IPSWICH-32B | IPSWICH-32B | IPSWICH-32B | IPSWICH-32B | 9/60: IPS - 32B |
| Nov-60 | STRATFORD-30A | STRATFORD-30A | STRATFORD-30A | MARCH-31B | IPSWICH-32B | IPSWICH-32B | IPSWICH-32B | IPSWICH-32B | IPSWICH-32B |

| | D5525 | D5526 | D5527 | D5528 | D5529 | D5530 | D5531 | D5532 | D5533 |
|---|---|---|---|---|---|---|---|---|---|
| Jan-59 | 3/59: MARCH - 31B | 3/59: STRAT - 30A | 3/59: STRAT - 30A | 4/59: NOR - 32A | 5/59: MARCH - 31B | 5/59: MARCH - 31B | 5/59: STRAT - 30A | | |
| Aug-59 | MARCH-31B | STRATFORD-30A | STRATFORD-30A | 6/59: MARCH - 31B | MARCH-31B | MARCH-31B | STRATFORD-30A | 6/59: IPS - 32B | 6/59: IPS - 32B |
| Nov-59 | MARCH-31B | 10/59: IPS - 32B | 10/59: IPS - 32B | 10/59: NOR - 32A | 10/59: NOR - 32A | 10/59: NOR - 32A | 10/59: IPS - 32B | IPSWICH-32B | IPSWICH-32B |
| Jan-60 | MARCH-31B | IPSWICH-32B | IPSWICH-32B | NORWICH-32A | NORWICH-32A | NORWICH-32A | IPSWICH-32B | IPSWICH-32B | IPSWICH-32B |
| Apr-60 | MARCH-31B | IPSWICH-32B | IPSWICH-32B | NORWICH-32A | NORWICH-32A | NORWICH-32A | IPSWICH-32B | IPSWICH-32B | IPSWICH-32B |
| Aug-60 | MARCH-31B | IPSWICH-32B | IPSWICH-32B | NORWICH-32A | NORWICH-32A | NORWICH-32A | IPSWICH-32B | IPSWICH-32B | IPSWICH-32B |
| Nov-60 | MARCH-31B | IPSWICH-32B | IPSWICH-32B | NORWICH-32A | NORWICH-32A | NORWICH-32A | IPSWICH-32B | IPSWICH-32B | IPSWICH-32B |

| | D5534 | D5535 | D5536 | D5537 | D5538 | D5539 | D5540 | D5541 | D5542 |
|---|---|---|---|---|---|---|---|---|---|
| Jan-59 | | | | | | | | | |
| Aug-59 | 6/59: MARCH - 31B | 6/59: IPS - 32B | 6/59: STRAT - 30A | 6/59: STRAT - 30A | 7/59: IPS - 32B | 7/59: IPS - 32B | 7/59: IPS - 32B | 7/59: IPS - 32B | 7/59: IPS - 32B |
| Nov-59 | 10/59: NOR - 32A | IPSWICH-32B | 10/59: IPS - 32B | 10/59: IPS - 32B | IPSWICH-32B | IPSWICH-32B | IPSWICH-32B | IPSWICH-32B | IPSWICH-32B |
| Jan-60 | NORWICH-32A | IPSWICH-32B | IPSWICH-32B | IPSWICH-32B | IPSWICH-32B | IPSWICH-32B | IPSWICH-32B | IPSWICH-32B | IPSWICH-32B |
| Apr-60 | NORWICH-32A | IPSWICH-32B | IPSWICH-32B | IPSWICH-32B | IPSWICH-32B | IPSWICH-32B | IPSWICH-32B | IPSWICH-32B | IPSWICH-32B |
| Aug-60 | NORWICH-32A | IPSWICH-32B | IPSWICH-32B | IPSWICH-32B | IPSWICH-32B | IPSWICH-32B | IPSWICH-32B | IPSWICH-32B | IPSWICH-32B |
| Nov-60 | NORWICH-32A | IPSWICH-32B | IPSWICH-32B | IPSWICH-32B | IPSWICH-32B | IPSWICH-32B | IPSWICH-32B | IPSWICH-32B | IPSWICH-32B |

| | D5543 | D5544 | D5545 | D5546 | D5547 | D5548 | D5549 | D5550 | D5551 |
|---|---|---|---|---|---|---|---|---|---|
| Jan-59 | | | | | | | | | |
| Aug-59 | 7/59: IPS - 32B | 8/59: IPS - 32B | | 8/59: IPS - 32B | 8/59: IPS - 32B | | | | |
| Nov-59 | IPSWICH-32B | IPSWICH-32B | 10/59: STRAT - 30A | 9/59: MARCH - 31B | 9/59: MARCH - 31B | 9/59: IPS - 32B | 9/59: IPS - 32B | 9/59: IPS - 32B | 9/59: IPS - 32B |
| Jan-60 | IPSWICH-32B | IPSWICH-32B | STRATFORD-30A | MARCH-31B | MARCH-31B | IPSWICH-32B | IPSWICH-32B | IPSWICH-32B | IPSWICH-32B |
| Apr-60 | IPSWICH-32B | IPSWICH-32B | STRATFORD-30A | MARCH-31B | MARCH-31B | IPSWICH-32B | IPSWICH-32B | IPSWICH-32B | IPSWICH-32B |
| Aug-60 | IPSWICH-32B | IPSWICH-32B | STRATFORD-30A | MARCH-31B | MARCH-31B | IPSWICH-32B | IPSWICH-32B | IPSWICH-32B | IPSWICH-32B |
| Nov-60 | IPSWICH-32B | IPSWICH-32B | STRATFORD-30A | MARCH-31B | MARCH-31B | IPSWICH-32B | IPSWICH-32B | IPSWICH-32B | IPSWICH-32B |

| | D5552 | D5553 | D5554 | D5555 | D5556 | D5557 | D5558 | D5559 | D5560 |
|---|---|---|---|---|---|---|---|---|---|
| Jan-59 | | | | | | | | | |
| Aug-59 | | | | | | | | | |
| Nov-59 | 9/59: IPS - 32B | 9/59: IPS - 32B | 10/59: IPS - 32B | 10/59: IPS - 32B | 10/59: IPS - 32B | 10/59: IPS - 32B | 10/59: IPS - 32B | 10/59: IPS - 32B | 10/59: IPS - 32B |
| Jan-60 | IPSWICH-32B | IPSWICH-32B | IPSWICH-32B | IPSWICH-32B | IPSWICH-32B | IPSWICH-32B | IPSWICH-32B | IPSWICH-32B | IPSWICH-32B |
| Apr-60 | IPSWICH-32B | IPSWICH-32B | IPSWICH-32B | IPSWICH-32B | IPSWICH-32B | IPSWICH-32B | IPSWICH-32B | IPSWICH-32B | IPSWICH-32B |
| Aug-60 | IPSWICH-32B | IPSWICH-32B | IPSWICH-32B | IPSWICH-32B | IPSWICH-32B | IPSWICH-32B | IPSWICH-32B | IPSWICH-32B | IPSWICH-32B |
| Nov-60 | IPSWICH-32B | IPSWICH-32B | IPSWICH-32B | IPSWICH-32B | IPSWICH-32B | IPSWICH-32B | IPSWICH-32B | IPSWICH-32B | IPSWICH-32B |

| | D5561 | D5562 | D5563 | D5564 | D5565 | D5566 | D5567 | D5568 | D5569 |
|---|---|---|---|---|---|---|---|---|---|
| Jan-59 | | | | | | | | | |
| Aug-59 | | | | | | | | | |
| Nov-59 | 10/59: IPS - 32B | 11/59: IPS - 32B | 11/59: MARCH - 31B | 11/59: MARCH - 31B | 10/59: MARCH - 31B | 11/59: HSEY - 34B | 11/59: HSEY - 34B | 11/59: HSEY - 34B | 11/59: HSEY - 34B |
| Jan-60 | IPSWICH-32B | IPSWICH-32B | MARCH-31B | MARCH-31B | 12/59: HSEY - 34B | HORNSEY-34B | HORNSEY-34B | HORNSEY-34B | HORNSEY-34B |
| Apr-60 | IPSWICH-32B | IPSWICH-32B | MARCH-31B | MARCH-31B | 4/60: NOR - 32A | 3/60: NOR - 32A | 3/60: NOR - 32A | 5/60: NOR - 32A | 4/60: NOR - 32A |
| Aug-60 | IPSWICH-32B | IPSWICH-32B | MARCH-31B | MARCH-31B | NORWICH-32A | NORWICH-32A | NORWICH-32A | NORWICH-32A | NORWICH-32A |
| Nov-60 | IPSWICH-32B | IPSWICH-32B | MARCH-31B | MARCH-31B | NORWICH-32A | NORWICH-32A | NORWICH-32A | NORWICH-32A | NORWICH-32A |

| | D5570 | D5571 | D5572 | D5573 | D5574 | D5575 | D5576 | D5577 | D5578 |
|---|---|---|---|---|---|---|---|---|---|
| Jan-60 | 12/59: MARCH - 31B | 12/59: MARCH - 31B | 12/59: MARCH - 31B | 12/59: MARCH - 31B | 12/59: NOR - 32A | 12/59: NOR - 32A | 12/59: NOR - 32A | 12/59: NOR - 32A | 12/59: STRAT - 30A |
| Apr-60 | MARCH-31B | MARCH-31B | MARCH-31B | MARCH-31B | NORWICH-32A | NORWICH-32A | NORWICH-32A | NORWICH-32A | STRATFORD-30A |
| Aug-60 | MARCH-31B | MARCH-31B | MARCH-31B | MARCH-31B | NORWICH-32A | NORWICH-32A | NORWICH-32A | NORWICH-32A | STRATFORD-30A |
| Nov-60 | MARCH-31B | MARCH-31B | MARCH-31B | MARCH-31B | NORWICH-32A | NORWICH-32A | NORWICH-32A | NORWICH-32A | STRATFORD-30A |

| | D5579 | D5580 | D5581 | D5582 | D5583 | D5584 | D5585 | D5586 | D5587 |
|---|---|---|---|---|---|---|---|---|---|
| Jan-60 | 12/59: STRAT - 30A | 12/59: NOR - 32A | 12/59: NOR - 32A | 2/60: IPS - 32B | 2/60: STRAT - 30A | 2/60: MARCH - 31B | 2/60: MARCH - 31B | 2/60: HSEY - 34B | 2/60: HSEY - 34B |
| Apr-60 | STRATFORD-30A | NORWICH-32A | NORWICH-32A | IPSWICH-32B | STRATFORD-30A | MARCH-31B | MARCH-31B | 5/60: C.YARD - 34G | 5/60: C.YARD - 34G |
| Aug-60 | STRATFORD-30A | NORWICH-32A | NORWICH-32A | IPSWICH-32B | 9/60: IPS - 32B | MARCH-31B | MARCH-31B | CLARENCEYARD-34G | CLARENCEYARD-34G |
| Nov-60 | STRATFORD-30A | NORWICH-32A | NORWICH-32A | IPSWICH-32B | IPSWICH-32B | MARCH-31B | MARCH-31B | CLARENCEYARD-34G | CLARENCEYARD-34G |

| | D5588 | D5589 | D5590 | D5591 | D5592 | D5593 | D5594 | D5595 | D5596 |
|---|---|---|---|---|---|---|---|---|---|
| Jan-60 | 2/60: HSEY - 34B | 2/60: HSEY - 34B | 2/60: HSEY - 34B | 2/60: HSEY - 34B | 2/60: HSEY - 34B | 2/60: HSEY - 34B | 2/60: HSEY - 34B | 2/60: HSEY - 34B | 2/60: HSEY - 34B |
| Apr-60 | 5/60: C.YARD - 34G | 5/60: C.YARD - 34G | 5/60: C.YARD - 34G | 5/60: C.YARD - 34G | 5/60: C.YARD - 34G | 5/60: C.YARD - 34G | 5/60: C.YARD - 34G | 5/60: C.YARD - 34G | 5/60: C.YARD - 34G |
| Aug-60 | CLARENCEYARD-34G | CLARENCEYARD-34G | CLARENCEYARD-34G | CLARENCEYARD-34G | CLARENCEYARD-34G | CLARENCEYARD-34G | CLARENCEYARD-34G | CLARENCEYARD-34G | CLARENCEYARD-34G |
| Nov-60 | CLARENCEYARD-34G | CLARENCEYARD-34G | CLARENCEYARD-34G | CLARENCEYARD-34G | CLARENCEYARD-34G | CLARENCEYARD-34G | CLARENCEYARD-34G | CLARENCEYARD-34G | CLARENCEYARD-34G |

| | D5597 | D5598 | D5599 | D5600 | D5601 | D5602 | D5603 | D5604 | D5605 |
|---|---|---|---|---|---|---|---|---|---|
| Jan-60 | 2/60: HSEY - 34B | 2/60: HSEY - 34B | 2/60: HSEY - 34B | 3/60: HSEY - 34B | 3/60: HSEY - 34B | 3/60: HSEY - 34B | 3/60: HSEY - 34B | 3/60: HSEY - 34B | 3/60: HSEY - 34B |
| Apr-60 | 5/60: C.YARD - 34G | 5/60: C.YARD - 34G | 5/60: C.YARD - 34G | 5/60: C.YARD - 34G | 5/60: C.YARD - 34G | 5/60: C.YARD - 34G | 5/60: C.YARD - 34G | 5/60: C.YARD - 34G | 5/60: C.YARD - 34G |
| Aug-60 | CLARENCEYARD-34G | CLARENCEYARD-34G | CLARENCEYARD-34G | CLARENCEYARD-34G | CLARENCEYARD-34G | CLARENCEYARD-34G | CLARENCEYARD-34G | CLARENCEYARD-34G | CLARENCEYARD-34G |
| Nov-60 | CLARENCEYARD-34G | CLARENCEYARD-34G | CLARENCEYARD-34G | CLARENCEYARD-34G | CLARENCEYARD-34G | CLARENCEYARD-34G | CLARENCEYARD-34G | CLARENCEYARD-34G | CLARENCEYARD-34G |

| | D5606 | D5607 | D5608 | D5609 | D5610 | D5611 | D5612 | D5613 | D5614 |
|---|---|---|---|---|---|---|---|---|---|
| Jan-60 | 4/60: HSEY - 34B | 4/60: HSEY - 34B | 4/60: HSEY - 34B | 4/60: HSEY - 34B | 4/60: HSEY - 34B | 4/60: HSEY - 34B | 4/60: HSEY - 34B | 4/60: HSEY - 34B | 4/60: HSEY - 34B |
| Apr-60 | 5/60: C.YARD - 34G | 5/60: C.YARD - 34G | 5/60: C.YARD - 34G | 5/60: C.YARD - 34G | 5/60: C.YARD - 34G | 5/60: C.YARD - 34G | 5/60: C.YARD - 34G | 5/60: C.YARD - 34G | 5/60: C.YARD - 34G |
| Aug-60 | CLARENCEYARD-34G | CLARENCEYARD-34G | CLARENCEYARD-34G | CLARENCEYARD-34G | CLARENCEYARD-34G | CLARENCEYARD-34G | CLARENCEYARD-34G | CLARENCEYARD-34G | CLARENCEYARD-34G |
| Nov-60 | CLARENCEYARD-34G | CLARENCEYARD-34G | CLARENCEYARD-34G | CLARENCEYARD-34G | CLARENCEYARD-34G | CLARENCEYARD-34G | CLARENCEYARD-34G | CLARENCEYARD-34G | CLARENCEYARD-34G |

| | D5615 | D5616 | D5617 | D5618 | D5619 | D5620 | D5621 | D5622 | D5623 |
|---|---|---|---|---|---|---|---|---|---|
| Jan-60 | 4/60: HSEY - 34B | | | | | | | | |
| Apr-60 | 5/60: C.YARD - 34G | 5/60: STRAT - 30A | 5/60: STRAT - 30A | 5/60: STRAT - 30A | 5/60: STRAT - 30A | 5/60: MARCH - 31B | 5/60: MARCH - 31B | 5/60: IPS - =32B | 5/60: IPS - =32B |
| Aug-60 | CLARENCEYARD-34G | STRATFORD-30A | STRATFORD-30A | STRATFORD-30A | STRATFORD-30A | MARCH-31B | MARCH-31B | 9/60: STRAT - 30A | 9/60: STRAT - 30A |
| Nov-60 | CLARENCEYARD-34G | STRATFORD-30A | STRATFORD-30A | STRATFORD-30A | STRATFORD-30A | MARCH-31B | MARCH-31B | STRATFORD-30A | STRATFORD-30A |

| | D5624 | D5625 | D5626 | D5627 | D5628 | D5629 | D5630 | D5631 | D5632 |
|---|---|---|---|---|---|---|---|---|---|
| Jan-60 | | | | | | | | | |
| Apr-60 | 6/60: IPS - 32B | 6/60: IPS - 32B | 6/60: IPS - 32B | 6/60: IPS - 32B | 6/60: IPS - 32B | 6/60: NOR - 32B | 6/60: NOR - 32B | 6/60: NOR - 32B | 6/60: STRAT - 30A |
| Aug-60 | IPSWICH-32B | IPSWICH-32B | IPSWICH-32B | IPSWICH-32B | IPSWICH-32B | 9/60: STRAT - 30A | NORWICH-32A | NORWICH-32A | STRATFORD-30A |
| Nov-60 | IPSWICH-32B | IPSWICH-32B | IPSWICH-32B | IPSWICH-32B | IPSWICH-32B | STRATFORD-30A | NORWICH-32A | NORWICH-32A | STRATFORD-30A |

| | D5633 | D5634 | D5635 | D5636 | D5637 | D5638 | D5639 | D5640 | D5641 |
|---|---|---|---|---|---|---|---|---|---|
| Jan-60 | | | | | | | | | |
| Apr-60 | 6/60: STRAT - 30A | | | | | | | | |
| Aug-60 | STRATFORD-30A | 8/60: STRAT - 30A | 8/60: STRAT - 30A | 8/60: STRAT - 30A | 8/60: STRAT - 30A | 8/60: STRAT - 30A | 8/60: C.YARD - 34G | 8/60: C.YARD - 34G | 8/60: C.YARD - 34G |
| Nov-60 | STRATFORD-30A | STRATFORD-30A | STRATFORD-30A | STRATFORD-30A | STRATFORD-30A | STRATFORD-30A | CLARENCEYARD-34G | CLARENCEYARD-34G | CLARENCEYARD-34G |

| | D5642 | D5643 | D5644 | D5645 | D5646 | D5647 | D5648 | D5649 | D5650 |
|---|---|---|---|---|---|---|---|---|---|
| Jan-60 | | | | | | | | | |
| Apr-60 | | | | | | | | | |
| Aug-60 | 8/60: C.YARD - 34G | 9/60: C. YARD - 34G | 9/60: C. YARD - 34G | 9/60: C. YARD - 34G | 9/60: C. YARD - 34G | 9/60: C. YARD - 34G | 9/60: C. YARD - 34G | 9/60: C. YARD - 34G | 9/60: C. YARD - 34G |
| Nov-60 | CLARENCEYARD-34G | CLARENCEYARD-34G | CLARENCEYARD-34G | CLARENCEYARD-34G | CLARENCEYARD-34G | CLARENCEYARD-34G | CLARENCEYARD-34G | CLARENCEYARD-34G | CLARENCEYARD-34G |

| | D5651 | D5652 | D5653 | D5654 | D5655 | D5656 | D5657 | D5658 | D5659 |
|---|---|---|---|---|---|---|---|---|---|
| Jan-60 | | | | | | | | | |
| Apr-60 | | | | | | | | | |
| Aug-60 | 9/60: C. YARD - 34G | | | | | | | | |
| Nov-60 | CLARENCEYARD-34G | 10/60: C.YARD - 34G | 10/60: C.YARD - 34G | 10/60: C.YARD - 34G | 10/60: MARCH - 31B | 10/60: MARCH - 31B | 10/60: MARCH - 31B | 10/60: MARCH - 31B | 11/60: MARCH - 31B |

| | D5660 | D5661 | D5662 | D5663 | D5664 | D5665 | D5666 | D5671 | |
|---|---|---|---|---|---|---|---|---|---|
| Jan-60 | | | | | | | | | |
| Apr-60 | | | | | | | | | |
| Aug-60 | | | | | | | | | |
| Nov-60 | 11/60: MARCH - 31B | 11/60: MARCH - 31B | 11/60: MARCH - 31B | 11/60: MARCH - 31B | 11/60: MARCH - 31B | 11/60: MARCH - 31B | 11/60: MARCH - 31B | 10/60: DARN - 41A | |

| | 1100hp Diesel D5900 | D5901 | D5902 | D5903 | D5904 | D5905 | D5906 | D5907 | D5908 |
|---|---|---|---|---|---|---|---|---|---|
| Jan-59 | 3/59: HSEY - 34B | | | 3/59: HSEY - 34B | 3/59: HSEY - 34B | | | | |
| Aug-59 | HORNSEY-34B | 5/59: HSEY - 34B | 5/59: HSEY - 34B | HORNSEY-34B | HORNSEY-34B | 5/59: HSEY - 34B | 5/59: HSEY - 34B | 5/59: HSEY - 34B | 5/59: HSEY - 34B |
| Nov-59 | HORNSEY-34B | HORNSEY-34B | HORNSEY-34B | HORNSEY-34B | HORNSEY-34B | HORNSEY-34B | HORNSEY-34B | HORNSEY-34B | HORNSEY-34B |
| Jan-60 | HORNSEY-34B | HORNSEY-34B | HORNSEY-34B | HORNSEY-34B | HORNSEY-34B | HORNSEY-34B | HORNSEY-34B | HORNSEY-34B | HORNSEY-34B |
| Apr-60 | 5/60: C.YARD - 34G | 5/60: C.YARD - 34G | 5/60: C.YARD - 34G | 5/60: C.YARD - 34G | 5/60: C.YARD - 34G | 5/60: C.YARD - 34G | 5/60: C.YARD - 34G | 5/60: C.YARD - 34G | 5/60: C.YARD - 34G |
| Aug-60 | CLARENCEYARD-34G | CLARENCEYARD-34G | CLARENCEYARD-34G | CLARENCEYARD-34G | CLARENCEYARD-34G | CLARENCEYARD-34G | CLARENCEYARD-34G | CLARENCEYARD-34G | CLARENCEYARD-34G |
| Nov-60 | CLARENCEYARD-34G | CLARENCEYARD-34G | CLARENCEYARD-34G | CLARENCEYARD-34G | CLARENCEYARD-34G | CLARENCEYARD-34G | CLARENCEYARD-34G | CLARENCEYARD-34G | CLARENCEYARD-34G |

| | D5909 | 1100hp Diesel D6100 | D6101 | D6102 | D6103 | D6104 | D6105 | D6106 | D6107 |
|---|---|---|---|---|---|---|---|---|---|
| Jan-59 | | 12/58: HSEY - 34B | 12/58: HSEY - 34B | 12/58: HSEY - 34B | | 2/59: HSEY - 34B | 3/59: HSEY - 34B | 3/59: HSEY - 34B | 3/59: HSEY - 34B |
| Aug-59 | 6/59: HSEY - 34B | HORNSEY-34B | HORNSEY-34B | HORNSEY-34B | 5/59: HSEY - 34B | HORNSEY-34B | HORNSEY-34B | HORNSEY-34B | HORNSEY-34B |
| Nov-59 | HORNSEY-34B | HORNSEY-34B | HORNSEY-34B | HORNSEY-34B | HORNSEY-34B | HORNSEY-34B | HORNSEY-34B | HORNSEY-34B | HORNSEY-34B |
| Jan-60 | HORNSEY-34B | HORNSEY-34B | HORNSEY-34B | HORNSEY-34B | HORNSEY-34B | HORNSEY-34B | HORNSEY-34B | HORNSEY-34B | HORNSEY-34B |
| Apr-60 | 5/60: C.YARD - 34G | 5/60: EFLD - 65A | 5/60: EFLD - 65A | 5/60: EFLD - 65A | 5/60: EFLD - 65A | 5/60: EFLD - 65A | 5/60: EFLD - 65A | 5/60: EFLD - 65A | 5/60: EFLD - 65A |
| Aug-60 | CLARENCEYARD-34G | EASTFIELD-65A | EASTFIELD-65A | EASTFIELD-65A | EASTFIELD-65A | EASTFIELD-65A | EASTFIELD-65A | EASTFIELD-65A | EASTFIELD-65A |
| Nov-60 | CLARENCEYARD-34G | EASTFIELD-65A | EASTFIELD-65A | EASTFIELD-65A | EASTFIELD-65A | EASTFIELD-65A | EASTFIELD-65A | EASTFIELD-65A | EASTFIELD-65A |

At one time the idea of there being no locomotive allocation at Doncaster would have been laughable, yet under dieselisation that is precisely what happened with no permanent allocation of engines at any point on the GN main line between London and York. Most passenger services originating from Doncaster were worked by multiple units from either Lincoln or Neville Hill whilst locomotives were provided by Immingham and Tinsley. Brush Type 2 D5671 of Sheffield passes behind the station with a trip working from Bentley Colliery to Tinsley in 1965.

The BTH D82xx 800hp Type 1's did not long outlive steam and all had gone by the early 1970's. For a time they, and the visually similar NB D84xx locomotives, played an important role in the London areas of the GN and GE systems, covering duties which did not call for a Type 2 locomotive. One of the Great Eastern allocation passes through Stratford with the 11.44 Temple Mills - Ripple Lane goods in 1965

| | D6108 | D6109 | D6110 | D6111 | D6112 | D6113 | D6114 | D6115 | D6116 |
|---|---|---|---|---|---|---|---|---|---|
| Jan-59 | | | | | | | | | |
| Aug-59 | 5/59: STRAT - 30A | 5/59: STRAT - 30A | 5/59: STRAT - 30A | 5/59: STRAT - 30A | 5/59: STRAT - 30A | 5/59: STRAT - 30A | 5/59: STRAT - 30A | 6/59: STRAT - 30A | 6/59: STRAT - 30A |
| Nov-59 | STRATFORD - 30A | STRATFORD - 30A | STRATFORD - 30A | STRATFORD - 30A | STRATFORD - 30A | STRATFORD - 30A | STRATFORD - 30A | STRATFORD - 30A | STRATFORD - 30A |
| Jan-60 | STRATFORD - 30A | STRATFORD - 30A | STRATFORD - 30A | STRATFORD - 30A | STRATFORD - 30A | STRATFORD - 30A | STRATFORD - 30A | STRATFORD - 30A | STRATFORD - 30A |
| Apr-60 | 5/60: EFLD - 65A | STRATFORD - 30A | STRATFORD - 30A | STRATFORD - 30A | STRATFORD - 30A | 6/60: EFLD - 65A | STRATFORD - 30A | STRATFORD - 30A | STRATFORD - 30A |
| Aug-60 | EASTFIELD - 65A | STRATFORD - 30A | 9/60: EFLD - 65A | 9/60: EFLD - 65A | 9/60: EFLD - 65A | EASTFIELD - 65A | 9/60: EFLD - 65A | 9/60: EFLD - 65A | 8/60: EFLD - 65A |
| Nov-60 | EASTFIELD - 65A | STRATFORD - 30A | EASTFIELD - 65A | EASTFIELD - 65A | EASTFIELD - 65A | EASTFIELD - 65A | EASTFIELD - 65A | EASTFIELD - 65A | EASTFIELD - 65A |

| | D6117 | D6118 | D6119 | D6120 | D6121 | D6122 | D6123 | D6124 | D6125 |
|---|---|---|---|---|---|---|---|---|---|
| Jan-59 | | | | | | | | | |
| Aug-59 | 6/59: STRAT - 30A | 6/59: STRAT - 30A | 6/59: STRAT - 30A | 7/59: IPS - 32B | 8/59: IPS - 32B | 9/59: IPS - 32B | 9/59: IPS - 32B | 9/59: IPS - 32B | 9/59: IPS - 32B |
| Nov-59 | STRATFORD - 30A | STRATFORD - 30A | STRATFORD - 30A | IPSWICH - 32B | IPSWICH - 32B | IPSWICH - 32B | IPSWICH - 32B | IPSWICH - 32B | IPSWICH - 32B |
| Jan-60 | 12/59: IPS - 32B | STRATFORD - 30A | 12/59: IPS - 32B | IPSWICH - 32B | IPSWICH - 32B | IPSWICH - 32B | IPSWICH - 32B | IPSWICH - 32B | IPSWICH - 32B |
| Apr-60 | IPSWICH - 32B | STRATFORD - 30A | IPSWICH - 32B | IPSWICH - 32B | 6/60: EFLD - 65A | IPSWICH - 32B | 6/60: EFLD - 65A | 5/60: EFLD - 65A | 5/60: EFLD - 65A |
| Aug-60 | 8/60: EFLD - 65A | 8/60: EFLD - 65A | 8/60: EFLD - 65A | 8/60: EFLD - 65A | EASTFIELD - 65A | 8/60: EFLD - 65A | EASTFIELD - 65A | EASTFIELD - 65A | EASTFIELD - 65A |
| Nov-60 | EASTFIELD - 65A | EASTFIELD - 65A | EASTFIELD - 65A | EASTFIELD - 65A | EASTFIELD - 65A | EASTFIELD - 65A | EASTFIELD - 65A | EASTFIELD - 65A | EASTFIELD - 65A |

| | D6126 | D6127 | D6128 | D6129 | D6130 | D6131 | D6132 | D6133 | D6134 |
|---|---|---|---|---|---|---|---|---|---|
| Jan-59 | | | | | | | | | |
| Aug-59 | | | | 10/59: EFLD - 65A | 10/59: EFLD - 65A | | | | |
| Nov-59 | 10/59: HSEY - 34B | 10/59: IPS - 32B | 10/59: IPS - 32B | 11/59: IPS - 32B | 11/59: IPS - 32B | 11/59: IPS - 32B | 11/59: IPS - 32B | 11/59: IPS - 32B | 11/59: IPS - 32B |
| Jan-60 | IPSWICH - 32B | IPSWICH - 32B | IPSWICH - 32B | IPSWICH - 32B | IPSWICH - 32B | IPSWICH - 32B | IPSWICH - 32B | IPSWICH - 32B | IPSWICH - 32B |
| Apr-60 | 5/60: EFLD - 65A | 5/60: EFLD - 65A | 5/60: EFLD - 65A | 6/60: EFLD - 65A | 5/60: EFLD - 65A | 6/60: EFLD - 65A | 6/60: EFLD - 65A | 5/60: EFLD - 65A | 6/60: EFLD - 65A |
| Aug-60 | EASTFIELD - 65A | EASTFIELD - 65A | EASTFIELD - 65A | EASTFIELD - 65A | EASTFIELD - 65A | EASTFIELD - 65A | EASTFIELD - 65A | EASTFIELD - 65A | EASTFIELD - 65A |
| Nov-60 | EASTFIELD - 65A | EASTFIELD - 65A | EASTFIELD - 65A | EASTFIELD - 65A | EASTFIELD - 65A | EASTFIELD - 65A | EASTFIELD - 65A | EASTFIELD - 65A | EASTFIELD - 65A |

| | D6135 | D6136 | D6137 | D6138 | D6139 | D6140 | D6141 | D6142 | D6143 |
|---|---|---|---|---|---|---|---|---|---|
| Jan-59 | | | | | | | | | |
| Aug-59 | | | | | | | | | |
| Nov-59 | 12/59: IPS - 32B | 12/59: IPS - 32B | 12/59: IPS - 32B | | | | | | |
| Jan-60 | IPSWICH - 32B | 1/60: IPS - 32B | 1/60: IPS - 32B | 2/60: KITTY - 61A | 3/60: KITTY - 61A | 3/60: KITTY - 61A | | | |
| Apr-60 | IPSWICH - 32B | IPSWICH - 32B | IPSWICH - 32B | KITTYBREWSTER - 61A | KITTYBREWSTER - 61A | KITTYBREWSTER - 61A | 4/60: KITTY - 61A | 4/60: KITTY - 61A | 4/60: KITTY - 61A |
| Aug-60 | 8/60: EFLD - 65A | 8/60: EFLD - 65A | 8/60: EFLD - 65A | KITTYBREWSTER - 61A | KITTYBREWSTER - 61A | KITTYBREWSTER - 61A | KITTYBREWSTER - 61A | 7/60: DUN - 62B | KITTYBREWSTER - 61A |
| Nov-60 | EASTFIELD - 65A | EASTFIELD - 65A | EASTFIELD - 65A | KITTYBREWSTER - 61A | KITTYBREWSTER - 61A | KITTYBREWSTER - 61A | KITTYBREWSTER - 61A | 8/60: TH JN - 62A | KITTYBREWSTER - 61A |

| | D6144 | D6145 | D6146 | D6147 | D6148 | D6149 | D6150 | D6151 | D6152 |
|---|---|---|---|---|---|---|---|---|---|
| Jan-60 | | | | | | | | | |
| Apr-60 | 4/60: KITTY - 61A | 5/60: KITTY - 61A | 5/60: KITTY - 61A | 5/60: KITTY - 61A | 6/60: KITTY - 61A | 6/60: KITTY - 61A | | | |
| Aug-60 | KITTYBREWSTER - 61A | 6/60: PTH - 63A | 6/60: INV - 60A | KITTYBREWSTER - 61A | KITTYBREWSTER - 61A | KITTYBREWSTER - 61A | 8/60: KITTY - 61A | 8/60: KITTY - 61A | 8/60: KITTY - 61A |
| Nov-60 | KITTYBREWSTER - 61A | 7/60: KITTY - 61A | 7/60: KITTY - 61A | KITTYBREWSTER - 61A | KITTYBREWSTER - 61A | KITTYBREWSTER - 61A | KITTYBREWSTER - 61A | KITTYBREWSTER - 61A | KITTYBREWSTER - 61A |

| | D6153 | D6154 | D6155 | D6156 |
|---|---|---|---|---|
| Jan-60 | | | | |
| Apr-60 | | | | |
| Aug-60 | 8/60: KITTY - 61A | 8/60: KITTY - 61A | | |
| Nov-60 | KITTYBREWSTER - 61A | KITTYBREWSTER - 61A | 11/60: KITTY - 60A | 11/60: KITTY - 60A |

**1000hp Diesel**

| | D8006 | D8010 | D8011 | D8020 | D8021 | D8022 | D8023 | D8024 | D8025 |
|---|---|---|---|---|---|---|---|---|---|
| Jan-58 | | 1/58: BRADFORD - 56G | 1/58: BRADFORD - 56G | | | | | | |
| Aug-58 | 10/58: KITTY - 61A | 2/58: To LM | 2/58: To LM | | | | | | |
| Jan-59 | 11/58: To LM | | | | | | | | |
| Aug-59 | | | | | | | | | |
| Nov-59 | | | | 10/59: HSEY - 34B | 10/59: HSEY - 34B | 10/59: HSEY - 34B | 11/59: HSEY - 34B | 11/59: HSEY - 34B | 11/59: HSEY - 34B |
| Jan-60 | | | | HORNSEY - 34B | HORNSEY - 34B | HORNSEY - 34B | HORNSEY - 34B | HORNSEY - 34B | HORNSEY - 34B |
| Apr-60 | | | | 5/60: C. YARD - 34G | 5/60: C. YARD - 34G | 5/60: C. YARD - 34G | 5/60: C. YARD - 34G | 5/60: C. YARD - 34G | 5/60: C. YARD - 34G |
| Aug-60 | | | | CLARENCE YARD - 34G | CLARENCE YARD - 34G | CLARENCE YARD - 34G | CLARENCE YARD - 34G | CLARENCE YARD - 34G | CLARENCE YARD - 34G |
| Nov-60 | | | | CLARENCE YARD - 34G | CLARENCE YARD - 34G | CLARENCE YARD - 34G | CLARENCE YARD - 34G | CLARENCE YARD - 34G | CLARENCE YARD - 34G |

| | D8026 | D8027 | D8028 | D8029 | D8030 | D8031 | D8045 | D8046 | D8047 |
|---|---|---|---|---|---|---|---|---|---|
| Jan-59 | | | | | | | | | |
| Aug-59 | | | | | | | | | |
| Nov-59 | 11/59: HSEY - 34B | 12/59: HSEY - 34B | 12/59: LEITH - 64H | 11/59: HSEY - 34B | 12/59: HSEY - 34B | 12/59: HSEY - 34B | | | |
| Jan-60 | HORNSEY - 34B | HORNSEY - 34B | 2/60: KITTY - 61A | 1/60: LEITH - 64H | 1/60: LEITH - 64H | 1/60: LEITH - 64H | 1/60: HSEY - 34B | 1/60: HSEY - 34B | 1/60: HSEY - 34B |
| Apr-60 | 5/60: C. YARD - 34G | 5/60: C. YARD - 34G | KITTYBREWSTER - 61A | 2/60: KITTY - 61A | 2/60: KITTY - 61A | 2/60: KITTY - 61A | 5/60: C. YARD - 34G | 5/60: C. YARD - 34G | 5/60: C. YARD - 34G |
| Aug-60 | CLARENCE YARD - 34G | CLARENCE YARD - 34G | KITTYBREWSTER - 61A | KITTYBREWSTER - 61A | KITTYBREWSTER - 61A | KITTYBREWSTER - 61A | CLARENCE YARD - 34G | CLARENCE YARD - 34G | CLARENCE YARD - 34G |
| Nov-60 | CLARENCE YARD - 34G | CLARENCE YARD - 34G | KITTYBREWSTER - 61A | KITTYBREWSTER - 61A | KITTYBREWSTER - 61A | KITTYBREWSTER - 61A | CLARENCE YARD - 34G | CLARENCE YARD - 34G | CLARENCE YARD - 34G |

| | D8048 | D8049 | 800hp Diesel D8200 | D8201 | D8202 | D8203 | D8204 | D8205 | D8206 |
|---|---|---|---|---|---|---|---|---|---|
| Jan-59 | | | | | | | | | 1/59: KITTY - 61A |
| Aug-59 | | | Ex LM | Ex LM | Ex LM | | | | KITTYBREWSTER - 61A |
| Nov-59 | | | 10/59: NOR - 32A | 10/59: NOR - 32A | 10/59: NOR - 32A | 12/59: NOR - 32A | 12/59: NOR - 32A | 12/59: NOR - 32A | 12/59: NOR - 32A |
| Jan-60 | 1/60: HSEY - 34B | 1/60: HSEY - 34B | 12/59: MARCH - 31B | NORWICH - 32A | NORWICH - 32A | NORWICH - 32A | NORWICH - 32A | NORWICH - 32A | NORWICH - 32A |
| Apr-60 | 5/60: C. YARD - 34G | 5/60: C. YARD - 34G | 2/60: NOR - 32A | NORWICH - 32A | NORWICH - 32A | NORWICH - 32A | NORWICH - 32A | NORWICH - 32A | NORWICH - 32A |
| Aug-60 | CLARENCE YARD - 34G | CLARENCE YARD - 34G | NORWICH - 32A | NORWICH - 32A | NORWICH - 32A | NORWICH - 32A | NORWICH - 32A | NORWICH - 32A | NORWICH - 32A |
| Nov-60 | CLARENCE YARD - 34G | CLARENCE YARD - 34G | NORWICH - 32A | NORWICH - 32A | NORWICH - 32A | NORWICH - 32A | NORWICH - 32A | NORWICH - 32A | NORWICH - 32A |

| | D8207 | D8208 | D8209 | D8210 | D8211 | D8212 | D8213 | D8214 | D8215 |
|---|---|---|---|---|---|---|---|---|---|
| Jan-59 | | 1/59: TH JN - 62A | | | | | | | |
| Aug-59 | | 2/59: To LM | | | | | | | |
| Nov-59 | | To LM | | 11/59: STRAT - 30A | 11/59: STRAT - 30A | 11/59: MARCH - 31B | 12/59: MARCH - 31B | 12/59: MARCH - 31B | |
| Jan-60 | 1/60: NOR - 32A | 1/60: STRAT - 30A | 1/60: STRAT - 30A | STRATFORD - 30A | STRATFORD - 30A | MARCH - 31B | MARCH - 31B | MARCH - 31B | 1/60: MARCH - 31B |
| Apr-60 | NORWICH - 32A | STRATFORD - 30A | STRATFORD - 30A | STRATFORD - 30A | STRATFORD - 30A | MARCH - 31B | MARCH - 31B | MARCH - 31B | MARCH - 31B |
| Aug-60 | NORWICH - 32A | STRATFORD - 30A | STRATFORD - 30A | STRATFORD - 30A | STRATFORD - 30A | MARCH - 31B | MARCH - 31B | MARCH - 31B | MARCH - 31B |
| Nov-60 | NORWICH - 32A | STRATFORD - 30A | STRATFORD - 30A | STRATFORD - 30A | STRATFORD - 30A | MARCH - 31B | MARCH - 31B | MARCH - 31B | MARCH - 31B |

| | D8216 | D8217 | D8218 | D8220 | D8221 | D8222 | D8223 | D8224 | D8225 |
|---|---|---|---|---|---|---|---|---|---|
| Jan-60 | 1/60: MARCH - 31B | 1/60: MARCH - 31B | 2/60: MARCH - 31B | 2/60: STRAT - 30A | | | | | |
| Apr-60 | MARCH - 31B | MARCH - 31B | MARCH - 31B | STRATFORD - 30A | 3/60: STRAT - 30A | 3/60: STRAT - 30A | 3/60: IPS - 32B | 4/60: IPS - 32B | 4/60: IPS - 32B |
| Aug-60 | MARCH - 31B | MARCH - 31B | MARCH - 31B | STRATFORD - 30A | STRATFORD - 30A | STRATFORD - 30A | IPSWICH - 32B | IPSWICH - 32B | IPSWICH - 32B |
| Nov-60 | MARCH - 31B | MARCH - 31B | MARCH - 31B | STRATFORD - 30A | STRATFORD - 30A | STRATFORD - 30A | IPSWICH - 32B | IPSWICH - 32B | IPSWICH - 32B |

| | D8226 | D8227 | D8228 | D8229 | D8230 | D8231 | D8232 | D8233 | D8234 |
|---|---|---|---|---|---|---|---|---|---|
| Jan-60 | | | | | | | | | |
| Apr-60 | 4/60: IPS - 32B | 5/60: IPS - 32B | 6/60: IPS - 32B | 6/60: NOR - 32A | 6/60: NOR - 32A | | | | |
| Aug-60 | IPSWICH - 32B | IPSWICH - 32B | IPSWICH - 32B | 9/60: MARCH - 31B | 9/60: MARCH - 31B | 8/60: NOR - 32A | 8/60: NOR - 32A | 9/60: STRAT - 30A | |
| Nov-60 | IPSWICH - 32B | IPSWICH - 32B | IPSWICH - 32B | MARCH - 31B | MARCH - 31B | 9/60: MARCH - 31B | 9/60: STRAT - 30A | STRATFORD - 30A | 10/60: STRAT - 30A |

| | D8235 | D8236 | 800hp Diesel D8400 | D8401 | D8402 | D8403 | D8404 | D8405 | D8406 |
|---|---|---|---|---|---|---|---|---|---|
| Jan-58 | | | 5/58: STRAT - 30A | 6/58: STRAT - 30A | | | | | |
| Aug-58 | | | STRATFORD - 30A | STRATFORD - 30A | 7/58: STRAT - 30A | 7/58: STRAT - 30A | 8/58: STRAT - 30A | 9/58: STRAT - 30A | 9/58: STRAT - 30A |
| Jan-59 | | | STRATFORD - 30A | STRATFORD - 30A | STRATFORD - 30A | STRATFORD - 30A | STRATFORD - 30A | STRATFORD - 30A | STRATFORD - 30A |
| Aug-59 | | | STRATFORD - 30A | STRATFORD - 30A | STRATFORD - 30A | STRATFORD - 30A | STRATFORD - 30A | STRATFORD - 30A | STRATFORD - 30A |
| Nov-59 | | | STRATFORD - 30A | STRATFORD - 30A | STRATFORD - 30A | STRATFORD - 30A | STRATFORD - 30A | STRATFORD - 30A | STRATFORD - 30A |
| Jan-60 | | | STRATFORD - 30A | STRATFORD - 30A | STRATFORD - 30A | STRATFORD - 30A | STRATFORD - 30A | STRATFORD - 30A | STRATFORD - 30A |
| Apr-60 | | | STRATFORD - 30A | STRATFORD - 30A | STRATFORD - 30A | STRATFORD - 30A | STRATFORD - 30A | STRATFORD - 30A | STRATFORD - 30A |
| Aug-60 | | | STRATFORD - 30A | STRATFORD - 30A | STRATFORD - 30A | STRATFORD - 30A | STRATFORD - 30A | STRATFORD - 30A | STRATFORD - 30A |
| Nov-60 | 10/60: IPS - 32B | 11/60: IPS - 32B | STRATFORD - 30A | STRATFORD - 30A | STRATFORD - 30A | STRATFORD - 30A | STRATFORD - 30A | STRATFORD - 30A | STRATFORD - 30A |

| | D8407 | D8408 | D8409 |
|---|---|---|---|
| Jan-58 | | | |
| Aug-58 | 9/58: STRAT - 30A | 9/58: STRAT - 30A | 9/58: STRAT - 30A |
| Jan-59 | STRATFORD - 30A | STRATFORD - 30A | STRATFORD - 30A |
| Aug-59 | STRATFORD - 30A | STRATFORD - 30A | STRATFORD - 30A |
| Nov-59 | STRATFORD - 30A | STRATFORD - 30A | STRATFORD - 30A |
| Jan-60 | STRATFORD - 30A | STRATFORD - 30A | STRATFORD - 30A |
| Apr-60 | STRATFORD - 30A | STRATFORD - 30A | STRATFORD - 30A |
| Aug-60 | STRATFORD - 30A | STRATFORD - 30A | STRATFORD - 30A |
| Nov-60 | STRATFORD - 30A | STRATFORD - 30A | STRATFORD - 30A |

| Shed | Aug-50 | Jan-51 | Aug-51 | Jan-52 | Aug-52 | Jan-53 | Aug-53 | Jan-54 | Aug-54 | Jan-55 | Aug-55 | Jan-56 | Aug-56 | Jan-57 | Aug-57 | Jan-58 | Aug-58 | Jan-59 | Aug-59 | Jan-60 | Aug-60 |
|---|---|---|---|---|---|---|---|---|---|---|---|---|---|---|---|---|---|---|---|---|---|
| Stratford | 2 | 2 | 2 | 2 | 11 | 14 | 11 | 12 | 14 | 13 | 19 | 37 | 46 | 47 | 47 | 52 | 57 | 55 | 54 | 51 | 52 |
| Edinburgh (SM) | | | | | | | | | | | | 3 | 4 | 3 | 3 | 4 | 12 | 19 | 25 | 26 | 51 |
| Clarence Yard | | | | | | | | | | | | | | | | | | | | | 34 |
| Darnall | | | | | | | | | | | | | | | | 5 | 9 | 16 | 25 | 29 | 34 |
| Immingham | | | | | | | | | | 3 | 12 | 8 | 14 | 14 | 18 | 22 | 25 | 29 | 32 | 32 | 33 |
| York | | | | | | | | | | | | | 7 | 10 | 10 | 10 | 10 | 10 | 18 | 20 | 32 |
| Daiycoates | | | | | 5 | 10 | 10 | 16 | 12 | 12 | 14 | 19 | 14 | 15 | 15 | 15 | 15 | 17 | 19 | 19 | 29 |
| March | 5 | 5 | 5 | 4 | 7 | 16 | 12 | 12 | 11 | 10 | 10 | 9 | 9 | 9 | 10 | 10 | 16 | 19 | 19 | 19 | 28 |
| Eastfield | | | | | | | | | | | | 1 | 3 | 4 | 6 | 14 | 13 | 13 | 13 | 13 | 24 |
| Thornaby | | | | | | | | | | | | | | | | | 13 | 14 | 15 | 17 | 23 |
| New England | | | | | | | | | 5 | 5 | 5 | 4 | 9 | 10 | 11 | 14 | 15 | 15 | 17 | 19 | 19 |
| Doncaster | | | | | | | | 1 | | | | 1 | | | 2 | 6 | 6 | 12 | 17 | 19 | 19 |
| Bradford | | | | | | | | | | | | | | | 3 | 7 | 6 | 6 | 4 | 9 | 19 |
| Norwich | | | | | | | | | | | 3 | 2 | 3 | 4 | 9 | 14 | 11 | 16 | 19 | 19 | 18 |
| Parkhead | | | | | | | | | | | | 3 | 4 | 4 | 6 | 5 | 7 | 7 | 7 | 7 | 17 |
| Kings Cross | | | | | 2 | 6 | 6 | 6 | 8 | 8 | 11 | 20 | 17 | 18 | 18 | 23 | 22 | 21 | 21 | 19 | |
| Darlington | | | | | | | | | | | | 18 | 18 | 18 | 18 | 7 | 6 | 7 | 7 | 7 | 16 |
| Thornton Jcn | | | | | | | | | | | | | 2 | 3 | 6 | 6 | 8 | 14 | 16 | 16 | 16 |
| Ipswich | | | | 1 | 1 | 1 | 1 | 2 | 5 | 4 | 6 | 9 | 9 | 11 | 11 | 11 | 10 | 14 | 14 | 14 | 14 |
| Gateshead | | | | | | | | | | | | | 6 | 6 | 5 | 8 | 8 | 7 | 7 | 13 | 13 |
| Lincoln | | | | | | | 3 | 3 | 5 | 4 | 3 | 3 | 4 | 4 | 4 | 4 | 8 | 9 | 10 | 13 | 13 |
| Harwich | | | | | | | | 4 | 10 | 10 | 15 | 15 | 15 | 15 | 15 | 15 | 17 | 13 | 13 | 13 | 13 |
| Springhead | | | | | | | | | | | | | | 4 | 3 | 9 | 9 | 11 | 12 | 10 | 13 |
| Kipps | | | | | | | | | | | | | | | 4 | 3 | 9 | 9 | 9 | 9 | 12 |
| Cambridge | | | | | | | | | | | | | | | | 6 | 9 | 11 | 12 | 10 | 11 |
| Heaton | | | | | | | | | | | | | | | | | | 12 | 10 | 9 | 11 |
| Boston | | | | | | | | | | | | | | 1 | 2 | 4 | 4 | 6 | 7 | 8 | 10 |
| Frodingham | | | | | | | | | | | | | | | | | | 12 | 11 | 10 | 10 |
| W. Hartlepool | | | | | | | 4 | 5 | 6 | 6 | 6 | 9 | 9 | 9 | 9 | 9 | 9 | 9 | 14 | 10 | 10 |
| Dundee | | | | | | | | | | | | 1 | 1 | 1 | 7 | 11 | 11 | 6 | 10 | 10 | 10 |
| Kittybrewster | | | | | | | | | | | | | | | | | | | | 1 | 9 |
| Ardsley | | | | | | | | | | | | | | | | | 9 | 9 | 9 | 10 | 9 |
| Retford | | | | | | | | | | | | | | | | | | 9 | 9 | 10 | 9 |
| Mexborough | | | 1 | 1 | 1 | 7 | 8 | 6 | 6 | 6 | 6 | 6 | 9 | | 10 | 10 | 10 | 8 | 9 | 9 | 9 |
| Goole | | | | | | | | | | | | | | | | | | 3 | 3 | 3 | 9 |
| Dunfermline | | | | | | | | | | | | | | | 5 | 7 | 8 | 9 | 9 | 9 | 7 |
| Hatfield | | | | | | | | | | | | | | | | 6 | 7 | 7 | 7 | 5 | 7 |
| Colwick | | | | | | | | | | | | | | | | | | | 7 | 7 | 7 |
| Hitchin | | | | | | | | | | | | | | | 1 | 2 | 2 | 5 | 5 | 6 | 6 |
| Lowestoft | | | | | | | | | | | | | | 1 | 1 | 1 | 2 | 2 | 4 | 4 | 6 |
| Percy Main | | | | | | | | | | | | 4 | 12 | 12 | 12 | 17 | | | | | 6 |
| Neasden | | | | | | | | | | | | | 3 | 5 | 5 | 5 | 5 | 5 | 5 | 5 | 5 |
| Blaydon | | | | | | | | | | | | | | | | | | 4 | 4 | 4 | 5 |
| North Blyth | | | | | | | | | | | | | | | | | | 5 | 5 | 5 | 5 |
| Haymarket | | | | | | | | | | | | | | | | | | 2 | 2 | 2 | 5 |
| Woodford H. | | | | | | | 5 | 5 | 5 | 4 | 4 | 4 | 5 | 4 | 4 | 4 | 4 | 4 | 4 | 4 | 4 |
| Neville Hill | | | | | | | | | | | | | | 5 | 5 | 5 | 5 | 5 | 4 | 4 | 4 |
| Yarmouth (ST) | | | | | | | | | | | | | | | | 1 | 1 | 1 | 2 | 3 | 3 |
| Sunderland | | | | | | | | | | | | | | | | | | | | 2 | 3 |
| Polmont | | | | | | | | | | | | | | 1 | 1 | 1 | 1 | 3 | 2 | 2 | 2 |
| Alloa | | | | | | | | | | | | | | | | | | | | 2 | 2 |
| Bathgate | | | | | | | | | | | | | | | | | 1 | 2 | 2 | 2 | 2 |
| Keith | | | | | | | | | | | | | | | | | | | | 2 | 2 |
| Hornsey | | | | 1 | 1 | 3 | 3 | 3 | 3 | 4 | 4 | 4 | 5 | 4 | 4 | 5 | 6 | 7 | 16 | 19 | 1 |
| Consett | | | | | | | | | | | | | | | | | | | | | 1 |
| S. Blyth | | | | | | | | | | | | | | | | | | 2 | 1 | 1 | 1 |
| Tweedmouth | | | | | | | | | | | | | | | | | | | | | 1 |
| Balloch | | | | | | | | | | | | | | | | | 1 | 1 | 1 | 1 | 1 |
| Yarmouth (V) | | | | 1 | | 1 | | 1 | | 1 | | 1 | | 1 | | 1 | | 1 | | | |
| Yarmouth (B) | | | | | | | | | | | | | | | | 1 | 1 | 1 | | | |
| Kings Lynn | | | | | | | | | | | | | | | | 5 | 5 | 5 | 5 | | |
| Melton C. | | | | | | | | | | | | | | | | 2 | 2 | | | | |
| South Lynn | | | | | | | | | | | | | | | | 2 | 2 | | | | |
| Spital Bridge | | | | | | | | | | | | | | | | | 4 | 2 | 3 | 3 | 3 |
| Middlesbrough | | | | | | | | | | | 2 | 8 | 9 | | | | | | | | |
| Newport | | | | | | | | | | | | | | | | | | 1 | | | |
| Dumbarton | | | | | | | | | | | | | | | | | | | | | |
| Total | 7 | 7 | 8 | 8 | 27 | 48 | 58 | 76 | 87 | 92 | 114 | 153 | 222 | 252 | 281 | 350 | 423 | 508 | 570 | 596 | 738 |

Regional distribution (end 1960): GN (143), GE (145), GC (104), NE (170), NB (164), GNoS (12)

Diesel shunting engines rarely aroused much interest yet the production of them - over 700 for the ex-LNER by 1960 - was an industry in its own right as indeed was the business of shunting, once the most commonplace activity on the railway system.

It is not simply the size of the fleet - the above was only about a quarter of BR's demand - but the use to which it was put which staggers the imagination. One might well wonder why Woodford Halse, popularly supposed a fairly quiet spot, should be given an allocation of five of BR's latest toys yet they were not actually enough to cover all the shunting at the location where the old and new yards required a total of four pilots and the West Junction and Wagon Shops a further two. In addition the passenger station was shunted during the late turn by a seventh pilot. On a proportional basis and assuming 350hp diesels were preferable to steam engines Woodford did rather better than Colwick, the GN yard for the Nottingham district, which had to wait until 1959 to get a paltry allocation of seven. In the light of the shunting commitment that Colwick had this was little short of astonishing; the loco being responsible for no less than sixteen full time pilots which included the yards at Colwick (9 engines), Nottingham Victoria, Basford and Daybrook (1 engine each) and London Road Goods, Nottingham (4 engines). Why the Nottingham district of the GN had to wait so long for diesel shunters cannot be recalled but the probability, as the 1950's progressed, of it being drawn into the London Midland web was no incentive.

A curious product of the programme concerned the Midland & Great Northern which - so far as shunting was concerned - may have a claim to be the first fully dieselised system in the country since all four of its pilots - two at South Lynn for the East and West yards respectively, one at Yarmouth Beach and two at Melton Constable (one of which performed at Norwich City) - went over to diesel working in February 1958. (As it happened, it was not the wisest of investments since, after spending a small fortune on driver training and the miscellany of alterations required for the reception of a new form of traction, the entire system was closed).

One of the earliest areas to be provided with diesel shunters was Hull where the three sheds provided no less than fifty-six daily pilots with a requirement for up to ten more when traffic was especially heavy. The heaviest burden fell upon Dairycoats shed which had to supply eleven locations with twenty-nine engines whilst Botanic Gardens, which existed primarily for passenger engines, sent a pair of shunters to Paragon station and Goole each plus one to Wilmington and a Sentinel to Stepney. Springhead and its sub-shed at Alexandra Dock, too often supposed to be a quiet backwater of the Hull and Barnsley, were not far behind Dairycoates and sent out twenty-one pilots, nine each for the Alexandra and King George Docks and three for the yard at Springhead. It is impossible to summarise in a paragraph the work these engines had to do but one measure is the basic service of principal goods trains from Hull each day which came to forty-three departures - roughly one every half an hour - consisting of one hundred and forty-three sections, all of which had to be put together with shunting engines. On top of that there was the mineral traffic....

Most shunting engines spent most of their lives in the yards to which they were allocated, only returning to the shed when required for maintenance: thus March acquired engines from Spital Bridge and Kings Lynn although it made little difference to the engines themselves. One interesting exception concerned the pilots at Kings Cross which provided twelve static pilots and fifteen run-round engines; the latter operating between Kings Cross Goods and Ferme Park to the direction of the Kings Cross traffic controller, much of whose time was spent trying to get a days work out of the Provender shunt or the North London Pilot. To the spectator the sight of an 0-6-0 (steam or diesel) blasting its way through Copenhagen tunnel with a trip from Five Arch to Clarence Yard seemed a pretty inspiring spectacle. It was only when one set foot inside the district control at Knebworth that one realised where the real noise came from as the section controller liverishly screeched at Inspectors, signalmen and guards in an effort to ensure that when the trip got to Clarence Yard, the engine went smartly down to Ashburton for a Ferme Park working without having to go back to Kings Cross for relief. Some of the most interesting work on the railway involved juggling with shunting engines.